Reader's Guide to

JUDAISM

ADVISORY BOARD

Reader's Guide to

JUDAISM

Editor

MICHAEL TERRY
Dorot Chief Librarian, Dorot Jewish Division,
The New York Public Library

FITZROY DEARBORN PUBLISHERS
CHICAGO • LONDON

CONTENTS

EDITOR'S NOTE

Aims, Scope, and Selection of Entries

The aim of the Fitzroy Dearborn Reader's Guides is to provide guidance to the secondary material in specific intellectual disciplines in brief bibliographic essays that analyze, interpret, and evaluate that material, succinctly presenting the student, teacher, researcher, and librarian with a selection of eligible candidates for further reading.

On the basis of a perusal of current academic publishers' catalogs, or a subscription to the *Times Literary Supplement,* or a stroll through the aisles of a national chain bookstore, the observer could hardly be faulted for taking Jewish Studies to be one of the primary categories of intellectual inquiry in the humanities. The boom in English-language Judaica publishing, however, is as novel as it is conspicuous. Still perceived, unlike Classics, as an interdisciplinary hybrid (albeit increasingly as a mark of esteem rather than a slight), Jewish Studies as a presence of any kind in English-speaking academe was little more than nominal before the second half of the 20th century. The seemingly breakneck pace of publishing activity a generation later, however, is less a matter of hybrid vigor than of gestation: in institutions of general learning, especially in the United States, there is now a full complement of practitioners, from callow youths to venerable emeriti as well as representatives of every degree of experience in between. Of course, the number of scholars, as much as the number of publications, is a function of a fundamental change of attitudes among readers as well as writers, Jews as well as non-Jews, reflecting the valorization of ethnicity and the study of alternative and minority experiences.

The Jewish national(ist) poet H.N. Bialik famously excoriated scholars of Judaism who elected to publish in the vernacular—rather than recognizing the claims of Hebrew as the holy, or literary, tongue—as enemies of the people and of posterity. The relative obscurity into which the writings of the 19th-century titans of the Wissenschaft des Judentums have fallen would seem to offer him some vindication, and it is not inconceivable that the labors of the English-speaking heirs of the German-speaking pioneers of the academic study of Judaism are flawed with an inherent obsolescence that does not mark the work of their Israeli colleagues. Prescinding, however, from speculation on the future history of the Jewish people or the English language, the fact remains that just now Jewish Studies in English, with its culturally specific nuances and interests, as well as a community of readers of its own, has burgeoned to become fully the counterpart of its Hebrew-language fraternal twin.

There is a mythic moment, corresponding to an actual turning point, in the emergence of a discipline when its adepts must give up on keeping abreast of new publications in the field, and thereafter on keeping abreast of new publications in increasingly specialized subfields. That moment is past for Jewish Studies in the English language, and this is what prompts the *Reader's Guide to Judaism.* There exist a number of one-volume Jewish encyclopedias—at least a couple of them extraordinarily good—and this compendium does not seek to function as another. What is currently lacking, and what this reference work attempts to supply, is a critical and explanatory signpost to the monographic literature on a wide range of subject matter within the study of Judaism. To that end, the field has been divided into almost 450 topics, and specialists have been invited to contribute signed bibliographic essays on the area of their expertise.

Each entry in the *Reader's Guide* consists of an essay preceded by a bibliographic headnote listing what the individual contributor deems the most valuable English-language works on the subject. Titles selected will all be available in English, whether originally or in translation, but, given the access services widely offered by contemporary libraries, they will by no means necessarily be in print. In the selection of titles, precedence has been given to books over articles, but essays or articles in journals or book-length collections have been included, especially where they offer important new interpretations or provide authoritative reviews of the literature on a subject. Typically, each essay in the *Reader's Guide* is around 1,000 words in length and discusses between five and nine titles. In certain cases ten or more items have seemed sufficiently important to require notice, and in these instances essays are 2,000 words in length. There are also a number of topics for which appropriate literature, at least in English, has proved severely limited, and here the reader is likely to find more extended discussion of fewer titles.

Naturally, the list of entries, developed in consultation with the project's advisers and contributing essayists, aspires to a balanced and authentic reflection of the scope of Judaism's preoccupations, but availability of scholarship, and specifically of scholarship in English, weighs very heavily here, since each topic needs to be the subject of sufficient worthwhile literature to allow for an expansive and somewhat comparative survey of the type that characterizes the *Reader's Guides*. While it is a cause for celebration that a work several times the present size could not begin to be exhaustive, many criminal omissions will undoubtedly be attributable to a lack of diligence on the part of the editor or a laspe of taste on the part of the contributors. On the other hand, one of the merits of a book like the *Reader's Guide* is its capacity to highlight surprising gaps. In the spirit of the *via negativa*, it may be hoped that the shortcomings of the present survey may stimulate here and there some localized bibliographic stocktaking.

Notwithstanding the generous proportions of the *Reader's Guide* and the avowedly selective and subjective approach of its essays, it has been necessary to restrict the range of topics covered, and as a result religious and ideological manifestations provide the primary focus. Insofar as the study of Judaism may be a narrower subject than Jewish Studies, it is the former that the *Reader's Guide to Judaism* purports to describe. It should also be noted that the *Reader's Guide* is a guide to secondary literature, and not to primary sources. There are two limited exceptions to this rule. An editorial introduction to a work by an important individual may be considered sufficiently valuable to justify inclusion in a case where the individual's own work would otherwise be excluded. Translations of portions of classical Jewish literature (e.g., Midrash Halakhah) have been included selectively, where the introduction, apparatus, or approach is such that the work may function as secondary literature in disguise.

Arrangement of the Entries

Entries appear in alphabetical order and a complete list can be found in the **Alphabetical List of Entries** (p. xv). Where there are several entries sharing the same general heading, the order does not normally proceed alphabetically, but from the more general to the more particular or from the earlier to the later, as appropriate (thus, "Holocaust: Responses" precedes "Holocaust: Film Treatments," and "Rabbinic Biography: Medieval" precedes "Rabbinic Biography: Early Modern").

While the overall arrangement of entries is alphabetical, there are other means of access to the contents of the *Reader's Guide*. These are:

1. **Thematic List** (p. xxi). This provides the reader with a list of entries arranged by broad subject area, specifically Arts and Material Culture, History, Individuals, Literature, Practice, References, and Thought. The criterion for the sometimes dubious distinction between topics assigned to Practice and those assigned to Thought is their degree of abstraction.
2. **Booklist Index** (p. 653). This lists in alphabetical order of author all books and articles discussed in any of the entries and can be used to locate discussion of the work of particular scholars. Occasionally books appear in more than one entry, and the reader can consult this index to locate multiple discussions of a particular title.

3. **General Index** (p. 687). This lists individuals, topics, and events mentioned in any of the entries. This index may be particularly useful for locating references to individuals, events, or other topics that have no entry of their own.
4. **Cross References.** At the end of many entries, there are *See also* notes that refer the reader to entries on related topics.

Format within Entries

Each entry begins with a list of the publications to be discussed by the essayist. Brief publication details are provided; normally dates are supplied for the first edition and the most recent revised edition, while paperback editions are omitted. In the text of each essay, the point at which each book or article receives its principal commentary is indicated by citation of the author's name in capital letters, although references to it may appear elsewhere in the essay. When more than one work by the same author is included, the name is capitalized at the beginning of the discussion of each book, followed by the date of publication in parentheses. Although the booklists in each entry proceed alphabetically by author, the order in which items are discussed has been left to the discretion of the individual essayists. The result is that a chronological approach has often been preferred, allowing discussion to reflect the evolution of a field of study; broader topics, however, have frequently found themselves best suited to thematic subgroupings.

Acknowledgments

Thanks are due to an array of congenial collaborators at Fitzroy Dearborn, and most especially to Robert M. Salkin, the commissioning editor, and Elizabeth Nishiura, my constant companions on this venture, and to their colleagues Alison Aves, Catherine E. Keich, Elizabeth Laskey, and Gretchen Willenberg. Much is owed also to a board of advisers who were lavish with good counsel during the planning stages. It remains only to acknowledge indebtedness to an extraordinary corps of contributing essayists. Some 200 strong, it is a group of considerable diversity: experientially, from doctoral candidates to senior faculty as near iconic as a relatively compact discipline allows; geographically, with preponderantly North American, Israeli, British, and Dutch contributors joined by others from a variety of countries with thriving Jewish Studies communities of their own, from Austria to Australia; and confessionally, with ordained contributors including rabbis of every stripe, a Franciscan friar, a Pentecostalist minister, and more. Their willingness to take time away from their respective projects to attend to these entries has regularly amazed, and collaborating with each has been a delight.

ADVISERS

Shulamith Berger
Nehama Edinger
Michael Fishbane
Arnold Franklin
David Goldenberg
Geoffrey Herman
Karina Martin Hogan

Menachem Kellner
Roger Kohn
Tzvi Langermann
Isaac Sassoon
Dan Sharon
Edward van Voolen
Barry Walfish

CONTRIBUTORS

Howard Tzvi Adelman
Rebecca Alpert
Eleanor Amico
Robert Ash
Shawn Zelig Aster
Fred Astren
Cynthia M. Baker
Carol Bakhos
Pamela Barmash
Judith R. Baskin
Leora Batnitzky
Wout Jacques van Bekkum
Dean Bell
Mara Benjamin
Philip J. Bentley
Shulamith Berger
Ellen Birnbaum
Laurie Blumberg
Julia Bock
Philip V. Bohlman
Alfredo Fabio Borodowski
S. Daniel Breslauer
Shannon Burkes
Deidre Butler
Hallie Lynn Cantor
Havva S. Charm

Judith R. Cohen
Alan D. Corré
Andrew Davies
Joseph M. Davis
Nachum Dershowitz
Eliezer Diamond
Marsha Bryan Edelman
Nehama Edinger
Laurence L. Edwards
Avrum Ehrlich
Carl S. Ehrlich
David Engel
Marc Michael Epstein
Peter R. Erspamer
Dina Ripsman Eylon
Michael V. Fox
Arnold Franklin
Lisbeth S. Fried
Dan Friedman
Baruch Frydman Kohl
Esther Fuchs
Zev Garber
Lloyd P. Gartner
Jane Gerber
Gary Gilbert
Pinchas Giller

Aubrey L. Glazer
Matthew Goff
Matt Goldish
Chanita Goodblatt
Sharon Green
Leonard J. Greenspoon
Kevin Edward Griffith
Sheila Dugger Griffith
Mayer Irwin Gruber
Peter Haas
Jacob Haberman
Schulamith Chava Halevy
Eric C. Helmer
Geoffrey Herman
Samuel Herzfeld
Richard Hirsh
Karina Martin Hogan
Leslie J. Hoppe
Timothy J. Horner
Sara R. Horowitz
Monika Humer
Charles David Isbell
Martin S. Jaffee
Julian Jakobovits
Barbara C. Johnson
Willis Johnson
Norma Baumel Joseph
S. Tamar Kamionkowski
Ephraim Kanarfogel
Dana Evan Kaplan
Gregory Kaplan
Jonathan Karp
Paul A. Kay
James A. Kelhoffer
Menachem Kellner
Ari Kelman
Joy Kingsolver
Samuel Z. Klausner
Mark Kligman
Cynthia A. Klíma
Rebbeca Kobrin
Samuel S. Kottek
Diane Kriger
Gail Labovitz
Hartley Lachter
Ruth Langer
Yaakov A. Lattes
Eric Lawee
Elliot Lefkovitz
Harris Lenowitz
Arthur M. Lesley
Alan Levenson
Mark LeVine
Bernard M. Levinson
Justin Jaron Lewis
Hilary Lieberman
Christopher A. Link
Shari Lowin
Edith Lubetski

George Mandel
Alisa Gayle Mayor
Rafael Medoff
David Meier
Marc Miller
Victor A. Mirelman
Alan Mittelman
Hillel C. Neuer
Scott B. Noegel
D.P. O'Brien
John T. Pawlikowski
Sarah Pessin
Sigrid Peterson
Lucy K. Pick
Judith S. Pinnolis
Sanford Pinsker
Paul A. Rainbow
Eric Reymond
Karyn Riegel
Ira Robinson
James T. Robinson
Fred Rosner
Jeffrey L. Rubenstein
William D. Rubinstein
Dominic Rudman
Leonard Victor Rutgers
Suzanne Rutland
Rachel Sabath
Angel Sáenz-Badillos
Ari Salkin-Weiss
Robert B. Salters
Gabriel Sanders
Jack T. Sanders
Roberta G. Sands
Marc Saperstein
Gad B. Sarfatti
Isaac Sassoon
Michael L. Satlow
Andrew Schein
Stuart Schoenfeld
Rebecca Schorsch
Emile G.L. Schrijver
Richard H. Schwartz
Roberta Hanfling Schwartz
Esther I. Seidel
Marc B. Shapiro
Brenda J. Shaver
Shmuel Shepkaru
Ita Sheres
Hayim Y. Sheynin
Colin Shindler
Adina Shoulson
Edward Silver
Rachel Simon
Alexej Michaelovitch Sivertsev
Abraham Socher
Adam Sol
Norman Solomon
Benjamin D. Sommer

Nanette Stahl
Leon Stein
Gillian D. Steinberg
Simon A. Steiner
Andrew E. Steinmann
Dennis Stoutenburg
Kenneth Stow
Adam Sutcliffe
Rivka B. Kern Ulmer
Ellen M. Umansky

Barry D. Walfish
Seth Ward
Arthur Waskow
Victoria R. Waters
Shalva Weil
David Weinberg
Libby White
Reena Zeidman
Walter P. Zenner

ALPHABETICAL LIST OF ENTRIES

THEMATIC LIST

Entries By Category

This outline is divided into the following seven sections, two of which are further divided into subsections:

ARTS AND MATERIAL CULTURE
HISTORY
INDIVIDUALS
LITERATURE
PRACTICE
REFERENCES
THOUGHT

ARTS AND MATERIAL CULTURE

Archaeology
Architecture, Synagogue: Late Antiquity
Architecture, Synagogue: Medieval and Modern
Art: Ceremonial
Art: Late Antiquity
Cemeteries: Antiquity
Cemeteries: Medieval and Modern
Costume
Film
Iconography
Ketubbah
Manuscripts, Hebrew
Music: Cantillation
Music: Cantorial Music
Music: Art Music
Music: American Jewish Music
Music: Ashkenazi Folk Music
Music: Sephardi Music
Music: Middle Eastern Music
Printing, Early Hebrew
Script and Scribal Practices
Theater

HISTORY

1) History by Period

History: Biblical Israel
History: Second Temple Period
History: Talmudic Era
History: Medieval
History: Modern

2) History by Phenomenon

Am Ha'arets
Anti-Judaism: Late Antiquity
Anti-Judaism: Middle Ages
Antisemitism
Apostasy
Assimilation
Ba'alei Shem
Black-Jewish Relations in the United States
Canaanites
Crusades
Crypto-Jews, Contemporary
Education

Emancipation
Exilarchate
Genizah, Cairo
Geonim
God-Fearers
Habad
Haskalah
Hellenism
Holocaust: Histories
Inquisition
Jewish Christians
Jewish Quarter
Jewish Studies
Karaites
Khazars
Lexicographers and Grammarians
Libels, Anti-Jewish: Medieval
Libels, Anti-Jewish: Modern
Marranism
Martyrdom
Medicine
Neturei Karta
Patriarchate
Pharisees
Philosemitism
Renaissance
Sadducees
Samaritans
Sanhedrin, Semikhah, and Rabbinate
Satmar
Scribes
Shtetl
Tabernacle
Temple and Temple Mount
Western Wall
Wissenschaft des Judentums
Women: Biblical
Women: Ancient and Modern
Women: Contemporary
Yeshivot: Medieval
Yeshivot: Modern

3) History by Region

Algeria
Ancient Near East
Ashkenazim
Australia and New Zealand
Babylonia
Baghdadi Jews of India
Balkans
Bene Israel of India
Canada
Central Europe
China
Cochin Jews
Egypt and Sudan
Elephantine
Ethiopia

France
Germany: Medieval
Germany: Modern
Great Britain
Hungary
India
Iran, Afghanistan, and Central Asia
Iraq
Israel, Land of: History
Israel, Land of: In Jewish Thought
Israel, State of: Judaism in Israel
Italy
Jerusalem
Latin America and the Caribbean
Libya
Lithuania
London
Middle East
Morocco
Netherlands, The
New York
North Africa
Poland
Portugal
Prague
Provence
Russia
Sephardim
South Africa
Spain
Syria
Temple and Temple Mount
Tunisia
United States: Community Histories
United States: General Histories
Venice
Western Wall
Yemen and the Arabian Peninsula

4) Universal Histories

History: Ideas of
History: General Histories, Premodern
    Authors
History: General Histories, Modern
    Authors

INDIVIDUALS

Abraham ben David of Posquières
Abravanel, Isaac
Abravanel, Judah
Abulafia, Abraham
Acosta, Uriel
Agnon, Shmuel Yosef
Ahad Ha'am
Akiba ben Joseph

LITERATURE

1) Bible

Exodus
Ezekiel, Book of
Ezra and Nehemiah, Books of
Five Scrolls
Flora and Fauna of the Bible
Genesis
Isaiah, Book of
Jeremiah, Book of
Job, Book of
Joshua, Book of
Judges, Book of
Kings, Book of
Lamentations
Leviticus
Masorah
Numbers, Book of
Pentateuch
Prophets, Former and Latter
Prophets, Twelve Minor
Proverbs
Psalms
Ruth, Book of
Samuel, Book of
Song of Songs
Wisdom Literature

2) Genres and Topics

Allegory
American Literature
Apocalyptic
Apocrypha and Pseudepigrapha:
    Translations
Apocrypha and Pseudepigrapha:
    Introductions
Ben Sira, Wisdom of
Christian Hebraists
Christian-Jewish Relations: Apologetics
    and Polemics
Dead Sea Scrolls
Ethical and Devotional Literature
Ethical Wills
Folktales
Gnosis and Early Mysticism
Haggadah, Passover
Halakhah: Introductions
Halakhah: Responsa
Hebrew Literature, Modern
Hellenistic Literature
Holocaust: Literature and Memoirs
Holocaust: Film Treatments
Homiletics
Judeo-Arabic Literature
Kabbalah: Translations
Kabbalah: Introductions
Ladino Literature
Literature, Jewish

Liturgy, History of
Liturgy, Reform
Midrash Aggadah
Midrash Halakhah: Translations
Midrash Halakhah: Introductions
Piyyut
Poetry: Biblical
Poetry: Medieval Hebrew
Poetry: Modern Hebrew
Poetry: American Jewish
Talmudic Literature: Translations
Talmudic Literature: Reference Tools
Talmudic Literature: Introductions
Talmudic Literature: Theology
Talmudic Literature: Hermeneutics
Targum
Women's Literature: Early Modern
Women's Literature: Modern and Con-
    temporary
Yiddish Literature
Zohar

PRACTICE

Abrogation of Law and Custom
Agricultural Laws
Agunah
Animals, Treatment of
Bar Mitzvah and Bat Mitzvah
Bioethics
Birth Control and Abortion
Charity
Circumcision
Conversion to Judaism
Death, Burial, and Mourning: Biblical and
    Talmudic
Death, Burial, and Mourning: Medieval
    and Modern
Dietary Laws
Divorce
Euthanasia
Festivals and Fasts
Magic and Superstition
Marriage
Mikveh
Passover
Priesthood: Biblical
Priesthood: Postbiblical
Sabbath
Script and Scribal Practices
Slavery
Sukkot
Synagogue
Tithes
Vegetarianism

REFERENCES

THOUGHT

A

Abraham ben David of Posquières
c.1120–1198

Provençal rabbinic authority

Cohen, Jeremy, "Rationales for Conjugal Sex in RaABaD's Ba'alei ha-Nefesh," *The Frank Talmage Memorial Volume,* edited by Barry Walfish, Haifa, Israel: Haifa University Press, 1992; Hanover, New Hampshire: University Press of New England, 1993

Scholem, Gershom, *Ursprung und Anfänge der Kabbala,* 1962; as *Origins of the Kabbalah,* edited by R.J. Zwi Werblowsky, Philadelphia: Jewish Publication Society, 1987

Silver, Daniel, *Maimonidean Criticism and the Maimonidean Controversy, 1180–1240,* Leiden, The Netherlands: Brill, 1965

Soloveitchik, Haym, "Rabad of Posquières: A Programmatic Essay," in *Studies in the History of Jewish Society in the Middle Ages and in the Modern Period,* edited by I. Etkes and Y. Salmon, Jerusalem: Magnes Press of Hebrew University, 1980

Twersky, Isadore, *Rabad of Posquières: A Twelfth-Century Talmudist* (Harvard Semitic Series, vol. 18), Cambridge, Massachusetts: Harvard University Press, 1962; revised edition, Philadelphia: Jewish Publication Society, 1980

Rabbi Abraham ben David of Posquières (known as Rabad) was one of the most important and prolific rabbinic figures in southern France during the second half of the 12th century. Born in Narbonne, he founded and supported an academy in Posquières using his personal wealth. A son-in-law and student of Abraham ben Isaac Av Beit Din of Narbonne and a student of Moses ben Joseph and Meshullam of Lunel, Rabad was held in the highest esteem by later rabbinic luminaries such as Nahmanides, Solomon ibn Adret (Rashba), and David ibn Abi Zimra (Radbaz).

TWERSKY's book is the definitive biography of Rabad and is a model for its genre. Twersky begins by noting the positions and spheres of influence that Rabad's teachers occupied, by characterizing the nature of rabbinic scholarship in Provence and the flow of Rabad's career and by depicting Rabad's personality. Subsequent chapters identify and describe Rabad's written works with particular emphasis on the glosses (*hassagot*) to Maimonides' *Mishneh Torah;* outline the sources that Rabad had at his disposal, including an important discussion of Rabad's attitudes toward post-talmudic rabbinic works and commentaries as a source of halakhic precedent; and highlight noteworthy disciples, followers, and descendants of Rabad. The final chapter explores Rabad's attitudes toward secular learning, philosophy, and Kabbalah. For Twersky, the glosses composed by Rabad to the works of Maimonides, Alfasi, and R. Zerahyah ha-Levi, along with a series of topical halakhic monographs, form the core of Rabad's creativity. In marked contrast to the assessments of 19th-century Wissenschaft scholarship, Twersky demonstrates that Rabad was familiar with philosophical teachings and terminology and was not hostile to rationalistic tenets and secular learning. Although a number of later kabbalists viewed Rabad as a link in the chain of esoteric studies and Rabad's son Isaac the Blind was a leading Provençal kabbalist, Twersky questions the depth of Rabad's commitment to this discipline and notes that, in any case, Rabad's halakhic scholarship and writings existed as an entity completely separate from any kabbalistic teachings and conceptions.

SCHOLEM, as part of a comprehensive survey on the origins of mystical study in medieval Europe, maintains that a series of formulations and phenomena attributed to Rabad by kabbalistic tradition suggest that Rabad, no less than other contemporary Provençal talmudists such as Rabbi Jacob the Nazirite, was significantly involved in the transmission of esoteric teachings. For example, Rabad expressed a view concerning proper mystical intentions during prayer, and he is cited by his grandson Rabbi Asher ben David with regard to the identity of the highest *sefirah* (mystical emanation). In addition, Rabad refers to esoteric notions about angels and the demiurge.

Based on the way that Rabad is cited in talmudic commentaries and codes, SOLOVEITCHIK argues that Rabad's *hassagot* to Mishneh Torah were little known and less influential in the medieval period than modern scholarship has assumed. Rabad was regarded by his contemporaries and successors primarily as the author of commentaries and other freestanding works, some of which have been lost. His intellectual independence led Rabad to free himself almost completely from the geonic orbit. Much of Rabad's interpretational insightfulness was absorbed and transformed by Nahmanides and ibn Adret, while late medieval halakhic writings preserved mainly the criticisms of Rabad and other Provençal talmudists, rather than their creativity. As a result, Rabad became known to later generations principally as the author of the *hassagot,* when in fact these *hassagot* were among the last things penned by Rabad. They were based largely on his earlier writings and were not meant to be systematic. Any evaluation of Rabad's impact on subsequent talmudic scholarship must take into account the full range of Rabad's rabbinic writings.

SILVER, in the context of an analysis of some of the issues involved in an early phase of the Maimonidean Controversy, compares the glosses of Rabad to Mishneh Torah, which Silver considers to be quite strident, to other contemporary critiques of Maimonides' halakhic thought. These include criticisms composed by Rabbi Moses ha-Kohen of Lunel and Rabbi Jonathan ha-Kohen of Lunel.

COHEN focuses on one of Rabad's topical treatises, *Ba'alei ha-Nefesh,* which deals with the laws and practices that govern family purity. In the final chapter of that treatise, Rabad enumerates a series of legitimate reasons for sexual relations between husband and wife. Cohen begins with a review of the scholarly assessments of Rabad's open discussion of the motivations for marital relations. Cohen notes that these assessments range from the claim that Rabad demonstrates a more permissive view of sexuality when compared to the mildly ascetic posture found within talmudic literature, to the suggestion that Rabad's approach was closer to the Aristotelian outlook of Maimonides, which adopted a relatively reserved approach concerning sexual relations. Cohen argues that by comparing the material in *Ba'alei ha-Nefesh* to discussions of conjugal sex in Christian writings throughout the medieval period, it is possible to understand better both the uniqueness of and the basis for Rabad's views. Cohen demonstrates that the four reasons given by Rabad correspond closely to those favored by Christian jurists in the mid-12th century. The reasons stemmed, at their core, from an Augustinian model, although, to be sure, Rabad stressed the relative merits of these motives rather than their sinfulness. Cohen's thesis has important implications for measuring the impact of Christian religious thought on medieval rabbinic literature in Christian Europe.

EPHRAIM KANARFOGEL

Abramovitsh, Sholem Yankev *see* Mendele Moykher-Sforim

Abravanel, Isaac   1437–1508

Portuguese-born financier, courtier, Sephardi leader, and theologian, died in Venice

Barzilay, Isaac E., "Isaac Abravanel (1437–1508)," in his *Between Reason and Faith: Anti-Rationalism in Italian Jewish Thought 1250–1650* (Columbia University, Publications in Near and Middle East Studies, series A, vol. 10), Paris and The Hague, The Netherlands: Mouton, 1967

Feldman, Seymour, "1492: A House Divided," in *Crisis and Creativity in the Sephardic World, 1391–1648,* edited by Benjamin R. Gampel, New York and Chichester, West Sussex: Columbia University Press, 1997

Gaon, Solomon, *The Influence of the Catholic Theologian Alfonso Tostado on the Pentateuch Commentary of Isaac Abravanel* (Library of Sephardic History and Thought, vol. 2), New York: Ktav, 1993

Kellner, Menachem Marc, "Introduction," in Abravanel's *Principles of Faith/Rosh Amanah,* Rutherford, New Jersey, and London: Farleigh Dickinson University Press, 1982

Lawee, Eric, "On the Threshold of the Renaissance: New Methods and Sensibilities in the Biblical Commentaries of Isaac Abarbanel," *Viator,* 26, 1995

Netanyahu, B., *Don Isaac Abravanel: Statesman and Philosopher,* Philadelphia: Jewish Publication Society of America, 1953; 5th edition, Ithaca, New York: Cornell University Press, 1998

Reines, Alvin Jay, "Introductory Essay," in *Maimonides and Abrabanel on Prophecy,* Cincinnati, Ohio: Hebrew Union College Press, 1970

Trend, J.B. and H. Loewe (editors), *Isaac Abravanel: Six Lectures by Paul Goodman, L. Rabinowitz (and Others) with an Introductory Essay by H. Loewe,* Cambridge: Cambridge University Press, 1937

As an influential government official and outstanding Jewish community leader and as one of the most prolific and versatile writers of premodern Judaism, Isaac Abravanel has attracted extensive attention from scholars of Jewish literature and history. Much of this attention, however, has taken the form of articles on specific themes rather than larger monographic studies.

TREND and LOEWE's collection of essays contains some of the best in the spate of mostly popular studies written in the years surrounding the quincentenary of Abravanel's birth. Different articles examine Abravanel's biography and such important and challenging subjects as his biblical scholarship and political thought. Leo Strauss's investigation of the latter has proved enduring and provides a valuable case study in Abravanel's relationship to Maimonidean, medieval Christian, and humanist thought as well.

GAON's book—a doctoral dissertation published a half-century after its completion (without updating)—argues, in large measure convincingly, for Abravanel's unstated reliance in his Torah commentaries on biblical exegesis found in works of the mid–15th-century Franciscan scriptural interpreter Alfonso de Madrigal "el Tostado." The historical and intellectual overviews found in the first part of the book must be used with great caution; the author's precise aim and point of view in drawing the connection between Tostado and Abravanel remain elusive, and the value of the book is further limited by the appearance of many untranslated Latin and Hebrew passages. Still, Gaon's book constitutes the only full-length account of a critical facet of Abravanel's sustained interaction with various strands of non-Jewish literature, works of Christian biblical interpretation among them.

NETANYAHU's book is the "great leap forward" in modern Abravanel studies. It remains indispensable especially for the vivid and generally dependable account of Abravanel's life and works contained in its first part. Here Netanyahu skillfully recaptures the drama of Abravanel's biography and the tumult of his times in a manner both academically rigorous and fully accessible to the general reader. This first part also intersperses an overview of Abravanel's wide-ranging literary corpus. Following the bio-bibliographic account comes the second part of the book, which seeks to reconstruct Abravanel's "world outlook." Its point of departure is Netanyahu's understanding that Abravanel was "the father of the [Jewish] messianic movements of the 16th and 17th centuries." Netanyahu's preoccupation with Abravanel's messianism is born of his Zionist orientation. In particular Netanyahu views Abravanel as a leader of a premodern Jewry that, in its expectation of supernatural deliverance, "breathed the atmosphere of dreams rather than reality." That is to say, he failed to actively undertake initiatives such as settlement of the land of Israel that would have placed the Jewish people's modern fate in its own hands. In all of this Netanyahu both overestimates the depth of Abravanel's messianic consciousness after the 1492 expulsion of Spanish Jewry and fails to substantiate his claims for Abravanel's decisive impact on early modern Jewish eschatological speculation and deed. Nonetheless, his book remains unquestionably the best choice for a detailed narration of Abravanel's life and for orientation into Abravanel's principal philosophic, historical, political, and messianic teachings.

BARZILAY synopsizes Abravanel's "antirationalism," a key component of his overall theological posture, viewed here from the peculiar angle (given Abravanel's predominantly Iberian religious formation) of Italian Jewish antirationalism. After sketching the emergence of this antirationalism in Abravanel's younger years, Barzilay unfolds Abravanel's more or less consistent rebuffs of philosophically oriented teachings as transmitted by such medieval predecessors as Maimonides and Gersonides. Following an impressive inventory of texts that attest Abravanel's opposition to, among other things, philosophic naturalism, allegorical interpretation, and soteriology, comes the surprising conclusion that Abravanel's antirationalism "seems to have been of a mere literary nature," a judgment that, if considerably overstated, does bear some weight.

REINES offers a sample of this antirationalism as it emerges in Abravanel's dialogue with his most revered medieval predecessor on the nature of prophecy. Reines describes with clarity Maimonides' naturalistic prophetology and Abravanel's rejoinder that prophecy is a miraculous creation by the special will of God, adeptly illuminating the highly technical topics attendant to this controversy in the process. Following his introductory essay, Reines provides annotated translations from Abravanel's commentary on the chapters devoted to prophecy in Maimonides' *Guide of the Perplexed.*

KELLNER's volume can be read profitably alongside Reines's since it, too, highlights Abravanel's tendency to take Maimonidean texts as a point of departure for theological reflection. Kellner's main contribution in his introduction is to suggest a solution for an obvious difficulty: Abravanel's study of Jewish dogma ends up providing a sharp dissent from the project of creed-formulation, even as the vast majority of Abravanel's work on the subject animatedly defends Maimonides' entry in this field, his famous 13 principles of faith. Kellner's solution, which lays to rest a problem that had long bedeviled scholars, is that Abravanel defended Maimonides' dogmatic principles only as "heuristic devices," while Abravanel's attack on creed formulation is directed "not at the principles as heuristic devices, but as axioms or dogmas the holding of which is necessary in order to merit life in the world to come." Following his introductory essay, Kellner offers an annotated translation of Abravanel's *Principles of Faith,* the only translation of a complete work of Abravanel available in English.

LAWEE's article reflects new emphases in historiography on Abravanel, who is here pictured as a scholar stimulated by a range of Renaissance and especially humanist trends. The article's threefold aim is to explore the impact of Renaissance "historical thinking" on Abravanel, to illustrate the impress of Renaissance sensibilities and methods on Abravanel's biblical exegesis rather than on aspects of his theology, and to argue for the influence of humanist critical categories on Abravanel's exegetical thought processes prior to his arrival in Italy in 1492. This article introduces one side of Abravanel's multifaceted biblical scholarship, an unjustly neglected topic.

Conversely, FELDMAN expresses reservations regarding the depth of Abravanel's embeddedness in a Renaissance milieu. Focusing on the question of his attitude toward philosophy and granting that Abravanel "was aware of some of the newer trends and ideas of the Renaissance," Feldman nonetheless emphasizes Abravanel's "essentially medieval mind," which he contrasts with that of Abravanel's eldest son, Judah, author of the famous Neoplatonic tract *Dialogues of Love.* Feldman suggests that it is the son and not the father who represents a "new era in Jewish social and intellectual history." Some may find this depiction of an Abravanel "house divided" too neat (and conventional), but Feldman makes his case with a combination of care and unapologetic gusto.

ERIC LAWEE

Abravanel, Judah c.1460–after 1522

Portuguese-born Italian philosopher and poet

Dethier, Hubert, "Love and Intellect in Leone Ebreo: The Joys and Pains of Human Passion," in *Neoplatonism and Jewish Thought* (Studies in Neoplatonism, vol. 7), edited by Lenn Evan Goodman, Albany: State University of New York Press, 1992

Feldman, Seymour, "1492: A House Divided," in *Crisis and Creativity in the Sephardic World, 1391–1648,* edited by Benjamin R. Gampel, New York and Chichester, West Sussex: Columbia University Press, 1997

Gershenzon, Shoshana, "The Circle Metaphor in Leone
Ebreo's *Dialoghi d'Amore*," *Da'at*, 29, Summer 1992

Guttmann, Julius, *Philosophies of Judaism: The History of
Jewish Philosophy from Biblical Times to Franz
Rosenzweig*, translated by David W. Silverman, New
York: Holt, Rinehart and Winston, and London:
Routledge, 1964

Ivry, Alfred L., "Remnants of Jewish Averroism in the
Renaissance," in *Jewish Thought in the Sixteenth
Century* (Harvard Judaica Texts and Studies, 2), edited
by Bernard D. Cooperman, Cambridge, Massachusetts:
Harvard University Center for Jewish Studies, 1983

Lesley, Arthur M., "The Place of the *Dialoghi d'amore* in
Contemporaneous Jewish Thought," in *Essential Papers
on Jewish Culture in Renaissance and Baroque Italy*
(Essential Papers on Jewish Studies), edited by David B.
Ruderman, New York: New York University Press, 1992

Lesley, Arthur M., "Proverbs, Figures, and Riddles: The
Dialogues of Love as a Hebrew Humanist Composition,"
in *The Midrashic Imagination: Jewish Exegesis, Thought,
and History,* edited by Michael Fishbane, Albany: State
University of New York Press, 1993

Milburn, A.R., "Leone Ebreo and the Renaissance," in *Isaac
Abravanel: Six Lectures by Paul Goodman, L.
Rabinowitz (and others) with an Introductory Essay by
H. Loewe; Edited by J.B. Trend and H. Loewe,*
Cambridge: Cambridge University Press, 1937

Nelson, John Charles, *Renaissance Theory of Love: The
Context of Giordano Bruno's "Eroici Furori,"* New York:
Columbia University Press, 1958

Perry, T. Anthony, "Introduction," in Leone Ebreo's
Dialogues d'amour (University of North Carolina Studies
in Comparative Literature, no. 59), Chapel Hill:
University of North Carolina Press, 1974

Perry, T. Anthony, *Erotic Spirituality: The Integrative
Tradition from Leone Ebreo to John Donne,* University:
University of Alabama Press, 1980

Pines, Shlomo, "Medieval Doctrines in Renaissance Garb?:
Some Jewish and Arabic Sources of Leone Ebreo's
Doctrines," in *Jewish Thought in the Sixteenth Century*
(Harvard Judaica Texts and Studies, 2), edited by
Bernard D. Cooperman, Cambridge, Massachusetts:
Harvard University Center for Jewish Studies, 1983

Scheindlin, Raymond P., "Yehuda Abravanel to His Son,"
Judaism, 41(2), Spring 1992

Scrivano, Riccardo, "Platonic and Cabalistic Elements in the
Hebrew Culture of Renaissance Italy: Leone Ebreo and
his *Dialoghi d'amore*," in *Ficino and Renaissance
Neoplatonism* (University of Toronto Italian Studies, 1),
edited by Konrad Eisenbichler and Olga Zorzi Pugliese,
Ottawa, Ontario: Dovehouse Editions Canada, 1986

Judah ben Isaac Abravanel was the son of Isaac Abravanel, the
outstanding Jewish leader in 15th-century Portugal, Spain,
and Italy, as well as a prolific Bible commentator. Judah was
born in Portugal and was active in Italy as a physician, philo-
sophical-religious writer, and poet. He is called Leone Ebreo
in the 16th-century editions of his surviving book, *The Dialogues of Love*. This is an encyclopedic work in the form of
three platonic dialogues between Philo and Sophia about love;
it became popular in Italian, Latin, French, and Spanish. The
authoritative studies of the author and his work are not in
English. An English reader can, however, gain an adequate idea
of the life of the writer, his work, and his influence from articles that should be generally available in university libraries
with a respectable Judaica collection.

The greatest task for understanding Judah is to decide in
which context he must be placed to be understood. Studies of
Judah and his work have generally approached him either historically, as a recipient or transmitter of influence, or through
philosophical analysis. Philosophical analyses have concentrated on connecting his statements either to ancient thinkers,
especially Plato and Plotinus; to the medieval Islamic and Jewish philosophers, mainly Averroës and Avicenna; or to Renaissance Christian contemporaries, especially Ficino, Pico, and
Bruno. More recently, he has been considered as a literary and
rhetorical author.

GUTTMANN's generally authoritative reference work,
dating from 1933, characterizes the *Dialogues* by contrasting
it with the medieval thinkers discussed in his survey, as well
as by connecting it with them. Judah derives from Hasdai
Crescas a conception of love that animates the static structures of medieval Aristotelian conceptions of the universe.
Knowledge in the *Dialogues* similarly becomes more than
discursive knowledge and enables the unification of humanity with God.

MILBURN balances intelligent discussion of Judah's biography, of central arguments of the *Dialogues*, and of the
book's influence on Italian, Spanish, and French thought and
literature. This is still the article with which to begin studying about Judah.

NELSON's summary of the main arguments of the *Dialogues* frequently quotes the book, in Italian and English, to
illustrate similarities and differences between statements in it
and statements in Renaissance philosophical love treatises by
Marsilio Ficino, Pietro Bembo, Baldassare Castiglione, and
Giordano Bruno.

PERRY's introduction to this 1974 edition of an early
French translation clearly and helpfully traces the argument
of the *Dialogues*, without reference to external sources. The
first chapter of PERRY (1980) clearly analyzes the arguments
of the *Dialogues*, and the second discusses the importance of
the dialogue form. Subsequent chapters examine the tradition
that Perry considers the *Dialogues* to have begun in the writings of French, Spanish, and English poets: Maurice Scève, Per-
nette du Guillet, Antoine Héroët, Jorge de Montemayor,
William Shakespeare, and John Donne.

PINES identifies and discusses Judah's references and allusions to specific medieval Arabic, Latin, and Hebrew philosophic texts. He shows that Avicenna's "Epistle on Love" is
the Arabic book that resembles the *Dialogues* most closely,
although it is not known to have been available to Judah. No
Christian thinker is mentioned in the *Dialogues*, but the contemporaneous writings of Marsilio Ficino, the Florentine
translator and commentator of Plato's Greek texts, obviously
are behind some of Judah's statements.

IVRY shows how the *Dialogues of Love* reflects late 15th-century Jewish discussion of the relation of philosophy to faith. He contrasts Judah, the representative of the Neoplatonic tendency of Jewish philosophy in Italy, to Elijah Delmedigo, an Averroist, to show the continuing importance of Averroism. More precisely, Ivry shows ways in which Judah harmonizes Platonic with Averroistic assumptions, methods, and conclusions rather than conforming exclusively to platonism.

FELDMAN contrasts the opinions of Judah with those of his father, specifically the ways in which they discussed creation and immortality. Judah's dialogue form aroused interest among Christians by discussing cosmology and the relation of philosophy to prophecy in terms of Eros, taken from Plato's *Symposium*. In contrast, Isaac's commentaries and treatises, being in Hebrew and using the manner and the range of philosophical reference of earlier Jewish philosophers, sought to address a Jewish, and even specifically Sephardi, audience.

GERSHENZON examines the concept of the circle, through which Judah described the operation of divine love throughout the universe. She examines the Christian humanist writings, particularly Ficino's commentaries on several of Plato's dialogues, to which Judah clearly alluded. She also shows that Judah occasionally employed the arguments of Giovanni Pico della Mirandola, another Florentine contemporary, to dispute Ficino's formulations.

DETHIER argues that the ways in which Judah discussed the interaction of human and divine intelligence, taken from Averroës and Avicenna, define the cosmos as unified in a pantheistic way. His demanding, allusive analysis shows the similarity of the most important parts of the *Dialogues* to passages in Plotinus and Ficino and contrasts Judah's intellectual love of God with Spinoza's.

SCRIVANO uses newly discovered documents to reopen biographical questions. He also tries to understand the teachings in the *Dialogues* as a confrontation between Jewish thought and European culture.

LESLEY (1992) analyzes the rhetorical situation of Judah at the end of the 15th century in Italy. Judah tried to unify a Jewish audience that was divided by fundamentally incompatible intellectual tendencies. LESLEY (1993) reconstructs the authorial choices that Judah faced in choosing to write in a particular form of dialogue about philosophy and Kabbalah. Use of the dialogue genre and rhetorical argumentation antagonized Jewish philosophers.

SCHEINDLIN translates and interprets the most substantial other writing by Judah that survives, a poetic complaint about fate from 1503. The poem is addressed to Judah's son, Isaac, who was converted to Christianity in Portugal. Scheindlin believes that "the poem's address to the boy appears not to be a mere rhetorical apostrophe but an actual address meant to be read by the addressee," and this shapes his sensitive translation.

ARTHUR M. LESLEY

Abrogation of Law and Custom

Ben-Menahem, Hanina, *Judicial Deviation in Talmudic Law: Governed by Men, not by Rules* (Jewish Law in Context, vol. 1), New York: Harwood Academic Publishers, 1991
Brooks, Roger, *The Spirit of the Ten Commandments: Shattering the Myth of Rabbinic Legalism*, San Francisco: Harper and Row, 1990
Fishman, Talya, *Shaking the Pillars of Exile: "Voice of a Fool," an Early Modern Jewish Critique of Rabbinic Culture* (Stanford Studies in Jewish History and Culture), Stanford, California: Stanford University Press, 1997
Jacobs, Louis, *A Tree of Life: Diversity, Flexibility, and Creativity in Jewish Law* (Littman Library of Jewish Civilization), Rutherford, New Jersey: Fairleigh Dickinson University Press, and London: Associated University Presses, 1983
Kirschenbaum, Aaron, *Equity in Jewish Law: Beyond Equity: Halakhic Aspirationism in Jewish Civil Law* (Library of Jewish Law and Ethics, vol. 18), New York: Yeshiva University Press, 1991
Scholem, Gershom, *The Messianic Idea in Judaism and Other Essays on Jewish Spirituality*, New York: Schocken, and London: Allen and Unwin, 1971
Weinstein, Sara, *Piety and Fanaticism: Rabbinic Criticism of Religious Stringency*, Northvale, New Jersey: Aronson, 1997

Abrogation refers to the temporary or permanent annulment of law and custom that has been rendered counterproductive or intolerable by changing circumstances. Common sense, inherited tradition, and judicial procedure alternately overturn and authorize the policies and programs of Judaism (Deuteronomy 17:8–11). Some interpreters deny that religious laws are abrogated per se since changes are legally justified (e.g., Eduyot 1:5); others demand that even biblical sanctions, if deemed unjust, be abrogated (e.g., Yebamot 89b). The dispute reveals a dilemma: regulated laws are mechanisms that refine custom, but regularized customs provide contexts in which law applies. This review considers studies of abrogation, obligation, and supererogation, bypassing discussion of the abundant polemical and apologetic exchanges with pagans, Christians, and Muslims on these issues of the scope of the law and its immutability.

The premise of JACOBS's elegant study is that a great variety of "opinions have had a voice in determining halakhah." He contends that any ordinance, except the most explicit of "blanket prohibition[s]" ratified by legislation, can be rejected or revised in "response to changed conditions and social needs"; other sanctions are "not abolished but circumvented" through legal fictions. But obligation deriving from nonlegal, aggadic sources invoking philosophy, mysticism, or moral psychology entails ambiguity: laws are "vehicles for the expression of . . . Jewish ideals and ideas," and yet are shaped by customary Jewish patterns of life to which they apply. The principle that custom can override law (Yebamot 12:1) suggests to Jacobs, perhaps too easily, that "the ultimate authority for determining which observances are binding . . . is the historical experience of the people Israel."

Abrogation in ritual and morality is probed by BROOKS. Citing the Mishnah and the Jerusalem Talmud, he explains how the spirit and underlying principles of Written Torah guide a legal process and dialectical exchange in Oral Torah. Brooks maintains that rabbinic "discourse educates and elevates one to new levels of holiness" while "allowing the law to continue to grow and encompass further areas of life in a practicable way." Means and ends of sanctification are ambiguous: "all that people observe in everyday life . . . exists within the realms of choices laid out by the Bible." On the other hand, this cogent but slim book adduces evidence that if one's intention was not to further the spirit of the Torah (in its narrowest sense), the law in fact might be abrogated.

Whereas Kirschenbaum's *Equity in Jewish Law: Halakhic Perspectives in Law: Formalism and Flexibility in Jewish Civil Law* (1991) surveys talmudic fairness and justice, KIRSCHENBAUM's companion volume treats exceptions and extensions of equity. Custom and law apply differently in varying situations because the "minimal requirements of the scriptural letter . . . justify rabbinic guidelines that 'deviate' from scriptural norms in order to achieve scriptural ideals."

BEN-MENAHEM identifies exemplary rabbinic figures who violated religious sanctions that conflicted with moral imperatives. He distinguishes positions proposing correctness of law and custom in theory as distinct from determining their effectiveness in practice. A "norm allowing departure . . . validates judicial decisions based on extra-legal considerations." According to this engaging study, judges may depart from previous abrogation as well as from prevailing rules.

WEINSTEIN gathers sources favoring the view that excessive devotion degrades, rather than enriches, religious law and custom. She posits that suspicions arise in the Talmud of attempts to combine humanity and divinity by making worship more prominent or rigorous than necessary. A pious individual imagines one can "better serve one's Creator by adopting a more difficult way of life." Weinstein warns that self-denial risks becoming self-aggrandizement by attracting attention, humiliating others, or diminishing the place of basic commandments. Opinions on ascetic behavior are presented ranging from legislating fasts that cause spiritual, if not physical, anguish to lifestyles shunning all but a few eccentric performances. Weinstein's point of view contends that "personal religious expression" should result in "being an especially kind person who is concerned with the welfare of others" and in zealotry in civil but not ritual matters, since humans understand themselves and each other better than they do God.

SCHOLEM keenly elucidates the "problem of the validity of all previous tradition." This crisis of early modernity comes to a head with the 17th-century messianic pretender Shabbetai Tsevi and his disciples, who claimed to anticipate, incite, or witness revolutionary transformation. A "sense of imminent catastrophe" prompted ancient exilic law and recent custom alike. A groundbreaking essay, "Redemption through Sin," argues that contradictions between inner sincerity and outward deception in *converso* experience led radicals to declare that public "violation of the Torah is now its true fulfillment." This attitude contrasts with the neutralization of messianism in a hasidic emphasis on salvation through quietist renewal instead of historical revolution. In all, traditional valorization

enables spontaneity in receptivity, allowing the anarchic breeze of mysticism and messianism to sweep through the well-ordered house of law and custom.

A vital historical account is presented in FISHMAN's vivid study and translation of the Venetian rabbi Leone Modena's 1623 enigma, *Kol Sakhal (Voice of a Fool)*. This anonymous essay, whose author's identity Fishman confirms, sets out to revamp, if not refute, rabbinic Judaism. According to Fishman, Modena appealed to reason and common sense rather than mysticism and messianism, distinguishing sharply between unambiguous legislation and more customary practices and "voluntary enhancement of religious performance." Fishman dissociates Modena's proposal from subsequent Reform and Orthodox movements: Modena sought to affirm the law by streamlining but not undermining it. Fishman's effort articulates a promising method of inquiry into texts that either "flirted with potentially disruptive approaches to interpretation or unequivocally violated the culture's juridical boundaries."

GREGORY KAPLAN

Abulafia, Abraham   c.1240–after 1291

Aragonese-born pioneer of "Ecstatic Kabbalah"

Idel, Moshe, *Kabbalah: New Perspectives*, New Haven, Connecticut: Yale University Press, 1988

Idel, Moshe, *The Mystical Experience in Abraham Abulafia* (SUNY Series in Judaica), Albany: State University of New York Press, 1988

Idel, Moshe, *Studies in Ecstatic Kabbalah* (SUNY Series in Judaica), Albany: State University of New York Press, 1988

Idel, Moshe, *Language, Torah, and Hermeneutics in Abraham Abulafia* (SUNY Series in Judaica), Albany: State University of New York Press, 1989

Idel, Moshe, *Hasidism: Between Ecstasy and Magic* (SUNY Series in Judaica), Albany: State University of New York Press, 1995

Kaplan, Aryeh, *Meditation and Kabbalah*, York Beach, Maine: Weiser, 1982

Scholem, Gershom, *Major Trends in Jewish Mysticism*, New York: Schocken, 1941; 3rd edition, New York: Schocken, 1954, and London: Thames and Hudson, 1955

Scholem, Gershom, *Kabbalah*, New York: New American Library, 1974

The Spanish Jewish mystic Abraham Abulafia broke with established kabbalistic circles that favored a long and rigorous course of study exploring the "true" nature of God. Abulafia's meditative science of letters did not necessitate a systematic approach to God through the study of the hierarchy of sefirot. Rather, Abulafia believed that knowledge of God could be obtained immediately through a technique of meditation upon all the letters of the Torah wherein the name of God was hidden. The recovery of Abraham Abulafia as a historical figure is largely due to the work of two scholars: Gershom Scholem and Moshe Idel.

SCHOLEM (1941) and SCHOLEM (1974) represent the essential point of departure for any study of Jewish mysticism in general and Abraham Abulafia in particular. Scholem places Abulafia and ecstatic Kabbalah within a sweeping historical context and, more particularly, within the context of 13th-century kabbalistic literature. Scholem's two surveys of the history of Jewish mysticism guide the reader through the various schools of Jewish mysticism. Scholem also allows the reader an insight into reactions to Abulafia's meditative science of the combination of letters, where the letters of the Torah are transformed into a divine music or a spiritual language that moves the devotee toward the name of God manifest in all creation. Within Scholem's systematic studies of Jewish mysticism, however, Abulafia's impact upon other early kabbalists is largely unnoticed. One of Scholem's students, Moshe Idel, has added a number of key works addressing the history of Jewish mysticism and Abulafia's historical significance.

IDEL (1989), drawing on the author's doctoral dissertation (Hebrew University of Jerusalem, 1976), reveals Abulafia's role in introducing to Jewish mysticism a more intense interest in language as a means of exploring a new realm of knowledge about the universe beyond the domains of the natural sciences or philosophy. As the putative language of God and the physical universe, Hebrew became the focal point for such discussions. Abulafia's hermeneutical system applied to the Torah, which reflected the intellectual structure of the universe and God himself, and constituted a significant departure from existing kabbalistic thought. Even so, Abulafian Kabbalah still accepted Torah as an allegorical process moving the mystic toward divine and intrasefirotic knowledge.

IDEL (1988b) and IDEL (1988c) promote the most in-depth analyses available of Abulafia as the founder of ecstatic Kabbalah. While rejecting possible links between Abulafia and the Cathars, Idel does offer tempting suggestions of connections between Abulafia and Sufi mysticism. Idel attributes Abulafia's breadth of influence to subtle dialogues that generated a blend of kabbalistic and Sufi thought in the Middle East. The best of contemporary scholars dealing with Abulafia, Idel demonstrates Abulafia's creative exploration of Maimonidean thought to break with traditional speculative Aristotelian philosophy as the means to the knowledge of God. Abulafian mysticism avoided the need for aesthetic discipline in favor of a strengthened intellect. All the while, Abulafia, who increasingly perceived himself in messianic terms and at one point traveled to Rome intent on confronting the pope, envisioned Judaism as the universal religion and disparaged Christianity and Islam. He believed that only through mystical experience induced through the impassioned intellectualized permutation of Hebrew letters into music and colors could the human intellect momentarily merge with God. Abulafia used erotic images as metaphors for the ecstatic consummation of human experience in union and in harmony with God as active intellect. Contrary to traditional Sefirotic Kabbalah, Abulafian mysticism focused on the benefits for the mystic and rejected any possibility of human influence upon God.

IDEL (1988a) and IDEL (1995) address Abulafia's place in a key chapter in the history of Jewish mysticism, namely, the development of Hasidism in the 18th and 19th centuries. In these studies, Idel continues his break with Scholem's more traditional historical line in favor of a more phenomenological approach to Jewish mysticism and Hasidism. Consequently, rather than viewing it as a direct response to Sabbatianism, Idel interprets Hasidism as an evolving, emerging force, drawing largely upon non-Lurianic schools, elements of magic, and Abulafia's ecstatic Kabbalah.

Within the merging streams of Jewish religious experience, Idel interprets the history of Jewish mysticism as a positive, creative interaction of schools of thought rather than a negative response to a misplaced messianism. As such, Abulafian Kabbalah is intimately tied to essential Judaism and specifically to extreme devotion to Jewish law and the growth of kabbalistic literature. Although Idel's coupling of Gnostic texts with Jewish speculative literature is arguably very weak, his works offer the reader an absorbing record of mystical practices applied by the Abulafian school. Furthermore, Idel provocatively interprets modern Hasidism as a merging of two schools of kabbalistic thought, allowing for a theological elite but opening the possibility of ecstatic experiences to the masses.

KAPLAN's popularizing anthology is short on analysis, but it does provide the English reader with a selection of primary source materials for the life and thought of Abulafia, along with a number of other classic texts of Jewish mystical spirituality.

DAVID MEIER

Acosta, Uriel 1583 or 1584–1640

Portugese-born Amsterdam theologian and critic of rabbinic Judaism

Altmann, Alexander, "Eternality of Punishment: A Theological Controversy within the Amsterdam Rabbinate in the Thirties of the Seventeenth Century," in *Essential Papers on Kabbalah*, edited by L. Fine, New York: New York University Press, 1995

Bergman, Peter M. (editor), *Uriel Acosta: A Specimen of Human Life*, New York: Bergman, 1967

Fishman, Talya, *Shaking the Pillars of Exile: 'Voice of a Fool,' an Early Modern Jewish Critique of Rabbinic Culture* (Stanford Studies in Jewish History and Culture), Stanford, California: Stanford University Press, 1997

Porges, Nathan, "Gebhardt's Book on Uriel da Costa," *Jewish Quarterly Review*, 19, 1928

Salomon, H.P. and I.S.D. Sassoon (editors), *Examination of Pharisaic Traditions/Exame das tradições phariseas: Facsimile of the Unique Copy in the Royal Library of Copenhagen, Supplemented by Semuel da Silva's Treatise on the Immortality of the Soul/Tratado da immortalidade da alma* (Brill Studies in Intellectual History, vol. 44), New York: Brill, 1993

Sassoon, I.S.D., "The Relevance for Today of Uriel da Costa's *Exame das tradições fariseas*," *Studia Rosenthaliana*, 28, 1994

Sonne, Isaiah, "Da Costa Studies," *Jewish Quarterly Review*, 22, 1932

Sonne, Isaiah, "Leon Modena and the da Costa Circle in Amsterdam," *Hebrew Union College Annual*, 21, 1948

Uriel Acosta (or da Costa or d'Acosta) gained fame as one of the most significant Jewish freethinkers before the modern era and as a possible influence on a far more important Jewish radical, Baruch (Benedict) Spinoza. Knowledge concerning this tragic figure changed considerably in the late 20th century due to the amazing discovery made by H.P. Salomon of a surviving copy of Acosta's book attacking rabbinic Judaism. This work was burned when it appeared, and until Salomon's discovery scholars assumed the entire edition was lost. With the examination of this find, much of the earlier Acosta scholarship has been superseded. A large amount of material on Acosta is available in addition to that listed above, but it is either unpublished (most important is material in Howard Adelman's 1985 Brandeis University Ph.D. dissertation on Leon Modena), not available in English (including work by C. Gebhardt, I.S. Révah, and H.P. Salomon), or scattered in books on other subjects.

SALOMON and SASSOON is clearly the place to begin any serious study of Acosta. Their book opens with a relatively short introduction dealing with biographical, philosophical, and historic topics pertaining to the thought of Acosta. A small bibliography follows, which will be particularly useful to those with additional language skills. The heart of the book is the facsimile edition of Acosta's *Examination of Pharisaic Traditions* followed by an English translation from the original Portuguese. Here Acosta develops what might be called his "early heretical" position against rabbinic theology and metaphysics, striking for its somewhat neo-Karaite biblicist position. After Acosta's treatise comes the earlier refutation penned by his adversary, the Hamburg physician Samuel da Silva, *Treatise on the Immortality of the Soul*, here presented in English alone, the Portuguese original being available as a companion volume. This is one of many works by scholars of the Western Sephardi diaspora defending the rabbinic position on the immortality of the soul. After da Silva's work there follows a group of appendixes, the most important of which is Acosta's autobiography, published by the Dutch theologian P. Van Limborch. This work, assumed to be genuine by most scholars, was allegedly left behind when Acosta committed suicide. It tells of Acosta's unhappy life, but it also incorporates a theological position far more radical than that for which he argued in the 1620s. The volume ends with Acosta family trees and indexes.

BERGMAN's volume consists entirely of primary sources concerning Acosta. It opens with the same autobiography found in Salomon and Sassoon's appendix. Next comes the highly important "Eleven Theses against the Tradition," a small work attributed by most scholars to Acosta, though it was composed anonymously. This composition, which was sent to the Venice rabbis, appears to contain the earliest known version of Acosta's antirabbinic position. Following are several documents surrounding Acosta's excommunications, at least one of which does not properly belong in this context. Some readers will find useful the preface by John Whiston to his English translation of the autobiography (1740), and Van Limborch's attempt to defend Christianity against Acosta's attack on religion.

PORGES offers a detailed critique of the most complete work on Acosta before Salomon and Sassoon, C. Gebhardt's *Die Schriften des Uriel da Costa mit Einleitung, Übertragung und Regesten* (Amsterdam, The Netherlands: Bibliotheca Spinozana, 1922). For the most part the design of his comments is to correct biographical and historical details where he feels Gebhardt erred. There are also substantive discussions, however, particularly regarding the terms "Sadducee" and "Pharisee" as they are used in the literature of the Acosta affair and the nascent biblical criticism as expressed by Acosta and Spinoza.

SONNE (1932) attempts to demonstrate that a famous work of Jewish radical thought called *Kol Sakhal (Voice of a Fool)*, found among the papers of Rabbi Leon Modena in Venice, was in fact a formulation of Acosta's position. Modena had been assigned by the Venice rabbinate to refute the "Eleven Theses" and had various contacts with Amsterdam Jewry.

SONNE (1948) attempts to defend his 1932 thesis and to add evidence in the form of a letter from Modena to the Amsterdam physician David Farrar, whom Sonne believes was connected with the Acosta affair. Farrar was then being accused of heresy in Amsterdam, and Modena comes to his defense. The evidence for Sonne's original thesis and his attempt to relate the Farrar-Modena correspondence to Acosta have both been matters of controversy in subsequent literature.

FISHMAN deals with Sonne's questions about the relationship between Acosta's critiques and the positions found in *Kol Sakhal* that resemble Acosta's in some ways. Fishman uses recent historiography to delve deeply into a comparison of doctrines expressed in each of Acosta's works and those in *Kol Sakhal,* and she treats theological positions as well as historic relationships in some detail. Much may be learned from this volume about early modern Jewish skepticism in view of a well supported understanding of both the Sephardi and Italian contexts, which goes far beyond Sonne.

ALTMANN's article does not deal for the most part with Acosta himself, but it supplies critical background for understanding the Acosta affair in the context of Amsterdam Jewry and the Western Sephardi diaspora. Altmann deals with the related rabbinic treatises on immortality of the soul, explaining among other things why this topic raised the hackles of former *conversos* in Amsterdam, Hamburg, and Venice so much. Whether or not any individual treatise was directed at Acosta himself, it is clear that the Acosta affair set the agenda for much of the ongoing debate about the soul, in which Amsterdam Sephardi manuscript collections are so rich.

SASSOON's short article is an attempt to define Acosta's theological views and to relate them to present-day theological controversies. The author's desire to welcome Acosta back into the Jewish fold is reminiscent of the annulment of Spinoza's excommunication by some 20th-century Zionists who saw him as an ideological ally. Sassoon's argument is undermined by the more radical position of Acosta in his autobiography.

MATT GOLDISH

Afghanistan *see* Iran, Afghanistan, and Central Asia

Aggadah *see* Midrash Aggadah

Agnon, Shmuel Yosef 1888–1970

Polish-born Israeli writer, Nobel laureate in literature

Aberbach, David, *At the Handles of the Lock: Themes in the Fiction of S.J. Agnon*, Rutherford, New Jersey: Fairleigh Dickinson University Press, 1983

Band, Arnold J., *Nostalgia and Nightmare: A Study in the Fiction of S.Y. Agnon*, Berkeley: University of California Press, 1968

Fisch, Harold, *S.Y. Agnon* (Modern Literature Monographs), New York: Ungar, 1975

Hochman, Baruch, *The Fiction of S.Y. Agnon*, Ithaca, New York: Cornell University Press, 1970

Hoffman, Anne Golomb, *Between Exile and Return: S.Y. Agnon and the Drama of Writing* (SUNY Series in Modern Jewish Literature and Culture), Albany: State University of New York Press, 1991

Katz, Stephen, *The Centrifugal Novel: S.Y. Agnon's Poetics of Composition*, Madison, New Jersey: Fairleigh Dickinson University Press, 1999

Patterson, David and Glenda Abramson (editors), *Tradition and Trauma: Studies in the Fiction of S.J. Agnon* (Modern Hebrew Classics), Boulder, Colorado: Westview, 1994

Shaked, Gershon, *Shmuel Yosef Agnon: A Revolutionary Traditionalist* (Modern Jewish Masters Series, 3), translated by Jeffrey M. Green, New York: New York University Press, 1989

Born in Galicia, Poland, Shmuel Yosef Agnon became the first Hebrew-language author to win the Nobel Prize for literature in 1966. His writings reveal rabbinic, hasidic, and modernist influences, while his style—a lyrical mixture of irony and dreamlike fantasy—invites a myriad of interpretations, including some comparisons with his contemporary, Franz Kafka. A number of critical studies of Agnon are available in English.

BAND's volume is one of the earliest English-language texts to provide a resume of Agnon's works and a review of the available critical studies. Published during Agnon's lifetime, and therefore an incomplete record of the author's career, this book nevertheless offers a vast, detailed, and well-researched survey of Agnon's literary devices and achievements. Noting such important facts as Agnon's meticulous editing of his own works and his quest for literary perfection, Band creates a multifaceted portrait of the writer's productive life. This book makes frequent references to Agnon's works and is best suited for readers with some previous knowledge of his writings.

HOCHMAN provides a good, basic overview of Agnon's work and worldview that includes pertinent insights about Agnon's roots. Hochman discusses, for example, the importance of the shtetl, which was in a state of decline by the time Agnon reached adulthood in prewar Europe but remained an institution that haunted Jewish thought and behavior. In such works as *The Bridal Canopy* (arguably his most famous novel), Agnon alludes to the shtetl to express an ambivalence toward the past, while invoking an atmospheric tone "permeated by a consciousness of how precarious tradition itself is, as well as how tenacious." Hochman also shows that the characters in Agnon's works are usually passive and alienated, drifting through life in search of meaning and identity. On the one hand, these characters cling to the safe but stagnant world of their ancestors; on the other hand, they feel the powerful pull of contemporary society, which, although dynamic, is morally and spiritually empty. Paradoxically, the characters' neurotic energy, generated as they seek a purpose in life, illuminates their inner spiritual world.

FISCH has written a helpful critical overview and introduction to Agnon. Like Hochman, Fisch stresses both the Eastern European social and cultural milieu that Agnon left behind and his ambivalent embrace of the State of Israel. Fisch does not trace the chronological development of Agnon's works, focusing instead on certain themes and stylistic modes; elaborating on common qualities found in Agnon's plots; and analyzing the threads that unify his work. Despite the lack of a full chronology, Fisch does explain how Agnon's biography and literary style converge.

SHAKED mixes biography and criticism while investigating the effects of Agnon's personal life on his literary production. The critic discusses how Agnon departs from themes and values familiar to East European culture, even as he simultaneously uses sacred Judaic references in his writings. Shaked also demonstrates that Agnon's complex literary persona, particularly as expressed through his "narcissistic stories" of the 1930s, reflects both the importance that the novelist attaches to Jewish history and his dual allegiance to the Zionist and secularist movements of the early 20th century.

ABERBACH explores the "salient psychological themes" of Agnon's works in a critical (but not historical) study. Drawing heavily on the work of Freud and other preeminent psychoanalysts, Aberbach argues that the hopeless immaturity of Agnon's characters results from oedipal conflict. Similarly, Aberbach contends that Agnon frequently uses gender-role reversals ("masculinized women" and latently homosexual men) and love triangles to depict a world replete with guilt, loneliness, and inadequacy, a world in which "the soul is missing." In fact, Aberbach identifies schizoid elements in Agnon himself, asserting that the author evinces a "false face, detachment from people, childishness, egocentricity, and a sense of inferiority." The dreamlike quality of Agnon's works, Aberbach concludes, points to a preoccupation with inner reality.

HOFFMAN goes one step further than Aberbach, for her study integrates psychoanalytic concerns from earlier intellectuals such as Jung and Freud with the more contemporary emphases of deconstruction and gender studies. This highly dense work places Agnon within the context of the 20th century, rather than discussing his intellectual debts to traditional literature, as Hoffman expounds on Agnon's use of language as a tool of modernist sensibilities. Hoffman offers refreshingly contemporary insights into Agnon's literary transformations, themes, and sources, and she shows how Agnon moves from his Eastern European origins to the broader canvas of Israeli life and culture by adapting his use of the Hebrew language. Hoffman further argues that the masculine/feminine imagery in Agnon's literature reflects patriarchal order. This book is not for the beginner; it demands knowledge of Hebrew language, literature, and culture, as well as a background in psychological and literary theories.

PATTERSON and ABRAMSON have edited an eclectic compilation of essays, which were originally presented at Mount Holyoke College in honor of the centenary of Agnon's birth. This book succeeds on many levels: it provides an introduction for the novice reader and deeper analyses for those already familiar with Agnon's style and messages. Aberbach analyzes the homosexual motif in Agnon's work, while Hoffman discusses the symbolism of the "Mad Dog" in Agnon's novel *Temol Shilshom (Only Yesterday)*. Contributions from Israeli critics as important as the novelist Aharon Appelfeld help make this book unique, as they offer perspectives rarely available to the English reader. Appelfeld movingly describes his friendship with Agnon, who had an immense influence on the author and his contemporaries: "He showed us that Jewishness is not an anachronism. It is possible to write about Jews in small towns and be a universalist. Jewishness is not an artistic obstacle—it is a richness to be sought."

KATZ draws on discarded and overlooked items from Agnon's archives (in search, he says, of the "ur-text," or original text) to argue that all of Agnon's published works convey related themes and similar characters. Each text illuminates the others, ultimately revealing something about Agnon himself, who deliberately blurs distinctions between his private and literary personas. His fiction serves to solidify his literary identity, enhancing his mythic stature among his reading public, particularly in Israel, where he is viewed as a "national treasure."

Considering Agnon's legacy, it is questionable whether the reputation of such a "national treasure" needs embellishment. Over the years, Jewish literature in Israel and the diaspora has flourished, but later generations of Jewish and Israeli writers, no matter how successful or innovative, must continue to acknowledge Agnon as their movement's most prolific and creative pioneer.

EDITH LUBETSKI

Agricultural Laws

Avery-Peck, Alan J., *The Priestly Gift in Mishnah: A Study of Tractate Terumot* (Brown Judaic Studies, no. 20), Chico, California: Scholars Press, 1981

Avery-Peck, Alan J., *Mishnah's Division of Agriculture: A History and Theology of Seder Zeraim* (Brown Judaic Studies, no. 79), Chico, California: Scholars Press, 1985

Brooks, Roger, *Support for the Poor in the Mishnaic Law of Agriculture: Tractate Peah* (Brown Judaic Studies, no. 43), Chico, California: Scholars Press, 1983

Fager, Jeffrey A., *Land Tenure and the Biblical Jubilee: Uncovering Hebrew Ethics through the Sociology of Knowledge* (Journal for the Study of the Old Testament Supplement Series, 155), Sheffield, South Yorkshire: JSOT, 1993

Grunfeld, Isidor, *Shemittah and Yobel*, London and New York: Soncino, 1972

Haas, Peter J., *A History of the Mishnaic Law of Agriculture: Tractate Maaser Sheni* (Brown Judaic Studies, no. 18), Chico, California: Scholars Press, 1980

Jaffee, Martin, *Mishnah's Theology of Tithing: A Study of Tractate Maaserot* (Brown Judaic Studies, no. 19), Chico, California: Scholars Press, 1981

Mandelbaum, Irving, *A History of the Mishnaic Law of Agriculture: Kilayim: Translation and Exegesis* (Brown Judaic Studies, no. 26), Chico, California: Scholars Press, 1982

Newman, Louis E., *The Sanctity of the Seventh Year: A Study of Mishnah Tractate Shebiit* (Brown Judaic Studies, no. 44), Chico, California: Scholars Press, 1983

Sarason, Richard S., *A History of the Mishnaic Law of Agriculture: Section Three, A Study of Tractate Demai* (Studies in Judaism in Late Antiquity, vol. 27), Leiden: Brill, 1979

The first 11 tractates of the Mishnah, known as Seder Zeraim, provide the primary source for agricultural law within Judaism. These tractates discuss the proper modes of producing, processing, distributing (to priests, Levites, and the poor), and consuming the produce of the Holy Land. Zeraim exists in Mishnah, Tosefta, and the Jerusalem Talmud; the Babylonian Talmud provides gemara only for the first tractate (Berakhot), which deals with blessings. This lack of Babylonian gemara is perhaps not surprising, as the laws pertain specifically to the Holy Land, not to agriculture as such.

In the late 1970s and early 1980s, Jacob Neusner at Brown University directed a number of graduate students in a systematic study of Mishnah Zeraim. Their common purpose was to understand what the law meant to the framers of Mishnah. That is, they were studying the social, political, and theological roots of rabbinic Judaism. A number of the dissertations produced in that effort have appeared in the Brown Judaic Studies series. While Neusner's views on the fundamental themes of Mishnah may be controversial, this collection of studies remains the most thorough treatment in English of agricultural law in Judaism.

AVERY-PECK (1985) summarizes the work of his colleagues, particularly focusing on the history and theology of the development of the Mishnaic text. Five themes, he says, are addressed in Zeraim: production of crops under conditions of holiness; conditions under which produce becomes subject to sanctification; designation of produce to be an agricultural offering; care and handling of holy produce; and eating food under conditions of holiness. The fundamental worldview, based on Scripture, is that God owns the land and has sanctified it; it, and its produce, are to be used accordingly. The major portion of the book classifies, tractate by tractate, the pericopes according to their "school" of origin: the "houses" (pre-70 C.E.), Yavneh (70 to 140 C.E.), or Usha (140 to 170 C.E.). This analysis reveals a shift from Yavnean concern with definitions of actions according to God's will to Ushan emphasis on human perceptions and intentions in determination of what is or is not permissible in sanctifying the land. In this way, Mishnah asserts that recent history (destruction of the Temple and the failure of Bar Kochba's revolt) notwithstanding, God's relationship to the land and to the people still holds. The people have the power to sanctify life and the land.

Common to all these studies in the Brown series is a form-critical approach to translation and exegesis, which stands in contrast to theologically based commentaries in traditional rabbinic sources. The authors' translations attempt to preserve formal traits of rhetoric. Interpretation is based on literary analysis, recognizing formal structures such as list, repetition, contrast, and dispute. Consideration of the arrangement of pericopes into larger units helps to discern the meaning of the whole tractate. Seven of the tractates in Zeraim deal with agricultural produce as related to Temple rites or tithing. JAFFEE treats the tractate on tithing (the first tithe, for the Levites), HAAS the tractate on the second tithe and its transportation to Jerusalem, and SARASON the tractate on doubtfully tithed produce. AVERY-PECK (1981) deals with the priests' portion of the harvest.

Three tractates address agricultural issues (that is, production) more directly. MANDELBAUM analyzes tractate Kilayim, dealing with permitted and prohibited mixtures of plants, animals, and fibers. The Mishnah supplements the scriptural sources by establishing criteria for distinguishing classes, defining what constitutes commingling, and determining how to keep categories distinct, all apparently with the purpose of maintaining an original orderly state created by God. BROOKS analyzes tractate Peah, which deals primarily with the harvest. The poor are entitled to gifts because they are without land yet under God's protection (much as the priests are). The offerings for the poor are treated in their order of separation during the harvest: the unharvested rear corner of the field; gleanings, forgotten sheaves, and separated grapes; defective clusters; and the poor tithe.

The sabbatical year (and the jubilee, the sabbatical of sabbaticals) have received more attention than the other laws of agriculture. While the call for fallow might have some ecological function, the sabbatical and jubilee had primarily socioreligious purposes. NEWMAN analyzes tractate Shebiit, which ordains a sabbatical for the land every seven years, analogous to the rest on the seventh day of creation. The laws of permitted and forbidden labor (beginning in the sixth year) and produce, and the requirement for remission of debts, are treated here. The reliance on scripture and the emphasis on the community's role in determining what constitutes sanctification together provided "a powerful statement that the holy life of Israel is eternal, that it remains essentially unaltered by the forces of history."

In contrast to the form-critical approach, which focuses on the historic development of a religious system, GRUNFELD writes strictly within a halakhic framework, presenting the current state of decided law. His main emphasis is on *shemittah* (the sabbatical year), the interpretation and application of its laws in modern times, instructions for observance within Israel, and implications for observant Jews elsewhere with regard to the produce of Israel. Like Newman and his colleagues, Grunfeld sees the purpose of the sabbatical as demonstrating the sanctity of the land, its produce, and people; it is an affirmation that God owns the land and cares for His people. Grunfeld sees the *shemittah* laws as part of the concerns of kashrut more generally; in fact, his treatment of these laws is also published under the title *Dietary Laws Regarding Plants and Vegetables, with Particular Reference to the Produce of the Holy Land,* as volume two of his compendium, *The Jewish Dietary Laws.*

FAGER addresses some of the same basic questions of Newman and Avery-Peck—how and why the jubilee exists—through the sociology of knowledge. He considers three social science models—structural functionalist, conflict, and symbolic—to consider the objective, expressive, and documentary meanings of the jubilee. He, too, concludes that the jubilee reinforced divine will, what ought to be in contrast to what is, with respect to relationships within society.

PAUL A. KAY

Agudat Israel *see* Haredim

Agunah

Aronoff, Susan and Rivka Haut, *Women in Bondage,* New York: Ktav, 1999

Biale, Rachel, *Women and Jewish Law,* New York: Schocken, 1984

Breitowitz, Irving, *Between Civil and Religious Law: The Plight of the Agunah in American Society* (Contributions in Legal Studies, no. 70), Westport, Connecticut: Greenwood, 1993

Bulka, Reuven, *Jewish Divorce Ethics: The Right Way to Say Goodbye,* Ogdensburg, New York: Ivy League, 1992

Globe, Leah Ain, *The Dead End: Divorce Proceedings in Israel,* Jerusalem: B.A.L. Mass Communication, 1981

Greenberg, Blu, *On Women and Judaism: A View from Tradition,* Philadelphia: Jewish Publication Society, 1981

Haut, Irwin, *Divorce in Jewish Law and Life* (Studies in Jewish Jurisprudence, vol. 5), New York: Sepher-Hermon, 1983

Haut, Rivka, "The Agunah and Divorce," in *Lifecycles,* edited by Debra Orenstein, Woodstock, Vermont: Jewish Lights, 1994

Jewish Law Annual, 4, 1981

Porter, Jack Nusan (editor), *Women in Chains: A Sourcebook on the Agunah*, Northvale, New Jersey: Aronson, 1995

Riskin, Shlomo, *Women and Jewish Divorce: The Rebellious Wife, the Agunah, and the Right of Women to Initiate Divorce in Jewish Law, a Halakhic Solution*, Hoboken, New Jersey: Ktav, 1989

Syrtash, John, *Religion and Culture in Canadian Family Law*, Toronto: Butterworths, 1992

An *agunah* (plural, *agunot*) is a woman who cannot remarry because her husband is unable or unwilling to give her a *get* (Jewish divorce). The term *agunah* actually means anchored or tied down and is first found in verb form in the biblical story of Ruth (1:13). The original talmudic use of the word was limited to cases in which the man had disappeared and literally could not act as a legal instrument in the Jewish divorce proceedings. Recently, popular usage has expanded the term to apply to all cases of women who are unable to remarry because their husbands will not acquiesce and give the *get*. Because the rabbinic court cannot compel the husband to authorize the writing of the *get*, and only a man can initiate the proceedings, problems arise most frequently for women, although the term *agun* can be applied to men.

BIALE's book on Jewish law introduces the topic of divorce and the *agunah* in two separate chapters. The author clearly presents the dominant classical texts, explicating the focal issues and describing the problem. She traces the historical development of the law beginning with the early rabbinic attempt to decrease the vulnerability of the women left in this uncertain state. The complex conditions of these situations have created a vast literature of rabbinic precedent and case law, which is difficult to negotiate. Following Biale through her explication of intricate legal matters associated with *agunah*, the reader can acquire a significant appreciation of Jewish law, its history, and its intersection with daily life.

BULKA has written an easy-to-read book that draws from both his rabbinic knowledge and his psychological training to clarify Jewish procedures and grounds for divorce and to delineate the rights and responsibilities of the parties involved. A practical guide to divorce, this book attempts to preserve marriage as well as prevent bitter disruptions and acrimonious litigation. The solutions offered emphasize ethical and emotional concerns, and the author does not analyze the history or content of Jewish law.

The *JEWISH LAW ANNUAL* devotes a special issue to a wife's right to divorce. This scholarly volume includes a series of historical articles by scholars in the various fields of ancient and medieval history discussing divorce in different cultures. Most of the authors do not approach the contemporary scene or present practical solutions. Instead, they delve into past examples of the law and known cognate cases and prototypes. A number of articles by scholars such as J. David Bleich, David Novak, and M. Chigier, however, do face current problems with visions of halakhic and legal solutions informed by historical and legal precedents. The conclusions of these authors are not necessarily compatible. The articles are dense, but the effort required to assimilate their contents is hand-somely repaid as they are filled with information that is otherwise very difficult to access.

Irwin HAUT, a lawyer and rabbi, has written an estimable book proposing a solution to the problem of the *agunah*. In a brief and reliable manner, Haut describes the Jewish law and presents the seriousness of the problem. The book includes a chapter on the search for equality in rabbinic responsa, a subject that is rarely treated in this context. Demonstrating his facility with comparative law, the author evaluates current civil and religious remedies and suggests a number of ways to resolve outstanding problems. Supported by his scholarship and experience in this area, Haut advocates that halakhic considerations incorporate a moral stance, and he optimistically looks forward to an enduring resolution.

RISKIN looks back into history to amplify the rights of Jewish women in divorce proceedings. He observes that early talmudic sources entertained the possibility that a woman might find her husband repulsive and seek a divorce, and, contradicting centuries of rabbinic responsa and many of his contemporaries, he argues that the geonic judgment allowing coercion of the husband to grant a divorce can still be applied in comparable modern cases. The book includes numerous relevant texts, translations, and a useful bibliography, all of which make the volume invaluable as a reference work.

BREITOWITZ has written an erudite and demanding book that compares the various secular and Jewish laws of divorce in the United States and focuses on procedures in Jewish contract law related to the *agunah*. The book is abundantly researched and provides hundreds of dependable footnotes. Breitowitz discusses New York *get* laws and explores concerns that arise in the U.S. context from the constitutional dictate prohibiting state interference in religious matters. As a resource the book is incomparable, filled with detail and analysis. Breitowitz's scholarship is apparent and should stand the test of time.

The only published description of the Canadian Jewish divorce law is found in SYRTASH's book on Canadian family law. Syrtash is a lawyer who was instrumental in changing the provincial and federal divorce acts to impart some protection to women bound by religious as well as secular laws. The section of the book dealing with Jewish divorce focuses on Ontario legislation and introduces the structure, format, and procedures of the federal law.

GREENBERG's chapter on Jewish attitudes toward divorce raises issues of ethics and equality. Beginning with a concise review of the topic, including a survey of the key talmudic text, the article assesses the positions of different denominations with regards to divorce. Greenberg casts her discriminating gaze at various solutions to the problem of *agunah*, and she seeks to acknowledge the importance of tradition without becoming an apologist for divorce laws that injure women. She raises the possibility of an amendment to the law that would enable a woman to "transfer a *get*," and she calls for an extension of the rabbinic law "limiting the husband's and expanding the wife's rights." Greenberg's arguments represent the views of many women whose devotion to halakhic Judaism is sorely challenged by the present process for divorce.

Rivka HAUT is an Orthodox activist whose essay reflects her years of experience working on behalf of *agunot*. Her piece delineates issues concerning rabbinic accountability and describes some important efforts to help *agunot*.

ARONOFF and HAUT describes many of the authors' experiences working with *agunot*. The book provides case studies presenting details about the abuses and other traumas suffered by *agunot* that have seldom been made available to a general readership.

GLOBE's short pamphlet also presents individual cases that illustrate the circumstances of *agunot*. The document focuses on cases in Israel and repudiates any contention that Israel is taking care of its *agunot*.

PORTER is a useful sourcebook and a collection of significant articles from all relevant sectors, including halakhic, secular, fictional, and journalistic sources from many parts of the world. The anthology contains selections from many of the authors listed above, and it recognizes that there are considerable areas of disagreement. It has a glossary, a useful bibliography, and a list of sources for help. Some of the essays are overpowering, but that is the nature of the topic.

NORMA BAUMEL JOSEPH

See also Divorce

Ahad Ha'am   1856–1927

Russian-born essayist and leader of cultural Zionist movement

Kornberg, Jacques (editor), *At the Crossroads: Essays on Ahad Ha-am* (SUNY Series in Modern Jewish History), Albany: State University of New York Press, 1983

Noveck, Simon (editor), *Great Jewish Thinkers of the Twentieth Century* (B'nai B'rith Great Books Series, vol. 3), Washington, D.C.: B'nai B'rith, Department of Adult Jewish Education, 1964

Roth, Leon, "Back to, Forward from, Ahad Ha-am?," *Conservative Judaism*, 17, 1960

Roth, Leon, *Judaism: A Portrait*, New York: Viking, and London: Faber, 1960

Simon, Leon, *Ahad Ha-am, Asher Ginzberg: A Biography*, Philadelphia: Jewish Publication Society, and London: East and West Library, 1960

Zipperstein, Steven J., *Elusive Prophet: Ahad Ha-am and the Origins of Zionism*, Berkeley: University of California Press, and London: Halban, 1993

Ahad Ha'am ("One of the People") was the pen name of the Russian Zionist Asher Ginzberg. He was the leader of cultural Zionism, as opposed to the political Zionism of Theodor Herzl. Ahad Ha'am viewed the mission of Zionism as the regeneration of the Jewish spirit in its restored homeland. He distinguished himself as an editor, an essayist, and one of the outstanding masters of Hebrew style.

NOVECK offers a useful and readable introductory presentation of the life and thought of Ahad Ha'am.

SIMON is an outstanding authority on Ahad Ha'am, and prior to writing this full-scale biography, he was the coauthor of a Hebrew study of the thinker as well as the translator into English of three volumes of his essays and letters. Simon's work is the most reliable interpretation of Ahad Ha'am's thought in English. Simon was also a disciple of the master since his student days at the University of Oxford and a personal friend from 1908 onward. The reader will have to determine for himself whether this friendship and admiration had a significant influence on the resulting portrait. At any rate, the picture that emerges from Simon's biography is that of a principled and austere keeper of the Zionist conscience whose fastidious vision of a morally regenerated Jewish people rose above the compromises and tumult of day-to-day politics.

ZIPPERSTEIN's portrait of Ahad Ha'am is diametrically opposed to that of Simon. Ahad Ha'am, according to Zipperstein, was politically ambitious, cunning, and duplicitous. He pretended to be a humble man, a mere journalist leaving policy decisions and leadership to others more worthy than himself. But his followers hero-worshiped him, and their adulation turned him into a secular, agnostic hasidic rabbi. Even his pen name Ahad Ha'am, "one of the people," is interpreted by Zipperstein as meaning one who is unique or special among the people, a snobbish leader of an intellectual elite. Thus what other scholars universally consider a modest pseudonym, Zipperstein views as a bid for leadership and primacy.

KORNBERG's collection includes 13 essays of generally high caliber in addition to the editor's introduction. These essays are divided into four groups, treating, respectively, Ahad Ha'am's role in the revival of Hebrew and as a Hebrew stylist; his political thought and activity; his controversies; and his influence and disciples. The first essay, by Alan Mintz, examines Ahad Ha'am's success as an essayist. According to Mintz, Ahad Ha'am's philosophical essays generally have a three-part structure. The thesis of an Ahad Ha'am essay opens with a striking challenge to accepted truths about human nature and history that is built around the tension between two concepts (priest and prophet, sacred and profane, imitation and assimilation, positive and negative). In the body of the essay these terms are elaborated by applying them either to various historic periods or across different realms of human activity. The essay concludes with the application of what has been described to Jewish history and to the contemporary Jewish situation. Mintz suggests that the structure of the essays is not only influenced by European models but also by the classical Jewish sermon. This is to say that Ahad Ha'am's model may have been homiletic midrash, with its preamble, or proem, which begins with a verse from the Hagiographa that, at first blush, is not at all related to the day's scriptural reading. As the preacher proceeds, however, it becomes quite obvious that the thought of the main text is clearly suggested, if not explicitly expressed. The obscure proem may have served as a device to stimulate greater attentiveness on the part of the congregation. Similarly, Ahad Ha'am would dazzle his readers with his acquaintance with the latest thinking in the sciences and social sciences and so establish his authority and gain assent to his viewpoint.

ROTH (1960a, 1960b) was the Ahad Ha'am Professor of Philosophy at the Hebrew University in Jerusalem for more than 25 years. His evaluation of Ahad Ha'am is significant, and since his two critical discussions supplement each other, they may conveniently be considered together. Roth attempts to answer the question: What is living and what is dead in Ahad Ha'am? Ahad Ha'am, he concludes, was not a philosopher and had no philosophy of his own; he was, rather, a philosophically minded essayist and a man of singular moral courage. Thus, Roth notes, he wrote a letter in his old age to the leading Jewish newspaper in Palestine to express his horror and shame at the killing of an innocent Arab boy by Jewish youths in retaliation for Arab attacks on Jews. Survival, he held, was not the be-all and end-all of building a Jewish homeland. There were prices that were too high to pay; it made no sense to try building a utopian state if in doing so Jews sacrificed the ethical teachings that had always inspired them. There was no pressing need for another small, corrupt, and strife-torn Levantine country just to excel in the export of citrus fruit. "If this be the Messiah," Ahad Ha'am exclaimed in talmudic idiom, "let him come, but let me not see him!" Commenting on Ahad Ha'am's ideas and his theory of Judaism, Roth finds value in his call for a world Jewish cultural center in Zion, the revival of Jewish values, and the concept of creating the "Jewish moral superman" who stands in apposition to the "secular Aryan superman," who is sensuous, power-laden, and capable of great demonic force. The "moral superman" of Judaism is to be the exemplar of social justice, for Ahad Ha'am identified the ethics of Judaism with the Hebrew Bible's demand for absolute justice, in contrast with the ethics of Christianity, understood by him as the ethics of love. In Roth's view, Ahad Ha'am's greatness lay in his attempt to recall Jewry to its ancient moral ideals, which he identified with the morality of the prophets.

While Roth shows some concern about Ahad Ha'am's formulations, his main reservation is not with the position itself but with the coherence it gives to Ahad Ha'am's own presuppositions. He depicts Ahad Ha'am as greatly influenced by the evolutionism of Herbert Spencer and the Spencerian French psychologist Frederic Paulhan, so that he views Judaism not as an eternal metaphysical essence but as a living growth rooted in the psychological organism, which is subject to change. There is thus a "national creative power" in the Jewish people that manifests itself in the Jewish "spirit," which in the past expressed itself in a primarily religious culture. But what is not clear is why, on Ahad Ha'am's evolutionary principles, Jews should continue to be bound by this view. The "spirit" may well evolve or the "national creative power" create something unfamiliar.

Twenty-four centuries ago Aristophanes, surveying the flux of events, remarked, "Whirl is king." But for Ahad Ha'am "Whirl" is emphatically not king. The keystone of his thinking is the absolute character of the moral law and the absolute character of the Jewish commitment to it. But according to the evolutionism of Spencer that Ahad Ha'am avowed, there cannot be such a thing as an absolute. So Roth exhibits Ahad Ha'am impaled on the horns of a dilemma: if his general theory is true, we have to abandon his moral outlook; if his moral outlook is true, we have to abandon his general theory.

JACOB HABERMAN

Akiba ben Joseph c.50–135 C.E.

Palestinian rabbi, scholar, and martyr

Aleksandrov, G.S., "The Role of Aqiba in the Bar Kokhba Rebellion," *Revue des Etudes Juives,* 132, 1973
Finkelstein, Louis, *Akiba: Scholar, Saint and Martyr,* New York: Covici, Friede, 1936
Goldin, Judah, "Toward a Profile of the Tanna, Aqiba ben Joseph," *Journal of the American Oriental Society,* 96, 1976
Guttmann, Alexander, "Akiba, 'Rescuer of the Torah'," in *Hebrew Union College Annual,* vol. 17, 1942–1943
Nadich, Judah, *Rabbi Akiba and His Contemporaries,* Northvale, New Jersey: Aronson, 1998
Primus, Charles, *Aqiva's Contribution to the Law of Zera'im* (Studies in Judaism in Late Antiquity, vol. 22), Leiden, The Netherlands: Brill, 1977
Sanders, E.P., "R. Akiba's View of Suffering," *Jewish Quarterly Review,* 63, 1972

Akiba ben Joseph was an eminent Palestinian rabbinic scholar, Torah teacher, and founder of a school in Bnei Brak. When the Roman government forbade the teaching of the Torah, Akiba publicly ignored the prohibition and died a martyr's death.

FINKELSTEIN's work is a learned biography that is also a good read and in places is more gripping than most historical novels. Finkelstein offers a striking portrait of Akiba and his times, his religious philosophy, his hermeneutical system, his contribution to the development of Jewish law, and his efforts on behalf of the survival and perpetuation of Judaism after the destruction of the Temple by the Romans. With sensitivity he traces Akiba's parentage and humble beginnings, his personal character and diligence, his romantic marriage, his relations with his colleagues and Bar Kokhba, whom he proclaimed as the Messiah, and his final martyrdom.

Finkelstein's account is pieced together from traditions, stray statements, maxims, and legal and homiletic discussions scattered throughout the vast talmudic-rabbinic literature. The thread that holds this scattered material together is the author's socioeconomic interpretation of Jewish history during the Second Commonwealth and the Talmudic period. According to Finkelstein's debatable theory, from the time of the Maccabees onward, there was a double social struggle in Judaism: that between the organized patricians, or Sadducees, and the scholars, or Pharisees; and that within the Pharisaic party itself, between the faction drawn from the patricians and provincial elite and those who came from a plebeian background. Armed with these quasi-Marxist assumptions and tools, Finkelstein interprets the life and activities of Akiba, whom he identifies as a champion of plebeian views, defending the economically and socially oppressed.

The sociological approach to Jewish history championed by Finkelstein was criticized by Gedalia Alon in a lengthy review of *Akiba* in a Hebrew journal. Alon did not dispute that an individual's economic background is an important influence on his point of view. What he did question was Finkelstein's exclusive reliance on this criterion to the neglect of all other factors. Jewish sages, like many others, he urged, frequently disagreed even when no economic issue was involved. In addition, the evidence, Allon maintained, is far more ambiguous and indecisive than Finkelstein represented it to be.

At times, Finkelstein accepts conjectures of other scholars as if they were proven and demonstrated beyond the shadow of a doubt. In a seminal lecture at the Hebrew University in 1929, Louis Ginzberg had suggested as a tentative hypothesis that for more than 150 years, up to the time of Hillel the Elder (an older contemporary of Jesus), leadership among the Pharisees was bipartisan, an aristocrat being president and a plebeian being head of the court, or vice versa. Finkelstein not only accepts this thesis as proven, but extends the principle of bipartisan leadership to a much longer duration, starting with Ezra and Nehemiah and ending with the compilation of the Mishnah at the beginning of the third century. Far too little is known about conditions during the Second Commonwealth to ascertain whether, for instance, Hillel was a typical plebeian and Shammai, who earned his livelihood as a carpenter, was a representative patrician. Despite these reservations, it can be said that Finkelstein has succeeded to a very large degree in sketching a fine portrait of a true religious genius who is described in the Talmud as "one of the fathers of the world."

NADICH relates the legends told by and about Akiba and his colleagues in classic rabbinic texts. The stories deal with the practical wisdom of the rabbis, the values they cherished, the standards of right conduct they advocated, and the sacrifices they made for the survival of Judaism. The volume is enhanced by a bibliography, a list of sources, and an index.

PRIMUS's work is a revision of a doctoral dissertation written at Brown University under the guidance of Jacob Neusner. Against the distinguished textual critic J.N. Epstein, who maintains that Akiba organized a collection of traditions that became the prototype of the Mishnah, Primus argues that neither the form nor the substance of the surviving material permits us to come to such a conclusion. Akiba's contribution to early rabbinic Judaism should be judged by the unfolding of the logic of legal concerns rather than by reference to the development of particular sorts of literature.

ALEKSANDROV argues that there is no indication in the sources that Akiba was the ideologue and instigator of the Bar Kokhba rebellion. Neither is there any indication in the sources that his numerous and wide travels were made to foment sedition and prepare for the rebellion as is contended by some modern Israeli scholars (Gedalya Allon, Samuel Yevin).

GUTTMANN contends that Akiba saved the Torah from oblivion in two respects: he was instrumental in organizing the oral tradition by subject matter, and he evaluated the vast material by arranging the halakhot (laws) in special compilations according to their importance in Jewish life as it evolved after the destruction of the Temple.

GOLDIN's thesis is that the ideal love relationship between husband and wife illuminates the intimate connection between Israel and God. Akiba interpreted the Song of Songs allegorically as Israel's proclamation to the Gentiles: I am His and He is mine.

SANDERS discusses Ephraim Urbach's thesis that the religious persecutions under the Roman emperor Hadrian prompted a new understanding of suffering, since this suffering was inflicted not for sins but for keeping the commandments. Akiba, therefore, taught that "sufferings are beloved" because they bring cleansing and atonement for sin, and he was able to see his own martyrdom as an expression of his love for God.

JACOB HABERMAN

Algeria

Amipaz-Silber, Gitta, *The Role of the Jewish Underground in the American Landing in Algiers, 1940–1942*, Jerusalem: Gefen, 1992

Bahloul, Joëlle, *The Architecture of Memory: A Jewish-Muslim Household in Colonial Algeria, 1937–1962* (Cambridge Studies in Social and Cultural Anthropology), New York: Cambridge University Press, 1996

Briggs, Lloyd Cabot and Norina Lami Guède, *No More for Ever: A Saharan Jewish Town* (Papers of the Peabody Museum of Archaeology and Ethnology, vol. 55, no. 1), Cambridge, Massachusetts: Peabody Museum, 1964

Chouraqui, André, *A Man in Three Worlds*, Lanham, Maryland: University Press of America, 1984

Epstein, Isidore, *The Responsa of Rabbi Simon b. Zemah Duran as a Source of the History of the Jews in North Africa*, London: Oxford University Press, 1930

Friedman, Elizabeth, *Colonialism and After: An Algerian Jewish Community* (Critical Studies in Work and Community), South Hadley, Massachusetts: Bergin and Garvey, 1988

Hershman, Abraham M., *Rabbi Isaac ben Sheshet Perfet and His Times*, New York: Jewish Theological Seminary of America, 1973

Rosenstock, Morton, "The House of Bacri and Busnach: A Chapter from Algeria's Commercial History," *Jewish Social Studies*, 14, 1952

Rosenstock, Morton, "Economic and Social Conditions among the Jews of Algeria, 1790–1848," *Historia Judaica*, 18, April 1956

Rosenstock, Morton, "The Establishment of the Consistorial System in Algeria," *Jewish Social Studies*, 18, 1956

Szajkowski, Zosa, "Socialists and Radicals in the Development of Anti-Semitism in Algeria (1884–1900)," *Jewish Social Studies*, 10, 1948

Szajkowski, Zosa, "The Struggle for Jewish Emancipation in Algeria after the French Occupation," *Historia Judaica*, 18, April 1956

A typical North African community, Algerian Jews were nonetheless unique in their almost complete French-style Westernization following the French occupation of 1830. Most of the community emigrated to France following Algeria's independence in 1962. Most of the relatively little research on Algerian Jews is in French and Hebrew.

The involvement of indigenous Algerian Jews in support of the American landing in Algiers in November 1942 is examined by AMIPAZ-SILBER. She describes the condition of Algerian Jews on the eve of World War II and how their life changed under Vichy rule with its anti-Jewish legislation, including the abrogation of their French citizenship. In this well-researched study, Amipaz-Silber details the establishment of the clandestine Jewish resistance movement and its contacts with U.S. representatives and examines the slow recovery of the political rights of the community following liberation.

Memories of Jewish-Muslim relations at home are examined by BAHLOUL on the individual case-study level: how Jewish and Muslim inhabitants of the same house in Sétif, eastern Algeria, remember in the 1990s their history as one of a multi-ethnic household, focusing mainly on the 1940s and 1950s. Bahloul, an ethnographer, is interested in collecting information about the lives of the various families and in the semantics and ethnography of memory. She examines the home and its memory as central to the construction of individual and group identity. Based mostly on interviews, the study provides a unique opportunity to examine close Jewish-Muslim relations and perceptions.

BRIGGS and GUÈDE conducted anthropological fieldwork among the Jews of the Algerian desert town of Ghardaia between 1947 and 1962, when the Jews fled upon the establishment of Algerian independence. The study describes the structure of the community, daily life, life cycles as relating to men and to women, education, religious practices, pilgrimage, and Jewish-Muslim relations. This is a unique study of a Jewish desert community that was quite different from those of the Frenchified coastal urban Algerian Jews. The absence of section titles and the lack of an index makes the location of specific topics difficult.

In his autobiography, CHOURAQUI provides his personal view of Jewish life in Algeria. Born in 1917 in Aïn Témouchent, Chouraqui describes his childhood and education against the background of his family's history and the condition of the Jewish community in Algeria, Jewish-Muslim relations, and Jewish-French relations. A lawyer and later a deputy mayor of Jerusalem, his memoirs reflect the life experience of an intellectual and political activist.

In this study of Jewish life in Algiers in the early 15th century, EPSTEIN uses more than 800 responsa by the Majorca-born Rabbi Simeon ben Zemah Duran, who fled to Algiers following the Iberian massacres of 1391 and served as chief rabbi there from 1408. Epstein examines the life of the Algerian community as reflected in Duran's responsa. Among the subjects dealt with are the political and social conditions of the Jews, taxation, cultural and religious issues, communal organization and institutions, education, and matrimony. Data on Duran and the rabbis who corresponded with him are also provided.

Based on interviews conducted in the mid–1970s with Algerian Jews from the small town of Batna who settled in Aix-en-Provence, France, following Algeria's independence, FRIEDMAN examines Jewish life in Batna and the life of these immigrants in France. Among the topics discussed are the influence of France on life in Algeria in general and the influence of French Jews on Algerian Jews in particular, the rise of antisemitism in colonial Algeria, the relations of the Jews of Batna with their Muslim and Christian neighbors, communal organization, family life, and the condition of the community during World War II and the Algerian War of Independence. Data on occupations and marriages are provided, including breakdown by gender and religion (Jewish and Christian).

The personality and contributions of Rabbi Isaac ben Sheshet Perfet are the subject of HERSHMAN's book. The Barcelona-born Perfet escaped in 1391 to Algiers, where he served as chief rabbi until his death in 1408. Perfet's responsa are utilized to examine Jewish life in both Spain and Algeria. Among the issues discussed relating to Algiers are polygamy, marriage, synagogues, religious services, and communal organization. While only part of the book deals with Algiers, the book is an important source on this little-researched period.

ROSENSTOCK (1952) discusses Jewish involvement in Algerian economic life in the 18th and early 19th centuries. He focuses on two Livornese Jewish families, Bacri and Busnach, who benefited from special economic and political privileges thanks to their foreign origin. Rosenstock examines their role in commerce and the services they provided to the local authorities, including their involvement in goods obtained through piracy. The declining position of these families following French occupation in 1830 is also charted.

ROSENSTOCK (1956a) explores the economic and social conditions prior to and following the French occupation of Algeria in 1830. Among the topics covered are communal organization, education, commerce, population, religious life, and the changes that took place during the transition from Ottoman to French rule.

ROSENSTOCK (1956b) examines the integration of Algerian Jewry in the Jewish consistorial system of France following the 1830 French occupation of Algeria. Rosenstock describes the efforts by French Jewry to organize the Algerian communities on a similar pattern to the French communities and to integrate them into the French system. He discusses French Jewry's efforts to carry on reforms, especially in education, among Algerian Jews. The activities of French Jewish public figures and organizations are reviewed, as are the reactions in Algeria regarding this involvement.

SZAJKOWSKI (1948) examines the development of antisemitism in Algeria in the late 19th century and the involvement of socialists and radicals in this process. Szajkowski explores the implications of the granting of French citizenship to Algerian Jews, as well as issues of class struggle and the Dreyfus Affair, on the growth of antisemitism among settlers in Algeria.

SZAJKOWSKI (1956) examines the process that led to the granting of French citizenship to most Algerian Jews in 1870. Based on French and Jewish sources, Szajkowski considers the reorganization of the Jewish communities in Algeria following the French occupation in 1830 as well as the political struggle in France and in Algeria that led to the changes in organization and status of Algerian Jews.

RACHEL SIMON

Allegory

Dawson, David, *Allegorical Readers and Cultural Revision in Ancient Alexandria,* Berkeley: University of California Press, 1992

Halkin, Abraham, "Ibn 'Aqnin's Commentary on the Song of Songs," in *Alexander Marx: Jubilee Volume on the Occasion of His Seventieth Birthday,* New York: Jewish Theological Seminary, 1950

Kugel, James, "The 'Bible as Literature' in Late Antiquity and the Middle Ages," *Hebrew University Studies in Literature and the Arts,* 11, 1983

Rosenberg, Joel, *King and Kin: Political Allegory in the Hebrew Bible* (Indiana Studies in Biblical Literature), Bloomington: Indiana University Press, 1986

Saperstein, Marc, *Decoding the Rabbis: A Thirteenth-Century Commentary on the Aggadah* (Harvard Judaic Monographs, 3), Cambridge, Massachusetts: Harvard University Press, 1980

Scholem, Gershom, *Zur Kabbala und ihrer Symbolik,* 1960; translated by Ralph Manheim as *On the Kabbalah and Its Symbolism,* New York: Schocken, and London: Routledge and Kegan Paul, 1965

Stern, Josef, *Problems and Parables of Law: Maimonides and Nahmanides on Reasons for the Commandments (ta'amei ha-mitzvot)* (SUNY Series in Judaica), Albany: State University of New York Press, 1998

Talmage, Frank, "Apples of Gold: The Inner Meaning of Sacred Texts in Medieval Judaism," in *Jewish Spirituality: From the Bible through the Middle Ages* (World Spirituality, vol. 13), edited by Arthur Green, New York: Crossroad, and London: Routledge and Kegan Paul, 1986

Wolfson, Harry Austryn, *Philo: Foundations of Religious Philosophy in Judaism, Christianity, and Islam* (Structure and Growth of Philosophic Systems from Plato to Spinoza, 2), 2 vols., Cambridge, Massachusetts: Harvard University Press, 1947, revised edition, 1963

The idea of allegory, a continuous or extended metaphor, developed in classical Greek rhetoric and criticism. Classical theories influenced, directly, the Greek-speaking Jews of Alexandria and, indirectly, medieval Jewish scholars in both Islamic lands and Christian Europe. Jews used allegory in poetry, storytelling, preaching, and correspondence and applied it to the interpretation of classical Hebrew and Aramaic writings. The allegorical method of exegesis was extremely productive—and controversial—throughout the medieval and early modern period, and modern literary scholars have revived the ancient and medieval traditions in their own attempts to explain Bible and Midrash. The following studies focus on the history of allegorical exegesis.

WOLFSON's monumental two-volume study of Philo, the cornerstone of the author's history of religious philosophy, laid the foundation for the modern study of Philo, whose theology, as expounded by Wolfson, used allegorical exegesis to harmonize the ideas of philosophy with the text of the Bible. Following a detailed analysis of the allegorical method, the bulk of Wolfson's study attempts to reconstruct the doctrines of this harmonized philosophy. Wolfson notably minimizes the influence of Homeric exegesis on Philo by emphasizing Philo's connection with a native Jewish midrash. Readers should consult the *Studia Philonica* (1972–1980) and *Studia Philonica Annual* (1989–) for critical evaluations of Wolfson and more recent bibliographies.

DAWSON places Philo squarely in the Hellenistic, rather than rabbinic, world by examining Philo's method of exegesis together with the pagan exegesis of Homer, the gnostic myth making of Valentinus, and the Christian exegesis of Clement of Alexandria. The author de-emphasizes formal literary analysis, philosophy, and apologetics while stressing the function of allegorical reading within a society or culture. He argues that allegory was a vital force in Hellenistic cultural criticism and revision and shows that although Philo, Valentinus, and Clement had very different ideas about Scripture and applied different methods of interpretation, they shared the same desire to reshape their communities through the reinterpretation of authoritative texts. Dawson also includes a full bibliography.

KUGEL extends the history of allegorical interpretation from ancient Alexandria to medieval and Renaissance Europe. In contrast to Wolfson, Kugel argues that Jewish and Christian interpreters made the Bible into their Homer and used the tools of classical criticism to demonstrate the Bible's literary merit and uncover its hidden wisdom. He emphasizes influence but also notes conflict and tension: for example, Christians tried to suppress classical literature, but they also cited it, and they used allegorical methods both to turn the Bible into philosophy and to interpret Virgil as Christian doctrine. Kugel closes with a brief examination of midrash that contrasts the traditional rabbinic exegesis with the Hellenistic traditions.

TALMAGE explains the methods and motives of allegorical interpretation in medieval Jewish philosophy and the Kabbalah. He discusses the apologetic motive for using allegories but emphasizes that the exegetes held more positive convictions as well. Philosophers and kabbalists truly believed that the Bible and rabbinic literature contained wisdom that was intentionally hidden to protect the multitudes from misunderstandings. Talmage also tries to flesh out the mentality of the culture in which allegory flourished, contrasting Eastern and Western societies, comparing the Jewish traditions with those of Christianity and Islam, and citing examples from art and architecture as well as literature. Talmage includes a bibliography.

HALKIN focuses on the allegorical interpretation of the Song of Songs. He briefly characterizes early interpretations—by rabbis and church fathers—before discussing the medieval commentary of Joseph ibn Aqnin and the philosophical tradition of Song of Songs commentary. Ibn Aqnin's *Revealing of the Secrets* explains the Song of Songs as a story about the soul's love for the active intellect and the soul's desire for union. *Revealing of the Secrets* was the first commentary to apply this particular allegory consistently, and Halkin gives examples that illustrate its content and method. He also compares this text to the later commentaries by Moses ibn Tibbon, Joseph ibn Kaspi, Immanuel of Rome, and Gersonides.

SCHOLEM represents the Kabbalah as a revolutionary yet paradoxically conservative transformation of religion in which the mystic expresses new, often radical, ideas using the traditional symbols of authoritative texts. To illustrate this process, Scholem discusses the kabbalistic theory of the Torah—as names of God, an organic unity, and a source of infinite meaning (or, at least, four senses, 70 faces, 600,000 aspects) —and then discusses kabbalistic myth and the creation of ritual. He emphasizes the importance of symbol, rather than allegory, but he also discusses the use of allegorical interpretation in the Zohar and the place of allegory in *pardes*, the fourfold interpretation of Scripture endorsed by the Kabbalah. Scholem's work is a classic, but the more recent work of Moshe Idel (e.g., *Language, Torah and Hermeneutics in Abraham Abulafia*, 1989) and Elliot Wolfson (e.g., *Along the Path*, 1995) should be consulted as well.

SAPERSTEIN argues that aggadic, or narrative, exegesis of the rabbis posed a particular challenge for the medieval Jewish scholar. The gross anthropomorphisms and strange stories in aggadah made it the object of antirabbinic criticism and a source of embarrassment for rationalistic Jews. He traces the history of Jewish response to this challenge—denying the authority of the aggadah, censoring offensive texts, or reinterpreting the texts—and then focuses on the commentary of Isaac ben Jedaiah. Saperstein examines Isaac's method of interpretation, emphasizing the different meanings of the Hebrew word *mashal* (allegory, parable, analogy, or metonymy) and distinguishing that term from *hash'alah* (metaphor or extended meaning). The author relates Isaac's method of interpretation to his theory of rabbinic language and esotericism. Saperstein also sets the commentary in historical context, reconstructing Isaac's philosophical views and legal interpretations and extracting material relating to contemporary Jewish life in 13th-century southern France.

STERN uses the idea of *mashal*—as parable or allegory—to analyze Maimonides' commentaries on biblical commandments. He argues that Maimonides' distinction between external and internal meanings in biblical stories and poems also applies to Maimonides' interpretation of the commandments, and Stern tests this theory by examining the philosopher's explanation of the rationale behind sacrifices, circumcision, and other laws. Arguing against the theory of Leo Strauss, who identifies Maimonides' dichotomy as a distinction between the exoteric and the esoteric, Stern claims that Maimonides' concept relates to the distinction between the welfare of the community—both social/political and intellectual—and the perfection of the individual.

ROSENBERG carries allegorical exegesis into the present age. Indeed, his book is an apology for allegory and a plea for allegorical reading. Following the lead of Philo, Maimonides, and Leo Strauss, and drawing from the theories of semiotics and deconstruction, the author interprets the stories of the Garden of Eden, the life of Abraham, and the monarchy of David as (interrelated) political allegory. He argues against advocates of source criticism and form criticism, as he contends that there is a literary unity in these stories that shows the conscious effort of an editor or redactor to advance a plot and present a specific argument. Although Rosenberg criticizes the theories of higher criticism, he does not reject its findings completely. Instead, he incorporates insights from these theorists into his own literary analysis, an approach that helps him to sustain the representation of allegory as a rich, allusive, and surprisingly complex species of discourse.

JAMES T. ROBINSON

American Literature

Berger, Alan L., *Children of Job: American Second-Generation Witnesses to the Holocaust*, Albany: State University of New York Press, 1997

Furman, Andrew, *Israel through the Jewish-American Imagination: A Survey of Jewish-American Literature on Israel, 1928–1995* (SUNY Series in Modern Jewish Literature and Culture), Albany: State University of New York Press, 1997

Guttmann, Allen, *The Jewish Writer in America: Assimilation and the Crisis of Identity*, New York: Oxford University Press, 1971

Kremer, S. Lillian, *Witness through the Imagination: Ozick, Elman, Cohen, Potok, Singer, Epstein, Bellow, Steiner, Wallant, Malamud: Jewish-American Holocaust Literature*, Detroit, Michigan: Wayne State University Press, 1989

Shechner, Mark, *After the Revolution: Studies in the Contemporary Jewish American Imagination*, Bloomington: Indiana University Press, 1987

Wirth-Nesher, Hana (editor), *What Is Jewish Literature?*, Philadelphia: Jewish Publication Society, 1994

For many scholar-critics, the "master story" of Jewish-American literature is the long 20th-century march toward assimilation. A literary experience that began amid the squalid conditions of a tenement Lower East Side continued as the sons of immigrants made their way to New York's City College and then into the cultural mainstream. Among this group, writers such as Philip Rahv, Irving Howe, and Alfred Kazin are emblematic of what came to be known as the "New York Jewish intellectuals."

Their counterparts among writers of fiction—notably, Delmore Schwartz, Saul Bellow, Bernard Malamud, and Philip Roth—helped to bring the rhythms of "Yinglish" to a wide public, and it is this *voice,* rather than their controversial assessments of Jewish life in America, that may yet become the New York Jewish intellectuals' greatest contribution to American literature.

When the immigrant world receded into dim memory, there were those—Irving Howe among them—who felt that a distinctly Jewish-American literature was no longer possible. Subsequent events have proved them wrong, and there is any number now of younger writers who are distinctly Jewish-American—some who explore their fractured identity as the sons or daughters of Holocaust survivors; some who have returned to the richness of Jewish history and thought; and some whose magical realism reinvents the American shtetl.

Granted, Jewish-American literature no longer seems as "hot" or as fashionable as it was during the decades between 1950 and 1980, but that dimension of literary politics is not, finally, as interesting as the work currently being done by dozens of talented and original Jewish-American writers.

GUTTMANN surveys the concerns and stylistic techniques that have energized Jewish-American writers from Abraham Cahan (whose 1917 *The Rise of David Levinsky* combined socio-realist description with a cautionary tale about American acculturation) to more recent writers such as Saul Bellow, Bernard Malamud, and Philip Roth. One of the earliest scholarly-critical explorations of Jewish-American fiction, Guttmann's categories (e.g., the movement from acculturation to assimilation) and his close readings of individual works remain influential.

SHECHNER sees Jewish-American literature as it reflects the movement away from radical politics and toward the promises of psychotherapy. Concentrating on Isaac Rosenfeld and Philip Roth, along with a handful of others, his purpose is not to present a comprehensive historical survey. Rather, he is interested in identifying the changing cultural milieu certain writers experienced as Marxism became yet another god that had failed. He also describes how a selected group of literary intellectuals tried, with varying degrees of success, to forge new themes, attitudes, and "voices" in a culture more prone to gestures of accommodation than to postures of alienation. Shechner describes his work as a "study of the Jewish intellectual's quest for a firm base of judgment and identity and his failure to maintain a steady relation to the world, immune from the shocks of the moment and the short-term fate of values and behavior under conditions of change and uncertainty."

Kremer and Furman both represent recent efforts to widen the concerns of Jewish-American literature from immigrant adjustment and the psychic battles waged under the banner of "alienation" to long-delayed ruminations about the Holocaust or the State of Israel. KREMER argues that the imagination can constitute an act of "witnessing" and that Jewish-American writers can make—indeed, have made—a significant contribution to Holocaust literature. She concentrates on writers such as Saul Bellow, Bernard Malamud, Edward Lewis Wallant, Leslie Epstein, and Cynthia Ozick. Kremer's important pioneering study has been expanded and updated by BERGER, who focuses on fiction by the American-born children of survivors such as Melvin Jules Bukiet, Julie Salamon, and Thane Rosenbaum.

FURMAN argues that "the Jewish-American writers' relatively new exploration of the fictional possibilities of Israel greatly contributes to the renaissance today in Jewish-American fiction as a whole," and to that end he devotes chapters that combine sociocultural history with close readings of Meyer Levin, Leon Uris, Saul Bellow, Philip Roth, Anne Roiphe, and Tova Reich. A groundbreaking and important study, it contrasts the concerns (and inevitable tensions) that preoccupied earlier writers with those that shaped Jewish-American views of Israel after the Six-Day War.

WIRTH-NESHER's anthology of criticism assembles the best that has been thought and said on the subject of what can or cannot be properly called Jewish literature. International in scope, there is, nonetheless, insufficient material devoted to Jewish-American literature by such distinguished writer-critics as Saul Bellow, Cynthia Ozick, and John Hollander. Wirth-Nesher's goal is less to offer readers an authoritative account of a subject still very much embroiled in controversy than to invite them into the debate: "By placing such divergent concepts of Jewish literature between the covers of one book, I have aimed to undermine any one essentialist view of Jewish culture, while at the same time tracing the distictinctive features of the act of self-definition in recent Jewish literary history."

SANFORD PINSKER

See also Poetry: American Jewish

Am Ha'arets

Cohen, Shaye, "The Place of the Rabbi in Jewish Society of the Second Century," in *The Galilee in Late Antiquity*, edited by Lee Levine, New York: Jewish Theological Seminary of America, 1992

Levine, Lee, "The Sages and the Ammei Ha-Aretz," in his *The Rabbinic Class of Roman Palestine in Late Antiquity*, New York: Jewish Theological Seminary of America, 1989

Nicholson, E.W., "The Meaning of the Expression *am ha-aretz* in the Old Testament," *Journal of Semitic Studies*, 10, 1965

Oppenheimer, Aharon, *The 'Am Ha-Aretz: A Study in the Social History of the Jewish People in the Hellenistic-Roman Period* (Arbeiten zur Literatur und Geschichte des hellenistischen Judentums, 8), Leiden: Brill, 1977

Zeitlin, Solomon, "The Am Haarez," *Jewish Quarterly Review*, 23, 1932

Am ha'arets, or "people of the land," is one of those peculiar social categories that has very little discernable content in itself but is instead a designation for an "other" outside of a Jewish "in-group." The reference appears numerous times in the Bible, often as a term by which Israelites are distinguished from either the indigenous people or from other colonizing populations of a land, especially Canaan. It is also frequently employed by the biblical authors to distinguish the Israelite populace itself from its own civic, military, and religious rulers. In later antiquity, the term is used throughout rabbinic literature to refer, exclusively and disparagingly, to the multitude of Jews who did not share emerging rabbinism's practices and prescriptions. It is in this latter usage that the term is most significant. With the ascendance of rabbinism in the early Middle Ages, the expression has, for the most part, become merely an epithet meaning "ignorant" or "uncultured" in a Jewish context.

The literature in English on the *am ha'arets* (plural: *ammei ha'arets*) is largely confined to one book, a small handful of articles, and LEVINE. While Levine's focus is the rabbis themselves, he makes frequent reference to the treatment in rabbinic texts of the *ammei ha'arets*—those for whom the rabbis reserve their most ferocious and vitriolic attacks. Levine reviews many of these acerbic remarks, as well as the earliest scholarly theories regarding the identity of the rabbis' intended targets. Unlike those who have identified the *ammei ha'arets* with specific sects or groups known from antiquity (identifications for which there exists no substantial evidence), Levine proposes that the rabbis are merely lashing out at the large segment of the Jewish population of Palestine that was uninterested, unsympathetic, and/or downright hostile to early rabbinic incursions into traditional Jewish communal institutions and practices. Over time, Levine suggests, there was a marked improvement in relations between the two sides, which is detectable in later strata of the rabbinic corpus. Levine's brief excursus serves as a useful encapsulation of the literature on the topic and alerts the reader to a few pertinent archaeological discoveries as well. His willingness to treat rabbinic accounts as, generally speaking, historically reliable and sufficient and his assumption that the rabbis were significant communal authorities in the earliest centuries of their movement does, however, set him at odds with much contemporary scholarship on this period.

COHEN's brief treatment of the topic represents a more critical and appropriately cautious approach than Levine's study. Cohen notes that while many of the traditions about the *ammei ha'arets* are attributed to Palestinian rabbis, the largest and most vicious body of such traditions is found exclusively in the Babylonian Talmud—a fact that raises serious doubt about these traditions' authenticity. In addition, Cohen observes that there is no evidence of mass outreach or educational initiatives on the part of the early rabbis, and a good deal of counter-evidence suggests that winning the mass of Jews over to their worldview and practices was not a goal of the small rabbinic coteries in Palestine in the early centuries of this era. Thus, in Cohen's view, insofar as *am ha'arets* refers to the great majority of Jews in antiquity, the general attitude of the earliest generations of rabbis toward them appears to be one of disdainful disinterest.

The only book-length study on the *ammei ha'arets* in English is OPPENHEIMER. While the book is extremely helpful as a thorough compendium of rabbinic references to the *ammei ha'arets*, it is by no means adequate as social history. After a brief review of prior scholarship and a general summary of the uses and history of the term *am ha'arets*, Oppenheimer turns to an extended discussion of tithes and ritual purity—the conceptual contexts within which the earliest rabbinic traditions about the *ammei ha'arets* appear. He then delineates a distinction between two kinds of *ammei ha'arets*: those who were not careful about performance of the commandments (*am ha'arets le-mitsvot*) and those who did not engage in rabbinic Torah study (*am ha'arets le-Torah*). Much of the remainder of the study is devoted to proposals regarding relations between the *ammei ha'arets* and the pre-rabbinic and rabbinic circles of sages. The book ends with a brief survey of "Galilean" versus "Judean" traditions and a consideration of the significance of the *am ha'arets* material with respect to Samaritanism and nascent Christianity. Absent from this rabbinically learned study is any awareness of the great variety and vitality that characterized non-rabbinic Judaism in these centuries or a recognition that the rabbis were the minority newcomers (sectarians?) to the Jewish landscape of the day. Hence, Oppenheimer (even more than Levine) confers upon

rabbinic dicta the status of historical truth and presumes throughout his analysis the legal and ethical normativity of all things rabbinic. This rather considerable shortcoming severely limits the usefulness of this study to that of an erudite compilation of primary material.

Finally, two older journal articles are worthy of mention. NICHOLSON's survey of the uses of the term *am ha'arets* in the Bible aptly concludes that the term's meaning changes so much from one biblical context to another that equating it with a fixed content is utterly inappropriate. ZEITLIN's far more dated piece is significant as an early scholarly attempt to consider rabbinic and non-rabbinic sources in dialog with each other. Today, Zeitlin's article serves merely as an interesting example of previous theories about the *ammei ha'arets*, virtually all of which have been summarily discredited by later critical inquiry.

CYNTHIA M. BAKER

Amoraim *see* Rabbinic Biography: Talmudic

Ancient Near East

Aldred, Cyril, *The Egyptians* (Ancient Peoples and Places, vol. 18), London: Thames and Hudson, and New York: Praeger, 1961; revised edition, London: Thames and Hudson, 1984; 3rd edition, New York: Thames and Hudson, 1998

Bottéro, Jean, *Mesopotamia: Writing, Reasoning, and the Gods*, Chicago: University of Chicago Press, 1992

Gordon, Cyrus H. and Gary A. Rendsburg, *The Bible and the Ancient Near East*, New York: Norton, 1997

Hallo, William W. and William Kelly Simpson, *The Ancient Near East: A History*, New York: Harcourt Brace Jovanovich, 1971; 2nd edition; Fort Worth, Texas: Harcourt Brace, 1998

Kramer, Samuel Noah, *From the Tablets of Sumer: Twenty-Five Firsts in Man's Recorded History*, Indian Hills, Colorado: Falcon's Wing, 1956; as *History Begins at Sumer*, London: Thames and Hudson, 1958; revised as *History Begins at Sumer: Thirty-Nine Firsts in Man's Recorded History*, Philadelphia: University of Pennsylvania Press, 1981

Kuhrt, Amélie, *The Ancient Near East, c. 3000–330 BC* (Routledge History of the Ancient World), 2 vols., London and New York: Routledge, 1995

Oppenheim, A. Leo, *Ancient Mesopotamia: Portrait of a Dead Civilization*, Chicago: University of Chicago Press, 1964, revised edition, 1977

Sasson, Jack M. (editor), *Civilizations of the Ancient Near East*, 4 vols., New York: Scribner, and London: Simon and Schuster and Prentice-Hall International, 1995

Shafer, Byron E. (editor), *Religion in Ancient Egypt: Gods, Myths, and Personal Practice*, Ithaca, New York: Cornell University Press, and London: Routledge, 1991

Silverman, David P., *Ancient Egypt*, New York: Oxford University Press, and London: Piatkus, 1997

Snell, Daniel C., *Life in the Ancient Near East, 3100–332 B.C.E.*, New Haven, Connecticut: Yale University Press, 1997

The ancient Near East is not easily synthesized into a single cogent literary, historical, social, or economic study without either oversimplifying or creating unwieldy tomes. The subject is vast and requires the command of numerous languages and disciplines. The regions that make up the ancient Near East are equally vast, including Mesopotamia, Egypt, Anatolia, Iran, and Canaan, to which some scholars would add the Aegean. Consequently, few works are able to bring together the expertise required for an intelligent comprehensive survey. With the rare exceptions noted here, the reader will benefit most by consulting works that limit their focus of study to one or two of the major regions.

ALDRED surveys the culture of ancient Egypt for the uninitiated in a readable and interesting manner. Moving chronologically from predynastic Egypt to the arrival of Alexander, he places in historical context the lives of pharaohs and commoners, taking periodic glances at their beliefs, art and architecture, and agriculturally based lives. Rich in photographic images, the work serves as an excellent introduction to the fundamental aspects of Egyptian culture. One of the work's greatest assets is its opening chapter on the loss and recovery of pagan Egypt, which outlines the discoveries and advances that aided in the Western realization of the character of ancient Egypt. The work moves beyond providing a mere historical skeleton of ancient Egypt by including in its final chapter extended discussions of Egyptian social groups, such as officers, military units, scribes, artisans, and peasants. Aldred includes a select bibliography for further research.

BOTTÉRO's essays highlight the living legacy of Mesopotamian "ways of thinking, analyzing, and organizing the universe." Bottéro sees here the first glimpses of what would become "Western" philosophy and science. An important contribution of this work is its discussion of the field of Assyriology. Bottéro is also noteworthy for his detailed description of the invention of writing and the eventual decipherment of cuneiform script. The book's approach is thematic and aims throughout to bring us closer to our cultural progenitors. Topics discussed include the divinatory sciences, the institution of divine kingship, law, sexuality, the religious system, the mythology of death, and "intelligence and the technical function of power." This work is distinguished by its thorough treatment of the intellectual history of ancient Mesopotamia.

GORDON and RENDSBURG offer one of the few surveys of biblical Israel as seen through the lens of the larger Mediterranean world. The work covers the patriarchal period, the Amarna Age, the importance of Ugaritic texts for shedding light on the Hebrew Bible, the development of the tribal league, monarchic and divided Israel, Mesopotamian invasions, and the eventual restoration of Jerusalem under Persian rule. The authors pay special attention throughout to the literary aspects of the Near Eastern texts in question and how they elucidate various aspects of the Hebrew Bible and its writ-

ers. One of the most important contributions of this work is its inclusion of Homeric literature for purposes of comparison with biblical and Near Eastern, especially Ugaritic, writings. Full of original insights, this work is immensely readable.

HALLO and SIMPSON outline the "political and cultural development of pre-classical antiquity," by which they intend primarily Mesopotamia and Egypt. The work covers the history of ancient Mesopotamia from the dawn of civilization to the conquest of Babylonia by the Persians in the sixth century B.C.E. Their treatment of Egyptian history covers the period from the appearance of writing, around 3000 B.C.E., to the conquest by Alexander in 322 B.C.E. The authors place emphasis on the political history of the two superpowers of the ancient world, while considering also the culturally, socially, and economically influential forces that shaped the respective entities. The resources that inform this work are more textual than archaeological. The book provides copious dynastic lists, photographs, and maps. Throughout the work there are demonstrations to be found of the authors' belief in the "underlying unity of the 'Ancient Near East.'"

KRAMER's unique study of the people credited with the invention of writing and a host of other cultural achievements has done much to put the great Sumerian culture on the map. While focusing on the various aspects of Sumerian culture, Kramer pays special attention to how the Sumerians contributed to the progress of world civilization. Among other things, the work discusses schools, international affairs, historiography, law, justice, social reform, agriculture and horticulture, cosmology and cosmogony, ethics, medicine, literature, and kingship. Kramer takes pains to point out many biblical parallels, though many of them are somewhat strained. Photographs, sketches, and maps assist the reader, as do an abundance of translations. While the book is in need of an update, it remains a classic first introduction to the Sumerians.

KUHRT's work is magisterial and exhaustive, providing informative background essays on various aspects of the greater Near East as well as countless maps and diagrams. While primarily a historical and, hence, chronological outline of rulers and events, the volumes also provide rich archaeological documentation for the periods in question. Filled with original insights into the many historical problems, the treatment is evenhanded and extraordinarily, even incredibly, readable. Kuhrt covers the civilizations of Mesopotamia and Egypt especially well, providing an excellent historical context for understanding the rise of biblical Israel. Her placement of biblical Israel within the larger Levant is indicative of a mastery of the historical context and is especially useful since it removes the Israelites and the Hebrew Bible from an isolation that all too often marks scholarship on the subject. Kuhrt's work highlights the continuities and interactions between periods and peoples of the ancient Near East.

OPPENHEIM offers a masterful, though dense, treatment of ancient Mesopotamia. The author's pessimism concerning the ability to reconstruct accurately ancient Mesopotamian culture is evident in the title and in the author's famous essay "Why a 'Mesopotamian Religion' Should Not be Written." Paradoxically, however, the work contributes so much to our understanding on the subject that it has yet to be rivaled. Oppenheim surveys the social and economic fabric, scribal activity and the various types of written sources, mathematics, astronomy, medicine, crafts, and the divinatory arts, as well as the differences between Babylonian and Assyrian cultures. He also offers an analysis of Mesopotamian psychology.

SASSON brings together the world's most prominent ancient Near East scholars for contributions on the subjects of their particular expertise. The encyclopedic format of the volumes allows readers ready access to up-to-date information on the most important aspects of ancient Near Eastern history and culture. Unique to these volumes is the extensive treatment of mid-Euphrates and Syrian sites such as Mari, Emar, Alalakh, and Ebla. The volumes include bibliographic references and indexes, and are divided into thematic units on the ancient Near East in Western thought, the environment, population, social institutions, history and culture, economy and trade, technology and artistic production, religion and science, language, writing and literature, and visual and performing arts.

The collection of essays edited by SHAFER touches upon the most fascinating aspects of ancient Egyptian religion, including in-depth analyses of Egyptian concepts of the divine, the gods, divine kingship, cosmogonies, and cosmology. It also delves more deeply than most treatments into such related subjects as concepts of order and misfortune, piety, decorum and morality, magic and divination, and experientiality. A host of well-known scholars are brought on board to tackle these issues, and the result is a readable exploration of the most salient aspects of Egyptian religion. While it is not meant to be exhaustive, the work serves as an excellent foray into the subject. Highly spiced with photographs, it also offers a useful bibliography.

SILVERMAN gathers 13 Egyptologists to explore the chief elements of ancient Egyptian culture. Space is devoted to all the major topics, including kingship, religion, pyramids and temples, the solar cult, gods and goddesses, beliefs and rituals, hieroglyphs, engineering, and astronomy. This collection of scholarly essays represents the latest thinking on these and other issues relating to ancient Egypt. Though useful and interesting as an introduction to ancient Egypt, the tome's hefty size makes it a cumbersome textbook.

SNELL's unparalleled work provides as exhaustive a history of the social and economic forces that influenced the lives of kings and commoners from Egypt to Anatolia as the non-technical reader could possibly desire. Unique to this work is Snell's effort to broaden the context of the ancient Near East by devoting discussion to comparisons with China, Etruria, India, and Greece. The book moves chronologically, pausing every five centuries or so to consider synchronic comparisons. The epilogue contains a useful review of previous social and economic studies of the ancient Near East, and the bibliography and footnotes are copious. Snell covers everything from trade and money to animal management and demography and focuses on the everyday life of the ancients. Bringing to bear a vast array of archaeological and textual evidence, he achieves a thoroughly intelligent restoration of the cultures of Western Asia.

SCOTT B. NOEGEL

See also Canaanites; History: Biblical Israel

Angels and Demons

Davidson, Gustav, *A Dictionary of Angels, Including the Fallen Angels*, New York: Free Press, 1967

Fossum, Jarl E., *The Name of God and the Angel of the Lord: Samaritan and Jewish Concepts of Intermediation and the Origin of Gnosticism*, Tübingen: Mohr, 1985

Gieschen, Charles A., *Angelomorphic Christology: Antecedents and Early Evidence* (Arbeiten zur Geschichte des antiken Judentums und des Urchristentums, 42), Boston: Brill, 1998

Isaacs, Ronald H., *Ascending Jacob's Ladder: Jewish Views of Angels, Demons, and Evil Spirits*, Northvale, New Jersey: Aronson, 1997

Langton, Edward, *Essentials of Demonology: A Study of Jewish and Christian Doctrine, Its Origin and Development*, London: Epworth, 1949; New York: AMS, 1981

Newsom, Carol, *Songs of the Sabbath Sacrifice: A Critical Edition* (Harvard Semitic Studies, vol. 27), Atlanta, Georgia: Scholars Press, 1985

Odeberg, Hugo (editor), *3 Enoch; or, The Hebrew Book of Enoch*, Cambridge: University Press, 1928; reprinted with new prolegomenon by Jonas C. Greenfield, New York: Ktav, 1973

Olyan, Saul M., *A Thousand Thousands Served Him: Exegesis and the Naming of Angels in Ancient Judaism* (Texte und Studien zum antiken Judentum, 36), Tübingen: Mohr, 1993

Schäfer, Peter, *The Hidden and Manifest God: Some Major Themes in Early Jewish Mysticism* (SUNY Series in Judaica), Albany: State University of New York Press, 1992

van der Toorn, Karel, Bob Becking, and Pieter W. van der Horst (editors), *Dictionary of Deities and Demons in the Bible*, Leiden and New York: Brill, 1995

The word "angel" is derived from *angelos,* the Greek term adopted to translate the Hebrew appellation *malakh* (messenger). As it originally appeared in Scripture, *malakh* could indicate any messenger whether human or heavenly, bearing good tidings or ill. Within a relatively short time, however, the term came to designate, more or less exclusively, the heavenly creatures acting in the service of (an increasingly transcendent) God.

A significant portion of the speculative lore surrounding angels is concerned with the origins and activities of the "fallen" angels—typically known as "demons." Derived (and freely adapted) from the Greek *daimon,* the classification of demon has variously been applied to destructive or malicious spirits *(mazzikin);* Babylonian sprites *(shedim);* the "evil inclination" *(yetzer hara);* and, of course, the fallen angels (commonly traced to the *Nephilim* of Genesis 6:4). Certain angelic figures, such as Satan and the Angel of Death, are viewed as ambiguously possessing both celestial and diabolical qualities.

Names, descriptions, and taxonomic designations for virtually innumerable angels and demons are readily found in a wide variety of scriptural, pseudepigraphic, rabbinic, and mystical texts. Accordingly, there exists an extensive array of textual viewpoints regarding the roles such creatures play in Jewish thought and related traditions. The ten texts selected here as representative of recent scholarship may be roughly grouped into four categories: general introductions (Isaacs, Langton, Davidson, van der Toorn); source materials with commentary (Odeberg, Newsom); comparative studies (Fossum, Gieschen); and systematic-exegetical studies (Schäfer, Olyan).

ISAACS is a useful beginning text for students and the general reader. The book's introduction boasts "sections on angels in the Bible, Talmud, Midrash, liturgy, Jewish philosophy, mysticism, and chasidic lore" as well as entries on "good and fallen angels, . . . the role of Satan, demons and evil spirits." This inventory, however, suggests much more than Isaacs is, in fact, able to provide in the space of this slim volume. The book is nevertheless an accessible (albeit considerably foreshortened) overview of Jewish perspectives on both angels and demons, containing "notable quotations and stories" that range from ancient tradition to present-day superstitions.

Researchers and students seeking a more specific, comprehensive resource regarding Jewish demonology will find that LANGTON's study remains one of the most informative introductions available. Inevitably, the 1949 text occasionally contains passages and perspectives that seem out-of-date or problematic. Readers may even contend with the book's leading premise—namely, that one can trace the evolution of a single, undifferentiated Jewish and Christian doctrine of demonology from ancient Semitic beliefs through the Hebrew Bible and Jewish apocryphal writings to the New Testament. Langton's evolutionary bias, however, provides an advantage of sorts to the text, which plainly recognizes the demonology of the New Testament as directly indicative of first-century Jewish beliefs and precedents. Moreover, the book provides fine, detailed expositions of the syncretic influences upon Jewish demonology while also giving extensive scriptural and rabbinical illustrations of the figures under consideration (Azazel, Lilith, Satan, the shedim, etc.).

DAVIDSON remains the best, most scholarly book of its kind. Consistently informative and responsible, this resource is also engaging and eminently useful for the specialist and casual reader alike. The extensively cross-referenced entries are culled from a rich and disparate body of sources. In addition to canonical, apocryphal, and mystical texts from Persian, Jewish, Christian, and Muslim traditions, the impressive bibliography also includes a great deal of the dubious (although fascinating) lore of occultism, as well as indispensable literary treatments by Dante, Milton, Blake, and others. Considered in its entirety, Davidson's book is a noteworthy chronicle of the power that angels and devils of all sorts have long held over the human imagination.

Another extremely helpful reference work—particularly for researchers whose primary focus is biblical scholarship—is the impressive *Dictionary of Deities and Demons in the Bible*, edited by VAN DER TOORN. Although restricted to article entries on demons and deities whose names can be found in the Bible (including the canonical Apocrypha), the book functions as an in-depth and inclusive "scholarly introduction to the religious universe which the Israelites and the Early Christians were part of." Indeed, the work features a broad, comparative perspective and offers entries not only for foreign deities (Baal, Marduk, Thoth, Zeus), but also for the numerous names and epithets of God (including metonymic designations such as "Face"), for various deified phenomena (Day, Death, Moon, Stars), for transfigured or glorified biblical characters (Enoch, Moses), and for miscellaneous spirits and heavenly beings of all kinds. Each entry begins with a detailed etymology and proceeds to an elaborate sociohistorical contextualization of the figure under consideration, both in terms of its originating background (Canaanite, Babylonian, Egyptian, Greek, etc.) and its biblical appropriation. Van der Toorn's excellent general articles on angels and demons should be among the first consulted for the beginning reader interested in these topics.

It is generally acknowledged that ODEBERG's problematic translation of 3 Enoch—one of the principal works of angelology in early Jewish mysticism—has been superseded by that of P. Alexander in Charlesworth's two-volume *Old Testament Pseudepigrapha*. Nevertheless, Alexander himself asserts that "despite its weaknesses [Odeberg's volume] remains valuable." In fact, Odeberg's excellent introduction continues to provide readers with essential, in-depth discussions of 3 Enoch's exceptionally elaborate angelology and demonology. Particularly important is his elucidation of the mysterious and powerful angel Metatron—the central figure of the text—who is explicitly identified with the biblical character Enoch (Genesis 5:18–24).

NEWSOM supplies readers with a remarkable critical edition of the Qumran angelic liturgy known as the *Shirot ʿOlat Ha-Shabbat*. Through the guidance of her meticulous reconstructive commentary, she makes it possible for advanced readers to trace the "form, content, and function" of these extremely fragmentary manuscripts. Readers lacking a rudimentary knowledge of Hebrew will encounter occasional difficulties with Newsom's text. The author's introduction—which includes a chapter on the detailed "priestly angelology" of this Qumran composition—is a helpful orientation to the fragments and their specifically liturgical context, which is described as "something like the cultivation of a mystical communion with the angels."

FOSSUM and GIESCHEN undertake thoroughgoing literary-historical examinations of Jewish and other Near Eastern angelologies in order to illuminate studies of related traditions. Their respective endeavors, therefore, are genuinely (and strikingly) comparative in nature, with angels and angelic characteristics serving as the primary means of exchange between disparate belief systems. Fossum's leading thesis is that the disputed theory of the Jewish origin of Gnosticism is sustained by a demonstration of the angelic—and thus Semitic—morphology of the Gnostic demiurge. Closely related to Fossum's project is Gieschen's, in which the evidence for an early "Angel Christology" is sought in the antecedent Jewish traditions of "angelomorphic divine hypostases" and "angelomorphic humans" (said to include "Patriarchs, Prophets, Kings, Apostles, and Elect Ones"). It is perhaps helpful to note that Gieschen studied under Fossum and that both authors share premises concerning the adaptability of Jewish angelic beliefs that are not universally conceded.

SCHÄFER provides a systematic investigation of the roles of God, angels, and human beings, as depicted in the documents of early Jewish mysticism. Close readings are given to five significant works of the *merkabah* ("throne-chariot") tradition: Hekhalot Rabbati, Hekhalot Zutarti, Ma'aseh Merkabah, Merkabah Rabbah, and 3 Enoch. Each text (or "macroform," Schäfer's preferred term for the "superimposed literary unit" of a composition with variable manuscripts) is explicated through a three-part analysis of its descriptive accounts of (1) God, (2) angels and the celestial hierarchy, and (3) the actual mystical experience of the individual human subject. Throughout, Schäfer offers substantial, well-argued interpretations of the various names of God and the angels, the functions of the angelic heavenly praises, and the evolving significance of theurgic magic in mystical praxis.

OLYAN's astute exegetical study opens with an extremely helpful survey of recent scholarship concerning the origins of speculative "notions about angels." His own analysis then proceeds with the most compelling of these hypotheses; namely, that discussions of angels gradually emerged out of the scrupulous rabbinic exegesis of the Hebrew Bible itself. Gracefully and systematically, Olyan demonstrates the "exegetical origins" of angelic designations through his own careful exegesis of various biblical cruces, each of which is shown to contain suggestive theophanic or angelophanic intimations. Strongly argued and subtly nuanced, this is a thoughtful, highly readable introduction to a far-reaching cluster of topics.

CHRISTOPHER A. LINK

Animals, Treatment of

Bleich, J. David, "Judaism and Animal Experimentation," in *Animal Sacrifices: Religious Perspectives on the Use of Animals in Science* (Ethics and Action), edited by Tom Regan, Philadelphia: Temple University Press, 1986

Cohen, Noah J., *The Concept of Tsa'ar Ba'ale Hayyim (Kindness, and the Prevention of Cruelty, to Animals): Its Bases and Development in Biblical, Midrashic and Talmudic Literature*, Washington, D.C.: Catholic University of America, 1953; as *Tsa'ar Ba'ale Hayim: The Prevention of Cruelty to Animals*, New York: Feldheim, 1976

Kalechofsky, Roberta (editor), *Judaism and Animals Rights: Classical and Contemporary Responses*, Marblehead, Massachusetts: Micah, 1992

Schochet, Elijah J., *Animal Life in Jewish Tradition: Attitudes and Relationships*, New York: Ktav, 1984

Contrary to the beliefs of many people, Judaism has beautiful and powerful teachings about the need to show compassion to animals. The following are a few examples: Moses and King David were considered worthy to be leaders of the Jewish people because of their compassionate treatment of animals when they were shepherds. Rebecca was judged suitable to be a wife of the patriarch Isaac because of her kindness in watering the ten camels of Abraham's servant, Eliezer. Of course, many Torah laws mandate proper treatment of animals. One may not muzzle an ox while it is working in the field nor yoke a strong and a weak animal together. Animals are to rest on the sabbath, the importance of this concept being suggested by its inclusion in the Ten Commandments. The psalmist indicates God's concern for animals, for "His compassion is over all his creatures" (Psalm 145:9). Additionally, there is a precept in the Torah to emulate the Divine compassion, as it is written: "And you shall walk in His ways" (Deuteronomy 28:9). Perhaps the Jewish attitude toward animals is best summarized by Proverbs 12:10: "The righteous person considers the soul (life) of his or her animal." In summary, the Torah prohibits Jews from causing *tsa'ar ba'alei hayim* (any unnecessary pain, including psychological pain, to living creatures). The works below expand substantially on this brief analysis.

COHEN provides a comprehensive, well-documented study of the "bases, development and legislation in Hebrew literature" related to the treatment of animals. This pioneering book refutes the philosopher Schopenhauer's assertion that the theory that animals have no rights is rooted in Judaism by presenting an abundance of Jewish teachings and stories to show that *tsa'ar ba'alei hayim* "is a Biblical concept and therefore embodied in Israel's institutional life." The book is very well organized and documented (the notes span nearly half the book). However, Cohen does not relate Jewish teaching to current abuses of animals. Instead, he concludes by defending *shehitah*, Jewish laws related to the slaughtering of animals and the consumption of meat.

SCHOCHET provides an extremely comprehensive, well-documented work (there are more than 1,500 notes) that covers all aspects of Jewish teachings related to the treatment of animals. The book is chronologically divided into three composite portraits: biblical, rabbinic, and medieval and modern. Many Jewish teachings on the proper treatment of animals are discussed, but the author states that Judaism considers animals as "useful property" and as "delicate tools" for the use of people. He also hedges about whether laws related to animals were given out of compassion toward animals or for other reasons, such as the preservation of species or to make animals more useful to people. While vegetarianism is called "the pristine scriptural ideal," the author also states that the practice "lacks mass appeal and fails to yield authority." He fails, however, to address the realities involved in the mass production and the widespread consumption of meat and their relationship to basic Jewish values.

KALECHOFSKY provides a wide variety of insightful essays by Jewish classical and contemporary writers on issues related to the modern treatment of animals. Many of the essays make a strong case for an end to the exploitation of animals. Part one ("The Way We Think") features an essay by Jacob S. Raisin on the "Humanitarianism of the Laws of Israel" that provides an excellent summary of Jewish teachings on compassion to animals. The essays in part two ("The Way We Eat") show the connections between Jewish teachings and vegetarianism. Especially valuable is an essay, "Vegetarianism from a Jewish Perspective," by Orthodox scholar Rabbi Alfred Cohen, that indicates that Jews need not eat meat today. Part three ("The Way We Are Now") is mainly composed of essays that provide moral and scientific arguments against vivisection.

The editor contributes introductions to each part that give a valuable overview of the issues to be discussed.

BLEICH brings excellent credentials as a scholar of Jewish law to his comprehensive essay. With great thoroughness, he considers Jewish teachings on compassion for animals as a prelude to his discussion of the permissibility of animal experimentation. It is significant that Bleich, a highly respected Orthodox nonvegetarian rabbi, makes strong statements on Jewish responsibilities toward animals; for example, "Judaism must perforce view compassion toward animals as a moral imperative," and "Judaism most certainly does posit an unequivocal prohibition against causing cruelty to animals." He concludes that animal experimentation is permissible when such experiments are directly connected to the preservation of human life, but experiments cannot be allowed for strictly educational purposes.

RICHARD H. SCHWARTZ

Anti-Judaism: Late Antiquity

Barrett, C.K., *The Gospel of John and Judaism* (Franz Delitzsch Lectures), Philadelphia: Fortress, and London: S.P.C.K., 1975

Brawley, Robert L., *Luke-Acts and the Jews: Conflict, Apology, and Conciliation*, Atlanta, Georgia: Scholars Press, 1987

Brown, Raymond E., *The Community of the Beloved Disciple*, New York: Paulist, and London: Chapman, 1979

Davies, Alan T. (editor), *Antisemitism and the Foundations of Christianity*, New York: Paulist, 1979

Gager, John G., *The Origins of Anti-Semitism: Attitudes toward Judaism in Pagan and Christian Antiquity*, New York: Oxford University Press, 1983; Oxford: Oxford University Press, 1985

MacLennan, Robert S., *Early Christian Texts on Jews and Judaism* (Brown Judaic Studies, no. 194), Atlanta, Georgia: Scholars Press, 1990

Meeks, Wayne A. and Robert L. Wilken, *Jews and Christians in Antioch in the First Four Centuries of the Common Era*, Missoula, Montana: Scholars Press, 1978

Richardson, Peter (editor) with David Granskou, *Anti-Judaism in Early Christianity*, vol. 1: *Paul and the Gospels*, Waterloo, Ontario: Wilfrid Laurier University Press for the Canadian Corporation for Studies in Religion, 1986

Ruether, Rosemary Radford, *Faith and Fratricide: The Theological Roots of Anti-Semitism*, New York: Seabury, 1974; London: Search, 1975

Sanders, Jack T., *The Jews in Luke-Acts*, Philadelphia: Fortress, 1987

Sanders, Jack T., *Schismatics, Sectarians, Dissidents, Deviants: The First One Hundred Years of Jewish-Christian Relations*, London: SCM, and Valley Forge, Pennsylvania: Trinity Press International, 1993

Sandmel, Samuel, *Anti-Semitism in the New Testament?*, Philadelphia: Fortress, 1978

Stern, Menahem (editor), *Greek and Latin Authors on Jews and Judaism*, 2 vols., Jerusalem: Israel Academy of Sciences and Humanities, 1974

Taylor, Miriam S., *Anti-Judaism and Early Christian Identity: A Critique of the Scholarly Consensus* (Studia post-Biblica, vol. 46), Leiden and New York: Brill, 1995

Wilson, Stephen G. (editor), *Anti-Judaism in Early Christianity*, vol. 2: *Separation and Polemic*, Waterloo, Ontario: Wilfrid Laurier University Press for the Canadian Corporation for Studies in Religion, 1986

Wilson, Stephen G., *Related Strangers: Jews and Christians, 70–170 C.E.*, Minneapolis, Minnesota: Fortress, 1995

For the period from the beginning of the Roman Principate until the rise of Islam, a few modern authors examine pagan hostility to Judaism, but most deal with Christian anti-Judaism. Among the latter, most concern themselves with early Christianity—before the end of the early rabbinic period (c.200 C.E.). Others examine later Christian anti-Judaism, and some the entire period.

One can find all the relevant texts having to do with Greek and Latin authors' views on Jews and Judaism in STERN's work. The texts appear here both in the original languages and in English translation, along with Stern's analysis. A reading of these texts shows that real hostility begins early in the Principate, but that earlier pagan writers had often either expressed sympathy for the Jewish way of life or merely commented on it objectively. Stern concluded that, in spite of hostility toward Jews, Jewish ideas and even the Jewish lifestyle had spread widely in Mediterranean societies. GAGER goes beyond Stern to demonstrate, in an excellent discussion, that pagan writers were normally well-disposed toward Jews and Judaism, and that major hostility appeared only in the period from circa 35 until circa 135 C.E.—that is, the time during which there were three Jewish revolts, two in Judah and one apparently empire-wide, against Roman rule. Even during this time, Gager shows, there were still pagan voices that spoke "against the stream." Furthermore, there is considerable evidence throughout the early Principate of pagans converting to Judaism or otherwise adopting Jewish ideas or practices. Thus Christian anti-Judaism is not the carrying over of pagan anti-Judaism into Christianity. Gager begins with the *Adversus Judaeos* literature and brings in evidence from Syrian Christianity in the fourth century that shows that even at that time all Christians cannot be said to have maintained a uniformly hostile attitude toward Jews and Judaism. He also finds varying degrees of hostility or even of accommodation in the New Testament. In a lengthy discussion of Paul, Gager proposes that Paul never intended to deny salvation to Jews as Jews but only insisted that gentiles need not become Jews to attain salvation. This explanation of Paul has not met with wide acceptance, and Gager is perhaps too inclined to emphasize the positive aspects of early Christian literature.

While Ruether was not the first Christian author to face the problem of the endemic nature of Christian anti-Judaism, she did so in a way that attracted attention and focused later debate. It seems best, therefore, to begin with her work and then to discuss others in chronological order.

RUETHER first presents an adequate discussion of pagan anti-Judaism, finding the pagan attitude toward Judaism ambivalent. She then proposes that this anti-Judaism cannot be the source of Christian anti-Judaism, which rested on a distinctively theological base. She examines the New Testament thoroughly and notes that it is general Jewish rejection of the Christian claim of Jesus' messiahship and lordship that leads to Christian claims of Jewish perversity and of Christian superiority to Judaism. The New Testament thus places the blame for the death of Jesus on Jews and endorses a Christology that is inescapably antisemitic. Next Ruether discusses the patristic literature of the *Adversus Iudaeos* type, where she finds a more systematic hostility, but one based on the New Testament.

This literature reads the Hebrew Bible in such a way that all the prophetic denunciations of wickedness are taken to apply to Jews, whereas all the prophecies of hope apply to gentile Christians. Jews are condemned for not following their Torah, but Christians are said to fulfill the Torah in a spiritual way. Following this, Ruether shows how this theological anti-Judaism became social policy once the empire became Christian early in the fourth century, and finally she proposes that modern Christianity could reverse its centuries-long anti-Judaism by emphasizing a theology of covenant.

BARRETT, in a book that was originally a lecture series in Germany, gives a fine review of scholarship on John in brief space and then addresses the relation of the Gospel of John to Judaism. Somewhat anticipating the theory of Raymond Brown (below), he understands the root of Johannine hostility to Judaism to lie in arguments between Christian Jews and other Jews that led to expulsion of the Christians from a synagogue. Barrett also makes the Jewish elements in the gospel clear. Uniquely, he finds the intellectual source of both Judaism and anti-Judaism in the gospel in John's own experience of both the reality of Judaism and the opposition between Judaism and Christianity. Thus the situation of Judaism, as of other elements, in John is paradoxical.

MEEKS and WILKEN approach the topic in a new way by examining the history of Jewish-Christian-pagan relations in one place—Antioch in Syria—over a period of several hundred years. First they sketch the history of Jews in Antioch—a large community that experienced some episodes of persecution during the period when there were Jewish revolts but that otherwise had apparently harmonious relations with their pagan neighbors. After Christianity began to spread in Antioch, there seems to have been no local conflict between Jews and Christians, and indeed from writers circa 110 and again circa 385 there is evidence of non-Jewish Christians' adopting Jewish practices. Christian leaders opposed this tendency. When Julian "the Apostate"—the Roman Emperor residing in Antioch—tried in the late fourth century to restore pagan religion to what was by then a Christian empire, he sought the support of Jews by also planning to rebuild the temple in Jerusalem so that Jews could again sacrifice to their god there. This pitted Christians against Jews, and John Chrysostom's sermons that so viciously attack Judaism come from this period. The book contains Chrysostom's anti-Judaic sermons as well as letters of about the same date from Libanius, a prominent pagan, to the Jewish patriarch. The letters are friendly and contrast strongly with Chrysostom's sermons. The book traces developments down to the early seventh century, when the Christian majority drove all the Jews out of Antioch.

The implication of Meeks's and Wilken's study is that Gager was correct in separating Christian anti-Judaism from possible pagan influence, but they further show that it was political events (not theology) that turned the Antiochene Christians against their Jewish neighbors, and that at least one early Christian community was not overtly anti-Judaic, whatever the Christian scriptures and leaders such as Chrysostom might say.

SANDMEL, in as irenic a way as possible, asks whether there was antisemitism or anti-Judaism in the New Testament, and he finds it everywhere, especially in the Gospels. The most notable points are that the New Testament makes Jews guilty of killing Jesus, even if they did not do the deed themselves, and that Paul makes of the Torah a useless and even vile thing. Sandmel's treatment is somewhat weakened by his tendency to cite many points of theological difference between Jews and Christians—such as the definition of Messiah (Christ)—as elements in early Christian antisemitism.

BROWN proposes a new understanding of the Gospel of John that reveals the social origins of the anti-Judaism there. According to Brown's theory, which has been widely accepted, one can see in John the history of a degenerating relationship between a minority of Christians in a Jewish congregation and the majority. At first there is a difference of opinion over the significance of Jesus, with many in the majority accepting that he was a good man who could perform healings. Later, the insistence of the Christians that everyone agree with them made it dangerous to be a Christian openly, so that there came to be a group of "crypto-Christians," and the majority expelled the Christians from the congregation. After this, the Christians turned more and more to non-Jews to seek converts and began to condemn Jews as a group.

The volume edited by DAVIES contains essays that respond to Ruether's book. The essays that consider late antiquity discuss the relation of pagan to Christian anti-Judaism, the Christian Christological rationale, how the Jews are presented in the Gospels and the Book of Acts, and anti-Judaism in the patristic period. The discussions of Matthew, Paul, and the patristic period are especially helpful, but the other discussions seem to betray some Christian defensiveness.

The volumes edited by RICHARDSON and GRANSKOU and by WILSON (1986) are the product of a seminar within the Canadian Society of Biblical Studies on the topic of early Christian anti-Judaism. They deal with relevant Christian—and to some degree Jewish—literature up until the year 200. Most of the essays explain what some might take to be anti-Jewish aspects of early Christian literature as being either directed to specific opponents (and thus not to be generalized) or the product of a particular situation where there was some hostility or competition between Christians and Jews. Several of the essays contain very keen observations, but the overall effect of the two volumes may be to obscure some of the harsher anti-Judaic tendencies in early Christianity.

SANDERS (1987) grapples with the problem in Luke and Acts (written by the same author) that the narrative often shows favorable or mixed interactions between Christians and Jews but that in the speeches—whether of Jesus in Luke or of the Apostles in Acts—Jews are routinely condemned. He notes that in Jesus' first speech and in Paul's last, Jews are condemned for not accepting Christianity, and furthermore that both speeches claim that this Jewish mistake was foretold in scripture, and Sanders concludes that the speeches present the author's attitude and that the author used the narrative to present a progressive justification for the condemnation in the speeches. Thus he finds Luke and Acts pronouncedly antisemitic.

BRAWLEY argues that Luke-Acts does not represent a theology of Christian supercessionism, that in fact the author tries to show how Judaism has its proper fulfillment in Jesus' messiahship. He proposes that the author was trying to reconcile feuding Jewish Christians and gentile Christians and to justify Paul's version of Christianity.

MacLENNAN focuses his attention on four *Adversus Judaeos* texts—the *Epistle of Barnabas,* Justin's *Dialogue with Trypho a Jew,* Melito's *Paschal Homily,* and Tertullian's *Answer to the Jews*—all from the second century. He emphasizes the particular situation of each text, bringing in archaeological evidence where it is available. In the end he finds that none of the texts is originally anti-Judaic, since each one is related to a particular Jewish situation, not to Judaism generally. In some cases, this seems to obscure the harshness of the rhetoric in these works.

SANDERS (1993) pays attention to what can be known about relations, not attitudes. He also brings in archaeological evidence, and he tries to understand everything in sociological perspective. Thus he strives for explanation as well as description. He understands the early Jewish sporadic persecution of Christians in terms of modern deviance theory and shows that most likely, every occurrence of such persecution closely followed a threat to Jewish identity (an exact dating is not always possible). He further shows that outside the context of Judea, there was little contact between Jews and Christians, but there were vigorous disagreements between Jewish Christians and gentile Christians. He understands this situation as the progress of disparate segments of a new religious movement groping toward just the level of accommodation and opposition to the larger society that will produce success.

While not discussing all the above works, TAYLOR attacks the underlying thesis of many of them, which is that Christian anti-Jewish statements grew out of specific situations. She agrees rather with Ruether that early Christian anti-Judaism has a symbolic or theological base, and she argues that to ignore that base in favor of the "conflict" model is to fail to come to grips with the heart of Christian anti-Judaism. Her slim volume merits most serious consideration.

WILSON's (1995) work, finally, has its greatest strength in being in effect a compendium of sources on early Jewish-Christian relations. It is also particularly valuable in presenting clearly the anti-Judaism of Luke-Acts and of Melito, in defining different types of Jewish Christians, and in detailing Christian appropriation and reinterpretation of Judaic tradition.

Perhaps the most important aspect of the works reviewed here is Christian willingness to confront the issue, even if the explanations that Christian scholars give often seem to absolve early Christian writers of antisemitism. The problem will doubtless continue to attract scholarly interest.

JACK T. SANDERS

See also Anti-Judaism: Middle Ages; Antisemitism

Anti-Judaism: Middle Ages

Chazan, Robert, *European Jewry and the First Crusade,* Berkeley: University of California Press, 1987

Cohen, Jeremy, *The Friars and the Jews: The Evolution of Medieval Anti-Judaism,* Ithaca, New York: Cornell University Press, 1982

Eidelberg, Shlomo, *The Jews and the Crusaders: The Hebrew Chronicles of the First and Second Crusades,* Madison: University of Wisconsin Press, 1977

Hsia, R. Po-chia, *The Myth of Ritual Murder: Jews and Magic in Reformation Germany,* New Haven, Connecticut: Yale University Press, 1988

Langmuir, Gavin I., *Toward a Definition of Antisemitism,* Berkeley: University of California Press, 1990

Oberman, Heiko, *The Roots of Anti-Semitism in the Age of Renaissance and Reformation,* Philadelphia: Fortress, 1984

Parkes, James, *The Conflict of the Church and the Synagogue: A Study in the Origins of Antisemitism,* London: Soncino, 1934; Philadelphia: Jewish Publication Society, 1961

Trachtenberg, Joshua, *The Devil and the Jews: The Medieval Conception of the Jew and Its Relation to Modern Antisemitism,* New Haven, Connecticut: Yale University Press, and London: Milford, Oxford University Press, 1943

Anti-Judaism in the Middle Ages, as at all times, was complex, dependent upon a variety of factors, and extremely volatile. Much like the later antisemitism associated with racial discussions in the 19th century, anti-Judaism was a manifestation of social, political, economic, and religious tensions, many of which had little to do with Jews inherently. Anti-Jewish sentiment and action were often the culminating expressions of attempts to define the medieval community by exclusion. After long periods of what might be termed "normal" relations, Jews could frequently be subject to legal and social discrimination and physical and spiritual attack. Notwithstanding recent discussions about how Jews fared in Islamic as opposed to Christian lands in the Middle Ages, it seems clear that the fate of Jews and Jewish communities everywhere was subject to the transformations within the host communities in which they resided, and could variously be good or bad at different times.

Anti-Judaism might be the manifestation of thought-out processes such as legal decrees that, among other restrictions, prohibited Jews from attending public baths; forced Jews to pay poll taxes; forced Jews to wear distinguishing clothes or markings; prohibited Jews from being in certain places at proscribed times; forced Jews to attend conversionary sermons; restricted Jewish religious practices; or hindered full Jewish participation in legal processes. But anti-Jewish actions could also result from more spontaneous outbursts among various strata of the population, resulting in expulsions, such as those in England, France, and numerous cities and territories in Germany; in massive pogroms throughout Islamic lands, for example in the Iberian peninsula and North Africa throughout the high Middle Ages; and in the violence of the Crusades.

Anti-Judaism could be a popular or an elite phenomenon: scholarly tracts could be written by theologians and legal scholars; anti-Jewish legislation could be drafted and enforced by territorial lords and monarchs. Often such "elite" culture could stimulate popular action against Jews. But popular culture in the form of stories, myths, and artistic representations might also disparage Jews and lead to serious consequences for Jewish communities.

The modern study of medieval anti-Judaism has been greatly affected by the perspective of 20th-century events and historiographic considerations. The multitude of books available on the subject, of which the following is only a very narrow sampling, exhibit a variety of understandings of Judaism and anti-Judaism and a diversity of sources and methods that reveal a great deal about Jewish culture as well as developments within non-Jewish society. The following studies show how Jews fared particularly in the European Middle Ages but also consider the intellectual and social milieu in which the Jews were conceived and written about.

TRACHTENBERG's classic text examines the demonization of the Jew in medieval Europe, particularly in associations of the Jews with the Devil; the image of the Jews as sorcerers, magicians, and poisoners; and the Christian theological attack against Jews as infidels and usurers. Trachtenberg is particularly interested in exploring the nature of medieval superstition and the ways in which medieval folk ideas have helped inform modern antisemitic representations of Jews and Judaism. The book examines the period between the 11th and 16th centuries, focusing more on popular and less on learned manifestations of anti-Judaism, and includes written sources as well as evidence gleaned from graphic arts. Not surprisingly, Trachtenberg finds that the accusations leveled against Jews had less to do with any Jewish practice of magic than with the beliefs and practices current among Christians.

PARKES's old but still important book spans late antiquity and the early Middle Ages. He surveys the position of the Jews in the Roman world, the clash between Christianity and Judaism (focusing in particular on the part played by Jews in the persecution of early Christians), and the position of Jews, especially their legal position, in Christian societies from the late Roman empire, the Byzantine empire, and the Visigothic kingdom. The volume also includes useful appendixes and extensive indexes.

EIDELBERG offers introductions to and translations of four Hebrew chronicles of the Crusades: *The Chronicle of Solomon bar Simson* written sometime in the early 12th century, which details the events of the attacks on the Jews in the First Crusade; *The Chronicle of Rabbi Eliezer bar Nathan,* which also chronicles the events of the First Crusade and seems to borrow from a parent source some of the same information as the previous chronicle; *The Narrative of the Old Persecutions,* or *Mainz Anonymous,* which also deals with the First Crusade, but offers additional information not found in the first two chronicles; and *Sefer Zekhirah,* or *The Book of Remembrances,* of Rabbi Ephraim of Bonn, a popular account by an important 12th-century scholar detailing the Second Crusade. The volume includes a general introduction to the subject and extensive explanatory footnotes.

CHAZAN offers a thorough presentation of the First Crusade and the Jews, including a general background to the Crusades and Jewish-Christian relations; an overview of the sources available (Christian and Jewish); a closer look at the actual violence and patterns of Jewish response; a study of the later Crusades; and a consideration of the position of the Crusades in the history of European Jewry. The volume includes extensive notes, bibliography, and index. Although Chazan rejects the idea that 1096 and the First Crusade marked a sharp turn in the Ashkenazi experience, he does argue that study of these events opens a number of broader questions regarding the history of the Jews in northern Europe during the Middle Ages, particularly the striking new developments of the 12th and 13th centuries.

Through an examination of a variety of manifestations of anti-Judaism in the Middle Ages, including legislation, politics, economy, religion, and irrational fantasies, LANGMUIR argues forcefully that Jews became the target of unusual hostility in northern Europe in the 12th and 13th centuries. Of particular interest is Langmuir's attempt to understand antisemitism more broadly through the medium of medieval manifestations of anti-Judaism and his analysis of the role of the irrational in medieval anti-Judaism.

COHEN investigates the theological status of the Jew in medieval Europe, noting that it is part of an elaborate web of Jewish-Christian relations. Of particular interest to Cohen is the importance of the Dominican and Franciscan friars who "directed and oversaw virtually all the anti-Jewish activities of the Christian clergy in the West." Cohen seeks to account for the anti-Jewish ideology of the friars and to understand it within the evolution of medieval Christian self-consciousness. He focuses on the emergence of anti-Judaism in mendicant theology, on the ideological refinement of anti-Judaism in the thought of Pablo Christiani and Raymond Martini, and on the development of mendicant anti-Judaism as reflected in the writings of Ramon Lull and a variety of other preachers. Cohen's book represents intellectual history at its best, with sharp analysis of medieval mendicant writing and broad understanding of the development of medieval culture.

OBERMAN, one of the great intellectual historians of the later Middle Ages and the Reformation, makes a sophisticated and important contribution to the discussion on anti-Judaism in the early formative years of Protestantism that offers a very detailed analysis of the theological and intellectual writings and arguments of a wide variety of central Reformation figures. Often this analysis results in a major reassessment of a particular author's position regarding Jews. The book offers also an important synthesis of material that has not often been taken as a whole or written about with great nuance. Oberman provides a useful biographical section on the primary scholars he examines as well as very thorough footnotes throughout. He discusses as well the later developments of what he calls the "Third Reformation," as he assesses the degree that one can speak about anti-Judaism and tolerance in early modern and, by extension, modern Europe.

In his very readable, well-researched, and suggestive study, HSIA attempts to understand the development and eventual decline in Germany of the legend of the Jewish ritual murder of Christian children for sacrificial purposes. According to Hsia, ritual murder accusations became widespread throughout Europe in the 13th century and reached their climax in the 15th and 16th centuries. They were particularly widespread in Germany. Rather than an attempt to refute the charges laid against Jews, Hsia uses the accusations as a means to "elucidate the production of social knowledge in its specific historical structure and to explain how cultural symbols acquired their power and signification." Hsia analyzes the major ritual murder trials leading up to the Reformation, and then assesses the effects that the Reformation, with its emphasis on religion over magic, had on ritual murder accusations. For Hsia, the Reformation brought about a divergence of learned and popular discourse about ritual murder, with popular culture retaining much of its earlier anti-Jewish virulence and learned culture becoming more legalistic and less persuaded by "popular superstitions."

DEAN BELL

See also Anti-Judaism: Late Antiquity; Antisemitism; Crusades; Inquisition; Libels, Anti-Jewish: Medieval

Antisemitism

Dinnerstein, Leonard, *Antisemitism in America,* New York: Oxford University Press, 1994

Gilman, Sander, *The Jew's Body,* New York: Routledge, Chapman and Hall, 1991

Goodman, David and Masanori Miyazawa, *Jews in the Japanese Mind: The History and Uses of a Cultural Stereotype,* New York: Free Press, 1995

Katz, Jacob, *From Prejudice to Destruction: Anti-Semitism, 1700–1933,* Cambridge, Massachusetts: Harvard University Press, 1980

Ruether, Rosemary Radford, *Faith and Fratricide: The Theological Roots of Anti-Semitism,* New York: Seabury, 1974; London: Search, 1975

Wistrich, Robert, *Antisemitism: The Longest Hatred,* New York: Pantheon, and London: Thames Methuen, 1991

The German journalist Wilhelm Marr coined the term "antisemitism" in 1897 as a synonym for "Judenhass" (Jew-hatred). Encompassing racial and political ideologies in addition to the many ancient accusations against Jews including deicide, antisemitism has protean meanings. Crossing the disciplines of history, anthropology, sociology, political science, literature,

psychology, and economics, the following six books explore antisemitism in Europe, the United States, and Asia. The half-dozen representative titles discussed here have been selected both for their intrinsic merits and for the diversity of their respective concerns and methodologies. Literature on the subject has been monitored in recent years in the excellent series *Antisemitism: An Annotated Bibliography* (New York: Garland, 1987–), edited by Susan S. Cohen for the Vidal Sassoon International Center for the Study of Antisemitism of the Hebrew University of Jerusalem.

WISTRICH offers a remarkably comprehensive overview of "the entire history of anti-Semitism from its beginnings until the present day, in a form accessible to the non-specialist reader." His collection contains an eight-chapter historical survey, from antiquity to beyond the Holocaust; six chapters of regional surveys ranging across Britain, North America, France, and Eastern Europe; and finally a section on the Middle East. Instead of providing a universal explanation for the phenomenon of antisemitism, Wistrich highlights the variety of stereotypes, fantasies, and obsessions that have revolved around Jews for more than 2,000 years. Analyzing economic, theological, cultural, and political beliefs, he explains antisemitism as simply the world's longest existing hatred. He argues that as early as the third century B.C.E., one can find the development of the main tenets of antisemitism: that Jews sacrificed non-Jews as part of religious rites, were snobbish and misanthropic, and produced nothing of value as a people. Yet, Wistrich maintains that meanings of antisemitism have not remained static through history. To strengthen his argument, Wistrich examines the different uses of antisemitism by Egyptians, Romans, Greeks, and Christians. Importantly for the contemporary reader, Wistrich analyzes how Christianity leveled charges of deicide and satanism against Jews. As a result, theological antisemitism, which held a component of inherited guilt for the death of Christ, was adopted by various Nazis, Bolsheviks, Muslims, and African Americans to justify their antisemitic beliefs. Existing as a "miasma of nightmarish paranoia, millennial fantasy, homicidal hatred, and sheer political cynicism," Wistrich asserts that antisemitism will continue to remain a destructive and divisive ideology for humankind.

RUETHER remains the most striking exploration of antisemitism within Christian theology. In her first chapters, she delves into ancient Greek, Roman, and Egyptian societies to show how non-Christian "pagan hate" for the Jews was not theological, but was rather a "consequence of religious sociology." Consequently, Ruether argues that antisemitism within Christianity is not an extension of classical antisemitism, but instead it is deeply rooted in the rejection of the Jews found in the New Testament Scriptures. Exploring the Christian Roman Empire, the Crusades, the Age of the Ghetto, the Enlightenment, and the Holocaust, Ruether contends that the Christian Church can not separate itself from its antisemitic heritage found in the New Testament and the negation of the Jews by the church fathers. Concerned with the historical culpability of Christianity against Judaism, Ruether calls for reforms in current Christian theological curricula in order for Christians to live without the need to destroy the teachings and people of Judaism.

KATZ chronicles the rise of modern antisemitism in intellectual thought from the end of the Middle Ages to the racial ideology of Nazi Germany. Importantly, Katz asserts that antisemitism, as a racial ideology, manifested itself as early as 1790. Unlike other scholars who date the emergence of racial antisemitism during the latter half of the 19th century, Katz attributes the initial development to antisemitic polemicists who took Johann Andreas Eisenmenger and Voltaire's writings out of context. Consequently, Katz argues that the bastardized versions of Eisenmenger and Voltaire's writings negatively influenced the social image of the Jew in Europe. Although Jews did receive rights during the period of emancipation, Katz suggests that "anti-Jewish animosity grew in strength, paradoxically just when in the wake of the Enlightenment and modern rationality one might have expected it to disappear." Katz not only traces the rise of modern antisemitism on an intellectual level; he also analyzes the political, cultural, and social attitudes toward Jews prevailing before, during, and after emancipation.

GILMAN analyzes the complex stereotypes of the male Jewish body found during the Christian Diaspora "as a means of comprehending the status as well as the representation of the Jew." In a series of essays, Gilman focuses on the stereotypes surrounding the foot, circumcised penis, nose, voice, skin color, and sexuality of Jewish men. Gilman argues that the representation of the Jewish male in society is the key to understanding the essence of Christian Jew-hatred and, consequently, racial antisemitism. Interpreting stereotypes of the Jewish body and psyche in speech, social constructs, psychology, gender, and race, Gilman demonstrates how the Jew is seen as "an Other, one of the 'ugly' race." Importantly, stereotypical images emerged when the science of race secularized many of Christianity's religious notions of the Jew. In addition, he contends that these stereotypes have led to the construction of the Jew's own identity, a blend of myth and realties producing a constructed difference between the sense of Jew and non-Jew in society.

DINNERSTEIN is the "first comprehensive scholarly survey of antisemitism in the United States." Providing a comprehensive overview from the colonial era to the present day (1607–1992), Dinnerstein devotes many of his chapters to 20th-century developments: post-World War I, the Depression, World War II, Southern antisemitism, and African American antisemitism. Dinnerstein dates the emergence of antisemitism in the United States to the last third of the 19th century when immigration soared; however, he asserts that a deeply ingrained hostility toward Jews already existed in the United States due to Christian theology. Dinnerstein argues that Christian heritage and teachings permeated U.S. society so thoroughly that even secular persons were influenced by Christian attitudes and beliefs. Yet he makes the distinction that to be Christian in the United States usually meant to be Protestant, and therefore Catholics also found themselves victims of discrimination. Moreover, Dinnerstein notes that Jews and Catholics have not been the sole targets of discrimination in the United States. The treatment of those considered racially different (African Americans, Asians, Native Americans, etc.) has been more severe than the treatment of those who were defined as whites. Dinnerstein notes, however, that many of these minority groups, notably African Americans, have engaged in antisemitism. After his analysis of Christian-Jewish relations and black-Jewish relations, Dinnerstein ends optimistically, asserting that antisemitism in the United States has been declining and will continue to do so.

GOODMAN and MIYAZAWA explore the existence of antisemitism and philosemitism in modern Japanese history. Although there are few Jews in Japanese society, Goodman and Miyazawa assert that the Japanese are both appalled and fascinated by Jews. With chapters ranging through all of modern Japanese history, the authors analyze the concept of the Jew in Japanese culture. Goodman and Miyazawa argue that the Japanese practice an antisemitism that is solely found in literature and thought, because they do not construct physical or social barriers to those Jews who live in Japanese society. Contending that the Japanese are a people with an "ethnic nationalist xenophobia," the authors explain how the Japanese notions of Jews stem from a 1000-year-old tradition of using images of all foreigners—the "other"—to define "Japaneseness." However, Japanese Christians in the early 20th century found racial and historical links between the Jews and the Japanese. Paradoxically, Goodman and Miyazawa state that while the Japanese see the Jews as the "other," who should therefore be feared and hated, the Japanese also see themselves as having a bond with God's "chosen people," who therefore should be admired and emulated. Citing many examples that illustrate the dual image of Jews in modern Japanese history, Goodman and Miyazawa contend that Japanese attitudes towards Jews reflect wider aspects of Japanese culture and history. By analyzing the dichotomy of Japanese antisemitism and philosemitism, Goodman and Miyazawa's book helps one understand "modern Japan, its development, its character, and its future promise."

LAURIE BLUMBERG

See also Anti-Judaism; Holocaust; Libels, Anti-Jewish: Modern

Apocalyptic

Coggins, Richard J., Peter R. Ackroyd, Anthony Phillips, and Michael A. Knibb (editors), *Israel's Prophetic Tradition; Essays in Honour of Peter R. Ackroyd*, Cambridge: Cambridge University Press, 1982

Collins, John J. (editor), *Apocalypse: Morphology of a Genre* (Semeia, vol. 14), Decatur, Illinois: Scholars, 1979

Collins, John J., *The Apocalyptic Imagination*, New York: Crossroad, 1984; 2nd edition, Grand Rapids, Michigan: Eerdmans, 1998

Collins, John J., *Apocalypticism in the Dead Sea Scrolls*, London and New York: Routledge, 1997

Hanson, Paul D., *The Dawn of Apocalyptic: The Historical and Sociological Roots of Jewish Apocalyptic Eschatology*, Philadelphia: Fortress, 1975, revised edition, 1979

Lambert, Wilfrid G., *The Background to Jewish Apocalyptic*, London: Athlone, 1978

Rowley, Harold H., *The Relevance of Apocalyptic: A Study of Jewish and Christian Apocalypses from Daniel to the Revelation*, London: Lutterworth, 1944; new and revised [3rd] edition, London: Lutterworth, and New York: Associated Press, 1963

Russell, David S., *The Method and Message of Jewish Apocalyptic, 200 B.C.–A.D. 100*, London: SCM, and Philadelphia: Westminster, 1964

Stone, Michael E., *Scriptures, Sects and Visions: A Profile of Judaism From Ezra to the Jewish Revolts*, Philadelphia: Fortress, 1980; Oxford: Blackwell, 1982

Once viewed as the poor relation of biblical literature, apocalyptic has been a subject of increased scholarly interest during the last two decades of the 20th century, with a particularly lively debate as to the origins of this genre of writing still ongoing. This interest seems likely to be maintained with the release of further material from Qumran.

STONE's book is a useful introductory guide to Judaism from the time of Ezra to the Jewish Revolts. Of particular relevance to apocalyptic are the chapters on the third century B.C.E. and the intellectual and cultural milieu in Palestine that led to the development of the apocalypse genre. Sections of the book also are dedicated to Enoch, apocalyptic origins, and the Qumran scrolls, as well as related topics such as pseudepigraphy and eschatology. Compact and lucid, this is a fine starting point for the general reader.

RUSSELL's book is in some respects dated but is still a useful source of reference for the general reader interested in the Jewish apocalyptic writings in the period from 200 B.C.E. to 100 C.E. Russell argues that apocalyptic writing arose out of the decline of traditional prophecy as the prophetic canon hardened around 200 B.C.E. At the same time, he claims, apocalyptic writing remains firmly embedded in prophecy. Both of these assertions would be accepted today by the vast majority of commentators, with the caveat that apocalyptic writing also belongs to a learned tradition, an aspect of the genre that receives less attention from Russell. Nevertheless, this remains an important book for its thorough treatment of the relationship between prophecy and apocalyptic writing.

COLLINS (1984) provides the best introduction to apocalyptic literature as a whole. He begins with important definitions of the terms "apocalypse" and "apocalypticism" and also gives some idea of the intellectual matrix and social settings from which they are derived. Thereafter, he adopts a largely chronological approach. Chapters focus particularly on Daniel and the early Enoch literature (as the earliest examples of true apocalypses); related genres such as the oracles and testamentary literature; and, importantly, the Jewish apocalyptic literature that emerged out of the destruction of Jerusalem in 70 C.E. and the diaspora. Again, this is a lucid work, accessible to nonspecialists but containing the best results of modern scholarship.

COLLINS (1997) also provides the best introduction to apocalyptic literature in the Qumran writings. Here, he approaches the subject of apocalypticism thematically, considering in turn topics such as creation and the origin of evil, the periodization of history in apocalyptic literature, messianic expectation, and resurrection. An outline of how each of these ideas is reflected in the apocalyptic literature from outside Qumran is provided, followed immediately by an examination of their occurrence in the Dead Sea Scrolls themselves. The concluding chapter, "The Apocalypticism of the Scrolls in Context," gives a fine, compact summary of the relationship between the scrolls, early Judaism, and formative Christianity (arguing convincingly against the minority of scholars who have attempted to see in the scrolls the authentic record of the latter).

COLLINS's (1979) collection of essays in the Semeia series is of particular importance for its presentation of A.J. Saldarini's essay "Apocalypses and 'Apocalyptic' in Rabbinic Literature and Mysticism," which discusses the reasons why Jewish apocalyptic literature appears to have died out following the revolts against Roman rule in the first and second centuries C.E. Saldarini argues that apocalyptic at this time was effectively transmuted into *merkabah* and *hekhalot* mysticism, and he goes on to discuss examples of these genres that fulfill the criteria for being termed an "apocalypse." Saldarini's essay concludes with an excellent bibliography for further reading in early Jewish mysticism and apocalyptic.

HANSON's work and its influence on subsequent discussions of the origins of the apocalyptic literature can hardly be underestimated. His basic thesis is that apocalyptic writing was born out of a conflict between a priestly (establishment) party and a disenfranchised visionary party in the early Persian period. It was the latter who were responsible for the prophetic literature (e.g., Joel, Zechariah 9–14, Isaiah 56–66), which is often argued to be behind the apocalyptic writings. Hanson's position has been strongly criticized in recent years but remains a landmark in the development of scholarly thought in this area, and almost any extended work on the origins of apocalyptic will make reference to it.

LAMBERT's work is an approachable consideration of the evidence that the Jewish apocalyptic genre may owe part of its origins to Persian (Zoroastrian) texts or to Babylonian *ex eventu* prophecy. An affirmative response to this question is put forward particularly in the case of the Book of Daniel, one of the earliest Jewish apocalypses.

ROWLEY's work, while in some respects dated, remains useful. This is particularly true of the first three sections, which focus on the rise of apocalyptic and then, in chronological order, give a *précis* of the main apocalyptic works from the third (or second) centuries B.C.E. to the end of the first century C.E. For Rowley, apocalyptic is the "child of prophecy and yet diverse from prophecy": a genre of consolatory literature arising out of the Antiochene persecution but using the prophetic idiom and incorporating foreign (notably Zoroastrian) elements.

COGGINS and associates' collection of essays is of importance for its presentation of M.A. Knibb's "Prophecy and the Emergence of the Jewish Apocalypses." This essay is an important and balanced review of the evidence surrounding the origins of apocalyptic literature, and it is ideal reading for a newcomer to the subject. Topics such as the difference between the terms "apocalypse," "apocalyptic," and "apocalypticism" are thoroughly dealt with, as well as the more significant theories such as Hanson's argument for the development of apocalyptic from "visionary" prophecy and von

Rad's suggestion that apocalyptic has its origins in wisdom literature rather than prophecy. The author's premise, that apocalyptic writing may be seen as a development of prophecy but in a learned or "scribal" tradition, is lucidly argued and reflects the current scholarly consensus on the subject.

DOMINIC RUDMAN

Apocrypha and Pseudepigrapha: Translations

Charles, R.H. (editor), *The Apocrypha and Pseudepigrapha of the Old Testament in English*, 2 vols., Oxford: Clarendon, 1913

Charlesworth, James H. (editor), *The Old Testament Pseudepigrapha*, 2 vols., Garden City, New York: Doubleday, and London: Darton, Longman, and Todd, 1983–1985

Metzger, Bruce M. (editor), *The New Oxford Annotated Bible with the Apocrypha*, New York: Oxford University Press, 1973, expanded edition, 1977

The New Interpreter's Bible: A Completely New Commentary in Twelve Volumes, Nashville, Tennessee: Abingdon, 1994–

The Parallel Apocrypha, New York: Oxford University Press, 1997

Sparks, H.F.D. (editor), *The Apocryphal Old Testament*, New York: Oxford University Press, and Oxford: Clarendon, 1984

Much of the extant Jewish literature written between 300 B.C.E. and 200 C.E. can be classified either as Apocrypha or Pseudepigrapha, but the line between the two categories is not universally agreed upon. Generally speaking, the term *Apocrypha* (Greek for "hidden works") designates those texts, mostly composed in Hebrew or Aramaic, that were included in the Septuagint (the Jewish translation of the Hebrew Bible into Greek) but were later excluded from the Jewish canon of Scripture. Many of these books are today considered deuterocanonical (secondarily added to the canon of inspired Scripture) by Roman Catholics, and each of the others is regarded as authoritative by some group of Eastern Orthodox Christians. *Pseudepigrapha* (Greek for "falsely attributed works") is a modern designation for a much larger group of books that were mostly composed by Jewish authors in the name of biblical heroes. These books were sometimes reworked by the Christian communities that preserved them but which generally did not consider them inspired Scripture. The books of 3 and 4 Maccabees, 1 Esdras, Psalm 151, and the Prayer of Manasseh (which were included in the Septuagint) and 2 Esdras (which was not) are sometimes numbered among the Apocrypha, but because of their disputed canonical status they are often classified as Pseudepigrapha.

The invaluable *Parallel Apocrypha* includes the Catholic *New Jerusalem Bible*, where the arrangement of the books is based on the Septuagint, so the deuterocanonical books (Apocrypha) are found in their traditional places among the books of the Hebrew canon. This arrangement is advantageous for the purpose of reading the Greek additions to Esther and Daniel in their original contexts, and it reveals something about how these books are thought to relate to the Hebrew canon (e.g., Tobit and Judith are grouped with Esther, Baruch with Jeremiah and Lamentations). Each book is accompanied by a concise introduction and detailed, illuminating annotations. Besides giving textual variants and alternative translations, these notes provide a good deal of historical, linguistic and philosophical background information and a modicum of literary analysis. Nevertheless, they are not free from Christian theological biases. The translations of the Apocrypha, however, reflect very accurately the Greek of the Septuagint, and an effort has been made to render key terms consistently. In some books (e.g., The Wisdom of Solomon), fidelity to the Greek has led to some awkward English constructions, but in general the translations manage to combine literalness with readability.

THE NEW INTERPRETER'S BIBLE, though not intended primarily for a Roman Catholic audience, also follows the order of the Catholic canon and does not include the books of the Apocrypha excluded from that canon. At the time of this writing, not all of the volumes containing books of the Apocrypha were yet available, but the series promises to be an invaluable reference tool when it is complete. *The New Interpreter's Bible* (NIB) presents two parallel translations for each book; for the Apocrypha these are the New Revised Standard Version (NRSV, the translation most often referred to by Christian biblical scholars) and the New American Bible (NAB, a less literal translation popular among American Catholics). The translations are divided into short sections, each accompanied by a fairly extensive scholarly commentary. Theological "reflections" are set apart from the running commentary, which is considerably more detailed than the notes in the NJB (or any other annotated Bible), but is nevertheless aimed at the general reader. The comments of Robert Doran on 1 and 2 Maccabees are especially clear and thoughtful.

METZGER provides the most complete collection of the Apocrypha (including the books not included in the Roman Catholic canon) in a separate volume from the canonical Scriptures. The translations follow the stylistic and methodological guidelines of the Revised Standard Version (RSV): using all available texts, they aim to produce an accurate reflection of the original without compromising readability. The annotations are brief and are mostly taken up with citing variants and biblical parallels, but sometimes they illuminate difficult passages. A slightly updated version of this work can be found in the Apocrypha section of the *New Oxford Annotated Bible with the Apocrypha* (NRSV), ed. Bruce M. Metzger and Roland E. Murphy, New York: Oxford University Press, 1991.

CHARLES's two-volume work is a milestone in the study of the Apocrypha and Pseudepigrapha: it is the first English translation of many of those works to be based on critical editions (for which Charles and his contributors were often themselves responsible). The Apocrypha volume contains most of the books included by Metzger, but the Pseudepigrapha volume is lacking many books found in the modern collections. Oddly, the latter volume does include the Mishnaic tractate Avot as well as the Story of Ahikar (a non-Jewish legend with affinities to Daniel 1–6, Esther, and Tobit). The style of the translations is generally graceful, if somewhat archaic, but the editor's principle of translating a hypothetical original text rather than following any of the extant versions seems dubious today. The extensive notes provide valuable information about the readings of the various versions, but they may be too technical to be helpful to the nonexpert. Perhaps the most dated aspect of Charles's collection is the patronizing attitude toward Judaism that comes across in many of the translators' introductions and notes.

Despite its misleading title, SPARKS provides a handy, single-volume collection of most of the complete books of the Pseudepigrapha. The accuracy and readability of the translations vary somewhat depending on the translator, but the volume is well-edited from a stylistic point of view. Sparks's aim is to provide the general reader with a smooth English translation of the Pseudepigrapha, unencumbered by scholarly annotations. Books that exist in multiple versions are represented by an eclectic type of text that does not give preference to any one version; only the most significant variants are noted. Because there are no interpretive notes, some translators compensate by adding interpretation to their translations, while others allow confusing passages to stand without explanation. In spite of its shortcomings from a scholarly point of view, Sparks's collection offers the most consistently accessible translations of the Pseudepigrapha.

The only complete translation of all the major Jewish and Christian pseudepigraphical literature of the modern period (apart from the Dead Sea Scrolls), including fragments of lost works quoted by later authors, is that of CHARLESWORTH. His approach is geared primarily to scholars, but the first-time reader of the Pseudepigrapha can also benefit from its thoroughness. Each book or fragmentary work is accompanied by an introduction that presents essential background information on the text and by extensive interpretive notes. Variant readings are clearly indicated, and if two significantly different versions of a text exist, the translations are printed side by side. Cross-references and biblical parallels appear in the margin. Hence, a page of Charlesworth's *Old Testament Pseudepigrapha* can manifest a layout almost as densely packed as a page of Talmud, making his collection more daunting than Sparks's. It may also be noted that the editor has not imposed stylistic restrictions on the work of the various translators. In any event, Charlesworth's translation is indispensable to anyone with a serious interest in the Pseudepigrapha.

KARINA MARTIN HOGAN

See also Apocrypha and Pseudepigrapha: Introductions

Apocrypha and Pseudepigrapha: Introductions

Collins, John J., *Jewish Wisdom in the Hellenistic Age* (The Old Testament Library), Louisville, Kentucky: Westminster John Knox, 1997; Edinburgh: Clark, 1998

Collins, John J., *The Apocalyptic Imagination: An Introduction to Jewish Apocalyptic Literature,* Grand Rapids, Michigan: Eerdmans, 1998
Freedman, David N. (editor), *The Anchor Bible Dictionary,* New York and London: Doubleday, 1992
Harrington, Daniel J., *The Maccabean Revolt: Anatomy of a Biblical Revolution* (Old Testament Studies, vol. 1), Wilmington, Delaware: Glazier, 1988
Jonge, M. de, *Outside the Old Testament,* Cambridge and New York: Cambridge University Press, 1985
Nickelsburg, George W.E., *Jewish Literature between the Bible and the Mishnah: A Historical and Literary Introduction,* Philadelphia: Fortress, and London: SCM, 1981
Stone, Michael E. (editor), *Jewish Writings of the Second Temple Period: Apocrypha, Pseudepigrapha, Qumran Sectarian Writings, Philo, Josephus* (Literature of the Jewish People in the Period of the Second Temple and the Talmud, vol. 2), Philadelphia: Fortress, 1984
Wills, Lawrence M., *The Jewish Novel in the Ancient World* (Myth and Poetics), Ithaca, New York: Cornell University Press, 1995

The Jewish Apocrypha and Pseudepigrapha form a group of compositions dating from the period 300 B.C.E. to 200 C.E.

NICKELSBURG offers the best general introduction to the Apocrypha and many of the Pseudepigrapha and also to their historical background. Most chapters begin with a historical survey of a particular period and proceed to discuss several works that were written in that context, often from widely divergent perspectives. The analysis of the texts, however, tends to be more literary than historical-critical, focusing on the peculiarites of each work that are likely to strike a first-time reader. In two chapters Nickelsburg departs from his chronological organization to compare works that share a common provenance (Egypt) or purpose (the exposition of biblical texts through expansion). While not comprehensive, Nickelsburg's book is engaging, thorough, and concise in its treatment of the most important Apocrypha and Pseudepigrapha.

STONE classifies the Apocrypha and Pseudepigrapha by literary genre, with a different scholar introducing each genre. This approach emphasizes the diversity of the texts under discussion and allows for a detailed comparison of similar works. Many of these texts contain elements of several genres, and therefore they receive differing, and even contradictory, treatments by two or more authors. Further, some chapters cover so many works that they are necessarily quite superficial, while other genres are represented by only a few examples that are explored in depth. The chapters titled "Historiography," "Testaments," and "The Sibylline Oracles" are especially useful as supplements to Nickelsburg's introduction.

FREEDMAN's dictionary contains introductions to each of the apocryphal and pseudepigraphical works as well as useful general essays on both categories of literature. The entries on the Apocrypha tend to be more detailed than those on the Pseudepigrapha because the former have received more attention from biblical scholars. All the entries, however, provide at least such basic information on a work as its genre, provenance, approximate date, and transmission history, as well as a summary of its contents.

For readers who want to get a general impression of the Pseudepigrapha, de JONGE's collection is a good point of entry. He has selected 12 pseudepigraphical works with broad appeal and asked leading scholars to translate excerpts from them and explicate these passages in a running commentary. Most of the scholars give a good general description of the work before presenting the excerpts, but the passages they choose do not always convey an accurate sense of the whole. Nevertheless, de Jonge's approach may be helpful to someone trying to decide which of the Pseudepigrapha to explore in depth.

Perhaps the most appealing genre of the entire apocryphal and pseudepigraphical literature is the so-called Jewish novel, the subject of WILLS's enjoyable book. Although the books he focuses on (both the Hebrew and expanded Greek versions of Daniel and Esther; Tobit, Judith, and Joseph and Asenath) are not much longer than modern short stories, Wills argues that they reflect the same artistic impulses as Hellenistic novels. In particular, the centrality of women characters and the attention to internal psychological states set the novels apart from other Jewish literature of the period. Although Wills employs a broad spectrum of literary theories and comparisons to interpret the novels, his discussions are lucid and his terminology is always clearly defined.

The most distinctive and extensive of pseudepigraphic genres is the apocalypse, to which COLLINS (1998) is the best introduction. Most scholars accept Collins's definition of apocalypse as "a genre of revelatory literature with a narrative framework, in which a revelation is mediated by an otherworldly being to a human recipient, disclosing a transcendent reality which is both temporal, insofar as it envisages eschatological salvation, and spatial, insofar as it involves another, supernatural world." After establishing the antecedents and social contexts of apocalyptic literature, Collins introduces each individual apocalypse, giving particular attention to the social and historical reality it reflects. Proceeding chronologically, he traces the development of the apocalypse genre, showing how it gave rise to related literature such as the Testaments and Sibylline Oracles. He also examines the influence of apocalyptic ideas on the Qumran sect and early Christianity.

COLLINS (1997) also provides an excellent introduction to the wisdom literature of the Hellenistic period, especially the important apocryphal books of Ben Sira and the Wisdom of Solomon. The introduction contrasts the general outlook of these books with that of Proverbs, Job, and Kohelet; the most important difference is that the Hellenistic books assume that the Torah is the primary source of wisdom, at least for Jews. The chapters on Ben Sira illustrate how the author, writing in Hebrew around 180 B.C.E., probably in Jerusalem, reworked the traditional forms and insights of Hebrew wisdom under the influence of Hellenistic culture. Collins argues that the apologetic and sometimes polemical tone of the Wisdom of Solomon reflects the struggle of an educated member of the Jewish community in Alexandria to uphold the values of his own culture as a model of the philosophical life valued by the elite of the dominant culture.

HARRINGTON contextualizes two difficult but very important historiographic works, 1 and 2 Maccabees. He uses the canonical Book of Daniel as a point of entry into the history of the Maccabean revolt, proceeds to the more novelistic account in 2 Maccabees, and afterward turns to the relatively dry 1 Maccabees. Gradually he fills in by this means a rough sketch of Jewish history from about 175 to 134 B.C.E., emphasizing how the various sources present the events rather than "what really happened" (about which one can only speculate). The reader is left with a vivid sense of the significance of this period for the formation of Judaism.

KARINA MARTIN HOGAN

See also Apocrypha and Pseudepigrapha: Translations

Apologetics *see* Christian-Jewish Relations: Apologetics and Polemics

Apostasy

Cohn, Leopold, *The Story of a Modern Missionary to an Ancient People,* Brooklyn, New York: American Board of Missions to the Jews, 1911

Endelman, Todd M. (editor), *Jewish Apostasy in the Modern World,* New York: Holmes and Meier, 1987

Katz, Jacob, *Exclusiveness and Tolerance: Studies in Jewish-Gentile Relations in Medieval and Modern Times* (Scripta Judaica, vol. 3), Oxford: Oxford University Press, and New York: Behrman, 1961

Klausner, Samuel Z., "How to Think about Mass Religious Conversion: Toward an Explanation of the Conversion of American Jews to Christianity," *Contemporary Jewry,* 18, 1997

Marrus, Michael Robert, *The Politics of Assimilation: A Study of the French Jewish Community at the Time of the Dreyfus Affair,* Oxford: Clarendon, 1970; as *The Politics of Assimilation: The French Jewish Community at the Time of the Dreyfus Affair,* Oxford: Clarendon, and New York: Oxford University Press, 1980

Rausch, David A., *Messianic Judaism: Its History, Theology and Polity,* New York: Mellen, 1982

Roth, Norman, *Conversos, Inquisition, and the Expulsion of the Jews from Spain,* Madison: University of Wisconsin Press, 1995

Tec, Nechama, *In the Lion's Den: The Life of Oswald Rufeisen,* New York: Oxford University Press, 1990

Zolli, Eugenio, *Before the Dawn: Autobiographical Reflections,* New York: Sheed and Ward, 1954

Apostasy is a pejorative term for the act of rejecting one religion in favor of another. In the Jewish/Christian case the Library of Congress subject heading is "proselyte" for a Christian who adopts Judaism and "convert" for a Jew who becomes a Christian. Apostasy may be thought of as an extension of structural assimilation into political, economic, and kinship institutions, in which Christianity is the regnant culture, as much as it may be viewed as joining a Christian religious community. Thus, the literature on religious apostasy is subordinate to that on assimilation, although the latter rarely deals with conversion. The literature on religious intermarriage, a meshing of Christian and Jewish kinship groups, is subordinate to both the assimilation and the apostasy literatures.

ROTH traces the conversion of Jewish leaders and tens of thousands of laypersons to Christianity in 14th- and 15th-century Spain, presenting problems in Jewish family law and around the conditions of return to Judaism for *conversos* who left Spain. By the 15th century the number of *conversos* was so large that distinctions were introduced between New and Old Christians, and conflict erupted between Jews and *conversos* over Jewish communal property. The friars' missionary efforts played no small role in this process, but so did the gradual decline in the quality of Jewish leadership, and Roth challenges the notion that large numbers of *conversos* continued Jewish practices.

KATZ authored a number of major historical studies of the assimilation of Western and Central European Jewry into their wider societies over the past 500 years. Here he describes the social and judicial separation between Jews and Christians, the issues arising from the Jews' talmudically imposed obligation to uphold the law of the land, and the way in which Jewish law affected economic relations between the groups. Katz further shows how in many cases the apostate was treated as a "sinning Jew" who did not lose his Jewish identity, a matter that raised problems with respect to spousal relations and to inheritance. The Jewish conception that gentiles were subject only to the Noachide laws is shown to have provided a basis for tolerance in the midst of exclusiveness. When Jews were coerced to apostatize, the rabbis are seen to have called increasingly for martyrdom. Ghettoization in the 16th century was accompanied by notions of essential differences between Jews and Christians calculated to make proselytization untenable. The 18th century, was characterized by an increasing sense of common humanity and tolerance between the communities.

MARRUS explains how the emergence of civil society in France during the 19th century occasioned greater social interaction between the Jewish and Christian communities. The antireligious sentiment in France is shown undermining Judaism as a faith and paving the way for conversions. The Jewish community was organized under a Consistoire Centrale, supported both by communal donations and government allocations, which supported the politics of assimilation. In this environment there developed political antisemitism epitomized by the Dreyfus case at the end of the 19th century. This environment also planted seeds of Zionist Jewish nationalism.

ENDELMAN has edited a collection of important papers dealing with issues of Jewish apostasy in the modern period. It includes an excellent report by Deborah Hertz titled "Seductive Conversion in Berlin, 1770–1809." Working with records archived by the Nazi Agency for Genealogical Research, she is able to estimate numbers and rates of conversion of Jews to Christianity in Berlin from the late 18th century until the establishment of the Third Reich. Endelman's own article examines conversion in Germany and England from 1870 to 1914, especially in relation to occupational advancement. William McCagg traces the number of Christians of Jewish descent in Hungary during the early 20th century in relation

to the national aim of "magyarization." Michael Stanislawski classifies Jewish apostates in czarist Russia in the late 19th and early 20th century by their social status and their motives for seeking conversion. Jeremy Cohen returns to Christian Spain for biographical accounts of Moses, who became Petrus Alfonsi; Judah ben David ha-Levi, who became Hermann of Cologne; and Saul of Montpelier, who became Pablo Christiani. Cohen discusses the significant role they played appealing to Spanish Jewry to convert.

A more contemporary autobiographical account is that of COHN, who describes his spiritual journey from Hungarian rabbi to founder of a Williamsburg mission to the Jews. ZOLLI, rabbi of Trieste and then chief rabbi of Rome, is a more academic than pastoral figure who describes a turbulent period of hiding from the Nazis in Rome during World War II, followed by a return to his pulpit, where he experienced a vision of Jesus calling to him at the end of a Yom Kippur service. By far the most sensitive and penetrating exploration of the soul of a contemporary convert is TEC's biography of Oswald Rufeisen, a Polish Jew who survived the Holocaust wearing a Nazi uniform and went on to become a Catholic monk living in a monastery in Haifa. Known to the wider world as Brother Daniel, Rufeisen's case gained notoriety through his unsuccessful efforts to persuade the Israeli courts to recognize him as a Jew by nationality.

KLAUSNER turns from the psychological study of individual converts to the sociological problem of mass religious conversions in which an entire society changes its religion. While aiming, ultimately, to understand the conversion of American Jews to Christianity, he explores a series of comparative cases such as the conversion of Egyptian Copts to Islam in the medieval period. The work explores autobiographies of Jews who became Christians and Christians who became Jews, and statistical data from the 1990 National Jewish Population Study on Jews who converted to Christianity and Christians who converted to Judaism is analyzed.

RAUSCH traces the history of Hebrew Christianity from its beginnings in the first century C.E. to its contemporary form as Messianic Judaism. Through doctrinal vicissitudes it has attempted to define a form of Judaism that includes a commitment to Christ along with the retention of some Jewish religious practices. The boundary between it as a separate movement and as a variant on Christian missions to the Jews has shifted from time to time. In its current incarnation as Messianic Judaism it has institutionalized specific centers of worship, some of which are federated in the Union of Messianic Jewish Congregations, and it tends to include a deep interest in Israel as a herald of the Second Coming. Leaders and followers have included both Jews who have "completed" their Judaism through acceptance of Christ and Christians who seek to reconstruct the historical Jewish roots of Christianity.

SAMUEL Z. KLAUSNER

Arabian Peninsula *see* Yemen and the Arabian Peninsula

Arama, Isaac c.1420–1494

Aragonese rabbi, scholar, and preacher

Feldman, Seymour, "The Binding of Isaac," in *Divine Omniscience and Omnipotence in Medieval Philosophy: Islamic, Jewish, and Christian Perspectives* (Synthese Historical Library, vol. 25), edited by Tamar Rudavsky, Boston: Kluwer Academic, 1985

Fox, Marvin, "R. Isaac Arama's Philosophical Exegesis of the Golden Calf Episode," in *Minhah le-Nahum: Biblical and Other Studies Presented to Nahum M. Sarna in Honour of his 70th Birthday* (Journal for the Study of the Old Testament Supplement Series, 154), edited by Marc Brettler et al., Sheffield, South Yorkshire: JSOT, 1993

Heller Wilensky, Sarah, "Isaac Arama on the Creation and Structure of the World," in *Essays in Medieval Jewish and Islamic Philosophy: Studies from the Publications of the American Academy for Jewish Research*, edited by Arthur Hyman, New York: Ktav, 1977

Kellner, Menachem, "Gersonides and His Cultured Despisers: Arama and Abravanel," *Journal of Medieval and Renaissance Studies*, 6, 1976

Munk, Eliyahu, *Aqaydat Yitzchaq: Commentary of Rabbi Yitzchaq Arama on the Torah*, 2 vols., Jerusalem: Mass, 1986

Pearl, Chaim, *The Medieval Jewish Mind: The Religious Philosophy of Isaac Arama*, London: Vallentine, Mitchell, 1971; Bridgeport, Connecticut: Hartmore House, 1972

Sirat, Colette, *A History of Jewish Philosophy in the Middle Ages*, Cambridge and New York: Cambridge University Press, 1985

Isaac Arama is best known for *Akedat Yitshak*, his philosophical and ethical commentary on the Torah. First published in Salonika in 1522, it has since appeared in many editions. It is usually printed along with *Hazut Kashah*, Arama's polemical essay against Averroistic tendencies in the Jewish communities of Spain, and his commentaries on the Scroll of Esther and the Book of Job.

MUNK has offered the only English translation of *Akedat Yitshak* to date. Unfortunately, the work is "translated and condensed," making it difficult for the reader to appreciate fully Arama's original text.

HELLER WILENSKY's essay, a summary of arguments from her doctoral dissertation, published in Hebrew as "R. Yitshak Arama umishnato hafilosofit" ("The Philosophy of Isaac Arama," 1956), is an excellent articulation of Arama's defense of the traditional doctrine of creation ex nihilo. Following the approach of Harry Wolfson, she systematically presents the philosophical and theological ideas scattered throughout Arama's commentaries. This article remains the finest comprehensive exposition of Arama's philosophical ideas.

PEARL offers a thorough but uninspired exposition of Arama's thought. Situating the philosopher within the general context of medieval Jewish culture, Pearl argues that he was a minor and unoriginal thinker interesting mainly for the fervor with which he defended traditional Jewish ideas. Although Pearl published his book almost 20 years after Heller Wilensky's major study, he does not refer to her work, nor to any secondary literature on medieval philosophy published after 1954.

In her excellent survey of medieval Jewish philosophy, SIRAT provides a fine summary of Arama and his six principles of faith—creation, divine omnipotence and miracles, prophecy and the revelation of Torah, providence, penitence, and the immortality of the soul—in the context of the debate in late medieval philosophy over Maimonides' 13 principles.

Both FELDMAN and FOX provide nuanced readings of Arama as a philosophical commentator on the Bible, pointing to the significance of the genre of philosophical exegesis that flourished in the medieval period. KELLNER shows how the reaction of people such as Arama against the Jewish Averroists became increasingly sophisticated, using Aristotelian methodology to undercut what was perceived in Aristotelianism as inimical to the faith.

BARUCH FRYDMAN KOHL

Aramaic Literature see Languages, Jewish; Targum

Archaeology

Bartlett, John Raymond (editor), *Archaeology and Biblical Interpretation*, London and New York: Routledge, 1997

Dever, William G., *Recent Archaeological Discoveries and Biblical Research*, Seattle: University of Washington Press, 1990

Finkelstein, Israel, *From Nomadism to Monarchy: Archaeological and Historical Aspects of Early Israel*, Washington: Biblical Archaeology Society, 1994

Fritz, Volkmar, *An Introduction to Biblical Archaeology* (Journal for the Study of the Old Testament Supplement Series, vol. 172), Sheffield, South Yorkshire: JSOT, 1994

Kenyon, Kathleen, *Archaeology in the Holy Land*, London: Benn, and New York: Praeger, 1960; 4th edition, London: Benn, and New York: Norton, 1979

Levine, Lee I. (editor), *Ancient Synagogues Revealed*, Jerusalem: Israel Exploration Society, 1981; Detroit, Michigan: Wayne State University Press, 1982

Mazar, Amihay, *Archaeology of the Land of the Bible, 10,000–586 B.C.E.* (Anchor Bible Reference Library), New York: Doubleday, 1985; Cambridge: Lutterworth, 1993

Meyers, Eric M. and James F. Strange, *Archaeology, the Rabbis, and Early Christianity*, Nashville, Tennessee: Abingdon, and London: SCM, 1981

Stern, Ephraim (editor), *The New Encyclopedia of Archaeological Excavations in the Holy Land*, 4 vols., New York: Simon and Schuster, 1993

Archaeology, the discipline that attempts to reconstruct the culture and history of antiquity through the excavation and reinterpretation of the material remains of ancient societies, is a relatively new field of study whose beginnings go back to the discovery of Troy by Heinrich Schliemann in 1870. The first to make a genuinely scientific endeavor of Syro-Palestinian or biblical archaeology was Flinders Petrie, who excavated at Tell el-Hesi in 1890. Until 30 years ago, Syro-Palestinian archaeology was the province of biblical scholars, who were principally concerned with demonstrating the historical value of narratives of the Hebrew Bible. Sites associated with early rabbinic Judaism or early Christianity received little attention by comparison, and remains from the Arab and Turkish periods were all but ignored. Today archaeologists working in the Middle East have much broader humanistic goals. The pace of excavation in the region quickened with the establishment of the State of Israel, whose Department of Antiquities oversees all archaeological projects in the country, as do similar departments in their respective countries in the Middle East.

STERN has edited a four-volume work that describes the results of excavations at 420 archaeological sites in Israel, Jordan, Syria, and the Sinai. Two hundred five archaeologists contributed the articles, most reporting on sites they excavated. The chronological scope of the articles extends from the beginning of human occupation to the Ottoman period (16th to 20th centuries C.E.). The reports are augmented by 4,000 charts, plans, maps, drawings, and photographs. Especially helpful to the nonspecialist is the glossary of archaeological, geographic, architectural, and art-historical terms found in the fourth volume.

Those interested in Syro-Palestinian archaeology mainly because of links with the Bible may find these volumes a disappointment. Although there is reference to a site's biblical connections, these volumes are not concerned with relating the archaeology to the Bible. For a connection to be made between an archaeological site and the Bible in these volumes, it is necessary that there be clear archaeological evidence of a connection. For example, the article on Sinai never mentions the Exodus because 13 years of careful excavation throughout the Sinai by several Israeli teams yielded no evidence of a mass migration through the Sinai Peninsula in the Late Bronze Age.

Most of the articles that appear in these volumes were written by the archaeologists responsible for the most recent excavations at the site about which they are writing. Discussion of the significance of the finds is minimal. The approach is technical and descriptive; those expecting a work directed at a more general audience will have to look elsewhere. These volumes reflect the sophistication of archaeology today, which is a scientific discipline in its own right. Its goals are not directly linked to solving problems of biblical interpretation, although biblical scholars cannot afford to ignore the work described in this encyclopedia. This is a most valuable reference work that archaeologists and biblical scholars will find essential in their research.

KENYON provides a more concise statement of the progress of archaeological investigation in the Syro-Palestinian area. She was responsible for the introduction of the methods of excavation and recording that are today's standard in Syro-Palestinian archaeology. The book presents data covering the beginnings of settled life in the region (9000 B.C.E.) to the exilic period (6th century B.C.E.). Its concern to reconstruct the history of the region with archaeological data reflects the dominant concern of Syro-Palestinian archaeologists as late as the 1970s. The volume is well illustrated with photographs and drawings. That this book went through four editions attests to how helpful students of archaeology have found it. It is a classic in the discipline.

While the goals of archaeology have broadened since Kenyon's time, her contribution to the methodology of excavation and recording has been decisive. Field archaeologists today still use procedures that she developed during her excavations at Tell es-Sultan (Jericho). What has changed since Kenyon's day are the techniques of interpreting the material recovered during excavation. These new techniques have enabled archaeologists to learn more from a site than the mere history of its occupation.

MAZAR offers readers a more current summary of archaeological activity in Israel and Jordan. This important Israeli archaeologist surveys the results of excavations at sites occupied in periods from the Neolithic Age (10,000 B.C.E.) to the end of Iron II (586 B.C.E.). Mazar's decision to end with Iron II unfortunately left much of the biblical period and all of the Second Temple period out of the discussion. Though Mazar describes archaeology as a "professional and secular discipline" that is "free from theological prejudices," his interpretation of the data sometimes does center on the question of the historicity of the Bible's narratives. For example, he asserts that details in the patriarchal narratives (Genesis 12–50) derive from Middle Bronze Age culture. Mazar is scrupulously fair in his treatment of the views of other archaeologists. In fact, the irenic tone of his book does not always make it clear how divergent are the interpretations of archaeological data.

The tone that Mazar tries to create in this work reflects the separation of the departments of archaeology and biblical studies in Israeli universities. This allows archaeologists to pursue their work independently of the agenda of biblical scholarship. The decision to take this approach has made it possible for Syro-Palestinian archaeology to make important contributions to understanding the world of antiquity, although Mazar himself tends to focus on the reconstruction of Israelite history.

FRITZ presents not just a summary of the progress of archaeological excavations, he also devotes about one-third of his work to introductory matters of geography, chronology, the methods of excavation, and the history of archaeological research in the region. While his summary of archaeological excavations is less thorough than those of Kenyon or Mazar, Fritz is more extensive. He includes a brief discussion of the Hellenistic and Roman periods.

This is a fine survey that can serve as a college textbook or as an introduction for the general reader interested in Syro-Palestinian archaeology. It is a manageable volume that acquaints readers with a discipline whose massive detail can overwhelm the beginner. The book contains 58 maps, drawings, and photographs, although still more helpful are the bibliographies that direct readers to more comprehensive works by leading archaeologists and historians.

The relationship of archaeology to biblical studies is an important methodological concern. DEVER, a leading advocate for archaeology's independence from biblical studies, still recognizes the contribution that archaeology can make to illuminating the biblical text. The first of the four essays in his book sets out Dever's views on how archaeology reveals the world of the Bible. The next two essays discuss two periods of biblical history that have been notoriously difficult to reconstruct: the settlement period and the period of the United Monarchy. The final essay deals with archaeological insights into ancient Israel's worship.

The discussion is fair, informed, and stimulating, though some familiarity with Syro-Palestinian archaeology is necessary to appreciate Dever's writings, the most controversial of which deals with the Israelite settlement in ancient Canaan. Here Dever reviews the current hypotheses that attempt to describe the settlement, none of which is completely persuasive. Dever does not suggest another alternative but rather proposes a synthesis that argues that Yahwism was the result of a new ethnic consciousness in central Palestine following the collapse of Canaanite society in the 12th century B.C.E. He takes pains to show how this conclusion can be integrated into a religious faith that believes the Israelite settlement in Canaan to be the work of God.

FINKELSTEIN has edited a volume of essays by Israeli archaeologists who offer studies on the transition from early Israelite society to the monarchy. The Bible itself does not offer a clear description of the socioeconomic considerations that led to the establishment of the ancient Israelite state. An important feature of several of the essays is the setting of this transformation in the larger cultural and political processes of the region. These essays offer a sociological model for understanding this transition as a supplement to the theological perspectives in the biblical text. The emergence of the Israelite national state, then, is seen as a process with discernible socioeconomic contours that are reflected in the archaeological record.

BARTLETT has edited a collection of essays covering much more of the history of ancient Israel, early Judaism, and early Christianity. Among the important topics treated here are the early settlement of Israel, early Israelite religion, the Dead Sea Scrolls, the Temple in Jerusalem built by Herod, and early Christian churches. One notable omission, however, is an article dealing with the synagogues. These essays show that archaeologists today are not focused solely on the reconstruction of history but have much broader social, political, and religious concerns. These are excellent studies that describe the results of important excavations.

For a long time, archaeologists working in Israel focused on sites from biblical antiquity since they wanted to show the historical reliability of Scripture. Sites related to postbiblical Judaism and early Christianity did not receive as much attention since theological rather than historical questions were deemed primary regarding these two religious traditions. MEYERS and STRANGE show the significance of archaeology for the study of Judaism and Christianity in Roman and Byzantine Palestine. They also introduce an important new idea in the interpretation of archaeological data: regionalism. This concept is illustrated by analysis of data that makes up

the cultural profile of ancient Galilee. Other topics covered in this survey are the languages of Roman Palestine, burial customs, art, and architecture. The authors conclude their work with reflections on the importance of the land of Israel in rabbinic and early Christian theology. Meyers and Strange provide a readable and informed summary of archaeological projects related to Roman and Byzantine Palestine. The book helps the reader appreciate the broader cultural goals of contemporary archaeology. The authors show how interpretation of the archaeological record can recreate the world of antiquity in a way that analysis of texts alone simply cannot.

When archaeologists began work on sites from the rabbinic period, their attention was drawn in particular to the excavation of synagogues. LEVINE has edited a collection of essays that show how the results of these excavations have raised new questions and have provided a new understanding of the contours of early rabbinic Judaism in Palestine. In particular, the essays deal with the origins of synagogue architecture and the dating of these structures. A specific issue that is still controversial is the dating of the synagogue at Capernaum. At one time, a consensus that dated the structure to the second or third century C.E. provided a benchmark for dating similar synagogues in Galilee. Loffreda's report on the most recent work on Capernaum, included in Levine's collection, indicates that the synagogue dates from the fourth or fifth century C.E., although essays by others in the volume voice vehement opposition. This well-illustrated compilation also testifies to the diversity of religious and aesthetic sensitivities among the Jews of Roman and Byzantine Palestine. Analysis of rabbinic texts alone does not show the religious diversity of Judaism in late antiquity in precisely the same way as does analysis of the material remains. This makes it clear that archaeology is not an interesting sidelight but an absolute necessity for a balanced view.

LESLIE J. HOPPE

Architecture, Synagogue: Late Antiquity

De Breffny, Brian, *The Synagogue*, New York: Macmillan, and London: Weidenfeld and Nicolson, 1978

Fine, Steven, *Sacred Realm: The Emergence of the Synagogue in the Ancient World*, New York: Oxford University Press, 1996

Foss, Clive, *Byzantine and Turkish Sardis* (Monograph–Archaeological Exploration of Sardis, 4), Cambridge, Massachusetts: Harvard University Press, 1976

Hanfmann, George M.A., *Sardis from Prehistoric to Roman Times: Results of the Archaeological Exploration of Sardis, 1958–1975*, Cambridge, Massachusetts, and London: Harvard University Press, 1983

Krinsky, Carol Herselle, *Synagogues of Europe: Architecture, History, Meaning*, Cambridge, Massachusetts: MIT Press, 1985; London: Constable, 1996

Levine, Lee I. (editor), *Ancient Synagogues Revealed,* Jerusalem: Israel Exploration Society, 1981; Detroit, Michigan: Wayne State University Press, 1982

White, L. Michael, *Building God's House in the Roman World: Architectural Adaptation among Pagans, Jews, and Christians* (ASOR Library of Biblical and Near Eastern Archaeology), Baltimore, Maryland: Johns Hopkins University Press, 1990

Wigoder, Geoffrey, *The Story of the Synagogue: A Diaspora Museum Book,* London: Weidenfeld and Nicolson, and San Francisco: Harper and Row, 1986

Wiseman, James, *Stobi: A Guide to the Excavations,* Belgrade: University of Texas Press, 1973

Little is known about the synagogue architecture of late antiquity, but since 1958 a number of ruins have come to light. Currently, there are excavations being carried out at Sardis (Turkey), Stopi (the former Yugoslavia), Ostia (near Rome), Hamman-Lif (near Tunis), and Dura-Europos (Syria). The Stopi and Ostia remains represent the only universally accepted synagogues discovered on the European continent. The synagogue at Ostia was discovered in 1961 during construction of a new autostrada to the Leonardo da Vinci Airport. In Sardis, archaeologists stumbled upon the exceptionally important remains of an ancient synagogue in the course of routine excavation in 1958. Because of recent excavations, a wider range of works that discuss the layout and architecture of synagogues in the diaspora has begun to appear. Indeed, many Jewish buildings unearthed have uncertain origins and their exact dating cannot be determined nor can their use specifically as a synagogue be ascertained. Many excavated synagogues have only a mosaic remaining, a tribute to a people who, despite many wars and much strife, continued to decorate their places of worship. One interesting architectural detail common among all five of the diaspora synagogues mentioned is that the interiors of the buildings are extensively decorated while the exteriors are notably nondescript, making much more difficult archaeologists' determination of whether a building was a synagogue or not.

DE BREFFNY states that, "Halakah, the laws, rules, and regulations which govern every phase of Jewish life and human relations, not only of religious but also domestic, social and political, govern only some specific aspects of synagogue design and are silent regarding the style and plan of the building." He notes, however, that according to the Tosefta, the synagogue was to be built on ground higher than that of surrounding buildings and it was to have windows that faced Jerusalem, with gates that opened toward the east. He discusses synagogue orientation and placement of the Torah ark, illustrated by the case of the synagogue at Dura-Europos (third century C.E.), where the wall containing the niche for the scrolls faced Jerusalem. While not restricted to ancient synagogues, this work contains illustrations of the layout of the synagogue at Sardis, photographs of many ancient synagogues, and a brief description of the synagogue at Stobi.

FINE provides a companion volume to the comprehensive exhibition on ancient synagogues mounted by Yeshiva University Museum in New York. A chronological history and a map of ancient synagogues in Israel precede the main text. The book supplies not only an archaeological introduction but also detailed drawings and photographs of ancient synagogue architecture. Of particular interest is his explanation of archaeological methods. Diaspora synagogues are briefly described in chapter one, along with a list of synagogues currently unearthed. The entire work is devoted to architecture of late antiquity in the Greco-Roman world, and the illustrations and photographs add greatly to an understanding of these structures.

FOSS discusses Sardis from 284 to 616 C.E. Although his treatment of the synagogue is brief, he furnishes the reader with a basic description of the colonnaded forecourt, the stucco walls, mosaic floors, and central fountain. There is further brief description of the various additions that took place from the fourth to the seventh century C.E. and much on the city of Sardis as a whole.

HANFMANN's work is a collection of essays that details results of archaeological digs at Sardis from 1958 to 1975. Of particular note is the essay entitled "The Synagogue and the Jewish Community," which describes the excavations, the forecourt, and the main hall of the Sardis synagogue as well as menorahs and inscriptions found there. The original plans and the early stages of synagogue construction are also clarified. A rich bibliography precedes the main body of the work, and the appendix contains notes to each chapter and a section devoted to illustrations and photographs.

KRINSKY divides her book into two parts. The first part presents general background material on the design of European synagogues. The second part offers descriptions of specific European synagogues that represent various architectural designs and styles. Of special note will be descriptions of the synagogues at Stobi, Sardis, Ostia, and Dura-Europos. The chapter titled "The European Synagogues from Antiquity to Modern Times" deals with rules regarding the location and characteristics of synagogues. The work is richly illustrated, and each chapter is followed by extensive notes.

LEVINE's collection of essays pertains to various synagogues around the world. Taken together, they provide a valuable overview of the archaeological and historical considerations at issue. G. Foerster's essay, "A Survey of Ancient Diaspora Synagogues," provides detailed descriptions of the floor plans at Stobi, Ostia, and Hamman-Lif. Levine admits that the magnificence of the synagogue at Duro-Europos "is not the building itself, but its art." The essay by A. Seager, "The Synagogue at Sardis," provides a detailed description of the layout of the Roman bath-gymnasium complex of which the synagogue is part.

WHITE argues that "the development of normative synagogue architecture through the fourth century C.E. paralleled (rather than preceded) that of Christian church building." This is proved by excavation at Dura-Europos. Chapter four details the transformation of a synagogue from residential domicile to house of worship. The synagogue at Sardis, with its basilican hall, was not originally a synagogue either and may well have been a private dwelling. White provides schematic plans of several synagogues, including Duro-Europos, Sardis, Stobi, and Ostia. There is limited detail on architectural design, but the floor plans offer the reader a clear picture of these early synagogues. Each synagogue is presented under a separate heading, and the significance of each is well demonstrated.

WIGODER suggests that toward the end of the second century C.E. the Roman attitude toward Jews relaxed and "relations with the Jewish community became more peaceful, the economic situation improved, and the next century saw a spate of building." He describes the orientation and interiors of synagogues and provides photographs depicting both the rich detail of the construction and the decorative mosaics. Of note are the plates showing model reconstructions of the synagogues at Dura-Europos and Sardis as well as column details in the Ostia synagogue.

WISEMAN supplies an in-depth description of the excavation and the architecture of the synagogue at Stobi. Distinctive here is the way in which this structure utilized some of the remaining walls of an earlier synagogue associated with Tiberius Claudius Polycharmus, "the father of the synagogue at Stobi."

CYNTHIA A. KLÍMA

See also Architecture, Synagogue: Medieval and Modern

Architecture, Synagogue: Medieval and Modern

De Breffny, Brian, *The Synagogue,* New York: Macmillan, and London: Weidenfeld and Nicolson, 1978

Folberg, Neil, *And I Shall Dwell among Them: Historic Synagogues of the World,* New York: Aperture, 1995

Kadish, Sharman, *Building Jerusalem: Jewish Architecture in Britain,* London and Portland, Oregon: Vallentine Mitchell, 1996

Kampf, Avram, *Contemporary Synagogue Art: Developments in the United States, 1945–1965,* Philadelphia: Jewish Publication Society, 1966

Krinsky, Carol Herselle, *Synagogues of Europe: Architecture, History, Meaning* (Architectural History Foundation Books, 9), Cambridge, Massachusetts: MIT Press, 1985; London: Constable, 1996

Piechotka, Maria, *Wooden Synagogues,* Warsaw: Arkady, 1959

Wigoder, Geoffrey, *The Story of the Synagogue: A Diaspora Museum Book,* San Francisco: Harper and Row, and London: Weidenfeld and Nicolson, 1986

Wischnitzer, Rachel, *Synagogue Architecture in the United States: History and Interpretation* (Jacob R. Schiff Library of Jewish Contributions to American Democracy), Philadelphia: Jewish Publication Society, 1955

Wischnitzer, Rachel, *The Architecture of the European Synagogue,* Philadelphia: Jewish Publication Society, 1964

The important works on synagogue architecture can be divided between historical works and photo essays. Both broad surveys and more localized studies are available. In the historical studies, the illustrative matter tends to be sparse and technical, but scholarly analysis abounds; by contrast, in photo essays one finds illustrations of the highest quality, often alongside texts of slender significance. Therefore, readers will fre-

quently find it helpful to use histories and photo essays together, for a survey may have only one dimly-lit photograph of an interior, while a plate in a popular photo essay may show under good light many salient details that one might otherwise miss. It should also be said that there are a number of works that bridge these two categories quite effectively.

The two classic works on synagogue architecture, which set the standard by which all others must be judged, are WISCHNITZER (1955) and WISCHNITZER (1964). These comprehensive and deeply serious volumes discuss the synagogue in its U.S. and European manifestations, respectively. Wischnitzer is known primarily for her work on iconography, and she applies the same acuity of vision as she situates each historical stratum of synagogue architecture within its appropriate social and intellectual context.

KRINSKY continues Wischnitzer's work in a well-conceived geography of Europe's synagogues. The most up-to-date work of architectural history reviewed here, Krinsky's book is organized by locale, and it includes a fine introduction as well as a useful bibliography for further research. The illustrations are disappointingly small and undistinguished, but still this work has great merit.

The books by DE BREFFNY and by WIGODER share a similar tone, which is substantially different from that of Wischnitzer. While Wischnitzer strives to place specific synagogues in historical context, De Breffny and Wigoder are interested, each in his own fashion, with the history of the synagogue as a sort of case study that illuminates the larger history of Jews from ancient to modern times. Thus, individual synagogues serve as illustrations for a broader historical lecture so that a synagogue used by the Jews of Spain becomes an opportunity for discussing the Spanish Jewish experience more generally. De Breffny features historical and contemporary photographs in his book, while Wigoder relies on photographs of the scale models of selected synagogues from Tel Aviv's Diaspora Museum. Both books are useful to scholars, but they are also suitable for general audiences.

Another classic and extremely useful work is PIECHOTKA's volume, which includes rare archival photographs of a specific class of synagogue structure, the wooden synagogues of Poland built from the late Middle Ages until World War II. These buildings were among the most architecturally fascinating, iconographically rich, and theologically complex edifices ever produced by Jews, and the photographs and architectural drawings in this book are an invaluable record of monuments that have been destroyed. The text, while sparse, contains as much information as one is now likely to find on these buildings.

KADISH writes a social history as well as an architectural history. Her well-written and finely illustrated volume does not attempt to cover all of synagogue architecture worldwide nor in a single country. Instead, it chronicles through architectural history the singular Jewish experience of London. Kadish's analysis has both breadth and depth, and it is sensitive to the nuance of social class, the character of individual neighborhoods, and intrareligious politics. The work should be considered a model for the next wave of scholarship in this field.

KAMPF's work is a product of its period—it is a positivist paean both to modernity and its redemptive possibilities, and to the Reform movement for its contributions to spiritual expression through architecture. Some readers may consider this perspective a flaw of the work, but nevertheless this is a beautifully produced book with superb black-and-white photographs, and it is certainly useful to scholars investigating this recent chapter of architectural history. Indeed, Kampf's book is a great boon, for it records a reaction expressed when these synagogues were new structures; unfortunately, similar documents are not available for synagogues built in earlier periods.

FOLBERG's opulent photo essay is so gorgeous that the reader may forgive the paucity of its text. The synagogues are often portrayed as unoccupied, testifying to the attrition or erasure of Jews in the areas in which the edifices are found. At the same time, the photographs of the buildings signify the presence, both liturgical and aesthetic, of Jewish culture and history. Thus, the volume captures the essence of the synagogue as a sacred space in a manner unparalleled by other, albeit more scholarly, works.

MARC MICHAEL EPSTEIN

See also Architecture, Synagogue: Late Antiquity

Aristotelianism

Fox, Marvin, *Interpreting Maimonides: Studies in Methodology, Metaphysics, and Moral Philosophy,* Philadelphia: Jewish Publication Society, 1989; London: University of Chicago Press, 1994

Guttmann, Julius, *Philosophies of Judaism: The History of Jewish Philosophy from Biblical Times to Franz Rosenzweig,* London: Routledge, and New York: Holt, Rinehart and Winston, 1964

Sirat, Colette, *A History of Jewish Philosophy in the Middle Ages,* Cambridge and New York: Cambridge University Press 1985

The heritage of philosophical thought bequeathed by Aristotle and its relationship to Jewish thought is tangled and often strongly opposed or rejected outright, and this for three primary but essentially linked reasons—Aristotle's doctrines of causation, necessity, and matter. Because Aristotle was convinced of the eternity of matter, his system neither needed nor allowed for a creator God, but posited merely a sufficient cause or force to set matter in motion, a force, one might be led to surmise, that would be subjected to change itself by the activity of setting things in motion. Further, necessity, ordering the intelligible regularity of cosmic events, linked together the chain of being, leaving no place within the scheme for outside intervention. These three items—the non-necessity of creation, the suggestion or hint of alteration within the first cause, and the impossibility of outside intervention—are all widely perceived to be deeply antithetical to Jewish religiosity. During the heyday of Jewish philosophy in medieval Europe, however, Aristotle's philosophy *was* philosophy and it could not be ignored. The system of philosophical theology developed in the late 12th century by Moses Maimonides is certainly prototypical of the kind of tension this complex situation engendered. To this day traditional opinion is divided as to whether this attempt is irredeemably heretical because it is entirely Aristotelian or whether it is the very model of conventional orthodoxy because it is actually a shrewd attack on Aristotle's system. Beyond a relatively brief period of glory at the beginning of the late Middle Ages, and due to this supposition of fundamental irreligiosity, Aristotelian philosophy is represented in the history of Jewish philosophy and religion almost wholly negatively or, at best when it is affirmed, with pronounced suspicion or hedged about with defensive gestures.

FOX's very evenhanded treatment of Maimonides deals with Maimonides' relationship to Aristotelian philosophy and theology with a fine appreciation for the whole of Maimonides' thought. Of particular interest are Fox's summary of the history of the question of this relationship within Jewish thinking and the sections dealing with Maimonides' metaphysical cosmology, specifically his accounts of divine causality, creation, and petitionary prayer, accounts that set Maimonides at odds with Aristotle. Fox takes the view that Maimonides was a thorough and unapologetic Aristotelian in all cases concerning the sublunary cosmos. Beyond the reach of human experience or prior to the instant of creation, however, Maimonides argued against Aristotle in favor of Plato (actually Neoplatonism) or prophetic insight. Indeed, medieval Aristotelianism as a matter of course combined some form of a Neoplatonic emanation scheme with Aristotle's notion of the eternity of matter.

SIRAT's account of Aristotelianism and its relationship to the development of Jewish philosophy is one of the few sustained treatments of the topic. It is important to bear in mind, especially with regard to the development of Jewish mystical thinking, that the texts of Aristotle along with commentaries were preserved through the early Middle Ages by Muslim philosophers. Prior to their translation into Latin or Hebrew they already had been used extensively in Arabic by Muslim, Christian, and Jewish Neoplatonists. Thus, a certain philosophical syncretism developed, combining an emanative scheme of orders or levels of creation with the notion of the eternity of matter. As Sirat points out, what distinguished an Aristotelian philosopher from a philosopher of another school was the greater number of strictly Aristotelian doctrines held and affirmed. The bulk of Sirat's chapter on the topic deals with the thought of the first strictly Aristotelian Jewish philosopher, the 12th-century Spanish scholar Abraham ibn Daud. She explains how the purpose of ibn Daud's text, *The Exalted Faith,* is to answer questions on the subjects of free will and determinism, and this in two sections: the first on proofs for the existence of the Prime Mover and the second on revealed religion. These two areas of inquiry, according to ibn Daud, come to the same thing. The world's amenability to scientific explanation, its intelligible causal relations as expression of the first cause, cannot be contradicted by revelation, and in truth biblical texts confirm and express the same truth as reason. Philosophy, meaning for ibn Daud the physical sciences, and religion are in fundamental agreement. Sirat is particularly helpful in explaining how the notion of form, passive and receptive in Plato, is transformed into an active and potent principle by the conjunction of Neoplatonism and Aristotelianism. It is this transformation that allows

Platonism and Aristotelianism to coexist fairly harmoniously in an emanative system. In this system, the eternity of matter is now understood as matter's position in a causally linked and teleologically ordered chain of emanations from an all-encompassing source, and matter is now derivative as well as originally "in" its eternal source.

GUTTMANN's chapter on Aristotelianism is the most detailed and exhaustive and therefore the most difficult summary of this complex subject. For the fullest understanding of his narrative, the reader should first peruse the prior chapters on the Kalam (Islamic philosophical theology) and Neoplatonism, for Aristotelianism figures within both. Guttmann begins with a very helpful overview of what he considers to be the source of a problem that will only increase in complexity, a dissonance between a "philosophical religion," intellectualist in orientation (that is, more forcibly Aristotelian), and revealed religion. "Jewish Aristotelians attempted to reconcile the oppositions on the basis of the Aristotelian system," a method that found its most successful champion in Maimonides and thereafter fell into disfavor. Following his general summary, Guttmann proceeds to discuss in greater detail particular problems such as the relationship of soul to body, the system of emanations and its connection to its source, the natural or supernatural relations of cosmic forces, and free will and predestination. These details are amplified as Guttmann examines the function of Aristotelianism in the thought of Abraham ibn Daud and Maimonides. The chapter concludes with a section on the 14th-century theologian Hasdai Crescas, who opposed Aristotelianism's concepts of space and infinity, which maintained the possibility of a vacuum, and Aristotelian necessity in favor of a voluntaristic notion of God's will. In this mode of thought, creation becomes the offspring of goodness rather than necessity.

ERIC C. HELMER

Art: Ceremonial

Grossman, Grace Cohen, *Judaica at the Smithsonian: Cultural Politics as Cultural Model* (Smithsonian Studies in History and Technology, no. 52), Washington, D.C.: Smithsonian Institution Press, 1997

Gutmann, Joseph (editor), *Beauty in Holiness: Studies in Jewish Customs and Ceremonial Art,* New York: Ktav, 1970

Israel Museum, *Architecture in the Hanukkah Lamp: Architectural Forms in the Design of Hanukkah Lamps from the Collection of Hanukkah Lamps at the Israel Museum* (Israel Museum Catalog, 186), Jerusalem: Israel Museum, 1978, 4th edition, 1983

Jacobs, Joseph and Lucien Wolf, *Catalogue of the Anglo-Jewish Historical Exhibition, Royal Albert Hall, London, 1887* (Publications of the Exhibition Committee, 4), London: Clowes, 1888

Kanof, Abram, *Jewish Ceremonial Art and Religious Observance,* New York: Abrams, 1969

Klagsbald, Victor, *Jewish Treasures from Paris: From the Collections of the Cluny Museum and the Consistoire,* Jerusalem: Israel Museum, 1982

Roth, Cecil (editor), *Jewish Art: An Illustrated History,* London: Allen, and New York: McGraw-Hill, 1961; revised edition, edited by Bezalel Narkiss, London: Vallentine, Mitchell, and Greenwich, Connecticut: New York Graphic Society, 1971

Sed-Rajna, Gabrielle, *Jewish Art,* New York: Abrams, 1997

It is difficult to define the category "Jewish ceremonial art": does it refer to ritual objects made by Jews, or for Jews, or does it include both types of cultural production? Such artifacts may also be cataloged in a variety of ways—by type of object, material of construction, or intended use; some analysts would also separate "folk" objects from "high" art. Scholars in this field debate why the aesthetic impulse of Jewish culture, when turned to the plastic arts, has primarily created objects that the majority culture might well regard as "minor," and they seek also to understand the relationship of Jewish ritual art to secular objects or to the Christian or Muslim liturgical objects that sometimes have influenced the style and form of Jewish creations. Additionally, scholars study how new vessels for new rituals may affect interpretations of Jewish ceremonial art.

The volumes by JACOBS and WOLF and by KLAGSBALD represent the most common approach to discussing Jewish ceremonial art: via the museum catalog. In these works, individual items are described and attributed to various locales—sometimes the categories are as broad as "Sephardi" or "Ashkenazi," and sometimes they are rendered more precisely. Read together, these two texts demonstrate the historical evolution of ideas about the role of the curator: while Jacobs and Wolf simply identify the objects in an exhibition, Klagsbald emphasizes description, comparison, and historical context, thus reflecting a greater cognizance of the intimate relationship between Jewish ceremonial art and Jewish history, which cannot be merely reduced to the object's liturgical purpose or aesthetic sensibility.

ROTH and SED-RAJNA both depart from the catalog format as they each present chapters on ritual objects within their magisterial and comprehensive surveys of Jewish art. These books share common themes—the functional properties of Jewish ritual art and the aesthetic elaboration of functional objects. Recognizing that Jewish tradition uses certain objects for the celebration of holidays and life-cycle events, these authors chronicle the ways in which various Jewish cultures have produced the required ritual items. Roth generally describes high art and fine examples, while Sed-Rajna is more interested in popular or folk creations. Both authors tend to use particular works of Jewish art to illustrate more general conclusions about Jewish praxis. These books are descriptive surveys, and they do not proceed to investigate essential questions concerning ceremonial art as the internal expression of Jewish cultural development in the diaspora.

As the title of his book implies, KANOF studies Jewish ceremonial art to illuminate Jewish practice, rather than placing ritual objects in the context of the communities that produced them. After dispensing with history in the introduction, Kanof organizes his book thematically by holidays, life-cycle events, and sacred space. The objects described serve as illustrations in a primer on Jewish observances, and differences between objects from different times and places are only considered when they illustrate the particular liturgical requirements of the communities that made them. Kanof does analyze contemporary Jewish ritual art, but he defines it as a new aesthetic approach to eternal ritual needs—old liturgy in new vessels. Therefore, he fails to consider how liturgical reform and innovation may affect the form of ceremonial objects. This omission may seem particularly egregious given that Kanof himself is rooted in the Reform tradition, but the book was produced in an era when Reform was presenting itself as conservative and mainstream rather than revolutionary.

GUTMANN's collection of essays represents a sampling of the opinions and preoccupations of mid-20th-century scholars of Jewish art. It considers the "problem" of the second commandment (which prohibits the creation of images), the origins of various ritual objects, and the relationship of ceremonial objects to Jewish custom. The anthology focuses on religious phenomenology more than historical context, although a couple of the articles do examine subjects (such as guilds, commissions, and artists' identities) that illuminate the social, as well as the liturgical, significance of ritual objects.

GROSSMAN's catalog does not merely describe objects or simply place them in historical context. Instead, she addresses certain essential issues related to Jewish ritual art, explaining how and why the collection in the Smithsonian Institution was created. The book offers an important historical and socioanthropological analysis of significant objects that Jews collect and display, and it contemplates how the Smithsonian Institution's status as the official site of U.S. culture affects perceptions of the items in the collection. Grossman examines the meaning of ritual art both for the Jews who originally used the objects and for the latter-day Jews (and non-Jews) who exhibit them as symbols of cultural identity.

The catalog from the ISRAEL MUSEUM raises issues of cultural identity similar to those considered by Grossman as it explores how the form of the Hannukah lamp incorporates architectural motifs and monuments from the wider secular environment. The text raises, although less explicitly than Grossman's catalog, issues of the relationship between majority and minority societies, comparisons between grassroots and "high" culture, and the place of the "profane" in cultural productions intended for holy purposes. The catalog leaves unexplored, however, how this particularly transparent example of cultural borrowing affects perceptions of the anti-assimilationist holiday of Hannukah. Despite this omission, this work, like Grossman's, helps to bring the insights of the emerging discipline of cultural studies to the analysis of Jewish ceremonial art.

Marc Michael Epstein

See also Art: Late Antiquity

Art: Late Antiquity

Goodenough, Erwin R., *Jewish Symbols in the Greco-Roman Period* (Bollingen Series, 37), 13 vols., New York: Pantheon, 1953–1968; abridged edition, edited by Jacob Neusner, Princeton, New Jersey: Princeton University Press, 1988; Oxford: Princeton University Press, 1992

Gutmann, Joseph (editor), *The Dura-Europos Synagogue: A Re-evaluation (1932–1972)* (Religion and the Arts, 1), Chambersburg, Pennsylvania: American Academy of Religion, 1973; as *The Dura-Europos Synagogue: A Re-evaluation (1932–1992)* (South Florida Studies in the History of Judaism, 25), Atlanta, Georgia: Scholars Press, 1991

Gutmann, Joseph, *Sacred Images: Studies in Jewish Art from Antiquity to the Middle Ages* (Variorum Reprint, CS303), Northampton, Northamptonshire: Variorum, 1989

Hachlili, Rachel, *Ancient Jewish Art and Archaeology in the Land of Israel* (Handbuch der Orientalistik, 7; Kunst und Archäologie 1.2.B/4), New York: Brill, 1988

Hachlili, Rachel, *Ancient Jewish Art and Archaeology in the Diaspora* (Handbuch der Orientalistik; Kunst und Archäologie 1.2.B/9), Boston: Brill, 1998

Levine, Lee I. (editor), *The Synagogue in Late Antiquity*, Philadelphia: American Schools of Oriental Research, 1987

Urbach, Efraim E., "The Rabbinical Laws of Idolatry in the Second and Third Centuries in the Light of Archaeological and Historical Facts," *Israel Exploration Journal*, 9(3–4), 1959

White, L. Michael, *Building God's House in the Roman World: Architectural Adaptation among Pagans, Jews, and Christians* (ASOR Library of Biblical and Near Eastern Archaeology), Baltimore, Maryland: Johns Hopkins University Press, 1990

White, L. Michael, *Texts and Monuments for the Christian Domus Ecclesiae in Its Environment* (Social Origins of Christian Architecture, 2), Valley Forge, Pennsylvania: Trinity, 1997

Relatively recent archaeological discoveries of synagogues have paved the way for the study of Jewish architecture in late antiquity, which, in turn, has revealed much about developments in Jewish art during this period. WHITE (1990) compares the parallel architectural developments in various ancient houses of worship during the first four centuries of the Common Era and focuses particular attention on Jewish, Christian, and Mithraic remains at Dura-Europos in Syria. WHITE (1997) offers more archaeological and epigraphic data to support his conclusions. Chapter four of his first volume and section three of his second volume focus on Jewish materials. His interest in relating archaeology to larger questions of social history has promising implications for future study of art in antiquity.

GOODENOUGH's pioneering and encyclopedic analysis, which appeared in 13 volumes (1953–1968), is a key text in the study of ancient Jewish art. Published under the same title in 1988, Jacob Neusner's single-volume introduction to and selective abridgment of volumes one, four, eight, nine, and ten makes the materials (including 91 illustrations) accessible to a much wider audience. One prominent theme in Goodenough's discussions concerns the relationship of Jewish artistic expressions to rabbinic opposition to art (cf. Exodus 20:4–6, Deuteronomy 4:15–18, 5:8–10, 27:15; contrast Exodus 31:1–11). His work certainly demonstrates that rabbinic teaching was not followed uniformly by diaspora Jews in the early centuries of the Common Era. It also raises lingering methodological questions both about interpreting the sometimes contrasting literary (e.g., rabbinic) and archaeological (e.g., synagogue artwork) evidence and about appreciating diversity of Jewish expression during this period. Goodenough also sees a connection between the mystical religion of Philo of Alexandria and the first followers of Jesus of Nazareth (i.e., Christian origins), on the one hand, and the Hellenistic Jews who, ignoring rabbinic prescriptions, made many splendid works of art, on the other. In studying their art, Goodenough also tries to learn about the mystical character of these Jews' religion that, in his view, gave rise to such creative expression. When evaluating issues of continuity and change in Judaism of this period, he examines the use of both distinctively Jewish (e.g., shofar) and Greco-Roman (e.g., astrological) symbols in synagogues. In this endeavor Goodenough is concerned not simply with interpreting Jewish art in light of biblical narratives or interpretations in rabbinic writings. Rather, he offers a comparative analysis of Greco-Roman and Christian evidence to ascertain the contemporary symbolic significance of various images for these Jewish communities.

Although Goodenough's work merits the lasting legacy of having opened up a new body of evidence that continues to attract scholarly attention, some of his interpretations have justifiably received pointed criticism. For example, URBACH rightly questions Goodenough's theses that prohibitions of Jewish art were absolute before 70 C.E. but of little or no consequence thereafter and that the spheres of influence of the Jewish "sages" (who allowed art) and the Sages, i.e., rabbis (who opposed it), were completely separate. On the latter point, funerary inscriptions on Jewish sarcophagi reflect contrasting perspectives on art—that is, copious ornamentation or a lack thereof. The fact that these sarcophagi were, nonetheless, buried in the same locations attests to an even wider diversity of opinion on this subject in Judaism. More significantly, Urbach offers an economic explanation for the prevalence of Jewish art in late antiquity: after the destruction of the Temple and the Bar-Kokhba revolt, much of the rural Jewish population migrated to cities. Because a larger number of Jews were exposed to life in the Greek polis, there was greater interaction with Greco-Roman and, later, Christian art. Moreover, Jewish craftsmen often found themselves in the sometimes precarious position of needing to work for non-Jews. An intriguing variety of rabbinic responses—ranging from outright condemnation of art to the giving of extraordinary dispensations to Jewish artists—attests to the then widely recognized and debated problem of Jewish artists' ostensibly assisting in the making of idols for pagans.

Continuing, expanding upon, and updating the work of Goodenough, HACHLILI (1988) discusses Jewish art and architecture in the land of Israel in the Second Temple period (part one) and in late antiquity until the time of the Arab conquest in the seventh century C.E. (part two). The second part of the volume deals exclusively with evidence from synagogues and includes chapters on iconography and symbolism; origins and sources of Jewish art; a comparison of Jewish and Christian art; distinguishing features of Jewish art; and the dating of synagogues. HACHLILI (1998) complements Hachlili (1988) and discusses Jewish art and architecture in synagogues of the diaspora. In general, Hachlili offers a balanced presentation of Jewish art, recognizing both decorative and iconographic functions as well as local influences and more wide-ranging motifs in synagogues. Of particular interest is her thesis that the same "general pattern books" were used by Jewish, Christian, and pagan artists and her support for Urbach's contention that Jewish artists worked regularly for non-Jewish as well as Jewish clients. Like Goodenough, however, Hachlili puts forth some controversial hypotheses. She maintains that in the Second Temple period Jewish art was limited to "aniconic, non-figurative designs." Only in the third century C.E. did art come to have symbolic significance, in part as a reaction to Christian influences. Like Goodenough, Hachlili posits that Jewish objects and elements (menorah, Ark of the Covenant) are said to have had a symbolic value, but unlike Goodenough, she claims that non-Jewish ones did not. Finally, Hachlili argues "that during late antiquity there evolved a specific Jewish art." Accordingly, Jewish artists always assumed a distinctively Jewish framework into which Oriental, Greco-Roman, and Christian elements were incorporated. Hachlili notes that what often differentiates Jewish art, especially in the diaspora, is the addition of Jewish symbols (frequently the menorah) to non-Jewish artistic motifs. Both of Hachlili's volumes include many photographs and illustrations.

Three other books merit brief mention here. Most pertinent for this subject in LEVINE are essays by Joseph Gutmann, Gideon Foerster, and Bezalel Narkiss; those by Foerster and Narkiss are complemented by illustrations at the end of the volume. Gutmann surveys the state of research subsequent to that of Goodenough on the Dura-Europos synagogue paintings (240s C.E.). Foerster examines the art and architecture of the synagogue in its late Roman setting and maintains that "Galilean synagogues . . . are a local, original, and eclectic Jewish creation," reflecting diverse influences of the second century C.E. Finally, Narkiss discusses pagan, Christian, and Jewish elements in the art of ancient synagogues. Particularly notable in Narkiss's essay is the Christian influence on Jewish art and vice versa: clearly neither Christians nor Jews lived in isolation from one another or from the influence of the greater Greco-Roman milieu. GUTMANN (1973) includes seven essays by seven scholars, including Gutmann, on various aspects of the paintings at the Dura-Europos synagogue. GUTMANN (1989) contains 17 of his other essays and articles (originally published between 1961 and 1988) on a variety of subjects related to Jewish art.

JAMES A. KELHOFFER

See also Art: Ceremonial

Asceticism

Biale, David, *Eros and the Jews: From Biblical Israel to Contemporary America,* New York: Basic Books, 1992

Boyarin, Daniel, *Carnal Israel: Reading Sex in Talmudic Culture* (The New Historicism, 25), Berkeley: University of California Press, 1993

Büchler, Adolf, *Types of Jewish-Palestinian Piety from 70 B.C.E. to 70 C.E.: The Ancient Pious Men* (Jews' College Publications, no. 8), London: Oxford University Press, 1922; New York: Ktav, 1968

Diamond, Eliezer, "Hunger Artists and Householders: The Tension between Asceticism and Family Responsibility among Jewish Pietists in Late Antiquity," *Union Seminary Quarterly Review,* 48, 1994

Fraade, Steven, "Ascetical Aspects of Ancient Judaism," in *Jewish Spirituality: From the Bible through the Middle Ages* (World Spirituality, vol. 13), edited by Arthur Green, New York: Crossroads, and London: Routledge and Kegan Paul, 1986

Fraade, Steven, "The Nazirite in Ancient Judaism (Selected Texts)," in *Ascetic Behavior in Greco-Roman Antiquity: A Sourcebook* (Studies in Antiquity and Christianity), edited by Vincent Wimbush, Minneapolis, Minnesota: Fortress, 1990

Jacobs, Louis, *Holy Living: Saints and Saintliness in Judaism,* Northvale, New Jersey: Aronson, 1990

Josephus, Flavius, *Works, English and Greek: Josephus, with an English Translation by Henry St. John Thackeray, Ralph Marcus, and Louis H. Feldman* (Loeb Classical Library, vols. 186, 203, 210, 242, 281, 326, 365, 410, 433, and 456), Cambridge, Massachusetts: Harvard University Press, and London: Heinemann, 1926–1963

Philo of Alexandria, *Works, English and Greek: Philo, in Ten Volumes (and Two Supplementary Volumes), with an English Translation by Francis Henry Colson and George Herbert Whitaker* (Loeb Classical Library, vols. 226, 227, 247, 261, 275, 289, 320, 341, 363, 379, 380, and 401), Cambridge, Massachusetts: Harvard University Press, and London: Heinemann, 1929–1962

Little has been written about Jewish asceticism, perhaps because it has been assumed generally that Judaism is devoid of or opposed to ascetic practices. As interest in the study of the human body generally and of asceticism specifically has recently grown, however, scholars have turned their attention to the ascetic aspects of Judaism. The following survey covers early reports of Jewish ascetics, as well as a pioneering study of Jewish asceticism and several more recent endeavors.

Perhaps the most famous descriptions of Jewish asceticism are by PHILO, a first-century C.E. Alexandrian Jew and a noted Platonist. In his writings he describes a group of Jewish ascetics called the Theraputae who practiced celibacy, followed a rigorous regimen of eating sparingly and infrequently, and spent much of their time in prayer and study. Philo has also left a written account of the best-known group of Jewish ascetics in late antiquity, the Essenes, whose practices included, at least for some, celibacy and the renunciation of private property. (See JOSEPHUS for another description of the Essenes by a contemporary of this Second Temple sect.)

Some 19th-century scholars suggested that those figures identified as "hasidim" in Second Temple and rabbinic literature were actually Essenes. For these scholars, the main implication of this identification was that nascent rabbinic Judaism was more heterodox than traditionalists would admit. Such an identification would also mean, however, that at least some Essenes traveled and were esteemed in the circles from which rabbinic Judaism grew. This fact, in turn, would imply a positive rabbinic attitude toward the ascetic practices of the Essenes. BÜCHLER vigorously rejects the identification of hasidim with the Essenes. He determines the characteristics of the hasid by examining the use of the term in both the Psalms of Solomon, written shortly after the beginning of the Roman occupation of Palestine in 63 B.C.E., and rabbinic sources. He concludes that in both contexts the hasid is characterized by extreme kindness and generosity toward others rather than by acts of self-denial. The conclusion to be drawn from Büchler's study, therefore, is that rabbinic praise of the pious does not include the celebration of asceticism, at least in its primary forms of self-denial.

More recently, however, scholars have reconsidered the question of asceticism within rabbinic Judaism, contending that, under the influence of Christianity, most studies of asceticism have focused on celibacy, thus excluding rabbinic Judaism, with its commitment to the commandment to "be fruitful and multiply," from analysis. In fact, contemporary students of asceticism have come to recognize increasingly that asceticism may exist in many different forms. FRAADE (1986) reviews earlier discussions of Jewish asceticism and then offers his own definition, which is broad enough to include behaviors other than celibacy in its purview but not so broad as to be meaningless. In light of this relatively expansive understanding of asceticism, Fraade reviews the evidence related to asceticism in pre-rabbinic and rabbinic Judaism. He finds scattered evidence of ascetic behavior in pre-rabbinic literature and evidence of what he calls "ascetic tensions" in rabbinic literature itself. In other words, he argues that although ascetic behaviors such as celibacy were not adopted by the rabbinic community, there were those within that community who were inclined to ascetic practices. FRAADE (1990) translates and comments on some of the central biblical and rabbinic texts relating to the nazirite, the clearest example of an ascetic persona in the Bible.

Perhaps the broadest, most ambitious study of Jewish asceticism is that of BIALE. Beginning with the Bible and ending with Woody Allen and Philip Roth, Biale identifies the rich variety of attitudes towards sexuality within Judaism. Most importantly, he emphasizes the degree to which rabbinic Judaism expressed ambivalence about sexuality, and he shows how that ambivalence resulted in limited celibacy among both Jewish mystics and some 18th-century hasidic circles. His discussion of the way in which, for the kabbalists, male-female sexuality is merely a reflection of the erotic union of the male and female aspects of the Godhead as well as an instrument for its realization is particularly fascinating. While in one sense this view heightens the significance of human sexuality, it also shifts the erotic focus of the kabbalistic male from the human to the heavenly realm, reducing his wife to the status of a necessary earthly means of achieving a cosmic end.

Talmudic attitudes toward sexuality are explored at some length by BOYARIN. He begins from the perspective that Judaism is much more "embodied" than Christianity; that is, Judaism, at least in its biblical and rabbinic formulations, views the human being as a body animated by a spirit rather than as a spirit trapped in a body. This perception is consistent with Judaism's emphasis on the importance of works generally and of procreation specifically, but the emphasis on embodiment leads to a stratification of the genders that gives greater status and power to males than it does to females. In particular, males are entrusted with the study and interpretation of Torah, the central commandment of rabbinic Judaism. The Talmud describes how in pursuit of study men often spent many years away from their wives and children, becoming, as Boyarin puts it, married monks. More provocatively, Boyarin notes the degree to which Torah study is eroticized in rabbinic sources, with the Torah being described as God's daughter and Israel's bride. In this sense, Torah is "the other woman," who draws scholars towards her and away from their flesh-and-blood mates. Thus, while rabbinic Judaism esteems the physical and regards procreation as God's will, it also creates a never-resolved tension between this obligation and that of Torah study.

As Biale and Boyarin imply, a crucial difference between Jewish and Christian ascetics is that Christians may choose celibacy, enabling them to remain solitary and familially unencumbered, while Jews may not avail themselves of this option, and therefore any asceticism on their part inevitably affects their families as well. DIAMOND has analyzed a number of talmudic narratives that consider the effects of the Jewish ascetic on his family. While a number of these texts are neutral or hostile towards the ascetic's impositions on his household, some narratives imply that he is doing his loved ones a service by assuring them a greater portion in the world to come. Once again, then, rabbinic sources reflect a deep ambivalence about asceticism.

While few works discuss biblical and rabbinic asceticism, even fewer deal with asceticism in the medieval and early modern periods. A notable exception is JACOBS, even though his work does not deal exclusively or even mainly with asceticism; its goal is rather to paint a vivid picture of Jewish saintliness throughout the ages, and ascetic behavior forms an important part of that portrait. In a chapter entitled "Saintly Extravagance," Jacobs describes the extremes to which Jewish saints, including hasidic masters and Lithuanian devotees of the Musar movement, went in matters of eating, sleeping, and sexual and social relations in order to attain and maintain their saintly state. His work clearly shows that at least among the Jewish spiritual elite, many forms of asceticism have been embraced as means toward the achievement of spiritual perfection.

ELIEZER DIAMOND

See also Dead Sea Scrolls

Ashkenazim

Agus, Irving Abraham, *The Heroic Age of Franco-German Jewry: The Jews of Germany and France of the Tenth and Eleventh Centuries, the Pioneers and Builders of Town-Life, Town-Government, and Institutions,* New York: Yeshiva University Press, 1969

Israel, Jonathan I., *European Jewry in the Age of Mercantilism, 1550–1750,* New York: Oxford University Press, and Oxford: Clarendon, 1985; 3rd edition, London and Portland, Oregon: Littman Library of Jewish Civilization, 1998

Patai, Raphael, *Tents of Jacob: The Diaspora, Yesterday and Today,* Englewood Cliffs, New Jersey: Prentice-Hall, 1971

Shulvass, Moses, *Between the Rhine and the Bosporus: Studies and Essays in European Jewish History,* Chicago: College of Jewish Studies Press, 1964

Szajkowski, Z., "Relations among Sephardim, Ashkenazim and Avignonese Jews in France from the 16th to the 20th Centuries," *Yivo Annual of Jewish Social Science,* 10, 1955

Weinreich, Max, *Geshikhte fun der Yidisher shprakh,* 1973; translated by Shlomo Noble with assistance of Joshua A. Fishman as *History of the Yiddish Language,* Chicago: University of Chicago Press, 1980

Zimmels, H.J., *Ashkenazim and Sephardim: Their Relations, Differences, and Problems as Reflected in the Rabbinical Responsa,* London: Oxford University Press, 1958; revised edition, Hoboken, New Jersey: Ktav, 1996

The term *Ashkenazim,* referring to Jews of North European descent, came first to be associated with the German lands and was later expanded to differentiate the culture, language, religious rituals, and other customs of Central and Eastern European Jews from those of the Spanish-Portuguese Sephardim. Until the 18th century, Sephardim were more numerous and more influential than Ashkenazim. Since that time, however, the position has been reversed, the disproportionate devastation of the Ashkenazim in the Holocaust notwithstanding.

The Ashkenazim originally settled an area of the land near the Rhine River that they called Loter (Lorraine) in about the 6th century C.E. By the 14th century their presence had expanded to encompass all the lands known now as Germany as well as parts of France, Austria, and Italy. Thereafter they moved primarily eastward to Poland, the Czech, Slovak, and Hungarian lands, Lithuania, the Ukraine, and Belorussia. From the Middle Ages to the age of the Enlightenment, the Ashkenazim in the cities frequently lived in a Jewish quarter. Eastern European Ashkenazi demography also featured the predominantly Jewish village, or shtetl. Torah and Talmud study were highly valued in both the cities and the villages, and centers of learning moved eastward from the Germanic lands through Poland and Lithuania as the Ashkenazim settled in these areas. From the 18th through the 20th century, Ashkenazim emigrated primarily to England, the Americas, Palestine/Israel, Australia, and South Africa.

WEINREICH presents a partial account of Ashkenazi Jewry through the history of the primary Ashkenazi language, Yiddish. He believes that "the history of Yiddish and the history of Ashkenaz are identical." Although his study focuses primarily on issues of structural linguistics, several chapters offer a clear description of how the Ashkenazim moved from the Germanic lands eastward and spread the use of Yiddish. Weinreich describes Jews in lands apart from Germany originally using other languages, with Yiddish slowly growing to achieve dominance as the Jews from the Germanic lands migrated to other areas in Europe and Eurasia. Weinreich uses maps and diagrams to show centers of Ashkenazi culture shifting from Worms and Regensburg to Prague, Brest-Litovsk, Krakow, and Vilna. For a general history of Ashkenazi migrations, these chapters serve as a particularly helpful and stimulating discussion.

PATAI offers an extremely useful survey of the main distinguishing features of Ashkenazi, Sephardi, and Oriental Jewry. In the first section of the book, he deals with issues of demography, migrations, language, and differences in culture and folk beliefs. His article on Jewish languages is particularly interesting and comprehensive. The second major division of the book deals with specific diaspora communities, Ashkenazi, Sephardi, and Oriental. In his extensive treatment of the Ashkenazim, he emphasizes the largest contemporary communities outside Israel, such as those of France, England, Russia, Argentina, and the United States. Although his book does not cover much of the traditional Central and Eastern European heartland, Patai is still able to balance his study between the historical development of Ashkenazi cultures and their current demographic features and status. In addition to the essays on Ashkenazim and Sephardim, the book also includes special sections on less well-known Jewish communities, such as those of Iraq, Iran, and the Caucasus. Because of its coverage of such a wide variety of Jewish communities, this book successfully points out the most distinctive features of Ashkenazi culture in contrast to those of other communities. In some cases, however, readers should watch for overly generalized statements about Jewish accomplishments in specific cultures.

AGUS focuses on the history of the earliest Ashkenazim, the German and French Jews in the tenth and 11th centuries. He posits that during this era, a "process of selection" occurred that guaranteed that the strongest members of the Jewish community would survive and thrive despite the constant chaos around them. The book is divided into 11 chapters, each of which explores a particular feature that helped to ensure the survival of the Franco-German Jewish communities. Agus devotes several chapters, for example, to business and trade and describes how Jewish merchants from different communities worked together and provided shelter for each other. He also provides detailed explanations of Jewish administrative autonomy, the strong community organization that created some kind of security, and the Jewish communities' relations with the gentile nobles who relied on them for business. Agus bases his study on rabbinic responsa, archival holdings, and other primary sources in addition to a vast variety of secondary literature. Although readers should be cautious about the Social Darwinist interpretations that Agus offers, this book is most valuable for understanding the roots and later growth of the Ashkenazim and their culture.

ISRAEL offers the most comprehensive history of European Jews, both Ashkenazi and Sephardi, for the early modern period in Europe. His discussion includes all relevant Eastern and Western European nations. He claims that, the great migrations eastward notwithstanding, Western European Jewry was also exceptionally vibrant during this period. Israel focuses on the economic and political roles conceived for Jews by ruling classes in different nations. He explains in detail the privileges granted to Jews by Rudolf II of Bohemia and by the Polish nobles in the late 1500s. He also deals with Jewish cultural and political autonomy, particularly in Poland, Lithuania, and Germany, and he argues that it was during the period 1550 to 1750 that Jewish culture experienced its highest level of cohesion and autonomy in Europe. Another highlight of this book is his extensive discussion of the role of Jewish financiers and military suppliers in different rulers' courts. Israel does a particularly good job of balancing materials on Jewish economic and cultural development and juxtaposing the history of Jewish autonomy with the history of the different nations in which they settled. The book contains extensive bibliographies of primary and secondary published sources and archival documents.

ZIMMELS offers a compelling study of the differences between theological beliefs and religious practices of Ashkenazim and Sephardim. His book is divided into three parts: a general survey and history of Ashkenazi and Sephardi religious thought; an outline of the most important divergences in the two subcultures; and a selection of topics covered by rabbis of both communities in their responsa. In the first section, Zimmels discusses the relations between Ashkenazi and Sephardi rabbinic leaders and documents 1,000 years of cultural exchange, influence, and tension. The remainder of the book details differences in practice, for example, in Hebrew pronunciation and script, or in customs relating to birth and death, marriage and divorce, or festivals and fasts. The communities' respective stringencies and leniencies are given special attention. The book is clearly intended for specialists, and it is well supported by extensive annotations. However, the lay reader also will find much of interest in this absorbing and felicitously written narrative.

SHULVASS focuses primarily on little-known aspects of Ashkenazi history. The essays in his book touch on both Western and Eastern European Jewry, the Ashkenazim in Italy, and the medieval Ashkenazi migration to Constantinople. Shulvass believes that the study of the "problems of communal reorganization and acculturation" faced by Ashkenazim "when they established a new life in Eastern Europe, in Italy, and on the Balkan peninsula" can provide significant insight into later Jewish migration to North America. He organizes his essays into three main topics: Germany and Western Europe, Eastern Europe, and Italy and farther south. After essays on the Ashkenazim during the crusades and the medieval Ashkenazi community, Shulvass reviews the rich history of the Ashkenazim in Poland, Lithuania, and Russia. Shulvass's essays on Eastern European Jewish history and Torah study provide a usefully concise overview of Jewish life in all the Eastern European lands. The other essays in his book focus on the Ashkenazim who chose to migrate to Italy, beginning in the 13th century C.E. He describes the strong cultural differences between the Ashkenazi emigres and the Sephardi and Italian Jewish communities in Italy. Shulvass writes in a colloquial, easy-to-read style, and his book is perhaps best for nonspecialists, for it does not include an index or footnotes.

SZAJKOWSKI also focuses on little-known aspects of the Ashkenazi experience. He deals with the strong cultural differences and disagreements that emerged among three distinct Jewish communities in France over the course of five centuries. Well buttressed with extensive references, Szajkowski's article explores issues of trade as well as culture among the Sephardi, Ashkenazi, and Avignonese Jews. He shows that the Sephardim at times had greater privileges in trade than the Ashkenazim. The article also offers details about the reactions of different Jewish communities to the antisemitism of Enlightenment figures such as Voltaire as well as members of mainstream Catholic French culture. The article ends with a study of the growth of the Ashkenazi population in France prior to World War II.

ALISA GAYLE MAYOR

See also Music: Ashkenazi Folk Music

Assimilation

Arendt, Hannah, *The Origins of Totalitarianism*, London: Secker and Warburg, and New York: Harcourt, Brace, 1951; expanded (3rd) edition, New York: Harcourt, Brace, and World, 1966; London: Allen and Unwin, 1967

Arendt, Hannah, *The Jew as Pariah: Jewish Identity and Politics in the Modern Age*, New York: Grove, 1978

Erspamer, Peter R., *The Elusiveness of Tolerance: The "Jewish Question" from Lessing to the Napoleonic Wars* (University of North Carolina Studies in the Germanic Languages and Literatures, vol. 117), Chapel Hill: University of North Carolina Press, 1997

Horkheimer, Max and Theodor W. Adorno, *Dialektik der Aufklärung: Philosophische Fragmente*, 1947; translated by John Cumming as *Dialectic of Enlightenment*, New York: Herder and Herder, 1972; London: Lane, 1973; new edition, London: Verso, 1979

Kristeva, Julia, *Étrangers à nous-mêmes*, 1988; translated by Leon Roudiez as *Strangers to Ourselves*, London and New York: Harvester Wheatsheaf, 1991

Sartre, Jean-Paul, *Réflexions sur la question juive*, 1946; translated by George Becker as *Anti-Semite and Jew*, New York: Schocken, 1948

Scholem, Gershom, *On Jews and Judaism in Crisis: Selected Essays*, New York: Schocken, 1976

Assimilation denotes the complete absorption of a minority into the dominant society. This essay will examine several critiques of the assimilation concept. In their 1947 tract, HORKHEIMER and ADORNO discuss with irony the difference between the liberal and the antisemite. According to Horkheimer and Adorno, for the liberal, the "Jewish question" was a mere pretext for discussion, while for the antisemite, the "Jewish question" was the most critical issue of the day. Liberal toleration was predicated on the belief that emancipation would eventually lead to the elimination of all cultural differences between Jews and gentiles and lead to the complete absorption of the Jews. Jews are seen as being part of a universal humanity who should erase the uniqueness of their culture. Antisemites, however, resent the continuing existence of Jewish cultural differences and the failure of Jews to completely assimilate. Antisemites have a consistent position: one of hatred. Liberals, on the other hand, are inconsistent.

ERSPAMER's study argues that those who seek to enter into a dialogue with "Otherness" must first resolve a dialogue within themselves. Efforts toward resolving this internal dialogue often result in an attempt to make the "Other" more similar to the self rather than an appreciation of the otherness for what it is and a resolution of the difference in a spirit of mutual respect.

ARENDT (1951) analyzes the internal contradictions inherent in the position of 18th-century advocates of tolerance: "The particularly tolerant, educated, and cultured non-Jews could be bothered socially only with exceptionally educated Jews. . . . Jews were exhorted to be educated enough not to behave like ordinary Jews, but they were, on the other hand, accepted only because they were Jews, because of their foreign exotic appeal." SCHOLEM contends that the willingness of reform-minded Germans to promote Jewish equality over the centuries came about "under the presupposition that Jews were willing to give themselves up as *Jewish* to an ever more progressive extent." To desire to "tolerantly" bring about the assimilation of the minority leads to an intolerant backlash when members of the minority group refuse to comply.

KRISTEVA points out that "the absorption of otherness proposed by our societies turns out to be unacceptable to the contemporary individual, jealous of his difference—one that is not only national and ethical but essentially subjective, insurmountable." Neither the principles of the antisemites nor those of the advocates of assimilation were acceptable to the Jewish community as a whole. According to SARTRE in his landmark study, the antisemite wishes to deny the Jew status as a human being and "leave nothing in him but the Jew, the pariah, the untouchable," whereas tolerant liberals wish to deny the Jews status as Jews and leave nothing in them but the human being, "the abstract and universal subject of the rights of man and the rights of the citizen." This leads to a difficult situation because, as Kristeva puts it: "A new homogeneity is not very likely, perhaps hardly desirable."

ARENDT (1978) points out that emancipation should have been "an admission of Jews *as Jews* to the ranks of humanity, rather than a permit to ape the gentiles or an opportunity to play the *parvenu*." In the absence of such full acceptance of otherness, Arendt argues, pariahdom is preferable to conformity to an unjust society. It accords a stance from which to criticize that society. The parvenu is not "born to the system, but chose it of his own free will, and . . . is called upon to pay the cost meticulously and exactly, whereas others can take things in stride." For Arendt, the question of being a parvenu or a pariah is nothing less than a choice between social ambition and political consciousness. Only a pariah can develop a true political consciousness because only pariahs can affirm their political identity and push for minority rights. Pariahs tend to be resisters, whereas parvenus are liable to be politically malleable.

PETER R. ERSPAMER

Astrology

Altmann, Alexander, "Astrology," in *Encyclopaedia Judaica*, Jerusalem: Encyclopaedia Judaica, 1972

Freudenthal, Gad, "Maimonides' Stance on Astrology in Context," in *Moses Maimonides: Physician, Scientist, and Philosopher*, edited by Fred Rosner and Samuel S. Kottek, Northvale, New Jersey: Aronson, 1993

Langermann, Y. Tzvi, "Maimonides' Repudiation of Astrology," in *Maimonidean Studies*, vol. 2, New York: Michael Scharf Publication Trust of Yeshiva University Press, 1991

Langermann, Y. Tzvi, "Some Astrological Themes in the Thought of Abraham Ibn Ezra," in *Rabbi Abraham Ibn Ezra: Studies in the Writings of a Twelfth-Century Jewish Polymath*, edited by Isadore Twersky and Jay M. Harris, Cambridge, Massachusetts: Harvard University, Center for Jewish Studies, 1993

Levy, Raphael, *The Astrological Works of Abraham Ibn Ezra: A Literary and Linguistic Study with Special Reference to the Old French Translation of Hagin*, Baltimore, Maryland: Johns Hopkins University Press, 1927

Levy, Raphael, *The Beginning of Wisdom, An Astrological Treatise by Abraham Ibn Ezra: An Edition of the Old French Version of 1273 and an English Translation of the Hebrew Original*, Baltimore: Johns Hopkins University Press, 1939; London: Oxford University Press, 1976

Ness, Lester John, "Astrology and Judaism in Late Antiquity," Ph.D. diss., Miami University, 1990

Sirat, Colette, *A History of Jewish Philosophy in the Middle Ages*, Cambridge and New York: Cambridge University Press, 1985

Stern, Josef, "The Fall and Rise of Myth in Ritual: Maimonides versus Nahmanides on the *Huqqim*, Astrology and the War against Idolatry," *Journal of Jewish Thought and Philosophy*, 6, 1997

Historically, Jewish outlooks on astrology have been as diverse as those of other cultures. While ancient and premodern scientists often treated astrology along with astronomy as a legitimate area of investigation, it eventually lost its place in the canon of mainstream science. And while many religious thinkers—even those denying fatalism—have embraced astrology as part and parcel of their theological world-views, many others have rejected it as a form of idolatry.

ALTMANN provides a useful reference guide to biblical, apocryphal, talmudic, midrashic, and later scholarly sources on astrology, including both philosophical and kabbalistic literature. Moving through the bulk of significant resources, he compiles a list of relevant figures and texts, drawing attention to a variety of passages and providing examples of many of the astrological beliefs held by Jews through the ages.

In his dissertation, NESS draws upon historical and archaeological data to argue that the Jews of late antiquity integrated many aspects of the surrounding polytheistic astral religion into their faith, but this synthesis was tempered by their commitment to monotheism. In effect, Ness asserts that the pagan astral gods were absorbed into Judaism during this period as astral angels subordinate to the single God of Israel. After charting the development of astrology from its origins in Mesopotamia through its treatment in the Greek world, Ness turns to an examination of this phenomenon in the Jewish world of late antiquity, and he ends his study with an analysis of a variety of Jewish "zodiac mosaics" that test his broader thesis. This study includes a very useful bibliography as well as extensive footnotes.

In the context of a chapter on Neoplatonism, SIRAT addresses the issue of astrology and Israel in the medieval context. While Sirat concludes that there is no particularly Jewish astrology, the reader is introduced to a number of uniquely Jewish applications of astrology, including a discussion of the talmudic claim that "Israel does not depend on a star" and the role of this statement in the medieval debate between Abraham bar Hiyya and Judah ben Barzillai regarding the status of astrology's permissibility and/or efficacy from a Jewish perspective. Sirat divides astrological discussion in Jewish texts into two main categories: using astrological information to chart Israel's historical progress toward the era of the Messiah; and turning to astrological considerations to explain some of the divine commandments. In light of these two groupings, Sirat offers details of the cosmologies and the ethics of Abraham bar Hiyya and Abraham ibn Ezra as examples of predominant Jewish proponents of astrology.

In his extended essay on astrology in Abraham ibn Ezra, LANGERMANN (1993) presents a picture of a Jewish figure whose astrological views reflect the general 12th-century Spanish intellectual culture, in which "astrology provided one of the primary mechanisms for naturalistic explanation." At the same time, however, Langermann cautions that ibn Ezra's astrological views may sometimes be overemphasized in assessments of his biblical commentary and overall thought. This latter point notwithstanding, Langermann makes clear the extent of ibn Ezra's astrological knowledge and analyzes his employment of astrological details in his exegetical work. Langermann considers ibn Ezra's discussions of climatological celestial influences and "astrological geography" (the idea that the land of Israel, by virtue of its spatial relation to a certain special celestial configuration, is holier than other places). The article also reviews ibn Ezra's claims about the impact on one's soul of stellar configurations at birth as well as his frequent explanations of biblical commands along astrological lines. Additionally, Langermann explores the extent to which ibn Ezra equates Jews and non-Jews with respect to celestial influence, noting his differences from Yehuda Halevi on this issue.

For an English translation of one of Abraham ibn Ezra's astrological works, see LEVY (1939) and LEVY (1927).

STERN presents a more detailed discussion of the use of astrology to ground the rationale of biblical commandments. In addition to exploring a variety of related issues, Stern's essay specifically addresses the debate between Maimonides and Nahmanides on the role of astrology within Judaism: where

Maimonides contests the truth and efficacy of astrology, Nahmanides supports them. Maimonides, focusing on the Sabian historical context of the early Israelites, sees certain commandments (specifically, the *hukkim*—that group of biblical prescriptions, such as the sending of a scapegoat, whose reasons are not apparent) as designed to wean Israel away from inefficacious pagan astral practices (where the name *hukkim* according to Maimonides highlights their role as negating the *hukkot ha-goyim* or "customs of the nations"). Nahmanides, instead, sees the *hukkim* as an acknowledgment within the Law of the efficacy of astral powers: for Nahmanides, the reason the Law prohibits certain forms of astrology and idolatry in general is precisely because they do represent real forces in the world. In effect, Stern discerns within Nahmanides' treatment of the *hukkim* a "vigorous anti-Maimonidean *defense* of the veracity of astrology."

Turning to Maimonides' views of astrology, FREUDENTHAL stresses the importance of distinguishing between "natural astrology" (the schema of Aristotelian cosmology and science), which Maimonides does not contest, and other types of astrology, which the philosopher rejects. By tracing the roots of astrology in medieval science, Freudenthal usefully reminds the reader who is unsympathetic to astrology that Maimonides' own opposition must be evaluated in its historical context, rather than according to modern standards. The author emphasizes that Maimonides' view was intellectually anomalous in his time, at odds with the beliefs of many mainstream rabbis and scientists, before offering two rationales for Maimonides' repudiation of astrology: first, astrology contradicts the fundamental notions of free will and "indeterminism" in Maimonides' thought; second, astrology is not compatible with Maimonides' epistemological skepticism.

LANGERMANN (1991) also evaluates Maimonides' unequivocal renunciation of astrology, dividing the philosopher's arguments along two major lines. First, Maimonides argues against astrology on the basis of a distinction between real science and pseudo-science—while true Aristotelian science is characterized by a firm grounding in first principles, the pseudo-science of astrology operates on the principle of induction (*tajribah*), drawing conclusions through repeated observations alone. The second line of argument that Langermann delineates in Maimonides' thought centers on the relationship between astrology and the forbidden practice of astral worship. Committed to defending God's unity and transcendence, Maimonides charges that the astrologers have wrongly confused physical astral powers with nonphysical efflux (*fayd*), and therefore they have mistaken the merely physical influence that the stars have on the earth for a far greater power. Furthermore, this very mistake has led to false reverence for the stars, which, in turn, has lent undue support to astral worship. Langermann concludes by examining how Maimonides' view of free will relates to his rejection of astrology. Langermann denies, however, that Maimonides' opposition to astrology is based on his rejection of determinism. The paper includes invaluable references to the primary and secondary scholarly literature as well as to pertinent manuscripts.

SARAH PESSIN

Atlases *see* Reference Works

Atonement *see* Festivals and Fasts; Sin and Atonement

Australia and New Zealand

Aron, Joseph and Judy Arndt, *The Enduring Remnant: The First 150 Years of the Melbourne Hebrew Congregation, 1841–1991*, Carlton: Melbourne University Press, and Portland, Oregon: International Specialized Book Services, 1992

Gluckman, Ann and Laurie Gluckman (editors), *Identity and Involvement: Auckland Jewry*, vol. 1, Palmerston North: Dunmore, 1990, vol. 2, 1993

Goldman, Lazarus Morris, *The History of the Jews in New Zealand*, Wellington: Reed, 1958

Mossenson, David and Louise Hoffman, *Hebrew, Israelite, Jew: The History of the Jews of Western Australia*, Nedlands: University of Western Australia Press, 1990

Porush, Israel, *The House of Israel*, Melbourne: Hawthorn, 1977

Rubinstein, Hilary L., *The Jews in Victoria, 1835–1985*, London: Allen and Unwin, 1985; Boston: Allen and Unwin, 1986

Rubinstein, Hilary L. and W.D. Rubinstein, *The Jews in Australia: A Thematic History*, 2 vols., Port Melbourne: Heinemann Australia, 1991

Rutland, Suzanne D., *Edge of the Diaspora: Two Centuries of Jewish Settlements in Australia*, Sydney: Collins, 1988; second revised edition, Rose Bay: Brandl and Schlesinger, 1997

Australia was the last continent where a Jewish community was established. Jews, estimated to number between six and 14, arrived as convicts on the First Fleet, which established the first European settlement on the continent in January 1788. Until 1933, the Jewish community, always numbering about 0.5 percent of the population, was predominantly British in origin and Orthodox in the British United Synagogue mold. Between 1933 and the early 1950s the size of the community doubled, from approximately 26,000 to approximately 52,000, chiefly through the extensive immigration of prewar German Jewish refugees and postwar Holocaust survivors. This growth resulted in a considerable religious diversification of Australian Jewry; a successful Jewish Reform movement was established at this time, and the Orthodox spectrum broadened to include strictly observant communities and other synagogues defined by their Religious Zionist orientation. The first full-time Jewish day schools were established in the 1940s in Sydney (Moriah College) and Melbourne (Mount Scopus College), the two main centers of Australian Jewish life. From the early 1950s until the end of the 1990s, the Jewish population of Australia doubled again, to approximately 105,000, through heavy immigration and internal growth. By 1999 there were approximately 65 synagogues in Australia, approximately 55

Orthodox (of varying types) and approximately ten Reform. There were no Conservative or Reconstructionist synagogues. More notably, Australia contains no fewer than 18 full-time Jewish day schools, with more than 10,000 students. Rates of intermarriage and assimilation among Australian Jews are remarkably low by diaspora standards, and Australia appears to be a diaspora community with a promising future.

New Zealand has always had a much smaller Jewish community than Australia, numbering no more than a few thousand. Refugee immigration during the Nazi period was minimal, and by the 1960s the community, centered in Auckland and Wellington, was in some danger of extinction. However, the recent immigration of ex-Soviet Jews and the foundation of day schools in Auckland and Wellington have contributed to a revival of the community, now numbering about 4,000.

Before the 1970s, histories of the Jews in Australia and New Zealand tended to be old-fashioned congregational narratives, often written by well-meaning amateurs. Since then, and especially since the mid-1980s, there has been an explosion of academic research on this subject, only some of which is highlighted here. The excellent *Australian Jewish Historical Society Journal,* published biannually, contains many articles, often on religious history, and reviews of all relevant new books. The main theme that has emerged from recent writings has been the sui generis but very successful adaptations of Jewish immigrants to the remote conditions of Australia. Most recent scholarship has discussed political and social questions; issues concerning the development of Judaism as a religion in Australia have perhaps been neglected, although as this survey shows, not ignored.

ARON and ARNDT have written a sophisticated commissioned history of the Melbourne Hebrew Congregation, a long-established synagogue associated with Melbourne's Jewish elite and old families, which recognized (until 1989) the British Chief Rabbi as its ultimate head. The authors trace the congregation's evolution into a less Anglo-Jewish, more broadly based institution under the impact of European immigration.

GOLDMAN, an English-born Orthodox rabbi in Melbourne from the 1930s until the late 1950s, wrote pioneering histories of Jews in Victoria (the state of which Melbourne is the capital) and in New Zealand. His history of New Zealand—now, unfortunately, a scarce collector's item—is a well-written general account, touching on all aspects of the development of the community.

The two volumes edited by GLUCKMAN and GLUCKMAN contain nearly 100 essays by Auckland Jews, ranging from general communal histories to individual biographies and reflections on the future of New Zealand Jewry. Perhaps ten of the articles deal directly with New Zealand Judaism and its evolution.

MOSSENSON's work is a history of the Jewish community in Western Australia. Remote not merely from the world's centers of Jewish life but also from the well-established communities of Melbourne and Sydney, Western Australia's community nevertheless developed in a way that was recognizably similar to Jewish societies in eastern Australia. Recently, Western Australia has experienced very rapid growth in its Jewish population, due especially to the heavy settlement of South African Jews.

PORUSH was a distinguished Orthodox rabbi who led Sydney's Great Synagogue in the postwar decades. The Great Synagogue, located in central Sydney, is often regarded as the most prestigious synagogue in Australia. Porush traces the history of the "Great" from the early 19th century to the 1970s, skillfully combining personal reminiscences with wider material on the evolution of Australian Jewry, especially in New South Wales.

Victoria has been the largest and most dynamic Jewish community in Australia during most of the 20th century, originating many trends imitated elsewhere. It is notable for the size and piety of its Orthodox community and for the quality of its secular Jewish leadership. RUBINSTEIN's history of the Victorian community was written on the 150th anniversary of European settlement in Melbourne, and it covers all aspects of religious life.

The two-volume history of Australian Jewry by RUBINSTEIN and RUBINSTEIN totals more than 1,200 pages. It is arranged thematically, with more than 200 pages devoted to the development of religious life. The history of each synagogue is given, and an account of all significant rabbis as well as a broader picture of the evolution of trends in Australian Judaism is included.

RUTLAND's book covers the whole history of the Australian Jewish community in all its aspects from 1788 until the late 1980s in nearly 500 pages. Great stress is placed on the broadening of the community as a result of the arrival of Holocaust refugees and survivors. The second edition of this work contains a 12-page summary of events from the mid-1980s until the mid-1990s.

WILLIAM D. RUBINSTEIN

Austria *see* Central Europe

Authority, Rabbinic and Communal

Agus, Irving, *Rabbi Meir of Rothenberg: His Life and His Works as Sources for the Religious, Legal, and Social History of the Jews of Germany in the Thirteenth Century,* Philadelphia: Dropsie College for Hebrew and Cognate Learning, 1947

Baer, Yitzhak F., "The Origins of Jewish Communal Organization in the Middle Ages," translated and adapted by Zipporah Brody, *Binah,* 1(4); originally published in Hebrew in *Zion,* 15, 1950

Baron, Salo, *The Jewish Community,* 3 vols., Philadelphia: Jewish Publication Society, 1942

Bonfil, Robert, *Rabbis and Jewish Communities in Renaissance Italy* (Littman Library of Jewish Civilization), translated by Jonathan Chipman, London: Oxford University Press, 1989

Elazar, Daniel J. (editor), *Kinship and Consent,* Philadelphia: Turtledove, 1981

Finkelstein, Louis, *Jewish Self-Government in the Middle Ages*, New York: Jewish Theological Seminary, 1924

Gitelman, Zvi (editor), *The Quest for Utopia: Jewish Political Ideas and Institutions through the Ages*, Armonk, New York, and London: Sharpe, 1992

Katz, Jacob, *Tradition and Crisis*, New York: Free Press of Glencoe, 1961; new translation by Bernard Cooperman, New York: New York University Press, 1993

Morrell, Samuel, "The Constitutional Limits of Communal Government in Rabbinic Law," *Jewish Social Studies*, 33, 1971

Studies of the Jewish community *(kehillah)* can be incredibly dry when approached from the vantagepoint of the many rabbinic and lay officials and their sundry tasks. A fascinating fundamental question, however, lurks behind these various studies that gets to the heart of matters of Jewish identity and survival: How much control did the Jewish community and/or the rabbis really have over the members of the community? That is to say, were the various sanctions and punishments described in the rabbinic literature and communal enactments *(takkanot)* actually carried out and, if so, by whom—the rabbis, the lay leaders, or the secular authorities?

There are several basic questions concerning the Jewish community that need to be answered not out of a sense of revisionism (which can be intellectually stimulating) but to honestly come to grips with the forces that controlled Jewish destiny over the centuries. First, what were the origins of the Jewish community? Do the various Jewish communities around the world represent examples of a universal continuity inspired by internal influences and rabbinic traditions, or do they reflect radical departures based on significantly different local circumstances? Second, can traditional Jewish communities be described as democratic? Or was leadership in the control of an intellectual or financial elite that allowed for very little popular input? Third, were the communities controlled by rabbinic or lay leaders? Although many of the sources were written by rabbis, did their ideal depictions of Jewish society reflect the political realities? These questions, often unstated in the hundreds of studies of various Jewish communities, are of more than academic interest because, whether discussed implicitly or explicitly, they probe the basic issues of Jewish originality, adaptation, and assimilation in addition to the specific problems of leadership, authoritarian or voluntary, and coercion, especially in matters of corporal and capital punishment. These matters are all connected to larger questions of whether the Jews constituted a polity since the destruction of the second Temple and whether they developed political theory and institutions during that period. These questions inform the often torturous discussions today about the nature of Jewish communities around the world, particularly in light of attempts to resuscitate Jewish political sovereignty in the State of Israel, an effort that has been marked by some success over the years.

AGUS presents an important but dated survey of the life of a major rabbinic figure, several studies on Jewish community self-rule, and a translation of a digest, often cited by later writers, of Rabbi Meir's responsa. Agus's book is marred by the outrageous theory that contends that questions about the origins of European urban societies can be explained by long-standing and unchanged democratic, free, just, and egalitarian Jewish influence on the development of aspects of these Christian institutions. Agus resolves important questions about rabbinic authority by concluding that the rabbis, unaided by secular authorities, wielded great moral authority in their communities. It was, however, the lay Jewish leaders who claimed coercive powers, including corporal punishment. Much of Agus's theory, however, is based on what seem to be tendentious assumptions about the dating of materials and parallelisms, which can hardly be evidence for influence. Reviewing Agus in *Speculum* (1967), the eminent medievalist Robert Sabatino Lopez notes, "The truth, [Agus] implies, is that the Jews have invented everything and surpassed everybody."

BAER, in one of his major ingenious but usually contradictory studies, tries to argue that Jewish communal organization was an immanent creation of Jewish history. He attempts to revise the then-current view that undermined the essential rabbinic aspects of the Jewish community and attributed them to external medieval contingencies. He argues that rabbinic law does recognize an organic communal unit. He also argues that the community, nevertheless, was never viewed by the sages of the Talmud as an autonomous unit with the right to make decisions by majority rule. It was, however, a concept found in ancient nonrabbinic Jewish literature, an assertion that he supports with extrarabbinic (Christian) texts and rabbinic archaeological inscriptions. Baer thus asserts that the idea of a *kehillah kedoshah*, a holy community, can be traced back prior to the destruction of the Temple and through talmudic literature, an assertion he seems to have negated earlier. Baer champions both the democratic and original nature of the Jewish community, demonstrating how it anticipated any such Christian developments in Europe, which by the 12th century overtook Jewish developments and influenced them. But like so many Jerusalem historians Baer resolves the tension between internal (acceptable) influence and external (unacceptable) influence by suggesting that the Jews ultimately only borrowed from the Christians those features that were inherent in earlier aspects of Judaism, in this case communal organization, making Christian culture nothing but a cryogenic freezer for storing Jewish artifacts until it was time for them to be revived as the situation required.

BARON, who, following Graetz and Dubnow, produced the greatest synthesis of Jewish history in the second half of the 20th century also published a classic three-volume study on the history of the Jewish community. The first volume traces the history of the Jewish community from biblical to modern times, the second examines specific themes, and the third contains notes and a bibliography of valuable sources on every pertinent subject. Baron's work is both balanced and blunt. He emphatically dismisses rhetoric about democratic features attributed to the Jewish community, preferring terms such as oligarchy, and acknowledges the lack of information concerning the origins of the Jewish community, the limited role of rabbis in Jewish communities, and the influence of external factors. Despite his profound attempt to minimize the role of the rabbis and traditional rabbinic law in Jewish communities and to stress the role of the wealthy members of the community, Baron accentuates the religious nature of the Jewish community. His descriptions of floggings, bans, and even capital punishment, however, may (following his own cautions) reflect more rabbinic theory than actual practice. Rabbinic theory, it must be remembered, was based not only on a polemic against powerful lay leaders but also on one against Christians who tried to diminish the dignity of Judaism by claiming, with allusion to Genesis 49:10, that the scepter had departed from Judah. Baron pays significant attention to the role of women, negating the presence of separate seating in early synagogues and affirming the role of women leaders of synagogues.

BONFIL studies the relationship between rabbis and lay leaders in early modern Italy. He notes the tension between established precedents, such as calling priests to the reading of the Torah first, and the desire of the rabbis to alter such traditions to enhance their prestige, e.g., by being called before the priests. Bonfil notes that in the serious matters of rabbinic authority such as adjudication, however, the authority of rabbinic autonomy, especially as a court with jurisdiction, was not recognized and that the rabbis functioned as judges only in matters of arbitration agreed upon in advance by both parties. The reason, he notes, was due to church objections to Jewish jurisdiction. According to Bonfil, the Jewish community also placed many obstacles in the way of the rabbis, such as decreasing their income and instituting an ever-higher minimum age of ordination, in order to limit their authority and their ability to control the community, sometimes by means of radical devices such as excommunication.

ELAZAR has collected a series of essays by leading scholars that focus on the central questions of rabbinic and communal authority throughout Jewish history. Bernard Susser and Eliezer Don-Yehiya note clearly the political agendas of authors when writing about Jewish political theory, especially regarding the use of the coercive powers of the host regime by an autonomous medieval community, which they characterize as a novelty in Jewish history. The juxtaposition of autonomous and host, however, seems to be slightly contradictory. Menahem Elon's essay touches on all the important historical matters related to questions of authority; however, his conception of historical development seems somewhat lacking in nuance. He posits monolithic centers of Jewish influence, massive transformations, and excessive communal autonomy, which he then goes on to undermine in more nuanced terms. Elon, like so many others who deal with the question of the use of force by the Jewish community to impose its will, cannot square theoretical with practical matters and so sidesteps the fundamental question by resorting to the expedient explanation of the community relying on moral authority. Gerald Blidstein provides one of the most thorough discussions of the basic texts about Jewish communal authority as well as the secondary literature.

FINKELSTEIN's classic study of the Jewish community introduces and reports in both English and Hebrew the basic texts of medieval Jewish communal life. Despite sound agnosticism on many of the important questions about the development of the Jewish community, Finkelstein, nevertheless, allows apologetics to fill some of the historical gaps. He does, therefore, see the Babylonian talmudic academies as exercising centralized authority over the Jews, a position that may

reflect more the aspirations of talmudic texts or Finkelstein himself than the reality of the period. He emphasizes that the origins of the Jewish community in Europe are obscure and that the Jews there had to develop their own courts, which administered civil and some aspects of criminal justice, again taking a moderate position in light of many of the more encompassing aspirations described in the rabbinic literature. He notes that there was no clear definition of the authority of the rabbis and traces some of the obscure origins of rabbinic authority outside of Palestine. In Babylonia these included simple recognition by the litigants in each case, authorization by the exilarch, or acceptance by the secular authorities. In Europe, however, the sources of rabbinic authority are less clear. Finkelstein suggests that it may have derived from early communal vows to of obedience or an ancient authorization by authorities in Palestine. Such a problem, he notes, was occasionally addressed by rabbis who attempted to introduce the institution of ordination in Europe. Classic examples of Finkelstein's apologetic include the artful dodge on the question of rabbinic authority by saying that the rabbis had no need for police power or physical force. Similarly, in referring to the 13th-century edict against wife beating by the French rabbinic authority Peretz bar Elijah of Corbeil, Finkelstein concludes, "This crime was one that rarely, if ever, gave trouble to the Jews of the Middle Ages." Responding to the same edict, Louis I. Rabinowitz notes in his *Social Life of the Jews of Northern France in the XII–XIII Centuries* (1938) that "the prohibition may have been the result of an addiction to the habit" and refers to "the prevalence of the custom of wife-beating." Similar apologetics on the parts of Finkelstein emerge when he discusses monogamy among the Jews and the medieval rabbis' ability to limit the unfair advantage the brother-in-law held over a childless widow, a position certainly belied by current practice today, which leaves many women chained as *agunot*.

GITELMAN collects several important essays that attempt to probe traditional Jewish texts for signs of political theory but usually find them wanting. Central to many of the essays is the attempt to wrestle with the question of the developmental nature of the texts and the applicability of traditional theoretical texts to real situations. In other words, the authors address the lack of not only a clear theory but a clear precedent so that over the ages Jewish communities had to formulate, often from scratch, principles such as discretionary powers to override traditional laws. Such a power to deal with immediate threats was indeed often seen as extending beyond the prerogatives of the court to members of the community.

KATZ is a classic study of a Jewish community, in this case the Jewish community of Eastern Europe at the end of the Middle Ages and the beginning of the modern period, the 16th to the 18th centuries. Key to Katz's book is precisely the question of the role of traditional Jewish law and rabbinic authority in the management of the community. As a result, he provides a magisterial account not only of the traditional texts but of the ways in which the Jewish community departed from them, both in matters of the rights of the minority, the development of customs, and the role of communal enactments. Katz's writing is incisive and his observations often stunning; in particular he notes many of the paradoxes of Jewish life.

One such example is the extent of Sephardi legal influence on the quintessentially Ashkenazi Jews of Lithuania and Poland, particularly in the manner in which informers were destroyed, following Katz's literal understanding of the texts. Key to understanding the nature of authority in Jewish community life in Eastern Europe is the fact that rabbis often served for very limited periods of time, having little opportunity to become an entrenched force in the community, or alternatively they bought their positions, enjoying the benefits of their office like a bishop would his bishopric but not necessarily for reasons of spiritual or intellectual attainments. Coercion, contrary to so many myths, was in the hands of the secular government, and, paradoxically, these powers were used by the Jews to support any independent authority they might have had. Similarly, most judicial decisions were rendered by lay leaders weighing the merits of the case rather than by a resort to rabbinic legal precedents, although excommunications were issued in cooperation with rabbinic leaders.

MORRELL draws on all previous studies of the Jewish community and the relationship of rabbis to it, reading the primary sources again very carefully. He asserts boldly that, although there were communal institutions in the time of the Talmud, rabbinic literature paid little attention to them. He demonstrates the attempt of later rabbinic authorities to reconcile the development of communal control with talmudic texts. The process that Morrell describes is one in which communal authority gradually shifts from the religious court to the lay leaders who gain the authority to overrule talmudic rulings or to justify practices such as majority rule that had no talmudic basis. He offers examples of texts that indicate that the rabbis have the ability to fine, ban, and flog, but the extent to which they exercised these abilities remains in question. Morrell compares the 13th-century views of the Ashkenazi authority Rabbi Meir of Rothenberg with the Sephardi Solomon ibn Adret as well as with later authorities in Italy, the Ottoman Empire, and Eastern Europe on the question of under what circumstances the majority of a community may impose its will on the minority, an important contribution to the study of the development of the idea of coercion in the Jewish community.

HOWARD TZVI ADELMAN

Autonomy, Personal

Borowitz, Eugene B., *Liberal Judaism,* New York: Union of American Hebrew Congregations, 1984
Borowitz, Eugene B., *Exploring Jewish Ethics: Papers on Covenant Responsibility,* Detroit, Michigan: Wayne State University Press, 1990
Eisen, Arnold M., *Taking Hold of Torah: Jewish Commitment and Community in America* (Helen and Martin Schwartz Lectures in Jewish Studies), Bloomington: Indiana University Press, 1997
Eisen, Arnold M., *Rethinking Modern Judaism: Ritual, Commandment, Community* (Chicago Studies in the History of Judaism), Chicago: University of Chicago Press, 1998
Meyer, Michael A., *Response to Modernity: A History of the Reform Movement in Judaism* (Studies in Jewish History), New York: Oxford University Press, 1988
Roof, Wade Clark, *A Generation of Seekers: The Spiritual Journeys of the Baby Boom Generation,* San Francisco: HarperSanFrancisco, 1993
Silverstein, Alan, *Alternatives to Assimilation: The Response of Reform Judaism to American Culture 1840–1930* (Brandeis Series in American Jewish History, Culture, and Life), Hanover, New Hampshire, and London: Brandeis University Press, 1994
Wertheimer, Jack, *A People Divided: Judaism in Contemporary America,* Hanover, New Hampshire: Brandeis University Press, 1997

One of the central issues in Judaism today is how to reconcile the autonomy of the individual with the needs of the community. For the U.S. Jewish community in particular, this challenge takes place on two levels. On one level, there is the question of whether individual Jews are entitled to make their own religious choices or whether they must obey external authorities. Must an individual observe kashrut (dietary laws), or is that a matter of personal choice? And if it is a matter of personal choice, does that decision have to be made on the basis of certain established criteria, or can the person make a personal decision based on completely subjective factors? On the second level, there are questions of how the Jewish community can and should orient religious belief and practice in the context of an open society such as the United States.

ROOF investigates these issues of autonomy as they reflect the concerns of U.S. Jews born after World War II. As the "Baby Boomer" generation has matured, becoming the parents of Jewish school children and forming the bulk of congregational membership in all U.S. Jewish denominations, members of that generation have brought liberal social perspectives to their respective religious institutions. Roof describes how these individuals grew up "in a post–60s culture that emphasizes choice, knowing and understanding oneself, the importance of personal autonomy, and fulfilling one's potential—all contributing to a highly subjective approach to religion." Roof argues that the Baby Boomers are a generation of seekers and that denominational loyalties that were once taken for granted can no longer be assumed.

Eugene Borowitz is a Reform Jewish theologian who has dealt with autonomy and related issues in great depth. In BOROWITZ (1984) he asks, "must we observe all the Commandments and traditions?" In response, he explains that in the Reform movement, the right of individual self-determination has always held a treasured place, but that in the late 20th century the concept of *mitsvah* in the sense of ceremonies and symbols commended if not commanded has become a more popular position in the movement.

In BOROWITZ (1990), the author addresses the inherent conflict between autonomy and tradition. Borowitz argues that "the Reform of Judaism to meet the situation of an emancipated Jewry became possible only when, even unconsciously, human autonomy could be asserted and given precedence over the authority of Jewish tradition." He explains that Moses

Mendelssohn asserted autonomy in the theological realm but remained orthoprax, while Israel Jacobson believed that it was the individual Jew's right, as well as his duty, to follow his conscience and that this autonomy was more important than conforming to the dictates of tradition.

While all of the Jewish denominations in the United States have had to deal with the question of autonomy versus conformity, the Reform movement has taken a particularly clear position on the issue. MEYER describes how that element of the Jewish community has attempted to meet the challenges of modernity and address conflicts between individuality and communal loyalty. Meyer asks, "What, after all this history and contemporary divergence, binds the Reform Movement together?" If each individual is entitled to use his or her personal autonomy to make independent religious decisions and groups of Jews in different communities, cities, or countries are free to move in dramatically different directions, then "where is its diachronic and synchronic continuity?" Meyer admits that "in some respects very little" holds the Reform community together, but he also explains that the early reformers believed that Orthodoxy could not meet the challenges of the modern world, and therefore the Reform movement developed a concept of an evolving Judaism as the best hope for Jewish religious survival. Personal religious autonomy lay at the heart of such a theological system.

SILVERSTEIN considers the theme of autonomy in the course of his study of the Reform movement in the United States from 1840 to 1930. He argues that scholars have taken two distinct approaches when evaluating the movement. Many earlier works focus on Reform as theology. This perspective led to studies focused on rabbinic leadership, ritual debates, and ideological platforms. In contrast to this approach, many of the more recent studies have concentrated on social and cultural changes and their impact on the Jewish community. The religious autonomy enjoyed by all U.S. citizens allowed for the development of a pluralistic religious system.

In the United States today, autonomy is taken for granted by most Jews. Even some participants in the contemporary Reform movement, while reiterating the centrality of religious autonomy for each individual and community, believe that there is a dire need for greater direction and structure in Jewish society. WERTHEIMER describes how the four principal U.S. Jewish denominations have met the challenges of post-World War II society, confronting the "fragmenting world of organized Judaism."

Arnold Eisen is one of the leading intellectuals seeking to provide Jewish theological responses to the challenge of individual and communal religious autonomy. In EISEN (1997), he argues that it is possible to revitalize Judaism in the United States by rebuilding a relationship with Jewish tradition. Eisen uses each of the five books of the Torah to demonstrate how Jews can find meaning in their tradition and hence choose to continue the covenant that their ancestors made with God.

In EISEN (1998), he argues that there has been a massive transformation of Jewish religious belief since the beginning of the 19th century and that these changes "continue to perplex Jewish communities and shape Jewish religious options today." Asserting that it may be more useful for the scholar to concentrate on the study of religious practice rather than that belief, he contends that contrary to many simplistic accounts, Jews did not go through a straightforward three-stage process of adopting Enlightenment ideas, casting off traditional Judaic beliefs, and then modifying or even rejecting the concept of the performance of the mitsvot. Rather, "Jews for the most part navigated their way through modernity's unfamiliar terrain much as we do today: via *eclectic patterns of observance and varied, often individual, sets of meanings* discovered in those patterns or associated with them" (emphasis in the original).

DANA EVAN KAPLAN

B

Ba'alei Shem

Adler, Hermann, "The Baal Shem of London," *Jewish Historical Society of England–Transactions*, 5, 1903

Alexander, Tamar, "R. Judah the Pious as a Legendary Figure," in *Mysticism, Magic, and Kabbalah in Ashkenazi Judaism* (Studia Judaica), edited by Karl-Erich Grözinger and Joseph Dan, New York: de Gruyter, 1995

Dov Baer ben Samuel, of Linits, *In Praise of the Baal Shem Tov (Shivhei ha-Besht): The Earliest Collection of Legends about the Founder of Hasidism*, edited and translated by Dan Ben-Amos and Jerome R. Mintz, Bloomington: Indiana University Press, 1970

Nigal, Gedalyah, *Magyah, Mistikah va-Hasidut*, 1992; translated by Edward Levin as *Magic, Mysticism, and Hasidism: The Supernatural in Jewish Thought*, Northvale, New Jersey: Aronson, 1994

Patai, Raphael, "Hayyim Shmuel Falck," in *The Jewish Alchemists: A History and Source Book*, Princeton, New Jersey: Princeton University Press, 1994; Chichester, West Sussex: Princeton University Press, 1995

Rosman, Murray Jay, *Founder of Hasidism: A Quest for the Historical Ba'al Shem Tov* (Contraversions, 5), Berkeley: University of California Press, 1996

Salzman, Marcus (editor and translator), *The Chronicle of Ahimaaz* (Columbia University Oriental Studies, vol. 18), New York: Columbia University Press, 1924

Literally "master of the Name," the designation *ba'al shem* (pl. *ba'alei shem*) first achieved a widespread currency among late 17th-century German-Polish Jews after they became acquainted with practical Kabbalah. Originally, the term applied only to distinctive men who were said to know God's secret name and to use that name for miraculous ends. The first man to bear the title proper was Elijah of Chelm, who flourished around 1500. Two centuries later, the phenomenon developed into a profession, with *ba'alei shem* wandering the countryside writing amulets, prescribing empiric medicines, performing miracles, and engaging in the casting out or summoning of spirits. The early 18th-century figure Rabbi Israel ben Eliezer—the Ba'al Shem Tov ("master of the good Name," an alternative form of the title)—was the founder of modern Hasidism, and he stands as the most prominent and best-known of the group.

NIGAL's treatment of Hasidism and hasidic stories represents the most comprehensive monographic introduction to the topic. In his first chapter, Nigal explains the term *ba'al shem* and introduces his readers to the types of miracles and personalities included under this designation. The following seven chapters address issues with which *ba'alei shem* dealt or that appear in hasidic stories about them. These include *kefitsat ha-derekh* (the miraculous reduction of long distances), transmigration, spirit possession and exorcism, intermarriage with demons, battles against the forces of evil, journeys to the Garden of Eden and back, and the power of amulets. Nigal includes accounts of early and later *ba'alei shem* as well as the negative responses of detractors as early as the preeminent medieval authorities, Hai Gaon and Maimonides. Some of the sources Nigal uses, such as *Ma'aseh Nissim*, are available only in Hebrew, and therefore the appearance of this work in translation holds an extra measure of importance for its English-speaking audience.

The earliest work to touch upon the subject of *ba'alei shem* and their powers is the *Chronicle of Ahimaaz*, a record of the internal affairs of an Italian Jewish family claiming to trace its lineage to the Judeans exiled to Italy by Titus. The chronicle also reports several accounts of miracles—exorcisms and transmutations—worked by holy men harnessing the power of God's secret name. Written by Ahimaaz ben Paltiel of Capua, the chronicle ends in 1054 in Byzantium, thus establishing a high medieval terminus a quo for *ba'al shem*-like activity in Europe. SALZMAN's English version includes a 60-page introduction in which the editor discusses the influence of Arabic poetry on Ahimaaz's literary style, provides a review of previous literature on the topic, attempts to reconcile the chronicle with history (a task that often proves impossible), and offers a valuable and informative analysis of the text as a genealogical and literary document.

Perhaps the best-known of books about *ba'alei shem* is DOV BAER of Linits's collection of stories about Israel ben Eliezer, the Ba'al Shem Tov (Besht), who is considered the founder of Hasidism. In 1814, Israel Yofeh of Kopys set the manuscript in type and added 17 pages on the Besht's mother, bringing the number of tales to 251. A few of these stories concern earlier *ba'alei shem*, such as Rabbi Adam and Rabbi Samuel. Ben-Amos and Mintz's modern English translation of this Yiddish-Hebrew work aims to preserve the original character of Dov Baer's manuscript; it shifts person where Dov

Baer shifted and repeats itself where he did. Ben-Amos and Mintz note that two images of the Besht emerge from Dov Baer's collection; one version portrays the Besht as a simple yet pious man whose greatness was kept secret until he reached his 30s. The other depicts a wandering *ba'al shem* whose supernatural gift was always known as he traveled the countryside performing miracles. Aside from such editorial comments, the work is valuable because it makes the tales of the Besht available to English readers.

ROSMAN's groundbreaking study of the Besht has an entirely different purpose. Where Dov Baer intended to publicize his master's miracles, Rosman approaches the Besht as the vehicle through which modern researchers can better understand Hasidim and, by extension, much of modern Jewish religion and experience. In his search for the historical Ba'al Shem Tov, Rosman discounts those sources that are the most susceptible to ideological interpolations and interpretations (such as Dov Baer's manuscript). Instead, Rosman relies on authenticated correspondence of the Besht, contemporary testimonies and texts, and posthumous letters. He also presents an analysis of the environment from which the Besht sprang, the 18th-century Polish town of Miedzyboz. As Rosman states, he is interested in the Besht's place in life, rather than in theology.

ADLER focuses his attention on "Dr." Samuel Falk (1710–1782), the Ba'al Shem of London. A friend of Moses David of Podhayce (the "Ba'al Shem of Podhayce") and a follower of Shabbetai Tsevi, Falk was in the business of contacting kings and other royal personages with offers of talismans, magic rings, and alchemical adventures. Later, he moved to London where he seems to have withdrawn increasingly from his public persona, preferring instead the quiet life of a private citizen, although he earned the title "Ba'al Shem of London" nonetheless. As he recreates Falk's life, Adler uses a number of sources in various languages, including letters from supporters, the writings of detractors (R. Jacob Emden and R. David Azulai), the memoirs of Benjamin Goldsmid (whose family held power of executor for Falk's estate), as well as Falk's diary, will, and epitaph. While later scholars tend to include Falk among the *ba'alei shem* without compunction, Adler retains more ambivalence, evidently regarding the title as one of high honor not to be accorded lightly: "Whilst on the one hand we dare not class him among worthies who have borne the designation of Baal Shem, it would be equally unjust to stigmatise him as a rank imposter." PATAI's chapter on Falk describes the exploits of the same individual from a different perspective. Patai bases his research on the diary of the Catholic Polish Count Rantzow, who recorded his firsthand experiences with the miracle-working Jewish alchemist in the mid-1730s.

ALEXANDER analyzes the tales of the exploits of R. Judah the Pious and his father Samuel, two of the earliest *ba'alei shem*, in terms of Hebrew hagiographic literature. Alexander notes that many of the activities attributed to Rabbi Samuel—riding a lion, creating a golem, his triumph over a priest using sorcery, and his rescue of a doomed Jewish community—conform to the Jewish and universal pattern of the legendary hero. The same point holds true for his son Rabbi Judah, who eclipses his older brother Rabbi Abraham and eventually becomes an even more potent *ba'al shem* than his father. Alexander aligns the Rabbi Judah stories with the four stages of the Jewish hero evident in Jewish hagiographic tales. Rabbi Judah, however, is not followed by his son, as is typical in Jewish hagiography. Rather, Rabbi Eliezer of Worms, Rabbi Judah's prize student who greatly toned down the behavior of his teacher, inherits the *ba'al shem* role for the next generation. This factor, combined with the problem that all these stories were composed some 300 years after Rabbi Judah lived, causes Alexander to question the authenticity of the tales, the manner in which they were composed, and the elements influencing their composition.

SHARI LOWIN

See also Israel ben Eliezer Ba'al Shem Tov

Ba'alei Teshuvah

Aviad, Janet, *Return to Judaism: Religious Renewal in Israel,* Chicago: University of Chicago Press, 1983

Danzger, M. Herbert, *Returning to Tradition: The Contemporary Revival of Orthodox Judaism,* New Haven, Connecticut: Yale University Press, 1989

Davidman, Lynn, *Tradition in a Rootless World: Women Turn to Orthodox Judaism,* Berkeley: University of California Press, 1991

Davidman, Lynn and Arthur L. Greil, "Gender and the Experience of Conversion: The Case of 'Returnees' to Modern Orthodox Judaism," *Sociology of Religion,* 54, Spring 1993

Kaufman, Debra Renee, *Rachel's Daughters: Newly Orthodox Jewish Women,* New Brunswick, New Jersey: Rutgers University Press, 1991

Ba'alei teshuvah, masters (or exponents) of return (or repentance) in the Hebrew idiom, are Jews who recommit to the strict practice of Judaism. The concept of *teshuvah* (return), which is grounded in the Torah and Talmud, refers to the process of repentance and atonement that makes it possible for those who have not been living religiously Jewish lives to affirm their religious commitment and identification with the Jewish community. Since the late 1960s, the term ba'alei teshuvah has been applied to Jews who have had little or no exposure to Judaism during childhood and thus are returning to their historic roots rather than a prior state of religiosity. The literature reviewed here consists primarily of social science research studies of the institutions that educate and socialize the returnees and the experiences of the men and women who return.

AVIAD describes the young people who attended ba'alei teshuvah yeshivot in Jerusalem in the late 1970s and the educational institutions themselves. Her examination is based on participant observation at the yeshivot, oral interviews, and a written survey of 375 students—66 percent males—some of whom were born in Israel and others in the diaspora. The American ba'alei teshuvah, as well as some of their counterparts from other parts of the world, were part of the youth culture that was disenchanted with materialism. The Israelis, on the other hand, were disillusioned with Zionism, which they associated with a secularism that produced social problems. Aviad notes the extent to which the ultraorthodox faculty of the yeshivot for ba'alei teshuvah disparage Western culture and are in some cases also anti-Zionist. She reports on the importance ba'alei teshuvah attach to being authentically Jewish, and she concludes that, for the most part, they come to feel more integrated and confident than they did before they became religious.

DANZGER covers much of the same ground as Aviad but provides a more comprehensive history and description of the American orthodox context. The author conducted more than 200 interviews in the United States and Israel and was a participant observer in ba'alei teshuvah yeshivot. He found that although secularism had a strong hold on American Jews, the civil rights movement of the 1960s, which emphasized ethnic identity, and the emergence of an antiestablishment counterculture spawned a group of Jewish hippies who were open to learning about orthodoxy. Orthodox groups in Israel and the United States responded by creating ba'alei teshuvah yeshivot and implementing strategies for recruitment: extending invitations to homes, instituting outreach programs for adults, and running special activities for young people. Danzger discusses typical curricular distinctions in the education of male and female ba'alei teshuvah, and cultural differences between "black hat" and "knitted kippah" yeshivot are also described.

Danzger identifies several themes in the "return" narratives of ba'alei teshuvah. Some find that what they considered success in their former lives is no longer meaningful. Others, described as seekers, see divine providence operating in their lives. Some ba'alei teshuvah become religious because of a fiancé, sibling, or other family member. The author also describes some of the difficulties ba'alei teshuvah face in orthodox life and belief, and he notes a tendency among them toward "exaggerated conformity." His informants stress that family relations can become problematic but that maintaining ties with parents and religious relatives as well as integration into orthodox communities is critical.

DAVIDMAN focuses on previously secular American women in the process of returning to Orthodoxy (ba'alot teshuvah). The participants in her ethnographic study were predominantly single women, some studying at Bais Chana, a Lubavitch residential seminary in St. Paul, Minnesota, and the others taking part in outreach activities sponsored by Lincoln Square Synagogue, a modern Orthodox congregation on the Upper West Side of Manhattan. The Bais Chana women were for the most part in their 20s, those at Lincoln Center about ten years older. Davidson immersed herself in these communities to learn firsthand about the processes of ideological conversion and socialization and to discover how women who were part of these communities viewed their experiences.

Both groups of women began to return to Orthodoxy in response to discontent and a subjective feeling of meaninglessness. The Lincoln Square women saw themselves as making a rational choice, whereas the Bais Chana women believed that their return was determined by divine providence. Similarly, the Lincoln Square participants were less likely than those from Bais Chana to express their religious turn in spiritual terms. The desire to live traditional lives as wives and mothers was a strong motivating factor for both groups of women. The religious leaders at Lincoln Square Synagogue accommodated to modernity whereas those at Bais Chana resisted it.

DAVIDMAN and GREIL investigate the impact of gender on the experience of return by comparing responses to interviews with 26 ba'alei teshuvah and 25 ba'alot teshuvah at Lincoln Square Synagogue. They describe three distinct search paths—accidental, casual, and committed—and identify gender differences in the paths taken. Women were somewhat more likely than men to have had an accidental search, whereas men were more likely to have had a committed search. Women were more likely than men to have discovered Lincoln Square through a personal contact. Both men and women were drawn to this Orthodox synagogue because of its sense of community. Men found particular satisfaction in participating in public worship. Women who were disturbed about gender roles in Orthodoxy were more likely to have left the synagogue or remained nonobservant than men who were uncomfortable with gender roles.

Like Davidman, KAUFMAN examines the lives of middle class ba'alot teshuvah. She had "loosely structured conversations" with 150 predominantly married, newly Orthodox women living in five U.S. cities. She found some differences in the socioeconomic backgrounds and spiritual orientations of the hasidic and nonhasidic participants. Even though many of these women did not identify with feminism, they incorporated many feminist values into their identities as Orthodox Jewish women. They celebrated their roles as wives and mothers and found meaning in living sex-segregated lives. Kaufman notes commonalities (as well as distinctions) between these newly Orthodox women and the trend in American feminism that has emphasized gender difference.

ROBERTA G. SANDS

Ba'al Shem Tov, Israel ben Eliezer see Israel ben Eliezer Ba'al Shem Tov

Babylonia

Brinkman, J.A., *A Political History of Post-Kassite Babylonia, 1158–722 B.C.* (Analecta Orientalia, 43), Rome: Pontificium Institutum Biblicum, 1968

Contenau, Georges, *Everyday Life in Babylon and Assyria,* London: Arnold, and New York: St. Martin's Press, 1954

Frame, Grant, *Babylonia, 689–627 B.C.: A Political History,* Istanbul: Nederlands Historisch-Archaeologisch Instituut te Istanbul, 1992

Hooke, S.H., *Babylonian and Assyrian Religion,* London and New York: Hutchinson's University Library, 1953

Neusner, Jacob, *A History of the Jews in Babylonia,* Leiden: Brill, 1965; 2nd edition, Chico, California: Scholars Press, 1984

Oates, Joan, *Babylon* (Ancient Peoples and Places, vol. 94),
    London: Thames and Hudson, 1979; revised edition,
    London and New York: Thames and Hudson, 1986
Saggs, H.W.F., *The Greatness That Was Babylon: A Sketch of
    the Ancient Civilization of the Tigris-Euphrates Valley,*
    London: Sidgwick and Jackson, 1902; New York:
    Hawthorn, 1962; revised as *The Greatness That Was
    Babylon: A Survey of the Ancient Civilization of the Tigris-
    Euphrates Valley,* London: Sidgwick and Jackson, 1988
Saggs, H.W.F., *Babylonians* (Peoples of the Past, 1),
    Norman: University of Oklahoma Press, and London:
    British Museum, 1995

The Southwest Asian empire of Babylonia flourished in the lower valley of the Tigris and Euphrates rivers from roughly 2100 B.C.E. to 689 B.C.E. and then again in the "Neo-Babylonian Period" as Chaldea from 625 B.C.E. to 538 B.C.E. The obvious importance of Babylonia for biblical studies and later Jewish history provided the original impetus for scholarly investigation of the history and culture of this region, but the continuing publication of cuneiform archival materials from Babylonia and its environs has made it the subject of serious study in its own right. In fact, while there remains a great deal we do not know about Babylonia, the very numerous studies that have been written from a wide variety of perspectives make it one of the most exhaustively studied cultural entities of the ancient world.

BRINKMAN investigates the political history of Babylonia from the second dynasty of Isin (c.1158 B.C.E.) to the death of Shalmanezzar V (c.722 B.C.E.). He considers the written and archaeological sources, establishes a chronological framework for the period including the proper dynastic sequence, and supplies a detailed diachronic narrative of political events. In addition, Brinkman provides an in-depth analysis of the role of large foreign populations such as Kassites, Sutians, Chaldeans, and Arameans. Since the last two of these peoples are especially prominent in the Hebrew Bible, this work will benefit students of biblical studies considerably. Moreover, it is an invaluable source of historical and political context for the events leading to the eventual destruction of Samaria. Brinkman also treats the government and army in a separate section of the book and supplies several useful appendixes and a lengthy bibliography.

CONTENAU's focus on the everyday life of the Babylonians makes this work unique among the sourcebooks on Babylonian history and culture. After establishing the geographic limits and the factors that shaped Babylonia, he explores the region's people and nearly every possible aspect of Babylonian life. Topics covered include the societal structure, family life, architecture and the plastic arts, homes and furnishings, clothing, food and drink, agriculture, business, and standards of exchange. In addition, Contenau provides an in-depth discussion of the intellectual achievements and religion of the Babylonians, devoting ample space to the Mesopotamian ontology and their belief in the power of words as well as to music and cultic practices. The subject matter and breadth of this pocket-size work breathes life into the ancient records, effectively presenting a people rather than a mere assemblage of cuneiform texts and ceramic wares.

FRAME details the written and archaeological sources for the period between 689 and 627 B.C.E. and discusses the various players of the period: Akkadians, Chaldeans, Aramaeans, Elamites, and others. The focus of his work is Babylon under the reigns of the Assyrian monarchs Sennacherib, Esarhaddon, and Ashurbanipal. Frame also examines the Babylonian state, the institution of the monarchy, the administration and military complex, as well as Babylonian foreign policy. Also supplied are several useful appendixes on economic texts, Babylonian officials, the difficulty of precise dating, and a few specific campaigns of Ashurbanipal. Frame's bibliography offers an impressive array of sources for advanced research. The period under Frame's microscope is an important one for biblical studies, and this work provides a richer context than can be found in comparative works attempting to cover a multiplicity of ancient Near Eastern societies.

HOOKE's small survey of the fundamental aspects of Babylonian and Assyrian religion is premised upon the author's assertion that "some knowledge of Babylonian religion is indispensable for a proper understanding of the development of Hebrew religion." Hooke's optimistic view concerning our ability to reconstruct the nuances of Babylonian religion and the importance of a full understanding of the religion for elucidating Israelite cultic and religious practice informs the subjects he discusses and the organization of the book. He outlines the textual and archaeological sources, the cultural background of the religion, the pantheon, temple buildings and personnel, rituals, Babylonian and Assyrian mythology, religion and daily life, divination, and astrology. Though it is somewhat naive in its monolithic treatment of the subject and is in need of an update, the book retains value both as a broad introduction to Babylonian religion and for its comparison of Babylonian and Assyrian religious practices. Hooke also supplies an appendix containing select ritual texts.

NEUSNER's chronologically presented series picks up where several of the other works cited here leave off, around 140 B.C.E. His historical study is divided into the following units: the Parthian period; the early Sasanian period; from Shapur I to Shapur II; the age of Shapur II; and later Sasanian times. Throughout, Neusner aims to "synthesize existing knowledge of the subject and, at a number of points, to add to that synthesis." He continues the works of previous scholars in tracking the influence of developing Parthian culture upon the Jews of Babylon. Omitted from his study are certain aspects of the history of Babylonia that are well treated elsewhere, for example, Parthian-Roman relations and Parthian cultural history. His work is filled with talmudic citations, many of which have seldom been interpreted historically.

OATES introduces readers to the chronology, geography, economy, people, and institutional powers of Babylon, as well as to the textual sources for its study. She divides her internal investigation of Babylon into four distinct periods: from Sargon of Agade to the Larsa kings, the Old Babylonian period, the Kassite and Chaldean period, and from the post-Kassite period to Hellenistic Babylon. One of the distinctive aspects of Oates's book is its reliance on both textual and archaeological evidence to tell a more complete story of Babylon. The nearly 140 illustrations distributed throughout the book also make for an interesting visual accompaniment and allow Oates to achieve her aim of leading "the general reader to further knowledge and the serious student to more analytical sources."

SAGGS (1995) focuses on the history and culture of ancient Babylon. Following a chapter on the rediscovery of Babylon, from which students of biblical studies will benefit much, Saggs clarifies the prehistory and later historical periods of Babylon. Though the book is organized according to the various periods into which scholars divide Mesopotamia in history, Saggs's emphasis is on the people and their culture, though Babylonian literature is given less space than the social, historical, and economic overviews of the city and its environs. With photographs, maps, chronological charts, and a select bibliography for advanced reading, this book is the perfect starting point for the study of Babylonia.

SAGGS (1902) is more comprehensive than the above introduction and also boasts a very large selection of high-quality photographs. After a chronological construction of the history of Babylon, Saggs develops several diachronic thematic studies on such topics as law and statecraft, administration and government, trade and commerce, magic and religion, the religious role of the king, literature, mathematics, astronomy, and medicine. Saggs concentrates to a greater degree than other works on this subject on the complex relationship between the powers of Babylonia and its northern neighbor and frequent aggressor, Assyria. In fact, this work is essentially a study of both ancient powers. This perspective allows Saggs to present the political history of the region with remarkable clarity. Two of the work's distinguishing features are a chapter devoted to the prehistoric period of the region and a chapter on the physical and intellectual legacy of ancient Babylon, both of which make accessible a larger context for understanding the city and its people. For students seeking a deeper knowledge of the subject, Saggs also provides a select bibliography at the end of the book divided by chapter.

SCOTT B. NOEGEL

Baeck, Leo 1873–1956

Posnan-born German rabbi and theologian

Altmann, Alexander, *Leo Baeck and the Jewish Mystical Tradition* (Leo Baeck Memorial Lecture, 17), New York: Leo Baeck Institute, 1973

Baker, Leonard, *Days of Sorrow and Pain: Leo Baeck and the Berlin Jews,* New York: Macmillan, 1978

Bamberger, Fritz, *Leo Baeck: The Man and the Idea* (Leo Baeck Memorial Lecture, 1), New York: Leo Baeck Institute, 1958

Friedlander, Albert H., *Leo Baeck: Teacher of Theresienstadt,* New York: Holt, Rinehart, and Winston, 1968; London: Routledge and Kegan Paul, 1973

Glatzer, Nahum N., *Baeck-Buber-Rosenzweig Reading the Book of Job* (Leo Baeck Memorial Lecture, 10), New York: Leo Baeck Institute, 1966

Homolka, Walter, *Jewish Identity in Modern Times: Leo Baeck and the German Protestantism* (European Judaism, vol. 2), Providence, Rhode Island: Berghahn, 1995

Wiener, Theodore, *The Writings of Leo Baeck, a Bibliography* (Studies in Bibliography and Booklore, vol. 1, no. 3), Cincinnati, Ohio: Hebrew Union College Press, 1954

Leo Baeck was born in Posen (Posnan) to a rabbinical family. His formal education prepared him to be a rabbi, but he emerged as a community leader, a teacher, and a philosopher as well. His intellectual capacity to rephrase the questions of Judaism and to provide contemporary answers, and his moral strength to share the fate of his community during the Holocaust made him the leader of German Jewry and an exceptional personality of the 20th century.

ALTMANN's subject is Baeck's relationship to the mystical tradition. Baeck discovered the significance of the mystical tradition in modern Jewish thought early in his career, but his attitude developed over the years from rejection to incorporation of this dimension into his theology. Altmann traces this development, showing how the Kabbalah was treated in Baeck's dissertation as a "mental delusion," and how this view remained the same in his published work *The Essence of Judaism.* During his debate with Protestant scholar Adolf von Harnack, Baeck is seen slowly recognizing the mystical trend of thinking. He explains that Jewish mysticism stems from the harshness of Jewish life and is a form of escapism. In an essay published in 1911, *Die Parteien im gegenwaertigen Judentum,* he differentiates between Jewish mysticism and so-called mere mysticism. He presents three major trends of postbiblical Jewish religious history: talmudic, philosophical, and mystical. He saw mysticism as part of normative Judaism. In *Wege im Judentum* he goes one step further: man for him become a cosmic being. He had discovered the essential nature of the Kabbalah. The second, much enlarged edition of *The Essence of Judaism* (1922) is shown by Altmann to represent a new orientation. His appreciation of mysticism and its relation to the ethical aspects of Jewish philosophy are expressed. "Mystery" is recognized as creating a fruitful polarity with "commandment," and a final statement of his view on mysticism is given in his last major work, *This People Israel.*

BAKER offers a full account of Leo Baeck, his career, his life, and his historical background. The thorough exploitation of extensive sources, including interviews, archival materials, memorabilia, Baeck's own writings, and secondary literature, makes this book a well-documented and intimate biography. The index and the detailed notes render the book additionally useful.

BAMBERGER's lecture introduces Baeck as a man. Beyond his public image, the reader becomes familiar with the personality of Baeck. Bamberger raises questions that contemporaries asked and answers them from the perspective of someone who knew Baeck well. Bamberger's point is that Baeck was not a popular speaker who offered easy or entertaining sermons; rather, he made heavy intellectual demands upon his congregation. This book presents a deeply personal picture of Baeck.

FRIEDLANDER's book on Baeck's theology also describes the Jewish community in which he worked—its institutions, factions, and orientations. He states that Baeck's greatest achievements were his contributions toward reestablishing

Jewish tradition, uniting the Jewish community, initiating a Jewish-Christian dialogue, and teaching the "real essence" of Judaism. According to Friedlander, Baeck was more of a rabbi and theologian than a philosopher and more of a leader of the Jewish community than a scholar, but this did not mean that he was not accomplished in all of these fields. The author goes into particular detail about Baeck's debate with the Christian theologian Adolf von Harnack. This book is not only important reading for those interested in Leo Baeck's life and accomplishments but also for anyone who wants to understand the intellectual history of Germany and the German Jews in the interwar period. A bibliography and index accompany the volume.

GLATZER discusses Baeck's interpretation of Job, which focuses on two points: the experience of mystery and the acceptance of the divine commandments. According to Baeck, the thinking process alone is not enough to describe man; revelation plays a part as well. At issue again is his interpretation of mystery as it developed through the years, from the first edition of *Essence of Judaism* to its fullest understanding in *This People Israel*.

HOMOLKA deals mainly with Baeck as a philosopher and particularly with the influences Baeck received and the responses he made in the field of religious philosophy during his career. He tracks both Baeck's philosophical development and his views on Christianity. His contribution to the Jewish-Christian dialogue started with the debate with Adolf von Harnack and continued with his analysis of Luther. Although his view supported the "classical" Jewish over the "romantic" Christian tradition, he was an initiator in the dialogue between synagogue and church. Homolka's work is short, well researched, and easy to follow. Each chapter promises and delivers a particular subject.

WIENER's bibliography was an attempt to compile a complete record of Baeck's literary activity, but since Baeck's personal library was destroyed during the Holocaust and it was difficult to access European publications at the time of the book's appearance in 1954, Wiener had limited success. He included lectures published in German-Jewish newspapers, but, with some exceptions demonstrating his organizational activities, the bibliography includes only Baeck's scholarly and theological writings. The works are arranged in chronological order. A separate list of books and periodicals can be found at the end of the bibliography, to which Baeck himself contributed.

JULIA BOCK

Baghdadi Jews of India

Elias, Flower and Judith Elias Cooper, *The Jews of Calcutta: The Autobiography of a Community, 1798–1972,* Calcutta: Jewish Association of Calcutta, 1974

Ezra, Esmond David, *Turning Back the Pages: A Chronicle of Calcutta Jewry,* 2 vols., London: Brookside, 1986

Hyman, Mavis, *Jews of the Raj,* London: Hyman, 1995

Jackson, Stanley, *The Sassoons,* New York: Dutton, and London: Heinemann, 1968; new edition, London: Heinemann, 1989

Musleah, Ezekiel N., *On the Banks of the Ganga: The Sojourn of Jews in Calcutta,* North Quincy, Massachusetts: Christopher Publishing House, 1975

Musleah, Rahel, *Songs of the Jews of Calcutta,* Cedarhurst, New York: Tara, 1991

Roland, Joan G., *Jews in British India: Identity in a Colonial Era* (Tauber Institute for the Study of European Jewry Series, vol. 9), Hanover, New Hampshire: University Press of New England, 1989; as *The Jewish Communities of India: Identity in a Colonial Era,* New Brunswick, New Jersey: Transaction, 1998

Roth, Cecil, *The Sassoon Dynasty,* London: Hale, 1941; New York: Arno, 1977

Slapak, Orpa (editor), *The Jews of India: A Story of Three Communities,* Jerusalem: Israel Museum, 1995

Solomon, Sally Luddy, *Hooghly Tales,* London: Ashley, 1998

"Baghdadi" was a self-designated label for Jews from the Middle East (Iraq, Syria, Persia, Yemen, etc.) who settled in Bombay and Calcutta during the British colonial period, from the mid–18th century until Indian independence in 1947. A small elite group made fortunes in textile production, jute, opium, and real estate, employing other Jews and establishing synagogues, schools, and charitable institutions for them. Numbering more than 5,000 at their height in the 1940s (slightly more in Bombay than Calcutta), they identified with the British and held themselves aloof from Bene Israel and Cochin Jews who had been in India long before them. After Indian independence almost all migrated to England and other English-speaking countries. The bulk of the research on Indian Baghdadis centers on Calcutta; more is needed on the community in Bombay and on connections to Iraqi Jewish communities in Burma, Hong Kong, and Shanghai.

ROLAND's solid historical study of Jewish identity under British colonial rule is the only book treating the Baghdadis of Bombay and Calcutta as one community with two branches. Extensive archival research and interviews in India, England, Israel, and the United States uncovered a wealth of detail about Baghdadi and Bene Israel life, and Roland's analysis is firmly grounded in a wider study of colonialism and Indian responses to British rule. She sees Baghdadi attempts to identify with the British (for political, economic, and social reasons) as fundamental to understanding their alienation from Bene Israel co-religionists and their eagerness to leave India for English-speaking countries after 1947.

ROTH, a noted English scholar, recounts the history of David Sassoon and his descendants. A Jewish merchant from Baghdad who founded a commercial empire in Asia, Sassoon and his sons dominated the international trade in opium, built cotton mills in Bombay, and established charities that aided the Jews of Bombay for generations. Roth's book and that of JACKSON document life among the wealthy cosmopolitan Baghdadi elite but give no information about middle class or poor Baghdadis and little sense of the Indian environment or wider Jewish life there (Bene Israel are mentioned once by Roth and not at all by Jackson).

E. MUSLEAH wrote the authoritative book on the Calcutta Jews, drawing on a variety of sources including Hebrew and Judeo-Arabic documents from the Sassoon Library and from collections in Calcutta. In more than 500 carefully documented pages, he recounts Calcutta Jewish history, describing formal institutions, intracommunal conflicts, and religious customs. The book is based on his doctoral dissertation for the Jewish Theological Seminary in New York, where he also received ordination. Born and brought up in a respected Baghdadi family in Calcutta, he returned there to serve as a rabbi from 1952 to 1964.

EZRA's first volume is a combined family memoir and history of the Calcutta Baghdadis, including historical anecdotes and short biographies of community leaders. It contains useful statistical tables on population, literacy, marriage, and occupations, as well as many photographs. The second volume is a compilation of detailed genealogical charts for many Calcutta families. A member of the prominent Ezra family of Calcutta industrialists, the author is a British-educated lawyer who practiced in Calcutta until 1967, when he returned to England.

ELIAS and COOPER, a Baghdadi mother and daughter from Calcutta, spent two years interviewing members of their community in England. From tape-recorded conversations they compiled this book on everyday Jewish life in Calcutta, consisting mainly of quotations about family, religion, customs, social life, education, and work. The final chapter on "identity" reveals varied responses to Baghdadi Jewish life in England as well as Calcutta.

HYMAN, another Baghdadi who grew up in Calcutta, effectively weaves together material from 80 interviews with her own reminiscences to paint a vivid picture of Calcutta Jewish life before, during, and after World War II—not only the synagogues, clubs, and schools, but also such informal institutions as a famous Jewish sweet shop and a village where families vacationed each year. She devotes a chapter to relations with servants and another to class differences and charity within the Jewish community. Material on Zionist organizing and the lives of early emigrants to Israel is particularly valuable. Informants were from England (mostly), Israel, Australia, Canada, and the United States.

SOLOMON also has written about growing up in the Baghdadi community of Calcutta. Hers is a light and charming personal memoir, illustrated with pencil sketches by her daughter. Beginning with early childhood memories and concluding in 1947 when she left Calcutta with her husband and first child, the book is filled with stories of family, neighbors, schools, camps, adolescent adventures, and the impact of World War II on her generation.

R. MUSLEAH has compiled 51 traditional *pizmonim* (songs of praise) of the Calcutta Jews, with words in Hebrew script and transliteration as well as English translation. The songs, transcribed in western-style musical notation, are categorized by occasion, for the sabbath and various holidays, and the user-friendly volume is illustrated with photographs from the Musleah family in Calcutta, where the author was born. The daughter of Rabbi Ezekiel Musleah, she is now a musician and journalist in the United States. A cassette tape of the *pizmonim* accompanies the book.

SLAPAK's Israel Museum exhibition catalogue contains color photographs and descriptions of Baghdadi ritual and material culture in Bombay and Calcutta, including synagogues, homes, ceremonial objects, domestic rituals, daily life, dress, customs, and ceremonies.

BARBARA C. JOHNSON

Balkans

Bar-Zohar, Michael, *Beyond Hitler's Grasp: The Heroic Rescue of Bulgaria's Jews*, Holbrook, Massachusetts: Adams Media, 1998

Beker, Avi, *Jewish Communities of the World*, Jerusalem: Institute of the World Jewish Congress, 1996; Minneapolis, Minnesota: Lerner, 1998

Benbassa, Esther and Aron Rodrigue, *The Jews of the Balkans: The Judeo-Spanish Community, 15th to 20th Centuries* (Jewish Communities of the Modern World), Oxford and Cambridge, Massachusetts: Blackwell, 1995

Bowman, Steven B., *The Jews of Byzantium, 1204–1453* (Judaic Studies), University: University of Alabama Press, 1985

Chasiotes, Ioannes K. (editor), *The Jewish Communities of Southeastern Europe: From the Fifteenth Century to the End to World War II*, Thessaloniki: Institute for Balkan Studies, 1997

Elazar, Daniel J. et al., *The Balkan Jewish Communities: Yugoslavia, Bulgaria, Greece, and Turkey*, Lanham, Maryland: University Press of America, 1984

Meyer, Peter et al., *The Jews in the Soviet Satellites*, Syracuse, New York: Syracuse University Press, 1953

Shaw, Stanford J., *The Jews of the Ottoman Empire and the Turkish Republic*, New York: New York University Press, and London: Macmillan, 1991

Jewish presence in the Balkans dates to antiquity. This essay considers books that trace the long history of Jewish communities in this area, as well as a number of works that focus on specific developments from the 20th century.

According to ELAZAR et al., "no region of Europe has a longer history of organized Jewish life" than the Balkans, and their text is a survey of that lengthy history. The authors assert that the first diaspora community outside of the Fertile Crescent was located in the Balkans, and they trace the lives of Balkan Jews under the successive regimes of pagan Rome, Christian Byzantium, the Muslim Ottoman Empire, and the Christian and Muslim states that replaced the Ottomans. The book also considers Jewish communities' struggles to survive after World War II, including discussion of Jewish life in the repressive Soviet satellite states.

BOWMAN describes Jewish life under the Byzantine Empire from the 13th century through the fall of Constantinople in the mid-15th century. Although integrated into the empire's Greek culture, Jews were its only non-Christian minority. Bowman demonstrates that Eastern Orthodox Christianity considered Judaism to be "accursed," and he explains how Byzantine emperors interfered with Jewish religious practices and promulgated codes restricting Jewish social, political, and economic activity.

SHAW investigates the history of Balkan Jews in the Ottoman Empire and under the Turkish Republic. He begins by considering Jewish life in the Byzantine era, discussing the large numbers of Jews who were forcibly converted to Christianity. He relates the history of the majority of the Jews who retained their identity in this relic of the Roman Empire, rabbanites who followed a "Romaniot" rite (Byzantium was the new Rome) and were influenced by Palestinian Judaism and by Hellenism, as well as by the Karaite minority. Shaw then argues that the Muslim conquest of Byzantium in the 14th and 15th centuries brought "instant liberation" for the Jews, who were naturally favored by Muhammad II over the Christians (Greek and Armenian) from whom he had wrested his new empire. The Ottoman lands became the destination of persecuted Ashkenazim fleeing Northern and Central Europe and Sephardim fleeing Iberia in the late 15th and 16th centuries. Eventually, the religious outlook of the Iberian immigrants and the Judeo-Spanish language became dominant over indigenous Jewish culture. Shaw deems 16th- and 17th-century Ottoman Jewry the largest and most prosperous Jewish society of its time. He designates this period a golden age as Jews settled in urban centers, such as Istanbul, Izmir, Salonika, and Sarajevo; enjoyed communal autonomy; became physicians at Court, bankers, and diplomats; and achieved such religious milestones as the publication of Joseph Caro's legal digests, *Shulhan Arukh*.

BENBASSA and RODRIGUE dispute Shaw's view of Ottoman-Jewish relations, which reflects traditional assumptions that Jews were treated well under the empire. They argue that the Iberians exaggerated their welcome and their success in the Balkans, asserting that, in fact, Jews did not generally flourish under Muslim rule. While a small Jewish elite grew politically influential and succeeded in some sectors of the economy (such as trade or cloth manufacture in Salonika), most Jews were involved in small-scale enterprises, and many were poor. According to Benbassa and Rodrigue, the Ottoman attitude toward Jews was dictated only by self-interest, tolerating them because "the Jews seemed reliable and possessed useful skills." Benbassa and Rodrigue trace the history of Balkan Jews through to the 20th century, discussing en route such topics as the decline of the Ottoman Empire and the inward turn of the Jewish community during the 17th century, which was accompanied by a rise in Jewish mysticism; the effects of the Enlightenment, modernization, and political, educational, and social reforms during the 18th and 19th centuries; the lives of Jews in the newly established Balkan nation-states after World War I; the rise of Zionism between the wars; and the impact of the Holocaust.

Several studies explore the recent past and present state of Jewish communities in the Balkans. Steven Bowman's essay in CHASIOTES examines the particular history of Greek Jews during the Holocaust, arguing that while the majority of Greek Jewry was lost, Greek officialdom did attempt to extend protection. BAR-ZOHAR investigates the unique situation of Jews in Bulgaria during World War II, showing that they were spared the fates that befell Jews in other Balkan nations because of the courage of King Boris and the church. MEYER et al. paint a grim picture of Jewish life under Balkan Soviet-style regimes after World War II, as all signs of separatism

were repressed. BEKER provides a survey of the current status of Balkan Jewries, arguing that Balkan societies, which have been subjected to warring nationalisms and revisionist histories, are discouraging venues for Jewish revival. Thus, the future of Balkan Jewries is at best uncertain.

LIBBY WHITE

Bar Kokhba, Simeon   d. 135 C.E.

Judean leader of revolt against Rome

Applebaum, Shimon, *Prolegomena to the Study of the Second Jewish Revolt (A.D. 132–135)* (BAR Supplementary Series, 7), Oxford: British Archaeological Reports, 1976

Marks, Richard G., *The Image of Bar Kokhba in Traditional Jewish Literature: False Messiah and National Hero* (Hermeneutics, Studies in the History of Religions), University Park: Pennsylvania State University Press, 1994

Yadin, Yigael, *Bar-Kokhba: The Rediscovery of the Legendary Hero of the Last Jewish Revolt against Imperial Rome*, New York: Random House, and London: Weidenfeld and Nicolson, 1971

Zerubavel, Yael, *Recovered Roots: Collective Memory and the Making of Israeli Tradition*, Chicago: University of Chicago Press, 1995

As leader of the remarkably unified Second Jewish Revolt against Rome (132–135 C.E.), Simeon Bar Kokhba (Shim'on bar Kosiva) served as the focus of the historiography of the period in its several genres, including social, intellectual, and military history, as well as in numismatics, rabbinics, polemics, fiction, drama, and poetry. The literature pertaining to Bar Kokhba attends to the history of his revolt on the one hand and to the reception of that history on the other. The first sort of literature may be further categorized as that which preceded the epigraphic and archaeological discoveries of 1951–1961 near the shores of the Dead Sea and that which followed those discoveries and their publication. The second sort of literature—that which deals with the reception of Bar Kokhba's story—may also be divided by date of publication according to whether it precedes or follows the second half of the 19th century, a period marked by the rise of Jewish interest in antiquity and by the rise of Zionism.

YADIN is a popular account, excitingly told, of his several discoveries, from that of the winter of 1951 through those of 1960–1961, of material related to Bar Kokhba and the revolt. He includes a description of another relevant find from the later expeditions: the archive of Babata, which contains material from the period of the revolt but is chiefly the "life story of Babata's family as well as that of her two husbands" and their property, from the Cave of Letters. The volume is illustrated with seven maps and dozens of spectacular illustrations, including photographs of objects, documents, and the expedition at work. The book deals only lightly with reception history (in chapter one, "Behind the Legend," and in the

"Appendix of references to Bar-Kokhba"), and the focus is exclusively on classical references, drawn from Jewish sources and from non-Jewish sources (accounts of the revolt from Dio Cassius, Eusebius, Jerome, and Epiphanius). He provides descriptions of objects and translations of letters—dictated, if not signed, by Bar Kokhba himself—that are essential to any understanding of the revolt and the Jewish parties to it, but he does not attempt to deal with their context or their relevance to the major questions of the history of the revolt. The figure of Bar Kokhba that emerges from the letters that Yadin presents shows him to have been a disciplinarian, restrained in his assumption of power, knowledgeable of the details of the campaign, and attentive to the minutiae of the government of his "Free Israel." He is also shown to have been interested in questions of husbandry and property and determined to maintain religious practices.

Yadin participates in the linkage of the revolt and the figure of Bar Kokhba with present-day Israel, relating his exposure of the discovery at the home of the president of Israel and in the presence of government officials, associating Bar Kokhba, "the last President of ancient Israel," with the current incumbent, Yitzhak Ben-Zvi. In a similar vein, others noted that the letters from the last chief of staff of the last national Jewish army, Bar Kokhba, had been revealed to Yadin, the first chief of staff of the new army of Israel. Yadin added to such romantic observations that, "Nothing remains here [at the caves] today of the Romans save a heap of stones on the face of the desert, but here the descendants of the besieged were returning to salvage their ancestors' precious belongings."

APPLEBAUM touches on the following historical questions: the cause(s) of the revolt; the number of Jews and Romans involved and the number of casualties; the extent of the fighting; the nature of Bar Kokhba's role (whether that of a messiah in a messianic war or not); and the effect of the revolt on Jewish populations and institutions in the north (the Galilee) and the south (Judaea, where almost all the action took place). There is no scholarly consensus on any of these questions, and in fact many scholars have changed their own opinions relating to them. Applebaum (amplified in his 1984 article in *Palestine Expeditionary Quarterly*), sees economic hardship, social inequity, and a continuous state of tension as the backgrounds to the revolt and appropriate to a messianic war led by a messiah. He describes the major cause of the revolt: Hadrian's policy toward the Jewish state—itself driven by other, nearly contemporary Jewish revolts. Hadrian's policies included the hellenization and romanization of Jerusalem, deification of himself and of homosexuality, and perhaps a ban on circumcision. According to Applebaum the number of soldiers and population groups involved was very large, with Jewish casualties alone reaching nearly 600,000. Judaea was repopulated by Jews within a few generations, though it never regained its power, while the Galilee was the immediate beneficiary of a refugee population.

Beyond the question of who Bar Kokhba really was—best answered by the letters and other documents—there remains to be considered the matter of his image and that of his revolt in the history of the Jewish people. This is the focus of MARKS, who describes how Bar Kokhba is viewed in the rabbinic literature as a flawed hero or a messianic imposter; by

two medieval writers living under the rule of Islam, with misgivings but with a melancholy appreciation of his messianic qualities; by Isaac Abravanel (and a variety of other Renaissance historians), with a saddened understanding of how the valorous Bar Kokhba (and Rabbi Akiba, his herald) turned out to be wrong, but for the best reasons, meaning, the relief of oppressed Jews and revenge against their oppressors; and by two kabbalists, Rabbi Hayyim Vital in the 16th century and Nathan of Gaza in the 17th century. The former understood Bar Kokhba as the metempsychosis of the messiah-soul who failed because of the weakness of his generation, while the latter believed that Bar Kokhba had been reborn as Shabbetai Tsevi, the messiah who would complete his task. Marks places these views of Bar Kokhba in their immediate contexts in terms of social, political, and intellectual history.

This work is brought into the present and focused on modern Jewish and Israeli devisements of Bar Kokhba by ZERUBAVEL in her post-Zionist consideration of Jewish memory and its reconstruction. Chapter five is devoted to the image of Bar Kokhba. Having begun with his elevation to the model hero of an armed struggle for national liberation, it proceeds to manipulate and diminish the significance of his defeat and ultimately to remove the memorialization of the disastrous end of the revolt from association with the fast of Tishah be-Av and to enshrine Bar Kokhba in memory as the victor celebrated in the festival of Lag ba-Omer.

HARRIS LENOWITZ

Bar Mitzvah and Bat Mitzvah

Davis, Judith, "Mazel Tov: The Bar Mitzvah as a Multigenerational Ritual of Change and Continuity," in *Rituals in Families and Family Therapy*, edited by E. Imber-Black, J. Roberts, and R.A. Whiting, New York: Norton, 1988

Davis, Judith, *Whose Bar/Bat Mitzvah Is This Anyway?: A Guide for Parents through a Family Rite of Passage*, New York: St. Martin's Griffin, 1998

Hartman, Ann, Sally Weber, and Stewart Vogel, "Celebration and Negotiation: Working with Separated, Divorced, and Remarried Families Approaching Bar/Bat Mitzvah Celebrations," *Journal of Jewish Communal Service*, 70 (2–3), Spring 1994

Holtz, Barry (editor), *Best Practices Project: The Supplementary School*, New York: Council for Initiatives in Jewish Education, 1993

Hyman, Paula, "The Introduction of Bat Mitzvah in Conservative Judaism in Postwar America," *YIVO Annual*, 19, 1990

Kahn, Nancy E., "The Adult Bat Mitzvah: Its Use in the Articulation of Women's Identity," *Affilia*, 10(3), 1995

Leneman, Helen (editor), *Bar/Bat Mitzvah Education: A Sourcebook*, Denver, Colorado: A.R.E., 1993

Salkin, Jeffrey K., *Putting God on the Guest List: How to Reclaim the Spiritual Meaning of Your Child's Bar or Bat Mitzvah*, Woodstock, Vermont: Jewish Lights, 1992, 2nd edition, 1996

Schein, Jeffrey and Susan Wyner, "Mediating the Tensions of Bar/Bat Mitzvah: The Cleveland Experience," *Journal of Jewish Communal Service*, 72, Spring 1996

Schoenfeld, Stuart, "Folk Judaism, Elite Judaism and the Role of Bar Mitzvah in the Development of the Synagogue and Jewish School in America," *Contemporary Jewry*, 9, Fall/Winter 1987–1988

Schoenfeld, Stuart, "Integration into the Group and Sacred Uniqueness: An Analysis of Adult Bat Mitzvah," in *Persistence and Flexibility: Anthropological Perspectives on the American Jewish Experience* (SUNY Series in Anthropology and Judaic Studies), edited by Walter Zenner, Albany: State University of New York Press, 1988

Schoenfeld, Stuart, "Some Aspects of the Social Significance of Bar/Bat Mitzvah Celebrations," in *Essays in the Social Scientific Study of Judaism and Jewish Society*, edited by Simcha Fishbane and Jack Lightstone, Montreal: Department of Religion, Concordia University, 1990

Schoenfeld, Stuart, "Interpreting Adult Bar Mitzvah: The Limits and Potential of Feminism in a Congregational Setting," in *Jewish Sects, Religious Movements, and Political Parties* (Studies in Jewish Civilization, 3), edited by Menahem Mor, Omaha, Nebraska: Creighton University Press, 1992

Schoenfeld, Stuart, "Ritual and Role Transition: Adult Bat Mitzvah as a Successful Rite of Passage," in *The Uses of Tradition*, edited by Jack Wertheimer, Cambridge, Massachusetts: Harvard University Press, 1992

Schoenfeld, Stuart, "Recent Publications on Bar/Bat Mitzvah: Their Implications for Jewish Education Research and Practice," *Religious Education*, 89, 1995

Sherwin, Byron, "Bar Mitzvah, Bat Mitzvah," in his *In Partnership with God: Contemporary Jewish Law and Ethics*, Syracuse, New York: Syracuse University Press, 1990

Bar mitzvah and bat mitzvah have legal, developmental, ceremonial, and celebratory dimensions. Scholarly work in English on each of these dimensions is available mainly in book chapters and journal articles, while the sources available in Hebrew are partial and dated. Medieval rabbinic Judaism used puberty, specifically the ages of 13 for boys and 12 for girls, as legal markers for adulthood. The Mishnah was invoked as the oldest textual source for what is now called bar mitzvah and bat mitzvah, although for some purposes other ages mark significant legal transitions. The idea that a significant psychological/moral transition also occurs at the age of bar mitzvah is developed in a number of midrashim. Since the 19th century, and especially since the mid-20th century, bar mitzvah and bat mitzvah have commonly become occasions when many guests are invited to witness a synagogue ceremony, often with associated elaborate social activities taking place from Friday night through Sunday night.

SHERWIN contains an overview and interpretation of many rabbinic sources and midrashim. Only in the early modern period does he find clear references to a synagogue ceremony and a subsequent celebration.

HYMAN has examined the introduction and spread of bat mitzvah in the Conservative movement, which became common in the 1950s and 1960s. Bat mitzvah is now common in all the branches of Judaism and in most Jewish communities.

SCHOENFELD (1995) uses what has been written on bar/bat mitzvah to identify common themes about the role of Judaism in the life of U.S. Jews. This article includes an extensive bibliography.

DAVIS (1998) provides the most important analysis of bar and bat mitzvah in current Jewish family life. While intended for a general audience, the book has its roots in DAVIS (1988), a contribution to the scholarly literature in the field of family therapy. Both sources examine how preparing for and celebrating these ubiquitous rituals are occasions for the family—as individuals and as a unit—to confront the meaning of Jewish identity. Families going through bar/bat mitzvah are forced to question the meaning of continuity from generation to generation, the transition into adolescence, extended family ties, gender identity, core values, and, of course, religious commitment. Throughout these analyses, Davis focuses on the possibility that the ritual can be an authentic expression of the family's values and emphasizes the cultivation of the skills needed to achieve that end.

SALKIN's book addresses families preparing for the event. It is distinguished from the numerous other practical guides on the market by its engagement with the challenge of cultivating spirituality in an event that is often focused on the party.

SCHOENFELD (1990), a study of the social celebrations that accompany the synagogue ritual, complements Salkin's approach. The social events, which often extend through the whole weekend, are secular rituals that dramatize the relationships among the child, the immediate family, the extended family, and the child's network of friends. These events express and interpret the child's entry into adolescence and the ambivalence of Jewish identity in the United States.

Studies by social workers and psychologists pay particular attention to relationships and issues that may potentially disrupt a psychologically successful ritual. HARTMAN, WEBER, and VOGEL, which analyzes strategies for working with families in which there has been separation, divorce, and remarriage is a good example of the work in this field.

Bar and bat mitzvah have also been closely tied to the emergence of the structure of Jewish education in North America. LENEMAN contains 50 chapters examining different dimensions of the link between bar/bat mitzvah and Jewish education. SCHOENFELD (1987–1988) documents the importance of bar mitzvah as an aspect of the folk religion of U.S. Jews and the strategy of the religious elite of requiring a minimal number of years of Jewish education before bar/bat mitzvah. It is clear from HOLTZ's study of "best practices" in supplementary education that preparing for the bar/bat mitzvah is a major task for Jewish education. Successful schools recognize the importance of these events as transitions into greater autonomy and responsibility. Religious educators struggle to ensure that the social agenda of bar/bat mitzvah does not overwhelm the religious one. SCHEIN and WYNER report on the experience of a Cleveland, Ohio, task force that worked with local congregations, rabbis, educators, and social workers to produce community guidelines and hold educational sessions for families.

Adult bar mitzvah and bat mitzvah—opportunities for adults to make symbolic statements about their identity by publicly demonstrating the skills of the early adolescent ritual—became common in the 1980s and 1990s. The innovation of adult bat mitzvah has been the object of several studies. KAHN shows how adult b'not mitzvah use the preparation and performance of the ritual to express complex identities. Three related articles, SCHOENFELD (1988), SCHOENFELD (1992a), and SCHOENFELD (1992b), contrast an individual adult bat mitzvah in a small independent synagogue with a group bat mitzvah in a large temple. The individual bat mitzvah used her ritual to affirm a personal spiritual journey before an assembly of family and friends. The author draws from Victor Turner's model of the stages of a rite of passage to analyze group bat mitzvah, which was experienced as an emotionally intense, successful ritual. The metaphor of a spiritual pilgrimage was pronounced in both experiences. While in both settings there was some hesitation about presenting adult bat mitzvah as a feminist ritual, in each case adult bat mitzvah successfully affirmed an active role for women as responsible members of the ritual community.

STUART SCHOENFELD

Bene Israel of India

David, Esther, *The Walled City,* Madras: Manas, 1997

Isenberg, Shirley Berry, *India's Bene Israel: A Comprehensive Inquiry and Sourcebook,* Berkeley, California: J.L. Magnes Museum, 1988

Israel, Benjamin Jacob, *The Bene Israel of India: Some Studies,* New York: APT, and London: Sangam, 1984

Kehimkar, Haeem Samuel, *The History of the Bene Israel of India,* London: Salby, 1937

Mahadevan, Meera, *Apana Ghara* [A Home of One's Own], New Delhi: Rajkamal Prakashan, 1961; as *Shulamith* (Indian Novels Series, vol. 7), New Delhi: Arnold-Heinemann, 1975

Roland, Joan G., *Jews in British India: Identity in a Colonial Era* (Tauber Institute for the Study of European Jewry Series, vol. 9), Hanover, New Hampshire: University Press of New England, 1989; as *The Jewish Communities of India: Identity in a Colonial Era,* New Brunswick, New Jersey: Transaction, 1998

Shaham, David (editor), *The Jews from the Konkan: The Bene Israel Community in India,* Tel Aviv: Beit Hatfutsoth, 1981

Slapak, Orpa (editor), *The Jews of India: A Story of Three Communities,* Jerusalem: Israel Museum, 1995

Strizower, Schifra, *The Bene Israel of Bombay: A Study of a Jewish Community,* New York: Schocken, 1971; as *The Children of Israel: The Bene Israel of Bombay,* Oxford: Blackwell, 1971

Weil, Shalva, "Bene Israel Indian Jews in Lod, Israel: A Study of the Persistence of Ethnicity and Ethnic Identity," Ph.D. diss., University of Sussex, 1977

The Bene Israel, centered in the state of Maharashtra and the city of Bombay (now Mumbai), form the largest of the three Indian Jewish communities. Originally they lived as oil-pressers in villages on the Konkan coast, but during British rule many moved to Bombay and other colonial cities, where they raised their economic and educational position dramatically. Research focuses on theories about their origin, history since the 18th century, relations with Indian "Baghdadi" Jews, impact of British colonial rule, communal organization, religious practices, Zionism, and life in Israel. Today there are fewer than 5,000 Bene Israel remaining in India and approximately 40,000 in Israel.

KEHIMKAR, an early Bene Israel intellectual and activist, completed in 1897 his ambitious study of the community's history and customs. Finally published in Palestine in 1937, it draws on earlier written accounts and on his own deep knowledge of Bene Israel traditions. Kehimkar argues that the community's ancestors, from the ten northern tribes, fled the Land of Israel in 175 B.C.E. and were shipwrecked off the Konkan coast. They preserved practices of the Second Temple period despite isolation from other Jews until their 19th-century religious "revival" under the leadership of Cochin Jews and their education by Christian missionaries. Kehimkar describes in rich detail their daily customs, life cycle rituals, holiday celebrations, service in the British Army, educational institutions, and communal organization; he argues against charges by Baghdadis that the Bene Israel are not pure Jews.

ISRAEL was a prominent 20th-century Bene Israel intellectual who wrote the essays in this collection between 1960 and 1984 after retirement from government service. He reviews and summarizes earlier origin theories, gives a helpful overview of the community's "religious evolution" after 1750, and analyzes demographic data from the 1961 and 1971 Indian census. Particularly important is his essay on the crisis surrounding religious discrimination against Bene Israel immigrants by Israeli rabbinical authorities in the early 1960s.

ISENBERG's substantial study is aptly subtitled "A Comprehensive Inquiry and Sourcebook." Meticulously researched and documented, it brings together material from Kehimkar, Israel, and many others with original archival research, interviews, participant-observation, and analysis, compiled over a period of more than 20 years. She includes valuable appendices, tables, photographs, and suggestions for further research. Isenberg is an American-born anthropologist who lived many years in India before settling permanently in Israel.

ROLAND's historical study analyzes Indian Jewish identity under 19th- and 20th-century British colonial rule, based on extremely thorough archival research (including Bene Israel periodicals in English and Marathi) and interviews in India, Israel, England, and the United States. She discusses both Bene Israel and Baghdadis, commenting on their complex relationships as well as their quite different responses to colonialism. Although many Bene Israel benefited from British rule through education and employment, most seemed secure in their Indian identity, and some became involved in nationalist organizing. In contrast, Baghdadi attempts to identify with the British can be seen as underlying their efforts to distance themselves socially and ritually from the Bene Israel, as well as underlying the Bene Israel resentment of the Baghdadis. Bene Israel Zionism and migration to Israel are analyzed in depth. Roland is an American scholar whose continuing work on the Indian Jews is highly recommended.

STRIZOWER's ethnographic study is based on fieldwork in India from 1959 to 1961, when about 13,000 Bene Israel remained, mostly in Bombay. Having participated in their religious and communal life, she describes it in detail, including marriage and the family, the synagogue, educational and charitable associations, and cliques and clubs. Her study includes review and analysis of their traditional history and relations with other Indian groups, Jewish and non-Jewish. The author is a European-born anthropologist teaching in Australia.

SHAHAM's volume is the catalog of an exhibit at the Diaspora Museum in Tel Aviv. It features artistic and informative photographs of the Bene Israel in India by Carmela Berkson, an American who has lived for many years in Bombay. The introductory essay by Shalva Weil gives a useful brief summary of Bene Israel history and culture.

MAHADEVAN's novel, the first by a Bene Israel author, tells the story of a traditional middle-class Bene Israel extended family in modern Bombay. The central character is Shulamith, whose husband has emigrated to Israel and left her to cope with three generations of this family as they struggle with changing women's roles, temptations of romance outside the community, class and religious issues within the community, and the decision of whether or not to emigrate. Originally written and published in Hindi, the English translation is a bit stiff, but the author gives a complex and invaluable glimpse of family and community life drawing on her own experience as a Bene Israel woman.

DAVID's recent novel addresses some of the same issues as Mahadevan's, also from the perspective of a Bene Israel woman, but this fictional character is a middle-aged unmarried woman in the small Bene Israel community of Ahmedabad in Gujarat. Separate from the center of Bene Israel life in Bombay and the Konkan, her family has grown gradually less observant of their Jewish traditions. Dramatic reminiscences of childhood and adolescence in her eccentric extended family bring to life the sounds, sights, fragrances, and religious influences of the Indian environment, where she was profoundly affected by intimate relationships with Hindu and Muslim servants, neighbors, and friends. A tone of melancholy and loss pervades the book, as she recalls the ghostly presence of previous generations, departures for Israel, and the death of loved ones.

WEIL is an Israeli anthropologist originally from England, whose doctoral dissertation is an important study of Bene Israel community life and ethnic identity in Israel. Grounded in three years of participant-observer research among 300 Bene Israel families in the city of Lod, she discusses their occupations, social characteristics, status in relation to other Israeli groups, communal organization (including active voluntary organizations), marriage and family, synagogue participation, and religious rituals and practices. The study is thoroughly researched and enjoyable to read.

SLAPAK's book on the three Indian Jewish communities contains many valuable photographs and descriptions of Bene Israel ritual and material culture in India, including synagogues, ceremonial objects, home rituals, daily life, dress, customs, and ceremonies.

BARBARA C. JOHNSON

Ben-Gurion, David 1886–1973

Polish-born Zionist leader and first prime minister of Israel

Bar-Zohar, Michael, *Ben-Gurion: A Biography*, London: Weidenfeld and Nicolson, 1978; New York: Delacorte, 1979

Gal, Allon, *David Ben-Gurion and the American Alignment for a Jewish State* (Modern Jewish Experience), Bloomington: Indiana University Press, 1991

Kurzman, Dan, *Ben-Gurion: Prophet of Fire*, New York: Simon and Schuster, 1983

Teveth, Shabtai, *Ben-Gurion and the Palestinian Arabs: From Peace to War*, Oxford and New York: Oxford University Press, 1985

Teveth, Shabtai, *Ben-Gurion: The Burning Ground, 1886–1948*, Boston: Houghton-Mifflin, and London: Hale, 1987

Teveth, Shabtai, *Ben-Gurion and the Holocaust*, New York: Harcourt Brace, 1996

Zweig, Ronald W. (editor), *David Ben-Gurion: Politics and Leadership in Israel*, London and Portland, Oregon: Cass, 1991

David Ben-Gurion was born David Joseph Green in Plonsk, Poland (Russian Pale of Settlement) on 16 October 1886. Claiming to be "a Zionist from birth," Ben-Gurion rose from his humble origins to embark on a quest to create a Jewish state for the Jews of Europe, whom he regarded as woefully mistreated and impossibly disunited. Ben-Gurion became president of the World Zionist Organization in 1946, and two years later he declared the establishment of the State of Israel. He not only became the first Israeli prime minister, but also served as the state's first foreign minister. His political career was frequently controversial. The legitimacy of his overriding objective in creating Israel was questioned, and it is claimed by many that he did not do enough to save Jews from their fate during World War II. Other scholars refute this claim, declaring that he was fully aware of Nazi activities but was unable to stop them. Ben-Gurion retired and then returned to politics several times during his life, permanently leaving the Knesset and public life by 1970. He died 1 December 1973 and was buried in Sde Boker in the Negev after a state funeral.

BAR-ZOHAR's biography is a translation of a work originally written in Hebrew and published after the deaths of Ben-Gurion and his wife Paula. The author worked closely with Ben-Gurion and had access to private archives that Ben-Gurion had never before opened to biographers. Included in these archives were very personal memoirs dealing with political as well as personal aspects of Ben-Gurion's life, and the biography reveals the very human side of the man. Bar-Zohar also uses Ben-Gurion's private diaries and unpublished documents to reveal previously concealed state secrets. The author presents detailed information about Ben-Gurion's political alliances, enlightening the reader about such issues as Ben-Gurion's heated feud with Chaim Weizmann, the Lavon Affair, and the Sinai Campaign. Photographs recording Ben-Gurion's political career and personal life complement the text.

GAL's book primarily concentrates on the years 1938 to 1942. These were the years during which the rift between Weizmann and Ben-Gurion widened, and the work offers a comparison of the political approaches of these two men. The main focus of this book, however, is Ben-Gurion's role as statesman and as diplomat. Gal reflects upon Ben-Gurion's stay in the United States from 1915 to 1918, when he participated in the organization of the American Jewish Congress, and describes his increasingly frequent visits to the United States in later years, in a period when pro-Zionist sentiment was growing in that nation. Gal's discussion of Ben-Gurion's fervent, ambitious desire to integrate Israel into the international democratic community is well executed. Several appendixes provide the reader with key statistics and with information on Ben-Gurion's policies. A glossary and extensive primary and secondary bibliographies round out the work.

KURZMAN spent 15 years conducting hundreds of interviews and undertaking extensive archival work to prepare for this biography. As the title of the work implies, he regards Ben-Gurion as a titan among Jewish leaders. Accordingly, the book is divided into sections entitled "Moses," "Joshua," and "Isaiah," and each section is divided into chapters based on biblical scriptures. Kurzman presents more intimate details about Ben-Gurion's birthplace, childhood, and teenage life than did Bar-Zohar. The volume contains extensive photographs, detailed notes, and an extensive bibliography that includes citations from newspapers, radio and television programs, unpublished documents, and oral histories.

TEVETH (1987) maintains that Ben-Gurion's story is too involved to cover completely all relevant points. Therefore, this work only recounts Ben-Gurion's life from his birth in Plonsk up to the founding of Israel. Teveth states that Ben-Gurion's life's work was "the founding of a secular authority, without which he could never have brought about the establishment of a state." The author further contends that Ben-Gurion was forced "to confront, helplessly, the destruction of European Jewry without losing faith in humankind and the Jewish people and without abandoning his confidence in the justice of the Zionist cause and its ultimate triumph." Extensive notes, a glossary, an index, and black-and-white photographs are included in the work.

TEVETH (1996) states that the aim of his work is "to examine the charges of collaboration and murderous indifference and to document Ben-Gurion's efforts to rescue the Jewish people." Critics charged that the Zionist leadership of Palestine ignored the fate of non-Zionist European Jews, and Ben-Gurion, as leader of the Zionist Labor Party, Mapai, was accused (along with other "singularly focused Zionist leaders") of being so preoccupied in the creation of a Jewish state that he was willing to sacrifice Eastern European Jewry to accomplish the goal. Teveth seeks to refute these charges and claims that his research, contrary to the claims of Ben-Gurion's critics, shows that as early as 1934, Ben-Gurion saw the ruination

of Europe's Jews and sought to keep them safe from the Nazis. His attempts to bring Jews out of Europe, whether to Palestine or elsewhere, were strenuous—indifference, especially in the United Kingdom and the United States, notwithstanding.

TEVETH (1985) traces Ben-Gurion's part in various stages of Jewish-Arab relations. Initially, Ben-Gurion's fervent dream of a Jewish land and his ties to Marxist utopianism were such that "he gave no thought to the Arabs, their problems, their social conditions, or their cultural life. Nor had he yet acquainted himself with the Jewish community of Palestine." Teveth describes clashes between Palestinian Arabs and immigrant Jews, as well as plans for peace and pan-Arabism. Although Ben-Gurion publicly denied that there was any opposition to Jewish settlement in Palestine, his diaries reveal his awareness of the extent of Arab resentment toward the immigrants. Teveth also suggests that Ben-Gurion did not believe that peace would ever be possible between the two peoples.

ZWEIG's compilation presents scholarly essays about various aspects of Ben-Gurion's life that were compiled to mark the centennial anniversary of Ben-Gurion's birth. The anthology includes essays by historians of international reputation as well as essays by lesser-known Israeli scholars; the articles cover areas of Ben-Gurion's life that previously have been discussed, along with newer areas of investigation, such as Ben-Gurion's role in developing the Israeli public education system. Contributors include Shimon Peres, Teveth, Gal, Uri Bialer, and Yehudit Auerbach. Extensive notes follow each essay.

CYNTHIA A. KLÍMA

Ben Sira, Wisdom of

Argall, Randal A., *1 Enoch and Sirach: A Comparative Literary and Conceptual Analysis of the Themes of Revelation, Creation and Judgment*, Atlanta, Georgia: Scholars Press, 1995

Beentjes, Pancratius C. (editor), *The Book of Ben Sira in Modern Research: Proceedings of the First International Ben Sira Conference, 28–31 July 1996, Soesterberg, Netherlands* (Beihefte zur Zeitschrift für die alttestamentliche Wissenschaft, 255), New York: de Gruyter, 1997

Blenkinsopp, Joseph, *Wisdom and Law in the Old Testament: The Ordering of Life in Israel and Early Judaism* (Oxford Bible Series), Oxford: Oxford University Press, 1983; New York: Oxford University Press, 1990; revised edition, 1995

Collins, John J., *Jewish Wisdom in the Hellenistic Age* (The Old Testament Library Series), Louisville, Kentucky: Westminster John Knox, 1997; Edinburgh: Clark, 1998

Crenshaw, James L., *Old Testament Wisdom: An Introduction*, Atlanta, Georgia: Knox, 1981; London: SCM, 1982; revised edition, Louisville, Kentucky: Westminster John Knox, 1998

Heaton, Eric William, *The School Tradition of the Old Testament: The Bampton Lectures for 1994*, Oxford and New York: Oxford University Press, 1994

Mack, Burton L., *Wisdom and the Hebrew Epic: Ben Sira's Hymn in Praise of the Fathers* (Chicago Studies in the History of Judaism), Chicago: University of Chicago Press, 1985

Sanders, Jack T., *Ben Sira and Demotic Wisdom* (Society of Biblical Literature Monograph Series, no. 28), Chico, California: Scholars Press, 1983

Skehan, Patrick W. and Alexander A. Di Lella, *The Wisdom of Ben Sira: A New Translation with Notes* (Anchor Bible, vol. 39), New York: Doubleday, 1987

The professional sage Simeon ben Jesus ben Sira, Jesus Sirach in Greek, compiled his book of proverbs around 180 B.C.E. in Jerusalem. His grandson later translated the book into Greek. This translation became part of the Christian Old Testament, where it acquired the name Ecclesiasticus. Today it appears only in Catholic Bibles, whereas Jews (who usually refer to the work as Ben Sira) and Protestants (who usually call it Sirach) relegate it to the Apocrypha. A total of about two-thirds of the original Hebrew document survives in several manuscripts, and all the Greek translation survives in a number of manuscripts. Since these manuscripts differ in some respects, one of the main issues that occupy scholars is establishing the original text. Aside from that, scholars have been primarily interested in understanding the book's principles of organization, its meaning, its relation to earlier Jewish writings and to foreign works, and the author's attitude to foreign cultures.

CRENSHAW discusses ben Sira's work within the context of ancient Israelite and Jewish wisdom books. He finds ben Sira's main innovation in his integration of sacred history and law into wisdom, whereas the older books, such as Proverbs, had been satisfied with nature study. Thus ben Sira emphasizes piety toward the Torah (the books of Moses), and he equates fear of God (i.e., obeying the Torah) with wisdom. Crenshaw sees that ben Sira readily borrows Greek ideas as long as he can "Hebraize" them. His book presents a good brief summary of the contents of the book of ben Sira.

Just under half COLLINS's book deals with ben Sira. He analyzes ben Sira's Hellenistic context (both political and intellectual), the subordinate relation of Torah to wisdom in the book, ben Sira's ethics, the problem of evil, and ben Sira's views on the history and destiny of Israel. The section on ethics emphasizes the individual and familial aspect of ben Sira's ethics and the author's eudaemonism and utilitarianism. Collins agrees with Burton Mack on ben Sira's view of the goal of history.

SKEHAN's and DI LELLA's commentary deals thoroughly with all aspects of ben Sira's work and its problems. A 90-page introduction discusses the title and contents of the book; ben Sira and his times; the canonicity of the book and its place in the canon of Scripture; literary genres; wisdom traditions in the Hebrew Bible; ben Sira's relationship to various books of the Hebrew Bible; ben Sira and non-Jewish literature; the original Hebrew text and ancient versions; the poetry of ben Sira; and the teaching of ben Sira. An English translation of the text that they established appears in brief sections, each section being followed immediately by textual and translational notes, and then by a substantive "comment" on the section. There is also an extensive bibliography. This work

provides an excellent clarification of the broad international and intellectual setting of the book, as well as of the author's meaning on many points. It generally agrees with Crenshaw on the analysis of different wisdom literary genres and with Jack Sanders on ben Sira's relation to earlier Judaic and foreign literature.

SANDERS analyzes the way in which ben Sira drew upon and adapted earlier Judaic tradition, especially that in the books of the Bible, and he then looks at the possibilities for ben Sira's inclusion of foreign material. He finds that quite a few of ben Sira's proverbs, especially having to do with friendship, came from the Greek author Theognis; and he finds some other evidence of Greek influence. Furthermore, he shows that ben Sira had relied on an Egyptian work in Demotic script, called today only *Papyrus Insinger*. Some of the more striking similarities are the presence in both works of images of 100 years as the limit of life and of the little bee that produces much honey. Both works also contain advice at or near the beginning on how to treat one's parents and a long hymn to God's creation at the end.

MACK examines in detail the long section at the end of the book in which ben Sira praises famous Jews of earlier years. He shows that the composition is related both to the preceding section praising God's creation and to the praise of the scholar in chapter 39. Further, the section betrays the influence of both Jewish wisdom texts and Greek literature. The section seeks to show that God's direction of history has led to the religiopolitical situation in ben Sira's time, when both worship and society focused on temple practice and the high priest.

HEATON begins with a brief analysis of ben Sira and with the observation that the author was a school master. He then shows ben Sira's indebtedness both to the international school (wisdom) tradition and to the traditions of Torah, prophets, and wisdom in the Bible, and he argues persuasively for the existence of a school tradition in ancient Israel. The existence of schools prior to ben Sira's time, however, remains a debated point among scholars.

While little of BLENKINSOPP's book deals directly with ben Sira, he presents an excellent analysis of the interaction between wisdom and law in ancient Israel and later Judaism. His section on Ecclesiasticus shows well how ben Sira assimilated Torah to wisdom.

The value of ARGALL's work is in drawing attention to the interaction between apocalyptic literature and wisdom literature and also in showing that both 1 Enoch and ben Sira deal with the themes of revelation, creation, and judgment in highly similar ways. Argall misunderstands ben Sira's attitude toward the Torah, however, and thinks that he draws revelation from the Torah. Skehan and Di Lella explain ben Sira's relation to the Torah more accurately.

The volume edited by BEENTJES contains essays presented by various scholars at a conference. Most essays deal with text, dating, and organization. One essay reviews recent research on the book through 1996; there are also especially noteworthy essays on ben Sira's use of the concept of "fear of the Lord" and on ben Sira's loyalty to the Jerusalem priesthood.

JACK T. SANDERS

Ben-Yehuda, Eliezer 1858-1922

Lithuanian-born Zionist ideologue and lexicographer, considered the father of Hebrew language revival

Avineri, Shlomo, *The Making of Modern Zionism: Intellectual Origins of the Jewish State*, New York: Basic Books, 1981; as *The Making of Modern Zionism: The Intellectual Origins of the Jewish State*, London: Weidenfeld and Nicolson, 1981

Ben-Yehuda, Eliezer, *A Dream Come True* (Modern Hebrew Classics), translated by T. Muraoka, edited by George Mandel, Boulder, Colorado: Westview, 1983

Fellman, Jack, *The Revival of a Classical Tongue: Eliezer Ben Yehuda and the Modern Hebrew Language* (Contributions to the Sociology of Language, 6), The Hague: Mouton, 1973

Hertzberg, Arthur (editor), *The Zionist Idea: A Historical Analysis and Reader*, Garden City, New York: Doubleday, 1959

Mandel, George, "Why Did Ben-Yehuda Suggest the Revival of Spoken Hebrew?" in *Hebrew in Ashkenaz: A Language in Exile*, edited by Lewis Glinert, New York: Oxford University Press, 1993

Silberschlag, Eisig (editor), *Eliezer Ben-Yehuda: A Symposium in Oxford*, Oxford: Oxford Centre for Postgraduate Hebrew Studies, 1981

Eliezer Ben-Yehuda—an early Zionist, Hebrew journalist, and leader of the movement for the revival of Hebrew as an everyday spoken language—was a highly controversial figure, and many texts about him are either hagiographic or the opposite, intentionally denigrating. Included in the former category is a full-length biography published in the 1950s that was, unfortunately, for many years the main source of information in English about Ben-Yehuda. Most of the authors of the hagiographic works were members of Ben-Yehuda's family or people associated with them, while many of the denigrators came from the ranks of the so-called Second Aliyah, the early socialist-Zionist pioneers who achieved a position of dominance in the Palestinian *yishuv* and who included the leading figures of the generation that eventually established the State of Israel. It is only since the 1970s that more dispassionate scholarly works about Ben-Yehuda have appeared. These texts' authors have tried to evaluate the facts of his life and work accurately and fairly, and they have been able to make use of a wide range of sources in Hebrew. Rather curiously—and fortunately for those readers who do not know Hebrew—many of these works were written in English; some of them have not been published in Hebrew.

The earliest work of scholastic quality is the study by FELLMAN, whose declared aim is to "examine the role played by Ben Yehuda in the revival of Hebrew and . . . to assess objectively the significance of his contribution in this sphere." Fellman rejects the school of thought that "considers Ben Yehuda in very simplistic terms a modern miracle maker who single-handedly revived the Hebrew language." In his view,

Ben Yehuda must be given the sole credit . . . for being the first to state the idea and the necessity of starting the revival and for being the first to show the feasibility of implementing it . . . however, Ben Yehuda needed and actively sought the help of many other interested parties who, mainly through their efforts and not those of Ben Yehuda, brought about the true revival of the language on a large scale.

In his book, Fellman discusses systematically the various activities of Ben-Yehuda that were intended to help bring about the revival, and the author concludes that Ben-Yehuda's most important contribution was his advocacy of the use of Hebrew as the language of instruction in Jewish schools in Palestine ("Hebrew through Hebrew"). Although Ben-Yehuda had suggested this method as early as 1880, even before he emigrated to Palestine, Fellman argues that the credit for its successful implementation actually belongs to the teachers in the agricultural colonies and not to Ben-Yehuda himself, who lived in Jerusalem and whose teaching career lasted for only about three months. Fellman's work remains the only serious full-length study of Ben-Yehuda in English. Although Fellman occasionally relies on sources of doubtful accuracy for certain minor conclusions and fails to provide an index, this work is indispensable for the study of its subject.

The ideological path taken by the young Ben-Yehuda on his way to Zionism became a subject of interest at the end of the 1970s, a century after he made his literary debut with an article advocating a Jewish national revival in the land of Israel. AVINERI, who devotes a chapter to Ben-Yehuda in his book on the intellectual origins of the Jewish state, argues that Ben-Yehuda began his inquiries as he became aware of the low artistic achievements of the Hebrew writers of his day, and he attributed this deficiency to the fact that Hebrew was not a spoken language. Influenced by the Russian populists, Ben-Yehuda believed that true literature could emerge only in a society that spoke the same language used for writing. He concluded that Hebrew literature could develop only in a society with a Jewish majority that used Hebrew as its living language of daily intercourse. The only way to create such a society was for Jews to emigrate in large numbers to Palestine and construct a Hebrew-speaking nation there. According to Avineri, Ben-Yehuda posited that the revival of spoken Hebrew was a means to an end (the creation of a superior Hebrew literature), while the settlement of the land of Israel by Jews would make that means possible.

Avineri's view is challenged by MANDEL, who argues that it was based on a misunderstanding of the single source that Avineri cited to support his argument—a brief letter by Ben-Yehuda to the editor of a Hebrew journal. Mandel also charges that Avineri ignored much evidence from other sources. According to Mandel, Ben-Yehuda was not mainly concerned with the quality of Hebrew literature. Instead, he feared for Hebrew's very existence because Jews were increasingly adopting the languages of the gentile majorities among whom they lived and ceasing to use Hebrew except as a language of prayer and religious study. Therefore, Ben-Yehuda decided that the only way to sustain Hebrew was to create a society in which Jews themselves formed the majority, and to this end large numbers of Jews needed to emigrate to the land of Israel. At a later stage of his life, Ben-Yehuda came to believe that even a Jewish majority in the land of Israel would not keep Hebrew alive unless it also became an everyday spoken language.

BEN-YEHUDA's memoir is an excellent starting point for anyone who wishes to learn about his early life. The text covers the years from his childhood to the birth of his first child in 1882, and it is therefore not a complete autobiography. However, it contains a great deal of important and interesting material, including a description of how Ben-Yehuda suddenly became convinced, while still at school, that the Jews needed a national revival in their ancestral homeland. This realization happened in 1877, four years before the great wave of pogroms in Russia that are usually regarded as the event that gave birth to Zionism, and nearly 20 years before the more famous conversion of Theodor Herzl. Ben-Yehuda became a "Zionist" (to use a word that, although not invented until the 1890s, is an accurate description of the views he held from 1877) at a time when very few, if any, other people held similar beliefs. Like Herzl, Ben-Yehuda arrived at his opinion independently and not because he was persuaded by anyone else's arguments, but Ben-Yehuda's reasons—unlike Herzl's—were not shaped by antisemitism. Because this memoir sheds light on Ben-Yehuda's conversion, it is obviously of interest to historians of Zionism.

The collection edited by SILBERSCHLAG contains a translation of Ben-Yehuda's first published article, "A Weighty Question" (1879), as well as four essays on diverse aspects of Ben-Yehuda's activities. In his collection of writings illustrating the historical development of Zionist ideology, HERTZBERG prints an 1880 letter by Ben-Yehuda to the editor of the Hebrew periodical *Ha-Shahar*. Like "A Weighty Question," the letter is a statement of Ben-Yehuda's reasons for advocating the settlement of Israel by Jews, but the letter was written about 18 months after the article, when his ideas had developed somewhat and become clearer and more straightforward.

GEORGE MANDEL

Bet Din *see* Sanhedrin, Semikhah, and Rabbinate

Bialik, Hayyim Nahman 1873–1934

Ukrainian-born poet, essayist, and editor

Aberbach, David, *Bialik* (Jewish Thinkers), New York: Grove, and London: Halban, 1988
Alter, Robert, "The Kidnapping of Bialik and Tchernichovsky," in his *After the Tradition: Essays on Modern Jewish Writing*, New York: Dutton, 1969
Breslauer, S. Daniel, *The Hebrew Poetry of Hayyim Nahman Bialik (1873–1934) and a Modern Jewish Theology* (Jewish Studies, vol. 10), Lewiston, New York: Mellen, 1991
Genn, Mordecai, "The Influence of Rabbinic Literature on the Poetry of Hayim Nahman Bialik," Ph.D. diss., Brandeis University, 1978

Leiter S. and Ezra Spicehandler, "Bialik, Hayyim Nahman," in *Encyclopaedia Judaica*, New York: Macmillan, 1972

Widely regarded as the greatest poet in the Hebrew language, Hayyim Nahman Bialik published his first poem, "To the Bird," in 1891. He lived in several small towns, villages, and cities of the Russian Jewish pale of settlement until he finally settled in the Land of Israel in 1924. A prolific editor, translator, and short story writer, he is best known for his longer epic poems, "Zohar," "The Pool," and "The Scroll of Fire."

ABERBACH's book, a volume in the Jewish Thinkers series, provides a short biography of Bialik. Aberbach consults previous studies of Bialik in Hebrew, as well as some of the few critical pieces in English, and offers his own interpretation of the poet's life. Aberbach's method grounds Bialik in the context of East European Jewry but also compares him with modernist poets such as W.B. Yeats and T.S. Eliot and offers something of a psychoanalytic approach to Bialik's works. He describes how Bialik, although very widely considered the national poet, felt highly ambivalent toward this role, and Aberbach sees this creating a tension in Bialik's work that is, he argues, the mark of his greatness.

The nonspecialist reader in search of an introduction to Bialik may also wish to consult LEITER and SPICEHANDLER. The first and larger part of this article, written by Leiter, offers a thorough biographical and bibliographic survey. Beginning with a description of Bialik's childhood, Leiter describes the events and people in the author's life that most influenced his artistic development: the time the young Bialik spent studying in the yeshivah at Volozhin, the influence of the great Zionist theoretician Ahad Ha'am on the young poet, the period spent in the great literary centers of Odessa and Warsaw, and the mature Bialik's decision to settle permanently in the Land of Israel in 1924. The second part of the essay, titled "Evaluation," is written by Spicehandler. After a few remarks surveying Hebrew poetry previous to the appearance of Bialik, Spicehandler demonstrates how Bialik's innovations of style, form, and subject represented a great change in Hebrew poetry. Basing his poems on European models and demonstrating complete command over the Hebrew language, Bialik, as viewed by Spicehandler, freed Hebrew poetry from its biblical roots and created the first works of truly modern Hebrew poetry.

ALTER looks at the ambivalent attitudes of modern Jewish writers toward the Jewish past and tradition. Alter deals in particular with Jewish authors writing in the United States, such as Saul Bellow and Bernard Malamud, and in Israel, such as S.Y. Agnon and H.N. Bialik. In his essay "The Kidnapping of Bialik and Tchernichovsky," which originally appeared in *Midstream* (June 1964), Alter points to ways in which he feels that these two giants of modern Hebrew poetry have been misinterpreted by many readers. Though he admits that several critics have indeed provided new and "useful" works on these two poets, he ends his essay on a pessimistic note: "the plight of Bialik and Tchernichovsky dramatically illustrates the need for enlightened, disciplined critics: only they can rescue the two great modern Hebrew poets from the hands of their abductors."

BRESLAUER's study is concerned with the relationship of traditional Judaism to the poetry of Bialik. Specifically, Breslauer looks at the particular brand of Judaism he sees inherent in Bialik's poetry. He makes it clear that he has no intention of denouncing Bialik for "secularizing" Judaism, as some previous critics have done. Rather, he points to Bialik's poems as new and individual attempts at a modern and alternative type of Judaism. Demonstrating a close familiarity both with Bialik's poetry and with the large body of critical literature in Hebrew, Breslauer advances the contention that Bialik's poetry serves "as the agenda for a contemporary Jewish theology."

GENN provides a detailed and comprehensive study of the influence of rabbinic literature on the poetry of Bialik. He argues that although previous works of this nature correctly identified many rabbinic sources in the poetry of Bialik, there are still many sources that have not been considered. It is Genn's purpose to fill this gap and to offer the reader a comparison between the rabbinic sources used by the poet and the poetry itself. The study consists mainly of close readings of the poems followed by an examination of rabbinic sources relating to the different poems and analysis of the relationships between poem and source. The author is appropriately steeped in both rabbinic literature and the large corpus of primary and secondary Bialik material.

MARC MILLER

Bible: Translations

Fox, Everett (translator), *The Five Books of Moses: Genesis, Exodus, Leviticus, Numbers, Deuteronomy; A New Translation with Introductions, Commentary, and Notes* (The Schocken Bible, vol. 1), New York: Schocken, and London: Harvill, 1995

Frerichs, Ernest S. (editor), *The Bible and Bibles in America* (The Bible in American Culture, vol. 1), Atlanta, Georgia: Scholars, 1988

The Holy Bible: Containing the Old and New Testaments [New Revised Standard Version Bible], New York and Oxford: Oxford University Press for the Division of Christian Education of the National Council of the Churches of Christ of the United States of America, 1989

Kee, Howard Clark (editor), *American Bible Society Symposium Papers on The Bible in the Twenty-first Century,* Philadelphia: Trinity, 1993

Orlinsky, Harry M. and Robert G. Bratcher (editors), *A History of Bible Translation and the North American Contribution* (Society of Biblical Literature Centennial Publications), Atlanta, Georgia: Scholars, 1991

Sheeley, Steven M. and Robert N. Nash, *The Bible in English Translation: An Essential Guide,* Nashville: Abingdon, 1997

Tanakh: The Holy Scriptures: The New JPS Translation According to the Traditional Hebrew Text, Philadelphia: Jewish Publication Society, 1985

Bible translations in English encompass a wide variety of translation philosophies and are targeted at diverse audiences, Jewish and Christian alike. While the most familiar English version is the King James Version of 1611, the 20th century has seen the production of more major English Bible translations than all previous centuries combined. Most of these were produced by Christian scholars for Christian readers. During the last half of the 20th century, however, Jewish scholars participated in ecumenical efforts to produce Bible translations as well as distinctly Jewish productions of English Bibles.

ORLINSKY and BRATCHER survey the history of Bible translation by dividing it into four great ages. The first great age of Bible translation stretches from 200 B.C.E. through the fourth century C.E. This age was dominated by two early Jewish translations: the Septuagint (Greek) and the Targums (Aramaic). The spread of Christianity gave rise to daughter translations of the Septuagint (i.e., translations of the Greek translation). The second great age of Bible translation begins in 400 and lasts until about 1500. The third great age of Bible translation runs from 1500 through 1960. Orlinsky and Bratcher concentrate on Bible translation in England and the United States during this age. This age saw the first great English translation, that of William Tyndale. In Orlinsky and Bratcher's opinion Tyndale is central to every English translation to this day. Tyndale, in turn, was enormously influenced by Martin Luther, whose translation of the Hebrew Bible was influenced by the commentary of the Jewish exegete Solomon ben Isaac (Rashi). The final age begins in 1960. In their discussion of the last two ages, the authors attempt to cover many of the Bibles produced in North America and provide comparisons and evaluations of them. Orlinsky and Bratcher's work is indispensable to anyone wishing to obtain more than a superficial understanding of the complex history of Bible translation.

FRERICHS assembles eight essays on the Bible in America. The second essay examines major translations produced by committees since 1900. It classifies them either as revisions of the King James Version or as new translations, and it evaluates them according to the degree that they communicate to their intended readers the emotional and cognitive message that was communicated to the original readers. Another essay provides an exhaustive survey of American Bible translations by individuals. A third essay surveys American Jewish Bible scholarship and translations, concentrating on the translations of Isaac Leeser (1806–1868), who produced a literal but wooden translation, and the versions issued by the Jewish Publication Society: *The Holy Scriptures* (1917), and its newer counterpart *Tanakh: The Holy Scriptures* (1985).

KEE contains a number of essays relevant to Bible translation. In particular, the essay titled "New Bible Translations: An Assessment and Prospect" explores the problems of modern Bible translations, asserting that the problem for translations into major European languages (English, French, German, etc.) is that the translators are well equipped with knowledge of the original Biblical languages but ill-informed of developments in linguistics, while for those producing translations in the indigenous languages of developing countries the opposite is true. Another essay examines the possibilities for breakthroughs in Bible translation and urges a more wholistic view of the translation task, including a greater understanding of the oral use of language and its effects upon the written word.

SHEELEY and NASH attempt to provide a guide for evaluating and choosing an English Bible translation. They begin by surveying the history of the Bible and its translation into English. Another chapter presents the challenges of translating the Bible. It divides translations into three categories that correspond to the approach to translation employed by the translators: verbal translations, dynamic translations, and paraphrases. Translations are categorized as verbal translations if they seek primarily to translate the Bible in a way that is faithful to the ancient words and forms of the Hebrew text. Dynamic translations are concerned with translating the meaning of the ancient text as faithfully as possible, even at the expense of the verbal forms. Paraphrase is the classification for Bibles that attempt to update the language of previous translations without consulting the text in the original language. Chapters on verbal translations and on dynamic translations and paraphrases evaluate a number of recent and widely available English Bible translations. A concluding chapter on choosing a Bible translation for personal use attempts to help readers in making this decision. Sheeley and Nash write for a general audience and do not hesitate to criticize various English translations for their shortcomings. They do, however, exhibit a bias toward verbal translations in general and the *New Revised Standard Version Bible* in particular.

THE HOLY BIBLE *(THE NEW REVISED STANDARD VERSION)* (NRSV) is an ecumenical Bible translation produced by approximately 30 scholars. It contains not only the Hebrew Bible but also the Christian New Testament and Apocryphal/Deuterocanonical books. Its Hebrew Bible committee included a Jewish scholar. The NRSV is a conscious continuation of the tradition of the King James Version. Among its controversial features is a commitment to gender-inclusive language even in some cases where it could be validly argued that the original language intended a gender-specific referent. The English rendering of the Hebrew Bible in the NRSV is more elevated and stately than its Christian New Testament counterpart. Undoubtedly, the NRSV is the most widely used modern English version among English-speaking biblical scholars.

TANAKH: THE HOLY SCRIPTURES is the most up-to-date Bible translation produced by a team of Jewish scholars. It consciously breaks away from the English of earlier translations but attempts to remain faithful to the Hebrew text. It is marked by the careful scholarship and thorough research that lies behind it. In any number of passages it offers fresh translations of high literary quality. In general it follows the Masoretic Text of the Hebrew Bible but does depart from it on a few occasions. It also contains quite a number of helpful notes for readers who seek further insight into ancient life and customs.

FOX presents a translation of the Torah along with extensive notes and commentary. It is marked by a translation philosophy that seeks to produce an English translation that preserves the literary features of the Hebrew text even at the expense of idiomatic English.

ANDREW E. STEINMANN

See also Bible: Criticism; Bible: Hermeneutics; Bible: Introductions; Bible: Law; Bible: Medieval Exegesis; Bible: Reference Tools; Bible: Theology

Bible: Reference Tools

Aharoni, Yohanan et al., *The Macmillan Bible Atlas*, New York: Macmillan, 1968; revised edition, London: Macmillan, 1978; 3rd edition, New York: Macmillan, 1993

Freedman, David Noel (editor), *The Anchor Bible Dictionary*, 6 vols., New York and London: Doubleday, 1992

Knight, Douglas A. and Gene M. Tucker (editors), *The Hebrew Bible and Its Modern Interpreters*, Philadelphia: Fortress, 1985

Kohlenberger, John R., III, *The NRSV Concordance Unabridged: Including the Apocryphal/Deuterocanonical Books*, Grand Rapids, Michigan: Zondervan, 1991

Matthews, Victor H. and Don C. Benjamin, *Old Testament Parallels: Laws and Stories from the Ancient Near East*, New York: Paulist, 1991, revised edition, 1997

Rogerson, John (editor), *Beginning Old Testament Study*, Philadelphia: Westminster, 1982; London: SPCK, 1983, revised edition, 1998

Thompson, Henry O., *Biblical Archaeology: The World, the Mediterranean, the Bible*, New York: Paragon, 1987

Zimmerli, Walther, *Old Testament Theology in Outline*, Atlanta, Georgia: Knox, 1978; Edinburgh: Clark, 1978

ROGERSON has edited a slim volume of essays to guide the beginner in the academic study of the Hebrew Bible. These essays give general orientations to the history of biblical studies, the methodology of biblical interpretation, the cultural world of the Bible, and some of the theological problems that readers today encounter when they begin to study the Bible systematically. The essays serve to dispel some popular myths about the Hebrew Bible and replace them with the results of scholarly consensus. This book shows that the Hebrew Bible deserves serious study because of compelling challenges it offers to readers today. This book is designed to make entrance into biblical studies easier for the general reader.

KNIGHT and TUCKER have edited a collection of essays that describe the present state of research into the Hebrew Bible in a clear and comprehensive fashion. Individual topics are discussed by some of the leading biblical scholars of the day. The authors not only review current scholarship but suggest some directions for future research. There is an excellent bibliography accompanying each article, enabling interested readers to probe more deeply into specific topics. In addition to articles that discuss the literature of the Hebrew Bible itself, there are articles on history, archaeology, the ancient Near Eastern environment, methods of biblical interpretation, ancient Israelite religion, the theology of the Hebrew Bible, and the relationship of the Bible to contemporary culture. This is a very useful volume since it provides the reader with a sense of trends in research, issues currently under study, and any consensus that has been attained. While the essays examine an enormous amount of secondary literature, the purpose is to show how scholarship has advanced. The authors do not burden the reader with a simple review of all the published literature but present to their readers important studies that have made significant contributions to the field.

A concordance, listing the place where a given word occurs in the Bible, is essential for the most basic analysis of the text because it helps the reader determine the usage, distribution, and context of the word in question. The concordance selected should correspond to the reader's chosen translation of the Bible. KOHLENBERGER's concordance to the *New Revised Standard Version* (*NRSV*) includes the apocryphal/deuterocanonical books along with those in the Hebrew canon. He also provides an index to the *NRSV* footnotes and a topical index. Concordances in book form, however, are becoming obsolete because computer-based technology allows for speed and a variety of searches using a concordance on a CD-ROM and a lexical analysis program such as those available from Logos Research Systems. There are several "bundles" of basic research tools available in CD-ROM format. These include various versions of the Bible, concordances, dictionaries, atlases, and commentaries.

Dictionaries of the Bible are invaluable as timesaving, informative resources. They give the reader a quick orientation to key words and concepts. There are several good one-volume and multivolume Bible dictionaries available. FREEDMAN's six-volume work is the most comprehensive, however, containing 6,200 entries written by 986 contributors. These statistics reflect the degree of specialization that has developed in biblical studies. Each major article and most others have helpful bibliographies attached. The volumes are amply illustrated. Little attention is given to the contemporary theological relevance of the topics discussed since both the contributors and the intended audience are so religiously diverse. This dictionary is also available on CD-ROM, which makes using it much simpler. The one-volume Bible dictionaries obviously cannot provide the detail of Freedman's *Anchor Bible Dictionary*, which will represent the gold standard for a long time to come.

ZIMMERLI offers a systematic presentation of the religious thought of ancient Israel as found in the Hebrew Bible. It deals with the central focus of that religious faith: the confession of the God of Israel under the name YHWH. Other topics include leadership, morality, liturgy, and eschatology. His presentation of ancient Israel's religious thought shows how this thinking found new expressions in new situations. Each section contains an extensive bibliography of studies in which fuller treatments of the topic can be found. The conclusions represent consensus viewpoints, but the discussion can be dense at times. It is a book for more advanced readers since it presupposes basic knowledge of the contents of the Bible.

The Bible did not emerge in a vacuum. Informed biblical study must consider the wider cultural context of the ancient Near East. Among the anthologies of ancient Near Eastern literature available, that produced by MATTHEWS and BENJAMIN may be most helpful to beginners. Ancient Near

Eastern texts are presented according to the books of the Hebrew Bible that they illuminate. The authors also give a sketch of ancient Near Eastern history and a good basic bibliography. The texts are not true translations but paraphrases. While they give the flavor of the ancient Near Eastern context, they do not provide the precise accuracy necessary for more specialized study. Still, this book provides the beginner with a good entry into the larger ancient Near Eastern world in which ancient Israel played a small part.

An atlas of the Bible is also necessary if biblical study is to recognize the cultural context that gave rise to the Bible. AHARONI provides readers not only with maps of the biblical world but with a historically oriented commentary to each map, along with references to biblical and extrabiblical texts related to each map. This volume, then, offers readers both an introduction to the geography of the biblical lands and a good sketch of their history. Atlases of the Bible are also available as part of computer-assisted biblical study programs.

The results of archaeological excavations supplement the picture of antiquity available through the analysis of its literary remains. Archaeology studies the material remains of the ancient world, and as such it too is essential to understanding the world of those who produced the biblical texts. THOMPSON orients the reader to archaeology as a field of study and then goes on to show how it can help in understanding the world of the Bible. The author also discusses how archaeology contributes to the religious understanding of those who accept the Bible as normative for faith and life.

LESLIE J. HOPPE

See also Bible: Criticism; Bible: Hermeneutics; Bible: Introductions; Bible: Law; Bible: Medieval Exegesis; Bible: Theology; Bible: Translations

Bible: Introductions

Anderson, Bernhard W., *Understanding the Old Testament*, Englewood Cliffs, New Jersey: Prentice-Hall, 1957, 4th edition, 1986; as *The Living World of the Old Testament*, London: Longmans, Green, 1958; 4th edition, Harlow, Essex: Longman, 1988

Ceresko, Anthony R., *Introduction to the Old Testament: A Liberation Perspective*, Maryknoll, New York: Orbis, and London: Chapman, 1992

Childs, Brevard S., *Introduction to the Old Testament as Scripture*, Philadelphia: Fortress, and London: SCM, 1979

Crenshaw, James L., *Story and Faith: A Guide to the Old Testament*, New York: Macmillan, 1986

Gottwald, Norman K., *The Hebrew Bible: A Socio-Literary Introduction*, Philadelphia: Fortress, 1985

Humphreys, W. Lee, *Crisis and Story: An Introduction to the Old Testament*, Palo Alto, California: Mayfield, 1979; 2nd edition, Mountain View, California: Mayfield, 1990

Laffey, Alice L., *An Introduction to the Old Testament: A Feminist Perspective*, Philadelphia: Fortress, 1988

Levenson, Jon D., *Sinai and Zion: An Entry into the Jewish Bible* (New Voices in Biblical Studies), Minneapolis, Minnesota: Winston, 1985

Rendtorff, Rolf, *The Old Testament: An Introduction*, London: SCM, 1985; Philadelphia: Fortress, 1986

J.G. Eichhorn published his *Einleitung in das Alten Testament* in 1783 and is considered the founder of the modern introduction to the "Old Testament." He attended to three questions: the growth of the canon, the history of the text, and the origin of the individual books of the Bible. RENDTORFF takes this classical model and modifies it in a creative way. Rather than focusing narrowly on the history of the text, Rendtorff uses the text to reconstruct the history of Israel before turning to extrabiblical material. He then shows how the biblical text is an expression of the life of ancient Israel. After describing how the individual texts became "literature," he discusses the biblical books in their present form. It is here that the author introduces the reader to the results of critical analysis of the individual books. He is careful to underscore the theological perspectives that characterized the canonical form of the individual books. Especially helpful are the cross-references he provides, directing the reader to related discussions elsewhere in the book. While this work was originally written in German, the excellent bibliographies provide the reader with direction to some works in English, even though German titles predominate. The book contains not a single illustration, map, chart, or photograph—an indication that the author sees his work as an introduction in the classical sense.

Though the cross-references in the margins of the text, the bibliographies, and indexes help make this book easier to use, the density of its presentation puts it beyond the reach of beginners. It is, however, a fine reference tool for the advanced student, who will find invaluable the author's accurate and balanced presentation of the state of scholarship regarding issues of history, the institutions of ancient Israelite society and religion, and the theological editing of the individual books in the canon. A particular issue that calls for some comment is the author's perspective on the origins of the Torah. He abandons the view of continuous sources combined by priestly circles. Rendtorff holds that the Deuteronomists gave the Torah its shape by combining fragments of earlier tradition and giving them a distinct theological interpretation.

ANDERSON has produced what has proven to be the most popular of these introductions among readers in the United States, having gone through four editions. The book is amply illustrated and engagingly written. The footnotes and bibliography direct the interested reader to important works of critical scholarship. Although the author sought to interweave the results of historical and archaeological research with literary criticism and biblical theology, the work is governed by the ideas of salvation history characteristic of the biblical theology movement. The problem is that focusing on "salvation history" makes some Hebrew Bible traditions marginal. For example, Anderson did not include a chapter on the psalms or the wisdom tradition in his first edition. This approach also is a distinctively Christian one that sees ancient Israel's destiny fulfilled in the life and ministry of Jesus, although this is not explicit in the book.

Throughout the four editions of his work, Anderson remained convinced of the historical value of biblical narratives. For example, he presented the patriarchal narratives (Genesis 12–50) as reflecting the cultural milieu of the Middle Bronze Age. He concludes, then, that these narratives are historical sources. Anderson's basic approach has not been affected substantially by the developments in biblical interpretation in the 40 years since his introduction first made its appearance. For example, he makes no use of the sociological and anthropological models that have proven their usefulness in offering new approaches to understanding the Bible. Still, each edition does show that—within his hermeneutical framework—Anderson has changed some positions. Thus, in the fourth edition he makes two significant changes. First, he advances his treatment of the Yahwist epic into the tribal era. He previously considered the Yahwist (author of the "J" source in the Pentateuch) to be the product of the Solomonic era, though a current tendency is to locate this material closer to the exile. Second, his presentation of the restoration places Ezra's mission before that of Nehemiah. In the first three editions, he held the opposite view.

LEVENSON offers an introduction to the Hebrew Bible that is explicitly Jewish in its approach. The first part of the book explores the covenant metaphor, showing that image at home in the culture of the ancient Near East. The section ends with a vigorous defense of the rabbis who have been accused of transforming this covenant ideal into legalism. The second part of the book explores the Zion metaphor and its implications for ancient Israel's liturgical life. The final section of the book argues against the notion that the Sinai tradition was dominant in the North while being displaced by Zion traditions in the South. This is less an introduction in the classical sense and more a theological essay on the significance of the Scriptures from a Jewish perspective.

The value of this work is that it offers a fresh theological interpretation that is not shaped by the categories of salvation history and the biblical theology movement that have dominated "Old Testament" interpretation until recently. It also adds an articulate and creative Jewish voice to a discussion that has been dominated by Christian interpreters. The author makes significant contributions for Jewish and Christian readers alike. For the former, he shows the value of a historical-critical approach to the Bible. For the latter, who tend to view prophets as the apex of ancient Israelite religion, he offers the twin foci of Torah and Temple as stimulating and engaging alternatives.

HUMPHREYS also makes the Moses/Sinai and David/Zion traditions linchpins for his presentation. He makes a conscious effort to augment the literary-critical scholarship of the classical introduction with results from the social-scientific methods in current vogue. This is a good introduction for those with little familiarity with the critical study of the Bible. This is not a theological essay like the one Levenson produced; it is clearly a textbook designed for beginning students. It has charts, maps, and photographs that enhance the content of a clearly written book. There are also select bibliographies of secondary literature in English.

Humphreys's book discusses three "crises" that led to the production of ancient Israelite and early Jewish literature: David's capture of Jebusite Jerusalem, the destruction of Jerusalem and its Temple by the Babylonians, and the First Revolt against Rome. In the course of describing the reaction to these crises, Humphreys introduces his readers to the biblical literature and noncanonical Jewish literature that were the products of theological reflection on these crises.

CRENSHAW provides an excellent resource for those disposed to a literary approach to biblical studies. After beginning with a short treatment of geography and history, the author, following the canonical ordering of the Hebrew Bible, considers each book in succession. He also includes a section that discusses the Apocrypha. The presentation is lucid and informed, although best suited for those who have some basic knowledge of the Bible, even though the book is intended as a college textbook. While Humphreys discussed the religious literature of ancient Israel and early Judaism as theological reflections occasioned by specific events in Jerusalem's history, Crenshaw approaches the Hebrew Bible and early Jewish religious texts primarily as literature. He focuses on the aesthetic rather than on the theological dimensions of the biblical material. Still, this is not purely a "Bible as literature" textbook. Crenshaw helps the reader appreciate the religious dimensions of the biblical text.

One shortcoming of a purely literary approach is that the results of archaeological work do not have much impact on the presentation. Also, the author may well give insufficient attention to certain topics. Apocalyptic, for example, was an important body of literature in early Judaism, but it receives minimal attention here.

CHILDS makes the cleanest break from the classical mold of "Old Testament" introductions. He is not interested in reconstructing the history of the text but in describing the theological meaning that the received text has for believers. The object of his study, then, is the Hebrew Scriptures as received by the synagogue and the church. He examines each book in canonical order by summarizing the literary-critical issues. The heart of his contribution, however, is his analysis of the canonical form of the books and the theological implications of this final form of the text. Appreciation of this book requires a level of sophistication that not all beginners will have. It is less an introduction than a reference work on the importance of the canon of Scripture in the life of believing communities. The value of Childs's work is that it shows how the Scriptures themselves grew out of a process of tradition and reinterpretation. With the formation of the canon, the results of that process became normative for the believing communities, whose reflections gave rise to the biblical text as it now exists.

GOTTWALD's work is also less an introduction than it is a reference tool. At the same time, it is clearly the most comprehensive introduction available. Gottwald goes into great detail, showing how the methods derived from the social sciences can relate to the literary-critical methods that have been characteristic of scholarly biblical interpretation. His understanding of the social process in ancient Israel clearly dominates the book. He sees ancient Israel's history as a by-product of social conflict between the rich and the poor. Though this struggle had religious overtones, it—not religious beliefs—shaped ancient Israel's life. Gottwald's views on the social process do not lead him to ignore the contributions of the historical-critical approach to the Bible. On the contrary, he provides readers with a most comprehensive treatment of the data that result from the application of this approach to the biblical text.

CERESKO wants to make the results of Gottwald's work available to a wider audience by showing the hermeneutical significance of his approach. Ceresko's introduction, then, explicitly shows the consequences of a liberation perspective on reading the Hebrew Bible. Though he achieves this goal, he neglects to fully inform his readers of the shape of current biblical scholarship in several important areas. Still, those looking for a readable and coherent introduction to the Hebrew Bible from a liberation perspective will appreciate this book. Unfortunately, it lacks the quantity and quality of illustrations that are so important in an introduction.

LAFFEY offers an approach similar to that of Ceresko. Similar to biblical interpretation from a liberation perspective, Laffey's feminist interpretation takes an "advocacy" stance. She helps readers see the ways that the biblical text has been shaped by the patriarchy and offers a reinterpretation of neglected or misinterpreted stories about women. This book is intended to supplement rather than supplant the standard introductions. It suffers from a shortcoming common to advocacy approaches whereby 20th-century motivations are read into some biblical texts at times. Still, the value of Laffey's approach is that it shows how the readers' social stance shapes their understanding of the Bible. This reinforces the notion that the reader is not a passive recipient of data—rather, he or she is an active agent in the process of interpretation.

LESLIE J. HOPPE

See also Bible: Criticism; Bible: Hermeneutics; Bible: Law; Bible: Medieval Exegesis; Bible: Reference Tools; Bible: Theology; Bible: Translations

Bible: Theology

Barr, James, *The Scope and Authority of the Bible* (Explorations in Theology, 7), Philadelphia: Westminster, and London: SCM, 1980

Barr, James, *Biblical Faith and Natural Theology: The Gifford Lectures for 1991, Delivered in the University of Edinburgh,* New York: Oxford University Press, and Oxford: Clarendon, 1993

Eichrodt, Walther, *Theologie des Alten Testaments,* 1933; translated by J.A. Baker as *Theology of the Old Testament,* 2 vols., Philadelphia: Westminster, and London: SCM, 1961

Goshen-Gottstein, Moshe, "Tanakh Theology: The Religion of the Old Testament and the Place of Jewish Biblical Theology," in *Ancient Israelite Religion: Essays in Honor of Frank Moore Cross,* edited by Paul D. Hanson, Patrick D. Miller, and S. Dean McBride, Philadelphia: Fortress, 1987

Greenberg, Moshe, *Studies in the Bible and Jewish Thought* (JPS Scholar of Distinction Series), Philadelphia: Jewish Publication Society, 1995

Kaufmann, Yehezkel, *Toldot ha-emunah ha-Yisre'elit*, 1937; translated and abridged by Moshe Greenberg as *The Religion of Israel: From Its Beginnings to the Babylonian Exile*, Chicago: University of Chicago, and London: Allen and Unwin, 1960

Knierim, Rolf, *The Task of Old Testament Theology: Substance, Method, and Cases: Essays*, Grand Rapids, Michigan: Eerdmans, 1995

Levenson, Jon, *Sinai and Zion: An Entry into the Jewish Bible* (New Voices in Biblical Studies), Minneapolis, Minnesota: Winston, 1985

Levenson, Jon, *The Hebrew Bible, the Old Testament, and Historical Criticism: Jews and Christians in Biblical Studies*, Louisville, Kentucky: Westminster/Knox, 1993

Ollenburger, Ben, Elmer Martens, and Gerhard Hasel, *The Flowering of Old Testament Theology: A Reader in Twentieth-Century Old Testament Theology, 1930–1990* (Sources for Biblical and Theological Study, 1), Winona Lake, Indiana: Eisenbrauns, 1992

von Rad, Gerhard, *Theologie des Alten Testaments*, 1957; translated by D.M.G. Stalken as *Old Testament Theology*, 2 vols., Edinburgh: Oliver and Boyd, and New York: Harper, 1962

Biblical theology—variously conceived as the attempt to describe biblical teachings concerning God and God's relation to the world and the community of believers, or as the project of constructing teachings about these issues on the basis of biblical texts—has not generally been a Jewish pursuit. However, while most "Old Testament" theologians speak from a Christian point of view, their work remains instructive for all students of Israelite religion. Moreover, in recent years some scholars have attempted to address the sorts of issues associated with biblical theology from a Jewish point of view. Finally, biases of biblical scholarship appear most clearly in biblical theology, and thus this field can elucidate not only the Bible but also modern scholarship.

Given the many volumes (usually of great length) devoted to biblical theology, students are greatly aided by the fine collection edited by OLLENBURGER, MARTENS, and HASEL. It presents excerpts from books by 20 biblical theologians (19 Christians and one Jew—a breakdown that accurately represents the field). Most authors are represented by two excerpts: a broad programmatic statement followed by a treatment of a specific topic. A short but helpful essay situates the selections in the context of each author's larger project and the field as a whole. Three essays by the editors survey the history of the field prior to the 1930s, its major currents since then, and its future. A 1787 essay by Johann Gabler, often considered the father of Old Testament theology, appears in an appendix.

EICHRODT sets out to provide an exposition of Old Testament thinking as a structural unity. Thus he claims to eschew both traditional Christian dogmatic theology (which prescribes rather than describes) and the history of Israelite religion (which studies variations that manifest themselves over time).

Rather than tracing the development of diverse schools of thought—a project he views as worthwhile but distinct from biblical theology—he finds a thread that holds the Old Testament together, to wit, the theme of covenant. He organizes his book around three categories: God and the People, God and the World, and God and Man. Eichrodt endeavors to show that the New Testament is fully consonant with the Old, and that the Old leads specifically to the New. Thus, while allegedly rejecting dogmatic theology and allowing the texts to speak for themselves, Eichrodt arrives at a classically Christian anti-Jewish conclusion (most evident in his famous description of postbiblical Judaism as "torso-like"). In spite of the chasm between his goal (allowing texts to speak for themselves) and his achievement (imposing Pauline views on them), Eichrodt's attention to the theme of covenant and his detailed considerations of many texts render his book a classic, albeit a deeply problematic and essentially anti-Jewish one.

VON RAD finds the fundamental element of the Hebrew Bible's worldview in the idea of "salvation history" (i.e., Israel's acknowledgement of God's saving actions). For von Rad, at the center of biblical theology stands history—in the sense not of events as they occurred but as remembered and confessed by Israel. True to his descriptive project, he emphasizes that the Hebrew Bible does not present a single theology but contains distinct and often competing sets of teachings, most of which share some element of salvation history. He approaches his exposition historically, attending to differences among prophetic, priestly, Deuteronomic, and wisdom viewpoints. He emphasizes the development of traditions within the Hebrew Bible and the crucial role that reinterpretation plays in it. In light of this tradition of reinterpretation, the New Testament continues the same stream as the Old Testament, and indeed culminates it. This is true even—or especially—when the New revises the Old. That the same claim can be made of rabbinic interpretation does not occur to von Rad. He fails to address why the culmination of this development is found in the Christian revision rather than any other postbiblical tradition.

KNIERIM envisions his work as descriptive, though engaged. In this book (more a collection of essays than a unified monograph), he highlights crucial questions often underplayed by other biblical theologians: the nature of revelation, the relationship between creation and revelation, and themes of justice, hope, sin, and spirituality. One chapter attends in particular to the problem posed for modern thinkers by the Old Testament's zeal for the expulsion or extermination of the Canaanites. Knierim repudiates the tendency of Christian thinkers, including Old Testament theologians, to subjugate the Old Testament to the New. He prefers to evaluate the varied theologies he finds in the Old Testament according to what he views as the most central biblical idea. Unsurprisingly, the idea he finds most central (YHWH's universal dominion in justice and righteousness) reflects his late-20th-century politics more than the texts themselves. Knierim dislikes the notion of the election of Israel, which he somehow wants to argue is alien to the core of Old Testament belief. In the end he differs from his Christian predecessors in imposing on the texts a modern liberal ideology rather than one taken from the New Testament.

BARR (1980) offers an entirely different approach to Old Testament theology and presents a useful polemic. Against much English-language biblical theology of the 1950s and 1960s, Barr argues that the theology of the Bible does not rest on the history underlying the stories but in the stories themselves. Historiography in the modern sense is not really present in the Old Testament; even to the extent that parts of Scripture depict events that actually occurred, the recounting of those events in Scripture is more oriented toward the future than the past. Thus biblical theologians would do better to be concerned with close readings of biblical texts than with defending the historical accuracy of biblical texts. Barr also addresses the question of the Bible's authority from a point of view that is neither fundamentalist nor relativist. Among other topics he addresses are the perils of politicized theologies (e.g., liberation theology) and the nature of "biblical" fundamentalism. These essays reflect his well-founded skepticism toward canonical approaches to Scripture and biblical theology.

BARR (1993) displays the author's constructive side, with a genuine command of both theological discourse and biblical studies (many biblical theologians have little expertise in the former and willfully forget much of the latter). Barr argues that biblical theology need not be opposed to natural theology—the idea that humans have a natural awareness of God or a capacity for such awareness—regardless of any special time-bound revelation that comes from the Bible or the Christian Church. On the contrary, some biblical texts themselves express a type of natural theology. Barr finds evidence of natural theology in various New Testament texts, in intertestamental Jewish texts such as the Wisdom of Solomon, in psalms (especially those concerned with nature or wisdom), in Proverbs and Job, in prophecy, and (less convincingly) in biblical law. Barr's argument is a polemic against the great Protestant theologian Karl Barth, who maintained that biblical revelation is incompatible with natural theology. This book is as much about Barth as it is about the Bible, which is entirely appropriate for an avowedly theological undertaking. This work does not claim to eschew concerns of Christian theology; instead, it does not limit itself to describing ancient ideas but addresses modern philosophical issues; it treats texts from the New Testament along with those from the Old. Yet this book is one of the few biblical theologies that is not in some way offensive to Jewish readers, and its insights into ancient Hebrew texts are just as promising for the construction of modern Jewish thought as they are for Christian theology. The book also includes a lengthy discussion of the Torah's commandment of genocide against Canaanites; Barr's treatment is honest and probing, though inconclusive.

These fairly representative examples suggest the questions: can there be a Jewish or non-Christian biblical theology? Should there be one? Why isn't there one? LEVENSON (1993) addresses these issues with uncommon clarity and élan, especially in the essay "Why Jews Are Not Interested in Biblical Theology." Levenson shows that Jews' aversion to the field does not result solely from the tendency of biblical theologians to denigrate postbiblical Judaism (as in the case of Eichrodt) or to ignore its existence (as does von Rad). For Jews, at least since the rabbinic period, religious discourse involves debate, novel interpretations appended to older ones, and multivocal-

ity. The structural unity or "center" that biblical theologians have tended to seek interests Jews less than it interests certain Christians. Jews traditionally read the Bible as a collection of distinct though interconnected utterances, and thus Jewish interpretations of the Bible contain piecemeal analyses rather than extended syntheses. Finally, for many modern Jews, the Bible is of mainly historical interest, and thus the timeless quality of theological approaches is not appealing.

Clearly, a Jewish biblical theology would look quite different from a Christian one, but this does not mean that it can never exist. KAUFMANN's history of Israelite religion might be thought of as a sort of descriptive theology. By emphasizing a central biblical idea (monotheism and the rejection of mythology), its growth, and its permutations, Kaufmann presents a work in some ways comparable to those of Eichrodt and von Rad (on Kaufmann's relationship to biblical theology, see Greenberg). An explicit attempt appears in LEVENSON (1985), who outlines a theologically sensitive description of biblical beliefs (note the plural) from a Jewish vantage point. He focuses on two covenant ideologies in the Hebrew Bible: Sinai covenant entails law and mitsvot; Zion covenant entails divine promise. These ideas are not mutually exclusive, although they are often in conflict with one another. They work together in the Hebrew Bible, as in later Judaism (which upholds the one in halakhah and the other in messianism). Texts that reflect Sinai covenant often mention and indeed are grounded in the covenant of promise. For Levenson, a Jewish biblical theology should be open to biblical texts as they stand (not only as viewed by rabbinic exegetes), to historical study of ancient Near Eastern backgrounds, and to the legacy of classical Jewish Bible commentary. The last element is rarely evident in Levenson's book, but this readable and erudite volume represents an important first step.

GOSHEN-GOTTSTEIN criticizes the affectations of biblical theology, which is far closer to dogmatic theology than it admits. The rubrics used to describe biblical thought owe more to Christian theology than to the emphases of the ancient Hebrew documents at hand. A theology (or "structural phenomenology") that reflects the Tanakh (Hebrew Bible) itself would afford more attention to God's self-revelation and withdrawal, to peoplehood (as opposed to the individual's relation to God), and to the land. Goshen-Gottstein specifies these themes because, as he points out, they are mentioned repeatedly in the Hebrew Bible. At the same time, the influence of later Jewish thought (Kabbalah, Zionism) is manifest in his list. In this sense his model is a specifically Jewish one. Nonetheless, he insists that Tanakh theology should not merely attempt to interpret in light of Jewish sources. The field of Tanakh theology belongs not only to Jewish Studies but also to biblical studies. A specifically Jewish perspective will help all scholars notice what they had neglected, just as the Christian field of Old Testament theology has made genuine contributions to the study of Hebrew Scripture in spite of its tendentious nature.

While GREENBERG does not describe his collection as a biblical theology, his essays present profoundly learned descriptions of biblical teachings and their relationship to Jewish tradition in a manner sensitive to contemporary concerns. As Greenberg examines narrow issues or elucidates specific passages (thus showing himself a typically Jewish exegete), he consistently sheds light on much larger questions. Thus his classic study of capital punishment in biblical and Mesopotamian law codes reveals central values of biblical thinking that were developed more fully in rabbinic literature. Other essays cover biblical notions of faith, prayer, and idealism; the tensions between nationalism and universalism in the Bible and postbiblical tradition; and the relationships among rabbinic, medieval, and modern interpretations of the Bible. It is indicative that this rich contribution to Jewish biblical theology emerges from a collection of essays that does not intend to be one.

BENJAMIN D. SOMMER

See also Bible: Criticism; Bible: Hermeneutics; Bible: Introductions; Bible: Law; Bible: Medieval Exegesis; Bible: Reference Tools; Bible: Translations

Bible: Hermeneutics

Alter, Robert and Frank Kermode (editors), *The Literary Guide to the Bible*, Cambridge, Massachusetts: Belknap Press of Harvard University Press, and London: Collins, 1987

Barton, John, *Reading the Old Testament: Method in Biblical Study*, Philadelphia: Westminster, and London: Darton, Longman and Todd, 1984; 2nd edition, Louisville, Kentucky: Westminster John Knox, and London: Darton, Longman and Todd, 1996

Brenner, Athalya (editor), *The Feminist Companion to the Bible*, Sheffield, South Yorkshire: Sheffield Academic Press, 1993, 2nd series, 1998

Brenner, Athalya and Carole Fontaine (editors), *A Feminist Companion to Reading the Bible: Approaches, Methods, and Strategies*, Sheffield, South Yorkshire: Sheffield Academic Press, 1997

Exum, J. Cheryl and David J.A. Clines (editors), *The New Literary Criticism and the Hebrew Bible* (Journal for the Study of the Old Testament Supplement Series, 143), Valley Forge, Pennsylvania: Trinity Press International, and Sheffield, South Yorkshire: JSOT, 1993

Fishbane, Michael, *Biblical Interpretation in Ancient Israel*, New York: Oxford University Press, and Oxford: Clarendon, 1985; reprinted with corrections, 1988

Mulder, Martin Jan (editor), *Mikra: Text, Translation, Reading, and Interpretation of the Hebrew Bible in Ancient Judaism and Early Christianity*, Minneapolis, Minnesota: Fortress, 1988

Schottroff, Luise, Silvia Schroer, and Marie-Theres Wacker, *Feministische Exegese*, 1995; translated by Martin and Barbara Rumscheidt as *Feminist Interpretation: The Bible in Women's Perspective*, Minneapolis, Minnesota: Fortress, 1998

Hermeneutics denotes the formulation and application of specific principles of interpretation, and hermeneutical approaches to the study of the Hebrew Bible are nearly as numerous as are interpreters. What is more, the field of hermeneutics continues to grow by leaps and bounds. In fact, although one can locate with relative ease works on the Hebrew Bible that adopt or betray one or another hermeneutic, general surveys on principles of biblical exegesis have appeared with relative frequency only in recent times. Hermeneutics as a subject of inquiry is a colossal topic, and it has undergone especially immense changes in the postmodern age. Postmodern methodologies have entered the world of biblical scholarship only slowly and not without controversy. Nevertheless, postmodern hermeneutical approaches are widely recognized to have brought a great deal of insight into biblical scholarship. The following attempts to represent the gamut of interpretive strategies, from ancient to modern, as well as works that couple a critical and historically contextual self-awareness with an even-handed treatment of their subject.

ALTER and KERMODE bring together more than 20 internationally known scholars for a penetrating and exhaustive look at the literary aspects of the Hebrew Bible and New Testament. The treatment of the New Testament along with the Hebrew Bible is both uncommon and enormously important, providing further impetus for comparative work. The encyclopedic format of the book makes it a handy reference for the general reader, and its keenly perceptive insights and broad scope make it also useful to the specialist. The guide will particularly benefit those who have some knowledge of the paths of biblical scholarship, but the uninitiated reader, religious or not, has much to gain as well. The book turns away from the general atomizing tendencies that have directed biblical scholarship for more than a century, and it is representative of a developing current of scholarship that makes a holistic approach to the text central to initial inquiry.

BARTON's eminently readable work outlines the major interpretive strategies that have shaped the study of the Hebrew Bible in the last century, and it offers discussions of the strategies' wider implications. Beginning with the literary critical approach, Barton moves on to form criticism, redaction criticism, the canonical approach, structuralist criticism, and then to the more recent postmodern critical approaches such as reader-response criticism and deconstruction. Barton supplements his discussions both with select bibliographies and with demonstrations of how each interpretive method can be applied to the Book of Ecclesiastes. Thus, Barton's work serves as an excellent "hands-on" primer.

BRENNER and FONTAINE's collection serves as an introduction to the ten-volume series edited by Brenner. This text does not focus on single books of the Bible. Instead, it examines "the structural and systemic issues of method that are largely glossed over or merely implied in most non-feminist works on the Bible." Thus, this work combines broad theoretical essays on feminist approaches to literature and non-feminist works relevant to feminist methodology. As the editors note, their volume embraces two concurrent trends emerging in biblical scholarship: feminist critical consciousness and literary theory. Brenner and Fontaine seek to engage, to excite, and to provoke student readers. Their goal, which is successfully realized, is to cause readers to evaluate critically the biases and methodologies with which they approach the Bible. While a few of the essays contain some Hebrew, most are accessible to lay readers. The work achieves the editors' aim of "maximizing and championing *difference*."

BRENNER explores biblical books and narratives from a feminist perspective. The series has ten volumes: Song of Songs; Genesis; Ruth; Judges; Samuel and Kings; Exodus to Deuteronomy; Esther, Judith, and Susanna; the Latter Prophets; Wisdom Literature; and references to the Hebrew Bible in the New Testament. Each work contains several essays by scholars who represent a balanced variety of methodologies. While the works do contain some Hebrew, primarily to elucidate periodic philological issues, the series is readable and enlightening.

EXUM and CLINES collect a number of diverse essays by renowned scholars representing the most recent and adventurous theoretical approaches to the biblical text, which the editors place under the rubric "The New Literary Criticism." The editors seek to distance the methodologies found in the book from the older literary-critical school that foregrounded the reconstruction of biblical history. In this work, it is the textuality of biblical literature that takes center stage; therefore, the perspective might be considered poststructuralist. The essays embrace a wide range of interpretive strategies and include intertextuality, reader-response criticism, deconstruction, psychoanalytic criticism, materialist and political criticism, ideological criticism, and feminist approaches. The entire biblical corpus is covered, from legal injunctions and narratives in the Torah to the Prophets and Writings. The collection demonstrates the impact of postmodern approaches on the biblical text and suggests multicontextual approaches to Scripture.

MULDER's collection of scholarly essays provides the most comprehensive survey of the early history of biblical interpretation. The work offers uniformly as much depth as it does breadth. It opens with a discussion of writing in ancient Israel and early Judaism in which all contextual aspects are examined (e.g., the alphabet and scripts, literacy and the centrality of the book in early Judaism, scrolls and codices, the development of the Hebrew canon, and the transmission of the biblical text from the pre-Masoretic period to recent printed editions). The chapters that follow discuss reading the Bible in the ancient synagogue, the Septuagint, the Samaritan Targum of the Pentateuch, Jewish Aramaic translations, the Peshitta, Latin translations, the interpretation of Scripture at Qumran, the use of scripture in the Apocrypha and Pseudepigrapha, the works of Philo, and the translation technique of Josephus. Other chapters are devoted to authority and exegesis in rabbinic literature, the Samaritan tradition, Gnostic literature, the New Testament, and the church fathers. In addition, this work contains a cumulative bibliography and an index of sources, making it an invaluable (and large) resource. Mulder's collection will benefit especially students who have some acquaintance with the subjects examined.

FISHBANE demonstrates the presence of exegetical practices and trends within the Bible, thus shedding light on the hermeneutics (and their ideologues) that influenced the composition of the Hebrew Bible and its eventual canonization. Fishbane explores the role of biblical law as a factor in the emergence of exegesis, and he provides ample detailed evidence for legal exegesis of various kinds in the Bible, such as verbatim exegesis, periphrastic exegesis, and pseudo-citations in historical sources. The major part of his work is divided into four sections that discuss different types of exegesis found in the Bible: scribal comments and corrections, legal exegesis, aggadic exegesis, and mantological exegesis. The unit on aggadic exegesis considers the law as found in the prophets, as well as narratives, liturgical and theological formulae, and various typologies. The unit on mantological, or prophetic, exegesis is especially useful to biblical scholars because it successfully places the exegetical traditions of biblical Israel and early Jewish commentators in historical context by comparing the strategies of these early interpreters with modes of interpretation found elsewhere in the ancient Near East, especially in Mesopotamia. This achievement also has the effect of highlighting the unique and important contributions of Israelite genius.

SCHOTTROFF, SCHROER, and WACKER offer an excellent outline of feminist exegesis, with each author taking a section of the book to discuss a different aspect of feminist interpretation. Wacker discusses the historical, hermeneutical, and methodological foundations of feminist exegesis. She first adopts a historical perspective and then distinguishes various approaches and categories of feminist exegesis before discussing the question of canon. Schroer authors a feminist reconstruction of the history of Israel. Her approach is first diachronic and then synchronic, allowing for a full exploration of the following topics: "Who is Eve?"; female sexuality; women and violence; access of women to the cultic sphere; and goddesses in ancient Israel. Schottroff contributes a feminist reconstruction of the history of early Christianity. Together, these authors provide a thorough historical and methodological context for current feminist engagement of the Bible.

SCOTT B. NOEGEL

See also Bible: Criticism; Bible: Introductions; Bible: Law; Bible: Medieval Exegesis; Bible: Reference Tools; Bible: Theology; Bible: Translations

Bible: Criticism

Alter, R., *The Art of Biblical Poetry,* New York: Basic Books, 1985; Edinburgh: Clark, 1990

Bar-Efrat, S., *Narrative Art in the Bible* (Journal for the Study of the Old Testament Supplement Series, 70), Sheffield, South Yorkshire: Almond, 1989

Brin, Gershon, *Studies in Biblical Law: From the Hebrew Bible to the Dead Sea Scrolls,* Sheffield, South Yorkshire: JSOT, 1994

Clines, David J.A., *Interested Parties: The Ideology of Writers and Readers of the Hebrew Bible* (Journal for the Study of the Old Testament Supplement Series, 205), Sheffield, South Yorkshire: Sheffield Academic Press, 1995

Fishbane, Michael A., *The Garments of Torah: Essays in Biblical Hermeneutics* (Indiana Studies in Biblical Literature), Bloomington: Indiana University Press, 1989

Gunn, D.M. and D.N. Fewell, *Narrative in the Hebrew Bible* (Oxford Bible Series), Oxford and New York: Oxford University Press, 1993

Jacobs, Louis (compiler), *Jewish Biblical Exegesis* (Chain of Tradition Series, vol. 4), New York, Behrman House, 1973

Krentz, Edgar, *The Historical-Critical Method,* Philadelphia: Fortress, and London: S.P.C.K., 1975

McKenzie, Steven L. and Stephen R. Haynes (editors), *To Each Its Own Meaning: An Introduction to Biblical Criticisms and Their Application,* Louisville, Kentucky: Westminster/Knox, and London: Chapman, 1993

Weiss, M., *The Bible from Within: The Method of Total Interpretation,* Jerusalem: Magnes, 1984

Approaches to biblical criticism have changed dramatically over the years, and any study must take into account a number of different techniques and methods. An excellent survey of most of the methods in current use in academic biblical studies may be found in the collection of brief introductory essays edited by McKENZIE and HAYNES, which deals with some 13 disciplines ranging from tradition history and source criticism to social-scientific criticism, feminist criticism, and poststructuralism. Each essay is the work of a leading scholar known for a special interest in the field under consideration and is illustrated with clear examples from the Hebrew Bible as well as the New Testament.

Pre-critical approaches to the Hebrew Bible are dealt with superbly by JACOBS, whose book is an anthology of selected passages from some of the great Jewish biblical interpreters from the 11th century onward, including ibn Ezra, Rashi, Kimhi, and Nahmanides. His selection excludes both the earlier rabbinic legal interpreters and later historical-critical approaches, so questions of authorial intent, historical accuracy, and the like are not covered at all. Jacobs claims that the authors he has chosen share a common interest in the application of the Bible to everyday life, not interpretation in the abstract. A number of different examples are offered for each selected author, who is introduced with a short biographical note, and these passages are commented on astutely by Jacobs, who regularly points out in particular the dual emphasis in these commentators on *derash,* "the meaning read into the text," and *peshat,* "the plain meaning of the text," as well as alerting his readers to each writer's unique style and characteristics.

FISHBANE's set of essays presents his thinking on Jewish hermeneutics and biblical criticism. He is particularly interested in the uniqueness of scripture, which he sees as "an ontologically unique literature" written principally "for the purpose of envisaging God" and by definition requiring reapplication and reinterpretation for each new generation. This he sees as the essential task of biblical criticism. In the first of three main sections of the book, he investigates the origins and intentions of biblical study, considering innerbiblical and extrabiblical exegesis (i.e., the internal reapplication of biblical truth and instruction to address new circumstances later in Israel's history as well as the interpretation of the whole corpus by later exegetes) and wonders how these pragmatic reapplications have transformed the doctrine and the understanding of Scripture.

Fishbane then proceeds in his second section to take two examples of this transformation in operation, as occasioned by the process of two dramatic changes in Israel—the development of ancient Yahwism in the face of conflict with pagan Canaanite religion and the growth of that ancient faith into rabbinic Judaism. He concludes by looking at a number of different examples of "making the pastness of texts present to us and part of our ongoing lives," considering excerpts from Martin Buber and Franz Rosenzweig and demonstrating how these two authors, among others, help their audiences read Scripture for its "inner power."

The mainstream historical-critical approach is dealt with well by KRENTZ, whose short introduction is intended to provide nonspecialist readers with a brief survey of the method. Krentz argues that the goal of the historical-critical method has never been to undermine the biblical traditions, but rather to gain an understanding of the facts of history: "[Historians are] concerned with more than the corpus of fact . . . [they want] to illuminate the past, to understand the events, and to interpret them." He also stresses what he sees as the neutrality of the method, arguing, "The task of the historian is not judgement, but description and explanation." This fails, however, to take into account the many value judgements the historical-critical method itself makes. Most of Krentz's examples are taken from the Christian New Testament, and the method he contends for is rapidly going out of use in more progressive academic circles. His book, nonetheless, remains probably the most useful short introduction to this discipline, which has shaped biblical studies in the 19th and 20th centuries.

ALTER was among the earliest critics to espouse a purely literary approach to the biblical text, rejecting the traditional methodologies. His work on poetry was written to supplement an earlier volume on biblical narrative, and it rapidly became one of the classic demonstrations of the immense literary skill exemplified in the Bible. The book strikes an excellent balance between theoretical chapters and practical analysis of the biblical text. After chapters on parallelism, the development of narrative elements in biblical poetry, and what Alter calls "structures of intensification,"—the manner in which "the artifice of form . . . becomes a particular way of conceiving relations and defining linkages, sequence and hierarchies in the reality to which the poet addresses himself,"—Alter turns to the biblical text and examines the use of these poetic devices in the books of Job, Psalms, Proverbs, Song of Songs, and also in the prophetic books, where he focuses particularly on Isaiah. A fascinating final chapter considers the "life" of the tradition of biblical poetry, surveying the history of its interpretation over the centuries and its reinterpretation in later poetry and hymnody.

Since so much of the Hebrew Bible consists of narrative, narratological criticism also has been of great importance. A classic introduction to this kind of study is that of BAR-EFRAT, who demonstrates well how interpreters may take account of textual features such as the narrator (overt or covert, omniscient or possessing limited knowledge), characters (how they are shaped and revealed, what factors distinguish major from minor characters, the difference between a "flat" and a fully rounded characterization), developments in the plot, and movements in time and space. Particularly useful are his chapter on narrative style, which considers stylistic and compositional devices, and the final chapter, where he demonstrates the insights narrative criticism has to offer in a lengthy exposition of the story of Amnon and Tamar.

WEISS covers much the same material but enters into a far more detailed analysis of the methods and approaches of this kind of biblical criticism (Weiss states plainly that his intention is "methodological rather than exegetical"). However, he proceeds to introduce the techniques of literary criticism by showing them in use on the biblical text, dealing first with the interpretation of contentious words within the text, then slowly broadening his view to take into account phrases, small-scale images, sentences, literary units, and finally the literary work as a whole. The practical outworking of Weiss's method is then demonstrated in a supplementary analysis of the story of Naboth's vineyard (I Kings 21), contributed by Yair Zakovitch. Seven appendixes also pick up on issues concerning some of the varied texts discussed in passing as part of the methodological essay.

GUNN and FEWELL, too, focus on literary perspectives on biblical narrative, but from a slightly more popular orientation and with excellent examples. Each methodological chapter is supplemented by a substantial literary reading of well-selected, important passages from throughout the canon, illustrating the technique featured in the theory section. While their chapter on characterization is particularly clear and detailed and deals at length with the special case of the characterization of God in biblical narrative, their major contribution—and the significant difference between their work and that of Weiss and Bar-Efrat—is their addition of material on two contemporary approaches: reader-response theory, which allows readers a significant role in the determination of the meaning of a text; and ideological criticism, which presumes that "particular readings imply certain values, stated and unstated" and investigates how the reader's own ideological presuppositions interact with those of the text, asking "what values are at work when we and others read and champion readings?" The book concludes with an excellent and extensive annotated bibliography.

One of the leading exponents of ideological criticism of the Hebrew Bible is CLINES, whose *Interested Parties* is a collection of some of his best work in this field over recent years, specifically dealing with "the impact of various ideologies upon the formation of the Hebrew Bible . . . by its writers and upon its reception by its readers." In an excellent introductory chapter that illustrates how anyone who comes to read the Bible does so as an "interested party," having a vested interest in the results of their reading, Clines questions the value and indeed the possibility of truly objective reading. This theme is taken up in the essays "Metacommentating Amos" and "Psalm 2 and the Moabite Liberation Front," which both examine how quick most commentators are to accept unquestioningly the ideology of the biblical text, even when that ideology is clearly problematic. A number of the other essays concentrate on asserting just how problematic biblical ideologies can be, subjecting Job, the Song of Songs, and Psalm 24 to reader-response and deconstructive critiques, which seek to demonstrate that sometimes the Bible can be a

rather dangerous book, despite its venerated status. Two further essays examine the characterization of God in the Pentateuch, suggesting that his behavior is not always what one might expect, and a "masculinist" critique of the presentation of King David, which illustrates as much about ancient Israelite attitudes to manhood as it tells of the character of Israel's greatest king.

BRIN's book deals with some of the problems that surround biblical law and its critical interpretation, first addressing some of the general difficulties posed by legal materials—for example, why do some laws detail at length the punishments described for breaking them, when others seem to have no sanctions attached? How did certain legal forms develop? To what extent is there a bias toward the poor in biblical law? He then investigates the whole issue of the legal status of the firstborn in ancient Israel, considering various angles such as the differing requirements for humans, clean and unclean animals, the inheritance laws, and the issue of royal succession. Of particular interest to many will be Brin's chapter on the legal traditions of the Dead Sea Scrolls, which shows how the authors of these traditions tried to disguise their authorship "behind a veil of pseudo-biblical composition" and sought to present their own legislation as mainstream, even Mosaic, and not sectarian.

ANDREW DAVIES

See also Bible: Hermeneutics; Bible: Introductions; Bible: Law; Bible: Medieval Exegesis; Bible: Reference Tools; Bible: Theology; Bible: Translations

Bible: Medieval Exegesis

Banitt, Menahem, *Rashi: Interpreter of the Biblical Letter*, Tel Aviv: Chaim Rosenberg School of Jewish Studies, Tel Aviv University, 1985

Baron, Salo W., "Restudy of the Bible," in his *A Social and Religious History of the Jews*, vol. 6, New York: Columbia University Press, 1952

Beattie, Derek Robert George, *Jewish Exegesis of the Book of Ruth* (Journal for the Study of the Old Testament Supplement Series, 2), Sheffield, South Yorkshire: Department of Biblical Studies, University of Sheffield, 1977

Eisen, Robert, *Gersonides on Providence, Covenant, and the Chosen People: A Study in Medieval Jewish Philosophy and Biblical Commentary* (SUNY Series in Jewish Philosophy), Albany: State University of New York Press, 1995

Gelles, Benjamin, *Peshat and Derash in the Exegesis of Rashi* (Études sur le judaïsme médiéval, 9), Leiden: Brill, 1981

Greenstein, Edward, "Medieval Bible Commentaries," in *Back to the Sources: Reading the Classic Jewish Texts*, edited by Barry W. Holtz, New York: Summit, 1984

Jacobs, Louis (compiler), *Jewish Biblical Exegesis* (Chain of Tradition, vol. 4), New York: Behrman House, 1973

Lockshin, Martin I. (editor and translator), *Rabbi Samuel ben Meir's Commentary on Genesis: An Annotated Translation* (Jewish Studies, vol. 5), Lewiston, New York: Mellen, 1989

Pearl, Chaim, *Rashi* (Jewish Thinkers), New York: Grove, 1988

Simon, Uriel, *Arba' gishot le-Sefer Tehilim,* 1982; translated as *Four Approaches to the Book of Psalms: From Saadiah Gaon to Abraham Ibn Ezra* (SUNY Series in Judaica), Albany: State University of New York Press, 1991

Talmage, Frank, *David Kimhi: The Man and the Commentaries* (Harvard Judaic Monographs, 1), Cambridge, Massachusetts: Harvard University Press, 1975

Talmage, Frank, "Apples of Gold: The Inner Meaning of Sacred Texts in Medieval Judaism," in *Jewish Spirituality: From the Bible to the Middle Ages* (World Spirituality, vol. 13), edited by Arthur Green, London: Routledge and Kegan Paul, and New York: Crossroad, 1986; reprinted in his *Apples of Gold in Settings of Silver: Studies in Medieval Jewish Exegesis and Polemics* (Papers in Mediaeval Studies), edited by Barry Dov Walfish, Toronto: Pontifical Institute of Mediaeval Studies, 1999

Walfish, Barry Dov, *Esther in Medieval Garb: Jewish Interpretation of the Book of Esther in the Middle Ages* (SUNY Series in Judaica), Albany: State University of New York Press, 1993

The medieval period of Jewish biblical exegesis began in the tenth century with Saadiah Gaon and the Karaites of Jerusalem and ended around the turn of the 16th century. As Frank Talmage has noted, medieval exegesis operated on many levels, according to the time, the place, and the predilection of the individual writer. In the later Middle Ages, some exegetes developed a four-fold system that was dubbed *pardes,* the acronym alluding to the four different exegetical approaches to the biblical text that were in vogue at the time. *Peshat* refers to the plain or contextual meaning, *remez* to the philosophical, *derash* to the homiletic, and *sod* to the mystical. During the rabbinic period and for much of the geonic period, the midrashic-homiletic approach to the Bible held sway, but in the geonic period, Jews began to study the Bible in new ways, including adopting a rationalist approach to exegesis that was influenced by the rationalist elements in Islamic culture. The story of this transformation is told in BARON.

GREENSTEIN is a lively and engaging introduction to medieval exegesis. He analyzes in detail a passage from Rashi as well as briefer passages from Rashbam and Abraham ibn Ezra. At the end of his article, he constructs an imaginary dialogue among these exegetes as they discuss the meaning of a verse in Genesis. The author provides a useful guide to further reading. Readers interested in a general survey of medieval exegesis will also be interested in JACOBS, which makes available extensive passages from the commentaries of most of the major exegetes and supplies brief introductions and extensive commentary. TALMAGE (1986) is a masterly study of the use of allegory in medieval exegesis that focuses on both philosophical and mystical texts. The analysis elucidates the prin-

ciple of freedom of interpretation of the biblical text that has characterized Judaism throughout the ages.

In addition to general discussions, readers can consult more specialized studies about particular commentators or about specific works of exegesis. SIMON presents an exhaustive detailed analysis of four radically different approaches to the Book of Psalms. It is the only extensive treatment in English of the exegetes of the Arabic period (Saadiah Gaon and the Karaites Yefet ben 'Ali and Salmon ben Yeruham), and the author also analyzes the commentary of Moses Gikatilla, an important but neglected Spanish *peshat* exegete. The bulk of the book is devoted to the exegesis of ibn Ezra, the most outstanding representative of the Spanish school of exegesis, which favored a rationalist approach to the Bible based on sound philological and grammatical foundations.

After Saadiah, few medieval philosophers wrote extensive biblical commentaries. The most notable exception is Rabbi Levi ben Gershom (Gersonides, Ralbag, 1280–1344), arguably the most important medieval Jewish philosopher after Maimonides. His commentaries span much of the Bible and are extremely prolix. They also contain a wealth of philosophical material that has never been subjected to scholarly analysis. EISEN's book attempts to begin to fill this gap by analyzing the development of Gersonides' philosophical ideas on providence, covenant, and chosenness in his biblical commentaries. This is an important, groundbreaking work that gives much insight into a major body of philosophical exegesis.

Rashi is undoubtedly the most widely read and studied medieval exegete. For an introduction to his exegesis, the chapter in PEARL is adequate and accessible. GELLES is devoted to elucidating a classic question in Rashi studies—the relationship between *peshat* and *derash* elements in his commentaries. Gelles provides a useful summary of the issues, and his assessment that Rashi had "a vision of Peshat yet unrealized" is probably the volume's most important insight.

The book by BANITT is a most unusual and original study of Rashi, but it is not for the novice. The author is a scholar of the Romance languages, and he argues that Rashi based much of his exegesis on a French vernacular tradition that had developed from the Greek and Latin (Vulgate) translations. According to Banitt, this tradition adhered to a literal interpretation of the Bible, based on the Greek versions, and therefore Rashi's *le'azim* (vernacular glosses) were not merely intended as additional comments for the French-speaking reader; instead, his exegesis was meant to correct or improve the already existing French translation. Banitt also tries to demonstrate with extensive examples and dazzling erudition that many of Rashi's comments were based on his belief in paronomasia (especially similarities in the sound of words in different languages). In some cases, the author may stretch his points, but many of his examples are quite convincing and deserving of further consideration.

Samuel ben Meir (Rashbam) was the most important representative of the Northern French School of *peshat* exegesis, which developed in the generation after Rashi. Rashbam's influence was relatively short-lived, spanning the 12th through the mid-13th centuries, and the best treatment of his commentaries available in English is found in LOCKSHIN. Another significant medieval commentator was David Kimhi, the principal representative of the Provençal school of exegesis, which combined philosophical sophistication with the Spanish approach of *peshat* interpretation based on grammar and philology. TALMAGE's (1975) chapter on "The Way of Peshat" is a definitive analysis of Kimhi's exegetical methodology.

BEATTIE is a pioneering introduction to the medieval exegesis of the Book of Ruth. The volume provides translations and analyses of several commentaries (including Yefet, Rashi, ibn Ezra, and Isaiah of Trani [erroneously labeled Pseudo-Kimhi]), but it suffers from the author's tendency to judge the value of the commentaries by the extent to which they address the prevalent concerns of modern biblical studies. This approach was common among earlier generations of scholars but has been generally replaced by a more sympathetic approach that endeavors to understand medieval exegetes and their work in their historical and cultural contexts.

WALFISH is the most ambitious study of the exegesis of a single biblical book. His work surveys and analyzes more than 25 Hebrew commentaries on Esther from 1100 to 1500, many of which are found only in manuscript and have never been studied before. This study makes a determined effort to place each exegete in his historical and cultural context. The first section of the book, which discusses the literary sources available to the exegete and reviews various exegetical methodologies, is a useful introduction to the medieval commentators, while the bio-bibliographical survey at the back provides additional information on the exegetes and their work. The second half of the book discusses the exegesis of Esther in its historical context, dealing with concerns such as antisemitism, Jewish-Gentile relations, and attitudes to the monarchy that are reflected in the commentaries.

BARRY D. WALFISH

See also Bible: Criticism; Bible: Hermeneutics; Bible: Introductions; Bible: Law; Bible: Reference Tools; Bible: Theology; Bible: Translations

Bible: Law

Daube, David, *Collected Works of David Daube*, vol. 1: *Talmudic Law* (Studies in Comparative Legal History, Robbins Collection), edited by Calum M. Carmichael, Berkeley: University of California Press, 1992

Finkelstein, J.J., *The Ox That Gored* (Transactions of the American Philosophical Society, vol. 71, part 2), Philadelphia: American Philosophical Society, 1981

Fishbane, Michael, *Biblical Interpretation in Ancient Israel*, New York: Oxford University Press, and Oxford: Clarendon, 1985

Greenberg, Moshe, *Studies in the Bible and Jewish Thought* (JPS Scholar of Distinction Series), Philadelphia: Jewish Publication Society, 1995

Hecht, Neil S. et al. (editors), *An Introduction to the History and Sources of Jewish Law* (Institute of Jewish Law, Boston University School of Law, no. 22), New York: Oxford University Press, and Oxford: Clarendon, 1996

Jackson, Bernard S., *Essays in Jewish and Comparative Legal History* (Studies in Judaism in Late Antiquity, vol. 10), Leiden: Brill, 1975

Kaufmann, Yehezkel, *Toldot ha-emunah ha-Yisre'elit mi-yeme kedem 'ad sof bayit sheni*, 1937–1956; translated and abridged by Moshe Greenberg from volume 8, book 4 as *The Religion of Israel: From Its Beginnings to the Babylonian Exile*, Chicago: University of Chicago Press, 1960

Levinson, Bernard M., *Deuteronomy and the Hermeneutics of Legal Innovation*, New York: Oxford University Press, 1997

Weinfeld, Moshe, *Deuteronomy and the Deuteronomic School*, Oxford: Clarendon, 1972; Winona Lake, Indiana: Eisenbrauns, 1992

Wellhausen, Julius, *Prolegomena to the History of Ancient Israel*, Edinburgh: Black, 1885; New York: Meridian, 1957

The study of biblical law is central to the emergence of modern biblical scholarship. A historical approach to the formation of the Pentateuch requires an analysis of how the content, assumptions, and sequence of composition of the three different law collections of the Bible relate to one another. The three law collections in question are the Covenant Code of Exodus 21–23, Deuteronomy 12–26, and the Holiness Code of Leviticus 17–26. This brief essay will focus on the development of the major models and methodologies used by scholars to investigate this material, emphasizing issues that touch upon the study of Judaism and framing the discussion along historical lines.

WELLHAUSEN offers a brilliantly argued example of a classical model of biblical scholarship known as the documentary hypothesis. He compares the legal collections of the Pentateuch both with one another and with the narrative works of the Deuteronomistic History (Joshua, Judges, Samuel, and Kings) and Chronicles. He accepts the hypothesis of prior scholars that Deuteronomy's call for the restriction of all sacrificial worship of God to one exclusive sanctuary (Deuteronomy 12) logically suggests that this legal corpus was closely tied to Josiah's reform of 612 B.C.E. (2 Kings 22–23) and was probably composed around that time. Viewed from that perspective, Wellhausen contends, Deuteronomy's requirements appear to have been a departure from tradition and not simply a reform in which the nation returned to older norms. He draws this conclusion because the requirement for cultic centralization in Deuteronomy contradicts the sanction commanding the worship of God at multiple altar sites evident both in law (e.g., Exodus 20:24) and in such narratives as Genesis 12, 1 Samuel 1, and 1 Kings 18. He therefore places the date of the Covenant Code prior to that of Deuteronomy and maintains that the priestly laws of the Holiness Code assumed centralization and therefore came after Deuteronomy, appearing in the postexilic period (fifth century B.C.E.). The author's model is rooted in the philosophy of German romanticism and consequently assumes that spontaneous religious spirit is more creative and meaningful than a religion that consciously employs literary activity and the intellect. The movement to law and to text is therefore viewed as the ossification of creative originality. This model thus entails an ill-conceived hierarchy that stigmatizes cultic law and pos-texilic Judaism as representing a decline from the previous heights of Israelite religion achieved in the age of the prophets. However, extensive literary remains from the ancient Near East, which were already beginning to emerge during the time that Wellhausen wrote, refute the author's conclusions on this subject, for this evidence demonstrates the antiquity of literacy, law, and cultic regulations in the region. Nonetheless, Wellhausen's theory still provides an indispensable, intellectually engaging analysis of the Pentateuch, one that is sensitive to how texts work and attentive to the ways in which the laws relate to and engage one another.

KAUFMANN challenges the classical model of the documentary hypothesis, although he does not reject it altogether, as some have done. He disputes the notion that the priestly literature (and the Holiness Code) represent a postexilic lapse, arguing to the contrary that the priestly literature preceded Deuteronomy and belonged to an early stage of the religion. The author denies any literary contact between the various legal strata of the Bible and also denies the dependence of Israelite law upon earlier Near Eastern sources, explaining all points of apparent similarity in terms of an alleged common tradition, out of which each body of legal literature arose as independent crystallizations. Although that approach has not proven tenable, Kaufmann helps open up a nonreductive approach to cultic and ritual law that saw that law as anchored in the ancient Near East. Equally important, his focus on the Torah as a body of literature expressing a coherent set of values that differ from those of prophetic literature provides a new approach to the classical documentary hypothesis that shows how prophecy often presupposes Pentateuchal norms while also making ethical law the dominant component of the covenant.

Accepting Kaufmann's position regarding the antiquity of the priestly literature (a theory that remains controversial), WEINFELD's important work on Deuteronomy has broad implications for the study of biblical law. He argues that the drafters of Deuteronomy were conversant with Hittite and, especially, contemporaneous neo-Assyrian state treaties. This theory has helped to establish interest in the phenomenon of direct or indirect contact between the creators of biblical and Near Eastern law, thereby encouraging an appreciation of the learned nature of Israelite legal writers. Weinfeld proposes that the writers of Deuteronomy were professional scribes attached to Josiah's court, and he posits that they drew on a wide range of biblical literature, both wisdom and law, to create their texts. Weinfeld's approach countered the then-dominant form-critical approach to Deuteronomy, which traced the text's origins to the oral preaching of the rural Levites. More important, his study provides an implicit challenge to the antitextual bias with which the discipline of form criticism was founded.

In a prolific career spanning many decades, DAUBE approached biblical law as a jurist trained in Roman legal history. He uses this expertise to show how the growth and structure of the biblical text can reflect developments in legal thought, thereby accounting for otherwise problematic constructions. For example, he argues that biblical legislators, like Roman lawmakers, would often add amendments or later reflections on a particular issue to the end of the original legal text as a coda. Daube also contends that the classical rabbinic techniques of legal reasoning (the hermeneutical "measures") were borrowed from the rhetorical conventions of Greco-Roman jurisprudence. With his capacity for interdisciplinary work, Daube has made important contributions to the study of Near Eastern, biblical, Jewish, and Roman legal history.

Most scholars have directed their attention toward reconstructing the correct sequence and development of the biblical legal collections in relation to one another and to the narrative strands of the Bible. In comparison to that valuable literary-historical enterprise, GREENBERG's essay remains an important attempt to articulate the meaning and significance of biblical law on its own terms. Focusing on the Covenant Code as the earliest legal source in the Bible, he contrasts its set of values with those of such great ancient Near Eastern legal collections as Hammurabi's Code (1752 B.C.E.), which it resembles both in form and in content. Two principles of sanction appear in each legal collection: either *talion* ("an eye for an eye") or financial compensation (a fine) may be imposed as penalties for wrongdoing. However, these principles do not operate identically within the two cultures. In the Babylonian context, *talion* may be imposed either for property crimes (such as theft) or for bodily injury; similarly, homicide is punishable either by financial compensation or by death, depending on the class of the victim. In the biblical context, by contrast, property crime is never punishable by execution of the thief, and bodily injury is never redressed in financial terms. The significance of this distinction is that the biblical legislator views *property* and *person* as separate legal and conceptual categories. Financial compensation marks property loss as finite and replaceable; *talion* marks the person as infinite in value and irreplaceable, which is to say, unique. The categorical distinction between the two categories is absent in cuneiform law.

Greenberg's argument initiated an ongoing debate about how to understand the biblical and cuneiform legal collections. (For the best edition of the latter, see Martha T. Roth, *Collections from Mesopotamia and Asia Minor* [1997].) JACKSON argues that it is invalid to make generalizations about cultural value on the basis of biblical law as codified in the Pentateuch. There is no evidence that those laws had operative force: at a number of points, other literary genres of the Bible, such as narrative and wisdom, presuppose sanctions and norms of redress inconsistent with the formal statements of the laws. Scholars such as Raymond Westbrook (in his essay "Biblical Law" in HECHT), working as jurists, have attempted to reconstruct the system of civil and criminal law that might have operated in ancient Israel. In a brilliant, posthumously published monograph, FINKELSTEIN raises the conceptual and methodological stakes in this debate. He contends that the conception of human value in modern Western culture corresponds to and derives from biblical law. This distinguished Assyriologist argues that ostensibly minute differences of sequence or legal sanction between biblical and Near Eastern law reflect the attempt of the drafter of biblical law to distinguish between person and property. In a richly suggestive analysis, he argues that the drafter's focus upon the category of *person* is apparent in the organization of the Covenant Code and even helps explain topical shifts in the biblical text that have otherwise been viewed as intrusive or secondary. Biblical law thus represents something similar to a philosophical argument that conceptualizes the autonomy and the sovereignty of the person. Finkelstein then follows the history of related ideas into the legal systems of antiquity, medieval Europe, and contemporary U.S. law.

This debate concerning whether Pentateuchal law reflects broader cultural norms and whether it had judicial force has inspired many avenues of research. Assyriologists have established that Hammurabi's Code was regarded as a literary classic for more than a millenium from the time of its composition, but it is never once cited in any of the thousands of actual court dockets that survive as reflections of actual legal practice in the ancient Near East; nor do actual penalties conform to its stipulations. On the basis of that sharp discontinuity between the literary formulation and the operation of law, many scholars regard the cuneiform legal collections as something closer to moral literature than positive law. That literary model may also be appropriate for biblical law, at least until the reconstruction after the Babylonian Exile when, under Persian rule, the postexilic community sought to reestablish itself by using the Pentateuch as a type of constitution.

FISHBANE, building on the insights of a number of other scholars, provides a new model for analyzing the composition and growth of biblical literature. He demonstrates the extent to which Israelite scribes and authors were constrained to comment upon, explicate, annotate, revise, refer to, and embellish earlier texts that occupied a privileged place in their culture. In doing so, Fishbane shows that the dynamic of tradition and interpretation is not only a postbiblical phenomenon but also occurs within biblical texts themselves. The continuities of literary form and exegetical technique, which reach from cuneiform literature through biblical texts to the Dead Sea Scrolls, imply that the exegetical techniques of rabbinic literature presuppose an immanent tradition of textual study and do not belatedly derive from the Greco-Roman culture of late antiquity. The book also establishes a continuity of form and scribal technique that spans the various literary genres of the Bible.

The standard view of Deuteronomy as one of the four documentary sources of the Pentateuch, dated to the late seventh century B.C.E., fails to explain either the book's similarities to or divergences from the Covenant Code. LEVINSON seeks to address these issues by arguing that the legal corpus reflects the struggle of its authors to introduce a radically new system of religious law that was viewed as essential for the nation's survival at the time of the neo-Assyrian crisis. Seeking to defend this transformation of prevailing norms, the reformers turned to earlier laws such as those in the Covenant Code, even when they disagreed with those laws, and revised the edicts in such as way as to lend authority to the reformers' new understanding of divine will. Passages in the legal corpus long viewed as redundant or displaced represent the attempt by Deuteronomy's authors to sanction their legal vision before the legacy of the past. This method of attributing an innovation to a tradition that is actually inconsistent with the reform represents a technique of authorship evident elsewhere in biblical and postbiblical literature, and understanding this process of revision helps open up a broader view of Israelite and Jewish religious history.

BERNARD M. LEVINSON

See also Bible: Criticism; Bible: Hermeneutics; Bible: Introductions; Bible: Medieval Exegesis; Bible: Reference Tools; Bible: Theology; Bible: Translations; Halakhah

Bibliographies *see* Reference Works

Bioethics

Abraham, A.S., *Medical Halachah for Everyone,* New York: Feldheim, 1980, 2nd edition, 1984

Bleich, J.D., *Judaism and Healing,* New York: Ktav, 1981

Bleich, J.D. and Fred Rosner (editors), *Jewish Bioethics,* New York: Hebrew Publishing, 1979

Feinstein, Moses, *Responsa of Rav Moshe Feinstein,* vol. 1: *Care of the Critically Ill,* translated and annotated by M.D. Tendler, Hoboken, New Jersey: Ktav, 1996

Jakobovits, Immanuel, *Jewish Medical Ethics,* New York: Bloch, 1959

Preuss, Julius, *Julius Preuss' Biblical and Talmudic Medicine,* translated and edited by Fred Rosner, Brooklyn, New York: Hebrew Publishing, 1978

Rosner, Fred, *Modern Medicine and Jewish Law,* New York: Yeshiva University, Department of Special Publications, 1972

Rosner, Fred, *Modern Medicine and Jewish Ethics,* Hoboken, New Jersey: Ktav, 1986, 2nd revised edition, 1991

Medicine's phenomenal growth in the second half of the 20th century was matched by a burgeoning interest in and development of medical ethics. The articulation of medical ethics in the authentic Jewish tradition has been rooted in teachings and texts that were produced over 3,000 years, as medical ethicists have probed these foundations to identify appropriate models for contemporary medical quandaries.

JAKOBOVITS remains the undisputed "father" of modern Jewish medical ethics. While focusing on the entire panorama of Jewish bioethics, the author develops this subject against the background of the principal teachings of other world religions. In this respect, the book remains unique. Jakobovits traces the evolution of Jewish attitudes from ancient to modern times, and he marshals a comprehensive bibliography documenting these developments. By stressing the moral and general ethical dimensions of Jewish teachings in addition to the minutiae of rabbinic opinion, he presents the topic in a modern light that emphasizes the unmistakable contemporary ramifications.

ROSNER (1972, 1991) is one of the most prolific English-language reviewers and compilers of Jewish bioethics. A full-time academic physician, his several books present brief chapters covering the entire gamut of the intersection of Judaism and medicine. His collaborative effort with J.D. Bleich, BLEICH and ROSNER, is also quite notable.

PREUSS provides a gold-mine of *materia medica* found in the ancient Jewish sources, including the Talmud and its contemporaneous works. While this text was not designed to discuss the ethical or moral questions of medicine, Preuss should be consulted by the serious student because he provides a historical dimension that illuminates the talmudic underpinnings of Jewish attitudes toward science and medicine.

Among the chief exponents of halakhic medical ethics is BLEICH, a professor of Talmud and Law at Yeshiva University. He is attentive to detail, his sources are comprehensive, and he aptly expresses the nuances of rabbinic thinking in contemporary legal terms. Often forceful in its views, Bleich's book is indispensable to the student of Jewish medical ethics and its application. Bleich takes a traditional view, arguing that halakhic criteria do not allow Jews to consider brain-death the equivalent to death.

As a biologist and rabbi, Tendler brings a desirable measure of expertise to his ethical analysis in his translation of FEINSTEIN, written by his late father-in-law. Rabbi Feinstein was regarded as the foremost halakhic authority of his generation. Tendler's familial associations undoubtedly afforded him a unique opportunity to observe and contribute to the development of halakhic attitudes to current problems. Always confident of his views, Tendler is known, in particular, for embracing the view that there is halakhic basis for equating mortality with brain-stem death, and he uses Rabbi Feinstein's writings to support this view. The Israeli Chief Rabbinate has adopted this position, thereby allowing Israel's leading hospitals to adopted standards similar to those used in U.S. medical facilities.

ABRAHAM belongs to a growing class of highly trained rabbi-physicians. His book, written for the layperson, is an excellent example of the growing number of texts on topics related to practical Jewish living.

JULIAN JAKOBOVITS

See also Birth Control and Abortion; Euthanasia; Reproductive Technologies

Birth Control and Abortion

Bleich, J. David, "Abortion in Halakhic Literature," in his *Contemporary Halakhic Problems* (Library of Jewish Law and Ethics), New York: Ktav, 1977

Feldman, David M., *Birth Control in Jewish Law: Marital Relations, Contraception, and Abortion as Set Forth in the Classic Texts of Jewish Law*, New York: New York University Press, 1968; as *Marital Relations, Birth Control, and Abortion in Jewish Law*, New York: Schocken, 1974

Jakobovits, Immanuel, "Controlling the Generation of Life," in his *Jewish Medical Ethics: A Comparative and Historical Study of the Jewish Religious Attitude to Medicine and Its Practice*, New York: Bloch, 1959

Rosner, Fred, "Contraception, Abortion and Pregnancy Reduction," in his *Modern Medicine and Jewish Ethics*, New York: Yeshiva University Press, 1986, 2nd edition, 1991

The biblical commandment of procreation is deemed technically fulfilled with the siring of two children. Another biblical precept, however, requires propagation of the race. Contraception, therefore, without specific medical or psychiatric indication, is not condoned in Judaism even after one already has two children. Several methods of contraception are discussed in the Bible and Talmud, including coitus interruptus (condemned by all the codes of Jewish law), the safe period, twisting movements following intercourse, an oral contraceptive potion (precursor of the "pill"), and an absorbent tampon during intercourse (precursor of the diaphragm).

The Jewish legal and moral attitude toward abortion based upon biblical, talmudic, and rabbinic sources including the responsa literature is discussed in detail by Feldman, Bleich, Jakobovits, and Rosner. They conclude that most rabbis permit and even mandate abortion when the health or life of the mother is threatened. Some authorities are stringent and require the mother's life to be in danger, however remote that danger, whereas others permit abortion for a less serious threat to the mother's health. Such dangers to maternal health may include deafness, cancer, pain, or psychiatric illness. The psychiatric indication for abortion must be certified by competent medical opinion or by previous experiences of mental illness in the mother, such as a postpartum nervous breakdown. If the mother becomes pregnant while nursing a child and the pregnancy changes her milk, thereby endangering the suckling's life, abortion is permitted.

The enormous rabbinic responsa literature dealing with contraception is presented in detail by FELDMAN in his now classic book. The author examines the rabbinic legal tradition that underlies Jewish values with respect to marriage, sex, and procreation, and he provides comparative reference to Christian tradition. He musters classical and contemporary sources not accessible to most English readers and collates these sources in a sequential pattern. The texts are allowed to speak for themselves, and the interpretations offered by Feldman are consistent with the process of legal and literary development in the codes of Jewish law, commentaries, and responsa. Feldman's presentation of halakhic (Jewish legal) material is totally adequate to address the "modern" societal themes of the sexual revolution, feminism, and population control.

Feldman finds the most lenient or permissive view regarding contraception to be that of 16th-century rabbi Solomon Luria, who allows the wife to apply a tampon before intercourse if conception and pregnancy would prove dangerous. Many subsequent writers support this view. On the other hand, there is a school of nonpermissivists who do not allow any impediment to natural intercourse. When pregnancy would be hazardous, the pessary or diaphragm is allowed by numerous authorities because it does not interfere with the normal coital act. This is not the case with the condom, which constitutes an improper interference and is strictly prohibited. Chemical spermicides and douches are other contraceptive methods that leave the sex act alone and thus are permitted by many responsa writers, although only in the case of danger to the mother from resulting pregnancy. As to whether spermicides or diaphragms are preferable, Feldman notes that this is a matter of debate. As for intrauterine contraceptive devices, recent medical evidence indicates that these prevent conception by inhibiting proper implantation of the fertilized ovum in the wall of the uterus. If this is so, then their abortifacient action would prohibit their use, as their action is akin to abortion.

In summary, Feldman's survey makes it clear that Jewish authorities prohibit contraception by any method when no medical or psychiatric threat to the mother or child exists. The duty of procreation, which is primarily a commandment to men, coupled with the conjugal rights of the wife in Jewish law, militates against the use of the condom, coitus interruptus, or abstinence under any circumstances. When pregnancy would be hazardous and when the use of birth control is given rabbinic sanction, a hierarchy of acceptability emerges from the talmudic and rabbinic sources. Most acceptable are contraceptive means that interfere least with the natural sexual act and the full mobility of the sperm and its natural course. According to Feldman, "Oral contraception by pill enjoys preferred status as the least objectionable method of birth control."

In his comparative and historical study of the Jewish religious attitude to medicine and its practice, JAKOBOVITS traces the development of Jewish and other religious views on contraception and abortion, among other medico-moral problems, from antiquity to the present day. His book, recognized as a classic and the pioneering work in its field, is profusely annotated with references to the original sources in religious, medical, legal, and historical literature. His special gift is for focusing authentic Jewish teachings on the complexities of modern medical practice.

BLEICH's approach to abortion is to present the variety of opinions and the multiplicity of voices, debates, and controversies so characteristic of the halakhic process. He endeavors to include as many opinions as he can among rabbinic authorities whose credentials are widely recognized and who are fully committed to halakhah. When he offers his own opinion, he does so authoritatively and with intellectual integrity.

ROSNER organizes a mass of halakhic material into concise and systematic presentations of medical-ethical subjects, including abortion and contraception. Like Feldman and Jakobovits, he discusses the attitudes of other religions to these subjects before presenting the Jewish view.

FRED ROSNER

See also Bioethics; Repoductive Technologies

Black-Jewish Relations in the United States

Berman, Paul (editor), *Blacks and Jews: Alliances and Arguments,* New York: Delacorte, 1994

Diner, Hasia R., *In the Almost Promised Land: American Jews and Blacks, l915–1935* (Contributions in American History, no. 59), Westport, Connecticut: Greenwood Press, 1977; Baltimore, Maryland, and London: Johns Hopkins University Press, 1995

Friedman, Murray, *What Went Wrong?: The Creation and Collapse of the Black–Jewish Alliance,* New York: Free Press, l995

Kaufman, Jonathan, *Broken Alliance: The Turbulent Times between Blacks and Jews in America,* New York: Scribner, l988

Salzman, Jack and Cornel West (editors), *Struggles in the Promised Land: Towards a History of Black–Jewish Relations in the United States,* New York: Oxford University Press, l997

The manner in which U.S. Jews and blacks are thought of and treated by the majority culture reveals a good deal about the gap between democratic ideals and American practice; how Jews and blacks regard each other is an important part of this complicated tale. Until the early 20th century, there was only minimal contact between the two groups. Nevertheless, many elements of the discrimination directed toward blacks could be, and often were, directed toward Jews. As blacks in ever-larger numbers moved north, Jews joined them in a common struggle for civil rights. The contribution of those Jews who helped to found the National Association for the Advancement of Colored People (NAACP) in 1909 is a matter of public record, as is the impact of Jewish philanthropists (particularly Julius Rosenwald) who gave millions of dollars to further black education, and the dedicated Jewish trade unionists who tried to unionize black workers.

But these longtime political allies did not share neighborhoods or come to know each other as individuals. In the late 1960s, a series of confrontations—everything from calls for black power to an insistence that black parents control their children's education—soon escalated into ugly instances of black antisemitism. As a result, some argue that the old "marriage" of blacks and Jews may have outlived its usefulness; others insist that reconciliation is both necessary and possible. Meanwhile, wedge issues such as affirmative action continue to drive the two constituencies apart even as calls for dialogue are repeated by well-meaning members of both groups.

DINER surveys the crucial years (1915–1935) during which the political alliance between blacks and Jews was formed. Chronicling the early years of the NAACP, she makes it clear just how much the fledgling organization depended on the money, dedication, and hard work of Jewish-Americans such as Joel and Arthur Spingarn, Louis Marshall, Jacob Schiff, Herbert Lehman, Herbert Seligman, and Jacob Billikopf. They served as dependable fund-raisers, high-ranking officers, and full participants in the organization's legal, political, and public educational efforts. At the same time, however, some blacks (W.E.B. DuBois most prominently) were ambivalent about this Jewish involvement. On one hand, these skeptics welcomed Jews' well-meaning support and especially their dollars; on the other hand, they resented what they viewed as the Jews' intrusiveness and overly aggressive personal styles. Diner's scholarly account remains the standard work on a subject that often generates more heat than carefully considered argumentation.

FRIEDMAN looks at black–Jewish relationships in terms of how and why the relationship seems to have turned sour. Black antisemitism—whether it appears in Nation of Islam publications and hate-mongering speeches by its officers, rallies on behalf of black control of the teachers (and increasingly the curriculum) in predominantly black urban schools, or the rioting in Crown Heights that set blacks against hasidic Jews—clearly worries Jewish liberals. Rather than editorialize, however, Friedman seeks to explain why the divergent paths that Jews and blacks have taken in the last three decades of the 20th century ended in political alliances of a very different sort than those that might have arisen from what appeared, at least on the surface, to be an abundance of common cause.

KAUFMAN, a reporter for the Boston Globe, was among the first to feel the sharply differing perceptions that often divide black reporters from their white counterparts. After Minister Louis Farrakhan gave a talk to the staff of the Globe, shouting matches erupted, and it did not take long before Jews were singled out for special abuse. How, black reporters asked, could Jews claim to be political allies but be so opposed to quotas and critical of affirmative action? How, Jewish reporters responded, could blacks be so blind to the impact of the Holocaust and brush off Jews' feelings of anxiety and vulnerability in the face of any antisemitic slur?

Kaufman was well aware of the psychic bonds that once linked Jews to blacks and blacks to Jews. James Baldwin wrote: "The Negro identifies himself almost wholly with the Jew. The more devout Negro considers that he is a Jew, in bondage to a hard taskmaster and waiting for a Moses to lead him out of Egypt"; and Kaufman celebrated a life's worth of Passover seders that made it clear that Jews were once slaves and thus uniquely positioned to empathize with blacks in their cries for social justice.

To better understand how and why the old alliance between blacks and Jews broke down, Kaufman reports "through a set of six serial biographies—the stories of five individuals and one family (three black and three Jewish) whose lives reflect the ebbs and flows, the triumphs and losses of black–Jewish relations over the past 30 years." His case studies on Paul Parks, Jack Greenberg, Rhody McCoy, Bernie and Roz Ebstein, Martin Peretz, and Donna Brazile serve as reminders that individual human beings, rather than competing ideologies and abstractions, are indispensable to understanding a very complicated social phenomenon.

SALZMAN and WEST have created an anthology meant to collect the most informed opinions of both blacks and Jews. Readers will learn from Thomas Cripps how blacks and Jews became "antagonist allies" in Hollywood, and from Jerome A. Chanes and Theodore M. Shaw why blacks and Jews see affirmative action policies quite differently. The collection of 21 essays ends with personal reflections on black–Jewish relations by Michael Walzer and Cornel West.

BERMAN's anthology is equally distinguished, including among its 19 black and Jewish contributors James Baldwin ("Negroes Are Anti-Semitic Because They're Anti-White" [1967]), Cynthia Ozick ("Literary Blacks and Jews"), and Julius Lester ("The Lives People Live"). Of special note, the collection reprints Norman Podhoretz's controversial 1963 essay, "My Negro Problem—and Ours," perhaps the article most prophetic of the smoldering black–Jewish hostility that would erupt only a few years later.

SANFORD PINSKER

Body

Boyarin, Daniel, *Carnal Israel: Reading Sex in Talmudic Culture* (The New Historicism, 25), Berkeley: University of California Press, 1993

Boyarin, Daniel, *Unheroic Conduct: The Rise of Heterosexuality and the Invention of the Jewish Man,* Berkeley: University of California Press, 1997

Eilberg-Schwartz, Howard, *People of the Body: Jews and Judaism from an Embodied Perspective* (SUNY Series, the Body in Culture, History, and Religion), Albany: State University of New York Press, 1992

Gilman, Sander, *The Jew's Body,* New York: Routledge, 1991

Kleeblatt, Norman, *Too Jewish?: Challenging Traditional Identities,* New Brunswick, New Jersey: Rutgers University Press, 1996

Critical theories about the Jewish body have emerged out of feminist theories of the female body that seek to account for gender-based stereotypes that make irrational claims about the nature of women's bodies and women's essential natures. Since the 1980s, scholars have applied the insights of these psychoanalytic and/or Marxist theorists to the history of antisemitic stereotyping of Jewish bodies. According to these scholars, the body is not defined simply as the physical body of flesh; it is also an imaginary cultural construction. This image of the body is more significant to the majority of observers than the biological body, and it shapes their perceptions of the physical entity. The power of fantasies, linking human identity to culturally mediated perceptions of the body, accounts for our discomfort when we are forced to see the body outside of its accustomed frames of reference. Thus, mutilation, deformity, dismemberment, autopsy, and the decomposition of corpses are unsettling precisely because they force us to relinquish cherished assumptions about identity and personhood. The theorists considered in this essay further contend that cultural constructions of the body must necessarily be shared by all members of the culture in which the constructions develop. Therefore, members of groups delimited by (generally) imaginary physical differences come, themselves, to identify with such differences, making them key parts of their own self-understanding. For this reason, studies of the stereotypes about the Jewish body incorporate both non-Jewish and Jewish ideas about such putatively

Jewish characteristics as large noses, male effeminacy, strong body odor, deformed feet, and abnormal genitals.

BOYARIN (1993) situates Jewish thinking about the body and sexuality within the context of the late Hellenistic cultures from which both rabbinic Judaism and Christianity emerged. He argues that the physical asceticism of early Christians, on the one hand, and the Jewish valorization of sexuality, on the other, were just two possible solutions to the set of cultural problems faced by the emergent faiths, and he posits that both solutions have had unfortunate consequences. Christians responded to socially divisive discourses of race, sex, and class by espousing a spiritual universalism in which all believers were one in the spirit. But this position left no room for desirable regional and ethnic differences, proposing in their place a universal Christian subject who was, by default, Roman, white, and male. Jews responded to exile and Christian polemic by valorizing genealogy and marital sexuality. But the logic of ethnic particularism and the increased emphasis on regulating women's sexuality eventually led to a loss of female autonomy and restrictions on the lives of Jewish women. Although Boyarin sometimes digresses into theoretical arguments of interest only to historians of the feminist movement, the book as a whole is very readable, and it is replete with fascinating quotations from a wide range of rabbinic discussions on the Jewish body.

BOYARIN (1997) documents how particular characteristics—softness, intellectualism, gentleness, abstraction, and anti-heroism—became associated with male Jews in early-modern Western Europe. The author contends that the Jewish "sissy" was a deliberate response to the anti-intellectual physicality of Christian romanticism. Jewish men, he argues, aspired to an ideal of masculinity that had evolved as a specifically Jewish alternative to Christian notions of manhood. If the ideal Christian man was broad-shouldered, strong, tanned and hard, then the ideal Jewish male body was lean, weak, pale, and soft. This argument is supported by a number of provocative illustrations.

EILBERG-SCHWARTZ collects articles on various aspects of the Jewish body that figure in antisemitic stereotypes and serve as markers of Jewish self-understanding. A helpful overview by the editor is followed by individual studies of sexuality in early Judaism; rabbinic sexuality and obesity; menstruation, pregnancy and childbirth; ascetic practices in 16th-century Kabbalah; God's body; physiognomy in medieval Jewish folk tales; antisemitic stereotypes about Jewish feet and noses; sexual ideology and practices among early Zionists; Jewish American "princesses"; and Jewish lesbians.

GILMAN is a particularly clear exposition of how the body is constructed by cultures in ways that seem arbitrary and strange to cultural outsiders. The author analyzes the work of 19th-century doctors, journalists, and anthropologists who attempted to describe the scientific differences between Jews and non-Jews, finding Jews pathologically inferior to non-Jews in many ways. These "experts" on racial difference claimed, *inter alia*, that Jewish noses and feet were malformed, that Jews were smelly and dirty, that Jewish men were effeminate and prone to hysteria, and that Jewish boys were sometimes born already circumcised. In the cultural logic of turn-of-the-century racial theory, Jewish men occupied an intermediate category between the truly male and the truly female. Gilman suggests

that modern antisemitism may have arisen as a fearful response to this imaginary emasculated Jewish man.

KLEEBLATT is a generously illustrated collection of essays primarily focused on artistic explorations of U.S. Jewish identity. Gilman's essay on Jewish bodies considers how the racist stereotyping of European antisemitism has shaped modern Jewish identities. Anthropologist Riv-Ellen Prell surveys 50 years of images of Jewish womanhood, contextualizing the stereotype of the Jewish American princess that has come to embody Jewish affluence and consumption. Maurice Berger asks why Jewish television writers and producers of the 1950s portrayed Jewish men in unflattering ways reminiscent of earlier antisemitic stereotyping. This anthology is the most accessible of the books listed here and would be a good starting point for anyone unfamiliar with cultural theory.

WILLIS JOHNSON

Books and Libraries

Alexander, Philip S. and Alexander Samely (editors), *Artefact and Text: The Re-creation of Jewish Literature in Medieval Hebrew Manuscripts: Proceedings of a Conference Held in the University of Manchester 28–30 April 1992*, Manchester, Greater Manchester: John Rylands University Library of Manchester, 1994

Brisman, Shimeon, *A History and Guide to Judaic Bibliography* (His Jewish Research Literature, vol. 1), Cincinnati, Ohio: Hebrew Union College Press, 1977

Gold, Leonard S. (editor), *A Sign and a Witness: 2,000 Years of Hebrew Books and Illuminated Manuscripts* (Studies in Jewish History), New York: New York Public Library/Oxford University Press, 1988

Gutmann, Joseph, *Hebrew Manuscript Painting*, New York: Braziller, 1978; London: Chatto and Windus, 1979

Hill, Brad S. (editor), *Miscellanea hebraica bibliographica*, London: British Library, 1995

Karp, Abraham J., *From the Ends of the Earth: Judaic Treasures of the Library of Congress: [Essays]*, Washington, D.C.: Library of Congress, 1991

Metzger, Thérèse and Mendel Metzger, *Jewish Life in the Middle Ages: Illuminated Hebrew Manuscripts of the Thirteenth to the Sixteenth Centuries*, New York: Alpine Fine Arts Collection, 1982

Narkiss, Bezalel, *Hebrew Illuminated Manuscripts*, New York: Macmillan, 1969

Offenberg, A.K. et al. (editors), *Bibliotheca Rosenthaliana: Treasures of Jewish Booklore, Marking the 200th Anniversary of the Birth of Leeser Rosenthal, 1794–1994*, Amsterdam: Amsterdam University Press, 1994, 2nd edition, 1996

Posner, Raphael and Israel Ta-Shema (editors), *The Hebrew Book: An Historical Survey*, New York: Amiel, 1975

Richler, Binyamin, *Guide to Hebrew Manuscript Collections* (Publications of the Israel Academy of Sciences and Humanities), Jerusalem: Israel Academy of Sciences and Humanities, 1994

Sed-Rajna, Gabrielle, *The Hebrew Bible in Medieval Illuminated Manuscripts*, New York: Rizzoli, 1987

As Posner and Ta-Shema write in their introduction, "Not for nothing has the Jewish people been known as the 'people of the book,'" for in addition to the centrality of the Torah, there are "thousands of books that are signposts on the long journey of the Jewish people." Numerous books and articles have appeared on the subject of books and libraries, generally consisting of a discussion of highlights from medieval Hebrew manuscript production and/or a chronological or geographical survey of the history of Hebrew printing. The works discussed here are selected for their fresh approach, their clear presentation, or their importance to the development of the field. All of the cited works contain long bibliographies with abundant references to other works, many of which would have been worthy of selection as well.

BRISMAN's introduction is an interesting combination of detailed bibliographical references and readable sections on the history of the field and its practitioners. He discusses all important general studies and most specialized catalogs of Hebrew and non-Hebrew Jewish books; he provides ample information on the lives and motifs of dozens of Hebrew bibliographers, both Jewish and non-Jewish; and he almost overloads his reader with statistical information on such technical details as the cataloging formats used in the various catalogs or the numbers of entries appearing in different bibliographies. This volume will be appreciated primarily by those who already have some familiarity with the huge body of literature on Jewish books. The interested lay person and bibliographical beginner may be best advised to limit themselves to reading the biographical sections and to use the work as a reliable tool of reference, rather than as a first introduction to Hebrew bibliography, in order to avoid being overwhelmed by the sheer amount of (admittedly impressive and reliable) detail.

POSNER and TA-SHEMA have brought together, edited, corrected, and augmented the many hundreds of articles about books that appear in the groundbreaking *Encyclopaedia Judaica* (Jerusalem, 1972). One of the great achievements of the editors is that they have succeeded in presenting these scattered texts in a clear, systematic manner. After a general introduction on writing and the importance of scrolls within Jewish tradition, the articles explore manuscripts, especially from the medieval era; discuss the science of the Hebrew book; and pay particular attention to printing. Chapters are devoted to major centers of Hebrew printing, Hebrew printers, the artistry of the book, and the "Love of the Book." This last chapter examines Hebrew book titles, approbations, colophons, censorship, the book trade, and other related topics. Two final chapters treat the "basic books" of Judaism (i.e., the Bible, Mishnah, and Talmud, Prayer Books, Mishneh Torah, Zohar, and Kabbalah, and the Haggadah) and Jewish libraries.

RICHLER's guide is the result of his decades of experience discovering, identifying, and describing Hebrew manuscripts in the Institute of Microfilmed Hebrew Manuscripts at the Jewish National and University Library in Jerusalem. Richler's main goal "is to enable the reader—novice and expert alike—to locate the manuscripts referred to in the scholarly literature and to provide him or her with the basic bibliographical

information concerning those manuscripts." The work contains information on libraries and their catalogs; public and private collections that have been dispersed or have changed ownership over the years; booksellers' and auction catalogs (an often forgotten source of information on Hebrew manuscripts); compilers of catalogs; abbreviations; geographical names; and cognomens (by which he means such designations as "the Golden Haggadah" or "the Amsterdam Mahzor.")

ALEXANDER and SAMELY deserve full credit for focusing scholarly attention on the important role that was played by Hebrew manuscripts in the literary transmission of classic Hebrew texts. Their proceedings are greatly augmented by an extensive introduction and may serve as a starting point for any serious student of Jewish literary transmission. Contributions include those of Israel Ta-Shema on "The 'Open Book' in Medieval Hebrew Literature: The Problem of Authorized Editions," Gabrielle Sed-Rajna on "The Image in the Text: Methodological Aspects of the Analysis of Illustrations and Their Relation to the Text," a groundbreaking article by Malachi Beit-Arié on "Transmission of Texts by Scribes and Copyists: Unconscious and Critical Interferences," Emile G.L. Schrijver on "Some Light on the Amsterdam and London Manuscripts of Isaac ben Moses of Vienna's 'Or Zarua,'" and Stefan C. Reif on "Codicological Aspects of Jewish Liturgical History." Appropriate indexes conclude this valuable work.

Among the many works on medieval Hebrew manuscript illumination, those by NARKISS (later published in a revised Hebrew edition, Jerusalem, 1984) and GUTMANN are generally considered to be classics. Both works provide fine typologies of representative selections of illuminated Hebrew manuscripts, with rich and attractive illustrations. Both are accompanied by reliable introductory chapters, and Narkiss's Hebrew edition contains numerous references to primary and secondary sources (many of which were written or edited by Narkiss himself).

Two other works on medieval Hebrew manuscript illumination employ entirely different approaches from that used in Gutmann or Narkiss. METZGER and METZGER start off with the question: "Was Jewish illumination sufficiently rich and diversified to afford a picture of Jewish life in the Middle Ages?" Although the work has been criticized by some scholars, the authors have managed to select hundreds of images from the considerable body of manuscripts available from the Middle Ages that illustrate such fascinating topics as the medieval Jew and the universe, the Jewish Quarter, the house, costume, the professional life of the Jewish community and its place in the medieval city, family life, and religious life.

SED-RAJNA's book, by contrast, finds its strength in its limitation. The author concentrates on diverse images of major biblical figures, such as Adam and Eve, Noah, the Patriarchs, Moses and Aaron, and David and Solomon, providing a surprisingly vivid comparative perspective on these characters.

GOLD is the catalog of a very successful 1988 exhibition at the New York Public Library that brought together a superb selection of medieval illuminated Hebrew manuscripts and early printed books. Apart from descriptions of all the books that were exhibited, the catalog contains articles by leading scholars in the field, including Malachi Beit-Arié, who explains the production process of medieval manuscripts; Evelyn M.

Cohen, who contributes a lucid article on medieval Hebrew manuscript illumination; and Michael W. Grunberger, who sheds new light on the publishing of Hebrew books in 19th-century Eastern Europe. Sharon Liberman Mintz's "Selected Bibliography of the Hebrew Book" is very useful.

KARP's book celebrates the 75th anniversary of the Hebraic Section at the Library of Congress. His approach is very literary, emphasizing the contents of the books or their role in Jewish cultural history more than their printing history or their visual splendor. As such, the work provides a highly inspired introduction to the fascinating world of Jewish literature in its widest possible sense. Worthy of particular mention is Karp's strong emphasis on books, journals, and graphic material pertaining to the history of U.S. Jewry, including biographical sketches and discussions of the works of such famous figures as Mordecai Manuel Noah, Isaac Leeser, and Leonard Bernstein.

The volume edited by OFFENBERG et al. celebrates the bicentennial of the birth of Leeser Rosenthal (1794–1868), the founder of the Bibliotheca Rosenthaliana in Amsterdam, the largest Jewish library on the European continent. The book aims to offer a "cross-section of the wealth of material at the Bibliotheca Rosenthaliana," and 54 of the most interesting items from the holdings of the library are reproduced and accompanied by short essays, usually written by renowned experts. The works are presented in chronological order, beginning with the 13th-century Mahzor from Esslingen, southern Germany, and concluding with a bibliophile's edition of poetry by the 20th-century Dutch-Jewish poet Saul van Messel (d. 1993; pseudonym of Jaap Meijer). Contributions include those of Menahem Schmelzer on the well-known medieval Ashkenazi legend of Rabbi Amnon, which first appeared in a 13th-century manuscript of Isaac ben Moses's *Or Zarua*; Malachi Beit-Arié on a mid-15th-century manuscript of a philosophical work by Averroës; Herbert Zafren on Elijah Levita's 1542 *Shemot Devarim*, printed at Isny, Bavaria; Richard Popkin on Spinoza; Yosef Kaplan, on the Sabbatean movement in Amsterdam; and Yosef Hayim Yerushalmi on Isaac Fernando Cardoso's *Las Excelencias de los Hebreos* (1679). Because of its rich and variegated content, the work can serve as an introduction to the diversity of Jewish booklore.

HILL's special issue of the *British Library Journal* contains nine articles by different authors. All of the contributions bear the mark of Hill's interests, either through their subject matter or through their editorial involvement. Especially useful contributions are Alan D. Crown's "Further Notes on Samaritan Typography"; Hill's "A Catalogue of Hebrew Printers" (the most important article in the volume); Hill and Leonard Prager's "Yiddish Manuscripts in the British Library"; and Hill's augmented version of Fred N. Reiner's account of the Shapira affair, in which the British Museum was offered a supposedly ancient Hebrew scroll by the Jerusalem book dealer Moses Wilhelm Shapira. The greatest merit of Hill's volume lies in its bibliographical wealth. Every article provides numerous footnotes, which often bring to light books and articles located in the most unexpected of publications that would otherwise have gone entirely unnoticed.

EMILE G.L. SCHRIJVER

See also Manuscripts, Hebrew

Buber, Martin 1878–1965

Austrian-born Israeli philosopher and theologian, Zionist thinker and leader

Aschheim, Steven, *Brothers and Strangers: The East European Jew in German and German Jewish Consciousness, 1800–1923*, Madison: University of Wisconsin Press, 1982

Buber, Martin, *Briefwechsel aus sieben Jahrzehnten*, 1972; translated by Richard Winston, Clara Winston, and Harry Zohn as *The Letters of Martin Buber: A Life of Dialogue*, edited by Nahum Glatzer and Paul Mendes-Flohr, New York: Schocken, 1991

Friedman, Maurice, *Martin Buber: The Life of Dialogue*, Chicago: University of Chicago Press, and London: Routledge and Kegan Paul, 1955; 3rd edition, Chicago: University of Chicago Press, 1976

Friedman, Maurice, *Martin Buber's Life and Work*, 3 vols., New York: Dutton, 1981–1983; London: Search, 1981–1988

Friedman, Maurice, *Encounter on the Narrow Ridge: A Life of Martin Buber*, New York: Paragon House, 1991

Horwitz, Rivka, *Buber's Way to "I and Thou": The Development of Martin Buber's Thought and His "Religion as Presence" Lectures*, Philadelphia: Jewish Publication Society, 1988

Katz, Steven, *Post-Holocaust Dialogues: Critical Studies in Modern Jewish Thought*, New York: New York University Press, 1983

Kepnes, Steven, *The Text as Thou: Martin Buber's Dialogical Hermeneutics and Narrative Theology*, Bloomington: Indiana University Press, 1992

Levenson, Jon Douglas, "The Hermeneutical Defense of Martin Buber," *Modern Judaism*, 11, 1991

Mendes-Flohr, Paul, *From Mysticism to Dialogue: Martin Buber's Transformation of German Social Thought* (Culture of Jewish Modernity), Detroit, Michigan: Wayne State University Press, 1989

Moore, Donald, *Martin Buber: Prophet of Religious Secularism*, Philadelphia: Jewish Publication Society, 1974; 2nd edition, New York: Fordham University Press, 1996

Schaeder, Grete, *The Hebrew Humanism of Martin Buber*, Detroit, Michigan: Wayne State University Press, 1973

Schmidt, Gilya Gerda, *Martin Buber's Formative Years: From German Culture to Jewish Renewal, 1897–1909* (Judaic Studies Series), Tuscaloosa: University of Alabama Press, 1995

Scholem, Gershom, *The Messianic Idea in Judaism and Other Essays on Jewish Spirituality*, New York: Schocken, and London: Allen and Unwin, 1971

Scholem, Gershom, "Martin Buber's Conception of Judaism," in *On Jews and Judaism in Crisis: Selected Essays*, edited by Werner J. Dannhauser, New York: Schocken, 1976

Silberstein, Laurence, *Martin Buber's Social and Religious Thought: Alienation and the Quest for Meaning* (Reappraisals in Jewish Social and Intellectual History), New York: New York University Press, 1989

Vermès, Pamela, *Buber on God and the Perfect Man*, Missoula, Montana: Scholars Press, 1980; London: Littman Library of Jewish Civilization, 1994

Vermès, Pamela, *Buber*, New York: Grove, and London: Halban, 1988

Martin Mordechai Buber has had a spectacularly wide influence on liberal Judaism in the 20th century, and his most famous book, *I and Thou*, remains a widely assigned work on modern religious thought. *I and Thou* marks a major turning point in Buber's intellectual development: all that comes after this work is filtered through the lens of the dialogic philosophy that it expounds. Buber made his mark in several areas. He was Western Zionism's most dramatic spokesman and most effective publicist in the years before World War I. His popularization of Hasidism for Western audiences took a generally despised movement and argued that it exemplified the best in Jewish spiritual striving. Buber's Bible translation, begun in 1925 with the aid of Franz Rosenzweig, certainly stands as a lasting monument to how German culture spurred Jewish creativity.

Maurice Friedman, a disciple, defender, and interpreter of Buber, presents the reader with an appropriate starting point. FRIEDMAN (1955) was an early foray in to Buber interpretation that launched many other (often more critical) appraisals. FRIEDMAN (1981–1983) should remain the standard for the foreseeable future, although further research prompted the author to write FRIEDMAN (1991), which incorporates much new data. Friedman presents Buber as a modern hero and a religious existentialist whose Jewishness in no way obscures his importance as a spokesperson for humanity in an inhumane age.

MOORE, written by a student of Friedman's and a Jesuit, embraces Buber as both an advocate and critic of any modern religion. Although the young Buber contrasted the creative impulse of religiosity with the stultifying forces of institutional religion, Moore focuses on the implicit necessity of religion in Buber's world-view. The key to Moore's view is expressed in the book's subtitle: Buber emerges as the modern prophet of religious secularism par excellence. Emphasizing Buber's engagement with society as a German Jew in the 1930s and as an Israeli in the 1940s–1950s, Moore argues that Buber considered grounding in a particular religious tradition as the basis for dialogue along the entire spectrum (politics, economics, etc.) of human existence.

SCHAEDER, the other major biographer of Buber, has the virtue of focusing more than is usual on Buber's mature Zionism, his dialogic vision of Jewish-Arab relations, and the conciliatory politics that inevitably resulted. "Hebrew Humanism," a term that Buber himself coined in opposition to the chauvinism of European nationalism, gives Schaeder her interpretative key. A succinct sketch by Schaeder can also be found in BUBER.

MENDES-FLOHR, like many other scholars, has focused particularly on Buber's early years. Mendes-Flohr considers the political anarchist and pacifist Gustav Landauer a major influence on the early Buber and argues that sociological studies such as Ferdinand Tonnies' *Society and Culture* have been underestimated as influences on Buber's development. For Mendes-Flohr, Buber's early thought was obsessed with the relationship of the individual and the community and this was not merely a post–*I and Thou* development. World War I emerges in this interpretation as a decisive move away from a romantic nationalism typical of the *fin de siècle*.

SCHMIDT has a good ear for romantic strains in early Buber that place him in the company of Friedrich Nietzsche, Carl Jung, and others. Schmidt states her thesis plainly: "Buber's interests were in German culture, in Jewish renewal and in the renewal of humanity, in that order." Schmidt stresses that Buber's early forays ("apprenticeships," in her words) were all preparatory to a synthesis he wished to bestow on German Jewry and that he was in the process of realizing before the Nazi takeover.

HORWITZ remains a critical reconstruction of the eight years between Buber's first drafting of his masterpiece and its appearance in 1923. Horwitz is particularly interesting when he points to Buber's lecture series "Religion as Presence," delivered at the Frankfurt Lehrhaus in 1922, as a breakthrough to the final form of *I and Thou*. Also interesting, although debatable, is her claim that Franz Rosenzweig's critique of Buber's use of language accelerated significantly Buber's break from key terms of an earlier *Erlebnismystik* and toward a mature articulation of his dialogic philosophy.

VERMES (1980) thoroughly explains the central terms in Buber's dialogic philosophy. VERMES (1988) is a reliable introduction to the man and his thought. Following Walter Kaufman's introduction to Buber's *I and Thou*, Vermes emphasizes the Jewish doctrine of repentance *(teshuvah)* as a central idea in Buber's book. Implicitly in Vermes and explicitly in Kaufman, this makes a case for *I and Thou* as a fundamentally Jewish book, Buber's influence on the Christian world notwithstanding.

ASCHHEIM deals with the *Ostjuden* (East European Jews) in the German Jewish mind and devotes an important chapter to Buber's key role in popularizing Hasidism. Beginning in 1906 with the appearance of the *Tales of Rabbi Nachman*, Buber published dozens of works on Hasidism, including several widely read translations of hasidic tales and several interpretive essays. Buber's representation of Hasidism probably has been his most debated legacy. The issue here, however, is not whether Buber played a huge role in bringing Hasidism to general attention (everyone concedes he did) but whether he did so responsibly.

SCHOLEM (1971 and 1976), Jewish mysticism's most important academic interpreter, accused Buber in a number of articles of presenting Hasidism in such a way as to bring it into close conformity with Buber's own affirmative, situational, existentialist, sacramentalizing view of life. Scholem scorned Buber for failing to admit his role as an interpreter of Hasidism and not just as a translator and presenter.

KATZ extends and sharpens Scholem's critique of Buber, noting that Buber underplayed the kabbalistic elements in the hasidic tales, the Jewishness of the terminology, and the positive content of the hasidic epiphany. This critique emerges from Katz's view of Buber's epistemology. Following Kant's approach to human autonomy as the ultimate deciding factor in religion and Kierkegaard's emphasis on the subjective nature of truth, Buber (in Katz's opinion) denudes the Jewish concept of revelation of any positive content. Additionally, this view compromises the communally binding force of tradition. What experience, Katz asks, binds the revelation of God to Moses on Sinai and the revelations experienced by the contemporary Jew?

SILBERSTEIN defends Buber's right as a creative interpreter of the biblical and hasidic texts. For Silberstein, as for Friedman, Moore, and Schaeder, Buber possesses one of the most original and important religious voices of the 20th century. Like these three scholars, Silberstein emphasizes Buber's continued attachment to the worldly role of religion, epitomized for Silberstein in Buber's post–1938 championing of Hebrew humanism. Silberstein's is also the first full-length work to discuss Buber's debt to critical theories of language, a debt elucidated by Kepnes.

KEPNES focuses on Buber's debt to the German tradition in the critical theory of language. The tradition of *verstehen,* perhaps rendered most simply as "deep, intuitive understanding," best explains the thrust of Buber's romantic hermeneutic. Wilhelm Dilthey and Hans-Georg Gadamer, and Max Horkheimer and Jürgen Habermas are presented here as Buber's decisive influences and intellectual fellow travelers. Yet Buber did not follow these figures slavishly. Kepnes shows that the dialogic and dynamic reading of the word behind the text (which Buber always emphasized in his Bible readings) may be contrasted to the static logos of Gadamer. In his final chapter, Kepnes explains that while narrative consistently remained Buber's primary mode of discourse, it was an "impure" narrative using philosophy and academic scholarship.

LEVENSON negotiates the Buber-Scholem controversy, probing the failures of an academic dialogue between those (Silberstein, Friedman) who see Buber as a creative religious thinker engaged in a "strong reading" of a previous text (a time-honored Jewish practice), and those (Scholem, Katz) who feel that Buber misrepresented the hasidic traditions that he did so much to popularize. Levenson concludes that Buber's dialogical approach really admits only an "I-Thou" approach. The "strong reading" approach advocated by the pragmatic philosopher Richard Rorty would necessarily involve Buber in an "I-It" reading, yet Buber always insisted that his was a reading of Hasidism that truly emerged from the sources. Implicitly, Levenson presents Buber as a thinker negotiating between modern and postmodern understandings of his task. Perhaps this helps explain Buber's relevance today.

ALAN LEVENSON

Burial *see* Death, Burial, and Mourning

C

Calendar

Burnaby, Sherrard B., *Elements of the Jewish and Muhammadan Calendars, with Rules and Tables and Explanatory Notes on the Julian and Gregorian Calendars,* London: Bell, 1901

Dershowitz, Nachum and Edward M. Reingold, *Calendrical Calculations,* Urbana: Department of Computer Science, University of Illinois, 1989; Cambridge: Cambridge University Press, 1997

Feldman, William M., *Rabbinical Mathematics and Astronomy,* London: Cailingold, 1931; New York: Hermon, 1965, 4th corrected edition, 1991

Levi, Leo, *Jewish Chrononomy: The Calendar and Times-of-Day in Jewish Law, Together with Extensive Tables,* Brooklyn, New York: Gur Aryeh Institute for Advanced Jewish Scholarship, 1967; as *Halachic Times for Home and Travel: World-Wide Times-of-Day Tables with Halachic and Scientific Foundations and Permanent Calendar,* Jerusalem: Mass, 1992

Maimonides, Moses, *The Code of Maimonides, Book Three, Treatise Eight: Sanctification of the New Moon* (Yale Judaica Series, vol. 11), translated by S. Gandz, commentary by J. Obermann and O. Neugebauer, New Haven, Connecticut: Yale University Press, 1956

Roth, Cecil (editor), *Encyclopaedia Judaica,* New York: Macmillan, 1971

Spier, Arthur, *The Comprehensive Hebrew Calendar: Its Structure, History, and One Hundred Years of Corresponding Dates: 5660–5760, 1900–2000,* New York: Behrman, 1952; as *The Comprehensive Hebrew Calendar: Twentieth to Twenty-Second Century, 5660–5860, 1900–2100,* New York: Feldheim, 1986

The Hebrew calendar is of the lunisolar type: months begin with the new moon, and years are kept in tune with the seasons by the intercalation of a leap month every two or three years. The calendar day begins at sunset. In ancient and classical times, the month began with the observation by at least two witnesses of the crescent moon; the Jerusalem authorities added leap months as the need arose. In the Bible, months are usually identified by number, beginning in spring; the Hebrew names for the months were replaced by the present names of Babylonian origin in antiquity.

The fixed calendar, attributed to the fourth-century patriarch Hillel II, is based on a mean month of 29 days, 12 hours, 44 minutes, and 3.33 seconds and on the 19-year Metonic cycle comprising seven leap years, each containing 13 months. The average year length is 365.2468 days, slightly longer than the mean tropical year; because of the accumulated discrepancy, Passover now often occurs more than a month after the vernal equinox. The fixed calendar also incorporates several rules for delaying the onset of the year, as a consequence of which common years have 353 to 355 days; leap years have 383 to 385 days; and Passover never begins on Monday, Wednesday, or Friday. The details of the fixed calendar were only finalized in the tenth century; the evolution of the calendar between the fourth and tenth centuries is still a matter of dispute.

In contrast to the Hebrew lunisolar calendar, the Gregorian calendar—designed at the end of the 16th century and used today throughout the world—is purely solar in nature. There were solar-based sectarian Jewish calendars in classical times, and there remain certain prayers that depend on the Julian (old-style) solar calendar. The Karaite lunisolar calendar is still observation-based.

Chapters six through ten of MAIMONIDES, composed in 1166, remain a classic exposition of the fixed calendar as used to this day, and resemble an earlier work on the calendar by Savasorda. The chapters preceding that section describe the procedures by which the Jerusalem court managed the observational calendar. The remaining chapters are astronomical in nature, based mainly on the work of the Muslim astronomer al-Battani. They provide arithmetical methods for determining the moment of first visibility of the lunar crescent (and its orientation), which would help enable a court to determine the plausibility of reported observations. This volume's introduction and notes by J. Obermann, notes by S. Gandz, and astronomical commentary by O. Neugebauer—as well as the notes by E. Wiesenberg in volume 14 of the same series—are indispensable.

BURNABY, containing more than 300 pages on the Hebrew calendar, offers the most detailed description in English. It includes historical details, methods of computation, an explanation of the formula for Rosh Hashanah propounded in 1802 by Karl Friedrich Gauss, various examples of erroneous dates in the literature, and a long list of festivals and other days of current or past significance.

FELDMAN explores all aspects of mathematics and astronomy in the Talmud and subsequent rabbinic literature and includes several chapters explaining Maimonides' method of calculating visibility. Chapter 17, on the fixed calendar, explains in detail the calculation of the time of mean conjunction, the four delays that may postpone Rosh Hashanah, and the resultant 14 types of years. That chapter also presents arithmetical rules for converting a Hebrew date into the corresponding Gregorian date, and it includes a discussion of various modern attempts to reform the calendar.

DERSHOWITZ and REINGOLD give precise algorithmic treatments of most of the major calendars of the world. Chapter nine describes easily programmed, simplified rules for the Hebrew calendar, for most of the Jewish and Israeli holidays, and for birthdays and *yahrzeits* (the anniversary of a person's death). It includes a brief history of the fixed calendar, as well as a description of the controversy between tenth-century Babylonian and Palestinian geonim regarding the exact parameters of delays.

SPIER is a standard work for converting dates between the Gregorian and Hebrew calendars, with tables for the 20th and 21st centuries. Sabbath Torah readings and holidays are noted. The book provides detailed rules for determining Hebrew birthdays and for *yahrzeit* according to prevailing Ashkenazi practice.

LEVI is most useful for determining times of day critical for ritual purposes, such as dawn and dusk, with tables for each degree of latitude and for 73 cities with large Jewish populations. Unlike most published tables, which use mean values for dawn regardless of season or location, the times in this work are derived from astronomical calculations of the depression angle of the sun. The English section of the book also includes a short chapter on the calendar and tables that allow conversion between Gregorian and Hebrew dates. It should be noted that there remain disputes about where to place the dateline for the purposes of religious observance and what times to use in polar regions. In practice, the international dateline is used and the times of prayer and observance at nearby synagogues below the Arctic Circle are followed.

ROTH prints a convenient calendar for the years 1920 through 2020, arranged by Gregorian year (and based on M. Greenfield's 150-year calendar, 1963) in the index volume. The corresponding Hebrew date is given for each Gregorian day. Dates of all holidays and fasts (and an indication of postponement, if any), as well as the Sabbath readings for the diaspora, are included. These accessible tables are ideal for determining the date for a bar mitzvah or bat mitzvah, as follows: look up the Hebrew date corresponding to the actual day of birth of the child; if the child was born after sunset, take the following day instead. The same Hebrew date 13 years later is the day of the bar mitzvah. For girls in Conservative and Orthodox practice, the bat-mitzvah is 12 years later. The event is usually celebrated on the first Saturday on or after that day, when the child is called to the Torah, but it can be postponed for convenience. Occasionally, the event may be celebrated before Saturday (but not before the actual Hebrew birthday)—on Monday or Thursday, or on a festival day, when there is also a synagogue Torah reading. Complications arise when the child was born in the Hebrew month of Adar, since there is an intercalary Adar every two or three years. If the child was born in Adar of a common year, or in Adar II of a leap year, then the bar mitzvah is in Adar in a common year, but in Adar II in a leap year. If the child was born in Adar I of a leap year, then the bar mitzvah is in Adar I of a leap year and in Adar in a common year. If the child was born on the 30th day of Heshvan, Kislev, or Adar I, then it may happen that in the year of the bar mitzvah the month has only 29 days, in which case the first day of the following month is used instead.

NACHUM DERSHOWITZ

Canaanites

Aubet, María Eugenia, *Tiro y las colonias fenicias de Occidente*, 1987; translated by Mary Turton as *The Phoenicians and the West: Politics, Colonies, and Trade*, Cambridge and New York: Cambridge University Press, 1993

Coogan, Michael David, *Stories from Ancient Canaan*, Philadelphia: Westminster, 1978

del Olmo Lete, Gregorio, *Canaanite Religion: According to the Liturgical Texts of Ugarit*, Bethesda, Maryland: CDL, 1999

Giveon, Raphael, *The Impact of Egypt on Canaan: Iconographical and Related Studies* (Orbis Biblicus et Orientalis, 20), Freiburg: Universitätsverlag, and Göttingen: Vandenhoeck and Ruprecht, 1978

Gray, John, *The Canaanites* (Ancient Peoples and Places, vol. 38), New York: Praeger, and London: Thames and Hudson, 1964

Gurney, O.R., *The Hittites*, London and Baltimore, Maryland: Penguin, 1952; 2nd edition, reprinted with revisions, London and New York: Penguin, 1990

Halpern, Baruch, *The Emergence of Israel in Canaan* (Society of Biblical Literature Monograph Series, no. 29), Chico, California: Scholars Press, 1983

Harden, Donald B., *The Phoenicians* (Ancient Peoples and Places, 26), New York: Praeger, and London: Thames and Hudson, 1962; reprinted with revisions, Harmondsworth, Middlesex, and New York: Penguin, 1980

Smith, Mark S., *The Ugaritic Baal Cycle: Volume 1, Introduction with Text, Translation and Commentary of KTU 1.1–1.2* (Supplements to Vetus Testamentum, vol. 55), New York: Brill, 1994

Tubb, Jonathan N., *The Canaanites*, Norman: University of Oklahoma Press, and London: British Museum Press, 1998

Biblical scholars have had a notoriously difficult time defining which group or groups compose the Canaanites and the geographic extent of their cultural and political influence. The biblical record is somewhat inconsistent in this regard as are extra-biblical sources, and with the exception of texts discovered at Ugarit (modern Ras Shamra in Syria), the Canaanites (including the later Phoenicians) have left no major archive that might enable us to answer these questions. Further, since

Ugarit is located so far north of Israel, some scholars feel that it should not be considered Canaanite at all. Others see the Ugaritic material as sharing enough correlates with what is known of the Canaanites from the Bible to warrant the label "Canaanite." The difficulty in defining precisely what is meant by Canaan and who the Canaanites were has stirred a great deal of debate, and consequently, despite their biblical fame, the Canaanites have few comprehensive scholarly studies devoted to them, unless one includes, as here, works devoted to Ugarit.

AUBET provides an up-to-date analysis of the historical and archaeological data that relate to the Phoenicians. In particular, she uses new archaeological evidence to reevaluate contemporary understanding of the Phoenician colonies and their relationship to local Iron Age communities. The focus of this work is the overseas expansion and Mediterranean trade network that the Phoenicians established from the eighth to the sixth century B.C.E. Aubet opens her work by examining the historical and cultural origins of the Phoenicians and then moves to an analysis of the bases for Phoenician expansion in the Mediterranean. Topics covered in this work include: Phoenician trade, exchange mechanisms and organization, the palace and the temple, routes of Phoenician expansion into the Mediterranean, the chronology and historiography of the Phoenicians in the west, Phoenician colonies, and the silver trade. A series of reflective essays synthesizes the contents of the book. Aubet includes several useful appendixes that discuss Phoenician Iron Age archaeology, the journey of Wen-Amon to Phoenicia, biblical oracles against Tyre, and the settlements of the central Mediterranean. At the end of the book she provides a bibliography for advanced research.

COOGAN's work offers readers a pocket-size translation of the four most important and complete Canaanite myths from Ugarit: the Tale of Aqhat, the Rephaim text, the Tale of Kret, and the Ba'al Myth. The introductions to each text are brief and footnotes are sparse, allowing for an extremely accessible read. Where Coogan does discuss a text's background, he seeks to juxtapose the Canaanite literature with biblical literature by pointing out linguistic, literary, and mythological parallels. In so doing, Coogan demonstrates for nonspecialist readers the profound impact of Canaanite culture and literature on the Israelites and the Hebrew Bible.

GIVEON's collection of essays is unique in that it takes as its point of departure the evidence for Canaanite contact with Egypt presented by objects of art. Since he transliterates and translates all Egyptian and Semitic words, the book can be used by specialists and interested lay readers. Giveon's essays explore the linguistic evidence for Egyptian contact in Canaan, Egyptian temples in Canaan, methodological issues in dealing with questions of interregional contact, the Samarian ivories, and literary evidence for Egyptian influence in Canaan and vice versa. Giveon also discusses the royal seals of the Egyptian 12th dynasty, Hathor as a goddess of music in the Sinai region, Egyptian mining in the Sinai, and the Phoenician sarcophagus of Ahiram. Combined, Giveon's essays demonstrate the important role that Egypt played in Canaan, and consequently, the impact of Egypt on ancient Israel.

GRAY outlines a vast array of ancient Near Eastern textual and archaeological sources that contain information about the society and culture of the Canaanites. Beginning with a discussion of the habitat and history of the Canaanites, Gray proceeds to explore daily life in Canaan as well as Canaanite religion, letters and literature, and art. His comparative approach allows the reader to draw parallels between the literary remains of Ugarit and Egypt and the Hebrew Bible, while preserving the essential and unique contributions of each culture represented by their respective literatures. Gray also provides a select bibliography for each chapter, making his book a useful first introduction to the Canaanites.

GURNEY's pocket-size outline of Hittite history includes sidebars on Achaeans and Trojans in Hittite texts and the Hittites in Canaan and ancient Israel. Gurney synthesizes previous German scholarship on the subject into a concise survey of the Hittite state and society, the Hittite economy, laws and legal institutions, warfare, language, religion, literature, and art. Since the Hittites played such an active role in Canaan and appear with relative frequency in the Hebrew Bible, the student interested in the Canaanites will gain much from this work. Numerous maps, photographs, diagrams, and indexes make the volume extremely useful as an introduction to the subject.

HALPERN brings together a vast array of literary, archaeological, and comparative sources to document the emergence of biblical Israel within Canaan. He is cautious in his treatment of the subject and continually seeks to distinguish the nuances in cult and authority that differentiate the various clans as well as the state from the general populace. Beginning with a discussion of the textual sources, their tendentiousness, and the context of Canaan during the Amarna period, Halpern moves to what he calls the "making of historical Israel." He sheds particular light on the organization of pre-monarchic Israel, the bases of its state and religious authority, the development of a national ethos characterized by religious affiliation, and the development of the Hebrew record that documents these changes. Just as importantly, Halpern offers a historical tour of the sociology of knowledge on the subject. While admitting that "historical Israel is not the Israel of the Hebrew Bible," Halpern nevertheless concludes that within Canaan "the Israel of the pre-monarchic period is not significantly different (except in the ways that one would ordinarily expect) from the picture painted in the biblical sources."

HARDEN offers a cultural survey of Phoenicia. He discusses the origins of the Phoenicians, provides a geographic description of the region under Phoenician influence, and outlines in broad strokes Phoenician history. Harden also provides discussions of Phoenician overseas expansion, the colony at Carthage, Phoenician government, social structure, religion, language, script, warfare, towns, industries, commerce, trade, and exploration. Though largely superseded by Aubet, the work remains a useful supplementary introduction.

SMITH makes accessible a critical edition, translation, and exhaustive commentary on one of the most important cycles of mythological texts from Canaan. While there is much in this work that is of particular benefit to scholars, the general reader will gain much from the comparative insights that Smith provides. He offers also a balanced discussion of the various interpretations of the myth, for example, ritual and seasonal theories, cosmogonic interpretations, historical and political views, and the limited exaltation of Ba'al. Numerous textual notes make this work an inexhaustible source of information for the interested comparatavist. Where appropriate, Smith also adds comments of a literary nature as well as comparisons with biblical, Akkadian, Sumerian, Egyptian, classical, Hittite, and even Indian texts. One of the most important aspects of Smith's work is that it sheds light from the Canaanite perspective on a god whom the biblical authors vilify. Smith also provides comprehensive citation, text, grammar, vocabulary, author, and general indexes.

TUBB provides the most up-to-date analysis of Canaanite culture. Paying special attention to archaeological data, Tubb surveys the various periods of Canaanite existence. Thus, with a few exceptions, the book's chapters cover specific archaeological periods (e.g., Bronze Age, Middle Bronze Age, Iron Age, etc.). Following a chapter on the Persian period, Tubb examines the Canaanite legacy as found in later Phoenician, Roman, and other Mediterranean cultures. By beginning with the Neolithic and Chalcolithic periods and concluding with the Neopunic period, Tubb demonstrates the continuity of Canaanite Levantine culture. Despite the presence of periodic small-scale incursions, especially in the third millenium B.C.E., Tubb argues for "a more or less uniform culture throughout the whole of the Levant in the Early Bronze, and perhaps even more so in the Middle Bronze Age." Despite the large-scale incursions of the Sea Peoples (among whom were the Philistines) and the pressing military influence of Egypt during the Late Bronze Age, Canaanite culture remained essentially consistent. Tubb's observations have implications for those historians who place the patriarchs and the social and tribal institutions they represent in the early Middle Bronze Age (a conclusion not shared by all scholars). If Canaanite culture is demonstrably continuous since the Early Bronze Age, "there is nothing to suggest that these institutions had not existed in Canaan from the inception of that period." Even during the early Iron Age, Tubb asserts, "the Canaanite ancestry of Israelite material culture is evident in nearly all of its aspects." In addition to many high-quality color and black-and-white photos of Canaanite material culture and archaeological sites, the book contains excellent maps, an ancient Near Eastern chronological chart, and a list of suggested readings.

DEL OLMO LETE's monograph opens with a useful history of the study of Canaanite religion. Moving from W.R. Smith and M.J. Lagrange to W.F. Albright, J.M. de Tarragon, and P. Xella, del Olmo Lete examines the sociology of knowledge on the subject and provides a concise context for his own work on Canaanite religion. The work focuses completely on information gleaned from the ritual and liturgical texts found at Ugarit. After providing philological and linguistic analyses, del Olmo Lete synthesizes the materials in an effort to uncover their underlying ideology. While certainly aimed at scholarly readers and thus filled with transliterations, the accompanying English translations and the insightful analyses make the book accessible to nonexperts as well. Among other topics included in this comprehensive study are discussions of sacred times and places, sacrificial rites, Canaanite mythology and epic, the pantheon, the funerary cult, festivals, processions, prayers and oracles, and magic. Del Olmo Lete emphasizes the cultic continuity and plurality shared with other second mil-

lenium sites in Syria and the legacy of Canaanite culture on the later Western world: "Rich and varied in its forms, it allows us to see the Canaanite religious universe beneath the Judaeo-Christian reaction against it, which in terms of culture makes clear the paganism underlying our own Western culture." This study offers the most comprehensive and up-to-date information available on the subject. It will not be surpassed for many years.

SCOTT B. NOEGEL

Canada

Abella, Irving, *A Coat of Many Colours: Two Centuries of Jewish Life in Canada*, Toronto: Lester and Orpen Dennys, 1990

Abella, Irving and Harold Troper, *None Is Too Many: Canada and the Jews of Europe, 1933–1948*, Toronto: Lester and Orpen Dennys, 1982; New York: Random House, 1983; 3rd edition, Toronto: Lester and Orpen Dennys, 1991

Brown, Michael, *Jew or Juif?: Jews, French Canadians, and Anglo-Canadians, 1759–1914*, Philadelphia: Jewish Publication Society, 1986

Elazar, Daniel and Harold Waller, *Maintaining Consensus: The Canadian Jewish Polity in the Postwar World*, Lanham, Maryland: University Press of America, 1990

Greenstein, Michael, *Third Solitudes: Tradition and Discontinuity in Jewish-Canadian Literature*, Kingston, Ontario: McGill-Queen's University Press, 1989

Rome, David, *Canadian Jewish Archives*, 48 vols., Montreal: Canadian Jewish Congress, 1974–1996

Rosenberg, Louis, *Canada's Jews: A Social and Economic Study of the Jews in Canada in the 1930s*, edited by Morton Weinfeld, Montreal and Buffalo, New York: McGill-Queen's University Press, 1993

Sack, B.G., *History of the Jews in Canada*, translated by Ralph Noveck, Montreal: Harvest House, 1965

Tulchinsky, Gerald, *Taking Root: The Origins of the Canadian Jewish Community*, Toronto: Lester, 1992

Tulchinsky, Gerald, *Branching Out: the Transformation of the Canadian Jewish Community*, Toronto: Stoddart, 1998

The earliest research on the Jews of Canada with lasting value had its origins at the Canadian Jewish Congress (CJC) in the 1930s and 1940s. It was the formation of the CJC in 1919 that consolidated the image of a united Jewry in the Dominion of Canada, and it was the CJC's revival in the 1930s that created both the archives essential for any scholarly study of Canadian Jewry and a cohort of dedicated researchers, who were also community activists. In that era, Canadian Jews, who were for the most part recent immigrants, were looked upon as marginal by the dominant groups within Canadian society—the English and French—and hence Jews were forced to create their own cultural space in Canada. It is no accident, then, that the first serious students of Canadian Jewry came from within the ranks of its own communal activists.

ROSENBERG was the most prominent among these activists. He must be considered the pioneer of social-scientific research into Canadian Jewry. His statistical tour de force, *Canada's Jews*, is still required reading for anyone seeking a clear and discriminating picture of Canadian Jewry in the interwar period, when it was establishing its character and institutions. The lasting importance of this book, originally published in 1939, is underscored by its republication in the 1990s with a stimulating introduction by Morton Weinfeld.

SACK was the first successful attempt at a comprehensive historical monograph devoted to the Canadian Jewish community. When it was written, originally in Yiddish, the subject was virtually uncharted territory. It was a history that had to be painstakingly assembled, reference by reference, by the author. The book has some of the faults as well as the virtues to be expected in a pioneering work. It examines the origins of Canadian Jewry in the 18th and 19th centuries, when the community remained relatively small, and it does not deal with the 20th century. Nonetheless, for the period it does cover, it may still be beneficially consulted.

The last of the great contributors to the study of Canadian Jewry stemming from the CJC is ROME, whose many years of service as head of the Congress's National Archives in Montreal facilitated the production of an enormous output of material, issued in a multivolume series titled *Canadian Jewish Archives*. The 48 volumes in the series explore numerous aspects of Canadian Jewish history and culture, with emphasis on transcriptions of and commentary on documentary sources. The series is particularly rich in dealing with the Yiddish-speaking immigrant milieu. Researchers in any aspect of the Canadian Jewish experience will find much valuable material for their studies in these volumes.

In recent decades, the locus of serious study of the Canadian Jewish experience has shifted to the universities. One of the first and arguably still the most prominent of the products of the academic study of this subject is ABELLA and TROPER. This masterful study of the antisemitism inherent in the Canadian polity and government, which resulted in Canada not offering refuge to Jews fleeing Hitler's Europe, achieved an extraordinarily wide influence in Canadian public discourse. Subsequently, BROWN published his book attempting to situate Jews historically in the evolving debate among Canadians on the nature of Canada: is Canada a pact between two founding peoples, English and French, or a mosaic composed of various groups of multiple origins?

GREENSTEIN constitutes the first major attempt to understand as a whole the literary output of 20th-century Canadian Jews, writing in English and French. The author's aim is clearly to establish Canadian Jewish literature as a subfield within the study of Canadian literature. Similarly, ELAZAR and WALLER seek to put Canada on the map of contemporary Jewish community studies as well as to alert Canadian students of political science to the rich organizational life of the Canadian Jewish community.

The increased scholarly interest of the 1970s and 1980s in the Canadian Jewish experience has brought about the possibility of creating synthetic narrative histories of great scholarly sophistication. ABELLA's book was written to accompany

a major museum exhibition on Canadian Jewry and admirably ties together its varied aspects. Less popular in tone is TULCHINSKY (1992), which traces the history of Canadian Jewry from its origins to the end of World War I. It stands as the most thorough examination of the subject to date, and it is especially strong in its coverage of the economic history of Canada's Jews. TULCHINSKY's (1998) sequel to *Taking Root* takes the narrative up to the contemporary period and is equally strong.

IRA ROBINSON

Caribbean *see* Latin America and the Caribbean

Caro, Joseph 1488–1575

Castilian-born codifier of Jewish law and kabbalist, died in Safed

Dorff, Elliot N. and Arthur Rosett, *A Living Tree: The Roots and Growth of Jewish Law,* Albany: State University of New York Press, 1988

Gordon, H.L., *The Maggid of Caro,* New York: Pardes Publishing House, 1949

Graetz, Heinrich, *History of the Jews,* vol. 4, Philadelphia: Jewish Publication Society, 1896

Lewittes, Mendell, *Principles and Development of Jewish Law: The Concepts and History of Rabbinic Jurisprudence from Its Inception to Modern Times,* New York: Bloch, 1987

Schechter, Solomon, "Safed in the Sixteenth Century," in *Studies in Judaism: Second Series,* Philadelphia: Jewish Publication Society, 1908

Werblowsky, R.J. Zwi, *Joseph Karo, Lawyer and Mystic* (Scripta Judaica, 4), London: Oxford University Press, 1962; 2nd edition, Philadelphia: Jewish Publication Society, 1977

Joseph Caro (also spelled Karo and Qaro) was born in 1488, probably in Toledo, Castile, left the peninsula with the exiles in 1492, and died in Safed in 1575. He is best remembered as the author of *Shulhan Arukh*, the principal code of Jewish law. This work is an abbreviation of his magnum opus, *Beit Yosef*. He was also a kabbalist who had frequent visitations from a *maggid*, a heavenly mentor construed as the personification of the Mishnah, and these encounters are described in his personal diary.

SCHECHTER has written an eminently readable account of 16th-century Safed, the "city of legists [i.e., legal scholars] and mystics" in which Caro spent the latter part of his life and of which he was perhaps the most eminent resident. The main discussion of Caro begins on page 210, but the entire essay gives an excellent account of the environment in which Caro flourished. The encyclopedic kabbalist Rabbi Moses Cordovero was a disciple of Caro, and his contribution is also discussed here, as is that of Rabbi Isaac Luria, known as Ari, "the

Lion." (The name *Loria,* to which the author frequently refers, is now usually transcribed Luria.)

In contrast to the above sympathetic account, GRAETZ in his magisterial history displays a strong animus against both the legalistic and mystical aspects of Caro's legacy, decrying his "sea of casuistical details and mere externals" as well as his "excited imagination," both of which offended Graetz's scientific approach to Jewish history. In some ways Graetz was a prisoner of the fashions of his time, and this is hardly a unique manifestation.

WERBLOWSKY offers here one of the best books in the area of Judaic Studies to be written in the 20th century. Although it modestly declares that "our survey was, perhaps, more of a preliminary reconnaissance than a definitive study," it covers thoroughly the inner life, very strange to the modern reader, of its subject, as well as various other aspects of his achievement and the development of his genius. The writer takes a distinctly scientific approach, but at the same time is respectful and avoids the tendentiousness of the 19th-century practitioners of the Wissenschaft des Judentums (a "science," or scientific approach to the study, of Judaism). Neophyte readers may do well to omit the highly technical third and eighth chapters, but careful reading of the remainder will repay them amply and give a clear insight into the subject and his times. These chapters provide a discussion of Caro's maggid; spiritual life in Safed; Caro's life and times; the doctrine of the *sefirot* (ten stages of divine emanation that manifest God in his various attributes); the *shekhinah* (originally the notion of divine immanence, developed by the kabbalists to mean the divine power closest to the created world, i.e., the tenth and last *sefirah*); the nature and fate of man in Kabbalah; and finally further discussion of Caro's *maggid* himself or herself.

LEWITTES, a progressive Orthodox Jew, and DORFF and ROSETT, traditional Conservative Jews, form a useful supplement to Werblowsky in assessing Caro's pivotal place in the development of Jewish law. Lewittes deals with Caro mainly in chapter nine, and Dorff and Rosett in topic nine. Both books avoid tub-thumping quite skillfully, although the genesis of Dorff and Rosett's book as the outline of a university lecture course is somewhat evident. No person of any religious persuasion can be totally dispassionate in assessing such complex and delicate matters. Both books, however, make a sincere effort and offer valuable information.

Before seeking out a copy of GORDON's book, readers are advised to see the review in the *Journal of Jewish Studies,* volume seven (1956), pages 119 to 121, which may help them decide not to do so. The author, however, and some of the authorities he cites have the merit of pointing out that it is very difficult to judge psychic manifestations belonging to a pre-scientific age, and he does give some insight into the contents of the diary. His book should not be rejected out of hand.

NASA spacecraft are routinely guided by three linked computers running the same program, which statistically reduces the chance of error to near zero. Caro the jurist uses a similar technique, funneling the true determination of the law through three leading medieval decisors, whose majority decision can, in his belief, hardly be in error. His Ashkenazi commentators do not much care for this approach, preferring the decision of the latest authorities. But the combination of his views and the

reactions he provoked has left a deep impression on Jewish culture, even that of those remote from their ancestral faith.

ALAN D. CORRÉ

Cemeteries: Antiquity

Bloch-Smith, Elizabeth, *Judahite Burial Practices and Beliefs about the Dead* (JSOT/ASOR Monograph Series, 7), Sheffield, South Yorkshire: JSOT, 1992

de Vaux, Roland, *Ancient Israel: Its Life and Institutions,* New York: McGraw-Hill, and London: Darton, Longman and Todd, 1961; 2nd edition, London: Darton, Longman and Todd, 1965

Gonen, Rivka, *Burial Patterns and Cultural Diversity in Late Bronze Age Canaan* (Dissertation Series/American Schools of Oriental Research, vol. 7), Winona Lake, Indiana: Eisenbrauns, 1992

Hachlili, Rachel and Ann Killebrew, "Jewish Funerary Customs during the Second Temple Period, in the Light of the Excavations at the Jericho Necropolis," *Palestine Exploration Quarterly,* 115, July–December 1983

Meyers, Eric, *Jewish Ossuaries: Reburial and Rebirth: Secondary Burials in Their Ancient Near Eastern Setting* (Biblica et Orientalia, 24), Rome: Biblical Institute Press, 1971

The interment of the dead was of great importance to the Jews in antiquity. Allowing the body to decay above ground was considered extremely dishonorable (e.g., 1 Kings 14:10–14). Because corpses were considered ritually impure, it was essential to bury them. The priority attached to proper burial and the maintenance of burial grounds is shown by the talmudic saying, "The Jewish tombstones are fairer than royal palaces" (Sanhedrin 96b; see also Matthew 23:29). The earliest Israelite graves apparently were family sepulchers, often caves as in the burial grounds of Abraham's family at Machpelah. Among the earliest biblical references to burial grounds set aside for commoners is 2 Kings 23:6.

GONEN provides an accessible survey of the archaeological evidence of cemeteries in Canaan in the late Bronze Age (c.1600–1200 B.C.E.). To date, there are more than 900 such burial sites known in Israel, which form a crucial antecedent to the development of Israelite burial customs. Gonen's analysis is broken down into several sections. One section examines burial caves, which normally have multiple interments; another section addresses pit burials, which normally have individual interments. Gonen also covers intramural burials, where the dead were buried inside a settlement, and foreign burials. Her study of cave cemeteries discusses the placement of corpses in order to determine if the dead were buried according to a particular plan. She gives extended consideration to the regional variety of burial types, and she explains how burial methods changed over time. Her last four chapters offer a thorough location-by-location account of Bronze Age burial sites in Israel.

BLOCH-SMITH presents an informative survey of biblical and archaeological evidence about funerary practices and beliefs in southern Israel during the Iron Age (1200–586 B.C.E.). She distinguishes eight different types of burial used in the 850 known Iron Age burial sites in the southern Levant. These types include cave tombs, cremation burials, and jar burials (which were used primarily for the interment of infants). Several charts help make more accessible the large amount of archaeological data covered in the book; some of these charts show how burial practices changed over time. Burial sites of both individuals and groups are reviewed. This work uses biblical depictions of death and burial to interpret the vast archaeological evidence about ancient burial sites. It includes as an appendix a long catalog of Iron Age burials, which is arranged so as to facilitate understanding of change over time.

DE VAUX's massive study of the institutions of ancient Israel includes an informative chapter on death and funeral rites. According to this chapter, the "normal type of Israelite tomb is a burial chamber dug out of soft rock, or making use of a natural cave." These tombs were often used by a family or clan for many generations. The poor who could not afford tombs were simply buried in the ground, while the wealthy would construct elaborate mausoleums, some of which can still be seen. According to the Bible, the kings of Judah had a necropolis inside Jerusalem (e.g., 1 Kings 2:10). Other burial sites were simply identified by a pillar. Jacob places such a pillar at Rachel's grave in Genesis 35:20. De Vaux speculates that the *bamot*, the "high places" that were sites of worship before the centralization of religion in Jerusalem, may have been burial sites as well.

MEYERS examines the practice of "secondary burials" in ancient Israel. In such burials, the bones were removed from a burial site and placed in a stone coffin or ossuary that was reburied in another location. While much of the scholarship on this phenomenon focuses on only one archaeological period, this work endeavors to show the "remarkable continuity in Palestine in the history of secondary burials from Chalcolithic times to Roman times." It also strives to reveal the theological implications of this form of burial depicted in the Bible and the Talmud (such as how these practices reflect conceptions of the afterlife). Meyers surveys the various Hebrew, Greek, and Aramaic words used in antiquity to describe secondary burials. By the time of Herod, it is clear that a secondary burial was often undertaken to relocate permanently in Israel the bones of Jews who died in the diaspora. While the work stresses that this aspiration is an ancient Israelite tradition, it does not examine the secondary burial of Jacob, who died in Egypt and whose bones were later brought to the family burial grounds of Machpelah (Genesis 50:13). The one shortcoming of this otherwise fine study is its failure to include or speculate on the date of this important biblical example.

HACHLILI and KILLEBREW present a comprehensive introduction to burial customs in Israel in the late Second Temple period (first century B.C.E. to first century C.E.). Their survey covers archaeological data, particularly a necropolis found in Jericho and the cemetery of the community at Qumran, where the Dead Sea Scrolls were found. Many of the cemeteries of this period were tombs (*kukhim*) carved into hillsides. The study also examines Jewish literature from this time that describes funerary practices. The most important textual sources are the Mishnah, which was written down around 220 C.E., and the writings of Josephus, a Hellenized Jew active in the second half of the first century C.E. For example, this study recalls the mishnaic rule that cemeteries must be placed outside town limits (Baba Batra 2:9). Also from the Mishnah, the reader learns that secondary burials were quite common: "When the flesh is completely decomposed the bones are gathered and buried in their proper place" (Sanhedrin 6:6). The study's examination of archaeological evidence suggests that secondary burials became more common at the end of the Second Temple period and that funerary methods in this period were heavily influenced by Hellenistic and Roman practices.

MATTHEW GOFF

See also Cemeteries: Medieval and Modern

Cemeteries: Medieval and Modern

Abrahams, Israel, *Jewish Life in the Middle Ages,* New York and London: Macmillan, 1896; new edition, London: Goldston, 1932

Grotte, Alfred, "Tombstones," in *The Universal Jewish Encyclopedia: An Authoritative and Popular Presentation of Jews and Judaism since the Earliest Times,* vol. 10, New York: Universal Jewish Encyclopedia, 1943

Kohler, Kaufmann, "Cemetery," in *The Jewish Encyclopedia,* 12 vols., New York and London: Funk and Wagnalls, 1901–1906

Lamm, Maurice, *The Jewish Way in Death and Mourning,* New York: David, 1969, revised edition, 1972

Safanov, Anatol, "Cemetery," in *The Universal Jewish Encyclopedia: An Authoritative and Popular Presentation of Jews and Judaism since the Earliest Times,* vol. 3, New York: Universal Jewish Encyclopedia, 1939–1943

Tagger, Mathilde A., *Printed Books on Jewish Cemeteries in the Jewish National and University Library in Jerusalem: An Annotated Bibliography,* Jerusalem: Israel Genealogical Society, 1997

Jews have buried or entombed their dead since ancient times. Early Jewish cemeteries consisted either of vaults in caves or of underground catacombs with niches for the dead. These vaults and catacombs can be found in the Middle East, Italy, and North Africa.

In the medieval period, Jewish cemeteries were usually outdoor spaces and were often called "Jews' gardens." Unlike the vaults and catacombs, which were divided into sections for families or groups, medieval cemeteries contained individual graves. Sephardi cemeteries tended to have plain, unadorned gravestones that lay flat on the ground, while Ashkenazi cemeteries usually had gravestones, sometimes elaborately carved, that stood upright. Gravestone inscriptions of the medieval period were mostly in Hebrew. In late antiquity, and again in the 17th century through more modern times, diaspora Jews made widespread use of vernacular languages and scripts for their funerary inscriptions.

KOHLER's article separates carefully the features of medieval Jewish cemeteries from those of modern ones. This article describes the layout of cemeteries, rules of proper conduct for visitors, and prayers to be read at the graveside. The article, although brief, also touches upon the subject of cemetery desecration. The bibliography is surprisingly extensive and names numerous sources that describe specific cemeteries in cities and countries throughout the world. The article also includes illustrations of cemeteries in Germany, Switzerland, Austria, and New York.

TAGGER offers an extensive bibliography and descriptive analysis of books available on specific Jewish cemeteries around the world, including ancient, medieval, and modern cemeteries. Her bibliography is based on the holdings of the national library in Jerusalem. She describes a total of 181 books relating to cemeteries in Europe, the Americas, the Middle East, and North Africa. Some of the titles listed by Tagger are catalogs of inscriptions or are directories of individuals buried in particular cemeteries, whereas others are general histories of cemeteries. Tagger indicates clearly the focus of each book, the languages in which it is available, and what sort of illustrations or other additional features are included. In an appendix, she provides genealogical tables for some of the most noted families whose histories are reflected in the books described. She also supplies two geographical indexes to assist identification of books on cemeteries in particular countries, regions, or villages. More than half the books mentioned by Tagger are in German, but 22 of the titles are in English, and there is material in 16 other languages (including Hebrew, French, Czech, Spanish, Russian, Yiddish, and Hungarian). The most popular cemetery to be examined, according to Tagger, is the old Jewish cemetery in Prague, the subject of 13 studies.

GROTTE surveys customs and art relating to Jewish tombstones from ancient to modern times. For medieval tombstones, he identifies and interprets some of the most commonly used symbols. Grotte believes that funerary art began to decline in the 19th century. Industrialization and mass production of tombstones displaced the artistic function, he claims. The article includes numerous photographs of different styles of tombstones, both medieval and modern, and a modest bibliography.

ABRAHAMS offers a brief survey of the conditions and foundation of Jewish cemeteries in medieval Europe. His survey notes the usual locations of cemeteries and the types of inscriptions and symbols typically found on tombstones. Later in the book, he describes the institution of the burial society as well.

SAFANOV offers a particularly clear and comprehensive survey of cemeteries from ancient and medieval to modern times. His article offers a plethora of examples from different countries to give a picture of Jewish burial customs and the growth and geographical distribution of the cemeteries. Safanov notes that in many European countries from the Middle Ages to the 18th century, Jews were given permission to have only one centralized cemetery. He describes the procedures for cemetery maintenance and includes several paragraphs on modern Jewish cemeteries, often sections of cemeteries that include burial plots for all faiths. The article also includes numerous photographs of cemeteries, including the old Jewish cemetery in Prague as well as others in Jerusalem, Morocco, Vienna, Berlin, and New York City. A short bibliography accompanies the article.

LAMM's description and explanation of contemporary burial customs encompasses the role of cemeteries. He contrasts recent developments in burial customs in the United States with what has hitherto been accepted as traditional. For example, he deals with the questions of the burial of spouses or children of different faiths and those who have died in war. Lamm also explains the rules pertaining to proper times for visiting the cemetery and for erecting the monument to the deceased. The book includes specific prayers to be read at the cemetery, describes mourning practices in detail, and offers reflections on the interpretation of death and immortality in Jewish philosophy.

ALISA GAYLE MAYOR

See also Cemeteries: Antiquity

Central Europe

Beller, Steven, *Vienna and the Jews, 1867–1938: A Cultural History,* Cambridge and New York: Cambridge University Press, 1989

Berkley, George E., *Vienna and Its Jews: The Tragedy of Success, 1880s–1980s,* Cambridge, Massachusetts: Abt, 1988

Dagan, Avigdor and Gertrude Hirschler, *The Jews of Czechoslovakia: Historical Studies and Surveys,* 3 vols., Philadelphia: Jewish Publication Society, 1968–1983

Don, Yehudah and Viktor Kárády (editors), *A Social and Economic History of Central European Jewry,* New Brunswick, New Jersey: Transaction, 1990

Iggers, Wilma Abeles, *The Jews of Bohemia and Moravia: A Historical Reader,* Detroit, Michigan: Wayne State University Press, 1992

Kieval, Hillel J., *The Making of Czech Jewry: National Conflict and Jewish Society in Bohemia, 1870–1918* (Studies in Jewish History), New York: Oxford University Press, 1988

Patai, Raphael, *The Jews of Hungary: History, Culture, Psychology,* Detroit, Michigan: Wayne State University Press, 1996

Central Europe is usually defined as the area containing the nations of the former Austro-Hungarian Empire, including Austria, the Czech Republic, Slovakia, and Hungary, as well as Galicia, Bukovina, and Sub-Carpathian Ruthenia. Central European Jewry has historically been as varied as the nations themselves. In the eastern part of the region, Jews shared many of the ways of their Eastern European counterparts, adhering to strict Orthodoxy. Further west, but especially in the Czech Republic and Austria, Jews were more often highly assimilated and active in secular society. In Vienna, many converted to Catholicism, while in the Czech lands there was a high rate of intermarriage between Jews and non-Jews. The

Jews of Budapest were active in the political affairs of the city, but a far greater percentage than in Vienna or Prague retained Orthodox ways. Jews in Vienna, Budapest, and Prague were great contributors to science, the arts, theater, and cultural life in general. Franz Kafka, Max Brod, Franz Werfel, Ludwig Winder, Jozsef Kiss, Arthur Schnitzler, Georg Lukacs, and Stefan Zweig are among a host of Jewish writers from Central Europe. The cultural, political, and social prominence of Jews in the cities of the region began in the 19th century and continued on a strong course until the end of World War I, with literature, music, and drama flourishing in large measure due to Jewish patronage and creativity. A major shift set in after the war, including dislocation in the East, the movement of many impoverished Jews to the cities where they found economic distress, a crescendo of antisemitism, and heavy emigration of the Jewish bourgeoisie. Zionism called many to Palestine, while others opted for life further to the west. Fully one quarter of Budapest inhabitants had been Jewish before World War I; more than 40,000 Jews had resided in Vienna, with 11,000 in Prague. These numbers dropped appreciably, and the vast majority of those who remained would later become victims of the Nazis. German and Soviet occupation has left the region a shadow of its former self, with not much more than a token Jewish presence.

BELLER's work investigates the cultural role of the Jews in Vienna. As Beller states, "The aim of this study is to clarify this question about the Jewish influence on Viennese culture and in Viennese culture." He asks whether the culture of fin-de-siècle Vienna was "Jewish," and what in fact was "Jewish" in Viennese culture? Contributions to art, architecture, music, theater, and opera are considered in detail. The work is divided into two sections: part one deals with the "Jewish question," and part two discusses the Jewish background of Vienna's culture. Beller provides tables illustrating the relative economic, social, and cultural participation in society of Jews and non-Jews, and he concludes that the fact that there was a large Jewish presence in Viennese culture is not accidental because the liberal educated classes were predominantly Jewish. His work poses many interesting questions and provides much new information and understanding.

BERKLEY explores the Austrian-Jewish mutual dynamic. Why did so many Jews flock to Vienna? Were the Austrians more antisemitic than the Germans? Berkley delves into the history of this symbiosis, tracing events from the era of Emperor Franz Josef to the presidency of Kurt Waldheim. The first chapter of the work, "Vienna, 1900: Dream and Reality," sets the stage for this work, portraying Vienna Gloriosa as the center of all that was beautiful, especially in art, literature, music, and architecture. Berkley unveils the darker side of Vienna in subsequent chapters titled "Divisions, Dissensions, and Doubts," "A New Kind of Anti-Judaism," and "The Solitary Scapegoat." He illustrates the rights stripped from Jews and details the spread of Jewish hate. It becomes difficult for the reader to grasp the Jewish attraction to such a city. Berkley's inspiration for this book was a remark made to him by a Viennese Jew who stated, "Before the war, I lived in a paradise." However, Berkley's research underscores the truism that all that glitters is not gold, as evidenced in chapters titled "The Spreading Swastika" and "Deportation and Destruction." In the last section of the work, devoted to postwar Vienna, Berkley writes, "When it comes to corruption, none of Europe's smaller countries seems to have equaled Austria's record . . ." Berkley's epilogue is especially provocative, for he attempts to find explanations for Austrian cruelty toward its Jews—a topic scholars may feel requires further exploration.

DAGAN and HIRSCHLER's three-volume work gives an excellent and in-depth investigation of Czech and Slovak Jews and their role in society, politics, and culture. Volume one begins with historical surveys of Bohemia, Moravia, Silesia, and Sub-Carpathian Ruthenia. Ruth Kestenberg-Gladstein's article discusses the position of the Jews between the Germans and the Czechs and the difficulties that they encountered, such as anti-German sentiment among the Czechs, who "regarded them [the Jews] as even more pro-German than they actually were." Aharon Moshe Rabinowicz provides a lengthy discussion of the legal position of Jews as they struggled for recognition as a nationality in the Czech and Slovak lands. The appendix to this article consists of legal documents and letters and is followed by a bibliography. Religious life in the Czech lands is covered by Gustav Fleischmann and Hugo Stransky. Joseph Pick comments on the economy and Jewish industrial activity from the time of the national revival until the 1930s. Discussions of literature, the newspaper press, book publishing, and music round out the offerings in this volume. Harry Zohn's "Participation in German Literature" and Egon Hostovsky's "Participation in Modern Czech Literature" provide the reader with fascinating comparisons between those Jews who identified themselves with Czech culture and those who felt kinship with German culture.

Volume two concentrates on the many movements in organized Jewish life: Zionism, the Czech-Jewish movement, the Jewish political arena (including Jewish political parties), and student organizations. Joseph Pick's article "Sports" offers interesting insight into a lesser-known area of Jewish life: Jews as pioneers in athletics, even serving as developers of the new school of gymnastics that later became known as "sokol." Religion, welfare, and education are covered across the entirety of the Czech lands. The section on art provides articles ranging from Jewish art in the Czech and Slovak lands to the architectural history of synagogues in Prague and Mikulov. This volume also contains many black-and-white photographs and line drawings, illustrating monuments of Jewish art and architecture throughout the country. The interwar transition in Jewish life completes this volume and includes a short discussion by Manfred Georg of refugees in Prague from 1933 to 1938.

Volume three reviews the Holocaust period and includes articles both on Terezin and on the anti-Jewish laws imposed in the Czech lands as early as 1938. Erich Kulka has contributed two articles, one on the annihilation of Czechoslovak Jewry and the other on Jews in the Czechoslovak armed forces. The interim period from 1945 to 1948 is treated in Kurt Wehle's article, "The Jews in Bohemia and Moravia: 1945–1948," which explores the reorganization of Jewish life in the Czech lands, the Jewish Religious Congregation, and the determination to rebuild the Jewish community. Hana Volavkova's article on the Jewish Museum of Prague describes the significance of the Prague Jewish Quarter and outlines the history and main features of the area. All three volumes feature bibliographies after each contribution and a full collective index for all three volumes, as well as an index of illustrations. The vast amount of research effort expended in preparing this work has rendered it an invaluable source.

DON and KARÁDY's compilation of articles by many different authors offers a variety of perspectives on Central European Jewry. The work is based on a conference held in France in 1986 about Jewish claims in Austria, Czechoslovakia, and Hungary. This collection seeks to define the economic role, the ideas, and the social and cultural activities of Central European Jewry. The authors admit that the economic role of the Jews is very complex, for their impact on the economy was positive in many ways, but it also turned the general population against them for perceived "encroachment." This fear brought with it a latent hostility, which blossomed during the interwar period. Yeshayahu Jelinek's article discusses the problem of Slovak Jewish identity and nationalism between the wars. The identity problem stemmed from the Slovak Jews' links to Hungarian Jewry. Social divisions, nationalism, and political life are thoroughly investigated. Nathaniel Katzburg's article portrays the role of Central European Jews as cultural and social intermediaries between Eastern and Western Europe. William McCagg traces the development of the Jewish communities of Prague, Budapest, and Vienna. He suggests that immediately after World War I, European Jewish life changed drastically and was seriously endangered from the outset. This collection offers the reader a well-rounded view of Central European Jewish life and brings to light several lesser-known aspects of the lives of Jews sandwiched between East and West.

IGGERS's lively and colorful compilation of short articles garnered from newspapers and journals is indicative of the great variety of Jewish life in the Czech lands. Her work is divided into five sections, spanning the eras from Maria Theresa through Stalin, as it "portrays the Jews of Bohemia and Moravia in their own words . . . " To this end, she assembles brief personal memoirs, family histories, and letters. Her intention is to reflect Jewish customs and lifestyle, on the one hand, and tensions in society, assimilation, nationality problems, and identity crises, on the other. Iggers also seeks to highlight the difference between German Jews and those in the Czech lands, and her general introduction is particularly helpful in this respect. Many of the articles, such as "The Jewish Flea Market," "A Teacher's Salary," and "A Jewish Junk Dealer," have unusual themes seldom represented in other historical works. Each section of the book begins with a historical discussion of the period at issue. Especially useful are a section of brief biographies of Jewish personalities and a gazetteer of towns and other Jewish geographical locations, such as certain suburbs and even streets, with their Czech and German names.

KIEVAL attempts to chart the multiethnic character of the Czech lands and to explain the implications for the Jews in modern Czech history. He identifies the linguistic problems in the area and does much to clarify conceptions of the place of the Jew in a Slavic milieu. Two topics specifically are discussed in the work: first, assimilation and language loyalty, and, second, the distinctive local character of Zionism here,

as an answer to the problem of identity amid a sea of Germans and Czechs. The differences between the Czech-Jewish movement and the Zionist movement are thoroughly defined in this work. Kieval reminds the reader, "Both the 'Czech Jews' and the Zionists deliberately distanced themselves from the liberal German consensus of the mid-19th century, seeking instead to create a modern Jewish culture more attuned to the multinational realities of East Central Europe." This work emphasizes how the various political agendas and social realities affected cultural development, especially in Prague. The comprehensive investigation of Zionism in the Czech lands includes discussion of the prominent role played by the Bar Kochba movement in such intellectual endeavors as publishing and reviews. Black-and-white portraits of various Jewish cultural figures such as Kafka and Siegfried Kapper are provided, as are photographs of the Josefov section of Prague.

PATAI's work is the result of massive learning on the subject of Hungarian Jewish life. His motive for producing this work is rooted in "the shabby treatment the Jews in Hungary have received at the hands of authors of the standard general histories of the Jewish people." The focus is mainly on Jewish cultural and literary production, for Patai contends that culture is key to the portrayal of a people and that Hungarian Jewish culture has for the most part been ignored. This work recounts Hungarian Jewish contributions to the sciences, the economy, and politics, but, as Patai states, "there can be no doubt that their most significant contributions were in the cultural fields of the arts, and especially literature." He also maintains, in keeping with some of his books on other subjects, that the psychology of the people needs to be investigated "to understand the motivations behind Hungarian Jews' overt reactions to the governmental, political, economic, social, and cultural forces affecting them." The book begins with a survey history dating from 103 B.C.E. through the Enlightenment to the 1848 Revolution and on to the fin de siècle. There is thorough discussion of the early 20th century, the Holocaust, and the era of reconstruction. This is an extremely ambitious, pioneering exploration of a much-neglected area of Jewish scholarship, and inevitably there are certain details in the mass of information presented that require revision. Patai inaugurates the process enthusiastically by including an appendix of animadversions by Professor Miklos Szabolcsi, which reached him when they could no longer be incorporated into the body of the text. A lengthy bibliography for each chapter is provided at the end of the book, although a great deal of the material consists of sources in Hungarian.

CYNTHIA A. KLÍMA

See also Hungary; Prague

Chagall, Marc 1887–1985
Russian-born French artist

Alexander, Sidney, *Marc Chagall: A Biography*, New York: Putnam, 1978; London: Cassell, 1979

Amishai-Maisels, Ziva, "Chagall's Jewish In-Jokes," *Journal of Jewish Art* 5, 1978

Compton, Susan P., *Chagall*, London: Royal Academy of Arts in association with Weidenfeld and Nicolson, and New York: Abrams, 1985

di San Lazzaro, G. (editor), *Hommage à Marc Chagall*, 1969; translated by Jacques Fermaud, Joyce Reeves, and Noel Burch as *Homage to Marc Chagall*, New York: Tudor, 1969

Kagan, Andrew, *Marc Chagall*, New York: Abbeville, 1989

Kamenskii, Aleksandr Abramovich, *Chagall: The Russian Years, 1907–1922*, London: Thames and Hudson, and New York: Rizzoli, 1989

Kloomok, Isaac, *Marc Chagall: His Life and Work*, New York: Philosophical Library, 1951

Meyer, Franz, *Marc Chagall, Leben und Werk*, 1961; translated by Robert Allen as *Marc Chagall, Writer on Art*, London: Thames and Hudson, and New York: Abrams, 1964

Wolitz, Seth, "Chagall's Last Soviet Performance: The Graphics for *Troyer*, 1922," *Journal of Jewish Art* 21–22, 1995–1996

The literature available on Russian-French artist Marc Chagall is wide-ranging in its treatment; readers can choose between narrowly focused articles and long biographies, between authors who write only about the Jewish quality of Chagall's art and those who skim over it, between picture books and critical studies. Few titles are both comprehensive and scholarly, but almost all include references to other studies on different aspects of Chagall's art.

The study by MEYER—the former husband of Chagall's daughter Ida—is the most comprehensive to date. His nearly 800-page text is divided into geographic/chronological sections, each of which is divided into many short chapters. It seeks "an understanding of Chagall's work in its entirety" and functions as both biography and art monograph while remaining easy to follow. Meyer sees Chagall's Jewish and Russian heritage as "factors in the artist's production [which] do not determine its nature," arguing Chagall's art was not intended for Jews alone. Included are an extensive index, a bibliography arranged chronologically, a chronological list of Chagall exhibitions, and a list of illustrations in the text.

ALEXANDER's biography of Chagall is a pleasure to read, although unlike Meyer's text it does little to advance serious scholarship about Chagall and his work. He weaves Chagall's autobiography with interviews with those who knew him and with descriptions of his life and work. Alexander questions the veracity of Chagall's self-description, and yet his own text sometimes seems far from factual, with no real notes and with citations woven in so seamlessly that it is easy to miss his sources. The text has a melodramatic quality to it, especially in describing Chagall's marriages to his second and third wives, but it contains a helpful bibliography for each chapter and a comprehensive index. Alexander treats Chagall's ambiguous yet important relationship with Judaism throughout the text, although it is not the focus of his biography.

In an often laudatory, abbreviated trip through Chagall's life, KAGAN highlights major events and influences on his art.

Chagall's Judaism is always present in the art discussed, especially in the images of Christ on the Cross, which are "distinctly Jewish." Kagan argues that "the floating, dreamy visions of Chagall's art have a background in Hasidic spirit, myth and lore." Of particular interest to scholars and general readers will be the appendixes, including "Artist's Statements," "Notes on Technique," "Chronology," a list of exhibitions and holdings in public collections, and a select but strong bibliography and index.

KLOOMOK's text is a heartfelt narrative account of Chagall's art that also weaves together biographical facts, Chagall's own words, and descriptions of his paintings. It moves chronologically through his life, emphasizing Chagall's Judaism and its important role in his work: Kloomok states that the "sources that nourish his genius are his childhood memories of Jewish life and his Jewish inheritance." This text reads as a personal, approving account of Chagall and concludes with a brief recapitulation of modern art and Chagall's important place in it.

DI SAN LAZZARO has edited a curious book, unscholarly yet multifaceted, that treats Chagall's Judaism intermittently. It is a compilation of articles by 13 different writers on aspects ranging from Chagall's imagination to his engravings and from his "love of the cosmos" to his ceramics and sculptures. The articles are interspersed with poetry by Chagall and his contemporaries, photographs, and images. Despite the book's lack of notes, bibliography, and other tools, the varying viewpoints add a vividness to the text, which may serve as a springboard for a range of further studies of Chagall.

AMISHAI-MAISELS's article interprets several of Chagall's paintings from three early stages of his career—his earliest work in Vitebsk, his Paris period after 1911, and his Russian period after 1914—through Yiddish idioms "hidden" in the paintings. She argues that Chagall's ambivalence about his religion and his status as an outsider—especially in France—impelled him to create mysterious works with Jewish meaning hidden in them. Amishai-Maisels sees the biting, elusive iconographic comments in his first Parisian paintings as Chagall's way of criticizing his new host country in a way only decipherable to Jews. She then argues convincingly that as Chagall reidentified with Judaism after moving back to his original home, Russia, he more directly conveyed his hidden meanings to help Jewish viewers identify—and identify with—his work.

KAMENSKII focuses less on Chagall's Judaism than on his identification as a Russian, which for Chagall "meant life which is pure and close to nature." This is a celebration of the joyous quality of Chagall's art and includes a continued discussion of the social, political, and artistic situation in Russia and of the Jews there, interweaving it with citations from Chagall's autobiography and writings, photographs, and artistic images. Particularly interesting are the pages framed with images from Chagall's contemporaries to deepen the reader's understanding of Chagall's art in its proper context. Kamenskii includes a helpful bibliography in English and Russian and an index of works by Chagall and others included in the text.

WOLITZ's article examines David Hofsteyn and Chagall's collaboration on *Troyer* (Grief) in Kiev in 1922, a poetic and graphic work lamenting Jewish victims of the Civil War pogroms of 1919 and 1920 and following the tragic journey into the "abyss" of Ukrainian Jews. Wolitz highlights Chagall's focus on rupture and the aftermath of violence and his use of Hebrew letters to heighten expression in focusing on the murder of Jews. Wolitz leads the reader through the poems and accompanying graphics, which represent Chagall's "farewell to the Soviet art world" and to Jewish modernist expressionism, and which Wolitz feels reveal him to be "quite devoid of nostalgia and full of indictment."

The comprehensive catalog edited by COMPTON for the major Chagall exhibit at the Royal Academy and Philadelphia Museum of Art in 1985 includes notes and essays by Compton and Norbert Lynton, as well as the plates and descriptions of all pieces included. The introduction highlights the central themes of Chagall's art—the circus, lovers, peasants, music, Christianity and Judaism, and suffering and death—the universal quality of his art, and the importance to him and his work of his Russian background. Compton includes a helpful Chagall chronology including major exhibits of his work and a short but important bibliography. Most helpfully, the catalog descriptions are separated into thematic categories: St. Petersburg, Paris, Russia and Berlin, France, the United States, France after 1948, theater, stained glass, prints, and books.

HILARY LIEBERMAN

Charity

Maimonides, Moses, *The Book of Agriculture* (Mishneh Torah, Book 7), New Haven, Connecticut: Yale University Press, 1979

Neusner, Jacob, *Tsedakah: Can Jewish Philanthropy Buy Jewish Survival?* (Basic Jewish Ideas), Chappaqua, New York: Rossel, 1982

Shear, Eli M. and Chaim Miller, *The Rich Go to Heaven: Giving Charity in Jewish Thought*, Northvale, New Jersey: Aronson, 1998

The Hebrew term for righteous giving (charity) is *tsedakah*, and in Judaism there is a large literature of popular stories that illustrate the benefits of tsedakah for both the donor and the recipient, as well as a body of laws and customs that encourage and regulate charitable giving as an essential means of strengthening individuals and the community.

One of the most important sources on tsedakah is found in MAIMONIDES' 12th-century code. This text presents the famous "Ladder of Charity," which describes eight levels of philanthropy, listed in descending order. The highest degree of charity is performed by one who strengthens a person so that he or she will no longer beg from others; in short, the recipient becomes self-sufficient. This self-sufficiency can be accomplished by the donor giving a person who lives in poverty a significant gift or a loan, or by entering into a partnership with the person. The degree of charity immediately below the highest level requires an environment of total anonymity; the donor does not know to whom the alms are given, nor does the recipient know who donated the alms. At this level the donor is fulfilling his or her religious duty for its own sake by contributing directly to the charity fund. The next levels of charity occur in situations in which either the donor or the recipient is not anonymous; persons who offer charity only when pressed reside at the bottom of the ladder. Maimonides' paradigm has often been used by later commentators to frame their own discussions of charity and to guide charitable giving.

NEUSNER comments on the role of tsedakah within the framework of Judaism, and he identifies acts deemed to constitute charity and righteousness in Jewish sources. The book explores teachings of the talmudic sages and Maimonides, and the author raises many questions about charity, among them, what particular acts of charity are people supposed to do? How do these acts help to define and express what kind of human beings the donors are? Neusner argues that Jewish laws of charity reinforce one fundamental point: the poor must be treated with dignity. Giving charity must be done in a sensitive manner, as both the donor and recipient are equally created in the image of God. Neusner emphasizes the validity and centrality of tsedakah as an instrument that presents an opportunity to lead a Jewish life by working for organizations and institutions that raise funds and distribute money for worthy causes, such as Jewish education, nursing homes, community programs, hospitals and hospices, and Israel. The book contains an appendix with the source texts in vocalized Hebrew and in translation.

The volume edited by SHEAR and MILLER addresses issues and sources similar to those discussed in Neusner. The contributors demonstrate that from the time of the Temple of Jerusalem, the charity fund was a center around which the Jewish community revolved. Welfare for the poor consistently included providing for clothing, education, dowries, Passover observance, and burials. Once a person resided in a Jewish community he was required to give to charity. Helping the poor was deemed the classic way of showing gratitude to God, and the book contains an extensive anthology of stories illustrating understandings of the concept of charity.

RIVKA B. KERN ULMER

China

Heppner, Ernest G., *Shanghai Refuge: A Memoir of the World War II Jewish Ghetto*, Lincoln: University of Nebraska Press, 1993

Leslie, Donald Daniel, *The Survival of the Chinese Jews: The Jewish Community of Kaifeng* (T'oung Pao Monographie, 10), Leiden: Brill, 1972

Maynard, Isabelle, *China Dreams: Growing up Jewish in Tientsin* (Singular Lives Series), Iowa City: University of Iowa Press, 1996

Pollak, Michael, *Mandarins, Jews, and Missionaries: The Jewish Experience in the Chinese Empire*, Philadelphia: Jewish Publication Society, 1980

Pollak, Michael, *The Jews of Dynastic China: A Critical Bibliography* (Bibliographica Judaica, 13), Cincinnati, Ohio: Hebrew Union College Press, 1993

Shapiro, Sidney (editor), *Jews in Old China: Studies by Chinese Scholars*, New York: Hippocrene, 1984

Sufott, E. Zev, *A China Diary: Towards the Establishment of China-Israel Diplomatic Relations,* London and Portland, Oregon: Cass, 1997

White, William Charles (compiler), *Chinese Jews: A Compilation of Matters Relating to the Jews of K'ai-fêng Fu,* Toronto, Ontario: University of Toronto Press, 1942; second edition, New York: Paragon, 1966

A considerable amount of modern research has been expended on the Jewish past in China, on their earliest settlement there and on the history of their Jewish identity in the face of assimiliation. A number of these studies will appeal to the interested layperson for the insight they provide into the history of a bygone symbiosis.

The voluminous work on the Jews of Kaifeng by WHITE is lavishly illustrated. First published in three volumes, it was reedited into one substantial tome of about 600 pages, with an introduction and an essay by Cecil Roth on an illuminated scroll of Esther, allegedly once owned by Jews in old China. White was bishop of Henan before he housed his Chinese collection at the Royal Ontario Museum, of which he became assistant director. The work is in three parts and deals with the history of the Kaifeng Jews, the community's Chinese stone inscriptions from the 15th to the 17th century, and genealogies constructed with reference to Hebrew and Chinese codices. Researchers will need to check White's abridged source materials carefully against the originals, even though some errors have been corrected by Donald Leslie.

LESLIE's comprehensive and scholarly study offers the first real synthesis of all the relevant Chinese, Hebrew, and Western primary sources. This standard work contains hundreds of bibliographical references and remains the prime text for all serious students of the subject. A careful evaluation of sources from "within" sheds light on the earliest traces of Jews in China and Kaifeng, their "discovery" and decline, their religion (synagogue, ritual, ethics), social structure, language, and writing; these are complemented by sources from "outside," such as travelers' reports and the accounts of Jesuits and of later informants, including native Chinese sources. To the scholarly apparatus have been added 37 plates and two maps.

POLLAK's (1980) critical and well illustrated study provides, not only for the student but also for the general reader, a "stepping stone to the more detailed investigations" of the history of the Jews in Kaifeng undertaken by Leslie. An account of their discovery by a Jesuit priest in 1605 is followed by an evaluation of the reactions in Europe, such as the curiosity and controversy this produced among Christian theologians, who, suspicious of the contents of the Hebrew Bible, now hoped to find new evidence of a "more truthful" version. These Jews did not surrender their Torah, however, until the advanced decline of their community led them to do so. Pollak surveys different theories about the beginnings of Jews in China, their relationship to their neighbors, and their Jewish way of life. He includes discussion of many of their customs and ethical values as expressions of their Jewish self-awareness. Finally, he considers their assimilation and ultimate absorption into the culture of their country.

Another most valuable contribution is POLLAK (1993), an updated and indexed companion volume to the 1988 reprint of the *Sino-Judaic Bibliographies* of R. Loewenthal. Surveying major and minor scholarly and more popular publications on the history of Jewish communities in China, it also includes studies on Jewish immigration since the Opium War, from Russia and from Nazi Europe. This survey of books, essays, and articles has been critically annotated by the author, who offers his "personal views regarding . . . quality and trustworthiness of the titles." The book brings together a large amount of material and facilitates research on a variety of themes within the rapidly expanding field of Chinese Jewish studies.

An unusual collection of studies, this time undertaken by Chinese scholars between 1897 and 1980, has been compiled by SHAPIRO, whose translated extracts and summaries are interspersed with his own comments and interpretations. The 13 individual contributions cover a wide range of subjects, which, given their various dates of publication, differ in reliability and quality of information. They range from a survey of religious sects in the Yuan Dynasty and more general discussions of Jews and Judaism in China to studies of individuals, including also interviews with the descendents of Kaifeng Jews conducted by the author in 1983. Here, basic statistics about occupations, marital and political status, standard of living, and religious beliefs and practices provide valuable information on the heirs of bygone Chinese Jewish life.

MAYNARD's lighthearted autobiography takes the reader to Tientsin where the author spent the first 19 years of her life, from 1929 to 1948. Her parents had fled Russia to escape Communism and antisemitism, and the family had to emigrate yet again under the Japanese occupation of Tientsin. The author's account is a description of a young girl's memories of her early life in a household crowded with Chinese servants about whom she knew next to nothing. Segregated from the Chinese population, but also from other Europeans, she can only convey to the reader occasional glimpses of the Chinese way of life. This honest and personal portrayal, however, does not lack self-criticism for her indifference, and there is plenty of comic relief. But above all, this is a description of emigration and refuge, of homelands lost and found, of alienation and the struggle for Jewish identity. A number of family photographs and official documents illustrate this now vanished world of 20th-century Jewish refugees for whom China provided, at least for a few years, a secure home.

HEPPNER's illustrated autobiography concentrates on Shanghai and provides an important historical record of Jewish life under the Japanese occupation. Bringing together personal memories and historical data, his life story starts in Germany with his childhood and education in the 1920s and 1930s. He describes the rise of antisemitism and the frantic search for refuge under the increasing threat of deportation until he was able to emigrate to China in 1938. Heppner gives a vivid account of Jewish life and Jewish-Chinese business in Shanghai. He considers to what extent the Joint Distribution Committee and, at least initially, the Japanese occupation forces helped the refugees until the Kempetai began to exercise more control and set up the ghetto in 1943. While the testimony of his personal odyssey also contains his first experiences in the United States, the main portion of Heppner's book records the daily struggles of this unique Shanghai community that existed for approximately one decade.

It was not until 1992 that diplomatic relations were established between China and Israel. SUFOTT, Israel's representative in the negotiations and subsequently her first ambassador to China, provides a most interesting description of the early and clandestine contacts between the two countries, revealing much about the mechanisms of both the Chinese decision-making process and the Jewish state's own modus operandi with regard to foreign policy. Sufott offers insight into the gradual progress of Israeli diplomacy as well as a fascinating account of both official and personal Chinese viewpoints on Israel, the Palestine Liberation Organization, and the Middle East peace process. The epilogue attempts an evaluation of China's stance toward Israel at the time of writing, without shirking the more sensitive issues that have created irritation in both China and Israel—notwithstanding an overall "consistent" policy during the first five years of diplomatic relationship.

ESTHER I. SEIDEL

Chosen People

Eisen, Arnold, *The Chosen People in America: A Study in Jewish Religious Ideology* (Modern Jewish Experience), Bloomington: Indiana University Press, 1983

Frank, Daniel H. (editor), *A People Apart: Chosenness and Ritual in Jewish Philosophical Thought* (SUNY Series in Jewish Philosophy), Albany: State University of New York Press, 1993

Novak, David, *The Election of Israel: The Idea of the Chosen People,* Cambridge and New York: Cambridge University Press, 1995

Wyschogrod, Michael, *The Body of Faith: Judaism as Corporeal Election,* New York: Seabury, 1983

A concept of Judaism with Pentateuchal roots and a controversial history is the docrine of election, the belief that God chose the people of Israel, out of all the peoples of the earth, for a distinct relationship. This particularist sense of being set apart has been bolstered by historical events, and it is symbolized and reinforced by the singularity of Jewish ritual life and customs.

EISEN's book focuses on Judaism in the United States, highlighting tensions between the idea of Jews as a chosen people and the U.S. beliefs in equality and personal freedom. The book discusses the views of several generations of U.S. Jews from a number of denominations, and Eisen analyzes the influence of social and cultural factors, arguing that in the U.S.-Jewish context, individualism and independent thought have become more highly valued than more separatist communal beliefs valorized by the institutions of Judaism.

FRANK's anthology of essays on chosenness, initially presented at a conference of the Academy for Jewish Philosophy in 1990, offers a philosophical analysis of the idea of election, analyzes Maimonides' views on chosenness, and debates aspects of chosenness that have caused controversies throughout history. Other essays focus on the idea of ritual, which the authors link to chosenness, given how much ritual has historically been vital in separating Jews from their host societies.

NOVAK explores the significance and merit of the idea that the Jews are chosen by God. His book is a theological and scholarly discussion of the importance of the concept of chosenness for Jewish identity, and it explores the paradox that Jews face as they are at once separate from and connected to the world. Novak argues that the election of Israel implies that the relationship between God and Israel is a historical, not natural or biological, bond, and he contends that its development is two-sided, for Israel is required to accept the chosen status that God confers. Novak analyzes the philosophies of Benedict Spinoza, Hermann Cohen, and Franz Rosenzweig, before concluding with discussions of biblical, rabbinic, and medieval thought.

WYSCHOGROD's brief theological investigation of the idea of chosenness challenges the traditional rationalistic interpretation of the concept identified with the thought of Maimonides and other medieval philosophers. While Wyschogrod maintains a connection with Jewish orthodoxy, he adds an existentialist turn to ideas about chosenness, emphasizing the events of Jewish history as the foundation for understanding Israel's election.

ELEANOR AMICO

Christian Hebraists

Daiches, David, *The King James Version of the English Bible: An Account of the Development and Sources of the English Bible of 1611 with Special Reference to the Hebrew Tradition,* Chicago: University of Chicago Press, 1941

Friedman, Jerome, *The Most Ancient Testimony: Sixteenth-Century Christian-Hebraica in the Age of Renaissance Nostalgia,* Athens: Ohio University Press, 1983

Hailperin, Herman, *Rashi and the Christian Scholars,* Pittsburgh, Pennsylvania: University of Pittsburgh Press, 1963

Lloyd Jones, G., *The Discovery of Hebrew in Tudor England: A Third Language,* Manchester, Greater Manchester, and Dover, New Hampshire: Manchester University Press, 1983

Loewe, Raphael, "Hebraists, Christian," in *Encyclopaedia Judaica,* vol. 8, Jerusalem: Keter, 1971

McKane, William, *Selected Christian Hebraists,* Cambridge and New York: Cambridge University Press, 1989

Christian Hebraists were scholars who explored the Jewish roots of European civilization. Beginning with the early Church fathers, such as Origen (c.185–254) and Jerome (Hieronymus; c.342–c.420), a primary motivation for the study of *Hebraica veritas* (Hebrew truth) was the production of biblical commentaries and translations. Two other goals have also been involved: the desire to convert the Jews by uncovering Christian truth in the Hebrew text; and the later Protestant interest in reforming the church by appealing to Luther's principle of *sola Scriptura* (the sole authority of

Scripture). Landmark texts include: Nicholas de Lyre's biblical commentaries, *Postillae Perpetuae* (1322–1330), which made extensive use of the works of the medieval Jewish exegete Rashi; Conrad Pellican's Hebrew grammar, *De Modo Legendi et Intelligendi Hebraeum* (1504); Johannes Reuchlin's Hebrew grammar and lexicon, *De Rudimentis Hebraicis* (1506); and the grammar, *Institutionum Hebraicarum Abbreviatio* (1528), and dictionary, *Thesaurus Linguae Sanctae Sive Lexicon Hebraicum* (1529) by Santes Pagnini.

Christian Hebraism also produced the first printing of important source books: Daniel Bomberg's rabbinic Bible (Hebrew text with parallel Jewish commentaries) in 1517 and 1518 and his complete editions of the two Talmuds, printed between 1520 and 1523; as well as the Complutensian Polyglot Bible, which was printed in 1517, containing (for the Hebrew Bible) parallel Hebrew, Latin, Greek, and Aramaic columns. Furthermore, Christian Hebraism ultimately filtered down from select scholars to affect Christendom at large, creating a new way of reading the Hebrew Bible that was incorporated into sermons and literary works.

LOEWE surveys Hebrew scholarship in the Christian world from the high Middle Ages (1100) until the development of widespread secular attitudes (1890). His essay provides a thorough chronological overview of this enterprise, noting significant landmarks such as the rise of the mendicant orders, the Renaissance and Reformation, and the Age of Printing. Loewe enriches this overview with a discussion of the various cultural contexts of Christian Hebraism, distinguishing three primary issues: the factors motivating Christian interest in the Hebrew Bible and in postbiblical Jewish institutions; the facilities for Christian scholarship, including the availability of sources of information, teachers, and libraries; and the occasions that offered opportunity for interaction between Jews and Christians (migrations, political changes, and linguistic developments). The article is embellished with an immense, all but exhaustive list of Christian Hebraist authors, replete with bio-bibliographic references.

HAILPERIN presents a study of two of the most important biblical exegetes of the Middle Ages: Rashi, a French Jew (1040–1105), and Nicholas de Lyre, a French Franciscan (c.1270–c.1349). He regards Nicholas's use of Rashi's biblical commentaries as a central chapter in the long history of Jewish-Christian intellectual encounters. Through careful comparative readings of the two commentaries, Hailperin emphasizes Rashi and Nicholas's mutual emphasis on the literal-historical—rather than the allegorical—meaning of the biblical text. The author also highlights the cultural and religious issues that gave rise to the need for such an emphasis, placing the study of biblical exegesis within a historical context.

McKANE singles out five Christian Hebraists, from the 12th through the 18th centuries, who contributed in different ways to the reception of the Hebrew Bible in the Catholic and Protestant Churches. He is primarily concerned with understanding how these scholars reconciled the historical and linguistic methods of exegesis they used to uncover the literal sense of the Hebrew text, on the one hand, with a Christological exegesis that disengages the Hebrew Bible from its specifically Jewish context, on the other. Closely examining translations of and commentaries on the Hebrew Bible, McKane reviews the theological and doctrinal shifts in the Christian understanding of the nature and authority of that text.

FRIEDMAN investigates the Christian Hebraica that developed in the first half of the 16th century, a subject that has not received sufficient scholarly attention. He first discusses three seminal scholars who represent different forms of nostalgic desire within Christian Hebraica of that time: Michael Servetus (c.1509–1553), Johannes Reuchlin (1455–1522), and Paul Fagius (1504–1549). Friedman then focuses on two major issues. The first involves the methods of scriptural exegesis and translation used by these Christian Hebraists, which were shaped specifically by their need to create a literal interpretation of the text that would place it in the context of accepted Christian prophecy rather than the Jewish historical context. The second issue involves the issue of Judaization, that is, the suspicions of these commentators' critics that Jewish religious sources inappropriately influenced the views of Christian Hebraists. Thus, Friedman considers how Christian Hebraica contributed to the intellectual climate of crisis and change during the period under study.

DAICHES spotlights one particular episode in Christian Hebraism—the creation of the King James (Authorized) English translation of the Hebrew Bible (1611). He first traces the history of English Bible translation from Tyndale (1523) to the King James Version. He then proceeds to place English Bible translation within the context of the Christian Hebraism of Europe in general and England in particular, demosntrating that this enterprise was the product of both the "back to the Bible" movement of the Reformation and the humanist scholarship of the Renaissance. Daiches then highlights the sources, equipment, and methods of the English translators by presenting a close textual analysis of the Book of Isaiah, collating English, Latin, Greek, Aramaic, and Hebrew divergences and elaborations.

LLOYD JONES extends Daiches's discussion of English Bible translation by exploring the comprehensive study of Hebrew in 16th-century England. Lloyd Jones considers various aspects of this enterprise, discussing the connection between English and continental Hebraic scholars, the common reasons for the flourishing of Hebrew studies (church reformation, Bible translation), and the development of a system of Hebrew studies in England (schools, universities, printing presses). He thus marshals afresh the existing evidence for the status of Christian Hebrew studies and scholars in Tudor England.

CHANITA GOODBLATT

Christian-Jewish Relations: Apologetics and Polemics

De Lange, Nicholas R.M., *Origen and the Jews: Studies in Jewish-Christian Relations in Third-Century Palestine*, Cambridge and New York: Cambridge University Press, 1976

Langmuir, Gavin I., *Toward a Definition of Antisemitism*, Berkeley: University of California Press, 1990

Lieu, Judith, *Image and Reality: The Jews in the World of the Christians in the Second Century*, Edinburgh: Clark, 1996

Maccoby, Hyam, *Judaism on Trial: Jewish-Christian Disputations in the Middle Ages* (Littman Library of Jewish Civilization), Rutherford, New Jersey: Fairleigh Dickinson University Press, and London: Associated University Presses, 1982

Setzer, Claudia, *Jewish Responses to Early Christians: History and Polemics, 30–150 C.E.*, Minneapolis, Minnesota: Fortress, 1994

Simon, Marcel, *Verus Israel: Étude sur les relations entre chrétiens et juifs dans l'Empire romain, 135–425*, 1948; translated by Henry McKeating as *Verus Israel: A Study of the Relations between Christians and Jews in the Roman Empire, 135–425* (Littman Library of Jewish Civilization), Oxford and New York: Oxford University Press, 1986

Wilken, Robert L., *John Chrysostom and the Jews: Rhetoric and Reality in the Late 4th Century*, Berkeley: University of California Press, 1983

Wilson, Stephen G., *Related Strangers: Jews and Christians, 70–170 C.E.*, Minneapolis, Minnesota: Fortress, 1995

Apologetic and polemical writings are those that either advocate a certain belief or practice (apologetics) or attempt to dismantle another's belief or practice through invective (polemics). Very little is known about how Jews perceived Christians, how they spoke about them, or even if they bothered to do so very much. Christianity, on the other hand, produced a substantial corpus of *Adversus Judaeos* material. Apparently, Judaism was a more heated topic for Christians than Christianity was for those Jews who generated religious writings. There is a great deal of development and variation within this Christian genre. There never was a single Christian approach to Jews and Judaism.

WILSON's study is the result of many years of careful and consistent work in the area of Christian-Jewish relations in the period following the New Testament writings. In this volume, Wilson's field includes not only canonical New Testament works (the Gospels and the Epistle to the Hebrews) but also noncanonical works such as the *Acts of Pilate*, the *Gospel of Thomas*, and the *Gospel of Peter*. Wilson also uses patterns of worship as a way of investigating the kinds of issues that may have been in dispute during this time. He sees in these kinds of issues an internal struggle for Christian self-definition in a Jewish context. The strength of this book lies in his lucid prose and the way he views this formative period in Christian-Jewish relations. Without the firm lines of canon (which did not exist during this time), a more varied picture of Christianity appears. There was no prevailing attitude toward Judaism. Various authors from different locations held very different views regarding Jews and Judaism.

The title of LIEU's book is an expression of the theory that runs through this examination of second-century Christian attitudes to Jews and Judaism. Her premise is that while the image of Jews or Judaism may appear artificial and contrived, the reality of the text lies in the context out of which these texts arose. Neither image nor reality are static concepts, but they can be distinguished from one another through a close reading of each text and other supporting information. These texts are carefully considered from a linguistic and historical point of view. Lieu also uses information, mostly archaeological, about Jews in Asia Minor as a way of putting the Christian sources in a historical context. Lieu's scholarship is very sound, and her attention to text and context is admirable. Anyone interested in early Christianity will benefit from this book, but for those interested in this particular field of study it is essential reading.

SETZER's topic is difficult to investigate because virtually all of the information we have about possible Jewish reactions to Christianity comes from Christian sources. This puts her at a disadvantage, but she nevertheless provides a helpful study of those passages or works from the first and second century C.E. that speak of Jewish reactions or opinions about Christians. The first part of the book is a survey of all those Christian writings, canonical and noncanonical, that mention how Jews reacted to early Christians. She concludes that virtually all the references about Jewish reactions are negative, but by the second century C.E. it appears that there was less direct animosity between Jews and Christians. The exchange becomes more removed and rhetorical in nature. Barriers to discovering information about Jewish reactions to Christians are formidable, but despite this she offers interesting and useful ways to read this highly emotive Christian material.

DE LANGE's book on Origen is an important text for understanding both Christianity and rabbinic Judaism in Palestine during the third century C.E. Both religions were in a state of flux and rapid development, and Origen's comments about Judaism provide a helpful perspective. De Lange sees Origen as a consummate academic who will not discriminate in his search for knowledge. Origen spoke to Christians, Jews, and heretics in his quest for knowledge about the biblical and Christian tradition. He was taught Hebrew for this purpose and was the first Christian scholar to undertake serious textual analysis of Scripture in Hebrew. Origen is an example of an early and extremely influential Christian scholar who was far more interested in scholarship than polemics. De Lange's study of his thought is a well written book that has yet to be equaled.

WILKEN's book seeks to explore Christian-Jewish relations through the eyes of one of the most revered writers of the high patristic period. John Chrysostom is mostly known for the eloquent sermons that he preached to his congregation in Antioch. This book is valuable because it attempts to understand Chrysostom's particular stance toward Judaism and his Christian audience in its late fourth-century C.E. context. Wilken is successful in transporting the reader back into the struggles facing Christianity. Christian history at this point was not a picture of steady success and world domination. Wilken examines Chrysostom in the light of Emperor Julian's anti-Christian agenda, Antiochene Jewry, the attractions of Judaism, and the unrest in his own church. His scholarship shows that Chrysostom is less concerned about Jews per se than he is about Christians who grant authority to the power of Jewish practice and worship. Wilken's style is clear and accessible to the nonspecialist reader.

SIMON's study has had a revolutionary effect on scholarship in this area. It challenged directly the long-held belief that Judaism buckled under the success of the Christian mission and became inverted and passive. Against the apparent silence of the Jewish sources, he posits the view that the only way to understand the intensity of the Christian sources is to assume an active and vigorous competition between Jews and Christians for converts. Christians produced *Adversus Judaeos* material because Jews were meeting Christians "blow for blow." Simon's view of mutual conflict has become quite popular in scholarship. This scenario is problematic because it assumes an active Jewish mission alongside the Christian mission and imposes Christian values (i.e., mission and conversion) on Judaism. This seminal work has recently come under fire because of these underlying assumptions, but it continues to stand as a central text in the field.

MACCOBY's book is a combination of commentary, history, and translation. He has chosen three of the chief Christian-Jewish debates staged in the Middle Ages: the Paris Disputation of 1240, the Barcelona Disputation of 1263, and the Tortosa Disputation of 1413–1414. Maccoby's explanations are clear and help the reader understand the Jewish communities and the individuals behind these disputations. In Paris it was a show trial with the Talmud in the dock. The Tortosa Disputation was characterized by terror and an inquisitional atmosphere. The disputation at Barcelona stands as the only occasion where moments of true debate occurred, and this is the debate that obviously holds Maccoby's imagination. His admiration for Nahmanides (the Jewish protagonist in the dispute) is obvious. The two accounts of this debate—Christian and Jewish—serve as helpful reminders of how accounts can differ based on one's perspective. This is a well written and accessible account of these influential disputations.

LANGMUIR brings together several articles published previously and a few new chapters to form his thesis on the development of antisemitism. The Holocaust plays a large role in this exploration. It is this eradicationist form of antisemitism that Langmuir sets out to trace. The chapters form a kind of journey of discovery that culminates in Langmuir's dating of antisemitism to the 12th century. Before this period there was a strong tradition of anti-Judaic teaching within the medieval church, but he sees two factors occasioning the shift to modern antisemitism: first, the economic explosion of the 12th century, when moneylending was one of the few vocations open to Jews; and second, the 12th-century renaissance, which raised serious doubts about the certainty of Christian doctrine and faith. Rumors that the Jews wanted to kill Christians or desecrate the host helped prove that Christ was indeed in the Eucharist and that Christianity was in fact right. Langmuir sees the level of hate in the late Middle Ages as essentially comparable to that of Nazi Germany and as such the starting point for modern antisemitism.

TIMOTHY J. HORNER

See also Christian-Jewish Relations: Contemporary Dialogue

Christian-Jewish Relations: Contemporary Dialogue

Fisher, Eugene J. (editor), *Visions of the Other: Jewish and Christian Theologians Assess the Dialogue*, New York: Paulist, 1994

Fisher, Eugene J., A. James Rudin, and Marc H. Tanenbaum (editors), *Twenty Years of Jewish-Catholic Relations*, New York: Paulist, 1986

Flannery, Edward H., *The Anguish of the Jews: Twenty-Three Centuries of Anti-Semitism*, New York: Macmillan, 1965; revised and updated edition, New York: Paulist, 1985

Gilbert, Arthur, *The Vatican Council and the Jews*, Cleveland, Ohio: World, 1968

Klenicki, Leon (editor), *Toward a Theological Encounter: Jewish Understandings of Christianity*, New York: Paulist, 1991

Oesterreicher, John M., *The New Encounter: Between Christians and Jews*, New York: Philosophical Library, 1986

Rittner, Carol and John K. Roth, *From the Unthinkable to the Unavoidable: American Christian and Jewish Scholars Encounter the Holocaust*, Westport, Connecticut, and London: Greenwood, 1997

Shermis, Michael and Arthur E. Zannoni (editors), *Introduction to Jewish-Christian Relations*, New York: Paulist, 1991

The last three decades of the 20th century witnessed a remarkable transformation of the relations between Christians and Jews. From the earliest centuries of the Christian era, Christianity fundamentally looked upon Jews as a rejected and despised people who had relinquished their role in the divine covenant by virtue of their rejection of Jesus as the promised Jewish Messiah. As a consequence, they have been subject to severe social and political restrictions and sometimes even to death, both during the Crusades and in a variety of subsequent pogroms.

For some Christians, especially those who had resisted the Nazis during the Holocaust, the evil of the traditional Christian approach to Jews and Judaism became very apparent. As a result, they launched an effort to refocus Christianity's approach to the Jewish people. Joining them were important leaders in the American churches who in the first half of the 20th century had begun working with Jews to combat economic injustices and racism. These forces coalesced in a powerful way at the Second Vatican Council, which issued a historic declaration on the church and the Jewish people in chapter four of its statement on non-Christian religions. This document also inspired similar responses from major Protestant denominations and ecumenical organizations such as the World Council of Churches. These official statements helped to generate a growing body of literature, some in a more popular vein and others decidedly scholarly in tone.

FISHER, who directs Catholic-Jewish relations for the National Conference of Catholic Bishops, has been a major contributor to the dialogue between Christians and Jews through his own writings as well as through the many volumes he has edited. Fisher's *Visions of the Other* contains four theological essays originally presented at the Ninth National Workshop on Christian-Jewish Relations in Baltimore (May 1986). The contributors are Irving Greenberg and David Hartman on the Jewish side and Paul van Buren and John T. Pawlikowski on the Christian side.

Greenberg, who has been one of the few Jewish scholars to address the theological role of Christianity from a distinctly Jewish perspective, stresses both the similarities and the differences in the roles that Judaism and Christianity play in the divine strategy of human redemption. He calls upon Jews today, despite the tragic history of Christian antisemitism, to recognize the sense of covenantal partnership. For Greenberg, one central implication of the covenant is the need for a plurality of legitimate symbols if God's interest is to elevate humanity to the fullest capacity of life.

Hartman, one of present-day Judaism's most creative thinkers, directs his thoughts toward the development of a spirit of pluralism in Judaism. This pluralism would allow Jews to rejoice in Christians' affirmation of their spiritual identities without feeling threatened about Jewish spiritual identity.

The two Christian contributions by van Buren and Pawlikowski both look to a new Christian theology of the Jewish people. Van Buren discusses a new Christian theology emerging from the dialogue, which recognizes the reality of a single covenant that has been substantially renewed on several occasions. One such renewal led to the emergence of the Christian Church. Pawlikowski focuses on the importance of the Holocaust experience for the meaning of the covenant today both in Judaism and Christianity.

The collection edited by FISHER, RUDIN, and TANENBAUM covers a broader range of topics. These range from an analysis of the first two decades of the Vatican II era (Rudin, Tanenbaum, and George Higgins), to the importance of the dialogue for biblical studies (Michael J. Cook and Lawrence Boadt), to liturgical and theological issues (Fisher, Pawlikowski, and Greenberg), and an analysis of official Catholic statements on Jewish-Christian relations (Fisher).

FLANNERY's volume, in its new updated edition, remains a popular classic in the field of Christian-Jewish relations. While not as scholarly a study as more recent works by Langmuir and others, it has been a challenging volume for many Christians since the original edition was published by Macmillan in 1965. Flannery has restored to Christian history pages thrown out for centuries and has forced the church to confront the dark side of its tradition. The volume chronicles the long history of antisemitism from its pre-Christian roots to the present day. Definitely, it is a book that has made a critical difference in the contemporary Christian-Jewish relationship.

GILBERT was one of the pioneers from the Jewish side in the dialogue with the Christians, and he was present at the Second Vatican Council. His book discusses the emergence of the conciliar text *Nostra Aetate*, whose fourth chapter produced the historic turnabout in Catholic-Jewish relations. He captures some of the delicate negotiations and compromises in formulating a text that had considerable initial opposition but which was strongly supported by the American hierarchy at the council.

KLENICKI, who has served for many years as the Director of Interreligious Relations for the Anti-Defamation League,

has edited (along with Eugene Fisher) several important volumes concerned with aspects of the dialogue. *Toward a Theological Encounter* is one of his most important contributions. Klenicki prodded a number of prominent Jewish scholars to begin to rethink the Jewish religious perspective on Christianity. It was not an easy task, and he had to reject some of the original contributions. But in the end, with essays by Klenicki himself and others such as Elliot Dorff, Walter Jacob, David Novak, Michael Wyschogrod, S. Daniel Breslauer, and David Dalin, he has assembled a comprehensive overview of Jewish viewpoints. This is one of the best and most comprehensive volumes on the subject.

OESTERREICHER's volume is a central contribution to an understanding of the development of Vatican II's declaration on the church and the Jewish people. While Arthur Gilbert was an observer at the council, Oesterreicher was an important architect of *Nostra Aetate*'s fourth chapter. A Jewish convert to Catholicism, Oesterreicher began to present an enhanced Christian understanding of Judaism through his publication *The Bridge*. While there were conversionist tendencies evident in Oesterreicher's early works, *The New Encounter* shows that he had moved beyond that approach. Clearly this is a major work by a person who, despite some valid criticism of his outlook, has contributed significantly to the remarkable transformation of Christianity regarding its Jewish question.

RITTNER and ROTH's book offers a comprehensive overview of major Jewish and Christian scholars' views on the theological significance of the Holocaust. It took some time for the Holocaust to surface in Christian-Jewish dialogue. Both Christians and Jews had a certain hesitation to raise the topic. But in recent years an increasing number of scholars have begun to recognize its central implications for contemporary theological reflection. The authors represent a good cross-section of contributors to the discussion. Susannah Heschel, Alan Berger, David Blumenthal, Richard L. Rubenstein, and Michael Berenbaum are major voices on the Holocaust in contemporary Judaism. The same holds true for the Christian contributors, who include Eva Fleischner, Harry James Cargas, Franklin Littell, Alice and Roy Eckardt, John Roth, and John Pawlikowski. This is an excellent volume for entering the world of religious reflection on the Holocaust.

The collection by SHERMIS and ZANNONI has become one of the more popular introductory volumes on the current dialogue. It includes essays by leading Jewish and Christian scholars. These essays cover a range of topics, most of which are central to the present-day Christian-Jewish conversation. Included are chapters on the Hebrew Scriptures and Jewish-Christian relations (Zannoni), on the New Testament and on Pharisaism (Cook and Pawlikowski), on the Holocaust (McGarry), on antisemitism (Athans), on intermarriage (Seltzer), on God (Culbertson), on feminism and the dialogue (Heschel), on the land tradition (Everett), and a final chapter on educational dimensions of the dialogue (Shermis). This is an excellent text for adult discussion groups as well as basic courses on Christian-Jewish relations.

JOHN T. PAWLIKOWSKI

See also Christian-Jewish Relations: Apologetics and Polemics

Chronicles

Auld, A.G., *Kings without Privilege: David and Moses in the Story of the Bible's Kings*, Edinburgh: Clark, 1994

Graham, Matt P., Kenneth Hoglund, and Steven McKenzie, *The Chronicler as Historian* (Journal for the Study of the Old Testament, Supplement Series, 238), Sheffield, South Yorkshire: Sheffield Academic Press, 1997

Japhet, Sara, *I and II Chronicles: A Commentary* (Old Testament Library), Louisville, Kentucky: Westminster/Knox, 1993

McKenzie, Steven L., *The Chronicler's Use of the Deuteronomistic History* (Harvard Semitic Monographs, no. 33), Atlanta, Georgia: Scholars Press, 1985

Myers, J.M. (editor and translator), *I Chronicles* (Anchor Bible, vol. 12), Garden City, New York: Doubleday, 1965

Myers, J.M. (editor and translator), *II Chronicles* (Anchor Bible, vol. 13), Garden City, New York: Doubleday, 1965

Williamson, H.G.M., *1 and 2 Chronicles* (New Century Bible Commentary), Grand Rapids, Michigan: Eerdmans, and London: Marshall, Morgan and Scott, 1982

Commentary on Chronicles has typically focused on several issues: the Chronicler's identity, the scope of the author's work, the purpose of the text, its sources, and the historicity of the events reported.

MYERS (1965a, 1965b) presents a standard commentary on Chronicles, offering an introductory essay and detailed explication of each chapter of the book as well as his own annotated translation of the Hebrew text, which attends to problems arising from the Hebrew idiom. Although he recognizes that there are discrepancies between the theology of Chronicles and that of Ezra-Nehemiah, Myers accepts the traditional view that these texts were written by a single author, perhaps Ezra himself, and argues that any differences between the books can be attributed to the passage of time. At the time of writing Chronicles, Myers contends, the chronicler was interested in the restoration of the kingdom with a Davidic scion at the head, while Ezra-Nehemiah evinces the same author's growing concern with the law, priesthood, and the temple. Myers also presents the traditional argument about the sources available to the chronicler, asserting that the chronicler knew the entire text that corresponds to the modern biblical books from Genesis to Kings. According to Myers, the chronicler added or subtracted from these biblical sources to support his ideology, using official lists, independent prophetic materials, and temple archives as supplementary sources to create what Myers assumes to be an accurate history.

WILLIAMSON's commentary also follows a traditional format, with an introductory essay and a detailed exegesis of each chapter of Chronicles. He does not provide a translation of the text but encourages the reader to consult the Revised Standard Version (RSV). Williamson's perspective is greatly influenced by an article by Sara Japhet, which argues that different authors wrote Ezra-Nehemiah and Chronicles and contends that the similarities of vocabulary and style between the two texts can be explained by the fact that the two authors shared a postexilic Hebrew idiom. While Myers asserts that Chronicles was written early in the Persian period, around 515

B.C.E. when the Daric (1 Chronicles 29:7) was minted, Williamson theorizes that time must have elapsed for this anachronism to be tolerated, and he concludes that the lack of evidence of Hellenistic influences on the text implies it was written later in the Persian period, perhaps in the fourth century B.C.E. Williamson does concur with Myers, however, when he assumes that Chronicles is based on historical sources and can provide reliable information for the reconstruction of Israelite history.

McKENZIE's study grew out of a Harvard doctoral dissertation he wrote under Frank Cross, and it clearly shows the influence of his mentor's theory of the double redaction of the Deuteronomistic History. McKenzie hypothesizes that the chronicler based his text on the first (not the second) redaction of the Deuteronomistic History, but the results of his analysis, while interesting, are not fully convincing. McKenzie demonstrates that Chronicles closely follows the history in Kings until the account of the death of Josiah, at which point the two accounts diverge. Therefore, McKenzie proposes, the version of Kings that the chronicler used must have been different from the modern text, ending with Josiah's demise (the very moment at which Cross contends that the first redaction of the Deuteronomistic History concludes). McKenzie argues, however, that many passages that Cross identifies as additions to Kings by the second redactor are, in fact, represented in Chronicles. In particular, he cites strong literary and theological evidence to suggest that four passages that Cross assigned to the second redaction actually were present in the first. These reassigned passages include references to exile, the conditional status of the Davidic covenant, the condemnation of Menasseh, and the peaceful fate of Josiah, and McKenzie uses these references to speculate that the first redaction is a postexilic text. If McKenzie is correct about this point, then traditional assumptions about both the Deuteronomistic History and the relationship between that history and Chronicles must be greatly revised.

Written from a conservative perspective, JAPHET's volume is far more comprehensive than other standard commentaries. It includes an introductory essay, detailed analyses of each chapter, the RSV translation, and notes on the Hebrew text and controversial elements of the RSV. Like Williamson, Japhet contends that Chronicles and Ezra-Nehemiah were written by different authors. Japhet further argues that Chronicles was written after Ezra-Nehemiah, proposing that these two books—along with the Pentateuch and Joshua through Kings, in their present form—served as major sources for the chronicler. Japhet also assumes that the chronicler had access to extrabiblical sources, and she suggests that the text provides authentic history. Disputing the theories of previous commentators who identify Chronicles with an earlier era, Japhet posits that the text was written around the end of the fourth century B.C.E., after the Persian domination but before Greek influence. She deduces the theology of the chronicler by tracing amendments that the author makes to his supposed original sources in the Deuteronomistic History. This hypothesis ignores McKenzie's work, which suggests that differences between Chronicles and Kings may result from the fact that the chronicler used a version of Kings that diverges from the modern text.

By contrast, AULD acknowledges the work of McKenzie in his monograph, which compares and contrasts passages from the Book of Kings to the text of Chronicles in order to theorize that both the Deuteronomistic historian and the chronicler inherited and revised a common text. Auld also argues that the theology of each of these authors can be derived from their additions to this shared text; he does not allow that the authors may have omitted parts of the original. This perspective provides a very different way of understanding both the chronicler and the Deuteronomistic History from that found in traditional commentaries, but it has found few adherents among other biblical scholars, most of whom still identify Kings as a source for Chronicles.

GRAHAM, HOGLUND, and McKENZIE present 11 essays that grew out of a colloquium on the topic of the historicity of Chronicles. All but one of the authors in this anthology conclude that the text adds little to the history gleaned from Kings, showing that scholarly opinion at the end of the 20th century differed radically from that expressed by Myers three decades earlier.

LISBETH S. FRIED

Chuetas *see* Crypto-Jews, Contemporary

Circumcision

Hoffman, Lawrence A., *Covenant of Blood: Circumcision and Gender in Rabbinic Judaism* (Chicago Studies in the History of Judaism), Chicago: University of Chicago Press, 1996

Isaac, E., "Circumcision as a Covenant Rite," *Anthropos: International Review of Ethnology and Linguistics*, 59, 1964

Lander, Janice et al., "Comparison of Ring Block, Dorsal Penile Nerve Block, and Topical Anesthesia for Neonatal Circumcision: A Randomized Controlled Trial," *Journal of the American Medical Association*, 278(24), 1997

Morgenstern, Julian, "The 'Bloody Husband' (?) (Exod. 4:24–26) Once Again," *Hebrew Union College Annual*, 34, 1963

Moss, Lisa, "Circumcision: A Jewish Inquiry," *Midstream*, 38, January 1992

Raul-Friedman, "A Rebuttal: Circumcision: A Jewish Legacy," *Midstream*, 38, April 1992

Romberg, Rosemary, *Circumcision: The Painful Dilemma*, South Hadley, Massachusetts: Bergin and Garvey, 1985

Schechter, Solomon, "The Child in Jewish Literature," in *Studies in Judaism*, Philadelphia: Jewish Publication Society, and London: Black, 1896

Snowman, Jacob, *The Surgery of Ritual Circumcision*, London: Medical Board of the Initiation Society, 1904, 3rd edition revised by Leonard Snowman, 1962

Wallerstein, Edward, *Circumcision: An American Health Fallacy*, New York: Springer, 1980

Circumcision, the excision of the foreskin of the male organ, is normally the first ceremonial act in which the male Jew participates, albeit unwittingly. It is known in Jewish tradition as *berit milah* (covenant of circumcision), usually abbreviated to *bris* by Ashkenazi Jews and to *milah* by Sephardim. This rite is ordained in Genesis 17:9–14, but circumcision was not invented at this juncture; rather a new spiritual meaning was breathed into a preexistent and quite widespread custom, as pointed out in the orthodox Pentateuch edited by J.H. Hertz in his commentary on this section. The medical benefits of the procedure are a matter of much controversy.

SCHECHTER limits his discussion to the social aspects of the rite in his classic *Studies in Judaism*. Although dated, these studies, written by a man who had an enduring influence on the development of Conservative Judaism, have continuing value. He sets the rite in its historical context, pointing out that from earliest times it was fulfilled with great joy, with individuals willing to undergo martyrdom in order to ensure its perpetuation. It is clear from his presentation that the *berit milah* is simply one constituent of the highly ritualized Jewish religion, albeit a very important one. It is an integral part of a nexus of custom and tradition that has ensured the continuance of the Jewish religion, without reference to its possible benefits or disadvantages in other respects.

MORGENSTERN's intent is to explain the mysterious passage in Exodus in which God seeks to kill Moses, and Moses is saved only by the intervention of his wife, who circumcises their son. In so doing, Morgenstern offers an explanation of the origins of the rite. He holds that performance of the ceremony at an early age, rather than at puberty, was original in the Semitic tribes and represents part of the taboo culture. Childbirth brought a state of impurity, which was purged by offering to the god or gods a portion of the tabooed object. Detachment of a part of the child's body and the shedding of his blood freed him from the possession of the spirits, and this is "quite manifestly" the origin of the rite of circumcision.

ISAAC offers a clear anthropological explanation with constant reference to Jewish sources. He holds that circumcision early in life is the original custom, but was delayed until after the first week, which was a taboo period.

The SNOWMANs were medical doctors and traditional *mohelim* (ritual circumcisers) who practiced for many years in England and circumcised members of the royal family. They expertly present the technical aspects of the operation.

MOSS writes a deeply felt plea to reevaluate circumcision in the light of modern findings, but her methodology is seriously flawed. She seeks halakhic reasons for the effective abolition of circumcision without any apparent awareness that conflict of laws is a normal situation in any legalistic context, and such conflicts—between federal mandates and states' rights, for example—are normally decided at some point for an enduring future. The fact that the halakhah may prohibit torturing a kitten or endangering the life of another human being simply does not pertain to circumcision which, by ancient consensus, clearly overrules these other principles.

RAUL-FRIEDMAN does not address the conflict issue in her rebuttal of Moss, but engages rather in a midrashic homily that expresses her passionate attachment to the "legacy" of circumcision.

HOFFMAN, an academic liturgiologist closely identified with Reform Judaism, offers one of the most recent extended studies of circumcision. This is a scholarly rather than a polemical work in which he addresses himself to a phenomenon that he finds puzzling. In 1843 a Jewish laymen's proposal to abolish circumcision as an outdated practice met with determined opposition on the part of rabbis who were inclined toward reform of the Jewish religion who had not balked at dispensing with Hebrew in Jewish prayer, cutting traditional ties with the Land of Israel, or rejecting the authority of the Talmud. Circumcision appears, then, as the sine qua non of Jewish identity. In his chapter "Reconstructing the Rite," Hoffman gives a detailed discussion of the rite as it exists now, quoting extensively from orthodox formulations, and shows that much of the liturgical material is medieval in origin. Hoffman goes on to discuss how circumcision fits into his perception of the rabbinic attitude toward gender differences: the strength of rabbinic men is that they control their impulses, and this is symbolized by circumcision. Women on the other hand are essentially uncontrolled; the spontaneous menstrual flow is symbolic of this. Hoffman discusses what he perceives as three categories that sum up modern uneasiness with circumcision. The first is the inherently sexist nature of the rite. He acknowledges this, but quotes with some approval the tendency to stress the covenantal aspect for both boys and girls at birth, making the actual operation in the case of boys secondary. The second is the fact that a fair amount of medical opinion considers circumcision unnecessary if proper hygienic practices are instituted. He offers no real response to this and indicates that it is difficult to justify automatic circumcision. The third is the moral argument that unnecessary pain is caused to the infant and thus to his parents. He indicates that the Jewish method is actually less painful than the use of clamps which is accepted medical procedure, a point made by several other writers. Hoffman does not really answer his original question, but this is hardly surprising, since the reasons why circumcision has had such a hold on moderns as well as primitives remain far from clear, despite the voluminous literature on the subject.

LANDER describes a controlled study of pain suffered by babies circumcised shortly after birth with the Gomco clamp and concludes that an anesthetic should be administered. Common Orthodox Jewish practice is to have a general anesthetic for children over the age of one year and a local anesthetic for adults. The use of a topical anesthetic for babies appears to be growing; in this case, the clamp is not used.

WALLERSTEIN and ROMBERG both write personal reactions to the question of whether circumcision should be continued, and they conclude that it should not. Raul-Friedman refers to Wallerstein as a circumcision expert, but in fact his expertise is self-taught. However, he has explored the subject thoroughly, and he gives many references for further reading.

To judge from these texts, it seems that Orthodox Jews will continue to practice circumcision along with all the other injunctions, which for them need no rational basis. Liberal Jews have the blessing and the curse of having to make a choice.

ALAN D. CORRÉ

Cochin Jews

Daniel, Ruby and Barbara C. Johnson, *Ruby of Cochin: An Indian Jewish Woman Remembers*, Philadelphia: Jewish Publication Society, 1995

Fuks, Suzon, *Keeping the Light: A Diary of South India*, Australia: published by the author

Johnson, Barbara C., " 'Our Community' in Two Worlds: The Cochin Paradesi Jews in India and Israel," Ph.D. diss., University of Massachusetts, 1985

Katz, Nathan and Ellen S. Goldberg, *The Last Jews of Cochin: Jewish Identity in Hindu India*, Columbia: University of South Carolina Press, 1993

Kushner, Gilbert, *Immigrants from India in Israel: Planned Change in an Administered Community*, Tucson: University of Arizona Press, 1973

Lord, J. Henry, *The Jews in India and the Far East*, Kolhapur: Mission, 1907; Westport, Connecticut: Greenwood, 1976

Mandelbaum, David, "Social Stratification among the Jews of Cochin in India and Israel," *Jewish Journal of Sociology*, 17, 1975; reprinted in *Jews in India*, edited by Thomas Timberg, New York: Advent, 1986

Segal, J.B., *A History of the Jews of Cochin*, London and Portland, Oregon: Vallentine Mitchell, 1993

Slapak, Orpa (editor), *The Jews of India: A Story of Three Communities*, Jerusalem: Israel Museum, 1995

Walerstein, Marcia S., "Public Rituals among the Jews from Cochin, India, in Israel: Expressions of Ethnic Identity," Ph.D. diss., University of California at Los Angeles, 1987

The Cochin Jews have lived for perhaps 2,000 years on India's southwest coast, now the modern state of Kerala. Residing in security under the friendly rule of Hindu maharajahs, they adapted to Indian culture but kept mainstream Jewish religious law and custom through contact with Middle Eastern and European Jews. Literature about them focuses mainly on historical origins, social relations among their internal factions, and recent life in Israel. Most migrated to Israel in the 1950s; there are now about 5,000 Cochinim in Israel and less than 50 in Kerala.

SEGAL, a British professor of Semitic languages, authored a comprehensive book on Cochin Jewish history, drawing on sources in English, Hebrew, and other languages. He begins with local origin legends; ancient trade between Kerala and the Middle East; the tenth-century royal copper plate document granting privileges to a well-established Jewish community in Cranganore (north of Cochin); and the 14th- to 16th-century exodus of Jews from Cranganore to Cochin and elsewhere in Kerala. The book is then divided into three periods of colonial rule in Kerala—Portuguese, Dutch, and British—echoing the centrality of colonial sources, and including new data from Portuguese archives. Other sources include travel writings, Hebrew documents by Cochin Jews, and the work of several generations of Indian and western scholars. Much of Segal's material is about the Paradesi or "white" Jews of Cochin, a separate congregation formed by post-15th-century immigrants from the Middle East and Europe (many of them Sephardi) who did not intermarry with the much larger and older group of Malabari or Kerala Jews, but who strongly identified with Kerala culture. As they were most active in international trade and favored by the colonial rulers, their story was more accessible to visitors and outside scholars.

LORD, a Church of England missionary who visited Cochin at the beginning of the 20th century, was the first outsider to give voice to the Malabari section of the community, reporting their version of their ancient origins. Through Lord, they rebutted the "white" claim that it was their ancestors who settled in Cranganore and that the Malabaris descend from slaves of these Paradesi ancestors.

MANDELBAUM, a noted American anthropologist and expert on Indian culture, wrote an influential article in 1939 on Cochin Jewish social structure, based partly on a brief visit to Cochin as a graduate student. In 1975 he revised and updated the study, setting forth a model of three Jewish castes in Cochin: the "white" (Paradesi), the "black" (Malabari), and the "brown" ("meshuhrarim" or manumitted slaves and their descendants in both factions). Grounded in his study of the larger Indian caste system, this model emphasizes ways in which Cochin Jews kept socially and ritually separate from each other, rather than the ways in which they were united. Though his article has affected almost all subsequent research on the Cochin Jews, Cochin Jews do not see themselves as constituting separate castes, nor do they use the term "brown" to refer to the so-called meshuhrarim.

DANIEL and JOHNSON coauthored this life story of Ruby Daniel, a Cochin Jewish woman who was born in 1912 in the Paradesi community. Daniel resoundingly challenges the labeling of her own family and others as meshuhrarim, and gives an alternative reading of Cochin Jewish history based on stories from her grandparents. She also tells about her own life; the first Cochin Jewish female to attend secondary school and college, she worked as a clerk and served in the Indian Navy during World War II before migrating to Israel in 1951 and settling on a kibbutz. The book includes translations of Malayalam-language Jewish songs sung by Cochin women, descriptions of holiday and life cycle celebrations from Daniel's childhood, and an introductory section by American anthropologist Johnson, who has studied the Cochin Jews for almost 30 years.

KUSHNER, an American applied anthropologist, carried out his study of planned change in an Israeli moshav (cooperative settlement) of Cochin immigrants from 1960 to 1961. Sympathetically describing the lives of the new immigrants (all Malabaris), he notes their transformation from small city or village merchants in Kerala to agricultural workers in the new Israel. This moshav was an "administered community" where few Cochini immigrants were yet taking initiative or responsibility for political or economic decision-making—in contrast to the later economic success of Cochini moshavim.

WALERSTEIN's folklore dissertation (based on extensive participant-observation) centers on more recent moshav-based Cochini life in Israel, focusing on public ceremonies (weddings, Simhat Torah, ceremonial vows in memory of a 17th-century holy man, Purim parties, synagogue dedications, a 30th anniversary celebration of Cochini aliyah) as expressions of ethnic identity. Her study is filled with ethnographic detail on Malabari life in Kerala and Israel, new information about

their immigration, and useful analysis of ritual change. Walerstein is an American scholar who lived for many years in Israel and developed close ties in the Cochini community.

JOHNSON's dissertation is an ethnographic study of the Paradesi community's transition from India to Israel, drawing on participant-observation in both countries. The Paradesis emigrated later than the Malabaris and now live scattered throughout Israel. Johnson describes past and contemporary life in Cochin, then analyzes how the Paradesis maintain a separate community identity in Israel despite their loss of geographical unity, by developing more flexible external boundaries, mutual aid and visiting patterns, and a new emphasis on community parties. Detailed comparison of Passover preparations in Cochin and Israel shows continuity and change. This study emphasizes women's central role in community preservation and social change.

KATZ and GOLDBERG (a professor of religion and a journalist from the United States, respectively) spent a year in the Paradesi community of Cochin not long after Johnson. Their book combines a thorough review of Cochin Jewish history with descriptions of daily life among the few Jews remaining there. Analysis of the ritual cycle of the Jewish year emphasizes parallels with Hindu beliefs and ritual practices, especially during the High Holy Days and Passover.

FUKS, a Belgian-born photographer, lived from 1993 to 1996 in Kerala. This book combines her exquisite photographs of the few Cochin Jews remaining in India with a handwritten diary of her experiences there. She combines artistry with personal and cultural sensitivity in intimate portraits of everyday life and special celebrations among Jews in Cochin, Ernakulam, and nearby villages. The historical introduction is by Samuel H. Hallegua, warden of the Paradesi synagogue.

SLAPAK's thorough study of Jewish material culture in India includes invaluable documentation and illustrations of Cochin Jewish synagogues, ceremonial objects, home rituals, daily life, dress, customs, and ceremonies.

BARBARA C. JOHNSON

Cohen, Hermann   1842–1918

German philosopher

Bergman, Samuel Hugo, *Faith and Reason: An Introduction to Modern Jewish Thought* (Hillel Little Books, vol. 5), translated and edited by Alfred Jospe, Washington: B'nai B'rith Hillel Foundations, 1961

Borowitz, Eugene B., *Choices in Modern Jewish Thought: A Partisan Guide*, New York: Behrman House, 1983; 2nd edition, West Orange, New Jersey: Behrman House, 1995

Poma, Andrea, *La Filosofia Critica di Hermann Cohen*, 1988; translated by John Denton as *The Critical Philosophy of Hermann Cohen* (SUNY Series in Jewish Philosophy), Albany: State University of New York Press, 1997

Rotenstreich, Nathan, *Jewish Philosophy in Modern Times: From Mendelssohn to Rosenzweig*, New York: Holt, Rinehart and Winston, 1968

Rotenstreich, Nathan, *Jews and German Philosophy: The Polemics of Emancipation*, New York: Schocken, 1984

Samuelson, Norbert, *An Introduction to Modern Jewish Philosophy* (SUNY Series in Jewish Philosophy), Albany: State University of New York Press, 1989

Schwarzschild, Stephen, *The Pursuit of the Ideal* (SUNY Series in Jewish Philosophy), edited by Menachem Kellner, Albany: State University of New York Press, 1990

Hermann Cohen was born in Coswig in 1842. He was the son of a cantor, and for a time Cohen studied to become a rabbi at the liberal Jewish Theological Seminary of Breslau before leaving to study philosophy, first at the University of Breslau and then at the University of Berlin. In 1865, he received his doctorate in philosophy from the University of Halle, and in 1873 he was appointed lecturer in philosophy at the University of Marburg. He became full professor in 1876 and taught at Marburg until 1912. From 1912 until his death in 1918, he taught at the Hochschule fuer die Wissenschaft des Judentums in Berlin.

At Marburg, Cohen was the founder of the very influential philosophical school known as Marburg neo-Kantianism. Claiming to have recovered the classical idealism of Plato, Leibniz, and Kant, Cohen attempted in particular to apply rigorously what he took to be Kant's transcendental method. Cohen's early works centered on a reinterpretation of Kant's three-part system. He published *Kant's Theory of Experience* in 1871, *Kant's Grounding of Ethics* in 1877, and *Kant's Grounding of Aesthetics* in 1889. With the publication of *Logic of Pure Cognition* in 1902, Cohen began to construct his own philosophical system. *Ethics of Pure Will* followed in 1904 and *Aesthetics of Pure Feeling* in 1912. Interpretations of Cohen's Jewish thought emphasize his final two major works: *The Concept of Religion in the System of Philosophy,* published in 1915, and *The Religion of Reason out of the Sources of Judaism,* published posthumously in 1919. In his introduction to Cohen's Jewish writings, Franz Rosenzweig argues that Cohen's late philosophy constitutes an existential break with his earlier idealist system, and the Jewish philosophical debate about Cohen continues to center on this issue of the philosophical relation of these later works on religion to Cohen's system as a whole. This debate also addresses broader questions concerning Cohen's respective relations with German and Jewish culture. Interpreters who argue that Cohen's writings on religion demonstrate a break with his idealist system tend to maintain also that this break marked his return to Judaism from a previous stage of alienation, while those who dispute the former contention also tend to dispute the latter, often arguing that Cohen never left the Jewish faith and that he never stopped identifying with the Jewish people.

BERGMAN argues that Cohen underwent a philosophical, social, religious, and existential change as a result of two experiences. First, when Heinrich von Treitschke published an antisemitic pamphlet in 1879, Cohen felt the need to defend Judaism publicly, publishing his own response, titled "The Jewish Question: A Confession," in 1880. Second, in 1914, Cohen traveled to Poland to lecture to Polish Jewry, and, according to Bergman, "these years brought a radical change in Cohen's philosophic orientation." Bergman acknowledges that Cohen himself was unaware of this change, but the author maintains that Cohen's writings on religion reflect an attempt to deal with the existential self, an issue that, Bergman contends, Cohen's earlier philosophical system could not approach.

ROTENSTREICH (1968 and 1984) offers a more technical analysis of Cohen's philosophy than Bergman, but he shares with Bergman the assumption that Cohen's writings on religion reflect an existential turn in the philosopher's system. Dividing Cohen's thought into two distinct periods, Rotenstreich examines the methodological change that (he claims) accompanies Cohen's conception of religion, asserting,

> In short, with the emphasis on the relation between religion and logic in his second period, Cohen had to make use of significant, real concepts; from the standpoint of method, he had to rely on experience as the source of important religious concepts, such as "I," sin, fellow man, love, suffering etc. . . .

More broadly, Rotenstreich maintains that Cohen's thought develops from and is the culmination of a broader German-Jewish philosophical effort to argue that Judaism is consonant with ethics. Accordingly, Rotenstreich discusses Cohen's conceptual relation to some basic tenets of the Reform Movement both in Germany and the United States. In particular, Rotenstreich explores Cohen's conception of Judaism's mission to the nations and the ways in which Cohen's view of Israel's historic fate has some fundamental affinity with the thought of David Einhorn (a central 19th-century exponent of reform in the United States).

SAMUELSON challenges the contention that there is a break in Cohen's system when the philosopher turns to the subject of religion, arguing that this mistaken position reflects the inability of interpreters to recognize the relation between the real and the ideal in Cohen's thought, particularly in his view of mathematics. To support this argument, Samuelson offers a detailed analysis of the interrelations among Cohen's mathematical, philosophical, and Jewish thought.

POMA's work offers the most comprehensive account of Cohen's thought available in the English language. This book bridges the issues that concern German, Israeli, and U.S. scholarship on Cohen. Against Rosenzweig in particular, Poma maintains that in the philosopher's religious writings, "Cohen further investigated problems that were already present in his system, and . . . his results were not a turning point, but a coherent further investigation of critical philosophy." Particular contributions of Poma's book are the author's lucid explanation of Cohen's logical conception of "conservation" and its relation to Cohen's arguments about messianic history, as well as Poma's convincing argument that for Cohen, the idea of God bridges logic and ethics. These points support Poma's argument for the continuity of Cohen's philosophical concerns and methods. Poma points out that Cohen's philosophy of religion, and his discussion of Jewish monotheism in particular, deals with "the problem of the limit," a problem that logic and ethics could only glimpse.

SCHWARZSCHILD rejects the notion that Cohen's *Religion of Reason out of the Sources of Judaism* constitutes an existential break with the philosopher's earlier system for both philosophical and biographical reasons. Schwarzschild uses Cohen's thought as the basis for his own philosophical arguments about the modern meanings of Judaism, art, ethics, and national identity. Summarizing Cohen's influence on his thought, Schwarzschild states that Cohen

> carried out the program in Jewish terms of philosophically restoring the "infinite" gap between ideality and reality and explicating in technical detail what the actionable consequences of that gap are for science, ethics, aesthetics, religion, and social policy.

Schwarzschild also endorses Cohen's controversial anti-Zionist claims.

BOROWITZ assesses the contemporary relevance for Cohen's thought within the context of the United States. The author explores Cohen's ethical monotheism and his defense of the particularity of Jewish identity, arguing that Cohen directly and indirectly influenced 20th-century U.S. Jewish thinking. A critic of Cohen's views of God and practice, as well as of his notion of Jewish peoplehood, Borowitz concludes that "Cohen's thought . . . remains a challenge to anyone who would assert that Judaism is essentially particularistic." Despite the contemporary relevance of Cohen's views about universalism, however, Borowitz maintains that it would be difficult to revive Cohen's philosophy today.

LEORA BATNITZKY

Commandments

Bazak, Jacob (compiler), *Mishpat va-halakhah, mivhar teshuvot*, 1971; translated by Stephen M. Passamaneck as *Jewish Law and Jewish Life: Selected Rabbinical Responsa*, 8 vols., New York: Union of American Hebrew Congregations, 1977

Chill, Abraham, *The Mitsvot: The Commandments and Their Rationale*, New York: Bloch, 1974

Maimonides, Moses, *The Commandments: Sefer Ha-Mitsvoth of Maimonides*, 2 vols., edited and translated by Charles Chavel, London and New York: Soncino, 1967

Neusner, Jacob, *Scriptures of the Oral Torah: Sanctification and Salvation in the Sacred Books of Judaism*, San Francisco: Harper and Row, 1987

Rabinowitz, Abraham Hirsch, *Taryag: A Study of the Origin and Historical Development, from the Earliest Times to the Present Day, of the Tradition that the Written Torah Contains Six Hundred and Thirteen Mitsvoth*, Jerusalem: Boys Town, 1967; as *TaRYaG: A Study of the Tradition that the Written Torah Contains 613 Mitsvot*, Northvale, New Jersey: Aronson, 1996

The Hebrew word *mitsvah* (plural: *mitsvot*), commonly translated into English as *commandment,* is used to imply something that has its origin in the divine that expresses the divine will for Israel. Chief among all the commandments are the Ten Commandments (Exodus 20:1–17 and Deuteronomy 5:6–21 and internalized in the ethical homily of Leviticus 19). The Ten Commandments stand apart from other laws both in terms of their rhetorical form and function. Popular tradition since tal-

mudic times has liked to regard the Pentateuch as legislating a total of 613 distinct commandments, although the specifics of this enumeration were a matter of keen medieval debate. Modern scholarship has stressed the similarity in form and content of biblical legislation to the legal systems of other ancient societies as well as the unique liturgical and spiritual function that commandments have performed in Jewish life.

MAIMONIDES discusses the basic principles used by the rabbis to determine which biblical precepts were to be included among the 613 mitsvot. The arbitrary-seeming number 613, alleged to comprise 365 negative mitsvot (corresponding to days in the solar year) and 248 positive mitsvot (corresponding to the putative number of parts of the human body), is manifestly less than the actual number of legal stipulations in Scripture. Maimonides seeks to explain and defend the number, however, and he offers classifications into which various mitsvot are to be divided. This exercise in the rationalization of an aggadic whim, in which Maimonides had been anticipated by such distinguished precursors as Saadia, constitutes one of the most influential schematizations in the history of Judaism.

RABINOWITZ begins his study with the time-honored assertion that the 613 mitsvot serve as a pedagogically perfect basis for learning about and understanding the heart of Judaism, in its written (biblical) and oral (rabbinic) dimensions. The Hebrew mnemonic *TaRYaG* (the numerical value of whose letters equals 613) thus becomes a symbol for the whole of the halakhic system. As Rabinowitz shows, the mitsvot have often been the subject of distinguishing categorization: mitsvot that derive directly from Scripture and mitsvot that derive from rabbinic discussion; less important mitsvot and more important mitsvot; rational mitsvot and revealed mitsvot; or mitsvot regulating conduct toward God and mitsvot regulating interpersonal relationships. Rabinowitz's viewpoint denies the value of such differentiations in favor of the mysticism of Mishnah Avot, where the view is expressed that no one can know the reward to be gained by the fulfillment of even the simplest precept.

NEUSNER considers the dual nature of Jewish revelation, written (biblical) and oral (rabbinic), highlighting a matter of fundamental importance in the study of Jewish law. Although the TaRYaG must be discerned in the written Torah itself, the meaning and significance of these "biblical" mitsvot cannot be understood unless one recognizes the process of continuing interpretation and disputation in which the rabbis were so assiduously engaged. Examining how Judaism ascribed the title of Torah to postbiblical literature such as the Mishnah, in effect elevating such literature to the status of revelation, Neusner posits that the rationale for this ascription is explained in the opening verse of Avot, an expression of the belief that the teachings of the rabbis of the Mishnah had been

> received in the chain of tradition from Sinai. And what they teach is Torah. Now the Mishnah . . . enjoys its standing and authority because it comes from sages, and, it follows, sages' standing and authority come from God.

Neusner contends that the work of these rabbis took a classical expression of the will of the divine and infused its principles into the realm of the mundane. The mitsvot taught in rabbinic literature are a compilation of the finest human expression of which the scholars and sages of their era were capable. But these teachings were not presented as mere options by the rabbis; they were weighted with authority virtually equal to that of biblical legislation. This presentation was possible because the rabbis met "the enormous challenge of finding warrant in the written Torah for the truth revealed in the oral Torah." Neusner concludes that the work of the rabbis shows how the principles of biblical mitsvot can be adapted to fit the needs of an era and a society radically different from that which was envisioned in biblical times.

CHILL addresses a central question facing modern Jews: "What value or purpose is there in the practical observance or the intellectual analysis of those mitsvot that seem to be outdated?" In his vigorously Orthodox defense of the mitsvot, Chill recognizes that the reasons for observing the commandments may at times seem "unappealing," but he insists that in such cases, "the reader should not arrogantly assume to himself the monopoly of wisdom and reject that rationale."

BAZAK, a Jerusalem judge and professor of criminology at Bar Ilan University, recognizes that a majority of Jews since the 19th century have viewed the mitsvot as unrelated to their lives and values. Searching through the legal opinions of the great rabbinic authorities of the 11th through the 15th centuries, Bazak focuses upon cases dealing with torts, while excluding opinions regarding ritual and family law. According to Passamaneck, the translator of this text, Bazak makes this selection because

> traditionally, a student of Talmud began his studies with chapters from the civil and commercial law . . . [because] the law, if it is to have meaning in society, must function in the heat and press of the marketplace, the shop, the hiring hall, and wherever men strive and strain to earn a livelihood.

Bazak successfully demonstrates that post-talmudic masters of Jewish law updated rabbinic interpretations of specific commandments yet held to the practical ideal of the mishnaic teachers underscored by Neusner. While Bazak, unlike Chill, does not attempt to offer reasons why modern Jews should adopt traditional ritual practices, he does present excellent examples of ancient commandments' relevance to contemporary circumstances that show the extraordinary richness of Judaism's legal corpus.

CHARLES DAVID ISBELL

See also Decalogue

Community *see* Authority, Rabbinic and Communal

Conservative Judaism

Cardin, Nina and David Wolf Silverman (editors), *The Seminary at 100: Reflections on the Jewish Theological Seminary and the Conservative Movement*, New York: Rabbinical Assembly and the Jewish Theological Seminary, 1987

Commission on the Philosophy of Conservative Judaism, *Emet Ve-Emunah: Statement of Principles of Conservative Judaism*, New York: Jewish Theological Seminary, 1988

Davis, Moshe, *The Emergence of Conservative Judaism: The Historical School in 19th Century America* (Jacob R. Schiff Library of Jewish Contributions to American Democracy, no. 15), Philadelphia: Jewish Publication Society, 1963

Dorff, Elliot, *Conservative Judaism: Our Ancestors to Our Descendants*, New York: Youth Commission, United Synagogue of America, 1977

Gillman, Neil, *Conservative Judaism: The New Century*, West Orange, New Jersey: Behrman House, 1993

Klein, Isaac, *A Guide to Jewish Religious Practice* (Moreshet Series, vol. 6), New York: Jewish Theological Seminary, 1979

Sklare, Marshall, *Conservative Judaism: An American Religious Movement*, Glencoe, Illinois: Free Press, 1955; new augmented edition, New York: Schocken, 1972

Waxman, Mordecai (editor), *Tradition and Change: The Development of Conservative Judaism*, New York: Burning Bush, 1958

Founded under the influence of the positive-historical school of Jewish studies that emerged in 19th-century Germany and then in the United States, the Conservative movement is now the largest Jewish denomination in the United States (constituting roughly 43 percent of all synagogue-affiliated Jewish households); the movement is also increasingly active (under the name "Masorti," or "Traditional") in South America, Europe, and Israel. Beginning formally in New York in 1887 with the establishment of the Jewish Theological Seminary to train rabbis and educators, the movement now encompasses five schools ordaining rabbis (in New York, Los Angeles, Jerusalem, Budapest, and Buenos Aires), as well as the Rabbinical Assembly, the United Synagogue of America, youth groups, day schools, summer camps, and other institutions. For many, the title of Mordecai Waxman's collection, *Tradition and Change*, has come to stand as the most succinct statement of the movement's ideology. Holding Jewish law to be central to Jewish religion and life (although practices among the laity vary widely), Conservative Judaism also brings to tradition a historical consciousness and awareness of the ways in which Judaism has changed in response to circumstances in the past, thus considering further change permissible and even desirable in the present.

DORFF is written for young adults in the movement's youth groups, and the book's tone reflects its audience. Adult readers overlooking this detail will find a fine overview of Conservative Judaism's history, institutions, and beliefs on such issues as law, theology, Jewish unity, and Zionism. Dorff carefully delineates the variety of outlooks contained within the movement, even providing a chart summarizing approaches of Orthodox, Reform, and differing strands of Conservative Judaism to revelation and law. Dorff's outline of the organizational structure of the movement is somewhat, but not overly, out of date, and focuses primarily on the U.S. arm of the movement.

DAVIS's book details the origins of the Conservative movement in the 19th century. The United States, with its commitments to religious equality and the separation of church and state, presented Jews with a historically unprecedented social situation, to which the "Historical School" offered one response. The Historical School was distinguished by its embrace of Emancipation and Enlightenment; its name marked both its adherents' commitment to Judaism as passed down through history and their awareness that Jewish practice had adapted over the course of that history to changing conditions. Davis traces the rise of Conservative Judaism as an organized denomination out of the Historical School, particularly emphasizing the founding and development of the Jewish Theological Seminary. Also included are short biographies of major figures in the Historical School and several significant documents of the period.

Writings by a number of the movement's forebears, as well as its more recent leaders (nearly all rabbis), are collected in WAXMAN's anthology. The historical section of the book focuses primarily on the late 19th and early 20th centuries; the mid-19th-century German and U.S. backgrounds of the movement are represented by a single selection each. The rest of the book consists of mid-20th-century Conservative Jewish thinkers' various approaches to issues such as the ideology of the movement, its liturgy, Jewish law, education and unity, and Zionism. Also included are legal responsa on two of the most controversial changes to Jewish law made by the Conservative movement, the relaxation of Sabbath prohibitions to allow unrestricted use of electricity and driving to the synagogue.

CARDIN and SILVERMAN have collected a number of informative articles that were written more recently than those in Waxman's anthology. A comparison of the authors and topics in the two collections is telling because it reveals changes that the movement underwent in the 30 years that passed between their publications. For example, Cardin and Silverman include eight female contributors (compared to Waxman's single woman author). The more recent anthology also contains a section on "Responding to Feminism"; as well as articles from laypersons, including a section on "The Making of Lay Leadership; and an article on "The Renewal of the Cantor." The institutional growth of the movement is reflected in Cardin and Silverman's articles on Ramah summer camps, the Jewish Museum in New York, and the Masorti Movement in Israel; the movement's continuing dedication to academic scholarship is demonstrated by this book in a section called "Symposium on Scholarship and Belief." Other articles grapple with the ideology of the movement, explore its commitment to pluralism, assess its successes and failures, and look toward its future.

SKLARE attempts to describe Conservative Judaism as lived and practiced by its members, rabbinic and lay. Sklare's unique and enduring insight is that Conservative Judaism has been shaped as much by sociological as ideological factors, reflecting particularly the interaction of U.S. Jews with their national milieu. Based largely on mid-20th-century research in suburban Conservative congregations around Chicago, this book has publicized the "insider's" view of the movement (notably documenting the low levels of ritual observance among the laity), and this perspective initially faced an ambivalent and occasionally hostile reception. A final chapter, added in 1972, helps to update the book. Many of the sociological factors that Sklare identified as affecting (Conservative) Judaism remain in force today, and his picture of the Conservative movement remains thoroughly relevant.

The movement's ideology is formally addressed by the COMMISSION ON THE PHILOSOPHY OF CONSERVATIVE JUDAISM. In this publication, a committee of scholars and lay members attempt for the first time to delineate the movement's stand(s) on a variety of issues, which are organized under three rubrics: "God in the World," "The Jewish People," and "Living a Life of Torah." While it is clear that this document was produced by committee, its form amply captures the diversity and pluralism of Conservative Judaism. *Emet Ve-Emunah* has been critiqued for a lack of specifics regarding Jewish practice and for a certain degree of (perhaps inevitable) self-contradiction; nonetheless, as Gillman states, "*Emet Ve-Emunah* . . . provides the first consistent and coherent theological groundings for much of what the Movement has said and done for generations."

KLEIN is the most complete source on Jewish law as understood by the Conservative movement. While obviously not up-to-date on the most recent writings and decisions on matters of law in Conservative Judaism, the volume is designed to be used as a handy reference on matters of religious observance as they arise. The particular tension of Conservative Judaism, "tradition and change," is highly evident in this work, as Klein is as likely to cite the writings and rulings of Conservative scholars and the movement's Committee on Jewish Law and Standards as he is to refer to classical codifications of Jewish law or responsa literature.

GILLMAN, a professor at the Jewish Theological Seminary, developed his book, in part, from his courses on Conservative Judaism for rabbinical students. Another overview of the movement's history, institutions and ideology, this volume's tone is very different from Dorff's study. Gillman subtitles his introduction "A Lover's Quarrel," stating that he writes as an insider and an advocate but also as a critic of Conservative Judaism. His most trenchant critique concerns the movement's reluctance for most of its history to articulate a coherent ideology. Gillman attempts to tease out the ideology of the movement's founders as displayed in their writings, and he devotes a chapter to the writing of *Emet V-Emunah*. The author does not shy away from other divisive issues that have recently challenged the movement, such as the roles and ordination of women, the place of homosexuals, the question of patrilineal descent, and the lack of observance of Jewish law among many of the movement's laypeople. A notable feature of this book is its generous use of visual materials. Finally, since Gillman's text is the most recent of the books surveyed here, it stands in a unique position to critique its precursors, an opportunity that the author seizes.

GAIL LABOVITZ

Continuity

Bayme, Steven (editor), *Facing the Future: Essays on Contemporary Jewish Life: In Memory of Yehuda Rosenman,* New York: American Jewish Committee, 1989

Cohen, Shaye J.D., *The Beginnings of Jewishness: Boundaries, Varieties, Uncertainties* (Hellenistic Culture and Society, 31), Berkeley: University of California Press, 1999

Cohen, Steven, *Content or Continuity?: Alternative Bases for Commitment: The 1989 National Survey of American Jews,* New York: American Jewish Committee, Institute of Human Relations, 1991

Sacks, Jonathan, *Will We Have Jewish Grandchildren?: Jewish Continuity and How to Achieve It,* London and Portland, Oregon: Vallentine Mitchell, 1994

Sarna, Jonathan D., "The Secret of Jewish Continuity," *Commentary,* 98(4), October 1994

Shrage, Barry, "A Communal Response to the Challenges of the 1990 CJF National Jewish Population Survey: Toward a Jewish Life Worth Living," *Journal of Jewish Communal Service,* 68(4), Summer 1992

Woocher, Jonathan, "Civil Religion and the Modern Jewish Challenge," in his *Sacred Survival: The Civil Religion of American Jews* (Jewish Political and Social Studies), Bloomington: Indiana University Press, 1986

Ever since Abraham, "the first Jew," confronted his mortality in the first book of the Bible, Jews have been greatly concerned about continuity, that is, the capacity to perpetuate the Jewish people as a clearly defined community. Most recently, scholars, religious leaders, and others have pondered how to maintain continuity in the distinctive social, economic, and political contexts of the modern world. In the United States, for example, the publication of the 1990 National Jewish Population Survey, which indicated a decline in the number of U.S. Jews, immediately became the focus of nearly every ensuing discussion on continuity. Issues for debate include the definition of Jewish identity, threats to continuity, and the viability of cultural and pedagogical programs intended to strengthen or enlarge the existing Jewish community.

WOOCHER defines the parameters of the debate over continuity in the contemporary U.S. Jewish community. The author asks and attempts to answer the central questions that faced the Jewish diaspora in the United States at the end of the 20th century: What defines Jewish identity in the U.S. context? Given the trends noted in population studies, is there any guarantee that there will be a viable Jewish community in the United States in the year 2020? Woocher argues that in the U.S. context, Jews may tend to eschew overtly religious aspects of Judaism, but some evidence suggests that a civil religion does help bind U.S. Jews into a community. For example, nonreligious Jews may express their Jewish identity by contributing to fund-raising efforts for Jewish causes. Woocher argues that the vibrant survival of the Jewish community is important to humanity as a whole, and he identifies specific practices that may enhance the possibilities of Jewish continuity.

BAYME's anthology, a volume published in honor of Yehuda Rosenman, contains essays by influential scholars on Jewish sociology, Jewish education, and the Jewish family, particularly in the North American context. The essays in this collection focus largely on evidence that the Jewish community in North America is in decline, and these articles, like the 1990 Population study and the ensuing commentary, suggest that the future viability of the Jewish community is highly doubtful.

Steven COHEN identifies the central issues that arose from the 1989 National Survey of American Jews. The author discusses "the concerns, attitudes and practices of American Jews, and identifies a gap between many Jews' professed belief in the importance and value of Jewishness and the minimal levels of Jewish content in their lives."

SHRAGE's article is one of the most important essays framing the debate and panic that followed the publication of the 1990 survey of the U.S. Jewish population. The author argues that Jewish federations across the United States should help provide synagogues with funding and support programs that target the moderately affiliated family. Shrage also urges Jewish organizations to create additional points of access to the Jewish community in order to strengthen the Jewish identity of U.S. Jews.

SARNA offers little in the way of recommendations for strengthening Jewish identity in the United States, but he does use the 1990 survey as a starting point for a thorough review of the trends of the Jewish community in the early 1990s.

SACKS concentrates on concerns over continuity among the Jews of England. Focusing on the miraculous aspect of Jewish survival, the author stresses the challenges of integration and survival for a Jewish community that has survived in previous ages in contexts of isolation. Sacks argues powerfully against the idea that segregation is the only key to Jewish continuity.

Shaye COHEN traces the discussion of Jewish identity back to its roots in ancient Palestine and the early diaspora experience. The author attempts to answer the questions of who was a Jew in antiquity and how Jewishness was defined. By delineating the boundaries that initially demarcated the Jewish community in antiquity, Cohen highlights the belief that the very definition of an ethnic unity depends upon a community's maintenance of boundaries and provokes questions of contemporary significance about the essential nature of Jewish identity. Cohen also contextualizes the variety of attitudes and practices that various modern Jewish communities use when potential converts seek to enter into the community and when Jews intermarry or elect to live in a non-Jewish community.

RACHEL SABATH

Conversion to Judaism

Bamberger, Bernard J., *Proselytism in the Talmudic Period,* Cincinnati, Ohio: Hebrew Union College Press, 1939

Eichhorn, David Max (editor), *Conversion to Judaism: A History and Analysis,* New York: Ktav, 1965

Epstein, Lawrence J., *Conversion to Judaism: A Guidebook*, Northvale, New Jersey: Aronson, 1994

Homolka, Walter, Walter Jacob, and Esther Seidel (editors), *Not by Birth Alone: Conversion to Judaism*, Herndon, Virginia: Cassell, 1997

Jacob, Walter and Moshe Zemer, *Conversion to Judaism in Jewish Law: Essays and Responsa* (Studies in Progressive Halakhah, vol. 3), Pittsburgh, Pennsylvania: Rodef Shalom, 1994

Rosenbloom, Joseph R., *Conversion to Judaism: From the Biblical Period to the Present*, Cincinnati, Ohio: Hebrew Union College Press, 1978

Scalamonti, John David, *Ordained to Be a Jew: A Catholic Priest's Conversion to Judaism*, Hoboken, New Jersey: Ktav, 1992

As Judaism has seldom regarded itself as a missionizing religion, books on conversion to Judaism in the past have been few and mostly have dealt with the history of conversion over the centuries. More recent studies, although they do not neglect the historical perspective, focus on the variety of reasons and personal motives for conversion and proceed to discuss the practical and theoretical requirements of the various streams within Judaism. Consideration is also given to the different answers in the current "Who is a Jew?" debate, which also affects the Law of Return and other matters of personal status in Israel.

BAMBERGER's scholarly and comprehensive study begins by tracing the origins of proselytism from the biblical period through the records of Jewish missionary activity in Hellenistic sources, before undertaking a thorough and exhaustive evaluation of the material presented in the talmudic literature. Here, numerous mistakes and misrepresentations of the Talmud in past studies are corrected. Special attention is given to the halakhic material given that it "represents the official Jewish attitude," determining the requirements for conversion as well as the reception and status of converts according to Jewish law. Favorable and adverse statements about converts follow, drawn from the purely rhetorical aggadah. A further chapter examines the actual circumstances of individual conversions mentioned in rabbinic literature, while the concluding survey demonstrates the rabbis' altogether favorable attitude to conversion throughout the talmudic period.

The general emphasis of ROSENBLOOM's study is historical-sociological, rather than theological, providing a synopsis of the course of conversion throughout Jewish history. He examines the process of conversion in the biblical and rabbinic periods and the reasons why conversion became restricted during the Middle Ages. The survey also covers the post-Enlightenment period and the contemporary situation. Accounts of group and individual cases of conversion throughout history successfully break up and illustrate the historical framework, while they also shed light on the sociological implications. References to statistics in Europe and the United States concerning intermarriage and conversion indicate new trends and more liberal attitudes to conversion in comparison with a past when attitudes were shaped by very different political and social circumstances.

The volume edited by EICHHORN also begins by tracing the subject of conversion to Judaism in Jewish classical sources from biblical to modern times, and it includes sections on individual and group conversions over the centuries. This is followed by analyses not only of the theological and sociological factors in conversion but also of the psychological state of the potential convert, while in a third part individuals give personal accounts with regard to their initial motivation for conversion and their experience of integration into their respective Jewish communities.

The volume edited by HOMOLKA, JACOB, and SEIDEL is a collection of studies only recently published in German and now available in an English-language version. Addressing interested laypersons, potential converts, and theologians active in interfaith work, the international team of contributors explores a variety of issues. The historical section surveys conversion from the Bible through the talmudic period and the Middle Ages to the present, while numerous testimonies by converts past and present make for lively reading. The section on current attitudes offers updates on the Jewish identity question in both Israel and the diaspora and describes the manifold theological, legal, sociological, and psychological aspects of conversion, undermining any residual impression that Jewish identity is conferred by birth alone.

EPSTEIN's recent guidebook is aimed at "those who are studying to become Jewish and . . . at those who have completed their conversion," but it also addresses those who wish to know about the manifold reasons that compel others to convert. This helpful volume encourages would-be converts to clarify their own motives for conversion and to consider carefully both their choice of denomination within Judaism and the effects of their conversion on family and wider society. The theoretical and practical requirements for the process of conversion are addressed, together with the possible psychological aspects of post-conversion integration experiences. The second part of the book provides a very basic introduction to Judaism's core beliefs and practices. It offers a summary of the leading classical Jewish texts together with a brief outline of Jewish history. Jewish practice is represented by a number of key prayers and an outline of Jewish holidays. Together with suggestions on further study through books and films, this manual concludes by providing the addresses of relevant Jewish organizations and guidelines for conversion published by the various Jewish movements in the United States.

The collection of essays edited by JACOB and ZEMER explores present-day conversion to Judaism by evaluating its past and present halakhic construction. The latter is constantly being revisited in accordance with the principles and theology of progressive Judaism, but, before the view of liberal halakhists is expounded, the volume surveys talmudic law and the subsequent rulings of orthodox halakhists. Among other issues, this volume assembles halakhic sources and rulings on the retroactive annulment of a conversion, examines the ambivalence to and the impact of sincere and ulterior motives for conversion, and discusses the ritual requirements for conversion laid down by Reform Judaism. A selection of contemporary Reform responsa to a variety of individual concerns with regard to conversion, brought about by unusual circumstances and borderline cases, concludes this topical volume, which reflects the current stage of the discussion within the progressive rabbinate.

SCALAMONTI's autobiography is representative of a more personal genre. It describes the conversion of a young Catholic priest to Judaism. Initially, the book provides an instructive insight into the regulated life of young seminarians: their hope and pride and their frustration at the restrictions imposed upon their daily lives, the rigidity of their study regimen, and the discouragement of questions and criticism. A period of profound disenchantment with the dogmatism of the Church and of severe inner doubt caused Scalamonti to rethink his vocation. While working as a waiter, he met an orthodox Jewish young woman who became the catalyst that helped transform his life. Comparing Catholicism with Judaism, he describes his own spiritual growth and "longing for a religion that would enable [him] to unite heart and mind," and how this search led him to embrace Judaism. This lively memoir will be of interest to anyone engaged in interfaith work, as it examines in a perceptive, albeit engaged, manner the differences between two major religions.

ESTHER I. SEIDEL

See also God-Fearers

Costume

Cohen, Abraham, "The Jewish Badge and Garb," in his *An Anglo-Jewish Scrapbook, 1600–1840: The Jew through English Eyes,* London: Cailingold, 1943

Goitein, S.D., *A Mediterranean Society: The Jewish Communities of the Arab World as Portrayed in the Documents of the Cairo Geniza,* vol. 4: *Daily Life,* Berkeley: University of California Press, 1983

Levine, Molly Myerowitz, "The Gendered Grammar of Ancient Mediterranean Hair," in *Off with Her Head!: The Denial of Women's Identity in Myth, Religion, and Culture,* edited by Howard Eilberg-Schwartz and Wendy Doniger, Berkeley: University of California Press, 1995

Ravid, Benjamin, "From Yellow to Red: On the Distinguishing Head-Covering of the Jews of Venice," in *The Frank Talmage Memorial Volume,* vol. 2, edited by Barry Walfish, Hanover, New Hampshire: University Press of New England, 1992

Rubens, Alfred, *A History of Jewish Costume,* New York: Funk and Wagnalls, and London: Vallentine Mitchell, 1967; revised edition, London: Owen, 1981

Zimmer, Eric, "Men's Headcovering: The Metamorphosis of This Practice," in *Reverence, Righteousness, and Rahamanut: Essays in Memory of Rabbi Dr. Leo Jung,* edited by Jacob J. Schacter, Northvale, New Jersey: Aronson, 1992

In biblical times, the daily costume of the Hebrews apparently did not differ much from that of neighboring peoples. The Bible refers to three basic garments, known in Hebrew as *simlah,* a long roll of cloth serving as an outer garment; *ezor,* a loincloth; and *ketonet,* a shirt-like garment corresponding to the Roman tunic. However, the Torah does prescribe a specifically ritual element of costume in the form of the *tekhelet* thread of Numbers 15.

From the postbiblical period through the modern era, the uniqueness of Jewish dress has frequently attracted the attention of Jewish and non-Jewish moralists, and RUBENS surveys the history of Jewish attire from antiquity through medieval and modern societies, Eastern and Western. One aspect of Jewish costume that stands out noticeably in Rubens's collection is the ubiquity of headgear, as nearly all the figures wear a head covering. This phenomenon conforms with the habits of surrounding societies, because in medieval times covering the head was the norm in both European and Eastern lands. Nevertheless, as several illustrations show, the Jews had a distinctive headgear, at least in parts of Latin Christendom, where their pointed hats were easily recognizable. The association of Jews with the wearing of a pointed hat partially explains why some scholars identify a pottery tomb figure from seventh- to ninth-century China with a Jewish peddler.

ZIMMER traces the practice of males covering their heads for religious purposes from the talmudic era through contemporary times. In the talmudic period, the common Jew was not particular about covering his head. Scholars were more meticulous, although they too were not entirely zealous followers of this custom. The Middle Ages also exhibits a dichotomy between the behavior expected of scholars and laymen, especially in Spain where there is evidence that this practice was not strictly followed. Similarly, in northern Europe, the 13th-century author of *Or Zarua,* Rabbi Moses ben Isaac of Vienna, criticized the Jews of France who recited benedictions with a bare head. However, evidence suggests that the German rabbis contended that covering one's head at all times was a recommended act of piety (*middat hasidut*). In the modern era, the nature of the debate has shifted. Reformers decided in the 19th century that head covering was no longer necessary under any circumstances, while conversely this practice became far more ubiquitous among Orthodox Jews. Indeed, perhaps as a backlash against the Reform movement, some Orthodox scholars demanded not one but two head-coverings. Contemporary Orthodox rabbis seem focused less on the question of whether or not a male should cover his head (a given) but rather on what should be the exact nature of this headcovering.

LEVINE studies comparatively the customs relating to the covering of women's hair in the ancient Greco-Roman world, ancient Jewish society, and contemporary Orthodox Jewish circles. In ancient Mediterranean societies, the hair of women often had both a metonymic and a metaphorical meaning. Hair symbolized the nature and restraints of a society, as well as a language of death and regeneration of the body. Levine notes the similarities between Greco-Roman practices and Jewish customs. For example, the Jewish wedding custom of *badeken,* where the groom lowers the veil over the bride's face, corresponds to the Greek *anakalupteria,* and Levine suggests that the original intention of both customs was the same: to permit the groom to see the bride in public for the first time in the presence of a supporting group of witnesses.

Thanks to the rich documents of the Cairo Genizah, more is known about the daily life of the Egyptian Jewish community of the Middle Ages than about any other medieval Jewish community. GOITEIN's classic study of this archive describes the clothing of the "Genizah people" in a highly detailed manner that far exceeds current knowledge of Jewish costume in any other medieval society.

The eighth-century Pact of Umar required that the clothing of tolerated non-Muslims (dhimmis) be distinguishable from that of their Muslim hosts. At first this requirement was hardly burdensome, as Jews dressed differently in any case. As time progressed, however, Jews began to dress in a manner apparently more similar to their hosts. The adoption of Arab dress eventually provoked decrees forcing Jews to wear a yellow badge (introduced in the year 850 by Caliph al-Mutawakkil) or to dye their outer garments.

Enforcement, however, was another matter. Although these dress requirements have been, in Goitein's words, "an obsession pestering Muslims" throughout their history, the Genizah shows no evidence of practical restrictions on the dress of non-Muslim people. Jews of all classes could be mistaken for their Muslim neighbors. One Muslim writer cited by Goitein lamented that,

> dhimmi women, when they leave their houses and walk in the streets are hardly to be recognized. . . . They go into the bazaars and sit in the shops of the merchants, who pay them respect on account of their fine clothes, unaware that they belong to the dhimmis.

Goitein does, however, find evidence pertaining to some distinctively Jewish garments among Genizah people. Thus, the Jewish prayer mantle had no fixed form in this period, and at least four different kinds of square outer garment could serve the purpose. Shawls with their accompanying ritual fringes were worn only during prayer, study, and banquets of a religious nature. They were worn in the street only when walking to and from the synagogue. Goitein speculates that Jewish women did have some particular tastes and styles in clothing. Thus, the jukaniyya (a house robe) and mukhlaf (a patchwork cloth) were garments perhaps favored only by Jewish women. Additionally, many women chose to decorate their clothes with a Jewish symbol such as a seven-branched candelabrum.

All the same, Goitein's research makes it clear that the daily garments of the Jewish community were generally very similar to the garments of their neighbors. An outer garment was the norm, as much a sign of respectability as for protection from the elements. Male and female fashions were not easily distinguishable, and at times husband and wife even shared clothes. In the Near Eastern quest for modesty, both men and women wore many layers of garments to conceal the body. These garments usually had wide and puffy sleeves, which also served a function similar to modern-day pockets. Head covering was worn at all times and by everyone, and often this was the most expensive element of a person's wardrobe. In general, the larger the head covering, the more prestigious the individual was considered to be.

Lastly, the prevalence of amulets should be noted among the jewelry worn by the Genizah people. Children as well as adults seem frequently to have been bedecked with ornaments that aspired to convey magical powers on the wearer.

Under Pope Innocent III, the Latin Church legislated at the Fourth Lateran Council (1215) that in order to prevent inadvertent sexual relations between Jews and Christians, Jews were to "be distinguishable from the rest of the population by the nature of their clothes." Aside from the stated reason for this decree, COHEN conjectures that the Church intended also simply to humiliate the Jewish people. Enforcement of this ordinance initially obligated Jews to wear a distinguishing yellow badge and later a Jewish hat, Judenhut. Cohen surveys the spread of this requirement through Latin Christendom, as well as implementation of the parallel decree under the Pact of Umar in Muslim lands. The Church's requirement continued through the early modern era. In Europe, only in England (after the readmission) and in the Netherlands were Jews spared the humiliation of this requirement. Cohen cites an English woman visiting Rome as late as 1826 who recounts that Jews were "obliged to wear a yellow ribbon as a mark of distinction when they mix among Christians."

Despite the fact that Jews were often embarrassed by the requirement to wear an identifying mark, the fact remains that many Jewish communities possessed, and still possess, a unique garb. Cohen suggests that the source of this practice lies in the nostalgia of displaced Jews who were reluctant to abandon the dress of their native land as they wandered from one country to another. This nostalgia, combined with Jewish isolation in ghettos and their fear of the attractions of apostasy, suffices to explain hesitation about embracing the latest fashions of their host country. Cohen describes the dress of a number of these communities: Polish Jews who wear the Russian fur cap and Polish black robe; Jews of Istanbul who don "a dingy-colored white cap, surrounded by a cotton shawl of a small brown pattern"; and Jews of Portugal whose "dress generally consists of a red cap, with a blue silken tassel at the top of it, a blue tunic girded at the waist with a red sash, and wide linen pantaloons or trousers."

RAVID's essay represents a case study of the enforcement of the requirement of a distinguishing Jewish garment in a single city, Venice, in the early modern period. The first charter permitting Jews to reside in Venice was granted in 1382, and soon after, in 1394, the city legislated that Jews must wear a visible yellow circle, the size of a loaf of bread, abc ᴄhe chest on their outer clothing. The color yellow in addition to being the traditional color assigned to Jews was also identified with other undesirable segments of society, such as prostitutes. Jewish neglect of this requirement caused the Venetian government to enact stricter legislation in 1496, requiring Jews to wear a yellow head covering at all times and in all places, and subjecting those who disobeyed this statute to a fine or imprisonment. However, Ravid shows that Jews continued to seek exemptions for themselves, and exemptions were granted to allow some to wear a black head covering when traveling or staying temporarily outside of the ghetto. Eventually, Venetian Jews, other than members of the Levantine community, changed from wearing yellow head coverings to wearing red ones, but exactly when and why this shift happened remains to be clarified. Ravid speculates that Jews might have preferred the color red because it lacked the negative connotations associated with the color yellow.

SAMUEL HERZFELD

Covenant

Heschel, Abraham Joshua, *God in Search of Man: A Philosophy of Judaism,* New York: Jewish Publication Society, 1955; London: Calder, 1956

Levenson, Jon D., *Sinai and Zion: An Entry into the Jewish Bible* (New Voices in Biblical Studies), Minneapolis, Minnesota: Winston, 1985

McCarthy, D., *Treaty and Covenant* (Analecta Biblica), Rome: Pontifical Biblical Institute, 1963, new edition, 1981

Mendenhall, George, "Covenant Forms in Israelite Tradition," *Biblical Archaeologist,* 17, 1954

Nicholson, E.W., *God and His People: Covenant and Theology in the Old Testament,* New York: Oxford University Press, and Oxford: Clarendon, 1986

Rosenzweig, Franz, "Revelation and Law: Martin Buber and Franz Rosenzweig," in *On Jewish Learning,* edited by N.N. Glatzer, New York: Schocken, 1965

A covenant is a contract, a formal and binding agreement, usually written, between two parties obliging them to perform or refrain from certain specified actions. Covenant *(berit)* is also the chief biblical model for describing the relationship between God and the people of Israel. The modern study of the concept of covenant between God and the people of Israel has undertaken two tasks, one historical and the other theological. The historical thrust has focused on questions of the origins of the concept of covenant and the date of the adoption of the idea of covenant as the prevalent model of the relationship with God. Modern Jewish theologians have sought to understand the significance of the concept of covenant for Jews in the aftermath of historical scholarship, insofar as it has shattered faith in the antiquity and uniqueness of the Israelite covenant and severed divine revelation from the Bible.

MENDENHALL focuses on the evidence of ancient Near Eastern suzerainty treaties and argues that the biblical descriptions of the covenant in the Decalogue (Exodus 20 and Deuteronomy 5) and elsewhere in the Book of Deuteronomy are modeled on the form and specific terminology of a Late Bronze Age (15th–13th century B.C.E.) Hittite treaty between an overlord and a vassal. The concept of covenant must, therefore, have been adopted by the Israelites about that time. The central features of a Hittite suzerainty treaty are the identification of the covenant giver; the historical prologue in which the overlord recounts his past deeds of benefit to the vassal; stipulations that the vassal is to obey; provision for deposit and periodic public reading; a list of witnesses to the treaty; blessings and curses; the ratification ceremony; and the reiteration of curses. Although the Decalogue itself contains only the first three elements, Mendenhall argues that the rest of the elements were part of the complex of traditions surrounding the founding of the ancient Israelite community even if they were put into written form later. Indeed, the provision for deposit and periodic public reading, list of witnesses, and the curses and blessings are absent from later treaty forms. Mendenhall identifies covenant-making as an activity undertaken when relations are forged between formerly separate groups, creating a new legal community. A covenant was the formal means by which the tribes, newly escaped from slavery in Egypt, were bound together in a religious and political community. The text of that covenant is the Decalogue.

McCARTHY argues on the contrary that the resemblance between Exodus 19–24 and Hittite suzerainty treaties is superficial because the biblical passage does not contain some essential features of a Hittite suzerainty treaty, such as a historical prologue and blessings and curses. In fact, Exodus 19–24 reflects a tradition of covenant-making by means of ritual, not the treaty-making tradition. Only in later texts, such as Deuteronomy, 1 Samuel 12, and Joshua 24, is the influence of ancient Near Eastern treaties—in this case Neo-Assyrian, not Hittite, treaties—manifest.

NICHOLSON assigns the concept of covenant to a later date, specifically to the time of the prophet Hosea (late 8th century B.C.E.). He maintains that the absence of the term *berit* (covenant) from any text that critical scholarship dates earlier than Hosea refutes any claim that the concept of covenant predates the late 8th century B.C.E. He argues further that the concept of covenant is the result of a decisive change innovated by the prophets, who challenged the existing social order by maintaining that the relationship between God and the people of Israel originated in free choice that had to be continually reaffirmed by adherence to the terms of the covenant. The concept of covenant received its fullest expression in Deuteronomy and the historical books—Joshua, Judges, 1 and 2 Samuel, and 1 and 2 Kings. For Nicholson, unlike Mendenhall and McCarthy, the significance of covenant lies in how it envisions Israel's relationship with and commitment to God. The covenant explicates what it means to be the people of God. Nicholson moves away from understanding the covenant as a means of uniting the tribes because none of the descriptions of covenant explain its purpose in such a way. Rather, the texts presuppose that the tribes belong together.

LEVENSON sketches the relationship of covenant theology to the other dominant theology in the Bible, Zion theology. In contrast to other scholars who believe that Zion theology superseded covenant theology or that Zion theology was prevalent in the southern kingdom while the concept of covenant persisted in the northern kingdom, Levenson argues that covenant theology and Zion theology coexisted and indeed transformed each other. Zion theology, with its emphasis on the cosmic importance of Zion, imbued the concept of covenant with universalistic import. Covenant theology, with its insistence on the fulfillment of covenantal obligations, qualifies the promise to the Davidic family of an everlasting monarchy by subordinating the fulfillment of the promise to obedience to divine commandments.

ROSENZWEIG believes that the concept of covenant does not appropriately describe the biblical description of the revelation and declaration of laws at Sinai. He argues that divine revelation was limited to the expression of God's commanding presence in relation to Israel. The spontaneous response reflected a feeling of obligation. When the original spontaneity dissipated, human beings transformed the feeling of obligation into impersonal laws encapsulated in books, devoid of any sense of personal relationship with God. Each individual Jew, therefore, must recapture the feeling of God's self-revelation and the natural response of obligation.

HESCHEL understands the Jewish people's participation in the covenantal process to be that of writing a midrash on revelation. In contrast to Rosenzweig, Heschel argues that divine self-revelation included specific content. Human beings, however, have no direct access to the pure form of God's will. Therefore, the Jewish community is forced to offer its best interpretation of God's will in every generation.

PAMELA BARMASH

Creation

Aviezer, Nathan, *In the Beginning: Biblical Creation and Science*, Hoboken, New Jersey: Ktav, 1990

Clifford, Richard J., *Creation Accounts in the Ancient Near East and in the Bible* (Catholic Biblical Quarterly Monograph Series, 26), Washington, D.C.: Catholic Biblical Association, 1994

Hess, Richard S. and David Tsumura, *I Studied Inscriptions from before the Flood: Ancient Near Eastern, Literary, and Linguistic Approaches to Genesis 1–11* (Sources for Biblical and Theological Study, 4), Winona Lake, Indiana: Eisenbrauns, 1994

Levenson, Jon D., *Creation and the Persistence of Evil: The Jewish Drama of Divine Omnipotence*, San Francisco: Harper and Row, 1988

Sarna, Nahum M., *Understanding Genesis* (Heritage of Biblical Israel, vol. 1), New York: Jewish Theological Seminary, 1966

Schroeder, Gerald L., *Genesis and the Big Bang: The Discovery of Harmony between Modern Science and the Bible*, New York: Bantam, 1990

Soloveitchik, Joseph, *The Lonely Man of Faith*, New York: Doubleday, 1992

The Book of Genesis contains two accounts of the creation of the world: an orderly and structured story of creation is presented in 1:1–2:3, and a slightly different story appears in 2:4–3:24. Most modern Jewish treatments on this topic compare these two stories to each other, to modern scientific theories of creation, or to other accounts of creation from the ancient world. Comparisons to scientific theories are usually designed to synthesize the biblical account of creation with modern ideas about evolution, and comparisons to other creation stories from the ancient world are usually designed to highlight the unique aspects of the biblical story.

LEVENSON presents a Jewish "biblical theology" of creation. He bases his study on comparisons between the biblical story of creation and other ancient Near Eastern accounts, examining the similarities and differences in the creation tales in order to discern how the ancient Israelites viewed creation and God's mastery of the universe. The author addresses the presence of evil in the creation story and investigates how biblical Israelites and later Jews dealt with this aspect of the biblical account. Levenson successfully melds literary and theological analysis in an insightful and compelling book.

Like Levenson, SARNA deals with both literary and theological issues in the biblical text. His treatment is briefer than Levenson's study (creation occupies only the first chapter of Sarna's book), and he deals with a broader range of questions. Sarna's chapter is appropriate for those seeking a readable introduction to the points of comparison between the biblical stories and other ancient Near Eastern creation accounts.

SOLOVEITCHIK's seminal essay is one of the more original treatments of the creation story. The article is a philosophical and theological discussion of the nature of religious existence, drawing on the story of creation. The author uses the differences between the two accounts of creation in Genesis as a springboard to contrast two different aspects of the human personality. He investigates dilemmas facing the person of faith in the modern world and debates whether the notion of religious surrender to God can be reconciled with modernity's orientation toward personal success. The essay is complex and demands a careful reading.

AVIEZER compares the biblical account of creation in Genesis to current scientific knowledge. He writes from the perspective of a physicist and deals with each of the days of creation recounted in the first chapter of Genesis in turn, discussing how modern scientists explain the origins of the various elements and entities identified in the biblical story. For example, his discussion of the second day in Genesis, when the firmament was created, is titled "The Formation of the Solar System." Aviezer consistently argues that the biblical account is not supplanted by modern science, choosing the views of eminent scientists who think that the "actual point of creation" is inexplicable by the ordinary rules of science. Aviezer's work is very useful for anyone seeking a way to synthesize the biblical story of creation with some perspectives of modern science.

SCHROEDER also seeks to harmonize the story of creation in Genesis with the conclusions of modern science. Writing both as a scientist and as a religious believer, he argues that the events that scientists theorize followed the big bang and the events described in the six days of Genesis are the same, although described in vastly different terms. His work is accessible to lay readers with a basic knowledge of modern science.

CLIFFORD writes from the perspective of a Roman Catholic, but his work is of great use to all readers interested in a clear and readable presentation of different accounts of creation found in various ancient Near Eastern texts (Mesopotamian, Egyptian, Ugaritic) as well as the different creation stories presented in the Bible. Clifford discusses not only the versions presented in Genesis 1 and 2, but also the other creation stories found in many of the Psalms, in Isaiah 40–55, and in Proverbs 8.

HESS and TSUMURA's anthology of academic essays presents 18 perspectives on the relationships between Genesis 1–11 and the ancient Near Eastern creation stories, including the Enuma Elish epic from ancient Mesopotamia. Two of the essays are introductory, surveying the field of comparative studies; the rest of the chapters deal with particular ancient

Near Eastern texts or specific elements of the Genesis story. The essays emphasize the sources of the biblical story and debate the ways in which ancient Near Eastern texts may have influenced the biblical account. Theological issues are not treated in these essays.

SHAWN ZELIG ASTER AND HILLEL C. NEUER

Crescas, Hasdai died c.1412

Catalan critic of Aristotelian philosophy

Lasker, Daniel J. (editor), *The Refutation of the Christian Principles by Hasdai Crescas*, Albany: State University of New York Press, 1992

Lasker, Daniel J., "Chasdai Crescas," in *History of Jewish Philosophy* (Routledge History of World Philosophies, vol. 2), edited by Daniel H. Frank and Oliver Leaman, London and New York: Routledge, 1997

Wolfson, Harry Austryn, *Crescas' Critique of Aristotle: Problems of Aristotle's Physics in Jewish and Arabic Philosophy* (Harvard Semitic Series, vol. 6), Cambridge, Massachusetts: Harvard University Press, 1929; London: Oxford University Press, 1971

Wolfson, Harry Austryn, *Studies in the History of Philosophy and Religion*, 2 vols., Cambridge, Massachusetts: Harvard University Press, 1977

LASKER (1992) translates and annotates Crescas's polemical anti-Christian work *The Refutation of the Christian Principles*. In a short foreword, Lasker describes the historical background that led to the writing of the book. He also outlines Crescas's biography and the main elements of his philosophy, and he provides data on the rest of Crescas's writings. He then discusses the original language of *The Refutation*, its title, date of composition, and Crescas's methodology. He considers relations between Crescas and Profiat Duran and discusses the disputed question of for whom the book was written.

LASKER (1997) gives a general evaluation of Crescas as "a fertile mind struggling to replace the accepted scientific verities of the day (Aristotelian philosophy) with traditionally religious (Jewish, rabbinic) nonphilosophical beliefs." He concludes that the result of Crescas's criticism of the rationalist thought of Maimonides and Gersonides was a philosophical system that could compete with Aristotelianism on its own terms. Given the paucity of Crescas's writings, however, and the contradictions between the opinions he articulates in his different works—even changing his mind within the same work—the nature, let alone the stature, of Crescas's thought is unclear.

Lasker describes the essence of each of Crescas's works separately. First comes *The Refutation of the Christian Principles,* in which Crescas sought to demonstrate that the principal beliefs of Christianity are contrary to reasonable thought. Crescas discussed ten such principal beliefs, analyzed their premises, and considered which of them were acceptable to both Jews and Christians and which were held by Christians alone. Lasker points out an important contradiction

between *Refutation of the Christian Principles* and Crescas's *Light of the Lord* concerning the question of creation ex nihilo: in the polemical work Crescas employed Gersonides' arguments against creation, while in the philosophical work he accepted the concept of creation and refuted Gersonides' arguments. Next Lasker discusses Crescas's *Sermon on the Passover,* which also includes statements that contradict his own opinions in *Light of the Lord,* for example on the issue of free will versus determinism. Finally, Lasker describes *Light of the Lord,* Crescas's major philosophical work. Crescas's intention was to overturn Maimonides' Aristotelian philosophy. His perception that rationalism weakened Jewish religion (or rather Jewish resistance to conversions and missionary activities) possibly played some role in this anti-Maimonidean critique. Crescas went as far as to reject Maimonides' 13 principles of Judaism. To replace them he formulated four categories of Jewish doctrine: roots, cornerstones, true doctrines or beliefs, and doctrines and theories. Maimonides believed that the existence of God is a revealed commandment, while Crescas argued that any revelation presupposes the existence of God, his unity, and his incorporeality. According to Crescas, this should be accepted as an axiom. He believed that God's unity is not given to rational proof; only reliance on revelation can guarantee the truth of the belief in one God. Maimonides believed that to define God is possible only by saying that which God is not, while Crescas argued that positive qualities can be attributed to God. Among his "cornerstones," Crescas listed six beliefs pertaining to divine revelation. He rejected the Aristotelian intellectualist approach to God's relation to the world and accepted biblical miracles literally, not figuratively as did the Aristotelians. Crescas believed in God's absolute knowledge of particulars and rejected free will. He ascribed a place of unrivalled preeminence to the Torah, which brings the believer to eternal life through love of God as expressed in observance of the commandments.

Crescas's "true beliefs" were creation ex nihilo, immortality, reward and punishment, resurrection, eternity of the Torah, the superiority of Mosaic prophecy, the efficacy of the *urim* and *tummim* (oracles) to learn the future, and the messiah. Any denier of even one of these principles is a denier of the whole Torah. The last portion of Crescas's *Light of the Lord* contains a number of short discussions of various topics that were commonplace in medieval philosophy, such as the eternity of the world, the possible existence of other worlds, and whether the heavenly spheres are intelligent living beings. In discussion of these topics, Crescas argued against the rationalist viewpoint. In the final analysis Lasker contends that although Crescas's philosophical contribution is undeniable, his works for many reasons did not exercise much influence on Jewish philosophy.

WOLFSON (1929) is one of the most fundamental treatments of Crescas's philosophy. Since the very core of Crescas's arguments was based on criticism of the philosophical background of the rationalist Jewish thought of Maimonides and Gersonides, refuting Aristotelian principles meant rejecting the main Jewish (and also Muslim and Christian) philosophies of the time. Crescas's "main object was to show that the Aristotelian explanation of the universe as outlined by Maimonides in his propositions was false and that the proofs of the existence of God which they were supposed to establish were groundless."

The same method that Crescas applied to the study of texts of others, Wolfson applies to the first 25 chapters of part one of book one of Crescas's *Light of the Lord*. These chapters were written in the form of "proofs" of the 25 propositions in which Maimonides summed up the main principles of Aristotle's philosophy. The first 20 chapters of part two of book one were written in the form of criticism of 20 of the 25 propositions. Wolfson deals with these two sets of chapters. Besides his analysis, he also offers a critical edition of the Hebrew text and a translation of the parts he discusses with extensive notes.

In his introduction, Wolfson scrutinizes Crescas's criticism of Aristotle in six chapters covering the following topics: sources, method, influence, and opposition; infinity, space, and vacuum; motion; time; matter and form; and foreshadowing a new conception of the universe. Wolfson states that no one before Crescas undertook the task of finding proofs for Aristotle's principles. All the commentaries on Maimonidean philosophy were explanations of Maimonides' own thought, ignoring its philosophical background. Crescas presented the Aristotelian explanation of the universe as outlined by Maimonides as false and groundless.

After scrutinizing the philosophical matter in Crescas, Wolfson describes Crescas's positive doctrines ("foreshadowing a new conception of the universe"). Crescas himself did not summarize these positive doctrines. He scattered separate statements that Wolfson gathers into a systematic unity. From this gathering emerges a new doctrine of the infinite universe that allows "incorporeal extensions" and the possibility of many worlds. A similar system was imagined by Giordano Bruno two centuries after Crescas. Moreover, Crescas corrected the very fallacies of the Aristotelian perception of celestial mechanics and made other advances in understanding the laws of nature that were proved by experiments three or four centuries later. This book can be recommended only to advanced readers familiar with the history of philosophy and science, and with some knowledge of Semitic languages.

WOLFSON (1977) includes the article *"Crescas on the Problem of Divine Attributes,"* which was written originally in 1916 and concerns the problem of universals. To Wolfson, the problem of attributes discussed in Jewish philosophy is a problem of universals in disguise. In chapter one of the article, Wolfson describes how Jewish and Muslim philosophers solved the problem before Crescas. In chapter two, he treats Crescas's solution of the problem in his criticism of Maimonides. Crescas, following logical reasoning, came to the inadmissibility of either positive or relative attributes. God's existence is necessary because it is not preceded by any prior cause but is causative because it is creative. Necessary existence means nothing but the absence of efficient causation. Crescas discussed the relation between essence and existence. Avicenna concluded that in God there is no distinction between essence and existence, while Averroes maintained that existence is identical to essence. The same difference of opinion exists between Avicenna and Averroes with regard to the

attribute of unity: Avicenna maintained that, like existence, unity is only accidental to essence, while Averroes, on the contrary, maintained that unity is identical to essence. In Jewish philosophy, Maimonides and his immediate disciples followed Avicenna, while all later Jewish philosophers accepted the view of Averroës. Crescas refuted both approaches by reducing their views to absurdity. Then Crescas worked out his own theory of attributes. He endeavored to prove that attributes are positive both in the sense that the divine substance is composed of essence and attribute, and in the sense that the predicate affirmed of God is a related term. Crescas especially mentioned the attributes of priority, knowledge, and power. The main advance in the thought of Crescas lay in his attempt to show the compatibility of essential attributes and absolute simplicity.

HAYIM Y. SHEYNIN

Crusades

Abulafia, Anna Sapir, "The Interrelationship between the Hebrew Chronicles on the First Crusade," *Journal of Semitic Studies,* 27(2), 1982

Chazan, Robert, *European Jewry and the First Crusade,* Berkeley: University of California Press, 1987

Chazan, Robert, *In the Year 1096: The First Crusade and the Jews,* Philadelphia: Jewish Publication Society, 1996

Eidelberg, Shlomo, *The Jews and the Crusaders: The Hebrew Chronicles of the First and Second Crusades,* Madison: University of Wisconsin Press, 1977

Goitein, S.D., "Contemporary Letters on the Capture of Jerusalem by the Crusaders," *Journal of Jewish Studies,* 3, 1952

Marcus, Ivan G., "From Politics to Martyrdom: Shifting Paradigms in the Hebrew Narratives of the 1096 Crusade Riots," in *Essential Papers on Judaism and Christianity in Conflict: From Late Antiquity to the Reformation,* edited by Jeremy Cohen, New York: New York University Press, 1991

Prawer, Joshua, *The History of the Jews in the Latin Kingdom of Jerusalem,* New York: Oxford University Press, and Oxford: Clarendon, 1988

Riley-Smith, Jonathan, "The First Crusade and the Persecution of the Jews," in *Persecution and Toleration: Papers Read at the Twenty-Second Summer Meeting and the Twenty-Third Winter Meeting of the Ecclesiastical History Society* (Studies in Church History, vol. 21), Oxford: Blackwell, 1984

The medieval military and religious movement known as the Crusades affected Jews living in Europe and the Holy Land, and several studies of its impact have centered around these two foci. More attention has been paid to attacks on Jews in Europe, especially those directed against Rhineland Jews and sparked by the call to the First Crusade in 1096. These studies have placed greatest weight on medieval Jewish reactions to and interpretations of the attacks, as described in a series of medieval Hebrew chronicles. The changing fate of Jews living in the Holy Land during this turbulent period has prompted a smaller but important group of studies.

EIDELBERG has translated into English four Hebrew chronicles of the First and Second Crusades. *The Chronicle of Solomon bar Simson, The Chronicle of Rabbi bar Nathan,* and *The Narrative of the Old Persecutions* (also know as *The Mainz Anonymous*) all recount attacks on Jews during the First Crusade; the *Sefer Zekhirah (The Book of Remembrance)* by Ephraim of Bonn describes events surrounding the Second Crusade in 1146 and 1147. Eidelberg gives brief introductions to each chronicle and highlights the liturgical quality of some sections. The general orientation that he provides suggests that attacks on Jews were primarily motivated by the antagonism and jealousy of Christian burghers toward wealthy Jews. He also contends that a better organized and prepared Christian elite was able to protect Jews more effectively from attacks in the wake of the call for the Second Crusade than it had been during the First Crusade. His translations have been criticized for using (without emendation) the faulty 1892 edition of the chronicles by Neubauer and Stern.

The three chronicles of the First Crusade share text and information, but untangling the exact nature of their relationship to one another has proved challenging because they exist only in late manuscripts (200 years and more after the events they describe) and because two of the chronicles exist only in a single copy. ABULAFIA describes the problems entailed in such investigations and outlines the solutions that have been proposed, providing a useful synoptic table. She hypothesizes that the three are directly related; that the so-called *Chronicle of Solomon bar Simson* is a compilation of the other two, with letters sent between affected Jewish communities; that this chronicle was written between 1140 and 1146; that Solomon bar Simson himself was not its author but only the name of one of the author's sources; that the *Chronicle of Rabbi bar Nathan* was written by Eliezer ben Nathan before 1146; and that the *Mainz Anonymous* was contemporary with the persecutions and possibly written by a Jew of Mainz.

MARCUS approaches these texts "as literary works, as fictions of a particular Jewish imagination," arguing that they are less useful and interesting as repositories of facts than as documents that reveal what cultural symbols Jews used to make sense of the horrific events of 1096. He highlights the liturgical and martyrological nature of sections of the chronicles and argues that when political intervention, which he calls the Esther paradigm, failed to protect the Jews, they turned to a new paradigm of sacrifice by relating the martyrdoms to the Temple cult in order to valorize what had happened.

RILEY-SMITH seeks to discern the relationship of the persecution of Jews in the First Crusade to the project of Crusade as a whole by comparing Christian and Jewish accounts of the attacks. He highlights the fact that the attackers were not gangs of peasants but crusaders under organized leadership, many of whom went on to successful careers in the Holy Land. He downplays as motives for attacking Jews both conversion of Jews by force and a wish to exact supplies by extortion and looting; he suggests instead that the primary motivating factor was a desire for vengeance against the perceived enemies of Christ.

CHAZAN (1987) argues that 1096 was not a catastrophic turning point in the history of Christian-Jewish relations and that Ashkenazi Jewry emerged intact from the terrible attacks. His important revisionist reading of the chronicles also suggests that, judging from their patterns of response to the violence, Ashkenazi Jews were better integrated into broader Christian society that has been assumed. The Jews' first response was to seek protection from Christian elites and from their neighbors. In some cases this was successful, but when it failed they either passively allowed themselves to be killed or killed their familes and themselves. The chronicles were written both to memorialize the victims and to reconcile the behavior of the voluntary martyrs with halakhic and aggadic norms. Chazan's translations of the *Mainz Anonymous* and the *Chronicle of Solomon bar Simson* supersede those in Eidelberg. CHAZAN (1996) presents the conclusions of his earlier book to a broader audience, deepening his discussion of the relationship of the events of 1096 to the problem of antisemitism.

GOITEIN translates and discusses two documents from the Cairo Genizah that reveal different aspects of the Jewish response to the Christian capture of Jerusalem in 1099. One describes relief work done for Jews displaced by the conquest. The second places the Frankish taking of the city within a broader context of struggles between Fatimids and Seljuks and shows its Jewish author to have had confidence that the Fatimids would soon retake the city.

PRAWER's work is a comprehensive history of the Jewish communities in the Holy Land from the Christian conquest in 1099 to the fall of the Latin Kingdom in 1291. He describes the initial destruction and dislocation of the Jewish communities after the conquest as well as their comparatively quick recovery. Although Jews were prohibited from living in Crusader Jerusalem, they were encouraged to settle in other cities and towns of the Latin East. They formed an especially strong and vibrant community in Acre in the 13th century. Prawer highlights the diverse origins of the communities in the Holy Land, noting that Jews from North Africa, Egypt, Yemen, and Iraq as well as from France, Spain, Italy, and Germany were attracted to come and join the nucleus already there.

LUCY K. PICK

Crypto-Jews, Contemporary

Bloomfield Ramagen, Sonia, "The Seridó: Refuge of the *Anussim*?," in *Land and Community: Geography in Jewish Studies* (Studies and Texts in Jewish History and Culture, 3), edited by Harold Brodsky, Bethesda: University Press of Maryland, 1997

Canelo, David Augusto, *Os ultimos cryptojudeus em Portugal,* 1987; translated by Werner Talmon-l'Armee as *The Last Crypto-Jews of Portugal,* Portland, Oregon: IJS, 1990

Haskell, Guy (editor), "Crypto-Jews of the American Southwest," *Jewish Folklore and Ethnology Review,* 18(1–2), 1996

Hernández, Frances, "The Secret Jews of the Southwest," in *Sephardim in the Americas* (American Jewish Archives, vol. 44, no. 1), edited by M.A. Cohen and A.J. Peck, Cincinnati, Ohio: American Jewish Archives, 1992

Patai, Raphael, *On Jewish Folklore*, Detroit, Michigan: Wayne State University Press, 1983

Santos, Richard G., "Chicanos of Jewish Descent in Texas," *Western States Jewish Historical Quarterly*, 15(4), 1983

Schwarz, Samuel, "The Crypto-Jews of Portugal," *Menorah Journal*, 12, 1926

The term "crypto-Jew" applies to persons who publicly profess another religion while privately practicing Jewish rituals, such as Friday-night candle lighting (perhaps unaware that family traditions are of Jewish origin), and to individuals who possess secret, transmitted Jewish identities (which may be unaccompanied by specifically Jewish practice). The word "marrano" is often used in the same sense, but it can carry a pejorative connotation. The Hebrew appellation "anusim" is more general, denoting Jews who adopted another religion under duress and their descendants who continue to belong to another faith, whether or not they maintain any Jewish traditions. In addition to short-lived instances of secrecy in Europe during the Nazi era, crypto-Judaism persisted into the 20th century among New Muslims, whose ancestors were forcibly converted in Persia in 1839, and among communities and individuals maintaining descent from New Christians, the Iberian Jewish majority who succumbed to the religious persecutions in Spain and Portugal between 1391 and 1497.

While countless descendants of the Iberian trauma the world over still maintain a Jewish heritage or identity, popular awareness of contemporary crypto-Judaism is limited primarily to groups in New Mexico and Belmonte, Portugal, and its significance is underrated, although there have been sporadic press reports on the topic since the early 1800s. The literature available in English remains scant, and much of it is anecdotal or amateur. Additional scholarly work is required to understand properly this subculture, particularly its prevalence among New Christians both during and after the Inquisition (which was abolished in the early 19th century). Important areas for research include the nature of crypto-Jewish religiosity and identity, attitudes of anusim toward the dominant religion, the history of particular Jewish customs that have been preserved, the process of identity transmission, and the art and literature of anusim (as well as any Jewish subtext therein). Also of interest are the crypto-Jews' reasons for remaining secretive after religious freedom has been granted; how the anusim have perceived normative Judaism; and the ways in which many modern-day crypto-Jews blend their Jewish heritage into a new, multifaceted identity. Research is hampered because crypto-Jews find it difficult to identify Jewish elements among customs remembered from home and because some have been too quick to attach Jewish meanings to certain customs or foods without adequate investigation. Furthermore, few scholars investigating this phenomenon have sufficient background in Jewish law and Sephardi customs to identify practices not mentioned in Inquisitorial documents. Appropriate methodology still needs to be developed, and the mixture of fact and fantasy in reports remains a serious problem.

While working as an engineer in Portugal in 1917, SCHWARZ was introduced to New Christians in the mountains of northern Portugal. In this sensitive, intelligent, and well-informed two-part essay (based on his unsurpassed book, *Cristãos-Novos em Portugal no Século XX*, Lisbon, 1925), he tells his story of getting acquainted with crypto-Jewish families in and around Belmonte. He describes their self-perception as well as how others saw them, demonstrates that numerous similar communities existed at the time, and notes that women were the torchbearers of tradition. Schwarz collected many of the secret prayers of crypto-Jews throughout the region, some of which appear in translation in the second part of the study. His work was instrumental in generating support for the emerging Jewish community of Oporto, headed by Captain Arturo Carlos de Barros Basto.

A more recent description of the crypto-Jews of Belmonte by CANELO, a school teacher in that town, is available in English. It begins with a compilation of historical information regarding the Jewish presence in Portugal as well as Christian attitudes toward the Jews, and it continues with a listing of customs and prayers based almost entirely on Schwarz's findings. He does, however, add a number of recently learned or composed prayers (e.g., a translation of the standard Friday night *kiddush*, presented as a crypto-Jewish Saturday night prayer) collected from a few community members since nearly half the formerly crypto-Jewish community adopted mainstream Judaism. The book suffers from inaccuracies of detail and translation, but the author's descriptions and personal observations afford the reader insight not only into the ritual life of this Portuguese community but also into how they are perceived by their Catholic neighbors.

Almost nothing has been written in English about contemporary crypto-Judaism in Brazil, where it appears to be widespread and in flux. BLOOMFIELD RAMAGEN is a professor of geography who, in her former capacity as an employee of the Israeli embassy in Brasilia, carried out extensive correspondence with anusim and wrote a masters thesis on the subject. In the published text, she considers one group from northern Brazil, their claim of transmitted Jewish identity, evidence they offer of their Sephardi roots, and reactions of scholars and representatives of Jewry and Israel. Her dispassionate examination gives the reader a glimpse into the problems inherent in the disparity between the folk-etymologies and historical theories that groups use to convince outsiders of the validity of their crypto-Judaism and the tools used by those outsiders who seek to verify the groups' status.

A folklorist of great eminence, PATAI collects in this volume various articles he wrote between 1936 and 1983. Section three ("The Marranos of Meshhed") is comprised of five chapters and offers a straightforward history of the "jedid al-Islam" crypto-Jews of Iran, which is based on oral histories and descriptions of that community's lifestyle. The final section ("On the Peripheries") investigates the newly formed organized communities of "Indian Jews" in Mexico who claim descent from anusim, as well as the New Christians ("Chuetas") of Majorca. Patai does not consider the latter to be crypto-Jews, both because they preserve no traces of Jewish heritage that he could identify and because even if they believe their Jewish ancestry was a secret, their Christian neighbors readily identified them as Jews based on their names and areas of residence.

Patai's two chapters on the Jewish Indians of Mexico are based on field trips taken in 1948 and 1964, during which he gathered oral testimony, mainly from community leaders, about their ethnohistory and observed their practices. He distinguishes between Adventist Protestants and crypto-Jewish Indians, but he suspects that the anusim have had a propensity to join Bible-reading and, later, Bible-observing Christian sects, once those options become available. Ultimately, Patai leaves the question of the origin of these communities (whether it was a "reawakening of the old faith which for many centuries had remained dormant" or merely "a pious fairy tale") unresolved; his main argument against their authenticity concerns the willingness of some community members to accept his advice and officially convert to Judaism in order to be recognized by the State of Israel. A remarkable polymath, Patai's judgment might have been rather different given greater familiarity with the history of the New Christian presence in Mexico and the beliefs and traditions reflected in Inquisition *processos*.

SANTOS, in one of the earliest attempts to grapple with the possibility of crypto-Judaism in the Southwestern United States, combines personal memories of foods and customs with some historical background, as the author seeks to demonstrate a likelihood of Jewish heritage among Texan Latinos. He concludes his essay with an emotional lament over the loss of crypto-Jewish tradition.

HERNÁNDEZ, a professor of English at the University of Texas, has compiled an extensive and eclectic list of all the elements believed in New Mexico to be of crypto-Jewish significance, based upon articles in the popular press and on interviews with Father C. Carmona, the historian L. Carrasco, New Mexico state archivist S. Hordes, and the latter's informants. Spanning the gamut from significant evidence of Jewish origins through tantalizing suggestions to fanciful signs, she discusses the history of the settlement of New Mexico; recounts the transmission of culture and the Penitente movement; lists "Jewish" names and surnames, artifacts, Sabbath and holiday customs, life-cycle rituals, and "Sephardi" foods; and identifies Jewish-seeming symbols on headstones and in Christian prayers, Ladino-sounding language, and Sephardi-sounding music. This work is the most comprehensive and vivid representation of crypto-Jewish self-perception as it has developed among a generation that has been influenced by external and often poorly informed Jewish sources.

The issue of *JFER* edited by HASKELL explores the controversy over the existence of contemporary crypto-Judaism in the Southwestern United States. The inclusion of two articles by Patai on the Mexican community of Venta Prieta attests to the editor's indecision as to whether the phenomenon of crypto-Judaism should be analyzed in geographically broad or specific terms. In her virulent contribution to this number, J. Neulander spends most of her time detailing the history of various "biblical churches," which she fails to connect convincingly with the claims of crypto-Judaism in New Mexico. The remainder of the issue contains several rejoinders to the conclusions of Neulander's article in an earlier issue of *JFER* (vol. 16, no. 1), in which she demonstrates that the popular *trompito* top—which resembles a *dreydl*—is unlikely to be a Jewish marker and then asserts that crypto-Judaism is a modern myth. T. Atencio, the son of a Hispanic Presbyterian minister who considers his family to be of Jewish descent, examines crypto-Jewish heritage in New Mexico—which he takes for granted—in the context of its role in the Manito culture and, eventually, in New-Mexican Chicano identity. S.C. Halevy, citing decades of earlier reports of a crypto-Jewish presence in the Southwest from retired rabbis and priests, reviews the nature of the surviving heritage. She presents evidence of rabbinic practices unrelated to Christian sectarian groups, including sweeping to the middle of the house, burning hair and nail trimmings, fasting on Mondays and Thursdays, soaking and scalding meat, avoiding meat-dairy combinations, and some mourning customs. In a contribution that shifts from personal reminiscence to the description of the general observances of a community, I. Medina-Sandoval gives a passionate account of her own heritage, placing her story in the context of what is known or believed regarding crypto-Judaism in the Southwest. The last article, by D.M. Gradwohl, raises succinctly the question of exceptionality: given the numerous past and present groups of Hispanic anusim throughout the world, why should their presence in the Southwest be so vehemently disputed?

SCHULAMITH CHAVA HALEVY

See also Marranism

Czech Republic *see* Central Europe; Prague

D

Daniel, Book of

Collins, John J., *Daniel: A Commentary on the Book of Daniel* (Hermeneia: A Critical and Historical Commentary on the Bible), Minneapolis, Minnesota: Fortress, 1993

Goldingay, John E., *Daniel* (Word Biblical Commentary, vol. 30), Dallas, Texas: Word, 1989

LaCocque, André, *Daniel in His Time* (Studies on Personalities of the Old Testament), Columbia: University of South Carolina Press, 1988

Montgomery, James A., *A Critical and Exegetical Commentary on the Book of Daniel* (International Critical Commentary, vol. 22), Edinburgh: Clark, and New York: Scribner, 1927

Wills, Lawrence M., *The Jew in the Court of the Foreign King: Ancient Jewish Court Legends* (Harvard Dissertations in Religion, no. 26), Minneapolis, Minnesota: Fortress, 1990

The Book of Daniel, found among the Writings in the Hebrew Bible, is a bilingual document written partly in Aramaic and partly in Hebrew. The first half of the book (chapters one through six) presents stories about Daniel and his companions, who rose to prominence at the Babylonian court after they were exiled following the destruction of Jerusalem, while the second half (chapters seven through 12) contains revelations given to Daniel about the future and the end of time. The form and content of these revelations have led scholars to regard the Book of Daniel as an apocalypse written sometime during the Maccabean period.

Among the most thorough studies of Daniel, COLLINS's commentary represents nearly 20 years of work on the subject. In the extensive introduction, Collins discusses the state of scholarly debate on the book's text, language, composition, genre, and setting, and he recounts the history of interpretation. The commentary also provides a substantial essay by Adela Yarbro Collins titled "The Influence of Daniel on the New Testament." The main part of the study moves systematically through the chapters of the book in both its Hebrew/Aramaic and Greek versions, the latter supplying the significant additions of the Prayer of Azariah and the stories of Susanna and of Bel and the Dragon. Important issues, such as the identity of the "Son of Man" mentioned in Daniel 7 and the idea of the resurrection of the dead present in Daniel 12, are discussed in greater detail in the excursuses that accompany the commentary on each of these chapters. Collins also draws heavily on the Dead Sea Scrolls, at least some of which were composed around the same time as the Book of Daniel and which reflect many of the same views.

GOLDINGAY has written a commentary intended for the scholar and nonspecialist alike. He provides a translation of the text followed by philological and textual notes, and he also addresses literary and historical questions. Goldingay accepts the popular thesis that the tales in Daniel 1–6 are pre-Maccabean and developed gradually, originating in the eastern diaspora. He regards the Book of Daniel as a creative amalgam of many traditions, asserting that the tales and visions can be read "as wisdom or as prophecy, as pedagogics or as eschatology, as halakah or as haggadah." Identifying Daniel as an early example of an apocalypse, Goldingay attributes the book to the Hasidim, exponents of a Jewish pietism active during the Maccabean period. Goldingay notes the differences between the Hebrew/Aramaic text and the Old Greek version, but he does not analyze them; similarly, he only refers in passing to the Maccabean setting of the visions in Daniel 7–12. Goldingay's use of the term "midrash" to describe some of the material contained in Daniel 1–6 and 10–12 is problematic. An extensive bibliography is provided at the end of the commentary.

LACOCQUE has produced an excellent introduction to Jewish apocalyptic literature by means of his thorough study of Daniel. LaCocque argues that the social milieu responsible for the apocalypses of the second century B.C.E. was that of the pacifist and anti-Hellenistic Hasidim. The Book of Daniel is addressed to the "faithful ones," the Hasidim, who risked their lives to uphold the Torah. LaCocque notes the close relationship between the Book of Daniel and the Dead Sea Scrolls and concludes that the community at Qumran constituted the true successors of the Hasidim. He argues that the stories about Daniel in chapters one through six are aggadic narratives, based on a core of legendary tradition, which served to exhort, inspire, and give hope to the persecuted faithful of the author's generation. LaCocque's interpretation of the Son of Man referred to in Daniel 7 is somewhat speculative. He opts for a conception of the Son of Man as High Priest, basing much of his interpretation on the scribal figure in Ezekiel 9–10, who he believes influenced the author of Daniel chapter seven. LaCocque concludes with an important discussion of the relationship of wisdom, prophecy, and apocalyptic in the Book of Daniel.

WILLS identifies the subject of his study as the "wisdom court legend," which he defines as "a legend of a revered figure set in the royal court which has the wisdom of the protagonist as a principal motif." He discusses many examples of this genre both within and outside of the Hebrew Bible, focusing on the Joseph, Esther, and Daniel stories, as well as a number of stories in Greek sources that are set in Near Eastern courts. Approximately one-third of the book is devoted to an analysis of the Daniel stories, especially chapters four, five, and six. Wills investigates the sources behind these stories and the history of their transmission; his arguments draw heavily from the Old Greek version, which Wills considers to be the best witness to the original form of the material. His use of the variant Greek texts of Daniel (and Esther) is especially commendable, for even when his conclusions about particular issues may be challenged, he has effectively demonstrated that the evidence of these versions can not be overlooked.

MONTGOMERY's scholarly commentary on Daniel is devoted primarily to philology. Preeminent in its comprehensiveness and balanced judgment, this study remains invaluable for its discussion of textual problems. Montgomery examines not only the Hebrew/Aramaic and Old Greek recensions of Daniel, but also the other Greek versions as well as the Latin, Coptic, and Syriac versions. Montgomery theorizes that the combination of languages in the Book of Daniel results from the incorporation of older Aramaic material into a work that was ultimately composed in Hebrew. Montgomery does not provide an English translation of the Book of Daniel, but his highly detailed textual and historical notes on each chapter or story are invaluable.

BRENDA J. SHAVER

Dead Sea Scrolls

Charlesworth, James H. (editor), *The Dead Sea Scrolls: Hebrew, Aramaic and Greek Texts with English Translations* (Princeton Theological Seminary Dead Sea Scrolls Project), 10 vols. projected, Louisville, Kentucky: Westminster/Knox, 1994–

Collins, John J., *Apocalypticism in the Dead Sea Scrolls* (The Literature of the Dead Sea Scrolls), London and New York: Routledge, 1997

Flint, Peter and James VanderKam (editors), *The Dead Sea Scrolls after Fifty Years: A Comprehensive Assessment*, 2 vols., Boston: Brill, 1998–1999

García Martínez, Florentino, *Textos de Qumrán*, 1992; translated by Wilfred G.E. Watson as *The Dead Sea Scrolls Translated: The Qumran Texts in English*, New York: Brill, 1994, 2nd edition, 1996

Schiffman, Lawrence H., *Sectarian Law in the Dead Sea Scrolls: Courts, Testimony, and the Penal Code* (Brown Judaic Studies, 33), Chico, California: Scholars Press, 1983

Schiffman, Lawrence H., *Reclaiming the Dead Sea Scrolls: The History of Judaism, the Background of Christianity, the Lost Library of Qumran*, Philadelphia: Jewish Publication Society, 1994

Shanks, Hershel (editor), *Understanding the Dead Sea Scrolls: A Reader from the Biblical Archaeology Review*, New York: Random House, 1992

Stegemann, Hartmut, *The Library of Qumran: On the Essenes, Qumran, John the Baptist, and Jesus*, Grand Rapids, Michigan, and Cambridge: Eerdmans, 1998

Ulrich, Eugene and James VanderKam (editors), *The Community of the Renewed Covenant: The Notre Dame Symposium on the Dead Sea Scrolls* (Christianity and Judaism in Antiquity Series, vol. 10), Notre Dame, Indiana: University of Notre Dame Press, 1994

VanderKam, James, *The Dead Sea Scrolls Today*, Grand Rapids, Michigan: Eerdmans, 1994

Vermes, Geza, *The Complete Dead Sea Scrolls in English*, New York: Lane/Penguin, and London: Lane, 1997

Wise, Michael, Martin Abegg, and Edward Cook, *The Dead Sea Scrolls: A New Translation*, San Francisco: HarperSanFrancisco, and London: HarperCollins, 1996

The Dead Sea Scrolls were certainly the best-publicized archaeological discovery of the 20th century, but much of the publicity has been tinged with sensationalism. A number of popular books on the scrolls have made claims that distort or disregard the findings of the majority of the careful scholars who have made scrolls research their life's work. In general, the media have tended to focus on the relevance of the scrolls to the history of Christianity, while overlooking their significance for understanding the history of Judaism. Although some of the books described here are addressed primarily to a Christian audience, all of them are informed by responsible scholarship and seek to place the scrolls in a Jewish context.

VANDERKAM offers a concise and balanced summary of the scholarly consensus on the main issues surrounding the scrolls. After a brief account of the discovery of the caves near Qumran that contained the scrolls and the excavation of the site, he briefly surveys the contents of the major scrolls. In the next two chapters, he defends the widely accepted hypothesis that the inhabitants of Qumran were Essenes, and he presents a detailed but cautious reconstruction of the history of that sect based on both textual and archaeological evidence. He then focuses on the impact of the discovery of the scrolls on the study of both the Hebrew Scriptures and the New Testament. His limited treatment of the recent controversies surrounding the scrolls is evenhanded, if somewhat protective of the original team of scholars to whom the publication of the scrolls was entrusted.

STEGEMANN takes a more outspoken approach than VanderKam to the task of introducing the scrolls. Stegemann devotes many pages to defending the original scrolls team and sharply critiquing several recent books alleging various conspiracies to keep the scrolls hidden from the public. The author's description of the excavations is colored by his unverifiable hypothesis that the Qumran settlement functioned primarily as a center of scroll production that served Essene communities throughout the land of Israel. He also puts forth the idiosyncratic theory that the Teacher of Righteousness (a key figure in the history of the community) served as high priest during the hiatus between Alcimus and Jonathan Maccabee (159–152 B.C.E.), before breaking away from the temple to found the Essenes. In spite of its polemical and speculative tendencies, Stegemann's book provides the most thorough and engaging descriptions of the contents of the scrolls of any introduction to date.

Another highly readable and informative introduction is that of SCHIFFMAN (1994). His stated purpose is to "correct a fundamental misreading of the Dead Sea Scrolls" by locating them in their Jewish context. His approach brings the scrolls into dialogue with other texts of Second Temple Judaism, on the one hand, and with the rabbinic literature, on the other. Chiefly on the basis of a comparison of the so-called Halakhic Letter (4QMMT) to rabbinic accounts of debates between the Pharisees and the Sadducees, he maintains that the Dead Sea community originated as an offshoot of the Sadducees. He contends that the scholarly consensus that the Qumran sect was Essene needs to be (at least) modified to take into account the sect's Saducean roots. In addition to exploring the Qumran community's distinctive halakhah, Schiffman treats a number of other issues that receive scant attention in other introductions to the scrolls, including prayer and ritual and the sect's attitudes toward gentiles and women.

In a collection of articles from the *Biblical Archaeology Review*, SHANKS presents a variety of approaches to the basic issues surrounding the scrolls, all geared to a general audience. Shanks was personally involved in the controversy over the delay in publication of the Cave 4 texts, so his introduction and choice of contributors betray a certain hostility toward the original team of scrolls researchers. (He includes the infamous interview that led to the removal of John Strugnell as chief editor of the scrolls.) Nevertheless, the articles are by experts, and most cover their subjects thoroughly. Some essays are on topics not treated in other introductions, such as the techniques used for reassembling fragmentary scrolls.

The most recent edition of VERMES's classic translation of the scrolls (first published in 1962) contains "all the texts sufficiently well-preserved to be understandable in English." It is certainly the most intelligible of the available translations, but its comprehensibility is partly the result of Vermes's maximalist approach to the reconstruction of fragmentary texts. In other words, wherever there are gaps in the recovered text, he has filled them with suppositions (indicating with square brackets where the reconstruction begins and ends) derived by analogy with similar texts, or at times by (admittedly highly educated) guesswork. This technique means that sometimes more than half of the words in a given translation represent Vermes's supplementation of the little that remains of the written scroll. He helpfully divides the documents into eight categories, although one might question why some of the "Biblically Based Apocryphal Works" were not included under "Apocalyptic Works" (as it stands, the latter is by far the smallest group represented). His introduction is lengthy (90 pages) and tends, like his translation, to be overconfident in reconstructing the history of the Qumran sect.

In recent years, many students of the scrolls have come to prefer the translation of GARCÍA MARTÍNEZ for a number of reasons. First, it is substantially complete, including all of the nonbiblical texts except those García Martínez considers too fragmentary to translate. For texts that are found in more than one of the scrolls, he translates each of the fragments separately rather than combining them into one composite version, as other translators do. He is much more conservative in his reconstructions than Vermes, supplying missing words only where there is a clear textual or contextual basis for doing so, and frequently using ellipses instead of offering conjectures. The resulting lack of fluency is compounded now and then by an infelicitous choice of words; the English version is a translation of the author's original translation into Spanish. Nevertheless, what it lacks in elegance, the translation makes up for in accuracy and consistency. García Martínez's organization of the texts into nine categories, however, often seems rather arbitrary, and his introductions to each category are too brief to be of much help to novices.

WISE, ABEGG, and COOK have opted to forego the thematic classification of the scrolls altogether, simply arranging them in numerical order. Moreover, they have given new names to many of the well-known documents (the Community Rule is titled "Charter of a Sectarian Jewish Association"); as a result, someone who has read an introduction to the scrolls might search their table of contents in vain for a familiar point of entry into the translation. Their introductions to the individual texts are sometimes informative, but they tend to emphasize points of contact with Christianity. The translations themselves are accurate and unbiased, and even more conservative than those of García Martínez, for the translators only represent words that are clearly legible on the Scroll fragments (indicating doubtful readings with square brackets and keeping reconstruction to a minimum).

For readers with some knowledge of the original languages of the scrolls, the series of editions and translations under the general editorship of CHARLESWORTH may prove to be very useful. (At this writing only three of the projected ten volumes are available.) Text and translation are attractively arranged on facing pages for ease of comparison, with textual variants noted on the text page and all other types of annotation (alternative translations, cross-references, exegetical comments, etc.) placed below the translation. The editors have been criticized for not making use of all the available scholarship, but this omission seems to be a conscious decision, in keeping with the editorial policy of minimizing reconstruction of the text. The translations aim to be as literal as possible, even following the word order of the original to the extent that English syntax will allow. The brief introductions to each text are densely packed with all sorts of information but offer very little interpretation. A reader with a serious interest in a particular scroll and a desire to form an independent opinion of it would do well to consult this series, although it could be years before the publication is complete.

Most scholars would define the Qumran community as a Jewish apocalyptic sect, even though they apparently did not compose any original apocalypses. COLLINS gives a succinct and lucid explanation of apocalypticism and its relationship to the scrolls. He illustrates the main features of apocalypticism with examples from two prototypical Jewish apocalypses, the Book of Daniel and I Enoch. He then traces several dominant apocalyptic themes through the Dead Sea Scrolls, including traditions about the origin of evil, the deterministic view of history, expectations about the messianic age and reward and punishment after death, and angelology. He concludes that while the beliefs of the Qumran community are illuminated by comparison to the apocalypses, the scrolls are innovative in many respects and contribute to a broader understanding of the social context of apocalypticism.

SCHIFFMAN's (1983) study of sectarian law was written before the discovery of 4QMMT (the Halakhic Letter) and therefore does not include his later claim that the halakhah of the Qumran sect is basically Sadducean. Yet in this volume, he already expresses doubts about the identification of the sect with the Essenes, because there are significant discrepancies between the laws of the sect and what is reported about Essene practice in external sources (particularly regarding celibacy and communal property). The focus of this volume is what would now be called "civil law" (roughly corresponding to the scope of the Mishnah's order Nezikin), although Schiffman convincingly demonstrates that the Qumran sect did not recognize a distinction between civil and ritual laws. Schiffman's thorough methodology, elucidating the halakhic reasoning of the Qumran sect by contrasting that reasoning with both biblical and rabbinic law, entails some quite technical discussions. Each chapter ends with a clear summary, however, making this book enjoyable reading for anyone with an interest in the development of halakhah.

The easiest way to get a sense of the different approaches taken by many of the major figures in scrolls research (at least in the early 1990s) is to read ULRICH and VANDERKAM's collection of essays. With only one or two exceptions, each of these articles is an excellent introduction to a prominent scholar's area of expertise. Some important issues are not covered, such as the sect's method of scriptural exegesis, whereas there are three overlapping discussions of messianism (out of a total of 13 essays). On the other hand, various methodologies are represented, and some of the authors openly disagree with one another (e.g., Baumgarten and Schiffman on Qumran law), making the collection as a whole more interesting than any of its parts.

The most far-reaching and up-to-date collection of scrolls studies available is found in the two volumes edited by FLINT and VANDERKAM. In the selection of contributors and topics, these volumes reflect an interest in both "past perspectives and future prospects" in scrolls research (to borrow from the subtitle of Jodi Magness's essay in volume one). Approximately half of the articles are by up-and-coming scholars who bring newer methodologies to bear on scrolls research. The first volume ranges from general surveys of the history of scholarship and archaeology of Qumran, through somewhat more concentrated studies of the main genres of Qumran texts, to highly specialized reports on techniques and technologies that have been or are beginning to be applied to scrolls research. The majority of the studies in the second volume are topical (e.g., "Holiness in the Dead Sea Scrolls," "The Demonology of the Dead Sea Scrolls," "Prophets and Prophecy at Qumran"). There are also two groups of three essays each under the headings "The Scrolls and Judaism" and "The Scrolls and Early Christianity." A comparison of these essays confirms that, in spite of all the changes over the course of the history of Qumran research, there is still a fundamental division between scholars who study the scrolls in the context of the history of Judaism and those who treat them as background to the history of Christianity.

KARINA MARTIN HOGAN

Death, Burial, and Mourning: Biblical and Talmudic

Bailey, Lloyd R., *Biblical Perspectives on Death* (Overtures to Biblical Theology, 5), Philadelphia: Fortress, 1979

Bloch-Smith, Elizabeth, *Judahite Burial Practices and Beliefs about the Dead* (Journal for the Study of the Old Testament Supplement Series, 123), Sheffield, South Yorkshire: JSOT, 1992

Feldman, Emanuel, *Biblical and Post-Biblical Defilement and Mourning: Law as Theology* (Library of Jewish Law and Ethics), New York: Yeshiva University Press, 1977

Lewis, Theodore J., *Cults of the Dead in Ancient Israel and Ugarit* (Harvard Semitic Monographs, no. 39), Atlanta, Georgia: Scholars Press, 1989

Schmidt, Brian B., *Israel's Beneficent Dead: Ancestor Cult and Necromancy in Ancient Israelite Religion and Tradition*, Tübingen: Mohr (Siebeck), 1994; Winona Lake, Indiana: Eisenbrauns, 1996

Spronk, Klaas, *Beatific Afterlife in Ancient Israel and in the Ancient Near East*, Neukirchen-Vluyn: Neukirchener Verlag, and Kevelaer: Butzon and Bercker, 1986

Tromp, Nicholas J., *Primitive Conceptions of Death and the Nether World in the Old Testament*, Rome: Pontifical Biblical Institute, 1969

Zlotnick, Dov, *The Tractate "Mourning" (Semahot): Regulations Relating to Death, Burial, and Mourning* (Yale Judaica Series, vol. 17), New Haven, Connecticut: Yale University Press, 1966

The traditions preserved in the Hebrew Bible are reticent regarding the subject of death. Academic inquiry into the topic therefore relies on mining the scattered references throughout the canon, comparison with other ancient Near Eastern cultures, and occasionally on archaeological data. It is a matter of current debate whether the Israelites, in spite of biblical prohibitions, engaged in ancestor worship or cults of the dead. Postbiblical Jewish approaches to death are less frequently discussed in the secondary literature, which focuses largely on contemporary mourning customs.

TROMP provides a detailed study, based on comparisons with Ugaritic terms, of the Hebrew words and phrases in the biblical corpus that refer to death and the realm of the dead. His method results in a largely philological project, one that focuses on text and language, particularly on the Bible's poetic compositions. Tromp concludes that the Israelite conception of the netherworld is closely related to the idea of the grave, and that it is often described as the negation of positive life experiences. His arguments here are persuasive, but his additional statement that death was regarded by the Israelites as a personal enemy is open to debate. While the subject of death probably does not, in the end, have the prominence in the

Hebrew Bible that he suggests, Tromp's study is an important contribution regarding the language of death in the biblical traditions.

BAILEY's book is part of the series "Overtures in Biblical Theology," and reflects the series' aim of discussing biblical themes in relation to the modern world. He begins with a brief reflection on modern thoughts about death, and then, in the bulk of the book, he studies several topics in a range of texts: attitudes toward death in the Hebrew Bible; the shift to new views of death with the rise of apocalypticism; death in post-biblical works including the Dead Sea Scrolls; and, finally, death in the New Testament. Bailey concludes by exploring the implications of these traditions for bioethics, for the modern fear of mortality, and for contemporary theology. His book does not provide a thorough scholarly analysis of the ancient texts but rather is aimed at a more general audience with an interest in modern theological questions.

SPRONK begins with an extensive survey of the history regarding scholarship on the question of whether a belief in the afterlife may be found in the Hebrew Bible. This is followed by a discussion of death in the cultures of the ancient Near East, including Egypt, Mesopotamia, Asia Minor, Greece, Syria, and Palestine. Spronk then moves on to ancient Israel and considers matters such as the culture's funerary customs, beliefs in the powerful dead, traditions about heaven, and the afterlife of the king. At the end of the book, he addresses a number of texts regarding notions of God's ability to rescue one from death. The evidence leads him to suggest that while Israelite Yahwism generally avoided the subject in order to resist Canaanite beliefs, there were still circles in Israelite folk religion in which the Canaanite views of death survived.

LEWIS readdresses the question of whether ancient Israel had a cult of the dead, which he defines in terms of acts intended to placate the dead or attain favors from them. He says that although many earlier scholars felt otherwise, in his opinion there is strong circumstantial evidence for death cult practices within the popular religion, practices that were rejected by the religious strand that eventually became normative Yahwism. He draws his evidence from a detailed analysis of recently published Ugaritic texts, and then he argues that similar traditions appear, or are forbidden, in a range of biblical materials including the Deuteronomistic, prophetic, and priestly literature. Lewis's study is most accessible to those with a background in Semitic languages, but his identification of a large number of biblical passages relevant to the death cult debate is useful for general readers.

BLOCH-SMITH examines Iron Age Judahite mortuary practices and beliefs, using both archaeological and literary evidence. She discusses the tomb types of the period, human remains, and the contents of the burials, and then she turns to the biblical texts for a short analysis. Her conclusion is that cults of the dead were a standard part of Judahite religious practice and were limited, but not utterly forbidden, by the Jerusalem priests and prophets beginning in the late eighth century B.C.E. The aim of these priests and prophets was to strengthen their own positions of power by reserving all forms of contact with the supernatural for themselves. An appendix of almost 100 pages catalogs Iron Age burials by time period and type and is followed by several illustrations and maps. Although Bloch-Smith considers literary materials, her book's focus and strength is the archaeology.

SCHMIDT questions what he describes as a recent academic consensus that some or most of Israelite society before the exile was involved in ancestor cults and necromancy. He provides a survey of Syro-Palestinian literary sources on the matter (from Ebla, Mari, Ugarit, Nuzi, and Emar) and then investigates biblical sources. He decides that while the texts show evidence for ongoing mortuary rites after burial, these rites affirm only a desire to take care of the dead or memorialize them and are not proof of actual ancestor cults. Neither pre-exilic Israel nor Judah appears to have believed in the dead's power to help the living, and when this belief did finally emerge in the tradition it was a late phenomenon, the source of which was Mesopotamian necromancy. Schmidt's work, read in conjunction with the opposing views above, shows the complexity involved in interpreting the data.

ZLOTNICK translates the "classic rabbinic text on death and mourning" from the Hebrew into English. While his book therefore consists largely of making available a primary source to an English audience, he provides a 30-page introduction that discusses the date of the tractate, its content, and its parallels with death customs in Greek and Roman texts. The translation itself follows, occupying 57 pages. Zlotnick's notes on the translation appear afterward and run to more than 70 pages, providing the reader with copious commentary on the primary source. A glossary and indexes follow, and the book concludes with a vocalized Hebrew text.

FELDMAN investigates biblical and rabbinic understandings of death and, more specifically, the content and ramifications of Jewish *tum'ah* (defilement) legislation. The first part of his study argues that in biblical and rabbinic thought, death is the highest state of desacralization, and that the defilement associated with death signifies alienation from God. The second half of the book studies talmudic mourning law, which functions, in his view, to represent the mourner's temporary separation from God, community, and self. He concludes with an analysis of all the rabbinic laments in the Talmud, presented with the Hebrew and Aramaic texts as well as English translations. Feldman's book is accessible to the general reader, and with its focus on rabbinic material, it is a rare investigation of postbiblical Jewish thinking about death.

SHANNON BURKES

See also Death, Burial, and Mourning: Medieval and Modern

Death, Burial, and Mourning: Medieval and Modern

Caro, Joseph, *Code of Hebrew Law/Shulhan 'Aruk*, translated by Chaim N. Denburg, Montreal: Jurisprudence, 1954

Cohen, Hershel and Victor M. Solomon, *Nahalat Shafrah: A Book of Eulogettes*, Hoboken, New Jersey: Ktav, 1990

Diamant, Anita, *Saying Kaddish: How to Comfort the Dying, Bury the Dead, and Mourn as a Jew*, New York: Schocken, 1998

Ganzfried, Solomon, *Code of Jewish Law/Kitzur Schulchan Aruch: A Compilation of Jewish Laws and Customs*, translated by Hyman E. Goldin, New York: Hebrew Publishing, 1927, annotated revised edition, 1963

Klein, Isaac, *A Guide to Jewish Religious Practice* (Moreshet Series, vol. 6), New York: Jewish Theological Seminary, 1979

Lamm, Maurice, *The Jewish Way in Death and Mourning*, New York: David, 1969; London: Kuperard, 1999

Maimonides, Moses, *The Code of Maimonides, Book Fourteen: The Book of Judges* (Yale Judaica Series, vol. 3), translated by Abraham M. Hershman, New Haven, Connecticut: Yale University Press, 1949

Rabinowicz, Tzvi, *A Guide to Life: Jewish Laws and Customs of Mourning*, London: Jewish Chronicle, 1964; New York: Ktav, 1967

Riemer, Jack (editor), *Jewish Reflections on Death*, New York: Schocken, 1974

Wieseltier, Leon, *Kaddish*, New York: Knopf, 1998; London: Kuperard, 1999

The laws of mourning apply when one of seven close relatives (father, mother, son, daughter, brother, sister, or spouse) passes away. Jewish tradition encourages simple funerals, and respect for the dead is considered the ultimate kindness.

MAIMONIDES, who wrote in the 12th century, and CARO, who wrote in the 16th, are the two chief codifiers of Jewish law. For the Sephardim, Maimonides and Caro are co-equal authorities. For the Ashkenazim, Caro's code, as supplemented by the 16th-century glosses of Moses Isserles (which incorporate the decisions, rulings, and customs of German and Polish scholars), is the ultimate authority. Should there be a conflict between Caro and Isserles, the rulings of the glossator govern for the Ashkenazim. In the 19th century, GANZFRIED wrote an abridgment of Caro's code and its commentaries. Because of their authoritative nature, these three codes are entitled to pride of place in any discussion of death, burial, and mourning in the Jewish tradition. However, law codes, by their very nature, tend to be dry and tedious reading, and therefore it may be preferable for the uninitiated to study the work of Lamm or Klein, which integrate Jewish law with Jewish values, before tackling these codes.

LAMM's pioneering study of Jewish laws and traditions pertaining to death and mourning is intended for the layman. Written from an Orthodox perspective, the laws are not simply ordered as a list but are interpreted as expressions of historic Jewish ideas and ideals. Lamm interprets traditional Jewish practice in a manner relevant to the average contemporary Jew. He aims to show that Judaism teaches the aching heart how to express its pain with love and respect and without vindictiveness or self pity. He makes interesting observations on the cathartic quality of the ritual tearing of garments prior to a funeral, the significance of the "filling-in" ceremony at the gravesite, the custom of washing one's hands upon returning from the cemetery, and other rituals associated with death and mourning.

RABINOWICZ presents a very useful compendium of the laws of mourning for the nonspecialist. The work is also valuable for scholars, for the author supports his statements with references to the Bible, talmudic and rabbinic texts, the standard codes, and the responsa literature. He points out that while the Jewish laws of mourning are many and detailed, they are inspired by a warm humanity. The guiding principle of the rabbis was always to adopt the "lenient view" when questions arose in connection with the laws of mourning. Particularly valuable is chapter 12, which is devoted to words of comfort from the Bible, the Talmud, and several modern writers.

KLEIN's code serves as a detailed and comprehensive guide for Conservative congregations and individuals sympathetic to the Conservative viewpoint. Like the rest of the work, the two chapters devoted to the laws of mourning consider traditional Jewish sources (Bible, Talmud, codes, responsa, etc.) and are fully referenced for further study. This text can also be used by Orthodox Jews because the author clearly indicates where the guidelines deviate from Orthodox practice, considering, for example, the Conservative practice that permits mourners to pin a symbolic black ribbon on their lapel for the *keriah*, which traditionally requires the rending of one's garment. Klein belonged to the right wing of the Conservative movement, and his views are more representative of the ritual practice endorsed by the Union of Traditional Judaism than that of the United Synagogue of Conservative Judaism.

DIAMANT aims to help non-Orthodox Jews, who view the halakhah as a reference point rather than a mandate, make Judaism's time-honored rituals into personal, meaningful sources of comfort. Every Jewish ritual and custom that surrounds death is guided by two principles: the requirement to show respect for the dead and the commandment to provide comfort for the bereaved. Diamant organizes her work on these dual cornerstones. Chapters discuss the Jewish funeral, the *shiva* period (the first week following a death, when community, friends, and family comfort and care for mourners), the needs of grieving children, mourning the death of a child, neonatal loss, suicide, and the death of non-Jewish loved ones.

RIEMER has edited an anthology of 23 selections by Jewish thinkers on the subject of death and dying. The contributors represent different religious perspectives, but all the authors have been shaped, at least in part, by the Jewish tradition. The texts are relevant because they wrestle with the Jewish tradition concerning death, the responsibility the living bear for the dead and the dying, and the particular issues these topics raise for contemporary Jews. Some of the essays probe the special problems posed by new medical technology and by other aspects of modern society. Riemer presents opposing views of euthanasia, the affirmative position being defended by Jeremy Silver and the negative by Hayim Greenberg. On a more personal level, Jacob Neusner writes movingly of his father-in-law's funeral in Jerusalem, and Deborah Lipstadt explains how mourning rituals helped her and her family cope at the time of her father's death. The book appropriately ends with a modern ethical will.

COHEN and SOLOMON view the Jewish eulogy as an opportunity for a spiritual leader to reach the mourners and community with a message that is both therapeutic and religious. Although solidly grounded in traditional Jewish sources, this collection of brief eulogies also incorporates contemporary views of grief psychology. Death affects everyone, regardless of religion or lifestyle, and the authors urge that every death be treated with respect and compassion. Even a person who subscribes to a different set of beliefs or engages in behavior considered deviant, deserves an honest eulogy that acknowledges his or her life and views without necessarily endorsing them.

WIESELTIER has edited the journal that he kept during the traditional year of mourning following the death of his father in March 1996. During this time, the author faithfully recited the Kaddish three times a day. The book has an existential as well as an intellectual dimension. The author, although not especially devout, poignantly recounts the continuity he sought with his father by reciting the prayer that has been aptly described as the handclasp of the generations. In addition, Wieseltier is an accomplished student of Hebrew literature, and his work is invaluable for its excerpts from, and analyses of, many medieval religious texts unavailable in English translation.

JACOB HABERMAN

See also Death, Burial, and Mourning: Biblical and Talmudic

Decalogue

Carmichael, Calum M., *The Origins of Biblical Law: The Decalogues and the Book of the Covenant*, Ithaca, New York: Cornell University Press, 1992

Goldman, Solomon, *The Ten Commandments,* Chicago: University of Chicago Press, 1956

Harrelson, Walter J., *The Ten Commandments and Human Rights* (Overtures to Biblical Theology, 8), Philadelphia: Fortress, 1980; revised edition, Macon, Georgia: Mercer University Press, 1997

Neusner, Jacob (editor), *How Judaism Reads the Torah,* New York: Lang, 1993

Nielsen, Eduard, *The Ten Commandments in New Perspective: A Traditio-Historical Approach* (Studies in Biblical Theology, 2nd series, no. 7), London: S.C.M., and Naperville, Illinois: Allenson, 1968

Phillips, Anthony, *Ancient Israel's Criminal Law: A New Approach to the Decalogue,* New York: Schocken, and London: Blackwell, 1970

Segal, Ben-Zion (editor), ʻAseret ha-dibrot be-reʼi ha-dorot, 1990; English edition edited by Gershon Levi as *The Ten Commandments in History and Tradition* (Publications of the Perry Foundation for Biblical Research), Jerusalem: Magnes Press of the Hebrew University of Jerusalem, 1990

Stamm, Johann Jakob with M.E. Andrew, *The Ten Commandments in Recent Research* (Studies in Biblical Theology, 2nd series, no. 2), London: S.C.M., and Naperville, Illinois: Allenson, 1967

Willams, Jay G., *Ten Words of Freedom: An Introduction to the Faith of Israel,* Philadelphia: Fortress, 1971

STAMM reviews the serious scholarship focused on the Decalogue during the first part of the 20th century. The introduction, which occupies half the book, discusses studies of the transmission, form, and origin of the Decalogue. Albrecht Alt's distinction between casuistic and apodictic laws and the covenant formulary receive the most attention here. In the next section, each commandment is discussed individually as exegetical studies on the commandments are summarized. The concluding chapter is a short discussion on the distinctive character of the Decalogue against the backdrop of ancient Near Eastern law codes. Stamm's book provides a convenient summary of the work done on the Decalogue primarily by German Protestant biblical scholars. Their work has been very influential in the development of scholarship on biblical law in general and the Ten Commandments in particular.

NIELSEN offers a hypothesis regarding the development of the Decalogue from its origins to it present literary setting in Exodus 20 and Deuteronomy 5. He suggests that the Decalogue was the basic law that defined the limits of royal behavior in the kingdom of Israel. Priests and elders produced these laws, which served as the basis for judicial decisions. After the fall of Israel to the Assyrians in 722 B.C.E., the Decalogue became a covenant document that served the cause of reform in Judah. In time, people came to regard it as a sacred tradition delivered by God. Nielsen denies that the Hittite treaties served as an analog in the development of the Ten Commandments.

PHILLIPS sees the origins in the Decalogue in ancient Israel's system of criminal law. Although the Ten Commandments do not contain sanctions, other laws mandate various penalties, including death, for individuals who violate laws similar to those found in the Decalogue. The original purpose of the Decalogue was to regulate conduct that was harmful to the community as a whole. Since any violation of the community's covenant with God was detrimental to the community's welfare, the Ten Commandments served to safeguard Israel's relationship with God.

CARMICHAEL makes an important connection between biblical laws and narratives. He argues that the origin of the laws found in the Bible was not a response to the social situation in ancient Israel; rather, biblical law developed out of scribal reflection on the narrative traditions of ancient Israel. The sources of biblical laws may be folk or scribal wisdom, custom, or ancient Near Eastern law codes, but the impetus for developing a distinctively Israelite code came from reflection on distinctive Israelite religious traditions. Carmichael illustrates this hypothesis regarding the Ten Commandments and other biblical laws by relating these laws to key moments in the stories about Jacob, Joseph, and Moses. This is a creative and engaging approach that not only provides a way to integrate biblical law and narrative but also helps contemporary believers see their experience as reflected in ancient narrative and legal texts.

NEUSNER, known for his translations of early rabbinic texts, offers a translation of the section of the Mekhilta of Rabbi Ishmael that deals with the Decalogue. In his prologue to the translation, Neusner provides a general introduction to the Oral Law of rabbinic Judaism and a more specific introduction to the Mekhilta, which has guided Jewish understanding of the Book of Exodus, including the Ten

Commandments. Shorter introductions to each section of the Mekhilta guide the reader through the ancient rabbinic work. Neusner's comments make it possible to appreciate early rabbinic discourse that, despite its importance and influence, may be unfamiliar and occasionally difficult for the modern reader.

At the time of his death, GOLDMAN was working on a multivolume commentary on the Hebrew Bible. His posthumously published study of the Ten Commandments was to be part of that work. In his commentary on Exodus 19–20, Goldman describes the giving of the Decalogue as a crucial step in transforming a band of freed Hebrew slaves into a civilized people. The commentary has two parts. The first offers a more general discussion of the religious and cultural significance of the Decalogue, while the second section deals with more technical, exegetical issues. Goldman was ahead of his time when he criticized the tendency of the scholars of his day to divide the biblical text into increasingly smaller fragments. He also found fault with the evolutionary framework within which some scholars placed the religion of ancient Israel. This is an excellent example of sound biblical scholarship at the service of a believing community.

HARRELSON writes on the Decalogue for a general and mostly Christian audience, although he does raise issues that relate to the Jewish community specifically. He sees the commandments as a charter of freedom rather than as restrictions on the human spirit. While Harrelson begins with issues that are of more interest to the scholar, such as the exegetical problems that call for a new study of the Decalogue as a whole, his most significant contributions are his lucid and insightful comments on each of the commandments and their importance in the contemporary world. He argues persuasively for the importance of moral imperatives, and he describes clearly the types of behavior that are harmful to humans.

WILLIAMS conceived his work as a response to what he saw as the post-Christian culture of the United States after the 1960s. He offers this line-by-line commentary on Exodus 20 as a way for believers to develop their identity in a secular culture. The commentary examines the meaning of the Decalogue in itself, in relation to other biblical motifs, and in relation to the contemporary scene. The basic assumption behind Williams's work is the enduring value of the Decalogue and the impossibility of exhausting its value for believers. While Williams writes for the general reader, he is not simply engaging in a homiletical exercise. The book is informed by critical scholarship but not limited by it. Williams wants to show how the Ten Commandments, critically understood, can shape the lives of believers in a time of cultural and moral relativity.

In SEGAL's collection, 17 Israeli students of the Bible, history, philosophy, liturgy, theology, music, poetry, and art have each approached the Decalogue from their individual perspectives. While the discussions follow the conventions of scholarly discourse, the book addresses itself to a broader audience. The first essay, Moshe Weinfeld's "The Uniqueness of the Decalogue and Its Place in Jewish Tradition," sets the tone for the volume. It weaves together biblical analysis with examples of how Jewish tradition has appropriated the "ten words." The final essay, Bezalel Narkiss's "Illustrations of the 10 Commandments in the Thirteenth Century Minute Mahzor," describes how medieval Jewish illuminated manuscripts depict the two tablets of the Law. All the essays in this collection are marked by careful scholarship, reverence for the tradition, and engaging discussion.

LESLIE J. HOPPE

See also Commandments

Demons *see* Angels and Demons

Deuteronomy

Carmichael, Calum M., *The Laws of Deuteronomy*, Ithaca, New York: Cornell University Press, 1974

Christensen, Duane L., *A Song of Power and the Power of Song: Essays on the Book of Deuteronomy* (Sources for Biblical and Theological Study, 3), Winona Lake, Indiana: Eisenbrauns, 1993

Mayes, Andrew David Hastings, *Deuteronomy* (New Century Bible Commentary), Greenwood, South Carolina: Attic, and London: Oliphants, 1979

McConville, J.G., *Law and Theology in Deuteronomy* (Journal for the Study of the Old Testament Supplement Series, 33), Sheffield, South Yorkshire: JSOT, 1984

Olson, Dennis T., *Deuteronomy and the Death of Moses: A Theological Reading* (Overtures to Biblical Theology), Minneapolis, Minnesota: Fortress, 1994

Polzin, Robert, *Moses and the Deuteronomist: Deuteronomy, Joshua, Judges,* New York: Seabury, 1980

von Rad, Gerhard, *Studies in Deuteronomy* (Studies in Biblical Theology, no. 9), Chicago: Regnery, and London: SCM, 1953

Weinfeld, Moshe, *Deuteronomy and the Deuteronomic School,* Oxford: Clarendon, 1972; Winona Lake, Indiana: Eisenbrauns, 1992

Weinfeld, Moshe, *Deuteronomy 1–11: A New Translation with Introduction and Commentary* (The Anchor Bible, vol. 5), New York: Doubleday, 1991

VON RAD's work represents the beginning of the modern study of Deuteronomy. The questions he asks deal with the sociological background of the text. He focuses on the book's social context by studying its style and forms of expression. He is struck by the variety of literary forms in the book and concludes that its complex literary structure must have been rooted in a ritual during which the clergy recited the laws of God. He identifies these reciters with the Levites and considers them to be the spokesmen of the Deuteronomistic movement. Especially influential is his thesis that the six books from Genesis through Joshua were simply the elaboration of what he calls "the short historical creed" found in Deuteronomy 26:5b–9. While scholars today have taken issue with some of von Rad's conclusions, his work remains seminal to the study of the Deuteronomic tradition. Von Rad's studies set the agenda of research into Deuteronomy for an entire generation of biblical scholarship.

Of the many full-scale commentaries on Deuteronomy, that of MAYES is clearly the most sober, engaging, and helpful to the general reader. The author is thoroughly familiar with current scholarship on Deuteronomy. He espouses no idiosyncratic positions but prefers to offer the reader the scholarly consensus, although he is fair in presenting the alternatives. The principal motif that is present throughout the commentary is Mayes's view that Deuteronomy conceives Israel as a community of brothers living in the land promised to their ancestors. This community expresses its unity through observing the laws given to it by its God. Because of Mayes's historical-critical concerns, he does pay some attention to the development of the book into its present form. Still, the history of the text is not the primary focus of this commentary; Mayes pays much more attention to the religious affirmations of the text. His commentary helps readers to appreciate Deuteronomy itself and also to see why many scholars consider the composition of Deuteronomy to be a turning point in Israelite religion, emphasizing as it does the central significance of a written authoritative law, the obedience of which will determine Israel's future.

Mayes examines carefully one of von Rad's most influential hypotheses about the development of Deuteronomy—that Deuteronomy is a product of ancient Israel's covenant tradition. While Mayes recognizes the connection between Deuteronomy and ancient Near Eastern covenant formularies, he asserts that the book is not a treaty document nor does it present itself as one. Mayes holds that the literary criticism of Deuteronomy must proceed independently of the covenant formulary.

OLSON provides a thorough presentation of Deuteronomy's theology by examining the full structure and movement of the book. Although this is a close literary reading of the text, Olson does not underplay the insights from historical criticism. The book's title comes from the author's assertion that the death of Moses is a significant motif throughout the Book of Deuteronomy, with important theological consequences. He sees Moses' death as a metaphor for the limits and inevitable losses of human life and power before God; the death has a positive function by offering a paradigm for the vocation of sacrificial giving. Olson studies Deuteronomy's religious ideas by focusing on the book as a whole rather than on the development of the book's theology through successive reinterpretations of traditional material.

Olson's work makes it clear that only thorough familiarity with Deuteronomy as a whole can allow appreciation of its components. His approach stands in contrast to attempts to reconstruct the history of Deuteronomy's formation as the result of a series of redactions, each with its editorial enrichments. This "archaeology" of Deuteronomy led to an elaborate conjectural reconstruction of ancient Israel's religious ideas and institutions.

POLZIN offers a synchronic study of Deuteronomy. He begins with a lengthy and dense discussion of his own literary approach. Polzin sees Deuteronomy as the result of a debate between proponents of the fixed Mosaic tradition and critics of that tradition. The latter offered a serious theological challenge to the Mosaic tradition by suggesting that the covenant should not be understood in a rigid, unconditional

manner. Israel's experience led the critics to suggest that Israel must depend upon divine mercy and not simply on its own achievements. Unlike some structuralists, Polzin is able to show how a close reading of the biblical text helps the student grapple with a crucial theological issue. He sees the existence of Deuteronomy as evidence of the freedom and multivalence of the ancient Israelite theological enterprise.

Polzin's work is a fine introduction to a contemporary literary critical approach to Deuteronomy. He appreciates the issues and concerns of historical criticism and does not engage in unnecessary diatribes against a historical approach to the book. His style is clear and persuasive and without the jargon that sometimes accompanies literary-critical studies. Polzin tests his hypothesis by examining the books of Joshua and Judges and sees the pattern found in Deuteronomy replicated in these first two components of the Deuteronomistic History.

WEINFELD (1972) tackles a most controverted issue in the study of Deuteronomy: the book's origins. He holds that Deuteronomy was the creation of scribal circles that began their literary project some time prior to the reign of Josiah (640–609 B.C.E.) and were still at work after the fall of Judah (587 B.C.E.). Although this hypothesis has not won wide acceptance, two aspects of Weinfeld's work that have been very helpful in the study of Deuteronomy are his analysis of the book's homiletic framework and of the book's legal code. He shows quite convincingly that the laws of Deuteronomy reflect a secular and humanistic perspective when compared to the laws of the Holiness (Leviticus 17–26) and Covenant (Exodus 20:22–23:33) Codes. He shows that the religious ideology and the didactic aims of Deuteronomy reflect the concerns of lay people rather than priests.

Some interpreters hold that the final forms of several books of the Hebrew Bible were the work of editors imbued with Deuteronomic theological perspectives. In an appendix to his book, Weinfeld assembles a list of what he considers "Deuteronomic phraseology" and the texts in the Hebrew Bible where these characteristic phrases occur. This provides the type of data necessary to evaluate any hypothesis regarding a supposed Deuteronomic redaction of other books.

WEINFELD (1991) has also completed one volume of a projected two-volume commentary on Deuteronomy for the Anchor Bible series. This format allows the reader to appreciate the author's skill as a translator, his insights as a historical critic, and his sensitivity as a biblical theologian. A principal achievement of this commentary is the consistency with which the author compares the words, literary forms, and theological ideas of Deuteronomy with other biblical texts, ancient Near Eastern works, classical Greek texts, the New Testament, and rabbinic literature. This helps clarify not only Deuteronomy's role in the development of ancient Israelite religion but also its significance as a religious text from the ancient Near East that helped shape both early Judaism and Christianity.

Weinfeld holds that the Book of Deuteronomy, while containing older traditions, took its shape during the time of Josiah. He sees the production of Deuteronomy as beginning the process of the canonization of Scripture. During the same period and for some time later, there were scribes who collected and edited traditions dealing with the settlement of the

Israelite tribes in Canaan and with the story of Israel's monarchy. In assembling these traditions, Weinfeld maintains, the scribes used the ideology of Deuteronomy as their unifying principle. The Book of Deuteronomy, then, was the text that changed the religion of ancient Israel into a religion of the book.

The essays collected by CHRISTENSEN include articles by several of the major scholars involved in the study of Deuteronomy. He has divided the book into five sections. The first deals with basic issues and the book as a whole; especially important here is Weinfeld's essay on the present state of research. The second part of the collection deals with the outer frame of Deuteronomy (i.e., chapters one through three and 31 through 34). The inner frame (chapters four through 11 and 27 through 30) is the subject of the third part. The fourth section is on the central core of the book (chapters 12 through 26). The essay by Braulik on the sequence of the laws is a significant contribution, and Polzin's essay on the compositional analysis of the Deuteronomistic History provides a good example of recent literary approaches to the book. The concluding section deals with new directions in the study of Deuteronomy.

As important as Christensen's book is, there are many other significant articles on Deuteronomy that could not be included in his collection. The Book of Deuteronomy has become a magnet, attracting the attention of many scholars who have made impressive gains in understanding and appreciating this book and its significance for the religion of ancient Israel and early Judaism. One may quibble about the inclusion of one or another of the essays in Christensen's volume, but as a whole it is an excellent entrance into the current state of research.

McCONVILLE takes the position that the laws of Deuteronomy are not simply one codification of ancient Israelite legal practice; he maintains that the Deuteronomic Code (Deuteronomy 12–26) is an expression of the book's theology. McConville focuses on cultic laws to prove this hypothesis. For example, he reads the laws of sacrifice less as technical directions on how sacrificial rituals are to be performed than as an illustration of Deuteronomy's view that the land is a gift that God has given to the people of Israel for their enjoyment. Earlier treatments of Deuteronomic laws study them as part of the history of Israelite religious practice. According to McConville, however, it is clear that in Deuteronomy the laws are theological statements.

Among the related issues that McConville discusses is the date of the composition of Deuteronomy. He rejects the common view that associates the book with Josiah's reform (seventh century B.C.E.); he sees the book taking final shape during the exile (sixth century B.C.E.). While others have believed the book to have undergone a long and complex literary development, McConville believes that a single author was responsible for the laws that deal with sacrifice and ritual. He considers his study to give credence to the possibility of a greater unity for the book than is usually allowed by historical critics.

CARMICHAEL also deals with the laws of Deuteronomy as he tries to fathom the principle of their arrangement, which many interpreters have regarded as haphazard. Carmichael suggests that Deuteronomy is not a legal code in the strict sense. Rather, it is a literary work that reinterprets the laws

and stories of Genesis, Exodus, Leviticus, and Numbers with the goal of religious reform. The laws of Deuteronomy make allusions to earlier traditions. While these allusions seem subtle, they were undoubtedly understood by the reformist circles for whom Deuteronomy was written. Carmichael rejects any suggestion that Deuteronomy is a composite work. Like McConville, Polzin, and Olson, Carmichael focuses on the unity of Deuteronomy rather than on attempting to reconstruct the literary history of the text. The tendency to view Deuteronomy as a literary whole is characteristic of contemporary approaches to the book. While it is difficult to deny that the book is, in some sense, a composite work, too little attention has been paid to the form that the text has in the canon.

LESLIE J. HOPPE

Devotional Literature see Ethical and Devotional Literature

Diaspora

Boyarin, Daniel and Jonathan Boyarin, "Diaspora: Generation and the Ground of Jewish Identity," *Critical Inquiry,* 19(4), 1993

Cohen, Robin, *Global Diasporas: An Introduction,* Seattle: University of Washington Press, and London: UCL, 1997

Dinur, Ben Zion, *Israel and the Diaspora,* Philadelphia: Jewish Publication Society, 1969

Dubnow, Simon, *Nationalism and History: Essays on Old and New Judaism,* edited by Koppel S. Pinson, Philadelphia: Jewish Publication Society, 1958

Eisen, Arnold M., *Galut: Modern Jewish Reflection on Homelessness and Homecoming* (Modern Jewish Experience), Bloomington: Indiana University Press, 1986

Patai, Raphael, *Tents of Jacob: The Diaspora, Yesterday and Today,* Englewood Cliffs, New Jersey: Prentice-Hall, 1971

Deriving from the Greek words meaning "to sow" and "over," diaspora refers to the state of Jewish people who live outside of the land of Israel. Since the destruction of the First Temple in 586 B.C.E., this has been the predominant mode of Jewish life and culture. Despite its centrality to Jewish history, there are few sustained studies of its specific impact on Jewish life and culture. What does diaspora mean to the people who live in Israel? Is it merely a waiting room for the prophetic "ingathering of the exiles?" Does it depend on a myth or movement of return to a homeland, or is it relatively autonomous? Or is it the circumstance of Jewish life and history, operating quite independently of a homeland? Finally, what can the diaspora tell us about Jewish history, culture, and life?

The first scholar to feature diaspora as a theoretical or methodological tool was DUBNOW, whose premise is that Jewish history is rooted primarily in diaspora, and yet it is not limited to persecution, exile, oppression, or waiting for redemption. Reading against the mainstream of Jewish historiography, Dubnow asserts that diaspora (rather than Israel) is a (if not the) crucial element in the perpetuation of Jewish cultural, scholarly, and communal life. According to his framework, Jewish life has organized itself historically around a progression of creative centers from Babylon to Spain to Poland (with other places in between). Dubnow argues that Jewish culture is a process of diaspora and that there is no preference given to a specific "home" over shifting or mobile ones. Although Dubnow was not a Zionist, he acknowledges the possibility of a Jewish state that could vie for (but would not be guaranteed) a central position in global Jewish life.

Following Dubnow, DINUR offers a historiographical study of the relationship between the diaspora and Israel. He suggests the term "Israel in the Diaspora" to convey that the diaspora is not a question of dispersion but a question of "Jewish continuity in the face of dispersion." Relying heavily on the "essential character," "emotional awareness," and "spirit" of the Jewish people, Dinur asserts that diaspora is a historical circumstance that is not necessarily one of persecution, migration, or oppression. Rather, diaspora is a historical condition that falls into the broader narrative of the "history of the Jews in their own land." As such, diaspora must necessarily contribute to its own demise either in the form of assimilation or through migration to the land of Israel. For Dinur, diaspora has been the historical circumstance for living out Jewish national destiny and maintaining Jewish political and administrative autonomy in the absence of a unified national framework.

PATAI believes that diaspora is the cultural trait that makes Jews unique among the people of the world, and he explores the impact of dispersion on Jewish culture. Dubnow and Dinur take historical approaches, while Patai's is anthropological. Following a broad historical survey of Jewish diasporas from Abraham onward, he turns briefly to the development of basic differences (e.g., language, folklore). The bulk of the book is dedicated to the study of a number of Jewish communities, including a historical overview of each and a short treatment of cultural practices that are shared among dispersed communities. He concludes that each Jewish community maintains a unique "cultural physiognomy" that is a distinct blend of "traditionally" Jewish and assimilated local cultures. This kernel of similarity that persists between dispersed communities is the essence of Jewish cultural survival. For Patai, the diaspora is a uniquely Jewish condition that demands of Jewish culture a balance between assimilation and retention, between creative innovation and Jewish tradition.

COHEN would disagree. In response to the proliferation of academic writing about diaspora, Cohen attempts a systematic analysis of diaspora, understood as a dynamic term that can be useful for describing or explaining numerous ethnic communities who live in diaspora in addition to Jews. Cohen establishes nine conditions for diaspora, which include dispersal (by trauma or in pursuit of work, colonies, or otherwise), a sense of ethnic solidarity, and the possibility of an enriching life in tolerant host countries. For Cohen, the Jewish diaspora is one among many and is unique, ironically, only insofar as its national return movement has succeeded. Cohen's nine features are a helpful guide for considering the extent to which diaspora has emerged to explain human migration and ethnic relationships in the contemporary world.

EISEN prefers "exile" to the "honorific" term diaspora, and his intellectual history of exile (which he considers to be nearly the same thing) is a brilliant and far-reaching survey of attitudes toward dispersion, tradition, and Jewish history. Eisen refuses the clichés that dominate so much of the literature in favor of an examination of the concept as it has been rendered from Genesis until the mid-1980s. The book, however, is much more than a survey of other writings, for Eisen establishes a pattern of evidence that exile is always both political and metaphysical. In this way, he resists the convenient tropes of exile and homecoming in favor of a complex and unstable notion of the relationship between diaspora and home that reflects both the historical conditions of Jews and the psychic, scholarly, cultural, religious, and political strategies for living Jewish lives. Organizing his study around delicate readings of classical Jewish texts (Genesis, Deuteronomy, the talmudic tractate Avodah Zarah, the Kuzari) and commentaries (Rashi, Isaac Luria, Ahad Ha'am, Herzl, Rosenzweig, and others), Eisen lays out the historical context that enabled each of these influential books to be written while suggesting how these contribute to our understanding of the contemporary world.

Finally, the most radical and, in some ways, most interesting discussion of diaspora comes from BOYARIN and BOYARIN, whose article offers a post-structural reading of diaspora both as a critique of nationalism and as the source of Jewish identity. Diaspora provides a theoretical model for Jewish creativity and survival based on exchange and interaction with neighboring communities rather than a national politics of self-determination based, as they see it, on separatism. Modeling Zionism after European nationalism spoils the redemptive power of its politics and ultimately condemns it as "a subversion of Jewish culture and not its culmination." They champion a Jewish collectivity that is flexible enough to share space and culture with other people as opposed to one based on territorial exclusivism. This radical critique of Israel and Zionism is a creative and rigorous evaluation of diaspora read through rabbinic literature and cultural studies and begins consideration of the political repercussions of diaspora and nation.

ARI KELMAN

Dictionaries *see* Reference Works

Dietary Laws

Douglas, Mary, *Purity and Danger: An Analysis of Concepts of Pollution and Taboo*, London: Routledge and Kegan Paul, and New York: Praeger, 1966; 2nd impression with corrections, London and Boston: Routledge and Kegan Paul, 1969

Douglas, Mary, "Deciphering a Meal," in her *Implicit Meanings: Essays in Anthropology*, London and Boston: Routledge and Kegan Paul, 1975

Grunfeld, Isidor, *The Jewish Dietary Laws*, 2 vols., London and New York: Soncino, 1972, 3rd edition, 1982

Karo, Joseph ben Ephraim, *The Kosher Code of the Orthodox Jew*, translated by S.I. Levin and Edward A. Boyden, Minneapolis: University of Minnesota Press, 1940

Katz, Jacob, *Exclusiveness and Tolerance: Studies in Jewish-Gentile Relations in Medieval and Modern Times* (Scripta Judaica, 3), Oxford: Oxford University Press, and New York: Behrman, 1961

Soloveitchik, Haym, "Can Halakhic Texts Talk History?" *AJS Review*, 3, 1978

GRUNFELD'S survey of the entire body of Jewish dietary laws draws upon traditional sources and is intended, in part, as a primer for those interested in the basic requirements of a kosher kitchen. Thus, in volume one, he reviews the general rules concerning the consumption of meat and fowl: animals that are forbidden to be eaten, the forbidden parts of permitted animals, conditions under which otherwise permitted animals are forbidden, and the final preparation of permitted meat. Additionally, Grunfeld summarizes the vast and highly complex laws concerning mixtures of meat and milk and the status of permitted foods that have contacted forbidden food (ta'aruvot). However, he correctly notes on two occasions that his elementary survey hardly does full justice to the intricate laws that govern this topic, which is traditionally one of the most complicated and detailed regions of rabbinic Judaism. Other topics covered in this first volume are the laws of leavened bread (hamets), which is forbidden on Passover; the permissibility of wine, cheese, milk, and bread that a gentile manufactures; and the requirement to inspect fruits and vegetables for insects and worms before consumption.

In addition to his introduction to the strict requirements of the dietary laws, Grunfeld also discusses the underlying reasons for these laws. Basing his analysis entirely on traditional Jewish sources, and especially on the writings of Samson Raphael Hirsch, Grunfeld offers religious, moral, and philosophical explanations for the seemingly idiosyncratic dietary requirements of the Jewish people. He favors the approach that contends that these dietary laws aim to exclude the spiritually harmful and morally dangerous influences of forbidden animals and forbidden parts of permitted animals from the body and soul of a Jew. Nonetheless, Grunfeld maintains that these dietary laws require observance simply because they were commanded to Jews by God.

Volume two discusses the dietary laws that relate to agriculture, especially the produce of the land of Israel. Here too, Grunfeld posits an ethical base for these restrictions: they are intended to inculcate the Jew with a high level of moral values—"such as kindness, charitableness, humility, helpfulness, fairmindedness, likability, sincerity, and confidence in the ultimate good of man." The survey of agricultural laws covers the laws of terumot and ma'aserot: that is, laws governing the tithes and donations that must be presented to the priests (kohanim) and Levites. Additionally, he surveys the laws governing orlah—the forbidden fruit of young trees; neta revaï—the produce of a tree in its fourth year of existence; hadash—the prohibition against eating new grain; kilayim—the injunction forbidding the mixture of different seeds, different kinds of animals, and wool with linen; and hallah—the requirement to remove a portion of kneaded dough. In all cases, Grunfeld considers the applicability of these laws in modern times and in places outside of the land of Israel.

The most extensive section of the second volume is Grunfeld's discussion of shemitah, that is, the prohibition on working the land of Israel once every seven years. There was heated discussion among rabbis of the 19th and 20th centuries concerning the nature of shemitah today, and whether one may use legal fictions such as the sale of the land of Israel (heter mekhirah) to escape some restrictions. Here too, Grunfeld's presentation is highly influenced by Hirsch, a vocal opponent of the heter mekhirah.

KARO is a translated version of the section known as "Laws of Terefah" of the Shulhan Arukh, the great code of Rabbi Joseph Karo. The rabbis understand the biblical injunction (Exodus 22: 31) against eating "any flesh that is torn of beasts in the field" to include any occasion in which the vital parts of an animal are punctured, missing, or broken. Thus, Mishnah Hullin lists 18 defects (terefot) that render an animal unfit for consumption. This number is not definitive, and one talmudic sage assumes that there are eight categories of terefot, while Maimonides rules that there are seventy. In addition to the negative injunction against eating a defective animal, the rabbis also define shehitah, a positive injunction requiring the proper slaughter of animals: a proper slaughter occurs when the majority of either the gullet or the trachea in a fowl, or the majority of both of these body parts in a quadruped, are severed in accordance with the law. The rabbinic discussion of laws relating to terefah and shehitah from talmudic times through the 15th century are codified in the first two sections of Yoreh Deah, the second of the four volumes of Shulhan Arukh. Levin and Boyden's literal translation also includes the 16th-century glosses of Rabbi Moses Isserles, which allows the code to accommodate northern European practice. Accompanying the translation are competent notes that reflect a portion of the vast and trenchant literature of commentary on Shulhan Arukh. These notes include the glosses of two 17th-century scholars: Rabbi Shabbetai Meir ha-Kohen and Rabbi David ben Samuel ha-Levi.

DOUGLAS (1966) argues against a long tradition that explains the biblical dietary laws of the Israelites as primitive, irrational, and inexplicable. She also rejects the use of allegory, as seen in the works of Philo, as a viable explanation of such laws. Instead, Douglas posits that the desire for holiness that the Bible declares is the ultimate aim of these putative restrictions, in reality demands that individuals seek out unity and perfection in their lives. Holiness is a matter of separating what should be separated, and the forbidden animals are those that do not conform to the expected norms of biblical society. Cloven-hoofed, cud-chewing ungulates are the model of the proper kind of food for a pastoralist. Assuming that the story of creation in Genesis lists the way animals are supposed to exist (fowl fly with wings; scaly fish swim with fins; and beasts hop, jump, and walk), Douglas argues that all other animals are unclean; "Any class of creatures which is not equipped for the right kind of locomotion in its element is contrary to holiness." The ultimate purpose of these dietary laws, then, is to inspire "meditation on the oneness, purity and completeness of God."

DOUGLAS (1975) responds to criticisms of her earlier position and reformulates her theory. She argues that the dietary rules of the Hebrews are consistent with the emphasis that Israelite religion places on purity and rejection of impurity; purity exists in the Hebrews' dietary laws, lineage rules, territorial boundaries, and animal sacrifices on their altars. She thus sees food restrictions as analogous to other prohibitions of mixtures. Douglas illustrates her revised theory with a novel but not entirely convincing reason for the injunction against eating pork. A pig, she claims, represents impurity and therefore is prohibited for three reasons: it is not an ungulate; it eats carrion; and non-Israelites raise it as food.

KATZ describes the function of dietary laws in the lives of medieval Jews. The Talmud forbids Jews from partaking in the bread, wine, oil, milk, and cheese of their gentile neighbors. However, the purpose of the talmudic prohibitions was largely to ensure the social cohesion of the Jewish community, while in the Middle Ages these same dietary requirements "became a method of personal conduct enabling the individual to preserve his inward sense of aloofness from those with whom he came into every day social contact." Consequently, Katz suggests that if there was an economic or social need to bend these restrictions, such powerful figures as Rabbenu Tam in the 12th century used casuistic arguments in order to protect the essential needs of the community. For example, the consumption of gentile bread was permitted by rabbinic figures after the 11th century because Jews could not practically rely upon Jewish bakers. Some figures, but not all, were lenient with respect to cooking done by a gentile (bishul nokhri), and eventually a middle position was found that allowed a gentile to do the actual work but required the Jew to maintain a fictional (Katz's term) involvement. The adjustment of dietary restrictions among the medieval rabbis thus supports Katz's overall view of the function of halakhah in that period: to achieve a balance between two opposing forces—the necessary realities of life and the maintenance of Jewish identity.

SOLOVEITCHIK discusses legal developments within the Franco-German culture of the high Middle Ages concerning the prohibition against drinking and trading wine that a non-Jew touched (yein nesekh). The subject of his study is the determination by medieval scholars of the exact moment in which the grape juice became wine and, consequently, became covered under the injunction of yein nesekh. The regnant practice in 11th- and 12th-century Germany was to prohibit gentiles from treading or touching the product even in the earliest step of wine production (i.e., while the grape pulp and juice remained in their original vat). However, the French view— beginning with Rashi (who hesitantly and ambiguously advanced this doctrine) and continued with far more certainty in his grandson, Rabbenu Tam—argued that so long as the wine remained in the cuvée in which it was originally trodden, it was immune from the qualifications of yein nesekh. The 12th-century Germans, led by the scholar Rabbi Shemaryah,

objected fiercely to this position. Indeed, the French never pursued their concession to its logical conclusion, which should have permitted gentile tub treading. Such a denial takes on even greater significance in light of the overwelming economic need for additional gentile labor. Soloveitchik argues that the prohibition against yein nesekh so strongly dominated the Ashkenazi mindset that any attempt to relax the restrictions on yein nesekh would have struck them with revulsion. Nevertheless, by the end of the 13th century, the stricter German position had given way to the more lenient French rulings.

SAMUEL HERZFELD

Divorce

Baskin, Judith R., "Rabbinic Reflections on the Barren Wife," *Harvard Theological Review*, 82, January 1989

Biale, Rachel, *Women and Jewish Law*, New York: Schocken, 1984

Bulka, Reuven P., *Jewish Divorce Ethics: The Right Way to Say Goodbye*, Ogdensburg, New York: Ivy League, 1992

Falk, Ze'ev W., *Jewish Matrimonial Law in the Middle Ages*, London: Oxford University Press, 1966

Freid, Jacob (editor), *Jews and Divorce*, New York: Ktav, 1968

Friedman, Mordechai, "Marriage as an Institution: Jewry under Islam," in *The Jewish Family: Metaphor and Memory*, edited by David Kraemer, New York: Oxford University Press, 1989

Hauptman, Judith, *Rereading the Rabbis: A Woman's Voice*, Boulder, Colorado: Westview, 1997; Oxford: Westview, 1998

Seltzer, Sanford, *When There Is No Other Alternative: A Guide for Jewish Couples Contemplating Divorce*, New York: Committee on the Jewish Family, Union of American Hebrew Congregations, 1990

The Babylonian Talmud (Gittin 90b) quotes the biblical prophet Malachi (2:13–14) in support of the assertion that "If a man divorces his first wife, even the altar sheds tears." There is little doubt that biblical and rabbinic traditions both view divorce as a tragic outcome antithetical to the joy that should accompany a marriage. Yet, Judaism permits divorce, uncertainly admitting that the alternative of an unhappy marriage may be even worse than the dissolution of the relationship. However, the ability to initiate divorce has always been a prerogative restricted to men: a divorced wife receives her get (divorce document) from her husband; she cannot be divorced from him if he is unwilling to end the marriage. In the contemporary era, this restriction continues to be a significant disability for women. While the frequency of divorce has fluctuated in various eras of the Jewish past, statistics indicate that recently married Jewish couples in contemporary North America have less than a 50 percent chance of sustaining their unions. Such findings are a cause for alarm in a Jewish community already gravely concerned about prospects for Jewish continuity.

The essays collected in FREID provide overviews of the ramifications of divorce in historical and contemporary settings from a range of denominational and disciplinary stances.

This useful volume includes discussions of divorce and divorce law in Jewish tradition, Judaism and human sexuality, and divorce and alienation in modern society, as well as several essays written from the field by Jewish social service professionals.

Feminist analyses of the development of Jewish divorce law from biblical legislation to rabbinic halakhah appear in both Biale and Hauptman. Quoting Deuteronomy 24, which forbids a divorced woman who has remarried and divorced again from remarrying her first husband, BIALE observes that the Hebrew Bible accepted divorce as a normal part of human life, effected when a man wrote a bill of divorcement, handed it to his wife, and sent her away to remarry as she pleased. Rabbinic discussion of divorce centered on defining the acceptable grounds for dissolving a marriage; the biblical given concluded that while a husband may divorce his wife for vaguely defined "unseemliness" a marriage was necessarily terminated by her sexual transgression. The halakhah does address the economic vulnerability of divorced women, obligating the husband to promise his wife a considerable minimum sum in case of divorce, a safety net extended by the rabbinic institution of the *ketubbah* (marriage contract). Biale also elaborates on the rabbinic provision that in the case of a woman's sexual or religious infractions, including refusing conjugal relations with her husband, she may be divorced without payment of her *ketubbah*.

Although divorce is a unilateral act reserved for men, the Talmud allows certain conditions when a woman may ask the court to compel her husband to divorce her. HAUPTMAN notes that by the Middle Ages, these conditions included a husband's repulsive physical condition, his violation of marital obligations, and, for some authorities, sexual incompatibility and physical abuse. The author stresses the ways in which the development of halakhic divorce legislation recognized women's suffering from male recalcitrance or capricious behavior and looked for ways to alleviate that distress. Thus, if a man cancelled a *get* without informing his wife, his marriage could be annulled by the court, while a man who falsely claimed that he issued a *get* under duress could be subject to corporal punishment. Similarly, Hauptman interprets rabbinic demands that a *get* be written with permanent ink on an enduring surface in a standard form as precautions intended to protect a woman against later claims that her divorce was not valid. Hauptman notes, however, that despite these rabbinic efforts to improve the wife's situation, she was still dependent on men to resolve her marital difficulties.

The halakhah rules that a man who lives with a woman for ten years in a childless marriage must either divorce her or take a second wife, for he is obligated to fulfil the commandment to procreate; the divorced wife may also try her luck with another spouse. BASKIN shows, however, that the aggadah undercuts this halakhic position by deprecating the dissolution of a stable marriage, insisting that barrenness is never more than a presumption, and relating tales of loving couples whose infertility was ultimately rewarded with children. Baskin argues that these aggadic stories offer an ethical and humane rebuttal to the halakhic insistence on divorce, constituting an extra-legal expression of concern for women and for the preservation of meaningful human relationships.

FRIEDMAN offers evidence from the Cairo Genizah that in the Islamic Middle Ages some Jews did not follow the unilateral rabbinic *ketubbah* issued in the husband's name but used an alternative *ketubbah* based on a statement of mutual obligations. These contracts, originating in the land of Israel, define marriage as a partnership and promise a wife the right to initiate divorce proceedings if she finds herself unable to live with her husband; this *ketubbah* was unknown among Jews in Christian countries and did not survive in mainstream Jewish practice.

FALK discusses two important reforms in divorce law enacted by the medieval Jewish communities of France and Germany. The first, attributed to Rabbi Gershom of Mainz in the 11th century ruled that a man could not divorce his wife against her will, an indication of the high status of women in this milieu. The second, probably dating from the 13th century, required that divorce become a public matter, approved by representatives of the community as well as by the couple involved; this development protected women by making divorce more difficult.

Seltzer, a Reform rabbi, and Bulka, an Orthodox rabbi and psychologist, have both produced books for divorcing couples and for those counseling such couples at this difficult juncture in their lives. SELTZER explores such topics as *shelom bayit* (domestic harmony), domestic abuse within Jewish families, the connection between the traditional *ketubbah* and alimony, difficulties for children, and the necessity of a *get*. BULKA provides comparable Orthodox perspectives.

JUDITH R. BASKIN

See also Agunah; Marriage

Djudezmo *see* Ladino Literature; Languages, Jewish

Dogmas

Abravanel, Isaac, *Principles of Faith=Rosh Amanah*, translated with an introduction and notes by Menachem Kellner, Rutherford, New Jersey: Farleigh Dickinson University Press, 1981

Baeck, Leo, "Does Traditional Judaism Possess Dogmas?" in *Studies in Jewish Thought: An Anthology of German Jewish Scholarship*, edited by Alfred Jospe, Detroit, Michigan: Wayne State University Press, 1981

Bleich, J. David, *With Perfect Faith: The Foundations of Jewish Belief*, New York: Ktav, 1983

Guttmann, Julius, "Establishing Norms for Jewish Belief," in *Studies in Jewish Thought: An Anthology of German Jewish Scholarship*, edited by Alfred Jospe, Detroit, Michigan: Wayne State University Press, 1981

Jacobs, Louis, *Principles of the Jewish Faith: An Analytical Study*, New York: Basic Books, and London: Vallentine,

Mitchell, 1964; reprinted with new preface, Northvale, New Jersey, and London: Aronson, 1988

Kellner, Menachem, *Dogma in Medieval Jewish Thought: From Maimonides to Abravanel* (Littman Library of Jewish Civilization), Oxford and New York: Oxford University Press, 1986

Margolis, Max L., *The Theological Aspect of Reformed Judaism*, Baltimore, Maryland: Friedenwald, 1904

Reines, Alvin J., "Reform Judaism," in *Meet the American Jew,* edited by Belden Menkus, Nashville, Tennessee: Broadman, 1963

Schechter, Solomon, "The Dogmas of Judaism," *Jewish Quarterly Review* (old series), 1, 1889; also published in *Studies in Judaism* (first series), Philadelphia: Jewish Publication Society, and London: Black, 1896

Shapiro, Marc B., "Maimonides' Thirteen Principles: The Last Word in Jewish Theology?" *Torah U-Madda Journal*, 4, 1993

Dogmas may be defined as a corpus of fixed beliefs authoritatively laid down for and subscribed to by members of a community. Since Judaism is known as a way of life rather than a mere creed, dogmas play a smaller role for Jews than they have, for example, in most traditional Christian denominations. As S.R. Hirsch aptly stated: "The catechism of the Jew is his calendar." It is significant that no creed has ever been practically employed as a test of membership in the Jewish community.

SCHECHTER's aim in his classic essay is twofold: to refute the contention of Moses Mendelssohn and his followers that Judaism has no dogmas; and to present in outline the historical development of dogmas in Judaism. Mendelssohn (in his *Jerusalem*, 1783, and elsewhere) refuses to base Judaism on doctrinal beliefs, asserting that Judaism is primarily a revealed legislation, a system of laws to be obeyed, not a system of articles of faith to be believed. Schechter makes it clear that Mendelssohn is not entirely consistent in his argument. At times, he asserts that Judaism does have dogmas, but those dogmas are more in harmony with reason than those of other religions. Furthermore, in a textbook for children, he includes the traditional Maimonidean creed found in the prayer book, but he changes the opening formula of each article from "I believe with perfect faith" to "I am firmly convinced." Schechter's rejection of "the great dogma of dogmalessness" is well reasoned, for subscription to revealed legislation is itself a dogma.

At the same time, however, Schechter's insistence that Judaism must have definite beliefs is not his last word on the subject. He argues that in the Bible humans are not commanded to believe in God, but rather the sacred writers operate with ideas that presuppose God's existence. Contrary to this assertion, some medieval Jewish authorities—including Maimonides, Nahmanides, and Halevi—interpreted the first of the Ten Commandments, "I am the Lord your God," as a command to believe in his existence. Additionally, Maimonides, in his Arabic Commentary on the Mishnah, when he reached the passage in tractate Sanhedrin that excludes unbelievers from a "share in the world to come," listed 13 principles of faith as criteria. These found their way into the prayer book and

thus obtained quasi-official sanction, becoming the first systematic presentation of a set of beliefs constituting the Jewish creed. But despite Maimonides' declaration in the epilogue to his 13 articles that membership in the Jewish community rests upon assent to the principles in their entirety—while the rejection of even one principle carries with it excommunication and classification as a heretic worthy of death—his formulation of the creed was not accepted by his medieval successors any more than it is today subscribed to by Reform, Conservative, or even most Orthodox Jews. Schechter presents a succinct yet densely informative survey of medieval reactions to Maimonides' formulation, down to the time of Abravanel.

The view of ABRAVANEL, elegantly rendered by Kellner, proves very interesting. The work is ostensibly devoted to defending Maimonides' 13 articles against his critics, but in his conclusion Abravanel states that Maimonides compiled these principles merely in accordance with the fashion of other nations, which set up fundamental axioms and theorems in their sciences, from which the investigators deduce propositions that are less evident. But Abravanel sees the Torah as a revealed code that does not rely on deductive reasoning; all of the Torah's commands are equally divine, and none of the edicts ought to be presumed more fundamental than any other.

BAECK clarifies Mendelssohn's view on dogmas and defends this position against Jewish reform critics such as David Einhorn, Samuel Holdheim, and Leopold Loew. Baeck contends that Judaism has no dogmas analogous to Christian authoritative formulations of faith such as the Apostles' Creed or Nicene Creed.

GUTTMANN, a historian of Jewish philosophy, wrote his study a generation after Schechter's famous essay, and they cover much of the same ground. Guttmann's discussion is more sophisticated than Schechter's, but it is much less readable.

BLEICH's useful anthology consists of selections from medieval philosopher-theologians arranged thematically under the rubrics of Maimonides' 13 principles. While a number of the selections have been translated especially for this work, Bleich frankly acknowledges that in other cases he had to use older and inferior translations because newer and superior versions were restricted by copyright considerations. There is a general introduction dealing with dogma in Judaism and briefer introductions to each of the 13 principles.

In his study of medieval Jewish dogmatic theology, KELLNER offers reliable translations, together with clear explanations and notes, of key passages from the works of both major and minor thinkers, beginning with Maimonides. Kellner's thesis is that creed-formulation arose in response to external influence and declined with the expulsion of the Jews from Spain.

MARGOLIS presents a scholarly critique, with immensely erudite footnotes, of the Maimonidean creed from the classic Reform Judaism perspective. The last part of the study is devoted to a proposed modern substitute for this creed. Margolis attaches an article on divine forgiveness as a correlate of divine justice to Maimonides' 11th principle. Discussing the fifth principle, he observes that a prayer recited on the Day of Atonement reads: "O Divine Mercy plead for us!"

JACOBS's interest in dogma is more theological than historical. He not only considers what Maimonides intended by his formulation in the Middle Ages; he also evaluates the relevance of that formulation for a modern-thinking Jew. In Jacobs's view, the first five principles present no offense at all to the modern mind, but the next four principles, especially the eighth (which asserts that the Torah has divine origins and was dictated by God to Moses), are not so clearly acceptable to modern Jews. Jacobs rejects the fundamentalist conception of revelation on the grounds that it is undermined and contradicted by the evidence of archaeology, anthropology, biblical criticism, and comparative religion. He contends that while "the Bible *contains* the Word of God, its own words are human." Throughout this learned and well-written book, Jacobs ably defends the position of Conservative Judaism.

SHAPIRO concludes that if rejection of one or more of Maimonides' principles equals heresy, then many of the greatest Jewish sages must be classed as heretics. The fourth principle affirms creation ex nihilo, but Abraham ibn Ezra and Gersonides taught creation from pre-existent matter. The eighth principle teaches that God revealed the entire Torah to Moses and that the Torah found today is identical to the Torah that Moses presented to the Children of Israel. But the Talmud notes that there were differences in Pentateuchal texts in Temple times, and there is also the view in the Talmud that Joshua wrote the last eight verses of the Torah. Ibn Ezra and other medieval exegetes suggested that certain verses in the Pentateuch are post-Mosaic. The tenth principle, that God knows the actions of individual men, was disputed by Gersonides and probably also by ibn Ezra.

REINES views Reform Judaism as a religious attitude without dogmas and without any clearly discernible outlines of belief or practice. Reform Judaism recognizes a sole regulative principle: every individual has an absolute right of religious self-authority and autonomy, provided he or she in turn respects the ultimate religious self-authority of every other individual. The quest for religious truth—the truth about the great themes of life and existence, God and the world, and good and evil—requires the radical personal freedom that is the hallmark of Reform Judaism. It is not clear what defines Reform Judaism, beyond freedom: Reines expressly affirms that Reform Judaism embraces different, contrary, incompatible, and mutually exclusive elements of belief. "Since no person or group of persons possesses absolute authority and the consequent right of dogmatization, Reform Jews, on principle, will subscribe to different views as their conscience, belief, and reason dictate." What distinguishes a Reform Jew from a Scientific Humanist or Ethical Culturist, for instance, is membership in a temple that, in the United States, is associated with one of Reform's three formal institutions: the Central Conference of American Rabbis (CCAR, the Reform rabbinical association); the Union of American Hebrew Congregations (UAHC, the Reform congregational association); or the Hebrew Union College-Jewish Institute of Religion (HUC-JIR, the Reform rabbinical seminary). Regardless of what an individual believes and practices or disbelieves and fails to practice, any member of a congregation affiliated with the UAHC, any member of the CCAR, or any member of the core HUC faculty is ipso facto a Reform Jew. Reines himself is a professor of philosophy at HUC-JIR in Cincinnati, Ohio, and an

authority on the philosophy of Maimonides, on whom he has written extensively.

JACOB HABERMAN

Dualism

Cohen Stuart, G.H., *The Struggle in Man between Good and Evil: An Inquiry into the Origin of the Rabbinic Concept of Yeser Hara'*, Kampen: Kok, 1984

Leaman, Oliver, *Evil and Suffering in Jewish Philosophy* (Cambridge Studies in Religious Traditions, 6), Cambridge and New York: Cambridge University Press, 1995

Levenson, Jon Douglas, *Creation and the Persistence of Evil: The Jewish Drama of Divine Omnipotence*, San Francisco: Harper and Row, 1988

Rosenberg, Shalom, *Good and Evil in Jewish Thought*, Tel Aviv: MOD, 1989

Segal, Alan F., *Two Powers in Heaven: Early Rabbinic Reports about Christianity and Gnosticism* (Studies in Judaism in Late Antiquity, vol. 25), Leiden: Brill, 1977

Dualism as a religious theory of two opposing entities or two conflicting elements has drawn considerable attention from scholars studying early Christianity, rabbinic Judaism, and gnosticism. Indeed, identification of the many manifestations of dualism in the writings of these sects may provide insight into the literature of a crucial turning point in world history. The following studies deal essentially with two types of dualism: theological dualism, the belief in two deities, one good and the other evil; and psychological dualism, the bad impulse versus the good impulse in the heart of a human being. Although it may seem paradoxical, admission of multiple forms of dualism enables the monotheistic believer to accommodate dualistic trends within the religion.

Psychological dualism, or the struggle between good and evil inclinations, is explored in COHEN STUART's detailed study, which deals with various sources dating from the Second Temple period, including the Dead Sea Scrolls. The book consists of two parts: part one discusses "the role of the evil inclination in the struggle in a human being between good and evil," and part two traces the development of the use of *yetzer* (inclination). Cohen Stuart asserts that the term *yetzer hara,* understood as the evil inclination, became popular only in the early Tannaitic period. In texts by Sirach and Philo, the evil inclination is identified as an impulse within a person and not as an outside force. However, in such writings, there is no mention of final judgment or what happens in the age to come. In Paul, IV Ezra, and rabbinic sources, evil inclination is similarly defined as an inner element, but these authors contend that a person has no control over it, and redemption is left in God's hands. In the Dead Sea Scrolls, Hermas, and the Testaments of the Twelve Patriarchs, the battle between good and evil is seen as a contest between two opposing spirits, while a person's decision to obey God appears to determine his or her fate in the age to come. Cohen Stuart concludes that the concept of the evil inclination grew out of the rabbis' struggles with dualism of body and soul (anthropological dualism) and dualism of God and Satan (cosmic dualism).

LEAMAN explores Jewish philosophical conceptions of good and evil, addressing these ideas systematically from the viewpoints of Philo, Saadya, Maimonides, Gersonides, Spinoza, Mendelssohn, Cohen, and Buber. His study begins and ends with discussions of the Hebrew Bible, particularly the Book of Job, and Leaman analyzes such issues as "how God relates to events in this world"; "what is Jewish philosophy"; and how that philosophy addresses evil and suffering. Leaman asserts that Jewish philosophers tend to consider diversified sources—biblical, legal, artistic, historical, ritual, and philosophical—when they discuss evil and suffering, and this practice enforces their arguments with religious and theological elements inherent in Jewish theodicy. For Leaman, one can solve the problem of the existence of evil in this world only by redefining and strengthening one's relationship with God, who is the source of any explanation for the way things are in the world. In his noteworthy chapter on the Holocaust, Leaman concludes that the phenomenon of evil and suffering during that period must be approached "on different lines from those acceptable in the past."

LEVENSON's book investigates the combination of theological dualism and psychological dualism and focuses primarily on the Hebrew Bible. The first few chapters, which deal with cosmogony and the persistence of evil and analyze their role in the Creation story of Genesis 1, are the most useful parts of the book. Parallels between the biblical account and the *Enuma elish* (the Babylonian Creation story) support Levenson's thesis that this particular creation theology is not "*creatio ex nihilo*," but the establishment of a "benevolent and life-sustaining order" by a God who can overcome all his opponents. Jewish apocalyptic literature and some rabbinic sources depict eschatological struggle on different levels between God and the evil power represented by Leviathan, Gog, Amalek, or the *yetzer hara*. Adherence to the divine commandments appears to enhance God's absolute victory over these evil forces. Levenson claims that this theology uses these assumptions to create a "semiotiose deity" who is still responsive to its cult and is able to rescue its believers. The author concludes that this type of theology has its roots in the 6th century B.C.E. and remains an important spiritual element in contemporary Judaism.

ROSENBERG explores the problem of good and evil in classical Jewish thought, although his notion of the classical ranges from the rabbinic period to the Holocaust. He presents a "history of ideas as a struggle" and distinguishes between "cosmic evil" and human ("anthropological") evil. Maimonides's views dominate Rosenberg's discussion, even in chapters that address other texts. Moreover, because the author interlaces both ancient and modern philosophical notions into his arguments, the reader can become somewhat bewildered.

SEGAL's book analyzes theological dualism, the belief in two opposing divine forces or deities. This belief was fiercely attacked by the rabbis, and out of that heresy Christianity and gnosticism eventually developed. According to Segal, both of these sects were affected by strong Hellenistic and Jewish apocalyptic influences that made it necessary for a mediating figure to come between believers and God. The rabbinic texts surveyed by Segal demonstrate that only among the rabbinic academies in Palestine of the Second Commonwealth was there a certain evolution in the identification and cataloguing of unwanted heresies. Segal proposes that gnosticism is a by-product of the "battle between the rabbis, the Christians and various other 'two powers' sectarians who inhabited the outskirts of Judaism." Initially, Segal surmised that the rabbinic reports about the "two powers in heaven" were "obscure." His conclusions confirm this supposition.

DINA RIPSMAN EYLON

E

Ecclesiastes

Barton, George A., *A Critical and Exegetical Commentary on the Book of Ecclesiastes* (International Critical Commentary, vol. 17), Edinburgh: Clark, and New York: Scribner, 1908

Crenshaw, James L., *Studies in Ancient Israelite Wisdom* (The Library of Biblical Studies), New York: Ktav, 1976

Crenshaw, James L., *Ecclesiastes: A Commentary* (Old Testament Library), Philadelphia: Westminster, 1987; London: SCM, 1988

Christianson, Eric, *Narrative Strategies in Ecclesiastes*, Sheffield, South Yorkshire: Sheffield Academic Press, 1998

Cohen, A. (translator), *Midrash Rabbah*, vol. 8, London: Soncino, 1939

Delitzsch, Franz, *Koheleth*, 1875; translated edition, Grand Rapids, Michigan: Eerdmans, 1989

Fox, Michael V., *Kohelet and His Contradictions* (Journal for the Study of the Old Testament Supplement Series, 71), Decatur, Georgia: Almond, 1989

Fox, Michael V., *Tearing Down and Building Up: A Rereading of Ecclesiastes*, Grand Rapids, Michigan: Eerdmans, 1999

Fox, Michael V., "Kohelet," in *Dictionary of Biblical Interpretation*, Nashville, Tennessee: Abingdon, 1999

Fredericks, Daniel C., *Coping with Transience: Ecclesiastes on Brevity in Life* (Biblical Seminar, 18), Sheffield, South Yorkshire: JSOT, 1993

Ginsburg, Christian David, *Coheleth: Commonly Called the Book of Ecclesiastes*, London: Longman, Green, Longman, and Roberts, 1861

Gordis, Robert, *Koheleth: The Man and His World*, New York: Jewish Theological Seminary of America, 1951; 3rd edition, New York: Schocken, 1968

Jarick, John, *Gregory Thaumaturgos' Paraphrase of Ecclesiastes*, Atlanta, Georgia: Scholars Press, 1990

Knobel, Peter (translator), *The Aramaic Bible*, vol. 15: *The Targum of Qohelet*, Collegeville, Minnesota: Glazier, 1991

Longman, Tremper, *The Book of Ecclesiastes* (New International Commentary on the Old Testament), Grand Rapids, Michigan: Eerdmans, 1998

Murphy, Roland E., *Ecclesiastes* (Word Bible Commentary, vol. 23A), Dallas, Texas: Word, 1992

Perry, T.A., *Dialogues with Kohelet: The Book of Ecclesiastes: Translation and Commentary*, University Park: Pennsylvania State University, 1993

Reichert, Victor and Abraham Cohen, "Ecclesiastes," in *The Five Megilloth*, edited by Abraham Cohen, London: Soncino, 1946, revised edition, 1984

Samuel ben Meir, *The Commentary of R. Samuel ben Meir, Rashbam, on Qoheleth*, translated by Sara Japhet and Robert Salters, Jerusalem: Magnes, and Leiden: Brill, 1985

Schoors, Antoon (editor), *Qohelet in the Context of Wisdom*, Louvain: Colloquium Biblicum, 1998

Seow, Choon-Leong, *Ecclesiastes: A New Translation with Introduction and Commentary* (Anchor Bible, vol. 18c), New York: Doubleday, 1997

Towner, W. Sibley, *New Interpreter's Bible*, vol. 5: *The Book of Ecclesiastes*, Nashville, Tennessee: Abingdon, 1997

Zuck, Roy B. (editor), *Reflecting with Solomon: Selected Studies on the Book of Ecclesiastes*, Grand Rapids, Michigan: Baker, 1994

The biblical book of Ecclesiastes (in Hebrew, Kohelet) is a puzzle full of contradictions, unevennesses, and unorthodox ideas, whose pessimism and skepticism seem contrary to the theology of other biblical books. As such, it has engendered much disagreement among scholars and a variety of approaches to dealing with these problems. Some commentators have sought to reconcile Kohelet with other biblical viewpoints, while others have highlighted—or exaggerated—his heterodoxy and regarded him as a deliberate polemicist. The latter approach is dominant in contemporary scholarship.

Commentaries are the starting point for a study of Kohelet. DELITZSCH's highly conservative commentary is still valuable, drawing on a profound (though outdated) knowledge of Hebrew and the classical commentaries. He is almost the only commentator to pay attention to the Masoretic accents. In spite of his conservatism, Delitzsch was able to lay down the arguments, which are still valid, for the book's late dating. Delitzsch reads Kohelet as "proof of the power of revealed religion which has grounded faith in God" but also of the inadequacy of Israelite religion. Several subsequent Christian commentators take this approach, explaining Kohelet's divergences from expected pieties and his apparent skepticism as proof that the faith of Israel was inadequate and awaiting completion in the gospel of the New Testament.

BARTON's commentary is valuable particularly as a representative of a once-influential approach that made Kohelet's thought internally consistent (but theologically more radical) by assigning numerous verses with apparently "orthodox" opinions to later writers. Kohelet's philosophy (after the excisions), though pessimistic and "hopeless" with its harsh and distant deity, is not immoral. He recommends healthy work and enjoyment of life. The teaching that remains is "to a Christian chilling and disappointing" but serves the purpose of clearing the ground for the new dispensation. The problem with removing some verses as doctrinal glosses is that there are so many apparent inconsistences in Kohelet that it is arbitrary to identify some statements as incompatible with the "real" Kohelet.

REICHERT and COHEN's commentary is the one commonly available in synagogues in the English-speaking world. It comments on the old Jewish Publication Society translation. It is succinct and simple, if rather pietistic, with a traditional Jewish orientation.

GORDIS's book was long the most popular commentary on Kohelet. It is clearly written and helpful to those with a modest command of Biblical Hebrew. But Gordis's analysis of Kohelet's thought is rather pedestrian and harmonistic.

CRENSHAW's (1988) commentary is valuable for its philosophical probing of Kohelet's thought, though his image of Kohelet seems too grim. Crenshaw describes the author as a radical, unrelenting polemicist struggling with the traditional beliefs of the wise.

MURPHY sees a more subtle interplay between Kohelet and the wisdom tradition, as Kohelet modifies and restricts some of its claims while affirming its basic validity. The commentary begins with valuable surveys of the state of research. According to Murphy, a variety of attitudes are heard in Kohelet. These are sometimes contradictory and sometimes in dialogue. Kohelet affirms the values of life, wealth, toil, and wisdom, but they prove inadequate when seen under the shadow of death. Kohelet is often in conflict with traditional wisdom teaching, especially with its claim to provide security, yet he affirms wisdom and remains within its traditions, employing its methods and literary genres. It is because Kohelet loves life and wisdom that he is grieved by death and by life's vanity.

FOX (1989; 1999a) takes as his starting point the contradictions that have long troubled commentators and argues that they are deliberate and should be interpreted rather than harmonized or eliminated. They show that Kohelet's central concern is the meaning of life—showing life's absurdity and pointing to ways meaning can be reconstructed. Even if the world as a whole lacks meaning, humans have the potential to experience passing moments of goodness and clarity. These are brief, limited, and uncertain, but they are enough to make life worth living. Fox's books include essays on Kohelet's vocabulary and thought as well as a commentary with a philological focus.

FREDERICKS's brief conservative commentary, aimed at a popular audience, paints the most optimistic picture of Kohelet. Kohelet confines his observations to the transient human realm and offers ways of coping with transience. Man's duty is to resign himself to God's will and accept circumstances beyond human control. Fredericks downplays Kohelet's pessimism and his bitterness about life's systemic injustices.

TOWNER's short and nontechnical commentary is aimed at a lay audience. Kohelet offers advice on living in a difficult, limited, and incomprehensible world. He teaches respect for an unknowable God, responsible use of limited human freedom, and the seizing of opportunities for happiness. Towner includes reflections on the present-day meaning of the book.

LONGMAN's approach is religiously conservative but innovative. He distinguishes Kohelet's message, which is skeptical and pessimistic, from the message of the author, which is that life is meaningless without God. The author gets the last word in the epilogues, 12:9–12 and 13–14. Kohelet's experience demonstrates the dangers of speculative skeptical wisdom. Longman's approach is based on a distinction drawn by Fox (1987) between Kohelet, a fictional persona, and the book's author. (Fox, however, thinks that the epilogue "buffers" rather than neutralizes the negativism of Kohelet's words.) Longman has studied Mesopotamian fictional autobiographies and locates Kohelet's words in that genre. It must be asked, however, whether the epilogues can cancel out a sense of skepticism and pessimism that dominates the book until the very end.

CHRISTIANSON applies a narrative-critical analysis to the book of Kohelet as a story and describes Kohelet as a persona, a literary character in his own right, rather than as the author. The formation and growth of the character of Kohelet is as important to the book as the ideas he expresses—which are not necessarily shared by the author himself, who speaks in the epilogue (12:9–14). Christianson's clearly written book examines a dimension of the book of Kohelet—its narrative character—that has been neglected until recently.

PERRY regards the epilogue as giving voice to the authoritative viewpoint. He distributes the entire book, down to parts of sentences, between two voices, a pious sage-narrator and a skeptical persona, Kohelet, the former transmitting and debating the wisdom of the latter. However, the way Perry assigns words to one voice or the other seems rather arbitrary.

SEOW's is the most valuable all-purpose commentary, offering a thorough examination of historical, textual, literary, and philological issues and extensive comparisons to other ancient Near Eastern literatures. Seow is almost alone in assigning Kohelet to the Persian, rather than the Hellenistic, period. Kohelet, according to Seow, is above all troubled by lack of human control of destiny. He teaches a spontaneous response to life, with an affirmative acceptance of both the possibilities and the limitations of being human.

Useful collections of essays on Kohelet, including some English translations of notable essays in German, are CRENSHAW (1976), ZUCK, and SCHOORS. For the history of Kohelet exegesis, see FOX (1999b). For a detailed summary of exegesis from ancient times to 1860, GINSBURG's survey is still unsurpassed.

Midrash Rabbah, available in the Soncino translation by COHEN, is a major compilation of early midrashic (homiletic) commentary that omits little of importance. The Targum (Aramaic translation) of Kohelet is more of a midrashic commentary than a translation; it is available in an English translation by KNOBEL. Little of medieval Jewish exegesis is available in translation, except for the innovative commentary of Rabbi SAMUEL BEN MEIR (Rashbam), which excels in attention to literary context and poetic features. Patristic exegesis is represented in JARICK's translation and discussion of Gregory Thaumaturgus's "Metaphrasis," while Murphy's commentary draws on ancient and medieval Christian interpretation.

MICHAEL V. FOX

Ecology

Bernstein, Ellen (editor), *Ecology and the Jewish Spirit: Where Nature and the Sacred Meet,* Woodstock, Vermont: Jewish Lights, 1998

Bernstein, Ellen and Dan Fink, *Let the Earth Teach You Torah: A Guide to Teaching Jewish Ecological Wisdom,* Wyncote, Pennsylvania: Shomrei Adamah, 1992

Cohen, Jeremy, *"Be Fertile and Increase, Fill the Earth and Master It": The Ancient and Medieval Career of a Biblical Text,* Ithaca, New York: Cornell University Press, 1989

Feliks, Yehuda, *Nature and Man in the Bible: Chapters in Biblical Ecology,* London and New York: Soncino, 1981

Hareuveni, Nogah and Helen Frenkley, *Ecology in the Bible,* Kiryat Ono: Neot Kedumim, 1974

Isaacs, Ronald H., *The Jewish Sourcebook on the Environment and Ecology,* Northvale, New Jersey: Aronson, 1998

Rabinowitz, Louis I., *Torah and Flora,* New York: Sanhedrin, 1977

Rose, Aubrey (editor), *Judaism and Ecology* (World Religions and Ecology), New York and London: Cassell, 1992

Troster, Lawrence and Miriam Wyman (editors), *Conservative Judaism* (special issue on Judaism and environment), 44(1), Fall 1991

Ecology encompasses both natural history (description of plants and animals) and scientific study of biological interactions with geologic, hydrologic, and atmospheric systems. Ecological issues such as changes in global environmental health and the imbalance of population growth and resource utilization have become the stuff of academic and popular debate and of international negotiations in the course of the late 20th century. Ecology is thus a subset of broader environmental thought, which encompasses perceptions of and approaches to issues such as management of natural and human systems. In this context the relationship of religion and environment has attracted considerable discussion. Some writers view western religion as the root cause of planetary despoliation, while others look to religion for a renewed environmental ethic. This essay addresses the environment and Judaism in the wider context.

Many books identifying plants or animals of the Bible are little more than catalogs and lack a particularly Jewish context. Three of the listed books illustrate ecology as natural history, in that they show how an awareness of flora and fauna helps elucidate the meaning of scriptural passages. HAREUVENI created Neot Kedumim, an environmental park near Tel Aviv, "to show the entire ecological framework of biblical and talmudic flora and fauna." This small book provides examples of nature-based similes, analogies, and metaphors, mostly from Prophets and Psalms. Hareuveni contends that an understanding of ecology helps decipher the symbolic meaning of these literary devices, and he argues further that Jewish practices, such as Shabbat and Sukkot observances, have preserved the symbolism of the ecological relationship of the people to the land.

RABINOWITZ's collection of weekly newspaper columns is arranged according to the cycle of torah or haftarah readings. Each short article (two to three pages) plays on some nature reference or imagery contained in the weekly reading. These little essays, representing "the fruit of personal observation," bespeak a love of the land of Israel and of the Scriptures. This book is not meant to be a systematic treatment of ecological matters.

FELIKS provides the most exhaustive treatment of the three. The more than 80 chapters (typically two to six pages long) proceed in an orderly fashion through Scripture. Feliks has two purposes: first, he applies philological and historical scholarship to the nature of the country at the time of Scripture's composition, in order to identify the species of flora and fauna mentioned in the texts. Second, he intends to recover both the symbol and the symbolism of the textual references, which are too often lost in translation. The result is ecology in the service of scriptural interpretation.

The other books on this list treat implications for environmental ethics, illustrating how Jewish texts teach respect for the environment and contribute to wise stewardship. Citation of proof texts from Scripture is a common device. Yosef Orr and Yossi Spanier (in Rose) summarize much of this genre: "sayings of the Jewish sages may serve as a constant source of encouragement and support" for conservation efforts. Bradley Shavit Artson (in Troster and Wyman) notes that most works "strain Jewish writings through the standards of the Green perspective to argue the relevance of Jewish tradition." BERNSTEIN and FINK's "guidebook for teaching Jewish perspectives on the human relationship with nature" is a good example of Artson's characterization. It comes from a grassroots organization in the United States aimed at developing programs to train Jewish leaders and lay people about environmental ideas. As such, it is full of proof texts, questions for discussion, and suggested activities on a variety of topics including the human place in creation, blessings and praise, waste reduction (based on the *bal tashhit* tradition), and social justice (based on the *tikkun olam* tradition). ISAACS provides an eclectic selection on ecology, nature, agricultural mitsvot, sabbath and holidays, folk remedies, songs, names for children, and so on. It is a sourcebook, not a reasoned consideration of environmental issues.

Contributions to the three edited volumes range from explorations of personal Jewish and environmental experiences to more scholarly considerations of closely defined themes. The volume by ROSE is one of several in a series on world religions and ecology. The 16 chapters are arranged in three sections: resources in Jewish teaching and tradition, Israel, and action. Noteworthy is Norman Solomon's exposition of Jewish attitudes to creation, a paradigm for the land and the people, specific examples of application to environmental laws, sample ethical problems relating to conservation, and a model Jewish statement on nature.

TROSTER and WYMAN assemble eight contributions from "Jews who see Judaism through their involvement in environmentalism and from Jews who see environmentalism through their involvement in Judaism." Noteworthy contributions include Troster's attempt to harmonize Jewish interpretation of "in the image of God" with Lovelock's Gaia hypothesis, and Artson's start at building a Jewish ecology from "an internal Jewish assessment of how our tradition and our God would have us relate to the world." Both of the books just mentioned include brief suggestions for individual and institutional environmental action.

The 37 contributions in BERNSTEIN are arranged into sections on sacred place, sacred time, and sacred community. Although uneven in scholarly depth and underpinnings, this is the foremost collection in English of the variety of thinking on environmental issues and Judaism. Many of the chapters, such as those by Neal Joseph Loevinger, Bradley Shavit Artson, Eliezer Diamond, and Lawrence Troster, illustrate well the interpretation of the enviornmental ethic from within Jewish tradition.

Standing apart on this list, as it is an extended academic exercise with a single focus, is COHEN's response to the frequent charge that the western environmental crisis has its origins in the grant of dominion to humans in Genesis 1:28. His close examination of the history of both Jewish and Christian interpretation and understanding of this verse indicates that it was rarely, if ever, read as a warrant for unrestrained exploitation of the world. That interpretation seems to be a product of the mid- to late 20th-century search for a source of current dysfunctional environmental behavior.

PAUL A. KAY

Economic Ideologies

Baron, Salo W., "The Economic Views of Maimonides," in *Essays on Maimonides, an Octocentennial Volume*, edited by Salo W. Baron, New York: Columbia University Press, 1941

Ginzberg, Eli, "Studies in the Economics of the Bible," *Jewish Quarterly Review*, 1932

Levine, Aaron, *Free Enterprise and Jewish Law, Aspects of Jewish Business Ethics*, New York: Ktav and Yeshiva University Press, 1980

Levine, Aaron, *Economics and Jewish Law, Halakhic Perspectives*, New York: Ktav and Yeshiva University Press, 1987

Levine, Aaron, *Economic Public Policy and Jewish Law*, Hoboken, New Jersey: Ktav, and New York: Yeshiva University Press, 1993

Neusner, Jacob, *Economics of the Mishnah*, Chicago: University of Chicago Press, 1990

Ohrenstein, Roman and Barry Gordon, *Economic Analysis in Talmudic Literature: Rabbinic Thought in the Light of Modern Economics*, Leiden and New York: Brill, 1992

Tamari, Meir, *With All Your Possessions: Jewish Ethics and Economic Life*, New York: Free Press, and London: Collier Macmillan, 1987

Tamari, Meir, *The Challenge of Wealth: A Jewish Perspective on Earning and Spending Money*, Northvale, New Jersey: Aronson, 1995

There are two basic issues in determining the ideology of an economic system. First, to what extent does the government allow private property? In a capitalist system, a large percentage of the resources of the country will be private property, while in a communist system there is no private property. Second, to what extent does the government intervene in the economic decisions of the people? In a market economy, there is relatively little intervention by the government, while in a planned or command economy the government is extensively involved with the economy. When discussing the question of economic ideologies in reference to religion, identical questions can be asked but with the religion and/or the religious authorities replacing the role of the government. In the classic texts of Judaism, there is no systematic discussion of these questions. However, there are discussions about issues and laws relevant to economics, and this allows inferences to be drawn about the underlying economic ideology of Judaism. The texts that are the basis for these inferences start with the Bible and continue through the modern era.

GINZBERG examines three sets of property laws recorded in the Bible: the laws of slavery, the sabbatical year, and the jubilee year. He argues that as "the notion of the Bible is that all beings owe their existence to God, there are laws for the manumission of slaves." Similarly, the laws of the sabbatical and jubilee years are based on the premise that God is the sole possessor of the land. Ginzberg also speculates about the historical reality of these laws, but many of his arguments rely on the assumptions of biblical criticism. The article ends with a critique of the view that the Bible supports communism.

NEUSNER compares the economic implications of laws recorded in the Mishnah (c.220 C.E.) with the economic theories of antiquity, especially those of Aristotle. Neusner gives a detailed explanation of several chapters in the Mishnah (principally chapters four and five in Tractate Baba Metsia) and concludes that the economic system envisioned by the Mishnah was a combination of a market economy and a planned economy (or what he terms a distributive economy). He claims that the assumption of the Mishnah is that while land is privately owned, it must be shared with God by donating the fruits of the land to God.

OHRENSTEIN and GORDON briefly review economic lessons to be learned from the Pentateuch and the book of Proverbs and then concentrate on economic ideas to be found in passages in the Talmud (c.500 C.E.). One of the fundamental ideas of a market economy is Adam Smith's doctrine of the "invisible hand," the idea that when people act in their own self-interest, they benefit society. Ohrenstein and Gordon contend that the Talmud anticipates this idea, which shows the Talmud's support for a market economy. In addition, they argue that many present-day economic ideas, such as game theory, opportunity cost, and human capital, can be found in the Talmud. They end with a brief look at the impact of

Judaism on the development of the European economy and capitalism.

BARON presents a lengthy essay on economic thinking that can be inferred from the writings of Maimonides. Maimonides was arguably the preeminent rabbinic jurist since the time of the Talmud and codified the laws of the Talmud. He addressed many issues that had economic ramifications. Baron notes that Maimonides, as opposed to Christian writers of his time, took for granted the institution of private property. "Maimonides, of course believed that God is the ultimate master of all things. But once acquired by an individual, such property is entirely his own and, subject to stated limitations, may be freely disposed of by him," writes Baron. These limitations are discussed in reference to the goods market, the money market, and the labor market. Baron argues that Maimonides sought a "proper balance between regimentation and freedom." Baron maintains that an important aspect of Maimonides' economic thought is that contrary to mystical approaches to religion, he stressed the importance of working and not living off charity.

LEVINE (1980, 1987, 1993), in a series of books that collects his articles, compares the approaches of a market economy and Jewish law to various economic issues, such as monopoly, competition, externalities, pricing, and taxation. The focus in each situation is whether and how Jewish law intervenes in the market. On each economic issue, Levine briefly presents the relevant economic theory, quotes the pertinent discussion in the Talmud, and then examines how these passages have been interpreted from the Middle Ages to the present. Levine infers that Jewish law rejects the idea of a completely free market economy, and he argues that Judaism attempts to promote social justice even if this is sometimes at the expense of economic efficiency and economic freedom.

TAMARI (1987, 1995) argues in both his books that there exists a separate and distinct "Jewish economic man," as Judaism places a religious and moral framework around the workings of the market economy. Not withstanding this framework, Tamari notes that while all wealth originates from God, "there is nothing intrinsically evil or sinful about pursing the accumulation of material assets and wealth." Tamari briefly quotes the argument that the biblical laws of the jubilee and sabbatical years support socialism. However, he dismisses this claim since "despite Judaism's insistence on economic justice, charity and mutual assistance, it also recognizes the legitimacy of private property, the profit motive, and the market mechanism." Tamari's books are similar in content, but the 1987 work concentrates more on economic issues, while the 1995 work places greater stress on ethical issues. Tamari covers many of the issues discussed by Levine, and both use similar sources for their inferences. The authors do differ in style, however; Levine generally provides a more detailed review of all the viewpoints, while Tamari includes more historical information.

ANDREW SCHEIN

Education

Adar, Zvi, *Ha-Hinukh ha-Yehudi be-Yisra'el uve-Artsot ha-Berit,* 1969; translated by Barry Chazan as *Jewish*

Education in Israel and in the United States, Jerusalem: Melton Center for Jewish Education in the Diaspora, 1977

Adelman, Howard, *The Jewish People: Teaching Jewish History, Social Studies, Israel, and the Holocaust in Religious Schools,* New York: Ktav, 1983

Adelman, Howard, *The Jewish Language: Teaching Hebrew in Religious Schools: Method, Motivation, and Materials,* New York: Ktav, 1984

Gartner, Lloyd P. (compiler), *Jewish Education in the United States: A Documentary History,* New York: Teachers College Press, 1969

Sarna, Jonathan D., *A Great Awakening: The Transformation That Shaped Twentieth Century American Judaism and Its Implications for Today,* New York: Council for Initiatives in Jewish Education, 1995

Schoem, David, *Ethnic Survival in America: An Ethnography of a Jewish Afternoon School,* Atlanta, Georgia: Scholars Press, 1989

Wolfson, Ron, *Shall You Teach Them Diligently?* (University Papers), Los Angeles: University of Judaism, 1983

Although Jews are extolled as People of the Book and are lauded for a strong commitment to religious education, the history of Jewish learning reveals that such characterizations remain more unfulfilled platitudes than regular aspects of reality, albeit with notable exceptions. Simhah Assaf and Nathan Morris amply illustrate these trends in their major multivolume Hebrew histories of Jewish education. Despite the vast amount of institutionally produced studies, curriculum guides, and model lessons, mixed with various attempts at theorizing and philosophizing about Jewish education and learning, the studies discussed in this essay have been chosen because they provide valuable insight into the eternal problems of Jewish education from historical, sociological, or programmatic points of view.

ADAR offers insight into the system of Jewish education in the United States and its shortcomings. Although reflecting the scene of the late 1960s and the mid-1970s, this book, like the impressions of North America presented by Alexis de Tocqueville or even earlier by J. Hector St. John de Crèvecoeur, stands as a classic statement about circumstances both before and after the time it was written—both because of its penetrating analysis of deep structures and because so little changes in Jewish education. Although Adar studies each denomination separately, many of his most important comments apply equally to all aspects of Jewish education. Particularly apt are his observations that most of the stated goals of Jewish education, both in Hebrew and English subjects, are unobtainable: the Hebrew because of a lack of time, interest, and teachers; and the English because advanced subjects are directed at children who are too young to appreciate them. Adar notes that students are not taught texts but are merely taught about texts, usually with apologetic meanings imposed on them. The lack of accumulation of skills, interest, and correlation with parental values places the school in an unreal realm that is not part of either U.S. or Jewish culture. A stinging critic of Hebrew supplementary schools for their failure to offer even a hint of historico-critical study, let alone to confront problematic aspects of Judaism, Adar was prophetic in predicting the success of the day school in U.S. Jewish life. This book, a product of the Samuel Mendel Melton Center for Jewish Education in the Diaspora at the Hebrew University of Jerusalem, represents many of the studies produced by this institution.

ADELMAN (1983, 1984) attempts to synthesize his experiences in the field of Jewish education as a teacher and principal with his graduate training in Jewish studies. In these pamphlets he offers a bluffer's guide intended to enable the novice to approach the Jewish classroom armed with ideas for understanding the dynamics of this particular setting as well as the subject matter being presented. He also provides an overview of the ingredients necessary for a professional Jewish educator to plan and implement a curriculum. These guides help teachers find a focus for presenting material and guiding students. In particular, they urge teachers to select aspects of the material that truly interest them and not to try to cover it all equally. Academics and professional teachers work this way with much success. Teachers are urged therefore to find key questions about Jewish history, life, and society in the various materials available rather than trying to work in sequence from a textbook. The pamphlets talk frankly about the limitations of the Jewish educational environment and the ways that an individual teacher can take control of the class using successful strategies of discipline, organization, and motivation. The pamphlet about teaching Hebrew is particularly specific about the necessity of offering honest motivations for the study of Hebrew, limited goals, and clear guidance for reaching them. One of the themes that emerge in Adelman's pamphlets is the need for both teachers and students to feel good about themselves and what they are doing. Whether they are studying Jewish history or Hebrew, therefore, they must feel that there is a manageable and interesting task before them in which they can succeed. In particular, teachers are urged not to badger students with corrections nor to demand perfection. In short, this approach comes from the realization that much of what does happen in Jewish education is affective rather than cognitive, and unfortunately it often can be negative rather than positive. By highlighting the ways in which teachers can create small communities with their classes, these pamphlets aim at building positive relations within Jewish education.

GARTNER provides a good foundation for a clear historical understanding of Jewish education in the United States. Although the book is a study of the development of Jewish education in the United States and may seem provincial for readers from other diaspora communities, it may, nevertheless, be highly instructive of the dynamics involved everywhere. These primary sources acquaint those interested in Jewish education with a real sense of the difficulties inherent in the enterprise, illuminating in particular the rocky beginnings, the difficulties in supporting and staffing institutions, and the financial, social, and cultural influences that have always played a part in the development of Jewish education. Some of the most salient features of the history of Jewish education include the fact that few Jews actually received a Jewish education; Jewish communities were unwilling to finance schooling; and few students made serious strides in their studies. Gartner regularly notes the role of the physical learning environment of the schools, the tensions between generations and between immigrant groups, the difficulties of learning Hebrew, the difficulty of finding teachers and paying them, the varying degrees of integration and exclusion of girls from Jewish education, and problems with discipline. One of the most interesting insights provided into the intellectual and religious underpinnings of U.S. Jewish education is the description of Rebecca Gratz, the founder of the first Jewish Sunday school. Gratz used a Christian catechism in her classes, but before class she had members of her family paste pieces of paper over answers unsuitable for Jewish children, an allurement to student interest and a token of the lack of specific Jewish cultural and religious content in the institution. One fascinating aspect of the various school reports concerns the amount of time spent studying maps of Palestine even prior to the rise of the Zionist movement.

SARNA, a scholar of American Jewish history, not only provides a clear reconsideration of Jewish history but also offers a paradigm shift in the study of Jewish education. Sarna demonstrates that toward the end of the 19th century (prior to the mass migration of Eastern European Jews), American Jews initiated a series of religious, cultural, and organizational changes. This kind of research is important for today's Jewish educators because of the picture it presents of the ability of Jews to reconstruct regularly the basic structures of educational and communal life itself. Sarna warns about the call for panaceas in Jewish schools.

SCHOEM, in a fascinating ethnographic study of one afternoon religious school, presents astute observations and interviews with all the major actors: the parents, teachers, children, rabbi, and principal. Although Schoem's work is well researched and contains an extensive bibliography, it appears that he was unaware of Adar's study, and thus he confirms many of Adar's findings independently, making his observations even more valuable. Schoem characterizes Jewish education as an inflexible and unreflective involvement in building an identity based on pride or guilt but not content. He sees this endeavor as geared to the formation of "anti-anti-semites" or "non-non-Jews." In other words, definitions of Jewish identity are based upon what one is not, often with the admixture of feelings of contempt and superiority. The values he identifies in the school—often a blurring of Jewish and secular values—include material prosperity, getting into college, and the family. Some of the key features of the culture of religious school include simple propinquity, the ritual of affiliation in an institution where everyone is Jewish, hating Hebrew school as a Jewish tradition, and the school as a place for participants to posture. The rhetoric of "a Jewish way of life" includes teachers who do not have any other connection with the Torah, Bible, or prayer book, who teach prayer without feeling comfortable at prayer themselves, and who continue the myth of learning Hebrew, practicing ethics, and joining a community. In short, Schoem documents with precision the diminution of standards of behavior and study at one religious school while at the same time acknowledging that the institution offers rich potential for building a community.

WOLFSON, in this pamphlet on family education, describes the current trend of the synagogue as the place parents go when they want to step out and do something Jewish. In other words, the synagogue and not the home constitutes the focal point for Jewish activities. Wolfson sharpens this thesis by noting that there are tensions between the home and the synagogue. Many parents, for example, do not want their children bringing religious values home from religious school. He contrasts the public Jewishness of the synagogue, the school, Jewish organizations, and Israel with the private Jewishness of home, identity, self-esteem, and cultural involvement. Wolfson concludes that religious schools provide only for public Jewishness, while the home provides for private Jewishness, thus bringing issues back to the parents. Wolfson offers quotations from three influential U.S. Jewish thinkers to support his point—A.J. Heschel, Robert Gordis, and Samuel Schaffler, each of whom articulates in his own way the current tendency of modern Judaism to be localized in the synagogue and the danger that this presents not only to Judaism in the home but to Judaism itself. As a solution, Wolfson suggests moving synagogue and school activities to the home, involving parents more, and developing vehicles for parental edification and leadership.

HOWARD TZVI ADELMAN

Egypt and Sudan

Cohen, Mark R., *Jewish Self-Government in Medieval Egypt: The Origins of the Office of Head of the Jews, ca. 1065–1126* (Princeton Studies on the Near East), Princeton, New Jersey, and Guildford, Surrey: Princeton University Press, 1980

El-Kodsi, Mourad, *The Karaite Jews of Egypt, 1882–1986*, Lyons, New York: Wilprint, 1987

Kasher, Aryeh, *The Jews in Hellenistic and Roman Egypt: The Struggle for Equal Rights*, Tübingen: Mohr, 1985

Krämer, Gudrun, *The Jews in Modern Egypt, 1914–1952*, Seattle: University of Washington Press, and London: Tauris, 1989

Landau, Jacob M., *Jews in Nineteenth-Century Egypt* (New York University Studies in Near Eastern Civilization, no. 2), New York: New York University Press, 1969

Laskier, Michael M., *The Jews of Egypt, 1920–1970: In the Midst of Zionism, Anti-Semitism, and the Middle East Conflict*, New York: New York University Press, 1992

Malka, Eli S., *Jacob's Children in the Land of the Mahdi: Jews of the Sudan*, Syracuse, New York: Syracuse University Press, 1997

Mann, Jacob, *The Jews in Egypt and in Palestine under the Fatimid Caliphs*, London: Oxford University Press, 1920; New York: Ktav, 1970

Modrzejewski, Joseph Mélèze, *Les Juifs d'Egypte, de Ramsès II à Hadrien*, 1991; translated by Robert Cornman as *The Jews of Egypt: From Rameses II to Emperor Hadrian*, Philadelphia: Jewish Publication Society, and Edinburgh: Clark, 1995

Shamir, Shimon (editor), *The Jews of Egypt: A Mediterranean Society in Modern Times*, Boulder, Colorado: Westview, 1987

One of the most ancient of Jewish communities, the Jews of Egypt were a very heterogeneous group and included a sizable Karaite community. The famed Cairo Genizah is a major source for research on regional medieval society. Being a venerable and major community, much scholarly attention has been paid to it, with publications mainly in Hebrew, English, and French.

Based primarily on Cairo Genizah documents, COHEN examines the origins of the office of Head of the Jews (*Ra'is al-Yahud; Nagid*), concentrating on the evolution of political power and authority rather than on the history of the title *Nagid*. Following an examination of Jewish autonomy under pre-Islamic regimes, Cohen focuses on the administration of several officeholders and provides much data and analysis on social and political issues relating to Jewish life in medieval Egypt and the life of minorities under Islam.

KASHER's study of the struggle for equal rights of Jews in Hellenistic and Roman Egypt does not regard it as a "war of emancipation," aspiring to citizenship in the polis. He believes that the equality that the Alexandrian Jews strove to obtain is to be conceived as an equality between two separate political bodies: the Jewish community and the Greek polis. The Jews fought for the right of self-organization within the polis on an equal footing with the Greeks, with this right being dependent on the central government rather than the polis. The study covers the period up to the Jewish rebellion of 115–117 C.E.

The Karaite community of Egypt, which was one of the world's major Karaite communities and an important component of Egyptian Jewry, is the subject of EL-KODSI's book, focusing on the years 1882 to 1986. As an active member of the community he had firsthand knowledge of its internal developments and access to Karaite archival sources and periodicals. Against the background of the origin of the Karaites and their history, El-Kodsi examines the community in Egypt: its structure and organization; relations with other Karaite communities and mainstream Judaism; its educational system, social services, liturgy, customs, traditions, and cultural and social activities; the impact of Zionism; and the exodus from Egypt after 1948.

KRÄMER provides a socioeconomic, political, and cultural history of the Jews of Egypt during the monarchy period, from 1914 until the Free Officers revolution of 1952. Based on Hebrew, Arabic, and foreign sources, the study is structured around a few major topics: communal structure and composition, socioeconomic and political change, Jewish reactions to political change, and the beginning of the end—the mass emigration that began in the late 1940s. Developments within the community are examined in relation to those in Egypt and the Middle East, and data is closely integrated into the analysis.

LANDAU includes a survey and a selection of documents on the Jews of Egypt from the fall of the Mamluk regime under Muhammad Ali in the first half of the 19th century until the end of World War I in 1918. Based on archival sources and publications in Hebrew, Arabic, and European languages, Landau's book examines the demography of the Jews and their occupations, their relations with gentiles, the spread of Jewish communities in Egypt, communal organization and institutions, education, intellectual and religious life, and early Zionism. Many sources are published in their original language.

LASKIER examines the Jewish community of Egypt during the period from 1920 to 1970 against the background of political developments in Egypt and in the Middle East. Based on extensive study of Egyptian publications and Israeli and international Jewish organizations' archival sources and publications as well as on interviews, Laskier provides a detailed description of the community. The implications of the Middle East conflict on the community are major themes, with discussion of Zionist underground activity, especially after 1948, in cooperation with Israeli institutions. Laskier also describes the secret efforts of international organizations to ameliorate the condition of the Jews of Egypt after 1948.

The modern history of the Jews of Sudan is the subject of MALKA's book. An indigenous businessman and the son of Sudan's chief rabbi, Malka left Sudan in 1964 and was one of the last members of the modern community formed following the 1898 defeat of the Mahdi. Using his own and his family's recollections as well as archival sources, Malka provides a vivid portrait of that community, its organization, and social, economic, and cultural life. Relations with the communities of Ethiopia, Aden, and Egypt as well as those of Europe and the United States are examined as are the conditions following Sudan's independence, which resulted in the departure of the Jews.

Based on Genizah documents and published sources, MANN examines Jewish life under Fatimid rule in Egypt and in Palestine from 969 to 1204. The first part of the study provides a chronological examination of the Jews in the regions under Fatimid rule, their communal organization, economic activity, social life, and major figures, including Maimonides, while numerous annotated documents are published in the second part. Considered a classic study of the period, Mann offers a carefully annotated and comprehensive examination.

MODRZEJEWSKI's study covers Jewish life in Egypt from biblical times to the annihilation of Egyptian Jewry following the 115–117 C.E. rebellion, focusing on the Hellenistic and Roman periods and emphasizing social change and institutional history. This meticulous study is based on literary sources and Greek papyri found in Egypt that provide much data on religion, administration, and everyday life of the Jews and the majority population. He examines a "Jewish Golden Age" in which Jewish life was enriched through the challenge posed by the advanced culture of the surrounding gentile environment.

The collection edited by SHAMIR covers the period from the Ottoman conquest in the early 16th century to the 1950s but focuses on the 20th century, discussing politics, economics, culture, and internal diversity. Several authors bring to light unknown state and private archival sources and provide some documents that are cited in their original languages. The role of the community and of individuals in the economic and cultural life of Egypt is discussed, highlighting Jews who were prominent in Egyptian Arabic theater, journalism, and literature. Other authors examine the evolution of the Egyptian nationality laws and their application to the Jews, the political participation of Jews between World War I and 1952, Rabbanite-Karaite relations, and images of Egyptian Jewry.

RACHEL SIMON

See also Genizah, Cairo

Elephantine

Kraeling, Emil G. (editor), *The Brooklyn Museum Aramaic Papyri: New Documents of the Fifth Century B.C. from the Jewish Colony at Elephantine* (Publications of the Department of Egyptian Art, Brooklyn Museum), New Haven, Connecticut: Yale University Press, 1953

Muffs, Yochanan, *Studies in the Aramaic Legal Papyri from Elephantine* (Studia et documenta ad jura Orientis antiqui pertinentia, vol. 8), Leiden: Brill, 1969; New York: Ktav, 1973

Porten, Bezalel, *Archives from Elephantine: The Life of an Ancient Jewish Military Colony,* Berkeley: University of California Press, 1968

Silverman, Michael H., *Religious Values in the Jewish Proper Names at Elephantine* (Alter Orient und Altes Testament, 217), Kevelaer: Butzon and Bercker, 1985

Yaron, Reuven, *Introduction to the Law of the Aramaic Papyri,* Oxford: Clarendon, 1962

The island of Elephantine is located in the Upper Nile at the First Cataract, across from the modern Egyptian city of Aswan (ancient Syene). Because of its strategic location near the Egyptian border with Nubia, the island was garrisoned in ancient times. During the period when Persian dominion stretched into Egypt, from the late sixth to the late fifth century B.C.E., Jewish mercenary troops and their families were stationed on the island. Aramaic papyri and ostraca, found in archaeological remains of the soldiers' homes, are among the few documents of Jewish origin to survive from this period, and they offer important insights into this chapter of Jewish history.

PORTEN presents the most comprehensive and in-depth treatment of Elephantine and its Jewish residents. The book is divided into three parts, each of which focuses on specific aspects of Elephantine life: politics and economics, religious worship, and communal relations. First, Porten surveys what is known about the immigration of Jews and Arameans to Egypt, exploring different theories as to when and why these population movements occurred. The second chapter treats the organization and administration of the Elephantine garrison. Detailed analyses of weights, measures, prices, food, and clothing give the reader a concrete idea of daily life in the community. Porten presents different hypotheses on the origin and nature of worship at Elephantine, theorizing that the Elephantine temple was created by certain alienated Jerusalemite priests who moved to Egypt in the seventh century B.C.E. He also carefully scrutinizes available evidence to argue that a limited number of Jewish residents participated in the cults of their Aramaic and Egyptian neighbors, a finding that might be expected in a remote area where Jews and non-Jews lived side by side. The following chapters of the book explore specific families and their interrelations as revealed in letters and legal documents. Thus, this accessible book not only illustrates the nuances of the legal system, it also portrays the individuals behind the texts. A final chapter considers the destruction and restoration of the temple of Elephantine. Porten elaborates on the tensions between the Jewish and pagan communities on the island as well as the relations of the Elephantine and Jerusalem Jews. The book is replete with footnotes, while a series of appendixes investigate specific topics that are primarily of interest to specialists.

KRAELING offers an introduction to the Elephantine documents that is shorter than Porten's treatment but is important nonetheless. Kraeling, like Porten, outlines different possible explanations for the origin of the Jewish colony and temple. His analysis, however, is more cautious than Porten's, and he is hesitant to isolate one explanation as more plausible than the others. Kraeling's introduction may be of particular interest to the general reader because it contains a history of the discovery and publication of Aramaic documents from Egypt that puts in perspective the textual finds from Elephantine. The introduction also contains a summary of the archaeological excavations on the island, something that is absent from Porten's work. The synopsis of excavations explains what is known of the architecture and layout of the city, while also demonstrating the random and reckless manner of the archaeologists, whose primary objective was the discovery of texts rather than the thorough preservation of the sites.

YARON directs his book to the reader, lay or professional, who wishes to learn more about specific legal practices at Elephantine but is unfamiliar with Aramaic. Yaron analyzes Elephantine law as a discrete entity, avoiding arguments about influences and origins. The benefit of this approach is that his focus stays on the Elephantine texts and does not get bogged down in the analysis of other legal systems. He attempts to reconstruct some of the laws that are only implicit in the texts themselves, suggesting, for instance, that eight witnesses were required for complicated legal procedures, while simpler procedures required only four witnesses. The study is broken down into chapters that discuss the form of the legal documents, court procedure, slavery, adoption, marriage, succession, and property. A final chapter briefly treats similarities between Elephantine, Egyptian, Babylonian, and later Jewish legal practices.

A much more detailed and specific treatment of law at Elephantine is provided in MUFFS, which analyzes the Aramaic texts in light of the legal tradition of ancient Mesopotamia. (The connection between the two traditions is a methodological premise of the study.) Muffs narrows his focus to a particular phrase found in ten individual Elephantine papyri that concern property rights. He methodically interprets each passage in which this expression appears and then compares this phrase to its Demotic and Akkadian counterparts. The goal of this study is, first, to demonstrate that this particular locution, dismissed by Yaron as superfluous, actually serves to indicate compensation. The wider objective is to establish the significance of the corresponding expressions in Demotic and Akkadian, thereby elucidating the relation between these legal traditions and Elephantine law.

SILVERMAN supplies a detailed analysis of Elephantine personal names in a book that surveys the chronological distribution and the languages of all the names found in the Elephantine texts. In addition, the author analyzes the morphology and meaning of all the West-Semitic names, asserting that the number of Akkadian names decreased over time, while the number of Egyptian and Hebrew-Aramaic names

increased. He suggests that pagan theophoric elements supplanted traditional Yahwistic elements in Jewish personal names as reverence felt for the appellations of God grew more intense. He posits that this trend prefigures transcendental conceptions of divinity peculiar to Egyptian Hellenistic Judaism.

ERIC REYMOND

Elijah ben Solomon of Vilna 1720–1797

Lithuanian talmudist

Brill, Allan, "The Mystical Path of the Vilna Gaon," *Jewish Thought and Philosophy*, 3, 1993

Cohen, Israel, *Vilna*, Philadelphia: Jewish Publication Society, 1943

Etkes, Immanuel, *R. Yisra'el Salanter ve-r'eshitah shel tenu'at ha-musar*, 1982; translated by Jonathan Chipman as *Rabbi Israel Salanter and the Mussar Movement*, Philadelphia: Jewish Publication Society, 1993

Fishman, David, *Russia's First Modern Jews*, New York: New York University Press, 1995

Ginzberg, Louis, *Students, Scholars, and Saints*, Philadelphia: Jewish Publication Society, 1928

Harris, Jay, *How Do We Know This?: Midrash and the Fragmentation of Modern Judaism*, Albany: State University of New York Press, 1995

Kaddari, Menahem, "Elijah ben Solomon Zalman," in *Encyclopaedia Judaica*, vol. 6, Jerusalem: Keter, 1971

Lamm, Norman, *Torah Lishmah: Torah for Torah's Sake in the Works of Rabbi Hayyim of Volozhin and His Contemporaries*, Hoboken, New Jersey: Ktav, 1989

Nadler, Allan, *The Faith of the Mithnagdim: Rabbinic Responses to Hasidic Rapture*, Baltimore, Maryland: Johns Hopkins University Press, 1997

Rosenblum, Yonason, *The Vilna Goan*, Brooklyn, New York: Mesorah, 1994

Schechter, Solomon, *Studies in Judaism*, Philadelphia: Jewish Publication Society, and London: Black, 1896

Schochet, Elijah J., *The Hasidic Movement and the Gaon of Vilna*, Northvale, New Jersey: Aronson, 1994

Rabbi Elijah ben Solomon Zalman of Vilna, popularly known as the Vilna Gaon (literally, "the genius of Vilna") or by the acronym Gra (Gaon Rabbi Elijah), was the outstanding rabbinic figure of the 18th century and the heroic model of non-hasidic Eastern European Orthodoxy in the following century. He was born in or near Vilna in 1720 and died there in 1797. His extreme precociousness (he is said to have delivered a learned talmudic discourse in the Great Synagogue of Vilna at age 6) led him to dispense with teachers at a very early age. This, in turn, allowed him to develop his own scholarly methods, which valued wide erudition and philological precision over the ingenious casuistry *(pilpul)* common among Ashkenazi talmudists at the time.

The Gaon led a reclusive and saintly life, supported by a modest stipend from the Jewish community of Vilna. He held no official position, but was nonetheless regarded as the leading rabbinic authority in Vilna, and indeed throughout much of the Ashkenazi world during the second half of the 18th century. His only real entry into the public sphere was in his unyielding opposition to the nascent hasidic movement, which he took to be dangerously anti-intellectual and antinomian. In providing the spiritual leadership for this opposition, the Gaon helped to found the Mitnagged (literally, "opposition") Orthodoxy of the 19th and 20th centuries. The nature and reasons for his opposition to Hasidism are discussed in each of the above listed entries. The most accessible and complete account of this phase of the Gaon's career is SCHOCHET, which includes many of the controversy's documents in elegant English translation.

There have been several biographies of the Gaon, beginning with the Hebrew hagiographies of the 19th century. SCHECHTER, GINZBERG, and the succinct essay by Menahem KADDARI in the *Encyclopaedia Judaica* are all distinguished attempts to provide critical biographical portraits. Ginzberg, himself a great philological master of the rabbinic tradition, makes some suggestions about the nature of the Gaon's scholarship, as does Schechter. COHEN, although dated, is useful for placing the Gaon's life within the communal setting of late 18th century Vilna. Each of these works necessarily draws on the hagiographical traditions. For a compendium of such folk traditions rendered in English and presented in the same pious spirit in which they originally arose, see ROSENBLUM. His portrait of the Gaon is more traditional and credulous than those of Schechter and Ginzberg.

Of course, the importance of the Gaon, even his saintly status, rests largely on his scholarly achievements, a fact that is crucial for understanding the Mitnagged subculture, for which he became a kind of intellectual icon. All of his works were published posthumously from marginal notations in the books of his personal library and from the notes of his sons and students. Among the most important of these are *Hagahot haGra*, textual glosses to the Babylonian Talmud; *Biur haGra*, a commentary on the *Shulhan Arukh*; *Aderet Eliyahu*, a commentary on selected passages throughout the Hebrew Bible; a homiletical commentary on the biblical Book of Proverbs; and a commentary on the early kabbalistic work *Sefer Yetsirah*. These works, which consist largely of terse commentary and philological emendations based upon the Gaon's encyclopedic erudition, do not lend themselves easily to translation or summary. For a brief but useful discussion of his work as a biblical exegete and his understanding of the nature of rabbinic interpretation, see HARRIS, which also traces the influence of the Gaon's approach.

Finally, there is the influence of the Gaon's thought and his image on Jewish ideologies of the 19th century. NADLER and LAMM both discuss the ideological roots of his opposition to Hasidism through careful interpretation of his students' work. Lamm focuses on the thought of the Gaon's greatest student, R. Hayyim of Volozhin, who founded the first modern yeshivah and gave theoretical articulation to Lithuanian Mitnaggedism in his religious writings. Similarly, Nadler is a thorough monograph on the religious thought of the Gaon's circle of followers, particularly that of the preacher Pinhas of

Plotsk, and the polemics of this line of thought with early Hasidism. Such studies are especially important since the Gaon's own work, while voluminous, was, as noted, restricted almost entirely to terse exegesis of classic texts. Hence, the more developed theoretical statements, sermons, and theological works of his students gain historical importance. Care should be taken, however, to distinguish the Gaon's thought from that of even his closest followers. BRILL is a useful short guide to the distinctive features of the Gaon's kabbalistic thought, coexistent with his antipathy to Hasidism.

Other 19th-century movements were also influenced by the Gaon, or at least they attempted to claim his influence. ETKES, the dean of Israeli scholars of the Gaon and Lithuanian Mitnaggedism, discusses the Gaon as a precursor to R. Israel Salanter, the founder of the Musar movement, a 19th-century movement of pietist asceticism. His portrait might be usefully compared with Nadler's. Less plausibly, early figures of the 19th-century Eastern European Jewish Enlightenment movement (Haskalah) also claimed the Gaon as an intellectual predecessor. They did so based upon his endorsement of a reformed Hebrew curriculum, the utility of certain forms of secular knowledge, and philological precision in talmudic studies. Historians of the 19th and early 20th century who were themselves champions of Haskalah, or their intellectual heirs, have taken such claims rather too seriously. Nadler convincingly rebuts this portrait. FISHMAN is the first study to focus on the most important source of this tradition, R. Barukh of Shklov and his circle. In the introduction to his translation of Euclid's *Elements* into Hebrew, Barukh recounted a conversation in which the Gaon purportedly commissioned the translation and discussed the importance of certain forms of secular knowledge.

Much of the scholarly literature on the Gaon, not to speak of the primary sources, is available only in Hebrew. The bibliographies of the *Encyclopaedia Judaica*, Etkes, Fishman, Lamm, Nadler, and Schochet will be of particular value in guiding the interested reader through this literature.

ABRAHAM SOCHER

Emancipation

Baron, Salo Wittmayer, *A Social and Religious History of the Jews*, 3 vols., New York: Columbia University Press, 1937, 2nd edition, 1962

Baron, Salo Wittmayer, "The Emancipation Movement and American Jewry," in his *Steeled by Adversity: Essays and Addresses on American Jewish Life*, Philadelphia: Jewish Publication Society, 1971

Birnbaum, Pierre and Ira Katznelson (editors), *Paths of Emancipation: Jews, States, and Citizenship*, Princeton, New Jersey: Princeton University Press, 1995

Duker, A.G. and M. Ben-Horin (compilers), *Emancipation and Counter Emancipation: Selected Essays from Jewish Social Studies*, New York: Ktav, 1974

Eisenbach, Artur, *The Emancipation of the Jews in Poland, 1780–1870* (Jewish Society and Culture), Oxford and Cambridge, Massachusetts: Blackwell, 1991

Endelman, Todd M., *The Jews of Georgian England, 1714–1830: Tradition and Change in a Liberal Society*, Philadelphia: Jewish Publication Society, 1979

Finestein, Israel, "Anglo-Jewish Opinion during the Struggle for Emancipation," in his *Jewish Society in Victorian England: Collected Essays*, London and Portland, Oregon: Vallentine Mitchell, 1993

Hertzberg, Arthur, *The French Enlightenment and the Jews*, New York: Columbia University Press, 1968

Hyman, Paula E., *The Emancipation of the Jews of Alsace: Acculturation and Tradition in the Nineteenth Century*, New Haven, Connecticut, and London: Yale University Press, 1991

Katz, Jacob, *Out of the Ghetto: The Social Background of Jewish Emancipation, 1770–1870*, Cambridge, Massachusetts: Harvard University Press, 1973

Katz, Jacob, *From Prejudice to Destruction: Anti-Semitism, 1700–1933*, Cambridge, Massachusetts: Harvard University Press, 1980

Marcus, Jacob R., *United States Jewry, 1776–1985*, 4 vols., Detroit, Michigan: Wayne State University Press, 1989–1993

Mosse, Werner E., Arnold Paucker, and Reinhard Rürup (editors), *Revolution and Evolution: 1848 in German-Jewish History*, Tübingen: Mohr, 1981

Rürup, Reinhard, "Jewish Emancipation and Bourgeois Society," *Leo Baeck Institute Year Book*, 14, 1969

Rürup, Reinhard, "Emancipation and Crisis: The 'Jewish Question' in Germany 1850–1890," *Leo Baeck Institute Year Book*, 20, 1975

Rürup, Reinhard, "German Liberalism and the Emancipation of the Jews," *Leo Baeck Institute Year Book*, 20, 1975

Rürup, Reinhard, "The Tortuous and Thorny Path to Legal Emancipation: 'Jew Laws' and Emancipatory Legislation in Germany from the Late Eighteenth Century," *Leo Baeck Institute Year Book*, 31, 1986

Salbstein, M.C.N., *The Emancipation of the Jews in Britain: The Question of the Admission of the Jews to Parliament, 1828–1860* (Littman Library of Jewish Civilization), Rutherford, New Jersey: Fairleigh Dickinson University Press, 1982

Schwarzfuchs, Simon, *Napoleon, the Jews, and the Sanhedrin* (Littman Library of Jewish Civilization), London and Boston: Routledge and Kegan Paul, 1979

Emancipation refers to the abolition of the distinctive, usually demeaning, legal and social status ascribed to Jews and the creation of laws that viewed Jews as citizens with rights equal to those accorded to other citizens. The social structure and political order in each country fixed the timing, character, and extent of Jewish Emancipation in the various nations. The change began in Great Britain and its colonies in the mid-18th century and slowly moved eastward across Europe and the Turkish empire, continuing after World War I and right up to the Polish constitution of 1931. By the 1870s, however, there was a full-scale antisemitic reaction in many nations against Jewish Emancipation. Over the past three centuries, scholars of Jewish history have repeatedly examined the struggle for Emancipation and its long-term results. Nineteenth-century Jews and most historians of that era regarded the age of Emancipation as a period of freedom and equality. Since about 1880, both the defects of Emancipation and the antagonism it evoked (culminating in the Holocaust) have brought about a much more critical view. The newer scholarship reacted against the utopian view of Emancipation by emphasizing that legal emancipation was not social emancipation and by arguing that extensive Jewish assimilation did not lead their host societies to regard Jews as true equals. The literature on Jewish Emancipation appears in many languages and is the subject of a host of scholarly articles.

One recent book of value is BIRNBAUM and KATZNELSON, which stress the plurality of emancipations. In addition to articles on the well-known cases of Germany (W.E. Mosse), France (P. Birnbaum), Britain (G. Alderman), and Italy (D. Segre), essays about cases less familiar to the English-language reader appear—The Netherlands (H. Daalder), Russia (M. Stanislawski), and Turkey (A. Rodrigue). Katznelson's article emphasizes the limits of Emancipation for Jews in the United States.

Selected articles from the journal *Jewish Social Studies* are gathered in DUKER and BEN-HORIN, which includes a large bibliography by Duker and an important essay titled "Impact of the Revolution of 1848 on Jewish Emancipation" by the renowned historian Salo W. Baron.

BARON (1937) and BARON (1971) both situate the history of the Emancipation of Jews in the United States in a comparative perspective. Baron posits that Jewish Emancipation did not occur as the result of Jewish efforts nor was it the product of ideologies concerning the Jews' place in society. Rather, he contends that Emancipation was the necessary corollary of revolutionary changes in France and elsewhere that replaced restrictive social classes and their legally defined privileges with equality. He recognizes the defects of Emancipation, but he stresses that Jews were not deluded when they sought equal rights. He also emphasizes that Emancipation pushed Jews to enter the modern world and adjust their religious and communal life to the demands of modernity. Another analysis of the Emancipation of Jews in the United States appears in MARCUS, which presents the U.S. case in full detail in a generally optimistic work that reflects the relatively positive U.S. experience.

Two works by a distinguished Israeli historian, KATZ (1973) and KATZ (1980), present a by-now-traditional view of Jewish Emancipation centered on events in Germany and the significance of ideological thought. Katz emphasizes that Emancipation was only partial, given half-heartedly, and always under attack. This view that Jewish Emancipation was fickle and ultimately false helped to inform Zionist ideology.

The best recent studies of Jewish Emancipation in Germany are the articles by RÜRUP (1969, 1975a, 1975b, 1986). In these essays and other studies not translated from his native German, Rürup connects the history of Jewish Emancipation to the evolution and decline of bourgeois liberalism in Germany.

The ramifications of German Jewish Emancipation are fully examined in the anthology edited by MOSSE, PAUCKER, and RÜRUP. After a broad survey of the German revolution by

Rürup, the collection includes studies of Emancipation as it affected population change (L. Schofer), rural Jews (M. Richarz), and the modern rabbinate (I. Schorsch). The anthology also contains a discussion by Mosse of the limits of Emancipation.

Emancipation in Britain necessitated mainly political emancipation. The fine work by ENDELMAN deals in an original fashion with the British social background, while SALBSTEIN treats in detail the parliamentary maneuvers and party politics that surrounded the Emancipation of British Jews. FINESTEIN raises a question that has yet to be properly studied: what did Jews think about Emancipation? Finestein's evidence suggests that the opinions of Anglo-Jewry were by no means unanimously favorable.

HERTZBERG maintains the controversial hypothesis that the leaders of the French Enlightenment pioneered secular antisemitism, but his account of the French Revolution and the Jews is brief and straightforward. SCHWARZFUCHS investigates the history of European Jews in the age of Napoleon. The author argues that the emperor was hostile to the Jews of France, although his relations with Jews elsewhere in Europe were less contentious. HYMAN's study of 19th-century French Jews in Alsace (the region with the highest Jewish population) shows that traditional ways persisted in private life and religion long after the Revolution.

EISENBACH's thorough study of the Emancipation of Polish Jews concerns the policies of the three powers, Austria, Prussia, and especially Russia, that governed over this population. The latter autocracy granted substantial rights to Jews, but only in its Polish lands.

LLOYD P. GARTNER

Emden-Eybeschütz Controversy

Cohen, Mortimer J., *Jacob Emden: A Man of Controversy*, Philadelphia: Dropsie College for Hebrew and Cognate Learning, 1937

Graetz, Heinrich, *History of the Jews*, vol. 5, Philadelphia: Jewish Publication Society, 1895; London: Jewish Chronicle, 1901

Schacter, Jacob Joseph, "Rabbi Jacob Emden: Life and Major Works," Ph.D. diss., Harvard University, 1988

The bitter 18th-century theological dispute between the German rabbis Jacob Emden and Jonathan Eybeschütz is, despite its profound impact on German Jewry, a sparsely researched topic that merits further attention from English-speaking scholars. Especially to be regretted is the fact that Emden's Hebrew-language autobiography, *Megillat Sefer,* has never been translated into English.

Emden was a prominent rabbinic scholar who was known for his traditionalist and elitist views and who viewed himself as a defender of the Jewish faith. Eybeschütz, a talmudist of comparable standing and an aficionado of the Kabbalah, was widely suspected of being a secret follower of the 17th-century messianic pretender Shabbatai Tsevi. A highly charismatic figure, Shabbatai set into motion a movement that would survive

his conversion to Islam and even his death, continuing to create a stir in surprising quarters well into the 18th century.

The outlines of the dispute are clearly recorded in GRAETZ. Graetz takes the position that Eybeschütz was indeed a Sabbatian. He acknowledges that Eybeschütz was a brilliant scholar but criticizes him for being seduced by "the crooked path of sophistry" and being "deeply committed to the Sabbatian heresy." In 1728 Eybeschütz was appointed preacher in Prague. His contacts with the Jesuits displeased many Jews. He was elected to the rabbinate of Metz, but the widow of the incumbent spoke out against it, because she believed him to be a heretic. Eybeschütz later exerted himself to become rabbi of the "three communities" (Altona, Hamburg, and Wandsbeck, the first of which was at that time under the sovereignty of Denmark). Emden was also a candidate for the rabbinate of the three communities and was aggrieved when Eybeschütz was chosen.

When Eybeschütz assumed the rabbinate, many Jewish women had been dying in childbirth. Eybeschütz provided expectant mothers with incantations for exorcising evil spirits. This left Eybeschütz open to the charge of heresy. Eybeschütz was accused of devising amulets with encrypted messages calling for Shabbatai Tsevi to intercede; Graetz believes that these accusations were well-founded.

Emden was very zealous in calling for the excommunication of Eybeschütz, and Emden tried to antagonize Eybeschütz's friends and supporters. Eybeschütz presented himself to his disciples as unjustly accused and railed against Emden's audacity. Eybeschütz had broad support within the Jewish community while Emden, the accuser, stood alone.

At first, public opinion was in Eybeschütz's favor. Eybeschütz denied charges of Sabbatianism and excommunicated his enemies. Emden was banished from Altona, but he refused to leave and became still more zealous in pressing his public accusations against Eybeschütz. A royal procurator declared that amulets devised by Eybeschütz contained Sabbatian writings. Riots broke out and Emden fled to Amsterdam.

Eybeschütz feared that Emden's presence in Amsterdam might prove dangerous for him, and he issued an encyclical that consisted of an exhortation to bear witness to his orthodoxy. He maintained that his amulets conformed to a deeply orthodox mysticism. A triumvirate of leading rabbis, including the revered Joshua Falk, published a decision declaring that the amulets were Sabbatian and that their author should be "cut off from communion with Israel." The case ended up in the Christian courts under the jurisdiction of King Frederick of Denmark, which decided in favor of Emden and against Eybeschütz. Eybeschütz was dismissed from his rabbinate and Emden was allowed to return to Altona. Eybeschütz continued to press his case with his followers and a heated controversy continued for a number of years. Finally, Eybeschütz's rabbinate was restored in a special election in 1753.

While Graetz believes that Eybeschütz was in fact a Sabbatian, COHEN argues that Eybeschütz was innocent of Sabbatianism. He points out that rabbis were expected to distribute amulets in the superstitious environment of 18th-century Germany. Those amulets that were demonstrably Sabbatian, argues Cohen, did not originate with Eybeschütz but were deliberately crafted to incriminate him. The mystical amulets that were of Eybeschütz's devising were subjected to a strained interpretation and falsely labeled as Sabbatian. Eybeschütz sought to prove the validity of his amulets and demonstrate that his enemies deliberately misconstrued them in order to force Shabbatai Tsevi's name into them. Furthermore, many of Eybeschütz's amulets may have been altered after he had written them.

Emden's written denunciations of Eybeschütz are, according to Cohen, full of invective and unsubstantiated charges; they represent scandal-mongering at its worst. Emden printed several pamphlets against Eybeschütz on his own printing press and distributed them throughout Germany. His vituperative attacks against Eybeschütz continued until Eybeschütz's death in 1764. After Eybeschütz's death, Emden attacked Frankism, and even the Zohar, with the same vigor with which he had attacked Sabbatianism. According to Cohen: "His contentious spirit made him prominent in his generation."

SCHACTER's massively researched study argues that even if the charges of Sabbatianism were true (and they may have been), Eybeschütz was not deserving of Emden's 13-year attack. He also concludes that Emden acted against his own interests in pursuing the matter to the extent to which he did. He finds it testimony to Eybeschütz's strength that he was able to have his rabbinate restored. Emden's contentiousness, on the other hand, is shown to have increased his marginalization within the Jewish community. Furthermore, the Emden-Eybeschütz controversy set a precedent for the persecution of other supposed heretics. In 1782, Napthali Hartwig Herz Wessely, a student of Eybeschütz who had become a leading proponent of Haskalah, was excommunicated for his book *Words of Peace and Truth,* although nothing in the book could have reasonably been considered heretical. Schacter argues that the great legacy of the Emden-Eybeschütz controversy was the installation of a profound fear of new ideas within the Jewish community.

PETER R. ERSPAMER

Encyclopedias *see* Reference Works

Epigraphy *see* Hebrew Alphabet

Eschatology

Bright, John, *Covenant and Promise: The Prophetic Understanding of the Future in Pre-exilic Israel,* Philadelphia: Westminster, 1976; London: SCM, 1977
Freedman, David N. (editor), *Anchor Bible Dictionary,* New York and London: Doubleday, 1992
Gowan, Donald E., *Eschatology in the Old Testament,* Philadelphia: Fortress, and Edinburgh: Clark, 1986
Hanson, Paul D., *The Dawn of Apocalyptic: The Historical and Sociological Roots of Jewish Apocalyptic Eschatology,* Philadelphia: Fortress, 1975, revised edition, 1979
Mowinckel, Sigmund Olaf Plytt, *Han som Kommer: Messiasforventningen i det Gamle Testament og pa Jesu tid,* Copenhagen: Gad, 1951; translated by G.W. Anderson as *He That Cometh,* New York: Abingdon, 1954; Oxford: Blackwell, 1956

The term *eschatology* usually is understood by biblical scholars to designate a literary genre or way of thinking about the world that refers not to a posited "end of time," but to any time in the future in which the course of history will be changed radically by the intervention of the deity. There is a scarcity of good literature dealing specifically with this topic.

FREEDMAN's dictionary is by far the best and the most up-to-date initial resource. D.L. Petersen's article, "Eschatology (OT)," provides a good, concise introduction to the sources out of which eschatological thinking arose. An outline of the historical development of eschatology through the preexilic and postexilic periods and some idea of its social setting is also provided. A more detailed article by G.W.E. Nickelsburg, "Eschatology (Early Jewish)," considers the eschatologies of the eighth-century prophets as well as the books of Jeremiah, Ezekiel, Isaiah 40–55, Isaiah 56–66, Isaiah 24–27, Haggai, and Zechariah. Perhaps more significant, however, is the section devoted to apocalyptic eschatology, which examines the early apocalyptic writings, including those from Qumran. Nickelsburg also explores the major themes associated with these texts (messianism, resurrection, eternal life, and the Kingdom of God) and the proposed historical/social setting for apocalypticism. A final section deals with the eschatologies of writings associated with the destruction of Jerusalem in 70 C.E. Together, these two articles provide a well-written, cogent, and accessible starting point for further study of the subject.

MOWINCKEL looks at the theme of kingship/messiahship in the Hebrew Bible and early Jewish writings with particular reference to how this was reflected in hope for the future (i.e., positive eschatology). Separate chapters survey the relevant material in the Hebrew Bible and explore the ideal of kingship in ancient Israel and how this ideal was expressed in expectations for the future. This then provides a basis for an assessment of the significance of the messianic idea in later Judaism. The development of the concept of the Son of Man and the application of Second Isaiah's Servant Songs in this context by Jewish and Christian groups are also discussed. While Mowinckel's work takes account only of one strand of eschatology in the Hebrew Bible and interprets the term in a more restricted sense than modern commentators would (by applying it to the end of days rather than to a radical future event), there is much that remains useful in this book. However, Mowinckel takes little account of the Qumran materials. Hence, some caution must be exercised in the use of this book, particularly as a resource for reconstructing messianic beliefs of the turn of the era.

As a starting point for discussion of the eschatology of the Hebrew Bible, GOWAN's slim volume focuses on traditions associated with Zion. Three main themes are discussed in detail: the transformation of human society, the transformation of the human person, and the transformation of nature. Each of these headings includes disparate ideas: for example, the chapter "Peace in Zion—The Transformation of Human Society" is divided into subsections on restoration to the promised land, the righteous king, and the transformation in the relationship between Israel and the nations (either by Israel's defeat of the nations on Mount Zion or by means of the pilgrimage of the nations to Zion). More controversial concepts also are introduced. Gowan asserts, for example, the idea of an "eschatological forgiveness" in the work of some prophets (e.g., Second Isaiah): a divine act of grace causing a fundamental change in the human recipient prior to God's transformation of society or nature. The third and final section of the book, on the transformation of nature, is considerably shorter. Generally, this is a useful book, rendered accessible to the general reader by its thematic approach. Unfortunately, the lack of chronological structure of the eschatology discussed results in little feeling of a historical development of these themes. Nor are the more negative eschatologies of preexilic texts given much consideration.

BRIGHT to some extent fills this gap by looking at the election of Mount Zion and David and the importance of these themes for the future expectations in Israel. He then goes on to examine the future hope as it appears in the work of the eighth-century prophets, and he traces this tendency toward positive eschatology, particularly in terms of the theme of covenant and promise, down to the exile. Like other authors, Bright tends to interpret the term eschatology in a positive sense, although not exclusively so: in this context he mentions the eighth-century prophets who spoke of Israel standing under God's judgment but who were able also to look forward to a time in the distant future when the projected punishment would be reversed (e.g., Amos, Isaiah). Probably most scholars would disagree with such dualistic readings of the preexilic prophets and argue that the positive eschatology in these books is representative of later (exilic) additions. Nevertheless, this remains a valuable work in that it approaches the subject with some degree of balance.

HANSON is more concerned with later developments and focuses on the literature of the earliest postexilic period. Essentially, he argues that the return of the exiles from Babylon at the end of the sixth century saw a seizure of religious power by a hierocratic "priestly" party (whose ideals are reflected in biblical texts such as Haggai, Zechariah 1–8, and Ezekiel 40–48). Over time, those who were disenfranchised by this seizure of power (particularly levitical and "visionary" prophetic groups) developed an increasingly eschatological outlook, calling on God to "rend the heavens and come down." Out of this conflict arose works such as Isaiah 56–66, Zechariah 9–14, Joel, and Malachi, and the apocalyptic worldview was formed. While it is true that Hanson's thesis as to the origins of apocalypticism has been strongly criticized, his book remains a useful discussion of the complex eschatologies of this period.

DOMINIC RUDMAN

Essenes *see* Asceticism; Dead Sea Scrolls

Esther, Book of

Bickerman, Elias J., *Four Strange Books of the Bible: Jonah, Daniel, Koheleth, Esther*, New York: Schocken, 1967

Brenner, Athalya (editor), *A Feminist Companion to Esther, Judith and Susanna*, Sheffield, South Yorkshire: Sheffield Academic Press, 1995

Day, Linda, *Three Faces of a Queen: Characterization in the Books of Esther* (Journal for the Study of the Old Testament Supplement Series, 186), Sheffield, South Yorkshire: Sheffield Academic Press, 1995

Fox, Michael V., *Character and Ideology in the Book of Esther* (Studies on Personalities of the Old Testament), Columbia: University of South Carolina Press, 1991

Larkin, Katrina J.A., *Ruth and Esther* (Old Testament Guides), Sheffield, South Yorkshire: Sheffield Academic Press, 1996

Levenson, Jon D., *Esther: A Commentary* (Old Testament Library), Louisville, Kentucky: Westminster John Knox, and London: SCM, 1997

Walfish, Barry Dov, *Esther in Medieval Garb: Jewish Interpretation of the Book of Esther in the Middle Ages* (SUNY Series in Judaica), Albany: State University of New York Press, 1993

The Book (or Scroll) of Esther, which is chanted in Jewish communities during the holiday of Purim, tells the story of a Jewish diaspora community under threat of persecution and of two heroes, Esther and Mordecai, who save their people from the evil vizier Haman. To some extent, this book has been a source of discomfort for Jews and Christians both because it never mentions God and because it seems to glorify violent revenge against gentiles. Nevertheless, this short biblical book has been the subject of numerous studies in recent years that point to new directions of interpretation.

BICKERMAN's book has become a classic among learned readers. He argues that there is a problem with the Book of Esther, namely, that there are two heroes: Esther and Mordecai. Bickerman posits that there were originally two independent stories, the tale of a queen who saves her people and the story of a new courtier who overthrows the wicked vizier. He writes:

> Having heard two parallel tales about a Jewish courtier and a Jewish queen who struggled with and overthrew the evil minister of their sovereign, the author of the Book of Esther thought that the stories represented two complementary versions of the same events and accordingly combined them.

Bickerman further asserts that the book was composed in order to explain the holiday of Purim, which already had a life of its own. Many readers disagree with his conclusions, but Bickerman's argument is filled with insights and interesting questions that are worthy of careful consideration.

FOX's book is intended both for the specialist and nonspecialist. Fox provides a fresh translation, literary commentary, and character analysis, in addition to chapters on dating, historicity, and genres. His methodology is based on "modernist" literary-critical approaches and character study. Fox's primary aim consists "in imparting the author's ideas about realities outside the book." For Fox, this means an exploration of the ideologies—national, religious, and ethical—of the book. Among his questions are: "How can Jews best survive and thrive in the diaspora?"; "What is the nature of the gentile world?"; and "Where do we see God?" Fox's analysis of Esther is based on the Hebrew (Masoretic) text; however, readers interested in the Greek versions should consult the final chapter, in which Fox summarizes his findings on this topic from his book, *The Redaction of the Books of Esther* (1991).

WALFISH addresses the role of the Book of Esther in the Jewish Middle Ages. The parallels between aspects of the Persian setting of Esther and the medieval conditions of Jewish life, such as persecutions in exile and the centrality of court life, made the Book of Esther particularly attractive to Jewish medieval exegetes. Walfish divides his study into two parts. In "The Work of the Exegete" he explores technical issues regarding sources, philology, and literary and theological issues. The second part, "The World of the Exegete," addresses issues more accessible to the nonspecialist, namely, what the Esther commentaries reveal about Jewish medieval life with respect to Jewish-gentile relations, antisemitism, the royal court, and the institution of the monarchy. This book is of greatest value for readers interested in the history of interpretation and/or Jewish medieval life.

BRENNER's volume is part of a series intended to amass both previously published and new critical articles on the books of the Bible from feminist-critical perspectives. Although this volume also contains studies on Judith and Susanna, it devotes the greater part of its pages to articles on the Book of Esther. The essays employ a range of methodologies and approaches, including folklore studies, literary criticism and intertextuality, visual arts, and midrash. The collection is to be commended for its diversity of approaches and its sophisticated level of discourse.

LARKIN impressively synthesizes a broad range of critical issues regarding the Book of Esther into a concise and readable introduction. She introduces the new student of Esther to the Greek versions of the book and highlights their most significant features. She provides brief introductions to early rabbinic debates regarding the authoritative status of Esther; discussions regarding the historical background of the story; the text's relationship to the Jewish holiday of Purim; and various hypotheses regarding the literary genre of Esther. Additionally, Larkin includes an initial bibliography for the reader who wishes to explore any of these issues in more depth.

DAY's work is less a study of the Book of Esther than it is a reevaluation of the characterization of Esther the queen. Opinions regarding Esther are quite varied: she has been characterized as flat, weak, and overly obedient; wise; tricky; a positive role model for women; and an oppressive example for women. Day reassesses these evaluations by considering not only the Hebrew (Masoretic) text but additionally the two extant Greek versions. Her analysis is based on the theory proposed in Seymour Chatman's *Story and Discourse: Narrative Structure in Fiction and Film* (Ithaca, New York: Cornell University Press, 1978), which conceives of character as a "paradigm of traits," that is, as a combination of traits that remain relatively stable throughout the unfolding of events. Day concludes that all three versions of Esther reflect "part of a general trend during the Hellenistic period to highlight female characters in literature." This book is also recommended for its extensive bibliography.

LEVENSON's commentary marks an important contribution to Esther studies. A commentary on the Book of Esther must include, essentially, two commentaries, because the Greek version (used in Catholic and Orthodox Bibles) and the Hebrew version (used in Jewish and Protestant Bibles) are radically different from one another. Levenson begins his commentary with a useful bibliography and an introduction outlining the basic features and problems of Esther. The translation integrates the Hebrew and Greek versions so as to yield a maximum of text, albeit with distinct sources clearly indicated. The commentary itself focuses on literary issues, with more attention given to rabbinic interpretation than is commonly found in critical Esther commentaries. Levenson's commentary also has the advantage of elegant prose that is clear enough for the nonspecialist.

S. TAMAR KAMIONKOWSKI

Ethical and Devotional Literature

Baskin, Judith R., "Jewish Women in the Middle Ages," in her *Jewish Women in Historical Perspective,* 2nd edition, Detroit, Michigan: Wayne State University Press, 1998

Dan, Joseph, *Jewish Mysticism and Jewish Ethics,* Seattle: University of Washington Press, 1986; 2nd edition, Northvale, New Jersey: Aronson, 1996

Dan, Joseph, *The Ancient Jewish Mysticism,* Tel-Aviv: MOD, 1993

Dishon, Judith, "Women in Medieval Hebrew Literature," in *Women of the Word: Jewish Women and Jewish Writing,* edited by Judith R. Baskin, Detroit, Michigan: Wayne State University Press, 1994

The word *devotional* does not turn up in a search of the CD-ROM edition of the *Encyclopaedia Judaica*. This can be taken as an index of the rarity, or nonexistence, of the category in Judaism. A modest presence of what is recognized in other religions as devotional literature occurs in Judaism in prayerbooks as optional readings, often in the vernacular rather than Hebrew and supplied as aids to contemplation. The process of anthologizing material for contemplation within the larger anthology that is the prayerbook remains largely unstudied.

Jewish ethical literature develops from the Wisdom Literature of the Hebrew Bible, organized around Wisdom personified, who becomes identified with Torah in both Hellenistic and rabbinic thought. This early form of ethical literature is expressed in collections of rabbinic sayings or in works probing the mysteries of God and of human responses. Similar works are part of the transition to a recognized literature that provides specifications for the human road to perfection. These ethical works, also dependent on Greek models and their adaptations in Islamic philosophy, entered Judaism in the medieval period.

DAN (1993) is a solid account of various kinds of Jewish mysticism in the talmudic and early medieval periods, before the flowering of Kabbalah. The history examines a number of Jewish spiritualities as recorded in literature, including Jewish Gnosticism, the Work of the Chariot/Hekhalot, Messianism, and the constructive mysticism of a book known as *Sefer Yetsirah*. Where possible, Dan develops what is known of the accompanying devotional practices, although what was involved is not always known. Instead, accounts of the conventional ways of reporting the results of those practices are available. Dan provides a readable and authoritative background in each of the methods and the literatures that developed out of them. Dan is a distinguished scholar of Jewish mysticism, but this book is a simple semipopular narrative account with minimal annotation.

DAN (1986) is a marvelous intellectual treat of a discussion that integrates Jewish mysticism with Jewish ethical literature. It manages to be profoundly interesting without demanding that the reader be an expert in the field. The author proceeds inductively by exploring the numerous ethical works that began in the medieval period and gradually took on a concern with the divine presence. Ethics, in the literature Dan surveys, becomes a way toward God so that ethical literature becomes the devotional literature of Judaism.

There is an interesting difference in the development of a secular literature in the 12th and 13th centuries. According to DISHON, "an entirely new literary genre, the debate about female virtues and vices, emerges at this time and continues well into the 17th century." While these works may be secular, they portray women in a world shaped by religious concerns about matters of life and death. To the extent that the depiction of positive and negative characteristics is a feature, this literature could be classified together with ethical literature. The various purposes of the ethical literature discussed by Dan, however, differ from the secular literature of vices and virtues discussed by Dishon.

Women's spiritual lives in the medieval period are the subject of BASKIN. She distinguishes between the lives of Jewish women in the Islamic world and those of Jewish women in Christian Europe, as represented by the Jewish communities known as the *Hasidei Ashkenaz*, German–Jewish pietists of the 12th and 13th centuries. In the case of the Islamic world, her source is the Cairo Genizah, whereas for the European world, she exploits accounts of women and their religious practices that can be gleaned from careful reading of *Sefer Hasidim*, the chief guide to religious practice of the pietists. To a considerable extent, however, what is known of the lives of medieval Jewish women indicates that they uniformly took as exemplary the (wise) woman of valor of Proverbs 31.

SIGRID PETERSON

Ethical Culture

Burtt, Edwin A., *Types of Religious Philosophy,* New York and London: Harper and Brothers, 1939; revised edition, New York: Harper, 1951

Friess, Horace L., *Felix Adler and Ethical Culture: Memories and Studies,* New York: Columbia University Press, 1981
Himmelfarb, Milton, *The Jews of Modernity,* New York: Basic Books, 1973
Kraut, Benny, *From Reform Judaism to Ethical Culture: The Religious Evolution of Felix Adler* (Monographs of the Hebrew Union College, no. 5), Cincinnati, Ohio: Hebrew Union College Press, 1979
Radest, Howard B., *Toward Common Ground: The Story of the Ethical Societies in the United States* (Ethical Culture Publications), New York: Ungar, 1969

Ethical Culture is a nontheistic religious movement inaugurated by Felix Adler in 1876. The movement is often viewed as a logical and natural development of classical Reform Judaism, and the leaders of Ethical Culture societies are often confused with radical reform rabbis.

KRAUT's study examines the relationship between Reform Judaism and the Ethical Culture movement of Felix Adler, whose dramatic public renunciation of Judaism shocked the Jewish community in the 1870s. From this full-scale biography there emerges the picture of a complex man. Adler was the descendant of rabbis on both paternal and maternal sides, closely related to the mystic Rabbi Nathan Adler of Frankfurt and Nathan Marcus Adler, chief rabbi of the British Empire. His father, Rabbi Samuel Adler, occupied the pulpit of the prestigious Reform congregation, Temple Emanu-El in New York City. After graduating from Columbia University, Felix was sent to Germany to study for the rabbinate with the intention of succeeding his father. At the Hochschule für die Wissenschaft des Judentums in Berlin he studied under Abraham Geiger and Herman Steinthal; while at the universities of Berlin and Heidelberg (which awarded him his doctorate) he studied Semitics, natural science, and philosophy. These studies undermined his faith in Judaism and supernatural religion. Kraut reports that Adler told one of his classmates at the Hochschule that on his return to New York he would stir things up.

When he returned in 1873, Adler was invited to preach in his father's temple, with a view to joining its ministry. In his trial sermon, he did not mention God but called for a "religion such as Judaism ever claimed to be—not by the Creed but by the Deed." When Adler was not offered the post of rabbi, he left the synagogue with a few sympathizers, and in May 1876 he founded the Society for Ethical Culture, dedicated to "the supreme importance of the ethical factor in all relations of life, personal, social, national and international, apart from any theological or metaphysical considerations."

Kraut shows that from its beginning, the movement, especially along the East Coast, drew its membership from among alienated Jews, and that throughout his life Adler was regarded as a radical, free-thinking rabbi by non-Jews. The Reform ministers are shown not to have repudiated Adler for two reasons. First, many of their congregants attended Adler's lectures and they did not want to offend those who underwrote their salaries. Second, they lacked Adler's training in religious scholarship, particularly in Bible criticism. Kraut finds only Kaufmann Kohler, the most intellectually able Reform theologian of the day, denouncing Adler as "a man who has deserted the Jewish flag and . . . blasphemes God and Judaism." With the passage of time, the Jewish establishment almost began to warm to Adler, and he was actively admired by many younger Reform rabbis concerned with social justice. Rabbi Stephen S. Wise, who officiated at Adler's funeral, hailed him as "Sinaitic in the clarity and radiance of his moral insight . . . treasurer and magnifier of the Hebrew prophets." Nevertheless, Adler remained a thorn in the side of the Reformers by exposing the patent contradiction in their position: on the one hand, they asserted Judaism's claim of religious universalism, while on the other hand, they affirmed the particularist mission theory, namely, the notion that Israel was God's chosen people, destined to remain separate for the sake of its priestly mission to spread its form of monotheism among the peoples of the world. Adler contended that since the Reformers regarded themselves as only a religious community, and since religious communities are held together by common religious beliefs, the Reformers should labor to bring about a fusion between themselves and liberal theists. According to Kraut, Ethical Culture pushed the Reform ideas of religious universalism and progressive human evolution to their logical conclusion.

RADEST examines from an Ethical Culture insider's perspective the rise of the movement that Kraut approaches from a Jewish point of view. These two works, therefore, complement each other. The later chapters of his book discuss the educational, philanthropic, and social reform activities of the society.

FRIESS, Adler's son-in-law, confidant, and disciple, provides an informative and useful portrait of Adler and his thought. He also describes the philosophy of the Ethical Culture movement, rooted in Adler's three fundamental tenets (postulates) of Ethical Culture: "the supremacy of the moral end of life above all other ends, the sufficiency of man for the pursuit of that end, and the increase of moral truth to be expected from loyalty in this pursuit."

BURTT devotes a chapter of his work to Adler's "religion of duty." Burtt highlights the main assumptions of Ethical Culture that have been subject to dispute and rejected by other religious philosophies. These disputed assumptions, dealing with man's moral situation, his social duty, and the possibility of metaphysical knowledge, are that man needs certainty by which to live; that he is capable of attaining this certainty in the form of a supreme principle of moral action; and that this principle is that inviolable worth attaches to every human personality, who must be treated accordingly.

HIMMELFARB observes that there has been a curious lack of objective inquiry into the social history of Ethical Culture. A question that particularly interests him is why so many Jews are attracted to Ethical Culture. Himmelfarb suggests that Ethical Culture serves as a decompression chamber, permitting apostasy to Christianity without feelings of guilt or anguish. The extended "baptism" may take place over several generations. Since membership in Ethical Culture societies has remained fairly constant at about 5,000 members, and since there is no natural increase due to the low birthrate of its members, there must be an influx of new members to make up for the loss in membership due to withdrawals and attrition. Membership in an Ethical Culture society is open to all with no formal conversion procedure, obviating the dramatic and possibly traumatic act of baptism and a Christian confession of faith. Nonpracticing Jewish parents bring up their children in Ethical Culture. Lacking any inhibitions not to do so, these children marry Episcopalians. Their children and grandchildren are likewise Christian. Here the cycle ends and a new group of ex-Jews enter the decompression chamber. This, in part, may explain the attraction of deracinated Jewish intellectuals to Ethical Culture, even though the ethical "postulates" of Felix Adler are as dogmatic and as little demonstrable as, say, the Mission theory of Reform Judaism advocated by his father.

JACOB HABERMAN

Ethical Wills

Dan, Joseph, "Ethical Wills," in *Encyclopaedia Judaica*, vol. 16, Jerusalem: Keter, 1971

Goldin, Judah, "Foreword," prefaced to reprint of *Hebrew Ethical Wills*, edited by Israel Abrahams, Philadelphia: Jewish Publication Society, 1976

Riemer, Jack, "Preface," in *Ethical Wills: A Modern Jewish Treasury*, New York: Schocken, 1983

Stampfer, Nathaniel, "Introduction," in *Ethical Wills: A Modern Jewish Treasury*, New York: Schocken, 1983

An ethical will is a literary device for leaving a moral legacy to one's descendants. Some scholars claim that such wills have an ancient pedigree, stemming from the oral testaments given by parents to their children as portrayed in the Bible. Ethical wills became a distinct literary genre, however, only in the European Jewish communities of the Middle Ages, taking their place alongside other ethical literary genres such as treatises, homilies, and monographs on various subjects. Unlike other types of ethical or moral literature, ethical wills are distinctive both in that they are written as lasting legacies for one's heirs rather than as works intended for a broader public, and in that generally they deal only with the traits necessary to lead a good life and not the philosophical or theological arguments behind these norms.

GOLDIN was the first contemporary scholar to analyze medieval Jewish ethical wills seriously as a distinct genre worthy of study. His major work on the subject appears as a foreword to the 1976 reprint of the first anthology of these texts, assembled by Israel Abrahams and originally published in 1926. It is in fact this book that brought the genre to public awareness for the first time. Accordingly, Goldin's foreword marks the beginning of serious scholarly treatment of this branch of moral literature. He notes that the writing of such wills in Judaism faces special problems. One problem is that what these texts have to say has been attempted many times before and so can rarely be new or unexpected. The other problem is that, aside from ethical wills, Jewish religious literature is replete with discussions of norms of behavior (i.e., halakhah). The ethical will thus developed, in his view, in order to stress in a new way the need to cultivate moral traits. From his perspective, it is not the content of these wills that is significant, then, but rather the rhetoric, the way they drive home their lesson as last testaments, exploiting the moral force of the deathbed.

DAN was the next significant scholar to take up the study of the genre. In his lengthy entry in the *Encyclopaedia Judaica*, he attempts to trace the major streams of the tradition of writing ethical wills. He adds considerably to knowledge of the historical development of the genre by mentioning the major writers and works that comprise this literature. Dan also alludes to some of the literary history of the genre, including the controversy surrounding the 13th-century ethical will of Joseph ibn Kaspi and its justification of philosophical speculation, and the family tradition of writing such wills as seen in several generations of the Horowitz family in Prague in the 17th century.

RIEMER and STAMPFER produced the only other significant book on ethical wills published in the 20th century. Published in 1983, theirs, like Israel Abrahams's, is a collection of significant ethical wills that is presumed to speak largely for itself. In his preface, Riemer notes that the editors have divided their material in such a way as to reflect the different experiences of Jews in this century: faith and piety, agony and anguish, return to power and statehood, and freedom. Despite their different provenances, however, all these wills, he claims, have a similar point to make, namely to call the readers to remembrance of what the people of Israel have stood for and suffered for. Stampfer's introduction raises some of the seminal questions that he sees arising from the collection and that in turn point the way for further research.

PETER HAAS

Ethiopia

Kaplan, Steven, *The Beta Israel (Falasha) in Ethiopia: From Earliest Times to the Twentieth Century*, New York: New York University Press, 1992

Leslau, Wolf, *Falasha Anthology* (Yale Judaica Series, vol. 6), New Haven, Connecticut, and London: Yale University Press, 1951

Parfitt, Tudor and Emanuela Trevisan Semi (editors), *The Beta Israel in Ethiopia and Israel: Studies on Ethiopian Jews*, Surrey: Curzon, 1999

Quirin, James, *The Evolution of the Ethiopian Jews: A History of the Beta Israel (Falasha) to 1920* (Ethnohistory Series), Philadelphia: University of Pennsylvania Press, 1992

Shelemay, Kay Kaufman, *Music, Ritual, and Falasha History* (Ethiopian Series Monograph, no. 17), East Lansing: African Studies Center, Michigan State University Press, 1986

Weil, Shalva (editor), *Ethiopian Jews in the Limelight*, Jerusalem: NCJW Research Institute for Innovation in Education, Hebrew University, 1997

Prior to the introduction of Christianity to Ethiopia in the third century C.E., Judaism had a considerable impact on the ancient Aksumite kingdom in that land. Biblical and Hebraic influences on early Ethiopian culture are well documented, and to this day, the Ethiopian Orthodox Church has adhered to Old Testament practices inspired by the Hebrew Bible. Against this backdrop, it is not surprising that a group of Ethiopian Jews, known as *Beta Israel* ("The House of Israel") or *Falashas* ("Strangers"), survived in Ethiopia from antiquity until the end of the 20th century, when the great majority of them migrated to Israel.

LESLAU, one of the greatest semitic linguists, displays a particular interest in the history of the Falashas of Ethiopia. His anthology provides rare translations from such sources of Falasha sacred literature as *The Death of Moses* and the *Apocalypse of Gorgorios*. In addition, Leslau's introductory chapter details in schematic fashion the life and customs of the Falashas as he found them in Ethiopia in 1947.

SHELEMAY's approach to the Falashas contrasts with that of many of her scholarly predecessors, who emphasize the Judaic aspects of Falasha tradition. Shelemay demonstrates their Ethiopian Christian heritage through an ethno-musicological analysis of Falasha liturgy, comparing the Falashas' liturgical cycle and literature with that of the Ethiopian Orthodox Church. She concludes that the extant Falasha tradition descends from a Judaized monastic tradition that emerged in the 14th and 15th centuries and was derived from Ethiopian Christian monks.

KAPLAN traces the history of the Beta Israel in Ethiopia. He mentions the existence of Jews in the early Aksumite kingdom, but he cannot identify any links between this early group of Jews and the *ayhud* (Jews, Judaizers) who emerged in Ethiopia sometime in the 14th century and became known as the Falashas. The author places this study of the Falashas in an Ethiopian context. He demonstrates that they cannot be a "lost tribe of Israel"; rather, he considers them to be an ethnic group that adopted its liturgy and specialized economy between the 14th and 16th centuries. He chronicles the development of this low-status group through the beginning of the 20th century, examining, in particular, the effect of the European missionaries and the impact of the Great Famine of 1888 through 1892 on the history of Beta Israel Judaism in Ethiopia.

QUIRIN's book is similar in scope to that of Kaplan's, but Quirin relies extensively on evidence from oral traditions to recount the development of the Beta Israel in Ethiopia from ancient times. Through careful historical reconstruction, the author demonstrates how the Jews of Ethiopia struggled to create and maintain their religious and ethnic identity in the face of external pressures, such as the loss of political independence in the 17th century and the arrival of Protestant missionaries in the 19th and 20th centuries. Quirin claims that the Beta Israel's strong sense of religious identity and their self-perception as a separatist group (together with their semi-independent material base as artisans) contributed to their emerging caste relationship with the dominant community, which prevented their assimilation in Ethiopian society.

PARFITT and TREVISAN SEMI's collection of articles, which arose out of the Society for the Study of Ethiopian Jewry (SOSTEJE) conference in Jerusalem in 1995, concentrates on the processes by which late 20th-century Ethiopian Jewish identity evolved. A group of original essays are devoted to documenting the lives of some of the Ethiopian Jews, such as Solomon Isaac and Hizkiahu Finkas, whom Jacques Faitlovitch, a 20th-century Polish Jewish "missionary," brought out of Ethiopia to be educated in Europe. Other essays are devoted to describing the changing identity of Ethiopian Jews in Israel, in the Israel Defense Force, in ritual situations, and in medical contexts.

WEIL's volume presents original contributions by eight leading scholars about the situation of the Ethiopian Jews both in Ethiopia and in Israel. Richard Pankhurst's essay, "The Beta Esra'el (Falashas) in their Ethiopian Setting," considers the similarities between Ethiopian Christianity and the Judaism practiced by the Beta Israel and argues that Westerners have distorted perceptions of Beta Israel religion. By contrast, an essay by Rosen refers to Ethiopian Jews in their Israeli setting, citing his own work as an Israeli government anthropologist to demonstrate how a better understanding of Ethiopian culture can help resolve practical questions the immigrants face in Israel. In her "Introduction: Ethiopian Jews in the Limelight," Weil contends that

> While [this volume is] tracing the emergence of a new identity for the Beta Israel as Ethiopian Jews in Israel, the newly-formed ethnic group could develop as a twilight group, straddling the boundaries of dark and light, black and white.

Survey results presented by Esther Benita and Gilah Noam show that an immigrant's length of time in Israel has been one of the factors that positively influences his/her employment and social integration opportunities.

SHALVA WEIL

Ethnology *see* Race, Jews as

Euthanasia

Abraham, A.S., "The Dying Patient and Euthanasia," in *The Comprehensive Guide to Medical Halacha,* New York: Feldheim, 1990

Herring, Basil F., "Euthanasia," in *Jewish Ethics and Halakhah for Our Time: Sources and Commentary,* 2 vols., New York: Yeshiva University Press, 1984

Jakobovits, Immanuel, "The Dying and Their Treatment," in his *Jewish Medical Ethics: A Comparative and Historical Study of the Jewish Religious Attitude to Medicine and Its Practice,* New York: Bloch, 1959

Rosner, Fred, "The End of Life," in *Modern Medicine and Jewish Ethics,* New York: Yeshiva University Press, 1986, 2nd edition, 1991

Jewish teaching in regard to mercy killing is based on the principle of the infinite value of human life. Hence, there is an obligation to provide all necessary care to patients even if they have only a few moments left to live. One is prohibited from doing anything that hastens death. Based on many sources, JAKOBOVITS, the father of modern Jewish medical ethics, concludes that any form of active euthanasia is strictly prohibited and condemned as plain murder; anyone who kills a dying person is liable to the death penalty as a common murderer. At the same time, he argues, Jewish law sanctions the withdrawal of any factor—whether extraneous to the patient himself or not—that may artificially delay the patient's demise in the final phase. Jakobovits is quick to point out, however, that all the rabbinic sources refer to a *goses*—an individual in whom death is believed to be imminent—as one whose life expectancy is three days or less. Thus, passive euthanasia for a patient who may yet live for weeks or months may not necessarily be condoned. Furthermore, in the case of an incurably ill person in severe pain, agony, or distress, the removal of an impediment to death, although permitted in Jewish law, may not be analogous to withholding the medical therapy that is perhaps sustaining the patient's life, albeit unnaturally. The impediments to death spoken of in codified Jewish law, whether far removed from the patient (as exemplified by the noise of wood chopping) or in physical contact with him (such as the case of salt on the patient's tongue), do not constitute any part of the therapeutic methods or equipment employed in the medical management of the case. For this reason, these impediments may be removed. Furthermore, in Jakobovits's view, it may be permissible to discontinue the use of instruments and machinery specifically designed and used in the treatment of incurably ill patients when it is certain that doing so will shorten the act of dying rather than interrupt life.

ABRAHAM takes the position that nothing may be done to a dying person that might hasten death. Since there are rare cases in which critically ill patients, for whom all hope has been abandoned, do nevertheless recover, it is the duty of the physician to continue treating a dying patient until the very end. This is equally valid if treatment may prolong life for only a short time, but not if the treatment would add suffering to a patient who has reached the natural end of the disease. Abraham further states that one may not hasten death, even that of a patient who is suffering greatly and for whom there is no hope of a cure, even if the patient asks that this be done. To shorten the life of a person, even a life of agony and suffering, is forbidden. To do so, albeit for reasons of compassion and even at the request of the patient, is equivalent to murder and is punishable accordingly. Under no circumstances does Jewish law permit escape from suffering at the price of human life. The value of life is infinite, and therefore the value of every part of it, however brief, is also infinite. Abraham concludes that denying the value of human life because of the nearness of death destroys the absolute value of all life and gives it instead a relative value only. Willingness to shorten, by however little, the life of a dying patient on the grounds that it is of no further value destroys the infinite value of all human life.

HERRING's approach to the subject is novel in its format in that he presents a brief introduction, a case illustration, sources, and a discussion of those sources in relation to the case. He has researched the contemporary halakhic literature and culled the most relevant and authoritative material bearing on euthanasia and related issues. He ably digests, summarizes, and popularizes his material so that it is accessible to the interested nonspecialist. The unusual format allows the reader to feel a sense of participation in the process of halakhic reasoning.

ROSNER draws heavily on the responsa of the late Rabbi Moshe Feinstein as well as classic sources in his exposition of the Jewish attitude toward euthanasia. He maintains that Jewish law requires the physician to do everything in his power to prolong life but prohibits the use of measures that prolong the act of dying. The value attached to human life in Judaism, he adds, is far greater than that in the Christian or Anglo-American common law traditions. To save a life, all Jewish law is automatically suspended, short of idolatry, forbidden sexual relations, and murder. Euthanasia, says Rosner, is opposed without qualification in Judaism, which condemns as sheer murder any active or deliberate hastening of death, done with or without the patient's consent. He notes that some rabbinic views do not allow any relaxation of efforts, however artificial and ultimately hopeless they are, to prolong life. Others, however, do not require the physician to resort to "heroic" methods, but sanction the omission of machines and artificial life-support systems that only serve to draw out the dying patient's agony, provided that basic care (such as food and good nursing) is provided.

Rosner stresses that the physician is given divine license to heal but not to hasten death. When a physician has nothing further to offer a patient medically or surgically, the physician's license to heal ends and he becomes no different from a lay person. Every human being is morally expected to help another human in distress; a dying patient is no exception to this entitlement to help. The physician, family, friends, nurses, social workers, and other individuals close to the dying patient are all obligated to provide supportive—including psychosocial and emotional—care until the very end. Fluids and nutrition are part and parcel of that supportive care, no different from washing, turning, talking to, singing with, reading to, or just listening to the dying patient. There are times when specific medical and/or surgical therapy is no longer indicated, appropriate, or desirable for an irreversibly ill, dying patient. However, under no circumstances can general supportive measures be abandoned to hasten the patient's demise.

FRED ROSNER

Exilarchate

Brody, Robert, *The Geonim of Babylonia and the Shaping of Medieval Jewish Culture*, New Haven, Connecticut: Yale University Press, 1998

Gil, Moshe, "The Exilarchate," in *The Jews of Medieval Islam* (Études sur le judaïsme médiéval, 16), edited by Daniel Frank, New York: Brill, 1995

Goode, A.D., "The Exilarchate in the Eastern Caliphate, 637–1258," *Jewish Quarterly Review* (new series), 31(2), 1940

Mann, Jacob, *Texts and Studies in Jewish History and Literature* (Abraham and Hannah Oppenheim Memorial Publications), 2 vols., Cincinnati, Ohio: Hebrew Union College Press, 1931–1935

Neusner, Jacob, *A History of the Jews in Babylonia* (Studia Post-Biblica, vols. 9, 11, 12, 14, 15), 5 vols., Leiden: Brill, 1965–1970

Wasserstrom, Steven, *Between Muslim and Jew: The Problem of Symbiosis under Early Islam*, Princeton, New Jersey: Princeton University Press, 1995

The Babylonian exilarchate, an office of Jewish authority held throughout late antiquity and the Middle Ages by a dynasty that traced itself to King David, was, along with the Yeshivot of Sura and Pumbedita, one of the major institutions of Jewish leadership in the geonic period. However, unlike the Babylonian academies, which were perceived as primarily religious institutions, the exilarchate was generally considered an institution of temporal authority. This perception left its mark in the sources available to historians and has had repercussions in secondary literature as well. While relatively abundant primary sources pertaining to at least certain aspects of the gaonate have survived—largely as a function of their continuing relevance to the development of halakhah—very little remains from the exilarchate itself. In fact, a large portion of the available information comes from geonic sources, which, far from being objective, are mainly interested in the occasions on which the exilarchate came into direct conflict with the academies. Two additional sources have helped to correct the skewed picture that emerges from the geonic sources: references to the exilarchate in Arabic literature and documents from the Cairo Genizah. For the most part, however, the history of the exilarchate has been told under the general rubric of geonic history, the dynamic relationship between it and the academies determining its place in scholarship.

MANN's work is based primarily on documents from the Cairo Genizah, a resource that has made significant contributions to practically every aspect of medieval Jewish history. Above all, Mann demonstrates that, despite its relatively weakened stature, the exilarchate continued to be a profoundly important force in the political life of medieval Jewry long after its supposed demise in the middle of the 11th century. Thus he devotes particular attention to the exilarchs who functioned in subsequent generations, as well as to the status and power attained by members of the exilarchal dynasty outside Babylonia. Illustrating a similar point, volume two of *Texts and Studies* contains considerable information on a particular branch of the exilarchal dynasty, the descendants of Anan b. David, who functioned for centuries as leaders within the Karaite community.

GOODE's article, while somewhat outdated, provides a useful chronological history of the exilarchate during the Islamic period. His account, essentially a synthesis of information gathered from medieval chronicles and to a lesser extent from Genizah documents, focuses on the disputes between exilarchs and geonim. An important aspect of this article is its periodization: by continuing his narrative down to the 14th century, Goode argues compellingly for the importance of tracing the institution's history even in its decline. The chronological chart at the end of Goode's article should be corrected on the basis of that given by Gil.

NEUSNER deals with the origins of the exilarchate as part of his general study of Babylonian Jewry in late antiquity. Through careful analysis of numerous references to the exilarchate in rabbinic literature, he attempts to reconstruct the social, political, and demographic factors that combined to bring about its establishment sometime around the end of the first century C.E. Following a familiar typology, Neusner sees the emergence of the exilarchate as the product of larger political forces acting outside the Jewish community. Thus, in his view, the exilarchate was the result of "a successful reorganization of Jewish affairs" by the Parthians, who were concerned to secure the loyalty of the potentially volatile Jewish community within Parthia's borders. Neusner's sensitivity to external influences is also evident in his analysis of the fate of the exilarchate under the radically different Sasanian dynasty. His analysis of the "uneasy alliance" between rabbis and exilarchs in the Talmud provides an important contextual backdrop to the conflicts that erupted between geonim and exilarchs during the medieval period.

GIL focuses on the exilarchate between the seventh and 11th centuries. He uses a variety of materials—medieval Hebrew chronicles, Arabic literature, and Genizah documents—to explore the sources of the exilarchate's authority, its functions, and its status in the Jewish and Muslim communities. Gil also sets out to clarify the thorny chronology of exilarchs in this period, a tedious but crucial first stage for serious historical research. A comparison of the articles by Gil and Goode reveals how much stands to be gained when Arabic sources and Genizah materials are incorporated into the study of the Jewish past. The article ends with a useful table of exilarchs that serves as a corrective to that given by Goode.

WASSERSTROM's book, unlike the other works discussed in this article, does not deal with the history of the exilarchate per se but instead with its function as a symbol within medieval cultural discourse. *Between Muslim and Jew* explores the complex synergistic relationship between Islam and Judaism in the Middle Ages. In particular, Wasserstrom is concerned with a process whereby each of the two sought to define and legitimate itself through its constructed image of the other. In a chapter devoted to the symbiosis between Judaism and Shi'ism, Wasserstrom considers a number of stories about the exilarchate that appear in Shi'ite texts. He shows that the figure of the exilarch actually plays a part in the polemical struggle between Sunnis and Shi'ites. Indirectly, Wasserstrom's chapter illustrates the unique popularity of and respect shown to the exilarchate in Muslim society.

BRODY's work, although devoted primarily to the Babylonian geonim, contains an important chapter in which the author dwells on the sources of the exilarchate's authority, its rights and responsibilities, and, in particular, its tense relationship with the gaonate during the Islamic period. Brody's concern is to flesh out the historical setting in which the geonim functioned, and as a consequence his treatment naturally focuses on the interaction between exilarchs and geonim. The reader will note that the delicate balance of power between exilarchs and rabbis depicted by Neusner for the pre-Islamic period continued, *mutatis mutandis,* in the competition for authority between exilarchs and geonim here described by Brody.

ARNOLD FRANKLIN

Exodus

Cassuto, Umberto, *Perush 'al sefer Shemot,* 1951; translated by Israel Abrahams as *A Commentary on the Book of Exodus,* Jerusalem: Magnes Press of Hebrew University, 1967

Childs, Brevard S., *The Book of Exodus: A Critical Theological Commentary* (Old Testament Library), Philadelphia: Westminster, 1974

Greenberg, Moshe, *Understanding Exodus* (Heritage of Biblical Israel Series, vol. 2), New York: Behrman House for the Melton Research Center of the Jewish Theological Seminary of America, 1969

Jacob, Benno, *The Second Book of the Bible: Exodus,* translated by Walter Jacob, Hoboken, New Jersey: Ktav, 1992

Sarna, Nahum M., *Exploring Exodus: The Heritage of Biblical Israel,* New York: Schocken, 1986

Sarna, Nahum M., *Exodus/Shemot: The Traditional Hebrew Text with the New JPS Translation* (JPS Torah Commentary Series), Philadelphia: Jewish Publication Society, 1991

Zakovitch, Yair, *"And You Shall Tell Your Son—":* The Concept of the Exodus in the Bible, Jerusalem: Magnes Press of Hebrew University, 1991

Inasmuch as the Book of Genesis recounts the origins and development of a family and its covenant relationship with God, the Book of Exodus describes the birth of a new people and their destiny *vis-à-vis* God. Exodus introduces the concept of a God who operates through history and the notion of a covenant expressed through law and sacred spaces and times. The Book of Exodus begins with the enslavement of the Israelites by the Egyptians and God's saving acts through his mediator, Moses, and concludes at Mount Sinai with the revelation of God and stipulation of the terms of the covenant.

CASSUTO's commentary, originally published in Hebrew in 1951 around the time of his death, reflects his encyclopedic knowledge and extreme sensitivity to the nuances of the Hebrew text. Rejecting the historical-critical approaches of his contemporaries for whom "the study of sources takes precedence over that of the book as we have it," Cassuto presents an exegesis of the received Hebrew (Masoretic) text whose primary aim lies in "elucidating and evaluating the work itself." Cassuto asserts that the Book of Exodus is based on an "ancient heroic poem," rather than the result of a weaving of separate sources. He does, however, concede in subtle ways to the source critics on a number of passages. Cassuto uses the format of a running commentary with the text of Exodus worked into his readings, which helps to make his commentary accessible to the nonspecialist. The greatest strengths of Cassuto's book are his insights into literary structure and ancient Hebrew literary techniques, such as the use of repetitions, the sequencing of sections, and the symbolism of numbers, particularly the use of the number seven as an organizing principle.

GREENBERG's book is the first volume of a planned multipart Exodus commentary for the Heritage of Biblical Israel series, the subsequent volumes of which were never published;

consequently, Greenberg's analysis of Exodus exists only through the narratives of the plagues. Greenberg applies a literary analysis to Exodus based upon the principle that a book is essentially "an organization of literary units meant to convey a complex ideational message." By ideational message he refers to the meaning of a book as it is reflected through the component parts into a coherent whole. His commentary operates on three levels: he analyzes the Book of Exodus as "an element in the Torah book"; he studies smaller literary units looking for themes and common structures; and he discusses the redactor's contributions in organizing the individual units into a coherent book. Greenberg shows how the Book of Exodus is not about conveying "the past historical but present affective," so that each generation of readers relives the saving acts of God. This short work is highly sophisticated yet readable and informative for the novice.

CHILDS's book may well be the definitive commentary on Exodus at present. Childs organizes his commentary into thematic units. Each unit contains a bibliography, translation, textual and philological notes, literary analysis, thematic interpretation, Hebrew Bible and New Testament contextual readings, and a history of exegesis. Childs's method is canonical; that is, he approaches the text as theological and canonical literature. Although he acknowledges that Exodus has a compositional history, he is interested in the final product that has shaped religious communities for generations. Unlike other interpreters who focus on the final product, Childs submits the text to a rigorous textual, philological, and source-critical analysis. Despite Childs's self-conscious reading as a Christian, Jewish readers can find a wealth of helpful information and insights into the text, particularly in his sections on thematic interpretation and the history of exegesis.

Sarna has published two books on Exodus that may be read concurrently. SARNA (1986) is intended for the nonspecialist curious about the historical and cultural background of Exodus. The book is highly readable, contains a helpful bibliography, and is filled with interesting information about the world of the ancient Israelites. Sarna has been criticized for overstating his case for the historicity of the exodus event when, for example, he discusses the atmospheric conditions at Mount Sinai and the geological background of the plagues. Readers should also be aware of Sarna's polemical attitude toward the uniqueness of ancient Israel in the ancient Near Eastern world. SARNA (1991), a contribution to the Jewish Publication Society's Torah Commentary series of which he is the general editor, is aimed at a popular Jewish audience and is particularly valuable for the novice. It is user-friendly, scholarly but not technical, and includes many gleanings from rabbinic and medieval Jewish commentators. His book also introduces background information from ancient Israel's surrounding cultures in a clear and effective manner. Finally, the excursuses at the end of the book provide excellent brief summaries of various themes and topics that emerge from the Book of Exodus.

JACOB's English commentary is based on his unpublished German manuscript, which was compiled during World War II. His son Ernest spent several years revising the book, and it was finally translated and edited by his grandson Walter. In some ways, Jacob paved the way for scholars such as Umberto Cassuto and Yehezkel Kaufmann in his repudiation of the historical-critical approaches of his contemporaries. Unfortunately, he gained many opponents as a result of the scathingly adversarial attitude reflected in his writing. Nonetheless, Jacob's work is intelligent and creative. The commentary is filled with traditional Jewish learning presented in a manner accessible to the nonspecialist. It also provides a window into early 20th-century pre-critical Jewish scholarship.

ZAKOVITCH's short book contains a number of studies on the Exodus motif throughout the Hebrew Bible. He is interested in various biblical viewpoints regarding the Exodus story. He addresses, for example, the following questions: Why were the Israelites enslaved in Egypt? How do the biblical books make reference to the Exodus account? What roles did the Exodus story play for ancient Israelites? Although not all scholars agree with his conclusions, this book should be of considerable interest to those who are looking for echoes of the Exodus motif throughout the Bible.

S. Tamar Kamionkowski

Eybeschütz, Jonathan *see* Emden-Eybeschütz Controversy

Ezekiel, Book of

Block, Daniel, *The Book of Ezekiel* (The New International Commentary on the Old Testament), 2 vols., Grand Rapids, Michigan: Eerdmans, 1997

Greenberg, Moshe, *Ezekiel 1–20: A New Translation with Introduction and Commentary* (Anchor Bible, vol. 22), Garden City, New York: Doubleday, 1983

Greenberg, Moshe, *Ezekiel 21–37: A New Translation with Introduction and Commentary* (Anchor Bible, vol. 22A), New York: Doubleday, 1997

Halperin, David J., *Seeking Ezekiel: Text and Psychology*, University Park: Pennsylvania State University Press, 1993

Klein, Ralph W., *Ezekiel: The Prophet and His Message* (Studies on Personalities of the Old Testament), Columbia: University of South Carolina Press, 1988

McKeating, Henry, *Ezekiel* (Old Testament Guides), Sheffield, South Yorkshire: JSOT, 1993

Torrey, Charles C., *Pseudo-Ezekiel and the Original Prophecy* (Yale Oriental Series), New Haven, Connecticut: Yale University Press, and London: Oxford University Press, 1930; reprinted with critical articles by Shalom Spiegel and Charles C. Torrey and prolegomenon by Moshe Greenberg, New York: Ktav, 1970

Zimmerli, Walther, *Ezekiel 1: A Commentary on the Book of the Prophet Ezekiel, Chapters 1–24* (Hermeneia: A Critical and Historical Commentary on the Bible), translated by Ronald E. Clements, Philadelphia: Fortress, 1979

Zimmerli, Walther, *Ezekiel 2: A Commentary on the Book of the Prophet Ezekiel, Chapters 25–48* (Hermeneia: A Critical and Historical Commentary on the Bible), translated by James D. Martin, Philadelphia: Fortress, 1983

The Book of Ezekiel is among the most provocative books in the Hebrew Bible. From grandiose divine visions to rational discourse and argumentation, from dramatic and unusual actions to a detailed utopian blueprint—all these seeming contradictions have evoked heated debates regarding authorship, dating, and provenance. The personality of the prophet also has intrigued readers for centuries and has led to a range of speculation concerning his prophetic experiences and state of mind.

TORREY wrote in the heyday of scholarly debate regarding the dating of the Book of Ezekiel. Based on a study of the language and references in the Book of Ezekiel, he maintains that Ezekiel was a pseudepigraph from the period of King Manasseh, reedited around the period of Alexander the Great. According to Torrey's thesis, the biblical book was given its Babylonian setting in order to promote what Torrey believed was the Chronicler's myth of an exile and restoration. Included in the 1970 reprint are refutations of Torrey's claims by Shalom Spiegel and a significant introduction by Moshe Greenberg. A late date for Ezekiel has been thoroughly debunked since Torrey's time, yet this work still marks an important chapter in Ezekiel scholarship.

ZIMMERLI's commentaries (1979 and 1983) provide the basis from which most other recent Ezekiel commentaries derive, and they are indispensable for the serious student of Ezekiel. The English editions are based on his German commentary, published in fascicles from 1955 to 1968. The layout of the English commentaries, determined by the editors of the Hermeneia series, begin with an extensive bibliography and introduction. The commentary on each unit is preceded by a translation side by side with extensive textual and philological notes. Following the translation and notes come sections on form, setting, interpretation, and aim. Zimmerli's work marks a change from earlier examinations of Ezekiel in that he redirects the focus of Ezekiel studies from dating and provenance to a form-critical approach. He devotes the greater part of his introduction to forms of prophetic speech, which lead him to conclude that "Undoubtedly the present Book of Ezekiel stems from the hand of the 'school of Ezekiel'." Zimmerli's focus on textual notes and on untangling the various editorial levels of the text, while valuable and of the essence to specialists, leads to an atomistic reading in which the text in its final form receives minimal attention.

GREENBERG's recent commentaries (1983 and 1997) are having an enormous impact on the direction of Ezekiel studies. Apart from the bold new approaches to which he subjects the text, Greenberg sets a standard for close readings of biblical literature. His commentaries are original, insightful, and well documented. He presents a "holistic" explication of the Book of Ezekiel, arguing that almost the entire book can be attributed to a prophet named Ezekiel who prophesied in Babylonia in the periods immediately preceding and following the capture and destruction of Jerusalem. In his introduction, he offers an incisive critique of critical-historical methodologies that slice texts into various layers based primarily upon modern assumptions of what constitutes good literature. Rejecting the position of an Ezekiel school, Greenberg proposes that the Book of Ezekiel "is the product of art and intelligent design" and that it reflects the work of "an individual mind of powerful and passionate proclivities." Whether or not one agrees that the entirety of the book is the direct product of Ezekiel himself, Greenberg's cautions regarding the evaluation of ancient literature through the eyes of a modern reader deserve serious consideration.

KLEIN's book, part of a series on biblical personalities, is nonetheless "not a biography but a literary and theological analysis of a biblical document" that "attempts to take seriously the present shape of the book, to decipher its imagery, to comment on its technical vocabulary, and to relate its several parts to one another." Klein stands between Zimmerli (with whom he studied) and Greenberg in that he supports theories of multiple redactions in composition but is most interested in the text in its final form. The book is organized around themes in the Book of Ezekiel such as the corruption of the Jerusalem Temple and its consequences, retribution and repentance, and visions of the future restoration of the people on its own land. This book is one of the few critical works on Ezekiel that is accessible to the nonspecialist searching for a serious engagement with the material. It is agreeably written and contains helpful summaries at the conclusion of each section.

McKEATING's brief book is a contribution to the Old Testament Guides, a series intended to provide the reader with "a short volume, concise and comprehensive, manageable and affordable, on the biblical book he or she is studying." Aside from some novel discussion of the last ten chapters of Ezekiel, McKeating concentrates more on a review of prior Ezekiel research and Ezekiel's place within prophetic traditions. He rejects the holistic approach of Greenberg in favor of a more historical-critical approach. This book is most valuable for the reader who seeks information on the history of scholarship, dating, composition, and redaction rather than on the literary and theological merits of the book itself.

HALPERIN's book is an interdisciplinary work that draws upon classic Freudian psychoanalysis to understand the eccentricities in the Book of Ezekiel. Salvaging and refining the initial arguments of Edwin C. Broome ("Ezekiel's Abnormal Personality," *Journal of Biblical Literature* 65, 1946), Halperin argues that problems in the text are best explained by positing that Ezekiel suffered from a mental disorder based upon childhood abuse by his parents resulting in "a frantic loathing of female sexuality." The first part of the book contains a refutation of Broome's critics and an assertion of the validity of psychoanalytic readings of biblical characters. Halperin's intent is "to make a case for the psychoanalytic perceptions of human nature and for its value as a tool for understanding literary creations of the remote past." His work raises crucial methodological questions that he does not adequately address: To what extent does a text reveal the internal life of its author? What is the place of a consideration of social contexts and literary techniques in a psychological approach?

BLOCK's commentary, a recent addition to the New International Commentary on the Old Testament series, is strongly influenced by Greenberg's work and Ellen Davies's claim that Ezekiel was a writing prophet, although Block writes that this "does not rule out editorial clarifications by later hands." The greatest strength of this commentary is its readability and its up-to-date bibliography. Block's introduction provides a lucid summary of issues such as historical and social background, literary style, and the theological claims of Ezekiel. Each section of the commentary has a discussion of style and structure, a translation and commentary, and an exposition of theological implications. The commentary is generally accessible to the nonspecialist, with technical language kept to a minimum.

S. Tamar Kamionkowski

Ezra and Nehemiah, Books of

Blenkinsopp, Joseph, *Ezra-Nehemiah: A Commentary* (Old Testament Library), Philadelphia: Westminster, 1988

Davies, P.R. (editor), *Second Temple Studies 1: Persian Period* (Journal for the Study of the Old Testament Supplement Series, 117), Sheffield: Sheffield Academic Press, 1991

Grabbe, Lester L., *Ezra-Nehemiah* (Old Testament Readings), London and New York: Routledge, 1998

Hoglund, Kenneth G., *Achaemenid Imperial Administration in Syria-Palestine and the Missions of Ezra and Nehemiah* (Society of Biblical Literature Dissertation Series, no. 125), Atlanta, Georgia: Scholars Press, 1992

Myers, Jacob M. (editor), *Ezra-Nehemiah* (Anchor Bible, vol. 14), Garden City, New York: Doubleday, 1965

Williamson, H.G.M., *Ezra, Nehemiah* (Word Biblical Commentary, vol. 16), Waco, Texas: Word Books, 1985

The books of Ezra and Nehemiah were originally considered one book, and they were probably produced by the same circle as the books of Chronicles, in about 400 B.C.E. There are many unresolved questions about the historical reliability of these books, including issues as basic as the existence and relative chronologies of the figures of Ezra and Nehemiah.

In a work intended for both the scholar and the lay reader, MYERS includes an introduction to the books of Ezra and Nehemiah, his own translation of the texts, notes on the Hebrew originals, and a commentary on each chapter. He takes a conservative approach to the text, but he also identifies issues of scholarly contention. Myers divides the two books in roughly the following way: a history (Ezra 1–6), an Ezra memoir (Ezra 7–10, Nehemiah 8–10), and a Nehemiah memoir (Nehemiah 1–7, 12–13), while Nehemiah 11 remains obscure. Myers asserts that the author of the first six chapters of Ezra was Ezra himself, who used available material to report accurately the history of the period. Myers suggests Ezra came to Judea after Nehemiah, in 398 B.C.E., the seventh year of the reign of Artaxerxes II, and not (as the biblical text implies) in 458 B.C.E., the seventh year of the reign of Artaxerxes I. His orders were to investigate the religious situation in Judea, bring contributions for the Temple, appoint magistrates, and teach the law. Myers notes a contradiction between Ezra's orders in the so-called rescript of Artaxerxes (Ezra 7:11–26) and his actions, the most famous of which was requiring all Israelite men to divorce their gentile wives. Unlike Ezra, Nehemiah was sent by Artaxerxes I as governor of Judea. His chief mission was to provide for the security of Jerusalem. Myers believes that Nehemiah replaced Sanballat, whom the biblical text portrays as his enemy.

In another commentary intended for scholarly and lay audiences alike, WILLIAMSON presents an introductory essay, his own translation of the text, notes on the Hebrew, and an extended analysis of each chapter. Like Myers, he asserts that the two books are structured in three parts, but he is not as conservative as Myers and does not assume Ezra to be the author of the first section. Williamson argues that knowledge of the operation of the Temple in the author's own day was enough to enable him to construct his narrative. He also disagrees with Myers about the timing of Ezra and Nehemiah's activities, concluding that Ezra returned (or was sent) from Babylon to Judea during the seventh year of the reign of Artaxerxes I and so preceded Nehemiah, but both authors do agree that the rescript of Artaxerxes is an authentic text that responds to a request from a Jew by incorporating the language of that request. Like Myers, Williamson notes the lack of agreement between Ezra's actions and his orders, and both commentaries conclude that Nehemiah was sent to be governor of Judea, succeeding Sanballat.

BLENKINSOPP's excellent commentary is written for both scholar and lay readers. Blenkinsopp assumes that Ezra preceded Nehemiah, but he differs from previous commentators by suggesting that the two men were active concurrently. Blenkinsopp agrees with Myers and Williamson that the rescript of Artaxerxes I is genuine. He compares Ezra's mission to that of Udjahorresnet in Egypt, arguing that Ezra was supposed to restore the Jerusalem Temple and endow the administration of Jewish law with the authority of the Persian emperor. Diverging from the opinions of previous commentators, Blenkinsopp argues that references to the punishments of flogging and confiscation of property show that the Persian penal code was invoked for infractions of Jewish religious law. Blenkinsopp follows the conventional wisdom asserting that Nehemiah was sent out to be governor of Judea, which was surrounded on all sides by hostile forces. He posits, however, that Tobiah was governor of Ammon, and he theorizes that Sanballat, Tobiah, Gashmu, and Nehemiah were all equal in status.

HOGLUND's important and original monograph employs a sociopolitical approach to the biblical text, based on work by S. Eisenstadt, to argue that the missions of both Ezra and Nehemiah should be seen as part of the overall imperial policy. For example, the author asserts that the prohibition against intermarriage instituted by both these men was not peculiar to their religious sensibilities as Jews; rather, the edict was ordered by the emperor and served the imperial purpose. Hoglund agrees with Blenkinsopp that Ezra's mission was comparable to Udjahorresnet's, and he proposes that both the transformation of the legal system and the imperial funding of scribal institutions in Egypt demonstrate how the empire established control over subject territories through laws and records. He further contends that Nehemiah's assignments to build the city's wall and the *birah,* or citadel, served imperial objectives. The *birah* was manned by imperial troops and located adjacent to the Temple. Its purpose was not only to protect a vulnerable portion of the city from outside attack but also to concentrate an imperial force where it would be most noticed by the city's inhabitants.

In his monograph, GRABBE presents a far more skeptical view of the historical authenticity of both Ezra and Nehemiah than previous writers have suggested. He does not view Ezra as a historical figure, and he argues that the rescript of Artaxerxes employs more recent forms of the Aramaic language than would be in evidence if it were a genuine source. He also charges that the huge sums of money that Ezra supposedly brought from Persia are preposterous; ridicules the story that Ezra did not request a guard as far-fetched; and asserts that the claim that Ezra had to resort to tearing his hair to enforce his legislation belies the fact a man in his position would have the power to appoint magistrates. According to Grabbe, Nehemiah was paranoid and the opposition to him was all in his head. Grabbe's nontraditional work certainly bears consideration.

The important book edited by DAVIES includes 11 sociopolitical essays about the books of Ezra and Nehemiah. Arguing that "Israel" is the subject, but not the author, of these books (since he views Israel as a literary construction rather than a historical phenomenon), Davies instructed each contributor to search the biblical text for evidence about the individuals and society that produced the works, as well as the audiences and the purposes of the literature. Each of the essayists succeeds in taking this approach to the text. In their contributions, Joseph Blenkinsopp and Richard Horsley argue that the Achaemenids (Persians) supported temples because temples were wealthy institutions with landholdings, work forces, capital, and the corresponding ability to function as banks. Furthermore, the temples' priesthoods, under the supervision of imperial officers, ensured that tribute went to the empire. Peter Ross Bedford cautions against comparing the Jerusalem Temple to other temples in the Persian empire, arguing that it was different because it did not own land and could not have acted as a bank. He does not offer data to support this claim, however. Kenneth Hoglund, using archaeological data, argues that not all of the Jews returning from Babylon went back to their original landholdings; instead, the number of settlements in Judea exceeded the number found prior to the exile. According to Hoglund, this fact implies that the empire instituted a policy of rural development in Judea in order to increase the flow of agricultural goods to the central government. He does not discuss, however, why the number of settlements in Samaria should have decreased under such an agricultural policy. Daniel L. Smith uses a comparative approach to suggest that the Israelite exiles in Babylon created a separate community with an independent ethos, occupied with self-preservation. In an original study, John M. Halligan contends that if the economy had deteriorated to the point described in Nehemiah 5:1–5, then it could not have been restored by forgiving debt and returning all forms of security, for the removal of the credit system would jeopardize all dependent commercial transactions and cause commerce to come to a standstill. Despite the apparent success of the essayists in fulfilling the assignment given to them by Davies, David Jobling complains in the closing essay that these articles do not demonstrate that a gap existed between the real world of the Second Temple and the representation of that era in the biblical texts.

LISBETH S. FRIED

F

Faith

Bergman, Samuel Hugo, *Faith and Reason: An Introduction to Modern Jewish Thought* (Hillel Little Books, vol. 5), translated and edited by Alfred Jospe, Washington: B'nai B'rith Hillel Foundation, 1961

Bleich, J. David (editor and translator), *With Perfect Faith: The Foundations of Jewish Belief*, New York: Ktav, 1983

Borowitz, Eugene B., *How Can a Jew Speak of Faith Today?*, Philadelphia: Westminster, 1969

Buber, Martin, *Zwei Glaubensweisen*, 1950; translated by Norman P. Goldhawk as *Two Types of Faith*, New York: Macmillan, and London: Routledge and Kegan Paul, 1951

Gurary, Natan, *The Thirteen Principles of Faith: A Chasidic Viewpoint*, edited by Moshe Miller, Northvale, New Jersey: Aronson, 1996

Jacobs, Louis, *Principles of the Jewish Faith: An Analytical Study*, New York: Basic Books, and London: Vallentine, Mitchell, 1964

Jacobs, Louis, *Faith*, New York: Basic Books, and London: Vallentine, Mitchell, 1968

Lamm, Norman, *Faith and Doubt: Studies in Traditional Jewish Thought*, New York: Ktav, 1971, 2nd edition, 1986

Scholars often define Judaism as featuring an "orthoprax" rather than an "orthodox" tradition, meaning that action defines Jewish obligations rather than belief. From at least the time of Philo of Alexandria in the Hellenistic period, however, Jewish thinkers have struggled with the faith that animates religious practice. Sometimes this concern has sought to understand the basic creeds or fundamental principles of Jewish belief; at other times the inner substance of religious sentiment is emphasized. Perhaps the most influential classical statement on Jewish faith was that of Moses Maimonides. In his commentary on the Mishnah, he enumerates 13 basic articles of faith that Jews must believe, and scholarship on Jewish faith often takes these as its point of departure.

BUBER introduces a classic distinction between what he thinks of as Judaic "faith" (trust in and reliance on God alone) and Hellenistic "belief" (acceptance of a particular doctrine). He argues that earliest Christianity continued the biblical tradition of faith as reliance upon the deity. He identifies Jesus' religious perspective with that of the Hebrew prophets and later Judaism. It was Paul, Buber contends, who introduced the nonbiblical idea of faith as belief or acceptance of a set of dogmas. Many contemporary scholars criticize this overly stark dichotomy. The distinction between Jewish and Christian faith is misleading and misrepresents the variety in both traditions.

JACOBS (1968) explores the dimensions of faith as a religious impulse. This book approaches the subject with sophistication, recognizing the modern debate over faith and the attacks on it from Marxist and Freudian analysis. Jewish faith is explained against the backdrop of key thinkers on religion such as Søren Kierkegaard and William James, as well as modern skepticism. Using copious examples from Jewish philosophers such as Maimonides, mystics such as Polish hasidim, and both biblical and rabbinic sources, the book explains how Jews have understood faith as a type of trust and as a basis for action and explores the relationship of faith to reason.

JACOBS (1964) takes a more historical approach. The book is organized around Maimonides' 13 articles of faith. Jewish philosophers such as Saadia, Maimonides, and Judah Halevi are discussed in connection with each article of this creed. The book's development, however, is more general than strictly philosophical. Discussion of philosophical faith is augmented with explanations of how Jewish mystics argue for faith from experience rather than from logic. Each chapter also takes up modern challenges to Jewish belief: Paul Tillich, Friedrich Nietzsche, Immanuel Kant, Ludwig Feuerbach, and modern biblical criticism figure in these discussions. Jacobs clearly seeks to defend these principles and establish their tenability for modern Jews based on the arguments developed in the past.

BLEICH provides translations of the major Jewish thinkers discussed by Jacobs. Like Jacobs, he organizes his work according to the 13 articles of faith of Maimonides. The book begins with a general discussion on articles of belief, including formulations not only by Maimonides but also by Joseph Albo and Isaac Abravanel. Bleich juxtaposes texts that often do not agree with one another or, at least, take different perspectives on the same article of faith. He shows that Jewish thinkers shared certain common themes or central concepts but also that they did not always present them in the same way. Students without knowledge of Hebrew will find these translations a useful guide to debates about faith within Jewish medieval thought.

GURARY retains the structural framework of the Maimonidean principles of faith, but these become a springboard from which he launches into a discussion of hasidic mystical belief. The book mixes reflections on classic texts from rabbinic literature, medieval writings, 18th- and 19th-century hasidic writings, and modern concerns. The author has a devotional and practical purpose in mind. His book seeks to evoke a response of faith from its intended audience. It goes beyond expository description to defend and advocate the faith it expounds. Some readers may be inconvenienced by the continual use of Hebrew terms, the meaning of which the author makes no attempt to explain.

LAMM offers a variety of perspectives from which to understand Jewish faith. The book begins with a theoretical reflection on the place of faith and doubt in Judaism. It suggests two major ways Judaism has responded to doubt—either with the advocacy of unquestioning trust and acceptance or with rationalistic argument. Lamm explicitly rejects Buber's view of two types of faith and substitutes a threefold category of cognitive, affective, and functional faith. The various studies included in this anthology of essays fall under one or another of these categories. Several essays focus on ethics, or functional faith, examining the moral revolution, ecology, and privacy in Jewish law and theology. Other essays examine cognitive issues such as the meaning of "synthesis," or the validity of Jewish monism, or the position of the human being in the cosmos. Affective faith receives treatment in an essay on scholarship and piety, which touches upon themes that Lamm examines in great detail in other works, themes associated with the Musar movement in Judaism.

The tension between faith and reason, between affective and cognitive faith, upon which Lamm touches, provides the unifying theme for BERGMAN. Modern Jewish thought, this book argues, moves between the poles of affective Judaic faith represented by thinkers such as Buber (but also Franz Rosenzweig and Abraham Isaac Kook) and cognitive faith defended by Hermann Cohen, A.D. Gordon, and Judah L. Magnes. The former group responds to modernity by deepening the affective elements in Judaism. The latter seek to strengthen arguments for Judaism's continuing validity. Zionists such as Gordon and Magnes confronted science as a challenge to religion and developed a rational faith despite the realities of modernity.

BOROWITZ focuses on the challenges of faith confronting modern liberal American Jews. The book raises questions about faith after the Holocaust, the meaning of revelation in a secular world, the viability of faith in the university, and the necessity for cooperation between all besieged communities of faith—in particular between Jews and Christians. Borowitz offers nontechnical discussions that are generally more accessible to the uninitiated reader than the other writings here discussed.

S. DANIEL BRESLAUER

Family

Bayme, Steven and Gladys Rosen (editors), *The Jewish Family and Jewish Continuity*, Hoboken, New Jersey: Ktav, 1994

Bermant, Chaim, *The Walled Garden: The Saga of Jewish Family Life and Tradition*, London: Weidenfeld and Nicolson, 1974; New York: Macmillan, 1975
Cohen, Shaye J.D. (editor), *The Jewish Family in Antiquity* (Brown Judaic Studies, no. 289), Atlanta, Georgia: Scholars Press, 1993
Cohen, Steven M. and Paula Hyman (editors), *The Jewish Family: Myths and Reality*, New York: Holmes and Meier, 1986
Fishman, Sylvia Barack, *A Breath of Life: Feminism in the American Jewish Community*, New York: Free Press, 1993
Hoobler, Dorothy, *The Jewish American Family Album*, New York: Oxford University Press, 1995
Kraemer, David (editor), *The Jewish Family: Metaphor and Memory*, New York: Oxford University Press, 1989
Linzer, Norman, Irving N. Levitz, and David J. Schnall (editors), *Crisis and Continuity: The Jewish Family in the 21st Century*, Hoboken, New Jersey: Ktav, 1995
Perdue, Leo G. and Carol Meyers (editors), *Families in Ancient Israel* (Family, Religion, and Culture), Louisville, Kentucky: Westminster/Knox, 1997

The family has been the central institution in all Jewish societies, and its particular structures, transformations, and tensions in various eras of the Jewish past are of increasing interest to historians and literary critics. Moreover, the Jewish family is also of significant contemporary concern to social scientists and communal leaders because its ability to withstand and adapt to the pressures and challenges of the present will determine Jewish survival in the future.

BERMANT provides a beautifully illustrated survey of the Jewish family through the ages intended for the general reader; the book's title, *The Walled Garden*, evokes the metaphor of the family as an enclosed and secure space but also raises the specter of the Jewish family's breakdown and collapse as a result of modern social change. Bermant believes the survival of the family is essential to the endurance of Judaism because the two are inextricably linked through faith and ceremony. His accessible text concentrates on the traditional roles of various family members and the rituals that have bound families together throughout Jewish history.

The books by Perdue and Meyers and by Cohen are both scholarly collections investigating the Jewish family in particular eras. PERDUE and MEYERS's volume contains essays by well-known scholars of the Hebrew Bible that discuss the family and family formation in early Israel, in the First Temple period (tenth to sixth century B.C.E.), and in the time of the Second Temple (fifth century B.C.E. to first century C.E.). A final chapter by Perdue draws theological and ethical implications from the biblical context for the family today.

The essays in COHEN's anthology concentrate on the Jewish family in late antiquity (first to sixth century C.E.) as portrayed in rabbinic texts, material culture, and in the Greek writings of the Hellenistic Jewish diaspora. Topics considered include parents and children in several different Jewish contexts—including a discussion of Jewish mothers and daughters in the Greco-Roman world, an examination of slavery in the ancient Jewish family, and a comparative study of Greek families in the same time period.

COHEN and HYMAN have collected well-documented essays that break ground in the scholarly study of the Jewish family. Chapters in the first part of the volume include studies of traditional Jewish family life in Eastern Europe and in North Africa; discussions of the family's transition to modernity both in Germany and during the Eastern European Jewish Enlightenment, and also as a result of emigration from Morocco to Israel; and images of the family and family members in various Jewish literary traditions. The volume's second half delineates a variety of contemporary Jewish families in Israel, Europe, and North America from various demographic and social science perspectives. A final chapter by Cohen evaluates "Vitality and Resilience in the American Jewish Family." As Hyman observes in her afterword, these essays demonstrate how family history can enrich understanding of the critical phenomena of modern Jewish history such as acculturation, Jewish identity, and social mobility.

KRAEMER's anthology offers a wide range of historical and literary studies of the Jewish family in both Muslim and Christian societies. While Cohen and Hyman arrange their volume chronologically, this collection is organized thematically around marriage, childhood, and adolescence; family and community; and the family as metaphor. The anthology's special contribution lies in its broad coverage of the rabbinic, medieval, and early modern periods, including a study of marital imagery in Jewish mysticism.

HOOBLER's compilation of personal stories of Jewish immigration to North America from the 18th century to the present is intended for young people and general readers. This well-illustrated collage of letters, diaries, newspaper articles, family photographs, and interviews provides a detailed and engaging picture of the adjustment of the immigrant family to the new realities of American society.

Most observers would agree that the contemporary Jewish family is facing hitherto unimagined and often conflicting demands. With the disappearance of the extended family, women's rapidly changing social roles, the rising divorce rate, and increasing societal tolerance of alternative life styles, traditional assumptions that Jewish families consist of child-rearing households led by a father and an at-home mother are no longer valid. The volumes edited by Bayme and Rosen and by Linzer, Levitz, and Schnall gather essays by social scientists and social-policy theorists assessing the state of the contemporary U.S. Jewish family in an era of such challenges as increasing intermarriage, advanced age of marriage, and a lower Jewish birthrate. Chapters in BAYME and ROSEN discuss adoption, abortion, and pornography; offer analyses of these phenomena; and prescribe policy measures that intend to support and preserve Jewish family structures.

LINZER, LEVITZ, and SCHNALL collect thoroughly referenced papers by clinicians and scholars from the Wurzweiler School of Social Work of Yeshiva University. The contributors argue that contemporary Jewish families are being undermined by an increasing acceptance of secular values, promoting individualism and pluralism and discouraging community connections. Essays address the impact of domestic violence, divorce, women's changing roles, the attractions of assimilation, the stresses of mid-life, and the challenges for families of caring for elderly parents, and the authors suggest some new approaches for dealing with these concerns. The authors are united by their commitment to the Jewish family as the ultimate guarantor of Jewish survival even as they caution against over-romanticizing Jewish families of the past.

FISHMAN examines the impact of two decades of feminism on the Jewish family in the United States, contending that the feminist movement has been a source of great moral vigor and religious renewal. However, she finds that Jewish women, encouraged to pursue higher education and career possibilities, are marrying outside their faith community more than ever before. Endogamous marriages, too, are taking place later than ever, and these delayed marriages are leading to a pattern of fewer children and an increase in infertility problems. Women's participation in the paid work force, often out of economic necessity, also impacts family planning decisions and Jewish communal involvement. In order to ensure Jewish continuity, Fishman argues that the U.S. Jewish community must recognize the implications of these social changes and respond in ways that are supportive of the contemporary needs of all Jewish families, including those who may be marginalized because of poverty, single parenthood, or parental lifestyle choices.

JUDITH R. BASKIN

Fasts *see* Festivals and Fasts

Feinstein, Moses 1895–1986

Russian-born American rabbi, decisor of Jewish law, and yeshivah principal

Eidensohn, Daniel (compiler), *Yad Moshe: Index to the Igros Moshe of Rav Moshe Feinstein*, Brooklyn, New York: Eidensohn, 1987

Feinstein, Moses, *Responsa of Rav Moshe Feinstein: Translation and Commentary*, vol. 1: *Care of the Critically Ill*, translated by Moshe Dovid Tendler, Hoboken, New Jersey: Ktav, 1996

Finkel, Avraham Yaakov, *The Responsa Anthology*, Northvale, New Jersey: Aronson, 1990

Finkelman, Shimon with Nosson Scherman, *Reb Moshe: The Life and Ideals of HaGaon Rabbi Moshe Feinstein* (ArtScroll History Series), Brooklyn, New York: Mesorah, 1986

Joseph, Norma Baumel, "Mehitza: Halakhic Decisions and Political Consequences," in *Daughters of the King: Women and the Synagogue: A Survey of History, Halakhah, and Contemporary Realities*, edited by Susan Grossman and Rivka Haut, Philadelphia: Jewish Publication Society, 1992

Joseph, Norma Baumel, "Jewish Education for Women: Rabbi Moshe Feinstein's Map of America," *American Jewish History*, special issue edited by Pamela Nadell, 1995

Joseph, Norma Baumel, "Separate Spheres: Women in the Responsa of Rabbi Moses Feinstein," Ph.D. diss., Concordia University, 1995

Joseph, Norma Baumel, "Hair Distractions: Women and Worship in the Responsa of Rabbi Moshe Feinstein," in *Jewish Legal Writings by Women,* edited by Micah Halpern and Chana Safrai, Jerusalem: Urim, 1998

Rosner, Fred (editor), *Medicine and Jewish Law,* vol. 2, Northvale, New Jersey: Aronson, 1990

There is a remarkable dearth of material about the work and impact of Rabbi Moses Feinstein, acknowledged by many as one of the greatest Jewish jurists and yeshivah educators of the 20th century. There have been a number of significant articles about his influence on specific topics but few books devoted to him. Nonetheless, in discussions of complex and contentious contemporary Jewish legal issues, his work is always cited. Born and trained in Russia, Rabbi Feinstein worked as head of a New York yeshivah, Mesivtha Tifereth Jerusalem. There he taught many generations of male students but achieved prominence through his collection of responsa. Thousands of his responses to individuals' questions on problems in Jewish law are collected in his eight-volume *Iggerot Moshe,* published in Hebrew between 1959 and 1996, the last volume posthumously. In accordance with his wishes, there has never been a comprehensive English translation of his work. Rabbi Feinstein also authored a series of talmudic interpretive texts known as *Dibrot Moshe.* These were published from 1947 to 1979. A volume of his sermons and original insights, *Darash Moshe,* was published posthumously by his family in 1988. Parts were translated into English in a book by the same title published in 1994.

FINKEL includes Rabbi Feinstein among the great authors of legal decisions from the sixth to the 20th century. Finkel's purpose is to reveal the breadth and depth of Jewish law and history. After a brief biographical sketch, Finkel presents his abridgement of seven of Rabbi Feinstein's decisions. From the seemingly trivial question of whether one can use paper cups for kiddush to the graver matter of heart transplants, the range presents a fair glance at the scope of Rabbi Feinstein's expertise. It does not, however, expose the reader to the complexity of the answers or to the brilliance of his reasoning and there is no accompanying analysis.

JOSEPH (1992, 1995a, 1995b, 1998) has explored Rabbi Feinstein's unique perspective on topics such as *mehitsah*, educating girls, hair as a distraction, and women's ritual involvement. The essays analyze Rabbi Feinstein's halakhic premises and methodologies, demonstrating some of his key concerns and identifying his influential role in the Jewish world. Joseph's doctoral dissertation investigates Rabbi Feinstein's approach to gender in constructing separate spheres. The analysis demonstrates that he had a particular conception of and contribution to Jewish life in the United States. His attitude toward rabbinic authority and halakhic change is also developed.

FINKELMAN wrote the only book-length biography of Rabbi Feinstein. This volume, written immediately after his death, was promoted as the official account by the Mesivtha Tifereth Jerusalem and the Yeshivah of Staten Island. The book is a sincere hagiography, filled with material gleaned from interviews with family, friends, and students. The stories told are filled with wonder and admiration. It is not an assessment of Rabbi Feinstein's teachings or legal decisions but rather is an appreciation of his moral character and devotion to the com-munity. He is presented as a saint, larger than life. Easy to read, Finkelman's book contains little commentary and is not an intellectual biography, but the stories do illuminate parts of his life and display the high regard in which he was held.

EIDENSOHN compiled a general index to *Iggerot Moshe* in both English and Hebrew. This book provides a quick search method, but there is neither an abstract of the discussions nor any indication of the decision rendered and the author insists that it is not to be used as an aid to personal halakhic decision-making.

ROSNER contains the proceedings of a conference on medicine and halakhah held in 1990. It is dedicated to the memory of Rabbi Feinstein, who was the *posek* (decisor) for the Association of Orthodox Jewish Scientists. The book includes two relevant essays. "Rabbi Moshe Feinstein's Influence on Medical Halachah," written by Rosner, is an appreciation of Rabbi Feinstein's decisions on medical issues. It is not a critical essay about those decisions and there is no background information. Rather, it summarizes decisions on a variety of medical issues ranging from contraception to dentistry, as well as sabbath rules for the doctor and for the patient. "Special Tribute to Rav Moshe Feinstein," written by his son-in-law Rabbi Moshe Tendler, explores the impact of several of these decisions. He cites some of the most momentous opinions in marital and medical matters and indicates the reasons for their great influence. This short essay is clear, reliable and informative.

The publication of FEINSTEIN is the first in a projected series. This volume is concerned with the care of the critically ill, focusing on Rabbi Feinstein's decisions about medical confirmation of time of death and organ transplants. The book begins with an important biographical essay presenting facts previously unknown, especially about his years in Russia. A major portion of the book is devoted to Rabbi Moshe Tendler's translation of key responsa from *Iggerot Moshe.* In order to clarify these difficult texts, Tendler analyzes the relevant talmudic sources. He also paraphrases and explains some of Rabbi Feinstein's meaning and methods. This volume attempts to define the issues while promoting Rabbi Feinstein's approval of organ donations. Aside from being very persuasive, Tendler displays his exceptional grasp of these decisions, their importance and impact. The concluding essay, coauthored by Fred Rosner, offers a succinct synopsis of Judaic sources on sanctity-of-life questions. The Hebrew texts of Rabbi Feinstein's responsa are included. It should be noted that J. David Bleich has written *Time of Death in Jewish Law* (1991), in which he also relies on Rabbi Feinstein, among others, to dispute use of brain death criteria as advocated by Tendler in this book.

NORMA BAUMEL JOSEPH

Feminism

Adler, Rachel, *Engendering Judaism: An Inclusive Theology and Ethics,* Philadelphia: Jewish Publication Society, 1998

Baskin, Judith (editor), *Jewish Women in Historical Perspective,* Detroit, Michigan: Wayne State University Press, 1991, 2nd edition, 1999

Baskin, Judith (editor), *Women of the Word: Jewish Women and Jewish Writing*, Detroit, Michigan: Wayne State University Press, 1994

Biale, Rachel, *Women and Jewish Law: An Exploration of Women's Issues in Halakhic Sources*, New York: Schocken, 1984; as *Women and Jewish Law: The Essential Texts, Their History, and Their Relevance for Today*, New York: Schocken, 1995

Cantor, Aviva, *Jewish Women/Jewish Men: The Legacy of Patriarchy in Jewish Life*, San Francisco: HarperSanFrancisco, 1995

Davidman, Lynn and Shelly Tenenbaum (editors), *Feminist Perspectives on Jewish Studies*, New Haven, Connecticut: Yale University Press, 1994

Fishman, Sylvia Barack, *A Breath of Life: Feminism in the American Jewish Community*, New York: Free Press, 1993

Greenberg, Blu, *On Women and Judaism: A View from Tradition*, Philadelphia: Jewish Publication Society, 1981

Hauptman, Judith, *Rereading the Rabbis: A Woman's Voice*, Boulder, Colorado: Westview, 1997; Oxford: Westview, 1998

Heschel, Susannah (editor), *On Being a Jewish Feminist: A Reader*, New York: Schocken, 1983

Koltun, Elizabeth, *The Jewish Woman: New Perspectives*, New York: Schocken, 1976

Levitt, Laura, *Jews and Feminism: The Ambivalent Search for Home*, New York: Routledge, 1997

Peskowitz, Miriam, *Spinning Fantasies: Rabbis, Gender, and History*, Berkeley and London: University of California Press, 1997

Peskowitz, Miriam and Laura Levitt (editors), *Judaism since Gender*, New York: Routledge, 1997

Plaskow, Judith, *Standing Again at Sinai: Judaism from a Feminist Perspective*, San Francisco: Harper and Row, 1990

Rudavsky, T.M. (editor), *Gender and Judaism: The Transformation of Tradition*, New York: New York University Press, 1995

Approaches to Jewish feminism have developed and evolved primarily since the 1970s. Early work in the field criticized what were seen as the patriarchal aspects of Jewish tradition, texts, and history because they accord a lower status to women than to men. Many early studies also sought to reform contemporary Jewish practices and to restore women's voices by recovering stories by and about Jewish women from the past. Later, Jewish feminist writing discovered additional ways of describing the experiences and cultures of Jewish women, both past and present, positing alternative histories alongside the available male-centered and male-authored studies. Some feminist scholars argue for gender equivalence in Jewish practice, while others advocate recognizing and honoring the difference of women's experiences. As feminist studies spawned the field of gender studies, scholars asked how incorporating women's perspectives, texts, and histories could reshape knowledge generally. In addition, they began to examine the nature of gender identity within the context of Jewish culture. Rather than regarding women's experiences as deviations from the normative male experience, scholars interpreted the construction and contexts of Jewish genders.

Among the earliest works of Jewish feminism, HESCHEL explores the implications of woman as "Other" in Judaism. The essays included here are by scholars and writers in diverse fields such as theology, history, literature, Bible studies, philosophy, and literature, and they approach their subject primarily from the standpoint of progressive Judaism. In different ways, the essays draw out the implications of the marginalization of women's perspectives, concerns, and voices in traditional Jewish texts written by men. Taken together, the collection reveals the extent of the conflict between Judaism and feminism, and it suggests some ways toward resolution through re-envisioning Jewish thought and practice.

The essays collected in KOLTUN, another early volume, offer an interdisciplinary snapshot of the beginnings of Jewish feminism in the United States. The book includes new rituals to mark events in Jewish women's lives, as well as assessments of the status of women in Jewish life and Jewish law, historical sketches of Jewish women and their significance, feminist readings of both traditional Jewish texts and contemporary writing, and explorations in feminist theology.

Several studies focus closely on the specific details of Jewish law as they relate to Jewish women. Writing from the perspective of an Orthodox feminist, GREENBERG brings feminism and traditional Judaism to bear on one another. Arguing that Jewish law evolves slowly over time, the book contemplates how and to what extent Judaism can absorb and respond to feminist critiques, particularly in education, liturgy, and areas of Jewish law that pertain to women, such as divorce. Rejecting the view that feminism is external and antithetical to Judaism and therefore poses a threat to Jewish survival and authenticity, the book asserts that feminism need not be incompatible with traditional Jewish values and practices. Greenberg insists on keeping as much of the tradition intact as possible, incorporating feminist concerns into the existing structures.

Advocating more strongly than Greenberg for reform of Jewish practice, BIALE offers an interpretive history of Jewish law as it pertains to women. Combining selections from classical Jewish legal sources, including the Bible, Talmud, and medieval codes, with an extensive commentary and explication, the book sees Jewish law as an evolving process which can and should respond to the challenge of contemporary Jewish feminism by absorbing feminist suggestions. Topics include marriage, divorce, sexuality, rape, abortion, and participation in Jewish ritual life.

In a sustained, detailed feminist reading of the treatment of women in the Talmud, HAUPTMAN demonstrates that the rabbis were attentive to the needs of women despite the patriarchal nature of society reflected both in the Bible and the Talmud. Focusing primarily on the Talmud's treatment of marriage, adultery, divorce, procreation, rape, and laws of inheritance and testimony, Hauptman traces significant changes in important aspects of Jewish law, which were enacted to accord women broader rights and higher status. Hauptman notes, for example, the gradual evolution of the institution of marriage from one of acquisition, in which a man purchased a woman from her father, into a relationship negotiated between the man and the woman herself.

In contrast, PESKOWITZ argues that rabbinic Judaism effaces and disempowers women, even when it strives to protect women's interests and raise their status. Integrating archaeological sources and contemporaneous writing into her interpretation of early rabbinic texts, Peskowitz exposes assumptions about gender in the development of rabbinic Judaism. By analyzing stories about the ordinary work of spinners and weavers, the book examines the construction of gender that becomes interwoven with and inherent in Judaism.

From a theological perspective, PLASKOW similarly critiques Judaism as a patriarchal tradition that has acknowledged the presence and Jewishness of women only with deep ambivalence. The book explores how Jewish ideas about God, Torah, justice, and Jewish communal values can be transformed through the active participation of contemporary Jewish feminists already working to reshape the tradition. Plaskow's analysis draws upon traditional Jewish texts as well as contemporary religious philosophers and feminist theologians and thinkers.

ADLER argues that contemporary Jewish communities that value the full and equal participation of women in all aspects of life "engender" Judaism in two senses. First, they shape the tradition they inherit. Second, they infuse Judaism with new practices and an understanding of the role of gender in Jewish law, learning, and practice. Retaining a connection with the ethical foundations of Jewish law and a knowledge of classical texts, Adler advocates a transformation of liturgy and of sexual relations and marriage. The book concludes with the development of a new wedding ceremony founded on a *Berit 'Ahuvim*, or Covenant for Lovers, which asserts a commitment to a relationship of equal partners and rejects the model of acquisition that defines the traditional Jewish wedding.

In contrast to Adler's formulation of a *Berit 'Ahuvim* to equalize the power relations in a Jewish wedding, LEVITT argues that the very basis for such contractual relationships rests on the inequality of the parties. While many of the earlier works on Jewish feminism center on exposing the patriarchal aspects of Jewish institutions and texts and advocate gender equality in Judaism commensurate with the values and sensibilities of contemporary liberal democracies, Levitt insists that the liberal state has not offered a secure home for Jewish women either as Jews or as women. The book traces the concept of the social contract as it affects Jews, and it analyzes the significance of marriage in the conception of Jews as citizens of the West.

Investigating the social and cultural history of Jewish women, scholars of the Jewish past in BASKIN (1991) apply gender as a category of analysis. They probe such issues as women's socioeconomic status, their relationship to Jewish law and Judaism, their responses to persecution, and domestic arrangements such as marriage, divorce, motherhood, widowhood, and inheritance. Arranged chronologically from biblical times to the 20th-century United States, the collected essays point to the limited opportunities for women in the realms of education, political power, and access to the public arena, as well as women's roles in the shaping, preservation, and transmission of Jewish identity.

From a sociological perspective, FISHMAN argues that feminism and the activism of Jewish women in the religious arena have revitalized Jewish life in the United States. Looking at women's participation in different facets of Jewish American life, Fishman points to the flourishing of new life-cycle rituals to mark the events in women's lives and to the burgeoning number of women in the rabbinate since the first Reform ordination in 1972.

CANTOR offers a broad-based analysis of the imprint of patriarchal values on Judaism and Jewish life and culture. The book is particularly interesting for its exploration of the ways in which internalized antisemitism fuels such modern stereotypes as the Jewish mother, affecting relationships between Jewish men and women and between generations.

A number of studies examine the impact of feminism on the academic study of Judaism. The first full-length work to examine the progress and influence of feminist scholarship within the many academic fields that constitute Jewish studies, the anthology edited by DAVIDMAN and TENENBAUM includes essays by feminist critics and scholars in a variety of disciplines, such as classical Judaism, film, literature, sociology, and history. The essays debate the patriarchal nature of Judaism, the status of women in Jewish law and Jewish communities, and the differences between the historical experiences of Jewish men and women.

Written by literary scholars, the essays in BASKIN (1994) explore the voices and experiences of Jewish women in a variety of cultures and languages from the Middle Ages to the present. Several of the essays focus on individual writers, while others explore the image of women in different literary contexts, such as medieval Hebrew or Yiddish literature, and broad themes such as women in the Holocaust and feminism in Israeli writing.

RUDAVSKY expands the scope of Jewish feminism. Building on earlier works that critique the silencing of women and the pervasiveness of patriarchal values in Judaism, the essays by scholars in a wide range of fields analyze the effects of modernity on Jewish women and men. Looking at historical and literary sources and evidence from popular culture, the essays explore what it means to think of oneself as a Jewish man or a Jewish woman.

PESKOWITZ and LEVITT acknowledge the pervasiveness of feminist and gender theory in contemporary Jewish studies. In the essays collected here, feminist critics and scholars in a variety of disciplines discuss the influence of feminism on the way they approach and think through Jewish academic work as well as the connections between their work and life. These essays implicitly debate the direction of feminism and gender studies and a variety of conflicts between feminism and Judaism, Jewish texts, practices, and identity. The volume examines the marginal, and potentially radical, position that both Jewish studies and feminist studies occupy in academic disciplines as well as the way each field has reshaped knowledge across disciplines.

Sara R. Horowitz

See also Women: Status

Fertility *see* Reproductive Technologies

Festivals and Fasts

Agnon, Shmuel Yosef, *Days of Awe,* New York: Schocken, 1946

Bloch, Abraham P., *The Biblical and Historical Background of Jewish Customs and Ceremonies,* New York: Ktav, 1980

Greenberg, Blu, *How to Run a Traditional Jewish Household,* New York: Simon and Schuster, 1983

Greenberg, Irving, *The Jewish Way: Living the Holidays,* New York: Summit, 1988

Heschel, Abraham Joshua, *The Sabbath: Its Meaning for Modern Man,* New York: Farrar, Straus, and Young, 1951

Ki Tov, Eliyahu, *Sefer ha-toda'ah,* 1958; translated as *The Book of Our Heritage: The Jewish Year and Its Days of Significance,* 3 vols., New York: "A" Publishers, 1968; adapted and expanded edition, New York: Feldheim, 1997

Knobel, Peter (editor), *Gates of the Seasons: A Guide to the Jewish Year,* New York: Central Conference of American Rabbis, 1983

Laskin, Martin, "Secular Holidays in Modern Israel: The Move toward Traditional Beliefs, Symbols and Rituals," *Conservative Judaism,* 46, Fall 1993

Vainstein, Yaacov, *The Cycle of the Jewish Year: A Study of the Festivals and of Selections from the Liturgy,* New York: Bloch, 1953; 2nd edition, Jerusalem: Department for Torah and Culture in the Diaspora, World Zionist Organization, 1964

Waskow, Arthur, *Seasons of Our Joy: A Handbook of Jewish Festivals,* New York: Bantam, 1982

All regular Jewish feasts and fasts are based on a 354-day lunar calendar year, adjusted from time to time to coincide with the seasons of the solar calendar year by means of a leap year of 13 months. More significant than the innovation of new festivals has been the imposition of new meanings, nowadays sometimes avowedly secular, on ancient holy days.

HESCHEL always expounds on his guiding axiom, "Judaism is a minimum of revelation and a maximum of interpretation." Working within a traditional framework, Heschel notes that all major world religions emphasize sacred spaces (e.g., religious sites, holy shrines, and temples). Judaism, however, focuses on sanctification of time in a unique manner. Heschel deals specifically with the sabbath as the point at which Jews usually either break from tradition or rejoin Judaism. For Heschel, Jews find definition in keeping the sabbath.

KI TOV expands Heschel's principle of sacred time by addressing the fasts and feasts of Jewish tradition throughout the cycle of the Jewish calendar. For Ki Tov, sacred time occurs again and again throughout the entire Jewish year, not just for a single day of the week. His work explains why Jewish feasts and fasts change their solar calendrical dates every year, and he also explains that the lunar calendar adds an extra month seven different times to its 19-year cycle to ensure seasonal continuity. Of the texts reviewed in this essay, Ki Tov most effectively presents the feasts and fasts, discussing how each

of them is observed according to tradition. A compendium of "insights and reasons, meanings, and allusions" addresses questions commonly asked about each holiday through comments drawn from midrashic sources and subsequent rabbinic authorities.

WASKOW also focuses on "holy time" and its spiritual meaning, hidden beneath the layers of traditional development. Waskow's interpretations sometimes seem as mythical as the traditions that he "demythologizes" by excluding them from discussion. Unfortunately, due to the vague references made to primary sources or the complete absence of any references whatsoever, the reader seldom knows whether Waskow is drawing from the deep wells of heritage or whether he is plumbing the depths of his own spirituality. Waskow does, however, include a bibliography after his discussion of each topic.

For the reader who wishes to know how to celebrate the festivals, Blu GREENBERG addresses the practical as well as spiritual dimensions of Jewish festive and holy days. Unlike Heschel and Ki Tov, Greenberg does not concern herself with the philosophical dimension, but her volume is one of the most useful texts for those seeking to put basic tradition into practice. Like Waskow, Greenberg encourages readers to consider the feasts and fasts in a hands-on manner. Both authors include recipes (and prayers in Hebrew, English transliteration, and English translation [in Greenberg only]) for each celebration. Greenberg provides a glossary and selected bibliography at the book's end.

BLOCH attemps to establish wherever possible the date of origin of elements of the feasts and fasts before tracing their development through the centuries. Bloch demonstrates how traditional interpretation and practice have changed in light of certain historical moments, including the emergence of the synagogue, the experience of exile, the encounter with Christianity and Islam, the Crusades, changing socioeconomic factors, the Holocaust, and the rebirth of Israel.

KNOBEL reflects Reform tenets pertaining to observance of the Jewish holidays, excluding the "second day" of diaspora observance as unnecessary and abandoning any traditional notion, in rabbinic or folk custom, of "unlucky days."

While somewhat pedantic at times, both Irving GREENBERG and VAINSTEIN offer most thorough treatments of the festivals from intellectual and liturgical perspectives, respectively. The reader is able to explore midrashic, talmudic, and other rabbinic discussions of the festivals and holy days by pursuing the meticulous citations provided by each author.

LASKIN describes how secular Israelis, many of whom had ceased to identify either with Judaism or even as Jews, are returning to the calendrical observance of a Jewish tradition whose symbols they find to be charged with meaning. Such renewed practice elicits beliefs that contradict the secular values of these modern Israelis and sometimes also the meanings ascribed to these practices by religious Jews.

AGNON's treatment of the High Holidays provides purple passages from nearly 300 ancient and modern sources, spanning more than 2,000 years of Jewish tradition. Outdoing Block and Weinstein's works in bibliographic eclecticism, Agnon regularly draws attention in his own critical commentary to what he terms "heathenish practices" contained within tradition.

Every author emphasizes the precedence of the sabbath over other holidays, and each offers an appreciation of the ancient year cycle, with its weekly, monthly, and annual rhythms. Ki Tov, Blu Greenberg, Irving Greenberg, Bloch, Vainstein, and Waskow also discuss postbiblical feasts and fasts.

DENNIS STOUTENBURG

See also Passover; Sukkot

Film

Berlin, Charles (editor), *Jewish Film and Jewish Studies*, Cambridge, Massachusetts: Harvard University Library, 1991

Desser, David and Lester D. Friedman, *American-Jewish Filmmakers: Traditions and Trends*, Urbana: University of Illinois Press, 1993

Erens, Patricia, *The Jew in American Cinema* (Jewish Literature and Culture), Bloomington: Indiana University Press, 1984

Friedman, Lester D., *The Jewish Image in American Film*, Secaucus, New Jersey: Citadel, 1987

Gabler, Neal, *An Empire of Their Own: How the Jews Invented Hollywood*, New York: Crown, 1988; London: Allen, 1989

Goldman, Eric A., *Visions, Images, and Dreams: Yiddish Film Past and Present* (Studies in Cinema), Ann Arbor, Michigan: UMI Research Press, and Epping, Essex: Bowker, 1983

Hoberman, J., *Bridge of Light: Yiddish Film between Two Worlds*, New York: Museum of Modern Art/Schocken, 1991

Kronish, Amy, *World Cinema: Israel* (World Cinema, 6), Madison, New Jersey: Fairleigh Dickinson University Press, and Trowbridge, Wiltshire: Flicks, 1996

Shohat, Ella, *Israeli Cinema: East/West and the Politics of Representation*, Austin: University of Texas Press, 1989

"We Jews are not painters," wrote Franz Kafka. "We cannot depict things statically. We see them as always in transition, as change. We are storytellers." As filmmakers, Jews may have learned to talk in pictures, but scholars of Jewish film continue overwhelmingly to favor literary analysis over strictly cinematic discourse, exploring representation and historical context more frequently than the complex interaction of form, style, and content. The substantial corpus of recent articles and dissertations adopting a broader perspective on Jewish media tend to provide greater theoretical complexity through interdisciplinary approaches.

The geographical contours of Jewish culture shape this survey of seminal book-length works into subsections on American-Jewish, Yiddish, and Israeli cinemas.

ERENS achieves the promise of her preface: to define, quantify, and trace comprehensively Jewish character and genre typologies in American films. Her diachronic examination of U.S. studio-produced features from 1903 (the earliest appearance of a Jewish character) to 1983 draws on rich archival and interview sources. Primarily an examination of film as text, Erens relies on literary theory to develop her discourse on positive, negative, and complex Jewish representation. The thorough filmography of works including Jewish characters and subjects provides a solid base for more specific studies.

GABLER explores the shtetl origins and vestigial quirks that render human such world powers as Harry Cohn (Columbia Pictures), Carl Laemmle (Universal Studios), and Louis B. Mayer (MGM). Drawing from extensive interviews and private documents, Gabler enlists juicy anecdotes about lifestyles and work to illustrate his thesis that assimilation-hungry outsiders constructed Hollywood's U.S. myth. Although he makes only passing reference to specific films, Gabler's study recounts the history of the immigrant Jews who created the Hollywood studio system in intimate detail.

In what is essentially a second edition of his *Hollywood Image of the Jew* (1983), FRIEDMAN considers Jewish agency in Hollywood production though a sociohistorical analysis of the explicit and tacit portrayals of Jewish characters and themes in mainstream U.S. films. The richly illustrated chapters are divided by decade (silent era to the 1980s) and provide theme, plot, and character analyses in varying depth for such films as *A Gentleman's Agreement*, *Fiddler on the Roof*, and *St. Elmo's Fire*. Friedman concludes that the range of Jewish presences on screen, from self-effacing comedian to complex and sensitive subject, serves to gauge the tensions between assimilation and otherness.

DESSER and FRIEDMAN set out "to situate a group of texts within a stream of social, cultural, historical, and ethnic factors," offering an auteuristic examination of "Jewishness" in the oeuvres of Woody Allen, Mel Brooks, Sidney Lumet, and Paul Mazursky. The authors begin their search for distinctively Jewish elements in the 1960s when, they note, ethnic diversity began to be represented more sensitively on the American screen. An awkward introduction attempts to classify as traditions in "Jewish Art" such elements as humor, social justice, the encounter with American life, and a concern with lifestyle trends. Stressing bodies of work over specific films, the bulk of the book examines the relationships that the directors maintain with their Jewish identity and concludes by predicting the loss of Jewish elements in American cinema as filmmakers become increasingly assimilated.

GOLDMAN takes the first substantive step toward the reevaluation of Yiddish film as both a popular and an artistic medium. The chapters, covering broad time periods, focus largely on sound film, with valuable studies of key figures such as Sidney Goldin and George Ulmer. Goldman also offers a detailed filmography.

Rigorously researched and brilliantly written, HOBERMAN's study stands with Nahma Sandrow's *Vagabond Stars: A World History of Yiddish Theater* (1977) as one of the preeminent histories of Yiddish art. Replete with information on such obscure movies as Grigori Roshal's *His Excellency* (1928) and the first filmed version of *The Yellow Passport* (1918), which featured a young Pola Negri, Hoberman locates Yiddish film within the context of world cinema through this comprehensive survey from the silent era through the postwar period. His careful attention to plot descriptions, production, distribution, exhibition, and reception spans low-budget melodramas (*shund* films), musicals, and art films from the United States, the Soviet Union, Poland, and Germany. Published in conjunction with the first major retrospective of Yiddish cinema, this richly illustrated volume is intelligently organized by national production periods, mapping a history of 20th-century Ashkenazi communal life and experience through the framework of cinematic production.

SHOHAT offers a richly nuanced, unabashedly political study that probes films as complex visual objects within the context of Israeli cinema. Anticolonial discourse (notably Edward Said's *Orientalism*) informs her diachronic examination of Ashkenazi/Western dominance, Sephardi/Eastern marginalization, and the exoticized, peripheral, and often invisible Palestinians/Israeli-Arabs. Five chapters delineate the slim corpus of Israeli cinema, beginning under the British mandate and extending through heroic nationalism, the *bourekas* genre of popular Sephardi films, the "personal cinema" of the 1970s, and trends of the 1980s such as the "Palestinian Wave." Each chapter combines analyses of individual films and genres with a politically critical approach to issues of production, spectatorship, and representation in Israeli film.

KRONISH looks at the history of film production as a building block of the Israeli nation-state. She traces government attitudes toward cinema, proffers a romantic analysis of pioneer culture's attitude toward film, and pays special attention to "artistic" developments in the 1970s, 1980s, and 1990s. Chapters on subjects including the post–Six-Day War period, women in Israeli film, and the individual in society are structured encyclopedically with well-organized treatments of directors, films, and historic events representative of these periods and themes. The comprehensive filmography is an excellent resource.

Published in conjunction with a conference organized to highlight Harvard's comprehensive Judaica videotape collection, BERLIN assembles four articles that may be most useful to students of Israeli media. Marilyn Gold Koolik's "Jewish Film Archives in Israel" recounts the institutional accumulation and use of newsreels, features, television, and multimedia, providing a finding aid for the most extensive collections. Igal Bursztyn's lucid and intelligent "Film in Israel: The Creation/Preservation of Jewish Culture" applies a Marxist-Barthian approach to the analysis of speech, art, and message in a series of film clips. In "The Role of Educational Television in Israel: The Sephardic Heritage," producer/director Haim Shiran discusses his own attempts to further pluralistic media representation. Bernard Cooperman's "The Uses of Film in Teaching and Research" champions the use of videos as pedagogic texts.

KARYN RIEGEL

See also Holocaust: Film Treatments

Five Scrolls

Crenshaw, James L., *Ecclesiastes: A Commentary* (Old Testament Library), Philadelphia: Westminster, 1987; London: SCM, 1988

Fox, Michael V., *Character and Ideology in the Book of Esther* (Studies on Personalities of the Old Testament), Columbia: University of South Carolina Press, 1991

Fuerst, Wesley J., *The Books of Ruth, Esther, Ecclesiastes, the Song of Songs, Lamentations: The Five Scrolls* (Cambridge Bible Commentary), Cambridge: Cambridge University Press, 1975

Gordis, Robert, *The Song of Songs: A Study, Modern Translation, and Commentary* (Texts and Studies of the Jewish Theological Seminary of America, vol. 20), New York: Jewish Theological Seminary, 1954

Nielsen, Kirsten, *Ruth: A Commentary* (Old Testament Library), Louisville, Kentucky: Westminster John Knox, and London: SCM, 1997

Westermann, Claus, *Die Klagelieder: Forschungsgeschichte und Auslegung*, 1990; translated by C. Muenchow as *Lamentations: Issues and Interpretation*, Minneapolis, Minnesota: Fortress, and Edinburgh: Clark, 1994

The Five Scrolls (in Hebrew, *megillot*) denote five short books collected near the end of the Hebrew Bible, each of which came to be read more or less widely during a particular festival in most Jewish communities. For Passover, celebrating the Exodus, the Song of Songs is read; for the Feast of Weeks (Shavuot), at the end of the harvest season and in memory of the giving of the law, Ruth is read; for the ninth of Ab, the day Jerusalem fell in 587 B.C.E., Lamentations is read; for Tabernacles (Sukkot), a celebration of the grape harvest, Ecclesiastes is read; and for Purim, when the people were saved from destruction, Esther is read.

FUERST addresses all five scrolls, following the same format in each case. He begins with a discussion of the book, including theories about most of the following topics: date and setting, formation, genre, structure, themes, history of interpretation within Jewish and Christian communities, relation to its festival, and comparison with other relevant biblical works. The text of each book follows, according to the New English Bible translation. At a series of junctures in the primary text under discussion, Fuerst provides a commentary on the foregoing section. He then offers a final discussion of the message of the scroll at hand. While a portion of Fuerst's book is devoted to providing the primary sources, his discussions offer a good survey of the main questions of interpretation and biblical scholarship on the texts in terms that are quite accessible for the nonspecialist.

GORDIS's book is devoted mostly to a detailed introduction to the Song of Songs, and a brief commentary follows the translation. His view of the text is that it is an anthology of various songs about love, nature, courtship, and marriage, which date from a period covering not less than the tenth to the fifth century B.C.E. He discusses several theories about the nature of the book, including allegorical interpretation, the view that it was a translation of a pagan cult liturgy, and the opinion that it represents an interchange between different characters in a drama, all of which he rejects. After discussing the Song of Songs in the context of wisdom literature, he goes on to defend his own view of it as a collection of lyrics, then discusses a variety of issues including its style and symbolism. Gordis offers a lucid discussion for the general reader, but with enough detail to be of use to the specialist.

NIELSEN presents a commentary on the Book of Ruth preceded by an extensive introduction. Her approach is to read Ruth intertextually, that is, in light of the other biblical narratives on which it relies. The explicit references to Rachel, Leah, Tamar, and Judah as well as the themes of famine and barrenness show that the reader is to understand Ruth as part of the patriarchal history and to make connections with the characters already established in this earlier tradition. The purpose of Ruth's extension of this history is to defend David's suspect genealogy through the Moabite Ruth and the even earlier ancestress Tamar. She rejects the view that Ruth is a post-exilic work and suggests that it was written in the monarchic period as a response to one of a number of crises requiring a defense of the Davidic dynasty. While these matters will continue to be debated, Nielsen's analysis is clear and readable.

WESTERMANN begins with a thorough discussion of how others have interpreted the Book of Lamentations, working through each scholar individually and then summarizing the academic consensus (or debates, as the case may be) by topic. He goes on to present his own analysis, which is that Lamentations is not preplanned literature but an immediate reaction to Jerusalem's destruction in 587 B.C.E., and that the book should be understood simply as a series of laments. These laments are communal in type and are distinctive in having adopted some of the themes of the dirge. They were originally oral and probably originated among eyewitnesses to the city's fall. Westermann offers an exegesis of the book and concludes by reflecting on its theological significance and its relevance to biblical theology. His study is particularly useful for those interested in the history of scholarship on Lamentations and the diversity of approaches to it.

CRENSHAW begins with a discussion of the themes of the Book of Ecclesiastes: human existence is without profit, one should enjoy life as much as possible before time runs out, and, in the end, chance and death are the driving forces of the world. God is distant, and there is no discernible pattern of order to be perceived in human life. Ecclesiastes is an example of biblical wisdom literature, but its worldview contrasts strongly with other biblical wisdom literature such as Proverbs. Crenshaw presents a detailed survey of scholarly approaches to the structure of Ecclesiastes and concludes that the book is largely unmodified by later hands. The date he suggests for its composition is 250 to 225 B.C.E., which he supports with various data including the late stage of the biblical Hebrew employed. The commentary that follows is detailed without being impenetrable, and it shows sensitivity to the melancholy quality of this unusual biblical book. Opinions as to the meaning, structure, date, and origins of Ecclesiastes are wide-ranging, but Crenshaw provides an even-handed presentation of the issues.

FOX furnishes a commentary on the Book of Esther in the first part of his study, but the real impact of his project lies in the thorough discussion of the characters—a discussion that aims not so much at the entertainment value to be discovered therein, but at understanding the ideology of Esther's author. Following the commentary, chapters on historicity, genres, and structures lead into the character analysis, which is provided one character at a time, with a chapter at the end of the book on the different text versions of Esther. Fox concludes that the book probably dates to the third century B.C.E. and possibly originates in Susa. Esther can properly be called a number of things with respect to genre: a diaspora story, a historical story, a festival etiology, and a festival lection. Its central theme is reversal, more specifically, that a plan to destroy the Jewish people results rather in the destruction of their enemies, and its theology is one of possibility. Fox's presentation is cogent and useful to readers of various backgrounds.

SHANNON BURKES

Flora and Fauna of the Bible

Feliks, Yehuda, *Ha-hai shel ha-Tanakh: sefer ha-zo'ologiyah ha-mikra'it*, 1954; translated by Pinhas Irsai as *The Animal World of the Bible*, Tel-Aviv: Sinai, 1962

Feliks, Yehuda, *Nature and Man in the Bible: Chapters in Biblical Ecology*, London and New York: Soncino, 1981

Moldenke, Harold Norman and Alma L. Moldenke, *Plants of the Bible*, New York: New York Botanical Garden, 1940

Møller-Christensen, Vilhelm and K.E. Jordt Jørgensen, *Encyclopedia of Bible Creatures*, edited by M. Theodore Heinecken, translated by Arne Unhjem, Philadelphia: Fortress, 1965

Pinney, Roy, *The Animals in the Bible: The Identity and Natural History of All the Animals Mentioned in the Bible* (Frontiers of Knowledge Series), Philadelphia: Chilton, 1964

Zohary, Michael, *Plants of the Bible: A Complete Handbook to All the Plants with 200 Full-Color Plates Taken in the Natural Habitat*, London and New York: Cambridge University Press, 1982

There are at least 150 species of animals and about 100 species of plants mentioned in the Hebrew Bible, a large number for what is usually thought of as a book of morality and religion. Interest in identifying these animals has been recorded since the dawn of biblical interpretation. In the Talmud and rabbinic literature, this interest was primarily halakhic, aiming at better application of biblical law. In medieval times, interpreters often found it excessively perplexing to identify biblical flora and fauna, and European translations sometimes resorted to guesswork in rendering obscure plants and animals. The interest in biblical flora and fauna in modern times comes from two sources. On one hand, the mid–19th-century explosion in ancient Near Eastern studies, coupled with traditional Protestant focus on Scripture's plain meaning, resulted in European interest in identifying the plants and animals of the Bible. On the other hand, the rise of Zionism with its biblical inspiration led to a rise in "Land of Israel" studies, and a preoccupation with the topography and natural history of the biblical world.

FELIKS (1954) deals with the larger issues connected with nature in the Bible. He aims to demonstrate that the profusion of both lofty and realistic descriptions of nature in the Hebrew Bible relates directly to the literary and theological message of the Bible: "A thorough knowledge of the surrounding scenery [of the biblical world] expands the breadth of our understanding of the text and deepens our feelings of identity with the Book of Books." He reviews more than 80 biblical passages, briefly identifying the plants and natural phenomena in each but focusing on the connection between the flora and fauna mentioned and the meaning of the passage. He demonstrates convincingly that understanding the plants and animals is critical in many passages to understanding the passages themselves.

ZOHARY documents 128 distinct plants, citing biblical passages. He identifies each on botanical grounds, citing the biblical and archaeological evidence for the identification, and provides the scientific name for each. He explains very briefly the significance of each species in its scriptural context. The book is written from the perspective of the botanist, rather than the biblicist, and includes many plates and figures.

MOLDENKE and MOLDENKE summarize previous research into the identity of the plants mentioned in the Bible and provide highly detailed botanical information, organizing plants into families. The literature on plants and botany in the ancient and classical worlds is surveyed extensively. The book is organized in a user-friendly way, but unfortunately it does not cite the plants by their Hebrew names.

FELIKS (1954) aims to provide zoological identification of the 150 animals mentioned in the Bible. He argues that such identification should take full account of traditional Jewish interpretation of the Bible, and it is for this reason that he has repeated recourse to rabbinic literature. He then discusses the habitat of these animals today, placing them in a modern Israeli setting.

MØLLER-CHRISTENSEN and JØRGENSEN discuss 65 animals in their popular work. Their method is to identify the animal, to cite some of the passages mentioning it, and to provide some information on the physical characteristics of each animal as known in modern times. Unfortunately, many of the biblical identifications are unduly speculative, with comparatively little use of other ancient Near Eastern references to these animals or to the original languages of the biblical text.

PINNEY's work discusses the animals of the Bible, grouping them by phylum and family and discussing their zoological characteristics: habitat, food, and physical description. He offers more zoological information than Møller-Christensen and Jørgensen but, like them, he does not take into account the results of ancient Near Eastern scholarship and tends to identify biblical animals with those found in the region today. The book contains 86 detailed and beautiful photographs, taken in Israel by the author, and it is chiefly useful for these.

SHAWN ZELIG ASTER

Folktales

Bar-Yitshak, Hayah and Aliza Shenhar-Alroy, *Jewish Moroccan Folk Narratives from Israel* (Jewish Folklore and Anthropology Series), Detroit, Michigan: Wayne State University Press, 1993
Rush, Barbara, *The Book of Jewish Women's Tales*, Northvale, New Jersey: Aronson, 1994
Sadeh, Pinhas, *Sefer ha-dimyonot shel ha-Yehudim: sipure 'am*, 1983; translated by Hillel Halkin as *Jewish Folktales*, New York: Anchor, 1989
Twerski, Abraham J., *Generation to Generation: Personal Recollections of a Chassidic Legacy*, Brooklyn, New York: Traditional Press, 1986
Weinreich, Beatrice Silverman (editor) and Leonard Wolf (translator), *Yiddish Folktales*, New York: Pantheon/Yivo Institute for Jewish Research, 1988

Daily conversation and moments of leisure in many Jewish communities have been great occasions for the telling of folktales, stories without a known author that are passed by word of mouth, often over many generations. The realm of folktales is one of cultural permeability: "Jewish" and "non-Jewish" folktales are often substantially identical, and Jews, spanning national boundaries, have played a significant role in transmitting folktales between non-Jewish groups. In contrast to the written texts of Jewish scholarship, folktales are shaped and transmitted largely by unlearned women and men. At the same time, given the high rate of literacy among Jews, Jewish stories readily pass from oral to written forms and back again. Boundaries are blurred further when stories of individual experiences are told alongside traditional folktales—as often happens—and when traditional stories are presented as individual experiences—as likewise they often are.

In the contemporary revival of storytelling as one of the performing arts, Jewish storytellers have been prominent and Jewish folktales have provided much of the source material. This is perhaps why so many English collections of Jewish folktales are now available. Some, however, include mainly literary material from written sources. Others present stories reworked to such a degree that one has to think of the authors as creative writers, using folktales as raw material. The collections reviewed here, presenting folktales from a variety of Jewish communities, are more authentic; most of their stories are based directly on oral tellings and are free of large-scale revisions. Several of the authors have made good use of the Israel Folktale Archives (IFA), which contain recordings of thousands of oral stories. The stories in these collections are intrinsically interesting and, for the storyteller, readily retellable.

Israeli novelist SADEH presents a rich selection of about 300 stories, some from "old . . . forgotten books" of legends and more from oral tellings in the IFA, with a substantial representation of Middle Eastern Jewish tales. Sadeh has chosen stories according to his literary taste, and he includes religious tales alongside those with a secular tone. He has grouped stories so that different versions of the same plotline follow each other and themes develop through several stories, giving the flavor of a long session of oral storytelling in which one tale sparks another. The spare writing style is not necessarily that of the original tellers, but it presents the stories clearly and without authorial intrusion, retaining occasional pious and proverbial phrases from the original tellings. Translator Halkin has provided a foreword introducing Sadeh and drawing attention to some differences between Ashkenazi and Middle Eastern Jewish folktales. Sadeh provides a reflective afterword, by turns informative and poetic. Only the source notes at the end of the book are inadequate, providing little information about the tellers or where the texts and recordings can be found.

RUSH draws entirely on stories recorded from oral tellings, some recounted to the author in person, many from the IFA. Some of the stories are personal experiences of women; others are traditional stories that also may have been told by men, but they appear here in versions that women have told to other women. The introductions by Rush and the important folklorist Dov Noy emphasize the role of storytelling as a way in which women teach each other, passing on messages of practical and spiritual wisdom. Seventy-three stories are included, in a variety of genres, told by women from a broad range of Jewish communities, including, for example, Bene Israel of India, Kurds, and Yemenites. The tales are grouped around themes such as stages of the female life cycle: birth, marriage, motherhood, aging, and death. There is introductory material for each story, including anecdotes about the storytellers and Rush's reflections on the message of the tale and, often, on how men's and women's tellings of the story differ. Rush, a professional storyteller, writes in a straightforward, lucid style.

BAR-YITSHAK and SHENHAR-ALROY present 21 stories told by Jews from Morocco, mostly elderly, living in Shlomi, Israel, a town of Moroccan immigrants. More than half the stories are told by women. Names and photographs of each storyteller are included, with information about his or her life and the contexts in which he or she tells stories. The tales are presented not in authorial revisions but in clear translations from the Arabic of the tellers. The distinctive verbal styles of the individual tellers are well represented, along with expressions characteristic of Moroccan Jewish storytelling in general. For example, any description of something as "big" is immediately qualified: "they had a big wedding, and there is no one greater than God." Several long wonder tales are included, their ornate plots enhanced by the flavor of oral expression. There are informative notes on folktales in Moroccan Jewish culture generally and in Shlomi specifically and on the themes of each story. This book gives a vivid picture of Jewish storytelling in a particular setting and by particular individuals, at the same time presenting highly readable and retellable stories.

WEINREICH presents a varied selection of 178 stories told in Yiddish in Eastern Europe and recorded especially in the 1920s and 1930s, a time when many nonspecialists as well as scholars were involved in collecting folktales and filling archives with thousands of stories, many of which escaped destruction. Weinreich provides introductory material for the book and for each chapter, discussing storytellers, types of stories, and the contexts of storytelling. The stories represent a variety of storytellers, "men and women of different age groups, professions and religious background," and genres, with each chapter devoted to a specific genre (allegorical tales,

children's tales, wonder tales, pious tales, humorous tales, and legends). The final section on supernatural tales concludes with an eyewitness account of a contest between a hasidic exorcist and a skeptic, with disturbing results, bringing into sharp focus some of the tensions between tradition and change that manifest themselves in the diversity of the other stories. The versions presented are direct translations from the Yiddish and include such features of oral telling as rhymes and, in one story, two melodies presented in musical notation.

Weinreich includes several striking examples of hasidic storytelling, an important component of the world of Yiddish folktales. Several collections of hasidic stories are available in English, but most are based on Hebrew books, at some remove from the language and contexts of oral telling. By contrast, TWERSKI, the son of a hasidic rabbi in the United States, Jacob Twerski of Milwaukee, recounts in his own words reminiscences of his family and their milieu and stories told to him by his parents, often about the hasidic rabbis in their ancestry. He intersperses his tales with comments reflecting both his training as a psychotherapist and also the hasidic tradition of interpreting the meaning of stories. This is a uniquely personal and living book of hasidic tales, and it includes several that are not available in other English collections.

JUSTIN JARON LEWIS

France

Adler, Jacques, *The Jews of Paris and the Final Solution: Communal Response and Internal Conflicts, 1940–1944* (Studies in Jewish History), New York: Oxford University Press, 1987

Albert, Phyllis Cohen, *The Modernization of French Jewry: Consistory and Community in the Nineteenth Century,* Hanover, New Hampshire: Brandeis University Press, 1977

Birnbaum, Pierre, *Anti-Semitism in France* (Studies in Social Discontinuity), Oxford and Cambridge, Massachusetts: Blackwell, 1992

Burns, Michael, *Dreyfus: A Family Affair, 1789–1945,* New York: HarperCollins, 1991; London: Chatto and Windus, 1992

Byrnes, Robert F., *Antisemitism in Modern France,* New Brunswick, New Jersey: Rutgers University Press, 1950

Cohen, Richard I., *The Burden of Conscience: French Jewish Leadership during the Holocaust* (The Modern Jewish Experience), Bloomington: Indiana University Press, 1987

Graetz, Michael, *The Jews in Nineteenth-Century France: From the French Revolution to the Alliance Israélite Universelle* (Stanford Studies in Jewish History and Culture), Stanford, California: Stanford University Press, 1996

Hertzberg, Arthur, *The French Enlightenment and the Jews,* New York: Columbia University Press, 1968

Hyman, Paula, *From Dreyfus to Vichy: The Remaking of French Jewry, 1906–1939,* New York: Columbia University Press, 1979

Hyman, Paula, *The Emancipation of the Jews of Alsace: Acculturation and Tradition in the Nineteenth Century*, New Haven, Connecticut, and London: Yale University Press, 1991

Hyman, Paula, *The Jews of Modern France* (Jewish Communities in the Modern World, 1), Berkeley: University of California Press, 1998

Malino, Frances and Bernard Wasserstein (editors), *The Jews in Modern France* (Tauber Institute Series, 4), Hanover, New Hampshire: University Press of New England, 1985

Marrus, Michael R., *The Politics of Assimilation: A Study of the French Jewish Community at the Time of the Dreyfus Affair*, Oxford: Clarendon, 1970; as *The Politics of Assimilation: The French Jewish Community at the Time of the Dreyfus Affair*, New York: Oxford University Press, 1980

Marrus, Michael R. and Robert O. Paxton, *Vichy France and the Jews*, New York: Basic Books, 1981

Weinberg, David H., *A Community on Trial: The Jews of Paris in the 1930's*, Chicago: University of Chicago Press, 1977

Wilson, Stephen, *Ideology and Experience: Antisemitism in France at the Time of the Dreyfus Affair* (Littman Library of Jewish Civilization), Rutherford, New Jersey: Fairleigh Dickinson Press, and London: Associated University Presses, 1982

The study of the Jews of modern France is a relatively recent phenomenon. While French Jewish scholars in the 19th century shared the German Haskalah's interest in Jewish history, their work was largely confined to unearthing early artifacts that demonstrated the antiquity of the Jewish settlement in France or disseminating medieval religious tracts and philosophical writings that were seen as cultural contributions to Judaism as a whole. Since the 1960s, however, the study of Franco-Judaica has gained respectability and importance as a distinct field of research, thanks in part to the revival of the French Jewish community, on the one hand, and the writings of an influential generation of postwar U.S. scholars, on the other. The result has been an impressive array of historical monographs that emphasize the distinctive role of French Jewry within both modern French and European Jewish history. These works have also challenged traditional assumptions about such widely diverse topics as the nature of modern Jewish identity, the process of assimilation, antisemitism and the Jewish response, and the relationship between Jews and the larger society in which they live.

HERTZBERG challenges the popular assumption that antisemitism emerged in large part as a reaction to the ideals of the Enlightenment and the French Revolution. In fact, the author maintains, many of the leading *philosophes* of the 18th century (including Voltaire, Diderot, and d'Holbach) personally hated Jews and actually laid the framework for what Hertzberg calls the revival of pagan antisemitism. Hertzberg contends that in the wake of the French Enlightenment, Jews were hated not only because of their religion and their rejection of Christianity but also because of their culture and ultimately their "biology." The work has not been without its

critics, who have argued that Hertzberg's arguments are often tendentious and ahistorical. Nevertheless, the book deserves to be read for its provocative analyses of both the roots of modern anti-Jewish hatred and the complex origins of Jewish Emancipation.

BYRNES remains the classic study of antisemitism in France, despite the fact that it is an old work. The book examines anti-Jewish sentiment from the establishment of the Third Republic in 1871 to the Dreyfus Affair, which preoccupied France at the end of the 19th century. As a product of the immediate postwar era, the book is strongly influenced by the experience of fascism in the 1930s and 1940s, which Byrnes saw as growing out of precisely such antidemocratic antecedents as antisemitism. The author never clearly explains the reasons for the rise of anti-Jewish sentiment, but his detailed discussion of the various attitudes and movements that arose in France on both the Left and the Right in the last quarter of the 19th century is unsurpassed. Byrnes intended to publish two other volumes dealing with the Dreyfus Affair and France after World War I, respectively, but the books were never completed.

BIRNBAUM's book takes up where Byrnes leaves off. Documenting how anti-Jewish attitudes were incorporated into France's major political battles throughout the late 19th and 20th centuries, the author seeks to counter Hannah Arendt's contention that antisemitism occurs primarily in "weak states." To the contrary, Birnbaum argues, "[i]t is the strength of the state and not its decline which caused political antisemitism to appear," and he supports this hypothesis by contrasting the often murderous policies of "strong-state" France with the relatively ineffectual social discrimination of "weak states" such as Great Britain and the United States. Assessing the political and economic turmoil in France in the 1970s and early 1980s, Birnbaum concludes that only deep political change will eliminate antisemitism and xenophobia in general as major forces in French society.

BURNS is a richly detailed history of the Dreyfus family. Far more than a simple recounting of the events of the Dreyfus Affair, the work attempts to break through the ideological abstractions of antisemitism, Zionism, and socialism to understand the attitudes and behavior of Alfred Dreyfus and his immediate family. Reading more like a 19th-century family novel than a historical work, the book examines the fate of the Dreyfus family from its assumption of citizenship after the French Revolution to its destruction during the Holocaust, thus shedding light on the nature of the identity of modern French Jews, in which "two faiths—religious and national . . . were often, though not always, in conflict."

WILSON's meticulously researched work places the rise of anti-Jewish sentiment and movements during the Dreyfus Affair in the general context of modernization in fin-de-siècle France. The author argues that antisemitism in late 19th-century France was more a response to changing social and economic conditions in the countryside than to any changes in the place of Jews within French society. In contrast to historians who have viewed anti-Dreyfusard propaganda as largely opportunistic, Wilson emphasizes the ideology of antisemitism, arguing that antisemitic movements during the Dreyfus Affair acted in ways similar to the behavior of modern-day sectarian religious movements, incorporating elements of unshakable belief, Manicheanism, and unremitting hostility toward their enemies into their ideologies.

ALBERT's work is a massive study of the major institution of French Jewry in the 19th century—the *Consistoire centrale*. While often tedious in its detail of the workings of the organization, the book effectively illustrates various aspects of Jewish life, especially in the years between 1830 and 1870, including demographic, geographic, and occupational changes; social and institutional transformations; and religious innovations. Albert contends that French Jewry in the post-emancipatory era possessed two characteristics that are hallmarks of modern society: a conscious reevaluation of traditional values and behavior, and a movement toward secularization. The work contains useful appendixes of demographic and occupational data on 19th-century French Jewry and texts of the major laws regulating the consistories.

HYMAN (1991) departs from standard studies of modern French Jewish history, which have largely limited themselves to the attitudes and behavior of urban elites. Instead, she examines the attitudes and behavior of the majority of 19th-century European Jews, the rural masses. Her study focuses on Alsatian Jewry, the first large traditional Jewish community on the European continent to experience the benefits and challenges of Emancipation and a force in the Paris community and elsewhere after 1870. By choosing to take a "grass-roots" approach that emphasizes socioeconomic developments rather than ideology, Hyman highlights the elements of continuity that accompanied the transformation of European Jewry from aliens to citizens in the period after Emancipation. Hyman's conclusion that the Jewish masses of Alsace maintained traditional beliefs and practices throughout the first half of the 19th century and responded cautiously to demands for modernization after 1848 not only helps to explain the relatively conservative nature of the French Jewish community but also illustrates the complex interweaving of tradition and change in the modernization of European Jewry as a whole.

MARRUS was one of the first historians to question the viability of the ideal of a French-Jewish symbiosis, which had formed the basis of French Jewish identity since the French Revolution. Strongly influenced by Hannah Arendt, who had repeatedly emphasized the shortsightedness and naiveté of Jewish community leaders in her writings on modern antisemitism, Marrus sharply criticizes French Jewry for being blind to the dangers of antisemitism during the Dreyfus Affair. By the end of the 19th century, he maintains, the Jews in France had lost their sense of community and had developed a political perspective that emphasized their loyalty to France at the expense of their right to be Jews. The result was that for most French Jews the onset of the Dreyfus Affair "appeared as only a ripple in the smooth course" of their lives. Marrus concludes his occasionally tendentious study with a paean to a small group of Zionists in late 19th-century France, who the author believes defied the views of the leaders of their community by proudly asserting their Jewish identity.

GRAETZ has countered Marrus's argument with an analysis that emphasizes the bonds that tied the Jews of 19th-century France together despite their strong assimilationist tendencies. Reflecting a strong Zionist perspective, the author contends that the 19th century witnessed the replacement of religious affiliation with nascent nationalist sentiments, as manifested in the activities of the *Alliance israélite universelle*. Graetz also insists upon the need to examine Jews on the periphery of communal life who, in their search to reconnect with Jewish life, provided emancipated Jewry with new forms of collective identification. In this sense, the author disputes the prevailing assumption that Emancipation necessarily led to assimilation and the disappearance of Jewish life.

HYMAN (1979) traces the response of French Jewry to the challenges of Eastern European Jewish immigration and antisemitism in the first three decades of the 20th century. Mirroring the arguments of Weinberg and others, Hyman maintains that fierce xenophobia (which arose in interwar France as a response to economic depression and social tensions) and the influx of significant numbers of immigrant Jews from Eastern Europe eroded the synthesis between French and Jewish values that had developed in the 19th century. Thus, an assertive and pluralistic community, which was far more vigorous in its own defense and which no longer rested exclusively on a religious definition of Jewish identity, emerged. Hyman concludes that these transformations enabled French Jewry to integrate 300,000 North African Jews in the 1960s and 1970s, becoming the largest Jewish community in contemporary Western Europe.

WEINBERG examines the often difficult relationship between Eastern European immigrants and native-born Jews in the period directly before the onset of the Holocaust. The book is divided into three sections: an examination of the population, professions, and organizations of Paris Jews in the 1930s; a study of the nature of Jewish identification; and a discussion of the contrasting analyses of antisemitism within the community and attitudes toward the question of a Jewish response. Like many of the works of young European Jewish historians in the 1970s, the book rests on the implicit assumption that, as in the United States, the classic assimilationist posture of established Jews weakened the community, while the influx of new Jewish immigrants helped to revitalize Jewish life. While Weinberg is often critical of the unwillingness of the Jews of Paris to act assertively against the threat of antisemitism in an era when the "Jewish question" existed but had not achieved a final solution, he nevertheless concludes that there was little that Jews could have done directly before or during the Holocaust to prevent their annihilation.

MARRUS and PAXTON attack the popular view that France was forced to engage in the deportation of its Jews during World War II because of pressure from the Nazi occupiers. The two authors claim that far from following the dictates of the Third Reich, the Vichy regime initiated its own anti-Jewish legislation that at times exceeded the policies of Nazi Germany in its stringency and brutality. Drawing heavily upon both German and French governmental archives, the work suggests that far fewer Jews living in France would have perished during the Holocaust if the Nazis had been obliged to carry out their murderous policies in France without the assistance of Vichy authorities. Rejecting the notion that Vichy represented a radical break from previous French governmental policies and popular attitudes, Marrus and Paxton stress the origins of the wartime regime's policy toward Jews in the anxiety and hostility surrounding Jewish refugees in the late 1930s. The book has created considerable controversy in France and has played an important role in that nation's painful reexamination of its myth of resistance to Nazism during World War II.

COHEN examines the difficult issues of collaboration and resistance facing the leaders of the French Jewish community during World War II. His study focuses on the activities of the *Union générale des israélites de France* (UGIF), an organization created by the Vichy government that was responsible for a variety of activities including carrying out government decrees, providing for the health and welfare of the community, and eventually overseeing deportations. Cohen challenges the often simplistic assumptions about Jewish behavior during the Holocaust by suggesting that the UGIF's response to Nazi and Vichy policies was complex and varied. While some individuals and groups in the organization followed government directives to the letter, others supported illegal activities, such as the housing of Jewish children in non-Jewish homes, assistance to Jews wishing to hide themselves, and the smuggling of refugees over the border to Spain and Italy. Throughout the ordeal, Cohen concludes, the UGIF remained true to two main ideals that often diminished its effectiveness: loyalty to French culture and a desire to maintain Jewish welfare services at all costs.

ADLER's work is a useful complement to Cohen's study and represents an extension of the studies by Weinberg and Hyman of the French Jewish community in the 1930s. Far more critical than Cohen of the activity of the UGIF, Adler examines the clashes between French-born and immigrant Jews, which had their origins in the interwar period. The author emphasizes how the Pétain regime exploited the divisions between the two groups, often pitting one segment of the population against the other by inciting controversy and lulling many Jews into a false evaluation of their situation. The book has been criticized for its overly negative assessment of the UGIF, but its examination of the activities of immigrant groups during Vichy, including most notably those of Jewish communists in occupied Paris, is of great value because these actions are generally ignored in the Cohen study.

MALINO and WASSERSTEIN's volume is a collection of essays drawn from a conference held at Brandeis University in 1975. Not surprisingly, it is an uneven work, reflecting the relatively new state of the field at the time that the conference was held. Among the many topics discussed are the mutual interaction between French history and Jewish history, the relationship between immigrant and native-born Jews, the attitudes of the French Left and Right toward Jews, and French Jewish historiography. Of particular value are Michael Marrus's essays on antisemitism and Nancy Green's article on Eastern European Jewish immigrants in Paris before World War I. The volume also contains a spirited debate over the value and significance of Emancipation for French Jewry, highlighted by an often obscure but fascinating essay by a leading French Jewish intellectual, Shmuel Trigano.

HYMAN (1998), a survey of modern French Jewish history, is an excellent synthesis of the scholarship of the last third of the 20th century. In a clear and concise presentation geared to the general reader, the author argues that the history of French Jewry is a microcosm of the modern Jewish experience in the West. Like other emancipated Jews in the 19th century, French Jews were compelled to construct new forms of identity and new communal institutions that would enable them both to maintain their distinctiveness and to participate in the larger society in which they lived. The history of French Jewry also reflects the polarities of assimilation and discrimination that characterize the modern Jewish experience. Similarly, the transformations in the French Jewish community highlight how mass migration can revivify Jewish communal life. Hyman also convincingly argues that the history of French Jewry reflects important dimensions of French history and culture, including the complex heritage of the Enlightenment, the strength and limits of the French state, the nature of the Right in national politics, and, most importantly, the attitude and behavior of the majority society toward minority groups within its midst.

DAVID WEINBERG

See also Provence

Frank, Jacob Joseph 1726–1791

Polish founder of neo-Shabbatean Frankist sect

Lenowitz, Harris, *The Jewish Messiahs: From the Galilee to Crown Heights,* New York: Oxford University Press, 1998

Mandel, Arthur, *The Militant Messiah: or, The Flight from the Ghetto: The Story of Jacob Frank and the Frankist Movement,* Atlantic Highlands, New Jersey: Humanities Press, 1979

Scholem, Gershom, "Redemption through Sin," in his *The Messianic Idea in Judaism and Other Essays on Jewish Spirituality,* New York: Schocken, and London: Allen and Unwin, 1971

Scholem, Gershom, "Frank, Jacob, and the Frankists," in *Encyclopaedia Judaica,* vol. 7, Jerusalem: Encyclopaedia Judaica, 1972

The 18th century saga that began in late 1755 with the proclamation of Jacob ben Leib (Jacob Joseph Frank's birth name) as the latest heir to the messiah Shabbetai Tsevi and with Frank's passage across the Dniester from Walachia into Poland, proceeded to feature two intra-Jewish public disputations and the conversion of hundreds of Jews to Catholicism, followed by the 13-year imprisonment of a now ennobled Jacob Joseph Frank. It ended in Offenbach on the Rhine in the early 19th century with the fiasco of his daughter Ewa's messiahship. This history collocates the Ottoman Empire and Eastern and Western Europe; normative Christianity, Islam, Judaism, and heretical movements in all three; the dismemberment of Poland and the heightening tension and complexity of the relationship of Germany, Austria-Hungary, and Russia; the French Revolution and the advancement of Jewish citizenship and civil rights. While Frankism cannot be seen as causative or even central to any of these, its history, documentation, and historiography reflect them all in a profound way.

MANDEL associates Frankism with Hasidism, decrying both and defaming the latter. The work particularly emphasizes the licentious and tyrannical nature of the leaders of these movements in constructing their practices. The author also recounts the militaristic tendencies of Frank in the organization and direction of his followers, and he associates the movement with other strains of Jewish nationalism that sought independent territories other than in the Land of Israel. Guided by the work of Jacob Katz and Gershom Scholem, Mandel spends nearly one-third of his brief study on the career of Moses Dobruschka, alias Junius Brutus Frey, a "nephew" (actually cousin) of Frank's, among the Jacobins.

Although Mandel is the single book-length work in English on Frank and the movement known as "Frankism," three long essays do present comprehensive depictions. Indeed, to the extent that Mandel is more than a lurid fantasy, it is dependent on SCHOLEM (1972) for the synthesis, rationalization, and updating of the work of earlier scholarship (although he does not acknowledge his dependency and seems unaware of other work in Hebrew). On the other hand, SCHOLEM (1971) is a work that is itself marked by an uncharacteristic passion and dependence on secondary sources of pronounced partiality and unsound scholarship. Opinions, theories, and ignorance have predominated in all but one of the synthetic works to the present (both those in English discussed here and those in other languages), perhaps because central issues of modern Jewish history are at stake: the history of Hasidism, mystic tendencies toward sexual license, Jewish millennialism, nationalism and Zionism, the determinative influence of disaster, and the very shape of modern Jewish history as it relates to the Shabbatean event of the previous century are some of the points overtly at issue. A more subtle and pernicious matter is the related characterization of East European Jewry as a dark and sullen medieval residue in the movement toward Jewish modernity.

Scholem (1971) is this great scholar's single most famous essay, composed in Hebrew in 1936. Its thesis is that Frank and Frankism display the disastrous end of the doctrines of the movement of Shabbetai Tsevi in an abhorrent nihilism that further develops the teachings of Baruchia Russo, one of his heirs. All norms of Jewish social behavior and religion are turned on their head, that which was illegal becoming obligatory as the final step toward gaining emancipation from all constraints on the natural life and achieving the apocalyptic millennium. This work and Scholem (1972) are concerned to show a relationship between Frankism, the Jewish Enlightenment, Hasidism, and the beginnings of Reform Judaism. Its quotations from Frank's own speeches are error-ridden, coming not from original documents but from translations done for him either from the Polish of an earlier study with its own limitations or by his wife from the Polish manuscripts. The outline of the history of Frank and the Frankist movement in Scholem (1972) came from earlier works by others (in German, Polish, and Hebrew) of a tendentious and polemic nature, but it is clearly expressed and dependable, grosso modo, these works having been attentively reconstructed by him.

LENOWITZ edits, translates, introduces, and focuses on Frank's dicta from the Polish manuscripts in order to substantiate and elucidate this messiah's theology, his literary output, and the conduct of his movement. It places Frank and his movement within the history of Jewish messiahs as not atypical expressions of the events and personalities associated with this history. It finds Frank a chameleon-like personality, living a life of extraordinary lability and innovating convincing literary creations suited to his time, following, and vision. Lenowitz brings Frank and his literary creations together with the hasidic "messiahs," particularly R. Nahman of Bratslav, and their literary remains.

HARRIS LENOWITZ

Frankel, Zacharias 1801–1875

Prague-born German rabbi and scholar, pioneer of positive-historical Judaism

Blau, Joseph L., *Modern Varieties of Judaism*, New York: Columbia University Press, 1966

Deutsch, Gotthard, *Zachariah Frankel*, New York, 1902

Ginzberg, Louis, *Students, Scholars and Saints*, Philadelphia: Jewish Publication Society, 1928

Rudavsky, David, *Emancipation and Adjustment: Contemporary Jewish Religious Movements, Their History and Thought*, New York: Diplomatic Press, 1967; as *Modern Jewish Religious Movements: A History of Emancipation and Adjustment*, New York: Behrman House, 1979

Schorsch, Ismar, "Zacharias Frankel and the European Origins of Conservative Judaism," *Judaism*, 30, 1981

Zacharias Frankel is considered the father of Conservative Judaism. He was the leader of the Breslau School, which combined observance of Jewish law with free inquiry into the historical development of talmudic traditions and the origin of Jewish ceremonies.

RUDAVSKY presents a clear and concise, but rather superficial, introduction to the thought of Frankel. The author discusses and examines how Frankel tried to distinguish between permanent and transitory values in Judaism.

DEUTSCH's monograph sketches the background, views, and accomplishments of Frankel, "the man of compromise." Frankel was born in Prague, a community noted for its culture, and throughout his career he played the part of a genuine ghetto patrician. His response in 1842 to the trustees of the first organized Reform congregation, the "Tempel" in Hamburg, regarding their revised prayer book is typical of the man. Theoretically, he did not believe in a personal Messiah, or in the return of all Israel to the promised land, but, practically, he wished all the prayers for the return to Palestine to be retained. In 1836 Frankel became rabbi of Dresden, a position he held for the next 18 years, during which time his views matured. While in Dresden, Frankel pursued his studies of the Greek translation of the Bible (Septuagint) and the talmudic literature, but he was by no means an ivory-tower scholar. He was, for instance, instrumental in securing abolition of *more Judaico*, the humiliating oath administered to Jews that implied that they were not to be treated like any other citizens.

A great step forward in Frankel's career came in 1854, when he was chosen as the president of the rabbinical seminary in Breslau, the first in all of Germany. Here he had a unique opportunity to disseminate his views. The school had been endowed from the legacy of a wealthy businessman in Breslau who was a friend and supporter of Abraham Geiger, the Reform leader, who expected to be invited to head the new seminary. The trustees of the legacy, however, felt that Geiger's views were too radical to win the confidence and support of the majority of congregations. The curriculum of the school included, besides the study of the Talmud and Codes, courses in Bible, Hebrew grammar, Jewish history, homiletics, and philosophy.

GINZBERG addresses the problem of how Frankel and the Breslau school could support freedom of inquiry while at the same time preserving and safeguarding Jewish tradition. Ginzberg finds the answer in the fact that Frankel never deduced the authority of Jewish law from the plenary inspiration of the Bible as the word of God. Thus a follower of Frankel could view the sabbath as originating from a Babylonian taboo-day and yet minutely observe all the sabbath laws practiced by the most strictly Orthodox. For an adherent of the Breslau school, the sabbath is holy not because its sanctity was proclaimed on Mount Sinai, but rather because it has become part of the authentic Jewish expression. It is the task of the historian to trace the beginnings and the development of Jewish customs and ceremonies; practical Judaism, on the other hand, is not concerned with origins, but regards institutions as they have come to be in the long quest of the Jewish people to discover the will of God.

Ginzberg gives a good summary of Frankel's major works, especially his introductions to the Mishnah and the Palestinian Talmud. At the end of his essay, Ginzberg, an outstanding talmudic scholar, compares the contributions of Frankel and Geiger to the study of the history of the halakhah. Geiger, he says, was superior as a critic of the development of Jewish law and its underlying principles, but Frankel greatly surpassed him as an interpreter of halakhic texts. Frankel's true preeminence lies in the harmonious union in himself of traditional Jewish learning and modern critical scholarship.

SCHORSCH covers much the same ground as Deutsch, but whereas Deutsch was born during Frankel's lifetime and often writes from personal knowledge, Schorsch writes as a trained historian working with documentary sources. He carefully explains the two adjectives in Frankel's concept of "positive historical Judaism." By "positive" Frankel meant in the first place the opposite of "negative," and he condemned the radical reformers, who saw in rabbinic Judaism nothing more than a mass of superstition and sacerdotal fraud, as being utterly negative. More importantly, "positive" carried a well-established technical connotation, implying either law in general or posited law as opposed to natural law. By choosing the adjective "positive," Frankel asserted the primacy of Jewish law and the fundamentally legal character of Judaism. By adding the adjective "historical" Frankel argued for a certain flexibility in the interpretation of Jewish law; the halakhah must be conceived in dynamic rather than static terms. If Jewish law was one pole of sanctity, history was most assuredly another, and it is this nonlegal dimension of Judaism that is designated "historical" in Frankel's classic phrase.

BLAU perceptively examines Frankel's position on moderate reform of Jewish religious beliefs and practices.

JACOB HABERMAN

G

Geiger, Abraham 1810–1874

German pioneer of Reform Judaism and
Jewish Studies

Geiger, Abraham, *Abraham Geiger and Liberal Judaism:
    The Challenge of the Nineteenth Century,* compiled by
    Max Wiener, translated by Ernst J. Schlochauer,
    Philadelphia: Jewish Publication Society, 1962
Heschel, Susannah, *Abraham Geiger and the Jewish Jesus*
    (Chicago Studies in the History of Judaism), Chicago:
    University of Chicago Press, 1998
Meyer, Michael, "Jewish Religious Reform and Wissenschaft
    des Judentums: The Position of Zunz, Geiger, and
    Fraenkel," *Leo Baeck Institute Year Book,* 16, 1971
Meyer, Michael, "Universalism and Jewish Unity in the
    Thought of Abraham Geiger," in *The Role of Religion in
    Modern Jewish History,* edited by Jacob Katz,
    Cambridge, Massachusetts: Association for Jewish
    Studies, 1975
Meyer, Michael, *Response to Modernity: A History of the
    Reform Movement in Judaism* (Studies in Jewish
    History), New York: Oxford University Press, 1988
Petuchowski, Jakob J., *New Perspectives on Abraham
    Geiger: An HUC-JIR Symposium,* Cincinnati, Ohio:
    Hebrew Union College-Jewish Institute of Religion, 1975

As the founding father of the Reform movement in Judaism,
Abraham Geiger ranks as one of the foremost German Jewish figures of the 19th century. His Judaism is a mixture born
of his traditional Orthodox upbringing and his secular German university education. While still a relatively young man,
Geiger began to feel that much of traditional Judaism was stifling, stagnant, and in need of change—a belief he carried with
him for the remainder of his life. As a solution to what he
viewed as the ossification of Judaism, he called for a reinterpretation of the tradition based on modern scientific analysis
of the texts (Wissenschaft). Although fellow reformers
embraced this position, it led to numerous, often rancorous,
arguments with traditionalists, most notably with his senior
colleague in the rabbinate of Breslau and the representative of
Orthodoxy, Solomon Tiktin. Geiger called for radical reform
throughout his life, but he nonetheless remained committed
to maintaining the unity of the Jewish community and often
tempered his behavior accordingly. When he died in 1874, he
left behind him a growing community of faith aligned with
the principles he had promoted so staunchly.

GEIGER constitutes the first major study of the man and his
philosophy. (The English translation represents a revision of the
German original.) The book consists of a substantial biographical sketch followed by excerpts from Geiger's letters, sermons, articles, and books (*The Science of Judaism, Judaism and
Its History,* and *The Original Text and Translations of the
Bible*), which illustrate his approach to Judaism as well as "the
vigor of his challenge." The editor, Max Wiener, charts Geiger's
life, from his Orthodox upbringing to his university education
to his pulpit in Breslau. Wiener also records in detail the controversies with Tiktin in Breslau that marked Geiger as a liberal. According to the editor, Geiger's greatness lay in his ideal
of religious reorganization deriving from spiritual and historical insight. Yet the editor also notes that, despite his philosophical innovations in this realm, Geiger never truly developed
into the kind of radical reformer for whom he called.

PETUCHOWSKI's book constitutes an amalgam of articles
on various aspects of Geiger's scholarship. David Weiss Halivni
looks at Geiger's critical approach to the Talmud and credits
Geiger for daring to interpret the Mishnah differently from the
way in which the rabbis of the Gemara did. Geiger's Talmud
criticism—his absolute refusal to subordinate scientific analysis to tradition—constitutes his major contribution to the field
of rabbinics. Nahum Sarna considers Geiger's Bible criticism,
which likewise called for a scientific analysis of the text. While
Protestant Bible criticism was already well established in
Geiger's time, Jewish scholarship avoided advanced Bible studies. Through his work, Geiger reclaimed Bible studies as a
legitimate concern of Jewish scholarship. Michael Meyer provides two articles in this compendium. The first consists of a
comprehensive bibliography of secondary literature on Geiger
in Hebrew, English, and German. Meyer's second contribution
addresses itself critically to Geiger's *Historical Judaism.*
Geiger's main failure, according to Meyer, was his inability to
distinguish between Jewish history and the history of Judaism.
For Geiger, they were one and the same, rendering the occur-
rences of Jewish history important only in the religious sense,
relevant to a people who make up a community of faith only.
In an appraisal of Geiger's prayer book reforms, Petuchowski
maintains that Geiger the extremely radical liturgical theoretician differed greatly from Geiger the liturgical practitioner.
While his rhetoric demanded much of Reform congregations
in terms of liturgical reform, in practice he elected to work

for change within the broad framework of unified Jewish congregations. Thus, his modified prayer book turns out to feature far fewer alterations of the text than one might expect.

MEYER (1975) likewise notes Geiger's commitment to Jewish unity, which the author links with Geiger's belief in universalism. As a young man, Geiger formed the belief that Jews could achieve a universal and universalist faith only by transcending Judaism, a faith he thought to be antithetical to universalism. The older Geiger, however, concluded that universalism was inherent only in Judaism. Thus, asserts Meyer, his early flirtation with schism gave way to a commitment to Jewish unity and the importance of the collective task, a stance he embraced until the end of his life. In his efforts to modernize Judaism and bring to light its universalist principles, Geiger was influenced by the Christian forms current in his day that stressed the universalization of Christianity. Notwithstanding this element of imitation, notes Meyer, Geiger maintained his claim that only Judaism was receptive to progress.

MEYER (1971) contrasts Geiger's ideology of religious reform with those of his reformist contemporaries, Leopold Zunz and Zacharias Frankel. This comparison provides the reader not only with an understanding of Wissenschaft according to Zunz and Frankel but also a deeper understanding of Geiger. Zunz, the nontheologian of the three, advocated strongly raising the Wissenschaft des Judentums—the scientific study of all, not just religious, Jewish texts—to the level of an academic discipline. Zunz's interests were the most clearly focused on the study of the Jewish past; like Geiger, this led Zunz to demand changes in the present state of Judaism, which he viewed as stagnant and backward. Although Frankel also supported the scientific study of religion, unlike Geiger and Zunz he insisted that Wissenschaft remain subservient to Judaism and not vice versa. Where Geiger occupied himself with a primary concern for revisiting philosophy and theology, Frankel insisted on reviewing practice, contending that the people were far more interested in changes in the demands of practice than they were in ancient Jewish philosophy and theology.

MEYER (1988) expands the comparison with Frankel in a larger treatment of the development of the Reform movement and Geiger's role therein. Meyer presents Geiger and Frankel as foils for one another, a surprising departure from the more common casting of Samson Hirsch in this role.

The latest monographic study of Geiger is HESCHEL's analysis of Geiger's study of the "Jewish Jesus." She draws an analogy to Manet's *Olympia,* whose direct stare at her audience discomforted a world used to the demure artistic portrayal of women. Similarly novel, Geiger's Jewish study of Jesus unsettled the Christian, or at the very least culturally Christian, academic world. According to Heschel, by reversing the situation in which Christians, especially the biblical critics of the age, wrote about Judaism to one where Jews wrote about Christianity, Geiger made a major adjustment to the power relations between the two religions. Where Christian theologians excoriated Pharisees and Pharisaism, Geiger argued purposely that Jesus was a Pharisee par excellence; the ideal that Jesus preached so steadfastly—the democratization of Jewish society—was the ideal championed by the Pharisees, unmistakably Jesus' teachers. Like Geiger's reversal of the scholarly gaze, his reincarnation of the Christian "mythic potential" under the most Jewish of auspices, namely the Pharisees as defined by the Christian theologians themselves, reclaimed power for the Jews in their academic and religious relationships with Christians.

SHARI LOWIN

Gender

Boyarin, Daniel, *Unheroic Conduct: The Rise of Heterosexuality and the Invention of the Jewish Man,* Berkeley: University of California Press, 1997

Eilberg-Schwartz, Howard, *The Savage in Judaism: An Anthropology of Israelite Religion and Ancient Judaism,* Bloomington: Indiana University Press, 1990

Hyman, Paula E., *Gender and Assimilation in Modern Jewish History: The Roles and Representation of Women* (Samuel and Althea Stroum Lectures in Jewish Studies), Seattle: University of Washington Press, 1995

Lassner, Jacob, *Demonizing the Queen of Sheba: Boundaries of Gender and Culture in Postbiblical Judaism and Medieval Islam* (Chicago Studies in the History of Judaism), Chicago and London: University of Chicago Press, 1993

Rudavsky, T.M. (editor), *Gender and Judaism: The Transformation of Tradition,* New York: New York University Press, 1995

Seidman, Naomi, *A Marriage Made in Heaven: The Sexual Politics of Hebrew and Yiddish* (Contraversions, 7), Berkeley: University of California Press, 1997

Wegner, Judith Romney, *Chattel or Person? The Status of Women in the Mishnah,* New York: Oxford University Press, 1988

Wolfson, Elliot R., *Circle in the Square: Studies in the Use of Gender in Kabbalistic Symbolism,* Albany: State University of New York Press, 1995

When God created human beings, the Hebrew Bible begins, he made them male and female. In the creation account in the next chapter, however, the narrative drops this nomenclature, preferring instead the terms *man* and *woman* in its description of the establishment of the social order. This terminological tension mirrors nicely the fundamental issues of gender. Males and females may be naturally differentiated by anatomy, but men and women are (or can be) culturally achieved states. Most cultures ascribe to a gender a wide range of characteristics, behaviors, and activities, and proper "men" and "women" are expected to conform to gender expectations. Feminist scholarship over the last 30 years has provided an array of methods for understanding how societies construct, reproduce, enforce, and violate gender boundaries. The relatively recent awareness of these issues not only has generated a burgeoning academic field, but it also has highlighted the gaps between modern values and traditional Jewish (and especially rabbinic) understandings of gender. There are now a number of valuable books that attempt to describe and analyze the ways in which Jews historically have constructed gender, and at the same time these studies have responded (if only implicitly) to the challenge that feminist scholarship has presented to modern Jewish communities.

RUDAVSKY presents a collection of essays by many of the leading scholars of gender and Judaism. The essays vary widely and are somewhat uneven. Nevertheless, they offer a good overview of different issues and approaches.

EILBERG-SCHWARTZ is not a book on gender per se, but his anthropological approach to the Hebrew Bible raises many issues that relate to how the different parties whose documents make up the Hebrew Bible constructed gender. Eilberg-Schwartz argues that the Hebrew Bible, especially within its rules concerning impure fluids, constructs a series of oppositions: men/women, life/death, control/lack of control. This dichotomized view of the world, in which gender plays a crucial role, is primarily the contribution of the Israelite priests, who attempted to construct a male community based on biological descent. For the priests, circumcision—the controlled release of blood from the organ of male reproduction—was the symbolic act par excellence in this construction.

Turning to early rabbinic literature, WEGNER employs a different approach. She examines how a single rabbinic document, the Mishnah (edited c.200 C.E.), constructs the legal status of women. Do these rabbis see a woman as an independent person (in the legal sense of the word) or as chattel, an object under the control of her father or husband? Wegner shows quickly that the binary nature of the question is misleading, for the Mishnah bifurcates the woman, regarding her as able to exert independent control in most areas of her life, with the significant exception of her sexuality. This bifurcation arose because the rabbis saw women as neither Self nor Other, but as ontologically ambiguous. Woman is thus an anomaly in the Mishnah, oscillating between two poles. Wegner's use of the term "chattel" is too strong (a woman's husband, for example, does not have the right to alienate her sexuality, i.e., to prostitute her), but her thesis deserves further consideration and testing in other rabbinic documents.

Instead of focusing on the way that law constructs and reproduces gender, LASSNER charts the history of exegesis of a single story—King Solomon's marriage to the queen of Sheba—from the Bible to the Middle Ages. Lassner demonstrates elegantly how in response to their perception of a tension between the biblical picture of a strong woman and their own understanding of the proper subordinate role for women, Jewish interpreters of the Bible increasingly tamed the queen of Sheba either by domesticating her or by demonizing her. By examining contemporary Islamic exposition of the same biblical story, Lassner also demonstrates that Jewish and Islamic exegetes were not working in isolation from each other but shared similar concerns about gender and even appropriated each other's readings of this story.

These later interpretations of the story of the queen of Sheba exemplify one strategy of reproducing gender roles and hierarchy, the creation of exempla or role models. WOLFSON examines a very different, and far more radical, strategy of constructing gender. According to Wolfson, many kabbalists (especially those who subscribed to Lurianic Kabbalah) understood gender constructions as ontological, based on the very nature of the divine. These kabbalists saw God as what Wolfson calls a "male androgyne." God is fully male, but folded within God's maleness is his female nature and attributes. The most striking kabbalistic image of this understanding is the portrayal of God's female nature as being embodied as the corona of his phallus. When God and the world are put right, female will be utterly assimilated into male. Despite the radicalism of this image, it reproduces an essentially conservative notion of gender: the male possesses power and the ability to act (the phallus), whereas the female is the passive receptacle of male activity. Wolfson's book is meticulously documented.

Language too can be gendered. In a short and interesting study, SEIDMAN discusses the gendering of Yiddish as a "female language" and of Hebrew as a "male language." The early Zionists and revivalists of Hebrew desired to see themselves and their activities as "masculine," which in turn led to their attaching a subordinate status ("female") to Yiddish. The construction of an "other" against which one can define oneself is of course not new, and perhaps it is not very surprising that the early promoters of Hebrew needed to demote Yiddish in order to define their own activity. What is more interesting here is that they chose gender as the vehicle for identification. It is not as if these Hebraists were entirely unaware of what they were doing; they describe their own linguistic activities using starkly masculine metaphors.

HYMAN provides a broader historical structure in which to view this phenomenon. She argues that Jewish assimilation in the 19th and 20th centuries must be viewed through the prism of gender. Jewish men and women, both in Western countries and in Eastern Europe, experienced assimilation differently, and these experiences led in turn to reassessments of gender roles and representations. In the West, for example, men and women assimilated in different frameworks. Jewish women, like their non-Jewish bourgeois sisters, were given responsibility for domestic life, including the moral and religious formation of children. Jewish men in the West, on the other hand, were expected to be more externally oriented. The material result of this division was that Jewish men assimilated more rapidly and radically than Jewish women. Yet this difference created a paradox: because women were responsible for the transmission of religious values, male assimilation was blamed on the failure of their mothers. In the East, on the other hand, where Jewish assimilation was harder to achieve, where Jewish women traditionally worked outside of the home, and where women were not valued as the sole transmitters of religious values, gender and gender roles were not seen as a significant category or subject of discussion. Eastern Jews brought this understanding of gender with them to the United States as immigrants at the beginning of the 20th century. These early Jewish immigrants adopted Western gender roles only in part, creating the image of the "Yiddishe Mamma," a domestic powerhouse who was a source of strength and support for her children.

Two factors, however, worked against the positive image of the strong Jewish mother. First was the antisemitic critique of Jewish masculinity, which dates from 19th-century Europe. Jewish men, antisemitic authors asserted, were not real men. Jewish men who were trying to assimilate could not ignore these attacks and responded by asserting their own masculinity, adopting the same gender values as their ambient cultures. This is the soil within which Zionism and the revival of Hebrew blossomed, and it explains the strong gender associations with these projects discussed by Seidman. The second factor in the United States was increasing assimilation. Sons and grandsons of these immigrants, caught between having lost their means for achieving Jewish status (through Torah study) and being denied status in the gentile world because of their Jewishness, turned against Jewish women. The result was the production of cultural stereotypes of the suffocating Jewish mother. "The baleboste gave way to the Jewish priestess in her home, and in the course of time the Yiddishe Mamma of song and story was transmuted into Sophie Portnoy."

Although the books surveyed above focus on vastly different times and places, their wider conclusions and implications are remarkably similar. All of these authors see gender as constructed, that is, as a malleable category that Jewish cultures throughout time have manipulated for a variety of reasons. Most of these Jewish constructions of gender have been nearly identical to those of proximate non-Jews. They also have been far from salutary for women. Nearly all of the authors discussed thus far reveal the androcentric nature of these gender constructions and the valuation of "male" as superior to "female." Lassner, Wolfson, and Hyman show most explicitly how uneasy many Jewish cultures felt at even the possibility of valuing female as higher than, or merely equal to, male.

On a deeper level, these books are wrestling not only with historical cultures, but with a very delicate issue: the role of modern Jewish women. While none of these books explicitly states it, all imply that past Jewish gender constructions are deeply flawed as models for modern Jewish life. Yet none takes the next step, explaining how modern Jewish society can understand gender. In a highly original and daring work, BOYARIN attempts to do exactly this. His argument is that from the rabbinic through the modern period, there have been Jews who had an alternative construction of gender that valorizes the "sissy," the feminized and eroticized Jewish male. Boyarin locates the origin of this gender construction in the rabbinic period, as a response to Roman colonization and hegemony, and he charts its survival in the Middle Ages (somewhat weakly argued with the example of Glikl of Hameln and more strongly illustrated with examples of art from the Passover Haggadah) and its flowering within later Ashkenazi culture. It is precisely this image to which both Zionism and Freud's theory of psychoanalysis attempted to respond. Boyarin wants to reclaim this gender construction, going so far as to suggest that the ideal of Jewish masculinity be seen in a woman, Bertha Pappenheim. Whether or not all or most of Boyarin's readings of this enormous range of sources are convincing or whether his ultimate suggestions become influential remains to be seen. What is clearer is that scholars now having exposed convincingly the androcentrism inherent in past Jewish gender constructions, Boyarin points the way to the next question: must responsible academic work restrict itself to the deconstruction of gender models, or can it contribute constructively to a modern, and passionate, debate?

MICHAEL L. SATLOW

See also Feminism; Sex; Women: Status

Genesis

Cassuto, Umberto, *Perush 'al Sefer Bereshit*, 1953; translated by Israel Abrahams as *A Commentary on the Book of Genesis*, 2 vols., Jerusalem: Magnes Press of Hebrew University, 1989

Gunkel, Hermann, *Die Sagen der Genesis*, 1901; translated by W.H. Carruth as *The Legends of Genesis: The Biblical Saga and History*, New York: Schocken, 1964

Leibowitz, Nehama, *Iyunim be-sefer Bereshit: be-'ikvot parshanenu ha-rishonim veha-aharonim*, 1966; as *Studies in Bereshit (Genesis) in the Context of Ancient and Modern Jewish Bible Commentary*, Jerusalem: World Zionist Organization, Department for Torah Education and Culture, 1974, 4th revised edition, 1993

Rendsburg, Gary, *The Redaction of Genesis*, Winona Lake, Indiana: Eisenbrauns, 1986

Sarna, Nahum, *Understanding Genesis* (Heritage of Biblical Israel, vol. 1), New York: Schocken, 1966

Sarna, Nahum, *Genesis/Be-reshit: The Traditional Hebrew Text with New JPS Translation* (JPS Torah Commentary), Philadelphia: Jewish Publication Society, 1989

Speiser, E.A. (editor and translator), *Genesis* (Anchor Bible, vol. 1), Garden City, New York: Doubleday, 1964, 3rd edition, 1979

von Rad, Gerhard, *Genesis: A Commentary*, Philadelphia: Westminster, and London: SCM, 1961; revised edition, Philadelphia: Westminster, 1973; London: SCM, 1985

The stories of Genesis have generated a library of commentaries and reflective works over the centuries. These works have examined Genesis from widely differing theological and methodological perspectives. During the 20th century, scholarly preference for understanding the book has shifted from one based on source-critical methodologies to one that treats the work essentially as a unity, whether written by one hand (a minority view) or compiled by a later redactor, dated to different periods and given different agendas depending on the scholar and his or her criteria.

CASSUTO's two-volume work can be credited, at least in part, with spearheading the initial forays into literary criticism of the Bible. Cassuto sifts a vast array of ancient Near Eastern sources and provides a careful and original study of the subtle nuances of the Hebrew text. In particular, he notes parallel units within the book of Genesis that possess a chiastic format, thus demonstrating a greater unity of the text than had been supposed by many scholars of his day. Where appropriate Cassuto also supplies information from the various other textual witnesses to illustrate how they differ from or elucidate the Hebrew text. The work was translated from Hebrew to English posthumously. Where Hebrew terms have been retained they are accompanied by transliteration and translation, making this a ready companion for students regardless of their knowledge of Hebrew. The champion of scholars who resisted the influential assumptions of Julius Wellhausen's Documentary Hypothesis, Cassuto offers a creative and scientific challenge to the atomization of the text. The two volumes cover Genesis from Adam to Noah and from Noah to Abraham, respectively.

GUNKEL's classic survey represents his reaction to and departure from Wellhausen's isolationist approach to the text. Gunkel, generally known as the founder of form criticism, treats the narratives of Genesis as a prose form of earlier poetic traditions. His work on Genesis is still regarded as an invaluable starting point.

LEIBOWITZ offers the text of Genesis in conjunction with selections from rabbinic commentaries and midrashim in Hebrew and English. In so doing, she makes accessible a world of early and diverse scholarship that is often unknown or unavailable. The work also lists at the end of each section a series of questions that challenge the reader to interrogate both the biblical text and the various commentators' positions and presuppositions. Leibowitz combines literary criticism, a feminist perspective, and traditional Jewish exegesis to make for original and engaging reading. Biographical notes on the commentators integrated into her work constitute a useful added feature.

VON RAD expands upon the theological implications of the earlier historical studies of Albrecht Alt and Martin Noth, aiming to "elucidate the relationship between Biblical historical and literary criticism and a Biblical theology of history." While adhering to the bare essentials of the Documentary Hypothesis, von Rad treats Genesis as a carefully composed "saga" and provides what is essentially a running commentary that separates the various narrative traditions (e.g., J, E, and P) while studying them within the context of a broader hexateuchal theology. Von Rad sees this as a preoccupation with a single and simple narrative theme: "God, the Creator of the world, called the patriarchs and promised them the land of Canaan. When Israel became numerous in the land of Egypt, God led the people through the wilderness with wonderful demonstrations of grace; then after their lengthy wandering he gave them under Joshua the Promised Land."

SARNA (1966) aims to elucidate the historical, philosophical, and sociological message of Genesis. He designed his work to "make the Bible of Israel intelligible, relevant and, hopefully, inspiring to a sophisticated generation, possessed of intellectual curiosity and ethical sensitivity." To this end, Sarna rejects the literalist interpretation of the Bible and instead places it in its appropriate cultural setting, treating the text as one would treat any historical document. Sarna distills for the nontechnical reader the advances of biblical scholarship, archaeology, and more recent techniques of critical analysis without leaning on jargon. While clarifying the broader cultural continuum that comprises the Near East, Sarna rightly emphasizes the differences as well, pointing out the distinguishing characteristics of Israelite religion and literature. He proceeds through the book of Genesis by pericope and cycle, providing separate treatments of creation, the flood, the Tower of Babel, the patriarchal period, the covenant, Sodom and Gomorrah, Isaac and the Akedah, Jacob and his relations with Esau and Laban, and finally the Joseph cycle.

Each page of SARNA (1989) provides Hebrew biblical text, interlinear translation, and a running commentary that highlights the most difficult and important verses. Sarna looks at Genesis with a literary eye and elucidates it with numerous references to ancient and modern scholarship. The commentary is transliterated when discussing particular words or phrases, rendering it useful to readers who are not familiar with Hebrew. Sarna's commentary represents a transitional phase in scholarship, one that links the early efforts at literary criticism of the Bible, and hence a holistic understanding of the received text, with a seasoned and cautious regard for the oral sources that comprise the narrative fabric.

SPEISER combines a mastery of ancient Near Eastern and traditional Jewish sources with the perspective of the school of higher criticism. In addition to providing a translation and thorough philological analysis of the more difficult aspects of the text, Speiser also delves into the redactional history of Genesis. In particular, he opines as to the various editorial strands that he sees layered into a semicohesive whole, which betray a number of hands as well as a grounding in pagan mythology. Throughout, Speiser provides archaeological and comparative evidence to elucidate the text. Though a few of Speiser's observations appear today somewhat dated and even somewhat presumptuous, his overall contribution to the study of Genesis cannot be overstated.

RENDSBURG expands upon the work of earlier literary critical scholars such as Cassuto in demonstrating how the entire work of Genesis forms a complex web of interconnected stories, held together by theme-words that link paired units. His book is divided into four major units—the primeval history, the Abraham cycle, the Jacob cycle, and the Joseph story—and considers also the parallels that connect each of the cycles. Rendsburg discusses the impact that the proposed redactional structuring has on source criticism and comments on a possible date for the book, which, based on literary parallels with Samuel and Kings, he places during the united monarchy, sometime in the tenth century B.C.E. His holistic approach to Genesis provides an insightful counterpoint to the atomizing tendencies of higher criticism.

SCOTT B. NOEGEL

Genizah, Cairo

Cohen, Mark R., *Jewish Self-Government in Medieval Egypt: The Origins of the Office of Head of the Jews, ca. 1065–1126* (Princeton Studies on the Near East), Princeton, New Jersey: Princeton University Press, 1980; as *Jewish Self-Government in Medieval Egypt: The Origins of the Office of the Head of the Jews,* Guildford, Surrey: Princeton University Press, 1980

Friedman, Mordechai A., *Jewish Marriage in Palestine: A Cairo Genizah Study,* 2 vols., New York: Jewish Theological Seminary of America, 1980

Gil, Moshe, *Documents of the Jewish Pious Foundations from the Cairo Geniza* (Publications of the Diaspora Research Institute, vol. 12), Leiden: Brill, 1976

Gil, Moshe, *Erets-Yisra'el ba-tekufah ha-Muslemit ha-rishonah (634–1099),* 1983; translated by E. Broido as *A History of Palestine, 634–1099,* Cambridge and New York: Cambridge University Press, 1992

Goitein, S.D., *A Mediterranean Society: The Jewish Communities of the Arab World as Portrayed in the*

Documents of the Cairo Geniza, 5 vols., Berkeley and Los Angeles: University of California Press, 1967–1988

Golb, Norman, "Sixty Years of Genizah Research," *Judaism,* 6, 1957

Mann, Jacob, *Texts and Studies in Jewish History and Literature* (Abraham and Hannah Oppenheim Memorial Publications), 2 vols., Cincinnati, Ohio: Hebrew Union College Press, 1931–1935

There is scarcely an aspect of the culture and history of medieval Near Eastern Jewry that has not been significantly impacted by the publication of materials discovered in what has come to be known as the Cairo Genizah. A *genizah* is a place to which written and printed Judaica and Hebraica—usually of at least a quasi-religious significance—is retired once it has become worn or unneeded, but the Cairo Genizah is the genizah par excellence, a quite singular example of such a repository, in almost constant use for close to 1,000 years before its "discovery" by European scholars in the 19th century. It would be impossible for a single article to embrace, in even the most cursory manner, all of the subjects—let alone the important publications—that fall within the purview of the present rubric. Subjects as disparate as biblical studies, rabbinics, Karaism, law, mysticism, philosophy, and poetry have all benefited from the discovery of these manuscripts. (See, for example, the update on research of genizah materials in the 1983–1985 yearbook of the *Encyclopaedia Judaica,* 163–171.) One field, however, may be said to owe its very existence to the discovery of the Cairo Genizah materials, namely the economic, political, and social history of medieval Near Eastern Jewry, especially in the period between the 11th and 13th centuries.

MANN focuses primarily on the religious and political institutions of the Jews. A number of the texts in this work reveal the complexity of the relations that existed between the central institutions of Babylonian authority (i.e., the academies and the exilarchate) and the newly emergent independent Jewish communities in North Africa and Europe. In this regard, Mann has played a critical role in demonstrating the usefulness of documentary material from the Cairo Genizah for Jewish history. Mann's interests, however, are not limited to the realms of social and political history, as various chapters of this work reveal. There are chapters that deal with the intellectual and cultural life of the Jews, and the first section of the work makes pioneering use of Genizah documents about the history of Jews in Europe, a path that has most recently been followed by Norman Golb.

GOLB's article, while now somewhat dated, is still a useful and entertaining introduction to the Cairo Genizah. In addition to describing the exciting events that led to Solomon Schechter's acquisition of the contents of the Genizah for the Cambridge University Library in 1896, Golb also gives the reader a sense of the important contributions to research that the Cairo Genizah has afforded since. In a clear and engaging style, he details numerous historical issues that have had to be revised and clarified in light of new information gleaned from sources discovered in the Genizah. Golb's article reviews the major fields of research that have been impacted by research on the Genizah materials and introduces the reader to many of the important scholars who have been involved in that enterprise.

GOITEIN's work is the masterful summation of a long and fruitful career of research into the economic and social history of Mediterranean Jewry based on documents from the Cairo Genizah. In five volumes of text, he recreates in particular the bustling Jewish society of Fustat (Old Cairo). But Goitein's work is neither a local history of Fustat nor of Egypt. The Jewish community that preserved the Genizah papers was, in Goitein's view, part of a much larger economic and cultural universe that transcended political and religious boundaries. Thus, Goitien states that his work is titled *A Mediterranean Society* "because the people described in it are to a certain extent representative of their class in the Mediterranean world in general, and its Arabic section in particular." For all of its breadth, however, Goitein's work does not ride rough-shod over the details of daily life; they are here in all of their vividness and complexity.

FRIEDMAN's work, like that of Gil (1976), is a close study of a corpus of documents all of a single type, in this case Palestinian marriage contracts. The discovery of the Cairo Genizah has shed light on the ancient religious tradition of Palestine, which differed on many points from that in practice in Babylonia, and Friedman's study uses Palestinian marriage contracts as a window onto that tradition. He notes a number of unique traits in these documents that point to a distinct Palestinian legal tradition, as well as certain scribal features that are particular to these documents. The second volume of this work contains edited transcriptions and translations of the documents upon which the study is based, together with helpful introductions and notes.

GIL (1976) is a study of documents pertaining to charitable institutions, similar in scope to Friedman's work on marriage contracts. Building on Goitein's preliminary investigations in the second volume of his *Mediterranean Society,* Gil extracts a wealth of data related to the economic and social conditions within the genizah community from 147 documents. In a lengthy introduction, he dwells on the various motivations, religious and economic, behind the endowment of these foundations and details their administration by the community. Gil also compares the role of these institutions within the Jewish community to that played by the *waqf* in Muslim society. Transcriptions and translations of the corpus of documents are offered in the second section of the work.

COHEN's book considers a crucial development in the political history of Egyptian Jewry. The author demonstrates how the documentary sources from the Genizah can serve as a historical corrective to the programmatic medieval chronicles upon which earlier generations of historians relied. Specifically, Cohen shows that the office of the Head of the Jews in Egypt came about as the end-result of a slow and protracted process originating within the Jewish community, and not by caliphal decree as described in medieval sources. He delves into the complex interpersonal relations among key players in this process, and he highlights similar developments of consolidation within Egypt's Coptic Christian community.

GIL (1983) is a synthetic treatment of the political, social, and economic history of Palestine. At the center of Gil's history of the Jewish community is the Palestinian yeshivah, an institution that was virtually unknown before the discovery of the Genizah and the research of Jacob Mann. Gil accords the yeshivah its rightful place among the international institutions of Jewish authority during the Middle Ages, alongside the exilarchate and the two academies in Babylonia. In addition to the wealth of data that it contains, Gil's book makes an important methodological statement by incorporating Genizah-based studies, usually of a narrowly Jewish nature, into a more comprehensive history of Palestine from the time of the Muslim conquest.

ARNOLD FRANKLIN

Gentiles

Katz, Jacob, *Exclusiveness and Tolerance: Studies in Jewish-Gentile Relations in Medieval and Modern Times* (Scripta Judaica, 3), Oxford: Oxford University Press, and New York: Behrman House, 1961

Katz, Jacob, *Goi shel Shabat*, 1983; translated as The *"Shabbes Goy": A Study in Halakhic Flexibility*, Philadelphia: Jewish Publication Society, 1989

Novak, David, *The Image of the Non-Jew in Judaism: An Historical and Constructive Study of the Noahide Laws* (Toronto Studies in Theology, vol. 14), New York: Mellen, 1983

Shahak, Israel, *Jewish History, Jewish Religion: The Weight of Three Thousand Years* (Pluto Middle Eastern Studies), London and Boulder, Colorado: Pluto, 1994

Although modern scholarship has amply documented the history of gentile attitudes toward Jews, the parallel topic of how Jews and Judaism have historically viewed gentiles remains largely neglected.

The work of Katz constitutes a partial exception. His studies of Jewish views of gentiles have been directed at two primary goals: first, to demonstrate how economic circumstances that condition Jewish-gentile relations have influenced the historical development of Jewish law (halakhah); and second, to show how varying demographic conditions and cultural orientations have shaped shifting Jewish perceptions of gentiles within the social-psychological sphere.

KATZ (1961) provides a broad survey of Jewish attitudes as they emerged in Christian Europe during medieval and modern times. In part one, Katz introduces readers to the kinds of tensions that arose in early medieval Europe between inherited rabbinic prohibitions on Jewish-gentile contact, on the one hand, and the needs of Jewish communities to maintain their economic viability through business relations with non-Jews, on the other. In part two, Katz explores a range of medieval Jewish "types"—such as proselytes, martyrs, pietists, and disputants—to demonstrate the wide variety of approaches toward Christians that existed within the same broadly-defined theological and legal value system. In part three, Katz traces how the shifting pressures of the early modern and modern periods of European history gradually transformed the attitudes expressed by Jews toward gentiles. Here the author posits that the cultural (and often

physical) isolation of Jewry in the 15th and 16th centuries contributed to a revision of Jewish perceptions of gentiles, whose intrinsic metaphysical natures, as well as their theological views, were now considered to differentiate them from Jews.

Ironically, this hardening of Jewish attributions of metaphysical "otherness" to non-Jews served as a prelude to the growth of greater tolerance within Judaism during the subsequent two centuries. As Katz emphasizes, this growth did not occur solely because of intrinsically theological criteria; rather, it developed for three other reasons. First, it was a response to occupational shifts mandated by the place of Jews in an expanding European mercantile economy. Second, tolerance among Jews rose amid other increased expressions of religious toleration by European Enlightenment movements during the 18th century. Third, Jews grew more tolerant in reaction to the new Emancipation contract established by the French Revolution. Nevertheless, Katz suggests that these pressures did not altogether eliminate the traditional anti-Christian (and more generally anti-gentile) spirit of Judaism, but rather forced Jews to adapt their attitudes to the orientations of various modern secular ideologies.

KATZ's (1983) analysis of the concept of the "sabbath gentile" avoids the weaknesses of over-generalization inherent in the broad focus of his earlier study. The "sabbath gentile," a non-Jew who performs certain work for Jews on the Jewish day of rest, was an institution that entered into the life of diaspora Judaism to resolve the problems created by the elaborate prohibitions in Jewish religious law against performing various functions construed as "work" on the sabbath. However, recourse to the use of gentiles to undertake necessary or desirable tasks—already problematic from the standpoint of mishnaic and talmudic law—created a host of novel halakhic problems, particularly as Jewish economic existence and business relations grew increasingly complex in Europe during the medieval and early modern periods.

Katz examines the various ways in which Jewish jurisprudence sought to accommodate itself to fundamental alterations in the character of medieval Jewish life, especially as a consequence of the shift in Jewish economy away from agriculture and toward trade, which occurred between the ninth and 12th centuries. In a fascinating exposition, he shows how rabbinic authorities justified practices already widely engaged in by Jewish communities, such as using gentiles to light fires, milk cows, transport goods, run shops, mint coins, and perform other tasks forbidden to Jews on the sabbath.

This phenomenon became much more prevalent in Poland during the later Middle Ages, as Jews in that nation leased farms, tolls, inns, and various other commercial franchises from noble landlords. The use of gentiles to maintain such enterprises on the sabbath was justified through legal fictions, such as the temporary "sale" or "rent" of the enterprise; on the basis of competing and overriding legal provisions; and on the grounds of legal distinctions, such as those between earning profit and avoiding loss. Nevertheless, as Katz shows, widely-deployed practices occasionally so exceeded the capacity of authorities to find loopholes that rabbis often found themselves condemning such practices without being able to stop them. In this manner, Katz uses the halakhic debates surrounding the sabbath gentile as a barometer to gauge the gradual breakdown of traditional Jewish authority under conditions of economic modernization.

NOVAK focuses on divisions in approach to the category of "righteous gentiles" within tannaitic, medieval philosophical, and kabbalistic literature. In premodern Judaism, the "righteous gentile" was a legal-conceptual, rather than a strictly ethical, category. Its origination during the tannaitic period produced a tripartite division separating Jews (those who adhere to the whole of Sinaitic revelation) from gentile idolaters (those who enjoy no part whatsoever in the Torah) and righteous gentiles (those who adhere to the seven "Noahide laws," which command the establishment of law courts and prohibit blasphemy, idolatry, sexual deviance, murder, theft, and eating the torn limb from a living animal, on the basis of the Sinaitic revelation). The creation of this third, "in-between" category led to debates within Judaism over whether or not gentile adherents of the Noahide laws can achieve divine salvation. Here, Novak explains, a rift emerged within Judaism that partially anticipated later divisions between Jewish philosophical and mystical traditions. It is in the latter, mystical, wing of Judaism that ontological distinctions between Jews and gentiles were most rigorously drawn. In contrast to Katz, who attributes this development to the "ghettoization" of late medieval and early modern Jewries, Novak posits that the demonization of the gentile dates back to various tannaitic traditions and evolved concurrently with the deepening of Jewish mystical orientations over the course of the Middle Ages.

Finally, SHAHAK presents a polemical overview of negative Jewish stereotypes of the gentile, loosely fitted into a broad historical framework. Shahak's approach is ideologically geared toward justifying an attack upon the political premises of Zionism and the constitutional prerogatives of modern Israel as the "Jewish State." While marked by broad overgeneralizations, occasional distortions, and sharp polemical broadsides, Shahak is largely right in his rejection of the apologetic emphases in mainstream academic Jewish historiography on the question of the gentile. Shahak thus provides a useful corrective to some of the weaknesses of the abovementioned works, one that underscores the need for extensive further research in this under-investigated field.

JONATHAN KARP

Geonim

Brody, Robert, *The Geonim of Babylonia and the Shaping of Medieval Jewish Culture*, New Haven, Connecticut: Yale University Press, 1998

Cohen, Gerson, "The Reconstruction of Gaonic History," in the introduction to the reprint edition of *Texts and Studies in Jewish History and Literature*, written by Jacob Mann, New York: Ktav, 1972

Gil, Moshe, *Erets-Yisra'el ba-tekufah ha-Muslemit ha-rishonah (634–1099)*, 1983; translated by E. Broido as *A History of Palestine, 634–1099*, Cambridge and New York: Cambridge University Press, 1992

Ginzberg, Louis, *Geonica* (Texts and Studies of the Jewish Theological Seminary of America), 2 vols., New York: Jewish Theological Seminary of America, 1909; 2nd edition, New York: Hermon, 1968

Groner, Tsvi, *The Legal Methodology of Hai Gaon* (Brown Judaic Studies, no. 66), Chico, California: Scholars Press, 1985

Malter, Henry, *Saadia Gaon: His Life and Works* (Morris Loeb Series), Philadelphia: Jewish Publication Society, 1921

Mann, Jacob, "The Responsa of the Geonim as a Source of Jewish History," in *The Collected Articles of Jacob Mann*, vol. 2: *Gaonic Studies*, Gedera: Shalom, 1971; New York: Behrman House, 1973

Sklare, David, *Samuel ben Hofni Gaon and His Cultural World: Texts and Studies* (Études sur le judaïsme médiéval, 18), New York: Brill, 1996

Most of the primary source material on the geonim—the spiritual leaders of early medieval Jewry—available to 19th-century historians pertained strictly to the geonim's public role as principals of the great academies, the yeshivot, in Babylonia and Palestine. It was thus through the prism of their institutional lives—reflected in the wealth of geonic responsa literature—that historical inquiry into the geonic period began. With the publication of materials found in the Cairo Genizah, however, new windows into the geonic period were opened. Besides a plethora of new responsa, commentaries, and legal treatises, the Genizah also provided letters and documents that allowed recent scholars to see beyond the abstract intellectual activity of the geonim and explore the sociological and political dimensions of the period. At the same time, the 20th century has seen a growing appreciation of the entrenchment of geonic history within contemporary Muslim society as well.

GINZBERG's work is a pioneering step in the study of geonic history both in its scope and the source material it uses. Based to a large extent on newly discovered responsa from the Cairo Genizah, it represents the first attempt to encompass the salient features of the geonic period in a work devoted exclusively to that subject. Ginzberg approaches his subject by focusing on the institution of the gaonate rather than searching for remarkable individuals. If the geonim themselves were for the most part less-than-monumental figures, he suggests, "the more important must have been the Gaonate to be able to impress its stamp upon several centuries." Ginzberg's study has produced a groundbreaking appreciation both of the sociological forces at play within the gaonate and of the long-overlooked political dimension of geonic history. However, it should be recognized that Ginzberg focuses almost exclusively on the halakhic activity of the geonim, obviously a perspective that skews the reader's impression of the period.

Owing to the relatively meager amount of biographical information available in the relevant sources, MALTER's work on Saadya is one of only a few works devoted to the lives of individual geonim. The comparatively large quantity of data available on Saadya's stormy public career, however, makes him one of the most suitable candidates for a monographic treatment of this sort. Malter regards Saadya as "the founder of a new epoch in Jewish history," whose main contribution lies in "the literary monuments [that he] left to posterity in nearly all branches of Jewish learning and literature." Malter insists that a "biography of [Saadya] should primarily be a record of his literary achievements and of his spiritual influence." Accordingly, the book's first part, which is devoted to Saadya's life, is offered as a backdrop to the discussion of Saadya's literary output, which is elaborated in the second part. The book's third section, a bibliography of modern scholarship on Saadya, was comprehensive in its day but is now sorely out of date.

MANN's study represents an important turning point in the study of the geonic period. His concern in this article (as in all of his works) is the realia of life as it had been lived by the common Jew. This orientation had already gained some following among Jewish historians, but it is innovatively applied to the geonic period by Mann. Acknowledging the inherent limitations of his sources, Mann nevertheless asserts that geonic responsa "are a real treasure trove for the knowledge of the life of the Jews of that period, especially in such points where the information to be obtained from external sources entirely fails." Critical of historians who, following blindly in the footsteps of Solomon Rappoport, treat the history of the geonic period as "a collection of biographies of the prominent spiritual and communal leaders," Mann extracts information from responsa literature about the lives of Jews in the various communities to which these communications were sent. The dense writing style that plagues this and many of Mann's other writings does not diminish Mann's profound insights.

COHEN's essay is an extremely informative overview of research in the field of geonic history. Ostensibly written as an introduction to the reprint of Jacob Mann's *Texts and Studies,* it is in fact a sweeping summary of 19th- and 20th-century scholarship on the geonic age and it pays close attention to the historiographical concerns of the authors it discusses. The reader of this essay will become acquainted with all of the major writers on the geonic period as well as the issues that occupied them. A useful bibliography is appended to the text.

GIL's work serves as an important corrective to the otherwise lopsided emphasis on the geonim of Babylonia in this article and in the field in general. Palestine was home to an academy of its own, which was also headed by individuals bearing the title "gaon." However, unlike the geonim of Babylonia, those in Palestine produced relatively little in the way of responsa. Thus, most of the information on the Palestinian geonim derives from personal letters and court documents found in the Cairo Genizah. The paucity of legal material produced by the Palestinian geonim has led historians to conclude that the Palestinian academy served primarily as an administrative center for the regions under its authority, and it was therefore comparable in many ways to the status of the exilarchate in Babylonia. Gil's work delineates the functions carried out by the Palestinian geonim during a period of nearly 200 years.

GRONER's work allows the reader to see in minute detail the process whereby the Babylonian Talmud achieved canonical status at the hands of the geonim. Groner examines the responsa that can be attributed with reasonable certainty to Hai Gaon—the largest number attributable to any one figure in the geonic period—with a view to extracting the hermeneu-

tical principles that underlie them. In particular, Groner demonstrates Hai's unwavering reliance on the Babylonian Talmud as the ultimate source of legal authority.

SKLARE's biographical study attempts to locate the early 11th-century figure Samuel ben Hofni, one of the last geonim of the Sura academy, within the general intellectual landscape of his time. Based on a close analysis of Samuel ben Hofni's works, some of which are published for the first time in this text, Sklare shows the close philological and conceptual affinity between these writings and those of contemporary Muslim mu'tazilite thinkers. Against the opposition of some conservative elements within the Jewish community, the rationalist spirit of the Muslims was embraced, albeit selectively, by Samuel and others like him who sought desperately to "revitalize and strengthen the intellectual life of the yeshivot and to maintain their central intellectual authority." Sklare's synchronic approach to the intellectual activity of the geonim represents a fresh new direction in research on the period.

BRODY offers an elegant and up-to-date synthesis of research on the major themes of the geonic period up to the 11th century. He considers the major accomplishment of the geonim to be their consolidation of Jewish culture along lines laid down in the canon of (Babylonian) rabbinic literature. This perspective is reflected both in the title of his book and the periodization that Brody employs. He develops his thesis by analyzing the various functions carried out by the geonim, paying particular attention to their literary and intellectual activity. The internationally recognized authority of the geonim within the Jewish world was critical to their success, and Brody explains how the geonim fought to maintain that status even as independent Jewish communities began to emerge in Europe and North Africa at the end of this period. In the book's final section, which dwells on the innovations introduced by Saadya and his successors, Brody conceives of these new developments as part of a desperate struggle by the geonim to retain their position in the face of a changing intellectual climate within the international Jewish community. Brody's patient discussion of the primary sources for the period, as well as his summaries of major points of scholarly debate, makes this a useful work for the advanced student and the beginner alike.

ARNOLD FRANKLIN

Germany: Medieval

Agus, Irving, *The Heroic Age of Franco-German Jewry: The Jews of Germany and France of the Tenth and Eleventh Centuries; the Pioneers and Builders of Town-life, Town-government, and Institutions,* New York: Yeshiva University Press, 1969

Breuer, Mordechai and Michael Graetz, *Tradition und Aufklärung 1600–1780,* 1996; translated by William Templer as *Tradition and Enlightenment, 1600–1780* (vol. 1 of *Deutsch-jüdische Geschichte in der Neuzeit–German-Jewish History in Modern Times,* edited by Michael Meyer and Michael Brenner), New York: Columbia University Press, 1996

Chazan, Robert, *European Jewry and the First Crusade*, Berkeley: University of California Press, 1987

Eidelberg, Shlomo, *Jewish Life in Austria in the Fifteenth Century as Reflected in the Legal Writings of Rabbi Israel Isserlein and his Contemporaries*, Philadelphia: Dropsie College for Hebrew and Cognate Learning, 1962

Hsia, R. Po-chia and Hartmut Lehmann, *In and Out of the Ghetto: Jewish-Gentile Relations in Late Medieval and Early Modern Germany*, Cambridge and New York: Cambridge University Press, 1995

Kisch, Guido, *Jewry-law in Medieval Germany: Laws and Court Decisions Concerning Jews* (Texts and Studies of the American Academy for Jewish Research, vol. 3), New York: American Academy for Jewish Research, 1949

Kisch, Guido, *The Jews in Medieval Germany: A Study of their Legal and Social Status*, Chicago: University of Chicago Press, 1949; 2nd edition, New York: Ktav, 1970

Shohet, David Menahem, *The Jewish Court in the Middle Ages: Studies in Jewish Jurisprudence According to the Talmud, Geonic, and Medieval German Responsa*, New York: Commanday-Roth, 1931

Straus, Raphael, *Die Judengemeinde Regensburg im ausgehenden Mittelalter, auf Grund der Quellen kritisch untersucht und neu dargestellt*, 1932; translated by Felix N. Gerson as *Regensburg and Augsburg* (Jewish Communities Series), Philadelphia: Jewish Publication Society, 1939

Zimmer, Eric, *Harmony and Discord: An Analysis of the Decline of Jewish Self-Government in Fifteenth Century Europe*, New York: Yeshiva University Press, 1970

Jews traveled through and perhaps even settled in Germany primarily as merchants in late antiquity and the early Middle Ages. There are references to Jews in the fourth century in the city of Cologne, for example. Still, there are no substantive records or indications of permanent Jewish settlement in Germany until the late tenth century. At that time a number of Jewish families made their way to Germany from Italy, among the most well-known being the Kalonymos family from Lucca, some of whom first settled in Mainz. Later, Jews moved to other Rhenish cities, including Speyer and Worms. In general, Jews found homes in old episcopal and trade centers and settled in the east, in Regensburg and Prague, as well. The famous invitation of the Bishop of Speyer to the Jews of Mainz in 1084 offered Jews numerous privileges for settling in the city at the same time that it made clear the economic benefit that the Bishop intended to reap from the Jews' activities. The charter was thus rather indicative of much of the later development of medieval German Jewry, and "charters" were soon offered to Jews in other cities, such as Worms in 1090. Owing to the favorable economic conditions and the settlement of important scholars, the Rhenish communities flourished during the high Middle Ages. Throughout the Middle Ages, however, Jews living in Germany had to navigate through complex relations with their local and imperial overlords as well as their Christian neighbors.

The majority of books available in English on the period focus on such relations, particularly at points of conflict, such as the crusades at the end of the 11th century; the increased restriction of Jewish social, political, and economic activity, especially in the 12th and 13th centuries; confrontations with the church; accusations of well poisoning during the time of the Black Death and the subsequent massacre and displacement of many Jewish communities; trials for alleged ritual murder and host desecration; and the eventual and almost systematic expulsion of the Jews from a variety of German cities in the 15th century and German territories in the 16th century. Less representative of the scholarship available in English, but certainly more central recently, is the internal history of the Jewish communities, in particular the growth of communal structures; the development of the rabbinate and the discussion over rabbinic ordination; as well as the intellectual accomplishments of the Hasidei Ashkenaz and the important rabbinic legal decisions of the 13th through the 15th century.

BREUER and GRAETZ focus on the 17th and 18th centuries, but the first portion of their work offers a general and very helpful overview of the history of the Jews in Germany from the beginnings of their settlement there through the 16th century. This first chapter would serve as a most useful introduction to the subject. The focus throughout is on both internal communal, cultural, and intellectual developments and on the impact of external forces on the Jews in Germany.

HSIA and LEHMANN present essays from a number of the most important international scholars of late medieval and early modern German Jewish history (from the 15th through the 18th century). While the volume addresses primarily the last phases of the Middle Ages, many of the contributors are important scholars in the more general field of medieval German Jewry, and the research presented is very current and multidisciplinary. The essays throughout the book present the history of the Jews from the "outside," that is, Jews seen from the Gentile world, as well as from the "inside," Jews looking out onto the non-Jewish world. The topics that receive the most attention are the effects of exclusion—imposed as well as self-imposed—of the Jews from the society around them; the social and economic structure of German Jewry; relations between Jews and their Christian neighbors and political lords; and representations of and prejudices against Jews.

AGUS, relying heavily on rabbinic responsa, discusses the early stages of settlement and development of the tenth- and 11th-century Franco-German (Rhenish) communities, which he considers the antecedents to a more modern conception of Ashkenazi culture that later, after the 14th century, spread to Eastern Europe. For Agus, the Franco-German communities of the tenth and 11th centuries enjoyed an improved condition over their Roman and Carolingian predecessors, featuring strong systems of education, economic opportunity, and autonomous self-government. Agus traces a number of significant aspects of the Jewish communal life of this period, especially business and economic practices, communal organization, domestic life, and relations with non-Jewish society.

SHOHET argues that Jewish life in Germany flourished in a uniquely Jewish fashion, which, although not "wholly uninfluenced by foreign ideals, was not moved nor dominated by them." The Italian and Spanish Jewish communities, on the other hand, were to a much larger degree influenced by the culture of their non-Jewish surroundings. Throughout, Shohet seeks to examine the adjustments in outward Jewish life as well as the attempts of Jewish authorities to harmonize Jewish law with the realities of life. Shohet's focus is on the juridical as well as the historical development of German Jewry in the Middle Ages. He asserts that the rabbinic Judaism of the period was less rigid and fixed than it subsequently became, and he insists that local customs and ordinances often took precedence in the legal decisions of Jewish courts. As Jewish contact with a vast non-Jewish world grew, the exigencies placed on the Jews themselves grew; thus, during the Middle Ages frequent rabbinical synods were called to discuss current issues and promulgate new ordinances as required. Shohet offers a classic description of some of the main internal Jewish institutions and customs from the perspective of the rabbinic literature of the period. Included for discussion are the definition, rights, and administration of the community; the synagogue; the various methods of assessing and collecting community and individual taxes; the legal relations of Jews to non-Jews and to non-Jewish courts; the organization of the Jewish courts, the extent of their legislative authority, and their ability to enforce their legislation; the status of informers against the community; and the use of evidence in legal proceedings.

CHAZAN argues that although modern historiography has viewed the events of the First Crusade in 1096 as a decisive and disastrous watershed in medieval Jewish history, the actual impact of crusader violence on European Jewry was rather limited. According to Chazan, the bulk of Ashkenazi Jewry emerged from the crusades unscathed to continue their rapid development, in terms of both economic growth and cultural creativity, with little hindrance and a fair degree of tolerance until the 13th century.

STRAUS presents and compares the historical developments of the Jewish communities in the Bavarian cities of Augsburg (in Swabia) and Regensburg (in Upper Palatinate). These two communities possessed large and significant Jewish communities in the Middle Ages, though both were devastated by misfortunes in the later Middle Ages. The Jews in Augsburg were expelled from that city during the Black Death massacres and then again in the fourth decade of the 15th century. The Jews of Regensburg were expelled in 1519 in the early phases of the Protestant Reformation. Combining a variety of archival material (for which Straus's work on the history of the Jews in Regensburg is well known in German) as well as chronicles and responsa literature, Straus offers a very full and detailed discussion of the political, economic, spiritual, and communal developments of the two communities, focusing on the period before the late medieval expulsions.

KISCH (1949b) offers the most thorough and significant study of medieval German Jewry-law available in any language. Since it first appeared in 1949, *The Jews in Medieval Germany: A Study of their Legal and Social Status* has exercised an enormous influence on legal history and even more so on the study of German Jewish history. Kisch's erudite and broad understanding of a variety of difficult medieval legal texts is truly impressive. Kisch argues that the admission of Jews as permanent settlers in Germany in the tenth century was indeed a watershed, but it was the rapid expansion of commerce and trade beginning in the 12th century that defined more precisely the rights and status of aliens and foreign merchants, at least in municipal, if not territorial, law. Jewry-law is, of course, non-Jewish in origin—the product of legislation, judicial administration, and legal theory in Christian states that confronted the issue of the legal status of the Jew and that typically treated Jews "as passive objects of legislation and law enforcement." Jewry-law saw and treated Jews as a collective separated from Christians in more than religious ways. In part one, Kisch reviews the vast history and literature on the subject and then discusses in detail the individual lawbooks and the specific Jewry-law regulations within them, as well as the scope of Jewry-law. In part two, Kisch assesses the legal status of the Jews in Germany, arguing that there were three primary legal developments in the protection of the Jews: special rights granted to Jews through privileges during the Carolingian period until the end of the 11th century; general and imperial protection of the Jews through land-peace legislation; and finally, perhaps most significantly, the Chamber Serfdom of the Jews after Frederick II's Jewry Privilege of 1236. In part three of the book, Kisch examines the specific applications of Jewry-law in penal, civil, criminal, and administrative law. Finally, in part four, Kisch presents reflections on the medieval conception and representation of the Jew. In the companion volume, KISCH (1949a) presents the German texts of passages dealing with Jews in a number of medieval lawbooks and jury-court decisions.

EIDELBERG offers a general history of the Jews in Austria in the 15th century, a period he considers to mark the decline of Austrian Jewry. After the 15th century the center of Jewish intellectual life shifted eastward to Bohemia, Hungary, and Poland. The study is based largely on the responsa of Rabbi Israel Isserlein, the last famous rabbinic scholar of medieval Austria, who died in 1460. After drawing a broad picture of Austrian Jewry in the period, Eidelberg focuses on Isserlein and what his writings reveal about the formal community structures and relations, moral conditions, customs, occupations, food, clothing, and housing of late medieval Austrian Jews.

ZIMMER examines the disintegration of the unique medieval Ashkenazi community at the end of the Middle Ages, owing to both external and internal factors. The autonomous Jewish communities that developed during the tenth through the 12th century were seriously challenged by the crusades as well as the growing role of Christian merchants, who eventually drove the Jews out of commerce and forced them into the profitable, if unreliable and dangerous, business of finance. Nevertheless, Jewish communities managed to retain a high degree of autonomy in attempting to define internal communal structures. Zimmer's expert handling of a variety of rabbinic sources, especially the responsa of such authorities as Meir of Rothenburg, Israel Bruna, Jacob Weil, Moses Minz, and Israel Isserlein, provides clear proof of the richness of the sources as well as the breadth of the internal rabbinic discussion of the later Middle Ages. The bulk of the book examines internal Jewish communal and legal administration, as well as the interrelation of various Jewish communities and the relationship between Jewish and non-Jewish civil society.

DEAN BELL

See also Germany: Modern

Germany: Modern

Brenner, Michael, *Nach dem Holocaust: Juden in
  Deutschland, 1945–1950*, Munich: Beck, 1995;
  translated by Barbara Harshav as *After the Holocaust:
  Rebuilding Jewish Lives in Postwar Germany*, Princeton,
  New Jersey: Princeton University Press, 1997
Gay, Ruth, *The Jews of Germany: A Historical Portrait*,
  New Haven, Connecticut: Yale University Press, 1992
Liptzin, Solomon, *Germany's Stepchildren*, Philadelphia:
  Jewish Publication Society, 1944
Mosse, George, *Germans and Jews: The Right, the Left, and
  the Search for a "Third Force" in Pre-Nazi Germany*,
  New York: Grosset and Dunlap, and London: Orbach
  and Chambers, 1970
Stern, Susan (editor), *Speaking Out: Jewish Voices from
  United Germany*, Chicago: Edition Q, 1995

Histories of the Jews of Germany tended for many years to emphasize the contributions of the Jews to both German and Jewish culture, the symbiosis of the German and Jewish experiences, and the tragic fate of German Jewry, the result of a legacy of German antisemitism and the Holocaust. In recent years some excellent studies have appeared that explore the experiences of German Jews after 1945 and, most recently, the situation of the Jews of Germany since reunification. New signs of the rebirth of Jewish life in that country have prompted an increased focus on contemporary developments.

BRENNER provides an in-depth survey of the restoration of Jewish life in Germany immediately after the Holocaust on two levels: a concise overview of developments in postwar Germany and extensive interviews with Jews active in helping to restore Jewish life in Germany. The author's family settled in Germany after the Holocaust, and Brenner characterizes his work as a "historian's interaction with his own history." The initial historical overview begins with the liberation of the Jews from the concentration camps, describes the difficult experiences in the Displaced Persons' camps, and catalogs the important cultural and organizational efforts of the Jewish remnant in creating a foundation for new Jewish beginnings. German antisemitism in the postwar decade is explored, as is the variety of Jewish responses. The excellent eyewitness accounts include perspectives from religious figures, Zionist activists, and community leaders such as Heinz Galinski and Ignatz Bubis. The final portion of Brenner's study surveys the last five decades of the 20th century, featuring topics that range from demographic developments and problems of Jewish identity to renewed religious and cultural endeavors. Fascinating anecdotes are offered throughout. Brenner concludes that there are signs of hope for a revival of Jewish life in Germany, but suggests that the questions of why and how Jews deal with their identity in a German environment will remain open for some time to come.

GAY has written an excellent, comprehensive survey of the Jews of Germany as well as a moving elegy on the creative interactions of the Jews with German culture, politics, society, and economy until the ultimate destruction of the Holocaust. After providing a workable background of the medieval and early modern period, Gay surveys the uneven and contradictory path of Jewish emancipation. German Jews created great works of pioneering scholarship in the study of Judaism and at the same time developed a passion for the humanistic side of German culture and strove desperately for acceptance by their Christian neighbors. But this was not to be, for Christian Germans, not German Jews, proceeded to posit the existence of "the Jewish question," with its suggestion that German Jews could never quite become acceptable, loyal Germans. Gay's study focuses on how German Jews lived, struggled, contributed, and achieved despite great odds. The book is beautifully illustrated and contains long and revealing quotes from the luminaries of German Jewry as well as from narratives of quite ordinary people. The book ends with stories of the emigration of German Jews from Nazi Germany to Palestine and with a moving farewell letter from the last entry in the minute book of the Jewish community of Insterburg in East Prussia, written on 24 April 1941, with its closing invocation, "Have mercy on us and have mercy on the whole Jewish people." Gay does not extend her story into the postwar period. This seems to indicate a belief that the great culture created by the Jews of Germany no longer exists, that the achievements of the German Jews constituted a world-enriching epic of a thousand years, abruptly ended by the Holocaust.

LIPTZIN conceived his study during the height of the mass murder of European Jews, setting out to explore the "tragic duality" of German and Jew. He sought to investigate how the great cultural figures of German Jewry reacted toward this duality as they struggled to define the problems not only of their Jewishness and their Germanness, but also of the larger question of Jewish relationships with non-Jewish neighbors in the modern world. In this pioneering study, Liptzin chose to approach the topic by developing a series of wonderful vignettes of important and representative German-Jewish authors, writers, and artists. The book is divided into a number of major topics: Jewish reactions to emancipation and modernity, the responses of assimilation and Zionism, the high points of Jewish achievement, the end of emancipation and the rise of Nazism, and the renaissance of Jewish religion and culture that began in the 1920s and continued despite the Holocaust. The reader will encounter such remarkable figures as Rahel Varnhagen in early 19th-century Berlin and the great writers Ludwig Boerne and Heinrich Heine. The German-Jewish pioneers of Zionism, Moses Hess and Theodor Herzl, are presented along with the tragic figures of Walter Rathenau and Theodor Lessing, so uneasy about their Jewish heritage. Some of the most fascinating chapters deal with Jewish Christians and the self-hating Austrian Jews Otto Weininger and Arthur Trebitsch who added to the Nazi storehouse of antisemitic stereotypes. The rediscovery of Judaism and the Jewish renaissance led by such figures as Martin Buber, and the emergence of "Pan-Humanists" including Erich Kahler and Kafka's first biographer, Max Brod, indicate for Liptzin a new synthesis of Judaism and humanism that would take the place of the shattered German-Jewish duality. It is remarkable that Liptzin realized in 1944 that Jewish life in a new Palestine would have to fashion a new amalgam of Judaism and humanism that could overcome a century of failed emancipation and the extreme responses of assimilation, surrender, and self-hatred. Although old, Liptzin's work turns out to be not only a perceptive study but also a historical document in its own right.

The "third force" to which MOSSE (one of the preeminent historians of German nationalism and antisemitism) refers in his subtitle is the 19th-century "Volkish" tradition in German nationalism that defined nationality on the basis of traditional links to the land and to the language, emotional ties, and later race and blood—as opposed to a conception of belonging based on civil rights, civic participation, and tolerance. This important force in German nationalism tended to exclude Jews, since German nationalists often associated Jews with the capitalism, liberalism, and materialism of modern, rather than traditional, society. Mosse argues that Jews were blamed by many German nationalists for the ills of modernity. Specific essays in Mosse's book develop variations on this theme. The chapter on the image of the Jew in German popular culture explores the stereotype of the Jew as greedy, dirty, and dishonest. Nevertheless, the German Volkish idea that a nation possessed a mystical folk soul influenced German Zionists and even Martin Buber, one of the preeminent Jewish theologians and cultural Zionists of the 20th century. Mosse's essays "Conservative Revolution" and "Fascism and the Intellectuals" illustrate how a deeply held antisemitism became fully integrated into German nationalism and prepared the way for the extremes of Nazism. The last essay in the book deals with left-wing Jewish intellectuals in the period of the ill-fated Weimar Republic. Many German Jews were attracted to the ethical idealism of humanitarian socialism, but this did not succeed in saving German democracy. Writing the book in the late 1960s, Mosse draws a parallel between these German-Jewish intellectuals and the young American "new left" radicals of the 1960s, who could be as impractical as their German counterparts and who similarly faced a society in turmoil that was turning to conservative solutions.

STERN is a British-born, American-educated Jew who has been living in Germany for more than 20 years. She exemplifies the kind of younger activist intellectuals who are participating in the new German-Jewish dialogue. She has edited an important collection of essays by 20 prominent German Jews. The unifying theme of the book explores the ways in which leading German Jews struggle to come to terms with themselves and their environment in the light of the recent past and of the new reunified Germany. For Ralph Giordano, a survivor and eminent novelist, the question, "Why have I remained," is crucial. Although critical of the problems of Germany, Giordano is hopeful that Jewish life will continue in a democratic framework. The historian Julius Schoeps deals with the guilt that some Jews feel for living in Germany, while other intellectuals and scholars affirm their ties with Germany. The problem of antisemitism is a recurrent theme in the book, and while leaders such as Ignatz Bubis are aware of the increasing respectability of antisemitism, others note the philosemitism of some Germans who look upon the Jews as a community of victims who can do no wrong, again creating a distorted image of Jews. Then there is the question of the transplanted Jews from the former Soviet Union, who comprise half of the 50,000 Jews living in Germany today. How will they come to define their Jewish identity? The final essays deal with the revival of Jewish religious and cultural life in Germany. Stern concludes that "there *is* Jewish life in contemporary Germany, and that this life is becoming ever more firmly established," both in the eyes of Jews and of non-Jewish Germans. The great value of this book is in the variety of perspectives it offers on the problems and the strengths of Jewish life in Germany today.

LEON STEIN

See also Germany: Medieval

Gershom ben Judah c.960–1028
Pioneer rabbinic authority and teacher of German Jewry

Agus, Irving, *The Heroic Age of Franco-German Jewry*, New York: Yeshiva University Press, 1969

Finkelstein, Louis, *Jewish Self-Government in the Middle Ages* (Abraham Berliner Series), New York: Jewish Theological Seminary of America, 1924; revised edition, New York: Feldheim, 1964

Grossman, Avraham, "The Historical Background to the Ordinances on Family Affairs Attributed to Rabbenu Gershom Me'or ha-Golah ('The Light of the Exile')," in *Jewish History: Essays in Honour of Chimen Abramsky*, edited by Ada Rapoport-Albert and Steven Zipperstein, London: Halban, 1988

Kanarfogel, Ephraim, *Jewish Education and Society in the High Middle Ages*, Detroit, Michigan: Wayne State University Press, 1992

Roth, Cecil (editor), *The World History of the Jewish People*, vol. 11: *The Dark Ages: Jews in Christian Europe, 711–1096*, New Brunswick, New Jersey: Rutgers University Press, and London: Allen, 1966

Talmudic thought in medieval Ashkenaz effectively begins with Gershom ben Judah, or Rabbenu Gershom as he is usually called. He headed the academy at Mainz and composed a talmudic commentary (embellished by his successors at Mainz) as well as liturgical poems and many responsa. Rabbenu Gershom is perhaps best known, however, for the series of ordinances attributed to him, which deal with a wide variety of issues including polygamy, personal privacy, and communal government.

AGUS traces the economic, social, and intellectual history of the Rhineland in the pre-Crusade period, utilizing the responsa and comments of Rabbenu Gershom and other rabbinic figures. Rabbenu Gershom dealt with the structure, parameters, and efficacy of *ma'arufiyya* (acquaintance), a monopolistic relationship in which a Jew had quasi-exclusive rights to business dealings and transactions with certain gentile clients. A great deal of trust between Jews was necessary in order to sustain this form of livelihood in early Ashkenaz, and the same can be said for Jewish involvement in moneylending at this time.

Rabbenu Gershom functioned as the leading scholar in his academy, to which students came from a very wide geographic area. At the same time, Rabbenu Gershom apparently decided matters of ritual and communal policy in consultation with a group of senior scholars and teachers. Agus notes that the writings of Rabbenu Gershom also suggest that at least one group of students in the academy consisted of adults who were already responsible for earning a livelihood for their families. The absence of a professional rabbinate, coupled with the goal of pursuing lifelong study nonetheless, typified early Ashkenaz in the pre-Crusade period. Agus also outlines the approaches of Rabbenu Gershom to domestic issues such as childlessness, divorce, and the payment of the ketubbah.

Many of these and other related issues are discussed briefly throughout the collection edited by ROTH. In addition, two chapters contributed to this volume by Agus, "Rabbinic Scholarship in Northern Europe" and "Rashi and His School," describe in some detail the rabbinic writings of Rabbenu Gershom and their place within the transmission of the study of the Oral Law. Included in this discussion are also a listing and a description of the ordinances (takkanot) attributed to Rabbenu Gershom. In the view of modern scholarship, these ordinances were not the product of one person. Several may have been enacted before Rabbenu Gershom; others were probably enacted in later centuries. The ordinances fall into three categories: regulation of marriage and divorce; the relationship of communities to nonmembers, new settlements, or other communities; and personal status (e.g., an ordinance against insulting penitent converts and another that protected the privacy of a person's letters). These ordinances were enforceable by means of anathemas or bans (such as *herem beit din* and *herem ha-yishuv*), procedures also attributed to Rabbenu Gershom. Rabbenu Gershom's contributions to the writing and interpretation of liturgical poetry and hymns are referred to in A.M. Habermann's chapter on the beginnings of Hebrew poetry in northern Europe and France.

FINKELSTEIN delineates the wide scope intended by Rabbenu Gershom's ordinances, the legal underpinnings of enacting ordinances, and the nature of the synods that promulgated them. He describes the provisions of the ordinances and reviews their attribution to Rabbenu Gershom. The best-known ordinance of Rabbenu Gershom forbade a man to marry more than one wife and was accepted throughout Ashkenaz and beyond. Bound to the ordinance that prohibited polygamy was another that prohibited contested divorce. The synods convened by Rabbenu Gershom became a model for supercommunal government throughout the Middle Ages. Finkelstein records the extant Hebrew versions of Rabbenu Gershom's takkanot and provides annotations and an English translation. Despite original publication some 75 years ago, this book remains a valuable textual resource.

GROSSMAN seeks to confirm that those ordinances that deal with familial issues were composed in 11th-century Ashkenaz, and in all likelihood by Rabbenu Gershom, by demonstrating that the social and religious milieu of this period comports quite well with the historical realia implicit in the ordinances. Grossman reviews and evaluates the factors that caused some historians to doubt even the attribution of the ordinance prohibiting polygamy to Rabbenu Gershom. He then demonstrates that monogamy was the accepted rule among Jews in Germany in the second half of the 11th century and that Ashkenazi sources from the mid-12th century explicitly mention Rabbenu Gershom as the author of the ordinance. Grossman discusses the historical motives and

developments that may have prompted this ordinance. Jewish husbands were often absent from their homes for long periods of time due to their involvement in trade and business. Grossman argues that this development also may have been a factor in the ordinance that prohibited divorcing a woman against her will and in the ordinance against reading another person's mail without permission. He further discusses the historical factors that support an 11th-century date for the ordinance concerning the breach of a betrothal.

KANARFOGEL includes a number of formulations by Rabbenu Gershom that relate to Jewish education and academies of higher talmudic studies. He reviews Rabbenu Gershom's rulings concerning the payment and support of the elementary-level tutor (melammed) and the teacher of older students. Kanarfogel also notes that pre-Crusade academies were typically identified with the city in which they were located rather than with a particular teacher, as was the case in the 12th century and beyond. References to Rabbenu Gershom and the academy at Mainz clearly reflect this distinction. In addition, Rabbenu Gershom and other pre-Crusade rabbinic scholars typically are shown issuing halakhic rulings based stylistically on biblical verses, another convention that was discontinued in the period following the First Crusade.

EPHRAIM KANARFOGEL

Ginzberg, Asher *see* Ahad Ha'am

Ginzberg, Louis 1873–1953

Lithuanian-born American scholar and interpreter of talmudic literature

Finkelstein, Louis, "Louis Ginzberg," *American Jewish Yearbook,* 56, 1955
Ginzberg, Eli, *Keeper of the Law: Louis Ginzberg,* Philadelphia: Jewish Publication Society, 1966
Golinkin, David, "Introduction," in *The Responsa of Professor Louis Ginzberg* (Moreshet, vol. 16), New York: Jewish Theological Seminary, 1996
Heller, Bernhard, "Ginzberg's *Legends of the Jews,*" *Jewish Quarterly Review,* 24 and 25, 1933–1934 and 1934–1935
Shargel, Baila R., "Louis Ginzberg as Apologist," *American Jewish History,* 79, 1989–1990
Spiegel, Shalom, "Introduction," in Ginzberg's *Legends of the Bible,* Philadelphia: Jewish Publication Society, 1968

FINKELSTEIN's portrait of Louis Ginzberg is representative of several short laudatory biographical sketches that eulogized the scholar of Jewish "Law and Lore." Finkelstein reflects upon the pious and intellectual life of the great talmudist, characterizing Ginzberg's five decades at the Jewish Theological Seminary in New York as a life devoted to the translation of both the Talmud and talmudic culture "into a philosophy of life capable of guiding the modern world." Finkelstein then describes Ginzberg's three primary concerns: research, guidance of others, and self-discipline, demonstrating that in each of these dimensions of his life, Ginzberg followed the model set for him by his illustrious ancestor, the Vilna Gaon.

Eli GINZBERG's loving memoir of his father offers the most extensive biographical account of the life of the scholar available in English. The author considers his work a memoir, rather than a biography, due to the selective nature of the tale. Although Eli Ginzberg draws upon several different sources for the portrait, he does not seek to investigate exhaustively all channels. For instance, he does not gather the perspectives of contemporaries and students of his father; Eli neither conducts interviews with these sources, nor does he write letters soliciting information from the many individuals whom his father trained and influenced. The author draws on an earlier Hebrew biography for which Louis provided material, autobiographical fragments that Eli's wife recorded while Louis was alive, letters, biographical details from Louis's academic publications, and Eli's personal recollections of conversations with and stories told by his father. The book moves chronologically from Louis's early youth through his years in academe at the Jewish Theological Seminary, at which point the author takes a more thematic approach, presenting chapters on friends, Zionism, Louis's wife, his views as a halakhic authority, and a final chapter titled "The Gentle Skeptic." This memoir is not a critical appraisal of Ginzberg's life and work, but a portrait in the form of a pastiche of stories, anecdotes, and letters.

GOLINKIN introduces the reader to a little-known dimension of Ginzberg's life work by publishing more than 100 of the scholar's responsa. After briefly describing Ginzberg's ancestry, upbringing, education, and innate genius—the ingredients that Golinkin proposes constitute the uniqueness of Ginzberg—and presenting a cursory sketch of Ginzberg's three areas of academic research, the author concentrates on introducing Ginzberg the halakhic authority and activist. Golinkin provides an overview of the contents of the responsa as well as of Ginzberg's legal approach. With the publication of this resource, Golinkin hopes to correct the mistaken scholarly assumption that faculty at the Jewish Theological Seminary in general, and Ginzberg in particular, were not actively engaged with the concerns of the community at large. This volume is an indispensable work for any serious student of Ginzberg.

HELLER's review of *The Legends of the Jews* is the only extensive analysis of this great work by Ginzberg. Heller categorizes the legendary material according to its different orbits of cultural influence, borrowing, and exchange. He discusses legends in relation to Egypt, Babylonia, Persia, India, classical antiquity, Jewish Hellenism, Christianity, and Islam, and he further divides Ginzberg's material according to folklore genres, such as myth, fable, and fairytale. When appropriate, Heller corrects Ginzberg's assumptions about borrowing and origins, and the author offers several pages of corrections to Ginzberg's notes, as well as additions to Ginzberg's already voluminous sources and traditions. Heller criticizes Ginzberg for failing to relegate consistently all the variants to the notes and challenges some of Ginzberg's specific decisions about which texts to place in the narrative section of the work. This essay is highly useful for anyone interested in assessing questions of Jewish legendary origins

and transmission. It does not, however, place the particular function and meaning of a folklore tradition in its literary and cultural context.

SHARGEL's article focuses on Ginzberg's work as a polemicist engaged in acts of communal self-defense. Ginzberg considered such polemics to be the proper task of the theologian, and Shargel relates his activism in this realm to his ambivalence about academia and his place within it. Shargel details "four separate occasions [when] he employed his erudition in the service of self-defense." Ginzberg twice defended Jewish ritual slaughter. Another time he wrote to dispel the faulty accusations at the heart of the infamous blood libel trial of Mendel Beilis in 1913. Fourth, he responded to Polish anti-Jewish propaganda circulating in the wake of World War I that sought to persuade Americans that the persecution of the Jews in Poland was a defensive measure. This article also offers a compelling historical explanation for Ginzberg's relative reticence regarding matters of apologetics.

In his introduction to the abridged version of Ginzberg's *Legends*, SPIEGEL begins with a broad overview of the meaning and history of Jewish legends and the variety of literary efforts to collect and organize them. He then briefly sketches Ginzberg's family lineage and education, singling out Ginzberg's doctoral dissertation titled "Haggadah in the Church Fathers" as the project marking Ginzberg's early interest in the recovery of lost aggadah. Spiegel then illustrates Ginzberg's work of recovery and reconstruction in *Legends*. In the second half of the essay, Spiegel discusses the etiology of Jewish legends, which he describes as a function of the dynamic interrelationship between Scripture and folklore, the work of the schools, and the common wisdom of the folk. Spiegel's portrait of this creative tension offers a much more dynamic and complicated relationship of folklore and the rabbis than the one glimpsed through Ginzberg's introductory remarks and notes to *Legends* (which are omitted from this one-volume edition). A classic piece on the history and nature of Jewish folkloric production and creativity, Spiegel's essay thus reframes as it introduces the original work.

REBECCA SCHORSCH

Glikl of Hameln   1645–1724

German memoirist

Abrahams, Beth-Zion (editor), *The Life of Gluckel of Hameln, 1646–1724, Written by Herself,* London: East and West Library, 1962; New York: Yoseloff, 1963

Bilik, Dorothy, "The Memoirs of Glikl of Hameln: The Archeology of the Text," *Yiddish,* 8, 1992

Davis, Natalie Z., *Women on the Margins: Three Seventeenth-Century Lives,* Cambridge, Massachusetts: Harvard University Press, 1995

Israel, Jonathan I., *European Jewry in the Age of Mercantilism, 1550–1750,* New York: Oxford University Press, and Oxford: Clarendon, 1985; 3rd edition, London and Portland, Oregon: Littman Library of Jewish Civilization, 1998

Schmelzer, Menahem, "Hebrew Printing in Germany," *Leo Baeck Year Book*, 33, 1988

Whaley, Joachim, *Religious Toleration and Social Change in Hamburg, 1529–1819* (Cambridge Studies in Early Modern History), Cambridge and New York: Cambridge University Press, 1985

Glikl of Hameln (also known as Glückel) was a 17th-century Jewish woman from Hamburg who wrote a lengthy memoir in Yiddish. While she was not a famous person in her time, Glikl's manuscript is both the most important document for European Jewish history of the late 17th and early 18th centuries and the earliest extant text by a Jewish woman. The memoir was passed down from her son to her grandson, who collaborated on copying the original text, which was later lost. In 1896, the distinguished scholar David Kaufmann published the first edition of Glikl's work in German, and reaction to its appearance was swift and impressive. For example, the first *Jewish Encyclopedia* (1901–1906) refers to Glikl in 11 different entries. Since then, translations have appeared in almost every decade, with the exception of the extended World War II period. There are editions available in each of the major languages of the Jewish people in the 20th century, and German and English readers can choose from several versions.

ABRAHAMS's translation of Glikl's work is the only English version adapted directly from the Kaufmann edition. Parts of her introduction, however, are dated since she wrote before important studies of life in 17th-century Hamburg were published in the late 20th century. The volume's 40 illustrations depicting the changing times in which Glikl lived contribute greatly to the book's worth. There are both engravings and woodcuts, a reflection of the fact that Glikl's life spanned these two artistic forms. The book also contains annotations and indexes of persons and places from Glikl's world.

BILIK emphasizes three issues crucial to the study of Glikl's autobiography and its historiography. First, she compares five different translations—two in German, two in English, and one in modern Yiddish, with emphasis on the first four versions. Second, the author examines Glikl's education in the context of early Yiddish writing for women. Finally, Bilik argues that an ethical will serves as the force that motivates Glikl's autobiography. The final word has not been written on any of these topics.

DAVIS's book on Glikl and two other 17th-century women has introduced many late 20th-century readers to Glikl's name. Davis analyzes many of the folktales in Glikl's text and identifies the wide-ranging sources from which she created her stories. The book highlights the last third of Glikl's life, which she spent in Metz, and the author reviews different naming practices used by Jews of that period, explaining how Glikl became Glückel von Hameln. The notes are rich with valuable information.

ISRAEL provides vital insights into the economic context of Glikl, her husband, Hayyim, and the network through which they conducted business, including a discussion of their connections to some "Court Jews." Their good fortune began to decline at the end of the 17th century, as changes in trading patterns, shifts in population, and new areas for economic expansion destabilized the existing economic situation.

SCHMELZER concentrates on the extraordinary efflorescence of Hebrew printing during Glikl's lifetime, thereby underscoring the religious-cultural dimensions of the society in which she wrote her memoir. While Glikl's formal education probably ended by 1660, her informal education could well have continued beyond that point as she maintained close contact with the Hamburg *shul* and traveled extensively to fairs and other sites where books were distributed. Schmelzer also argues that Jews of Glikl's class, including rabbis, those connected to the *klaus*, and *parnassim,* typically owned many books, and therefore Glikl probably had access to literary works possessed by her father and other relatives.

WHALEY's outstanding analysis of primary and secondary sources on Hamburg provides an original description of political and religious realities faced by non-Lutherans in that city during Glikl's lifetime. Lutheran clergy and lay adherents of the state religion discriminated against Catholics, Calvinists, and both Sephardi and Ashkenzi Jews, and this monograph explains the expulsion of Ashkenazim, Glikl's family included, as well as their later return. Whaley emphasizes the overall economic motivation for keeping Jews in the cosmopolitan port city, the role of the burghers, and changing tax demands during this era.

ROBERTA HANFLING SCHWARTZ

Gnosis and Early Mysticism

Dan, Joseph, *ha-Mistikah ha-'Ivrit ha-kedumah*, 1989; as *The Ancient Jewish Mysticism* (Broadcast University Series), Tel-Aviv: MOD, 1993

Halperin, David J., *The Faces of the Chariot: Early Jewish Responses to Ezekiel's Vision* (Texte und Studien zum antiken Judentum, 16), Tübingen: Mohr, 1988

Schäfer, Peter, *Der Verborgene und offenbare Gott*, 1991; translated by Aubrey Pomerance as *The Hidden and Manifest God: Some Major Themes in Early Jewish Mysticism* (SUNY Series in Judaica), Albany: State University of New York Press, 1992

Scholem, Gershom, *Jewish Gnosticism: Merkabah Mysticism, and Talmudic Tradition,* New York: Jewish Theological Seminary, 1960, 2nd edition, 1965

Wolfson, Elliot R., *Through a Speculum That Shines: Vision and Imagination in Medieval Jewish Mysticism*, Princeton, New Jersey: Princeton University Press, 1994

Recognition that Jewish mysticism has more ancient postbiblical sources than the early kabbalistic literature is a fairly recent development. Prior to the groundbreaking work of Gershom Scholem in the 1950s, the body of literature now considered to be evidence of early Jewish mysticism, the Hekhalot corpus, was regarded as part of the talmudic tradition. The esoteric character of these texts had been recognized, but, for the most part, neither their antiquity nor their uniqueness had been suspected. Scholem claimed, however, that the texts originated in the first or second century C.E., and this hypothesis is now generally accepted, although some recent authors argue for a later date. The texts that belong to the Hekhalot literature are *Hekhalot Rabbati (The Greater Palaces), Hekhalot Zutarti (The Lesser Palaces), Ma'aseh Merkabah (The Working of the Chariot), Merkabah Rabbah (The Great Chariot)*, and the so-called Hebrew book of Enoch, also known as 3 Enoch. Two other texts, *Re'uyyot Yehezqel (The Visions of Ezekiel)* and *Masekhet Hekhalot (The Tractate of Palaces)*, have a more tenuous relationship to the corpus. For the most part, the texts of the Hekhalot corpus document the visionary experiences of the *yored merkabah,* the one who "descends" (that is, ascends) to the chariot (merkabah) and journeys through the seven heavenly palaces (hekhalot) to witness the enthronement of God. Hence, the type of mysticism expressed by these texts is called merkabah mysticism. In addition to God and the initiate who makes the journey, the texts are populated with myriad angels of various ranks, special seals, dangerous tasks, divine names, and magical words and actions. The form of mysticism under consideration is also referred to as theosophic, for the literature explores the mysteries of the divine life and the reciprocity of the relationship between the divine and human worlds. The texts suggest that divine life influences creation, but humans also influence the divine, creating a relationship that perhaps results in theurgy—the coercion, manipulation, or mastery of God. In this respect, the Hekhalot texts have an air of Gnosticism about them: they embody secret knowledge of an esoteric, partisan nature that is secured by way of illumination. Scholars continue to debate, however, whether the texts can be classified as Gnostic per se and whether they suggest that Gnosticism arose from within Judaism.

DAN presents a fine summary of the elements of early Jewish mysticism, beginning with a chapter discussing the history and composition of the Hekhalot texts (including a helpful survey of the relatively brief history of interpretation of the literature) and concluding with a chapter setting out his understanding of the essence of ancient Jewish mysticism. Dan also presents chapters devoted to aspects and themes that appear in the various texts such as the merkabah itself, the anthropomorphism of *Shi'ur Komah* (a tradition of gross speculation about God's physique), the Prince of the Torah, the angel Metatron (i.e., Enoch), and the character and itinerary of the one who "descends" to the chariot. Dan takes a reasoned approach to the particular issue of Gnosticism and the possibility that Gnosticism arose from within the Jewish world during the late Second Temple era. Although it remains a matter of speculation whether Christian forms of Gnosticism originated from within the Mandaean sect rather than in Gnostic trends within Judaism, Dan doesn't entirely discount the possibility. The Mandaean community clearly predated the rise of Christianity, had close ties to the Jewish community in Jerusalem (before fleeing to Transjordan and then to Iraq), and perhaps observed Jewish traditions such as the dietary laws. It is not known, however, whether the late literature of this sect reflects its origins. Dan also addresses the mysticism of the Hekhalot literature and its relation to Gnosticism, but here again he concludes that it is impossible at this time to determine the direction of influence. Although it is possible that the traces of Gnosticism in merkabah mysticism were stimulated by explicitly Jewish Gnostic sources, such texts have not been discovered. Therefore, the most that can be said

is that the Hekhalot texts and merkabah mysticism participate in the overall spirit of Gnosticism. Because other works on early Jewish mysticism are rather specialized, this book is recommended as a sound general introduction to the topic and the current state of research.

HALPERIN's extraordinary book brings the reader into immediate contact with the mysteries and dangers of the merkabah. Indeed, while this text is a work of remarkable scholarship, it sometimes takes on the character of a mystery novel as the author seeks to explain why the vision of Ezekiel's chariot so fascinated early rabbinic Judaism. Halperin reminds the reader that this vision once inspired such pronounced awe and fear that warnings were issued that its exposition in unlearned hands might result in death or disease. The central topic that occupies Halperin is the merkabah itself. In fact, this mysterious chariot plays a very minor role in the Hekhalot literature, whereas in the secondary literature about the ascension of the mystic, rabbinic allusions to the merkabah and the Hekhalot material are nearly always linked. In order to begin to untangle these puzzling associations, Halperin examines the source of the tradition, Ezekiel 1 and 10, through a psychoanalytic theory of desire and dread. This approach has aroused the suspicions of some of Halperin's critics, who accuse him of inappropriately applying (post)modern methods to ancient materials, but Halperin contends that rabbinic exegesis resembles psychoanalysis, for forms of interpretation work by both associations and linkages rather than by direct linear reference. According to Halperin, the "associative wires that gave the *merkabah* its extraordinary charge of excitement and fear" must be traced back to "something which [the rabbis] found inherently thrilling or appalling." Halperin argues that the key to unlocking the mystery of the merkabah is found in the prohibitions that regulated the exposition of the merkabah. While some readers may find Halperin's revelations controversial (even outrageous), there is more than enough in this fine book to satisfy any reader interested in a close and imaginative reading of the texts that produced merkabah mysticism.

SCHÄFER's book is the product of many years of acclaimed work on the literary aspects of the Hekhalot literature. The author strives to allow these works to determine their own themes, rather than imposing modern questions upon them as, according to Schäfer, Scholem did when he argued that the texts mainly concern the ascent of the mystic and the final vision of the enthroned king. Schäfer insists that the Hekhalot texts themselves do not speak with one voice (he refers to the texts as macroforms, that is, crystallized forms of smaller literary units), and he contends that they do not demonstrate a consistent vision, but he nevertheless finds three central themes that are elaborated, although without unanimity, throughout the literature—conceptions of God, angels, and humanity. The central sections of the book explore and elaborate how these conceptions are expressed in the literature and how the themes stand in relation to one another. The author offers abundant quotations from original sources to assist readers without access to the primary literature. The concluding chapter is especially important because it sets the terms for all subsequent debates concerning the nature and meaning of merkabah mysticism and the Hekhalot texts, particularly as they relate to God's character and position relative to Israel, questions of the magical or theurgic elements found in the literature, and the use of secret names to command angels, the Torah, and perhaps even God. Schäfer concludes that the Hekhalot literature gives evidence of a plurality of views on the themes considered, and he contends that this complexity stems from an as-yet unidentified community's struggle to formulate a new and revolutionary conception of God as both essentially hidden and simultaneously manifest.

SCHOLEM's book is the first scholarly work to explore the Hekhalot literature and advance an argument for its distinct status as early Jewish mysticism. In 1957, Scholem delivered the Israel Goldstein Lectures at the Jewish Theological Seminary in New York. This book is based on those lectures and includes several appendixes, one of which is the first publication of *Ma'aseh Merkabah*. At the time when Scholem originally presented his lectures, the Dead Sea Scrolls and the Gnostic texts from Nag-Hammadi had just been discovered, and scholars were hotly debating whether Judaism and Christianity had Gnostic origins. Scholem reorients this debate in two ways. First, he contends that the Hekhalot texts represent an esoteric Jewish tradition that originated contemporaneously with the emergence of Gnostic traditions in Christianity (not during the Middle Ages, as had been previously assumed). Second, Scholem argues that merkabah mysticism cannot be classified as Gnostic, even though the Hekhalot texts promote a secret and dangerous knowledge and offer procedures for a mystical flight through heavenly palaces. Scholem's call for a new evaluation of the inner development of Judaism continues to inspire scholars.

WOLFSON's book is one of the most lushly written, meticulously researched scholarly works to appear in recent memory in any field. The subject matter—the tension between iconic (visual, corporeal) and aniconic representations of God in Jewish mysticism—is difficult and controversial, but Wolfson manages to produce a text that is a model of clarity and economy. The author argues that the tension between iconic visionary forms of mystical experience and other forms (such as aural) is an essential component of mystical speculation. Wolfson claims that "literary evidence attests that the religious experience described in the different currents of Jewish mysticism from Late Antiquity through the Middle Ages is overwhelmingly visual." Ironically, the aniconic bias of the Hebrew biblical corpus helps to provide the context for the obsession of early Jewish mystics with imagistic visualization of the divine form, the body of God. Wolfson primarily concentrates upon the development of mystical theosophies in the High Middle Ages, but chapters three and four contain a fascinating discussion of the nature of visions in the Hekhalot mystical literature. Contrary to other interpreters (such as Scholem), Wolfson argues that visions of glory such as those recorded in this literature refer to the transcendent God in essence and not merely a luminous reflected glory. There is, in these texts, the suggestion that the essentially invisible God can be seen by humans, although he simultaneously remains hidden. Wolfson contends that this paradox of "seeing" God should remain in tension and not be resolved one way or another, for this tension generates and tolerates a discursive experience that simultaneously reveals what cannot be seen and conceals what must not be seen. Perhaps Wolfson's most singular contribution to the study of early Jewish mysticism is his use of an erotic mythology to interpret the paradoxical vision of the divine form in light of a prohibition against uncovering the divine phallus. Wolfson also takes up the challenge of determining how these traditions find their place within normative rabbinic Judaism. The copious notes and bibliography that accompany the text are especially valuable for any reader wishing for an exhaustive guide to the literature of early mysticism.

ERIC C. HELMER

God, Doctrines and Concepts of

Dorff, Elliot N., *Knowing God: Jewish Journeys to the Unknowable,* Northvale, New Jersey: Aronson, 1992

Goodman, Lenn Evan, *Monotheism: A Philosophic Inquiry into the Foundations of Theology and Ethics* (David Baumgardt Memorial Lectures), Totowa, New Jersey: Allanheld, Osmun, 1981

Kaplan, Mordecai, *The Meaning of God in Modern Jewish Religion,* New York: Behrman's Jewish Book House, 1937

Katz, Steven T. (editor), *Jewish Ideas and Concepts,* New York: Schocken, 1977

Mason, Richard, *The God of Spinoza: A Philosophical Study,* Cambridge and New York: Cambridge University Press, 1997

Marmorstein, Arthur, *The Old Rabbinic Doctrine of God,* vol. 1: *The Names and Attributes of God,* London: Oxford University Press, 1927; New York: Ktav, 1968

Marmorstein, Arthur, *The Old Rabbinic Doctrine of God,* vol. 2: *Essays in Anthropomorphism,* London: Oxford University Press, 1937; New York: Ktav, 1968

Sonsino, Rifat and Daniel B. Syme, *Finding God: Ten Jewish Responses,* New York: Union of American Hebrew Congregations, 1986

While doctrines of God may have been formulated as dogmas in order to sustain a theological framework, concepts of God are more flexible in nature as they continue to be discussed with the aim of providing an intellectually coherent and meaningful idea of God as an integral part of Jewish belief and practice.

A guide to the fundamental concepts of Judaism has been edited by KATZ, collecting for the most part material written for the *Encyclopaedia Judaica*. The resultant topical approach, together with notes, glossary, biographical index, and bibliography, is particularly suitable as an introductory work for the nonspecialist. Two of the three sections focus on "God" and on "God and the Jew." While the latter examines the relationship between God and the individual in Judaism through concepts such as covenant, chosen people, revelation, Torah, mitsvot, piety, and study, part one explores the concept of God in the Bible and Talmud, in medieval Jewish philosophy and Kabbalah, and in modern Jewish thought. It further examines the names given to God and God's attributes, such as providence, justice, and mercy, and it addresses the referential designations, such as Ruah ha-Kodesh and Shekhinah, in their significance as divine manifestations. Altogether, this volume provides a clear overview of the different shades of meaning of the "God" concept as reflected in classical, medieval, and modern Jewish sources.

The manual by SONSINO and SYME also addresses "the different ways Jews have spoken of God throughout history," and it presents ten "options," all of which grapple with the questions: How can God be defined and named? How can we know God, and what is God's relationship to the world in general and to the Jews in particular? How can God allow evil to happen, and how can we act in accordance with God's will? The authors look at concepts of God in the Bible and in rabbinic literature, as well as those held by Jewish theologians from Philo of Alexandria via Maimonides, Isaac Luria, and Spinoza to Buber, Steinberg, Kaplan, and Fromm. Each period or individual is given a brief introduction, which is followed by a number of theses encapsulating the quintessence of each position, before a conclusive summary is added for the benefit of the uninitiated reader. In spite of its conciseness, this small book should stimulate and encourage the beginner to reflect upon challenging questions and answers regarding past and present discussions of Jewish ideas of God.

The concept of God is central to the thought of Spinoza to such an extent that he has been hailed as a "God-intoxicated man," while he also has been accused of atheism for chosing to live outside any religious community. Bringing together the philosopher's fundamental conclusions about God and religion, MASON's clear and carefully reasoned book "is the fullest study in English for many years on the role of God in Spinoza's philosophy." While the first part of this study examines God's existence, nature, and relationship to the world in terms of causality and is, "of necessity, more philosophically technical, the conclusions should be of interest to theologians and philosophers of religion as well as to philosophers." The second part deals with Spinoza's judgment of religion in general, its origins, history, and practices, while the third part addresses Spinoza's ideas on religious freedom. Some of Mason's conclusions challenge the stereotype of Spinoza as a rationalist and emphasize his commitment to consistency in an overall immanent worldview. This commitment is apparent in Spinoza's identification of the study of nature with the study of God: only if we understand the world's phenomena scientifically, he maintains, can we achieve a proper, God-like view of the universe.

GOODMAN's profound and compelling study responds to the equation of empiricism and atheism of British philosophers such as Sir Alfred Ayer. Based on his Baumgardt lectures at Oxford, it is addressed to the philosophically literate reader. The chapter titled "The Logic of Monotheism" analyzes God with reference to Greek ideals of divinity and value judgments and compares them with the Hebrew tradition and its innovative "moralization" of the notion of the divine. Goodman claims that, by introducing ethical standards of behavior, the Hebrews met the challenge "to retain the divine within the range of human grasp" and yet managed to work out a coherent concept of divine absoluteness. The second chapter examines philosophical arguments for the existence of God, while the last chapter, on monotheism and ethics, addresses moral obligations and standards of morality in view of God's transcendence and demonstrates "how moral rules are made possible in a monotheistic conceptual framework."

MARMORSTEIN's comprehensive work "endeavours to present the doctrine of God according to the sources of information as preserved in the ancient writings of the rabbinic teachers and sages, homilists and thinkers." This thorough, in-depth study of a vast corpus of original source material has become a standard work indispensable to all serious students for its eloquent demonstration of how the various theological conceptions must be judged in relation to the time and country of their teachers. The first volume deals with the use of the old biblical names and attributes of God, which were "of the utmost influence on human society and institutions." The second volume comprises five essays covering "some of the aspects of rabbinic teachings and speculations on the subject of anthropomorphism, anthropopathism," and the imitation of God. It examines ideas put forward by Philo and the aggadah, such as the (in)visibility of God, as well as the terminology of the literalist and the allegorical interpretations of the Bible and the discussions between these two schools.

A modern understanding of belief in God, together with a whole new approach to Judaism, is presented by KAPLAN in what has become a fundamental text for the Reconstructionist movement. Although first published in the 1930s, it should still be of great interest to the present-day reader searching for a meaningful concept of God. "Designed to reinterpret the idea of God in such a way as to render it spiritually exalting, intellectually acceptable and ethically potent," Kaplan construes God as "a power that makes for salvation." This idea of God attempts to achieve personal regeneration by releasing the potentialities of ethical personality for a better social life and thereby an improving social order. Jewish "peoplehood" and the "God-idea" are therefore linked, and God functions as an affirmation of life's value and holiness. Kaplan's methodological approach has been called a "predicate theology," emphasizing that God should be thought of not as a being or as a philosophical idea, but as a power radiating divine qualities. This study is less concerned with what God is or with describing God than with offering a view of what it means in practice to believe in God.

The uncertainty of the modern Jew concerning what to make of belief in God lies at the heart of DORFF's study. Without assuming of his readers a background in philosophy, Dorff skillfully takes them through some of the major traditional and modern options and examines their "soundness" as sources of knowledge about God. Motivated by the need to explain to himself intellectually how his belief in God relates to his traditional practices, this study is also a record of Dorff's own personal quest. Using the *Shema* as a leitmotiv, Dorff examines how one can serve God through heart (intellect), soul (emotions), and might (bodily strength). He probes into what can be known about God through the experience of prayer, through human reason and conduct, and, more importantly, through divine revelation and divine action, while not shunning the problem of evil and its apparent contradiction of God's justice and goodness. This clearly articulated personal odyssey of faith concludes with a discussion of the function, truth, and authority of images of God.

ESTHER I. SEIDEL

See also God, Names of

God, Names of

Kaufmann, Yehezkel, *Toldot ha-emunah ha-Yisre'elit*, 1937; translated by Moshe Greenberg as *The Religion of Israel: From Its Beginnings to the Babylonian Exile*, New York: Schocken, and London: Allen and Unwin, 1960

Marmorstein, Arthur, *The Old Rabbinic Doctrine of God*, vol. 1: *The Names and Attributes of God*, London: Oxford University Press, 1927; New York: Ktav, 1968

Scholem, Gershom, *Major Trends in Jewish Mysticism* (The Hilda Stich Stroock Lectures), New York: Schocken, 1941; 3rd edition, New York: Schocken, 1954; London: Thames and Hudson, 1955

Scholem, Gershom, "The Name of God and the Linguistic Theory of the Kabbalah," *Diogenes*, 79–80, 1970

Trachtenberg, Joshua, *Jewish Magic and Superstition: A Study in Folk Religion*, New York: Behrman, 1939

Wolfson, Elliot R., "Occultation of the Feminine and the Body of Secrecy in Medieval Jewish Kabbalah," in his *Rending the Veil: Concealment and Secrecy in the History of Religions*, New York: Seven Bridges, 1999

Extracting a name's meaning from its multilayered valences involves a struggle to reveal that name's concealed essence. The power that such a quest still exerts in particular regarding the names of God, and the field of semiotics in general, is evinced in the perpetual struggle to stabilize momentarily a concealed essence through the act of writing. In its most essentialized form, the Ineffable Name of God conceals so as to retain its primordial sacredness. The (un)veiling of signifier from signified comes to the fore as the Name can only be uttered in full by the High Priest yearly from within the Holy of Holies of the Jerusalem Temple. Thus, a substitute name must take its place the remainder of the year. Ultimately, there are not Names, but the Name: the very name that is written as YHWH is pronounced Adonai. As E. Wolfson has articulated it: the inexpressibility of the inexpressible is preserved only through that which is expressed. While such a nominal interplay pervades much of Jewish praxis and dogma, it also explains much of the hermeneutic obsession with reading, writing, and the recitation of text that marks this age.

KAUFMANN's classic work offers a demythologization of biblical Israel's conception of God as the Name. Israelite folk religion evidently passes through polytheistic and monolatrous stages of naming before attaining the transcendence of biblical thought. Even isolated traces of pagan mythology do not counter the biblical contention that its subject matter is a relation of the Name to its creation. Any theophanic encounters are not aspects of God's life, but rather are external adjuncts of the Name's self-revelation within the world. Contrary attributes, which in paganism constitute opposing divine realms, are united in the Name. Kaufmann's thesis demonstrates how the tetragrammaton is shown to be titular syncretism and not mythological. The underlying assumption is an amalgam of natures and roles as only possible in an unfettered, transcendent Name.

MARMORSTEIN focuses on the rabbinic doctrine of the names of God. He traces prohibitions on the use of the Tetra-grammaton back as far as the third century B.C.E.; this interdiction is shown to apply in conversation, in greetings, and in the notarization of documents alike. Marmorstein proceeds to collect and assess an array of rabbinic traditions such as the claim that after the death of Simeon the Just, the priests ceased to use the Name in pronouncing blessings; that inside the Holy of Holies the priests would utter the Name according to its writing, whereas outside by its substitute; and that even in its pronunciation within the Temple precincts, utterance was not distinct enough to be discernable. Marmorstein also explores the extent to which rabbinic lore discerns a dualistic naming: that God (the Tetragrammaton) connotes mercy, whereas "Power" (*Elohim*) connotes judgment. This nearly Gnostic interpretation of names typifying rabbinic monotheism is one facet of Marmorstein's elaborate picture. Although rabbinic tradition commonly speaks of 70 names, Marmorstein assembles and alphabetizes a total of 91, documenting his sources carefully. The author's traditionalist standpoint seems to predispose this important study to both an early historical dating of the various names and to the rejection of any possibility of syncretism.

TRACHTENBERG redresses the general neglect of the folk religion of Judaism, whose casuistic counterpoint has dominated scholarship. Limited to the literature of medieval Germanic Jewry, his scope excludes the influential corpus of Lurianic mysticism emanating from 16th-century Safed. Nevertheless, this study remains an invaluable standard account, with useful appendixes of Jewish sorcery, magic, amulets, folk medicine, divination, astrology, and dream interpretation, each of these fields being heavily contingent upon conceptions about the names of God. The expansion of the Tetragrammaton is traced in names composed of from eight to 72 letters or syllables, and here Trachtenberg's reliance on the compilation efforts of Nathan Hannover, a 17th-century composer of mystical prayers, is marked. Trachtenberg fills to the brim a diverse bag of tricks from which the Jewish magician can draw, depending on the existential moment.

SCHOLEM (1941) surveys the history of Jewish mysticism in nine lectures, touching repeatedly on transmutations in the understanding of the names of God. Merkabah mysticism focuses on God as King in glory, where the master of the secret names transforms mysticism into a theurgic affecting of the supernal realm. From the end of the 13th century, prophetic kabbalism, a contemplation of letters and their permutations, marks an ecstatic path transforming the ineffable name into the object of meditation. At the same time, Zoharic theosophy conceptualizes the whole Torah as a corpus symbolicum of the concealed name in its ten emanations, awaiting elucidation by the mystic. In the 16th and 17th centuries, Lurianic Kabbalah envisions a harmonic restoration, repairing the damage inflicted by the primordial catastrophe through a praxis of continually unifying shards of the divided name. SCHOLEM (1970) describes an implicit hermeneutic system that views the Name as the original source of all language. While the Name bears no concrete signification, in projecting beyond meaning it invites infinite interpretations in a way that typifies a hermeneutic of Jewish thought.

WOLFSON revises visions of Jewish hermeneutics in particular and semiotics in general. In the former he builds on

Scholem's research, while in the latter he extrapolates principles from the name's secrecy. Wolfson's rigorous investigation of the Zohar reveals an "othering" of the feminine aspect of the Godhead (in all of its emanatory denominations) to be evaluated strictly from the Zohar's phallocentric point of view. Through the apt lens of contemporary feminist reflection, Wolfson returns to the rabbinic paradox explored by Marmorstein and pervading the Zohar: how the two names are one. For the Zohar, the ultimate secret is the mystery that marks the path of secrecy, centering around an occlusion of the feminine whose femininity is no longer ontologically distinct from the male. The erotic nature of the names' union necessitated concealment of the exposed, underscoring the dialectical tension of concealment and disclosure. In much of modern scholarship, this secret has translated into a fear of uncovering the hidden in the symbol of the concealed woman. It transpires from Wolfson's work that the secret of the names of God has hidden itself precisely from the very scholars who have undertaken the systematic exposure of the mysteries of the tradition.

AUBREY L. GLAZER

See also God, Doctrines and Concepts of

God-Fearers

Feldman, Louis H., *Jew and Gentile in the Ancient World: Attitudes and Interactions from Alexander to Justinian*, Princeton, New Jersey: Princeton University Press, 1993

Hengel, Martin and Anna Maria Schwemer, "Excursus I: The Problem of the 'Sympathizers' and Jewish Propaganda," in their *Paul between Damascus and Antioch: The Unknown Years*, Louisville, Kentucky: Westminster John Knox, and London: SCM, 1997

Kraabel, A.T., "The Disappearance of the 'God-Fearers,'" *Numen*, 28, 1981

Lieu, J.M., "The Race of the God-Fearers," *Journal of Theological Studies*, 46, 1995

Millar, Fergus, "Gentiles and Judaism: 'God-Fearers' and Proselytes," in *The History of the Jewish People in the Age of Jesus Christ (175 B.C.-A.D. 135)*, vol. 3, part 1, by Emil Schürer, revised by Géza Vermès, Fergus Millar, and Martin Goodman, Edinburgh: Clark, 1986

The Acts of the Apostles in the New Testament speaks 11 times of "those who fear God" (10:2, 22, 35; 13:16, 26) or "those who reverence [God]" (13:43, 50; 16:14; 17:4, 17; 18:7). In four instances they form a group of attendees at a synagogue, distinct from the Jewish members (13:16, 26, 43; 17:17). Most readers to the present day have understood that undefined numbers of Gentiles in the Mediterranean world of the first century C.E. were attracted to Judaism and went regularly to their local synagogues to hear the scriptures read and expounded, without becoming proselytes by circumcision. Presumably some undertook to keep more of the commandments than others.

Since the 1980s scholars have debated whether the so-called God-fearers actually existed, and if so, what prompted them to associate with Jews and why they had reservations about converting. The issue of the God-fearers bears on larger questions: how Jews were perceived by Greco-Roman society, whether they missionized, and how they defined membership of their own people. Since important books now cover these related matters (e.g., Menahem Stern, editor, *Greek and Latin Authors on Jews and Judaism*, 3 vols., Jerusalem: Israel Academy of Sciences and Humanities, 1974–1984; E.P. Sanders, editor, *Jewish and Christian Self-Definition*, 3 vols., Philadelphia: Fortress, and London: SCM, 1980–1982; David Rokeah, *Jews, Pagans, and Christians in Conflict*, Jerusalem: Magnes Press of Hebrew University, and Leiden: Brill, 1982; John G. Gager, *The Origins of Anti-Semitism: Attitudes toward Judaism in Pagan and Christian Antiquity*, Oxford and New York: Oxford University Press, 1983; Lawrence H. Schiffman, *Who Was a Jew?: Rabbinic and Halakhic Perspectives on the Jewish Christian Schism*, Hoboken, New Jersey: Ktav, 1985; Martin Goodman, *Mission and Conversion: Proselytizing in the Religious History of the Roman Empire*, Oxford: Clarendon, and New York: Oxford University Press, 1994), each of which has a long bibliography in its own sphere, the present review focuses on selected literature about the God-fearers themselves, most of which is in scholarly journals or book chapters.

KRAABEL presents the most outspoken challenge to the traditional consensus. While teaching Classics at the University of Minnesota and specializing in archaeology, Kraabel came to suspect that the God-fearers might be a figment of Acts' imagination. Two factors suggested this. The archaeological data, in his view, contained no trace of Gentile "God-fearers," although six excavated synagogue sites with more than 100 inscriptions were known at the time he wrote his article. Also, a critical stance toward Luke-Acts had recently come into vogue, according to which the author sometimes played fast and loose with the facts of history in order to get across his theological message. Part of his message was the idea that Christianity developed out of Judaism in natural stages, its acceptance by Gentiles in synagogues being an intermediary step. In this way the author tried to reconcile the church's Gentile constituency with Christianity's claim to rootedness in God's revelation to Israel.

By the time his iconoclastic article came out, Kraabel knew of the discovery five years earlier of an inscription at Aphrodisias in Caria, which, after its full publication in 1987 (Joyce Reynolds and Robert Tannenbaum, *Jews and God-Fearers at Aphrodisias: Greek Inscriptions with Commentary: Texts from the Excavations at Aphrodisias Conducted by Kenan T. Erim*, Cambridge: Cambridge Philological Society, 1987), would turn the judgment of the scholarly world against his skepticism. A year before the final report, MILLAR, one of the world's foremost experts on the history of Judaism in late antiquity, put the great weight of his reputation behind Acts and the tradition on the basis of the same datum. The inscription lists the names of people who contributed to the foundation of something, presumably a building. A first group includes many Hebrew names. After a one-line break, a subheading reads, "and such as are God-fearers," followed by a list containing names that are not Hebrew. "The new inscription thus provides the conclusive evidence for the reality of a defined category of gentile 'God-fearers' attached to a Jewish community"; indeed, he concludes that "it would be difficult to imagine clearer evidence."

To date, the most complete assemblage of data bearing on the issue is the chapter-length treatment by FELDMAN. He agrees with Kraabel that Acts requires independent confirmation and should not be used as the control for other potentially relevant data. Therefore he marshals other sources: "circumstantial" evidence, by which he means the analogy of degrees of conversion in other religions ancient and modern; Greek and Roman references to pagan sympathizers with Jews; Jewish references (in Philo, Josephus, the apocrypha and pseudepigrapha, and talmudic writings); Christian references other than those in Acts, taken mainly from the early church fathers; and the evidence of inscriptions and papyri (of which Feldman finds perhaps as many as 14, including those from Aphrodisias, in contrast to Kraabel's none). Feldman simply lays out the facts with minimal comment. The effect is to place the Acts material in a wide context of converging lines. Feldman goes on to enumerate several dozen factors that likely attracted pagans or Christians to Judaism. Among them were its antiquity, the Jews' respect for law and order, and their ethical behavior, as well as social, political, and business concerns. Reasons why sympathizers did not convert varied; some may have wanted to avoid being accused of atheism for not worshiping pagan deities.

LIEU offers a postmodern perspective on the problem. She lays aside the historical questions of whether and why the "God-fearers" existed; instead, she asks what rhetorical benefits people gained by applying the adjective to themselves. (Curiously, she criticizes scholarship for not distinguishing between *theosebes,* "God-fearing," and the Greek participial expression *hoi sebomenoi ton theon,* "those who fear God"; she is interested only in the former, which is not in Acts, and so sidesteps the book of Acts altogether.) She concludes that "God-fearing" Jews or Christians wished to be regarded as pious and to exclude each other from that honor, and to be regarded as religious rather than atheistic or superstitious in the face of pagan charges.

HENGEL adds his authority to that of Millar and Feldman in accepting ancient testimony concerning the God-fearers. But in analyzing what drew pagans of high standing to synagogue worship, Hengel puts his finger on an obvious theological matter that Feldman seems to have overlooked: simply that Jewish scripture readings and sermons taught ethical monotheism.

PAUL A. RAINBOW

Golem

Bilski, Emily D., *Golem! Danger, Deliverance, and Art,* New York: Jewish Museum, 1988

Goldsmith, Arnold L., *The Golem Remembered, 1909–1980: Variations of a Jewish Legend,* Detroit, Michigan: Wayne State University Press, 1981

Idel, Moshe, *Golem: Jewish Magical and Mystical Traditions on the Artificial Anthropoid* (SUNY Series in Judaica), Albany: State University of New York Press, 1990

Kieval, Hillel J., "Pursuing the Golem of Prague: Jewish Culture and the Invention of a Tradition," *Modern Judaism,* 17(1), 1 February 1997

Scholem, Gershom, "The Idea of the Golem," in his *On the Kabbalah and Its Symbolism,* New York: Schocken, and London: Routledge and Kegan Paul, 1965

Sherwin, Byron L., *The Golem Legend: Origins and Implications,* Lanham, Maryland: University Press of America, 1985

Winkler, Gershon, *The Golem of Prague,* New York: Judaica Press, 1980

The figure of the golem–an anthropoid created and animated by human magic–has evolved beyond its origins in the Jewish mystical tradition into one of the most potent and ubiquitous legends of contemporary folklore. The history of golem-making has attracted the attention of leading scholars of Jewish mysticism, while an extensive literature also exists on the diverse cultural representations of this legend over the past 150 years. There remains considerable uncertainty and controversy regarding the relationships among late antique, medieval, and modern notions of the golem. However, the diversity of analytical approaches taken to this theme–textual-critical, philosophical, historical, visual, and literary–generally complement rather than directly conflict with each other.

SCHOLEM's pioneering essay, first published in 1955 in German, remains the most elegant and accessible study of the history of the golem in Jewish mysticism. He traces the subject from the biblical and talmudic discussions of God's creation of Adam (which the magical process imitates) to Jacob Grimm's 1808 account of golem-making among Polish Jews. The author focuses on the exegesis of the late antique *Sefer Yetsirah* by the French and German Hasidim of the 12th and 13th centuries, who interpreted this text as a magical manual for the creation of life. In this period, he argues, a standard ritual for golem-making emerged, involving the kneading of earth and water and the mystical recitation of combinations of the Hebrew alphabet. According to Scholem, this procedure was understood as a mystical representation of the creative act, intended to induce ecstatic experience rather than the actual creation of life. His taut historical account explains that the Safed kabbalists of the 16th century abandoned these rituals and considered the golem only as a theoretical notion, whereas early modern German and Polish Jews for the first time conceived of the golem as a mechanical automaton, capable of performing tasks and even of overpowering its master.

IDEL provides by far the most detailed textual study of this subject. He acknowledges his profound debt to Scholem but takes issue with what he sees as the earlier historian's overly unified account of the evolution of a single "idea" of the golem. Idel also queries Scholem's sharp differentiation of Jewish beliefs from pagan astrology and animation of statues, as well as Scholem's claim that all medieval golem practices were oriented towards mystical experience. Idel argues that while the Sephardi ecstatic Kabbalah strongly privileged spiritual over material creation, the golem-making of the Hasidei Ashkenaz can be more plausibly interpreted as a magical ritual. He also gives more credence than Scholem to the possibility that there was a subterranean transmission of the tradition from late antiquity to the medieval period, and to the variegated influence of Neoplatonic and Aristotelian ideas on Jewish mysticism. Based on the close reading of source texts, from which he quotes extensively, Idel advances a subtle analysis of both the theosophical and experiential dimensions of golem beliefs, from the ancient period to contemporary ultra-orthodoxy. However, despite his critique of Scholem's historical schema, Idel by no means conclusively displaces the earlier paradigm.

SHERWIN's brief study covers both the textual origins and 20th-century significance of the golem. He summarizes the ancient and medieval sources and 18th-century coalescence of the legend around the 16th-century figure of Rabbi Judah Loew, the Maharal of Prague. The author then turns to a philosophical consideration of these narratives in the context of recent understandings of the possibilities and perils of human creativity. Rabbinic discussions of such issues as whether a golem can be included in a quorum are related to 20th-century debates on genetic engineering, *in vitro* fertilization, and artificial intelligence. Diverging considerably from his starting-point, Sherwin thoughtfully explores the inner significance of the legend.

BILSKI's volume is the catalog for an exhibition on the golem mounted at the Jewish Museum in New York, and it is lavishly illustrated with images from all media inspired by this theme. Bilski's own essay comprehensively traces the visual history of the golem, from late 19th-century drawings and early 20th-century film, theater, and opera to abstract and installation art of the late 1980s. A separate essay by Elfi Ledig is devoted to Paul Wegener's three *Golem* films (1915–1920). Idel contributes a historical overview, which usefully summarizes the arguments of his book. However, the volume focuses primarily on the impact of the Golem motif on the visual imagination of the 20th century.

GOLDSMITH usefully complements Bilski, providing a roughly parallel account of 20th-century literary representations of the golem. He notes the irony that the Maharal, a determined opponent of magic, has become the primary figure associated with the creation of a golem. The author closely examines the two texts most responsible for popularizing this myth: Rabbi Yudl Rosenberg's publication, in Hebrew and Yiddish, of a purported eyewitness account of Rabbi Loew's golem-making (1909), and Chayim Bloch's German re-telling of these tales (1919). Goldsmith also offers a perceptive reading of Gustav Meyrinck's febrile, "psychological gothic" novel *The Golem* (1915), as well as interpretations of later golem literature, including poetry by Jorge Luis Borges and John Hollander.

WINKLER's volume should be approached with caution. In defiance of almost all scholarly opinion, he argues that Rosenberg's text was based on a genuine and authoritative manuscript account of the Golem of Prague. Although this claim can be safely discounted, he nonetheless provides a readable–but modified–version of these influential stories, together with a non-historical summary of the place of the golem in Jewish teachings on magic, witchcraft, and the occult.

Finally, KIEVAL's article usefully illuminates the history of the association of the Maharal of Prague with the golem legend. While acknowledging the uncertainty that still surrounds this issue, he dates the beginnings of the charismatic veneration of the Maharal to the early 18th century and traces the literary debut of the Golem of Prague to two texts from the 1840s. The most noteworthy and influential innovation in Rosenberg's version, Kieval notes, is that the golem is cast as the protector of a Jewish community threatened from outside, in contrast with the traditional understanding of golem-making as a reminder of the dangers inherent within the creative process itself.

ADAM SUTCLIFFE

Gordon, Judah Leib 1830–1892

Lithuanian-born Hebrew poet and champion of Haskalah

Rhine, Abraham Benedict, *Leon Gordon: An Appreciation*, Philadelphia: Jewish Publication Society, 1910

Slouschz, Nahum, *The Renascence of Hebrew Literature (1743–1885)*, Philadelphia: Jewish Publication Society, 1909

Spiegel, Shalom, *Hebrew Reborn*, Philadelphia: Jewish Publication Society, 1930; London: Benn, 1931

Stanislawski, Michael, *For Whom Do I Toil? Judah Leib Gordon and the Crisis of Russian Jewry* (Studies in Jewish History), New York: Oxford University Press, 1988

Waxman, Meyer, *A History of Jewish Literature from the Close of the Bible to Our Own Days*, vol. 3: *From the Middle of the 18th Century to the Year 1880*, New York: Bloch, 1930–1941

Judah Leib Gordon is renowned as a Hebrew poet, journalist, and exponent of Jewish Enlightenment in Russia. Gordon is preeminent in 19th-century Hebrew literature as a master of language, as a poet, and as a humorist.

SLOUSCHZ's account of the revival and renaissance of Hebrew letters in the 18th and 19th centuries contains an early appreciation of Gordon. The chapter devoted to Gordon discusses his place in the resuscitation of Hebrew poetry.

RHINE's pioneer biographical sketch of Gordon is also useful, but it is very dated as to the cultural background material. The last two chapters on Gordon's epic and lyric poetry are well worth reading, however, and contain some excellent translations.

WAXMAN's standard history of Jewish literature includes an account of Gordon that is largely dependent on Rhine. It may be consulted, however, by those who have no access to Rhine's monograph.

STANISLAWSKI's work is the first full-length biography of Gordon in any language. The author is more interested in Gordon the thinker than in Gordon the poet. His study places Gordon in the twin contexts of 19th-century Russian and Jewish history. Stanislawski shows the interplay between Russian intellectual and political developments and the emergence of modern Jewish cultural and national consciousness. Gordon holds a unique position among the men who made the Jewish Enlightenment movement (Haskalah) a success. He played a prominent part in the battle against the exclusiveness of traditional Judaism and advocated the adoption of European modes of life and thought. Gordon championed a humanist and liberal approach to all the major questions facing the Jews in their tortuous transition to modernity: the religious reform of Judaism, the attractions and limits of political liberalism, the relation of Jews and gentiles, the nature of modern antisemitism, the status of women in Jewish society, and many other burning questions and issues that remain largely unresolved. Gordon's slogan, "Be a man outside and a Jew at home" taken from his poem "Awake My People" (c.1862) is usually interpreted in an assimilationist fashion. Gordon, it is generally said, advocated a split in Jewish identity between formal religious observance limited to the private domain of the home and synagogue, and suppression of all outward manifestation of Jewishness in deference to the host culture. Stanislawski, on the contrary, argues that Gordon had something far more noble in mind: continued adherence to Jewish values, in both the religious and national sense, accompanied by openness to general European culture, to which, indeed, the Jews had much to contribute. Gordon's slogan "therefore, was a call not for the bifurcation of Jewish identity, but for its integration." The watershed pogroms of 1881, the emergence of European nationalism, and antisemitism rendered Gordon's worldview irrelevant, and he died an isolated and disappointed man.

SPIEGEL is a very perceptive critic. Gordon believed that his satire "The Point of the Yod," loosely translatable as "The Dot on the I," was his most successful poem. The poem is directed against the rigorous interpretation of the law by narrowminded rabbis who are insensitive to the hardships and sufferings they cause. It is also a plea for the emancipation of Jewish women. The story sounds like a soap opera. The beautiful Bat-Shua is married to Hillel, an ugly, unmanly, and unworldly weakling who has never learned anything but Talmud. She lives with her husband for three years, giving birth to two children and supported by her father. When this subsidy runs out, her husband leaves her to seek his fortune abroad. At first she receives letters from him regularly; then he stops writing, all trace of him is lost, and Bat-Shua becomes a grass widow. She is able to eke out a living by painful toil and pours out all her love on her children. Salvation comes in the person of Fabi, an engineer, who supervises the construction of a railway line in town. Fabi is an enlightened Jew, educated, intelligent, handsome, and generous. He falls in love with Bat-Shua and learns of her plight. Through a friend in Liverpool, Fabi discovers that the faithless husband is peddling there and would be willing to divorce his wife for a consideration of $500, with which he intends to go to America. The writ of divorce is properly drawn up, attested to by the local rabbinical court, and sent to the wife. Finally it seems that Bat-Shua will enjoy the happiness that she has amply merited. But alas, the course of true love does not run smoothly. After taking the payoff Hillel embarks for America, but his vessel is shipwrecked and all on board are lost. When the divorce arrives, the local rabbi, a rigid legalist, insists that the name of Hillel should have been written *scriptio plena* with the vowel letter i (yod), even though this dogmatism offends the elementary laws of Hebrew grammar.

He declares the divorce invalid, and since Hillel is dead and cannot correct the scribal error, the talmudic law applies: "the wife of a man lost in bottomless waters cannot remarry." Thus is the happiness of Bat-Shua shattered forever by the jots and tittles of an inhumanly rigorous legalism.

Spiegel considers Gordon's extravagant satires directed at rabbinic despotism to be artistic failures—gross caricatures that lack even poetic verisimilitude. The tragedy of the Jewish woman as described by Gordon is superficial and contrived. The poet rants and raves against heaven because his heroine cannot marry a wealthy man, and he defames religious leaders by drawing a hate-distorted picture of rabbinic cruelty. Spiegel notes that in another poem Gordon shows an appreciative understanding for the necessities of the non-Jewish Russian law: the law may have prescribed certain formalities in order to prevent fraud and must be obeyed despite any individual hardships it may cause. Spiegel notes Ahad Ha'am's opinion that Israel Zangwill's novel *The Children of the Ghetto* more fairly presents the problem of the conflict between the proscriptions of a rigid code lagging behind the developing social conscience because there, the heroine's happiness is destroyed not by a narrow-minded fanatic but by her own doting father.

JACOB HABERMAN

Graetz, Heinrich 1817–1891

German *Wissenschaft* scholar and leading interpreter of Jewish history

Baron, Salo W., *History and Jewish Historians: Essays and Addresses,* edited by Arthur Hertzberg and Leon A. Feldman, Philadelphia: Jewish Publication Society, 1964

Herlitz, G., "Three Jewish Historians: Isaak Markus Jost, Heinrich Graetz, Eugen Taeubler: A Comparative Study," *Yearbook of the Leo Baeck Institute,* 9, 1964

Schorsch, Ismar, "Introduction," in Heinrich Graetz's *Die Konstruktion der jüdischen Geschichte* (1936), translated by Ismar Schorsch as *The Structure of Jewish History, and Other Essays* (Moreshet, vol. 3), New York: Jewish Theological Seminary, 1975

Heinrich Graetz was one of the foremost German Jewish historians of the 19th century. Partially self-taught, Graetz served as a professor at the Jewish-Theological Seminary at Breslau (now Wrocław, Poland). Graetz was also a prolific writer who produced, in addition to many well-researched essays, an 11-volume history of the Jewish people (1853–1876) that represents the first comprehensive treatment of this subject according to modern scholarly standards. (The work appeared in English translation in 1891 in a five-volume version titled *History of the Jews.*) Having been influenced as a historian by the ideas of the German philosopher G.W.F. Hegel, Graetz became a pivotal figure in the attempt of German Jews to reshape their identity in the wake of their societal emancipation.

BARON presents a short biographical sketch of Graetz's life and work. While essentially descriptive, Baron discusses briefly

Graetz's stand concerning Orthodox Judaism and Reform Judaism and his "proto-Zionist" leanings. Baron also includes remarks on Graetz's critics and on those writers who influenced Graetz most, for example, Hegel and Leopold von Ranke.

HERLITZ places Graetz's writings in the larger context provided by the writings of Isaak Markus Jost and Eugen Taeubler, two eminent Jewish historians that preceded and succeeded Graetz, respectively. In addition to providing some biographical details, Herlitz analyzes Graetz's conception of Jewish history, liberally citing his writings. Herlitz is primarily interested in Graetz's shortcomings as a historian and remains fairly superficial in his descriptive analysis.

SCHORSCH offers an excellent and detailed introduction to the writings and thinking of Graetz and also provides annotated selections from Graetz's oeuvre (especially his essays), many of which are presented here in English for the first time. Schorsch is particularly interested in the ideological forces at work in the writings of Graetz and in the question of how Graetz's ideas related to the events that shaped Jewish life in 19th-century Germany.

LEONARD VICTOR RUTGERS

Grammarians *see* Lexicographers and Grammarians

Great Britain

Alderman, Geoffrey, *Modern British Jewry,* New York: Oxford University Press, and Oxford: Clarendon, 1992

Black, Eugene, *The Social Politics of Anglo-Jewry, 1880–1920,* Oxford and New York: Blackwell, 1988

Cesarani, David (editor), *The Making of Modern Anglo-Jewry,* Oxford and Cambridge, Massachusetts: Blackwell, 1990

Endelman, Todd, *The Jews of Georgian England, 1714–1830: Tradition and Change in a Liberal Society,* Philadelphia: Jewish Publication Society, 1979

Gartner, Lloyd, *The Jewish Immigrant in England, 1870–1914,* Detroit, Michigan: Wayne State University Press, and London: Allen and Unwin, 1960

Katz, David, *The Jews in the History of England, 1485–1850,* New York: Oxford University Press, and Oxford: Clarendon, 1994

Lipman, V.D., *Social History of the Jews in England, 1850–1950,* London: Watts, 1954

Mundill, Robin, *England's Jewish Solution: Experiment and Expulsion, 1262–1290* (Cambridge Studies in Medieval Life and Thought), London and New York: Cambridge University Press, 1998

Richardson, H.G., *The English Jewry under Angevin Kings,* London: Methuen, 1960

Notwithstanding the discovery in England of minor Jewish artifacts dating from Roman times, the presence of a Jewish population in Britain in Roman or Saxon times remains an issue of speculation. The first substantial Jewish population arrived following the Norman conquest in 1066.

A standard work on the history of medieval English Jews is RICHARDSON. Concerned mainly with the reigns of Henry II and his successors, this work represented, in its day, a significant reappraisal of the medieval Jewish experience, and it has not been rendered obsolete by subsequent scholarship. Richardson corrects widespread misunderstandings concerning the situation of Jews in England and presents a balanced account of Jewish-Christian relations. He goes to considerable trouble to make it clear that the Expulsion of 1290, which brought to a close medieval English Jewish life, was not the outcome of radical shifts in the economic situation. Jews were not as heavily engaged in money-lending as had been portrayed, nor had they been taxed into poverty. To the contrary, evidence suggests a significant diversity of economic activity among medieval English Jews. In Richardson's view, the expulsion arose from a growth of intolerance and oppression directed toward those represented as heretics or infidels.

A more recent treatment of the situation of medieval English Jewry and the expulsion is MUNDILL. This work has a more modern feel to it than Richardson's account, reflecting the influence of contemporary social sciences on the writing of history. Mundill's examination of the complex currents of events, both in England and on the European continent, in the decades prior to 1290 shows that the expulsion was part of a larger pattern of discriminatory acts against Jews. The analysis of King Edward's situation lends substantial credibility to Mundill's surprising conclusion that the expulsion was executed virtually on a whim and because "the time was right."

For three and a half centuries following the expulsion, there were virtually no Jews in England, save for clandestine visitors or illegal immigrants whose presence the authorities often ignored. The stereotype Jew, however, survived during this period as a figure of English legal discourse and literature, and the Israeli historian KATZ broke new ground in the writing of Anglo-Jewish history by "tracing the Jewish thread throughout English life between the Tudors and the beginning of mass immigration in the mid-nineteenth century." Many of Katz's contemporaries viewed the work of earlier generations of Anglo-Jewish historians as flawed, being little more than "Whig history," that is, an optimistic and teleological account of events culminating in the admission of the first Jewish member to Parliament in 1858. Katz counters the assumptions of such earlier works as he takes a novel approach to English Jewish history that looks for explanations of events less in the circumstances of the Jews than in the circumstances of the Christian majority of England and their attitudes regarding Jews and Judaism. Katz's book displays immense learning combined with great storytelling skill.

The Jewish population in Great Britain grew steadily beginning in the early 18th century. ENDELMAN comprehensively documents the experiences and concerns of Anglo-Jews in the 18th and early 19th centuries, presenting a highly readable account of the struggle of some Jews to remove the (not very onerous) civil disabilities under which they, as well as other nonconformists, labored. Endelman produces important insights into both the internal politics of Anglo-Jewry and

Jewish relations with the developing liberal state during a period that has had a long-term impact upon the subsequent development of Anglo-Jewish institutions and social life.

Although LIPMAN is dismissed by some as belonging to the older generation of "Whig" historians, this judgment is too harsh. Lipman was one of a small number of English historians who pioneered the writing of the history of late 19th- and 20th-century Jewish immigrants and who depicted Jewish life in the East End of London. His book on Anglo-Jewish social history from 1850 to 1950 remains a reliable account of a key period during which Anglo-Jewish life was transformed. His descriptions of the demographic changes; occupational and economic structures; and the development of charitable, educational, and religious institutions in Anglo-Jewry are models of clarity.

GARTNER's monograph remains the definitive work on immigrant Jews in England, and it has contributed greatly to the development of a critical historiography of Anglo-Jewry. Gartner conjures up the world of the mainly poor and uneducated Eastern European immigrants who crowded into London's East End. In an intensely moving account, Gartner documents the almost relentlessly grim daily life of the immigrants, as they struggled first to survive and then to better themselves, eventually laying the foundation for contemporary Anglo-Jewish prosperity.

BLACK focuses on the world of social relations among different groups of Jews and between Jews and others in England. The author is at his best when he contrasts the milieu of the established, Anglicized, and wealthy Jews with the world of the newly arrived ethnics from Eastern Europe. Black creates beautifully drawn vignettes of Anglo-Jewish life, such as accounts of the Anglo-Jewish aristocracy, who took very seriously their mission of socializing the immigrants and turning them into members of the "respectable poor" who would embrace the virtues of self-help and upward mobility.

CESARANI's volume is not a general history of Anglo-Jewry but a collection of essays on (often neglected) aspects of the community, including discussions of trade unions, women, and the household economy. The collection reflects contemporary historians' increased focus on issues such as class, ethnicity, and gender. It is ideologically the opposite of "Whig history," for it stresses diversity and rejects a view of history as moving in linear fashion from intolerance to inclusion.

ALDERMAN's concerns as a scholar of government and politics are reflected in his fine study of political relations within the modern Anglo-Jewish population and the Jewish community's relationship to the British state. Of particular interest are the final two chapters of Alderman's history, which set recent debates and divisions within Anglo-Jewry into clear relief, mapping the community's trend toward both fragmentation and pluralism within an overall context of gradual numerical decline in the Anglo-Jewish population.

ROBERT ASH

See also London

H

Habad

Deutsch, Shaul S., *Larger Than Life: The Life and Times of the Lubavitcher Rebbe Rabbi Menachem Mendel Schneerson,* 2 vols., New York: Chasidic Historical Productions, 1995

Ehrlich, Avrum M., *Leadership in the HaBaD Movement,* Northvale, New Jersey: Aronson, 2000

Elior, Rachel, *The Paradoxical Ascent to God: The Kabbalistic Theosophy of Habad Hasidism* (SUNY Series in Judaica), Albany: State University of New York Press, 1993

Foxbrunner, Roman A., *The Hasidism of Rabbi Shneur Zalman of Lyadi,* Tuscaloosa: University of Alabama Press, 1994

Friedman, Menachem, "Habad as Messianic Fundamentalism: From Local Particularism to Universal Mission," in *Accounting for Fundamentalisms: The Dynamic Character of Movements* (Fundamentalism Project, vol. 4), edited by Martin E. Marty and R. Scott Appleby, Chicago: University of Chicago Press, 1994

Levin, Shalom, *History of Chabad in the Holy Land: 1777–1950,* Brooklyn, New York: Kehot, 1988

Levin, Shalom, *History of Chabad in the U.S.A.: 1990–1950,* Brooklyn, New York: Otsar ha-Hasidim, 1988

Levin, Shalom, *History of Chabad in the U.S.S.R.: 1717–1950,* Brooklyn, New York: Kehot, 1989

Loewenthal, Naftali, *Communicating the Infinite: The Emergence of the Habad School,* Chicago: University of Chicago Press, 1990

Habad is the name of a hasidic school of thought founded in White Russia around the turn of the 19th century by Rabbi Shneur Zalman of Lyadi in reaction to accusations that Hasidism was suitable only for the unlearned simpleton. The movement sought to sow a dimension of scholarship, sophistication, and methodic mysticism into the hasidic revolution. The name *HaBaD* in itself indicates the movement's purpose: the term is an acronym for *hokhmah* (wisdom), *binah* (understanding), and *da'at* (knowledge). In its origin, the role of the rebbe was significantly different in Habad thought from the role played by the rebbes in other hasidic groups. He was a teacher and guide more than a miracle-worker and saint. The

Habad movement is more famous today for the social role it played among Russian Jewry and later among Jews in the United States and Israel than for its scholarly origins. Habad hasidic thought has become synonymous with the Lubavitch dynasty of rebbes because they were the most effective in disseminating the school's philosophy. A clear continuum of ideas and philosophy from the early days of the movement until the present does not exist, however. Following his appointment in 1951, a messianic cult began to develop around the personality of the seventh Lubavitcher rebbe, Menahem Mendel Schneersohn, reaching extreme levels of hope and disappointment upon his death in 1992. The movement has not appointed a new rebbe and presently remains split between messianic elements and less defined groups.

DEUTSCH's two-volume work on the life and times of Schneersohn is not purely academic in tone, and it is troubled by unnecessary errors, unprofessional editing, and a lack of objective commentary. Despite these problems, it is indispensable to an understanding of the leadership of the seventh Lubavitcher rebbe, and it offers indirect insights into the Lubavitch movement and the evolution of what is known today as modern Habad Hasidism. Particularly valuable is the information that Deutsch found in the private files of the dynasty. The study is important for sociologists and historians alike. Volume one covers the early years of Schneersohn's life by drawing from documentary sources and interviews with acquaintances of the family. Deutsch discusses the political circumstances of the period, the difficulties that Jewry and Habad Hasidism encountered, and the reasons that Schneersohn was chosen to marry the sixth Lubavitcher rebbe's daughter. Volume two continues in this strain; included are fascinating interviews with leading religious figures in American Jewry that illuminate Schneersohn's personality. Descriptions of Deutsch's personal life, his break with Lubavitch, and his claims to be a contemporary Habad rebbe add a curious dimension to this work.

EHRLICH has written the most comprehensive work on the history of Habad leadership; it draws from the rebbes' published writings and from primary and secondary sources, interviews, private diaries, and oral traditions. Describing the various leaderships of the respective Habad rebbes, Ehrlich theorizes about how they rose to leadership and recounts what they did with the mantle of authority. While quite a few works address the early period of Habad, little information exists about the intermediate period. Ehrlich summarizes the process of transferring authority, including the arguments and splits that took place in the Habad movement from its inception under the leadership of Rabbi Shneur Zalman until the election of Rabbi Menahem Mendel Schneersohn in 1951. The author considers how the Lubavitch dynasty emerged as the sole surviving Habad subgroup and tries to identify leadership patterns. The book is presented in three sections: a general study of the principles of Jewish, hasidic, and Habad leadership; a summary of all the successions and leadership struggles in Habad history; and a study of how Schneersohn became the seventh Lubavitch rebbe. As the bibliography of political, sociological, historical, and theological sources suggests, this work is a study of leadership dynamics as much as it is an analysis of the Habad movement.

ELIOR's work focuses primarily on the first and second generations of Habad philosophy, and it does not address the modern movement or the dramatic later shifts in Habad thinking. The author analyzes early influences on Habad and the paradoxical nature of the complex habadic view of God and the world. She describes the interaction between Habad and more traditional schools of thought; explores the differences between Habad and other hasidic schools; and identifies the essential novelty of the habadic endeavor as the movement's effort to design a spiritual process and paradigm that facilitated a refined religious consciousness while demanding scholarship, piety, and an unceasing commitment to activism and halakhah within the "lower worlds." Elior also addresses the relationships among different categories of mystical thought and explains the way in which these ideas are reflected in community life.

FOXBRUNNER's work on the philosophy and method of Rabbi Shneur Zalman's mysticism is exhaustive. Focusing almost entirely on the founder's beliefs, the author tries to place these ideas into broad religious-ethical categories. Foxbrunner's work lacks a critical dimension, but it is a good overview of the concepts of early Habad mysticism and the personal religious aspirations of Rabbi Shneur Zalman.

FRIEDMAN, an authoritative sociologist of religious movements, traces the evolution Lubavitch from the local dynasty led by the fifth rebbe through its emergence as a worldwide religious movement inculcating extreme messianism under the seventh rebbe. The author presents various interesting theories regarding the evolution of Habad thought, and he tries to understand the present movement in light of its history.

LEVIN (1988a, 1988b, 1989), chief librarian at the Habad headquarters in Brooklyn and the ultimate Habad historian, is the author of three monumental volumes on modern Habad history that are a veritable treasure chest of materials culled from the library he heads. These works are based on official Habad sources and have undergone censorship, but Levine nevertheless provides highly scholarly discussion on potentially controversial subjects; the careful reader will appreciate these studies.

LOEWENTHAL's work on the first two generations of Habad leadership is notably comprehensive, well organized, and thoroughly scholarly as it presents important names, dates, maps, and other details relevant to the subject. Loewenthal deals with social and political dimensions of Habad thought and development, including discussions of such topics as war,

poverty, persecution, the use of printed matter, and the fight over the future leadership. He identifies different hasidic populations with different needs and describes how the Habad movement catered to the various groups. In addition, he describes the broad and original theological contributions that Habad made to the hasidic world. His endnotes are scrupulously written and fascinating in their own right.

AVRUM EHRLICH

Haggadah, Passover

Freedman, Jacob (editor), *Polychrome Historical Haggadah for Passover,* Springfield, Massachusetts: Jacob Freedman Liturgy Research Foundation, 1974

Glatzer, Nahum Norbert, E.D. Goldschmidt, and Jacob Sloan (editors), *The Passover Haggadah*, New York: Schocken, 1953, new expanded edition, 1996

Goodman, Philip, *The Passover Anthology* (JPS Holiday Series), Philadelphia: Jewish Publication Society, 1961, paperback edition with new introduction by Ellen Frankel, 1993

Raphael, Chaim, *A Feast of History: Passover through the Ages as a Key to Jewish Experience; with a New Translation of the Haggadah for Use at the Seder,* New York: Simon and Schuster, 1972; as *A Feast of History: The Drama of Passover through the Ages; with a New Translation of the Haggadah for Use at the Seder,* London: Weidenfeld and Nicolson, 1972

Steingroot, Ira, *Keeping Passover: Everything You Need to Know to Bring the Ancient Tradition to Life and Create Your Own Passover Celebration,* San Francisco: HarperSanFrancisco, 1995

Yerushalmi, Yosef Hayim, *Haggadah and History: A Panorama in Facsimile of Five Centuries of the Printed Haggadah from the Collections of Harvard University and the Jewish Theological Seminary of America,* Philadelphia: Jewish Publication Society, 1974, 2nd edition, 1997

The Passover Haggadah—a compilation of biblical passages, prayers, hymns, and rabbinic literature—was probably assembled sometime during the Second Temple period in Palestine and is read during the Passover Seder, the ceremonial meal held in Jewish homes to commemorate the Israelite redemption from Egypt in biblical times. The earliest extant version appears in a tenth-century prayerbook from Babylonia (modern Iraq). The Haggadah became an especially cherished text for Jews all over the world, and nowhere is this high regard more evident than in the illustrations lavished on it by generations of Jewish artists from medieval times to the present. These illuminations represent biblical scenes as well as images based on rabbinic legends.

The first printed version of the Haggadah appears to have been published in Guadalajara in 1482, ten years before the expulsion of the Jews from Spain. One cannot be certain, however, because no place or date of publication is given in the text. The first illustrated Haggadah printed in Hebrew that has survived in its entirety was produced in Prague in

1526. This influenced a long line of illustrated Haggadot, a tradition that continues to this day.

In modern times, the Haggadah has taken on a new significance as Jewish life has changed and evolved. The text and the illustrations that were fixed for centuries have started to vary as the Haggadah has begun increasingly to reflect not only Israel's ancient history but also contemporary Jewish agendas and events. Some of the most interesting modern Haggadah editions come from Israel, where the importance of the return to Zion predominates as a theme both in the text and in the illustrations. The various movements in the lives of American Jews have produced Haggadot that reflect their own vision of Judaism and their understanding of themselves as American Jews. Jewish artists such as Arthur Szyk, Ben Shahn, and Yaakov Agam have further enriched the modern repertoire with their illustrated Haggadah editions.

YERUSHALMI surveys the development of the printed Haggadah over the last five centuries. He does so by means of facsimile pages from representative editions found in the libraries of Harvard and the Jewish Theological Seminary of America. Each facsimile page is accompanied by a discussion of the history and important features of the particular edition. The book appeared in 1975, and thus only Haggadot printed before that date are surveyed. Yerushalmi includes a lengthy and informative introduction, which provides an overview of the history of the Haggadah from its earliest development to the present. This book, unique in its approach, is an erudite and fascinating study by an eminent American scholar of Jewish history.

GOODMAN devotes two chapters to the discussion of the Haggadah in the context of his book on the Passover festival. Chapter five is concerned with the development of the Passover Haggadah. The chapter traces the evolution of the text and analyzes its relationship to the Bible, the Mishnah (the primary rabbinic legal text), and the Midrash (rabbinic exegesis of the Bible). He then reviews the history of the printed Haggadah, its commentaries and translations, and concludes with a look at modern variations of the traditional text. Chapter 16 examines Haggadah illustration. Written by Rachel Wischnitzer, a noted historian of Jewish art, the chapter traces manuscript Haggadah illumination through a study of the development of several themes: the sages in Bnei Brak, the family seder, the four sons, the Exodus, and various other biblical motifs. She also examines the illustrations of the early editions of the printed Haggadah and concludes with a discussion of the revival of Haggadah illustration in modern times. Goodman's book originally was published in 1961 and is, therefore, not current. It is, however, an excellent resource for the historical study of the Haggadah and of Haggadah illustration.

RAPHAEL's book consists of the full text of the Haggadah in Hebrew and in English translation and an examination of its history. Chapter one discusses the Haggadah in modern times and focuses on its adaptability to modernity. Chapter three, *The Development of the Haggadah*, traces the evolution of the text from postbiblical times through the 17th century. He discusses the Haggadot of the medieval period and provides many illustrations of the superb art that accompanied these manuscripts. He continues with a review of the early printed Haggadah editions. Raphael's book is a resource for the study of the Haggadah in medieval and early modern times, with the profuse visual material significantly enhancing the text.

GLATZER presents the traditional Hebrew text of the Haggadah with a facing-page English translation that attempts to imitate the elevated tone of the Hebrew. It thus uses archaic English forms (such as "thee" and "thou") and is not gender neutral. The introduction, running commentary, and explanatory notes are based largely on the writings of Ernst Daniel Goldschmidt, one of the great scholars of Jewish liturgy. Assembled for this edition are additional readings: "Legends and Teachings," "Readings on the Holocaust," and "Some Contemporary Seder Thoughts." Also included are a guide to names, works, and terms, and illustrations from Haggadot of the past.

FREEDMAN's work derives its title from the manner in which the editor attempts to highlight by means of color the era from which each stratum of the Haggadah text derives. He uses colored squares at the head of paragraphs and sections to indicate the era when they were introduced and presents parts of the text in different colors in order to indicate their source. It is an innovative if at times confusing way of presenting the Hebrew text of the Haggadah. This edition is, thus, a good choice for readers with some knowledge of classical Jewish texts who wish to gain a better understanding of the Haggadah's textual sources. In addition to the English translation and the many explanatory notes, the volume includes numerous black-and-white and colored plates of medieval illuminated manuscripts and early printed Haggadot.

STEINGROOT discusses the Haggadah in chapter five of his book. He notes its sources and provides a rather modern and even hip commentary on the text. He concludes with what must be the most exhaustive catalog of extant Haggadah editions that currently exists in English. The list covers Haggadot produced by the three main modern movements in Judaism (Orthodox, Conservative, and Reform) as well as alternative versions such as feminist, secular, and even Christian Haggadot. His comments on each of the more recent editions are meant to assist in the choice of a Haggadah edition for use at the seder.

NANETTE STAHL

Halakhah: Introductions

Elon, Menachem, *Ha-mishpat ha-Ivri,* 1973; translated by Bernard Auerbach and Melvin J. Sykes as *Jewish Law: History, Sources, Principles,* 4 vols., Philadelphia: Jewish Publication Society, 1994

Hecht, Neil S., Bernard Jackson, Stephen Passamaneck, Daniella Piatelli, and Alfredo Rabello (editors), *An Introduction to the History and Sources of Jewish Law* (Boston University, Institute of Jewish Law Publication no. 22), New York: Oxford University Press, and Oxford: Clarendon Press, 1996

Herzog, Isaac, *The Main Institutions of Jewish Law,* 2 vols., London and New York: Soncino, 1936–1939, 2nd ed., 1965–1967

Jackson, Bernard (general editor), *The Jewish Law Annual,* Leiden: Brill, 1978–

Jackson, Bernard (editor), *Modern Research in Jewish Law* (Jewish Law Annual Supplement, no. 1), Leiden: Brill, 1980

Jackson, Bernard (editor), *Jewish Law in Legal History and the Modern World* (Jewish Law Annual Supplement, no. 2), Leiden: Brill, 1980

Urbach, Efraim E., *Halakhah, mekoroteha ve-hitpathutah*, 1984; translated by Raphael Posner as *The Halakhah: Its Sources and Development* (Yad La-Talmud), Ramat Gan: Masadah, 1986

Until the late 20th century, introductions to halakhah— identifying the basic concepts operative in Jewish law and tracing their historical evolution concept-by-concept and institution-by-institution—were severely limited in quantity and quality. What few attempts there were in English were often the work of practicing lawyers equipped with a greater or lesser degree of traditional Jewish learning. These amateur if worthy efforts generally left much to be desired. Aside from academic method, there was lacking both the breadth of erudition to allow for a genuinely comparative perspective and a proper recognition of the ongoing evolution of halakhic ideas. Menachem Elon notes that "most scholarly activity in the field was confined to the Biblical and Talmudic periods," and he attributes this shortcoming in large measure to "the failure to appreciate the significance of the juridical autonomy enjoyed in most Jewish population centers from the time of the Talmud until the eighteenth century (and in certain 'eastern' Jewish communities even later) and the consequent widespread ignorance of the continuous creativity and development of Jewish civil administrative, public, and even criminal law throughout that long period."

One notable pioneering exception was the two-volume work produced by HERZOG, the first chief rabbi of Israel, while he was still chief rabbi of Ireland. Volume one is devoted to the law of property and volume two to the law of obligations. Original and profound, the book remains of much more than historical interest, but it is also a good deal harder going than the best of introductions that have followed in its wake. Even the author himself is willing to admit the scale of the challenge involved when he writes "Only experts who know from first-hand study the intricate, the bewildering, semi-enigmatic nature and often semi-chaotic state of so much of the stupendous mass of material of which this work forms the methodised, reasoned quintessence, presented in Westernised and modernised form, will be able to gauge the mental effort which this must have entailed."

In subsequent decades, in line with an emphasis on an expanded canon, the academic study of halakhah has undergone a radical transformation, with activity centered around the law faculty of the Hebrew University of Jerusalem, as well as the law schools of British and American universities, chiefly among the faculty inspired by the charismatic teacher of Roman law, David Daube. The exhilarating new research that has ensued has largely taken the form of articles and conference proceedings, and the main vehicle of dissemination has been Bernard JACKSON's *Jewish Law Annual*, published since 1978 under the auspices of the International Association of Jewish Lawyers and Jurists, and latterly in conjunction with the Boston University School of Law. The first issue announced that the series would "seek to promote research in Jewish

Civil Law; to foster interest in the Jewish legal system among comparative lawyers and secularly-trained Jewish lawyers; and to provide a medium for communication between lawyers and students of halakhah, and between Israel and the Diaspora." Jackson went on to state that "by and large, the halakhah has served as a unifying force for the Jewish intelligentsia throughout the centuries." He admitted that "Jewish emancipation and secularisation have posed major problems in this regard," but he aspired nonetheless to witness a restoration of the status quo ante through the application of modern scholarly methods. If this has not fully come to pass it is only because the hope was so extravagantly ambitious. For its part, the annual has established itself as a hardy perennial, consistently delivering a remarkably high number of important contributions to knowledge across an often startlingly broad range of Jewish and cross-cultural inquiry.

In later issues a tripartite format has emerged. A typical issue will comprise studies relating to a single if loose theme, usually the topic of the association's annual conference; a "chronicle" surveying major recent developments in "hot" areas of halakhah (e.g., women's rights in the custody of children, or the determination of brain death); and finally an exceedingly thorough "survey of recent literature," in which an impressively inclusive range of relevant monographs and articles appearing in the journals (irrespective of language) are classified by subject and admirably abstracted.

The cadre of adepts responsible for this distinguished journal is also to be credited with three related publications, two of them published as supplements to the *Jewish Law Annual*. The first supplement (JACKSON 1980a) is a discussion of methodologies in this emerging specialty. Supplement two (JACKSON 1980b) includes contributions by David Daube and Shelomo Goitein as well as Israeli Supreme Court Justice Haim Cohn.

The third volume, edited by HECHT et al., sets out to fill "a serious gap" in terms of the lack of "a single-volume introduction to Jewish Law, designed especially to provide essential background information for those seriously encountering Jewish Law for the first time." It need hardly be said that this collaborative effort is a triumph of good judgment, a consistently pleasant read of assimilable size yet detailed enough to be both useful and satisfying. Each contributor to the 16 essentially chronological chapters remarks on "the political and juridical background of the particular period, the character of the sources from it, and some salient features of its substantive law and legal practice," and also presents "a brief list of major authorities of the period and a basic bibliography." A notable feature of Hecht's volume is its inclusion of sections on developments at the margins of the mainstream: notice is taken of the Aramaic papyri, the Apocrypha and Pseudepigrapha, and the Dead Sea sectaries, and there are whole chapters on Samaritan and Karaite halakhah.

ELON's summa—at over 2,300 pages in four large-format volumes, no other word will do—is indisputably the standard comprehensive work. This is not a compilation of contributions by a multitude of specialist hands, but a tour de force of rather 18th-century proportions on the part of its single author, a long-time law professor at the Hebrew University and latterly deputy president of the Israeli Supreme Court. Elon is best known for his work in the field of *mishpat 'Ivri* ("Hebrew jurisprudence"), especially in terms of the integration of halakhic concepts and values within the framework of the fundamentally English legal heritage of the "Jewish State," and this is central to his final volume here. Conversely, he also considers the novel implications of Israeli sovereignty, which called into being a legislative authority, the Knesset, sanctioned to enact what is in a sense "Jewish law" without recourse to halakhic tradition.

Of the earlier volumes, the first comprises: (1) an extended introduction to "The History and Elements of Jewish Law" (Elon's discussion includes chapters on such crucial topics as "The Oral Law: Definitions and General Principles" and "The Prerogatives of the Halakhic Authorities," as well as a review of the history of the academic study of halakhah); and (2) a section on "The Legal Sources of Jewish Law: Exegesis and Interpretation," an introduction to the legal hermeneutics of the rabbis. This section is particularly valuable for the extent to which it goes beyond the principles of midrash well-covered elsewhere, to discuss such issues as the interpretation not of Scripture but of communal enactments. In volume two, Elon continues to review legal (i.e., conceptual) sources of Jewish law, specifically in terms of legislation, custom *(minhag)*, precedent *(maʿaseh)*, and legal reasoning or logic *(sevarah)*. Volume three provides a historical review of halakhic literature by genre: commentaries, novellae, codes, and responsa, as well as reference tools and secondary literature.

The author's clarity of exposition is remarkable enough in itself, but his work is rendered still more accessible by its exemplary front and end matter. A summary of contents listing volumes, parts, and chapters is followed by a fuller table of contents in which analysis is carried beyond chapters to sections and subsections. Volume four ends with three appendixes (a "Cross-reference Table" correlating decisions in Maimonides' and Joseph Caro's codes; "Comparisons of the Language and Style" of the chief medieval codifiers; and a bibliography of collected responsa), a handy glossary, bibliography, and indexes of sources and subjects.

Finally, mention must be made of a substantial tome that makes a monumental contribution to the field, and, in a handsome translation, to the literature in English, even if its scope is less comprehensive than its sweeping title may suggest. URBACH promises to treat *The Halakhah: Its Sources and Development*, but he elects to arrest that development around the fifth century C.E. with the redaction of Talmud. Unlike the authors of the works described above, Urbach belongs (in terms of academic pigeonholing) to the department of Talmud rather than to the law school, but it is not a matter of disciplinary propriety that induces him to exclude from consideration both the earlier and the later medieval periods, the epochs of the geonic responsa and of the great enterprises of codification, two golden ages of halakhic development. After all, Urbach's own study of the Tosafists, still available only in Hebrew, is among the most valuable contributions that Jewish studies has made to an understanding of the evolution of halakhah in the Middle Ages. Rather, the cut-off is dictated by his assigned role in contributing to a series aimed at putting the fruits of the scientific study of Judaism at the disposal of lay people whose lifestyle includes the traditional component of Talmud study.

To that end, Urbach offers a grand historical survey of the budding and flowering of the legal categories invoked by the rabbis and their Pharisaic progenitors that is awesome in its apparent simplicity. "The discussions of the various halakhic subjects in this volume are based on the opinions of many generations of scholars who have applied scientific, philosophical and historical methodology to this study of talmudic literature," he writes. "However, since this present work is intended to be a wide-ranging summary, I have also offered my own solutions to various problems, without going into details of why I reject the opposing views, although I have always tried to indicate such in the footnotes. In the body of the book, I have let the sources speak for themselves—more perhaps than is usual—with only necessary explanations." Urbach is a model of conservatism in the best sense. The writing here of this leading Israeli scholar feels almost as if it were crafted to represent an unspoken repudiation of Jacob Neusner, the dominant presence in contemporary U.S. Talmud scholarship, whose voluminous publications feature a bizarre mix of extreme skepticism in theory and extreme confidence in practice. By contrast, Urbach is deliberate in judgment and at pains to avoid harmonizing his sources any more than he is compelled to believe that they allow. That, however, is a good deal, for the halakhic sphere is shown to reflect broad consensus (lawyers, after all, must agree upon basic principles). Urbach does not dwell on rabbinic hermeneutics, the mechanics of midrashic justification for legal constructions, a matter for quasi-literary scholarship, but he brings his skills as a preeminent historian of talmudic ideas to bear on a great range of larger concepts. Among them are "regulations and ordinances" (for which no biblical sanction is claimed), "the place of custom in halakhah"; the history of law courts and the punishments they administered; precedent; testimony; theory and practice; legal argumentation and decision-making; legal fictions; and equity. He tries "to place the laws discussed within the general framework of Jewish social and cultural history" and to trace "the influences of laws and commandments and the everchanging stream of life in the hope of revealing how the personalities of the Halakhah succeeded in coping with new conditions."

Urbach's best-known work, *The Sages: Their Concepts and Beliefs*, to which the present work serves as a counterpart, is an attempt to synthesize the notoriously unhomogenous theological beliefs of these same rabbis. Given the centrality and the priority that these sages ascribed to halakhah, however, perhaps the title given to his work on the aggadah would have served better to convey the content of his statement on the halakhah.

ARI SALKIN WEISS

Halakhah: Responsa

Agus, Irving, *Urban Civilization in Pre-Crusader Europe: A Study of Organized Town-life in Northwestern Europe during the Tenth and Eleventh Centuries Based on the Responsa Literature*, 2 vols., New York: Yeshiva University Press, and Leiden: Brill, 1965

Freehof, Solomon B., *The Responsa Literature*, Philadelphia: Jewish Publication Society, 1955

Groner, Tsvi, *The Legal Methodology of Hai Gaon*, Chico, California: Scholars Press, 1985

Haas, Peter J., *Responsa: The Literary History of A Rabbinic Genre,* Atlanta, Georgia: Scholars Press, 1996

Jacobs, Louis, *Theology in the Responsa,* London and Boston: Routledge and Kegan Paul, 1975

Lauterbach, Jacob, "She'elot u-Teshubot," in *The Jewish Encyclopedia,* vol. 2, New York: Funk and Wagnalls, 1901

Mann, Jacob, *The Responsa of the Babylonian Geonim as a Source of Jewish History,* Philadelphia: Dropsie College, 1917; reprint, New York: Arno, 1973

Roth, Joel, *The Halakhic Process: A Systemic Analysis,* New York: Jewish Theological Seminary of America, 1986

Responsa are legal rescripts written by recognized rabbinic authorities in response to questions put to them by other rabbis or communal leaders. First appearing in about the ninth century, the genre soon spread throughout the Mediterranean basin, and by the 11th century responsa could be found coming from, or being addressed to, rabbinic authorities in virtually every corner of the Jewish world. Such texts became a standard vehicle for the dissemination of rabbinic legal decisions and continue to be written in the present day. Although usually dealing with practical matters connected with the application of Jewish law, especially in cases involving civil disputes, responsa have in fact been written on virtually every aspect of Jewish life and thought. The responsa literature thus offers a rich source for reconstructing the history of rabbinic law as well as for illuminating the details of day-to-day life in Jewish communities.

LAUTERBACH presents the first "scientific" overview of the genre. He takes for granted the traditional view that responsa represent a specifically Judaic type of literature that has its origins in biblical times and stands behind much of what appears in the Talmud. He proceeds to reconstruct the subsequent development of the literature by identifying six periods of historical development: the geonic period (seventh to ninth century), the rise of local responsa (tenth to 11th century), the first rabbinic (11th to 12th century), the second rabbinic (13th to 14th century), the third rabbinic (15th to 18th century), and the fourth rabbinic periods (19th century to the present). In each case he notes the paradigmatic writers and the important social and political conditions that shaped their activities.

MANN follows Lauterbach's lead by using responsa as historical sources to reconstruct Jewish life in geonic times, which he defines as the seventh through the mid-11th century. In a series of articles first published in various installments in *The Jewish Quarterly Review* between 1917 and 1921 and collected in this volume, Mann undertakes a largely philological investigation of the responsa literature, discussing the probable provenance of the materials found in the medieval collections of geonic responsa, the apparent method by which these texts were preserved and collected, and various critical issues connected with use of language. Throughout the book, a number of responsa are presented in the original without translation and then are subjected to detailed literary analysis so as to throw light on various aspects of Jewish life in Babylonia.

FREEHOF is largely responsible for reviving the responsa as a subject of scholarly investigation. He himself became interested in the literature as a result of his experiences as an army chaplain during and immediately after World War II. He became involved in helping recover lost Jewish libraries and developed a large personal collection of responsa literature and subsequently revived the art of responsa writing in the Reform movement all but single-handedly. Freehof's book is an attempt to introduce the genre to a wider public. His review of the history of responsa is largely a repeat of Lauterbach's seminal encyclopedia piece. The rest of the book is an exploration of the depth and richness of the literature. In such chapters as "Widespread Debates," "History in the Responsa," "Modern Inventions," and "Curious Responsa," Freehof shows that the responsa literature is a gold-mine of information that throws light on countless aspects of Jewish studies beyond the development of Jewish law. He also provides brief biographies of some major responsa writers and offers some translated sections of selected responsa.

AGUS's two-volume study of pre-Crusade Jewish life in Europe is one of the first major studies since Mann's to take responsa seriously and systematically as historical, not just legal, source materials. His study reconstructs various aspects of Jewish life on the basis of rulings and discussions in the responsa literature of the time. Included in his work are not just business and economic issues, but also matters of family life, education, and relations between Jews and their non-Jewish neighbors. One of Agus's most important contributions is to offer translations of the responsa on which he bases his work, thus making this literature available for the first time to an English-speaking audience.

JACOBS's study should be seen as part of his larger project of developing a systematic statement of Jewish belief and theology. His interest in the literature is primarily in showing that speculation on philosophical or theological issues was not alien to rabbinic activity. Beginning with geonic responsa and then arranging his material by century, Jacobs leads the reader through the world of Jewish thought by examining the responsa of major thinkers who deal with more theoretical or philosophical issues, especially those regarding fundamental principles of Jewish faith.

ROTH published his study on the occasion of the centenary of the Jewish Theological Seminary of America, the central training institution for Conservative rabbis. The Conservative movement has always been concerned with the process by which Jewish law is authentically changed, and Roth uses his study to throw light on the inner workings of this process. By reading responsa as one would court briefs, Roth attempts to extract from them a sense of the inner logic of the Jewish juridical process. His book thus covers such themes as judicial discretion and precedent, sources of rabbinic authority, the role of custom, and the use of extralegal sources in decision-making. In this effort he draws on Bible, Mishnah, Talmud, commentaries, and a melange of responsa from various times and places to trace the intellectual limits of what he regards as a single and unitary legal system.

GRONER's study, which developed out of his doctoral dissertation at the Hebrew University, is a much more modest and methodologically controlled attempt to adduce the principles behind Jewish jurisprudence. Groner limits his interest to the legal methodology of the Babylonian Geonim, and in fact focuses on only one of these: Hai Gaon, who lived from 939 to 1038 and who served as the last great head of the talmudic academy in the Babylonian town of Pumbeditha. This gaon was not only in a position to have a major influence on Jewish legal thought in the crucial transition from geonic authority (centered in the academies of Babylonia) to more local rabbinic authority, but also has had a large body of his responsa preserved. Groner's study shows the extent to which the jurisprudence of the Geonim was an extension of the Talmud.

HAAS's review of the history of the responsa genre is the first comprehensive look at the literature and its history since Lauterbach. Haas, a Reform rabbi, is interested in the diversity of forces and ideas that have shaped the history of Jewish law. For purposes of this study, he has divided the genre into six groupings: geonic, early Spanish, early German and French, classical Rabbinism, modern Orthodox, and modern English-language. He then proceeds in each case to place the constituent responsa into their historical, social, and political context and to adduce how that context shaped the legal rhetoric of that age. Through an analysis of the shifting rhetoric of the responsa genre, Haas attempts to articulate different underlying theories of authority and conceptions of law that have operated at different times and places in Jewish history.

PETER HAAS

Hanukkah *see* Festivals and Fasts

Haredim

Goldberg, Hillel, *Israel Salanter, Text, Structure, Idea: The Ethics and Theology of an Early Psychologist of the Unconscious*, New York: Ktav, 1982

Heilman, Samuel, *Defenders of the Faith: Inside Ultra-Orthodox Jewry*, New York: Schocken, 1992

Helmreich, William, *The World of the Yeshiva: An Intimate Portrait of Orthodox Jewry*, New York: Free Press, and London: Collier Macmillan, 1982

Hundert, Gershon D. (editor), *Essential Papers on Hasidism: Origins to Present* (Essential Papers on Jewish Studies), New York: New York University Press, 1991

Jung, Leo (editor), *Jewish Leaders, 1750–1940* (Jewish Library, vol. 6), New York: Bloch, 1953

Nadler, Allan, *The Faith of the Mithnagdim: Rabbinic Responses to Hasidic Rapture*, Baltimore, Maryland: Johns Hopkins University Press, 1997

Haredim, the preferred designation for ultraorthodox Jews, is best translated as "fearful ones" or "shakers." The Quakers also acquired their name from the same phrase in Psalms, "to be fearful (or shake or quake) before God", and the piety of their respective lifestyles is comparable. The term Haredim satisfies the need of others to describe the phenomenon of black hats and coats and a fierce observance of Jewish ritual law, but it obscures the nuances that constitute the many strains of ortho-

doxy, with their respective theologies, practices, ethnic origins, and social structures. Haredim are not homogenous, although the founding of a political organization, Agudat Israel, in 1912 helped forge unity. The holocaust in the Haredi heartland, however, and internal dissension have left Agudist ranks decimated. Schisms brought the defection of rejectionists of accommodation to Zionism (Neturei Karta), and of Mitnaggedim (Degel HaTorah, rejecting hasidic dominance) and Sephardim (Shas, rejecting Yiddish-oriented Ashkenazi dominance). At present, the term Haredim loosely describes three major groupings united by piety yet almost as strongly opposed to each other: the hasidic movement with its subgroups, the Lithuanian-style Mitnaggedim (or opponents of Hasidism) who developed their own style of spirituality alongside Hasidism, and the emerging community of Sephardi Haredim, newly organized in Israel in the image of both Mitnaggedim and Hasidim. No academic studies have been written to date about Shas; it reflects primarily an Israeli phenomenon and has only recently come to be a force within ultraorthodoxy.

GOLDBERG's work is one of the first academic studies of the 19th-century rabbi Israel Salanter's life, thought, and contribution to nonhasidic Orthodox continuity. So far as an understanding of community hierarchy and leadership and ideology enable an understanding of the Haredi community, a study of one of its early proponents is important. As founder of the Musar movement, Salanter established a spiritual discipline of ethical self-improvement intended to maintain a vigil against the growing attraction of Hasidism. Arguably, by affirming his ethical teaching and ideological foundation it became unnecessary for Mitnaggedic orthodoxy to define itself purely as a reaction to Hasidism. Goldberg seeks to portray Salanter as an early psychologist who recognized the benefits of certain religious habits for the welfare of the individual, including the study of the Torah, tight communal life, and obedience to the law. Goldberg describes Salanter's essential ideas concerning the nature of the soul, good and evil, reward and punishment, and the struggle of mind over heart, which remain prevalent today among Haredim of the Mitnaggedic persuasion. Goldberg assesses the extent to which a continuity of Salanter's teachings exists in the contemporary Orthodox world and to what extent it has passed, recognizing that there are many who will argue that the Musar movement ended with the death of its founder.

HEILMAN, an anthropologist and ethnographer, admits that his interest in Haredim was entwined with his personal search for the utopian past of his ancestors, a search that he concludes was in vain. Heilman briefly describes the Haredi world and then outlines its social history. He focuses on three subjects: community, education, and passages (e.g., matchmaking, weddings, and funerals). He also looks at the sexual habits of Haredi communities. While this work purports to analyze the general subject of the ultraorthodox, Heilman's subjects are mainly from hasidic sects and less from the Mitnaggedim. This in itself may be a legitimate reflection of the diminished sociological differences between the two.

JUNG collects essays describing and representing a cross-section of Jewish spiritual leaders from Eastern Europe, the United States, and England from the mid-18th century until the 1940s. While the figures discussed here represent strict

Orthodox traditions, not all are considered Haredi. This, however, is primarily because of changing trends and the success of one group in establishing a broader following rather than the unorthodox nature of the other's teachings or activities. The spectrum of people discussed is impressive and includes Elijah ben Solomon of Vilna, Shneur Zalman of Lyadi, Akiba Eger, Moses Sofer, Menahem Morgenstern of Kotzk, Samson Raphael Hirsch, Israel Salanter, Ezriel Hildesheimer, Marcus Horowitz, Hayyim Ozer Grodzinski, Israel Meir Hacohen, and others. While Jung tries to emphasize certain ethical standards championed by these individuals, and in doing so sets them up as role models to inspire Jewish continuity, he also provides a glimpse into the desired ethos of a community as illustrated by leaders who by their communities' acclamation are their representatives.

HELMREICH provides insight into the world of the Haredim by offering a portrait of life in their chief educational instrument, the yeshivah. He interviews renowned deans and spiritual leaders of these academies including Rabbis Moshe Feinstein, Yitzhak Hutner, Shneur Kotler, and Joseph Soloveitchik. He offers a sketch of the historical development of the yeshivah, but the value of this work is in his description of various contemporary American yeshivot. He discusses the various styles of yeshivah and their hierarchal structure. Helmreich looks at the types of people likely to go to a yeshivah and quotes interviews with some; he also focuses on the relationship that students have with their parents and particularly with their teachers. Helmreich's investigation of students' extracurricular activities, the particular nature of peer pressures, and the formula for social success in the yeshivah are poignant. While Helmreich is writing as a sympathetic insider, almost as an apologist, his observations of the pervasive influence of the yeshivah and the absolute halakhic authority it enjoys in the eyes of the students and parents is crucial to understanding the development of Haredi society.

HUNDERT brings together an impressive collection of essays on all facets of Hasidism including studies of its social and religious origins, teachings and customs, social and ideological development during the 19th century, and modern manifestations. The contributors are leaders in their fields, with each offering his or her perspective on an aspect of Hasidism. The collection provides insight into the academic debate regarding the development of hasidic thought.

NADLER's work is a rare academic study dedicated to Mitnaggedic ultraorthodoxy. Despite the fact that half of today's ultraorthodox Jews are Mitnaggedim, virtually nothing has been written about them, while an abundance of research has emerged around the study of Hasidism. He warns against viewing ultraorthodox Haredism as a religious monolith and encourages the detection of significant distinctions. One senses Nadler's engagement as he bemoans the academic trend to see Hasidism as an almost organic continuity from the rich Jewish mystical tradition instead of a deviation from tradition. He proceeds to elucidate the theological and historical differences that make Mitnaggedism the quintessential continuation of tradition. Nadler's work can be summed up as an analysis of the major works of three Mitnaggedic proponents: Elijah ben Solomon of Vilna, Hayyim of Volozhin, and Phinehas of Polotsk. But he does have a good deal to say about the hasidic

portraits of spirituality, if only to demonstrate how Mitnaggedic views differ. By describing how their perspectives on Kabbalah, prayer, asceticism, and scholarship are at variance, he bolsters his thesis that the Mitnaggedim represent a classical tradition and Hasidism deviates from it. This work is an important contribution to the study of Haredim for its sharp and critical attack on the perception of homogeneity and harmony that might otherwise be suggested by the blanket term ultraorthodoxy.

AVRUM EHRLICH

Hasidei Ashkenaz

Cronbach, Abraham, "Social Thinking in the *Sefer Hasidim*," *Hebrew Union College Annual*, 22, 1949

Dan, Joseph, *Jewish Mysticism and Jewish Ethics*, Seattle: University of Washington Press, 1986; 2nd edition, Northvale, New Jersey: Aronson, 1996

Kanarfogel, Ephraim, *Jewish Education and Society in the High Middle Ages*, Detroit, Michigan: Wayne State University Press, 1992

Kramer, Simon, *God and Man in the "Sefer Hasidim," Book of the Pious*, New York: Bloch, 1966

Marcus, Ivan, *Piety and Society: The Jewish Pietists of Medieval Germany*, Leiden: Brill, 1981

Schäfer, Peter, "Ashkenazic Hasidism," *Jewish History*, 4(2), 1989

Scholem, Gershom, *Major Trends in Jewish Mysticism*, New York: Schocken, 1941, 3rd edition, 1954; 3rd edition, London: Thames and Hudson, 1955

Soloveitchik, Haym, "Three Themes in the *Sefer Hasidim*," *AJS Review*, 1, 1976

The Hasidei Ashkenaz, or German Pietists, appeared at the end of the 12th and beginning of the 13th centuries in the Rhenish communities and in Regensburg, and thereafter spread throughout Germany and France. It has been argued that the Hasidei Ashkenaz were influenced by internal Jewish developments dating back to eighth- and ninth-century Italy. It also has often been assumed that they were affected by external Christian traditions, including monastic, mendicant, German pietist, and even troubadour movements. Frequently it has been asserted that they developed in response to the violence against the Jews during the crusades. More recently this theory has been viewed as insufficient, although it could be argued that it is precisely in the period after the crusades that the Pietists attained a mature, solid, and recognizable identity. It is clear, in any event, that the theology of the Hasidei Ashkenaz shows important strands deriving from Jewish *hekhalot* and *merkabah* literature as well as Christian Neo-Platonism.

The Pietists often gathered around a leading figure, a pietist sage, and at times were pitted against the traditional leadership of the communities in which they lived. On the one hand, the Hasidei Ashkenaz sought positions of leadership and service within the Jewish communities; on the other hand, at times they secluded themselves from the community. The most prominent early members of the Hasidim were Samuel ben

Kalonymos he-Hasid, Samuel's son Judah ben Samuel he-Hasid, and Judah's relative and pupil, Eleazar ben Judah Kalonymos of Worms. Among the important works produced by the Hasidim are the *Sefer Hasidim* and the *Rokeah*. Although Hasidic thought evolved over a long period of time, certain generalizations are typically made about the Pietists' religious observance and theology. Like their Christian pietist peers, they feared sin and sought to live according to a simple but strict fashion, noting that the inner or "true" belief was more important than external appearance. The Hasidim produced both ethical and theological works, and throughout they stressed the unity and incorporeality of God, even though they subscribed to the idea that there exist intermediary powers between God and man. They believed that mortification of the body could serve as a method of repentance, and they argued that *kiddush ha-Shem* (martyrdom) was a most worthy act. The Hasidim stressed the importance of overcoming physical temptation, and they emphasized both the power and danger of love and sexuality in a language that is frequently cited as erotic.

MARCUS presents the most thorough discussion of the Hasidei Ashkenaz available in English. He avoids the discussion of historical causation by not focusing on the "alleged" historical factors that affected the German Pietists, such as Christian influence, anti-Jewish persecution, or even the challenge of northern French Jewry's talmudic scholasticism (tosafism). Instead he emphasizes the previously unnoticed differences among the Pietist authors in order to understand the developments within the pietistic movement. In his "Introductory Perspectives," Marcus offers an extensive summary and assessment of the work that has been done to date on the Hasidei Ashkenaz, particularly that of Yitzhak Baer, Gershom Scholem, and Joseph Dan. Marcus then quickly jumps into the dense pietistic literature to explore what he terms the first medieval European Jewish religious revival and adjustment. He finds that although Samuel, Judah, and Eleazar agreed that the ideal Jew (i.e., the *hasid*) should pursue the personal goal of otherworldly salvation, they differed regarding the social implications of that ideal. Little information is available about Samuel, so, accordingly, Marcus focuses on Judah and Eleazar. In Judah's *Sefer Hasidim*, Marcus explores the ways in which the Pietists interacted with non-Pietist Jews, who often expressed contempt for them. But Judah's attempt to forge a community of "Jewish saints" lasted only briefly. It was not until Eleazar that elements of Pietism became "respectable" even among non-Pietist Jews. Eleazar codified pietistic behavior into daily life, and thus "European Jewish piety was reshaped by the practices and norms that had formerly been characteristic of the Pietist fellowship alone."

SCHOLEM's work on Jewish mysticism is the classic text on the subject. As would be expected in the context of the larger work, Scholem's discussion of the Hasidei Ashkenaz moves from a general discussion of the rise of Hasidism in medieval Germany to a fuller consideration of the mystical tradition in German Jewry—eschatology, ascetics, magical power, the mysteries of prayer, and the conception of God—focusing on the *Sefer Hasidim*.

SCHÄFER notes recent research that, unlike the earlier work of Baer and Scholem, argues that the ethical code of the German Pietists had substantial Jewish roots and motivations, particularly in the early mystical *hekhalot* literature. The ethical codes of the Pietists, therefore, cannot be seen as deriving solely from contemporary Christian influences.

KANARFOGEL uses rabbinic literature and focuses on the various facets of education in the world of the Ashkenazi talmudists, the tosafists, between 1096 and 1290. He explores elementary education and the attitudes toward childhood and the educational process, the economic considerations of higher education, and the relationship between talmudic academies and the communities in which they were located, as well as the intellectual milieu of the academies. The final chapter of the book looks more specifically at the educational theory and practice of the German Pietists.

DAN is one of the acknowledged leaders in the field of medieval Jewish intellectual history, and his writings are much cited. In this essay, Dan focuses on the strict ethical system created by the Hasidei Ashkenaz and argues that the mystical element within their system of thought made their rigorous ethics bearable by creating a bilateral movement between human and spiritual realms.

SOLOVEITCHIK offers a close reading and expert analysis of the *Sefer Hasidim*, particularly in assessing the apparent disparity between rabbinic and hasidic norms. In the end, Soloveitchik asserts that the Hasidei Ashkenaz movement ran into difficulty when it coupled extreme spirituality with an ideology of public service. He argues also that the Hasidei Ashkenaz must be understood against the backdrop of the 12th-century intellectual revolution of the tosafists.

CRONBACH notes that the *Sefer Hasidim* does not deal with spiritual matters alone. In this book he analyzes the earthly matters discussed throughout the *Sefer Hasidim*, such as sales, loans, investments, business ethics, charity, community management, and ransoming prisoners, and he offers translations of the relevant parts of the book.

KRAMER also focuses on the *Sefer Hasidim*, but with an eye to uncovering the ethical teachings of the 13th and 14th centuries, particularly in the context of the relationship between man and God, focusing on the precepts of fear and love of God. Ethical goals may be achieved, according to the author of *Sefer Hasidim*, by holding the same standards of behavior for oneself as for others; appealing to practical reason; resisting evil with all one's strength; and realizing that the power and responsibility of proper ethical decision making lies in one's own hands.

DEAN BELL

Hasidic Thought

Buber, Martin, *The Origin and Meaning of Hasidism*, New York: Horizon, 1960

Idel, Moshe, *Hasidism: Between Ecstasy and Magic* (SUNY Series in Judaica), Albany: State University of New York Press, 1995

Jacobs, Louis, *Hasidic Prayer* (Littman Library of Jewish Civilization), London: Routledge and Kegan Paul, 1972; New York: Schocken, 1973

Loewenthal, Naftali, *Communicating the Infinite: The Emergence of the Habad School,* Chicago: University of Chicago Press, 1990

Schatz Uffenheimer, Rivka, *ha-Hasidut ke-mistikah,* 1968; translated by Jonathan Chipman as *Hasidism as Mysticism: Quietistic Elements in Eighteenth Century Hasidic Thought,* Princeton, New Jersey: Princeton University Press, 1993

Scholem, Gershom G., *Major Trends in Jewish Mysticism* (Stroock Lectures, 1938), New York: Schocken, 1941; London: Thames and Hudson, 1953; 3rd revised edition, New York: Schocken, 1954; London: Thames and Hudson, 1955

Scholem, Gershom G., "Devekut, or Communion with God," in his *The Messianic Idea in Judaism and Other Essays on Jewish Spirituality,* New York: Schocken, and London: Allen and Unwin, 1971

Wertheim, Aaron, *Halakhot va-halikhot ba-Hasidut,* 1960; translated by Shmuel Himelstein as *Law and Custom in Hasidism,* Hoboken, New Jersey: Ktav, 1992

Modern Hasidism originated in rural areas of Poland and Ukraine during the 18th century and has inspired a number of very complex interpretations. It has been labeled ecstatic, quietistic, gnostic, messianic, and spiritualistic; it also has been labeled the antithesis of each of these qualities. Even the movement's first two generations, with unitary leadership under Rabbi Israel ben Eliezer Ba'al Shem Tov and the Maggid of Mezhirech, respectively, are viewed by scholars in widely divergent ways.

Scholarly inquiry into Hasidism began during the 19th century, but it was not until 1906 that a wider community of scholars and readers noticed the movement with the first of philosopher Martin Buber's publications. Buber was attracted to Hasidism by the many legends told by and about its charismatic leaders, and he began to translate them into German. Over time, Buber came to believe that the society that produced these tales was "the greatest phenomenon in the history of the spirit, greater than any individual genius in art and in thought." The way that a hasidic community achieved a "hallowing of the everyday" struck Buber as a model for modern life. BUBER seeks to communicate to the wider world the message that he feels is contained in Hasidism. The author, however, is criticized for allowing his own existentialism and his passion for that message to impair his analysis of Hasidism, causing him to ignore its historical context and its otherworldly tendencies.

Gershom Scholem, who initially agreed with Buber that in Hasidism "personality takes the place of doctrine," eventually turned to the extensive homiletic literature of the hasidic masters and concluded that Hasidism was a doctrinally innovative branch of Jewish mysticism. His chapter on Hasidism in SCHOLEM (1941) is from an early period, when he writes: "In the place of the theoretical disquisition, or at least side by side with it, you get the Hasidic tale." Later, after much study of the theoretical literature, he concludes that the innovation of Hasidism lies not in folktales and hagiography but in creating and recasting mystical doctrine. SCHOLEM (1971) is an example of this later thinking.

SCHATZ UFFENHEIMER, a student of Scholem, has written a comparative study of early hasidic quietism, or reaching God through abandonment of the self. Her study extends Scholem's view in that she often portrays the hasidic masters as theological innovators. The book has the feel of a collection of essays, but the translation is exacting and there is a great deal of documentation.

IDEL wishes to stand "on the shoulders" of the giants—Buber and Scholem—and to supply readers with "another vision of Hasidism." Idel is a scholar of Jewish mystical literature, and he aims to show that the origins of Hasidism are much more complicated than most would suppose. Previously, scholars assumed that the mystical basis of Hasidism was the Kabbalah of Rabbi Isaac Luria and his school and that the early modern messianic tragedies of Sabbatianism and Frankism were crucial to understanding Hasidism. Idel seeks to revise this by rejecting what he calls "proximism," in this case the view that relatively recent events in history (e.g., Sabbatianism) and in mysticism (Luria) are necessarily more important to Hasidism than older trends. He proposes a "panoramic" approach that reveals the indebtedness of Hasidism to early Castilian Kabbalah, ecstatic Kabbalah, Rabbi Moses Cordovero, the Maharal of Prague, and other mystical and magical sources, all widely available in 18th-century Poland. Interestingly, Scholem's essay on *devekut, imitatio Dei* with aspirations to *unio mystica,* cites some of the sources that Idel claims have been ignored. Idel's book is dense but invaluable.

LOEWENTHAL has written a very readable book on what he calls "the communication of the esoteric" in Hasidism. Until now, he writes, Hasidism has been studied either as a sociopolitical phenomenon that succeeded in reordering Eastern European Jewish life during a period of turmoil or as a mystical phenomenon, drawing attention to its doctrinal variations, mystical forebears, and the theological debates among contemporaries. Yet neither method accounts for the extent and manner of communicating mystical teachings within the hasidic group. In one group, these teachings may be kept to a select few; in a second group, they may be hinted at only in the form of tales; and in a third they may be explained to all in printed form. These differences in the ethos of communication combine social and mystical elements. Loewenthal shows how the communication ethos of Habad Hasidism differed from that of its hasidic precursors and how it developed internally. While some premises remain unexamined, this is a good case study in an area ignored by most scholars of hasidic texts; there is little that is abstract or musty here.

JACOBS has also written an excellent volume on a specific and important aspect of Hasidism, namely prayer. The fine introduction, lucid prose, and extensive quotation show how hasidic prayer in all its variety was often, by its very centrality, revolutionary. Besides showing the scale of innovation, the book is a comprehensive treatment of a variety of hasidic attitudes toward Jewish prayer. It is not overly theoretical nor is it polemical as are some works on Hasidism. Neither Jacobs nor Loewenthal seeks to prove either side of the protracted debate between partisans of Buber and those of Scholem. Jacobs's and Loewenthal's works use both tales and homilies, demonstrating that neither source is self-sufficient for understanding a phenomenon as complex as Hasidism.

WERTHEIM's unique work presents hasidic thought as more than theoretical and mythological; the author maintains that in a thousand ways it has affected everyday Jewish customs with which its academic interpreters have not always been familiar. This compendium of such changes, presented in their incredibly detailed context, helps readers grasp how much hasidic thought has transformed Jewish life and practice.

SIMON A. STEINER

Hasidic Music *see* Music: Ashkenazi Folk Music

Haskalah

Erspamer, Peter R., *The Elusiveness of Tolerance: The "Jewish Question" from Lessing to the Napoleonic Wars*, Chapel Hill: University of North Carolina Press, 1997

Katz, Jacob, *Out of the Ghetto: The Social Background of Jewish Emancipation, 1770–1870*, Cambridge, Massachusetts: Harvard University Press, 1973

Meyer, Michael A., *The Origins of the Modern Jew: Jewish Identity and European Culture in Germany, 1749–1824*, Detroit, Michigan: Wayne State University Press, 1967

Sorkin, David Jan, *The Transformation of German Jewry, 1780–1840*, New York: Oxford University Press, 1987

The Haskalah was the movement among Central European Jews of the 18th and 19th centuries to modernize their religion and make it more cosmopolitan by adopting the standards of the Western European Enlightenment. It soon spread from Central Europe to Eastern Europe. Haskalah (the Hebrew term for Enlightenment) is acknowledged as a major movement of Jewish transformation.

In his leading study of 1967, MEYER examines the work of several major figures of the Haskalah, including Moses Mendelssohn, David Friedländer, and Saul Ascher. Meyer describes Moses Mendelssohn as an amazing and paradoxical figure who exerted a modernizing influence on German Jewry by championing the nascent German culture of the 18th century. Meyer rightfully describes Mendelssohn as a "master of German prose" at a time when most German Jews spoke Yiddish instead of German. Meyer points to the priority Mendelssohn placed on being accepted by the German intellectual elite. He viewed his acquaintance with such non-Jewish intellectual luminaries as Gotthold Ephraim Lessing, Friedrich Nicolai, Christoph Martin Wieland, and Johann Gottfried von Herder as among the great fortunes of his life.

Mendelssohn viewed morality as the cornerstone of any religion, and his personal practice of virtue made him much admired by Christian society and added to his reputation as an intellectual meriting wide attention. The cultivation of virtue seemed to him, says Meyer, "the most effective assault upon the stereotype of the greedy moneylender."

Mendelssohn's recognition by non-Jewish society led to pressure to convert to Christianity from the Swiss theologian Johann Caspar Lavater. Meyer describes Mendelssohn's resis-

tance to this pressure: "since God desires only the best for man [Mendelssohn found] it is inconceivable that He should, as Christianity claims, make salvation dependent upon a revelation bestowed only on a small percentage of the human race."

In his examination of David Friedländer, Meyer describes differences in viewpoint between Friedländer and his mentor Mendelssohn. Friedländer found less value in Jewish ceremonial law than did Mendelssohn, and he wished to see it abolished altogether. He viewed Jewish ceremonial law as keeping Jews in an infantile state and hindering their emancipation.

Saul Ascher, bookdealer and political journalist of the late 18th and early 19th century, is also examined by Meyer. He concentrates on Ascher's 1792 tract, *Leviathan; or, On Religion with Respect to Judaism*. Ascher defends Judaism as a religion with dogmatic content: he sees no schism between natural religion (religious morality based on rationalistic principles) and dogmatic religion based on mysticism and ceremony. Meyer touts Ascher as a highly unusual figure who merits further examination.

The Haskalah is also examined in depth by KATZ, who is interested in the historical sociology of the Jewish Emancipation movement and its relationship to the Haskalah. He describes Moses Mendelssohn and the Mendelssohn circle as a phenomenon that reduced the degree of separation between Jewish and Gentile societies. At the same time, Katz notes that the acceptance of Jews such as Mendelssohn into Christian society was based on the belief that they would convert. Katz examines the influence of the Enlightenment on Jewish thinkers in terms of their desire to influence their fellow Jews. He discusses the "spreading of Enlightenment to Jewish communities" by writers, educators, and reformers working to better the lot of their Jewish coreligionists. The Enlightenment is seen as an important locus of communication between Jewish and non-Jewish intellectuals.

SORKIN incisively examines the ideology of emancipation. His central thesis is that emancipation was conceived in terms of a quid pro quo: Jews were to reform and modernize themselves in exchange for increased rights. Sorkin examines the writings of Napthali Hartwig Herz Wessely in terms of Wessely's dissatisfaction with traditional Jewish intellectual and religious life. He explains that for Wessely there are two realms of knowledge: the particular and the religious. The particular realm of knowledge deals with teachings of man, and the religious realm of knowledge deals with teachings of God. The teachings of God are not bound by the laws of reason; the teachings of man are, however, bound by the laws of reason and are fundamental to all societies. The teachings of man cover such issues as etiquette and civility and technical and scientific knowledge.

Wessely believed that Jews and Judaism should conform to universal standards dictated by the teachings of man. This constitutes a break with the rabbinic literature that denoted that divine law was the source of all values. Wessely's writing is tinged with vague notions of a tutelary state because he sees monarchs as educators. Jews' ills demanded a nonreligious remedy. He discusses educational reform: he feels that Jews should give up Yiddish and speak proper German. Sorkin sees David Friedländer as a key figure in developing the notion that the state should play a tutelary role in the reform of the Jews.

ERSPAMER discusses some figures of the Haskalah not covered by other authors, including Elcan Isaac Wolf and a writer known only as Arenhof. Wolf wrote a book of medical advice for his Jewish coreligionists titled *On the Illnesses of the Jews*. In this book of medical advice, Wolf draws a close correlation between the adverse medical circumstances faced by the Jews and their problematic social and political situation. He maintains that the contemporary situation of the Jews is not as bad as in earlier times, but that current illnesses are a product of past adversities faced by the Jewish people. This is a subtle rhetorical device for pointing out how restrictive social circumstances harm the Jews without appearing to be critical of the current government or society.

Erspamer also examines one of the few pieces of "fictional" literature of the Haskalah, Arenhof's drama *Some Jewish Family Scenes* (1782). The play, written in the wake of Hapsburg Emperor Joseph II's tolerance patent of 1781, argued that the emancipatory reforms enabled the Jews to take their place as Germans without abandoning their Jewish identity. The play reflects the great hopes and expectations with which members of the Haskalah greeted the tolerance patent. It gave Jewish intellectuals a feeling that they, too, belonged to the dominant Austrian society.

PETER R. ERSPAMER

Hebrew Alphabet

Cross, Frank Moore, "The Development of the Jewish Scripts," in The Bible and the Ancient Near East, edited by George Ernest Wright, Garden City, New York: Doubleday, and London: Routledge and Kegan Paul, 1961

Driver, Godfrey Rolles, *Semitic Writing*, Oxford: Oxford University Press, 1948; as *Semitic Writing from Pictograph to Alphabet*, edited by S.A. Hopkins, London and New York: Oxford University Press, 1976

Gelb, Ignace J., *A Study of Writing*, Chicago: University of Chicago Press, and London: Routledge and Kegan Paul, 1952; new edition, Chicago: University of Chicago Press, 1969

Healey, John F., "The Early Alphabet," in *Reading the Past: Ancient Writing from Cuneiform to the Alphabet*, London and New York: Guild, 1990

Naveh, Joseph, "Alphabet, Hebrew," in *Encyclopaedia Judaica*, Jerusalem: Encyclopaedia Judaica, 1972

Naveh, Joseph, *Early History of the Alphabet: An Introduction to West Semitic Epigraphy and Palaeography*, Jerusalem: Magnes, and Leiden: Brill, 1982; 2nd revised edition, 1987

The article by HEALEY gives a very clear picture of the origins and development of the Hebrew alphabet as one of the scripts used in the Syro-Palestinian area from the beginning of the second millennium B.C.E. Shortly before the third millennium B.C.E. the two great ancient civilizations of the Middle East, the Akkadian (Mesopotamian) and the Egyptian, were using word-syllabic writing. In such a system, each sign (grapheme) stands for a syllable or for a whole word; the Egyptian script also had a set of 26 uniconsonantal signs, but not much use was made of them. From the early second millennium B.C.E. a number of inscriptions were found from Sinai and Palestine in an alphabetic writing—a writing in which each sign stands for one sound (phoneme) only. The advantage of an alphabetic script is quite clear, because it makes it possible to write all the words of a language using a small number of signs. The first texts of this kind that are known to scholars are the Proto-Sinaitic inscriptions of c.1700 B.C.E. Scholars do not know (and probably will never know) where and by whom the West Semitic script was created. Over the course of a few centuries, the Phoenician, Hebrew, and Aramaic alphabets (and others) stemmed from this script, and the Greeks learned the alphabet from the Phoenicians. The signs of the West Semitic script indicated only the consonants of the words, leaving out the vowels. In the beginning it was pictographic and acrophonic, each sign representing a concrete object and standing for the first sound of the name of this object: *b* from *baytu* (house), *k* from *kappu* (palm of hand), *m* from *mayyuma* (water), *r* from *ra'shu* (head), and so on. This system of writing was inspired by the set of uniconsonantal Egyptian signs. The pure consonantal character of the West Semitic script caused ambiguity in the reading of many words; to obviate this shortcoming, beginning about the eighth century B.C.E. and maybe earlier, some letters (*w, y, h,* and later ' [*aleph* = glottal stop]) were used also as vocal signs. Much later, around the seventh or eighth century B.C.E., Hebrew (as well as Syriac and Arabic) adopted a set of special signs (vowel points) that were added to the letters in order to indicate the vowels. The beginning of the alphabet is detailed much more thoroughly by DRIVER within the general picture of the scripts of the Semitic languages.

GELB puts forth a complete theory of the beginning and evolution of writing, and in this framework he deals also with the Hebrew alphabet. He takes the view that because the West Semitic script is purely consonantal, it is not in fact a true alphabet but should be regarded as a syllabic writing in which each sign stands for a consonant followed by any vowel. According to him the first real alphabetic writing is the Greek script, because when the Greeks adopted the Phoenician script they changed the meaning of some letters from consonants into vowels.

NAVEH (1982) traces the evolution of alphabetic writing from its inception up to the crystallization of modern Semitic scripts and deals also with its adoption by the Greeks, which according to him happened in the eighth century B.C.E. The Hebrew as well as the Aramaic alphabets stem from the Phoenician alphabet, having developed in slightly different ways. After the Babylonian captivity the Jews discarded their traditional script and adopted a new one stemming from the Aramaic script: Naveh calls the old script "Hebrew script" and the new one (usually called "square script") "Jewish script."

NAVEH (1972) traces the history of the Hebrew alphabet to the present day, specifying the different types of script according to their chronological and geographical distribution.

CROSS summarizes our present knowledge of the early square Hebrew script of the last centuries B.C.E. and first centuries C.E., relying on the Qumran material and on various inscriptions. He gives a detailed description of the different types of script according to epochs, such as Hasmonean, Herodian, and post-Herodian, and according to scribal traditions, such as formal, protocursive, and semicursive hands.

GAD B. SARFATTI

See also Hebrew Language

Hebrew Language

Ben-Hayyim, Zeev and Uzzi Oman, "Hebrew Grammar," in *Encyclopaedia Judaica,* vol.8, Jerusalem: Encyclopaedia Judaica, 1972

Brovender, Chaim, Joshua Blau, Esther Goldenberg, Uzzi Oman, and Eli Eytan, "Hebrew Language," in *Encyclopaedia Judaica,* vol. 16, Jerusalem: Encyclopaedia Judaica, 1972

Brown, Francis, S.R. Driver, and Charles Briggs, *A Hebrew and English Lexicon of the Old Testament,* Boston: Houghton Mifflin, 1891; Oxford: Clarendon, 1892; as *The Brown-Driver-Briggs Hebrew and English Lexicon,* Peabody, Massachusetts: Hendrickson, 1996

Joüon, Paul, *Grammaire de l'Hébreu Biblique,* 1923; translated and revised by T. Muraoka as *A Grammar of Biblical Hebrew,* 2 vols., Rome: Pontificio Istituto Biblio, 1991, corrected edition, 1993

Kautzsch, E. (editor), *Gesenius' Hebrew Grammar,* London: Asher, and Andover, Massachusetts: Draper, 1880; 2nd American edition, Boston: Bradley, 1898; 2nd English edition, Oxford: Clarendon, 1910

Koehler Ludwig and Walter Baumgartner, *The Hebrew and Aramaic Lexicon of the Old Testament,* 3 vols., Leiden and New York: Brill, 1994

Rosen, Haim B., *Contemporary Hebrew,* The Hague: Mouton, 1977

Sáenz-Badillos, Angel, *Historia de la lengua hebrea,* 1988; translated by John Elwolde as *A History of the Hebrew Language,* Cambridge and New York: Cambridge University Press, 1993

Segal, M.H., *A Grammar of Mishnaic Hebrew,* Oxford: Clarendon, 1927

The Hebrew language is 3,000 years old. It was a spoken and written language from the beginning of the first millennium B.C.E. to about 200 C.E., then only a written language until the beginning of the 20th century, when it was revived also in speech. Modern Israeli Hebrew is remarkably close to biblical Hebrew in its basic morphological structure and in its vocabulary. Nevertheless, Hebrew has known many changes during its long life, so a detailed study is usually divided according to its different chronological layers: biblical Hebrew, mishnaic or rabbinic Hebrew, medieval Hebrew, and modern Hebrew. Biblical Hebrew has been painstakingly studied (by Jews and non-Jews) over the centuries; the scientific study of mishnaic Hebrew began only in the 20th century and so, necessarily, did that of the modern language. The medieval period still lacks a detailed and comprehensive description. The best

introduction to the study of Hebrew is the study of its history. Dictionaries and grammars of the biblical stratum detail its basic structure, its place in the Semitic family, and its relationship to other languages.

SÁENZ-BADILLOS begins with the earliest discernible layers of the language in its Semitic origins and continues through the period of the Bible, the rabbinic writings, the rich medieval literature, and up to the astonishing revival of the spoken language in recent times.

The first modern grammar of biblical Hebrew was Gesenius's *Hebraeische Grammatik.* First printed in 1813, it appeared in German in 29 editions revised by various scholars. It was translated into English by G.W. Collins and A.E. Cowley (1898), and this translation was published again (1910) as revised by Cowley according to the 28th German edition by KAUTZSCH. In spite of its age it is still a useful basic reference book. BROWN, DRIVER, and BRIGGS, based on Gesenius's lexicon, is still a reliable and useful tool. KOEHLER and BAUMGARTNER is the English translation of the third German edition of the lexicon by these two scholars. To date, three volumes have appeared, containing all the Hebrew material except for the last two letters of the alphabet. It is detailed and up to date. This dictionary is alphabetically ordered by words and not by roots, as Brown, Driver, and Brigg's work is, so that is easier for the beginner to use.

JOÜON, published in French in 1923, was very well received by scholars, especially its third part, on syntax. T. Muraoka's English translation, published in 1991, is a revision of the original book that takes into consideration documents and languages (such as Ugaritic and Eblaite) made known to scholars after Joüon's publication. This revision, in the form of added footnotes, rewriting of paragraphs, and sometimes deletion of a whole paragraph or insertion of a new one, makes this the most up-to-date work on the subject.

SEGAL is the only modern book completely devoted to mishnaic Hebrew. Since it appeared it has been the target of criticism, mainly because it does not distinguish between the different chronological layers within mishnaic Hebrew and because it relies on the printed text of the Mishnah (which differs in may points from the ancient manuscripts, whose language is presumably nearer to the original). A more modern and sound approach can be found in BROVENDER et al.'s chapter on mishnaic Hebrew in the article "Hebrew Language" in the *Encyclopaedia Judaica.* This monograph-length article describes the various periods of the Hebrew language. It was coauthored by various scholars, each an expert in a given field, and it is a main source of information on medieval Hebrew. Modern Hebrew is also described in detail by BEN-HAYYIM and ORNAN.

Modern Hebrew is the subject of ROSEN's brilliant and original work, which is particularly remarkable for its fourth chapter, "Content and Lexicon," dealing with semantic topics.

GAD B. SARFATTI

See also Hebrew Alphabet; Languages, Jewish

Hebrew Literature, Modern

Abramson, Glenda and Tudor Parfitt (editors), *The Great Transition: The Recovery of the Lost Centers of Modern Hebrew Literature*, Totowa, New Jersey: Rowman and Allanheld, 1985

Bargad, Warren, *From Agnon to Oz: Studies in Modern Hebrew Literature* (South Florida Studies in the History of Judaism, 126), Atlanta, Georgia: Scholars Press, 1996

Domb, Risa, *Home Thoughts from Abroad: Distant Visions of Israel in Contemporary Hebrew Fiction*, London and Portland, Oregon: Vallentine Mitchell, 1995

Fischman, Naomi, *Western and Eastern Cultures Reflected in Modern Hebrew Literature*, Jerusalem: Jerusalem Academic Press, 1976

Fuchs, Esther, *Israeli Mythogynies: Women in Contemporary Hebrew Fiction* (SUNY Series in Modern Jewish Literature and Culture), Albany: State University of New York Press, 1987

Hakak, Lev, *Equivocal Dreams: Studies in Modern Hebrew Literature*, Hoboken, New Jersey: Ktav, 1993

Halkin, Simon, *Modern Hebrew Literature: Trends and Values*, New York: Schocken, 1950; as *Modern Hebrew Literature, from the Enlightenment to the Birth of the State of Israel: Trends and Values*, New York: Schocken, 1970

Mintz, Alan (editor), *The Boom in Contemporary Israeli Fiction* (Tauber Institute for the Study of European Jewry, 24), Hanover, New Hampshire: University Press of New England, 1997

Shaked, Gershon, *The Shadows Within: Essays on Modern Jewish Writers*, Philadelphia: Jewish Publication Society, 1987

Modern Hebrew literature, in the limited sense of the body of fiction written in Hebrew primarily by Jews since the waning of the Haskalah period at the end of the 19th century, has its roots in Jewish Europe and is characterized by a secularist impetus and the adaptation of Western literary forms.

BARGAD's methodology of literary criticism is constructed along the lines of the stylistic and linguistic theories of the Russian Formalists. As such, it brings something fresh to the supersaturated study of modern Hebrew literature. Noteworthy is his essay on the "binary oppositions," the "semantic structures of equivalence or opposition," in the poetry of Amir Gilboa. Bargad concludes that by implementing these binary oppositions, Gilboa's poetics bring the reader closer to the poems' beauty and innovation.

MINTZ's collection of five essays covers the Israeli literary scene from 1973 to 1993, a short period that witnessed "an explosion of literary creativity" unparalleled in the history of Hebrew literature. Mintz contends that the political, social, and economic developments of the time can be interpreted as sets of opposites—male/female, Ashkenazi/Sephardi, religious/secular, land of Israel/diaspora, collectivism/individualism, native Israelis/Holocaust survivors—that are then reflected in literary works by various Israeli authors. This volume focuses on the creation of the "new Jew" in Israel, who challenges gender roles and imposes new meanings onto traditional values.

Anne Golomb Hoffman's essay examines two major novelists, Yaakov Shabtai and A.B. Yehoshua, asserting that Shabtai works his "way out of an oppressive masculinity," while Yehoshua "engages the dynamics of gender and sexuality on an interpersonal level that resonates with implication for the history of the nation." Gender issues are also addressed in Yael Feldman's essay, which evaluates the work of Amalia Kahana-Carmon, Shulamith Lapid, Shulamith Hareven, and Ruth Almog and identifies two major trends, "feminist romance" and "masked autobiography," in the literature by these female writers. Additionally, Berg investigates how Sephardi literature has moved from the margins to the mainstream with the rise of such writers as Sami Michael, Amnon Shamosh, Yehoshua, Shimon Ballas, and Dan Seri, who have developed the genre of "immigrant literature" and the political novel.

DOMB discusses the theme of displacement in six Israeli novels, five of which were published in the 1980s and are charged with politics, ideology, and social realism. Rather than analyzing "protagonists who are expatriates," Domb focuses on "those who leave and then return, and . . . novels where the tension between home and abroad is manifested in the dialectics of inside and outside." The study examines the works of Yehoshua, Almog, Benjamin Tammuz, Shlomo Nitzan, and Yehuda Amichai. Domb's broad vision and clarity make this short work a valuable contribution to the literary criticism of modern Hebrew literature.

FISCHMAN investigates the outcome of the encounter between Ashkenazi and Sephardi cultures as reflected in contemporary Hebrew fiction. The study explores the romantic aspects of exoticism (that is, " the total feelings and emotions that are aroused by the encounter with new countries and their inhabitants") that are evoked in fictional characters of Yemenite and Sephardi descent. The works of five authors are evaluated according to their ability to "paint" Yemenite or Sephardi cultures. In particular, Haim Hazaz and Mordecai Tabib are the featured as the "painters of Yemenite life." Hazaz, an Ashkenazi Jew, felt the allure of the Yemenite Jews, whose culture differed so from his inherited perspective. Tabib, a native Israeli of Yemenite descent, writes about the interrelationship between Yemenites and Ashkenazim, which is what Fischman sees as making his account so fascinating and exotic.

FUCHS surveys the Israeli fiction scene from the late 1950s to the early 1980s, including the works of Yehoshua, Amos Oz, and Kahana-Carmon, from a feminist literary viewpoint. Fuchs coins several new terms in her literary criticism: mythogyny, "the patriarchal myth(s) of womanhood"; gyniconologies, "androcentric representations of womanhood"; and gynography, "revisionary writing that subtly parodies the patriarchal mythogynies." Despite a literary climate that devalues women writers and women protagonists, Fuchs is able to penetrate the sociopolitical realities of the Jewish women who are portrayed by mainstream Israeli authors.

ABRAMSON and PARFITT's collection of essays contributes much to the establishment of context by concentrating on the shifting importance of various literary centers in the historical development of modern Hebrew literature, emphasizing in particular communities in Central and Eastern Europe and in Israel. The anthology traces developments chronologically, beginning with the transition from Austria and Germany to Odessa and Vilna as the foci of Hebrew literary activity and concluding with the establishment of a literary community by the early settlers in Palestine at the dawn of the 20th century. Especially noteworthy are the chapters devoted to the often-overlooked importance of Odessa as an important Hebrew cultural center.

HAKAK divides his book between a study of S. Agnon, on the one hand, and interpretations of the literature of Yehoshua and the poetry of David Vogel, Nathan Alterman, Nathan Zach, Aharon Almog, and Erez Biton, on the other. Hakak uses Agnon's "Simple Story" as the basis for a critical analysis of the motif of the cock-*gever* (male), which runs through the story and "makes the reading process particularly intensive and creative." In another interesting chapter devoted to Agnon, the author compares Agnon's "In the Forest and in the City" and Charles Dickens's *Great Expectations*, arguing that these texts not only have similar characters, settings, and plots, but also share common themes and social ideologies. The book ends with a chapter about the poetry written by Sephardim; valuable in itself, it makes for an abrupt conclusion when an overall summation is so palpably called for.

HALKIN surveys the history of modern Hebrew literature as it reflects "the socio-historical forces which have motivated Jewish life during the last two centuries." Clearly, this is a shift from literary criticism to a historical and ideological study. Halkin moves from Haskalah literature to the new Israeli fiction, insisting that a "thread of continuity" has run through the centuries, enabling the restoration of an independent Jewish state, and he asserts that "the symbol of this spiritual thread of continuity has been the Hebrew language."

SHAKED stresses that his collection of essays tells "the story of a spiritual emigration from Jewish Europe." Modern Hebrew literature has its roots in the diaspora and even in Israel it still reflects the lives of both the new immigrants and their ancestors. Shaked explains that his generation of authors, like other generations of Hebrew writers since the Middle Ages, went through an identity crisis that involved internal and external struggles. More specifically, he claims that modern Hebrew fiction assimilated literary forms, such as the novel, the short story, and even fairy tales, from external cultures, but he also argues that this assimilation is not complete because traditional elements of rabbinic and hasidic literature continue to exert enormous influence. In fact, as the tension between the traditional and Western components increases, this literature becomes more interesting and complex.

DINA RIPSMAN EYLON

Hellenism

Bickerman, Elias J., *The Jews in the Greek Age*, Cambridge, Massachusetts: Harvard University Press, 1988

Cohen, Shaye J.D., *From the Maccabees to the Mishnah* (Library of Early Christianity, 7), Philadelphia: Westminster, 1987

Davies, W.D. and Louis Finkelstein (editors), *The Cambridge History of Judaism*, vol. 2: *The Hellenistic Age*, Cambridge and New York: Cambridge University Press, 1984

Feldman, Louis H., *Jew and Gentile in the Ancient World: Attitudes and Interactions from Alexander to Justinian*, Princeton, New Jersey: Princeton University Press, 1993

Grabbe, Lester L., *Judaism from Cyrus to Hadrian*, vol. 1: *The Persian and Greek Periods*, Minneapolis, Minnesota: Fortress, 1992; London: SCM, 1994

Hengel, Martin, *Judentum und Hellenismus*, 1969; translated by John Bowden from the second German edition as *Judaism and Hellenism: Studies in Their Encounter in Palestine during the Early Hellenistic Period*, 2 vols., Philadelphia: Fortress, and London: S.C.M., 1974

Kraft, Robert A. and George W.E. Nickelsburg (editors), *Early Judaism and Its Modern Interpreters* (The Bible and Its Modern Interpreters, 2), Atlanta, Georgia: Scholars Press, 1986

Modrzejewski, Joseph M., *Les Juifs d'Egypte, de Ramsès II à Hadrien*, 1991; translated by Robert Cornman as *The Jews of Egypt: From Rameses II to Emperor Hadrian*, Philadelphia: Jewish Publication Society, and Edinburgh: Clark, 1995

Tcherikover, Avigdor, *Hellenistic Civilization and the Jews*, Philadelphia: Jewish Publication Society, 1959

The cultural, social, and political interchange that marked Hellenism was by no means a uniquely Jewish experience, but the records for Jewish interaction with the West are more extensive than for other ancient peoples of the Near East. In recent decades researchers have been busy retranslating and reinterpreting long-known documents (such as the books of Maccabees), analyzing new archaeological discoveries (notably the Dead Sea Scrolls), and integrating all of these materials in accordance with long-established as well as recently developed methodologies and approaches. Because the Hellenistic era is a pivotal one in Jewish history and shares many characteristics with the modern age, scholars have not been reluctant to apply critical appraisals to aspects of Hellenism they perceive as fruitful syntheses or momentous crises.

TCHERIKOVER's volume is the oldest of the books under review aimed primarily at a scholarly audience. At this level, it represents both a masterful presentation of consensus views at the middle of the 20th century and a springboard for some of its author's creative and still-influential hypotheses, especially in regard to the complex events leading up to the Maccabean Revolt. Although more than four decades of exciting new discoveries and reinterpretations pertaining to the Hellenistic era separate today's readers from Tcherikover and his contemporaries, his well-written and vigorously argued study is essential reading for anyone with a serious interest in the history of Jews and Judaism during this period.

BICKERMAN's account of Hellenistic Judaism was designed primarily for the general reader. For such an audience, it constituted a fine synthesis of pre-1950 scholarship. Although the copyright date of Bickerman's book is four decades later, its contents draw heavily on two earlier works: a 1949 essay entitled "The Historical Foundations of Postbiblical Judaism," and his controversial 1937 monograph, *Der Gott der Makkabäer*. Bickerman's mastery of the material and his easy-to-follow style have contributed to the continued popularity of this work among nonscholars. It should, however, be supplemented by more recent nonspecialist publications, some of which are described below.

HENGEL's two volumes had their genesis in the 1966 thesis that the author presented to the Faculty of Protestant Theology in Tübingen, Germany. As indicated by the book's subtitle, the primary historical focus of Hengel's work is on the first half of the Hellenistic period through the mid–second century B.C.E. But Hengel's focus is broader than history, encompassing just about every imaginable aspect of the Jewish-Greek encounter. The scholarly structure upon which Hengel built his analysis is unusually impressive and solid: the 320 or so pages of text in the first volume are matched by an equal number of pages of notes, bibliographies, and indices in the second volume. It is for this reason, among others, that subsequent scholars over the past 25 years have continued to mine (if not always mind) Hengel's interpretations and the sources upon which he relied.

DAVIES and FINKELSTEIN's edited volume on Judaism in the Hellenistic period is in general on the same lofty and weighty level as other studies in the "Cambridge History" series. Themselves superb scholars, Davies and Finkelstein have assembled a stellar group of colleagues to compose authoritative essays on the major topics and movements of relevance to the study of this period. These studies are not, however, as up-to-date as the volume's copyright would indicate, since there was an unusually long delay (even by scholarly standards) from the time articles were submitted to their eventual publication. Nonetheless, it remains the case that no one, from advanced undergraduate to senior specialist, can afford to overlook the various contributions in this collection.

KRAFT and NICKELSBURG edited their volume as part of the centennial celebration initiated by the Society of Biblical Literature in 1980. With few exceptions, the 17 essays that make up the collection also date from that year, even though another half-decade passed before publication. The term "early Judaism" is here taken to encompass the period from Alexander the Great through the Roman emperor Hadrian. Thus, some of these chapters are not immediately relevant to the Hellenistic period, though all cover historical, literary, numismatic, and other phenomena of singular importance for an understanding not only of Hellenism, but also of its antecedents and successors. Perhaps the greatest merit of this volume is the authors' shared determination to allow the ancient documents to speak for themselves, revealing strengths and especially weaknesses in previous scholarly consensuses and also the fluid, often dynamic character of ancient Jewish society and religion in their relations with other peoples and cultures. With its lack of a subject index or cross references, this volume is not nearly as user-friendly as it could be, even for advanced scholars, but the richness of its contents at least partially justifies the extra effort such shortcomings entail.

COHEN's book would function well in many classroom or study group settings, since its author envisions such an audience in his preface and, as is all too rare these days, actually keeps this general audience in mind throughout. He includes a minimum of footnotes and technical language, does not presuppose extensive prior knowledge on the part of his readers, and refers the interested to well-chosen resources for further study. Cohen has not organized his book in terms of an overall chronological structure, with the first chapter dealing with the earliest events and the last with the latest. Instead, most of his individual thematic chapters, which deal with history, religion, communal institutions, sectarian movements, and canonization, are themselves structured chronologically. This will put a bit of a burden on the reader with exclusive interests in Hellenism. However, there is nothing daunting about Cohen; his erudition is as deep as it is wide, and many of his readers may end up being led by him to expand the horizons of their interest.

GRABBE's two-volume discussion and analysis of Judaism from the mid–sixth century B.C.E. to the mid–second century C.E. is, in a word, superb. It is, in fact, difficult to imagine any one, from out-and-out beginner to well-traveled veteran, who will not benefit enormously from working through relevant sections of Grabbe's erudite and exceptionally well organized tomes. Although only a portion of one of his volumes deals specifically with Hellenism, the same lustrous quality of presentation is apparent throughout. For most chapters—including the two devoted to Alexander, the Ptolemies, the Seleucids, the Maccabean Revolt, and the Hasmoneans—Grabbe begins with a short section discussing and evaluating major secondary studies. This is followed by a full appraisal of primary sources, not only literary but also archaeological and artifactual (to use Grabbe's term). He then focuses on important individual events or phenomena, especially those that have occasioned substantial previous debate. Each of Grabbe's chapters ends with an extensive synthesis, which itself concludes with his own interpretation and reconstruction. These will not always garner immediate assent, but they will inevitably command respect. Through a detailed system of cross-referencing, readers can easily move from one topic to another and from one era to preceding and subsequent ones.

FELDMAN's substantial volume is focused, in the words of its subtitle, on attitudes and interactions, both positive and negative, between Jews and non-Jews throughout the ancient world. On the one hand, his chronological boundaries are far wider than the Hellenistic period; on the other, his emphasis does not allow for a discussion of a wide range of phenomena in antiquity, though this last remark is in no sense a criticism, since Feldman never intended this particular work to function in that way. After detailing Jewish-Gentile relationships in the land of Israel and in the Diaspora, he looks at evidence of anti-Jewish bigotry or prejudice from governments, the general populace, and the intellectual classes. Feldman balances these three chapters of negatives with three further essays on the attractions of Jews, namely, their antiquity (this was so even in the ancient world), the cardinal virtues, and Moses as an ideal leader. These are in turn followed by chapters on the success Jews enjoyed in winning converts and sympathizers. It was Feldman's perception of Jewish success in these latter areas, in spite of often bitter opposition, that led him to construct this massive study in the first place. Feldman's presentation is vigorous and his annotation extensive. His work has been criticized on several different levels by many of his fellow scholars, but in any case it is well worth consulting, even if (or, perhaps, precisely because) it does not represent the current consensus.

MODRZEJEWSKI's comprehensive study of the Jews in Egypt first appeared in French in 1991. Its prompt translation and appearance in English are especially welcome; there is nothing else that compares to its scope and elegance of presentation. Ptolemaic (Hellenistic) Egypt occupies the middle of Modrzejewski's volume; befitting an era he titles "the Zenith," it receives the bulk of the author's attention. In successive chapters, Modrzejewski addresses topics relating to Alexandrian Judaism; Jews outside of the capital, including those in military service; the Septuagint, law, and justice; the Jewish temple at Leontopolis; and texts and incidents that lie "at the wellsprings of pagan anti-Semitism" (to use the author's phrase). Modrzejewski's prose (as translated) is eminently readable; his annotations and bibliographical references are full and up-to-date; his glossary, calendars, conversion charts for weights and measures, and related material are all very helpful; and the numerous illustrations, often depicting little-known artifacts, are well chosen and beautifully reproduced. In many ways, Jews in Hellenistic Egypt enjoyed a veritable Golden Age. It is fortunate for them and for us that Modrzejewski has chosen to be one of its chroniclers.

LEONARD J. GREENSPOON

See also Hellenistic Literature; History: Second Temple Period

Hellenistic Literature

Charlesworth, James H. (editor), *The Old Testament Pseudepigrapha*, 2 vols., Garden City, New York: Doubleday, and London: Darton, Longman and Todd, 1983–1985

Goldstein, Jonathan A., *1 Maccabees* (Anchor Bible, vol. 41), Garden City, New York: Doubleday, 1976

Goldstein, Jonathan A., *2 Maccabees* (Anchor Bible, vol. 41A), Garden City, New York: Doubleday, 1983

Moore, Carey, *Judith: A New Translation with Introduction and Commentary* (Anchor Bible, vol. 40), Garden City, New York: Doubleday, 1985

Mulder, Martin J. (editor), *Mikra: Text, Translation, Reading and Interpretation of the Hebrew Bible in Ancient Judaism and Early Christianity*, Minneapolis, Minnesota: Fortress, 1988

Nickelsburg, George W.E., *Jewish Literature between the Bible and the Mishnah: A Historical and Literary Introduction*, Philadelphia: Fortress, and London: SCM, 1981

Schiffman, Lawrence H., *Reclaiming the Dead Sea Scrolls: The History of Judaism, the Background of Christianity, the Lost Library of Qumran*, Philadelphia: Jewish Publication Society, 1994

Stone, Michael E. (editor), *Jewish Writings of the Second Temple Period: Apocrypha, Pseudepigrapha, Qumran Sectarian Writings, Philo, Josephus*, Philadelphia: Fortress, 1984

Wills, Lawrence M., *The Jewish Novel in the Ancient World* (Myth and Poetics), Ithaca, New York: Cornell University Press, 1995

A wide array of genres and themes awaits the reader of literature produced by and for Jews during the Hellenistic period. Some of this is canonical for Jews and Christians; other works, although not included in any known canon, nonetheless had wide circulation and authority. Recent decades have seen the discovery and publication of hitherto unknown documents or new versions of well-known Hellenistic literature. In many cases it is necessary to work back to the original or earliest recoverable form (in Greek or Hebrew/Aramaic) by retroversion from one of the more "exotic" ancient languages or by stripping away Christian accretions from earlier Jewish writings. There is also increased interest in phenomena such as audience reaction and interplay between Jewish and non-Jewish literature of this era.

Stone and Mulder's collections, which are part of the authoritative Compendia Rerum Iudaicarum ad Novum Testamentum series, form indispensable starting points for anyone with a serious interest in literature produced within Jewish communities during the Hellenistic period. The material gathered together by STONE is most relevant for this purpose. Specialists deal with biblical (understood in its most inclusive signification) materials; historical documents; examples from wisdom, testamentary, oracular, and apocalyptic literature; and sectarian texts from Qumran (the Dead Sea Scrolls). The discussions are well balanced, fully documented, and aimed at a sophisticated but not specialist audience. There is an extensive (one is tempted to say exhaustive) bibliography for the volume as a whole, as well as for individual chapters, and the indices of sources and of ancient names and subjects are satisfyingly ample. All in all, the editor and contributors to this volume have done everything possible to disseminate knowledge and facilitate further research.

MULDER's volume is as reliable, well organized, and complete as Stone's. Like Stone's, it covers areas not directly relevant to the study of Hellenistic literature. Mulder's volume is especially strong in its examination of translations of Scripture (*Mikra*), such as the Septuagint and the Targumim, and its varied interpretations at Qumran, in the Apocrypha and Pseudepigrapha, and in the fragmentary works of a handful of Hellenistic poets and historians. Both the biblical text and its exegetical authority among the Samaritans are given due notice and analysis.

NICKELSBURG's study is another point of entry into Hellenistic literature, more accessible for the general reader than the two volumes just described. Nickelsburg, a widely respected scholar of this period and a contributor of two chapters to the volume edited by Stone, manages with remarkable success to remain true to all three elements in his subtitle: although literature is the main topic, he provides ample historical background to contextualize the many texts he mentions. Moreover, he neither forgets nor talks down to the general reader who forms his intended audience. Like the Stone and Mulder volumes, this work covers more than Hellenistic literature, which may induce users to move beyond the consideration of strictly Hellenistic documents.

CHARLESWORTH has produced a magisterial two-volume collection that all researchers, from tyros to veterans, will need to consult at some point. A worthy successor to the earlier collection by R.H. Charles, the Charlesworth volumes contain authoritative translations of key documents (Hellenistic and later) within the general categories of apocalyptic literature and testaments (volume one) and expansions of the Hebrew Bible and assorted other works (volume two). Each translation is fully annotated with both textual and exegetical comments and is preceded by a full introduction, which summarizes the work and provides an in-depth presentation from many perspectives of nearly every issue relevant to a correct understanding and appreciation. A combined index of topics and names for both volumes can be found at the end of the second volume. For the many individuals with a deep interest in Hellenistic literature but without the linguistic facility to read the documents in their original (or at least ancient) forms, Charlesworth's volumes are as close an encounter as they are likely to experience.

SCHIFFMAN's wide-ranging and vigorously argued book is essential reading for anyone who wishes for an in-depth understanding of the Dead Sea Scrolls, most of which were produced in the second and first centuries B.C.E. It is Schiffman's contention that the bulk of previous scrolls research, focusing as it did almost entirely on their relationship to early Christianity, failed even to begin to do justice to the Jewish context(s) in which the scrolls were produced. Only by restoring these documents, including sectarian regulations and biblical (re)interpretations, to their rightful place in the history of Judaism will their full significance become clear—for believing Jews and Christians and anyone else with a lively interest in the history of religions. Given the fragmentary nature of many of the documents and the many unanswered (and perhaps ultimately unanswerable) questions about the identity of those who authored the scrolls, their connection with the site at Qumran, and the inner connections between one scroll and another, it is inevitable that many of Schiffman's interpretations are speculative and controversial. But he remains faithful to the text and to his readers, who are well served by the overall organization as well as the discrete discussions that constitute this volume.

WILLS's focus is also on a body of literature, but one united—in his analysis—by genre rather than by place of discovery. He makes cogent and imaginative arguments in favor of an understanding of Daniel (in its fuller Septuagint form), Greek Esther, Tobit, Judith, and Joseph and Aseneth as ancient Jewish novels. As such, these works (all of which, except Joseph and Aseneth, are contained in the fuller canon of Roman Catholicism and Eastern Orthodoxy) should not be used as sources for valid historical information (as would be the case with historical novels, a related but separate genre exemplified by 2 and 3 Maccabees), nor should they be criticized or even ridiculed for supposed historical bloopers, often of mammoth proportions. Rather, they are to be enjoyed by audiences today, as presumably they were by a growing Jewish middle class in the Hellenistic period and later, for their exciting narratives; their extraordinary interest (especially by comparison with earlier biblical texts) in the inner or emotional lives of their characters, in particular female ones; and other related entertainment-enhancing elements.

MOORE's commentary on Judith both anticipates and expands upon many of the insights Wills expresses. Unlike many other volumes in the well-known Anchor Bible series,

Moore's really does have something important to say to the general readers who were the original target audience for the series. Like Wills, Moore seems genuinely to enjoy the material he is commenting on; additionally, he is exceptionally adept at conveying that sense of enjoyment to his audience as he writes about everything from historicity to canonicity, from sex to text. He is especially effective when he discusses the literary qualities of Judith, among which irony stands preeminent as the key that unlocks many hitherto obscure and frequently surprising elements in this book. Moore's translation reads well, and he provides a plethora of useful notes and stimulating commentary. In short, this is a charming introduction to the story of one of Hellenistic Judaism's most extraordinary female characters.

GOLDSTEIN's two volumes of commentary, one each on 1 and 2 Maccabees, are amazingly full compendia (with a total of more than 1,100 pages) of knowledge and insight on these two influential books of the Apocrypha. The two volumes are intended to be used together not only because of their common subject matter (although often differing perspectives), but also because Goldstein has chosen to "introduce" both 1 and 2 Maccabees in the first volume. This does not, however, deter him from providing 2 Maccabees with a separate and extensive—more than 100 pages—introduction of its own. Although he does not neglect the work of others, Goldstein's strength lies in his ingenious, although not always widely accepted, solutions to many of the major historical and literary puzzles that have vexed generations of researchers. For this reason, readers of Goldstein will probably also wish to consult other works discussed if their goal is, for example, to follow the thread of scholarly interchange on particular topics. But Goldstein does succeed, in both introduction and in commentary, in provoking thought about the nature of ancient historical writing and modern interpretations of this important genre.

LEONARD J. GREENSPOON

See also Hellenism

Herzl, Theodor   1860–1904

Austro-Hungarian ideologue and organizer of political Zionism

Bein, Alex, *Theodore Herzl: A Biography*, translated by Maurice Samuel, Philadelphia: Jewish Publication Society, 1941; new edition, London: East and West Library, and Philadelphia: Jewish Publication Society, 1956

Brude-Firnau, Gisela, "Theodor Herzl Writes the Manifesto *The Jewish State*," in *Yale Companion to Jewish Writing and Thought in German Culture, 1096–1996*, edited by Sander L. Gilman and Jack Zipes, New Haven, Connecticut: Yale University Press, 1997

De Haas, Jacob, *Theodor Herzl: A Biographical Study*, 2 vols., Chicago: Leonard, 1927

Elon, Amos, *Herzl*, New York: Holt, Rinehart and Winston, 1975; London: Weidenfeld and Nicolson, 1976

Handler, Andrew, *Dori: The Life and Times of Theodor Herzl in Budapest (1860–1878)*, Tuscaloosa: University of Alabama Press, 1983

Kornberg, Jacques, *Theodor Herzl: From Assimilation to Zionism* (Jewish Literature and Culture), Bloomington: Indiana University Press, 1993

Pawel, Ernst, *The Labyrinth of Exile: A Life of Theodor Herzl*, New York: Farrar, Straus, and Giroux, 1989; London: Collins-Harvill, 1990

Anyone who decides to study Theodor Herzl will not suffer from a lack of interesting biographies of this charismatic figure. The first major biography to appear in English was that of DE HAAS, an important Zionist leader in his own right and a close associate of Herzl. His biography gains from a firsthand familiarity with many of the events he describes, including the six international Zionist Congresses over which Herzl presided. He also discusses Herzl's negotiations with the Grand Duke of Baden, Kaiser Wilhelm II, and Sultan Abdul Hamed II of Turkey for the establishment of the Jewish State in Palestine, with the knowing way of one of the Zionist movement's insiders. De Haas's biography confines itself to Herzl's political life, whereas other biographers are interested in the impact on Herzl's developing thought of his childhood, education, family life, and prezionist professional life as a minor playwright and successful journalist.

De Haas, however, begins his biography with the journalist Herzl's coverage of the Dreyfus Affair, which encouraged Herzl to become an activist for the establishment of a Jewish State. De Haas has written a fine biography, well worth reading for its in-depth coverage of early Zionism and Herzl's seminal role in making it into a movement of major political significance. Archival materials, including letters from Herzl and important documents of early Zionism, complement the book as illustrations.

BEIN's biography is a thorough examination of the Zionist leader in remarkably well written prose. The work is frequently criticized for the extreme admiration that Bein lavishes on his subject. One example of this is the way Bein describes the pre-Zionist playwright Herzl as a literary genius, whereas most modern scholars would characterize him as at best a middlebrow writer whose Zionist writings have substantial political and historical interest but whose earlier writings are not particularly significant.

Noted novelist and biographer PAWEL is aided by a dramatic style that makes his work accessible to a wide readership. It is nonetheless a rigorous examination of Herzl as a political leader and the developments that brought him to that point. His presentation is balanced and in no way suffers from hero worship. Much of Pawel's biography is based on speculation, and the craft of the experienced novelist is well in evidence. The work contains extensive analysis of Herzl's personal life and marital problems; elements of psychobiography give the work considerable deftness.

Pawel maintains that the rejection of Herzl's play against antisemitism, *The New Ghetto* (1894), helped move him in the direction of becoming a Jewish political leader. Pawel sees additional motivation in the failure of Herzl's meeting with Baron Maurice de Hirsch, in which Herzl discussed the founding of a Jewish state for the first time. De Hirsch's rejection of the idea prompted Herzl to write his major manifesto of Zionism, *The Jewish State*. In describing *The Jewish State*, Pawel remarks, "The measure of a manifesto is not its intellectual profundity but its emotional impact," and Pawel credits it with having been more emotionally persuasive than the earlier Zionist efforts of Leo Pinsker and Moses Hess. The work had its greatest impact not on the wealthy whom Herzl was trying to influence but on the masses of poor Jews.

Similarly, in ELON's biography, the author points out that Herzl did not invent Zionism but "he forged the instruments that would put Zionism into practice." Elon remarks, "There is always a trace of quixotism when devotion to a cause is extreme, logical, and saintlike. . . . He [Herzl] walked a tightrope between charlatanism and genius." Elon stresses how for Herzl the Jewish state could have been established anywhere Jews could acquire territory, not necessarily Palestine. However, the bulk of his followers, notably Martin Buber, were in favor of establishing a Jewish state only in the biblical homeland of Palestine. The Zionist movement was tragically split by Herzl's negotiations with the British to establish a Jewish state in Uganda, and the resulting quarrels inside the movement may have hastened Herzl's death of heart failure at the age of 44.

HANDLER concentrates on Herzl's childhood and student years. It is a highly speculative account of the influence that Hungarian/Magyar (as opposed to German) culture may have had on Herzl's life, given his childhood in Budapest.

KORNBERG presents an incisive account of Herzl from his 18th to his 36th year, when he converted to Zionism. The study contains an interesting critique of Herzl's play, *The New Ghetto*. According to Kornberg, the play argues that assimilation of Jews into German society leads toward contempt of all things Jewish (i.e., Jewish self-hatred). Jacob's assimilation into non-Jewish society is a tragedy that brings about his early death in a duel. Dueling is a gentile custom that Jacob accepts in order to bring about his acceptance into gentile society, but in fact it only hastens his death.

BRUDE-FIRNAU points out in her article that while Herzl was covering the Dreyfus Trial for *Die neue Freie Presse*, his dispatches reflected on the resolute character of the maligned defendant, and this brought him closer to assuming a role as a political leader. She provides a concise and readable outline of Herzl's biography, based on his primary writings and diaries. She maintains that Herzl's meetings with Sultan Abdul Hamed II were important despite the sultan's refusal to cede Palestine for the building of a Jewish state. These meetings helped Zionism to become an international political force by inspiring others to take it seriously.

PETER R. ERSPAMER

Heschel, Abraham Joshua 1907–1972

Polish-born American theologian, social activist, and teacher

Fierman, Morton C., *Leap of Action: Ideas in the Theology of Abraham Joshua Heschel,* Lanham, Maryland: University Press of America, 1990

Friedman, Maurice, *Abraham Joshua Heschel and Elie Wiesel: You Are My Witnesses,* New York: Farrar, Straus, and Giroux, 1987

Kaplan, Edward K., *Holiness in Words: Abraham Joshua Heschel's Poetics of Piety* (SUNY Series in Judaica), West Fulton: State University of New York Press, 1996

Kasimow, Harold, *Divine-Human Encounter: A Study of Abraham Joshua Heschel,* Washington, D.C.: University Press of America, 1979

Kasimow, Harold and Byron L. Sherwin (editors), *No Religion Is an Island: Abraham Joshua Heschel and Interreligious Dialogue,* Maryknoll, New York: Orbis, 1991

McBride, Alfred, *Heschel: Religious Educator,* Denville, New Jersey: Dimension, 1973

Merkle, John C., *The Genesis of Faith: The Depth Theology of Abraham Joshua Heschel,* New York: Macmillan, and London: Collier Macmillan, 1985

Perlman, Lawrence, *Abraham Heschel's Idea of Revelation* (Brown Judaic Studies, no. 171), Atlanta, Georgia: Scholars Press, 1989

Abraham Joshua Heschel made a lasting impression on a generation of thinkers in every sphere of American Jewish religious life. He influenced Reform, Conservative, and Orthodox Jewish leaders as they sought to develop an authentic American Judaism. He inspired Jews to undertake social projects and to join with non-Jews in seeking to remedy the "insecurity of freedom." He also expounded a biblical philosophy of Judaism that has influenced the way both Jews and non-Jews think about religion. The many writings about the man and his work reflect the multiplicity of facets in his achievement.

FIERMAN offers a useful introduction to Heschel's work. The author had been studying Heschel for 23 years, and this considered work synthesizes the various monographs and papers that have evolved from that early interest. The book was written primarily for the author's students studying Heschel, but it has a secondary purpose of introducing the breadth and depth of this thinker to anyone beginning to read of him. Heschel's theology was distinctive, and the book includes studies of Heschel's ideas on prayer, faith, humanity, Israel, the Sabbath, the prophets, the Bible, and religious action generally. Heschel's social activism appears in chapters on freedom, peace, racism, justice, and brotherhood. Heschel the teacher is introduced in a chapter on education. A moving epilogue, "Moments of Remembrance for Dr. Heschel," helps readers catch a glimpse of the human being behind the theologian and activist. The book remains expository and descriptive. The author summarizes Heschel's ideas, paraphrasing them in simpler terms. For the beginner who wants to decode Heschel, this book is a helpful guide.

MERKLE offers a more sustained and critical analysis of Heschel's thought. He summarizes Heschel's major ideas, cites his sources at length, and takes on other interpreters of the thinker. He provides a clear account of Heschel's life, of his theological concerns, and of his relationship to the Jewish tradition. This sophisticated introduction to Heschel's major concepts begins by looking at Heschel's life, ecumenical impact, and depth-theology, which is an outgrowth of his universalism. The central section looks at general theological ideas such as God and the divine mystery and at more specifically Jewish theological concerns such as faith, revelation, the Bible, the rabbis, the Torah, and the people of Israel. Interestingly, the study ends with what Heschel regards as the preconditions of faith, the "antecedents" of belief on which all religion depends. This organization of the book shows how Heschel's thinking depends on his phenomenological analysis of human faith.

Merkle is a Christian and his interest in Heschel shows the ecumenical scope of his influence. KASIMOW also recognizes this aspect of Heschel's writing and provides a thorough introduction to Heschel's thought. His work is more rigorous and academic and contains copious citations from Heschel's writings, from other modern thinkers such as Martin Buber, and from classic medieval Jewish writers such as Maimonides. This makes the work an excellent preparation for someone who wants a firm basis on which to understand Heschel. One important and often overlooked theme covered here is Heschel's thought in relationship to non-Jewish religions, an implication Kasimow sees as making a crucial difference in modern life. KASIMOW and SHERWIN develop this idea through the many essays in their edited anthology. This anthology demonstrates how Heschel's influence has touched various religious thinkers across several traditions.

While several books provide a guide to Heschel's thought, KAPLAN enables readers to understand just why Heschel is often so frustrating to read, even when he is most inspiring. Kaplan explores Heschel's strategy in evoking faith from a reader and provides readers with a sophisticated investigation of Heschel's means of creating empathy together with critical awareness. He leads the reader through Heschel's philosophical concerns and social activism to a consideration of major modern theological problems such as the Holocaust and "modern miracles" such as the rebirth of the Jewish state. He concludes by reflecting on "Heschel's unfinished symphony"—the enduring significance of his personality and writings. Kaplan addresses serious theological issues in a technical way that is often illuminating. Some readers may find Kaplan's own use of language daunting, but the struggle to discover his insights will be rewarded.

PERLMAN offers an equally technical introduction to one of the major ideas in Heschel's theology—that of revelation. Perlman reviews the ideas of earlier commentators on Heschel and places his theology in the wider context of religious philosophy by looking at the thought of Baruch Spinoza, Edmund Husserl, and Emannuel Levinas. He also shows how Heschel uses rabbinic teachings about revelation as a foundation for his own thought. A good grounding in philosophy is a prerequisite for profitable reading of this technical book, which illuminates Heschel's place in the general development of modern thought. It may be too detailed for some readers, but it offers a persuasive account of Heschel as a careful theologian and not merely as a master of language.

FRIEDMAN is better known as an expositor of Martin Buber than of Heschel or Elie Wiesel, who are the subjects of this book. His friendship with Heschel, their shared social concerns, and his early writings on Heschel combine, however, to make this volume a valuable window to Heschel's genius. While the book does review much that Friedman has written elsewhere about Heschel's thinking, it also adds personal touches such as descriptions of Heschel's home life and family. The book includes citations from Heschel's published and unpublished writings that make it useful for understanding the nature of Heschel's public declarations. The final pages in this book note how Heschel and Elie Wiesel collaborated on several occasions and how their "witness" for the modern world converges in a significant way.

Heschel's role as a teacher cannot be overestimated. First at Hebrew Union College in Cincinnati and then at the Jewish Theological Seminary in New York, Heschel impressed his view of religious education on his students. McBRIDE addresses this facet of Heschel in his early study. While later writers also touch on Heschel as educator, this book explores his themes at length and then applies them to the teaching of Christianity. Such an application underscores the way in which Heschel's work is accessible to non-Jews.

S. DANIEL BRESLAUER

Hirsch, Samson Raphael 1808–1888

German rabbi and ideologue of separatist
Neo-Orthodoxy

Breuer, Mordechai, review of *Tradition in an Age of Reform: The Religious Philosophy of Samson Raphael Hirsch,* by Noah H. Rosenbloom, *Tradition: A Journal of Orthodox Thought,* 16(4), 1977
Haberman, Jacob, "Kaufmann Kohler and His Teacher Samson Raphael Hirsch," *Leo Baeck Institute Yearbook,* 43, 1998
Hirsch, S.A., "Jewish Philosophy of Religion and Samson Raphael Hirsch," in his *A Book of Essays,* London: Macmillan, 1905
Liberles, Robert, "Champion of Orthodoxy: The Emergence of Samson Raphael Hirsch as Religious Leader," *AJS Review,* 6, 1981
Liberles, Robert, *Religious Conflict in Social Context: The Resurgence of Orthodox Judaism in Frankfurt am Main, 1838–1877,* Westport, Connecticut: Greenwood, 1985
Rosenbloom, Noah H., *Tradition in an Age of Reform: The Religious Philosophy of Samson Raphael Hirsch,* Philadelphia: Jewish Publication Society, 1976

Samson Raphael Hirsch was a prominent rabbi, author, and spokesman for Neo-Orthodox Judaism. Hirsch defended orthodoxy in a manner that appealed to educated, cultured, and intelligent people. He founded a separatist congregation in Frankfurt am Main because he felt that the general community did not sufficiently protect the interests of the Orthodox.

HIRSCH, no relative, produced his portrait shortly after the death of his famous namesake. He gives a brief biographical account of his subject and a summary of his main works, together with extensive quotations from them. He correctly sees the keystone of Hirsch's religious philosophy in the extended comparison of the two revelations of God, in nature and in Torah. Nature and Torah (so the argument runs) are both parts of the total reality of which God is the author; in both one must discriminate between the facts and interpretations or explanations of the facts; in both the adequacy of an explanation depends on its covering the facts concerned, or of the facts fitting into the explanation; whether a satisfactory explanation of the facts has been discovered or not, the reality of the facts is beyond dispute; hence the ordinances of the Torah remain the law for us, even if we do not comprehend their reason and purpose.

ROSENBLOOM has written a comprehensive study of Hirsch's life and thought. The work is divided into three parts. Part one deals with the intellectual temper of the age, the background of Hirsch's family, his education, and a detailed account of the various rabbinic positions he occupied in Oldenburg, Emden, Nikolsburg, and finally in his separatist congregation in Frankfurt am Main. Parts two and three analyze respectively two of Hirsch's most important works, *The Nineteen Letters,* dealing with the challenges posed to traditional Judaism by the Emancipation and the modern secular world, and *Horeb,* a compendium of Jewish laws and observances with particular emphasis on their underlying ideas. Rosenbloom stresses the limited secular and religious education acquired by Hirsch. Hirsch attended the University of Bonn for only 18 months and left without obtaining a degree. Rosenbloom even raises doubts about whether Hirsch ever received the traditional rabbinic ordination *(semikhah).* He did study for barely over a year at the yeshivah headed by the renowned Jacob Ettlinger in Mannheim, but it is hardly likely that the latter would have conferred the title of rabbi on a student whose talmudic knowledge was at best limited and superficial. The letter of recommendation that Hirsch received from Nathan Adler for the rabbinic position in Oldenburg, which the latter was relinquishing, referred to Hirsch as "the young man" rather than by the title rabbi, which the occasion would have warranted. Possibly, Rosenbloom suggests, Hirsch was ordained subsequently while serving as a rabbi.

In analyzing *The Nineteen Letters,* Rosenbloom argues that Hirsch nurtured a secret ambition to become a modern Maimonides, as suggested by the Hebrew title of this work, *Iggerot Zafon* (Letters to the North), which parallels Maimonides' *Iggeret Teman* (Letter to the South). Rosenbloom finds that Hirsch's differentiation between the negative investigation of Judaism from without and the positive investigation from within was akin to Hegel's distinction between comprehension of a thing *für uns* and *für sich.* According to Hegel, an appreciative understanding of an attitude or position cannot be satisfied by a mere external response but requires an effort to discover the intrinsic meaning and inner spirit of that point of view.

BREUER contests some of the conclusions of Rosenbloom. He maintains that the correct vocalization of the title of Hirsch's work in Hebrew is not *Iggerot Zafon,* but *Iggerot Zafun* (Letters of the Concealed One, i.e., one who writes under a pseudonym, in this case "Ben Uziel"). This undermines the argument that Hirsch aspired to the mantle of Maimonides. Breuer further finds the evidence for the supposed influence of Hegel forced and unconvincing. There is no direct evidence in Hirsch's writings to enable judgment of how far he was influenced by Hegel's philosophy. The principle of the self-sufficiency of Judaism that Hirsch espoused makes it unlikely that he viewed his work as an exposition of Hegel's philosophy.

LIBERLES's (1981) essay emphasizes the importance that Mount Horeb plays in Hirsch's writings from the mid-1830s to the early 1850s. Hirsch's work on Jewish law, *Horeb,* was actually written before *The Nineteen Letters,* but, at the request of the publisher, the shorter and more popular work was published first. While Horeb as a Deutoronomic synonym for Mount Sinai, the site of the divine revelation of the Torah to Israel, was appropriate enough as the title of a work on Jewish law, that interpretation does not fully convey the symbolic significance of that mountain for Hirsch himself. Considerable evidence from Hirsch's writings bears witness that Hirsch identified Horeb less with the theophany at Sinai than with the dialogue between God and Elijah at Horeb. Just as in the days of the monarchy, Israel forsook God's covenant and worshiped idols and only Elijah remained loyal, so in his own age only Hirsch remained loyal to the Torah and its teachings.

LIBERLES (1985) reveals the context in which Hirsch established Neo-Orthodoxy, as head of the separatist Israelite Society of Religion (Israelitsche Religionsgesellschaft) in Frankfurt. The debate between Hirsch and Rabbi Seligmann Baer Bamberger of Wuerzburg regarding secession from the community is examined in detail. Liberles conveys the acrimony by reporting that when Hirsch appealed to the rabbinic dictum that if a sage has declared something forbidden—in this instance, remaining in the community with the Reformers—his colleague is not allowed to declare it permitted, Bamberger replied that the rule applies only when both authorities have equal standing, but if one is superior in learning he can reverse the decision of a lesser scholar. Liberles refutes the exaggerated claims about the decline of orthodoxy in Frankfurt before Hirsch's arrival and the myth of ten founders of the separatist congregation. On the other hand, the secession of Hirsch's Religionsgesellschaft from the community is shown to have had a moderating effect on the majority, who thereafter paid greater attention to the needs of the Orthodox.

HABERMAN believes that any analysis of Hirsch that does not see in him a man of faith and a charismatic leader does not do him justice and is false. He points out that some of the greatest Jewish thinkers of the 19th and early 20th centuries, such as Hermann Cohen, Graetz, and Steinschneider, came under his spell, and that more than a century after his death there are vibrant Orthodox communities modelled on his teaching of "Torah plus secular culture." Hirsch, then, may be viewed as the most successful Jewish controversialist in modern times. He also maintained good relations with the non-Jewish majority, declaring Jew and Gentile equally precious to God in his direction of world history, whereas Geiger, the spokesman of the Reformers, had to attack Christianity vigorously, sometimes to the extent of distorting its teachings, because after discarding Jewish laws and rituals there was otherwise little to differentiate Reform Jews from their neighbors.

Haberman further emphasizes that Hirsch did not antagonize the East European and Palestinian Orthodox establishment either, because he maintained that his synthesis was meant for Germany and Western Europe and was not necessarily valid elsewhere. Thus Hirsch won the support of East European rabbis (even if behind his back they may have whispered that he was a lightweight and a "prayer-book scholar"), while his contemporary Esriel Hildesheimer who tried to export his own version of Neo-Orthodoxy to Hungary and Jerusalem was denounced as a heretic and excommunicated.

Haberman underscores a surprising feature of Hirsch's personality: his tolerance for the ideological shortcomings of his students. When young Kaufmann Kohler came to him with his doubts, Hirsch told Kohler not to worry, that everything would turn out just fine, and that a journey around the world involves passing the torrid zone.

Hirsch's comparison of God's revelation in Nature and in the Torah is examined in detail by Haberman, who finds three aspects of the comparison to have merit. First, Hirsch correctly discerned that modern science, and the modern temper in general, is empirical in its approach rather than a priori. Second, it may be necessary methodologically to prescind from the question of the origin of the Torah and concentrate instead on the type of personality that is molded by adhesion to its way of life. In this, Hirsch anticipated the phenomenalists and their concept of "bracketing." Finally, Hirsch made the study of Torah acceptable in a scientific age, arguing that the conceptual methods used to study Torah and science are in many respects analogous, both representing intellectually respectable systems. The theological assumptions of halakhic laws are the counterpart of the metaphysical assumptions of the laws of physical nature. The observer in both cases attempts to rationalize the phenomena he sees, in a manner consistent with the basic principles he assumes. The comparison, however, is shown to founder on an equivocation of the word "law." Hirsch, after all, is confusing a "law" of the Torah, a clearly prescriptive command that such-and-such an action be done (or not done), with a "law" of nature, which is merely descriptive (or statistical) and which simply cannot be "broken."

JACOB HABERMAN

History: Ideas Of

Baron, Salo, *History and Jewish Historians: Essays and Addresses,* Philadelphia: Jewish Publication Society, 1964

Funkenstein, Amos, *Perceptions of Jewish History,* Berkeley: University of California Press, 1993

Meyer, Michael A., "Introduction," in his *Ideas of Jewish History* (Library of Jewish Studies), New York: Behrman, 1974

Neusner, Jacob, "The Religious Uses of History: Judaism in First-Century A.D. Palestine and Third-Century

Babylonia," in his *Talmudic Judaism in Sasanian Babylonia: Essays and Studies* (Studies in Judaism in Late Antiquity, vol. 14), Leiden: Brill, 1976

Schorsch, Ismar, *From Text to Context: The Turn to History in Modern Judaism* (Tauber Institute for the Study of European Jewry Series, 19), Hanover, New Hampshire: University Press of New England, 1994

Van Seters, John, "Israelite Historiography," in his *In Search of History: Historiography in the Ancient World and the Origins of Biblical History,* New Haven, Connecticut: Yale University Press, 1983; London: Yale University Press, 1986

Yerushalmi, Yosef Hayim, *Zakhor: Jewish History and Jewish Memory* (Samuel and Althea Stroum Lectures in Jewish Studies), Seattle: University of Washington Press, 1982

The notion that "ideas of history" might constitute a worthwhile field of study is a relatively recent intellectual innovation and even more so for Jewish approaches to history. With the exception of biblical historiographic surveys, which generally focus on the Bible's Near Eastern context, scholarship on Jewish philosophies of history is only now beginning to come of age.

BARON's collection of essays, while dated, provides a solid foundation for more recent scholarship on Jewish historiography and ideas of history. His concerns are, in fact, surprisingly current in their focus and scope; he opens with a discussion of Jewish identities and evaluates various kinds of historical inquiry in terms of their ability to serve the particular characteristics of the Jewish past. The second section analyzes Maimonides and his conception of history. Finally, Baron turns to Azariah dei Rossi, Jost, Graetz, Steinschneider, and Herzfeld, all of whom were important contributors to Jewish ideas of history, thinkers whose work still lacks thorough examination by scholars.

MEYER's introduction to his compilation of primary sources delineates some basic theoretical issues pertinent to Jewish philosophies of history, such as periodization and historical continuity. His essay provides a useful outline of Jewish historiographic documents from the Bible through the 19th century. Except for a brief eruption of historical works in the 16th century (including works focused on non-Jewish histories), the late Middle Ages and the early modern periods are for Meyer bereft of historical thought, especially in Northern Europe. He applauds the invention of a critical historical tradition in the 19th century and devotes much of his attention to its practitioners and their heirs: Krochmal, Zunz, Graetz, Dubnow, Baeck, and Rivkin.

YERUSHALMI's well-known, even paradigmatic essay is a model of sophisticated but accessible scholarship on Jewish historical thinking. Animated by the tension between the biblical injunction to "remember" and the striking ahistoricity of the traditional Jewish worldview, Yerushalmi's text divides the Jewish past into the biblical and rabbinic, medieval, post-Spanish Expulsion, and modern periods. He argues that although one can find the seeds of historiographic scholarship in the premodern age, these authors are not the intellectual forebears of modern Jewish historiography. Rather, only in the modern period can Jewish contemplation of the past properly be called "historical." As they applied the innovations of scientific history (*Wissenschaft*) to the Jewish past, Jewish historians opened up new perspectives and opportunities for self-criticism. However, Yerushalmi argues, modern historiography is antithetical to traditional Jewish understandings of the past. Modern Jews may know more about their history than their ancestors, but this knowledge comes at the price of alienation.

While SCHORSCH's focus is limited to the development of a modern, self-critical historical tradition in the 19th and 20th centuries, this book nonetheless contributes invaluably to an understanding of the Jewish historical enterprise in general. The division of the study into two main sections, "Emancipation and Its Aftermath" and "Thinking Historically," reveals Schorsch's concern with the political causes and ramifications of the Jewish turn to historical scholarship. Yet Schorsch relies primarily upon Jewish sources and explanations, rather than taking a comparative approach. Perhaps that focus explains why he sees Jewish historicism as considerably less problematic than Yerushalmi does; for Schorsch, historical thinking is liberating, "the intellectual counterpart to the political freedom of emancipation."

FUNKENSTEIN's work, while serving as a critique of and response to Yerushalmi's essay, has a much greater scope than that text had. Funkenstein's premise is that historical consciousness and collective memory can be distinguished from one another, but they are by no means dichotomous. He demonstrates convincingly that although historiographic literature is the exception in traditional Jewish sources, historical reflection abounds in premodern halakhic and exegetical Jewish literature. This work is greatly strengthened by its comparative focus (Funkenstein is particularly adept with medieval Christian as well as Jewish sources) and by its extensive reliance on political, religious, and social thought. Rather than a mere cataloguing of "philosophies of history," this exceptionally erudite volume engages other themes as well, all of which shed light on the Jewish historical enterprise: the history of antisemitic and anti-Christian polemics; Jews' perception of their own election and uniqueness and their simultaneous challenge to Christian theology and history; past and present forms of messianism in relation to historical consciousness; and the role of historical thinking in the rise of modern nationalism.

NEUSNER juxtaposes the highly historical books from the biblical period (such as Samuel and Kings) and the utter lack of historical interest manifested during the rabbinic period. Using two eras each immediately following political catastrophe as case studies, Neusner investigates the relationship among messianism, politics, and historical thinking. He argues that the rabbis encouraged a mythic understanding of the past, but this interest served mainly to defuse eschatological fervor in the present, for the focus on individual acts of piety and study reframed the causes of the current situation as sociological rather than historical. Interestingly, Neusner concludes that the lack of historical inquiry during the rabbinic period was due to a sense that history had exhausted its pedagogical purposes and that the task at hand demanded a more useful enterprise. Although this article is far from exhaustive, it offers a provocative starting point for future investigations of rabbinic ideas of history.

The strength of VAN SETERS's section on Israelite historiography lies in his attention to theoretical and scholarly approaches (in subsections titled "The Critical Issues" and "Narrative Forms") as well as his presentation of general tropes in biblical histories and in the biblical idea of history. Where most treatments of this topic tend toward the highly technical language of the higher critics, Van Seters presents the issues of authorship, the evaluation of the various biblical histories, and questions of biblical "philosophies" of history in straightforward and accessible terms. He offers his own assessment of the value of comparative and literary approaches to ancient historiography while acknowledging the presence of scholarly debate on these approaches. This essay is followed by separate chapters devoted to the historiography of the books of Joshua, Samuel, and Kings.

MARA BENJAMIN

See also History: Biblical Israel; History: General Histories, Modern Authors; History: General Histories, Premodern Authors; History: Medieval; History: Modern; History: Second Temple Period; History: Talmudic Era

History: General Histories, Premodern Authors

Funkenstein, Amos, *Perceptions of Jewish History*, Berkeley: University of California Press, 1993

Meyer, Michael A. (compiler), *Ideas of Jewish History*, New York: Behrman House, 1974

Rapoport-Albert, Ada (editor), *Essays in Jewish Historiography* (History and Theory, Beiheft 27), Middletown, Connecticut: Wesleyan University, 1988

Yerushalmi, Yosef Hayim, *Zakhor: Jewish History and Jewish Memory*, Seattle: University of Washington Press, 1982

The study of premodern historiography constitutes an important exercise in Jewish history. The distinguishing feature of these early texts is the search for meaning on the part of the writer, rather than simply the accumulation of historical facts—what could be called positivism. Indeed, because so much of the efforts of the writers are devoted to the understanding of the historic events, the reports are often filled with invented materials that could be called fiction. The intent of such a mixture of fact and fiction is not, as is commonly held, due to ahistorical tendencies but to a desire to place the events in a larger matrix, one that is based upon archetypes and paradigms of meaning derived from biblical and rabbinic texts. Most recently, especially following Yosef Yerushalmi's seminal study, *Zakhor*, the discourse over Jewish historiography has revolved around the concepts of history and memory as if they were polar opposites. Such categories have been applied to the classic sources of ancient and medieval Jewish history such as Josephus, the anonymous Seder Tanna'im ve-'Amora'im, Iggeret Rab Sherira Gaon, Maimonides' Iggeret Teman, the anonymous Yosippon, Abraham ibn Daud's Sefer ha-Kabbalah, the Hebrew Crusade Chronicles, and the Memorbücher. They have also informed debates over whether the Jewish historio-

graphic texts of the 16th century, such as Solomon ibn Verga's *Shebet Yehudah*, Abraham Zacuto's *Sefer Yuhasin*, Elijah Capsali's *Seder 'Eliyahu Zuta*, Samuel Usque's *Consolacam as Tribulacoens de Israel*, Joseph Kohen's '*Emeq ha-Bakha*, Gedaliah ibn Yahia's *Shalshelet ha-Kabbalah*, Azariah dei Rossi's *Me'or 'Einayim*, and David Gans's *Zemah David*, constitute new directions or a continuation of the medieval genre, with the major break coming only in the 19th century, if at all. One often-overlooked source of Jewish historiography in the medieval and early modern period is the writings of Jewish travelers such as Eldad ha-Dani, Nathan ha-Bavli, the correspondence between Hasdai ibn Shaprut and the Khazar kings, the chronicle of Ahimaaz, the itinerary of Benjamin of Tudela, the travels of Petahiyah of Ratisbon, the letters of Obadiah di Bertinoro, and the travel diary of David Reuveni.

YERUSHALMI's modern classic in Jewish historiography has inspired an entire generation of Jewish historians to respond not only to his brilliant thesis but also to the rabbinic, medieval, and early-modern Jewish historiographic texts he treats. Yerushalmi begins with a very personal appreciation of and lament over the role of the professional historian, the separation between history and memory, and the difference between the traditional concern of Jews with history and "our own"—he does not specify to whom he is referring. He repeatedly rephrases the distinction between Jewish memory and the study of history, historiography, and curiosity about the past. He continually reverts to a standard for judging historical merit based on the needs of modern scholarship from a very positivistic sense: "the history of the Talmudic period itself cannot be elicited from its own vast literature, [nor even] an elementary retrieval of what occurred." Here Yerushalmi is almost paraphrasing Leopold von Ranke: *Wie es eigentlich gewesen* ("as it actually was"). One might wonder, however, whether scholars can learn something about the history of the talmudic period through the use of anachronism in rabbinic literature and whether something can be revealed about this history in the difference between the biblical and the talmudic versions of events. For example, the story about Moses visiting the academy of Rabbi Akiba does not constitute a fact but reports the historiographic orientation of the rabbis. The rabbis may not have written postbiblical history, but they made it; their concerns with the meaning of history, therefore, constitute historiography. By taking the rabbis to task for not reporting events as historians report battles—in chronicles, in chronological order, in narrative form—is to impose upon them a definition of history that was not their own. When writing about works from the Middle Ages, Yerushalmi attempts to evaluate the intentions of the authors in his own terms, dismissing a wide range of materials because of what he sees as the authors' intentions. He is assuming objective historicism for its own sake as the gold standard of historiography; yet, as others have argued, all history is contemporary. When Maimonides draws on historical evidence with considerable freedom, therefore, one may look to him not as an archivist but as a participant whose use and phrasing is of major importance to subsequent generations. If Maimonides expressed contempt for historical works—while citing historical events—this is itself historiographic. Yerushalmi argues that memories are preserved in ritual and liturgy, rendering them historiographical, a case he made splendidly in his own book *Haggadah and History* (Philadelphia, 1975). However, he also demands accuracy of his sources, succumbing to what R.G. Collingwood once criticized as the desire of some historians for the chronicler or even the poet to do the work of the historian. Both the chronicler and the poet produce what can be the raw data of the past. The attempt to understand it must be left to the historian's efforts and imagination. Furthermore, in Collingwood's view, history is interpreted not as a story of successive events but as an expression of thoughts. Yerushalmi rejects these expressions of thought and looks for facts about events. He continues to assert that the standard for evaluating the authors is their relation to historical knowledge when in fact they must be seen as a source of thought, which according to Collingwood is historical. Yerushalmi tests 16th-century Jewish historical writing against the other historical writing of the era and finds the Jewish efforts wanting. Nevertheless, he finds some changes in terms of a new appreciation of events for the present and future. Here he overlooks the fact that for medieval Jews their archetypal and midrashic presentation of events gave them meaning for the present and the future as well. Yerushalmi is stuck on the idea that in the 16th century there were Jewish historians, but in fact there were not—there were rabbis and poets who wrote historical books.

FUNKENSTEIN, picking up on criticism of the aspects of many implicit or explicit critiques of the distinction between history and memory, adds a third category to these discussions of history and memory: historical consciousness and awareness, or the creative imagination of the historian or writer. He argues that despite the absence of historiography, Jews never stopped thinking about history and that such thinking was not alien to collective memory. Following many writers on the personal nature of collective memory, such as G.W.F. Hegel and Maurice Halbwachs, Funkenstein argues that collective memory based on language expresses personal consciousness, distinct from both collective memory and historical memory. Historical consciousness begins with the present, so that the past is the remembered present and the future is the anticipated past. Funkenstein questions the notion that there was a rupture between historical consciousness and modern historiography. He dismisses Jewish medieval political history, because the Jews saw themselves as objects rather than subjects, a position that can be questioned by reading the various travelers' accounts. He also diminishes the importance in Jewish historiography of the role of archetypes and typologies in ancient and medieval Jewish literature, except in the works of Nahmanides. Funkenstein finds that historical detail plays a role in halakhic literature. The remainder of the book offers a fascinating discussion of the paradoxes and pitfalls of biblical, medieval, and modern historiographic writing.

In this important study of Jewish historiography, MEYER offers an introductory essay that traces the development of Jewish historiography from the ancient period through the Middle Ages, then focusing on the 16th and 17th centuries and including also the classics of 19th-century *Wissenschaft*, before concluding with recent Israeli and American writers. In his essay Meyer identifies the major themes of the material: the collective nature of Jewish identity, the theological component, problems of periodization, rabbinic interpretation,

and secularization. The bulk of the book is devoted to examples from each of the writers, many translated here for the first time. Meyer's introductions to each of the sections contain biographical as well as contextual information. Although many contemporary scholars have offered radical postmodern critiques of premodern Jewish historiography, Meyer's work endures as a classic introduction to the field.

RAPOPORT-ALBERT's collection of essays includes contributions on Jewish historiography by leading historians; three in particular are of importance in evaluating the views of Yerushalmi's work. Jacob Neusner notes that while the talmudic period was rich with historical crises, it produced what he calls an ahistorical canon or philosophical system. At first he searches rabbinic literature for useful historical information in the positivistic sense, the kind of information a military historian would look for: great affairs, vast territories, movements of men and nations, and individual motivations. Neusner, however, ends up using the word historical in two different senses, designating one "manifest" and the other "latent." He does recognize the Talmud as a profound statement of latent history, although he dismisses the Talmud as a historical document, that is, a source of positivistic information. By "latent history" he means trends and issues, and discussions of imagination, emotion, reason, and thought—in short, what could be called the collective mentality of the people.

Without using the actual term, Robert Chazan's essay suggests that medieval Jews had a sense of historical consciousness, seeing themselves as part of a tradition that stretched from Abraham to contemporary polemics concerning the true Israel. As examples of specific but eclipsed elements in this consciousness, he lists the land of Israel, the Davidic dynasty, and the Hebrew language. Details of all three facets of medieval Jewish life are consciously, perhaps not always realistically, described in travelers' accounts, which Chazan dismisses as a far-from-riveting depiction of daily events, suggesting that their authors did not see these elements as suspended but very much alive. Chazan sees the medieval Jewish historiographic enterprise as based on the use of biblical and rabbinic archetypes. He draws examples from liturgical compositions addressing Abraham's sacrifice of his son Isaac. Chazan does, however, carefully note in medieval texts instances of consciousness of discontinuity between contemporary events and previous periods, devoting particular attention to such aspects of Maimonides' writings.

Robert Bonfil's contribution offers one of the most critical approaches to Yerushalmi's book. He notes the absence of a definition of history and historiography in Yerushalmi, questions his assertion that Jewish historiography and history are relatively new products of the 19th century, and notes Yerushalmi's failure to write about external influences on Jewish historiography. Bonfil thus highlights Yerushalmi's notions that there was a sharp break in continuity between the premodern and modern world and that Jewish group memory is decaying. Thus Bonfil asserts that, according to Yerushalmi, in the premodern period history was subordinate to memory, a position that has reversed itself. He then presents Yerushalmi's discussion of Jewish historiography in the 16th and 17th centuries as an exception, the origins of which Yerushalmi attempts to explain as a result of the expulsion of the Jews from Spain, rather than analyze as a phenomenon. He then proceeds to demolish the notion that many of the titles referred to by Yerushalmi actually constitute works of history according to the standards of the period. Bonfil, however, falls into the positivistic trap of basing his definition of a work of history on whether it contains accurate facts and reads like a historical chronicle, specifically mentioning the examples of political and military history, rather than whether it was written with the purpose of explaining Jewish life.

HOWARD TZVI ADELMAN

See also History: Biblical Israel; History: General Histories, Modern Authors; History: Ideas of; History: Medieval; History: Modern; History: Second Temple Period; History: Talmudic Era

History: General Histories, Modern Authors

Baron, Salo Wittmayer, *A Social and Religious History of the Jews*, 3 vols., New York: Columbia University Press, 1937, 2nd edition, 18 vols., 1952–1983

Baskin, Judith (editor), *Jewish Women in Historical Perspective*, Detroit, Michigan: Wayne State University Press, 1991, 2nd edition, 1998

Ben-Sasson, Haim Hillel, *Toldot 'Am Yisra'el*, 1969; as *A History of the Jewish People*, Cambridge, Massachusetts: Harvard University Press, and London: Weidenfeld and Nicolson, 1976

Dubnow, Simon, *Istoriia evreiskogo naroda na vostoke*, n.d.; as *History of the Jews*, translated by Moshe Spiegel, 5 vols., South Brunswick, New Jersey: Yoseloff, 1967–1973

Finkelstein, Louis (editor), *The Jews: Their History, Culture, and Religion*, 2 vols., New York: Harper, 1949; 3rd edition, 1960; reprinted in 3 vols. as 4th edition, New York: Schocken, 1970

Graetz, Heinrich, *History of the Jews*, 6 vols., Philadelphia: Jewish Publication Society, and London: Nutt, 1891

Seltzer, Robert M., *Jewish People, Jewish Thought: The Jewish Experience in History*, New York: Macmillan, 1980

Stillman, Norman A., *The Jews of Arab Lands: A History and Source Book*, Philadelphia: Jewish Publication Society, 1979

GRAETZ is the premier example of 19th-century Jewish historiography and is one of the earliest and most significant Jewish histories written by a modern author. Originally written in German in 11 volumes, the English translation is condensed to six volumes that omit footnotes. While the German edition only goes as far as 1848, the English edition includes material up until 1870. A historical positivist who was influenced by Hegel and committed to the *Wissenschaft des Judentums*, the Jewish Enlightenment movement for the scientific study of Jewish history and literature, Graetz interprets Jewish history as revealing the destiny of a people. Jewish suffering, which

Graetz views as greater than that of any other historical group, is one significant mark of Jewish messianic destiny. Although Graetz was personally committed to Jewish emancipation, he firmly believed in Judaism's national character, evinced in what he views as the Jewish people's mission as living bearers of the unique religious and moral message of Judaism. Graetz was harshly criticized by virtually every intellectual faction in 19th-century Europe. His criticism of Christianity and Reform Judaism naturally alienated German Christians as well as prominent Reform Jews. German nationalist antisemitic thinkers used his argument that Judaism was a national religion as proof that Jews could not be integrated into the German nation. Orthodox leaders also criticized Graetz, denouncing him as an infidel and despising his historical analysis of Jewish law. Notwithstanding Graetz's interpretative biases, his *History of the Jews* endures as a pioneering monument of Jewish historiography.

The most recent edition of DUBNOW covers biblical times to the 1930s and concludes with material on American Jewry, the emergence of Nazism, and the Zionist settlement of the land of Israel. Dubnow describes his approach to Jewish historiography as sociological and universal, arguing that Jewish history is integral to the history of civilization as a whole. Like Graetz, Dubnow emerges from the *Wissenschaft des Judentums* tradition, stressing that Judaism can be formulated scientifically and that Jewish history can be understood as a process. Dubnow critiques Graetz's approach, however, arguing that Graetz reduces history to the two dominant motifs of Jewish martyrdom and intellectual creativity. The sociological method is presented as the appropriate corrective for what Dubnow views as a distortive and limited methodology. Dubnow conceives of the Jewish people as a nation but rejects political Jewish nationalism. As such, he maintains that Jewish history is both spiritual and social; Jews were a nation perhaps without a homeland, but they certainly had a national history and identity. In Dubnow's terms, the object of Jewish historiography is "the people, the national entity, its origin, growth, and struggle for existence," and the maintenance and defense of national integrity is the dominant theme of Jewish history. Dubnow is most commonly criticized by historians for disregarding contemporary Western European social scientific methodology in his historiography and for failing to substantially appreciate the effects of external forces on Jewish history. Dubnow's contribution to the development of Jewish history is particularly important as he provided a transition from 19th-century Jewish historiography (with its emphasis on historical process) to later 20th-century Jewish histories, which reject the assumption that Jewish history can furnish a unified interpretative structure.

BARON surveys Jewish history from ancient times until the late medieval period. The revised edition updates many of the sources and reevaluates some of Baron's historical analyses, particularly after the ancient period. Divided into three epochs, "Ancient Times," "High Middle Ages," and "Late Middle Ages and the Era of European Expansion," the history is incomplete, ending before consideration of the modern period. Individual volumes are not precisely chronological; instead, the organization prioritizes thematic analyses. Baron's emphasis is on the social, economic, political, and intellectual influences of Jewish history. For example, an entire volume is devoted to "Philosophy and Science" in the High Middle Ages, and a volume titled "Citizen or Alien Conjurer" focuses on Jewish social and political marginalization in the Late Middle Ages. Baron is especially interested in institutional and official influences. Several later historians balance this emphasis by exploring how closely different elements of society reflect official church or government interests. The sheer scope of this enormous history allows Baron to explore historical particularities and commonalities. He is appropriately sensitive to the national contexts in which Jewish communal histories emerge and is generally precise in limiting historical explanations and interpretations to specific countries during particular historical periods.

FINKELSTEIN ambitiously assumes the task of comprehensively offering an overview not only of Jewish history but also of culture and religion. This collection of essays by experts is divided into an extremely concise history of the Jewish people from the biblical period until 1945; an extensive section titled "The Role of Judaism in Civilization"; a fascinating albeit obsolete section on Jewish sociology; and an oddly brief section (composed of only one article by Finkelstein) titled "The Jewish Religion." The first section, which is oriented toward American Jews of Ashkenazi origin, includes essays on the biblical period, postbiblical Judaism, the talmudic period, European Jewish history until 1648, Jewish Western European history from 1648 until the beginning of World War II, and the Holocaust. As the chancellor of the Jewish Theological Seminary of America, Finkelstein's editorial voice speaks to an American Jewish community in welcome terms: rational faith, the miracle of Jewish survival, the contribution of the Jewish people to civilization, and the place of American Jews within the history of Jewry. While Finkelstein's work is in no way formative in terms of the development of Jewish historiography (as are the works of Graetz or even Dubnow), it was extremely influential during an important stage in the formation and evolution of the American Jewish community's self-identity in the 1960s and 1970s.

SELTZER presents an accessible and broad one-volume general history of the Jewish people. Beginning with the origins of the Israelites, this chronological history moves through the ancient, late antique, medieval, early modern, and modern periods. The discussion of each period is complemented by historical maps and chronological tables comparing general and Jewish history. Seltzer introduces the major philosophical and religious thinkers of each historical period, focusing on those persons, events, and movements that Jewish historians have traditionally positioned as significant. The author also comments on the development of Jewish historiography, relating the evolution of this discipline to historical events and intellectual movements. He demonstrates the synergistic relationship between Jewish history, the Jewish people's understanding of that history, and the development of Jewish historiography. Seltzer's strength is his ability to introduce the reader to Jewish history by framing that history in terms of particular biographies, schools of thought, or political movements. While this strategy risks being distortive as elitist, Seltzer conscientiously balances this tendency by expanding his discussion to include groups that resist or are unaffected by social, religious,

and intellectual reforms. The result is a succinct and balanced overview of political, social, cultural, religious and intellectual Jewish history.

BEN-SASSON offers an overview of Jewish history from the biblical period to the 20th century. Focusing on religious, political, social, and economic factors, the text is organized into six individually authored, chronological sections. Essays on the ancient and classical periods—from before the Israelite conquest of Canaan through the postbiblical and talmudic eras and closing in 640 C.E.—are essentially chronological. The chapters dealing with the medieval and modern period are thematic. Thus, in the Middle Ages section, the author (Ben-Sasson himself) includes a chapter on Jewish communal autonomy, and in the modern period section the author (S. Ettinger) includes a chapter on antisemitism and the appearance of antisemitic political parties. The well-formulated medieval section emphasizes cultural history, particularly the tensions and interplay between Jews and gentiles. Almost one third of the more than 1,100 pages is devoted to the comprehensively chronicled modern period. Ettinger surveys modern Jewish history from the late 17th century until the Yom Kippur war of 1973. As a whole, the global perspective of Ben-Sasson's collection and the attention paid to recent scholarship has contributed to its well-deserved status as one of the standard modern works of Jewish history.

STILLMAN presents an excellent overview of Arab Jewry until the beginning of the modern period, which he addresses specifically in his sequel, Jews of Arab Lands in Modern Times. He presents an illuminating selection of previously unavailable archival sources, along with photographs, letters, diary entries, newspaper articles, and government documents, offering a richly textured portrait of the Jewish experience in Islamic societies. Beginning with Muhammad and early Muslim attitudes toward Jews, Stillman's historical narrative moves through the Middle Ages and closes with the 19th century. Stillman focuses on the development of Jewish communities, with attention to how Arab culture, thought, and history shaped the Jewish experience in these areas. He is particularly effective in his historical presentation of the development of tensions between Arab and Jewish communities. Stillman's portrayal of the diversity and vibrancy of these Arab Jewish communities makes for an accessible and engaging narrative that has quickly become the standard work on Arab Jewry and has been lauded as much for its balanced tone as for its deft presentation of an extremely complex set of relationships.

BASKIN is the only substantial text to present the history of Jewish women from the biblical period until the 20th century. While the essays are not chronologically comprehensive, they are extremely successful as a whole in pointing out the breadth of the history of Jewish women. The collection unites the work of many preeminent scholars working in areas relating to women and Judaism, and it addresses topics and themes from throughout Jewish history, including biblical, rabbinic, medieval, and modern material from both the Sephardi and Ashkenazi traditions in key Jewish communities ranging from Eastern and Western Europe to North America and Israel. The variety of Jewish women's experiences is selectively explored, combining intellectual, social, cultural, and political histories. The second edition underscores this diversity by adding four essays that explore specific cultural histories, namely Israeli, English, French, and Eastern European experiences. It is unfortunate that Joan Ringelheim's "Women and the Holocaust: A Reconsideration of Research," which appeared in the first edition, is omitted in the second; the collection would be complemented by an essay exploring the gendered experiences of the Holocaust. Nevertheless, both the study of women and Judaism and Jewish historical scholarship are much enhanced by this remarkable anthology.

DEIDRE BUTLER

See also History: Biblical Israel; History: General Histories, Premodern Authors; History: Ideas of; History: Medieval; History: Modern; History: Second Temple Period; History: Talmudic Era

History: Biblical Israel

Ahlström, Gösta W., *The History of Ancient Palestine from the Palaeolithic Period to Alexander's Conquest*, Sheffield, South Yorkshire: JSOT, 1993; as *The History of Ancient Palestine*, Minneapolis, Minnesota: Fortress, 1993; 2nd edition, 1994

Bright, John, *A History of Israel*, Philadelphia: Westminster, 1959; London: SCM, 1960; 3rd edition, 1981

Freedman, David Noel and David Frank Graf (editors), *Palestine in Transition: The Emergence of Ancient Israel* (Social World of Biblical Antiquity Series, vol. 2), Sheffield, South Yorkshire: Almond, 1983

Fritz, Volkmar and Philip R. Davies (editors), *The Origins of the Ancient Israelite States*, Sheffield, South Yorkshire: Sheffield Academic Press, 1996

Grabbe, Lester L. (editor), *Can a "History of Israel" Be Written?*, Sheffield, South Yorkshire: Sheffield Academic Press, 1997

Hayes, John H. and James Maxwell Miller (editors), *Israelite and Judaean History*, Philadelphia: Westminster, and London: SCM, 1977

Miller, James Maxwell and John H. Hayes, *A History of Ancient Israel and Judah*, Philadelphia: Westminster, and London: SCM, 1986

Noth, Martin, *The History of Israel*, New York: Harper and Row, and London: Black, 1958; 2nd edition, 1960

Two assumptions undergird BRIGHT's history of Israel. First, he is confident that the Bible is a legitimate source for reconstructing the history of ancient Israel. Second, he believes this confidence to be supported by the results of archaeological excavations that Bright understands as supporting the historical value of biblical narratives. The consequences of Bright's approach is most obvious in his presentation of the patriarchal narratives (Genesis 12–50). He concludes that the biblical narratives are historical works since they reflect the social and economic situation of the second millennium B.C.E. as reflected in ancient Near Eastern sources. Although none of these sources mentions any of the patriarchs, Bright maintains that there is a "balance of probability" indicating that the bib-

lical patriarchs were historical figures. While Bright asserts that it is not possible to be too precise in reconstructing the events that led to the settlement of the Israelite tribes in Canaan, he clearly favors the conquest model.

Bright does more than offer a reconstruction of ancient Israelite history, he also sketches the development of ancient Israelite theology. The contours of the picture Bright draws show his debt to the biblical theology movement, which considers it axiomatic that the events narrated in the Bible actually happened and that the history of ancient Israel be regarded as "salvation history." Bright characterizes both Judaism and Christianity as two possible "destinations" for ancient Israel's history. While Bright's contribution to this history of Israel was an important one in his day, the value of his approach to ancient Israelite history needs careful reexamination in light of the current state of both historical and archaeological scholarship. Its theological orientation makes this work still very influential, however, among more conservative Christian readers.

NOTH offers a perspective on the history of early Israel far different from that of Bright. He believes that the traditions about the patriarchs and Moses offer nothing that the historian can use in reconstructing the history of Israel. This sharp divergence from Bright's approach spawned what became an acrimonious debate between the two scholars that was broken off after Bright accused Noth of historical nihilism for his refusal to consider the stories of the patriarchs and the Exodus as historical in the technical sense. Noth indeed considered the history of Israel as beginning with the tribal league.

The most distinctive and influential feature of Noth's history of Israel is his theory of an Israelite amphictyony. He holds that Israel's tribes organized themselves in a federal structure analogous to the classical amphictyony (an association of neighboring states in defense of a religious center). This theory enables Noth to discuss the settlement period, a notoriously difficult component of Israelite history. In addition, the amphictyony supplies a context within which to locate Israelite religious, social, and political institutions as well as the early stages of the formation of the Pentateuch. Noth considers premonarchic Israel to be a religious entity—the covenant people of God. The theory of an Israelite tribal league makes it possible for Noth to describe an institutional form for this religious entity. While scholars have not abandoned Noth's theory of an Israelite amphictyony completely, they do not use it as comprehensively as he did. Current scholarship has focused its attention on the family and the clan rather than on the tribe as the basic social units of premonarchic Israel.

There have been several attempts to write a history of Israel without the theological biases evident in the Bible. The most comprehensive of these is the posthumously published work of AHLSTRÖM. Still, this book is markedly traditional in its basic understanding of history as an idealistic account of the political and military activities of significant individuals. This is precisely the way the Bible presents the story of Israel. Since there is no corroboration for the biblical account of the premonarchic period, the author asserts that the historian is not on firm ground until the time of David and Solomon. His reconstruction of the early history of Israel differs substantially from the biblical account, while his reconstruction of the time of the monarchy is less radical than other recent histories.

Ahlström devotes three full chapters to the Bronze Age in Palestine. The data presented in these chapters is almost exclusively archaeological. He does discuss Abraham in an excursus and concludes that the biblical stories about him come from a much later date and do not reflect the sociopolitical situation of Bronze Age Palestine. Particularly telling in the patriarchal narratives is the absence of any allusion to Egyptian hegemony in the region. The distinctive feature of Ahlström's presentation is his consistent emphasis on seeing the history of ancient Israel against the wider backdrop of ancient Near Eastern history.

HAYES and MILLER have edited a volume of essays that discuss the problems in writing a history of ancient Israel. Individual essays cover each period from the patriarchs to the coming of the Romans. Two periods that receive attention are the patriarchal and settlement periods—eras that continued to raise difficulties for historians. After an essay by John Hayes on approaches to reconstructing Israel's history, from the earliest attempts to current endeavors, the problems of writing the history of early Israel become evident. While William Dever and W. Malcolm Clark find archaeological data sufficient to conclude that the Middle Bronze Age provides the background for the patriarchal narratives, Thomas Thompson holds that these stories are late literary inventions. J. Maxwell Miller provides a convenient summary of theories regarding the Israelite occupation of Canaan; he asserts that the process by which Israel acquired the land was not a pan-Israel invasion and took place over a long period, though the core of the Israelite community was settled in Canaan by 1200 to 1000 B.C.E. The essays dealing with periods from the monarchy to the coming of the Romans to Palestine show that these eras do not involve such serious methodological issues as does the early history of Israel. The principal issue is how to integrate the results of archaeology into any historical reconstruction, but several of the essays make little or no reference to archaeological data. Their historical reconstructions depend solely on literary sources: the Bible and ancient Near Eastern texts.

While the essays in the Miller and Hayes collection show that there are some methodological issues that any historian of ancient Israel needs to face, GRABBE has edited a volume of essays originating in a seminar that dealt directly with methodological concerns. Lester Grabbe's own essay asserts that a history of Israel can be written with the Bible as a resource. Still, he notes the difficulties attendant to using the Bible for historical reconstruction and suggests that historians indicate the probability of any reconstruction. Other essays describe developments in the field of historiographical study and the ambiguity of terms such as "Israel" and "history writing." Herbert Niehr's essay differentiates among the various sources that the historian can use and the methodological issues related to each type of source. In many instances biblical texts are secondary or even tertiary sources. Highlighting the problems that come with basing any historical reconstruction solely on written sources, this volume underscores the need for developing a more archaeologically and geographically based historiography, as suggested by Thomas Thompson's essay.

In addition to the collected essays they edited, MILLER and HAYES have produced a history of Israel from the period of the Judges to the fall of the Persian Empire. They forego any attempt at reconstructing the patriarchal and Mosaic periods after discussing the problems that face the historian. For the most part, this is a history of the ancient Israelite nation states. This volume is geared toward nonprofessionals and is augmented by many charts, maps, illustrations, and translations of relevant ancient Near Eastern texts that illuminate the authors' narrative. They use the Bible as one source in their historical reconstruction, but they do depart from its presentation when other sources require it. They are also careful to include data from archaeology when appropriate. While this volume does not deal directly with the methodological issues raised by the Grabbe volume, it does not use the Bible as uncritically as earlier histories tended to do.

FREEDMAN and GRAF have edited a collection of essays that deal with the differing historical reconstructions of how the ancient Israelites came to control the land that became the locus of their subsequent history. There are essays by William Stiebing, John Halligan, Norman Gottwald, and Marvin Chaney. These essays are sympathetic to the hypothesis of George Mendenhall, who holds that there was no violent conquest of Canaan. Ancient Israel emerged as the result of a peasants' revolt against social, political, and economic exploitation by the city-states of Canaan. The final essay is by Mendenhall, who describes how he has refined his original thesis and why he rejects the development of his views by Norman Gottwald, who uses a Marxian model for interpreting the early history of Israel. One feature that all the essays share is the attempt to place the developments in 13th- and 12th-century Canaan into a larger historical, geographical, and sociological framework.

While Mendenhall's hypothesis has proven to be an attractive alternative to the conquest model defended by Bright and the infiltration model offered by Noth, there are questions about the viability of his reconstruction of the situation in Canaan in the Late Bronze Age. There simply does not seem to be enough evidence of a disaffected peasant population that was ready to withdraw its loyalty from the political structures of Canaan. Similarly, questions arise about how Israel emerged from a supposedly diverse body of disaffected peasants. Another question raised by Mendenhall's hypothesis is the origin of the idea of an invasion from abroad, which is central to the biblical presentation of the settlement.

While the question of Israelite origins occupied historians for most of the 20th century, a new issue has stirred up much controversy among both historians and archaeologists. It is the issue of the "united monarchy." FRITZ and DAVIES have edited a collection of essays focusing on the formation of the Israelite and Judean states. Some scholars hold that there was a united kingdom, composed of the Israelite and Judahite tribes, extending its influence through most of the eastern Mediterranean region in the tenth century B.C.E. This united kingdom later split into two states: a northern and a southern kingdom. Others maintain that the biblical narratives about Saul, David, and Solomon are fiction and that the kingdoms of Israel and Judah were never united. Essays by Thomas Thompson and Baruch Halpern are methodological discussions about archaeology, literature, and history. Three essays deal with the social organization of the Israelite state.

Christa Schäfer-Lichtenberger compares the sociological and biblical views of the early Israelite state. Niels Peter Lemche asserts that the patronage society—not the nation state—was the next stage in complexity after the Israelite tribal society. David Hopkins discusses the problems in reconstructing the economic system of an ancient society. The collection concludes with five essays that center on the principal biblical characters of the early monarchy: Saul, David, and Solomon. The essays in this volume offer sharply divergent viewpoints. This reflects the current state of scholarship on the early Israelite monarchy. There is little consensus on even the most basic questions. The debate has become more intense since the discovery of an inscription at Tel Dan, which is read by some as referring to a king of the "house of David." Questions have been raised not only about the reading of the inscription but also about its authenticity.

LESLIE J. HOPPE

See also History: General Histories, Modern Authors; History: General Histories, Premodern Authors; History: Ideas of; History: Medieval; History: Modern; History: Second Temple Period; History: Talmudic Era; Israel, Land of: History

History: Second Temple Period

Cohen, Shaye J.D., *From the Maccabees to the Mishnah* (Library of Early Christianity, 7), Philadelphia: Westminster, 1987

Feldman, Louis H., *Josephus and Modern Scholarship (1937–1980)*, New York: de Gruyter, 1984

Hengel, Martin, *Judaism and Hellenism: Studies in Their Encounter in Palestine during the Early Hellenistic Period*, 2 vols., Philadelphia: Fortress, and London: SCM, 1974

Kraft, Robert A. and G.W.E. Nickelsburg (editors), *Early Judaism and Its Modern Interpreters* (The Bible and Its Modern Interpreters, 2), Atlanta, Georgia: Scholars Press, 1986

Kuhnen, Hans-Peter, *Palästina in Griechisch-Römischer Zeit*, Munich: Beck, 1990

Schürer, Emil, *The History of the Jewish People in the Age of Jesus Christ (175 B.C.–A.D. 135)*, edited by Géza Vermès and Fergus Millar, 3 vols., Edinburgh: Clark, 1973–1986

Stemberger, Günter, *Jewish Contemporaries of Jesus: Pharisees, Sadducees, Essenes*, Minneapolis, Minnesota: Fortress, 1995

VanderKam, James C., *The Dead Sea Scrolls Today*, Grand Rapids, Michigan: Eerdmans, 1994

The "Second Temple period" spans almost 600 years between the rebuilding of the Temple of Jerusalem by Jewish exiles who had returned from Babylonia in the 530s and 520s B.C.E. and the destruction of the Temple by the Romans in 70 C.E. Characteristic of this period of Jewish history is the continuous interaction between Jewish and other civilizations (most prominently Hellenism) in both the political and the cultural

arena. A study of this interaction, and especially of the rich variety and dynamic nature of Jewish responses to the demands of an increasingly cosmopolitan world, has long occupied a central place in scholarly studies devoted to this period.

COHEN investigates the period from the 160s B.C.E. to the early second century C.E. in a very readable and up-to-date study aimed at both beginning students and well-advanced scholars. In addition to describing the political events that mark this period, Cohen provides insightful discussions of Jewish religious practices and beliefs during this time, the history of the various Jewish communal institutions and sectarian movements, and an elucidation of the complicated issue of the canonization of Scripture. With a glossary and suggestions for further reading, this book succeeds in drawing a truly accessible and comprehensive picture of the transformations in the Jewish community from post-exilic times to the emergence of rabbinic Judaism.

FELDMAN presents a thorough critical bibliography of modern scholarship on Josephus, the author whose writings form the single most important source of literary information on the Second Temple period. Arranged topically, this rich bibliography addresses all the major aspects of Josephus's work, including his accomplishments as a historian, his activities as a "rewriter" of the Hebrew Bible, his relationship to and depiction of Jewish law and Jewish religious practices, as well as the various text editions and the history of transmission of Josephus's writings. Each item includes a summary of the book or article cited, providing readers with a quick and reliable means to familiarize themselves with the various issues addressed by Josephus and with recent scholarly discussions on the ways in which Josephus has treated such issues.

HENGEL's lengthy study argues that the cultural differences between the Jewish communities in the Land of Israel and those in the diaspora (particularly in Egypt) were much smaller than has commonly been assumed. Presenting a systematic analysis of practically all the available primary sources, Hengel also argues that a substantial Hellenization of the Jews in the Land of Israel had occured long before the Maccabean Revolt. Written in the 1970s with an eye to a scholarly audience, this study continues to occupy a central place in the study of the Hellenization of Second Temple Judaism.

KRAFT and NICKELSBURG have published a collection of essays by leading scholars in the field of Second Temple Judaism. Subject headings include "Historical Settings," "Recent Discoveries," and "The Literature." Each scholar presents an up-to-date review of the state of knowledge in his or her respective field of expertise, with excellent references to further scholarly literature. Especially useful is the easy access it provides to the various types of literature deriving from this period, including rewritten bibles, the so-called testament literature, apocalyptic, wisdom literature, and Jewish historiography. Also included is a short discussion of the Samaritans and an extensive survey of Jewish numismatics.

KUHNEN has composed a richly illustrated and bibliographically well documented study of the archaeology of the land of Israel during the Hellenistic and Roman periods. Discussing monumental architecture, including palaces and theaters, domestic architecture, funerary architecture, and small finds, in addition to questions of chronology, Kuhnen documents the interaction between local and Greco-Roman civilization on the level of material culture over a period that spans almost a millennium. Kuhnen furthermore elaborates on the history of archaeological research in this part of the ancient Near East. In the appendixes, discussions of Jewish numismatic evidence and of the physical remains bearing on the Nabateans have been included.

SCHÜRER's classic study of the history of the Jews in the time of Jesus, which was originally published in German in 1886 and which has since been translated into English and thoroughly updated by a team of well-known scholars, provides readers with a systematically arranged account that addresses virtually all aspects of Jewish history during the Second Temple period. It includes discussions of the political developments that affected the Jewish community and the various types of literature produced at the time, and it also includes an extensive, up-to-date presentation of the evidence bearing on the Dead Sea Scrolls and the Qumran community. Of encyclopedic scope and generally reliable, Schürer's three-volume *tour de force* is a work originally conceived from a Christian theological point of view onto which has been grafted comprehensive nonpartisan modernization in the form of massive footnoting.

STEMBERGER has written a study that critically investigates the present state of knowledge concerning the various Jewish sectarian groups that are known to have played a role in the history of the land of Israel during first centuries B.C.E. and C.E. Discussing at length the evidence contained in the writings of Josephus, the New Testament, and rabbinic literature and using this evidence to describe the ways in which Pharisaic, Sadducean, and Essene ideology and theology differed, Stemberger also presents a sensible discussion of the question of whether the rabbis of the post–70 C.E. era should be regarded as the direct successors to and intellectual heirs of the Pharisees. Concision notwithstanding, this is one of the most balanced accounts of this issue currently available.

VANDERKAM presents an easy-to-read introduction to the study of the Dead Sea Scrolls. Addressing all the major issues, VanderKam first describes the discovery of these documents and the archaeological methods used to reconstruct them, and then proceeds to present a systematic discussion of the contents of various manuscripts retrieved in and around Qumran. VanderKam also explores the strengths and weaknesses of the theory that associates the Qumran community with the so-called Essenes. He concludes his survey with a discussion of how the Qumran discoveries have affected understanding of the text of both the Hebrew Bible and the New Testament. Each chapter contains a bibliographical note with suggestions for further reading.

LEONARD VICTOR RUTGERS

See also History: Biblical Israel; History: General Histories, Modern Authors; History: General Histories, Premodern Authors; History: Ideas of; History: Medieval; History: Modern; History: Talmudic Era; Israel, Land of: History

History: Talmudic Era

Alon, Gedalia, *Toldot ha-Yehudim be-Erets-Yisra'el bi-tekufat ha-Mishnah veha-Talmud,* 1952; edited and translated by Gershon Levi as *The Jews in Their Land in the Talmudic Age (70–640 C.E.),* 2 vols., Jerusalem: Magnes Press of Hebrew University, 1980

Hauptman, Judith, *Rereading the Rabbis: A Woman's Voice,* Boulder, Colorado: Westview, 1997

Jaffee, Martin, *Early Judaism,* Upper Saddle River, New Jersey: Prentice-Hall, 1997

Kalmin, Richard, *The Sage in Jewish Society of Late Antiquity,* New York: Routledge, 1999

Kraemer, Ross, "Jewish Women in the Diaspora World of Late Antiquity," in *Jewish Women in Historical Perspective,* edited by Judith Baskin, 2nd edition, Detroit, Michigan: Wayne State University Press, 1998

Neusner, Jacob, *A History of the Jews in Babylonia,* 5 vols., Leiden: Brill, 1965–1970

Peskowitz, Miriam B., *Spinning Fantasies: Rabbis, Gender, and History,* Berkeley: University of California Press, 1997

Schiffman, Lawrence H., *From Text to Tradition: A History of Second Temple and Rabbinic Judaism,* Hoboken, New Jersey: Ktav, 1991

Yerushalmi, Yosef Hayim, "Biblical and Rabbinic Foundations: Meaning in History, Memory, and the Writing of History," in his *Zakhor: Jewish History and Jewish Memory,* Seattle: University of Washington Press, 1982

The talmudic era, beginning with the Second Temple's destruction in 70 C.E. and extending to the Islamic conquest of Mesopotamia in 634, is the common focus of the diverse studies considered here. Four are comprehensive treatments; the others are more specialized. All represent historical approaches to Judaism in a broad sense that does not entail a narrative of events. As Yerushalmi notes, "the history of the talmudic period itself cannot be elicited from its own vast literature."

SCHIFFMAN provides the most comprehensive history, beginning with the Hebrew Bible and ending with the Talmud and Midrash. His is the most straightforward chronological narrative and is easy to read. The author provides tables, notes, and a glossary as well as the expected index and bibliography.

ALON was constructed by his students out of lecture notes that cover the historical outline of the period and include detailed discussions of subjects that interested the rabbis. The English translation is clear, with a minimum of unexplained terms. There is no glossary, however, and some passages may be hard going for the uninitiated. Alon wrote when most scholars assumed that the rabbis ruled in this era, that the only Judaism was rabbinic Judaism. While the subject matter is determined by rabbinic literature, Alon brings vast erudition in other sources from the period, including Greek and Latin literature and documentary papyri. His topical approach tends to leave some periods uncovered and to assume that the details are valid for the whole period unless contradicted by other evidence.

JAFFEE defines the period 450 B.C.E. to 650 C.E. as the era of early Judaism, and he examines Judaism in a frame that is geographically the broadest of the four general histories discussed here. His short book is notable for recognizing that Jewish history includes both men and women. Jaffee is committed to the topical approach, by which he conveys the changing religious worlds of the varieties of Judaism. His topics include social and political aspects as well as the symbolic structure implied by conceptions of Judaism. Jaffee covers ritual spaces and performances; traditional text as written and transmitted; and the transformative knowledge of sages, mystics, and visionaries.

KRAEMER also takes a sophisticated look at topics, with ensuing difficulties similar to those faced by Alon and Jaffee. Her topics are determined by the available nonrabbinic information. Kraemer introduces the reader to a number of women by name, as they are known from inscriptions, papyri, and literature. Areas discussed include women's economic lives, education, synagogue life and other religious practices, and public activity. The usual topics of marriage, motherhood, male–female relationships, and control by men are also considered. Kraemer is concerned with the reliability of her evidence as history, and her article is interspersed with brief methodological discussions.

PESKOWITZ writes about women as well as men in Judaism of the Roman period. She considers both "a history in which women were present and a historiography in which women have been absent." Her book is an intriguing if meandering conversation about historical topics made new by the way in which she asks questions of the material. Peskowitz develops a delightful invitation to participate in thinking through the implications of historical evidence for the period. She is careful to explain any terms that might be unfamiliar; she demands of her readers a great deal of thought rather than a great deal of erudition.

KALMIN is a straightforward attempt to persuade the reader of his thesis. He argues (in contrast to Neusner's portrayal of close and constant contact, as discussed below) that the rabbis of the Babylonian Talmud were much more aloof from the nonrabbinic classes than the rabbis portrayed in the Palestinian Talmud. He points out that the pervasive differences between the two Talmuds support the historicity of the contrasting traditions in each. According to Kalmin, though, the precise extent of the differences is difficult to gauge. Kalmin's style is clear and almost lawyerly: he lays out his thesis at the beginning of the work, and each chapter buttresses his points from a different perspective. To add strength to his argument, Kalmin explores the interpretive, or exegetical, differences between the Jewish communities of Babylonia and those of Israel, discussing the rabbis' literary treatment of David, Moses, and Ahitophel. Kalmin does demonstrate that there are differences, although this is not the strongest aspect of his discussion.

NEUSNER has anticipated Kalmin's question about the degree of separation of the talmudic sages from the rest of Jewish society, and Neusner has come to a different answer. In his dissection of the chronological layers of the Babylonian Talmud, Neusner narrates a history derived from the Talmud but woven together with nontalmudic information about the Parthian and Sassanian (post–224 C.E.) rulers of Persian Babylonia and their culture. He notes that rabbinic

leaders held positions that entailed supervising the markets, for example, which would not tend to isolate them within their own aristocratic class. Neusner's five volumes provide a coherent narrative of the development of rabbinic Judaism in Babylonia from the late Persian Period through the final redaction of the Babylonia Talmud (circa 600 C.E.). As a coherent narrative, it is a worthwhile aid to cognitive appropriation of the activities and concerns of the rabbis; it is by no means a work of demonstrable historical truth, and Neusner himself has famously come to doubt the possibilities for historical reconstruction entertained by his early publications.

HAUPTMAN's understanding of history is indexed by change observed at particular points over several millennia. She typically compares original biblical expressions of the law with later interpretations, noting changes and transformations in interpretation representative of the talmudic era. She demonstrates that within the limits of their patriarchal system, the rabbis sought to lessen the severity of laws dealing with women. Her style is wonderfully open; she represents the positions of others with care and appreciation of valid if uncongenial arguments.

YERUSHALMI provides a summary essay covering a very long span of time with memorable phrases and sentences on every page. Yerushalmi enjoins the reader to remember and yet there is no history and no memorized narrative sequence past the time that the Bible ends. The extant sources, after Josephus (c.37–101 C.E.), are not concerned with narratives of events. As Yerushalmi interprets it, history is made plain in the prophetic telling of God's role in biblical events. Without the prophetic voice telling the story of God and God's people, there is no narrative history.

SIGRID PETERSON

See also History: Biblical Israel; History: General Histories, Modern Authors; History: General Histories, Premodern Authors; History: Ideas of; History: Medieval; History: Modern; History: Second Temple Period

History: Medieval

Ashtor, Eliyahu, *The Jews of Moslem Spain,* 3 vols., Philadelphia: Jewish Publication Society, 1973–1984

Baer, Yitzhak F., *Toldot ha-Yehudim bi-Sefarad ha-Notsrit,* 1959; translated by L. Schoffman as *A History of the Jews in Christian Spain,* 2 vols., Philadelphia: Jewish Publication Society, 1961–1966

Chazan, Robert, *European Jewry and the First Crusade,* Berkeley: University of California Press, 1987

Cohen, Gerson D. (editor), *A Critical Edition with a Translation and Notes of the Book of Tradition (Sefer ha-qabbalah),* Philadelphia: Jewish Publication Society, 1967; London: Routledge and Kegan Paul, 1969

Cohen, Jeremy, *The Friars and the Jews: The Evolution of Medieval Anti-Judaism,* Ithaca, New York: Cornell University Press, 1982

Cohen, Mark R., *Jewish Self Government in Medieval Egypt: The Origins of the Office of the Head of the Jews*

(Princeton Studies on the Near East), Princeton, New Jersey, and Guildford, Surrey: Princeton University Press, 1980

Goitein, Shelomo Dov, *A Mediterranean Society: The Jewish Communities of the Arab World as Portrayed in the Documents of the Cairo Geniza*, 6 vols., Berkeley: University of California Press, 1967–1993

Katz, Jacob, *Exclusiveness and Tolerance* (Scripta Judaica, 3), London: Oxford University Press, and New York: Behrman House, 1961

Langmuir, Gavin, *History, Religion, and Antisemitism*, Berkeley: University of California Press, and London: Tauris, 1990

Langmuir, Gavin, *Toward a Definition of Antisemitism*, Berkeley: University of California Press, 1990

Marcus, Ivan G., *Piety and Society: The Jewish Pietists of Medieval Germany* (Études sur le judaisme médiéval, 10), Leiden: Brill, 1981

Stillman, Norman, *The Jews of Arab Lands: A History and Source Book*, Philadelphia: Jewish Publication Society, 1979

Stow, Kenneth, *Alienated Minority: The Jews of Medieval Latin Europe*, Cambridge, Massachusetts: Harvard University Press, 1992

Jewish life during the Middle Ages took place in three distinct spheres: Italy and Northern Europe, the Iberian Peninsula, and the Islamic world stretching from Baghdad to Morocco. The historiographies of these three regions differ sharply, but in all three cases historians generally recount a story of initial religious toleration eventually followed by assault and expulsion. In these standard histories, the Jews are portrayed as fundamentally passive, and the internal life of Jewish communities is typically depicted as hermetically sealed, virtually untouched by cultural exchanges. These images require, and are slowly achieving, revision in order to acknowledge dialectical interaction between Jewish and non-Jewish communities on all planes. Similarly, the histories of Islamic territories that describe tranquil relationships between Jews and Muslims until the dawn of early modern times must be modified to recognize more fully the tensions in the Judeo-Islamic experience.

BAER's comprehensive work discusses Jewish communal, intellectual, and political life, with extensive coverage of religious issues. Baer contends that there is a unity of the Jewish people in all ages and that their entire "history . . . constitutes an organic unit." Furthermore, he assumes a moralizing position, asserting that the wealthy are skeptics, Aristotelians, and prone to conversion, while the poor are pious, mystical, and faithful. Although it has been the subject of a number of articulate challenges, this text remains worthwhile and provocative.

Gerson COHEN's rewarding translation of a traditional chronicle includes highly erudite footnotes and copious endnotes, as well as an exemplary introduction and further discussion. He paints a lasting portrait of Spanish Jewish grandeur in the so-called Golden Age, even as he emphasizes

the significance of tensions and crisis, rather than dwelling on specific cultural achievements or moments of glory.

ASHTOR's idealized descriptions are less insightful than the analysis offered by Gerson Cohen, but GOITEIN's enormous survey of all aspects of Mediterranean Jewish life is a synthesis of great and enduring value that organizes a vast quantity of difficult-to-read documentation in Judeo-Arabic drawn from the Cairo Genizah. Goitein's attempts to reconstruct Jewish family life in volume three are seemingly descriptive, but they also effectively answer the basic questions posed by other scholars studying the history of the family and provide a foundation for an array of detailed future research projects.

A judicious collection of documents and commentary, STILLMAN's work excels in its description of the conflict between Muhammad and the Jews, a little-known episode that is pregnant with implications for modern Jewish-Muslim relations.

Mark COHEN's history of Egyptian Jewry in the High Middle Ages may be the sole in-depth study of Jewish communal control in a specific Judeo-Islamic setting. Based on rabbinic literature and Genizah documents, the book probes traditional questions of social organization and studies the respective status of Jews and Muslims in the region.

STOW presents the first overview of European Jewish life in the Middle Ages (including Italy and sometimes Spain) since Ben-Sasson's dramatic nationalistic accounts of the 1960s, which depicted a church-driven history of cultural exchanges alternating with persecution. Stow portrays Jewish life against the background of Christian piety; discusses the significance of the emergence of monarchies whose foundations were at least as spiritual as they were secular; and analyzes the Jewish immersion (albeit not submersion) in medieval culture as a whole.

KATZ's classic study of Jewish-Christian relations traces Ashkenazi attitudes toward Christianity, emphasizing in particular how Jews moved from perceiving Christianity as a kind of idolatry toward recognizing Christian monotheism. Katz identifies the dangers inherent in this change and explains why Jews at the turn of the 14th century were not quick to accept its first expressions by Menahem Me'iri.

Jeremy COHEN's book has garnered enormous attention for its thorough discussion of Christian Hebraist products of the 13th century. Especially useful are lengthy excerpts from the *Pugio fidei* (1278) of Ramon Marti (Raymond Martini). Much debate has been inspired by Cohen's insistent statement of the thesis that the mendicant orders aroused Christian society against Judaism, as the orders sought to convert the Jews or have them expelled.

LANGMUIR (1990a, 1990b) must be seen as two halves of a whole. The first book is a long, sociological attempt to identify the seat of antisemitism in what Langmuir defines as the irrational, specifically in accusations of ritual murder leveled against Jews. While Langmuir is perhaps overly careful in the distinction he draws between the "irrational" and the "nonrational" elements of the anti-Jewish myths and canards of the Middle Ages, the often brilliant essays in his second volume are not limited by such strict definitions. It is debatable, however, whether the sharp break Langmuir would make between anti-Judaism and antisemitism helps or hinders his analysis.

MARCUS presents a thorough study of the doctrine and social organization of the Hasidei Ashkenaz. The book investigates two competing theses: first, that these "Hasidim" (not to be confused with the modern hasidic movement) were a continuity of early Italo-Ashkenazi culture; second, that they were extremists, propagating wholly untenable pietistic ideals, which Eleazar of Worms eventually domesticated, thereby introducing an ascetic element into later Ashkenazi practice.

Surprisingly, CHAZAN is the first book to deal at length with the history of the First Crusade and the Jews. Its intensive exposition of Hebrew texts brought the topic to the attention of a wide audience for the first time; previously, only a few readers of late-19th-century German editions and translations were aware of the relevant literature. Chazan's readings are highly faithful to the literal meanings of the medieval chronicles, but this faithfulness often results in interpretative inconsistency.

KENNETH STOW

See also History: Biblical Israel; History: General Histories, Modern Authors; History: General Histories, Premodern Authors; History: Ideas of; History: Modern; History: Second Temple Period; History: Talmudic Era

History: Modern

Goldscheider, Calvin and Alan S. Zuckerman, *The Transformation of the Jews* (Chicago Studies in the History of Judaism), Chicago: University of Chicago Press, 1984

Hyman, Paula, *Gender and Assimilation in Modern Jewish History: The Roles and Representation of Women* (Samuel and Althea Stroum Lectures in Jewish Studies), Seattle: University of Washington Press, 1995

Katz, Jacob, *Out of the Ghetto: The Social Background of Jewish Emancipation, 1770–1870*, Cambridge, Massachusetts: Harvard University Press, 1973

Mendes-Flohr, Paul and Jehuda Reinharz (editors), *The Jew in the Modern World: A Documentary History*, New York: Oxford University Press, 1980, 2nd edition, 1995

Neusner, Jacob, *Death and Birth of Judaism: The Impact of Christianity, Secularism, and the Holocaust on Jewish Faith*, New York: Basic Books, 1987

Sachar, Howard, *The Course of Modern Jewish History*, Cleveland, Ohio: World, and London: Weidenfeld, 1958; new revised edition, New York: Vintage, 1990

Modern Jewish experience is frequently dated to radical transformations in an influential host culture, whether to Napoleon's dismantling of the ghettos of Western Europe at the end of the 18th century or back still further to the development of modern economic institutions in the mercantilist culture of 17th-century Amsterdam.

SACHAR's historical survey of the modern period begins with these developments and clearly presents the major historical factors that shaped modern Jewish life in both Eastern and Western Europe. He successfully highlights the different experiences of modernity in these two regions and provides small human details that bring the narrative to life for the reader. Dominant modern concepts such as Jewish Emancipation, antisemitism, liberalism, capitalism, and Zionism are presented in terms of their historical context and influence. The latter third of the text (in the revised edition) is devoted to the second half of the 20th century. The Holocaust is treated succinctly in two chapters that focus respectively on the historical antecedents of Nazism and the war years. Unusual among general modern Jewish histories, the text also includes one brief chapter on the history of Jews in Canada, Australia, South America, and South Africa. The revised volume closes with three chapters on the State of Israel from its earliest stages, through the Arab-Israeli wars, to the political challenges in the late 1980s to the settlement and limited annexation of the West Bank. Overcoming the difficulties of compiling a general history of this complex period, this text is one of the few works that effectively present an overview of modern Jewish history from its precursors to the end of the 20th century.

KATZ confines his study to the period he considers the first century of modern Jewish history, 1770 to 1870. Like Sachar, Katz emphasizes the differences between Western and Eastern European experiences of modernity. However, Katz also contends that European Jews in both the East and West shared many common experiences as a consequence of modernity, with their increased participation in the wider secular society. Focusing on the interplay between Jews and non-Jews, Katz skillfully illustrates various reactions to the social, cultural, intellectual, and economic changes of the early modern period. He is especially adept at tracing the ebb and flow of the forces that were operating in the bid for Jewish Emancipation. Katz outlines how both Jewish and non-Jewish communities were divided on the issue of Emancipation, and he explores how opponents and proponents took advantage of legal and cultural factors to advance their positions. While each European nation was subject to distinctive dynamics, Katz concludes that, despite these variations, Emancipation in each instance was fueled by the common forces of nationalism, rationalism, and humanism. Although Katz may tend to represent disproportionately the history of the intellectual elite at the expense of other groups, this minor difficulty is outweighed by his ability to convey deftly the complexity of the particular historical contexts and processes of Jewish Emancipation in an accessible manner.

NEUSNER examines the question of the transformation of Jewish faith during the modern period. Noting that both Judaism and Christianity were fragmented when each religion's respective claim to self-evident authority was undermined by 19th-century scholarship, he contends that the modern epoch in Jewish history is chiefly distinguished by a plurality of types of Judaism: the Orthodox, Reform, and Conservative movements, Yiddishism, Socialism, and Zionism, and, lately, the Judaism of Holocaust and Redemption. Each of these variants operates as a cultural system that responds to the challenges of modernity, such as secularism, assimilation, or the Holocaust. Neusner investigates how each form of Judaism explores such issues, emphasizing the various movements' historical developments, their respective claims to represent a self-evident truth, and their relative successes as cultural adaptations. This theoretical model offers an unusual view of modern Jewish history in which ideological and religious communal affiliation is the primary category of analysis.

GOLDSCHEIDER and ZUCKERMAN emphasize the process of modernization in their treatment of this period. The authors' methodology is less historical than sociological. They compare Jewish communities' responses to modernization and argue that the social cohesion of ethnic communities, such as Jewish communities, is not inevitably bound to break down due to modernization. Rather, they contend, modernization works as a process: modifying or transforming, strengthening or weakening, social structures. In this argument, ethnicity is regarded as a continuous social force that operates throughout history. Modernity is not the antithesis of ethnicity, and secularism is not the necessary end result of modernization. The authors apply this theoretical framework to Jewish communities throughout Europe, the United States, and Israel, from the premodern period through the late 20th century. Drawing on myriad sources including demographic data, political speeches and platforms, religious ideology, and economic and political theory, this project presents an original view of modern Jewish communities, which has in recent years transformed the model of modern Jewish history.

HYMAN focuses on gender as a significant and largely overlooked category of analysis in the study of modern Jewish history. This brief book is not a general history, but it is included here as a corrective for general histories that tend to efface the presence of women in history. This work is clearly limited in its scope, focusing exclusively on the theme of assimilation during the period 1850 to 1950 in Europe and the United States. The author does not address the Holocaust or the period considered in Katz's work. Hyman revisits traditional analyses of Jewish assimilation as a major feature of the modern period, positing that gender differences are manifest in the differing ways that women and men experienced and responded to the challenges of modernity. The author's skillful use of little-known sources, such as speeches, institutional publications, and memoirs, combines with incisive analysis and argumentation. Hyman frames the question of assimilation broadly, enabling her to touch on virtually every major theme of modern Jewish history, including antisemitism, Zionism, capitalism, secularism, and religious diversity.

MENDES-FLOHR and REINHARZ offer a comprehensive collection of sources for the study of modern Jewish history. Arranged chronologically and spanning the entire modern period, this collection includes virtually every type of written source, including many texts that had not previously been available in English. Each source is concisely annotated with sufficient information to place the selected passage in its historical context, and chapters are introduced with a succinct overview of the historical period or theme at issue. The diverse selection of texts demonstrates the editors' critical sensitivity to the multiplicity of Jewish experiences in the modern period. However, this sensitivity is marred by certain conspicuous deficits. The editors have consciously included more texts relating to Jewish women's experiences in the second edition, but there remains an unfortunate paucity of material pertaining to women or gender issues. Similarly, important non-American, non-European texts related to modern Jewish history are not well represented, and the coverage of Arab Jewish experiences of modernity (especially prior to the emergence of the State of Israel) is notably inadequate. Still, the value of this rich documentary history to the student of modern Jewry cannot be overestimated.

DEIDRE BUTLER

See also History: Biblical Israel; History: General Histories, Modern Authors; History: General Histories, Premodern Authors; History: Ideas of; History: Medieval; History: Second Temple Period; History: Talmudic Era

Holiness

Douglas, Mary, *Purity and Danger: An Analysis of Concepts of Pollution and Taboo*, New York: Praeger, and London: Routledge and Kegan Paul, 1966

Eilberg-Schwartz, Howard, *The Savage in Judaism: An Anthropology of Israelite Religion and Ancient Judaism*, Bloomington: Indiana University Press, 1990

Frank, Daniel H. (editor), *A People Apart: Chosenness and Ritual in Jewish Philosophical Thought* (SUNY Series in Jewish Philosophy), Albany: State University of New York Press, 1993

Hoffman, Lawrence A., *Beyond the Text: A Holistic Approach to Liturgy* (Jewish Literature and Culture), Bloomington: Indiana University Press, 1987

Jacobs, Louis, *Holy Living: Saints and Saintliness in Judaism*, Northvale, New Jersey: Aronson, 1990

Knohl, Israel, *Mikdash ha-demamah*, 1992; translated as *The Sanctuary of Silence: The Priestly Torah and the Holiness School*, Minneapolis, Minnesota: Fortress, 1995

Levenson, Jon D., *Sinai and Zion: An Entry into the Jewish Bible* (New Voices in Biblical Studies), Minneapolis, Minnesota: Winston, 1985

Neusner, Jacob, *A History of the Mishnaic Law of Purities* (Studies in Judaism in Late Antiquity), 22 vols., Leiden: Brill, 1974–1977

Rose, Gillian, *Judaism and Modernity: Philosophical Essays*, Oxford and Cambridge, Massachusetts: Blackwell, 1993

Holiness (*kedushah*) conveys ultimate meaning and supreme authority in religious life. Jewish people, texts, events, places, rituals, and symbols associate sanctity with worldly life (Genesis 2:3; Psalms 19) for groups (Exodus 19:6, Deuteronomy 7:6) and individuals (Deuteronomy 5:23–26). Such expressions and performances praise the elemental conditions of life in a world that is given to humanity's care (Isaiah 6:3), and they convey hope for improving the scarce chances of the human lot (Isaiah 19:2). Judaism finds holiness both in familiar, partially exhibited social and natural worlds, and in unique, all-encompassing realms of mystical experience. With holiness, one aspect of life is set apart from the rest of life in order to be rendered perfectly whole and complete (Leviticus 11:44–47).

Paradoxically, what is reckoned holy authorizes reality by supplanting life's "profane" terms, just as it transforms that reality by converting into "ordinary" life. The confluences and tensions in this paradox vary according to contexts in which holiness is set and uses to which it is put.

DOUGLAS's work correlates ritual institutions, creation myths, and classifications of good and right in the sacred. The author uses anthropological tools to argue that such ritual "abominations" as eating pork express symbolically the ideology of priests of the Book of Leviticus, sketching a "moral map" of their society. Douglas's theorem "where there is dirt, there is system" encapsulates the belief that sacrificial rites cleanse impurities and impose order in response to untidy distinctions and practical blunders (such as those that can arise when the priests deal with anomalous species that do not conform to generic classes of living creatures). Like cleanliness, holiness protects life as it expels waste. Social arrangements and moral codes placate anxieties about confusion and imperfection. They contain and constrain life at its boundaries in order to attain the "unity, integrity, perfection of the individual and of the kind." Purity that abolishes malfeasance and dissonance is paradoxically ordered by systems or bodies of thought and practice it displaces, for without the existence of profane elements, the distinction "holiness" would not have any significance.

NEUSNER places the dialectic of holiness and profanity in an evolutionary schema in his comprehensive exposition of the Mishnah's order of Purities. He contrasts the biblical priests' view of holiness as governed by sacrificial rites with the holiness expressed in the richly layered symbols and gestures of rabbinic Judaism, and he contends that the rabbis' examination of foods on the table and fluids in the body demonstrates their concern for the purity of the home, where "the sacred abides, if not wholly as it did in the Temple." As familiar blessings replaced exceptional sacrifices as holy rituals, "intentions of ordinary people living commonplace lives" established "a sacred structure held together by hope." Neusner explains the changing view of what constitutes holiness by examining the different historical conditions and social concerns faced by biblical Israel and rabbinic Judaism.

KNOHL investigates changing accounts of holiness within the Bible's priestly writings themselves. Elucidating cultic terminology and technique, he argues that the Holiness Code (Leviticus 19–26) is a late composition that integrated priestly legislation with its subsequent critique by the prophets, and he thus identifies the distinct yet compatible conceptions of holiness found in different periods in the history of priestly texts. For early priests, the holy withdraws from ordinary life, denoting the abstraction of divinity as "wholly other." In the later "holiness school," however, purification rites mesh with human purposes such as social justice, bringing holiness into every mode of life through blessings and deeds. The locus of holiness shifted, for instance, when sabbath replaced sacrifice as a central rite: the latter's "sanctuary of silence," which entreated awesome power, evolved into the sabbath's "temples in time," which linked high moral purpose with domestic, worldly institutions. Once viewed as whole and imposing, holiness becomes partial and familiar in later priestly accounts.

Rich evocations of holiness appear in LEVENSON's study of biblical poetry, narrative, law, and architecture. Bringing harmony to discordant voices, the book focuses on the Torah received at Mount Sinai and the Temple erected on Mount Zion. The author shows that the Sinaitic covenant set Israelites into personal relationships with God through an "ever-renewed" contract, in which specific religious deeds (mitsvot) commemorated events in "the intersection of love and law . . . the link between a past together and a future together." In addition, Zion provided divinity with permanent residence in the Temple or images of Messiah. Transcending history, sacrifice articulated "a theology of creation . . . where the costs exacted by the harshness of normal life are not paid" and life obtained "a higher degree of reality." The sacred resided in unity distinct from the evolution of creation, yet partial indications of sanctity pervaded all elements of worldly life.

Some baser aspects of purity are exposed by EILBERG-SCHWARTZ. Sex and violence in Jewish law and lore show that claims to moral integrity can create or reproduce systems of social power as they address concerns about natural dangers. Besides reflecting social interests, the act of purification "symbolically enacts" the experience of communal identity: such rites, which can be as diverse as animal sacrifice, circumcision, or prayer, encourage social and cultural coherence rather than conflict among community members. Noting that a body politic is maintained despite or because of competition for scarce resources and skirmishes over boundaries, the author argues that holy objects and performances formally equate the structure of a society with that community's mythic conception and original moral code. The book effectively summarizes issues of embodiment and power in ancient Judaism, but the author fails to scrutinize the enlightened gaze through which anthropology identifies certain behaviors as savagery.

HOFFMAN focuses on the specific contexts in which the blessings of holiness are performed. Detailed research into liturgical changes in modern Reform Judaism accompanies broad discussions of ancient myth and ritual, situating the "sacred" in specific vocabularies and cultural settings. The author contends that public ceremonies differentiate holy from profane in order to bestow "meaning, pattern, composition, and rhythm . . . on human existence in the world." By contrast, esoteric practices identify sanctity with cosmic forces (Isaiah 6:3), allowing "the mystic to escape the fetters of mundane reality and to enter the realm of the numinous." The study's anthropological views of worship illustrate varieties of holiness in historical and social contexts.

Culling vivid portraits of extraordinary individuals from Jewish literature from the Bible through the writings of Hasidism and the Musar movement, JACOBS gleans historical reversals in the meanings of tsaddik and hasid, which can attribute holiness to either a pious person who resides within prescribed and proscribed activities or an exceptional individual who exceeds the insufficient if necessary boundaries of legality. Thus, both regulated and free acts can be seen to sanctify reality, as holy persons embody such divergent qualities as erudition and innocence, simplicity and extravagance, equanimity and rapture, or isolation and participation. The author asserts that Judaism offers many routes to holiness, as it "counts the world well lost in the attempt to come closer to God."

The essays collected by FRANK explore arguments for Jewish separateness in pursuit of holiness. The contributors examine sanctified communities (Exodus 19:6; Deuteronomy 7:6) and sanctifying commandments (Leviticus 19:2, 21:6). L.E. Goodman maintains that Saadya and Maimonides believed that moral perfection is intrinsically rational for humans, although its applications are shaped by specific dictates of the good life. He concludes that ritual invests social convention with "a borrowed sanctity" that "modulates" individual Jewish lives so that "the whole life of Israel becomes the symbol of God's holiness." Moshe Sokol argues that ritual metaphorically restructures the experience of divinity differently in different contexts. Norbert Samuelson contends that political and theological lines of meaning do not converge in rabbinic, medieval, and modern systems of thought, suggesting that the object of worship is ambiguous. The volume helpfully evaluates evidence of holiness in diverse communal sensibilities and ritual performances.

Most studies have not considered sanctity a modern problem. ROSE corrects this oversight, exploring currents of holiness in Jewish engagements with recent European enlightenment ideologies and emancipatory schemes. Each essay draws the reader into a masterly polemic arguing that philosophy has failed to show how modernity and Judaism are split equally between a "moral discourse about rights and actual systems in power" and are broken by the "interference of meanings" whenever societies and communities intervene between intentions and activity. Sharp analyses show how those like Buber, Rosenzweig, and Levinas simultaneously oppose and reconcile ethical values and conventional norms. Caught in the middle, holiness "elevates what it would exclude as its Other" and imagines law and morality only where "the world . . . is dangerous: its *dominium* that of an apparently independent 'power' which is in effect dependent on the defeat of its others, and is therefore rigidly enforced but unstable and reversible." This ties a sacred history to its holocaust (eradication). Rather than improvise a single term between divinity and creation, Rose reconstructs modern Judaism as a worldly ideal that mediates states of practice, always discovering greater meanings and values. This brings the reader full circle in seeking out the diverse contexts and purposes that render ultimate significance and power in Judaism.

GREGORY KAPLAN

Holocaust: Histories

Bauer, Yehuda, *A History of the Holocaust,* New York: Watts, 1982

Dawidowicz, Lucy S., *The War against the Jews, 1933–1945,* New York: Holt, Rinehart and Winston, 1975

Gilbert, Martin, *The Holocaust: A History of The Jews During the Second World War,* New York: Holt, Rinehart, and Winston, and London: Weidenfeld and Nicolson, 1975; 10th anniversary edition, 1985, with new intro. and biblio., New York: Seth, and Harmondsworth: Penguin, 1986

Goldhagen, Daniel Jonah, *Hitler's Willing Executioners: Ordinary Germans and the Holocaust,* New York: Knopf, and London: Little, Brown, 1996

Hilberg, Raul, *The Destruction of the European Jews,* New York: Harper and Row, and London: Allen, 1961; revised and definitive edition, 3 vols., New York: Holmes and Meier, 1985

Poliakov, Leon, *Breviaire de la haine: Le IIIe Reich et les Juifs,* Paris: Calmann-Levy, 1951; as *Harvest of Hate: The Nazi Program for the Destruction of the Jews of Europe,* Philadelphia: Jewish Publication Society, 1954; London: Elek, 1956; revised and expanded edition, New York: Holocaust Library, 1979

Weiss, John, *Ideology of Death: Why the Holocaust Happened in Germany,* Chicago: Dee, 1996

Yahil, Leni, *The Holocaust: The Fate of European Jewry, 1932–1945,* New York: Oxford University Press, 1990

The Holocaust—the intended total destruction of the European Jews by the German Nazis and their European collaborators—has resulted in the creation of at least 10,000 books and articles, most of them written in the past 20 years. In the first decade after the end of World War II, a few very fine histories and personal accounts appeared, but they were largely ignored. It was only after the trial of Adolf Eichmann in the early 1960s that serious research on a wide variety of topics began. More books on the Holocaust were produced in the 1970s and a flood of material appeared in the two decades that followed. The realization had taken hold that the Holocaust was a defining event of the 20th century, a turning point in human affairs of the greatest magnitude. But it took at least a generation after the event for the Holocaust to achieve this centrality.

BAUER is perhaps the leading Israeli historian of the Holocaust. His fine survey appeared in 1982 after much research on various aspects of the Holocaust had enabled such a comprehensive synthesis to be done. It was one of the first works on the Holocaust to begin with the question, "Who are the Jews?" This enabled the non-Jewish reader to achieve a multicultural perspective, viewing the Jews as people as well as victims. Bauer begins his story early, in the time of emerging Christianity. He paces the reader through the Middle Ages, the Renaissance and Reformation, the Enlightenment, and the 19th century. This has the effect of combining Jewish history with the broader developments of Western civilization. Excellent chapters on World War I, the Weimar Republic, and the context of Nazi Germany set the stage for the story of the Holocaust. Here, the Jewish response, including resistance, is covered thoroughly. Chapters on the behavior of the Allies and the possibility of rescue are very informative. Bauer views the Nazi intention of total eradication as ideologically motivated, and he presents his case very well. This fine history is studded with helpful maps and contains a detailed and most informative diagram of the Auschwitz concentration and death camp.

DAWIDOWICZ presented her history of the Holocaust in the mid-1970s, at a point when interest in the event had begun to escalate. The book is very well written, and its first part focuses on a detailed analysis of Hitler and Nazi Germany, the SS (*Schutzstaffeln,* the Nazi secret service), Nazi foreign policy, and the annihilation camps. Dawidowicz portrays Hitler convincingly as obsessed with the "Jewish problem" above all other considerations. The second portion of the book deals with the reactions of the victims and presents their story most eloquently. The behavior of the Jews in the ghettos, the heroic attempts of Jews to sustain community and cultural life in the midst of hellish conditions, the resistance of the ghettos in the face of the greatest of odds, the horrendous choices faced by individuals, and finally the ability of the victims to maintain their decency are rendered with great skill. The book concentrates mainly on Poland, while the fate of the Jews in other countries is summarized not in the text proper but in a massive appendix. Dawidowicz's omission of the failure of the Allies to intervene and the lack of an assessment of the significance of the Holocaust in human affairs make this book less comprehensive than Bauer's. Still, the book provides a moving human record of the Jewish people during the most trying chapter of their long history.

GILBERT presents his work in the style of history as chronicle, in the manner of earlier classic historians. His book, much longer than the histories of Bauer and Dawidowicz, presents the story of the Holocaust month-by-month. Although short on analysis, the chronicle is overwhelming in its detail, unforgettable in its focus on riveting episodes. The victims are not anonymous; wherever possible Gilbert provides their names to record that real individuals lived, struggled, and died during this period. Gilbert's use of sources is masterful and includes much new material not available in previous histories. One striking example is that of Salmen Lewenthal, a member of the "Sonderkommando" [Special Squads] in Auschwitz. He witnessed the arrival of the transports, the revolt of the inmates in October 1944, and the terrible fate of the children. Lewenthal's manuscript was discovered in 1962 in a jar buried in the ground near Crematorium III, where he worked. He did not survive, but he left an invaluable testimony. Gilbert's narrative history is among the most gripping of the general chronicles of the Holocaust.

The young scholar GOLDHAGEN has written one of the most controversial books about the Holocaust to have appeared to date. He set out to prove that ordinary Germans from all walks of life were able to kill because "ideas about Jews that were pervasive in Germany and had been for decades, induced ordinary Germans to kill . . . systematically and without pity." Moreover, they enjoyed themselves while doing it. The author argues that a specific, "eliminationist" type of antisemitism had developed in modern Germany. He shows, for example, that of 51 antisemitic publications that appeared between 1861 and 1895 in Germany, almost one-half called for the physical elimination of the Jews. Goldhagen would only have strengthened his case had he discussed the Austrian antisemites. Once the Nazis came to power, the killer instinct was liberated, and during the Holocaust ordinary Germans, including police battalions, Hitler youth, and even army musicians, participated in the killing until the last day of the war. Goldhagen seems, however, to have underestimated the role of Hitler and the bureaucracy, the impact of constant indoctrination, and the force of totalitarianism. He overlooks the existence of some democratic and humanistic elements in Germany that refused to succumb to hate. Still, Goldhagen has produced a stimulating and courageous work of scholarship that succeeds in showing how millions of ordinary people

internalized obsessive stereotypes and were able to kill with glee and abandon. Jewish survivors have welcomed this book more warmly than most historians have, as the survivors experienced the actions of these "ordinary Germans" firsthand.

HILBERG produced one of the seminal books of 20th-century scholarship. A work of massive, thorough research, it is a book about a process, about how the European Jews were destroyed. The focus is on those who carried out the Holocaust: "Lest one be misled by the word 'Jews' in the title, this is not a book about the Jews. It is a book about the people who destroyed the Jews. Not much will be read here about the victims. The focus is placed on the perpetrators." Still, Hilberg discusses the precedents that led to the Holocaust. Medieval exclusion of the Jews was followed by expulsion and then in modern times by racist ideas of extermination. As a political scientist, Hilberg argues that once the German Jews lost their civil rights in 1933, their right to live became questionable. This enormous study is divided into the steps of the destruction process starting with Nazi definition of the Jews, then covering expropriation, concentration, mobile mass shootings, deportations and, finally, the vast network of industrialized camps of death. Hilberg illustrates that for the first time in history, the killers overcame all obstacles to genocide, and a vast bureaucracy of death was established. The Holocaust can be a warning, said Hilberg, but it can also be a precedent. Despite the great studies of Jewish spiritual and physical resistance published since 1960, Hilberg held in his 1985 revised edition to his original assertion that Jewish resistance was negligible. His focus was on how 6 million people could be destroyed by a modern state in a short period of time, and this contribution to modern understanding will be of lasting value.

POLIAKOV, a foremost historian of antisemitism, wrote his work in French in 1951 when the word "Holocaust" had not yet been applied to the Jewish catastrophe. This was the first major survey of the history of the Holocaust. Despite later scholarship on resistance, European collaborators, the role of the professions and of ordinary people, and non-Jews who saved Jews, this book was a milestone in the history of Holocaust scholarship. Its findings and conclusions still hold up very well. Poliakov was an observer at the Nuremberg trials and had access to many captured Nazi documents. He traced the development of the Holocaust from the beginnings of Nazi persecution through pillage (which only recently has become an area of widespread interest), to the ghettos, massacres, and death camps. He includes a chapter on resistance. What was most innovative about his work was his attention to the bystanders and the churches and especially to the non-Jewish victims of the Holocaust. Poliakov was one of the rare observers to realize early on that the Holocaust was the most extreme manifestation of genocide in a century of what later came to be called "ethnic cleansing." Even so, he realized that the Holocaust was powered not by self-interest but by fanaticism and irrationality. The killing of the Jews became an end in itself, and that put the Holocaust in a class by itself.

WEISS published his study shortly after Goldhagen's book appeared, and it is the perfect companion work to the Goldhagen thesis. Like Goldhagen, Weiss asserts that antisemitism in Germany was different from that in other countries: it was more pervasive, more philosophical, and wedded to German nationalism. Unlike Goldhagen, Weiss develops a linear history of a unique antisemitism in both Germany and Austria. He draws from a wide variety of sources—intellectual history, social movements, political parties, and influential elites. He shows how this antisemitism came to advocate extermination and became radicalized in the 20th century. He proves how the Nazis were able to tap into a popular wellspring—the Holocaust required the complicity of tens of thousands of Germans from all walks of life—notwithstanding that after the war many Germans preferred to absolve themselves and their peers from the mass murders they had committed. Unlike Goldhagen, who is a child of survivors, Weiss notes that he is of Austrian Catholic ancestry, an example of the distinguished Christian historians who are producing works on the Holocaust of first importance.

YAHIL, like Bauer, is a distinguished Israeli historian of the Holocaust. Her massive history complements the other major surveys; it explores aspects of the Holocaust that are treated lightly or passed over in other works. For example, Yahil provides in-depth accounts of the organizations of German Jews, their reactions to persecution, and their specific problems of prewar emigration. In the course of her account of the Holocaust proper, Yahil provides close-grained accounts of lesser-known ghettos in the Radom district and eastern Upper Silesia. Exploration of such intriguing topics as "The Orthodox Jew and the Struggle for Survival," "Efforts to Get People Released" from the labor and extermination camps, the behavior of neutral Switzerland and Spain, and "Escape Routes to the Far East" all provide extremely valuable insights on the Holocaust that are lacking in other works. Although this sometimes results in choppy organization, the book is ideal territory for browsing and for filling gaps in both regional and topical coverage.

LEON STEIN

See also Holocaust: Film Treatments; Holocaust: Literature and Memoirs; Holocaust: Responses to the Holocaust

Holocaust: Literature and Memoirs

Bosmajian, Hamida, *Metaphors of Evil: Contemporary German Literature and the Shadow of Nazism,* Iowa City: University of Iowa Press, 1979

Brenner, Rachel Feldhay, *Writing as Resistance: Four Women Confronting the Holocaust: Edith Stein, Simone Weil, Anne Frank, Etty Hillesum,* University Park: Pennsylvania State University Press, 1997

Ezrahi, Sidra DeKoven, *By Words Alone: The Holocaust in Literature,* Chicago: University of Chicago Press, 1980

Flanzbaum, Hilene, *The Americanization of the Holocaust,* Baltimore, Maryland: Johns Hopkins University Press, 1999

Friedländer, Saul (editor), *Probing the Limits of Representation: Nazism and the "Final Solution,"* Cambridge, Massachusetts: Harvard University Press, 1992

Halperin, Irving, *Messengers from the Dead: Literature of the Holocaust,* Philadelphia: Westminster, 1970

Hartman, Geoffrey (editor), *Holocaust Remembrance: The Shapes of Memory,* Oxford and Cambridge, Massachusetts: Blackwell, 1994

Horowitz, Sara R., *Voicing the Void: Muteness and Memory in Holocaust Fiction* (SUNY Series in Modern Jewish Literature and Culture), Albany: State University of New York Press, 1997

Kremer, S. Lillian, *Witness through the Imagination: Ozick, Elman, Cohen, Potok, Singer, Epstein, Bellow, Steiner, Wallant, Malamud: Jewish-American Holocaust Literature,* Detroit, Michigan: Wayne State University Press, 1989

Lang, Berel (editor), *Writing and the Holocaust,* New York: Holmes and Meier, 1988

Langer, Lawrence L., *The Holocaust and the Literary Imagination,* New Haven, Connecticut: Yale University Press, 1975; London: Yale University Press, 1977

Langer, Lawrence L., *Versions of Survival: The Holocaust and the Human Spirit* (SUNY Series in Modern Jewish Literature and Culture), Albany: State University of New York Press, 1982

Langer, Lawrence L., *Admitting the Holocaust: Collected Essays,* New York: Oxford University Press, 1995

Mintz, Alan, *Hurban: Responses to Catastrophe in Hebrew Literature,* New York: Columbia University Press, 1984

Patterson, David, *The Shriek of Silence: A Phenomenology of the Holocaust Novel,* Lexington: University Press of Kentucky, 1992

Rosenfeld, Alvin H., *A Double Dying: Reflections on Holocaust Literature,* Bloomington: Indiana University Press, 1980

Roskies, David G., *Against the Apocalypse: Responses to Catastrophe in Modern Jewish Culture,* Cambridge, Massachusetts: Harvard University Press, 1984

Sicher, Efraim (editor), *Breaking Crystal: Writing and Memory after Auschwitz,* Urbana: University of Illinois Press, 1998

Young, James, *Writing and Rewriting the Holocaust: Narrative and the Consequences of Interpretation,* Bloomington: Indiana University Press, 1988

Because the extremity of Nazi atrocity struck many as incompatible with the aesthetic concerns of literature, and the need to assert the facts of the Nazi genocide seemed at odds with the license of the literary imagination, Holocaust literature was not taken seriously by scholars for several decades after World War II. Among the first book-length studies of Holocaust literature, LANGER (1975) opened the field in important ways to literary analysis. Based on an exploration of literary techniques developed in individual literary works, the book establishes an aesthetics of atrocity and argues for the role of the literary imagination in conveying difficult aspects of Nazi horror. Like works that follow it, the book argues against political philosopher Theodor W. Adorno's assertion of the incompatibility of the Holocaust and the poetic imagination.

While acknowledging a discomfort with applying the tools of literary criticism to works depicting massive suffering and death, ROSENFELD ultimately sees critical methodologies as vital in understanding the complicated import of significant writing by Holocaust survivors. Taking as its central theme the double death inflicted by the Nazis during the Holocaust—the annihilation of European Jewry and the destruction of dearly held ideas about humanity and inherited traditions of meaning—the study explores the perspectives and literary strategies of Holocaust literature. Probing the implications of that double destruction for literature and culture, the book argues that one must think through criteria for distinguishing good representations from bad or exploitative ones, criteria that open on aesthetic as well as moral categories.

Similarly asserting that one needs to unravel the complexities of literary style and structure in order to understand the important ideas that underlie works of Holocaust literature, BOSMAJIAN explores the connections between history, myth, atrocity, and language in postwar German literature. The study focuses on the attempts to struggle against the legacy of the Nazi era and the particular challenges it poses for the German language and literary tradition. The book argues for the predominance of irony in Holocaust literature.

Asserting the place of imaginative literature about the Holocaust as a form of testimony, EZRAHI surveys and categorizes a broad spectrum of Holocaust writing according to mode of presentation, placing each work along a continuum of "realism" ranging from diaries and memoirs, to documentary fiction, to mythical representation. Underlying each mode, the analysis discerns an ideological or ethical interpretation of these historical events and the way they must be remembered.

For HALPERIN, in a less literary and more straightforward reading of these works, Holocaust writing serves primarily as a moral vehicle, a means by which authors instruct readers in the moral implications of the Holocaust. Examining diaries, memoirs, and fiction by survivors, the book evaluates them according to ethical rather than literary criteria, reading the works as straightforward reflections on the history of the Nazi genocide and the lessons to be gleaned from it.

In a collection of essays primarily by creative writers and literary scholars, LANG questions the role of imaginative writing in Holocaust representations. From different perspectives, the essays address aesthetic and ethical limitations of Holocaust writing of all kinds—literary, historical, philosophical. They consider as well the way that evil is conceptualized in writing about the Holocaust.

The essays in FRIEDLÄNDER, too, consider the difficulties raised by the representation of the Holocaust across disciplines. Historians, historiographers, philosophers, and literary scholars probe issues such as historical relativism and ideological interpretation with relation to the Holocaust and the problems of aesthetic representation of the Holocaust, seeking the ethical limits and particularly the appropriateness and usefulness of postmodernism in representing the events of the Nazi genocide. Several of the essays focus specifically on literature, addressing such topics as the Holocaust in Israeli literature and the poetry of Paul Celan, and the volume as a whole tackles issues that bear on the understanding of the complexities of Holocaust literature, such as the shaping of cultural memory and the appropriation and misappropriation of the Holocaust.

Several studies examine Holocaust literature not only as testimony but also as a form of reflection on some of the complicated issues that arise in Holocaust studies. Using the theme of muteness as a central term of analysis, HOROWITZ traces the tension between the said and the unsaid in Holocaust fiction. Reading a wide range of narratives, the book demonstrates that Holocaust fiction uses different forms of muteness to address and help resolve the central issues that arise in Holocaust studies, such as the difficulty in adequately representing the Nazi genocide, the dangers of Holocaust fiction, and the limitations of historical narrative. When embedded in a literary work, muteness can paradoxically express the confrontation with the void—meaninglessness, the shattering of the self, death. The book presents both a theoretical framework for reading Holocaust fiction and a series of close readings of individual works.

Rather than seeing Holocaust literature as a vehicle for history, PATTERSON focuses on literature's ability to convey truths that are not necessary factual. Thus, the book argues, literature is the medium best suited to conveying the dehumanization and confrontation with meaninglessness experienced by victims of the Nazi genocide. Using a Bakhtinian analysis and attentive to the theological implications of the Holocaust, the book focuses on the Holocaust novel as a dialogic encounter.

Similarly focusing on ethical issues, BRENNER explores the diaries of four Western European women who perished during the Nazi years: Edith Stein, Simone Weil, Anne Frank, and Etty Hillesum. She argues that each of these women saw the Holocaust as a threat not only to her existence but to the liberal, universal values that gave moral order to her world. These women were assimilated, secularized Jews or Christians who had converted (or whose parents had converted) from Judaism prior to the Holocaust. The book views the women's very act of writing about this as a form of resistance to Nazism.

Rather than looking at Holocaust literature exclusively and across cultures, MINTZ examines imaginative responses to the Nazi genocide in Hebrew literature in the context of responses to catastrophe in Hebrew literature and in the Jewish tradition. Looking at catastrophe as an event defined not only by pain and death but also as one that engenders a crisis of continuity for the culture, this study explores the way Hebrew literature struggles with such issues as the Jewish community's sense of itself, its role in history, its connection to God and the covenant—in short, the paradigms of meaning by which it understands itself.

Working in a similar vein, ROSKIES discusses Holocaust writing by victims and survivors in the context of Jewish responses to catastrophe over time. Arguing against seeing the Holocaust as an apocalyptic event without analogy, Roskies examines ghetto diaries, as well as poetry and art by survivors, in light of traditional Jewish liturgical expressions of lamentation and the acknowledgment of divine transcendence. Seeing precedents in these religious writings as well as in the more secular body of writing that depicts violent pogroms, the book asserts an inner continuity as the Jewish tradition absorbs, mourns, and transcends the Nazi genocide.

In HARTMAN, essays by creative writers, historians, literary critics, and art historians consider the different ways in which the Nazi genocide has been remembered and interpreted and contemplate the shape memory will take as more time passes. Examining material as diverse as ghetto diaries, survivor writing and oral testimony, monuments, painting, film, and concentration camp architecture, the essays examine the complications of remembering and transmitting a history of atrocity and trauma.

YOUNG argues that the past becomes known and remembered through its various representations in historical and literary narratives, poetry, written and oral recollections, and official memorials. Examining a wide range of material, the book explores the kinds of understanding of the past implicated in different forms of historical representation, collective and personal memory, and imaginative reflections.

LANGER (1982) argues that the different ways in which survivors recollect and narrate the memories of their experiences during the Nazi genocide not only reveal what happened but also frequently reflect a need to reaffirm values shaken by the Holocaust. Analyzing fiction by Tadeusz Borowski, Elie Wiesel, and others, memoirs by Primo Levi, poetry by Gertrud Kolmar and Nelly Sachs, books by Bruno Bettelheim and Viktor Frankl, and other writing, the study traces the way psychology, language, art, and literature have confronted the difficult issues raised by the Holocaust. LANGER (1995) continues to explore this theme, focusing on the reluctance of much Holocaust literature and film to see the Nazi genocide for what it was. Instead, the book argues, these works tend to depict the Holocaust in ways that reaffirm treasured ideals—such as the triumph of the human spirit over evil, the innate goodness of people, and the ability of art to transcend even the harshest reality.

Several works focus on Holocaust writing by people who did not themselves experience Nazi atrocity. Carrying further the idea that imaginative literature can serve as a form of Holocaust testimony, KREMER argues that those who are neither survivors nor eyewitnesses may bear witness through the imagination. Thus, U.S. writers who were not personally threatened by the European Jewish catastrophe have, through a combination of research, empathy, and moral engagement, created a body of literature that represents the Nazi genocide and struggles with its implications. The volume offers close readings and analyses of ten Jewish American novelists.

Focusing exclusively on writing and art by the post-Holocaust generation in Israel, the United States, and elsewhere, SICHER explores issues of collective memory and trauma as Holocaust representation passes from the domain of survivors and eyewitnesses into history and cultural memory. The multidisciplinary collection of essays by scholars in literature, film, history, psychology, American studies, and cultural studies examines the uses and interpretations of the Holocaust half a century later.

The essays collected in FLANZBAUM analyze the central position of the Nazi genocide in the American imagination, and they interpret the proliferation of Holocaust imagery in high and popular culture. Written by scholars in a variety of disciplines, the essays examine the Americanization of the Holocaust by looking at contemporary poetry, fiction, theater, film and television, museums, memorials, and visual arts.

SARA R. HOROWITZ

See also Holocaust: Film Treatments; Holocaust: Histories; Holocaust: Responses to the Holocaust

Holocaust: Responses to the Holocaust

Berkovits, Eliezer, *Faith after the Holocaust,* New York: Ktav, 1973

Fackenheim, Emil, *To Mend the World: Foundations of Future Jewish Thought,* New York: Schocken, 1982

Garber, Zev, *Shoah: The Paradigmatic Genocide: Essays in Exegesis and Eisegesis* (Studies in the Shoah, vol. 8), Lanham, Maryland: University Press of America, 1994

Garber, Zev with Alan L. Berger and Richard Libowitz (editors), *Methodology in the Academic Teaching of the Holocaust* (Studies in Judaism), Lanham, Maryland: University Press of America, 1988; London: University Press of America, 1989

Greenberg, Irving, "Religious Values after the Holocaust: A Jewish View," in *Jews and Christians after the Holocaust,* edited by Abraham J. Peck, Philadelphia: Fortress, 1982

Littell, Franklin H., *The Crucifixion of the Jews,* New York: Harper and Row, 1975

Rosenbaum, Irving J., *The Holocaust and Halakhah* (Library of Jewish Law and Ethics), New York: Ktav, 1976

Rubenstein, Richard L., *After Auschwitz: Radical Theology and Contemporary Judaism,* Indianapolis, Indiana: Bobbs-Merrill, 1966; revised as *After Auschwitz: History, Theology, and Contemporary Judaism,* Baltimore, Maryland: Johns Hopkins University Press, 1992

Ruether, Rosemary Radford, *Faith and Fratricide: The Theological Roots of Anti-Semitism,* New York: Seabury, 1974; London: Search, 1975

Schindler, Pesach, *Hasidic Responses to the Holocaust in the Light of Hasidic Thought,* Hoboken, New Jersey: Ktav, 1990

Wiesel, Elie, *Night,* New York: Hill and Wang, 1958; London: Macgibbon and Kee, 1960

Wiesenthal, Simon, *The Sunflower,* London: Allen, 1970; New York: Schocken, 1976, revised edition, 1997

If Elie Wiesel is correct that the Holocaust, or Shoah, transcends history and that the living are neither capable nor worthy of recovering its mystery, then responses to the Shoah say more about the fears and concerns of the respondents than about the event itself. Religious and theological response to the Shoah is an excruciating experience, but it is nevertheless necessary. Wiesel himself relates witness stories promoting Jewish survival as an unshakable dogma after Auschwitz. The theocentric religious philosophies of Emil

Fackenheim, Eliezer Berkovits, and Irving Greenberg talk respectively of an obligatory 614th commandment (no posthumous victory for Hitler), encounter theology, and voluntary covenant, which together represent a mending of the Jewish world. Richard L. Rubenstein demands a letting go of traditional Judaism's doctrine of God for a new symbol of God's reality conducive to the lessons learned from Auschwitz. In contrast, Irving J. Rosenbaum and Pesach Schindler show how rabbinic responsa and Hasidism maintain classical Orthodox belief rooted in spontaneous religious experience in dealing with the Holocaust. Franklin H. Littell and Rosemary Radford Ruether speak of the iniquity of the Shoah as the indelible stain on the Christian world made near-permanent by the nearly 2,000 years of a hermeneutics of hate. Simon Wiesenthal and Zev Garber raise issues of identity and ethics.

The position taken by GARBER, BERGER, and LIBOWITZ is not a historical approach alone, since that may hinder student comprehension of the event. They present a wide range of literary, pedagogical, and theological concerns and approaches that attempt to pinpoint ways in which it is possible to remain human and seek meaning in an age of technologically administered mass death.

WIESEL's writings have made him the messenger of the Jewish Holocaust victims and the prophetic muse of the post-Holocaust age. This fact may explain why he composed his first published memoir, *Night,* in Yiddish, the *lingua franca* of murdered European Jewry, rather than in French, the language in which he usually works. Wiesel writes masterfully, and in *Night* he describes the death camp horror that turns a young Jewish boy into a witness to the death of his family, his innocence, and his God.

> Never shall I forget that night, the first night in camp which has turned my life into one long night. . . . Never shall I forget the little faces of the children, whose bodies I saw turned into wreaths of smoke beneath a silent blue sky. Never shall I forget those flames which consumed my faith forever. Never shall I forget that nocturnal silence which deprived me, for all eternity, of the desire to live. Never shall I forget those moments which murdered my God and my soul and turned my dreams to dust. Never shall I forget these things, even if I am condemned to live as long as God Himself. Never.

Wiesel's manifesto does not diminish the paradox of the Shoah but serves to make the issue more troubling, and therefore also more full of hope. Wiesel has strongly advocated that the specific lessons of the Shoah should never be lost. His eyewitness approach to the event, which is rooted in the redemptive quality of memory, carries the message that one can survive with morality, a message that appeals to all who have suffered or will suffer.

FACKENHEIM attempts to show how the Jew gains authenticity and respectability after Auschwitz. He explores the options in Jewish thought caused by modernity and reflected in the writings of Baruch Spinoza and Franz Rosenzweig. According to him, the Holocaust experience makes folly both of Spinoza's absolute of reason and of Rosenzweig's "anti-speculative" existentialist thought. He posits that Jewish survival cannot be seen in physical terms nor in ahistorical thinking. Rather, the survival of the Jews is learned from the everyday acts of prisoners in the death camps nurtured and sanctified by the way of Torah. Thus, the standard for millions of Jews trapped in Hitler's inferno was neither nihilism nor despair nor suicide but the practice of Judaism to the extent possible under such horrendous conditions. This behavior, identified by Fackenheim as *tikkun 'olam* ("mending the world"), points the way to healing the rupture of the Jewish people after the Shoah. In sum, Jews must survive as Jews—morally, ethically, and ritually—and under no circumstances must a posthumous victory be granted to Hitler (Fackenheim's "614th Commandment").

BERKOVITS understands well the limits of theology, what it can and cannot do in explaining the effect of the worst catastrophe in Jewish history on the faith of Israel. The two principal approaches, complete submission to the Shoah as a manifestation of divine will or a total rejection of beneficent providence, are both acceptable within reason. In his radical Orthodoxy, the basics of Judaism are derived from an encounter between God and Israel begun at Sinai and renewed during centuries of prophetic leadership and later rabbinic thought. God is a creator God and the world of his creation is purposefully designed as less than perfect, for if it were perfect there would be no need of history or of the finite realm. God is not the elusive "absolute" of philosophers, but, as in the biblical-rabbinic imagery, he is involved in history and cares for his creation. He shows his loving concern through ethical-religious channels. Man, made in the image of God, properly lives that image only by performing Godlike actions of mercy, justice, and righteousness. God purposefully hides his face *(hester panim)* so that humanity can exercise freedom of ethical choice, thereby becoming a partner—albeit subordinate—with him in bringing about a universal era of peace and redemption. Shoah is a dramatization of faith shattered when humanity fails and *hester panim* prevails. Berkovits acknowledges this and his encounter theology treats all who died in the European hell, believers and non-believers alike, as *kedoshim* (saints, martyrs). From this recognition comes the breakthrough of faith after the Shoah.

GREENBERG holds that in view of what the Shoah presents, the murder of millions coupled with a horrifically hidden God, the role of Israel's covenant and the nature of Israel's election must be revised, reevaluated, and renegotiated. He is willing to acknowledge that the Imposed Covenant of Sinai is no longer valid after Auschwitz. It cannot be otherwise; it has failed. Centuries of persecution have chipped away at its words, and the flames of the Shoah have obliterated its authoritative voice that "descended in fire" (Exodus 19:18); it is "the shattered paradigm." Yet, in its place, a new covenant has arisen by virtue of the actions of survivors and other Jews who chose not to assimilate, die, or forget but to survive as a people. Jewish survival by any means necessary, including "secular" activity, is the central tenet of the new Voluntary Covenant; the rest of the Jewish way is commentary. Greenberg is not willing to sacrifice the unity of Judaism any more than the unity of God. By propounding a shift in the image of the covenant from imposed to voluntary, he is responding to today's religionless Jew, who lives Judaism either by being, or by being in the process of becoming, but not necessarily by doing the Torah of Sinai. Covenant living in the image of God, not logic or straight belief, is Greenberg's new theology ("holy secularity") for shaping Jewish values after the Shoah.

RUBENSTEIN's enlarged and updated version of *After Auschwitz*, published 26 years after the first edition appeared, follows the form but not necessarily the content of his seminal work, which many agree "invented Holocaust theology." The kaleidoscope of information therein includes: (1) rethinking the death of a theology that teaches God chose Israel, sustained her in history, and abandoned her in Auschwitz; (2) reinterpreting belief and tradition for an increasingly post-traditional Judaism freed from the mass of fundamental legalism and ethnic parochialism; and (3) more generally, reflecting on noteworthy current events at the crossroads of three continents in terms of Holy War and ethnic cleansing.

Rubenstein questions unabashedly the principle of divine activity in history. He asks why the Guardian of Israel did not impede the senseless slaughter of millions of Jews, including 1.5 million children. Likewise shocking and tragic to him is the suggestion that Nazi atrocity is a just compensation for collective Jewish sins or a wake-up call against a far worse collective punishment and devastation. He opines that the evil that the Nazis unleashed against the Jewish people, coupled with a seemingly nonintervening deity, requires as a basic minimum that Jews give up any notion that they are the Chosen People of God. Rubenstein's invitation to seek God beyond the God of theism forces us to confront the results of belief in the biblical God of merit and promise, reward and punishment. He proposes a new framework for Shoah theology, and he begins with a frank acknowledgment of a basic insufficiency of Jewish doctrine to explain Jewish tragedy. The eclipse of trust and the absence of convincing theistic answers contribute to Rubenstein's modus operandi. He replaces the biblical-rabbinic Lord of History with the kabbalistic doctrine of Holy Nothingness. That is to say, the essence of God as known to God is neither material nor personal. "To speak, admittedly in inadequate language, of God as the "Nothingness" is not to suggest that God is a void; on the contrary, the Holy Nothingness is a *plenum* so rich that all existence derives therefrom. God as the "Nothing" is not absence of being, but a superfluity of being. . . . The infinite God is not a thing; the infinite God is nothing."

Contra his critics, Rubenstein never wrote of the "death of God" but only "the time of the death of God," meaning, "the absence of God in contemporary culture." Nor does he maintain that people exist by their own resources (wit and animalistic instinct to survive as a group or race). Rather, he writes that life is more than narrow individualism and group chauvinism when dealing with ethical and moral issues. Thus, psychoanalysis, sociology, and political theory—rather than traditional categories of biblical and rabbinic belief—can best explicate Judaism and the Jewish people after Auschwitz.

ROSENBAUM draws on the responsa of the rabbis from the Shoah, particularly the multivolume *She'elot u-Teshuvot mi-Ma'amakim* by Rabbi Ephraim Oshry of Kovno, and he discusses religious problems caused by the Shoah for the whole gamut of Jewish law: domestic relations, financial affairs, observance of kashrut, sabbath, festivals, and other religious duties, and life and death issues. The disturbing ethical and moral question of who shall live and who shall die and related dilemmas are eclectically chosen from this literature and commented upon. Examples of human courage and Jewish solidarity, generally unknown to the nonspecialist, are lucidly presented in this volume.

Though others have written on oral and literary responses to Jewish martyrdom and suffering or have authored responsa on the Shoah, SCHINDLER seeks out the hasidic response: how aspects of classic hasidic thought imbued with Kabbalah permeated the belief and behavior of the hasidim of Belz, Bratslav, Gur, Lubavitch, and other dynasties and prepared them to face life and death during the European *hurban* ("destruction"). Each chapter examines the effects of a specific problem resulting from the kabbalistic-hasidic *Urglaube* regarding the symbiotic interaction of God and Man, in which the actions of *etaruta deletata* (Lower World) have an impact on *etaruta dele'ela* (Upper World). The problems are: evil and suffering; punishment and exile, redeemed by chastisement and redemption; *Kiddush ha-Shem* and *Kiddush ha-Hayyim* (sanctification of God's name in death and life); cofraternal roles of zaddik and hasid, leader and follower; and the realized tension between the activist and quietist schools of hasidic response to the trauma of *di milhomeh yohren* ("the war years"). Schindler explores the full range of hasidic *hutzpah* and *'ahavat Yisrael* (respectively, courage bordering on the reckless and love of the Jewish people), and he shows how hasidic faith and rabbinic halakhah fashioned the single-mindedness of most hasidim, who defiantly opposed Nazi evil decrees, but, in the end, accepted joyously the divine decree.

LITTELL's title suggests that Christians have made much of the cross and crucifixion but it is the Jews who have lived it. Whether or not there is a direct link between 2,000 years of Christian supersessionism and the Shoah, Christian culpability in the destruction of European Jewry cannot be denied. Littell, dean of Christian scholars of the Shoah in the United States, was among the first to question the credibility of Christianity in the wake of the Shoah. He asks how Christianity can claim moral credibility, let alone superiority, if in the heart of Christendom thousands of baptized Christians and other leaders consented to the mass murder of Jews contrary to doctrinal statement and confession of faith. He calls on Christians to unload their theological antisemitism by rejecting age-old *Contra Judaeos* preaching and teaching. Death begets rebirth, and implicit in the Jewish people's return to history (resurrection) after the Shoah (crucifixion) is the humbling of Christianity. "If we who profess Christ, do not when push comes to shove care whether Jews live or die . . . our 'dialogue' is but foolishness, out utterances but a tickling of jaded ears." Littell concludes that only full fraternity of the Christian Church with the Jewish people, inaugurated by confession of Shoah guilt, can begin the process of *teshuvah* ("return") to an old-new common tradition of remembrance.

RUETHER's work is considered among the most radical in exposing the anti-Jewish tendencies in the New Testament, which became the basis of hostile teachings among the Church Fathers and in later ecclesiastical education. She calls antisemitism "the left hand of Christology" and maintains that Christian "messianic absolutism . . . generated Christian totalitarianism and imperialism," which is the bedrock of the *Adversus Judaeos* tradition. By historicizing the eschatological and by spiritualizing the historical, the New Testament writers interpret the positive prophetic texts as fulfilled in Jesus and, by extension, the Church as the "new Israel," and the negative prophetic texts as fulfilled in the "old Israel." This recasting of sacred history is possible only if Jesus is perceived as the absolute and only way to God and salvation. Ruether argues that this is historically flawed and religiously absurd. Further, this saga of Christian triumphalism justifies for many Christians their active participation in the Shoah. Hitler (baptized a Roman Catholic and never excommunicated by the Church), for example, when asked by a group of Methodist deaconesses in 1933, "Herr Reichskanzler, from where do you get the courage to undertake the great changes in the whole Reich?" responded with a New Testament in hand, "From God's word." The way out of this morally and theologically alarming situation, Ruether suggests, is (1) to rethink the exclusive Christ of faith in full view of the Jewish Jesus of history, and (2) to see Christian sancta as parallel to, not above, the Jewish experience. Ruether's proposals constitute an important step forward in amending the tradition of anti-Judaism in Christian theology that contributed to the Shoah.

WIESENTHAL tells of a Nazi, a participant in the slaughter of innocents, terrified of dying with the burden of his guilt. He asks forgiveness from a Jewish concentration camp survivor, one who knows well the meaning of the Jewish moral dilemma when victim-survivor shakes hands and makes peace with the enslaver-destroyer. The Jew listens with horror and feeling to the German's deathbed plea, and walks quietly out of his presence without giving absolution. The author's moral dilemma now becomes the reader's as the latter is asked to confront the question, "What would I have done?" A collection of 32 responses from Jews and non-Jews alike then follows, providing the reader with a situation that must be entered, analyzed, and internalized.

GARBER provides information about the challenge to Jewish and Christian self-identity and theology presented by the Shoah. He summarizes his philosophy about teaching and learning from the Shoah as "Sinai, not cyanide." In other words, Garber maintains that a moral and ethical standard must prevail over a philosophy of survival at any price. He believes that passionate objectivity—not a controlled and distant objectivity—is the only way to avoid becoming a mere teller of facts. The Shoah requires passion and a broad, philosophical approach—"historiosophy"—so as not to diminish the event.

ZEV GARBER

See also Holocaust: Film Treatments; Holocaust: Histories; Holocaust: Literature and Memoirs

Holocaust: Film Treatments

Avisar, Ilan, *Screening the Holocaust: Cinema's Image of the Unimaginable* (Jewish Literature and Culture), Bloomington: Indiana University Press, 1988
Colombat, André, *The Holocaust in French Film* (Filmmakers, no. 33), Metuchen, New Jersey: Scarecrow, 1993
Doneson, Judith, *The Holocaust in American Film*, Philadelphia: Jewish Publication Society, 1987
Insdorf, Annette, *Indelible Shadows: Film and the Holocaust*, New York: Vintage, 1983; 2nd edition, Cambridge and New York: Cambridge University Press, 1989
Loshitzky, Yosefa (editor), *Spielberg's Holocaust: Critical Perspectives on "Schindler's List,"* Bloomington: Indiana University Press, 1997
Santner, Eric L., *Stranded Objects: Mourning, Memory, and Film in Postwar Germany*, Ithaca, New York: Cornell University Press, 1990

Perhaps because Nazi Germany made pervasive and concerted use of the film industry as a tool of ideological persuasion, or perhaps because the Allied forces liberating the concentration camps at the war's end could not believe what they saw, cinema has been an important vehicle for representing the Holocaust since the mid-1940s. Included under the rubric of Holocaust films are documentaries (which may rely upon original Nazi or Allied film footage and photographs, retrospective testimony, or journeys back to the site of atrocity), docudramas, feature films, and experimental cinema. Critical consideration of film as a serious genre for reflection on the Nazi past, the implications of that past, and the cultural lenses through which it is viewed, took on greater importance at the end of the 20th century.

A comprehensive overview of films dealing with the Holocaust, INSDORF covers a wide range of genres—including documentary, docudrama, and feature films—in a variety of languages. Organizing the films according to genre, subgenre (such as the personal documentary, the montage, or black humor), and theme (such as the child, identity, or German guilt), the book covers more than 100 titles produced from the 1940s through the 1980s. In addition to summarizing the plot of each film, Insdorf articulates what she considers as its central thesis, compares it to other films in its category, and offers some details related to its production.

Focusing solely on film produced in the United States, DONESON examines fewer films than Insdorf but does so in greater depth. The book not only explores the ways in which U.S. cinema and television attempt to represent the Holocaust but also investigates the U.S. slant of these representations. The book places each film in the context of the cultural moment in which it was produced, discussing, for example, the changing stature and concerns of the U.S. Jewish community and the development of "Americanized" meanings for the Holocaust.

AVISAR similarly analyzes the motivations and interpretations implicit in cinematic representations of the Holocaust. Arguing that film can contribute meaningfully to discourse on the Nazi genocide by both representing the Holocaust and reflecting upon its meaning, Avisar arranges Holocaust film first by genre—documentary and narrative (feature) film—then by nation, with a chapter each on Czech and U.S. cinema: the former is interpreted as complex if sometimes flawed, while the latter is regarded as a failed enterprise, both morally and aesthetically.

Like Doneson, COLOMBAT focuses on the representation of the Holocaust in the cinema of a single nation—in this case, France. The first third of the book analyzes almost five decades of French films in light of French antisemitism during and after World War II and evolving attitudes toward complicated issues of French complicity and resistance, with respect to political issues current during film production. The last two-thirds of the study offer close analyses of particular films (including *Night and Fog, Mr. Klein,* and *Weapons of the Spirit*) and the work of Marcel Ophüls and Louis Malle.

SANTNER does not focus on representations of the victims of the Nazi genocide; instead he studies how postwar German cinema performs and depicts the *Trauerarbeit,* or the psychological expression in the German national psyche of the legacy of Nazism and the Holocaust. By looking closely at the works of two filmmakers, Edgar Reitz *(Heimat)* and Hans Jürgen Syberberg *(Our Hitler),* the book explores the successes and failures of individual and national attempts to integrate the memory of loss, destruction, and disorientation.

In an anthology about what may be, arguably, the most influential representation of the Holocaust in a feature film, LOSHITZKY provides multiple ways to consider Steven Spielberg's *Schindler's List.* Written by scholars in fields as diverse as history, literature, cultural studies, film studies, and communication, the essays examine the reception of the film in the United States, Germany, France, and Israel, evaluating its success as a representation of the Holocaust. Several of the essays discuss its use of antisemitic imagery, while others explore the place of popular culture in interpreting and transmitting collective memory.

SARA R. HOROWITZ

See also Holocaust: Histories; Holocaust: Literature and Memoirs; Holocaust: Responses to the Holocaust

Holy Places *see* Veneration of Saints, Pilgrimages, and Holy Places

Homiletics

Bettan, Israel, *Studies in Jewish Preaching: Middle Ages,* Cincinnati, Ohio: Hebrew Union College Press, 1939; London: University Press of America, 1988

Friedenberg, Robert V., *"Hear O Israel": The History of American Jewish Preaching, 1654–1970* (Studies in Rhetoric and Communication), Tuscaloosa: University of Alabama Press, 1989

Ruderman, David (editor), *Preachers of the Italian Ghetto,* Berkeley: University of California Press, 1992

Saperstein, Marc, *Jewish Preaching, 1200–1800,* New Haven, Connecticut: Yale University Press, 1989

Saperstein, Marc, *"Your Voice Like a Ram's Horn": Themes and Texts in Traditional Jewish Preaching* (Monographs of the Hebrew Union College, no. 18), Cincinnati, Ohio: Hebrew Union College Press, 1996

The word *homiletics* is generally understood to refer to the art of preaching. In the present context, it is used in a broader sense to cover the history of Jewish preaching, entailing the sermons delivered by Jews, usually in the context of public worship, and the texts (printed books or manuscripts) in which a record of such oral communication was preserved. There is evidence of an ongoing tradition of Jewish preaching from the rabbinic period through the early Middle Ages. However, the earliest extant texts of actual Jewish sermons written by identifiable authors date from the 13th century.

BETTAN, a professor of homiletics at the Hebrew Union College in Cincinnati, Ohio, was the first to publish critical investigation of medieval and early modern Jewish preachers in English. His volume of studies is composed of articles published in the *Hebrew Union College Annual* during the 1930s, supplemented by an introductory essay on "Early Preaching in the Synagogue" and a brief conclusion. These studies focus on the printed oeuvre of seven European preachers, from Jacob Anatoli in the 13th century through Jonathan Eybeschuetz in the 18th. Most of the chapters follow a common format: an introduction, a biographical and bibliographical section, a treatment of the preacher's biblical exegesis and other homiletic techniques, and a topically organized reconstruction of the preacher's religious worldview. For this purpose, Bettan weaves together passages from all the sermons written by the preacher. He provides sound introductions to these seven figures, although he provides little clear sense of what any one actual sermon was like.

In a sense, FRIEDENBERG's book continues Bettan's project, taking up in the 18th century where the earlier book left off and shifting the purview from Europe to North America. The author reveals an interest in rhetorical technique and in the relationship of the preachers and their sermons to the American historical context. The first chapter, on colonial and Revolutionary America, highlights the Sephardi clergyman Gershom Mendes Seixas; the second, on Jacksonian America, treats the German immigrant Isaac Leeser; the third, on the Civil War period, analyzes a sermon by the Swedish-born New York rabbi Morris Raphall that refutes the abolitionist claim that slavery is condemned as a sin in sacred scripture. An extensive discussion of the preaching of Isaac Mayer Wise, founder of the institutions of American Reform Judaism, shows the influence on Wise of Hugh Blair's rhetorical theory. The author then reviews the preaching of the Zionist rabbis Stephen S. Wise and Abba Hillel Silver. The final chapter discusses sermons of five "elder statesmen," representing Orthodox, Conservative, and Reform Judaism in the post–World War II generation. The many sermons by American preachers published in Yiddish or Hebrew are not addressed. An epilogue discusses homiletic training in American rabbinical seminaries in the 1980s.

RUDERMAN has edited, introduced, and contributed to a collection of essays on the Italian Jewish community, primarily in the late 16th and early 17th centuries. Marc Saperstein provides an overview of the topic, raising such issues as the paucity of texts preserved and the absence of bibliographic studies, the relationship between a native Italian homiletic tradition and the impact of the Spanish émigrés, the influence of Christian homiletics, the training of Jewish preachers, and the writing and printing of sermon collections (including the shift from Hebrew to vernacular texts). Moshe Idel treats the Mantuan rabbi Judah Moscato; his analysis of passages in two of Moscato's sermons points to the significant influence of Hermetic views and thus the powerful impact of Renaissance culture on Moscato's thought. Robert Bonfil discusses sermons by Judah del Bene, recorded by an educated listener, to illustrate the role of preaching as a mode of mediating between the elite culture of the intellectual and the popular culture of the average congregant. Ruderman's own contribution documents the use of scientific knowledge and medical analogies in the sermons of Azariah Figo. Joanna Weinberg analyzes the sermons of the Venetian polymath Leone Modena and the possible influence of a homiletic work by the Italian bishop Panigarola. Elliott Horowitz analyzes the emergence of the eulogy as a major genre of Italian preaching beginning in the 16th century. A common theme in many of these studies is the effect of Renaissance culture and the role of kabbalistic and scientific doctrines in these sermons.

SAPERSTEIN (1989) was the first comprehensive study of medieval and early modern Jewish homiletics published in English since Bettan. A substantial introduction discusses the nature of the source materials, including the problematic relationship between the oral sermons and the texts in which they were preserved, the settings and occasions for Jewish preaching, the interaction between preachers and their congregations (especially when sermons of rebuke were being delivered), the ways in which preachers organized and structured their material, and the value of sermons as evidence for Jewish history and as a genre of Jewish literature. The individual sermon, rather than the collection gathered over many years, is the focal point. Examples of such sermons by 16 preachers over six centuries are translated and analyzed, all for the first time in English, four of them from manuscript. The book concludes with a collection of briefer sources pertaining to the history and theory of Jewish preaching.

SAPERSTEIN (1996) contains a number of thematic studies of traditional Jewish preaching from the Middle Ages through the 18th century. These themes include homiletic motifs in sermons for the Days of Awe and Passover; exegesis of biblical and rabbinic texts and the popularization of philosophical material by the preachers; Jewish-Christian relations as revealed in the preaching of both sides; sermons of rebuke as a reflection of points of tension in Jewish society; and occasional sermons in times of national crisis or celebration as evidence for an incipient sense of patriotism. The book also contains a number of homiletic texts published for the first time, including the earliest known Jewish instructions on the art of preaching and several significant examples of the eulogy genre.

MARC SAPERSTEIN

Homosexuality

Alpert, Rebecca, *Like Bread on the Seder Plate: Jewish Lesbians and the Transformation of Tradition,* New York: Columbia University Press, 1997

Balka, Christie and Andy Rose (editors), *Twice Blessed: On Being Lesbian, Gay, and Jewish,* Boston: Beacon, 1989

Beck, Evelyn T. (editor), *Nice Jewish Girls: A Lesbian Anthology,* Watertown, Massachusetts: Persephone, 1982; revised and updated, Boston: Beacon, 1989

Lamm, Norman, "Judaism and the Modern Jewish Attitude to Homosexuality," in *Encyclopaedia Judaica Year Book,* Jerusalem: Encyclopaedia Judaica, 1974

Matt, Herschel, "Sin, Crime, Sickness or Alternative Life-Style?: A Jewish Approach to Homosexuality," *Judaism,* 27(1), 1978

Moore, Tracy (editor), *Lesbiot: Israeli Lesbians Talk about Sexuality, Feminism, Judaism and Their Lives,* London and New York: Cassell, 1995

Raphael, Lev, *Journeys and Arrivals: On Being Gay and Jewish,* Boston: Faber, 1996

Shokeid, Moshe, *A Gay Synagogue in New York,* New York: Columbia University Press, 1995

The intersection of religion and sexuality is a small but growing field of investigation. While there have been many studies of the legal prohibitions against male homosexuality found in ancient Jewish texts, female homoeroticism in ancient periods has been ignored by commentators. There are few works considering Jewish themes from a gay or lesbian perspective, and the genre of the coming-out story, chronicling the personal struggles and creative experiences of individuals trying to reconcile their homosexual and Jewish identities, has been the most popular vehicle for Jewish gay and lesbian self-expression.

In a thorough and clear discussion of all relevant references in Jewish legal literature, LAMM presents a standard Orthodox approach to the issues of Judaism and homosexuality. Like a number of other authors writing from an Orthodox or Conservative perspective, he contends that contemporary Jews should condemn homosexuality as something that defies Jewish law and nature.

MATT is the first Conservative rabbi to break from the tradition that condemns homosexuality as a sin, crime, or sickness. Arguing that homosexuality is not a choice, he supports the integration of gay men and lesbians into mainstream Jewish religious life, as congregants, rabbis, and teachers. Matt also reasons that if God fashions people with same-sex desires, then these desires must be a natural part of the order of creation. His writing has influenced many Jewish communities to accept gays and lesbians, while also inspiring liberal rabbinical seminaries to accept them for training.

SHOKEID, an Israeli anthropologist, offers a sympathetic ethnographic account of several years that he spent attending Congregation Beit Simchat Torah, a gay and lesbian synagogue in New York City. Although the congregation includes both men and women, the author neglects gender issues, focusing primarily on the men who started the congregation, and exploring how they reconcile their Jewish and gay identities through religious activities of study and prayer.

BECK provides the first book that concentrates entirely on the stories of Jewish lesbians coming to terms with their identities. Most of the contributors to this anthology came out as lesbians during the second wave of the feminist movement in the United States in the 1970s. Discovering that lesbian feminism is not always sympathetic to religion in general and to Jewishness in particular, the authors began reclaiming their connection to their Jewish roots. Using personal narratives, poetry, and fictional accounts, the contributors to this volume break new ground by making lesbians visible in the Jewish community for the first time in history. Several ultraorthodox groups have responded by excommunicating the editor and contributors and burning copies of their book.

BALKA and ROSE offer the first collection including the perspectives of both gay men and lesbians. This series of essays contains coming-out stories; academic studies on gay men and lesbians in different historical periods; discussions of contemporary issues of gay and lesbian synagogues; and analyses of homosexuals' involvement in the world of U.S. Judaism. The authors present a powerful and influential set of arguments for the inclusion and visibility of gay men and lesbians in the Jewish community, as well as practical suggestions for involving homosexuals in synagogue life. The volume also incorporates the views of feminists and Jews with disabilities. A poignant essay by a closeted lesbian rabbi illuminates issues of discrimination in the Jewish community, while an account of a gay commitment ceremony raises the issue of gay marriage.

RAPHAEL's series of personal essays is the only available full-length treatment of the conflicts and connections between gay and Jewish identities. As a child of Holocaust survivors, Raphael is particularly effective when discussing contemporary Jewish and gay issues related to that trauma. He also examines the difficulty of writing fiction and prose with gay and Jewish themes and reviews the reception that his work receives from particular audiences.

MOORE uses interviews from a number of Israeli lesbians to reveal the complexities of their position in Israeli society. Although the interviews are limited to speakers of English, they create a broad and complicated picture of Israeli lesbian life and the changes that have been taking place as a public gay rights movement has emerged.

ALPERT's book elaborates on neglected Jewish texts about female homoeroticism and uses midrashic techniques to suggest ancient and modern texts that might be relevant to lesbian Jewish life. She evaluates issues that concern religious lesbians, such as how to celebrate holidays and mark life-cycle events in a Jewish context. The book also examines the importance of Jewish lesbian fiction for creating positive images for Jewish lesbians.

REBECCA ALPERT

Human Rights

Cohn, Haim H., *Human Rights in the Bible and Talmud,* Tel Aviv: MOD, 1989

Falk, Ze'ev, *Law and Religion: The Jewish Experience,* Jerusalem: Mesharim, 1981
Konvitz, Milton R., *Judaism and the American Idea,* Ithaca, New York: Cornell University Press, 1978
Sharfman, Daphna, *Living without a Constitution: Civil Rights in Israel,* Armonk, New York: Sharpe, 1993
Sidorsky, David (editor), *Essays on Human Rights: Contemporary Issues and Jewish Perspectives,* Philadelphia: Jewish Publication Society, 1979
Zamir, Itzhak and Allen Zysblat, *Public Law in Israel,* New York: Oxford University Press, and Oxford: Clarendon, 1996

The fundamental tension in the slender and inadequate literature on Judaism and human rights involves the fervent belief that Jews as a minority around the world are entitled to human rights, while as a majority in the Jewish state they are entitled, out of regard for traditional religious sensibilities, to limit the rights of minorities, whether Muslim, Christian, or Jewish. Key to following the fundamental problems in most literature on Judaism and human rights, therefore, is the paradox of secular Jews using religious texts abroad to enhance arguments for human rights and religious Jews using secular politics at home in Israel to limit them. In particular, the literature on Judaism and human rights regularly tries to show the Jewish origins of democratic principles, while Israel to this day lacks a constitution because of the objections of religious Jews whose hostility toward democratic principles can be chronicled throughout history. For the most part, it seems that Israeli writers treat this subject, especially with regard to problems in Israel, with much more honesty and sophistication than writers in the diaspora, who tend to be apologetic or in denial.

COHN's judicial career has been brilliant, but when he attempts to write on Judaism and human rights in this and other books, he falls into the same trap as many others. This book is apologetic and polemical at the same time, trying to both demonstrate pride in the glorious religious tradition of the Jews and to show that some of the major desiderata on human rights can be filled from within the tradition. Cohn attempts to create an imaginary case for human rights in Judaism based on the assumption that biblical and talmudic texts were normative and not countered by any subsequent legal developments or interpretive traditions. Thus, he presents a picture unconnected with history, tradition, or reality. Unfortunately, Cohn quotes out of context and without citation, and he suggests that his readers find the sources using dictionaries and concordances, leaving them at the mercy of his impressionistic and selective renderings. Indeed, he emphatically states that he is not an apologist, noting that aspects of the tradition are discriminatory, untenable, and archaic, but he assures readers that in their day these aspects of the tradition were progressive. Cohn tries to convince his readers that the Torah serves as a constitution that guarantees human rights, but later in the book he celebrates the uncompromising nature of ancient Judaism against the threats of other religions, noting bans on doing business with idolaters. Cohn apparently sees no contradiction in championing Torah Judaism as a guarantor of human rights and its allowing the murderer of a non-Jew to receive his punishment from God rather than in a court of law. The argument often deals entirely with generalities and not specific cases. Cohn's Jewish information is often deficient, to the detriment of his argument. For example, he attributes only to God the right to kill extra-judicially or without trial, ignoring long-standing valorization of dispatching the *moser* (informant), Amalek, and the seven nations of Canaan. Basing equality of the sexes in Judaism on God's having created men and women in his image is either delusional or wishful thinking in light of traditional Judaism. In his zealous enthusiasm to demonstrate the fact that discrimination against women in Judaism is to their benefit, Cohn asserts that a husband cannot impose work on his wife, contradicting Maimonides' instructions that a woman who refuses to do housework is to be beaten with a rod (Mishneh Torah, Ishut 21:10). Similarly, of the three passages in the Mishnah that deal with forcing a man to divorce his wife, one against it (Yebamot 14:1) and two in favor of it (Gittin 9:8 and Arakhin 5:6), Cohn mentions only the one against it. Similarly, he refers to the ban of Rabbenu Gershom on divorcing a woman without her consent, without mentioning all the exceptions to it that have accumulated over the centuries.

FALK presents a notably serious and reasoned approach. In his chapter on democracy he forthrightly asserts that both law and religion subordinate the wishes of the individual, that there are inherent tensions between religion and democracy, and that there can be no easy synthesis between Judaism and democracy. On this point he invokes the thought of Yeshayahu Leibowitz, who asserts that democracy, which is anthropocentric, is based on the Kantian idea of human autonomy, while religion, which is theocentric, is based on heteronomy. Nevertheless, acknowledging that some spokesmen for Orthodox Jewry see democracy and Judaism as incompatible, Falk raises the possibility that this may not be the case and traces arguments from Jewish history and religious texts for both sides. This leads to his view that Judaism, especially as practiced under state control in Israel, must make some serious concessions concerning autonomy for the two to be compatible. Unlike others, who deny any conflicts between Judaism and democracy, Falk argues soundly and cogently that many Jewish ideals of equality and human rights, despite biblical precedents sanctioning the oppression of various groups, were meant for a glorious egalitarian future. His chapters often, therefore, have more of a hortative than a historical quality to them.

KONVITZ, a major figure in the study of human rights, presents an unfounded, tendentious, contradictory, and apologetic masterpiece that deserves careful reading to learn how myths are created. Konvitz establishes a priori categories to explain Jewish existence: Israel does not place its own national existence or honor as an absolute; the "essence" of the Hebrew scriptures (selectively equated with Judaism) represents a universal ethical system of thorough egalitarianism; principles of the Torah and the U.S. Constitution are so close that he can speak of an "American-Hebraic idea"; and Israel has a unique sense of purpose among the nations. Anyone who looks beyond these comforting notions, especially with regard to what happens in Israel, is guilty of sympathizing with the murderous aspirations of the Palestine Liberation Organization. Konvitz's enthusiasm for his idealized vision of the United States leads him to conclude that the United States has resolved issues concerning racial segregation and abortion not by violence and mob action but through the rule of law. He next considers Israel, where he concludes that the eventual constitution will be based on the spirit of the Torah, which will put some actions beyond the power of any human institution. So, the United States must live by the law, a law derived from Judaism, but Israel is destined to be a theocracy. Konvitz has little patience, therefore, for those who question the segregation of the sexes at the Western Wall in Jerusalem and are not sensitive to the traditional needs of those religious Jews who enforce the segregation. At one point, however, Konvitz unexpectedly admits that he has been nurtured by both cultures. This constitutes a surprising assertion because all along he has been attempting to convince readers that Judaism and Western democracy represent one and the same culture. He sees the all-male prayer groups at the Wall as representing all Jews praying in one place at one time and revels in the diversity of those different kinds of Jews with whom he can pray—omitting women and liberal Jews. Konvitz's sympathy for civil rights evaporates entirely as he relates a critical experience in which he encountered a Jew at the Wall trying to stop another Jew from taking a photograph on the sabbath, which Konvitz views enthusiastically as the effective expression of group consciousness.

SHARFMAN, an instructor at the University of Haifa who is involved in the Israeli civil rights movement, places Israel's lack of a constitution in the context of the history of the state and the ongoing development of particular laws involving various freedoms such as freedom of the press and freedom of association and the problems posed by both religious and security considerations. At the center of her deeply impressive historical argument stand developments in Jewish Palestine from the 1920s on, especially the emphasis placed by David Ben-Gurion, Golda Meir, the Histadrut, and kibbutzim, and even by Vladimir Jabotinsky and the Revisionists on centralization of power, bureaucratization, control by an elite, and the lack of acceptance of the role of the individual. Sharfman documents compellingly the hostility of pioneer politicians to press freedom (and the very idea of broadcasting) as well as their sympathy for the use of coercion and even violence to settle controversies. She describes one of the first collisions between the religious groups and democratic principles, which involved the right of women to vote and to serve on the Representative Assembly and the National Committee. In 1922, because religious Jews would not sit with women, the Representative Committee did not meet for almost a year. With the founding of the State, both Ben-Gurion's party, Mapai, for opportunistic reasons, and the National Religious Party, out of commitment to the authority of the Torah, opposed a constitution, and for this reason, the Ben-Gurion government maintained the Emergency Powers Act imposed by the British. Sharfman refers to the government's treatment of new immigrants as "a hierarchical system of dependence" by operated by "petty tyrants" and "thugs." Moshe Sharett, acting prime minister, referred to new immigrants as "children," incapable of exercising any judgment, and Ben-Gurion called them "human dust." Arab minorities were subject to the military government until 1966, a rule that many in the government saw as corrupt, an obstacle to the development of true democracy in Israel, and a useful tool for enemy propaganda. The religious establishment, through political coalitions, gained control of all Jewish marriages and divorces as well as the supervision of many other matters. Ben-Gurion noted: "The freedom of religion and conscience that the religious party demands for itself is not something it is prepared or capable of granting to others." Sharfman notes the inherent contradiction between the position of religious Jews who do not accept the right of a secular majority to rule over them and their view of their right as a minority to impose their views on the majority. In other words, Jewish law does not recognize moral autonomy, only obedience. Attempts to put forward basic laws of human rights, even when they do not grant freedom of worship to all religions and branches of Judaism, have been opposed by the religious parties who want to protect their control over determining matters of personal status. Sharfman cites quotations from religious leaders indicating that recognition of human worth and human freedom reflects an antireligious and even racist mentality. She shows that secular parties, both on the right and on the left, have accepted the religious status quo both out of practical necessity to maintain power and support coalition governments and out of the desire to preserve images of national unity. Sharfman reports early misgivings expressed by Supreme Court Justice Haim Cohn about the exclusive jurisdiction of religious courts, Ben-Gurion's resistance to change, the hope expressed by a minister of religious affairs that Jewish law could be modernized, and Ben-Gurion's deathbed regret that he had not followed Cohn's advice.

For many of the authors represented in SIDORSKY's collection, the concept of human rights does not extend beyond what Jews are entitled to receive. They do not appear to believe that when Jews are in power, they are obligated to extend rights to others. Leslie C. Green's essay cites the 1950 Israeli Law of Return as an example of respect for human rights, clearly confusing Jewish rights with human rights. The essay goes on to argue that Israeli courts have ensured that there is no religious discrimination and that tolerance and equality are maintained among all religious groups, a statement that is contradicted by the many laws in Israel that discriminate against Reform and Conservative Jews. Similarly, Yoram Dinstein's essay notes that the Six-Day War marked a turning point for the treatment of Jews in the Soviet Union, oblivious to the fact that it also marked a turning point for many Arabs in the territories occupied by Israel that year. Shimon Shetreet deals squarely with issues in Israel, acknowledging the presence of religious coercion in Israel with the subjection of citizens to the religious courts for marriage and divorce. In another essay on Israel, drawing heavily from materials in the *Israel Yearbook on Human Rights,* Jerome J. Shestack tries to diminish most charges of human rights violations against Israel, including allegations of torture. He suggests that in 1967 Jews found themselves ruling over others for the first time and that it was "a strange and unwanted role for the Jews," although since the founding of the State, Jews had ruled over many thousands of Arabs. Ultimately, when Shestack has exhausted all dodges, including the improvements in human rights enjoyed by the Arabs, he deals with censorship, economic standards, administrative detention, treatment of detainees, deportations, the demolition of homes, and the building of settlements. Most of these practices he attributes to the need to counter Palestinian terrorism and support Israeli security needs. Shestack ends, however, by making it clear that occupation is repugnant to what he calls Jewish values, although its biggest supporter is the National Religious Party, and he asks what engaging in such an occupation will do to Israeli society. In his essay, the great Jewish historian Salo Baron confirms that as democracy spread through Europe during the 18th century, Jewish elites were afraid that egalitarianism would weaken traditional Jewish communal control and threaten their leadership role. Contrary to the apologetics about the compatibility of Judaism with democracy and the Torah with constitutions, Baron shares a Yiddish joke from the time that explains the word for constitution, *Konstitutsie,* as *konst du, tist du,* "if you can, you do," pointing to the fear that constitutions would enable an expansion of individual liberties, something that traditional Judaism was not prepared to accept.

ZAMIR and ZYSBLAT offer a collection of Israeli Supreme Court decisions with introductions that nicely supplement Sharfman's book, particularly her final chapters on the Israeli Supreme Court and various freedoms. Zysblat's introduction, however, diverges sharply from some of the points made by Sharfman. He asserts that constitutions are not necessary to establish democracies: totalitarian regimes can exist with them, and democracies, such as Great Britain, can exist without them. He also casts the traditional Jewish community and the Zionist movement as having long-standing traditions of democracy. Indeed, contradicting one of Sharfman's major points, Zysblat asserts that the proportional representation system in national elections, which requires such delicate coalitions, is in fact the major guarantee of democracy in Israel. His main point, however, agreeing with Sharfman, is that the Supreme Court, by creatively interpreting the law, is the ultimate protector of civil rights in Israel. Some of the classic cases discussed include the Kol Ha'am case of 1953, which concerned the closing of a newspaper for attacking Abba Eban's supposed offer to put 200,000 Israeli troops at the side of the Americans in the event of a war with the Soviet Union; the Kach case of 1987, which concerned the obligation of public television to carry information relating to the incitements to racism of Rabbi Meir Kahane; and the Elon Moreh case, involving the question of Jewish expropriation of Arab land on the West Bank for ideological rather than security reasons, the only reasons allowed by law and international convention. David Kretzmer, a professor of law at the Hebrew University and a member of the United Nations Commission on Human Rights, confirms that the most adamant opposition to civil rights legislation in Israel comes from the religious parties. In particular, he notes that the 1992 Basic Law of Human Rights does not allow judicial review of existing legislation, which he feels indicates a lack of confidence that this legislation would meet the basic standards of human rights. Kretzmer's article makes it clear that there is a basic conflict between Israel being a Jewish and a democratic state, evidence that Judaism is not essentially committed to human rights and that democratic institutions did not spring forth from Jewish tradition.

HOWARD TZVI ADELMAN

Humor

Ausubel, Nathan (editor), *A Treasury of Jewish Humor*, New York: Crown, 1948

Cohen, Sarah Blacher (editor), *Jewish Wry: Essays on Jewish Humor* (Jewish Literature and Culture), Bloomington: Indiana University Press, 1987

Davidson, Israel, *Parody in Jewish Literature* (Columbia University Oriental Studies, vol. 2), New York: Columbia University Press, 1907

Dundes, Alan and Thomas Hauschild, "Auschwitz Jokes," *Western Folklore*, 42(4), 1983

Greenstein, Edward L., "Humour and Wit," in *The Anchor Bible Dictionary*, vol. 3, edited by David Noel Freedman, New York and London: Doubleday, 1992

Harris, David A. and Izrail Rabinovich, *The Jokes of Oppression: The Humor of Soviet Jews*, Northvale, New Jersey, and London: Aronson, 1988

Jason, Heda, *Studies in Jewish Ethnopoetry: Narrating Art, Content, Message, Genre* (Asian Folklore and Social Life Monographs, vol. 72), edited by Lou Tsu-k'uang in collaboration with Wolfram Eberhard, Taipei: Orient Cultural Service, 1975

The study of Jewish humor is a relatively new field. The first important book about biblical humor was *Humour and Irony in the Bible* (London: Luzac, 1891) by Rabbi Joseph Chotzner (1849–1914), rabbi of Belfast and a former housemaster at Harrow. The next important book on this subject was Edwin M. Good's *Irony in the Old Testament* (London: SPCK, 1965). Since the 1980s, however, humor in the Hebrew Bible has been analyzed in detail in scholarly articles and monographs. The author of seminal studies on humor in both Hebrew Scripture and other literatures of the ancient Near East, GREENSTEIN traces the history of research and describes succinctly the seven major forms of humor manifest in the Hebrew Bible: sarcasm, ridicule, satire, parody, trickery, verbal wit, and proverbial humor.

DAVIDSON, best known for his classic studies on medieval Hebrew poetry, focuses his analysis on parody. He calls attention to two parodies in the Jerusalem Talmud (Pesahim 3:7 and Nedarim 6:8); discusses the Samaritan high priest Phinehas ben Abisha's (1376–1440) fascinating treatise on Samaritan eschatology that takes the form of a parody on the biblical story of Noah and the Ark (Genesis 6:13–8:11); and surveys more than 500 parodies from Jewish literature spanning the 11th to the 19th century. Davidson shows that Jewish parodists were preachers disguised as jesters, and he contends that most Jewish parodies were recognized for what they were and never swallowed whole. He argues, however, that parody did perform important social functions. For example, when Joseph Perl of Tarnopol aped the famous Latin anticlerical satires of 16th-century German Christian humanists in his 1819 book *Megalleh Temirin* (*Revealer of Secrets*), he succeeded in exposing the vices of hasidic leaders and the foolishness of their followers. Davidson declares with misplaced modernist optimism that Hasidism "might have withstood anathemas indefinitely, but it could not endure the lash of ridicule and exposure very long."

In a book published before the collapse of the Soviet Union, HARRIS and RABINOVICH posit that for many Russian Jews poking fun at the foolishness of Communist officials is "a treasured, if largely private, means of conveying anger, frustration or criticism in an often hostile environment." Through his personal use of Soviet Jewish humor, the proverbial Soviet Jew "manages to face life with endless reserves of common sense and optimism." He becomes "the irrepressible foil of the world's most powerful repressive society."

AUSUBEL's English-language anthology contains humorous stories and poems by 72 authors; most of the selections come from Yiddish-speaking Ashkenazi Jewry of the 18th to 20th centuries, although the volume also includes texts by three medieval Jews from Spain (Abraham ibn Ezra, Judah Al-Harizi, and Shem Tov Falquera) and a selection from the apostate Bar Hebraeus (1226–1286), who became head of the Jacobite Church in Syria and who wrote in Arabic. Still, this collection belongs to a genre of anthologies of Jewish humor that perpetuate the simplistic notion that Jewish humor is largely limited to humor in a Yiddish milieu.

JASON's analysis of the humor of Middle Eastern Jews corrects this distorted impression. She also argues that the stories of the foolish sages of Chelm belong to a genre of "numskull tales" that are found in non-Jewish and Jewish cultures alike. "Numskulls," she asserts, "are not a mirror ridiculing human society but are perceived by the narrating society as part of the universe of beings, real and imaginary, which populate the normal world." The imaginary realm ruled by fools who think they are wise is identified, to the chagrin of the real inhabitants of the place in question, with a real place: for example, Schildau in German folklore, Gotham in English folklore, or Chelm in Yiddish folklore. Following the dean of Israeli folklore studies, Dov Noy, Jason also argues that "parodies on Jewish traditional literary style are the only "special kind of joke [that] has not been found (until now) in non-Jewish cultures." Contrary to this claim, however, even these jokes, as Davidson's seminal study explains, have their counterparts in other cultures, such as 11th-century B.C.E. Babylonia where the famous "Dialogue of Pessimism" parodies well-known works that were part of the literary canon studied in the scribal academies.

COHEN assembles 14 scholarly yet eminently accessible essays. These studies demonstrate that Jewish humor worthy of study is confined neither to the vanished world of East European Jewry nor to the literary parodies of medieval Iberian Jewry. Topics treated include female Jewish comedians in the United States; Israeli humor; Canadian Jewish humor; and Woody Allen. The volume contains a comprehensive bibliography of Jewish humor.

DUNDES and HAUSCHILD investigate jokes about Jews circulating in Germany since the Holocaust. Commenting on examples of antisemitic humor collected by Hauschild in 1982, folklorist Dundes accepts the view that jokes told about the members of a particular ethnic, national, or religious group may offer a socially sanctioned outlet for the expression of aggression toward that group, and he surmises further that the concept of self-hatred may adequately explain why Jews tell antisemitic jokes.

MAYER IRWIN GRUBER

Hungary

Braham, Randolph (editor), *Hungarian-Jewish Studies*, 3 vols., New York: World Federation of Hungarian Jews, 1969

Braham, Randolph, *The Politics of Genocide: The Holocaust in Hungary*, 2 vols., New York: Columbia University Press, 1981, revised edition, 1994

Braham, Randolph and Attila Pók (editors), *The Holocaust in Hungary: Fifty Years Later* (Eastern European Monographs, no. 477), New York: Rosenthal Institute for Holocaust Studies, Graduate Center of the City University of New York, 1997

Braham, Randolph and Bela Vago (editors), *The Holocaust in Hungary: Forty Years Later* (Eastern European Monographs, no. 190), New York: Social Science Monographs, 1985

Carmilly-Weinberger, Moshe (editor), *The Rabbinical Seminary of Budapest, 1877–1977: A Centennial Volume*, New York: Sepher-Hermon, 1986

Dalmat, Dan, *Bibliographia Hungarica-Judaica (Magyar-Zsidó Bibliográfia, 1945–1990)*, Budapest: Géniusz, 1991

Dán, Róbert (editor), *Occident and Orient: A Tribute to the Memory of Alexander Scheiber*, Budapest: Akadémiai Kiadó, and Leiden: Brill, 1988

Don, Yehudah and Viktor Kárády (editors), *A Social and Economic History of Central European Jewry*, New Brunswick, New Jersey: Transaction, 1990

Handler, Andrew (editor), *Ararát: A Collection of Hungarian-Jewish Short Stories*, Rutherford, New Jersey: Fairleigh Dickinson University Press, 1977

Handler, Andrew, *From the Ghetto to the Games: Jewish Athletes in Hungary* (East European Monographs, no. 192), Boulder, Colorado: East European Monographs, 1985

Katzburg, Nathaniel, *Hungary and the Jews: Policy and Legislation, 1920–1943*, Ramat Gan: Bar-Ilan University Press, 1981

Komoróczy, Géza (editor), *Jewish Budapest: Monuments, Rites, History*, New York: Central European University Press, 1999

McCagg, William O., Jr., *Jewish Nobles and Geniuses in Modern Hungary* (East European Monographs, no. 3), Boulder, Colorado: East European Quarterly, 1972

Patai, Raphael, *The Jews of Hungary: History, Culture, Psychology*, Detroit, Michigan: Wayne State University Press, 1996

Perlman, Robert, *Bridging Three Worlds: Hungarian-Jewish Americans, 1848–1914*, Amherst: University of Massachusetts Press, 1991

Sanders, Ivan, "Jewish Revival in Central Europe: A Survey of Recent Hungarian Judaica," in *Jewish Book Annual*, 1991–1992

Scheiber, Alexander, *Jewish Inscriptions in Hungary, from the 3rd Century to 1686*, Budapest: Akadémiai Kiadó, and Leiden: Brill, 1983

Silber, Michael K. (editor), *Jews in the Hungarian Economy, 1760–1945: Studies Dedicated to Moshe Carmilly-Weinberger on His Eightieth Birthday*, Jerusalem: Magnes Press of Hebrew University, 1992

Vago, Bela and George Lachmann Mosse (editors), *Jews and Non-Jews in Eastern Europe, 1918–1945*, New York: Wiley, 1974

Yaron, Baruch (compiler), *Jews and Judaism in East European Publications, 1945–1970: A Bibliography*, edited by Benjamin Pinkus, Jerusalem: Hebrew University, Centre for Documentation of East European Jewry, 1972

Although there is considerable literature available on the history of Jews in Hungary, it is mostly in Hungarian, German, and Hebrew. For the English reader, there is only one comprehensive monograph available, written by Raphael Patai. Other scholarship is also available on this topic, but it is published in different collections of essays or as chapters in general history books on Hungary and Central Europe. The following survey considers studies of Hungarian Jewish history on a large scale and includes descriptions of the political, social, cultural, religious, and economic status of Hungarian Jews. Among these topics, literature on the Holocaust and on the period between World War I and World War II are numerically overrepresented, a reflection not only of the available literature in English but of the enormous impact of the Holocaust as a subject of scholarship.

BRAHAM (1981) is a full account of the events of the Hungarian Holocaust. The introduction presents the political characteristics of the Hungarian Jewish past; special attention is paid to the interwar period of Hungarian and international politics. The text, which is thoroughly documented with evidence and facts, is arranged chronologically but is often interrupted by analysis of different institutions created by the Nazis to destroy Hungarian Jewry (for example, chapters on the organization of forced labor, the ghetto, and the administrative aspects of deportation). The appendix provides further information on the special regulations regarding the status of Jews, the chronology of the period between 1867 and 1965, and the names of authors whose works were prohibited during the Holocaust. BRAHAM and VAGO and BRAHAM and PÓK update the literature on the Holocaust in Hungary. Both volumes offer essays on the postwar impact of the Holocaust on Hungarian society.

BRAHAM's (1969) three-volume set contains essays written by several Hungarian Jewish authors. The aim of the first two volumes is to provide literature on various aspects of the history of Hungarian Jews. Among the subjects covered are the history of Jewish settlement; an overview and bibliography of the political and social integration of Hungarian Jewry; the destruction of Jews in Transylvania and in Carpato-Ruthenia; research facilities in Hungary concerning the Holocaust period; Hebrew poetry in Hungary; the history of the Jewish Congress of 1868–1869; a historical study of the economic life of Hungarian Jews; a good guide to Hungarian Jewish art and culture; the Jewish policy of the Kallay government; the role of the Jewish Council in the Holocaust; and the war crimes trials relating to Hungary. The third volume is devoted entirely to the Holocaust. Its main focus is on providing primary sources and personal accounts.

The collection of essays edited by CARMILLY and contributed by prominent historians and rabbis is more than its title suggests. The rabbi-professors in the Rabbinical Seminary of Budapest were the spiritual leaders of the country's Neolog (progressive) Jewish community and the main contributors to Jewish scholarship in Hungary for more than 100 years. Two heavily annotated essays deal with Hungarian and Transylvanian Jewish historiography. The other essays cover the history of the seminary, the seminary's relations with the Jewish world, and the scholarly contributions of its professors. The book contains lists of seminary-related publications and of the names of faculty members and graduates. Some photographs also accompany the volume.

The volume edited by DÁN collects essays written by a number of distinguished scholars as a tribute to the memory of Alexander Scheiber, the director of the seminary and the leader of the Neolog community in Hungary for three decades. Although the majority of articles offer contributions on different issues in general Jewish history, the book features additional information on the following topics of specific concern to Hungarian history: the history of the Jews of Buda, the Jewish tax collectors, and an important essay on Jewish communal organizations.

In the volume edited by DON and KARÁDY, a few essays deal specifically with Hungary. Katz's article discusses some unique characteristics of Hungarian Jewish history: Hungary's relatively high percentage of Jews compared to neighboring countries and the official split between Neolog and Orthodox communities that created different answers to the call for participation in the economic and cultural life of Hungary. A few articles deal with the special effects of the dissolution of the Austro-Hungarian Dual Monarchy on the status of the Jews. Don discusses how this period brought about the end of a pattern of consistent liberal policies toward Jews. Nathaniel Katzburg states that the Dual Monarchy as a multinational state provided an opportunity to exercise independent Jewish policies, and he notes that growing antisemitism in the interwar period slowed the assimilation process. William O. McCagg, Jr., points out that after World War I, the ultraleft revolution destroyed the alliance between the democratic urban classes, and the repression of the revolution destroyed the prestige and participation of the entire political left. With the Treaty of Trianon, a great number of Orthodox communities became part of the successor states that acquired Hungarian territory, and thus the Neologs' influence became stronger within Hungary. McCagg notes that Jews' continued involvement in the Hungarian political system had a negative impact on their relationship to Jews in other Central European countries. Karády suggests certain topics for further studies concerning comparative sociology in the region. Lengyel and Kovacs deal with the survival pattern and the ethnic composition of the economic elite. Kovacs describes the status of Jewish lawyers in the interwar period. Comparing their position to that of doctors, she shows that since lawyers received protection from their professional associations, they were much less likely to lose their status. The decline came after the war, when lawyers could no longer keep their professional associations.

The literary anthology edited by HANDLER (1977) presents Jewish literature from the interwar period. Although the choice of authors could have been broader, this collection is the only source of its kind.

The overrepresentation of Jewish athletes in winning Olympic medals for Hungary is the subject of HANDLER (1985). The book examines the period between 1896 and 1968. The phenomenon is a telling aspect of the Hungarian Jewish community's special achievements. The author mentions his difficulties with collecting data; some athletes significantly preferred not to reveal their Jewishness to the public.

KATZBURG presents official policy and legislation on the status of Jews in the interwar period. The orientation of each government and policies of the various parties are discussed. While describing the special laws, the author explains their effects on different aspects of Jewish life. The volume concludes with an excellent summary and a small collection of contemporary diplomatic documents.

McCAGG examines the causes of the social stratification of the Jews and their elevation to the Hungarian nobility. The excellent portraits of individuals and families provide a selection of stories on the merging of the business world with nobility, which caused economic, social, cultural, and political mobility. The author is fascinated by the great number of geniuses that have emerged from Hungary and searches for a correlation between their achievements and the ennoblement of Hungary's Jewish capitalists.

PATAI's work is mostly a cultural history. Scattered data have been collected and organized to form a continuous history of Jews in Hungary. The book provides a wealth of information but it does not discuss such aspects of Jewish history as the settlement of different communities, their institutions, the economic and social status of the Jewish people in Hungary, the reasons for the weakness of the Hungarian Zionist movement, or the role of orthodoxy. It is a well-written and interesting book and is a remarkable source for English readers with an interest in Hungarian Jewish history.

PERLMAN searches for the distinctive characteristics of Hungarian Jewish immigration to the United States. His goal is to understand the causes of a certain invisibility of Hungarian Jews as a group on the way to making it in the United States. The causes can be traced to the fact that they were listed either as Hungarian or as German and Austrian immigrants. Furthermore, the majority of Jewish immigrants did not recognize them either, on account of their lack of "Yiddishkeit." Perlman discusses the different waves of emigration, and a detailed bibliography on Hungarian Jewish emigration accompanies the book.

SANDERS's article provides a description of literary life after the war, the atmosphere, the question of identity, and the main themes chosen by Jewish authors. Readers will become familiar with the most important names and works in contemporary Hungarian Jewish literature.

SCHEIBER's collection of Jewish inscriptions from the territory of greater Hungary makes accessible sources for the study of the history of settlement and of the level of Hebrew culture in the region. Scheiber describes and presents photographs of a variety of artifacts, from tombstones to textiles. Although the book may appear too technical for the general reader, it offers tangible evidence of an early Jewish presence in Hungary. A finding list, inventory numbers, and references complete the volume.

SILBER's collection takes on the task of describing the socioeconomic aspects of Jewish life in Hungary. The book is dedicated to Moshe Carmilly-Weinberger, whose biography and bibliography are also presented in this volume. Comparing Jews with other ethnic groups, the question of the disproportionate role of Jews in the economy is discussed in the introduction by Silber. He explains the phenomenon in connection with social dimensions—their minority status, the large population of peasants, the politically powerful nobility, and the weak urban class—rather than in terms of particular ethnic or cultural orientation. While economic backwardness in Hungary triggered participation, political backwardness had negative effects. Emancipation came late, the royal towns often exercised their right not to tolerate Jews, and, as essays by Hanak and Katus point out, occupational restrictions forced Jews to accept a socially disadvantaged status. By analyzing Jewish participation in the economy and especially in the commercial sector, Don concludes that Jews preferred to operate in the competitive market. Jews constituted almost one-quarter of the capital's population, and the high proportion of Jews among Hungary's urban professionals is the subject of Katus's essay. As Katus's data show, from the middle of the 19th century, new fields started to open for Jews in agriculture and the free professions. Three scholars, Bacskai, Puskas, and Komlos, warn against the overestimation of the role of the Jewish entrepreneur. Puskas examines the changing patterns in land leasing and sees scope for a much more integrated Jewish role in the whole development of the Hungarian economy and society. Komlos examines the standard of living of the Jewish population. Karady notes that regional variation also played an important role. Neolog strongholds were located in urban areas and the Orthodox remained in the villages and underdeveloped regions. The opportunity for Jewish personalities to emerge and their growing influence in national organizations are the subjects of the studies of Voros, Deak, and Varga. Kovacs investigates the question of how antisemitism affected engineers; compared to doctors and lawyers (discussed in Don's book), this group suffered most from discrimination. Ranki examines the common characteristics of Jewish occupational structure in 20th-century Central Europe.

VAGO and MOSSE have edited a collection of comparative essays focusing on the sociopolitical aspects of Jewish history. The volume is a result of an international symposium, held in Haifa, emphasizing the interaction between Jews and non-Jews in Eastern Europe. Major issues raised include the different degrees of assimilation and dissimilation, identity, and the role and treatment of Jews in different East European societies. A significant portion of the volume is comprised of essays on Hungary.

DALMAT's bibliography surveys only books published in Hungary between 1945 and 1990. The entries are arranged chronologically by subject. YARON's parallel bibliography covers books and periodical articles that appeared between 1945 and 1970.

KOMORÓCZY's volume is the result of a team effort. The content is very rich, examining all aspects of Jewish life in Budapest. Starting with the first signs of a Jewish presence in Roman times, the growing Jewish involvement in the capital is illuminated. The illustrations of prominent people and buildings present the reader with a good sense of the community's ethos; the bibliography provides access to a wealth of information; and descriptions of the life in certain areas traces the uniqueness of Hungarian Jewish experience.

JULIA BOCK

I

ibn Daud, Abraham c.1110–1180

Spanish historian and Aristotelian philosopher

Cohen, Gerson D. (editor), "Introduction, Analysis and Interpretation," in his *A Critical Edition with a Translation and Notes of the Book of Tradition (Sefer ha-qabbalah) by Abraham ibn Daud*, Philadelphia: Jewish Publication Society, 1967; London: Routledge and Kegan Paul, 1969

Cohen, Gerson D., "The Story of the Four Captives," in his *Studies in the Variety of Rabbinic Cultures* (JPS Scholar of Distinction Series), Philadelphia: Jewish Publication Society, 1991

Eran, Amira, "Abraham Ibn Daud's Definition of Substance and Accident," *Arabic Sciences and Philosophy*, 7, 1997

Frank, Daniel H. and Oliver Leaman (editors), *History of Jewish Philosophy* (Routledge History of World Philosophies, vol. 2), London and New York: Routledge, 1997

Guttmann, Julius, *Ha-Filosofyah shel ha-yahadut*, 1951; translated by David W. Silverman as *Philosophies of Judaism: The History of Jewish Philosophy from Biblical Times to Franz Rosenzweig*, New York: Holt, Rinehart and Winston, and London: Routledge, 1964

Husik, Isaac, *A History of Mediaeval Jewish Philosophy*, New York: Macmillan, 1916, new edition, 1930

Samuelson, Norbert M., "Ibn Daud's Conception of Prophecy," *Journal of the American Academy of Religion*, 45 (Supplement), 1977

Samuelson, Norbert M., "Causation and Choice in the Philosophy of Ibn Daud," in *The Solomon Goldman Lectures*, vol. 2, edited by Nathaniel Stampfer, Chicago: Spertus College of Judaica Press, 1979

Sirat, Colette, *A History of Jewish Philosophy in the Middle Ages*, Cambridge and New York: Cambridge University Press, 1985

Smidt van Gelder-Fontaine, Theresia Anna Maria, *In Defence of Judaism: Abraham Ibn Daud, Sources and Structure of ha-Emunah ha-Ramah* (Studia Semitica Neerlandica), Assen: Van Gorcum, 1990

Ibn Daud is generally considered the first Aristotelian among medieval Jewish philosophers. He also distinguished himself as a chronicler and historian, and his *Book of Tradition* was the standard source for the history of the talmudic–early medieval period until well into the 20th century.

COHEN (1967) in his extensive introduction deals with the very limited biographical information available regarding ibn Daud and the cultural environment and background of the *Book of Tradition*. Cohen's penetrating analysis discusses ibn Daud's overwhelming influence not only on medieval and early modern Jewish historiography, but also on its more recent counterpart, generally called *Wissenschaft des Judentums*, as it developed in the 19th and the first half of the 20th centuries among such Jewish and non-Jewish scholars as Graetz and Halevy in Germany and George Foot Moore at Harvard. In his "Analysis and Interpretation," Cohen examines the structure of the *Book of Tradition*, ibn Daud's sources, his conception of the symmetry of history, his views of the four empires and Jewish history, and his typology of the rabbinate. Cohen discusses the ostensible reason for his chronicle: the challenge to rabbinic Judaism from the Karaite schismatics, whom ibn Daud portrays as malicious, fraudulent, and traditionless heretics whose arguments carry no weight whatsoever.

Two caveats may be entered against Cohen's otherwise excellent work: first, his patronizing and condescending attitude to ibn Daud, and second, the extreme historical relativism espoused by him. Cohen repeatedly uses such expressions as "preposterous arguments," "fantastic blunders," "howlers," and "glaring contradictions and discrepancies." His relativist position is clearly stated in the opening pages of his introduction. Here he espouses the view that until recently ibn Daud was a primary source of information on the talmudic and geonic period and on Jewish settlement in the Iberian Peninsula, but that with the new Genizah material and other sources on the Jews of Spain, the work is now virtually "worthless" as "a source of historical information on earlier periods," even if it remains "one of the finest introductions to the Jewish community of 12th-century Spain." Cohen views himself as standing outside of the stream of history, and his historical relativism is a self-defeating assumption. However, because of the wide range of authorities, both primary and secondary, utilized by Cohen, his flawed methodological assumptions do not undermine his analysis of ibn Daud's work as a basic introduction to the way of life, tensions, and achievements of the rabbinic civilization that flowered under the protection and stimulus of Islamic domination.

COHEN (1991) is a detailed study, with 255 wide-ranging and erudite footnotes, of ibn Daud's account of the capture, redemption, and rise to fame of four scholars, the renowned tale of "The Four Captives" recounted in the final section of ibn Daud's chronicle. Cohen views the tale as a historical romance composed to explain the transfer of rabbinic authority from Babylonia to Muslim Spain and the West.

GUTTMANN and HUSIK offer the standard histories of medieval Jewish philosophy. Each has his champions among the outstanding authorities in the field. Harry Wolfson valued Husik's *History* very highly, while Georges Vajda of the Sorbonne preferred the work of Guttmann. The chapter on ibn Daud's philosophy in both of these works may be consulted with profit, as may the newer summation of SIRAT. Samuelson has contributed the chapter on ibn Daud to a 1997 collective work on Jewish philosophy edited by FRANK and LEAMAN.

SMIDT VAN GELDER-FONTAINE offers a detailed examination of ibn Daud's philosophical work, *The Exalted Faith*, which he wrote in Toledo in 1160–1161, at about the same time that he wrote his historical work, *The Book of Tradition*. The two works belong together and form an integrated apologia that a modern editor might have issued under the title *The Defense of Judaism through Reason and History*. Smidt van Gelder-Fontaine's work is a revised version of her doctoral dissertation at the University of Amsterdam. She felt moved to write it because *The Exalted Faith* is usually neglected, and ibn Daud is either portrayed merely as the forerunner of Maimonides or as a not very original thinker. Hers is a thematic investigation of *The Exalted Faith*. Each chapter gives a summary of ibn Daud's discussion of a theme and its interrelation with other topics discussed, the Jewish and Islamic sources on which he drew, and the way in which he incorporates the philosophy of the Islamic Aristotelians al-Farabi and ibn Sina into his own thought. She pays careful attention to ibn Daud's use of biblical verses to show that the Bible and philosophy are in agreement.

In contrast to the view of Guttmann and others who believe that free will plays only a marginal role in *The Exalted Faith*, and that in fact the work is primarily concerned with the relation between philosophy and religion in general, Smidt van Gelder-Fontaine believes that free will is central to the work. Although freedom of the will is dealt with in only five of its 104 pages, consideration of the treatise's complete structure makes it clear that the question of whether man is free or determined in his actions really dominates ibn Daud's thinking. The free will problem may appear only at the end of the work, but as ibn Daud puts it, in an Aristotelian idiom popular among medieval Jewish thinkers (it is found even in the second stanza of Solomon Alkabez's famous Sabbath hymn), free will is first in thought but last in action. In other words, the author's main point is left to the end with the whole argument gradually leading up to it.

ERAN shows the indebtedness of ibn Daud to his Muslim predecessors and demonstrates his literal dependence on Avicenna for his definitions of substance and accident.

SAMUELSON (1979) discusses in detail ibn Daud's defense of freedom and its relation to divine foreknowledge and providence. Ibn Daud raises the difficulty that if God knows what man will do throughout his life, it is hard to see how he can be blamed and punished for his sinful acts. Ibn Daud's answer is that some actions fall into the category of the "possible" whose outcome God himself does not know. If God knew all future events, then all events would be necessary, and if everything is necessary, then human labor and petitionary prayer would be futile. To this answer Samuelson raises the objection that even if humans were to grant the assumption that people will labor and pray only if they believe that their efforts can change something, God could still choose a world in which He knows everything, but does not allow human beings to know that He knows everything. The knowledge of future contingents is one of the hardest knots in philosophy and has troubled logicians to the present time. Indeed, modern logicians have given future contingents an intermediate truth-value similar to what ibn Daud calls the "possible."

SAMUELSON (1977) examines the place that ibn Daud's theory of prophecy occupies in his philosophical system, the pre-conditions for attaining prophecy, the grades of prophecy, and the sense in which ibn Daud describes prophecy as a natural phenomenon. The article includes a comparison of ibn Daud's theory of prophecy with that of Maimonides, ibn Daud building his apologia on the publicity attached to the miracles related in the Torah and the uninterrupted continuity and incorruptibility of the unbroken chain of tradition going back to Sinai. If the report of a particular event derives from only a single person, doubt is justified, but when a mass of 600,000 prophets (witnesses) guarantee the authenticity of that event, every doubt is excluded. This argument proves the authority of the Sinai revelation somewhat cavalierly by assuming the accuracy of the biblical narratives in which it is conveyed.

JACOB HABERMAN

ibn Ezra, Abraham   c.1090–1164

Spanish-born poet, grammarian, astrologer, and propagator of Sephardi culture

Díaz Esteban, Fernando (editor), *Abraham ibn Ezra y su tiempo: Actas del simposio internacional (Abraham ibn Ezra and His Age: Proceedings of the International Symposium)*, Madrid: Asociación Española de Orientalistas, 1990

Friedländer, Michael (editor and translator), *The Commentary of ibn Ezra on Isaiah* (Publications of the Society of Hebrew Literature), London: Trübner, 1873; reprint, New York: Feldheim, 1960

Friedländer, Michael, *Essays on the Writings of Abraham ibn Ezra* (Publications of the Society of Hebrew Literature), London: Trübner, 1877; reprint, Jerusalem: Mitshuf, 1963

Lipshitz, Abe, *The Commentary of Rabbi Abraham ibn Ezra on Hosea*, New York: Sepher-Hermon Press, 1988

Simon, Uriel, *Arba' gishot le-sepher tehilim me-R. Saadya Gaon 'ad 'Avraham ibn 'Ezra'*, 1982; translated by L. J.

Schramm as *Four Approaches to the Book of Psalms: From Saadiah Gaon to Abraham ibn Ezra*, Albany: State University of New York Press, 1991

Twersky, Isadore and Jay M. Harris (editors), *Rabbi Abraham ibn Ezra: Studies in the Writings of a Twelfth-Century Jewish Polymath*, Cambridge, Massachussetts: Harvard University Center for Jewish Studies, 1993

The multiple facets of this polymath, as poet, biblical exegete, grammarian, mathematician, astronomer, astrologer, and philosopher, and some aspects of his life, both in Islamic Spain and in Christian Europe, have attracted the attention of many scholars.

FRIEDLÄNDER (1877) discusses the philosophy and theology of ibn Ezra and analyzes his biblical commentaries. The first essay deals with ibn Ezra's cosmogonic ideas as expressed, above all, in his exegetical works; the author notes that the first verses of Genesis describe for ibn Ezra the transformation of preexistent chaos into the universe. He elucidates his anthropological ideas, which, following a neoplatonic pattern, are centered on the theory of the microcosm. The divine and immortal soul is a stranger and a prisoner in the body, desiring to return home to its heavenly abode and to know God through the study of His works in the universe. Friedländer also discusses ibn Ezra's views on revelation and inspiration. The second essay includes a detailed description of his biblical commentaries, which, although needing to be complemented by more recent scholarship, offers a comprehensive picture that still has much to offer by way of useful information about the contents and characteristics of ibn Ezra's exegetical works. Friedländer describes briefly some of the manuscript versions of the commentaries and supercommentaries (i.e., commentaries written by later authors in explication of ibn Ezra's own commentaries).

FRIEDLÄNDER (1873) features an introduction dealing with the biography of ibn Ezra, notes on the authors quoted in the *Commentary on Isaiah*, ibn Ezra's philosophical and theological ideas, and a description of his writings and of some of the manuscripts. The first volume includes an annotated English translation of the commentary; the Hebrew text, edited from manuscripts, is in the third volume, which also includes a useful glossary, while the second volume has the King James version of Isaiah revised according to the interpretation of ibn Ezra. Even if Friedländer's biography of ibn Ezra includes some uncritical or scarcely proved observations, the translation of the commentary is accurate and true to the Hebrew text, and the notes constitute an important aid, replete with references. Of the biblical commentaries by ibn Ezra available in English, it remains perhaps the most valuable edition.

LIPSHITZ offers an introduction, a critical Hebrew text of the *Commentary on Hosea*, and an English annotated translation. The introduction deals briefly with the activities of ibn Ezra as biblical exegete and his influence on future generations, among Christian scholars as well as Jews. The Hebrew text, based on six manuscripts, was superseded not long after its publication by the superior 1989 edition of Uriel Simon (*Abraham Ibn Ezra's Two Commentaries on the Minor Prophets: An Annotated Critical Edition* [Hebrew]), which also added a second and previously unknown commentary on Hosea by ibn

Ezra. Lipshitz's English translation, however, is true to the text and is supplemented with many observations on the history of exegesis in general, intended to make the complex language and thought of ibn Ezra accessible to today's readers.

SIMON discusses four different Jewish commentaries on Psalms by Saadia ben Joseph Gaon, the Karaites Salmon ben Yeroham and Yephet ben Ali, and by Moses Gikatilla and Abraham ibn Ezra. He presents the peculiarity of ibn Ezra by contrasting him with the preceding authors: the Book of Psalms was for Saadia, a second Pentateuch; for the Karaites, prophetically ordained liturgy; for Gikatilla, nonprophetic prayers and poetry; while for ibn Ezra it is prophetic and sacred poetry. Simon compares the preserved parts of the two versions of the commentary written by ibn Ezra, the first one from Italy, and the second (standard) one, from France. The prologue to the "First Introduction" deals with the character of the Psalms as sacred poetry designed to be sung with instrumental accompaniment, while the introduction to his standard Psalms commentary discusses only the question of authorship and the holiness of the Psalms. Simon analyzes ibn Ezra's opinion about the writing and editing of Psalms, about the prophetic function of the psalmists, and the possible late date of composition of some psalms. Simon underlines ibn Ezra's differences with the Karaites and discusses his views about the order of Psalms and the meaning of the strange terms that appear in their headings. It is an excellent book by one of the leading experts on the exegetical activity of ibn Ezra.

DÍAZ ESTEBAN collects the Proceedings of the International Symposium on ibn Ezra that took place in Madrid, Tudela, and Toledo in February 1989. Of the 45 papers, 24 are in English and deal with diverse aspects of ibn Ezra's life and work: ibn Ezra's biography and his world, biblical exegesis, Hebrew grammar, Hebrew poetry, and the history of science and of philosophy. There are contributions from T. Alexander (folktales), A. Yitzhak (Saadia), L.A. Feldman (Nissim Gerondi), L. Glinert (syntax), R. Goetschel (the golden calf), E. Gutwirth (supercommentaries), E. Hazan (poetry), M. Itzhaki (riddles), I. Lancaster (creation), N.R.M. de Lange (Byzantium), I. Levin (a synoptic evaluation), R. Loewe (ibn Gabirol), Z. Malachi (astronomy and astrology), S. Regev (reasons for the commandments), S.C. Reif (*Commentary on Canticles*), T. Rosen (*muwashshahat*), M. Saraf (North African literature), G. Sed-Rajna (Hebrew manuscripts), H. Shai (Judeo-Arabic commentaries), E. Silver (ibn Ezra's early life), U. Simon (harsh language and humor), A. Tanenbaum (the soul in his poetry), Y. Tobi (poetry), and Y. Yahalom (the poetics of Spanish *piyyut*).

TWERSKY and HARRIS present a compilation of essays in English and Hebrew about different aspects of the work of ibn Ezra. The English section of the book includes studies by N. Sarna, U. Simon, T. Langermann, and J. Harris. Sarna underlines ibn Ezra's unique place in the history of Jewish exegesis, starting with linguistic analysis and intellectual coherence, and describes the main features of his work, such as the emphasis on grammatical questions and rhetoric, and ibn Ezra's respect for the classical Sages accompanied by irreverent detachment from the post-talmudic exegetes. Langermann deals with the role of astrology in ibn Ezra's philosophical outlook, focusing on passages in which an astrological interpretation is evident, such as treatments in his biblical commentaries of animal sacrifices, the holidays, the scapegoat, the peculiar properties of the land of Israel, free will and determinism, and the special status of the Jewish people. Simon explains the technique followed by ibn Ezra's interpreters in their supercommentaries. He offers a historical review of such writings, from the earlier period (13th century), in which many supercommentaries were written and lost, through the so-called ibn Ezra Renaissance in the second half of 14th century. Harris discusses the meaning of ibn Ezra in modern Jewish history, from Spinoza on, according him an enigmatic and protean profile and a central role in historical debates. He reviews the reactions to ibn Ezra's exegetical work among Christians (such as Richard Simon) and Jews (M. Mendelssohn, A. Geiger, M. Schreiber, etc.). Also discussed are responses to his philosophical views (Krochmal, Jastrow, Rosin). Ibn Ezra is shown to be of crucial symbolic significance for later generations, a pioneer of Bible criticism and a truly modern metaphysician. As such he is adored by progressives and regarded with considerable misgivings by hardline traditionalists.

ANGEL SÁENZ-BADILLOS

ibn Ezra, Moses   c.1055–after 1135

Andalusian poet, literary scholar, and philosopher

Allony, Nehemiah, "The Reaction of Moses Ibn Ezra to 'Arabiyya," *Bulletin of the Institute of Jewish Studies*, 3, 1975

Brann, Ross, "Structure and Meaning in the Secular Poetry of Moshe Ibn Ezra," Ph.D. diss., New York University, 1981

Brody, Heinrich, "Moses Ibn Ezra: Incidents in His Life," *Jewish Quarterly Review*, 24, 1933–1934

Brody, Heinrich (editor), *Selected Poems of Moses ibn Ezra*, translated by Solomon Solis-Cohen, Philadelphia: Jewish Publication Society, 1934

Dana, Joseph, "Natural Qualifications of a Medieval Poet According to Moshe Ibn Ezra," *Journal of Semitic Studies*, 41(2), 1996

Fenton, Paul, "Gleanings from Mošeh Ibn 'Ezra's Maqalat al-hadiqa," *Sefarad*, 36, 1976

Scheindlin, Raymond P., "Rabbi Moshe Ibn Ezra on the Legitimacy of Poetry," *Medievalia et Humanistica*, 7, 1976

Tanenbaum, Adena V., "Poetry and Philosophy: The Idea of the Soul in Andalusian Piyyut," Ph.D. diss., Harvard University, 1993

Of the many activities of the notable Andalusian Jew Moses ibn Ezra, scholars have paid particular attention to his poetry, his work on literary criticism (*Kitab al-Muhadara wa-al-Mudhakara*, "Book of Discussion and Conversation"), and his philosophical views. Additionally, historians have investigated concrete aspects of ibn Ezra's life. Some of his poems can be read in Heinrich BRODY (1934) and in Raymond Scheindlin's *Wine, Women and Death* (1986) and *The Gazelle* (1991).

BRODY (1933–34) comments on one of the most obscure aspects of ibn Ezra's life: his alleged love affair with his niece, which has been interpreted as the cause of the poet's voluntary exile from Granada. Although some scholars accepted this hypothesis proposed by Samuele Davide Luzzatto, Brody asserts that the romance is just a fable because the known facts preclude it. Both poetry and letters show that ibn Ezra left Granada later than his brothers, around 1095; he moved to Christian Spain because he did not feel safe in Andalusia. The specific incident that made him leave Granada and in which his niece (Isaac's daughter) was apparently involved remains undetermined, but Brody is certain that it was not a love affair. Brody's article is a classic exposition of the life of the poet by one of the great scholars of the first half of the 20th century, who knew and used the sources in a very convincing way. It is still well worth reading.

ALLONY examines the attitude of ibn Ezra toward Arabic culture, in the light of the ideological trends that prevailed during ibn Ezra's lifetime. Allony emphasizes that the poet, like other Jewish intellectuals of his time, was aware of two social forces operative in the Muslim world and in particular in Andalusia: the 'arabiyya, and the shu'ubiyya. The first doctrine, defended by many learned and educated Muslims, asserted the superiority of Arabia, the Arabs, Muhammad, the Kuran, and Arabic language and poetry, while the second started as the reaction of the people of many of the conquered countries, aiming to obtain equal rights and promoting their own cultures as equally valuable to that of the Arabs. For Allony, these two currents inspired many of the Jewish cultural and literary polemics that originated during the Middle Ages. Ibn Ezra admired Arabic culture much more than other Jewish intellectuals of his time, but because he was a loyal, traditional Jew, he was not completely carried away by this admiration. He defended the aesthetic and rhetorical values of the Bible and Hebrew language, and he wrote poetry only in Hebrew. Allony offers an interesting perspective on the intellectual attitude of this author.

FENTON, who has recently published a book in French on ibn Ezra's *Maqalat al-hadiqa* (1996), offers in this article an extract from his doctoral dissertation (Sorbonne, 1976), which provides important information about this little known work that completes the *Kitab al-Muhadara*. When he wrote the article, Fenton had no access to one of the two manuscripts of the book, held in the Russian National Library in St. Petersburg, but his study of the other manuscript, preserved in Jerusalem, allowed him to present the contents of the book: a demonstration that the Hebrew Scriptures possess their own elaborate system of rhetoric and a polemic against the supremacy and inimitability of the Kuran, plus an analysis of biblical metaphors. Fenton draws attention to aspects of the book that bear important literary or philosophical (Neoplatonic) significance, analyzing some of its Jewish and Greco-Arabic sources. A pioneering study of this rediscovered, fundamental work of ibn Ezra, the article should be of considerable interest to philosophers and historians of literary criticism alike.

TANENBAUM interprets the ideas on the soul found in two liturgical poems by ibn Ezra. She shows that many images of wandering, displacement, and captivity in the secular poems he wrote after leaving Granada were often employed in his piyyutim in order to evoke both the plight of the Jewish nation and the odyssey of the soul. Tanenbaum analyzes in particular a long, strophic poem of repentance, which refers in several stanzas both to Israel and to the soul. The poet defines "exile" as the soul's separation from her source, because she has an essential affinity with God, is linked to Him with bonds of passionate love, and is engaged in the quest for reunion. Through philosophical study, the soul may attain ultimate felicity, the contemplation of the divine. Readers interested in liturgical poetry and philosophy will enjoy this meaningful inquiry.

SCHEINDLIN analyzes the views on the nature of poetry and its place among the activities of the intellect expressed by ibn Ezra in his *Book of Discussion and Conversation.* Scheindlin describes the contents of the book both analytically and from a global perspective. He concludes that this work does not resemble the Arabic *artes poeticae.* It is a defense of Jewish culture, a redemption of the honor of the Hebrew language, and its main concern is the legitimacy of Arabic-style Hebrew poetry. Ibn Ezra's book contains a mixture of positive and negative evaluations of poetry. The contradictions can only be explained with reference to the peculiar cultural situation of ibn Ezra's circle. Traditional talmudists opposed Arabic-style poetry, reacting against the use of the holy tongue for secular purposes and against the sensual way of life and the social setting of poetry. Furthermore, subjecting Hebrew to the patterns of Arabic could be seen as a kind of subversive act, a celebration in Hebrew of Arabic culture. Ibn Ezra critiques and defends poetry; he did not stop writing poetry, but he did turn to philosophy in old age. A very personal and original interpretation of this crucial and difficult work, Scheindlin's study is especially recommended.

DANA studies the qualifications of the poet according to the *Kitab al-Muhadara*: natural gift, ethnic and geographic origin, and creative talent. For ibn Ezra, poetry is not an art that can be acquired, for it presupposes a natural talent. The Arabs were naturally eloquent, and their geographical proximity to cultured countries helped them to develop their talent in the same way that the tribes of Judah and Benjamin, who dwelled in Jerusalem, excelled intellectually (as seen in their descendants, the Jews of Spain). The poet has an imagination that enables him to experience visions and distinguishes him from other men, but poetry requires labor and skill, too. Creativity as an effect of inspiration makes poetry into humanity's ideal intellectual achievement. Dana offers a clear and accurate presentation of the subject with constant references to Arabic literature.

BRANN qualifies ibn Ezra as "the most conservative of the Andalusian Hebrew poets to compose poetry on the model of Arabic prosody and poetics." This is not necessarily a negative evaluation because, as Brann also remarks, ibn Ezra was considered "the consummate Hebrew poet, the embodiment of the traditions and ideals of the school." Brann translates several paradigmatic poems; analyzes their structure and literary strategies in search of the interplay of formal elements;

and shows that the poet, who respects the complex of traditional norms of composition, has made an intense personal investment in his creations. Brann views ibn Ezra as a true master of technique and makes it clear that in this poetry the important element is not thematic subjectivity (the reflection of the personal experiences of the poet), but ibn Ezra's embellishment of tropes and figures. Ibn Ezra's poetry is interpreted as a practical application of the literary theory expressed by the poet in his *Kitab al-Muhadara.* His originality lies in his structural mastery over traditional forms of composition. Brann's book is quite demanding, but the well-prepared reader, with some knowledge of literary criticism, will appreciate a fine and precise analysis that is an extremely valuable introduction to the world of medieval Hebrew poetry.

ANGEL SÁENZ-BADILLOS

ibn Gabirol, Solomon c.1020–c.1057

Andalusian poet and Neoplatonist philosopher

Bargebuhr, Frederick, *The Alhambra: A Cycle of Studies on the Eleventh Century in Moorish Spain,* Berlin: de Gruyter, 1968

Loewe, Raphael, *Ibn Gabirol* (Jewish Thinkers), London: Halban, 1989; New York: Grove Weidenfeld, 1990

Myer, Isaac, *Qabbalah: The Philosophical Writings of Solomon Ben Yehudah Ibn Gebirol, or Avicebron,* Philadelphia: Isaac Myer, 1888; 2nd edition, New York: Weiser, and London: Stuart and Watkins, 1970

Scheindlin, Raymond P., "Ibn Gabirol's Religious Poetry and Arabic *Zuhd* Poetry," *Edebiyat,* 4(2), 1993

Scheindlin, Raymond P., "Ibn Gabirol's Religious Poetry and Sufi Poetry," *Sefarad,* 54(1), 1994

Scheindlin, Raymond P., "Poet and Patron: Ibn Gabirol's Poem of the Palace and Its Gardens," *Prooftexts,* 16(1), 1996

Sirat, Colette, *A History of Jewish Philosophy in the Middle Ages,* Cambridge and New York: Cambridge University Press, 1985

Tanenbaum, Adena V., "Poetry and Philosophy: The Idea of the Soul in Andalusian Piyyut," Ph.D. diss., Harvard University, 1993

The exceptional significance of the role played by the Andalusian philosopher and Hebrew poet Solomon ibn Gabirol in medieval Jewish culture has attracted the attention of many scholars interested in the different aspects of his personality and work. Only a part of his poetic oeuvre can be read in English translation: in 1923 there appeared Israel Zangwill's rendering of *Selected Religious Poems* by ibn Gabirol. Raymond Scheindlin's *Wine, Women and Death* (1986) and *The Gazelle* (1991) both contain exquisite English versions of some of the poems, accompanied by helpful commentaries.

The excellent and expert scholarship of LOEWE yields a fine overview of ibn Gabirol's manifold production and his interesting personality. Loewe presents in 200 pages ibn Gabirol's ethics and metaphysics on the one hand and his secular ("social") and liturgical poetry on the other. The author is aware that, due to editorial requirements, his study is too short to deal adequately with all the pertinent subjects, and he humbly contents himself with providing "an appetizer," encouraging his readers to address themselves seriously to more technical works. Nevertheless, no important detail about ibn Gabirol's life and times, including his philosophical and poetic activities, has been neglected. Loewe furnishes several good poetic translations (with original text), including the complete *Royal Crown*, with useful commentaries. Loewe suggests that ibn Gabirol is "the greatest of the Spanish-Jewish poets." A personal, original, and very valuable synthesis of the many facets of this Jewish author, this is the best comprehensive introduction to ibn Gabirol's work.

BARGEBUHR, who has published another notable book in German on ibn Gabirol, argues that the palace of the Alhambra is the site of ibn Gabirol's poem describing an Andalusian mansion. Bargebuhr constructs a whole theory about this poem and its "Solomonic symbolism," which assumes that the poet did not die in 1052 or 1057, as is usually thought, but around 1070 (following the view of the Renaissance Jewish historian Abraham Zacuto) and that ibn Gabirol spent a long time in Granada. Ibn Gabirol wrote this particular panegyric when his patron, Yehosef ibn Nagrela, constructed his splendid palace. Its remains can be seen in the excavated structures of the 11th-century Alhambra; the fountain described by the poet would be the extant Fount of Lyons. The book tries to reinforce this theory with many arguments derived from art history and Hebrew poetry, and it includes translations of several descriptive poems of ibn Gabirol accompanied by commentary. This is a very learned book written in an almost belligerent style. The author's central thesis, however, is not accepted by many serious scholars.

SIRAT's survey of the history of Jewish medieval philosophy constitutes the best available introduction to this subject for a wide audience. Ibn Gabirol is included in the chapter titled "The Neoplatonists." The author comments briefly on ibn Gabirol's philosophical works, centering her attention on his *Fountain of Life*, "a good illustration of the nonconfessional character of philosophy when the philosophy in question is a science [the science of matter and form], and not the application of this science to a revealed religion." Sirat describes ibn Gabirol's thought as one of the most striking and original philosophies produced by a medieval Jew, even if he followed Neoplatonic ideas when he analyzed the mechanism of creation. Among ibn Gabirol's main contributions, Sirat emphasizes the importance he accorded to knowledge, the human being as microcosm, the concept of the three souls, his doctrine of the divine will, and the ascent toward the divine. Sirat argues that ibn Gabirol had a limited influence on later Jewish philosophers because he did not treat the most urgent problem for the Jews of subsequent generations: the relationship between philosophy and faith. But she emphasizes also that, in spite of the attacks of the Aristotelians, his ideas, "destined to misinterpretation," can still be found in the works of the Spanish kabbalists. This is an excellent general presentation of his philosophical significance.

A curious early work, MYER dedicates more than 500 pages to the study of ibn Gabirol's philosophy, searching for the connection between his writings and the Kabbalah (in particular the Zohar) and other esoteric (even Chinese, Egyptian, and Mexican) literature. From today's perspective, the book is a strange mixture of learned but uncritical philosophical and mystical references, with almost no practical value. Those who do choose to read it will need to apply constant vigilance, continually contrasting it with the new data and more authentic perspectives that have accrued after more than a century of research.

TANENBAUM devotes a large section of her doctoral dissertation to the study of the soul and the notions of retribution in the *Royal Crown* and in one of ibn Gabirol's liturgical poems of admonition. Tanenbaum posits that the incorporation of speculative ideas into his poetry is one of ibn Gabirol's most significant innovations. From his Neoplatonic perspective, ibn Gabirol integrates traditional and new philosophical concepts and redefines some of the fundamental assumptions and symbols of classical Judaism. The soul may be seen as a divine emanation, and it must return to its source. Ibn Gabirol set trends that would dominate Andalusian piyyut through the middle of the 12th century. This study coordinates in a very clear way the decisive philosophical and poetic elements of ibn Gabirol's work.

Scheindlin, in several articles and in sections of his books, has interpreted masterfully several aspects of ibn Gabirol's poetic work. Comparing his liturgical poems, and in particular his *reshuyot*, with Arabic *zuhd* poetry (SCHEINDLIN [1993]) and with Sufi poetry (SCHEINDLIN [1994]), Scheindlin notes that *zuhd* (ascetic) poetry is not a forerunner of Sufi poetry, and he demonstrates that none of these poets directly influenced ibn Gabirol. He also asserts that these genres cannot be taken as sources for ibn Gabirol's innovations in the sphere of Hebrew liturgical poetry. The intimate tone of his poems, their references to the love of God, and the new individual voice are closer to some kinds of Arabic private prayer of the time. SCHEINDLIN (1996), an analysis of ibn Gabirol's poem on the palace and its gardens, proposes a literary reading of the verses as a true panegyric in accordance with the classical rules. (This interpretation is far-removed from Bargebuhr's thesis, which Scheindlin rejects in this article and in other publications.) The poem, with its movement from light to darkness and back to light, deals ostensibly with palaces and gardens, but it is really about a patron. The transition verse allows the poet to disclose the patron's power as creator of the animating soul of the palace and the garden. This is a wonderful approach to ibn Gabirol's creative literary imagination, and it is particularly recommended.

ANGEL SÁENZ-BADILLOS

ibn Nagrela, Samuel 993–1055 or 1056

Andalusian poet and courtier

Ashtor, Eliyahu, *The Jews of Moslem Spain*, vol. 2, Philadelphia: Jewish Publication Society, 1979

Bargebuhr, Frederick, *The Alhambra: A Cycle of Studies on the Eleventh Century in Moorish Spain*, Berlin: de Gruyter, 1968

Brann, Ross, "Textualizing Ambivalence in Islamic Spain: Arabic Representations of Ismail ibn Naghrilah," in his *Languages of Power in Islamic Spain* (Occasional Publications of the Department of Near Eastern Studies and the Program of Jewish Studies, Cornell University, vol. 3), Bethesda, Maryland: CDL, 1997

Hamori, Andras, "Rhetoric and the Succession of Themes in a Poem by Samuel Hanagid," *Prooftexts*, 16(1), 1996

Rosen, Tova, "The Hebrew Mariner and the Beast," *Mediterranean Historical Review*, 1–2, 1986

Schirmann, Jefim, "Samuel Hannagid, The Man, The Soldier, The Politician," *Jewish Social Studies*, 13, 1951

Segal, David Simha, "Ben Tehillim of Shmuel Hanagid and the Book of Psalms: A Study in Esoteric Linkage," Ph.D. diss., Brandeis University, 1975

Wasserstein, David, *The Rise and Fall of the Party-Kings: Politics and Society in Islamic Spain 1002–1086*, Princeton, New Jersey: Princeton University Press, 1985

Samuel ibn Nagrela, known also as Samuel ha-Nagid, the title he received as leader of the Andalusian Jewish communities, was the vizier of the Berber kings of Granada, Habus and Badis, and was one of the most significant personalities of al-Andalus in the 11th century. His productivity in numerous and diverse disciplines has earned the attention of many scholars interested in literature and history. Some of his poems are available in English, thanks to books by Leon Weinberger, *Jewish Prince in Moslem Spain: Selected Poems of Samuel Ibn Nagrela*, (University: University of Alabama Press, 1973), and Peter Cole, *Selected Poems of Shmuel HaNagid* (Princeton, New Jersey: Princeton University Press, 1996).

SCHIRMANN, in a classic essay, offers a comprehensive picture of the rich personality of ibn Nagrela that, after the passage of some decades, has retained its full value. The great teacher of the present generation of historians of Jewish medieval literature, Schirmann presents with precision the most important aspects of the life of the Nagid; his political and military career; his polemical, halakhic, and philological writings; and his poetry. The article is historically oriented, offering a good conspectus of the main data contained in the war poems without paying extended attention to their literary aspects. One might quibble over occasional small details in the course of the many questions so masterfully covered in this study, but this is indispensable reading.

ASHTOR dedicates a long chapter of his notable book to Samuel ha-Nagid and his son, Jehoseph ha-Nagid. Ashtor's presentation of these characters has all the virtues and limitations of the rest of his book: a learned use of contemporaneous Arabic and Hebrew sources; a precise description of the political, sociological, economic, and spiritual atmosphere of the epoch; sharp historical judgement; and excessive reliance on imagination to explain minor details on points where current knowledge is limited. All of these characteristics combine to give the most detailed biography of the Nagid available. It is necessary to read the text from a rigorously critical perspective, but it can even be enjoyed as a novel.

WASSERSTEIN includes a chapter on the Jews in his excellent study of the Muslim Taifa states, and the pages devoted to ibn Nagrela are particularly illuminating. The activity of the Nagid is depicted within the framework of a detailed and well-constructed examination of the epoch. Wasserstein investigates ibn Nagrela's polemical controversy with ibn Hazm and the problem of the employment of highly qualified Jews in the courts of the Muslim kings. This is a sober and very objective picture of the role played by ibn Nagrela in Granada's government and is highly recommended.

BARGEBUHR studies the palace of the Alhambra. Examining ibn Gabirol's poem describing an Andalusian mansion and its "Solomonic symbolism," Bargebuhr maintains that the poem was written when Jehoseph ibn Nagrela, the son of the Nagid, erected a splendid palace on the hill of the Alhambra. The Nagid had called ibn Gabirol to Granada to help educate his son. Jehoseph's palace, Bargebuhr claims, coincides with the excavated structures of the 11th-century Alhambra, and the fountain described by ibn Gabirol corresponds to the extant Fount of Lyons. The book tries to reinforce this theory with many arguments taken from art history and Hebrew poetry, and it describes in detail the atmosphere of Granada in the time of the Nagid and his son. This very learned book adopts an almost belligerent tone in defense of its author's central thesis, which is not widely accepted today.

BRANN rereads the conflicting literary representations of the Nagid by the Arabic writers of his time, searching for their textual environment in order to illuminate some of the subtleties of the paradoxical relations between Muslims and Jews in al-Andalus, which were characterized by extended periods of tolerance punctuated by occasional outbreaks of hostile reaction. He explores in these sources how the members of the two communities thought of each other and lived together, asking: how is it that positive representations of Jewish courtiers such as the Nagid and vicious attacks on the Jews were written at the same time? Furthermore, why do scholars reading the same sources find in them quite different perspectives? The Hispano-Arabic sources, Brann argues, can be read as a textualization of the fluctuating and ambivalent relations between Muslim and Jew. The presentation and interpretation of the sources here is simply excellent, and the more familiar readers are with the milieu, the more intensely they are likely to relish this article.

SEGAL's unpublished doctoral dissertation compares *Ben Tehillim* by the Nagid with the book of Psalms and scrutinizes the esoteric codes that allow a medieval author to establish parallels among different texts. After a typological comparison of the poems of both books, Segal establishes a full and clear linkage between eight poems of the Nagid and an equal number of Psalms. Ibn Nagrela, who chose to conceal a body of poetry closely related to Psalms within his *Diwan*, fashioned not a few of his war (or "martial") and nature poems after models in the Psalter, and these poems can be identified as belonging to the esoteric corpus called *Ben Tehillim*. Thus, ibn Nagrela employed specific cues, or literary devices, to lead the "extremely discerning reader" to discover the concealed textual references. Segal contends that "most likely the Nagid wrote his 'psalms' for recitation in the soon-to-be rebuilt Temple" and that this context could be the "primary reason for his veiling of the exact nature and locus of *Ben Tehillim*," but this conclusion (and Segal's messianic evaluation of the Nagid's poetry) is not clearly justified. In fact, the book is not free from controversy in several aspects, but Segal presents a very suggestive theory, well worth the consideration of well-informed readers.

ROSEN translates and comments on the Nagid's poem about the sea-monster, "in many respects, the strangest poem in the *Diwan.*" After examining its factual probability, she searches for similar motifs in Arabic literature, concluding that in this first sea poem of Hebrew medieval literature, the Nagid leaned heavily on an established tradition (including that of Sinbad), in particular in his account of the beast. The fact that very similar images are found in work by a later Arabic poet allows her to infer the existence of an earlier common tradition. As in the Nagid's later war poems, the narrative sequence (similar to the description of the battle) is framed in a "religious" prologue and epilogue. This is a simple, clear, and well-crafted analysis of the poem and its parallels.

HAMORI analyzes and comments on the war poem written by the Nagid in 1039 celebrating the victory against the troops of ibn 'Abbad of Seville. Hamori distinguishes 11 thematic sections in the poem and pays particular attention to the forms of parallelism and symmetry that mark the conclusion of each section. He supports his explanations with references to Arabic and biblical texts employed by the poet. The Nagid's rhetorical practice in the verses appears in the numerous isomorphic structures, above all at the boundaries of the thematic segments found in the composition. An illuminating interpretation of the poem, this will be particularly appreciated by specialist readers.

Angel Sáenz-Badillos

Iconography

Cohen, Richard I., *Jewish Icons: Art and Society in Modern Europe*, Berkeley: University of California Press, 1998

Epstein, Marc Michael, *Dreams of Subversion in Medieval Jewish Art and Literature*, University Park: Pennsylvania State University Press, 1997

Goodenough, Erwin Ramsdell, *Jewish Symbols in the Greco-Roman Period* (Bollingen Series, 37), 13 vols., New York: Pantheon, 1953–1968; abridged edition, Princeton, New Jersey: Princeton University Press, 1988; Oxford: Princeton University Press, 1992

Gutmann, Joseph (editor), *No Graven Images: Studies in Art and the Hebrew Bible,* New York: Ktav, 1971

Huberman, Ida, *Living Symbols: Symbols in Jewish Art and Tradition,* Ramat-Gan: Massada, 1988

Kochan, Lionel, *Beyond the Graven Image: A Jewish View,* New York: New York University Press, and London: Macmillan, 1997

Narkiss, Bezalel et al., *Index of Jewish Art: Iconographical Index of Hebrew Illuminated Manuscripts,* Jerusalem: Israel Academy of Sciences and Humanities, 1976–

Analysis of Jewish iconography must ask whether there should be Jewish art at all, given the prohibition on image-making in the second commandment, and this question has indeed preoccupied many Jewish-art historians. Scholars at the end of the 20th century, however, began emphasizing other issues as well.

GUTMANN's collection accords clear priority to the relationship between the second commandment and the production of Jewish art. Despite the biblical prohibition, Jews have created art since earliest antiquity, and their work has naturally been influenced by the artistic styles of their non-Jewish neighbors. The essays in this volume generally take the position that art that exhibits the style of the surrounding culture must necessarily imply a certain degree of assimilation by the minority community. Some Israeli scholars have disputed this assumption, however, positing lost Jewish antecedents for the Christian art that later Jewish art seems to emulate. This debate is perhaps an example of the intellectual conflict between diasporism and nationalism.

A substantial counterweight is provided by the classic, 13-volume work by GOODENOUGH (1953–1968).He attributes the existence of Jewish art to assimilation and heterodoxy, but he also argues that an analysis of Jewish art, beginning with the ancient period, can help explain the culture and its aesthetic impulse. Goodenough moves beyond debating whether Jewish art has a biblical "right" to exist, impressively investigating a host of other issues in these volumes, which are arranged by topic. A useful abridged edition of the arguments from the multivolume magnum opus appeared in 1988.

KOCHAN represents the interest of recent art theory in the philosophical rationales for prohibiting or justifying the creation of graven images. The author considers the history of changing definitions of the term "graven image" and presents comparisons between Jewish and Byzantine iconodulism and iconoclasm as he seeks to describe a Jewish aesthetic and explain how it emerges and develops in history.

The massive index of Jewish art edited by NARKISS is the product of the labor of numerous young art historians in Jerusalem who are attempting to create a catalog of monuments of Jewish art and architecture around the world. Each card in the index records one iconographic motif from a manuscript or ritual object. This documentation is meticulously thorough, creating a very useful research tool, but the attention to detail also means that the project will proceed slowly and coverage will long remain very partial.

COHEN effectively charts the attitudes of early modern and modern Jews toward art and particularly toward its political uses. In a work that is large in scope, yet detailed both in language and ideas, Cohen argues that the study of visual culture can help explain the formation of modern Jewish identity from the court Jews through Zionism. This book excels at analyzing the connections between Judaism's visual and political cultures.

HUBERMAN presents an unsatisfactory concordance of images and texts, iconological in its approach and quite inattentive to history. She juxtaposes each image in her book with an "appropriate" biblical or midrashic text, thereby implying that the images express an ahistorical, universal message. In fact, images rarely convey the same meaning across all contexts, and it is important to be cautious instead of jumping to conclusions about an icon's significance, even when a text accompanies an image. Thus, oblivious to the possibility of ambivalence or subversiveness, Huberman notes the juxtaposition of a synagogue painting of an Austro-Hungarian eagle with a verse from Deuteronomy 32:11 describing God's protection of Israel. Taken at face value, this combination of image and text assuredly implies that the icon serves as a patriotic symbol of the loyalty of the Jews to the Austro-Hungarian Empire. Huberman does not explain, however, that some observers would recognize that the imagery of the icon also evokes the text of Obadiah 1:4 (which depicts the eagle as a symbol of an empire destined to be destroyed by God). Thus, the same illustration can be interpreted by "insiders" as presenting a message that radically challenges the verse so diplomatically cited.

As an antidote to the sort of approach typified by Huberman, EPSTEIN discusses the medieval use of iconography to formulate dreams of subverting or protesting against the majority culture. In the Middle Ages, the art of Jews seems indistinguishable (except for the language of the manuscripts) from the art of non-Jews, but Epstein argues that careful attention to the distinctive text-culture of the original audience for medieval Jewish art can reveal a sort of symbolic secret language that displaces the surface meaning of the images.

MARC MICHAEL EPSTEIN

Identity

Boyarin, Jonathan and Daniel Boyarin (editors), *Jews and Other Differences: The New Jewish Cultural Studies,* Minneapolis, Minnesota: University of Minnesota Press, 1997

Dawidowicz, Lucy S., *The Jewish Presence: Essays on Identity and History,* New York: Holt, Rinehart and Winston, 1977

Gilman, Sander L. and Jack Zipes (editors), *Yale Companion to Jewish Writing and Thought in German Culture, 1096–1996,* New Haven, Connecticut, and London: Yale University Press, 1997

Gorni, Yosef, *The State of Israel in Jewish Public Thought: The Quest for Collective Identity,* New York: New York University Press, and Basingstoke, Hampshire: Macmillan, 1994

Rubin, Barry, *Assimilation and Its Discontents,* New York: Times/Random House, 1995

Yudkin, Leon Israel, *Jewish Writing and Identity in the Twentieth Century,* New York: St. Martin's Press, and London: Croom Helm, 1982

Identity is a term that ordinarily suggests a quality of stability, equality, or unchanging internal substance or essence. Contemporary notions of personal and cultural identity, however, suggest certain vexing problems, not the least of which is that the modern mind must come to some appreciation of notions of mobile or constructed—hence fundamentally malleable and relational—forms of identity. The human, natural, and physical sciences, though disagreeing in many significant ways, all have contributed to modern theories of identity a tendency toward an evolutionary and differentially constituted formulation. Personal, social, and cultural identities are understood under these terms to be eminently historical, thoroughly mate-

rial products of the interplay between multiple forces that, though they include the individual, are often considered to be beyond the individual's ken or control. Simply put, identity becomes an ongoing achievement, something like a conversation, rather than a fixed core around which change occurs. The theme of identity is perhaps best understood when counterposed with sameness, otherness, and difference, raising the question of how something remains identifiably the same while undergoing significant alteration.

In their remarkably well wrought, beautifully textured work, GILMAN and ZIPES have overseen the production of a millennial monument to German Jewish identity. It is an exceptional achievement of coordination, structure, and selection featuring the historical-critical work of 119 eminent contributors of topical or historical essays, which have been arranged in chronological order. Each essay can be likened to a partial diagnostic examination of a complex system. Each measures the pressure of a particular moment in time under the guidance of the following symptomatic question: "what is 'Jewish' about 'Jewish' writing in 'German-speaking countries'?" Regarding this question the following issues seemed paramount: language and discourse, ideal and actual geography, Diaspora as exile and achievement, survival and separation, and integration and acculturation. As the editors note, the volume addresses this complexity; it does not resolve it. Some essays focus on a political or historical event, others on an author or group of authors, still others on cultural, artistic, religious, or literary movements. Found here, for instance, are essays by Paul Mendes-Flohr on Franz Rosenzweig's 1914 essay "Atheistic Theology"; Susannah Heschel on Abraham Geiger's 1857 ground-breaking *Urschrift und Übersetzungen der Bibel*; Klaus Berghahn on Lavater's attempt to convert Moses Mendelssohn in 1769; and any number more. Each article ends with a fine bibliography. This volume should find its place as a standard reference on a great many shelves.

In a work that is sure to arouse a passionate response in the reader, BOYARIN and BOYARIN argue that Jews and Jewish culture are ripe for cultural studies. They wonder, however, whether "Jewishness is up to the challenge." The authors realize that the intentional embrace of a cultural studies purview would situate Jewish cultural identity within a broader cultural-comparative framework, hence perhaps introducing the thesis of a specific (and philanthropically supportable) "Jewishness" to its own demise. The editors and contributors argue otherwise, countering that opening up to the Other what has been largely an internecine debate on the question of Jewishness is a "move toward the recognition of Jewish culture as part of the world of differences to be valued and enhanced" and a way to "avoid being consumed by a liberal universalist ethos." Contributions include Benjamin Orlove's examination of ethnographic notions of selfhood as multiple and fragmentary; Chana Kronfeld's essay, which asks whether modernism's penchant for privileging marginal literature as the voice of the revolutionary Other may not in fact be the substitution of one marginalizing criteriology for another; and Vivian Patraka's discussion of the use of the term Holocaust in public discourse, arguing that it functions performatively and strategically as a meaning-making term and not solely as the name for a historical fixity, and that it evinces a representative mobility that ensures both the necessity and the impossibility of its remembrance. A number of authors embrace a deconstructivist approach, which, one might argue, is an eminently Jewish form of interpretation and argument.

RUBIN's work on assimilation is rich with historical detail and filled with anecdotal accounts, first-hand testimonies, summary biographies, and personal observations, a combination that makes his book on this most difficult of subjects a surprisingly lively read. Major and minor figures, movements, and events from all sides of the issue, both Jewish and non-Jewish, are given voice and juxtaposed so that the result seems more like a living and vigorous conversation than a presentation of categories, arguments, and positions. Indeed, one will search the book in vain for a conclusive determination on the issue since, as Rubin takes pains to point out, assimilation historically has been a double-edged sword with both remarkably beneficial and disastrous results. Throughout the text, the reader will be confronted with the paradoxical and incongruous modalities of life and thought that mold the identity of Jewish difference. These modalities derive from what Rubin seems to argue is the natural teleological force or direction of assimilation, which is the eventual (possibly salvific) total interiorization of Jewish difference under the sign of a universal difference. Such a result, of course, tends to leave the defense and support of a Jewish specificity speechless and perhaps finally vacuous. Such impossibilities and actual contradictions are at the heart of the matter, and Rubin does not shy away from depicting the reality of these entanglements or from exposing the consequences.

GORNI's text begins with a statement of difference: the difference between notions of essential identity and "the essence of contemporary Jewish identity." He argues that the goals of emancipation have in large measure been achieved in this century's movement of the diasporic community to the United States and in the creation of the State of Israel. Today it is the link between the two that "confers collective identity on this multiform entity. The Jews as a group have no other real identity." For Gorni, the "real identity" of contemporary Jewry is found in the explication of this division, for it is the question of Jewish identity that divides them and, one might say, keeps them together. The United States and Israel are differentiated centers of Jewish identity. Each side of the divide is further differentiated by a multiplicity of intellectuals, academics, and public figures, constituting a heterogeneous and contentious mix that ensures that the debate remains ongoing and malleable. Gorni tracks the permutations of the debate through four phases that span the years 1942 to 1987, starting with the question of normalization that began with the creation of Israel up to the present preoccupation with the question of equal status between diasporic and Israeli Jewry. The utility of Gorni's presentation is the determination of categories or principles equipped with which the reader may understand what might otherwise appear to be a wholly acrimonious debate. In Gorni's afterword, the category that becomes the most determinate way to preserve Jewish distinctiveness is a form of Cultural Zionism adequate to the times, to wit "the Jews of the Diaspora must promote the center" and "Israel must encourage autonomous, cultural and ideological trends in the Diaspora."

In a compendium of DAWIDOWICZ's previously published essays, the reader will find her sketch of "the odyssey of American Jews in search of themselves." The essays are divided into four sections. The first concerns the meaning of modern American Jewry; the second describes Judaism in terms of its religious forms; the third explores the continuity between a large part of modern Jewry and its East European roots; and the fourth takes up the Holocaust as it continues to set Jewish priorities and definitions. Dawidowicz will not define Jewish identity by birth alone but maintains that the conditions of modernity dictate that Jewishness must also be a matter of choice. Early on, Erik Erikson's theory of identity formation is given a positive review, a theory that holds that identity or "selfhood" is an interactive accomplishment, an "intersection of individuality, culture and history." Within this mixture, a contemporary Jewish distinction requires profession, commitment, and a mobilized community. In other words, Jewishness must not only be a given, it must also be sought after and affirmed. Dawidowicz is convinced that Jewish identity will persevere even under conditions of increasing secularization and shifting Jewish values because religious identity, which she continues to believe is essential, "does not necessarily affirm a personal commitment to Judaism, but rather to membership in the Jewish people."

The relationship between Jewish identity and Jewish writing is YUDKIN's target. For the Jewish people, a people of the text and hence a written and writing people, the supposition of just such an equation has long been formative for Jewish identity. But this is no simple coincidence. The first chapter, "A Jewish Literary Identity," sets the tone for what follows. Over the course of a chapter that darts from author to author, language to language, place to place, period to period, and finds no unifying theme, Yudkin states his thesis: "These are Jewish writers carving out literature from an experience, sometimes changing course, country, language, opinion and objective. They reflect the pattern of Jewish life made articulate." Jewish identity as written becomes the articulation of the conditions within which Jews find themselves, conditions of mobility, discomfort, alienation, and, perhaps, nonidentity or marginal identity. The experience of Jewish writers and the corpus produced is paradoxically the writing of an identity in continual search of itself. The table of contents reflects this theme. The terms "between," "revolution," "exile," "periphery," and "fringes" in search of "home," "centre," "Europe," and "new beginning" are definitive. Yudkin finds that such conditions have afforded the Jewish writer an extraordinary freedom and power to render Jewish existence in unflinching detail. Yudkin considers the work of a large number of writers from Europe, America, Russia, and Israel and successfully renders each author's unique voice and purpose.

ERIC C. HELMER

Idolatry

Cross, Frank Moore, *Canaanite Myth and Hebrew Epic: Essays in the History of the Religion of Israel*, Cambridge, Massachusetts: Harvard University Press, 1973

Frymer-Kensky, Tikva, *In the Wake of the Goddesses: Women, Culture, and the Biblical Transformation of Pagan Myth*, New York: Macmillan, 1992

Halbertal, Moshe and Avishai Margalit, *Idolatry*, translated by Naomi Goldblum from unpublished lectures, Cambridge, Massachusetts: Harvard University Press, 1992

Kaufmann, Yehezkel, *Toldot ha-emunah ha-Yisre'elit*, 1937; translated and abridged by Moshe Greenberg as *The Religion of Israel: From Its Beginnings to the Babylonian Exile*, Chicago: University of Chicago, and London: Allen and Unwin, 1960

Kochan, Lionel, *Jews, Idols and Messiahs: The Challenge from History*, Oxford and Cambridge, Massachusetts: Blackwell, 1990

Patai, Raphael, *The Hebrew Goddess*, New York: Ktav, 1967; 3rd edition, Detroit, Michigan: Wayne State University Press, 1990

Smith, Mark S., *The Early History of God: Yahweh and the Other Deities in Ancient Israel*, San Francisco: Harper and Row, 1990

As a monotheistic faith, Judaism always has presented itself as rejecting idolatry, by which it means the worship of deities other than the one God. The polemic in the Hebrew Bible against idolatrous worship has been taken up again and again in later writings. Yet modern scholarship shows that idolatry—broadly understood—has surfaced again and again in Jewish religious life and, in fact, was not absent from biblical faith. Several modern thinkers, of whom Nietzsche was the most prominent, reverse the biblical appraisal of idolatry and see in it a positive religious value.

KAUFMANN offers the classical description of idolatry as anathema to Jewish religious life. He surveys the polemics against idolatry in the Hebrew Bible and notes that the biblical authors misunderstood the religious dimension of idolatry. The misrepresentation of idolatry as the worship of wood and stones, rather than the gods they represented, and the mocking characterization of idolatry in the Bible, he insists, demonstrate that biblical religion stood at an opposite end of religious life from that represented by idolatry. Belief in a single creator divinity makes the worship of any created thing incomprehensible. Kaufmann rejects modern scholarship that sees traces of ancient myth and polytheistic belief in biblical narratives. He suggests that biblical religion fails to come to grips with idolatry precisely because it is out of the range of its theological spectrum; it is too alien even for understanding. This approach has been highly influential and continues to dominate many treatments of the Hebrew Bible.

CROSS uses both comparative ancient Near Eastern data and internal evidence from the Bible to show that biblical religion was more complex than Kaufmann suggests. Much of the epic material in the Hebrew Bible is shaped by the mythic themes of polytheism. The recognition of several divine beings surfaces in many biblical passages, and kings who seek to return to archaic and primal traditions often evoke a pluralistic sense of divine powers. The deep imprint of such archaic religion on the Bible suggests that the exilic and postexilic periods were not characterized by an automatic rejection of polytheism or idolatry. Tension between portrayals of Israel's God,

YHWH, as a warrior or as a creator give evidence of the way in which the Bible sought to synthesize the variety of divine entities that tradition had authorized.

SMITH attributes the development of biblical monotheism to two opposite tendencies—that of absorbing and assimilating the religion of the polytheistic environment and that of separating Israelite identity from that of the polytheistic culture. These two movements resulted in creating the image of a single divine being who combines the various potencies and attributes of several diverse deities. Achievement of this result also stimulated a polemic against those cultures that retained separate gods to serve different purposes. Smith seems to agree with Kaufmann that by the end of the process shaping the Hebrew Bible, idolatry became a focus for polemical self-identification. The Bible defines its religion in opposition to idolatry. Yet, like Cross, Smith finds the acceptance of polytheism and idolatry throughout the early history of Israel.

PATAI offers an anthropologist's argument for the existence not only of biblical polytheism but also for the continued worship of several divine forces throughout the Jewish experience. He suggests that the biblical record shows continued devotion to the Hebrew Goddess Asherah. Thereafter, he claims, the Goddess reappears in rabbinic texts and in mystical texts such as the Zohar. The image of Lilith, for example, appears to him as no less a reflection of the female divinity than the Shekhinah, God's indwelling presence. This book uses scholarship accrued from secondary sources even though it includes copious references to original texts. As such, many scholars look on it with distrust and think that it offers an uncritical approach. Readers, however, are likely to be grateful for the many passages that Patai presents in translation and for the range of his interests. He emphasizes the omnipresence of the Goddess not only in biblical times but in later periods of Judaism as well.

FRYMER-KENSKY provides a more detailed and scholarly account of the marginalization of the Goddess in biblical religion. She offers a survey of various goddesses in the ancient world and reflects, as a feminist, on the relationship of theology to women and gender. She interprets the monotheistic emphasis on a single, abstract divinity as a metaphor for the social inequality of the genders in daily life. Nevertheless, she sees prophets who imagine Zion as a mother, daughter, or bride as reviving a more active and dignified view of women. While they remain monotheists, they prepare the way for seeing wisdom as a feminine manifestation of the divine. Frymer-Kensky sees the recapture of the feminine and its integration into a biblically based religious perspective as a major modern challenge.

The challenge of modernity is at the heart of KOCHAN. After sketching the social and historical background of Jewish messianism at the dawn of modernity in the 17th through the 19th century, he turns attention to the rhetoric of opposition to idolatry used in response to it. He surveys the discussions of idolatry in rabbinic material and the medieval period and identifies the view that idolatry is not only worship of material objects and natural phenomena but most essentially is the attempt to create a human reality that displaces God's world. He claims that all attempts to eradicate this idolatrous impulse have ultimately failed. The modern period has proven even more susceptible to the temptation to substitute a humanly constructed ideal for God's actual world. Even religious Zionism continues the utopian hope that animates idolatry as understood in the modern period.

All these themes find a place in the magisterial work of HALBERTAL and MARGALIT. This book offers a definitive treatment of idolatry from early biblical writings through the modern period, tracing the biblical use of idolatry as a metaphor for betraying national values. Halbertal and Margalit show how idolatry came to refer to any representation of things in the world. The book explores understanding idolatry as error, as myth, as immorality, and as political betrayal. The book concludes by reviewing the modern revaluation of idolatry as a positive way for humanity to assert control over itself and the world.

S. DANIEL BRESLAUER

Impurity *see* Holiness

India

Abraham, Margaret, "Ethnic Identity and Marginality: A Study of the Jews of India," Ph.D. diss., Syracuse University, 1989

Beth-Hillel, David d', *Unknown Jews in Unknown Lands,* New York: Ktav, 1973

Bhende, Asha and Ralphy E. Jhirad, *Demographic and Socio-Economic Characteristics of Jews in India,* Bombay: Organisation for Educational Resources and Technological Training, India, 1997

Katz, Nathan (editor), *Studies of Indian Jewish Identity,* New Delhi: Manohar, 1995

Lord, J. Henry, *The Jews in India and the Far East,* Kolhapur: Mission, 1907; Westport, Connecticut: Greenwood, 1976

Rabinowitz, Louis, *Far East Mission,* Johannesburg: Eagle, 1952

Slapak, Orpa (editor), *The Jews of India: A Story of Three Communities,* Jerusalem: Israel Museum, 1995

Timberg, Thomas A. (editor), *Jews in India,* New York: Advent, 1986

There are three distinct groups of Jews in India. While the Cochin Jews of Kerala and the Bene Israel of Maharashtra are thoroughly Jewish in heritage and religious practice, both are also well integrated into their very different regional, ethnic, and linguistic Indian identities. Both groups descend from Jews who settled in India many centuries ago (perhaps 2,000 years ago in the case of Kerala), whereas the ancestors of the Baghdadi Jews in Bombay and Calcutta migrated from Iraq and other Middle Eastern countries from the 18th to the 20th century, during the period of British rule. Since Indian independence in 1947, almost all the Cochin and Baghdadi Jews have left India—the Cochinis for Israel, where about 5,000 are found today, and most of the several thousand Indian Baghdadis for English-speaking countries. About 5,000 Bene Israel remain in India, and about 40,000 are found today in Israel. Much of the literature on Indian Jews concentrates on just one or two of these groups; this entry reviews books reporting on all three.

SLAPAK offers the most comprehensive introduction to the three Indian Jewish communities. Her lavishly illustrated volume is more than a catalog of the ambitious 1995 exhibition that she curated at the Israel Museum in Jerusalem. It begins with useful historical introductions to the three groups by scholars Shirley Isenberg, Barbara Johnson, and Joan Roland, then features Slapak's own meticulously researched articles on the synagogues, ceremonial objects, home rituals, daily life, dress, customs, and ceremonies of each community, plus an article by Shalom Sabar on illuminated Indian *ketubbot.* Slapak's ethnographic material is drawn from Hebrew and English sources and from her many years of research among the Indian Jews in Israel.

BETH-HILLEL's book, notable among the various travelers' reports on the Jews of India, is an edition by W. Fischel of his early-19th-century book. Rabbi David d'Beth-Hillel was an Ashkenazi traveler from Safed who wrote and published the original book in Madras, India, as an English translation of portions of his much longer (and now lost) Hebrew manuscript. He spent eight years traveling in the Middle East and Asia, and from his four years in India he reported on the history and customs of the Jews in Cochin and of the Bene Israel and some newly arrived "Arabian" (Baghdadi) Jews in Bombay. Though this was a time when many emissaries from Eretz Israel were traveling in Asia, Beth-Hillel represented no one but himself; he was motivated by a personal search for remnants of the Ten Lost Tribes, which he claimed to find in questionable places. His views on the Baghdadi Jews in Bombay are thoroughly negative, but he is much more positive about the Bene Israel. In Cochin he reports on the economic decline of the so-called white Jews—a separate congregation of Sephardi and other immigrants who had arrived in Kerala during relatively recent centuries—in contrast to the greater stability that he perceived among the larger and more ancient Jewish group in Kerala.

LORD was a Church of England missionary who worked among the Bene Israel from 1882 to 1924 and who also visited and studied the Cochin Jews. This is a reprint of several of his articles that thoroughly review and evaluate the available literature on both communities. His account of the Cochin Jews is particularly important for its attention to the more ancient Malabari section of the community (sometimes labeled "black Jews") and their own version of their origins. The book has several appendixes, including an extensive bibliography and demographic statistics on the three communities.

RABINOWITZ, a chief rabbi of South Africa who later became a leading rabbinic figure in Jerusalem, traveled to India in the early 1950s when many of the Jews there were awaiting migration to Israel. He takes a scholarly interest in the history of the communities, weaving historical information into this lively account of his visit. He does not hesitate to point out political conflicts among various Indian factions and Zionist emissaries, nor to criticize the over-dependence of many Baghdadi Jews on charitable trusts established by a few wealthy families; and his report on Cochin is offensively gossipy in places. However, the book is valuable in offering a unique overview of the Indian Jews during this important period in their history, and of the Zionist efforts to arrange for their emigration.

TIMBERG compiled the first anthology of articles on the three Indian communities, combining new scholarly writings with reprints of classic sources—earlier articles by David Mandelbaum and Myron Weinstein and a hard-to-find translation from Portuguese of the 1686 DePaiva report on the Cochin Jews (edited by S.S. Koder). The Cochin section includes articles written in the 1980s on songs and legends, comparison of Kerala Jews and Christians, and Cochin weddings in Israel. The Bene Israel articles are historical, focusing on 19th- and 20th-century issues; Shalva Weil's bibliographical overview of research on the Bene Israel is particularly valuable. Timberg himself wrote both historical articles on the Baghdadis.

The KATZ anthology is a collection of more recent articles on the three Indian communities by some of the same scholars. Katz and Goldberg compare Cochin Jewish rituals with Hindu customs of Kerala, and Johnson discusses cultural continuities between Cochin and Israel as seen in community parties. Isenberg writes about changes in culture and identity among Bene Israel villagers, including excerpts from oral histories. Roland and Timberg both discuss the evolution of Indian Jewish identity during the British colonial period, Roland concentrating on the Bene Israel and Timberg on the Baghdadis. Ruth Cernea's article on the Jews of Burma notes historical connections with India. Abraham's article summarizes her research on ethnic identity among the three communities.

BHENDE and JHIRAD analyze results of a professional demographic survey of 81 percent of the Jewish population of India (5,271 in the 1991 census), looking at age and sex ratios, family structure, marriage, education, occupation, and health. Almost half the book consists of statistical tables.

ABRAHAM, an Indian Christian, is the first social scientist to carry out systematic ethnographic research among all three Indian groups. Her sociology dissertation explores ethnic identity and marginality among Bene Israel, Cochin Jews, and Calcutta Baghdadis in India, and among Bene Israel and Cochin Jews in Israel—concluding that they have experienced dual ethnicity in India and dual marginality as Jews in India and as Indians in Israel. Carrying out this ambitious project of interviews and participant-observation in two countries within 16 months limited her sample of sites and interviewees, making it difficult for the reader to assess whether her generalizations would hold for a larger sample. She began the research in India, deriving Israeli informants from those preliminary contacts. Thus, for example, her concentration on white Jews in Cochin may have led to limited contact with the Malabaris who make up the vast majority of Cochinis in Israel.

BARBARA C. JOHNSON

See also Baghdadi Jews of India; Bene Israel of India; Cochin Jews

Inquisition

Beinart, Haim, "The Converso Community in 16th and 17th Century Spain," in *The Sephardi Heritage: Essays on the Historical and Cultural Contribution of the Jews of Spain and Portugal*, vol. 1: *The Jews in Spain and Portugal before and after the Expulsion of 1492*, edited by Richard Barnett, London: Vallentine, Mitchell, and New York: Ktav, 1971

Beinart, Haim, *Anusim be-din ha-Inkvizitsyah*, 1965; translated as *Conversos on Trial: The Inquisition in Ciudad Real* (Hispania Judaica, 3), Jerusalem: Magnes Press of Hebrew University, 1981

Beinart, Haim, "The Conversos and Their Fate," in *Spain and the Jews: The Sephardi Experience in 1492 and After,* edited by Elie Kedourie, London: Thames and Hudson, 1992

Beinart, Haim, "The Conversos in Spain and Portugal in the 16th and 17th Centuries," in his *Moreshet Sepharad: The Sephardi Legacy*, vol. 2, Jerusalem: Magnes Press of Hebrew University, 1992

Beinart, Haim, "The Expulsion from Spain: Causes and Results," in his *Moreshet Sepharad: The Sephardi Legacy,* vol. 2, Jerusalem: Magnes Press of Hebrew University, 1992

Beinart, Haim, "The Great Conversion and the Converso Problem," in his *Moreshet Sepharad: The Sephardi Legacy,* vol. 1, Jerusalem: Magnes Press of Hebrew University, 1992

Kamen, Henry Arthur Francis, *The Spanish Inquisition,* New York: New American Library, 1956; London: Weidenfeld and Nicolson, 1965; revised as *The Spanish Inquisition: An Historical Revision,* London: Weidenfeld and Nicolson, 1997; New Haven, Connecticut: Yale University Press, 1998

Lea, Henry Charles, *A History of the Inquisition of the Middle Ages,* 2 vols., New York: Macmillan, 1887; London: Sampson Low, 1888

Melammed, Renée Levine, "Judaizing Women in Castile: A Look at Their Lives before and after 1492," in *Religion in the Age of Exploration: The Case of Spain and New Spain* (Studies in Jewish Civilization, 5), edited by Bryan F. LeBeau et al., Omaha, Nebraska: Creighton University Press, 1996

Netanyahu, Benzion, *The Origins of the Inquisition in Fifteenth Century Spain,* New York: Random House, 1995

Netanyahu, Benzion, *Toward the Inquisition: Essays on Jewish and Converso History in Late Medieval Spain,* Ithaca, New York: Cornell University Press, 1997

Roth, Cecil, *The Spanish Inquisition,* London: Hale, 1937; New York: Norton, 1964

Zorattini, P.C. Ioly, "The Jews and the Inquisition of Aquileia and Concordia," in *Jews and Conversos: Studies in Society and the Inquisition: Proceedings of the Eighth World Congress of Jewish Studies Held at the Hebrew University of Jerusalem, August 16–21, 1981,* edited by Yosef Kaplan, Jerusalem: World Union of Jewish Studies, 1985

Research into the complex set of problems presented by the Inquisition started several centuries ago and has produced a vast body of literature representing a great variety of views. Such questions as the true faith of the conversos (converts to Christianity), the reasons for establishment of the New

Spanish Inquisition, the roles of state and church, and the degree of cruelty exercised by the inquisitors remain subjects of debate. The majority of publications on this topic have appeared in historically Catholic countries in Spanish, Portuguese, French, Italian, and German. This essay chiefly discusses recent English-language academic works that represent different schools and opinions. Two multivolume works on the Spanish National Inquisition are omitted deliberately—Henry C. Lea's *A History of the Inquisition of Spain* and Haim Beinart's edition of *Records of the Trials of the Spanish Inquisition in Ciudad Real*. These publications are too rich and too detailed to address in a short survey, but they should be consulted by anyone interested in the topic. Numerous works of local history, including works on the Inquisition in the New World and in different Spanish and Portuguese colonies, also fall beyond the scope of this review. Readers may wish to refer additionally to works that focus primarily on *conversos,* as this subject is intimately connected to the history of the Inquisition. Information on the Inquisition also is included in a variety of publications on the expulsion of the Jews from Spain, in general Jewish and Spanish histories, and in biographies of Spanish monarchs, politicians, and 15th-century Jewish personalities.

Readers should differentiate between the medieval inquisition, a church institution established by Pope Gregory IX in the 1230s to fight various anti-Catholic heresies, witchcraft, satanism, and blasphemy across Europe, and the New Spanish Inquisition (or Spanish National Inquisition) that was sanctioned by Pope Sixtus IV but was essentially a judicial organ (tribunal) that gave to Ferdinand and Isabella the power to interfere in affairs of any class or group in Castile, Aragon, or Andalusia. The Spanish monarchs controlled appointments to the post of Inquisitor General and shared with the church the proceeds from confiscated property. This essay focuses mainly on works about the New Spanish Inquisition and refers to publications about the earlier papal inquisition only in those cases when the discussion is connected to Jewish affairs.

LEA's study of the medieval inquisition is based on extensive research in various archives. The scope of subjects and the wealth of factual information are breathtaking. The inquisition mostly prosecuted Christian heretics, but Lea also chronicles many instances in which Jews were targeted and Jewish texts were destroyed or censored. It transpires that some of the medieval translations from Hebrew were ordered specifically to determine the anti-Christian contents of the books under suspicion.

ROTH is a survey of the Spanish Inquisition. The author provides an overview of the history of the Jews in Spain, and he offers a short excursus into the history of the punishment of Christian heretics from 385 C.E. through the Episcopal (or General) Inquisition to the Papal Inquisition, noting that the use of torture was officially authorized by a papal bull in 1252 and that in both the Papal and the New Spanish inquisitions, inquisitors had the power to confiscate the property of their victims. The accused were not allowed recourse to defense counsel, and the names of witnesses were concealed from the accused. Roth describes the evolution of the Spanish Inquisition, beginning with the first Grand Inquisitors Tomas de Torquemada and Diego de Deza and covering the entire history of the institution, including

the activities of the Holy Office in the New World. He supplies detailed accounts of pogroms and propaganda, and he explores the lives and legal and religious status of conversos, declaring, without offering proof, that the great majority of the New Christians were crypto-Jews (individuals who live as Jews in private and as Christians in public). Roth also identifies a number of New Christians who achieved high positions in Spanish government and society. He argues that there are many similarities between 15th-century Spain and Germany during the Nazi regime.

BEINART (1971) examines the lives of conversos in Spain after the expulsion of the Jews in 1492. He argues that conversos played the same role in Spanish society as the Jews did before the expulsion, and he maintains that for the most part the conversos were crypto-Jews. These conversos struggled to stay separate from the gentile population, marrying within the converso group and educating their children outside of church schools. Beinart considers the impact of the Inquisition on the converso population, demonstrating that there was hardly a family of conversos from which one or more members did not appear before a court of the Inquisition. The author also addresses the arrival in Spain at the end of the 16th century of a great number of conversos from Portugal, noting that the immigrants strengthened the Spanish converso communities. He also examines the rise of a number of messianic movements, usually involving a young female prophet who related her visions of redemption, at the beginning of the 16th century. Beinart cites liturgical pieces found in the archives of the inquisitions that reveal the daily sorrows and hopes of the conversos and show how conversos preserved and disseminated their knowledge of Hebrew and religious texts and tried to fulfill clandestinely the precepts of the law of Moses.

BEINART (1981) presents the conclusions from his study of Spanish Inquisition archives. Both the life and attitudes of the conversos, on one hand, and all the processes and methods of the Inquisition, on the other, are described. Beinart investigates the public and social image of the conversos, recounts their meetings and prayers, and evaluates their attitudes toward Christianity and toward life and death.

BEINART (1992d) describes the growth of antisemitism in Spain, beginning with an account of the pogroms of 1391 that started in Seville. One-third of the entire Jewish population—those who refused to surrender their religion—were killed, and approximately another third were forced to convert to Catholicism. In 1412 another wave of incitements and pogroms forced mass conversion. These mass conversions created considerable problems: on the one hand, some conversos expected to be able to return to their ancestral faith when circumstances allowed. On the other hand, many Spaniards were unwilling to integrate New Christians into the emerging Spanish nation. Beinart discusses riots, trials, pedagogical projects, proposals for segregating or expelling conversos, propaganda, and other 15th-century responses to the New Christians. The essay concludes with a discussion of the actions and methods of the Spanish National Inquisition.

BEINART (1992c) begins with an account of the marriage (in 1469) and coronation (in 1474) of Isabella and Ferdinand, which led to the unification of Castile and Aragon. Beinart explains how the monarchs sought to pacify their nation and quell opposition to their reign through several anti-Jewish decisions, including one related to Jewish moneylenders and another forcing Jews to wear a special badge and clothing of particular colors and fabrics. Beinart also provides details of Ferdinand and Isabella's journey to Andalusia, where complaints that conversos were actively returning to Judaism with the help of local Jews led the monarchs to send a formal request to Pope Sixtus IV to establish a National Inquisition based in Seville. The article covers the implementation of additional anti-Jewish measures and the solidification of the monarchs' power; discusses the history of the segregation and expulsion of Spanish Jews; and reviews the edict of the expulsion itself.

BEINART (1992b) describes the life of the conversos in Portugal and Spain and traces the various attitudes of different monarchs. The establishment of the Inquisition in Portugal was delayed until 1531, and its operations did not commence until 1539. After the unification of Spain and Portugal in 1580, their inquisitions remained separate institutions. This article surveys crypto-Jewish life throughout the Iberian peninsula, relates information on prophetic movements, and investigates the emigration of conversos to the Low Countries, Italy, Turkey, France, and Portuguese colonies in the New World and Africa. The essay also analyzes evidence from the files of the Inquisition of Jewish practices among the conversos in the 16th and 17th centuries.

BEINART (1992a) systematically surveys the history of the conversos from their appearance as a significant group in 1391 up to the abolishment of the Inquisition in Spain in 1834. He divides this history into three periods: the pogroms of 1391 through the expulsion of the Jews in 1492 and the forced conversion in Portugal in 1497; converso life in Spain and Portugal from the 1490s to 1580; and 1580 to the end of inquisitorial activity. In the first section, the author discusses the foundation of the Spanish National Inquisition, and activities of both the inquisitors and the conversos are related throughout all the periods.

NETANYAHU (1995) is the most comprehensive, innovative, and independent research on the subject of the origin and the first phase of the Spanish Inquisition's history to be produced in recent decades. Originally formulated in the 1950s, the author's conclusions have been deeply controversial but equally influential. Netanyahu argues that previous studies of the Inquisition have failed to explain its origins, and he traces the historiography surrounding this topic, contending that the prevailing assumption that the Inquisition responded to the significant presence of Jewish practices and beliefs among the conversos was based on insufficient research and faulty reasoning. In fact, he posits, documents demonstrate that by 1460 the majority of conversos were willing assimilationists who desired to merge with the Christian majority. Over time, the number of sincere Christians among the conversos increased while the crypto-Jews gradually vanished. Therefore, the Inquisition could not have been a response to Judaizing and must be explained in other terms. Accordingly, Netanyahu analyzes an impressive array of primary sources, including documents independent of the official Inquisition records including Jewish, Marrano, and Old Christian sources, and he evaluates socioeconomic, political, intellectual, and theological factors that contributed to the emergence in the mid–15th century of the notion of the conversos as a group that was racially distinct from other Spaniards. Netanyahu's thinking has for its point of departure the observation that until the establishment of the Inquisition, virtually all Jewish authorities in Spain and outside of Spain regarded the Marranos as renegades, apostates, or gentiles. It could not have been in the interests of the Jews to maintain this view if the truth about the New Christians' affiliations had been otherwise. The author proceeds to a minute examination of the massive corpus of New Christian apologies and Old Christian accusations, and he comes to the conclusion that the standard accusation that the Marranos were Jews or Judaizers was a weapon of a vilifying propaganda representing a flowering of an ancient tradition of antisemitism. From this legacy of hate, according to Netanyahu, emerged the Inquisition's racist obsession with "blood purity."

NETANYAHU (1997) is a collection of the author's essays that originally were published in different periods of his scholarly career. These articles criticize certain theories and doctrines employed by historians to explain the origins of the Spanish Inquisition and the racist prosecution of the conversos. Some Christian scholars have claimed to find such racist notions as blood purity in Jewish sources, but Netanyahu refutes such theories and demonstrates that these scholars have misinterpreted Jewish sources. He concludes that the primary reason that the New Spanish Inquisition was established was the rising tide of antisemitism.

The most recent, significantly revised edition of KAMEN presents a balanced picture of the Spanish Inquisition. The author describes a gradual change in attitudes of the Christian majority toward religious minorities in Spain from *convivencia* to religious tension, ideological intolerance, and crusades of persecution. Kamen attributes the Christian hostility to their resentment of Jews, and subsequently ex-Jews, who made up a professional class comprising translators, physicians, diplomats, suppliers to the army, and especially tax collectors. He describes the fury of the anti-Jewish pogroms of 1391, the mass conversions and creation of the class of New Christians, anti-Jewish riots in the 15th century, and anti-Jewish measures enacted by the crown. He also examines regional and historical variations in the quality of relations between conversos and Christians and between conversos and Jewish communities. Kamen's study continues through the expulsion of the Jews (this section is troubled by the fact that by simply counting surviving tax returns, he probably underestimates significantly the number of Jews in Spain on the eve of the expulsion in 1492), depicts the public activities and religious beliefs of conversos, chronicles in detail the activities of the Inquisition, and evaluates the motives of the various parties involved. Kamen identifies numerous conversos who held the highest positions in the state and church hierarchies. "At the end of the 15th century the principal administrators of Aragon were conversos. At the very moment that the Inquisition began to function, five conversos . . . held the five most important positions in the kingdom." En route to his conclusion that cupidity motivated the Inquisition, Kamen surveys the anti-Jewish and anti-converso writings, attempts to ascertain the true nature of the New Christians, and discovers identical heretical opinions among New Christians and Old Christians, for which only the New Christians were prosecuted.

Kamen concludes that the "converso danger" was invented to justify spoliation of conversos and that there was no systematic "converso religion" in the 1480s to justify the creation of an Inquisition.

For the first five years all the operations of the National Inquisition were limited to the politically sensitive region of Andalusia; a nationwide operation was not yet given serious consideration. Kamen argues that the broadening of the Inquisition and the creation of its new tribunals was probably the result of the plots of would-be inquisitors trying to find good reasons for expanded repression. He points to how the cruelties and iniquities of these inquisitors led to the famous Bull of 1482 issued by Pope Sixtus IV, in which the pope protested wrongful persecution, lust for wealth, false testimony, torture, confiscation of property, and unjust executions—a document that the pope then revoked under pressure from King Ferdinand.

MELAMMED examines a group of archives of the Spanish Inquisition pertaining to trials of New Christian women accused of observing the Jewish sabbath, holidays, customs, and dietary laws. Some of these women were hosting prayer groups in their homes and instructing other conversas in Judaism. Before the expulsion of the Jews, conversas received many forms of assistance from the local Jewish community. Melammed demonstrates that the contents of the files include very detailed, precise claims about the Jewish life of the conversas and their families. The archives also show the inquisitors' thoroughness and the extent of the suffering caused by the Inquisition.

ZORATTINI uses nearly 2,000 trial records from the bishop's court of Udine to examine the trials of Jews by the Holy Office of Aquileia and Concordia from the middle of the 16th to the end of the 18th century. He provides details of a number of notable cases, including the trial of a Jewish banker accused of converting the son of a local cobbler and that of a country priest accused of playing chess with a local Jew in his shop. Trials of the Judaizers were relatively rare in northern Italy, and punishments against those convicted were milder than in Spain, a fact that the author explains by noting the small number of Jews resident in Friuli. As a tiny minority, the Jews in that region were not seen as a threat to Catholicism, nor were their assets substantial enough to covet unduly.

HAYIM Y. SHEYNIN

Iran, Afghanistan, and Central Asia

Brauer, Erich, "The Jews of Afghanistan: An Anthropological Report," *Jewish Social Studies,* 4, 1942

Fischel, Walter J., "The Jews of Central Asia (Khorasan) in Medieval Hebrew and Islamic Literature," *Historia Judaica,* 7, 1945

Fischel, Walter J., "The Jews of Persia, 1795–1940," *Jewish Social Studies,* 12, 1950

Fischel, Walter J., "New Sources for the History of the Jewish Diaspora in Asia in the 16th Century," *Jewish Quarterly Review,* 50, 1950

Fischel, Walter J., "Azerbaijan in Jewish History," *Proceedings of the American Academy for Jewish Research,* 22, 1953

Fischel, Walter J., "Isfahan: The Story of a Jewish Community," in *The Joshua Starr Memorial Volume,* New York: Jewish Social Studies, 1953

Loeb, Laurence D, *Outcaste: Jewish Life in Southern Iran* (Library of Anthropology), New York: Gordon and Breach, 1977

Moreen, Vera Basch, *Iranian Jewry's Hour of Peril and Heroism: A Study of Babai ibn Lutf's Chronicle, 1617–1662* (Texts and Studies, vol. 6), New York: American Academy for Jewish Research, 1987

Patai, Raphael, *Jadid al-Islam: The Jewish "New Muslims" of Meshhed* (Jewish Folklore and Anthropology Series), Detroit, Michigan: Wayne State University Press, 1997

Shaked, Shaul (editor), *Irano-Judaica: Studies Relating to Jewish Contacts with Persian Culture throughout the Ages,* Jerusalem: Ben Zvi Institute, 1982

Soroudi, Sorour, "Jews in Islamic Iran," *Jerusalem Quarterly,* 21, 1981

Yeroushalmi, David, *The Judeo-Persian Poet Emrani and His "Book of Treasure,"* Leiden and New York: Brill, 1995

Iranian Jews are an ancient community, unique in their life under Shi'i Islam, and have been westernized only in small part during the 20th century. Much of the research on the community deals with its literature in Judeo-Persian. Historical reseach in Hebrew and English has been published mainly as articles.

BRAUER's report focuses on the communities of Herat, Kabul, and Balkh, where most of the Jewish population of Afghanistan lived in the 1940s. He describes their economic position in the 20th century following attempts to establish a state monopoly over foreign trade. Brauer provides much information on marriage customs, the position of women and children, communal organization, religious life, and belief in magic.

FISCHEL's 1945 article deals with the Jews of Khorasan, the easternmost part of the ancient Persian empire. Following a discussion of the sources used, Fischel describes the distribution of the Jewish communities in Khorasan (mainly in the towns of Merv, Balkh, Ghazna, and Herat). He examines the population of these communities, economic conditions, relations with the authorities, and cultural and religious life in medieval times.

Another article by FISCHEL (1950b) examines the Jewish communities of Hormuz, Kung, and Malacca from 1548 to 1551 based on documents from the archive of the Society of Jesus in Rome and other sources. Jews, mainly of Portuguese origin, settled in Hormuz following the Portuguese conquest in 1507. They joined an existing Babylonian Jewish community of great antiquity and played an important role in the economic life.

Another of FISCHEL's articles (1950a) focuses on Iranian Jews during the Qajar period (1796–1925) and that of Reza Shah Pahlavi (1925–1940). The examination is chronological and is divided according to the reigns of the monarchs and important political and socioeconomic events. Fischel examines the position of the community, economic activities, internal developments within the community, relations with the authorities and society at large, and attempts at foreign intervention in favor of Iranian Jews, mainly since the late 19th century.

FISCHEL's survey (1953b) of the Jews of Isfahan starts with an examination of the origins of the Jewish community there. Most of the article deals with the Muslim period: Isfahan under the caliphate, the Safavid Dynasty, and the Qajar Dynasty. Special attention is given to the persecution and forced conversion of the Jews of Isfahan in the 17th century.

FISCHEL's article (1953a) on the Jews of Azerbaijan, the northwestern province of Iran, shows the early settlement of Jews there, based on Cairo Genizah documents. He examines the changing influence of Jews in Azerbaijan, especially in Tabriz, under the Mongol rulers (1258–1335). Their political and economic power is detailed as is their contribution to Persian historical writing. Fischel also provides data on the Jews from the 16th to the 19th century.

The Jews of Shiraz in southern Iran are the subject of LOEB's book, based on a field study conducted in Iran and Israel in 1967 and 1968. Following a short survey of the history of the Jews in Iran, and especially in Shiraz, and examining Shi'i Islam's attitude toward Jews, Loeb provides a detailed examination of the Shirazi Jewish community in the late 1960s. Among the subjects dealt with are social and economic life, education, arts, amusements, leisure time, and special local customs. Loeb's book provides a unique opportunity to learn about the daily life of a well-defined urban Jewish community and how the community reacted to modernization under the shah prior to the Islamic revolution.

MOREEN examines an important Judeo-Persian poetic source dealing with Jewish life in Iran during the 17th century. *Kitab-i Anusi* (Book of a Forced Convert) by Babai ibn Lutf is a major source for this period and deals primarily with persecutions of the Jews. Following a political survey of the Safavid Dynasty, Moreen examines the life and work of the author. She analyzes his book in the context of Iranian and Jewish historiography as well as the literary characteristics of the work and its linguistic peculiarities. Moreen also examines the importance of the book in Safavid history and the history of Iranian Jews.

SHAKED's serial publication includes numerous annotated scholarly articles, mostly in English, by leading experts in the field. It contains studies on literature, linguistics, history, and religion and focuses on Jewish-Persian contacts.

The fate of the Jews of Meshhed, one of the few Jewish communities anywhere that were forced to convert to Islam, is examined in detail by PATAI. Following a brief history of Iranian Jews and an examination of the status of Jews under Shi'i Islam, Patai focuses on the attack against and forced conversion of Meshhedi Jews in 1839 and their clandestine Jewish life thereafter. Among the subjects dealt with are the impact of Zionism and the emigration of Meshhedi Jews in the 20th century. The book includes tales and legends as well as an examination of the customs and institutions of the community. The study is based on interviews that Patai conducted in the 1940s with Meshhedi Jews living in Jerusalem and on published sources.

SOROUDI surveys the status of Jews under Islam in Iran until the beginning of the Islamic Republic, relating to the special attitude of Shi'i Islam to the Jews. Soroudi examines the persecutions and restrictions of the Jews under the Safavid Dynasty (1500–1736). The author also discusses the role of the mullahs under the Qajar Dynasty (1796–1925) and the implications of that role for the Jews as well as the influence of relations with the West during the 19th century. This is contrasted with the position of the Jews under the Pahlavi Dynasty (1925–1978), which advocated secular nationalism, Westernization, and close relations with the State of Israel.

The "Ganj-name" (Book of Treasure) by the 15th-century Judeo-Persian author Emrani is analyzed by YEROUSHALMI. Following a discussion of Emrani's life and works, Yeroushalmi summarizes the Book of Treasure, a book of counsel and advice as well as a commentary on the mishnaic tractate Avot. The text is provided in full in the original Judeo-Persian and in English translation, and both are heavily annotated. Yeroushalmi examines the literary and linguistic aspects of Emrani's book, and his work is of value to those interested in Judeo-Persian and Persian literature and linguistics as well as in the cultural history of Persian Jews.

RACHEL SIMON

Iraq

Brauer, Erich, completed and edited by Raphael Patai, *The Jews of Kurdistan*, Detroit, Michigan: Wayne State University Press, 1993

Gat, Moshe, *The Jewish Exodus from Iraq, 1948–1951*, London and Portland, Oregon: Cass, 1997

Haddad, Heskel M., *Flight from Babylon: Iraq, Iran, Israel, America*, New York: McGraw-Hill, 1986

Hillel, Shlomo, *Operation Babylon*, Garden City, New York: Doubleday, 1987; London: Collins, 1988

Melamed, Ora (editor), *Annals of Iraqi Jewry* (Publication Series on Communities of Israel), Jerusalem: Eliner Library, 1995

Rejwan, Nissim, *The Jews of Iraq: 3000 Years of History and Culture*, London: Weidenfeld and Nicolson, and Boulder, Colorado: Westview, 1985

Sassoon, David Solomon, *A History of the Jews in Baghdad*, Letchworth, Hertfordshire: S. D. Sassoon, 1949

Sassoon, David Solomon, "The History of the Jews of Basra," *Jewish Quarterly Review*, 17, 1927

Sawdayee, Maurice M., *The Baghdad Connection*, Locust Valley, New York: Sawdayee, 1991

Sawdayee, Max, *All Waiting to Be Hanged: Iraq Post-Six-Day War Diary*, Israel: Levanda, 1974

Shiblak, Abbas, *The Lure of Zion: The Case of the Iraqi Jews*, London and Atlantic Highlands, New Jersey: Al Saqi, 1986

One of the most ancient of Jewish communities, the Jews of Iraq were urban and rural, with the former undergoing modernization in the 20th century. Most of the community emigrated in the 1950s. Much research has been conducted on the community, mostly in Hebrew.

BRAUER's book is an ethnological study of the Jews of Kurdistan, based on interviews conducted in Jerusalem in the 1930s with Kurdish Jewish immigrants. The work was published posthumously in Hebrew in 1947, and this is a revised edition by Patai. Brauer examines previous studies of Kurdish Jews, their environment, and history. He pays special attention to their material culture, the family, life cycle, women, economic life, social organization, education, the synagogue, the sabbath, and holidays. Brauer's detailed description serves as an invaluable source about an extinct Jewish rural community.

The mass Jewish emigration from Iraq in the late 1940s and early 1950s is the focus of GAT's book, which is based on archival material from Israel, the United Kingdom, and the United States and on published sources. Against the background of the socioeconomic conditions of the community, its modernization, and involvement in Iraqi life, Gat examines the implications of the 1941 anti-Jewish riots (Farhud) for the community and the establishment of the clandestine Zionist movement with its defense operations. Gat details the secret emigration and discusses the involvement of Israeli emissaries and of Iraqi and Iranian personalities. He believes that there was no connection between the bombings in Baghdad and the exodus. This is a detailed, thoroughly researched study of the Iraqi Jewish mass emigration.

HADDAD, a Baghdadi Jewish ophthalmologist, tells about his life in Iraq and his experiences in Israel and the United States following immigration. He provides a vivid description of his family, the community, education, the 1941 anti-Jewish riots (Farhud), his involvement in clandestine Jewish defense activities, and the Jewish mass emigration through Iran to Israel. His memoirs provide a very personal insider's view of the turbulent 1940s.

HILLEL's book focuses on the Jewish mass emigration from Iraq in the late 1940s and early 1950s. Iraqi-born Hillel was sent from Israel to Iraq to help organize the covert emigration, which took place mostly through Iran. Hillel, one of the main figures involved in this operation, tells about the organization of the emigration; negotiations with Iraqi and Iranian politicians; Iraqi government decisions regarding the status of Iraqi Jews and their emigration; the bombings in Baghdad and the reaction of the Jews to them; the trials and hangings of accused Jews; and international reactions to these events. This is an important detailed testimony by one of the major organizers of the Iraqi emigration.

MELAMED's book includes numerous descriptions, mainly by Iraqi Jewish emigrants, reflecting on daily life in the community. Among the issues discussed are childhood memories, folklore, relations between Jews and gentiles, religious scholarship and customs, economic activity, communal administration, and education. Special chapters describe Zionist activity, the 1941 anti-Jewish riots (Farhud), the mass emigration, absorption in Israel, and the Iraqi diaspora. The testimonies, journalistic reports, and photographs provide interesting source material on the Iraqi community.

REJWAN surveys the history of the Jews of Iraq from biblical times to the mass emigration of the early 1950s. Based on published sources and his own first-hand knowledge of the later period, Rejwan examines Iraqi Jewish history, culture, and society and provides a chronology. He divides the survey into three parts: from the Assyrian captivity to the Arab conquest (731 B.C.E.–641 C.E.); the encounter with Islam (641–1850); and a century of radical change (1850–1950). Rejwan provides a useful comprehensive historical survey of Iraqi Jews and contributes new information mainly for the 1930s and 1940s, during which he was active in Iraqi intellectual and political life as well as Jewish communal life.

SASSOON's (1927a) book covers the history of the Jews of Baghdad from earliest times to the first decades of the 20th century. He provides much information on important rabbis and families and examines the structure of the community in the late 19th century, religious life, educational developments, welfare services, liturgy, customs, superstitions, proverbs, and printing. A special section deals with settlements of Baghdadi Jews in the Far East. Much of the information is based on personal knowledge not available elsewhere.

SASSOON's (1927b) article covers the history of the Jews of Basra from the 9th to the early 20th century, focusing on the 19th century. Numerous sources, many in Hebrew and Judeo-Arabic, are cited with English translation and detail the structure of the community, its leaders, economic conditions, and relations with the authorities and foreigners.

SAWDAYEE (1991) provides an examination of the impact of modern education on the Jewish community of Iraq, with special reference to Baghdad, against the background of developments in society at large during the 19th and 20th centuries. He describes the various school systems that became available to Jews due to external interventions (Ottoman, British, and Arab as well as French-Jewish and Anglo-Jewish) and internal efforts, including those of wealthy Iraqi immigrants in Europe and the Far East. Sawdayee describes the cultural, economic, social, and political impact of these developments on the Jews of Iraq and the reasons for their mass emigration.

SAWDAYEE (1974) is a diary of the author that details the condition of the Jews of Iraq during and following the 1967 Israel-Arab Six-Day War. Sawdayee was one of some 3,000 Jews who remained in Iraq following the mass emigration of the early 1950s. He describes their harsh conditions, especially following the Arab defeat in 1967, and focuses on the clandestine escape of some 95 percent of the Jews in 1970, leaving only 250 in Iraq.

SHIBLAK examines the reasons behind the mass emigration of Jews from Iraq, mostly to Israel, in the early 1950s. The study opens with an examination of social, economic, and political developments in Iraq in the first half of the 20th century. This is followed by a discussion of the involvement of Jews in Iraqi society, the implications of the Palestine issue for Iraqi politics, and the role of Zionism among Iraqi Jews. Because Jews were deeply involved in Iraqi life and the role of Zionism was weak, Shiblak explains how it was the events culminating with bombings in Baghdad, trials, activities of Israeli emissaries in Iraq, and the denaturalization law that eventually led to the mass exodus.

RACHEL SIMON

Isaiah, Book of

Childs, Brevard S., *Isaiah and the Assyrian Crisis* (Studies in Biblical Theology, 2nd series, vol. 3), London: SCM, and Naperville, Illinois: Allenson, 1967

Conrad, Edgar, *Reading Isaiah*, Minneapolis, Minnesota: Fortress, 1991

Darr, Katheryn Pfisterer, *Isaiah's Vision and the Family of God*, Louisville, Kentucky: Westminster/Knox, 1994

Friedländer, Michael (editor), *The Commentary of Ibn Ezra on Isaiah*, London: Society of Hebrew Literature, 1873; New York: Feldheim, 1960

Hayes, John H. and Stuart A. Irvine, *Isaiah, the Eighth-Century Prophet: His Times and His Preaching*, Nashville, Tennessee: Abingdon, 1987

Miscall, Peter D., *Isaiah* (Readings, a New Biblical Commentary), Sheffield, South Yorkshire: JSOT, 1993

Seitz, Christopher R., *Zion's Final Destiny: The Development of the Book of Isaiah: A Reassessment of Isaiah 36–39*, Minneapolis, Minnesota: Fortress, 1991

Sweeney, Marvin A., *Isaiah 1–39: With an Introduction to Prophetic Literature* (The Forms of the Old Testament Literature, vol. 16), Grand Rapids, Michigan: Eerdmans, 1996

Watts, John D.W., *Isaiah 1–33* (Word Biblical Commentary, vol. 24), Waco, Texas: Word, 1985

Watts, John D.W., *Isaiah 34–66* (Word Biblical Commentary, vol. 25), Waco, Texas: Word, 1987

Williamson, H.G.M., *The Book Called Isaiah: Deutero-Isaiah's Role in Composition and Redaction*, Oxford and New York: Oxford University Press, 1994

Since the magisterial commentary of Bernhard Duhm written late in the 19th century, Isaiah has been treated by biblical critics as three books in one. First Isaiah, chapters one to 39, originated in the eighth century B.C.E. and is a record of the ministry of the prophet Isaiah of Jerusalem himself. Second Isaiah, chapters 40 to 55, often said to have originated in Babylon, is seen as an exilic work. The last eleven chapters, which comprise Third Isaiah, are said to date from the very early restoration period, the late sixth century B.C.E. In modern academic tradition the three sections of the book have been treated as separate but related works, but approaches to the interpretation of Isaiah have been transformed in recent times by the growing realization that whatever the diverse origins of the various hypothetical sections of the text, the book as it exits now is a unity, in terms of presentation if nothing else. A number of monographs have sought to investigate, quantify, and explain this unity.

WILLIAMSON acknowledges with regret the dichotomy that he claims has arisen between the older historical-critical exegetical methods and the newer approaches of literary criticism. He states his desire to try to bridge that gap by proposing an explanation for the combination of Deutero-Isaiah in the first 39 chapters of the book that both historically-oriented and literary scholars will find attractive. Choosing not to complicate his study further by taking the work of Trito-Isaiah into account, Williamson presumes that "approaches to the unity of Isaiah should be pursued by way of a more intense appli-

cation of traditional methods rather than ignoring or bypassing of them." In particular he sets himself three tasks: to investigate to what extent (if any) Deutero-Isaiah may have been written in "conscious dependence" upon Proto-Isaiah; to consider what purpose and function the links between the two sections identified by other scholars serve; and to examine the possibility of "converse influence," in other words, to quantify the influence of later passages of the book upon earlier ones. Williamson's detailed and convincing analysis leads him to conclude that Deutero-Isaiah was especially influenced by the writings of Proto-Isaiah, and that he deliberately sought to build upon the earlier work, which the later author believed had special significance for his own time. To make that influence plain, Deutero-Isaiah then edited and adapted the writings of Isaiah of Jerusalem to serve as part of his new prophetic history and vision of the future.

SEITZ is concerned with two important questions: how the message of Isaiah of Jerusalem came to be taken up and expanded so dramatically by later generations, and in what form the book of Isaiah originally circulated before it was combined with later material. Seitz suggests that the obvious place to start to answer both these questions is the end of First Isaiah. In chapters 36 through 39, which deal with God's intervention to save Jerusalem from Assyria during the reign of Hezekiah, he identifies the most important link between the two main sections, chapters one through 39 and chapters 40 through 66. Since the motif of "concern over the destiny of Zion" is fundamental to chapters 36 through 39, he suggests that this theme may well be the structuring device of the book in its present form. It explains how Second Isaiah deals with some of the important theological issues raised by the deliverance of Jerusalem, bringing the earlier tradition to culmination. Chapters 36 through 39 are therefore the "pivot on which the entire tradition process turns" and determine "most of the shape and character of Second Isaiah."

WATTS's (1985, 1987) two-volume commentary presents a unique approach to all 66 chapters of Isaiah. Since all of the historical events of the book are presented as past history, Watts postulates a very late date for the book. He sees it as an authorial unity that comprises earlier materials but dates in its present form from Jerusalem in the fifth century B.C.E. He sees Isaiah as a vision, which he defines as a prophetic drama, and he divides the book like a play into acts and scenes, ascribing different lines of speech or narration to different speakers and characters within the drama. The theme of this drama, according to Watts, is God's strategy for human history—it seeks to remind its listeners of God's past intervention on Israel's behalf and thereby assure them of his future interest in their safety and blessing. Even if his admittedly rather curious presentation of the text is unconvincing, Watts' philological, translational, and textual notes are of immense value, as are his bibliographies (which appear before each major section). The way the commentary is divided into two sections—a short "comment" on notable verses or clauses and a larger-scale "explanation" that covers the wider perspective of the text—makes it very useful for study and reference.

MISCALL's commentary sets out to be a "reading of the text of Isaiah as a whole" rather than a commentary in the traditional sense of the word, and it pays no attention to philological, textual, or historical details. He shares Watts's view that the book of Isaiah in its present form must date from the postexilic era, but beyond that Miscall refuses to consider its composition, authorship, or provenance, leaving aside even the question of which oracles are authentic to Isaiah and which should be seen as later additions. While Miscall recognizes that the book has an obvious historical reference, he chooses not to interpret the book in relation to its historical context but rather in relation to itself and its readership. Thus, rather than seeing sin and punishment as a feature of Israel's past and blessing and privilege as their future destiny, he argues that all events in the book speak directly to the time of the author and his contemporaries, as well as later readers. Miscall's intent is to present an overview of the text, a guidebook to lead readers through the web of intertextuality that is Isaiah, pointing to many features of interest and difficulty along the way. Again like Watts, Miscall views Isaiah as a vision, "a panorama of God and world," but understands this to mean that Isaiah presents a particular future that Israel can choose, something to be sought out and worked for rather than just borne in mind, and Miscall highlights the stark choice Isaiah presents between the destiny of the righteous and of the wicked.

Much contemporary research into the Book of Isaiah presumes this literary unity. CONRAD's work is typical of the newer literary-critical approaches to Isaiah for a number of reasons. First, he treats the book as a single entity and is unconcerned with the question of its origins. Although he still feels such issues have their place, Conrad is more concerned with the reception of the text than its formation. Second, he argues that the role of the readers of the book is far more important than scholarship has traditionally acknowledged, and that the modern context is really the only one readers can use to interpret the text with any degree of confidence. He maintains that readers actually know nothing about the real or implied author and his original audience and that readers cannot be sure how the biblical text relates to actual historical events and individuals, if indeed it has any historical reference at all. In the center of his book, Conrad applies his literary methodology to the text and considers the royal narratives, the "we" passages, and the passages that would appear to imply that YHWH has a strategic plan for the future of world history by considering the effect of such passages on the reader.

Another interesting reader-response study of the book, much more cautious than Conrad's and written from a feminist perspective, is that of DARR, who considers the reception of Isaiah's family imagery from the perspective of a hypothetical knowledgeable ancient reader. While her work on the text itself is insightful and thought-provoking, it is largely descriptive, and Darr's great strength lies in the way she demonstrates the "determinative power" of the biblical text, how it directs its readers and "invites [them] to particular perceptions of reality."

Two additional important commentaries deserve mention. Although SWEENEY is noted for his literary and redactional studies of the book, his commentary is significant as the only purely form-critical one for many years. He focuses on the smallest literary units, paying attention to their structure,

genre, setting, and intention, as well as the historical development of the Isaianic tradition where appropriate. Sweeney's is not, therefore, an exegetical commentary and needs supplementing with other sources of information, but it provides an excellent counterbalance to the literary commentaries already discussed. The usefulness of the book is increased further by its helpful introduction to the form-critical categories that relate to prophetic books, narratives, and speech forms, and an excellent glossary.

FRIEDLÄNDER's work is an annotated translation of the great commentary on Isaiah by ibn Ezra, arguably one of the most important (and interesting) of all precritical commentaries on the prophets. A short biography precedes the commentary itself, where, while the editor's explanatory comments are helpful and insightful, ibn Ezra's own understanding of the text is allowed to shine through, revealing some fascinating interpretative insights and raising questions that often seem remarkably modern. At the same time, his background in rabbinic interpretation also is obvious in the style and form of the commentary.

It is also worth noting that despite recent controversy over the extent of the work of Isaiah of Jerusalem, much interest in the historical individual remains. CHILDS presents one of Isaiah's most important early works. What exactly happened during Hezekiah's revolt and Sennacherib's 701 B.C.E. campaign into Judah has long puzzled scholars, since neither the Bible nor the extrabiblical evidence is quite clear. Childs acknowledges that this is the case and suggests it will always be so. To his mind, the difficulty is insoluble without additional external information, and therefore he makes no proposals as to the real events of that year. A second issue is that of the preaching of Isaiah—what was his response to the crisis at the time, and what course of action did he advocate before and after? Once again Childs suggests that no definitive answer is possible, and having rejected other attempts at reading things into the mind of the prophet, he restricts himself to a purely form-critical analysis of the texts from Isaiah and the biblical histories that address the Assyrian crisis, in an endeavor to demonstrate the different kinds of source material available to contemporary scholars. The diversity Childs notes in these sources would no doubt be labeled inconsistency by more skeptical scholars: whereas he admits that the message of hope and the message of judgment in Isaiah offer "two strikingly different portrayals" of the prophet's ministry that "simply cannot be harmonized," Childs refuses to choose between them because he sees them both as employing ancient traditions. His intention, as one reviewer has said, is to cross-examine the witnesses rather than hand down a verdict.

HAYES and IRVINE also concern themselves with the historical question and are much more positive than most biblical historians as to what can really be known about Isaiah's ministry. They suggest that virtually all of chapters one through 39 should be ascribed to the preaching of Isaiah of Jerusalem, and, equally controversially, they argue that with a few minor exceptions the material is arranged in chronological order with very little editorial adaptation. After a detailed survey of what is known of the history of the period and a summary of Isaiah's theological and religious context, Hayes and Irvine proceed to comment on the text section by section, giving particular attention to the historical context of the various speeches and narratives. Although their argument is perhaps taken too far, their stress on the authenticity of most of first Isaiah serves as a welcome rejoinder to some of the more extreme form-critical studies.

ANDREW DAVIES

Islamic-Jewish Relations

Bat Ye'or, *Le dhimmi,* 1980; translated by David Maisel, Paul Fenton, and David Littman as *The Dhimmi: Jews and Christians under Islam,* Rutherford, New Jersey: Fairleigh Dickinson University Press, and London: Associated University Presses, 1985

Bat Ye'or, *Les Chrétientés d'Orient: entre jihâd et dhimmitude: VIIe–XXe siècle,* 1991; translated by Miriam Kochan and David Littman as *The Decline of Eastern Christianity under Islam: From Jihad to Dhimmitude: Seventh–Twentieth Century,* Madison, New Jersey: Fairleigh Dickinson University Press, 1996

Cohen, Mark R., *Under Crescent and Cross: The Jews in the Middle Ages,* Princeton, New Jersey: Princeton University Press, 1994

Goitein, S.D., *Jews and Arabs: Their Contacts through the Ages,* New York: Schocken, 1955, revised edition, 1974

Stillman, Norman A., *The Jews of Arab Lands: A History and Source Book,* Philadelphia: Jewish Publication Society, 1979

Stillman, Norman A., *The Jews of Arab Lands in Modern Times,* Philadelphia, Jewish Publication Society, 1991

Wasserstrom, Steven M., *Between Muslim and Jew: The Problem of Symbiosis under Early Islam,* Princeton, New Jersey: Princeton University Press, 1995

The relationship between Judaism and Islam, and between those who practice these religions, is necessarily complex, spanning 14 centuries, diverse cultures, Arabs and non-Arabs, religion, philosophy, and politics. For most of this period, Jews were a small but important minority within the Islamic world, but Islam continued or absorbed many elements of Judaism, which itself was greatly influenced by surrounding Islamic religion, culture, and intellectual life. Contemporary Middle Eastern realities bespeak relations that are much different; the rise of Israel and of modern Islamic nation-states has necessarily colored the way all or almost all 20th-century authors write on this subject, even when relating only to pre-modern times. The numerous works that deal specifically with aspects of Israel in the Middle East or other contemporary issues are not discussed here (nor are works that specialize in one country or region). The last part of the 20th century has also seen a dramatic rise in the Islamic communities of Europe and the Americas; Jewish-Islamic relations in these areas, however, have hardly begun to be studied.

GOITEIN's major contribution to medieval Jewish studies is his massive *A Mediterranean Society;* many Jewish-Islamic themes surface in that work as well as in his short *Jews and Arabs.* Originally written in 1955, Goitein revised *Jews*

and Arabs several times and included a chapter bringing the story past the Six Day War. In this work, Goitein suggests reasons for spiritual affinities but also finds great differences between Islam and Judaism in the speed of religious development, the different ways of life in the religions' formative stages, in attitudes toward language, and in their perception of their prehistory. Goitein goes on to summarize legal and economic situations and modalities of the "Jewish-Arabic symbiosis," including language, philosophy, mysticism, messianism, ritual, and poetry. His remarks on Arab literature and journalism after 1967 are of great interest. He saw Arab attitudes of fierce resistance to Israel borne not out of persecution and decay (as seems to explain the quiescence of the Middle Eastern Jewish communities) but out of ascent and prosperity. Throughout, this book is informed with an optimism that might seem quaint. Although it is clearly tinged with realism, few others allowed themselves so positive a view about prospects for contemporary intellectual and cultural interaction between Muslims and Jews until the Oslo accords, a process that commenced over two decades after the final words of *Jews and Arabs* were written.

WASSERSTROM is perhaps the most successful of the many writers who have weighed in on the question of the "symbiosis" of Judaism and Islam in the early Muslim centuries, the term popularized by Goitein in the work noted above and elsewhere. Wasserstrom discusses the borrowing of cultural imagery from one religious community by another while noting that the cultural loan hardly has "the same sense as when a lender lends to a debtor." Rather, continued borrowing resulted in a tremendously creative manipulation of common, mutually intelligible social and cultural languages of theology, messianism, and eschatology. Wasserstrom notes Jewish influences during the formative years of what became a world civilization, within the context of the Jews' social, religious, and intellectual contributions. Of particular interest are his treatment of the Jewish-Islamic symbiosis in the story of the Jewish Messianic Abu 'Isa al-Isfahani and his exploration of Shi'i-Jewish contacts, both in history and in the construction of myth. Also extremely suggestive are his treatments of interfaith contacts in exegesis, chronicles, and eschatology. This book, with its lyrical writing and breadth of reference, is an important addition to the intellectual and religious history of both Judaism and Islam and to the study of how this history has been perceived.

COHEN argues that any description of the status of Jews within Islamic society must strike a firm balance between the myth of an interfaith utopia and the "neo-lachrymose counter-myth" of never-ending persecution. To do so, Cohen describes and contrasts Jewish status in Islam with that in medieval Europe, displaying a deep familiarity with both modern and medieval sources in European languages, Hebrew, and Arabic. Beyond a reexamination of legal status, he discusses economic integration and social concerns such as hierarchy, marginality, ethnicity, and sociability. Polemics and the historiography of persecutions occasion a balanced evaluation of intellectual historians' views of collective memory and identity, anti-semitism, and Jewish attitudes toward the authorities in the many lands of their dispersion. Cohen probes deeply into some fundamental concerns of Jewish life in the Middle Ages and reminds readers that it is inappropriate to read the history of Jewish-Islamic relations with monolithic, preconceived notions.

STILLMAN's (1979, 1991) two-volume set provides a series of essays tracing the history of the Jews of Arab lands from earliest times to the contemporary world, accompanied by a substantial selection of English translations of the most important primary sources, many from the Genizah. The documents in both volumes cover the full gamut of genres: some texts are legal or literary, including laws and edicts and a fairly lengthy selection from Maimonides' *Letter to Yemen;* others are more personal, including marriage documents, letters, and lists. The historical chapters provide a narrative context for the history of the Jews in the Islamic world, following such items as economic and political integration, internal leadership, polemics, and interreligious discourse. Stillman devotes a chapter to "the long twilight" starting in the 13th century, in which the status of the Jewish communities worsened and the relationship between Jews and Muslims became one of persecution. For the modern period in the Middle East, of course, the dominant issues are nationalism, antisemitism, and especially Zionism. Readers of Stillman's essays will get a good sense of the great differences between various Arab countries and regions. The author carefully but briefly gives an overview of Jewish institutions, economics, and status in each of the major centers of Jewish life. In the second volume, he stresses the many differences between Arab countries in their attitudes toward Zionism and other Jewish movements and toward the role of the Jews in their midst.

BAT YE'OR's (1980, 1991) books, like Stillman's, each include two sections, the first being a monograph on the history of non-Muslims in Islamic lands, the second a substantial collection of documents. Gisele Littman's Hebrew pen name means "Daughter of the Nile"; she was born in Egypt, which she left in the humiliating mass exodus of 1956. The historical surveys are well written and researched, although clearly organized to present the narrow point of view that Jews (and Christians) in Islamic lands are victims of *jihad* and must be considered "oppressed" or "subjugated original populations." The accurately translated documents provide a substantial selection and represent important materials often not available elsewhere in English. Both volumes include Christianity within their scope; the status of Jews and Christians was at least in theory identical, and treating them together helps elucidate some points. Yet there is little about the theological, cultural, or administrative developments within either community: the focus is on the history of subjugated status. Bat-Ye'or clearly sees contemporary events in the light of the continuity of the Islamic institution of jihad, carried on by all means possible, including terrorism, diplomacy, and war. Readers will find her works challenging and constructive, but they should approach them with care, remembering Cohen's caveat about one-sided interpretations of Jewish-Islamic relations.

SETH WARD

Israel, Land of: History

Avigad, Nahman, *Discovering Jerusalem*, Nashville, Tennessee: Nelson, 1983

Avi-Yonah, Michael, *Bi-yeme Roma u-Bizantiyon*, 1946; as *The Jews under Roman and Byzantine Rule: A Political History of Palestine from the Bar Kokhba War to the Arab Conquest*, New York: Schocken, 1984

Devir, Ori, *Off the Beaten Track in Israel: A Guide to Beautiful Places*, New York: Adama, 1985

Parkes, James, *A History of Palestine from 135 A.D. to Modern Times*, New York: Oxford University Press, 1949

Smith, Charles, *Palestine and the Arab-Israeli Conflict*, New York: St. Martin's, 1988, 3rd edition, 1995

Zerubavel, Yael, *Recovered Roots: Collective Memory and the Making of Israeli National Tradition*, Chicago: University of Chicago Press, 1995

Most of the major works on the history of the land of Israel consist of multivolume series in Hebrew, which are often exhaustively detailed and devoted to a particular period or place. Some works are guides to specific locations and discuss historical, archaeological, natural, and recreational aspects. In addition, many studies offer reevaluations of historical, cultural, and archaeological trends, often centered around specific events in the history of the land of Israel, such as the Maccabean revolt, the discovery of the Dead Sea Scrolls, the destruction of Jerusalem, the Bar Kokhba revolt, the Crusades, the battle of Tel Hai, and the Israeli-Arab wars. The books discussed in this essay are representative works in English from each of these categories.

AVIGAD's book is a systematic study of Jerusalem through many of the stages of its development. In particular, Avigad writes as an archaeologist involved with the excavations in Jerusalem from 1969 to 1980. The book is filled with aerial photographs, maps, old photographs, pictures of recent discoveries, and sketches offering plausible reconstructions of historical sites. The text provides a historical as well as an archaeological narrative. Avigad reports on the discoveries from the periods of the first and second temples, including inscriptions, city walls, coins, pottery, weapons, mosaic floors, and wall frescoes, some of which bear evidence of the fire and devastation of 70 C.E. Based on a map of Jerusalem from the Byzantine period, Avigad and his crew also discovered the ruins of several massive churches and the ancient Roman road, the Cardo, running through the city. Avigad's account ends with several important discoveries from the period of the Crusades.

AVI-YONAH begins with a brief survey of the Persian period, covers the Hasmonean rule, and then discusses the Roman conquest and subsequent wars with the Jews. Among little-known features of his story is the extent to which Jews continued to practice temple rituals after the sanctuary in Jerusalem was destroyed in 70 C.E. Avi-Yonah draws on Jewish, Roman, and Christian sources. He offers detailed accounts of specific events, often discussing a range of scholarly opinion about them. Some of his characterizations of early Jewish-Christian relations may be slightly lacking in nuance, but in other matters, such as the rebellion of Patricius and the plans of Julian the Apostate to rebuild the temple, he is nuanced in the extreme. Shortcomings include Avi-Yonah's claim that women were confined to the balconies of the synagogues, which contradicts Shmuel Safrai's important 1963 article concerning the topic. Similarly, he traces the roots of the development of Hebrew poetry, *piyyut*, to the ban on Torah study imposed by the Byzantine emperor in the early seventh century, another view that has been challenged by other scholars.

DEVIR's exceptional travel guide, translated from Hebrew and based on an Israeli television show, divides the country into seven regions and discusses approximately a dozen little-known sites of historical significance in each region. Devir devotes two pages to each site and includes photographs, a map, and a historical essay for each. Among the sites profiled are forts, aqueducts, mountains, lakes, streams, waterfalls, monuments, ancient synagogues, ruined cities, battlefields, churches, and gorges. Many of these sites are not typical tourist destinations, and some, therefore, are not maintained or easily accessible.

PARKES offers one of the few one-volume English-language histories of the land of Israel. His early works on the relationship of the church and the synagogue and on the medieval Jewish community, as well as his studies of antisemitism and his advocacy of Jewish causes during the 1930s and 1940s, made him a philosemitic pioneer among Christian clergymen and scholars. In this book Parkes also embraces the Jewish cause, often without considering Arab interests or Muslim sensibilities. Despite the stridency of this polemic as well as an occasional overabundance of details and a lack of clear design, Parkes provides a valuable and insightful survey of the global and local forces during each period of the history of the land. Each chapter contains incisive observations for formulating an appreciation of the scholarly controversies that surround each period. Parkes asserts (and many now agree) that Hadrian's decrees were not meant to be anti-Jewish. His comments on anti-Christian formulations, presumably the *birkat haminim*, drawn up by the rabbis at Yavneh, may assume more than the data allow, but he does make the important point that Jews were as aggressively anti-Christian in late antiquity as Christians were anti-Jewish. Parkes describes in detail a Jewish revolt against the Romans in 350 that was led by Patricius, an event that often goes unreported but contributes much to understanding the continued rebelliousness of the Jews of Palestine. He dates the often unnoticed return of Jews to Jerusalem after the Hadrianic expulsion to the fifth century, during the time the Empress Eudocia was living in the city. Parkes pays attention to cultural and religious developments in Palestine, as reflected in rabbinic and patristic literature. As Parkes traces the subsequent occupations of Palestine by the Persians, Arabs, crusaders, Mameluks, and Turks, he does not pay significant attention to Islamic accomplishments and is wont to dismiss Muslims out of hand as being responsible for destruction, devastation, and depopulation. In particular, he asserts that the sacred graves often taken over by Muslims began as Jewish or Christian shrines, although the scholarly consensus today often asserts that Jewish and Christian pilgrims appropriated Muslim tombs. Parkes provides a fascinating survey of modern Palestine including Napoleon's campaign, the role of natural disasters, missionaries, archaeologists, philanthropists, and con-

suls and the rise of Arab nationalism and the Zionist movement. In addition, Parkes regularly inserts information about all the various minorities in the land of Israel: Bosnians, Druze, Circassians, Egyptians, Samaritans, Karaites, and Bahai.

SMITH presents a valuable synthesis of literature written by authors of many different sympathies. He begins with a survey of the history of Palestine, quickly moving to Turkish rule. Smith repeatedly shows how events in the region are results of earlier developments elsewhere in the world among Jews, Muslims, and Western powers. A regular phenomenon in his account involves politicians, including Western diplomats, Israelis, and Arabs, lying in order to advance their own personal agendas at the expense of national policy. In controversial matters all sides find different levels of meaning in statements made by members of the opposing sides. All sides routinely hope that expectations for peace will not be met and peace negotiations will fail.

ZERUBAVEL focuses upon three major events in the history of the land of Israel, which she does not treat in chronological order: the battle of Tel Hai, the Bar Kokhba revolt, and the fall of Massada. She discusses each event in the context of the development of Zionist historiography and Jewish collective memory in the land of Israel and abroad. She thus locates the origins of each myth and their depictions in literature, ritual, and commemoration, and discusses the current political and national aspects of each myth. One of the most intriguing features of the book is the way in which Zerubavel shifts the object of her study from the events of history themselves to the different ways in which meaning is attached to them. Thus, unlike most people for whom the tour guide serves as a major source of historical information, she makes the tour guide into an object of study as an agent of collective memory, demonstrating that history and memory are not always identical but exist in a creative tension. She reports that one tour guide told her how he was taught to give different versions of the Massada story to Israeli and to foreign tourists. In one anecdote Zerubavel reports that David Ben-Gurion chided Bar Kokhba and his followers for having written in Aramaic and not Hebrew. One of the most fascinating aspects of the book is the description of the development during the 20th century of the myths associated with Massada as Jews developed the site for visits. Zerubavel also incorporates the role that these myths play in contemporary jokes. When Zerubavel's book first appeared, it received particular attention because it offered a revision of Joseph Trumpledor's famous last words at the battle of Tel Hai in 1920. According to legend he said in Hebrew, "*Tov lamut baad artzenu*" ("It is good to die for our country"). Questioning not only his level of Hebrew but the naturalness of such a sentiment, Zerubavel reports that a countermyth developed in which his final words were the similar sounding Russian curse, "*uob tzoyu mat*" ("f—k your mother"). The book ends with a discussion about the invention of tradition and the multiple meanings of memories, important concepts for studying any aspect of the history of the land of Israel.

HOWARD TZVI ADELMAN

See also Israel, Land of: In Jewish Thought; Israel, State of: Judaism in Israel; Jerusalem

Israel, Land of: In Jewish Thought

Buber, Martin, *Bein Am Learzo* (1944); as *On Zion: The History of an Idea,* New York: Schocken, and London: Horovitz, 1973

Davies, W.D., *The Gospel and the Land: Early Christianity and Jewish Territorial Doctrine,* Berkeley and London: University of California Press, 1974

Davies, W.D., *The Territorial Dimension of Judaism,* Berkeley: University of California Press, 1982

Halkin, Abraham (editor), *Zion in Jewish Literature,* New York: Herzl, 1961; London: University Press of America, 1988

Heschel, Abraham Joshua, *Israel: An Echo of Eternity,* New York: Farrar, Straus and Giroux, 1969

Hoffman, Lawrence (editor), *The Land of Israel: Jewish Perspectives* (University of Notre Dame Center for the Study of Judaism and Christianity in Antiquity, no. 6), Notre Dame, Indiana: University of Notre Dame Press, 1986

The Land of Israel fosters tension in Jewish thought. The sacred geography of the Land and the "holy city" of Jerusalem have been integral to the memories and aspirations of the Jewish people; many of the commandments of the Torah can be observed only within the boundaries of the Land. Yet Jewish communities have lived and thrived outside the Land for millennia. To maintain the centrality of the Land without subverting the possibility of creative Jewish life outside it was the challenge faced by Jewish thinkers of the diaspora in all generations.

BUBER's book was first published in Hebrew in 1944 under the title *Bein Am Learzo* (Between a People and Its Land). The structure of the book set the pattern for later treatments. It begins with a section on the Bible, exploring motifs such as the prayer of the first fruits (Deuteronomy 26:1–10), in which the gift of the Land betokens the unity of the God of history and the God of nature, the promise of the Land in the covenant, and the idea of Zion as the center of a future redeemed world. Buber then analyzes interpretations of these motifs in rabbinic literature. A section on "The Voice of Exile" includes ideas of the Land in the Zohar, in Judah Halevi's Kuzari, and in Judah Loew (Maharal) of Prague, to whom he attributes the "beginning of the national idea." Also included is the account of the hasidic rebbe Nahman of Bratslav's visit to Palestine. Turning to the Zionist idea, he treats Moses Hess, Leo Pinsker, Theodor Herzl (the rather critical discussion of whom reflects Buber's own reservations about political Zionism), Ahad Ha'am, Rabbi Abraham Kook, and Buber's special hero, A.D. Gordon, whom he calls "the most remarkable" of the pioneers. In the diversity of these medieval and modern thinkers, the material looks less like a history of an idea than variations and transformations of a theme.

The essays edited by HALKIN cover similar ground while focusing on the themes of exile and redemption. In his own contribution, Halkin insists that "Zion is the central theme of the Bible": its gift from God to the chosen people, its loss, and its (future) restoration. Gerson Cohen, noting that "fully one third of the Mishna, and hence of all Jewish law, is inextri-

cably connected with the land of Israel," discusses legislation regarding emigration from the Land and rabbinic treatment of the rights to the Land. Essays on medieval literature return to the themes of exile and the attempts to transcend it in liturgical poetry by Palestinian, Ashkenazi, and Spanish poets and in prose texts, including the Zohar and works by Halevi, Maimonides, and Nahmanides. Two final essays treat modern Hebrew poetry and prose, both emphasizing the power of the exile motif recovered (after its abandonment by the Jewish Enlightenment) by the Zionists, who repudiated the traditional claim of its penitential value. Only rarely are issues such as the possibilities of full spiritual life in the diaspora or the possibility of exile in the Land of Israel itself given serious attention.

HESCHEL's work is characteristically lyrical and rhapsodic, suffused with biblical language. It is deeply engaged, with the author rhetorically speaking on behalf of the Jewish people in history: "Why did our hearts throughout the ages turn to Erets Israel? . . . We have lived in some parts of Europe for nearly two thousand years." This book is explicitly set in the immediate aftermath of the Six Day War, which is juxtaposed contrapuntally with the Holocaust. Heschel does not abandon the assertion made in earlier writings that, unlike paganism, Judaism finds holiness in time rather than space. Yet in the wake of emotions generated by a Jewish return to the site of the Temple Mount following the dreadful anxiety of May and early June 1967, he apparently concluded that he gave insufficient emphasis to the role of sacred geography in Jewish experience. An earlier work proclaims, "The sanctity of time came first, the sanctity of man came second, and the sanctity of space last." Here the emphasis is different: "The history of Jerusalem is endowed with the power to inspire such moments [of holiness], to invoke in us the ability to be present to His presence."

DAVIES's (1974) extensive study treats in great detail the significance of the Land of Israel in Hebrew Scriptures, extrabiblical Jewish sources, and the New Testament. DAVIES (1982), a considerably shorter book, is also more sweeping, setting out to determine whether the territorial dimension, specifically the attachment to the Land of Israel, is essential or accidental and peripheral to Judaism. After a section on biblical and extrabiblical and rabbinic sources that summarizes much of the earlier book, Davies continues through the Middle Ages to the Zionist movement and modern religious thinkers, although here the treatment is far more sketchy. Despite abundant textual evidence for the centrality of the Land, Davies notes the diversity of Jewish expressions on this subject, such as the texts that shift the focus away from Jerusalem or spiritualize it, the transformation of Torah into a "portable land," or the varied historical experiences of diaspora Jewish communities. His conclusion is that living in the Land is not absolutely essential to Judaism in the way that the Torah is, that "Judaism is not a territorial religion."

HOFFMAN's edition of scholarly essays reveals the academic outlook a generation after Halkin's book. The biblical scholar Harry Orlinsky argues from a precise analysis of legal terminology that the assignment of the Land of Israel to the Jewish people was a fundamental "cornerstone" of the covenant between God and Israel. The article that follows, on

Land theology in Philo and Josephus, explores the rather different treatments by two leading diaspora thinkers of Hellenistic Judaism. Two essays on the Mishnah grapple with problems such as the borders of the Land, the status of the laws bound up with the Land for gentiles living in it and for Jews living outside it, and—more abstractly—whether the sanctity of the Land can be transferred to other places. Five essays on the "medieval" period dealing with legal, polemical, philosophical, kabbalistic, hasidic, and artistic texts reveal a panoply of attitudes—including attempts to spiritualize the Land often associated exclusively with Christian doctrines—that belie simplistic ideological pronouncements. Three contributions on the modern period treat the "demystification, resymbolization, and politicization" of the Land, and the knotty problem of whether the return of the Jewish people to the Land and the reestablishment of a Jewish state there should be viewed as part of the process of messianic redemption or in strictly historical categories. This is the best summary in English of current, nuanced, nonideological, and nonpolemical investigation into an abundance of Jewish sources.

MARC SAPERSTEIN

See also Israel, Land of: History; Israel, State of: Judaism in Israel; Jerusalem

Israel, State of: Judaism in Israel

Leibowitz, Yeshayahu, *Judaism, Human Values, and the Jewish State,* edited by Eliezer Goldman and translated by Eliezer Goldman and Yoram Navon, and by Zvi Jacobson, Gershon Levi, and Raphael Levy from portions of the author's *Yahadut, 'am Yehudi, u-medinat Yisrael* (1976) and *Emunah, historiyah, va-arakhim: Ma'amarim ve-hartsa'ot* (1982), Cambridge, Massachusetts, and London: Harvard University Press, 1992

Liebman, Charles S. and Eliezer Don-Yehiya, *Religion and Politics in Israel* (Jewish Political and Social Studies Series), Bloomington: Indiana University Press, 1984

Litvin, Baruch and Sidney B. Hoenig (editors), *Jewish Identity: Modern Responsa and Opinions on the Registration of Children of Mixed Marriages; David Ben-Gurion's Query to Leaders of World Jewry: A Documentary Compilation,* New York: Feldheim, l965

Luz, Ehud, *Makbilim nifgashim: Dat u-le'umiyut ba-tenu'ah ha-tsiyonit be-mizrah Eiropa be-re'shitah (1882–1904),* 1985; translated by Lenn J. Schramm as *Parallels Meet: Religion and Nationalism in the Early Zionist Movement (1882–1904),* Philadelphia: Jewish Publication Society, 1988

Newman, David (editor), *The Impact of Gush Emunim: Politics and Settlement in the West Bank,* London: Croom Helm, 1985

Ravitzky, Aviezer, *Kets ha-meguleh u-medinat ha-Yehudim,* 1996; translated by Michael Swirsky and Jonathan Chipman as *Messianism, Zionism, and Jewish Religious Radicalism,* Chicago and London: University of Chicago Press, 1996

Sobel, Zvi, *A Small Place in Galilee: Religion and Social Conflict in an Israeli Village* (New Perspectives Series), New York: Holmes and Meier, 1993

Sobel, Zvi and Benjamin Beit-Hallahmi (editors), *Tradition, Innovation, Conflict: Jewishness and Judaism in Contemporary Israel* (SUNY Series in Israeli Studies), Albany: State University of New York Press, 1991

Sprinzak, Ehud, *Brother against Brother: Violence and Extremism in Israeli Politics from Altalena to the Rabin Assassination,* New York: Free Press, 1999

Urian, Dan and Efraim Karsh (editors), *In Search of Identity: Jewish Aspects in Israeli Culture* (Cass Studies in Israeli History, Politics, and Society, no. 7), London and Portland, Oregon: Cass, 1999

Zipperstein, Steven J., *Elusive Prophet: Ahad Ha'am and the Origins of Zionism,* Berkeley: University of California Press, and London: Halban, 1993

Since the birth of modern Zionism over a century ago, the question of what role Judaism would play in the building of a Jewish national homeland has been surrounded by unremitting controversy. Was Zionism a European nationalist movement representing something fundamentally new in Jewish culture? Or rather, was it an outgrowth of Judaism's 2000-year commitment to return to Zion? Throughout the transformation of Zionism from an ideology into a movement and finally into a modern nation-state, the question of the role of Judaism has always been of the essence. The debates over the role of Judaism in Zionism and the State of Israel have also attracted scholarly attention for decades. Through a review of some of the scholarship concerning the role of Judaism in Zionist ideology, Israeli political culture, and Israeli popular culture, this survey highlights the way that questions concerning Judaism and Israel are central to many aspects of current research on the State of Israel.

One cannot appreciate current discussions concerning the status of Judaism within the State of Israel without viewing it within the context of Zionist ideology at the end of the 19th century. Since the birth of modern Zionism, the question of Judaism and modern Jewish national identity has been at the center of the Zionist effort to define itself. Was Israel to be a state for Jews? Or a Jewish state? LUZ addresses these question by arguing that Zionism sprang up in the late 19th century in order to address the tension created between "religion and life," or tradition and modernity. Luz mainly explores the position taken by secular circles in Eastern Europe concerning the relationship of Judaism and Zionism and unfortunately does not contextualize the views of these circles by juxtaposing their opinions with those of Zionists in the religious camp.

The main secular ideologue who dealt with the complex relationship of Judaism to a prospective state of Israel was Asher Ginzberg, commonly known as Ahad Ha'am. ZIPPERSTEIN explores Ahad Ha'am's writings within the context of his complex relationship to Judaism and the general background of Jewish life in Odessa in the late 19th century. Ahad Ha'am saw Zionism as a Judaic cultural renaissance, and without Judaism at the center of the new Jewish homeland, the dreams of modern Zionists would ultimately fail. While Zipperstein highlights the weaknesses in Ahad Ha'am's writing (he often used his conclusions as evidence in his arguments), Zipperstein does not deal with why Ahad Ha'am was so popular in his day. Nonetheless, Zipperstein raises critical questions in connection with his subject's contention that a state for Jews could never exist without a central role for Judaism.

Raising similarly troubling questions concerning the relationship of Judaism and the State of Israel is the late-20th-century philosopher Yeshayahu LEIBOWITZ. In his incisive yet somewhat repetitive collection of essays, Leibowitz argues that Judaism and the State of Israel must be separate entities for the sake of both. Leibowitz maintains that Judaism makes demands of humans but does not bestow upon them benefits. Political involvement corrupts Judaism by not focusing on the demands that Judaism makes of its believers but rather on Judaism's utility. Leibowitz believes that any link between Judaism and the State of Israel both debases Judaism and endangers the state, for politicized religion is not religion and can be used improperly to justify any act.

Other late-20th-century approaches to the role of Judaism within the State of Israel are presented in RAVITZKY. An intellectual historian, Ravitzky argues that after the founding of the state, "the religious mind found it difficult to view Zionism and messianism as two unrelated phenomena." It was this troubled religious mind that could not ratify a constitution for the State of Israel that was not based on Torah law. Ravitzky shows how some Orthodox Jews insisted that the State of Israel embodied messianic redemption, while others, such as the Satmar hasidim, saw its creation as an act of Satan and refused to recognize Jewish sovereignty in the land of Israel. Ravitzky does clarify the multiple and competing ideologies of Orthodox Jewry concerning the question of the relationship of Judaism and the State of Israel. However, ideologies do not develop within a social or political vacuum, and Ravitzky fails to contextualize his discussion within the greater context of Israeli society. Consequently, Ravitzky does not provide a framework to explore all the complexities of the relationship of Judaism to the State of Israel.

There are several collections of articles that examine the question of Judaism and the State of Israel from a legal or sociopolitical perspective. The classic and pioneering work on this topic is LITVIN and HOENIG, which provides many basic insights into this complex relationship. However, over the last 30 years much has changed in Israeli society, causing parts of their study to become outdated. Articles in SOBEL and BEIT-HALLAHMI examine how Judaism is often the arena for social conflict on the communal level in Israel, as can be seen from several case studies that the book presents and from the dilemmas faced by religious "dissenters" (such as Reform or Conservative Jews) in Israel. This collection provides the greater context for the findings of SOBEL's community case study of Yavneel, in which he uses the events in one small village in the Galilee as a lens to see how Judaism becomes the focal point for social conflict in the State of Israel.

Also utilizing a case study approach, LIEBMAN and DON-YEHIYA explore such issues as religious parties in Israel and religious extremism, yet their most provocative analysis concerns Jewish identity among secular Israelis. They maintain that Israelis' national identity reinforces their Jewish identity and that Israelis affirm the value of a Jewish state that is based

on a recognizable religious culture. Israelis, it transpires, generally believe that there must be some relationship between Judaism and the State of Israel. If Israelis ever question the centrality of Judaism to the State of Israel, it is chiefly because they are practically inconvenienced by coercive religious legislation mandated by religious extremists as the price of their participation in Israel's perpetual coalition governments.

Using cultural studies as their framework for analysis, URIAN and KARSH present a series of articles dealing with the numerous conflicts arising from "the problematic continuum between Israeliness and Jewishness." The great value of their collection is their exploration of the *Kulturkampf* between religious and secular Israelis as reflected in contemporary Israeli cinema and theater. A number of provocative essays on topics such as images of religious Jews and *ba'alei teshuvah* in the theater demonstrates how the study of Israeli arts and culture offers substantial insight into the dilemmas shaping Israelis' understanding of the relationship of Judaism to the State of Israel.

The value of NEWMAN's case study of Gush Emunim, the ultranationalist post-1967 settler faction within the National Religious Party, is that it brings to bear both sociological and ideological analysis on the question of religious extremism and the State of Israel; however, this collection is problematic since Newman overstates the impact Gush Emunim has had on Israeli society and political culture. Gush Emunim is just one manifestation of what can result from the combination of Judaism and politics in the contemporary State of Israel. The violent results of the current debate concerning the role that Judaism should play in the State of Israel is addressed in SPRINZAK, which explores intra-Jewish violence throughout the history of Israel. The assassination of Yitzhak Rabin by a religious Zionist prompted Sprinzak's examination of Jewish violence, which is basically a compendium of intra-Jewish violent conflicts in Israel. While not directly addressing the question of the role of Judaism in the State of Israel, Sprinzak places recent violence, which was driven in large part by the question of the role of Judaism in Israel, within the historical context of intra-Jewish conflict in Israel. Sprinzak's discussion of contemporary conflicts exposes certain biases, yet his overview of the sporadic violence of some ultraorthodox Jews in response to decisions of Israel's democratic government and of haredi desire for a greater role for Judaism in the State of Israel (or at least the land of Israel) is illuminating for anyone who wants to understand the recent violence within its proper historical perspective.

REBECCA KOBRIN

See also Israel, Land of

Israel ben Eliezer Ba'al Shem Tov
c.1700–1760

Podolian founder of modern Hasidism

Ben-Amos, Dan and Jerome R. Mintz (translators and editors), *In Praise of the Baal Shem Tov [Shivhei ha-*

Besht]: *The Earliest Collection of Legends about the Founder of Hasidism*, Bloomington: Indiana University Press, 1970

Buber, Martin, *Erzählungen der Chassidim*, 1947; translated by Olga Marx as *Tales of the Hasidim*, New York: Schocken/Farrar, Straus and Young, 1947; London: Thames and Hudson, 1956

Kaplan, Aryeh, *The Light Beyond: Adventures in Hassidic Thought*, New York: Maznaim, 1981

Rosman, Murray Jay, *Founder of Hasidism: A Quest for the Historical Ba'al Shem Tov* (Contraversions, 5), Berkeley: University of California Press, 1996

Sears, Dovid, *The Path of the Baal Shem Tov: Early Chasidic Teachings and Customs*, Northvale, New Jersey: Aronson, 1997

Healer, seer, master of prayer, storytelling, and song, spiritual guide, model of open-hearted, life-affirming religion, Israel Ba'al Shem Tov ("Master of the Good Name") was one of the most influential teachers and leaders in Jewish history. He stands at the source of and continues to inspire the hasidic movement, which despite Jewish secularization and the destruction of its Eastern European homeland remains a growing and confident trend in Orthodox Judaism and a vital source of ideas and inspiration for unorthodox Jews. His written legacy, however, is minimal, consisting of a few letters to relatives. He is known through the writings of disciples and through stories retold and, indeed, increasing in number over successive generations.

BEN-AMOS and MINTZ have translated and annotated *Shivhei ha-Besht,* important as the major source for attempts to reconstruct the life of the Ba'al Shem Tov and as the first printed book of hasidic tales. First published in 1814, 54 years after the death of its subject, the book is steeped in early hasidic oral tradition; nearly every story begins by noting from whom the author heard it. The translation is straightforward and, explicitly and appropriately, does not aim for more aesthetic appeal than the original. As a result, the nonhistorian may find this book uneven reading and spiritually less than uplifting. The focus of most of the stories is on rather crude miracles, as well as scattered, frustratingly brief recollections of a variety of incidents. It rewards a patient reading, however, with its glimpses of a very human Ba'al Shem Tov, seen at times angry, afraid, or jocular. The translators have included appendixes that are useful for the study of the stories, including a recapitulation of the original work's notes on informants, and an index to folkloric motifs. There is one glaring misjudgment in the translation whereby the Tetragrammaton is spelled out with vowels, contrary to Jewish practice and certainly not reflecting the original text.

BUBER, writing in German, was one of the first to introduce Western European and North American readers to the hasidic traditions of Eastern Europe and to draw on hasidic inspirations in constructing a contemporary and unorthodox approach to Judaism. Buber drew on extensive reading in hasidic literature, although unfortunately without noting his sources. His retellings of stories are usually closely based on the original versions, but they have a distinctively polished literary quality, well reflected in Olga Marx's English translation.

At times, in keeping with his intuitive sense of their meaning, Buber changed stories in subtle but far-reaching ways. Most of Buber's hundred or so stories about the Ba'al Shem Tov are drawn from *Shivhei ha-Besht,* so that the reader of Ben-Amos and Mintz's translation can readily discern Buber's hand at work. Drawing on other sources as well, Buber constructs a version of the Ba'al Shem Tov that remains accessible to many contemporary readers, with miracles downplayed and the intensity of human relationships highlighted. Buber has smoothed over some of the Ba'al Shem Tov's rough edges seen in *Shivhei ha-Besht,* creating, surprisingly, a more saintly figure than in the original hasidic texts.

ROSMAN undertakes a serious and thorough attempt to discover all that can be known historically about the Ba'al Shem Tov. With appropriate skepticism and a wide use of sources, he surveys earlier scholarship, draws on evidence previously unconsidered or undervalued, and arrives at new, potentially controversial conclusions. In particular, he makes use for the first time of the Polish archives of the town of Miedzyboz, the Ba'al Shem Tov's home. These records establish the historical existence of the Ba'al Shem Tov (which some scholars had questioned); he is referred to as the "kabbalist" and "doctor." The archives yield information about his family and associates, his status in the Jewish community, and the general economic and political context of his time. The chapter significantly titled "A Person of His Time" offers Rosman's tentative reconstruction of the Ba'al Shem Tov's historical role. He sees the Ba'al Shem Tov as a transitional figure: a recognized mystic and healer, supported by the Jewish establishment of his community, who practiced the pietism of his time in a way that lent itself to greater popularization. In this view the Ba'al Shem Tov did not found a new movement; rather, when the hasidic movement began, its leaders saw him as their predecessor and inspiration. The final chapter analyzes the editorial decisions made by the printer of *Shivhei ha-Besht* as an early example of the use of stories of the Ba'al Shem Tov in supporting new developments in Hasidism.

The hasidic works devoted to teachings attributed to the Ba'al Shem Tov are not available in translation. Excerpts of his teachings, however, can be found in Kaplan and Sears, both of whom, though from Orthodox perspectives, are following Buber in presenting the Ba'al Shem Tov in a way that is meant to be useful to contemporary spiritual seekers.

To this end SEARS's book contains two main sections: a selection of teachings and anecdotes grouped according to themes, and a section of customs and recommendations for the daily routine and the holidays. The translations are clear, although some readers will find the transliteration of Hebrew terms according to a modified Ashkenazi pronunciation to be confusing. As Sears acknowledges, attribution of most of these teachings to the Ba'al Shem Tov himself is dubious; the selection draws on a wide variety of sources including some from long after the Ba'al Shem Tov's time.

KAPLAN was an important Orthodox outreach teacher, oriented, as his introductory sketch of the Ba'al Shem Tov's life suggests, toward meditative practice. He provides clear English paraphrases (not literal translations) of selections from classic hasidic books, arranged by such themes as "Meditation and Prayer" and "Life and Society." Teachings attributed to the Ba'al Shem Tov are well represented, more than those of any other master. There are footnotes on the Hebrew sources and on parallel texts. Neither Sears nor Kaplan has attempted to sift out what is more or less likely to be historically authentic; rather, the Ba'al Shem Tov is presented as later generations of hasidim remembered him.

JUSTIN JARON LEWIS

See also Ba'alei Shem

Italy

Bonfil, Roberto, *Ha-Rabanut be-Italyah bi-tekufat ha-Renesans*, 1979; as *Rabbis and Jewish Communities in Renaissance Italy*, London: Littman Library of Jewish Civilization, 1993

Bonfil, Roberto, *Jewish Life in Renaissance Italy*, Berkeley: University of California Press, 1994

Roth, Cecil, *The History of the Jews of Italy*, Philadelphia: Jewish Publication Society, 1946; Westmead: Gregg, 1969

Roth, Cecil, *The Jews in the Renaissance*, Philadelphia: Jewish Publication Society, 1959

Shulvass, Moses A., *Haye ha-yehudim be-Italyah bi-tekufat ha-Renesans*, 1955; as *The Jews in the World of the Renaissance*, Leiden: Brill, 1973

Simonsohn, Shlomo, *The Apostolic See and the Jews*, vol. 7 (Studies and Texts Series, 109), Toronto: Pontifical Institute of Mediaeval Studies, 1991

Toaff, Ariel, *Love, Work, and Death: Jewish Life in Medieval Umbria*, London and Portland, Oregon: Littman Library of Jewish Civilization, 1996

Jews have lived in Italy since the Roman period, and the scholarship on their history covers a broad range of topics from many historiographic perspectives. There are scholars who prefer a documentary history centered on specific archives and others whose content is regulated by a predetermined topic. Historians may favor working with Christian sources, or prefer instead Jewish internal records, or be happy to use both. Of course, there are studies that survey the development of the Jewish presence in Italy throughout history and others that stress a particular period.

ROTH (1946) is one of the most basic texts in the field. Its purpose is to survey the entire Jewish history of Italy in a manner that is accessible to nonspecialists. This is also its fault; there is neither a comprehensive bibliography nor footnotes, so its academic usefulness is limited. Roth compresses a vast amount of scattered material in one book, however, starting from the Roman period and continuing to the 20th century. He covers much ground at high speed. His point of view is classical and his book describes a history of events and personages.

SHULVASS describes Jewish history in Italy during the Renaissance with special attention given to such topics as the characteristics of the Jewish population and its geographical dispersion, the evolution of the community, economic life, family and social life, literature, the fine arts, the world of sci-

ence, and finally the Renaissance in daily life. Shulvass argues that the Renaissance is regarded as one of the most significant eras in human history because men began to perceive the world more consciously in all its vastness and beauty. This work is an important contribution to the comprehension of what is therefore a central period in Jewish history. It is readable by anyone, specialist or layperson.

SIMONSOHN's book is a summation of the six great volumes of archival documents he has published in this series. As he states in the introduction, the book is an attempt to trace the history of the papacy's policy toward Jews from its inception to the Counter-Reformation. Thus, the book covers more than 1,000 years of history, from the adoption of Christianity by the Emperor Constantine through the Middle Ages to the 16th century. It traces the unfolding of Christian-Jewish relations as viewed by the papacy and depicted in the records of the Vatican Archives. Topics examined in this study include the Inquisition and its attitude toward Jewish literature, the prosecution of Jewish converts, polemics and disputations between Jews and Christians, and Jewish banking.

ROTH (1959) is a classic text on the cultural aspects of Italian Jewish history from the 14th to the 16th century. It analyzes the non-Jewish context of Renaissance Jewish life as well as the influence of non-Jewish scholars on Jewish culture. As Roth wrote, "this work is an experimental study of the interaction of two societies and of two cultures at one of the seminal periods of the world's history." In his opinion, the Jews not only participated in Renaissance culture, but they also made essential contributions to what was, in consequence, a "golden age" of Jewish-Christian relations. Perhaps this picture is idyllic, but until a few decades ago this was the main trend of Jewish historians, and Roth was an important representative of this reading.

BONFIL (1979) deals with the shape of the institution of the rabbinate–one of the central topics in Jewish history–during the Renaissance. This monograph describes such topics as the social meaning of rabbinic ordination, the judicial function of the rabbis, and the cultural world of the rabbis. It analyzes the application of Jewish law and the role of the rabbis within the community structure. Bonfil pays much attention to the cultural aspects of rabbinic activity, such as literary and philosophical production, according them equal weight with juridical and social aspects.

TOAFF concentrates on the Jews of Umbria, although his book is also an essay on the specific historiographic question of whether Jewish history should be studied from Jewish sources only or seen through the eyes of outsiders. Toaff's thesis is that to form a true picture of Jewish life one must take account of all the pressures and contradictions acting from within and without. In his opinion, it is not acceptable to disqualify Christian sources as tendentious in order to give credence to the image of a homogeneous Jewish society. Toaff wants to present a picture of everyday life instead of the intellectual history hitherto in fashion, and therefore his book deals with such topics as love and marriage, foodways, magic and ritual beliefs, patterns of discrimination, and employment opportunities for Jews.

BONFIL (1994) deals with the "fundamental opposition between the world of the Christian majority, and that of the

Jewish minority." In fact, Bonfil wants to suggest a partial revision of current historiography so as to present the history of Renaissance Italian Jewry from the inside. In his opinion, a history seen from the inside implies "coming to awareness of the self in the act of specular reflection in the other." This book is a major essay on historical theory, dealing with issues of time and space, sound and silence. At the same time, it is crammed with information about such topics as Jewish occupations, education, and culture.

YAAKOV A. LATTES

See also Venice

J

Jabès, Edmond 1912–1991

Egyptian-born French writer and thinker

Boyarin, Jonathan, "Jewish Ethnography and the Question of the Book," in his *Storm from Paradise: The Politics of Jewish Memory*, Minneapolis: University of Minnesota Press, 1992

Gould, Eric, *The Sin of the Book: Edmond Jabès*, Lincoln: University of Nebraska Press, 1985

Motte, Warren F., *Questioning Edmond Jabès*, Lincoln: University of Nebraska Press, 1990

Stamelman, Richard, "The Graven Silence of Writing," in *From the Book to the Book: An Edmond Jabès Reader*, Hanover, New Hampshire: University Press of New England, 1991

Wolfson, Elliot R., "From Sealed Book to Open Text: Time, Memory, and Narrativity in Kabbalistic Hermeneutics," in *Interpreting Judaism in a Postmodern Age* (New Perspectives on Jewish Studies), edited by Steven Kepnes, New York: New York University Press, 1996

Born in Cairo to an upper-middle-class Jewish family of Italian nationality, the mistaken declaration of his birth two days earlier forever marked Edmond Jabès. His identity as a Jew and as a poet was no longer singular but was invaded by an "other" who shared his name and existence. The first manifestation of existence, for the Jew and for God, is marked by an absence carried within the name. These ensuing realities of lack, absence, otherness—all major themes of Jabès's oeuvre—appear to have been marks of his being from birth. Toward the creation of a new language of mystical Jewish humanism in aphoristic poetry and prose, Jabès counters these terrifying realities with fragmentary poems and commentaries of hope that prioritize love for the stranger; the incarnation of difference in the face of every human being; the desire for love and sharing; the importance of hospitality; and longing in the absence of the other for God. As much as any kabbalist, this Jewish poet was passionately consumed with the magical power of letters to write the universe anew. His death marked the close of a great sequence of books that continue to call all into question and, with special force, to challenge the persistence of antisemitism and racism throughout the world.

GOULD reprints in translation two important European essays by M. Blanchot and J. Starobinski, while also assembling some of the foremost interpretations of Jabès by North American critics, poets, and novelists. Gould's introduction furnishes the reader with broad strokes on the Jabèsian canvas, especially in its tentative delineation of the contributors into four possible circles of interpretation: boundaries; exile, humanist, Jew; reading the question; and displacements. The commentary beginning in section two introduces Blanchot's category of interruption as a rupture in the word of the broken tablets where the renewed history of a people folds in on itself. Blanchot's category is further investigated by Handelman and Stamelman (via Scholem) in their application of Isaac Luria's apophatic system of contraction, exile, and restoration to the Jabèsian project for purposes of comparison and elucidation. Handelman follows the Lurianic thread in presenting a comparison to Rabbi Nahman of Bratslav, whose visions of God's exile pushed Hasidism to its limits, just as Jabès pushes postmodernism to its limits. Handelman posits Jabès as having met Scharlemann's challenge of formulating a postmodern theology that questions theism in order to incorporate time and negation back into the deity. What ensues—a decentering bordering on nihilism—is challenged by Kaplan as an act of post-Nietzschean humanist faith preserving the play of desire in the Book as question. The third section of Gould's work addresses the literary qualities of this questioning, which are held to be exegetical or midrashic. Endless subversions of the signified, both oedipal and Lurianic, belie the investigation of Waldrop (Jabès's foremost translator). The fourth section dwells on the controversy of the Book and certain possible directions in post-Holocaust Jewish writing. Lang posits that Jabès is not writing *about* the Holocaust but is writing *in* the Holocaust, collapsing subject and medium.

STAMELMAN provides a rich introduction to the scope of Jabès's thought as it appeared in 17 books published between 1943 and 1985. From the very first page of the Jabèsian book, Stamelman encapsulates the poet's oeuvre as that of an exile who offers testimony to the loss of life, family, and homeland. Reading Jabès involves becoming aware of a scream; the poet's words resonate with the lamentations of exile, with the ashes of Auschwitz, with the voice of humanity separated from a withdrawn God, with the cry of unending questions. Language as the root of all existence allows Jabès to find all of reality within the Book. However, the errancy of words reveals the incompleteness of every book. Despite the reality of the forever deferred work, the Book of books, there resonates beneath all writing a messianic text of a withdrawn God awaiting revelation. Each (re)reading and (re)writing of a book reveals another book in the offing. Reduplication of signs fosters continuous revelation in the book. The tissue of signs that enshrouds Jabès's oeuvre (Jew, God, book, desert, stranger, threshold, vocable, question, etc.) while circling in a never-ending repetition always reveals another facet of the exilic condition. The ephemeral answer, however, is merely another question, in a chain of interminable self-interrogation. Questioning is a mode of being in the world. It underlies the Jewish quest for identity.

MOTTE constructs a matrix for reading the self-interrogation that Jabès demands of all readers as well as the author.

BOYARIN elaborates this Jabèsian quest for Jewish identity in constructing a new discipline called Jewish ethnography, deriving its structure from the poet. Boyarin's fourth chapter, "Jewish Ethnography and the Question of the Book," undergirds each of Boyarin's idiosyncratic case studies, which seek to demystify and invigorate the contemporary practice of anthropology by revealing the link between knowledge and power. This link reveals the dualism of approaches to integration in anthropological studies, being either spatial or temporal. Boyarin redresses this oversight with his threefold concern: to create a choice beyond either self-representation as a specialist in an unrecognized area of research or abandonment of any professional relationship to a particular group in order to focus on pure theory; to critically engage the ignored or patronized status of Jewish ideas in elite intellectual discourse; and the well-being of the Israeli Jewish and Palestinian Arab peoples. The consideration of a distinctive Jewish ethnography builds on this threefold concern by relating to integral aspects of both Jewish cultural dynamics and postmodern thought about writing. Boyarin draws upon Jabès as both a Jew and as an ethnographer and on Jabès's writing as exemplary of postmodern Jewish self-expression. Further, Jabès is seen to challenge the rabbinic substitution of ritual solidarity for material community. The proposed hermeneutical community collapses with the modern period and its revolution against an elite rabbinic community of textual desire. Neither the book nor the land alone can sustain both the moral exigency and the historical contingency that together constitute Jewishness. The proposed solution to this overt spatial or temporal priority is a negative ethnography, since time and space are being constantly reinvented.

WOLFSON's project of re-visioning kabbalistic hermeneutics is continually guided and undergirded by the subtextual poetry of Jabès. God's linguistic self-disclosure (both graphic and phonic), a predominant motif in the Jabèsian oeuvre, is traced by Wolfson throughout the work of the 18th-century Lithuanian talmudist and kabbalist R. Elijah ben Solomon Zalman, the Gaon of Vilna. Jabès proposes to imagine the fabric of the world and human existence as textual. Writing, from Jacques Lacan on, has its ontic ground in the phallus. Thus, language is more than the house of being—it is the very being itself. This linguistic unveiling, of and through the Hebrew Scriptures, is the time of being's becoming. In framing his analysis of the Gaon through Jabès, Wolfson reveals the essential connection between the book and time. Both textuality and temporality disclose the dialectic of hiddenness and manifestation. The revelation of the hidden thread through dissimulation is intrinsic both to the text and its divine counterpart. Sealing one's fate in the engraving of time that ensues from the veiled disclosure of the exposed concealment is the challenge of writing.

AUBREY L. GLAZER

Jeremiah, Book of

Carroll, Robert P., *From Chaos to Covenant: Uses of Prophecy in the Book of Jeremiah*, London: SCM, and New York: Crossroads, 1981

Carroll, Robert P., *Jeremiah: A Commentary*, London: SCM, and Philadelphia: Fortress, 1986

Carroll, Robert P., *Jeremiah* (Old Testament Guides), Sheffield: JSOT Press, 1989

Holladay, William L., *Jeremiah: A Commentary on the Book of the Prophet Jeremiah*, 2 vols., Philadelphia: Fortress, 1986, 1989

McKane, William, *A Critical and Exegetical Commentary on Jeremiah*, 2 vols., Edinburgh: Clark, 1986, 1996

Nicholson, Ernest W., *Preaching to the Exiles: A Study of the Prose Tradition in the Book of Jeremiah*, Oxford: Blackwell, and New York: Schocken, 1970

Overholt, Thomas W., *The Threat of Falsehood: A Study in the Theology of the Book of Jeremiah*, London: SCM, and Naperville, Illinois: Allenson, 1970

The Book of Jeremiah attracted increasing critical interest in the last two decades of the 20th century, particularly with respect to questions of authorship and formation. The lively debate that ensued has been marked by the publication of a number of significant commentaries and monographs.

CARROLL (1989) is probably the best general introduction to the critical problems associated with Jeremiah, and it claims to presuppose of the reader no prior knowledge other than having read the biblical text. It gives a fine overview of the contents, structure, and what is termed the "theopolitics" of the work. For Carroll, "argument and ignorance" are the defining characteristics of Jeremiah scholarship: little, he thinks, can be known of Jeremiah the man, nor which sections (if any) of the book that bears his name he wrote, nor even to what time the book should be dated. Carroll's approach in this work is therefore to review the various debates surrounding the book without reaching firm conclusions.

CARROLL's (1981) own approach finds much firmer expression in his monograph. The emphasis in this work is on the idea that the Book of Jeremiah is the result of a "Jeremiah Tradition" rather than the work of the prophet himself. However, Carroll does argue that much of the poetic material in chapters one through 25, if not written by the prophet himself, at least provides the starting point for the accretion of prose traditions by the editors of the book. Probably the most important of these editors would in fact have been the Deuteronomists—the group responsible for writing the so-called Deuteronomistic History. For Carroll, it is this school that should be credited for much of the present form of the book. This is a detailed and helpful work that provides information on the various genres and editorial intentions of the material and gives a wealth of detail on the historical background to many of the texts.

CARROLL's (1986) commentary on Jeremiah provides more detailed analysis of the text than his other two works and is therefore best approached last. It is, if anything, more outspoken than his previous monograph, attacking the "dogma of Jeremiah studies" that the prophet himself may have produced the poetic oracles in the book. Thus, these oracles are just as likely a product of the Jeremiah tradition as the prose sermons in the book, and the "historical" Jeremiah (if such a thing can be said to exist) is utterly obscured behind a tradition that has created the Jeremiah of the book that bears his name. This is an excellent commentary, with an extensive and useful introduction.

McKANE approaches the text in a way similar to Carroll. Yet, whereas Carroll is cautious about ascribing Jeremianic authorship to any text, McKane takes the position that the poetry in the first half of the book may be seen as the original Jeremianic nucleus of the work, to which other (non-Jeremianic) oracular material was added over the course of time. The book of Jeremiah is thus an example of what he terms a "rolling corpus," evoking the image of a snowball rolling down a hill, gathering extra layers of snow as it goes. This is not an easy work to read, emphasizing as it does questions of language and different traditions represented by the secondary translations (especially the Greek Septuagint). Nevertheless, it is an extremely important work, and students of Jeremiah should aspire to read it.

HOLLADAY takes a much more traditional approach to the Book of Jeremiah, adopting the position that it is possible to establish the data for reconstructing the chronology of Jeremiah's career with some degree of accuracy. This is done in the first volume of his commentary in a preliminary survey. The main significance of Holladay's position, expounded in more detail in the second volume, is that he disagrees with those commentators (e.g., Carroll, McKane) who see the prose sections of the book as representative of a strong Jeremiah tradition and in particular as having been shaped by the Deuteronomists. While some expansion to the text of Jeremiah occurred during and after the exile, the Deuteronomistic elements in Jeremiah's writing may be seen as the prophet's counterproclamations to a posited preexilic septennial recitation of Deuteronomy. Indeed, argues Holladay, much of the characteristically "Deuteronomistic" terminology of Jeremiah can in fact be shown to be distinctively Jeremianic. Examples of such language in other works are claimed to have been composed later than the Book of Jeremiah and hence influenced by the prophet. Thus, the distinctive voice of the prophet can be said to extend beyond the poetic oracles into the sermonic prose of the latter portion of the book.

NICHOLSON takes up a middle position between the extremes represented by commentators such as Carroll and Holladay. Nicholson's approach examines the Jeremianic prose tradition in turn from literary, theological, and historical perspectives, concluding that these portions of the book are the product of exilic writers' attempts "to draw out, expand, or otherwise develop for their own situation and time, the significance of his oracles and sayings." As such, even the prose elements may well be based on authentic sayings of the prophet. Although somewhat dated, this monograph remains a useful and sensible guide to the critical problems of the text.

OVERHOLT represents a holistic approach to the Book of Jeremiah that takes less account of questions of authorship or setting, concentrating instead on a particular theme in the book: that of falsehood. He argues that the Book of Jeremiah is concerned with three main types of falsehood: the false sense of security of the people threatened by Babylon; the falsehood of the prophetic opponents of Jeremiah, who encouraged the Judean people to resist the Babylonian might; and the falsehood of idolatry, which led ultimately to divine punishment and the destruction of Judah. Although the complex questions of authorship are not addressed, this monograph gives a good overall picture of the theology of the book that bears the prophet's name.

DOMINIC RUDMAN

Jerusalem

Armstrong, Karen, *Jerusalem: One City, Three Faiths*, New York: Knopf, and London: HarperCollins, 1996

Avigad, Nahman, *Ha-'Ir ha-'elyonah shel Yerushalayim*, 1980; translated as *Discovering Jerusalem*, Nashville, Tennessee: Nelson, 1983; Oxford: Blackwell, 1984

Bahat, Dan, *The Illustrated Atlas of Jerusalem*, New York: Simon and Schuster, 1990

Benvenisti, Meron, *City of Stone: The Hidden History of Jerusalem*, Berkeley: University of California Press, 1996

Geva, Hillel (editor), *Ancient Jerusalem Revealed*, Jerusalem: Israel Exploration Society, 1994

Gilbert, Martin, *Jerusalem: Rebirth of a City*, New York: Viking, and London: Chatto and Windus, 1985

Gilbert, Martin, *Jerusalem in the Twentieth Century*, New York: Wiley, and London: Chatto and Windus, 1996

Hammer, Reuven (editor), *The Jerusalem Anthology: A Literary Guide*, Philadelphia: Jewish Publication Society, 1995

Levine, Lee I. (editor), *Jerusalem: Its Sanctity and Centrality to Judaism, Christianity, and Islam*, New York: Continuum, 1999

Shanks, Hershel, *Jerusalem: An Archaeological Biography*, New York: Random House, 1995

Yadin, Yigael (editor), *Jerusalem Revealed: Archaeology in the Holy City, 1968–1974*, Jerusalem: Israel Exploration Society, 1975; New Haven, Connecticut: Yale University Press, 1976

Despite its location in a semi-arid and mountainous region, without natural resources or a port, Jerusalem has been one of the world's most celebrated and contested cities, a critical element in the sacred geography of Judaism, Christianity, and Islam. Jerusalem's rise began in the 11th century B.C.E. when David established it as his political capital. His son Solomon constructed the First Temple, consolidating Jerusalem's status as Judaism's spiritual center. For almost a millennium, Jews brought their sacrificial offerings to Jerusalem, until the destruction of the Second Temple in 70 C.E. For the next 1,900 years, successive groups, including Romans, Byzantines, Arabs, Crusaders, Ottomans, and the British, governed the city, each leaving an indelible mark on its identity. In 1948, the newly founded state of Israel and Jordan divided Jerusalem into two cities, the latter acquiring possession of the Old City and its holy sites. Nineteen years later, Israel unified the city under its sole authority. Jerusalem has been venerated as the city of God's presence, of messianic redemption, and of eschatological hope. A city intimately entwined with the sacred legends and heroes of three religious traditions, Jerusalem arouses deep feelings that have contributed to its prestige and beauty but have also figured in its contentious and sometimes bloody history.

BAHAT, a leading archaeologist of Jerusalem, begins with brief discussion of the topography of Jerusalem and the major archaeological excavations conducted since the 19th century. In the following chapters, he maps out the boundaries of the city and the locations of its major structures. In addition to the maps and the many valuable line drawings and plans of major buildings, Bahat provides a history, drawing on both the archaeological finds and the literary records of Jerusalem from its prehistory to the 1970s.

SHANKS presents some of the most significant archaeological discoveries that illuminate the history of Jerusalem from the time of David to the destruction of the Second Temple. Hundreds of photographs and drawings augment his lively descriptions of Hezekiah's tunnel, the Herodian Temple, and the Garden of Gethsemane, among other sites. He also includes a briefer treatment of the major monuments built during the Byzantine, Islamic, and Crusader periods.

AVIGAD, director of the archaeological excavations of the Upper City beginning in 1969, reports on the many important discoveries unearthed in a decade of work, which was often conducted in the midst of controversy. Among the highlights in this richly illustrated book are the discovery of the Israelite wall, which demonstrates that the ancient city covered part of the western hill; the excavation of the Burnt House, which provides vivid testimony to the devastation that consumed Jerusalem in 70 C.E.; and the identification of the once magnificent Nea Church built by Justinian in the sixth century C.E.

YADIN and GEVA are two volumes that together collect more than 70 articles originally published in the Hebrew-language archaeological journal *Kadmoniyot*. The volumes offer the most detailed reporting in English on the archaeological excavations conducted in Jerusalem between 1967 and 1992. Each book includes general articles on various areas of the city and more detailed studies on specific subjects such as buildings, tombs, and seals. As one might expect, both volumes are richly illustrated with photographs of the sites and artifacts, maps, and floor plans. Geva includes a list of all major archaeological activities in Jerusalem from 1967 to 1992 and a brief description of the most important discoveries associated with each dig.

HAMMER collects more than 200 passages culled from a diverse array of Jewish writings on Jerusalem, including folktales, songs, and prayers, and excerpts from prophets, rabbis, philosophers, mystics, travelers, historians, Zionists, politicians, poets, and novelists. The collection offers a rich section on modern writers, some pieces appearing in English for the first time. More than 100 maps, photographs, and paintings enhance the literary descriptions. The book emphasizes "the way in which the Jewish consciousness has perceived Jerusalem, has been created by it, and has in turn created a Jerusalem that includes streets and alleys but goes beyond that into feelings, values, beliefs, and prophetic hopes."

Gilbert presents vivid histories of Jerusalem during the 19th and 20th centuries. In GILBERT (1985), he traces the emergence of Jerusalem from a small, backward town into a thriving, if miniature, metropolis by the end of the 19th century, and he includes many of the earliest photographs of Jerusalem. Working from an array of contemporary documents, Gilbert not only tells the history of the city, but also conveys a sense of life in Victorian Jerusalem. GILBERT (1996), also drawing on numerous eyewitness accounts, examines the tremendous geographic expansion of the city, the growing division between Jews and Palestinians, and the volatile history of Jerusalem in the 20th century.

BENVENISTI, former deputy mayor of Jerusalem, offers a highly informed study of contemporary Jerusalem. His synchronic approach to the history of this conflict-riven city, particularly since 1967, engages several contested issues including the management of the holy sites; the political implications involved in drawing boundaries; the difficulties of establishing an effective and equitable municipal government; the unique linkage between urban planning and political goals; and the spatial, economic, and cultural distinctions that have left the city greatly divided and have contributed to hostility, fear, and prejudice among its inhabitants. Throughout the 20th century, Jews and Palestinians mined the chronicles of Jerusalem to construct myths that "aid them in their present-day quarrels." In order to deal with the conflict, he advocates an incremental, process-oriented approach that stresses remedies to immediate controversies rather than grandiose plans designed to meet a predetermined solution. Despite the tumultuous history of the city, Benvenisti looks forward to a time of peace and reconciliation among the various groups who call Jerusalem home.

ARMSTRONG chronicles the history of Jerusalem as a holy place, a city of mythical status, and a symbol of the divine for Jews, Christians, and Muslims. She describes how the city has undergone religious, political, linguistic, and cultural transformations, and she examines how each successive culture has used its sacred myths and architecture to justify its claim to the city and to shape Jerusalem's religious identity. She closes with a critique of those groups who have employed a "religion of hatred," controlling the city through violence and by displacing others.

LEVINE has collected 33 essays written by outstanding scholars that explore the central ideas, events, monuments, and institutions that define the sacred character of Jerusalem for Jews, Christians, and Muslims and that identify the place of Jerusalem in medieval Jewish and Christian traditions. The contributors examine how each religious community made its unique mark on the city and how each defined Jerusalem to suit its own religious, political, and social agendas.

GARY GILBERT

See also Temple and Temple Mount; Western Wall

Jesus and Judaism

Borowitz, Eugene B., *Contemporary Christologies: A Jewish Response,* New York: Paulist, 1980

Charlesworth, James H. (editor), *Jesus' Jewishness: Exploring the Place of Jesus within Early Judaism* (Shared Ground among Jews and Christians, vol. 2), Philadelphia: American Interfaith Institute, 1991

Crossan, John Dominic, *The Historical Jesus: The Life of a Mediterranean Jewish Peasant,* San Francisco: HarperSanFrancisco, and Edinburgh: Clark, 1991

Meier, John P., *A Marginal Jew: Rethinking the Historical Jesus* (Anchor Bible Reference Library), 2 vols., New York: Doubleday, 1991

Thoma, Clemens and Michael Wyschogrod (editors), *Parable and Story in Judaism and Christianity,* New York: Paulist, 1989

Vermès, Géza, *The Religion of Jesus the Jew,* Minneapolis, Minnesota: Fortress, and London: SCM, 1993

Young, Brad H., *Jesus and His Jewish Parables: Rediscovering the Roots of Jesus' Teaching,* New York: Paulist, 1989

Zannoni, Arthur E. (editor), *Jews and Christians Speak of Jesus,* Minneapolis, Minnesota: Fortress, 1994

A most remarkable transformation in scholarship has taken place in recent years regarding the Jewishness of Jesus. Only a few decades ago, following the lead of Rudolf Bultmann, the primary thrust was on Jesus' uniqueness and his universalism. But over the last several years a growing body of literature has stressed instead the deep positive connections between Jesus and the Judaism of his time. While this new scholarship has taken many different turns in likening Jesus to his Jewish contemporaries, there remains through all the volumes the common thread that it is impossible to understand Jesus and his renewal movement today without situating them squarely within the Judaism of the period. Most of the new scholarship has been undertaken by Christians, but some Jews also have looked anew at the significance of Jesus' teaching for Judaism.

BOROWITZ's analysis of contemporary Christologies is one of the best books to come from a Jewish perspective. With his customary critical openness Borowitz surveys the thought of important Christian theologians such as John Knox, Karl Barth, Wolfhart Pannenberg, Rosemary Ruether, Dorothee Soelle, Karl Rahner, Jurgen Moltmann, James Gustafson, and Reinhold Niebuhr. Borowitz's last two chapters ask whether Christology automatically leads to antisemitism, or, as Ruether has termed it, whether antisemitism is Christology's "left hand." Borowitz argues that it is not. In his reflective conclusion he expresses gratitude for the opportunity to interact with these theologians, and he invokes a Jewish blessing upon them. This volume remains a seminal work in the Christian-Jewish dialogue. While there is need for further reflection from the Jewish perspective, Borowitz has laid a solid foundation.

CHARLESWORTH has been one of the most prolific contributors to the rethinking of Jesus' Jewish context, both as an author and as an editor. In this volume he acts as both. In addition to writing two fine essays titled "The Foreground of

Christian Origins and the Commencement of Jesus Research" and "Jesus, Early Christian Literature, and Archaeology," Charlesworth has assembled a notable array of Jewish and Christian scholars such as John P. Meier, Géza Vermès, Daniel Harrington, David Flusser, Harvey Cox, Hans Kung, Ellis Rivkin, and Allan F. Segal. This is a superb introduction to the field.

CROSSAN's book, the central work of an ever-expanding corpus, has been much discussed, both in academic and popular circles. Because of the extensive publicity it has generated, it has probably been read by more nonscholars than any other volume on the subject. It is a scholarly work but is written in an idiom that effectively communicates with the nonspecialist. Crossan has been a preeminent member of the Jesus Seminar, a group of scholars that has aimed at identifying the authentic gospel sayings of Jesus. Crossan himself maintains that the so-called "gospel tradition" is not limited to the four canonical gospels alone but is found in other texts from the period as well. It is vital to bring all of these together to arrive at any coherent picture of Jesus. Crossan does this in this volume, although not to the satisfaction of some important New Testament scholars.

Crossan's picture of Jesus is that of a peasant Jewish Cynic whose appeal came from his actions more than his words. Jesus was part of the ideological orientation and pastoral missionary perspective of inclusive Judaism and cannot be properly understood apart from that context. Clearly this volume demands attention even if one ultimately disagrees with Crossan's methodology and some of his basic conclusions.

MEIER's volumes, while they have not achieved the same popular notoriety as Crossan's works, have received a somewhat more positive evaluation in scholarly circles. While Meier recognizes the need to turn to noncanonical sources for a full picture of Jesus and his activities, he believes far more than Crossan in the historicity of the gospel accounts themselves. In volume one, Meier discusses sources, methodology, and what he terms the "roots of the person" of Jesus. He ends with a chronology of Jesus' life. Volume two is more thematic, focusing on Jesus' stance toward the Mosaic law and other questions. For Meier, Jesus emerges as a "marginal Jew" who, while passionate in his Jewish beliefs and committed to Jewish religious practice, was nonetheless willing to criticize a corrupt clergy and thereby invoke the ire of the upper-level priests.

For those previously unacquainted with the literature, a reading of the Crossan and Meier volumes will provide a good cross-section of contemporary Jesus scholarship. Despite their serious methodological differences, Crossan and Meier both agree on the profound linkage between Jesus and the Judaism of his day.

For many years in biblical studies and still today in some circles, the parables of Jesus were seen as unique to his preaching and as a means whereby he drew a line in the sand between his vision and that of his Jewish colleagues. Recent scholarship has begun to change that perspective dramatically, insisting that the parable was a quite commonplace literary device in Jesus' time and that the parables of Jesus insofar as they critique Jewish practice, do so out of a Jewish perspective. In a collection dedicated to a rethinking of the parables,

THOMA and WYSCHOGROD have brought together a respectable group of Jewish and Christian scholars such as David Flusser, David Stern, Aaron A. Milavec, and Lawrence Boadt to complement their own contributions. This volume is a good place to begin a consideration of the parable as a uniting, rather than a divisive, force in Christian-Jewish relations.

VERMÈS is one of the most noteworthy Jewish scholars on the New Testament. While not all other scholars, either Jewish or Christian, would subscribe to some of his conclusions in *The Religion of Jesus the Jew* and other works, his research must be acknowledged in any serious discussion of the Jewish context of Jesus' teachings. Vermès is very positive in his assessment of Jesus' links to the reformist Judaism of his day. Following a rather general Jewish line of argument, he accuses Paul of shifting Jesus' emphasis on God the Father, an emphasis in which *teshuvah* (repentance) and *emunah* (faith) were key to a direct relationship with God, to a focus on the risen and glorified Lord without whose meditation it is impossible to reach God.

YOUNG, an evangelical Christian scholar, has done important research in lining up Jesus' parables with the Jewish tradition. In the manner of Thoma, he has gone against the prevailing scholarly grain in his approach. This work, rooted in an important way in the work of Young's Jewish mentor David Flusser, argues that the "kingdom of heaven" theme, a central focus of Jesus' teaching, is not an eschatological concept but rather a technical term Jesus used to designate God's reign as a present reality among those who have accepted the call to obey the divine will.

Finally, ZANNONI's edited volume includes prominent scholars such as Shaye Cohen, E.P. Sanders, Paula Fredericksen, John Donahue, Alan Segal, and Monika Hellwig addressing Christological issues in the context of the Jewish-Christian dialogue. This is an excellent introduction to the array of perspectives on one of the central issues in the contemporary dialogue, the theological significance of Jesus.

JOHN T. PAWLIKOWSKI

Jewish Christians

Daniélou, Jean, *The Theology of Jewish Christianity* (The Development of Christian Doctrine before the Council of Nicaea, vol. 1), translated and edited by John A. Baker, London: Darton, Longman and Todd, and Chicago: Regnery, 1964

Lüdemann, Gerd, *Ketzer*, 1995; translated by John Bowden as *Heretics: The Other Side of Early Christianity*, London: SCM, and Louisville, Kentucky: Westminster John Knox, 1996

Pines, Shlomo, *The Jewish Christians of the Early Centuries According to a New Source* (Proceedings of the Israel Academy of Sciences and Humanities, vol. 2, no. 13), Jerusalem: Academy of Sciences and Humanities, 1966

Pritz, Ray A., *Nazarene Jewish Christianity: From the End of the New Testament Period until Its Disappearance in the Fourth Century* (Studia Post-Biblica, vol. 37), Leiden: Brill, and Jerusalem: Magnes, 1988

Rowland, Christopher, *Christian Origins: An Account of the Setting and Character of the Most Important Messianic Sect of Judaism*, London: SPCK, 1985

Taylor, Joan E., *Christians and the Holy Places: The Myth of Jewish-Christian Origins*, Oxford: Clarendon, and New York: Oxford University Press, 1993

Wilson, Stephen G., *Related Strangers: Jews and Christians, 70–170 C.E.*, Minneapolis, Minnesota: Fortress, 1995

Jewish Christians can be defined as that group of ethnic Jews who were the first to believe that Jesus was the messiah. They considered themselves Jews and followed the Mosaic law as they had always done. They are classically associated with Peter and John of the Jerusalem Church. There is some evidence that this form of Christianity/Judaism continued into the fourth century C.E. This group is not to be confused with later Christians of non-Jewish descent who were attracted to Judaism and its practices or teachings—the so-called Judaizers. There are certainly attestations of Jewish Christian groups, but what they believed, where they lived, or how they behaved is extremely difficult to discern in great detail.

WILSON is a large work that covers more than Jewish Christians. Two chapters, however, are particularly helpful in exploring some of the historical factors that had a bearing on Jewish Christianity. Wilson believes that there was a strong and fairly well-defined form of Christianity that appears, from a modern perspective, to blur the lines between Judaism and Christianity. His research tracks the movement of these Jewish Christians and the possible reasons for their marginalization in Christianity. He grants a certain degree of validity to the supposed exodus of Christians (of Jewish origin) from Jerusalem to the city of Pella, part of the Roman Decapolis. This occurred shortly before the Jewish War of 66–70 C.E. This is a highly disputed historical account, but Wilson takes a mediating line, reading the account in the light of other associated historical phenomena. The fact that the Jerusalem bishops appear to be non-Jewish after this time points away from an influential Jewish presence in the Jerusalem church after 70 C.E. The shift from Sabbath to Sunday is also explored. These topics are covered in the chapter on Christian worship.

LÜDEMANN's book is organized principally around Paul and the varied reactions to his work. The book is thick with footnotes and scholarly accoutrements. At times, the prose is unabashedly partisan, and there are also points at which he is overly general. This does not, however, detract from the interesting scenario he lays out or from his engaging style. By his reckoning, the apostle Paul was the first Christian heretic. It was the Jewish Christians of Jerusalem who first rejected Paul because of his teachings and expelled him from their ranks. Paul's life and ministry are interpreted as basically fruitless and troubled. Those who came after Paul used his teaching in different ways. The battle was waged over who owned Paul, and the once-orthodox Jerusalem Church (i.e., Jewish Christians) became the heretics. This theory is speculative and fragile, but it is also a helpful counter to some overly homogenized accounts of early Christianity.

The subtitle of ROWLAND's book sets the stage for his approach to the emergence of Christianity. This book is helpful because it spends a luxuriant amount of time discussing the nature of Judaism before the emergence of Christianity. Rowland's survey covers a wide range of topics, from attitudes toward the temple to ideas surrounding angelic mediators. What links Rowland's thinking is the genre of Apocalyptic. This fiery vision of Christianity counters the popular notion that Christianity sprang fully formed from the womb of proto-rabbinic Judaism. Rowland forwards the notion that Christianity arose as an apocalyptic Jewish sect that expected the imminent return of Jesus, the proclaimed Messiah. Rowland also attempts to track the shift from a loosely formed group defined by freedom and expectation to the less expectant but better organized group of believers who became known as the Christians. Thus, this book sheds very helpful light on Jewish Christianity.

PINES provides an extended and erudite article on what he feels is an authentic piece of evidence for the existence of Jewish Christianity up until the fifth century. Besides the many references to various Christian groups in Christian writings, there are virtually no sources that can be attributed to these groups, save the Pseudo-Clementine tradition. Pines attempts to show that beneath a tenth-century Arabic polemic against Christianity lie ancient fragments of a Jewish Christian document. The attempt is limited by Pines's understanding of early Christianity and the generalizations he sometimes employs. Even if his thesis is overly enthusiastic, it remains an interesting example of a literary excavation that does shed some light on the beliefs and attitudes of ethnically Jewish groups who were messianic in their thinking and completely Jewish in their practice.

PRITZ attempts to fill a gap in the scholarship on Jewish Christianity by focusing on the Jewish Christian group referred to as the Nazarenes. Many times various Jewish Christian groups are thrown into one group, but a closer examination reveals that such a conflation is the product of Christian apologetic and scholarly habit, rather than actual similarity. Pritz admits that tracing such a group is a difficult process. His work catalogs ancient sources that refer to the Nazarenes. Pritz concludes that this is the name of the most primitive group of Christians. The name existed even before Christians were called such. He reckons that this is the group that fled Jerusalem around the time of the Jewish War (70 C.E.). Caught between the Jews and the Christians, they were forced out of both communities.

TAYLOR's book is a systematic refutation of the theory that Christian holy sites were established by early Jewish Christians based on their first-hand knowledge of the places where Jesus prayed, was crucified, and was buried. The author challenges this idea by questioning the presumption of a strong and constant Jewish Christian presence in Jerusalem up until the Jewish revolt of 135 C.E. The book illustrates that there is a great deal of disparity between the literary sources for Jewish Christianity (almost entirely Patristic) and the archaeological material. She asserts that much archaeological material has been falsely dated (making it appear much older) and much of the symbolism has been misread in order to make it fit into a scholarly construct called Jewish Christianity. She concludes that it is the influence of Constantine in the fourth century C.E. and his attempt to establish Christianity as the preferred religion that is responsible for the Christian veneration of holy places, not Jewish Christians.

The foundational work of DANIÉLOU has advanced this field to a great degree. His book is a compendium of all possible sources, organized around theological themes. Daniélou's work constructs a theology from very disparate elements. It is pure theology in that he does not consider the historical question of whether there was any one group who ever believed in these ideas. This book should be read with the full knowledge that what Daniélou describes are aspects of early Christianity that have Jewish components. It does not describe the theology of a single group called Jewish Christians, neither does it establish the existence of Jewish Christians. If read with this understanding, however, the work is a rich tapestry of detail and an interesting analysis of fine theological points. His analysis is linguistic and exacting at times, but it is organized topically so the reader can choose particular subjects with ease. This is a book for the reader who is serious about delving into the theological aspects of Jewish Christian beliefs.

TIMOTHY J. HORNER

See also Apostasy

Jewish Quarter

Dagan, Avigdor and Gertrude Hirschler, *The Jews of Czechoslovakia: Historical Studies and Surveys,* 3 vols., Philadelphia: Jewish Publication Society, 1968–1983

Dubnow, S.M., *History of the Jews in Russia and Poland from the Earliest Times until the Present Day,* 3 vols., translated by I. Friedlaender, Philadelphia: Jewish Publication Society, 1916

Green, Nancy L., *The Pletzl of Paris: Jewish Immigrant Workers in the Belle Epoque,* New York: Holmes and Meier, 1986

Iggers, Wilma Abeles, *The Jews of Bohemia and Moravia: A Historical Reader,* Detroit, Michigan: Wayne State University Press, 1992

Israel, Jonathan I., *European Jewry in the Age of Mercantilism, 1550–1750,* New York: Oxford University Press, and Oxford: Clarendon, 1985; 3rd edition, London and Portland, Oregon: Littman Library of Jewish Civilization, 1998

Michman, Jozeph, *The History of Dutch Jewry during the Emancipation Period, 1787–1815: Gothic Turrets on a Corinthian Building,* Amsterdam: Amsterdam University Press, 1995

Patai, Raphael, *Tents of Jacob: The Diaspora, Yesterday and Today,* Englewood Cliffs, New Jersey: Prentice-Hall, 1971

Patai, Raphael, *The Vanished Worlds of Jewry,* New York: Macmillan, 1980; London: Weidenfeld and Nicolson, 1981

Sadek, Vladimír, Jiřina Šedinová, and Jiří Macht, *Prague Ghetto,* Prague: Olympia, 1991

The term "Jewish quarter" usually refers to the area of a large city, such as Prague, Budapest, or Warsaw, where Jews have made their homes and created their businesses. Some Jewish quarters were quite elegant, such as those of Vienna or Budapest, and many others were slums until sanitation brigades cleaned out dangerous buildings and abandoned homes, as was the case of the old Prague Jewish quarter in the latter half of the 19th century. Some Jewish quarters were voluntary communities, and others were the result of forced segregation, such as the ghettos of early modern Italy or the mellahs of Morocco, where Jews continued to be locked up at night in the 20th century. In countries where policies of ghettoization applied, Jewish quarters were a feature not just of major cities but of the remotest small towns as well. Voluntary or not, the Jewish quarters represented to some degree a haven for diaspora Jewry.

Many Jewish quarters repeatedly suffered destruction and rebuilding during the course of the centuries. The best-preserved Jewish quarter in Europe today is that of Prague. Most were all but eradicated by the Nazis during World War II; since the fall of the Berlin Wall, however, a number of these quarters are experiencing restoration as a function of new interest in the former Jewish presence.

DAGAN and HIRSCHLER's compilation, a comprehensive history of the Jews of the Czech Republic and Slovakia, does not treat the Jewish quarter as an explicit theme in much depth. However, Hans Kohn's chapter in volume one, titled "Before 1918 in the Historic Lands," relates the history of the Prague Jewish quarter, or Josefov. In Ruth Kestenberg-Gladstein's article, "The Jews Between Czechs and Germans in the Historic Lands, 1848–1918" (also in volume one), there is significant discussion not only of the cultural contributions made by Jews once they were free to leave the Prague ghetto, but also of the prejudices and other obstacles they encountered as "strangers" in the Czech lands. Volume two contains Hugo Stransky's chapter, "The Religious Life in Slovakia and Subcarpathian Ruthenia," which provides valuable descriptions of the Jewish quarter of Bratislava, the center of religious authority in the area, as well as that of Kosice in Eastern Slovakia and of Mukacevo in Subcarpathian Ruthenia.

DUBNOW's work consists of two volumes of text plus a third volume of indexes, which are very helpful in locating information on various aspects of life in the Polish Jewish quarters. Chapter two of the first volume, "The Jewish Colonies in Poland and Lithuania," relates the historical background of the arrival of Jews in Poland and the steady flow of Jews into the Polish lands from Bohemia and Germany due to persecution. The rise of Casimir the Great, "the peasant king" who believed the Jews had a special role in developing Poland economically, and the history leading to the development of Cracow's Kazimierz Jewish quarter are amply discussed.

GREEN's book provides a contrast to studies of the Jewish quarters of Central and Eastern Europe, bringing to light the history of the old Jewish quarter of Paris, the Marais, known also since the Middle Ages by the Yiddish appellation, Pletzl. Green seeks to define the social and economic impact of the arrival in the late 19th century of Eastern European Jews, where there was already an established community of French Jews. She traces the history of the labor movement within the community, describing such features as the tension between immigrant Jewish workers in the garment industry and their employers, also immigrants. The book details the

inner workings of the Jewish quarter, with much material on political activity and religious life. Maps of the Pletzl are provided as well as charts of the social and political composition of the quarter.

IGGERS's anthology of newspaper articles, letters, and selections from memoirs details lesser-known aspects of Czech Jewish life, particularly in the Jewish quarter of Prague, from personal points of view. There is important material here on the legends of Rabbi Loew, the history of the cemetery, the dissolution of the ghetto in 1852, and the partial demolition of the old Josefov district. Most significant, however, are the personal feelings about the Jewish quarter revealed in this collection.

ISRAEL's work focuses on the participation of Jews in European economic life together with their gravitation to cities and areas of cities where many Jews already resided. The "program of ghettoization" is also discussed admirably, using the examples of Rome, Venice, and Mantua. There is a fascinating bibliography with an enormous range of references that run the gamut of European languages.

MICHMAN's research is particularly interesting for its insights into the complex fragmentation of the Dutch Jewish quarter concerned. He describes the Dutch government's dealings with the two Jewish communities in Amsterdam, Sephardi and Ashkenazi (or rather, Portuguese and High German), and the Jewish political activities within the two distinct camps. Also discussed are the newspapers of the communities, the languages, and the adoption of Sephardi customs within a new community of more liberal Ashkenazi Jews in direct opposition to the traditionalist old community. In particular, Michman discusses the controversies that raged between these communities, most importantly the matter of "the feasibility and justifiability of a continued observance of religious precepts," which caused a deep rift during the "French Era" of Napoleonic occupation of the Netherlands.

PATAI (1971) and PATAI (1980) devote much space to tracing the historical development of the Jewish quarter and capture the old world in photographs of the inhabitants as well as buildings that frequently no longer exist or remain today only as abandoned shells. The author focuses on Eastern and Southern Europe, North Africa, and Southwest Asia. He provides a wide perspective on the Jews in these areas and the communities that they formed; Sephardim and Ashkenazim are both well represented.

SADEK, ŠEDINOVÁ, and MACHT have compiled an interesting volume that is first and foremost a photographic survey of the Josefov section of Prague, the former Jewish quarter. The book provides an in-depth report on the architecture and decoration of many of the synagogues, among them structures dating from the Gothic, Renaissance, and Baroque periods. The work also includes a substantial history of the Prague ghetto in an appendix.

CYNTHIA A. KLÍMA

See also Venice

Jewish Studies

Adelman, Howard, "Is Jewish Studies Ethnic?," in *Ethnicity, Women, and the Liberal Arts Curriculum,* edited by Johnnella E. Butler and John C. Walter, Albany: State University of New York Press, 1991

Cohen, Shaye J.D. and Edward L. Greenstein (editors), *The State of Jewish Studies,* Detroit, Michigan: Wayne State University Press, 1990

Myers, David N., *Re-Inventing the Jewish Past: European Jewish Intellectuals and the Zionist Return to History,* New York: Oxford University Press, 1995

Schorsch, Ismar, *From Text to Context: The Turn to History in Modern Judaism,* Hanover, New Hampshire: Brandeis University Press, 1994

The history of Jewish studies has not yet been written. Scholars engaged in this field, however, are beginning to subject it to searching analysis. Pertinent articles have appeared that offer two extreme positions on the recent development of Jewish studies. One stresses the increased interest in Jewish studies as a result of heightened Jewish self-awareness beginning in the late 1960s because of the Six-Day War, growing interest in the Holocaust, and the influence of African American and ethnic consciousness that resulted in the establishment of new academic programs and a diversification of the curriculum. The other, usually a reaction to the first view, argues that the study of Hebraica and Judaica has held an ancient and honorable place in the traditional university curriculum. The truth, of course, lies somewhere in the middle. Jewish studies, by which is meant the critical study of the history, literature, and thought of the Jewish people since the biblical period, has an ancient pedigree that is far from unbroken or unblemished. On the other hand, the field continues a scholarly tradition that stretches back to periods earlier than the consciousness-raising events of the late 1960s, particularly to 19th-century Germany, turn-of-the-century America, and mid-20th-century Palestine.

ADELMAN, tracing most of the literature on the history of the field, shows that while Jewish studies has had a long history, it has had an erratic pattern of growth and, even after its establishment, course offerings in Jewish studies have been and still are regarded as dispensable. He notes that the appearance of Jewish studies seems to correlate more with the personal needs of the practitioners—Christian or Jewish students, teachers, and alumni—than with what schools have considered to be their essential curricular needs. Although making substantial academic contributions, medieval European and colonial American Christian pioneers in Hebraica, Judaica, and rabbinica pursued their work for the furtherance of Christianity, often at the expense of Judaism. Adelman maintains that the early pioneers of *Wissenschaft des Judentums,* "the science of Judaism," had a mixed agenda with two incompatible goals: Jewish survival and ethnic pride and objective nonpartisan scholarship. The failure of Jewish studies to find acceptance at universities until the late 20th century can be viewed as being as indicative of the nature of the field as it is of the universities. Having developed in other contexts, most notably rabbinical seminaries and Jewish communal institutions, Jewish studies has acquired contours that still make it difficult for it to fit into the secular collegiate curriculum, according to Adelman. The burden of adjustment, however, does not fall exclusively on Jewish studies. He proposes that one of the essential aspects of Jewish studies is a challenge to the nature and structure of Western higher education. One of the tensions present when Jewish studies is introduced as a field is whether it or the traditional curriculum is in fact ethnic. Ironically, writers on Jewish studies typically want to distance their field from the "ethnic" label, which often evokes partisan associations, while at the same time they list all the benefits that the Jewish community derives from the academic study of Judaism. Adelman points out that they argue that Jewish studies should be objective and should not be a partisan enterprise, and they overlook the fact that the academic process has always been committed to fostering particular values whether they are nationalistic, religious, gendered, or racial. Adelman maintains that the ultimate defense against ideological forays into the classroom is the academic process itself, which is based on rigorous disciplinary and methodological questioning of all data, assumptions, and conclusions. If such tests are not applied, the fault does not lie with a particular field but with the academic process itself. According to Adelman, the task before Jewish studies, therefore, is not the repression of identity, community, or social concerns, but the creation of a methodology that will help these matters find expression among many disciplines and departments on campus. Indeed, he argues, the articulation of Jewish considerations in the curriculum provides an opportunity not only for those involved in academics but also for those committed to the ethnic community. The critical academic study of the Jewish people is the only opportunity to challenge tendentious, polemical, and self-serving interpretations of the Jewish experience. Thus, writes Adelman, Jewish studies offers a valuable way to invigorate a sense of cultural creativity and to develop critical thinking in the Jewish community.

COHEN and GREENSTEIN's collection contains articles on the state of various fields within Jewish studies, written by leading scholars and including insightful responses by their colleagues. In Greenstein's overview of recent biblical scholarship, one argument may serve as a significant point of departure, embracing many views toward the study of the Bible. Although the camel has been seen as the biblical animal par excellence, scholars have questioned when the camel was actually domesticated and whether references to it in Genesis were anachronistic. Greenstein presents views dating the appearance of the camel from as early as 1200 B.C.E. to as late as 600 B.C.E. In his response, Jon D. Levenson offers, among many interesting comments, the remarks of a 14th-century supercommentary to Abraham ibn Ezra's Pentateuch commentary in which ibn Ezra suggested that anachronisms in the Torah may undermine the idea that Moses wrote it: "What should I care," the supercommentator asks, "whether it was Moses or another prophet who wrote it, since the words of all of them are true and inspired?" Such a comment both refutes and accepts the basic critical premise of ibn Ezra. In his essay "The Modern Study of Ancient Judaism," Cohen formulates a profound response to many of the questions that haunt Jewish studies: "History, like most of the humanities, is an art, not science. Its results are conditional, not inevitable; conjectural, not empirical. Historical truths are not 'discovered' so much as 'created' by the interpreter." Cohen adds another analytical gem with his introduction of the distinction between scholarly "unifiers" and "separators." These approaches represent the attempts by scholars either to find a consistent unity in the work of an author or to see inconsistencies, contradictions, and developments in the work of a particular writer or a text. Cohen applies this model to the study of texts by Philo and Josephus as well as the Dead Sea Scrolls, and by extension it may be applied to all of Jewish studies. Finally, Cohen raises the issue, often implied but rarely confronted, of internal versus external influences on Jewish development. In his response, Richard S. Sarason pursues this issue by trying to establish criteria for determining influence beyond superficial parallelisms. Ivan Marcus's "Medieval Jewish Studies: Towards an Anthropological History of the Jews" raises many important interpretive matters concerning the intersection of social history, literary criticism, religious studies, and anthropology. Marcus offers two phrases worthy of repetition that mark attempts to find nuances and ambiguity: "surface bumpiness," rather than the "smoothness of the text," and "the weirdness of a cultural phenomenon," which he uses to characterize his readings of medieval Jewish texts, aided in the former case by the medieval commentaries of Rashi and in the latter by Clifford Geertz and Victor Turner.

MYERS picks up the development of Jewish studies in 19th-century Europe and follows it into Palestine. He traces the transformation of *Wissenschaft* in German to Jewish studies in Hebrew and the change in agenda behind such a transformation, most notably from justifying Jews and Judaism to German culture and society to the invention of a national identity in Palestine and the construction of a new historical memory. At the center of this book is the story of the development of the Institute for Jewish Studies at the Hebrew University, which opened in 1924. Two of the key features of Myers's argument are that such a transformation, from *Wissenschaft des Judentums* to *Hokhmat Yisrael*, was never complete and that a so-called Jerusalem school of Jewish studies never created a monolithic point of view. One of the ultimate paradoxes of the development of Jewish studies in such a national environment was the expressed hope of many of the practitioners to free Jewish studies and Jewish identity from external influences, forces that were not only the hallmark of Jewish development in the diaspora but in Palestine as well. Instead, what was stressed was internal essence, inner continuity, and organic development, embodied in common memory, Hebrew, habits, and rituals. Biblical criticism, therefore, proved particularly troublesome throughout the early history of the university, and Jewish history and general history were taught in separate departments. Others, however, often tried to incorporate the influence of external forces and stressed, particularly in fields such as medieval Spanish Hebrew poetry, Jewish philosophy, and Haskalah literature, the high level of influence of the non-Jewish environment. Myers reports that the Yivo Institute was created in Vilnius by anti-Zionists in response to the opening of the Hebrew University and the opposition to the study of Yiddish there. Paradoxically, it was the German Jews of Palestine who supported the study of Yiddish as part of their sympathies with cultural pluralism in Palestine, while the native

Yiddish speakers with their newfound loyalty to Hebrew formed the opposition to Yiddish studies. In Jerusalem as well as in Germany, Jewish studies were, therefore, caught between personal, national, and communal concerns and the requirements of objective scholarship.

SCHORSCH notes that from 1812 to 1822, Prussian authorities declared Jews eligible to hold academic posts, and Jewish intellectuals in Europe turned to the *Wissenschaft des Judentums*, calling for critical study of Jewish history, the Bible, rabbinics, literature, theology, law, and even contemporary statistics. This was a movement that attracted young Jewish intellectuals, primarily students at the new University of Berlin, whose feelings toward their own people had been awakened by contemporary criticism, popular anti-Jewish movements, and the indifference, estrangement, or apostasy of many young Jews. They hoped that such a purely scholarly, objective study of the Jewish past would awaken in Jews a sense of pride; produce educational, communal, and religious reform; help foster Jewish survival; and cause non-Jews to develop a more favorable opinion of Jews. These goals extended beyond disengaged scholarship and reflected the sometimes ambiguous direction of the movement, which included preference for Sephardi over Ashkenazi culture, Reform over rabbinic Judaism, and the rational over the mystical. Schorsch traces the development of the thought and activities of several of the pioneers of *Wissenschaft* (some of whom would later convert, finding it impossible to pursue a career at German universities). Leopold Zunz, who resolutely remained in the field but never in a university position, had become frustrated with the anti-Jewish views of his professor, Christian Friedrich Ruehs, which may have inspired his own Jewish writings in reaction. Moritz Steinschneider, who devoted his long life to prodigious Jewish scholarship but also never held a real academic position, offered the following sobering observation: "One cannot teach Jew-haters, least of all through history." Heinrich Heine, although he converted, is discussed in the context of his early association with *Wissenschaft* and his hostility to some of its approaches, which led him to write the "Rabbi of Bacharach." He noted later in life that kugel (noodle pudding) had done more to preserve Judaism than all the issues of the *Zeitschrift für die Wissenschaft des Judentums*.

HOWARD TZVI ADELMAN

See also Wissenschaft des Judentums

Job, Book of

Gordis, Robert, *The Book of God and Man: A Study of Job*, Chicago: University of Chicago Press, 1965

Habel, Norman C., *The Book of Job: A Commentary* (Old Testament Library series), Philadelphia: Westminster Press, 1985

Leaman, Oliver, *Evil and Suffering in Jewish Philosophy* (Cambridge Studies in Religious Traditions, no. 6), Cambridge and New York: Cambridge University Press, 1995

Murphy, Roland E., *Wisdom Literature: Job, Proverbs, Ruth, Canticles, Ecclesiastes, and Esther* (The Forms of the Old Testament Literature, vol. 13), Grand Rapids, Michigan: Eerdmans, 1981

Pope, Marvin H., *Job: A New Translation with Introduction and Commentary* (Anchor Bible, vol. 15), Garden City, New York: Doubleday, 1965

Westermann, Claus, *The Structure of the Book of Job: A Form-Critical Analysis*, Philadelphia: Fortress, 1981

One of the most complicated books of the Bible and full of highly enigmatic poetry, the Book of Job explores human suffering as well as God's justice, foreknowledge, and power. As a result of a contention between God and Satan over Job's fidelity, Job is beset with loss of wealth, family, and health. His friends counsel him to repent of the sins that must have caused his suffering, while Job maintains his innocence and calls on God to explain his hardships. A young man, Elihu, also challenges Job when Job's friends run out of words. Finally, God addresses Job in two dramatic scenes but never attempts to justify his actions. Instead, God calls on Job to contemplate his finite humanity as compared to divine omnipotence and wisdom. In the end, Job is pronounced righteous by God and his health and prosperity are restored.

Job has been an intensely studied book. Scholars have challenged its unity, some defending it as a composition by one author, others seeing it as a compilation of several sources. Nor is there agreement on the book's main message or even genre.

MURPHY explores the various units that make up the book. After analyzing the structure of the book as a whole (which he divides into 31 sections) as well as exploring issues of genre and setting, he concludes that the overall intention of the book is to show the inadequacy of the theory that God always punishes evil people and always rewards those who do good. Instead, the book defends God's mysterious freedom to act as he wants in the world. Murphy then offers a structural analysis of each section of Job with short discussions of the genre, setting, and intent of these sections.

WESTERMANN argues that the Book of Job is organized around Job's lament, "Why must I suffer?" He contends that the narrative portions of Job that introduce the book and conclude it are integral to the message of the work as a whole and are part of the skillful crafting of the author. After making this assertion, Westermann analyzes individual sections of Job as different genres (disputation, praise, lament, etc.) and shows how they fit into the author's construction of the book.

POPE offers a translation of Job and a detailed commentary. He views the book as a compilation of compositions by various authors with a central core revolving around the dispute between Job and his friends. Despite this patchwork of sources, the book exhibits a high degree of unity of thought. The book itself fits into no category neatly but combines features of several genres. Pope argues that the most likely date for the composition of the core of the book is the seventh century B.C.E. Overall, Job presents several conflicting views of the problem of divine justice in conflict with purposeless human suffering. At times it argues for a view of suffering as always owing to God's just punishment of evildoers. At other times it argues that Job is an exemplar of trust in God, even as Job's suffering cannot be explained. Other passages suggest

that the problem of human suffering is beyond human understanding. Still other passages suggest that human suffering can also be a warning to righteous people about potential and latent sins.

HABEL defends the coherence of the Book of Job in his commentary by arguing that the book is organized as an extended metaphor. The comparison is to a lawsuit. Job first contemplates filing a lawsuit, then challenges his accuser, seeks an arbiter, and submits testimony. Then Job takes an oath and presents his challenge, receives a verdict, is challenged by God, retracts his litigation, and is vindicated. This lawsuit plays itself out in three movements: God afflicts the hero, the hero challenges God, and God challenges the hero. However, Habel admits that the lawsuit metaphor does not answer the question of God's justice, which is the focus of much of the book. Instead, through the lawsuit Job comes to transcend the moral order by his innocent suffering. Habel declines to settle on a date for the composition of the book, presenting arguments for dates anywhere between the tenth and fourth centuries B.C.E. However, he favors a date in the fifth or fourth centuries.

GORDIS views Job as the foremost achievement of Hebrew wisdom. He asserts that the author understood human suffering as a moral discipline. Neither God nor his world can be judged fairly from the perspective of human suffering and need, as Job attempted to do. The author of Job offers no justification that will make sense to human logic; the author was too religious to believe that any neatly articulated system of human thought could explain creation's beauty or the tragedy of human existence. Gordis argues that the book possesses an organic unity and denies the claims of scholars who would view the book as a compilation by various authors. However, he does admit that some passages in the Hebrew text may have suffered from corruption during the centuries of its transmission. Gordis includes a second section in his book, offering his own creative and insightful translation of Job.

LEAMAN treats the problem of suffering and its relation to evil in the world not only in the Book of Job but also in Jewish thought through the centuries. He examines the problem of suffering in Job as handled by Philo, Saadia ben Joseph Gaon, Maimonides, Gersonides, Baruch de Spinoza, Moses Mendelssohn, Hermann Cohen, Martin Buber, and several modern writers on the Holocaust. In all these he explores the question of how God could allow evil in the world and concludes that questions about evil and suffering are not only important in their own right but also serve to direct people to try to understand their relationship with God.

ANDREW E. STEINMANN

Johanan ben Zakkai first century C.E.

Pioneer of rabbinic Judaism in Roman Palestine

Alon, Gedalia, *Jews, Judaism, and the Classical World: Studies in Jewish History in the Times of the Second Temple and Talmud*, translated by Israel Abrahams, Jerusalem: Magnes Press of Hebrew University, 1977

Alon, Gedalia, *Toldot ha-Yehudim be-Erets-Yisrael bi-tekufat ha-Mishnah veha-Talmud*, 1952; translated by Gershon Levi as *The Jews in Their Land in the Talmudic Age: 70–640 C.E.*, Jerusalem: Magnes Press of Hebrew University, 1980; Cambridge, Massachusetts: Harvard University Press, 1984

Cohen, Shaye J.D., "The Significance of Yavneh: Pharisees, Rabbis, and the End of Jewish Sectarianism," *Hebrew Union College Annual*, 55, 1984

Dubnow, Simon, *History of the Jews*, vol. 2: *From the Roman Empire to the Early Medieval Period*, South Brunswick, New Jersey: Yoseloff, 1967

Graetz, Heinrich, *History of the Jews*, vol. 2, London: Nutt, 1891–1892; Philadelphia: Jewish Publication Society, 1891–1898

Neusner, Jacob, *A Life of Rabban Yohanan Ben Zakkai, ca. 1–80 C.E.* (Studia Post-Biblica, vol. 6), Leiden: Brill, 1962

Neusner, Jacob, *Development of a Legend: Studies on the Traditions Concerning Yohanan ben Zakkai* (Studia Post-Biblica, vol. 16), Leiden: Brill, 1970

Neusner, Jacob, *First Century Judaism in Crisis: Yohanan ben Zakkai and the Renaissance of Torah*, Nashville, Tennessee: Abingdon, 1975

The destruction of the Second Temple, the center of Jewish political and religious life, in 70 C.E. was a watershed event that necessitated a restructuring of Judaism and of Jewish leadership. According to traditional accounts, Johanan ben Zakkai stands out during this period as a leader with foresight and initiative who guided the Jewish people and Judaism through a potentially catastrophic crisis. Classical scholarship tends to rely on these traditional sources and views Johanan as a national and religious hero. Newer scholarship, however, is more critical of rabbinic sources and challenges many of their basic assumptions. Because Johanan is seen as instrumental in the creation of diaspora Judaism and the foundation of "normative" rabbinic Judaism, his activities remain more or less pertinent to the study of all subsequent phases in the development of Judaism.

GRAETZ's portrayal of Johanan and the institution he established at Yavneh reflects Graetz's overall historiographic program. Although a product of the Wissenschaft school, he used its methodology conservatively in reaction to the radical scholarship associated with religious reformers such as Abraham Geiger. Graetz's primary focus is on the continuity of Judaism as a religion, so that what matters to him here is Johanan's role in establishing Yavneh as a new spiritual center and in creatively maintaining religious traditions despite new political circumstances. Graetz dwells on the hermeneutical approach of Johanan and his unique ability to connect oral tradition and contemporary conditions to the written law.

DUBNOW's perspective similarly reflects his programmatic ideology. For Dubnow, Jewish continuity was based primarily on national identity rather than religion, and this identity could be preserved perfectly well in the diaspora. Accordingly, Dubnow praises Johanan for the establishment in Yavneh of a new social and political center and for creating "the foundation of future Jewish autonomy."

Alon's scholarship is distinguished by his critical use of both traditional Jewish texts and classical literature. His research on Johanan offers new conclusions based on a questioning of accepted theories and a reconsideration of fundamental assumptions. Based on the broader political situation and evidence offered by Josephus, ALON (1977) claims that Yavneh was a Roman internment city to which Johanan was exiled. In light of the fact that the Roman goal was to destroy Jewish autonomy, Alon dismisses the possibility that Johanan was able to convince the Romans to hand over Yavneh for the establishment of a new Jewish center: "the only concession [Johanan] could obtain from the Romans was to save some lives—his own life and the lives of his disciples and friends and relatives." The English version of Alon's work also provides a complete translation of the rabbinic sources that reveal divergent traditions regarding Johanan's departure from Jerusalem and his meeting with Vespasian.

As in his earlier book, ALON (1980) is particularly interested in Johanan's leadership role before and during the war with the Romans and his status in the period that followed. Alon identifies Johanan as a leader of the Pharisees who was a realist regarding relations with Rome and resisted the rebellious tactics of the Zealots. Alon argues that following the war Johanan was not accepted universally as the leader of the community, and it is not at all clear that he filled the role of patriarch. In fact, Johanan faced a great deal of opposition from the masses and from the other leaders. Yavneh, Alon contends, only became the locus of a strong central authority when Rabban Gamliel, a descendant of Hillel, was appointed as head of the court there.

Neusner's work on Johanan is particularly interesting because his methodology and conclusions have changed through the course of his long career. NEUSNER (1962), his first book, and its popular version, NEUSNER (1975), rely heavily on rabbinical sources—midrash, Mishnah, and Talmud—and he treats the information he finds there uncritically. He assumes that all these texts contain reliable and historically accurate information about the life and actions of Johanan. Through these sources Neusner attempts to construct a biography of Johanan, a task previously unattempted. As the title of the popularized version implies, Neusner explores the life of Johanan within the context of the political and religious crises facing the Jews in the first century as the result of Roman rule. He traces Johanan's move from the Galilee to Jerusalem, his ascent within the Pharisaic sect, his homiletic and interpretive style, and his constant struggle with the Sadducees and Temple priests. According to Neusner, Vespasian knowingly and strategically allowed Johanan to establish an academy in Yavneh. In keeping with Neusner's understanding of Roman policy, Vespasian did not wish to inflict utter destruction but wanted to quell the rebellion and to reestablish a limited and loyal Jewish self-government. Johanan succeeded in consolidating the power of the Pharisees who came to represent establishment Judaism while marginalizing the other sects. By assuming religious and legal authority, he reshaped the religious cult and facilitated the survival of Judaism and Jewish autonomy in the post-Temple period.

NEUSNER (1970) serves as a corrective to the methodology of his earlier work. Here, he pioneers his form-critical and source-critical approach, which acknowledges the complex relationships between various rabbinic texts and questions the historical reliability of these texts. Using his new methodology, which categorizes sources according to particular forms and traces the developments and additions that appear in later texts, Neusner observes the growth of a tradition. He draws interesting conclusions about the development of rabbinic literature and about rabbinic perceptions of Johanan through different generations but finds he can say little about the figure of Johanan himself. Neusner concludes that Johanan was opposed to war with the Romans and that he was responsible for the promulgation of numerous decrees following the destruction of the temple. This amounts to a much less colorful picture of Johanan than that portrayed in Neusner (1962), certainly more cautious and in all probability more accurate.

COHEN offers an entirely different perspective on Yavneh and its meaning that seems to have ramifications for, if not roots in, the fragmented nature of late-20th-century Jewry. Cohen bases his revisionist theory on a reexamination of the familiar sources and an analysis of new evidence such as Patristic writings and data from Qumran. Despite the trauma experienced by the loss of the temple, Cohen maintains that the destruction did not mark a crisis. In the years leading up to the destruction, the proliferation of sects and cultic practices that did not revolve around the temple prepared the rabbis and the general population for this very situation. This being the case, the contribution of Johanan was not that he provided an alternative to temple Judaism. Rather, Cohen praises Johanan and his contemporaries in Yavneh for creating an inclusive society that abolished the sects that were so prevalent in the previous period. Perhaps in search of a pluralistic model for the present, Cohen argues that sectarianism was brought to an end in Yavneh not by the increased exclusivity and dominance of one group but by a conscious effort on the part of the scholars to "agree to disagree." Contra Neusner, Cohen dissociates the rabbis and the Pharisees; unlike the Pharisees, the rabbis were not interested in creating a leadership clique that dubbed dissenters heretics. With the destruction of the temple, the source of a monolithic understanding of Judaism was gone and a pluralistic conception of Judaism evolved.

ADINA L. SHOULSON

Josephus, Flavius   c.38–after 100

Judean patriot turned Roman historian of the Jews

Attridge, H.W., "Josephus and His Works," in *Jewish Writings of the Second Temple Period: Apocrypha, Pseudepigrapha, Qumran, Sectarian Writings, Philo, Josephus* (Literature of the Jewish People in the Period of the Second Temple and Talmud, 2), edited by Michael Stone, Philadelphia: Fortress, 1984

Bilde, Per, *Flavius Josephus between Jerusalem and Rome: His Life, His Works and Their Importance* (Journal for the Study of the Pseudepigrapha, Supplement Series, 2), Sheffield, South Yorkshire: JSOT, 1988

Cohen, Shaye J.D., *Josephus in Galilee and Rome: His Vita and Development as a Historian* (Columbia Studies in the Classical Tradition, vol. 8), Leiden: Brill, 1979

Grabbe, Lester L., *Judaism from Cyrus to Hadrian*, Minneapolis, Minnesota: Fortress, 1992; London: SCM, 1994

Rajak, Tessa, *Josephus, the Historian and His Society*, London: Duckworth, 1983; Philadelphia: Fortress, 1984

Schwartz, Seth, *Josephus and Judaean Politics* (Columbia Studies in the Classical Tradition, vol. 18), New York: Brill, 1990

The Jewish historian Flavius Josephus was a priest, an alleged Pharisee, commander of rebels defending Galilee during the Great Jewish Revolt, and a beneficiary of the patronage of the Flavian dynasty following the war. He is undoubtedly one of the most important and most perplexing sources of information about Jewish communities in the Roman Empire during the late Second Temple period.

Although Josephus refers to a number of literary projects in his writings, only four texts are extant. The *Jewish War*, completed within a decade of the destruction of the Temple by Titus in 70 C.E., strives to correct public misconceptions about the events that led to the Great Jewish Revolt and to rehabilitate the martial reputation of the Jewish defense (his own role included) during the war and its immediate aftermath. *Jewish Antiquities*, written during the early 90s, presents a history of the Jews from the biblical account of Creation up to the events preceding the Revolt. The *Life*, which was issued as an appendix to *Antiquities*, responds to personal attacks against Josephus by his various rivals and gives a further account of his conduct during the war and his fortunate treatment by Vespasian and Titus, the details of which sometimes conflict with the description in *War*. *Against Apion*, clearly written for a non-Jewish audience, contrasts Judaism and Jewish history with Greek civilization; it may be the only extant example of an early Jewish apology.

For readers unfamiliar with Josephus's writings, GRABBE provides a brief yet critical resume of his life, followed by an overview of each of his four extant works. Grabbe also evaluates Josephus as a historian and suggests general considerations that will help the novice to interpret Josephus's historical and personal claims.

In another text intended for nonspecialists, RAJAK concentrates mostly on Josephus's early life and writings. She discusses the plausibility of Josephus's assertions about his family pedigree, his traditional Jewish education, and his experiences in the world of the priestly social elite. She generally accepts Josephus's claim that he experimented with several forms of Judaism when he was 16 years old and his contention that he spent three years in the wilderness during his adolescence. Rajak then examines Josephus's interpretation of the Great Jewish Revolt, considering his biases as a member of the priestly elite and the tension between his adoption of Hellenistic historiographical conventions, on the one hand, and his traditional Jewish notion of Providence and his preoccupation with collective suffering for national sins, on the other. The author closely scrutinizes the occasionally divergent accounts in *War* and *Life* of Josephus's controversial actions in Galilee.

She asserts that the latter account is generally more reliable, although it does not clearly reveal Josephus's true intentions with regards to the revolt. In *War,* Rajak claims, Josephus sought to ingratiate himself with the more moderate Jews, who must have been highly suspicious, their moderation notwithstanding, of the circumstances behind his survival and subsequent prosperity. *Life,* according to Rajak, addressed fellow Jews who lived through the same events, as Josephus worked to rescue his reputation as military commander from charges of gross incompetence stemming from his dismissal.

COHEN critically reconstructs the events of Josephus's Galilean campaign from the conflicting accounts in *War* and *Life.* The author argues that Josephus intentionally obscured the early course of the rebellion in *War,* alleging a period of moderation and legitimacy sandwiched between periods of terror and anarchy. By dividing the early history of the war into two parts, the tyrannical first period followed by the legitimate second period, Josephus was able simultaneously to condemn the fomenters of the war and to justify his own involvement. Cohen postulates that the outbreak of the war occurred spontaneously, without plans or leaders, and that Josephus willingly participated in the war from its chaotic inception, having been sent with two other priests to prepare the district of Galilee for the Roman onslaught. Josephus failed, however, to incite the nonbelligerent Galilean population, who deserted at the first sign of Vespasian's advent, and he was finally compelled to enter Jotapata, where, after a brief resistance, he was captured. After this point, Josephus served the Romans as propagandist, guide, and interpreter. At the same time, his views, as depicted in *Antiquities* and *Life,* became distinctly pro-Pharisaic as Josephus aligned himself with the rabbis, who were increasing in influence, perhaps even attaining some measure of official recognition for their academy at Yavneh.

Many scholars tend to limit their studies of Josephus to particular events or specific time periods, but BILDE offers a comprehensive biography, covering events prior to the war, Josephus's exploits in Galilee in 66 and 67, his life as a captive in a Roman camp, and his later history as a client of the Flavian dynasty. Bilde willingly accepts Josephus's claims in *Life* about his motives and pacifist attitudes during the campaign in Galilee, thus challenging Cohen's assumption that Josephus initially supported the Revolt wholeheartedly. Bilde treats Josephus as a creative author with artistic ambitions (as well as obvious political and theological intentions) who faithfully transcribed essential data from his sources. Understanding *Against Apion* as the key to all of Josephus's writings, Bilde contends that Josephus aimed to reestablish and maintain the rights and status of the Jewish people within the Roman Empire in the precarious situation following the war, while at the same time seeking to encourage his coreligionists to cooperate openly with the Roman government and with Greco-Roman civilization.

Concurring with Rajak and Bilde, ATTRIDGE understands Josephus as a member of the Jerusalem aristocracy who therefore would have received an education both in Jewish traditions and in (at least) the rudiments of Greek learning. However, Attridge is more skeptical than these other historians about Josephus's account of his adolescence in *Life,* asserting that his description of the formative influence of the various schools of Jewish thought appears rather artificial. Specifically, Attridge questions how easily Josephus could have been exposed to the three dominant Jewish schools of thought during his youth if much of this period was also devoted by him to desert asceticism, and the author notes that Josephus's tale has plenty of parallels in other stories of philosophers' quests. Thus, the account is probably a literary invention that serves to indicate that Josephus made an informed choice when he opted for the Pharisees. Unlike Bilde, Attridge contends that the inconsistencies between the accounts in *War* and *Life* about Josephus's activity during the early war years in Galilee present certain knotty problems for the modern interpreter. In *War,* Josephus is a noble warrior elected by the people of Jerusalem, and a worthy adversary of Rome who ultimately bows to necessity and to the evident will of God by conceding to Titus and the power of Rome. *Life,* Attridge submits, serves primarily as an apologia for the historian against the attacks of Justus of Tiberias, who leveled charges of warmongering and tyranny. Attridge's most useful contribution in this study is the delineation of the distinctive tendencies in each of Josephus's extant works.

SCHWARTZ studies the intellectual development of Josephus during the years between completion of his two major works, *War* and *Antiquities.* Schwartz stresses that Josephus was a public figure, interested and informed about political developments in Rome and Judea, and Schwartz argues that many features of Josephus's historiography can be best explained against the background of his shifting political concerns and social connections. Schwartz observes, for instance, that references in *War* to biblical stories do not demonstrate any depth of knowledge, but they do express a reverence for the cult and the Temple, which points to Josephus's affiliation with the upper-class Jerusalem priesthood. Thus, *War* reveals Josephus's concern for the interests of the Herodians and high priestly families, the traditional Judean aristocracy who remained the most powerful people in Jewish Palestine. In *Antiquities,* however, Josephus suddenly exhibited great familiarity with, and willingness to report accurately, the contents of the Jewish Scriptures, and he also abandoned the highly peculiar stories of *War.* Schwartz speculates that this change may signify that by the 90s Josephus no longer supported the traditional priestly regime. Rather, the more rabbinic descriptions of Jewish law in *Antiquities* probably functioned as propaganda to promote the sages, who had now begun to consolidate their leadership in Jewish Palestine.

D.P. O'BRIEN

Joshua, Book of

Boling, Robert and G. Ernest Wright, *Joshua* (Anchor Bible, vol. 6), Garden City, New York: Doubleday, 1982
Butler, Trent C., *Joshua* (Word Biblical Commentary, vol. 7), Waco, Texas: Word, 1983
Cohen, A., *Joshua and Judges* (Soncino Books of the Bible), London: Soncino, 1950; New York: Soncino, 1982

Davis, Avrohom Yosef, *The Book of Joshua* (Metsudah Tanach Series), Brookline, Massachusetts: Israel Book Shop, 1997

Drucker, Reuven, *Yehoshua/The Book of Joshua* (ArtScroll Tanach Series), Brooklyn, New York: Mesorah, 1982

Nelson, Richard D., *Joshua: A Commentary* (The Old Testament Library), Louisville, Kentucky: Westminster John Knox, 1997

Rosenberg, A.J. and Sidney Shulman, *The Book of Joshua* (Judaica Books of the Prophets), New York: Judaica, 1980

In recent years the Book of Joshua has garnered considerable scholarly attention centering on theological issues (for example, the justice or lack thereof in so-called holy warfare), historical concerns (what, if anything, can be recovered concerning an Israelite influx into, if not invasion of, Palestine), and literary matters (the book's inclusion in the larger work of the Deuteronomist[s] and its overarching themes when read synchronically, among others). For more than a millennium, Jewish interpreters, reading the text of Joshua with great care and sensitivity, have noted many of the same phenomena as their modern counterparts as well as others that escape contemporary notice. Because there is no single commentary on Joshua that encompasses all these insights and approaches, it is necessary to consult a number of volumes in order to appreciate this book at its fullest.

BOLING and WRIGHT have combined their respective talents and expertise to produce one of the best commentaries on the Book of Joshua. Wright, a colleague of W. F. Albright and a pioneer in biblical archaeology, wrote the introduction, which he completed shortly before his death in 1974. Since Boling chose not to update it, the synthesis that Wright achieved could not have taken into account any of the developments that occurred during the decade between his death and the book's publication. Boling, who also wrote the Anchor Bible commentary on Judges, was very familiar with textual and literary matters. He is generally successful in combining diachronic and synchronic insights in the production of a new translation and full textual and exegetical annotations. Although Boling sometimes puts forth interpretations that are idiosyncratic and a bit off center, overall this volume is a clear and trustworthy reflection of mainstream biblical scholarship on the Book of Joshua at the end of the 1970s.

BUTLER's volume appeared in the Word Biblical Commentary series just a year after Boling and Wright's. Some readers may be put off by its inclusion in a series sponsored by a conservative Christian publisher (Word Books). They should not be. In many ways, Butler's is the finest one-volume commentary accessible for the general reader. Although he tends to be most comfortable with traditional interpretations that favor the historicity of the Joshua narrative, he is not dogmatic and retains the rare ability to give ample space to opposing points of view. Butler is especially sensitive to the structure and texture of the Hebrew of the Masoretic Text and has many acute, even arresting comments to make in this regard. His bibliographies are remarkably complete and up-to-date, and his volume is user-friendly both in its overall organization and its individual units. It should be noted that, like Boling and Wright, Butler lacks any special training in traditional Jewish exegesis or scholarship.

NELSON's treatment is among the very best and clearest expositions of those spawned by the recent renewal of interest in the Book of Joshua. Like many contemporary scholars, Nelson does not believe that this biblical book contains or communicates much (if any) valid historical information about the period of Joshua or an Israelite "conquest" of Palestine. Rather, the book as it exists now is the end product of a complex process of composition, transmission, collection, and redaction. At each stage of this development, as Nelson expounds upon it, authors or redactors sought to address questions of vital concern to their own generation. Although such a focus on Nelson's part might have led to the slighting of a synchronic appreciation of the finished product, this is fortunately not the case here. Nelson also pays considerable attention to the Septuagint version of Joshua and the differences between this Greek text and the Masoretic Text. Nelson does not, however, deal with traditional Jewish sources; those interested in such matters will of necessity turn to commentaries such as those evaluated below.

COHEN's commentary on Joshua reproduces the Jewish Publication Society's English translation of 1917 along with the Hebrew text. The revision of Cohen's work in the early 1980s was primarily directed toward the elimination of non-Jewish sources contained in Cohen's original edition. The overall goal of this Soncino series is to acquaint the general reader with many of the main strands of traditional Jewish biblical interpretation. Given the extent and vastness of such exegesis, Cohen was necessarily selective in the material he included. His exegetical stance is decidedly conservative: the Book of Joshua is a single literary composition by an eyewitness contemporary with the events described. Moreover, as viewed by Cohen, there are no contradictions within the Book of Joshua or between this book and other parts of the Hebrew Bible, especially the Book of Judges. Cohen is thus free to concentrate on the truths, spiritual and otherwise, that are divinely revealed through this text.

ROSENBERG and SHULMAN have produced a unique volume on the Book of Joshua. In addition to printing the Masoretic Text, they also include an Aramaic Targum and the standard collection of classical Hebrew commentaries found in rabbinic bibles. The Masoretic Text receives a new English translation as does all of the commentary of Rashi, the most influential medieval Jewish exegete. Many other well-known Jewish commentators are quoted extensively in English, and select portions from talmudic and midrashic sources are also cited. All of this conforms to and confirms the value of the rather lengthy subtitle of this volume: *A New English Translation of the Text, Rashi and a Commentary Digest*. The exegetical stance of the volume's editors is highly conservative, but there is an awareness on their part of at least some elements of the modern critical approach to the Hebrew Bible.

DRUCKER was entrusted with the preparation of the Joshua commentary for ArtScroll. Every ArtScroll volume (there are now more than 400 of them, encompassing a wide variety of Jewish texts and themes) is carefully prepared from an aesthetic as well as a theological perspective. In the case of Joshua, those competent in Hebrew are treated to an easy-to-read font, and all users benefit from an array of maps that is all too rare even in books devoted to such geographically rich narratives as Joshua. In keeping with other ArtScroll productions, the divine name is represented by the term Hashem (literally, the Name). ArtScroll translations seek to bring out the theological and philosophical implications of the Hebrew as God's word, an enterprise that is enhanced and enriched by extensive (albeit necessarily anthologized) citations from traditional Jewish sources. Although not to everyone's liking, the ArtScroll phenomenon is a growing presence within North American Jewry and not just in the Orthodox community.

DAVIS's volume, as is made clear through its subtitle, is distinguished by its new linear translation of the biblical text and of Rashi. The top portion of each page contains a series of brief lines (one to five words each) from the traditional Hebrew text of the Book of Joshua with an English rendering opposite. The bottom half of the page follows the same columnar format, but with lines from Rashi (in Hebrew and in English) rather than from the biblical text. Rashi's paramount influence not only among subsequent Jewish interpreters but also on Christian exegetes and bible translators fully justifies the attention lavished on him in this work. English readers are now also in a position to compare the work of Rashi as Davis presents it with the earlier translation furnished by Rosenberg and Shulman. Davis's translation maintains proper names in a form closer to the Hebrew than is usually found (for example, Moshe and Yehoshua). In many other ways also, in the introduction and in the translation itself, readers are ushered into the world of Joshua as understood by the rabbis.

LEONARD J. GREENSPOON

Judah Halevi c.1070–1141

Spanish Hebrew poet and theologian

Baron, Salo W., "Yehudah Halevi, an Answer to an Historic Challenge," *Jewish Social Studies*, 3, 1941

Brann, Ross, "Judah Halevi: The Compunctious Poet," *Prooftexts*, 7(2), 1987

Goitein, Shelomo Dov, *A Mediterranean Society: The Jewish Communities of the Arab World as Portrayed in the Documents of the Cairo Geniza*, vol. 5: *The Individual: Portrait of a Mediterranean Personality of the High Middle Ages as Reflected in the Cairo Geniza*, Berkeley and London: University of California Press, 1988

Hamori, Andras, "Lights in the Heart of the Sea, Some Images of Judah Halevi's," *Journal of Semitic Studies*, 30, 1985

Kayser, Rudolf, *The Life and Time of Jehudah Halevi*, translated by Frank Gaynor, New York: Philosophical Library, 1949

Pines, Shlomo, "Shi'ite Terms and Conceptions in Judah Halevi's *Kuzari*," *Jerusalem Studies in Arabic and Islam*, 2, 1980

Scheindlin, Raymond P., "Contrasting Religious Experience in the Liturgical Poems of Ibn Gabirol and Judah Halevi," *Prooftexts*, 11(3), 1991

Silman, Yochanan, *Philosopher and Prophet: Judah Halevi, the Kuzari, and the Evolution of His Thought* (SUNY Series in Judaica), Albany: State University of New York Press, 1995

Sirat, Colette, *A History of Jewish Philosophy in the Middle Ages*, Cambridge and New York: Cambridge University Press, 1985

Strauss, Leo, *Persecution and the Art of Writing*, Glencoe, Illinois: Free Press, 1952

Yahalom, Joseph, "Diwan and Odyssey: Judah Halevi and the Secular Poetry of Medieval Spain in the Light of the New Discoveries from Petersburg," *Miscelanea de Estudios Arabes y Hebraicos*, 44, 1995

One of the greatest personalities of Jewish Middle Ages, Judah Halevi was at the same time an immensely popular poet and a rather conservative thinker, whose magnum opus, the *Kuzari*, pioneered opposition to philosophical interpretations of Judaism. The poetic and philosophical aspects of his work have been highlighted in both earlier and recent studies about him. Numerous studies have been dedicated to the life of Halevi and in particular to his eventual journey to Jerusalem. Some of his poems are translated into English in *Selected Poems of Jehudah Halevi*, edited by Heinrich Brody and translated by Nina Salaman (Philadelphia: Jewish Publication Society, 1928).

Biographical insights are offered by Baron, Kayser, Goitein, and Yahalom. BARON presents a valuable sketch of Halevi, reviewing this rich personality's experiences against the background of his age. In the space of a few pages, Baron describes the political and cultural context in which Halevi created his poetical and philosophical oeuvre. Baron considers the meaning of Halevi for Jews in the 1940s, and the author underlines, among other traits, Halevi's great perseverance in times of crisis, his courage, his clarity of purpose, and his firm belief in the Palestinian ideal. The article was written before the discovery and publication of important materials, but it remains very interesting as a general evaluation of Halevi's personality and period.

KAYSER's book gives the classic precritical perspective on the epoch and the circumstances of Halevi's life, unfortunately with a heavy admixture of inexact details. The author was a well-known German literary journalist who was persecuted by the Nazis. In the language of his era, Kayser presents Halevi as "one of the mightiest religious poets [that] any race and any century has ever produced," and "the greatest symbol of medieval Judaism." Due to a lack of critical principles, Kayser fails to distinguish between documented data and legends about famous authors, including Halevi. Some of his assertions are careless impossibilities; he maintains, for instance, that Halevi heard as a boy of "the atrocities perpetrated by the Almohades." Nor is Kayser necessarily helpful when he describes Halevi's "metamorphosis from mundane minstrel to religious bard" as a deepening and widening of his character. However, some of Kayser's descriptions of the poet's work and personality are still acceptable. The book has to be read critically, because many of its views have been refuted by new data, but it projects an infectious enthusiasm for Jewish civilization that one can admire to this day.

GOITEIN, after protracted study of the Judeo-Arabic materials of the Cairo Genizah, was able to publish several very important new documents about Halevi and in particular about his last days in Egypt and his journey to Jerusalem. In the last of his five magisterial volumes on medieval Jews along the Mediterranean, Goitein devotes 20 pages to the discussion of several letters connected with Halevi. In the first letter, written in Granada in 1130, a young friend described Halevi as "an illustrious scholar of unique and perfect piety." Goitein studied the archives of Abu Sa'id Halfon ben Nethanel ha-Levi, a Cairene businessman who visited Spain many times and became a good friend of Halevi. These archives have yielded more than 20 letters from or about Halevi; five are holographs that the poet himself wrote in Spain, with important allusions to the redaction of the *Kuzari*; there are also letters with references to his stay in Egypt, his presence on board the ship that would bring him to Palestine, and his death in the summer of 1141. Goitein translates and comments on these texts; his quite new and critical data is presented in exemplary fashion by a true master.

YAHALOM offers a new perspective on the last years of Halevi's life, employing only recently accessible materials from the Second Firkovich Collection of the Russian National Library in St. Petersburg. These documents enable a new evaluation of the poet's metaphorical language, which challenges the view of the life of the poet generally accepted since the essay published by Jefim Schirmann in 1938 ("The Life of Judah Halevi," [Hebr.], *Tarbiz* 9). Yahalom's article presents new hypotheses, for instance, about the time of Halevi's visit to al-Andalus: Halevi was still living in Christian Spain, and it was there that he met Moses ibn Ezra after ibn Ezra left Granada, close to 1095. Once Halevi came to al-Andalus in search of the great sages, he would never return to Christian Spain; the eruption of invaders from North Africa prompted him instead to actualize his life's dream by going to the land of Israel. Yahalom comments also on new materials that throw light on the last months of Halevi in Egypt and his failed attempt to go to Palestine overland. He is able to offer as well a new outlook on the transmission history of Halevi's poems, thanks to hundreds of manuscript pages from St. Petersburg. The article uses important, previously unknown materials, and it offers a multitude of interesting new insights, although some interpretations are still open to discussion.

Among commentaries on Halevi's philosophical activity are Sirat, Strauss, Pines, and Silman. SIRAT's presentation of Halevi's thought occupies a section of the most comprehensive English introduction to the history of Jewish medieval philosophy available. The study identifies the significance of Halevi's *Kuzari* for the history of Jewish thought, without elaborating on the role the text played in future anti-rationalistic movements. After explaining in a clear and thorough way the main lines of debate between various religions presented in the *Kuzari*, Sirat analyzes Halevi's approach to the problem of universalism as opposed to particularism and the central position Halevi attributed to Israel. Sirat additionally examines Halevi's proposal that the way to God is through prophecy, not philosophy. She

maintains that Halevi chose in many points the most particularist interpretations of Judaism, even when Jewish tradition included other more liberal or inclusive opinions. The chapter offers a clear and precise exposition of Halevi's central ideas. Written very objectively, it is recommended for readers of all kinds.

STRAUSS's essay on the "Law of Reason" in the *Kuzari* is part of a celebrated volume on the relationship between philosophy and politics in Jewish thought. The problematic has to do with the *ius naturale* and the distinction between "rational laws" and "revealed laws." Strauss argues that the *Kuzari*, addressed to naturally pious people in a state of doubt, is primarily a defense of Judaism against philosophy, because Halevi thought that a true philosopher can never become a genuine convert to Judaism. The main part of the study is dedicated to the philosopher's and religionist's evaluations of the Law of Reason. These rational laws are a complete theologico-political code—the religion of philosophers and the rules of conduct that a philosopher must observe in order to become capable of contemplation. Halevi's basic objection to philosophy was not particularly Jewish: rather, it was a defense of morality, which, he believed, is necessarily connected to revealed religion. This article remains a valuable analysis of the problem seen from a general philosophical perspective, even if other experts would prefer a more historical treatment, with references to Arabic sources.

PINES, another colossus of the history of philosophy, discusses some of the main terms employed by Halevi in the conceptual framework of the *Kuzari*. Pines argues that these terms appear with the same (or very similar) meanings in Shi'ite, and more concretely in Ismai'li, texts. Although it is not clear how and where Halevi came to know these concepts, what is clear is that they influenced him very deeply. Pines proves also that while book one of the *Kuzari* seems to invoke ibn Bajja's theories, some sections of book five are based on Avicenna's conception of the soul, which suggests a considerable interval of time between the redaction of the two parts of Halevi's book. Pines's very technical study requires a good background in Arabic and Jewish philosophy for full comprehension, but it must be considered a turning point in the study of the philosophical conceptions of Halevi's apologetic and polemical work.

SILMAN investigates the *Kuzari* from a historical point of view, trying to distinguish Halevi's earlier and later thought. Offering a very acute analysis, Silman identifies at least three distinct strata in the development of Halevi's thought. The first is a kind of Aristotelian position that predates the writing of the book. The second is an early anti-Karaite stage, in which Halevi still maintained an Aristotelian point of view, trying to interpret Jewish tradition from this perspective. This stage is reflected in some parts of the *Kuzari* (part three and certain sections of parts one and two). Finally, there is a later strand to his thought, represented in other sections of the book (parts four and five, along with the rest of parts one and two), that emphasizes concrete human experience, and in particular the historical experience of the Jewish people. In the last stage, Halevi abandoned the principles of Aristotelian philosophy in an effort to resolve the tensions and internal contradictions of his system. Although he catalogs these clearly defined stages of evolution, Silman defends (in a rather artificial way) the internal dialectical unity of Halevi's book. This is a very systematic study of Halevi's thought, in spite of all Halevi's vacillation and inconsistencies. However, the division that Silman proposes is not the only possible one, and the different attitudes of Halevi toward philosophy could also be interpreted (in a quite different chronological sequence) as an answer to his Arabic sources. Still, this is important reading for adequately prepared readers.

Brann, Hamori, and Scheindlin all have much of importance to say about Halevi's poetry. BRANN investigates in this article, as he does in his excellent book *The Compunctious Poet* (1991), a well-known topos in Arabic and Hebrew literature: the "compunctious poet." By this term, he alludes to the poet's contradictory attitudes toward poetry, which he interprets as a sign of the conflicts inherent in living in two quite different worlds. Hebrew poets tried to be true to Jewish tradition without renouncing the ideals of Arabic education. This cultural ambiguity is reflected in the phenomenon of the repentant poet, who regrets in his old age that he composed poetry in Arabic style when young, but who never ceases to write. Brann applies this general theory to Halevi, presenting an alternative to the traditional views (based on the "conversion theory"), which posit that Halevi was the darling of Andalusian Jewish society in his youth but began to renounce the ideals of al-Andalus and determined to set out for Palestine and a life of religious devotion when he was about 50 years old. Brann demystifies the conventional view of Halevi's posture with respect to poetry, showing the poet's ambivalent attitude toward Hebrew verse. Until the last days of his life, Halevi remained an Andalusian and a compunctious Hebrew poet conflicted about the ambiguity of his literary identity. Brann performs an excellent analysis of the sources, succeeding in finding a new and deeply perceptive interpretation of the texts.

HAMORI, a notable scholar in the field of Arabic and Hebrew poetry, comments on a poem by Halevi in which a physical odyssey and a spiritual journey run parallel courses, with the description of a storm and the calm that follows reassuring both the actual and the mental traveler. Some images of purification and illumination and the final allusion to the conjunction of the heart with nature are symbolically and philosophically interpreted by Hamori. He compares these images with some assertions of the philosopher and the rabbi in the *Kuzari*, and he shows how Halevi turned a Neoplatonic series of images, known among Arabic thinkers, into poetry. This study is an ingenious and attractive discovery of coincidences between the poetic and the philosophic work of Halevi.

Scheindlin, a great expert on Jewish medieval poetry, has translated and commented on several secular and liturgical poems of Halevi in his two splendid books, *Wine, Women and Death* (1986) and *The Gazelle* (1991). In SCHEINDLIN, he contrasts the individual vision and religious experience reflected in Halevi's liturgical poetry with that of ibn Gabirol. The comparison of poems of the two authors, who employed very similar words, reveals that although both were grounded in Neoplatonic psychology, they were in fact far removed from each other's thinking. Ibn Gabirol's speaker was active and bitter, while Halevi's voice was much more submissive and accept-

ing. Halevi attributed greater importance than ibn Gabirol did to the distance between God and humanity, or divine transcendence. Without abandoning the rabbinic religious ethos, Halevi introduced in his poems a climate of tranquil confidence in God, a passive acceptance of his will, that seems to have its main sources in Arabic religious poetry. Scheindlin's precise and appealing analysis shows in a very convincing way that Halevi was influenced by Sufism and the Islamic pietism of his age.

ANGEL SÁENZ-BADILLOS

Judah Loew ben Bezalel c.1525–1609

Talmudist, theologian, and rabbi of Prague

Bokser, Ben Zion, *From the World of the Cabbalah: The Philosophy of Rabbi Judah Loew of Prague*, New York: Philosophical Library, 1954; London: Vision, 1957; as *The Maharal: The Mystical Philosophy of Rabbi Judah Loew of Prague*, Northvale, New Jersey: Aronson, 1994

Buber, Martin, "The Beginning of the National Idea: The High Rabbi Liva," in *On Zion: The History of an Idea*, translated by S. Godman, New York: Schocken, and London: East and West Library, 1973

Elbaum, Jacob, "Rabbi Judah Loew of Prague and His Attitude to the Aggadah," *Scripta Hierosolymitana*, 22, 1971

Goldsmith, Arnold, *The Golem Remembered, 1909–1980: Variations of a Jewish Legend*, Detroit, Michigan: Wayne State University Press, 1981

Kleinberger, Aaron Fritz, "The Didactics of Rabbi Loew of Prague," *Scripta Hierosolymitana*, 13, 1963

Kulka, Otto Dov, "Comenius and Maharal: The Historical Background of the Parallels in Their Teaching," *Judaica Bohemiae*, 27, 1991

Safran, Bezalel, "Maharal and Early Hasidism," in his *Hasidism: Continuity or Innovation?* (Harvard Judaic Texts and Studies, 5), Cambridge, Massachusetts: Harvard University Press, 1988

Sherwin, Byron L., *Mystical Theology and Social Dissent: The Life and Works of Judah Loew of Prague* (Littman Library of Jewish Civilization), Rutherford, New Jersey: Fairleigh Dickinson University Press, and London: Associated University Presses, 1982

Judah Loew ben Bezalel (called Maharal) was one of the leading thinkers of 16th-century Judaism. He is also an enigmatic and paradoxical figure, and interpretations of his thought differ widely. Furthermore, he is the hero of a well-known legend, the story of the Golem of Prague. GOLDSMITH discusses the origins of this legend, and its many versions in 19th- and 20th-century Jewish literature. Titles discussed, however, will focus on the historical rather than the legendary Maharal.

SHERWIN provides the best survey of the known facts of Maharal's life, which are relatively few. Sherwin also surveys

Maharal's formal theology and shows Maharal's dependence on medieval Spanish Kabbalah. He demonstrates conclusively the links between Maharal's kabbalistic theology, particularly his belief in a metaphysical difference between Jews and non-Jews, and his stringent halakhic views concerning non-Jews. Sherwin also argues (as the historian Yizhak Baer did concerning Moses de Leon and other kabbalists in late 13th-century Spain) that Maharal's kabbalistic theology was linked to a critique of the wealthy leaders of the local Jewish community.

BOKSER's attempts to contextualize Maharal in 16th-century history, whether Jewish or European, are not accurate. Moreover, his survey of Maharal's life and thought has in most respects been superseded by Sherwin's biography. In one respect, however, Bokser's biography is still superior: namely, it gives the reader a good sense of the range of Maharal's thinking, including such topics as the nature of man, the nature of the Jews and the Jewish nation, education, the meaning of Jewish history, the problem of miracles, the messianic age, and the interpretation of the Bible and talmudic legends. Like Sherwin, Bokser points to the roots of Maharal's theology in Kabbalah. His interpretations of Maharal's kabbalistic views, however, tend to make them sound like those of a good-hearted, liberal Jew of the 1950s (that is to say, like Bokser himself).

BUBER places Maharal in a very different context and emphasizes another aspect of his thought. The crucial dimension in Maharal's thinking, according to Buber's interpretation, is his understanding of the Jews as a physical as well as a metaphysical people and of the return to Zion as a natural as well as a miraculous process. Since the land of Israel is the natural home of the Jewish people, Maharal argued, the state of exile is in some sense unnatural and, therefore, temporary. Buber compares Maharal briefly to certain Christian political thinkers of the 16th and 17th centuries and points to certain resemblances between Maharal and Jean Calvin. Maharal insisted rationally, Buber claims, on the rights of all nations and on that basis on the rights of the Jewish nation, including its right to independence. He believed superrationally in the unique holiness of the Jewish people and the land of Israel. For Buber (whose career as a Zionist had important links to Prague), Maharal was a forerunner of the "spiritual Zionism" that Buber believed in and developed.

KLEINBERGER surveys Maharal's proposed reforms of Jewish education and points to the many resemblances between Maharal's views and those of the famous Czech educational reformer of the 17th century, Johann Comenius. Kleinberger is the only one of the writers discussed here who ignores the superrational and kabbalistic elements of Maharal's teachings. He argues that Maharal, like Comenius, adhered strictly to a natural view of education, that is, one in which the method and the subject matter are chosen in light of the nature of the individual student, and in particular are graded according to the student's abilities.

KULKA's essay supplements both Buber's and Kleinberger's. Kulka suggests that the Protestant sect known as the Moravian Brethren may have been the proximate source of some of Maharal's novel ideas on education and nationality. In spite of Maharal's antagonism toward Christianity and his stress on the differences between Jews and non-Jews, Kulka suggests that his contacts with non-Jews, and with Brethren in particular, may have been extensive.

ELBAUM discusses another phase of Maharal's creative reinterpretation of Judaism: his allegorical reading of talmudic legends. Maharal polemicized against those who interpreted the legends as merely accurate or, worse still, inaccurate historical accounts. As Elbaum illustrates, Maharal reinterpreted each detail, nearly each word, of each talmudic legend as a part of his ethical, theological, and mystical system. Elbaum locates the roots of this hermeneutical stance in the kabbalistic tradition and, more distantly, in Maimonides.

SAFRAN's essay is the most adequate study of Maharal's mysticism as well as of his later influence. Safran explicates Maharal's vision of the mystical path. It is based on a distinction between a "natural" and a "supernatural" frame of vision. The shift from the former to the latter leads ultimately to the annihilation of the sense of self. Stemming from that defeat of the egotistical, judgmental self is an ethics of humility, patience, and charity. Safran then shows the influence of Maharal's thought on certain 18th- and early 19th-century hasidic leaders.

JOSEPH M. DAVIS

Judaism, Introductions to

Blau, Joseph L., *Modern Varieties of Judaism* (Lectures on the History of Religions Sponsored by the American Council of Learned Societies, new series, no. 8), New York: Columbia University Press, 1966

Fackenheim, Emil L., *What Is Judaism?: An Interpretation for the Present Age,* New York: Summit, 1987

Garber, Zev (editor), *Methodology in the Academic Teaching of Judaism* (Studies in Judaism), Lanham, Maryland: University Press of America, 1986; London: University Press of America, 1987

Garber, Zev (editor), *Academic Approaches to Teaching Jewish Studies,* Lanham, Maryland: University Press of America, 1999

Hertzberg, Arthur (editor), *Judaism* (Great Religions of Modern Man), New York: Braziller, and London: Prentice-Hall International, 1961; new edition, New York: Washington Square, 1963

Heschel, Abraham Joshua, *The Sabbath: Its Meaning for Modern Man,* New York: Farrar, Straus, and Young, 1951

Holtz, Barry W. (editor), *Back to the Sources: Reading the Classic Jewish Texts,* New York: Summit, 1984

Jaffee, Martin S., *Early Judaism,* Upper Saddle River, New Jersey: Prentice-Hall, 1997

Neusner, Jacob, *The Way of Torah: An Introduction to Judaism,* Belmont, California: Dickenson, 1970; 6th edition, Belmont, California: Wadsworth, 1997

Seltzer, Robert M. (editor), *Judaism: A People and Its History* (Religion, History, and Culture), New York: Macmillan, and London: Collier Macmillan, 1989

Sherwin, Byron L. and Seymour J. Cohen (editors), *How to Be a Jew: Ethical Teachings of Judaism*, Northvale, New Jersey: Aronson, 1992

Siegel, Richard, Michael Strassfeld, and Sharon Strassfeld (editors), *The Jewish Catalog: A Do-It-Yourself Kit*, Philadelphia: Jewish Publication Society, 1973

Wouk, Herman, *This Is My God: The Jewish Way of Life*, Garden City, New York: Doubleday, 1970; London: Collins, 1973; revised edition, New York: Pocket Books, 1974; London: Fontana, 1976

Different disciplines have their own patterns of thinking, inquiry, and information processing. Scientific inquiry, for example, calls for classification, explanation of technical processes, detailed statements of fact often containing a definition or statement of principle, problem solving, and experiment reporting, which involves discriminating observation, careful explanation, and considered conclusions. The academic study of Judaism exposes the reader to an appreciation of the Jewish religious heritage in all its aspects and helps foster an understanding of the contributions of that heritage to world civilization in general, and to Western culture in particular. As such, the Jewish religious tradition addresses peoplehood, worldview, and lifestyle, and "Introductions to Judaism" is an instructional form of the humanities characterized by that branch of learning's emphasis on reading, writing, and reasoning. How and why are explained and discussed at length by GARBER (1986 and 1999).

SIEGEL, STRASSFELD, and STRASSFELD write out of a commitment on the part of the editors and contributors to raise Jewish consciousness and to explore how Jews can find meaningful ways to express and experience Jewish religious identity and values. The work suggests that Jewish norms, traditions, and culture have been compromised massively by American Jews in their attempt to assimilate; that Judaism is often seen as no longer an option by assimilated Jews, which requires analysis of the problems that Jewishness presents in contemporary society; and that the Jewish heritage can be saved in the diaspora by stressing personal involvement and the aesthetic value of *Yiddishkeit* over abstract philosophical and metaphysical discussions. The spirit of the articles, with many accompanied by relevant illustrations, range from sublime and learned to humorous and pop. The barely hidden agenda—namely, to push the idea that being Jewish is enjoyable and that Jewish renewal is possible by the transmission of Judaism through living experiential role models—is by and large successful and contagious. The prime audience for this comprehensive guide in "how to" Judaism is neither the totally committed nor the lost of the Jewish community but the very large group of younger Jews who are open to an appreciation of their people's vast cultural heritage—however defined. The criticism of the Jewish establishment, with its preference for outer image tied to progress over inner essence defined by tradition, makes for a Jewish subculture, if not counterculture. In sum, these volumes are a reflection of and guide to a new quest for an old identity through Jewish Americana.

Whereas other manuals of "how to" Judaism suggest involvement in aesthetic Judaism to counter assimilation, SHERWIN and COHEN, following the direction of 16th-century Jewish mystic Judah Loew of Prague (Maharal) and the late-16th- and early-17th-century Polish talmudist Samuel Edels (Maharsha), discuss personal, religious, and moral virtues in three sections (God, Self, Self and Others), each containing five chapters. Combining selections from classical and modern ethicists with comments of their own, the authors examine a plethora of Jewish values, such as belief, Torah, repentance, health, death, parenthood, philanthropy, and sexual ethics. They suggest that Jewish ethical literature offers a "road map for the individual committed to the creation of the supreme art-form—one's own life." As pointers toward this goal, Sherwin and Cohen provide a vocabulary for "how to be—alive as—a Jew" (i.e., guidance in the basic understanding of explicit and implicit traditions of Jewish moral principles and practice). The message conveyed is akin to what the prophets taught: the Jewish people living according to the plan of the Torah demonstrates the surest proof of God's ethics, Israel's uniqueness, and man's humanity.

The Koran speaks of the Jews as a "People of the Scripture," but in the modern period Jews have largely lost direct contact with the Bible and the classical literature of Judaism that has emanated from it. HOLTZ's guide to these classics is an impressive step toward rectifying this lacuna. In a series of reader-friendly, hands-on teaching sections, American scholars write on selected passages from the Bible, Talmud, midrash, medieval biblical exegesis and medieval philosophy, Kabbalah, Hasidism, and the liturgy. What is of value here is not so much the corpus of facts or descriptive data presented but the invitation to learn by engaging the primary source material on its own terms and in the context of sacred Jewish literary tradition. Learning involves not only information given and received but the recipient's discovery of what that knowledge means. The learning exchange would be incomplete if one were to prevail without the other. This thoughtful book captures the excitement when both prevail.

HERTZBERG's handbook, part of the Great Religions of Modern Man series, is an account of the origin and development of key ideas of Judaism extrapolated from an extensive selection of Jewish writings dating from the biblical era to our own. His chapters are a synthesis of ideas and beliefs that describe the parameters of the Jewish value system: God, Torah (teaching and commandments), people (chosen and covenant), land (holy and home), doctrine (life and death, man, messiah, morality, etc.), holy space and time, and prayer. He does not present a comprehensive discussion of items and issues, and what he does say has been superseded by others. Nonetheless, his grasp of what is meant by Jewish religion and traditions, and what can be learned from them, is commendable.

WOUK, Pulitzer Prize-winning author of *The Cain Mutiny* and other epics, explores the central teachings of Judaism against a brief historical background. The author's goal is to explain the ancient traditions of the religion and their contemporary meanings. Wouk invites the reader, Jew and non-Jew alike, not only to read about the faith of the Jews but also to confront the process itself. He moves through Jewish ethics and symbols (e.g., clothing, diet, shelter), rites of passage, and the liturgical year painlessly, pausing whenever he wishes to illustrate a lesson, taking what appears to be a detour and then bringing the reader back to the true course, enhanced by the sights seen. Though Wouk recognizes in the modern era multiple forms of dissent from the biblical consent of *na'aseh venishma* (we shall do and obey), he argues that the point of departure for all of these voices is the classical teaching from Sinai. He offers a strong testimony of Orthodox faith, which reasons that Torah and Western culture are compatible.

FACKENHEIM's interpretation of Judaism is founded on profound knowledge of Jewish habits and customs, doctrines and practices, values and ideals, outlook and philosophy. After discussing the religious situation of the contemporary Jew, he examines concepts, issues, and meanings gleaned from both the religious and secular spheres of the Jewish experience: God, Torah, peoplehood, Zionism, antisemitism, prayer, repentance, and the meaning of Messiah for today's Jew. In Fackenheim's view, the theme of transition from homelessness to homeland is particularly real and important, and a major section of the volume is devoted to the Jewish State where generations of Jewish thought and practice are being digested, accepted, challenged, preserved, and renewed day by day. This is a salutary work whose commitment to unity is marked by creative diversity.

The age of European Enlightenment and emancipation brought a radical departure from traditional thought patterns and aspirations. Emancipation destroyed the authority of the Jewish community, and the Enlightenment offered an ideological justification for the surrender of the authority of Jewish tradition in modern Jewish history. BLAU's volume successfully reviews the many adjustments that Judaism has made in response to the challenge of modernity, including changes in the *kehillah* (community) and the synagogue as well as in ideological approaches, doctrinal and educational viewpoints, leadership, and the basic dynamics of European and American Judaism. His thesis that all varieties of Jewish religion and Jewish nationalism are responses aiming to avoid destroying continuity with tradition (e.g., Jews in a free society remain attached to Torah more in morality than in ritual) amounts, however, to a Western cross-cultural exploration of Jewish beliefs and practices.

SELTZER attempts to give some much-needed direction to important problems that arise in a serious study of Judaism in the context of phenomenology and the history of religions. The articles, reprinted from *The Encyclopedia of Religion* (Macmillan, 1987), examine "religious behavior, thought, literature, symbolism, and society" and are arranged in five groups of essays. Each chapter is topically focused and shares a number of methodological directives: identify the problem, search for different schools of interpretation, elucidate advantages and disadvantages connected with each school, and provide an agenda and annotated bibliography for further study and discussion. Careful scholarship and useful information, albeit extremely compressed, can benefit college-oriented classes and informed adults, the readers toward whom this anthology is directed.

NEUSNER is one of the 20th century's great Judaic scholars, whose prolific publishing on the literature of the talmudic era has earned him worldwide acclaim. His careful step-by-step form-critical methodology portrays the history and structure of Judaism academically with little room for partisanship. Immanence and transcendence within Judaism are depicted in categories of the shape of faith—God, man, rites of passage, festivals, community—and the dynamics of faith—religious commitment and social problems, contemporary values and the present state of Jewish belief. Neusner does not see Judaism "merely [as] the evanescent culture of the Jewish group." Rather, he maintains that Judaism, the religion, can and must be discussed and analyzed by the same accepted methods and procedures applied to other religions. His history of religion approach provides an alternative to the school of "ethnic Judaism" in understanding the Jewish religious experience.

JAFFEE presents the development of Judaism from the end of the Israelite epoch (c.450 B.C.E.) to the start of the Middle Ages (c.650 C.E.). The book's participatory style permits the reader to confront the dynamics of text and traditions in the political and social history of the Jews in and outside the Land of Israel during this time. Each chapter presents ideas and issues, charts and illustrations, notes and reference material. Taking the position that early Judaism was a mosaic of worldviews struggling to be Israel in a world created and governed by the God of Israel, Jaffee demonstrates that serious scholastic inquiry may be iconoclastic and even troubling, but it is ultimately liberating and invigorating.

HESCHEL, identified by Neusner as the single most influential theologian of Judaism of the 20th century, asserts the centrality of God to all life and God's need of humans ("Divine Pathos"). He maintains that revelation in the Jewish religion is expressed in terms of *mattan Torah* (the giving of Torah) by God in consonance with "the receiving of Torah" voluntarily by the people. Heschel's brief monograph (136 pages), written in image-laden cadences and considered one of the most important of his writings, captures eloquently the intent and spirit of the sabbath as understood in rabbinic, kabbalistic, and hasidic writings and especially as practiced by religiously observant Jews of Eastern Europe—an ethos all but destroyed in the Shoah. He explains how the sabbath emerged as a bulwark against the passage of time, including death, and has become an echo of eternity. His aphoristic essay is poetic, philosophical, and quotable. As an institution the sabbath represents the quintessential introduction to Judaism, and Heschel expresses powerfully its values of amity not animosity and conformity not conflict between humankind and nature as recorded in the Torah of Moses and taught by the sages of Israel.

ZEV GARBER

Judeo-Arabic Literature

Blau, Joshua, *The Emergence and Linguistic Background of Judaeo-Arabic: A Study of the Origins of Middle Arabic* (Scripta Judaica, 5), London: Oxford University Press, 1965; 2nd edition, Jerusalem: Ben-Zvi Institute, 1981

Blau, Joshua and Simon Hopkins, "On Early Judaeo-Arabic Orthography," *Zeitschrift für Arabische Linguistik*, 12, 1984

Blau, Joshua and Simon Hopkins, "Judaeo-Arabic Papyri: Collected, Edited, Translated and Analysed," *Jerusalem Studies in Arabic and Islam*, 9, 1987

Drory, Rina, "Bilingualism and Cultural Images: The Hebrew and Arabic Introductions of Saadia Gaon's Sefer ha-Egron," in *Language and Culture in the Near East* (Israel Oriental Studies, 25), edited by Shlomo Izre'el and Rina Drory, New York: Brill, 1995

Halkin, Abraham S., "Judeo-Arabic Literature," in *The Jews: Their History, Culture, and Religion* (The Gitelson Library), edited by Louis Finkelstein, Philadelphia: Jewish Publication Society, 1949; 3rd edition, London: Owen, 1961; 4th edition, New York: Schocken, 1970

Hary, Benjamin, *Multiglossia in Judeo-Arabic: With an Edition, Translation and Grammatical Study of the Cairene Purim Scroll* (Études sur le judaïsme médiéval, 14), New York: Brill, 1992

Steinschneider, Moritz, *An Introduction to the Arabic Literature of the Jews*, London: 1901

Stillman, Norman, *The Language and Culture of the Jews of Sefrou, Morocco: An Ethnolinguistic Study* (Journal of Semitic Studies Monograph, 11), Manchester, Greater Manchester: University of Manchester, 1988

A major concern of scholarship on Judeo-Arabic has been the points of contact between it and other languages such as Classical Arabic, Colloquial Arabic, Hebrew, and Aramaic. To a large extent, the continuing debate over whether Judeo-Arabic constitutes a distinct language hinges on the precise nature of these relationships. Late 19th- and early 20th-century scholars maintained that the Arabic used by Jews was in its essentials undifferentiated from that employed by Muslims. More recently, however, this view has been challenged by Blau and others who maintain that Judeo-Arabic represents a linguistic development all its own. Often such assessments have repercussions for the broader question concerning Jewish participation in the general culture of Arabic-speaking societies.

STEINSCHNEIDER's lectures, originally published in serial form, are a natural outgrowth of the great bibliographer's incomparable mastery of the manuscript collections of Europe, coupled with his lifelong concern with the history of Jewish participation in Islamic culture. Unlike other pioneers of the *Wissenschaft des Judentums*, Steinschneider emphasized Judaism's embeddedness within the surrounding non-Jewish environment, in particular that of the Islamic world. "Arabic and German are the only languages and nationalities which have been of essential and continuing influence on Judaism," he insists. Steinschneider devotes the first part of his work to an exhaustive catalog of the Arabic names borne by Jews, which he painstakingly culls from the printed and manuscript resources at his command. In the second part, he offers some general observations on the position of Jews within medieval Muslim society, the major genres represented in Judeo-Arabic literature, and some of the salient features of the Arabic used by Jews. In this volume, as in all of his work, Steinschneider's dry exposition is amply compensated for by his remarkably fastidious attention to detail.

HALKIN provides a useful introduction to some of the main genres of Judeo-Arabic literature, including Bible translations, commentaries, grammatical treatises, halakhic monographs, and philosophical works. However, Halkin's description is heavily colored by a somewhat outdated supposition that the orientation of medieval Jewish culture in Spain and the East was predominantly rationalist. This bias is apparent in his emphasis on the philosophical works written in that period and in his sweeping dismissal of the literature produced in the post-medieval period. Moreover, unlike Blau (who stresses the distinctness of Judeo-Arabic from classical Arabic and, by implication, the cultural separation of Jews and Muslims), Halkin sees in Judeo-Arabic an expression of the close affinity that existed between the two cultures: "[T]his unhesitating readiness to write in a language other than Hebrew demonstrates of course an identification with environment which was not reached in other lands."

BLAU's work gives a linguistic history of classical (i.e., medieval) Judeo-Arabic that focuses on its emergence within the context of the general development of the Arabic language. Blau considers Judeo-Arabic to be a manifestation of Middle Arabic, which emerged after the Arab conquests of the seventh century in the newly founded urban centers of the Near East. Accordingly, Blau emphasizes the importance of Judeo-Arabic for a proper appreciation of the development of modern Arabic dialects from classical Arabic. At the same time, Blau insists that because of its unique orthographic, linguistic, and thematic features, Judeo-Arabic "must be accorded the status of a language in its own right." He draws sociological conclusions about the interaction between Jewish and Muslim society on the basis of this linguistic distinctiveness, asserting that "[t]he general use of Hebrew script clearly shows the barrier that separated the bulk of the Jewish population from Arab and Islamic culture."

Blau and Hopkins's pair of articles examine a number of ninth-century Judeo-Arabic papyri that exhibit an orthographic tradition different from that used almost universally in works written after the tenth century. Unlike Classical Judeo-Arabic Spelling, which is based on "a more or less mechanical transfer of classical Arabic orthography into Hebrews letters," this newly discovered orthographic system, which the authors designate Early Vulgar Judeo-Arabic Spelling (EVJAS), exhibits "a phonetic rendering of the Arabic sounds through the medium of Hebrew script." EVJAS's freedom from classical Arabic orthography leads Blau and Hopkins to the conclusion that it was a system used primarily by uneducated members of the Jewish community "who lacked accomplishment in literary Arabic." The authors attribute the disappearance of EVJAS after the tenth century to the enormous popularity of Saadya's Pentateuch commentary, which used classical Judeo-Arabic orthography and exerted a profound cultural influence on all strata of contemporary Jewish society. The general conclusions of this study are succinctly described in BLAU and HOPKINS (1984), while transcriptions, translations, and annotations of the papyri can be found in BLAU and HOPKINS (1987).

STILLMAN's book is the fruit of an intensive study of the dwindling Jewish community of Sefrou, Morocco, conducted in 1971 and 1972. While the centerpiece of the book is a close analysis of the unique dialect of Judeo-Arabic spoken by Sefrou's Jews, Stillman's concerns go beyond the parameters of pure linguistics. Assuming the "intimate, indeed inseparable, link between culture and language," he considers the distinctive Judeo-Arabic dialect of the Sefrou community as an important window onto its cultural life. The second part of the book is a collection of orally transmitted texts, in transliteration and translation, which help to fill out the sketch of the Sefrou Jewish community and its language as drawn in the book's first section.

HARY's study is a pioneering attempt at incorporating the wealth of Judeo-Arabic literature produced after the Middle Ages into the purview of scholarly research. Hary bemoans the general neglect of what he terms Later and Modern Judeo-Arabic—even among leading scholars of the field—out of a preference for the classical Judeo-Arabic of the medieval period. Building on linguistic research in Arabic, Hary emphasizes the element of multiglossia in Judeo-Arabic and identifies five distinct stages, each with its own multiglossic structure. The centerpiece of Hary's book is a critical edition, translation, and analysis of the Cairene Purim Scroll, a Judeo-Arabic text commemorating the miraculous deliverance of Cairo's Jewish community in 1524. Hary's grammatical study of the Purim Scroll locates that work within the multiglossic history of Judeo-Arabic that he proposes.

DRORY's brief but interesting article explores the cultural context underlying the bilingualism of Jewish literature in the medieval Islamic world. She begins with what she regards as the deliberate choice of Jewish writers to use either Arabic or Hebrew in their works, contending that this choice was determined by "a clear-cut division of functions . . . between the two languages." Arabic, she argues, was used for straightforward expression, serving what Roman Jakobson has termed the "referential function." Hebrew, on the other hand, filled a "literary-aesthetic function" and was used to produce texts that would arouse admiration. Moreover, she insists that each language was laden with its own unique "repertoire of culturally constructed images." As an illustration, Drory compares the Hebrew and Arabic introductions to Saadya's *Sefer ha-Egron* and shows how in each case the choice of language suggested wholly different models of reality.

ARNOLD FRANKLIN

Judeo-Spanish *see* Ladino Literature;
Languages, Jewish

Judges, Book of

Alt, Albrecht, "The Settlement of the Israelites in Palestine," and "The Formation of the Israelite State in Palestine," in his *Essays on Old Testament History and Religion*, translated by R.A. Wilson, Oxford: Blackwell, 1966; Garden City, New York: Doubleday, 1967
Boling, Robert G. (editor), *Judges* (Anchor Bible Series, vol. 6A), Garden City, New York: Doubleday, 1975
Burney, C.F., *The Book of Judges: With Introduction and Notes*, London: Rivingtons, 1918, 2nd edition, 1920; as *The Book of Judges, with Introduction and Notes, and*

Notes on the Hebrew Text of the Book of Kings, with an Introduction and Appendix, New York: Ktav, 1970
Fishelis, Avraham and Shmuel Fishelis, *Judges: A New English Translation* (Judaica Books of the Prophets Series), edited by A.J. Rosenberg, New York: Judaica Press, 1983
Klein, Lillian R., *The Triumph of Irony in the Book of Judges* (Journal for the Study of the Old Testament Supplement Series, 68), Sheffield, South Yorkshire: Almond, 1988
Malamat, Abraham, "The Period of the Judges," in *The World History of the Jewish People*, vol. 3: *Judges*, edited by B. Mazar, New Brunswick, New Jersey: Rutgers University Press, and London: Allen, 1971
Slotki, Judah J., "Introduction and Commentary on Judges," in *Joshua and Judges* (Soncino Books of the Bible Series), edited by A. Cohen, London: Soncino, 1950
Soggin, J. Alberto, *Judges: A Commentary* (Old Testament Library), translated by John Bowden, Philadelphia: Westminster, and London: SCM, 1981

Seventh of the 24 books of the Hebrew Bible, according to the traditional Jewish count, the Book of Judges is the second book of the "Nevi'im Rishonim" or "Historical Prophets." Judges covers the period from the death of Joshua to the eve of the monarchy. The date of the historical events it describes is much debated, but they probably took place sometime between 1300 and 1000 B.C.E. The "judges" of the book are political, military, or prophetic leaders who arise in time of political crisis in order to save one or more of the Israelite tribes from enemy oppressors. The book narrates the careers of six such leaders in detail and six others much more briefly. These judges differ from kings in that they are nondynastic and attain leadership solely because of popular support. The units in chapters three to 16 frequently follow a cycle: the Israelites worship idols rather than God, an enemy oppressor gains the upper hand, and the Israelites cry out to God, who sends a judge to redeem them. Freed from oppression, the Israelites resume their sinful ways. Chapters one and two of the book contain a recapitulation of the conquest, and chapters 17 to 21 contain narratives of particular tribes. The Gideon and Abimelech stories in chapters six to 11 argue strongly against monarchy as an institution. In contrast, chapters 17 to 21 describe political chaos using the refrain "in those days there was no king in Israel."

BOLING has written an omnibus commentary, dealing with philological as well as theological and archaeological issues. The work is well structured, containing a translation followed by a section of largely philological notes, followed by a "comment" section dealing with thematic and theological issues. This division makes the work useful both to interested but casual readers and to advanced students. The introduction deals with the historical background, describing society in the land of Israel as it might have looked at the time of the judges, based on ancient Near Eastern sources. Throughout, Boling uses current knowledge of ancient Near Eastern society to highlight theological messages in the text.

KLEIN shows how important the technique of irony is in the Book of Judges. Because this technique is so pervasive in

Judges, she covers most of the issues of literary art in this biblical book. Influenced by modern narratology, she reads Judges not as an ancient Near Eastern historical text but as literature, to be investigated for its narrative craftsmanship. The ancient Near Eastern context is referred to only to provide background for the irony in the book. Klein is concerned with wordplay and other subtle ways in which irony is present in the story, when subjected to a close reading. This work is useful for casual readers and serious students.

ALT attempts to relate the early history of Canaan (known from extra-biblical sources) to the political structures described in Judges. Many of Alt's conclusions cannot be proven, but the essays are useful summaries of what is known about Canaan in the period described in Judges. Alt argues that the Israelite tribes absorbed many non-Israelite city-states in the monarchy period, and that this was decisive in changing the political character of Israel.

MALAMAT's essay provides more solid treatment of the relationship between the Book of Judges and ancient Near Eastern texts. He recognizes that in fact there is "a complete lack of extra-biblical sources directly pertaining to the historical events of the period of the Judges." He focuses on reconstructing the history of this period by distinguishing between historical and ahistorical sections of the book, arguing that the original story is often historical, but that it is edited into a theological (and ahistorical) framework in order to serve didactic purposes.

SLOTKI provides the best Jewish commentary on Judges available in English, designed to make the text accessible and acceptable to contemporary Jewish readers with little background in Bible. He draws primarily on traditional Jewish commentators and secondarily on modern non-Jewish commentators. His comments focus on difficult words or unfamiliar terms in the text, on points where the plot seems disjointed, and on passages that might be found objectionable by the modern reader, such as Judges 1:6, which speaks of the mutilation of a Canaanite king by the tribe of Judah: "Mutilation does not otherwise seem to have been practised by the Israelites. The same cannot be said for other nations of antiquity. . . ." His commentary also notes verses of particular significance to postbiblical Jewish tradition, for example the connection between Judges 21:19 and the celebration of the 15th of Av. The commentary is brief and well written.

The work of FISHELIS and FISHELIS is primarily an English summary of midrashic, didactic, and homiletical material collected from rabbinic sources and the popular Judeo-Spanish anthology, Me'am Lo'ez. It tends to shy away from the classic medieval Jewish *pashtanim* (plain-sense interpreters) who are the mainstay of other volumes in this series, and whose comments elucidate genuine difficulties in the text. Like the other books in this series, however, it does present the Hebrew text of the Bible, along with Targum Pseudo-Jonathan, Rashi, Kimhi, Gersonides, and the Metsudot (the commentaries contained in the Lublin Rabbinic Bible) and on the facing page, an English translation of the biblical text, together with an English digest of traditional Jewish commentary. This particular volume's approach to its selection of commentary is foreshadowed by the simplistic approach expressed in the introduction: "The main lesson of the book, in short, is to teach us that we are completely under God's supervision." One wonders why 21 chapters of highly sophisticated prose and two millennia of interpretation are necessary if the plain sense of the narrative can be adequately distilled in this one-sentence moral lesson.

BURNEY's commentary is a classic product of early-20th-century biblical scholarship. He is concerned with determining authorship of different sections of the book, with the book's structure, and with establishing the "original" text of Judges. He also devotes much space (chiefly in the introduction) to "external information bearing on the period." He summarizes a great deal of ancient Near Eastern research, some of which is really more relevant to Kings, and much of which was only thought to be relevant at all in the excitement that accompanied 19th-century discoveries of Assyrian, Babylonian, and Egyptian texts. Several useful maps integrating then-new knowledge of biblical geography are included, showing sites thought in 1918 to be identifiable with events of Judges.

SOGGIN's commentary is chiefly of use to those versed in academic biblical scholarship. It contains extensive discussions aiming to establish the "correct" text of Judges, based on the Septuagint and other ancient versions. Discussions are often philological or structural and tend to ignore narrative studies and theology. The commentary integrates some material from ancient Near Eastern studies. The book contains a translation, a verse-by-verse commentary, and a discussion of each chapter's structure.

SHAWN ZELIG ASTER

Justice *see* Sanhedrin, Semikhah, and Rabbinate

K

Kabbalah: Translations

Dan, Joseph and Ron Kiener (editors), *The Early Kabbalah* (Classics of Western Spirituality), New York: Paulist, 1986

Englander, Lawrence A. with Herbert W. Basser, *The Mystical Study of Ruth: Midrash HaNe'elam of the Zohar to the Book of Ruth* (South Florida Studies in the History of Judaism, no. 75), Atlanta, Georgia: Scholars Press, 1993

Fine, Lawrence, *Safed Spirituality: Rules of Mystical Piety, the Beginning of Wisdom* (Classics of Western Spirituality), New York: Paulist, 1984

Gikatilla, Joseph ben Abraham, *Gates of Light/Sha'are Orah* (Bronfman Library of Jewish Classics), translated by Avi Weinstein, San Francisco: HarperCollins, 1994

Ginsburg, Elliot K. (editor), *Sod ha-Shabbat/The Mystery of the Sabbath: From the Tola'at Yáaqov of Meir ibn Gabbai* (SUNY Series in Judaica), Albany: State University of New York Press, 1989

Green, Arthur, *Keter: The Crown of God in Early Jewish Mysticism*, Princeton, New Jersey, and Chichester, West Sussex: Princeton University Press, 1997

Krassen, Miles (editor), *The Generations of Adam* (Classics of Western Spirituality), New York: Paulist, 1996

Matt, Daniel Chanan, *Zohar: The Book of Enlightenment* (Classics of Western Spirituality), New York: Paulist, and London: SPCK, 1983

Matt, Daniel Chanan, *The Essential Kabbalah: The Heart of Jewish Mysticism*, San Francisco: HarperSanFrancisco, 1995

Scholem, Gershom, *Zohar: The Book of Splendor* (Schocken Library, 19), New York: Schocken, 1949; London: Rider, 1977

Sperling, Harry, Maurice Simon, and Paul P. Levertoff (editors), *The Zohar*, 5 vols., London: Soncino, 1931–1934; New York: Bennet, 1958; 2nd edition, London: Soncino, 1984

Tishby, Isaiah and Yeruham Fischel Lachower, *Mishnat ha-Zohar*, 2 vols., Jerusalem: Mosad Bialik, 1969; translated by David Goldstein as *The Wisdom of the Zohar*, 3 vols., Oxford: Oxford University Press, 1991

Verman, Mark, *The Books of Contemplation: Medieval Jewish Mystical Sources* (SUNY Series in Judaica), Albany: State University of New York Press, 1992

Wald, Stephen G., *The Doctrine of the Divine Name: An Introduction to Classical Kabbalistic Theology* (Brown Judaic Studies, no. 149), Atlanta, Georgia: Scholars Press, 1988

Kabbalistic texts are difficult. They are often characterized by dense, allusive writing styles. The central kabbalistic work, the Zohar, is written in a particularly obscure Aramaic, so that from the very first century of its circulation, sections of it were translated into Hebrew for the edification of larger segments of the populace. As the Zohar and other works circulated through the West during the Renaissance, they were the object of intense interest. Italian Neoplatonists, working in conjunction with kabbalists who were flirting with apostasy, translated the Zohar, Joseph Gikatilla's *Gates of Light*, and other important works into Latin. In all these cases, the simple assumption was that if the canon of Jewish mysticism were only translated, it would thereby become accessible. In fact, this has seldom been the case, and certain source texts in Kabbalah may arguably be untranslatable, owing to their various levels of nuance, pun, and concrete poetic meaning. Nonetheless, ever since the Renaissance, issues of style have not prevented a few idealists from attempting to render the teachings of Jewish mysticism in various other vernaculars.

Today, with the flowering of interest in spiritual traditions, the process of translation continues unabated. The following comprise a selection of some of the better translations of kabbalistic works. In referring to them as such, it must be stressed that an important body of mystical writings, namely the literature of Hasidism, falls outside of this category and rightfully occupies a niche all its own in Jewish literature.

The literature of the early Kabbalah is represented in three studies. Mark VERMAN's edition of *The Books of Contemplation* was the first critical edition in any language of these important works. Selections from these works as well as the most representative texts of the first flowering of Kabbalah in Provence and Gerona are available in DAN and KIENER's *The Early Kabbalah*, which also has impressive notes. GREEN's *Keter* is an important study of the process through which ancient postbiblical motifs of the divine monarch gave way to the theoretical portrayal of this realm of monarchy as synonymous with the highest emanation (*sefirah*) of existence, the aforementioned *Keter*. Verman and Green's translations are academic studies in their own right, while Kiener and Dan's work represents a popular edition with scholarly proprieties, in line with the editorial policies of the Paulist Press *Classics of Western Spirituality* series.

SPERLING, SIMON, and LEVERTOFF's translation of the Zohar, the central work of Jewish mysticism, covers about half the full work and features some erroneous translations. It seems that the translators' understandings of the work's symbolic nuances were incomplete. Far superior is TISHBY and LACHOWER's *The Wisdom of the Zohar*, which includes extensive topical introductions and excellent translations of a number of sections. MATT (1983) and SCHOLEM have produced popular editions, each of which consists of short, widely circulated sections. Matt's work is distinguished by a readable introduction and excellent notes. WALD provides a good translation of an obscure yet important passage from the Zohar; this work also serves as the first critical edition of any Zoharic text. ENGLANDER's translation of the Zohar on Ruth presents a previously unavailable section of that work. GIKATILLA's aforementioned *Gates of Light*, a work from the same medieval milieu as the Zohar, has been rendered in an excellent translation, with good notes, by Weinstein.

The vast literature of the period following the publication of the Zohar has been particularly neglected by the academy. Three volumes are of particular importance, in that they reproduce works influenced by the Zohar. GINSBURG's translation of Meir ibn Gabbai's *Sod ha-Shabbat (The Mystery of the Sabbath)* is the first example of post-Zoharic mysticism to reach a general audience. FINE's book has made available a number of writings of the Safed mystics, highlighting the severe and bleak asceticism that lay at the heart of much of their thought. KRASSEN has produced an important translation of a section of *Shenei Luhot ha-Berit (The Two Tablets of the Covenant,* also known as *Shelah)*, a widely circulated early 17th-century work drenched in the teachings of the Safed renaissance. Finally, for the reader wishing to take a few first steps in the mystical orchard, MATT (1995) provides the best introduction to the texts.

PINCHAS GILLER

See also Kabbalah: Introductions; Zohar

Kabbalah: Introductions

Fine, Lawrence (editor), *Essential Papers on Kabbalah* (Essential Papers on Jewish Studies), New York: New York University Press, 1995

Ginsburg, Elliot K., *The Sabbath in the Classical Kabbalah* (SUNY Series in Judaica), Albany: State University of New York Press, 1989

Halamish, Mosheh, *An Introduction to the Kabbalah* (SUNY Series in Judaica), Albany: State University of New York Press, 1999

Halperin, David, *The Faces of the Chariot: Early Jewish Responses to Ezekiel's Vision* (Texte und Studien zum antiken Judentum, 16), Tübingen: Mohr, 1988

Idel, Moshe, *Kabbalah: New Perspectives*, New Haven, Connecticut: Yale University Press, 1988

Liebes, Yehuda, *Studies in Jewish Myth and Jewish Messianism* (SUNY Series in Judaica), Albany: State University of New York Press, 1993

Scholem, Gershom, *Major Trends in Jewish Mysticism* (Hilda Strook Lectures), New York: Schocken, 1941; 3rd edition, New York: Schocken, 1954; London: Thames and Hudson, 1955

Scholem, Gershom, *Ursprung und Anfänge der Kabbala*, 1962; translated by Allan Arkush as *Origins of the Kabbalah*, edited by R.J. Zwi Werblowsky, Princeton, New Jersey: Princeton University Press, 1987

Scholem, Gershom, *On the Kabbalah and Its Symbolism*, New York: Schocken, and London: Routledge and Kegan Paul, 1965

Scholem, Gershom, *Kabbalah* (Library of Jewish Knowledge), New York: Quadrangle/New York Times, 1974

Scholem, Gershom, *On the Mystical Shape of the Godhead: Basic Concepts in the Kabbalah*, New York: Schocken 1991

Wolfson, Elliot, *Through a Speculum That Shines: Vision and Imagination in Medieval Jewish Mysticism*, Princeton, New Jersey: Princeton University Press, 1994

Wolfson, Elliot, *Along the Path: Studies in Kabbalistic Myth, Symbolism, and Hermeneutics*, Albany: State University of New York Press, 1995

Wolfson, Elliot, *Circle in the Square: Studies in the Use of Gender in Kabbalistic Symbolism*, Albany: State University of New York Press, 1995

Among the major achievements of Jewish studies has been the reintroduction of Kabbalah to the spiritual and scholarly discourse of modernity. Kabbalah was much maligned by Heinrich Graetz and other exponents of the *Wissenschaft* school of thought characteristic of 19th-century Jewish scholarship. Hasidism, which Graetz viewed as a melange of superstition and social recidivism, was reappraised by the existentialist philosopher Martin Buber and by Hillel Zeitlin, martyr of the Warsaw ghetto. Kabbalah was similarly due for reappraisal, and a redeemer arose in the mid-20th century in the form of Gershom Scholem of the Hebrew University of Jerusalem.

SCHOLEM (1941) is a seminal linear presentation of the development of Jewish mysticism, tracing Kabbalah from its origins in the mystery traditions of antiquity through its flowering in the Zohar and the teachings of the Safed mystics into the present-day hasidic movement. Scholem's elegant study is undisputedly the prerequisite work for the beginning student of Kabbalah.

Scholem's 1941 work, however, neglects the mysterious recrudescence of Kabbalah in 12th-century Provence and Catalonia and it does not discuss the influence of the mysterious book *Bahir,* the subject of Scholem's doctoral thesis. These desiderata were rectified in SCHOLEM (1962). SCHOLEM (1974) reproduces all the articles Scholem contributed to the *Encyclopaedia Judaica*, and, as a monograph, this compilation may be too dense for the lay reader. Two English works, SCHOLEM (1965) and SCHOLEM (1991), together translate Scholem's Hebrew work *Essential Chapters in the Understanding of the Kabbalah and Its Symbolism.*

After Scholem's death, a new generation of scholars began to reexamine his portrayal of kabbalistic history and to develop some new ideas. The first and most self-conscious reassessment is that of Moshe Idel. Idel has written extensively on the neglected oeuvre of the 13th-century kabbalist Abraham Abulafia. In his comprehensive statement on Kabbalah, IDEL questions the historiographical premises of Scholem's work, particularly the latter's portrayal of later Kabbalah as a messianic juggernaut fueled by a response to history. Idel elevates the theoreticians of mystical speculation, whom Scholem considered somewhat ancillary, to a central role in kabbalistic history, emphasising the influence of figures such as Abulafia, Moses Cordovero, and Menahem Recanati. He argues for the continuing relevance of these mystics in such later phenomena as Hasidism.

A more traditional approach to continuing Scholem's research is evident in LIEBES. Liebes has chosen the central canonical traditions of Kabbalah, namely the Zohar, the Lurianic tradition, and the best known hasidic masters, as his areas of specialization. His research posits a messianic tradition whose origins are in the Zohar itself. This tradition extends through the Safed renaissance, the Sabbatian heresy, and into Hasidism. In Liebes's view, this tradition bifurcates into a continuing struggle between light and darkness, in which Shabbetai Tsevi's mystical heresy evolved into a satanic force that vanquished such original hasidic masters as the Ba'al Shem Tov and Rabbi Nahman of Bratslav.

Wolfson has adopted Scholem's method of examining given ideas and phenomena as they evolve through the historical processes of Jewish thought. WOLFSON (1994) is a sweeping work that moves toward identifying an underlying myth in Kabbalah that is sharply divergent from the portrayals of earlier scholars. In this work as well as in the articles collected in WOLFSON (1995a and 1995b), one may chart his progress towards this understanding. According to Wolfson, the inner mystique of Kabbalah is the process in which enlightenment brings on a crossing of gender boundaries, so that the masculine becomes the feminine and vice versa. This process of "oracular phallocentrism" comprises at the very least a crucial dimension of Jewish esotericism.

HALAMISH provides an overview of Kabbalah with particular attention to the philosophical issues. Halamish's approach is phenomenological and serves as a refreshing counter to the historiographical thinking so prevalent among Scholem's students. This work addresses aspects of the kabbalistic tradition in light of their relationship to general Jewish thought, as opposed to their role in the phenomenology of mysticism, collecting important sources from across the historical development of Kabbalah.

FINE includes a number of important essays by distinguished contributors to the contemporary discourse on Jewish mysticism. Two key essays included in this collection are Daniel Chanan Matt's inquiry into the concept of the mystical void in Jewish mysticism, "Ayin: The Concept of Nothingness in Jewish Mysticism," and an excellent article by Chava Weissler on Ashkenazi women's spirituality.

Certain studies provide cogent introductions to specific areas within the field of Kabbalah broadly conceived. HALPERIN is an engrossing portrayal of the early period of Jewish mysticism rooted in contemplation of the *merkabah*, the chariot described in the oblique first chapter of the Book of Ezekiel. Halperin's work portrays the *merkabah* tradition as the esoteric core of Pharisaism and analyzes the revelation experience of these talmudic mystics of Roman Palestine in bold psychological terms.

GINSBURG reviews the mystical underpinnings of traditional Jewish sabbath observance. His study concludes before the innovations of the Safed renaissance, concentrating on the teachings of the Zohar and of the mystics of the first generations after the Zohar's appearance. Ginsburg defines the mystical conception of the sabbath and its rituals in terms of the creation of sacred space, a notion that has had considerable resonance in the study of world religions.

PINCHAS GILLER

See also Kabbalah: Translations; Zohar

Kahane, Meir 1932–1990

American-born Israeli vigilante and political activist

Cohen-Almagor, Raphael, *The Boundaries of Liberty and Tolerance: The Struggle against Kahanism in Israel*, Gainesville: University Press of Florida, 1994

Dolgin, Janet L., *Jewish Identity and the JDL*, Princeton, New Jersey: Princeton University Press, 1977

Friedman, Robert I., *The False Prophet: Rabbi Meir Kahane, from FBI Informant to Knesset Member*, Brooklyn, New York: Lawrence Hill, and London: Faber and Faber, 1990

Mergui, Raphaël, *Meïr Kahane: Le rabbin qui fait peur aux juifs*, 1985; translated by Philippe Simonnot as *Israel's Ayatollahs: Meir Kahane and the Far Right in Israel*, London and Atlantic Highlands, New Jersey: Saqi, 1987

Shamir, Michal, "Kach and the Limits to Political Tolerance in Israel" in *Israel's Odd Couple: The 1984 Knesset Elections and the National Unity Government*, edited by Daniel Judah Elazar and Shmuel Sandler, Detroit, Michigan: Wayne State University Press, 1990

Sprinzak, Ehud, *The Ascendance of Israel's Radical Right*, New York: Oxford University Press, 1991

Meir Kahane was born Martin David Kahane into a rabbinical yet highly nationalist family. His father adhered to Revisionist Zionism rather than the more moderate Religious Zionism of the Mizrachi movement. Kahane grew up in the subculture of Betar, the Revisionist Zionist youth group, and idolized its founder, Vladimir Ze'ev Jabotinsky, the archetypal fin de siècle Jewish intellectual. Jabotinsky had been a role model for a generation of youth including Menahem Begin and Avraham Stern. His advocacy of a proud nationalism, his celebration of military prowess, his promotion of *hadar* ("dignity") and ritual, and his elevation of individualism attracted them. Betar, however, had become far more radical than its mentor and was heavily influenced by a Zionist far right as well as the authoritarianism of statist European regimes of the 1930s. Kahane's coming of age coincided with the revelations of the Holocaust and the struggle for an independent Jewish state. All of this helped to forge a social container for his insecurities and aimlessness, endowing him with a sense of purpose as well as delusions of political grandeur.

FRIEDMAN documents these early years in a revealing account in the tradition of investigative journalism. Friedman is particularly illuminating in detailing Kahane's alternate life as the bareheaded, secular Michael King, provider of information for the Federal Bureau of Investigation and intrepid sexual explorer. Friedman also documents the sources of financial support for Kahane's activities and projects, including the comedian Jackie Mason and New York's Syrian Jewish community.

It was perhaps his admiration for Jabotinsky that drew Kahane toward the world of journalism and polemicism. In the 1960s he began a long association with the ultraorthodox, far-right Brooklyn-based *Jewish Press*. His regular broadsides against liberals, leftists, assimilationists, secularists, opponents of orthodoxy, and perceived enemies of the Jewish people made a significant contribution in developing the paper's popular appeal.

Half of MERGUI's journalistic account is devoted to a long interview with Kahane, concentrating in particular on Kahane's views on Israel as a Torah state and his assertion that Judaism and democratic values are in opposition. In the 1980s Kahane wrote several tracts on relations between Jews and non-Jews, but long before, in 1968, he had founded the Jewish Defence League (JDL) in response to an explosion of black militancy with its demand for affirmative action and community control.

Kahane's talent for public relations and the marketing of images and slogans as well as the vigilante character of the JDL attracted large numbers of youth. It propelled Kahane and his approach into the national arena and offered a magnetic alternative to the pedestrianism of the Jewish establishment. DOLGIN argues cogently that this approach provided a way of life, a mindset, and an identity for many disaffected young Jews from a variety of backgrounds. By 1970 the JDL had embarked on a campaign of hit-and-run violence, which included plans to bomb Soviet institutions and black community centers, assassinations of PLO officials, and the hijacking of an Egyptian airliner. The retaliation by the authorities to these events led many members of the JDL, including Kahane, to depart for Israel.

SPRINZAK's book on the Israeli far right contains the best analysis in English of Kahane's sojourn in Israel and his Kach party. Sprinzak writes that Kahane was able to "attract bitter and insecure people who project a sense of failure: failure in the Israeli economy, failure to identify with the nation's symbols of legitimacy." Sprinzak examines Kahane's theory of revenge and the call for Jewish isolationism, catastrophic messianism, xenophobia, social Darwinism, and racist symbolism. Kahane's election to the Knesset in 1984 came at a time when the idea of "transferring" the Palestinians out of Israel and the West Bank was beginning to gain political credence. SHAMIR details the political constellation of social forces in the 1984 election, which permitted Kach—a quasi-fascist movement, according to Sprinzak—to gain national legitimacy with a seat in the Knesset. Although opinion polls indicated growing support for Kahane, the Central Elections Commit-

tee disqualified Kach two weeks before the 1988 election. This move relegated Kach once more to a vociferous extraparliamentary group. Even so, its activities in the 1980s aroused the increasing concern of intellectuals and educators who viewed Kahanism as a racist pollutant in Israeli life. These activities also provoked profound discussions in legal circles on the status of such a movement in the Jewish state, an issue that COHEN-ALMAGOR expounds at length. As all non-hagiographic studies indicate, Kahane was an unstable figure who did not possess the intelligence of Jabotinsky or the political ability of Begin. Despite his undeniable charm, Kahane exuded a propensity to fantasize and possessed an inability to work as a team player. Inevitably, he disagreed and argued with those who could have assisted him and his movement to gain legitimacy and power.

COLIN SHINDLER

Kaplan, Mordecai Menahem 1881–1983

Lithuanian-born American rabbi, founder of the Reconstructionist movement

Breslauer, S. Daniel, *Mordecai Kaplan's Thought in a Postmodern Age* (South Florida-Rochester-Saint Louis Studies on Religion and the Social Order, vol. 8), Atlanta, Georgia: Scholars Press, 1994

Goldsmith, Emanuel S., Mel Scult, and Robert M. Seltzer, *The American Judaism of Mordecai M. Kaplan* (Reappraisals in Jewish Social and Intellectual History), New York: New York University Press, 1990

Gurock, Jeffrey S. and Jacob J. Schacter, *A Modern Heretic and a Traditional Community: Mordecai M. Kaplan, Orthodoxy, and American Judaism*, New York: Columbia University Press, 1996

Libowitz, Richard, *Mordecai M. Kaplan and the Development of Reconstructionism* (Studies in American Religion, vol. 9), New York: Mellen, 1983

Scult, Mel, *Judaism Faces the Twentieth Century: A Biography of Mordecai M. Kaplan* (American Jewish Civilization), Detroit, Michigan: Wayne State University Press, 1993

Mordecai Kaplan's life and thought have recently been the subject of renewed interest, following a period of quiescence immediately after his death in 1983. The Reconstructionist Jewish movement that he started has expanded to become a fourth denomination in North American Jewish life, and as the movement has evolved in new directions, a number of studies have examined Kaplan's unique American Judaism.

Kaplan's program of Reconstructionism represented a uniquely American approach to the problems of adjusting Judaism to the modern, secular, and scientific norms of the 20th century. He remained ambivalent throughout his life about whether his program constituted the seeds of a fourth Jewish denomination alongside Reform, Conservatism, and Orthodoxy or was instead a "school of thought" designed to be applied across the spectrum of the existing movements. But

Kaplan was unambiguous and unrelenting in his insistence that a supernatural Judaism could not survive. His thinking proceeds from the assumption that Judaism is the evolving religious civilization of the Jewish people rather than the supernatural revelation of God. All of the specific categories of Kaplan's thought and program flow from this fundamental and radical revision of the claims of inherited tradition.

SCULT's biography investigates the life and thought of Kaplan through 1934. Scult describes Kaplan's family of origin and his adult relationships, adding vivid private details to the better-known story of Kaplan's public and intellectual life. Scult's extensive use of Kaplan's diaries is a major strength of this sympathetic treatment, for these diaries reveal Kaplan's feelings of insecurity, uncertainty, and apprehension regarding his literary abilities and his chosen professional path. Scult's treatment of Kaplan's acceptance, vacillation, and then rejection of his appointment to head the Jewish Institute of Religion sheds new light on a well-known career crisis in Kaplan's life. The author's analysis represents a revision of several commonly held assumptions about Kaplan, both in intellectual and personal terms. For example, Scult disputes arguments that Kaplan's thought was derivative of the work of Emile Durkheim and John Dewey. In general, the author argues that Kaplan's thought was original and that he was an intellectual pioneer, rather than the eminent synthesizer of emerging intellectual trends typically described in other accounts.

LIBOWITZ's insightful study offers an intellectual analysis of the major streams of Jewish and general academic thought that were synthesized in the emerging Kaplan program of Reconstructionism. While Scult argues for the originality of Kaplan's thinking, Libowitz supports the more common view that he was a derivative albeit creatively synthetic thinker; for example, Libowitz argues that Kaplan relied on the sociology of Emile Durkheim, a hypothesis that Scult challenges.

GUROCK and SCHACTER, writing from the perspective of contemporary Orthodoxy, are less sympathetic than Scult and Libowitz toward Kaplan's naturalistic treatment of Judaism as the product of the Jewish people and his rejection of the doctrine of scriptural revelation. The study covers the early years of Kaplan's rabbinic career, follows him through his gradual break with Orthodoxy between 1915–1922, and then argues that Kaplan and the leadership of Orthodoxy continued to interact thereafter. Kaplan maintained an almost unique position as an English-speaking, Orthodox-trained rabbi who was able to speak to the children of Orthodox immigrants, and this fact partially explains why certain Orthodox lay leaders indulged Kaplan's increasingly public deviance from traditional thought and practice.

BRESLAUER's book challenges the common assumption that Kaplan's thought is uncritically steeped in the assumptions of modernity and consequently only interesting as a particular example of an eclipsed era in U.S. Jewish thought. Breslauer asserts that the framework and content of Kaplan's thought are uniquely open to the insights of postmodernism, an intellectual movement that Kaplan anticipated by several generations.

GOLDSMITH, SCULT, and SELTZER have edited a comprehensive analysis of the major categories of Kaplan's thinking, with contributions from 19 scholars under five headings:

"Contexts," "Stages in a Life," "Intellectual Contemporaries," "Reinterpreting Judaism," and "The Ideologist." This anthology complements Ira Eisenstein and Eugene Kohn's earlier study, *Mordecai M. Kaplan, An Evaluation* (1952); read together, these two texts chronicle Kaplan's life and explain his very considerable influence on 20th-century U.S. Judaism.

RICHARD HIRSH

Karaites

Ankori, Zvi, *Karaites in Byzantium: The Formative Years, 970–1100*, New York: Columbia University Press, 1959

Birnbaum, Philip (compiler), *Karaite Studies*, New York: Hermon, 1971

Gil, Moshe, *A History of Palestine, 634–1099*, Cambridge and New York: Cambridge University Press, 1992

Mann, Jacob, *Texts and Studies in Jewish History and Literature*, vol. 2: *Karaitica*, Cincinnati, Ohio: Hebrew Union College Press, 1931

Miller, Philip E., *Karaite Separatism in Nineteenth-Century Russia: Joseph Solomon Lutski's "Epistle of Israel's Deliverance,"* Cincinnati, Ohio: Hebrew Union College Press, 1993

Nemoy, Leon, *Karaite Anthology*, New Haven, Connecticut: Yale University Press, 1952

Polliack, Meira, *The Karaite Tradition of Arabic Bible Translation*, New York: Brill, 1997

Wieder, Naphtali, *The Judean Scrolls and Karaism*, London: East and West Library, 1962

The Karaites are a Jewish sect whose teachings reject the authority of Rabbanite tradition and leadership, refuting the concept of the Oral Law and talmudic literature and recognizing the Hebrew Bible as the only divinely revealed authoritative source for law. Karaism emerged, along with a number of other non-rabbinic Jewish groups, in the Islamic Middle East during the eighth and ninth centuries, and the sect posed a serious challenge to Rabbanite leadership in the tenth and 11th centuries. Subsequently, small but flourishing Karaite communities were found at various times in Constantinople, the Crimea, and Poland-Lithuania. Karaism still exists, mainly in Israel. Most significant contemporary studies of Karaism are published in journal articles, but there are a number of important books on the topic.

MANN's massive collection presents a wide range of studies covering all periods of Karaite history, accompanied by Karaite texts in English translation. Avoiding the difficult question of Karaite origins, the book is divided into three major sections. In the first section, Mann deals with the important early period, from the ninth through the 11th century, when Karaites settled in Palestine (especially Jerusalem) and developed a "keen intellectual rivalry [with the rabbis] concerning the theological ideas of Judaism and the interpretations of the Bible." Section two investigates the Karaites of Byzantium, Turkey, and the Crimea, focusing on the 16th through the 18th century. The third section discusses the Karaites in Lithuania and Poland, with special attention given to communal organization, economics, and relations with the Rabbanites. This book remains a foundation for serious inquiry into Karaism.

NEMOY's book is the best introduction to Karaism, both for the general and the academic reader. Its chapters on individual Karaite thinkers are arranged in chronological order, starting with the eighth-century figure Anan ben David, who is acknowledged by many Karaites as the movement's founder, and concluding with the 15th-century codifier of Karaite law, Elijah Bashyazi. Each chapter introduces a Karaite author and provides a selection from his texts in English translation. This work is Nemoy's only book on Karaites, although his journal articles are among the most important in the field.

WIEDER tackles the difficult problem of possible connections between the Dead Sea Scrolls and Karaite religious thought, noting their similar ideologies, exegetical methods, and phraseologies. According to Wieder, these correspondences suggest that contributors of the first-century C.E. Qumran community survived into the ninth century and influenced early Karaites. Wieder's theory has influenced some subsequent scholarship, but it remains controversial. This is the best book-length treatment of the subject.

GIL's book on Palestine covering the period from the rise of Islam until the Crusades covers much more than the history of the Karaites, but his chapter titled "Karaites and Samaritans" is the only up-to-date, synthetic treatment of Karaite florescence in the early period. In addition to this chapter, references to the Karaites abound throughout this major work. Gil presents the problem of Karaite origins with care, demonstrating the issue's complexity by identifying many possible antecedents to fully developed medieval Karaism. His carefully researched footnotes provide the reader with a complete introduction to scholarship on Karaites.

POLLIACK focuses on Karaite translation of the Bible into Arabic in the early period, while directing the reader's attention to large ideological issues. She demonstrates that the methodology of Karaite translators reflected scripturalist attitudes toward the biblical text and rejected much traditional (usually rabbinic) biblical interpretation. The Karaites valued direct interrogation of the text, while reacting against Rabbanite interpretive notions and translation techniques. These Karaite attitudes led to a kind of medieval individualism based upon technical linguistic expertise, which resulted in multiple voices within Karaism. Polliack also argues that these methods have antecedents in pre-Karaite Jewish traditions. This important contribution to Jewish Bible studies in the Middle Ages assumes of the reader an acquaintance with classical Hebrew grammar background.

ANKORI investigates the transfer of Karaite scholarship and leadership from the Islamic world to the Orthodox Christian domains of the Byzantine Empire. Drawing from primary sources that range from the tenth through the 15th century, he interprets several Karaite manuscripts that had been overlooked by other scholars. Ankori demonstrates that Byzantine conquests of Muslim territories in the tenth century led to an influx of Karaite Jews into Constantinople, where they embarked on a massive "Hebrew literary project" to translate their texts from Arabic into Hebrew and to transform their ideology. He carefully contextualizes this centuries-long process against the background of Christian dominion and Rabbanite dominance. Sometimes very technical in its presentation, this is an important work of Karaite studies and requires careful reading.

MILLER's work is the only book-length study in English that deals with the Karaites of Eastern Europe in a balanced manner. The Eastern European Karaites' movement away from Jewish identity since the early 19th century has inspired an apologetic and polemical literature based on questionable scholarship. Miller critically examines the beginnings of Russian Karaite separatism in the wake of the partition of Poland in 1795, demonstrating that the widening of the rift originated when Simhah Babovich, a Crimean Karaite leader, traveled to St. Petersburg in 1827 to seek an exemption for the Karaites from czarist anti-Jewish legislation. The successful outcome of this mission laid the foundations for Karaite institutional separation from Rabbanite Judaism, which in the 20th century encouraged the Karaites to assimilate their religion to European models and establish an ethnic identity based upon non-Judaic characteristics.

BIRNBAUM collects seven of the most important journal articles on Karaism into his volume. Three of these essays, including the book-length article "The Karaite Literary Opponents of Saadia Gaon," are by Samuel Poznanski, the founder of 20th-century Karaite studies. Other topics covered here include Karaite liturgy and the reading of the Torah (by Jacob Mann); the historical evidence for Anan ben David (by Leon Nemoy); and a comparison of Karaite halakhah with the halakhah of the Sadducees, the Samaritans, and Philo (by Bernard Revel). Birnbaum's volume is essential to Karaite studies.

FRED ASTREN

Kashrut *see* Dietary Laws

Kaufmann, Yehezkel 1889–1963
Ukrainian-born Israeli biblical historian

Greenberg, Moshe, *Studies in the Bible and Jewish Thought* (JPS Scholar of Distinction Series), Philadelphia: Jewish Publication Society, 1995.

Kaufmann, Yehezkel, *Toldot ha-Emunah ha-Yisre'elit*, 1937; translated and abridged by Moshe Greenberg as *The Religion of Israel: From Its Beginnings to the Babylonian Exile*, Chicago: University of Chicago, and London: Allen and Unwin, 1960

Kaufmann, Yehezkel, *Ha-Sipur ha-Mikra'i 'al kibush ha-arets*, 1955; translated by M. Dagut as *The Biblical Account of the Conquest of Canaan*, Jerusalem: Magnes Press of Hebrew University, 1985

Kaufmann, Yehezkel, *History of the Religion of Israel*, vol. 4: *From the Babylonian Captivity to the End of Prophecy*, translated by C.W. Efroymson, New York: Ktav, 1977

Kaufmann, Yehezkel, *Christianity and Judaism: Two Covenants,* translated by C.W. Efroymson, Jerusalem: Magnes, 1988, 2nd edition, 1996

Knohl, Israel, *Mikdash ha-demamah,* 1992; translated by Jackie Feldman and Peretz Rodman as *The Sanctuary of Silence: The Priestly Torah and the Holiness School,* Minneapolis, Minnesota: Fortress, 1995

Levenson, Jon, "Yehezkel Kaufmann and Mythology," *Conservative Judaism,* 36(2), 1982

Potok, Chaim, "The Mourners of Yehezkel Kaufmann," *Conservative Judaism,* 18(2), 1964

Schwarz, Leo (editor), *Great Ages and Ideas of the Jewish People,* New York: Random House, 1956

Talmon, Shemaryahu, "Yehezkel Kaufmann's Approach to Biblical Research," *Conservative Judaism,* 25(2), 1971

Tigay, Jeffrey, *You Shall Have No Other Gods: Israelite Religion in the Light of Hebrew Inscriptions* (Harvard Semitic Studies, 31), Atlanta, Georgia: Scholars Press, 1986

Yehezkel Kaufmann, a leading scholar of Bible and Jewish history and professor of Bible at the Hebrew University in the last years of his life, exerts a vast influence on modern Jewish biblical scholarship. His eight-volume magnum opus, *Toldot ha-Emunah ha-Yisre'elit* (History of Israelite Religion), published between 1937 and 1957, has been central in setting the agenda of Israeli biblical criticism. The first seven volumes of this work (covering the period from Israel's origins to the beginning of the Babylonian exile—that is, up until the prophet Ezekiel) are abridged and translated in KAUFMANN (1960). The last volume (covering the late exilic and postexilic era—that is, from Deutero-Isaiah through the end of the biblical canon) is translated in its entirety in KAUFMANN (1977). A convenient summary of Kaufmann's approach appears in his own contribution to SCHWARZ's collection, and a portrait of this lonely but much admired scholar emerges from the touching article by POTOK.

Kaufmann's thesis in his classic work is in part a response to earlier biblical critical theories, especially those associated with the seminal work of Julius Wellhausen. Kaufmann maintains that Israelite religion was monotheistic from a very early period. He rejects the view that monotheism emerged only in the exilic period as the result of a long development from paganism. According to Kaufmann, even Israelite folk religion was monotheistic well before the period of the monarchy. By monotheism, Kaufmann means not only the belief in one God, but moreover the belief that this one God is supreme over nature, unaffected by magic, and beyond mythology. So unfamiliar were Israelites with paganism that they completely misunderstood the nature of idolatry, thinking that pagans actually worshiped wood and stones rather than the gods represented by them. The many biblical diatribes against foreign religions testify to the completely monotheistic religion of the Israelites precisely because these diatribes misrepresent the worship and faith of Israel's neighbors; had the Israelites actually participated in that worship, they could not possibly have portrayed it so inaccurately. Because he insists that Israelites were so little tainted by paganism, Kaufmann must deny the portrayal of backsliding Israelites found in many biblical texts.

The prophets and the authors of Kings exaggerate the extent of polytheism among Israelites, partly as a result of their need to justify the punishment the Israelites faced. While Kaufmann asserts that monotheism's emergence represented a revolutionary change rather than an evolutionary process, he emphasizes an evolution within Israelite monotheism from early priestly texts to later prophetic ones. Earlier texts do not fully develop the implications of monotheism, but classical prophets such as Isaiah and Jeremiah espouse ideas that follow from the radical monotheism of the Bible, such as the eventual recognition of the one God by all humanity and the primacy of morality over cult.

Kaufmann departs from earlier and contemporary biblical critics especially in one other way: he dates all the sources of the Pentateuch to the preexilic period. Wellhausen and his followers viewed the priestly sections as the Pentateuch's latest strand, reflecting the degeneration of pristine prophetic religion into dry and lifeless legalism. Kaufmann critiques the proofs Wellhausen used to support his late dating and consequently views priestly texts as among the very earliest Israelite documents that have survived. Thus these clearly monotheistic texts help testify to the original and central role that monotheism played throughout Israelite history.

Another aspect of Kaufmann's insistence on the absolute separation between Israelite religion and its pagan neighbors appears in KAUFMANN (1955). There he argues that the general picture in the Book of Joshua is accurate: the Israelites entered Canaan from the outside and conquered its highlands in a swift military campaign. Consequently, relatively little intercourse between Israelites and Canaanites took place at the outset of Israel's history, and thus the Israelites knew little of paganism.

Kaufmann's proposals have been variously received. Many contemporary scholars agree that priestly material is early, but a majority continue to view it as late. KNOHL presents what amounts to a synthesis of the two positions: he shows that the central stratum of priestly legislation and narrative is early, but he also identifies a distinct stratum in Leviticus and Numbers that was composed during the late preexilic and exilic periods. Much of Wellhausen's evidence for the lateness of priestly texts in fact comes from this separate document. Knohl's work also contains a useful bibliography on the voluminous literature relating to the dating of priestly material in the Pentateuch. Kaufmann's insistence (in conflict with both modern scholarship and the testimony of prophets such as Hosea and Jeremiah) that few Israelites actually prayed to gods other than YHWH has received support from TIGAY. He notes that archaeological evidence does not support the claim that ancient Israelites were polytheistic; Israelite names found on ancient artifacts and documents refer often to YHWH but almost never to non-Israelite gods. Nonetheless, Kaufmann's notion of an absolute break between paganism and monotheism is probably overstated. LEVENSON points out that the inaccuracy of biblical portrayals of idolatry may result not from ignorance but from the tendentious and polemical nature of these texts. Moreover, he shows that elements of mythology are more common in the Bible than Kaufmann acknowledges. Kaufmann's assertions regarding the conquest of Canaan have found few adherents.

Helpful discussions of Kaufmann's work on the Bible, its contributions and its limitations, appear in TALMON and in GREENBERG.

Earlier in his life, Kaufmann wrote a four-volume work, *Golah ve-Nekhar* ("Exile and Alienation"), published in 1929–1930, which examines the life of the Jewish people in exile from a sociological and philosophical point of view. Three chapters of this work are available in English in KAUFMANN (1988). While *Golah ve-Nekhar* as a whole discusses the reasons for the survival of the Jews as a nation during the exile (due to the "iron barrier" of their religion), the chapters translated by Efroymson focus on Christianity and Islam. These two religions continue Judaism's fight against paganism, and Kaufmann acknowledges the integrity of the religious polemics of each of these three monotheistic faiths. He examines the origins of Christianity as a Jewish messianic movement and its separation from Judaism. In the last chapter, he examines the nature of Jewish identity in its ethnic and religious dimensions, the relationship of Judaism and Greek culture, and the persecution of Jews at the hands of Christians and Muslims.

BENJAMIN D. SOMMER

Ketubbah

Davidovitch, David, *The Ketuba: Jewish Marriage Contracts through the Ages,* Tel Aviv: Lewin-Epstein, 1968; New York: Adama, 1985

Diamant, Anita, *The New Jewish Wedding,* New York: Summit, 1985

Epstein, Louis M., *The Jewish Marriage Contract: A Study in the Status of the Woman in Jewish Law,* New York: Jewish Theological Seminary, 1927

Friedman, Mordechai Akiva, *Jewish Marriage in Palestine: A Cairo Genizah Study,* vol. 1: *The "Ketubba" Traditions of Eretz Israel,* New York: Jewish Theological Seminary, 1980

Friedman, Mordechai Akiva, *Jewish Marriage in Palestine: A Cairo Genizah Study,* vol. 2: *The "Ketubba" Texts,* New York: Jewish Theological Seminary, 1980

Gaster, Moses, *The Ketubah,* Berlin: Rimon, 1923; 2nd edition, New York: Hermon, 1974

Leifer, Daniel I., "On Writing New *Ketubot,*" in *The Jewish Woman: New Perspectives,* edited by Elizabeth Koltun, New York: Schocken, 1976

Sabar, Shalom, *Ketubbah: Jewish Marriage Contracts of the Hebrew Union College Skirball Museum and Klau Library,* Philadelphia: Jewish Publication Society, 1990

Sabar, Shalom, *Mazal Tov: Illuminated Jewish Marriage Contracts from the Israel Museum Collection,* Jerusalem: Israel Museum, 1993

Satlow, Michael, "Reconsidering the Rabbinic *Ketubah* Payment," in *The Jewish Family in Antiquity* (Brown Judaic Studies, no. 289), edited by Shaye J.D. Cohen, Atlanta, Georgia: Scholars Press, 1993

The *ketubbah* (plural, *ketubbot*) is the Jewish marriage contract, traditionally written in Aramaic and presented by the groom to the bride as a guarantee of her maintenance and conjugal rights during marriage and financial support at its end, whether by divorce or death of the husband. The wife is granted a stipulated sum secured by a lien on the husband's property, and the fact that the wife may collect the sum in the event of divorce generally has been interpreted as protection for women against hasty divorce action by husbands. Although talmudic sources debate whether the ketubbah's general authority is rooted in biblical law or is a rabbinic enactment, the rabbinic texts agree that its implementation in the particular form of a lien on the husband's property can be attributed to Simeon ben Shetah in the second century B.C.E. More recent scholarship, however, has questioned this attribution. Once a "live" contract between the parties stipulating carefully negotiated financial details of the marriage (such as dowry), the use of the traditional ketubbah in Jewish weddings has become largely symbolic since medieval authorities prohibited divorce without the wife's consent and still more so since Jews have generally come to accept secular laws regulating marriage. Some modern Jews, however, are attempting to revive the contract's significance by creating new, personalized ketubbot.

GASTER's work is marked by dated assumptions regarding gender roles and relations, the reliability of rabbinic narratives as sources for history, and the moral superiority of Jews and Jewish marriage practices. Gaster's description of the history of the ketubbah has influenced later works, but the author's main interest is the ketubbah as a potential source for historians, not the history of the ketubbah itself. The bulk of his work is dedicated to highly overstated, but not completely inaccurate, claims about the usefulness of ketubbot for the study of Jewish settlement patterns, onomastics, genealogy, economic and material conditions, art history, and other topics.

EPSTEIN's book represents the most comprehensive single work about the ketubbah. The book is a legal history, rather than an exploration of the religious significance of the ketubbah, and most of the text is dedicated to detailed explorations of provisions long out of use. The study is dated in ways similar to Gaster's monograph but with far less detriment to its scholarship. Thus, Epstein, like Gaster, relies heavily on the authority of rabbinic sources (accepting the facticity, for example, of the rabbinic accounts of Simeon ben Shetah's institution of the ketubbah), but Epstein's analysis of those sources is commendably thorough, as he weaves the multiple accounts into a plausible composite.

FRIEDMAN (1980a, 1980b) has analyzed fragments of 65 ketubbot found in the Cairo Genizah and dating to the tenth and 11th centuries. The first volume of the study contains the analysis; the second offers the documents themselves in Hebrew and English translation. Friedman reconstructs early Palestinian ketubbah traditions in which the text was far more fluid than the formulaic document of Babylonian tradition, thus creating a seriously altered picture of the history of the ketubbah. (Previous scholars, who were generally unaware of or unfamiliar with the Cairo documents, frequently assigned the standardized formulation of Babylonia to a very early date.) Moreover, there are elements in the Cairo documents that take the form of a mutual contract between husband and wife and include provisions for divorce initiated by the wife, thereby calling into question the picture of gender relations presented in other studies.

SATLOW, reviewing earlier scholars' reliance on rabbinic traditions regarding the origins of the ketubbah, states that "to move from the traditions' understanding of history to history itself is a logical leap not justified by the evidence." Instead, Satlow dates the institution of the ketubbah (as opposed to other forms of marriage payments such as bride price or dowry) to the rabbis themselves, in the period just following the destruction of the Second Temple. He notes that no earlier Jewish document (biblical, apocryphal, or Greco-Roman) refers to a "ketubbah," and he argues that most of a number of earlier examples of Jewish marriage contracts only contain references to dowries; at a minimum, he shows that none of the earlier documents can be proven conclusively to include ketubbah payments.

As demonstrated by Davidovitch and Sabar, ketubbot were often lavishly illuminated, and these documents therefore constitute a significant part of the corpus of Jewish art. The collections reproduced in these authors' studies include ketubbot from a variety of places and times (other fine collections are excluded from this essay because of their parochial focus), many in vivid color. The most extensive historical introduction appears in SABAR (1990), which emphasizes Italian ketubbot. In this volume and in SABAR (1993), which takes the fascinating tack of arranging materials and discussion by common artistic motifs rather than provenance, the author exhibits caution, refusing to affirm that the ketubbah as now known has antecedents prior to the talmudic period in Babylonia. DAVIDOVITCH's introduction appears to have been written in Hebrew and then translated into English (versions in both languages appear, at opposite ends of the book); the author draws the history of the ketubbah primarily from Gaster (itself problematic) and quotations from that work are retranslations of the Hebrew translation rather than citations of the original English. All three of these volumes discuss the development and transmission (or lack thereof, in some locales) of Jewish decorative arts as evidenced in the ketubbah; notable for the length and depth of its text is Sabar's second volume. Davidovitch's book includes the fewest plates of the three.

LEIFER outlines three reasons for drafting a new form of ketubbah: the lack of mutuality and equality of legal status [in the traditional ketubbah]; the change in a woman's economic and social situation; and the legal irrelevance of the economic aspects of the traditional *ketubah*. Leifer, a rabbi who worked with a number of couples to create ketubbot, suggests some personal and subjective guidelines for those wishing to do likewise, and he offers two examples in Hebrew and English. Because of the highly individualistic and personalized nature of this new practice, there is no organized collection of these texts available. DIAMANT includes several examples in her book, a guide for Jewish brides and grooms, in the section dedicated to the ketubbah. Unfortunately, the cited texts appear only in English, and Diamant gives no indication if Hebrew versions are available.

GAIL LABOVITZ

Khazars

Barthold, W. and P.B. Golden, "Khazars," in *The Encyclopaedia of Islam, New Edition*, vol. 4, Leiden: Brill, 1979

Brook, Kevin A., "A Brief History of the Khazars," in *The Kuzari: In Defense of the Despised Faith*, by Judah ha-Levi, translated and annotated by N. Daniel Korobkin, Northvale, New Jersey: Aronson, 1998

Dunlop, D.M., *The History of the Jewish Khazars*, Princeton, New Jersey: Princeton University Press, 1954

Golb, Norman, *Jewish Proselytism: A Phenomenon in the Religious History of Early Medieval Europe*, Cincinnati, Ohio: Judaic Studies Program, University of Cincinnati, 1987

Golb, Norman and Omeljan Pritsak, *Khazarian Hebrew Documents of the Tenth Century*, Ithaca, New York: Cornell University Press, 1982

Golden, Peter B., *Khazar Studies: An Historico-Philological Inquiry into the Origins of the Khazars*, 2 vols., Budapest: Akadémiai Kiadó, 1980

Pritsak, Omeljan, "Khazars," in *Dictionary of the Middle Ages*, vol. 7, edited by Joseph R. Strayer, New York: Scribner, 1986

In the middle of the tenth century, the mysterious story of the conversion to Judaism of the Khazars, nomads and seminomads of the Caspian steppes, became known to Jewish communities from Constantinople to Spain. In the 12th century, the great poet and philosopher Judah Halevi penned *Kuzari* (or the Khazarian Book), a series of dialogues between the Jewish scholar and the Khazarian king in which the scholar aims to persuade the king that Judaism is the highest form of religion, superior to Islam and Christianity. Since then, Jewish authors have frequently addressed the subject of the Khazars.

A new wave of research into the Khazars and Khazaria commenced in the second half of the 19th century, especially after the discovery of Hebrew correspondence between Umayyad vizier Hasdai ibn Shaprut of Cordova and the Khazarian king Joseph of Atil (c.960). The development of oriental studies in the 19th century resulted in the publication of many additional sources on the Khazars and Khazaria in the languages of Central Asia, the Caucasus, and Middle East, reflecting the fact that the Khazars interacted with neighbors, allies, enemies, and traders, many of whom left records of Khazaria in their chronicles. During the 19th and 20th century, some research about the Khazars was motivated by political or antisemitic reasons: for example, the Karaites sought to avoid disabilities imposed on Jews by the Russian czarist government and to escape Nazi persecution by claiming that they were descendants of Khazarian or Turanian (i.e., non-Semitic) people. After World War II, certain scholars and pseudoscholars tried to disconnect Ashkenazi Jews from the rest of the Jewish community by asserting that Ashkenazim are descendants of Khazars and therefore have no hereditary title to the land of Israel.

There are tremendous obstacles to study of the Khazars. First, few archaeological artifacts from Khazarian societies are available. Second, it is very difficult to locate Khazarian cities, battlefields, or other relevant places, and excavations of those sites that have been found have not provided much definitive evidence of Khazarian history. Third, very few words are preserved from the Khazars' language, and many of these words are only preserved in descriptions in other languages, which may have corrupted the terms and names they cite. Nevertheless, today the literature on the Khazars is voluminous, is written in many languages, and covers different aspects of Khazarian history and culture. Most scholarship occurs in nations that historically had contact with the Khazars (including Russia, China, Bulgaria, Ossetia, Georgia, Armenia, Daghestan, Azerbaijan, and Turkey), although Western scholars have also investigated some issues, particularly those that relate to Arab, Byzantine, and Iranian sources. This essay focuses on recent English-language studies based on primary sources.

DUNLOP presents the first full-scale history of the Khazars, based on different groups of historical sources. He discusses the place of the Khazars in history, noting that predecessors of this group prevented the advance of the Arabs over the Caucasus Mountains in the seventh century and stemmed the eastward spread of Byzantium. The author analyzes the theory of the Uigur origin of the Khazars, and he examines hypotheses concerning the consolidation of the Khazar state in the middle of the seventh century. He also traces the Khazar-Arab wars; the Khazar conversion to Judaism; the 200 years in which the Khazar Empire flourished and expanded; relations between Khazars and Russians; and the decline and fall of the Khazar state.

BARTHOLD and GOLDEN's article concisely presents research findings up to 1978. They discuss the emergence of the Khazar tribe in the sixth century, the rise of the Khazar Empire, its wars and political relations with neighboring communities (including the Byzantine Empire), the Khazars' conversion to Judaism near the beginning of the ninth century, their economic activities, and their language. In Barthold and Golden's analysis of the Khazars' conversion, the authors explore a variety of sources that present conflicting accounts about the dates of the conversion and the number of people involved.

GOLB discusses several instances in which Gentiles converted to Judaism in the Middle Ages; he seeks to explain through the investigation of Hebrew manuscripts the attraction of non-Jews to Jewish monotheism. Golb divides his discussion into six sections. In the first five, he describes separate cases of conversion recorded in the manuscripts of the Cairo Genizah, and in the sixth section, he provides an account of the conversion of the Khazars and rebuts the views of several writers who use Khazar history to advance such political agendas as anti-Zionism. Golb also criticizes scholars who suggest that conversion to Judaism was limited only to the Khazar king's court or to residents of the capital city; he argues that manuscript evidence clearly demonstrates that rabbinic Judaism was widely practiced in Khazaria and that Jewish teachers emigrated to Khazaria from Palestine, Babylonia, Iran, Byzantium, and other lands. He also cites Abraham ibn Daud (c.1160), who met Khazar rabbinic scholars who traveled to Toledo.

GOLB and PRITSAK publish and discuss a previously unknown document, the letter of a rabbinic Jewish community of Kiev that was written in archaic Hebrew, with the words transcribed in Turkic runes. Six Khazarian Turkic personal names are intermingled with the signatures of Hebrew names on this letter. Golb discusses Hebrew evidence, while Pritsak deals with Turkic references. Pritsak concludes that the Kievan letter was written while the Khazarian administration was still in effect, that is, before the Rus' conquest of Kiev, which Pritsak tentatively dates by comparing different Russian chronicles. Based on documentary evidence, he dates the letter to around 930.

In the second part of the book, Golb presents a new edition of the diplomatic correspondence of Hasdai ibn Shaprut of Cordova edited by P.K. Kokovcov in 1932, as well as S. Schechter's version of the text and a historical and geographical evaluation of the Schechter text.

GOLDEN's comprehensive and penetrating historico-philological research is exemplary. He delves into the complex questions concerning the identification and etymology of all Khazarian words and names preserved in multiple sources and written in a variety of languages. He also supplies complete texts of these sources. The author not only employs medieval sources and modern Western research, but also refers to some Eastern European publications. This work is one of the most valuable resources available to philologists, linguists, and anthropologists studying the Khazars.

PRITSAK offers an overview of the history of the Khazars that differs in some respects from that presented in the Barthold and Golden study. For example, he places the first seat of the Khazars in Daghestan, and he identifies the Iranian Varaz tribe as the group that founded the dynasty of kings to which King Joseph, the correspondent of Hasdai ibn Shaprut, belonged. Pritsak calls the first Khazarian king who converted to Judaism "the majordomo" (he came from a social group from which majordomos to Khazarian kings were recruited) and hypothesizes that the date of his private conversion was 731, decades before he imposed the Jewish religion on the kaghanate at the end of the eighth century. Pritsak examines the ideological foundations for the conversion, explains the empire's sources of wealth, evaluates the factors that led to the empire's collapse, and investigates the fates of the various factions that emerged after the empire fragmented.

In his introduction to Halevi and in his subsequent monograph, *The Jews of Khazaria* (Northvale, New Jersey: Aronson, 1999), BROOK summarizes very accessibly the history of the Khazars from their settlement in the steppes north of the Caucasus sometime before the fifth century. Formerly nomadic, the Khazars adopted a settled lifestyle and were occupied with fishing, crafts, and agriculture. They harvested grapes, barley, rice, wheat, and vegetables. Other members of the tribe maintained the Turkic warrior tradition of expert horseback archery. Brook also considers their conversion to Judaism, discusses their relationships with Turkic tribes of the Caucasus and Central Asia, and offers exceptionally clear information about the decline of the Khazar state, its intermingling with other Turkic tribes, and the final destruction of the Khazar kingdom by Mongols in the 1230s. Brook apparently accepts most of Judah Halevi's book as a reliable historical source, incorporating statements from the philosopher's presentation into an exposition of Khazarian history based on the work of more recent historians.

HAYIM Y. SHEYNIN

Kibbutz

Ben Rafael, Eliezer, *Crisis and Transformation: The Kibbutz at Century's End* (SUNY Series in Israeli Studies), Albany: State University of New York Press, 1997

Infield, Henrik, *Cooperative Living in Palestine* (Rural Settlement Institute Research Series on Cooperation), New York: Dryden, 1944

Kats, Yosef, *Between Jerusalem and Hebron: Jewish Settlement in the Hebron Mountains and the Etzion Bloc in the Pre-State Period*, Ramat-Gan: Bar-Ilan University Press, 1998

Kimmerling, Baruch, *Zionism and Economy*, Cambridge, Massachusetts: Schenkman, 1983

Leon, Dan, *The Kibbutz: A New Way of Life* (The Commonwealth and International Library), New York and Oxford: Pergamon, 1969

Maron, Stanley, *Kibbutz in a Market Society*, Israel: Yad Tabenkin, 1993

Near, Henry, *The Kibbutz Movement: A History* (Littman Library of Jewish Civilization), 2 vols., Oxford and New York: Oxford University Press, 1992–1997

Shafir, Gershon, *Land, Labor, and the Origins of the Israeli-Palestinian Conflict, 1882–1914* (Cambridge Middle East Library, 20), Cambridge and New York: Cambridge University Press, 1989; updated edition, Berkeley: University of California Press, 1996

Since the beginning of the 20th century, the kibbutz has been one of the most important symbols of the ethos and practice of the Zionist resettlement of Palestine. Born on the shores of the Sea of Galilee in 1910 out of a desire of Jewish laborers to "be autonomous and work without overseers or external control" (as a founder of the first kibbutz described it), by 1940 there were 82 kibbutzim with more than 26,000 members; by 1992 the number had reached 269, with a population of 128,000. Throughout its history, what distinguished the kibbutz from other forms of cooperative Jewish agricultural settlement, such as the *moshav* and *moshav-ovdim,* has been the notion of "complete collectivism" in property, production and labor, consumption, and living arrangements.

Analyzing the roots and ramifications of this collectivist ideology has long been a central goal of scholarship on the kibbutz. An early example of this focus is INFIELD. This book exhibits several characteristics of kibbutz historiography, including detailed descriptions of and statistics about the kibbutz way of life as a guide to explaining the movement's success, discussions of the relationship between the major kibbutz federations and the Zionist agencies, and comparisons with the *moshav* and *moshav-ovdim.* Moreover, Infield provides an early example of the focus on education and the "remodeled family" (i.e., sexual equality and innovative methods of child-rearing) that is common to most analyses of the kibbutz, while his discussion of the contradictions inherent in the "Arab dilemma" illustrates how kibbutzniks early on experienced the discontinuity between their socialist and nationalist visions, which led some to "despair of building their new home on the basis of social justice."

LEON appeared just as the growing industrialization of the kibbutz economy was fundamentally changing consumption patterns, living standards, and lifestyles on the kibbutz. It thus presents a good snapshot of the late 1960s socioeconomic and ideological position of the kibbutz within Israeli society. Focusing on the largest of the four national kibbutz federations, Kibbutz Artzi-Hashomer Hatzair, Leon's discussion of the "dominant question" of women and their work roles and his argument that sexual equality and separate children's quarters had achieved the "destruction . . . of the patriarchal foundation of the family" epitomize the classic Jewish historiography of the kibbutz during this period.

NEAR's two volumes undoubtedly constitute the most comprehensive study of the phenomenon in English. Volume one examines the origins and growth of the kibbutz movement during the years 1909 to 1929. The emergence of kibbutz-type settlements out of the early communes of the second aliyah is described in detail, as is the crystallization of three interrelated groups *(kevutsot)* focused on defense, work, and settlement—the central components of kibbutz ideology and praxis by the end of the "experimental stage" of smaller scale settlements. Also documented thoroughly is the recognition of the kibbutz as an integral part of the *yishuv* in the 1920s. Near explains that an important reason for the growth of the kibbutz was its relationship to the pioneering youth movements in the diaspora, which encouraged thousands of young, trained immigrants to join the kibbutzim by the 1930s, just when rising rates of Jewish-Palestinian violence and the possibility of partition between the two groups increased the importance of the kibbutz as a means to "create facts" on the ground in Palestine.

Near's second volume investigates the crises and achievements of the kibbutz movement during the years 1939 to 1995. The first half documents the political, strategic, and military roles of the kibbutz (particularly in the growth and activities of the Haganah) during the last decade of the British Mandate, from World War II through the War of 1948. While the kibbutzim served as vital training and supply areas for the Haganah during the War of Independence, Near explains that their vaunted strategic function as facts on the ground in Arab regions was a failure, as 71 kibbutzim were left in Arab territory in the final UN Partition Plan. The second half of the volume deals with the crisis that arose with the "end of pioneering" in the 1950s, when the kibbutzim failed to absorb or integrate the new immigrant population, instead becoming embroiled in the ideological and political turmoil that plagued the Mapai and Mapam parties (with whom most kibbutzim were affiliated) during the next decade.

Near concludes with a discussion of developments during the last 30 years of the 20th century that can only be regarded as cursory. More general problems with both volumes are their overly descriptive (as opposed to analytical) style and an avoidance of sources and studies critical of the traditional Labor Zionist historiography (even hagiography) of the kibbutz. As a result, it is difficult for the reader to process the vast information Near presents or to understand how the dynamics of earlier periods have influenced, and can help contemporary scholars understand, the challenges currently before the kibbutz movement.

KATS is perhaps the only monograph in English to examine the features of the religious kibbutzim in significant detail. The book deals with the debates surrounding the establishment and subsequent experiences of several religious kibbutzim in the Hebron mountains and the region south of Bethlehem (the Etzion bloc) during the last decade of the Mandate period. These settlements were part of the effort by Jewish land-purchasing bodies such as the Jewish National Fund to move beyond the historical focus on settling the coastal plains and to begin purchasing large tracts of land in the hilly regions of central Palestine, home to the bulk of Palestine's Arab population.

As Kats explains in rich detail, the initial reluctance by settlers to move to this seemingly harsh territory "gradually gave way to a genuine sense of attachment" as they became acclimated to their surroundings and achieved sometimes impressive successes in making the kibbutzim economically and socially viable enterprises. His detailed descriptions of the hard work needed to reclaim the land for farming paint a vivid portrait of the daily life of the settlers, including their economic and political struggles both with the national Zionist bodies and the local Arab populations. Most importantly, Kats's analysis also demonstrates that however much kibbutz ideology was predicated on agricultural pioneering, from the beginning geographical and political circumstances forced the settlers to move into nonagricultural activities, such as stone quarrying and summer guest housing for religious Jews, in order to survive. This transformation would be repeated by secular kibbutzim as the Israeli economy liberalized in the decades after achieving sovereignty.

Kats draws from many underutilized archives associated with religious Zionism to shape his narrative, but he does not examine the relations between these religious settlers and their secular kibbutz counterparts. Furthermore, because he used no non-Jewish sources (such as the United Kingdom's Public Records Office or the Palestinian Arab press), British and Arab voices never appear to add context or provide an alternative point of view to his protagonists. Moreover, like the other works discussed here, Kats uncritically accepts the traditional Zionist/Israeli description of Palestine, and specifically the territory on which kibbutzim were established, as neglected and stagnant prior to its "reclamation" by Jews. Research of the last two decades of the 20th century, however, has shown this description to be both inaccurate and ideologically motivated.

Despite the absence of their voice in the narrative, however, Arabs remain a constant presence—for example, in the centrality of the theme of security or the importance of road-building (today's "bypass roads") to enhance settlement activity. But a different methodological and even epistemological grounding is required to reveal the constitutive role played by the indigenous Palestinian population and its implied yet conflicted relationship with the burgeoning Jewish community in the creation and development of the kibbutz as a socioeconomic, political, and military institution. Kimmerling and Shafir both provide this alternative perspective, examining the etiology and transformation of the kibbutzim from a critical political economy perspective. SHAFIR's analysis focuses on the pre–World War I era, which he sees as the formative period for the ideology and practice of the Labor movement out of which the kibbutz was born. His investigation demonstrates that the need for collective agricultural settlement resulted from the difficulties individual settlers had

adapting to strenuous agricultural labor and from the struggles of Jewish laborers against both the low wages paid by the Jewish planters and the Palestinian workers who accepted them. Out of these struggles the concept of *kibbush 'avodah* ("conquest of labor") was born, in which the incipient Labor movement struggled to secure large-scale employment of Jews in the existing Jewish-bourgeois economy. Yet by 1909—one year before the establishment of the first kibbutz—this strategy had proven an "abysmal failure." The labor movement began to understand that it could only secure jobs for Jewish workers within a socioeconomic system under its control, which in turn necessitated control over a defined territory in which such an economy could be established. Thus, the object of conquest was transformed from the labor market to the land itself, and the ideology of *kibbush karka'* or the "conquest of land," was born. The kibbutz soon emerged as a central player in the struggle to conquer both land and labor for Jewish workers.

KIMMERLING examines the dominant strains of Zionist economic ideology and the Zionists' interaction with the actual economic reality in Palestine/Israel, and he reaches a similar conclusion to that of Shafir. Kimmerling's analysis of the kibbutz begins with the industrial revolution in the kibbutzim that commenced in the late 1950s. This resulted not just from the changing demography and human geography of the country that accompanied the influx of hundreds of thousands of immigrants from Middle Eastern countries; more specifically, the process emerged from the aging of the kibbutz population, the need to find less physically demanding occupations for that population, and the need to raise standards of living and preserve the kibbutz's socioeconomic status as Israel industrialized.

This process of industrialization represented a major departure from the historic kibbutznik denigration of manufacturing as a primary cause of the unequal distribution of resources and undemocratic social hierarchy characteristic of modern capitalism. Kimmerling also demonstrates how the shift to industry signified the diminished ideological position of the kibbutz—and thus Labor Zionism—within Israeli society, which culminated in the 1977 Likud victory and accelerated the marketization and consumerization of Israeli society.

Maron and Ben Rafael both describe the roots and ramifications of these transformations in the kibbutz and Israeli society at large. MARON's study examines how the kibbutz system has adapted to an increasingly consumerist and market-oriented culture and political economy in Israel while remaining true to its collectivist roots. According to Maron, the kibbutz emphasis on rootedness and continuity has conflicted with the stress on personal mobility and individual movement inherent in contemporary market societies. This conflict has led to several adaptations in the kibbutz organization, such as the expansion of personal (versus communal) budgets, and more significantly, the development of a more "family friendly" atmosphere (in contrast to the earlier belief that the discrete familial unit was a threat to the solidarity of the kibbutz), which has in turn transformed the educational system and the position of the ideological bellwethers of the kibbutz—its women.

BEN RAFAEL similarly describes the "malaise" suffered by the kibbutz community in the late 1980s and 1990s and the "de-collectivization" that has occurred as members no longer interact with the same frequency and intimacy as they did, for example, when parents met nightly in the now-abandoned "children's houses." His review of the great body of contemporary anthropological field work on the kibbutz reveals that today there is less fraternity and more instrumentalism in the way members treat each other than there was previously; moreover, the "kibbutz capitalism" that has emerged during the last several decades and the concomitant "embourgeoisement" of kibbutzniks have been fraught with contradictions that have further strained the system, leading central kibbutz institutions such as children's houses, schools, and collective dining rooms to lose their unique kibbutz character.

Despite these problems, Maron argues that the kibbutz continues to offer an important "alternative to the city" as Israel, like so much of the world, becomes more urbanized and more market- and consumer-oriented. Maron and Ben Rafael's discussions highlight both the obstacles that the kibbutz will face in coming decades and the potential of the kibbutz to constitute an alternative ideological, socioeconomic, and political model for Israeli society.

MARK LEVINE

Kimhi Family

Chomsky, William (editor), *David Kimhi's Hebrew Grammar (Mikhlol) Systematically Presented and Critically Annotated*, Philadelphia: Dropsie College for Hebrew and Cognate Learning, 1933

Kimhi, Joseph, *The Book of the Covenant*, translated by Frank Talmage, Toronto: Pontifical Institute of Mediaeval Studies, 1972

Kimhi, Moses, *Commentary on the Book of Job* (South Florida Studies in the History of Judaism, no. 64), edited by Herbert Basser and Barry D. Walfish, Atlanta, Georgia: Scholars Press, 1992

Talmage, Frank Ephraim, *David Kimhi: The Man and the Commentaries* (Harvard Judaic Monographs, 1), Cambridge, Massachusetts: Harvard University Press, 1975

Talmage, Frank Ephraim, *Apples of Gold in Settings of Silver: Studies in Medieval Jewish Exegesis and Polemics* (Papers in Mediaeval Studies), edited by Barry Dov Walfish, Toronto: Pontifical Institute of Mediaeval Studies, 1999

The Kimhi family immigrated from Spain to Provence in the mid-12th century, in the wake of the Almohade persecutions, and established themselves in Narbonne. The family brought with them the rationalist intellectual tradition that they had absorbed in their native land. The father, Joseph (c.1105–c.1170), and his two sons, Moses (who died c.1190) and David (c.1160–c.1235), dedicated their scholarly lives to three areas of study: grammar, exegesis, and polemics. Joseph wrote a polemic, *The Book of the Covenant,* which seems to have been directed at apostates from Judaism in an attempt to convince them to return to the fold. His grammar books,

Sefer Zikaron and *Sefer ha-Galui,* laid the foundation for the work of his son David. Moses wrote commentaries on the Books of Proverbs and Job as well as a grammar book, *Mahalakh shevilei ha-da'at (The Course of the Paths of Knowledge).* David attained the greatest renown, as a grammarian, biblical exegete, and as representative of the rationalist tradition in medieval Jewish intellectual circles. He was a staunch defender of Maimonides and even undertook a strenuous journey in his later years to plead the cause of his master during the first Maimonidean Controversy in 1232.

A number of 19th- and early 20th-century scholars studied the Kimhi family, but no one devoted more energy to them than Frank Talmage, who served as a professor at the University of Toronto until his death in 1988. Talmage wrote his dissertation on David Kimhi, and many of his early publications were devoted to David and his father Joseph.

Talmage's introduction to his translation of Joseph KIMHI's polemic situates the work in its time and in relation to other medieval polemical literature. It also summarizes the basic biographical and bibliographical information on Joseph. TALMAGE (1999) reprints several of the author's important articles about the members of Kimhi family. In "Rabbi Joseph Kimhi: From the Dispersion of Jerusalem in Sepharad to the Canaanites in Zarephath," Talmage concentrates on a single aspect of Joseph's intellectual persona—his extreme biblical purism—and shows how this factor influenced his exegesis and his reading of the text of the prayerbook. This analysis shows clearly the cultural differences between the Jews of Spain and those of France, including southern France where the Kimhis settled. As an immigrant, Joseph must have had a particularly difficult time adjusting to a milieu that did not share his values in linguistic and other intellectual matters.

Other essays in Talmage's 1999 collection help round out the picture of the family. "David Kimhi and the Rationalist Tradition" provides a detailed discussion of the philosophical background of David's work and analyzes his views on a number of key issues, explaining how he was thoroughly grounded in Maimonidean Aristotelianism. A second essay on the same subject, "David Kimhi and the Rationalist Tradition, II: Literary Sources," examines the rationalist sources David used in his commentaries and provides a picture of his intellectual formation. The essay on "R. David Kimhi as Polemicist" discusses David's commentaries in the context of other polemical literature of the period. The very fact that he incorporated polemical material in his commentaries assured their availability and popularity in religious debates. Much evidence exists to demonstrate the continued popularity and use of his work throughout the Middle Ages and the Renaissance.

TALMAGE (1975) supplies additional insights into David's life and work in an excellent intellectual biography of this important representative of the rationalist school in medieval Judaism. A child of Joseph's old age, David lost his father at the age of ten. His brother Moses, who was considerably older, became his surrogate father and directed his education. The first chapter describes the cultural milieu in Narbonne and gives a detailed portrait of David's educational curriculum. Chapters two and four discuss his views on the exile, redemption, and eschatology. Chapter three, the largest chapter, is devoted to a detailed and masterly exposition of David Kimhi's exegetical methodology, especially his relationship to rabbinical midrash.

Those interested in learning about David Kimhi's grammatical work would profit from consulting CHOMSKY's book, a reorganized annotated edition of David's *Mikhol*, a highly influential Hebrew grammar. The introduction to this work gives a fair assessment of Kimhi's achievement as a grammarian.

The little that is known about the elder son, Moses KIMHI, is summarized in Walfish and Basser's introduction to his commentary on the Book of Job. The introduction also gives some insight into Moses' exegetical methodology.

BARRY D. WALFISH

Kings, Book of

Aharoni, Yohanan, *Erets-Yisra'el bi-tekufat ha-Mikra: ge'ografyah historit,* 1962; translated and edited by Anson F. Rainey as *The Land of the Bible: A Historical Geography,* London: Burns and Oates, 1962; Philadelphia: Westminster, 1967; 2nd edition: London: Burns and Oates, 1978; Philadelphia: Westminster, 1979

Bright, John, *A History of Israel,* Philadelphia: Westminster, 1959; London: SCM, 1960; 3rd edition, 1981

Cogan, Mordechai and Hayim Tadmor, *II Kings: A New Translation* (Anchor Bible Series, vol. 11), Garden City, New York: Doubleday, 1988

Gray, John, *I and II Kings: A Commentary* (Old Testament Library), Philadelphia: Westminster, 1963; London: SCM, 1964; 2nd edition, Philadelphia: Westminster, 1970; 3rd edition, London: SCM, 1977

Hochberg, Reuven and A.J. Rosenberg, *I Kings: A New English Translation* (Judaica Books of the Prophets), New York: Judaica Press, 1980

Montgomery, James A., *A Critical and Exegetical Commentary on the Books of Kings* (International Critical Commentary, vol. 10), edited by Henry Snyder Gehman, Edinburgh: Clark, and New York: Scribner, 1951

Rosenberg, A.J., *II Kings: A New English Translation* (Judaica Books of the Prophets), New York: Judaica Press, 1980

Slotki, I.W., *Kings: Hebrew Text and English Translation* (Soncino Books of the Bible, vol. 4), London: Soncino, 1950; New York: Soncino, 1978; revised edition, 1990

Thiele, Edwin R., *The Mysterious Numbers of the Hebrew Kings,* Chicago: University of Chicago Press, 1951; revised edition, Exeter, Devon: Paternoster, 1966; new revised edition, Grand Rapids, Michigan: Kregel, 1994

Walsh, Jerome T., *1 Kings* (Berit Olam Series), edited by David W. Cotter, Collegeville, Minnesota: Liturgical Press, 1996

Ninth of the 24 books of the Hebrew Bible (according to the traditional Jewish count), the Book of Kings is the fourth book of the Prophets and the last of the "Nevi'im Rishonim" or "Historical Prophets." Kings, appearing nowadays as First and Second Kings, is first found divided in the Septuagint. It recounts the political history of Israel from David's death to the destruction of the first temple, roughly 960 to 586 B.C.E. First Kings chapters two to 11 tells of Solomon's reign and the building of the first temple; after Solomon's death, the kingdom split into the northern kingdom of Israel and the southern kingdom of Judah. First Kings 12 through Second Kings 17 details the political and military history of the divided kingdoms and the careers of Elijah and Elisha, the northern prophets. In 722 B.C.E, the kingdom of Israel came to an end. Second Kings chapters 18 through 25 depicts the last 140 years of Judah. History in Kings is consistently recounted with a didactic and theological slant, aiming to prove that loyalty to the God of Israel leads to political success. Much modern research on Kings is supplemented by Assyrian, Babylonian, and North-West Semitic texts discovered by archaeologists that assess the history of this period from the point of view of the nations surrounding Israel.

COGAN and TADMOR have produced what is undoubtedly the best modern commentary on the Book of Kings. The volume, which is devoted to Second Kings, includes an English translation, while the accompanying commentary focuses primarily on textual and historical problems. Information gleaned from Assyrian, Babylonian, and other ancient Semitic cultures is brought to bear on the text, and the chronology of Kings is correlated with that of the kings of Assyria and Babylonia. The wealth of comparative Semitic material in this volume makes it more useful to the scholar than to the layperson, but the work can effectively introduce the interested nonspecialist to the comparative method. A complete bibliography is included. The book's only shortcoming is that literary studies of the narrative sections of Kings are not as well integrated into the text as they might have been. The Anchor Bible volume on First Kings has not yet appeared.

WALSH, conversely, covers only First Kings. His book proves a valuable complement to Tadmor and Cogan, as he focuses exclusively on "literary art" and ignores nearly all of the historical and archaeological issues in Kings, as well as many of the theological ones. The commentary provides a good close reading of the narrative in Kings, highlighting points of irony, structure, language, and perspective that might escape the casual reader but are central to the message and ideology of the book. The volume does not supply the biblical text itself.

AHARONI's work is by no means a commentary on Kings, but the last third of his book deals with the archaeological and epigraphic evidence for the period covered by Kings. Aharoni integrates biblical sources with ancient Assyrian, Egyptian, Israelite, and other extra-biblical texts, and he carefully surveys the history of the period. One of his prime concerns is to locate accurately the sites of particular events and in so doing to create a "historical geography" of the Bible.

BRIGHT's work is a popular summary of biblical history and chapters six to eight deal with the period covered by Kings. Bright presents history as a running narrative, includes social history, and is eminently readable. Unfortunately, some of Bright's data come from texts while some conclusions are based on deduction, and he does not always distinguish clearly between the two approaches.

THIELE presents a particularly original and unusual study of the chronology in Kings. Working with the biblical text, as well as with ancient Assyrian sources, he provides dates for the reigns of all the biblical kings that accord with both the biblical and extra-biblical data.

The volumes by HOCHBERG and ROSENBERG and by ROSENBERG present the best available summary for the non-specialist of 2000 years of Jewish interpretation of Kings. These works present the Hebrew text of Kings, together with Targum Pseudo-Jonathan and the commentaries of Rashi, Kimhi, Gersonides, and the Metsudot (reproduced from the Lublin Rabbinic Bible), while an English translation of the biblical text, together with a digest of the traditional commentaries, appears on the adjacent page. The selection from the commentaries focuses on points in the text that the modern reader is likely to see as difficult. Most of the commentators selected concern themselves with contextual, plain-sense interpretation, and the rabbinic sources on which these medieval commentators draw are also presented. The different commentaries are well-translated, and they are organized so as to form a coherent discussion without obscuring differences of opinion between commentators. Reasons for the traditional commentators' differing views are discussed in Rosenberg and Hochberg's notes. These are extremely useful works for those interested in explaining traditional commentary.

SLOTKI aims at the Jewish layperson, integrating some material from studies of the ancient Near East with traditional Jewish commentary. The Hebrew text is presented together with a good English translation and a brief but helpful commentary that relates passages in Kings to other biblical passages and tries to make the biblical idiom comprehensible to the modern reader.

GRAY's work contains an English text and commentary, and it is generally a model of critical Bible scholarship. His commentary confronts questions of authorship and philological and theological issues. The commentary integrates some material from ancient Near Eastern studies, but these sources are not a prime focus of the commentary, as they are in Cogan and Tadmor's work. Gray uses ancient Near Eastern texts to note similarities between royal behavior in Israel and in neighboring countries, a point often ignored by other writers. This is a comprehensive commentary, covering everything except narrative studies and traditional Jewish interpretation. Gray footnotes some of the more important scholarly works on related questions, but he provides too few suggestions for further reading to be very useful to the advanced student. The commentary is most useful to readers with some basic knowledge of Hebrew.

MONTGOMERY's commentary extensively analyzes "lower criticism," attempting to establish the original version of the text of Kings by reference to the Septuagint and other ancient versions. He uses some material from the ancient Near East to show parallels between biblical and ancient Near Eastern practices, but he does not discuss chronologies or correspondences between the events of Second Kings and events described in Assyrian and Babylonian texts, nor is there much sophisticated concern with issues of literary art.

SHAWN ZELIG ASTER

Kingship

Goodblatt, David, *The Monarchic Principle: Studies in Jewish Self-Government in Antiquity* (Texte und Studien zum antiken Judentum, 38), Tübingen: Mohr (Siebeck), 1994

Grabbe, Lester L., *Priests, Prophets, Diviners, Sages: A Socio-Historical Study of Religious Specialists in Ancient Israel,* Valley Forge, Pennsylvania: Trinity Press International, 1995

Halpern, Baruch, *The Constitution of the Monarchy in Israel* (Harvard Semitic Monographs, no. 25), Chico, California: Scholars Press, 1981

Ishida, Tomoo, *The Royal Dynasties in Ancient Israel: A Study on the Formation and Development of Royal-Dynastic Ideology* (Beiheft zur Zeitschrift für die alttestamentliche Wissenschaft, 142), New York: de Gruyter, 1977

Polish, David, *Give Us a King: Legal-Religious Sources of Jewish Sovereignty,* Hoboken, New Jersey: Ktav, 1989

Whitelam, Keith, *The Just King: Monarchical Judicial Authority in Ancient Israel* (Journal for the Study of the Old Testament Supplement Series, 12), Sheffield, South Yorkshire: JSOT, 1979

It is a historical fact that during the better part of four centuries, monarchs governed biblical Israel. However, scriptural attitudes toward monarchy seem to range from outright disdain (1 Samuel 8:7–18; Hosea 3:4, 13:10–11) to enthusiasm bordering adulation, notably in the so-called royal Psalms (e.g., Psalms 45, 110). The ambivalence is epitomized in the talmudic dispute (Sanhedrin 20b) regarding the significance of the king provisions of Deuteronomy 17:14–20. Should these passages be read as promoting, or even commanding, the appointment of a king, or does the appointment of a monarch indicate nothing more than a concession to a misguided Israel? Modern scholars recognize the dissonance between royalist and antiroyalist stances in the biblical literature, and historians have attempted to map out the respective evolutions of the two positions as well as their relationship to one another, while at the same time paying due attention to the wider socioreligious context, including attitudes toward kingship in Israel's ancient Near Eastern environment.

GRABBE emphasizes the Israelite king's cultic function. The author dedicates only one of eight chapters on an assortment of religious specialists to the king, but because the source material is meager, Grabbe is able within that brief space to marshal all important references to kings performing sacral duties. He brings to the reading and analysis of the texts a declared skepticism akin to that of scholars such as Robert Carroll, Philip R. Davies, and Niels Peter Lemche, contending that "we cannot be sure that the Israel of the texts was historical, or to . . . what extent the historical people of central Palestine corresponded with the entity described in the biblical literature." Even as he recognizes the limitations of the textual evidence of the king's priestly role, however, he also identifies enough references (including such difficult readings as "David's sons were priests" [2 Samuel 8:18]) to suggest that prior to the exile, when priesthood became monopolized by

Aaronites, Israelite kings officiated at the altar as a matter of course.

POLISH's aim is not primarily history for its own sake. Rather, he delves into ancient sources in search of an explanation for the contemporary Israeli *kulturkampf* regarding the nature of Jewish sovereignty. As he sees it, as a modern Jewish state becomes a reality, "Suddenly the theoretical speculations of ancient scholars take on compelling and intimidating relevance." He traces the roots of modern debates about political authority from the Bible's ambivalence toward kingship, through Pharisaic and talmudic attitudes to the Hasmoneans, and beyond. At the heart of this age-old tension, Polish identifies a fundamental question—is the state supreme, or is it always subservient to what the rabbis called the Kingdom of Heaven? In the process of exploring this issue, he provides a comprehensive overview of Jewish sociotheological evaluations of kingship, particularly as they relate to hopes for the ideal messianic king. Whether or not one accepts its central hypothesis, this book is a mine not merely of invaluable source material but also of some acute insights.

HALPERN seeks "to isolate the structure of the ascension process in Israel and to coordinate it with the sacral concepts that informed it." The first two chapters are especially rewarding, as Halpern discusses the tension between the position advocating the establishment of a royal dynasty and the position supporting the election of individuals to fill the office of king. (This tension is epitomized in the pentateuchal king law that insists that the king shall be an individual divinely chosen [Deuteronomy 17:15] but then goes on to envisage a royal line [verse 20].) For instance, Halpern charts the process of election through the evolution of the title *nagid*, concluding that "the forms of dynasty enforced in Israel a reduction of 'divine' influence over the succession." Much of the in-depth philological discussion is obviously oriented toward specialists in the discipline. Overall, this book is an ambitious work that somehow manages to tackle the nitty gritty while keeping a constant eye out for the underlying concepts. There is plenty here for serious students to get their teeth into—and mastication will be amply rewarded.

ISHIDA concentrates on the topic of dynasty, in a study that complements Halpern's treatment of the hereditary aspect of kingship. Like Halpern, Ishida asks, what room is there for divine election once a royal dynasty has been established? In the case of Assyria, Ishida suggests, "One of the reasons for laying stress on divine election in Assyria can be found in the custom that the right of primogeniture was not regarded as the absolute basis for royal succession." The author also investigates why the throne of the Northern Kingdom of Israel (as well as the Edomite throne [Genesis 36: 31–39]) was marked by such frequent changes of royal line, thus contradicting the supposition that kingship is inherently hereditary. Ishida acknowledges the views of those scholars who believe that "the principle of dynastic succession was not acknowledged as licit by the people of Israel . . . since monarchy was based on 'charismatic leadership'," although he favors alternative explanations. He surveys dynastic styles not just of Mesopotamia, but also of Egypt and the Hittite empire.

WHITELAM ensures that the king's judicial role is not overlooked. Throughout history, many kings have eschewed the responsibility of adjudication and been satisfied with a military or military-cum-ceremonial function, but Whitelam cites ample biblical and extrabiblical sources (Mesopotamian, Syro-Palestinian, and Egyptian) to show that in the ancient Near East "it was the king's primary duty to guarantee the true administration of justice throughout the land." Drawing from the available evidence, the author explains in socioreligious terms why certain cultures would expect more direct judicial involvement on the part of their king than would other cultures. A helpful feature of his work is its end-of-chapter summaries.

The inclusion here of GOODBLATT may seem odd, for the title of his work does not refer to the kingship of biblical Israel. Rather, the author primarily investigates the postexilic high priesthood and the patriarchate and exilarchate of rabbinic times. His work is relevant, however, because he argues that these hieratic leaders enjoyed in their day an acclaim and loyalty parallel to that of the biblical kings. He demonstrates that "the hope for a restoration of Davidic kingship can be traced in literature of the Second Temple period," and he contends that "we can discover in certain sources an ideology justifying priestly monarchy and bestowing on it a legitimacy in terms of Judean concepts."

ISAAC SASSOON

Klezmer *see* Music: Ashkenazi Folk Music

Kook, Abraham Isaac   1865–1935
Latvian-born mystic and chief rabbi of Palestine

Agus, Jacob B., *Banner of Jerusalem: The Life, Times, and Thought of Abraham Isaac Kuk, the Late Chief Rabbi of Palestine*, New York: Bloch, 1946

Ben Shlomo, Yosef, *Poetry of Being: Lectures on the Philosophy of Rabbi Kook*, Tel Aviv: MOD, 1990

Gellman, Ezra (editor), *Essays on the Thought and Philosophy of Rabbi Kook*, Rutherford, New Jersey: Fairleigh Dickinson University Press, 1991

Kaplan, Lawrence and David Shatz (editors), *Rabbi Abraham Isaac Kook and Jewish Spirituality* (Reappraisals in Jewish Social and Intellectual History), New York: New York University Press, 1995

Neriah, Moshe Zvi, *Moʻade ha-Reʻiyah*, 1979; translated by Pesach Jaffe as *Celebration of the Soul: The Holidays in the Life and Thought of Rabbi Avraham Yitzchak Kook*, Jerusalem: Genesis Jerusalem Press and Feldheim, 1992

Rabbi Abraham Isaac Kook was the first chief rabbi of Palestine and a renowned halakhist, mystic, poet, and public figure. He was born in Grieve, Latvia, and spent the formative years of his scholarly training at the famed yeshivah of Volozhin, studying under Rabbi Naphtali Tsevi Yehudah Berlin. Kook's rabbinic career took him from the small towns of the Russian Pale of Settlement to Jaffa, London, and eventually to Jerusalem, where he reorganized the rabbinate. Kook was a critical figure in the Jewish community of mandatory Palestine in virtue of his fusion of profound Zionist and Orthodox commitments. His vision of the future of the land of Israel had secular pioneers playing as crucial a role as the religious community in the rebirth of the Jewish nation in its homeland.

AGUS, who was rabbi of a large Conservative congregation in suburban Baltimore, is the author of the classic biography of Rabbi Kook. It remains the best place to begin, both for its wealth of details and for its delightfully clear style. The first half of the work is dedicated to the details of Kook's extraordinarily active life, while the second half focuses on his intellectual endeavors (insofar as there can be any hard-and-fast division between the two subjects). The more strictly biographical chapters provide a colorful picture of Kook's young life in the Pale of Settlement and his development into a celebrated Talmud scholar and budding Zionist activist. A brief intellectual history of the period of his youth follows, and Agus explains how such trends as the "Jewish Enlightenment" and 19th-century nationalism influenced Kook's thought. Chapters three and four conclude the biographical account with Rabbi Kook's activities as a leader in Palestine, featuring discussions of some of his most controversial opinions, his most vociferous opponents, and his hopes for a united Jewish community in the land of Israel. The latter portion of the work introduces the reader to Kook's mystical and philosophical insights, covering a wide variety of topics including the "nearness of God" and its central role in spiritual life, Torah, Israel (the people and the land), prayer, evil, and evolution. While Agus argues that one should not "expect to discover a complete system of philosophy in Kook," this biography certainly conveys the depth and breadth of Kook's contribution to Jewish thought.

BEN SHLOMO is a professor of Jewish philosophy at Tel Aviv University, and his book is based on a series of radio lectures that he gave as part of the Broadcast University's offerings. Unlike Agus, Ben Shlomo maintains that underneath the unsystematic surface of Rabbi Kook's writings lies a unified philosophy that can indeed be described as a system. This system is a dialectical one that allows all aspects of existence to have a positive role in the ongoing perfection of the universe; even phenomena that at first appear dark or evil are actually catalysts for the development of their more positive counterparts. Ben Shlomo develops this central theme throughout his book, with discussions ranging from the role of the divine will in creation to the unified multiplicity of the natural world, the existence of evil, and the final redemption of humankind.

GELLMAN's book is a collection of previously published essays by academics, rabbis, and independent scholars. Also included at the end of the book are two excerpts from Kook's own writings, on the renewal of the Jewish people and on the commandments. Gellman's goals for the volume were "to include those essays which touched upon the broader and more universal aspects of Rabbi Kook" and to provide the reader with "the basics of his philosophy." In line with these aims, the collection opens with an essay by Norman Lamm stressing the kabbalistic concept of unity as an overarching theme of Rabbi Kook's philosophy. This piece turns out, as expected, to define

the tenor of the rest of the collection, inasmuch as unity in all its forms (cosmic, religious, and national, to name but a few) appears as an important element in the discussions of almost every subject. The contextualization of Rabbi Kook's ideas within the various streams of traditional Jewish thought (see especially Yaron's article) and analysis of Kook's ideas as they relate to the spiritual and national situation of Jewry in the 20th century both receive secondary emphasis.

KAPLAN and SHATZ have compiled an excellent group of academic studies on Kook, many of which have not appeared elsewhere. The work is divided into three topical sections and ends with a comprehensive bibliography of primary and secondary materials. The authors represented in this collection present often differing interpretations of Kook's thought, providing a glimpse of some of the major hermeneutical problems regarding his work. Part one treats Rabbi Kook's relationship to Jewish traditions, with essays on his transformations of Kabbalah and Hasidism, his relationship to the legacy of Maimonides, and his contributions as poet and halakhist. As evident from Agus, Ben Shlomo, and Gellman, Kook's notions of unity and the dialectical processes of history and spiritual life figure largely in his thought, and part two is dedicated to discussions of how these elements appear in his thinking on tolerance, the sacred and the profane, belief, and the overcoming of death. Part three, the shortest section of the book, is titled "Zionism, Messianism, and the State of Israel," and it explores the role of Kook's dialectics in his thought on the land of Israel as well as the practical implications of his views for the Jewish polity.

NERIAH, in contrast to all of the authors reviewed above, gives the reader an "insider's" view of Rabbi Kook. His book is organized thematically, each chapter focusing on a different holiday or period of the Jewish year. The chapters are comprised of quotations from Rabbi Kook's writings and speeches together with a multitude of anecdotes about him told by his followers and friends. They transmit a sense of Kook's powerful personality and the impact he had on those who came under his spell. A glossary of Hebrew and Aramaic terms is provided, along with an appendix of short biographies of leading protagonists in the story of his life.

VICTORIA WATERS

Kotsk, Menahem Mendel of *see* Menahem Mendel of Kotsk

Krochmal, Nachman   1785–1840

Galician idealist philosopher of history and *Wissenschaft* scholar

Cooper, Eli Louis, *Am Segullah: A Treasured People*, New York: Vantage, 1983

Harris, Jay, *Nachman Krochmal: Guiding the Perplexed of the Modern Age* (Modern Jewish Masters Series), New York: New York University Press, 1991

Rotenstreich, Nathan, *Jewish Philosophy in Modern Times: From Mendelssohn to Rosenzweig*, New York: Holt, Rinehart and Winston, 1968

Schechter, Solomon, "Nachman Krochmal and the 'Perplexities of the Time'," in his *Studies in Judaism*, Philadelphia: Jewish Publication Society, 1915

Schorsch, Ismar, "The Philosophy of History of Nachman Krochmal," *Judaism*, 10, 1961

Schorsch, Ismar, "Zunz as Krochmal's Editor," *Leo Baeck Institute Yearbook*, 31, 1986

Spiegel, Shalom, *Hebrew Reborn*, New York: Macmillan, 1930; London: Benn, 1931

Nachman Krochmal was one of the first Jewish thinkers to integrate the study of history into his philosophical system. In *Moreh Nevukhei ha-Zeman* (Guide to the Perplexed of Our Time), edited by Leopold Zunz and published posthumously in 1851, Krochmal describes the eternal essence of the history of the Jewish people using the vocabulary of contemporary idealist philosophy. Much of the literature on Krochmal and his work has been sparse and haphazard. Some scholars have discussed Krochmal within the context of larger studies covering many modern Jewish thinkers, often drawing on just one aspect of his philosophy in order to support a particular thesis. Others have focused primarily on the secular philosophical influences on Krochmal. Harris offers the most comprehensive treatment of Krochmal's intellectual legacy to date.

Although only an impressionistic sketch, SCHECHTER's pioneering article was one of the earliest works on Krochmal. His engaging prose provides a glimpse of Krochmal's life and his conception of history. Schechter explains why Krochmal's unprecedented foray into the field of Jewish history earned him the title Father of Jewish Science.

SPIEGEL analyzes Krochmal's work in the context of numerous other works written in Hebrew during the period of the Haskalah and thereafter. Taking a Zionist perspective, he claims that all Hebrew writings, even those whose authors were heretics, have religious content and lead "slowly but surely towards a revival of Jewish religious values." Krochmal's *Moreh* serves as an example that proves this theory. Although Krochmal was an observant Jew, his use of secular philosophy and treatment of contemporary issues removed his thinking from the realm of tradition. Nevertheless, Spiegel maintains that Krochmal's introduction of a historical sense into Jewish thought and his empirical study of Jewish rites and practices were aimed at preserving tradition. Spiegel argues that Krochmal "provided a foundation for Judaism in the empirical reality of all the spiritual creations of the Jewish genius."

SCHORSCH (1961) provides an important contribution to the discussion of Krochmal's intellectual heritage. He argues that although clearly influenced by Georg Wilhelm Friedrich Hegel, Krochmal's philosophy of history is not identical to that of his German predecessor. The article explores Krochmal's attempt to resolve the tension between tradition and history through a philosophic concept of immanence that states that the resolution of all conflicts is inherent in the Torah as given at Sinai. Schorsch compares Krochmal's Absolute Spirit and Hegel's World Spirit, pointing out several crucial distinctions.

According to Hegel, there is an end to history—a point at which man can escape it and achieve a complete understanding of the spirit. Krochmal, however, did not believe that most humankind would ever be able to comprehend the infinite spirit. The nation of Israel, nonetheless, was the one people that was not entirely controlled by these patterns of history. Because Israel's national spirit is the Absolute Spirit, the "study of Jewish history has become the door into the nature of the Absolute Spirit."

ROTENSTREICH is interested in the "transfer of philosophical concepts to traditional religious discourse" that results from the confrontation between traditional religious trends and philosophical systems. Rotenstreich's discussion of Krochmal is included within his discussion of Solomon Formstecher and Samson Raphael Hirsch because all three consider Judaism a religion of the spirit. Unlike the latter two thinkers, however, Krochmal's conception of spirit is transcendent, encompassing ethics. For him, Judaism, like all religions, does not occupy its own sphere; rather, it is subsumed by the greater totality of the Absolute Spirit. According to this view, explains Rotenstreich, "the religious sphere is a transitional stage on the road to complete, philosophical knowledge, just as the religious concept of God is a transitional stage to the perfect concept of God, that is, the 'absolute spiritual'." Perfection is achieved only through the comprehension of the absolute spiritual, which is expressed through history. Rotenstreich's discussion is somewhat cumbersome, however, particularly because his treatment of Krochmal relies on his discussion of Formstecher and Hirsch.

COOPER uses Krochmal's philosophy of history in order to support his thesis that the Jews are an eternal people and that the basis for their perseverance is the human-divine relationship. In this short book, he adopts Krochmal's assertion that the Jews are an eternal people and sees in Hasidism an instructive example of their characteristic endurance through history. Although his discussion is ideologically driven by a preconceived understanding of the eternal relationship between God and the Jewish people, Cooper does provide the most detailed overview of Krochmal's summary of the cycles of Jewish history.

SCHORSCH (1986) moves away from analysis of the intellectual content of Krochmal's writings and provides a refreshing perspective on his work. Because Krochmal died before completing his manuscript, Leopold Zunz, whom Krochmal personally requested to be his editor, faced the difficult task of organizing his work. In this article, Schorsch prints 29 letters connected to the preparation and publication of Krochmal's *Moreh*, which he found in Zunz's papers taken out of Germany in 1938. The letters themselves are written in German and Hebrew, but in his English-language introductory article Schorsch discusses the value of these letters in helping to identify Zunz's contributions to the original manuscript as well as in pointing to the concerns and influence of Krochmal's family members. Although none of these letters were penned by Krochmal himself, they contribute significantly to a vivid picture of the man and his intellectual legacy.

HARRIS has written "a biography of the mind that produced the great work," meaning, the *Moreh*. He accomplishes this task by challenging Krochmal's ideas with the philosophies of the thinkers whose ideas contested the traditional Jewish under-standing of God, history, the Bible, rabbinism, and the aggadah (Harris devotes one chapter to each of these topics). Harris is very clear in his presentation of the theories of these fashion-able European thinkers, demonstrating how they contest tra-ditional views and then explaining how Krochmal resolved these conflicts. He emphasizes repeatedly Krochmal's unique approach in which he subverts the very language and criteria of his opponents in order to support his own claims. Thus Krochmal, while accepting Herder's and Hegel's notion of his-torical cycles in which each nation experiences an era of supremacy and is then superseded, aims to demonstrate, through his lengthy discussion of the Jewish renaissance dur-ing the Second Commonwealth, how the Jewish people can never be superseded. Harris organizes Krochmal's ideas clearly and vividly depicts the Jewish and European intellectual milieux to which he was reacting. As a conservative 19th-century Wissenschaft thinker, Krochmal advises the perplexed of his time to embrace new intellectual currents because all of mod-ern scholarship is contained within traditional Jewish thought.

ADINA L. SHOULSON

L

Labor *see* Social Ethics

Ladino Literature

Alexander, Tamar, "A Judeo-Spanish Traditional Play (Salonica, 1932)," in *The Jewish Communities of Southeastern Europe: From the Fifteenth Century to the End of World War II*, edited by Ioannes K. Chasiotes, Thessaloniki: Institute for Balkan Studies, 1997

Altabé, David Fintz, "Konsezho a Tomar: A Haskalah Work in Judeo-Spanish," *Tradition*, 15(4), Spring 1976

Altabé, David Fintz, "The Romanso, 1900–1933: A Bibliographical Survey," *Sephardic Scholar*, 3, 1977–1978

Altabé, David Fintz, "Parallels in the Development of Modern Turkish and Judeo-Spanish Literatures," in *Studies on Turkish-Jewish History: Political and Social Relations, Literature, and Linguistics: The Quincentennial Papers*, edited by Altabé, Erhan Atay, and Israel Katz, New York: Sepher-Hermon for the American Society of Sephardic Studies, 1996

Altabé, David Fintz, "Reflections of Sephardic Life in the Ottoman Empire in Two Judeo-Spanish Novels," in *Studies on Turkish-Jewish History: Political and Social Relations, Literature, and Linguistics: The Quincentennial Papers*, edited by Altabé, Erhan Atay, and Israel Katz, New York: Sepher-Hermon for the American Society of Sephardic Studies, 1996

Angel, Marc D., "The Pirkei Abot of Reuben Eliyahu Israel," *Tradition*, 11(4), Spring 1971

Angel, Marc D., "Judeo-Spanish Drama: A Study of Sephardic Culture," *Tradition*, 19(2), Summer 1981

Angel, Marc D., *La America: The Sephardic Experience in the United States*, Philadelphia: Jewish Publication Society, 1982

Armistead, Samuel G., "Judeo-Spanish Traditional Poetry in the United States," in *Sephardim in the Americas: Studies in Culture and History* (Judaic Studies Series), edited by Martin A. Cohen and Abraham J. Peck, Tuscaloosa: University of Alabama Press, 1993

Armistead, Samuel G. and Joseph H. Silverman, *The Judeo-Spanish Ballad Chapbooks of Yacob Abraham Yoná* (Folk Literature of the Sephardic Jews, vol. 1), Berkeley: University of California Press, 1971

Armistead, Samuel G. and Joseph H. Silverman, "Sephardic Folkliterature and Eastern Mediterranean Oral Tradition," *Musica Judaica*, 6(1), 1983–1984

Armistead, Samuel G., Joseph H. Silverman, and Israel J. Katz, *Judeo-Spanish Ballads from Oral Tradition* (Folk Literature of the Sephardic Jews, vol. 2), Berkeley: University of California Press, 1986

Armistead, Samuel G., Joseph H. Silverman, and Israel J. Katz, *Judeo-Spanish Ballads from Oral Tradition II: Carolingian Ballads (1): Roncesvalles* (Folk Literature of the Sephardic Jews, vol. 3), Berkeley: University of California Press, 1994

Benardete, Maír José, *Hispanic Culture and Character of Sephardic Jews*, New York: Hispanic Institute in the United States, 1953; 2nd corrected edition edited and augmented by Marc D. Angel, New York: Sepher-Hermon, 1982

Benmayor, Rina, "Social Determinants in Poetic Transmission: The Sephardic *Romancero*," in *The Sepharadi and Oriental Jewish Heritage: Studies*, edited by Issachar Ben-Ami, Jerusalem: Magnes Press of Hebrew University, 1982

Bunis, David M., "Pyesa di Yaakov Avinu kun sus izus (Bucharest 1862): The First Judezmo Play?," in *History and Creativity in the Sephardi and Oriental Jewish Communities*, edited by Tamar Alexander, Abraham Haim, Galit Hasan-Rokem, and Ephraim Hazan, Jerusalem: Misgav Yerushalayim, 1994

Bunis, David M., "Modernization and the Language Question among Judezmo-Speaking Sephardim of the Ottoman Empire," in *Sephardi and Middle Eastern Jewries: History and Culture in the Modern Era*, edited by Harvey E. Goldberg, Bloomington: Indiana University Press, 1996

Cohen, Judith, "Women's Role in Judeo-Spanish Song," in *Active Voices: Women in Jewish Culture*, edited by Maurie Sacks, Urbana: University of Illinois Press, 1995

Cohen, Judith, "Evolving Roles of Women in Judeo-Spanish Song," in *Hispano-Jewish Civilization after 1492*, edited by Yom Tov Assis and Galit Hasan-Rokem, Jerusalem: Misgav Yerushalayim, 1997

Díaz Más, Paloma, *Los Sefardíes*, 1986; translated by George K. Zucker as *Sephardim: The Jews from Spain*, Chicago: University of Chicago Press, 1992

Filippis, Dimitrios, "An Introduction to the Sephardic Language and Literature of the Spanish-Speaking Jews of Thessaloniki," in *The Jewish Communities of*

Southeastern Europe: From the Fifteenth Century to the End of World War II, edited by Ioannes K. Chasiotes, Thessaloniki: Institute for Balkan Studies, 1997

Halio, Hank, *Ladino Reveries: Tales of the Sephardic Experience in America,* New York: Foundation for the Advancement of Sephardic Studies and Culture, 1996

Hemsi, Alberto, *Cancionero Sefardí* (Yuval Music Series, 4), Jerusalem: Jewish Music Research Centre, the Hebrew University of Jerusalem, 1995

Kobrin, Nancy H., "Holocaust Literature in Judeo-Spanish, Portuguese and Spanish," *Tradition,* 18(3), Fall 1980

Lévy, Isaac Jack, *And the World Stood Silent: Sephardic Poetry of the Holocaust,* Urbana: University of Illinois Press, 1989

Loewenthal, Robyn Kay, "Elia Carmona's Autobiography: Judeo-Spanish Popular Press and Novel Publishing Milieu in Constantinople, Ottoman Empire, Circa 1860–1932," Ph.D. diss., University of Nebraska-Lincoln, 1984

Mirrer, Louise, "Reinterpreting an Ancient Legend: The Judeo-Spanish Version of the Rape of Lucretia," *Prooftexts,* 6(2), May 1986

Mirrer, Louise, "Adultery, Intermarriage, and the Theme of Group Destruction in the Judeo-Spanish Ballad Tradition of Seattle and Los Angeles," in *History and Creativity in the Sephardi and Oriental Jewish Communities,* edited by Tamar Alexander, Abraham Haim, Galit Hasan-Rokem, and Ephraim Hazan, Jerusalem: Misgav Yerushalayim, 1994

Nar, Albertos, "Una pastora yo ami: An Oriental Sephardic Folksong and Its Origins," in *The Jewish Communities of Southeastern Europe: From the Fifteenth Century to the End of World War II,* edited by Ioannes K. Chasiotes, Thessaloniki: Institute for Balkan Studies, 1997

Refael, Shmuel, "The Judeo-Spanish 'Romance': The Characteristics and Uniqueness of the Genre in Salonica," in *The Jewish Communities of Southeastern Europe: From the Fifteenth Century to the End of World War II,* edited by Ioannes K. Chasiotes, Thessaloniki: Institute for Balkan Studies, 1997

Romero, Elena, "Literary Creation in the Sephardi Diaspora," in *Moreshet Sepharad: The Sephardi Legacy,* vol. 2, edited by Haim Beinart, Jerusalem: Magnes Press, Hebrew University, 1992

Salama, Messod, "Rabbinical Exegesis in the Judeo-Spanish Romancero," in *Hispano-Jewish Civilization after 1492,* edited by Yom Tov Assis and Galit Hasan-Rokem, Jerusalem: Misgav Yerushalayim, 1997

Vidakovic Petrov, Krinka, "Sephardic Folklore and the Balkan Cultural Environment," in *History and Creativity in the Sephardi and Oriental Jewish Communities,* edited by Tamar Alexander, Abraham Haim, Galit Hasan-Rokem, and Ephraim Hazan, Jerusalem: Misgav Yerushalayim, 1994

Vidakovic Petrov, Krinka, "The Sephardim in Yugoslavia: Playwrights, Plays, and Performances," in *Hispano-Jewish Civilization after 1492,* edited by Yom Tov Assis and Galit Hasan-Rokem, Jerusalem: Misgav Yerushalayim, 1997

Weich-Shahak, Susana, "Musico-Poetic Genres in the Repertoire of the Saloniki Sephardic Jews," in *The Jewish Communities of Southeastern Europe: From the Fifteenth Century to the End of World War II,* edited by Ioannes K. Chasiotes, Thessaloniki: Institute for Balkan Studies, 1997

Weich-Shahak, Susana, "Stylistic Features of the Sephardi Copla," in *Hispano-Jewish Civilization after 1492,* edited by Yom Tov Assis and Galit Hasan-Rokem, Jerusalem: Misgav Yerushalayim, 1997

Research into Ladino literature, conducted mostly in Spain and Israel, is a field of study all but unexplored before the late 20th century. Older publications were essentially bibliographies or anthologies. The first monograph dealing with a large body of Judeo-Spanish literature was published in Spanish only several years ago (Elena Romero's *La creación literária en lengua sefardí,* Madrid: Mapfre, 1992). Only a few English-language studies exist, and they are generally confined to only one literary work or one aspect of literature, most often the Sephardi ballads known as romances. The works reviewed in this essay are recent studies in English on Eastern Judeo-Spanish literature. Readers are cautioned that this survey does not cover the full breadth of the literary production of Spanish-speaking Sephardim. Nor does this essay consider works on Western Sephardi literature, because such works were not written in Ladino but in Castilian Spanish or in Portuguese.

ALEXANDER presents her literary analysis of Shlomo Merkado Reuben's play *Ester* (Esther), which was written and performed in Salonika (Thessaloníki) in 1932. Alexander begins by discussing the tradition of biblical dramas in Jewish society and provides background material about forms of Purim celebration. She also provides a biographical sketch of Reuben. She discusses the play's music, the original choreographer, and the circumstances of the play's production. She also analyzes different versions of the text, the structure of the play, its performance, and the sources Reuben drew from in writing the play. She concludes by discussing French playwright Jean Racine's influence on Reuben.

ALTABÉ (1976) analyzes an anonymous autobiographical story printed serially in a Ladino journal in Vienna. The story takes place in about 1880 and is set in Istanbul. It describes the first 35 years of the author's life in a traditional Sephardi community. The author paints a vivid yet critical portrait of the society and its superstitions. Altabé summarizes the contents and compares the ideas of the author with the aims of the Alliance Israélite Universelle.

ALTABÉ (1996a) compares events in Turkey and in Sephardi communities during the 17th to 19th centuries. Around 1840 the first Turkish and the first Judeo-Spanish newspapers began to appear. Translations of French literature became available in both cultures as well. In 1873 the first patriotic Turkish play was staged. Similarly, Sephardi communities began performing Judeo-Spanish plays, religious dramas, and secular plays (mostly those of Molière or Racine) at the Alliance schools. Outstanding original Judeo-Spanish playwrights included Abraham Capon and Shabbetay Djaen of Yugoslavia.

Two other works of Altabé are worthy of note. ALTABÉ (1996b) discusses the novel *Rafael i Miryam* by B. Sacerdote (possibly a pseudonym of B. Hakohen) and the autobiography of Elia Carmona, which not only uses the devices of fiction but in many ways resembles a picaresque novel. ALTABÉ (1977–1978) lists original Judeo-Spanish works and translated novels published from 1900 to 1933 and provides statistical data.

ANGEL (1971) offers a biographical sketch of Rabbi Reuben Eliyahu Israel of Rhodes, bibliographic information on his works, and literary analysis. Angel praises his subject's translation of Mishnah Avot, published in 1924, and discusses some of his translation methods.

ANGEL (1981) describes the beginnings of the modern study of Sephardi culture in Spain as a prologue to his review of Elena Romero's important 1979 study of the dramatic literature of the Eastern Sephardim, *El Teatro de los Sefardies orientales*. Romero lists 684 original and translated plays. Angel summarizes Romero's research and notes that the dramatic repertoire of Judeo-Spanish theaters in the United States should be added to this list.

ANGEL (1982) is a biography of Moise Gadol, the editor of *La America*, the first Judeo-Spanish newspaper published in the United States (1910–1925). Gadol and his newspaper played a central role in New York City's Sephardi community, and the newspaper reported on and documented the community's activities and concerns. Using *La America* as his main source (other sources include interviews with Gadol's friends and acquaintances), Angel chronicles Gadol's life in the larger context of the Sephardi immigrant community. Most of the Judeo-Spanish intellectuals living in the United States from 1910 to 1941 are mentioned in the book, as are other Judeo-Spanish newspapers, particularly *La Vara*, a major competitor of Gadol's paper.

ARMISTEAD, one of the most distinguished American researchers of Judeo-Spanish folk literature, presents a short description of an ambitious team project he carried out with Joseph H. Silverman and ethnomusicologist Israel J. Katz. He supplies introductions to and examples of each genre of the literature in romanized Judeo-Spanish and in English translation. ARMISTEAD and SILVERMAN (1983–1984) provide a useful introduction to the study of Judeo-Spanish folklore, concentrating mostly on ballads and *coplas* and their connections with Greek, Turkish, and Serbo-Croat counterparts.

In the introduction to their study, ARMISTEAD and SILVERMAN (1971) make a serious attempt to compile a biography of the poet and collector of Judeo-Spanish folk poetry, Jacob Abraham Jona of Salonika (Thessaloníki). They supply a list of his chapbooks and a bibliography of the romances published in these pamphlets. In the introduction to ARMISTEAD, SILVERMAN , and KATZ (1986), the authors consider the traditional types of Sephardi ballad and their importance in research on medieval Spanish balladry. They describe how they collected and collated versions of texts as they conducted their fieldwork from 1957 to 1978 in different Sephardi communities. They also compare their findings to Ramon Menendez Pidal's collection of ballads from the Iberian Peninsula and review most other published collections. In the introduction to ARMISTEAD, SILVERMAN, and KATZ (1994), the authors discuss separate thematic aspects of the traditional ballads of the Sephardim, going back to Car-

olingian ballads and their Spanish derivatives, connected to the defeat of the French at Roncesvalles. The authors discuss particular ballads and their forms, tracing their evolution from medieval Spain to versions current among their Balkan Sephardi informants.

BENARDETE presents a useful introduction to Judeo-Spanish culture and provides historical and social background for the emergence of Judeo-Spanish literature, as well as documenting Sephardi contacts with Spain and tracing the decline of Sephardi communities. He examines the role of Hebrew and Judeo-Spanish languages in Jewish society, noting the influence of Sephardi Hebrew literature on the emerging Judeo-Spanish literature and arguing that Hebrew stood in the way of Judeo-Spanish evolving as a literary language. He discusses some early Sephardi and Marrano literati of the Ottoman Empire, such as Rabbi Moses Almosnino and Amatus Lusitanus. Other topics he covers include Judeo-Spanish books from the first half of the 16th century, the composition of the popular homiletical digest *Me'am Lo'ez*, translations of the Bible dating from before the expulsion as well as later translations of the 18th century, the impact of the establishment of modern schools by the Alliance Israélite Universelle, and Judeo-Spanish newspapers. He asserts that Christian missionaries played a positive role in educating Jewish boys and girls and by translating the Bible into Judeo-Spanish. Benardete concludes with a discussion of Sephardi communities in the United States and their social and cultural problems.

BENMAYOR analyzes the modern study of Sephardi ballads (romances), noting differences in methodology and goals, and calls for an integration of the research. She outlines key social issues confronting the Sephardim in the Ottoman Empire, the role oral poetry played in social functions, and how social factors influenced the history of folk literature.

BUNIS (1996) describes the language problems that began to arise in Sephardi communities in the Ottoman Empire as the influence of Western culture increased. Bunis notes that debates published in the Judeo-Spanish press are very important both to the study of the sociology of the Sephardim and to the study of the literary process in Judeo-Spanish literature. The article discusses two aspects of these debates: arguments regarding replacement of the language and arguments regarding normalization of the language. To help illustrate the differing attitudes toward Judeo-Spanish, Bunis notes that the same language was known by different names (e.g., Judezmo) and that its scripts and orthography were extremely varied.

BUNIS (1994) discusses Moshe Shemuel Kofino's play *Pyesa di Yaakov Avinu kun sus izus*, which was performed in Bucharest in 1862 and which the author contends may be the first Judezmo play. The play dramatizes the biblical story of Joseph being sold into slavery by his brothers. Bunis analyzes the play's language, content, and literary features and also includes a transcription of the play.

COHEN (1995) discusses women in their role as performers and transmitters of Judeo-Spanish songs. Previous researchers dealt with text or music only. Cohen outlines various genres of Judeo-Spanish song, and then she describes the function of each genre. She also describes the almost spontaneous process of "dechristianization" and adaptation of non-Jewish content to make it reflect Jewish values. Cohen also acknowledges the role recent scholars have played in the reshaping of the Judeo-Spanish repertoire, particularly the cadre of women scholars who both conduct ethnomusicological research and also act as consultants to performers. COHEN (1997) describes women's role in the selection, performance, and preservation of the character of Judeo-Spanish songs and compares and contrasts the heroines of these songs with modern women performers.

Chapter four of DÍAZ MÁS's book offers the most complete English-language survey of Judeo-Spanish literature to date, although it still does not cover the entire spectrum. The chapter is an excellent place for beginners to gain a familiarization with the literature. The chapter is divided into the following subsections: "The Bible and Religious Literature," "The Coplas," "Traditional Genres: Proverb, Popular Story, Ballad," and " 'Adopted Genres': Journalism, Narrative, Theater, Autograph Poetry."

FILIPPIS sets down some basic facts on the Judeo-Spanish of Salonika (Thessaloníki) and discusses the names of the language and its elements, speech, and scripts. He also discusses literary genres of Judeo-Spanish literature and their relationship to Balkan literatures. He discusses Me'am Lo'ez and other literary works, the influence of the Alliance Israélite Universelle on education and literary tastes, and the development of a prolific Judeo-Spanish press. The author notes the influence of translations of Western novels and of the modernization of Sephardi life, especially after the Greek annexation of the city in 1912, on Judeo-Spanish literature. Filippis concludes by outlining the causes of the crisis in Sephardi society—the disintegration of its traditional structure, the community's identity crisis, the language problem, and finally the consequences of the Holocaust.

HALIO's book is a collection of his columns published in the *Sephardic Home News* beginning in 1986, when the Judeo-Spanish language was dying and some older Sephardim, mostly born in the United States, demonstrated a curiosity about their parents' or grandparents' native tongue. Halio writes on a wide variety of subjects including the history of Spanish Jews, the identity of the Sephardim, the beauty of Judeo-Spanish, Ladino proverbs, poetry, fables, loan words in Judeo-Spanish (e.g., from Turkish or English), and the difficulties Sephardi immigrants experienced in learning English.

In a new edition of HEMSI's collection of Judeo-Spanish folk songs of the eastern Mediterranean region, Edwin Seroussi evaluates the compilation, citing the opinions of such experts as Samuel G. Armistead and Joseph H. Silverman and ethnomusicologist Israel J. Katz. He describes the original layout and its genre and thematic divisions, followed by a description of the present edition. Seroussi also discusses the history and conception of Hemsi's collection, including some quotes from Hemsi's autobiographical writings, and evaluates Hemsi as a musicologist. Introducing the liturgical section of the collection, Seroussi comments on seven songs included in the section and cites their sources. The songs he discusses were all translated from Hebrew or Aramaic and became traditional through their performance on holidays. Paloma Díaz Más provides the historical background for Hemsi's work and ranks him among other researchers of Sephardi romances. She analyzes his methods and the ways in which he built his col-

lection. Then she examines the content, themes, and motifs of the romances in the collection and discusses the originality of the ballads. José M. Pedrosa discusses versions of songs recorded by Hemsi and notes their value for researchers. He finds in the collection the following genres: birth songs, lullabies, love songs, wedding songs, entertainment songs, and death songs. Pedrosa considers the relationship between *romanceros* (ballads) and *canciones* (songs) and also discusses the geographical or ethnic origins of songs. Elena Romero introduces *coplas* (rhymes). She points out that *coplas* were written down, whereas *romanceros* and *canciones* were transmitted orally. She mentions that *coplas* owe less to Hispanic influences and may be viewed as original Sephardi creations. She discusses *coplas* with biblical themes and a few that are of religious or national interest. One of the *coplas* contains a reference to the false messiah Shabbetai Tsevi. In his discussion, Armistead notes the value of the Hemsi collection and the importance of the present edition. He observes that the collection preserves numerous Turkisms and Balkanisms. Regarding the literary process in oral poetry, the collection is valuable for the study of contamination (combining diverse components of unrelated narrative poems). He illustrates the ethnically varied character of Sephardi songs by pointing out loan words borrowed from Greek, Turkish, and Albanian.

KOBRIN brings to light some neglected works of Holocaust literature. Among the works she discusses are Isaac Benrubi's *El Sekreto del mudo*, a novel about two Sephardi inmates in Auschwitz, and a communal history, *Zikhron Saloniki: Grandeza i Destruyicion de Yeruchalayim del Balkan*, edited by David A. Recanati. Although only a very small part of *Zikhron Saloniki* is written in Judeo-Spanish, even this part is not original.

In the preface and introduction to his anthology of poetry, LÉVY brings together historical and literary data related to the fate of those who were part of the Sephardi diaspora during World War II, particularly those living in Greece. In a special introductory chapter "Hatred Hurt Them into Poetry," he analyzes poems written by Sephardi inmates of Auschwitz and other camps and Sephardi survivors of the Holocaust and identifies the poems' principal ideas and motifs. The anthology itself includes poems in the original Judeo-Spanish with parallel English translations.

LOEWENTHAL presents a biographical sketch of Elia Carmona, a major figure among modern Sephardi writers and journalists. She also provides an introduction to the history of the Judeo-Spanish press and transliterates Carmona's autobiography.

MIRRER (1986) analyzes an old Judeo-Spanish ballad based on the ancient Roman legend of Lucretia, the virtuous Roman matron, and the Roman king Tarquin. In all the Sephardi versions of this ballad, Lucretia is a Jewish queen and Tarquin is a Christian king who attempts to seduce her. Pride in Jewish identity prompts Lucretia to give up her life rather than dishonor her kinsmen. Mirrer uses this romance as an example of how literary processes may reshape history.

MIRRER (1994) suggests the vividity with which Sephardim continue to view the Spain of their ancestors as a point of reference. She discusses a particular group of romances, involving themes of adultery and intermarriage, that are sung in

Seattle and Los Angeles. She argues that these medieval texts serve a contemporary social function because adultery and intermarriage are major threats to the stability of the American-Sephardi subculture.

NAR discusses one of the best-known Sephardi folk songs, "Una pastora yo ami," providing its original Judeo-Spanish text and an English translation. He traces the song's origins to the Greek poem "The Kiss" by the 19th-century Greek poet Georgios Zalokostas. Nar discovers that the poem became popular through theatrical performances and was then reworked into a Judeo-Spanish context.

REFAEL concentrates on ballads. He summarizes the results of his research on some 356 ballads of Salonika (Thessaloníki), discussing their classification and the tasks of his project.

ROMERO surveys Judeo-Spanish literature from the 16th through the 19th centuries. She discusses biblical translations and liturgical works, religious ethics and halakhah, the works of Rabbi Abraham Asa and Me'am Lo'ez, the Judeo-Spanish press from the mid-19th century to the present, and Judeo-Spanish theater, a field in which Romero is a pioneering researcher. Romero concludes by discussing the factors that brought about the decline and demise of Judeo-Spanish literature in the 20th century.

SALAMA criticizes earlier scholars for concentrating on Spanish sources of Judeo-Spanish ballads and neglecting Jewish ones. He discusses the biblical romances and their popularity in different Jewish communities. Salama suggests that rabbis or learned laymen may have extemporized midrash-based elaborations of the original Iberian Peninsula romances. These midrashic interpretations were later memorized by female singers and became a major source of popular literature. Most of the rabbinic material were borrowed from Me'am Lo'ez or from Pirke Avot; the rest comes largely from Sefer ha-Yashar and Pirke de Rabbi Eli'ezer. Salama asserts that almost all of the deviations or additional details in biblical romances can be explained by finding the sources in this midrashic literature.

VIDAKOVIC PETROV (1994) describes the ethnic diversity of the Balkan peninsula and the social conditions of the Sephardi communities and how these circumstances influenced Sephardi popular literature. The beliefs, superstitions, and popular customs of Balkan gentiles found their way into Judeo-Spanish oral and literary texts. Vidakovic concludes with a discussion of two Sephardi documents, a manuscript from Bosnia dated 1820 and a notebook of David Kamhi of Sarajevo. Both documents show that the Sephardim were bilingual, at home in Serbo-Croat as well as Spanish, and familiar with local folklore. Processes of assimilation and interaction had been at work all through the Ottoman period, and they intensified during the middle of the 19th century. By the end of the 19th century, some Sephardi writers wrote in Serbo-Croat, while others continued to write in Judeo-Spanish until World War II.

VIDAKOVIC PETROV (1997) is a survey, beginning in 1625, of dramas performed among the Sephardim of Italy and Yugoslavia. Most of the plays—comedies and tragedies—were biblical narratives related to particular holidays such as Purim or Passover. Vidakovic also discusses a number of theaters, actors, and playwrights in Yugoslavia.

WEICH-SHAHAK (1997a) discusses Judeo-Spanish romanceros, cancioneros, and coplas. The emphasis in her article is on the classification and definition of these genres. She analyzes the social function and the prosody and literary features of the poems in conjunction with their musical structure. She also notes Eastern influences. WEICH-SHAHAK (1997b) defines the Sephardi copla genre and analyzes content, structure, versification, rhyme schemes, and musical structure.

HAYIM Y. SHEYNIN

Lamentations

Hillers, Delbert R. (editor), Lamentations (Anchor Bible, 7A), Garden City, New York: Doubleday, 1972, 2nd edition, 1992

Provan, Iain, Lamentations (New Century Bible Commentary), Grand Rapids, Michigan: Eerdmans, and London: Pickering, 1991

Rosenberg, Abraham J., The Five Megilloth, vol. 2: Lamentations and Ecclesiastes, New York: Judaica, 1992

Salters, Robert B., Jonah and Lamentations (Old Testament Guides), Sheffield, South Yorkshire: JSOT, 1994

Westermann, Claus, Lamentations: Issues and Interpretation, Minneapolis, Minnesota: Fortress, and Edinburgh: Clark, 1994

The Book of Lamentations is a collection of five poems, traditionally held to be the work of the prophet Jeremiah; indeed, the Greek translation of the book has a superscription that identifies not only the author but the time in which the book was written: just after the fall of Jerusalem in 586 B.C.E. This identification is further emphasized by the location of the book within the Greek Bible, where it is juxtaposed with Jeremiah. Four of the five poems are in acrostic form, while the fifth, although not an actual acrostic, has 22 lines (the number of letters in the Hebrew alphabet). The questions that arise in the book are those of origin, authorship, function, background, and theology, and some of the publications described below deal with these issues. The traditional view that Jeremiah was the author has been abandoned by all but the most conservative biblical scholars, but there are those who would argue that the book is, nevertheless, a unity, whoever the author was.

WESTERMANN's highly interesting book is true to its subtitle: the text covers the issues and provides interpretation. While there is a translation and a commentary on the text, there is also an invaluable section (chapter two) that puts the reader in the picture by tracing the history of the interpretation of Lamentations from the turn of the century up to 1985. Westermann then deals with the date of composition, the place of composition (probably Judah), the question of authorship, and the unity of the book (several authors and not a unity). Westermann's first chapter is a discussion of various views on the idea that Lamentations may be modeled on a foreign (Sumerian) lament over the city of Ur and so is a literary construction. The argument that prevails is that the genre of the five poems is largely that of the communal lament seen in various ancient Near Eastern cultures and most familiarly in the Book of Psalms. Westermann holds that the acrostic pattern has been imposed on the poems, thereby giving the impression that there is a unity of sorts, but that the sentiments are, for the most part, a collection of actual expressions of grief and lamentation from those who witnessed the fall of Jerusalem. In a section titled "The Theological Significance of Lamentations," he observes that God is depicted as directing history—not just the history of Israel but that of all peoples, at least in their relation to Israel. The book also shows that the authors, who attribute the fall of Jerusalem to the sins of the people of Judah, are in agreement with the prophetic message represented by Jeremiah.

SALTERS's book is not a commentary; it is a guide to Lamentations and is primarily aimed at the general reader or student. Salters believes that all five poems have as their starting point the tragedy of the fall of Jerusalem and its aftermath, and he feels it is important to offer a chapter on the historical background to this event—the rise of the kingdom of Babylon, the rebellion by Zedekiah, etc.—to set the scene. He also supplies an outline of the book before discussing traditional issues such as authorship (not Jeremiah and probably not one author), the acrostic phenomenon (employed as an artistic device and not as an aid to memory or to teach the alphabet), and the poetry in the book. He believes that the book was written and used to commemorate the disaster of 586 B.C.E.—the fact that the poems differ from the laments in the Book of Psalms points to the sheer magnitude of the tragedy, calling forth a special kind of composition.

In the second edition of HILLERS's commentary, he says that he writes "primarily for the general reader," and this is indeed so, although it should be noted that Hillers does provide technical support both for his views and for his translation. Subsequent to the publication of the first edition, a fragment of the Hebrew text of Lamentations was discovered among the documents of the Dead Sea Scrolls, and in the second edition Hillers discusses its quite considerable divergences from the Masoretic Hebrew text. Hillers is a cautious scholar, but this is one of the very best English-language treatments of Lamentations.

PROVAN's book is a good traditional commentary. The main difference from, say, Hillers' lies in Provan's belief that the poems may not have originated in the aftermath of 586 B.C.E. He argues that others have accepted the traditional standpoint (at least in part) without proper examination of the evidence. There are no dates or names given in the book to link the poems with any period in particular. The author, he argues, is given to hyperbole, which makes any attempt at interpretation a risky business.

ROSENBERG's book may, at first sight, alarm the general reader, but in fact a lot of what he says is quite digestible. It is true that the Hebrew text is accompanied by the Targum and several medieval Hebrew commentaries, but it is not necessary to read Hebrew or Aramaic to understand much of the accompanying material. Rosenberg offers a new English translation of Lamentations and a translation of the commentary by the medieval exegete Rashi (a valuable contribution in itself), which is supplemented with quotations and observa-

tions from midrashim and other medieval works, some of which are not available elsewhere in English translation. If the reader is searching for a modern approach to Lamentations this is not the place to look—Rosenberg simply assumes that Jeremiah is the author and that the fall of Jerusalem and its aftermath has caused him to write in this way—but Rosenberg approaches the text in such a way that the mood of lament comes across vividly to the reader. In fact, the medieval emphasis makes this book a good complement to Westermann's history of modern interpretation.

ROBERT B. SALTERS

Languages, Jewish

Ahroni, Reuben, "Some Observations on the Judeo-Arabic Dialect of the Jews of Aden," in his *The Jews of the British Crown Colony of Aden: History, Culture, and Ethnic Relations,* New York: Brill, 1994

Avishur, Yitzhak, "Some New Sources for the Study of the Text and Language of Saadya's Translation of the Pentateuch into Judeo-Arabic," in *Genizah Research after Ninety Years: The Case of Judaeo-Arabic: Papers Read at the Third Congress of the Society for Judaeo-Arabic Studies,* edited by Joshua Blau and Stefan C. Reif, Cambridge and New York: Cambridge University Press, 1992

Besso, Henry V., "Judeo-Spanish: Its Growth and Decline," in *The Sephardi Heritage,* edited by R.D. Barnett, New York: Ktav, 1971

Birnbaum, Salomo, "Jewish Languages," in *Essays in Honour of The Very Rev. Dr. J.H. Hertz,* edited by I. Epstein, E. Levine, and C. Roth, London: Goldston, 1942

Blau, Joshua, *The Emergence and Linguistic Background of Judaeo-Arabic,* London: Oxford University Press, 1965; 2nd edition, Jerusalem: Ben-Zvi Institute for the Study of Jewish Communities in the East, 1981

Blau, Joshua, "On a Fragment of the Oldest Judeo-Arabic Bible Translation Extant," in *Genizah Research after Ninety Years: The Case of Judaeo-Arabic: Papers Read at the Third Congress of the Society for Judaeo-Arabic Studies,* edited by Joshua Blau and Stefan C. Reif, Cambridge and New York: Cambridge University Press, 1992

Blau, Joshua and Simon Hopkins, "On Early Judeo-Arabic Orthography," in Blau's *Studies in Middle Arabic and Its Judaeo-Arabic Variety,* Jerusalem: Magnes Press of Hebrew University, 1988

Bunis, David M., "The Language of the Sephardim: A Historical Overview," in *Moreshet Sepharad: The Sephardi Legacy,* vol. 2, edited by Haim Beinart, Jerusalem: Magnes Press of Hebrew University, 1992

Bunis, David M., "Judezmo and Its Hebrew and Aramaic Component: An Introduction," in his *A Lexicon of the Hebrew and Aramaic Elements in Modern Judezmo,* Jerusalem: Magnes Press of Hebrew University [and] Misgav Yerushalayim, 1993

Chetrit, Joseph, "Judeo-Arabic and Judeo-Spanish in Morocco and Their Socio-linguistic Interaction," in *Readings in the Sociology of Jewish Languages*, edited by Joshua A. Fishman, Leiden: Brill, 1985

Cohen, D. and Joshua Blau, "Judeo-Arabic," in *The Encyclopaedia of Islam*, edited by E. van Donzel, B. Lewis, and Ch. Pellat, vol. 4, new edition, Leiden: Brill, 1978

Drory, Rina, " 'Words Beautifully Put': Hebrew Versus Arabic in Tenth-Century Jewish Literature," in *Genizah Research after Ninety Years: The Case of Judaeo-Arabic: Papers Read at the Third Congress of the Society for Judaeo-Arabic Studies*, edited by Joshua Blau and Stefan C. Reif, Cambridge and New York: Cambridge University Press, 1992

Fishman, Joshua A. (editor), *Never Say Die!: A Thousand Years of Yiddish in Jewish Life and Letters*, New York: Mouton, 1981

Fitzmyer, Joseph A., *A Wandering Aramean: Collected Aramaic Essays*, Missoula, Montana: Scholars Press, 1979

Greenfield, Jonas C., "The Genesis Apocryphon: Observations on Some Words and Phrases," in *Studies in Hebrew and Semitic Languages Dedicated to the Memory of Prof. Eduard Yechezkel Kutscher*, edited by Gad B. Sarfatti et al., Ramat-Gan: Bar-Ilan University Press, 1980

Harris, Tracy K., *Death of a Language: The History of Judeo-Spanish*, Newark: University of Delaware Press, and London: Associated University Presses, 1994

Jerusalmi, Isaac, "Ladino, Our Language," in his *From Ottoman Turkish to Ladino: The Case of Mehmet Sadik Rifat Pasha's Risâle-i Ahlâk and Judge Yehezkel Gabbay's Buen Dotrino* (Ladino Books), Cincinnati, Ohio: Jerusalmi, 1990

Komlosh, Yehudah, "The Etymological Basis of Certain Translations in the Targum Jonathan to the Twelve Prophets," in *Studies in Hebrew and Semitic Languages Dedicated to the Memory of Prof. Eduard Yechezkel Kutscher*, edited by Gad B. Sarfatti et al., Ramat-Gan: Bar-Ilan University Press, 1980

Kutscher, Edward, "Aramaic," in *Encyclopaedia Judaica*, vol. 3, Jerusalem: Keter, 1971

Kutscher, Edward, *Hebrew and Aramaic Studies*, Jerusalem: Magnes Press of Hebrew University, 1977

Lazard, G., "Judeo-Persian: Language," in *The Encyclopaedia of Islam*, edited by E. van Donzel, B. Lewis, and Ch. Pellat, vol. 4, new edition, Leiden: Brill, 1978

Paper, Herbert H. (editor), *Jewish Languages: Theme and Variations*, Cambridge, Massachusetts: Association for Jewish Studies, 1978

Schussman, Aviva, "An Iraqi Judeo-Arabic Version of Ma'aseh Avraham: Some Literary and Linguistic Features," in *Genizah Research after Ninety Years: The Case of Judaeo-Arabic: Papers Read at the Third Congress of the Society for Judaeo-Arabic Studies*, edited by Joshua Blau and Stefan C. Reif, Cambridge and New York: Cambridge University Press, 1992

Shaked, Shaul and Amnon Netzer (editors), *Irano-Judaica*, 3 vols., Jerusalem: Ben-Zvi Institute for the Study of Jewish Communities in the East, 1982–1994

Shy, Hadassa, "Taqdir and Its Counterparts in Mediaeval Judeo-Arabic," in *Genizah Research after Ninety Years: The Case of Judaeo-Arabic: Papers Read at the Third Congress of the Society for Judaeo-Arabic Studies*, edited by Joshua Blau and Stefan C. Reif, Cambridge and New York: Cambridge University Press, 1992

Sokoloff, Michael, "Notes on the Vocabulary of Galilean Aramaic," in *Studies in Hebrew and Semitic Languages Dedicated to the Memory of Prof. Eduard Yechezkel Kutscher*, edited by Gad B. Sarfatti et al., Ramat-Gan: Bar-Ilan University Press, 1980

Weinreich, Max, *History of the Yiddish Language*, translated by Shlomo Noble with the assistance of Joshua A. Fishman, Chicago: University of Chicago Press, 1980

Wexler, Paul, "Recovering the Dialects and Sociology of Judeo-Greek in Non-Hellenistic Europe," in *Readings in the Sociology of Jewish Languages*, edited by Joshua A. Fishman, Leiden: Brill, 1985

Zafrani, H., "Judeo-Berber," in *The Encyclopaedia of Islam*, edited by E. van Donzel, B. Lewis, and Ch. Pellat, vol. 4, new edition, Leiden: Brill, 1978

Jewish languages is not a well-established linguistic category. Not all linguists accept this division on the grounds that this group includes languages that belong to different families. Many linguists resent classification of languages according to religious criteria. In addition, the Hebrew script cannot be the sole criterion, because the form is secondary to the language structure. Most modern scholars accept the idea of studying "languages of the Jews" as sociolects, while some others prefer to see the so-called Jewish languages as dialects of the languages of the majority in a particular geographic region; thus they see in Judeo-Spanish a dialect of Castilian, in Yiddish a dialect of German, in Judeo-Persian a dialect of Persian. There is more consensus in relation to European Jewish languages, although scholars are divided in identifying and counting these languages. Some think they number more than a dozen, while others count more than two dozen. The assessment of primary data is still in its infancy. From time to time, new Jewish languages and dialects are reported (e.g., Judeo-Persian dialects of the Jews of Arbīl and Hamadān or different dialects of Judeo-Arabic in Iraq, which were recognized during the 1980s). The disagreements relate also to the names of languages. Not all Jewish languages have been investigated to the same degree, some have not been researched at all, and others are known only in general. Very little of the linguistic research has concerned itself with the history of all Jewish languages, with even the best studies limited to a description of one or a group of Jewish languages or dialects. The greatest number of research works on the subject are in Hebrew, German, French, Italian, Spanish, Dutch, Czech, Hungarian, Russian, and Polish; some recent studies have also appeared in Arabic, Persian, Turkish, and Japanese. This essay, however, focuses on a limited selection of relatively recent English works and stresses the better-known Jewish languages.

BIRNBAUM deals with the classification of Jewish languages. He discusses different categories that linguists in the past ascribed to them. He rejects the categories "mixed languages" or "creolized languages" as irrelevant in relation to Jewish languages, stating that most known languages can be regarded as mixed. The term dialects is less derogatory to Jewish languages, but it implies a connection to a particular geographic area. The terms formed with *Judeo-* prefixed to the name of the non-Jewish majority language, for example, Judeo-Aramaic, Judeo-German, and Judeo-Spanish, are not linguistically and sociologically precise. Scholars still use these terms, but they are gradually being replaced by names such as Judezmo and Yiddish. Birnbaum himself suggests names such as Jevanic for Judeo-Greek, Zarphatic for Judeo-French, Italkian for Judeo-Italian, Farsic for Judeo-Persian, Maaravic for the Judeo-Arabic of the Maghreb, and Arvic for the Judeo-Arabic of western Asia, although by the close of the 20th century it appeared that only one of his suggestions—Farsic—was (partially) accepted, because it happened to approximate the name the language's speakers used. In the rest of the article, Birnbaum discusses factors involved in the formation of the entire group of Jewish languages and considers and rejects such factors as race and national spirit. He notices common trends in the group, namely, conservatism on many levels of the language and both phonological and lexical archaisms. He mentions the influence of religion and script on Jewish languages, noting, however, that religion and script alone do not define the language. He also notes that some of the Jewish languages are largely secularized.

PAPER's collection considers a number of Jewish languages: Hebrew, Aramaic and its dialects, Yiddish, Judeo-Romance languages, Ladino language and literature, Judeo-Persian, medieval Judeo-Arabic, and the languages used in Palestine from 200 B.C.E. to 200 C.E.

Semitic (Afro-Asian) Languages

Judeo-Aramaic

KUTSCHER (1972), the most important scholar of Aramaic, provides a survey of the entire Aramaic branch of Semitic languages. Among different languages and dialects, many are Judeo-Aramaic. Among the earliest Jewish texts in Aramaic are long passages in the biblical books of Ezra and Daniel (fourth to second centuries B.C.E.), which represent varieties of ancient and official Aramaic. Another significant group includes ancient Aramaic texts that originated in Elephantine (a Jewish colony in southern Egypt that flourished during the sixth and fifth centuries B.C.E.) and in other areas of Egypt (e.g., Hermopolis, fifth century B.C.E.) and Jerusalem inscriptions dating from the Second Temple period. Kutscher discusses Judeo-Aramaic varieties together with non-Jewish Aramaic.

KUTSCHER (1977) is a collection of the author's linguistic studies. Kutscher discusses the language of many ancient texts in Judeo-Aramaic, for example, Jerusalem inscriptions and the Genesis Apocryphon (a long midrash on Genesis found among the Dead Sea Scrolls). Kutscher reviews Aramaic influences on mishnaic Hebrew; the Jerusalem Talmud and aggadic midrashim; Samaritan Aramaic; and major research tools (especially lexicographic works). GREENFIELD clarifies some Aramaic terms used in the Genesis Apocryphon in two particular semantic fields: legal terminology and exorcism terminology.

KOMLOSH illustrates the various ways in which Targum Jonathan has been translated. Sometimes the translation is literal, sometimes associative, sometimes contextual (translating a word so that it fits in the context of the preceding and the following words), sometimes midrashic.

SOKOLOFF discusses a number of Aramaic words from the Vatican codex of *Bereshit Rabbah* and interprets the passages in which these words appear. Some of the words cited have never been registered in any dictionaries and some are written differently from the known forms. In cases in which there are parallels in other Aramaic dialects, Sokoloff cites them. This work clarifies the semantics of many words and is a useful aid in understanding Aramaic texts.

There are several relevant essays in FITZMYER's collection. In the chapter on the languages of Palestine, he describes materials written in Palestinian Aramaic dating from the first century B.C.E. to the second century C.E. The materials include scrolls found in Khirbet Qumran: the Genesis Apocryphon, the Prayer of Nabonidus, the Description of the New Jerusalem, the Elect of God text, parts of the Testaments of the Twelve Patriarchs, Pseudo-Daniel, Targums of Job, Tobit, Targum of Leviticus, a text mentioning "the Son of God" and "the Son of the Most High," legal documents from the wadis Murabba'at, Habra, and Seiyâl. He also discusses phases of the Aramaic language and traces linguistic developments.

Judeo-Arabic

In COHEN and BLAU's entry on Judeo-Arabic in *The Encyclopaedia of Islam*, Cohen summarizes the results of research in Judeo-Arabic dialects. He stresses that there is no one form common to all Arabic-speaking Jews. Judeo-Arabic dialects are as varied as those characteristic of different groups of Muslims. In most of the regions of the Near East, the differences between Muslim and Jewish dialects are minor, sporadic, and unstable, except in southern Iraq and the Maghreb. Cohen demonstrates the peculiarities of the Baghdadi Judeo-Arabic dialect on phonetic and morphological levels. He then presents details of several Maghrebine dialects (those of Fez, Marrakesh, and Debdou in Morocco as well as those of Tlemcen [Algeria] and Tunisia). Cohen attempts to find explanations for the differentiation of the speech between Muslims, Christians, and Jews. Blau, one of pioneers in research of medieval Judeo-Arabic, clarifies the origins of Judeo-Arabic immediately after the great Arab conquests. As soon as Muslim citizens of the towns started to speak Middle Arabic, the Judeo-Aramaic speakers of the same towns also started to speak Arabic, although preserving some elements of their Aramaic speech. In writing, the Jews employed different languages for different purposes: prose was written in Judeo-Arabic, poetry in Hebrew, and the liturgy in Hebrew and Aramaic. Literary Judeo-Arabic is based mainly on Middle Arabic with some blending of Classical Arabic. Most of the features of Judeo-Arabic are also characteristic of Middle Arabic dialects.

The general use of Hebrew script clearly shows the barrier that separated the bulk of the Jewish population from Arab and Islamic cultures. Judeo-Arabic writers tended to feel that they were writing in a language separate from Arabic. BLAU (1981) summarizes the results of the author's research in written Judeo-Arabic. He stresses that Jews, like Christians, were less inclined to use Classical Arabic than their Muslim contemporaries; their writing contains features of Middle Arabic mixed with some Classical Arabic elements. The most prominent features of medieval Judeo-Arabic are the disappearance of final vowels and the weakening of short vowels, the weakening and disappearance of the glottal stop, the reduction of *status constructus*, and the replacement of the dual form by the plural.

BLAU (1992) attempts linguistic analysis of the Cambridge Genizah fragment T-S Ar. 53.8, whose orthography is archaic and influenced by Hebrew orthography rather than by Arabic. After comparison to other Judeo-Arabic texts, Blau concludes that this fragment is older than Saadia's translation and that it is apparently the oldest Judeo-Arabic translation extant. Blau offers examples of the peculiarities of the orthography and includes annotations on the text.

BLAU and HOPKINS considers spellings in Judeo-Arabic before 1000 B.C.E., which they term Early Vulgar Judeo-Arabic, based on early Judeo-Arabic papyri (documents and private letters). The spellings found in these papyri differ from those of Classical Judeo-Arabic in that they do not follow the letter rendering of Arabic script but rather represent a phonetic transcription of the sounds of the speech.

In his study of Saadia's Judeo-Arabic translation of the Pentateuch, AVISHUR asserts that there is no adequate edition of this text. The language of Saadia is so rich that it is necessary to compare many sources fully to understand his words and constructions. In the Yemenite manuscripts used by most editors, the Persian words that abound in Egyptian, Iraqi, and Syrian manuscripts were replaced by Arabic words. To determine the form and meaning of these words, Avishur suggests that both Persian lexicography and the Judeo-Persian translations need to be consulted. Avishur makes the important point that Persian words entered Judeo-Arabic in three different ways. Some entered from literary Arabic, others came from spoken Iraqi Arabic, and still others first entered the Aramaic language and from there entered Saadia's language. Avishur also points out that in addition to his use of literary Arabic, Saadia used some dialectal forms. Because Saadia was exposed to Arabic in three different parts of the Near East— Egypt, Palestine, and Iraq—he heard three different Judeo-Arabic dialects. Noting that the Iraqi elements of Saadia's language are often not recognized, Avishur attempts to address this by offering some examples.

DRORY presents the actual linguistic situation in tenth-century Mesopotamia and notes a language shift from Aramaic to Arabic. At the time, the tension between Aramaic and Hebrew was being replaced by a tension between Arabic and Hebrew. She describes Hebrew/Aramaic and Hebrew/Arabic diglossia, noting a division of functions between Hebrew and Arabic.

SHY studies the use and meaning of several technical terms in Judeo-Arabic exegetical literature. She exemplifies her points by citing the works of Classical Judeo-Arabic writers including Saadia ben Joseph Gaon, Ibn Janah, Gikatilla, Judah ibn Bal'am, Maimonides, and Tanhum ha-Yerushalmi.

SCHUSSMAN analyzes a late Iraqi version of *Ma'aseh Abraham* (the Abraham-Nimrod legend) printed in Baghdad in 1890. She states that the language of this folk text is closer to literary Judeo-Baghdadi than it is to colloquial speech. She notes as well some peculiarities of this dialect.

AHRONI, himself a speaker of the Judeo-Arabic dialect of Aden, studies native speakers of the dialect who live in Israel and England. Among his observations he notes the wide divergence of this dialect from other Judeo-Arabic dialects, including the dialects of the Yemenite Jews. It is so interspersed with Hebrew and Aramaic words and phrases that it is not intelligible to non-Jewish Arabic-speakers. He also describes the multilingual roots of this dialect. Ahroni's glossary demonstrates his points and describes some of the typical ways spoken Jewish languages of Semitic stock have developed.

Hellenic Languages

Judeo-Greek

WEXLER traces Judeo-Greek dialects in Greek and formerly Greek-dominated areas. He also discusses the relationship of Judeo-Greek to other Jewish languages in the region. Then he explains how Judeo-Greek elements made their way into different families of Jewish languages.

Romance Languages

Judeo-Spanish (Ladino, Judezmo)

BUNIS (1992) briefly traces the history of Judeo-Spanish, discussing the complex web of contacts of the Sephardim with their Muslim and Christian neighbors and the names of the language, alphabet, and writing system. Then he speaks about different varieties of Judeo-Spanish and classifies the language at different stages of its development according to particular phonetic, morphological, or lexical changes. He also points out how Judeo-Spanish differs from Castilian.

BUNIS (1993) provides a historical overview of Judeo-Spanish. He traces the survival and development of the language for nearly 500 years in the Ottoman Empire and North Africa, observing a gradual bifurcation of the Ottoman and North African varieties. The latter developed into a full-fledged independent Jewish language (Haketia), while Ottoman Judeo-Spanish survived in many dialects, albeit forming two groups: those used in southeastern (modern Turkey and Greece) and northwestern (the former Yugoslavia) areas. In addition, he describes distinctive Israeli and Middle Eastern dialects. According to Bunis, the history of the language may be divided into distinct periods: Old Judezmo (current from the 11th century to about 1547), Middle Judezmo (c.1547 to 1820), and Modern Judezmo (c.1820 to the present). He discusses the characteristic linguistic features of each period.

Although BESSO considers questions similar to those explored in Bunis's 1992 article, the two works are complementary because they consider different sources and cite different examples. Bunis's article is more systematic and centers on language development, while Besso offers readers a broader overview.

HARRIS's work, based on her doctoral dissertation, is the only English-language book on the history of Judeo-Spanish, although her emphasis is on the social history of the language rather than its linguistic history. Taking as her focus the "death of a language" phenomenon, Harris discusses the history of

Judeo-Spanish in parallel with the history of its speakers in Spain before the time of the expulsion and in the Sephardi diaspora up to the present. She makes exhaustive use of the historical, statistical, demographic, and sociological data of recent researchers. Harris notes that in the Ottoman Empire the Sephardim spoke a regional dialect, but a Castilian dialect was accepted as the official language. Linguistic unity was achieved about half a century after exile (i.e., dialect differences were reduced or assimilated into Castilian). Harris discusses the various scripts used for Judeo-Spanish. Although "rabbinic" semicursive or "Rashi script" *(ketav Rashi)* was generally used for writing and for printing Judeo-Spanish texts, Harris demonstrates how extensively other scripts were also used: quadrate script *(ketav merubba)* was employed in the printing of some books and for handwritten official documents, while the *solitreo* script was used for notes and letters. The connection between Rashi, the archetypical Ashkenazi, and distinctively Sephardi script is also explained: the semicursive handwriting now known as Rashi script was a Sephardi manuscript hand that had been in use for a century or two before the first dated Hebrew printed book appeared in Reggio di Calabria (1475). The book in question was Rashi's Torah commentary, the type selected emulated Sephardi handwriting, and the association stuck.

As a factor in the development of Judeo-Spanish, Harris notes the isolation of Judeo-Spanish speakers from Spain and points out the various independent formations and transformations influenced by local and foreign languages. During the migrations from region to region, local words and expressions, as well as morphological and syntactic influences, began to infiltrate Judeo-Spanish speakers' speech. Thus Turkish, Greek, Slavic, and Arabic words expressing new concepts entered Judeo-Spanish. Harris also documents the influence of Western languages such as Italian and French, entering Judeo-Spanish through the schools in which Sephardi children were educated. In the Balkans, Judeo-Spanish remained the principal language of the Sephardim from the settlement in 1492 to World War II. However, as a result of the Greek annexation of Salonika in 1912 and unfavorable socioeconomic conditions from the 1920s onward, Sephardim from the Balkan countries began to immigrate to the United States, Latin America, and Palestine. The second wave of Sephardi immigration occurred after World War II when survivors of the Holocaust went to the United States and Israel. Most Judeo-Spanish speakers today live in Israel and the United States, and most are over 50 years old. According to Harris's estimation, in the 1990s not more than 60,000 people still spoke the language. Since it is not being passed on to younger generations, the author concludes that the language is dying. Harris devotes significant attention to the different names of the language and the social conditions of the use and decline of the language, noting circumstances such as the rise of nationalism in Turkey and the Balkan countries, the rise of Zionism, and Western educational influences in Sephardi communities. According to Harris, the final blow was the Holocaust, during which many Judeo-Spanish speakers perished.

JERUSALMI's piece is part of the introduction to a volume containing a Judeo-Spanish translation of a book on moral values. Nevertheless, it offers a significant amount of information about the Ladino language and its history. Jerusalmi points out that for half a millennium Ladino speakers were isolated from outside Hispanic influences. He suggests that during this time conscious efforts were made to maximize the interchangeability between Hebrew/Aramaic and Ladino. Jerusalmi refutes the opinions of scholars who assert that these efforts resulted in extremely literal Ladino translations of the Bible. Jerusalmi contends that this extreme literalness is due to a desire to approximate "*la verdad Hebrayca*" (the truth behind the Hebrew). Jerusalmi also discusses the Ladino characteristic of coining new words to parallel Semitic concepts. He maintains that Hebrew script did not fit the language and that it impeded learning and reading for pleasure and endorses the switch to Roman script that followed in the wake of Atatürk's eurocentric realignment of Turkish. Jerusalmi argues against making a sharp distinction between Ladino and Judeo-Spanish and against the use of both the terms Judeo-Spanish and Judezmo. He asserts that Ladino is the traditional and ideal name for the language, justifying his opinion by quoting 12 prominent rabbis, authors, and translators. In a section on grammar, Jerusalmi points out some linguistic patterns in the text that differ greatly from newer texts influenced by French or other Western European languages.

Germanic Languages

Yiddish

Of all the Jewish languages, Yiddish—the Jewish language of the Ashkenazim—has received the most scholarly attention. It also achieved the widest dissemination. Before the Holocaust Yiddish was spoken by more than 11 million people, throughout most of Europe and the Americas, with the highest concentration of speakers in Eastern Europe. WEINREICH describes the emergence and development of Yiddish in the Rhine Valley (the Jewish name for the area is Loter) among local Gallic and Germanic tribes around the year 1000. He describes how different tribes in Europe were assimilated and absorbed into a new ruling majority following conquests or migrations. The same patterns can be seen in Jewish communities. The Jews arrived in an area with a vernacular and acquired a new language based on the language of the ruling majority, but also incorporating elements of their vernacular. Subsequent migrations brought them into contact with other tribes, resulting in further modifications in the language. Weinreich insists that one of the major factors in the development of Yiddish was "the way of the ShaS" (i.e., the idiom and cadences of Talmud study). The center of Ashkenazi settlement gradually moved toward Eastern Europe, and by the 17th century most Ashkenazim lived on Polish lands. Weinreich also points out that the history of Yiddish reflects the history of the Ashkenazim. Weinreich identifies four periods in the development of Yiddish: Earliest Yiddish (c.1000–1250); Old Yiddish (1250–1500); Middle Yiddish (1500–1750); and Modern Yiddish (1750–present). Analogy was very important in the shaping of the language at different stages of its development. It worked on many levels of the language but is most recognizable in the formation of words using particular models and morphemes, especially suffixes. Weinreich also touches upon the formation of Yiddish dialects and the development of the language through literature and social change.

FISHMAN's collection contains many essays on multiple aspects of Yiddish. Weinreich's "The Reality of Jewishness versus the Ghetto Myth: The Sociolinguistic Roots of Yiddish" and Yudel Mark's "The Yiddish Language: Its Cultural Impact" both offer important data on the history of the language. Weinreich suggests that exploring the historical development of linguistic processes in different Jewish ethnic groups will reveal many analogies and similarities. According to Weinreich, the persistence of the ghetto throughout early modernity and into the 19th century was chiefly responsible for the divergence of the Yiddish language from standard German. Weinreich demonstrates how autonomous Jewish communal institutions not only contributed to the vitality of ghetto society but also played an important role in the development of Yiddish.

Judeo-Iranian Languages

Judeo-Persian

LAZARD discusses the great value of Judeo-Persian texts for researching the history of Persian and for the study of its dialects. Lazard notes that the Jewish texts are very close to the language of everyday speech and that Judeo-Persian literature is not linguistically homogeneous. Lazard delineates the dialectal differences in four groups of Judeo-Persian texts: (1) the Dandan-Uylik letter is remarkable for its archaisms (e.g., the use of the *idafa* particle to denote the relative, as in Middle Persian), the paucity of Arabic words and the presence of some Sogdian words; (2) a group of Bible translations and paraphrases (e.g., British Library manuscripts of a commentary on Ezekiel and the story of Daniel, a translation of the Pentateuch preserved in the Vatican, and a few other texts) reflect dialects of the south of Iran (Khūzestan and Fārs); (3) literature, especially poetry (14th to 18th centuries), is generally free from dialectal characteristics; (4) the literary and exegetic texts produced in Bukhara (primarily 17th to 19th centuries) are written in Judeo-Tajik, which is very similar to modern Tajik.

SHAKED and NETZER's series deals with Jewish-Iranian relations in a broad sense. Among the materials presented in these collections are literary and folkloric Judeo-Persian texts. In volume three of the series, Haide Sahim's article, "The Dialect of the Jews of Hamedan," deals with the spoken Judeo-Persian of Hamedan (otherwise known as Hamadan, ancient Ecbatana, capital of Media). The author discusses the biblical record of the transfer of the northern kingdom of Israel's population in 721 B.C.E. to this area. He notes that Israelites most likely settled there long before that date, or at the very least, caravans of Israelite merchants passed through the city. Until 1900, the city was home to a Jewish population larger than those in Teheran or Işfahán. Today almost all native speakers of this dialect have emigrated from the city, many to Teheran, and the dialect seems on its way to extinction. Sahim's research was conducted with informants before 1970, when there were still about 350 speakers of the dialect in the city. The residents of Hamedan referred to their language as 'Ebri (i.e., Hebrew), or ancient Persian. According to Sahim, however, the language contains very few Hebrew words.

Berber Languages

Judeo-Berber

ZAFRANI reports on the dialects of the Berber-speaking Jews (Shleuh) who lived in secluded communities in the valleys of the Anti-Atlas mountains in the region near the Wadi Sous and on the fringe of the Sahara Desert. Most of the residents of these communities immigrated to Israel. While a majority of these communities were bilingual (Berber and Arabic), others were strictly Berber speaking, as at Tifnut. In the valley of the Todgha (Tinghir) and elsewhere, Berber was used not only for communication among families and in economic transactions but also as a language of culture and traditional instruction and alongside Hebrew in religious life, giving rise to traditional translations of sacred texts, liturgies, and especially the Passover Haggadah.

CHETRIT describes the interaction of three Jewish languages in Morocco: Judeo-Berber, Judeo-Arabic, and Judeo-Spanish (Haketia). He explores such phenomena as bilingualism and migration, noting especially the impact on North Africa of successive waves of Spanish refugees, as major factors in the development of Moroccan Jewry's polyglot diversity.

HAYIM Y. SHEYNIN

Latin America and the Caribbean

Avni, Haim, *Argentina and the Jews: A History of Jewish Immigration,* Tuscaloosa: University of Alabama Press, 1991

Cohen, Robert, *Jews in Another Environment: Surinam in the Second Half of the Eighteenth Century,* Leiden and New York: Brill, 1991

Elkin, Judith L., *Jews of the Latin American Republics,* Chapel Hill: University of North Carolina Press, 1980; 2nd edition as *The Jews of Latin America,* New York: Holmes and Meier, 1998

Emmanuel, Isaac and Suzanne Emmanuel, *History of the Jews of the Netherlands Antilles,* 2 vols., Cincinnati, Ohio: American Jewish Archives, 1970

Lesser, Jeffrey, *Welcoming the Undesirables: Brazil and the Jewish Question,* Berkeley: University of California Press, 1995

Levine, Robert M., *Tropical Diaspora: The Jewish Experience in Cuba,* Gainesville: University Press of Florida, 1993

Mirelman, Victor A., *Jewish Buenos Aires, 1890–1930: In Search of an Identity,* Detroit, Michigan: Wayne State University Press, 1990

Jewish life in Latin America and the Caribbean spans half a millennium, from the time of the conquistadors to the present, and also a vast geographical area, from Mexico to the southern tip of Argentina and Chile. It includes large countries with substantial Jewish minorities as well as small island nations with a tiny Jewish presence.

ELKIN has written a very inclusive one-volume description of Jewish life in the region that gives a taste of the range of experiences throughout successive periods and in the various countries. The work is largely based on secondary sources but manifests a comprehensive understanding of the issues. After a short chapter on the colonial period, the book presents important survey chapters on Jewish immigration to the different independent republics, the development of Jewish agricultural colonies, the economics of Jewish life in the continent, and a survey of Jewish cultural and religious endeavors. Of considerable interest is the last section, which places Jewish life in Latin America within several contexts, such as the culture of each independent state and interrelationships with world Jewry, Zionism, and Israel.

While there was in effect no Jewish life in the Spanish and Portuguese colonial territories in Latin America because Jews were prohibited from entering them, there were centers of Jewish life in the Dutch domains. Chief among these was the island of Curaçao, and EMMANUEL and EMMANUEL have provided a detailed history of internal developments within the Jewish settlement there, as well as in the other Dutch islands, most importantly St. Eustatius. Migrations, the economy, religious life, including the appointment of rabbis and cantors, and especially the links with the mother community in Amsterdam are narrated in abundant detail. COHEN's work is more narrowly focused, limiting itself to describing Jewish life in Surinam, a Dutch colony on the South American mainland facing the Caribbean, specifically during the second half of the 18th century. He places the Jews, a small community throughout the period, in the context of the life of the general population, dwelling on issues such as immigration; the environment and the deep effects it had on the economy and health of the immigrants; the urbanization and impoverishment of the plantation owners (both Jews and non-Jews); relations between Sephardi Jews and their mulatto children; and the colony's sudden but short-lived cultural life. Cohen's comparative approach helps clarify the role of the Jews of Surinam among white plantocrats and slave owners.

The Jewish presence in Argentina is by far the largest and most vibrant in Latin America. The studies by Avni and Mirelman are based on thorough research in the most pertinent archives in Argentina, Israel, the United States, and Europe. They focus, however, on different issues. AVNI gives a detailed history of Jewish immigration to the country from its wars of independence from Spain to the 20th century, placing it in the context of Argentine and world history. The various chapters deal with the issue of legitimization of the Jewish presence in the country, reaction to the promotion of Jewish immigration at various times, the attitudes of established Jews to the newly arrived, and efforts to integrate them into their adoptive country. Legal impediments and stumbling blocks due to antisemitic postures are analyzed. Important chapters deal with the periods of large Jewish immigration during the two decades before and the two decades after World War I, including the establishment of Jewish agricultural colonies in the hinterland under the sponsorship of the Jewish Colonization Association, the closing of the gates during the Nazi era, and the trickle of Jewish newcomers in the aftermath of World War II. The epilogue reveals that immigration gave way to emigration, due on the one hand to ideological motivations such as settling in Israel, and on the other to political reasons such as the growing antisemitism during the Eichmann capture and trial, the Proceso and Dirty War years, and the economic stagnation that ensued.

MIRELMAN's work concentrates on Jewish life in the capital city of Buenos Aires, where the vast majority of the Jews finally made their homes. It is also limited to the major formative period of Jewish Buenos Aires, which ended in 1930. While the book contains major chapters on immigration and Jewish-gentile relations, including the week of physical violence against Jews during the Semana Tragica of 1919, its emphasis is on internal Jewish developments. There are significant discussions of the various Sephardi groups and their involvement in all aspects of Jewish life. Chapters deal with religious institutions and observances; Zionist and leftist activities; Jewish education along ideological lines; the development of Jewish culture in Yiddish, Hebrew, and Spanish; the rise of the first generation of Jews educated in the country; and the valiant fight against coreligionists involved in prostitution and the white slave traffic. A final chapter describes the centralizing forces in the Jewish community and the development of the Kehilla, a major characteristic of Jewish political organization not only in Argentina but also throughout Latin America.

LEVINE, basing his study mainly on secondary sources and an impressive array of interviews, explores in some detail the major aspects of the Jewish experience in Cuba up until the present. Aware of the contrasts with other Latin American diasporas, Levine makes interesting comparisons with Mexican and Argentine Jewries. There are vivid descriptions of the way the relatively small Jewish community was affected by major issues in Cuban history. Important chapters are devoted to the St. Louis incident in 1939, the question of refugees during the Nazi period, and the way in which Cuban Jewry weathered World War II. Internal Jewish matters, such as the tensions between religion and secularism and between Zionism and socialism, are also discussed. The question of antisemitism and reactions to the Castro revolution and its aftermath are also dealt with in some detail.

Brazil is the largest and most populous country in Latin America, and its Jewish community is second only to Argentina's in size. LESSER, in a study based on research carried out in archives in the United States, Israel, England, and Brazil, presents a detailed account of Brazilian immigration policy from the interwar period to the immediate postwar years. He amply describes the cultural context, the political calculations, and the practical results of a policy that welcomed Jewish immigrants in spite of an order prohibiting the issuance of visas to people of Semitic origin. Using comparative methods to gauge racial considerations, Lesser interprets dictator Getulio Vargas's strategy regarding immigration as intent on not stirring up criticism among nativists and at the same time gaining favor with the Vatican, the United States, and Britain.

All the works cited include elaborate bibliographies in their respective fields.

VICTOR A. MIRELMAN

See also Inquisition

Leone Ebreo *see* Abravanel, Judah

Levi ben Gershom   1288–1344

Provençal astronomer, Aristotelian philosopher, and
biblical commentator

Bleich, J. David, *Providence in the Philosophy of
    Gersonides*, New York: Yeshiva University Press, 1973

Eisen, Robert, *Gersonides on Providence, Covenant, and the
    Chosen People: A Study in Medieval Jewish Philosophy
    and Biblical Commentary*, Albany: State University of
    New York Press, 1995

Goldstein, Bernard R., *The Astronomy of Levi ben Gerson
    (1288–1344): A Critical Edition of Chapters 1–20 with
    Translation and Commentary*, New York: Springer-
    Verlag, 1985

Levi ben Gershom, *The Commentary of Levi ben Gerson
    (Gersonides) on the Book of Job*, translated by Abraham
    L. Lassen, New York: Bloch, 1946

Levi ben Gershom, *The Wars of the Lord*, translated by
    Seymour Feldman, 3 vols., Philadelphia: Jewish
    Publication Society, 1984–1999

Levi ben Gershom, *Commentary on Song of Songs*,
    translated by Menachem Kellner (Yale Judaica Series, vol.
    28), New Haven, Connecticut: Yale University Press,
    1998

Manekin, Charles H., *The Logic of Gersonides: A
    Translation of Sefer ha-Heqqesh ha-Yashar (The Book of
    the Correct Syllogism) of Rabbi Levi ben Gershom*,
    Dordrecht and Boston: Kluwer, 1992

Samuelson, Norbert Max (editor and translator),
    *Gersonides' The Wars of the Lord, Treatise 3: On God's
    Knowledge* (Mediaeval Sources in Translation, vol. 19),
    Toronto: Pontifical Institute of Mediaeval Studies, 1977

Staub, Jacob J., *The Creation of the World According to
    Gersonides*, Chico, California: Scholars Press, 1982

Levi ben Gershom, known in English as Gersonides and in
Hebrew by the acronym Ralbag, was one of medieval
Judaism's most creative and wide-ranging thinkers. A native
of Provence and a critical admirer of both Maimonides and
Averroës, he was a philosopher, exegete, halakhist, and logi-
cian, as well as an astronomer and mathematician of major
historical significance. In philosophy he wrote an independent
treatise, *Wars of the Lord*, and many supercommentaries on
the commentaries of Averroës to Aristotle. His Bible commentaries went through many editions and several of them are
included in standard rabbinic Bibles.

BLEICH translates the fourth treatise of Gersonides' *Wars
of the Lord,* devoted to the question of providence. His introduction places Gersonides' discussion in its philosophical context, and his many annotations make Gersonides' often
difficult text much clearer. Gersonides presents a very mech-
anistic vision of providence, according to which human beings
who perfect themselves intellectually protect themselves
thereby from the evils that befall the ignorant and can thus be
said to be providentially guided and protected without any
actual divine intervention.

EISEN studies the problem posed for Gersonides by the
notion of the chosen people. Providence, Gersonides holds,
attaches only to individuals and in varying degrees, depending upon their intellectual attainments. How, then, can it guide
and protect a whole nation? A detailed study of Gersonides'
Bible commentaries, especially those on Genesis and Exodus,
leads Eisen to Gersonides' idea of "inherited providence,"
according to which the people of Israel are protected by the
special providence extended to the Patriarchs Abraham, Isaac,
and Jacob.

GOLDSTEIN has pioneered the study of Gersonides'
astronomy. Gersonides' major work in astronomy was
included in the medieval manuscripts as the first section of
part five of *Wars of the Lord*, but the printed editions of the
work never included it. Goldstein rescued the work from
oblivion, and in this book he provides an edition of the
Hebrew text of the first 20 (of 136) chapters, noteworthy for
the description of the observational instrument invented by
Gersonides, the Jacob Staff, which came into general use by
mariners. In his introduction, Goldstein situates Gersonides
in the history of astronomy, examining the influence of his
predecessors upon him and his influence upon later
astronomers.

LEVI BEN GERSHOM (1998), Gersonides' commentary
on Song of Songs, is perhaps the most philosophical of all
his Bible commentaries. This is a consequence of Gersonides' claim that of the whole biblical canon, only Song of
Songs has no benefit for the masses. Other biblical books
teach philosophy, but they also teach history, ethics, and,
of course, law. Song of Songs teaches only philosophy, its
surface meaning having no benefit to the reader. Gersonides
reads Song of Songs as a handbook in epistemology, describing the hylic intellect's great desire to reach perfection and
the stages of study (mathematics, physics, and metaphysics)
that lead to that perfection. Kellner's translation includes
an introduction placing the commentary in the context
of Gersonides' life and times, and extensive annotations on
the text.

LEVI BEN GERSHOM's (1984–1999) magnum opus, *The
Wars of the Lord*, contains six treatises devoted to human
immortality, prophecy, God's knowledge, providence, astronomy and astrology, and creation and miracles. Never previously
translated in its entirety into any language, this high-water
mark of Jewish Aristotelianism is handsomely served by Feldman's clear, idiomatic English, which hides much of the grace-
lessness of the Hebrew original. Feldman has added to his
translation long introductions and an important appendix on
Gersonides' exegesis. Feldman's work is also, in effect, a critical edition of the Hebrew text, since he includes lists of variant readings that underlie his translation.

LEVI BEN GERSHOM (1946), Gersonides' commentary
on Job, interprets the book as an analysis of the doctrine of
providence. In this he follows in the footsteps of Saadia and
Maimonides. His commentary parallels his discussion of providence in the fourth treatise of *Wars of the Lord* and he shows
how his extremely untraditional view of providence can be
read out of the book of Job. Lassen's clear translation includes
a very brief introduction and some source notes.

MANEKIN presents a translation of Gersonides' *Book of
the Correct Syllogism* with an extensive introduction, detailed
commentary, and analytical glossary. Gersonides' book, which

Manekin characterizes as arguably the greatest work on logic written in Hebrew, attempts to construct a theory of the syllogism free of the errors that Gersonides detected in Aristotle as interpreted by Averroës. Manekin's long introduction and wealth of annotations make Gersonides' otherwise forbidding work accessible.

SAMUELSON presents a very heavily annotated literal translation of *Wars of the Lord*, which deals with the question of God's knowledge of particulars. It is here that Gersonides' most daring theological claim—that God does not know individuals (including human beings, even the most saintly of them) as such—is worked out in careful argumentation with Aristotle and Maimonides. The treatise itself is short, if dense, and Samuelson's commentary, which carefully situates Gersonides' discussion in the history of western philosophy, makes up the bulk of this book.

STAUB takes up another of Gersonides' notorious claims: that God did not create the world ex nihilo, but, rather, from preexisting matter. Staub's long introduction, literal translation of the relevant chapters from the second part of the sixth treatise of *Wars of the Lord*, and extensive commentary follow Gersonides' complex arguments with Aristotle and Maimonides on the issue of creation.

MENACHEM KELLNER

Levi Isaac of Berdichev c.1740–1810

Galician hasidic saint and teacher

Blumenthal, David R., *God at the Center: Meditations on Jewish Spirituality*, San Francisco: Harper and Row, 1988

Buber, Martin, *Tales of the Hasidim*, translated by Olga Marx, New York: Schocken/Farrar, Straus and Young, 1947; London: Thames and Hudson, 1956

Dresner, Samuel H., *Levi Yitzhak of Berditchev: Portrait of a Hasidic Master*, New York: Hartmore House, 1974; updated edition, New York: Shapolsky, 1986

Kaplan, Aryeh, *The Light Beyond: Adventures in Hassidic Thought*, New York: Maznaim, 1981

Wiesel, Elie, *Célébration hassidique: portraits et légendes*, 1972; translated by Marion Wiesel as *Souls on Fire: Portraits and Legends of Hasidic Masters*, New York: Random House, and London: Weidenfeld and Nicolson, 1972

The most beloved of the hasidic masters—even mentioning his name, so it is said, opens the heavenly gates of love—Levi Isaac ben Meir of Berdichev is the subject of surprisingly few English works, and his own major book, *Kedushat Levi* (Holiness of Levi) has not appeared in translation. The works reviewed below, however, are good sources for stories and excerpts from his written teachings.

BUBER, writing originally in German, retold hasidic stories with close attention to the Hebrew and Yiddish sources, though he introduced subtle variations based on his modern literary and spiritual sensibilities. He was among the very first to introduce Levi Isaac and the other hasidic masters to Western European and North American readers. This classic book includes 65 stories and brief teachings about Levi Isaac; the emphasis is on his emotional candor and intensity. The poetic clarity of Buber's style is well communicated in Olga Marx's English translation.

DRESNER is the major source in English on Levi Isaac, highlighting his love for all Israel and his fervor in prayer and Jewish observance. Essentially this is a work of hagiography but one founded on historical research and attention to the sources. It includes many tales about Levi Isaac as well as brief selections of teachings from *Kedushat Levi* and from other hasidic sources in which he is cited. Dresner makes use of other historical evidence as well, including a contemporary nonhasidic description. A narrative of Levi Isaac's often difficult career is accompanied by chapters on themes such as prayer, observance of commandments, and love of Israel.

WIESEL retells stories of a number of hasidic masters and reflects on who they were and what they meant to him in his hasidic childhood and in his adult life as a survivor and memorializer of the Holocaust. Most of the stories in the short chapter on Levi Isaac are also found in Buber and Dresner, but Wiesel distinctively highlights an aspect of "despair and revolt" in Levi Isaac. Thus, he dwells on Levi Isaac's nervous breakdown, which incapacitated him for a year, and even more so on his famous arguments with God, which Wiesel speculatively locates in the last years of Levi Isaac's life, after his return to health. Wiesel has surely read much of himself into Levi Isaac, but his intuitive approach creates a memorable picture of the man.

"The general principle," *Kedushat Levi* begins, "is that the blessed Creator created all and is all." KAPLAN's introductory notes describe *Kedushat Levi* as lucidly written, working kabbalistic teachings into advice for day-to-day spiritual living, and as one of the most popular books in hasidic life. In his own lucid style, Kaplan provides English paraphrases (though not literal translations) of selections from a variety of classic hasidic books, accessibly arranged by themes such as "Meditation and Prayer" and "Life and Society." *Kedushat Levi* is well represented, with some 60 pages of excerpts, several of them substantial at three or four pages long. Kaplan provides footnotes on Hebrew sources and parallel texts, with some useful explanatory remarks.

BLUMENTHAL is the author of a significant work of original theology, *Facing the Abusing God* (1993), and also this earlier work of personal theology, presented in the quintessentially Jewish form of commentary. The texts commented on here are passages from *Kedushat Levi*, which Blumenthal presents in paraphrase and occasionally in translation together with his own reflections. Through his role as selector of the material and commentator, often speaking in personal tones, the dominant voice is Blumenthal's, but he presents Levi Isaac's ideas with humility and sympathy. Blumenthal calls attention to concepts he finds profound and to how Levi Isaac's teachings can be applied today, often in ways that challenge common complacencies and pat solutions.

JUSTIN JARON LEWIS

Levinas, Emmanuel 1906–1995

Lithuanian-born French thinker

Aronowicz, Annette (translator), "Translator's Introduction," in Levinas's *Nine Talmudic Readings*, Bloomington: Indiana University Press, 1990

Bernasconi, Robert and Simon Critchley (editors), *Rereading Levinas* (Studies in Continental Thought), Bloomington: Indiana University Press, and London: Athlone, 1991

Critchley, Simon, *The Ethics of Deconstruction: Derrida and Levinas*, Oxford and Cambridge, Massachusetts: Blackwell, 1992

Davis, Colin, *Levinas: An Introduction*, Notre Dame, Indiana: University of Notre Dame Press, and Cambridge: Polity, 1996

Derrida, Jacques, "Violence and Metaphysics: An Essay on the Thought of Emmanuel Levinas," in his *Writing and Difference*, translated by Alan Bass, Chicago: University of Chicago Press, and London: Routledge and Kegan Paul, 1978

Eaglestone, Robert, *Ethical Criticism: Reading after Levinas*, Edinburgh: Edinburgh University Press, 1997

Peperzak, Adriaan Theodoor, *To the Other: An Introduction to the Philosophy of Emmanuel Levinas* (Purdue Series in the History of Philosophy), West Lafayette, Indiana: Purdue University Press, 1993

Stone, Ira, *Reading Levinas/Reading Talmud: An Introduction*, Philadelphia: Jewish Publication Society, 1998

Born in Kaunas, Lithuania, in 1906, Emmanuel Levinas has become one of the most important contemporary philosophers. Originally known to Jean-Paul Sartre and others in the 1930s as an early French expositor of Edmund Husserl, Levinas was later regarded by an increasing number of readers as the 20th century's foremost philosopher of ethics. Despite not moving to France until 1923, he wrote his mature work primarily in French and much remains to be translated. His initial audience was in France, and, although books about him in English are increasingly available in the form of original texts and as translations of non-English texts, the best books on Levinas are still unavailable in English. There is no biography of Levinas in English, and even the most reliable biography in French (Marie-Anne Lescourret, *Emmanuel Lévinas*, Paris: Flammarion, 1994) is already out of date.

The most important advocate of Levinas's centrality to ethical thought in the post-structuralist period has been Jacques Derrida. CRITCHLEY's aim is to show that, contrary to accusations of its tendency to encourage personal and political quietism based on ontological indeterminacy, deconstruction has always inherently needed or implied "the ethical." In this book, deconstruction, as disseminated by Derrida, and the ethical philosophy of Levinas are explicitly linked. Although not free of the technical vocabulary that is necessary to represent the ideas of these two men, the book opens by asking, on the reader's behalf, why one should read Levinas or Derrida. It does a convincing job of answering its own question by arguing that Levinasian ethics may provide a way to reincorporate

the deconstruction of Derrida, Lacoue-Labarthe, and Nancy into discourse and so provide a compelling account of justice and a just polity.

At the time of writing, DERRIDA's book-length eulogy to Levinas (*Adieu*, Paris: Galilee, 1997) is untranslated, but his essay from 1964 is available. The essay is the earliest major article about Levinas accessible in English. In it Derrida puts the Levinasian project into perspective by explaining how it questions the Greek tradition that formed the thought of Western Europe, including that of Levinas's two early mentors, Husserl and Martin Heidegger. Derrida demonstrates the way in which the traditions Levinas uses are at constructive odds and what effects that has had on contemporary French philosophy. The piece is typical of Derrida's dense writing style and presupposes a familiarity with, if not the texts, at least the contexts of his work.

After being introduced to Levinasian ideas through Derrida, scholars of literary criticism have shown a profound interest. EAGLESTONE gives an account of the history of ethics in critical theory and outlines the reasons why contemporary philosophy is deeply implicated in the current practices of the discipline. Trying to avoid tritely "applying" Levinas, Eaglestone explains how Levinas might permit a redefinition of approach that would allow for a reintroduction of ethics into criticism.

DAVIS provides the clearest general introduction to Levinas that currently exists in English. It is brief and acknowledges that it cannot adequately explain each of its topics, but it lives up to its billing as an introduction. It gives the reader a short biography and then expands, in a more accessible way, upon the themes that Derrida began meditating upon in "Violence and Metaphysics": the relation to Husserlian and Heideggerian phenomenology; the repression of the "Other" as a form of the "Same"; the development of an ethics beyond phenomenology; the place of the Jewish tradition in tension with the Christian and Greek traditions of thought; and finally the influence that Levinas has had on contemporary French philosophers and literary critics. Davis uses his historical perspective to examine the problems that French philosophy has had in reading Levinas, namely, it is unable to incorporate him into a tradition or understand his difference. Davis's book contains remarks on most topics in Levinas's thought but does not go into great detail about any of them, an attribute that is mirrored by the daunting bibliography that contains an impressive array of books but little way of choosing between them. For more detailed analyses than Davis provides, BERNASCONI's collection has short essays by many of the major commentators on different aspects of Levinas's philosophical work as well as four essays on Levinas's influence on Derrida and Blanchot.

PEPERZAK is a comprehensive and technical introduction to Levinas's philosophy. Peperzak comments at length on the 1957 essay "Philosophy and the Idea of the Infinite" as a way of beginning to deal with Levinas's first major work, *Totality and Infinity*, which he then proceeds to discuss. Peperzak assumes that the reader has little prior knowledge of the texts but still manages to lay out in some detail Levinas's main contributions to philosophy without excessively simplifying the difficulties of his work. Peperzak reaches only the second major work, *Otherwise than Being; or, Beyond Essence*, in his final chapter, and it is at this point that he overreaches and in the space he has allowed himself can no longer lucidly convey the complexities of the philosophy and the vast context of the traditions within which Levinas worked. The book contains a useful preliminary bibliography of Levinas's philosophical oeuvre and early work in English about him.

Levinas himself separated the two branches of his work—the philosophical and the confessional—from one another while acknowledging that they have a "common source of inspiration." This bifurcation has affected the reception of his work: his confessional work (centered on talmudic interpretation) has provided the focus for Jewish scholars, and the philosophical work developing out of his work on Husserl and Heidegger has provided material for philosophers and literary critics. It is the latter that has produced the most material, but the framework and background of his confessional work is succinctly described by ARONOWICZ in the translator's introduction to a volume that includes some of the best examples of that work in English. STONE, however, takes more time to expand upon Levinas's approach to talmudic interpretation from a rabbinic point of view and to explain as well as demonstrate Levinas's methodology.

DAN FRIEDMAN

Leviticus

Douglas, Mary, *Purity and Danger: An Analysis of Concepts of Pollution and Taboo*, London: Routledge and Kegan Paul, and New York: Praeger, 1966; 2nd impression with corrections, London and Boston: Routledge and Kegan Paul, 1969

Hartley, John E., *Leviticus* (Word Biblical Commentary, vol. 4), Dallas, Texas: Word Books, 1992

Knohl, Israel, *Mikdash ha-demamah: 'iyun be-rovde ha-yetsirah ha-kohanit sheba-Torah*, 1992; translated by Jackie Feldman and Peretz Rodman as *The Sanctuary of Silence: The Priestly Torah and the Holiness School*, Minneapolis, Minnesota: Fortress, 1995

Levine, Baruch A., *Leviticus/Va-yikra: The Traditional Hebrew Text with the New JPS Translation* (JPS Torah Commentary Series), Philadelphia: Jewish Publication Society, 1989

Milgrom, Jacob, *Leviticus 1–16: A New Translation with Introduction and Commentary* (Anchor Bible, vol. 3), New York: Doubleday, 1991

Wright, David Pearson, *The Disposal of Impurity: Elimination Rites in the Bible and in Hittite and Mesopotamian Literature* (Society of Biblical Literature Dissertation Series, no. 101), Atlanta, Georgia: Scholars Press, 1987

Since late antiquity it has been increasingly standard for Jews to see in the Pentateuch and oral tradition a total of 613 commandments. Two-hundred-forty-seven of these, which is to say slightly more than 40 percent, are contained in the Book of Leviticus. The first ten chapters of Leviticus deal with the sacrificial service of the Temple. Chapter 11 establishes the basis for the dietary laws; chapters 12 through 16 lay down other rules of purity; and chapter 23 prescribes the sabbath and festivals.

For Christians—which is to say for the majority of persons who believe in the Bible, study the Bible, and teach the Bible—the Book of Leviticus is an enigma because at least 17 of its 27 chapters deal wholly with subjects that Christianity, from its inception, has declared obsolete. It is not surprising, therefore, that the Christian-dominated Anchor Bible series would find it appropriate to assign the Book of Leviticus to MILGROM, a Jewish scholar, to explain this strange (from a Christian perspective) book of the Jewish Torah. When called upon to say something meaningful about Leviticus, earlier generations either treated its rules and regulations as arbitrary, or they superimposed fanciful allegorization upon the unfamiliar rites and ceremonies of the biblical Tabernacle and Temple. As a Semitist of the first rank with a thorough grounding in comparative religion, anthropology, Second Temple literature, and rabbinics, however, Milgrom reveals for the first time in perhaps two and a half millenia the abiding message contained in the symbolic world set forth in Leviticus and its cognate literature. One of the crowning achievements of his distinguished scholastic career is his exciting 1163-page commentary on Leviticus 1–16. Seeing how much light Milgrom has shed on the unknown in this first volume, scholars, clergy, students, and lay Bible readers look forward to seeing how much further illumination will be forthcoming when he publishes his commentary on Leviticus 17 through 27, chapters that contain, inter alia, "Love your neighbor as yourself" (Leviticus 19:18).

Milgrom has produced a number of first-rate graduate students who have followed his lead in delving into and explaining in the light of comparative religion and comparative Semitics the intricacies of Leviticus's symbolic rites. One of the most important works produced by a Milgrom student is WRIGHT, the first serious attempt to analyze Leviticus's rules of disposal, such as the scapegoat (Leviticus 16) and the rites for purification of the recovered leper (Leviticus 14). Wright also offers original insights when treating phenomena of exclusion and restriction as a body and assessing which ideas are expressed symbolically by these rites. Employing the method of contrastive comparison, Wright unpacks Leviticus's rites for the disposal of impurity through an in-depth study of comparable rites described in cuneiform tablets from the ancient Near East and through a careful consideration of exegetical insights contained in rabbinic literature and medieval Jewish biblical commentary. Wright shows that in other ancient Near Eastern civilizations impurity stemmed from a variety of sources (including angry deities, demonic attacks, witchcraft, sorcery, and sickness), but Leviticus and its cognate biblical literature limit the sources of evil to ritual impurity and human transgression, a message of considerable importance.

It is difficult to imagine that Milgrom would have found an audience, lay or scholarly, for his analysis of the symbolism behind the rules and regulations of Leviticus before the anthropologist DOUGLAS broke thoroughly new ground in her study, which rejects both of the medieval apologies for Jewish dietary laws—arbitrary fiats of the divine legislator and considerations of hygiene—and seeks, with the aid of anthropological method and parallels from Hinduism, to find Scripture's own rationale. That rationale proves to be a matter of order vs. disorder, and Douglas allows the reader to see how it is played out in the warp and woof of Leviticus's laws of purity. She concludes that "the dietary laws would have been like signs which at every turn inspired meditation on the oneness, purity and completeness of God."

LEVINE has made excellent use of an important opportunity to popularize his own discoveries as well as those of his mentors H. L. Ginsberg and Cyrus H. Gordon and his distinguished contemporaries, including Milgrom, Haran, Knohl, Schwartz and the late Moshe Held. Especially significant is Levine's transmission in lucid English of many important insights from David Tsevi Hoffmann's monumental commentary, until now only available in its German original (1905–1906) and in a Hebrew translation. This volume represents the first time that a professional Jewish biblical scholar of the first rank has written a commentary on the Book of Leviticus geared to the needs of laity and clergy.

While Levine writes for a specific (i.e., Jewish) audience whose intellectual and spiritual thirst has long been neglected, HARTLEY addresses a much larger audience of students and scholars of every denomination and persuasion, who can now for the first time identify the important issues in Leviticus at a glance. Thus, for example, there is a clear presentation of the deliberate use of neutral, nonsexist language by the author(s) of Leviticus, one of many discoveries by linguists and theologians who have tended to publish such findings only in obscure professional journals and festschriften. Hartley's comprehensive commentary provides a masterful summary of the full range of ancient, medieval, and modern exegesis, both Jewish and Christian, covering historical, philological, and theological issues. He succeeds in the avowed goal of the series of which this volume is part: making technical and scholarly approaches to a theological understanding of Scripture comprehensible to educated laypersons, beginning students, clergy, and a broad range of professional scholars. He repeatedly demonstrates that frequently the most recondite current biblical scholarship contains insights that can enrich both the inner and the public life of contemporary men and women.

In 1878, Julius Wellhausen published his monumental *Prolegomena to the History of Ancient Israel*, which gave the widest possible currency to the theory that the Pentateuch had been redacted from four main documents, designated J, E, D, and P. That same year A. Klostermann published an article in which he separated from P (the supposed source of all of Leviticus) a further documentary source: the Holiness Code contained in Leviticus 17–26. A century later, KNOHL, one of the young superstars of contemporary Israeli biblical scholarship, clearly distinguishes and examines in detail the distinct languages, symbolic worlds, and ideologies that set apart the Priestly Code (P) contained, inter alia, in Leviticus 1–16 from the Holiness Code contained in Leviticus 17–26 and from additional passages produced by what he calls the Holiness School that are scattered throughout the books of Exodus and Numbers. In Knohl's reading, the detachment of the cult from public morality is one of many expressions of the Priestly Code's deanthropomorphism. Another such expression is the absence of prayer from cultic worship as prescribed in

P. Likewise, Knohl argues that the Holiness Code and the related Holiness School, which he dates to the period of Isaiah (second half of the eighth century B.C.E.), foster a much more intimate relationship between every human being and the deity. Such a relationship is reflected in the frequent declarations, "I am the LORD your God" (Exodus 6:6, 8; 7:4, 5; Leviticus 17:10; 23:5; etc.) as well as in frequent references to God's body parts. Feldman and Rodman's English translation of his remarkable opus provides the key to unlocking one of the Bible's best-kept secrets: that it contains a treasure trove of ancient Hebrew symbology, which adumbrates the famous theological debate as to whether God is the unmoved mover (Maimonides, anticipated by the Priestly School) or the most moved mover (Heschel, anticipated by the Holiness School).

MAYER IRWIN GRUBER

Lexicographers and Grammarians

Amzalak, Moses Bensabat, *Portuguese Hebrew Grammars and Grammarians*, Lisbon: [s.n.], 1928

Chomsky, William, *Hebrew: The Eternal Language* (Gitelson Library), Philadelphia: Jewish Publication Society, 1957

Eldar, Ilan, "The Grammatical Literature of Medieval Ashkenazi Jewry," in *Hebrew in Ashkenaz: A Language in Exile*, edited by Lewis Glinert, New York: Oxford University Press, 1993

Fellman, Jack, *The Revival of a Classical Tongue: Eliezer Ben Yehuda and the Modern Hebrew Language* (Contributions to the Sociology of Language, 6), The Hague: Mouton, 1973

Galliner, Helmuth, "Agathius Guidacerius 1477?–1540: An Early Hebrew Grammarian in Rome and Paris," *Historia Judaica*, 2(2), October 1940

Goshen-Gottstein, Moshe, "Foundations of Biblical Philology in the Seventeenth Century Christian and Jewish Dimensions," in *Jewish Thought in the Seventeenth Century* (Harvard Judaic Texts and Studies, 6), edited by Isadore Twersky and Bernard Septimus, Cambridge, Massachusetts: Harvard University Center for Jewish Studies, 1987

Hirschfeld, Hartwig, *Literary History of Hebrew Grammarians and Lexicographers, Accompanied by Unpublished Texts* (Jews' College Publications, no. 9), London: Oxford University Press, Milford, 1926

Skoss, Solomon L., "A Chapter on Permutation in Hebrew from David ben Abraham Al-Fasi's Dictionary Jami 'Al-Alfaz," *Jewish Quarterly Review*, 23, 1932–1933

Skoss, Solomon L., *Saadia Gaon, the Earliest Hebrew Grammarian*, Philadelphia: Dropsie College Press, 1955

Wechter, Pinchas, *Ibn Barun's Arabic Works on Hebrew Grammar and Lexicography*, Philadelphia: Dropsie College for Hebrew and Cognate Learning, 1964

The development of Hebrew grammar and lexicography took place over a period of more than 1,000 years, involving a great number of scholars who produced thousands of titles. The literature discussing original works is rather extensive, although most of the important research was published in Hebrew, German, French, or Spanish, and only a few works are available in English. The Cairo Genizah material is still explored only partially. Many important medieval and early modern linguistic works are still in manuscript.

HIRSCHFELD's short book offers a cursory outline of the history of Jewish linguistic literature from Saadia Gaon to Samuel ben Elhanan di Archivolti and Leone Modena. Hirschfeld supposes that the first Hebrew grammarians were the Karaite scholars of the Scriptures, since the biblical text, stripped of rabbinic tradition and strictly construed, was the only material they claimed to admit as a guide to religious life. He mentions only a few names of the Karaite grammarians who lived prior to Saadia Gaon, however, and his discussion of Saadia is little more than a brief overview of his work. SKOSS (1955) provides a much fuller and more detailed treatment of Saadia's linguistic works. Hirschfeld describes the tenth-century North African scholar Judah ibn Kureish as the father of comparative Semitic philology, although modern scholars may not agree with this attribution. Still, ibn Kureish was one of the first grammarians to treat the relation of Hebrew to Aramaic and the relation of Arabic to Hebrew.

SKOSS (1932–1933) devotes the introduction to his partial edition of David ben Abraham al-Fasi's dictionary to the analysis of his views on the phenomenon of permutation in Hebrew. This Karaite scholar was not the first to notice the phenomenon. A large portion of the article examines the exploitation of permutation in the Talmud and midrash. Skoss also describes the views of Aaron ben Asher, Saadia Gaon, Judah ibn Kureish, Dunash ben Labrat, Menahem ben Saruk, and others concerning permutation.

WECHTER devotes his principal research work to a study of ibn Barun's *Book of Comparison between the Hebrew and the Arabic Languages* (c.1085), surviving parts of which were edited by P.K. Kokovtsov (Kokowtzoff) of the Russian Academy of Sciences and appeared in 1893 and 1916. In chapter one Wechter cites Hebrew-Arabic comparisons in the Talmud and midrash as well as in medieval Hebrew works by grammarians, exegetes, and lexicographers; in chapter two he tries to establish some biographical facts and dates; and in chapter three he speaks about the sources and influence of Isaac ibn Barun. The rest of the book contains descriptions of ibn Barun's grammar and lexicon and annotated English translations of the fragments published by Kokovtsov.

CHOMSKY begins with an examination of the semantics and grammar presupposed in rabbinic midrash. He continues with a discussion of Saadia Gaon's role as the father of Hebrew grammar. Chomsky's next section is devoted to the Spanish school of Hebrew grammarians. Most of the great innovations in the analysis of Hebrew grammar belong to this school, and Chomsky summarizes the achievements of the best-known grammarians from Menahem ben Saruk and Dunash ben Labrat to Judah Hayyug, Jonah ibn Janah, Samuel ha-Nagid, Abraham ibn Ezra, and the Kimhi family. He describes in detail a controversy between ibn Janah and Samuel ha-Nagid and speaks of the popularizing activities of Abraham ibn Ezra. Chomsky, a specialist on David Kimhi (the

collector and interpreter of much of the grammar and lexicography of the Spanish school), next evaluates Kimhi's linguistic activities, noting Kimhi's "fine sense of system and organization and deep insight into the language and its structure." Since Kimhi worked after the close of the "Golden Age," Chomsky summarizes by way of background the contributions of the early medieval grammarians and then describes the reaction to the Maimonidean Controversy and the subsequent regress of grammatical studies among the Jews, while also tracing the emergence of Hebrew grammatical studies in the Christian world. Finally, he discusses some Jewish grammarians of the Enlightenment.

AMZALAK surveys the Hebrew grammars written in Hebrew, Latin, and Portuguese by Portuguese authors, and authors of Portuguese extraction, from the 15th century to 1914. Among the grammarians whom he notes, the most important are: (1) David ben Solomon ibn Yahya, author of *Leshon limmudim* (published in Constantinople in 1506); (2) Moses ibn Habib, best known for his Aristotelian poetics, *Darke no'am* (1486), who also wrote *Perah Shoshan* (1484), a longer grammar influenced by Efodi, and a shorter grammar, *Marpe lashon,* based on sources such as ibn Hayuj, ibn Janah, Abraham ibn Ezra, and Efodi; (3) David ben Joseph ibn Yahya whose grammatical works, sometimes cited by Christian Hebraists who were his pupils, are still in manuscript; (4) Solomon de Oliveyra who published a number of books on questions of Hebrew philology including *Yad lashon* and *Dal sefatayim*, which were published in one volume as *Livro da gramatica hebrayca e chaldayca* (1689); (5) Menasseh ben Israel who wrote a compendium of Hebrew grammar, *Safah berurah*, which remains in manuscript; (6) José Vieira who wrote *Compendio de gramatica hebrea*; (7) Moses ben Gideon Abudiente, author of a long and erudite Hebrew grammar; (8) Moses Raphael Aguilar who wrote *Epitome de grammatica hebraica* (published in Leiden in 1660); and finally (9) Baruch Spinoza, whose *Compendium grammatices linguae Hebraeae* (1677), suggestively stresses the importance of the noun above all other parts of speech. The rest of the grammarians Amzalak lists are Christian Hebraists. All the grammars discussed in his handy but characteristically superficial study are not so much original contributions to theory as textbooks that served the educational needs of their time.

ELDAR deals with the beginnings of grammar study among Ashkenazim in parts of eastern France and Germany. He lists eight grammatical writings of the Ashkenazi school, which are still in manuscript, and identifies ten Ashkenazi grammarians whose works have been lost. Then he summarizes the content of each of the eight preserved writings. Grammatical study in Ashkenaz was concerned primarily with the correctness of the biblical text and with the proper pronunciation of it. Eldar acknowledges that the Azhkenazi school did not produce significant advances in Hebrew grammar but notes the sharp logical insights of certain individuals.

GALLINER traces the origins of Hebrew studies among Christians in the late Renaissance, arguing that the extent to which these studies were taken up at the behest of the *ecclesia militans* rather than under the influence of humanism has been understated. Galliner elucidates the activities of 16th-century Catholic scholar Agathio Guidacerio who held professorial positions in Rome and Paris. In his *Grammatica Hebraicae linguae* (1518), Agathio felt it necessary to justify the learning of Hebrew by quoting from Saint Augustine and Saint Jerome. He also praised Pope Leo X for his work in behalf of the study of Oriental languages. Agathio studied for seven years under the learned Rabbi Jacob Gabbai and used the grammar of Moses Kimhi. The content of Agathio's short book is based on the first chapter of David Kimhi's grammar *Mikhlol*. In 1529 he published a larger book on Hebrew grammar, *Institutiones grammaticae Hebraicae linguae*. However, the summation of his achievements as a Hebrew grammarian is presented in his *Grammaticae in sanctam Christi linguam institutiones* (Paris, 1539). Of course, Agathio's importance also rests upon the fact that he taught Hebrew to hundreds, and perhaps thousands, of Christians, some of whom became either important theologians, humanists, or leaders of the Counter-Reformation. His last works were an edition of Hebrew text of the Song of Songs and Ecclesiastes with Latin translation (1539) and an edition of Kimhi's *Mikhlol* (1540).

GOSHEN-GOTTSTEIN discusses contact among Jewish teachers and Christian scholars, including Obadiah Sforno who taught Johannes Reuchlin and Elia Levita (Eliyahu Bahur) who taught Hebrew grammar to many leading Christian scholars. He observes that whereas the first two generations of Christian Hebraists studied under Jewish teachers, by the third generation study of Hebrew had become so well established among Christians that many were taught Hebrew by other Christian Hebraists. Following the period of Levita, Jewish learning was sufficiently accessible to Christian scholars that Jews were increasingly not aware of subsequent developments in Hebrew philology (and in a broader sense, biblical studies) in Christian scholarly circles. Also of great interest is Goshen-Gottstein's discussion of Menahem Lonzano's and Jedidiah Norzi's reaction to Daniel Bomberg's *Biblia Rabbinica* (1525) and the theological motives of the Christian Hebraists.

In his volume devoted to the great Jewish linguist Eliezer ben Yehuda, FELLMAN describes the lexicographical work of the man who almost single-handedly realized an exhaustive multivolume dictionary of the Hebrew language of all periods that includes a great number of neologisms of his devising to address the needs of his contemporaries. According to Abraham Berliner, "What the French Academy did for French, what the Grimm brothers did for German, Ben Yehuda did for our holy tongue."

HAYIM Y. SHEYNIN

Libels, Anti-Jewish: Medieval

Chazan, Robert, *Medieval Stereotypes and Modern Antisemitism*, Berkeley: University of California Press, 1997

Hsia, R. Po-Chia, *The Myth of Ritual Murder: Jews and Magic in Reformation Germany*, New Haven, Connecticut: Yale University Press, 1988

Langmuir, Gavin, *Toward a Definition of Antisemitism*, Berkeley: University of California Press, 1990

Rubin, Miri, *Gentile Tales: The Narrative Assault on Late-Medieval Jews*, New Haven, Connecticut, and London: Yale University Press, 1999

Schreckenberg, Heinz, *The Jews in Christian Art: An Illustrated History*, New York: Continuum, and London: SCM, 1996

Trachtenberg, Joshua, *The Devil and the Jews: The Medieval Conception of the Jew and Its Relation to Modern Antisemitism*, New Haven, Connecticut: Yale University Press, and London: Milford, Oxford University Press, 1943; 2nd edition, Philadelphia: Jewish Publication Society, 1983

Several folk motifs or myths that circulated between the middle of the 12th century and the beginning of the 18th are treated collectively as a set of antisemitic libels. Although this designation implies that the accusations were promulgated by people who knew them to be false, the scholarly consensus is that many medieval Christians honestly believed that Jews ritually murdered young boys, tormented consecrated hosts, and poisoned wells. Recent studies have focused on the ways in which such beliefs emerged from learned literature and popular culture, on methods of transmission, on the psychological context in which such convictions helped people make sense of their world, on the manipulation of these motifs by interested parties (both non-Jewish and Jewish), and on the circumstances under which such beliefs could lead to violence. Some of the most important recent work on this subject has appeared in Hebrew and German. In addition to the books cited above, readers should look for forthcoming translations of works by Wolfgang Treue, Friedrich Lotter, and Israel Yuval.

CHAZAN claims that modern antisemitism is part of the "ideational legacy" of the 12th and 13th centuries—a legacy that includes the whole range of medieval libels. The emergence of these new ways of understanding and characterizing Jews during the Middle Ages is the primary focus of his book, which begins with a brief sketch of the migration of Jews northward from the Mediterranean basin in the ninth and tenth centuries. The new Jewish immigrants were conspicuously wealthy, sophisticated aliens in the culturally and economically backward river valleys of northern France and Germany. They were thus uniquely prepared to prosper during the social, economic, and cultural efflorescence that has been called the 12th-century renaissance. Chazan surveys the major models adduced by historians for understanding the ensuing deterioration in Jewish-Christian relations and cites the most important primary sources. His analysis of Crusader violence and Jewish responses to such assaults is particularly helpful. This is a good, concise introduction to the subject.

HSIA argues that the belief that Jews ritually extracted the blood of Christian boys at Easter emerged from a prior belief that Jews practiced magic. The Jewish magician had been a feature of Christian legend since antiquity. In German-speaking lands, legends of Jewish magic, folk beliefs about the magical powers of blood, and the church's new emphasis on the salvific potency of the blood of Christ thought to be present in the host merged with the new myth of ritual murder to form the blood libel. Hsia charts the rapid spread of the blood libel for 200 years, beginning in the 13th century, and then traces its gradual decline, which he attributes to fading consensus about the veracity of the institutions that had created the blood libel as a new kind of social knowledge, and to the ebbing belief in magic. This book is almost exclusively concerned with events in Germany.

LANGMUIR's collected essays constitute the most elaborate and carefully theorized analysis of ritual murder and the blood libel to have appeared in English. He interprets these medieval libels psychoanalytically, as symptoms of an irrational Christian reaction to repressed doubts about the truth of Christian doctrine, and he argues that the very idea of ritual murder, as well as its subsequent elaboration in blood libels and claims of host desecration, emerged from pervasive doubt about the Catholic doctrine of transubstantiation. Fantasies of Jews mocking Christ's passion and tormenting consecrated hosts helped buttress Christian beliefs by suggesting that, deep down, Jews acknowledged the centrality of Christ and the reality of transubstantiation, their perverted protestations to the contrary notwithstanding.

RUBIN traces the emergence and evolution of Christian claims that Jews tormented consecrated communion wafers. She locates the earliest of such stories in Paris in the year 1290 and maps the spread of the tale throughout Europe. Her approach is grounded in the work of recent French historians who have studied the ways in which discourse shapes and reflects the social world. She draws her evidence from a very wide range of sources, including Latin and vernacular chronicles, Hebrew responsa and liturgy, and Christian art and folk tales. Tracing the frequently lethal social consequences of the spreading stories about host desecration, Rubin paints a vivid picture of the mental world of late-medieval Europe that emphasizes the impact of narratives constructed from folk motifs and from learned theology. An interesting appendix translates the text of a medieval Jewish response to Christian claims of host desecration.

SCHRECKENBERG is a pictorial survey of the representation of Jews in Christian art. Included in its encyclopedic coverage are many of the medieval libels. Each of the more than 1,000 pictures is briefly discussed, but the volume is primarily a collection of images. It is the first place to look for depictions of medieval Jews.

TRACHTENBERG wrote his popular work in the early days of World War II, and it reflects the passion and anguish of U.S. Jews as they learned of events in Europe. The author's style of engaged scholarship is currently out of fashion, but this book continues to be cited by academics. It draws on both learned and popular sources to document its central claim that many medieval and early-modern Christians thought of Jews as demonic—either as allies of Satan or as demons themselves. The imagined Jewish penchants for sorcery, ritual murder, well poisoning, usury, and host desecration were understood as signs of this special relationship with the devil. The text, which is sometimes weakened by ahistorical generalizations (such as claims about the universality of Jewish suffering) is enhanced by more than 20 illustrations.

WILLIS JOHNSON

See also Anti-Judaism: Middle Ages

Libels, Anti-Jewish: Modern

Carmichael, Joel, *The Satanizing of the Jews: Origin and Development of Mystical Anti-Semitism*, New York: Fromm International, 1992

Cohn, Norman, *Warrant for Genocide: The Myth of the Jewish World-Conspiracy and the Protocols of the Elders of Zion*, New York: Harper and Row, and London: Eyre and Spottiswoode, 1967; new edition, London: Serif, 1996

Gross, John, *Shylock: A Legend and Its Legacy,* New York: Simon and Schuster, 1992

Lindemann, Albert, *The Jew Accused: Three Anti-Semitic Affairs (Dreyfus, Beilis, Frank), 1894–1915,* Cambridge and New York: Cambridge University Press, 1991

Seiden, Morton Irving, *The Paradox of Hate: A Study in Ritual Murder,* South Brunswick, New Jersey: Yoseloff, 1968

In late antiquity, Jews were accused of unsociability, fanaticism, and pride. In the Christian Middle Ages they were charged with deicide, ritual cannibalism, well-poisoning, and witchcraft. All these accusations carried over into the modern era. New libels, however, were added as well: In the modern era, Jews were accused of being evil capitalists or loathsome communists, not only practitioners of an evil religion but an accursed race of traitors and conspirators. These modern libels adapted, expanded, and radicalized the older characterizations of the Jews as an evil people to explain the problems of modern times.

CARMICHAEL provides an excellent overview of the "objectification" of the irrational hatred of the Jews at the core of antisemitism. He describes how the Jew became the theological symbol and later the racial incarnation of the Devil. This libel began with the charge of deicide and survived into modern times as a "mystical" concept. It differed from conventional libels or ethnic slurs directed against minority groups, taking on a "cosmic magnitude" in representing the Jew as all-powerful, diabolical evil. In modern times this libel became entirely secularized. The very survival of the Jews in the face of great odds was explained by antisemites as evidence of their mysterious power. The Jew became the secular Anti-Christ responsible for a host of modern ills. The images of the Wandering Jew, of Shylock, of the arch-capitalist and the arch-communist, and, finally, of the incurably evil race all represented modern elaborations on older religious themes. The new forms of antisemitic libel came together in Nazism as a response to the extreme cumulative traumas of modernity in 20th-century Germany. Stalinist Russia also exploited modern antisemitic libels. Carmichael ventures the hope that the impact of the Holocaust will discredit mystical antisemitism and that Christians will discard their traditional fondness for scapegoating.

COHN has written the best book on the sources, significance, and impact of the myth of a Jewish world conspiracy. He was led to his conclusion that the idea of a Jewish world conspiracy was such a supremely powerful and deadly modern anti-Jewish libel in 1945 while scouring the Nazi literature about Jews. From there he went on to trace the origin of these ideas in the early Christian era and the medieval period, finding the origins of the myth to lie in the charge that the Jews plotted to kill Jesus and then proceeded to plot ritual murders, desecrations, and plagues. In modern times, the Jews were accused of conspiring to bring about the French Revolution, and they were charged with running both modern banking and industry and the revolutionary movements of modern times. By the 1880s these ideas were taking shape in France, England, and Germany, but they achieved a "classic" and systematic expression in the *Protocols of the Learned Elders of Zion* in the czarist Russia of 1905. This text was modeled on a collection of forgeries and especially a pamphlet directed against Napoleon III by his critic Maurice Joly written in 1870. The *Protocols* accused the Jews of being behind every conceivable problem of modern times. By 1920 new libels were added, blaming the Jews for World War I and the Bolshevik Revolution. During the 1920s the *Protocols* was translated into an array of languages and printed in a great number of editions. Henry Ford subsidized U.S. editions, while the tract had great influence in Nazi Germany. It was a "warrant for Genocide" because it claimed that the Jews, being eternal conspirators who used diabolical means to master the world, had to be destroyed by any measure, however drastic. After 1945 the *Protocols* continued to circulate in the Soviet Union, the Arab countries, and among sundry movements of the radical right, and it has exhibited remarkable longevity and staying power to this day.

GROSS traces the legend and legacy of the figure of Shylock through the many and fascinating forms it has taken in the literature of modern times. The author approaches the literary character of Shylock as an economic, psychological, and cultural symbol. Immortalized in Shakespeare's 1598 play, *The Merchant of Venice*, the ancestry of Shylock can be traced back to a 14th-century Italian characterization of a Jewish money lender. A number of English versions preceded Shakespeare's play, most notably Chrisopher Marlowe's *The Jew of Malta* of 1589. In Shakespeare's drama the craven and vengeful Jew Shylock is contrasted to the honest and generous Venetian merchant, Antonio. Shakespeare represented Shylock as the personification of Judaism as a "pseudoreligion"—materialistic, legalistic, and lacking in spirituality. Shylock's only redeeming feature is his love for his daughter Jessica. At the end of the play, Shylock is forcibly converted to Christianity, then banished unceremoniously. Gross guides the reader through later interpretations of the story, in which Shylock emerges as a persecuted and more sympathetic figure. By the 20th century, Freud was able to view Shylock as a tragic father figure, although antisemites of left and right continued to find the grasping Shylock a convienient and time-honored weapon. A still more sympathetic Shylock emerged after 1945, but Gross maintains that Shakespeare never intended Shylock to be a "Jewish villain." Whatever the case, the playwright's masterpiece is shown to have added a powerful stereotype to the arsenal of modern anti-Jewish libels.

LINDEMANN has written an important comparative history of three significant anti-Jewish "affairs," in France, Russia, and the United States at the turn of the 20th century: Alfred Dreyfus was accused of treason, Mendel Beilis of ritual murder, and Leo Frank of rape and murder. Dreyfus was convicted and later pardoned and rehabilitated and Beilis was acquitted by a jury of Russian peasants, while Frank was lynched by a mob that feared his acquittal. In each of these cases modern antisemites attempted to harness public outrage for their own purposes. The author seeks to separate myth from reality in all three episodes and explains how Jews fought back. He shows how the three historical incidents were not only expressions of established antisemitic libels, but were also rooted in modern crises and in "real" conflict between Jews and non-Jews. In France, for example, the Dreyfus affair was instigated by reactionary elites hostile to liberalism; in Russia a backward autocracy sought to stir up antisemitism in order to distract its people from domestic and international crises, and in the Southern United States populist antisemites used the Jews as a symbol of Yankee capitalism. Lindemann argues that these affairs drew on older libels but were modern in their appeal to mass passions and their relation to social and economic problems. He also stresses the role of personalities in history. Some traditional antisemites came to the defense of Dreyfus and Beilis, while Frank was prosecuted by a philosemite who happened to believe him guilty. Ironically, violent antisemitism continued in France and Russia but declined in the United States.

SEIDEN offers an interesting Freudian explanation for the rise and persistence of anti-Jewish libels, developing his thesis through a detailed analysis of ten antisemitic documents covering 2,000 years of Western history. The roots of anti-Jewish libels in the West, he maintains, lie in the accusation that the religion of the "father" (Judaism) murdered the founder of the new religion (the "son") that the father helped to create. Thus, the Jews are accused of committing a "ritual murder" of the son of God, who is also their own son. Herein lies the "irrational hatred and irrational guilt" that permeates antisemitism. Anti-Jewish libels can result from the conflict between a demonic primordial father and an innocent and pure primordial son. The Jews become the "primordial cosmic scapegoat." For Seiden, this horrendous drama was enacted in the mind of Hitler and his concentration camps. The selected antisemites whose writings are analyzed include Cicero, Tacitus, Augustine, Martin Luther, Henry Adams, H.L. Mencken, and Hitler himself. The legends of the Jew as financial wizard, eternal wanderer, and demonic father—along with more than 50 additional ugly stereotypes—-are extracted from these readings. Seiden illustrates as well the bitter irony that while the antisemites suffered from feelings of inadequacy and self-hate, some Jews too came to accept and explain their own sufferings as deserved, natural, and inevitable.

LEON STEIN

See also Antisemitism

Libya

Applebaum, Shimon, *Jews and Greeks in Ancient Cyrene* (Studies in Judaism in Late Antiquity, vol. 28), Leiden: Brill, 1979

De Felice, Renzo, *Jews in an Arab Land: Libya, 1835–1970*, Austin: University of Texas Press, 1985

Goldberg, Harvey E., *Cave Dwellers and Citrus Growers: A Jewish Community in Libya and Israel*, Cambridge: Cambridge University Press, 1972

Goldberg, Harvey E., *Jewish Life in Muslim Libya: Rivals and Relatives*, Chicago: University of Chicago Press, 1990

Hakohen, Mordechai, *The Book of Mordechai: A Study of the Jews of Libya*, edited and translated by Harvey E. Goldberg, Philadelphia: Institute for the Study of Human Issues, 1980; London: Darf, 1993

Simon, Rachel, *Change within Tradition among Jewish Women in Libya*, Seattle: University of Washington Press, 1992

Libyan Jews are unique among modern North African Jews in their Italian influence. Since the 1950s, most of the community immigrated to Israel and Italy. Relatively little research has been conducted on Libyan Jews, most of it published in Hebrew, English, and Italian.

APPLEBAUM examines the first phase of Jewish existence in Cyrenaica, eastern Libya. Following a description of the land and a survey of Greek colonization, including Ptolemaic and Roman rule in the region, as well as the economy and agriculture of ancient Cyrene, Applebaum focuses on the Jewish community. He examines the circumstances of their settlement and their spread across the region in towns and rural areas and describes the organization of their communities. Applebaum then proceeds to examine the background to the Jewish revolt in Cyrenaica under Trajan (115–117), which shook the Roman empire and had devastating results for the Jews. He provides a detailed, annotated description of the revolt in Cyrenaica and its spread to Egypt, Cyprus, Mesopotamia, and Palestine. As a result of the revolt, the Jewish communities of Cyrene, Egypt, and Cyprus were destroyed, to be renewed only much later by new waves of immigration. This is the main study on the topic and includes detailed information followed by analysis and bibliography.

DE FELICE examines Jewish life in Libya under several regimes: the second Ottoman administration (1835–1911), the Italians (1911–1943), the British (1943–1951), and Arab independent rule prior to Qadhdhafi's revolution (1952–1969). The book's main contribution relates to the Italian period, examining changes in Jewish communal organization, the impact of fascism on Jewish life, and especially their condition during World War II. De Felice provides much information on the deterioration of Jewish-Muslim relations in the 1940s and on the mass migration of the late 1940s to early 1950s, during which time most of Libya's Jews left for Israel. Conditions under Arab rule, the Jews' final departure, mainly to Italy, following the 1967 Arab-Israeli War, and Qadhdhafi's ascent to power in 1969 are also examined. Based on Italian, British, and Jewish archival materials as well as numerous publications, this is the most comprehensive study of Libyan Jewry in modern times, though it is occasionally difficult to use.

GOLDBERG (1972) examines the continuity and the change that the rural Tripolitanian Jewish community of Gharian experienced in the course of immigrating to Israel. Because most of the original community settled together in a rather homogenous village, Goldberg could compare their social, economic, cultural, and communal interrelations in both places. The first part of the book, based on published sources and the testimonies of immigrants, focuses on the community before emigration: its structure and relations with the authorities, with the Muslim neighborhood, and with other Jewish communities and the Jewish leadership, as well as economic, cultural, and social issues. Goldberg then examines the immigration process and settlement in a cooperative village in Israel and provides a detailed examination of life there, based on field research conducted between 1963 and 1965. Although most of the study deals with the period after immigration, this is an important book examining a Jewish rural community and the implications of immigration for its life.

GOLDBERG (1990) analyzes from historical and anthropological perspectives the changing relations between Jews and Muslims in Libya from the early 19th century to the mid-20th century. He examines the mutual influence of Jews and Muslims living in close proximity for generations while keeping their individual characters and specific social and economic roles in the society as a whole. Special chapters deal with Jewish life in Muslim Tripoli in the late Karamanli period (early 19th century); cultural sources of the Jewish wedding in Libya; the changing role of itinerant Jewish peddlers in Tripolitania at the end of the Ottoman period and under Italian rule; Jewish-Muslim religious rivalry in Tripolitania; a cultural analysis of the Tripolitanian anti-Jewish riots of 1945; and historical and cultural process with regard to change and stability in the perception of Jews in Libyan society. The book includes a bibliography on Libya as well as more generally on North Africa and the Middle East and on anthropology.

HAKOHEN includes selections from the Hebrew original *Higid Mordekhai*, which was written at the beginning of the 20th century by a Tripolitan Jew based on his own observations and on older manuscripts. Being a well-versed individual who was involved in Jewish communal and educational life in Tripoli and who traveled in the Tripolitanian hinterland, Hakohen includes invaluable information in various fields, including history, demography, linguistics, social and economic life, folklore, anthropology, religion, and interfaith relations. Though only parts of the original Hebrew manuscript were translated, it is still a very important source for the study of the Jews of Libya in the framework of the gentile environment prior to the Italian occupation. The importance of the book is further enhanced by the notes and introductions furnished by Goldberg, who puts the indigenous phenomena into a broader Jewish framework and adds an extensive bibliography.

The slow, evolutionary change in the status of Jewish women in Libya in the 19th and 20th centuries is examined by SIMON. Based on archival and published sources, the book shows how social, economic, and political changes in Libya affected the Jews, including women, and analyzes developments in women's social position, family life, education, and public life. Economic deterioration and foreign penetration opened new work opportunities for women, which gradually allowed them to become wage earners outside the home. Economic needs, on the one hand, and the wish of many Jews who had economic and social ties with Europe to imitate Europeans socially and culturally, on the other, resulted in the provision of formal education for women. Consequently, Jewish women were exposed exclusively to modern secular education whereas men studied in both traditional and modern schools. Despite all the changes, the Jewish community remained traditional and the principles upon which it operated did not change drastically. Thus, the male power structure did not alter in the private or the public domain and the position of women changed little within these spheres despite the expansion of opportunities for women in education and economic life. This book is the first comprehensive study of Jewish women in a modern Middle Eastern or North African land.

RACHEL SIMON

Lieberman, Saul 1898–1983

Belorussian-born American textual scholar of talmudic literature

Marx, Alexander, "Dr. Lieberman's Contribution to Jewish Scholarship," *Proceedings of the Rabbinical Assembly of America,* 12, 1949

Neusner, Jacob, *Why There Never Was a "Talmud of Caesarea": Saul Lieberman's Mistakes,* Atlanta, Georgia: Scholars Press, 1994

Sigal, Phillip, "The Scholarship of Saul Lieberman: Reflections on His First Yahrzeit," *Judaism,* 33(2), Spring 1984

Saul Lieberman ranks as one of the 20th century's most important scholars of rabbinic literature. His critical editions and books have become standard reference tools. He is particularly known for his innovative studies of the influence of Hellenistic culture on rabbinic Judaism. Many of Lieberman's works were written in Hebrew and remain untranslated. He was born in Motol, Belorussia, and was ordained at the yeshivah of Slobodka in 1916. He studied talmudic philology and Greek literature at the Hebrew University, and he graduated with a master of arts degree in 1931 and was hired as a lecturer. In 1940 Lieberman began teaching at the Jewish Theological Seminary, becoming its dean in 1949. He was president of the American Academy for Jewish Research, and in 1971 he became the first non-Israeli to win the Israel Prize for Jewish Studies. Lieberman died on 23 March 1983, aboard an El Al airliner bound for Israel.

MARX's essay is the transcript of an address given in 1948 at a convention in Chicago of the Rabbinical Assembly of America. This address is an informative survey of Lieberman's works. It is perhaps most useful for its review of many of Lieberman's studies that are written in Hebrew and not otherwise accessible to English readers. For example, it summarizes Lieberman's critical edition of the Tosefta, a collection of rabbinic literature with secondary canonical status. It examines his treatment of manuscript variants and his theories of how and when different Tosefta manuscripts were produced. Marx also reviews some of Lieberman's studies in Hebrew on the Jerusalem Talmud. Lieberman helped discredit the view that the Jerusalem Talmud was a uniform text. Rather, he

argued that it was a compilation of material from different rabbinic schools that were produced in different times. Marx discusses Lieberman's 1944 essay, "The Martyrs of Caesarea," written in English, which compares accounts of the persecution of the Jews at the time of Hadrian to accounts of the persecution of Christians. Also discussed are studies on such subjects as Yemenite midrash, Maimonides, and the Karaites.

SIGAL's article is a helpful general introduction to Lieberman's scholarship. Sigal surveys briefly Lieberman's chief works and the principles that guided his studies. He describes Lieberman as the "outstanding practitioner" of the analysis of rabbinic literature with modern historical critical methods. His ideas on how texts developed over time into their present form are very influential. Sigal suggests that perhaps Lieberman's most important contribution to the study of rabbinic literature is his case for the extent to which the Tosefta and Palestinian Talmud, which are often neglected by students of the Mishnah and Babylonian Talmud, must be taken into consideration. Lieberman's critical editions make much of this "deutero-canonical" rabbinic literature accessible to scholars. Sigal also provides examples that show the breadth of Lieberman's erudition. He had a command not only of rabbinic literature but also of the Dead Sea Scrolls, classical and Hellenistic literature, and New Testament and early Christian writings as well.

NEUSNER critiques Lieberman's thesis that three tractates of Nezikin in the Palestinian Talmud (Yerushalmi), Baba Kamma, Baba Metsia', and Baba Batra (the Baba'ot), were the product of the rabbinic academy in the coastal city of Caesarea. The conventional view is that the entire Yerushalmi was edited in Tiberias. Lieberman's proposal is found in his monograph "The Talmud of Caesarea" (*Supplements to Tarbiz,* vol. 2, no. 4, Jerusalem, 1931). Lieberman developed this theory to explain long-noted differences of style, content, and terminology between the Baba'ot and the rest of the Yerushalmi. For example, this would account for the unusually large number of Greek words in the Baba'ot, since Caesarea was an extremely Hellenized city. Neusner argues that it is not necessary to explain the Baba'ot's peculiarities by positing their provenance in this city. Instead, he argues that the relationship between the Baba'ot in the Yerushalmi and the rest of its tractates is analogous to the relationship between the Baba'ot of the Babylonian Talmud and the rest of its tractates. Neusner proceeds to accuse Lieberman of not understanding the logic underpinning these talmudic tractates. While it is healthy to subject propositions made by preeminent scholars to scrutiny, in this case such an accusation is conspicuously unpersuasive.

MATTHEW GOFF

Lineage

Cohen, Shaye J.D., *The Beginnings of Jewishness: Boundaries, Varieties, Uncertainties,* Berkeley: University of California Press, 1999

Goodblatt, David, *The Monarchic Principle: Studies in Jewish Self-Government in Antiquity* (Texte und Studien zum antiken Judentum, 38), Tübingen: Mohr (Siebeck), 1994

Ilan, Tal, *Jewish Women in Greco-Roman Palestine* (Texte und Studien zum antiken Judentum, 44), Tübingen: Mohr (Siebeck) 1995; Peabody, Massachusetts: Hendrickson, 1996

Kalmin, Richard, "Genealogy and Polemics in Rabbinic Literature of Late Antiquity," *Hebrew Union College Annual*, 67, 1996

Kalmin, Richard, "Relationships between Rabbis and Non-Rabbis in Rabbinic Literature of Late Antiquity," *Jewish Studies Quarterly*, 5(2), 1998

Lewis, I.M., "Descent," in *Encyclopedia of Social and Cultural Anthropology*, edited by Alan Barnard and Jonathan Spencer, London and New York: Routledge, 1996

The chain of father-child or mother-child relationships that establishes a person's descent from specific ancestors is an apt means of defining identity. A genealogy may refer to biological facts, but very often it is a more or less mythical construction handed down from generation to generation in order to provide a specific identity for a person or group. Genealogies appear worldwide in many different forms, which can be roughly divided into two categories: *cognate* genealogies, which put equal weight on each parent's families, and *unilineal* genealogies. The latter can be divided again into two patterns: *patrilineal* genealogies, highlighting the importance of descent from the father and his male ancestors, and *matrilineal* genealogies, emphasizing descent from the mother and her ancestresses as crucial for the child's identity. The unfolding of theories concerning lineage and descent groups is one of the traditional domains of social anthropology. The reference article by LEWIS gives a sound survey of the history and contemporary state of lineage theory.

In antiquity as well as in the present, the societies of the Middle East generally emphasize patrilineality. An individual is rooted in his or her group by endless chains of sons and fathers that recede into the group's mythical past. This pattern is also true for biblical genealogies, where membership of the people of Israel is defined through patrilineal descent from the patriarchs and one of the 12 tribes that the patriarchs begat. Patrilineality thus is the determining factor of family, tribal, and ethnic affiliations. Affiliation with a certain Israelite patrilineal tribe or tribal segment is especially important where priestly and levitical descent is concerned. In these cases, descent implies additional religious rights and responsibilities, as well as restrictions concerning marriage.

The Jewish people, however, broke with the Middle Eastern tradition of unequivocal patrilineality and introduced matrilineality as a consideration. Thus, matrilineality and patrilineality have different social functions in Jewish social practice. The matrilineal pattern matters only in cases of intermarriage with non-Jews; it helps determine ethnicity, thereby governing relations between Jews and gentiles. One halakhically Jewish grandparent is the criterion of automatic entitlement to Israeli citizenship, but an amendment stipulating matrilineal descent remains high on the Orthodox agenda. Patrilineality retained its effect only for social status inside the Jewish community: rabbinic rulings since late antiquity try to downplay biblical notions of patrilineality, interpreting them

as relating to an intra-Jewish context. In any case, for the rabbis it was not descent from an esteemed or wealthy lineage that conferred honor but accomplishments in the study and practice of Torah. Rabbinic texts, therefore, rather neglect genealogical considerations. Because of this virtual absence of sources, little scholarly work has been produced on patrilineality in the Jewish context.

COHEN is the most important contemporary scholar analyzing rabbinic notions of matrilineal descent. His work, here and in scattered articles, is both comprehensive and vital to the discussion because it summarizes the few previous relevant works on the topic and combines them with the crucial primary sources to formulate a new and fruitful synthesis. How, when, and why, Cohen asks, did the rabbis depart from the biblical social patterns of unequivocal patrilineality in order to adopt the opposing principle of matrilineality? In the biblical and Second Temple periods, it was an individual's patrilineal genealogy that determined his or her identity as a Jew. The child of a Jewish male was a Jew. A mother of non-Jewish origin joined her husband's patrilineal clan by marriage, at the same time becoming a member of the Jewish people. Ritual conversion of women was neither known nor thought necessary. Rabbinic halakhah, however, stated that only the child of a Jewish female was a Jew, and in accordance with this new emphasis, the rabbis introduced rituals of conversion for gentile women who wished to be Jewish.

While Cohen comes close to a satisfactory answer to the questions of how and when the rabbis introduced the shift, he decides to leave the question of why open for the time being. He argues that this transformation did not happen before the time reflected in the Mishnah (second century C.E.) and that the earliest evidence of matrilineality as part of Jewish marital law is found in Mishnah Kiddushin 3:12. But why did the rabbis depart from the biblical law of patrilineality, which was, after all, social practice all over the Middle East? In Cohen's view, there are two reasonable explanations for this development. First, the rabbis may have extrapolated to human unions the mishnaic understanding of the biblical law of *kilayim* (forbidden mixtures), which stated for example that the offspring of the union of a horse with a donkey must be judged matrilineally. The second hypothesis, which Cohen finds more convincing, concerns the influence of the Roman law of intermarriage. Roman law held, in principle, that the status of offspring of any union in which one parent was not a full-fledged Roman citizen was determined by the mother's lineage. (Later, however, the Romans declared that such offspring should follow the parent of inferior status, who may not necessarily be the mother.) Cohen concludes that the crucial rabbinic source, Mishnah Kiddushin, may express a combination of these two factors, as the rabbinic concept of kilayim facilitated the influence of the Roman law.

The introduction of matrilineality split the group affiliations of a Jew: ethnicity was now governed by female descent, while family and (where relevant) tribal affiliation stayed within the domain of patrilineality. The relevance of patrilineality has been shown by ILAN in her study of Jewish women's lives in antiquity. On the one hand, descent defined an individual's eligibility for marriage; on the other hand, marriage was a means of conserving lineage purity. Rabbinic literature provides a number of texts pertaining to preferred and forbidden matches among Jews of different family or tribal descent. Patrilineages of high esteem favored marriage within the family in order to avoid the complications of marrying outsiders. Thus, the texts advocated such endogamous practices as marriage between first cousins and the union between a man and his sister's daughter. Ilan explains that in the Second Temple period, when priestly power was flourishing, it was predominantly families from the tribe of Levi who used endogamy to keep their lineage pure. Early rabbinic texts, such as passages in Mishnah Kiddushin, chapter four, still deal with such questions as who is allowed to marry a woman of priestly stock—an important issue in a patrilineal society in which a woman's children belong to her husband's lineage. After the destruction of the Temple, priorities concerning whose lineage purity was of the highest value changed. The newly powerful lay scholars paid little respect to the old tribal pedigrees, and scholarship became a determinant for marriageability in the rabbinic world. When the Babylonian Talmud (Pesahim 49b) catalogs desirable marriage partners, scholars rank the highest, while priests do not appear on this list. The sages and their offspring, however, soon formed patrilineal clans of their own, affiliation with which was an important factor in one's status and marriageability. Thus, kinship as a basic principle remained effective.

Kalmin's research on Jewish societies of the classical rabbinic period similarly emphasizes the history of patrilineality. In several articles, notably KALMIN (1996) and KALMIN (1998), he examines the importance of pedigree as a means of distinction between rabbinic and non-rabbinic families. Kalmin explores the regional divergence of Jewish social traditions, highlighting the differences between Palestinian and Babylonian Jewish societies as reflected in rabbinic texts: Babylonian rabbis pronounced the importance of lineage purity for rabbinic families and advocated a clear-cut, almost caste-like separation between themselves and "ordinary" Jewish families, while Palestinian rabbis of the same period were much more permissive. According to Palestinian sources, casual everyday contact and intermarriage between members of rabbinic and non-rabbinic lineages are permissible and sometimes even desirable. Kalmin links this striking difference to the different social environments in which the two Jewish communities lived. The non-Jewish Persian majority in Babylonia attached much importance to questions of lineage purity and the segregation of social classes, and Kalmin suggests that under this influence Babylonian rabbinic circles came to fear that casual relations with non-rabbinic families would open the way for intermarriage and compromise their lineage purity. In Palestine, however, the non-Jewish majority reflected the Greco-Roman cultural pattern in which stratification was much weaker. Rigid class and lineage boundaries were not considered desirable form, and again the attitude of the dominant culture influenced the Jewish minority.

GOODBLATT's study of Jewish views on monarchy provides another strong argument for recognizing the importance of patrilineality in postbiblical and rabbinic times. Unlike Ilan and Kalmin, Goodblatt studies dynasties of pre- and non-rabbinic "nobility." Nevertheless, he comes to similar conclusions, while questioning the common scholarly tendency to analyze the political and social ideologies expressed in rabbinic texts without discussing the historical context in which the rabbis lived. He argues that rabbinic texts do not reflect the extent to which Jewish societies of postbiblical times were still strongly committed to those ideologies of patrilineality that supported priestly status or that of Davidic royalty. Goodblatt makes his point through an analysis of three Jewish monarchies: the priestly monarchy of Second Temple times; the Palestinian patriarchate from the House of Gamaliel (second to fifth century C.E.); and the exilarch in Babylonia (second to 13th century C.E.). All three exemplify how a constructed patrilineal genealogy can serve political purposes. The priestly monarchs claimed descent from the High Priest Aaron of the tribe of Levi, while the patriarchal and the exilarchal ruling lineages founded their political claims on descent from the royal House of David as the noblest lineage of the tribe of Judah. Focusing on the case of the Palestinian patriarchate (which is the least studied of the three institutions), Goodblatt demonstrates how the Roman-backed family of Gamaliel had to construct a Davidic pedigree in retrospect in order to be respected by its Jewish subjects. Furthermore, Jews at that time acknowledged that the patriarchate and the exilarchate shared a genealogically based hierarchy, with the exilarchate deemed superior to the patriarchate. This arrangement was reflected in the ascription of the patriarch's descent from David through females, while the exilarch traced Davidic descent through males. This hierarchy illustrates the deeply rooted pattern of patrilineality in Jewish society: descent from a male line proves much more highly esteemed than affiliation through matrilineage.

Thus, like Kalmin, Goodblatt explains that the Jews of late antiquity used the concept of "pure" patrilineal lineage to stratify society. He concludes with the view that the strikingly few references in rabbinic literature to the importance of genealogy do not by their scarcity prove that lineage was unimportant for Jewish life. Instead, the omissions reveal that the talmudic masters had little interest in these matters on ideological grounds.

MONIKA HUMER

Literature, Jewish

Burnshaw, Stanley, Carmi Charny, and Ezra Spicehandler (editors), *The Modern Hebrew Poem Itself*, New York: Holt, Rinehart, and Winston, 1965

Mintz, Alan, *Hurban: Responses to Catastrophe in Hebrew Literature*, New York: Columbia University Press, 1984

Roskies, David G., *Against the Apocalypse: Responses to Catastrophe in Modern Jewish Culture*, Cambridge, Massachusetts: Harvard University Press, 1984

Scheindlin, Raymond P., *Wine, Women, and Death: Medieval Hebrew Poems on the Good Life*, Philadelphia: Jewish Publication Society, 1986

Waxman, Meyer, *A History of Jewish Literature*, 5 vols., New York: Yoseloff, 1960

Zinberg, Israel, *A History of Jewish Literature,* 12 vols., translated by Bernard Martin, Cleveland, Ohio: Press of Case Western Reserve University, 1972

The study of Jewish literature, from the narratives of the Tanakh to the poetry of the generation of Palmah, can be a fascinating and compelling source of enjoyment. Contrary to conventional wisdom, Jewish literature, rather than simply representing details of Jewish life in a positivistic or ethnographic sense, has often been influenced greatly by the surrounding culture and represents a polemic against traditional piety and popular values. Jewish literature has been produced in Jewish languages such as Hebrew, Aramaic, and Yiddish as well as many other languages.

BURNSHAW serves the autodidact's pursuit of Hebrew poetry. Turning to the back of the book, the reader will find an introductory essay on the history of modern Hebrew poetry by Ezra Spicehandler. He proceeds from the poetry of Spain to the creativity of Hayyim Nahman Bialik and Saul Tchernichowsky in Europe and early developments in 20th-century Palestine, and finally to post-State developments in Israel. Benjamin Hrushovski traces the development of Hebrew poetics from the Bible through the Middle Ages to the modern period, and he includes discussions of modern Hebrew meter, pronunciation, rhythm, and rhyme. The book contains discussions of 69 poems, most chosen for their aesthetic qualities. The book presents the poems in Hebrew, transliteration, and translation; the renderings of the poems are followed by biographical information on the poet and analyses by various scholars and poets. Burnshaw also provides useful information concerning biblical and historical allusions. The material moves from the classics of Bialik and Tchernichowsky to the major figures of modern Israel including poets involved in the Canaanite movement, an attempt to distance Israeli culture from Judaism. The work includes poetry by women and poetry written in reaction to the Holocaust.

MINTZ offers a historical monograph on a specific topic—catastrophe—in a specific type of literature—Hebrew—dealing with a set of authors ranging from biblical through rabbinic, medieval, and modern to contemporary Israeli writers. Beyond the impressionistic glimpses of authors found in general surveys and encyclopedias, Mintz compares the way in which writers approach a common theme. He presents not only a compelling introduction to each author and his texts but also supplies historical background relevant to both the events and the mentality of the authors and their original readers. Of particular importance is Mintz's development of what he calls the *mikdash* (sanctuary) paradigm in discussing Jewish depictions of suffering as sacrifice during the Middle Ages. One of Mintz's most astounding literary-historical discoveries appears in his discussion of Bialik's reaction to the Kishinev pogrom of 1903. In his "Be'ir haharegah" ("In the City of Slaughter"), Bialik condemns the Jews in vitriolic language for not defending themselves in the face of the attack. What Mintz discovered was that after the pogrom a committee was formed to investigate the violence. In reading their unpublished report, Mintz learned that the committee knew about Jewish self-defense efforts during the pogrom. He concludes, therefore, that Bialik's poem was founded upon a lie—

Bialik himself was not only a member of the committee, but it was he whom the committee sent to investigate on site in Kishinev and he who wrote the report.

ROSKIES treats the same subject as Mintz but from a different perspective (the Holocaust) and by making use of other (primarily Yiddish) materials. One of the central questions he deals with is the question of the continuity and uniqueness of the Holocaust and the usefulness of traditional archetypes. To answer this he suggests that the Holocaust was actually anticipated by the artistic process. Roskies does not deal with his material chronologically, purposely avoiding what he calls seamless progressions, and instead treats it thematically. The book is filled with fascinating asides about most major modern Hebrew and Yiddish writers. His central thesis revolves around the relationship of ancient archetypes, scriptural and midrashic, to Jewish collective memory. Roskies notes that traditional Jewish archetypes of sacrifice and martyrdom were collective rather than individual. Subsequent Jewish memory appropriated and often altered these archetypes, the most famous alteration being that Abraham actually sacrificed Isaac, an image that was actualized by Jewish parents during some of the eruptions of anti-Jewish violence in the Middle Ages. The remainder of the book focuses on the ways that individual authors, often survivors of the Holocaust, drew on these traditions. The final chapter elaborates a significant theme in modern Jewish literature and art: the appropriation of the crucifixion as a symbol of Jewish catastrophe, a trend that he traces back in Yiddish literature to 1909 and in Hebrew literature to 1923, when the nationalist poet Uri Zvi Greenberg wrote a poem in the shape of a cross. The book closes with a discussion of Marc Chagall's Crucifixions. Although Chagall painted them as early as 1912, it was not until the 1930s that he connected them with Jewish suffering. Mixing the study of history and literature effortlessly, Roskies uncovers an amazingly sobering fact: the Nazi officer in charge of the liquidation of the Vilna ghetto had spent three years pursuing Jewish studies at the Hebrew University of Jerusalem. Joining the roster of so many scholars of the Bible, Semitics, and even rabbinics who wrote denunciations of the Jews during the 19th century, this officer's immersion in Jewish studies and Jewish life in the land of Israel leaves readers with serious questions about whether such studies and relationships offer any real hope for better relations.

SCHEINDLIN has produced an accessible masterpiece on a splendid period in the development of Jewish literature. After an introduction about the context of Hebrew poetry in Muslim Spain and a few words on the major poets, each section of the book begins with an introduction to one of the selected genres of poetry: wine, love, and death. Scheindlin presents examples of each type of poem in both Hebrew and English translation and then analyzes each poem. He stresses that his approach highlights not what is unique about Judaism but what Judaism shares with general culture, and it illustrates how the poetry constitutes a unique cultural synthesis between Jewish traditions and those of Islamic Spain, including meter, rhyme, and literary conventions. His masterful translations convey these features felicitously in English. The three themes that Scheindlin selects constitute not mere examples but significant vantage points on the cultural world of the Jews of

Spain, especially since these genres, particularly hedonistic drinking songs and love poems sometimes addressed to men by men, are not a regular feature of Jewish culture in other periods. His discussion of these is nuanced and sensitive to the literary and social forces involved. On one matter Scheindlin's presentation appears contradictory. When discussing the wine poetry, he regularly asserts that these poems document a social reality and are not simply literary conventions copied from the works of Arab contemporaries. When he discusses the love poetry, however, he argues that it is conventional and stylized, and thereby he undermines the positivistic possibility of finding hard autobiographical data. When arguing for a difference in social realities behind these two types of poems, however, Scheindlin does make the profound observation that if Jews imitated some conventions and not others, that reveals a telling cultural choice on their part. Such an approach may offer a more intriguing and consistent direction of study than the attempt to correlate one genre with social reality at the expense of another.

WAXMAN actually wrote most of his work between the late 1920s and the early 1940s, later adding a supplementary volume covering the period from 1935 to 1960. Thus, much of Waxman's work represents not an improvement over Israel Zinberg's work (discussed below) but rather an alternative approach. Waxman covers a much broader expanse of literature, beginning earlier and extending his coverage wider geographically and later chronologically, with considerably more attention to rabbinic and religious literature. He presents his material thematically, and thus discussion of major authors may be spread out over several sections. However, each section pulls together and shapes diverse material into a coherent unit. Waxman offers plot summaries of important works with very few quotations. The work is composed of nine books bound in the first four volumes, with each volume containing supplements and excursuses on various topics. A brief outline of the book indeed serves as an outline of the contours of Jewish literature. The first book contains units on apocryphal, rabbinic, and Hellenistic literature. Books two and three include several units on medieval Jewish literature divided chronologically, and discussions of grammar, biblical exegesis, and Hebrew poetry beginning with the *piyyut* of the land of Israel. Further units include medieval rabbinic literature (arranged by category: talmudic commentaries, law codes, and responsa). These units are followed by chapters on philosophy and theology, ethics, mysticism, Karaite literature, materials on history, geography, travel, science, fables, proverbs, satire, Kabbalah, autobiography, polemics, and early Yiddish literature. In book four Waxman traces the development of modern Jewish literature, beginning with hasidic literature and then turning to Haskalah. Book five treats the 19th century including various Jewish movements, Jewish science, Jewish thought, and rabbinic literature. Book six offers an introduction to the renaissance of modern Hebrew literature at the end of the 19th century, with discussions of authors and genres. Book seven traces Yiddish and then European Jewish vernacular literature in a similar manner. Book eight returns to the modern manifestations of the medieval categories such as biblical exegesis, rabbinic literature, history, geography, autobiography, philosophy, theology, and ethics. Book nine treats American Jewish literature written in English, Yiddish, and Hebrew, and it then surveys American accomplishments in classical Jewish scholarship of the Bible, rabbinics, and Jewish law. The fifth volume of Waxman's collection offers updates, by genre and author, on Hebrew and Yiddish poetry, short stories, novels, and essays and also offers units on more traditional categories such as the Bible, rabbinics, history, biography, autobiography, philosophy, and theology. The work ends with an update on American scholarship in Hebrew literature, Jewish studies, and Jewish thought.

ZINBERG's work is a multivolume history of Jewish literature and culture, originally written in Yiddish. Trying to formulate a secular vision of Jewish culture, he concentrates primarily on poetry, ethics, mysticism, philosophy, and polemics and excludes most aspects of medieval rabbinic and religious literature. The volumes follow a chronological and geographical order. Each chapter usually focuses on a leading individual as well as other literary figures around him and only sometimes pulls together material by theme, rarely by genre. During the 1960s this work was translated into Hebrew, accompanied by additional notes. The English translation of the 1970s does not have all the material of the Hebrew translation. Zinberg, with his extensive quotations, is best viewed as an introduction and as providing a sometimes cumbersome approach for situating authors and locating sources, rather than as the final word on any subject. His work is perhaps most profitably consulted alongside Waxman, by way of a second opinion.

HOWARD TZVI ADELMAN

See also American Literature; Hebrew Literature; Hellenistic Literature; Judeo-Arabic Literature; Ladino Literature; Languages, Jewish; Poetry; Women's Literature; Yiddish Literature

Lithuania

Cohen, Israel, *Vilna*, Philadelphia: Jewish Publication Society, 1943, facsimile edition, 1992

Goldstein, Sidney, *Lithuanian Jewry, 1993: A Demographic and Sociocultural Profile* (Jewish Population Studies, no. 28), Jerusalem: Avraham Harman Institute of Contemporary Jewry, Hebrew University of Jerusalem, 1997

Greenbaum, Masha, *The Jews of Lithuania: A History of a Remarkable Community, 1316–1945*, Jerusalem: Gefen, 1995

Hundert, Gershon David and Gershon C. Bacon, *The Jews in Poland and Russia: Bibliographical Essays* (The Modern Jewish Experience), Bloomington: Indiana University Press, 1984

Schoenburg, Nancy and Stuart Schoenburg, *Lithuanian Jewish Communities* (Garland Reference Library of the Humanities, vol. 1321), New York: Garland, 1991

Jews first began migrating to Lithuania in the 1300s and became a major presence there after about 1365. To an extent, Jews in Lithuania enjoyed greater security and social and economic freedom than those in other medieval European nations because some leaders of Lithuania demonstrated greater religious and cultural tolerance. Nevertheless, the frequent subjugation of Lithuania in wars between larger states created severe crises for Lithuanian Jewry over the centuries, from restrictive legal measures to show trials and pogroms. In the 1500s, Jews were granted freedom of movement and employment, and they became a particularly important force in trade. Two major European centers of Jewish social and cultural activity from the 17th century to World War I were Vilnius (Vilna) and Kaunas (Kovno). From 1795 to 1918, after Russia had annexed a large portion of Polish territory, Lithuania formed a part of the Russian Empire. During this time, Lithuania was a major center of Jewish culture with numerous yeshivot, rabbinic authorities, and scholars, and Vilnius was viewed as "the Jerusalem of Lithuania." After World War I, newly independent Lithuania lost Vilnius to Poland. Jewish autonomy eroded in the Lithuanian republic of the 1920s and 1930s, and during World War II Nazis and Lithuanians destroyed most of the country's Jewish population. The government of the Soviet Union, which took over Lithuania after World War II, largely prohibited religious expression. After the dissolution of the Soviet Union and the emergence of the new Lithuanian republic after 1991, the Jewish community experienced some signs of a rebirth.

GREENBAUM gives a clear and well-written overview of Lithuanian Jewish political, social, and cultural history from the Middle Ages to 1945. She focuses on cultural institutions and social phenomena, such as the older yeshivot in Lithuanian territories, Jewish councils, and the Jewish Bund. Throughout the book, historical narrative is amplified by descriptions and explanations of the great Jewish cultural achievements of each period. Greenbaum points to the highlights of Jewish life in the medieval period under the different rulers of Lithuania, and she provides a particularly interesting survey of Jewish cultural life in the 18th-century Enlightenment period, noting especially the differences between hasidim and their opponents in Lithuania and Poland. In her examination of Lithuanian Jewry under Russian rule from the late 18th century to World War I, she alternates between describing the largely intolerant policies of the czars and the Jews' own increasing attempts to secure greater freedoms or to assimilate to Russian life. The book ends with a review of Jewish national autonomy in the free Lithuanian republic that lasted until World War II and a section on the near-liquidation of Lithuanian Jewry during the Holocaust. There are numerous sources in a variety of languages in the bibliography, and the notes for each chapter are particularly clear and detailed.

COHEN views Lithuanian Jewish history through the prism of the Jewish community of Vilnius. His book traces the political, social, demographic, and cultural history of Vilnius and Lithuanian Jewry from 1350 to the beginning of World War II. The book intertwines narration of historical developments under Lithuania's different rulers with descriptive sections on the Jewish community's customs and self-government. Cohen does a particularly good job of sorting out the financial and external relations of the Vilnius Jewish ruling body, or Kahal, with both the Lithuanian Jewish community as a whole and with the Polish and Russian rulers of Lithuania. He also devotes some attention to the Karaite group in Vilnius and

Lithuania and to notable Lithuanian Jewish cultural and artistic figures. The book contains useful illustrations of Vilnius's Great Synagogue and the ghetto. Although this book has a bibliography, Cohen does not supply footnotes, so this book may not lead directly to other sources for those readers who are researching more specific topics.

HUNDERT and BACON present a set of bibliographical essays that will be useful for readers studying Jewish life in both Poland and Lithuania or in Lithuania as part of the Soviet Union. For those studying Lithuania alone, there are some relevant references but not many. Nevertheless, the book's division into two long essays with bibliographies at the end of each helps to establish the context of, and interconnections between, Lithuanian-Jewish, Polish-Jewish, and Soviet history. The book notes reference works, surveys, studies of cultural and political history, and journals devoted specifically to individual countries. The only real shortcoming of this book is the lack of a comprehensive index of minor or individual topics.

SCHOENBURG provides a unique perspective on Lithuanian Jewish history and culture through the prism of genealogy as well as history. Originally geared toward readers tracing their roots to specific Lithuanian Jewish families or villages, it offers useful insights into the life of the Lithuanian shtetl as well as life in the larger cities such as Vilnius and Kaunas. The book begins with a condensed but informative history of Jewish life in Lithuania from the 1300s to the end of World War II. A large portion of the book describes specific towns, villages, and Jewish communities in Lithuania, which it lists with their Yiddish and alternative names. Most entries in this section of the book offer a brief history of each town, a description of Jewish life and the most important buildings there, and a list of the leading Jewish families in the town, as established from archival sources. An appendix shows each town on exhaustive maps. Other appendixes include lists of Lithuanian Jewish names that emerged from specific towns, lists of Lithuanian Jewish Holocaust survivors, and a bibliography of other works relating to Lithuanian Jewish history and genealogical research. This book is particularly useful for readers who wish to form a general understanding of the workings of Lithuanian Jewish village and community life or to study population patterns and customs in different regions of Lithuania.

GOLDSTEIN updates the information available on Lithuanian Jewry to provide a demographic profile of this population in the post-Soviet era. Goldstein writes that his purpose was to determine whether international sources could help to revive Jewish life and culture in Lithuania today. He provides a thorough and valuable analysis of numerous facets of the experience of current Lithuanian Jews, whose numbers have declined from about 30,000 after the Holocaust to 6,500 as of 1993. Analyzing the data derived from surveys and interviews with more than 4,000 Lithuanian Jews, Goldstein explores everything from issues of marriage, housing, professions, and economic factors to issues of ethnic conflict and the observance of specific Jewish traditions and rituals. Numerous charts, tables, and graphs throughout the book illustrate Goldstein's statistical findings. One notable finding is that Lithuanian-born Jews residing in Lithuania are more likely to identify themselves as Jewish than are Russian-born Jews residing in Lithuania. Perhaps more predictably, he also finds that those who identified themselves as Jews in terms of religion are more likely to be observant of Jewish traditions and customs than those who identified themselves as Jews by ethnicity or birth. Goldstein concludes by encouraging increased international involvement with Lithuanian Jews, as the presence of a larger international Jewish community helped smaller Jewish populations in countries such as Denmark to retain their identity and cohesiveness. The main focus of this book, however, is on the demographic charts.

ALISA GAYLE MAYOR

Liturgy, History of

Bradshaw, Paul F. and Lawrence A. Hoffman (editors), *The Making of Jewish and Christian Worship*, Notre Dame, Indiana: University of Notre Dame Press, 1991

Elbogen, Ismar, *Der Jüdische Gottesdienst in seiner geschichtlichen Entwicklung*, 1913; translated by Raymond P. Scheindlin as *Jewish Liturgy: A Comprehensive History*, Philadelphia: Jewish Publication Society, 1993

Heinemann, Joseph, *Ha-tefilah bi-tekufat ha-Tana'im veha-Amora'im*, 1962; translated by Richard S. Sarason as *Prayer in the Talmud: Forms and Patterns* (Studia Judaica, vol. 9), New York: de Gruyter, 1977

Hoffman, Lawrence A., *The Canonization of the Synagogue Service* (Studies in Judaism and Christianity in Antiquity, no. 4), Notre Dame, Indiana: University of Notre Dame Press, 1979; London: University of Notre Dame Press, 1986

Idelsohn, A.Z., *Jewish Liturgy and Its Development*, New York: Holt, 1932; London: Constable, 1995

Kohler, Kaufmann, *The Origins of the Synagogue and the Church*, edited by H.G. Enelow, New York: Macmillan, 1929

Langer, Ruth, *To Worship God Properly: Tensions between Liturgical Custom and Halakhah in Judaism* (Monographs of the Hebrew Union College, no. 22), Cincinnati, Ohio: Hebrew Union College Press, 1998

Reif, Stefan C., *Judaism and Hebrew Prayer: New Perspectives on Jewish Liturgical History*, Cambridge and New York: Cambridge University Press, 1993

Zahavy, Tzvee, *Studies in Jewish Prayer* (Studies in Judaism), Lanham, Maryland: University Press of America, 1990

Modern study of the history of the liturgy began with the 19th-century *Wissenschaft des Judentums* school. Scholars from Leopold Zunz on, using primarily philological methods, proposed reconstructions and datings of the earliest versions of rabbinic prayers. The discovery of the Cairo Genizah and Qumran complicated and enriched these efforts and led eventually to a methodological shift, led by Joseph Heinemann, who posited that early liturgy was so fluid that no reconstruction or dating was possible. Most recently, Ezra Fleischer has published a series of articles in Hebrew questioning Heine-

mann's conclusions. This debate remains unresolved, impeded not just by the complete lack of any prayer books predating the ninth century but also by evolving methodologies in the study of rabbinic literature as a whole. Medieval and modern liturgical developments have generally received much less attention, as have non-Ashkenazi rites.

The oldest, most valuable comprehensive history of the liturgy is ELBOGEN, first published in German in 1913 and translated into English with the updates of the 1972 Hebrew edition. Part one surveys the components of the liturgy, including a description of each prayer, its putative origins and development, and the differences between various rites; part two presents a history of the liturgy as a whole; and part three discusses the synagogue context of the liturgy. While Elbogen's descriptions and references remain invaluable, his historical interpretations have been superseded. Aware of the early findings from the genizah, he still assumed a discrete date of promulgation for each prayer. His discussions of liturgical poetry, as indicated by the long 1972 additions, are fundamentally flawed. His understanding of the contribution of mysticism is also limited.

Most of KOHLER's posthumous work dedicates chapters to the development of the synagogue and its liturgy and to the various groups that shaped them in the Second Temple period. While, like Elbogen, he shies away from suggesting original texts of the prayers, he does give detailed datings of each segment with attention to possible borrowings and influences from surrounding cultures. While he criticizes Elbogen's interpretations, Kohler perpetuates many of the same methodological flaws, including, especially, insupportable assumptions about the realities of Second Temple religious life.

IDELSOHN embeds these same sorts of assumptions about the early liturgy in his sequential, historically oriented description of the traditional liturgy. Prefacing this description are chapters tracing the development of Jewish worship from the First Temple to the compilation of the ninth-century *Seder Rav Amram Gaon* as well as discussions of liturgical poetry, the influence of Kabbalah, and medieval regional developments. The final chapter of the book discusses Reform liturgy. His medieval historical observations, although incomplete, are more reliable than his early materials; his discussion of liturgical poetry, while more accurate than Elbogen's, is incomplete in light of more recent discoveries.

HEINEMANN's revolutionary study, published in Hebrew in 1962 and integrating the evidence of Qumran, applies the tools of form criticism to the existing data on the early history of the liturgy. Heinemann suggests persuasively not only that fixed authoritative texts for synagogue prayer were nonexistent in the Second Temple period but also that the prayers as they are known now may not have existed then. He suggests, rather, that vocabularies and syntaxes of prayer were gradually developing independently in different social contexts: the synagogue, the study hall, the temple, the law court, and the private realm. Only gradually in the rabbinic period and after do these crystallize into the known rites. Speculation about dates of and motives for the composition of specific prayers is thus inappropriate. Critics of Heinemann question whether rabbinic liturgy could have functioned without fixed texts; it is also unclear whether the pre-rabbinic synagogue was a place of prayer at all.

HOFFMAN, following Heinemann, analyzes the evidence for the formalization of the liturgy in the geonic period, the point at which there begins to be clear insistence on fixed prayer texts. Hoffman collects and interprets the geonic responsa and legal literature on the various parts of the liturgy and then concludes with an analysis of the factors motivating various geonim to move toward "canonization" of the liturgy. While canonization reflects more what certain geonim wanted than what they achieved, Hoffman's work provides crucial insights into a critical period.

ZAHAVY's seriously flawed volume employs a novel reading of early rabbinic history, suggesting that the various parts of the liturgy originated with rival political factions in post-destruction Judaism. While intriguing, his arguments are poorly supported and documented and hence unconvincing.

REIF's important survey of the entire history of Jewish liturgy constitutes a dialogue with his predecessors and a programmatic call for future research. Methodologically, he follows Heinemann. Not an introductory text, it is best read after Elbogen, Heinemann, and, ideally, Fleischer (Hebrew). Particularly significant are Reif's chapter on talmudic liturgical issues, his history of the prayer book as a literary text, and his chapters on medieval liturgical developments. His notes and bibliography provide important reference to the rich periodical literature not discussed here.

BRADSHAW and HOFFMAN include contributions on methodology and history that, while not groundbreaking, are accessible to the nonspecialist and up-to-date. Hoffman reads liturgy through the lens of anthropological ritual studies; Zahavy makes the same historical claims as above; Chiat discusses archaeological contributions. Reif and Friedland divide their historical survey at the geonic emergence of the prayer book. Like Kohler, this volume presents Jewish liturgical history in dialogue with its Christian counterpart.

LANGER looks not at prayer texts but at the development of the legal framework governing them. Beginning with an analysis of the development of talmudic liturgical law and a summary of its principles, she then studies the changing application of several of these principles in the medieval world. Addressed are issues of the fixity and authority of received prayers and proper venues for their recitation. She studies the acceptance of post-talmudic blessings, the integration of liturgical poetry, and the private recitation of angelic liturgies. Each case and its resolution reflect shifting balances between rabbinic legal decrees and actual communal practice, factors that have been largely ignored in previous liturgical histories.

RUTH LANGER

See also Liturgy, Reform

Liturgy, Reform

Blau, Joseph L. (compiler), *Reform Judaism: A Historical Perspective: Essays from the Yearbook of the Central Conference of American Rabbis*, New York: Ktav, 1973
Bradshaw, Paul F. and Lawrence A. Hoffman (editors), *The Changing Face of Jewish and Christian Worship in North America* (Two Liturgical Traditions, vol. 2), Notre Dame, Indiana: University of Notre Dame Press, 1991
Elbogen, Ismar, *Der Jüdische Gottesdienst in seiner geschichtlichen Entwicklung*, 1913; translated by Raymond P. Scheindlin as *Jewish Liturgy: A Comprehensive History*, Philadelphia: Jewish Publication Society, 1993
Friedland, Eric L., *"Were Our Mouths Filled with Song": Studies in Liberal Jewish Liturgy* (Monographs of the Hebrew Union College, no. 20), Cincinnati, Ohio: Hebrew Union College Press, 1997
Hoffman, Lawrence A. (editor), *Gates of Understanding: A Companion Volume to Shaarei Tefillah, Gates of Prayer*, New York: Union of American Hebrew Congregations, 1977
Meyer, Michael A., *Response to Modernity: A History of the Reform Movement in Judaism* (Studies in Jewish History), New York: Oxford University Press, 1988
Petuchowski, Jakob J., *Prayerbook Reform in Europe: The Liturgy of European Liberal and Reform Judaism*, New York: World Union for Progressive Judaism, 1968
Plaut, W. Gunther, *The Rise of Reform Judaism: A Sourcebook of Its European Origins*, New York: World Union for Progressive Judaism, 1963
Plaut, W. Gunther, *The Growth of Reform Judaism: American and European Sources until 1948*, New York: World Union for Progressive Judaism, 1965
Reif, Stefan C., *Judaism and Hebrew Prayer: New Perspectives on Jewish Liturgical History*, Cambridge and New York: Cambridge University Press, 1993

Despite the continuing centrality of liturgical change as a primary mode of theological self-definition in Reform Judaism, relatively little has been written on the subject. Not only do major prayer books lack significant scholarly analysis, but the vast treasuries of liturgy written for particular communities have gone largely unexamined in the various efforts to understand the history of the movement.

The most significant exception to this generalization is PETUCHOWSKI. Based on an analysis of the weekday and Sabbath services in the surviving 171 European Reform and Liberal prayer books that he was able to identify, ranging from 1816 to 1967 (and listed in a bibliography in chapter one), Petuchowski describes and explains the development of European Reform liturgy. Although acknowledging the interdependence of these reforms with those occurring contemporaneously in North America, Petuchowski was required by his sponsors to maintain a strictly European focus. Five chapters treat aspects of the process of reform, examining the various social and intellectual forces shaping the changes. Eight chapters then focus on the approaches taken to the reforming of some of the individual topics of the liturgy that the Reform world found most troubling, such as particularism, ties to Zion, and restoration of the sacrificial cult. These more-focused studies include aspects of the High Holy Days liturgy, including a detailed look at the memorializing of the dead. Throughout, Petuchowski has included generous citations of the original sources, including the Hebrew of the prayer texts. The volume also contains a valuable bibliography of European non-Reform and North American prayer books and of secondary writings about Jewish prayer.

The other exception, FRIEDLAND's volume, comprises the author's collected articles. This melange, in general more descriptive than analytic, includes a brief survey of medieval developments; studies of specific early North American Reform prayer books; thematic studies on innovative Hebrew prayers in Reform worship, on Sephardi and mystical influences, and on theologies of death, messianism, and vengeance in certain holiday liturgies; and the author's reviews of various Reform and Reconstructionist prayer books that have appeared since the mid-1970s. While the bulk of Friedland's writings focus on the texts of the North American Reform movement, his volume does not fill the gaps left by Petuchowski's European emphasis. He provides neither a broad historical discussion of North American developments nor penetrating analysis of many important theological issues. For instance, there is no direct discussion of the prayer book that dominated the North American Reform movement for most of its history, the *Union Prayer Book*, and no formal discussion of the impact of Zionism or feminism. His discussions, however, are important collections of the relevant data needed for some more analytical treatments.

Less consistently academic but still important is HOFFMAN's collection of essays published to accompany the 1975 *Gates of Prayer* (the revision of the *Union Prayer Book*). The first three sections of this book gather previously published essays, or selections from essays, by major reform thinkers on the history, theology, and praxis of Reform worship. Notable here is the subtle editorial creation of a discussion of the major innovation of this new prayer book—its retreat from any attempt to propound a unified theological statement for the entire movement. The fourth section consists of Hoffman's own essay, "The Liturgical Message," which presents an important analysis of the history of Reform liturgy and proposes a mode of understanding the new prayer book that moves away from dependence strictly on the rational interpretation of the verbal texts to the admission of more symbolic and affective modes of interpretation. The final section provides an introduction and explanation of the new text.

A few of the general histories of Jewish liturgy have included sections on Reform. ELBOGEN's classic text devotes its entire discussion of "The Modern Period" to three brief chapters on Reform. The book, published originally in 1913, reflects historically and critically, yet clearly as a partisan apologist, on the 19th-century development of the movement, primarily in Germany and North America. The 1993 date of the English edition is somewhat misleading, for it simply translates the 1913 original, adding only the emendations, presumably here by Petuchowski, to the 1972 Hebrew edition. These additions largely summarize Petuchowski's own work. While important, this text is dated.

More recently, REIF's comprehensive liturgical history devotes its final two chapters to the modern world. Reif's discussion of Reform itself is somewhat superficial and presents no new material. However, because he does not focus exclusively on the Reform movement, he offers valuable insights into the contexts in which various reforms occurred. His interests in methodology lead him to pose many penetrating questions for future study.

Some collections of articles contain relevant materials. BLAU includes a section titled "On Ritual and Worship," which reproduces important articles by Kaufmann Kohler (1907), W. Gunther Plaut (1965), Samuel S. Cohon (1928), and Israel Bettan (1930) on, respectively, the necessity of reformed ceremonial observances, the Sabbath, and two critiques of the *Union Prayer Book*. While these articles may be read as scholarly reflections on contemporary problems, they may also fruitfully be employed as primary sources for the theology of Reform liturgy.

BRADSHAW and HOFFMAN include a brief article by A. Stanley Dreyfus that summarizes the history of liturgical reform and that concludes with an analysis of the recent "Gates" series of Reform prayer books. Michael Signer's essay on the "Poetics of Liturgy" may be read as a critique of the contemporary liturgical situation in the Reform world. The other articles in this collection, devoted to issues in various Christian settings, provide valuable counterpoint to the Jewish experience and point to glaring gaps in the literature about Reform liturgy, such as the absence of any serious study about the impact of feminism.

A significant portion of the reforms of the Reform movement have expressed themselves liturgically. Hence, any history of the movement necessarily discusses liturgical issues. MEYER's authoritative, well-indexed history contains no extended discussion of liturgy but rather incorporates rich quantities of material into its larger analysis. No serious study of Reform Judaism can ignore this volume. PLAUT's (1963, 1965) two-volume history includes sections devoted to matters of synagogue and liturgy. Each section includes introductory material followed by selections from documents.

RUTH LANGER

See also Liturgy, History of; Reform Judaism

London

Alderman, Geoffrey, *The Jewish Community in British Politics*, Oxford: Clarendon, and New York: Oxford University Press, 1983

Alderman, Geoffrey, *London Jewry and London Politics, 1889–1986*, London and New York: Routledge, 1989

Alderman, Geoffrey, *Modern British Jewry*, Oxford: Clarendon, and New York: Oxford University Press, 1992

Brook, Stephen, *The Club: The Jews of Modern Britain*, London: Constable, 1989

Fishman, William J., *East End Jewish Radicals, 1875–1914*, London: Duckworth, in association with the Acton Society Trust, 1975

Kosmin, Barry A., and Nigel Grizzard, *Jews in an Inner London Borough: A Study of the Jewish Population of the London Borough of Hackney Based on the 1971 Census*, London: Research Unit, Board of Deputies of British Jews, 1975

Kosmin, Barry A., and Caren Levy, *Jewish Identity in an Anglo-Jewish Community: The Findings of the 1978*

Redbridge Jewish Survey, London: Research Unit, Board of Deputies of British Jews, 1983

Roth, Cecil, *The Great Synagogue, London, 1690–1940,* London: Goldston, 1950

Rubinstein, W. D., *A History of the Jews in the English-speaking World: Great Britain,* Basingstoke, Hampshire: Macmillan, and New York: St. Martin's Press, 1996

There is no evidence of Jews in Roman or Saxon London, but William of Malmesbury notes that William the Conqueror brought Jews from Rouen to London in the wake of the Norman Conquest of 1066. In the reign of Henry I (1100–1135), the establishment of a Jewish quarter *(vicus Judaeorum)* is first noted, followed a couple of years later by the first blood libel against the Jews, with a fine of £2000 levied against the community. Several scholars visited London in the 12th century, and Abraham ibn Ezra wrote his *Iggeret ha-Shabbat* and *Yesod Mora* there during the reign of Henry II (1154–1189). The persecutions in France in the 1170s led to an influx of scholars such as Yom Tov of Joigny. The coronation of Richard I in 1189 was marked by the first massacre of Jews in London and followed by the first charter granted to the community. A series of worsening incidents involving further blood libels, pogroms, and economic and religious discrimination led to the expulsion of England's Jews by Edward I in 1290. Jews from Spain and Portugal were the main visitors thereafter, and a small community of Marranos existed until the English republic under Oliver Cromwell tacitly re-admitted the Jews in 1656. The establishment of an Ashkenazi community in 1690 followed the original Sephardi settlers from the Netherlands. The history of Anglo-Jewry is somewhat the history of the Jews of London. Indeed the London Committee of Deputies became the representative body of British Jewry in 1760.

ROTH's classic history of the Great Synagogue documents the development of the Ashkenazi community, its rabbis and lay leaders. Completed just before the destruction of this historic building by German bombers in 1941, it projects an informative and colorfully descriptive account.

Alderman, a historian of the successor generation, is more analytical in his own work and highly critical of the public relations agenda of Roth and his time. In particular ALDERMAN (1992) emphasizes the diversity and lack of uniformity within Anglo-Jewry. For example, the class structure of London Jews in 1882 suggests 42.2 percent were middle class and 23.6 percent were paupers. The great immigration from Russia and Poland after 1881, however, threatened all that and produced an antipathy on the part of anglicized West End Jews and their United Synagogue toward the poverty-stricken immigrant Jews in London's East End and the alarmingly ethnic premises where they met for prayer and study. The latter, as described in detail by Alderman, developed into the Federation of Synagogues. Alderman is also incisive on the transformation of the office of Chief Rabbi into a Jewish counterpart to the Archbishop of Canterbury for British society at large. He charts the genesis in London of different Jewish denominations: Reform (1840), Liberal (1902), and most recently the Masorti followers of Rabbi Louis Jacobs, a leading talmudic scholar effectively expelled from the United Synagogue in the 1960s for expounding a qualified interpretation of traditional doctrines of revelation.

RUBINSTEIN is particularly interesting for taking issue with the view (of Geoffrey Alderman and Richard Bolchover, among others) that London Jewry was docile and ineffective during the Holocaust period and could have done more. Rubinstein contends that "hindsight is not historical evidence."

London Jewry has a radical political tradition of liberalism, socialism, anarchism, communism, and Trotskyism, which has emanated essentially from London's East End. In 1876 Aron Lieberman established Agudat ha-Sotsyalistim ha-'Ivriim be-London (London Hebrew Socialist Union), and Morris Winchevsky's publication *Der Polisher Yidl* followed shortly afterward. FISHMAN details these early years of Jewish radicalism and especially the life and work of Rudolf Rocker, a German Catholic who developed and led the Jewish anarchist movement and devoted many years to the Jewish working class of London's East End.

Since World War II, London's changing Jewish population has been swollen by migration to the capital from other British cities as well as from Israel and South Africa and from former British colonies. At the same time, the population has been diminished by emigration to Israel, Australia, Canada, and other English-speaking countries as well as by a much-increased rate of assimilation and exogamy. Today London Jews account for a probable two-thirds of British Jews. During the last quarter of the 20th century, demographic analysis carried out by KOSMIN and GRIZZARD and by KOSMIN and LEVY established a factual picture of London Jewry firmly based in social scientific research. The Board of Deputies of British Jews and the Institute for Jewish Policy Research regularly produce demographic and general research on the changing patterns of London Jewry.

BROOK has written a journalistic account of Anglo-Jewry and its institutions that is critical, iconoclastic, and sharply observant. Unusually for a book on this subject, it has been reviewed widely in the national press in Britain and gone into a second edition. ALDERMAN (1983 and 1989) examines contemporary Jewish policy and national issues. His analysis of Jewish voting patterns is particularly interesting and suggests that the central issue for London Jews, as for non-Jews, is their socioeconomic situation rather than any specific Jewish agenda. He does, however, note that in Margaret Thatcher's heavily Jewish constituency of Finchley, the Jewish vote for the Conservatives ought to have been higher, and he sees here a possible reflection of disagreement with her social and foreign policies. Even so, Alderman concludes that any connections with the radicalism of the days of Jewish anarchism and domination of the London region of the Communist Party are long gone.

COLIN SHINDLER

Lubavitch *see* Habad

Luria, Isaac 1534–1572

Charismatic Palestinian pioneer of messianic Kabbalah

Fine, Lawrence, "Maggidic Revelation in the Teachings of Isaac Luria," in *Mystics, Philosophers, and Politicians: Essays in Jewish Intellectual History in Honor of Alexander Altmann* (Duke Monographs in Medieval and Renaissance Studies, no. 5), edited by Jehuda Reinharz, Daniel Swetschinski, and Kalman Bland, Durham, North Carolina: Duke University Press, 1982

Fine, Lawrence, *Safed Spirituality*: *Rules of Mystical Piety, the Beginning of Wisdom* (The Classics of Western Spirituality), Ramsey, New Jersey: Paulist Press, 1984

Fine, Lawrence, "The Contemplative Practice of Yihudim," in *Jewish Spirituality: From the Sixteenth-Century Revival to the Present* (World Spirituality, vol. 14), edited by Arthur Green, New York: Crossroad, 1987; London: Routledge and Kegan Paul, 1988

Jacobs, Louis (editor and translator), *The Palm Tree of Deborah* [Tomer Devorah by Moses ben Jacob Cordovero], London: Vallentine, Mitchell, 1960; New York: Sepher-Hermon, 1981

Schechter, Solomon, "Safed in the Sixteenth Century," in his *Studies in Judaism,* vol. 2, Philadelphia: Jewish Publication Society, 1908

Scholem, Gershom, *Major Trends in Jewish Mysticism* (Hilda Strook Lectures), New York: Schocken, 1941; 3rd edition, New York; Schocken, 1954; London: Thames and Hudson, 1955; with new foreword by Robert Alter, New York; Schocken, 1995

Isaac Luria, the *Ari* (acronym for Adonenu ["Our Master"] Rabbi Isaac), was the most influential Jewish mystic of the Renaissance and modern times. His system of Kabbalah took on the stature of a revealed religion for his followers, as they believed it to have originated with a direct communication from the prophet Elijah. Despite its quiet beginnings, within 30 years Luria's teaching had become central among the mystics of the land of Israel, and within 50 years it was to become the single most powerful force in Kabbalah. Luria's life story, particularly as presented in such enthusiastic works as *Shivhei ha-Ari* and *Toledot ha-Ari,* provided a legendary context for his theoretical teachings. (Limited selections from *Shivhei ha-Ari* have been published in English as *Tales in Praise of the Ari,* translated by Aaron and Jenny Klein, Philadelphia: Jewish Publication Society, 1970.) A cult of personality, modeled on the Zohar's veneration of Simeon bar Yohai, was carried over into Luria's circle and from there to the movements that accompanied the messianism of Shabbetai Tsevi and the sages of Polish Hasidism. Evident in Luria's writings is a growing sense of psychological dread. SCHOLEM interprets this sense of catastrophe and dread as a response to the expulsion of the Jews from Spain in 1492. According to him, Luria's worldview was meant as nothing less than "a mystical interpretation of Exile and redemption, or even as a great myth of Exile. Its substance reflects the deepest religious feelings of the Jews of that age." Lurianic speculative literature took shape over several generations in the writings of a number of authors and editors led by Hayim Vital. Vital's pre-

sentations of the Lurianic system were variously combined and successively revised to make up what is commonly referred to as *Kitvei ha-Ari,* the Lurianic canon. During the first 200 years after Luria's death, only two compositions from the canon were formally published, while hundreds of manuscripts circulated, transmitting teachings identified as his in dozens of formats. Many of the Lurianic texts were not available in print until the 19th century. This resulted in the circulation of many secondary and tertiary recensions and summaries of the Lurianic doctrine.

For Western readers, the first sympathetic exposition of Luria's teaching and of the Safed renaissance in general was SCHECHTER's essay. This work, like much of Schechter's literary production, is semi-apologetic but portrays the energy and pathos of the Safed experience in ways that would be influential for later scholars.

Modern studies of Luria have been dominated by the research of Yosef Avivi, Ronit Meroz, and Lawrence Fine. Avivi and Meroz have both produced taxonomic analyses of the Lurianic canon, building on the foundation of Scholem's pioneering research, and especially his bibliographical work in which he attempts to differentiate true and false attributions to Luria. Unfortunately, the work of these two Israeli scholars has not yet been translated into English. Lawrence Fine takes a phenomenological approach, concerning himself with Luria's mystical practices. Through the practice of these mystical *kavvanot,* or "intentions," the mystic took an active role in bringing together the shattered metaphysical superstructure, mending the "broken vessels." In FINE (1987) and FINE (1982), the author discusses another way that Lurianic doctrine influenced the methodologies for the shamanistic, visionary practices that some of the kabbalists who gravitated to Safed brought with them from the diaspora.

It remains a matter of debate whether the most distinguished figure of the Safed renaissance was Isaac Luria or the great teacher whose reputation he eclipsed, Moses Cordovero. Cordovero synthesized a unified approach to the various traditions that comprised the legacy of the medieval Kabbalah, drawing upon the Zohar, the teachings of Abraham Abulafia and other strands, and combining them into a vast baroque system. Cordovero has been largely inaccessible in English writings, and a translation of the groundbreaking Hebrew studies of his thought by Bracha Sack is particularly to be desired. Still, a good sense of Cordovero and the milieu he fostered in the Galilee, out of which the dynamic personality of the Ari emerged, can be garnered from JACOBS and from FINE (1984). Jacobs presents a lucid translation of Cordovero's manual of "kabbalistic ethics," prefaced by an extended and thorough introduction that sets out the kabbalistic preconceptions implicit in this statement of moral theology. Fine's accessible and illuminating introduction to the ethos of Safed contextualizes and annotates selected supererogatory rituals fostered by Abraham Galante, Abraham Berukhim, and Joseph Karo, as well as Cordovero and Luria. The book also features a popular period abridgement of Elijah de Vidas's enormously influential *Beginning of Wisdom,* a visceral summons to the good life pietistically construed.

PINCHAS GILLER

Luzzatto, Moses Hayyim   1707–1746

Italian-born kabbalist, moralist, poet, and playwright, died in Acre

Bindman, Yirmeyahu, *Rabbi Moshe Chaim Luzzatto: His Life and Works,* Northvale, New Jersey: Aronson, 1995

Carlebach, Elisheva, "Redemption and Persecution in the Eyes of Moses Hayim Luzzatto and His Circle," *Proceedings of the American Academy for Jewish Research,* 54, 1987

Gallant, Batya, "The Alleged Sabbateanism of Rabbi Moshe Hayyim Luzzatto," *Tradition,* 22, 1986

Ginzburg, Simon, *The Life and Works of Moses Hayyim Luzzatto, Founder of Modern Hebrew Literature,* Philadelphia: Dropsie College for Hebrew and Cognate Learning, 1931

Roth, Cecil, *The History of the Jews of Italy,* Philadelphia: Jewish Publication Society, 1946; Westmead: Gregg, 1969

Moses Hayyim Luzzatto was the preeminent kabbalist and Hebrew poet of the 18th century. English-language scholarship on him includes three general works (Roth, Ginzburg, and Bindman) that offer a biographical and bibliographical description and two others (Carlebach and Gallant) that deal with specific aspects of his life and work.

ROTH presents, in very condensed form, a survey of Italian Jewish history, but he does succeed in giving the reader a fair amount of basic information about Luzzatto and his times. Roth claims that "Luzzatto is one of the most important names in Jewish literature and links the poetical tradition of the Middle Ages with that of today." The book presents briskly the figure of Luzzatto, his writings, and his studies in Kabbalah, as well as his esoteric self-image as Messiah, which caused a major dispute within the Jewish community and compelled him to flee Padua.

GINZBURG's book is substantially a biography of Luzzatto and a survey of his writings. The book is divided into two parts. The first section deals with the life of Luzzatto, and the second concerns his works and is divided into three areas: the kabbalistic and rabbinic field, the dramas and the poems in terms of their content, and questions of literary style and meter. In particular, Ginzburg describes the polemical stories that arose in Padua about Luzzatto, his messianism, his mystical revelations, and his ensuing persecution. In his literary analysis, Ginzburg compares Luzzatto's theatrical works with those of the non-Jewish writers of the Italian Baroque. Naturally, Ginzburg's work does not reflect subsequent trends in literary criticism, and it is also somewhat dated by his unfamiliarity with the many dramas by Jewish authors published from manuscript only in recent years, which nevertheless exercised considerable influence on the work of Luzzatto.

BINDMAN's book is not intended to be a scientific study. It does not include a bibliography or footnotes and is essentially just a popular biography of Luzzatto. It consists of very brief chapters dealing with the various aspects of Luzzatto's life and work. The book's approach is a little superficial, although it does offer a general survey of the subject for non-specialist readers. Naturally, one should not look for a deep analysis of Luzzatto's writings in this work, but in spite of that, the book does present the distinctive religious experience of Luzzatto. At the end there is a selection of brief quotations from Luzzatto's writings to illustrate, according to Bindman, "the range of key points in the subject matter."

GALLANT's brief article studies substantially the accusation of Sabbatianism that the rabbis of Venice leveled against Luzzatto. Gallant summarizes Luzzatto's attitude to Sabbatianism and Tishbi's opinion that Luzzatto's teacher, Rabbi Isaiah Bassan himself, brought these charges of Sabbatianism against him. In conclusion, Gallant analyzes and critiques Tishbi's thesis. This study enlightens a central aspect of Luzzatto's thought and reviews the most important secondary literature on the subject.

CARLEBACH analyzes some of the philosophical conceptions that emerge from Luzzatto's literary endeavors. According to Carlebach, Luzzatto inhabited a richly imaginative inner spiritual world, and he believed himself chosen for a special destiny. For this mission he took steps to prepare himself, registering his experiences in a diary. In Carlebach's opinion, these mystical experiences influenced Luzzatto's other writings. In this important article, Carlebach also surveys other texts that affected Luzzatto's imagination, and she gives a sharply defined picture of Luzzatto's mystical thought.

YAAKOV A. LATTES

Luzzatto, Samuele Davide   1800–1865

Italian biblical commentator, pioneer of *Wissenschaft,* and theologian

Baron, Salo W., "The Revolution of 1848 and Jewish Scholarship," *Proceedings of The American Academy for Jewish Research,* 18, 1949

Gopin, Marc, "The Religious Ethics of Samuel David Luzzatto," Ph.D. diss., Brandeis University, 1993

Harris, Monford, "The Theologico-Historical Thinking of Samuel Luzzatto," *Jewish Quarterly Review,* 52, 1962

Margolies, Morris B., *Samuel David Luzzatto, Traditionalist Scholar,* New York: Ktav, 1979

Morais, Sabato, *Italian Hebrew Literature,* Julius H. Greenstone, editor, New York: Jewish Theological Seminary, 1926

Rosenbloom, Noah, *Luzzatto's Ethico-Psychological Interpretation of Judaism: A Study in the Religious Philosophy of Samuel David Luzzatto* (Studies in Torah Judaism, 7), New York: Yeshiva University Department of Special Publications, 1965

Roth, Cecil, *The History of the Jews of Italy,* Philadelphia: Jewish Publication Society, 1946; Westmead: Gregg, 1969

Slymovics, Peter, "Romantic and Jewish Orthodox Influences in the Political Philosophy of S.D. Luzzatto," *Italia,* 4, 1985

Theologian, biblical scholar, grammarian, liturgiologist, poet, and charismatic pedagogue, Samuele Davide Luzzatto is the defining thinker of modern (i.e., post-Emancipation) Italian

Judaism. The various studies on Luzzatto have treated his literary production (Slymovics), his thought (Gopin and Harris), and his historical context (Baron), while other writers have taken a more biographical approach.

ROTH's book is a general survey of Italian Jewish history, and therefore it supplies only very basic information about Luzzatto. Roth does, however, describe the intellectual activity of Luzzatto and his milieu in Italy as well as abroad. For this reason, his book is a fundamental work for the comprehension of this corner of history, even if it has been superseded in its historiographic approach by newer studies. It is of very limited value for scientific research because it does not note its sources, but it is a good and stimulating read nonetheless.

MORAIS describes the Jewish cultural context of the period as well as Luzzatto's family background. The work covers the mentality of the time and the intellectual activity of Luzzatto in defending the Jewish religion from criticism and in perpetuating and spreading the knowledge of sacred literature. Morais includes an account of Luzzatto's efforts to cultivate scholars at the Rabbinical College in Padua and a description of his various works.

MARGOLIES's study is perhaps the most detailed and comprehensive biography of Luzzatto. It discusses the different aspects of Luzzatto's life: his background and his influences, his religious inner world, his relationship with his contemporaries, and his poetry. Furthermore, it analyzes Luzzatto's exegesis, thought, and linguistic studies. In particular, this work provides an interesting description of Luzzatto's intellectual and personal commitments, such as his approach to the Bible based on linguistics and philology, and also the scholarly activity reflected in his enormous correspondence with the most eminent minds of the period. One chapter is dedicated to the Italian Hebrew literature that inspired Luzzatto's own poetry and to the estimation of his poetry by his contemporaries.

ROSENBLOOM's book analyzes a specific aspect of Luzzatto's thought: his efforts to reconcile traditional Judaism with the rationalist philosophy of the 19th century and thus to interpret it in light of his post-Enlightenment age. Rosenbloom argues that Luzzatto's purpose was to demonstrate that the Torah can be reconciled with the categories of reason and principles of logic. In fact, Luzzatto interpreted Jewish tradition as an ethical and ethnic culture, and he published a number of books that expounded a view of Judaism that emphasized particularly its ethical rather than speculative aspect.

GOPIN discusses the religious philosophy of Judaism as developed by Luzzatto. In his opinion, the Jewish thought of Luzzatto was unique in the context of the period because he based his analysis on moral sense theory, similar to the approach to ethics of Hume, Rousseau, and other European thinkers. This work studies the different editions of Luzzatto's autobiography, the collections of his Italian and Hebrew letters, and other writings. Its aim is to demonstrate the interaction of Luzzatto's personal history and the development of his ethical thought, as well as the relationship between Luzzatto and rabbinic Judaism. Gopin concludes that Luzzatto incorporated rabbinic Judaism into his ethics, although he evaluated the rabbis critically in the light of personal sentiment, in particular toward non-Jews.

BARON's article is an important contribution to understanding Luzzatto's historical and social background. It analyzes the influence on Jewish scholars of revolutionary ideas and movements at the beginning of the 19th century and also their participation in the revolutions of 1848. He considers the Jewish scholars who participated in the struggle for Jewish emancipation, notably Luzzatto, and who contributed immense activity and vast correspondence to furthering the cause. This article therefore takes a wide perspective on the political context in which Jewish intellectuals worked.

SLYMOVICS's article is a philosophical analysis of Luzzatto's thought. Its purpose is to examine the conception of Judaism as it emerged in his writings and the different cultural trends that influenced him. Through comparison of the thought of Luzzatto with that of Rousseau, Slymovics demonstrates the similarities of their religious and social conceptions. In Slymovics's opinion, both Luzzatto and Rousseau were Enlightenment figures who severely criticized the rationalistic tendency of their day. He also analyzes their shared concept of law and politics as rooted in morality, as well as their view of history. This article is learned and technical, and as such will be mainly of interest to scholars of Jewish philosophy.

HARRIS's work analyzes Luzzatto's thought and his intellectual achievements to reveal a "coherent approach to historical scholarship and to Jewish tradition." Harris notes the emphasis Luzzatto placed on the distinction between Greek and Jewish mentalities. He also illuminates Luzzatto's inner world as a theologian and the grounds for his strenuous opposition to Kabbalah in general and his debunking of the Zohar in particular. In spite of this antimystical tendency, in Harris's opinion Luzzatto had great respect for Christianity and saw a need for Jewish-Christian dialogue.

YAAKOV A. LATTES

M

Magic and Superstition

Ben-Ami, Issachar, *Saint Veneration among the Jews in Morocco*, Detroit, Michigan: Wayne State University Press, 1998

Grözinger, Karl Erich and Joseph Dan (editors), *Mysticism, Magic, and Kabbalah in Ashkenazi Judaism: International Symposium Held in Frankfurt a.M. 1991*, New York: de Gruyter, 1995

Idel, Moshe, *Hasidism: Between Ecstasy and Magic*, Albany: State University of New York Press, 1995

Nigal, Gedalyah, *Magic, Mysticism, and Hasidism: The Supernatural in Jewish Thought*, Northvale, New Jersey: Aronson, 1994

Patai, Raphael, *The Jewish Alchemists: A History and Source Book*, Princeton, New Jersey: Princeton University Press, 1994

Ruderman, David B., *Kabbalah, Magic, and Science: The Cultural Universe of a Sixteenth-Century Jewish Physician*, Cambridge, Massachusetts: Harvard University Press, 1988

Seidel, Jonathan Lee, "Studies in Ancient Jewish Magic," Ph.D. diss., University of California at Berkeley, 1996

Sharot, Stephen, *Messianism, Mysticism, and Magic: A Sociological Analysis of Jewish Religious Movements*, Chapel Hill: University of North Carolina Press, 1982

Sperber, Daniel, *Magic and Folklore in Rabbinic Literature*, Ramat-Gan: Bar-Ilan University Press, 1994

Swartz, Michael D., *Scholastic Magic: Ritual and Revelation in Early Jewish Mysticism*, Princeton, New Jersey: Princeton University Press, 1996

Trachtenberg, Joshua, *Jewish Magic and Superstition: A Study in Folk Religion*, New York: Behrman's Jewish Book House, 1939

Evidence of the use of magic is abundant in the Jewish literature of late antiquity and the Middle Ages, even though there is much confusion as to what the word *magic* means, and scholars debate how to apply the term within the realm of religion. Many issues regarding the significance of magic and superstition for Judaism remain unsettled, for numerous ancient sources containing relevant texts written in Hebrew, Aramaic, and other languages remain in manuscript and have not been studied or translated.

Much of what is known about antique Jewish magic stems from the Hekhalot ("Chambers of Heaven") literature. The focus of Hekhalot is ritual—it is a literature of Jewish magic and phenomenology. Many theories abound regarding the historical origin of the Hekhalot literature, and the great authority Gershom Scholem considered it to be vital to the evolution of Jewish mysticism. One text in this literature, the Sar-Torah, depicts an angel who transformed ancient conjurers into learned rabbis. Rabbis of the time were responsible for memorizing incantations for use in many areas, such as health, love, prosperity, childbearing, and improvement of memory. Superstitious features of this literature include belief in the rabbis' ability to bring the dead back to life and in their power to battle evil. Conjuring the name of God, uttering magic spells, and calling angels for divine intervention were all conceived as part of the rabbi's job description.

It is not impossible that the themes of the Hekhalot literature and the attendant rituals may help explain why Jews were accused of magic and dark deeds for many centuries. The growing segregation of Jews only reinforced public opinion against them, and accusations of sorcery, ritual murder, magic, and consorting with demons were commonplace—biblical and talmudic injunctions notwithstanding.

BEN-AMI's exhaustive work on modern Jewish saint worship in Morocco is the culmination of 10 years of research and includes a list of 656 saints, 25 of whom are women. Ben-Ami does not present a historical study of saint veneration; instead he compiles and interprets the relevant folklore. He has divided his work into five categories: folktales, descriptions of miracles, dreams, descriptions of experiences while paying homage to saints, and related traditions. Magic in ceremonies and rituals and notably in the exorcism of evil spirits is well represented in this book, and the author describes the perception that magic and superstition offered the Jews essential protection against an evil environment comprising a fundamentally hostile Islamic majority. Visits to saints' tombs offered Moroccan Jews "a heightened sense of Jewish unity and identity," and Ben-Ami argues that "The powerless minority seeking security found a highly effective protective mechanism in the countless miracle tales of punishments inflicted on Muslims who harmed Jews or Jewish saints." The author describes Moroccan Jews' beliefs regarding saintly powers, such as the abilities of saints to cure sickness, converse with plants and animals, and tame wild beasts. He also includes numerous photographs of saints' tombs and a glossary that will be helpful to those uninitiated in Jewish culture. The reader will find both French and English sources in the bibliography.

GRÖZINGER has compiled a collection of essays from a conference on mysticism, magic, and Kabbalah in Ashkenazi Judaism that took place in Frankfurt in 1991. Many of the essays in this volume deal with medieval Jewish mysticism in Germany and surrounding areas of central Europe. This work is especially valuable because most scholarship has concentrated on mysticism in southern Europe. The history of Kabbalah in Germany is addressed as are more sectarian manifestations of mysticism such as Sabbatianism. Grözinger's own essay, "Between Magic and Religion: Ashkenazic Hasidic Piety," evaluates the relationship between magic and religion, using the talmudic and Hekhalot literature, along with later medieval sources, to illustrate intimate links between the two realms. Most essays are in English, with a few articles written in German interspersed throughout the volume. Grözinger also offers studies of individuals as prominent as Judah Loew ben Bezalel and as obscure as Meyer Heinrich Hirsch Landauer.

IDEL seeks to define the roles of magic and mystical practice in Hasidism. He attempts to answer several questions concerning Hasidism by looking at clues in earlier forms of Jewish literature. He argues that the *zaddikim* or rebbes did not seek ecstasy as their ultimate goal, but they did endeavor to bring divine power into their midst to benefit the community, and religious ecstasy was widely perceived as the precondition for wonder-working. Idel introduces the reader to several models of Hasidism and devotes one chapter to the mystico-magical model. In chapter four, titled "Mystical and Magical Prayer in Hasidism," Idel presents a thorough explanation of the Lurianic method of prayer, or *kavannot*. Appendixes offer the reader further assistance in understanding aspects of Kabbalah, Lurianic theosophy, and magical power. A rich bibliography will prove invaluable for the scholar seeking further insight into the role of magic and superstition in Hasidism.

NIGAL begins his work with the first of the hasidic storytellers, the Ba'al Shem Tov, considered a worker of wonders who conjured up miracles to heal the sick and to bless couples with fertility. The background of the Ba'al Shem's ministry is discussed, as well as the use of amulets used by the Ba'al Shem himself. The second chapter discusses the concept of *kefitsat ha-derekh*, a kind of magical time travel that enabled adepts to shorten the duration of a journey. Other areas explored within the work are reincarnation, exorcism, demons, and magic formulae. Nigal recounts numerous traditional stories to exemplify the use of magic and superstition, interpreting them from a historical and sociological perspective with notable clarity.

Jews were widely perceived as a community of alchemists in the Middle Ages and early modernity, largely as a function of their great repute in the sciences of the time, specifically medicine and astrology. PATAI introduces the reader to the various definitions of alchemy, from its consideration as a legitimate, albeit misdirected, attempt to turn base metals into gold to the belief that it could transform the imperfect human soul into a "more perfect spiritual entity." Two basic versions

of alchemy are identified: alchemy as science and alchemy as magic. Patai explains the work of the Jewish alchemists, and he notes ironically that while Kabbalah and Hasidism enjoyed a rehabilitation in the last half of the 20th century, alchemy was not so fortunate, perhaps because it demands too much specialized training. Earlier scholars had been unable to find proofs of Jewish alchemical activity prior to the Renaissance in Jewish or European literature, but Patai claims to have found such evidence. This material is arranged in chronological order, from biblical, Hellenistic, and talmudic evidence through the 19th century. Patai, the pioneering polymath of Jewish studies in the late 20th century, has rendered a signal service by locating and assembling references to alchemy and its Jewish connection in European as well as in Jewish literature. A very useful alchemical vocabulary follows the text, and illustrations are provided throughout the work.

RUDERMAN considers relationships among science, magic, and Judaism in 16th-century Europe. The study centers on the world of Abraham ben Hananiah Yagel (1553–c.1623), a Jewish magician, kabbalist, and physician, and the author investigates how magic figured in the medicine of the time and considers how Yagel's own religious beliefs affected his scientific research. Ruderman states,

> As a religious thinker, he [Yagel] sought to reshape Jewish culture by underscoring the religious value of comprehending the natural world, by reformulating kabbalistic tradition in the language of scientific discourse so as to promote it as the highest form of human knowledge, and by pushing Jewish religious sensibilities to their limits in advocating the legitimate role of the magical arts as the ultimate expression of human creativity in Judaism.

Ruderman analyzes Yagel's work *Ya'ar ha-Levanon*, in which Yagel encourages his readers to use magic for human benefit and to unlock the secrets of the divine body. Ruderman's elucidation of the role of magic in past medical practice provides an interesting insight into the background and development of modern medicine.

SEIDEL's ambitious dissertation examines "the historical development of the conceptualization of Jewish magic," focusing on the word *magic* and on magic as a field. He argues that scholars have traditionally scoffed at the possibility that magic was widely used in early Judaism because "early evidence was indeed against" this supposition. Many Jewish *Wissenschaft* scholars downplayed magic's role in Judaism because they believed that the presence of magic was indicative of degeneracy. Seidel rejects such claims, as well as the theory that magic is merely a vestige of more primitive times. He contextualizes his research by investigating the history of the discourse about magic, studies the term *magic* in ancient Near Eastern contexts, and emphasizes the social role of magic in biblical, Greco-Roman, and rabbinic contexts.

SHAROT offers the reader some interesting historical background on magical religion in the established Jewish community and various millenarian movements in the diaspora, Sabbatianism, and Hasidism. The theurgic orientation of the millenarian movements is noted, manifested, for example, in their elaborate after-meal liturgies. Sharot's concluding chapter, a summary of the major arguments of the work, is a tour de force.

TRACHTENBERG's work remains the definitive effort to clarify aspects of magic and superstition and their relationship to Judaism. Practitioners of Judaism have often been accused of practicing sorcery in virtue of the ritualistic character of the religion. Even the task of house-cleaning for Passover was sometimes perceived by non-Jews as strange and therefore magical. By way of distinction, Trachtenberg defines the bona fide Jewish magician as "a scholar by vocation, a practitioner of the mystical-magical arts by avocation." The power of the "the word" and the role of evil and demons, numerology, dreams, nature, and medicine are clearly discussed. The book provides a marvelous overview of the interconnected roles that magic, superstition, and religion play. The reader is well-advised to consult this general survey of research into magic and its role in Judaism before embarking on more specialized studies.

SPERBER's study investigates the place of magic in the midrashic and talmudic literature. Sperber divides his work into five areas: folklore, magic, historical allusions, midrashic texts, and specifically Palestinian rabbinical texts. Areas of discussion include Greek magical terms, amulets, incantations, and fantastic creatures. A useful index of rabbinic sources is appended.

SWARTZ provides an estimable guide to the concepts and rituals embedded in the Hekhalot literature. He analyzes the Sar-Torah and other texts and argues for its continuity with the mysticism of the early talmudic sages. This extensive study explores the forgotten rituals of ancient Jewish mysticism and themes that relate to memory and the role of magic. Swartz seeks to define the patterns of the Sar-Torah narratives, and he provides copious translations in which rituals and prescriptions for purification are well represented. Also very helpful to the reader are Swartz's detailed annotations and thorough bibliography.

CYNTHIA A. KLÍMA

Mahzor see Liturgy, History of; Liturgy, Reform

Maimonidean Controversy

Chavel, Charles B., *Ramban: His Life and Teachings,* New York: Feldheim, 1960
Dienstag, Jacob I., *Eschatology in Maimonidean Thought: Messianism, Resurrection, and the World to Come: Selected Studies, with an Introduction and a Bibliography,* New York: Ktav, 1983
Sarachek, Joseph, *Faith and Reason: The Conflict over the Rationalism of Maimonides,* Williamsport, Pennsylvania: Bayard, 1935
Septimus, Bernard, *Hispano-Jewish Culture in Transition: The Career and Controversies of Ramah* (Harvard Judaica Monographs, 4), Cambridge, Massachusetts: Harvard University Press, 1982

Shrock, Abe Tobie, *Rabbi Jonah ben Abraham of Gerona: His Life and Ethical Works,* London: Goldston, 1948
Silver, Daniel Jeremy, *Maimonidean Criticism and the Maimonidean Controversy, 1180–1240,* Leiden: Brill, 1965
Talmage, Frank, *David Kimhi: The Man and the Commentaries* (Harvard Judaica Monographs, 1), Cambridge, Massachusetts: Harvard University Press, 1975
Twersky, Isadore, *Rabad of Posquières: A Twelfth-Century Talmudist,* Cambridge, Massachusetts: Harvard University Press, 1962; revised edition, Philadelphia: Jewish Publication Society, 1980

The Maimonidean Controversy refers to several related episodes through most of the 13th century, beginning during the lifetime of Moses ben Maimon (Maimonides) and extending for about a century after his death—some of them having little or nothing to do directly with Maimonides. It includes arguments over halakhic authority, the comprehensive claims of the Mishneh Torah, the doctrine of resurrection, and the appropriate place of philosophy in Jewish discourse. The dramatic peak of the controversy was the burning of Maimonides' *Guide of the Perplexed* in 1232. Daniel Jeremy Silver observes that Maimonides' opponents praised him as much as his supporters did, and the controversy ultimately inscribed Maimonides' prestige "indelibly in the ledgers of Jewish literature."

Sarachek and Silver have produced the only book-length studies of the controversy. Other volumes reviewed here are primarily studies of some of the key players (apart from Maimonides himself). Although not reviewed here, consideration should also be given to works of general Jewish history by Yitzhak Baer, Heinrich Graetz, and Julius Guttmann.

SARACHEK's pioneering effort to summarize events on the basis of available sources sets the conflict against the background of an "age of intellectual expansion" for Islam, Christianity, and Judaism. It was triggered in part by the fall of Constantinople to the crusaders in 1204 (the year of Maimonides' death) and a resultant availability of the works of Aristotle. While far less polemical than earlier historians (such as Graetz), Sarachek still has a tendency to view the Maimonidean camp as enlightened and progressive and its critics as reactionary and retrograde. Rabbi Abraham ben David of Posquières (known as Rabad), for example, is rendered as a one-dimensional opponent, a characterization later contested by Isadore Twersky. Sarachek accepts the traditional sequence of events leading to the burning of Maimonides' works, arguing that the *Moreh* and the *Sefer ha-Madda* were denounced to Catholic Church authorities by "the strict traditionalists," but he dissents from earlier accounts that name Rabbi Solomon ben Abraham of Montpellier as the direct instigator.

SILVER goes further: clearly Solomon ben Abraham, David ben Saul, and Jonah Gerondi were active and public in their opposition to philosophical trends represented by Maimonides. "There is, however, every reason to doubt their being the actual agents of denunciation," writes Silver. He focuses on a narrower period of the controversy. Whereas Sarachek sets the dispute against the historical background of "intellectual expansion," Silver hypothesizes that the looming danger of the newly militant church was the primary cause of the dispute's intensity. The church directly involved itself in Jewish affairs, with disputations, missionizing, and critiques of the Talmud by converts to Christianity. In more normal times, new questions would have been assimilated and answered. In these conditions of fear, however, philosophy and its attendant questioning became suspect: "Today's youthful questioner might be tomorrow's convert and . . . informer."

Silver therefore posits a group of "restless and rootless anonymous men" as the source of the Maimonidean Controversy. Few of them had actually read the *Moreh*, but they were happy to believe that it justified their abandonment of Jewish observance. These anonymous intellectuals had wealth and connections but were alienated from Jewish tradition. According to Silver, "It is always dangerous for a people when an alienated intelligentsia develops alongside an equally intelligent authoritative leadership with whom it can hardly communicate." Further, given that the church was newly militant and missionary, this group of rootless cosmopolitans seemed to expose the community to the risk of widespread apostasy. This is why "men of faith" set themselves to prevent "defection and defamation."

DIENSTAG assembles material that sheds light on one of the major issues that engaged some of the disputants: eschatology. Especially useful are the brief biographical sketches of some of the principals, along with bibliographical notes, contained in the introduction.

Nahmanides was an important participant in one phase of the controversy, and CHAVEL, who has devoted much work to Nahmanides, provides a helpful, if eulogistic, survey of the basic biographical facts. The second half of the book synopsizes Nahmanides' views on various aspects of Jewish teaching. Similar in structure is the work of SHROCK on R. Jonah Gerondi, another major combatant.

The works of Twersky, Septimus, and Talmage do not differ significantly on the general outline of events, but they offer striking detail about several of the principals and render the cultural context with much richer complexity. TWERSKY's brilliant study of Rabad offers a remarkable view not only of its central subject, but also of the broader background of 12th-century talmudic culture. Clarifying what most talmudists of that period were trying to accomplish, Twersky brings into vivid relief the revolutionary achievement of Maimonides in the Mishneh Torah.

While sharply critical of Maimonides for failing to cite sources, even accusing him of having "an overbearing spirit," Rabad nevertheless holds Maimonides' achievement in high regard. Rabad initiated the *hassagot* literature, glosses now scattered throughout printed editions of the Mishneh Torah, which are "both criticism and commentary, dissent and elaboration, stricture and supplement." Twersky's careful analysis emphasizes that, contrary to a widespread perception of Rabad as solely a critic of Maimonides, he was often eager to support Maimonides' view when he found it convincing.

Rabad's critique of the Mishneh Torah certainly lent support to opponents of Maimonides by raising questions about Maimonides' halakhic mastery. Yet it seems more likely that Rabad's own motivations had more to do with his sense of the appropriate direction of halakhic research, his "critico-conceptual approach" to Talmud. Above all, Rabad wished to prevent the stagnation that might overtake talmudic study if the Mishneh Torah became established as authoritative. This is in agreement with Silver's view that Rabad's primary concern was "the integrity of his halachic world," and that while Rabad is an important critic of Maimonides, he certainly did not start the controversy.

Rabbi David Kimhi (Radak) and Rabbi Meir ben Todros ha-Levi Abulafia (Ramah) were partisans on opposite sides of the conflict. TALMAGE bases much of his study on extensive readings of Radak's biblical commentaries, combing this material for useful biographical insights. According to SEPTIMUS, the vehemence of the controversy in the 1230s reflects a shift in the cultural arena. Earlier arguments over philosophical rationalism had been confined to Judeo-Arabic culture. Now Spain was looking toward Europe and so was setting up the first direct engagement between Franco-German talmudic Jewry and Spanish philosophical rationalism. Septimus also detects elements of "sociocommunal struggle" and takes issue with Gershom Scholem's contention that the antirationalists were closely connected with the Kabbalah.

LAURENCE L. EDWARDS

See also Moses ben Maimon

Maimonides *see* Moses ben Maimon

Maimonides Family

Fenton, Paul (editor and translator), *The Treatise of the Pool/Al-Maqāla al-Ḥawḍiyya*, London: Octagon, 1981

Fenton, Paul, "The Literary Legacy of David ben Joshua, Last of the Maimonidean Negidim," *Jewish Quarterly Review*, 75, 1984

Goitein, S.D., *A Mediterranean Society: The Jewish Communities of the Arab World as Portrayed in the Documents of the Cairo Geniza*, Berkeley and London: University of California Press, 1967–1988

Mann, Jacob, *Texts and Studies in Jewish History and Literature*, 2 vols., Cincinnati, Ohio: Hebrew Union College Press, 1931–1935

Rosenblatt, Samuel (editor and translator), *The High Ways to Perfection of Abraham Maimonides* (Columbia University Oriental Studies, vol. 27), New York: Columbia University Press, 1927

Moses ben Maimon (Maimonides, 1135 or 1138–1204?) never accepted the formal title of "Nagid" as head of the Jewish community of Egypt, but he and his descendants served in this capacity until the late 14th century. The preservation of personal letters, literary works, and historical traditions by and about members of the Maimonides family allows a unique glimpse of the intellectual life, social and family relations, and communal roles of Maimonides himself, his father, his brother, his in-laws, and his descendants. His father, Maimon "the Judge," was himself the author of an important work, the *Letter of Consolation*. Moses' son Abraham (1186–1237) served as Nagid most of his adult life; Abraham's son David (1222–1300) succeeded his father as Nagid. Although Moses ben Maimon was perhaps the most prominent exponent of the rationalist-philosophical trend within Judaism, his son and some of his descendants were more closely associated with mystical tendencies, especially with Jewish Sufi-style mysticism. Abraham is remembered not only for championing and defending his father's works but also for his attempts to reform the prayer service and for his magnum opus, the *Kifāyat al-'Abidīn* (discussed below), a manual for following the mystic path. His son Obadiah (1228–1265), David's younger brother, is also known for his mystical work. The last of Maimonides' descendants to serve as Nagid were Joshua (1309–1355) and his son David (1335–1415), who apparently served until the 1370s and also wrote on mystical topics. Although much is known about the Maimonidean dynasty, relatively little has been written in English, and little of that in book form. Several items selected here are English-language introductions to editions of works by Maimonides' descendants.

GOITEIN had a lifelong fascination with Abraham Maimonides. He translated Abraham's responsa from Arabic into Hebrew, published major articles on his work, and saw Abraham—more than his father—as the archetypal man of medieval Jewish civilization represented in the Genizah materials. There is material on Maimonides' family relationships in volume two of Goitein's *Mediterranean Society* and elsewhere in this important work. But, most importantly, the final sections of Goitein's fifth volume, delivered to the printer just before he died, summarize his lifework on Abraham and refer to every important document and study of Abraham that he published. Here and elsewhere, Goitein discusses Abraham's pietism (although he was not interested in a philosophical analysis), his activism and leadership within the pietist movement, and his constant involvement in community affairs, including attention to minute administrative details, which presumably made it difficult for him to complete his works. Goitein saw the focus of his *Mediterranean Society* as continuing only to the rise of the Mamluk regime; in consequence, there is much about Moses ben Maimon and his son Abraham but little on subsequent members of the family.

MANN's work on Genizah material revolutionized understanding of geonic times, Karaism, and medieval Egyptian Jewry. His classic Texts and Studies includes references to Maimonides family members and descendants throughout the two-volume collection. Among its pearls is a short narrative on "The Egyptian Negidim of Maimonides' Family," which is, despite its brevity, still among the most substantive histories of the family in English. Readers should be aware, however, that research after Mann's time has filled in some of the missing data and has identified some works that were unknown to Mann.

ROSENBLATT edited and translated into English the ninth and final surviving section of Abraham Maimuni's *Kifāyat al-'Abidīn*, naming it *The Highways to Perfection*. Maimuni also wrote works defending his father and a commentary on the Bible that he completed only as far as the middle of Exodus. Other portions of the *Kifāyat al-'Abidīn* have come to light since Rosenblatt's edition. Maimuni describes traits necessary to achieve perfect moral character, such as faith in God, asceticism, and prayer. Maimuni lauds the Sufi way of life and, as Rosenblatt points out, makes scriptural arguments to justify his views that the Sufis merely continued the ancient ways of the prophets, which had been lost within the Jewish community. The goal is described as *wuṣūl*, which Rosenblatt usually translates as "union" with God; this was the subject of the tenth and concluding section of Maimuni's work, which did not survive.

FENTON's (1981) introduction gives a detailed history of the Egyptian pietist movement, providing information on some of the individuals who moved through Egypt, family relations within the Egyptian hasidim, and a resumé of the views and practices of the group. Fenton describes how Obadyah quotes liberally from his father's and grandfather's works, such as the *Mishneh Torah*, the *Commentary on Mishnah Avot*, and the *Kifāyat al-'Abidīn*. Like his grandfather, he seeks a goal of perfecting the intellect's perception of Reason and claims that his treatise is written in such a way as to conceal some of its most important insights—except from those initiates who study the work carefully. Yet, as Fenton notes, the work is much more practically oriented than Moses ben Maimon's *Guide of the Perplexed*. Obadyah stresses the need to shun corporeal necessities, practice solitude, marry late, and be firmly grounded in the exoteric law before seeking to "enter Paradise" by pursuing the mystic path to gain the "favor of Reason."

FENTON's (1984) article on David ben Joshua includes some biographical narrative but is largely bibliographical; it nevertheless provides English readers with a fair idea of the scope of David's oeuvre and the nature of his thought. In this article, Fenton sets forth his reason for identifying David ben Joshua as the author of the *Murshid ilā al-tafarrud* (Guide to Detachment), a Jewish Sufi-style work first described by Franz Rosenthal. (Fenton includes a more substantial biographical narrative and description of the contents of the *Murshid*, an ethical manual on the stations needed to reach the exalted plane of *hasidut*, in the Hebrew introduction to his Hebrew translation of this work.) In this article, Fenton also describes at some length David's most outstanding composition, *Tajrīd al-haqā'iq al-nazariyya* (Abstract of Speculative Truth), and, in briefer fashion, his other works, some 17 in all. Fenton's list of the sources known to David gives an idea of the tremendous breadth of his personal library and his interests in science, philosophy, and even the Zohar and other kabbalistic literature.

SETH WARD

See also Moses ben Maimon

Manuscripts, Hebrew

Beit-Arié, Malachi, *Hebrew Codicology: Tentative Typology of Technical Practices Employed in Hebrew Dated Medieval Manuscripts* (Institut de recherche et d'histoire des textes: Etudes de paléographie hébraïque), Paris: Centre National de la Recherche Scientifique, 1976

Goldstein, David (editor), *The Ashkenazi Haggadah: A Hebrew Manuscript of the Mid-15th Century from the Collections of the British Library,* New York: Abrams, and London: Thames and Hudson, 1985; new edition, London: Thames and Hudson, 1997

Gutmann, Joseph, *Hebrew Manuscript Painting,* New York: Braziller, 1978; London: Chatto and Windus, 1979

Metzger, Thérèse, and Mendel Metzger, *Jewish Life in the Middle Ages: Illuminated Hebrew Manuscripts,* New York: Alpine Fine Arts Collection, 1982

Narkiss, Bezalel, *Hebrew Illuminated Manuscripts,* New York: Amiel, 1969

Sabar, Shalom, *Ketubbah: Jewish Marriage Contracts of the Hebrew Union College Skirball Museum and Klau Library,* Philadelphia: Jewish Publication Society, 1990

Hebrew illuminated manuscripts from the Middle Ages are a rich but under-investigated resource, ripe to be mined for insights into the inner landscape of medieval Jewish society, and for revelations about the world views of the documents' creators, patrons, and intended audience. Several anthologies of medieval manuscript art have been created, offering samples that may be studied in order to gauge the broad parameters of the field, differences among schools, and geographical and chronological distinctions.

NARKISS's survey provides an introductory historical chapter, followed by one-page analyses of a considerable number of monumental examples of Hebrew manuscript illumination. Each page of description includes a discussion of iconography and faces a full-page, full-color example from the manuscript in question. Manuscripts are identified by title (for example, "The Golden Haggadah"), as well as by call-numbers of the repsective libraries. The titles applied by Narkiss have become commonplace, although they are not necessarily historically authentic. The work represents a considerable effort to gather and characterize a large number of manuscripts and to delineate a field of research around them. The problems with the volume are obvious—due to both the paucity of surviving manuscripts and the fact that Narkiss shows only a single page from each of the selected manuscripts (which are replete with many other fascinating iconographies); the selection is rather arbitrary in its scope, partially obscuring the importance of items that it does not, or cannot, show.

The format of GUTMANN's smaller, less elegant work resembles the organization of Narkiss's compilation, although the layout makes the information it contains less accessible than in Narkiss. This volume is part of a more general series, and the effect is to place Hebrew manuscript illumination in the context of a broader universe of discourse and to impose some uniformity on the volume.

In general, the works by Narkiss and Gutmann complement each other. The authors mostly discuss different manuscripts, and when the two texts do analyze the same document, they provide illustrations of different folios from the manuscripts in question. The scholarly differences between the backgrounds of Gutmann, a U.S. scholar, and Narkiss, an Israeli, are revealed in the distinctive themes that the authors identify in their introductions. Gutmann focuses on the biblical prohibition against the production of graven images and considers the general problem of Jewish art that surrounds that edict (a preoccupation also found in many of his other works), while Narkiss concentrates on the historical antecedents for Hebrew manuscript illumination. Both works emphasize, to differing degrees, the possibility that a lost tradition of early Jewish manuscript painting informed the creation of medieval Christian art. Both books also stress the stylistic similarities between Hebrew manuscripts and their contemporary Christian and Muslim counterparts, and as a result, the authors do not effectively explain which characteristics, aside from the Hebrew script and the occasional manifestation of midrashic allusion, may distinguish the Hebrew manuscripts from those of the majority cultures. This problem has been addressed by more recent work in the field of iconography.

The METZGERs' work occupies a unique position among surveys of Hebrew manuscript illumination. Organized by topic, the work considers many more manuscripts than the volumes by Gutmann and Narkiss, including secular manuscripts written in Hebrew besides religious texts. Following the direction established by the earliest forays into the topic, they regard medieval Hebrew art as a rich historical resource for scholars of medieval Jewish life, and the authors provide a charming glimpse into some of the ways in which medieval Jews, or the artists they commissioned, wished to represent their culture. The Metzgers are rather naïve, however, to assume that these images present an accurate or factual image of contemporary Jewish life. Still, their work contributes much toward a more complete, if not entirely objective, idea of medieval Jewish clothing, home furnishings, rituals, and holiday celebrations. The index of manuscripts (including documents that were not cited in the volume as well as cited sources) is a major accomplishment, which provides concise and precise information about most extant illuminated Hebrew manuscripts, organized by library and call-number.

The best way to appreciate Hebrew illuminated manuscripts is, of course, to examine an entire manuscript, rather than a single folio or a cropped image. GOLDSTEIN's complete edition of a 15th-century Haggadah is a model presentation of such a complete document. While quite a few rare and very expensive collector's facsimiles exist, Goldstein's beautiful edition is an example of a number of recent publications that are widely available, affordable, scholarly, and comprehensive. The full text of this Haggadah and its commentaries is provided, and the iconography of each folio is fully described. Complete bibliographical, provenance, and codicological details are included. Working with this kind of a facsimile is the next best thing to seeing the original in the British Library.

BEIT-ARIÉ is a masterpiece of codicological information, essential for anyone who wants to date or classify Hebrew manuscripts. The work is unsurpassed in detail, clarity, and precision, providing up-to-date information on all physical aspects of the Hebrew manuscript book. The text is accompanied by clear illustrations that exemplify the topics under discussion.

SABAR's catalog of marriage contracts is an example of trends in art history scholarship at the end of the 20th century. A comprehensive catalog of a single collection, the work evaluates one of the more easily researched and presented genres within the field of illuminated manuscripts: marriage contracts are by nature dated, and each contract is a single folio. Therefore, the original provenance of these objects is known, and the manuscript can be fully reproduced as well as described. Sabar applies sociological insights as well as aesthetic criteria to the evaluation of these documents, with great success.

MARC MICHAEL EPSTEIN

See also Books and Libraries; Printing, Early Hebrew; Scribes; Script and Scribal Practices

Marranism

Baer, Yitzhak, *A History of the Jews in Christian Spain,* 2 vols., Philadelphia: Jewish Publication Society, 1961–1966

Cohen, Martin, *The Martyr: The Story of a Secret Jew and the Mexican Inquisition in the Sixteenth Century,* Philadelphia: Jewish Publication Society, 1973

Henningsen, Gustav and John A. Tedeschi, *The Inquisition in Early Modern Europe: Studies on Sources and Methods,* De Kalb: Northern Illinois University Press, 1986

Netanyahu, Benzion, *The Marranos of Spain, from the Late XIVth to the Early XVIth Century, According to Contemporary Hebrew Sources,* New York: American Academy for Jewish Research, 1966

Rivkin, Ellis, "The Utilization of Non-Jewish Sources for the Reconstruction of Jewish History," *Jewish Quarterly Review,* 47, 1956–1957

Rivkin, Ellis, *The Shaping of Jewish History: A Radical New Interpretation,* New York: Scribner, 1971

Roth, Cecil, *A History of the Marranos,* Philadelphia: Jewish Publication Society, 1932; 3rd edition, New York: Harper and Row, 1966

Yerushalmi, Yosef Hayim, *From Spanish Court to Italian Ghetto: Isaac Cardoso: A Study in Seventeenth-Century Marranism and Jewish Apologetics,* New York: Columbia University Press, 1971

Beginning in 1391, Jews in Spain were drawn to the baptismal font in large numbers, both voluntarily and involuntarily. In the course of the next century, especially as these conversos and their descendants, the New Christians, prospered, their loyalty to Catholicism was questioned by Spanish Old Christians. By the end of the century the Inquisition was put into place by the Spanish authorities. The ostensible purpose of the Inquisition in Spain, and later in Portugal, was to uproot the Judaizing practices of the New Christians, regarded as crypto-Jews and commonly called *Marranos.* Scholars have, however, questioned whether the Inquisition was really driven by religious motivations or by social and racial designs against the New Christians as a class or race. Chief among the concerns of scholars studying the Inquisition, therefore, is the question of the reliability of the dossiers produced by its tribunals. On the one hand, it is easy to ascertain that many of those who were most skeptical of the reliability of inquisitional sources had

used them the least. On the other hand, it must be stressed that until the relatively recent opening of Spanish society to outside scholars and a new historiographic interest in such documents, very few historians actually used the inquisitional sources extensively, and it does not appear that those who did use them did so with much caution. In addition, 20th-century manifestations of supposedly crypto-Jewish practices in Portugal, and more recently the Southwestern United States, have served to complicate the issue by offering, to some observers, evidence of the viability of the Marrano movement and the reliability of charges against them.

BAER betrays a major inconsistency between his enthusiastic acceptance of inquisitional documents when they demonstrate the loyalty of New Christians to Judaism and his rejection of them as biased when they do not. Baer recognizes that the Inquisition produced information that was not always true, because it relied upon torture to force confessions or because it encouraged people to slander their neighbors. Nevertheless, even when he raises the possibility that the records of the Inquisition were unreliable, Baer always concludes with a dogmatic affirmation of the Jewishness of the New Christians. Although Baer tries to show religious motivation for the behavior of both New Christians and Inquisitors, he repeatedly undermines this position by raising the possibility that the Inquisition was economically rather than religiously motivated.

RIVKIN (1956–1957) issues a startling challenge to several central tenets of the conventional wisdom of Jewish historiography concerning the New Christians or conversos of Spain and Portugal, asserting that they were loyal Christians and were not persecuted because of their secret Judaism. He also asserts that the Inquisition was not established to destroy a danger to the Catholic faith and that the dossiers of the Inquisition cannot be used as evidence for the religious life of the conversos. In addition to denying that the majority of the New Christians practiced Judaism in secret, Rivkin challenges the basic methods employed by Jewish historians by claiming that the primary sources available to the historian cannot be relied upon literally. In this historiographic work, Rivkin does not build from archival inquisitional documents but rather tears down the rickety edifices constructed by previous scholars of the Inquisition who, he contends, accepted the inquisitional documents as valid sources for reconstructing the life of the New Christians. RIVKIN (1971) elaborates the view that the decision by New Christians to adopt Judaism in the Ottoman Empire was based on the business opportunities available to them as Jews and not on any feelings for Judaism they had nurtured in Spain or Portugal. He argues that it was the Inquisition that created the Jewish consciousness in some New Christians by identifying them with Jews and Judaism, although such charges may have been unfounded. He also asserts that the Ottoman sultan realized that it was in his best interest for the New Christians who settled in the empire to embrace Judaism openly. Rivkin's views align him with the Portuguese historian Antonio José Saraiva, whose evisceration of the spiritual pretensions of the uniquely far-reaching Portuguese Inquisition are presented in a comprehensively expanded and updated English version by Herman Prins Salomon and Isaac Sassoon, forthcoming from E.J. Brill.

In the introduction to his 1964 translation of Samuel Usque's *Consolation for the Tribulations of Israel,* Martin Cohen confirmed Rivkin's views by asserting that the wealth and influence of the Spanish New Christians was the reason they were accused of practicing Judaism in secret. He argues that false charges were made in order to fan popular hatred against the New Christians and to justify their liquidation. Cohen, nevertheless, appears to part company with Rivkin by asserting that the majority of Portuguese New Christians remained true to Judaism. COHEN's book on the activities of the Inquisition in the New World presents Rivkin's views at length, but Cohen diverges from Rivkin on the reliability of Inquisitional sources, describing his own account as "entirely factual," with every "detail, description, and transcribed conversation . . . found in the trial records of the Inquisition or other unimpeachable primary or secondary sources."

HENNINGSEN and TEDESCHI bring together many studies of the Inquisition done during the 1970s and 1980s by scholars who used inquisitional documents, and they show that critics of previous historiography on New Christians were correct: most of the victims were probably loyal to Christianity. Even those who managed to leave the Iberian peninsula by no means always returned to Judaism, and those who did were not always steadfast in their Jewishness. Many chose to return home to Spain and Portugal. Others became very critical of rabbinic authority. Nevertheless, there were some New Christians who returned to Judaism—often women—whose Inquisition dossiers show that members of their families had been watched for several generations by the Inquisition because of Judaizing practices. The recent scholars represented in this collection have demonstrated that the authors of the monumental older works on the Inquisition possessed only impressionistic knowledge of the available materials, that on most major questions concerning these materials historians today are still ignorant, that inquisitional materials must be used in conjunction with other contemporary evidence, and that it is necessary not only to record information from the inquisitional archives but to reconstruct it critically. These later scholars note that the information in inquisitional dossiers may have passed through several filters: language differences between the interrogated and the Inquisition, gaps in education between the tribunal and the interrogated, and scribal conventions that standardized testimony. In one recent study of the Spanish Inquisition it was discovered that of the approximately 44,000 trials around the world between 1540 and 1700, only 40 percent were devoted to major heresies, among which Judaizing represented only a small part. Thus 60 percent of the inquisitors' efforts went to prosecuting heretical propositions (about priests, the pope, or the Virgin Mary), blasphemy, bigamy, crimes against the Holy Office, premarital intercourse, homosexuality, sodomy, bestiality, sexual solicitations by clergy during confession, magic, witchcraft, astrology, necromancy, sorcery, and superstition; these charges were usually leveled against "Old Christians," who were often uneducated and rural. These charges reflected more the post-tridentine fear of medieval Catholicism than any fear of Judaism. Furthermore, only 1.8 percent of the accused were put to death, an average of about five per year. For some earlier tribunals, however—for example, the one held in Valen-

cia from 1478 to 1530—there was a much higher percentage of Judaizers tried (up to 90 percent), and about 30 percent were killed. Recent scholars of the dossiers notice that the Inquisition always was on the lookout for Judaizers and readily found them during various waves of interest in Judaizers, which continued up to the 18th century. Often during the late 16th century, entire communities were discovered, sometimes even in monasteries. Despite their difficulty in identifying what they were looking for, the Inquisition did not have to fabricate their findings. Their files, however, are not easy to interpret because they represent the complexities of both crypto-Judaism and a secretive bureaucracy. Most researchers now feel that by understanding the filters through which inquisitional materials passed—the structures of New Christian life and inquisitional procedure—they have access to rich, reliable, and detailed sources.

The views contained in NETANYAHU's magnum opus go back to his 1947 dissertation on Don Isaac Abravanel, which was published in 1953. Netanyahu claims that most New Christians had no loyalties to Judaism except for a few vestigial habits. Following Baer's characterization of the Jews of Spain as religiously lax because of the philosophical influence of Averroës, Netanyahu argues that as New Christians they certainly had even less interest in practicing Judaism in secret. By falsely accusing the New Christians of Judaizing, the Inquisition was motivated by racial, political, and economic considerations and not by religious zeal. Netanyahu also sees that Baer's characterizations of Spanish Jewry's religious laxity were not consistent with his enthusiastic description of their crypto-Judaism. Netanyahu's attempt to show that rabbinic literature of the period for the most part dismissed the Jewishness of the conversos produced a spate of attention to this question that also drew further study of Rivkin's views, although Netanyahu does not address Rivkin's work explicitly. One of the major criticisms of Netanyahu's thesis is that the rabbinic writings from the Sephardi diaspora on which he relied included negative characterizations of Iberian New Christians that were written for local audiences. Often the purpose was to make matters easy in cases of marriage and inheritance for Jews who had fled Spain. For these reasons rabbinic responsa were often as contradictory, tendentious, polemical, and unreliable as Netanyahu claims the inquisitional sources are.

ROTH sees his subject as a romantic episode and testimony to the tenacious desire of the crypto-Jews to transmit their religion in secret. Thus, concerning the attachment of New Christians to Christianity, some were sincere converts, but the vast majority remained completely loyal to Judaism, keeping all of the traditional observances. While doing so they managed to prosper because of the new economic opportunities open to them and the high level of intermarriage with Old Christian families. With the establishment of the Inquisition, according to Roth, many Judaizers were caught and burned; he rarely mentions trumped-up charges or confessions made solely due to torture. Roth's work is filled with subtle contradictions. It is only when he describes crypto-Judaism in Portugal that he indicates that Spanish crypto-Judaism was much weaker and that Marranism would have died out during the 16th century had it not been for the Portuguese Inquisition. Similarly, he admits that the majority of those who died at the stake denied Judaism while they lived and that denunciations were based on trivial lapses into old habitual actions, thus diminishing his assertions of widespread sincerity. Roth concedes that dossiers of the Inquisition cannot be relied upon implicitly. He describes the religion of the Marranos as narrow and atrophied but claims that it preserved all the basics of traditional Judaism. From Roth it appears that the major goal of the Inquisition remained always to ferret out Judaizers, despite its interest in others such as Muslims, Protestants, bigamists, sorcerers, and witches. He concludes that the number of Judaizers killed in Spain and Portugal exceeded 30,000. However, in 1958 Roth conceded in the foreword to a new edition of his book that ". . . very important research has been done recently on the early days of crypto-Judaism in Spain, on the origins of the Inquisition, and on various aspects of the history of the Marrano Diaspora. Years have diminished, though it is to be hoped not entirely obliterated, the author's high romanticism of a quarter-century ago. . . ."

YERUSHALMI offers a major study of the New Christians based on dossiers of the Inquisition, and he begins with an incisive summary of Rivkin's arguments and then a refutation of them. Yerushalmi's attention to Rivkin's thesis is striking because of his profound disagreement with it and the significant research he has produced based on the very inquisitional documents discounted by Rivkin. The bulk of the book is devoted to following sample migrations of New Christians from Spain to Italy. In the course of presenting a compelling narrative, Yerushalmi pulls together all the forces in early modern Jewish history, including the rise of the Sabbatian movement.

HOWARD TZVI ADELMAN

See also Crypto-Jews, Contemporary

Marriage

Baskin, Judith (editor), *Jewish Women in Historical Perspective*, Detroit, Michigan: Wayne State University Press, 1991, 2nd edition, 1999

Diamant, Anita, *The New Jewish Wedding*, New York: Summit, 1985

Epstein, Louis M., *Marriage Laws in the Bible and the Talmud* (Harvard Semitic Series, vol. 12), Cambridge, Massachusetts: Harvard University Press, 1942

Friedman, Mordechai Akiva, *Jewish Marriage in Palestine: A Cairo Genizah Study,* 2 vols., New York: Jewish Theological Seminary of America, 1980

Goitein, S.D., *A Mediterranean Society: The Jewish Communities of the Arab World as Portrayed in the Documents of the Cairo Geniza*, vol. 3: *The Family*, Berkeley: University of California Press, 1978

Lamm, Maurice, *The Jewish Way in Love and Marriage*, San Francisco: Harper and Row, 1980; London: Harper and Row, 1982

Sabar, Shalom (editor), *Ketubbah: Jewish Marriage Contracts of the Hebrew Union College Skirball Museum and Klau Library,* Philadelphia: Jewish Publication Society, 1990

In 1997–1998, the Israel Museum in Jerusalem staged an exhibition on marriage among Afghan Jews during the late 19th and early 20th centuries. The exhibition was striking for two reasons. First, by presenting the Jewish wedding customs and rituals alongside the wedding customs of their non-Jewish neighbors, the exhibition highlighted the extensive similarities of the weddings and marital understandings of the Jewish and non-Jewish communities. Second, simply by graphic demonstration of Jewish weddings that seem bizarre to most moderns, the exhibition emphasized the discontinuites of Jewish marriage. Afghan Jews, like modern Jews, shared the cultural ideals of their host community and also attempted to make it "Jewish" by incorporating some unique legal institutions or rituals (e.g., gift-giving between the betrothed couple's families on Jewish rather than Moslem holidays).

Unfortunately, there is no English version of the catalog for this exhibition. The issues that it raises, however, can be traced in other ways. One of the most common elements of a Jewish marriage, from late antiquity to the present, is the marriage contract, or ketubbah. Because it combines traditional legal language with artistic adornment, the ketubbah is an important source for the study of Jewish assimilation and self-identity. SABAR documents the collection of 271 ketubbot from the Skirball Museum, dating from the 14th to the 20th century from all over the world. The descriptions and photographs are accompanied by a short commentary, mostly dealing with the artistic aspects of the ketubbot. The ketubbot themselves are, for the most part, highly ornate, but the chronological presentation, by location, of these ketubbot highlights the lack of a uniform artistic ketubbah tradition. When artists looked for methods or models for illustrating ketubbot, they turned to the artistic world around them rather than to earlier Jewish ketubbot. For example, an image of hands about to deliver the priestly blessing appears in a ketubbah from Italy dated 1775 and in another from Brazil dated 1911. Neither the artistic rendition of the hands nor their symbolic meanings are similar: in the former ketubbah they indicate the marriage of a member of a family claiming priestly descent, while in the latter they are simply a sign of good wishes, an invocation of blessing. Likewise, priestly hands and indeed all human and animal representations are absent from ketubbot from countries under Islamic rule, while some Italian ketubbot contain lavish baroque images of men and women in various states of undress.

Despite its mainly symbolic function today, the ketubbah originated as an enforceable legal document, and its language contains or alludes to the legal rights and obligations of marriage as understood by the rabbis. FRIEDMAN examines both the legal and linguistic aspects of the ketubbah. This two-volume study has become the standard academic reference work on the ketubbah and, therefore, also on the traditional legal structure of Jewish marriage. The first volume is devoted to analysis of and commentary on the different clauses of the ketubbah, tracing their development from rabbinic sources (or sometimes earlier) to their presence in the Palestinian ketubbot from the Middle Ages found in the Cairo Genizah. In the second volume, Friedman publishes these medieval ketubbot from the Genizah. Friedman demonstrates that even the language of these ketubbot was not always uniform, having frequently been adapted for the particular situations of their authors.

Whereas Friedman focuses on the legal aspects of the ketubbot, GOITEIN provides a social-historical synthesis of the marriages of the "Genizah people." This highly readable scholarly masterpiece combines legal material with data gleaned from sermons and letters to present a rich picture of how these Jews understood and practiced marriage. Here too, little distinguished the marriages of Jews from those of the non-Jewish majority. Goitein's study is the most complete account of marriage in any premodern Jewish community.

EPSTEIN straddles the line between offering a legal history of Jewish marriage and a historical explanation for the development of Jewish laws of marriage. He deals with a wide range of legal issues relating to marriage, tracing each of them from the Bible to the 19th century. His results are dated and his historical conclusions suspect, but in the absence of a more recent comprehensive study of Jewish marriage law, this remains a useful reference.

BASKIN is a collection of essays dealing with the historical experience of Jewish women, not with marriage per se. Nevertheless, many of the essays here at least touch upon Jewish marriage in different historical periods. Of particular note is the essay by Deborah Hertz, "Emancipation through Intermarriage in Old Berlin," in which she explores the odd fact that an extraordinary proportion of Jewish women from the aristocratic Jewish families of Berlin at the turn of the 19th century married non-Jews, at least for their second marriages.

Today, Jews continue to adopt the marriage customs, rituals, and understandings of those around them, modifying them in order to assert Jewish identity. DIAMANT and LAMM offer two examples of this phenomenon. Both are "how-to" books primarily for American Jews, step-by-step guides to creating a Jewish marriage. Diamant writes from a more liberal perspective, showing greater concern with integrating egalitarianism and modern conceptions of marriage (e.g., an important goal of marriage is the fulfillment of personal happiness) than with legal aspects. Lamm details the legal aspects of marriage as they are commonly accepted in Orthodox communities today and attempts to show the relevance of traditional practices (some of which are not particularly old) for modern Jewish marriages. Ultimately, however, they both struggle with the same issue, that of what it means for highly assimilated American Jews to have "Jewish" marriages. The visions of marriage that they offer are as close to each other, and to those of many non-Jewish Americans, as they are different from those, for example, of the Jews of Afghanistan.

MICHAEL L. SATLOW

See also Divorce; Ketubbah

Martyrdom

Agus, Ronald E., *The Binding of Isaac and Messiah: Law, Martyrdom, and Deliverance in Early Rabbinic Religiosity* (SUNY Series in Judaica), Albany: State University of New York Press, 1988

Chazan, Robert, *European Jewry and the First Crusade*, Berkeley: University of California Press, 1987

Droge, Arthur J. and James D. Tabor, *A Noble Death: Suicide and Martyrdom among Christians and Jews in Antiquity*, San Francisco: HarperSanFrancisco, 1992

Levenson, Jon Douglas, *The Death and Resurrection of the Beloved Son: The Transformation of Child Sacrifice in Judaism and Christianity*, New Haven, Connecticut: Yale University Press, 1993

Marcus, Ivan G., "From Politics to Martyrdom: Shifting Paradigms in the Hebrew Narratives of the 1096 Crusade Riots," in *Prooftexts*, vol. 2, Baltimore, Maryland: Johns Hopkins University Press, 1982

Soloveitchik, Haym, "Religious Law and Change: The Medieval Ashkenazic Example," *AJS Review*, 2, 1987

Spiegel, Shalom, *Me-agadot ha'-akedah*, 1950; translated by Judah Goldin as *The Last Trial*, New York, Pantheon, 1967

The Talmud requires Jews to give up their life in cases of idolatry, forbidden sexual relations, and bloodshed. Along with this basic halakhic instruction, rabbinic texts narrate the martyrdoms of rabbis executed by Romans. In midrashic literature, these rabbis are known as the Ten Martyrs (*asarah haruge malkut*). The term *kiddush ha-Shem*, or the Sanctification of the (divine) Name, has come to designate this phenomenon of voluntary death in the name of God. Large-scale Jewish martyrdom arose during the crusades together with complex religious and moral dilemmas. Despite the controversy, *kiddush ha-Shem* remained an integral part of the Jewish experience in Europe.

AGUS opens with the story of the anonymous mother and her seven martyred sons found in the Second Book of Maccabees. Agus understands this "typological story" to be a form of rationalization of martyrdom. He proceeds with "a comparative study of the story's configuration in several versions with an eye to understanding its early rabbinic manifestation," which also incorporates the biblical story of the binding of Isaac (the *Akedah*). Through careful examination of early rabbinic texts, Agus unravels the rabbinic understanding of the dialectical relationships between martyrdom and the Law, and the tension existing between the course of history and personal biography. What leads Israel to actual martyrdom, according to Agus, is "Israel's shrugging off the yoke of the Law," while readiness to suffer for the Law eliminates the need for martyrdom. Piety—a combination of personal suffering and constant repentance—neutralizes the need for actual martyrdom and thus provides Jews with the spiritual alternative of "vicarious martyrdom." As the story of the Akedah demonstrates, suffering for the Law leads to personal salvation and self-realization in the present. Abraham and Isaac should thus inspire every Jew as they also inspire the Messiah. "The messiah is an Abraham sacrificing his son Isaac, the promise of the future, in the conviction that a heroic embracing of the present is an embracing of God and His deliverance." The Messiah therefore delivers every Jew not by dying for his nation, but by cleaving to a life of suffering in exile.

CHAZAN meticulously and thoughtfully analyzes the complex relationship between Franco-German Jews and Christians during the First Crusade. Relying on both Hebrew and Latin sources, the author identifies the major players in the assaults and explores the different Jewish patterns of response to the crusaders' slogan, "death or conversion," paying a great deal of attention to the controversial and disturbing reaction of (passive and active) Jewish martyrdom. Chazan contends that these patterns of attack and response represent new styles of persecution and martyrdom, and in his search for a historical explanation of the changes, he describes in impressive detail the innovative martyrological behavior of medieval Ashkenaz as well as the imagery and radical ideology that characterized the milieu. Despite the high number of casualties, Chazan does not treat the First Crusade as a major turning point in Jewish-Christian relationships; instead he delineates the return of Ashkenazi Jewry to normal and prosperous life after the conflict, although he also contends that these martyrdoms were not forgotten, remarking that "A significant new dimension had been added in 1096 to the legacy of *kiddush Ha-Shem*." Readers who do not know Hebrew will appreciate the appended English translations of two medieval texts pertaining to the events. Students of medieval history and Jewish martyrdom will find Chazan's book both fundamental and illuminating.

DROGE and TABOR provide a comparative study of voluntary death in antiquity, arguing that it was a popular concept among pagans, Jews, and early Christians. In the authors' opinion, the Book of Daniel demonstrated the belief that voluntary death in the name of God may bring redemption and salvation, which was later developed in other, noncanonical Jewish documents, such as the Assumption of Moses and the Books of the Maccabees. The authors also rely heavily on Josephus' accounts to support their arguments. For Droge and Tabor, Josephus represents "the beginning of the philosophical discussion of voluntary death in the Jewish sources," although a generation earlier Philo of Alexandria provides another philosophical treatment of voluntary death, which echoes the legacy of Socrates. The authors conclude their analysis of Jewish sources with a short survey of voluntary death in rabbinic literature, positing that the practice is considered common and acceptable behavior in early rabbinic texts.

LEVENSON's book is not a work on Jewish martyrdom per se, but his treatment of the all-important story of the Akedah explains why the biblical story retained a central role in Jewish and Christian martyrology. In contrast to the prevailing view, he suggests that the pagan ritual of child sacrifice had also been practiced among the ancient Israelites on some occasions. Attempts were made to curb this ritual, but the primordial belief in its benefits was not completely forgotten. This hypothesis leads Levenson to regard the archetypal story of the near-sacrifice as the "seed" that inspired the theology of Jewish martyrdom as it evolved in the aftermath of Antiochus's attempt to suppress Judaism. This seed, Levenson continues, "would be watered by the blood of Jewish martyrs," from the

Second Temple to the First Crusade and beyond. Although the story of the Akedah is not the only source of Jewish martyrdom, students interested in the Jewish martyrological phenomenon will find Levenson's contribution of value.

MARCUS's important article brings attention to the fictional aspects of the Hebrew narratives of the First Crusade. He sees in these narratives a creative literary response to the tragic events. In his opinion, the narratives combine two "acts": political and martyrological. The purpose of the latter is to explain, through "Jewish religious imagination," the Jewish failure to secure protection from political authorities. While the political sections of the narratives are "predictable," the martyrological scenes are "spontaneous." These spontaneous scenes provided a theodicy designed to overcome the Jewish political defeat. The literary shift from politics to martyrology, Marcus argues, defines the narratives of 1096 as a body of religious polemics.

SOLOVEITCHIK focuses on the legal works of the tosafists that attempt to bridge the gap between halakhah and medieval reality. The many instances of Jewish active martyrdom, which the author labels "suicides," during the crusades serve as Soloveitchik's case studies. He tries to understand how the tosafists legitimized self-killing and the killing of fellow Jews, acts that one may define as suicide and murder. His answer: the tosafists could find justification for suicide by employing canonical and semi-canonical literature, as well as aggadah, but even these radical thinkers found it difficult to defend the killing of others. Soloveitchik associates the inclination of Ashkenazi Jews toward extreme behavior with their self-image as an ideal religious society.

SPIEGEL explores rabbinic approaches to the biblical story of the Akedah in antiquity and the Middle Ages. In his view, the Bible introduced the Akedah story mainly to abolish the pagan ritual of human sacrifices. Genesis 22:19 ("So Abraham returned [alone] to the young men"), however, opened the door to legends of actual sacrifice on Mount Moriah. Such exegesis leads Spiegel to conclude that "some leftover of belief" from the pagan world can be traced in Amoraic texts, "if not earlier." He argues that it is possible that the "Haggadah recovered for Judaism something of that legacy the Torah wished to renounce, or at least to subdue." Although other midrashim endeavored to uproot this foreign influence, stories of Isaac's actual sacrifice evolved throughout the early rabbinic period. The aggadic version of the biblical story "became the favorite one in the medieval time." It is Abraham and Isaac of the midrash who became the Ashkenazi archetype and inspiration during the crusades. From the early midrashim, medieval narratives recovered the hope that the merit of their numerous Akedot would sustain the nation. Spiegel concludes his classic work with his translation of the *Akedah*, a poem by Rabbi Ephraim ben Jacob of Bonn.

SHMUEL SHEPKARU

Masorah

Breuer, Mordechai (editor), *The Masorah Magna to the Pentateuch*, 2 vols., New York: Lehmann Foundation, 1992

Ginsburg, Christian D., *Jacob ben Chajim's Introduction to the Rabbinic Bible, Hebrew and English*, London: Longman, Green, Longman, Roberts, and Green, 1865; as *Jacob ben Chajim Ibn Adonijah's Introduction to the Rabbinic Bible, Hebrew and English* (Library of Biblical Studies), New York: Ktav, 1968

Ginsburg, Christian D., *Introduction to the Massoretico-Critical Edition of the Hebrew Bible*, London: Trinitarian Bible Society, 1897; New York: Ktav, 1966

Gordis, Robert, *The Biblical Text in the Making: A Study of the Kethib-Qere*, Philadelphia: Dropsie College for Hebrew and Cognate Learning, 1937, augmented edition, New York: Ktav, 1972

Kahle, Paul, *The Cairo Geniza* (Schweich Lectures of the British Academy), London: Oxford University Press for the British Academy, 1947; 2nd edition, Oxford: Blackwell, 1959; New York: Praeger, 1960

Kelley, Page H., Daniel S. Mynatt, and Timothy G. Crawford, *The Masorah of Biblia Hebraica Stuttgartensia: Introduction and Annotated Glossary*, Grand Rapids, Michigan: Eerdmans, 1998

Wickes, William, *Two Treatises on the Accentuation of the Old Testament* (Library of Biblical Studies), edited by Harry M. Orlinsky, prolegomenon by Aron Dotan, New York: Ktav, 1970

Yeivin, Israel, *Mavo la-Masorah ha-Tavranit*, 1971; translated by E.J. Revell as *Introduction to the Tiberian Masorah* (Masoretic Studies, no. 5), edited by Harry M. Orlinsky, Missoula, Montana: Scholars Press for the Society of Biblical Literature and the International Organization for Masoretic Studies, 1980

The Hebrew term *masorah* is an alternative form of the Hebrew term *masoret*, which referred initially to a canonical version of the consonantal Hebrew text of Holy Scriptures. In rabbinic literature, the purely consonantal—and thus ambiguous—written text was distinguished from the vocalized and more unequivocal orally transmitted pronunciation of the consonantal text. The oral pronunciation was called in Hebrew *mikra*, literally, "what is read (chanted) aloud."

There are three main theories as to the etymology of masorah/masoret in relation to editions of the Hebrew Scriptures and their apparatuses. The most plausible view is that the term derives from Biblical Hebrew *masoret* (bond) (Ezekiel 20:37) and that it refers to the binding character (i.e., the inerrant authority) of the canonical consonantal text of the Bible. Another plausible theory holds that the term derives from a rare meaning of the verb *masar* (to count) and that it refers to the activity of fixing the number of letters of each biblical book in order to guarantee preservation of the integrity of the text. It is widely assumed, however, that masoret is derived from the more common definition of the verb *masar* (that is, "to hand over") and that the noun means "tradition."

This folk etymology obscures rabbinic Judaism's distinction between the written word of God (Scripture) and tradition, a distinction that is reflected in the antithetical pair *masoret-mikra*, in which it is *mikra* that represents oral tradition.

At some point between the 6th and 9th centuries C.E., masorah or masoret came to refer not only to the consonantal text of Hebrew Scripture but also to a series of apparatuses apparently created by expert masoretes. These apparatuses include: the vowel points; the so-called masoretic accents, which are a highly sophisticated system of punctuation interpreted also as musical phrasing for the chanting of Scripture in public worship; and three separate collections of text-critical notes. The first of these collections is called the small masorah (Hebrew *Masorah Ketanah* or *Masoret Ketanah*; Latin *Masorah Parva*). It is a series of marginal notes to the biblical text. These notes point to peculiar words; peculiar spellings of common words; such phenomena as blank spaces in the middle of a verse; words that appear in the text but are not read aloud; and words that are read aloud although they do not appear in the text. The second set of notes, called the large masorah (Hebrew *Masorah Gedolah*; Latin *Masorah Magna*), is a detailed explanation of the laconic notes found in the small masorah with many additional notes as well. A third collection of notes, extant in several distinct versions, is also referred to as the large masorah. This last form of masoretic apparatus notes peculiarities in the biblical text either topically or according to the order of books in Hebrew Scripture and their respective subdivisions.

C.D. Ginsburg's magnum opus was a brilliant critical edition of the Hebrew Bible based upon the biblical text published in Venice by Daniel Bomberg in his so-called Second Rabbinic Bible (1524–1525). In a companion volume, GINSBURG (1897) explains the Western (Palestinian) and Eastern (Babylonian) recensions of the Hebrew Bible; examines the differences between the Western recensions of Aaron Ben-Asher (c.900–940 C.E.) and Moses Ben-Naphtali; and identifies the Second Temple–era roots of masoretic activity. The author surveys the important medieval biblical manuscripts known to Western European scholars in his time, and he traces the history of the printing of the Hebrew Bible through Bomberg's third quarto produced in Venice between 1525 and 1528. This Bible was used by Luther and other reformers, who translated the Bible into the major modern languages of the Western world.

While recent works listed here discuss some of the fine points concerning masorah in all its ramifications that were discovered in the 20th century, the two 16th-century works published in GINSBURG (1865) preserve what was known and believed about masorah at the dawn of the modern era, when Hebrew Scripture was first printed with movable type.

In chapter two of his study, KAHLE discusses the history of the Hebrew text of the Bible and identifies the masoretes. He recounts his 1926 discovery of the early-11th-century Leningrad Codex B19A, the oldest complete text of the Hebrew Scriptures, and he tells how he persuaded Rudolph Kittel to use this version of the Hebrew text as the basis of the third edition of *Biblia Hebraica* (Stuttgart: Württemburg Bibelanstalt, 1937).

Drawing from older and better manuscripts that were unknown to Ginsburg, YEIVIN explains the history of masorah and evaluates its significance. He considers in detail the masoretic terminology of the Tiberian masoretes that is reflected in the Ben-Asher codices, and he traces the roots of masoretic activity in the wider contexts of both Hellenistic-Roman-Byzantine culture and rabbinic halakhah.

KELLEY, MYNATT, and CRAWFORD present a lucid and comprehensive dictionary in straightforward English of the abbreviations employed in the marginal masorah printed in the *Biblia Hebraica Stuttgartensia* (Stuttgart: Deutsche Bibelgesellschaft, 1967). This handy volume, complete with introduction and extensive bibliography, enables students, scholars, and the curious layperson to learn from this ancient critical apparatus.

There are 1,350 places in the Hebrew Bible where the marginal masorah indicates that one is to read a word other than that found in the body of the text. The word to be read is called *keri*, the Aramaic imperative "read," while the unread word is called *ketib*, the Aramaic for "it was written." Examining the many theories proposed to account for this phenomenon, GORDIS concludes that the *ketib* in all instances reflects an archetypal text of the Hebrew Bible selected during the reign of Queen Salome Alexandra of Judah (76–67 B.C.E.) while the *keri* is drawn from an ancient collection of variants from other manuscripts.

BREUER, recognized by religious and academic authorities alike as a foremost expert on the text of the Hebrew Bible, presents a complete edition of the *masorah magna* of Ms. L^M of the Pentateuch and the Former Prophets. This manuscript was produced by the same Samuel ben Jacob who produced Ms. L B19A, which is the basis of the third edition of *Biblia Hebraica* and *Biblia Hebraica Stuttgartensia*. Breuer's English introduction identifies different mistakes that the scribe makes in each of the two manuscripts, thus demonstrating evidence of human frailty as well as prodigious skill in these texts.

Children preparing for Bar/Bat Mitzvah learn that the printed Bible in Hebrew contains signs that are interpreted as musical phrases. These masoretic accents serve also as a highly sophisticated system of punctuation and as indicators of which syllables are to be stressed. WICKES explains the intricacies of two distinct systems of these accents—one for Psalms, Proverbs, and Job 3:2–42:6 and another for all the rest of Hebrew Scripture. Wickes summarizes the most important information in two brief tables, one for each of the two systems.

MAYER IRWIN GRUBER

Medicine

Avalos, Hector, *Illness and Health Care in the Ancient Near East: The Role of the Temple in Greece, Mesopotamia, and Israel* (Harvard Semitic Monographs, no. 54), Atlanta, Georgia: Scholars Press, 1995

Brim, Charles J., *Medicine in the Bible,* New York: Froben, 1936

Kottek, Samuel S. (editor), *Medicine in Bible, and Talmud* (Proceedings, 2nd International Symposium on Medicine in Bible and Talmud), *Koroth* special issue 9(1–2), Fall 1985

Preuss, Julius, *Biblisch-talmudische Medizin*, 1911; translated by Fred Rosner as *Julius Preuss' Biblical and Talmudic Medicine,* New York: Sanhedrin, 1978

Rosner, Fred, *Medicine in the Bible and the Talmud: Selections from Classical Jewish Sources,* New York: Ktav, 1977; augmented edition, New York: Yeshiva University Press, 1995

Even if "the Jewish element in medicine has been present since antiquity and has made itself felt in various ways in medical history" (G. Rosen), there is, nevertheless, no specifically Jewish medicine. Much might be said of Jewish physicians through the ages, Jewish medical ethics, medicine and Jewish law, and Jewish medical institutions; this essay, however, is limited to the topic of medicine in ancient Jewish sources. Even thus restricted, this is a field of inquiry that has been extensively plowed, though mainly by antiquarian hobbyists and/or from an apologetic point of view. Nevertheless, collaborative ventures among trained historians of medicine and of ancient cultures, philologists, classicists, Assyriologists, and cultural anthropologists are developing and should lead to a renewed evaluation of the data.

PREUSS's epoch-making work remains unsurpassed as regards its scope and cautious, critical, scholarly approach. Still, this does not mean that the work could not bear some revision, whether in light of modern medicine or of advanced biblical and talmudic scholarship. Preuss attests judiciously that "there is no Jewish medicine in the sense that we speak of an Egyptian or a Greek medical science." No less important is his premise that although Bible and Talmud are religious writings, "for historical research, however, religious feelings should play no role at all." His book is divided into 18 chapters: on the physician, anatomy and physiology, pathology and therapy, special pathology, injuries, and malformations; thence to the specialties: ophthalmology, dentistry, oto-rhinology, nervous and psychiatric disorders, skin diseases, gynecology, and obstetrics; and finally materia medica, forensic medicine, dietetics, and regimens of health. The bibliography has unfortunately not been updated, but in Fred Rosner's English version the index of passages cited has been revised and the general index considerably enlarged. One may regret that the glossary of Hebrew and Aramaic terms compiled by Loewinger, although incomplete and even questionable at times, has not been included. This glossary was appended to the German-language version reprinted in New York in 1971. Once corrected, it would be a very valuable resource for Hebrew- and Aramaic-reading scholars, including talmudists. One problem of Preuss's work is that biblical and talmudic data are closely interwoven, too closely if one considers the span of time between the biblical and talmudic eras. Still, Preuss was quite right when he subtitled his book "Contributions to the History of the Science of Healing and of Culture in General." (This subtitle has unfortunately disappeared in the English translation.) Paraphrasing a statement of a talmudic sage, Preuss acknowledges at the end of his introduction that he is only a collector and an organizer. Manifestly, he did much more than that, and no publication in this field can omit a reference to his magnum opus.

BRIM's study was restricted to the Pentateuch, scanned through the eyes of medieval commentators, Rabbi Solomon Yitshaki (Rashi) in particular. If the author's aim was "the exposition of the science of medicine in the Torah," his approach was definitely apologetic and uncritical. The strange transliteration of the Hebrew terms is also problematic. Although completely outdated since the translation of Preuss's work into English, the fact that this book deals only with the Pentateuch allows one to find the relevant biblical data with greater ease. The work was obviously addressed to (physician) readers of the Bible, not to scholars of ancient medicine.

ROSNER's own book on biblical and talmudic medicine was published one year before his translation of Preuss's work came off the press. A number of chapters are directly inspired by Preuss, such as data on diseases (rabies, hemophilia, scurvy, gout, heatstroke, etc.) and on organs (heart, spleen, gallbladder). A chapter on the talmudic scholar-physician-astronomer Mar Samuel is added to a more general section on physicians in the Talmud. There is also a chapter on ethics and prayers for the physician, and more miscellaneous items, such as sex determination, forensic medicine, suicide, and anesthesia. Ethical and halakhic dimensions are also addressed in Rosner's compilation. He has collected and organized wide-ranging data, drawing heavily on medieval commentators and on rabbinic literature. This is perhaps not very sound historically, but it is the accepted way of traditional Jewish cultural studies and is thus adapted to the broader public.

The essays in KOTTEK's collection were read at the Second International Symposium on Medicine in Bible and Talmud (Jerusalem, 1984). Twenty-seven brief papers deal mainly with talmudic medicine and include renewed considerations of pregnancy and fertility, pestilence, water supply, ecology, and alcohol consumption. Other essays discuss biblical topics, such as tsara'at (the so-called biblical leprosy), ritual impurity, toxicology, and baldness. The four keynote essays deal with rabbinic law as related to medical data; talmudic medicine and Greek sources; the concept of "disease" in the Talmud; and a reappraisal of Preuss's work. K. Codell Carter argues in his paper that in the Talmud "health and long life were construed preeminently as consequences of conformity to social and religious norms." S. Newmyer shows that "while talmudic medicine certainly does not eschew magic, it shows to a significant degree the rationalism of Greek medicine." S. Kottek gives evidence of various influences on the phenomenology of disease, including theoretical, empirical, and popular sources. Two other special issues of Koroth (now Korot) cover the Proceedings of the First and Third Symposia (1981 and 1987, published 1982 and 1988). These international meetings attest to the wide range of scholars involved in an area of research that is obviously multidisciplinary.

AVALOS's approach to illness and health care is original and stimulating. The author does not restrict his research to ancient Israel but extends it to the ancient Near East—to Greece and Mesopotamia in particular. His thesis is that the temple has a central role to play in this comparative approach. Avalos's methods are those of cultural anthropology. He relies heavily on biblical criticism. His scholarship in Assyriology and ancient lore more generally and his comprehensive analysis of biblical topics such as tsara'at allow him to come to tentative conclusions that go beyond Preuss's cautious claims. Avalos argues that in case of disease there was "a dichotomous system of options in Israel." Disease was either a punishment by the Lord or was "arbitrary" (he does not mention the concept of

"trial"). The Priestly Code represents an "official religion," while it seems that Israelites used "illegitimate options" quite frequently. Thus Avalos uses the categories of medical anthropology in order to discuss the socio-religious framework of Israelite (biblical) health care. When he speaks of "medical theology," however, one may feel somewhat uneasy. This may be a misleading way of unifying two different themes: the theological meaning of disease and the theological context of healing. It seems, moreover, excessive and unfounded to argue—as some cultural anthropologists have—that God was the only accepted healer, whereas human healers were frowned upon. The moral (and judicial) duty to heal (admittedly in a context of assault and injury in Exodus 21:19), and the famous encomium of the physician by Ben Sira (chapter 38), can hardly be considered marginal.

SAMUEL S. KOTTEK

See also Bioethics; Reproductive Technologies

Menahem Mendel of Kotsk
1787 or 1789–1859

Polish hasidic leader and moralist

Feinberg, Chaim, *Leaping Souls: Rabbi Menachem Mendel and the Spirit of Kotzk*, Hoboken, New Jersey: Ktav, 1993

Fox, Joseph, *Rabbi Menachem Mendel of Kotzk: A Biographical Study of the Chasidic Master*, Brooklyn, New York: Bash, 1988

Heschel, Abraham Joshua, *A Passion for Truth*, New York: Farrar, Straus and Giroux, 1973

Oratz, Ephraim (translator), *And Nothing but the Truth: Insights, Stories, and Anecdotes of Rabbi Menachem Mendel of Kotzk*, New York: Judaica, 1990

Raz, Simcha (editor), *The Sayings of Menahem Mendel of Kotsk*, translated by Edward Levin, Northvale, New Jersey: Aronson, 1995

Menahem Mendel Morgenstern, the Kotsker rebbe, was the fiery leader of a hasidic movement that originated in the Polish town of Kotsk in the mid–19th century. He was an often harsh and dynamic individual committed unwaveringly to personal integrity. "Who is the 'man of truth'?" he asked. "One who takes pains and labors to say only true things." His brand of Hasidism, which emphasized brutal honesty and total self-nullification, revolutionized the hasidic movement of Eastern Europe, particularly in Poland, where his numerous disciples (including the rebbes of Gur and Alexander) synthesized rigorous talmudic study with spiritual fervor.

The Kotsker rebbe left only a very limited body of written works (having destroyed most of his own writings); it is chiefly his sayings that have survived. Trenchant and often abrasive, these sayings indicate the sharp mind that shaped them, and they are the basis for the materials that have become available in English about the Kotsker rebbe.

HESCHEL provides a study comparing the Kotsker to his contemporary Søren Kierkegaard, a Christian mystic and the father of existentialism. There are indeed similarities in their sober views of humanity and their low tolerance for moral imperfection. They also shared certain personality traits (sarcasm, alienation), behaviors, and ascetic practices. Kierkegaard remained a bachelor; the Kotsker went into virtual seclusion during the last two decades of his life. The fact that the two men moved in completely different orbits, however, raises questions regarding Heschel's contention that the similarities he identifies are meaningful. Also questionable is the author's recourse to modern psychological theories to analyze the Kotsker. Conflicts between the rebbe's exacting principles and his human frailty might have plagued the Kotsker and contributed to his withdrawal from society, but Heschel's labeling these thoughts and actions as manic-depressive tendencies imposes a materialistic reading on the mind of a spiritual giant. Nevertheless, this book is passionate and moving.

FOX attributes the Kotsker's breakdown and withdrawal to his frustration over his inability to reconcile the inherent contradictions of his philosophy. The author vividly recreates the Kotsker's dramatic moment of collapse, which shocked and disillusioned many followers, including Rabbi Mordecai Joseph, who broke away and founded the Izbica system. Fox is also unsparing in his depiction of the Kotsker's difficult personality. As a result, this book may upset some readers. Nevertheless, it is highly valuable for its extensive coverage of the Kotsker's life and historical background. Fox depicts the events leading up to the founding of the hasidic movement by the Ba'al Shem Tov, discussing the Chmielnicki massacres of 1648, the cold elitism of the Jewish intelligentsia, the messianism of Shabbetai Tsevi, and the disillusionment and demoralization of the Jewish masses in Poland. Also explored in depth are the teachers and other figures who influenced the Kotsker rebbe (for example, the "Holy Jew," the Seer of Lublin) and the Kotsker's warm relations with his foremost disciple Rabbi Isaac Meir, who became the first rebbe of Gur. This book fits the Kotsker rebbe squarely within the context of Jewish and East European society, showing him as very much a person of his times.

ORATZ does not mention the Kotsker's more controversial actions, but he does examine why the Kotsker's demanding credo produced such ambivalence and hostility among his contemporaries. In his introduction, Oratz vigorously defends the Kotsker, while arguing that the rebbe's unrelenting rebukes left many feeling angry and defensive. "Kotsk stripped the false and fraudulent gentility from those who paraded as venerable and esteemed persons," he writes. "Is there any wonder that this generated opposition?" The introduction also contains a biography of the Kotsker and an overview of his basic principles, such as self-analysis and criticism. The rest of the book presents Kotsker quotes and anecdotes, centered on three facets of truth—man and God, man and himself, man and the world—and supplemented with scholarly insights.

FEINBERG touches briefly on the Kotsker's personal life and focuses mainly on the teachings, as he traces the Kotsker's spiritual path. Each chapter discusses a specific aspect of the Kotsker philosophy (e.g., faith, humility), showing how these principles lead progressively to self-renewal and transforma-tion. The Kotsker's sayings are smoothly integrated within a florid narrative. This book, written during an illness that claimed the author's life, is not only a tribute to a powerful leader, but clearly a labor of love. It is also a linear, instructional blueprint of the Kotsker worldview.

The sayings of the Kotsker rebbe reveal so much about the man himself that they can occupy a book of their own. In an excellent translation, RAZ arranges the Kotsker's incisive words according to theme and lets them speak for themselves. The introduction provides a good overview of the Kotsker's life and philosophy and uses quotations from the Kotsker himself to illuminate his role not as a benign mascot but as a stern spiritual guide:

> One who seeks to be a Rebbe must ascend mountains and descend valleys, seek hidden treasures, and knock on the gates, many gates, until the heart breaks, until the body crumbles, until the heaven and earth collapse, while he maintains his way.

More than any other statement, these thunderous words reveal the Kotsker's turbulent soul. If self-improvement was the Kotsker rebbe's goal, it is the fear of heaven that was his motivation and his obsession. This fear hovered over the lives of those around him, consuming them, stimulating them, and revitalizing Jewry with intellectual energy.

HALLIE LYNN CANTOR

Menasseh ben Israel 1604–1657

Portugese-born Dutch preacher, writer, and leader

Berg, Johannes van den and Ernestine G.E. van der Wall (editors), *Jewish-Christian Relations in the Seventeenth Century: Studies and Documents* (International Archives of the History of Ideas, 119), Boston: Kluwer Academic, 1988

Kaplan, Yosef, Henry Méchoulan, and Richard Popkin (editors), *Menasseh ben Israel and His World* (Brill's Studies in Intellectual History, vol. 15), New York: Brill, 1989

Katz, David S., *Philo-Semitism and the Readmission of the Jews to England, 1603–1655* (Oxford Historical Monographs), Oxford: Clarendon, and New York: Oxford University Press, 1982

Manasseh Ben Israel, *The Hope of Israel*, translated by Moses Wall, 1650; edited by Henry Méchoulan and Gérard Nahon, Oxford and New York: Oxford University Press, 1987

Roth, Cecil, *A Life of Menasseh ben Israel: Rabbi, Printer, and Diplomat*, Philadelphia: Jewish Publication Society, 1934

Wolf, Lucien (editor), *Menasseh Ben Israel's Mission to Oliver Cromwell: Being a Reprint of the Pamphlets*

Published by Menasseh ben Israel to Promote the Re-Admission of the Jews to England, 1649–1656, London: Macmillan, 1901

Menasseh ben Israel's life brings together elements of the Portuguese Marrano experience, the beginnings of Amsterdam Jewish life, and the spadework for the readmission of Jews to England. The child of a family that had returned to Judaism after fleeing Portugal, Menasseh received a traditional Jewish education, entered the rabbinate, and became a scholar, printer, and prolific and diverse author. Notably, he reached out to Christian scholars, entering into correspondence with a number of philosemites both on the European continent and in England. Although his mission to England ended in qualified failure and he died disappointed and destitute, Menasseh left behind a rich heritage of writings and ideas that influenced the intellectual ferment of the Baroque among Jews and Christians alike.

ROTH's classic work remains the only complete biography of Menasseh, and undergraduates and lay readers will find it well worth consulting, although it lacks the insights of later researchers who have uncovered much material unseen by Roth. This highly readable book traces Menasseh's life from his Marrano background in Portugal and his youth in the emerging Jewish community of Amsterdam; discusses his experiences, positive and negative, as a rabbinic leader; reviews his career as a printer and author; and describes his Jewish and non-Jewish friends. A chapter is dedicated to Menasseh's influential little book, *The Hope of Israel,* and the biography concludes with an account of his failed mission to England. Roth presents Menasseh's many vicissitudes with great sympathy, creating a rounded portrait supported by appropriate bibliography and endnotes.

KATZ has written a number of important works bearing on the life of Menasseh. In his introduction to the most directly pertinent of these studies, Katz stresses that his aim is to sum up the key intellectual movements of the period, and he proceeds to describe the ferment of ideas that led Menasseh to undertake his mission to England as well as the events surrounding the mission's failure. Katz concentrates on the more speculative theological issues: Judaizers and the Mosaic law; the supernatural qualities of Hebrew; matters millenarian; and the ten lost tribes. He demonstrates the growth of philosemitic movements in England from the time of James I through the Civil War to the Commonwealth period and then analyzes events following Menasseh's arrival in England in 1655 and the presentation of his seven-point petition. While the final chapters focus on the events of the Whitehall Conference more than on Menasseh himself, Katz's exemplary use of contemporary sources illuminates brilliantly the framework in which Menasseh operated. A detailed bibliography and footnotes add to the value of this publication.

KAPLAN, MÉCHOULAN, and POPKIN, representatives of the scholarship of Israel, Europe, and the United States, respectively, present an important collection of papers from a conference on "Menasseh ben Israel and His World" held in Israel. These offerings explore "Menasseh ben Israel in terms of Portuguese expectations, Scottish millenarianism, various Dutch movements, various English thinkers and politicians, in terms of both the Jewish and Christian contexts." Kaplan's historio-graphical introduction is very helpful, and the collection of work by both Jewish and general historians sheds much light on Kabbalah, Jewish messianism, Christian Neoplatonism, and millenarianism. While this collection of papers presents a great deal of new research, it remains a matter of debate whether the parallel growth of Jewish messianism and Christian millenarianism in the 16th and 17th centuries was essentially coincidental or much more interdependent, as Michael Heyd points out in his concluding comments. The publication fails to arrange the papers in the most logical order, and as a result the volume is somewhat disjointed and is less accessible to nonspecialist readers than it might have been.

Complementing the above, BERG and VAN DER WALL's compilation on Jewish-Christian relations in the 17th century is divided into two sections: studies and documents. In the studies section, R. Popkin's chapter titled "Jewish-Christian Theological Interchanges in Holland and England" offers the most explicit discussion of Menasseh. P. van Rooden's chapter on the Dutch theologian and rabbinic scholar Constantijn L'Empereur, and van der Wall's essay on the millenarian Petrus Serrarius, also illustrate the claim that Menasseh was "the father of Judeo-Christian friendship." The second half of the book presents many valuable sources, including Menasseh's preface to the vocalized Mishnah (1646), the Latin contents of his *Nishmat Hayyim,* and his *Compendium Kabbalae.* The careful scholarship enhances significantly the reader's appreciation of Menasseh's many contributions to the developing Christian-Jewish dialogue of the 17th century.

Méchoulan and Nahon's edition of MANASSEH's *Hope of Israel* includes informative introductory sections on the Jews of Amsterdam and Menasseh's life and scholarship. It also provides notes and a detailed introduction. In addition, Popkin contributes an interesting note on Menasseh's English translator, Moses Wall. This edition makes a key primary resource for early modern Jewish history readily accessible to a general audience, and it is essential reading for anyone who wishes to understand Menasseh's life and writings.

Similarly, WOLF's classic edition of Menasseh's writings and pamphlets requesting the readmission of the Jews to England is of the greatest value. Published in 1901, it remains a basic work.

SUZANNE D. RUTLAND

Mendele Moykher Sforim 1835–1917

Russian pioneer of modern Hebrew and Yiddish literature

Aberbach, David, *Realism, Caricature, and Bias: The Fiction of Mendele Mocher Sefarim,* London and Washington, D.C.: The Littman Library of Jewish Civilization, 1993

Frieden, Ken, *Classic Yiddish Fiction: Abramovitsh, Sholem Aleichem, and Peretz* (SUNY Series in Modern Jewish Literature and Culture), Albany: State University of New York Press, 1995

Madison, Charles A., *Yiddish Literature: Its Scope and Major Writers,* New York: Ungar, 1968

Miron, Dan, *A Traveler Disguised: A Study in the Rise of Modern Yiddish Fiction in the Nineteenth Century*, New York: Schocken, 1973

Miron, Dan and Ken Frieden (editors), *Tales of Mendele the Book Peddler: Fishke the Lame and Benjamin the Third* (Library of Yiddish Classics), introduction by Dan Miron, translations by Ted Gorelick and Hillel Halkin, New York: Schocken, 1996

Zuckerman, Marvin, Gerald Stillman, and Marion Herbst (editors), *Selected Works of Mendele Moykher-Sforim* (The Three Great Classic Writers of Modern Yiddish Literature, vol. 1), [Malibu, California]: Joseph Simon/Pangloss Press, 1991

Novelist, essayist, social critic, and reformer, Sholem Yankev Abramovitsh took his pen name from the fictional narrator of his novels, Mendele Moykher Sforim (Mendele the Book Peddler). The author, known as the father of both modern Yiddish and modern Hebrew literature, had a genius for language, creating a Yiddish fiction whose realism was influenced by Dickens and Gogol. Abramovitsh began his career as a Hebrew writer but switched to Yiddish early on in order to reach a wider audience. Toward the end of his life, Abramovitsh returned to writing in Hebrew. Translating his own novels from Yiddish into Hebrew, he crafted a modern Hebrew literary prose where previously there had been none, this at a time when Hebrew was not once more a spoken language. The focus of Abramovitsh's writing was on the teeming, desperately poor Jewish communities of the Russian Pale of Settlement. Although he viewed Jewish life in Eastern Europe with a critical eye, he tempered his satiric censure by sympathetic identification with the poignant human plight of the *shtetl* world.

ABERBACH's book begins with a comparative study of the five novels that Abramovitsh wrote in Yiddish and translated into Hebrew in the latter part of his career and goes on to explore the interwoven strands of realism, social criticism, Jewish self-hate, satire, and autobiography in Abramovitsh's writing. The book includes a bibliography of Abramovitsh's works and a bibliography of secondary sources.

FRIEDEN devotes the first section of his study of the three greatest Yiddish writers to Abramovitsh. Beginning with a chronology and short biography of Abramovitsh's life, he continues with a literary analysis of the author's fictional work by focusing on the evolution of Abramovitsh's literary alter ego, Mendele the Book Peddler. The persona of Mendele appears in all of Abramovitsh's novels, and although some critics claim that Mendele is a static figure, Frieden maintains that he evolves over the course of Abramovitsh's career. As Frieden sees it, the author altered the Mendele persona in his Hebrew stories, "retaining his irony but rendering the overall effect less subversive." He concludes with a short survey of critical views of Abramovitsh. The book provides both an overview and a close reading of Abramovitsh's fiction. Drawing upon historical, political, social, and religious events, Frieden provides the background that situates Abramovitsh in a time and place. The book includes a bibliography of primary and secondary sources and a list of English translations.

MADISON discusses Abramovitsh's work in the context of the development of Yiddish literature. In chapter two, which he devotes to the author, he gives an overview of Abramovitsh's work while placing him in the overall tradition of Yiddish writing. Although Madison discusses Abramovitsh's literary output, his approach is more historical than literary. He focuses on the social conditions of the Jews in the Russian Pale of Settlement and demonstrates how Abramovitsh responded in his works to the misery he saw around him. Madison's chapter is useful as a brief introduction to the study of Abramovitsh. A bibliography of Yiddish writings in English translation and a bibliography of source materials are included.

MIRON and FRIEDEN's book is part of the Library of Yiddish Classics series, edited by Harvard Yiddish scholar Ruth R. Wisse. The tales included in the book are English translations of *Fishke the Lame* and *The Brief Tales of Benjamin the Third*. Miron's informative introduction examines Abramovitsh as a cultural and literary figure whose linguistic and literary innovations pointed the way for the Yiddish and Hebrew writers who followed. Miron argues that Abramovitsh projected for the first time in modern literature "the historical presence and unique lifestyle of the traditional premodern Eastern European Jewish community as a total, complex, and aesthetically balanced and self-contained 'world.'" Miron discusses Abramovitsh's evocation of the shtetl world through his literary creation of the three prototypical small towns of Glupsk (Kesalon in Hebrew), Tuneyadevka (Betalon), and Kabtsansk (Kabtsiel). These towns represent the entire Russian Jewish Pale of Settlement where living conditions were abysmal and the spiritual and intellectual life of its inhabitants, in Abramovitsh's view, were backward and stifling. The depiction of this imaginary geographical space whose very names are comical—Foolsville, Idleville, and Paupersville—provides the canvas for Abramovitsh's biting satire, according to Miron. Against this Jewish mass stands the author's other brilliant creation, the figure of Mendele the Book Peddler, who is of the shtetl world but also has distance from it as a result of his trade—he is on the road all the time. He thus serves as the perfect mouthpiece for Abramovitsh. The two ably translated novels included in this volume serve as models of Abramovitsh's art.

MIRON'S book examines the rise of modern Yiddish literature in the 19th century through an analysis of the fictional figure of Mendele the Book Peddler. "The rhetorical position of the figure of Mendele and its function as an ironic persona are analyzed as indication of a historical-cultural-literary situation, not as mere specimens of the art of storytelling," writes Miron. The book presents a far-reaching discussion of the strategies employed by Abramovitsh—the harsh critic of Jewish life in the Pale—in order to make it possible for his social, reformist agenda to coexist with his equally compelling artistic, literary impulse. It is indispensable reading for anyone interested in Abramovitsh's literary enterprise in particular and in the development of 19th-century Yiddish literature in general. The book includes several pages of illustrations and an extensive bibliography.

The anthology edited by ZUCKERMAN, STILLMANN, AND HERBST is the first extensive collection in English translation of the most important parts of Abramovitsh's literary output. It includes two complete novels, excerpts from several others, a short story, a memoir, a brief biography, a chronology, a selective bibliography, and a glossary of the Yiddish and Hebrew terms retained in the translations. Each work in the anthology is preceded by an introduction by one of the editors. The extensive background material combined with the large number of Abramovitsh's translated works makes the book an invaluable resource. It is highly recommended as a starting point in any study of Abramovitsh.

NANETTE STAHL

Mendelssohn, Moses 1729–1786

German Enlightenment philosopher, theologian, and advocate of civil rights

Altmann, Alexander, *Moses Mendelssohn: A Biographical Study*, London: Routledge and Kegan Paul, and Philadelphia: Jewish Publication Society, 1973

Arkush, Allan, *Moses Mendelssohn and the Enlightenment* (SUNY Series in Judaica), Albany: State University of New York Press, 1994

Breuer, Edward, *The Limits of Enlightenment: Jews, Germans, and the Eighteenth-Century Study of Scripture*, Cambridge, Massachusetts: Harvard University Press, 1996

Katz, Jacob, *Tradition and Crisis: Jewish Society at the End of the Middle Ages*, New York: Free Press of Glencoe, 1961

Lowenstein, Steven M., *The Berlin Jewish Community: Enlightenment, Family, and Crisis, 1770–1830* (Studies in Jewish History), London and New York: Oxford University Press, 1993

Meyer, Michael, *The Origins of the Modern Jew: Jewish Identity and European Culture in Germany, 1749–1824*, Detroit, Michigan: Wayne State University Press, 1967

Sorkin, David, *Moses Mendelssohn and the Religious Enlightenment*, Berkeley: University of California Press, and London: Halban, 1996

There has been a palpable surge of interest in Moses Mendelssohn in recent years. This development no doubt has been occasioned, at least in part, by the burgeoning of the field of Holocaust studies and the attention this relatively new field has focused on the German-Jewish relationship generally. Whether one views this relationship as hostile by definition or as something more benign, Mendelssohn emerges as a key figure. Discussions of Mendelssohn tend to conform to an agreed formula: thinker torn between two worlds. Where scholars differ is in the way they choose to people and color these worlds.

KATZ's subtitle is misleading, for when he speaks of the Middle Ages he is not using the standard European periodization. The focus of this classic study is on the disintegration of the traditional Jewish world, a process Katz locates between the 16th and 18th centuries. The book operates at a significant level of abstraction, focusing more on institutions than on individuals. Indeed, Katz's treatment of Mendelssohn in the book's closing sections is really more an analysis of the Haskalah than it

is a discussion of the thinker. This metonymy allows Mendelssohn to emerge as larger than life. He becomes a symbol perched somewhere between the old world and the new.

MEYER's book, although now more than 30 years old, remains a serviceable introduction to the dynamic period in German-Jewish history between 1750 and 1825. The first two chapters provide a concise yet learned introduction to Mendelssohn's life and thought. The book's focus is on the question of what happens to Jewish life once it comes to occupy just one segment of a person's existence. The split here is between Mendelssohn the philosopher and Mendelssohn the Jew. The author's treatment of the thinker is ultimately colored by the book's progression toward the 19th century's more romantically inspired conceptions of Judaism. Mendelssohn's rational synthesis of Judaism and Enlightenment is thus deemed "an ephemeral solution."

ALTMANN's is the most comprehensive book on Mendelssohn ever published in any language. Now more than a quarter-century old, it remains the standard work. Altmann's is the only English-language book that claims to present a life of Mendelssohn. Altmann deems Mendelssohn German Jewry's patron saint, at once emphasizing his contributions to German language and culture and crystallizing his reputation as devoted Jew, philosopher of Judaism, and advocate of Jewish civil rights. Although today's scholars have begun to move away from Altmann's bifurcated approach, his book nevertheless continues to set the tone of much Mendelssohn research. Scholars will use Altmann's work as the foundation for more focused studies. Important as it is, however, this is a long (900 pages) and unwieldy book without an easily discernible argument.

LOWENSTEIN stresses that "this study does not seek to answer the ideological questions underlying much of the debate over the Berlin Haskala. Its purpose, rather, is to give a clear picture of the nature of the events that took place among Berlin Jewry in the late eighteenth and early nineteenth centuries." Lowenstein's focus on the day-to-day helps highlight those aspects of Mendelssohn's career that are often overlooked by more philosophically oriented studies. Lowenstein sheds light, for instance, on Mendelssohn's involvement in the silk trade, a connection he maintained through much of his life. The author's approach is also valuable in showing how Mendelssohn, who was at some points a catalyst for change and at others a conservative force, was often out of step with his community.

ARKUSH rejects the notion that Mendelssohn was torn between Judaism and Enlightenment philosophy. "Mendelssohn was able, with little difficulty, to harmonize the doctrines of natural religion with the tenets of Judaism," writes Arkush. He identifies two alternative sources of tension in Mendelssohn's defense of the Jewish Bible: Mendelssohn's espousal of liberal politics, on the one hand, and the still more difficult problems posed by Spinozan historical criticism, on the other. Arkush claims that Mendelssohn was aware of the flaws of his defense, but he cynically papered them over so as to preserve his credentials as a loyal Jew. The book is a Straussian attempt to view the surface of Mendelssohn's work as in conflict with its subtext. As such, it is not entirely convincing.

SORKIN's book is, in part, a response to "the need for a succinct and accessible interpretation of Mendelssohn's Jewish thought." Sorkin maintains that this body of work, much of which was written in Hebrew, has been largely ignored by scholars, and what has emerged as a result is a distorted understanding of Mendelssohn's oeuvre. The author's focus on the Hebrew works helps bring to light Mendelssohn's debt to the Andalusian tradition, an approach developed in medieval times in which sacred texts are seen not as vessels of esoteric truth but as sources of practical knowledge, best understood literally. The book unfolds in three roughly chronological sections devoted to Mendelssohn's philosophy, exegesis, and politics, respectively. Throughout, the author shows how Mendelssohn privileged practical concerns over speculative ones in both his Hebrew and German works. In so doing, and through depicting Mendelssohn as a religious Enlightener, Sorkin narrows the gap between Mendelssohn's "two faces."

BREUER lays bare what is perhaps the Haskalah's central irony: that the Jewish Enlightenment was at once an attempt to emulate contemporary European thinking and at the same time a harking back to medieval exegetical traditions. The book's early chapters juxtapose the long history of Jewish Bible commentary with the younger tradition of text-critical methods of interpretation. In this context, Breuer introduces his analysis of Mendelssohn's Bible translation, "the most important and enduring scholarly work of the German Haskala." Breuer succeeds in locating Mendelssohn's project between no fewer than four coordinates: new European trends, revived medieval methods, the tradition-bound rabbinate of Mendelssohn's day, and those acculturated Jews who had already turned their backs on Judaism completely. Breuer's narrowly focused approach allows a very complex and nuanced Mendelssohn to emerge.

GABRIEL SANDERS

Messer Leon Family

Carpi, Daniel, "Notes on the Life of Rabbi Judah Messer Leon," in *Studi sull'ebraismo italiano: in memoria di Cecil Roth,* edited by Elio Toaff, Rome: Barulli, 1974
Messer Leon, Judah, *Nofet tsufim,* c.1474–1477; translated and edited by Isaac Rabinowitz as *The Book of the Honeycomb's Flow/Sepher Nopheth Suphim,* Ithaca, New York, and London: Cornell University Press, 1983
Tirosh-Rothschild, Hava, *Between Worlds: The Life and Thought of Rabbi David ben Judah Messer Leon* (SUNY Series in Judaica), Albany: State University of New York Press, 1991

Two members of the Messer Leon family have been studied in depth. Judah ben Jehiel Rofeh, known as Messer Leon (c.1420–1497/1499), was a rabbi and head of yeshivot in Ancona, Padua, Bologna, Mantua, and Naples as well as a physician and a productive philosophical writer. His son, David ben Judah Messer Leon (c.1460–after 1530), was a rabbi and philosophical writer about Jewish religious belief. Most scholarship on the two is in German

and Hebrew, but two important recent books about them are in English.

Judah (Leon), born in northern Italy around 1420, was a physician. In 1452, probably because of his medical activity, the emperor and pope conferred on him the title of "Master," which became added to his name as "Messer Leon." Messer Leon was the head of the yeshivah in Ancona by 1454. He was active in Padua in 1470, in Venice and Bologna in 1471–1472, and in Naples from about 1480 to 1495.

Messer Leon wrote commentaries on Yedaiah Bedersi's *Behinat Olam;* on Aristotle's logical treatises, *Isagoge, Categories,* and *De interpretatione;* on four books of Aristotle's *Physics* and his *Posterior Analytics;* and on Maimonides' *Guide for the Perplexed.* He also wrote supercommentaries on Averroës's commentaries on Aristotle's *Prior Analytics* and *Ethics.* He wrote a Hebrew grammar book, *Livnat ha-Sapir,* a logic textbook, *Mikhlol Yofi,* and a book on rhetoric for Hebrew, *Nofet Tsufim,* translated here as *The Book of the Honeycomb's Flow.* This, the first Hebrew book by a living author to appear in print, was published in Mantua, probably between 1474 and 1477, without Judah's supervision.

CARPI publishes some Latin and Hebrew documents about Judah's activities.

The scholarship on Judah is collected in Rabinowitz's introduction to MESSER LEON, a systematic account of the art of rhetoric. Rabinowitz's text and translation of *The Book of the Honeycomb's Flow* occupy most of the book. Messer Leon wrote the Hebrew rhetoric manual as a service to his yeshivah students, many of whom also studied medicine at the Italian universities. Rhetoric, like grammar and logic, was a liberal art that all medical students were required to study. Messer Leon equally intended to demonstrate his belief that the Hebrew Bible was the source of all learning, including the art of rhetoric, as well as being the highest example of rhetorical expression. The book is organized on the pattern of two main precedents: the Middle Commentary of Averroës on Aristotle's *Rhetoric* and a classical Latin book, the *Rhetorica ad Herrennium,* that medieval scholars thought was written by Cicero. Messer Leon illustrated all these authors' arguments with examples from the Hebrew of the Bible, so that the book presents rhetorical analysis of many biblical passages. The first part of Messer Leon's book defines rhetoric and the good orator. The second part discusses the ways to organize the three different kinds of rhetorical argument: courtroom pleading, political deliberation, and praising or blaming. The third part discusses the different kinds of human character and the different emotions. The fourth part presents the possible figures of speech, each one exemplified by biblical illustrations.

David, Messer Leon's son, was born in Venice, ordained a rabbi in Naples at the age of 18, was active in Istanbul (1496–1497), Salonica (Thessaloníki, c.1504), and Valona (in what is now Albania, 1510), and probably died in Salonica during the 1530s. TIROSH-ROTHSCHILD provides the only intellectual biography of David, and she and Carpi dispute several of Rabinowitz's conclusions, notably the dates of David's birth, of Judah's travels, and of important letters. Four of the seven chapters of the book integrate the events of his life into their social and cultural background, and the last three chapters analyze the doctrines in his writings. Tirosh-Rothschild emphasizes the importance of the background to David's activity. He became a leader in a Jewish community at a time when major upheavals destroyed some Jewish communities, led to the creation of others, and compelled Jewish scholars to reformulate their beliefs under new circumstances. David was among the teachers whose work enabled Kabbalah, previously known only to small numbers of devotees, to be integrated into general Jewish belief, along with philosophy.

Tirosh-Rothschild's first chapter sketches the economic, social, and political settings of Jewish life in Italy at the time of David's birth as well as the activity of his influential father, Judah. The second chapter reconstructs David's education, which combined Jewish law, Latin and Greek literature, philosophy, and Kabbalah. He studied in Padua and Naples, but, after the French invasion of 1495, he went to the Ottoman Empire. There he had to defend his Italian version of Jewish learning against the opposition of the majority of the Jewish population, new émigrés from Spain.

Chapter three traces his encounter with Ottoman Jewish life in Constantinople. There, his Italian manner of preaching led him to lose his rabbinic post. His request for financial support from a Jewish patroness in Florence was the occasion for his writing a book, *Shevah ha-Nashim* (*In Praise of Women*), which is in manuscript.

Chapter four surveys other controversies in which David was involved. He supported the Romaniot (Greek) Jewish authority, Rabbi Moses Capsali, in 1496–1497. In Valona, in about 1510, he disputed with Sephardi Jews. David wrote accounts of these disputes in two books of responsa, one of which was published in the 19th century as *Kevod Hakhamim* (*The Honor of Scholars*), and another that remains in manuscript. His commentary on Maimonides' *Guide of the Perplexed*, called *Ein ha-Kore* (*The Eye of the Reader*), in manuscript, records his defense of Maimonides in 1506 while in Salonica.

Chapter five presents the configuration of David's learning that made him a *hakham kolel*, a "complete" or "comprehensive scholar," who was competent in all branches of knowledge, including philosophy and theology. David harmonizes reason and revelation in his book *Magen David (Shield of David)*.

Chapters six and seven explain the systematic theology presented in David's book *Tehillah le-David (David's Praise)*. Chapter six summarizes his theology, notably his definition of the dogmas of Judaism. In contrast with such formulations of Jewish dogma as Maimonides' 13 principles, David argues that the three essential dogmas of Judaism are creation *ex nihilo*, prophecy, and miracles.

Chapter seven explains divinity: the existence and attributes of God, the essence of God, and divine knowledge and providence. The arguments and conclusions combine Kabbalah with Aristotelianism, as refracted through Thomas Aquinas.

ARTHUR M. LESLEY

Messiah and Messianism

Charlesworth, James H. (editor), *The Messiah: Developments in Earliest Judaism and Christianity* (The First Princeton Symposium on Judaism and Christian Origins), Minneapolis, Minnesota: Fortress, 1992

Ravitzky, Aviezer, *Messianism, Zionism, and Jewish Religious Radicalism* (Chicago Studies in the History of Judaism), translated by M. Zwirsky and J. Chipman, Chicago: University of Chicago Press, 1996

Saperstein, Marc (editor), *Essential Papers on Messianic Movements and Personalities in Jewish History* (Essential Papers on Jewish Studies Series), New York: New York University Press, 1992

Scholem, Gershom G., *Sabbatai Sevi: The Mystical Messiah, 1626–1676*, Princeton, New Jersey: Princeton University Press, and London: Routledge and Kegan Paul, 1973

Solomon, Norman, *Judaism and World Religion* (Library of Philosophy and Religion), New York: St. Martin's, and London: Macmillan, 1991

Urbach, Efraim E., *Hazal, pirke emunot ve-de'ot*, 1969; translated by Israel Abrahams as *The Sages: Their Concepts and Beliefs*, 2 vols., Jerusalem: Magnes Press of Hebrew University, 1975; Cambridge, Massachusetts: Harvard University Press, 1987

The biblical Hebrew word *mashiah* ("Messiah") means "anointed"; both high priests (Exodus 29:7) and kings (1 Samuel 10:1) were inducted into their sacred callings by ceremonies of anointment. Deutero-Isaiah refers to Cyrus, king of Persia, as "anointed," meaning that he was fulfilling, albeit unwittingly, God's mission to restore Israel (Isaiah 45:1).

By the first century B.C.E., the concept had arisen that an anointed descendant of David would arise to defeat the Lord's enemies, restore Israel to its land, free the world from war and want, and rule over a redeemed humanity. This idea, destined to play a significant role in the development of Judaism as well as Christianity, is a conflation of various biblical prophecies such as those in 2 Samuel 7:9, Ezekiel 37:21, Joel 3:14, Amos 5:18, Isaiah 11 and 27:13, and Zechariah 9:9–10, 14:9.

CHARLESWORTH's collection of papers presented at a Princeton Symposium on Judaism and Christian Origins contains a wealth of up-to-date scholarship on the development of the Messiah concept from its genesis in the Hebrew scriptures to its flowering in the first and second centuries C.E., both in early Christianity and in rabbinic culture. Full consideration is given to the evidence from the Apocrypha, the Pseudepigrapha, and the Dead Sea Scrolls. Controversial issues, including the significance of the varied titles applied to Jesus, such as "Son of Man," are handled sensitively and with authority, and there is a wealth of penetrating studies on topics such as the Messianic Banquet, the relationship between conversion and messianism, and messianic figures and movements in first-century Palestine. Charlesworth himself contends that the common portrayal of the Jewish world in the time of Jesus as feverishly obsessed with messianic expectation is wide of the mark; such fervor, he maintains, was largely confined to small apocalyptic groups. The Jewish philosopher and contemporary of Jesus, Philo of Alexandria, seems, on the surface, unconcerned with messianic issues; yet Peter Borgen, in a penetrating study of Philo's political theory, demonstrates how deep-seated are the messianic elements in Philo's expectation of an ideal emperor with a universal mission.

RAVITZKY, a leading Israeli academic and philosopher, brings to his book the unique insights of one who has worked in the political arena to combat the excesses of radical messianism that he perceives as an aberration in contemporary Jewish Orthodoxy. His description of how the 19th-century religious "harbingers of Zion" such as Judah Alkalai and Tsevi Hirsch Kalischer, under the influence of burgeoning European nationalisms, moved from a passive "yearning for Zion" to an active, even radical, political program, is vivid yet unfailingly careful in its scholarship. It prepares the way for him to assess the dilemma of Orthodoxy, which now has to relate itself to a Jewish state that, contrary to messianic prediction, remains secular and has not brought the expected era of peace, ingathering of the exiles, and rebuilding of the Temple. Many readers will be particularly fascinated by Ravitzky's assessment of the Lubavitch movement and the tensions and radicalism generated first by the response of its fifth rebbe, Joseph Isaac Schneersohn, to secular Zionism, and more recently by the messianic claims made openly since 1992 for its last rebbe, Menahem Mendel Schneersohn, who died in 1994.

SAPERSTEIN's collection of seminal essays written over the past 75 years commences with studies of the "Second Commonwealth," including the time of Jesus, but deals mostly with later developments in Judaism up to the present day. In his introduction he notes the intermittent appearance of messianism in the Jewish world; the archetypal career of the pseudo-Messiah Shabbetai Tsevi in 1666; and the rise of Reform Judaism, socialism, and Zionism as "redemptive" movements. A penetrating essay by Eliezer Schweid further examines the metamorphosis of the messianic idea into contemporary political forms, while Menachem Kellner focuses on "Messianic Postures in Israel Today." Other sections of the book contain important essays on early Islamic (Shiite) influences on Jewish sectarianism, on Jewish pseudo-Messiahs in the period of the Crusades, on the origins of "Acute Apocalyptic Messianism" (Isaiah Tishby) after the 1492 Expulsion from Spain, and on Sabbatianism, Hasidism, and Zionism. Bat-Zion Eraqi contributes a fascinating chapter on the little-known 19th-century Yemenite pseudo-Messiah Shukr Kuhayl II.

SCHOLEM's monumental work on Shabbetai Tsevi remains the most detailed and cogent account available of any Jewish pseudo-Messiah. With profound scholarship and acute insight, he places the Sabbatian movement within the social and intellectual context of 17th-century Jewry. Shabbetai's subversion of Lurianic Kabbalah is clear; however, Scholem's contention that the antinomian tendency within Sabbatianism contributed to the rise of Reform Judaism has been doubted by some more recent scholars.

SOLOMON argues that though there is no consistent rabbinic concept of Messiah, traditional views may be conveniently expressed along seven parameters. To what extent is Messiah within or beyond the normal historical process? Is there a fixed time for his coming or does it depend on human action? Is Messiah a person or rather a "golden age"? Is his mission political or spiritual? Is it particular (directed to Israel) or universal (to humankind as a whole)? Will his advent be a catastrophic or an evolutionary process? How much detail can be put into the picture? The maximal view is that the messianic advent is "not of this world"; it will come about at a predetermined time; Messiah is a preexistent son of David on whom God's glory will descend, because God, not the Messiah, is the actual Redeemer; Israel will be delivered from its enemies, and the exiles, including the Ten Tribes, will be gathered to the land of Israel, and exercise spiritual dominion over humankind; and the coming will be a "catastrophic" event, brought about by divine intervention in history. On the minimal view, no personal Messiah will arise, no catastrophic event will take place; if and when Israel repents, its political independence will be restored, and Jerusalem will become a spiritual center for mankind. Solomon asks how much of this, beyond the general confidence in a better future, still makes sense within a modern world view; for instance, does any "ultimate solution" make sense when we think in terms of billions rather than thousands of years? He notes also the paucity of conception of what things will actually be like when the Messiah comes; how will the administration work, for instance?

URBACH's masterly study of the thought of the rabbis was first published in Hebrew in 1969, and much of the detail of its scholarship has been superseded. However, it remains one of the best and most readable introductions to classical Jewish thought, and the chapter relating to Messiah, together with other references easily traced through the index, helps to place rabbinic thinking on this subject in its broad context.

NORMAN SOLOMON

Middle East

Ben-Zvi, Itzhak, *The Exiled and the Redeemed,* Philadelphia: Jewish Publication Society, 1957; 2nd edition, Jerusalem: Ben-Zvi Institute, 1976

Cohen, Hayim J., *The Jews of the Middle East, 1860–1972,* New York: Wiley, 1973

Cohen, Hayim J. and Zvi Yehuda, *Asian and African Jews in the Middle East, 1860–1971: Annotated Bibliography,* Jerusalem: Ben-Zvi Institute, 1976

Deshen, Shlomo and Walter P. Zenner (editors), *Jewish Societies in the Middle East: Community, Culture, and Authority,* Washington, D.C.: University Press of America, 1982

Deshen, Shlomo and Walter P. Zenner (editors), *Jews among Muslims: Communities in the Precolonial Middle East,* New York: New York University Press, and Houndmills, Basingstoke, Hampshire: Macmillan, 1996

Fischel, Walter J., *Jews in the Economic and Political Life of Mediaeval Islam,* London: Royal Asiatic Society, 1937; New York: Ktav, 1969

Landshut, S., *Jewish Communities in the Muslim Countries of the Middle East,* London: Jewish Chronicle, 1950; Westport, Connecticut: Hyperion, 1976

Patai, Raphael, *The Seed of Abraham: Jews and Arabs in Contact and Conflict,* Salt Lake City: University of Utah Press, 1986

Schechtman, Joseph B., *On Wings of Eagles: The Plight, Exodus, and Homecoming of Oriental Jewry,* New York: Yoseloff, 1961

Stillman, Norman A., *The Jews of Arab Lands: A History and Source Book*, Philadelphia: Jewish Publication Society, 1979

Stillman, Norman A., *The Jews of Arab Lands in Modern Times,* Philadelphia: Jewish Publication Society, 1991

The first Jewish diaspora was in the Middle East, which hosted major Jewish communities until the mid-20th century, when most Jews emigrated these communities, mainly to Israel as well as to Western Europe and the Americas. Much research has been conducted on Jews in the region as a whole and on individual countries, much of it in Hebrew as well as in English, French, and local languages. Important bibliographies have also been compiled.

BEN-ZVI examines several Oriental Jewish communities, mostly in the Middle East. In the first part he studies ancient communities (Yemen, North Africa, Iraq, Caucasia, Georgia, Bukhara, Crimea, and Iran) and proceeds to describe a number of Jewish sects (Samaritans, the Sabbatian Dönmeh of Salonica, and Karaites), Jewish traditions among Muslim tribes, Oriental travel journals, and Jewish sovereign states in the diaspora. The study is augmented by interviews with members of Middle Eastern Jewish communities before and after their immigration to Israel, with whom Ben-Zvi, the second president of Israel, had close and warm relations.

COHEN's study covers the modern Middle East from the late 19th century to the 1970s. Following a historical survey up to 1870, Cohen devotes separate chapters to political, demographic, economic, and educational-cultural developments, each chapter subdivided by country. The last chapter deals with social change and examines morals and criminality, religion, and the status of women. The book includes much data and analysis, is easy to use, and deals with several major issues governing Jewish life in the region.

COHEN and YEHUDA's useful bibliography of monographs and articles has two parts: the first deals with Asian and African Jews in Israel, and the second covers the Jews of the Muslim Middle East (Egypt, Syria and Lebanon, Iraq, Kurdistan, the Arabian Peninsula, Turkey, and Iran). Each country chapter in the second part is further subdivided as follows: general works on the country; general works on its Jews; travels; demography, health, and economics; education; status of women; culture and literature; religion and customs; Jewish organizations; political situation; Zionism; aliyah; Jewish diaspora of the country in question; and bibliography. Author and place indexes are included. Most of the entries are in Hebrew but many are in English, French, and German.

DESHEN and ZENNER (1982, 1996) have edited two collections of articles on Jews in the Middle East. Both include an introductory section covering the region as a whole, followed by articles on Morocco, Tunisia, Tripolitania, Syria, Iraq, Yemen, and Iran. Among the topics dealt with are the move from tradition to modernity, communal life, social structure, relations with Muslim neighbors and colonial authorities, and religious life with special reference to women, folk songs, and education. Recommended readings for the region and by

country are included. These are valuable collections, even though they do not cover the whole region, focusing instead on specific topics.

FISCHEL's book examines the economic and political role of Jews in the region from Egypt to Iran from the eighth to the 14th century and is based on Arabic and Jewish sources. The study is divided chronologically based on the Islamic regimes that governed the region and is subdivided by leading Jewish personalities whose economic activities are examined along with their political power, their dependence relations with the rulers, and their relations with the Jewish community. The study is of importance for Jewish, as well as general economic, political, and cultural history.

LANDSHUT's survey was prepared in 1950 for the American Jewish Committee and the Anglo-Jewish Association. It opens with a historical introduction on population, relations with Muslim authorities, communal organization, and the effects of colonialism and nationalism on the Jews. This is followed by country-by-country surveys covering the Middle East and North Africa, with the exception of Tunisia, Algeria, and Morocco. A general Jewish population table, map, and bibliography are included. The book provides a succinct and comprehensive survey of the Jews in the early 1950s.

PATAI provides a historical and anthropological description of Jews in Arab lands and their relations with the Muslim majority from the rise of Islam to the 1980s. He examines the representation of Jews in Arab tradition, compares the life of Jews in Yemen and Morocco, and pays special attention to Jewish and Arab folklore, Middle Eastern perceptions of the feminine in the divine, and the status of women. Written by an anthropologist, this work provides much comparative data on everyday life and culture.

SCHECHTMAN focuses on the Jewish mass migration from the Middle East and North Africa to Israel in the late 1940s and early 1950s, providing a country-by-country examination of the phenomenon. Each chapter describes the history and conditions of the community prior to emigration, examines the emigration itself and its organization, and provides data on those who stayed. The concluding segment examines the integration of the immigrants in Israel. Schechtman's book is an important and comprehensive early study on the last phases of Jewish life in the Middle East and North Africa.

STILLMAN (1979) includes a survey and sources on Jews in Arab lands from the rise of Islam in the seventh century until the beginning of modernization in the 19th century. The survey starts with the encounter of Muhammad and the Jews, continues through the first three centuries under Islam to the Islamic high middle ages, and ends with the Mamluk empire and the Ottoman empire at the dawn of modern times. The sources follow the same order as the historical portions and are all annotated and published in English. An extensive bibliography and an index are included. Stillman provides an indispensable comprehensive examination and documentation of Jewish life in Arab lands.

STILLMAN (1991) is structured like his 1979 book and covers the period from the early 19th century to the almost complete exodus of Jews from Arab lands in the mid-20th century. The survey starts with the impact of the West on the region, examines social transformations, colonialism and nationalism, the influence of Zionism on Middle Eastern Jews, and the deteriorating condition of Jews in the 1930s. The survey ends with the condition of Jews during World War II and the mass migration thereafter. The sources are very rich and cover all aspects of the survey. Like Stillman's earlier volume, this is essential reading for people interested in the Middle East and North Aftrica, the status of minorities, and the implications of colonization and decolonization for the region.

RACHEL SIMON

See also Algeria; Egypt and Sudan; Iran, Afghanistan, and Central Asia; Iraq; Libya; Morocco; North Africa; Syria; Tunisia; Yemen and the Arabian Peninsula

Midrash Aggadah

Boyarin, Daniel, *Intertextuality and the Reading of Midrash* (Indiana Studies in Biblical Literature), Bloomington: Indiana University Press, 1990

Braude, William (translator), *Pesikta Rabbati: Discourses for Feasts, Fasts, and Special Sabbaths* (Yale Judaica Series, vol. 18), 2 vols., New Haven, Connecticut: Yale University Press, 1968

Braude, William and Israel Kapstein (translators), *Pesikta de-Rab Kahana: R. Kahana's Compilation of Discourses for Sabbaths and Festal Days,* Philadelphia: Jewish Publication Society, and London: Routledge and Kegan Paul, 1975

Freedman, H. and Maurice Simon (editors), *Midrash Rabbah,* London: Soncino, 1939; 3rd edition, London and New York: Soncino, 1983

Friedlander, Gerald (editor), *Pirke de Rabbi Eliezer,* London: Paul, Trench, Trubner, and New York: Bloch, 1916; 4th edition, New York: Sepher-Hermon, 1981

Ginzberg, Louis, *The Legends of the Jews,* 7 vols., Philadelphia: Jewish Publication Society, 1909

Goldin, Judah (translator), *The Fathers according to Rabbi Nathan* (Yale Judaica Series, vol. 10), New Haven, Connecticut: Yale University Press, 1955

Hartman, Geoffrey H. and Sandford Budick (editors), *Midrash and Literature,* New Haven, Connecticut: Yale University Press, 1986

Kalmin, Richard, "Patterns and Developments in Rabbinic Midrash of Late Antiquity," in *Hebrew Bible, Old Testament: The History of Its Interpretation,* vol. 1, edited by Magne Sæbø, Göttingen: Vandenhoeck and Ruprecht, 1996

Kugel, James, *In Potiphar's House: The Interpretive Life of Biblical Texts,* San Francisco: HarperSanFrancisco, 1990; 2nd edition, Cambridge, Massachusetts: Harvard University Press, 1994

Kugel, James, *The Bible as It Was,* Cambridge, Massachusetts: Belknap Press of Harvard University Press, 1997; revised as *Traditions of the Bible: A Guide to the Bible as It Was at the Start of the Common Era,*

Cambridge, Massachusetts: Harvard University Press, 1998

Mack, Hananel, *The Aggadic Midrash Literature* (Broadcast University Series), Tel-Aviv: MOD, 1989

Spiegel, Shalom, *Me-agadot ha-'akedah,* 1951; translated as *The Last Trial: On the Legends and Lore of the Command to Abraham to Offer Isaac as a Sacrifice: The Akedah,* Philadelphia: Jewish Publication Society, 1967

Stern, David, *Parables in Midrash: Narrative and Exegesis in Rabbinic Literature,* Cambridge, Massachusetts: Harvard University Press, 1991

Strack, Hermann Leberecht and Günter Stemberger, *Einleitung in Talmud und Midrasch,* 1982; translated by Markus Bockmuehl as *Introduction to the Talmud and Midrash,* Edinburgh: Clark, 1991, 2nd edition, 1996

The study of midrash aggadah (the classical rabbinic interpretation of Scripture for any purpose other than elucidation of the law—be it moral exhortation or popular storytelling) may be approached from various perspectives, and the meaning of aggadah itself has given rise to a plethora of scholarly works. In addition to synchronic compilations of aggadot, recent publications include diachronic analyses of the development of particular stories and folklore. Furthermore, there is a keen interest among postmodern literary theorists in the study of midrash as literary discourse. In a similar vein, midrashic scholars have used literary theory to understand not only the use of certain exegetical techniques but also the meaning of midrash as a literary and cultural artifact.

BOYARIN's work, dealing primarily and explicitly with midrash through a postmodern critical lens, is an invaluable contribution to the field of midrashic studies. Scholars consider his introduction a groundbreaking, masterful exposition of midrash as an interpretative discourse that is historically and ideologically situated. Boyarin exploits the concept of intertextuality to describe both the Bible itself and the rabbinic code used to interpret the text. Through a study of the Mekhilta and its use of quotations, he illustrates how rabbinic interpretation is both the continuation and disruption of tradition. Although the work deals with an essentially halakhic corpus, on a more general level, it attempts to determine "what sort of theory would allow [the rabbis] to make the interpretive moves they make."

HARTMAN and BUDICK's collection of essays discussing the nature of midrash is a felicitous entry into the study of midrash as literature. The anthology is particularly useful to those readers interested in examining the relationship between midrash and contemporary literary inquiry. The work in general draws attention to the ways in which midrash reads Scripture. It is important to note, however, that some of the studies in this compilation are more relevant than others. One of the most significant essays is Heinemann's "Nature of the Aggadah," where he discusses aggadah as a method of "creative genesis," a means by which the rabbis used Scripture to wrestle with contemporary issues. Goldin's essay, "Freedom and Restraint of Haggadah," conceives of aggadah as the essential counterpart to halakhah and focuses on the necessity of their interplay, for "they are an articulation of the fundamental, universal, interminable combat of obedience and individual conceit." In addition to these articles, Fishbane's "Inner Biblical Exegesis: Types and Strategies of Interpretation in Ancient Israel," James Kugel's "Two Introductions to Midrash," and Frank Kermode's "Plain Sense of Things" help illuminate various aspects of the nature of midrash aggadah.

STERN's in-depth analysis provides the reader with a clear understanding of the function of the *mashal* (parable) in rabbinic literature. Stern explores the compositional and exegetical techniques of the mashal, its rhetoric, and its role in midrashic discourse. He claims that parables about kings constitute the preeminent form of narrative in rabbinic literature, and he argues that this form provides a point of entry into nearly every aspect of this literature and its interpretation. Stern only analyzes meshalim found in Midrash Lamentations Rabbah, but his treatment provides readers not only with a great appreciation for the structure of these texts, but also with a model of how to approach midrash as a whole. That is, he examines meshalim as both narrative and exegesis; at the same time he takes into account the historical context in which they were created. Although he emphasizes the mashal, Stern also examines other literary forms such as the *petihta* (the proem of a homiletic midrash), and the *ma'aseh* (reportage). This work is an important resource not only for those examining the mashal in particular, but also for those desiring a better sense of the literary character of midrash aggadah.

MACK's work is an excellent introduction to the various corpora and exegetical methods of midrash aggadah. In addition to an important exposition of the meaning and nature of aggadah, the work includes a lucid discussion of related topics such as the historical context that gave rise to this form of literature. One welcome feature of Mack's work is its successful attempt to cover several, if not all, aspects of midrash aggadah in a comprehensive yet concise manner.

In his review essay on midrash, which includes an exhaustive bibliography on midrashic studies, KALMIN discusses the most salient features of midrash and pays special attention to the differences between the midrash of Palestine and Babylonia, the two centers of rabbinic Judaism. This article also surveys works that deal with such issues as the relationship between the diverse exegetical schools and the *Sitz im Leben* of rabbinic exegesis. Kalmin concludes with an instructive examination of a midrashic text found in "chronologically and geographically diverse rabbinic compilations." His balanced perspective, which takes into account both the literary and historical aspects of midrash, is a significant contribution to the field.

SPIEGEL's work is a perspicacious examination of various ancient texts that interpret the *akedah* (the binding of Isaac in Genesis 22). The author not only examines postbiblical writings such as the works of Philo, midrashim, talmudic sources, the gospels, and patristic literature, he also gives serious consideration to traditional biblical commentary and higher criticism. First written in Hebrew, this study was originally designed to serve as an introduction to "The Akedah," a 12th-century poem by Rabbi Ephraim of Bonn, which Spiegel, primarily a scholar of medieval Hebrew poetry, edited and analyzed for publication. The volume is a rich resource for anyone interested in literature on the *akedah* trope. The

sophistication and magnitude of the author's work is universally recognized by scholars of midrash.

KUGEL (1990) examines a series of stories pertaining to the Joseph narrative and seeks "to present a methodological model for reading early biblical interpretation." The author devotes part one of the study to various exegetical motifs underlying narrative expansions of the Joseph story in Jewish sources; Kugel also makes some references to relevant Christian and Muslim texts. In part two, he deals with a variety of stories and motifs. He discusses, for example, biblical texts of a nonlegal character such as the tale of Lamech and Psalm 137, and he examines the injunction of Leviticus 19:17, "You shall not hate your brother in your heart; you shall surely reproach your neighbor, and you shall bear no sin because of him." To illustrate how early exegetes dealt with this verse, Kugel draws on such works as the Wisdom of Ben Sira, the Testaments of the Twelve Patriarchs, the Damascus Document (one of the many writings of the Qumran community), and the Sifra, a compilation of tannaitic midrashim on Leviticus. At the end of part two, after having examined the ways in which exegetical motifs develop, Kugel formulates nine theses, "general conclusions about the workings of biblical exegesis as a whole," that are essential to understanding the creation and development of postbiblical exegesis. The glossary familiarizes the reader with important terms and sources related to the study of midrash aggadah.

The unprecedented work of GINZBERG, the aggadic scholar par excellence, is the most comprehensive collection of aggadic material extant. His compilation of folklore, tales, and legends is not limited to rabbinic literature but draws also from targumim and medieval biblical commentaries. The first four volumes provide the general reader with hundreds of legends. Volumes five and six contain notes to the previous volumes and are replete with rabbinic and pseudepigraphic parallels as well as references to the writings of the church fathers, and volume seven provides an index to this mine of aggadic material.

Although not of the same magnitude as Ginzberg's work, KUGEL's (1997; revised, 1998) work is also a synchronic collection of biblical interpretation. Kugel limits the scope of his work to the centuries just before and after the beginning of the common era, from approximately 200 B.C.E. to 150 C.E., and he deals with motifs and interpretations based on two dozen stories found in the Torah. The work attempts to reconstruct the Bible as it was understood in this period, a daunting task. Kugel successfully elucidates how these ancient biblical interpretations "came to cling to the biblical text." The author examines texts culled from such sources as Philo, Josephus, the Dead Sea Scrolls, and the rabbis, and he offers an erudite commentary on the selected material. He explains the interpreter's modus operandi and demonstrates how particular exegetical techniques gave rise to crucial transformations in the meaning of a biblical story. This work, an expanded version of his *The Bible as It Was*, is useful to the general reader and the biblical expert alike.

First published in 1887, STRACK's bibliographic guide remains invaluable as a result of STEMBERGER's complete revision. The book briefly introduces each work and refers the reader to extant manuscripts, printed editions, translations, and secondary literature. Each rabbinic work is also discussed in terms of its history, character, and date of origin. Scholars in the field readily acknowledge the scope of Strack and Stemberger's contribution to rabbinic studies. Their introduction is a superb point of entry into the vast material of rabbinic literature.

FREEDMAN and SIMON have edited the standard English translation of the Midrash Rabbah. Replete with extensive notes and indexes, this ten-volume work, the first of its kind, attempts to be both faithful to the original text and intelligible to the common reader. Each component work is preceded by an introduction that discusses the putative dating and possible place of origin as well as the fundamental features and distinguishing characteristics of the individual compilation.

GOLDIN's translation of Avot de Rabbi Natan, the earliest extant commentary on the mishnaic tractate Avot, is a significant addition to the rich library of rabbinic texts in English translation. His work, the first English translation of this text, is based on Solomon Schechter's edited text, which was first published in 1887. The synopsis of each chapter is a helpful guide for those unfamiliar with Avot. Goldin draws upon the works of traditional commentators of both Avot and Avot de Rabbi Natan to provide the reader with copious notes that not only facilitate the reading of the work but also contribute to an understanding of the transmission and inner workings of rabbinic literature.

FRIEDLANDER's translation of Pirke de Rabbi Eliezer, a composite aggadic work redacted in the ninth century, is meticulous and draws upon a wide range of primary and secondary sources. Friedlander bases his translation on an unedited manuscript belonging to Abraham Epstein of Vienna, but he also consults Genizah fragments and other manuscripts including those edited by Horowitz. The extensive footnotes refer readers to parallel sources, explain ambiguous allusions in the text, indicate manuscript variants, and give historical, theological, and literary references that place the work within the broader contexts of Judaism, Christianity, and Islam.

BRAUDE's two-volume English rendering of Pesikta Rabbati is exemplary in its scope. The translator has an acute awareness of textual nuance. He points out variants among the manuscripts, and his notes render obscure comments comprehensible. Moreover, his discussion of the distinguishing characteristics of Pesikta Rabbati is substantive and especially useful to those unfamiliar with its content and method.

Braude's talent for translating ancient sources is also apparent in BRAUDE and KAPSTEIN, a compilation of homiletic midrashim from Pesikta de-Rab Kahana. The introduction offers a thorough analysis of the Pesikta's contents and its structure, style, and textual history. More important, the translators exhibit a precision and sensitivity to language subtleties, evidenced in the translation itself and in the detailed footnotes, that are quite exceptional.

CAROL BAKHOS

Midrash Halakhah: Translations

Basser, Herbert W. (editor and translator), *Midrashic Interpretations of the Song of Moses*, New York: Lang, 1984

Hammer, Reuven (editor and translator), *Sifre: A Tannaitic Commentary on the Book of Deuteronomy* (Yale Judaica Series, vol. 24), New Haven and London: Yale University 1986.

Lauterbach, Jacob (editor and translator), *Mekilta de-Rabbi Ishmael* (Schiff Library of Jewish Classics), 3 vols., Philadelphia: Jewish Publication Society, 1933-35.

Levertoff, Paul (editor and translator), *Midrash Sifre on Numbers: Selections from Early Rabbinic Scriptural Interpretations*, New York: Macmillan, and London: Society for Promoting Christian Knowledge, 1926.

Neusner, Jacob (editor and translator), *Sifre to Numbers: An American Translation and Explanation* (Brown Judaic Studies, no. 118–119), 2 vols., Atlanta, Georgia: Scholars Press, 1986

Neusner, Jacob (editor and translator), *Sifre to Deuteronomy: An Analytical Translation* (Brown Judaic Studies), 2 vols., Atlanta, Georgia: Scholars Press, 1987

Neusner, Jacob (editor and translator), *Mekhilta according to Rabbi Ishmael: An Analytical Translation* (Brown Judaic Studies, no. 148), Atlanta, Georgia: Scholars Press, 1988

Neusner, Jacob (editor and translator), *Sifra: An Analytical Translation* (Brown Judaic Studies, no. 138–140), 3 vols., Atlanta, Georgia: Scholars Press, 1988

Neusner, Jacob (editor and translator), *The Components of the Rabbinic Documents: From the Whole to the Parts*, vol. 12, pts. 1–3: *Sifre to Numbers* (South Florida Academic Commentary Series, nos. 104–106), Atlanta, Georgia: Scholars Press, 1998

Translation of halakhic midrash is a paradoxical enterprise insofar as the results are most usable by those who need them least. The idiom of this literature, even in translation, demands an intimacy with the rabbinic mind, its legal categories and methods of scriptural interpretation. To anyone else the works will appear as so much foolishness and have sometimes been categorized as such by those who have an insufficient grasp of antique exegesis in general and the rabbis, their methods, and objectives in particular. This is also true of the narrative sections of midrashic literature, but an ability to spot the mechanics of rabbinic interpretation at work is even more indispensable when it comes to the extrapolation of detailed law from Scripture. No translation will suffice to convey this aptitude, which requires extended study and experience. With the premise that all these translations will be of value only in proportion to the familiarity that the reader brings to the literature, some general appraisals of what is available are presented below.

HAMMER's translation of Sifre, the halakhic midrash on Deuteronomy, shows much industry in finding the proper English idiom to render technical Hebrew vocabulary. The problem is that his work is very uneven and has a number of gross misunderstandings of complex legal terminology. His rendition of the narrative portions also fails to hit the mark in a number of instances. The upshot is that the translation is unreliable in its details but acceptable in the main as a plausible representation of the gist of Sifre Deuteronomy.

NEUSNER (1987) has followed his predecessor (giving acknowledgement) and corrected a number of Hammer's mistranslations in the legal portions, but Neusner has introduced a number of debatable renderings himself. In his introduction to the large section of narrative in Sifre Deuteronomy he acknowledges that Herbert W. Basser's *Midrashic Interpretations of the Song of Moses* (see below) provides a much better understanding in difficult places than Hammer's work. Having realized this, he nevertheless follows Hammer almost exclusively to the detriment of his rendition.

NEUSNER (1988a) fares better with his translation of the halakhic midrash on Exodus, but then again LAUTERBACH has produced a first-rate translation for him to consult. Neusner's work lacks notes and commentary, a necessity that all other translators provide, and as a result Neusner leaves the reader inevitably bemused at times. Midrash halakhah is often predictable and similarly often a very complex and obscure genre that absolutely demands some kind of commentary. Lauterbach includes some notes and references in his edition, as well as his own critical edition of the Hebrew text as a basis for the translation.

NEUSNER (1986) has the rather poor model of LEVERTOFF for some of the work he presents on Sifre on the Book of Numbers. He does not have even Levertoff as a model for the balance of the text of Sifre Numbers. NEUSNER (1998) presents the completion of his Sifre Numbers. This contribution is not nearly as readable as his translations of midrash for which he had the benefit of consulting earlier works in English. Nonetheless, it is an attempt at literal rendition.

NEUSNER (1988b) translates the halakhic midrash on Leviticus, a project in which Neusner has invested much effort. Like much of his Sifre Numbers, he has had to do the work without benefit of an English model to consult. The result is that a number of passages require revision and the work is too uncertain to consult with confidence. In general, the major problem with Neusner's work is that he has not studied the rabbinic commentaries, which often clarify quite convincingly the sense of the laconic wordings of halakhic midrash. A further major drawback of his work is that it is not at all indexed; other translators have provided not one but often several useful indexes, enhancing the utility of their work by providing access points by way of sources, parallels, and topics. Neusner's trademark penchant for breaking up sentences into what he considers logical units is interesting, but here one meets problems of consistency. Why does one item in a list deserve a full sentence while several other items in the same list are lumped together in another sentence, even though everything suggests that the midrash treats all equally? Still, since Neusner ensures that each unit is numbered, it does make for easy reference for any discussion that might ensue around his translations.

Only full translations into English have been considered thus far, but one should note that there are translations of sections of these midrashim in English and full translations in European languages. BASSER's study referred to above is limited to the "halakhic midrash" on a non-halakhic passage, chapter 32 of the Book of Deuteronomy, but it is remarkable for the erudition and understanding that the editor brings to the methodology and context of this form of rabbinic literature.

It is not envisioned that these translations will be of much benefit to those who are not able to read the Hebrew originals, but as a guide to accompany scholars and students as they navigate their way through difficulties, each translation is of potential use. In the final analysis, the greatest problem in producing a competent translation lies in the ability of the translator to comprehend the original text. Most of the translations considered here have relied upon extant critical—but not necessarily final—editions and the notes—valuable but far from exhaustive—found within these editions. There is much important work to be done.

REENA ZEIDMAN

See also Midrash Halakhah: Introductions

Midrash Halakhah: Introductions

Boyarin, Daniel, *Intertextuality and the Reading of Midrash* (Indiana Studies in Biblical Literature), Bloomington: Indiana University Press, 1990

Fraade, Steven, *From Tradition to Commentary: Torah and Its Interpretation in the Midrash Sifre to Deuteronomy* (SUNY Series in Judaica), Albany: State University of New York Press, 1991

Goldin, Judah, *The Song at the Sea: Being a Commentary on a Commentary in Two Parts*, New Haven, Connecticut: Yale University Press, 1971

Goldin, Judah and Reuven Hammer, *The Classic Midrash: Tannaitic Commentaries on the Bible* (Classics of Western Spirituality), New York: Paulist, 1995

Hammer, Reuven, *Sifre: A Tannaitic Commentary on the Book of Deuteronomy* (Yale Judaica Series, vol. 24), New Haven and London: Yale University 1986.

Herr, Moshe David, "Midreshei Halakhah," in *Encyclopaedia Judaica*, Jerusalem: Keter, 1971

Horovitz, Saul, "Midrash-Halakah," in *The Jewish Encyclopedia: A Descriptive Record of the History, Religion, Literature, and Customs of the Jewish People from the Earliest Times to the Present Day*, New York and London: Funk and Wagnalls, 1901

Lauterbach, Jacob, *Mekilta de-Rabbi Ishmael* (Schiff Library of Jewish Classics), 3 vols., Philadelphia: Jewish Publication Society, 1933-35.

Neusner, Jacob, *Sifre to Deuteronomy: An Analytical Translation* (Brown Judaic Studies, nos. 98 and 101), 2 vols., Atlanta, Georgia: Scholars Press, 1987

Neusner, Jacob, *Sifre to Deuteronomy: An Introduction to the Rhetorical, Logical, and Topical Program* (Brown Judaic Studies, no. 124), Atlanta, Georgia: Scholars Press, 1987

Neusner, Jacob, *Mekhilta According to Rabbi Ishmael: An Analytical Translation* (Brown Judaic Studies, no. 148), Atlanta, Georgia: Scholars Press, 1988

Neusner, Jacob, *Sifra in Perspective: The Documentary Comparison of the Midrashim of Ancient Judaism* (Brown Judaic Studies, no. 146), Atlanta, Georgia: Scholars Press, 1988

Neusner, Jacob, *The Canonical History of Ideas: The Place of the So-Called Tannaite Midrashim: Mekhilta*

Attributed to R. Ishmael, Sifra, Sifre to Numbers, and Sifre to Deuteronomy (South Florida Studies in the History of Judaism, no. 4), Atlanta, Georgia: Scholars Press, 1990

Neusner, Jacob, *The Components of the Rabbinic Documents: From the Whole to the Parts,* (South Florida Academic Commentary Series, nos. 75–84, 89, 94–98, 100–106), 12 vols. in 23 pts., Atlanta, Georgia: Scholars Press, 1997–1998

Strack, Hermann Leberecht and Günter Stemberger, *Einleitung in Talmud und Midrasch,* 1982; translated by Markus Bockmuehl as *Introduction to the Talmud and Midrash,* Edinburgh: Clark, 1991, 2nd edition, 1996

Midrash halakhah denotes the corpus of interpretation by the rabbis of the first two centuries of the Common Era, aimed for the most part at extrapolating law from the biblical books of Exodus, Leviticus, Numbers, and Deuteronomy. Since Genesis and Exodus 1–11 do not teach many laws, there is no legal midrash to them. The date of the compilation of these exegetical compendia remains guesswork for the most part, but it may be safely assumed that the traditions themselves are no later than the third century C.E. These midrashim are sometimes denoted by the name "tannaitic midrashim" since the authorities to whom these interpretations are attributed are exclusively the tannaim of first through early-third-century Palestine. There are very few works in English that introduce the contents and composition of tannaitic midrash.

These works are referred to as "Mekhilta according to Rabbi Ishmael," "Mekhilta according to Rabbi Simeon bar Yohai" (both on Exodus), "Sifra" or "Torat Kohanim" (on Leviticus), "Sifrei Debei Rav" (on Numbers and Deuteronomy); there is also a work that survives in fragments known as "Mekhilta on Deuteronomy." To this list one might add "Sifrei Zuta" on the Book of Numbers, although the bulk of the text is evidently lacking and the date of this work is still largely a matter of conjecture. In STRACK and STEMBERGER, the classic old introduction to the full range of rabbinic literature by Strack, who provided succinct characterizations of the halakhic midrashim along with a thorough bibliography, has been invaluably updated by Stemberger, whose judicious summaries and assiduous bibliographic intelligence brings the scholarship up to date as far as 1995.

The most comprehensive studies in English come from the pen of Jacob Neusner, who provides a mass of translations and analysis of the materials in his many works. NEUSNER (1997–1998) provides methodological studies in the rhetoric and topics of each of the halakhic midrashim. Besides translating the major midrashim, he has written extensive introductions to these works in separate monographs: NEUSNER (1987a, 1987b, 1988a, 1988b, 1990). In all these cases, he isolates particular forms used in the various midrashim and correlates these forms to specific messages that he sees embedded in these works, one predominant form and message per work. For example, Sifrei Deuteronomy has a separate authorship from the other works. Likewise Sifrei Numbers and Sifra are separate works addressing unique problems each in their own way. Neusner compiles impressive arrays of statistics correlating form and message. He concludes that apart from the Mekhilta according to Rabbi Ishmael, each midrash aims to present a coherent and cohesive approach to a specific issue.

Neusner's approach, although industrious and probing, has not been well received by scholars of halakhic midrashim. Neusner delineates separate literary forms and decides that the form most used in a compilation is the form uniquely suited to that authorship for his message. Virtually every midrash scholar in the 20th century, as discussed by HOROVITZ and by HERR, has accounted for the same observations in a much simpler way. Legal materials in the halakhic midrashim are considered as mainly the product of the hermeneutic rules of one school, while narrative midrashim are usually the product of those of another school. These scholars do not doubt that the style and structure of the biblical verses being commented upon determine the form and preoccupation of the commentary in the midrashim as a whole. They do not study individual authorships of any midrashic compendium but attempt to account for the features of the literature as a whole. For them, midrash responds to the biblical texts in light of some particular wording in the Bible and in light of its genre (legal or narrative). The midrashim themselves have no message beyond elucidating the subjects of the biblical text in accordance with specific school traditions. Neusner's method forces him to articulate imprecise categories and then to fit every compilation into a straitjacket such as "God loves Israel" or "Scripture defeats logic." These are much too vague to work as fine classifications. In the end his proliferation of messages is not as useful as the more elegant division into two schools. Neusner had hoped to establish a paradigm shift but so far there has not been much affirmation from the scholarly world.

Other works incorporate introductions to halakhic midrashim incidental to their aim of explaining midrash aggadah (the ethical rather than legal exposition of Scripture). Among the better treatments are the translations and commentaries of select sections of midrash with incisive, subtle, and informed introductions offered by GOLDIN and by GOLDIN and HAMMER. Among the weaker offerings one might note the overpraised studies by FRAADE and by BOYARIN. These works, while popular in academic circles, fail to provide a lucid approach to the materials. Instead they offer an array of flashy interpretations that resonate in a convoluted way with current literary fads while making no attempt to address the real concerns of the rabbis and ignoring the transmitters of the texts throughout the ages. These traditional approaches to the meaning of the text are, however, entertained in the introductions to the translations by HAMMER and by LAUTERBACH as well as by Neusner.

REENA ZEIDMAN

See also Midrash Halakhah: Translations

Mikveh

Kaplan, Aryeh, *Waters of Eden: An Exploration of the Concept of Mikvah: Renewal and Rebirth,* New York: National Conference of Synagogue Youth of the Union of

Orthodox Jewish Congregations of America, 1976, 2nd edition, 1982

Neusner, Jacob, *A History of the Mishnaic Law of Purities* (Studies in Judaism in Late Antiquity), vols. 13–14, Leiden: Brill, 1976; as *The Judaic Law of Baptism: Tractate Miqvaot in the Mishnah and the Tosefta: A Form-Analytical Translation and Commentary and a Legal and Religious History* (South Florida Studies in the History of Judaism, no. 112), Atlanta, Georgia: Scholars Press, 1995

Slonim, Rivkah and Liz Rosenberg (editors), *Total Immersion: A Mikvah Anthology*, Northvale, New Jersey: Aronson, 1996

A *mikveh* (Hebrew: gathering) is a pool of water used for ritual immersion. NEUSNER's two volumes on the development of the rabbinic laws of the mikveh contain translations of the relevant passages in their historical context and his perceptive commentaries. At first glance, the mishnaic laws primarily supplement the biblical laws of purification by providing additional details, but Neusner underscores the extent to which the mishnaic laws express the innovations of the rabbis. This study is the foremost scholarly treatment of the subject of mikveh; Neusner translates and analyzes complex passages from the Mishnah, Tosefta, Maimonides, and other rabbinic texts concerning the construction of a mikveh, the water supply, and the immersion of people and utensils in the purifying waters.

KAPLAN's study of the mikveh includes an exploration of its biblical roots. The author observes that the first step in the consecration of Aaron and his sons as priests involved immersion in a mikveh. This immersion was not, however, for purification purposes; rather, the purpose was to effect a change in status (Ex. 29:4). Kaplan also explains that in the Mishnah's account of the Temple, the mikveh played an important role on the Day of Atonement, for on that day, the high priest immersed himself in a mikveh each time he changed his vestments. The high priest was not considered impure nor unclean; he used the mikveh to change his status. In a similar manner, the mikveh may change the spiritual status of other individuals; most dramatically, when a non-Jew converts to Judaism, the mikveh marks his or her transformation. Kaplan summarizes the rules of the mikveh and gives some mystical explanations underlying its function. For example, a mikveh is comparable to a womb and enables one to have a "spiritual rebirth," although the ultimate source of purification is God, not the ritual.

The volume by SLONIM and ROSENBERG on ritual immersion in a mikveh consists of 47 essays by different authors. The book is divided into three parts: "In Theory and Practice," "Voices," and "Memories and Tales." Slonim's introduction explains in simple language the purpose of a mikveh from a contemporary Orthodox perspective, emphasizing that, although observant Jews typically use an artificial construction as their mikveh, natural bodies of water are also mikvehs and have the power to purify. Slonim also discusses the regulations for constructing, maintaining, and using a mikveh.

The book includes a discussion of "family purity," personal accounts of mikveh experiences, practical guidelines, and a list of addresses of mikvehs.

RIVKA B. KERN ULMER

Miracles

Borodowski, Alfredo F., "Isaac Abravanel on Miracles: The Tension between Biblical Exegesis and Philosophy," Ph.D. diss., Jewish Theological Seminary, 1997

Eisen, Robert, *Gersonides on Providence, Covenant, and the Chosen People: A Study in Medieval Jewish Philosophy and Biblical Commentary* (SUNY Series in Jewish Philosophy), Albany: State University of New York Press, 1995

Heller, Joseph, "Maimonides' Theory of Miracle," in *Between East and West: Essays Dedicated to the Memory of Bela Horovitz*, edited by Alexander Altmann, London: East and West Library, 1958

Kellner, Menachem, "Gersonides and His Cultured Despisers: Arama and Abravanel," *Journal of Medieval and Renaissance Studies*, 6, 1976

Kellner, Menachem, "Gersonides on Miracles, the Messiah and Resurrection," *Da'at*, Winter 1980

Kellner, Menachem, "Gersonides on the Problem of Volitional Creation," *HUCA*, 1980

Ravitzky, Aviezer, "The Anthropological Theory of Miracles in Medieval Jewish Philosophy," in *Studies in Medieval Jewish History and Literature*, vol. 2, edited by Isadore Twersky, Cambridge, Massachusetts: Harvard University Press, 1984

Reines, Alvin J., *Maimonides' Concept of Miracles*, Cincinnati, Ohio: Hebrew Union College Press–Jewish Institute of Religion, 1975

Schweid, Eliezer, "The Belief in Miracles as an Article of Faith," in his *Feeling and Speculation*, Ramat Gan: Masadah, 1970

Urbach, Efraim E., *Hazal, pirke emunot ve-de'ot*, 1969; translated by Israel Abrahams as *The Sages: Their Concepts and Beliefs*, 2 vols., Jerusalem: Magnes Press of Hebrew University, 1975; Cambridge, Massachusetts: Harvard University Press, 1987

The rabbinic dictum, "Do not rely on a miracle" (*Pesahim* 64b) seems to have resonated with subsequent Jewish scholars, none of whom has produced a comprehensive study of miracles in Judaism. Even Maimonides and Gersonides, who dealt with topics such as prophecy and providence, omitted a systematic treatment of miracles. The few articles on this subject limit themselves to general surveys or particular ideas of individual thinkers, mostly from the medieval period. Consequently, those in search of a full and systematic treatment of the supernatural will have to piece together scattered fragments on this subject.

URBACH's classic work on the thought of the rabbis includes a chapter titled "Magic and Miracles." There he delves into a wide range of topics and their relationships to miracles. These include miracles as proof of prophecy, as promoters of faith, as ethical vehicles, as a confirmation of the truth of Israel's election and of the Torah, as deliverers of individuals and communities, and as manifestations of the doctrine of reward and punishment. Urbach also addresses the correlation of miracles and magic and of miracles and Jewish Law. He concludes that the problem of the relationship between the laws of nature and miracles did not preoccupy the sages. The change in the order of the universe was not usually considered to be a miracle; on the contrary, this order itself was viewed as the greatest of miracles and as a testimony to God's power. The fulfillment of commandments and acts of kindness were understood as being central in a way that reliance upon the supernatural was not. Urbach attests that this approach toward miracles was one of the divisive points between Jews and early Christians, who preferred to emphasize the supernatural. In his usual style, Urbach includes a vast number of rabbinic sources that may assist future research.

SCHWEID analyzes the positions of particular medieval thinkers, most of whom maintained that belief in miracles is a principle of the Jewish faith and who inherited the biblical view of a Creator who intervenes directly in the world's affairs. These thinkers were confronted both by the philosophical doctrine of the eternity of the universe and by its corollary: the contention that natural laws are inviolable. Schweid begins with Saadia Gaon and his rejection by Neoplatonists such as Bahya ibn Pakudah, Solomon ibn Gabirol, and Abraham ibn Ezra. He proceeds to an analysis of Judah Halevi, Maimonides, Shem Tov ibn Falaquera, Isaac Albalag, and Hasdai Crescas, among others. The main contribution of this study is that it frames each thinker within broad philosophical trends. Thus, for instance, Crescas's theory is not studied in isolation or as a reaction to his Jewish predecessors but primarily as a rejection of Aristotelian philosophy. In other words, although Schweid explores the development of perspectives of the supernatural among Jewish thinkers, he emphasizes their connection to general philosophy. This approach imbues the reader with an understanding of the main philosophical problems confronted by these thinkers and places each doctrine within the context of philosophical discussion of the supernatural.

RAVITZKY's article is dedicated to the study of what he calls the "anthropological school of miracles." This school, which maintains that miracles are a phenomenon of nature produced by a special human being, was ignored by Maimonides and Halevi and rejected by Gersonides and Crescas. However, it was adopted by many other significant thinkers such as Abraham ibn Daud, Abraham ibn Ezra, Joseph Kaspi, Abraham Abulafia, Isaac ibn Latif, and Jacob Anatoli. Ravitzky succeeds not only in illustrating its development and systematizing the different positions, but also in tracing their roots to Islamic philosophy, mainly to Avicenna, with whom it originated. Moreover, he analyzes the critique of this position, which began in the 14th century with Kalonymus ben Kalonymus, Simeon ben Tsemah Duran, and Abra-

ham Bibago among Jewish thinkers, and Aquinas and Nicole Oresme among Christian scholastics. The final section of the study concentrates on this viewpoint's resurrection under different premises in the 15th century by Zerahiah Halevi, Mattathias Hayishari, and Joseph Albo. More than being just an excellent overview of the anthropological school, this study serves as a good general introduction to the problem of the supernatural. Its rich footnotes will be invaluable to those who want to research the subject further.

HELLER's article serves as a basic and succinct introduction to Maimonides' view of miracles. In just over 15 pages, the piece analyzes the incongruities between Maimonides' views in his *Commentary to the Mishnah* and in the *Guide of the Perplexed*, discusses miracles and creation, Shekhinah (divine immanence), prophecy, providence, and the nature and meaning of divine attributes, and culminates with the influence of Maimonides' theory. Although those who expect an in-depth analysis may find it superficial, those who possess some philosophical background and wish to avoid an intricate discussion about the notoriously elusive Maimonides will be rewarded with a concise view of what are regarded as his key positions.

REINES's article offers a thorough analysis of Maimonides' view of miracles. Subscribing to the school that distinguishes between an exoteric and esoteric understanding of Maimonides, Reines provides two opposite interpretations of Maimonides' position: the "apparent" and the "modified" conception of miracles. According to the first, intended for the masses who understand Scripture literally, miracles are events produced by a special will of God, who suspends the laws of causation. The "modified" or philosophical position, on the other hand, affirms that, although a rare occurrence, miracles were programmed into the essence of things to occur in the future as any other natural phenomena. Reines, who endorses the "modified" theory, offers a fair analysis of both.

Three articles by Menachem Kellner provide an overview of Gersonides' conception of the supernatural. For instance, KELLNER (1980a) underlines one of the basic principles of Gersonides' theory of the supernatural: the greatness of a prophet is proportional to the greatness of his miracles. Similarly, KELLNER (1980b) explores Gersonides' ideas concerning whether and how a timeless and immutable being can intervene in ever-changing history. KELLNER (1976) offers the author's most complete and systematic treatment of the supernatural. This article, which revolves around the interpretation of Joshua 10:13—a verse that became one of the foci in the medieval discussion of miracles—serves as a case study that explores and contrasts most of Gersonides', Arama's, and Abravanel's views of the supernatural.

EISEN's book represents the first in-depth study of the correlation between Gersonides' exegetical and philosophical corpora. While exploring the topic of particular providence, the main expression of which is found in miracles, Eisen offers a detailed account of how numerous biblical miracles, especially those that occurred during the exodus from Egypt, are interpreted in Gersonides' biblical commentary and in his *Wars of the Lord*. He concludes that, contrary to common belief, which based upon his philosophical writings ascribes to this philosopher a rejection of individual providence, his exegesis recognizes a variation called "inherited providence" bestowed upon the Israelites in Egypt in virtue of Abraham's merits. Eisen concludes that the exegetical and philosophical writings complement each other and must be correlated in order to obtain a full understanding of Gersonides' views. This study will not only provide a systematic interpretation of Gersonides' view of the supernatural but will serve as a matrix for those who want to investigate the connection between exegesis and philosophy.

BORODOWSKI's dissertation entails a comprehensive study of the nature of the relationship between Abravanel's philosophical corpora and his vast exegetical writings. Focusing on the topic of miracles, this work explores how Abravanel's philosophical treatise, *Mifa'lot Elohim* (a book that concentrates on the greatest of miracles, Creation, and includes a chapter on the theory of the supernatural), correlates with his interpretation of the biblical counterparts. Abravanel's methodology is characterized by prefacing each discussion with an extensive list of questions on the biblical text as well as a summary and critique of his predecessors. This approach is echoed in Borodowski's work, which, prior to analyzing Abravanel's theory, offers a general discussion of the main issues relating to the topic of miracles as well as an assessment of Maimonides' and Gersonides' and other philosophers' views through the prism of Abravanel's critique. Thus, more than a study of Abravanel, this work serves as an introduction to the study of the supernatural as well as a systematic overview of miracles in medieval Jewish philosophy. Special emphasis is placed on how the different philosophical positions influenced the interpretation of rabbinic sources on miracles. Arranged thematically, the dissertation contains, among others, the following chapters: "The Concept of Miracle: The Possible and the Impossible," "Miracles and the Possibility of *Ex-Nihilo* Creation," "Miracles and Free Will," "Agency and Purpose of Miracles," and "Prophecy and Miracles."

ALFREDO FABIO BORODOWSKI

Mitnaggedim *see* Haredim

Modena, Leone   1571–1648

Italian rabbinical scholar, controversialist, writer, and promoter of Jewish music

Adelman, Howard Ernest, "New Light on the Life and Writings of Leon Modena," in *Approaches to Judaism in Medieval Times*, vol. 2 (Brown Judaic Studies, no. 57), edited by David R. Blumenthal, Chico, California: Scholars Press, 1985
Cohen, Mark R., "Leone da Modena's *Riti*: A Seventeenth Century Plea for Toleration of Jews," *Jewish Social Studies*, 34(4), 1972
Cohen, Mark R. (editor and translator), *The Autobiography of a Seventeenth-Century Venetian Rabbi: Leon Modena's* Life of Judah, Princeton, New Jersey: Princeton University Press, 1988
Fishman, Talya, *Shaking the Pillars of Exile: "Voice of a Fool," an Early Modern Jewish Critique of Rabbinic Culture* (Stanford Studies in Jewish History and Culture), Stanford, California: Stanford University Press, 1997
Ravid, Benjamin, "The Prohibition against Jewish Printing and Publishing in Venice and the Difficulties of Leone Modena," in *Studies in Medieval Jewish History and Literature* (Harvard Judaic Monographs, no. 2), edited by Isadore Twersky, Cambridge, Massachusetts, and London: Harvard University Press, 1979
Rivkin, Ellis, *Leon da Modena and the Kol Sakhal*, Philadelphia: Dropsie College, 1948

Leone Modena (also known as Leon[e] da Modena and Leon[e] Modena da Venezia), the best-known Venetian rabbi of the 17th century, was a preacher, teacher, writer, poet, legal functionary, printer, and much else. His legacy, however, remains mysterious. His writings define not only his personal views but the entire Italian Jewish culture of his time. The literature published in English on Modena examines some of these writings and their publication history and presents a debate over his authorship of the controversial text *Kol Sakhal*, a harsh critique of the rabbinic Judaism of which Modena himself was a leading exponent.

RIVKIN's brief text argues that Modena, a protagonist of rabbinic Judaism, could not have authored *Kol Sakhal*. He discusses the rise of heresy in the 17th century as well as the strong position of the Jewish community of Venice, arguing that Venetian Jews were in a unique position to crush the heresy arising in other European cities. Rivkin's complimentary portrait of Modena sees him as a champion of enlightened Rabbinism and of the superiority of the Jewish religion and Hebrew language. Rivkin uses stylistic and thematic evidence to argue that Modena could not have been the author of such a "vitriolic attack against Rabbinical Judaism." Rivkin takes issue with the greatest of 19th-century authorities who link *Kol Sakhal* with Modena's name, blasting Isaaco Reggio's study as "worthless" and "invalid," criticizing the "baselessness" and "irresponsible method" of Abraham Geiger's work, and citing the inconclusive arguments of scholars subsequent to Reggio and Geiger on both sides of the debate.

FISHMAN's recent and more lengthy study argues that Modena was indeed the author of *Kol Sakhal*. She refutes proposals by previous scholars and concludes that Modena composed the text under a pseudonym, a common practice in the age in which he wrote. She examines the text in light of the political, religious, and cultural contexts of the time, discusses the treatise's revisionist view of Jewish law, and reflects on the text's significance within the history of Jewish thought. Fishman also analyzes the work within the context of Venice's struggle with Rome and the Papacy. Although she cannot find concrete reasons as to why Modena would have written the text, Fishman argues, using philological evidence, that Modena is unequivocally the text's author. Certainly she detects stylistic patterns and wording not found before Modena's time to tie its creation to his lifetime and to Venice. Her bibliography is lengthy and very helpful.

ADELMAN's brief study separates the legend of Modena from the historical counterpart, focusing its argument on the authorship of *Kol Sakhal*. Adelman interestingly discusses the reasons for the creation of this legend and how it has prevented scholars from truly understanding Modena. As examples, he discusses the theories of four scholars—Reggio, Samuele Davide Luzzatto, Geiger, and Heinrich Graetz—who, in contradictory ways, all tried to prove Modena was the author of *Kol Sakhal*. He then profiles the reality of Modena's situation, claiming Modena devoted his life to serving the Jews of his generation by enriching Jewish literature and defending the principles of rabbinic Judaism from threats from all sides. Adelman separates legend from history regarding Modena to demonstrate his true "unhappy but productive life," stressing the importance of Modena's autobiography for understanding his actual, historic self and his link to *Kol Sakhal*.

That autobiography is presented by COHEN (1988) in an accessible manner for the first time in English. This *Life of Judah*, found in manuscript in the Biblioteca Ambrosiana in Milan, first came to the attention of scholars in the 19th century. It is invaluable for understanding the unhappiness Modena endured, the gambling he used as an escape from his life, and the hard work and despair he suffered during the 31 years over which he wrote this memoir. Cohen and his colleagues, Theodore Rabb, Adelman, and Natalie Davis, present a sympathetic view of this character through their introductory essays. Cohen and Rabb use the autobiography as a means of viewing "northern Italian Jewish life in general from the sixteenth and seventeenth centuries"; Adelman argues that the autobiography gives a fascinating yet partial glimpse of the life of this exceedingly active and complex man; and Davis proposes viewing the autobiography in the context of other early modern European autobiographies to see how those of Jews differ from those of Christians. The text brings to life much of the scholarly debate over Modena.

In a brief study, COHEN (1972) discusses Modena's *Historia de' riti hebraici* in a new light, as an apologetic text to highlight Jews' virtues and refute Johannes Buxtorf's 1603 negative portrayal of Jews in his *Synagoga Judaica*. Cohen convincingly sees Modena's text as a reaction to 16th-century Europe's negative portrayal of Jews as mystics. Cohen concludes that the rhetoric of the text is not unlike that of the 18th- and 19th-century Jewish emancipation literature and claims the *Riti* was an attempt at advancing social integration in repressive, Counter-Reformation Venice. He calls for investigation of the scholars who read Modena, such as Selden, Basnage, Calmet, and Grégoire, to examine the *Riti*'s effect on Christian attitudes toward Jews.

RAVID's article revisits the Venetian prohibition of Jewish involvement in printing. His intriguing study uses documents from the Venetian State Archives to establish the date of the original prohibition as 1548, not 1571 as long assumed. He also shows that the prohibition may not have been aimed at Jews directly, but rather was designed to prevent importation and printing of Protestant books within Venice's Counter-Reformation culture. However, Ravid also

cites three Jews active in printing whose success may have aroused the resentment of Christian competitors. He discusses the creation of a printers' guild to ensure Catholic dominance of the field, a guild from which Jews were banned. Ravid cites a passage from Modena's autobiography regarding his grandson's imprisonment in 1634 for printing as the impetus for Jews having sought a modification of the prohibition against them. He establishes that, while legislation technically prevented their involvement in printing, Jews actually continued their printing activity until the end of the Venetian Republic.

HILARY LIEBERMAN

Modern Orthodox Judaism

Bernstein, Louis, *Challenge and Mission: The Emergence of the English Speaking Orthodox Rabbinate*, New York: Shengold, 1982

Bulka, Reuven P. (editor), *Dimensions of Orthodox Judaism*, New York: Ktav, 1983

Heilman, Samuel C., *Synagogue Life: A Study in Symbolic Interaction*, Chicago: University of Chicago Press, 1976

Heilman, Samuel C. and Steven M. Cohen, *Cosmopolitans and Parochials: Modern Orthodox Jews in America*, Chicago: University of Chicago Press, 1989

Joselit, Jenna Weissman, *New York's Jewish Jews: The Orthodox Community in the Interwar Years* (Modern Jewish Experience), Bloomington: Indiana University Press, 1990

Sacks, Jonathan (editor), *Orthodoxy Confronts Modernity*, Hoboken, New Jersey: Ktav in association with Jews' College, London, 1991

"The Sea Change in American Orthodox Judaism: A Symposium," *Tradition*, 32(4), Summer 1998

Soloveitchik, Haym, "Rupture and Reconstruction: The Transformation of Contemporary Orthodoxy," *Tradition*, 28(4), Summer 1994

Wurzburger, Walter S. (editor), "Symposium: The State of Orthodoxy," *Tradition*, 20(1), Spring 1982

Modern Orthodox Judaism designates the faith of those individuals and institutions that affirm traditional Jewish beliefs, such as the divine revelation of the Torah; observe Jewish ritual laws; have a positive attitude toward secular education and engage in various professions such as law and medicine; and emphasize the matters that they have in common with all other Jews rather than those that separate them from all other Jews. While Modern Orthodoxy is a 20th-century religious movement, its antecedents go back to Samson Raphael Hirsch's 19th-century attempt to synthesize Jewish tradition and modern culture, as articulated in his slogan, "Torah with the way of the land."

BULKA collects a series of essays on Orthodox Judaism. Of particular interest is Charles Liebman's contribution, "Orthodoxy in American Jewish Life," which first appeared in the *American Jewish Year Book* of 1965. Liebman's considered judgment is that the only remaining bastion of Jewish passion resides in the Orthodox community. This landmark piece brought the demographic, communal, and institutional aspects of Orthodox Judaism to the fore. The essay contains a large section on Modern Orthodoxy that discusses the organization and ideology of this movement. Although its statistics are hopelessly out of date, this seminal essay still bears careful study. In "The Ambiguous Modern Orthodox Jew," Lawrence Kaplan focuses on the issue of how the Modern Orthodox Jew relates, or does not relate, the component elements of his identity, modernity and Orthodoxy, to one another. He asks whether the word *modern* in the appellation *Modern Orthodox Jew* modifies the adjective *Orthodox* or the noun *Jew*. His essay examines the profound ideological and religious implications of fusing together various dimensions. The dean of the right-wing Telshe Yeshiva in Chicago offers a detailed point-by-point analysis of the divergent viewpoints of Modern Orthodoxy and the Torah True Judaism he represents. At the beginning of his essay, he quotes the remark of his sainted rebbe: "We no longer have to fear Conservatism—that is no longer the danger. Everyone knows that it is *avodah zarah* [idolatry]. What we have to fear is Modern Orthodoxy." The author of this essay, Chaim Dov Keller, is a graduate of Yeshiva University, an institution prominently identified with Modern Orthodoxy. In general, critics on the right censure the typical Jew who populates many Modern Orthodox synagogues as a poker-playing, disco-dancing, synagogue-schmoozing, marginal Orthodox Jew who rarely, if ever, opens up a gemara. He is lax in observance: he will eat hot dairy food in a nonkosher restaurant when with a business client, and his wife is not likely to use a mikveh.

BERNSTEIN describes the struggles of the nascent Modern Orthodox rabbinate to establish itself. With the passage of time, its rabbinic organization, the Rabbinical Council of America, became the largest rabbinic body in the world. When it was first organized in 1935, however, a spokesman for the more traditional Union of Orthodox Rabbis (Agudat Harabbonim) declared that only members of that organization were true rabbis, while all others were deceiving the public. The traditional rabbis particularly resented the council's involvement in kashrut, an area that it considered its own preserve. The prestige of the Rabbinical Council was greatly enhanced in the mid-1950s when Rabbi Joseph Soloveitchik became chairman of its Halakha Commission. The Rabbinical Council is a strong supporter of the Jewish state and, unlike rabbinic organizations to the left or right, is a staunch ally of the Chief Rabbinate of Israel. In the matter of cooperation with the non-Orthodox, the position of the council (on the advice of Rabbi Soloveitchik) is as follows: when representation of Jews and Jewish interests vis-à-vis the non-Jewish world are involved it fully cooperates with other groups and presents a united front, but in matters concerning Jewish law, synagogues, and education, it does not join groups that deny the foundations of its viewpoint.

HEILMAN and HEILMAN and COHEN usefully supplement each other. Heilman's 1976 ethnographic study describes from the perspective of a participant-observer the inner life of a Modern Orthodox synagogue in metropolitan "Sprawl City," a large Northeastern municipality. Heilman calls this synagogue Kehillat Kodesh, "holy community," and enhances his book with lively anecdotes gathered from several years of involvement in the activities of the congregation. An interesting feature of Heilman's work is his analysis of gossip. Conversation, gossip, and joking, which are often overlooked as a characteristic of informal social life, are viewed here not as idle talk but as an activity with many social functions. Gossip acts as an upholder of traditional standards, since it is a reflection of public opinion, community sentiments, beliefs, and values. Heilman and Cohen's work analyzes the behavior and attitudes of Modern Orthodox Jews in a survey based largely on members of New York City's Lincoln Square Synagogue. The Modern Orthodox are engaged in a delicate balancing act between segregation and integration, caught between the conflicting demands of Jewish parochialism and secular cosmopolitanism. The authors conclude that while triumphalism is hardly inherited, there is a future for Modern Orthodoxy in the United States. First, intensive Jewish education has become de rigueur in Orthodox circles. Second, the fact that most Orthodox young people will attend such schools will further network relations among them. Finally, it is likely that women will play an increased and influential role in Modern Orthodox Jewish life.

JOSELIT's fascinating book deals with modern "Americanizing Orthodox Jews" and concentrates on two rabbis and their affluent congregations in two upscale Manhattan neighborhoods: Joseph Lookstein of Kehillat Jeshurun and Leo Jung of the Jewish Center. She contends that the level of observance was far from high. For example, the Jewish family purity laws were widely disregarded and in effect fell into disuse.

SOLOVEITCHIK explores the recent changes in Modern Orthodoxy and its movement to the right. He traces this to a shift from a mimetic tradition of transmitting the ways of religious life—children absorbing patterns of conduct by observing adult and peer behavior at home and in the street, synagogue, and school—to a text-based culture, where a plethora of legal codes and guides to religious practice and observance dictate correct religious performance. The shift of authority to texts and their enshrinement as the sole source of authenticity has caused power to shift from the congregational or communal rabbi to acknowledged masters of talmudic law who are relatively insulated from the larger community and the day-to-day experience of most Orthodox Jews. Lacking the religious experience of God and the numinous in this secular age, Orthodox Jews seek to ground their spirituality in ritual observance of the minutiae of the halakhah. Soloveitchik poignantly concludes that Modern Orthodox Jews "having lost the touch of His presence . . . seek now solace in the pressure of His yoke."

Tradition magazine is a publication of the Rabbinical Council of America. In the early 1980s and again in the late 1990s, it devoted an entire issue to the condition of Modern Orthodoxy, inviting a number of its leading exponents to respond to some fundamental questions. In recent years Orthodoxy in general has become self-confident and buoyant as a result of its newfound strength and vitality. Yet the Modern Orthodox respondents to these symposia (WURZBERGER and "THE SEA CHANGE IN AMERICAN ORTHODOX JUDAISM") manifest many signs of a failure of nerve: a sense of inferiority vis-à-vis the right-wing Orthodox and a loss of self-confidence in their way of life, which is viewed as second-class Orthodoxy. The very legitimacy of Modern Orthodoxy is categorically denied in right-wing circles. One symposiast (David Singer) confesses that he is stranded with a handful of Orthodox intellectuals while the Orthodox community as a whole goes marching off in a traditionalist direction. As an undergraduate at Yeshiva University in the 1960s, Singer writes that the mood was euphoric. Modern Orthodoxy was about to sweep all before it. Twenty years later he looks back with bitterness and admits defeat: "We are pathetically few in number, lack a sound institutional base, and are largely without leadership." His final judgment is that "History has almost certainly passed us by." The Modern Orthodox rabbinate has been marginalized with the death of its mentor, Rabbi Joseph Soloveitchik, in 1993. As Heilman notes in the second symposium, the Modern Orthodox rabbi of the Rabbinical Council is viewed by the yeshivah world as a kind of red heifer, at best, purifying the "impure" moderns but contaminating the "purer" yeshivah people and, at worst, as part of the "other side," the devil's domain of which the kabbalists speak.

SACKS, the chief rabbi of the United Hebrew Congregations of the British Commonwealth, has gathered together ten essays, which had their genesis in the conference "Traditional Alternatives: Orthodoxy and the Jewish Future," convened by Jews' College, London, in May 1989. All the contributors, including the chief rabbi, are adherents of modern or centrist Orthodoxy. They include such leading exponents of Modern Orthodoxy as Norman Lamm, Charles Liebman, Shlomo Riskin, Reuven Bulka, and David Hartman. The essays deal with such themes as the future of Modern Orthodoxy, women's equality and Judaism, religion and politics in Israel, and the encounter of Orthodoxy with secular culture. Collectively, these essays show how avowed spokesmen of Modern Orthodoxy face and confront formidable spiritual challenges.

JACOB HABERMAN

Momigliano, Arnaldo 1908–1987

Italian-born British ancient historian

Berti, Silvia, "Introduction," in Arnaldo D. Momigliano's
    Essays on Ancient and Modern Judaism, Chicago:
    University of Chicago Press, 1994
Rivista Storica Italiana, 100(2), 1988
Steinberg, Michael P. (editor), *The Presence of the
    Historian: Essays in Memory of Arnaldo Momigliano*
    (History and Theory Beiheft, 30), Middletown,
    Connecticut: Wesleyan University, 1991

Arnaldo Momigliano was one of the most important ancient historians of the 20th century. Of Italian Jewish descent, Momigliano served as a professor at the universities of Rome and Turin, moving to England upon the promulgation of the racial laws in 1938. He took a post at University College, London, and remained there until his retirement. Momigliano

was a visiting professor at various universities in the United States and Italy. A recipient of 16 honorary degrees, Momigliano was a prolific writer who published works on many aspects of Greek and Roman history. He also developed a profound interest in the history of Judaism and early Christianity, even though he is best known for his insightful studies on ancient and modern historiography.

BERTI provides a short and easy-to-read biography that describes Momigliano's career as a scholar, his research interests, and his reaction to the writings of Jewish contemporaries such as Leo Strauss and Gershom Scholem. The other essays collected in Berti's volume illustrate Momigliano's characteristically straightforward way of dealing with the topics selected; these essays provide a good overview of and introduction to his contribution to Jewish studies, with special emphasis on his historiographic perspective.

The RIVISTA STORICA ITALIANA's special issue on Momigliano contains contributions (written in Italian) by Momigliano's friends and colleagues. The essays highlight different aspects of Momigliano's life and work including discussions of Momigliano's studies on ancient Rome, his interest in historiography, and his analysis of the writings of German historians. Additional essays explore Momigliano's relationship with British culture as well as his work on the history of Judaism. Written primarily for scholars, this collection provides a good introduction to Momigliano's thinking. The essays are especially useful for gaining a better understanding of Momigliano's interest in historiography.

STEINBERG's collection of scholarly essays, which includes translations of some of the *Rivista Storica Italiana* pieces, evaluates different aspects of Momigliano's contribution to the field of ancient history. The pieces address Momigliano's views on the history of historiography; his contribution to the study of the interaction between pagan, Jewish, and early Christian culture; his interest in biography; his relationship with the writings and thinking of Ernesto de Martino; and an appreciation of Momigliano's years in England.

LEONARD VICTOR RUTGERS

Montagu, Lily 1873–1963

British social worker and pioneer of Liberal Judaism

Conrad, Eric, *Lily H. Montagu: Prophet of a Living
    Judaism*, New York: National Federation of Temple
    Sisterhoods, 1953
Kuzmack, Linda Gordon, *Woman's Cause: The Jewish
    Woman's Movement in England and the United States,
    1881–1933*, Columbus: Ohio State University Press, 1990
Meyer, Michael A., *Response to Modernity: A History of
    the Reform Movement in Judaism* (Studies in Jewish
    History), New York: Oxford University Press, 1988
Montagu, Lilian H., "Spiritual Possibilities of Judaism
    Today," *Jewish Quarterly Review*, 11, January 1899
Montagu, Lilian H., *Thoughts on Judaism*, London:
    Johnson, 1904

Montagu, Lilian H., *The Faith of a Jewish Woman*, London: Allen and Unwin, 1943

Umansky, Ellen M., *Lily Montagu and the Advancement of Liberal Judaism: From Vision to Vocation* (Studies in Women and Religion, vol. 12), New York: Mellen, 1983

Umansky, Ellen M., "Liberal Judaism in England: The Contribution of Lily H. Montagu," *Hebrew Union College Annual*, vol. 55, Cincinnati, Ohio: Hebrew Union College-Jewish Institute of Religion, 1985

Umansky, Ellen M. (editor), *Lily Montagu: Sermons, Addresses, Letters, and Prayers* (Studies in Women and Religion, vol. 15), New York: Mellen, 1985

Lillian Helen Montagu was a British social worker, writer, suffragist, religious organizer, and spiritual leader who founded and long remained the driving force behind the Liberal Jewish movement in England, established in 1902. She later conceived of and, in 1926, helped create the World Union for Progressive Judaism, an organization intended to unite Liberal Jews and to promote the growth of Liberal Judaism as an international movement. From 1928 until her death in 1963, she also served as lay minister for London's West Central Liberal Jewish Congregation. To date, relatively little has been published on Montagu, perhaps because no book-length study has yet focused on either Liberal Judaism in England or the World Union. However, there are a number of works, including several by Montagu herself, that shed considerable light on her understanding of Judaism as personal religion, her communal activities and concerns, and her historical significance.

Montagu was not the first within the late 19th-century Anglo-Jewish community to identify herself as a Liberal Jew. She was, however, the first to issue a concrete "call to action." MONTAGU (1899) describes the depth of the spiritual degeneration of Anglo-Jewry and calls upon religiously committed Orthodox, Reform, and Liberal Jews to join an association aimed at reviving the community's religious life. Montagu advocates the establishment of weekly Liberal Jewish worship services and the publication of pamphlets through which the teachings of Liberal Judaism might be spread, and she proposes that membership in the association be open to all Jews sympathetic to the association's goals and to Montagu's belief in Liberal Judaism's ability to attract and reawaken the religiously disaffected. The interest generated by this essay later led Montagu to view its publication as the Liberal Jewish movement's true beginning.

MONTAGU's (1943) autobiography is a revealing account of her spiritual journey from the religious Orthodoxy of her father to a more personally meaningful sense of Jewish self-identity. Her chapters on the founding of the Jewish Religious Union (JRU), the organization out of which the Liberal Jewish movement in England emerged, and the World Union for Progressive Judaism are particularly valuable in detailing the specific roles that Montagu played in their creation, ideological goals, and organizational development.

MONTAGU (1904) is the author's first full discussion of her understanding of Judaism and the significance of religious faith. Montagu explicitly acknowledges her indebtedness to the writings and personal influence of Claude Montefiore, an early proponent of Liberal Judaism and president of the JRU, and she emphasizes the necessity of grounding theological ideas in one's own lived experiences. Montagu's personal struggle to assimilate religious concepts into her life illustrates the book's underlying theme that experience alone convinces people of God's existence.

CONRAD's short biography of Montagu was published in honor of her 80th birthday. It is a loving, intimate, and at times, reverential portrait of Montagu as social worker and religious leader, written by her nephew and designated literary executor. Although the book contains a few minor historical inaccuracies, Conrad's many personal details and small vignettes provide a rare view of Montagu's private life. Noteworthy too are the book's photographs and its foreword, written by Leo Baeck.

UMANSKY (1983) is, to date, the only book-length critical study of Montagu as religious organizer, leader, and thinker. Following an introduction that clarifies the book's historiographical assumptions and relationship to other studies of Anglo-Jewry, part one traces the historical, religious, and intellectual settings in which Montagu rose to prominence. Part two traces her family background, early achievements as an author and pioneer in the British club movement, and the spiritual awakening that led Montagu to devote her life to the Liberal Jewish cause. Including lengthy discussion of her role in the organization and development of Liberal Judaism, the book ends with an assessment of Montagu's historical significance. Umansky also shows ways in which a study of Montagu's life provides general insights into the religious possibilities and dilemmas faced by many modern Jewish women, as women and as Jews.

UMANSKY (1985a) delineates Montagu's contribution to Liberal Judaism in England. Without minimizing the important contributions of either Montefiore or Israel Mattuck, the movement's two other early leaders, the author carefully traces the origins of the Liberal Jewish movement, revealing Montagu's significance as its founder and the individual most responsible for its organizational growth. It also reveals the extent to which Montagu, along with Montefiore and Mattuck, helped provide the movement with its early spiritual vision.

UMANSKY (1985b) contains almost 50 of Montagu's previously unpublished writings, including those of greatest historical significance, such as the letter that directly led to the founding of the JRU, the first sermon that Montagu delivered at the Liberal Jewish Synagogue, and the sermon she delivered in 1928 at the first World Union conference in Berlin. The anthology also includes Montagu's personal letters to family members and colleagues, outlines of special religious services that she created, and prayers that she wrote and incorporated into communal worship.

KUZMACK's history of the Jewish women's movement in the United Kingdom and the United States during the late 19th and early 20th centuries offers substantial information on the Jewish League for Woman's Suffrage, founded in 1912, which sought to secure religious, communal, and secular voting rights for Jewish women in Britain. Included is a lengthy description of Montagu's activities as the League's vice president and spiritual advisor. Noteworthy too is Kuzmack's fine section on Jewish women's philanthropic and social groups, which provides insight into the importance of Montagu's work as leader of the West Central Girls' Club, England's "first multi-purpose Jewish girls' educational and social club and settlement house."

MEYER critically examines the Reform movement from its early-19th-century origins through the late 1980s. Impressive for both its breadth of material and its depth of analysis, the book details Montagu's central role in the creation and development of Liberal Judaism in England. It also mentions her work on behalf of the World Union for Progressive Judaism to establish Liberal congregations in Australia, New Zealand, Brazil, and South Africa. Meyer's discussion of Montagu is relatively brief, but it clearly establishes her significance within the history of Reform Judaism.

ELLEN M. UMANSKY

Morocco

Ben-Ami, Issachar, *Saint Veneration among the Jews in Morocco* (Raphael Patai Series in Jewish Folklore and Anthropology), Detroit, Michigan: Wayne State University Press, 1998

Brown, K.L., "Mellah and Madina: A Moroccan City and Its Jewish Quarter (Salé ca. 1880–1930)," in *Studies in Judaism and Islam,* edited by Shelomo Morag, Issachar Ben-Ami, and Norman A. Stillman, Jerusalem: Magnes Press of Hebrew University, 1981

Corcos, David, *Studies in the History of the Jews of Morocco,* Jerusalem: Mass, 1976

Deshen, Shlomo, *The Mellah Society: Jewish Community Life in Sherifian Morocco* (Chicago Studies in the History of Judaism), Chicago: University of Chicago Press, 1989

Gerber, Jane S., *Jewish Society in Fez 1450–1700: Studies in Communal and Economic Life* (Studies in Judaism in Modern Times, vol. 6), Leiden: Brill, 1980

Laskier, Michael M., *The Alliance Israélite Universelle and the Jewish Communities of Morocco, 1862–1962* (SUNY Series in Modern Jewish History), Albany: State University of New York Press, 1983

Romanelli, Samuel, *Masa ba-'Arav,* 1853; translated and edited by Yedida K. Stillman and Norman A. Stillman as *Travail in an Arab Land* (Judaic Studies Series), Tuscaloosa: University of Alabama Press, 1989

Schroeter, Daniel J., *Merchants of Essaouira: Urban Society and Imperialism in Southwestern Morocco, 1844–1886* (Cambridge Middle East Library), Cambridge and New York: Cambridge University Press, 1988

Serels, M. Mitchell, *A History of the Jews of Tangier in the Nineteenth and Twentieth Centuries,* New York: Sepher-Hermon, 1991

Stillman, Norman A., *The Language and Culture of the Jews of Sefrou, Morocco: An Ethnolinguistic Study* (Journal of Semitic Studies Monograph, no. 11), Manchester: University of Manchester Press, 1988

As home to a major indigenous Jewish population that absorbed a large number of exiles from medieval Spain, the once very substantial Jewish community of Morocco is still active despite large-scale emigration since 1948, mainly to Israel, France, and North America. Much research has been conducted on the community, mainly in Hebrew and French, as well as in English.

Saint veneration, a major characteristic of Moroccan society, is examined by BEN-AMI, who focuses on its Jewish aspects. The first part of the book is an analytical survey, starting with an examination of the genesis of a saint, families of saints, and saints from the land of Israel. He then examines the relations between saints and their disciples, saints as miracle workers, and the relations between saints and the world of nature. Ben-Ami describes visits of the faithful to the saints and the organizing work involved in this. Relations between Jews and Muslims with regard to saint veneration are examined, as is the development of saint veneration among Moroccan Jews in Israel. Here Ben-Ami considers old and new saints and sites. The second part of the book examines the tales and legends related to specific saints, including women saints. Combining analysis, description, and data, this is the major work on the subject.

BROWN examines how French colonialism influenced cultural, social, economic, and political developments among the Jews and Muslims of Salé. Following a description of the Jewish quarter (mellah) in Salé and the character of this port town, Brown considers how Westernization influenced Jewish life and relations with the Muslims. The impact of the West is seen to have spurred Zionism among the Jews and Moroccan nationalism among the Muslims, gradually pulling both groups in different directions.

CORCOS is a posthumous collection of the gentleman-scholar's engaging and informative journal articles on Moroccan Jewry that include three historical surveys of successive periods of the Middle Ages and studies of local given and family names. Note, however, that whereas three of the articles are in Hebrew and three in French, only his valuable study of the Marinide era (13th to 15th centuries) appears in English.

DESHEN surveys life within the urban Moroccan Jewish quarter (mellah) during the 18th and 19th centuries, based on writings of indigenous Jews, including correspondence, rabbinic responsa, and communal archives. Deshen deals with Jewish-Muslim relations, economic life, relations between individuals in the community and its leaders, internal taxation and charity, scholars, synagogues, and family life. Deshen's study contributes much to the understanding of Jewish life in Morocco in precolonial times and is of importance for students of both Jewish and Moroccan history and society.

GERBER's study on the Jews of Fez focuses on the organization and economic life of the community from 1450 to 1700. Following a discussion of the political context and the history of the community, Gerber examines the organization of the community, its structure, functionaries, economic life, and taxation. Special attention is paid to the impact on the community of Fez of the arrival of the Sephardim. The study is based primarily on Jewish sources as well as Arabic and European documents. Focusing on just one community over a period of two and a half centuries enables Gerber to paint a very vivid picture.

LASKIER examines the implications of the activities of the Alliance Israélite Universelle (AIU) in Morocco during the 100 years since it started operating there. He begins by describing the Jewish community of Morocco before the AIU became involved and the background to the establishment of the AIU in 1860 by French Jews. Laskier then discusses the educational operations of the AIU in Morocco, its relations with the French protectorate authorities between 1912 and 1956, and how its attitude changed as a result of World War II and the establishment of the State of Israel. The examination covers educational, cultural, social, economic, and political issues, including Jewish-Muslim relations, and uses much archival material, especially from the archives of the AIU itself.

Mantua-born ROMANELLI was a man of the Enlightenment and the age of revolution who was in Morocco from 1786 to 1790. His book, originally written in Hebrew, focuses on the Jews of Morocco and was intended for Jewish readers. It combines his personal tribulations with a vivid and detailed description of Moroccan Jewry, highlighting numerous details of daily life and customs. He taught himself the Jewish vernacular and was able to provide information unknown to outsiders. His skill as a storyteller coupled with the information he provided made his book a very popular and important source on the community at the end of the 18th century. The translators' notes and bibliography enhance the value of the book still further.

While examining the society of Essaouira as a whole, SCHROETER's book is especially important for the study of Moroccan Jews because of their great numbers in Essaouira and their major role in its economic life, a result of their special status based on British protection. Using extensive and diverse sources, Schroeter provides a rich analysis of mercantile life in Essaouira and its place in international trade and the role of Jews in these fields.

The Jews of the international city of Tangier are the subject of SERELS's book. Following a short survey of the town's history and growth until the late 19th century, European attempts at its internationalization are examined against the background of political and economic developments. Most of the study deals with the 20th century and the implications of internationalization for the Jews. The organization of the community is examined, as are its economic, social, and cultural conditions. Serels based his book on archival sources, oral histories, and published accounts and includes biographical sketches of prominent members of the community. The book adds to the short list of monographs on specific urban Maghrebi Jewish centers.

STILLMAN's book is an ethnolinguistic study of the Judeo-Arabic vernacular of the Jews of Sefrou and is accompanied by transcribed texts and their annotated English translations. Following a historical, social, economic, and cultural survey of the community, Stillman proceeds to his examination of Sefriwi Judeo-Arabic. This is followed by stories about saints and scholars, folk beliefs, folk medicine, reminiscences of the past, and studies of local vernacular Scripture translations and poetic texts. This book is of great importance to linguists, folklorists, and historians.

RACHEL SIMON

Moses ben Maimon   1135 or 1138–1204?

Cordoba-born physician, philosopher, theologian, and rabbinic authority, died in Egypt

Altmann, Alexander, "Free Will and Predestination in Saadia, Bahya, and Maimonides," in his *Essays in Jewish Intellectual History*, Hanover, New Hampshire: University Press of New England, 1981

Fox, Marvin, *Interpreting Maimonides: Studies in Methodology, Metaphysics, and Moral Philosophy*, Philadelphia: Jewish Publication Society, 1989; London: University of Chicago Press, 1994

Goitein, Shelomo D., "Moses Maimonides, Man of Action: A Revision of the Master's Biography in Light of Geniza Documents," in *Hommage à Georges Vajda: Études d'histoire et de pensée juives*, edited by Gérard Nahon and Charles Touati, Louvain: Peeters, 1980

Guttmann, Julius, *Philosophies of Judaism: The History of Jewish Philosophy from Biblical Times to Franz Rosenzweig*, translated by David W. Silverman, New York: Holt, Rinehart and Winston, and London: Routledge, 1964

Haberman, Jacob, *Maimonides and Aquinas: A Contemporary Appraisal*, New York: Ktav, 1979

Hartman, David, *Maimonides: Torah and Philosophic Quest*, Philadelphia: Jewish Publication Society, 1976

Heschel, Abraham Joshua, *Maimonides*, 1935; translated by Joachim Neugroschel as *Maimonides: A Biography*, New York: Farrar, Straus, Giroux, 1981

Heschel, Abraham Joshua, "Hahe'emin ha-Rambam shezakhah linevu'ah?" in *Louis Ginzberg: Jubilee Volume on the Occasion of His Seventieth Birthday*, 2 vols., New York: American Academy for Jewish Research, 1945; translated by David Wolf Silverman as "Did Maimonides Believe That He Had Attained the Rank of Prophet?" in Heschel's *Prophetic Inspiration after the Prophets: Maimonides and Other Medieval Authorities*, Hoboken, New Jersey: Ktav, 1996

Husik, Isaac, *A History of Medieval Jewish Philosophy*, New York: Macmillan, 1916, new edition, 1930

Husik, Isaac, "A Question of Logic in Maimonides," in his *Philosophical Essays, Ancient, Mediaeval and Modern*, edited by Milton C. Nahm and Leo Strauss, Oxford: Blackwell, 1952

Kravitz, Leonard S., "The Revealed and the Concealed: Prophecy, Miracles and Creation in the *Guide*," *Central Conference of American Rabbis Journal*, 16, October 1969

Kravitz, Leonard S., *The Hidden Doctrine of Maimonides' "Guide for the Perplexed": Philosophical and Religious God-Language in Tension*, Lewiston, New York: Mellen, 1988

Leaman, Oliver, *Moses Maimonides*, London and New York: Routledge, 1990; revised edition, Richmond, North Yorkshire: Curzon, 1997

Pines, Shlomo, "Introduction," in Maimonides' *The Guide of the Perplexed*, Chicago: University of Chicago Press, 1963

Ravitzky, Aviezer, "Samuel Ibn Tibbon and the Esoteric Character of *The Guide of the Perplexed*," *AJS Review*, 6, 1980

Ravitzky, Aviezer, "The Secrets of *The Guide of the Perplexed*: Between the Thirteenth and Twentieth Centuries," in *Studies in Maimonides*, edited by Isadore Twersky, Cambridge, Massachusetts: Harvard University, Center for Jewish Studies, 1990

Roth, Leon, *The Guide for the Perplexed*, London and New York: Hutchinson's University Library, 1948

Strauss, Leo, *Philosophie und Gesetz*, 1935; translated by Eve Adler as *Philosophy and Law: Contributions to the Understanding of Maimonides and His Predecessors*, Albany: State University of New York Press, 1995

Strauss, Leo, "On Abravanel's Philosophical Tendency and Political Teaching," in *Isaac Abravanel: Six Lectures by Paul Goodman, L. Rabinowitz (and others) with an Introductory Essay by H. Loewe*; edited by J.B. Trend and H. Loewe, Cambridge: Cambridge University Press, 1937

Strauss, Leo, *Persecution and the Art of Writing*, Glencoe, Illinois: Free Press, 1952

Strauss, Leo, "How to Begin to Study *The Guide of the Perplexed*," in Maimonides' *The Guide of the Perplexed*, edited by Shlomo Pines, Chicago: University of Chicago Press, 1963

Tchernowitz, Chaim, *Maimonides as Codifier* (Maimonides Octocentennial Series, pamphlet 3), New York: Maimonides Octocentennial Committee, 1935

Twersky, Isadore, *Introduction to the Code of Maimonides (Mishneh Torah)* (Yale Judaica Series, vol. 22), New Haven, Connecticut: Yale University Press, 1980

Yellin, David and Israel Abrahams, *Maimonides*, London: Macmillan, and Philadelphia: Jewish Publication Society, 1903; revised as *Maimonides: His Life and Works*, New York: Hermon, 1972

Moses ben Maimon, also known as Maimonides and by the Hebrew acronym Rambam (Rabbi Moses *ben* Maimon) was an outstanding rabbinic authority, codifier, religious philosopher, and communal leader. Both in medieval and modern times there has been wide disagreement surrounding his philosophic system. Some critics perceive a unity between his philosophic and legal works, while others insist that there is a duality between the two, with the philosophic works containing heterodox views on creation, prophecy, the efficacy of prayer, and the resurrection of the dead, among other subjects.

HESCHEL (1935) has provided an introduction to Maimonides that tries to interweave his biography and his thought. For this integrated portrait, Heschel quotes extensively both from Maimonides' correspondence and from relevant portions of his philosophical and legal writings. Some of Heschel's insights first mentioned in this study were later expanded by him into full-length monographs. For example, his theory that Maimonides aspired to prophetic inspiration is more fully discussed in HESCHEL (1945). In his 1935 biography, Heschel makes some shrewd psychological observations throughout, for instance on how Maimonides was affected by the death of his younger brother, David, in a shipwreck. (He asserts that Maimonides had feelings of guilt over his self-centeredness in allowing David to support the family and endangering himself in the process.) As in all his books, Heschel writes in a unique, lively, and passionate style. Heschel has possibly done a disservice, however, to both Maimonides and serious scholarship by giving credence to a number of pious legends. Thus Heschel relates that on the night after Maimonides finished his code, the *Mishneh Torah,* he dreamed that his father Rabbi Maimon came to visit him with a stranger whom he introduced as "Our Teacher Moses, the son of Amram." Maimonides was apprehensive, but Moses told him that he had come to look at his code. After examining the work, Moses said: "Congratulations, may your strength increase!" It need only be said that legend likewise recounts that when Aquinas finished the *Summa,* the figure on the crucifix in his cell spoke to him, saying, "Master Thomas, you have written well about me; your teachings are true Catholic doctrine." Both Maimonides and Aquinas can shine by their own lights and do not need such hagiographic embellishments to add brilliance to their reputations.

YELLIN and ABRAHAMS's biography of Maimonides was written by Abrahams and based on a Hebrew biography by Yellin published in 1898. Both authors were important scholars, and Abrahams writes in an easy-flowing, graceful style. Separate chapters are devoted to different stages in Maimonides' life, as well as to his major works, the *Commentary on the Mishnah, Mishneh Torah,* and *The Guide of the Perplexed.* The revised edition features a valuable introduction and bibliography and important supplementary notes by Jacob Dienstag, a leading authority on Maimonides. Some of the more significant notes deal with Maimonides' attitude toward Islam; literature discussing the myth of the apostasy of Maimonides; and reference to an article refuting statements in Abrahams's text (as well as in Heschel's biography) that Maimonides was the court physician of Saladin and that he was invited by Richard I, the Lionheart, to treat him.

GOITEIN begins his article by referring to the complaint of Georges Vajda of the Sorbonne that there is no satisfactory biography of Maimonides—even the date of his birth and death are uncertain. Goitein partially attempts to remedy this defect on the basis of his study of the vast Genizah material, most of which was recovered at the end of the 19th century from the store-chamber of the medieval synagogue in Old Cairo (also known as Fustat). Many of the documents show that Maimonides was not a cloistered scholar but a consummate "man of action." In November 1168, the town of Bilbeis, which harbored an important Jewish community and served as the Egyptian terminal of the caravan route between Palestine and Egypt, was stormed and captured by the crusaders and many Jewish inhabitants were taken prisoner. Goitein shows that extraordinary efforts and enormous sums were needed to ransom the captives. The ransom for a prisoner, 33 and one-third gold dinars, was more than many craftsmen or shopkeepers could save in a lifetime. Maimonides sent circulars to numerous communities to help raise the money and at times was personally involved in its collection. Maimonides' swift rise to the office of Head of the Jews so soon after his arrival in Egypt (which is documented in Genizah sources) was due, at least in part, to his tireless efforts on behalf of the captives of Bilbeis.

ROTH presents, in broad outline and simple language, the life, work, and influence of Maimonides. The author has produced a brief, reliable interpretation of Maimonides akin to what is found in such series of semipopular monographs as "Past Masters," "90 Minutes," or "The Spirit of Philosophy," with a concise, lucid, and authoritative introduction to the philosopher's ideas and extensive quotations from his writings.

TCHERNOWITZ's pamphlet is also semipopular in nature but specifically presents a brief analysis of the method and scope of Maimonides' work as codifier of Jewish law. Although Tchernowitz was a leading authority on the development of halakhah and later wrote a multivolume Hebrew work on the subject, he wore his learning lightly, and this essay is truly a sketch by the hand of a master. Among the topics covered are the influence of Maimonides' predecessors; the purpose of the *Mishneh Torah* (according to Tchernowitz it was mainly educational—Maimonides wanted to compile a Jewish pandect); Maimonides' methodology or how he arranged the material of his code; its sources; Maimonides' system of interpretation; critics and commentators on the code; and the influence of Maimonides on later codifiers.

TWERSKY, famously tough and exacting on his students at Harvard, emerges through his 640-page analysis of Maimonides' *Mishneh Torah* as at least as demanding on himself. Some of his learned footnotes could easily be expanded, if not into doctoral dissertations, then certainly into masters' essays. He has observed the two commandments addressed to scholars: "Thou shalt work at the sources" and "Thou shalt acquaint thyself with work done before thee and beside thee." It would be difficult to find a significant article on Maimonides' code that Twersky has not seen or reckoned with. Twersky covers not only the same ground as Tchernowitz in much greater detail but also topics not considered by Tchernowitz, such as the language and style of the code, to which he devotes a chapter. Some of his conclusions may be questioned by other scholars, as for example his contention that Maimonides was not significantly influenced by Islamic thought and law, but all future scholars will have to reckon with this monumental study. Additional consequence is added to the book by Twersky's acknowledgement in his preface of the help he received from his father-in-law, the great Maimonidean authority Rabbi Joseph Baer Soloveitchik, with whom he discussed many of the issues raised.

Twersky considers the question of why Maimonides wrote his code, and he is rightly critical of scholars who would like to substitute their own conjectures in place of the reasons given by Maimonides himself, conjectures such as that he attempted to refute the Karaites or that he wanted to write the Constitution for the imminent Messianic Kingdom of Israel. On the other hand, even Twersky is not entirely above reproach in the matter of Maimonidean scholarship attempting to "improve" on Maimonides. Thus, he uses the word *diwan* repeatedly to characterize this Hebrew work in terms of its Arabic literary milieu, whereas Maimonides is invariably content to refer to his work as *al-hibur* or *al-talif*.

GUTTMANN presents a summary of Maimonides' philosophical system and finds his significance in establishing the biblical Creator-God within the framework of philosophical cosmology, and thus achieving a true philosophical synthesis between biblical religion and Aristotelianism with its conception of God as the necessary cause of the world.

HUSIK (1916), although reflecting an earlier phase of research, discusses (as does Guttmann) Maimonides' views on the existence and attributes of God, the origin of the universe, prophecy, providence, and ethics, but he is more skeptical than Guttmann of the resulting synthesis.

HUSIK (1952) in his charming four-page essay (originally written in 1923) spells out his misgivings about Maimonides' synthesis very clearly. In the *Guide*, Maimonides criticizes the Kalamists (Islamic dialectical theologians) for proving the existence of God by arguing that the world is not eternal and therefore must have been created, and since nothing can create itself, it must have been created by God. Maimonides argues that the major premise, namely that the world is not eternal, has not been scientifically proven and is doubtful. He therefore adopts the Aristotelian proof based upon motion, on the assumption (tentatively held and rejected afterward) that motion and, hence, the world are eternal. "Be prepared for either case," could well be Maimonides' motto. If the world is created, the Kalamists are proven correct, and if the world is eternal, Aristotle is proven correct; in either case the existence of God is firmly established. Husik, however, wonders if it is quite that simple. Is not an elementary blunder in logic committed if one reaches the same conclusion whether the major premise is affirmative or negative? To take the most famous of all syllogisms: all men are mortal; Socrates is a man; therefore Socrates is mortal. This is a valid argument; the conclusion follows necessarily from the premises. But if the major premise is changed to the counter-proposition, all men are immortal, then the conclusion obviously would be Socrates is immortal. How, then, can Maimonides reach the same conclusion proceeding from contradictory major premises? Husik answers simply that Maimonides does not. An unmoved mover is not the Maker of heaven and earth, and the God of Aristotle and the philosophers is not the God of the Hebrew Bible; an unbridgeable gulf extends between them.

In his various studies, STRAUSS (1935, 1937, 1952, 1963) gave a new turn to the study and interpretation of Maimonides' philosophy. The views of PINES, professor of Jewish and general philosophy at the Hebrew University and translator of the *Guide* into English, closely parallel those of Strauss. According to Strauss, the *Guide* is an esoteric work whose real message is presented between the lines, and that message is that reason and revelation are not fully reconcilable. According to Maimonides, this realization must be concealed from the "vulgar masses," who must observe the precepts of the Torah to prevent social anarchy. The basic critical canon of interpretation used by Strauss is that a seemingly casual contradiction of a conventional belief (or of a necessary presumption or consequence of such a belief) is what Maimonides really wishes to maintain, while repeated affirmations and reaffirmations of orthodox dogmas, if they are surreptitiously contradicted, are merely sops thrown to the "vulgar." Since secrecy can to some extent be identified with rarity, of two contradictory statements in the *Guide*, that which occurs least frequently (or only once) represents the true view of Maimonides.

RAVITZKY (1980) shows that Strauss's way of interpreting the *Guide* is very similar to that of Samuel ibn Tibbon, offered during Maimonides' lifetime. Abraham Maimuni,

Maimonides' son, acknowledged that his father considered ibn Tibbon, who translated the *Guide* into Hebrew, to have penetrated and fathomed his teachings. The fundamental methodological principles of this esoteric interpretation are: highlighting the role of intentional contradictions in the text; identification of the concealed truth with a rare or unique statement appearing in the text; a search for the esoteric context of comments that seem out of place; and special attention to chapters whose subject matter breaks the continuity of a series of chapters.

RAVITZKY (1990) widens the scope of his inquiry beyond ibn Tibbon to include other commentators and interpreters of the *Guide* and lends further support to Strauss's reading of Maimonides.

ALTMANN argues that in the *Guide*, Maimonides contradicts doctrines affirmed in his more popular works. It can be shown that in the *Guide*, Maimonides tacitly replaces the absolute freedom of the will expressed in his dogmatic works by a deterministic theory that must be considered to represent his esoteric doctrine.

HARTMAN's book is a persuasive defense of the unity of Maimonides' thought, seeking to prove that he "chose the way of integration" and achieved a genuine synthesis between philosophy and Jewish law. But is Hartman successful? Perhaps the most competent critical evaluation of his study is the one given by Shlomo Pines in his foreword. He says that Hartman's interpretation "seems to engender more difficulties than it solves, and some of these may prove to be insurmountable." Pines, gentleman that he was, does not insist on spelling out these difficulties, but they are in any case all too evident from the introduction to his translation of the *Guide*, referred to above: "Maimonides had very strong convictions concerning the utility and even necessity of an official system of religious beliefs for the preservation of communal obedience to the law. What is more, he lived up to his convictions by formulating in his commentary on the Mishnah the thirteen principal dogmas of Judaism. *Many of these dogmas run counter to philosophic truth*" (emphasis added).

FOX has written with a twofold aim: (1) to mount a sustained attack on the Maimonidean scholarship of Leo Strauss and his school, and (2) to offer alternative interpretations of Maimonides' views on key issues. Fox is correct in maintaining against Strauss that precisely because the *Guide* is a Jewish book, it cannot at the same time also be a thoroughly philosophic book. (Thus, Leibniz's respect for the work of Maimonides was that of one philosopher for another, despite the fact that the *Guide* was a Jewish book.) Fox has also made the correct methodological observation that one cannot simply classify all statements in the *Guide* that are in any way inconsistent with each other as "contradictions." Rather, one must distinguish carefully between contraries, subcontraries, and other inconsistencies.

Finally, Fox is correct in observing that some of Strauss's interpretations are somewhat nebulous and problematic and carry with them certain inherent dangers. In his essay of 1963, for example, Strauss analyzes the first 49 chapters of the *Guide*, which are devoted to the theme of God's incorporeality and problems connected with it. Most of these chapters are devoted to expounding the true, deeper meaning behind such biblical metaphors as God's face, eyes, or feet, or locutions used to describe his actions. Strauss notes that the term "hand," which occurs repeatedly in the Bible, is not analyzed by Maimonides at all, but that in chapter 14 Maimonides interrupts his discussion of verbs and other parts of speech that refer to place and turns to an explanation of "man." According to Strauss this is not an accident. He observes that the Hebrew word for hand, *yad,* has a numerical equivalent of 14, and that the hand is the characteristically human organ by which man is distinguished from the rest of creation. By metonymy "hand" stands for "man," while the number 14 is closely associated in Maimonides' works with Torah. His code is divided into 14 books (in fact, rabbinic writers generally refer to the code by the name *Yad*). In the *Book of Commandments,* Maimonides sets out "14 roots of the commandments," and in the *Guide,* he divides the commandments into 14 classes. Maimonides, in the characteristic Straussian view disparaged by Fox, was sending a hidden message to initiates, a message that he felt was not suitable for the general public—namely, that the commandments of the Torah are man-made, and the Torah has a human, rather than divine, origin.

It seems true that Strauss's earlier studies are more solid than his later speculations. The earlier studies are based on a clear methodology and logical analysis, and the later, while certainly not irresponsible kabbalistic interpretations or undisciplined, extravagant imaginings, are creative reconstructions that by their very nature are not provable. Still, Fox's critique of Strauss does not affect the main thrust of Strauss's Maimonidean scholarship. Worse, Fox disregards the more recent investigations by the late Abraham Nuriel of Bar-Ilan University (unfortunately available only in Hebrew), which lend strong support to Strauss. After a careful study of the methodological approach of Maimonides, Nuriel comes to the conclusion that of two contradictory statements, the one that is formulated with a misplaced keyword is the one that Maimonides considers false. In light of his theory, Nuriel examines the use of the expression "the Creator" *(ha-Bore')* in the *Guide*. He notes that this term never appears in those passages where Maimonides expresses his positive opinion on the creation of the world. Conversely, in each and every instance that this word appears, Nuriel finds that it serves to appease the censorious opinions of the vulgar. He therefore concludes that Maimonides explained the first verse of the Bible as referring to creation from preexistent matter.

Fox's positive contributions seem more perplexing than guiding. Consider creation versus eternity. In the *Guide* (2:32), Maimonides mentions a link between the "three opinions concerning the eternity of the world or its creation in time" and "three opinions concerning prophecy." Commentators have been baffled with the problem as to which of the three opinions concerning creation represents the "real" Maimonides and what his corresponding opinion is with regard to the problem of prophecy. There are at least nine hypothetical solutions to this riddle, and in actuality there are many more because different interpretations are put on the various views. (This writer is familiar with 16 proposed "solutions"; besides those discussed here, the reader may refer to the articles of Davidson [1979], Harvey, and Kaplan listed in the bibliography of Leaman's book.) To the three views mentioned by Maimonides on that occasion, namely, the Platonic, Aristotelian, and Jewish, Fox adds that of the Kalam, discussed by Maimonides elsewhere, making the minimum number of solutions 12 rather than nine. According to Fox, Maimonides effects a "syncretistic unification" of elements drawn from all four positions. He contends that "Maimonides sees a useful counterweight to the Aristotelian theory in the Kalam affirmation" and that Maimonides picks and chooses "desirable" and "positive" features of the Kalam and Aristotle, while rejecting "undesirable" and "negative" features. However, the "Great Eagle" who soared to the heavens on the wings of understanding was capable of more than this seam-bursting eclecticism of the jackdaw that is of little philosophical consequence. If this were truly Maimonides' opinion, he would himself deserve the scorn he heaped on the Kalamists, whose premises and arguments were driven by a desired outcome rather than by a regard for the truth (1:71). Questions are not answered and problems are not solved by claiming that Maimonides deliberately maintained "a dialectical tension between diverse positions."

Even recourse to a "severe dialectical tension" does not solve the problem of petitionary prayer in Maimonides' system. Did Maimonides believe that prayer falls into the category of "necessary beliefs" or did he believe that God answers prayers? Maimonides' doctrine of the divine immutability and absolute transcendence suggest the former. Maimonides goes as far away as possible from the anthropomorphic pitfall, resting uneasily on the very edge of the agnostic pitfall on the other side. Maimonides' conception of God as the Unknowable Negation of Privation does not satisfy the religious instinct. Mankind seeks the assurance of a loving, caring God—a refuge, the everlasting arms, or a Friend behind phenomena (to use Edwyn Bevan's apt phrase), not an undifferentiated ooze. Fox attempts to settle the matter by claiming that Maimonides' attitude to verbal petitionary prayer may be illuminated by his private practice. To commemorate his delivery from a life-threatening storm at sea, Maimonides vowed to keep its anniversary as a fast, in his words "seeing nobody, and praying and reading in solitude the entire day." "This," declares Fox, "is hardly the thinking or the practice of man who holds that prayer is intended only for the protection of the masses from heresy, while the truly educated should serve God exclusively through the activity of the intellect." Such anecdotal evidence is at best of limited biographical interest and does not resolve any philosophical issue. Even an advanced thinker on the positive side of agnosticism may spend a day in silent adoration and contemplative reverence of a power not human that makes for righteousness. What is more, in the very source cited by Fox, this story serves to illustrate not Maimonides' attitude to petitionary prayer but his love and attachment to the Holy Land: the day of the tempest was observed as a fast-day, while the day of his arrival in Palestine was celebrated as a day of feasting and rejoicing.

KRAVITZ (1969) is one of the most persuasive interpreters of Maimonides in the Straussian tradition. Kravitz develops the pregnant thesis that Maimonides himself has provided the key to understanding the *Guide* in his method of reading the Book of Job, particularly in his interpretation of the speeches of Elihu, which superficially seem merely to repeat what the other three comforters have said but which in reality disclose quite

untraditional views. For many, this essay will mark a Copernican revolution in their understanding of Maimonides. Students often feel that modern critics read their own heterodox views into the *Guide*, and that they have darkened counsel by words without understanding. Kravitz will convince them that the critics are on to something significant that cannot be evaded or ignored: "According to Maimonides' *philosophy*, Israel's *history* did not occur as reported in the Bible."

KRAVITZ (1988) is the author's definitive study of the *Guide*. According to Kravitz the *Guide* reflects the central problem of medieval theology, that of correlating a conceptual system drawn from one world with a textual system drawn from another. That problem finds its specific focus in *theos*, on what is meant by God. For the conceptual system drawn from Greek philosophy, God is an idea, the Ultimate Form; for the textual system drawn from the world of the Bible, God is a person, the Ultimate Will. For the philosophers, forms are as they are and do not change; hence, God is and cannot change; for the religionists, God acts and responds and hence, in some manner, changes. The textual system was the basis of the religious life; it did not present a problem to those whose mindset was formed by it, and it did present a problem to those who were entranced by the conceptual system. They were perplexed by the relation of one system to the other.

Maimonides wrote the *Guide* to provide guidance by interpreting the words of the Torah using the notions of the philosophers. In a most careful manner, Maimonides gradually moved the reader for whom the book was intended from the denial of the Deity being corporeal, to the denial of the Deity acting in a corporeal manner, to a denial of the Deity acting; or to put it in another manner, Maimonides sought to move the astute reader to the notion that the Deity eternally acted, and hence, paradoxically, never changed. Since the Deity did not change, the reader had to change; by activating his intellect, by following the philosophers' curriculum of the study of mathematics, physics, and metaphysics, the reader was to achieve the true wisdom that is the correct understanding of the Deity. That true wisdom was, however, not attainable by most people; hence, the *Guide* was carefully written to hide its meaning from those who could not use it and who, like a baby trying to eat steak, would be harmed by it. Even so, those who do not "get it" can still gain something from the book, for as Maimonides indicated by quoting the phrase "A word fitly spoken is like apples of gold in fittings of silver," those who cannot apprehend the gold of the book can learn something from the silver.

HABERMAN is interested in the question of how rationalist thinkers, such as Maimonides and Aquinas, could make room for supernatural revelation within their philosophical systems. Aquinas accepts Aristotle's psychology and his reliance on sense data and combines it with the Neoplatonic goal of a mystical union with God. In taking his theory of man's goal from the Neoplatonists and his account of man's nature from the Aristotelians, Aquinas was left with a huge gap, which he neatly filled with the Christian revelation and its promises. According to Maimonides, the prophet is a philosopher-king in the Platonic sense, and the supreme prophet, Moses, "the man of God," was that charismatic prophet-lawgiver/philosopher-king all in one, who achieved intellectual completeness and was able to promulgate the perfect and eternal law designed for the physical and spiritual perfection of the individual and society.

Maimonides agrees with Plato that there are certain beliefs that ought to be propagated by rulers whether they are in fact true or known to be false, on the grounds that they are valuable instruments for the promotion of good conduct on the part of the mass of the population. The question suggests itself as to whether intellectuals would support such a scheme to preserve the social order from the corrosive acids of rationalist philosophy. The simple answer is that they had no choice. There were no secular alternatives in Maimonides' age; the only alternatives were religious, and the other monotheistic religions affirmed the same dogmas as Judaism, plus others that could not readily be reconciled with Aristotle's philosophy. Moreover, religious skepticism will often ally itself with political conservatism. Since there can be no rational ground for preferring one set of dogmas over another, one may as well become a conformist and adhere to the rules and customs of one's own group in order to safely pursue philosophic inquiry. This, of course, has no bearing on the question of whether the philosopher in his study ought to believe in, say, the 13 principal dogmas of Judaism. He ought only to believe what is either self-evident, capable of certain or probable proof, or verifiable by sensible or introspective perception.

Haberman examines on their merits Maimonides' views on all major questions such as the existence and attributes of God, creation, the nature of prophecy, and divine providence, assuming that they were advocated because Maimonides was convinced that they were true. Only when such a reading is precluded by the ordinary canons of criticism and when they differ markedly from those Maimonides expressed elsewhere, as in the *Treatise on Resurrection,* is interpretation geared to these views' social utility and political usefulness. Critics generally have found Haberman's study useful and solidly documented, but some reviewers have objected to his participation in the argument. Zwi Werblowsky, in *The Jewish Journal of Sociology* (volume 23, June 1981), wrote, "[T]he reader sometimes gets the impression that there really are three great philosopher-theologians: Maimonides, Aquinas, and Haberman. Lest this sound unkind, let me hasten to add that the book is well-written, extremely readable, and exhibits considerable erudition which, together with a certain charming frankness, goes a long way towards reconciling the reader with the author's occasionally implicit arrogance."

LEAMAN interprets Maimonides as falling squarely within the tradition of philosophy as it developed in the Islamic world. There is much merit to this approach, but Leaman overdoes it. After all, any Muslim philosopher who would assert, as Maimonides repeatedly does, that Moses was the greatest of all prophets, both of those who preceded and those who followed him (i.e., including Muhammad) would have been summarily executed and his books burned. Still, Leaman avoids technical scholarly jargon and has interesting things to say on a number of topics. In regard to creation versus the eternity of the world, for instance, he discusses what he terms the "Maimonides Principle," namely that the laws of nature that govern the universe need not have been in force when the present order of events came into existence. This principle does, after all, find some support from the Big

Bang cosmological theory according to which matter, energy, space, and time were indeed created during a primeval explosion lasting less than a trillionth of a second some 15 billion years ago.

JACOB HABERMAN

See also Maimonidean Controversy

Moses ben Nahman 1194–1270

Catalan-born talmudist, theologian, mystic, and controversialist, died in Palestine

Chavel, Charles, *Ramban, His Life and Teachings,* New York: Feldheim, 1960

Chazan, Robert, *Barcelona and Beyond: The Disputation of 1263 and Its Aftermath,* Berkeley: University of California Press, 1992

Funkenstein, Amos, *Perceptions of Jewish History,* Berkeley: University of California Press, 1993

Kanarfogel, Ephraim, "On the Assessment of R. Moses b. Nahman and His Literary Oeuvre," *Jewish Book Annual,* 54, 1997

Twersky, Isadore (editor), *Rabbi Moses Nahmanides (Ramban): Explorations in His Religious and Literary Virtuosity,* Cambridge, Massachusetts: Harvard University Press, 1983

Wolfson, Elliot, "By Way of Truth: Aspects of Nahmanides' Kabbalistic Hermeneutic," *AJS Review,* 14, 1989

A leading Spanish talmudist, Moses ben Nahman, also known as Nahmanides and by the acronym Ramban (Rabbi Moses ben Nahman), was the intellectual and communal leader of Catalan Jewry during a crucial period. His writings reflect a synthesis of the dialectical tradition of the tosafists in northern France with the geonic-Andalusian traditions of analytical scholarship and literary culture. The broad scope of Nahmanides' learning enabled him to provide a measure of stability in the face of conflicts that arose from within Jewish society and from the Christian world as well.

CHAZAN's study focuses on Moses ben Nahman's disputation with Pablo Christiani at Barcelona in 1263. Chazan begins by reconstructing the debate and its strategies on the basis of the brief Latin report produced by a Christian observer as well as the Hebrew narrative that Nahmanides himself composed. In doing so, Chazan evaluates the goals and methods of both of these accounts and compares and contrasts their findings, exploiting very effectively the significant differences in style and substance to clarify Nahmanides' aims and tactics. Chazan then moves on to consider the aftermath of the disputation from several perspectives. The "victory" secured by Ramban was followed by new Christian missionizing pressures against which Ramban sought, in turn, to reassure his fellow Jews. His efforts were centered on the interpretation of certain aggadic passages and biblical texts utilized by Christians for polemical purposes. In addition, Ramban wished to demonstrate the certainty and predictability of the messianic redemption. Chazan notes that while Nahmanides is considered to be somewhat conservative with regard to his kabbalistic teachings, his messianic calculations and interpretations possess an innovative flair.

FUNKENSTEIN discusses Nahmanides' penchant for typological symbolism in his biblical commentary against the backdrop of contemporary Christian typological exegesis. A number of the prefigurations of subsequent biblical developments found in Ramban's Torah commentary reflect a recognizable measure of Christian influence. To be sure, Ramban does not divulge the Christian origins of these interpretations, and many of Nahmanides' typologies are structured to counter Christian constructions. Moreover, Nahmanides' limitation of his use of typology to the patriarchal narratives was due perhaps to his awareness of the importance of this method for Christian interpretation. As a kabbalist, Nahmanides preferred to find biblical symbolism linked to letters and names rather than to events and persons. In his discussion, Funkenstein raises the issue of the relationship between the straightforward approach to biblical exegesis (peshat) and the kabbalistic approach (sod). He suggests that these categories almost never overlap in Ramban's commentaries.

TWERSKY introduces a rich collection of essays by pointing to the diversity of Nahmanides' achievements and by stressing, against the tendency in earlier historiography, that the corpus of Ramban's writings must be considered as a comprehensive oeuvre and should not be fragmentized. Bernard Septimus's opening essay demonstrates the degree to which Nahmanides remained faithful to the Andalusian tradition even as he was exposed to the very different methodologies and ideals of Ashkenazi scholarship and culture. This loyalty is evident in the style of his writing; in the nature of his citations in his biblical and talmudic commentaries; and in the nuanced positions that he took with regard to philosophy and science during the Maimonidean controversy and with regard to the use of aggadah at the Barcelona disputation. As an inheritor of the Geonic-Andalusian tradition, Nahmanides never accepted the absolute authority of all aggadah, nor did he see kabbalistic interpretation as the universal key to the understanding of aggadah. In a brief essay, Ezra Fleischer sketches the parameters of Nahmanides' small but impressive poetic output, which reflects the salient characteristics of the Gerona school of Hebrew poetry. Moshe Idel links the relatively meager output of Ramban in terms of kabbalistic literature to the fact that Ramban was a conservative kabbalist. He was prepared to formulate or record only those kabbalistic interpretations that he had received from his teachers. Even those interpretations suggested by fellow members of the Gerona school of Kabbalah were not accepted by Ramban unless he was certain that they had emerged from a reliable kabbalistic tradition. He took a stand in marked contrast to the approach of other members of the Gerona school who favored direct and open dissemination of kabbalistic teachings. Bezalel Safran compares and contrasts Ramban's views on the sin of Adam and the fall of man to those of another member of the Gerona school, Azriel. Safran notes in passing that Ramban's endorsement of a limited asceticism was linked in his writings to achieving communion with the divine (devekut). David Berger argues that Ramban was much more familiar with aspects of Aristotelian thought and other philosophical systems and literature than has been imagined. This assessment leads Berger to a reconsideration of Nahmanides' view of nat-

ural law. In addition, Berger and Septimus both point to numerous instances in Ramban's Torah commentary in which peshat and sod do coincide.

WOLFSON maintains that Nahmanides was, in his biblical commentary, a kabbalist first and foremost, and a not-so-conservative kabbalist at that. His warning against speculation about kabbalistic secrets and ideas is overshadowed by the fact that he alludes to these secrets in his commentaries, thereby bringing this material to the attention of a general audience. Ramban employed a dynamic kabbalistic hermeneutical method. In the realm of esoteric interpretation, Ramban followed both a theosophical system as well as a mystical tradition that read the text of Scripture as a matrix of divine names. This tradition is but one example of a mystical doctrine found in Ramban's writings that originated with the German Pietists. In Wolfson's view, Nahmanides did not differentiate between rabbinic and kabbalistic modes of biblical and talmudic interpretation. Moreover, he considered aggadic interpretation to be a key to the understanding of Kabbalah. At the same time, Ramban's rejection of certain aggadic passages at Barcelona (and even in his Torah commentary) is readily understood. Even as aggadah was critical to Ramban's understanding of Kabbalah, he did not have to accept all aggadic statements as binding.

CHAVEL has written a basic biography of Rabbi Moses ben Nahman that describes his familial background and identifies his major teachers and students. Chavel also reviews Ramban's many compositions, grouping them under the headings of halakhic treatises and collections, works written in defense of earlier authorities, and talmudic novellae and responsa. The book concludes with a survey of Ramban's views on various matters of religious thought and faith, but it lacks the sophisticated level of analysis that characterizes some of the more recent studies of Ramban.

KANARFOGEL reviews the surge of writings about Ramban produced in the last 20 years, noting the vast difference between these studies and the efforts of historians writing at the dawn of modern Jewish historiography. In addition to focusing on many of the issues discussed above, Kanarfogel deals with Nahmanides' approaches to halakhic formulation and talmudic interpretation and with the diverse figures and movements throughout medieval Europe that may have influenced Nahmanides' thinking in a number of disciplines.

EPHRAIM KANARFOGEL

Mourning *see* Death, Burial, and Mourning

Muhammad and Judaism

Ahmad, Barakat, *Muhammad and the Jews: A Re-Examination*, New Delhi: Vikas, 1979

Firestone, Reuven, *Journeys in Holy Lands: The Evolution of the Abraham-Ishmael Legends in Islamic Exegesis*, Albany: State University of New York Press, 1990

Geiger, Abraham, *Was hat Mohammed aus dem Judenthume aufgenommen*, 1833; as *Judaism and Islam*, Edinburgh: Williams and Norgate, 1896; New York: Ktav, 1970

Katsh, Abraham, *Judaism in Islam: Biblical and Talmudic Backgrounds of the Koran and Its Commentaries*, New York: Block, 1954; 3rd edition, New York: Sepher-Hermon, 1980

Lewis, Bernard, *The Jews of Islam*, Princeton, New Jersey: Princeton University Press, and London: Routledge and Kegan Paul, 1984

Newby, Gordon, *A History of the Jews of Arabia: From Ancient Times to Their Eclipse under Islam* (Studies in Comparative Religion), Columbia: University of South Carolina Press, 1988

Rosenthal, E.I.J., *Judaism and Islam* (Popular Jewish Library), New York and London: Yoseloff, 1961

Torrey, Charles Cutler, *The Jewish Foundation of Islam* (The Hilda Stich Stroock Lectures), New York: Jewish Institute of Religion Press, 1933

Wasserstrom, Steven M., *Between Muslim and Jew: The Problem of Symbiosis under Early Islam*, Princeton, New Jersey: Princeton University Press, 1995

Watt, W. Montgomery, *Muhammad at Medina*, Oxford: Clarendon, 1956; New York: Oxford University Press, 1981

The abundant literature on Muhammad and Judaism reflects the continuing scholarly controversy regarding the formative role played by Judaism in the shaping of Islam. More than a century after Western scholars first suggested Muhammad's indebtedness to Judaism, the subject of Judaism's influence on Islam is still largely a matter of heated disagreement. For those who adhere to the tenets of Islam, the entire issue is incomprehensible: Islam represents the original and perfect faith, and Judaism is but an imperfect reflection and distortion of that true faith. For scholars outside of the Islamic tradition, the degree of Islam's indebtedness to Judaism and the relative influences of Christianity and Judaism are at the heart of the debate.

The pioneering work on the subject of Islam's debt to Judaism is GEIGER's study, in which he highlights Kuranic stories, motifs, and concepts that probably derived from Judaism. Since the appearance of Geiger's book, many studies have been written to support or elaborate upon his conclusions, while other authors have sought to prove that Christianity, and not Judaism, was the main source of inspiration for the founder of Islam. In the 1970 reprint of Geiger's classic, Moshe Perlmann provides a good introduction to the literature on the various theories about the influences on Muhammad.

A sophisticated and nuanced analysis of the many issues involved in the relationship between Islam and Judaism can be found in the study by WASSERSTROM, who argues that the model of "borrowing" should be abandoned in favor of a paradigm that analyzes the process of "accommodation of the other" that occurred among both Jews and Muslims in response to one another. Wasserstrom is interested in the creative interplay that resulted from this accommodation, a process that yielded what he terms "products of mutuality." Each of the six chapters in this book investigates the process of self-definition by which both Judaism and Islam sought to legitimate themselves through their interpretations of the other religion.

Most discussions of Judaism and Muhammad accord centrality to Muhammad's relations with the Jews while he served as lawgiver and arbitrator in Medina. WATT examines the relations between the prophet and the powerful Jews of that city after Muhammad's departure in 622. Watt notes in the early part of Muhammad's career in Medina a "tendency to make his religion similar to that of the Jews and to encourage his Medinan followers to continue Jewish practices which they had adopted." The author attributes to this policy such practices as the original orientation of Muslim prayer toward Jerusalem, the license to eat the food of the "People of the Book," and the Kuranic permission allowing male followers of Muhammad to marry Jewish women. Despite Muhammad's efforts, the Jews of Medina rejected his overtures to create a religious and political union. According to Watt, once Muhammad was rebuffed, he understandably began to assert his independence from the Jews, adopting a new policy that culminated in both intellectual and physical attacks on his former prospective allies.

Less is known about Muhammad's contact with Judaism in Mecca, the commercial hub and pagan cultic center of Arabia in which Muhammad began his ministry, than is known about his time in Medina. TORREY proposes that Muhammad derived many of his earliest monotheistic views from an unidentified Jewish community in Mecca. The author contends that this community can be traced back to the sixth century B.C.E., and he argues that it was thoroughly familiar with the Bible, Jewish oral law, and the aggadah. Torrey claims that Muhammad not only learned the rudiments of Judaism from these Jews, he also learned a censored version of Christianity. By emphasizing the rabbinic Jewish origins of Islam, Torrey rejects the views of scholars subsequent to Geiger, such as Wellhausen and Andrae, who argue that Christianity had a more dominant role than Judaism in the formation of Islam. Torrey's thesis is highly speculative and has accordingly been dismissed by most modern scholars. Nevertheless, his work raises the important question of Jewish settlement in the Arabian peninsula, and it seeks a historical basis for the philological claims first put forward by Geiger.

NEWBY considers the relationship of Muhammad to Arabian Jewry in a comprehensive overview of Jewish history in the Arabian peninsula. Disputing the reliability of the Arabic historiographical tradition on the origins of Arabia's Jews, Newby stresses the importance of linguistic evidence, from which he concludes that there must have been a well-integrated Jewish presence in the Arabian peninsula in the early seventh century. An existing Arabian Jewish community was considerably augmented by Jews fleeing Palestine after the failure of the Bar Kokhba revolt in the second century C.E., and, according to Newby, "it is after this that Arabian Judaism begins to flourish." Newby relates the story of Arabia's Jews beyond the death of Muhammad, tracing continual Jewish settlement in Arabia well into the Middle Ages.

Perhaps the most telling examples of cultural borrowing between Islam and Judaism can be found through textual analysis of the Kuran and the Islamic legal system. Illustrative of the approach of comparative textual criticism is the work by KATSH. His close study of verses from chapters two and three of the Kuran stresses evidence that Muhammad borrowed extensively from Jewish material. Moreover, on the basis of the rabbinic sources that he finds embedded in the Kuran, Katsh rejects earlier views that characterized the Jews of Arabia as ignorant and removed from the flourishing centers of rabbinic Judaism in Palestine and Babylonia.

FIRESTONE draws conclusions similar to those of Katsh based upon a close reading of medieval Islamic exegesis of the Abraham/Ishmael tradition. Firestone argues that biblical legends were originally brought by Jews and Christians to the Arabian peninsula where they were then transformed. In this regard, Firestone sees the development of the Abraham/Ishmael legends in Islam as an example of the "clear continuity between Islam and pre-Islamic religious ideas and institutions." At the same time, however, Firestone insists that the Islamic traditions are more than simple borrowings, for "[j]ust as they display continuity from earlier and contemporaneous literature, they also exhibit originality as new literary works."

Muslim scholarship does not acknowledge this debate regarding the sources of Islamic traditions. For Muslims, Muhammad is the Prophet of God, and the Kuran is eternal and uncreated. If there are common elements in the two traditions, this similarity is explained as the result of a common divine source. Where the sources differ, Muslims explain the discrepancies as a result of the distortions and corruptions that the Jews introduced into the original Islamic revelations. Questions of chronology and the knowledge that Judaism antedates Islam by 2,000 years do not enter into Islamic discussion. AHMAD provides a rare English-language treatment by a Muslim of the interaction of Muhammad and Judaism.

Although modern Muslim scholars usually do not approach their traditional sources in order to examine critically parallels and mutual relationships between Islam and other faiths, medieval Islamic jurists were frequently interested in the question of so-called Judaizing practices or Jewish influences. The initial acceptance, followed by repudiation, of Jewish practices and narrative traditions marked the early legal traditions of Islam. Initially, sayings of the *Banu Isra'il* (Children of Israel), known as the *Isra'iliyyat,* circulated freely. Permission to embrace such traditions was eventually revoked by Islamic authorities, who also prohibited the study of Jewish Scriptures by Muslims. ROSENTHAL offers an introductory discussion of parallel legal developments in Judaism and Islam, without making hasty judgements about the direction of influence.

LEWIS's elegant, succinct, and persuasive book offers the best one-volume overview of the entirety of the Jewish-Muslim historical encounter. Lewis seeks to examine the complex relationship between Judaism and Islam in terms of the more general question of Islam's relationship to minority religious groups. He begins by identifying two common stereotypes that have dominated the discourse on Islam's relationship with other religions: on one hand, Islam is viewed as fanatically uncompromising in its opposition to other faiths, and, on the other hand, Islamic society is imagined as an "interfaith utopia." Lewis rejects both of these assumptions in this well-balanced study of what he terms the "Judaeo-Islamic" tradition.

JANE GERBER AND ARNOLD FRANKLIN

Musar

Eckman, Lester, *The History of the Musar Movement: 1840–1945*, New York: Shengold, 1975

Eckman, Lester, *The Teachings of the Fathers of the Musar Movement*, New York: Shengold, 1990

Etkes, Immanuel, *Rabbi Israel Salanter and the Mussar Movement: Seeking the Torah of Truth*, Philadelphia: Jewish Publication Society, 1993

Goldberg, Hillel, *Israel Salanter, Text, Structure, Idea: The Ethics and Theology of an Early Psychologist of the Unconscious*, New York: Ktav, 1982

Levinas, Emmanuel, "In the Image of God, according to Rabbi Hayyim Volozhiner," in *Beyond the Verse*, translated by Gary D. Mole, Bloomington: Indiana University Press, and London: Athlone, 1994

Levinas, Emmanuel, "Useless Suffering," in *Entre Nous: On Thinking-of-the-Other,* translated by Michael Smith and Barbara Harshav, New York: Columbia University Press, 1998

Musar can be rendered as "ethics" or as "ethical self-improvement." The Musar movement, a religious trend among Jews in 19th- and 20th-century Eastern Europe, specifically Lithuania, that emphasized ethical exercises and contemplation and that arose in response to the challenges to rabbinic Judaism posed by the twin threats of hasidic pietism and the secularizing intellectualism of the Haskalah, had a significant impact on the development of Judaism. Many of the teachings of the movement are based on the medieval and early modern literature devoted to the cultivation of *middot* (personality traits), and M.H. Luzzatto's *Mesillat Yesharim*, or *The Path of the Just*, is especially valorized. The Musar movement also created its own texts that sought to map the essential nature of the human being, on the one hand, and the good life, on the other, and the founder of the Musar movement, Israel Salanter (1810–1883), can be credited with one of the most original and influential reconceptualizations of Jewish thought in the modern period.

ECKMAN (1990) outlines the origins of the Musar movement and emphasizes its successes. Based on the letters and published works of the leaders of the Musar movement, this work is a clear, although not entirely academic, analysis of the various schools of Musar. The author initially focuses on one of Salanter's students, Isaac Blaser (1837–1907), and then devotes individual chapters to other teachers and schools, including Simcha Zissel (1829–1898), another prominent student of Salanter. Eckman addresses the recurrent preoccupations of the movement: prayer, morality, psychology, knowledge, and education. He also explains that the curricula of the various Musar yeshivot differed in their emphasis of study and practice. For example, the Kelm curriculum was weighted toward religious, as opposed to secular, studies, although, as the author is careful to note, the Kelm school did not see the study of secular subjects as a necessary evil. "On the contrary," Eckman asserts, the school believed that "understanding science and the general environment was necessary, not only for better living, but better to comprehend religious teachings." Each chapter is replete with many details and references to primary sources, but the author often fails to convey the intensity of the conflicts among the leaders of the Musar schools, and the study lacks critical analysis of the sources it cites. ECKMAN (1975) similarly tends to emphasize positive accomplishments and discount disputes within the movement.

GOLDBERG is a thorough treatment of the central ideas and methodologies of the movement as expounded in the writings of Salanter. Highlighting the central questions that the Musar pedagogues sought to answer, the author leads the reader through the initial political, intellectual, and spiritual development and expansion of the Musar movement as a Jewish response to modernity.

ETKES is the most significant scholarly analysis of the roots and development of the Musar movement. The book guides English-language readers through some of the most obscure and difficult texts and terminology of the movement. The volume also makes the material accessible to those unfamiliar with this period of Jewish history, for the author presents a history of the intellectual, spiritual, and historical development of Musar that begins by tracing the individuals who most significantly influenced Salanter's thinking. Etkes argues that Salanter's most unique and important contribution to Judaism was his transformation of the issues of ethics from the domain of theology to the realm of psychology, and the author explains the essential connections between modern psychology and the traditional understanding of personal ethical development. Chapters eight through ten provide the basis for a thorough grasp of the radical nature of Musar as well as the impact that the movement has had on all ensuing discussions of ethics and human nature in Judaism. Etkes does not refrain from evaluating the successes and failures of the various Musar schools, and he comments on the extent to which they reflected the teachings of Salanter. He insists that the religious-cultural tendency "embodied in the writings of the Gaon, given systematic formulation by Rabbi Hayyim, and again embodied in the person of Rabbi Zundel Salant" provides a clear precedent for Salanter's conception of the human being.

The influential French Jewish philosopher LEVINAS (1994, 1998) makes an explicit attempt to situate many of the themes of the Musar movement in a completely modern and not necessarily religious or Jewish context. Focusing on the interpersonal experiences of the individual, the author stresses the interdependence of humans, and he examines the ethical necessity of experiencing the suffering or pain of the other. He writes, "It is in the interhuman perspective of my responsibility for the other, without concern for reciprocity, in my call for his or her disinterested help, in the asymmetry of the relation of one to the other, that I have tried to analyze the phenomenon of useless suffering."

RACHEL SABATH

Music: Cantillation

Binder, Abraham Wolf, *Biblical Chant*, New York: Philosophical Library, 1959; London: Owen, 1960

Idelsohn, Abraham Zebi, *Thesaurus of Oriental Hebrew Melodies*, Berlin: Harz, 1923–1933; as *Thesaurus of Hebrew Oriental Melodies*, New York: Ktav, 1973

Jacobson, Joshua R., "Ta'amey Hamikra: A Closer Look," *Journal of Synagogue Music*, 22(1–2), July/December 1992

Rosenbaum, Samuel, *A Guide to Haftarah Chanting*, New York: Ktav, 1973

Rosenbaum, Samuel, *A Guide to Torah Reading: A Manual for the Torah Reader*, New York: Ktav, 1982

Rosowsky, Solomon, *The Cantillation of the Bible: The Five Books of Moses*, New York: Reconstructionist Press, 1957

Spiro, Pinchas, *Haftarah Chanting*, New York: Board of Jewish Education of Greater New York, 1964, revised edition, 1994

Weil, Daniel Meir, *The Masoretic Chant of the Bible*, Jerusalem: Mass, 1995

Wickes, William, *A Treatise on the Accentuation of the Twenty-One So-Called Prose Books of the Old Testament, with a Facsimile of a Page of the Codex Assigned to Ben-Asher in Aleppo*, Oxford: Clarendon, 1887; with prolegomenon by Aron Dotan, New York: Ktav, 1970

Cantillation involves the reading of biblical texts according to a system of diacritical markings known as *ta'amei hamikra'*. These *ta'amim* appear as dots, lines, and other symbols above and below the verse, and they serve three purposes. Their primary functions are to indicate syntax and the correct accentuation of individual words. In addition, they have a musical function, as these accents guide the reader in the appropriate chanting of the text. Books and articles about cantillation focus variously on one, two, or all three of these functions.

WICKES adopts a primarily grammatical approach in his scholarly work, which offers a thorough discussion of the relationship of the *ta'amim* to Hebrew syntax and includes rules for parsing, based upon the markings in the text. Wickes's study remains the only book of its kind available in English, although recent works in Hebrew may offer more accessible reference to the grammatical underpinnings of cantillation.

IDELSOHN devotes space in each of the ten volumes of his monumental work to a discussion of the musical aspects of cantillation found in each of the Jewish subcultures that he studied. Idelsohn notes structural similarities among the disparate traditions, concluding that all Jewish music is based upon common roots in biblical chant.

ROSOWSKY presents the first major work in English devoted exclusively to cantillation. In this exhaustive yet accessible study, Rosowsky clearly sets out the grammatical structures that guide the employment of each accent in a clause, dividing them into "servants" and "lords," which function interdependently and appear in predictable sequences. He also dedicates extensive space to a patient and thorough exposition of the manner of chanting each accent according to the Lithuanian tradition imported to the United States. Rosowsky offers examples of the adaptation of each neume (musical symbol) to words of one to seven syllables, providing real illustrations of each possibility drawn from actual biblical verses. The volume is available in many school and synagogue libraries, and it should be consulted by any serious student of the subject.

While Rosowsky went to elaborate lengths to expound the Eastern European tradition, BINDER took just 125 pages to explore the Central European tradition preferred by his students at the Reform movement's Hebrew Union College. Binder's more compact treatment is a thorough and extremely practical survey of the basics. In addition, Binder offers instructions for dealing with the musical "detours" or irregularities in the Pentateuch, as well as information about all the Ashkenazi variations employed in chanting the Prophets and Five Scrolls. Binder concludes his slim volume with a comparative chart of all six cantillation systems.

Several volumes intended primarily for lay readers offer some introduction to the history of biblical chant and the organization of the accents into clauses. SPIRO's text is clearly meant for use in instructional settings, and it is especially well suited for use by adolescents preparing for Bar and Bat Mitzvah ceremonies. A supplemental "Guide for the Junior Torah Reader" provides a brief introduction to the Torah service, including charts for each kind of scriptural chant.

Rosenbaum was for many years the executive vice president of the Conservative movement's Cantors Assembly, and both ROSENBAUM (1973) and ROSENBAUM (1982) are as reader-friendly as Spiro's work, offering practical information for prospective chanters.

WEIL has authored an exhaustive study of cantillation whose syntactical/grammatical system presents the accents of the 21 prose books of the Bible in groups of "leaders" and "suspense" (an organization not unlike the division of accents maintained by Rosowsky into the classical "lords" and "servants"). Weil also investigates the original musical content of the now-universal Tiberian system of accentuation. Unfortunately, all of his research is predicated not only on the reader's prior knowledge of basic principles of cantillation, but also on familiarity with the work of a variety of other authors on the subject (notably M. Breuer) that is not readily available, at least in English. Weil's scholarship may be pioneering, but it is also highly abstruse, and therefore it is of little use to most students of the tradition of biblical chant.

JACOBSON's journal article is noteworthy, for it offers a comprehensive overview of several issues relating to cantillation. Jacobson starts by exploring the interrelationship between biblical texts and the uses of the *ta'amim*, in order to facilitate the proper setting of those same texts in liturgical compositions. He then turns his attention to the grammatical and syntactical uses of the accents, illustrating how various sentences could be misread if the punctuation provided by the *ta'amim* were ignored. Jacobson also provides an introduction to the syntactical division of Scripture that the experienced reader can use to predict the appearance of the correct accent. His article concludes with a brief bibliographic survey of books on cantillation and a call for greater diligence on the part of music professionals in the performance and practice of this sacred art. While the presentation of this article is marred by various printer's errors, this flaw should not detract from Jacobson's scholarship.

MARSHA BRYAN EDELMAN

See also Music: American Jewish Music; Music: Art Music; Music: Ashkenazi Folk Music; Music: Cantorial Music; Music: Middle Eastern Music; Music: Sephardi Music, Music: Views on Music

Music: Cantorial Music

Cohon, Baruch Joseph, "The Structure of the Synagogue Prayer-Chant," *Journal of the American Musicological Society*, 3(1), 1950

Gradenwitz, Peter, *The Music of Israel: From the Biblical Era to Modern Times*, Portland, Oregon: Amadeus, 1996

Idelsohn, Abraham Zebi, *Jewish Music in Its Historical Development*, New York: Holt, 1929; as *Jewish Music: Its Historical Development*, London: Constable, 1992

Levine, Joseph A., *Synagogue Song in America* (Performance in World Music), Crown Point, Indiana: White Cliffs Media, 1989

Rothmüller, Aron Marko, *The Music of the Jews: An Historical Appreciation*, London: Vallentine, Mitchell, 1953; New York: Beechhurst, 1954; revised edition, Cranbury, New Jersey: Barnes, 1967

Sendrey, Alfred, *The Music of the Jews in the Diaspora (up to 1800): A Contribution to the Social and Cultural History of the Jews*, New York: Yoseloff, 1971

Slobin, Mark, *Chosen Voices: The Story of the American Cantorate* (Music in American Life), Urbana: University of Illinois Press, 1989

Werner, Eric, *The Sacred Bridge: The Interdependence of Liturgy and Music in Synagogue and Church during the First Millennium*, vol. 1, New York: Columbia University Press, and London: Dobson, 1959; vol. 2, New York: Ktav, and London: Dobson, 1984

Werner, Eric, *A Voice Still Heard: The Sacred Songs of the Ashkenazic Jews* (Leo Baeck Institute Series), University Park: Pennsylvania State University Press, 1976

Treatment of the literature on cantorial music as a topic might encourage the reader to surmise that there is just one such genre. In fact, while the term refers to the ritual melodies performed by a Jewish precentor, there is immense variety in the global spectrum of cantorial music. Allowing for any number of subtler regional variations, we can divide the Jewish musical traditions of the world into three cultural subsets: Oriental or Middle Eastern music, which denotes by and large the repertoire of Jews living in Islamic lands; Sephardi music, which encompasses the traditions of Jews who lived in medieval Spain or Portugal and the lands of the Sephardi diaspora since the end of the Middle Ages; and Ashkenazi music, which denotes the musical output of the Jews with origins in Central and Eastern Europe.

Since the great majority of Jews in English-speaking countries are Ashkenazim, it is primarily their cantorial music that has received treatment in English-language studies, although there are innumerable books of actual cantorial music, noting the traditions of Jews from a variety of regions, Oriental and Sephardi included.

IDELSOHN, the first Jewish ethnomusicologist, devotes much of his landmark synthesis to discussion of cantorial music from the biblical period through the dawn of the 20th century. Chapters 4 through 16 of part 1 (more than 250 pages) provide a thorough overview of the history of synagogue music and its evolution from unrhythmical chant to art music. Idelsohn's prose is dry, and many of his musical illustrations, and the observations accompanying them, will be lost on the uninitiated. This remains, however, a first stop for any serious student of cantorial music.

Idelsohn was followed by a fairly long list of Jewish music historians eager to contribute their understandings to the literature. Of necessity, cantorial music is featured in their work, since (with only local exceptions) it and the folk music which it influenced were the sole extant Jewish musical forms until the 19th century. While none of these focuses exclusively or even disproportionately on cantorial music, the surveys by SENDREY, ROTHMÜLLER, and GRADENWITZ are among the most comprehensive, and each is well worth examination.

Eric Werner, by contrast, devoted much of his career to championing a thorough understanding particularly of Jewish liturgical music and the factors that influenced its development. Since the Ashkenazim lived in constant contact with their Christian neighbors, it is not surprising that Jewish and non-Jewish music should have cross-pollinated extensively. WERNER (1959) describes the results of this intermingling of traditions, exploring the maze of similarities and borrowings back and forth between the two forms. A more detailed examination specifically of the Jewish music that resulted is presented in WERNER (1976). The author places his study in a context of the many influences—internal and external—that affected the practice of cantorial music. He tends to assume considerable knowledge of both Judaism and music on the part of his readers, and sometimes it will be difficult for the non-specialist to follow. On the other hand, his understanding of the scope of Jewish history and literature is impressive, and the thoughtful reader will gain much from these volumes.

The important article by COHON contributes a clear and concise yet comprehensive understanding of "The Structure of the Synagogue Prayer-Chant." Following a brief explication of the distinction between a traditional "scale" and the "modes" employed in synagogue song, Cohon then discusses the four modes on which traditional Ashkenazi synagogue music is based: *Adonoy Molokh, Ahavoh Rabboh, Mogen Ovos,* and Psalm Mode. Each of these is utilized in unique ways for different times of day and/or different liturgical seasons, resulting in distinctive musical flavors. Cohon carefully charts the classical motives employed in each manifestation of the mode. While his article is, of necessity, somewhat technical and best understood by readers with some musical literacy, it is nevertheless easy enough to follow and provides a wonderful introduction to the world of cantorial music.

The only recent book to deal with the relationship between traditional and contemporary cantorial music is LEVINE. He provides a comprehensive survey of the subject, from Temple days to the modern American synagogue, and includes useful discussion of the primary modes utilized in Ashkenazi cantorial music, as well as extensive illustrative material. Unfortunately, Levine's tone varies from accessible and even mildly humorous to professorial and esoteric. In addition, especially in discussing more contemporary music (for which he barely attempts to disguise his disdain), Levine reaches some of his predetermined conclusions only by taking several examples out of any practical context. Despite its uneven presentation, this is a one-of-a-kind treatment of the subject, and it remains an essential element in the effort to understand the evolution of cantorial music.

One last volume must be added to the list of indispensable references for an appreciation of cantorial music: SLOBIN. While surveying the role of the cantorate in American Jewish life, he coincidentally traces the evolution of synagogue musical practice. No study of cantors could be complete without some consideration of their music, and Slobin does not disappoint, discussing traditional *nusach* as well as art music written especially for the modern synagogue. This book contributes the context for appreciating cantors and their music, and it is a valuable addition to the literature.

MARSHA BRYAN EDELMAN

See also Music: American Jewish Music; Music: Art Music; Music: Ashkenazi Folk Music; Music: Cantillation; Music: Middle Eastern Music; Music: Sephardi Music; Music: Views on Music

Music: Art Music

Bohlman, Philip V., *The World Centre for Jewish Music in Palestine, 1936–1940: Jewish Musical Life on the Eve of World War II*, New York: Oxford University Press, and Oxford: Clarendon, 1992

Brod, Max, *Israel's Music*, Tel Aviv: Sefer, 1951; expanded by Yehuda Walter Cohen as *Die Musik Israels*, London: Bärenreiter, 1976

Fleisher, Robert, *Twenty Israeli Composers: Voices of a Culture,* Detroit, Michigan: Wayne State University Press, 1997

Hirshberg, Jehoash, *Music in the Jewish Community of Palestine, 1880–1948: A Social History,* New York: Oxford University Press, and Oxford: Clarendon, 1995

Karas, Joza, *Music in Terezín, 1941–1945,* New York: Beaufort, 1985

Keren, Zvi, *Contemporary Israeli Music: Its Sources and Stylistic Development,* Ramat Gan: Bar-Ilan University Press, 1980

Ringer, Alexander L., *Arnold Schoenberg: The Composer as Jew,* New York: Oxford University Press, and Oxford: Clarendon, 1990

Tischler, Alice, *A Descriptive Bibliography of Art Music by Israeli Composers* (Detroit Studies in Music Bibliography, no. 62), Warren, Michigan: Harmonie Park, 1988

Weisser, Albert, *The Modern Renaissance of Jewish Music: Events and Figures, Eastern Europe and America,* New York: Bloch, 1954; reprint with new introduction, New York: Da Capo, 1983

Art music assumes three different but related forms in Jewish history and culture. First, composers create a music with distinctively Jewish themes, with resonances both inside and outside Jewish society. Second, composers with Jewish identities create works that express that identity, either through historical circumstances or because of conscious decisions to ascribe Jewish meaning to a composition. Third, particular works of music develop symbolically Jewish identities because of their reception history, and the Jewish identity of the composers in such instances may or may not be relevant to that history. Art music becomes Jewish, therefore, for both textual and contextual reasons.

WEISSER was the first music scholar to outline the conditions for Jewish art music. The Jewish composers generating the "modern Renaissance"—from the late 19th century into the 1920s—came of age at a high point of Russian nationalism, and they correspondingly developed their "Jewishness" by collecting and setting Jewish folk songs through the St. Petersburg Society for Jewish Folk Music. Jewish art music emerged at the interstices between tradition and modernity. A Jewish music theory took shape through investigations of intrinsically Jewish musical traits, such as those in the ritual of the synagogue, and their reformulation into modern compositional techniques. Weisser devotes separate chapters to Joel Engel, Joseph Achron, Moses Milner, Lazare Saminsky, Alexander Krein, and Michael Gniessen, and he closes the book with a chapter on the movement's influence in America.

RINGER makes a bold and controversial case for establishing the attributes that mark a composer as Jewish. As the leading figure of European musical modernism, Arnold Schoenberg is usually interpreted as a composer more concerned with the independence of music from internal and external identities. This book brings an alternative perspective to the composer, first, by arguing that Schoenberg intensified his treatment of Jewish themes throughout his life, and second, by establishing parallels between Schoenberg's aesthetic approaches and Jewish mystical traditions. Schoenberg's obsession with number theory, for example, is likened to Kabbalah. Ringer's major contribution is the musical portrait of Schoenberg as a complex figure, whose musical activities ranged from the most esoteric domains to popular musics such as cabaret.

HIRSHBERG writes the first comprehensive music history of the *yishuv*, the period of resettlement in Palestine prior to Israeli statehood in 1948. He employs a sociological methodology, examining cultural institutions and musical change more extensively than the music itself. The period unfolds as one marked by struggle and experimentation yet fundamental to the emergence of a national music culture. Each chapter encompasses a historical moment in or a significant influence on the music of Israel. The social history of music in the book portrays music as a means of accommodating differences among the ethnic communities and establishing a distinctive 20th-century voice.

BOHLMAN translates and edits the documents of the first art music society in the land of Israel, the World Centre for Jewish Music in Palestine (WCJMP), which flourished briefly on the eve of World War II. Organized by three European immigrants—Salli Levi, Joachim Stutschewsky, and Hermann Swet—the WCJMP established contacts with Jewish musicians throughout the world, attempting to centralize Jewish musical activity in the *yishuv* by founding the journal *Musica Hebraica,* organizing concerts and festivals, and publishing new compositions. The documents in the book give voice to many Jewish musicians as the specter of the Holocaust continued to grow, and the interpretive chapters examine the difficulties, personal and musical, of creating a national music culture in Israel.

KARAS has written the first major English-language study of music in the Nazi concentration camp of Theresienstadt (Terezín) in the northwestern part of Czechoslovakia. Terezín was somewhat unusual insofar as the prisoners were allowed to continue artistic activities, even in the midst of brutal deprivation. Concerts continued, and several of Central Europe's most distinguished Jewish composers—Pavel Haas, Gideon Klein, Hans Krása, and Viktor Ullmann among others—were active in the camp's musical life before deportation to the Auschwitz extermination camp. Karas portrays Terezín's musical culture very lucidly, and several works, such as Krása's children's opera, *Brundibár,* receive in-depth treatment. Though the book does not dwell on Jewishness in Terezín's music culture, it becomes clear that many composers intensified the Jewish qualities in their works while in the camp.

BROD has written an in-depth historical study of art music in Israel at the end of the *yishuv* and the beginning of statehood. An immigrant from Prague, Brod provides a sensitive portrait of the accomplishments of the immigrant generation, framing it as an in-gathering of diverse cultures. Jewish music and art music in Israel, therefore, reflect this diversity and are aesthetically the products of historical circumstances in the diaspora and in Israel. When the first edition appeared, art music in Israel was also benefiting from integration into a wide range of other cultural activities, from radio to dance and theater, with which Brod himself was associated. The first edition, which appeared only in English translation, quickly became a classic music history. The expanded edition retained the German in which Brod wrote and included an extensive update by Yehuda Walter Cohen, who gives an account of the subsequent quarter century of Israel's music history.

KEREN approaches the music culture of Israel in the 1960s and 1970s by laying out a broadly historical background. Though his subject is art music in Israel, the influences he considers make it clear that his subject is also Jewish music in a narrower sense because of the ways religious traditions, Jewish folk music, and the Hebrew language naturally influence the composer. The presentation and analysis of contemporary Israeli music rely almost entirely on musical style, with biography and historical context kept to a mininum. Each discussion of musical style is illustrated with several musical examples, a total of 187 of which fill the book's 181-page appendix.

TISCHLER provides a bibliography of works by composers active in Israel from the *yishuv* period until 1986, when she completed her research. For each work she includes not only the bibliographical citations but also information about first performances, manuscripts, and availability of taped or other recordings. The entries are organized by composer, and each composer is introduced with a biographical sketch, which is followed by a complete listing of compositions. The research for the book took place in libraries and archives primarily in the United States, Europe, and Israel, and researchers who want to pursue these sources will find the way well paved. Though the book stems primarily from institutional materials, it opens up many other possibilities for further research.

FLEISHER has gathered interviews from 20 of Israel's most distinguished composers, organizing them into three generations: immigrants who developed their compositional vocabularies prior to settling in Israel, a second generation that came of age during early statehood, and a third group whose musical voices developed after Israel became a nation. Fleisher has meticulously researched each composer and his or her works, making the reference aspects of the book as up-to-date as possible. The interviews are not presented in journalistic format but rather as narratives that allow each composer to speak as eloquently as possible. An American composer, Fleisher has taken great pains to ensure that his book is not simply a history but rather an ethnographic entry into the art-music scene of Israel in the late 20th century.

PHILIP V. BOHLMAN

See also Music: American Jewish Music; Music: Ashkenazi Folk Music; Music: Cantillation; Music: Cantorial Music; Music: Middle Eastern Music; Music: Sephardi Music; Music: Views on Music

Music: American Jewish Music

Baumgarten, Murray (general editor), "Klezmer: History and Culture, A Conference," *Judaism: A Quarterly Journal of Jewish Life and Thought*, 47(1), Winter 1998

Fromm, Herbert, *On Jewish Music: A Composer's View*, New York: Bloch, 1978

Heskes, Irene, *Passport to Jewish Music: Its History, Traditions, and Culture* (Contributions to the Study of Music and Dance, no. 33), Westport, Connecticut: Greenwood, 1994

Kanter, Kenneth A., *The Jews on Tin Pan Alley: The Jewish Contribution to American Popular Music, 1830–1940*, New York: Ktav, 1982

Levine, Joseph A., *Synagogue Song in America* (Performance in World Music Series), Crown Point, Indiana: White Cliffs Media, 1989

Shelemay, Kay K., *Let Jasmine Rain Down: Song and Remembrance among Syrian Jews* (Chicago Studies in Ethnomusicology), Chicago: University of Chicago Press, 1998

Slobin, Mark, *Tenement Songs: The Popular Music of the Jewish Immigrants* (Music in American Life), Urbana: University of Illinois Press, 1982

Slobin, Mark, *Chosen Voices: The Story of the American Cantorate* (Music in American Life), Urbana: University of Illinois Press, 1989

A comprehensive study of American Jewish music in all its facets has yet to be written. General Jewish music histories devote little attention to understanding the profound effect of the American experience on Jewish music. When transplanted to the United States, classic sacred and folk traditions from the Ashkenazi and Sephardi communities evolved in a wide range of directions. Genres from synagogue song to klezmer music were markedly influenced by American culture. Jewish music also became woven into the cultural and economic fabric of the American concert hall, theater, films, and the recording industry, as Jewish musicians reached outward from immigrant beginnings, creating a musical synthesis that inextricably linked American culture and the Jewish world. The readings listed above represent areas of recent study related to American Jewish music in its diverse forms—sacred and secular, deeply traditional and radically innovative.

HESKES provides an excellent overview of American Jewish music in a section titled "Three Hundred Years of Jewish Music in America" that examines the "complex legacy" of influences and traditions that Jews brought to the North American continent, and she provides summary highlights of major events and turning points in that history. The author focuses on significant artistic practices and mentions regional as well as national figures, including composers, cantors, organists, choir directors, and musical organizers. She covers musical theater, popular song, cantorial and choral synagogue song, klezmer, labor songs, and Yiddish popular music. Heskes also outlines the careers of major Jewish composers such as Ernest Bloch, Darius Milhaud, Arnold Schoenberg, and Leonard Bernstein, and she considers Jewish dimensions of their lives and music. A brief chapter on popular songwriters such as Irving Berlin, Jerome Kern, and George and Ira Gershwin provides perspective on the increasing allure of secular American culture for Jewish artists.

SHELEMAY offers a case study of *pizmonim* (songs) of a Syrian Jewish community, based on ethnographic research involving field recordings and interviews, primarily with subjects in Brooklyn, New York, although she also documents musical connections between this community and other Syrian Jewish communities. Shelemay explains in detail how this music reflects an array of cultural processes involved in the transmission of Middle Eastern folk and sacred musical traditions. She explores the intricate workings and daily practices of cultural memory through music.

FROMM captures the American Jewish music world through the eyes of a musician practicing in a Reform synagogue. The essays, many of which had been previously published over the span of Fromm's career, outline the composer's views as he tackles the hard questions regarding the definition of Jewish music and the practical aspects of routine temple musicianship. Fromm elucidates not only the attitudes of his time but also the goals and ideas behind his own synagogue compositions. He discusses the works of many other composers and contemporaries. Especially useful are his reviews of books and particular synagogue works and other Jewish compositions.

LEVINE has produced the best work outlining how Americans practice the art of synagogue song. He primarily focuses on technical musical analysis of traditional synagogue chants, including extensive examples of cantorial styles that cover the arts of improvisation and prescribed motifs. He reveals his views of the influences of folk, pop, rock, and jazz on Jewish liturgical music, and in the conclusion, he evaluates the Americanization of Ashkenazi musical tradition.

SLOBIN (1989) provides a highly readable book of applied ethnomusicology that serves also as a historical and sociological study of Jewish music in the United States. The author presents Jewish community and musical life through anecdotes and extensive quotations from primary sources. Through these sources, Slobin traces the evolution of the role of the American cantor, emphasizing the extent to which cantors played a crucial part in the survival of Jewish sacred music across denominational lines. He discusses the first major waves of Jewish immigration from Europe, during which the cantor served as a primary religious leader; the early days of phonograph recordings, when select cantors became Jewish celebrities; and the modern era, when the cantorate became professionalized. Slobin discusses the current nature of the cantor's job, and he examines new trends in the profession including the recent inclusion of women. Specific musical examples reveal how the basic repertoire can provide clues to the significance and responsibilities of the cantor in various historical periods.

SLOBIN (1982) explores the popular secular works of music created by Jews during the great period of immigration at the turn of the 20th century. Millions of Jews from Europe brought their folk cultural legacy and Yiddish language to North American shores. Popular Jewish songs, sentimental ballads, and melodrama expressed ethnic identity and reflected the concerns and passions of that immigrant population. Slobin expounds the beliefs, the social and economic milieu, and the organizational life that encompassed these new immigrants. He explains the roles of various types of musicians including cantor, meshoyrer, and klezmer musicians. The accomplishments of Yiddish theater musicians such as Goldfaden, Mogulesco, Perlmutter, Rumshinsky, and Secunda are detailed. These and other prolific Yiddish theater composers set the stage for later American musical theater. Slobin also discusses the stylistics of Yiddish sheet music.

KANTER contends that the participation of Jewish composers, performers, agents, producers, and publishers played a prominent role in shaping the development and course of popular song in the United States. In the first section of the book, Kanter traces Jewish participation in American popular music through the songs of musicians such as Henry Russell and John Howard Payne. He chronologically outlines the contributions of numerous Jews involved in minstrel shows, the song repertoire of the Civil War era, parlor songs of the gay nineties, burlesque, and vaudeville. The second major section of the book is devoted to chapters offering biographies of notable American musicians such as Henry Russell, Monroe Rosenfield, Charles Harris, Irving Berlin, Lorenz Hart, Richard Rodgers, Oscar Hammerstein, Jerome Kern, and George and Ira Gershwin. Kanter concludes with a selection of illustrated covers of American Jewish sheet music.

BAUMGARTEN, the general editor of *Judaism*, oversaw a special section to volume 47 that contains selected conference papers from the Klezmer Research Conference at Wesleyan University. The collection explores the phenomenal recent revival in klezmer music and includes a history of klezmer in the United States, detailed analyses of influences on and by klezmer music, a discussion of the argot peculiar to this musical subculture, and insiders' views of the vibrant nature of the current klezmer music scene.

JUDITH S. PINNOLIS

See also Music: Art Music; Music: Ashkenazi Folk Music; Music: Cantillation; Music: Cantorial Music; Music: Middle Eastern Music; Music: Sephardi Music; Music: Views on Music

Music: Ashkenazi Folk Music

Cahan, Yehuda Leyb, *Yidishe folkslider mit melodien* [Yiddish Folk Songs with Melodies], edited by Max Weinreich, New York: Yivo Institute for Jewish Research, 1957

Coopersmith, Harry (editor), *Songs of Zion*, New York: Behrmans Jewish Book House, 1942

Flam, Gila, *Singing for Survival: Songs of the Lodz Ghetto, 1940–1945*, Urbana: University of Illinois Press, 1992

Heskes, Irene, *Yiddish American Popular Songs, 1895 to 1950: A Catalog Based on the Lawrence Marwick Roster of Copyright Entries*, Washington, D.C.: Library of Congress, 1992

Nathan, Hans (editor), *Israeli Folk Music: Songs of the Early Pioneers*, Madison, Wisconsin: A-R Editions, 1994

Rubin, Ruth (editor), *A Treasury of Jewish Folksong*, New York: Schocken, 1950

Sharvit, Uri, *Chassidic Tunes from Galicia*, Jerusalem: Renanot, 1995

Slobin, Mark (editor and translator), *Old Jewish Folk Music: The Collections and Writings of Moshe Beregovski*, Philadelphia: University of Pennsylvania Press, 1982

Vinaver, Chemjo, *Anthology of Hassidic Music*, edited, introduced, and annotated by Eliyahu Schleifer, Jerusalem: Jewish Music Research Centre, Hebrew University, 1985

In the broadest sense, Ashkenazi folk music includes the vernacular, popular, and oral traditions of the Jewish communities of Central and Eastern Europe, where Yiddish or German was commonly a lingua franca, alongside the various national languages and regional dialects. Ashkenazi folk music is both secular and sacred, and its history often unfolds as a documentation of the tensions between these domains in Jewish society. Different tensions result from the ways in which folk music forms at the fault lines between rural and urban, oral and written, and Jewish and non-Jewish cultural practices. Studies and collections of Ashkenazi folk music often narrate such tensions, and they document moments of historical change, notably the challenge of modernity to traditional Jewish life, the immigration of Ashkenazi Jews to North America and Israel, the pressures of antisemitism, and the destruction of Ashkenazi civilization through pogroms and the Holocaust.

HESKES provides synopses of 3,427 Yiddish songs published in the United States during the first half of the 20th century, which constituted a golden age for the Yiddish stage and for Yiddish popular music. Though each song is documented with detailed information about its composition, publication, and musical content, Heskes' approach is that of a social historian, using song to illuminate the culture of the Ashkenazi immigration to North America. The introductory essays, Yiddish guide, bibliographies, lists of sources, and illustrations from Yiddish sheet music make this volume very accessible for anyone with an interest in Ashkenazi oral and popular traditions. The volume stands also as crucial documentation of the Jewish contribution to American popular song.

CAHAN was the most important collector of Ashkenazi folk music from the turn of the century until the 1920s. This volume contains repertoires from different projects undertaken by Cahan throughout East and East-Central Europe. This edition follows several earlier editions, in Lithuania and New York, and it is one of the most comprehensive of all collections of Ashkenazi folk music from pre-Holocaust Europe. The bulk of the texts and commentaries are in Yiddish, but Max Weinreich introduces the volume in English, and the song texts are romanized. In addition to the 205 pieces with transcribed melodies, folk poetry and other song texts appear, organized according to genre and function. The volume is crucial to understanding Ashkenazi folk music in the decades prior to the Holocaust.

NATHAN gathers an anthology of folk-song settings commissioned by the Keren Kayemet (Jewish National Fund) in the late 1930s. The folk songs themselves were collected on kibbutzim and were usually poems by such distinguished poets as Nathan Alterman and Hayyim Nahman Bialik. The composers accepting the invitation to create a national art song were Aaron Copland, Paul Dessau, Artur Honegger, Darius Milhaud, Erich-Walter Sternberg, Ernst Toch, Kurt Weill, and Stefan Wolpe, and their compositions in this volume reflect their individual interpretations of Jewish music as well as their perceptions of unifying national traits. The volume opens and closes with historical and analytical essays by Philip V. Bohlman, whose concluding afterword is an extensive study of the relation between Jewish folk and art music.

COOPERSMITH compiles a volume of 209 songs in a work that enjoyed enormous success in the 1940s. The songs reflect the time of their compilation, particularly the emigration from Europe to North America and Palestine and the in-gathering and formation of new communities and traditions. The songs are divided between folk traditions (126 Yiddish and Hebrew folk songs, many with Zionist themes) and religious functions, most of them intended for holidays. Coopersmith was the most important Jewish music educator in the United States during the mid–20th century, and the book is conceived in such a way as to be profitably used in Jewish education. The songs and melodies lend themselves to easy performance, with many also in English translation.

FLAM draws on exhaustive interviews with survivors of the Łódź ghetto and on archival sources in Israel, Europe, and the United States to create a historical portrait of song in one of the ghettos formed by the Nazis. The interaction between folk and popular song traditions provided a narrative continuity to ghetto life, connecting the Jews of Łódź to their pasts, while at the same time providing them with a common set of experiences that allowed some form of survival. Flam follows certain songs as they unfolded in a history of their own, which simultaneously reflected the social changes in the ghetto. Just as some songs passed from domestic use to the workplace and public stage, others circulated as street songs or chronicled particular figures in the ghetto, especially Chaim Rumkowski, the political leader of the Jewish community. Folk and popular song provides a lens for drawing the reader closer to the everyday world of the Łódź ghetto.

VINAVER gathers folk songs from the Eastern European hasidic communities in which he worked as a collector and folklorist prior to his immigration to the United States in the late 1930s. Although Vinaver did not restrict himself to religious folk music—he was especially interested in the music for the Yiddish stage—his hasidic collections are the first to establish a framework for explicitly religious songs as folk music. The religious folk music of the hasidim, Vinaver found, spilled out of the synagogue and reflected the distinctive history of the Eastern European sects. The genres recognized by Vinaver, for example, the textless *nigun* (literally, "something played," a "melody"), have become standard symbols of the folk culture of Ashkenazi Jews, especially in the revival of Ashkenazi folk music at the end of the 20th century. Eliyahu Schleifer not only gathers together a superb anthology from Vinaver's collections and publications, but he also provides splendid musicological commentary.

SLOBIN translates and edits some of the core work of Moses Beregowski (1892–1961), the most important Soviet folk-music scholar and ethnologist, whose research examined Jewish traditions in different parts of the Soviet Union but focused on the most intensely Jewish regions of Ukraine. This volume contains both analytical essays and Beregowski's transcriptions, most of them published previously but here available in the West and with English translations for the first time. Beregowski struggled against Soviet authorities and scientific ideologies throughout his life, but he succeeded nonetheless in amassing large collections, several of which are under study and being prepared for publication. Beregowski's scientific perspectives were distinctive in the Jewish music scholarship of his age, particularly his recognition that Jewish folk music did not exist in a cultural vacuum and that it reflected fairly widespread cultural exchange.

RUBIN gathers Jewish folk songs, most of them Ashkenazi and from Eastern European sources, in one of the first popular collections compiled after the Holocaust and Israeli statehood. The selection and format of the volume reflect folklore theory of the mid-20th century, with the first part devoted to events in the life of the Jewish community, the second part to holidays, and the third part to historical events (songs of partisans and of Israel). The tone of Rubin's introduction and of her commentaries is nostalgic, and she regards the volume as preserving traces of a way of life that has been lost or destroyed. This collection of folk songs, however, has become a classic and has been particularly influential on Ashkenazi folk music in North America.

SHARVIT brings an ethnomusicological and analytical approach to folk songs and dances from Galicia, a thoroughly

Yiddish-speaking Jewish region that included parts of modern Poland and Ukraine. The volume includes melodies from genres across the Jewish culture of Galicia: synagogue and liturgical music; *Tischlieder* (table songs) and other songs from the home; and song and dance for hasidic celebration. Sharvit analyzes the modal infrastructure of these repertoires, and he presents this as a typology that represents a musical and cultural unity in the region. The tunes appear as transcriptions from collections gathered by the author's father, Elazar Sharvit (Schwerd), a Galician hasid himself and descended from a notable hasidic lineage. The volume, therefore, has a broader ethnographic and deeper personal quality than most collections of hasidic song and dance.

PHILIP V. BOHLMAN

See also Music: American Jewish Music; Music: Art Music; Music: Cantillation; Music: Cantorial Music; Music: Middle Eastern Music; Music: Sephardi Music; Music: Views on Music

Music: Sephardi Music

Adler, Israel, *Musical Life and Traditions of the Portuguese Jewish Community of Amsterdam in the XVIIIth Century* (Yuval Monograph Series, 1), Jerusalem: Magnes Press of Hebrew University, 1974

Adler, Israel, *The Study of Jewish Music: A Bibliographical Guide,* Jerusalem: Magnes Press of Hebrew University, 1995

Bunis, David, *Sephardic Studies: A Research Bibliography Incorporating Judezmo Language, Literature and Folklore, and Historical Background* (Garland Reference Library of the Humanities, vol. 174), New York: Garland, 1981

Cohen, Judith R., "Judeo-Spanish Songs in the Sephardic Communities of Montreal and Toronto: Survival, Function and Change," Ph.D. diss., Université de Montréal, 1989

Cohen, Judith R., "Women's Role in Judeo-Spanish Song," in *Active Voices: Women in Jewish Culture,* edited by Maurie Sacks, Urbana: University of Illinois Press, 1995

Cohen, Judith R., "Sonography of Judeo-Spanish Song," *Jewish Folklore and Ethnology Review,* 18(1–2), 1996

Dorn, Pamela J., "Change and Ideology: The Ethnomusicology of Turkish Jewry," Ph.D. diss., Indiana University, 1991

Etzion, Judith and Susana Weich-Shahak, "The Music of the Judeo-Spanish Romancero: Stylistic Features," *Anuario Musical,* 43, 1988

Hemsi, Alberto and Edwin Seroussi (editors), *Cancionero Sefardí,* Jerusalem: Jewish Music Research Center of Hebrew University, 1995

Katz, Israel Joseph, *Judeo-Spanish Traditional Ballads from Jerusalem: An Ethnomusicological Study,* 2 vols., recording, Brooklyn, New York: Institute of Mediaeval Music, 1972–1975

Katz, Israel Joseph, "Pre-Expulsion Tune Survivals Among Judeo-Spanish Ballads? A Possible Late Fifteenth Century French Antecedent," in M. Gerli and H. Sharrer, eds. *Hispanic Medieval Studies in Honour of Samuel G. Armistead,* Madison: Hispanic Seminary of Medieval Studies, 1992

Seroussi, Edwin, *Mizimrat Qedem: The Life and Music of R. Isaac Algazi from Turkey,* with 2 cassettes, Jerusalem: Renanot, 1989

Seroussi, Edwin, "New Directions in the Music of the Sephardi Jews," *Studies in Contemporary Judaism* 9, 1993

Seroussi, Edwin, "Sephardic Music: A Bibliographic Guide with a Checklist of Notated Sources," *Jewish Folklore and Ethnology Review,* 15(2), 1993

Seroussi, Edwin, *Spanish-Portuguese Synagogue Music in Nineteenth-Century Reform Sources from Hamburg: Ancient Tradition in the Dawn of Modernity* (Yuval Monograph Series, 11), Jerusalem: Magnes Press of Hebrew University, 1996

Shiloah, Amnon, *Jewish Musical Traditions* (Jewish Folklore and Anthropology Series), Detroit, Michigan: Wayne State University Press, 1992

Weich-Shahak, Susana, *Judeo-Spanish Moroccan Songs for the Life Cycle* (Yuval Music Series, 1), with cassette, Jerusalem: Jewish Music Research Center of Hebrew University, 1989

Weich-Shahak, Susana, "Adaptations and Borrowings in the Balkan Sephardic Repertoire," *Balkanistica,* Spring 1998

This survey concentrates on studies of the song repertoire in Judeo-Spanish (popularly known as "Ladino," a term that technically refers to literal translations from classic Hebrew texts rather than to a vernacular). The published research in this field is mostly in Spanish, and many of the most important contributions are found as journal articles, book chapters, encyclopedia entries, and even liner notes accompanying sound recordings rather than as monographs. This list, then, reflects a small sample, concentrating on material in book form and available in English. Musical anthologies (Manuel Alvar, Arcadio de Larrea Palacin, Isaac Levy, Leon Algazi) have not been included, but most are listed in the bibliographies in Seroussi 1993 and Cohen 1989. Musical analysis of Judeo-Spanish song has lagged behind textual analysis, so that many more titles are available that discuss the song texts only, with little or no reference to the music. With respect to Balkan Sephardi music, articles by Ankica Petrovic (Bosnia), Nikolai Kaufman (Bulgaria), Gisela Sulteanu (Romania), and S. Kaludova must also be mentioned, though they are not discussed here.

ADLER (1974) gives a good general idea of liturgical and art music in 18th-century Amsterdam's Sephardi community. His book also serves as a useful reference tool, giving the musical incipits of many melodies. ADLER (1995) is an important recent reference work, although not, of course, restricted to Sephardi music.

BUNIS surveys only the period up to the early 1980s, but he does include some out-of-the-way articles, and he also provides valuable information about early (78 rpm) recordings of Ottoman Sephardi singing.

COHEN (1989) focuses on Sephardi communities in Canada, primarily from Spanish-speaking northern Morocco (reflecting a significant part of the Canadian Sephardi community), with some material from the eastern Mediterranean as well. The dissertation offers historical background, a review of the literature, and a discussion of the songs in their social context. Also included are several brief oral histories and character sketches. Cohen proposes a reclassification of Judeo-Spanish song, downplaying the emphasis on the ballad corpus (romancero) and giving full attention to other genres, both life cycle and year cycle songs of considerable antiquity and newer aspects of the repertoire: lyric, topical, and recreational songs. Specifically musical aspects discussed include performance practice (with comparisons of current performance traditions and early-20th-century transcriptions) and some melodic analysis. Some 70 songs appear with musical transcriptions, and there is a concordance facilitating comparisons with other published versions. Cohen also has published a number of articles and book chapters; in addition she has produced recordings of Judeo-Spanish songs, as a soloist as well as with the Moroccan Sephardi ensemble *Gerineldo*, directed by Oro Anahory-Librowicz. Anahory-Librowicz herself has published widely on Judeo-Spanish song texts and other traditional literature.

COHEN (1996) updates earlier versions (appearing in 1993 and 1995 in *Jewish Folklore and Ethnology Review*) of a sonography of Judeo-Spanish song, listing 78 rpms, LPs, cassettes, CDs and some films and videos, with brief commentaries. This work is probably the most complete published discography available at the time of writing. Several documentary recordings are given special attention. Another version, with fewer entries but more information on selected items, may be found in the second edition of *World Music: The Rough Guide* (London: World Music Network, 1999).

Women have been the main singers and transmitters of Judeo-Spanish song; COHEN (1995) examines their role in detail. The article discusses the changing roles for women, who in a more traditonal setting would have transmitted songs to their daughters but now transmit them to noninsider singers and scholars, who often assume a variant of a daughter's role.

DORN follows several intriguing articles with her dissertation, an informative overview of musical life in the Sephardi communities of Turkey with a strong anthropological orientation. Included are discussions of disemia, culture contact, and epistemological aspects of change. The community is described in historico-political and ethnographic detail, providing a solid context for discussions of influences from Balkan, Greek, Turkish, and Western musical cultures on the song repertoire and performance styles. Both traditional and new styles are given serious attention. More musical transcriptions would have been welcome, but those that are provided are well chosen and cogently discussed.

The article by ETZION and WEICH-SHAHAK, one of a small group of studies carried out by these two Israeli scholars, reflects their respective expertise in early Iberian musicology and in Judeo-Spanish song. Their articles comprise the first serious treatment of concrete musical relationships between the Sephardi and early Spanish *romanceros,* using systematic analysis of a defined corpus.

A select team of specialists in different aspects of Judeo-Spanish traditional literature, headed by ethnomusicologist Edwin Seroussi, has produced HEMSI and SEROUSSI, a landmark critical edition of Hemsi's early-20th-century transcriptions/arrangements of eastern Mediterranean Judeo-Spanish songs. This edition includes a detailed account of Hemsi's life and work and discussions of the different song genres in the edition (for another view of classification, see Cohen 1989). The small, seldom-discussed corpus of Ladino prayers is also included, as are Hemsi's previously unpublished melodies and commentaries, as well as useful concordances and other reference materials. Susana Weich-Shahak provides related song versions from her field collections at the National Sound Archives in Jerusalem, and Samuel G. Armistead, the "dean" of Judeo-Spanish studies, ends the volume with an erudite but highly readable postscript. Paloma Díaz-Más, José Manuel Pedrosa, and Elena Romero seldom publish in English, so their contributions here are another boon of this publication; an accompanying recording would have been ideal.

Katz may be considered the pioneer of a serious ethnomusicological approach to Judeo-Spanish song. His numerous articles and analyses of Judeo-Spanish and Iberian music are scattered over a wide range of monographs, journals, and conference proceedings, but KATZ (1972–1975), a two-volume work, is the only book-length publication of which he is the sole author. Katz is known particularly for his collaboration in studies of the Judeo-Spanish *romancero* by Samuel G. Armistead and Joseph Silverman, notably the monumental, ongoing series *Folk Literature of the Sephardic Jews* (University of California). His work with both medieval Iberian music manuscripts and regional traditions has added to the value of his publications, which focus on painstaking, systematic musical transcriptions and analyses, particularly of the romances, rather than on social context and personalities. In this book Katz gives a historical introduction and review of the literature—to that point, some 25 years ago—and a very detailed musical examination of ballads recorded from eastern Mediterranean traditional singers in Jerusalem. The second volume consists of comparative transcriptions of the variants of five ballads. A small soft-plastic phonograph recording is included, particularly valuable in that it was recorded in the 1960s, when very few documentary recordings were made. For another approach to the question of Sephardi–early Iberian musical links discussed by Etzion and Weich-Shahak, and others, see KATZ (1992).

SEROUSSI (1996) explores a little-known aspect of Sephardi music, that of the community of Hamburg, providing thorough historical background, musical transcriptions, and analysis. It is a short but thoroughly researched and densely packed study that should stimulate further research on the music of the Portuguese Jewish communities of Western Europe and their relationship to Jewish musical traditions of Spain and Portugal, on the one hand, and to those of North Africa and the former Ottoman lands, on the other.

SEROUSSI (1989) is a monograph that accompanies the welcome remastering of 78 rpm phonograph recordings by the great Turkish Sephardi singer and cantor Isaac Algazi. The two cassettes include material in Hebrew and Judeo-Spanish, as well as some in Turkish. The Judeo-Spanish songs are sung in virtuoso Turkish style, in *maqam* (the complex system of Middle Eastern musical modes) and with unobtrusive instrumental accompaniment, often on the *oud* (lute). The monograph gives musical and text transcriptions, as well as biographical and historical background and musical analysis; the set is invaluable for understanding the Ottoman Sephardi musical tradition.

SEROUSSI (1993b) is a very useful bibliography, referring both to Judeo-Spanish and to "Sephardi" music in the broader sense of the term. Seroussi has written extensively on the contemporary state of the Judeo-Spanish tradition; see, for example, SEROUSSI (1993a).

SHILOAH is a valuable guide to the music and musical life of a wide variety of Jewish communities. Rather than organize the study geographically or by culture, the author examines different aspects of musical life, referring in each chapter to a wide range of Jewish cultures. Inevitably, with this sort of wide-ranging study, there is no shortage of omissions, but Shiloah's expertise and experience make this a very important reference and a stimulating point of departure for the discussion of how to approach the study of Jewish music. Again, a recording would have enhanced the book's value greatly.

Weich-Shahak has produced a plethora of articles, scholarly anthologies, and documentary (and more recently semidocumentary) recordings based on her extensive field collection of Judeo-Spanish songs, part of the National Sound Archives at the Hebrew University of Jerusalem. WEICH-SHAHAK (1989) is in book form, with a cassette of documentary recordings of Judeo-Spanish life cycle songs from Morocco, mostly performed by women now living in Israel. One key singer was recorded two decades earlier by both Henrietta Yurchenco (CD "Alegrias y Duelas de la Novia," Global Village 145) and Manuel Alvar (unpublished, Arias Montano Institute, Madrid); this offers an unusual opportunity to compare the singer's style over a 20-year range. The book includes—as do almost all of Weich-Shahak's publications—detailed musical and text transcriptions, along with background material.

WEICH-SHAHAK (1998), a valuable counterpart to the Moroccan study of 1989, is a long article that examines Balkan, particularly Bulgarian and Greek, sources for Judeo-Spanish songs and follows logically from her earlier articles on Bulgarian Sephardi song (*Orbis Musicae* 1979–1980 and 1981–1982; *Revista de Dialectologia y Tradiciones Populares* 44, 1989) and the documentary recordings from her field collection (AMTI, Hebrew University of Jerusalem and Tecnosaga, Madrid).

JUDITH R. COHEN

See also Music: American Jewish Music; Music: Art Music; Music: Ashkenazi Folk Music; Music: Cantillation; Music: Cantorial Music; Music: Middle Eastern Music; Music: Views on Music

Music: Middle Eastern Music

Dorn, Pamela J., "Change and Ideology: The Ethnomusicology of Turkish Jewry," Ph.D. diss., Indiana University, 1991

Halper, Jeff, Edwin Seroussi, and Pamela Squires-Kidron, "Musica Mizrakhit: Ethnicity and Class Culture in Israel," *Popular Music*, 8(2), 1989

Hirshberg, Jehoash, *Music in the Jewish Community of Palestine, 1880–1948: A Social History,* New York: Oxford University Press, and Oxford: Clarendon, 1995

Horowitz, Amy, "Performance in Disputed Territory: Israeli Mediterranean Music," *Musical Performance,* issue title: *The Performance of Jewish and Arab Music in Israel Today,* 1(3), 1997

Idelsohn, Abraham Z. (editor), *Thesaurus of Oriental Hebrew Melodies,* 10 vols., Berlin: Harz, 1914–1932; New York: Ktav, 1973

Idelsohn, Abraham Z., *Jewish Music in Its Historical Development,* New York: Holt, 1929

Kligman, Mark, "Modes of Prayer: Arabic Maqamat in the Sabbath Morning Liturgical Music of the Syrian Jews in Brooklyn," Ph.D. diss., New York University, 1997

Seroussi, Edwin, "The Turkish *Makam* in the Musical Culture of the Ottoman Jews: Sources and Examples," *Israel Studies in Musicology,* 5, 1990

Seroussi, Edwin, "Sephardic Music: A Bibliographic Guide with a Checklist of Notated Sources," *Jewish Folk and Ethnology Review,* 15(2), 1993

Sharvit, Uri, "The Musical Realization of Biblical Cantillation Symbols *(Te'amim)* in the Jewish Yemenite Tradition," *Yuval,* 4, 1982

Shelemay, Kay Kaufman, *Music, Ritual, and Falasha History,* East Lansing: African Studies Center, Michigan State University, 1986

Shelemay, Kay Kaufman, *Let Jasmine Rain Down: Song and Remembrance among Syrian Jews,* Chicago: University of Chicago Press, 1998

Shiloah, Amnon, *The Musical Tradition of Iraqi Jews: Selection of Piyyutim and Songs,* Or Yehuda: Iraqi Jews' Traditional Culture Center, 1983

Shiloah, Amnon, *Jewish Musical Traditions,* Detroit, Michigan: Wayne State University Press, 1992

Shiloah, Amnon, *The Dimension of Music in Islamic and Jewish Culture,* Brookfield, Vermont, and Aldershot, Hampshire: Variorum, 1993

Tasat, Ramon Alberto, "The Cantillations and the Melodies of the Jews of Tangier, Morocco," D.M.A. diss., University of Texas at Austin, 1993

The use of "Middle Eastern" for the present summary denotes Jewish life in the lands to the south and east of the Mediterranean. The term "Oriental" was commonly used in earlier studies denoting these non-European regions, but "Middle Eastern" is more to the point. Arabic and Turkish styles in this region are the predominant influences in music and other aspects of cultural life. Two areas on the periphery of this region, Yemen and Ethiopia, are also included. Studies of the music of Jews living in the Middle East, and those from the Middle East living in other areas, are few. No comprehensive or comparative studies exist. Research has focused on particular communities, and most are even more specialized, investigating music in a particular context.

SEROUSSI (1993) provides a general bibliography of Sephardi music, Middle Eastern traditions included.

Idelsohn was among the first to study this region. IDELSOHN (1914–1932) covers music practiced in many areas and the practice of these traditions in Palestine. The traditions, as labeled by Idelsohn, are Yemenite, Babylonian, Persian, Bukharan, Dagestani, Oriental Sephardi (including Syrian and Egyptian), and Moroccan. Idelsohn noticed similarities in the practice of Jews from Syria, Egypt, and Lebanon. This practice by the mid–20th century was combined and is known as the *Yerushalmi-Sephardi* tradition, the music common to the Levantine Sephardim of Jerusalem. The monumental work of Idelsohn has been the source material for other scholars ever since. These volumes include explanations of the music, historical and theoretical material, and transcriptions of melodies he heard.

One attempt to look comparatively at Jewish musical practices in order to theorize a common origin was undertaken by IDELSOHN (1929). He looked particularly at Torah cantillation practice in various communities and noted similarities. SHILOAH (1992) provides a critical assessment of Idelsohn's approach in light of recent findings and methodology. Both are broad studies dealing with Middle Eastern as well as European music and provide a fundamental basis for the study of Jewish music.

Documentary sources are usually limited, if available at all, due to the largely oral transmission of these traditions. SEROUSSI (1990) investigates the *makam* (Middle Eastern musical modes) and *piyyut* (paraliturgical religious text singing) practices in the Ottoman region. *Piyyut* texts often provide indications for the origins of the music. SHELEMAY (1986) focuses on the history of the Beta Israel, or Falasha, community in Ethiopia through their liturgy, noting the similar practices of Ethiopian Christian monks. A range of historical issues and concerns related to Middle Eastern Jews is offered in SHILOAH (1993), including use of musical instruments, similarities to Arabic and Islamic practice, religious attitudes toward music, and mysticism. This publication is a collection of his articles and essays.

Most regional studies discuss the interrelationship of Jewish music to that of the local Turkish or Arabic styles. Thus, Seroussi (1990) looks at the similarities to Turkish music of *piyyut* singing in the Ottoman Empire, noting its decline in the 1920s. DORN looks broadly at the range of music among Jews in Turkey during the 1980s. She shows how the Turkish (*a la Turka*) and European (*a la Franka*) styles are blended with a preference for the latter, since it is considered modern. Singing in the synagogue is an exception, and more Turkish, less European melodies are favored.

The music of Syrian Jews has been studied outside of its native context. SHELEMAY (1998) researched Syrian Jews in Brooklyn, New York, Mexico, and Israel, focusing on *pizmonim*, non-synagogal *piyyutim*. This tradition includes the singing of Hebrew texts to known Arabic melodies. Her focus is on the lives of the individuals who perpetuate this tradition. Issues such as history and memory, tradition and change, transmission, ethnicity, and immigration frame her work. KLIGMAN focuses on the Sabbath liturgy of Syrian Jews in Brooklyn. Arabic music, singing styles, and aesthetics are incorporated into the liturgy on many levels. The *makamat* (plural of *makam*)

serve as the bridge; the weekly Torah reading is associated with a *makam* that becomes the central mode of liturgical singing for that day. The synthesis of Arabic musical styles in a Jewish religious context is used in Kligman's approach for an ethnomusicological study dealing with culture contact.

The music of Morocco is studied by TASAT, who focuses on the liturgical music of Tangier Jewry. He shows the range of musical styles, European and Maghrebi, common in this region. Tasat includes musical examples and descriptions of the liturgical contexts. Studies of other regions, not as comprehensive, include SHILOAH (1983) on the Iraqi tradition, where musical transcriptions make up the bulk of the study along with historical and stylistic comments; and SHARVIT on Yemenite Torah cantillation. The range of chants employed in the course of Torah study and public Torah reading in this tradition are compared.

Other studies focus on the incorporation of Middle Eastern musical styles in new contexts. HIRSHBERG looks at contemporary Israeli art music in its earliest years of formation, noting how European immigrant composers adapted Middle Eastern music into a Western context. Studies of popular music, found in HALPER, SEROUSSI, and SQUIRES-KIDRON and in HOROWITZ, focus on the growth of *muzikah mizrakhit yam tikhonit* (Eastern music of the Mediterranean) from an informal context in the 1970s into an industry. The music is a pan-ethnic style that integrates Hebrew lyrics that commingle with Arabic, Persian, Kurdish, and Turkish texts, and Eastern European, Greek, Turkish, or Arabic tunes and musical styles. Halper, Seroussi, and Squires-Kidron focus on the history of the genre and on Ashkenazi-Sephardi tensions in Israel. Horowitz shows how local aesthetic markers draw in Egyptian, Jordanian, Lebanese, Syrian, and Palestinian listeners.

MARK KLIGMAN

See also Music: American Jewish Music; Music: Art Music; Music: Ashkenazi Folk Music; Music: Cantillation; Music: Cantorial Music; Music: Sephardi Music; Music: Views on Music

Music: Views on Music

Gradenwitz, Peter, *The Music of Israel: Its Rise and Growth through 5000 Years,* New York: Norton, 1949; as *The Music of Israel: From the Biblical Era to Modern Times,* Portland, Oregon: Amadeus, 1996

Idelsohn, A.Z., *Jewish Music in Its Historical Development,* New York: Holt, 1929; as *Jewish Music: Its Historical Development,* London: Constable, and New York: Dover, 1992

Maimonides, Moses, *The Responsum of Maimonides (1135–1204) Concerning Music,* translated by Boaz Cohen, New York: Posy-Shoulson, 1935

Mendelsohn, Ezra (editor), *Modern Jews and Their Musical Agendas* (Studies in Contemporary Jewry, vol. 9), New York: Oxford University Press, 1993

Sendrey, Alfred, *Music in Ancient Israel,* New York: Philosophical Library, and London: Vision, 1969

Sharvit, Uri (editor), *Jewish Musical Culture: Past and Present,* special edition of *The World of Music,* 37(1), 1995

Shiloah, Amnon, *Jewish Musical Traditions* (Jewish Folklore and Anthropology Series), Detroit, Michigan: Wayne State University Press, 1992

Werner, Eric, *Hebrew Music,* Cologne: Arno Volk Verlag, 1961

The extensive literature devoted to views on Jewish music falls into two larger ontological and aesthetic categories. First, scholars concern themselves with the fundamental questions of what Jewish music really is, or even if it has a metaphysical presence of its own. Crucial to this first area of concern is the acceptability of music in Jewish religious practices. Second, there is considerable tension between views on Jewish music that regard it as bounded and those that regard it as unifying. The former position considers Jewish music to be a set of repertoires and practices that lend themselves to definition, and the latter sees it as diverse and responsive to the changing contexts of history and diaspora. Writings on Jewish music are therefore split according to views that argue for exclusivity and those that espouse inclusivity. Modern ethnomusicological scholarship increasingly embraces the diversity of Jewish music and music cultures, preferring to celebrate the ways it represents the different communities of Israel and the diaspora.

The most influential writer of the Middle Ages on almost all aspects of Jewish life, MAIMONIDES' views on music are no exception. Echoed by other medieval Sephardi decisors and still more widely honored in the breach, his position reflects a general rabbinic ambivalence toward the arts. Against a background in which Arabic music-making, with its largely amatory thematic conventions, enjoyed immense popularity and was feared liable to distract if not debauch, he draws a distinction between secular and sacred music, ruling against the former "be it unaccompanied, accompanied, or purely instrumental" while approving the latter for its capacity to "heighten the spiritual emotions of joy and sorrow." Maimonides' writings also connect the use of specific repertoires to the various liturgies and holidays of the Jewish calendar.

SENDREY surveys concepts and uses of Jewish music from biblical times through rabbinic sources until the sixth century. Drawing on his other bibliographic projects, Sendrey organizes this large book historically and according to the textual and contextual functions of music. The book is remarkable for the breadth of its scope. Not only does Sendrey consider every type of ancient text in which Jewish music of any kind might appear, but he also considers Jewish music in cultural processes that are by no means exclusively Jewish. Non-Jewish influences are seen to be critical as early as biblical times because of the extent of contact with neighboring cultures. The conceptual breadth of the book is most fully evident in sections devoted to dance, instrumental music, and women, subjects rarely included in earlier books on Jewish music.

IDELSOHN drew upon his experiences as a cantor and musicologist, his comparative studies of European Jewish liturgical and folk music, and, most significantly, years of pioneering fieldwork in Palestine to write the classic historical study of Jewish music. The title of the book clearly points to Idelsohn's belief that Jewish music developed historically, that is, has responded to the different conditions in the places and times in which Jews live. Jewish music is therefore dynamic, and it is not restricted to specific genres or even religious settings. Idelsohn concerns himself with a wide range of modal, liturgical, and functional frameworks, especially those of Ashkenazi traditions in the post-Haskalah era but also the Sephardi and Eastern communities of the early 20th century. This book offers an extremely valuable point of departure for any reader wanting to understand Jewish music in its variety.

WERNER employs the methods of comparative musicology to show the ways in which Jewish melody disseminates throughout the diaspora, retaining certain core similarities but acquiring variants that distinguish one community and its repertoires from another. Morphological tables make it possible to group variants so that their similarities unify them, often with certain variants presented as if they were original or authentic within the grouping. Methodologically, Werner treats all repertoires and genres in the volume as if they were traditional, which primarily means that they were transmitted orally. Accordingly, his concept of "Hebrew music" embraces cantillation, Psalm tunes, prayer, and folk music.

GRADENWITZ proposes several imaginative root metaphors (e.g., the flute-playing shepherd in the desert) to give unity to a sweeping history of music in "the eternal land." The book is broadly comparative, but in a style inherited from European comparative musicology prior to World War II, and many comparative assertions are therefore very tendentious. The author has, nonetheless, gathered an extraordinary amount of information, and as one of Israel's foremost music publishers during the early decades of statehood, he has access to many details about the formation of individual and national compositional styles. The biographical sketches of Israeli composers are complemented by focused discussions of noteworthy works. Though the author's perspectives are highly personal and somewhat biased, the book provides a detailed introduction to Jewish music and to the music of Israel for the reader with little previous knowledge of these areas.

MENDELSOHN gathers seven essays in a symposium to investigate the ways in which Jews and Jewish communities have used music to respond to the pressures of modernity. Topics examined here range from assimilation to Zionism to Israeli nation-building to the preservation of Sephardi traditions. The concept of music itself varies from one "musical agenda" to the next, revealing both aesthetic breadth and a high degree of ambivalence about music's Jewishness. In each essay music contributes substantially to Jewish identity and empowers the transformation of Jewish communities in their diverse responses to modernity. Essays by Ezra Mendelsohn, Philip V. Bohlman, and Judit Frigyesi consider the presence of music as a form of Jewish identity in 19th- and early 20th-century Europe. Edwin Seroussi, Natan Shahar, Jehoash Hirshberg, and Lionel Wolberger examine the proliferation of distinctive genres in modern Israel.

SHILOAH views diversity and an extensive capacity to change and respond to new cultural contexts as fundamental to the wide range of traditions that represent Jewish music in the late 20th century. Musical pluralism is no less a factor in Israel, where Jewish musical traditions have been concentrated since statehood, than in the diaspora, where Jewish music continues to reflect the entire range of Jewish ethnic and religious diversity. Shiloah employs the methodologies of modern ethnomusicology, thereby dividing the book's chapters according to music's genres, functions, and contexts. Jewish music history, therefore, does not adhere to a central core and teleology of return, but rather it consists of myriad historical processes. His treatment of mystical and paraliturgical traditions, as well as Sephardi and Middle Eastern Jewish communities, is particularly valuable.

SHARVIT gathers five essays from distinguished Jewish-music scholars Eliyahu Schleifer, Edwin Seroussi, Kay Kaufman Shelemay, Mark Slobin, and Sharvit himself, who examine the problems and methods of studying Jewish music in its cultural contexts. Unifying the essays is the attempt to distinguish the realities of Jewish music, especially variation and difference, from the myths about it, especially its presumed unity and capacity to connect the present to the past. All the essays examine the ways Jewish music shapes and is shaped by the experiences of diaspora; they also examine how music is a powerful form of responding, even adapting, to the shifting contexts of non-Jewish cultural surroundings. As a whole, the volume provides a superb set of new approaches for the modern and postmodern study of Jewish music.

PHILIP V. BOHLMAN

See also Music: American Jewish Music; Music: Art Music; Music: Ashkenazi Folk Music; Music: Cantillation; Music: Cantorial Music; Music: Middle Eastern Music; Music: Sephardi Music

Mysticism *see* Gnosis and Early Mysticism; Kabbalah

N

Nahmanides *see* Moses ben Nahman

Nahman of Bratslav 1772–1811
Podolian hasidic saint and messianic theologian

Green, Arthur, *Tormented Master* (Judaic Studies Series),
  University: University of Alabama Press, 1979
Kaplan, Aryeh, *Until the Mashiach: Rabbi Nachman's
  Biography: An Annotated Chronology,* edited by Rabbi
  Dovid Shapiro, Brooklyn, New York: Breslov Research
  Institute, 1985
Sternharz, Nathan, *Tzaddik: (Chayey Moharan): A Portrait
  of Rabbi Nachman,* translated by Avraham Greenbaum,
  New York: Breslov Research Institute, 1987

Considering the importance of Rabbi Nahman as a Jewish
leader and thinker, the dearth of biographies or even biographical material on him is somewhat surprising. The Breslov
Research Institute deserves credit for the little material that
does exist. However, many of their publications are reprints of
Nahman's own songs and stories rather than books about him.
The original source for information about the life of Nahman
is his closest disciple, Nathan STERNHARZ. Sternharz deifies
Nahman to an almost blasphemous degree. He writes, "Who
can describe . . . all the great and awesome wonders performed
by our leader, teacher and Rebbe, light of lights. . . . He raised
one up from the dust and dunghill and brought me to himself.
In his love he drew me closer than anyone else, and appointed
me to receive and write down his Torah teachings." The book
takes an unabashedly subjective, highly laudatory approach to
the rabbi, intended to bring the nonbeliever closer to God. In
many ways it reads like a messianic text, promising that Nahman will save those who come to his graveside, donate money
to charity in his name, and recite ten psalms he had prescribed.
At the same time, though, and in spite of the often overzeal-
ous voice of the author, the book opens readers to the teachings of Nahman because of its straightforward organization
and pithy presentation of his words. Segments of Nahman's
teachings, for example, "His Wit," "His Devotion to God," and
"His Spiritual Struggles," allow readers to come to grips with
Nahman, Sternharz himself, and some of the fundamentals of
Bratslav Hasidism. As the translator points out in his introduction, some readers may have trouble believing that Sternharz's words represent the absolute truth, although the depth
of his faith is unquestionable. For readers who are new to the
ideas of Rabbi Nahman, though, the sections "Conversations
Relating to His Lessons" and "Conversations Relating to His
Stories" are particularly useful; in both sections, Sternharz
plays the part of the simpleminded student and asks the rebbe
questions for the benefit of the reader. This book cannot function as a modern critical biography of Nahman, but as a historical text and as an introduction to Bratslav thought, it is of
central importance.

A similar but more recent volume is KAPLAN. Also published by the Breslov Research Institute, this volume
approaches Nahman similarly. It includes a very brief history
of the Haskalah (Jewish Enlightenment movement) and a
sketch of shtetl life in the Pale of Settlement in order to set a
backdrop for the story of Rabbi Nahman. Unlike Sternharz's
book, though, Kaplan's biography is based less upon Nahman's
own stories and more upon chronology; it is structured by a
day-to-day timeline of events. Much of the information is ultimately the same as the information in *Tzaddik*—and *Tzaddik*
was clearly one of Kaplan's primary texts in researching his
own volume—but the book as a whole resembles a sort of
third-person diary rather than a traditional biography. The
appendixes may be worth examining. They include several
maps, Nahman's letters, a list of other tzaddikim, descriptions
of important centers in Eastern Europe and the Holy Land as
they were at the time of Nahman, a comprehensive list of Nahman's writings, and a glossary of Yiddish and Hebrew terms.
The bulk of the book, though, directly echoes Sternharz's earlier writings.

GREEN is the only critical biography of Nahman available. He has taken on a daunting task, as he points out in
his introduction, because almost all his evidence comes from
Nahman himself or from Sternharz or from subsequent Bratslav hasidim. Green takes it as a given that hasidic texts
about the rabbis are "embellished," often because "there is
a worry that the master will be degraded as he is humanized." In this version, the rabbi is indeed humanized through
a psychological reading of his life and teachings. He is not,
however, degraded and is instead approached as a vitally
important leader, thinker, and, most interestingly, man. The
deified Nahman portrayed by both Sternharz and Kaplan is
not the subject of Green's book; his Nahman is a brilliant,
learned, widely influential man, but a man nonetheless.

This biography also includes an account of "messianic strivings" prior to Nahman and a fascinating chapter on Nahman's journey to the land of Israel. Because this book encompasses and interprets all previous material in a sensitive and effective way, and because it corresponds to what most contemporary readers would expect of a biography, this is probably the most useful place to begin.

GILLIAN D. STEINBERG

Nasi Family

Garshowitz, Libby, "Gracia Mendes: Power, Influence and Intrigue," in *Power of the Weak: Studies on Medieval Women*, edited by Jennifer Carpenter and Sally-Beth MacLean, Urbana: University of Illinois Press, 1995

Ravid, Benjamin, "Money, Love and Power Politics in Sixteenth Century Venice: The Perpetual Banishment and Subsequent Pardon of Joseph Nasi," *Italia Judaica*, Rome: Ministero per i beni culturali e ambientali, 1983

Roth, Cecil, *The House of Nasi: Dona Gracia*, Philadelphia: Jewish Publication Society, 1948

Roth, Cecil, *The House of Nasi: The Duke of Naxos*, Philadelphia: Jewish Publication Society, 1948

Salomon, Herman Prins and Aron di Leone Leoni, "Mendes, Benveniste, De Luna, Micas, Nasi: The State of the Art (1532–1558)," *Jewish Quarterly Review*, 88, 1998

Saperstein, Marc, "Martyrs, Merchants and Rabbis: Jewish Communal Conflict as Reflected in the Responsa on the Boycott of Ancona," *Jewish Social Studies*, 43, 1981

The Nasi family was one of the wealthiest and most powerful families in Jewish history. The story of the Nasi family has been reconstructed from sources such as diplomatic correspondence, personal diaries, Hebrew chronicles, and rabbinic literature. Dona Gracia Nasi, born Beatrice de Luna in Portugal in 1510, married Francisco Mendes (or Benveniste) who, in partnership with his brother Diogo, maintained major business ties in Antwerp. Francisco died in 1535, leaving Dona Gracia a large estate. She soon left Portugal with her sister, Brianda de Luna, her daughter (Ana, Brianda, or Reina, depending on the author), and her nephews Samuel and Joseph Nasi, born Bernardo and Joao Micas (Miques or Miguez). In Antwerp, after marrying Brianda (with whom he had a daughter, Beatrice), Diogo died in 1543. He left Dona Gracia Nasi, in addition to several other guardians, in charge of the entire family's financial and charitable enterprises, devoting resources to resettle conversos as the Inquisition encroached upon them. Gradually, she moved her family from Flanders through France to Venice. After they arrived in Venice, living outside the ghetto as Christians, Brianda (Dona Gracia's sister and Diogo's widow), resented Dona Gracia's control of the family fortune and denounced her for Judaizing. The Turks, thereupon, interceded to save Dona Gracia and her huge fortune while she fled to Ferrara. There she reverted to Judaism, may have changed her name, and worked with other former New Christians in communal and cultural matters such as publishing. With the sultan's support, the entire family arrived in the Ottoman Empire where Dona Gracia supported many Jewish activities. The studies that have emerged concerning the family have successively built upon and critiqued their predecessors. The information offered in these endeavors, from mundane matters of spelling to the identification of significant individuals, constitutes a vague and sometimes contradictory mass of information from which it is difficult to draw definitive conclusions. The classic studies in English represent not a summation of the material but only a raw beginning.

GARSHOWITZ provides a summary of all previous research on Dona Gracia Mendes. In particular, Garshowitz touches on the fascinating questions in Jewish law concerning the validity of Catholic marriages of New Christians and the nature of inheritance among them. Her documentation on this aspect of the Nasi family history is rich in primary and secondary sources.

RAVID's study draws on his meticulous archival research to re-create the story of Joseph Nasi's abduction of his cousin Beatrice in order to save her from suitors outside the limited family circle and to protect both the family's assets and its religious secrets. Beyond the abduction, marriage, consummation, and ban passed on Joseph, Ravid explores the subsequent reconciliation between Joseph Nasi and the Republic of Venice. Ravid's study, however, leaves some questions unanswered. Where was Dona Gracia during this intrigue? How does his account reconcile with the fact that most writers have Beatrice eventually marrying Bernardo Micas (Samuel Nasi) and Joseph marrying Reina (Ana), Dona Gracia's daughter?

ROTH's (1948a, 1948b) reluctance to document his sources, his overblown prose, his gratuitous and often misguided judgments, and his lack of precision (mixed with a sentimental and romantic approach) diminish the contribution of much of his work. In particular, Roth tries to depict Joseph Nasi, especially his plans to resettle Tiberias, as an early Zionist, intent on solving the Jewish question of his day. These reservations do not reflect recent changes in historical sensibilities or the nature of scholarly writing but were expressed as early as 1948 in Ellis Rivkin's review in the *Jewish Quarterly Review*. He noted Roth's inflation of meager sources, repetitiousness, subjective asides, and extraneous references. Rivkin, an astute observer, noted that Roth depicted Don Joseph as vacillating, whimsical, arbitrary, unpredictable, and flamboyant. These characterizations are not only tedious but inaccurate and inconsistent with Roth's attempt to paint him as a powerful leader of the Jewish people. The failure of Jews to sustain the community in Tiberias reflects a lack of Jewish interest in maintaining settlements in the land of Israel and is not, as Roth suggests, a symptom of Arab and Christian abuse of the land.

SALOMON and LEONI have done a splendid job of combing the world for information about the career of the Nasi family. This article includes new material concerning many fascinating aspects of the history of the family and rereadings of earlier articles. The finds include the 1531 letters that King João III of Portugal and his wife Catarina wrote to Emperor Charles V protesting the arrest and expropriation of the property of Diogo Mendes. The bold revisions that the article proposes to the often hazy morass of names and dates connected with this family cannot always be accepted. For example, if it is certain that Dona Gracia left with her household for Constantinople during the summer of 1552, it is not clear how the abduction of young Beatrice by João Micas could have taken place in January 1553 with her mother's secret connivance. Given the confused nature of the data that all the scholars are working with, referring to reconstructions by others as "aberrations" and suggesting that they contain "howlers" may be not only harsh but wrong.

SAPERSTEIN reviews the account of Pope Paul IV's initiation in July 1555 of an action in Ancona against Judaizing New Christians who were living under the protection of previous papal privileges. About 100 individuals were arrested and their property confiscated, although around 30 escaped. The rest were tortured by inquisitional tribunal. In the autumn of 1555 and spring of 1556, Dona Gracia tried to intervene and had Sultan Süleyman I send an envoy to Ancona for the protection of Turkish subjects. The Inquisition found many of those arrested guilty: 38 returned to the church, 26 were sent to row galley ships as punishment, and 24 or 25 were sentenced to strangulation and then burning, which took place over several days in April and June of 1556. In April 1556 the idea was raised that all Jewish merchants of the Ottoman Empire boycott the port of Ancona and use instead Pesaro. This would both punish the pope and prove to the duke of Pesaro, Guidobaldo II, that he would be better off with Turkish Jewish trade than with good relations with the pope. Dona Gracia and her nephew Joseph tried to get all the rabbis—most of whom were paid by them—to support the boycott by imposing a ban against anyone who traded with Ancona. There was some support for this, especially by rabbis of Iberian origin who thought that such a movement would protect Sephardim everywhere from similar treatment. Similarly, the Jews of Pesaro supported the boycott, because they did not want to anger the duke if the boycott failed after he had gone against the pope. Opposition, however, grew in Italy, especially among Italian Jews of Ancona who feared that they would be ruined and blamed for the losses of the whole city and who claimed that the treatment of the Jews in Pesaro had been no better than in Ancona. The boycott thus soon collapsed and the duke of Pesaro expelled many Jews. An attempt by the Jews to organize a similar boycott against products from Nazi Germany in April 1933 failed for very similar reasons and a comparison of the two events is highly instructive.

HOWARD TZVI ADELMAN

Nehemiah, Book of *see* Ezra and Nehemiah, Books of

Neoplatonism

Altmann, A. and S.M. Stern (editors), *Isaac Israeli: A Neoplatonic Philosopher of the Early Tenth Century; His Works Translated with Comments and an Outline of His*

Philosophy (Scripta Judaica, 1), London: Oxford University Press, 1958; Westport, Connecticut: Greenwood, 1979

Goodman, Lenn E. (editor), *Neoplatonism and Jewish Thought* (Studies in Neoplatonism, vol. 7), Albany: State University of New York Press, 1992

Idel, Moshe and Bernard McGinn (editors), *Mystical Union and Monotheistic Faith*, New York and London: Macmillan, 1989

Matt, Daniel C., "*Ayin*: The Concept of Nothingness in Jewish Mysticism," in *The Problem of Pure Consciousness: Mysticism and Philosophy*, edited by Robert K.C. Forman, New York: Oxford University Press, 1990

Sells, Michael A., *Mystical Languages of Unsaying*, Chicago: University of Chicago Press, 1994

Wolfson, Harry Austryn, *Philo: Foundations of Religious Philosophy in Judaism, Christianity, and Islam* (Structure and Growth of Philosophic Systems from Plato to Spinoza, 2), 2 vols., Cambridge, Massachusetts: Harvard University Press, 1947, 4th edition, 1968

Neoplatonism, while difficult to systematize, officially begins with the Platonic innovations of the Greek philosopher Plotinus in the third century C.E. Following Plato's doctrine of the unity of the divine, Neoplatonism considers the nature or essence of the divine One; the nature of the One's self-relation; the One's relation to the created cosmos; the relations among the things that are not the One; and the identities of singular and composite things. These matters are commonly understood according to a descending hierarchy of levels or orders of creation, each level outflowing or overflowing into the one following, a scheme that is usually characterized by the term "emanation." A restricted view of Neoplatonism will understand it to have ended with the closing of the Platonic Academy in Athens by Justinian in 529 C.E.; a periodized view will understand it according to founders, schools, and successors such as the theurgical Syrian school of Iamblichus and his followers (245–325 C.E.); a broader view will consider the affinities between Neoplatonic metaphysics, ontology, and cosmology, and modern and postmodern philosophies and religions.

GOODMAN, in the preface to the volume of essays deriving from the International Conference on Neoplatonism and Jewish Thought held in 1987, makes the bold claim that "it would not be an exaggeration to say that Neoplatonism was the philosophy that was most influential upon the formation of Jewish thought" during the Hellenistic, Roman, and medieval periods, and that it plays "a significant role, if not the dominant role, in the whole development of modern Jewish thought." The essays are arranged chronologically beginning with David Winston's article on Philo and concluding with Richard Popkin's piece on Spinoza, with an additional essay by Robert McLaren devoted to the whole of Jewish Neoplatonism and the question of its psychodynamic propaedeutic, its service to and by the heart. Although the articles cover a wide variety of themes, texts, and authors (with a number devoted to Maimonides), it would be appropriate to say that the notion of mediation holds them together: each essay explores the problem of the affirmation of an absolutely transcendent deity, of God's radical separation from the created order, and the ways in which Neoplatonism's dialectical innovations on the problem have been appropriated by and integrated into Jewish philosophy and religion. Bernard McGinn's article on "Ibn Gabirol: the Sage among the Schoolmen" is instructive. Interest in the number three certainly is not a Christian innovation. Philosophies grounded in Neoplatonism often propound a triadically arranged system. In Gabirol, for instance, one finds the science of matter and form, the science of Will, and the science of First Essence. Since the oneness of the One and the otherness of the cosmos are basic convictions, any relationship between them must be mediated by or through some third thing or essence or combinatory element, something one might call a one-many. The nature of this third thing and its relationship to both sides of the dialectic and its self-relation is a constant matter of dispute primarily for the reason that the One can never be, but somehow always is, a related member. For Plotinus this third was Nous; for ibn Gabirol it was Will or *voluntas*. According to McGinn, ibn Gabirol's "fundamentally Jewish concern with protecting divine transcendence" produces the principle that the Will is actually and not only potentially multiple, thereby assuring that the First Essence is strictly and absolutely unknowable.

The preface to the volume of essays edited by IDEL and McGINN explains that its occasion was a series of invited lectures on the theme of Kabbalah held at the Jewish Theological Seminary in New York in 1985. The expressed purpose of the lectures was to relate to Moshe Idel's then forthcoming text, *Kabbalah: New Perspectives* (Yale University Press, 1988), in which he argues against the notion "that there is little, if any, talk of mystical union among the Jewish Mystics." In Idel's own contribution to the lecture series, "Universalization and Integration: Two Conceptions of Mystical Union in Jewish Mysticism," he furthers his argument, in particular by focusing upon the term *devekut,* which, he claims, is "a term whose large mystical semantic field includes a variety of meanings, from imitating divine behavior to total fusion with the divine." Idel reduces these meanings to two, reflected in the essay's title: *universalization,* referring to imitation, and *integration,* referring to fusion or, as he puts it in a subtitle, entering God. Idel directly attributes this latter possibility to "the role played by the Neoplatonic conception of the basic affinity and even the continuity of the divine and the human spiritual powers" and the influence of these conceptions upon Jewish mysticism.

MATT provides the reader with an excellent survey of key Neoplatonic themes that have influenced Jewish philosophy and Jewish mysticism. He uses as his rubric an analysis of the kabbalistic notion of *ayin,* nothingness, and its functional place within the emanatory system of the *sefirot,* within which *ayin* is associated with *keter 'elyon,* the highest crown or first *sefirah.* Here one learns how Plato's positive notion of creation by design was reversed by Plotinus, who insisted that nothing positive could be said about the divine, it being absolutely One without internal division or attribute, without the will to create an absolute limit to comprehension. One will therefore find in all Neoplatonically influenced discourses an emanation scheme of levels or orders of creation that, in effect, maintains

an absolute separation between the One and the created order. Therefore, *nothing,* paradoxically, becomes a certain sort of positively negative attribute of the divine that one may indicate only through a process of negation, a process that may be characterized as a return to or unification with nothing—the One. Matt traces this method of negative theology through the philosophy of Philo, the formative Christian mysticisms of Pseudo-Dionysius, John the Scot Eriugena, Meister Eckhart, and certain Islamic versions, into the works of Maimonides and medieval Jewish mystics such as Moses de Leon and Azriel of Gerona. Finally Matt considers the vital and allegedly self-annihilating interiorization of the notion of *ayin* in Hasidism. Matt concludes: "The reality that animates and surpasses all things cannot be captured or named, but by invoking *ayin* the mystic is able to allude to the infinite, to *alef* the ineffable." The reader should pay particular attention to Matt's notes, which contain important references and helpful additional commentary.

In the important volume by SELLS, which is not devoted to Neoplatonism per se but to the discursive process of *apophasis* (the process of speaking away or unsaying objectifying propositions or names meant to identify the divine), the interested reader will find an essential guide to understanding the peculiar referential logic of philosophical or mystical texts influenced by Neoplatonism. Over the course of a work that begins with Plotinus, considers and analyzes the works of Dionysius, Eriugena, ibn 'Arabi, Marguerite Porete, and finally Meister Eckhart, Sells argues steadily and persuasively for the reasonableness of apophatic language, a discursive logic that includes an anarchic (without first principle or origin) meaning event. Such a meaning event in fact ensures the integrity of apophatic language rather than draining it of meaning and sense, a charge often dismissively leveled against discourses that move according to a logic of negation or contradiction. Sells finds such a meaning event in the logic of the *epistrophe* or the "turning back" of a first proposition upon itself by another, a semantic movement that produces "a semiotic spiral motion ever deeper into the pre-referential ground (or groundlessness) of the discourse." Such a gesture can be found in the Plotinian notion that all things are in and from the One without duality for the very reason that there is nothing in the One. The second statement turns against the first and unsays it, a turn that does not annihilate its sense but instead poses a dilemma of fused and split references within which distinctions are made and broken down. Sells notes and analyzes other strategies such as "regress from reference," "double-proposition semantics," "subject-predicate fusion," "ingress into symbol," and others that thereafter become the lenses through which the authors named above are read. Sells's endnotes are rich and exhaustive, and they should not be missed. The connections made between apophasis and postmodern discourses, particularly those of Jacques Derrida and (by this author's lights) Emmanuel Levinas, are provocative and telling.

ALTMANN and STERN's text on Israeli, perhaps the earliest Jewish Neoplatonist (c.855–c.955 C.E.), consists of two parts: the first is a translation of and commentary on Israeli's *Book of Definitions,* fragments of the *Book of Substances,* the *Book on Spirit and Soul,* and the *Chapter on the Elements.* Not included is Israeli's *Book on the Elements.* The texts were originally written in Arabic, though there are Hebrew and Latin translations. Those works still available in Arabic were translated from the Arabic, though most are based on a Hebrew translation of an Arabic original. The second part of the work, perhaps of most interest to readers, is a survey of Israeli's complete philosophy, which the authors divide into two parts titled "The Downward Way" (from the creator to the elements and composite substances) and "The Upward Way" (which concerns the process of purification toward union with the divine). The prefatory material includes a basic introduction to the texts and a biographical note on what may be known of Israeli's life and influence. It is undoubtedly true that Israeli's *Chapter on the Elements* (also known as the *Mantua Text* for the Italian city in which the single extant fragment is preserved) was formative for the rise of Kabbalah in the 13th-century Gerona circle. Ezra ben Solomon cites it, as does Azriel of Gerona, though they were probably unaware that the text was Israeli's, since the text seems ascribed to Aristotle, though it is actually a commentary upon a pseudo-Aristotelian text. The Jewish mystics of Gerona were intrigued by the affinities between Israeli's Neoplatonic doctrine of emanation and their system of the sefirot. Maimonides also mentions Israeli, although only to censure his work as primitive and lacking philosophical sophistication.

WOLFSON'S magisterial commentary on Philo of Alexandria remains unparalleled with respect to the ground it covers, the way it seeks to systematize Philo's evolving thought, and its grand arrangement of the material within a stated framework of philosophical problems common not only to Philo but to "religious philosophies" spanning the following 17 centuries. It is both an exegesis of Philonic philosophy and an unrepentant history of big and transcending ideas. Today this style of philosophy appears rather suspect with its uncritical endorsement of an intellectual world of pure and co-implicated ideas, but it is nonetheless breathtaking in scope and in the grandiosity of its claims. A reader's reward continues to be found in Wolfson's exegetical and interpretive labors, which are meticulously informed and clearly presented. One will leave Wolfson's *Philo* with the distinct impression that a certain Neoplatonically construed metaphysical framework may be the very philosophical theology by which the three monotheisms are most implicitly ecumenical. In a certain respect it is also a testimony to Philo's understanding of the universal implications of Judaism. Volume one considers Philo's historical situation within Hellenistic Judaism and his biblical-allegorical philosophical method, God, the intelligible world and the logos, creation, the logos immanent to the world and the laws of nature, the nature of the soul, and the freedom of the will. Volume two considers types of knowledge and the functions of prophecy, Philo's proofs for the existence of God, the role and status of divine predicates with respect to the tenet of the unknowability of God, and Philo's moral and political philosophies. Wolfson concludes with a section on Philo's innovations.

ERIC C. HELMER

Netherlands, The

Blom, J.C.H., Renate Fuks-Mansfeld, and I. Schöffer (editors), *The History of the Jews in the Netherlands*, Oxford: Littman Library of Jewish Civilization, 1999

Bloom, Herbert I., *The Economic Activities of the Jews of Amsterdam in the Seventeenth and Eighteenth Centuries*, Williamsport, Pennsylvania: Bayard, 1937

Bodian, Miriam, *Hebrews of the Portuguese Nation: Conversos and Community in Early Modern Amsterdam* (Modern Jewish Experience), Bloomington: Indiana University Press, 1997

Frank, Anne, *The Diary of a Young Girl: The Definitive Edition*, edited by Otto Frank and Mirjam Pressler, translated by Susan Massotty, New York: Doubleday, 1995; London: Viking, 1997

Gans, Mozes Heiman, *Memorbook: History of Dutch Jewry from the Renaissance to 1940*, London: Bosch and Keuning, 1977

Leydesdorff, Selma, *Wij hebben als mens geleefd: Het joodse proletariaat van Amsterdam, 1900–1940*, 1987; translated by F. Henry as *We Lived with Dignity: The Jewish Proletariat of Amsterdam, 1900–1940*, Detroit, Michigan: Wayne State University Press, 1994

Michman, Jozeph, *The History of Dutch Jewry during the Emancipation Period, 1787–1815: Gothic Turrets on a Corinthian Building*, Amsterdam: Amsterdam University Press, 1995

Moore, Bob, *Victims and Survivors: The Nazi Persecution of the Jews in the Netherlands, 1940–1944*, New York and London: Arnold, 1997

The story of Jews in the Netherlands spans from a still obscure medieval presence to an apogee of dazzling Baroque creativity and on to tragedy in the 20th century, followed by the regrouping of survivors. The Portuguese Marranos who settled in Amsterdam in the 16th and especially 17th centuries and proceeded to recreate their Sephardi traditions were joined in the mid-17th century by Ashkenazi refugees fleeing the massacre of Polish Jews by the Cossacks in 1648 and 1649 and the persecution of Lithuanian Jewry following Sweden's invasion of that nation in 1655. Jews in the Netherlands enjoyed comparative tolerance and security and the community flourished, attracting further Jewish immigration. By 1933, the Jewish population of the country had grown to 110,000, and during that decade it was supplemented by an additional 30,000 Jewish refugees from Germany and other parts of Nazi-dominated Europe. Between 1942 and 1945, 107,000 of the 140,000 Jews in Holland were deported by the Nazis, moving by rail directly from the internment camp of Westerbork to the death camps at Auschwitz and Sobibor; a mere five percent survived. At the end of the 20th century, the Dutch Jewish community numbered around 30,000 residents.

The substantial volume edited by BLOM, FUKS-MANSFELD, and SCHÖFFER offers the one comprehensive survey of the whole of Dutch Jewish history through the end of the 20th century. The book, a collection of studies on successive periods by some of the most accomplished scholars in the field, makes clear its aim of strenuously avoiding original research in favor of a clear synopsis of the state of the art. Schöffer's introduction reviews the historiography of the Jews of the Netherlands. He is followed by B.M.J. Speet on the Middle Ages, D.M. Swetchinski's "Between the Middle Ages and the Golden Age, 1516–1621," Jonathan Israel's "Economic Activities in the Dutch Republic until c.1750," and Y. Kaplan's "Religious, Cultural and Social Life, 1600–1750." Next comes Fuks-Mansfeld's extensive treatment of the little-known history of the period from 1750 through 1870, followed by Blom's absorbing study of the decades from 1870 to the Nazi occupation. F.C. Brasz's discussion of the postwar period brings to a close a useful and distinguished compilation.

GANS covers the history of Dutch Jewry from the Renaissance to 1940. For the period up to the eve of the decimation of the community by the Nazis, it offers a comprehensive picture, superbly constructed, beautifully illustrated (with a total of 1,100 images), and highly readable. Each chapter commences with a series of quotations that provide insight into the key themes. At the end of the book, there is a short historical summary, endnotes, a detailed names index, and a shorter subject index. (The table of contents appears on the very last page of the book.) Because of its bulk (852 folio pages), this book is probably more useful as a reference work than as an introductory text , but it is nevertheless a must for lay reader and scholar alike.

BLOOM's book on the economic activities of the Jews of Amsterdam illuminates an important facet of Dutch Jewish history. While there are a great many books dealing with the intellectual accomplishments of Amsterdam Sephardim, this book offers the most detailed analysis of their economic activities. Bloom provides a comprehensive outline of the trades and crafts that Jews developed in the city (such as the silk industry and the sugar, diamond, tobacco, printing, and book trades), and he identifies the trade routes in Europe, the Middle East, and the New World (both India and the Americas) that Jews helped expand. His final chapters examine trade in money and securities and discuss the affluence and subsequent decline of Dutch Portuguese Jewry. Bloom's fascinating study of the socioeconomic status of the Sephardim, which is contrasted with that of Amsterdam's Ashkenazim, as well as his detailed use of sources, facts, and figures makes this book an invaluable resource.

BODIAN's study of the Portuguese conversos (descendants of Jews who had converted to Christianity) who settled in Amsterdam beginning in the late 16th century is a seminal work. Drawing on recent research by scholars such as I.S. Revah, Y.H. Yerushalmi, Yosef Kaplan, and Jonathan Israel, as well as a careful study of the relevant primary sources, the author has created a clear and incisive picture of the complex Jewish identity of the conversos. Following a superb introductory chapter analyzing the nature of Marrano life in the Iberian peninsula, Bodian discusses the formation of the Jewish community in Amsterdam; the Dutch context; the continuing influence of the Jews' Iberian and New Christian heritage; the conflictual process of re-Judaization; and the continuing links that ex-conversos, or the "Nation," maintained with conversos both in Amsterdam and across Europe. Bodian has managed to achieve her aim of breaking "out of the mold of

converso research" by highlighting the double dichotomy of a highly complex identity: Portuguese and Dutch, Catholic and Jewish.

MICHMAN has written a detailed history of the emancipation of Dutch Jewry from 1787 to 1815, including the key Napoleonic period of the Batavian Republic and Kingdom of Holland (1795–1815), which was previously all but ignored in the English-language literature on Dutch Jewry. In his preface, Michman states that he hopes the book will ensure that Dutch Jewry's story during this "momentous period" will claim its "rightful place in Jewish historiography," and he has definitely met his objective through his careful scholarship, detailed discussion, and intelligent analysis of events, which is amply supported by his footnotes. This is a book more suited to the scholar than the general reader.

LEYDESDORFF has produced a sensitive, well-crafted sociological study of the Jewish proletariat of Amsterdam, examining their lifestyles, their areas of settlement, and the assistance provided to the poor. Drawing from oral histories and writings from the period 1900 to 1940, she seeks to recreate a world destroyed by the Holocaust. The introductory chapter includes a valuable discussion of memory and the significance of oral history.

FRANK's diary, which has been translated into more than 50 languages, has been described by Bob Moore as "an icon of the Holocaust." While providing invaluable insights into the conditions experienced by Jews hiding from the Nazis in Amsterdam, this personal perspective does not, of course, offer a complete picture of Dutch Jewry during the Holocaust or the circumstances surrounding Frank's tragedy. MOORE, on the other hand, is a major systematic study of the Jews of the Netherlands during the Holocaust. The book focuses on the historical debate over the Netherlands' record during the Holocaust, examining such facts as the high mortality rate of Dutch Jewry (compared to Jews in other Western European nations) that challenge the picture of strong Dutch resistance that emerged after World War II. Moore's approach is basically chronological: he begins by placing the Dutch Jews in both their historical and social context before discussing the stages after May 1940 of identification, isolation, and deportation. He also examines survival strategies, such as legal exemptions and hiding, and he evaluates the roles of those Dutch who assisted their Jewish neighbors as well as the fates of foreign Jews. There is a chapter dealing with the persecutors and an account of liberation. While Moore's analysis is weakened by his failure to provide a distinct section on the Dutch Nazi Party, he has synthesized recent scholarship to produce an accessible, cogently argued, and readable book, which should certainly be consulted by lay and academic readers.

SUZANNE D. RUTLAND

Neturei Karta

Domb, Jerahmeel Israel Isaac, *The Transformation: The Case of the Neturei Karta*, London: Domb, 1958; 2nd edition, Brooklyn, New York: Hachomo, 1989

Lamm, Norman, "The Ideology of the Neturei Karta:
According to the Satmarer Version," *Tradition*, 12, Fall
1971

Landau, David, *Piety and Power: The World of Jewish
Fundamentalism*, New York: Hill and Wang, and
London: Secker and Warburg, 1993

Marmorstein, Emile, *Heaven at Bay: The Jewish
Kulturkampf in the Holy Land*, London and New York:
Oxford University Press, 1969

The Neturei Karta (Aramaic for "Guardians of the City") is an anti-Zionist, ultra-Orthodox, extremist Jewish group that does not recognize the State of Israel. While the overwhelming majority of Eastern European rabbinic authorities initially opposed political Zionism and even Religious Zionism (Mizrachi), they came to an accommodation with the State of Israel once it was established. The Neturei Karta, however, has consistently opposed the State of Israel and has professed support for the Palestine Liberation Organization (PLO) and called for the internationalization of Jerusalem.

DOMB has written an ardent and passionate manifesto in support of Neturei Karta. He describes the origins of this group in the early 1940s, when Amram Blau and others left Agudat Israel because they felt that it had compromised its viewpoint with the ideology of secular Zionism. The partisan nature of Domb's advocacy is evident in his celebration of how, in the War of Independence, the Old City of Jerusalem "miraculously" remained in Jordanian hands "in order to prevent the eventual profanation of the place of the Holy Sanctuary which might have taken place, had it been included in the Zionist redemption." (In the aftermath of the Six Day War in 1967, when Jerusalem was reunited and the Western Wall became accessible, a revisionist explanation would be offered stating that "miracles" are miracles only when they occur in conformity with the Torah and Jewish law; otherwise like the legerdemain of the miracle-workers in Pharaoh's Egypt, they are deceptions of Satan.)

LAMM demonstrates that the views of Neturei Karta are not without basis in classical Jewish sources, but he contends that the texts have been interpreted in a one-sided and sometimes arbitrary manner. In addition, texts that are of a homiletic nature have been interpreted as if they were legal pronouncements. The locus classicus on which Neturei Karta relies is a passage in the Talmud (Ketubot 111a) that states that at the time of the destruction of the Temple and the beginning of the exile, God administered three oaths to the Jews to govern their survival in the diaspora: God adjured Israel (1) not to use force to enable a mass return to the land of Israel; (2) not to rebel against the nations among which they are dispersed; and (3) not to take the initiative in hastening the advent of the Messiah prematurely. At the same time God adjured the gentile nations that they should not oppress Israel beyond their endurance. All authorities now agree that the gentile nations violated their oath. The question then arises as to the status of the three oaths that Israel took. Some eminent talmudists, such as Rabbi Meir Simhah of Dvinsk, maintain that the oaths are interdependent, and that since the gentiles violated their oath, Israel is released from its oaths. Neturei

Karta, and their great collaborator and ideologue, Rabbi Yoel Teitelbaum of Satmar, strongly disagree with this interpretation and consider the various oaths as independent covenants. Either way, however, the Balfour Declaration and the United Nations vote of 1947 would seem to negate the assertion that Zionism violates the oaths forswearing rebellion against gentile governments and forcible immigration to Palestine. Lamm sums up the major thesis of Neturei Karta as follows: there can be only divine, not human, political initiative; spiritual return must precede political redemption; the agents of redemption must be the pious—those committed to God and Torah; and the Jewish State must be a thorough theocracy, not a democracy.

MARMORSTEIN provides an answer to the question of why Neturei Karta, whose numbers probably never exceeded 3,000, had at one time such a powerful influence over religious society in the State of Israel. He thinks it is misleading to envisage the religious struggle as one of a monolithic group of believers waging war against a group of militant secularists in defense of their religious views and principles. Rather, he considers the religious camp as a three-tiered structure. He compares the religious situation in Israel to a territory under siege. The citadel is manned by zealots, while the metropolis itself is inhabited by fervent, if less flamboyant, believers. The population of the area between the metropolis and the border is familiar with the modes of expression and conduct prevalent on both sides of the frontier and is sensitive to variations. Proximity to people outside the territory, as well as a prevalence of professional skills and broad cultural interests, fosters an attitude of tolerance, if not respect, for outsiders on the part of the borderers. There is a continuous stream of traffic in and out of the borderland. Defectors are replaced by new arrivals. Sometimes the children of borderers who have been sent to the metropolis for their religious education and spiritual advancement are reluctant to leave; and indeed, a trickle of recruits for manning the citadel come from their ranks.

In this extended analogy, Neturei Karta, the Guardians of the City, represent the shock troops who man the citadel; the ultraorthodox Agudat Israel and its offshoots represent the metropolis; and the former Mizrachi or National Religious Party (NRP), representing the Modern Orthodox Religious Zionists, constitute the borderers. Now, in theory, the common enemy of all religious parties are the secularists, but in practice, claims Marmorstein, the real enemy is the group slightly to the left on the spectrum. Thus Neturei Karta assails Agudat Israel for accepting government subsidies for their schools, while Agudat Israel vociferously attacks the NRP for permitting mixed swimming in their rural settlements. Finally, the NRP is inhibited from engaging in dialogue and cooperating with secular elements. The effect, therefore, of Neturei Karta's stance is an overall shift to the right.

LANDAU examines some of the reasons for the decline of the influence of Neturei Karta after 1967, and why its dwindling numbers have been marginalized even by the ultraorthodox, noting five factors. First, some of its positions have become too extreme and extravagant. For example, the unification of Jerusalem and access to the Western Wall, the holiest shrine in Judaism, was welcomed by the Agudah-type of ultraorthodox who flocked there from the moment it was captured, while Neturei Karta called for the internationalization of Jerusalem. Second, there has been no colorful and charismatic leader of the group since the death of Rabbi Amram Blau in 1974. Third, financial support has dwindled since the death of Rabbi Yoel Teitelbaum in 1979. Fourth, the group has lost credibility with its intemperate attacks on Rabbi Eliezer Menahem Shach, the venerable head of the famous Ponevezh yeshivah and spiritual leader of the Degel Hatorah Party, himself widely considered to be something of an extremist. Finally, Neturei Karta's very success has led to its marginalization. The initiative for street campaigns and demonstrations on religious issues, for example, has passed from Neturei Karta to the religious parties of the ultraorthodox "establishment."

JACOB HABERMAN

New York

Encyclopaedia Judaica, 16 vols., Jerusalem: Keter, 1971

Franks, Abigail, The Lee Max Friedman Collection of American Jewish Colonial Correspondence: Letters of the Franks Family, 1733–1748 (Studies in American Jewish History, no. 5), edited by Leo Hershkowitz and Isidore S. Meyer, Waltham, Massachusetts: American Jewish Historical Society, 1968

Glazer, Nathan and Daniel P. Moynihan, Beyond the Melting Pot: The Negroes, Puerto Ricans, Jews, Italians, and Irish of New York City, Cambridge, Massachusetts: MIT Press, 1963, 2nd edition, 1970

Goren, Arthur A., New York Jews and the Quest for Community: The Kehillah Experiment, 1908–1922, New York: Columbia University Press, 1970

Grinstein, Hyman B., The Rise of the Jewish Community of New York, 1654–1860, Philadelphia: Jewish Publication Society, 1944

Gurock, Jeffrey S., When Harlem Was Jewish, 1870–1930, New York: Columbia University Press, 1979

Hershkowitz, Leo (editor), Wills of Early New York Jews, 1704–1799 (Studies in American Jewish History, no. 4), New York: American Jewish Historical Society, 1967

Howe, Irving, World of Our Fathers, New York: Harcourt Brace Jovanovich, 1976; as The Immigrant Jews of New York, 1881 to the Present, London: Routledge and Kegan Paul, 1976

Jackson, Kenneth T. (editor), The Encyclopedia of New York City, New Haven, Connecticut: Yale University Press, 1995

Kessner, Thomas, The Golden Door: Italian and Jewish Immigrant Mobility in New York City, 1880–1915 (Urban Life in America Series), New York: Oxford University Press, 1977

Moore, Deborah Dash, At Home in America: Second Generation New York Jews (Columbia History of Urban Life), New York: Columbia University Press, 1981

Poll, Solomon, The Hasidic Community of Williamsburg, New York: Free Press of Glencoe, 1962

Rischin, Moses, The Promised City: New York's Jews, 1870–1914, New York: Harper and Row, 1962

Sanders, Ronald, The Downtown Jews: Portraits of an Immigrant Generation, New York: Harper and Row, 1969; London: Constable, 1987

Wenger, Beth S., New York Jews and the Great Depression: Uncertain Promise (Yale Historical Publications), New Haven, Connecticut: Yale University Press, 1996

The largest urban Jewish community in the world and in Jewish history is New York City. Its estimated 1,765,000 Jews in 1927 constituted 29.5 percent of the city's population and reached 2,035,000 in 1937, about 28 percent of the city's population. This was probably the high point of Jewish population, and there were 1,335 congregations. There were only an estimated 1,048,000 New York City Jews in 1995, a decrease due to large-scale movement to the suburbs and to emigration as well as a low birthrate. The Jews of New York have maintained a vast assortment of organizations for religion, culture, education, charity, defense, Zionism, and trade unionism, as well as Jewish theaters and newspapers. They weigh heavily in the city's economy, particularly in commerce, finance, and the professions, and are influential in the city's politics. Jews occupy a central position in the city's renowned cultural life.

Basic reference works such as the ENCYCLOPAEDIA JUDAICA and JACKSON contain numerous articles pertaining to the Jews of New York, including personalities, institutions, and general themes. Works on American Jewish history refer constantly to New York, as the center of American Jewry and by far its largest community.

Two books, FRANKS and HERSHKOWITZ, provide close views of New York Jewish life, especially its social and economic aspects, during the city's colonial era, thanks to their detailed notes and introductions. For the early period GRINSTEIN remains the standard, detailed institutional history, written from an Orthodox perspective and now somewhat dated. Grinstein also deals with social welfare, religious observance, and conversion. The major phase of New York City Jewish history occurred during the East European mass immigration from 1881. Several substantial works examine this central period when the Jewish population boomed from about 80,000 in 1870 to 1,765,000 in 1927 and continued to rise.

RISCHIN is a basic work on the city's immigrants. He treats admirably their economic and social history and trade union movement and sets them within the broadening parameters of urban society. It is implicit in his view that Jewish developments parallel those of general urban life during the Progressive era; his book, however, is short on religious and communal history.

What Rischin abbreviates or omits is thoroughly discussed in GOREN. This is an excellent study of the communal and cultural life of masses of "downtown" immigrants and the relations between them and "uptown" Americanized middle-class Jews. Goren relates the significant but in the long run unsuccessful attempt to unite New York Jews in one communal organization (kehillah).

Not to be overlooked is the large, famous work by HOWE, which narrates with deep sensitivity the story of the East European immigrants from their departure from Russia and

Poland to their arrival and life of struggle in New York City. Individual memoirs presented with psychological insight are central to Howe's narrative. He is particularly attentive to Yiddish culture and socialism somewhat at the expense of more conservative movements.

SANDERS, a readable and lively book, concentrates like Howe on the Yiddish cultural and socialist environment of the immigrants, especially the press. A significant study of Jewish immigrant mobility, placed in a fruitful comparative context, is KESSNER.

An excellent study of a "second settlement" neighborhood is GUROCK. It uses to good effect printed and manuscript data of the United States census alongside more customary press and institutional records.

The vast generational cohort that made the transition from immigrants to natives between 1920 and 1940 is skillfully presented in the imaginative work by MOORE. It emphasizes the prosperous 1920s rather than the depressed 1930s. This shortcoming is more than compensated for by the excellent study of WENGER, which deals mainly with social and economic problems of the 1930s. The Jews of New York City since 1945 have yet to receive the attention of historians.

Several studies have been devoted to the ultraorthodox, including hasidic, groups. An early, effective example is the sociological study of POLL. The Jews' place among the city's ethnic and racial groups is analyzed in the lively study by GLAZER and MOYNIHAN, who regard ethnicity not as transitory but as a permanent factor in New York City's life.

LLOYD P. GARTNER

New Zealand *see* Australia and New Zealand

Nieto, David 1654–1728

Italian-born London rabbinical leader, philosopher, theologian, and controversialist

Gaster, Moses, *History of the Ancient Synagogue of the Spanish and Portuguese Jews, the Cathedral Synagogue of the Jews in England, Situate in Bevis Marks*, London, 1901

Goldish, Matt, "Newtonian, Converso and Deist: The Lives of Jacob Henrique de Castro Sarmento," *Science in Context*, 10, 1997

Loewe, Raphael, "The Spanish Supplement to Nieto's *Esh Dath*," *Proceedings of the American Academy for Jewish Research*, 48, 1981

Petuchowski, Jakob J., "Haham David Nieto and Deistic Trends in Eighteenth-Century Judaism," *Journal of Jewish Studies*, 5, 1954

Petuchowski, Jakob J., *The Theology of Haham David Nieto: An Eighteenth Century Defense of the Jewish Tradition*, New York: Bloch, 1954; revised edition, New York: Ktav, 1970

Roth, Cecil, "Haham David Nieto," in his *Essays and Portraits in Anglo-Jewish History*, Philadelphia: Jewish Publication Society, 1962

Roth, Leon, "David Nieto and the Orthodoxy of Spinozism," *Chronicum Spinozanum*, 1, 1928

Ruderman, David, "Jewish Thought in Newtonian England: The Career and Writings of David Nieto," *Proceedings of the American Academy for Jewish Research*, 58, 1992; as chapter 11 in *Jewish Thought and Scientific Discovery in Early Modern Europe*, New Haven, Connecticut: Yale University Press, 1995

Solomons, Israel, *David Nieto and Some of His Contemporaries*, London: Spottiswoode, Ballantyne, 1931

David Nieto was haham (rabbi) of London's Portuguese Jewish community from 1701 until his death in 1728. A Sephardi physician and scholar from Italy with wide interests, he found himself the spiritual leader of an unruly congregation of former conversos recently returned from Catholicism. His writings offer a unique window into the problems of Jewish tradition in Newtonian England, though they had relatively little influence either on subsequent generations or in other communities. Haham Nieto appears to have possessed a mild character, but his convictions were strong and his best-known works are polemical in character.

SOLOMONS remains the most important biographer of Nieto. He deals with Nieto's life in detail and explains the basic background behind his various writings. He also disentangles the publication history of these works, much of which was previously unclear. An especially useful feature of this study is the inclusion of key documents in English translation. At the end Solomons includes an extremely detailed bibliography of Nieto's works and a series of appendixes dealing with important personalities in Nieto's circle.

GASTER, though an older and more popular work than those of Solomons and Petuchowski, still contains some details of Nieto's biography and thought that are useful and of interest to those seeking a complete picture of Nieto.

Cecil ROTH offers another brief biographic study of Nieto, based mainly on Solomons and Petuchowski but not lacking in his own keen observations. Roth, a pioneering historian of the former conversos and of Italian Jewry, presents Nieto's life and works in a characteristically readable and easily accessible manner.

PETUCHOWSKI (1954b) remains the only monograph on Nieto's thought. As a reform theologian, Petuchowski is particularly interested in the forms of Jewish heterodoxy that arose among the London Portuguese former conversos and in Nieto's attempts to combat these doctrinal deviances. Following a biographic summary, Petuchowski enters into a detailed discussion of the various challenges to traditional Judaism offered by both rationalists and mystics among the Portuguese Jews. He then turns to Nieto's responses to these challenges, which he characterizes as reflecting a "scientific" approach. Nieto's views on traditional doctrines of revelation, the oral law, the talmudic sages, and God are examined, and a chapter is added on Nieto's place in the history of Judaism. Much research has been done on attitudes toward these issues in the period since Petuchowski wrote, but his book still holds up remarkably well and remains the standard work on Nieto's theology.

PETUCHOWSKI (1954a) presents a more specific interdisciplinary study about one major episode in Nieto's London career: the accusation of heresy leveled at him by certain congregants in 1703. Despite Nieto's exoneration by the great Haham Tsevi Ashkenazi, Petuchowski contends that in his claim that "God is nature and nature is God," there is still ample evidence that Nieto was indeed influenced by the deism. He adduces assorted evidence to this effect.

Leon ROTH simply published a critical document in the aforementioned debate over Nieto's orthodoxy, an English translation of Haham Tsevi's responsum exonerating Nieto from the charge. There is nothing more to the article, but Roth's title, "David Nieto and the Orthodoxy of Spinozism," indicates clearly that Roth saw Nieto's position on God and nature as Spinozist. This differs from Petuchowski's view that Nieto was a deist, but they share a common view that Nieto's accusers were somehow correct about his heterodoxy.

LOEWE's important article was the first in a long while to advance materially understanding of Nieto and his milieu. The subject of this study is a short manuscript supplement to Nieto's work *Esh Dat*, a polemic against the Sabbatian kabbalist Nehemiah Hayun. Loewe transcribes and translates the supplement, and he offers a penetrating analysis of its significance. He claims that the deep concern Nieto expressed over the Hayun affair was mainly the result of his fear that the Jews' somewhat tenuous settlement rights in England would be threatened if Hayun's messianic heterodoxy became known to the authorities.

RUDERMAN's interest in Nieto concerns an area mainly overlooked by previous scholars: Nieto's deep preoccupation with science, which figures significantly in all his works. Ruderman offers convincing arguments that Nieto, in attempting to impress sophisticates in his congregation as well as to satisfy his own curiosity, absorbed much of the "Newtonian synthesis" between science and religion then current in England. The ideas expressed in the Boyle Lectures delivered by Samuel Clarke, a leading student of Newton and proponent of the Newtonian synthesis, appear to have been most influential on Nieto. While he may or may not have come in direct contact with these lectures, Nieto's thinking is unquestionably in harmony with Clarke's design argument and Newtonian proofs for divine providence.

Prompted by Ruderman's study, GOLDISH investigates the impact of Nieto's "Jewish Newtonian synthesis" on his leading student, Jacob de Castro Sarmento. Goldish contends that Nieto's scientific proofs of Jewish doctrine exercised a powerful but temporary influence over the brilliant Sarmento, who abandoned Judaism little by little after Nieto's death.

MATT GOLDISH

North Africa

Abitbol, Michel, *The Jews of North Africa during the Second World War*, Detroit, Michigan: Wayne State University Press, 1989

Attal, Robert, *Les Juifs d'Afrique du Nord: Bibliographie*, Jerusalem: Ben-Zvi Institute, 1973

Chouraqui, André N., *Between East and West: A History of the Jews of North Africa*, Philadelphia: Jewish Publication Society, 1968

Cohen, Mark R. and Abraham L. Udovitch (editors), *Jews among Arabs: Contacts and Boundaries*, Princeton, New Jersey: Darwin, 1989

Goitein, Shlomo Dov, *A Mediterranean Society: The Jewish Communities of the Arab World as Portrayed in the Documents of the Cairo Geniza*, Berkeley: University of California Press, 1967–1993

Hirschberg, Haïm Zeev, *Toldot ha-Yehudim be-Afrikah ha-Tsefonit*, 1965; as *A History of the Jews in North Africa*, 2 vols., Leiden: Brill, 1974–1981

Laskier, Michael M., *North African Jewry in the Twentieth Century: The Jews of Morocco, Tunisia, and Algeria*, New York: New York University Press, 1994

Seminar on Muslim-Jewish Relations in North Africa, *Proceedings of the Seminar on Muslim-Jewish Relations in North Africa*, New York: World Jewish Congress, 1975

Slouschz, Nahum, *Travels in North Africa*, Philadelphia: Jewish Publication Society, 1927; as *The Jews of North Africa*, Philadelphia: Jewish Publication Society, 1944

Throughout the Middle Ages, North Africa absorbed large numbers of Sephardim, who greatly shaped the character of its ancient indigenous Jewish communities. Another major influence since the 19th century resulted from French cultural intervention and political involvement. Most Jews emigrated in or after 1948, mainly to France, Israel, and the Americas, though sizable communities remain in Morocco and Tunisia. Much research has been conducted on the region as a whole and even more on individual communities, especially on Morocco, mainly in Hebrew and French as well as in English.

ABITBOL divides his book on the Maghreb during World War II into three chronological parts. In the first he examines the position of the Jews in Morocco, Algeria, and Tunisia on the eve of World War II, paying special attention to French-Jewish and Muslim-Jewish relations and to antisemitism among European settlers. He then discusses the anti-Jewish legislation under the Vichy regime and its implementation in each country as well as the impact of the German presence, especially as it relates to Tunisia. Among the issues dealt with are help for refugees (mainly from Europe), work camps, internment, and the attitude of the Muslims toward the condition of the Jews. The third part analyzes the reasons for and the process of the slow recovery following the Allied landing and liberation.

ATTAL's bibliography includes more than 10,000 entries on North African Jews. The bibliography starts with the region as a whole, followed by sections on Libya, Tunisia, Algeria, and Morocco. Each part is divided into sequences documenting literature in Hebrew and Roman script, and its arrangement is alphabetical by author and chronological for entries with no known author. Author and subject indexes in Hebrew and Roman script are included, and the sequence of items for the region and country in question is printed at the bottom of each index page to facilitate the search. This is the major bibliography on the subject. Though most entries are in Hebrew and French, many are in English.

CHOURAQUI provides a historical survey of North African Jews as well as an examination of their communal life. The survey starts with the Carthaginian through Roman periods but focuses on the Muslim and colonial eras. The earlier periods are discussed generally, whereas the later ones are divided by specific countries. Much attention is given to cultural issues, population trends, and the intellectual, social, economic, and political impact of the West on North Africa in general and on the Jews in particular. Chouraqui deals also with the impact of nationalism—Arab and Jewish—on the region, the mass Jewish emigration following the establishment of the State of Israel, and the struggle for independence culminating in the establishment of independent Maghrebi states. Statistical data and bibliography are included.

COHEN and UDOVITCH's collection includes six articles exploring the experience of Jewish communities of North Africa and Iraq in the 19th and 20th centuries as an example of interaction between a religio-ethnic group and the dominant Arab-Muslim society. The articles examine the practical and symbolic exchanges between communities, shared traditions and cultural forms, and the boundaries between the communities. The articles deal with literature, marriage celebrations, foodways, language, and trade. Although limited in the number of countries and subjects covered, this collection includes important studies and new approaches for an understanding of the life of minorities.

GOITEIN's pioneering work based on the Cairo Genizah documents examines the medieval Mediterranean society and is considered a classic. The study deals both with the Jewish communities and with the gentile societies among which they lived. It opens with a discussion of the Cairo Genizah itself and a survey of the historical, economic, and social background. Among the main topics of the study are economic life, communal organization, education, interfaith relations, daily life, family life, the home, and the individual—a portrait of a Mediterranean personality of the high Middle Ages. The six-volume study concludes with a volume of cumulative indexes covering text and notes. In its wealth of data and depth of analysis, this work is indispensable for the study of Jewish and gentile Mediterranean medieval society and is a must-read even for those focusing on the modern period.

HIRSCHBERG's two-volume book is the broadest study, both geographically and chronologically, on Maghrebi Jews: it covers the region from Morocco to Libya from antiquity to the 1950s. Based on numerous publications in Hebrew and European languages, Hirschberg discusses developments in communal organization, economic and spiritual life, and the implications of political changes for the Jews. For the period after the 16th century, the countries are treated separately. Although many monographs have been published since Hirschberg's book using archival sources that have subsequently become available, it remains the most comprehensive survey on North Africa as a whole.

Based on a wide range of public and private archival sources as well as on numerous publications in several languages, LASKIER examines the political history of Maghrebi Jews before, during, and following colonial rule. Among the issues examined are the condition of the Jews during World War II, Zionism, emigration (including clandestine operations), the involvement of international organizations (primarily Jewish) in favor of Maghrebi Jews, Jewish-Muslim relations, Jewish self-defense operations, and Jewish relations with the nationalist movements. This study adds much new information on North African Jews in an integrated, analytical way.

The SEMINAR ON MUSLIM-JEWISH RELATIONS IN NORTH AFRICA was one of the first meetings focusing on Maghrebi Jews in which leading figures in the field participated: S.D. Goitein, N.A. Stillman, J. Gerber, and R. Press. They examined aspects of Jewish-Muslim relations during the medieval and modern periods, mainly in Morocco, and their articles reflect various points of view. The discussion that followed included several remarks by people originating from the Maghreb who added their own impressions regarding Jewish-Muslim relations as they experienced them or heard about them.

SLOUSCHZ's 1927 book describes his travels among the Jewish communities of the four countries comprising North Africa during the years 1906 to 1914. He visited the major urban centers and smaller hinterland communities and benefited from the information provided by indigenous Jewish scholars. The book starts with Slouschz's visit to Tripoli and its surroundings as well as the Tripolitanian Saharan communities. This is followed by his visits to Tunisia (including the island of Djerba), Algeria, and Morocco. The book examines the history of the communities, their organization, customs, and social, economic, and cultural life. Slouschz, an epigraphist, is especially interested in Jewish antiquities and the Jewish origin of local peoples. The book was republished in 1944 as *The Jews of North Africa*, unchanged except for the title.

RACHEL SIMON

See also Algeria; Libya; Morocco; Tunisia

Numbers, Book of

Douglas, Mary, *In the Wilderness: The Doctrine of Defilement in the Book of Numbers* (Journal for the Study of the Old Testament Supplement Series, 158), Sheffield, South Yorkshire: JSOT, 1993

Hackett, Jo Ann, *The Balaam Text from Deir 'Alla* (Harvard Semitic Monographs, no. 31), Chico, California: Scholars Press, 1984

Levine, Baruch A., *Numbers 1–20: A New Translation with Introduction and Commentary* (Anchor Bible, vol. 4A), New York: Doubleday, 1993

Milgrom, Jacob, *Numbers/Ba-midbar: The Traditional Hebrew Text with the New JPS Translation* (JPS Torah Commentary Series), Philadelphia: Jewish Publication Society, 1990

Olson, Dennis T., *Numbers* (Interpretation: A Bible Commentary for Teaching and Preaching), Louisville, Kentucky: Knox, 1996

The fourth book of the Bible, the Book of Numbers, has been perceived widely as the Bible's basement, into which an editor, divine or human, has dumped all the laws and stories that do not seem to fit anywhere else. Applying the literary methods in vogue in the academic study of the Hebrew Bible at the close of the 20th century, however, OLSON succeeds in demonstrating that the very structure of the Book of Numbers, far from being haphazard, is a work of art crafted to express a series of messages. Drawing from the full gamut of contemporary Jewish and Christian exegesis of Numbers as well as ancient exegesis contained in such places as the rabbinic and patristic corpora, Olson provides for each and every pericope a clear exposition both of its probable original meaning and of its contemporary relevance to such issues as setting boundaries, showing respect for leaders, and the need for those leaders to be open to their own flaws.

If Olson seems to draw out for his target audience of preachers and teachers the eternal verities contained in the Book of Numbers read in light of an exegetical consensus, MILGROM demonstrates that modern biblical studies is a field of exciting new discoveries and debates in which there are winners and losers. For example, he goes to great lengths to explain how Mayer Gruber's findings put to rest the scholarly myth that ancient Israel was peopled with sacred prostitutes (women who engaged in extramarital sex at temples and elsewhere in order to increase by sympathetic magic the fertility of the land). By summarizing and explaining major issues in the ancient, medieval, and modern study of the Book of Numbers, Milgrom shows that vital issues in religion and life are contained in the fourth book of the Bible.

In contrast to Milgrom's nontraditional Jewish commentary, LEVINE provides a detailed, nonsectarian scholarly analysis of Numbers. (Interestingly, the two authors switch roles when commenting on Leviticus; in that instance, Levine writes for a Jewish audience, while Milgrom offers the nonsectarian interpretation.) Notwithstanding their continual disagreement over issues very important to them and to other professional biblical scholars—notably the relative dating of Leviticus and Deuteronomy—Milgrom and Levine epitomize a rare and vanishing breed of Jewish scholar, whose native language is English but who are steeped in Hebrew of all periods, acquired (like their Yiddish) in childhood. Both are ordained Conservative rabbis whose mastery of Semitic languages and literatures has earned them international reputations. Both, however, have devoted much of their energy in recent years to expounding the message of the Bible to the People of the Book and disseminating ancient and modern Jewish exegesis to the larger world of academicians, students, and educated laity.

If the works by Milgrom and Levine successfully combine summaries of their respective contributions with a fair hearing to other biblical scholarship on the Book of Numbers, the works by Douglas and Hackett are uniquely significant contributions on specific issues. The importance of these two studies to the Book of Numbers and to 20th-century biblical scholar-ship is amply demonstrated by the attention they receive in the other works cited here. Going beyond her seminal contribution almost 30 years before of an anthropological perspective on the dietary laws of the Book of Leviticus, DOUGLAS's work makes sense of much of the Book of Numbers that previously had been discussed, allegorized, diagrammed, or condemned all without being understood. Christian Bible criticism has often taken for granted that the purity laws characteristic of Leviticus and Numbers were Judaism's strategy for turning away from other nations. This corollary was drawn by Max Weber in *Das antike Judentum* (1921), where he contended that "the negative attitude of the Jews themselves was rather the decisive factor for anti-semitism in antiquity." Douglas's work demonstrates, however, that in Leviticus and Numbers "defilement is caused not by contact with other people; it comes out of the body, or it comes out of moral failure. Everybody is liable to be defiled or to defile. This should be totally unexpected to the anthropologist used to purity codes in other religions." In addition, Douglas contends that Hebrew Scripture's concept of defilement can be elucidated most clearly by treating the Book of Numbers as a literary unit rather than as the Bible's junk room.

In 1967 an Arab worker at Deir 'Alla in Jordan discovered a set of tablets among material that archaeologists had thrown onto the refuse pile. Inscribed on the tablets in black and red ink in early-seventh-century B.C.E. Ammonite script and in a South Canaanite dialect was a brief narrative concerning a diviner named Balaam, son of Beor. While Palestinian archaeology has shed much light on the material culture of Iron-Age Israel, it is still quite infrequent that inscriptions from the ancient Near East actually refer by name to some person heretofore known only from the Bible. In fact, the Deir 'Alla Balaam tablets are the only extant Iron-Age texts that refer by name to a personality mentioned in the Pentateuch. Thus, these tablets seem to preserve a record of how Iron-Age non-Israelites viewed the very Balaam who receives a mixed reception from Israelites in the biblical books of Numbers and Deuteronomy. HACKETT's work is the single most comprehensive and levelheaded treatment in English of these ancient texts. Hackett's edition, translation, and commentary on the Balaam texts therefore forms part of the necessary background for reading the Book of Numbers and its religious messages in its ancient context.

MAYER IRWIN GRUBER

Numbers and Numerology

Abrams, Daniel, "From Germany to Spain: Numerology as a Mystical Technique," *Journal of Jewish Studies,* 47(1), Spring 1996

Levias, C., "Gematria," in *The Jewish Encyclopedia,* vol. 5, edited by Isidore Singer, New York and London: Funk and Wagnalls, 1901, new edition, 1925

Lieberman, Stephen J., "A Mesopotamian Background for the So-Called Aggadic 'Measures' of Biblical Hermeneutics," *Hebrew Union College Annual,* 58, 1987

Locks, Gutman G., *The Spice of Torah—Gematria,* New York: Judaica Press, 1985

Scholem, Gershom, "Gematria," in *Encyclopaedia Judaica*, vol. 7, edited by C. Roth, Jerusalem: Keter, 1971

Wolfson, Elliot R., "Letter Symbolism and Merkavah Imagery in the Zohar," in *'Alei Shefer, Studies in the Literature of Jewish Thought*, edited by Mosheh Halamish, Ramat-Gan: Bar Ilan University Press, 1990

Corresponding in turn to the numbers one through ten, to multiples of ten through 90, and to multiples of 100 through 400, the 22 letters of the Hebrew alphabet have been used as hermeneutical tools by which words are given numerological values and compared with the values assigned to other words.

Gematria, the calculation of the numerical value of letters, is the 29th of the 32 hermeneutical rules countenanced by the rabbis for valid aggadic interpretation of the Torah, but it is by no means a strictly Jewish notion. To the contrary, there is evidence of gematria in the Greek tradition, in cuneiform hermeneutic texts, and in Christian commentary on the Hebrew Bible. Some scholars trace the etymology of the term to the Greek *geometria* (or to the related notion of geometrical number); others contend that the root of the word is found in the Greek *grammateia*, from *grammateus* (secretary or scribe), or directly from *gramma* (letter). In the Jewish mystical tradition, there are as many as 75 different varieties of gematria. Consult LEVIAS for the best current enumeration of some of these many varieties.

SCHOLEM's short encyclopedia entry on gematria is a concentrated repository of relevant distinctions as well as primary and secondary source materials. Scholem draws attention to the variety of types of gematria, and he outlines—and briefly explains—seven of the nine kinds listed by Moses Cordovero in *Pardes Rimmonim*. With respect to the influence of gematria on early kabbalistic literature, Scholem notes that it was "not considerable on the greater part of the Zohar and on the Hebrew writings of Moses b. Shem Tov de Leon" and that the impact is seen instead in the latter half of the 13th century, especially in the works of Abraham Abulafia. Scholem also notes that Joseph Gikatilla—a student of Abulafia—made extensive use of gematria, and that the influence can be seen in later zoharic literature (but not the Zohar itself).

In his article on letter symbolism, WOLFSON offers a detailed, essentially linguistic (that is to say, letter-focused) discussion of medieval interpretations of the chariot (*merkabah*) imagery of Ezekiel chapter 1. The article's focus on the importance of letters to the *merkabah* speculation of Joseph Gikatilla and of Moses de Leon in his writings prior to the appearance of the Zohar helps to reveal the extent of the numerological significance of those letters in these early texts, as well as in the Zohar itself. As such, Wolfson's discussion suggests the emergence of a decidedly numerological underpinning to the Zohar and pre-Zohar Sephardi mystical texts. This numerological slant may be seen specifically in the employment and analyses of *merkabah* imagery in Gikatilla and de Leon. Both employ cosmological systems in which the relation between the divine unity—the charioteer—and the plurality that follows—the chariot—is defined (at least partially) through specific recourse to, among other things, the numerological value of the tetragrammaton in the case of de Leon, and involving a mode of letter permutation in the case of Gikatilla.

ABRAMS's article, as its title suggests, examines possible textual links between the Ashkenazi and Sephardi mystical traditions in the Middle Ages. Focusing on the use of numerology in both of these traditions, the author discusses the greater numerological focus found in the Ashkenazi mystics, finding in Abraham Abulafia alone a real extension of the German approach among the Sephardim. The article analyzes the experiential role of numerology, in which the repetitious act involved in calculating the numerological values of words, rather than the values of the words per se, is understood as the primary means by which the mystic seeks to achieve a mystical experience in the form of a heightened spiritual (or altered mental) state.

LOCKS provides a manual for numerological analysis of biblical texts. His volume lists each word that occurs in the Pentateuch in numerical order—that is, according to the numerical value of its letters. The book starts with the number three and ends with 1,500, and under each numerical value, Locks presents the relevant words in order of their first occurrence in the biblical text. Each word entry is presented in fully vocalized Hebrew script accompanied by an exact citation and an English translation. The work also includes a very useful introductory chapter by Immanuel Schochet.

LIEBERMAN demarcates the analogues of gematria in cuneiform, Greek, Arabic, and other texts, noting that the earliest recorded occurrence of gematria is attributed to an eighth-century B.C.E. Assyrian king. The author distinguishes between constitutive and interpretational uses of gematria: the latter method uses numerological techniques to interpret words, and the former method employs numerology to select a name, a term, or a spelling (e.g., Eleazar of Worms named his book *Rokeah* because that title shares the numerical equivalent of 308 with his own name, Eleazar). In addition to the naming of books, Lieberman also discusses the implications of numerological considerations for the processes of indicating calendrical dates and naming years, and he recounts the general connection between numbers and letters in many textual traditions. Lieberman concludes that, given the employment of numerological techniques before and during the composition of the Hebrew Bible, it is entirely possible that gematria (as well as *notarikon*, the interpretation of selected words in the biblical text as if they were acronyms) was employed within the Bible itself, encoding hidden messages into the text that were to be discovered by employment of gematria or notarikon analysis (the *at-bash* code of the Book of Jeremiah being a case in point).

SARAH PESSIN

O

Onomastics

Beider, Alexander, *A Dictionary of Jewish Surnames from the Russian Empire*, Teaneck, New Jersey: Avotaynu, 1993

Demski, Aaron, Joseph Reif, and Joseph Tabory (editors), *These Are the Names: Studies in Jewish Onomastics,* Ramat-Gan: Bar-Ilan University Press, 1997

Fowler, Jeaneane D., *Theophoric Personal Names in Ancient Hebrew: A Comparative Study* (Journal for the Study of the Old Testament Supplement Series, 49), Sheffield, South Yorkshire: JSOT, 1988

Grabbe, Lester L., *Etymology in Early Jewish Interpretation: The Hebrew Names in Philo* (Brown Judaic Studies, no. 115), Atlanta, Georgia: Scholars Press, 1988

Guggenheimer, Heinrich W. and Eva H. Guggenheimer, *Jewish Family Names and Their Origins: An Etymological Dictionary,* Hoboken, New Jersey: Ktav, 1992

Kaganoff, Benzion C., *A Dictionary of Jewish Names and Their History,* New York: Schocken, 1977; London: Routledge and Kegan Paul, 1978

Kolatch, Alfred J., *Complete Dictionary of English and Hebrew First Names,* Middle Village, New York: David, 1984

Mettinger, Tryggve N.D., *Namnet och närvaron: Gudsnamn och Gudsbild i Böckernas Bok,* 1987; translated by Frederick H. Cryer as *In Search of God: The Meaning and Message of the Everlasting Names,* Philadelphia: Fortress, 1988

Tigay, Jeffrey H., *You Shall Have No Other Gods: Israelite Religion in the Light of Hebrew Inscriptions* (Harvard Semitic Studies, 31), Atlanta, Georgia: Scholars Press, 1986

Onomastics (from the Greek *onoma*) is the study of names. An examination of the name that an individual bears can reveal much information concerning that person's origin, identity, religious worldview, social status, and mores. As the following works make clear, playing "Jewish geography" can also be an academic enterprise.

KAGANOFF is one of the best starting points for the layperson interested in learning about Jewish names and onomastics. In the first part of the book, Kaganoff presents a general introduction to the study of Jewish names, tracing both the history of Jewish naming practice and the history of Jewish names. Two slightly subversive conclusions may be drawn from this section: first, that there is no standard Jewish way of naming, and second, that many of the names that are considered typically Jewish in the modern world actually originated in non-Jewish contexts. The second part of the book provides a short dictionary of Jewish family names that complements the discussion in the first section. Kaganoff's presentation of these names emphasizes their meanings and derivations. His work, however, has been criticized as superficial by professional onomasticians.

KOLATCH has made a career of publishing reference books on names for a popular Jewish audience. The main body of this catalog of 11,000 first names in use in both the English- and Hebrew-speaking worlds alphabetically lists boys' and girls' names. Kolatch includes each name's meaning and variant forms (for example, Moe and Moyse for the English Moses and its Hebrew equivalent Moshe), and an appendix organizing Hebrew names according to their English definitions will assist readers seeking Hebrew equivalents for "secular" names. An introduction provides a brief overview of how names developed and how Jews in particular have chosen names over the course of time.

BEIDER's major scholarly work is devoted to the cataloging and analysis of some 50,000 Jewish surnames from the Russian Jewish Pale of Settlement. In the first part, the author introduces the reader to the study of Jewish onomastics; analyzes the primary data according to source language, type, and linguistic criteria; and places the material in a historical context. The second part of the volume lists the names with their translations, geographic distribution, and possible etymologies. Because the various languages use diverse methods to transcribe Jewish names, the third part provides a phonetic key to finding name listings. Thus, one can find the surname of the painter Marc Chagall, even though it is spelled Shagal according to Beider's system of transcription.

The dictionary by GUGGENHEIMER and GUGGENHEIMER is broader than Beider's work in scope but not in depth. The Guggenheimers list and give etymological explanations for the surnames employed by Ashkenazi, Sephardi, Oriental, and Israeli Jews in the modern world. While the authors treat the first two categories as comprehensively as possible, they admit that their access to sources for Oriental surnames was limited and that they were unable to include

Ethiopian surnames in their work. The book includes a brief introduction, followed by the distinctive dictionary that offers Yiddish-, Hebrew-, Arabic-, and some Russian-derived names in the original script of the respective languages.

DEMSKI, REIF, and TABORY's collection of essays delivered at a conference on Jewish onomastics at Bar-Ilan University includes five essays written in English along with four articles in Hebrew that are summarized in English. There are four essays on Jewish names in antiquity; four more on names and naming patterns among Sephardi and Yemenite communities, particularly during the 19th and 20th centuries; and one article on the anthropology of Jewish names. The centerpiece of the book, however, is an annotated bibliography on Jewish onomastics, which concentrates mainly on works in English. Overall, the volume is an accessible scholarly source for those desiring to delve deeper into the subject.

More specialized studies include TIGAY's controversial attempt to reconstruct the history of Israelite religion on the basis of the contemporaneous extrabiblical onomasticon. According to Tigay's analysis, close to 50 percent of the approximately 1,200 names known from ancient Hebrew inscriptional sources contain theophoric or divine elements, the overwhelming majority of which allude to the tetragrammaton. Less than six percent refer to other gods. Tigay therefore concludes that ancient Israelite religion, at least during the eighth through sixth centuries B.C.E., was overwhelmingly monotheistic. It should be noted that his conclusions diverge from the theory supported by most contemporary biblical researchers, namely that the religion of Israel prior to 586 B.C.E. and the Babylonian Exile was polytheistic or just possibly monolatrous, a system pledging allegiance to one deity without denying the existence of other gods.

FOWLER is an exhaustive study of Hebrew names from biblical times that include either direct or implicit references to God. Drawing from both the biblical onomasticon and names found in ancient Hebrew epigraphic sources, Fowler identifies the elements that refer to God in the first part of her work, while in the second part she subjects the various theophoric names to a rigorous semantic analysis. The final sections of the study compare the religious concepts that the author derives from the biblical onomasticon with those that she identifies from other ancient Semitic onomastica. Like Tigay, Fowler challenges the preeminent view in modern biblical studies as she concludes that the evidence of the biblical onomasticon supports the traditional contention that Israelite religion was monotheistic and in many respects distinct from other religions in its ancient Near Eastern environment.

METTINGER is a work of Christian biblical theology that nonetheless conveys some very useful information concerning the names and designations of God in the Hebrew Bible. Mettinger surveys the philology, history, and theological meaning of the various divine names in the Bible, including YHWH, *'el(ohim)*, and *'el-shadday*, and he places these names into a relatively conservative reconstruction of the history of the religions of Israel and its neighbors in antiquity. He also analyzes the import of various divine designations, including *YHWH tseva'ot*, *'elohim hayyim*, and God as "king," "redeemer," "savior," and "creator." His concluding sections deal with the images of God in the book of Job and the issue of God-language and gender studies.

GRABBE explores how the Hellenistic-Jewish philosopher Philo used etymologies in his allegorical method of scriptural interpretation. Grabbe has isolated 166 biblical names for which Philo presents etymologies. These go beyond the level of the purely etiological and appear influenced more by the Hellenistic (rather than the Jewish) sphere. Yet, unlike his Hellenistic intellectual forebears, Philo draws from a tradition that had knowledge of the Jewish languages of his time, namely Hebrew and Aramaic. Philo did not know these languages himself, however, and Grabbe therefore posits that the philosopher had at his disposal a preexisting onomasticon, albeit corrupted in the course of its scribal transmission.

CARL S. EHRLICH

Oral Tradition

Elman, Yaakov, *Authority and Tradition: Toseftan Baraitot in Talmudic Babylonia*, Hoboken, New Jersey: Ktav, 1994

Faur, José, *Golden Doves with Silver Dots: Semiotics and Textuality in Rabbinic Tradition* (Jewish Literature and Culture), Bloomington: Indiana University Press, 1986

Fraade, Steven D., *From Tradition to Commentary: Torah and Its Interpretation in the Midrash Sifre to Deuteronomy* (SUNY Series in Judaica), Albany: State University of New York Press, 1991

Gerhardsson, Birger, *Memory and Manuscript: Oral Tradition and Written Transmission in Rabbinic Judaism and Early Christianity*, foreword by Jacob Neusner, Copenhagen, Denmark: Munksgaard, 1961; as *Memory and Manuscript: Oral Tradition and Written Transmission in Rabbinic Judaism and Early Christianity; with, Tradition and Transmission in Early Christianity*, Grand Rapids, Michigan: Eerdmans, 1998

Neusner, Jacob, *Oral Tradition in Judaism: The Case of the Mishnah* (Garland Reference Library of the Humanities, vol. 764), New York: Garland, 1987

Zlotnick, Dov, *Iron Pillar–Mishnah: Redaction, Form, and Intent*, New York: Ktav, 1988

The study of oral tradition in Judaic cultures has proceeded within a number of disciplines and focused on a wide variety of topics. The present essay addresses a setting of special interest to historians of the religious dimension of Judaic culture—the relation of ancient oral tradition to the surviving records of the classical rabbinic writings of late antiquity (c.200–650 C.E.). Such writings include, most famously, legal compendia such as the Mishnah and the Tosefta, various collections of biblical interpretation known as Midrash, and the Talmuds of Palestine and Babylonia.

In these writings, and especially in later medieval theological, jurisprudential, and historical thought, rabbinic knowledge regarding law, history, and biblical interpretation is commonly termed "Oral Torah." That is, rabbinic tradition is viewed as stemming from a primordial revelation on Sinai that complements the "Written Torah" of Moses himself. The rabbinic understanding is that Moses transmitted this Oral (unwritten) Torah by word of mouth to his disciples and they to theirs, in an unbroken line of transmission. According to rabbinic thought, this Oral Torah survives more or less intact in the extant rabbinic writings of antiquity.

Most modern students of the rabbinic writings of late antiquity are prepared to doubt that much, if any, rabbinic Oral Torah originates in Mosaic revelation. Of much greater interest is the degree to which the surviving writings can provide access to earlier, exclusively oral forms of rabbinic or even pre-rabbinic traditions of the Second Temple or early post-Temple periods. Similarly, many are interested in the role that oral mastery and performance of rabbinic tradition played in the intellectual and moral formation of rabbinic disciples. There are at present no comprehensive treatments of all the issues relating to rabbinic oral tradition in late antiquity, nor does any one book even consider the entire surviving literature from the perspective of oral tradition. But the books discussed here constitute important steps in opening the topic to disciplined academic inquiry.

GERHARDSSON, despite huge theoretical paradigm shifts in rabbinic studies since he wrote, remains the most important first introduction to the various issues surrounding rabbinic oral tradition. The new edition of his book, with Jacob Neusner's foreword, is most welcome. Gerhardsson gathers exhaustively the most important rabbinic sources that shed light on the oral dimension of rabbinic tradition. His main concern is to recover the pedagogical and mnemonic methods by which oral tradition was composed, mastered, and transmitted in the circles of rabbinic discipleship. The chief flaws in Gerhardsson's work are theoretical: his way of citing rabbinic sources obscures the degree to which later, theologically motivated perspectives on oral transmission might shape descriptions of early practices, and he implicitly assumes that rabbinic tradition circulated in an exclusively oral form prior to its transcription in writing.

Jacob Neusner, in reviews and other articles, has become the most important critic of these theoretical weaknesses (although he appears to have repented in his foreword to the new edition of Gerhardsson). NEUSNER offers a comprehensive profile of the mnemonic system of the Mishnah in particular, focusing on such issues as the way literary forms serve to shape conceptual contents, the role of formulaic patterns in aiding memorization, and the degree to which the Mishnah, as a memorized text, gave birth to (rather than grew out of) an oral tradition. In his view, the act of writing down rabbinic traditions has profoundly altered them: "Those who wish to trace the history of oral tradition cannot find an exemplary case in the Mishnah. Those who propose to explain how a statement in oral form takes shape and enters into a continuous tradition by contrast will find in the Mishnah's later history a source of probative examples indeed."

ZLOTNICK's volume focuses on the Mishnah as well, offering an overall introduction to the history of the mishnaic tradition and the nature of the Mishnah as a literary work. His conception of the relation of the extant mishnaic text to antecedent rabbinic oral tradition, however, represents a methodological step backward from Neusner's achievement,

failing to refute or even to address any of Neusner's major theoretical proposals. Nevertheless, Zlotnick's discussions of the mnemonic traits of mishnaic discourse are astute and insightful on their own terms. The book offers a useful contrast to the formalistic analyses preferred by Neusner.

ELMAN's work is by far the most sophisticated in its use of contemporary anthropological and literary-historical approaches to orality as a route into interpreting the earliest history of rabbinic oral tradition. He addresses the Tosefta, a legal compendium roughly contemporary with the Mishnah and parallel to it in style and content. His penetrating comparisons of texts preserved in extant manuscripts of the Tosefta with their parallels in the two Talmuds yields the claim that the Tosefta benefited from transmission as both an oral and a written text. The written rendering is of Palestinian provenance and represents an earlier form of the text than its orally transmitted Babylonian counterpart. Elman cautiously avoids generalizations about whether this dual track transmission characterizes all rabbinic texts. His work constitutes a crucial turn in the discussion of the nature of rabbinic literary tradition as found in the Mishnah and Tosefta, and it has important implications for other compilations as well.

FAUR's theoretical point of departure is in semiotics. From this vantage he offers a global theory of rabbinic literature as a medium of oral and written communication. A key contribution is his mining of the rich medieval rabbinic tradition for insights into how the tradition itself understood the implications of the dual media of textual transmission. Despite a tendency to accept at face value the rabbinic mythologization of oral tradition as revelation, Faur's is an informative and stimulating investigation into the oral dimension of rabbinic textuality.

FRAADE's work focuses on an important midrashic text of the early rabbinic period. While not primarily concerned with problems of oral tradition per se, the volume offers numerous stimulating observations regarding the performative dimension of rabbinic text-making. Fraade sees the composition of midrashic texts as a way of embodying key rabbinic values and of participating in the production of Torah. The interpretive process of the midrashic text represents for Fraade "the literary face of an otherwise oral circulatory system of study and teaching by whose illocutionary force disciples became sages and sages became a class that could extend their teachings . . . into Jewish society more broadly."

MARTIN S. JAFFEE

Orthodox Judaism *see* Haredim; Modern Orthodox Judaism

Ozick, Cynthia 1928–

American novelist and critic

Bloom, Harold (editor), *Cynthia Ozick* (Modern Critical Views), New York: Chelsea House, 1986

Cohen, Sarah Blacher, *Cynthia Ozick's Comic Art: From Levity to Liturgy* (Jewish Literature and Culture), Bloomington: Indiana University Press, 1994

Friedman, Lawrence S., *Understanding Cynthia Ozick* (Understanding Contemporary American Literature), Columbia: University of South Carolina Press, 1991

Kauvar, Elaine M., *Cynthia Ozick's Fiction: Tradition and Invention* (Jewish Literature and Culture), Bloomington: Indiana University Press, 1993

Kielsky, Vera Emuna, *Inevitable Exiles: Cynthia Ozick's View of the Precariousness of Jewish Existence in a Gentile Society* (Twentieth Century American Jewish Writers, vol. 2), New York: Lang, 1989

Lowin, Joseph, *Cynthia Ozick* (Twayne's United States Authors Series, 545), Boston: Twayne, 1988

Pinsker, Sanford, *The Uncompromising Fictions of Cynthia Ozick* (Literary Frontiers, no. 29), Columbia: University of Missouri Press, 1987

Strandberg, Victor, *Greek Mind/Jewish Soul: The Conflicted Art of Cynthia Ozick* (Wisconsin Project on American Writers), Madison: University of Wisconsin Press, 1994

Walden, Daniel (editor), *The World of Cynthia Ozick* (Studies in American Jewish Literature, vol. 6), Kent, Ohio: Kent State University Press, 1987

Cynthia Ozick is unique among American writers, particularly Jewish-American writers, for her synthesis of Jewish ideals with secular mores and her presentation of Judaica within all contexts—religious, cultural, and ethnic. Her fiction, laced with irony and mordant satire, chiefly revolves around two themes: the age-old struggle between Judaism (monotheism) and Hellenism (paganism); and contemporary Jewry's reconciliations with the post-Holocaust world. The growing number of scholarly works devoted to Ozick acknowledge her literary achievement.

BLOOM's compilation of essays provides a "representative selection" of criticism of her work and thought. Arranged chronologically up to the year 1983, it contains two reviews of *Trust*, Ozick's first novel, and her shorter works (i.e., *Pagan Rabbi, Bloodshed and Other Novellas*). Bloom's book is a good introduction to Ozick's fiction and its recurrent influences—biblical, midrashic, and mythological.

Another compilation of essays can be found in the journal issue edited by WALDEN and devoted entirely to Ozick. Articles by prominent critics cover all her works up to *The Messiah of Stockholm*, published in 1987, and delve into various topics—for example, the "hasidic voice" in Ozick's prose, her use of memory, and, inevitably, her broad use of Jewish lore and literature.

PINSKER explores the dilemmas of being both a Jewish writer and a Jewish-American writer. He discusses comparisons between Ozick and Flannery O'Connor as well as Ozick's admiration of Henry James, whose style she emulated and incorporated into *Trust*. While learning the craft of writing in the English language from gentile writers, Ozick tried to forge at the same time a literary English that could serve as a "new Yiddish," concerning herself with things religiously Jewish and expanding the concept of a Jewish-American writer in ways that differed radically from her predecessors, Philip Roth, Saul Bellow, and Bernard Malamud.

LOWIN also examines the issues concerned with being Jewish and being a writer and provides a good overview of Ozick's works, with a lengthy bibliography at the end. He arranges her work chronologically (up to 1987) in order to show its evolution of style and prose. Lowin praises Ozick for her intensity "about conveying a greater understanding of the role Judaism has played—and continues to play—in the development of Western civilization." Lowin views many of Ozick's stories as "polemics against storywriting," since the inherent imagination, in Ozick's view, risks transgressing the biblical injunction against idol worship.

KIELSKY concentrates on the moralism behind Ozick's fiction, discussing her condemnation of the diaspora mentality and how resulting attempts at assimilation have been disastrous for the Jewish people. Kielsky asserts that the failure of Ozick's characters to transform themselves into modern Hellenists serves to call for a return to the ways of the forefathers—the path of Torah—which Ozick stresses as the salvation of Jewry.

The raging conflicts within Ozick's fiction also provide the springboard for FRIEDMAN, who declares assimilation "anathema, involving as it does the yielding up of Jewish identity, the homogenization of Jewish uniqueness . . . the Jewish writer must resist aping Gentile culture." Even while combining Jewish and Greek symbols in her work, Ozick views their cultures as fundamentally incompatible, and her characters' internalization of moral dilemmas shows the futility of trying to escape ancestral roots. The bibliography at the end of this book is useful and extensive.

KAUVAR discusses Ozick's Jewish sources—Torah, Talmud, Kabbalah—as well as Jewish philosophers and gentile authors. The critic compares Ozick's novella *The Cannibal Galaxy* not only to Henry James but also to Nathaniel Hawthorne; she likens *The Messiah of Stockholm* to the work of authors such as Pär Lagerkvist, Julian Tuwim, and Balzac. This is a broad and rigorously academic work covering virtually all the writings that influenced Ozick.

While COHEN acknowledges Ozick's debt to earlier masters, she concentrates mainly on Ozick's unique comedic gifts. This exuberant book discusses how "in her originally clever fashion, she tells the whole embarrassing truth, which the art of comedy is dedicated to telling." Ozick's pathetically confused, "self-deluded characters" serve as symbolic weapons with which to mock and attack not only human foibles but what she views as intellectual presumptuousness and artistic hubris.

STRANDBERG provides a dense but comprehensive overview of all of Ozick's works—not only her fiction but also her essays and critical works. He analyzes the recurrent themes, for example the fusion and conflict between Jewish identity and secular culture and Ozick's use of Judaic and pagan symbols, and he lauds her intellectual rigor and mastery of style.

Ozick's praise is much deserved. Only a master storyteller such as Ozick, so steeped in Jewish and secular learning, can combine both worlds with such skill and display the Jewish paradox, and ultimately, the human condition.

EDITH LUBETSKI

P

Pappenheim, Bertha 1859–1936

Austrian-born German social worker and leader of
German Jewish feminist movement

Freeman, Lucy, *The Story of Anna O.*, New York: Walker,
    1972; London: Aronson, 1994
Kaplan, Marion A., *The Jewish Feminist Movement in
    Germany: The Campaigns of the Jüdischer Frauenbund,
    1904–1938* (Contributions in Women's Studies, 8),
    Westport, Connecticut: Greenwood, 1979
Rosenbaum, Max and Melvin Muroff (editors), *Anna O.:
    Fourteen Contemporary Reinterpretations*, New York:
    Free Press, 1984

A pioneering Jewish German feminist who founded the German Jewish feminist movement in the late 1920s and initiated relief efforts on behalf of the Jewish community after the rise of Nazism in the late 1930s, Bertha Pappenheim also launched a campaign against the "white slavery" commerce in young Jewish and non-Jewish girls in Eastern Europe between the two world wars. A scholar, public speaker, and translator, she is also known as one of Sigmund Freud's earliest patients, under the pseudonym of Anna O.

KAPLAN offers a brief biography of Bertha Pappenheim and an analysis of the goals and achievements of the Jewish feminist movement in Germany in the first three decades of the 20th century. She investigates the conflicts and tensions between Jewish and German feminism and explains the structure and functions of the German Jewish feminist movement; she discusses Pappenheim's campaign against the clandestine commerce in prostitution in the Jewish and non-Jewish sectors; and she describes Pappenheim's critique of the male leadership of the Jewish community in Germany. In the Nazi era, the Jewish Feminist Bund (JFB) focused on relieving the distress of both men and women in the face of intensifying persecutions, and it carried on social and cultural activities until it was outlawed. Kaplan shows the extent to which Pappenheim was an admirer and friend of the philosopher Martin Buber and argues that she was equally committed to feminism and to her Jewish heritage. In addition, Kaplan discusses Pappenheim's "career" as a patient of Freud, and she notes that Pappenheim was a writer and a scholar as well as a translator. Among her translations into German was Gluckel of Hamelin's Yiddish biographical memoir and Mary Wollstonecraft's *A Vindication of the Rights of Woman*. Kaplan's account of Pappenheim's life is the most informative and detailed available to date.

FREEMAN uses fictional reconstruction in her attempt to introduce Bertha Pappenheim as the psychiatric patient who may have helped to constitute the "talking cure" as the foundation of modern psychoanalysis. Freeman traces the development of Anna O.'s speech from disconnected memories and hallucinations to more focused language, and she describes Anna O.'s paralyzing symptoms and their gradual disappearance. Freeman describes Pappenheim's growing interest in rendering social services for the poor and needy, and she highlights Pappenheim's work in various orphanages, her eventual discovery of feminism, and her work organizing a federation for women, which is correlated to journeys she undertook to Eastern Europe, Turkey, and Palestine. Freeman also discusses Pappenheim's struggle against Nazi oppression. This fictional biography is not a scholarly study, but it is worthy of examination given the relatively limited number of historical works.

ROSENBAUM and MUROFF offer a collection of essays on various aspects of Bertha Pappenheim's role as the psychiatric patient Anna O. The essays range from biographical and historical treatments to cultural and psychological reconstructions. Several essays argue that Anna O.'s psychiatric illness should be understood as a result of the historical and cultural strictures placed on women's lives at the turn of the 20th century. The introduction and the conclusion offer information on Josef Breuer, Anna O.'s first psychiatrist, who hypnotized his patient in an attempt to induce her to speak about her repressed desires and memories. The book sheds light, too, on the hysterical symptoms of Anna O., who as a patient in a Swiss psychiatric hospital developed a hysterical pregnancy. The volume as a whole emphasizes Anna O.'s contribution to the development of the "talking cure" as one of the basic methods pioneered first by Breuer and later by Freud. The collection attests to scholarly interest in the contribution that Anna O. made in her capacity as a patient, but it would seem that more work needs to be done to explain the mysterious link between the hysterical patient and the vibrant social activist.

ESTHER FUCHS

Papyri *see* Elephantine

Passover

Bokser, Baruch M., *The Origins of the Seder: The Passover Rite and Early Rabbinic Judaism,* Berkeley: University of California Press, 1984

Gaster, Theodor H., *Passover: Its History and Traditions,* New York: Schuman, 1949; London: Abelard-Schuman, 1958

Kitchen, K.A., *Pharaoh Triumphant: The Life and Times of Ramesses II, King of Egypt,* Warminster: Aris and Phillips, 1982

Saldarini, Anthony, *Jesus and Passover,* New York: Paulist, 1984

Sarna, Nahum M., *Exploring Exodus,* New York: Schocken, 1986

Passover is the festival of redemption and renewal: it marks the start of the biblical year, and it is associated with a story that may be considered the beginnings of Jewish communal history. The holiday is an identification with the events of the Israelites' enslavement in Egypt and, more specifically, with their exodus. God is portrayed in the Passover story as directly intervening to enable the Israelites' liberation, while, on a more secular level, Moses is the hero of the exodus, acting as God's prophet and undertaking the Herculean task of releasing the Hebrews from their bondage. The main ritual of Passover is the recitation of the story of Egyptian enslavement, particularly to inculcate in the young a sense of obligation to God the emancipator; that ritual emphasizes the act of redemption and includes a presentation of various symbolic foods related to the drama of the exodus.

GASTER focuses on the remote origins of Passover, arguing that it can be traced to an ancient pattern of seasonal rituals that celebrate the beginning of the agricultural year. The author maintains that the central feature of the entire ancient ceremony is a common meal eaten by all members of a family at full moon; indeed, the Israelite writers who describe the tradition warn that those who abstain from the ritual will cut themselves off from the rest of the people. Gaster contends that the real significance of Passover lies in the idea of freedom: as the holiday celebrates the physical and social emancipation of a particular people from bondage, it becomes a festival celebrating the ideal of liberty. Additionally, Gaster posits that, while family reunion and celebration are essential to the holiday, it is also important to understand the role of the supernatural in this particular tradition. God is clearly united with humans during the recitation of the story of the exodus, and the Passover feast of reunion seeks divine alliance and assistance in the coming year. Gaster describes the essence of the seder recital and ritual; he recounts the narrative text of the Haggadah, which is based on the story of the escape of the Israelites from Egypt as summarized in the Book of Deuteronomy, and he traces the history of the Haggadah from its probable origins in the first century C.E. through its completion in the 15th century.

BOKSER dedicates his book to the origins of the seder and particularly to its relation to Mishnah Pesahim chapter 10; he focuses his argument on the authors of that Mishnah and their understanding of the Passover evening celebration.

Bokser contends that the seder exemplifies the rabbis' "program for a religious life without a central cultic temple," for the participants in the seder ritual manage to accomplish in the home practices that are full of cultic meaning. Although he primarily emphasizes the Mishnah and the efforts of the rabbis to restructure the rites and ideological meaning of Passover, the author also examines how the wider Hellenistic environment may have affected the seder and its rituals, particularly the emphasis on banquets and fraternal meals. Finally, Bokser analyzes the meaning of the prescribed recitation of the exodus experience, suggesting that the ritual is an intellectual experience for adults as well as children. Moreover, he notes that the various blessings included in the Passover Haggadah deepen the practitioners' sensitivity to the divine dimension of the event.

SALDARINI interprets the significance of Passover in a Christian framework. He identifies descriptions of Passover in the New Testament, specifically reviewing the possibility that the Last Supper was a Passover meal, but he cautions that the New Testament references should not be viewed as descriptions of a Jewish holiday. The gospels do not portray the Passover meal as a celebration of the exodus; instead, they reinterpret the ritual to relate it to Jesus' death and the future of Christianity. Thus, the unleavened bread that symbolizes deliverance in the original story becomes the salvational body of the Messiah, and the wine becomes his sacrificial blood, the sign of redemption. Saldarini demonstrates that early Christians did not focus on the exodus; rather, he contends that they converted the Last Supper into an event that anticipated the salvation of the community. The gospels concentrate their attention on Jesus' death as a permanent sacrifice and his message to his disciples that they must await the coming salvation. By comparison, the rabbis suggested that by eating the Passover meal, the Jews were partaking in the experience of salvation.

In a study that accepts the basic historicity of the events remembered in the Passover celebration, SARNA investigates distinctive themes and motifs in the Book of Exodus. He posits, that, unlike the gods of the pagans, the God of Israel is outside and above nature; thus, God uses the plagues depicted in the exodus story to illustrate his supernatural power. Sarna also argues that the text introduces God as an entity that cannot be defied by humans, even though they do have free will, and he explores how the Book of Exodus demonstrates that history is not haphazard and accidental; rather, it unfolds as God's grand design to redeem humans from injustice and oppression. Sarna explains, too, how the exodus affects the religious calendar and ritual practices of Israel: the new year begins in the spring; the sabbath is linked to the Israelites' liberation from Egypt; and foodways are related to that great event. Finally, Sarna asserts that the motif of the exodus serves as a motivation for ethical behavior, for God's redemptive acts require that humans imitate him and attempt to live justly.

Like many other scholars, KITCHEN notes the very strong written and oral exodus traditions related to the celebration of Passover and its many rituals, and he argues that these traditions are sufficient proof that the exodus story is grounded in historical fact. He admits that there is no independent historical evidence to verify the biblical story of the plight of the Israelites and their exodus, but he claims that there is sufficient evidence in the text of the Book of Exodus to speculate that the events did in fact occur in Egypt. He contends that the book demonstrates an understanding of uniquely Egyptian labor and magic practices, and he posits that the exodus route described in the text fits very well with other geographical descriptions of the region from the 13th century B.C.E. Also, the status of Moses suggests a cosmopolitan New Kingdom environment for the story, and the various techniques associated with the building of the tabernacle and the portable ark also appear to be Egyptian in origin, dating from the late second millennium B.C.E. Kitchen argues that the fact that there is no Egyptian record of the exodus or of the Israelites proves nothing, because the Egyptians would not necessarily have recorded a loss of the magnitude that the Book of Exodus describes.

For Kitchen, the presence of so many Egyptian references in the book not only suggests that the book has some historicity, it also reflects a literary triumph for Pharaonic culture. While the Israelites claim the moral high ground and exhibit military might, Kitchen proposes that the textual evidence shows that Exodus historians were deeply affected by Egyptian influences.

ITA SHERES

See also Haggadah, Passover

Patriarchate

Alon, Gedalia, *Toldot ha-Yehudim be Erets-Yisra'el bitekufat ha-Mishnah veha-Talmud*, 1980; translated by Gershon Levi as *The Jews in Their Land in the Talmudic Age (70–640 C.E.)*, 2 vols., Jerusalem: Magnes, 1980–1984; Cambridge, Massachusetts; Harvard University Press, 1989

Avi-Yonah, Michael, *The Jews of Palestine: A Political History from the Bar Kokhba War to the Arab Conquest*, Oxford: Blackwell, and New York: Schocken, 1976

Goodman, Martin, "The Roman State and the Jewish Patriarch in the Third Century," in *The Galilee in Late Antiquity*, edited by Lee Levine, New York: Jewish Theological Seminary, 1992

Levine, Lee I., *The Rabbinic Class of Roman Palestine in Late Antiquity*, Jerusalem: Yad Izhak Ben-Zvi, and New York: Jewish Theological Seminary, 1989

Mantel, Hugo, *Studies in the History of the Sanhedrin* (Harvard Semitic Series, 17), Cambridge, Massachusetts: Harvard University Press, 1961

There is no single book in English that focuses exclusively on the history of the Jewish patriarchate, but several works dealing with the history of Palestine in the rabbinic period provide extensive albeit often diffuse discussion of the patriarchal office, usually noting its relationship to the world of the talmudic sages. There are two major groups of sources on the Jewish patriarchate. Rabbinic texts by and large reflect the sit-

uation of the second and third centuries C.E. and depict the patriarchs essentially as talmudic sages wielding considerable administrative power. Roman and Byzantine sources stem from the late third through the fifth century C.E. and concentrate on patriarchal status in relation to the imperial government. Both the chronology and the content of these sources can be contradictory, creating difficulties for contemporary scholars. Modern historians have tended to regard the patriarchs as part of the rabbinic elite, almost always relying on the rabbinic texts and their view of patriarchs as the starting point for historical analysis. The works of Avi-Yonah and Mantel reflect this more traditional way of understanding the place and function of the patriarchate in Jewish society. Both authors depict the patriarch as wielding centralized power over Jewish communities in both Palestine and the diaspora, and they contend that the office represented the Jews in dealings with the Roman government and also supervised judicial appointments on the local level. This view has been substantially challenged in recent studies, however, which tend to downplay the role of the rabbis in general, and that of the patriarch in particular, in running Jewish communities of that period. Instead, the revisionist scholars suggest that from the very beginning Jewish communities had a considerable autonomy that they struggled to preserve. The consequences of this approach for the study of the patriarchate are especially clear in the works of Goodman. In recent years the more traditional approach has been steadily abandoned because of serious methodological problems.

ALON discusses various issues pertaining to the early history of the Jewish patriarchate (second and third centuries C.E.). He maintains that the office of the patriarch originated immediately after the destruction of Jerusalem by the Romans in 70 C.E. He also argues that Rabban Johanan ben Zakkai was the first person to exercise the functions of patriarch, subsequently stepping down in favor of Rabban Gamaliel from the dynasty of Hillel. The author discusses the alleged patriarchate of Rabban Johanan in some detail, paying special attention to Jewish opposition to his rule and the reasons for his ultimate replacement by Rabban Gamaliel. Although Alon clearly recognizes the contradictions and inconsistencies contained in the stories about Rabban Johanan, he still contends that one can use these tales as historical sources. This work is therefore important because it represents one of the rare attempts to evaluate rabbinic sources critically without completely rejecting them as historically unreliable. Alon depicts the rabbinic movement as by no means unanimous; rather, he asserts that it consisted of various, often antagonistic, factions. As a result, he analyzes the patriarchate as part of the complex of relationships among the different groups of the Jewish population in Palestine.

AVI-YONAH describes the history of Palestine in the second through seventh centuries C.E. and devotes a significant part of his book to the analysis of the Jewish patriarchate. He singles out two main periods in its history. The first started immediately after the Bar Kokhba rebellion with the election of Simeon ben Gamaliel as patriarch. According to Avi-Yonah, it was Rabban Simeon, rather than Judah the Patriarch, who took the crucial steps toward becoming an absolute ruler of the Jewish people. In many respects, the rule of Rabbi Judah the Patriarch resembled that of a king. He had absolute authority to appoint judges in the Jewish community, and he wielded power not only in Palestine but also in the diaspora. During this period, the interests of the patriarch and the rabbis usually coincided, and in fact the former helped to secure rabbinic authority among the Jewish people. During the second period, which started in the middle of the third century, patriarchal power considerably decreased. The ordination of judges passed from the patriarchs to the Sanhedrin, comprising the leading sages of that time. The sages took over leading positions at the court and often rebuked patriarchs for their incompetence. The abolition of the patriarchate was caused by the attempts of the Christian imperial government to undermine Jewish positions in Palestine and to further conversion among the Jewish population of the empire. Despite his extensive use of sources, Avi-Yonah's work is very much out-of-date in terms of its methodology. It is based on the uncritical assumption that the rabbis were in charge of communal life in Palestine from the third century on. The patriarchate is seen as first and foremost a rabbinic institution, inaugurated by the decision of the Sanhedrin and afterward carefully supervised by scholars. Avi-Yonah accepts the idea of a highly centralized Jewish government in this period, with administrative power concentrated in the hands of the patriarchs and legislative power held by the Sanhedrin. His picture of the activities of the Roman government is overtly polemical and one-sided. Avi-Yonah clearly favors rabbinic narratives and usually accepts them as historically reliable.

GOODMAN has called into question a number of assumptions usually made about the patriarch. He does not think that sufficient evidence supports the hypothesis that the rise to power of the patriarchs occurred earlier than the time of Judah the Patriarch (who is the first patriarch about whose status we have indisputable information), and he argues that even in the cases of Judah the Patriarch and his third-century successors, the power wielded by the patriarchs and their courts was far from absolute. Goodman doubts whether the office of patriarch was officially recognized by Roman authorities prior to the fourth century, asserting that before the reign of Constantine, the Romans tended to turn a blind eye to the activities of the patriarchs, regarding them as unofficial leaders of the Jews. Goodman also questions whether patriarchs ever supervised such essential administrative tasks as the collection of taxes. Instead, he posits that the power of the patriarch was largely based on his economic standing as a rich landowner and his recognition within the Jewish community. Goodman maintains that the social structure of ancient Galilee was, as a whole, based on relatively independent and self-sufficient rural communities, which opposed any interference in their affairs either by the Galilean cities or by the patriarchs. Hence, he concludes that one should not exaggerate the power of the patriarch even within Galilean Jewish society, let alone in the diaspora. Goodman's approach reflects tendencies in modern scholarship to critically revise previous claims about uncontested and centralized rabbinic leadership in Palestine in the third through the fifth centuries.

LEVINE offers one of the most recent attempts to synthesize the history of rabbinic Judaism in Roman Palestine. He devotes a significant part of his book to the discussion of the role of the patriarchs in Jewish society, concentrating on their standing relative to the sages, as well as to the local Jewish aristocracy. The scope of Levine's work is limited to the third century C.E., although he makes occasional reference to later periods. As a result, he uses rabbinic texts as his major sources, checking them now and again against later non-rabbinic material. According to Levine, the patriarchs were crucial throughout the period under discussion. They wielded considerable power in Jewish internal affairs both in Palestine and in the diaspora, and they granted appointments to the sages, fixed the Jewish calendar, and collected taxes for the Roman government. At the same time, individual sages (such as Rabbi Johanan) played a prominent role at the patriarchal court: supervising appointments, advocating the interests of other sages before the patriarch, and furthering patriarchal interests among the sages. Despite occasional quarrels between patriarchs and sages, the relationship between them was one of close cooperation. In terms of social status, however, the patriarchs were part of the rich, urban aristocracy, maintaining close and amicable contacts with others of this class. For the period under discussion, Levine calls into question the very existence of the Sanhedrin, which has been seen as an alternative source of power rivaling that of the patriarchs, and thus denies that there was any sustained rabbinic opposition to patriarchal rule. As a result, the patriarchate becomes in his account the one and only central Jewish institution of that period, acting on the behalf of the rabbinic sages, as well as the lay Jewish aristocracy.

MANTEL analyzes the history of the patriarchal office in terms of its relationship to the Sanhedrin, examining interactions between these two bodies of Jewish self-government and their respective roles in running Jewish communal life. The author considers a tremendous volume of material, but his final conclusion does not go beyond the fact that "the relations between the Nasi and the Sanhedrin were highly complex." He observes that their functions often overlapped, thus causing friction between the two institutions. According to Mantel, the patriarch wielded exclusive power to appoint the sages, intercalate the calendar, excommunicate, lift bans of excommunication under certain circumstances, and collect funds. The patriarch maintained his influence in the diaspora by sending his messengers to collect funds and preside in the courts if necessary. Mantel portrays the Jewish leadership of that period as highly centralized, placing both Palestine and the diaspora (with some reservations) under the sway of patriarchal authority. The Nasi firmly belonged to the class of rabbinic scholars and as such participated in sessions of the Sanhedrin, whose functions and standing relative to the patriarch Mantel fails to determine. As a whole, Mantel's research strongly reflects a romantic perception that late antique Jewish society in Palestine was ruled by scholars. Mantel does use non-Jewish sources, but he derives his conclusions largely from the rabbinic material without calling into question this material's basic reliability. Therefore, the methodological value of his work is highly questionable. On the other hand, the number of accumulated and analyzed sources (both rabbinic and Roman) makes this book extremely valuable for any new research in the field.

ALEXEJ MICHAELOVITCH SIVERTSEV

Paul and Judaism

Boyarin, Daniel, *A Radical Jew: Paul and the Politics of Identity* (Contraversions, 1), Berkeley: University of California Press, 1994

Davies, W.D., *Paul and Rabbinic Judaism: Some Rabbinic Elements in Pauline Theology*, London: S.P.C.K., 1948; 3rd edition, London: S.P.C.K., 1970; 4th edition, Philadelphia: Fortress, 1980

Hengel, Martin with Roland Deines, *The Pre-Christian Paul*, Philadelphia: Trinity Press International, and London: SCM, 1991

Hengel, Martin with Anna Maria Schwemer, *Paul between Damascus and Antioch: The Unknown Years*, Louisville, Kentucky: Westminster John Knox, and London: SCM, 1997

Montefiore, Claude, "The Genesis of the Religion of St. Paul," in his *Judaism and St. Paul: Two Essays*, London: Goschen, 1914; New York: Dutton, 1915

Sanders, E.P., *Paul and Palestinian Judaism: A Comparison of Patterns of Religion*, Philadelphia: Fortress, and London: SCM, 1977

Sanders, E.P., *Paul, the Law, and the Jewish People*, Philadelphia: Fortress, 1983; London: SCM, 1985

Sandmel, Samuel, *The Genius of Paul: A Study in History*, New York: Farrar, Straus and Cudahy, 1958

Schoeps, H.J., *Paulus: Die Theologie des Apostels im Lichte der jüdischen Religionsgeschichte*, 1959; translated by Harold Knight as *Paul: The Theology of the Apostle in the Light of Jewish Religious History*, Philadelphia: Westminster, and London: Lutterworth, 1961

Segal, Alan, *Paul the Convert: The Apostolate and Apostasy of Saul the Pharisee*, New Haven, Connecticut: Yale University Press, 1990, new edition, 1992

Stendahl, Krister, "The Apostle Paul and the Introspective Conscience of the West," *Harvard Theological Review*, 56, 1963; reprinted in *Paul among Jews and Gentiles, and Other Essays*, Philadelphia: Fortress, 1976; London: SCM, 1977

Westerholm, Stephen, *Israel's Law and the Church's Faith: Paul and His Recent Interpreters*, Grand Rapids, Michigan: Eerdmans, 1988

During the present century many scholars have challenged the common view of an irreconcilable opposition between Paul's inherited Judaism and his eventual Christianity. Several leading Jewish authors have attempted sympathetic readings of Paul as a Jew, while Christian Paulinists strive to leave behind a jaundiced outlook on Judaism.

MONTEFIORE was a Jewish liberal who, at the dawn of the 20th century in Britain, broke with tradition and expressed admiration for Paul. Although modest about his learning—his gentlemanly prose breezes along with only occasional erudite references or footnotes—his monograph-length essay swept aside ancient Jewish-Christian polemics and prepared the ground for fruitful dialogue among Pauline specialists of both faith communities. It has been immensely influential. After castigating Jewish and Christian contemporaries for lack of mutual sympathy, the essay asks against which form of first-century Judaism did Paul react. A summary of talmudic religion follows, designed to lay to rest Christian distortions of rabbinic Judaism based on Paul's epistles rather than on living experience. A rabbi of 500 C.E. would have viewed God as warm and close, the Torah as a gift and a privilege, the commandments as a joy to keep, and human failings as reparable by prayer and repentance. To judge from Paul's views on corresponding points, the apostle could not have known such a happy religion prior to his conversion. Paul must therefore have been raised in a poor kind of Hellenistic Judaism. Like many Christian scholars of the "history of religions" school of thought, Montefiore held that Paul gathered many of his Christian ideas from paganism.

DAVIES's work, a landmark in the field of Pauline studies (passing through four editions), was created in the middle of the 20th century, when "history of religions" scholars were turning from pagan Hellenism to Palestinian Judaism, Hellenized to some degree, to mine for parallels that might shed light on Paul. An opening chapter sharply questions Montefiore's thesis that Paul was unfamiliar with Pharisaism, as well as its underlying assumption that the rabbinic, apocalyptic, and Hellenistic types of Judaism were clearly distinct. The chapters that follow isolate important Pauline concepts such as the flesh and sin, Adam, Christ as the divine Wisdom, the Spirit, the atonement on the cross, and the resurrection, and find corresponding categories in rabbinic writings. Davies, a Christian, concludes that Paul was basically a Pharisee who never gave up his rabbinic modes of thought even after he became convinced that the messiah had come in Jesus.

SANDMEL offers a wide-ranging, nontechnical, careful study of Paul by a prominent Jewish historian of religion and expert on Philo of Alexandria. Paul was a Jew of the diaspora, concludes Sandmel, but contrary to the opinion of Montefiore this does not imply a negative value judgment about Paul's Judaism. Neither Philo nor Paul absolutized the Torah, although Paul's reason for limiting it was a personal (and unPhilonic) chafing under its demands (Romans 7). Disputes with Palestinian Christians who held to the eternal validity of the Torah colored some of the apostle's more bitter statements on the subject. In spite of his mistakes, Paul remains a genius whose positive legacy was a powerful critique of institutionalized religion of all forms and a championing of the rights of the individual conscience.

STENDAHL's now classic essay was first published in Swedish in 1960. Himself a Lutheran minister (later briefly a Swedish bishop) and a Harvard academic, Stendahl boldly critiqued the Reformation notion of Paul as Luther's prototype. Because Paul, looking back, could say that he had been "as to righteousness under the Torah blameless" (Philippians 3:6), his conversion, argues Stendahl, was not in fact motivated by a tormented conscience before God, but by an objective call to preach Christ to the gentiles. On this showing, the Pauline doctrine of justification by faith apart from works of Torah was an answer, not to the soteriological problem of how sinful humanity can find a gracious God but to the missionary problem of how gentiles as such, without undergoing proselytization, can have full status among God's people. The essay engages with secondary literature in footnotes but was first delivered as a lecture to the American Psychological Association and remains, in revised form, accessible to the nonspecialist.

In SCHOEPS's scholarly monograph, a fully equipped Jewish historian of religion seeks to put something like Montefiore's general outline in a more scientific context. The product has been widely hailed as a major contribution to Pauline studies. The complete round of possible religious influences on Paul are surveyed—mystery religions, Gnosis, Hellenistic Judaism, Palestinian exegesis, and apocalyptic ideas—and none excluded, although Paul is seen as a diaspora Jew. Overall Schoeps shows by detailed comparisons how "the theology of the apostle Paul arose from overwhelmingly Jewish religious ideas." The two exceptions, decisive for Paul's break with mainline Judaism, were his Christology and his view of the Torah. Paul's idea of a divine redeemer is alien to Judaism and finds its natural antecedents in pagan myths. The (mis)translation of *torah* in the Greek Septuagint by *nomos* ("law") and of *berit* by *diatheke* ("disposition") obscured for Paul the Jewish view of the divine-human covenant as a reciprocal relationship within which performance of the commandments takes on its meaning, and it left Paul free to oppose the saving covenant to the killing letter of the Law. When the Christian Church adopted Paul as its theological fountainhead, its misunderstanding of Judaism was fated from the beginning.

SANDERS (1977), building on the work of Davies, was the chief catalyst in bringing about the current "new perspective" on Paul among New Testament scholars and won for its author, who describes himself as a secularized Protestant, a deserved place in the front rank of his field. Although few of its main points were new, Sanders documented his case with a range and a vigor, and he took his colleagues to task with a vehemence that seized their attention and inaugurated a paradigm shift in mainline Anglo-American New Testament scholarship. The book is a comparative study of the way to salvation in ancient Judaism and Christianity. Nearly three-quarters of its 550 pages are devoted to Jewish sources dating from between roughly 200 B.C.E. and 200 C.E., presented with a view to demolishing a caricature of Judaism that had established itself in Germany through the influence of F. Weber, E. Schürer, W. Bousset, R. Bultmann, and others and erecting in its place a construction drawn from the sources themselves. This is the part of the book that has made its mark. Gone is the view of Judaism as a religion of works-righteousness wherein a fearful human suppliant performs the commandments to earn merit and wrest favors from a cold, calculating deity; instead Judaism appears much as Jewish apologists such as Montefiore or Christians such as G.F. Moore had long been presenting it. In comparing patterns of religion, Sanders asks of Judaism and of Christianity respectively what it takes to get into the divine-human covenant and to remain within it. He concludes, broadly speaking, that in either religion one gets in by divine grace (election) and stays in by good works. On that score, he thinks, there was little difference between Hillel and St. Paul. Thus for Sanders the question becomes acute why Paul turned from Judaism to Christianity. He supposes that Paul had no complaint about Judaism. Rather, taking Christ and especially the cross as his starting point and reasoning backward from solution to plight, Paul came to hold that salvation is solely in Christ.

SANDERS (1983) expands on Paul's tension with his fellow Jews. Insisting on a distinction between Paul's arguments and his real reason for conversion, Sanders produces a Paul who basically criticized his kinsmen for two things: lack of faith in Christ and relegating gentiles to an inferior status outside of the covenant. Paul denounced the Torah not on the grounds that it led to self-righteousness or was unfulfillable, but only insofar as it was a symbol of Jewish exclusivism.

WESTERHOLM is a young Christian New Testament specialist. The first half of his technical monograph surveys 20th-century research into Paul's view of the Torah, judiciously selecting and reviewing contributions by W. Wrede, A. Schweitzer, C.G. Montefiore, H.J. Schoeps, W.G. Kümmel, K. Stendahl, R. Bultmann, U. Wilckens, E.P. Sanders, J.W. Drane, H. Hübner, and H. Räisänen. The second half of the monograph (with frequent Greek quotations and footnotes) gives Westerholm's own view. Westerholm adopts the post-Sanders new perspective on ancient Judaism, with the proviso that even after Christian accounts of Paul's ancestral religion have been purged of inaccuracies, Judaism remains more positive about human moral ability than Paul is. For Paul sin is an intractable, ontological trap, and therefore the failure of the Torah is really the failure of fallen human nature to perform it. Hence only God's grace, available through the atoning death of Christ, can undertake to provide a redemption in which humans cannot effectively cooperate under the mere letter of the Torah. This neo-Lutheran reading of Paul represents the measured reception that Sanders and his followers have found among German critics as well as in conservative Protestant circles in Britain and the United States.

SEGAL presents a fresh reading of Paul by a young Jewish historian of religion who has a special interest in describing varieties of early Judaism that after 100 C.E. got branded as heretical by the rabbis. Joining those who have abandoned theories of Paul's nurture in Hellenistic Judaism, Segal takes seriously Paul's own claims to have been a thoroughly trained Pharisee. He compares Paul's visions of the risen Christ to heavenly revelations reported by Jewish mystics in, say, the Merkabah tradition. A sociological model of conversion sheds light on the radical about-face that ensued for Paul's beliefs and community membership and goes far to explain many of Paul's extreme Christian positions. Perhaps Segal's most signal contribution is his methodological reclamation of Paul as a major source for understanding first-century Judaism as such in several ways. Parallels in Paul can warrant early dates for some otherwise undateable rabbinic traditions. Enough of the Pharisee remains in the apostle to enable scholars to ferret out, with care, data for pre-70 C.E. Pharisaism. Paul the apocalyptist and Christo-mystic, who never saw himself as anything other than a faithful Jew, illustrates one more fascinating item on the menu of pre-Orthodox Jewish options.

Two recent monographs on Paul with Martin Hengel as their principal author aim to correct lingering distortions of the older "history of religions" school. Hengel represents the most learned of moderately conservative but critical scholarship in his field. With a characteristic wealth of primary documentation and copious endnotes, Hengel combs over the Pauline corpus for tidbits about Paul's early life, conversion, and early development as a Christian, and he draws a portrait resting on the New Testament sources and credible in Paul's Greco-Roman-Jewish context. Hengel believes that the evidence, if not dismissed in favor of pet hypotheses, points firmly to Paul's having been raised by Aramaic-speaking, observant Jewish parents. Paul became a Pharisee under the guidance of Rabban Gamaliel in Jerusalem but broke from the moderation of his master in order to persecute zealously the fledgling Jewish-Christian movement on the charges that it questioned the permanence of Temple and Torah and proclaimed a crucified messiah. During this period Paul was confident in his Pharisean piety. Only an encounter with the risen Christ reversed his view of Jesus and provoked a rethinking of many details of his beliefs while leaving the Jewish structure of his thought intact. All the main features of Pauline theology derive from Hellenized Palestinian Judaism (HENGEL and DEINES), and not from some syncretistic religion of Tarsus or Antioch (HENGEL and SCHWEMER).

BOYARIN calls himself a talmudist and postmodern Jewish cultural critic. His concern is for justice toward marginalized persons, especially for Jews and women in western countries, and for Arabs in the state of Israel. Boyarin's utopia would be a multicultural society free of hierarchies, in which no group dominated another. Current obstacles to such a utopia are an ethnocentrism that excludes the Other, exemplified by Israeli policies, and a cultural imperialism that absorbs all and subordinates (or eradicates) people who persist in being genuinely different. The latter, typical of Christian culture, is the more dangerous error, for it led to the Holocaust, and Boyarin traces its roots back to Paul, admitting it runs contrary to Paul's own intentions. The essay is not a historical description of Paul as he was but rather a postmodernist conversation with Paul as the author reads him, one possible reading among others. Not because Paul himself says so, but because Boyarin considers it morally and politically urgent, the key to Paul is found in his statement that in Christ there is no Jew or Greek, neither male nor female (Galatians 3:28). Boyarin takes this to mean that Paul's gospel of universal salvation tended to obliterate people's peculiarities. Paul supported it by allegorizing the scriptures (e.g., circumcision becomes baptism) and by valuing the soul at the expense of the body. Paul, a Hellenistic Jewish monotheist, came to this position through an insight that Jesus is now the universal Lord, after a period of being troubled by Jewish nationalism and its lack of concern for gentiles. Hence Paul too was a cultural critic addressing Jews of his day from within Judaism, as he saw it. Even though Paul's Platonizing solution to the dilemma of universality and particularity unwittingly contained the seeds of antisemitism and so must be rejected, his profound wrestling with the issue can still challenge Jews to move toward a pluralism that retains Jewish identity but remains open to others. One chapter in Boyarin's work is devoted to a selective survey of recent contributions on the subject of Paul and Judaism by, among others, J. Gager, L. Gaston, J.D.G. Dunn, and F. Watson.

PAUL A. RAINBOW

Peace *see* **War and Peace**

Pentateuch

Blenkinsopp, Joseph, *The Pentateuch: An Introduction to the First Five Books of the Bible* (Anchor Bible Reference Library), New York: Doubleday, and London: SCM, 1992

Campbell, Antony and Mark O'Brien, *Sources of the Pentateuch: Texts, Introductions, Annotations,* Minneapolis, Minnesota: Fortress, 1993

Carpenter, J. and G. Harford-Battersby, *The Hexateuch According to the Revised Version,* 2 vols., London and New York: Longmans, Green, 1900

Cassuto, Umberto, *Torat ha-te'udot ve-siduram shel sifre ha-Torah: Shemonah shi'urim,* 1941; translated by Israel Abrahams as *The Documentary Hypothesis and the Composition of the Pentateuch: Eight Lectures,* Jerusalem: Magnes Press of Hebrew University, 1961

Crüsemann, Frank, *The Torah: Theology and Social History of Old Testament Law,* translated by Allan Mahnke, Minneapolis, Minnesota: Fortress, 1996

Habel, Norman, *Literary Criticism of the Old Testament* (Guides to Biblical Scholarship), Philadelphia: Fortress, 1971

Kaufmann, Yehezkel, *Toldot ha-emunah ha-Yisre'elit,* 1937; translated and abridged by Moshe Greenberg as *The Religion of Israel: From Its Beginnings to the Babylonian Exile,* Chicago: University of Chicago, and London: Allen and Unwin, 1960

Knohl, Israel, *Mikdash ha-demamah,* 1992; translated by Jackie Feldman and Peretz Rodman as *The Sanctuary of Silence: The Priestly Torah and the Holiness School,* Minneapolis, Minnesota: Fortress, 1995

Noth, Martin, *Überlieferungsgeschichte des Pentateuch,* 1948; translated by Bernhard Anderson as *A History of Pentateuchal Traditions,* Englewood Cliffs, New Jersey: Prentice-Hall, 1972

Rendtorff, Rolf, *Das Überlieferungsgeschichtliche Problem des Pentateuch,* 1977; translated by John Scullion as *The Problem of the Process of Transmission in the Pentateuch* (Journal for the Study of the Old Testament Supplement Series, 89), Sheffield, South Yorkshire: JSOT, 1990

Tigay, Jeffrey (editor), *Empirical Models for Biblical Criticism,* Philadelphia: University of Pennsylvania Press, 1985

Wellhausen, Julius, *Prolegomena to the History of Ancient Israel,* Edinburgh: Black, 1885

Whybray, R.N., *The Making of the Pentateuch: A Methodological Study,* Sheffield, South Yorkshire: Sheffield Academic Press, 1987

The Pentateuch is an unusually diverse anthology containing cultic ordinances, narratives, civil and criminal law, architectural directions, genealogies, travel itineraries, and poems. It invites many different types of analysis, and the scholarly approaches that have been applied to it are as varied as its contents. Consequently, the study of the Pentateuch must overlap many areas of biblical scholarship, such as the study of biblical narrative, the investigation of biblical law, and the history of Israelite religion.

BLENKINSOPP provides an excellent introduction to the wide-ranging field of modern Pentateuchal studies. His first chapter reviews the last two centuries of scholarship in a readable fashion. Subsequent chapters treat the structure of the Pentateuch as a whole, its major sections, and its overarching themes. Significantly, he does not limit his holistic reading to the narrative material (as many other scholars do), and he attends to covenantal and legal aspects of the work as well.

Pentateuchal scholarship in the last two centuries has been dominated by source criticism—that is, the attempt to identify the various documents or sources from which the Pentateuch is built and to use the study of those documents to understand how the religion of Israel developed. The most well-known source-critical theory is the Documentary Hypothesis, according to which four main documents comprise the Pentateuch (or perhaps the Hexateuch, since many scholars believe that the Book of Joshua was originally part of the literary collection that includes Genesis, Exodus, Leviticus, Numbers, and Deuteronomy). These sources are usually referred to by the sigla J, E, P, and D.

A readable introductory summary of the Documentary Hypothesis is found in HABEL (who refers to source criticism as "literary criticism," by which he means the attempt to discover the literary sources of the Pentateuch, not the attempt to interpret its texts). He analyzes the first nine chapters of Genesis in order to exemplify how the theory works. Subsequently, he summarizes the salient characteristics and attitudes of the P and J sources. Habel does not, however, offer a detailed defense of the theory. His book allows the reader to become familiar with the main outlines of the Documentary Hypothesis but not to form an opinion as to whether the theory is accurate.

For a defense of the Documentary Hypothesis one can, however, turn to CARPENTER and HARFORD-BATTERSBY. The first volume of their work sketches the development of the theory in great detail, starting with medieval Jewish scholars who began tentatively to question whether the theory of Mosaic authorship was tenable, through the seminal work of Spinoza, and into the full flowering of the Documentary Hypothesis in the mid–19th century. Carpenter and Harford-Battersby then offer an extensive treatment of the evidence in favor of the theory, a description of the various sources (along with lists of their characteristic vocabulary), and a discussion of the redaction of the documents into the Hexateuch as we know it. The second volume consists of a translation of the Hexateuch in which the assignment of each passage, verse, or word to a source is made clear and is defended in considerable detail.

Not all scholars have accepted the classical Documentary Hypothesis in the form it took during the middle and late 19th century. NOTH doubts the existence of a five-part Pentateuch, arguing that Deuteronomy originally was written as an introduction to the historical writings in the Books of Joshua, Judges, Samuel, and Kings. While he agrees that the preceding four books (or Tetrateuch) were built from the J, E, and P sources, he does not always agree with his predecessors regarding the nature and extent of those sources. Moreover, he emphasizes the documents' prehistory, and he attempts to reconstruct the traditions on which they were based. These traditions were often peculiar to a particular tribe or region; they were brought together at an early period of Israelite history and were then used as the basis for each of the written sources, which in turn were later combined to form the Tetrateuch and Deuteronomy.

A synopsis of Noth's source-critical theory is given in the convenient work by CAMPBELL and O'BRIEN, which presents translations of Noth's P, J, and E separately, along with discussion of each. Campbell and O'Brien disagree with Noth on several points: for example, they point out that E has a great many gaps, and therefore they (like many other scholars) view E not as a separate source but as a supplement to J. They emphasize the use that Noth's source-critical model has for a literary reader—for one who looks at the patterns and ideas in the final form of the Torah, which (they assert) achieves unity from its diversity.

RENDTORFF represents a more radical break from the Documentary Hypothesis. He follows Noth and others in emphasizing the history of traditions underlying the Pentateuch and concludes that a traditio-historical analysis in fact undermines the notion that one can find four main sources that run from beginning to end of the Pentateuch or Tetrateuch. Rather, the main thematic and narrative units (such as the primeval history, the Abraham stories, and the Moses stories) arose independently and were combined to form the Pentateuch. A postexilic priestly editor added final touches; these editorial additions resemble but are far shorter than the classical P source.

Some scholars, especially of a more conservative bent, reject the source-critical model altogether. CASSUTO maintains that many contradictions noticed by source critics are not contradictions at all, and he wonders whether any texts in the ancient world were actually composed by the cumbersome combination of originally disparate documents; after all, no copies of J, E, P, or D have ever been found, and their existence is a matter of scholarly speculation.

Similarly, WHYBRAY argues that the Pentateuch was composed in the exilic period by a single author who used a very large number of older texts and traditions. Thus he suggests a fragmentary rather than a documentary basis for the Pentateuch, acknowledging that a redactor used older texts but denying that these older texts were discrete and recoverable wholes. Moreover, Whybray (like Cassuto) emphasizes the creative role of the redactor/author. The very fact that redactors put these texts together into a narrative whole shows that what appear to be inconsistencies to modern readers were not necessarily viewed as such by ancient readers, authors, and editors; consequently, one cannot be sure that an apparent contradiction or repetition really does show the existence of more than one author. Rather, modern readers need to become more familiar with the poetics of ancient narrative.

This line of reasoning, however, fails in light of careful attention to ancient Near Eastern texts and their literary history. TIGAY collects a number of studies that provide an empirical basis for the source-critical model. These studies show that ancient Near Eastern writers did produce new texts by combining older ones that are known to archaeologists. He shows, for example, that originally separate tales about Gilgamesh known from early-second-millennium Mesopotamian tablets were brought together to form the Old Babylonian Gilgamesh epic extant in tablets dating to the mid–second millennium. Subsequently, additional stories known from independent mythological texts (for example, the story of the flood, which is found as a freestanding narrative on various tablets) were added to the epic. As a result, the first millennium (or "Standard") copies of the epic differ significantly from the Old Babylonian version. The late or Standard version displays precisely the sort of terminological and stylistic variation that source critics claim to find in the Pentateuch, and those differences can be traced in the late text to their sources in the earlier texts. For example, the phrasing used to introduce a character's speech varies in the late epic. This stylistic variation might lead a source critic to suspect that two documents have been combined to form the late epic, especially since one form of phrasing appears only in sections dealing with the flood while the other never appears there. This source-critical hypothesis is confirmed by an examination of older documents: one form of phrasing appears consistently in the Old Babylonian epic, the other in the originally independent flood story. Tigay's work does not prove the existence of J, P, or E, but it does show that the sort of composition through combination and editing posited by scholars of the Pentateuch did occur in the world of ancient Israel, and it demonstrates that the editorial process left differences of wording and style in the original texts largely intact.

A central debate in Pentateuchal studies involves the dating of the P source, which seems to give structure to the Pentateuch as a whole and provides much of the Pentateuch's cultic and ritual material. WELLHAUSEN argues that P is the latest source and dates it to the exilic or postexilic period. He points out that P reflects the most highly developed (and hence the latest) legal and cultic system. This highly artificial system appears divorced from the agriculturally based and spontaneous religion of the pre-exilic era. Wellhausen's position is summarized in Carpenter and Harford. Others scholars (especially Israeli and Jewish ones) argue that P is the earliest source or that P was composed over a long period of time beginning as early as the premonarchic era. Highly developed legal and ritual systems, after all, are known from ancient Near Eastern cultures older than Israel, and Wellhausen's description of the P source as artificial and lacking spontaneity reflects his own religious prejudice rather than an ancient Israelite worldview. The classic exposition of this thesis appears in KAUFMANN; a more recent argument appears in Knohl (with important bibliographic references to other research on the dating of P). This debate does not merely pertain to one Pentateuchal source but has implications for the history and nature of Israelite religion. Scholars who date P to the exile imply (or assume) that the cultic and legalistic concerns of the Torah were not original to the religion of Israel; those who believe that P is early uphold the view that law and ritual were central to Israel's relationship with its God from the beginning of the nation's existence.

Many studies provide literary or exegetical analyses of the Pentateuch. Attention to the legal and cultic framing of the Five Books as a unit is less frequent but no less important given the predominance of legal and cultic material in the Pentateuch. KNOHL examines the tension between two strands within the priestly source. He shows that one older strand shuns popular forms of religion (which may be tainted by paganism), emphasizes the transcendence of God, and recoils from any form of anthropomorphism. Further, this austere strand argues that the cult must be practiced for its own sake, not for any hope of divine reward, and thus it separates morality from the cult. A later strand is more open to popular practices, which it reinterprets in a monotheistic fashion. It attempts to justify legal practices rather than seeing them as ends in themselves; it stresses the reciprocal nature of God's relationship with Israel and links morality and cult. Because priestly literature provides the framework for the Pentateuch, Knohl's analysis of the tension between these priestly schools has important repercussions for an understanding of the Pentateuch as a whole.

CRÜSEMANN also attends especially to the legal shape of the Pentateuch. He argues that the identification of the law with revelation at Sinai is a late development in the tradition-history of the Pentateuch. Much of his book examines the relationships among the four law codes found in the Pentateuch. While his dating of the codes is not novel, his attention to the social setting from which the codes arose is of particular interest. Thus the covenant code (Exodus 20:22–23:33) stemmed from northern Israel, while Deuteronomy was promoted by free landholders. Crüsemann argues that the Pentateuch as a whole combines contradictory materials in order to forge a united authoritative text for the postexilic nation attempting to remain distinct while living under largely benign Persian rule.

BENJAMIN D. SOMMER

Peretz, Isaac Leib 1852–1915

Polish Yiddish and Hebrew writer

Frieden, Ken, *Classic Yiddish Fiction: Abramovitsh, Sholem Aleichem, and Peretz* (SUNY Series in Modern Jewish Literature and Culture), Albany, New York: State University of New York Press, 1995

Howe, Irving and Eliezer Greenberg, "Introduction," in *Selected Stories [of I.L. Peretz]*, New York: Schocken, 1974; London: Elek, 1975

Samuel, Maurice, *Prince of the Ghetto*, New York: Knopf, 1948; London: University Press of America, 1988

Wisse, Ruth R., "Introduction," in *The I.L. Peretz Reader* (Library of Yiddish Classics), New York: Schocken, 1990

Wisse, Ruth R., *I.L. Peretz and the Making of Modern Jewish Culture* (Samuel and Althea Stroum Lectures in Jewish Studies), Seattle: University of Washington Press, 1991

Yiddish and Hebrew poet and author Isaac Leib Peretz is, along with Mendele Moykher-Sforim and Sholem Aleichem, one of the three so-called "classic" Yiddish writers. Born in Zamosc, Poland, Peretz eventually settled in Warsaw, where he lived most of his adult life. Peretz made his literary debut in Yiddish in 1888 with the poem "Monish," after first writing in Polish and Hebrew. An experimenter in several different literary genres, Peretz is best known for his short stories such as "Bontshe the Silent" and "If Not Higher," and his plays *The Golden Chain* and *At Night at the Old Market*.

In his introductory survey of modern Yiddish literature and its three founding fathers, Mendele Moykher-Sforim, Sholem Aleichem, and I.L. Peretz, FRIEDEN discusses the place of Peretz in the Yiddish canon and his influence as a cultural activist, as the first writer of psychological fiction in Yiddish, and as the first exponent of Yiddish literary modernism. This book is a well documented and admirable introduction to the beginnings of modern Yiddish literature. Frieden gives a detailed chronology of events in the life of Peretz and a valuable interpretative survey of his works.

Literary critic and anthologist HOWE and GREENBERG, a Yiddish poet and critic, together assembled several volumes of Yiddish prose, poetry, and essays and did much to introduce Yiddish writers to an English reading audience. In this short yet valuable essay they offer useful biographical and analytical remarks on Peretz and consider his role as a cultural hero. Their work demonstrates a clear familiarity with both primary and secondary sources as they situate Peretz within the contexts of Jewish belles lettres and American and European literature. They view Peretz's later works, in particular his collections *Hasidic* and *Folk Tales,* as his best works and see his earlier stories as weak.

SAMUEL recreates some of Peretz's most famous stories, taken in particular from Peretz's books *Hasidic* and *Folk Tales.* He accomplishes this by retelling many of these stories through his own free translation and interpretation. The stories are interspersed with critical commentary and analysis.

WISSE (1991) argues the case for Peretz's central role in the creation of modern Jewish culture. Wisse posits that through his contribution to Yiddish literature, Peretz attempted to develop a creative and unifying tool for Jews, people with neither a land of their own nor collective political power. Wisse claims that Peretz wanted literature to fill these voids in Jewish life and to offer some form of empowerment. Wisse's careful analysis of Peretz's writings demonstrates a comprehensive knowledge not only of Peretz's oeuvre in Yiddish and Hebrew but also of the large corpus of secondary literature on the author. She examines the great influence of Peretz on succeeding generations of writers as well as the authority he wielded over a large segment of the Jewish people during his lifetime. Peretz was a humanist who believed that antisemitism could be overcome and rapprochement attained between Jews and gentiles. Through cultural advancement, Peretz believed that Jews could become more secular and therefore acceptable to the non-Jewish world. Wisse concludes that Peretz's optimism was belied and his influence curtailed by subsequent events: "While Peretz was shaping an earthly culture that outrivaled heaven's in its goodness, others were shaping an earthly culture that outrivaled hell's in its venom. The school children of Vilna and of all Poland were murdered with the words of Peretz on their lips."

WISSE (1990) is the introduction to an anthology of writings by Peretz in English translation, which forms part of Schocken's Library of Yiddish Classics, of which Wisse is the editor. Her introduction begins with the claim that "Isaac Leib Peretz was arguably the most important figure in the development of modern Jewish culture." Wisse explains that Peretz, the first Yiddish literary modernist, differed from the other two fathers of modern Yiddish literature in that he felt more of a need to express himself as an individual and break from the traditional Jewish collective. After a short yet comprehensive account of Peretz's formative years, Wisse turns to his writing and shows in particular his use of traditional Jewish sources, such as the Yiddish folktale and the hasidic story, as the tools of his literary craft.

MARC MILLER

Pharisees

Baumgarten, A.I., "The Name of the Pharisees," *Journal of Biblical Literature*, 102(3), 1983

Bowker, John, *Jesus and the Pharisees*, Cambridge: Cambridge University Press, 1973

Cook, Michael J., *Mark's Treatment of the Jewish Leaders* (Supplements to Novum Testamentum, vol. 51), Leiden: Brill, 1978

Goodblatt, D., "The Place of the Pharisees in First Century Judaism: The State of the Debate," *Journal for the Study of Judaism*, 20, 1989

Neusner, Jacob, *The Rabbinic Traditions about the Pharisees before 70*, 3 vols., Leiden: Brill, 1971

Saldarini, Anthony J., *Pharisees, Scribes and Sadducees in Palestinian Society: A Sociological Approach*, Wilmington, Delaware: Glazier, 1988

Sanders, E.P., *Judaism: Practice and Belief, 63 BCE–66 CE*, Philadelphia: Trinity Press International, and London: SCM, 1992; 2nd impression with corrections, 1994

Schwartz, D.R., "Josephus and Nicolaus on the Pharisees," *Journal for the Study of Judaism*, 14, 1983

Smith, Morton, "Palestinian Judaism in the First Century," in *Israel: Its Role in Civilization*, edited by Moshe Davis, New York: Seminary Israel Institute of the Jewish Theological Seminary of America, 1956

Telford, W.R., "Review of *Mark's Treatment of the Jewish Leaders*, by M. Cook," *Journal of Theological Studies*, 31, 1980

The Pharisees were one of many Jewish sects that existed in Palestine during the late Second Temple period. Within the extremely variegated Judaism of the time, the Pharisees are perhaps the most widely represented Jewish group in extant sources. Indeed, two authors important for any reconstruction of the social and historical dimensions of Judaism, Flavius Josephus and Paul of Tarsus, claim membership in the Pharisaic party. Nevertheless, the available information on the Pharisees is quite sparse. Furthermore, the modern researcher faces the added difficulty of sifting through often conflicting accounts of the Pharisees presented in the three major primary sources: Flavius Josephus, the New Testament, and rabbinic literature.

BAUMGARTEN discusses the meaning of the name "Pharisees." Many scholars have supposed that the name derives from the Hebrew *perushim*, "separatists," in either an approbative or a derogatory sense. After a lexical analysis of the term *akribeia*, "accurate," in the Greek sources, which is used in connection with the Pharisees by Josephus, the Acts of the Apostles, and Nicolaus of Damascus, Baumgarten proposes that the Hebrew root *prs* was probably understood by the Pharisees and their opponents as "to specify," even if the root's original etymology conveyed a different meaning. Thus, the Pharisees presented themselves as the "specifiers" to indicate that they could provide precise knowledge of the law. Baumgarten's article may provide valuable evidence of the way that the Pharisees wanted to be seen by their contemporaries in an age when exact knowledge of the law was prized.

SMITH's article is a seminal challenge to the scholarly consensus that the Pharisaic variety of Judaism constituted an orthodox or normative Judaism. According to Smith, the Pharisees were simply one of several sects—albeit the "largest and ultimately most influential"—that were competing for the attention of the unaffiliated majority. He notes that Josephus's summaries of Pharisean influence and control are not substantiated by individual accounts. A critical rereading of Josephus, which takes into account the omission of any description of the influence of the party in his *Jewish War* (in contrast to *Antiquities*), suggests that Josephus was attempting to persuade the Roman authorities to entrust the leadership of the Jewish population to the Pharisees by overstating the latter's influence. Similarly, Smith posits that the description of Pharisees in rabbinic literature needs to be reinterpreted in light of its distinct bias in favor of the Pharisees.

The rabbinic traditions about the Pharisees of the Second Temple period have been systematically collected and analyzed from redactional and literary-critical perspectives by NEUSNER. In his three-volume work, Neusner catalogs the types and forms of rabbinic traditions about the Pharisees and compares them with traditions about other groups in ancient Judaism. Neusner concludes that the rabbinic traditions pertain chiefly to the half-century that preceded the destruction of the Temple. At that time, the Pharisees were primarily a society for table-fellowship, which functioned as "the high point of their group." This transition from a political party during the Hasmonean period to a table-fellowship sect was largely the work of Hillel, who directed the Pharisees into more passive and quiescent paths, enabling them to survive the reign of Herod.

SCHWARTZ offers two theses that challenge the views of Neusner and others who argue that the Pharisees, who had been politically active in the Hasmonean period, withdrew from politics in the time of Herod and remained withdrawn until the destruction of Jerusalem in 70 C.E., after which they renewed their bid for political power. First, he insists that most of Josephus's sources on the Pharisees can be attributed to Nicolaus of Damascus and were not created for propaganda reasons. Second, Schwartz asserts that the historians' claims that the Pharisaic center at Yavneh was recognized by the Roman government and that negotiations for this recognition were carried on in the 90s "rest on virtually nothing." In conclusion, Schwartz proposes that Josephus created his "incorrect but safe" portrayal of the Pharisees in his *Jewish War* as uninvolved in politics—and, therefore, uninvolved in rebellion—in the anti-Jewish political climate that immediately followed the First Jewish Revolt against Rome. By the time

Josephus wrote his *Antiquities*, the political climate was less hostile to Jews and, hence, Josephus felt freer to use other sources that indicated Pharisaic involvement in politics and even in rebellion.

GOODBLATT usefully summarizes the views of different scholars on the debate about the political influence of the Pharisees in first-century C.E. Judaism. He challenges Schwartz's proposal that the very fact that Josephus in his *Jewish War* describes the Pharisees as the "first sect" implies that they exercised considerable political influence. In addition, he maintains (again *contra* Schwartz) that he can find no explanation of Gamaliel's rise to power after 70 except that he received a Roman appointment. This thesis is based on his understanding of the Roman policy of interventionism in the internal affairs of subject peoples.

COOK applies source-critical analysis to the Gospel of Mark as he seeks to determine how familiar Mark was with different Jewish groups and how he obtained his information about them. Cook contends that the Evangelists themselves were unclear about the identities of the various Jewish groups, including the Pharisees, active in Jesus' time. The Evangelists did not adequately define and distinguish between the different Jewish groups because they could not make such categorizations. The treatments of Jewish leadership groups in the Gospels of Matthew and Luke are essentially no more than preservation and occasionally free embellishment of the Markan account. Thus, the appearance of a given Jewish leadership element in the later synoptic gospels does not necessarily enhance current knowledge of that group or even confirm Mark's assumption that such a group confronted Jesus during his ministry.

TELFORD, while agreeing overall with Cook's case, challenges him in three areas. First, Telford disputes Cook's argument that the Gospel writers could not have known about the Jewish groups in Jesus' time. According to Telford, this conclusion is largely based on debatable presuppositions regarding the provenance of the synoptic gospels, including the unconvincing dismissal of the possibility of a Palestinian provenance for the Gospel of Mark. Furthermore, Cook's suggestion that Matthew's treatment of the leadership groups is simply an embellishment of the Markan account fails to take into account some distinctly Matthean passages that cannot easily be treated as revisions of Mark. Second, Cook's claim to isolate specific controversial sources is based on one factor alone—the distribution of group titles—without taking linguistic and theological factors into account. Third, Cook's assertion that "scribes" and "Pharisees" are synonymous fails to take into account the more difficult reference in Mark to "the scribes of the Pharisees."

SANDERS's substantial and sympathetic work on the practice and beliefs of Judaism in the late Second Temple period includes two chapters devoted to the history and practice of the Pharisees. He carefully distinguishes between the popularity of the Pharisees and their ability to control official and public events. When describing Pharisean beliefs, Sanders resorts to rabbinic literature, particularly tannaitic midrashim, thereby linking Pharisaism and Rabbinism. Sanders concludes that the beliefs and practices of the Pharisees fit into a theological rubric of what he terms "covenantal nomism." Sanders challenges the assumption by many earlier scholars that the Pharisees believed that the common people were excluded from the sphere of the divine and sacred. Rather, the "people of the land" were one step lower on the purity ladder than the Pharisees themselves, who were one step below the priests outside the temple.

BOWKER has conveniently collected all the primary references to the Pharisees from Josephus and rabbinic literature. Bowker intends his introductory book "to serve as a companion to studies of the Pharisees." Included in his book is a very useful chapter on the problems of identifying the Pharisees in extant sources. Bowker's great contribution is his reexamination of the scholarly assumption that the *perushim* of rabbinic literature actually do refer to the pre-70 C.E. Pharisees. It is, he contends, equally possible that the term *perushim* refers to individuals or groups who separated themselves in some manner but were not a clearly defined sect. In effect, Bowker questions the thesis that the perushim of the late Second Temple period were the ancestors of the rabbis of Yavneh and beyond.

SALDARINI dismisses the reconstructions of first-century Pharisaism by many scholars who have based their results on literary criticism without taking into account the social conditions in which Palestinian Jews lived under the Roman Empire. Challenging reconstructions centered on the rabbinic material, Saldarini notes that the tannaitic authors did not identify themselves as Pharisees. He assumes that, after the losses of the Temple, the Jerusalem leadership, and the clear political identity of Jews, there must have been major adjustments to the Jewish understanding of the world and to Judaism's symbolic systems, behavioral patterns, and values. The scarcity of evidence about Pharisees in the primary sources means that the few references must be interpreted in a larger historical and sociological context, and this is precisely what Saldarini aims to do in his study. He concludes that the Pharisees were a literate, corporate, voluntary association that constantly sought influence with the governing class. Thus, Saldarini rejects Neusner's description of the Pharisees as a sect-like table-fellowship. The Pharisee association probably functioned as a social movement seeking to change society and establish a new communal commitment to a strict Jewish way of life based on adherence to their covenant.

D.P. O'BRIEN

Philo of Alexandria c.20 B.C.E.–c.50 C.E.

Neoplatonist philosopher and Bible commentator

Belkin, Samuel, *Philo and the Oral Law: The Philonic Interpretation of Biblical Law in Relation to the Palestinian Halakah* (Harvard Semitic Series, vol. 11), Cambridge, Massachusetts: Harvard University Press, 1940

Birnbaum, Ellen, *The Place of Judaism in Philo's Thought: Israel, Jews, and Proselytes* (Brown Judaic Studies, no. 290; Studia Philonica Monographs, 2), Atlanta, Georgia: Scholars Press, 1996

Borgen, Peder, *Philo of Alexandria: An Exegete for His Time* (Supplements to Novum Testamentum, vol. 86), New York: Brill, 1997

Cohen, Naomi G., *Philo Judaeus: His Universe of Discourse* (Beiträge zur Erforschung des Alten Testaments und des Antiken Judentums, vol. 24), New York: Lang, 1995

Colson, F.H., G.H. Whitaker, and Ralph Marcus (translators), *Philo in Ten Volumes (and Two Supplementary Volumes)* (Loeb Classical Library), Cambridge, Massachusetts: Harvard University Press, and London: Heinemann, 1929–1962

Goodenough, Erwin R., *By Light, Light: The Mystic Gospel of Hellenistic Judaism,* New Haven, Connecticut: Yale University Press, and London: Oxford University Press, 1935

Goodenough, Erwin R., *The Politics of Philo Judaeus: Practice and Theory,* New Haven, Connecticut: Yale University Press, and London: Oxford University Press, 1938

Goodenough, Erwin R., *An Introduction to Philo Judaeus,* New Haven, Connecticut: Yale University Press, and London: Oxford University Press, 1940; 2nd edition, New York: Barnes and Noble, and Oxford: Blackwell, 1962

Haase, Wolfgang (editor), *Religion: Hellenistisches Judentum in römischer Zeit: Philon und Josephus (Aufstieg und Niedergang der römischen Welt: Geschichte und Kultur Roms im Spiegel der neueren Forschung,* part 2, vol. 21, section 1), New York: de Gruyter, 1984

Mendelson, Alan, *Philo's Jewish Identity* (Brown Judaic Studies, no. 161), Atlanta, Georgia: Scholars Press, 1988

Morris, Jenny, "The Jewish Philosopher Philo," in *The History of the Jewish People in the Age of Jesus Christ, (175 B.C.–A.D. 135): Volume 3, Part 2,* by Emil Schürer, revised and edited by Géza Vermès, Fergus Millar, and Martin Goodman, Edinburgh: Clark, 1987

Radice, Roberto and David T. Runia, *Philo of Alexandria: An Annotated Bibliography: 1937–1986,* New York: Brill, 1988, 2nd edition, 1992

Runia, David T., "How to Read Philo," *Nederlands Theologisch Tijdschrift,* 40, 1986; reprinted in his *Exegesis and Philosophy: Studies on Philo of Alexandria,* Aldershot, Hampshire: Variorum, and Brookfield, Vermont: Gower, 1990

Runia, David T., *Philo of Alexandria and the Timaeus of Plato* (Philosophia Antiqua, vol. 44), Leiden, The Netherlands: Brill, 1986

Runia, David T., "Philo in a Single Volume," *Studia Philonica Annual,* 6, 1994

Sandmel, Samuel, *Philo of Alexandria: An Introduction,* New York: Oxford University Press, 1979

Sterling, Gregory E. (editor), *Philo of Alexandria Commentary Series,* Notre Dame, Indiana: University of Notre Dame Press, forthcoming

Tobin, Thomas H., *The Creation of Man: Philo and the History of Interpretation* (The Catholic Biblical Quarterly Monograph Series, no. 14), Washington D.C.: Catholic Biblical Association of America, 1983

Winston, David, *Logos and Mystical Theology in Philo of Alexandria,* Cincinnati, Ohio: Hebrew Union College Press, 1985

Wolfson, Harry A., *Philo: Foundations of Religious Philosophy in Judaism, Christianity, and Islam* (Structure and Growth of Philosophic Systems from Plato to Spinoza, 2), 2 vols., Cambridge, Massachusetts: Harvard University Press, 1947, 4th edition, 1968

Yonge, C.D. (translator), *The Works of Philo: Complete and Unabridged,* Peabody, Massachusetts: Hendrickson, 1993

Philo of Alexandria, also called Philo Judaeus, is the most prominent example in antiquity of a writer who brought together Jewish tradition and Greek philosophy. Some authors, in fact, have debated which influences are more predominant, the Jewish or the Greek. Well-acquainted with both Jewish and Greek culture, Philo has been considered from multiple perspectives—as a Greek philosopher, mystic, Jew, biblical interpreter, allegorist, and rhetorician, among others. Not only has Philo generated interest in his works for their own sake, but scholars have also been drawn to him for the light he sheds on such varied topics as Greek philosophy, the history of Judaism, Hellenistic and Roman culture, ancient Alexandria, Gnostic thought, the New Testament, and writings of the Church Fathers. In recent decades, studies on Philo have proliferated, leading some to speak of a "Philo renaissance." As a result, those interested in Philo will find many resources at hand to assist their pursuits.

English-language readers can acquaint themselves with Philo's writings in a 12-volume translation by COLSON, WHITAKER, and MARCUS. For those who would like Philo's (nearly) complete works in one volume, YONGE is also available. This translation, however, is problematic for a number of reasons, as detailed by RUNIA (1994). At least one new English translation, edited by STERLING, is being planned, though this will likely not be published in its entirety for several years. This series will represent a collaborative effort by several scholars to publish translations of and commentaries on Philo's writings. Whichever translation one uses, any student of Philo—whether novice or veteran—will benefit from consulting RUNIA's article (1986a) on how to read Philo.

In the introduction to their indispensable annotated bibliography, which includes works from 1937 through 1986, RADICE and RUNIA describe the flourishing of Philonic scholarship in the late 20th century. The bibliography—which aims to be comprehensive, at least in English—is indexed according to authors, reviewers, biblical passages, Philonic passages, subjects, and Greek terms. Each year the bibliography is updated in a publication titled *The Studia Philonica Annual.* In this journal, readers will also find articles—generally in English—covering Philo from several points of view. Similarly, the volume edited by HAASE collects a number of essays in English on different subjects, providing a good illustration of the multifaceted approaches in Philonic research.

GOODENOUGH (1962) emphasizes the human factors involved in becoming acquainted with Philo—factors that pertain to Goodenough himself as the author, to the reader as a unique individual, and to Philo the man. Explaining his own predilections about religion, Goodenough views Philo as a mystic whose Judaism departed from " 'normative' Judaism," because Philo's Judaism was influenced by "the pagan idea of salvation, that is, that the spirit be released from the flesh in order to return to its spiritual source in God." Cautioning that any reader of Philo will view him in terms of his or her own personal proclivities, Goodenough offers some useful methodological guideposts. Among these is the need to pay attention to the context of Philo's works, specifically their purpose and likely intended audience. Besides its emphasis on method, another strength of this introduction is its express purpose "of helping the beginner to make a start in an intelligent reading of Philo"; to this end, Goodenough suggests a program of reading to guide the learner through Philo's various works. In other chapters, he discusses Philo as a political thinker, Jew, philosopher, and mystic.

GOODENOUGH (1935) sets forth the hypothesis for which he is perhaps best known, namely, that Philo was but one representative of a Hellenized, mystical Judaism, the goal of which was to rise above the created, material world in pursuit of knowledge of God, the Absolute. Arguing that Philo was writing for potential proselytes as well as for Jews, Goodenough spells out the details of what he calls the Jewish "Mystery," based upon Philo's allegorical commentaries. To support his contention that there existed a wider, non-"normative" Judaism, he supplements the evidence from Philo with a discussion of non-Philonic writings.

GOODENOUGH (1938) argues that Philo was strongly influenced by Hellenistic notions of the ideal king, though he stopped short of ascribing divinity to any ruler. Best known for his high esteem of contemplation, Philo was nevertheless also active in the political life of his Jewish community and often stressed the importance of cultivating both the practical and the theoretical life. Of special interest is the way Goodenough analyzes Philo's works with an eye toward understanding their aims and audiences. For example, Goodenough uses this approach to explain why in one set of works Philo portrays the figure of Joseph as an arrogant politician, while in another set of works he depicts Joseph as an ideal ruler. Also, Goodenough concludes that Philo's two extant political treatises (several others were lost) were written for non-Jewish rulers as a warning that their potential success or failure depended upon how well or badly they treated the Jews.

SANDMEL, writing some 40 years after Goodenough, his teacher, aims at a simpler presentation of Philo that incorporates scholarship from the intervening four decades. Sandmel focuses upon Philo's use of allegorical interpretation, explaining that Philo viewed biblical narrative as an allegory of "the spiritual journey which each of us can make." With this useful orientation, Sandmel guides the reader through Philo's works and thought with additional chapters devoted to Philo and Palestinian Judaism, Philo and Gnosticism, Philo and Christianity, and a consideration of Goodenough's position on Philo. While agreeing with Goodenough's evaluation of Philo's Hellenized mystical religiosity, Sandmel believes Goodenough went too far in positing the existence of a more widespread, marginal Judaism.

MORRIS's extended essay offers a careful and worthwhile synthesis of scholarship through the mid-1980s on a variety of issues but especially on matters related to Philo's individual treatises. She emphasizes that most of these treatises are commentaries on Jewish Scripture, a feature that underscores Philo's commitment to Jewish tradition. Noting that as an expositor of Scripture, Philo did not offer a systematic presentation of his ideas, Morris briefly comments on his most prevalent notions pertaining to God; divine intermediaries and the divine Logos; the creation and preservation of the world; theory of man; and ethics.

WOLFSON's Philo is very much a systematic philosopher whose Judaism was "of the same stock" as the Judaism of his Pharisaic contemporaries. Paying little heed to Philo's mystical side, Wolfson masterfully collects and organizes his positions on a wide array of philosophical topics, showing continuities and discontinuities with earlier and contemporary positions. As the finest representative of the Hellenistic Jewish endeavor to harmonize the truths of Scripture and philosophy, Philo, according to Wolfson, established a trend that was continued by the Church Fathers and medieval Jewish, Christian, and Muslim thinkers, to be overturned only centuries later by Spinoza. No one interested in Philo's philosophy can ignore Wolfson's work, but readers should keep in mind that Wolfson's systematization is more characteristic of his own way of thinking than of that of Philo.

WINSTON highlights both the philosophical and the mystical bents of Philo's writings. He focuses upon Philo's Logos concept, arguing that according to Philo one cannot approach God directly but only through the Divine Mind, or Logos. Describing Philo as "an unabashed Platonist," Winston sees the purpose of Philo's scriptural commentaries as "to trace the return of the human soul to its native homeland by means of the allegorical method of interpretation." Although the inherently individualistic mystical goal of knowledge of God through the Logos was supremely important to Philo, Winston also sees in his thought a tension between "nationalism and universalism, the mystical and the this-worldly."

RUNIA (1986b) recognizes in Philo a complex mixture of philosopher, exegete, mystic, and Jew, characterizing him primarily as a "philosophically orientated exegete of Scripture." Runia investigates in impressive detail the ways in which Philo understood and used the *Timaeus* of Plato. Concerned with the origins of the world, the *Timaeus* provided Philo with an important exegetical tool with which to understand and elucidate the structural framework and thought of the writings of Moses and to demonstrate the harmony between philosophy and Scripture. Acknowledging that Philo undoubtedly had Jewish exegetical predecessors, Runia calls him a pioneer who was the first to bring together "in a grand scale" Greek philosophical thought and the biblical view of God's activity in history.

TOBIN sees Philo as a scriptural exegete who was not completely original but stood within a tradition of interpretation. Based upon Philo's discussions of the creation of man in Genesis 1–3, Tobin identifies layers of interpretations with the aim of "sort[ing] out what is Philo and what is traditional material." While many scholars have recognized that Philo must certainly have used traditional elements in his writings, Tobin's work is significant for its effort to identify these elements and to correlate them with contemporary philosophical currents in Alexandria. He concludes that Philo's exegesis

incorporates an earlier "consistent, Platonically oriented interpretation of the creation of man" and that Philo himself introduced the allegory of the soul, whereby events in the biblical account are understood to describe internal conflicts and activities within the individual, especially within the soul.

BORGEN portrays Philo as "an exegete for his time" by showing that his scriptural interpretations were integrally related to the contemporary political and social background and that they paralleled, in content and form, other ancient Jewish and Christian interpretations. According to Borgen, Philo's view that the Mosaic laws embodied the universal cosmic law suggested that the Jews had a universal purpose: to bring proselytes into the nation. In Borgen's detailed presentation of Philonic exegetical levels and forms, readers may find certain categorizations somewhat general and may wish for more discussion of the significance of identifying the forms. Nonetheless, Borgen's correlations between Philonic interpretations and contemporaneous political and social factors, while necessarily speculative at times, are frequently suggestive, refocusing our attention upon a valuable and often neglected dimension of Philo's writings.

MENDELSON explores Philo's identity as a Jew in relation both to other Jews and to non-Jews. Among Jews, Philo was an "elitist" who expounded the esoteric meaning of Scripture through allegorical interpretation, albeit for the benefit of anyone capable of understanding this meaning. Nonetheless he also remained deeply committed to the entire Jewish polity, and Mendelson outlines in noteworthy detail the beliefs and practices that would have constituted "the minimum requirements" for belonging to this Jewish polity. Responding to negative perceptions by non-Jews, Philo emphasized the openness and humanity of his people, Mendelson claims, but when speaking of pagan beliefs and practices, he adopted a sense of spiritual superiority.

BELKIN focuses upon Philo's knowledge of Jewish law, arguing that his interpretations are largely in accord with Palestinian tannaitic halakhah. In this opinion, Belkin stands apart from other scholars who emphasize the differences between Philo and the Palestinian rabbis on legal matters. The only book-length study on this subject in English, Belkin's work must be used with caution. Because he wrote before the Dead Sea discoveries, he does not include valuable sources for this period, and the later rabbinic works he does use are not infallible witnesses to first-century practices. Until it is replaced, however, this volume introduces English-language readers to an important issue in Philonic studies.

COHEN, like Belkin, compares Philo with Palestinian sources in an attempt to portray him as "thoroughly Jewish (in the traditional sense)." Positing what she calls the "Palestinian/Diaspora midrashic tradition," Cohen argues that Philo was familiar with this common treasury of Jewish interpretations—both legal and nonlegal. She also maintains that Philo used a special "Judeo-Greek vocabulary," the words of which carry specifically Jewish nuances alongside their generally accepted, and occasionally philosophical, meanings. Some, but not all, of Cohen's evidence is convincing. A recent example of the longstanding effort to establish a link between Philo and other Jewish sources, this book shows that effort to be worthwhile but challenging.

BIRNBAUM examines how Philo evaluated the importance of being a Jew in relation to the potentially universal, philosophical goal of "seeing God" and also to the biblical claims that God chose the particular nation of Israel to be his special people. Noting that Philo understood "Israel" to mean "one that sees God," Birnbaum studies his different uses of the words "Israel," "Jew," and "proselyte," as well as his approach to such notions as the covenant and the chosen people. In contrast to authors who assess Philo's Jewishness by comparing him with other Jewish and Greek sources, Birnbaum focuses on Philo's own thought to understand how and why Judaism was important to him. She concludes that for Philo, believing in, or "seeing," God was paramount—a goal attainable by non-Jews as well as Jews. Although Philo's special devotion to Judaism and the Jews was profound, this devotion, Birnbaum claims, is not ultimately explained by his thought, which emphasized a potentially universal goal, but by his life, which was clearly marked by an active concern for and participation in the particular community of the Jews.

ELLEN BIRNBAUM

Philosemitism

Bevan, Edwyn R. and Charles Singer (editors), *The Legacy of Israel,* Oxford: Clarendon, 1927

Braybrooke, Marcus, *Children of One God: A History of the Council of Christians and Jews,* London and Portland, Oregon: Vallentine, Mitchell, 1991

Edelstein, Alan, *An Unacknowledged Harmony: Philo-Semitism and the Survival of European Jewry* (Contributions in Ethnic Studies, no. 4), Westport, Connecticut: Greenwood, 1982

Grose, Peter, *Israel in the Mind of America,* New York: Knopf, 1983

Katz, David, *The Jews in the History of England, 1485–1850,* New York: Oxford University Press, and Oxford: Clarendon, 1994

Kobler, Franz, *The Vision Was There: A History of the British Movement for the Restoration of the Jews to Palestine,* London: Lincolns-Prager, 1956

Lindemann, Albert S., *The Jew Accused: Three Anti-Semitic Affairs (Dreyfus, Beilis, Frank) 1894–1915,* Cambridge and New York: Cambridge University Press, 1991

Rappaport, Solomon, *Jew and Gentile: The Philo-Semitic Aspect,* New York: Philosophical Library, 1980

Rubinstein, William D. and Hilary L. Rubinstein, *Philosemitism: Admiration and Support in the English-Speaking World for Jews, 1840–1939,* London: Macmillan, 1999

Philosemitism is a complex notion, but it may be defined as admiration for Jews by non-Jews as well as support for Jews by non-Jews during times of antisemitic oppression. There was an early, fairly well-examined tradition of Christian philosemitism from medieval times through the Enlightenment, which often emphasized tolerance for the Jews (or their restoration to Palestine) as a necessary prelude to the Second Coming. Philosemitism in the post-Enlightenment period stemmed from a variety of sources, especially from liberal and progressive activists and theorists, from many Christians, especially Protestants, from gentile Zionists, and from a surprising number of political conservatives who viewed the Jews as a worthy, time-honored elite group. The assumption that most philosemites have been Christian conversionists with an ulterior motive to their Jewish sympathies is naive: surprisingly early, many viewed Judaism as deserving of respect for being the ancestral religion of Christianity, while many Protestants associated antisemitism with medieval persecutions carried out by the Catholic Church, which they deplored.

Philosemitism is arguably a much more important phenomenon in the modern history of the Jews than is generally credited. For instance, the warmth of the United States government and most Americans for the State of Israel has its origins in a remarkable tradition of American support for Jewish resettlement in Palestine that predates the Herzlian Zionist movement by many decades; a similar tradition can be found in Britain. The centrality of antisemitism for modern Jewish history, culminating in the Holocaust, has regrettably caused the strength of philosemitism to be downplayed or, indeed, denied altogether. The subject of philosemitism remains exceptionally unexplored and manifestly underresearched and is one in which scholars have the opportunity of producing work of considerable importance and originality.

BEVAN and SINGER is a collection of 13 essays, mainly by non-Jewish British academics, about the Jewish contribution to Western civilization. Typical essays include "The Debt of Christianity to Judaism," by F.C. Burkitt of Cambridge, and "The Influence of the Old Testament on Puritanism," by W.B. Selbie of Oxford. A somewhat surprisingly early volume of its kind to come from the Oxford University Press, its essays are still valuable.

BRAYBROOKE surveys the history of the (British) Council of Christians and Jews. Founded in 1942 as a response to the Holocaust, it met early opposition from Roman Catholics and Orthodox Jews and in recent decades has faced considerable left-wing Christian opposition on account of Israel's Palestinian policies. Nevertheless it has become a prime focus of Britain's interfaith dialogue.

EDELSTEIN's pioneering work appeared two years after Solomon Rappaport's. It is a more comprehensive work, tracing philosemitism from the Middle Ages to the contemporary period and attempting an analysis. Its most provocative thesis is that the survival of the Jews in Europe depended in large measure on Christian admiration and support.

GROSE demonstrates the long-standing support given by American elites and opinion-leaders to the creation of a Jewish state in Palestine, support that long predates the Zionist movement. Founded in Protestantism and liberalism, it helps to explain America's strong support for the State of Israel since 1948.

KATZ's comprehensive history of the Anglo-Jewish community from the 15th to the mid-19th century summarizes the author's important research on the role of philosemitism in the readmission of Jews to England by Oliver Cromwell in 1656 and discusses subsequent British philosemites. Its very complete bibliography refers to numerous other publications on this subject.

KOBLER's work was an early attempt to examine the long history of proto-Zionism by British gentiles, a tradition that was highly relevant to the promulgation of the Balfour Declaration in 1917. Kobler does not conceal the variety of motives among early restorationists, including conversionism, but also emphasizes its philosemitic aspects.

LINDEMANN's very controversial study of three celebrated antisemitic affairs of the 1894–1915 period (in France, Russia, and the United States) attracted both widespread praise and considerable hostility from critics. Lindemann emphasizes the ambiguousness of the allegedly antisemitic component of these incidents, as well as the real contribution of each of the protagonists to his own tragedy. Its relevance here lies in the author's pioneering study of the very wide philosemitic support received by Dreyfus, Beilis, and Frank, often from the most unlikely sources.

RAPPAPORT is probably the first modern account of philosemitism and its dimensions. The work, by a Vienna-born South African rabbi, consists of 11 essays on philosemitism, covering the medieval and modern periods. Useful distinctions are made, while the ambiguities in the stances of philosemites are not glossed over.

RUBINSTEIN and RUBINSTEIN analyze philosemitism in the English-speaking world since the Damascus Affair of 1840, based largely upon primary and contemporary sources. Their book examines the philosemitic response of many prominent gentiles during well-known antisemitic crises up to and including the Nazi period and offers a typology of philosemitism: liberal and progressive, Christian, Zionist, and elitist/conservative.

WILLIAM D. RUBINSTEIN

Philosophy: General

Blau, Joseph L., *The Story of Jewish Philosophy*, New York: Random House, 1962

Cohn-Sherbok, Dan, *Fifty Key Jewish Thinkers* (Key Concepts Series), London and New York: Routledge, 1997

Frank, Daniel and Oliver Leaman (editors), *History of Jewish Philosophy* (Routledge History of World Philosophies, vol. 2), London and New York: Routledge, 1997

Guttmann, Julius, *Philosophies of Judaism: The History of Jewish Philosophy from Biblical Times to Franz Rosenzweig*, London: Routledge, and New York: Holt, Rinehart and Winston, 1964

Katz, Steven, T. (editor), *Jewish Philosophers*, New York: Bloch, 1975

Seeskin, Kenneth, *Jewish Philosophy in a Secular Age*, Albany: State University of New York Press, 1990

Seltzer, Robert M., *Jewish People, Jewish Thought: The Jewish Experience in History*, New York: Macmillan, 1980

Historians of Jewish philosophy have two options: to survey, in chronological order, the work of individual thinkers or periods of thought through the centuries; or to focus on specific philosophical concepts central to Jewish thought and trace their development and relevance today.

BLAU's survey is a successful attempt to address, in clear and simple language, the interested layperson rather than the specialist. Instead of offering an in-depth study of selected issues, Blau presents the very broad range of Jewish philosophy with emphasis on "the continuities and changes that have taken place in Jewish philosophic thought from the Bible to the 20th century." The book's easy legibility does not preclude its seriousness, and it certainly covers much ground: the reader is taken from a discussion on the nature of philosophy itself and a comparison with biblical ethics, via an exposition of the wisdom of the prophets and the Jewish encounter with Hellenism, to rabbinic modes of thought and on to the Kabbalah. Also discussed are the great Jewish medieval philosophers, Renaissance thinkers, and Spinoza and how Enlightenment thought led to Reform Judaism and, eventually, to Jewish existentialism. This is a most useful introductory overview for the beginner.

Another introductory survey, quite different in style and content, is the panorama of 50 key Jewish thinkers (philosophers, theologians, kabbalists, and theoreticians of Zionism) presented in alphabetical order and selected by COHN-SHERBOK for their "importance in the history of Judaism from post-biblical times to the present day." This manual devotes no more than three pages to each of its 50 thinkers, and it is therefore primarily a reference book and of special interest to the layperson seeking a quick overview of a particular thinker. The summary of each thinker's work also contains a biographical sketch and select bibliography of primary and secondary sources.

Contributions on individual Jewish philosophers prepared as articles for *Encyclopaedia Judaica* (Jerusalem, 1972) have been collected and edited by KATZ into an illustrated, comprehensive history of Jewish philosophers, to which Katz himself has added a survey of Jewish thought since 1945. The glossary, biographical index, and bibliography will assist readers at an introductory level to engage the major Jewish philosophers as well as the theological traditions from which "the hybrid known as Jewish philosophy" emerged.

GUTTMANN's masterly critical history of Jewish philosophy has remained the standard work by a single author written for the serious student. Surveying the period from biblical times to Franz Rosenzweig, it aims at an impartial analysis and a methodological description of Judaism in terms of its correspondence to philosophical categories. Using philosophical tools to elucidate the content of Judaism, Guttmann follows Immanuel Kant's demand for a separation of the religious concept of truth from the metaphysical concept of truth. This being the task of reason itself, Guttmann's history of philosophy is essentially a history of rational Jewish philosophy. Certain to remain authoritative and indispensable, this survey not only provides a profound analysis of Judaism and its philosophies but also demonstrates how closely bound they remained to the non-Jewish sources from which they originated and drew much inspiration.

The recently published voluminous, comprehensive, chronological survey edited by FRANK and LEAMAN is bound to become a new standard work in the field, presenting in a collection of essays all major and minor philosophers of Judaism according to their respective schools of thought. The essays are written by an international team of experts and feature extensive bibliographies. Contributions range from a discussion of the nature of Jewish philosophy itself and its beginnings in the Bible to a forecast of its future. This substantial volume encompasses the whole range of Hellenistic, medieval, modern, and contemporary Jewish thought and covers present-day issues such as nationalism, Zionism, feminist and postmodern Jewish thought, and the Holocaust. Emphasis is given throughout to the dialectical interchange between Jewish ideas and influential non-Jewish sources in their parallel development. The result is a unique approach to the history of Jewish philosophy that covers an unprecedented variety of perspectives and ideas and helps significantly to establish Jewish philosophy as a discipline in its own right rather than as a mere addendum to Jewish religion or general philosophy. This is an indispensable reference book for serious study of Jewish philosophy.

SEESKIN offers a careful analysis of selected philosophical issues central to Jewish thought that addresses the notion of Jewish philosophy itself. He goes on to deal with past and present discussions of such issues as divine attributes, creation, revelation, the problem of evil and the Holocaust, the idea of God, and autonomy and ethics. The author's aim is to trace a dialogue between great Jewish and non-Jewish philosophers across the ages (Maimonides, Halevi, Spinoza, Cohen, Buber, Rosenzweig and Plato, Aristotle, Descartes, Kant, and Kierkegaard). He claims that this dialogue remains relevant and seeks to encourage secular philosophers "to pay more attention to Jewish philosophy and to get Jewish philosophers to pay more attention to secular philosophy." Although this problem-oriented study is clearly written, a reader with some background in both Jewish and secular philosophy is most likely to be stimulated and to benefit from the constructive solutions it offers.

SELTZER's voluminous contribution can best be characterized as a history of ideas of the Jewish people from earliest times to the present, documenting "periods of conscious encounter with the most sophisticated general modes of philosophy and scientific thought." The emphasis is clearly on the history, with the ideas themselves occupying a subordinate role. Yet this comprehensive study does offer a concise description of philosophical developments through the ages and may therefore serve as a useful introduction to Jewish philosophy by illuminating the historical framework that has shaped philosophical considerations over time.

ESTHER I. SEIDEL

See also Philosophy: Medieval; Philosophy: Modern

Philosophy: Medieval

Bleich, J. David (editor), *With Perfect Faith: The Foundations of Jewish Belief*, New York: Ktav, 1983
Husik, Isaac, *A History of Mediaeval Jewish Philosophy*, New York: Macmillan, 1916, new edition, 1930

Hyman, Arthur and James J. Walsh (editors), *Philosophy in the Middle Ages: The Christian, Islamic, and Jewish Traditions*, New York: Harper and Row, 1967; 2nd edition, Indianapolis, Indiana: Hackett, 1983
Jacobs, Louis (compiler), *Jewish Ethics, Philosophy and Mysticism* (The Chain of Tradition Series, vol. 2), New York: Behrman House, 1969
Kellner, Menachem, *Dogma in Medieval Jewish Thought: From Maimonides to Abravanel* (Littman Library of Jewish Civilization), Oxford and New York: Oxford University Press, 1986
Lasker, Daniel J., *Jewish Philosophical Polemics against Christianity in the Middle Ages*, New York: Ktav, 1977
Sirat, Colette, *A History of Jewish Philosophy in the Middle Ages*, Cambridge and New York: Cambridge University Press, 1985

There are different ways to approach medieval Jewish philosophy, which by nature is closely bound and subservient to religion. Histories of medieval Jewish philosophy provide surveys covering the whole spectrum of Jewish thought from the ninth to the 15th century in varying detail. Other studies are arranged according to the central issues discussed by Jewish medieval thinkers. The view that Jewish philosophy proper can only be identified as a phenomenon of the Middle Ages and that it never went beyond that period has been challenged by recent studies.

Since its first publication in 1916, HUSIK's "history of medieval Jewish rationalistic philosophy" has gone through a number of reprints and remains a popular work, both for the intelligent nontechnical reader and for the professional student. The discussion ranges chronologically from Isaac Israeli in the ninth century to Joseph Albo in the 15th century, covering all the major Jewish thinkers of the Middle Ages and aiming "to interpret their ideas from their own point of view as determined by their history and environment and the literary sources, religion and philosophy, under the influence of which they came." The result is a readable and objective, albeit not too critical, exposition, based largely on the study of the original sources, with a synoptic introduction and valuable conclusions as to the nature of Jewish philosophy, which, according to Husik, "never passed beyond the scholastic age."

A broader range of Jewish medieval philosophy, which includes the Italian Jewish philosophers of the Quattrocento, is expounded by SIRAT, who, in additon to the main discussions of the thought of the great Jewish medieval thinkers, also devotes much attention to lesser-known authors. Reflecting on the different and wider connotations the word *philosophy* comprised across the centuries, Sirat also includes in her discussion astrology and Kabbalah, for "as long as traditional texts were referred to in order to justify a philosophical doctrine . . . one can speak of Jewish philosophy." The comprehensive bibliography, together with lengthy quotations often from little-known works in manuscript, which are commented upon critically and placed within their historical and philosophical context, make this study not only a thorough introduction but also an indispensable reference tool for the serious student of medieval Jewish thought.

Anyone interested in a wider view of medieval philosophy in general, within which Jewish philosophy occupies only a part, should look to the volume edited by HYMAN and WALSH, which has become, since its first appearance in 1967, "a standard work for teaching medieval philosophy." This study is the result of a laudable attempt to focus on the large area of philosophical common ground between Christianity, Judaism, and Islam, exemplified to a great extent by their respective representatives of Neoplatonism and Aristotelianism. Although the section on Jewish philosophy only comprises Saadiah, ibn Gabirol, Maimonides, Gersonides, and Crescas, the careful choice of primary sources not only offers a valuable introduction to each individual thinker but also reflects issues of general relevance to all three faiths, with discussions of such topics as causality, God's knowledge, and the divine attributes. This important anthology, although "not intended as a substitute for a fully fledged history of medieval philosophy," offers an understanding of the issues common to all three faiths and highlights their "different theological commitments" and their respective contributions to the philosophical discussion.

JACOBS's introductory study offers short selections in modern translation from the works of great medieval Jewish thinkers. It is subdivided into three sections, each prefaced by a short introductory note. The extracts are interspersed with Jacobs's own commentaries and interpretation, and the concise and clear language used throughout will help both the general reader and the beginner in their approach to medieval text study. The three sections focus, repectively, on ethics (which is defined in contrast to Jewish law and is represented here from ten different sources, chiefly from the Musar literature), philosophy (addressing creation, the concept of God, and free will), and mysticism. This last topic is often excluded from historical surveys of philosophy because of its highly speculative nature. Here it is introduced by the teachings of leading kabbalists, from the Zohar via the hasidic movement to A.I. Kook, exemplifying various "contemplative exercises on God's nature in His relationship to the created world."

"Representative selections from the writings of major medieval Jewish philosophers" are also at the heart of the volume edited by BLEICH. Although, regrettably, Bleich was obliged to use some older and less reliable translations of the material here presented, this collection of a wide range of primary sources provides a valuable text base for undergraduate students. Selections are organized around Maimonides' Thirteen Principles of Faith and enable the student to draw comparisons between the arguments of the great medieval thinkers with respect to each of those principles: God's existence, unity, incorporeality, eternity and omniscience, prayer, prophecy, revelation, reward and punishment, belief in the Messiah, resurrection, and the immutability of the Torah. Bleich's introduction discusses the development of and opposition to dogmatic principles within Judaism, while the selections themselves are representative of the medieval systematic approach to the essential notions of Jewish belief still relevant today.

The systematic development of creed formulation in Judaism, initiated by Maimonides, is also addressed by KELLNER. Demonstrating the background against which Maimonides elaborated his principles and tracing their pervasive influence, Kellner's study follows the responses to this challenge in the writings of Duran, Crescas, Albo, Abravanel, and a number of lesser-known figures down to the 16th century. This thoughtful book will appeal to philosophers and theologians alike, as it provides a successful argumentation that the dispute concerning the nature of dogmas or principles of faith "makes sense primarily in the context sufficiently influenced by Greek philosophical categories to understand the content of faith in propositional, not attitudinal terms." Kellner also addresses the reasons why philosophical reflection declined in popularity, and with it "Jewish dogmatics."

LASKER's study is a systematic investigation of Jewish anti-Christian literature. It examines the relationship between Judaism and Christianity from the perspective of the Jewish polemical literature of the Middle Ages that attempted to use tools of philosophy to cement faith and to refute accusations against it. Lasker carefully considers the various types of argument employed in a number of polemical sources. He examines the use of reason in religious debates and expounds various Jewish refutations of such key Christian doctrines as trinity, incarnation, transubstantiation, and virgin birth. The concluding chapter considers the role of philosophy in Jewish-Christian polemics and advances general conclusions about the nature of those polemics. With scholarly notes citing sources in their Hebrew and Arabic original, a comprehensive bibliography, and an index of citations, this is a masterly study of great benefit to anyone interested in philosophical critiques of Christianity, in Jewish-Christian relations, or in the differences between the two religions.

ESTHER I. SEIDEL

See also Philosophy: General; Philosophy: Modern

Philosophy: Modern

Baeck, Leo, *Das Wesen des Judentums,* 1905; translated by Victor Grubwieser and Leonard Pearl as *The Essence of Judaism,* London: Macmillan, 1936; revised by Irving Howe, New York: Schocken, 1948

Buber, Martin, *Ich und du,* 1923; translated by Walter Kaufmann as *I and Thou,* New York: Scribner, and Edinburgh: Clark, 1970

Cohen, Hermann, *Die Religion der Vernunft aus den Quellen des Judentums,* 1919; translated by Simon Kaplan as *Religion of Reason out of the Sources of Judaism,* introductory essay by Leo Strauss, New York: Ungar, 1972; new introductory essays by Steven S. Schwarzschild and Kenneth Seeskin, Atlanta, Georgia: Scholars Press, 1995

Fackenheim, Emil L., *To Mend the World: Foundations of Future Jewish Thought,* New York: Schocken, 1982; as *To Mend the World: Foundations of Post-Holocaust Jewish Thought,* New York: Schocken, 1989

Guttmann, Julius, *Die Philosophie des Judentums,* 1933; translated by David W. Silverman as *Philosophies of Judaism: The History of Jewish Philosophy from Biblical Times to Franz Rosenzweig,* New York: Holt, Rinehart and Winston, and London: Routledge, 1964; as *The Philosophy of Judaism: The History of Jewish Philosophy from Biblical Times to Franz Rosenzweig*, London and Northvale, New Jersey: Aronson, 1988

Heschel, Abraham, *God in Search of Man: A Philosophy of Judaism*, New York: Jewish Publication Society, 1955; London: Calder, 1956

Kaplan, Mordecai M., *Judaism as a Civilization: Toward a Reconstruction of American-Jewish Life*, New York: Macmillan, 1934; enlarged edition, New York: Reconstructionist Press, 1957

Levinas, Emmanuel, *Totalité et Infini: Essai sur l'extériorité*, 1961; translated by Alphonso Lingis as *Totality and Infinity: An Essay on Exteriority* (Duquesne Philosophical Series, vol. 24), Pittsburgh, Pennsylvania: Duquesne University Press, 1969

Mendelssohn, Moses, *Jerusalem, oder Über religiöse Macht und Judentum*, 1783; as *Jerusalem, or, On Religious Power and Judaism*, Hanover, New Hampshire: University Press of New England, 1983

Rosenzweig, Franz, *Der Stern der Erlösung*, 1921; translated by William W. Hallo as *The Star of Redemption*, New York: Holt, Rinehart and Winston, and London: Routledge and Kegan Paul, 1971

Spinoza, Benedictus de, *The Chief Works of Benedict de Spinoza*, vol. 1: *Tractatus Theologico-Politicus*, translated by R.H.M. Elwes, London: Bell, 1883, revised edition, 1900; as *The Chief Works of Benedict de Spinoza*, vol. 1: *Theologico-Political Treatise*, New York: Dover, 1951

Modern Jewish philosophy, sometimes referred to as modern Jewish thought, can be understood as a conversation between modern Jews and the modern world. The subjects of this conversation include both the philosophical and the Jewish, or the secular and the religious.

SPINOZA is sometimes considered the earliest exponent of modern Jewish philosophy, although this claim is debatable. On the one hand, this 17th-century philosopher lived before the "modern" era had clearly begun; he was excommunicated from the Jewish community, and he did not clearly present himself or his thought as Jewish. On the other hand, Spinoza's approach may be considered modern in its commitment to a rational exploration of theology; he was a Jew, and there are major Jewish influences in his thought. Unlike later modern Jewish philosophers from the 18th and 19th centuries who attempt to harmonize Jewish thought with Western philosophical notions in order to vindicate the rationality or morality of Judaism, Spinoza develops a religious philosophy that is grounded in the Hebrew Bible without explicitly advocating Judaism. Blending biblical exegesis and political treatise in order to argue for freedom of thought and religious practice, Spinoza rejects the medieval goal of harmonizing revelation and reason, for he contends that philosophy searches for truth, while religion promotes acceptance and obedience. He argues that the Bible has a social and pedagogical function as it teaches ethics to the pious masses; the philosophically minded person, however, can learn the "habit" of virtue through reason alone. Spinoza further rejects all anthropomorphic or androcentric ideas of God, insisting that God can only be conceptualized as the apotheosis of universal, rational law.

Living almost a century after Spinoza, MENDELSSOHN is often cited as the first modern Jewish philosopher. The most persuasive voice for Jewish emancipation of his time, Mendelssohn wrote for both Jewish and non-Jewish audiences. He argues that both religion and the state, when grounded in reason, share the same ultimate goal of promoting human happiness. Neither the state nor religion has the authority to constrain personal freedom of thought and conviction, though the state does have the right to prohibit atheism because atheism is injurious to the public good. This treatise is often polemical when it compares Judaism to Christianity. Disputing the assertion that Christianity liberates its adherents from the burdensome laws and rituals of Judaism, Mendelssohn argues that Christianity actually limits freedom of thought through its coercive dogmas, which deny that God's incontrovertible existence is discoverable through reason, independent of revelation. He argues that Christianity claims to be the exclusive bearer of revelation, but Judaism claims only that Jewish law is incumbent on the Jewish people, providing the Jewish path toward salvation. The corollary of this assertion is that Jews must be emancipated so they may be full members of society while continuing to observe that law that applies particularly to them.

Many modern Jewish philosophers have been inspired by COHEN's argument that what makes Jewish philosophy specifically Jewish is its concern for ethics. Strongly influenced by Immanuel Kant, Cohen argues that religions must be evaluated scientifically on the basis of their rationality. Accordingly, Judaism is conspicuous for its ideal moral conception of God that humans are expected to emulate. While Christianity has a modified form of monotheism that reifies the Holy Spirit, the essence of Judaism is moral and rational because of its emphasis on the ethical, as exemplified in the writings of the prophets. The rationality of Jewish texts is what gives them their qualitative edge. For Cohen, one's ethical relationship with other people is inseparable from one's relationship with God. The Spirit of Holiness (*ruah ha-kodesh*) between humans and God is a manifestation of their essential relation or correlation with one another. Humans become co-creators with God through the covenant of their relation. Cohen optimistically believes in human perfectibility and judges that it is humanity's task to transform the natural relationships among humans into ethical relationships where humans exist in loving, covenantal communion with one another.

Written and published decades before he was interned in the Theresienstadt concentration camp, BAECK's treatise is implicitly a polemical response to *The Essence of Christianity*, by liberal Protestant thinker Adolf Harnack. Baeck creates a typology of Judaism in which he outlines the essential elements of Jewish faith and existence, and he contends that the primacy of ethics in Judaism makes that religion unique. He argues that Jews understand themselves to be in continuity with other Jews in history, insisting that membership in this Jewish world places a person in the minority, often persecuted, always different. The intellectual, moral, and spiritual consciousness that emerges from this experience distinguishes Judaism from other religions. Intellectually, Jews have always needed to adapt in order to survive as a minority. Morally and spiritually, Judaism's ethical monotheism, as epitomized in the prophets, derives from the Jews' realization that moral law is absolute and that God is the source of that law. Baeck concludes that monotheism is the logical result of Judaism's ethical optimism: there is good; God is the source of good; humans have the power and potential to realize that good.

A dominant theme in modern Jewish philosophy is the phenomenological premise that the self exists in relationships and that relationships among humans can be correlated with relationships with God. BUBER's definitive and influential exploration of the theme of relationality is presented in three parts. In part one, Buber introduces the argument that all experience is relational, as he presents the ideal language of relationships. Buber differentiates among types of relationships by using the word pairs I/It and I/Thou. I/It relationships are mundane relationships, operating at the cognitive rather than the ethical level, while I/Thou relationships occur between persons; they are ethical, reciprocal, mutual, and transformative. Part two refines the discussion of relationality by philosophically examining relationships in terms of human history, which, Buber argues, demonstrates the continual natural devolution of I/Thou relationships into I/It relationships. In part three, Buber explores humanity's relationship with God, asserting that God, unlike people, cannot be reduced to an object in an I/It relationship. God is always Thou, and humans glimpse this ultimate relationship in all their other I/Thou relationships with persons. Thus, Buber sees interpersonal relations as extraordinarily empowering because they illuminate relations with the divine.

Like Buber, LEVINAS stresses that the ethical is located in the interpersonal relationship. While Buber contends that the I/Thou relationship is mutual, however, Levinas uses the model of the face-to-face encounter to stress the asymmetry of ethical relationships. Levinas understands the self to be in an obligatory relationship with a wholly other person, and he uses a phenomenological approach to present the Other as feminine, represented by the biblical archetype of "the poor, the widow, the orphan." While the vulnerability of this figure prompts the self to feel radical responsibility for the Other, Levinas argues that the Other is actually "higher" than the self. It is in fact the height of the Other, glimpsed as Infinity in the Face of the Other, that commands the self to act responsibly, as master and teacher. This relationship, then, extends to community when a third person enters into the relationship, for each human is capable of assuming the roles of self, Other, and third person. Thus, the responsibility the self experiences is also experienced by the Other or the third person. Like Buber, Levinas understands that one's relationship with other persons is the prerequisite to a relationship with God. He stresses that there can be no knowledge of the relationship with God except through the establishment of interpersonal relationships.

While its difficult prose has made it inaccessible to many readers, ROSENZWEIG's text is widely respected as one of the great works of modern Jewish philosophy. The treatise is divided into three parts, each of which is in turn divided into three books. Through a method he calls "absolute empiricism," Rosenzweig develops a philosophy based on experience, which he uses to disclose the three essential elements discussed in part one: God, world, and humans. Part two examines God's creation of the world; God's revelation to humans; and humanity's redemption of the world. Part three considers the roles of Jewish and Christian communities in redemption. Unlike Cohen and other rationalists, Rosenzweig gives extraordinary primacy to the experience of revelation. Defining revelation as God's loving encounter with the self, which is immediately recognized in the form of commands, he asserts that redemption occurs when a person who has experienced God's loving revelation turns toward others, breaking down the existential isolation that all persons experience. Like Buber and Levinas, Rosenzweig argues that the interpersonal relationship is the model of the relationship between God and humans.

FACKENHEIM's systematic response to the Holocaust considers and rejects the positions of both Jewish and non-Jewish philosophers as the author seeks a philosophical foundation for the spiritual, cultural, and historical survival of the Jewish people. He begins from a position of faith, asserting that the God of Israel acts in history and that Jewish history is marked by such epoch-making events as the exodus from Egypt, the revelation at Sinai, and the destruction of the First and Second Temples. In the modern period, Fackenheim identifies Emancipation, the Holocaust, and the creation of the State of Israel as epoch-making events of equal importance to those of biblical times, for these unique modern episodes similarly usher in new phases in Jewish history by changing the ways in which Jews reflect back and understand their own past. Most importantly, each epoch-making event imposes new demands on the Jewish people, as well as upon humanity as a whole. Fackenheim concludes with a passionate and compelling affirmation of the importance of *teshuvah* (literally, "return"), which he identifies as the underlying theme of this work. Fackenheim describes *teshuvah* throughout his text as the divine-human turning toward each other, and he contends that Jews and humans as a whole must not only turn toward God but they must also work toward *tikkun 'olam*, the Jewish mystical goal of mending the world.

A sequel to his work, *Man Is Not Alone: A Philosophy of Religion*, HESCHEL's popular and often poetic text is divided into three sections, God, Revelation, and Response. Heschel discusses religion and the Bible; examines humanity's relationship with God; and concludes that because Jews must be understood as living in a sacred or holy dimension, the preservation of Judaism is a spiritual act. Contending that the central message of the Hebrew Bible is that God expresses his love by choosing the Jewish people, Heschel proposes that Jews can only understand their common history, from biblical misfortunes to the horrors of Auschwitz, in terms of that divine loving choice. The Jewish history of survival, Heschel argues, teaches that one must move beyond ordinary standards of behavior in order to achieve genuine humanity; similarly, Jews need to be more than a people: they must be a holy people. Being chosen by God requires self-transcendence on the part of the individual and of the people as a whole.

KAPLAN's magnum opus focuses on the question of Jewish continuity. Rather than defining Judaism as a religion, Kaplan characterizes it as the evolving religious civilization of the Jewish people, and he proposes a philosophy for understanding and developing the next stage of this civilization. Asserting that Jewish civilization includes those religious and cultural features that are essentially Jewish (language, history, folk arts, social structures, spiritual ideals, and standards of conduct), Kaplan states that the protection and promotion of these features are essential to the continuity of Judaism both in the diaspora and in a Jewish homeland. However, Kaplan does not think that Judaism need be homogenous, as no single pattern of Jewish life is adequate to meet the needs of diverse Jewries. He argues that the future continuity of Jewish civilization cannot depend on blind acceptance of traditional beliefs; instead, it must rest on the vital study of, and interest in, those elements of Jewish literature, such as the Torah and Talmud, that are central to traditional belief. Repudiating the doctrine of being the chosen people as an elitist notion that leads to bigotry, Kaplan advocates the reconstruction of Judaism through an engagement with evolved intellectual, socioeconomic, political, ethical, and religiocultural ideals.

GUTTMANN's volume presents both the earliest major scholarly analysis of modern Jewish philosophy and Guttmann's own modernist philosophical position. The third and last section of the text deals exclusively with modern Jewish philosophy, examining the views of well-known thinkers, such as Mendelssohn, Cohen, and Rosenzweig, as well as less familiar figures, such as Solomon Formstecher, Nachman Krochmal, and Moritz Lazarus. Guttmann places all these thinkers in the wider context of modern Jewish philosophy, identifying their original contributions to the field as well as their intellectual debts to other philosophers. The result is an insightful overview of the dominant themes of Jewish philosophy prior to the 20th century.

DEIDRE BUTLER

See also Philosophy: General; Philosophy: Medieval

Pilgrimages *see* Veneration of Saints, Pilgrimages, and Holy Places

Piyyut

Elbogen, Ismar, *Jewish Liturgy: A Comprehensive History*, translated by Raymond P. Scheindlin based on the author's *Der judische Gottesdienst in seiner geschichtlichen Entwicklung* (1913) and the annotated Hebrew translation *ha-Tefilah be-Yisra'el be-hitpathutah ha-historit* (1972), Philadelphia: Jewish Publication Society, 1993
Hoffman, Lawrence A., *The Canonization of the Synagogue Service*, Notre Dame, Indiana: University of Notre Dame Press, 1979
Petuchowski, Jakob J., "The Poetry of the Synagogue," in *Literature of the Synagogue*, edited by Petuchowski and Joseph Heinemann, New York: Behrman House, 1975
Petuchowski, Jakob J., *Theology and Poetry* (Littman Library of Jewish Civilization), London and Boston: Routledge and Kegan Paul, 1977
Scheindlin, Raymond P. (compiler), *The Gazelle: Medieval Hebrew Poems on God, Israel, and the Soul*, Philadelphia: Jewish Publication Society, 1991
Spiegel, Shalom, "On Medieval Hebrew Poetry," in *The Jews: Their History, Culture, and Religion*, edited by Louis Finkelstein, 3rd edition, New York: Harper, 1960
Weinberger, Leon, *Jewish Hymnography* (Littman Library of Jewish Civilization), London and Portland, Oregon: Vallentine Mitchell, 1998

Hebrew devotional poetry, known as *piyyut* (plural *piyyutim*), is an important part of the synagogue service. Liturgical poems were written to be recited during the service and follow specific forms and deal with specific themes. From the inception of the piyyut tradition and through medieval times, piyyutim were written by payyetanim, professional poets who were also cantors and rabbis. Their poetic creations were recited publicly in the communal prayer service. This tradition was widely practiced and each community composed unique piyyutim. The use of religious poetry in the synagogue service continues today, but public recital of new and original verse is a custom that has all but vanished.

Since recorded information about ancient prayer services is scarce, the exact beginning of piyyut is unknown. Many issues concerning the early use of piyyut in the service remain problematic. For this reason, several theories exist explaining the initiation of piyyut.

For a general overview of the evolution of piyyut, ELBOGEN's comprehensive history of Jewish liturgical life is ideal. Originally published in German in 1913, this English translation includes notes from the 1972 Hebrew edition. The notes correct and update the original text with scholarship based primarily on discoveries from the Cairo Genizah. New datings and supplementary information on poets and their work contribute significantly to the chapters on piyyut.

Elbogen analyzes the development of piyyut and reviews the major liturgical poets of Palestine, Christian Europe, and Spain. Concerning the origins of piyyut, he distinguishes two distinct periods—a period in which prayer was established and a period for the development of piyyut. The fixed standard prayers were established at the close of the talmudic period, and piyyut developed later as an adornment to the prayers. In addition, Elbogen believes that piyyutim were never used as actual prayers but were attachments recited in addition to the standard prayers.

SPIEGEL, whose narrative style makes for easy reading, discusses the origins of synagogue poetry, illustrates the way that piyyutim thematically correspond with the prayers, and reviews the major liturgical poets and their contributions. Ascribing great antiquity to piyyut, he argues, in contrast to Elbogen, that standard prayer and synagogue poetry developed simultaneously. The original choice for liturgical poetry was the Psalms, but communities felt they had new things to say. Ancient rabbis desired to preserve an element of spontaneity in the prayers and paved the way for new liturgical poetry. During the Middle Ages some rabbinic authorities discouraged the addition of piyyutim. However, the charm and excitement inherent in the addition of new piyyutim to the fixed formula of the synagogue service overcame these objections, and this freer form of religious expression flourished.

HOFFMAN focuses on the medieval controversy concerning the use of piyyutim. Citing geonic sources from the ninth and tenth centuries, he contextualizes the issue as one which was, in fact, part of the struggle between Palestinians and Babylonians for hegemony in the Jewish world. The objections to piyyut, according to Hoffman, reflect the conflict between Palestinian custom and Babylonian authority. Since piyyutim were Palestinian in origin, Babylonian authorities attempted to bar their use. The resistance of the geonim finally ended with Saadia Gaon, who included Palestinian piyyutim as well as his own compositions in the prayer book that he compiled.

By far the most comprehensive and thorough overview, in English, of the entire history of piyyut is WEINBERGER. Arranged historically and by region, the book outlines the innovations of each period, analyzing the particular contributions of the individual poets in terms of language and style. The development of different genres of synagogue poetry is clearly laid out, with explanations of the function, theme, and placement of each type of poem in the liturgy. Of particular interest are the chapters on the poets of Byzantium, the Ottoman Empire, and the Karaite community. The inclusion of this material is an important contribution.

A close examination of individual piyyutim can be found in PETUCHOWSKI (1975), which includes a selection of 15 piyyutim translated into English. The translations are literal rather than poetic, shying away from recreating the original poetic styles. This exciting selection of poems from different ages is arranged chronologically; it begins with an example of an ancient piyyut from the Cairo Genizah and ends with an example from 12th-century France. Each poem is introduced with biographical data about the poet and a discussion of the poem's liturgical use. Notes on each poem comment on biblical and literary allusions in the text. In addition, the essay provides a succinct summary of the Hebrew scholarship on piyyut, posing some major questions and explaining the views of Mirsky, Schirmann, and Fleischer.

PETUCHOWSKI (1977) assembles a selection of synagogue poems that express "unconventional and daring theological ideas." Each poem is preceded by a brief history of the religious concept it conveys. The Hebrew poem is followed by an English translation and commentary. Subjects such as anthropomorphic descriptions of God, God's suffering, and Israel's redemption are considered. This study reveals the varied theological views expressed and tolerated in the long-standing "Orthodox liturgical tradition."

The piyyutim of Golden Age Spain ushered in a new approach to Hebrew language. Before this period, poets made extensive use of biblical quotations and midrashic allusions. In Spain, however, the language of the Bible was freed from its original context and used to express new themes. SCHEINDLIN presents a selection of these poems, with each Hebrew piyyut set on the page facing that of its English translation. A short explanatory essay follows each poem. These poems amply illustrate the degree of cultural integration achieved in the Golden Age. Golden Age poets successfully merged Jewish literary tradition with the science and philosophy of the surrounding Arabic culture and thereby created a new type of synagogue poetry. Surprisingly, the same style and language utilized in Hebrew secular love poems was also used by the Spanish poets to convey a religious message in sacred poetry. Scheindlin divides the poems

into two groups. In one, romantic images are used to depict God's relationship with the collective community of Israel. In the other, this imagery is used to express the individual's love for God.

NEHAMA EDINGER

Poetry: Biblical

Alter, Robert, *The Art of Biblical Poetry*, New York: Basic Books, 1985; Edinburgh: Clark, 1990

Berlin, Adele, *The Dynamics of Biblical Parallelism*, Bloomington: Indiana University Press, 1985

Berlin, Adele, *Biblical Poetry through Medieval Jewish Eyes* (Indiana Studies in Biblical Literature), Bloomington: Indiana University Press, 1991

Coogan, Michael David, *Stories from Ancient Canaan*, Philadelphia: Westminster, 1978

Freedman, David Noel, *Pottery, Poetry, and Prophecy: Studies in Early Hebrew Poetry*, Winona Lake, Indiana: Eisenbrauns, 1980

Hrushovski, Benjamin, "Note on the Systems of Hebrew Versification," in *The Penguin Book of Hebrew Verse*, edited by T. Carmi, New York: Viking, and London: Lane, 1981

Kugel, James, *The Idea of Biblical Poetry: Parallelism and Its History*, New Haven, Connecticut: Yale University Press, 1981

Lowth, Robert, *Lectures on the Sacred Poetry of the Hebrews*, London: Johnson, 1787; new edition, New York: Leavitt, 1829; 4th edition, London: Tegg, 1839

Parker, Simon (editor), *Ugaritic Narrative Poetry* (Writings from the Ancient World, vol. 9), Atlanta, Georgia: Scholars Press, 1997

Petersen, David and Kent Richards, *Interpreting Hebrew Poetry* (Guides to Biblical Scholarship, Old Testament Series), Minneapolis, Minnesota: Fortress, 1992

Watson, Wilfred G.E., *Classical Hebrew Poetry: A Guide to Its Techniques* (Journal for the Study of the New Testament Supplement Series, 26), Sheffield, South Yorkshire: JSOT, 1984, 2nd edition, 1986

The modern study of biblical poetry is generally thought to begin with the work of LOWTH, professor of poetry at Oxford and later bishop of London. Lowth identified "parallelism," rather than strict meter familiar from classical verse, as the main structure of biblical poetry. He showed that most lines of ancient Hebrew verse consist of two or three members (or half-lines) that echo each other on a semantic level. Lowth's identification of three types of parallelism in many ways continues to set the agenda. These categories are: synonymous parallelism, in which the second half-line echoes the first; antithetical, in which the second opposes the first; and synthetic, in which the nature of the semantic parallel is not obvious.

Subsequent scholars have attempted to find other structures that work with or even instead of parallelism. Some maintain that biblical poems use a stress or accent-based meter, in which each half-line has a set number of stressed syllables; others (especially FREEDMAN) count all syllables (stressed and unstressed), arguing that each line contains two members with an equal number of syllables. Successive lines, however, do not necessarily have the same number of syllables. These metrical explanations of Hebrew verse are vitiated by the lack of definite knowledge regarding Hebrew pronunciation during the biblical period and by the failure of biblical authors to follow the rules decreed by these scholars. Indeed, the scholars in question are frequently compelled to emend texts or remove "prose accretions" in order to demonstrate that their theories work (see especially the discussion in Kugel).

HRUSHOVSKI emphasizes that parallelism involves not only semantic counterparts (which at times fail to appear, as Lowth was loath to admit; note his catch-all third category) but also equivalences of syntax, accent, and phonology. In light of the latter equivalences, the attempts to find a strict metrical basis for biblical poetry fall away; they are revealed to be an occasional result of parallelism of accent.

BERLIN (1985) applies perspectives from theoretical linguistics to the study of parallelism (primarily, but not exclusively, in poetic texts), demonstrating that parallelism often exists within a line's deep grammatical structure. Like Hrushovski, she notes the existence of phonological parallels involving assonance and sound-play. These other forms of parallelism show the phenomenon to be more prevalent than some scholars have recognized and allow more meaningful substitutes for Lowth's synthetic category.

In the first chapters of their respective books, KUGEL and ALTER emphasize the dynamic nature of the parallel line, in which the second half not only reiterates the first but also intensifies or specifies it. Thus they move decisively beyond Lowth in arguing that parallel lines are forceful because of their attempts to move beyond their own parallelism. However much they agree on the dynamic nature of parallelism in their highly readable yet sophisticated discussions, Kugel and Alter debate the meaning of the term poetry itself. Alter finds the term useful, but Kugel argues that no clear distinction exists between prose and poetry in biblical texts; rather, the texts usually called "poetry" display certain rhetorical features with great regularity (e.g., in the Book of Psalms), while the passages normally labeled as "prose" display those features only sporadically (e.g., most examples of narrative prose in Genesis). Other texts lie in the middle of a continuum (e.g., many prophetic texts, such as parts of Ezekiel, the classification of which as prose or poetry has been an area of disagreement among scholars; and texts such as Genesis 1:1–2:4a that are unusually rhythmic and majestic, though not quite as regular in their parallelism as a psalm). The attempt to categorize these "in-between" texts as either prose or poetry is, according to Kugel, so much striving after the wind.

In the remainder of his book, Alter proceeds to offer very sensitive readings of ancient Hebrew poems from the Book of Psalms, wisdom literature, and prophecy. In these readings (which show affinities to New Criticism) Alter richly demonstrates the relevance of his observations on the structure of the poetic line from the outset of his book. In spite of their own linguistic sensitivity, it should be noted that neither Kugel nor Alter requires knowledge of Hebrew on their readers' part.

The remainder of Kugel's book traces the history of the poetics of biblical poetry—how ancient, medieval, and some modern readers have understood or forgotten the system of ancient Hebrew poetry Kugel describes at the outset of his book. Another detailed discussion of medieval Jewish approaches to biblical poetry, including precursors to Lowth's theory, is found in BERLIN (1991), which contains a history of scholarship and analyses of medieval Jewish texts in relationship to their own historical settings and to modern work on poetry. In the second half of this book, Berlin provides translations with introductions of several important medieval Jewish texts that provide theoretical discussions of biblical poetry.

While the amount of scholarship on ancient Hebrew poetry is vast, students are aided by the existence of several helpful overviews of the field. PETERSEN and RICHARDS have provided an admirable and readable introductory work. A far more detailed discussion (yet well organized and hence readily usable) is found in WATSON. Watson's book is outstanding not only for its comprehensive review of the field and its copious examples but also for its attention to the strong points of contact between biblical and other ancient Near Eastern poetry, especially that of ancient Ugarit (a topic treated to some extent by Kugel and Freedman as well). Translations of Ugaritic poems, whose connections to biblical poetry are readily evident, are found in PARKER and in COOGAN; the former also contains the Ugaritic texts and detailed notes, while the latter's introductions are geared more toward the reader with no prior knowledge.

BENJAMIN D. SOMMER

Poetry: Medieval Hebrew

Brann, Ross, *The Compunctious Poet: Cultural Ambiguity and Hebrew Poetry in Muslim Spain,* Baltimore: Johns Hopkins University Press, 1991

Carmi, T. (editor and translator), *The Penguin Book of Hebrew Verse,* Harmondsworth, Middlesex, and New York: Penguin, 1981

Hamori, Andras, *On the Art of Medieval Arabic Literature,* Princeton, New Jersey: Princeton University Press, 1974

Pagis, Dan, *Hebrew Poetry of the Middle Ages and the Renaissance,* Berkeley: University of California Press, 1991

Scheindlin, Raymond, *Wine, Women, and Death: Medieval Hebrew Poems on the Good Life,* Philadelphia: Jewish Publication Society, 1986

Scheindlin, Raymond, *The Gazelle: Medieval Hebrew Poems on God, Israel, and the Soul,* Philadelphia: Jewish Publication Society, 1991

Schippers, Arie, *Spanish Hebrew Poetry and the Arab Literary Tradition: Arabic Themes in Hebrew Andalusian Poetry,* Leiden and New York: Brill, 1994

Schirmann, Jefim, "The Function of the Hebrew Poet in Medieval Spain," *Jewish Social Studies,* 16, 1954

Schirmann, Jefim, "Problems in the Study of Post-Biblical Hebrew Poetry," *Proceedings of the Israel Academy of Sciences and Humanities*, 2(12), 1967

Schirmann, Jefim, "Introduction," in reprint of Israel Davidson's *Otsar ha-shirah veha-piyut: Thesaurus of Medieval Hebrew Poetry*, vol. 1, New York: Ktav, 1970

Stern, Samuel Miklos, *Hispano-Arabic Strophic Poetry: Studies*, selected and edited by L.P. Harvey, Oxford: Clarendon, 1974

Scholarship on the Hebrew poetry of the High Middle Ages typically stresses one of three topics: continuity with older Hebrew liturgical poetry, the innovative aspects of the new kind of Hebrew poetry written in Arabic meter that was created and developed in Muslim Spain, or the history of Hebrew poetry in Italy.

CARMI's excellent bilingual anthology of Hebrew poems from the Bible to the present time offers in the introduction a general perspective on the history of Hebrew poetry. The author underlines that poems have been written in Hebrew virtually without interruption for 3,000 years, moving from one center to another and usually assimilating the thematic and prosodic conventions of the surrounding culture. He describes the flowering of liturgical poetry in Palestine and the radical innovations of the Andalusian school and its continuation in Christian Spain, among other distinct historical periods of Hebrew literature. A short but very adequate description of the characteristics of poetry in the Middle Ages is complemented by a "note on medieval Hebrew genres," limited to the main types of liturgical poetry as well as a "note on the systems of Hebrew versification," written by B. Hrushovski. The selection of poems is very judicious, and the translation, in prose, reproduces the content with precision and without being unduly literal.

Schirmann was the teacher of several generations of scholars in the field of medieval Hebrew poetry. Most of his works are written in Hebrew, but the three articles selected here are among his most famous contributions in English. SCHIRMANN (1970) deals with the emergence of research on Hebrew poetry, particularly during the 19th and early 20th centuries. He offers an appreciation of the work of pioneers such as Zunz, Delitzsch, Dukes, Kaempf, Sachs, Geiger, and Luzzatto, and he discusses the significance of the great reference work prepared by Davidson, indexing more than 36,000 Hebrew poems. SCHIRMANN (1967) is a reflection on the main difficulties faced by scholars of medieval Hebrew poetry, such as its chronological and geographical diffuseness, the number of manuscripts, the lack of critical editions, and the need for knowledge of many ancillary subjects. He argues the need for describing the history of Hebrew literature from a new viewpoint, clarifying the milieu in which each poet lived, his cultural inheritance, and the special traits that are attributable to his character and the influences to which he was exposed. SCHIRMANN (1954) was the first important sociological study of Hebrew poetry. It explores the ethos of commitment to poetry as a profession and clarifies the origins and circumstances of the poets and their readers and hearers. Also treated are the differences between secular and liturgical poetry, the phenomenon of wandering poets, the relationship between the poet and his patron, the role of music in the recitation of poetry, and the collection and dissemination of poems.

PAGIS's posthumously published book includes three lectures on different technical aspects of medieval and Renaissance poetry: individuality and stylization; imagery; the conviction that poetry is not only a game but also an essential vehicle for expression and characterization; and the merging of convention and experience in the premodern Hebrew love poetry of Spain and Italy. As in Schirmann's studies, Pagis underscores here the confluence of tradition and innovation in this poetry and its readiness to absorb foreign influences, whether Arabic or, later, Spanish and Italian. Pagis was one of the great experts on medieval Hebrew secular poetry, as amply demonstrated by his many books and articles in Hebrew. Even though the volume under discussion does not provide a systematic exposition, his erudition and refined sensibilities are evident in these interesting English lectures, full of brilliant, incisive remarks and well-chosen examples.

Scheindlin elaborates a new image of the Hebrew Andalusian poets, opening fresh paths for research in the comparative fields of Arabic and Jewish poetry. SCHEINDLIN (1986) contains a selection of poems written in those circles of "wealthy Jews, thoroughly educated in Arabic language and literature . . . who were also pious, learned, and fiercely loyal to Jewish interests." Accepted in Muslim society, "the price was acculturation, not conversion." These Jews assimilated the Arabic literary tradition and synthesized it with their own literary heritage. The poets, according to Scheindlin, kept religion and social life carefully separated in their work. Their courtly poems, about conventional themes, deal with the pleasures of life such as wine parties, love, and desire, or are reflections on the brevity of life and display "the aristocratic ideals of harmony, balance, and control in the medium of rhythm and rhetoric." After an informative general introduction, each section presents the peculiarities of a particular genre, and there is a bilingual selection of 31 poems featuring beautiful translations and brief commentaries that afford easy reading even for nonspecialist readers.

SCHEINDLIN (1991) complements the first book and deals with topics related to Hebrew-Andalusian synagogal poetry. Both Scheindlin's works have in common a profound comprehension of the Arabic and the Jewish cultural world of the Middle Ages, and the two books share a similar approach. *The Gazelle* examines the introduction of Arabic secular imagery into the closed world of Jewish liturgical prayer in al-Andalus. The author asks himself how the same poets could write both classes of poetry—secular poems for Jewish courtiers and liturgical poems for the synagogue. From a very modern perspective, Scheindlin poses the question of how much non-Jewish culture a Jew could in conscience adopt in the Middle Ages and to what extent he could arrive at a kind of cultural symbiosis, belonging at the same time to Israel and to the international class of intellectuals. The introduction, dealing with the spiritual atmosphere and the innovations of the Spanish school of synagogal poetry, is followed by two main sections, about "God and Israel" and "God and the Soul," with an annotated translation of 30 liturgical poems written by Solomon ibn Gabirol, Moses ibn Ezra, Judah Halevi, Isaac ibn Ghayyat, Levi Altabban, and Abraham ibn Ezra. The exquisite precision of his translation is counterbalanced by a technical, enlightening, well-elaborated explanation of the poems, which takes into consideration not only the subject matter but also the literary form of the compositions. The poems are interpreted with reference to the spiritual atmosphere of the epoch, and frequent comparison is made to the Arabic models.

BRANN offers a highly original panorama of the spiritual and cultural atmosphere in which the Andalusian Hebrew poets lived among their Muslim neighbors. Two processes, urbanization and Arabization, transformed the Jews under medieval Islam. Secular Hebrew poetry became one of the most significant manifestations of the "cultural *convivencia*" for Jews and Muslims in al-Andalus and for Jews and Christians in Christian Spain; it may be described as a Hebrew subcultural adaptation of Arabic poetry carried out by the so-called courtier-rabbis, Jews educated both in their own tradition and in the dominant Arabic culture of the court. According to Brann, Hebrew secular poetry represents the "fusion of Arabic prosody, form, and style with biblical Hebrew diction and imagery." The main part of Brann's book is devoted to the study of the topos of the "compunctious poet": "it serves as an emblem of the poet's contradictory attitudes toward poetry and as a sign of the ambiguities and conflicts inherent in their culture." The poets lived in two cultural worlds governed by systems of values that were very different and sometimes opposed; they tried to be true to Jewish tradition without renouncing the ideals of their Arabic education. This cultural ambiguity is reflected in the curious attitude of the repentant poet, who regrets in his old age having composed poetry in Arabic style when young but never ceases to write. The topic, also known among Arab poets, is examined in the Jewish tradition, in particular among great Andalusian poets such as Moses ibn Ezra and Judah Halevi, and in other poets of the Christian kingdoms, such as Shem Tov ibn Falaquera, Meshullam de Piera, and Todros Abulafia. Brann's very suggestive book can serve as an excellent introduction to the world of Hebrew-Spanish poetry for the uninitiated and has much that is new to say to readers at all levels of expertise.

STERN was, prior to his early death in 1972, one of the most outstanding scholars of Arabic and Hebrew strophic poetry (*muwashshah*), and he revolutionized knowledge of the field by deciphering the Romance final refrains (*kharja*) found in some of these compositions. This volume, which appeared after his death, contains some of his periodical articles in English and an abridgment of his unpublished doctoral dissertation on strophic poetry in al-Andalus. Even with the passing of the years, his observations on the history of this kind of poetry originating in Muslim Spain, his readings of the Romance *kharjas*, his studies on a more popular kind of Arabic strophic poetry, the *zajal*, and his reflections about the possible connections between the Islamic literary world and the literary atmosphere of medieval Western Europe remain indispensable for any reader interested in the field.

HAMORI provides a general study of some essential aspects of medieval Arabic poetry, and his penetrating, acute, and delightful exposition of the character and evolution of the genres and techniques used by the Arabic poets is a great help for understanding Andalusian Hebrew poetry, too, written as it was in the same cultural atmosphere. In his analysis of the

theme of time, Hamori includes a fine commentary on a Hebrew descriptive poem by Samuel ibn Nagrella ha-Nagid. The book is written for the student of literature as well as for the specialist in Arabic or Hebrew, and it deals with the transformations from the sixth to the tenth century in poetic genres and in the poets' attitudes toward time and society. Some questions about poetic technique and methods employed in the composition of prose also are addressed.

SCHIPPERS offers a survey of the poetic themes and motifs occurring in Hebrew Andalusian poetry that were borrowed from Arabic literature, in particular during the 11th century. He concentrates on the work of the four main Hebrew poets of the Golden Age—Samuel ha-Nagid, Solomon ibn Gabirol, Moses ibn Ezra, and Judah Halevi—and he presents Hebrew poetry as an imitation of Arabic poetic genres, images, and motifs in a revived Classical Hebrew language. The study begins with some consideration of convention, imitation, and originality, followed by a sketch of the social and historical situation of Jews and Muslims in Spain. The main part of the book deals with the comparison of the genres employed in Hebrew and those of Arabic poetry: the themes of wine, love, and nature, descriptions of war, laudatory compositions, elegies, and poems about poetry itself. The underlying idea is that the Hebrew poets were in essence not very different from the Arabic poets, lived in the same cultural atmosphere, and employed similar techniques, even if they had some distinctive views and methods. The war poems of Samuel ha-Nagid and the elegies also have many parallels in Arabic poetry. The author underlines how oriental Arabic poets, such as al-Mutanabbi, exerted a great influence in Muslim Spain, serving as models even for the Hebrew poets, although each poet showed his own originality in his personal elaboration of the standard topics.

ANGEL SÁENZ-BADILLOS

Poetry: Modern Hebrew

Halkin, Simon, *Modern Hebrew Literature*, New York: Schocken, 1950, new edition, 1970

Jacobson, David C., *Does David Still Play before You? Israeli Poetry and the Bible*, Detroit, Michigan: Wayne State University Press, 1997

Kohn, Murray, *The Voice of My Blood Cries Out: The Holocaust as Reflected in Hebrew Poetry*, New York: Shengold, 1979

Kronfeld, Chana, *On the Margins of Modernism: Decentering Literary Dynamics* (Contraversions, 2), Berkeley: University of California Press, 1996

Preil, Gabriel, *Israeli Poetry in Peace and War* (Herzl Institute Pamphlet, no. 13), New York: Herzl, 1959

The rise of modern Hebrew poetry is generally associated with the emergence of a secular Jewish culture among Eastern European Jewry in the 1880s. This development principally manifested itself in the circle of Ahad Ha'am, who advocated "cultural Zionism"—a movement that promoted the revival of Jewish literary creativity in the Hebrew language. The movement bore its first fruit in the highly original verse of Hayyim Nahman Bialik and Saul Tchernichovsky, who quickly established themselves as the leading poetic voices of the Hebrew revival. By the 1920s, the center of poetic creativity had shifted to Palestine, where Hebrew was already established as the language of daily discourse, thus becoming a natural medium for poetic expression. Nathan Alterman, Leah Goldberg, and Abraham Shlonsky were leading poets of this period, and their verse mirrored a new Jewish identity taking root in its original homeland. When the State of Israel was declared in 1948, Hebrew poetry became an integral part of Israeli cultural life, reflecting the nation's struggles, triumphs, and contradictions. In recent years, the poet Yehuda Amichai has been widely regarded as Israel's unofficial poet laureate, perhaps because he manages to capture in his modernist verse the conflicting sides of contemporary Israeli life. His poems combine heroic defiance, subdued idealism, and existential doubt, while simultaneously reflecting the spiritual realities of an often turbulent history.

HALKIN provides a good introduction to the study of modern Hebrew poetry, devoting almost a third of his book to a discussion of the social and political forces that led to the creation of a distinctly modern literature in Hebrew. Halkin proceeds both chronologically and thematically, linking the work of some of the first modern Hebrew poets through, for example, their common tendency to portray the individual Jew as physically heroic. He then explores some of the experimental features of the verse written in the pioneering era that preceded the founding of the State of Israel. Chapters seven through nine discuss the various ways in which Hebrew poets responded in verse to the tragic fate of the Jews in Nazi Europe, and the book concludes with a penetrating analysis of the prevalence of religious themes in modern Hebrew poetry by apparently secular poets. This latter discussion is one of the most valuable aspects of the book, for it treats a subject that has received little attention from other literary historians.

Although short on words, PREIL's book is long on content. In a mere 33 pages, he provides an incisive analysis of some of the major themes in modern Hebrew poetry. The first half of the essay discusses the work of three poets—Uri Zvi Greenberg, Goldberg, and S. Shalom—and cites the work of such major influences as William Butler Yeats and Walt Whitman in order to place the three authors in a larger context. In the second half, Preil compares Hebrew poetry written during Israel's War of Independence in 1948 to similar texts composed in other difficult times, including critical moments of the biblical era and of the Jewish experience in medieval Spain. Through this comparison, Preil brings to light the ways in which modern poets both absorb and transform the traditions of earlier generations.

KRONFELD applies postmodernist literary theory to modern Hebrew poetry. Concerned with the apparent contradictions in such notions as "marginality" and "canonization" as they apply to belles lettres, Kronfeld attempts to redefine the terms through her study of Hebrew (and Yiddish) poetry. The book is marked by substantial use of technical language, but Kronfeld's interpretations of individual poems by writers such as Esther Raab, David Fogel, and Amichai are both discerning and instructive.

JACOBSON's book focuses on the use of biblical sources in modern Hebrew poetry. His study is limited primarily to lyrical poetry written after Israeli independence, from the late 1940s to the early 1990s. Dividing the chapters along topical lines, Jacobson concentrates on contemporary issues such as the Israeli-Arab conflict and the tension between religion and secularism in Israel. Jacobson's book has a clear political agenda, seeking to dispute "the assumption of many religious Jewish Israelis that territorial compromise with the Arabs is in violation of biblical teachings." Unfortunately, the polemical nature of this book detracts from its usefulness as an objective source, marring what is otherwise a thorough and enlightening analysis of biblical motifs in modern Israeli poetry.

KOHN investigates how modern Hebrew poets have responded in verse to the destruction of European Jewry during World War II. He identifies the poems according to "psychological" categories and divides his chapters accordingly, employing such headings as "The State of Shock," "Despair," and "Confession." Of particular value are the citations from poems written by lesser-known Hebrew poets from within the ghettos of Nazi Europe. Unfortunately, Kohn cites only portions of the poems under discussion, rather than presenting works in their entirety. This approach leaves the reader uncertain as to whether Kohn's interpretations are sustainable. This book also lacks an index, which, given the admirable breadth of material that Kohn treats, would have made it considerably more useful for reference purposes.

SHARON GREEN

Poetry: American Jewish

Bloom, Harold, "The Sorrows of American Jewish Poetry," *Commentary*, 53(3), March 1972

Gitenstein, R. Barbara, *Apocalyptic Messianism and Contemporary Jewish-American Poetry* (SUNY Series in Modern Jewish Literature and Culture), Albany: State University of New York Press, 1986

Gitenstein, R. Barbara, "American-Jewish Poetry: An Overview," in *Handbook of American-Jewish Literature: An Analytical Guide to Topics, Themes, and Sources*, edited by Lewis Fried, New York: Greenwood, 1988

Hollander, John, "The Question of Jewish American Poetry," *Tikkun*, 3(3), May/June 1988

Liptzin, Solomon, *The Jew in American Literature*, New York: Bloch, 1966

Mersand, Joseph, *Traditions in American Literature: A Study of Jewish Characters and Authors*, New York: Modern Chapbooks, 1932

Pacernick, Gary, *Sing a New Song: American Jewish Poetry since the Holocaust* (Brochure Series of the American

(Routledge History of World Philosophies, vol. 2), edited by Daniel H. Frank and Oliver Leaman, New York and London: Routledge, 1997

Sharkansky, Ira, *Israel and Its Bible: A Political Analysis* (Garland Reference Library of Social Science, vol. 1031), New York and London: Garland, 1996

Walzer, Michael, *Exodus and Revolution,* New York: Basic Books, 1985

Wildavsky, Aaron, *The Nursing Father: Moses as a Political Leader,* University: University of Alabama Press, 1984

Wildavsky, Aaron, *Assimilation Versus Separation: Joseph the Administrator and the Politics of Religion in Biblical Israel,* New Brunswick, New Jersey: Transaction, 1993

It is natural to begin with the question of whether there is any such thing as Jewish political theory. If by this term we would designate a uniform body or tradition of political philosophy, then the answer would have to be, "No." Jewish sources are rich in political insight and teaching, but they do not express that teaching in unambiguous political-philosophical treatises corresponding to Plato's *Republic* or Aristotle's *Politics*. Political teaching can be found in the Bible, in the aggadic and halakhic writings of the rabbis, in medieval philosophy and commentary, as well as in other settings. Why no political-philosophical treatises as such?

MELAMED, in his useful survey of medieval and Renaissance Jewish political thought, suggests that the writing of a treatise presupposes the distinctiveness of the political realm vis-à-vis other fields of human endeavor, as well as vis-à-vis the spiritual realm. This was possible in a Christian setting where a City of Man was juxtaposed to a City of God (and consequently politics could be distinguished as a discrete and inferior dimension), but not in a Jewish (or Muslim) setting where revelation was purported to legislate for the whole of life. Revelation, given in the form of a holy law, has as its object the creation of a holy commonwealth. Revelation is thus fundamentally political in Judaism: it intends an ideal Jewish polity as its goal.

In a sense, then, Jewish political theory is less a discrete body of thought within Judaism than simply a way of understanding Jewish thought. Whenever Jewish thinkers try to apply biblical and rabbinic teaching to the classic dilemmas of social life (individual vs. community, rights vs. duties, consent vs. dissent, grounds of legitimate authority, power and its uses, forms of governance, etc.), they are somehow employing "Jewish political theory." Yet this claim may seem too broad, for it fails to distinguish political theory from ethics or law. Although these fields of inquiry certainly overlap, some distinction is possible. For moderns, a distinguishing factor has been that political theory has had to do with the state. For Jews, however, this referent is not necessarily helpful. Jews have long lived in political communities far more compact and with considerably less power than states. Yet Jews have continued to reflect thoughtfully about what the meaning of their political experience has been. Jewish political theory is concerned with political institutions, thought, and behavior in a variety of political contexts, not just in states.

As a point of departure for constituting a broadly inclusive yet distinctive Jewish political theory, let us turn to a remark-able phenomenon: the return to the Bible as a source of political wisdom. Modern political theory began, in a sense, with the rejection of Scripture as an authoritative source of political teaching. Early modern political philosophers such as Thomas Hobbes, John Locke, and Baruch de Spinoza had to engage the Bible (the common coin of intellectual discourse in their cultures), but they did so largely to dismiss it. They wanted to found a new political teaching on a "scientific" basis. In the works considered in this article we have a late modern reversal of this early modern abandonment. Scripture, studied through the lens of traditional Jewish commentary, once again receives a politically sensitive reading. Let us consider the interpretations of four leading political scientists who, in returning to Scripture, have returned to their Jewish roots.

Wildavsky's works arise from the twin convictions that the Bible has much to say to modern political scientists and that modern political science can illuminate biblical teaching. WILDAVSKY (1984) sees the Torah as, in effect, a treatise on how Moses learned to become a leader. As a theorist, Wildavsky argues that leadership is tied to the political culture or regime in which leaders operate. Moses operated under four successive regimes, finally crafting a mixed regime of equality and hierarchy as the ideal political framework for his people. Wildavsky seeks to show how existing political theorizing on leadership can learn from Mosaic teaching and how biblical study can be enriched by attention to the political teaching embedded in the text.

WILDAVSKY (1993) contrasts the revolutionary statesman, Moses, with Joseph. Joseph represents the path not taken, an antitype to Moses. Joseph, faithful servant to Pharaoh who despoiled and enslaved the entire Egyptian people, represents the dangers of assimilation to an invidious political and religious system. While Moses led his people out of Egypt, Joseph led them in. Joseph helped to lay the basis for the despotic Egyptian regime that later enslaved Israel. In both of these books, Wildavsky sees the basic problem of Jewish history as a problem of how to participate in politics (in order to survive) without losing identity based on faith in God (and thus ceasing to survive). Using midrash, critical biblical commentary, and contemporary political theory, Wildavsky produces a reading in which sacred and secular elements are mutually supportive.

WALZER's project resembles Wildavsky's in that he also finds two basic tendencies in Jewish political experience: Exodus politics and its intemperate opposite, messianic politics. Walzer shows how the Exodus narrative is the basis of the Western radical tradition. Moses led a revolutionary regime out of which emerged a covenantal nation with its own understanding of freedom, responsibility, and social justice. This covenantal culture has been committed to the long march through history. Opposed to this is an apocalyptic mentality that wants liberation not just from historical injustice and political oppression but from history as such. This abiding temptation is a root of the mystical, radical nationalism found in some segments on the right of the Israeli spectrum today.

SHARKANSKY also orients his study of the political themes of the Bible to the situation in Israel in the 1990s. He relates traits of Israeli political culture, such as morally charged public criticism of officials, to traits of biblical political culture, such as prophecy. Taking a less reverent, more forthrightly secular approach to the Bible, Sharkansky claims that the Bible has no unambiguous political principles or teaching. Its authors and editors are responsible for a contradictory, dissonant text. That, indeed, is the Bible's greatest strength: it engendered a moral and political Jewish culture able to cope with contradiction, paradox, and compromise. Jewish political thought from the Bible on is characterized by pragmatic coping.

ELAZAR's work is the first of a four-volume historical-theoretical study of the covenant tradition in politics. The Bible is informed by a dominant albeit contested idea: covenant. Free people form themselves into a nation through voluntary association based on shared moral and religious ideals. Elazar traces the presence of significant covenantal themes in many biblical books, writes a history of biblical regimes in relation to the ideals of covenantalism, and continues the story through subsequent Jewish history. Elazar, the founder of modern Jewish political studies, has written a foundational text.

It is too early to know whether this return to Scripture is the beginning of a trend or just an idiosyncratic event. At any rate, it does constitute, in the aggregate, a Jewishly engaged expression of political theorizing.

ALAN MITTLEMAN

Portugal

Altabé, David Fintz, *Spanish and Portuguese Jewry before and after 1492,* Brooklyn, New York: Sepher-Hermon, 1993

Beinart, Haim, "The Conversos in Spain and Portugal in the 16th to 18th Centuries," in his *Moreshet Sepharad: The Sephardi Legacy,* vol. 1, Jerusalem: Magnes Press of Hebrew University, 1992

Bodian, Miriam, *Hebrews of the Portuguese Nation: Conversos and Community in Early Modern Amsterdam* (Modern Jewish Experience), Bloomington: Indiana University Press, 1997

Herculano, Alexandre, *Historia da origem e estabelecimento da Inquisicao em Portugal,* 1852; translated by John C. Branner as *History of the Origin and Establishment of the Inquisition in Portugal* (Stanford Studies in History, Economics, and Political Science, vol. 1, no. 2), Palo Alto, California: Stanford University Press, 1926

Kaplan, Yosef, "The Intellectual Ferment in the Spanish-Portuguese Community of Seventeenth Century Amsterdam," in *Moreshet Sepharad: The Sephardi Legacy,* vol. 1, edited by Haim Beinart, Jerusalem: Magnes Press of Hebrew University, 1992

Lipiner, Elias, *Two Portuguese Exiles in Castile: Dom David Negro and Dom Isaac Abravanel* (Hispania Judaica, 10), Jerusalem: Magnes Press of Hebrew University, 1997

Nahon, Gérard, "From New Christians to the Portuguese Jewish Nation in France," in *Moreshet Sepharad: The Sephardi Legacy,* vol. 1, edited by Haim Beinart, Jerusalem: Magnes Press of Hebrew University, 1992

Raphael, David (editor), *The Expulsion 1492 Chronicles: An Anthology of Medieval Chronicles Relating to the Expulsion of the Jews from Spain and Portugal,* North Hollywood, California: Carmi House, 1992

Yerushalmi, Yosef Hayim, *The Lisbon Massacre of 1506 and the Royal Image in the Shebet Yehudah* (Hebrew Union College Annual: Supplements, no. 1), Cincinnati, Ohio: Hebrew Union College-Jewish Institute of Religion, 1976

Information about the first Jewish settlements in the Iberian Peninsula is sketchy, but by the time that the separate Portuguese state emerged in the 12th century, Jewish communities had been established in the territory for centuries. From the 12th century to 1497, Jews enjoyed a relatively tranquil life, living in *judarias* and usefully serving the monarchy, both as taxpayers and as court physicians, astrologers, astronomers, cosmographers, mathematicians, and polyglots. In return, many of them enjoyed individual privileges, concessions, and exemptions. The Portuguese Jews were organized in corporations called *comunas,* which were governed by the *arrabi mor* (chief rabbi), who had supreme authority over the Jews of the whole kingdom, and by *arrabis menores* (lower judges). Some restrictions on the liberty of the Jews were declared as early as the establishment of the separate kingdom, but these rules were not strictly enforced. Prior to 1497, many Jews occupied important positions: for example, Moses Navarro was chief treasurer of the kingdom during the reign of Alfonso IV (1325–1357) and Pedro I (1357–1367). His successor was Judah Aben Menir. The most famous personality in the history of Portuguese Jewry was Isaac Abravanel, who, in addition to his scholarly activities as prominent theologian and Bible commentator, was counselor and favorite of King Alfonso V (1438–1481). In 1497, capitulating to pressure from Spain, the Portuguese government mandated the conversion of its Jewish subjects to Catholicism. The later history of Portuguese Jewry is therefore divided between the story of New Christians who remained in Portugal and the experiences of those who emigrated.

In the majority of non-Portuguese books on the history of Jews in Portugal, that history is described jointly with that of Spain. The works devoted solely to Portuguese Jewry are few, and they usually focus on one aspect, one particular event, or one personality instead of providing a broad survey. This essay reviews some of the most recent English-language works on the topic, giving priority to the most broadly informative studies.

ALTABÉ describes some aspects of Jewish life in Portugal, emphasizing events between 1492 and 1497 and the lives of conversos (Jews who converted to Christianity, variously designated New Christians, Marranos, or Crypto-Jews) in the centuries following those years of persecution. He identifies several ways that Portuguese Jews were able to preserve their Jewish identities after the forcible conversion of 1497, some by escaping Portugal, some by leading double lives.

LIPINER collects and comments upon Portuguese documents from the Arquivo da Torre do Tombo related to the events that forced two important 15th-century Jewish figures, David Negro and Isaac Abravanel, to flee from Portugal to Castile. The author also provides a useful overview of the history of the Jews of Portugal, in order to place the contents of the documents in historical perspective.

BODIAN's history of Portuguese Jewry in Amsterdam begins with an account of the Portuguese conversos prior to their arrival in the Netherlands. The author does not focus on the details of historical events; instead, she concentrates on analyzing the historical meanings of the term "nation" as it was used in the Iberian Peninsula to distinguish the conversos from other Christian residents. Tracking the emergence of the converso class from the Spanish pogroms of 1391, the author demonstrates that the status of converso became an inherited condition for several generations before the anti-converso violence of the late 15th century. Activities of the Inquisition and the Spanish decrees of expulsion from Spain in 1492 and of mass conversion in Portugal in 1497 triggered a new wave of conversions, and the experiences of persecution and violence prompted the New Christians to solidify their sense of shared identity apart from the rest of the population. Meanwhile the Iberian use of the term *los de la nación* (those of the nation) to refer to the conversos emphasized their purported ethnic or racial traits. Beginning in 1449, the racist "estatutos de limpieza de sangre" (laws regulating the "purity" of bloodlines) were instituted in Castile and later adopted by the Portuguese. Moreover, in Portugal, the application of the term "nation" to describe the conversos directly referred to the idea that Jews have historically constituted a distinct people. Following this important introductory account of the history of the conversos in Portugal, Bodian devotes the bulk of her perceptive study to the dynamic history of emigrants from that community who settled in Amsterdam, beginning in the early 17th century.

YERUSHALMI documents a tragic event in the history of the New Christians of Lisbon: the massacre perpetrated by a Christian mob in April 1506 in which between 1,200 and 1,930 conversos were killed. He compares the historical accounts of the violence in the Hebrew chronicle *Shevet Yehudah*, by Solomon ibn Verga, and the German account *Von dem christenlichen Streyt*, by an anonymous writer who reported the massacre immediately after the event. A number of King Manuel's letters and edicts concerning the episode and punishment of the perpetrators are appended to the volume.

HERCULANO's book is dated, but, with the exception of chapter one (which has been supplanted by later research), the volume remains an important source. Herculano was a pioneer in the study of the history of the Inquisition in Portugal. This study is confined to the initial period of persecution, from 1492 to 1547, but for this period, the author provides very complete and fully documented coverage, focusing objectively on such issues as King Manuel's orders concerning the abduction and baptism of Jewish children in the 1490s and their seclusion on the equatorial island of São Tomé for Catholic reeducation. The preface by Y.H. Yerushalmi clarifies important themes and motifs used by the author, providing proof of the study's historical and moral credibility.

RAPHAEL publishes numerous historical chronicles from 1492 and the period thereafter, including a few texts related to events in Portugal. For example, the Portuguese chronicles of Rui de Pina and Garcia de Resende describe conditions imposed on the Jews expelled from Spain who wished to enter

Portugal; the accounts by Abraham Zacuto, Samuel Usque, Damião de Góis, and Jerónimo Osório recount tragic events that occurred between December 1496 and February 1497, including the forced baptism of Jewish children, the forced conversion of adult Jews, and the ensuing wave of suicides. Other selections (by Elijah Capsali, Abraham ben Solomon, and Abraham Saba) depict tortures of those Jews who refused to convert. The edict outlawing Judaism in Portugal and its territories is reprinted among other appendixes.

BEINART considers the status of conversos who remained in Spain and Portugal after Catholic conformity had been imposed across the peninsula. Topics discussed include the Spanish royal proclamation that promised Spanish exiles in Portugal that their property would be restored if they returned to Spain as converts; the gruesome events of December 1496 through Passover 1497; and the transformation of the entire Iberian Jewish population into a converso class after 1497. Following anti-converso rioting in 1506, King Manuel granted the conversos permission to emigrate from Portugal on 1 March 1507. Between 1507 and 1521, the conversos enjoyed a period of relative tranquility, but by 1540 a national inquisition had been established, initiating a new age of unprecedented persecution of the conversos that lasted until 1821. Although the majority of the conversos were sincere Christians, some of the documents and other putative evidence of the Inquisition suggest that among them lived some Crypto-Jews (that is, those who secretly maintained a Jewish identity or observed Jewish customs).

At different times, special permissions were given to particular conversos or entire groups of conversos to travel or to emigrate from Portugal, and many used these permissions, creating new Portuguese communities outside of Portugal. One of these communities—in France—is described in a very informative article by NAHON. He relates how the new immigrants obtained permission to settle in France and recounts how eruptions of popular antisemitism sometimes forced the conversos either to leave their towns of residence or to face severe repression. Although the Portuguese were legally permitted to settle anywhere in the French kingdom, they chose primarily to reside in such cities as Bayonne, Bordeaux, and Auch in southwestern France. Additional communities were settled on the Atlantic coast from Saint Jean de Luz to Rouen, and several small communities were established in the French interior.

KAPLAN deals with another—and undoubtedly the greatest—of such communities of Portuguese emigrants, that of Amsterdam, where many conversos were able to return to Judaism. Among those of Portuguese Jewish descent in Amsterdam were observant Jews, intellectuals who disputed rabbinic views, and atheists. The spectrum of religious and philosophical views of many conversos who grew up in a Catholic culture influenced by the thought of Aquinas and Erasmus contradicted the views of traditional Judaism to which most Portuguese emigrants returned when they settled in Amsterdam. In some cases, new immigrants refused circumcision, and a number of individuals in the Amsterdam community, such as Juan de Prado, David Farrar, and Uriel da Costa, were accused of harboring Karaite leanings. Kaplan contends that the opposition of these intellectuals to the oral tradition reflects

Protestant influence on their beliefs, and he identifies the responsa of Leone Modena, the intellectualist rabbi of Venice, as a key source for grasping many of the theological controversies that arose among the Portuguese in Amsterdam.

HAYIM Y. SHEYNIN

Prague

Altshuler, David (editor), *The Precious Legacy: Judaic Treasures from the Czechoslovak State Collections*, New York: Summit, 1983

Cohen, Gary, "Jews in German Society: Prague 1860–1914," *Central European History*, 10, 1977

Dagan, Avigdor et al. (editors), *The Jews of Czechoslovakia: Historical Studies and Surveys*, 3 vols., Philadelphia: Jewish Publication Society, 1968–1983

Demetz, Peter, *Prague in Black and Gold: Scenes from the Life of a European City*, New York: Hill and Wang, 1997

Kieval, Hillel, *The Making of Czech Jewry: National Conflict and Jewish Society in Bohemia, 1870–1918* (Studies in Jewish History), New York: Oxford University Press, 1988

Muneles, Otto (editor), *Prague Ghetto in the Renaissance Period* (Jewish Monuments in Bohemia and Moravia, vol. 4), Prague: Orbis, 1965

Neher, André, *Jewish Thought and the Scientific Revolution of the Sixteenth Century: David Gans (1541–1613) and His Times* (Littman Library of Jewish Civilization), translated by D. Maisel, Oxford and New York: Oxford University Press, 1986

Pawel, Ernst, *The Nightmare of Reason: A Life of Franz Kafka*, New York: Farrar, Straus, Giroux, and London: Harvill, 1984

For the thousand-year history of the Jews of Prague, there are two survey works, both of which are useful as a point of departure.

DEMETZ surveys all of Prague history, not only the history of its Jews. He provides a series of vignettes and studies of crucial periods in Prague's history, highlighting two features in particular. The first is the multicultural (Czech, German, Jewish, Italian) character of Prague and its long history of intergroup tensions and violence. The second is a tradition of thought, from the Middle Ages to the turn of the 21st century, that Demetz characterizes as rationalistic, practical, socially progressive, and reformist. He contrasts this tradition with the image created by other writers (as well as by the Prague tourist industry) of "Magical Prague" or "Mystical Prague." Demetz pays considerable attention to the Jewish community. His treatment of Jewish history is especially strong on the Middle Ages.

A second survey work is ALTSHULER. It is a catalog of an exhibition from the Jewish Museum in Prague and includes hundreds of exceptionally beautiful illustrations, a visual history of the community that complements the written record. It also contains a lengthy essay on the history of the Jews in

Prague by Hillel Kieval. Kieval covers the history of the Prague Jewish community from its medieval origins and through the Holocaust and beyond. He discusses communal organization, politics, economics, and culture. His interpretation is upbeat, showing the vitality and cultural creativity of the Prague Jewish community and its generally positive interactions with the Christian milieu. He plays down the theme of persecution. In general the relative importance of persecution and tolerance, exclusion and assimilation has been the major focus of scholarly debate over the history of the Prague Jews.

Two periods of Prague Jewish history have attracted special attention, the Golden Age (roughly 1570 to 1620) and the period from 1870 to 1918. During the last decades of the 16th century, Prague was home to the court of the Hapsburg emperor Rudolph II, and as such the city became a center of European art and science. In the Jewish community, the Golden Age was the period of Rabbi Judah Loew ben Bezalel (Maharal).

NEHER's biography of David Gans studies one of the outstanding scholars of the Jewish community in the time of Maharal. Gans was a historian and an astronomer who worked briefly with the Danish astronomer Tycho Brahe. Like Kieval, Neher stresses the theme of tolerance. Brahe was happy to discuss astronomy with his Jewish colleague; Gans was openminded toward the new astronomy of Copernicus; and the Jewish community was accepting of Gans's interest in science.

The essays collected by MUNELES discuss the social and cultural history of the Prague Jews in this period. In keeping with the tendencies of Marxist history (the volume was produced under Communist rule), individual personalities, such as Maharal and Gans within the Jewish community and Rudolph II outside it, are not emphasized. Two essays on social history document the polarization of Prague Jewry during this period into the very wealthy and the very poor. They also stress the ongoing hatred of Jews among the Christian population of Prague. Two other essays briefly survey the religious and artistic works produced by Prague Jews in this period. This is practically a "coffee-table book"; there are many beautiful illustrations but no footnotes.

The second period that has attracted extensive scholarly attention, the turn of the 20th century, roughly 1870–1920, is the period of Franz Kafka. KIEVAL presents the story of the Jewish community in this period as a classic Zionist narrative. The period of political liberalism in the mid-19th century was accompanied by widespread Jewish assimilation. Assimilation in Bohemia could move, however, in either of two directions: toward German culture or toward Czech culture. The surge of political antisemitism in about 1890 brought about the rise of Zionism in Prague and Bohemia and a renewed consciousness of Jewish national identity.

COHEN, by contrast, regards the trend toward assimilation into German culture as the predominant one in this period. He warns against a tendency to assign Czech and Jewish national identities to 19th-century Prague Jews. People should, he argues, see them as they saw themselves, that is, as Germans who happened to be Jewish by religion.

Much of the study of Prague Jews in this period centers around Kafka, and his life provides insight into the Jewish community of the period. PAWEL locates Kafka within a social context of Jewish family, friends, and fellow writers, and Pawel provides sketches of a great many of them. He also shows Kafka's contacts with the larger world of Jewish culture: the visiting Yiddish theater, the Zionist movement, and the Hasidim whom Kafka met at Czech health resorts. In Pawel's view, however, Kafka's contact with Jewish religion was quite minimal and overwhelmingly negative. He suggests a reading of Kafka (and by extension, of a large part of Prague Jewry) close to Isaac Deutscher's model of the "non-Jewish Jew."

The major work on the period 1918 to 1948, including the Holocaust period, is DAGAN's three-volume collection of essays. The essays are very diverse and focus generally on Czechoslovakian Jewry, rather than specifically on Prague Jewry. They survey, among other topics, the arts, literature, music, sports, the Zionist movement, synagogues, the legal status of Jews and Judaism, and Jewish involvement in the Czech economy and politics. The essays are long on facts and lists and short on interpretation. Prague Jews occupy a dominant place in many of these essays; in some (such as the essay on literature), nearly everyone discussed is a Prague Jew. The excellent essays on the Holocaust period (volume three) provide a detailed narrative of the destruction of Prague Jewry and their road, together with the other Jews of Bohemia and Moravia, through Terezin to the death camps. An essay by Erich Kulka tells the much less widely known story of armed resistance to the Nazis among Czechoslovak Jews.

JOSEPH M. DAVIS

Prayer *see* Liturgy, History of; Liturgy, Reform

Priesthood: Biblical

Blenkinsopp, Joseph, *Sage, Priest, Prophet: Religious and Intellectual Leadership in Ancient Israel* (Library of Ancient Israel), Louisville, Kentucky: Westminster/Knox, 1995

Grabbe, Lester L., *Priests, Prophets, Diviners, Sages: A Socio-Historical Study of Religious Specialists in Ancient Israel*, Valley Forge, Pennsylvania: Trinity Press International, 1995

Haran, Menahem, *Temples and Temple-Service in Ancient Israel: An Inquiry into the Character of Cult Phenomena and the Historical Setting of the Priestly School*, Oxford: Clarendon, 1977; as *Temples and Temple-Service in Ancient Israel: An Inquiry into Biblical Cult Phenomena and the Historical Setting of the Priestly School*, Winona Lake, Indiana: Eisenbrauns, 1985

Knohl, Israel, *Mikdash ha-demamah*, 1992; translated as *The Sanctuary of Silence: The Priestly Torah and the Holiness School*, Minneapolis, Minnesota: Fortress, 1995

Levine, Baruch, *Numbers 1–20: A New Translation with Introduction and Commentary* (Anchor Bible, vol. 4), New York: Doubleday, 1993

Milgrom, Jacob, *Leviticus 1–16: A New Translation with Introduction and Commentary* (Anchor Bible, vol. 3), New York: Doubleday, 1991

Priests *(kohanim)* were the primary actors in the biblical pattern of divine worship. Although all Israel was intended to form a "kingdom of priests and a holy nation" (Exodus 19:6), the sanctity of the people was symbolized by the priesthood, which became a basic element of ancient Israelite civilization. The kohanim were distinguished from the tribe of Levi, which was recognized as having a special religious status secondary to that of the priests. As evidenced by the common use of the term *khn*, the institution of the priesthood was widespread in the ancient Near East, although the qualifications and purposes of such priests may have been different in each religion.

In the biblical period, the tasks of the kohanim included officiating at rituals connected to the sacrificial system; blessing the people; sounding the trumpets on festivals and new moons; blowing the *shofar* on Yom Kippur of the Jubilee year as well as on the first day of the seventh month and whenever the Ark of the Covenant was moved; ascertaining the will of God through oracular means; determining and treating impurities on the skin, clothing, or buildings; working with the elders to judge the people; and more generally preserving traditions and instructing the people.

While in the age of the Tabernacle and Temple, the kohanim were essential to the sacrificial ritual; following the destruction of the Temple, the role of the kohanim was significantly altered. Their presence was not necessary for public prayer to take place in the synagogue. Nonetheless, a restricted status for kohanim was preserved because it was assumed that the holiness of the kohanim did not end with the destruction of the Temple. The priests were given both social and legal recognition that has continued, in some form, throughout Jewish history.

HARAN discusses the history of the priesthood and the cult of ancient Israel. He explores the history of the priesthood and contends that in open cultic areas outside of cities, there was neither regular sacrifice nor priestly officiants. Permanent sanctuaries, however, were the domain of the priests and were not places of community worship. Haran examines the differences among various biblical sources regarding the relationship between the Levitical tribe and the priests. He differentiates sharply between the hypothetical documents posited by higher criticism as biblical source material. Thus, he maintains that in P sources, the Levites were always set aside as a priestly tribe and that the Zadokite priesthood was not a predecessor to the Aaronide priesthood but a refinement of it. On the other hand, he identifies a common orientation to the priesthood in J, E, and D: all males from the tribe of Levi were eligible to serve as priests, but only if they were in the chosen place.

KNOHL suggests that the Holiness Code (H) is not merely a literary unit that forms part of the Priestly Source (P). Instead, H represents a later effort by the priests to fuse the realm of ritual with legal and social rules. The priesthood responded to the prophetic critique of the religious and social problems of the eighth century B.C.E. by infusing holiness with moral content, applying it to the whole community (not just the priests) and extending it to the entire land of Israel (not only the sanctuary). MILGROM agrees with Knohl's dating and situating of H, but he argues that the cultic-ritual legislation of the first part of Leviticus encompassed ethical elements, so that this characteristic of the Holiness Code was not a radically new development. He disputes Knohl's contention that the priesthood was a closed group that barred the laity from access to the sanctuary. To the contrary, Milgrom argues that while elitists formed a zealous hereditary elite, they ensured that the ordinary householder was given a degree of access to elements of the Israelite cult without parallel in the ancient Near East. Following Yehezkel Kaufmann, Milgrom contends that only the sacrificial act was carried out in silence and that the evidence is compelling that music, psalms, and the priestly blessing were used as part of the cult. Knohl, however, argues that the entire sanctuary ritual was conducted in silence to distinguish it from the magical incantations associated with other ancient religions.

In LEVINE's commentary, he argues that Numbers is not an idealized and unrealistic source of information about the kohanim. To the contrary, Numbers reflects a dimension of religious praxis that is far more realistic than are prophetic pronouncements. Levine contends that the Tabernacle traditions and other compilations of priestly material are later developments, for other sources do not refer to the priest-Levite stratification that he traces to the exilic policy of Ezekiel 44. He also argues that the Levites in Leviticus may not be different from Deuteronomy, in which priests and Levites are interchangeable terms.

In the course of a "history from below," GRABBE examines the priests, one of many classes of "religious specialists" in ancient Israel. He recognizes the methodological difficulties of reconstructing the history of the Bible, but he claims that textual hints, cross-cultural comparisons, and some "authentic" texts allow for the writing of social history. He reviews numerous biblical references to priests as well as cross-cultural parallels in order to articulate a description of the functions, duties, and structure of the priesthood. Grabbe notes that while cultic functions were exclusive to the priests, the duties and skills of the kohanim occasionally overlapped with those of the diviner and the sage, and he posits that some priests were also prophets and scribes, resulting in a complex pattern of interaction among various religious authorities.

BLENKINSOPP also presents a social history of the intellectual leadership in Israel as exercised by sage, priest, and prophet, but he emphasizes the difficulty in tracing the history of the priesthood and the particular challenges presented by ancient sources as a basis for an anthropologically grounded history. Echoing Max Weber, Blenkinsopp notes that the crucial difference between prophet and priest is that the priest alone is appointed, so his salvific authority is derived by virtue of office and not through charisma. The role of the priest was to facilitate ritual and to maintain the continuous operation of the cult with its sacred norms, places, and times. This role required specialized training and resulted in an intellectual tradition particular to the priesthood. Priests also served as diviners and teachers, but not preachers. The relationship between the Aaronide, Zadokite, and Levite priesthoods is presented as being complex and uncertain, and the gradual demise of the priesthood after the destruction of the Second Temple is discussed as part of a transition to the nascent rabbinic tradition.

BARUCH FRYDMAN KOHL

See also Priesthood: Postbiblical

Priesthood: Postbiblical

Cohen, Stuart A., *The Three Crowns: Structures of Communal Politics in Early Rabbinic Jewry,* Cambridge and New York: Cambridge University Press, 1990

Goodblatt, David, *The Monarchic Principle: Studies in Jewish Self-Government in Antiquity* (Texte und Studien zum antiken Judentum, 38), Tübingen: Mohr (Siebeck), 1994

Liver, Jacob, " 'The Sons of Zadok the Priests' in the Dead Sea Sect," *Revue de Qumran,* 21(6), 1967

Olyan, Saul M., "Ben Sira's Relationship to the Priesthood," *Harvard Theological Review,* 80(3), 1987

Schürer, Emil, *The History of the Jewish People in the Age of Jesus Christ (175 B.C.–A.D. 135),* vol. 2, revised and edited by Geza Vermes and Fergus Millar, Edinburgh: Clark, 1979

Schwartz, Seth, *Josephus and Judaean Politics* (Columbia Studies in the Classical Tradition, 18), New York: Brill, 1990

Smallwood, E.M., "High Priests and Politics in Roman Palestine," *Journal of Theological Studies,* 13, 1962

Stern, M., "Aspects of Jewish Society: The Priesthood and Other Classes," in *The Jewish People in the First Century* (Compendia rerum Iudaicarum ad Novum Testamentum), vol. 2, edited by Stern and S. Safrai, Assen: Van Gorcum, 1975

Priesthood emerged from the biblical period to become a dominant factor in Jewish society during the Second Temple era. To a large extent, a study of the vicissitudes of the priesthood is necessarily a study of the political and social history of the Jewish people in Judea during the Second Temple period.

The state of the priesthood during the early Hellenistic period is addressed by OLYAN in his discussion of the relationship between the Book of Ben Sira and the priesthood. Beginning with the premise that Ben Sira was himself a priest, the author attempts to locate Ben Sira in his priestly context. Olyan argues that on the issue of priesthood, Ben Sira's ideology was faithful to the priestly writings of the Pentateuch. Ben Sira supported the pan-Aaronide priesthood and wrote polemics against other views of the priesthood, such as the exclusionary Zadokite and inclusive Levite ideologies.

LIVER examines the unique degree of authority and leadership ascribed to the sons of Zadok in the literature of the Dead Sea Sect (DSS). He also discusses some of the issues surrounding the priesthood in general relating to the DSS, noting that references to the sons of Zadok appear frequently in, and seem to be peculiar to, the sectarian literature. Zadokite lineage is generally assumed to be an important component in the origins of the DSS, and many scholars suppose that the DSS split from the wider community on the basis of a claim that the Hasmonean clan lacked the legitimate Zadokite lineage required by custom to fulfill their leadership role in the temple. Liver compares other sources that stress the sons of Zadok, such as the Books of Ezekiel and Ben Sira. He concludes that references to sons of Zadok reflect both the prominence of the Zadokite line in the era when the literature was written and the importance of members of Zadokite descent among the founders of the DSS, but, he argues, there is insufficient evidence to prove that sectarian opposition to the Hasmoneans was based on the claim that the Hasmoneans were not Zadokites. His analysis suggests that references to the sons of Zadok in the literature of the DSS do not imply controversy over, or opposition to, other priestly categories. In general, Zadokite priests are mentioned in conjunction with their position of authority within the sect and not in relation to cultic matters. In short, there is no sign of a polemical tone in the references to the sons of Zadok.

GOODBLATT theorizes that priestly, monarchic hegemony was the rule throughout the Second Temple period, thereby disputing the widely held view that a national council, sometimes called the *gerousia* or Sanhedrin, shared leadership roles with the high priesthood and occasionally surpassed that office in importance during this period. This council was at most, he argues, a local Jerusalem council, not a national institution. His source analysis is systematic and thorough. His discussion of priestly ideology is particularly fascinating. Further studies may lead to a more nuanced conclusion, but Goodblatt's research has greatly challenged the theory that the council and high priesthood shared authority. This volume is rich in source material; the author's style is a little wordy, but the book is very readable.

The updated and revised edition of SCHÜRER's monumental history contains a detailed account of the priesthood throughout the Second Temple period and describes the social stratification of the priesthood. The book provides an informative, systematic description of the Temple and its administration and offers an excursus on the evolution of the various priestly entitlements and emoluments. The copious notes help to make this book a reservoir of source material and relevant scholarly research.

The social and political influence of the priesthood as a class are probed by STERN. Although his essay concentrates on the first century C.E., the author also examines issues pertaining to the rise in priestly hegemony in the previous centuries, especially around the time of the Hasmonean revolt. Stern highlights the internal aspects of the priestly divisions, such as the family ties that helped determine priestly allegiances, in particular among the high priestly families, and he evaluates how these relationships colored the social interactions and politics of the time.

SMALLWOOD considers the role of the high priesthood in the politics and intrigue of the period between the end of Herod's reign and 70 C.E. Josephus recorded two very different accounts of the part played by the high priesthood in the revolt against Rome of 66–70 C.E. In his earlier account, *The Jewish War*, Josephus intentionally cleared the high priests of active complicity in the actions of the Jewish war camp, but he contradicts this account in his later depiction of the events, *Jewish Antiquities*. Smallwood examines these discrepancies and concludes that high priests were more involved in the anti-Roman politics before and during the revolt than Josephus was eager to acknowledge.

Like Smallwood, SCHWARTZ seeks to understand why Josephus excuses high priests from direct culpability in the revolt in *The Jewish War*, which was written around 80 C.E., whereas in *Antiquities of the Jews*, written nearly 20 years later, Josephus practically goes out of his way to incriminate the priesthood. Schwartz argues that the differences between the two chronicles reflect Josephus's changing assessment of the relative influence exerted by the various leadership groups, including the high priestly oligarchy, after 70 C.E., as well as corresponding changes in Josephus's expectations, hopes, and fears. Schwartz also discusses the integration of priests into the evolving rabbinic movement. Although Josephus abandons the cause of the high priestly families, the upper priesthood, with whom he identifies, still continues to enjoy his support.

The history of the priests after Josephus's account ends has not enjoyed a full scholarly treatment. Nevertheless, several important studies of this topic have appeared in Hebrew in recent years, and COHEN is an attempt to digest these studies and develop them into a coherent account. This book is essentially a work on Jewish political theory in the early centuries of rabbinic Judaism. Cohen describes leadership conflicts in which the rabbis emerge as the ultimate victors. The title of the volume refers to the notion that within Jewish society there were three separate "crowns," that is, competing claimants for terrestrial power: the priesthood, royalty, and the possessors of Torah scholarship. Royalty was represented by the various claimants to Davidic lineage: the Patriarchs in Palestine and the Exilarchs in Babylonia. According to Cohen, the priests began to decline in influence following the destruction of the Temple. This decline was gradual, however, and priests competed with the rising rabbinic ethos for a couple more centuries. Much remains to be studied in this fascinating period of change, and the author's tripartite model may well be too simplistic to account for all the diversity that characterized Jewish society in late antiquity. Recent epigraphic discoveries in Palestine, as well as studies on *piyyut* (liturgical poetry) and Genizah documents all raise the possibility that priests may have continued contending for the leadership in Jewish society for many more centuries than Cohen admits.

GEOFFREY HERMAN

See also Priesthood: Biblical

Printing, Early Hebrew

Amram, David W., *The Makers of Hebrew Books in Italy: Being Chapters in the History of the Hebrew Printing Press*, Philadelphia: Greenstone, 1909; London: Holland, 1963

Hill, Brad S. (editor), *Incunabula, Hebraica and Judaica: Five Centuries of Hebraica and Judaica, Rare Bibles, and Hebrew Incunables from the Jacob M. Lowy Collection: Exhibition Catalogue*, Ottawa, Ontario: National Library of Canada, 1981

Hill, Brad S., *Hebraica (Saec. X ad Saec. XVI): Manuscripts and Early Printed Books from the Library of the Valmadonna Trust: An Exhibition at the Pierpont Morgan Library New York,* London: Valmadonna Trust Library, 1989

Hill, Brad S., *Books Printed on Vellum in the Collections of the British Library,* compiled by R.C. Alston, with a Catalogue of Hebrew Books Printed on Vellum compiled by Brad Sabin Hill, London: British Library, 1996

Offenberg, A.K., *Hebrew Incunabula in Public Collections: A First International Census* (Bibliotheca Humanistica and Reformatorica, vol. 47), Nieuwkoop: De Graaf, 1990

Offenberg, A.K., "The Spread of Hebrew Printing," in *The Image of the Word: Jewish Tradition in Manuscripts and Printed Books: Catalogue of an Exhibition Held at the Jewish Historical Museum, Amsterdam (14 September–25 November 1990),* Amsterdam: Amsterdam University Library and Jewish Historical Museum, 1990

Offenberg, A.K., *A Choice of Corals: Facets of Fifteenth-Century Hebrew Printing* (Bibliotheca Humanistica and Reformatorica, vol. 52), Nieuwkoop: De Graaf, 1992

Popper, William, *The Censorship of Hebrew Books,* New York: Knickerbocker, 1899; reprint, with introduction by Moshe Carmilly-Weinberger, New York: Ktav, 1969

The apostles of Gutenberg's epoch-making invention of 1450 were itinerant Germans who carried their printing presses throughout the Holy Roman Empire and over the Alps. Within 20 years their apprentices had come to include Jews, and specifically German Jewish refugees in Italy, who had begun to apply the technology of movable type to the dissemination of Hebrew literature. The decades that followed proved among the most eventful in Jewish history, and, particularly as a result of the ensuing dislocations, the earliest printing in many parts of the world, from Portugal and North Africa to the Balkans and the Middle East, was in Hebrew.

OFFENBERG (1990b) covers more than five centuries of Hebrew printing and provides a well-structured, if somewhat staccato, general introduction to the field. The presentation is primarily chronological, secondarily geographical. All major Hebrew printing centers, printers, and important printed editions are mentioned, and the article provides a number of useful bibliographical references.

Another general introduction to early Hebrew printing (in the 15th and 16th centuries) is HILL's (1989) tastefully executed catalog of Hebraica from the Valmadonna Trust Library. This work represents both the personal bibliophilic interests of the London-based collector, Jack V. Lunzer, and Hill's scholarly concerns. Almost all of the books discussed in the catalog reflect Lunzer's love of special copies (that is, those with special provenance, executed on special materials such as colored papers or parchment, or exquisitely bound), and the volume demonstrates Hill's sound knowledge of the history of Hebrew bibliography, his ability to indicate new possible areas of research, and his awareness of the importance for Hebrew bibliography of flawless indexes.

HILL (1981) is a catalog from an exhibition at the National Library of Canada in Ottawa, where the author served as curator of the Jacob M. Lowy Collection from 1979 to 1989. The volume presents a thematic overview of the history of Hebraic and Judaic books and may be considered as an incunabulum of Hill's bibliographic oeuvre.

Two works by Offenberg are important examples of modern research into Hebrew incunabula. OFFENBERG (1990a) lists 139 editions of Hebrew books that can safely be assumed to have been printed before 1501. Approximately 40 presses in Italy, Spain, Portugal, and Turkey printed these editions. Somewhat more than 2,000 copies are extant, in more than 150 collections worldwide. The census provides as much information on the individual copies as possible, and a sound introduction and indexes augment it.

OFFENBERG (1992), which borrows its title from a medieval work by Solomon ibn Gabirol, contains revised versions of seven of the author's articles about 15th-century printing, originally published between 1969 and 1990. Chapters include a highly informative overview titled "Literature on Hebrew Incunabula since the Second World War" and "A List of Copies of Hebrew Incunabula, Disappeared from Public Collections since the Outbreak of the Second World War." The value of the volume is augmented by the many x-ray photographs of watermarks related to the various works under discussion.

HILL (1996), a catalog of Hebrew books printed on vellum in the British library, is more limited in scope than the other two texts of his reviewed here. The introduction explains the chronology of printing of Hebrew texts on this deluxe material and deals with the subjects of vellum, Jewish languages, Judaica on vellum, marginal annotation, format, and provenance. The catalog contains 75 entries and includes ample bibliographical references. The Hebrew incunabula appear in a separate listing of incunabula printed on vellum, which is based on data from the British Library's automated incunabula catalog. Regrettably, this source uses different headings and slightly different romanizations than those used by Hill.

Although not always very reliable and somewhat outdated, AMRAM's work is still the only introduction to Hebrew printing in its most important center, Italy. After an introductory chapter, Amram discusses the pioneers of Hebrew printing in Italy between 1475 and 1482 (overlooking the fact that the first Hebrew incunabula were produced in Rome between 1469 and 1472). The author then considers the Soncino dynasty of printers, the famous Christian printer Daniel van Bomberghen of Venice, and Hebrew printing in other Italian towns. An especially interesting chapter is devoted to the public quarrel of the two Venetian printers Giustiniani and Bragadini over an edition of Maimonides' *Mishneh Torah,* a dispute which would eventually lead to the condemnation of the Talmud by the Catholic Church and a halt to Hebrew printing in the city of Venice.

Christian reservations about the publication of Jewish books is the topic of POPPER's fascinating and groundbreaking work on censorship, which provides a detailed, if often outdated, discussion of the strategies of the Inquisitions, as well as of the reactions of the Jews. Special attention is paid to the late 16th and early 17th centuries (what Popper calls the "Golden Era") in Italy, during which time most Hebrew books that came from Italian presses were checked and often expurgated by such Christian censors as Camillo Jaghel and Luigi da Bologna. Popper's illustrated list of Italian censors, with identifications of their often hardly legible signatures, is particularly useful. Carmilly-Weinberger's introduction to the 1969 reprint updates Popper's insights, placing his work in a wider historical perspective and discussing the significance of Jewish self-censorship in early modern times.

EMILE G.L. SCHRIJVER

Prophecy

Aune, David, *Prophecy in Early Christianity and the Ancient Mediterranean World*, Grand Rapids, Michigan: Eerdmans, 1983

Barton, John, *Oracles of God: Perceptions of Ancient Prophecy in Israel after the Exile*, London: Darton, Longman, and Todd, 1986; New York: Oxford University Press, 1988

Blenkinsopp, Joseph, *A History of Prophecy in Israel from the Settlement in the Land to the Hellenistic Period*, Philadelphia: Westminster, 1983; London: SPCK, 1984; 2nd edition, Louisville, Kentucky: Westminster John Knox, 1996

Heschel, Abraham J., *The Prophets*, 2 vols., New York: Harper and Row, 1962

Heschel, Abraham J., *Prophetic Inspiration after the Prophets: Maimonides and Other Medieval Authorities*, edited by Morris Faierstein, Hoboken, New Jersey: Ktav, 1996

Kaufmann, Yehezkel, *Toldot ha-emunah ha-Yisre'elit*, 1937; translated and abridged by Moshe Greenberg as *The Religion of Israel: From Its Beginnings to the Babylonian Exile*, Chicago: University of Chicago Press, and London: Allen and Unwin, 1960

Kaufmann, Yehezkel, *History of the Religion of Israel*, vol. IV: *From the Babylonian Captivity to the End of Prophecy*, translated by C.W. Efroymson, New York: Ktav, 1977

Scholem, Gershom, *Sabbatai Sevi: The Mystical Messiah, 1626–1676*, Princeton, New Jersey: Princeton University Press, and London: Routledge and Kegan Paul, 1973

Sommer, Benjamin, "Did Prophecy Cease? Evaluating a Re-evaluation," *Journal of Biblical Literature*, 115(1), 1996

von Rad, Gerhard, *The Message of the Prophets*, New York: Harper and Row, 1965; London: SCM, 1968

Wilson, Robert, *Prophecy and Society in Ancient Israel*, Philadelphia: Fortress, 1980

Several book-length discussions of biblical prophecy and the work of individual prophets are available. VON RAD begins with a discussion of general issues: the literary and theological traditions within which individual prophets worked, major concepts running through most of the prophetic literature, and speculation regarding the nature of prophets' experiences and of their claims to knowledge of the divine will. Discussions of the classical or literary prophets follow, focusing on the message of each prophet rather than on the literary history of each text (though he does not completely ignore the latter issue). Von Rad pays little attention to preclassical prophets such as Elijah and Elisha in this book.

HESCHEL (1962) devotes a great deal of attention (especially in his second volume) to the nature of the revelations the biblical prophets experienced. He examines the philosophical implications of their utterances and of their claims to have had contact with the divine. Further, he analyzes the image of God that emerges from the prophetic corpus; this part of his discussion has many points of contact with his works on rabbinic and modern Jewish thought. Heschel's first volume includes summaries of the messages of selected prophetic books; as in von Rad, scant notice is given to the preclassical figures. Although he is aware of questions regarding the composition of prophetic books, Heschel devotes his energies to elucidating the texts themselves, not to reconstructing their history. His presentations of these texts are vivid and readable.

A very different approach emerges from the work of BLENKINSOPP. He is especially interested in the connections among preclassical, classical, and post-exilic prophecy, and thus he provides more of a historical narrative on the growth and changes within Israelite prophecy and less of a theological work than von Rad or Heschel. He also provides an excellent history of scholarship, reviewing in a clear and lively fashion the various trends that have emerged since the mid–19th century. Blenkinsopp is especially interested in the redaction of the biblical texts. He devotes a great deal of attention to three questions: How much of a prophetic book is likely to record the actual teachings of the prophet? To what extent did later disciples or editors alter or enlarge the text, and to what ends? What is the relation between a prophet and the book that bears the prophet's name?

A significant counterbalance to Blenkinsopp's approach appears in the work of KAUFMANN (1937). Writing decades before Blenkinsopp, Kaufmann responds to the assumptions underlying the later scholar's work. He provides strong arguments that most prophetic books underwent little editorial revision after they were composed by the prophet (though he acknowledges, of course, that some books—for example, Isaiah—are composite works). His discussions of individual books, in which he focuses on their historical setting as well as their place in the development of Israelite religion, are exemplary. Each figure emerges from his presentation as an individual; Kaufmann does not neglect the extent to which prophets took issue with each other and with other streams of biblical tradition. His treatment of prophets up until Ezekiel appears in his 1937 work; he discusses prophets after Ezekiel in KAUFMANN (1977).

WILSON is also interested in the development of prophecy and Israelite religion, but he uses a more anthropological and sociological approach. He emphasizes the social location of each prophet, the extent to which the prophet was part of the power structure of his day or was a peripheral figure, and the support groups that allowed the prophet to function. His descriptions of two main streams of Israelite prophecy may not be valid, but his review both of the history of biblical scholarship on prophecy and of anthropological descriptions of prophets and mediums throughout the world is enormously helpful. Further, he includes an excellent discussion of prophecy in the ancient Near Eastern societies out of which Israel grew.

Prophecy remains a relevant topic for Jewish studies outside the biblical period. BARTON describes how prophetic texts became canonical in the Second Temple period (indeed, his discussion of the formation of the biblical canon is one of the finest available), and he shows how other literature, such as apocalyptic texts, took the place of prophecy. AUNE presents early Christianity as a prophetic movement, emphasizing points of contact between early Christians on the one hand and biblical prophecy, apocalyptic and messianic prophets of the Second Temple period, and Greco-Roman prophetic figures on the other. He also argues against the position (found in Kaufmann [1977]) that biblical prophecy declined early in the Second Temple period and maintains that prophets continued to flourish up until and after the destruction of the Second Temple. A similar thesis appears in HESCHEL (1996), who contends that the prophetic spirit remained active in medieval Judaism as well. Prophetic elements were particularly strong in medieval Jewish mystical circles (especially those of a messianic character), but these elements also appear on rare occasion even in halakhic literature. SOMMER argues against this thesis, however. He shows that prophecy was viewed as dormant in the various forms of Judaism that existed in the late Second Temple period, though Jews generally acknowledged that prophecy would reappear with the coming of the Messiah. An example of the resurgence of prophecy (or of the belief that prophecy had reappeared) in a messianic movement is examined by SCHOLEM in his study of the Sabbatians. Adherents of this group, like the early Christians before them, surmised that prophecy had returned along with the Messiah, who, inconveniently, committed apostasy and died. A more recent example of this sort of belief can be found among some Lubavitch hasidim, whose zeal for their dead messiah-prophet will no doubt be the topic of forthcoming studies.

BENJAMIN D. SOMMER

Prophets, Former and Latter

Brenner, Athalya (editor), *A Feminist Companion to the Latter Prophets* (The Feminist Companion to the Bible, vol. 8), Sheffield, South Yorkshire: Sheffield Academic Press, 1995

Bronner, Leila Leah, *The Stories of Elijah and Elisha as Polemics against Baal Worship* (Pretoria Oriental Series, vol. 6), Leiden: Brill, 1968

Carroll, Robert P., *When Prophecy Failed: Reactions and Responses to Failure in the Old Testament Prophetic Traditions,* London: SCM, 1979

Gunn, David M., *The Fate of King Saul: An Interpretation of a Biblical Story* (Journal for the Study of the Old Testament Supplement Series, vol. 14), Sheffield, South Yorkshire: JSOT, 1980

Long, V. Philips, *The Reign and Rejection of King Saul: A Case for Literary and Theological Coherence* (Society of Biblical Literature Dissertation Series, vol. 118), Atlanta, Georgia: Scholars Press, 1989

Rost, Leonhard, *Die Überlieferung von der Thronnachfolge Davids,* 1926; translated by Michael D. Rutter and David M. Gunn as *The Succession to the Throne of David,* Sheffield, South Yorkshire: Almond, 1982

Watts, James W. and Paul R. House (editors), *Forming Prophetic Literature: Essays on Isaiah and the Twelve in Honor of John D.W. Watts,* Sheffield, South Yorkshire: Sheffield Academic Press, 1996

Wilson, Robert R., *Prophecy and Society in Ancient Israel,* Philadelphia: Fortress, 1980

The very different types of literature in the Former and Latter Prophets sections of the canon have resulted in sharply differing approaches being used to interpret them. Much of the recent research on the former prophets, for example, has consisted of narrative-critical studies and detailed analyses of major characters within the narrative.

LONG's doctoral dissertation considers the 1 Samuel account of the life of King Saul from a narratological perspective, and it is typical of the new-critical, narrative-based analysis that was common in the 1970s and 1980s. Long identifies a number of key historical and theological issues provoked by the Saul texts, which have proven troublesome to interpreters for many years—particularly the interpretative crux of 1 Samuel 10:7–8 and the claim of Saul's rejection by God—and suggests that these problems result from difficulties with the literary interpretation of the text. Having considered some specific features of Hebrew narrative style, he then proceeds to use the insights of contemporary literary approaches and concludes that 1 Samuel is broadly neutral on the question of kingship in general and rather critical of Saul himself, but that it holds an extremely negative view of the people's request for a king. Long takes account of the work of Gunn but differs from him on a number of points of detail, and in particular he sees little reason to blame God for his treatment of Saul. Rather, in his view it is the people who are to blame for their unreasonable request.

GUNN sees the story of King Saul's life as a work of high tragedy in the same tradition as *King Oedipus, Macbeth, Tess of the D'Urbervilles*, and the like, and also as a piece of writing exhibiting immense literary skill and a highly significant moral dimension. Gunn is troubled by God's treatment of Saul, whom he sees as doomed to failure not because of his own waywardness or disobedience but largely because of the intervention in Saul's life of "forces beyond his control." Israel's first king therefore becomes a victim of circumstance—and of the deity—as much as of his own stupidity. In particular, he has to deal with many more obstacles to and restrictions upon his rule than his successor David. Gunn traces these themes throughout the life of Saul and concludes by summarizing the characterization of Saul and God in the Deuteronomistic History. He examines in particular Saul's jealousy and his knowledge of his rejection and God's readiness to condemn Saul, even to manipulate him by sending an evil spirit upon him.

Although his suggestions have come under increasing criticism in recent years, ROST is a classic and is fundamental for any study of the united monarchy. Based on a detailed source-critical analysis of Samuel and Kings, Rost postulates an originally independent Succession Narrative written early in Solomon's reign, presumably by an author from within the court, and demonstrates how it seeks to justify the ascent of Solomon to his father's throne. The Succession Narrative along with the story of the ark and Nathan's prophecy to David in 2 Samuel 7 are then examined in detail in a masterpiece of "tendency criticism," as Rost investigates the historical circumstances of the end of David's reign and the beginning of Solomon's and outlines the distinctive theological perspectives of the various authors.

BRONNER seeks an explanation for the strong miraculous element in the biblical narratives concerning Elijah and Elisha. Rejecting the scholarly tendency to rationalize the miracle stories away or see them as legendary and secondary additions to the genuine historical data contained in the narratives, she argues that they have a vital role to play. She sees the battle for ascendancy between Ba'al and YHWH as being a key theme of the biblical text, and she suggests that these "wonder stories" feature strongly in the comparison of YHWH, the living and active God, and the inactive, impotent, and incompetent Ba'al. They are primarily a polemic against paganism. The miraculous elements of the text are therefore essential to the author's rhetorical strategy and serve to magnify the deity rather than his servants the prophets. In support of her thesis, Bronner finds parallels in Ugaritic literature that confirm her suspicions, noting how both Elisha and Elijah seem to have powers that in the pagan sources are ascribed to Ba'al alone, such as control over the weather, the ability to resurrect the dead, the privilege of ascending to heaven, and so on. By giving YHWH authority over these powers, the biblical narrator is seeking to reject the claim of Ba'al to any sort of authority and thus to undermine popular conceptions of Canaanite mythology.

Turning to the latter prophets, a number of important works have enhanced understanding of what prophecy is and how it relates as a phenomenon both to ancient Israel and to biblical scholars and faith communities today. CARROLL's classic book uses the social-psychological concept of cognitive dissonance to seek an explanation for the surprisingly large number of apparent "failed" prophecies in the Hebrew Bible. Dissonance theory considers the result of a subject holding two mutually contradictory beliefs or pieces of data and examines how such scenarios are resolved or avoided. In terms of biblical prophecy, Carroll demonstrates how failed prophecies may be reinterpreted by the community and examines the response of believers within and without the text to "disconfirmed" or contradicted predictions and statements, looking at their attempts to bridge the gap between expectation and reality. Working from the observation that "dissonance gives rise to hermeneutic," Carroll shows how religious communities have dealt with cognitive dissonance by qualifying and reinterpreting one or other of the cognitions, by appealing to the need for faith, or by understanding their circumstances differently or working to change them to avoid dissonance in the first place. He concludes that popular frustration at this continuing reinterpretation may have been among the causes of the rapid demise of classical prophecy after the exile and the move toward the less easily verifiable apocalyptic.

WILSON's book is perhaps one of the clearest and most thorough of the many great introductions to the prophetic phenomenon that have appeared in the second half of the 20th century. Writing again from a sociological perspective, he stresses the need for an interdisciplinary approach to understanding biblical prophecy, one that will stretch across the boundaries of time and location as well as social context. Wilson examines apparently prophetic or mystic figures in contemporary societies, considering whether concepts of possession, divination, and manticism prevalent in tribal societies today are able to throw any light on biblical understandings of the prophet as an intermediary between God and humans. He then applies those conclusions to the available extrabiblical evidence from the ancient Near East before applying the results of his background research to an analysis of prophetism in Israel and Judah, which reveals a number of notable differences in prophetic activity between the twin states. Wilson also establishes a distinction between the central prophets, who apparently desired to work within the system for change (or sometimes to maintain the status quo), and peripheral prophets, who rejected the traditions and ideologies of their society to the extent that they became outcasts and found it necessary to critique their nation from outside. Wilson's work offers helpful insights into prophetic origins and development, and it provides convincing explanations for the different functions of some prophetic figures within the text and the contrasting ways in which they appear to be received by their audiences.

How prophetic books actually came into being is an entirely different question, however. It is very difficult to classify the prophetic books in terms of a common genre and equally hard to explain their historical development, how they came to be the kind of books they are now, and even how they came into existence. The series of essays collected by WATTS and HOUSE seeks to address such questions as these, regarding the nature and formation of prophecy in its literary form from a number of different methodological standpoints, including those of textual criticism, close synchronic reading of the text, tradition history, and redaction criticism. This diversity of approaches results in a wide variety of conclusions that highlight still further the very real problems that need to be tackled by any explanation of the origins of the prophetic books.

BRENNER's book, one of a series on the various subsets of the Hebrew canon, consists of a number of essays written by feminist or feminist-influenced biblical scholars. It is divided into three sections. The first considers the case of Hosea and his marriage to Gomer, which often has presented scholars with an ethical dilemma. Brenner's second section turns to the problem of "pornoprophetics," the vivid and explicitly sexual imagery that appears in many prophetic texts, often seeming to glorify sexual and physical assault and the brutal humiliation of women for the pleasure and fantasy of men. A third section consists of a solitary essay by Nancy Bowen on the characterization of God in the prophetic books that questions his trustworthiness as a character, especially when he appears intent on deception.

ANDREW DAVIES

Prophets, Twelve Minor

Barton, John, *Amos's Oracles against the Nations: A Study of Amos 1.3–2.5* (Society for Old Testament Study, vol. 6), Cambridge and New York: Cambridge University Press, 1980

Carroll R[odas], Mark Daniel, *Contexts for Amos: Prophetic Poetics in Latin American Perspective* (Journal for the Study of the Old Testament Supplement Series, vol. 132), Sheffield, South Yorkshire: JSOT, 1992

Hasel, Gerhard F., *Understanding the Book of Amos: Basic Issues in Current Interpretations*, Grand Rapids, Michigan: Baker Book House, 1991

House, Paul R., *The Unity of the Twelve* (Journal for the Study of the Old Testament Supplement Series, vol. 97), Sheffield, South Yorkshire: Almond, 1990

King, Philip, *Amos, Hosea, Micah: An Archaeological Commentary*, Philadelphia: Westminster, 1988

Nogalski, James, *Literary Precursors to the Book of the Twelve* (Beihefte zur Zeitschrift für die alttestamentliche Wissenschaft, vol. 217), Berlin and New York: de Gruyter, 1993

Nogalski, James, *Redactional Processes in the Book of the Twelve* (Beihefte zur Zeitschrift für die alttestamentliche Wissenschaft, vol. 218), Berlin and New York: de Gruyter, 1993

Person, Raymond Franklin, *In Conversation with Jonah: Conversation Analysis, Literary Criticism, and the Book of Jonah* (Journal for the Study of the Old Testament Supplement Series, vol. 220), Sheffield, South Yorkshire: Sheffield Academic Press, 1996

Sherwood, Yvonne, *The Prostitute and the Prophet: Hosea's Marriage in Literary-Theoretical Perspective* (Journal for the Study of the Old Testament Supplement Series, vol. 212), Sheffield, South Yorkshire: Sheffield Academic Press, 1996

Smith, George Adam, *The Book of the Twelve Prophets, Commonly Called the Minor*, London: Hodder and Stoughton, and New York: Armstrong, 1896; revised edition, New York and London: Harper and Brothers, 1940

Much recent interest in the minor prophetic books has focused on their unity. Scholars have begun to question why the Book of the Twelve is considered a single entity in the canon of the Hebrew Bible, what binds it together, and what the individual books actually have in common. HOUSE bemoans the paucity of treatments of the Minor Prophets as a whole, pointing out that although they have long been designated one book they have hardly ever been treated as such. He is interested in how they came to be associated and what it means for their interpretation that they are now one book. House believes study of the final canonical form of the books offers some key interpretative insights, and he advocates the use of canonical criticism because he feels it "asks the right questions to discover unity," although it is unable to answer them all. He also favors the application of literary criticism, North American formalism in particular, which has even more to offer because it "provides the actual means of uncovering unity." He then proceeds to demonstrate the advantages his method offers students of the Minor Prophets, as he explores the various genres and subgenres of prophetic literature. His formalistic approach, in conjunction with an awareness of theological ideas such as sin, punishment, and restoration as major structural devices, is used to delineate the structure of the prophetic corpus. Further chapters consider the plot, which he identifies as the "natural outworking" of the structure, and the characterization of God, the prophets, Israel, and the nations in the Book of the Twelve.

NOGALSKI (1993a, 1993b) also considers the origin of the Book of the Twelve in his two books, which together represent the fruit of his doctoral studies. Not unlike House, his particular interest is in identifying "the techniques employed in the combination of the prophetic writings and their possible consequences for the individual books," especially in determining "how this unification affected the shape and content of the original writings." Nogalski suggests the books are unified by the use of catchwords, where "the end of one writing contains several words and phrases that reappear in the beginning units of the adjacent writing," and he proceeds to demonstrate how this is true, before turning his attention to the origins of these catchwords—are they authorial, redactional, the work of the collector, or accidental? His work demonstrates very effectively the intertextual relationships that exist between the minor prophetic books.

The Book of Amos has been the subject of more critical analysis than most of the Minor Prophets, and a very substantial number of important monographs have been published in recent years. In the light of this glut of scholarship, HASEL provides an excellent orientation to Amos study, examining current scholarly opinion on some ten key interpretative issues within the book, including consideration both of the prophet's background (his profession, social context, and approach to prophecy) and of his literary and theological gifts (taking account of such concerns as his oracles against the nations, his social critique, and his eschatology). Under each chapter heading, Hasel considers the contributions of a number of leading commentators and scholars on the issues in question, comparing and contrasting their conclusions before siding with one view or another (sometimes rejecting them all and providing his own alternative). Perhaps the greatest asset of Hasel's work is its breadth of scholarship, as it takes into account material from all kinds of sources, some of which is unlikely to be readily available to English readers. His work therefore provides a useful source text for current opinion on the interpretation of one of the most extensively discussed minor prophets.

CARROLL's revision of his doctoral thesis is notable for its fascinating dual focus on two concerns. First, he is interested in reading the Bible from the perspective of his native Guatemala, seeking to identify and quantify the unique contribution Latin America has to offer to biblical studies and to understand how biblical and theological scholarship can relate to and interact with Latin American culture, especially given the current Western/Anglo bias typical of most academic dialogue. Second, Carroll seeks to formulate a context-based approach to the Bible that emphasizes the importance of the text itself but still seeks to relate that text to the world of the interpreter. After an introductory section that considers anthropological and sociological studies of prophecy and other attempts at reconstructing the ministry and message of Amos, this double emphasis is worked out fully on the basis of the presumption that "a poetic reading within a rich understanding of the [interpreter's] cultural context" is the best way to proceed. Carroll stands in a tradition similar to that of Liberation Theology: he portrays the prophetic text as being in itself a call for believers to stand up against injustice and work toward the creation of a new kind of society. At the same time, however, he wishes to move beyond the simple call to social action and sees "prophetic" ministry as something much broader. He seeks to establish the foundations for a contemporary prophetic ministry in Latin America based on his reconstruction of the meaning of Amos for today.

BARTON's short monograph treats two particular issues that concern Amos's oracles against the nations. First he asks, "Why does the book of Amos begin with a series of oracles against Israel's neighbours, and only then turn to denounce the prophet's own people?" Barton sees three possible options here. Either these oracles are reminiscent of the very oldest, highly nationalistic type of prophecy evidenced in the story of Balaam and Egyptian execration texts; or Amos is among the first to offer the radically new insight that all nations are under the control and direction of one God; or, possibly, the oracles merely serve as a literary device to draw attention to the fate of Israel and Judah and thus carry little theological import. He then proceeds to ask himself, "Why does Amos think that these other nations are accountable for their atrocities?" and concludes that Amos "was appealing to a kind of conventional or customary law about international conduct which he at least believed to be self-evidently right." Barton also observes that this conclusion has implications for current understanding of Amos's ethics, noting that the fact that "he sees moral conduct as a matter of conformity to a human convention . . . rather than to the overt or explicit demands of God" implies that Amos's ethical system is "not simply a question of theonomy, as it is quite widely thought to be."

KING is noted as an archaeologist of great erudition and insight, as well as a biblical scholar of high sensitivity to the text, and his archaeological commentary demonstrates both qualities. King's intention in this work is to demonstrate how archaeology can illuminate (not prove) the Bible, and he moves in this direction by highlighting some key discoveries that bear on the interpretation of Amos, Micah, and Hosea. He provides much information and many photographs and drawings. King makes use of all that is known of the historical and geographical setting of the books, such as the position, structure, and social organization of the cities and nations mentioned in the eighth-century prophets, as well as offering some significant insights into such topics as ancient warfare and defense, religious worship and practice, and agriculture and herdsmanship. King shows very plainly how the archaeologists' reconstruction of life in ancient Israel can then be used to elucidate the biblical text.

Perhaps one of the most important commentaries on the Minor Prophets in the history of their interpretation is the famous study by SMITH. This two-volume work deals with the books in chronological order, providing each book with an introduction dealing with critical issues such as authorship,

date, and the like, and a couple of chapters of thorough exposition, based upon Smith's own translation, supplemented with detailed critical and explanatory notes. Rather than verse-by-verse exegesis, Smith prefers to comment on the text in its larger individual units, which means he avoids the tendency to atomize and retains a good holistic view of the books.

Contemporary literary-critical approaches also have been applied recently to the prophetic books. An excellent illustration of this can be found in the work of PERSON, who views the Book of Jonah in the light of theories of narrative art and through the reading process developed with the aid of conversation analysis, the critical study of conversations. He argues that in Jonah, "the narrator satirically manipulates readers in the selection and arrangement of the characters' speeches," and he proceeds to justify his thesis in a verse-by-verse exposition of the book, which demonstrates effectively how the conversations "contribute to the development of the different narrative elements of plot, character, atmosphere and tone." Person also includes a different reading of Jonah, written from the perspective of the reader-response theory of Wolfgang Iser, and this adds further to the value of his work.

Another interesting example of the application of radical literary criticism to the prophetic books is provided by SHERWOOD. Her book highlights the difficulties posed by the account of Hosea's marriage (Hosea 1–3) and treats the story from four different literary perspectives, those of ideological criticism, semiotics, deconstruction, and feminist criticism. Sherwood provides a thorough and often entertaining introduction to each of these approaches in turn before applying them to her chosen text and drawing out their implications for biblical studies in general. She concludes that "Hosea 1–3 is a text that exists primarily to 'contend' with and provoke a 'controversy' with its implied audience," and she suggests that literary study of the text is better able than many methods to highlight these "shocking strategies." This is because her approach sees the difficulties in the text, its "disjunctive style and its capacity to subvert itself" not as problems, but as moments of opportunity, "a way of suggesting different meanings." Sherwood also sees a number of correspondences between prophecy and postmodern styles of writing, noticing that the capacity and desire to shock readers, which directs much postmodern fiction, can certainly be identified in Hosea, too.

ANDREW DAVIES

Proselytizing *see* Conversion to Judaism;
God-Fearers

Provence

Calmann, Marianne, *The Carrière of Carpentras* (The Littman Library of Jewish Civilization), Rutherford, New Jersey: Fairleigh Dickinson University Press, and London: Associated University Presses, 1983

Golb, Norman, "New Light on the Persecution of French Jews at the Time of the First Crusade," *Proceedings of the American Academy for Jewish Research*, 34, 1966

Grayzel, Solomon, "The Avignon Popes and the Jews," *Historia Judaica*, 2(1), 1940

Grayzel, Solomon, "The Confession of a Medieval Jewish Convert," *Historia Judaica*, 17(2), 1955

Herskowitz, William K., "Judeo-Christian Dialogue in Provence as Reflected in *Milhemet Mitzva* of R. Meir Hameili," D.H.L. diss., Yeshiva University, 1974

Kober, Adolf, "Jewish Converts in Provence from the Sixteenth to the Eighteenth Century," *Jewish Social Studies*, 6(4), 1944

Nirenberg, David, *Communities of Violence: Persecution of Minorities in the Middle Ages*, Princeton, New Jersey: Princeton University Press, 1996

Shatzmiller, Joseph, "Contacts et échanges entre savants juifs et chrétiens à Montpellier vers 1300," in *Juifs et judaïsme de Languedoc XIIIe siècle–début XIVe siècle*, edited by Marie-Humbert Vicaire and Bernhard Blumenkranz, Toulouse: Privat, 1977

Shatzmiller, Joseph, "Tumultus et Rumor in Sinagoga: An Aspect of Social Life of Provençal Jews in the Middle Ages," *AJS Review*, 2, 1977

Szajkowski, Zosa, "The Decline and Fall of Provençal Jewry," *Jewish Social Studies*, 6(1), 1944

Szajkowski, Zosa, "Relations among Sephardim, Ashkenazim and Avignonese Jews in France from the 16th to the 20th Centuries," *Yivo Annual of Jewish Social Science*, 10, 1955

Szajkowski, Zosa, "The Comtadin Jews and the Annexation of the Papal Provence," *JQR*, n.s. 46, 1955–1956

Twersky, I., "Aspects of the Social and Cultural History of Provençal Jewry," in his *Studies in Jewish Law and Philosophy*, New York: Ktav, 1982

Academic research on the Jews of Provence started in the 19th century and was done mostly by French scholars. Some work has appeared in Israel in Hebrew. This essay covers only English-language works and emphasizes the most recent and the most informative ones.

CALMANN's state-of-the-art monograph is based largely on three archives in Carpentras (documents for the years 1277 to 1789) and two archives in Avignon. It aims "to discover the pattern of life within the *carrière* [Provençal for Jewish quarter; more precisely, street] of Carpentras, the relations of its inhabitants with one another and with the Christians, with the people of the Comtat and beyond, and with their ultimate rulers, the popes." The analysis is thematic, comprising ten chapters: the origins of the *carrière*; people and buildings; everyday life; a state within the state; the finances of the community; the economic history of the *carrière*; language, literature, and learning; the church and conversion; relations between Jews and Christians; and the revolution and after. Calmann's work, although academic in method and approach, is written in clear language avoiding technical jargon and can be recommended equally for scholars and general readers.

GOLB has reexamined and reedited a previously only partially published Cairo Genizah letter mentioning a pogrom in a French community during the Middle Ages. He emends the reading of a geographical name and determines that the event—in which many Jews were killed, their children captured to be raised as Christians, and their houses plundered—took place in the town of Monieux, in the Vaucluse near Carpentras. Basing his work on internal and external evidence, Golb has been able to determine that a wave of pogroms hit the Jews of Provence some time before October 1096, just as in northern France and Germany.

After examining a large amount of Vatican material, GRAYZEL (1940) states with certainty that the Avignon popes employed the services of Jews on a large scale. Grayzel also describes restrictions upon Jewish life such as the enforcement of the Jewish badge, the prohibition of the employment of Christian servants and nurses and certain measures of ghettoization. A considerable number of papal documents of the 13th and 14th centuries are examined that refer to converts and conversion, particularly to converts who relapsed into Judaism. Practicing Jews are depicted as repeatedly having been accused of influencing these reversions, while the popes of Avignon, particularly John XXII, emerge as quite zealous in converting the Jews.

GRAYZEL (1955) depicts the social conditions of Jews in Provence, particularly in the vicinity of Toulouse, but typical for all of Western Europe in the 14th century. Although the article focuses on a specific case, it gives a broad picture of forced conversion and the persecution of Jews by the Catholic Church at the beginning of the 14th century. As such, the importance of this article goes far beyond appearances, and it stands as a significant treatment of the whole phenomenon of forced conversion and relapse.

NIRENBERG deals with the problem of persecution of minorities in Christian Europe, mainly in 14th-century Aragon, but some parts of his book concern the Jews of France. Basing his work on medieval Jewish and Christian chronicles, he describes how the so-called Shepherds' Crusade originated in Normandy, reached Paris, and rapidly moved to Provence and Languedoc. Despite Pope John XXII's objections to massacres of the Jews, the local townsfolk and municipal officials supported the shepherds' atrocities. At places where the pope's orders were routinely obeyed, it was possible to stop the massacres and even to drive the perpetrators out of the area, as was the case in Carcassonne. The author tries to offer reasons why common folk supported the shepherds and their violent actions against the Jews. He argues that by attacking the Jews, the shepherds indirectly attacked the French crown, because "the Jews in France were considered fiscal agents of the monarchy, occasionally serfs of the king." Nirenberg shows a different kind of anti-Jewish attack following the so-called Lepers' Plot of 1321; these attacks were committed not by an ignorant mob but by the urban populace encouraged by the local officials. Also the alleged guilt of the Jews was different in nature; now they were accused of participating in a plot with the lepers and the Muslim king of Granada to poison Christendom. Nevertheless, the results were similar: in both cases hundreds of Jews were massacred, burned, or forced to commit group suicide. In the epilogue, Nirenberg treats cases of violence against the Jews during the Black Death (1348) in the south of France (Carcassonne, Narbonne, and in certain towns of Roussillon). This time most of the attacks against the Jews took place beyond the Pyrenees, in Aragon and Catalonia, where again hundreds of Jews were killed under suspicion of treason and poisoning the waters. It does not mean that similar events did not happen in Provence. As in many other cases, there are no historical sources for Provence in this respect.

HERSKOWITZ has edited the Hebrew text of the first section of *Milhemet Mitsvah* by Rabbi Meir ben Simeon HaMeili of Narbonne, a polemical anti-Christian work. This section is devoted to debates between the author and various clergy, including the archbishop of Narbonne, who later became Pope Gregory IX. In his introduction, Herskowitz collects historical, political, economic, and religious facts pertaining to conditions of the Jews in Provence in the 13th century from published Jewish and Christian sources.

KOBER notes that after the forced baptisms prevalent during the 15th century and the expulsion of Jews from Provence at the end of the 15th century, Provence faced the same problem with its Neophytes as Spain with its Marranos, or New Christians. King René (1431–1480), benevolent toward the Jews for financial reasons, at the same time did everything in his power to induce them to embrace Christianity. He accorded special privileges to Jews who consented to be baptized. After 1481, however, there were numerous incidents of forced baptism. The Jews expelled in 1500 fled to the neighboring Comtat Venaissin, and some made their way to Italy and Turkey. Their property was confiscated and incorporated into royal holdings.

Because of the grand scale of voluntary conversions in the 15th century, however, the Provençal parliament found it necessary to pass the law of 24 May 1542, forbidding under dire penalty any discrimination against Neophytes on account of their former affiliations. But particular incidents Kober describes show that this law was not strongly enforced, so that in 1611, for example, the advocate general, de Monier, laid before King Henri IV false charges against members of parliament of Jewish ancestry, drawing attention to this common feature. Only in 1778 was the distinction between the various leading families of Provence—between those who were originally Christian and those who descended from Jewish or Muslim ancestry—legally abolished.

Kober writes about papal policy toward the Jews of Comtat Venaissin from the 16th to the 18th century, when the Vatican introduced different measures to encourage the baptism of Jews. One of them was compulsory and frequent attendance at conversionist sermons. Despite all the measures attempted, there were very few converts until the later half of the 18th century. It was only at this time that the conditions of Jewish life in Provence approached the intolerable, with forced baptisms of Jewish children without parental consent becoming an almost daily occurrence. In the end many Jews left the region to save their offspring.

SHATZMILLER (1977b) describes the central role of the synagogue in medieval Provence, concentrating particularly on the town of Manosque. The preeminent historian of medieval Provençal Jewry, the author discusses several incidents of personal assault, strife, commotion, and dispute at the synagogue, which he traces in local court documents and finds paralleled in other locations. Shatzmiller shows how different Jewish communities dealt with dissent and disagreement between members. He also explains the relationship of the town authorities to the Jewish community and how they maintained public order.

SHATZMILLER (1977a) demonstrates that there was significant contact and even cooperation between medieval Jewish and gentile scholars in Provence, particularly in Montpellier. These contacts took different forms but most often it was that of translations of scholarly literature from Hebrew to Latin or from Latin to Hebrew. He cites a number of examples from the years 1299 to 1306.

SZAJKOWSKI (1944) stresses that the relationship of Christians to converts in the papal enclave was markedly different from that in the rest of Provence. The baptized Jews here became real Christians, and the hostility toward them ceased. But unconverted Jews, on the contrary, experienced a greater hostility and were in fact despised, so that in the 17th century the gentry of Comtat Venaissin demanded the expulsion of the Jews. In 1768 the Comtat Venaissin was united with France, and the Jews felt more comfortable, with fewer limitations and restrictions, but antisemitic accusations and occasional publications continued to harass them. Thus even in 1789, the year of the French Revolution, antisemitic charges were brought up for discussion in the National Assembly and espoused in the speech of the Provençal deputy Charles François Bouche.

SZAJKOWSKI (1955) describes the demography of the Jews in Provence after the French Revolution. He discusses patterns of emigration from the four older communities of Carpentras, Cavaillon, Avignon, and L'Isle-sur-la-Sorgue; economic and social status; trades and professions; religious and civic life; education; cultural life; and finally the disappearance of the communities from the midst of an often quite hostile environment.

SZAJKOWSKI (1955–1956) summarizes the political history of the annexation of the papal province by France during the last quarter of the 18th century and describes how the changes affected its Jewish residents beginning with the first printed request for annexation, which included a proposed review of the status of Jews bristling with antisemitic charges.

TWERSKY singles out the period from the middle of the 11th to the early 14th century as the most important in development of the intellectual activities of Provençal Jewry. He notices the "remarkable efflorescence" of Jewish culture in Provence in rabbinics, philosophy, mysticism, ethics, exegesis, polemics, apologetics, grammar and lexicography, poetry, and belles lettres in relatively favorable social, political, and economic circumstances. All this was achieved, on the one hand, by preserving and transmitting the accumulated philosophic and scientific learning of Arabic-speaking Jewry and, on the other hand, by interpreting and disseminating it and mixing it with elements that either appeared first in Provence or were absorbed from the culture of Ashkenazi Jewry.

HAYIM Y. SHEYNIN

See also France

Proverbs

Alshekh, Moses, *Rav Peninim be'ur Mishle Shelomoh*, 1592; translated by E. Munk as *The Book of Proverbs with Rav Peninim: Commentary*, Brooklyn, New York: Spiegel, 1991

Brenner, Athalya and F. Van Dijk-Hemmes, *On Gendering Texts: Female and Male Voices in the Hebrew Bible* (Biblical Interpretation Series, vol. 1), Leiden and New York: Brill, 1993

Brown, William P., *Character in Crisis: A Fresh Approach to the Wisdom Literature of the Old Testament*, Grand Rapids, Michigan: Eerdmans, 1996

Bryce, Glendon E., *A Legacy of Wisdom: The Egyptian Contribution to the Wisdom of Israel*, Lewisburg, Pennsylvania: Bucknell University Press, 1979

Camp, Claudia, *Wisdom and the Feminine in the Book of Proverbs*, Decatur, Georgia: Almond, 1985

Camp, Claudia, "What's So Strange about the Strange Woman," in *The Bible and the Politics of Exegesis: Essays in Honor of Norman K. Gottwald on His Sixty-Fifth Birthday*, edited by David Jobling et al., Cleveland, Ohio: Pilgrim, 1991

Clifford, Richard, *Proverbs* (Old Testament Library), Louisville, Kentucky: Westminster John Knox, 1998

Cook, Johann, *The Septuagint of Proverbs: Jewish and/or Hellenistic Proverbs?: Concerning the Hellenistic Colouring of LXX Proverbs* (Supplements to Vetus Testamentum, vol. 69), New York: Brill, 1997

Delitzsch, Franz, *Biblical Commentary on the Proverbs of Solomon*, Edinburgh: Clark, 1874; Grand Rapids, Michigan: Eerdmans, 1950

Fontaine, Carole, *Traditional Sayings in the Old Testament: A Contextual Study* (Bible and Literature Series, 5), Sheffield, South Yorkshire: Almond, 1982

Fox, Michael V., *Proverbs 1–9* (Anchor Bible), Garden City, New York: Doubleday, 1999

Golka, Friedemann W., *The Leopard's Spots: Biblical and African Wisdom in Proverbs*, Edinburgh: Clark, 1993

Harris, Scott L., *Proverbs 1–9: A Study of Inner-Biblical Interpretation* (Society of Biblical Literature Dissertation Series, no. 150), Atlanta, Georgia: Scholars Press: 1995

Malbim, Meir Loeb ben Jehiel Michael, *Malbim on Mishley: The Commentary of Rabbi Meir Leibush Malbim on the Book of Proverbs*, translated by Charles Wengrov, New York: Feldheim, 1982

McKane, William, *Proverbs: A New Approach* (Old Testament Library), Philadelphia: Westminster, and London: SCM, 1970

Murphy, Roland E., *The Tree of Life: An Exploration of Biblical Wisdom Literature* (Anchor Bible Reference Library), New York: Doubleday, 1990; 2nd edition, Grand Rapids, Michigan: Eerdmans, 1996

Newsom, Carol A., "Woman and the Discourse of Patriarchal Wisdom: A Study of Proverbs 1–9," in *Gender and Difference in Ancient Israel*, edited by P.L. Day, Minneapolis, Minnesota: Fortress, 1989

Perdue, Leo G., *Wisdom and Creation: The Theology of Wisdom Literature*, Nashville, Tennessee: Abingdon, 1994

Toy, Crawford H., *A Critical and Exegetical Commentary on the Book of Proverbs* (International Critical Commentary, vol. 16), New York: Scribner, and Edinburgh: Clark, 1899

Van Leeuwen, Raymond, *New Interpreter's Bible*, vol. 5: *Proverbs*, Nashville, Tennessee: Abingdon, 1997

Visotzky, Burton L., *The Midrash on Proverbs* (Yale Judaica Series, vol. 27), New Haven, Connecticut: Yale University Press, 1992

von Rad, Gerhard, *Weisheit in Israel*, 1970; translated by James D. Martin as *Wisdom in Israel*, London: SCM, and Nashville, Tennessee: Abingdon, 1972

Westermann, Claus, *Roots of Wisdom: The Oldest Proverbs of Israel and Other Peoples*, Louisville, Kentucky: Westminster/Knox, and Edinburgh: Clark, 1995

Whybray, R.N., *The Composition of the Book of Proverbs* (Journal for the Study of the Old Testament Supplement Series, 168), Sheffield, South Yorkshire: JSOT, 1994

Whybray, R.N., *The Book of Proverbs: A Survey of Modern Study* (History of Biblical Interpretation Series, vol. 1), New York: Brill, 1995

Williams, James G., *Those Who Ponder Proverbs: Aphoristic Thinking and Biblical Literature* (Bible and Literature Series, 2), Sheffield, South Yorkshire: Almond, 1981

The biblical Book of Proverbs (in Hebrew, Mishlei) belongs to wisdom literature, a genre cultivated throughout the ancient Near East. A number of important studies of wisdom literature include discussions of Proverbs. Most important is VON RAD's theological-philosophical reading of Israel's experiential wisdom (regrettably published in a contorted English translation). Another valuable synthesis of wisdom thought is PERDUE's, which describes wisdom as a dialectic between anthropology (with its focus on the practicalities of life and the secular world) and cosmology (the affirmation of a just and beautiful cosmic order created by God). MURPHY provides a helpful introduction to wisdom literature, giving considerable attention to Proverbs. He places unusual emphasis on the "faith experience" underlying wisdom.

WHYBRAY (1995), a topical history of Proverbs study in the modern period, is an excellent place to start for an orientation to the field. His survey also includes summaries of important works in French and German.

Premodern exegesis of Proverbs has not been properly studied or translated into English. Elements of Hellenistic Jewish exegesis can be inferred from the ancient Greek translation, the Septuagint, which COOK's detailed and technical study analyzes. Very little of the rich traditional Jewish exegesis is available in English. The translation of ALSHEKH's commentary is partial and paraphrastic, but it does give the gist of his literary and homiletic insights. VISOTZKY's translation, introduction, and annotations of a rich ninth-century compendium of exegesis, homilies, and legends grant a wide audience access to an important midrash. There is also an abridged translation of the commentary by MALBIM, a traditionalist 19th-century scholar with a keen sensitivity to the nuances of words and phrases.

DELITZSCH's dense commentary, while dated, religious, and moralizing, is still valuable. Delitzsch understands wisdom as drawn from the religion of Israel but cast in a universalistic, humanistic form intended to demonstrate that Israelite religion is fit to become a world religion. One of the few commentators to consider the implications of the Masoretic accentual system for exegesis, his comments are based on a deep knowledge of Hebrew but are limited by an obsolete philological method.

TOY's dry and academic exegesis is useful for its philological and textual notes as well as for its effort to restate precisely the surface meanings of the proverbs. Like Delitzsch's work, this analysis is dated in many ways, especially in its treatment of the ancient translations.

McKANE's commentary is somewhat difficult to read because of its nonsequential exegesis. It is also hindered by an idiosyncratic (but in some ways perceptive) historical schema that arranges the sayings of Proverbs in three hypothetical stages of development: an old, secular wisdom; a community-centered wisdom; and a Yahwistic-pietistic reinterpretation. Nevertheless, the work is characterized by sensible judgment and is based on a thorough knowledge of language and text.

For a number of decades, there were few good commentaries available in English. Some major commentaries, however, have recently appeared or are about to appear.

CLIFFORD's commentary aims at an educated lay readership but includes some technical notes. It gives special attention to rhetoric and forms of communication.

VAN LEEUWEN writes for a broader readership, and the presentation is nontechnical. The editor has a Christian orientation, but he does not impose it on the text, which includes two English translations, a literary commentary, and an exposition with "reflections" that uses Proverbs to explore contemporary realities. Van Leeuwen takes issue with the notion that Proverbs is somehow less "religious" than the rest of the Bible or divorced from biblical Yahwism.

FOX's commentary on chapters one through nine is designed for both a general and an academic audience. (A volume on chapters ten through 31 is in progress.) The extensive discussion of philological and textual issues will primarily interest scholars, but the body of the exposition and some topical essays are accessible to a broader audience. The commentary is a study in intellectual history, emphasizing comparisons between Proverbs and wisdom literature from elsewhere in the Near East, particularly Egypt. Proverbs' innovative claim, Fox argues, is that the human intellect, founded on fear of God and tutored in traditional teachings, is the prime virtue of character and as such is the necessary (and almost sufficient) means for creating a life of material, physical, social, and moral success.

BRYCE traces the Egyptian influences on Israelite wisdom, stressing the way in which Proverbs 22:17–23:11 draws upon the Instruction of Amenemope. The author examines the textual parallels in detail and distinguishes three stages of borrowing and development: adaptation, assimilation, and integration. He also discusses the Egyptian background of the royal and political wisdom of Proverbs 25–27. This book does not require knowledge of Hebrew or Egyptian and is a valuable introduction to the question of the foreign background of Israelite wisdom.

HARRIS's intertextual study seeks allusions to other biblical books in Proverbs 1:8–19, 1:20–33, and 6:1–19. He finds deliberate reuse of elements from the Joseph story and from Jeremiah's career (Jeremiah 7 and 20). Of the various parallels he suggests, the most convincing is the prophetic background of the figure of wisdom in Proverbs 1:8–19.

WHYBRAY (1994) investigates the development of Proverbs from its original short units to its present form—a very difficult task, given that the book is compiled from different sources. In chapters one through nine, he identifies ten originally independent instructions (as many scholars do), which, he contends, were elaborated in a couple of later redactions, one concerned with wisdom, the other with Yahwistic religion. (Separating these layers presupposes a rigorous, one-dimensional consistency on the original author's part, because otherwise the author could have introduced the wisdom and Yahwistic motifs himself.) Whybray notes that the rest of the Book of Proverbs is composed mostly of individual sayings, which, he argues, were progressively gathered and organized by associative principles. A number of scholars are currently looking for patterns in Proverbs, but significant patterns remain elusive in chapters ten through 29. Whybray's study is a feasible but rather strained approach to this issue.

WILLIAMS attends to the philosophical basis of aphoristic wisdom, which he describes as the attempt to find and construct meaning in "fragments of experience." He regards aphorisms not only as a literary type but also as a way of constructing and conveying a view of reality. For Williams, the key concept is order, and he examines how aphoristic wisdom serves to establish—and sometimes undermine—order through tradition and experience.

BROWN's readable and innovative study identifies character formation as the primary goal of wisdom literature. He argues that Proverbs, particularly chapters one through nine, seeks to inculcate character virtues in a family context, hoping that adults will then use these values to promote their community's welfare. While the thesis as stated is an overgeneralization for wisdom literature as a whole, it is a valuable corrective to the older view of Proverbs (e.g., that presented by Toy), which construed the book as aimed at individual success alone.

FONTAINE introduces a new consideration into the study of biblical proverbs: proverb performance. Sayings are first of all a form of speech, intended for use in everyday discourse, although they are also purposive and have functions in literary contexts (which can be explored by examination of proverb use in biblical narrative). It remains to be seen to what degree the sayings in the Book of Proverbs can be explained in performance terms. Whatever their origins, however, the collected sayings in their current form are purely literary and detached from actual use.

Both WESTERMANN and GOLKA also investigate the social functions of traditional sayings in oral transmission and use. They detach preexilic Israelite wisdom from the social locations to which it is usually assigned, the scribes of the royal court and a hypothetical wisdom school. Instead, they describe this older Israelite wisdom, found primarily in Proverbs ten through 29, as oral folk wisdom, whose purposes and social setting can be better elucidated by comparison with African proverbs than with ancient Near Eastern wisdom. Westermann in particular reconstructs a congenial picture of simple village life, which he believes is the context of the folk sayings. These arguments about the relevance of the African parallels are, however, not fully convincing, and the derivation of the mass of Proverbs from a village setting may seem an oversimplification. Still, the focus on the folk/oral origins of some of the sayings of Proverbs is a welcome correction of the earlier, overly scholastic and literary point of view.

CAMP's (1985) study of the feminine in Proverbs is the most important of the numerous feminist studies of the book. It seeks to explain the origin and meaning of feminine imagery in the book, examining in particular the personification of wisdom as a woman (Proverbs 8) who mediates between the divine and the human. This image is based on the various roles and values associated with women in ancient Israel, and Camp shows that wisdom's female qualities are as essential as its abstract symbolic significance to the ethos of Proverbs. She further considers the relevance of the feminine in the shaping of the book as a whole.

Several feminist studies have focused on images of women in Proverbs one through nine, especially the "strange woman," the seductress of chapter seven. In their ideologically charged study, BRENNER and VAN DIJK-HEMMES identify a female speaker in parts (perhaps all) of Proverbs one through nine. This speaker, Brenner contends, internalizes masculine values implicit in the patriarchal effort to control female sexuality. Van Dijk-Hemmes, however, claims that the female voice partially "deconstructs its own position" and thus reduces its subservience to patriarchy.

Less convoluted are CAMP (1991) and NEWSOM's essays, which describe the strange woman as a representative of the "other" and a symbol of all dangers, chaotic powers, and/or marginalized groups or discourses. One may wonder, however, whether these works are historical analyses or modern allegorizations of a portrayal of ordinary adultery, which was deemed a sufficient evil to warrant grim warnings.

MICHAEL V. FOX

Psalms

Allen, Leslie C., *Psalms 101–150* (Word Biblical Commentary, vol. 21), Waco, Texas: Word, 1983; Milton Keynes, Buckinghamshire: Word, 1987

Craigie, Peter C., *Psalms 1–50* (Word Biblical Commentary, vol. 19), Waco, Texas: Word, 1983

Gruber, Mayer I., *Rashi's Commentary on Psalms* (South Florida Studies in the History of Judaism, no. 161), Atlanta, Georgia: Scholars Press, 1998

Keel, Othmar, *Die Welt der altorientalischen Bildsymbolik und das Alte Testament: am Beispiel der Psalmen,* 1972; translated by Timothy H. Hallett as *The Symbolism of the Biblical World: Ancient Near Eastern Iconography and the Book of Psalms,* New York: Seabury, and London: S.P.C.K., 1978

Rendsburg, Gary A., *Linguistic Evidence for the Northern Origin of Selected Psalms* (Monograph Series/Society of Biblical Literature, no. 43), Atlanta, Georgia: Scholars Press, 1990

Sarna, Nahum M., *Songs of the Heart: An Introduction to the Book of Psalms,* New York: Schocken, 1993

Simon, Uriel, *Arba' gishot le-Sefer Tehilim,* 1982; translated by Lenn J. Schram as *Four Approaches to the Book of Psalms: From Saadiah Gaon to Abraham Ibn Ezra* (SUNY Series in Judaica), Albany: State University of New York Press, 1991

Tate, Marvin E., *Psalms 51–100* (Word Biblical Commentary, vol. 20), Dallas, Texas: Word, 1990

Among the larger books of the Hebrew Bible, Psalms is commonly divided into 150 distinct compositions distributed among five separate books, probably on the analogy of the five books of the Pentateuch. Superscriptions contained in the Book of Psalms attribute 73 of the compositions to King David, while 24 of the psalms are not assigned to any author.

In the Pentateuch and the Prophets, notes SARNA, God reaches out to human beings, whereas in the Psalms, by and large, it is human beings who reach out to God. In his 20-page introduction and in the essays discussing ten representative psalms (Psalms 1; 8; 15; 19; 24; 30; 48; 82; 93; and 94) that follow, Sarna regards the Book of Psalms as an anthology of prayers deemed eternally relevant. He summarizes the gamut of ancient, medieval, and modern exegesis, including his own discoveries amassed during a lifetime of researching and teaching Psalms. He shows how the details that occupy biblical scholars can add to the value of specific psalms as devotional literature for contemporary readers.

Christian scholars emanating from traditions in which a hymnal (with or without a prayerbook) is used at worship services have often suggested that the Book of Psalms was the hymnal of Second Temple Judaism. Unsurprisingly, some Protestant groups have insisted that no hymn that was not based on Psalms—the hymnbook provided, as it were, by God—should be sung in church. Such a notion was anticipated by some medieval Karaite Jews who, seeing the Book of Psalms as a book of prayers, concluded that it, rather than the rabbinic liturgy, was the divinely sanctioned order of public worship. SIMON shows that such an idea is spelled out in detail by the 10th-century Karaites Japheth ben Ali and Salmon ben Jeroham. Moreover, Simon demonstrates that it is by way of a heated response to this Karaite view that Saadia, a contemporary of Japheth and Salmon, insists that the Book of Psalms is not a book of prayers addressed to God but rather another form of Torah in which God speaks, this time not through Moses but through King David. Simon shows how Abraham ibn Ezra wends his way between the Scylla of Japheth ben Ali's and Salmon ben Jeroham's liturgical dogma and the Charybdis of Saadia's prophetic dogma, attempting to return exegesis of the Psalter to rationality by suggesting, as had Rashi and before him the rabbis of the Talmud, that the Book of Psalms is in fact an anthology of numerous poetic genres, most but not all of them forms of prayer composed over the period of time between the dawn of Israel's history and the Babylonian exile.

CRAIGIE, TATE, and ALLEN succeed in what some modern biblical scholars like to call "total interpretation," which is to say that they bring to bear upon each psalm every possible discipline that might shed light upon the words, phrases, and messages of these ancient poems: philology, archaeology, form criticism, and newer forms of literary criticism. Their truly comprehensive bibliography is a gold mine for scholars, students, clergy, and teachers, as well as for lay Bible readers of every persuasion.

If these three volumes give us a little of everything, RENDS-BURG satisfies a different type of curiosity: the attempt to demonstrate that within the Psalter one can in fact find what ibn Ezra's teacher Moses ha-Cohen ibn Gikatilla sought in his own time, namely the identifying marks of psalms composed in a particular time and place. Rendsburg exemplifies the linguistic orientation of recent generations of American Jewish biblical scholars. He argues on the basis of phonological, orthographic, morphological, and syntactic features, as well as 41 lexical elements, a few word-pairs shared with Phoenician and Ugaritic, and references to Northern Israelite place names, that Psalms 9–10; 16; 29; 36; 42–50; 53; 58; 73–85; 87–88; 116; 132; 133; and 140–141 were composed in the Northern Kingdom during the two hundred years of its existence as a distinct political entity (922–722 B.C.E.). Rendsburg has absorbed well the teaching of his mentor Cyrus Gordon and of the latter's contemporaries, mostly now deceased, that it is the task of the exegete to clarify what the biblical text says and why and to leave what that text means to the heart and mind of the intelligent and sensitive reader.

KEEL is a biblical scholar who has attracted the admiration of archaeologists for bringing to bear the findings of archaeology on the understanding of the Bible. He demonstrates again and again that strange turns of phrase in various psalms refer to objects that can be identified in the artifactual legacy of the ancient Near East. He manages to make the metaphors and similes and references to ancient material culture found in the Book of Psalms regularly intelligible to the modern reader. Typical is his illustration of Psalm 105:18 ("His feet were bound in fetters, his neck was put in a collar of iron") with a detail from a bas relief from the palace of Sargon II of Assyria, depicting a prisoner bound with handcuffs and leg irons in use in the time of Isaiah. Another typical illustration

pairs Psalm 57:1 ("In the shadow of his wings I will take refuge") with an ivory carving from eighth-century B.C.E. Arslan Tash, 40 kilometers east of Carchemish. The artwork here portrays an individual protected by the enormous wings of two anthropoid deities.

GRUBER presents a reliable Hebrew text of Rashi's commentary on Psalms 1–89 together with a translation into modern idiomatic English and a supercommentary on Rashi's commentary in the form of endnotes on each psalm. Making use of specialized studies of Rashi and Gruber's own discoveries, these notes pinpoint the interpretive problems that Rashi's exegesis and eisegesis confront, place Rashi's commentary in dialogue with other ancient, medieval, and modern commentators, identify Rashi's sources, and shed light on his language. Rashi's commentary reveals its author to have been the ideal teacher who struck the proper balance between providing what every educator wants students to know about Hebrew grammar and syntax and what the average student really wants to know about the meaning of the psalms now. Gruber's concise but informative introduction provides a decent funeral for the claim made by several scholars that Rashi neither noticed nor understood one of the characterstic features of ancient Hebrew poetry, synonymous parallelism. A forthcoming second volume will present the Commentary on Psalms 90–150 in both Hebrew and English together with English supercommentary and a new introduction.

MAYER IRWIN GRUBER

Pseudepigrapha see Apocrypha and Pseudepigrapha

Punishment see Authority, Rabbinic and Communal; Sanhedrin, Semikhah, and Rabbinate

Purity see Holiness; Mikveh

R

Rabbinic Authority *see* Authority, Rabbinic and Communal

Rabbinic Biography: Talmudic

Bader, Gershom, *Unzere gaystige riezen,* 1934; translated by Solomon Katz as *The Encyclopedia of Talmudic Sages,* Northvale, New Jersey: Aronson, 1988

Finkelstein, Louis, *Akiba: Scholar, Saint and Martyr,* New York: Covici, Friede, 1936

Gilath, Itzchak, *R. Eliezer Ben Hyrcanus: A Scholar Outcast,* Ramat Gan: Bar-Ilan University Press, 1984

Green, William Scott, "What's in a Name?: The Problematic of Rabbinic 'Biography'," in *Approaches to Ancient Judaism: Theory and Practice* (Brown Judaic Studies, vol. 1), Missoula, Montana: Scholars Press, 1978

Neusner, Jacob, *A Life of Rabban Yohanan ben Zakkai, ca. 1–80 C.E.,* Leiden: Brill, 1962; 2nd edition, 1970; abridged as *First Century Judaism in Crisis: Yohanan ben Zakkai and the Renaissance of Torah,* Nashville, Tennessee: Abingdon, 1975

Neusner, Jacob, *Development of a Legend: Studies on the Traditions Concerning Yohanan ben Zakkai* (Studies Post-Biblica, vol. 16), Leiden: Brill, 1970

Steinberg, Milton, *As a Driven Leaf,* New York: Behrman House, 1939

Rabbinic literature contains no complete biographies as found in classical literature but rather numerous brief traditions of the deeds and sayings of sages scattered among legal and exegetical compilations. The two dominant approaches to these biographical traditions can be designated "synthetic" and "analytic." Synthetic rabbinic biography proceeds by collecting disparate biographical traditions about a sage from all rabbinic sources and integrating them to fashion a coherent life. Similarly, all legal opinions and ethical teachings attributed to a sage are collected in order to determine his legal and moral visions. This method essentially accepts rabbinic traditions as reliable historical sources, although the biographer exercises critical judgment when faced with contradictions or blatantly supernatural features. Analytic rabbinic biography, a method pioneered by Neusner, is skeptical of the historical accuracy of rabbinic biographical traditions, for reasons detailed below by Green. The goal is to understand the function and meaning of biographical traditions within rabbinic compilations. Analytic biography seeks to discern the development of the image of a sage in rabbinic group memory rather than to reconstruct his life as actually lived. In recent years most critical scholars have abandoned the synthetic method because of severe methodological problems.

BADER synthesizes brief biographical sketches of about 90 of the leading sages of the first six centuries C.E. The length of his entries varies greatly. Bader assembles the main biographical traditions about each sage, strings them together into a loose narrative framework, and adds data about teachers and disciples together with a character sketch. He paraphrases important or unusual legal opinions and theological statements. The work is thoroughly "traditional"; it is based exclusively on rabbinic sources even when they contain obviously incorrect information, such as mistakes about the chronology and acts of Roman emperors. It makes no attempt to understand the sages within any larger economic, social, or cultural context. Talmudic accounts of the sages performing miracles are presented as fact. The book should not be read as a lesson in history. Rather, it provides convenient summaries of traditional images of the leading sages in line with those prevalent in the Middle Ages and among traditional religious circles today.

FINKELSTEIN constructs a synthetic life of Rabbi Akiba, probably the most influential sage of the second century C.E. Finkelstein devotes considerable attention to the economic situation, social structure, and cultural state of second-century Palestinian Jews. He quotes Akiba's sayings copiously, both in order to manifest his character and to reconstruct the events and contexts in which they were first uttered. The book contains a lengthy appendix assessing Akiba's legal opinions and arguing that they represent "plebeian" positions against the interests of aristocratic landowners. Finkelstein's attention to wider economic, social, and historical contexts constitutes a considerable advance over previous biographies (as exemplified by Bader), which did little more than place biographical traditions in a rough sequence and collect important sayings. Yet despite his attempts at a neutral perspective, Finkelstein's biography is thoroughly hagiographic, depicting Akiba as a hero in his lifetime and a model for generations to follow. His Marxist-oriented readings of Akiba's teachings in particular, and rabbinic conflicts in general, are not persuasive. Because of the dearth of information in the sources, Finkelstein engages in much more imaginative reconstruction than is ordinarily found in biographical writing.

STEINBERG relates the life of Elisha ben Abuya, known as Aher, "the Other," a famous sage of the second century C.E. This extremely readable book is a historical novel that supplements rabbinic traditions with "free interpretation"—it is not a work of critical historical scholarship. While taking artistic license, Steinberg has "attempted throughout to be true in spirit to the ancient world both Hellenistic and Jewish." He vividly depicts the intellectual conflicts between rabbinic ideas and Greek philosophical teachings that characterized Hellenistic-Roman times. He portrays Elisha as a sage struggling to make religious and intellectual sense of the world under the pressures of these two world views. The book is highly recommended for those interested in gaining a sense of the tensions probably experienced by many Jews in Hellenistic-Roman times.

GILATH presents an intellectual or halakhic biography of Rabbi Eliezer ben Hyrkanos, a leading sage of the early second century C.E. Eliezer's corpus of teachings expresses an idiosyncratic and generally strict system of law. The book collects Eliezer's legal traditions, describes his modes of biblical exegesis, assesses the role of reasoning in his legal vision, and compares his views with the more widely accepted positions of his colleagues. Gilath offers a comprehensive analysis of Eliezer's legal system and attempts to determine its provenance and place in the history of Jewish law. He also discusses important biographical traditions of Eliezer's early life, relationships with other sages, and conflicts. This book provides a superb description of the distinctive legal system of one sage and its place in the historical development of law. It is also a challenge to the contentions of Green and Neusner that rabbinic traditions are unreliable and that attributions cannot be trusted, for Eliezer's traditions in fact yield a consistent and coherent legal system.

GREEN discusses the methodological considerations regarding the use of rabbinic traditions for biographical writing. He notes that the "literature of rabbinic Judaism offers no systematic or coherent biographies of its important sages" and proceeds to explain why in "the strict sense of the term, rabbinic biography is an impossibility." Biographical traditions appear in works redacted centuries after the events they describe and cannot be considered historically accurate. Moreover, the authors or redactors of rabbinic works shaped the material to a considerable extent. They selected traditions important to them and discarded other traditions, so there is no representative body of the teachings of a given sage. Rabbinic literature uses a limited number of rhetorical patterns or forms, which destroy the unique modes of expression of a sage and "thereby conceal distinctive elements of personality, character and intellect." Different rabbinic works attribute the same tradition to different sages, and the names vary in different manuscripts of the same work. This makes it impossible to determine with certainty what a given sage did or said. Green argues that synthetic biography must be replaced by the study of how rabbinic traditions "change and develop across documents and through time." He suggests that "the basic problematic of rabbinic 'biography' ought to be conceived in terms of understanding the dynamics of tradition rather than the recovery of an individual life or a particular period in the history of Judaism."

NEUSNER (1975) is a popularized revision of his earliest work on rabbinic biography, first published in 1962, before he despaired of writing synthetic biography (see Neusner 1970). Here Neusner provides a synthetic reconstruction of the life of Rabban Johanan ben Zakkai, one of the leading architects of rabbinic Judaism who survived the destruction of the Temple in 70 C.E. To create contexts for Johanan's experiences, Neusner adopts historical and sociological models, including Max Weber's theories concerning tensions between charisma and routine in religious life. He describes Johanan's career in the context of the challenges and changes following the Roman conquest. Neusner also organizes and summarizes Johanan's main teachings, including his political and religious views. The book offers a highly readable portrait of a leading sage during the founding era of rabbinic Judaism.

NEUSNER (1970) is the scholarly book in which he first carried out his analytic approach to rabbinic biography by studying the traditions of Rabban Johanan ben Zakkai, on the basis of which he had written a synthetic biography (see Neusner 1975). Neusner begins with a discussion of methodology that articulates the problems regarding the nature of rabbinic biographical traditions, the accuracy of attributions, and the degree of historical reliability. He then collects all traditions concerning Johanan ben Zakkai, analyzes each one on its own terms, and compares the different versions of the same saying or story. Neusner is particularly interested in the forms of the traditions and the "life-situations" that underlie them. He pays attention to the role played by later redactors or editors in changing earlier traditions for their own purposes. Systematic comparison of traditions from early and later rabbinic collections demonstrates that the later versions result from literary processes of reworking and embellishing and cannot be accepted as independent historical witnesses. In the final section Neusner assesses how the legend of Johanan's life developed and changed over the course of time and in different rabbinic circles. He concludes that scholarship cannot say too much with certainty about a sage's "real" life or opinions, but it can shed light on the "mind of the immediate disciples and those who followed in later schools and communities," including their views of earlier heroes and their religious values. This is a book that is intended for scholars and those who wish to learn about methodological issues in great detail.

JEFFREY L. RUBENSTEIN

See also Rabbinic Biography: Early Modern; Rabbinic Biography: Medieval; Rabbinic Biography: Modern

Rabbinic Biography: Medieval

Agus, Irving, *Rabbi Meir of Rothenburg: His Life and His Works as Sources for the Religious, Legal, and Social History of the Jews of Germany in the Thirteenth Century,* 2 vols., Philadelphia: Dropsie College for Hebrew and Cognate Learning, 1947; 2nd edition, New York: Ktav, 1970

Bonfil, Roberto, *Rabanut be-Italyah bi-tekufat ha-Renesans,*
1979; translated by Jonathan Chipman as *Rabbis and
Jewish Communities in Renaissance Italy* (Littman
Library of Jewish Civilization), Oxford and New York:
Oxford University Press, 1990

Chavel, Charles B., *Ramban: His Life and Teachings,* New
York: Feldheim, 1960

Malter, Henry, *Saadia Gaon: His Life and Works,*
Philadelphia: Jewish Publication Society, 1921

Netanyahu, Benzion, *Don Isaac Abravanel: Statesman and
Philosopher,* Philadelphia: Jewish Publication Society,
1953; 5th edition, Ithaca, New York: Cornell University
Press, 1998

Septimus, Bernard, *Hispano-Jewish Culture in Transition:
The Career and Controversies of Ramah* (Harvard
Judaica Monographs, 4) Cambridge, Massachusetts:
Harvard University Press, 1982

Steiman, Sidney, *Custom and Survival: A Study of the Life
and Work of Rabbi Jacob Molin (Moelln) Known as the
Maharil (c.1360–1427), and His Influence in Establishing
the Ashkenazic Minhag (Customs of German Jewry),*
New York: Bloch, 1963

Talmage, Frank, *David Kimhi: The Man and the
Commentaries* (Harvard Judaica Monographs, 1),
Cambridge, Massachusetts: Harvard University Press,
1975

Twersky, Isadore, *Rabad of Posquières: A Twelfth-Century
Talmudist,* Cambridge, Massachusetts: Harvard
University Press, 1962; revised edition, Philadelphia:
Jewish Publication Society, 1980

In the early Middle Ages, the title of rabbi designated a person of scholarly standing and perhaps social reputation, but did not of necessity indicate a position within the community hierarchy. For most of the Middle Ages, the position of rabbi was not that of a salaried or official public position. Scholars who filled the position of rabbi typically did so on a part-time basis and made their careers through their own professions, often as businessmen or physicians. As communal institutions began to deteriorate, the role of the rabbi, particularly the local rabbi, took on greater significance within the communities, although there often were power struggles between rabbis and influential lay leaders, as well as among the rabbinic leaders themselves. By the 14th century in both Sephardi and Ashkenazi lands, a procedure to measure talmudic and halakhic knowledge and to provide a diploma of *semikhah,* or rabbinic ordination, was introduced, though not without opposition. Beginning in the 14th century, the idea of the *mara de-'atra,* literally "master of the place," gained ground, and local rabbinic figures attained greater authority and prestige. Rabbis might be appointed to a communal position by their teachers, especially if the teacher was powerful, or be invited by the ruling members of the community. Rabbis did exercise a certain amount of power within the community, even if that power often seemed more theoretical than real. Rabbinic authorities could, for example, impose the *herem* (ban of excommunication), restraining dissenting members of the community from communal functions and interaction with community members. In many places, the bulk of the extant internal records for the Jewish communities are rabbinic responsa—written answers to a variety of legal questions asked of a particular rabbi.

By the 16th century, rabbinic contracts become more common. A contract between the community in Friedberg and its rabbi is extant, which among other things stipulates that the rabbi would receive a yearly salary as well as fees for marriages and divorces; would not move for a certain number of years; and significantly, would not act against the authority of the community. For the biographies of rabbis of the early and high Middle Ages, numerous philosophical and theological sources have been thoroughly mined and at times supplemented from information gathered from the responsa literature.

Although old, MALTER's book on the great linguist, exegete, philosopher, and head *(gaon)* of the important Babylonian yeshivah of Pumbedita, Saadia ben Joseph al-Fayyumi (Saadia Gaon; 882–942), is nevertheless an excellent study that presents much detail about Saadia's early environment and education, his appointment as gaon (928), and his controversies with the exilarch as well as the Karaites. The book also offers a useful overview of Saadia's writings and his influence on later generations. Saadia's philosophical magnum opus, *The Book of Beliefs and Opinions,* is also available in an excellent English translation by Samuel Rosenblatt (New Haven, Connecticut: Yale University Press, 1948).

NETANYAHU's classic two-part study traces the career and movements of the great Spanish financial adviser and exegete Isaac Abravanel (1437–1508) from birth to his final years in Italy. Netanyahu explores Abravanel's central theological concepts—for example, his thinking on revelation, history, and messianism. According to Netanyahu, Abravanel is the last outstanding Jewish figure of the Middle Ages, a true statesman (as royal treasurer and an outspoken defender of the Jews), a philosopher who lived at a pivotal period of Jewish history—before, during, and after the expulsion of the Jews from Spain—and the author of a variety of theological works that exerted great influence during the 16th century and since.

Written by one of the most important 20th-century scholars of medieval Jewish intellectual history, TWERSKY follows the career of the important and prolific talmudist from 12th-century Provence, Rabbi Abraham ben David (Rabad) of Posquières (c.1120–1198). Particularly interesting are Twersky's comments on Rabad's criticism of Maimonides' *Mishneh Torah* and on Rabad's relationship to Kabbalah.

TALMAGE traces the life and career of the Provençal exegete and grammarian David Kimhi (Radak; c.1160–c.1235). Talmage focuses on Radak's childhood in Narbonne and his development as a mature scholar who emphasized the *peshat,* or plain sense of scripture, and relied heavily on the grammatical skills evident in his famous work *Mikhlol.* Talmage also includes a very useful bibliographic note.

CHAVEL, perhaps the most influential exponent of his subject in the 20th century, offers a brief but very readable biography of Rabbi Moses ben Nahman (Ramban; 1195–1270), one of the most illustrious of Jewish exegetes, proto-kabbalists, and apologists. Ramban spent the last few years of his life in Palestine after his disputation with the Jewish apostate Pablo Christiani in Barcelona. Part one of the book treats the life of Ramban, while part two explores his theological reflections upon such topics as creation, miracles, the land of Israel, and redemption.

SEPTIMUS studies the somewhat obscure figure of Rabbi Meir ha-Levi Abulafia (Ramah; c.1165–1244) in an effort to understand better the Hispano-Jewish culture that underwent rapid and profound transition in the 12th and 13th centuries as Spanish Jewry was being transferred from Muslim to Christian rule. Ramah himself was a formidable scholar—a leading talmudist and the initiator of European polemic over Maimonidean rationalism. He also was an accomplished poet and community leader.

AGUS offers a very informative overview of Meir of Rothenburg (Maharam; c.1215–1293), focusing on his early life, education, and intellectual and communal influence. The bulk of the two volumes consist of translations of Maharam's exceedingly rich responsa dealing with a variety of issues such as prayer and ritual; sabbath and holiday observance; dietary laws; mourning; marriage; divorce; inheritance; and legal procedure. Agus's work includes extensive indexes. Maharam was perhaps the foremost of medieval German rabbis, and his decisions were cited throughout the later Middle Ages.

STEIMAN details the historical background, life, and teachings of Rabbi Jacob ben Moses ha-Levi Molin of Mainz (Maharil; late 14th to mid-15th centuries). Steiman is particularly concerned with the evolution of Ashkenazi *minhag* (custom) within the school of Maharil and his disciples, such as Zalman of St. Goar and Jacob Weil. Steiman sees in Maharil an important link in the chain of Ashkenazi rabbinic development from the 12th to the 18th centuries. Relying heavily on Maharil's responsa, Steiman creates an especially rich portrait of late medieval German Jewish communal life.

BONFIL presents a detailed and significant study of the institution of the rabbinate, in particular its relationship to and position within the communities of Italy during the Renaissance. Bonfil explores the social and cultural background to the development of the rabbinate; the status, authority, and decline of the prestige of rabbinic ordination; the local conditions of the community-appointed rabbi; and the legal and cultural world of the rabbis themselves.

DEAN BELL

See also Rabbinic Biography: Early Modern; Rabbinic Biography: Modern; Rabbinic Biography: Talmudic

Rabbinic Biography: Early Modern

Barzilay, Isaac E., *Yoseph Shlomo Delmedigo, Yashar of Candia: His Life, Works and Times*, Leiden: Brill, 1974

Cohen, Mark (editor), *The Autobiography of a Seventeenth-Century Venetian Rabbi: Leon Modena's "Life of Judah,"* Princeton, New Jersey: Princeton University Press, 1988

Cohen, Mortimer J., *Jacob Emden: A Man of Controversy*, Philadelphia: Dropsie College for Hebrew and Cognate Learning, 1937

Eidelberg, Shlomo, *R. Juspa, Shamash of Warmaisa (Worms): Jewish Life in 17th Century Worms*, Jerusalem: Magnes, 1991

Roth, Cecil, *A Life of Menasseh ben Israel: Rabbi, Printer, and Diplomat*, Philadelphia: Jewish Publication Society, 1934

Ruderman, David, *The World of a Renaissance Jew: The Life and Thought of Abraham ben Mordecai Farissol*, Cincinnati, Ohio: Hebrew Union College Press, 1981

Sherwin, Byron, *Mystical Theology and Social Dissent: The Life and Works of Judah Loew of Prague*, London: Associated University Presses, and Rutherford, New Jersey: Fairleigh Dickinson University Press, 1982

Werblowsky, R.J.Z., *Joseph Karo: Lawyer and Mystic*, London: Oxford University Press, 1962; 2nd edition, Philadelphia: Jewish Publication Society, 1977

Like many aspects of Jewish history, Jewish experience in what has come to be called the early modern period (though the term is used more frequently within Western, non-Jewish history) was a complex mixture of events and cultures that one might more appropriately term both medieval and modern. For present purposes, one may consider early modern that period extending from the massive forced expulsion of Jews from Spain and much of Germany (and the subsequent "eastward migration") to the legislation of the Napoleonic period. It is quite difficult to draw generalizations regarding the development of rabbinic institutions and personalities in this 300-year period, particularly given the geographic and cultural distance of the Jewish populations within the diaspora. The dispersion of Sephardi Jews, for example, forced the integration of earlier Iberian customs with local Jewish cultures encountered in other parts of Europe (in Amsterdam, Hamburg, and Venice, for example), in North Africa, and in the Ottoman Empire. In some places, communities and communal customs merged, taking on new accents; in other places, immigrant communities became dominant, eventually displacing or absorbing local communal customs and traditions; in still other places, rival communities developed, with their own unique customs and social structures, and often with their respective rabbinic leaders vying for authoritative control of the religious and communal practices of the area. This is also the period of the embryonic communities in North America (in New York and Philadelphia, for example). The selection of biographies offered here is of rabbis exclusively from Europe. Nevertheless, these biographies present a wide variety of personalities and indicate the scope and breadth of rabbinic activities and influences in the early modern period.

Religious practice, individual personality, and the larger environment (both Jewish and gentile) all combined to affect Jewish identity and communal structure. As the position of the rabbi became more professionalized and established in certain places, it also became more and more subject to restrictions imposed by local Jewish lay leaders and communal expectations. Detailed rabbinic contracts (in Germany in the 18th century, for example) stipulated the remuneration due to rabbis for their services, but also dictated the extent of rabbinic power and privilege.

In his classic account, WERBLOWSKY presents the life and thought of one of the most profound of Jewish thinkers and systematizers, Rabbi Joseph Karo (1488–1575), author of *Beth Yosef* and *Shulhan Arukh*, eventually considered the summa of rabbinic Judaism. Karo was also a kabbalist of great renown, both before and after his time in Safed, who authored *Maggid Mesharim* in which he described mystical revelations from a heavenly mentor *(maggid)*. *Maggid Mesharim* is a mystical diary of kabbalistic doctrines and rules for ascetic life revealed in nightly visitations over the course of 50 years. After establishing Karo's authorship of *Maggid Mesharim*, Werblowsky offers a comprehensive assessment of Karo's kabbalistic theology, situating it within the context of 16th-century Safed and Karo's own life in Spain, the Balkans, and the land of Israel.

SHERWIN reconstructs the historical events of the life, thought, and social concerns of the enigmatic and mystical Rabbi Judah Loew of Prague (Maharal, born between 1512 and 1526 and died in 1609). Maharal was descended from prominent rabbis and was himself an esteemed talmudist, moralist, and mathematician. He served as *Landesrabbiner* of Moravia in Nikolsburg and later founded a yeshivah in Prague, a city to which he returned frequently throughout his career, eventually as chief rabbi. In this book, Sherwin offers a lucid analysis of the legends and historiographic depictions of Maharal, an investigation into questions of Maharal's date of birth and the order of his written works, and an extensive bibliography. The body of the book explores Maharal's broad but unsystematic writings in relation to the following topics: God, Torah, Israel (in particular Jewish-gentile relations), theological anthropology, messianism, and social concern.

With extensive notes, bibliography, and appendixes, RUDERMAN examines the life of Abraham ben Mordecai Farissol (c.1451–c.1525), covering his beginnings in Avignon, his time in Mantua, and finally his settlement in Ferrara, and offering along the way rich contextual information. In Ferrara, Farissol served as a cantor, mohel, scribe, and educator. In the true spirit of the Italian Renaissance, Farissol combined an aptitude for biblical commentary with polemical skills—as evidenced in disputations with Christians and in defense of Jewish moneylenders—and significant abilities in the physical and natural sciences. Farissol was a particularly important geographer, writing the first modern Hebrew work on the subject.

Mark COHEN offers a full treatment of the autobiography of Leone (Judah Aryeh) Modena (1571–1648), including a complete English translation of the text and extensive historical notes and introductory essays by a number of experts in the history of early modern Jewry as well as early modern cultural history. Modena was a major figure of his time, an established rabbinic authority in Venice and a prolific writer and learned scholar who wrote well in Italian and Latin as well as Hebrew. He published numerous works, including a bitter attack against the Marrano Uriel da Costa and a qualified defense of the oral tradition and talmudic writings. Modena wrote anti-Christian polemics but severely criticized Jewish kabbalists as well. His autobiography is a revealing entrance into the complex world of Renaissance Jewry; it demonstrates the variety of occupations in which the rabbi could be involved, from moneylending to writing and translating. It also reveals something of the intricate relations between Jews and Christians in Italy and offers glimpses of the multifaceted life within the Venetian ghetto.

BARZILAY offers a detailed look at the famous rabbi, philosopher, and mathematician Joseph Solomon Delmedigo (1591–1655). The son of the celebrated Rabbi Elijah Delmedigo, he frequently visited Leon Modena while studying medicine at Padua, and he traveled widely throughout Europe. He was accomplished in a variety of academic fields and languages, combining scholarship of the classics with Kabbalah, which he criticized sharply. Barzilay's book examines the life, career, and writings of Joseph Delmedigo. It first traces Delmedigo's background, upbringing, and travels throughout the Middle East, Poland, Germany, and the Low Countries; it next reviews his published works; then it investigates his secular, philosophical, and kabbalistic studies; and finally it assesses his relations to rabbinic and Karaite Judaism and to non-Jews. In the appendixes, Barzilay speculates on Delmedigo's date of departure from his birthplace of Candia (Crete) and offers details about his numerous unprinted works. The book ends with an extensive and very useful bibliography.

ROTH offers the standard biography of the great leader of Dutch Jewry in the 17th century, Menasseh ben Israel (1604–1657). He succeeds in depicting Menasseh as a complex figure; born a Marrano, he was very successful in the yeshivot of Amsterdam and eventually succeeded Rabbi Isaac Uzziel as the preacher of the Neveh Shalom congregation. He authored a number of important talmudic and linguistic works in Hebrew and Spanish and gained a reputation within both Jewish and Christian circles. His later works were particularly directed at non-Jews, among whom Menasseh had many important friends including Grotius and Rembrandt. Menasseh is also shown as a savvy politician who helped pave the way for the return of the Jews to England. Roth discusses various aspects of Menasseh's life, including his Marrano background; his rabbinic training and career; his accomplishments as a writer and as a printer (he printed what may have been "the first scientific issue" of the *Mishnah*, with his own brief marginal notes, in 1631–1632); his famous work *The Hope of Israel*, which described the purported discovery of the Ten Lost Tribes in South America; and his political work in England.

EIDELBERG offers a very brief introduction to, and the full texts of, three works written by Juspa Shammash (Joseph the Sexton, 1604–1678) of Worms. The three texts are *Minhagim di-Kehillah Kedoshah Warmaisa* (Custom Book of Worms); *Ma'asei Nissim* (Book of Wonder Stories); and *Pinkas ha-Kehillah* (Ledger of Commercial Contracts). Eidelberg offers full English translations, copies of the original manuscripts, and modern Hebrew editions of all three texts. Juspa was born in Fulda (Hesse) of a middle-class family and moved later to Worms to study in the yeshivah of the famous Rabbi Elijah Loanz. Juspa soon married into a reputable Worms family and was able to attain the position of shammash (sexton) and scribe of the community, a position he held for 40 years that required him to record important communal events, provide services for the rabbinic court, prepare a variety of documents such as marriage contracts and bills of divorce, and sign documents as a witness to their binding legality. Juspa's writings reveal the rich texture of Jewish life in Germany in the 17th century: internal business, religious and social relations and relations with non-Jews that fluctuated between peaceful coexistence and oppressive persecution.

Mortimer COHEN's book on Jacob Emden (1698–1776) is the classic account of a stormy figure in 18th-century Germany. Cohen divides the life of Emden into marked phases: childhood and youth; marriage and wandering; the brief service as rabbi in Emden; the stormy years in the "Three Communities" (Altona, Hamburg, and Wandsbeck), including Emden's well-known and inflammatory controversy with Jonathan Eybeschuetz, who was rabbi of the Three Communities between 1750 and 1764; and his final years. As Cohen notes, this study originated as an investigation into the great controversy between Emden and Eybeschuetz. Throughout Cohen is also concerned with the personality of Emden, emphasizing his strong anti-Sabbatian polemics, his antiphilosophical stance, and a number of unusual halakhic opinions and character traits.

DEAN BELL

See also Rabbinic Biography: Medieval; Rabbinic Biography: Modern; Rabbinic Biography: Talmudic

Rabbinic Biography: Modern

Ellenson, David, *Rabbi Esriel Hildesheimer and the Creation of a Modern Jewish Orthodoxy* (Judaic Studies Series), Tuscaloosa: University of Alabama Press, 1990

Etkes, Immanuel, *R. Yisra'el Salanter ve-r'eshitah shel tenu'at ha-musar*, 1982; as *Rabbi Israel Salanter and the Mussar Movement: Seeking the Torah of Truth*, Philadelphia: Jewish Publication Society, 1993

Green, Arthur, *Tormented Master: A Life of Rabbi Nahman of Bratslav* (Judaic Studies Series), University: University of Alabama Press, 1979

Klugman, Eliyahu Meir, *Rabbi Samson Raphael Hirsch: Architect of Torah Judaism for the Modern World* (ArtScroll History Series), Brooklyn, New York: Mesorah, 1996

Shapiro, Marc B., *Between the Yeshiva World and Modern Orthodoxy: The Life and Works of Rabbi Jehiel Jacob Weinberg*, London and Portland, Oregon: Littman Library, 1999

Biographies of modern rabbinic personalities are nothing new, but English-language biographies of Orthodox rabbinic figures (the focus of this essay) are a relatively recent phenomenon. While books recounting the lives of these rabbinic figures abound, they are virtually all hagiographic and must be approached with great caution, both for what they include and for what they omit. These books are written to inspire piety and respect for the rabbi and have a specific ideological agenda. Although they deserve study in their own right, they cannot properly be considered biographical.

The chief distributor of hagiographic literature in contemporary Orthodoxy is the ArtScroll imprint, and KLUGMAN appears under these auspices. However, Klugman's book is of a completely different genre, and it is therefore regrettable that the work did not appear under the aegis of another press. Because of the publisher, it is likely that Klugman will be ignored by many scholars. However, once one gets past some minor pious trappings, one finds a comprehensive and authoritative biography of one of the most significant Orthodox rabbis in modern times. Samson Raphael Hirsch, as the creator of a new form of Orthodoxy that integrated the best of worldly culture, has been subject to a variety of interpretations as well as revisionism. Klugman avoids tendentious interpretation and portrays Hirsch's life and thought in a manner that both laypeople and scholars will find appealing. The major criticism of Klugman's work is that because he is not a trained historian, he is ill-equipped to deal with the larger historical issues taking place in Hirsch's time, not to mention the complicated question of Hirsch's indebtedness to contemporary German philosophy. That having been said, it is remarkable that a nonprofessional could produce what must be regarded as a first-class biography.

The life and work of Nahman of Bratslav have been popularized by Elie Wiesel and continue to fascinate readers of all religious backgrounds. GREEN offers a complete biography of this most enigmatic of hasidic leaders. His study must of necessity deal with issues of psychohistory, as Nahman's life virtually cries out for this type of examination. Green skillfully shows the guilt, inner struggle, and doubt found in this hasidic master. In an excursus, Green discusses how to make use of Nahman's tales, in many ways his most enduring achievement. Another excursus, devoted to the issues of faith, doubt, and reason in Nahman, is a fine exercise in how unsystematic teachings and reflections, such as were offered by Nahman, are to be used with profit by the intellectual historian.

ETKES provides a comprehensive biography and study of the contributions of Israel Salanter, founder of the 19th-century Musar movement, which was devoted to strengthening piety and ethical conduct through self-examination. Along the way Etkes illuminates a great deal about traditional Eastern European Orthodoxy and thus places Salanter's innovative movement in its proper context. In the course of his study, in which he shows the intellectual sources for Salanter's Musar thought, Etkes also disposes of some of the hagiography that has arisen around Salanter (e.g., that he preceded Freud in discovering the unconscious). Relevant to Salanter's life are the activities of the maskilim (in particular their involvement in the creation of a rabbinical seminary), the opening of the first *kollel*, and the founding of *Tevunah*, the first Torah periodical. Etkes discusses Salanter's involvement with all of these endeavors as well as his other communal activities.

ELLENSON offers a very readable study of Esriel Hildesheimer, the great halakhic scholar, devotee of *Wissenschaft des Judentums*, builder of institutions of learning, battler against Reform, and supporter of Jewish causes the world over. Ellenson examines in close detail Hildesheimer's life and work with emphasis on the institutions that Hildesheimer built in Hungary and Germany, which were the backbone of Neo-Orthodoxy. Ellenson is particularly strong in describing the various struggles and successes of Hildesheimer, perhaps the loneliest of the great rabbinic figures of the 19th century, who stood virtually alone against great opposition throughout his life and yet refused to waver. Although Ellenson's book is a great contribution to German Jewish history, as a biography it is somewhat lacking. For example, Ellenson provides an excellent portrait of Hildesheimer the builder, teacher, and shaper of events; however, one would also have liked to see more appreciation of Hildesheimer the scholar, both in the areas of *Wissenschaft* and halakhah. Ellenson is only interested in the latter when it has some relevance to the issue of Orthodox-Reform disputes.

SHAPIRO offers a complete study of the life and works of Jehiel Jacob Weinberg, one of the most important halakhists of 20th-century Orthodoxy. In addition to illuminating Weinberg's life, Shapiro also discusses a number of other aspects of Jewish history, such as the Lithuanian yeshivot, the Musar movement, Eastern European Jews in Weimar Germany, varying conceptions of *Torah im derekh erets* (the synthesis of religious and secular values), Orthodox attitudes toward *Wissenschaft des Judentums,* and the special problems of Orthodox Jews in Nazi Germany. Weinberg's major claim to fame is his halakhic writings, and Shapiro focuses on what he regards as the most significant facet of these writings, namely, how Weinberg integrated aspects of the modern world into the halakhic system. This approach was based on the notion that reform, within limits, is a crucial element to the success of Orthodoxy. Weinberg is shown to follow in the path of his predecessors in Germany who believed that when confronted with faltering religious observance, traditional Orthodox practices must be modified in a liberal direction in order to increase their appeal. This contradicts the approach of the influential Rabbi Moses Sofer who not only argued against any liberalization but also advocated increased stringencies as a means of countering spreading irreligiosity. One of the book's appendixes contains, in English translation, a lengthy and fascinating 1933 letter to Hitler written by several German Orthodox leaders.

MARC B. SHAPIRO

See also Rabbinic Biography: Early Modern; Rabbinic Biography: Medieval; Rabbinic Biography: Talmudic

Rabinovitch, Sholem *see* Sholem Aleichem

Race, Jews as

Alcalay, Ammiel, *After Jews and Arabs: Remaking Levantine Culture,* Minneapolis: University of Minnesota Press, 1993

Fishberg, Maurice, *The Jews: A Study of Race and Environment,* New York and London: Scott, 1911

Gilman, Sander, *The Jew's Body,* New York: Routledge, 1991

Kautsky, Karl, *Are the Jews a Race?,* London: Cape, and New York: International, 1926

Patai, Raphael and Jennifer Patai, *The Myth of the Jewish Race,* New York: Scribner, 1974; revised edition, Detroit, Michigan: Wayne State University Press, 1989

Zollschan, Ignaz, *Jewish Questions: Three Lectures,* New York: Bloch, 1914

Race is not a static category but a historical discourse used to differentiate strategically one group from another. Indebted as much to anthropology as it is to biology, racial determination is always fraught with instability and is often bolstered by class, gender, linguistic, labor, or cultural differences. Jews, as a people living among (and tending to resemble) other peoples, are confronted with a troubling question of difference: how can Jews be considered a single people (generally a racial determination) while they appear to be so diverse? In other words, are Jews a race? More interesting than any simple yes or no answer are the ways in which this question has been framed and asked historically in order to discuss the issues at stake in the determination of Jewish identity according to race, rather than seeking to definitively establish its characteristics.

GILMAN's landmark work is an insightful and invaluable contribution to the study of Jews as a race. He examines representations of Jewish male bodies in Europe during the 18th and 19th centuries. Focusing on particular body parts and characteristics, Gilman masterfully examines racial stereotypes ranging from the Jewish nose to the Jewish genius. His analysis focuses on the determination and characterization of a Jewish race primarily by German scientists, anthropologists, and intellectuals. This book succeeds on two levels. First, it lays out clearly the historical circumstances of the racialization of Jews in Europe, including discussions of criminology, demography, and immigration. Second, it exposes the roots of the question and offers an incisive, well documented, and clearly explicated critique.

ZOLLSCHAN was a Jewish physician whose book is largely a response to the highly charged antisemitic climate of fin-de-siècle Vienna. Employing a scientific concept of race, Zollschan addresses Aryan claims of Jewish racial inferiority. His book is divided into three parts: the first is an evaluation of race science; the second explores historical (as opposed to "purely" genealogical) factors that influence the formation of a race, including immigration, miscegenation, and assimilation; and the third section is an argument for the contributions of the Jewish race to humanity. For Zollschan, the problem of race is a problem of antisemitism, and therefore the only cure lies in the establishment of a Jewish state. Zollschan denied any physical difference between Sephardi and Ashkenazi Jews in the interests of racial (and national) unity and a future of national rebirth. Zollschan's application of race science in the name of Zionism is crucial to understanding the power of this discourse in the formation of Jewish identities.

Also extremely critical of race-based antisemitism, the German socialist KAUTSKY's study fails to discover a set of racial characteristics shared by Jews. In stark contrast to Zollschan, Kautsky is highly critical of Zionism, which he views as an offshoot of antisemitism: both seek separatism, both aspire to racial distinction, and both rely on the racialization of the Jews in order for their respective projects to succeed. Kautsky offers a broad critique of race as inherently "in flux and transition" and therefore qualitatively unhelpful. For Kautsky, the only solution for the race problem is proletarian rebellion. His critique of race science is interesting not so much for its hopeful prescription but for the way in which it illustrates the connections between race and nationalism and warns against its dangers.

Kautsky owed a great debt to FISHBERG's study of the Jews. For many years, Fishberg's work stood as the authoritative anthropological study of the Jews as a race. His goal was to solve the "problem" of assimilating a vast number of immigrants into the United States and England. Taking a primarily morphological approach, Fishberg compared numerous Jewish populations along a variety of axes, both genetic and social (from height and weight to criminality and "political condition"), in order to determine whether or not Jews constituted a distinct racial group. For Fishberg, the Jews do not constitute a distinct race, as they tend to adopt not only the behavior but the appearance of the larger community in which they live. Ironically, his claim that Jews alone possess this ability to adapt to their milieu is insufficient evidence to establish a Jewish race. Therefore, they can be safely assimilated into the "Anglo-Saxon body politic." Read as a historical document, this book is an invaluable resource as it succinctly and unselfconsciously situates the discourses of race and Jewish identity within the continually contested bounds of nationalism, immigration, science, and culture.

Taking a similar approach to that of Fishberg, PATAI and PATAI understand race as fundamentally a question of blood purity. Complete with 16 pages of head-shots of Jews from around the world, the Patais employ historical and genetic data to prove that Jews do not constitute a race, concluding that there is no morphological continuity between Jews of different lands. They do, however, establish that although Jews do not constitute a single race, there is evidence—in the form of seven polymorphic genes—indicating a common Mediterranean origin. They are careful to reiterate that this common origin does not establish racial continuity. The 1989 edition includes a chapter refuting the claim that "Zionism is racism" on the basis that there is no such thing as a Jewish race.

Finally, ALCALAY's analysis of Levantine literature approaches race in a dramatically different way. Through literary theory, Alcalay reads Jewish studies into a Middle Eastern context in order to interrogate the axiom of fundamental racial difference between Jew and Arab. Alcalay's cogent critique of European Zionist racism against Jews from Arab lands vigorously challenges claims of Jewish racial unity and offers a regional-cultural rather than racial framework for studying Jews, Arabs, and those for whom both categories apply. Alcalay's work does not address the topic of race explicitly, but it is significant here for its broad and flexible reworking of the boundaries of racial identity and its reevaluation of accepted notions of racial difference. Using literature as opposed to science or anthropology enables Alcalay to shed some much-needed critical light on the issue of race in the Middle East.

ARI KELMAN

See also Race, Views on

Race, Views on

Aschheim, Steven, *Brothers and Strangers: The East European Jew in German and German Jewish Consciousness, 1800–1923*, Madison: University of Wisconsin Press, 1982

Efron, John, *Defenders of the Race: Jewish Doctors and Race Science in Fin-de-Siècle Europe*, New Haven, Connecticut: Yale University Press, 1994

Gilman, Sander, *Freud, Race, and Gender*, Princeton, New Jersey: Princeton University Press, 1993

Kleeblatt, Norman L. (editor), *Too Jewish?: Challenging Traditional Identities*, New Brunswick, New Jersey: Rutgers University Press, 1996

Pellegrini, Ann, *Performance Anxieties: Staging Psychoanalysis, Staging Race*, New York and London: Routledge, 1997

Since the Holocaust there has been a great reluctance to use race-based science in discussions of identity. Nevertheless, race remains one of the primary categories of personal and political identification and affiliation. There is no single, monolithic Jewish opinion of race, and it is important to remember that the question is not whether there is or is not such a thing as Jewish thinking about race, because it is clear that at various times in history there have been a range of ideas on the subject and at other times no consciousness of it. Due to the flexibility of the term, Jews have long held highly ambivalent attitudes toward the category of race and have both suffered and benefited from its use. The issue at stake here is how Jews have negotiated their own racialization and the racialization of others.

For ASCHHEIM, race lies at the center of Europe's Jewish question. He examines carefully the role of race in the immigration and absorption of Polish and Russian Jews into German-Jewish communities during the late 19th and early 20th centuries. Whereas antisemites employed race to elide cultural differences between the immigrant and established Jewish communities (thus to condemn all Jews in one breath), German Jews adopted race to differentiate themselves from the Eastern Jews, whom they saw as uncultured, unenlightened, and otherwise backward. Yet, at the same time, generally they felt an affinity toward their coreligionists and organized extensive assistance programs for them. For these Jews, race was the vehicle for reaffirming their German identity while it also became the conduit for the expression of a quasi-national Jewish bond. This ambivalence is tied firmly to the German Jews' self-perception as enlightened, modern citizens of the state, which, for them, transcended (Jewish) race and reinscribed it along national (German) lines. Race was so tightly woven into their self-conception and political goals that their views on it were rarely expressed as such and took more subtle and at times contradictory forms, which Aschheim brings to light.

Examining much the same time and place, EFRON considers the lives of Jewish doctors and their work with respect to race science. Writing against the notion that postwar European decolonization was the first challenge to traditional anthropology, Efron's careful study provides an account of oppositional racial discourse during the late 19th and early 20th centuries as practiced by European Jewish doctors. For Jews generally and Jewish physicians in particular, to deploy race science was a strategic manipulation of current discourse rather than the wholesale purchase of a biased science. Efron asserts that none of his subjects employed race in a chauvinistic manner; instead, he argues that race science was an available means for raising ethnic pride and unity under the specter of European antisemitism. He adds that almost all the Jewish doctors whom he studied acknowledged the great significance of history and culture in the formation of the Jewish people, yet each still returned to race as the final determinant. Efron's study is an account of the salience of race science, insufficient as it was (and is) to prove conclusively the existence of a Jewish race.

Looking at race during the same period, GILMAN's work on Sigmund Freud makes an invaluable contribution to the Jewish discourse on race for its analysis of the intersection of race and gender. Gilman claims that Freud's Jewish identity was both defined and disturbed by European race science. Freud's anxiety regarding his race was aggravated by the popular cultural feminization of Jewish men, which he sought to ameliorate by projecting it onto women and other perceived inferiors. By providing a survey of the medical literature of the time, Gilman illustrates both the role of gender in establishing and fixing racial difference and also Freud's ambivalence about this (gendered) racial categorization. Gilman provides a detailed framework and solid evidence for a racial analysis that not only includes but relies on gender, based on the particular experience of Jews in Vienna.

PELLEGRINI picks up where Gilman leaves off. Rooted in psychoanalysis and performance theory, she offers a reading of race that is from the outset infused with gender. Fully aware of its social construction, her analysis of race explores its instability and ambivalence to determine how it works in contemporary society. Brilliantly, she details the interaction between "Jewishness," "Blackness," and "womanliness" as they have been constructed, performed, and maintained by Freud, Frantz Fanon, Albert Memmi, Sandra Bernhardt, and Anna Deveare Smith. Race, for Pellegrini, is not a biological fact but a social performance—one that is mediated by racial and gendered difference and one that is never complete. Like Gilman, she does not accept race as a static category but rather examines how it is always infused with performances of gender. As such, race and racial performance becomes, for Jews, a strategy of articulation, disavowal, resistance, and reinforcement. Pellegrini's poststructuralism is both a critique of race science as well as an investigation of the ongoing significance of race as a social category.

The themes of nation and gender that gird any discussion of race are provocatively engaged in the art and essays assembled by KLEEBLATT in a companion volume to the exhibition of the same name mounted by the Jewish Museum in New York in 1996. Insofar as stereotypes are racially motivated (under the assumption that cultural behavior is linked to certain biological traits), each of the authors and artists engages representations of Jewishness with a particular focus on bodily function and appearance. Some authors and artists trace this genealogy more conceptually, as in Margeret Olin's essay where biology becomes the common ancestor of racism and

formalist criticism. Others, such as Riv-Ellen Prell and Maurice Berger, examine the ways in which gender behaves as the fulcrum for the perpetuation of Jewish racial stereotypes. The artists exhibited are equally incisive in their critical deployment of Jewish iconography from rhinoplasty to Barbara Streisand to sewing samplers. While not all are concerned with race per se, the attitude of each toward Jewish identity is undergirded by a sense of exploration, and they often deal with issues of the body, appearance, and racial "passing." Race is a key factor in the book, but its meaning is undetermined. The artists and authors of Kleeblatt's volume seek to undermine any sense of racial typology in favor of a fungible, unstable, and playful configuration of Jewish belonging.

ARI KELMAN

See also Race, Jews as

Rashi *see* Solomon ben Isaac

Reconstructionist Judaism

Alpert, Rebecca T. and Jacob J. Staub, *Exploring Judaism: A Reconstructionist Approach,* New York: Reconstructionist Press, 1985

Berkovits, Eliezer, "Reconstructionist Theology: A Critical Evaluation," in his *Major Themes in Modern Philosophies of Judaism,* New York: Ktav, 1974

Eisenstein, Ira, *Reconstructing Judaism: An Autobiography,* New York: Reconstructionist Press, 1986

Kaplan, Mordecai M., *The Future of the American Jew,* New York: Macmillan, 1948

Liebman, Charles, "Reconstructionism in American Jewish Life," in his *Aspects of the Religious Behavior of American Jews,* New York: Ktav, 1974

Raphael, Marc Lee, "Institutions and Organizations: 1922–1983" and "[Reconstructionism:] Origins and Ideology," in his *Profiles in American Judaism,* San Francisco: Harper and Row, 1984

Rosenthal, Gilbert S., "Reconstructionism: History" and "Reconstructionism: Ideology," in his *Contemporary Judaism: Patterns of Survival,* New York: Human Sciences Press, 1986

Wertheimer, Jack, "The Reconstruction of Kaplanian Reconstructionism," in his *A People Divided: Judaism in Contemporary America,* New York: Basic Books, 1993

Reconstructionist Judaism is a 20th-century North American Jewish movement with an ideology and program rooted in humanism, naturalism, democratic theory, pragmatism, and the historical method of analysis. The movement has undergone two primary periods of development. The first is associated with the work of the movement's founder, Rabbi Mordecai Kaplan (1881–1993). Kaplan's philosophy and program are the basis of Reconstructionist Judaism, although Kaplan resisted efforts to define Reconstructionist Judaism as a fourth movement or denomination in North American Judaism. A leader of the left-wing of Conservative Judaism, he preferred to think of his program as a "school of thought," despite his efforts to organize liturgy, publications, foundations, and other institutions normally associated with a movement. The second period of development includes the founding of the Reconstructionist Rabbinical College in 1968 and the consequent emergence of the movement as a fourth denomination.

KAPLAN's exposition represents the most comprehensive statement of his program and thinking. Building on his earlier work, *Judaism as a Civilization; Towards a Reconstruction of American-Jewish Life* (New York: Macmillan, 1934), this book shows how Kaplan and others of his generation positioned the emerging movement. Kaplan regards Judaism not as a religion but as a civilization or culture. He views Judaism as the natural historical product and project of the Jewish people, rather than as a revealed religious system handed down by God at Mount Sinai, as the Bible presents it. According to Kaplan, God is not a supernatural being but a power or process that provides meaning and human fulfillment. Jewish law, especially as applied to ritual, must be seen as a pluralistic pattern of custom rather than a uniform expectation of law-fulfillment. Judaism is not an unchanging system of faith and law, Kaplan argues, for it has undergone change and development in every generation, and the religion must continue to evolve—now rationally and self-consciously—if it is to survive the challenges of modernity.

EISENSTEIN's autobiography offers a historical-personal narrative about the development of Reconstructionist Judaism. A member of the generation that followed Kaplan's, Eisenstein is recognized as the founder of Reconstructionism as a movement. He was the preeminent disciple, as well as son-in-law, of Kaplan, and he served as co-rabbi in Kaplan's congregation. He was also editor of *Reconstructionist* magazine and the founding president of the Reconstructionist Rabbinical College. Eisenstein's book documents the inside story of the emergence of Reconstructionism as an independent movement, reflecting the author's own valuable perspective on both the ideology and architecture of the movement.

BERKOVITS provides a dated but still valuable critique of Kaplan's religious thinking, focusing specifically on his claims that God can be understood as process or power rather than as being. Berkovits's Orthodox identification establishes him as an inevitable critic of Reconstructionism, but his criticisms stress weaknesses in Kaplan's own thinking instead of simply using the Orthodox perspective to disavow Kaplan's non-Orthodox thinking.

LIEBMAN published his study just as the Reconstructionist seminary was first opening its doors, the moment that defined the independence of the movement. While the author's analysis of the state and strength of the movement is valuable and interesting, it is now completely out of date and should be interpreted as a historical snapshot of the movement at the critical juncture between the Kaplan incarnation and the stage that would soon follow. Liebman's study is famous for its claim that most American Jews (at least in 1968) identified with positions that were clearly Reconstructionist but very few of those Jews called themselves Reconstructionists. Liebman suggests that the movement's expression of popular views may be one of its weaknesses, indicating that Reconstructionism articulates the status quo rather than envisioning what Judaism should be. He also argues that Reconstructionism may represent what sociologists call "folk religion," while traditional Judaism is an "elite religion."

The strength of ROSENTHAL's treatment is its succinct analysis and presentation of admittedly complex Kaplanian ideas. The concise study is weakened, however, when it subsumes or ignores valuable nuances and distinctions between Kaplan's thinking and Rosenthal's critique of that thinking. Rosenthal's analysis of the movement itself is more contemporary than that of Liebman, although he presents only the beginnings of the developments of the 1970s and 1980s.

RAPHAEL investigates the new concerns of Reconstructionism that emerged in the early- to mid-1980s. He identifies such central trends of this period as the movement's interest in mystical and hasidic thought, its attraction to spiritual disciplines and new rituals, and the rethinking of Kaplanian concepts. Organizational developments are also noted: the study covers the move of the seminary to a new campus and its adoption of a more stable and structured program; the development of a Reconstructionist Rabbinical Association (1974); and the consolidation, realignment, and expansion of the movement's publications and congregational organization. Raphael's treatment concludes with the beginnings of what would prove to be the movement's major project, product, and statement of its second stage: the new prayer-book series titled *Kol HaNeshamah*.

Reconstructionism, as a small movement unencumbered by historical structure and precedent, found itself responding rapidly in the 1980s to challenging societal changes as refracted through the Jewish community. A Conservative Jewish thinker, WERTHEIMER critically discusses the Reconstructionist movement's embrace of equality for gay and lesbian Jews; its sympathy toward spirituality; its liberal approach to the reality of intermarriage via outreach and welcome to interfaith families; and its position that rabbi and laity should democratically share decision-making power. Wertheimer suggests that in its rush to embrace progressive positions, Reconstructionism is open to the charge that it has abandoned Kaplan's core concepts and program.

ALPERT and STAUB, two mid-1970s graduates of the Reconstructionist Rabbinical College, present both the Kaplanian background and contemporary formulations of Reconstructionism. The authors provide a valuable portrait of a movement that is rooted in one man's thinking but has grown to meet the needs of Jews three and four generations removed from that of Kaplan—generations living in a different setting and tackling different questions.

RICHARD HIRSH

Reference Works

Aharoni, Yohanan and Michael Avi-Yonah, *The Macmillan Bible Atlas*, New York: Macmillan, 1968; revised as *The Modern Bible Atlas*, London: Allen and Unwin, 1979; 3rd edition as *The Macmillan Bible Atlas*, New York: Macmillan, 1993

Aumann, Moshe et al., *Carta's Historical Atlas of Israel: A Survey of the Past and Review of the Present*, Jerusalem: Carta, 1983

Avi-Yonah, Michael, *The Madaba Mosaic Map*, Jerusalem: Israel Exploration Society, 1954

Bacon, Josephine and Martin Gilbert, *The Illustrated Atlas of Jewish Civilization*, London: Deutsch, 1990

Bahat, Dan, *Atlas Karta le-toldot Yerushalayim*, Jerusalem: Carta, 1983; as *The Illustrated Atlas of Jerusalem*, translated by Shlomo Ketko, New York: Simon and Schuster, 1990

Brisman, Shimeon, *Jewish Research Literature*, vol. 1: *A History and Guide to Judaic Bibliography* Cincinnati, Ohio: Hebrew Union College Press, 1977

Brisman, Shimeon, *Jewish Research Literature*, vol. 2: *A History and Guide to Judaic Encyclopedias and Lexicons*, Cincinnati, Ohio: Hebrew Union College Press, 1987

Cutter, Charles and Micha Falk Oppenheim, *Jewish Reference Sources: A Selective, Annotated Bibliographic Guide* (Garland Reference Library of Social Science, vol. 126), New York: Garland, 1982; 2nd edition, as *Judaica Reference Sources: A Selective, Annotated Bibliographic Guide*, Juneau, Alaska: Denali, 1993

De Lange, Nicholas Robert Michael, *Atlas of the Jewish World*, Oxford: Phaidon, and New York: Facts on File, 1984

Friesel, Evyatar, *Atlas of Modern Jewish History*, Oxford and New York: Oxford University Press, 1990

Gilbert, Martin, *Jewish History Atlas*, New York: Macmillan, and London: Weidenfeld and Nicolson, 1969; 4th edition, London: Weidenfeld and Nicolson, 1992; as *The Atlas of Jewish History*, New York: Morrow, 1993

Gilbert, Martin, *Atlas of the Holocaust*, London: Joseph, 1982; as *The Macmillan Atlas of the Holocaust*, New York: Macmillan, 1982; 2nd edition, as *The Dent Atlas of the Holocaust*, London: Dent, 1993; as *Atlas of the Holocaust*, New York: Morrow, 1993

Hyman, Paula E. and Deborah Dash Moore (editors), *Jewish Women in America: An Historical Encyclopedia*, 2 vols., New York: Routledge, 1997; London: Routledge, 1998

Jacobs, Louis, *The Jewish Religion: A Companion*, Oxford and New York: Oxford University Press, 1995

Kaganoff, Nathan, *Judaica Americana: An Annotated Bibliography of Publications from 1960–1990*, 2 vols., Brooklyn, New York: Carlson, 1995

Marcus, Jacob Rader (editor), *The Concise Dictionary of American Jewish Biography*, 2 vols., Brooklyn, New York: Carlson, 1994

New York Times Company, *Israel, the Historical Atlas: The Story of Israel from Ancient Times to the Modern Nation*, New York: Macmillan, 1997

Singerman, Robert, *Judaica Americana: A Bibliography of Publications to 1900*, 2 vols., New York: Greenwood, 1990

Werblowsky, R.J. Zwi and Geoffrey Wigoder (editors), *The Oxford Dictionary of the Jewish Religion*, New York: Oxford University Press, 1997

Vilnay, Zev, *Atlas Tav Shin Kaf Het*, 1968; translated by Moshe Aumann as *The New Israel Atlas: Bible to Present Day*, London: Humphrey, 1968; New York: McGraw-Hill, 1969

As a humanistic discipline (and a small one at that), Jewish studies was only modestly affected by new media in the late 20th century. The limited ability of computers to search non-Roman scripts proved an additional inhibiting factor. Certainly, the advent of electronic mail encouraged communication and a wide sharing of scholarly notes and queries, but the most significant developments were at an evolutionary rather than a revolutionary level, with the conversion of existing reference works or ongoing bibliographic projects to electronic formats. With the concurrent appearance at the very end of the 20th century of the two chief encyclopedic and bibliographic resources in Jewish studies—*Encyclopaedia Judaica* and the Jewish National and University Library's Index of Articles on Jewish Studies (RAMBI)—on CD-ROM and online via the website of the Hebrew University of Jerusalem, respectively, the days of similar works (as opposed to monographic literature) on the inflexible medium of paper seem numbered. The following remarks, therefore, describe in some detail the range of atlases—as reference literature where traditional printed format continues for the moment to retain a certain appeal—but move briskly over the territory of bibliographies, encyclopedias, and dictionaries. The latter are understood not as language tools but as one-volume encyclopedias supplying summary definitions of concepts, people, and places significant to the study of Judaism.

If the particular state of flux in a kind of literature that is in any case especially susceptible to obsolescence is one reason for brevity, there are two further, equally compelling reasons. One is the sheer vastness of the literature, while the other is more comforting—the job has already been done to perfection in the two volumes by Shimeon Brisman and the volume by Charles Cutter and Micha Oppenheim. BRISMAN (1977, 1987) is primarily an important and pleasurable history of Jewish research literature, but his treatment of the major and minor monuments of reference publishing in Jewish studies, which proceeds by genre and then chronologically within each genre, is laid out in such a way as to function as a superb bibliography of bibliographies, in the case of volume one, and of encyclopedias and lexicons (again, lexicons of Judaism to the exclusion of lexicons of Jewish languages) in volume two. Brisman's discussion of a major work may run to several pages, and the author manifests quite exceptional sensitivity to the needs of researchers in the mass of illuminating information he assembles. In particular, his work makes visible the enduring potential in obscure and otherwise forgotten publications often from the 19th century.

Volume one covers general and subject-specific bibliographies of Hebraica and of European-language Judaica; published catalogs of major libraries' collections of Jewish literature; bio-bibliographical works; bibliographical periodicals; and indexes to periodicals and monographs. Brisman remarks in his preface that

> during the last two and a half centuries numerous efforts have been made—with ranging degrees of success—to

bring the fast-growing Jewish literature under biblio-graphic control. During his years as a Jewish studies librarian and lecturer in Hebrew bibliography, the author has noticed with disappointment that the average Jew-ish scholar, student, or even librarian is totally unaware of the existence of such tools; but he has been pleasantly surprised as a lecturer to notice students' fascination with Jewish bibliography, a subject usually considered dry. It seems that Jewish bibliography, when presented in the realm of Jewish cultural and literary history, can become an exciting topic for scholars and students.

In view of the preeminence accorded to bibliographic intelli-gence by the "information age," perhaps Brisman need not have worried, but his books—anything but dry—certainly make his point and richly repay cover-to-cover reading.

CUTTER and OPPENHEIM offer a guide to the reference lit-erature of Jewish studies that is quite different from Brisman and is equally invaluable. A straightforward bibliography by subject and by genre within subjects, it offers brisk, informed annota-tions that are typically descriptive rather than evaluative, never devoting more than a paragraph to a single work and occa-sionally not more than a couple of lines. The authors identify a staggering 888 reference books. The clarity and simplicity of the layout ensures that the reader can hardly fail to find immediate assistance and a dependably exhaustive set of pointers. This small book can be relied upon without fear of a daunting over-load on the one hand or oversight of key resources on the other. The work is also notable for being more up-to-date: Cutter and Oppenheim's second edition (which renders entirely obsolete their more modest first edition of 1982) appeared some 15 years after Brisman's volume on bibliography, and much had appeared in the intervening years. Their book is also distinctive for the range of reference tools it distinguishes and describes, among them biographical dictionaries, calendars, filmographies, travel guides, and all manner of directories and yearbooks.

To indicate the frenetic pace of production during the 1990s of reference works in Jewish studies, it may suffice merely to mention half-a-dozen outstanding examples. SINGERMAN accomplishes an extraordinary feat of bibliography, identify-ing and indexing 5,892 American Jewish books and 479 ser-ial titles published through 1900. This achievement is complemented by KAGANOFF, who devotes two further vol-umes that resemble Singerman's and bear the same title as his. Kaganoff lists American Jewish books and articles for the years 1960 through 1990—some 7,427 in total. Both compi-lations feature an invaluable subject index.

In terms of encyclopedias and dictionaries published during the 1900s, it is necessary to mention Marcus and also Hyman and Dash Moore. MARCUS provides the briefest of bio-graphical entries for close to 24,000 prominent American Jews, supplying place and date of birth, education, profession, communal involvement, and field of distinction, before listing references to ampler treatments elsewhere. It is, therefore, a central clearinghouse for the published but scattered data of American Jewish biography—a cumulative index, inter alia, to any number of ephemeral directories and *Who's Who*s.

HYMAN and MOORE offer full encyclopedic treatment for 800 individual American Jewish women, with an additional 110 topical entries. These cover institutions such as the can-torate and organizations such as Hadassah, as well as broader treatments of the women's "club movement" or "fiction." Replete with excellent photographs and an exemplary bibli-ography, this magnificent review of the state of knowledge fills a grievous gap and is bound to be the point of departure for much further research.

Finally it should be said that while a good many of the numerous lexicons of Judaism are at best uninspired, two new publications, one appearing in 1995 and the other in 1997, tower over the field, offering intelligibility to guide the inex-pert and a discriminating combination of information and interpretation to assist, interest, and frequently to stimulate Jewish studies professionals, sometimes even in their own area of immediate expertise. Jacobs, on the one hand, and Werblowsky and Wigoder, on the other, might appear to be in competition with each other, a curious circumstance given that both books are published by the same press. The books cover much the same ground, limiting themselves to explicitly reli-gious dimensions of the Jewish experience, but with one major difference. WERBLOWSKY and WIGODER have totally trans-formed an older work, their dated and less valuable *Encyclo-pedia of the Jewish Religion* (1965), by successfully galvanizing a large team of experts to produce the entries, which are use-fully signed, their brevity notwithstanding. JACOBS has pro-duced a tour de force, an alphabetized conspectus of Judaism as he compellingly sees it. Both this personal—but unfailingly unexceptional—statement of Jacobs and the collective wisdom of so many of his most distinguished contemporaries in Werblowsky and Wigoder are essential reference tools.

References to maps date back to biblical times. In Ezekiel 4:1, the prophet engraves the plan or map of the city of Jerusalem in preparation for a siege. Similar maps have been found on Babylonian monuments. The earliest real maps—the remarkably accurate Portolano maps—were designed for nav-igation of the coasts of the Mediterranean during the Second Crusade of Louis IX of France in 1270. The only pertinent ancient map that has been preserved in its original format is the Madaba mosaic, which depicts parts of Egypt, the Sinai peninsula, the land of Israel, and Southern Syria. It was orig-inally part of the floor of a Byzantine church built in the 6th century C.E., located in present-day Jordan, and is available in facsimile with a meticulous commentary and introduction by AVI-YONAH.

AHARONI and AVI-YONAH trace the history of ancient Israel from the Canaanite period through the Bar-Kokhba revolt in more than 260 maps that are unfailingly clear, dependable, and useful, if graphically dreary from the per-spective of subsequent advances in production values.

AUMANN is a short, concise, and comprehensive atlas of the land of Israel from ancient times to the 1980s that encom-passes in texts and maps the entirety of Jewish history in the region. A section titled "Israel—Today" contains graphs and maps depicting the topography, vegetation, social structure, communities, and religious life of Israel. There are also sta-tistics on youth activities, sports and physical fitness, and pri-vate enterprise.

Tracing the development of the Jewish people from biblical times to the establishment of the State of Israel, BACON and

GILBERT's atlas is a pleasant popular account of Jewish communities worldwide. The chapters titled "The Jewish Enlightenment to the Eve of the Holocaust" and "The Dark Side: Anti-Semitism" are especially noteworthy. Numerous photographs and historical maps accompany this text, creating an impression reminiscent of a slide show.

DE LANGE's perspective is innovative and somewhat more original than those provided in the Aumann and the Bacon and Gilbert atlases. He investigates the evolution of the Jewish people, exploring "who they are, and how they have come to be where they are today." Because, writes De Lange, no precedents existed for this sort of publication, he constructs his own "perhaps idiosyncratic form of presentation," in which each of the atlas's three parts features a "different approach" to the Jewish world. Part one concentrates on migration and social conditions; part two contains a collection of general essays dealing with Jewish cultures; and part three depicts the Jewish world of today, highlighting both its dispersion and its centers around the globe. The volume concludes with a glossary, list of illustrations, bibliography, gazetteer, and a limited index.

Martin Gilbert has produced a number of successful historical atlases, for example on British history and Russian history, consistently emphasizing clarity above all else, which he achieves by opting for broad strokes discriminatingly chosen. This is true for GILBERT (1969), a lightly annotated atlas that "traces the world-wide migrations from ancient Mesopotamia to modern Israel," while attempting to "avoid undue emphasis" on the painful events in Jewish history, which sometimes seem to overshadow the many cultural achievements, bravery, and resistance of the Jewish people. Gilbert also portrays obscure episodes and communities in Jewish history, shedding light on the Jews of India, 175 B.C.E.–1795 C.E.; Jewish converts to Christianity, 45–300 C.E.; and the Karaites, 700–1960 C.E. Discussions of recent events such as the Jewish emigration from Russia and Operation Moses, in which thousands of Ethiopian Jews were brought to Israel, are also included in the atlas. A short bibliography provides sources for further study.

GILBERT (1982) manages to retain the uncluttered feel that characterizes all his atlases, but this time without any loss of detail. This is because the topic is relatively limited in time and space, with the anti-Jewish measures of 1933 to 1945 being illustrated in some 316 maps as against the 123 maps devoted to the entire Jewish experience in his general work. As a result, he is able to present, with his customary flair for succinct graphic eloquence, a great range of information, frequently of an illuminatingly microcosmic or local character, as in the typical full-page maps titled "Nine Deportations to Belzec, 7 September 1942" or "Jews, Greeks and Italians Drowned off Polegandros, 6 June 1944."

If Gilbert's productions are notably clean and make an excellent introduction, FRIESEL, again an atlas by a highly renowned modern historian, goes for richness of detail at the expense of soothing white space. Limited to the modern period, it does not offer significant coverage of events until the second half of the 19th century. For subsequent years, however, it is a treasure trove of demographic data: population growth, occupational distribution, exogamy, urbanization, migration, languages, and religious and intellectual differences are admirably presented. Names of institutions are occasionally rendered somewhat impressionistically, but caution is appropriate in approaching all these sweeping summaries of a world of history and does very little to diminish the value of an exceptionally suggestive and informative work of reference.

The NEW YORK TIMES COMPANY's historical atlas is a valuable, unique work that appropriately positions itself along "that often disputed border where history meets journalism." Nine reporters who have served as *Times* correspondents in Israel and the Middle East since 1948 each contribute a judicious and succinct essay on subjects from ancient times through the assassination of Yitzhak Rabin in 1995 and the establishment of a Likud government in 1996. If it is more journalism than history, it is also more history than atlas. Still, the volume does present many colorful photographs and more than 50 small but useful maps illustrating historical developments, including the Desert Storm military operation in Iraq, the Intifada, settlements in contention, and emerging Palestinian autonomy. The atlas ends with a section of biographical sketches titled "National Builders: Leaders Who Shaped Israel."

Although VILNAY's atlas purports to depict the "new Israel," it is now outdated and could be classified as a historical atlas because it only reflects events up to the Six-Day War of 1967. Nevertheless, it remains an exceptionally useful tool, largely for its unconventional and sometimes idiosyncratic choice of subject matter. The work is arranged in four sequences. "Modern Israel" covers the basics of the physical and political geography of the State of Israel before proceeding to illustrate cartographically such intriguing sidelines as settlements named after Christian friends of Israel, benefactors, and soldiers. Other maps identify holy places, and the various religious minorities are given due attention. Another map locates the yeshivot of Israel; sketchy and dated, it is of limited use today, but, typical of Vilnay, this is a neat idea. The second sequence, "The Struggle for Independence," covers developments during the British Mandate and the early years of statehood. The third section offers a brisk march through the history of the land of Israel from Joshua's conquest, by way of Romans, Crusaders, Ottomans, and Napoleon, to Allenby; the volume concludes with a useful fourth section devoted to the depiction of the assorted plans for creating a Jewish state that were drafted before and during the British Mandate. Although spelling, notably of the names of individuals, is not all that it might be, this is quite a useful publication.

A more modern, more academically sophisticated, and much more detailed historical treatment specifically of Jerusalem is offered by BAHAT. As comprehensive and informative as could be hoped for in its presentation of the earlier strata of the city's exceedingly complex past, it is relatively—disappointingly—brisk in its treatment of developments once Saladin succeeds in evicting the Crusaders.

DINA RIPSMAN EYLON AND ARI SALKIN-WEISS

See also Bible: Reference Tools; Talmudic Literature: Reference Tools

Reform Judaism

Borowitz, Eugene, *Reform Judaism Today,* 3 vols., New York: Behrman House, 1977

Martin, Bernard (editor), *Contemporary Reform Jewish Thought,* Chicago: Quadrangle, 1968

Meyer, Michael, *Response to Modernity: A History of the Reform Movement in Judaism,* New York: Oxford University Press, 1988

Neusner, Jacob (editor), *The Reformation of Reform Judaism* (Judaism in Cold War America, 1945–1990, vol. 6), New York: Garland, 1993

Showstack, Gerald, *Suburban Communities: The Jewishness of American Reform Jews* (Brown Studies on Jews and Their Societies, vol. 5), Atlanta, Georgia: Scholars Press, 1988

Silverstein, Alan, *Alternatives to Assimilation: The Response of Reform Judaism to American Culture, 1840–1930* (Brandeis Series in American Jewish History, Culture, and Life), Hanover, New Hampshire: University Press of New England, 1994

Reform Judaism was a modernizing effort within Central and Western European Judaism in response to the Enlightenment and the abolition of the medieval ghettos in the late 18th century. By the 1830s it had taken on the form of an organized movement. It was brought to the New World by German Jewish immigrants arriving in the decades before the U.S. Civil War, and it became the dominant form of American Jewish life until the influx of traditional Eastern European Jews beginning in the 1880s. The Reform movement has continued to be a major presence in American Judaism, comprising some 30 to 40 percent of all affiliated Jews. Since World War II and the Holocaust, Reform Jews have been moving toward the incorporation of more traditional European Jewish customs.

BOROWITZ provides a three-volume series of small books designed to spell out "the state of the question" in Reform Judaism as it seemed in 1973 (a *Leader's Guide* prepared by Joel Soffir constitutes a fourth volume). The occasion for this series was a broad-ranging self-evaluation within the American Reform movement undertaken on the centenary of the founding of the Reform seminary, Hebrew Union College, in 1873. The movement sought a reevaluation of the meaning of Reform in light of the Holocaust and the establishment of the State of Israel. In volume one *(Reform in the Process of Change)*, Borowitz rehearses both the lessons that he felt Reform had taught modern Jews and the lessons that the Reform movement had learned over the century that had elapsed. Volume two *(What We Believe)* builds on these lessons to reflect on what affirmations a Reform Jew can or must make. Volume three *(How We Live)* looks at how Borowitz thinks Reform Jews should live in the world and especially their religious duties, their stance toward the State of Israel, and their relationship to other people. In the end, he concludes that the task facing Reform is to learn how to live with diversity.

MEYER has written the first comprehensive history of the Reform movement since the beginning of the 20th century. By the mid-1980s the turmoil of the 1970s had passed and the meaning of Israel and the Holocaust had been squarely faced by Reform Jews. Meyer's history moves away from the essentials and the apologetics of earlier treatments of the history of Reform and draws attention instead to the dynamic tensions to which the creators of the movement were responding. The result is a thick history of the Reform movement that firmly embeds its development in the social and political realities out of which the movement grew and developed. The book ends with the convulsions of the mid-1970s, including the effects of the anti-Vietnam War movement, the Civil Rights struggle, and Jewish confrontation with Israel and the Holocaust.

NEUSNER has put together what could be an interesting companion to Meyer's history. Neusner's work is a collection of articles and essays by significant contemporary Reform thinkers on various aspects of Reform Jewish life. The collection is part of a ten-volume series that deals with the various manifestations of modern U.S. Judaism. The particular essays brought together here were written between 1951 and 1989 and were chosen because they represent a broad perspective on the Reform consideration of the situation of modern Jewish life.

MARTIN has brought together a collection of essays by Reform Jewish leaders and thinkers dealing with central issues of Reform Jewish belief. All were written by rabbis who were alumni of Hebrew Union College, the Reform seminary, and so represent the thinking of leaders of American Reform Judaism. Most of the essays were written for this volume, the remainder having been originally published elsewhere, usually in the official publications of the Reform rabbinate. The point was to begin the process of articulating a theology for American Reform Judaism. The collection opens with an essay on theological methodology by Eugene Borowitz, the major American Reform Jewish theologian. Other essays deal with Reform concepts of God, with Reform and traditional Jewish normative practice (halakhah), and the question of Jewish chosenness and destiny. The last essay, written by the editor, sums up the current state of Reform theology as he sees it.

SILVERSTEIN approaches the situation of contemporary Reform by asking how the movement got to where it is. His study looks at the various influences on Reform Jews in America from 1840 until the 1930s. He finds a community that was anxious to maintain its Jewish identity but was looking for a way of doing so compatible with the American context. The result was the creation of a particular style of American Reform synagogue that offered a place for Judaism to be celebrated, but in a voluntaristic institutional setting that mirrored American social and corporate values. For Silverstein, the structure of the American Reform synagogue movement, including its national organizations, has been the most complete example of the creation of an ethnic Jewish lifestyle within an American cultural framework.

SHOWSTACK discusses what has become the major concern within the Reform Jewish community of the 1980s and 1990s: how to hold onto Jewish identity in a community that is rapidly assimilating into American culture. Showstack's book is an in-depth analysis of the sociological and demographic situation of American Reform Jews. What he documents is that Reform Jews (and American Jews in general) have to a large extent succeeded in "making it" in America, but have maintained, or developed, along the way a strong sense of having a distinct ethnic identity. The sense of the book is that the future of Reform will devolve more and more into serving this ethnic definition of Jewishness.

PETER HAAS

See also Liturgy, Reform

Renaissance

Bonfil, Roberto, *Gli Ebrei in Italia nell'epoca del Rinascimento*, 1991; translated by Anthony Oldcorn as *Jewish Life in Renaissance Italy*, Berkeley: University of California Press, 1994

Cohen, Mark R. (editor and translator), *The Autobiography of a Seventeenth-Century Venetian Rabbi: Leon Modena's Life of Judah*, Princeton, New Jersey: Princeton University Press, 1988

Fishman, Talya, *Shaking the Pillars of Exile: 'Voice of a Fool,' an Early Modern Jewish Critique of Rabbinic Culture* (Stanford Studies in Jewish History and Culture), Stanford, California: Stanford University Press, 1997

Ravid, Benjamin and Robert Davis, *The Jews of Venice*, Baltimore, Maryland: Johns Hopkins University Press, 1999

Ruderman, David B., *Kabbalah, Magic, and Science: The Cultural Universe of a Sixteenth-Century Jewish Physician*, Cambridge, Massachusetts: Harvard University Press, 1988

Jews have lived in Italy without interruption since antiquity. Until the high Middle Ages, Italian Jewry was concentrated in the southern part of the peninsula. By the 13th and 14th centuries, however, with hostile papal policies in the south and favorable treatment in the north, the Jews began to flourish in many of the cities and small towns of northern Italy, primarily as loan bankers but also as merchants. As antagonism toward the Jews increased in France and the Germanic lands, many fled to take advantage of the opportunities in Italy. Spanish Jews began to migrate to Italy after the persecutions of 1391 and continued for several centuries, even after they, or their ancestors, had converted to Catholicism. Since the Jews provided valuable services, they often received generous charters allowing them to live comfortably. Prosperous, connected with all levels of Christian society, and living in relatively small Jewish communities, these Jews cultivated the tastes and culture of bourgeois Christians. These tendencies became particularly pronounced during the Renaissance, a time when cultural creativity also flourished among the Jews of Italy. At various times, despite intermittent expulsions, their protectors included the popes in Rome, Ancona, and Bologna, the Medici in Florence, the Gonzaga in Mantua, the Este in Ferrara, the Sforza in Milan, and the Republic of Venice.

BONFIL's contribution provides a fresh study of an often misunderstood period of Jewish history and offers a pioneering model of the application of the *Annales* or *mentalité* model of history writing to the study of Jewish history. Bonfil wrestles with two equally stimulating questions: (1) to what extent was the history of the Jews in Italy during the Renaissance different from that of the Middle Ages, and (2) how does the historian discover and describe the mentality of Jews living in different periods of history. For Bonfil, these questions are more significant than the conventional preoccupation with the extent to which the Italian culture of the Renaissance influenced the Jews; for him this conventional thinking assumes that there were two distinct cultures, an assumption he will not accept. He argues that the Jews of Italy shared many ideas, social relations, and even sexual intimacies with their Christian neighbors, without reducing the gap between the two religions or peoples. One of the contributions of this view is to show that a structure shared with other peoples, common in Jewish history, is not the same as assimilation. These shared structures produced a Jewish mentality different in Italy than in other parts of the world at the same time and different during the Renaissance from what preceded it in Italy. Regularly he singles out for strong criticism the writing of Cecil Roth, whose research on the Jews during the Renaissance is widely known. Readers may derive more benefit from Bonfil's stunning analysis by turning first to the second section of the book.

COHEN's collaborative work treats Leone Modena's Hebrew autobiography, *Hayyei Yehudah*, "The Life of Judah." Modena (1571–1648), the outstanding Venetian rabbi of the early modern period, wrote a great number of Hebrew works in many of the literary genres of Renaissance and Baroque Italy and personally engaged in polemics with Jews and Christians about the nature of rabbinic Judaism. Although he wrote many responsa, letters, and poems, central to an understanding of his thought are works that he never explicitly prepared for publication, which in addition to his autobiography include his attacks on Kabbalah—particularly his scholarly assault on the antiquity of the Zohar and Christian use of it for missionary activity—and his presentation of a powerful critique of rabbinic Judaism, *Kol Sahal*. In addition to translating and editing the autobiography, Cohen discovered that the interlinear interpolations are in a different ink from the rest of the text, indicating that the author later revised his work to modify or intensify his reactions to the events described. Cohen and Theodore Rabb place the work in the context of early modern Jewish and general history. Natalie Zemon Davis, drawing on the canons of autobiographical criticism, insightfully characterizes the work as "Fame and Secrecy," as part of a program, conscious or not, of posturing, confessing, bragging, and repenting. Her essay places the autobiography in the context of early modern life-writing. Benjamin Ravid provides archival materials in Italian from the Venetian State Archives relevant to Modena and Venetian Jewish history. Howard Adelman compares the autobiography with Modena's other writings, especially his letters. Adelman and Ravid's historical notes can be read sequentially after reading the entire autobiography.

FISHMAN has written a brilliant study of *Kol Sahal* that sheds much light on the enigmatic but well-documented personality of Leone Modena as well as on the nature of rabbinic Judaism itself. As Fishman correctly notes, reactions to *Kol Sahal* for the past century and a half have been based on the Jewish denominational preferences of the historian. Some have tried for various reasons either to identify Modena not only as the editor and copyist of the work, about which there can be no dispute, but also as its author, either vindicating their own desire to undermine rabbinic authority or else Modena's position as a rabbi. Fishman draws on a comparison between passages in Modena's oeuvre and in *Kol Sahal* to reach the conclusion that Modena was indeed the author of *Kol Sahal*. Fishman raises the possibility that Modena donned a mask when writing *Kol Sahal*, a work she characterizes as an "invention." This thesis becomes especially convincing when comparing *Kol Sahal* to Modena's autobiography, *Hayyei Yehudah*. This latter work can easily seduce the reader into thinking that he or she has access to the facts of its author's life and that the author may not have been a particularly happy, successful, or endearing personality. This creates what could be called a false positivism because, especially when compared to his other writings, the apparently straightforward factual nature of his autobiographical narrative proves to be falsified by other competing facts. A similar conclusion emerges when comparing Modena's autobiography with that of Abraham Yagel's contemporaneous *Gei Hizzayon*, a work that clearly mixes dream sequences with descriptions of what seem to have been actual events, heightening the question not of how to separate fact from fiction, but rather why autobiographical writers mix them so effortlessly in their constructions of their selves.

RAVID and DAVIS have gathered some of the most recent and interesting scholarship on the history of the Jews of Venice, which sheds much light on Renaissance Jewry. Ravid traces parliamentary discussions and legal development pertaining to the presence of Jews in Venice. Calabi offers a synchronic study of the ghetto as the "City of the Jews." Malkiel examines the legal relationship between the Jewish community and the Republic of Venice. Arbel extends the discussion to Jews living in Venetian territories abroad. Pullan presents the financial aspects of Jewish moneylending. Roberto Bonfil's presentation covers aspects of rabbinic authority—or lack of it—and mysticism. Ioly Zorattini draws on the records of the Venetian Inquisition to present a social and religious history of popular religious practices that came to the attention of the authorities. Harran's essay examines in depth the musical contribution of Leone Modena in its larger context. Adelman shows the relationship between matters of gender and family in the Jewish community and major moments in Venetian and world history. Horowitz offers a social history of the public aspects of the Jewish community. David Ruderman elucidates aspects of Jewish medicine and scientific thought.

RUDERMAN's study of the life and literary production of Abraham Yagel creates an insightful description of the intellectual currents among Italian Jewry in the late 16th and early 17th centuries. The title may suggest—especially in light of popular notions of Italian Jewish history as well as of Kabbalah, magic, and science—that the book is about marginal or exotic aspects of Jewish life. However, Ruderman establishes conclusively that the major Jewish figures of the period were influenced by trends in the general Renaissance to pursue these subjects, even though they did so as an expression of their attachment to traditional rabbinic values and practices. Ruderman asserts that *Gei Hizzayon*, a detailed account by Yagel of his misfortunes, which Ruderman also translated, edited, and published as *Valley of Vision: The Heavenly Journey of Abraham ben Hananiah Yagel* (Philadel-phia: University of Pennsylvania Press, 1990), was an unprecedented attempt at Jewish autobiography in premodern Hebrew literature, and he argues that it reflected a growing awareness of the self. Many of the very features in *Gei Hizzayon* that might lead one to think that it is not an autobiography, such as descriptions of dreams, discussions with the dead, and adventures of the soul outside the body, are in fact also found in Modena's *Hayyei Yehudah*. Moreover, it is these inventive aspects that must be considered essential to an autobiography. Beyond each of their pioneering attempts at writing Hebrew autobiographies, Yagel's and Modena's lives are amazingly similar to each other in many areas, specifically those that have led scholars to place them at the periphery of Jewish life: Yagel was often dismissed as an apostate—for no valid reason according to Ruderman—and Modena has been dismissed as a heretic, also for no valid reason. Financial failures, unsuccessful business partnerships, and much anxiety marked both men's lives. Both were concerned with a wide range of illnesses, especially "melancholia," Yagel as a professional physician and Modena as a professional patient. Very few of either man's major works were published in his lifetime, and the works that were published were of limited scope and importance, although not without significance as regards their attempts to popularize Judaism. The unintended consequence of both men's work is that they continue to provide fascinating, detailed information about Jewish life during the Renaissance and the development of a sense of self among Jews during the early modern period.

HOWARD TZVI ADELMAN

Renewal

Adler, Rachel, *Engendering Judaism: An Inclusive Theology and Ethics*, Philadelphia: Jewish Publication Society, 1998

Alpert, Rebecca, *Like Bread on the Seder Plate: Jewish Lesbians and the Transformation of Tradition* (Between Men–Between Women), New York: Columbia University Press, 1997

Angel, Leonard, *The Book of Miriam*, Buffalo, New York: Mosaic, 1997

Balka, Christie and Andy Rose, *Twice Blessed: On Being Lesbian, Gay, and Jewish*, Boston: Beacon, 1989

Berman, Phyllis and Arthur Waskow, *Tales of Tikkun: New Jewish Stories to Heal the Wounded World*, Northvale, New Jersey: Aronson, 1996

Berrin, Susan, *A Heart of Wisdom: Making the Jewish Journey from Midlife through the Elder Years*, Woodstock, Vermont: Jewish Lights, 1997

Bloch, Chana and Ariel Bloch, *The Song of Songs: A New Translation with an Introduction and Commentary*, New York: Random House, 1995

Brener, Anne, *Mourning and Mitzvah: A Guided Journal for Walking the Mourner's Path through Grief to Healing*, Woodstock, Vermont: Jewish Lights, 1993

Cooper, David A., *God Is a Verb: Kabbalah and the Practice of Mystical Judaism*, New York: Riverhead, 1997

Cowan, Paul and Rachel Cowan, *Mixed Blessings,* New York: Doubleday, 1987

Dekro, Jeffrey and Lawrence Bush, *Jews, Money, and Social Responsibility: Developing a "Torah of Money" for Contemporary Life,* Philadelphia: Shefa Fund, 1993

Eisenberg, Evan, *The Ecology of Eden,* New York: Knopf, 1998

Elon, Ari, *From Jerusalem to the Edge of Heaven: Meditations on the Soul of Israel,* Philadelphia: Jewish Publication Society, 1995

Falk, Marcia, *The Song of Songs: Love Poems from the Bible,* New York: Harcourt Brace Jovanovich, 1977; Sheffield, South Yorkshire: Almond, 1982; revised as *The Song of Songs: A New Translation and Interpretation,* San Francisco: HarperSanFrancisco, 1990

Falk, Marcia, *The Book of Blessings,* San Francisco: HarperSanFrancisco, 1996

Feld, Merle, *A Spiritual Life: A Jewish Feminist Journey* (SUNY Series in Modern Jewish Literature and Culture), Albany: State University of New York Press, 1998

Fink, Nan, *Stranger in the Midst: A Memoir of Spiritual Discovery,* New York: Basic Books, 1997

Firestone, Tirzah, *With Roots in Heaven: One Woman's Passionate Journey into the Heart of Her Faith,* New York: Dutton, 1998

Fox, Everett, *The Five Books of Moses* (Schocken Bible, vol. 1), New York: Schocken, and London: Harvill, 1995

Frankel, Ellen, *The Five Books of Miriam: A Woman's Commentary on the Torah,* New York: Putnam, 1996

Green, Arthur (translator and editor), *Upright Practices: The Light of the Eyes* (Classics of Western Spirituality), New York: Paulist, 1982

Green, Arthur, *Seek My Face, Speak My Name: A Contemporary Jewish Theology,* Northvale, New Jersey: Aronson, 1992

Green, Arthur (editor), *The Language of Truth: The Torah Commentary of the Sefat Emet, Rabbi Yehudah Leib Alter of Ger,* Philadelphia: Jewish Publication Society, 1998

Heschel, Susannah (editor), *Moral Grandeur and Spiritual Audacity: Essays,* New York: Farrar, Straus and Giroux, 1996

Hyman, Naomi, *Biblical Women in the Midrash: A Sourcebook,* Northvale, New Jersey: Aronson, 1997

Kamenetz, Rodger, *The Jew in the Lotus: A Poet's Rediscovery of Jewish Identity in Buddhist India,* San Francisco: HarperSanFrancisco, 1994

Kamenetz, Rodger, *Stalking Elijah: Adventures with Today's Jewish Mystical Masters,* San Francisco: HarperSanFrancisco, 1997

Kushner, Lawrence, *God Was in This Place and I, I Did Not Know,* Woodstock, Vermont: Jewish Lights, 1991

Lerner, Michael, *Jewish Renewal: A Path to Healing and Transformation,* New York: Putnam, 1994

Matt, Daniel, *Zohar: The Book of Enlightenment* (Classics of Western Spirituality), New York: Paulist, and London: SPCK, 1983

Matt, Daniel, *The Essential Kabbalah,* San Francisco: HarperSanFrancisco, 1995

Mirel, James L. and Karen Bonnell Werth, *Stepping Stones to Jewish Spiritual Living: Walking the Path Morning, Noon, and Night,* Woodstock, Vermont: Jewish Lights, 1998

Mitchell, Stephen, *Into the Whirlwind: A Translation of the Book of Job,* Garden City, New York: Doubleday, 1979; as *The Book of Job,* San Francisco: North Point, 1987; London: Cathie, 1989

Omer-Man, Jonathan, *Worlds of Jewish Prayer: A Festschrift in Honor of Rabbi Zalman M. Schachter-Shalomi,* Northvale, New Jersey: Aronson, 1993

Orenstein, Debra, *Lifecycles,* Woodstock, Vermont: Jewish Lights, 1994

Petsonk, Judy, *Taking Judaism Personally: Creating a Meaningful Spiritual Life,* New York: Free Press, 1996

Piercy, Marge, *He, She, and It,* New York: Knopf, 1991

Piercy, Marge, *The Art of Blessing the Day: Poems with a Jewish Theme,* New York: Knopf, 1999

Pitzele, Peter, *Our Fathers' Wells: A Personal Encounter with the Myths of Genesis,* San Francisco: HarperSanFrancisco, 1995

Plaskow, Judith, *Standing Again at Sinai: Judaism from a Feminist Perspective,* San Francisco: Harper and Row, 1990

P'nai Or Religious Fellowship, *Or Chadash: A Guide to Shabbat Celebration,* Philadelphia: ALEPH (Alliance for Jewish Renewal), 1987

Prager, Marcia, *The Path of Blessing: Experiencing the Energy and Abundance of the Divine,* New York: Bell Tower, 1998

Raphael, Simcha Paull, *Jewish Views of the Afterlife,* Northvale, New Jersey: Aronson, 1994

Rapoport, Nessa, *A Woman's Book of Grieving,* New York: Morrow, 1994

Schachter-Shalomi, Zalman, *Paradigm Shift,* Northvale, New Jersey: Aronson, 1993

Schwartz, Richard H., *Judaism and Vegetarianism,* Smithtown, New York: Exposition, 1982; 2nd edition, Marblehead, Massachusetts: Micah, 1988

Shapiro, Rami, *Wisdom of the Jewish Sages: A Modern Reading of Pirke Avot,* New York: Bell Tower, 1995

Waskow, Arthur, *Seasons of Our Joy,* New York: Bantam, 1982

Waskow, Arthur, *These Holy Sparks: The Rebirth of the Jewish People,* San Francisco: Harper and Row, 1983

Waskow, Arthur, *Down-to-Earth Judaism: Food, Money, Sex, and the Rest of Life,* New York: Morrow, 1995

Waskow, Arthur, *Godwrestling: Round 2: Ancient Wisdom, Future Paths,* Woodstock, Vermont: Jewish Lights, 1996

Weissler, Chava, *Voices of the Matriarchs: Listening to the Prayers of Early Modern Jewish Women,* Boston: Beacon, 1998

Wiener, Shohama, *The Fifty-Eighth Century: A Jewish Renewal Sourcebook,* Northvale, New Jersey: Aronson, 1996

Winkler, Gershon, *Sacred Secrets: The Sanctity of Sex in Jewish Law and Lore,* Northvale, New Jersey: Aronson, 1998

The movement called by its participants "Jewish renewal" is chiefly but not exclusively made up of North American Jews. It originated in the 1960s and 1970s and consists of the intertwining of three strands of Jewish rethinking: the neo-Hasidism of Martin Buber, Abraham Joshua Heschel, Shlomo Carlebach, and Zalman Schachter-Shalomi; the emergence of informal prayer groups *(havurot)* and similar forms of Jewish community that were participatory, intimate, and deeply engaged in the progressive political energies of the period from 1967 to 1975; and the emergence of a movement for equality of women and men in existing Jewish life and in shaping what Judaism is to become, including the insights of feminist Judaism. During the 1980s and 1990s, other strands became increasingly important parts of the weave of Jewish renewal: the knowledge and practice of forms of meditation used in Eastern spiritual traditions, the rediscovery of meditative traditions in Judaism, and a spiritually rooted concern for the endangered web of life on this planet, leading to a conscious eco-Judaism. Most Jewish-renewal people, though committed to nurturing exploratory institutions such as ALEPH: Alliance for Jewish Renewal, also see Jewish renewal as a process reaching beyond all denominational boundaries and institutional structures. This process is going on in Jewish music, liturgy, midrash, art, education, and politics. It takes place in synagogues of all denominations as well as in *havurot*, in "secular" and in communal settings, in ashrams and on Broadway. At the heart of Jewish renewal is an understanding of Jewish history as a series of encounters with God, the experiences of a community once again renewed in contemporary times after the crisis of the Holocaust and the seeming triumph of modernity in both its creative and destructive aspects.

Several books use biography and history to describe the movement. KAMENETZ (1994) is the story of a meeting in India between rabbis and the Dalai Lama, with an exploration of the encounter's deeper meaning and results. KAMENETZ (1997) is the story of the more mystical and meditative aspects of Jewish renewal, especially focusing on several individual teachers and rabbis. PETSONK tells the story of her own life journey into Jewish renewal. She discusses key aspects and describes meetings with important teachers of the movement. WASKOW (1983) is an interpretive history that chronicles the movement from its origins in the late 1960s to 1982.

Several books describe the major theological and practical positions of the movement. SCHACHTER-SHALOMI offers a collection of crucial essays on crossing the river into a new form of Judaism for the 21st century and far beyond. The essays explore the nature of Jewish community and history, an experiential approach to prayer, or "davvenology," and the possibilities of a new outlook on Jewish law (the "psycho-halakhic process"). WASKOW (1996) looks at the changing faces of the Torah as renewal communities wrestle and dance with it. It includes a theology of human and Jewish history and discusses why the movement for Jewish renewal has appeared at this historical moment. It also addresses the nature and future of the State of Israel and the meaning of the Holocaust. In addition, it discusses the biblical concept of jubilee applied to high-tech society, ways to understand and deal with the present environmental crisis, prayer forms that emerge from new ways of connecting with God, and other crucial con-

cerns of *tikkun 'olam*, which can be understood as the advancement of social justice. Despite its title, LERNER's book is not a definitive or comprehensive statement on Jewish renewal. It takes one important stance within the movement, focusing on issues of public policy and psychological transformation. Beginning with a psychologically rooted analysis of the God of love and why the Bible sometimes portrays God as cruel, the book moves into a political analysis of modern malaise and discusses how to draw on religious and spiritual practice to heal society.

PLASKOW reexamines Judaism from a feminist perspective. Assuming the full inclusion of women and their life experience, she asks how Judaism might look in the three classic categories of God, Torah, and Israel. ADLER looks especially at how halakhah, prayer, and marriage might be addressed in a Judaism as inclusive of women as of men. Both OMER-MAN and WIENER are collections of Festschrift essays by students of Zalman Schachter-Shalomi that point toward emerging directions in the "new paradigm" of Judaism. PIERCY (1991) is a novel set in the mid-21st century; it concerns a Jewish-renewal community of free humans and a free android/golem who live in a world of corporate feudalism and global scorching. The plot is intertwined with a retelling, through a woman's eyes, of the story of the Golem of Prague. GREEN (1992) is an exploration of many new metaphors for God and their implications for the practice of Judaism.

Much energy has been brought to the study of the Torah both through new translations of biblical, rabbinic, kabbalistic, and hasidic texts and through new midrashic approaches. The most important of the translations is FOX, which comes far closer to the meaning, poetry, wordplay, and cadences of the Hebrew than any previous English translation of the Pentateuch. The translations of the Song of Songs by FALK (1977) and by BLOCH and BLOCH are extraordinary openings to the sensuality of the Hebrew text. MITCHELL makes the intense drama of Job accessible to contemporary ears. SHAPIRO is a translation of Pirke Avot with a Jewish-renewal overtone to his understanding of the rabbis.

Several translations of kabbalistic and hasidic material have been of special importance to the Jewish-renewal community. GREEN (1982) brings Menahem Nahum of Chernobyl into English, and GREEN (1998) does the same—along with Green's own comments—for the Gerer Rebbe, Judah Leib Alter. MATT (1983 and 1995) presents powerfully poetic translations of key kabbalistic texts.

One emerging form of Jewish-renewal midrash is a synthesis of the old midrashic method, which lived totally inside the text, and the old historical-analytical form, which treated the text as only an inert object to be dissected. The Jewish-renewal synthesis uses the historical method to understand the text more deeply as part of a spiritual search. Far from being treated as dead, the text becomes all the more alive because it is about the ways in which the seeker's progenitors responded to the great historical and personal upheavals of their lives. One important example of this approach is EISENBERG, which draws on contemporary ecology and archaeology to see the Torah as, in part, a profound spiritual and political response to the agricultural revolution. Another is ANGEL, an intriguing quasi-factual report on how a group of women in Jerusalem are carrying forward the study of an ancient text that their female ancestors had studied for centuries, a text that presents itself as the Torah taught by Miriam. The text is feminist and eco-sensitive, seeing ancient Israel as a shepherd people deeply critical of ownership-agriculture. FRANKEL imaginatively weaves midrashic comments by real and archetypal women into biblical texts. HYMAN brings ancient rabbinic midrash about the women of the Bible face-to-face with midrash written by women of the renewal generation. KUSHNER weaves his own midrash together with a series of rabbinic and hasidic commentators, creating a rich tapestry of meaning through this juxtaposition.

During the mid-1990s the process of midrashic renewal moved into an unprecedented arena: midrash not only on biblical but also on talmudic stories. ELON intertwines his own understanding of a number of talmudic texts with his life experience in the Israeli army and the peace movement. BERMAN and WASKOW write new midrashic tales to heal wounded aspects of biblical and rabbinic tradition, addressing, in particular, the absence of women. The Jewish-renewal movement took the entire notion of midrash in a new direction, beyond words—creating midrash-in-action, as people played the various parts in biblical stories and filled in gaps in the tales through their own improvisational drama. This approach was called by some of its practitioners "drushodrama" and by others "Bibliodrama." PITZELE raises the process to a high art, and in his book he tells some of the stories that emerged from Bibliodrama sessions.

Much of Jewish-renewal thought has focused on new approaches to prayer, meditation, and celebration of festivals and life-cycle events. WASKOW (1982) is a guide to walking the festivals as a spiritual path that evokes both nature and history, intertwined with an explanation of millennial change in the festivals as an index to the spiritual growth of the Jewish people as a whole. There have been two major efforts to reconceive the prayer book to address God in nonhierarchal terms: the compendium issued by the P'NAI OR RELIGIOUS FELLOWSHIP and FALK (1996). The P'nai Or publication also shows how to use dance, meditation, dialogue, and other nonverbal or interpersonal techniques as part of prayer. PRAGER explores the depths of meaning in just six words—the formula with which blessings in rabbinic Judaism begin. WEISSLER rescues from oblivion and translates from Yiddish the *tkhine*—a form of prayer of the heart that Ashkenazi women uttered and often wrote. She then brings the *tkhine* process into the current generation by including some contemporary women's prayers, and she ends with a brilliantly self-reflective look at her role as a feminist scholar researching the past and creating a new future in the process. COOPER has made publicly available new forms of meditation that are rooted in ancient but almost forgotten practices of the kabbalists and are now being used by the Jewish-renewal community. New approaches to life-cycle rhythms are exemplified in the books by ORENSTEIN and BERRIN. Each is an anthology of new writing on spiritual aspects of the life cycle that have previously been celebrated only rarely. MIREL and WERTH's book takes the reader through a weekday with the same celebratory care that has usually been devoted only to Shabbat. BRENER, RAPHAEL, and RAPOPORT all focus

on the spiritual meaning of death and grief. Today, renewal Jews live in the most cross-communal atmosphere that has existed in about 2,000 years. As a result, the question of inter-religious households has been of great interest and is explored from a renewal standpoint in COWAN and COWAN. FINK explores conversion to Judaism from the convert's standpoint.

A number of books appeared in the late 1980s and 1990s that addressed Jewish-renewal approaches to infusing the practices of daily life with holiness. WASKOW (1995) draws on the past and imagines the future of Jewish ways of making holy daily practices regarding food, money, sex, and rest. For example, he offers suggestions for eco-kosher ways of consuming not only food but also energy resources. In addition, he presents ideas about new Jewish sexual ethics, the socially responsible use of money, and the crucial element of rest in healing a production-addicted society. DEKRO and BUSH focus on the creation of a Torah morality of money. BALKA and ROSE's work and ALPERT's book explore the implications of the full visibility of gay men and lesbians in Jewish life and religious practice. WINKLER not only translates a major treatise on Jewish sexual ethics by the 18th-century rabbinic authority Jacob Emden but he examines its origins and implications as well. SCHWARTZ develops a theme concerning food—vegetarianism—that has been of great interest to many renewal Jews. HESCHEL brings together the spiritual search and the political commitment of her father, Abraham Joshua Heschel, in a way that shows how deeply his work toward an everyday/holy Judaism both influenced and was influenced by the Jewish-renewal generation. FIRESTONE's brilliantly written memoir recounts the passionate and turbulent spiritual journey of her life. FELD weaves midrash, poetry, and family memoir together into a characteristically Jewish-renewal way of dancing with the Torah. PIERCY (1999) is a collection of the author's earthy Jewish poetry—some of it extremely funny, some of it awe inspiring, some of it warm and caressing, and much of it prayerful and explicitly intended for liturgical use.

ARTHUR WASKOW

Reproductive Technologies

Bleich, J. David, "In Vitro Fertilization: Maternal Identity and Conversion," in his *Contemporary Halakhic Problems* (Library of Jewish Law and Ethics), New York: Ktav, 1977

Feldman, Emanuel and Joel B. Wolowelsky, *Jewish Law and the New Reproductive Technologies*, Hoboken, New Jersey: Ktav, 1997

Grazi, Richard V. (editor), *Be Fruitful and Multiply: Fertility Therapy and the Jewish Tradition*, Spring Valley, New York: Feldheim, 1994

Jakobovits, Immanuel, "Artificial Insemination, Test Tube Babies and Host Mothers," in his *Jewish Medical Ethics: A Comparative and Historical Study of the Jewish Religious Attitude to Medicine and Its Practice*, New York: Bloch, 1975

Rosner, Fred, "Artificial Insemination, In Vitro Fertilization, Surrogate Motherhood, and Sex Organ Transplants," in his *Modern Medicine and Jewish Ethics*, New York: Yeshiva University Press, 1986, 2nd edition, 1991

Artificial insemination, in vitro fertilization, surrogate motherhood, and cryopreservation of sperm, eggs, or fertilized zygotes for later use are all strongly opposed by some rabbis on moral and halakhic grounds, and just as strongly justified by others.

According to JAKOBOVITS, human procreation should not be converted into the "manufacture" of progeny. The intimacy of husband and wife should not be broken by the "biologization" of family life. He further posits that:

> . . . artificial insemination utilizing an outside donor (AID) is considered to pose grave moral problems. Such operations, even if they may not technically constitute adultery, would completely disrupt the family relationship. Moreover, a child so conceived would be denied its birth-right to have a father and other relations who can be identified. Altogether, to reduce human generation to "stud-farming" methods would be a debasement of human life, utterly repugnant to Jewish ideals and traditions.

Jakobovits concludes that a balanced judgment on these moral issues cannot rest only on medical evidence or opinion, nor can he agree to leave the decision as to who will sire a child simply to the discretion of doctors or laboratory technicians. This would erode the sanctity of the marriage bond and violate the Jewish concept of an intimate personal partnership with God in the generation of life. To abort a mother's naturally fertilized egg and to re-implant it into a "host-mother" as a convenience for women who seek the gift of a child without the encumbrance and disfigurement of pregnancy is, he maintains, offensive. Likewise, to use another person as an incubator and then take from her the child she has carried and delivered for a fee is a revolting degradation of maternity and an affront to human dignity.

Far less critical of assisted reproduction is GRAZI, whose book is the first English work of its kind to deal exclusively with issues of fertility therapy in the Jewish tradition. The book provides an extensive survey of the relevant medical data and halakhic sources based on professional expertise and the verdicts of many rabbinic authorities. The sources and thought processes that lead to the diverse conclusions are as interesting as the rulings themselves. Several contributors to Grazi's book provide sensitive and scholarly insight into the medical and psychological as well as halakhic aspects of infertility and new assisted reproductive technologies.

ROSNER's analysis of Jewish views on artificial insemination, in vitro fertilization, surrogate motherhood, and sex organ transplants points out that in Judaism infertility is considered to be an illness—physiological, emotional, or both—and the physician's duty and mandate is to heal illness and to overcome, if possible, the somatic and emotional strains related to the illness. To help a couple to have their own child through the modern technologies of artificial insemination or in vitro fertilization seems to him to be within the physician's purview and, he argues, may even strengthen the bonds of the marriage and the family structure. While the use of host or surrogate mothers for the convenience of couples able to conceive by normal coitus cannot be condoned, an infertile Jewish couple may, he contends, have recourse to the new reproductive technologies. This includes the use of a surrogate mother in the absence of alternatives, in order to effect pregnancy and by so doing preserve their marriage and bring themselves happiness.

Most rabbinic authorities rule that parturition serves to establish the maternal relationship so than in situations of surrogate motherhood, the birth mother is legally considered the mother. BLEICH, however, raises the possibility that Jewish law may recognize a second maternal relationship based upon donation of an ovum. He adds that it is also possible that an additional nongenetic and nonparturitional relationship, or even multiple relationships of that nature, may be established on the basis of gestation. Bleich further rules that a child born of an in vitro procedure in which the ovum was donated by a non-Jewish woman requires conversion. Although their grounds are not entirely clear, some authorities maintain that, in such cases, immersion for purposes of conversion must be performed after birth and cannot be accomplished on behalf of the child by immersion of the mother during pregnancy. Whether or not there exists a maternal relationship between the Jewish birth mother and the child converted after birth is a matter of some dispute, and Bleich concludes that these issues represent matters of grave halakhic and moral significance requiring informed rabbinic guidance.

FELDMAN and WOLOWELSKY have published a compilation of eight articles by Bleich and others on Jewish law and the new reproductive technologies. These appeared originally in the journal *Tradition*. They underscore the perception that until recently it was man, woman, and God who joined to create a new human child. Now the doctor-scientist has joined the team so that humans are not only controlling nature, but creating it as well.

FRED ROSNER

See also Bioethics; Birth Control and Abortion

Revelation *see* Oral Tradition

Rosenzweig, Franz 1886–1929

German philosopher and theologian

Berkovits, Eliezer, *Major Themes in Modern Philosophies of Judaism*, New York: Ktav, 1974

Buber, Martin and Franz Rosenzweig, *Scripture and Translation* (Indiana Studies in Biblical Literature), Bloomington: Indiana University Press, 1994

Gibbs, Robert, *Correlations in Rosenzweig and Levinas*, Princeton, New Jersey: Princeton University Press, 1992

Mendes-Flohr, Paul (editor), *The Philosophy of Franz Rosenzweig* (Tauber Institute for the Study of European Jewry Series, 8), Hanover, New Hampshire: University Press of New England, 1988

Mendes-Flohr, Paul, *Divided Passions: Jewish Intellectuals and the Experience of Modernity* (Culture of Jewish

Modernity), Detroit, Michigan: Wayne State University Press, 1991

Miller, Ronald Henry, *Dialogue and Disagreement: Franz Rosenzweig's Relevance to Contemporary Jewish-Christian Understanding*, Lanham, Maryland: University Press of America, 1989

Mosès, Stéphane, *System and Revelation: The Philosophy of Franz Rosenzweig* (Culture of Jewish Modernity), Detroit, Michigan: Wayne State University Press, 1992

Novak, David, *Jewish-Christian Dialogue: A Jewish Justification*, New York: Oxford University Press, 1989

Rosenzweig, Franz, *Franz Rosenzweig: His Life and Thought*, edited by Nahum Glatzer, New York: Farrar, Straus and Young, 1953; 3rd edition, Indianapolis, Indiana: Hackett, 1998

Rosenzweig, Franz, *On Jewish Learning*, edited by Nahum Glatzer, New York: Schocken, 1965

Franz Rosenzweig, who died in 1929 at age 43, could easily have been lost to Jewish tradition; an assimilated German Jew, he managed, however, to find his way back to a committed, observant, and unorthodox Jewish identity. Rosenzweig's philosophical magnum opus, *The Star of Redemption*, drafted on German army postcards during World War I, is a notoriously difficult work. His poetical and liturgical translations from Hebrew to German, especially his collaboration with Martin Buber on the translation of the Hebrew Bible, seemingly had their fate tied to the community for which he wrote and struggled, and that was either murdered or dispersed by the Nazis. His institutional legacies, most notably the Free Jewish Lehrhaus, an innovative program in Jewish adult education, achieved some success but were also shut down with the Nazi takeover. How then, does one account for the fact that among committed liberal Jews, especially within the rabbinate, Rosenzweig is fairly well known and extremely influential? The answer is simple: Rosenzweig's recognized greatness as a Jewish thinker owes much to the devotion of his immediate disciples.

ROSENZWEIG (1953) and ROSENZWEIG (1965) offer accessible and moving writings as well as a good starting point. Although editor Nahum Glatzer has attempted to gloss over Rosenzweig's indifference to Zionism and to downplay his mystical tendencies (which Rosenzweig both displays and derides), it is less an interpretation than a presentation designed to render Rosenzweig accessible to an English-speaking audience.

MOSÈS offers the best guide to Rosenzweig's *The Star of Redemption*, which has been translated into English by William Hallo, a scion of the Rosenzweig circle. Influenced throughout by Emmanuel Levinas, a philosopher who also helped promote Rosenzweig's importance, Mosès explicates the central categories of Rosenzweig's *Star*: world, man, God, creation, revelation, and redemption. Translated ably from the French, Mosès implicitly makes a case for treating Rosenzweig as a systematic theologian rather than as a mystic, although it is clear that both tendencies are found in *The Star*.

GIBBS makes a case for Levinas as a Jewish thinker and Rosenzweig as a philosopher of the first rank. Countering the prevailing tendency of ignoring Rosenzweig the thinker for Rosenzweig the educator, activist, and "returned Jew" (*ba'al teshuvah*), Gibbs tries to show how the two categories inter-

penetrate and inform each other. Gibbs also takes issue with the common presentation of Rosenzweig as a religious existentialist.

BERKOVITS contends that Rosenzweig, imprisoned by the racist and Christologically triumphalist culture of modern Germany, imposes essentially foreign categories on Judaism and imagines a theological cosmic collaboration between the two religions where none exists. The Rosenzweigian portrayal of Judaism as beyond the ordinary operations of time and history appears to Berkovits untrue to Judaism's this-worldly stance.

MILLER vigorously champions Rosenzweig's views on the interrelationship between Judaism and Christianity, seeing in Rosenzweig a Jewish voice opposing religious exclusivism and the doctrine of biblical inerrancy. His book is a good representative of what several Christian thinkers have found attractive in Rosenzweig.

NOVAK steers a midway course between Berkovits and Miller, employing Rosenzweig's thought as a platform for his own justification. Noting Rosenzweig's own acceptance of the eternal enmity between Jews and Christians, Novak terms Rosenzweig's discussion "an important ground-clearing operation" but not itself a Jewish justification for interreligious dialogue.

MENDES-FLOHR (1988) is a critically judicious balance of articles on Rosenzweig, most of which the average reader may find too academic. More accessible are the essays on Rosenzweig in MENDES-FLOHR (1991). One essay details Rosenzweig's rejection of the historicism adumbrated by Hegel (the subject of Rosenzweig's doctoral dissertation and first book) and developed further by many others, including Friedrich Meinecke, a professor of Rosenzweig's who urged him (unsuccessfully) to pursue an academic career. Another essay, "Rosenzweig and Kant: Two Views of Ritual and Religion," analyzes Rosenzweig's unique view of halakhah. Spurred by Buber's essay "Herut," Rosenzweig gave mature expression to his philosophy of mitsvah observance in "The Builders." Mendes-Flohr explicates Kant, Buber, and Rosenzweig on the mitsvot and gives a strong defense of Rosenzweig's final position, which may be categorized as expressing an experiential imperative. Rosenzweig's attempt to blend the objective and subjective dimensions of mitsvah observance gets rougher treatment in Berkovits.

BUBER and ROSENZWEIG cast light on Rosenzweig's importance as a translator of the Bible and prayer book. The introductory essays by Everett Fox and Lawrence Rosenwald are very helpful in explaining Rosenzweig's pathbreaking views on language, his collaboration with Martin Buber, and the incredible care that went into their monumental Bible translation. Along with Fox's introduction, the translated essays, previously unavailable in English, call attention to Buber and Rosenzweig's emphasis on the oral nature of Scripture, the use of theme words (*Leitwoerter*) as links in the unfolding of the biblical story, and the narrative importance of the Hebrew etymologies, especially of personal and place names.

ALAN LEVENSON

Rosh Hashanah *see* Festivals and Fasts

Rossi, Azariah dei   c.1511–c.1578

Italian historian and humanist

Baron, Salo Wittmayer, *History and Jewish Historians: Essays and Addresses,* Philadelphia: Jewish Publication Society, 1964

Bonfil, Robert, "Some Reflections on the Place of Azariah de Rossi's *Meor Enaim* in the Cultural Milieu of the Italian Renaissance Jewry," in *Jewish Thought in the Sixteenth Century*, edited by Bernard Dov Cooperman (Harvard Judaica Texts and Studies, 2), Cambridge, Massachusetts: Harvard University Center for Jewish Studies, 1983

Morais, Sabato, *Italian Hebrew Literature,* edited by Julius H. Greenstone, New York: Jewish Theological Seminary, 1926

Roth, Cecil, *The History of the Jews of Italy,* Philadelphia: Jewish Publication Society, 1946; Westmead: Gregg, 1969

Segal, Lester A., *Historical Consciousness and Religious Tradition in Azariah de' Rossi's Me'or 'Einayim,* Philadelphia: Jewish Publication Society, 1989

Veltri, Giuseppe, "The Humanist Sense of History and the Jewish Idea of Tradition: Azaria de' Rossi's Critique of Philo Alexandrinus," *Jewish Studies Quarterly* 2, 1995

Weinberg, Joanna, "'The Voice of God': Jewish and Christian Responses to the Ferrara Earthquake of November 1570," *Italian Studies* 46, 1991

Studies on the Italian rabbinical scholar and humanist Azariah dei Rossi are of two kinds: the general-biographical and those that treat a specific issue. Any book on Jewish history in Italy during the Renaissance must dedicate some space to the figure of dei Rossi, and such is the case with Morais and Roth. The other titles discussed here are specific essays on dei Rossi, describing his conception of history, his religious thought, and his account of the Ferrara earthquake as compared with that of other witnesses.

MORAIS's book is a general biographical study of several leading Italian Jewish figures. It provides the background to and the contents of dei Rossi's famous book *Meor Enayim,* which takes its inspiration from the earthquake of Ferrara and discusses first the philosophical aspect of this event, debating whether it is best seen as the result of natural causes or of the invisible hand of God. The second part of dei Rossi's work is a translation of the Letter of Aristeas on the origin of the Septuagint, and the third section contains an encyclopedic survey of Jewish history.

ROTH, in his general book, surveys a whole list of Jewish authors and scholars in very few words. Roth gives a brief description of dei Rossi's writings and their origin in the Ferrara earthquake. According to Roth, *Meor Enayim,* which revisits traditional Hebrew historiographic sources in the light of late antique Greek literature, represents the first application of the new, critical methodology of the Renaissance to Jewish history. The main advantage of Roth's account is its brevity, which may be suited to nonspecialist readers.

SEGAL analyzes the historiographic views of dei Rossi, his approach to secular knowledge, and his critical attitude to aggadah. Segal's opinion is that the work of dei Rossi is different from other Jewish historical literature of the 16th century, for his thinking is conditioned by the authoritative continuity of classical Jewish teaching in some respects but is also historically oriented with respect to other traditional components of Judaism. Segal describes the opposition to secular learning in certain quarters of Italian Jewry, and he surveys the intellectual milieu of dei Rossi's historiographic work. His purpose is to understand dei Rossi's pioneering inquiry into rabbinic tradition and the distinction he draws between the halakhic and the nonjuristic material. Segal's brief book offers a summary of dei Rossi's thought as well of the literature about him.

BARON's study is one of the first and most basic introductions to dei Rossi's historiographic work. Baron dedicates only three chapters to dei Rossi: the first offers an intellectual biography and surveys his writings; the second analyzes dei Rossi's conception of life and his thinking on such issues as religion, philosophy, and science as it emerges from his works; and the third chapter is an important essay on dei Rossi's historical method. In this chapter Baron reconstructs the Jewish historiographical tradition as well as Italian historical conceptions that influenced dei Rossi. In Baron's opinion, dei Rossi laid the foundations for a major revolution in Jewish historical consciousness.

VELTRI's study is a further exploration of dei Rossi's concept of history. Veltri briskly surveys the biography of dei Rossi as well as the scholarly literature about him. But the main point of this brief article is the investigation of dei Rossi's attitude toward Philo of Alexandria. Veltri analyzes the Renaissance scholarly understanding of the figure of Philo and dei Rossi's emphasis on Philo's faults, such as his lack of knowledge of Hebrew.

WEINBERG's brief essay deals with the different accounts of the earthquake that occurred in Ferrara in 1570 and to which dei Rossi devoted the first section of *Meor Enayim.* There are in fact many descriptions of the scene of the city of Ferrara in ruins that try to determine the earthquake's cause and the extent of the damage. Weinberg stresses that dei Rossi adds many Jewish sources to the general discussion, lending a new dimension to these reflections on the earthquake, particularly regarding the interpretation of its cause. In spite of the fact that writings of contemporary non-Jewish scholars in response to the earthquake frequently cite Aristotle, the conclusion of all of them was the same as dei Rossi's—that the earthquake was one of God's ways of admonishing the wicked and an exhortation to repentance.

BONFIL argues that the strong opposition to *Meor Enayim* was connected to its opponents' perception of the book as deeply radical. He tries to analyze both sides of this famous controversy and thus come to a conclusion about dei Rossi's intellectual milieu. Bonfil surveys the many reactions of the Establishment against the book, and he concludes that dei Rossi remained unique in his time. The article contributes much to an understanding of the intellectual climate in which *Meor Enayim* was published.

YAAKOV A. LATTES

Russia

Baron, Salo W., *The Russian Jew under Tsars and Soviets,* New York: Macmillan, 1964, 2nd edition, 1976

Dubnow, Simon M., *History of the Jews in Russia and Poland from the Earliest Times until the Present Day,* translated by I. Friedlaender, 3 vols., Philadelphia: Jewish Publication Society, 1916–1920

Greenberg, Louis, *The Jews in Russia: The Struggle for Emancipation,* New Haven, Connecticut: Yale University Press, 1966

Hundert, Gershon David and Gershon C. Bacon, *The Jews in Poland and Russia: Bibliographical Essays* (The Modern Jewish Experience), Bloomington: Indiana University Press, 1984

Levin, Nora, *The Jews in the Soviet Union since 1917: Paradox of Survival,* 2 vols., New York: New York University Press, 1988; London: Tauris, 1990

Levitats, Isaac, *The Jewish Community in Russia, 1844–1917,* Jerusalem: Posner, 1981

Luckert, Yelena, *Soviet Jewish History, 1917–1991: An Annotated Bibliography* (Garland Reference Library of Social Science, vol. 611), New York: Garland, 1992

Pinkus, Benjamin, *The Jews of the Soviet Union: The History of a National Minority* (Soviet and East European Studies), Cambridge and New York: Cambridge University Press, 1988

Ro'i, Yaacov, *Jews and Jewish Life in Russia and the Soviet Union* (Cummings Center Series), Ilford, Essex, and Portland, Oregon: Cass, 1995

Jews first began migrating to the territories of Russia around the sixth century C.E. They moved northward from the Crimea to Kievan Rus', where a pogrom took place in the 12th century. Throughout the Middle Ages, Jews typically endured great intolerance and torments from Russian rulers based in Moscow, and they were more inclined to settle in Poland or Lithuania. In the early 18th century, Peter I and Elizabeth demonstrated particular intolerance toward Jews and expelled them from Russia, but Catherine II later acquired large areas of Polish territory where many Jews had settled. In the 1790s Catherine set the first Pale of Settlement, legislating the specific regions of the Russian Empire in which Jews were permitted to live (except for those who had a special permit to live elsewhere in the empire). These regions were largely those of Poland, Ukraine, Bessarabia, White Russia, and Lithuania; with variations from time to time, this policy remained in effect until 1915.

Jews played a prominent role in the Russian Revolution of 1917 and most czarist policies against Jews were abolished at that time. Nevertheless, the Soviet regime's antireligious policy took hold in the 1920s, and Jewish traditions were almost completely discouraged after 1930. The Stalinist period was characterized by numerous episodes of antisemitism, including purges of prominent Jewish intellectuals, involvement in the atrocities of the Holocaust in Soviet territories, and the trials of prominent Jewish doctors who were accused falsely of plotting against the Soviet state in 1953. In the latter part of the 20th century before the breakup of the Soviet Union, many Jews emigrated from Russia to other countries outside the Soviet Union, but those who were detained became the focus of world attention on account of human rights issues. After 1985, Gorbachev's new policy of *glasnost* allowed the expansion of religious life once again, and a partial revival of Jewish culture has taken place since the breakup of the Soviet Union in 1991 and 1992.

DUBNOW's three-volume history of the Jews in Russia and Poland was one of the groundbreaking works of the 20th century on the topic, and it still retains much relevance for today's readers who are interested in the Jews of the Russian Empire before the Soviet era. The history offers separate chapters and divisions on Russia and Poland. Beginning with the Crimean diaspora in the sixth century C.E., he traces the Jews' movements northward and eastward. He then focuses primarily on the periods between the Middle Ages and World War I. In his analysis of the Jews in czarist Russia, Dubnow stresses the "conflict between [Russia's] anti-Jewish traditions and the necessity of harboring in her dominions the greatest center of the Jewish Diaspora," namely, the lands of Poland and Lithuania that became part of Russian czarist territories in the late 18th century. He also covers the most important aspects of antisemitism in czarist Russia, such as ritual murder trials and pogroms. This history deserves much merit for its range and scope, but more recently it has been criticized for the fact that it completely separates its analysis of the inner life of the Jewish community from the study of Jews in the face of Russian czarist law or the outside world. Later histories analyze interaction between the two dimensions in much greater detail.

BARON presents one of the few surveys that cover both Russian and Soviet Jewish history. This book gives a shorter survey of Jews in Russia before the 18th century than Dubnow but then devotes significant space to handling the different policies of each Russian ruler toward the Jews. Between the chapters on the status of the Jews in imperial Russia and Soviet Russia, Baron provides several chapters dealing with specific customs and ways of life in the Russian Jewish communities. The chapters on the Soviet era cover everything from government policies to Soviet Jewish cultural and artistic accomplishments. Throughout the book, Baron deals especially well with demographic and migration issues and gives precise figures on the Jewish population of different regions of Russia at significant periods of transition throughout history. He also offers a unique description of Jewish socioeconomic issues in the 20th century before World War I as well as significant discussion of the Soviet-era Jewish agricultural communities and the project of the autonomous Jewish republic of Birobidzhan in the Far East. The book contains detailed endnotes and a generally comprehensive index as well.

HUNDERT and BACON present a set of bibliographical essays that are potentially useful for readers studying Jewish life in territories ruled by the Russian Empire, such as Poland, as well as imperial and Soviet Russia. The book is divided into two long essays with bibliographies at the end of each essay. The book examines reference works, surveys, journals devoted specifically to individual countries, cultural history, and political history by periods. For czarist Russia, the second essay highlights topics such as education, Jewish political parties, antisemitism, and World War I. The Soviet period is covered by sections on religion, culture, the Soviet territories intended for Jews, and late 20th-century Soviet Jewry. The only real difficulty of this book is that it does not contain a comprehensive index of minor or individual topics.

LEVITATS presents an interesting view of Jewish life in imperial Russia through his survey of a vast corpus of documentary records as well as other histories. Rather than giving a general account through the eyes of the chief leaders, he presents a history of the interactions between the Jewish community and the czarist government through specific court cases, Jewish council records, manuscripts, and legal resolutions. Issues covered in this book include marriage law, property, taxation, military service, the use of specific languages in education, and Jewish autonomy. For readers interested in such things, this book offers more answers about the workings of Russian czarist law and Jewish councils than most general histories can provide. Levitats also supplies an extensive bibliography of the primary and secondary sources that he used for his work.

GREENBERG focuses on Russian Jewish legal and political history from the 19th century to the beginning of the Russian Revolution. His work analyzes how Jews in the intelligentsia interacted both with the Russian ruling class and with the Russian Jewish community as a whole. He interweaves issues such as assimilation, nationalism, and the revolutionary movements to develop a complex picture of the general status and problems of the Jewish population in Russia through the early 20th century. Unlike Simon Dubnow, Greenberg also offers an unusually detailed study of the ways that the Jewish minority was viewed in the Russian Duma, or parliament, between the first revolts in 1905 and the Russian Revolution. In addition, Greenberg deals with the increasing emigration of Russian Jews from 1881 onward and British and American responses to the issue of human rights in Russia at that time. His work includes a comprehensive index and a good selected bibliography on topics ranging from agriculture and the economy to culture and education.

LUCKERT offers an excellent bibliography on Soviet Jewish life, history, and culture that is a must for those who are dealing with Russian Jews in the Soviet period. This bibliography is divided into extremely helpful groupings both by theme and by period. Sections of special importance include those on human rights; Soviet-Israeli relations; emigration and Jewish dissidents and refuseniks; and Jews in the cultural life of Russia and the Soviet Union. The bibliography includes books, articles, testimonies, political propaganda, government documentation, and even relevant works of literature and music by Soviet Jewish authors. The works cited in the bibliography are in ten languages, including English, with English translations for some of the titles of works in Russian and other languages.

PINKUS provides a particularly systematic history of the minority status of Jews in the Soviet Union from 1917 to 1983. The introductory section of his book gives a useful description of previous research on Soviet and Russian Jewry and a brief sketch of the legal position of the Jewish minority in Russia before the 1917 Russian Revolution. Throughout the book, Pinkus divides Soviet Jewish history into three clear periods: the period of construction (1917–1939), the period of destruction (World War II to the death of Stalin in 1953), and the period after Stalin (from 1953 to the 1980s). For each period, Pinkus details Soviet theory on national minorities and compares the case of the Jewish minority to others in the Soviet Union. Then he analyzes how specific regulations and elements of legislation during these successive periods affected Jews' education, culture, and sense of identity as Soviet citizens. Finally, each section includes an analysis of interactions between Soviet Jews and the international Jewish community. Pinkus gives particularly detailed treatment to questions of antisemitism in the Soviet Union from 1947 to 1953, including an analysis of the portrayal of Jews in the media during that period and careful discussion of the 1948 attacks on "cosmopolitans" and the 1953 Doctors' Plot. He also gives a detailed analysis of the changes in the attitudes of leaders toward the Jewish minority, from Khrushchev to Andropov. This book includes detailed notes and a select bibliography as well.

LEVIN offers a comprehensive study of the experience of Jews in the Soviet Union on both a general and specific level. In her preface, she notes that she aimed to study elements of Soviet Jewish history that had previously been neglected, such as Lenin's low regard for Jewish nationalism and the resettlement of Jews to rural areas in the 1920s. Nevertheless, her work blends the newly researched information with an overarching history of the Jewish population in the Soviet Union. Key topics emphasized in this book include the Jewish Section of the Communist Party, Jewish farm colonies in Ukraine and other areas, Jews in heavy industry under the five-year plans, Yiddish culture, the Holocaust in the Soviet lands, and Soviet Jewish emigration. Levin includes information on relatively recently discovered atrocities of the Holocaust on Soviet soil, such as the massacres of Babyi Iar' in Ukraine and Ponary in Lithuania. She also pays much attention to the difficulties experienced by dissidents such as Anatolii Shcharanskii, Ida Nudel, and Vladimir and Maria Slepak. Levin's work includes detailed maps and tables as well as numerous documentary photographs, an extensive section of endnotes, and a full bibliography.

RO'I offers a collection of essays by historians who use new data to supplement and update what can be learned in other histories. This collection deals primarily with Soviet Jewry, but it also has some essays that reanalyze important issues regarding the status of Jews in the Russian Empire. The essays are divided into categories that include: the czarist legacy in the treatment of Jews, the Bolshevik approach to the minority question, World War II, the status of religion in the Soviet Union, demography and emigration, and the Soviet and international Jewish communities. Eli Lederhendler's article titled "Did Russian Jewry Exist Prior to 1917?" explores the cultural and political differences that sometimes divided the Polish, Ukrainian, Belarussian, and Lithuanian Jews in the territories of the Russian Empire. Naomi Blank's article titled "Redefining the Jewish Question from Lenin to Gorbachev: Terminology or Ideology?" explores the depictions of Jews as a minority in Soviet politics and media and the effects of political decisions on everyday life for Soviet Jews. The articles by Iakov Etinger and Alexander Lokshin provide an unusual analysis of the Doctors' Plot of 1953 from two points of view: that of an eyewitness who was arrested in connection with this case and that of an outside historian. Mordechai Altshuler and John Garrard explore the issues of Soviet Jewish resistance to the Holocaust and Soviet journalism on the Holocaust, while Ro'i and Lili Baazova provide updated analyses of religious activity and the suppression of Judaism in Russia and Georgia. Other essays explore the correlation of Jewish emigration with Soviet-Israeli diplomatic relations and with U.S. policy from Richard Nixon to George Bush.

ALISA GAYLE MAYOR

Ruth, Book of

Brenner, Athalya (editor), *A Feminist Companion to Ruth* (Feminist Companion to the Bible, 3), Sheffield, South Yorkshire: Sheffield Academic Press, 1993

Fewell, Danna Nolan and David Miller Gunn, *Compromising Redemption: Relating Characters in the Book of Ruth* (Literary Currents in Biblical Interpretation), Louisville, Kentucky: Westminster/Knox, 1990

Hals, Ronald M., *The Theology of the Book of Ruth* (Facet Books Biblical Series, 23), Philadelphia: Fortress, 1969

Kates, Judith A. and Gail Twersky Reimer (editors), *Reading Ruth: Contemporary Women Reclaim a Sacred Story*, New York: Ballantine, 1994

Larkin, Katrina J.A., *Ruth and Esther* (Old Testament Guides), Sheffield, South Yorkshire: Sheffield Academic Press, 1996

Sasson, Jack M., *Ruth: A New Translation with a Philological Commentary and a Formalist-Folklorist Interpretation* (Johns Hopkins Near Eastern Studies), Baltimore, Maryland: Johns Hopkins University Press, 1979; 2nd edition, Sheffield, South Yorkshire: JSOT, 1989

The Book of Ruth is frequently referred to as one of the greatest literary masterpieces in the Hebrew Bible. With only four chapters, the book leads its readers through a complex interweaving of themes and character relations. The variety of interpretations of this short work is a testament to its artistry. The Book of Ruth provides a commentary, for example, on the importance of *hesed* (loving-kindness), on the tenuous position of the outsider, on relationships between women, on the Davidic genealogy, and on God's hiddenness. The various Christian canons place Ruth next to Judges, reflecting the period in which this tale is set; however, the Hebrew Bible positions Ruth in the Writings, as one of the Five Scrolls.

HALS devotes his short monograph to the theology of the Book of Ruth. The absence of explicit reference to God in this biblical book has led many scholars to regard it as secular literature, but Hals, along with a handful of other scholars, maintains that the author of Ruth is making a theological statement about the hiddenness of God. Hals places Ruth in the same genre as the court history of David and the Joseph story—all narratives in which God does not appear—and argues that these texts provide a model of a deity who leads characters in subtle, nonmiraculous ways. Hals further argues

that the Book of Ruth should be dated to the period of the Solomonic Enlightenment, a time marked by a fascination with God's role in the lives of ordinary people and banal events. This claim about the theological milieu of the Solomonic era and the date of Ruth is disputed; nevertheless, Hals is one of only a handful of modern scholars who submit the text to careful theological inquiry.

Conversely, SASSON regards the Book of Ruth as secular literature, whose primary theme is how Ruth secures Boaz as Naomi's redeemer. On the basis of the categories fashioned by the Russian folklorist Vladimir Propp (*Morphology of the Folktale*, 2nd edition, 1968), Sasson shows how the Book of Ruth follows the folktale genre. He contends that the story's primary purpose is to legitimize the Davidic dynasty. Among Sasson's most intriguing claims is his rejection of levirate marriage as the legal background for the book. Additionally, he argues that the genealogy of chapter 4:18–22 is original and not a later editorial addition. The first section of Sasson's commentary contains a fresh translation with extensive philological notes. Noteworthy is his expertise in northwest Semitic languages. In his 1989 edition, Sasson acknowledges the limitations of Propp's Russian folktale categories for ancient Semitic literature.

FEWELL and GUNN are the editors of the series Literary Currents in Biblical Interpretation, to which this study belongs. This book, as the series title suggests, reflects literary trends shaped by the postmodern milieu. Fewell and Gunn claim that their reading of Ruth "subverts" conventional character and genre types. The first section of the book takes a radical turn from conventional biblical studies. They present a creative retelling *(midrash)* of the Book of Ruth committed to filling in gaps in the text and exploring the psychological motivations and perspectives of each character. The second section offers a literary analysis of Ruth. Within debates concerning the primacy of text or reader, Fewell and Gunn come down unambiguously on the side of the reader. Readers sympathetic to the general perspectives of postmodernism are likely to respond to this book favorably.

BRENNER's volume is from a series the purpose of which is to amass both previously published and new critical articles on the books of the Bible from feminist-critical perspectives. The Ruth collection is divided into four sections that represent the various directions of Ruth studies among feminist scholars. The presupposition of the first section, subtitled "Gendered Reading Perspectives," is that "filling in the gaps is not simply a matter of interpretative discretion. It constitutes a necessity for understanding the story and its plot." The second section explores the possibility of female authorship, a question that has also arisen regarding the Song of Songs. The final two sections touch upon postbiblical interpretation and Ruth in the arts. Efforts at bringing feminist criticism into mainstream biblical scholarship have been finding growing success and Brenner's series is quickly becoming an indispensable resource.

KATES and REIMER have assembled a collection of brief commentaries, interpretive essays, short stories, poetry, and meditations on the Book of Ruth from feminist perspectives. The contributors are noted Jewish feminists from a variety of vocational backgrounds and Jewish affiliations. The articles range in orientation from academic to personal, from critical to creative. The basic premise of this collection is that "it is interpretive traditions more than biblical texts that leave women feeling excluded," and the aim of the book is that "Jewish women will redefine a space initially created by other hands, creating a space in which other women can feel they belong." Each section of the book is inspired by a specific verse in Ruth, although many of the essays deal with broader themes. Overall, the contributions offer insights and perspectives that have been overlooked by both traditional and critical commentators. The collection is geared to a popular audience, but any serious reader of Ruth will find useful insights in these pages.

LARKIN's work provides clear and concise introductions to the essential critical questions regarding the Book of Ruth. She presents the positions of key scholars in an accurate and fair manner. Larkin addresses the book's date, the debate regarding the legal background of the story, issues of text and canon, literary topics such as genre, and the theological dimensions of the book. Unfortunately, the growing body of critical feminist literature on Ruth receives only minimal attention. Still, nonspecialists looking for a brief introduction to the state of scholarship on Ruth will find this book informative and highly readable.

S. TAMAR KAMIONKOWSKI

S

Saadia ben Joseph Gaon 882–942

Egyptian-born Babylonian rabbinic authority, Bible translator and commentator, liturgist, and controversialist

Baron, S.W., "Saadia's Communal Activities," in *Saadia Anniversary Volume* (American Academy for Jewish Research, Texts and Studies, vol. 2), edited by Boaz Cohen, New York: Jewish Publication Society, 1943

Brody, Robert, *The Geonim of Babylonia and the Shaping of Medieval Jewish Culture*, New Haven, Connecticut: Yale University Press, 1998

Davidson, Israel (editor and translator), *Saadia's Polemic against Hiwi al-Balkhi: A Fragment* (Texts and Studies of the Jewish Theological Seminary, vol. 5), New York: Jewish Theological Seminary, 1915

Goodman, Lenn Evan (translator), *The Book of Theodicy: Translation and Commentary on the Book of Job* (Yale Judaica Series, vol. 25), New Haven, Connecticut: Yale University Press, 1988

Malter, Henry, *Saadia Gaon: His Life and Works*, Philadelphia: Jewish Publication Society, 1921

Rosenblatt, Samuel (translator), *The Book of Beliefs and Opinions* (Yale Judaica Series, vol. 1), New Haven, Connecticut: Yale University Press, 1948

Skoss, S.L., "Saadia Gaon, the Earliest Hebrew Grammarian," *Proceedings of the Academy for Jewish Research*, 21–23, 1952–1954

Saadia ben Joseph, Gaon of Sura, was a pioneering scholar who ranks as the outstanding Jewish spiritual and intellectual leader of the early Middle Ages. He fused Greco-Arabic philosophy with the accepted manner of studying scripture and rabbinic law, and he broadened the horizons of medieval secular arts and sciences within the Jewish milieu. He was a master of Hebrew philology and also had a profound grasp of Aramaic and Arabic, as demonstrated by his multifaceted literary activity. *The Book of Beliefs and Opinions* can be considered the most comprehensive and coherent representation of Saadia's thinking on the relationship between *ratio* and *religio*; it is the first great philosophical summa in Judaism.

BARON's essay emphasizes the commitment to communal leadership that runs through every aspect of Saadia's career, permeating even his most abstruse philosophical writings. Above all else, however, Baron stresses the importance of two public controversies in properly assessing Saadia's life: his conflict over the computation of the Jewish calendar with Aaron ben Meir and his dispute with the exilarch David ben Zakkai. In dealing with these episodes, Baron repeatedly goes beyond the internal workings of the Jewish community in order to stress the importance of the surrounding Muslim context. Thus, as a backdrop to Saadia's efforts to reunify the Jewish community in the East, Baron repeatedly highlights the contemporary political disintegration of the Abbasid Empire, under which much of the Jewish community in the East lived. In a similar vein, he explains various developments in the Jewish community in light of factors affecting the Muslim government bureaucracy.

BRODY's book is a masterful survey of the geonic period to the 11th century. The final third of the book is devoted to an examination of the ways in which Saadia, who functioned as Gaon of the Sura yeshivah from 928 until his death in 942, revolutionized the cultural world of the Babylonian academies. One of Saadia's achievements in this regard was to expand Babylonian intellectual pursuits to include such Palestinian disciplines as linguistics, liturgical poetry, and theology. Similarly, Saadia was responsible for bringing the Palestinian Talmud into the intellectual horizon of the Babylonian geonim and for cultivating such new disciplines as biblical and talmudic exegesis. Above all, however, Saadia's impact on the cultural world of the geonic academies was felt in his far-reaching literary contributions to the field of talmudic law. In this area Saadia and his successors are credited with the formulation of systematic halakhic monographs that seem to be modeled upon scientific writings from the surrounding Arabic culture.

DAVIDSON translates a large section of Saadia's polemical response to the heretical "questions" raised by Hiwi of Balkh against the authority of the Hebrew Bible. Saadia's text, written in verse, is today the main source for Hiwi's views, the intellectual roots of which remain obscure and a matter of disagreement. Among other things, Hiwi objected to the biblical idea that God commands man to offer sacrifices, the Bible's frequent use of anthropomorphic language, and the biblical notion of reward and punishment. Saadia's response to Hiwi relates most directly to his tireless efforts at stamping out heresy, a campaign that also led him to attack Karaism. But it reveals other sides of his creative spirit as well, among them his aesthetic appreciation of poetry and his strong commitment to the study and elucidation of the Hebrew Bible.

GOODMAN presents a fine example of Saadia's activities as translator into Arabic and commentator on the books of the Hebrew Bible, in this case the Book of Job. Saadia's intention was to provide the eastern Jewish communities with standardized Judeo-Arabic versions of Hebrew Scripture; the swift and widespread adoption of his *Tafsir,* an Arabic translation of the Pentateuch, attests to the achievement of this purpose. The commentaries accompanying the translations were clearly meant to present a biblical text that could withstand the test of logic and could come to the defense of the traditional rabbinic faith, whose precepts were being undermined at the time by the growing power of the Karaites and other heterodox groups. The polemical interests that stimulated Saadia's textual studies are transcended by his search for thematic coherence in Scripture by way of logic, grammar, philosophy, science, and, of course, rabbinic tradition. His Arabic translation of Job, together with his systematic commentary, is central in this regard. Goodman shows in this edition how Saadia's creative and reconstructive work as a philosopher and a grammarian sustained and guided his reading and understanding of Job.

MALTER's book, though somewhat dated, is still the most comprehensive introduction to Saadia's multifaceted career. Fortunately, a relatively large amount of biographical information on Saadia is available, and Malter uses this data in the first part of his book to sketch a compelling narrative of the Gaon's life. In this section Malter deals with Saadia's education in Palestine, his emigration to Babylonia, his clashes with other communal leaders (e.g., Aaron Ben Meir and David Ben Zakkai), and his tireless struggle against Karaism and heresy. In the second part of the book Malter surveys Saadia's literary output, which he justly regards as Saadia's most significant contribution to Jewish history.

ROSENBLATT's scholarly translation of Saadia's *Kitab al-amanat wa'l-i'tiqadat (The Book of Beliefs and Opinions)* introduces the reader to Saadia's philosophical magnum opus. This work constitutes the first comprehensive presentation of Judaism as a system of beliefs consistent with the dictates of reason and logic. In terms of both its composition and apologetic style of argumentation, *The Book of Beliefs and Opinions* reflects the influence of the contemporary Muslim school of thought known as Mu'tazilism. The work is composed of ten treatises that deal with the following topics: (1) the creation of the world, (2) God's unity and divine attributes, (3) the commandments, (4) human free will, (5) virtue and vice, (6) the human soul, (7) resurrection, (8) the messianic age, (9) reward and punishment, and (10) the golden mean.

SKOSS offers an overview of Saadia's major grammatical work, *Kitab fasih lughat al-'ibraniyyin (The Book of the Eloquence of the Language of the Hebrews).* Saadia's linguistic studies, which bear the unmistakable influence of methods developed by Arabic grammarians, represent a marked advance over the work of his predecessors, the Masoretes, who were primarily concerned with the proper vocalization of the biblical text. While later medieval Hebrew grammarians often criticized his views, Saadia is to be credited with inaugurating the scientific study of the Hebrew language. Although Saadia composed a number of works specifically dealing with linguistic questions, matters of language also played an important role in his biblical commentaries, his theological studies, and even his polemical writings.

ARNOLD FRANKLIN
AND WOUT JACQUES VAN BEKKUM

Sabbath

Eskenazi, Tamara C., Daniel J. Harrington, and William H. Shea, *The Sabbath in Jewish and Christian Traditions,* New York: Crossroad, 1991

Greenberg, Irving, "The Dream and How to Live It: Shabbat," in his *The Jewish Way: Living the Holidays,* New York: Summit, 1988

Heschel, Abraham Joshua, *The Sabbath: Its Meaning for Modern Man,* New York: Farrar, Straus and Giroux, 1951, expanded edition, 1952

Katz, Jacob, *Goi Shel Shabat,* 1983; translated by Yoel Lerner as *The "Shabbes Goy": A Study in Halakhic Flexibility,* Philadelphia: Jewish Publication Society, 1989

Klein, Isaac, "The Sabbath (I): Liturgy," and "The Sabbath (II): Prohibition against Work," in his *A Guide to Jewish Religious Practice* (Moreshet Series, vol. 6), New York: Jewish Theological Seminary of America, 1979

KLEIN provides an excellent overview of the observance of the sabbath as a day of rest according to Jewish law. He gives a detailed description of the liturgy of the home and synagogue as well as explaining the theological underpinnings of the prohibition of work. In place of an extensive discussion of the 39 categories of forbidden work as defined in classical rabbinic sources, he emphasizes areas of sabbath rest most probably relevant to the largely urbanized circumstances of English-speaking Jewry in the late 20th century: carrying, traveling, the use of electrical appliances, the rabbinic interdiciton of handling any objects not intended for sabbath use, the requirement of withdrawal from activities that are not congenial to the spirit of the sabbath, the question of sports, and the case of a non-Jew working for a Jew.

KATZ, one of the most distinguished Jewish historians of the 20th century, provides an instance of how economic and technological change has forced Jewish practice to accept what had heretofore been forbidden. Jewish law did not permit non-Jews to work for Jews on the sabbath. Indeed, the rationale for the commandment to rest on the sabbath in the Decalogue in Deuteronomy 5 is to secure rest for household servants. The only leniency permitted is the hiring of a non-Jew to perform work for a Jew where the non-Jew has the option of doing the work on a day of the week of his choosing; if perchance the work is done on the sabbath, the Jew is not liable for violating the sabbath since the timing was the choice of the person hired. Katz shows how this stringency became impractical in the mid- to late Middle Ages because of changes in living conditions. For example, Jews who needed to travel had to board barges that sailed on the major rivers of Europe. The barge might stop at a certain destination only on the sabbath, forcing Jewish travelers to avail themselves of the work of the barge's crew in helping passengers and their baggage disembark.

The volume by ESKENAZI, HARRINGTON, and SHEA consists of papers and responses delivered at a symposium about the sabbath at the University of Denver. The papers offer a variety of analyses of the development of the sabbath in the biblical and rabbinic eras as well as offering theological and liturgical perspectives on the sabbath. The volume concludes with papers on the legal problems encountered by those who celebrate the sabbath on Saturdays, both Jews and Seventh-day Adventists.

GREENBERG, a modern Jewish theologian, argues that the sabbath is an expression of dialectic living, accepting and embracing the world as it is while setting up a weekly return to perfection. "[The sabbath] is the temporary anti-reality of perfection. For approximately twenty-five hours, all things are seen through the eyes of love, as if all of nature were perfect, in harmony with itself and with humanity, respecting creation." Greenberg explores how the sabbath undermines the pathologies of power in which profit possesses the highest status. He concludes his discussion with a pluralistic approach to the sabbath, one that can be shared across a wide spectrum of observance regardless of denominational affiliation. He bases this approach on the recognition of the sabbath as a shift in the mode of being. Each individual experiences this transformation in different ways.

HESCHEL's book has been called the most significant writing about the sabbath since the Enlightenment. Heschel focuses on the emotive aspects of Jewish religious experience rather than on the reasonability of the sabbath or on its law and history. For him, the essence of spiritual living is to face sacred moments. He identifies the sabbath as a sanctuary in time, the coronation of a day in the spiritual wonderland of time. "The meaning of the Sabbath is to celebrate time rather than space. Six days a week we live under the tyranny of things of space; on the Sabbath, we become attuned to *holiness in time*. It is a day on which we are called upon to share what is eternal in time, to turn from the results of creation to the mystery of creation." The sabbath comes of its own accord into human lives and, unlike a geographic sanctuary, cannot be conquered or lost. The sabbath is universal because all human beings encounter time as intrinsic to all experience and transcending all experience. Unlike space, time belongs to no one. The sabbath possesses a profoundly ethical dimension in that it is a day shared with all humanity. The sabbath embodies the belief that all human beings are equal and that the equality of human beings entails the nobility of human beings. The sabbath, to Heschel, is "a day of armistice in the economic struggle with our fellow men and the forces of nature—is there any institution that holds out a greater hope for man's progress than the Sabbath?" The sabbath is not primarily a symbol of creation but a memorial of redemption, a time to remember the day of the Exodus from Egypt, the day when Israel stood at Sinai, and the day of the messiah. Heschel also draws attention to the fact that comfort and pleasure are an integral part of sabbath observance. The sabbath is a day for the body as well as for the soul.

PAMELA BARMASH

Sabbatical Year and Jubilee *see* Agricultural Laws

Sacrificial Cult *see* Priesthood: Biblical

Sadducees

Daube, David, "On Acts 23: Sadducees and Angels," *Journal of Biblical Literature,* 109, 1990
Goodman, Martin, "Sadducees and Essenes after 70 C.E.," in *Crossing the Boundaries: Essays in Biblical Interpretation in Honour of Michael D. Goulder,* edited by Stanley E. Porter, Paul Joyce, and David E. Orton, Leiden and New York: Brill, 1994
Grabbe, Lester, *Judaism from Cyrus to Hadrian,* 2 vols., Minneapolis, Minnesota: Fortress, 1992; London: SCM, 1994
Lightstone, Jack, "Sadducees versus Pharisees," in *Christianity, Judaism and Other Greco-Roman Cults,* edited by Jacob Neusner, Leiden: Brill, 1975
Saldarini, Anthony J., *Pharisees, Scribes and Sadducees in Palestinian Society: A Sociological Approach,* Wilmington, Delaware: Glazier, 1988

The Sadducees were one of many Jewish sects that existed in Palestine during the late Second Temple period; they may also have survived into early rabbinic times. It is difficult to reconstruct the Sadducees' social status and distinct religious beliefs, in part because the treatment of the sect in the works of Josephus, the Gospels, and rabbinic literature is consistently hostile and polemical. Furthermore, none of the sect's own writings have survived to the present day. Modern secondary literature on the Sadducees, particularly in the English language, is relatively scarce in comparison to recent scholarly treatments of some of the other Jewish sects of the period, such as the Pharisees and Essenes. Jean Le Moyne's *Les sadducéens* (1972) is the only major study on the Sadducees. There are, however, some very useful articles and essays that critically investigate the meager references to the Sadducees in ancient sources.

For an up-to-date overview of modern scholarship on issues concerning the Sadducees (including German and French works) and a brief evaluation of the ancient sources, one should consult GRABBE's handbook. He tentatively theorizes that the Sadducees first appeared as more of a political than a religious entity, and he hypothesizes that there may have been some sort of connection between the Sadducees and the priestly establishment. As depicted in ancient sources, the sect's biblical interpretation and beliefs also suggest the Sadducees' connection to priestly concerns. Grabbe follows Josephus in suggesting that the Sadducees were identified with the upper socioeconomic class, although the author does not conclude that all Sadducees were priests, and he does not contend that they were all wealthy.

SALDARINI draws from the methods of social science to place the Sadducees in the context of Palestinian Jews living in the Roman Empire. He challenges the description of the Sadducees by Josephus and many modern scholars as a sectlike group. If the Sadducees were from the governing class, as stated by Josephus, then they were probably not a protest group in a proper sense; rather, Saldarini speculates, they were likely a small group of Jews with particular ideas on how to live the Jewish life. Saldarini is rightly cautious about depending too much on the veracity of the ancient sources in the reconstruction of Saducean beliefs and practices. The New Testament and Josephus agree that, unlike the Pharisees, the Sadducees did not believe in the resurrection. Beyond this observation, the sparse references to the Sadducees in these sources reveal very little. Indeed, Saldarini criticizes the standard treatments of the Sadducees that differentiate them from the Pharisees on the basis of the Sadducees' insistence on literal interpretation of Scripture and their rejection of Oral Torah, arguing that these accounts are either misleading, or they are not explicitly supported by the ancient evidence. The author contends that all Jews had, in a sense, their own Oral Torah and their own laws and customs that developed over many years. The Sadducees' disputes with the Pharisees only reveal that the Sadducees observed biblical laws as they interpreted them and that they rejected some of the Pharisaic interpretations.

DAUBE proposes a new interpretation of a particular passage in the Acts of the Apostles that has, in the past, been used by scholars to support the notion that the Saducean denial of angels and resurrection was the basis of the contention between the Sadducees and Pharisees noted in that passage. Daube argues that, in light of the angelology found in parts of the Hebrew Scriptures, it is unlikely that the Sadducees could have denied outright the existence of angels. Drawing on other New Testament passages, 1 Enoch, and rabbinic literature, Daube postulates that the reference to angels in the passage in question concerns the interim state of the deceased person between death and resurrection and is not an example of angelology as such. Daube also finds allusions to the disputed angelic existence of the deceased in the interim period in Josephus's depiction of the contention between Sadducees and Pharisees where, according to the former sect, the soul perishes with the body, while the latter group maintains that the soul survives, and reward or punishment is meted out according to previous conduct on earth, with the virtuous eventually receiving a new body at the resurrection.

GOODMAN's article looks into the question of the fate of the Sadducees (and Essenes) after the destruction of the Temple in 70 C.E. He challenges the standard assumption that these Jewish groups disappeared soon after this time by citing patristic and rabbinic sources that give faint hints that the groups may have survived. Indeed, Goodman hypothesizes that Jewish groups and philosophies known before 70 C.E., possibly including the Sadducees, continued for years, perhaps centuries, after the Temple's destruction. To support this claim, Goodman suggests that the Sadducees seem to have based their group's identity on particular ideas—whether theological or halakhic—rather than organizational structures or buildings, and therefore the sect need not have been rendered moribund after the destruction of the Temple. He posits that

the relative silence that we find in rabbinic and patristic sources concerning the Sadducees can be attributed to the rabbis' disinterest in non-rabbinic Jews (a similar observation can be made to explain the rabbis' inattention to Christianity). He attributes the scarcity of information about the Sadducees in Christian texts to the fact that the Christian writers were interested in Jews only in the context of biblical Israel, the life of Jesus, or the problem of Jewish practices in the church.

LIGHTSTONE investigates salient tannaitic sources for insights into the controversies between the Sadducees and Pharisees. After analyzing seven pericopes in which the sources juxtapose both parties, Lightstone notes that most of these references rhetorically vilify the Sadducees. He concludes that there is no evidence that any theological or halakhic rubric formed the basis of the supposed conflict between Sadducees and Pharisees. Indeed, according to Lightstone, it is quite possible that the tannaim projected some of their laws on the Pharisees when they suggested that those laws were the basis for the inter-party conflict. Like Goodman, Lightstone suggests that there is evidence that the Sadducees survived and may even have remained a prestigious group for some time after the fall of Jerusalem in 70 C.E.

D.P. O'BRIEN

Saints *see* Veneration of Saints, Pilgrimages, and Holy Places

Samaritans

Bowman, John, *Samaritan Documents: Relating to Their History, Religion, and Life* (Pittsburgh Original Texts and Translation Series, 2), Pittsburgh, Pennsylvania: Pickwick, 1977

Coggins, R.J., *Samaritans and Jews: The Origins of Samaritanism Reconsidered* (Growing Points in Theology), Atlanta, Georgia: Knox, and Oxford: Blackwell, 1975

Crown, Alan D. (editor), *The Samaritans*, Tübingen: Mohr (Siebeck), 1989

Crown, Alan D., Reinhard Pummer, and Abraham Tal (editors), *A Companion to Samaritan Studies*, Tübingen: Mohr (Siebeck), 1993

Garber, Zev, "The Samaritan Passover," in *Experiencing the Exodus from Egypt*, edited by Duane L. Christensen, Berkeley, California: BIBAL, 1988

Gaster, Moses, *The Samaritans: Their History, Doctrines and Literature* (Schweich Lectures, 1923), London: Oxford University Press for the British Academy, 1925

Gaster, Moses, *Samaritan Eschatology* (Samaritan Oral Law and Ancient Traditions, vol. 1), London: Search, 1932

Montgomery, James A., *The Samaritans, the Earliest Jewish Sect: Their History, Theology and Literature* (Bohlen Lectures, 1906), Philadelphia: Jewish Publication Society, 1907; with introduction by A.S. Halkin, New York: Ktav, 1968

Purvis, James D., *The Samaritan Pentateuch and the Origin of the Samaritan Sect* (Harvard Semitic Monographs, vol. 2), Cambridge, Massachusetts: Harvard University Press, 1968

Tsedaka, Benyamin, "Samaritan Holidays and Festivals," in *Encyclopaedia Judaica*, vol. 14, Jerusalem: Keter, 1978

The Samaritans, who call themselves *Shamerim* or *Shomerim al ha-'emet* (keepers of the truth) and who are called *Kutim* in rabbinic literature, believe that they are the true guardians of the Torah of Moses and the true descendants of the people of the biblical kingdom of Israel. In the first century C.E. the Samaritans may have numbered more than a million people dwelling throughout the land of Israel. However, centuries of conflict, intermittent war, and coercive religious decrees, including forced conversion to Christianity and Islam, decimated their numbers to 146 at the end of Ottoman rule (1917). Soon after, Samaritan births increased (marriages to female "converts" from Judaism is said to be a factor contributing to the rise in population), and by 1948, the population had doubled. Today the Samaritans number more than 600 persons, living primarily in Kiryat Luza on Mt. Gerizim, Nablus, and Holon. Recent discussion in Samaritan studies have increased knowledge in areas of archaeology, epigraphy, paleography, linguistics, history, literature, religion, and theology.

CROWN presents a major tome on the state of Samaritan studies today. Chapters by leading Samaritanologists include essays on Samaritan history (Persian to modern periods); material remains (archaeology, numismatics, inscriptions); chronicles (historical literature); eschatology, sects and movements; literature (pentateuchal, halakhic, liturgical); languages (Hebrew, Aramaic, Arabic); calendar; ritual and customs; music; manuscripts; and select bibliography. The anthology lacks essays on Samaritan folklore and theology, but anyone interested in obtaining information on Samaritan civilization in general and on current research in particular should begin with this collection of lengthy, encyclopedia-style articles. The companion volume, an encyclopedic dictionary edited by CROWN, PUMMER, and TAL, provides summaries and evaluations of key words, ideas, and concepts, as well as biographical data related to the growing field of Samaritanology.

MONTGOMERY's book seeks to answer the question, who are the Samaritans? He surveys three centuries of Western discovery and interest in the Samaritans, and he presents his views on the history of the Samaritans to his own day (the early 20th century). This volume is the first attempt to assess critically their languages and literature, liturgy, and theology in a single study. Also included are Jewish, Christian, and Muslim references and an annotated translation of *Massekhet Kutim*, a noncanonical rabbinic tractate on Jewish dealings with the Samaritans. Montgomery's chapters are comprehensive and suggestive, and his work is rightly referred to by Alan Crown as "a classic text-book that has never been superseded."

GASTER (1925) was originally presented as the Schweich Lectures for 1923 at the British Academy. The first lecture evaluates the importance of Samaritans for biblical history and reviews biblical history in light of the Samaritan tradition. Disputations and hostility between Jews and Samaritans and the legal status of both groups under Roman rule are chronicled. In the second lecture, Gaster argues that Samaritan doctrines and religious practices represent a stage in Israelite tradition that developed before the formation of sects or political parties. Their strict adherence to the Torah of Moses, their rites of passage, and their views of sacred place and time reveal commonality as well as differences with the practices and beliefs of the Sadducees, Pharisees, and Essenes. Additionally, there is no trace of paganism or syncretism in Samaritan religion, a fact that Gaster uses to portray the Samaritans as a distinctively Jewish sect. The third lecture introduces a wide spectrum of Samaritan texts, manuscripts, commentaries, midrashic interpolations, liturgy, poetry, and mystical and eschatological writings. Especially noteworthy are the discussion of the Scroll of Abisha', Gaster's consideration of the relation of the Samaritan Pentateuch to the Masoretic Text and Septuagint, and his analysis of the poems of the foremost hymnologist, Markah (third or fourth century C.E.).

GASTER (1932) probes the Samaritan beliefs in immortality and resurrection, reward and punishment, the Taheb (a Samaritan Messiah), and the Second Kingdom. Citing previously unedited manuscripts, he shows that Samaritan eschatology is intimately bound up with the commandments, ordinances, and rules of the Torah. Gaster argues that Jews and Samaritans are "rivals in claims [that they possess the authority of Moses], but linked in spirit." His pioneer research has helped pave the road for later academic studies of the Samaritans.

PURVIS's monograph links the origin of the Samaritan sect to the redaction of the Samaritan Pentateuch contemporaneous to the destruction of the Samaritan Temple by John Hyrcanus (128 B.C.E.). He advances this thesis by noting differences in the orthographic traditions of the Samaritan Pentateuch and Jewish writings of the Hasmonean period. Historically, religious disputes (over issues such as the rival claims to sanctity of Mt. Moriah and Mt. Gerizim, and their respective priesthoods) divided the two groups, and political strife in the late Hasmonean period prevented any steps toward reconciliation. The proclamation of the Samaritan Pentateuch registered Samaritan opposition to both the Hasmonean conquest and the Judaization of Judea, and it signaled the emergence of the Samaritans as a separate monotheistic community.

COGGINS rejects the traditional stance of Jews and Samaritans with regard to the origins of Samaritanism. The author proposes that Samaritan origins date back to the fall of Samaria to Assyria (722–721 B.C.E.) and that the Samaritans are a mixture of the remnant native population and foreigners who accompanied the Assyrian conquerors. This theory contradicts the Samaritans' contention that the separation began when Eli led many Israelites astray by moving from Shechem to Shiloh, thereby contaminating the purity of the Northern cult, of which the Samaritans are sole guardians. Coggins also rejects the views of schismatic theorists (i.e., those who trace Samaritan origins to a dispute with other Jews), whose data is founded more on anti-Samaritan polemic than on hard evidence. Indeed, "schism" is only possible if an "orthodoxy" exists, and until the rabbinic era, no such norm existed in Judaism. The Hebrew Bible contains no explicit negative allusion to the Samaritans, but, beginning with the Book of Ben Sira, which refers to "the foolish people [Samaritans] that live in Shechem," (Sir. 50:26), one can find numerous disparaging references. The different eschatological, religious, and theological assertions in such references resemble charges made in the conflict between Pharisees and Sadducees. Demonstrating that continual, heated disputes over the priesthood and the true sanctuary helped augment Judeo-Samaritan hostility and their ultimate parting of the ways, Coggins concludes that the formative period for the rise of Samaritanism was the last three centuries before Christianity.

BOWMAN examines passages of Samaritan literature relating to their understanding of themselves as a religion and a people. There are six sections with selections: Torah (creation and Decalogue), chronicles (Tolida or Genealogy, Book of Joshua, "Chronicle Adler," and Kitab al-Ta'rih by Abu al-Fath), biblical commentaries in Arabic illustrating halakhic and aggadic matter, aggadic midrash (examples from Abu l-Hasan al-Suri on angels and from Memar Markah on the "Day of Vengeance" [Deuteronomy 32:33; Masoretic reading "vengeance is Mine"]), Samaritan *Hillukh* (code of laws) on marriage and divorce, and four short public prayers (weekday, festival, sabbath). This study explores Samaritan religious beliefs, practices, apologetics, and polemics, demonstrating how the life of the Samaritans diverges from standards authorized by Jewish orthodoxy. For example, the expansion of the Samaritan Tenth Commandment with reference to Mt. Gerizim (e.g., Deuteronomy 11:29b; 27:2b-3a, 4–7, etc., in the Samaritan Pentateuch, is viewed by Bowman as a response to the destruction of the Samaritan Temple in the late Hasmonean period.

TSEDAKA is a leader of the Holon Samaritan community, director of the Samaritan Research Institute there, and editor of *Aleph Beth Hadashot Ha-Shomronim* (*A.B.: The Samaritan News*), which publishes Samaritan texts, news items, and statistical data, as well as selections from scholarly articles about the Samaritans, with sections in English and Arabic as well as modern Hebrew and Samaritan (Paleo-Hebrew) scripts. His essay provides a clear, concise account of the Samaritan year cycle and religious ceremonies. His traditio-historical view, which presents more community-focused information than critical evaluation, proposes that holy time and rites of passage are the matrix around which Samaritan ideology, identity, and memories are spun. For example, he posits that communal participation in the Passover sacrifice on Mt. Gerizim is a major sign that Samaritan corporate identity extends back to the exodus from Egypt and forward to settlement within the land of Israel.

GARBER's eyewitness account of the Samaritan Passover explains the holiday's significance. He identifies Samaritan readings of biblical texts, as well as creeds and practices, that conflict with normative rabbinic traditions, and he argues that Samaritans celebrate Israel's ongoing freedom story on Mount Gerizim as a way of affirming that the Samaritan identity is not merely a vestige of a generally forgotten past but a dynamic force in the minds of people today.

ZEV GARBER

Samuel, Book of

Berlin, Adele, *Poetics and Interpretation of Biblical Narrative*, Sheffield, South Yorkshire: Almond, 1983

Fokkelman, J.P., *Narrative Art and Poetry in the Books of Samuel: A Full Interpretation Based on Stylistic and Structural Analyses*, 4 vols., Assen: Van Gorcum, 1981–1993

Garsiel, Moshe, *The First Book of Samuel: A Literary Study of Comparative Structures, Analogies, and Parallels*, Ramat-Gan: Revivim, 1983; Winona Lake, Indiana: Eisenbrauns, 1990

Goldman, S., *Samuel: Hebrew Text and English Translation with an Introduction and Commentary*, London and New York: Soncino, 1949

McCarter, P. Kyle, *I Samuel: A New Translation* (Anchor Bible, vol. 8), Garden City, New York: Doubleday, 1980

McCarter, P. Kyle, *II Samuel: A New Translation with Introduction, Notes, and Commentary* (Anchor Bible, vol. 9), Garden City, New York: Doubleday, 1984

Rosenberg, A.J., *Samuel I: A New English Translation of the Text and Rashi, with a Commentary Digest* (Judaica Books of the Prophets), New York: Judaica, 1976

Rosenberg, A.J. and Moshe Ch. Sosevsky, *Samuel II: A New English Translation of the Text and Rashi, with a Commentary Digest* (Judaica Books of the Prophets), New York: Judaica, 1978

Eighth of the 24 books of the Hebrew Bible, according to the traditional Jewish count, third book of the Prophets and of the *Nevi'im Rishonim* (Historical Prophets), the Book of Samuel was divided into First and Second Samuel as early as the Septuagint. The book recounts the political history of Israel from the beginning of the monarchy to the end of David's reign, as well as the personal histories of Samuel, Saul, and David. National and personal histories are mixed together throughout the book. Samuel is considered the zenith of biblical narrative, due to its artful and intricate storytelling and its use of a wealth of narrative techniques.

FOKKELMAN's four-volume commentary, which is published without a translation of the Hebrew text, is one of the most voluminous biblical commentaries ever written. The length of the work is all the more remarkable because Fokkelman deals only with literary issues, ignoring the historical questions surrounding the book. Volume one is entitled "King David" and examines 2 Samuel 9–20; volume two, "The Crossing Fates," considers 1 Samuel 13–31 and 2 Samuel 1; volume three, "Throne and City," focuses on 2 Samuel 2–8 and 21–24; and volume four, "Vow and Desire," deals with 1 Samuel 1–12. Almost every detail of the text is analyzed in terms of its contribution to the literary whole. This commentary is intended for the serious student, but it is surprisingly readable for a work of this scope.

McCARTER (1980, 1984) is an omnibus commentary, using all the tools of modern biblical research and exploring issues of source criticism, text criticism, and historical geography, as well as lexical, syntactic, and exegetical concerns. A translation is presented for each section of the book, followed by notes and commentary on that section. McCarter's work is aimed at readers with some knowledge of biblical scholarship. The commentary does not emphasize literary issues as fully as might be desirable.

GOLDMAN's work is the best short introduction to the Book of Samuel for the reader with limited or no knowledge of Hebrew. The brief commentary is attuned to the needs of modern readers, focusing primarily on points in the text or in the plot that the layperson is likely to find troubling or difficult to understand. Little attention is paid to those issues of source criticism, comparative studies, or historical geography that are likely to be of more interest to the specialist than the general reader. The commentary draws on both Jewish and non-Jewish expositors but is designed to give a Jewish perspective on the text. A useful index to names, subjects, and themes in the Book of Samuel concludes the work.

ROSENBERG's edition of 1 Samuel and ROSENBERG and SOSEVSKY's edition of 2 Samuel present the Hebrew text of the Bible together with the commentaries of Rashi, David Kimhi, Gersonides, Joseph Kara, David Altschuler, and the Targum on one page, with an English translation of the biblical text and of selections from the various commentaries on the facing page. This format allows the English reader access to the traditional commentaries. The editors have taken care to select from the commentaries only those passages that help the modern reader to understand the text, omitting long midrashic expositions.

GARSIEL deals only with the first five chapters of Samuel in his brief book, which cites many verses but does not provide the entire text in Hebrew or English. He presents a literary study that focuses on comparisons between these chapters and other biblical narratives, and he emphasizes that such comparisons are built into the narratives, as the Samuel stories often refer to other biblical stories. He further explains that character opposition is a central facet of Samuel's narrative, with Samuel and his parents contrasted with Eli and his sons, for example. This volume is highly readable and valuable to anyone interested in the Bible or in literature, although knowledge of Hebrew is necessary for the fullest understanding of this book.

BERLIN's work discusses the literary techniques of biblical narrative in general, but most of the author's examples are drawn from Samuel, a fact that is unsurprising as that book is widely regarded as the outstanding example of narrative art in the Bible. Her sections on "Character and Characterization" and "Point of View" are particularly rich in discussions of Samuel. This work will prove especially rewarding for readers with some familiarity with the Bible, as well as some background in narratology.

SHAWN ZELIG ASTER

Sanhedrin, Semikhah, and Rabbinate

Ehrlich, Avrum M., *Sanhedrin Studies,* Cambridge: Cambridge University Press, 2000
Elazar, Daniel J. (editor), *Authority, Power, and Leadership in the Jewish Polity,* Lanham, Maryland: University Press of America, 1991

Gitelman, Zvi (editor), *The Quest for Utopia: Jewish Political Ideas and Institutions through the Ages,* Armonk, New York, and London: Sharpe, 1992
Mantel, Hugo, *Studies in the History of the Sanhedrin,* Cambridge, Massachusetts: Harvard University Press, 1961
Newman, Jacob, *Semikha: A Study of Its Origins, History and Function in Rabbinic Literature,* Manchester, Greater Manchester: Manchester University Press, 1950
Schwarzfuchs, Simon, *A Concise History of the Rabbinate,* Oxford and Cambridge, Massachusetts: Blackwell, 1993
Sicker, Martin, *The Judaic State: A Study in Rabbinic Political Theory,* New York: Praeger, 1988

The study of rabbinical office and its juridical function has many aspects, among them the history of the ancient Sanhedrin, the evolution of the rabbinate as an institution, and the study of present-day Jewish religious life involving sociological, theological, and political dimensions. The studies discussed in this essay are selected more for the political philosopher than for the historian, for these works struggle with the history of Jewish institutions primarily as a way to understand present debates about the idea of Jewish authority.

EHRLICH translates, discusses, and annotates a Hebrew discourse by Yehudah Leib Maimon entitled "Renewal of the Sanhedrin in our Restored State," published in 1951. This work is particularly important because it integrates the subject of Sanhedrin and authoritative religious leadership into a discussion of the State of Israel, halakhic reform, and modernization. Included in this work is a review of the debate between two 16th-century rabbis, Jacob Berab, who sought to renew the antique *semikhah* (ordination) and reconvene the Sanhedrin, and Levi ibn Habib, who opposed Berab's proposals. The introduction and footnotes to this work are instructive to those interested in the emerging discipline of Jewish political philosophy.

ELAZAR's collection of essays on Jewish authority presents a survey of views from the ancient period to the present. Elazar outlines the disciplines that encompass the study of Jewish authority as both political science and Jewish studies, and he argues that the basic assumptions upon which this concept rests are the Torah, the priesthood, and kingship. The editor selects essays on leadership in late antiquity and the Middle Ages, as well as studies of the views of authority held by French, British, and American Jews. He also includes essays on the subjects of ethics and national power, revolution, and education.

GITELMAN has compiled philosophical essays about the nature of authority in Jewish politics. The essayists express differing viewpoints, but Gitelman contends that the Jewish political tradition is united in a search for utopian standards. Views of the Jewish polity have ranged from a desire to be a holy community to the rule of halakhic law and order. Historically, Jewish authority often depended entirely on the goodwill of civil governments in regions where the Jews resided, and obedience to the rabbis was often fueled by the Jewish community's sense of self-preservation. West European Jewish communities separated their religious identities from their national ones, but their utopias resembled Western models. The ways in which these discussions on the Jewish polity represent authority are interesting and subtle.

MANTEL's work deals with the history of the Sanhedrin in Israel from the Second Temple period through the decline of its authority in the fourth century C.E. The author summarizes various views on the nature of the Sanhedrin, and he explores such issues as the number of sanhedrins, the number of their judges, the scope of their jurisdictions, and their functions. He also discusses the nature of Sanhedrin politics and tensions between the Sanhedrin as parliament and various kings, tyrants, high priests, and ruling bodies. Mantel describes how the Sanhedrin interacted with scholars and its relationships with Jewish communities in Israel and the diaspora. He also explains the duties and authority of the Sanhedrin's president in economic, social, and moral matters, as well as the president's travel habits, religious jurisdiction, and administrative work. The bibliography thoroughly covers the range of works written on the subject.

NEWMAN remains one of the few studies that focus entirely on the subject of the ultimate form of Jewish authority, *semikhah,* or ordination. The author surveys the biblical origins of semikhah, the qualifications demanded of candidates, the debate over the precise jurisdiction of an ordained rabbi, and the various rituals and ceremonies of ordination. He also discusses how and when the semikhah ceased and describes various historical attempts to renew it. Newman tries to identify a continuity in the semikhah process from biblical times to the period of the Sanhedrin and the Second Temple. He argues that although the honorific titles and job descriptions of Jewish leadership often changed, the semikhah always existed during the period under discussion. Newman's description of the 16th-century debate between Jacob Berab and Levi ibn Habib over the renewal of semikhah is especially interesting. More generally, the volume provides the groundwork for further studies of semikhah and Sanhedrin, particularly as they relate to the State of Israel.

SCHWARZFUCHS's book is the first significant history of the rabbinate from its beginnings until the present. In concise chapters, the author discusses such topics as the reasons for the emergence of the rabbinic model of leadership and the causes of its changing functions. Schwarzfuchs views the rabbinate as a continually evolving institution of judicial and religious authority that uses anachronistic titles but adapts to address the ever-emerging needs of the community. The author shows that although the use of the title *rav* or *rabbi* began in the late Second Temple period, it was only in the Middle Ages that this title referred to a particular community function and institutionalized authority. Schwarzfuchs discusses the interaction of the rabbinate with Christian rulers and investigates the role of the chief rabbis in the collection of taxes, the legislation of ordinances, and the official representation of the needs of the Jewish community. He quotes contracts for rabbinic employment to demonstrate what communities expected from their rabbis, and he explains revolutions in rabbinic leadership and variations in Ashkenazi, Sephardi, and hasidic concepts of rabbinic authority. He also discusses the emergence of a modern model of rabbinic leadership, the founding of seminaries for rabbinic training and ordination, selected contemporary problems, and the future of the rabbinate.

SICKER offers a thorough study of ancient Jewish political institutions: the priesthood, prophecy, the monarchy, and the judiciary. While some of these roles are biblical in origin, Sicker studies them from the perspective of rabbinic commentary dating from the Talmud to the 19th century. He scours hundreds of rabbinic commentaries and Jewish philosophical works, presenting the political thinking of different communities and rabbis throughout the diaspora. He portrays rabbinic thinking as possessing a wealth of experience on such questions of government as the separation of powers, checks and balances, and civil duties. His endnotes and references are extensive and very useful.

AVRUM EHRLICH

See also Authority, Rabbinic and Communal

Satmar

Eisenberg, Robert, *Boychiks in the Hood: Travels in the Hasidic Underground,* San Francisco: HarperSanFrancisco, 1995; new edition, London: Quartet, 1996

Finkel, Avraham Yaakov, *Contemporary Sages: The Great Chasidic Masters of the Twentieth Century,* Northvale, New Jersey: Aronson, 1994

Kranzler, George, *Hasidic Williamsburg: A Contemporary American Hasidic Community,* Northvale, New Jersey: Aronson, 1995

Poll, Solomon, *The Hasidic Community of Williamsburg,* New York: Free Press of Glencoe, 1962

Rubin, Israel, *Satmar: Two Generations of an Urban Island,* New York: Lang, 1997

Satmar is a hasidic group with tens of thousands of adherents that was founded by Rabbi Yoel Teitelbaum and, since his death in 1979, has been led by his nephew Rabbi Moshe Teitelbaum. Based in the Williamsburg section of Brooklyn, with other major centers in the hasidic village of Kiryas Yoel in Orange County, New York, as well as in London, Antwerp, and Jerusalem, the movement aspires to recreate the pre–World War II lifestyle of the pious Jews of Transylvania and Sub-Carpathian Ruthenia. Within the variegated hasidic movement, it is the largest and most influential grouping. It has not, however, sought to gain either publicity or influence in the world at large, and as a result it is little known and often stereotyped. These books by sympathetic outsiders go beyond the stereotypes.

The widespread impression of Satmar as a hermetically sealed, embattled community is undermined by the ease with which EISENBERG was able to write his book. His physical appearance and minimal Jewish identity are radically unhasidic, but Eisenberg is fluent in Yiddish and has some hasidic relatives, and he found no difficulty gaining access to opinions and information. His first chapter describes a visit to the Satmar community in Williamsburg, interspersing brief but vivid pictures of various individuals, including rebels, with analyses that tend to emphasize the controversial but also show admiration. Satmarers appear repeatedly throughout the remainder of this entertaining book, which serves to provide some context for the distinctive elements of their way of life. While various authors have given differing accounts of the transition from the late, intensely beloved rebbe to his successor, Eisenberg contrasts the existence of an organized movement of dissidents opposed to the new rebbe with the emerging sense of others within the community that "there can be Satmar without the Satmar Rebbe."

POLL's work, written in the early 1960s, is a highly readable account of hasidic life in Williamsburg that remains a largely accurate description. Poll mentions Satmar (and other groups) by name only in passing, but most of his general statements apply to Satmar in particular. Poll focuses on the facets of hasidic life most likely to strike an outsider as strange, providing useful insights into underlying values and historical background. He gives little sense of the lives or characters of specific individuals, but he paints striking pictures of social types, especially in chapter seven, "The Social Stratification of the Hasidic Community." He also conveys a sense of hasidic voices through translations of newspaper advertisements, fundraising letters from impoverished rabbis, and similar documents of daily life. The mingling of religious principle with ordinary routine is described engagingly, especially in the references to the effects of particularly stringent observance of the dietary laws. Only the historical background (in the first five chapters) is a little too narrowly focused, and as a result, the book could convey the false impression that all hasidim are from Hungary and live in Williamsburg.

KRANZLER's book is a sequel to his *Williamsburg: A Jewish Community in Transition* (1961), which traced developments in Jewish Williamsburg that began before the postwar hasidic immigration. In the sequel, he studies hasidic Williamsburg as a whole, but he emphasizes the leading role of Satmar and its rebbes. Based on written surveys and interviews, the book includes many quotations from and descriptions of ordinary hasidim as well as leaders of the community. Relatively long and concisely written, this study includes much information on various aspects of the Satmar community, from the family (chapter four) to the broader social structure (chapter five) and interactions with the outside world through political and economic activity (chapters two and eight). A hagiographic account of the late rebbe is also included (Appendix B). Kranzler writes with unreserved admiration for Satmar; he dismisses as unimportant the tensions around the succession of the new rebbe and other potentially controversial issues.

RUBIN's book, devoted specifically to Satmar, revises his *Satmar: An Island in the City* (1972): each of the original chapters is followed by a supplement assessing changes in the intervening years. Based on interviews and the author's personal observations of the community, this book offers pictures painted in broad strokes rather than detailed analysis. The organization by topic is similar to Kranzler's arrangement, although Rubin treats historical background and religion more thoroughly. Rubin evinces admiration for Satmar, but he has a more critical eye than Kranzler; in particular, Rubin gives greater weight to internal struggles in the community following the succession of the new rebbe and to the changes that may result (such as greater independence from the rebbe in individual decision-making). Rubin also discerns evidence of slow and subtle Americanization, which he sees as exemplifying the "ubiquity and inevitably of sociocultural change" in even the most conservative communities.

FINKEL presents biographical summaries, selected teachings, and photographs of 37 hasidic rebbes of the 20th century. The brief chapter on "Rabbi Yoel Teitelbaum of Satmar—Reb Yoilish, the Satmarer Rebbe" includes a photograph of the late rebbe's soulful face, information on his lineage and early years, and a summary of the growth of Satmar Hasidism in New York and its many educational and charitable institutions. Most importantly, it presents the only selection of Satmar teachings available in English, giving some sense of the forcefulness of the rebbe's words and of the theological underpinnings of Satmar's controversial opposition to Zionism ("Don't Leave Prematurely" and "Unexpected Redemption").

JUSTIN JARON LEWIS

Schechter, Solomon 1847?–1915

Romanian-born Anglo-American *Wissenschaft* scholar, essayist, and theologian

Bentwich, Norman De Mattos, *Solomon Schechter: A Biography*, Cambridge: Cambridge University Press, and Philadelphia: Jewish Publication Society, 1938
Ginzberg, Eli, *Keeper of the Law: Louis Ginzberg*, Philadelphia: Jewish Publication Society, 1966
Ginzberg, Louis, "Solomon Schechter," in his *Students, Scholars and Saints*, Philadelphia: Jewish Publication Society, 1928
Karp, Abraham J., "American Rabbis for America: Solomon Schechter Comes to the Seminary," in his *Jewish Continuity in America: Creative Survival in a Free Society*, Tuscaloosa: University of Alabama Press, 1998
Kripke, Myer S., "Solomon Schechter's Philosophy of Judaism," *The Reconstructionist*, 3(12–13), 22 October and 5 November 1937
Marx, Alexander, "Solomon Schechter," in his *Essays in Jewish Biography*, Philadelphia: Jewish Publication Society, 1947; London: University Press of America/Eurospan, 1986

Schechter was a rabbi, textual scholar of rabbinic literature, leader of Conservative Judaism, and discoverer of an invaluable treasure trove of Hebrew manuscripts, which he rescued from the storage room of a Cairo synagogue and brought to Cambridge University, where he served as "Reader in Talmudic." In 1902 he became president of the Jewish Theological Seminary of America in New York, a post he held until his death in 1915.

MARX's essay serves as a good introduction to Schechter's life and his contribution to Jewish scholarship. Marx recounts how impressed he was by Schechter's generosity of spirit and impulsive nature. The two first met in Cambridge in 1898, when Marx came to collate the manuscripts of a book. After welcoming Marx, Schechter revealed that he had intended to edit the work himself and had already made copies of some important manuscripts and had begun to write notes on the text. Since he had abandoned the project, Schechter presented all this material, the results of considerable effort, to Marx, a total stranger. Marx asserts that this remarkable act of generosity expressed Schechter's personality.

BENTWICH offers the only full-length biography of Schechter. Bentwich had known and revered Schechter when he lived in England. Schechter's widow and his son, Frank, made letters, documents, and papers available to Bentwich, and Frank Schechter reviewed the manuscript shortly before he died. The resulting biography displays the merits and shortcomings of such an arrangement. Although the volume lacks critical analysis, Bentwich successfully captures Schechter's personality, sparkling wit, and charisma. Bentwich is thoroughly at home and reliable when describing the period in which Schechter resided in England. He is not on such safe ground when he describes Schechter's arrival in the United States and activities at the seminary. Bentwich's biography should thus be read in conjunction with more recent studies covering the last part of Schechter's life.

KARP studies the protracted negotiations leading to Schechter's departure for the United States. Schechter's reasons for wanting to immigrate to the United States included his desire to live and raise his children in a Jewish environment; his wish to provide them with a good education, which was not possible given his salary at Cambridge; and his embarrassment that a major part of that salary was subsidized by Claude G. Montefiore, a radical reformer who favored Sunday services. In the United States, messianic expectations were aroused by Schechter's imminent arrival. Karp addresses the question of why Jacob Schiff, the financier, and a group of wealthy German Jews who belonged to the leading Reform temple in the United States, Temple Emanu-El, decided to support the reorganization of the traditionally oriented Jewish Theological Seminary and underwrite Schechter's coming to the United States. Bentwich argues that the group was concerned that Reform had gone too far and saw the urgency of erecting a bulwark for traditional Judaism, but this is patently absurd. Karp contends that the real concern was a fear of political radicalism. Schiff, Louis Marshall, the Lewisohns, the Guggenheims, and their group were anxious lest the newly arrived East European immigrants turn to socialism and anarchy. The wealthy German, uptown Jews saw signs of a decline in the Jewish character—a loosening of family ties and a rise in offenses against the law of the land, such as increasing involvement in gambling and prostitution. According to Karp, it was this that spurred them to support Schechter's coming to the United States.

In his memorial address honoring Schechter, Louis GINZBERG, master teacher of Talmud at the Jewish Theological Seminary of America for more than half a century, expresses the opinion that the key to Schechter the scholar was Schechter the man. Schechter's inclusive notion of "Catholic Israel" reflected his soul, and nothing Jewish was alien to him. Ginzberg notes that Schechter contributed to an extraordinary range of Jewish learning, including studies of pre-talmudic literature and sects, Talmud and midrash, law and legend, and Karaite polemics and geonic apologetics. He also reviews Schechter's ideas concerning the intellectual and spiritual activity of Jews in Palestine during the 16th century and points out that there is hardly a branch of Jewish literature that Schechter did not enrich.

Eli GINZBERG states that in later years his father (Louis Ginzberg) completely changed his view of Schechter—not Schechter the man, but Schechter the scholar. The younger Ginzberg observes that time alters a man's views. Perhaps the senior Ginzberg felt that the writer of a memorial address, like the writer of an epitaph, is not "on oath." Louis Ginzberg's final judgment is that Schechter was incompetent as a scholar and temperamentally incapable of serious scholarship. In the last years of his life, he dictated his reminiscences to his daughter-in-law, Ruth Szold Ginzberg, on one occasion remarking:

> Schechter was a Rumanian who had never had a proper modern education. . . . He didn't have the patience necessary for a scholar. He had intuition but not the essential knowledge. . . . At one time intuition was sufficient for scholars. A century ago knowledge was very limited, but in our times one must be a philologist as well; one must have a sense of economics, of archaeology, etc.

KRIPKE, in his critique of Schechter's theology, notes that nowhere did Schechter make a complete and finished statement of his philosophy of Judaism. It is therefore difficult, if not impossible, to determine Schechter's stand on many problems of primary importance. One of his favorite words was aspects, and his major synthetic work was called Some Aspects of Rabbinic Theology. Aspects is a comfortable word, permitting the writer to dwell upon what is congenial to him and to omit what is not—for example, a coherent discussion of the place of revelation in Jewish theology. The impression Kripke gives is that Schechter did not take the doctrine of revelation literally. Instead of revelation, the ultimate source of authority for Schechter was the conscience of "Catholic Israel," a term he used to indicate the spirit of the Jewish people as a whole. He maintained that Judaism "has distinct precepts and usages and customs, consecrated by the consent of Catholic Israel through thousands of years." The will of Catholic Israel is the final authority. Kripke argues that Schechter's acceptance of Judaism as a revealed religion is inconsistent with his acceptance of Catholic Israel as the criterion of authenticity of a belief or practice; for if a matter is divinely revealed, it is clearly unchangeable for all time. It cannot be changed, even with the consent of the entire people; after all, the worship of the golden calf was the result of the common consent of the people. Moreover, it is exceedingly difficult to see how any change may take place if Catholic Israel is the authority. No one can be the first to change anything since the weight of Catholic Israel is against the individual. With the best will in the world one cannot probe too deeply what Schechter means by viewing Judaism as a living organism developing from age to age.

JACOB HABERMAN

Schoenberg, Arnold 1874–1951

Austrian-born American composer

Cooper-White, Pamela, Schoenberg and the God-Idea: The Opera Moses und Aron (Studies in Musicology, no. 83), Ann Arbor, Michigan: UMI Research, 1985

MacDonald, Malcolm, *Schoenberg* (Master Musicians Series), London: Dent, 1976

Ringer, Alexander, *Arnold Schoenberg: The Composer as Jew,* New York: Oxford University Press, and Oxford: Clarendon, 1990

Smith, Joan Allen, *Schoenberg and His Circle: A Viennese Portrait,* New York: Schirmer, and London: Collier Macmillan, 1986

Sterne, Colin C., *Arnold Schoenberg: The Composer as Numerologist,* Lewiston, New York: Mellen, 1993

Stuckenschmidt, H.H., *Arnold Schoenberg,* Zurich: Atlantis, 1957; London: Calder, 1959; New York: Grove, 1960

Stuckenschmidt, H.H., *Schoenberg: His Life, World, and Work,* New York: Schirmer, 1974; London: Calder, 1977

Most of the literature on Arnold Schoenberg focuses more on his music and his 12-tone system than on the man himself. The books surveyed here, however, deal primarily with Schoenberg the man, even though they have much to say about his music theories as well. The latest research on all aspects of Schoenberg's life and work can be monitored by consulting the *Arnold Schoenberg Institute Journal,* published by the University of Southern California. Few of the books listed here are straight biographies; most of them approach Schoenberg from a particular angle. Of the chronological biographies, MacDONALD's is straightforward and easy to read. It distances itself from most of the more personal aspects of Schoenberg's life and instead focuses on the development of his musical style, the public reception of his work, and some explanation of his musical theories.

STUCKENSCHMIDT (1957) is similar to MacDonald. It offers interpretations of Schoenberg's major works and analyzes his compositions. It also discusses his life as a young musician and some of his early influences. However, for a truly comprehensive Schoenberg biography, readers must turn to STUCKENSCHMIDT (1974). Stuckenschmidt opens this volume with an apologetic note about how much material was absent from the first biography. That problem does not plague him again, though; this biography includes absolutely every detail of Schoenberg's life, from his deepest thoughts to the dates of every performance and composition to word-for-word documentation of important conversations. The scope of the work is remarkable.

Although Stuckenschmidt's treatment is comprehensive and exemplary, several other books develop certain specific areas of Schoenberg's life. Schoenberg's later influences are interestingly documented by SMITH, who explores the cultural environment in which he lived and the people with whom he kept company. She also includes information on Schoenberg as a teacher and performer. Smith's book has some transcriptions of conversations between Schoenberg and his contemporaries and a very thorough appendix with brief biographies of the central figures in Schoenberg's life.

Of the books with particular arguments and angles, STERNE's is one of the most interesting. With a forward by composer John Cage, the book asserts that Schoenberg composed his music based on numerology. Schoenberg was concerned with numbers from early childhood, and Sterne includes many charts plotting the way Schoenberg put music together. Sterne proves his point with examples from a variety of compositions and shows Schoenberg's pervasive interest in numerology through the numerological games he played with names and dates as well as with music. Although at times the charts and numbers in this book are overwhelming and somewhat cryptic, they do provide new insights into the workings of Schoenberg's mind. Studied in conjunction with Ringer's or Cooper-White's book about Schoenberg as a Jew, this book is liable to prompt questions about the extent to which this preoccupation with numerology derives from or parallels Jewish mysticism.

Two studies address Schoenberg as Jew directly. RINGER views Schoenberg as a highly influential figure not only in the music of the 20th century but more generally in its aesthetics. His book explores the values of a man who felt himself culturally bound to Germany yet forced out because of his Jewishness. The volume is actually composed of essays written over a period of 15 years and therefore shows a developing conception of Schoenberg as Jew. Some of the essays consider his interactions with other Jewish composers, while others deal with his place in the history of Nazi Germany and his struggle to escape persecution. Two particularly notable segments are the chapter that examines Schoenberg's relationship with Rabbi Stephen Wise and the essay about the idea of "Jewish music," both of which raise interesting philosophical points. Ringer also includes several fascinating appendixes, including Schoenberg's own "Four Point Program for Jewry," which sheds much light on Schoenberg's sense of a Jewish identity.

COOPER-WHITE approaches Schoenberg's Judaism by analyzing the composition most obviously influenced by the Bible. In addition to documenting the creation of the opera, its musical composition, and how Schoenberg came up with the idea, Cooper-White also explores the environment in which a biblical opera could be written and the significance of its being composed by a Jew. She includes sections on Schoenberg's religious growth, possible kabbalistic influences on his work, and his relationship with Judaism in light of the rise of Nazism. Separate sections also focus on the libretto, the music, and the leitmotiv. Overall, this is a remarkable and detailed study of one work from a variety of angles.

GILLIAN D. STEINBERG

Scholem, Gershom 1897–1982

German-born Israeli pioneer of the academic study of Kabbalah

Biale, David, *Gershom Scholem: Kabbalah and Counter History,* Cambridge, Massachusetts, and London: Harvard University Press, 1987

Bloom, Harold (editor), *Gershom Scholem,* New York: Chelsea House, 1987

Dan, Joseph, *Gershom Scholem and the Mystical Dimension of Jewish History,* New York: New York University Press, 1987

Mendes-Flohr, Paul (editor), *Gershom Scholem: The Man and His Work*, Albany: State University of New York Press, 1994

Schweid, Eliezer, *Mysticism and Judaism According to Gershom G. Scholem*, Jerusalem: Magnes Press of Hebrew University, 1983; as *Judaism and Mysticism According to Gershom Scholem*, Atlanta, Georgia: Scholars Press, 1985

Gershom Scholem is generally regarded as the founder of the modern academic study of Jewish mysticism. His research touches upon all areas of Jewish mysticism and is rooted in detailed philological analysis of the enormous array of manuscripts and texts related to the field. His work has made a lasting impression not only within the field of Jewish mysticism but also in other areas of research in Judaic studies, including history, philosophy, and literature.

BIALE analyzes the assumptions and influences that lie behind Scholem's historiography and his conception of Judaism. The author points out that Scholem was a Zionist who immigrated to Palestine as early as 1923 and who rejected, both politically and culturally, the German Jewish world that created the *Wissenschaft des Judentums*. Biale also explains that when Scholem returned to an identification with Judaism he did not adopt a traditional framework; instead he was inspired to create his own response to the rationalist theology that dominated German Jewish thought of the 19th century. Many scholars from the *Wissenschaft* school saw mysticism as an impediment to the progress of Jewish history. They regarded mysticism, with its nonrational way of thinking and its mythical symbolism, as a corruption of proper religious experience, which was best exemplified in Judaism by the Aristotelian philosophy of the Middle Ages. Rejecting this position, Scholem designated the esoteric mystical dimension of Judaism as the key to its future. Scholem took up the task of writing a "counter history" of Judaism as a protest against both the Orthodox and Enlightenment traditions, and Biale compares Scholem's work to the similar projects of Martin Buber and Micha Josef Berdyczewski. The author posits that, unlike Buber and Berdyczewski, who were heavily influenced by Nietzsche, Scholem advocated a return to the sources of Jewish mysticism in an effort to set a course for a future Judaism based on the spirit of the Jewish mystical past.

SCHWEID evaluates Scholem's views on mysticism and Jewish history. Critically examining the larger picture of Judaism and Jewish history that emerges from Scholem's works, Schweid argues that Scholem's analysis of Judaism is guided by his preference for the mystical and gnostic elements of the Jewish tradition and his rejection of both halakhic Judaism and liberalism. In his theoretical discussions of the history of religious evolution, Scholem designates mysticism as the third and final stage in the progression of the religious consciousness within a given religious tradition. Schweid contends that by privileging the mystical dimension of religion, Scholem sets out to marginalize other forms of religious experience, such as legal praxis, that have played a crucial role within Judaism. In chapter seven, the author further criticizes Scholem's sympathetic treatment of Shabbetai Tsevi, which depicts his failed messianic movement in the 17th century as a significant development of the mainstream of Jewish mystical consciousness. Schweid argues that the Sabbatian heresy was a dangerous perversion of Jewish thinking and cannot be placed within the history of legitimate Jewish religious experience.

DAN stresses that the main thrust of Scholem's work as the scholar himself envisioned it was to clarify the history of Jewish mysticism. Dan summarizes Scholem's elaborate presentation of this history from the origins of Jewish mysticism in the Hekhalot and Merkabah literature through the development of kabbalistic schools in Safed in the 15th and 16th centuries and on to the Sabbatian and hasidic movements of early modernity.

BLOOM's volume brings together an eclectic assortment of studies dedicated to the analysis of not only Scholem's scholarly work but his personality and religious thought as well. Scholem's views on Sabbatianism and Hasidism and his reconstruction of the early stages of the Kabbalah are discussed. Additional essays reflect on Scholem's views on Judaism, Gnosticism, history, language, Zionism, and theology. Also included in this volume are discussions of Scholem's lasting influence on the academic study of Judaism.

MENDES-FLOHR's book is a collection of eight essays that touch upon various themes in Scholem's life, thought, and scholarship. Mendes-Flohr assesses Scholem's spiritual and philosophical orientation toward Judaism and religion. E.E. Urbach analyzes Scholem's understanding of Jewish studies and its role in history. I. Tishby discusses Scholem's contribution to the study of the Zohar. J. Dan describes Scholem's understanding of Hasidism and argues that it reflects the scholar's own idealism. N. Rotenstreich addresses Scholem's conception of Jewish nationalism. Finally, M. Beit-Arié describes Scholem's love of bibliographic research.

HARTLEY LACHTER

Science and Religion

Carmell, Aryeh and Cyril Domb, *Challenge: Torah Views on Science and Its Problems*, London: Association of Orthodox Jewish Scientists, and New York: Feldheim, 1976; new edition, New York: Feldheim, 1988

Feldman, W.M., *Rabbinical Mathematics and Astronomy*, London: Cailingold, 1931; New York: Hermon, 1965, 4th edition, 1991

Ruderman, David B., *Jewish Thought and Scientific Discovery in Early Modern Europe*, New Haven, Connecticut: Yale University Press, 1995

Samuelson, Norbert M., *Judaism and the Doctrine of Creation*, Cambridge and New York: Cambridge University Press, 1994

Schroeder, Gerald L., *Genesis and the Big Bang: The Discovery of Harmony between Modern Science and the Bible*, New York: Bantam, 1990

The Bible is in no way a textbook of science, but many of its chapters demonstrate a sophisticated knowledge of the environment: for instance, Leviticus 18 presupposes a careful classification of living creatures; Job 28 reveals a knowledge of mining; and Isaiah 41 hints at ancient Israelite agriculture and arboriculture. Several rabbis of the Talmud are said to have excelled in science or medicine, and the Jews of the Middle Ages played a significant role in mediating the scientific knowledge of the Muslim world to the West, thus stimulating the Renaissance. Yet the rise of science in early modern times shattered the assumption that all knowledge, including scientific knowledge, was to be found in revealed texts. The new knowledge did not appear to be in Scripture; similarly, information previously gleaned from Scripture did not seem to accord with the findings of the scientists. The radical transformation of science in the 20th century, particularly through relativity and quantum mechanics, has encouraged some authors to seek a new conformity between religion and science, but this endeavor may well prove illusory.

CARMELL and DOMB are respectively an Orthodox realtor and rabbi and an Orthodox physicist; both are pioneers in the Association of Orthodox Scientists. In this collection of essays, they assert that religious truth is in conformity with contemporary science; thus, the authors self-consciously follow in the footsteps of German Orthodoxy, whose symbiosis of Torah and culture ("Torah im derekh erets") was exemplified in the Bund jüdischer Akademiker (Association of Jewish Academics) of the pre-Nazi era. The first section of the book, "Areas of Interaction," is devoted to the broad relationship between religion and science. Part two focuses on creation and evolution, and it opens with a fascinating selection of traditional sources (from the early rabbinic onward) that appear to interpret the Genesis stories of creation along evolutionary, or at least developmental, lines. The section concludes with a summary of opinions on evolution voiced at sessions of a panel convened by the Association of Orthodox Scientists in 1971 and 1972 to respond to students' questions. Part three, "The Secular Bias," attempts both to discredit historical criticism of the Bible and to establish the rationality of belief in God. Several contributors argue that sciences such as quantum mechanics lend themselves to interpretations of nature that are congruent with a belief in the divine. Part four, "Ethical Problems," is concerned with practical matters such as the ethics of population control, medical experimentation on humans, and organ transplants. Carmell's own final essay, "Judaism and the Quality of the Environment," is notable as one of the earliest attempts by a modern writer to articulate a distinctly Jewish religious viewpoint on human responsibility for the environment.

FELDMAN's volume owes much to the research of a previous generation of German scholars, such as Mahler and Baneth. It is perhaps the first work of significance in this field to be published in English, and it deservedly has been reissued, but unfortunately not revised, in recent years. Feldman, who was senior physician at a London hospital, focuses on mathematical and astronomical passages in the Talmud and later rabbinic literature, relating these texts both to the Ptolemaic astronomy of the rabbinic period and to the more modern astronomy of Johannes Kepler and Sir Isaac Newton. Much of the book is devoted to expounding Jewish calendrical calculations, which depend on a complex relationship between the apparent motions of the sun and the moon; Feldman gives one of the few clear accounts available in English of Maimonides' perplexing treatise on the subject.

RUDERMAN's volume is much more than the historical investigation of a previously neglected topic. By analyzing the way that Jews responded to, or even participated in, the European scientific revolution of the 17th century, he is able to articulate the problems and dilemmas that challenged the worldview shared by Jews and Christians in the Middle Ages and ultimately shaped modernity. How, for instance, did Jews react to Copernicus's refutation of Ptolemy's geocentric universe? Did the Jewish establishment, like the Catholic hierarchy, censure those who upheld the new theories? The range of attitudes is encapsulated in the debates of 17th-century Italian Jews. Leone Modena, for instance, is portrayed as "an intellectual fully committed to integrating rabbinic culture with the secular world and to explaining it . . . in terms comprehensible to human reason and experience." Like his contemporary Joseph Delmedigo, Modena was ready to welcome the new scientific achievements. On the other hand, men such as Moses Hayyim Luzzatto and Moses Zacuto emphasized the study of Kabbalah, and while they were not necessarily hostile to the scientific study of nature, they rejected the historical critique of traditional rabbinic and kabbalistic sources. Ruderman's fascinating book contains an essay on the 16th-century community of converso physicians, including the noted physiologist Zacutus Lusitanus, and a chapter on "science and skepticism" in the work of Simone Luzzatto. The concluding bibliographical essay on the study of nature in ancient Judaism is particularly helpful.

SAMUELSON argues that there is congruence, or at least compatibility, between modern cosmology and biblical and later Jewish accounts of creation. He contends that the "creation myth" of Genesis has frequently been interpreted in traditional Jewish philosophy in terms deriving from Plato's *Timaeus*, the best and most influential premodern creation story. Now, however, it is the task of theologians to interpret Genesis in terms of the story told by contemporary science, and the "myth" offered by science expresses the Genesis concept even better than Plato's myth did. Samuelson devotes the opening chapter of his book to an exposition of the doctrine of creation in Franz Rosenzweig's *Star of Redemption*. Samuelson himself reads Genesis as "a narrative of creation . . . divided into seven atemporal units"; in other words, a single act of God, performed upon a single, undifferentiated space, is separated into distinct domains. Furthermore, the universe exists not for the sake of its creatures, but for the service of God, while creation and revelation point forward to redemption in an "asymptotic" process—that is, a process that has direction but no beginning or end. Four aspects of the Jewish concept of creation interface with contemporary scientific cosmology: the nature and origin of the universe in relation to time; the role of space in the story of creation; the relation of the actual physical universe to other possible universes; and the relationship between the domains of science and ethics from a religious perspective. Samuelson articulates this interface by reference to theories of parallel universes, inflationary universes, quantum mechanics, and the reversibility of time. The book opens avenues for exploration, and it provides a useful introduction to some of the classical Jewish sources on creation, particularly Gersonides, as well as to Plato's *Timaeus* and Rosenzweig's *Star of Redemption*.

SCHROEDER, a nuclear physicist and oceanographer and an aspiring theologian who resides in Jerusalem, wrote this book in response to probing questions from his children. The question that apparently worried him most was how to reconcile the opening pages of Genesis that describe the creation of the earth in six days less than 6,000 years ago with the scientific theories that the universe is roughly 15 billion years old; the earth is five billion years old; and hominid history stretches back a few million years. He argues that the billions of years that have followed the Big Bang, according to cosmologists, and the events of the first six days of Genesis are "identical realities that have been described in vastly different terms." The key lies in the relativity of time: six days as seen by God, who was the only observer of pre-Adam creation, are equivalent to five billion years viewed from a human perspective. This thesis might seem naïve if Schroeder did not cloak it in learned quotations from Maimonides and the Talmud and in a great deal of superfluous physics liable to impress the non-scientist. The book will not satisfy the serious theologian, but it is well worth reading as an example of a current trend in Jewish fundamentalist writing.

NORMAN SOLOMON

Scribes

McCarthy, Carmel, *The Tiqqune Sopherim and Other Theological Corrections in the Masoretic Text of the Old Testament* (Orbis Biblicus et Orientalis, 36), Freiburg: Universitätsverlag, 1981

Mulder, Martin Jan, *Mikra: Text, Translation, Reading, and Interpretation of the Hebrew Bible in Ancient Judaism and Early Christianity* (Compendia rerum Iudaicarum ad Novum Testamentum, section 2, vol. 1), Minneapolis, Minnesota: Fortress, 1988

Tov, Emanuel, *Bikoret Nusah ha-Mikra: Pirke Mavo*, 1989; translated as *Textual Criticism of the Hebrew Bible*, Minneapolis, Minnesota: Fortress, 1992

Weingreen, Jacob, *Introduction to the Critical Study of the Text of the Hebrew Bible*, New York: Oxford University Press, and Oxford: Clarendon, 1982

Würthwein, Ernst, *The Text of the Old Testament: An Introduction to the Biblia Hebraica*, Grand Rapids, Michigan: Eerdmans, 1979; London: SCM, 1980; 2nd edition, Grand Rapids, Michigan: Eerdmans, 1995

Yeivin, Israel, *Mavo la-Masorah ha-Tavranit*, 1971; translated as *Introduction to the Tiberian Masorah* (Masoretic Studies, no. 5), Missoula, Montana: Scholars Press, 1980

The scribes (Hebrew: *soferim*) referred to in this essay are the disciples, and their successors, of the biblical scribe Ezra, who were active in the periods of the Second Temple and the Talmud. In the Babylonian Talmud (Kiddushin 30a), it is written that "the early scholars were called 'Soferim' because they used to count all the words of the Torah" (the statement is a play on the two meanings of the Hebrew root *spr*, "to count" and "to copy"). As McCarthy has noted, later

scholars have sought to discover the exact role of these scribes in the transmission of the Hebrew Bible. Talmudic and medieval texts allude to or imply earlier versions of certain scriptural passages, and scholars seek to determine what the scribes may have added to or subtracted from these previous versions; to establish when the scribes intervened; and to understand their motives.

McCARTHY discusses in great detail the Tikkunei Soferim, an authoritative listing of 18 scribal emendations to the biblical text, summarizes the history of their study, and provides abundant references to earlier literature on the topic and on related subjects, such as the use of euphemism in the Hebrew Bible and the nature of the amended texts in the older versions, such as the Greek Septuagint. This work, originally published as a dissertation, pays full attention to technical, textual details, but it does not really provide the historical framework needed by novices in the subject.

WEINGREEN, by contrast, does address the general reader, as he aims "to present an acceptable scheme and a practical apparatus for the critical study of the text of the Hebrew Bible." He claims that the "miscopying" of the biblical text should ultimately be "attributed to human fallibility and misunderstanding." His work's main merit is that it puts the conscious and unconscious interventions of the scribes in their proper historical perspective. The book also presents a fair judgment of the activities of the scribes, based on modern conceptions of textual criticism, concluding that "axioms recorded in the Talmud relating to the serious study of the Hebrew Bible represent a sensible approach, expressing basic postulates which are highly acceptable to the textual critic today."

YEIVIN's classic on the Tiberian Masorah, "the collected body of instructions used to preserve the traditional layout and text of the Bible unchanged," deserves special mention here, even though it centers on the Masoretes (the natural successors of the scribes), rather than the scribes themselves. Especially in part two of the work, titled simply "The Masorah," the reader will find numerous direct and indirect references to the work of the scribes, which illustrate the meticulous care with which the scribes performed their duty.

In addition to Yeivin, two other introductions to the Masoretic Text of the Hebrew Bible also provide information about the work of the scribes. WÜRTHWEIN considers the role of the *soferim* in his discussion of the canonization of the consonantal text and the conscious interventions in passages in the original text that were motivated by those passages' supposedly problematic content. He also explains in some detail the notation of textual changes by the *soferim* in the critical apparatus of the Masoretic Bible.

TOV's work is an impressive and comprehensive study covering the state of research in textual criticism of the Hebrew Bible. Especially in chapter one and in his discussion of "Hebrew Witnesses" in chapter two, "Textual Witnesses of the Bible," Tov evaluates the work of the scribes and provides up-to-date bibliographical references.

MULDER's huge volume includes an article by Meir Bar-Ilan titled "Scribes and Books in the Late Second Commonwealth and Rabbinic Period." This essay is the only source discussed here in which the soferim's identities, employers, methods, and social status, as well as the practicalities of their work, are addressed in detail. This encyclopedic volume contains numerous other articles that touch upon the work of the scribes and a wealth of additional bibliographical information; it should be consulted by any serious student of the textual criticism of the Hebrew Bible.

EMILE G.L. SCHRIJVER

See also Masorah; Script and Scribal Practices

Script and Scribal Practices

Beit-Arié, Malachi, *Hebrew Codicology: Tentative Typology of Technical Practices Employed in Hebrew Dated Medieval Manuscripts* (Etudes de paléographie hébraïque), Paris: Centre National de la Recherche Scientifique, 1976
Beit-Arié, Malachi, *Hebrew Manuscripts of East and West: Towards a Comparative Codicology* (Panizzi Lectures, 1992), London: British Library, 1993
Beit-Arié, Malachi, *The Makings of the Medieval Hebrew Book: Studies in Palaeography and Codicology*, Jerusalem: Magnes Press of Hebrew University, 1993
Beit-Arié, Malachi et al., *Specimens of Mediaeval Hebrew Scripts*, vol. 1: *Oriental and Yemenite Scripts*, Jerusalem: Israel Academy of Sciences and Humanities, 1987
Birnbaum, Solomon, *The Hebrew Scripts*, 4 vols., London: Palaeographia, 1954–1957
Richler, Binyamin, *Hebrew Manuscripts: A Treasured Legacy*, Cleveland, Ohio: Ofeq Institute, 1990
Yardeni, Ada, *Sefer ha-ketav ha-'Ivri: Toladot, yesodot, signonot, 'itsuv*, 1991; translated as *The Book of Hebrew Script: History, Palaeography, Script Styles, Calligraphy and Design*, Jerusalem: Carta, 1997

RICHLER's publication is an introduction to the study of Hebrew manuscripts intended to serve both scholar and layperson. It provides basic and easily accessible information on practically every aspect of the modern study of the handwritten Hebrew book: the existence of autograph manuscripts of great scholars, ancient Hebrew writings, the Dead Sea Scrolls, colophons, codicology, paleography, scribes, the subject matter of the manuscripts, illuminated manuscripts, manuscript collections, the Cairo Genizah, some famous Hebrew manuscripts, catalogs, the importance of manuscripts, and the future of manuscript research. The work is supplemented by a chapter on the Cairo Genizah by Robert Brody, a glossary, a selected bibliography, and an invaluable selection of sample transcriptions of various Hebrew scripts.

BIRNBAUM's study is considered a classic. It divides the Hebrew scripts into 26 geographically distinguished "types," for which Birnbaum has coined several designations based on Hebrew terms, including: Italkian, from the word *Italki* (Italian); Temanic, from *Temani* (Yemenite); and Yevanic, from *Yevani* (Greek). For the different modes of script he uses the terms "square," "scroll square" (a variant form used for Torah

and Esther scrolls), "cursive," and the intermediate "mashait." (Birnbaum resented the common application of the term "rabbinic" to semicursive hands, since "the 'rabbis' had, of course, no closer connection with this style than with square and cursive"). Birnbaum's is the first comprehensive work on the subject, and it is still of great value, partly because it includes postmedieval scripts. His peculiar terminology, however, has never really been accepted, especially because his introductory remarks—in which one might seek a thorough explanation of his method—are rather brief.

YARDENI's work is as comprehensive in its coverage of different historical periods as Birnbaum's study, but her approach is entirely different from his. A renowned expert on Hebrew paleography, especially of the earlier, premedieval periods, Yardeni is also an acclaimed designer of modern typefaces. Her book reflects both her scholarly knowledge and her design expertise as it directs the reader's attention to the various shapes of the individual letters and to the intricacies, both historical and technical, of the letters' development. The work has much to offer both the layperson and the specialist. The uninitiated reader will be especially interested in part one, which discusses historical and palaeographical background, and part four, on calligraphy, script-composition, and the designing of typefaces. The expert will appreciate Yardeni's specialized knowledge of Hebrew paleography, demonstrated in part two, and the treatment of script styles and the script charts in part three. The book offers hundreds of illustrations, many of which Yardeni drew herself. Although the reproductions are relatively poor, especially when compared to the quality of the illustrations in the 1991 Hebrew edition, they are a delight for any lover of the Hebrew script.

The first volume of a new series investigating medieval Hebrew scripts, prepared under the supervision of BEIT-ARIÉ (1987), fills a noticeable gap in the literature on Hebrew scripts. The book contains charts with Hebrew alphabets from the Orient and Yemen meticulously copied from selected dated manuscripts, including a number from the Cairo Genizah. Each alphabet is accompanied by a photograph of a page from the source manuscript. In addition to recording the *lettre moyenne* of the specific manuscripts, the charts also depict the variant forms of the letters that inevitably occur in a handwritten text. This single volume will primarily interest paleographers and scholars specializing in this region. As the series develops to include additional volumes covering other regions, it should become an indispensable tool for a far larger audience of historians and philologists of the Middle Ages who seek to localize and decipher Hebrew scripts.

In addition to the volume discussed above, Beit-Arié has made a number of other important contributions to the field of Hebrew manuscript research. Among these works, the one that has had the strongest impact on the development of the field is without doubt BEIT-ARIÉ (1976). It is based on limited data retrieved from the Hebrew Palaeography Project (HPP), initiated by Beit-Arié and the French scholar Colette Sirat in 1965 and sponsored by the Israel Academy of Sciences and Humanities and France's Centre National de la Recherche Scientifique (Institut de Recherche et d'Histoire des Textes). HPP's main goal was, and still is, "to collect all information available on dated Medieval Hebrew Mss., to classify the data and establish standards for dating and locating undated Mss." Beit-Arié's volume provides detailed information on writing materials (parchment and paper); the structure of quires; means of preserving the order of quires, sheets, and leaves; ruling and pricking techniques; and devices employed to produce straight left-hand margins. There is a separate chapter on the adoption of local codicological practices by immigrant scribes. Although Beit-Arié has stressed on a number of occasions that the book is out of date, based as it is on only limited data, the volume can still serve as an excellent introduction to the field of medieval Hebrew codicology for the novice, and it is an indispensable handbook for the specialist.

BEIT-ARIÉ (1993b) collects numerous important articles by the author on Hebrew manuscripts of the Middle Ages. The volume, which also contains addenda and corrigenda to the articles, is subdivided into four sections: part one discusses methodology, offering information about identifying and cataloging manuscripts that will greatly interest specialists in the field. The second section, titled "Medieval Scribes: Personal Manifestations and Common Practices," contains a detailed study of the itinerant 15th-century scribe Joel ben Simeon Fayvesh Ashkenazi and a very illuminating essay titled "Stereotype and Individuality in the Handwriting of Medieval Scribes." In this article, Beit-Arié points out that paleographical identification on the sole basis of the shape of the Hebrew letters is seriously hampered by the medieval scribes' aspiration to copy the hand of their masters (the ideal of stereotype). At the same time, however, other so-called parascriptural elements, such as the shape of the grapheme used for the Divine Name, the ligature of the letters *alef* and *lamed*, and the shape of so-called graphic fillers (signs commonly written against the left-hand margin and used to fill the line that would otherwise be left empty) offer ample opportunity to identify scribal individuality. Part three consists of codicological descriptions and paleographic analyses of five important medieval Hebrew manuscripts, most of which have appeared in facsimile reproductions. They are the Damascus Pentateuch, the Valmadonna Pentateuch, the Worms Mahzor, the Rothschild Miscellany, and the Washington Haggadah. The final section, titled "The Beginning of Printing and Scribal Tradition," contains only one article, which deals with the relationship between early Hebrew printing and handwritten books, an area of incunable research that has moved more to the center of scholarly attention since Beit-Arié first published his findings in the original Hebrew version of this article in 1975. (The English translation in this collection has been revised.)

Beit-Arié's impressive work in Hebrew manuscript research includes comparative studies that situate those manuscripts in the context of surrounding book cultures. BEIT-ARIÉ (1993a), comprising his Panizzi Lectures at the British Library, is devoted entirely to exploring the significance of such comparisons. The volume's three chapters deal with "Medieval Hebrew Manuscripts as Cross-Cultural Agents"; "The Art of Writing and the Craft of Bookmaking"; and "Scribal Re-Making: Transmitting and Shaping Texts." The first two chapters are important updates and re-statements of Beit-Arié's favorite research themes: the idiosyncrasies of medieval Hebrew manuscripts and their correspondences with other book cultures; the need for a statistical approach when localizing and dating Hebrew manuscripts; and the process of redefining the different types and modes of medieval Hebrew scripts. The third chapter brings to the fore the internal development in Beit-Arié's oeuvre. It discusses the effect that the dynamics of handwriting had on the transmission of medieval text in general and medieval Hebrew texts in particular. The author posits that "the fundamental difference between Hebrew and Latin, Greek and to some extent Arabic book production" can be traced to "two cardinal factors of medieval Jewish life in the East and West—general literacy and the lack of political organization," and he discusses the demand for Hebrew manuscripts, the varying degrees of professionalism found among Hebrew scribes, and the process of copying manuscripts, which introduced both intentional and unintentional changes in the texts. He concludes that "What medieval Hebrew copyists did while copying was indeed to deconstruct the text and then reconstruct it." This third chapter provides a particularly powerful example of Beit-Arié's work.

EMILE G.L. SCHRIJVER

See also Masorah; Scribes

Secularism

Birnbaum, Pierre and Ira Katznelson (editors), *Paths of Emancipation: Jews, States, and Citizenship*, Princeton, New Jersey: Princeton University Press, 1995

Cohen, Steven, *American Modernity and Jewish Identity*, New York: Tavistock, 1983

Eisen, Arnold, *Rethinking Modern Judaism: Ritual, Commandment, Community* (Chicago Studies in the History of Judaism), Chicago: University of Chicago Press, 1998

Endelman, Todd, *Radical Assimilation in English Jewish History, 1656–1945* (Modern Jewish Experience), Bloomington: Indiana University Press, 1990

Goldscheider, Calvin, *Jewish Continuity and Change: Emerging Patterns in America* (Jewish Political and Social Studies), Bloomington: Indiana University Press, 1986

Goldstein, Joseph, *Jewish History in Modern Times*, Brighton, East Sussex: Sussex Academic Press, 1995

Goodman, Saul (editor), *The Faith of Secular Jews* (Library of Judaic Learning), New York: Ktav, 1976

Katz, Jacob, *Out of the Ghetto: The Social Background of Jewish Emancipation, 1770–1870*, Cambridge, Massachusetts: Harvard University Press, 1973

Sharot, Stephen, *Judaism: A Sociology*, Newton Abbot, Devon: David and Charles, and New York: Holmes and Meier, 1976

Secularization refers to the process by which the cultural values of societies become increasingly oriented toward the material while emphasis on the spiritual declines. Secularism is often regarded as a hallmark of modern societies, accompanying the spread of science, the political changes of the French Revolution, and its theoretical precursor, the Enlightenment.

For European Jews, the Haskalah brought in its wake various forms of secularism.

The doyen of late 20th-century Israeli historians, KATZ, has traced the journey of some European Jews from the fringes of European society to its mainstream, describing with insight and detachment the upheaval and disintegration of much of traditional Jewish society and the concurrent transformations in religious belief and practice during the century from 1770 to 1870. Katz documents changes in communities, education, and occupations; traces the decline of traditional religious forms and the birth of Reform Judaism; and examines the reactions of non-Jews to Jewish emancipation.

In a work that is too brief to do full justice to the author's ambitious aims, SHAROT attempts to develop a sociology of modern Judaism. Using a chronological framework, he briefly, but competently, surveys Judaism across a wide range of times and places. He deals with the subjects of secularism and secularization throughout the book, devoting the final chapter in particular to these topics.

In his remarkably lucid exposition of modern Jewish history, GOLDSTEIN identifies five trends and developments—what he terms "historical processes"—that characterized the 19th and 20th centuries: migration, emancipation, cultural revolution, antisemitism, and Zionism and the State of Israel. Goldstein sees the impact of secularism on the Jews as nothing less than a revolution in their culture, the origins of which he traces to the Enlightenment.

ENDELMAN's book on the assimilation of Jews in England represents an important historical case study of Jews in a single nation and their "careers" out of Judaism. Such studies of the experience of individual societies are instructive, for the experience of Jewish life in one society is frequently quite different from that in others. England was a nation in which the forces of secularism were at work from early in the modern period, given great impetus by, for example, Henry VIII's secularization of church lands through the Act of Dissolution of 1536. English Jews were affected by the secularist trajectory of the society around them, and, as Endelman notes, they were the first Jewish community in history whose circumstances dictated that its identity was established on a purely voluntary basis.

BIRNBAUM and KATZNELSON's anthology analyzes the distinctive histories of different Jewish societies. The wide-ranging collection of studies examines the experience of Jewish emancipation in Europe (including Russia and Turkey) and the United States. The primary focus is on the impact of liberal, republican, and Enlightenment ideas on the development of nation-states and notions of citizenship, and the consequences of these innovations for the Jews in each nation. The essays demonstrate that Jewish experiences not only varied from nation to nation, they also varied among different communities and classes within individual nations.

Both Cohen and Goldscheider base their studies of contemporary U.S. Jewry on the important statistical studies of Boston Jews undertaken by the Combined Jewish Philanthropies of Greater Boston in 1975. COHEN's brief study tackles the evolving sense of identity of late 20th-century U.S. Jews, most of whom were several generations removed from direct contact with the immigrant experience and integrated thoroughly into mainstream U.S. society. GOLDSCHEIDER,

an expert demographer, meticulously details the socioeconomic profile of contemporary U.S. Jews. As economic and social status increased, traditional religious observance declined, and expressions of religion became more secular, but both studies contend that the United States' complex and often unconventional Jewish population has a secularized but still strong sense of Jewish identity.

GOODMAN's collection of essays on the paradoxical topic of the faith of secular Jews is diverse and challenging. The anthology is framed by the question, what does it mean to be both a Jew, maintaining a distinctive and separate identity, and a member of secular society, accepting claims of universal rationality and the uniform character of human nature? In the 19 selections, which date from the late 19th and 20th centuries, the secular Jew appears as a product of the modern world, whose identity is thoroughly at odds with the Jewish tradition of the premodern world. Many strands of Jewish thought and secularist impulse are represented in these writings, and as a result, no singular, definitive vision of the interplay between secularization and Judaism emerges.

EISEN's analysis of contemporary Judaism and his critical review of important modern and postmodern thought are impressive. The study is an erudite and objective anthropological account of Judaism, exploring patterns of religious observance and secularization with greater depth than most studies of its type.

ROBERT ASH

Semikhah *see* Sanhedrin, Semikhah, and Rabbinate

Sephardim

Angel, Marc D., *Voices in Exile: A Study in Sephardic Intellectual History* (Library of Sephardic History and Thought), Hoboken, New Jersey: Ktav, 1991

Ashtor, Eliyahu, *Korot ha-Yehudim bi-Sefarad ha-Muslemit*, 1960; as *The Jews of Moslem Spain*, 3 vols., Philadelphia: Jewish Publication Society, 1973

Baer, Yitzhak, *Toldot ha-Yehudim bi-Sefarad ha-Notsrit*, 1959; as *A History of the Jews in Christian Spain*, 2 vols., Philadelphia: Jewish Publication Society, 1961

Brann, Ross, *The Compunctious Poet: Cultural Ambiguity and Hebrew Poetry in Muslim Spain* (Johns Hopkins Jewish Studies), Baltimore, Maryland: Johns Hopkins University Press, 1991

Dobrinsky, Herbert C., *A Treasury of Sephardic Laws and Customs: The Ritual Practices of Syrian, Moroccan, Judeo-Spanish and Spanish and Portuguese Jews of North America*, New York: Yeshiva University Press, 1986, revised edition, 1988

Elazar, Daniel J., *The Other Jews: The Sephardim Today*, New York: Basic Books, 1989

Gerber, Jane, *The Jews of Spain: A History of the Sephardic Experience,* New York: Free Press, 1992

Goodblatt, Morris, *Jewish Life in Turkey in the Sixteenth Century, as Reflected in the Legal Writings of Samuel de Medina,* New York: Jewish Theological Seminary, 1952

Kaplan, Yosef, *Mi-Natsrut le-yahadut: hayav u-pe'ulav shel ha-anus Yitshak Orobiyo de Kastro,* 1982; as *From Christianity to Judaism: The Story of Isaac Orobio de Castro* (Littman Library of Jewish Civilization), Oxford and New York: Oxford University Press, 1989

Netanyahu, B., *The Marranos of Spain: From the Late 14th to the Early 16th Century, According to Contemporary Hebrew Sources,* New York: American Academy for Jewish Research, 1966; 3rd edition: Ithaca, New York: Cornell University Press, 1999

Samuel ha-Nagid, *Jewish Prince in Moslem Spain: Selected Poems of Samuel Ibn Nagrela* (Judaic Studies, 3), translated by Leon Weinberger, University: University of Alabama Press, 1973

Scheindlin, Raymond, *Wine, Women, and Death: Medieval Hebrew Poems on the Good Life,* Philadelphia: Jewish Publication Society, 1986

Scheindlin, Raymond, *The Gazelle: Medieval Hebrew Poems on God, Israel, and the Soul,* Philadelphia: Jewish Publication Society, 1991

Yerushalmi, Yosef, *From Spanish Court to Italian Ghetto: Isaac Cardoso, a Study in Seventeenth-Century Marranism and Jewish Apologetics* (Columbia University Studies in Jewish History, Culture, and Institutions), New York: Columbia University Press, 1971

Zimmels, H.J., *Ashkenazim and Sephardim: Their Relations, Differences, and Problems as Reflected in Rabbinical Responsa* (Jews' College Publications, new series, no. 2), London: Oxford University Press, 1958; revised edition, Hoboken, New Jersey: Ktav, 1996

Sephardim (from *Sepharad,* the biblical place-name that came to be associated with Spain in the Middle Ages) form one of the two major divisions of the Jewish people. Spanish Jews liked to view themselves as descendants of the Jerusalem elite of priests and aristocrats exiled by King Nebuchadnezzar in 586 B.C.E. During their long residence in Iberia, the Jews experienced periods of intense persecution as well as eras of creativity and tranquility. Living primarily under Islamic rule from 711 to 1147, Iberian Jews explored new areas of knowledge in science, philosophy, and above all, Hebrew poetry and linguistics. Drawing inspiration from Muslim poets and courtiers, Jews forged a sophisticated and urbane civilization in the Umayyad court of Cordoba (especially in the tenth-century reign of Abd-el-Rahman III) and the subsequent petty Berber kingdoms. Sephardi identity is intimately connected with this period of cultural efflorescence. By the mid-13th century, the majority of the Sephardim lived under Christian rule, where they suffered a steady decline, ultimately ending in forced conversion and expulsion.

GERBER provides a handy single-volume synthesis of the Sephardi experience from antiquity to the present time. Her textbook chronicles the life of Sephardi Jewry and the development of Sephardi civilization prior to 1492 and in the post–1492 Sephardi dispersion. It also analyzes the intimate connections between Sephardi and Middle Eastern Jews.

The classic study of Islamic Spain is the three-volume work by ASHTOR, whose extensive use of Arabic documents enlivens his occasionally fanciful account. His book ends with the Christian reconquest of Toledo in 1085, although Jewish life in Islamic Spain continued to flourish under the stability maintained by the Almoravides until the middle of the 12th century. The 1992 reprint of Ashtor's dated but still essential work features a critical introduction by David Wasserstein.

Islamic Spain is best remembered in Jewish history for the remarkable Hebrew secular and religious poetry that it fostered. The best anthology of texts and translations from the secular repertoire of the Sephardim is SCHEINDLIN (1986), while the liturgical poetry produced during the Golden Age is treated in SCHEINDLIN (1991). The judiciously selected and elegantly translated poems in these two volumes are supplemented with helpful commentaries that offer the reader a window into the cultural world of the Andalusian courtier class.

A critical analysis of some of the tensions that the courtier class of Jewish poets and leaders experienced is provided by BRANN. He examines the ambivalent attitudes of Spanish Jewish poets toward their secular poetry, interpreting the common typology of "the compunctious poet" as "an emblem of the conflicts inherent in Andalusian Jewish culture and society."

SAMUEL HA-NAGID is an English translation of a wide range of the poetry written by the courtier-poet-statesman Samuel ibn Nagrela. In an introductory chapter, the translator, Leon Weinberger, describes the Andalusian world of ibn Nagrela for the reader, paying special attention to developments in Hebrew poetry that were a product of that culture.

The Christian reconquest of Spain began with the capture of Toledo in 1085 and concluded with the fall of Granada in 1492. During the centuries of reconquest, Jews experienced major changes, and BAER is unrivalled as the classic survey of evolving Jewish life in Christian Spain.

By the 13th century, developments in the Catholic Church, especially the growing influence of the mendicant orders, began to have a deleterious effect upon the well-being of Iberian Jews. After the disputation of Barcelona in 1263, Christian missions among the Jews led to a steady erosion of Jewish self-confidence. The crises of the 14th century, particularly the devastation wrought by the Black Death and the perception that the Jews had caused the plague by poisoning wells, led to a drastic decline in the status of Spanish Jews. That decline accelerated in the aftermath of the great pogroms of 1391. In the course of the year-long violence, Jews were offered the choice of conversion or death. Many chose conversion, and one of the most controversial issues in Sephardi historiography is the question of the residual Jewish identity of the forced converts, known as conversos. The classic study of the conversos is NETANYAHU. Netanyahu makes a powerful case that crypto-Judaism had actually died out among the conversos within a single generation. Subsequent charges of Judaizing behavior, Netanyahu argues, were fabricated in order to destroy the converso class in Spanish society.

The "problem" of the conversos and their alleged Judaizing activities ultimately led to the establishment of a national Inquisition in 15th-century Spain and the cataclysmic expulsion of the Jews in 1492. Following their departure, Sephardi refugees scattered throughout the Mediterranean and the New World, flocking to the expanding Ottoman Empire by the thousands. Smaller numbers of refugees found asylum in North Africa and Italy, establishing Sephardi communities among the indigenous Jewish populations. The 16th century witnessed a renaissance of Jewish life in many of the centers of Islamic civilization in North Africa and the Near East. Everywhere that the Sephardim settled, they introduced a great deal of ferment. Their distinctive customs and great pride were frequent sources of dissension.

In the 16th and 17th centuries, many New Christians sought to return to Judaism after the trauma of conversion in Spain and Portugal. The fascinating life of one such seeker, Isaac Cardoso, is reconstructed in YERUSHALMI. By tracing Cardoso's career and transformation of consciousness, Yerushalmi makes an eloquent attempt to refute the contention of Netanyahu that the conversos of Spain were thoroughly Christian by the middle of the 15th century.

GOODBLATT is a good introduction to Sephardi life in 16th-century Turkey. His account, which is based on the legal writings of the Salonican rabbi Samuel de Medina (1506–1589) and two of his colleagues, is a fine example of the effective use to which responsa literature can be put in writing social and economic history. From this material, Goodblatt successfully teases out information on the economic, political, and religious life of Turkish Jewry. As an appendix the author offers translations of 18 illustrative responsa.

For discussions of the Sephardi diaspora in the Netherlands and the intellectual climate among the Portuguese Jews in 17th-century Amsterdam, see KAPLAN. His book focuses on the life of a Portuguese converso who, in 1662, in the middle of his career as a physician, came to Amsterdam and returned to Judaism. Isaac Orobio de Castro's dramatic change of identity was part of a general trend throughout the 17th century that witnessed the migration of Spanish and Portuguese New Christians to the religiously tolerant atmosphere of the Netherlands. Kaplan examines the forces that motivated Orobio and others like him to make the move back to Judaism and evaluates the unique sense of Jewish heritage that was forged by these Jews in the process of reconciling their dual identities.

ANGEL offers a general introduction to the neglected field of the intellectual history of the Sephardi diaspora. In a series of studies, the author surveys various aspects of the creativity of Sephardim since the expulsion of 1492. Among the themes he examines are the spiritual and theological reactions of Sephardim to the expulsion, the decline of rationalism and the rise of mysticism, and various attempts by Sephardi leaders to accommodate to modernity.

An overview of contemporary Sephardi communities and a personal analysis of differences between Ashkenazim and Sephardim can be found in ELAZAR.

ZIMMELS's erudite and elegant study illuminates numerous major and minor differences between Ashkenazi and Sephardi

practice. The author begins by identifying seven historical periods in the relationship between the legal traditions of Ashkenazim and Sephardim, distinguishing these periods according to the direction of influence from one group to the other. The second part of the book examines specific areas in which Ashkenazi and Sephardi practice diverge, while the third part offers translations of six rabbinic responsa that directly address matters related to these differences.

DOBRINKSY presents a manual on the differences in ritual practice among various Sephardi traditions, represented by the Moroccan, Syrian, Judeo-Spanish (i.e., Balkan), and Spanish and Portuguese Jewish communities in contemporary North America. He examines the customs of these four communities in three spheres: matters concerning life-cycle events and family life, daily worship, and sabbath and holiday observance.

JANE GERBER
AND ARNOLD FRANKLIN

Sex

Biale, David, *Eros and the Jews: From Biblical Israel to Contemporary America,* New York: Basic Books, 1992; Berkeley: University of California Press, 1997

Boyarin, Daniel, *Carnal Israel: Reading Sex in Talmudic Culture* (The New Historicism, 25), Berkeley: University of California Press, 1993

Brenner, Athalya, *The Intercourse of Knowledge: On Gendering Desire and "Sexuality" in the Hebrew Bible* (Biblical Interpretation Series, vol. 26), New York: Brill, 1997

Cohen, Jeremy, *"Be Fertile and Increase, Fill the Earth and Master It": The Ancient and Medieval Career of a Biblical Text,* Ithaca, New York: Cornell University Press, 1989

Eilberg-Schwartz, Howard (editor), *People of the Body: Jews and Judaism from an Embodied Perspective,* Albany: State University of New York Press, 1992

Epstein, Louis M., *Sex Laws and Customs in Judaism,* New York: Bloch, 1948

Feldman, David M., *Birth Control in Jewish Law: Marital Relations, Contraception, and Abortion as Set Forth in the Classic Texts of Jewish Law,* New York: New York University Press, 1968; as *Marital Relations, Birth Control, and Abortion in Jewish Law,* New York: Schocken, 1974

Satlow, Michael L., *Tasting the Dish: Rabbinic Rhetorics of Sexuality,* Atlanta, Georgia: Scholars Press, 1995

The concept of sexuality emerged in Europe around the beginning of the 20th century as a means of identification as well as an object of intense discussion and scrutiny. In this era, some sexual behaviors—and the individuals who practiced them—were deemed "deficient" or "unhealthy," while other behaviors and persons were sanctioned. Many European scholars, including a number of Jews, created the concept of "Jewish sexuality," which described certain "Jewish" sexual practices that were categorized among the unhealthy types of sexuality. Not surprisingly, many Jewish scholars fought this categorization by producing a voluminous body of apologetic literature, which argues that rabbinic legislation (halakhah) on sexuality actually reflects the high moral character of "Jewish sexuality."

Most of this apologetic literature is only available in German, but its flavor can be sampled in EPSTEIN. Written for both a scholarly and general audience, this work is among the first texts in English to present a history of rabbinic legislation on sexuality. Epstein's topics are somewhat eclectic, and his tone can at times be annoyingly apologetic (as it responds to polemics with which most readers will not be familiar), but the book remains useful for its summary of the historical development of many halakhic issues dealing with sexuality.

Although FELDMAN's history of halakhah similarly has an apologetic tone, his work is more sophisticated than Epstein's. Feldman emphasizes the development of one particular aspect of rabbinic legislation, that related to birth control and non-procreative sex, but this topic is so broad that he ultimately discusses much of the halakhah on sexuality. The book focuses on finding the "correct" halakhic solutions to problems, rather than explaining the historical reasons why the halakhah developed as it did. The last chapter analyzes some of the issues raised by advances in bioresearch, but treatment of these issues is still rather superficial, even though an appendix has been added to the second edition.

COHEN also engages in a historical survey, but his concern is the history of the exegesis of Genesis 1:28—God's command to the first humans. Examining interpretations of this text from the ancient and medieval periods, Cohen demonstrates that both Jews and Christians saw in Genesis 1:28 the divine blessing for human procreation. Although these two communities used different idioms to express the nature of that blessing and its relationship to the divine covenant, both faiths were also confronting the human dilemma of standing between the beasts and the angels (to use a rabbinic phrase).

The remaining books employ a different approach than the texts reviewed above. Rather than analyzing halakhah or exegesis from the classical period to the present, they attempt to explain how Jews within particular historical and cultural contexts constructed, or understood, their sexuality. The earliest fruits of this approach are Biale and Eilberg-Schwartz. BIALE presents "snapshots" of Jewish approaches to sexuality from the Bible to *Portnoy's Complaint*. He emphasizes the profound ambivalence that many Jewish communities have shown toward sexuality. His chapters on Hasidism and Zionism are particularly enlightening. EILBERG-SCHWARTZ's superb collection of essays displays a similar range, touching on aspects of Jewish views of the body and sexuality from the Bible to modernity. Gary Anderson's essay, for example, studies early Jewish answers to the question of whether Adam and Eve had sex in the Garden of Eden, and in the process he explores how their answers relate to much wider theological concerns.

BOYARIN stresses the extent to which classical rabbinic culture insisted on an embodied perspective of human nature that consciously rejected the Hellenistic body/soul dualistic anthropology. Boyarin explores, among other topics, the transmission of sexual knowledge among the rabbis; the "sexualization" of Torah study; and the role of women in rabbinic society. Most chapters provide close extended readings of particular talmudic stories. Like Biale, Boyarin is sensitive to points of disjuncture where the rabbis express ambivalence about sexuality. Boyarin correctly links rabbinic understandings of sexuality to their stances on gender, and he concludes that, as misogynistic as the rabbis sometimes appear to have been, they never elevated misogyny to a core value.

SATLOW also concentrates on the rabbinic period. His book analyzes the rhetoric that the rabbis used to convince people to follow sanctioned sexual mores in such areas as incest, non-procreative sex, homoeroticism, and marriage. He concludes that Palestinian and Babylonian rabbis had radically divergent understandings of sexuality, as each group's views had more in common with their ambient cultures than with each other.

BRENNER interprets some of the ways in which the Hebrew Bible constitutes gender and sexuality. More precisely, these provocative essays ask how the Hebrew Bible "genders" sexual desire and behaviors. The Hebrew Bible, Brenner argues, does not have a category equivalent to the modern notion of sexuality. "Sexuality in the ancient world is subsumed under other, more important social requirements such as survival, procreation, internal and external boundaries," writes Brenner, and in these "more important" matters, men are understood as the primary actors and initiators.

Brenner maintains that sexuality is not a discrete cultural construct that can simply be divorced from other societal issues. Jewish understandings of sexuality throughout the ages have been related to material conditions, power, and issues of gender and identity. If one conclusion emerges clearly from all of the works reviewed here, it is that there is not (and never was) a single "Jewish" view of sexuality.

MICHAEL L. SATLOW

Shabbetai Tsevi 1626–1676

Izmir-born messianic pretender and catalyst of the antinomian Sabbatian movement

Carlebach, Elisheva, *The Pursuit of Heresy: Rabbi Moses Hagiz and the Sabbatian Controversies,* New York: Columbia University Press, 1990

Idel, Moshe, " 'One from a Town, Two from a Clan': The Diffusion of Lurianic Kabbala and Sabbateanism: A Re-Examination," *Jewish History,* 7, 1993

Liebes, Yehuda, *Studies in Jewish Myth and Jewish Messianism,* Albany: State University of New York Press, 1993

Scholem, Gershom Gerhard, *Major Trends in Jewish Mysticism,* New York: Schocken, 1941; 3rd revised edition, 1954

Scholem, Gershom Gerhard, *Shabbatai Sevi veha-tenu'ah ha-shabbeta'it bi-yemei hayyav,* 1957; revised and augmented as *Sabbatai Sevi: The Mystical Messiah* (Bollingen Series, 93), Princeton, New Jersey: Princeton University Press and London: Routledge and Kegan Paul, 1973

Scholem, Gershom Gerhard, *The Messianic Idea in Judaism and Other Essays on Jewish Spirituality,* New York: Schocken, and London: Allen and Unwin, 1971

Shabbetai Tsevi was the central figure of "Sabbatianism," the most important messianic movement of the diaspora phase of Jewish history. In 1648 he proclaimed himself Messiah, and he attracted great numbers of followers across Europe, North Africa, and the Middle East before his imprisonment in Istanbul in 1666 and conversion to Islam. The most comprehensive studies on this subject, those of Gerhard Scholem, together describe every aspect of the Sabbatian movement and provide a profound analysis of its ideological and theological background. Other scholars' works have been more specific, probing particular aspects of this movement.

SCHOLEM (1957) is without doubt the most important and complete work on the subject. He explains, first of all, in great depth, the historical, sociological, and cultural background both of the Sabbatian movement and of the conception of messianism in rabbinic Judaism and Kabbalah. The book examines both the personal history of Shabbetai Tsevi, his sickness and his mystical manifestations, and also the development of the Sabbatian movement and its influence on the Jewish world until the time of Shabbetai's death. Scholem's intention was to continue the study of the movement after this point, but he did not succeed. This monumental tome is based on a vast array of documents otherwise unpublished.

SCHOLEM (1941) surveys the different movements in Jewish mysticism in each of the various periods of the past 2,000 years. The first chapter addresses the general characteristics of Jewish mysticism, and it is therefore a good introduction to Sabbatianism. Subsequent chapters, although not describing the movement, also present necessary background to the topic. The seventh chapter, "Sabbatianism and Mystical Heresy," describes the development of the movement and analyzes Sabbatian ideology and its connections with the Kabbalah.

SCHOLEM (1971) is the perfect introduction to this theme. This book deals with many aspects of the concept of messianism in Judaism, including the conflict between Jewish and Christian messianism, the idea of redemption through sin, and the messianic idea in Kabbalah. A great part of the book is dedicated to the Sabbatian conception of Messiah, before and after Shabbetai's conversion to Islam, and to the legacy of his life in the various religious trends that perpetuated Sabbatian innovations. Scholem analyzes the development of the idea of messianism in Jewish sources and gives the reader a vivid understanding of this element in Jewish culture.

CARLEBACH studies in particular the development of Sabbatian heresy after Shabbetai's death. She describes the messianic atmosphere in Jerusalem in the 17th century, which influenced Moses Hagiz, one of the seminal figures in the post-Sabbatian controversies. Shabbetai's heresies produced a great many ideological rifts among Jewish communities around the world, and this book describes those consequences of the Sabbatian movement in diverse places. It analyzes the many books published in this period in connection with these controversies, as well as the various rabbinical figures who took part in these disputes. It is, thus, in a real sense, a continuation of Scholem's work.

LIEBES's book on the development of Jewish myth has two chapters that deal with Sabbatian Kabbalah and its messianic and theoretical foundations. In the first chapter Liebes analyzes the roots of Jewish messianism as well as the mystical conceptions of the main figures of this movement: Shabbetai himself, Nathan of Gaza, and Miguel Cardozo. In the second chapter, Liebes studies various theological issues in Sabbatianism and problems concerning the religious faith of Shabbetai himself, such as his apostasy, which was interpreted as a form of punishment for Israel.

IDEL's article examines some theses adduced by Scholem relating to the linkage between Sabbatianism and Lurianic Kabbalah. Scholem thought that Lurianic teaching was widely diffused in the generation before the appearance of Shabbetai, and thus its doctrine influenced the Sabbatian movement. Idel examines the spread of Lurianic mysticism in the 17th century and concludes that Scholem overemphasized its role. Therefore, this work is, on one hand, a revision of Scholem's explication of Shabbetai's movement, and, on the other hand, an independent study of the history of the influence of the Kabbalah on the Jewish world.

Yaakov A. Lattes

Shavuot *see* Festivals and Fasts

Shoah *see* Holocaust

Sholem Aleichem 1859–1916
Ukranian-born Russian Yiddish author and humorist

Frieden, Ken, *Classic Yiddish Fiction: Abramovitsh, Sholem Aleichem, and Peretz* (SUNY Series in Modern Jewish Literature and Culture), Albany, New York: State University of New York Press, 1995

Miron, Dan, "Shalom Aleichem," in *Encyclopaedia Judaica*, Jerusalem: Keter, 1971

Miron, Dan, *Sholem Aleykhem: Person, Persona, Presence* (Uriel Weinreich Memorial Lecture, 1), New York: Yivo Institute for Jewish Research, 1972

Ozick, Cynthia, "Sholem Aleichem's Revolution," *New Yorker*, 64, 28 March 1988

Roskies, David (editor), "Sholem Aleichem: The Critical Tradition," *Prooftexts* special issue, 6(3), 1986

Along with Mendele Moykher Sforim and Isaac Leib Peretz, Sholem Aleichem is one of the three so-called "classic" writers of modern Yiddish literature. Sholem Aleichem began his writing career in Hebrew, as did many Eastern European Yiddish writers of the 19th century. *Two Stones*, his first Yiddish work, was published in 1883 under his given name, Sholem Rabinovitch. Later that year he adopted the salutation "Sholem Aleichem" ("peace upon you") as a nom de plume, using it for the first time in the feuilleton "The Elections." Sholem Aleichem went on to write poetry, journalism, novels, plays, short stories, and monologues. It is in these last two genres that the writer exhibited his greatest talents. His major works include *Tevye the Dairyman, Menakhem Mendl, Motl the Cantor's Son*, and *From the Fair*.

Using parody as the starting point for his introduction to modern Yiddish literature, FRIEDEN devotes the largest section of his book to a study of Sholem Aleichem and his place in the modern Yiddish canon. He builds upon the work of previous critics of Yiddish literature, such as Shmuel Niger, Y.Y. Trunk, and Dan Miron, and applies to Yiddish writings the ideas of literary theorists such as M.M. Bakhtin and Wayne Booth. Frieden's solid introduction is strengthened by a thorough bibliography of both primary and secondary sources for Sholem Aleichem in several languages as well as a comprehensive chronology of events in the life of the author. This is a valuable complement to Frieden's insightful readings of the primary sources and of the extensive body of criticism on Sholem Aleichem in English, Hebrew, and Yiddish. Frieden also examines the interesting personal and professional relationships between the three authors of classic Yiddish fiction.

ROSKIES has edited an issue of the journal *Prooftexts* devoted to the critical tradition on Sholem Aleichem's work. These essays, most of them translated from the Yiddish, were (with the exception of the essay by Michael Stern) originally intended for a book collecting and comparing criticism of Sholem Aleichem written through the course of the 20th century. The issue features such classic studies of Sholem Aleichem as the 1908 article by the Yiddishist critic Bal Makhshoves, regarded as having launched the field of literary criticism of Sholem Aleichem. This volume also includes works by two of the most talented Soviet Yiddish critics of the interwar period, Meyer Viner and Max Erik, as well as a more recent article by Roskies himself, who takes a new and fresh approach to Sholem Aleichem's semi-autobiographical novel *From the Fair*.

MIRON (1972a) is composed of two sections. The first part of the article, titled "Life and Works," provides a succinct yet comprehensive account of Sholem Aleichem's biography. In the second section, "Development of His Works," Miron divides the author's writing into four chronological periods. During the first period, 1883–1890, Sholem Aleichem began his Yiddish literary career in two main genres, the novel and feuilleton; it was in the latter genre, Miron argues, that the young Sholem Aleichem excelled and created works of significant and lasting influence. In the second period, 1892–1898, Miron writes that Sholem Aleichem "began to consolidate his position as the most important comic author in Jewish literature." This was the period in which the author wrote the first installments of his great works *Tevye the Dairyman* and *Menakhem Mendl*. According to Miron, the third period, 1899–1905, brought about the refinement of the central genres in the oeuvre of Sholem Aleichem, the monologues, the "fantastic" tales, the stories for Jewish holidays, the children's stories, and the stories of his archetypal shtetl, Kasrilevke. The fourth and last period, 1906–1916, was spent writing novels, a return to an earlier, neglected genre, as well as the continued development of major works such as *Tevye* and *Menakhem Mendl,* and the beginning of new and large projects that would remain unfinished at the time of the author's death, such as *Motl the Cantor's Son* and the semiautobiographical *From the Fair*.

MIRON (1972b) is a pivotal study explaining not only the significance of the author's chosen name but also its effect and influence on popular readings of his work. Miron shows how this was not merely a pen name but rather a presence that transcended historical boundaries and enabled Sholem Rabinovitch to create through his creation, Sholem Aleichem. Miron demonstrates how this invented presence almost swallowed the historical man, so that eventually the author signed his own last will and testament with both his given name and the name by which he had come to be known.

OZICK's well-crafted and jargon-free article shows how Sholem Aleichem almost single-handedly transformed the status of Yiddish from a medieval language, seen as inferior by Jews as much as gentiles, into a modern language capable of sustaining and nurturing a literature comparable to the modern literatures of Europe. The second half of this essay is a glowing review of the first volume to appear in Schocken's Library of Yiddish Classics, an English translation of Sholem Aleichem's *Tevye the Dairyman* and *Railroad Stories*. The article also contains Ozick's own interesting and erudite interpretation of these works.

MARC MILLER

Shtetl

Beller, Ilex, *La Vie du Shtetl: La Bourgade juive de Pologne en 80 tableaux*, 1986; translated by Alastair Douglas Pannell as *Life in the Shtetl: Scenes and Recollections*, New York: Holmes and Meier, 1986

Cohen, Chester G., *Shtetl Finder: Jewish Communities in the 19th and 20th Centuries in the Pale of Settlement of Russian and Poland, and in Lithuania, Latvia, Galicia, and Bukovina, and with the Names of Residents*, Los Angeles: Periday, 1980

Hoffman, Eva, *Shtetl: The Life and Death of a Small Town and the World of Polish Jews,* Boston: Houghton Mifflin, 1997; London: Secker and Warburg, 1998

Neugroschel, Joachim (editor and translator), *The Shtetl*, New York: Marek, 1979

Pinchuk, Ben-Cion, *Shtetl Jews under Soviet Rule: Eastern Poland on the Eve of the Holocaust* (Jewish Society and Culture), Oxford and Cambridge, Massachusetts: Blackwell, 1991

Roskies, Diane K. and David G. Roskies, *The Shtetl Book*, New York: Ktav, 1975, 2nd revised edition, 1979

Schoenfeld, Joachim, *Shtetl Memoirs: Jewish Life in Galicia under the Austro-Hungarian Empire and in the Reborn Poland, 1898–1939,* Hoboken, New Jersey: Ktav, 1985

Sternberg, Ghitta, *Stefanesti: Portrait of a Romanian Shtetl*, Oxford and New York: Pergamon, 1984

Zborowski, Mark and Elizabeth Herzog, *Life Is with People: The Culture of the Shtetl*, New York: Schocken, 1962

The Yiddish term *shtetl* (pl. *shtetlekh*) is a diminutive of the word "Stadt" (German for "city") and describes a small and mainly Jewish town, frequently of less than 10,000 inhabitants. The very mention of the word shtetl evokes deep emotion and memories for those who grew up in such villages.

Each shtetl had its own unique history, culture, values, and traditions, and so commanded considerable loyalty from its inhabitants and former inhabitants. Even language could vary from one shtetl to the next. Shtetlekh were located for the most part in Eastern Europe—Russia, Ukraine, Poland, Slovakia, Romania—and no two were quite alike. Herein lies the difficulty in describing a "typical" shtetl, for no such entity existed. Nevertheless, most shtetlekh did consist of ramshackle houses lined up along very narrow dirt, or sometimes cobbled, streets. There was a central marketplace that was the hub of trade and social activity. A world of its own, the inhabitants were forced to lead lives separate from an outside world that frequently took out its frustrations on the defenseless shtetl dwellers. That outside world was changing and the shtetl was in constant fear of being invaded and destroyed by (among others) those who could not accept people who refused to change with the times. The government became more hostile after the assassination of Czar Alexander II on 7 March 1881. Along with great political unrest came a dramatic increase in pogroms against Jews. The remaining shtetlekh were eradicated under Nazi occupation. Most of the villagers met their end in concentration camps or migrated to distant lands. What remains of the shtetl, then, is a culture that lives in a literature of vivid characters and lively wit. It is the literature of and about the shtetl that nourishes the spirit of Yiddishkeit in a world that has changed drastically since World War II.

BELLER's collection of images reflects the memories of his own shtetl, which he left when he was 14 years old. His paintings serve as a chronicle of life in the Polish community of Grodzisko. With colorful, sometimes dramatic, sometimes peaceful depictions of shtetl life, the artist recreates from memory the sweet and simple everyday activity of a vanished past. This profoundly considered documentation provides a precious glimpse of customs, costumes, and tradition. In the preface, Charles Dobzynski states, "There will always be those who shy away from the simplicity of the pictures, pointing out how naïve and crude they are, but in fact, their most important feature is that they are accurate representations." Each painting is accompanied by narrative, a caption, or a poem. Beller yearns to capture not only the visual shtetl but the emotional shtetl as well. His paintings represent births, weddings, deaths, holidays, and the demise of shtetl life. Of particular note is the artist's personal essay, "At My Grandfather's Graveside in Poland," in which he recounts his first visit to his shtetl in 54 years. The only remaining sign of Jewish life is his grandfather's gravestone, too heavy for the Nazis to remove.

COHEN's compilation provides the names of Jewish communities in Eastern Europe around the year 1900. A map is included, facilitating location of these towns. With more than 2,000 entries, the scope is fairly comprehensive. Shtetlekh that only came into existence in the 20th century, however, are not mentioned. Cohen maintains that memorial books for destroyed communities are often very vague about the date of establishment of a shtetl. His sources were 19th-century Hebrew and Yiddish newspapers and books and especially rabbinical directories. His main list of shtetlekh is arranged alphabetically, with location information and the names of prominent residents. A supplemental list is appended at the end of the work. The compilation is helpful in locating former settlements because it includes the names of existing towns nearby. It is also of value for family historians. Cohen furnishes a list of obituaries from the Hebrew newspaper *Hatsefirah*.

HOFFMAN states that her work "is a book of memory and about memory—or rather, of and about multiple layers of memory." The book is primarily about the quest for information on the vanished Jews of the Polish shtetl of Bransk. Basing her text on the views expressed in a documentary film by Marian Marzynski, Hoffman confronts many villagers still living in Bransk and encounters a wide array of townspeople, from avowed antisemites to individuals who are brought to tears as they tell the stories of their murdered neighbors and friends. Hoffman describes one independent local activist, Zbigniew Romaniuk, who is attempting to revive consciousness of the town's Jewish past and who has created a makeshift Jewish cemetery using stones from the original graveyard destroyed by the Nazis. The work traces the history of Bransk's Jews from the time of their arrival. Through the skillful use of diplomatically conducted interviews, a startling vision of the earlier village unfolds. Hoffman seeks to understand the Polish hostility toward Jews and to make sense of seemingly normal people turning suddenly against one another, to the point when, as Hoffman puts it, "I can see such a man, in such a time, slipping into the kind of darkness in which a fatal betrayal might be perpetuated, or a murder committed, quite casually, in the light of day."

NEUGROSCHEL's anthology is an attempt to show the diversity of Jewish life in Eastern Europe. The book begins with tales from medieval times and ends with the demise of the shtetl in World War II. All the stories reflect some aspect of shtetl life and are meant variously to entertain, teach, remind, chide, or poke fun. The stories open up the world of the shtetl in effectively realistic fashion. Part one contains stories that describe the religious culture. Part two deals with the Jewish Enlightenment (Haskalah) and points out the "backwardness" of shtetl life. Yisroel Aksenfeld's "The Headband" is a good example of the pessimistic treatment of the shtetl. Stories in part three concern tradition and modernization, from tales of traditional marriage to those that reflect encroachment of the new and disintegration of the old through intermarriage and conversion. The stories in part four illustrate Jewish fears of military conscription and the agony of being separated from the religious life of the shtetl, as illustrated by Fischel Bimko's "The Draft." Especially representative of the end of shtetl life is Avrom Reyzen's "Acquiring a Graveyard," in which shtetl residents plan the establishment of a town cemetery, only to have their shtetl become its own burial ground with the arrival of Russian soldiers.

PINCHUK's work chronicles the history of shtetl life in eastern Poland between September 1939 and June 1941. He analyzes the relations between Jews and the Red Army on the brink of the Soviet takeover of Eastern Europe, admitting to holes in his research due to the inaccessibility of Soviet archives and the wartime destruction (or simple nonexistence) of statistics. By way of background, Pinchuk discusses the multi-ethnic atmosphere in this area of Poland. Chapter two, titled "Shtetl Jews," provides a valuable outline of the history of small-town life in eastern Poland. Pinchuk links the depressed economic status of the Jews to their subjugation under independent Poland. He further discusses what followed the Soviet conquest: the transformation of Jewish life through assimilation to the structure of the Soviet state and through acceptance of loyalty not to the Old World but to the New Order.

ROSKIES and ROSKIES select a model shtetl called Tishevits in Lublin Province, Poland, in order to provide the reader with an in-depth description of life in such a town. As American-born scholars, the Roskies have no direct experience of the shtetl, but they are "determined not to make do with generalizations and sentimentalism." Because of the vast amount of written material concerning their chosen shtetl, the Roskies are able to give the reader a comprehensive view of Jewish life in this market town. As the work concerns itself with Yiddish-speaking Jews, a basic Yiddish vocabulary is provided, phonetically transliterated. The introductory chapter, "How the Jews Came to Poland," provides three different stories relating to the arrival of Jews in the area. The Roskies have also included several maps with detailed keys, as well as many black-and-white photographs of Jewish life in Tishevits. Their overview also includes documents, folk songs, proverbs, and many short stories, which not only add details of everyday life, but also are arranged in an attractive order that leaves the reader with a strong sense of the vivacity of shtetl life. Many other facets are covered, such as growing up as a shtetl Jew, relations with non-Jews, and dialects of Yiddish.

SCHOENFELD's work is a recollection of his own youth and a world destroyed by the Holocaust. He focuses mainly on Hapsburg Galicia, part of the Austro-Hungarian Empire. Schoenfeld provides firsthand testimony of the poor treatment of shtetl Jews by Poles and Ukrainians alike. With remarkable detail, he paints a portrait of the brutality inflicted upon Jews by townspeople and points a finger at the church for its encouragement as well. In strong contrast to Hoffman's work, which tries to comprehend the cruel behavior of villagers, Schoenfeld's account does not seek excuses for evil. His work recounts bitter confrontations with non-Jews and details the brutal acts committed against himself and his neighbors. Descriptions of occupations, superstitions, education, family life, holidays, and social occasions brighten the work considerably and at times are presented with humor.

STERNBERG has recreated the Romanian shtetl of Stefanesti through the use of personal recollection, interviews, photographs, and archival documentation. Located at the periphery of the Yiddish-speaking heartland, Romanian was the primary language, seen as the vehicle of upward mobility. Sternberg maintains that life in the Romanian shtetl was not as economically depressed as in the shtetlakh of Poland and the Russian Pale of Settlement. The author also makes clear that a shtetl is not a ghetto, "for it was voluntary rather than forced segregation." The geographic, historical, social, and economic background of Stefanesti is described in minute detail. Differences in family life in the shtetlakh of Romania and the shtetlakh of the Pale of Settlement are explained along with differences in religious traditions. This explanation is perhaps the most important section of the work for a comparative study of shtetl life. An entire chapter is devoted to songs (in Romanian or Yiddish with English translations) for many different occasions. Sternberg also relates many interesting superstitions and proverbs of Stefanesti. A glossary, a list of Yiddish and Romanian terminology, and an extensive appendix further complement this appealing work.

ZBOROWSKI and HERZOG's book is disputed territory. Critics claim that this work, which is dependent on personal memoirs of former shtetl dwellers, represents a overly romanticized version of shtetl life. Others decry the patchwork method that authors used to create a "model shtetl," a composite that never existed. The work relies on novels, memoirs, histories, films, and previous studies in order to create the feeling and the atmosphere of a shtetl. The hypothetical shtetl duly emerges, a kaleidoscope of various genres interwoven with memory, both accurate and fading. Zborowski and Herzog readily admit the limitations of their study: "the culture portrayed is that of the shtetl and not that of all Jews," and "the effort is to portray the living culture rather than to trace the origin of its manifestations." This disavowal of historicism, however, means that the shtetl takes on a life of its own—there is no right or wrong when describing a typical shtetl. The authors are nothing if not aware of the controversial character of their project, conceding that "The problem of whether *Life Is with People* offers an accurate portrait of the shtetl notwithstanding, there remains a larger issue. Is the shtetl, a highly-charged literary and historiographic construction with a life of its own, the most productive point of departure for an anthropology or a history of East European Jewish life?" Zborowski and Herzog have attempted valiantly to use various means to capture the spirit and the heart of the shtetl, however, and it is not without some justification that this work remains a definitive publication in the minds of many.

CYNTHIA A. KLÍMA

Siddur *see* **Liturgy, History of; Liturgy, Reform**

Sin and Atonement

Cohen, Hermann, *Die Religion der Vernunft aus den Quellen des Judentums*, 1919; translated by Simon Kaplan as *Religion of Reason out of the Sources of Judaism*, New York: Ungar, 1972

Milgrom, Jacob, *Leviticus 1–16: A New Translation with Introduction and Commentary* (Anchor Bible, vol. 3), New York: Doubleday, 1991

Miller, Patrick D., *Sin and Judgment in the Prophets: A Stylistic and Theological Analysis* (Society of Biblical Literature Monograph Series, no. 27), Chico, California: Scholars Press, 1982

Schechter, Solomon, *Some Aspects of Rabbinic Theology*, New York: Macmillan, and London: Black, 1909

Steinsaltz, Adin, *The Thirteen Petalled Rose*, translated by Yehuda Hanegbi, New York: Basic Books, 1980

The biblical basis for contemporary categories of sin and atonement may be found in two originally quite divergent groups of texts. One thread of tradition is based in the legislation governing the operation of the sacrificial cult. Read chronologically, these materials exhibit a growing willingness to transpose the categories of holiness and defilement from the temple sanctuary to the sphere of social relations. In tandem with this development, the prophetic writings are increasingly able to link particular indictments of antisocial behavior to a broader system of values and to an explicit concept of sin. After the destruction of the Second Temple, the rabbis expanded these two strands into a rich ethical anthropology. The commandments of the Torah and general expectations of propriety in human activity were alike construed as mitsvot. On the other hand, the human urge to transgress and be selfish was understood to derive from a fundamental inclination toward error, called the *yetser*. Atonement was effected in one of two ways. First, it could be achieved through the careful and attentive cultivation of the moral self through adherence to the mitsvot and relentless attention to transgressions against others. More broadly, however, it could be achieved through participation in the evolving rituals of the "Days of Awe" or "High Holidays." The atonement liturgy was the product of active rabbinic adaptation of temple rituals of expiation to provide an ongoing mechanism for forgiveness for unintentional transgressions against divine commandments.

The monumental commentary by MILGROM on the first 16 chapters of Leviticus contains a wealth of information on the priestly writings. Its detail and elaboration may strike the non-specialist as daunting, but its discussion of sin and repentance and expiation/atonement are an excellent introduction to the priestly theology and its development. Careful consideration must be given to Milgrom's willingness to read textual ambiguities through the lens of later rabbinic theology. Still, his citation of ancient Near Eastern ritual and conceptual parallels is exhaustive and invaluable.

MILLER surveys the pre-exile prophetic literature to create a typology of transgression and punishment. He finds links of correspondence, consequence, and retributive justice to proliferate as conceptual bonds that tie sin and subsequent judgment together. The persistence of such links, he suggests, provides one with a basis for comprehending the prophetic understanding of reciprocity between human action and effect. As such, it allows readers to perceive the minimum conditions for a developing theology of judgment and repentance in these writings. His study is valuable not only for its analysis and arrangement of a diverse body of material but also for its careful and nuanced presentation of a variety of exemplar texts that relate to prophetic indictments of sin.

In rabbinic Judaism, the prophetic doctrine of sin and retribution and the priestly ideas of transgression and atonement find their synthesis in the theology of the *yetser* and atonement. The presentation by SCHECHTER of the rabbinic sources is succinct but satisfying. Some may be put off by his synthesis of diverse strands of tradition into a deceptively unanimous theological system or by a certain bias against his midrashic sources. Still, the depth of detail and the perceptiveness of his interpretations make this book a valuable resource, and his felicitous style is legendary. Schechter notes a growing tendency toward conceptualization of the *yetser* as a personalized and autonomous force with which each individual must contend.

Although this is a development away from the biblical concept of the *yetser* as an internal faculty, he is careful to stress that the reader should understand this development as conceptual rather than substantive. He continues by outlining the varieties of rabbinic understandings of sacrificial atonement. Blood sacrifice comes to be not unique but to stand alongside fasting, suffering, charity, and Torah study as means of expiating guilt, and none of these is effective without repentance. In Schechter's discussion, repentance comes to stand alongside the mitsvot as a formative principle in the cosmos, acknowledging the gap between human will and divine command and providing a means of bridging the two.

COHEN develops a subtle theology that places atonement and redemption at the center of humanity's relations with God. Reclaiming much of the conceptual ground from standard Christian theologies of sin and atonement, he develops his own theological position through a careful reading of the prophets and the Psalms. The apex of biblical ethics, in his estimation, is found in Ezekiel, who was most able to elevate the prophetic critique of collective sin to a specific indictment for personal transgression. With this development, a theological position is facilitated wherein individuals stand accountable for personal activity and must interrogate the basis of their transgressions, confess their sins before their fellows, and take an active role in their own redemption. Cohen's book stands as a masterpiece of synthetic theology, and his particular formulation of the problem of sin and the necessity of atonement is indispensable.

STEINSALTZ develops a theology of repentance that is grounded in kabbalistic cosmology. He suggests that human behavior cannot be understood as relevant only in an interpersonal or an ethical sense. Instead, actions taken have a metaphysical significance, and the mitsvot are treated as fundamental ordering principles of the cosmos. Transgression is not merely personally relevant, it has a powerful effect on the world in which one lives. Individual human souls are interconnected and woven in with the fabric of the divine creation, and sin damages the integrity of that fabric. Thus, Steinsaltz suggests that repentance has an import that exceeds the personal. Its highest form is as an act of *tikkun*, or reparation. It is rooted in personal choice, but it extends outward to strengthen the cosmos in the face of the damage done to it by sin. Steinsaltz is an eloquent advocate of kabbalistic theology and writes with careful awareness of the need to make its theological subtleties meaningful for the contemporary reader.

EDWARD SILVER

Singer, Isaac Bashevis 1904–1991

Polish-born American Yiddish novelist and journalist

Hadda, Janet, *Isaac Bashevis Singer: A Life* (Studies in Jewish History), Oxford and New York: Oxford University Press, 1997

Landis, Joseph C. (editor), *Aspects of I.B. Singer,* New York: Queens College Press, 1986

Miller, David Neal, *Fear of Fiction: Narrative Strategies in the Works of Isaac Bashevis Singer* (SUNY Series in Modern Jewish Literature and Culture), Albany: State University of New York Press, 1985

Miller, David Neal (editor), *Recovering the Canon: Essays on Isaac Bashevis Singer* (Studies in Judaism in Modern Times, vol. 8), Leiden: Brill, 1986

Sanders, Ronald, *The Americanization of Isaac Bashevis Singer* (B.G. Rudolph Lectures in Judaic Studies), Syracuse, New York: Syracuse University Press, 1989

Zamir, Israel, *Avi, Yitshak Bashevis-Zinger,* 1994; translated by Barbara Harshav as *Journey to My Father, Isaac Bashevis Singer,* New York: Arcade, 1995

Yiddish author of short stories, novels, journalism, and literary criticism, and younger brother of Yiddish novelist Israel Joshua Singer, Isaac Bashevis Singer was awarded the Nobel Prize for Literature in 1978, the only Yiddish writer ever to receive this honor. His first literary efforts were poems and short stories written in Hebrew at a very young age. His debut in Yiddish came in 1925 with the story "In Old Age," published in the Warsaw literary journal for which he was a proofreader. He signed this story with the name "Tse." Later that same year he wrote the story "Wives" and, for the first time, employed the name "Isaac Bashevis," which he would use for his Yiddish belletristic works until his death. This name was based on his mother's name, Bas-sheva (Bathsheba), "Bashevis" meaning "Bathsheba's." Singer's first novel, *Satan in Goray,* was published serially in 1934 and in book form the following year. Among Singer's most famous works are the stories "Gimpel the Fool" and "Yentl the Yeshiva Boy," as well as the novels *The Family Moskat* and *Enemies, a Love Story.*

HADDA's comprehensive study demonstrates great familiarity with the large corpus of Singer's writings both in the original Yiddish and in the numerous English translations. Moreover, she presents her interesting and insightful findings based upon many hours of interviews with friends and family members of Singer. This is all done within the framework of a literary biography that often turns to psychoanalysis as a methodological model.

The essays in the volume edited by LANDIS deal with various phases in the life and work of Singer and are culled from issues of the literary journal *Yiddish,* which Landis edited. In addition to an article by Landis, there are essays by the Yiddish writer and critic Aaron Zeitlin and the Yiddish literary critic Shmuel Niger. This collection is complemented by a selection of writings by Singer himself.

Responding to the fact that more attention has been paid to English translations of Singer's works than to the Yiddish originals, MILLER (1985) concentrates his monograph on those works that remain untranslated. This volume is informed by the author's knowledge of the wider Yiddish canon, but it makes reference to works by other authors only when absolutely necessary. The focus here is almost exclusively on Singer and his narrative strategies.

MILLER (1986) aims to make a contribution to the discussion of canon formation in literary studies, with particular focus on a somewhat neglected aspect of this field, namely "the role of the author in shaping the perception of his or her oeuvre, on the one hand, or in championing the candidacy of that oeuvre for acceptance into the broader canon." The essays in this volume all focus on Singer and are written by an international team including Miller and fellow American Seth Wolitz; Israeli scholars Hana Wirth-Nesher, Leonard Prager, and Khone Shmeruk; and the Yiddish poet and critic Yankev Glatshteyn.

SANDERS's lecture discusses issues of categorization, considering why Singer has traditionally been considered an American writer. Sanders pinpoints several factors that led to the "Americanization" of this writer of Polish-Jewish origin. For example, the short story "Gimpel the Fool" was translated by Irving Howe and inspired a large English reading audience for Singer in the United States. Singer then became increasingly involved in the translation of his own works into English. The film version of his novel *Enemies, A Love Story* earned him even wider acclaim and popularity in the United States. Sanders agrees that Singer is properly designated an American writer, ending his lecture with the judgment: "I think that, by this time, we can call the only Yiddish winner of the Nobel Prize an American national treasure."

Israeli journalist ZAMIR offers an honest and unpretentious look at his relationship with his world-famous father. In the author's own words: "This is neither a biography of my father nor an evaluation of his literary work. That has been done by others more qualified than me. This is, rather, a personal account of what started as a failed father-son relationship and ended in a mature friendship." Zamir writes that Singer left Warsaw for New York in 1935, when Zamir was six years old, and the two did not meet again until 20 years later. This book provides an intriguing glimpse of the writer from the uniquely personal perspective of his son.

MARC MILLER

Slavery

Chirichigno, Gregory C., *Debt-Slavery in Israel and the Ancient Near East* (Journal for the Study of the Old Testament Supplement Series, 141), Sheffield, South Yorkshire: JSOT, 1993

Flesher, Paul Virgil McCracken, *Oxen, Women or Citizens?: Slaves in the System of the Mishnah* (Brown Judaic Studies, no. 143), Atlanta, Georgia: Scholars Press, 1988

Mendelsohn, Isaac, *Slavery in the Ancient Near East: A Comparative Study of Slavery in Babylonia, Assyria, Syria, and Palestine, from the Middle of the Third Millennium to the End of the First Millennium,* New York: Oxford University Press, 1949

Urbach, E.E., "The Laws Regarding Slavery as a Source for Social History of the Period of the Second Temple, the Mishnah and Talmud," in *Papers of the Institute of Jewish Studies, London,* vol. 1, edited by J.G. Weiss, Jerusalem: Magnes Press of Hebrew University, 1964; Lanham, Maryland: University Press of America, 1989

Zucrow, Solomon, *Women, Slaves, and the Ignorant in Rabbinic Literature, and Also the Dignity of Man,* Boston: Stratford, 1932

An unusual feature of Jewish slavery law is the distinction made between the Hebrew slave, who serves for a limited term, and the non-Hebrew (often called "Canaanite") slave, who is more like a permanent chattel. The regulations regarding such slaves are far from consistent. Among the more complex issues are the divergences among the biblical slave laws, including three apparently conflicting manumission laws in Exodus, Leviticus, and Deuteronomy, and the further differences between these biblical slave laws and the later rabbinic rules. Scholars debate the extent to which such textual differences reflect changes in the nature and function of slavery as actually practiced in the ancient Near East.

ZUCROW, in the second part of his work, provides an overview of both biblical and rabbinic slave law. His approach is ethical rather than historical, with the aim of revealing attitudes toward slaves. Dividing the relevant texts into four broad types—patriarchal (the biblical Genesis narratives), post-patriarchal (other biblical books), talmudic (tannaitic and amoraic texts), and post-talmudic (the works of Maimonides and other codifiers)—he reviews the key features of slave law in each. Zucrow argues that the biblical passages give a sense that the master's power over the slave, both Hebrew and non-Hebrew, was to be restrained. In talmudic law, however, the attitude toward the non-Hebrew slave has deteriorated, whether due to foreign influence or misguided exegetical activity on the part of the sages; such slaves were considered "mere asses," among other degradations. Though selective, Zucrow's work is a lucid introduction to the intricacies of slave law.

Certain of the biblical slave rules are remarkably similar to the slave laws of other ancient Near Eastern cultures, particularly Mesopotamia. Such parallels are drawn by some scholars to suggest the existence of a common law or school tradition from which these regulations developed. Two studies on biblical slavery adopt such a comparative approach.

MENDELSOHN attempts a historical outline of slavery—its sources, legal status, and economic role—among the Israelites and other ancient Near Eastern cultures. The Israelite case is derived from a philological analysis of relevant biblical passages, supplemented in some cases with archeological evidence; gaps in the biblical record are filled in with evidence from Mesopotamia and Ugarit. The author concludes that most slaves in Israelite society were Hebrews forced into service to pay off debts; it is to these that the laws of Exodus and Deuteronomy are addressed, while the later Leviticus law covers those who sold themselves into slavery. Though some of the research used by the author has now been superseded or at least challenged, the study remains broadly useful as an introduction to the main issues of ancient slavery and to the cultural milieu within which the biblical rules operated.

CHIRICHIGNO focuses on the three biblical manumission laws, with the aim of explaining their purpose within the socioeconomic circumstances of Israelite society. First, the author summarizes prior scholarly opinion on the development of social stratification and the nature of debt-slavery in Mesopotamia and then relates these conclusions to the Israelite situation through an analysis of relevant biblical terminology. The remainder of the book provides a detailed structural and philological analysis of the three manumission laws. In contrast to the thesis that these laws stem from different textual traditions, Chirichigno posits that they all were part of a comprehensive social welfare scheme designed to restrict the permanent enslavement of Israelites and their dependents for debt as well as the permanent alienation of patrimonial land. He further suggests that these rules could all have been operative at a very early period. The book is directed at the specialist reader well versed in biblical Hebrew but is also valuable as a general reference tool, with its summaries of prior research and its comprehensive bibliography covering the economies of the ancient Near East and aspects of biblical law and interpretation.

Within the great mass of rabbinic literature (particularly Mishnah, Tosefta, and the Palestinian and Babylonian Talmuds), the numerous inconsistencies in slave law pose a challenge to scholars and incite a degree of controversy regarding the most appropriate approach. URBACH contends that one may detect in these contradictions a development and reinterpretation of the law that can be directly related to changing historical conditions. Selecting from among the many rabbinic discussions on slaves and hypothesizing the historical context surrounding them, he posits an outline of the course of slavery among Jews from the Second Temple period onward. He argues that in the period following Nehemiah, Hebrew slaves constituted the main source of slavery, while non-Hebrew slaves increased with the Maccabean wars and Hasmonaean conquests. Earlier postbiblical laws focused on integrating such non-Hebrew slaves into the community, while following the destruction of the Second Temple rules were designed both to prevent the assimilation of those of dubious status as well as to favor an increase in slave trading. Though Urbach's methodology has been challenged, this detailed article is useful as a source for rabbinic citations on slavery and offers insight into the many layers of which rabbinic slave law is composed.

FLESHER examines the slave rules found in one particular rabbinic work, the Mishnah. He argues that this text must be approached as a system unto itself, and, contrary to Urbach, that its rules are purely "utopian" and cannot be taken as direct evidence of historical reality. Flesher posits that in contrast to the biblical slave system, which distinguishes between Hebrews and non-Hebrews, the Mishnah's primary slave system ignores the slave's genealogy and defines his slave status in terms of the control exercised over him by a male Israelite householder. The nature of this control is then explored and used to illustrate the slave's similarity to both inanimate property and other humans as well as the slave's place in the cult. Flesher contrasts the status of the "freedman" and concludes with a detailed definition of the Mishnah's concept of "freedom." Highly theoretical, the book is an interesting and methodical application of the systemic approach favoured by Jacob Neusner. It is complemented by a list of Mishnah passages dealing with slaves and a bibliography covering aspects of the study of ancient slavery and rabbinic Judaism.

DIANE KRIGER

Social Ethics

Breslauer, S. Daniel, *Contemporary Jewish Ethics: A Bibliographical Survey* (Bibliographies and Indexes in Religious Studies, no. 6), Westport, Connecticut: Greenwood, 1985

Dorff, Elliot and Louis Newman (editors), *Contemporary Jewish Ethics and Morality: A Reader*, Oxford and New York: Oxford University Press, 1995

Herford, R. Travers (editor), *Pirke Aboth: The Tractate "Fathers," from the Mishnah, Commonly Called "Sayings of the Fathers,"* New York: Jewish Institute of Religion Press, 1925; as *The Ethics of the Talmud: Sayings of the Fathers*, New York: Schocken, 1962

Isbell, Charles David, *Malachi: A Study Guide Commentary*, Grand Rapids, Michigan: Zondervan, 1980

Kroloff, Charles A., *When Elijah Knocks: A Religious Response to Homelessness*, West Orange, New Jersey: Behrman House, 1992

Novak, David, *Jewish Social Ethics*, New York: Oxford University Press, 1992

Plaut, W. Gunther and Mark Washofsky, *Teshuvot for the Nineties: Reform Judaism's Answers to Today's Dilemmas*, New York: Central Conference of American Rabbis, 1997

Vorspan, Albert and David Saperstein, *Jewish Dimensions of Social Justice: Tough Moral Choices of Our Time*, New York: UAHC, 1998

Social ethics is viewed by all branches of Judaism as a critical area of life and study. The earliest biblical texts include injunctions against harming other human beings both within and outside the boundaries of Israelite society proper. Biblical and all subsequent Jewish legislation emphasizes the importance of individual and societal protection for the weak and powerless, stressing the fact that even kings and other high-ranking members of society are accountable to God for proper personal ethics as well as for ethically sound public policies. The classical prophets, especially Amos, Micah, and Isaiah, interpreted the true essence of Mosaic ("traditional") religion to be a type of socially responsible conduct that promised justice and equality across a wide spectrum of early Israelite society.

ISBELL examines the ethical message of a lesser-known prophet, Malachi, who preached to the community of Jews newly returned to Jerusalem from Babylonian captivity. The author shows how the prophet interprets such issues as marriage and divorce, acceptable contributions to charitable causes, and proper relationships between parents and children. Isbell demonstrates that Malachi uses these common social themes as the key to understanding the nature of God, the definition of the people Israel, and the basis for a covenantal relationship between God and Israel.

HERFORD provides both a readable English translation of and a running commentary on the mishnaic tractate *Avot*, which is generally considered to be the first specifically ethical compilation in postbiblical Judaism. Classical ethical thought in Judaism is deemed by the author to deal with practical deeds rather than with speculative systems of philosophy.

Throughout the book, Herford offers excellent insight into these ordinary, daily concerns of the early rabbis—such as hospitality to strangers, respect between student and teacher, and relations with evil people.

The studies by BRESLAUER and by DORFF and NEWMAN consider the significance of basic biblical and mishnaic concepts in the modern era. The modern examples these authors choose serve to underscore the genius of the classical texts, which isolated for examination the core issues of all societal groups in all eras.

By contrast, NOVAK expands the list of ethical issues facing contemporary Jews to include topics that could not have been anticipated in earlier times. Among his ten seminal essays are discussions of subjects such as the ethical treatment of AIDS patients, proper consideration for social minorities, ecology for a shrinking planet, and war and peace in the nuclear age. The strength of Novak's work is that he approaches these new issues by constant reference to the old sources, seeking to discern in classical Jewish literature the principles that have abiding value even after the specificity of their own era has been lost. Successfully combining theoretical analysis with practical modern concerns, Novak makes a significant contribution to Jewish theology. His work is also important because it engages certain Christian ethical thinkers in dialogue. Without minimizing the theological differences that divide the two traditions, Novak places the field of Jewish ethics in a broader social and religious matrix.

VORSPAN and SAPERSTEIN center their discussion around issues that divide persons of good will and reason. There is virtually no debate, for example, about the postulate that one ought to deal kindly and fairly with others. But when specific issues, such as abortion, capital punishment, criminal justice, or homosexuality, become the focus, differences abound regarding how to apply this general ethical rule. Vorspan and Saperstein attempt, with varying degrees of success, to show how Judaism informs the current debates about these "tough moral choices." Two things become clear when reading their work. First, Judaism has a long history of facing thorny ethical issues and debating them openly and honestly. Second, there is seldom the luxury of a consensus among Jewish thinkers about difficult moral and ethical issues. The authors conclude that a specifically Jewish approach to ethical questions must encourage Jews to tackle hard choices, allowing the possibility of more than one morally acceptable position and understanding that such debates must be continual and situational rather than dogmatic and definitive.

PLAUT and WASHOFSKY consider a wide variety of ethical issues from the perspective of Reform Judaism. Some parts of the book address ritual and synagogue politics, but the majority of the 75 questions that the authors investigate concern ethical issues of wide public interest, such as HIV testing, abortion, gossip, and customs of marriage and divorce. In fact, although their final chapter is specifically titled "Social Issues," all of the preceding chapters of the book also deal more with social issues than with any other subject, a focus that underscores the significance of social ethics in Jewish life.

KROLOFF offers a fine example of the way in which Judaism can focus upon a single issue of social ethics. The author aims to demonstrate that homelessness is not merely a political or economic problem; it also involves profoundly religious and ethical challenges. By examining the problem of homelessness within a framework of religious obligation, Kroloff provides a distinctively Jewish perspective on a modern issue. He also shows how Jewish theology passes the ultimate test of its classical system of social ethics, the ability to move from theory to practical application in a socially responsible fashion.

CHARLES DAVID ISBELL

Sociology of Religion

Levine, Hillel and Lawrence Harmon, *The Death of an American Jewish Community: A Tragedy of Good Intentions,* New York: Free Press, 1992

Neusner, Jacob, *The Social Study of Judaism: Essays and Reflections* (Brown Judaic Studies Series, 162), vol. 2, Atlanta, Georgia: Scholars Press, 1988

Novak, David, *Jewish Social Ethics,* New York: Oxford University Press, 1992

Sharot, Stephen, *Judaism: A Sociology,* New York: Holmes and Meier, and Newton Abbot, Devon, England: David and Charles, 1976

Sklare, Marshall (editor), *The Jewish Community in America* (Library of Jewish Studies), New York: Behrman House, 1974

The sociology of religion has its historical moorings fairly well anchored in the work of three major figures who flourished in the late 19th century: Emile Durkheim, Karl Marx, and Max Weber. Each of them, though for differing reasons and with differing results and for good or ill, believed that religious phenomena play a wide-ranging, formative, and authoritative role in the production of individual and collective identities, ideas, norms, values, and feelings. The sociology of religion brings to bear upon religious collectivities the questions, methods, and theories developed within sociology. What are the dynamics of social change? How do societies move from one form of organization to another? How do forms of religion contribute to individual, collective, and institutional identity? With rapid advances in technological sophistication, secularization, and globalization, does religion fall by the wayside or is it a continuing force for revolutionary change?

Until recently the sociology of religion has tended to focus on the processes of secularization and the increasing insignificance of religion, a focus that has made the continuing worth of the sociology of religion itself questionable. This is changing, however, as the sociology of religion becomes comparative rather than insular, opening itself to, rather than avoiding, the contributions of other religious studies disciplines.

SHAROT's introduction acknowledges the unique way in which a sociology whose target is Jewish life and history is simultaneously and foremost a sociology of religion. Again a consequence of the diaspora, says Sharot, it is also a comparative analysis "of a *single* religiously distinctive ethnic group in a number of societies." This peculiar sociological admixture, the thesis of a singular difference that traverses multiple

national, cultural, and temporal boundaries, perhaps could only be ventured when directed toward Judaism. Though it is debatable whether modern Jewish life is either identical with Jewish religion or identifiable as a cohesive, transnational ethnic culture, at the same time an affirmation of both suppositions seems equally necessary in order that there be the possibility of a sociology of Judaism. Since it appears to be a modern fact that it is possible to be socially and culturally quite imperceptibly Jewish, the sociology of Jewish religion in certain respects remains an analysis of the coercive pressures, both subtle and extreme, brought to bear by a wider or "host" culture against Jewish religio-culture, pressures that ensure a continuing identity of varying states of integrity. The social study of Jewish religion is therefore a study of marginality, separation, and adaptation. It is thus not surprising that Sharot's main concerns are the variables associated with acculturation, assimilation, and secularization, as these, according to their times and places, have historically informed the pragmatics of Jewish affiliation. Considering the necessarily circumstantial particularity of these variables, Sharot's work recommends itself as one of the few sociologies of Judaism that attempts a cross-cultural historical and comparative analysis that begins with premodern Judaism and ends with 20th-century Judaism in England and the United States. In line with certain Weberian claims advanced and modified by Peter Berger (see, for example, his *Social Construction of Reality, The Sacred Canopy,* and *A Rumor of Angels*), Sharot finds a complicity between Jewish religion and practice and the process of secularization.

NEUSNER addresses, perhaps uniquely, the social order of Judaism in terms of its classical literature, in particular the Mishnah, as it expresses a programmatic "social system, politics, economics and philosophy." This contextual, historical approach is in line with Neusner's all but innumerable other works in the systematic study of religion as exemplified by Judaism. In this volume, however, the questions directed at the text differ in that they derive from the larger questions brought to bear upon a religious community by the social sciences, questions such as Weber's hypothesis of a link between Western systems of religious belief and "rational" economic action—i.e., capitalism. Neusner claims that the Mishnah sets forth the terms and structure of a political economy that has been definitive for that social entity which constitutes Judaism. "I see," he says, "the politics as a concrete and material statement of the social entity of the system; the economics as the equally practical expression of its way of life; and the philosophy, of course, as the agenda through which the prevailing world-view addresses concrete and urgent questions of mind." The book is structured around a series of essays that address the political economy of Judaism in general and the Mishnah in particular; the politics and theological anthropology of Judaism; the philosophy of Judaism given principle by the Mishnah; and the situation of Jews and Judaism in the global social order.

LEVINE and HARMON's book is an ethnographic study of a particular case of urban ethnic relations—those between blacks and Jews in the Boston, Massachusetts, suburbs of Dorchester, Mattapan, and Roxbury from the early 1950s to the early years of the 1970s, a period during which these communities witnessed a complex transformation from predominately Jewish to African-American neighborhoods. While this is not a novel phenomenon, it had previously been understood according to a "succession" theory that held that Jews, fleeing an inner-city ethnic neighborhood, would sell to blacks. The remaining Jews would be composed of shopkeepers and slumlords. Levine and Harmon instead focus on the forces brought to bear against the Jewish community by bankers and real estate agents who conspired—by the use of specious financial incentives to minorities and by intimidation and threats to "loosen up" properties—to redline those districts. The book challenges the thesis that the breakdown of the historic alliance between blacks and Jews is wholly attributable to forces internal to these communities. "There is growing evidence," they say, "that elusive forces external to the black and Jewish communities also played a role in undermining their relationship, and that opportunities were lost for positive contact between blacks and Jews at the neighborhood level." The authors focus on the ways bankers used federal loan programs for low-income residents, and they look in particular at the Boston Banks Urban Renewal Group, composed of the heads of 22 savings banks, which created an inner-city district within which "and only within which" blacks could obtain these attractive terms.

The ethical basis for normative Judaism, so often construed in terms of a system of inexorable laws, does not, according to NOVAK's important reading of Jewish social ethics, illuminate itself. "The Law is, rather, a divinely grounded *and* historically developing system that subjects the most cogently argued theory to the collective precedents of the centuries-old community." With such an understanding of Jewish law as principle rather than rule, a Jewish social ethics is the ongoing result of a hard-won, responsibly engaged communitarian dialogue and the expression of a "historical continuity between the development of Jewish life" and Jewish law. Because Jewish social ethics is the expression of such covenental, other-obligated responsibilities, it is, according to Novak, "essentially a theological ethics." It must evidence responsibility to Torah as revelation, as a historically mediated, peopled tradition, and as a response to present concerns such as the actual political and social liberation of the Jewish people and the protection of the interests and rights of every other. The book affirms some fairly startling approaches, such as the Christian theologian Paul Tillich's theonomous ethical theory grounded in desire for the good and the Catholic thinker John Courtney Murray's Thomistic natural law theory, then adjusts these theories by an appraisal of distinctively Jewish ethical dilemmas.

SKLARE's edited volume of essays, a companion to *The Jew in American Society,* which focused upon the individual American Jew, here considers the communal aspects of American Jewry according to five categories: the informal community, the formal community, religious movements, Jewish education, and the Jewish community and general society. The authors, for the most part, present their findings in terms of a narrative analysis of historical and statistical data, and most follow a stage-model format to display, arrange, and understand the social structure of a community according to certain standard organizational-developmental models. The need for the attention to Jewish communal life reflected in this volume is critical, according to Sklare, since "the American Jewish community . . . has become crucial to the future of the Jewish people." There is a profound urgency subtending the articles to spell out anomic and separatist forces that work to threaten the survival of Jewish life. Charles Liebman's essay on "Orthodoxy in American Jewish Life," for instance, differentiates Orthodoxy from Reform and Conservative forms by its weak coordination in associations and groups and by its European origins, both of which contribute to its sectarian insularity. On the other hand, he also highlights forces for stabilization, growth, and cohesion.

ERIC C. HELMER

Solomon ben Isaac 1030 or 1040–1105
French pioneer Bible and Talmud commentator

Banitt, Menahem, *Rashi: Interpreter of the Biblical Letter,* Tel Aviv: Chaim Rosenberg School of Jewish Studies, Tel Aviv University, 1985

Catane, Mochè, *Recueil des Gloses: Les Gloses françaises dans les commentaires talmudiques de Rachi d'apres l'ouvrage d'Arsène Darmesteter et D.S. Blondheim (1929),* Tel Aviv: Gitler, 1984, revised edition, 1988

Doron, Pinhas, *The Mystery of Creation According to Rashi: A New Translation and Interpretation of Rashi on Genesis I–VI,* New York: Maznaim, 1982

Hailperin, Herman, *Rashi and the Christian Scholars,* Pittsburgh, Pennsylvania: University of Pittsburgh Press, 1963

Saltman, Avrom and Sarah Kamin, *Secundum Salomonem: A Thirteenth Century Latin Commentary on the Song of Solomon,* Ramat Gan: Bar-Ilan University Press, 1989

Solomon ben Isaac, commonly known by the acronym Rashi (Rabbi Solomon ben Isaac), was born in Troyes, the capital of the Champagne region of northern France. Founder of an illustrious family of rabbis, several of whom contributed commentaries of enduring value on both the Hebrew Bible and the Babylonian Talmud, Rashi himself penned the most famous and influential Hebrew commentaries on both of those corpora. Part of the standard curriculum of Jewish schools to this day, Rashi's biblical commentaries exercised an enormous influence on Christian exegetes such as Hugh of St. Victor, Nicholas de Lyre, and Martin Luther. Rashi also authored liturgical poems and numerous legal responsa. Unfortunately, much of the literature about Rashi is highly sentimental, reflecting the view in many quarters that his commentaries are virtually holy writ, from which Jewish literature is forbidden to dissent. At the same time, the modern Jewish scholars of the Wissenschaft des Judentums seem to have found in Rashi—with his use of French, his anti-Christian diatribes, and his way of being quoted extensively by Christian exegetes—a considerable cultural hero who, no less than the poets and exegetes of Spanish Jewry's Golden Age, provided a model for modern Judaism's search to live comfortably both with the totality of

Jewish spiritual-literary baggage and with Western culture. It is no accident, therefore, that academic scholarship on Rashi in English and French places disproportionate emphasis on points of contact between Rashi and Western Christendom, just as the literature prepared for the yeshivot tends to treat Rashi's commentaries exclusively as an outgrowth of his familiarity with talmudic literature. The stature of Rashi as a commentator on both Bible and Talmud lies in his careful synthesis of what the reader ought to know of philology and grammar and what the reader would like to know of the eternal verities that transcend the exegesis of a text.

Rashi's commentaries on the Bible contain 4,382 glosses written in various European languages, mostly in Old Northern French, while his commentaries on the Babylonian Talmud contain 2,475 such glosses. Among the most important surviving testimonies written in Old Northern French, these precious glosses were largely overlooked by readers of Rashi's commentaries after the beginning of the 14th century, when the Jews were expelled from France, and French ceased to be a language spoken by Jews for many centuries. Early in the 20th century, Arsène Darmesteter and David Blondheim published comprehensive lists of these glosses, establishing—with the assistance of medieval manuscripts and early printed editions of the commentaries—the correct spelling of each gloss in both Hebrew and Latin characters. BANITT argues convincingly that most of the glosses in Rashi's biblical commentaries serve to correct what Rashi believed to have been errors in the then-conventional Jewish translation of the Scriptures into spoken Old Northern French, which had been passed down from parents to children and from teachers to pupils over several generations. (An analogous traditional Jewish translation of the Scriptures—in this case into an antiquated form of Italian—was studied in the schools that the great Bible scholar Umberto Cassuto attended as a child just over a century ago. Similar oral transmissions of Talmud and Scripture in Yiddish continue to survive in some Jewish primary and secondary schools.) Banitt argues further that many characteristic Hebrew expressions that make their first appearance in Rashi's commentaries are best understood as Gallicisms, which is to say Rashi's rendering in written Hebrew of thoughts formed in the language of everyday speech, namely Old Northern French.

In the milieu of the yeshivah and elsewhere in modern Jewry, the study of Rashi's Talmud commentary is both a liturgical act (analogous to Christian "Bible study") and an academic exercise (analogous to obtaining a bachelor's degree) requisite to becoming a master of the cultural canon. CATANE has rendered yeoman service to people who study Rashi's commentary on the Talmud. He provides, on the basis of the findings of Darmsteter, Blondheim, and other luminaries, a comprehensive list of the French and other European-language glosses in Rashi's Talmud commentaries, together with the correct spelling in both Hebrew and Latin script and, where warranted, a concise explanation of what precisely the gloss is meant to add to Rashi's analysis of the talmudic passage in question. The numbered list, arranged according to the order of the Babylonian Talmud, is supplemented by alphabetic indexes in both Hebrew and Latin script and by concise, user-friendly introductions to the volume in English, French, and Hebrew.

To this day, students in Jewish day schools learn Rashi's methodology by osmosis, plowing through all his commentaries on the Pentateuch and much of the Prophets until the words and methods have been thoroughly absorbed by the student. For a more systematic approach to understanding Rashi, contemporary students will do well to make use of DORON's handy volume. The author applies his thorough grounding both in rabbinic lore and in the modern philological-historical study of the Hebrew Bible to Rashi's text. Doron's work contains the Hebrew text of Rashi, a lucid English translation, and a brilliant English supercommentary on Rashi's commentary, albeit only on the first six chapters of Genesis.

HAILPERIN's work is the most sophisticated and complete discussion yet produced both of Rashi and of Rashi's commentaries in their historical context. Doron and Catane's manuals are meant primarily for students, and the works by Saltman and Kamin and by Banitt are suited especially to scholars, but Hailperin's monumental volume has abiding interest for students, scholars, and laity. Hailperin presents in one handy volume: i) the most valuable biography of Rashi and his family; ii) flawless English translations of passages from Rashi's commentaries on the Pentateuch, the Prophets, and the Psalms, selected for their bearing on the major theme of the book, namely, the ongoing argument between Judaism and Christianity as to which of these two communities of faith reflects the authentic continuation of the religion of ancient Israel; and iii) lucid footnotes and appendixes, shedding light on a great array of people and issues. Hailperin set a new standard for the treatment of a Jewish culture-hero, who both before and since has been treated unremittingly much as George Washington was in the famous biography by Parson Weems. Unquestionably, the few scholars who have contributed books and articles of abiding worth on Rashi in English stand firmly on the shoulders of Hailperin.

Kamin was one a small handful of people who have demonstrated the necessary profundity to advance the study of Rashi very significantly beyond Hailperin. Tragically, Kamin's career was just getting off the ground when it was cut short by cancer. Her swan song, SALTMAN and KAMIN, demonstrates most lucidly what can be seen less clearly from Hailperin's book and from the well-known work of Beryl Smalley: the tremendous (quite immediate) impact that Rashi had on Christian exegesis of Scripture. Rashi, as Kamin expounded on several occasions, sought to show that Jewish allegorical interpretation of the Song of Songs (like Judaism itself) constituted a truth deeper than that found in Christian allegorical interpretation because the Jewish allegorical reading, as presented by Rashi, stood on the firm foundation of scientific lexicography, morphology, and syntax. The anonymous 13th-century Christian exegete who produced the Latin commentary published and analyzed by Saltman and Kamin accepted Rashi's argument and set out to produce a Christian allegorical commentary on the Song of Songs that copies much from Rashi but tries also to create a new Christian allegory based on scientific philology. The book contains a brilliant introduction presented in both Hebrew and English, a critical edition of the Latin text of the Christian commentary, and a rendering of that text in Hebrew and English. In addition, Saltman and Kamin make available here a reliable text of Rashi's commentary on the Song of Songs that avoids the mass of human errors that mark previous editions.

MAYER IRWIN GRUBER

Soloveitchik, Joseph Baer 1903–1993

Polish-born American theologian and
rabbinic authority

Agus, Jacob, *Guideposts in Modern Judaism: An Analysis of Current Trends in Jewish Thought,* New York: Bloch, 1954

Angel, Marc D., *Exploring the Thought of Rabbi Joseph B. Soloveitchik,* Hoboken, New Jersey: Ktav, 1997

Borowitz, Eugene, *Choices in Modern Jewish Thought: A Partisan Guide,* New York: Behrman House, 1983; 2nd edition, West Orange, New Jersey: Behrman House, 1995

Goldberg, Hillel, *Between Berlin and Slobodka: Jewish Transition Figures from Eastern Europe,* Hoboken, New Jersey: Ktav, 1989

Goldy, Robert G., *The Emergence of Jewish Theology in America* (Modern Jewish Experience), Bloomington: Indiana University Press, 1990

Hartman, David, *A Living Covenant: The Innovative Spirit in Traditional Judaism,* New York: Free Press, and London: Collier Macmillan, 1985

Kaplan, Lawrence, "The Religious Philosophy of Rabbi Joseph Soloveitchik," *Tradition,* 14, Fall 1973

Lichtenstein, Aharon, "Joseph Soloveitchik," in *Great Jewish Thinkers of the Twentieth Century* (B'nai B'rith Great Books Series, vol. 3), edited by Simon Noveck, Washington, D.C.: B'nai B'rith, Department of Adult Jewish Education, 1963

Munk, Reinier, *The Rationale of Halakhic Man: Joseph B. Soloveitchik's Conception of Jewish Thought* (Amsterdam Studies in Jewish Thought, vol. 3), Amsterdam: Gieben, 1996

Ziegler, Aharon, *Halakhic Positions of Rabbi Joseph B. Soloveitchik,* Northvale, New Jersey: Aronson, 1998

The scion of an illustrious rabbinical family, Rabbi Joseph B. Soloveitchik was the acknowledged leader of centrist Orthodoxy in the second half of the 20th century and was recognized both as a preeminent talmudic scholar and as a highly original interpreter of Jewish thought and theology. Beginning in 1941, Soloveitchik served as the master teacher of Talmud at Yeshiva University's affiliated Rabbi Isaac Elchanan Theological Seminary and chairman of the halakhah commission of the Rabbinical Council of America for more than 40 years. He was affiliated with Agudat Israel in the 1930s and addressed its national conventions during those years; in the 1940s, he identified with religious Zionism, and, until his death, he was honorary president of Mizrachi.

LICHTENSTEIN has drawn a very appealing portrait of Soloveitchik in the first systematic English-language presentation of his ideas. This essay helps the reader appreciate why Soloveitchik was revered by thousands of students and fol-

lowers as "the Rav," the rabbi's rabbi, a role model among interpreters of Jewish law and theology. According to Lichtenstein, Soloveitchik's personal demeanor demonstrated that "Halakhic Man" (Soloveitchik's term) can be creative, open-minded, and compassionate, profoundly committed to the Torah and at the same time a sophisticated modern thinker.

BOROWITZ, a leading Reform Jewish theologian, provides a clear, nontechnical study of Soloveitchik in what may be the most satisfactory introduction to this seminal thinker who tried to build bridges between Orthodox Judaism and the modern world. According to Borowitz, Soloveitchik expresses greater confidence in human reason than does Martin Buber; he is in closer communication with the thoughtful but uncommitted inquirer than is A.J. Heschel; and he is more intellectually sophisticated than Mordecai Kaplan. One possible misconception that may arise from this analysis should be clarified. Borowitz worries that there is a certain ambiguity in Soloveitchik's concept of the Halakhic Man. Sometimes he implies that Halakhic Man is a pure type that is not intrinsically linked to Judaism, which leads Borowitz to ask if a learned Jesuit can be a halakhic personality, given that the Society of Jesus puts an emphasis on intellectualism and observance that appears to be akin to halakhic piety. On other occasions, Soloveitchik seems to believe that Halakhic Man is a category limited to Jews of a particular type. In that case, Borowitz contends, Soloveitchik reveals a certain elitism, dividing this small coterie of men from ordinary Jews and the rest of humanity. In fact, the ambiguity may not be quite so pronounced or so problematic as Borowitz suggests: Halakhic Man par excellence is the rabbinical scholar, but in a wider sense Soloveitchik uses the term at least to embrace any Jew who guides his life by the principles of the halakhah. Borowitz's general criticism of the use of pure types in Soloveitchik's writings is more significant. Soloveitchik structures his thoughts around an entire galaxy of ideal types (including Halakhic Man, Scientific Man, Religious Man, Mystic Man, and Lonely Man of Faith, among others), and Borowitz indicates how difficult it is to apply such typologies to real situations: "Typologies may illuminate, but it is never clear whence the types arise; why these and not others are selected; how the types used for various situations relate to one another; and what gives the total universe of types its integrity."

KAPLAN, a rabbi and a professor of Jewish studies at McGill University, has translated Soloveitchik's *Halakhic Man* into English and written about him repeatedly. His essay presents a rounded picture of Soloveitchik's religious philosophy and is particularly valuable for its extensive quotations from works only available in Hebrew. Kaplan maintains that while Soloveitchik's understanding of Halakhic Man is essentially valid, it sometimes needs to be qualified. For example, Soloveitchik contends that his protagonist does not view the regulations of the Torah as an alien law, imposed on him from the outside, but treats it as an internalized creation performed in perfect freedom. We must distinguish, says Kaplan, between the study and observance of halakhah, however: the halakhic personality experiences the Torah as his own creation and possession when he studies it, but when he has to put the halakhah into practice, he does feel the "yoke of the commandments."

ANGEL, rabbi of the Spanish and Portuguese Synagogue in New York, has edited a collection of 14 valuable essays previously published in *Tradition,* a journal of Orthodox Jewish thought, to which he has added a general introduction and an overview of the individual contributions. The essays are well written and discuss many aspects of Soloveitchik's wide-ranging thought. Marvin Fox and Moshe Sokol come to opposite conclusions as to whether or not there is a unity to Soloveitchik's philosophy. Sokol contends that the existentialism of *The Lonely Man of Faith* is altogether different from the rationalist, neo-Kantian structure of *Halakhic Man,* while Fox finds a unifying principle in Soloveitchik's thesis that halakhah is the only legitimate source of Jewish doctrine. Jonathan Sacks, the chief rabbi of the Commonwealth and a former teacher of philosophy, discusses Soloveitchik's early epistemology, identifying parallels between his thought and the works of the philosophers Hans-Georg Gadamer and Richard Rorty.

GOLDBERG offers a sensitive and penetrating analysis of the unresolved inner tensions in Soloveitchik's thought and the effects of those tensions on his students and disciples. According to Goldberg, "The upshot of Rabbi Soloveitchik's life and thought is the impossibility of harmony in life or thought, neither the living harmony of oscillation between struggle and tranquility, nor even the intellectual harmony of dialectic balance between polar concepts."

Just as the successors of G.W.F. Hegel can be divided into Right and Left Hegelians, so the followers of Soloveitchik can be separated into right-wing and left-wing factions. The right-wing followers include the *rebbeim* (Talmud teachers) at the Rabbi Isaac Elchanan Rabbinical Seminary affiliated with Yeshiva University, while those of the left-wing include Irving Greenberg, Emanuel Rackman, Avi Weiss, Walter Wurzburger, and HARTMAN. Hartman is the founder and director of the Shalom Hartman Institute for Advanced Jewish Studies, a senior lecturer in the Department of Jewish Thought and Philosophy at the Hebrew University of Jerusalem, and an accomplished talmudist, who for many years attended the talmudic discourses of Soloveitchik. Hartman asserts that the writings of Soloveitchik demonstrate a shift in attitudes. Hartman argues that in the earlier works, Soloveitchik advocates the synthesis of Jewish thought and modern culture, while in his later writings, he expresses an ambivalence and hesitation, which Hartman finds regrettable. Hartman concludes that Soloveitchik became concerned "that if there were a total translation of the halakhic experience into Western rational categories, commitment to the halakha would be weakened."

A leading Conservative rabbi, who for many years had studied the Talmud and the philosophy of Maimonides under Soloveitchik, AGUS raises two objections to his teacher's position as espoused in *Halakhic Man* (the only work by Soloveitchik that had been published at the time Agus's criticism first appeared). First, Agus posits that Soloveitchik has failed to establish the independence and self-sufficiency of the halakhah, and he is therefore forced to bring in philosophical and kabbalistic concepts to explicate his philosophy of the halakhah. Second, Agus disputes Soloveitchik's contention that halakhic concepts are a priori in nature, charging that Soloveitchik improperly uses the term *a priori* in a dogmatic, Pickwickian sense. If one employs the term accurately to designate knowledge that is independent of experience and there-

fore held to be indubitable, then, Agus argues, halakhic principles in all their minutiae and particularity could never be regarded as a priori constructions. This argument, if sustained, undermines both Soloveitchik's apologia for Orthodox Judaism and his implied critique of the poisonous subjectivism of non-Orthodox varieties of Judaism.

GOLDY traces the influence of Protestant theologians on the thought of Soloveitchik, beginning with Søren Kierkegaard and Rudolf Otto, and particularly such neo-Orthodox exponents of crisis theology as Karl Barth and Paul Tillich. Goldy detects an inconsistency in Soloveitchik's openness to continuing dialogue between traditional Judaism and modern culture and thought, on the one hand, and his anti-ecumenical stance and unswerving opposition to interfaith theological dialogue, on the other. There is indeed this inconsistency in Soloveitchik's philosophy, but that fact does not necessarily constitute a genuine problem, for Soloveitchik is a self-avowed dialectical thinker who has pointed out that the Judaic dialectic, unlike the Hegelian, lacks the third stage of reconciliation *(aufhebung).* His anti-ecumenical views may therefore flow dialectically from his clear vision of the station and duties of Halakhic Man and actually reinforce his conception.

MUNK has written a very scholarly study of Soloveitchik's thought, which includes the only detailed critical examination of his doctoral dissertation on Hermann Cohen's epistemology and ontology. Munk concludes that Soloveitchik's critique demonstrates a fundamental and unbridgeable difference between his philosophy and that of Cohen regarding the character and methodology of thought and the correlation of thought and actuality. The dissertation also reveals the influence of Nicolai Hartmann and Max Scheler, among others, on Soloveitchik, while his later writings show that the impact of these phenomenologists grew more pronounced as his thinking developed. Successive chapters expound and analyze Soloveitchik's major philosophical works. Munk is reluctant to draw overall conclusions about Soloveitchik's thought because only a small fraction of his extensive, fragmentary, and sometimes incoherent oeuvre has been published. Munk does contend, however, that Soloveitchik's fine delineation and characterization of the *lamdan* (talmudic scholar), a type not exactly found in any other social group or religious community, is a significant contribution of lasting value.

ZIEGLER has formulated some of Soloveitchik's halakhic decisions in a manner suitable for the lay reader. In general, the rulings do not differ from those of the traditionalist rabbinic authorities, although there are two possible exceptions: first, Soloveitchik declares that it is mandatory, not merely permissible, for men who do not wear beards to shave on the intermediate days of Passover and Sukkot so as not to appear unkempt on the holidays. Second, he views Thanksgiving as a civil, and not a religious, holiday and permits its celebration. Unfortunately, Ziegler's work lacks a discussion of Soloveitchik's "modern" positions relating to the significance of the State of Israel, his advocacy of intensive Talmud study by women, and his endorsement of secular studies and philosophy.

JACOB HABERMAN

Song of Songs

Bloch, Ariel and Chana Bloch, *The Song of Songs: A New Translation with an Introduction and Commentary,* New York: Random House, 1995

Brenner, Athalya (editor), *A Feminist Companion to the Song of Songs* (Feminist Companion to the Bible, 1), Sheffield, South Yorkshire: Sheffield Academic Press, 1993

Falk, Marcia, *Love Lyrics from the Bible: A Translation and Literary Study of the Song of Songs* (Bible and Literature Series, 4), Sheffield, South Yorkshire: Almond, 1982; revised as *The Song of Songs: A New Translation and Interpretation,* San Francisco: HarperSanFrancisco, 1990

Fox, Michael V., *The Song of Songs and the Ancient Egyptian Love Songs,* Madison: University of Wisconsin Press, 1985

Pope, Marvin H., *Song of Songs* (Anchor Bible, 7C), Garden City, New York: Doubleday, 1977

Perhaps no other book of the Bible has elicited as much comment as the Song of Songs. The variety of interpretation is not merely the product of recent times, for diverse interpretive strategies were present already in antiquity, as the debate over whether the poem should enter the canon of Scripture demonstrates. The discovery of ancient Near Eastern texts since the mid-19th century has opened new corridors of interpretation. Yet, despite the wealth of comparative material, no consensus has been reached with regard to the Song's overall meaning, purpose, history, or original context.

As the entries below will attest, scholars have studied the eight-chapter poem from a variety of perspectives and have brought a variety of theoretical frameworks to bear upon the Song. Most of the important analyses and discussions of the Song remain largely inaccessible to a lay public, scattered as they are in scholarly journals and technically erudite monographs. Even some of the entries below, which are exceptionally accessible to general readers, contain some technical linguistic and philological data. Nevertheless, these works are representative of the most important advances in current understanding of the Song of Songs.

The recent translation of the Song by BLOCH and BLOCH benefits from the expertise of a world-renowned Semitist and a first-class poet. The result is a sensuous account of sexual awakening. The Hebrew text accompanies both the English translation and the commentary at book's end, and the frequent use of transliterations helps make the Song completely accessible to nonscholars. No conjectures are offered as to authorship, although linguistic evidence is used to place the date of the Song in the third century B.C.E. The commentary discusses the Song's place in the canon of Scripture and the history of its interpretation. This translation uniquely represents the passionate love described in the poem not as unrequited, but as consummated. The sexual delights in the Song are presented as reciprocal, tender, and erotic. Eros fills the Israelite landscape, and the lovers celebrate it. Although not portrayed as a drama, the poem carries dramatic effect, and Bloch and Bloch treat it not as an anthology of poetic snippets, but as a unity.

BRENNER's inaugural volume of the Feminist Companion to the Bible series is a collection of essays that investigate the Song from a variety of feminist critical perspectives. Written by a diverse array of scholars, the selections are generally cohesive and accessible to nonscholars. The articles are grouped into six units: the history of feminist readings of the Song; female authorship and culture; intertextual connections and the critique of patriarchy; structure and discourse; genre interpretation; and a scholarly retrospective. Each of the 20 essays offers a unique and insightful contribution to current understanding of the poem. Topics addressed in the essays run the complete gamut of historical inquiry on the Song, including the poem's female voice, audience, sexual imagery, and eventual canonization. The essays represent the most recent advances in feminist scholarship on the Song and demonstrate a fruitful union between feminist approaches to text and other interpretive strategies.

FALK offers an English translation along with a discussion of the Song's context, genre, themes, and motifs. Her translation, while at times straying from the Hebrew original, nonetheless captures the rapturous beauty of the poem. Her approach is primarily literary, paying special attention to the poem's structure. Falk sees no reason to treat the poem as a single text, opting instead to view the book as a collection of 31 lyric poems. In the analytic section of the book, Falk challenges the notion that the Song contains "bizarre, comical, and puzzling" imagery in those units of the Song commonly called *wasfs,* poetic sections that elaborately describe the human body. Falk contends that "sexist interpretation of the *wasf . . .* and of the Song in general is a striking example of how the text can be distorted by culturally biased reading." She also argues, for a variety of reasons, that the composition was penned by a woman and concludes that the Song itself speaks to mutuality and balance between the sexes.

FOX offers the only major study of the poem's relationship to Egyptian love poetry. Based on his comparisons, Fox argues that the Song of Songs "though often considered a loose collection of short songs, is in fact an artistic unity." He replaces the popular allegorical interpretation of the text with one that understands the poem as simply exploring the subject of sexual love between human beings. In addition to an in-depth commentary, examination of the Song's social setting, and compositional analysis, Fox provides a comprehensive discussion of the Egyptian materials and appends hieroglyphic transcriptions of the Egyptian texts themselves. These features make Fox's study valuable to scholar and nonscholar alike.

POPE's hefty volume remains the most comprehensive study of the poem to date. Virtually every aspect of the poem is discussed, from the ancient translations and the date of the book, to prosody, generic classification, and the medieval commentaries. One of Pope's most important contributions is his discussion of the history of interpretation of the Song, which covers a great deal of territory, from the early allegorization of the poem and later dramatic and mystical interpretations, to more recent feminist and psychoanalytical approaches. Based on a wealth of comparative data, especially from Mesopotamia and Ugarit, Pope concludes that the Song originally served as a cultic hymn for use in non-Israelite fertility worship. While some of this work, especially the commentary section, is philologically and linguistically oriented, the great majority is accessible to a general audience. It also provides a wealth of bibliographic information on the Song.

SCOTT B. NOEGEL

South Africa

Abrahams, Israel, *The Birth of a Community,* Cape Town: Cape Town Hebrew Congregation, 1955

Hellig, Jocelyn, "The Jewish Community in South Africa," in *Living Faiths in South Africa,* edited by Martin Prozesky and John de Gruchy, New York: St. Martin's Press, and London: Hurst, 1995

Hoffmann, N.D., *Seyfer ha-zikhroynes,* 1916; translated as *Book of Memoirs: Reminiscences of South African Jewry,* Cape Town: Kaplan Centre for Jewish Studies and Research, University of Cape Town, 1996

Shain, Milton, *The Roots of Antisemitism in South Africa,* Charlottesville and London: University Press of Virginia, 1994

Shimoni, Gideon, *Jews and Zionism: The South African Experience (1910–1967),* Cape Town: Oxford University Press, 1980

Suttner, Immanuel (editor), *Cutting through the Mountain: Interviews with South African Jewish Activists,* Johannesburg: Viking, 1997

The study of the Jews of English-speaking countries has achieved a new prominence in the aftermath of the destruction of European Jewry in the Holocaust. Although the Jewish community in the United States is clearly the most studied English-speaking community, Jews in Canada, New Zealand, Australia, Great Britain, Zimbabwe, and South Africa have also merited the attention of historians and sociologists. The number of Jews in South Africa peaked at 118,000; since the 1970s, many South African Jews have immigrated to Australia, the United States, and Israel, and the Jewish population in that nation is currently around 85,000. Because of the historical context of apartheid, the history of the Jews of South Africa has a character that is unique in modern Jewish history. In order to understand the full picture of how Jews have interacted with modernity in different social and political contexts, it is critical for the scholar to take into account the South African Jewish experience.

One of the classic books on the Jewish experience in South Africa is SHIMONI, a detailed account of the Jewish community in South Africa up to 1967 that places that community's history in the context of Zionism. The author covers most of the important political issues and particularly emphasizes the relationship between the Jews and the ruling groups in the country.

One of the best overviews for those seeking information about the Jewish community in South Africa in the 1990s is HELLIG, which was published as part of a collection of articles on all of the major religions in the country. Hellig adeptly gives a brief outline of the historical background of South African Jewry and presents a vivid picture of the different aspects of Jewish life in contemporary South Africa. Particularly interesting is her account of the unobservant Orthodox Jews who constitute the majority of the South African Jewish community. Nevertheless, Hellig correctly points out that there has been a tremendous revival of Torah study, worship, and observance, particularly in Johannesburg. She describes the development of small, informal prayer groups evoking the Eastern European *shtiebl* that have gained popularity at the expense of large institutionalized synagogues.

One of the most interesting historical documents of South African Jewry is a memoir by HOFFMANN that was written in Yiddish and originally published in 1916. The author describes the origins of the community and evaluates relations between Jews and Afrikaners. He also presents a great deal of information about the lives of South African blacks, although he displays a prejudiced perspective characteristic of his time. This document can be read in conjunction with ABRAHAMS's history of the Jews in the Western Cape Province until the end of the Anglo-Boer War in 1902. Other classics of South African Jewish history include Louis Herrman's *A History of the Jews in South Africa* (1930), and Gustav Saron and Louis Hotz's *The Jews in South Africa: A History* (1955).

SHAIN is a masterpiece describing the history of antisemitism in South Africa up to 1930. His work is particularly important because, although the history of racism in South Africa has long been recognized, historians before Shain typically suggested that antisemitism was a foreign phenomenon that was introduced into South Africa in the 1930s through Nazi propaganda. Shain shows, however, that antisemitism had deep roots in South African society that dated back to the late 19th century. Using not only the expected political sources but also plays, novels, caricatures, and jokes, Shain's book serves as a central source for the history of Jewish-Christian relations in South Africa.

Since the end of apartheid, there has been an increasing interest in the role that Jews did or did not play in the struggle to end institutionalized racism. SUTTNER presents a collection of interviews with South African Jewish activists; the book is named for a statement in the Talmud that insists "let justice cut through the mountain." The collection includes interviews with many of the most important antiapartheid activists, including Joe Slovo and Ronnie Kasrils, both of whom were important figures in the armed struggle of the African National Congress against the apartheid government. Also included are interviews with the Nobel Prize-winning author Nadine Gordimer, musician Johnny Clegg, politician Helen Suzman, and Rabbi Ben Isaacson. The book is a very rich source of material on Jewish activists and can form the basis for a great deal of future analysis.

DANA EVAN KAPLAN

Spain

Aronsfeld, C.C., *The Ghosts of 1492: Jewish Aspects of the Struggle for Religious Freedom in Spain, 1848–1976* (Jewish Social Studies Monograph Series, no. 1), New York: Conference on Jewish Social Studies, 1979

Ashtor, Eliyahu, *Korot ha-Yehudim bi-Sefarad ha-Muslemit,* 1960; as *The Jews of Moslem Spain,* 3 vols., Philadelphia: Jewish Publication Society, 1973

Avni, Haim, *Spain, the Jews, and Franco,* Philadelphia: Jewish Publication Society, 1982

Bachrach, Bernard S., *Early Medieval Jewish Policy in Western Europe,* Minneapolis: University of Minnesota Press, 1977

Baer, Yitzhak, *Toldot ha-Yehudim bi-Sefarad ha-Notsrit,* 1959; as *A History of the Jews in Christian Spain,* 2 vols., Philadelphia: Jewish Publication Society, 1961

Carpenter, Dwayne E., *Alfonso X and the Jews: An Edition of and Commentary on Siete Partidas 7:24 "De los Judíos"* (University of California Publications in Modern Philology, vol. 115), Berkeley: University of California Press, 1986

Chazan, Robert, *Daggers of Faith: Thirteenth-Century Christian Missionizing and Jewish Response,* Berkeley: University of California Press, 1989

Cohen, Jeremy, *The Friars and the Jews: The Evolution of Medieval Anti-Judaism,* Ithaca, New York: Cornell University Press, 1982

Kamen, Henry, *The Spanish Inquisition,* New York: New American Library, 1956; London: Weidenfeld and Nicolson, 1965; as *The Spanish Inquisition: A Historical Revision,* London: Weidenfeld and Nicolson, 1997; New Haven, Connecticut: Yale University Press, 1998

Katz, Solomon, *The Jews in the Visigothic and Frankish Kingdoms of Spain and Gaul* (Monographs of the Mediaeval Academy of America, no. 12), Cambridge, Massachusetts: Mediaeval Academy of America, 1937

Lea, Henry Charles, *A History of the Inquisition of Spain,* 4 vols., New York and London: Macmillan, 1906–1907

Netanyahu, B., *The Origins of the Inquisition in Fifteenth Century Spain,* New York: Random House, 1995

Roth, Cecil, *The Spanish Inquisition,* London: Hale, 1937; New York: Norton, 1964

Septimus, Bernard, *Hispano-Jewish Culture in Transition: The Career and Controversies of Ramah* (Harvard Judaic Monographs, 4), Cambridge, Massachusetts: Harvard University Press, 1982

Wasserstein, David, *The Rise and Fall of the Party-Kings: Politics and Society in Islamic Spain, 1002–1086,* Princeton, New Jersey: Princeton University Press, 1985

The sojourn of the Jews in Spain lasted at least 1,500 years, producing a vibrant and sophisticated culture inherited to a greater or lesser extent by Jews the world over. Their history is generally divided into periods according to the regnant religion of the peninsula: Visigothic Christians ruled from the fourth through seventh century; Ummayad Muslims reigned from the eighth through the tenth century and were followed by division into several Berber Islamic kingdoms; and medieval Christian kingdoms ultimately joined forces and secured control of all of Spain in 1492. After the expulsion of the Jews in that year, organized Jewish life ceased to exist in Spain until the 20th century.

During the period of Visigothic rule in Spain, the Iberian peninsula gradually moved from an attitude of tolerance toward the Jews to one of repeated and virulent persecution. Anti-Jewish laws punctuate many of the seventh-century reigns, which succeeded one another in rapid succession. Useful discussions of Visigothic anti-Jewish policies are found in the studies by Bachrach and by Katz. KATZ's treatment, while informative, manifests all the signs of what Salo Baron referred to as the "lachrymose conception of Jewish history." Katz summarizes the period as follows: "The persecution of the Jews was due to the union between Church and State . . . for a century and a quarter kings and bishops united in an effort to convert the Jews of Spain or to drive them from the kingdom."

BACHRACH attempts to move away from the historiographical model represented by Katz and others in this field by offering a general survey of the early medieval policy of Western European governments toward Jews "from the perspective and aims of its formulators." Bachrach's sober assessment of Visigothic anti-Jewish policy leads him to challenge the received wisdom that Jews living in the Visigothic realm were subjected to an unrelenting series of anti-Jewish laws promulgated by a united church and monarchy. Insofar as such legislation was enacted, Bachrach argues that the noteworthy role played by the Jewish population in assisting the Arab conquerors indicates the utter failure of the Visigothic reign to break the political power of the Jewish community.

The Jews of Islamic Spain prior to the fall of Toledo in 1085 are the subject of ASHTOR's three-volume study. The author occasionally indulges in imaginative speculation in order to piece together a coherent narrative, but he nevertheless provides a good introduction to the dominant personalities and themes of the period.

Spanish history between the fall of Cordoba and the fall of Toledo, known as the period of the "party kings," is the subject of the close study by WASSERSTEIN. In a chapter on the Jews, Wasserstein describes Jewish life under these Berber rulers. In particular, he notes the increased political activity of the Jews and their assimilation of Islamic cultural patterns during this period. Wasserstein investigates the career of Samuel ibn Nagrela, who served as the vizier for the Zirid dynasty that ruled Granada.

The two-volume history by BAER is the standard work on the Jewish experience in Christian Spain. Baer punctuates his work with generous quotations from a wide variety of primary sources that provide the reader with a good sampling of the many areas of literary expression cultivated by Spanish Jewry.

SEPTIMUS analyzes the transition from Islamic to Christian rule through the career of a rabbinic leader who bridged the two civilizations, Rabbi Meir ha-Levi Abulafia (Ramah). Septimus focuses on Ramah's involvement in the controversy over Maimonidean rationalism, which, in many ways, exemplified the cultural clash between "Spanish intellectuals saturated with Greco-Arabic philosophy" and "northern French talmudists totally innocent of philosophical thought" that characterized this period of change.

As the Christian kingdoms gained control over the Iberian peninsula in the 13th century, they promulgated new laws to regulate the position of the Jews. CARPENTER presents a useful English translation of the laws of Alfonso the Wise.

For two significant and contrasting interpretations of the origins and scope of the missionary efforts aimed at the Jews and Muslims in the 13th century, see the books by Cohen and Chazan. COHEN argues that in the 13th and early 14th centuries, Franciscan and Dominican friars developed a "new Christian ideology with regard to the Jews, one that allotted [the Jews] no legitimate right to exist in European society" and constituted a radical break with patristic theology. Cohen attributes this new attitude to a sense of outrage that accompanied the Christian discovery of the Talmud's existence, a discovery that in the minds of the friars forfeited the Jews' right to legal protection in Christendom as the bearers of the Old Testament. CHAZAN, on the other hand, dismisses the notion that the mid-13th century saw the emergence of an altogether new ideology. The necessary ideological ammunition to justify the repudiation of the Jews, he argues, could be found in the venerable Augustinian doctrine. Chazan locates the intensification of Christian missionary efforts among the Spanish Jews within "a broader campaign to engage the non-Christian world in spiritual encounter," made possible by a new material and spiritual vigor and driven by a sense of theological anxiety and insecurity.

The operations of the Inquisition loom large in the destruction of the Jews of Spain. The classic study of the history, methods, and chief actors of the Spanish Inquisition is LEA's four-volume work. NETANYAHU's monumental study of the Inquisition and the Jewish question traces antisemitism in Spain from antiquity through the Middle Ages, examining the Inquisition as a racist, antisemitic institution. This volume supplements the author's earlier work in which he examined the Hebrew sources relating to the expulsion. ROTH's work, although somewhat dated, is still useful. He examines the events leading up to the establishment of the Inquisition in the 15th century and follows its evolution through to its demise in the 19th century. KAMEN offers a broader view of the interaction of the Inquisition with Spanish politics, literature, and religion. He stresses that Spain's decision to expel its Jews was neither surprising nor extraordinary. In describing the historical context for the expulsion, Kamen argues that "the expulsion was, in its widest interpretation, an attempt by the feudalistic nobility to eliminate that section of the middle class—the Jews—which was threatening its predominance in the state."

The lingering echoes of the expulsion in the Spanish historical consciousness are examined by ARONSFELD, who traces the vicissitudes of the debate over abrogation of the expulsion decree and the continuing anti-Jewish forces in the Spanish parliament. Aronsfeld recounts how liberal-minded Spanish politicians who joined forces with Jewish leaders from other countries to seek the readmission of Jews repeatedly encountered strong resistance due to the enduring legacy of the racist doctrines of the expulsion.

AVNI offers a reassessment of Spain's role in rescuing Jews during World War II. While acknowledging that "the Spanish authorities did not discriminate against Jews when they were among large numbers of French, Polish, Dutch, and other refugees illegally crossing the Spanish border," Avni argues that when the fate of Jews alone was at stake Franco's regime reduced its rescue efforts to the barest minimum, with the tacit approval of the Allies.

JANE GERBER
AND ARNOLD FRANKLIN

Spinoza, Baruch de 1632–1677

Dutch philosopher

Allison, Henry E., *Benedict de Spinoza*, Boston: Twayne, 1975; as *Benedict de Spinoza: An Introduction*, New Haven, Connecticut, and London: Yale University Press, 1987
Curley, Edwin, *Behind the Geometrical Method: A Reading of Spinoza's Ethics*, Princeton, New Jersey: Princeton University Press, 1988
Garrett, Don (editor), *The Cambridge Companion to Spinoza*, Cambridge and New York: Cambridge University Press, 1996
Hampshire, Stuart, *Spinoza* (Pelican Philosophy Series, 1), Harmondsworth, Middlesex: Penguin, 1951; New York: Barnes and Noble, 1956; revised edition, Harmondsworth, Middlesex, and New York: Penguin, 1987
Harris, Errol E., *Spinoza's Philosophy: An Outline*, Atlantic Highlands, New Jersey: Humanities, 1992
Harris, Errol E., *The Substance of Spinoza*, Atlantic Highlands, New Jersey: Humanities, 1995
Lloyd, Genevieve, *Routledge Philosophy Guidebook to Spinoza and the Ethics*, London and New York: Routledge, 1996
Mason, Richard, *The God of Spinoza: A Philosophical Study*, Cambridge and New York: Cambridge University Press, 1997
Norris, Christopher, *Spinoza and the Origins of Modern Critical Theory* (Bucknell Lectures in Literary Theory, 5), Oxford and Cambridge, Massachusetts: Blackwell, 1991
Silverman, R.M., *Baruch Spinoza: Outcast Jew, Universal Sage* (Jews in Modern Culture), Northwood, Middlesex: Symposium, 1995
Smith, Steven B., *Spinoza, Liberalism, and the Question of Jewish Identity*, New Haven, Connecticut: Yale University Press, 1997
Strauss, Leo, *Spinoza's Critique of Religion*, New York: Schocken, 1965
Wolfson, Harry A., *The Philosophy of Spinoza: Unfolding the Latent Processes of His Reasoning*, 2 vols., Cambridge, Massachusetts: Harvard University Press, 1934
Yovel, Yirmiyahu, *Spinoza and Other Heretics*, vol. 1: *The Marrano of Reason*, Princeton, New Jersey: Princeton University Press, 1989; Oxford: Oxford University Press, 1992
Yovel, Yirmiyahu, *Spinoza and Other Heretics*, vol. 2: *The Adventures of Immanence*, Princeton, New Jersey: Princeton University Press, 1989; Oxford: Oxford University Press, 1992

Countless studies testify to the worldwide importance and influence of Baruch (Benedictus) de Spinoza, who has remained nevertheless a figure of disputed significance within Jewish thought. He has been ostracized as a bitter critic of religion and celebrated as a pioneer of secular Judaism, hailed as a "God-intoxicated man" and excoriated as an atheist. This small selection from a vast secondary literature attempts to bring together classic studies and recent publications relating to Spinoza's *Ethics* and to both his *Tractatus Theologico-Politicus (TTP)* and his *Tractatus Politicus (TP)*. Some of these studies adopt a broad perspective, while others are in-depth treatments of particular themes, especially his controversial position within, or rather at the margin of, Jewish thought.

HAMPSHIRE's original edition has gone through many reprints and a few revisions since 1951. His clearly articulated study of Spinoza's thought aims "to give such a critical exposition of his most important doctrines as will be intelligible and interesting even to the non-specialist without any sacrifice of accuracy or completeness: so far as possible to abstain from technical jargon, but also to avoid undue simplification." After elucidating Spinoza's philosophical background, the study follows Spinoza's own order of exposition in *The Ethics* and expounds his metaphysical doctrine of the one substance, God or Nature, as the central feature of his all-embracing framework. Hampshire then describes and assesses Spinoza's ideas on the nature of knowledge and freedom, the existence of God, ethics and politics, and mind and matter, in an attempt "to keep the balance between the theoretical and the metaphysical interests of . . . *The Ethics* and the practical and political reasoning in the *TTP* and in the *TP*." The appendix provides a brief account of Spinoza's life.

Another excellent general introduction to the life and work of Spinoza is ALLISON's study, "intended primarily for the general reader or student with some background in philosophy," but, at the same time, also addressing "the more advanced student and perhaps even the specialist." His lucid presentation of "an exacting overview of Spinoza's entire philosophy" aims both at breadth and at depth. A brief account of Spinoza's life is followed by a presentation of the main features of 17th-century thought that are relevant to an understanding of Spinoza's ideas today. Allison examines critically the chief doctrines of *The Ethics*, closely following "the actual course of [the] arguments" in the primary text in order to assist "the reader who is struggling to follow the often tortuous course of Spinoza's thought." Discussion of the notion of freedom leads to an exposition of Spinoza's political philosophy, and the final chapter considers his views on religion, together with his revolutionary biblical criticism.

HARRIS (1992) is a serious yet "simplified introductory presentation of the major branches of Spinoza's philosophy" that will help beginning students gain access, in plain language, to the main ideas and line of reasoning Spinoza expounded, without being overburdened with a scholarly apparatus. The introduction considers the current appeal of Spinoza's thought and advances the view that his system resulted from the exertions of a man of great integrity and moral sincerity, and that it can still provide practical guidance for contemporary problems of human existence. Separate chapters explore Spinoza's deductive reasoning, his idea of God, and his "reconciliation" of mind and body, time and eternity, teleology and freedom, and good and evil. Finally Harris addresses Spinoza's views on pol-

itics and religion, whereby the latter is transformed into a form of consciousness that "embraces all time and all existence in an eternal concept of the whole."

LLOYD's accessibly written introductory manual will appeal to any beginning student who seeks to be led through the complex text of Spinoza's *Ethics*. This brief but thorough guide deals with the key issues of Spinoza's thought, evaluating his arguments in their historical context before assessing them for their continuing relevance to contemporary philosophy. It also introduces the uninitiated reader to the many angles from which *The Ethics* can be approached by providing an overview of other scholars' critical interpretations. In a clearly structured and concise way, Lloyd examines Spinoza's ideas on God, minds and bodies, freedom, knowledge, and love of God. The final chapters pay special attention to Spinoza's ideas on the eternity of the mind and address the question, "What makes *The Ethics* an ethical work?"

CURLEY provides the advanced student with a substantial introduction to *The Ethics*. Reworked from his Jerusalem Spinoza lectures of 1984, it is the fruit of 25 years of study of Spinoza. This volume by the renowned editor and translator of Spinoza's collected works is addressed both to the professional Spinoza scholar and to anyone who is prepared to read carefully and who has some knowledge of the thought of Descartes and Hobbes. Curley's masterly reading of *The Ethics* falls into two sections: the first part follows Spinoza's own arguments and shows how they originated from his study of Descartes and Hobbes; the scholarly notes constituting the second part attempt to support some of the more controversial conclusions advanced in the first part, with abundant references to recent commentators on Spinoza.

WOLFSON's two magisterial volumes on Spinoza's philosophy have remained a standard work in spite of some recent criticism (from Curley among others) for relating Spinoza more to scholastic thought than to the thought of his immediate predecessors. Primarily based upon *The Ethics*, Wolfson's study aims to relate the explicit Benedictus to the implicit Baruch, "the first of the moderns" to "the last of the medievals." Following Spinoza's own method, he traces the philosopher's building blocks backward, analyzing them both for their detailed meaning and for their wider connotations for his whole system. Wolfson's work can therefore be read as a running commentary on *The Ethics* or as a rich source book of ideas and their development in the history of philosophy, including discussions of the thought of Maimonides, Crescas, and Spinoza's other Jewish sources. Spinoza's definitions of substance, mode, attributes, and other terms and concepts are all given a thorough analysis, and the last chapter assesses the innovations and radicalism of Spinoza's thought.

Spinoza's concept of "substance" lies at the heart of the collection of essays by HARRIS (1995), which aims at clarifying some of the more vexing problems in Spinoza's thought. Harris addresses the relationship between Spinoza's methodology and the metaphysical content of his philosophy, present in notions such as the finite and infinite. He examines the meaning of the infinity of the divine attributes and the doctrine of the mind-body relationship, the order of ideas and things, the human mind, and God's mind. The second part deals with Spinoza's politics and religion and his ideas of natural law and contract, before taking issue with Strauss's suggestion of an esoteric doctrine in the *Tractatus Theologico-Politicus*. The final part looks at Spinoza's spiritual relationship with Leibniz and assesses his influence on Fichte, Schelling, and Hegel, and their criticisms of him. The emphasis in Harris's study is on "Spinoza's holism and its implications both within and beyond Spinoza's own writings," and the work is addressed to the more advanced student.

The collection of essays written by an international team of scholars and edited by GARRETT is one in a series of Cambridge companions to major philosophers, aimed at the non-specialist as well as the advanced student. Each of the essays provides a clear and systematic approach to a different aspect of Spinoza's thought, covering his metaphysics, epistemology, psychology, and political theory and his revolutionary ideas on religion and biblical criticism. His controversial image is discussed along with his achievements, the reception of his thought and influence, and some more recent perspectives on his life and works. Other contributions throw new light on Spinoza as a keen scientist and consider his influence on psychology and also on political thought (Henry Kissinger claimed to have been influenced by some of Spinoza's "Machiavellian" ideas). This up-to-date study, to which has been added a substantial bibliography, will serve as a useful reference work on recent developments in the interpretation of Spinoza's thought.

NORRIS emphasizes the lasting influence of Spinoza's thought for poets and literary theorists, after considering his invigorating influence on the Enlightenment. His study has three aims: to establish "that nearly all the great debates in present-day literary theory have their origin in one or another aspect of Spinoza's work," to trace Spinoza's influence on French movements of thought over the past three decades (from Althusserian Marxism to hermeneutics, deconstruction, narrative poetics, new historicism, and thinkers such as G. Deleuze), and most importantly, to demonstrate that Spinoza's work "may help us to perceive some of the fallacies . . . of foreshortened historical perspective that have characterized the discourse of literary theory in its latest post-modern phase." Norris's book is therefore addressed primarily to the student of French poststructuralism and its offshoots, rather than to Spinoza specialists.

STRAUSS's thorough and scholarly study of Spinoza's religious philosophy draws conclusions that remain controversial and challenging (see, for example, Harris [1995] and Donagan in Garrett). Its central theme is the critical presentation of Spinoza's *Tractatus Theologico-Politicus*. Strauss maintains that Spinoza was inconsistent and contradicted himself on numerous occasions, charging him with deliberately discrediting traditional Judaism and with undermining the authority of Scripture. He addresses Spinoza's critique of Maimonides' and Calvin's thought, then examines Spinoza's political doctrines such as his theory of natural right and the social function of religion. He considers both Spinoza's interest in and his indifference to the Bible as well as his philological and historical criticism of it. The thoughts of Spinoza's forerunners, Uriel da Costa and Isaac de la Peyrère, and their critique of religion are also expounded, together with aspects of Hobbes's attitude toward religion.

A liberal Jewish approach to Spinoza is undertaken in SILVERMAN's study, which portrays Spinoza's thought as representative of "both a radical break with traditional norms and a dependence upon them." An introductory sketch looks at "how Spinoza has been received by Jews and non-Jews of various outlooks." Addressing the magnitude of Spinoza's legacy in the 20th century, its relation to Judaism, and the current challenge offered by his thought, Silverman demonstrates how Spinoza can be shown to reflect traditional Jewish values and takes a fresh approach with regard to his reputed "heresies." Silverman gives credit to Spinoza's Bible criticism and its impact on the Reform movement, and he outlines Spinoza's political theory in terms of its influence on current secularist thinking in Israel. Spinoza studies aside, this lively book should appeal to anyone interested in an unprejudiced critical analysis of many of the conceptual building blocks that make up Judaism.

YOVEL's (1989a, 1989b) erudite and richly informative volumes present Spinoza "as the most outstanding and influential thinker of modernity." The first volume examines the world of the Marranos and is indispensable for an understanding of Spinoza's background and his break with the Amsterdam Jewish community. Yovel clarifies how the crypto-Jewish life of generations of Marranos undermined both Judaism and Christianity, leading to skepticism and secularism. Providing fascinating insight into the patterns of the Marrano mind and experience, Yovel portrays Spinoza in a newly secularized context before examining his significance for contemporary Jewish thought. Surveying the thought of Kant, Hegel, Heine, Marx, Nietzsche, Freud, and Einstein for their indebtedness to Spinoza, Yovel demonstrates in his second volume how all these thinkers shared the essentials of Spinoza's notion of immanence and reveals the extent to which this idea has left its mark on modern culture as a major liberating force.

SMITH's lucid, comprehensive, and scholarly book is the first study to connect two strands of Spinoza's thought: first, he portrays Spinoza as a politically engaged thinker who "advocated and embodied a new conception of the emancipated individual" and who influenced political movements as diverse as the Enlightenment, liberalism, and political Zionism. Second, and more importantly for Judaism, Smith considers how the liberal solution has affected the Jewish question. He argues with regard to the *Tractatus Theologico-Politicus* that Spinoza was the first Jewish thinker who made the civil status of Jews essential to modern political thought by recasting Judaism "to include the liberal values of autonomy and emancipation from tradition." Spinoza's powerful statements for freedom of thought and expression and his theories of right and contract earn him "a rightful place in the history of political thought as one of the leading philosophical founders of modern liberalism." This book probes deeply into the relationship between Judaism and liberalism and successfully demonstrates that it was Spinoza who "made the Jewish question an essential ingredient of modern political thought."

The concept of God is central to the thought of Spinoza to such extent that he has been celebrated as a "God-intoxicated man," while he has also been accused of atheism for choosing to live outside any religious community. Bringing together the philosopher's fundamental conclusions about God and religion, MASON's clear and carefully reasoned book "is the fullest study in English for many years on the role of God in Spinoza's philosophy." While the first part of this study examines God's existence, nature, and relationship to the world in terms of causality and is, "of necessity, more philosophically technical, the conclusions should be of interest to theologians and philosophers of religion as well as to philosophers." The second part deals with Spinoza's judgment of religion in general, its origins, history, and practices, while the third part addresses Spinoza's ideas on religious freedom. Some of Mason's conclusions challenge the stereotype of Spinoza as a rationalist and emphasize his commitment to consistency in an overall imma-nent worldview, so apparent in Spinoza's identification of the study of nature with the study of God: only if the world's phe-nomena can be understood scientifically, he maintains, can a proper, God-like view of the universe be achieved.

ESTHER I. SEIDEL

Steinberg, Milton   1903–1950

American theologian

Cohen, Arthur A., "Introduction," in Steinberg's *Anatomy of Faith,* New York: Harcourt, Brace, 1960
Cohen, Arthur A., "Judaism in Transition," in his *The Natural and the Supernatural Jew: An Historical and Theological Introduction,* New York: Pantheon, 1962; London: Vallentine, Mitchell, 1967; 2nd edition, New York: Behrman House, 1979
Goldy, Robert G., *The Emergence of Jewish Theology in America* (The Modern Jewish Experience), Bloomington: Indiana University Press, 1990
Noveck, Simon, *Milton Steinberg: Portrait of a Rabbi,* New York: Ktav, 1978
Noveck, Simon, "Kaplan and Milton Steinberg: A Disciple's Agreements and Disagreements," in *The American Judaism of Mordecai M. Kaplan* (Reappraisals in Jewish Social and Intellectual History), edited by Emanuel S. Goldsmith et al., New York: New York University Press, 1990

Milton Steinberg was a noted Conservative rabbi with Recon-structionist leanings, an author and theological writer. His lit-tle book *Basic Judaism* was justly praised as one of the best presentations of the Jewish religion, and his novel *As a Driven Leaf* had a certain vogue and still remains in print.

NOVECK (1978) was a former student of Steinberg at the Jewish Theological Seminary, and he then served as Stein-berg's assistant at the Park Avenue Synagogue in New York. In 1950, after Steinberg's death at the early age of 46, Noveck became his successor, serving in that capacity until the fall of 1956. This perceptive and meticulously researched biography concentrates on three areas in which Steinberg distinguished himself, and in which he was regarded as a paradigm of what a rabbi should be: the congregational rabbinate, writing, and teaching. Noveck describes a Steinberg who grew up in Syra-cuse, New York, and excelled early in his academic studies. His

parents had largely given up Jewish observances, but the fam-ily lived with his maternal grandparents, and Steinberg fondly remembered the religious atmosphere of the home. When he was a teenager, Steinberg's family moved to New York City, where they joined a Conservative synagogue. There Steinberg came under the influence of its rabbi, Jacob Kohn, who dis-cussed religious philosophy with him and encouraged him to practice traditional Judaism.

At City College in New York, Steinberg was intellectually stimulated by the courses in philosophy that he pursued under Morris Raphael Cohen, a naturalist, who was highly critical of theism and organized religion. Noveck clearly portrays the bat-tle going on in Steinberg's mind between Cohen and Kohn: the secularist arguments of the one and the religious counterargu-ments of the other. Steinberg studied for the rabbinate at the Jewish Theological Seminary but was disappointed in his hope that his studies would help him resolve his theological doubts. He was on the verge of withdrawing from the seminary on half a dozen occasions, and he would have done so were it not for Mordecai Kaplan, the Morris Cohen of the seminary faculty. Kaplan was a disabuser and a cleanser of inherited prejudices and unexamined assumptions, but, unlike Cohen, he was not merely critical and negative. Kaplan wanted to refashion and revitalize Judaism for the modern world, and toward that end he founded the Reconstructionist movement, which Steinberg joined and in which he was active. Steinberg was renowned for his thought-provoking sermons, which were a model of clar-ity, relevance, and beauty. He realized that many of his listen-ers did not have the philosophical background to follow all his ideas, but he felt that the pulpit was a place from which one should draw not only stimulus and courage, but also knowl-edge and guidance. Steinberg's sermons dealt with three major topics: problems of Zionism and Jewish survival, doctrines and beliefs, and social problems in the light of Jewish tradition. Some representative sermons are titled: "Intermarriage: Is It Wise? Is It Right?" "Lessons from Germany," "Can We Be Orthodox?" "What Value Has Prayer?" "Mercy Killings," and "The Dilemma of the Pacifist." Steinberg loved the congrega-tional ministry, and people from all walks of life perceived him to be a charismatic and extraordinarily sensitive leader.

Steinberg's first book, *The Making of the Modern Jew,* pub-lished in 1934, attracted wide attention as a discussion of the factors of Jewish survival in the face of persecution. Its sequel, *A Partisan Guide to the Jewish Problem* (1945), which had a great impact, makes it clear that to Steinberg the most ten-able theory of Jewish life in America is that of living in two civilizations, being at home in both American and Jewish cul-ture. In a particularly eloquent epilogue, Steinberg replies to the question, "Why be Jews?" with a ringing affirmation that, despite misery and persecution, Jewish life is infinitely worthwhile. Steinberg's semiautobiographical historical novel, *As a Driven Leaf* (1939), dealt with the conflict in the soul of a first-century talmudic sage, Elisha ben Abuyah, who was drawn to both Hellenism and Hebraism, and whose struggle to live in two worlds destroyed his ability to live in either. Elisha is emblematic of Steinberg himself and his family in many ways.

Steinberg somewhat complacently took it for granted that the deep, demonstrated roots of his own faith would be transmitted automatically to his two sons, Jonathan and David. They were given only a spotty, sporadic Jewish education and were not required to observe Jewish law. In the year before his death, Steinberg began to work very closely on Latin with his older son Jonathan, and during his father's funeral, Jonathan suddenly stepped forth and read one of his father's favorite passages from the *Meditations* of Marcus Aurelius. When interviewed by Noveck, Steinberg's son, by then a professor of history at Cambridge University and completely alienated from Jewish life, remarked ruefully that his father was too permissive and that if he had been stricter things might have turned out differently. Perhaps Rabbi Steinberg himself was somewhat ambivalent and uncertain about the synthesis he tried to achieve between Jewish values and American ideals. Like his fictional hero, Elisha, Steinberg came to appreciate the centrality of faith in human life. Noveck ends his study with a touching story. Just before he finished his book, Noveck visited Steinberg's grave in Westchester County, north of New York City. His tombstone contains the words "Faith and Reason," which his wife had chosen, but the word "Reason" is covered with foliage, and now, from a distance, nothing remains but "Faith."

Cohen was a student and admirer of Steinberg during the last five years of Steinberg's life. His two essays supplement each other and can be considered together: COHEN (1960) is expository and summarizes Steinberg's views, while COHEN (1962) is a critical evaluation of those views. In Cohen's judgment, Steinberg was not a theological pathbreaker and made no significant contribution to American Jewish thought in the 1930s and 1940s. Steinberg's novel, *As a Driven Leaf*, marks a turning point in his thinking. Toward the end of his life, he criticized Reconstructionism as being unyielding to theological speculation and closed to the requirements of poetry. In particular, Steinberg became highly critical of Kaplan's conception of God as the sum total of those forces that enhance life and make for salvation. He raised the following objections and reservations to this view: it is not clear whether God is the Supreme Being, an entity that really exists, an aspect of reality, an abstract metaphysical principle, or merely a useful fiction. Steinberg pointedly asked: "Who adds up 'the sum' in 'the sum total of forces that make for salvation?' Is the sum added up 'out there' or in the human imagination?" Further, this conception comes close to tribalism in religion because of its relativism and parochialism in time and space.

NOVECK (1990) examines the different approaches to the problem of God as conceived by Steinberg and Kaplan. Kaplan prefers to speak of God as a process or force rather than an entity or being. He rejects the latter idea because he sees in it a remnant of anthropomorphism and mythology. For Kaplan "God" is not a substantive noun, such as "gold" or "silver," but a functional noun, such as "president" or "ruler." God is, therefore, a correlative noun, with salvation or human fulfillment as the correlate. The term "God" for Kaplan denotes the power or process both in the cosmos and in man that makes for human fulfillment (or salvation) in the pursuit of the ideals of truth, goodness, and beauty, interwoven in a pattern of holiness. Steinberg's theology is more traditional in its approach to belief in God. For him God is a personal being, a supreme existential reality; a God who is merely an aspect of reality, the sum of those forces that make for the enhancement of life, is not enough of a God. For Steinberg, belief in God is a hypothesis to be tested, like any other hypothesis. The theistic explanation of the world and the human situation fits the facts better than any rival theory. Noveck minimizes the differences between Kaplan and Steinberg, seeing the areas of agreement between them as far greater than the areas of disagreement. Noveck denies that Steinberg was distancing himself from Kaplan, and that if he had lived, he would have disassociated himself entirely from Kaplan and from the Reconstructionist movement. He tried to reconcile a more traditional metaphysics with the reconstruction of Jewish life in the modern world. It is not entirely clear, however, how Steinberg, for example, can speak of "God as a lawgiver" and yet accept Kaplan's approach to Jewish ritual as religious folkways.

GOLDY examines the relationship between Steinberg and Will Herberg. When Herberg became disillusioned with Marxism and turned instead to Jewish theology for guidance, Steinberg helped him gain a forum and respectability in rabbinic circles. Herberg, for his part, influenced Steinberg to question the religious liberalism that he espoused and to study the work of Jewish existentialists, especially Martin Buber and Franz Rosenzweig. While Steinberg was undeniably rethinking his position and turning in a new direction, it may be wondered whether this move was really in the direction of religious existentialism or rather toward the process theology of Whitehead and Hartshorne. Steinberg's untimely death preempted articulation of his mature standpoint.

JACOB HABERMAN

Sudan *see* Egypt and Sudan

Suicide

Droge, Arthur J. and James D. Tabor, *A Noble Death: Suicide and Martyrdom among Christians and Jews in Antiquity*, San Francisco: HarperSanFrancisco, 1992

Goldstein, Sidney, *Suicide in Rabbinic Literature*, Hoboken, New Jersey: Ktav, 1989

Hankoff, Leon D., "Judaic Origins of the Suicide Prohibition," in *Suicide: Theory and Clinical Aspects*, edited by Leon D. Hankoff and Bernice Einsidler, Littleton, Massachusetts: PSG, 1979

Reines, Ch. W., "The Jewish Attitude toward Suicide," *Judaism*, 10(2), 1961

Rosner, Fred, "Suicide in Biblical, Talmudic and Rabbinic Writings," *Tradition: A Journal of Orthodox Thought*, 11(2), 1970–1971

Shapiro, Marc B., "Suicide and the World-to-Come," *AJS Review*, 18(2), 1993

Siegel, Seymour, "Religion: A Jewish View," in *Suicide: Theory and Clinical Aspects*, edited by Leon D. Hankoff and Bernice Einsidler, Littleton, Massachusetts: PSG, 1979

Halakhic Judaism generally distinguishes between two forms of intentional death. One who agrees to be killed in order to avoid idolatry, incest (to include adultery), and bloodshed is described as *mekaddesh ha-Shem* (sanctifying God's name); one who intentionally kills himself for personal reasons may be viewed as *me'abbed 'atsmo beda'at* (destroying himself wittingly). While the former is praised and venerated as a holy devotee, the latter is condemned and scorned as a selfish transgressor. According to the post-talmudic tractate Semahot, unsanctioned acts of voluntary death deny the dead ordinary burial rites. Subsequent popular perceptions deprived self-destroyers of a place in the world to come.

HANKOFF argues that the prohibition against suicide originated in the Bible. In his view, the generic prohibition against spilling blood in Genesis 9:4–6 includes self-killing. God's rejections of Jonah's, Elijah's, and Job's wishes to end their lives prematurely connote, in Hankoff's opinion, such a ban. Hankoff associates the prohibition against voluntary death with the Semites' belief that blood carries the soul and bonds the tribe's sacred relationships. Blood, as a sacred property, could be shed only with communal consent. Individuals who shed their own blood were acting alone, thus jeopardizing the social structure and violating the tribe's covenant with the divine. Hankoff therefore considers the Gileadites' burning of Saul's body a form of communal undoing of the king's illegal spilling of his blood. He views cases of self-destruction that did not involve actual bloodshed as "less heinous." Hankoff reaches these conclusions at the same time that he acknowledges that the Bible does not explicitly condemn or ban self-destruction.

According to DROGE and TABOR, the Bible neither condemns nor bans suicide at all. Samson's honorable burial by his family and Ahitophel's burial in his fathers' tomb do not indicate that an unusual treatment of suicides was practiced. According to the authors, the Bible presents Samson's (Judges 16:23–31) and King Saul's (1 Samuel 31:13; 2 Samuel 21:12–14) deaths as noble. What determines the biblical attitude toward self-killing is the circumstances that lead to the act rather than the act itself. In the Hellenistic and Roman periods, the perception of self-killing as a noble act further increased. The authors discuss extensively Josephus Flavius's descriptions of self-inflicted deaths during military and political events. They downplay Josephus's view of self-killing as an act of madness, which leads suicides to the "darker regions of the nether world." Josephus's remarks that self-killers are not to be buried until sunset (like criminals) and that children suffer for their parents' self-destructive acts (*Jewish War*) are ignored. Despite Genesis Rabbah's (34:13) and Rabbi Eleazar's prohibition against injuring oneself (Baba Kamma 91b) and the caveat not to see the grave as a place of refuge (Abot 4:22), the authors argue that the Talmud does not oppose taking one's own life. Moreover, they suggest that the desire to enter the world to come served as a motivation for self-killing. The Talmud, however, does not present entry to the world to come as the motivation for deliberate deaths even in cases of martyrdom, and some tragic stories (Berakhot 23a; Hullin 94a) are mentioned in order to prevent circumstances that might lead to self-killing. While one may occasionally disagree with the authors' interpretations, this stimulating book is nonetheless an essential contribution. Through their fresh methodology, the authors have done much to clarify the role and scope of this puzzling phenomenon in antiquity.

SIEGEL relies on the assumption that the value of human life has always been a central motif in Judaism. Using the term suicide in a pejorative sense, the article views self-killing as a denial of divine providence. King Saul constitutes an exception, for his death was decreed by God and foretold by Samuel. Hanina ben Teradyon's story (Avodah Zarah 18a–b) serves the author as a paradigm of religious devotion. Despite the cases of Saul and the 400 youths who chose self-drowning (Gittin 57b), Siegel holds that normative Judaism rarely permits self-killing even when religious and moral danger is imminent. Such acts would display a denial of hope in the Omnipotent. For this reason, he argues, rabbis did not approve self-killing in Nazi ghettos. In line with current rabbinic consensus, Siegel concludes that normative Judaism today views most suicides as individuals who destroyed themselves "unwillfully." Thus, as tractate Semahot instructs, they cannot be held culpable, and the usual rites of burial abide. Only suicides that "consciously" challenge the boon of life and the existence of their Creator do not merit the rites for the dead.

REINES introduces discussion of sociological, psychological, and philosophical aspects of suicide. He views suicide as an offense against the protagonist and humanity. From a social viewpoint, individuals lack the right to self-destruct. In his view, the Jewish unequivocal condemnation of suicide as a sinful act against God inspired Christianity and Islam. Based on the biblical stories of voluntary death that were committed under political and military duress, Reines argues that rabbis made exceptional decisions in similar situations. Yet he infers that suicide was unknown to the Israelites. Reines concludes with a useful observation: the treatment of suicides in rabbinic literature may seem rigid and dogmatic, but in actual practice the rabbis understood suicide's psychology and thus "exercised realistic flexibility."

ROSNER begins with the biblical stories of suicide, leaving out the case of Abimelech. Short rabbinic commentaries follow Saul's and Zimri's stories. Next Rosner skims through the Apocrypha and also adds brief descriptions of Job's near suicide and Josephus Flavius's reports on Jotapata and Masada. He continues with examples of suicide in talmudic, midrashic, and late rabbinic material. The article concludes with the section "Martyrdom in Judaism." Rosner could have avoided many of his inaccurate statements if he had set for himself definitions of suicide and martyrdom. He mentions the stories of Hanina ben Teradyon, the archetype of martyrdom in Judaism, and the 400 youths (Gittin 57b) in his section "Suicide in the Talmud," instead of in his section on martyrdom. Yet he determines that "Judaism regards suicide as a crime and strictly forbidden by Jewish law." His talmudic illustrations do not justify such a strict assertion. He inappropriately analogizes the suicide with "one who burns a Sefer Torah," and unfoundedly concludes in the name of the rabbis that "he who willfully destroys himself has no share in the world to come." Another erroneous statement is that "martyrdom includes the ending of one's own life." Nowhere in the Talmud is taking one's life as an act of martyrdom explicitly approved. Rosner's example of Hanina ben Teradyon contradicts his own conclusion.

GOLDSTEIN thoroughly covers suicidal incidents from biblical through recent times and reviews the diverse commentaries they have triggered. His attempt to arrive at a halakhic definition of suicide is useful in understanding various rabbinic decisions. Goldstein's classifications of suicides clarify why talmudic rabbis exonerated numerous cases. When self-destruction resulted from poverty, humiliation, mental illness, or personal stress, rabbis exercised leniency and often found the suicides inculpable. Such suicides thus are not denied burial rites. But no unanimous ruling exists. Chapter six, "Suicide as an Act of Martyrdom," views the acts of suicide it describes as praiseworthy and meritorious. Although technically correct, from the halakhic viewpoint, the Hebrew terms for *suicide* and *martyrdom* constitute a contradiction. Excursus 1, "Mourning Procedures for an Intentional Suicide," sheds more light on suicides' burial rites. The many quotations in the appendix reinforce Goldstein's exhaustive study.

SHAPIRO convincingly demonstrates that the rabbinic maxim "those who commit suicide have no share in the world to come" has no halakhic foundation. He traces the earliest mention of this notion to a 14th-century Bible commentary by the Yemenite Rabbi Nethanel ben Isaiah. Shapiro suggests a possible Islamic influence on Nethanel. From the 16th century the notion gained momentum, and by the 18th century it had become widespread both in Ashkenazi and Sephardi circles. Despite the parallels between this maxim and the Christian view on suicide, Shapiro contends that the expression in question "arose out of an interpretation of the various *halakhot* connected to suicide." The article is an important reminder that Judaism did not always perceive suicide as a heinous sin.

SHMUEL SHEPKARU

See also Martyrdom

Sukkot

Donin, Hayim Halevi, *Sukkot* (Popular History of Jewish Civilization), New York: Amiel, 1974

Drucker, Malka, *Sukkot: A Time to Rejoice*, New York: Holiday House, 1982

Gaster, Theodor H., "The Feast of Booths," in *Festivals of the Jewish Year: A Modern Interpretation and Guide*, New York: Sloane, 1953

Goldwurm, Hersh et al., *Succos: Its Significance, Laws, and Prayers: A Presentation Anthologized from Talmudic and Traditional Sources* (ArtScroll Mesorah Series), Brooklyn, New York: Mesorah, 1982, 2nd edition, 1989

Goodman, Philip (editor), *The Sukkot and Simhat Torah Anthology*, Philadelphia: Jewish Publication Society, 1973

Rubenstein, Jeffrey L., *The History of Sukkot during the Second Temple and Rabbinic Periods* (Brown Judaic Studies, no. 302), Atlanta, Georgia: Scholars Press, 1995

Schauss, Hayyim, *The Jewish Festivals: From Their Beginnings to Our Own Day*, New York: Union of American Hebrew Congregations, 1938

Sukkot (Tabernacles) is the last of the three annual pilgrimage festivals. Celebrated at the close of the agricultural year in the fall, at the time of the fruit, olive, and grape harvests, Sukkot is the most joyous festival of the year. During the Second Temple Period, worshipers gathered at the Jerusalem Temple for a week-long complex of rituals including processions, water libations, sacrifices, and all-night merrymaking. Scholars have applied several methods of religious studies to shed light on different aspects of the festival. Comparative religion and anthropology illuminate the diverse and colorful rituals practiced at the Temple. Historians of religion seek to understand the rabbinic reinterpretations and transformations of the festival after the destruction of the Temple in 70 C.E. Popular books generally concentrate on the *lulav* (festal wand) and *sukkah* (booth), the two main rituals to survive the destruction, and describe the liturgy and customs practiced in the past and today.

DONIN's book is a comprehensive and straightforward account of the history, customs, and traditions of Sukkot. He includes the main laws of the sukkah and the four species together with descriptions of how the rituals have been observed at different points in history. Donin offers an excellent summary of the significance of the festival within Jewish tradition and a fine discussion of its spiritual motifs. Numerous photographs and illustrations enhance the book. This work is recommended for anyone seeking a readable overview of almost every aspect of the festival.

DRUCKER explains the festival and its customs on an elementary level. The book contains brief historical summaries but primarily describes Sukkot as it is celebrated today. It contains recipes, activities, and instructions on how to build and decorate a sukkah. The book is for those interested in learning how to celebrate at home or in the synagogue and is appropriate for children.

GOODMAN provides an extensive anthology that includes biblical, talmudic, medieval, and other historical sources concerning the festival; summaries of important laws and customs; translations of prayers and liturgical poetry; and descriptions of the colorful festival rituals. There are brief accounts of the historical development of the festival and its rituals and of the nature of Sukkot celebrations in disparate Jewish communities. Goodman also includes short stories, poems, humorous anecdotes, and recipes related to the festival. This is a valuable compendium of a great number of diverse sources.

GASTER's chapter on Sukkot applies sociological and anthropological approaches to the study of religion in order to interpret the customs and rituals of the festival. He describes Sukkot in terms of seasonal festivals occurring at set points of the agricultural cycle. Gaster employs cross-cultural comparisons to shed light on fertility and rain-making rituals and points out pagan influences. His main emphasis is the festival as celebrated in biblical and ancient times, especially the festivities at the Jerusalem temple. While many of Gaster's interpretations are speculative, he offers rich and interesting comparative perspectives on the festival and its customs.

GOLDWURM's book, a volume of the ArtScroll Mesorah Series, offers an Orthodox manual for understanding and celebrating the festival. The first section contains moral and spiritual insights related to Sukkot and its rituals, essentially a collection of sermonic points culled from various sources. The second section defines commandments and customs. The third section is a digest of laws divided into 124 sections, a how-to manual for the interested observer. The fourth section contains liturgy and blessings in both Hebrew and English with a commentary. The book is intended as a practical guide for the contemporary Orthodox Jew.

RUBENSTEIN presents a scholarly analysis of the development of the festival and its rituals from late biblical times through the end of the talmudic period. The work reconstructs the festival as celebrated in the Jerusalem Temple and studies the changes that occurred when the Temple was destroyed. The first half collects and discusses references to Sukkot in sources from the Second Temple era, including Josephus, Philo, and the Qumran scrolls. The second half provides a detailed legal history of rabbinic laws related to the festival and discusses midrashic traditions that express the rabbinic interpretations of the symbols and rituals. The book is intended for scholars, particularly those interested in history.

SCHAUSS includes three chapters on Sukkot. The first two provide narrative accounts written in the present tense of Sukkot celebrations in the Jerusalem Temple and in Eastern Europe; these chapters offer vivid, imaginative descriptions of what an eyewitness might have observed. The third chapter explains the origins and significance of the principal rituals.

JEFFREY L. RUBENSTEIN

Symbols and Symbolism

Altmann, Alexander (editor), *Biblical Motifs: Origins and Transformations* (Philip W. Lown Institute of Advanced Judaic Studies, Studies and Texts, vol. 3), Cambridge, Massachusetts: Harvard University Press, 1966

Ginsburg, Elliot K., *The Sabbath in the Classical Kabbalah* (SUNY Series in Judaica), Albany: State University of New York Press, 1989

Goodenough, Erwin R., *Jewish Symbols in the Greco-Roman Period* (Bollingen Series, 37), 13 vols., New York: Pantheon, 1953–1968; abridged edition, edited by Jacob Neusner, Princeton, New Jersey: Princeton University Press, 1988; Oxford: Princeton University Press, 1992

Kanof, Abram, *Jewish Symbolic Art,* Jerusalem and Woodmere, New York: Gefen, 1990

Neusner, Jacob, *Symbol and Theology in Early Judaism,* Minneapolis, Minnesota: Fortress, 1991

Although Judaism, rooted in the aniconism of the Second Commandment, has traditionally expressed some ambivalence about the use of symbols, there is still a rich history of Jewish symbolism through the ages. Both figurative painting and relief carvings, especially dating from the third century C.E. onward, have been found in synagogue excavations. From antiquity to the present, symbolism has played an important part in Jewish religious life, both in the home and in places of worship.

The most elaborate of works on Jewish symbolism is the 13-volume set by GOODENOUGH (1953–1968), who examined the archaeological evidence from the Greco-Roman world, documenting the symbols found in synagogues from that time and place, including artifacts from Dura Europos in Syria. Not content merely to collect and document, however, Goodenough applies a striking interpretation to the images he assembled. Until his study, it was generally believed that Judaism in late antiquity was a nonvisual culture adequately described by the rabbinic works of the time. Goodenough posits, however, that there were actually two forms of Judaism at this time: that defined by the rabbis, and a more popular and mystical form, influenced by Hellenistic ideas and somewhat similar to the Judaism of Philo, and represented in the surviving synagogue art. His conclusions, however, are still disputed. The final two volumes of the series contain summary and conclusions, and indexes and maps, respectively. Published posthumously, they provide invaluable assistance in approaching such a massive amount of information.

The 1988 edition of Goodenough is an abridgement of his findings, edited and condensed by Jacob Neusner into a single volume. Neusner makes much of the most striking information collected by the author easily accessible to the general reader; the abridgement is also valuable because most of the original 13 volumes are now out of print. Included are both archaeological material and Goodenough's interpretations of it. In addition, the editor provides a foreword that outlines Goodenough's work and discusses the views of those who have disputed his conclusions.

NEUSNER's own study of early Jewish symbolism is heavily influenced by Goodenough's material and his readings of it. In fact, Neusner presents his book as exploring the work of Goodenough and that of the interpreter of early rabbinic theology, Max Kadushin. The author emphasizes that symbolism appears not only in frescos and mosaics but also in literary material, stressing that words, including the words of the rabbis, also can be highly symbolic, more concerned with evoking attitudes and emotions—which is (Neusner claims) the purpose of symbols—than is generally supposed. This very dense book then looks at both literary and artistic materials from early Judaism before coming to the conclusion that the kinds of symbols found in the ancient synagogues can also be found in the rabbinic writings of the time.

KANOF offers a simple yet highly perceptive and richly informative survey of current knowledge of the range and distribution of Jewish symbols in late antiquity and the Middle Ages. The various forms and their likely significance are discussed by type, in chapters concentrating on messianic symbols, the symbolic significance of the temple, temple vessels, the menorah, flora, fauna, and the signs of the zodiac. With further contextualizing chapters on religious symbolism in general and "pagan" (i.e., Greek) symbolism in particular, and at less than 100 pages of text with more than 100 helpful illustrations, this modest book provides an excellent introduction.

ALTMANN's collection of essays comes from the 1962 and 1963 Lown Institute research colloquia titled "Images and Symbols: Studies in the Origins and Transformations of Biblical Motifs." The erudite essays cover a variety of topics relating to biblical and early Jewish symbolism, such as a discussion of the differences and interdependence between Jewish and Zoroastrian dualism, studies of symbolism in the Pentateuch, and consideration of the apparent contradictions between the finds in the Dura Europos synagogues and the evidence from talmudic literature.

GINSBURG limits his study to the symbolic representations of the sabbath in the Kabbalah. For this mystical tradition in Judaism and especially for the powerful strain that developed in Safed in the 16th century, the sabbath took on a highly figurative and deeply emotional meaning. Ginsburg first provides a discussion of the Kabbalah and its history and practice, preparing the reader to delve more specifically into ideas about the sabbath. The author then surveys sabbath ideology prior to that of the kabbalists, including analysis of biblical and talmudic beliefs. He discusses the elaborate preparations for the sabbath practiced by the kabbalists and examines the Saturday night rituals and prayers that allowed the practitioner to separate from this highly emotional time, which was seen as a living expression of a union with God, as well as (inevitably) a marriage ceremony of the masculine and feminine aspects of God.

ELEANOR AMICO

Synagogue

Brooten, Bernadette J., *Women Leaders in the Ancient Synagogue: Inscriptional Evidence and Background Issues* (Brown Judaic Studies, no. 36), Chico, California: Scholars Press, 1982

Elbogen, Ismar, *Der Jüdische Gottesdienst in seiner geschichtlichen Entwicklung*, 1913; translated by Raymond P. Scheindlin as *Jewish Liturgy: A Comprehensive History*, Philadelphia: Jewish Publication Society, 1993

Fine, Steven (editor), *Sacred Realm: The Emergence of the Synagogue in the Ancient World*, New York: Oxford University Press and Yeshiva University Museum, 1996

Fine, Steven, *This Holy Place: On the Sanctity of the Synagogue during the Greco-Roman Period* (Christianity and Judaism in Antiquity Series, vol. 11), Notre Dame, Indiana: University of Notre Dame Press, 1997

Grossman, Susan and Rivka Haut (editors), *Daughters of the King: Women and the Synagogue: A Survey of History, Halakhah, and Contemporary Realities*, Philadelphia: Jewish Publication Society, 1992

Heilman, Samuel C., *Synagogue Life: A Study in Symbolic Interaction*, Chicago: University of Chicago Press, 1976

Korros, Alexandra Shecket and Jonathan D. Sarna, *American Synagogue History: A Bibliography and State-of-the-Field Survey*, New York: Wiener, 1988

Prell, Riv-Ellen, *Prayer and Community: The Havurah in American Judaism*, Detroit, Michigan: Wayne State University Press, 1989

Urman, Dan and Paul V.M. Flesher (editors), *Ancient Synagogues: Historical Analysis and Archaeological Discovery*, 2 vols., New York: Brill, 1995

Wertheimer, Jack (editor), *The American Synagogue: A Sanctuary Transformed*, Cambridge and New York: Cambridge University Press, 1987

The synagogue, as an institution of Jewish life dedicated to the reading and teaching of Scripture, was well established by the first century C.E., but its functions shifted dramatically in the centuries following the destruction of the Temple. Probably by the end of the second century, it was also becoming a place of communal prayer under rabbinic direction. By the late rabbinic period, it had become a place of holiness, marked by the permanent presence of the Torah scroll and Temple imagery. Rabbinic literature and archaeology are the primary sources for information about the origins of the synagogue. While archaeologists have focused on architectural and decorative features of the synagogue, textual study has investigated the development of rabbinic liturgy.

URMAN and FLESHER's volume represents a state-of-the-art survey of the synagogue in late antiquity, including new material and collecting and translating (where necessary) essential previously published articles. Section four, "The Synagogue's Nature and the Jewish Community," addresses the social functions of the synagogue most directly. The extensive bibliography points the reader to all relevant earlier work, including the important collections of English articles edited by Joseph Gutmann, Rachel Hachlili, and Lee Levine.

FINE (1996) centers on architectural analysis, but it also includes articles by Fine on the holiness of the synagogue and by Shinan on the liturgical life of the synagogue. FINE (1997) brings the textual and archaeological evidence into dialog in order to document and explain the transition of the synagogue from an early tannaitic meeting place of tentative sanctity to the fully holy place reflected in evidence from the fourth century onward. He argues that the synagogue's holiness, while deriving in part from appropriation of Temple images and ideas, comes primarily from "the community and its sacred scrolls." In the course of this study, he charts the emerging role of the synagogue in Jewish life under rabbinic guidance and in its Greco-Roman and Babylonian contexts.

BROOTEN, examining primarily diaspora inscriptions, finds evidence that women held official roles in ancient synagogues. In the course of her discussions, she examines necessarily the meanings of the various titles held, thus providing an important survey of current knowledge of male leadership at the time. The second half of the book explores background issues, especially the women's gallery and, more briefly, women's prayer, philanthropy, and proselytism.

There exists no adequate study of the development of the medieval synagogue as an institution. Information may be gleaned here and there in the various works on medieval synagogue architecture and on medieval liturgy or medieval society in general. The most comprehensive, if somewhat dated, discussion may be found in the third section of ELBOGEN. Significant articles, however, are included as well in GROSSMAN and HAUT's collection. This volume is divided into three sections. The first, "History," contains studies of women's public religious life from the Jerusalem Temple through the synagogues of various parts of the medieval Jewish world. The second, "Halakhah," presents discussions of the legal issues that have most affected women's roles in the synagogue, including Orthodox and non-Orthodox voices. The third, "Contemporary Realities," offers both scholarly studies of Mediterranean, Persian, and American Jewish women's synagogue experiences and personal vignettes by women who have filled various roles in the synagogue.

Grossman and Haut's collection is also conspicuous for the significant degree to which it examines the synagogue experience of non-Western Jews; most contemporary work in English has focused on the U.S. experience. For example, WERTHEIMER's volume consists of a series of 14 commissioned essays by leading scholars. After an introductory overview, the essays consider the history of the U.S. synagogue from both denominational and thematic perspectives. The latter group of essays includes histories of individual yet paradigmatic congregations, as well as discussions of the immigrant experience, synagogue seating, music, and the non-liturgical educational and social functions of the synagogue in the United States. Those interested in pursuing research on individual U.S. communities should consult KORROS and SARNA, which also includes comprehensive introductory essays.

The social sciences have contributed significantly to understanding of the U.S. synagogue experience. HEILMAN's volume reports the results of a participant-observer study of a modern Orthodox congregation in the northeast. Here, Heilman is concerned less with the religious life of the synagogue than with the human interactions surrounding the formal activities of prayer and study. Beyond the expected chapters on synagogues as houses of prayer, study, and assembly, Heilman includes studies of factors shaping the community of the synagogue, such as gossip and joking, and markers of social boundaries and of subgroups in the synagogue. Thus, he takes note of aspects such as choral singing, swaying during prayer, participation in appeals, and the resolution of arguments.

PRELL's book, in contrast, derives from her research as a participant-observer in an informal havurah-style community in Los Angeles in the mid-1970s. Unlike Heilman's Orthodox Jews, whose religious expression is dictated by tradition and law, these Jews are searching for religious expression consonant with their secular countercultural commitments. While also sensitive to social issues, Prell's study examines how the dialogue between received ritual and modernity shapes the religious life and identity of this community. In so doing, she provides both important background on the general U.S. synagogue scene against which the havurah communities rebelled and a theoretical structure by which the ritual performances of other synagogues may be analyzed.

RUTH LANGER

See also Architecture, Synagogue

Syria

Deshen, Shlomo and Walter P. Zenner, *Jews among Muslims: Communities in the Precolonial Middle East,* New York: New York University Press, and Houndmills, Basingstoke, Hampshire: Macmillan, 1996
Frankel, Jonathan, *The Damascus Affair: "Ritual Murder," Politics, and the Jews in 1840,* Cambridge and New York: Cambridge University Press, 1997

Harel, Yaron, "Temurot be-Yahadut Suriah, 1840–1880," Ph.D. diss., Bar-Ilan University, 1992
Marcus, Abraham, *The Middle East on the Eve of Modernity: Aleppo in the Eighteenth Century,* New York: Columbia University Press, 1989
Shelemay, Kay Kaufman, *Let Jasmine Rain Down: Song and Remembrance among Syrian Jews,* Chicago: University of Chicago Press, 1998
Stillman, Norman, *The Jews in Arab Lands in Modern Times,* Philadelphia: Jewish Publication Society, 1991
Sutton, Joseph A.D., *Magic Carpet: Aleppo-in-Flatbush: The Story of a Unique Ethnic Jewish Community,* New York: Thayer-Jacoby, 1979
Sutton, Joseph A.D., *Aleppo Chronicles: The Story of the Unique Sephardeem of the Ancient Near East, in Their Own Words,* New York: Thayer-Jacoby, 1988
Williams, Bill, *The Making of Manchester Jewry: 1740–1875,* Manchester: Manchester University Press, and New York: Holmes and Meier, 1976
Zenner, Walter P., *Global Community: The Jews of Aleppo, Syria,* Detroit, Michigan: Wayne State University Press, 2000

The study of Syrian Jews, like that of other Middle Eastern Jewish communities, is still in a formative stage. While these communities have a venerable history, reaching back to the beginnings of the Jewish dispersion, the Eurocentric nature of Judaic scholarship has led to neglect of these communities in more recent times. Forty years ago, an English-speaking student wishing to learn about the Jews of Syria had to rely on encyclopedia articles, accounts by travelers and missionaries, and the *American Jewish Yearbook,* published by the American Jewish Committee and the Jewish Publication Society of America, which gave an annual account of events in various countries. Only if the reader knew Hebrew or French was it possible to find some original sources and scholarship. The situation has changed, but it is still necessary to look for material in places other than books devoted solely to this topic. This survey will deal with books on the Jews of Syria as well as works on their descendants who have emigrated. These Syrian Jewish communities outside of Syria have become quite important during the 20th century. Several of the volumes listed here are overviews of Middle Eastern Jewry as a whole. Others are works on Jewish communities with a significant Syrian-Sephardi component.

STILLMAN provides a brief history and selection of sources on Jews in Arab lands in his volume. Several of these documents give reports of the Jews in Syria in recent times. They are drawn from European and Jewish sources, including Hebrew rabbinic literature. They provide illustrations of dramatic events (such as the Damascus affair of 1840) and general social conditions (such as a rabbinic comment on female dancers). Some of the sources from Egypt refer apparently to immigrants from various countries including Syria.

MARCUS describes Middle Eastern urban life in 18th-century Aleppo on the eve of the full incorporation of this Ottoman city into the European-dominated capitulations system. The book is about Aleppo as a whole, not only its Jews. Marcus has utilized Hebrew sources as well as documents in

Arabic, French, English, and Turkish. He helps significantly to place the Jews in the broader context of Syrian life.

HAREL's doctoral dissertation was written in Hebrew but with a lengthy English summary. This book is based on primary documentary material, and it covers social, economic, and political institutions and events during the period from 1840 to 1880. Harel is in the process of publishing his research on the Jews of Damascus and Aleppo in a variety of English as well as Hebrew journals.

DESHEN and ZENNER's collection consists of articles dealing with Middle Eastern Jewish society just before European colonization. Most of the articles deal with a specific Jewish community (Morocco, Tunisia, Syria, Iraq, Iran). There are two articles on Syria by Zenner. One deals with the external relations of the Jews with their non-Jewish neighbors, the government, and the economy. The other article discusses primarily the family and community in Aleppo and Damascus in the 19th and early 20th centuries. A bibliography referring to periodical literature and some primary source material in English, Hebrew, and other languages is included.

FRANKEL tells the story of the accusation of ritual murder against the Jews of Damascus in 1840 as an episode in European history. He does provide the local background in addition to the global political context, but his study focuses attention on the European consuls, especially the French consul, rather than on local Christians, as prime movers in the affair. He provides portraits of individual actors in the event, including Moses Abulafia, a rabbi who was tortured into becoming a witness for the prosecution of Jews and whose son was a prominent Damascus rabbi in the next generation. Still, it should be noted that Syrian Jewry is not at the center of his account of this incident.

WILLIAMS's book describes the growth of the Jewish community in Manchester, England, prior to the Russian immigration in the 1880s. Again, the Syrian Jewish immigrants play only a small role in the overall picture. He does, however, describe them vividly and shows how the various segments of the Manchester Jewish community—English, German, Greek-Sephardi, and Syrian-Sephardi—interacted in the late 19th century. Williams places the Syrian-Sephardi immigrants into the broader context of the British cotton trade and a growing middle-class Jewish community.

SUTTON (1979) describes the New York (Brooklyn) Syrian Jewish community, treating all phases of its life, from its origins in immigration to business, the family, synagogues, resorts, and portraits of individuals. He also includes material on Aleppo, whence much of the Brooklyn Syrian community originates.

SUTTON (1988) includes a long overview of the community plus oral histories that he recorded in New York City. These include the recollections of early emigrants from Syria, later émigrés, and people who lived in other communities, including Egypt, Brazil, Mexico, Britain, Israel, and various locations in the United States. Most of those who had lived outside New York City at one time in their lives, however, were residents of Brooklyn or Deal, New Jersey, by the time they were recorded.

SHELEMAY, an ethnomusicologist, looks at the Syrian Jewish tradition of writing Hebrew hymnody (*pizmonim* and *bakkashot*) to fit Arabic melody-types. She analyzes the recent development of this tradition among Jews from Syria living in Brooklyn, Mexico, and Israel and places it into the general development of these Syrian Jewish communities. She also shows how singers from the Syrian communities have kept the tradition of singing these songs alive in several different countries under a variety of circumstances. She demonstrates how Syrian Jews have managed to maintain separate communities but how they have also perpetuated selected elements of their Middle Eastern Jewish culture and adapted them to their Israeli and diaspora societies.

ZENNER is preparing for publication a book that deals with Jews from Aleppo, both in Syria and in their dispersion in recent times to England, the United States, Latin America, and Israel. He stresses the relationship between the economic roles played by Jews from Aleppo and their changing ethnic identities. He makes an effort to explain why certain communities have perpetuated stronger communal structures and identities than others.

WALTER P. ZENNER

Szold, Henrietta   1860–1945

American Zionist and humanitarian

Dash, Joan, *Summoned to Jerusalem: The Life of Henrietta Szold,* New York: Harper and Row, 1979

Gidal, Tim, *Henrietta Szold: A Documentation in Photos and Text,* New York: Gefen, 1997

Lowenthal, Marvin, *Henrietta Szold: Life and Letters,* New York: Viking, 1942

Shargel, Baila Round (editor and translator), *Lost Love: The Untold Story of Henrietta Szold: Unpublished Diary and Letters,* Philadelphia: Jewish Publication Society, 1997

Henrietta Szold was a leading American-born Zionist activist; an important figure among exponents of Jewish studies; an influential teacher; the founder of Hadassah, the women's division of the Zionist movement; and the founder of Youth Aliyah, an organization that facilitated the emigration to Palestine of thousands of young Jews before and during the Holocaust. In the United States, she dedicated herself to a scholarly, pedagogic, and editorial career, while in Palestine she focused on organizational and social service activities.

LOWENTHAL presents the first comprehensive biography of Szold. His book traces Szold's life, beginning with her early years and education in Baltimore, Maryland, and her decision to found a night school for Russian Jewish immigrants. It describes her conversion to Zionism and her 26-year career as the editorial secretary of the Jewish Publication Society. Lowenthal recounts the founding of Hadassah and Szold's work in Palestine as the director of the organization, with its special commitment to the provision of medical services, which would lead to the founding of the Hadassah hospital in Jerusalem. The book provides a detailed chronology of Szold's activities, reconstructing the main events and developments in her life through letters and speeches. Lowenthal emphasizes Szold's achievements, but he describes as well her difficulties and frustrations.

DASH follows a geographical rather than a chronological paradigm in her account of Szold's life. She focuses on the major personal influences in Szold's life, such as Louis Ginzberg, her admired and beloved mentor at the Jewish Theological Seminary in New York. Dash reveals that Szold was not just the editor and translator of Ginzberg's multi-volume scholarly work, *Legends of the Jews*, but that she also developed a passionate attachment to Ginzberg, a sentiment that was not reciprocated. Dash emphasizes the intellectual and ideological dimensions of Szold's development as a Zionist thinker. Bringing her subject to life, Dash offers detailed descriptions of Szold's meetings with key Zionist leaders, social gatherings, and relationships with family members. This biography presents Szold as a vulnerable and complex woman.

GIDAL creates a more popular overview of Szold's life using photographs and excerpts from letters. There are only a few photographs of Szold, but many pictures capture the new life of young immigrants to Palestine during the late 1930s. Especially striking are photos of the "Teheran children," who were smuggled out of Nazi-occupied Europe and reached Palestine thanks to Youth Aliyah. Some photographs document Szold's strong friendship with Judah Magnes, the leader of Berit Shalom, the political organization that advocated peace with the Palestinians. The narrative in this book is not excessively informative, and it does tend to glamorize Szold, emphasizing the visionary who was personally involved in her projects and cared deeply for the people whose lives she helped change.

SHARGEL focuses on Szold's relationship with Louis Ginzberg against the background of New York in the first decade of the 20th century. Shargel introduces excerpts from Szold's previously unpublished diary in addition to previously unpublished correspondence between Szold and Ginzberg. Numerous letters refer to professional issues and transactions between Ginzberg and his devoted translator-editor. A good number of letters also confirm a sentimental attachment on Szold's part that goes far beyond professional devotion. Diary entries are especially revealing in this regard, exposing the turbulent emotions with which Szold was struggling especially when she heard news of Ginzberg's European fiancée and relating to his subsequent marriage. Shargel suggests that the unrequited love and the deep disappointment Szold suffered may have led to her decision to emigrate to Palestine and immerse herself in Zionist activities. The book rejects previous idealizations of Szold's life, and its contention that Szold's unrequited love may have led to her brilliant political career is somewhat controversial.

ESTHER FUCHS

T

Tabernacle

Cross, Frank Moore, "The Tabernacle," *Biblical Archaeologist*, 10(3), September 1947

Haran, Menahem, *Temples and Temple-Service in Ancient Israel: An Inquiry into the Character of Cult Phenomena and the Historical Setting of the Priestly School*, Oxford: Clarendon, 1977; as *Temples and Temple-Service in Ancient Israel: An Inquiry into the Biblical Cult Phenomena and the Historical Setting of the Priestly School*, Winona Lake, Indiana: Eisenbrauns, 1985

Morgenstern, Julian, *The Ark, the Ephod and the "Tent of Meeting"* (Henry and Ida Krolik Memorial Publications, vol. 2), Cincinnati, Ohio: Hebrew Union College Press, 1945

Onians, John, "Tabernacle and Temple and the Cosmos of the Jews," in *Sacred Architecture in the Traditions of India, China, Judaism, and Islam* (Cosmos, 8), edited by Emily Lyle, Edinburgh: Edinburgh University Press, 1992

Strong, James, *The Tabernacle of Israel in the Desert*, Providence, Rhode Island: Harris, Jones, 1888; as *The Tabernacle of Israel: Its Structure and Symbolism*, Grand Rapids, Michigan: Kregel, 1987

The Tabernacle (*mishkan*) is the tent sanctuary that God commanded the Israelites to build when they were in the wilderness. The word derives from the Latin *tabernaculum* (tent), which was used in the Vulgate Bible. The sanctuary is also referred to as the "tent of meeting" (*'ohel mo'ed*) and, less frequently, as the "tent of testimony" (*mishkan ha'edut*). In Exodus 26, Moses is instructed how it should be built. It is constructed and consecrated in Exodus 40. It was considered the locale of God's physical presence and the designated place where Moses spoke with God. After the arrival of the Israelites in the promised land, the Tabernacle resided in the sanctuary at Shiloh (Joshua 18:1). When Solomon consecrated the Temple in Jerusalem, the priests brought the Tabernacle into it (1 Kings 8:4).

STRONG provides a thorough study of the descriptions of the Tabernacle in the Bible. His first chapter is a brief survey of the Tabernacle's history. His second focuses on the material description of the Tabernacle and has numerous helpful illustrations. He speculates on how it was dismantled for transportation and describes the arrangement of the tribes, each of which had a designated location in relation to the Tabernacle

both when marching and at camp. He also summarizes the description of the Holy of Holies. It was separated from the rest of the Tabernacle with screens and contained such sacred objects as the mercy seat, the cherubim, and the Ark of the Covenant. Strong's third chapter speculates on the symbolic significance of such features as the Tabernacle's symmetry and measurements. His book concludes with a discussion of the ways in which the deity manifests himself at the Tabernacle.

CROSS offers an archaeological and historical study of the Tabernacle. He sees in the biblical accounts of the Tabernacle several authentic details about how the Israelites worshiped in the desert. He argues, however, that these authentic details have been combined with "heavily idealized" depictions of the Tabernacle, which come from a later stage of Israelite religion. He considers the biblical descriptions of the Tabernacle in their present form as having been edited substantially in the time of David. David established Jerusalem as the political and religious center of the monarchy, and Cross argues that in bringing the Ark into Jerusalem, David tried to establish the city as a legitimate center of the religion by presenting it as heir to the tradition of the Tabernacle. This argument, however, while plausible and intriguing, cannot be proved.

MORGENSTERN provides examples of desert sanctuaries from Islamic cultures that have affinities with the descriptions of the Tabernacle and the Ark in the Bible. This suggests that the Bible's account is at least in part historically accurate. He aims to find in the Bible and in forms of worship among Muslims "the period and practices of pre-Islamic, ancient Semitic religion." Among his examples is the Bedouin *kubbe*, a holy tent made of red leather. He is of the opinion that the two main Hebrew terms that are translated by the word *Tabernacle* (*mishkan* and *'ohel mo'ed*) refer to different shrines from different periods of Israelite history. He argues that the *'ohel mo'ed* was understood to be merely the site of divine manifestation, whereas the *mishkan*, representing a later stage, was thought to be the actual residence of God. Thus, he argues, we can see in the terminology of the Tabernacle stages of a transition of the status of the sanctuary in Israelite religion, evolving from desert shrine toward the Temple of Jerusalem.

The collection of papers read at a 1991 conference on Architecture and Traditional Systems of Belief and edited by Emily Lyle offers insightful discussions on sacred architecture in several religious traditions. Among the essays is ONIANS's. His contribution focuses not on the historical veracity of the

Tabernacle but rather on how, as an idea, it contributes to the stability of Judaism. He argues that one way in which Judaism was able to withstand the destructions and desecrations of the Temple was by developing sacred edifices that existed solely in textual form. While physical buildings could be destroyed, the Tabernacle and the Temple could survive in the Bible as verbal constructs. Thus he dates composition of the biblical descriptions of the Tabernacle to the period after Nebuchadnezzar's destruction of the Temple in 586 B.C.E. While the Tabernacle is undoubtedly important as a textual construct, the essay's complete dismissal of a historical basis for the Tabernacle seems too extreme. As other scholars have observed, there is evidence that some elements of the biblical depiction of the Tabernacle are based on a kernel of truth.

HARAN surveys the origins of the Israelite priesthood and the Temple and how this history has influenced the composition of biblical texts. Guiding his studies is the conviction that the priestly texts of the Bible are often archaic, whereas other scholars often assume that many of them were heavily edited or composed much later, around the time of the consecration of the Second Temple. Haran dedicates three chapters to the Tabernacle. The first covers the biblical account of the material composition of the Tabernacle and its contents. The second chapter is on the priestly injunctions regarding the Tabernacle aimed at protecting its sanctity, such as the prohibition of nonpriests from approaching the vicinity of the shrine. His third chapter discusses the commonly accepted view that the biblical account of the Tabernacle is an idealized account based on the Temple of Jerusalem. To assert the antiquity of the pentateuchal account he argues that much of it is related not to the Jerusalem Temple but to legends about the ancient Israelite sanctuary in the town of Shiloh (Joshua 18:1). Like many scholars, he feels that the Bible's description of the Tabernacle contains some authentic information from ancient layers of the religion. He argues, however, that more texts of the Bible reflect these early materials than many other scholars would claim.

MATTHEW GOFF

Talmudic Literature: Translations

Epstein, Isidore (editor), *The Babylonian Talmud: Seder Nezikin, Translated into English with Notes, Glossary and Indices,* London: Soncino, 1935–1952

Goldwurm, Hersh and Yisroel Simcha Schorr (editors), *The Talmud/Talmud Bavli: The Schottenstein Edition* (ArtScroll Series), Brooklyn, New York: Mesorah, 1990–

Neusner, Jacob, *The Talmud of the Land of Israel: A Preliminary Translation and Explanation* (Chicago Studies in the History of Judaism), Chicago and London: University of Chicago Press, 1982–1993

Neusner, Jacob, *The Talmud of Babylonia: An American Translation* (Brown Judaic Studies), Chico, California: Scholars Press, 1984–1993

Neusner, Jacob, *The Talmud of Babylonia: An Academic Commentary* (South Florida Academic Commentary Series), Atlanta, Georgia: Scholars Press, 1994–

Steinsaltz, Adin, *The Talmud/Talmud Bavli: The Steinsaltz Edition,* 21 vols., New York: Random House, 1989–2000

Audio recordings: CD-ROM, published by Torah Communications Network, 1618 43rd St., Brooklyn, NY 11204, (718) 436-4999; tapes, published by Torah Tapes, Inc., 1814 50th St., Brooklyn, NY 11204, (718) 438-3904

Translations are generally described as either "literal" or "dynamic-equivalent." Literal translations stay as close as possible to the word-for-word meaning of a text and in the process lose elements of the original that depend on larger patterns of literary, logical, idiomatic, or philosophical meaning. Dynamic-equivalent translations strive to replicate these larger patterns of meaning but in the process may move very far from the literal meaning of the words. The careful positioning of a translation between these two stylistic poles is the most difficult work of a translator, and when done well it is invisible. The Talmud may be a uniquely challenging text to translate because its meaning depends equally on a precise terminology and on large rhetorical and logical structures that often span several pages of the original. The translations discussed here address this challenge in different ways and serve the needs of different audiences. They are listed in order from the most literal to the most dynamic-equivalent.

EPSTEIN is the first complete translation of the Babylonian Talmud into English. It is generally a close, literal translation of the standard printed text. It is a good place to look for a precise translation of the often-difficult Aramaic of the Bavli. The standard biblical and talmudic cross references are also translated in concise footnotes, and some censored material is restored. Although it is unexcelled in the accuracy of its literal translation, Epstein generally fails to represent the logical structure of the talmudic argument. It is, however, the standard English translation, and it is suitable for quotation in scholarly writing. Epstein's version is frequently referred to by the name of the publishing house—"Soncino."

NEUSNER (1982–1993) is the only available translation of the Palestinian Talmud (Yerushalmi). It is a more dynamic-equivalent translation than Epstein, following an innovative format that arranges the text on the page as an outline of the talmudic argument. Each tractate is situated within its order, then outlined chapter by chapter according to the unfolding of the argument. This translation emphasizes the broad shape of the argument, its context, and the conceptual units from which it is constructed.

NEUSNER (1984–1993) is a full translation of the Babylonian Talmud that resembles Neusner (1982) in style and format. It is most useful when read in conjunction with Epstein. NEUSNER (1994–) is intended to replace Neusner (1984–1993). It is more analytic than the previous edition in its arrangement of the text and supplies useful introductions and running commentaries. It is a fully dynamic-equivalent translation, focusing on the rhetorical, conceptual, and juristic content of the Talmud rather than the literal meanings of the individual words.

STEINSALTZ is an English translation of selected tractates from his ongoing project to translate the Babylonian Talmud into modern Hebrew. It combines both literal and dynamic-equivalent translations on a single page, together with a vocalized version of the original Hebrew and Aramaic text. While only four tractates are available in English, these provide the best introduction to reading the Talmud in the original.

GOLDWURM and SCHORR aims primarily at Orthodox-identifying Jewish students and should serve them well. It translates the Mishnah and Gemara, generally following the interpretation of Rashi. Parallel notes offer further interpretation and clarification, drawn largely from other medieval commentaries (e.g., Tosafot, Rashba, Meiri). Comments not directly concerned with elucidating the flow of the text are usually halakhic in nature. They will be helpful to observant Jews who want to deepen their understanding of halakhah but may be otherwise confusing as the presentation is ahistorical. The English text is printed facing a reproduction of the corresponding page from the Vilna edition, with the translated section on each page highlighted. Like Steinsaltz, this translation is intended for beginning to intermediate students who are learning to read the Talmud in Aramaic, and the translators carefully foreground the logical structure as it unfolds. It should be noted that the vocalization of the original is idiosyncratic, representing not the grammatically normative form of the words but the pronunciation current in Ashkenazi yeshivot. As a dynamic-equivalent translation, Goldwurm and Schorr is excellent, but readers in search of a more academic or critical translation would be better served by Epstein or Neusner (1994). Goldwurm and Schorr is frequently referred to by the name of its underwriter, "Schottenstein."

Audio recordings of classes on the entire Babylonian Talmud are distributed on tape and CD-ROM. Each class is about one hour long, covering a single folio of the Talmud. The recordings are intended in the first instance to promote participation in daf yomi—a program in which students worldwide read the same leaf of Talmud every day, taking about seven and one-half years to complete the cycle. In the course of each class, the relevant folio is translated and discussed. The classes thus move very quickly and are suitable for intermediate to advanced students experienced in reading the Talmud in the original. The translation and commentary are similar to those in Goldwurm and Steinsaltz.

WILLIS JOHNSON

See also Talmudic Literature: Hermeneutics; Talmudic Literature: Introductions; Talmudic Literature: Reference Tools; Talmudic Literature: Theology

Talmudic Literature: Reference Tools

Carmell, Aryeh, *Aids to Talmud Study*, London: East End Jewish Scholarship Centre, 1974; 3rd edition, New York: Feldheim, 1975; as *Aiding Talmud Study*, 5th edition, London: East End Jewish Scholarship Centre, and New York: Feldheim, 1991

Frank, Yitzhak, *The Practical Talmud Dictionary*, Spring Valley, New York: Feldheim, 1991, 2nd edition, 1994

Frank, Yitzhak, *Grammar for Gemara: An Introduction to Babylonian Aramaic*, Jerusalem: Ariel, United Israel Institutes, 1992, new edition, 1995

Krupnick, Eliyahu, *The Gateway to Learning: A Systematic Introduction to the Study of Talmud*, New York: Feldheim, 1981

Perlmutter, Haim, *Tools for Tosafos*, Southfield, Michigan: Targum, 1996

Steinsaltz, Adin, *The Talmud: The Steinsaltz Edition: A Reference Guide*, New York: Random House, 1989

Strack, Hermann Leberecht, *Introduction to the Talmud and Midrash*, Philadelphia: Jewish Publication Society, 1931; revised by Günter Stemberger and translated by Markus Bockmuehl, 2nd edition, Edinburgh: Clark, 1996

The study of the Babylonian Talmud is regarded as the most prestigious activity by observant Jewish communities. This study has traditionally been reserved almost exclusively for men and taught as the culmination of an educational process that begins with instruction in biblical Hebrew and codified halakhah. Since the 1970s, however, the Ba'alei Teshuvah movement has led a large number of newly observant, English-speaking adults with no prior background in rabbinic culture to begin studying Talmud. Several introductions have been written specifically for this adult audience, and collectively they constitute a huge advance in talmudic pedagogy. Although the Talmud remains an oral tradition best learned from a teacher, it is now possible for a diligent adult to do much toward attaining talmudic literacy on his or her own. Audio recordings are also available of expertly taught classes on every page of the Talmud.

CARMELL is among the best guides available in English. It has been through five editions and presents the bare bones of what a beginner needs to know as he or she sets out in Talmud study: the most common talmudic phrases and abbreviations; a basic Aramaic vocabulary; and tabular summaries of semi-cursive script, *gematria* (rabbinic numerology), the Hebrew calendar, and talmudic weights and measures. The appendix and charts showing the chronology and interrelationships of the Talmud's major protagonists are especially useful.

FRANK (1992) is an introduction to the grammar of Babylonian Aramaic, the principal language of the Babylonian Talmud and the basis of much rabbinic Hebrew. Although the study of grammar has been discouraged in traditional yeshivot, adult readers coming to the Talmud may find a formal presentation helpful. This book is a comprehensive but not exhaustive survey that presents all the grammar a talmudist will need in a format that is clear and well-organized. It includes a section of exercises that can be studied by individuals or in a classroom. The full paradigms of 30 common Aramaic verbs are particularly helpful.

FRANK (1991) is not a complete dictionary of talmudic Hebrew and Aramaic. It is restricted to the key words and phrases that signal the logical and rhetorical structure of the talmudic argument. Covering an extensive vocabulary, the dictionary translates these terms literally, providing information on grammatical forms and roots and giving extended explanations and examples of how the phrases function in context. Frank concludes with a substantial dictionary of rabbinic abbreviations as well as tables of talmudic weights, measures, coins, and numbers. Practically speaking, this is the single most useful book reviewed in this article.

The range of coverage in KRUPNICK is similar to that found in Carmell, but Krupnick is organized as a textbook for adult beginners. The book's strengths lie in the clarity of its discussion of the structure of talmudic arguments and the way in which it illustrates the function of key Aramaic terms. The examples are well chosen, but they are not extensive enough for this book to stand alone as an introduction to reading the Talmud. The brief discussion of the rules of Rashi's Talmud commentary and of Tosafot, the classic medieval glosses on Rashi, is however exceptional for its clarity.

PERLMUTTER introduces the intermediate student to the character of the Tosafot. The ability to understand a talmudic text together with Tosafot constitutes basic talmudic literacy. Although this volume is the most conceptually advanced of the books under review, it is a model of clarity. In a series of short chapters, Perlmutter explains everything one needs to know to read Tosafot, from vocabulary and syntax to rhetorical structure to hermeneutic strategies and assumptions.

STEINSALTZ was written to accompany the ongoing translation of the entire Talmud into modern Hebrew and of selected tractates into English. It covers much of the same material as Carmell, but it also includes a helpful glossary titled "Halakhic Concepts and Terms." This text is suitable for absolute beginners but it does not stand alone as an introduction to reading the Talmud.

STRACK, which first appeared in German in 1887, is the authoritative academic introduction to talmudic literature. Stemberger's updated edition includes massive revision and correction. It has a more scholarly tone than the other books discussed in this article, with exemplary bibliographies (current as of the early 1990s) of primary and secondary materials, including valuable comments on the merits of different editions of rabbinic texts. A concise historical survey is followed by chapters on the rabbinic school system, rabbinic hermeneutics, the nature of oral law, and biographies of major talmudic rabbis. The chapter on the languages of rabbinic literature is an excellent orientation to the subject. The fine treatment of talmudic literature is followed by a valuable survey of midrashic literature. Strack is not intended as a first guide for students learning to read Talmud, but readers with an academic bent will find it fascinating.

WILLIS JOHNSON

See also Talmudic Literature: Hermeneutics; Talmudic Literature: Introductions; Talmudic Literature: Theology; Talmudic Literature: Translations

Talmudic Literature: Introductions

Holtz, Barry (editor), *Back to the Sources: Reading the Classic Jewish Texts*, New York: Summit, 1984
Neusner, Jacob, *Invitation to the Talmud: A Teaching Book*, New York: Harper and Row, 1973; revised edition, San Francisco: Harper and Row, 1984
Neusner, Jacob, *Invitation to Midrash: The Workings of Rabbinic Bible Interpretation: A Teaching Book*, San Francisco: Harper and Row, 1989

Safrai, Shemuel (editor), *The Literature of the Sages*, Philadelphia: Fortress, 1987
Steinsaltz, Adin, *The Essential Talmud*, New York: Basic Books, and London: Weidenfeld and Nicolson, 1976
Strack, Hermann Leberecht, *Introduction to the Talmud and Midrash*, Philadelphia: Jewish Publication Society, 1931; revised by Günter Stemberger and translated by Markus Bockmuehl, 2nd edition, Edinburgh: Clark, 1996

One can speak of two types of introductions to talmudic literature. One type typically provides historical background, a survey of the literature's contents, and brief biographies of some of the leading rabbinic figures. The second type introduces the reader to the methodology of rabbinic literature in action. A beginning student of rabbinic literature should consult at least one introduction of each type; for the reader's convenience the two groups of introductions will be discussed separately.

The classic introduction to rabbinic literature is by STRACK and STEMBERGER. Originally written in 1887 by Hermann Strack, a German Protestant professor of Old Testament, and first translated into English in 1931, the work was exhaustively revised and updated by Günter Stemberger in 1982, 1991, and again in 1995. The work is both concise and comprehensive, and it includes a brief overview of the history of the rabbinic period as well as thumbnail biographies; a discussion of rabbinic education and methodology; and separate introductions to the Mishnah, the Tosefta, the Palestinian and Babylonian Talmuds, the later tractates, and the various genres of midrashic works. The information here is as up-to-date as one could hope for—there is even an appendix surveying the electronic resources available for the study of Talmud and midrash—and each section is accompanied by an extensive bibliography.

Another fairly comprehensive introduction to rabbinic literature is SAFRAI. This collection of essays by various scholars begins with a presentation of the historical background of the rabbinic period, followed by a discussion of two concepts—Oral Torah and halakhah—that undergird all of rabbinic discourse and literature. Safrai then presents essays on the Mishnah (with a separate essay for the nonlegal Tractate Avot), Tosefta, Palestinian Talmud, Babylonian Talmud, and the later tractates. There is also a final essay titled "Post-Talmudic Literature in the Land of Israel." Unfortunately, volume two of this work, which will cover midrashic literature, is not yet available.

Although the aforementioned books overlap and agree in many respects, there are subtle but significant differences between them. Among scholars of rabbinic literature, Israeli scholars such as Hanoch Albeck, Efraim Elimelech Urbach, and, to a lesser degree, J.N. Epstein have tended to be more trusting of rabbinic statements and traditions as being historically reliable, while in the United States Jacob Neusner and his disciples have been more skeptical. Although Stemberger and Safrai have consulted both schools of thought, Stemberger leans toward the Neusnerian school while Safrai and his colleagues are members of the Israeli school. Thus, for example, the essay on the Mishnah in Safrai accepts as historically accurate rabbinic statements about the Mishnah's prehistory that Stemberger presents much more provisionally.

STEINSALTZ is significantly different from the previously mentioned works in that it is written from an avowed spiritual perspective rather than from a scholarly one. It is meant to encourage the reader to make Talmud study part of a personal spiritual discipline by introducing the concerns and, much more cursorily, the methods of the Babylonian Talmud. A brief historical section at the beginning of the book cites rabbinic traditions as matters of fact, such as the story of Rabbi Akiba growing up an ignoramus and beginning to study only at age 40. The bulk of the work is actually an outline of the content of the six orders of the Mishnah rather than that of the Babylonian Talmud itself. Perhaps the most moving sections of the book are the last three chapters. Here Steinsaltz argues that a Talmud scholar must not only grow intellectually but also must transform his entire personality in accord with rabbinic teaching. He then argues that the Talmud has not simply been the preserve of the learned but has had a deep influence on the entire Jewish people. Finally, he provides a reminder that "the Talmud has never been completed," and he invites the reader to participate in the ongoing conversation that is talmudic study. In short, while this work is not reliable as a historical and scholarly guide, it provides a powerful argument for the devotional study of rabbinic literature.

There are also works that introduce the reader to rabbinic literature inductively by leading him or her through sample passages of rabbinic works. A pioneer in this regard is Jacob Neusner. NEUSNER (1973) conducts the reader through the relatively brief eighth chapter of Tractate Berakhot, analyzing and comparing the material in the Mishnah, Tosefta, Palestinian Talmud, and Babylonian Talmud. The final chapter draws theological conclusions from the material studied. As always, Neusner finds religious significance not only in the material's content but also in its form. He shows that among other concerns the rabbis are interested in finding the connection between the mundane and the sublime and in facing the tension between logic and life. In his conclusion he argues that Talmud study is an excellent preparation for learning to make decisions in the face of modernity's relativism.

NEUSNER (1989) provides a similar introduction to both the legal and narrative midrashim. In a concluding chapter, Neusner presents his understanding of the larger theological agenda informing the midrashic process. He believes that it is intended to uncover the relevance of the truths contained in Scripture as they apply to the life and times of those engaged in midrash.

Finally, there are the chapters on Talmud and midrash in HOLTZ. After a brief introduction to the background and terminology of rabbinic literature, Robert Goldenberg guides the reader through the first pages of the Babylonian Talmud in order to acquaint him or her with the types of issues that occupied the rabbis and the methods they used to address them. Holtz, after defining midrash and classifying its genres, introduces sample midrashic texts and explains both their methods and their messages.

Eliezer Diamond

See also Halakhah: Introductions; Talmudic Literature: Hermeneutics; Talmudic Literature: Reference Tools; Talmudic Literature: Theology; Talmudic Literature: Translations

Talmudic Literature: Theology

Kadushin, Max, *The Rabbinic Mind*, New York: Jewish Theological Seminary, 1952; 3rd edition, New York: Bloch, 1972

Kraemer, David Charles, *The Mind of the Talmud: An Intellectual History of the Bavli*, New York: Oxford University Press, 1990

Kraemer, David Charles, *Reading the Rabbis: The Talmud as Literature*, New York: Oxford University Press, 1996

Moore, George Foot, *Judaism in the First Centuries of the Christian Era: The Age of Tannaim*, Cambridge, Massachusetts: Harvard University Press, 1927

Neusner, Jacob, *Invitation to the Talmud: A Teaching Book*, New York: Harper and Row, 1973; revised edition, San Francisco: Harper and Row, 1984

Neusner, Jacob, *Invitation to Midrash: The Workings of Rabbinic Bible Interpretation: A Teaching Book*, San Francisco: Harper and Row, 1989

Schechter, Solomon, *Some Aspects of Rabbinic Theology*, New York: Macmillan, 1909; as *Aspects of Rabbinic Theology*, New York: Schocken, 1961

Urbach, Efraim Elimelech, *Hazal, pirke emunot ve-de'ot*, 1969; as *The Sages: Their Concepts and Beliefs*, Jerusalem: Magnes Press of Hebrew University, 1975; Cambridge, Massachusetts: Harvard University Press, 1987

Constructing a rabbinic theology is difficult for at least two reasons. The first is that we have no theological treatises from the talmudic era. Instead, statements of theological import are sprinkled in among the rabbis' legal discussions. Second, the rabbis favor legal, hermeneutical, and narrative discourse, rather than philosophical interchange. Nonetheless, there are some fine studies of rabbinic theology. Most are topically arranged, but some modern studies have focused on the theology implicit in the mode of rabbinic discourse itself.

A pioneering study of rabbinic theology is that of SCHECHTER. He outlines rabbinic views on God and God's relationship to Israel and the world; the centrality of law to rabbinic Judaism; the problem of sin and evil; and the importance and means of repentance. Especially important is a chapter entitled "The Joy of the Law." Here Schechter seeks to dispel the mistaken notion that Judaism is a religion of joyless legalism. Schechter, citing talmudic and medieval sources, shows that for the rabbis there is a joy inherent in the fulfillment of the commandments, in particular because they lead to a profound intimacy with God.

MOORE is the first Christian scholar to have written a theology of Judaism in English based primarily on rabbinic sources rather than the Apocrypha and Pseudsepigrapha. He does so in order to provide the reader with a picture of "normative" Judaism, as Moore puts it, a notion much criticized by other scholars. He provides a survey of all the sources available for deriving Jewish theological views. He then presents rabbinic views from the first two centuries of the Common Era on revelation, God, sin and atonement, observance, morals, piety, and the afterlife. For all Moore's efforts to present an "authentic" picture of Judaism, his presentation, by concentrating mainly on issues of belief, underemphasizes the importance for the rabbis of observance in all areas of life.

A difficult but important work is that of KADUSHIN. He addresses the issue raised earlier by Schechter, namely that there is no systematic theology within rabbinic Judaism and that conflicting views often are presented without resolution. Responding to this observation, Kadushin seeks to explain rabbinic theology in its own terms rather than trying to fit it artificially into a structure more suitable for Christian theology. He proposes that rabbinic ideology consists of what he calls "value-concepts" to which the sages refer with one or more "value-terms," such as Malkhut Shamayim (the kingship of Heaven) and Kiddush Hashem (the sanctification of God's name). These terms and concepts are intentionally left vague, says Kadushin, both so that they can be applied in many different situations with various shades of meaning and so that individuals may understand these concepts and terms according to their own lights. Because of the importance of language for rabbinic thought, moreover, one must be aware that when key rabbinic terms are translated into English their import may be altered significantly. Kadushin also makes extended reference to the social and biological sciences in order to frame his thesis in a more universally accessible form. Although the works to which he refers are now outdated, one must give Kadushin credit for his efforts at synthesizing rabbinic thought and the scientific theories of his day.

More recently URBACH has written a comprehensive review and analysis of rabbinic theology. In his introduction Urbach reviews and critiques the work of his predecessors. His major contribution—which he finds previous studies lacking—is a nuanced, historically aware presentation of rabbinic thought. This means, first of all, recognizing that there are often minority views alluded to or merely hinted at that must be teased out of the rabbinic sources. Often this can be done by consulting the Apocrypha or Qumran literature. Moreover, a study of these works as well as Christian literature makes it clear that rabbinic statements are often responses to views expressed by other groups. An example of this is his comparison of rabbinic and Christian exegesis of the Song of Songs. Finally, by paying close attention to the dating of rabbinic dicta one can trace ideological shifts over time in rabbinic thought (sometimes in response to evolving Christian thought).

NEUSNER (1973, 1989) offers an approach to the study of rabbinic theology that is significantly different from that of his predecessors. He is extremely skeptical about the reliability of the attributions in rabbinic literature and concludes, therefore, that it is not possible to offer a trustworthy survey of the theological views of particular sages. What is feasible, in his opinion, is to derive the theology of various "authorships": that is, the editors of the Mishnah, the editors of the Babylonian Talmud, and so on. For the most part the theology that Neusner derives from these documents is not from the avowedly theological statements in each work but from the type of issues it chooses to discuss and the manner in which it chooses to discuss them. Neusner notes, for example, that the mishnaic preoccupation with the effect of human intention on the ritual status of objects indicates its belief in the efficacy and importance of human will. Neusner understands numerous stories about sages in the Jerusalem Talmud as presenting the sage as an embodiment of Torah. He suggests that the Babylonian Talmud's greater use of Scripture relative to the Jerusalem Talmud and its organizing of discussions around scriptural verses shows its intention of integrating the Oral Torah of the rabbis with the Written Torah of Scripture, thereby giving rabbinic teachings the same status and authority as the Bible.

KRAEMER's (1990, 1996) important contribution is the examination of the basic methodology of rabbinic literature and argumentation, particularly as found in the Babylonian Talmud, so as to show its theological import. He demonstrates that in Babylonia there was an ever-growing interest in the mechanics and possibilities of disputation and that this coincided with an increasing recognition that ultimate truth was not available in any verifiable sense. This bred a love for dialectic coupled with the humility born of realizing the limitations of human intellect. It is this humility, in Kraemer's view, that is rabbinic Judaism's strength and saving grace.

ELIEZER DIAMOND

See also Talmudic Literature: Hermeneutics; Talmudic Literature: Introductions; Talmudic Literature: Reference Tools; Talmudic Literature: Translations

Talmudic Literature: Hermeneutics

Boyarin, Daniel, *Intertextuality and the Reading of Midrash* (Indiana Studies in Biblical Literature), Bloomington: Indiana University Press, 1990

Goldin, Judah, *The Song at the Sea: Being a Commentary on a Commentary in Two Parts,* New Haven, Connecticut: Yale University Press, 1971

Holtz, Barry (editor), *Back to the Sources: Reading the Classic Jewish Texts,* New York: Summit, 1984

Jacobs, Louis, *Studies in Talmudic Logic and Methodology,* London: Vallentine, Mitchell, 1961

Jacobs, Louis, *The Talmudic Argument: A Study in Talmudic Reasoning and Methodology,* Cambridge and New York: Cambridge University Press, 1984

Mielziner, Moses, *Introduction to the Talmud,* Chicago: Bloch, 1894; 2nd revised edition, London: Funk and Wagnalls, 1903; 5th edition, New York: Bloch, 1968

Neusner, Jacob, *Invitation to the Talmud: A Teaching Book,* New York: Harper and Row, 1973; revised edition, San Francisco: Harper and Row, 1984

Neusner, Jacob, *Invitation to Midrash: The Workings of Rabbinic Bible Interpretation: A Teaching Book,* San Francisco: Harper and Row, 1989

Porton, Gary, *Understanding Rabbinic Midrash: Texts and Commentary,* Hoboken, New Jersey: Ktav, 1985

Steinsaltz, Adin, *The Talmud, the Steinsaltz Edition: A Reference Guide,* New York: Random House, 1989

Steinsaltz, Adin, *The Talmud/Talmud Bavli: The Steinsaltz Edition,* 21 vols., New York: Random House, 1989–2000

The hermeneutics of rabbinic literature refers both to the methods used by the rabbis to interpret biblical and other rabbinic sources and the various methods that have been proposed to understand rabbinic methodology itself. Because it is difficult to distinguish between these two topics in practice, and because the works reviewed below deal with both issues, the term "hermeneutics" is used in this essay to encompass both types of methodologies. On the other hand, talmudic and midrashic hermeneutics are distinct (although related) disciplines; therefore, this survey addresses works on each of these areas separately, beginning with talmudic hermeneutics.

One of the earliest English introductions to rabbinic hermeneutics is MIELZINER. The first section is comprised of a brief review of the Babylonian Talmud, cognate works, and the Talmud's major medieval commentators; a listing of manuscripts, printed editions, and translations of the Talmud; a bibliography; an impassioned defense of the Talmud against its detractors; and a powerful invitation to the reader to take up Talmud study. The second and third sections are more directly relevant to the subject at hand. The second, which is titled "The Legal Hermeneutics of the Talmud," explains the major methods used by the rabbis to interpret scripture, while the third section, "Talmudical Methodology and Terminology," surveys the various types of rabbinic discourse and the terms used by the rabbis to signal the different types of interchange. Although Mielziner first cites each term in its original Hebrew and Aramaic, he also provides an English translation for each phrase. Furthermore, he provides examples from rabbinic literature for each term. This work brings the reader as close to the spirit of talmudic argumentation as is possible without studying the Talmud itself.

Most of the other works under discussion introduce talmudic methodology inductively, as they investigate some portion of the Babylonian Talmud. For example, Robert Goldenberg (in HOLTZ) translates and analyzes the opening few pages of Berakhot, the first tractate in the Talmud. NEUSNER (1973) is a much broader undertaking than Goldenberg's effort; it offers a comparative presentation of the eighth chapter of Berakhot as it appears in the Mishnah, the Tosefta, the Jerusalem Talmud, and the Babylonian Talmud. In this way, Neusner not only introduces the hermeneutics of the Babylonian Talmud; he also explains that text's role as interpreter of earlier material contained in the Mishnah and Tosefta, and he identifies the differences in style and substance between the Babylonian and Jerusalem Talmuds.

STEINSALTZ (1989–2000) is a highly ambitious work of talmudic hermeneutics; it aims to make talmudic literature accessible to the English-speaking student who is unfamiliar with the rabbinic corpus. Steinsaltz's edition (which translates four out of 37 tractates—Baba Metsia, Ketubbot, Taanit, and Sanhedrin—in 21 volumes) includes a literal translation of the original text of the Talmud (which is included), as well as an expanded translation-commentary, which explains the methods and assumptions behind talmudic discourse. Other useful features include footnotes summarizing selected glosses of the classical medieval commentators, summations of Jewish law that derive from the passage under discussion, side notes on language and terminology and on the social and material world in which the Talmud was composed, and brief biographies of the sages mentioned in each passage.

STEINSALTZ (1989) is intended to facilitate use of Steinsaltz's multivolume work described above. This volume includes thumbnail biographies of the major Palestinian and Babylonian rabbis of the talmudic period as well as listings and explanations of the major terms used in rabbinic discussion and scriptural interpretation. Unfortunately, these lists are of limited use to the reader who does not know Hebrew: although the explanations are in English, the terms themselves are listed in Hebrew, without transliterations.

The studies by Louis Jacobs provide general introductions to talmudic methodology, which are illustrated with examples from specific passages. JACOBS (1961) is divided into two sections: the first consists of essays about various aspects of rabbinic logic. It includes comparisons of rabbinic methodology to Greek logic and to the methodology of the English philosopher John Stuart Mill, as well as an analysis of the relative authority accorded by the rabbis to logic and to Scripture. The book's second half presents a study of a number of talmudic passages that demonstrates some of the literary tools used to construct talmudic discourse. JACOBS (1984) contains an excellent introduction to the methods of argumentation employed in the Talmud; it offers analyses of selected talmudic passages from both conceptual and literary perspectives.

BOYARIN provides an extremely sophisticated introduction to midrashic hermeneutics. He employs contemporary literary theories to explain the intent and method of midrash. This work is difficult to read, especially because Boyarin uses the complex vocabulary of literary criticism extensively, but the reader will be amply rewarded for the effort.

Holtz engages midrashic methodology with his translation and explication of some representative midrashim from the various genres. NEUSNER (1989) analyzes a significant number of selections from the major legal and narrative midrashim in his introductory text. He supplements his discussion of particular midrashim with a review of the agendas and methods of each of the midrashic compilations that he cites.

PORTON cites and glosses selections from the early legal midrashim and two of the early narrative midrashim, Genesis Rabbah and Leviticus Rabbah. His analyses are extremely detailed; they enable the reader to follow each step of the midrashic process of reasoning and interpretation. GOLDIN is a commentary on the portion of the Mekhilta (an early rabbinic midrash on Exodus) that examines the Song at the Sea, the poem recited by Moses and Israel to celebrate the miracle that allowed them to cross the sea on dry land while the Egyptians who pursued them drowned. He provides both an elegant translation and incisive glosses.

ELIEZER DIAMOND

See also Talmudic Literature: Introductions; Talmudic Literature: Reference Tools; Talmudic Literature: Theology; Talmudic Literature: Translations

Tannaim *see* Rabbinic Biography: Talmudic

Targum

Cathcart, Kevin J., Michael Maher, and Martin McNamara (editors), *The Aramaic Bible*, Edinburgh: Clark, and Wilmington, Delaware: Glazier, 1987

Diez Macho, Alejandro, "The Recently Discovered Palestinian Targum and Its Relationship with Other Targums," in *Congress Volume: Oxford, 1959* (Supplements to Vetus Testamentum, vol. 7), edited by G.W. Anderson, Leiden: Brill, 1959

Drazin, Israel, *Targum Onkelos to Deuteronomy,* New York: Ktav, 1982

Drazin, Israel, *Targum Onkelos to Exodus,* Hoboken, New Jersey: Ktav, 1990

Drazin, Israel, *Targum Onkelos to Leviticus,* New York: Ktav, 1994

Shinan, Avigdor, "Live Translation: On the Nature of the Aramaic Targums to the Pentateuch," *Prooftexts,* 3(1), 1983

Sperber, Alexander, *The Bible in Aramaic: Based on Old Manuscripts and Printed Texts,* vol. 4, B: *The Targum and the Hebrew Bible,* Leiden: Brill, 1973

York, Anthony D., "The Targum in the Synagogue and in the School," *Journal for the Study of Judaism,* 10, 1979

As Aramaic replaced Hebrew as the language of everyday life for Jews during the Babylonian exile (beginning in 597 B.C.E.) and Second Temple period (515 B.C.E.–70 C.E.), it became increasingly necessary to translate the Bible—and especially those parts of the Bible formally read during synagogue services—into Aramaic. The result is called *targum* (plural *targumim*), the Aramaic word for "translation." A number of written targum texts have been preserved: Targum Onkelos; Targum Neofiti; the Fragmentary Targum; Targum Pseudo-Jonathan; and various Cairo Genizah fragments of targumim, all on the Pentateuch; a distinct Targum Pseudo-Jonathan on the Prophets; and separate targumim on Psalms, Proverbs, Job, Song of Songs, Ruth, Lamentations, Ecclesiastes, Esther (three), and Chronicles. These targumim vary considerably in style and theological content.

Scholars have focused on eliminating scribal and printing errors as well as deliberate interpolations that have crept into published targum texts; they have analyzed the interpretative stances and theology of individual targumim; and they have worked to determine whether particular targumim are of Babylonian or Palestinian origin.

CATHCART, MAHER, and McNAMARA and their collaborators are in the process of translating all the targumim into English. Most of the targumim have never been translated before, and this project is a considerable undertaking. Each volume contains a translation of one of the targumim on a biblical book, along with commentary, textual notes, and an introduction to that particular targum and its interpretive stance. Both the translations in this series and their introductory essays are generally high in quality.

A series of commentaries on the targumim has also commenced with contributions to date from DRAZIN (1982, 1990, 1994), as well as M. Aberbach and B. Grossfeld.

SHINAN explores the practice of targum as an actual activity that occurred in synagogue, and he tries to recreate the concerns that a *meturgeman* (reciter of targum) would have while he worked. The meturgeman was a professional, who apparently made a living from his craft. He would stand beside the Torah reader and recite the Aramaic translation by heart. The close resemblance of the Hebrew and Aramaic languages inspired the meturgeman to create word-plays based on the Hebrew and to diverge from Aramaic grammatical conventions in order to remain close to the Hebrew text of the Bible. The meturgeman was a mediator between rabbinic culture and the masses and incorporated the values of both. The targumim abound in folk beliefs and angelology, and they include a strong didactic emphasis on the rewards of Torah study and fulfillment of commandments, as well as praise for the power of prayer. The fact that the congregation listened to the meturgeman, instead of following a text directly, is reflected in the addition of interjections that were designed to inspire greater attention before important verses. Similarly, curses were changed from second-person to third-person to prevent confusion in the mind of a listener, who might misapprehend and think the curse was directed at him.

SPERBER distinguishes clearly between targum as an institution and targum as a literary document, noting that 1,200 years passed between the initial formulation of the oral targum tradition and the transcription of the oldest extant targum text. He argues that Targum Onkelos is a conflation of the products of two schools of translators, emphasizing the evidence of doublets (that is, two translations of the same unit of text) and sharp differences in style: one school adheres to literal translation as much as possible, deviating only to clarify an idiom or to demonstrate the validity of rabbinic interpretation, while the other school uses a freer, midrashic interpretative stance. Sperber speculates that the more literal elements were of Babylonian origin and the more interpretative parts emanated from the Palestinian tradition. He insists that close attention be paid to the style of targumic translation—it was never simply word-for-word—and he underscores the extent to which targum changes the biblical text when the original text contains ideas that run counter to the views of the period in which it was translated. For example, biblical anthropomorphisms were regularly rewritten. Thus, the idiomatic Hebrew expression "to walk before God" was rendered as "to serve God," while biblical mentions of other gods were changed to refer to idols. Sperber stresses that targum was aimed at the level of common folk: therefore, it contained explanations and revisions of difficult passages, and it included clarifications of grammatical problems.

DIEZ MACHO has published Targum Neofiti, a complete targum to the Pentateuch, which he discovered in the Vatican Library. This targum is an example of the Palestinian tradition, and Diez Macho argues that the fact that it was based on a Hebrew text that differed substantially from the Massoretic Hebrew Bible proves that it was compiled in either the first or second century B.C.E. Targum Neofiti, therefore, is a pre-Christian translation and older than Targum Onkelos.

YORK analyzes rabbinic references to targum and argues that targum was as important in the school as it was in the synagogue. The elementary-school curriculum accorded pride of place to instruction in targum. This fact is not in itself surprising, for there was a close relationship between school and synagogue, and the school with its *hazzan* (or superintendent) was typically housed in the synagogue. But the schools regarded targum not merely as important but also as inspired. Indeed, it was the targum's status as part of the corpus of Oral Torah that explains the strictures that delayed the act of committing targum to written form for so many centuries.

PAMELA BARMASH

Temple and Temple Mount

Ben-Dov, M., *Hafirot Har ha-Bayit*, 1982; translated as *In the Shadow of the Temple: The Discovery of Ancient Jerusalem*, New York: Harper and Row, 1985

Comay, Joan, *The Temple of Jerusalem*, New York: Holt, Rinehart and Winston, and London: Weidenfeld and Nicolson, 1975

Haran, Menahem, *Temples and Temple-Service in Ancient Israel: An Inquiry into the Character of Cult Phenomena and the Historical Setting of the Priestly School*, Oxford: Clarendon, 1977; as *Temples and Temple-Service in Ancient Israel: An Inquiry into Biblical Cult Phenomena and the Historical Setting of the Priestly School*, Winona Lake, Indiana: Eisenbrauns, 1985

Hayward, Robert, *The Jewish Temple: A Non-Biblical Sourcebook*, London and New York: Routledge, 1996

Levenson, Jon D., *Sinai and Zion: An Entry into the Jewish Bible* (New Voices in Biblical Studies), Minneapolis, Minnesota: Winston, 1985

Mazar, Benjamin, *The Mountain of the Lord*, Garden City, New York: Doubleday, 1975

Ritmeyer, Leon and Kathleen Ritmeyer, *Secrets of Jerusalem's Temple Mount*, Washington, D.C.: Biblical Archaeology Society, 1998

Rosen-Ayalon, Myriam, *The Early Islamic Monuments of Al-Haram Al-Sharif: An Iconographic Study*, Jerusalem: Institute of Archaeology, Hebrew University of Jerusalem, 1989

For a millennium, Jews worshiped God on the Temple Mount, home to Jerusalem's First and Second Temples. The area, known as Mount Moriah, occupies the highest elevation on ancient Mount Zion and enters Jewish history during the time of King David, who acquired the land from the Jebusites. The honor of building the First Temple, however, fell to David's son, Solomon. Approximately 70 years after that temple's destruction in 586 B.C.E., the Second Temple was erected on the same site. This structure underwent numerous renovations, most stunningly during the time of Herod, who expanded the Temple Mount to its largest proportions, approximately 170,000 square yards, or 40 acres. In 70 C.E., the Roman army destroyed the Second Temple, but the Temple has endured as a revered image in Jewish literature and thought. Byzantine rulers left the Temple Mount desolate as proof that God had abandoned the Jews. In the seventh century, Arab Muslims captured Jerusalem and began transforming the Temple Mount into an Islamic holy site with the construction of the al-Aqsa mosque and the Dome of the Rock. Built over the

area once occupied by the two successive Temples, the golden Dome stands today as the most recognizable feature of the Jerusalem skyline. Modern archaeological investigations conducted in the 19th and 20th centuries have made substantial contributions to knowledge of the Temple Mount's appearance and function.

COMAY recounts the history of the Temple Mount within the context of Jewish history from the time of Abraham to the early 1970s. Her book provides an accessible description of the Solomonic Temple, the sacrificial rituals performed there, the priesthood, and the Herodian expansion and renovations. She briefly describes the Islamic transformation of the sacred precinct and the Western Wall. Numerous reproductions of medieval and Renaissance illuminated manuscripts and paintings enliven the narrative.

LEVENSON examines the complex and complementary relationship between the two holy mountains in Jewish tradition, Sinai and Zion. In addition to representing the everlasting covenant with the house of David, Mount Zion serves as the location where the voice of God, heard first on Mount Sinai, continues to be experienced. Levenson describes the way in which the Temple occupies a central place in Jewish theology, functioning as the "conduit through which messages pass from earth to heaven"; it is the atemporal location forestalling a collapse into chaos and a spatial microcosm of the universe itself. The Temple, always more than a physical location, was able to transcend its destruction when Judaism transposed its sanctity onto other venues and activities, including prayer, study, synagogue, and the domestic table.

HARAN's detailed study of temple worship in ancient Israel focuses on four topics: the role of the temple in Israelite religion; the priesthood; the rituals; and the pilgrimage festivals, especially Passover, which were major occasions for temple worship. Although he also describes numerous other temples that existed in ancient Israel, the author concentrates on the Temple in Jerusalem. He argues that the Priestly source (P), one of the hypothetical source documents believed to have been used to compose the Pentateuch, should be dated to the First Temple period. (Many scholars dispute this early dating of P.) From this controversial position, Haran believes that the priestly account can be used as a reliable source of information about the operation and ideology of the First Temple.

HAYWARD has selected eight texts written in the Second Temple period that express "what the Temple service meant to Jews of the Second Temple times." These writings reflect the tremendous value and respect Jews attached to the Temple. Hayward allows each text to speak for itself but also provides a brief introduction in which he identifies five recurrent themes related to the Temple: along with its rituals, the Temple establishes and secures order in the cosmos; it acts as a microcosm for the entire universe; it serves as the earthly counterpart to the heavenly angelic worship; it marks the site where Israel seeks God's blessings; and it is prominently associated with light, particularly as a symbol of God's presence.

BEN-DOV presents a richly illustrated history of the Temple Mount and those areas that stood in its shadow from the time of David to the Ottoman Empire, highlighting the tremendous architectural developments introduced during the Herodian, Byzantine, and Umayyad periods. He supplements this narrative with a history of the archaeological excavations, often told through dramatic anecdotes taken from his own experiences at the site. He describes in detail the buildings, bridges, arches, gates, walls, porticos, tunnels, drainage system, and cisterns that made up the Temple Mount, along with the pottery, coins, and other small artifacts that have contributed to a better understanding of the Temple's functions.

MAZAR, who supervised the archaeological excavations conducted around the Temple Mount beginning in 1968, opens his book with a brief summary of the surveys conducted in the 19th and 20th centuries. He then weaves together the literary record and the archaeological data to tell the story of the Temple Mount and surrounding areas of Jerusalem from the earliest construction to the destruction of the Second Temple. The book focuses on the architecture of the First and Second Temples along with the associated structures located on the Temple Mount and in the City of David. The author concludes with an examination of the Islamic holy sites constructed during Umayyad period and subsequent changes introduced by Crusaders, Mamluks, and Turks. Mazar includes hundreds of photographs of the Temple Mount, the excavation sites, and the artifacts uncovered.

Leon Ritmeyer served as the architect involved with the archaeological excavations south of the Temple Mount from 1973 to 1978. Based on the discoveries from these excavations and the reports compiled by 19th-century archaeologists, RITMEYER and RITMEYER identify the probable location of the First and Second Temples (immediately below the current site of the Dome of the Rock) and reconstruct the layout of the Temple Mount before it was devastated by the Roman army. The numerous drawings provide a vivid depiction of the ways the Temple Mount may have looked during the biblical, Hasmonean, and Herodian periods.

ROSEN-AYALON studies the transformation of the Temple Mount into *al-Haram al-Sharif*, an Islamic holy site. With particular focus on the Dome of the Rock and the al-Aqsa mosque, she concludes that the buildings of the Haram were not constructed in a haphazard manner but were "positioned in accord with a well thought-out plan." She demonstrates that the axial relation between the al-Aqsa mosque and the Dome, not to mention the Dome itself, was inspired by the Basilica and Rotunda of the Church of the Holy Sepulchre in Jerusalem in an effort to overshadow the Christian shrine and thereby promote the Islamic identity of the city. In addition, she shows how the Dome's rich decorations were meant to evoke the long-standing identification of Jerusalem as the earthly paradise.

GARY GILBERT

See also Tabernacle; Western Wall

Theater

Beck, Evelyn Torton, *Kafka and the Yiddish Theater: Its Impact and His Work*, Madison, Wisconsin, and London: University of Wisconsin Press, 1971

Ben-Ari, Raikin, *Habima*, translated by A.H. Gross and I. Soref, New York: Yoseloff, 1957

Cohen, Sarah Blacher (editor), *From Hester Street to Hollywood: The Jewish-American Stage and Screen* (Jewish Literature and Culture), Bloomington: Indiana University Press, 1983

Isser, Edward, *Stages of Annihilation: Theatrical Representations of the Holocaust*, Madison, New Jersey: Fairleigh Dickinson University Press, and London: Associated University Presses, 1997

Kaminska, Ida, *My Life, My Theater*, edited and translated by Curt Leviant, New York: Macmillan, 1973

Klima, Cynthia Ann, "A Tricultural Theatrical Tradition: The History of the German Theater in Prague, 1883–1938," Ph.D. diss., University of Wisconsin at Madison, 1995

Lifson, David S., *The Yiddish Theatre in America*, New York: Yoseloff, 1965

Sandrow, Nahma, *Vagabond Stars: A World History of Yiddish Theater*, New York: Harper and Row, 1977

Jewish theater is a multifaceted art whose form depends on the country where the theater is located and on the audience attracted to such theater. Naturally, Yiddish theater is primarily associated with the Jews of Poland, Russia, and Lithuania. It was originally an unsophisticated form of theater presented by wandering troupes subsisting on very little and often playing for free in cafes and small restaurants. The plays were simple in form, yet it was precisely this simplicity that conveyed lessons to audiences so easily and subtly. Yiddish theater was brought to New York by Eastern European immigrants, and its eventual demise was due to the obliteration during World War II of Eastern European Jewish life, specifically obliteration of the shtetl, which was the primary inspiration for the milieu of Yiddish theater.

The endeavors of the acting company Habima provided a Hebrew-language venue for Jewish theater. Like the Yiddish theater, Habima troupes traveled extensively, often performing in front of audiences that understood little or no Hebrew. Habima's creative roots were in Russia, but finally it found repose in Israel. In Western Europe, there were several small Jewish theaters, but more significant was Jewish involvement in the general theater community. Jewish participation in the cultivation and preservation of drama on stage helped theaters such as the New German Theater (Neues Deutsches Theater) in Prague and theaters in Vienna and Germany to survive even when financial times were catastrophic. Performances of German classics such as *Maria Stuart, Emilia Galotti, Faust,* and *Nathan der Weise* were supported greatly by Jewish cultural societies. Following World War II, a new form of Jewish theater began to emerge—the Holocaust drama. This genre was slow to catch on after the war, but in the 1960s interest in such works proliferated. Finally, dramatists such as Wendy Wasserstein, Neil Simon, Lillian Hellman, and Paddy Chayefsky are among the numerous modern Jewish playwrights whose plays have been recognized with various accolades and whose contributions to the great quilt of U.S. culture are considered invaluable.

BECK's work focuses on Franz Kafka's relationship to Yiddish theater. A major change occurred in Kafka's writing around 1912, a year that coincides with his first experience with Yiddish theater in Prague, where performances took place in the modestly decorated Café Savoy. Dramatic elements and clearly defined characters began to make their appearance in his works, and thus his writing became more adaptable to the stage. Beck concentrates on revealing the differences in Kafka's writing prior to and following the year 1912 as well as the transformation of his prose into stageable drama.

BEN-ARI's work traces the history of the first Hebrew acting company, Habima, from its inception as a cooperative community theater to its designation as a state theater in Russia and finally to its reconstitution in Israel. Ben-Ari, a former member of the troupe, lends firsthand knowledge of a theater created to give Jews a sense of identity and to relate the richness of Jewish culture on stage in the original language of the Jews. The chapters "The Habima and Theatrical Theory" and "The Stanislavsky System" describe the implementation of Stanislavsky's acting techniques by Habima's actors. Black-and-white photographs of individual actors, of the acting troupes, and of scenes from plays complement the work. Inspirational and at times emotional, the work is the story of a troupe that triumphed in the face of monetary, political, and social hardships.

COHEN's compilation contains articles reflecting the different facets of Jewish theater, from immigrant Yiddish theater to the contemporary U.S. scene with its themes ranging from the Jewish folklore-laden vision of Isaac Bashevis Singer to the Holocaust. Several playwrights are well represented in the book, including Lillian Hellman, Paddy Chayevsky, Clifford Odets, Neil Simon, Jules Feiffer, and Saul Bellow. Because the work encompasses many areas of Jewish theater, it is well suited to those readers who desire a good overview of the history, development, and modern forms of the medium. Of particular note is Nahma Sandrow's "Yiddish Theater and the American Theater," which follows Yiddish theater from Eastern Europe to New York. In addition, a discussion of Jewish comedy is featured in the work.

ISSER states that his work "seeks to identify emerging patterns and correlations among dramatic texts written on the topic" of the Holocaust. In addition, he makes the case that this delicate subject must not be manipulated for artistic or political purposes, for such treatments are an invitation to historical revisionists. The book is divided into ten chapters, describing plays written to relate the Holocaust to U.S. audiences and discussing various playwrights, such as George Bernard Shaw and Arthur Miller, and their diverse relationships to the theme of Holocaust drama. Chapter five is devoted to German theatrical responses to the Holocaust, and it treats such topics as Peter Weiss's documentary theater and Berthold Brecht's Marxist interpretations of the subject. Isser divides Holocaust drama into two categories: death camp drama and survivor drama. He also addresses the issue of "theatrical space"—that is the victims and the enemy, both on stage and "potentially in the audience." This work provides references to many plays and thoughtful insight into an area of drama that is highly compelling and worthy of further study.

KAMINSKA's memoirs describe her life as a child actress sharing the stage with her mother, Esther Rachel Kaminska, the "Mother of Yiddish Theater." She recounts a life of travel from Warsaw to St. Petersburg, experiencing the Revolution in Russia, antisemitism in Poland, and the Yiddish performance scene in New York. Kaminska relates the hardships of traveling in such a theatrical troupe, including troubles with local authorities, government censors, and war. She details her brush with the Nazis, her life under Communism, European tours in the 1950s, and her jump from stage to celluloid. The book provides valuable insight into people who suffered for their art and who labored to perfect something for which they had immense passion.

KLIMA's dissertation begins with a background sketch of Jewish Prague and the history of Czechs, Germans, and Jews in the city. While the work does not deal specifically with Jewish theater, it does explore the important role Jews played in saving and preserving German drama in Prague. Several Jewish playwrights and their plays are discussed in the work. Included is an extensive appendix that lists newspaper articles about plays, plays performed in German-language theaters, and cafés where Jewish intellectuals gathered to share ideas regarding the Prague literary scene. Also provided is an outline of the stages in Prague. A thorough bibliography makes this work a valuable source for further information on Jewish involvement in the world of Prague German drama.

LIFSON's work traces the historical background of Yiddish theater and shows how many forms of drama, including German expressionism and French impressionism, were imported to the United States by Yiddish acting troupes. Extensively discussed too is the shtetl of Eastern Europe, whose life is thematically central to the spirit of Yiddish theater and whose language "is a dialect of the human soul." Lifson explains why Yiddish theater thrived in New York. Playwrights, their plays, Yiddish actors, the audience, drama clubs, the Folksbiene, and the Jewish Art Theater are treated in separate chapters. Lifson's final chapter outlines the decline of Yiddish theater, which he attributes to the destruction of the shtetl during World War II. Included are black-and-white photographs of dramatic scenes on stage and of notable actors.

SANDROW insists that her purposes are "historical, not critical." The work chronicles the Yiddish theater, from the biblically based dramas of the 17th century to the theaters of New York. She also examines the entry of secular learning into the realm of Yiddish theater during the Haskalah, or Enlightenment. The work encompasses many aspects of Yiddish drama, including German classics translated into Yiddish, and there is a chapter on Avrom Goldfadn, the "Father of Yiddish Theater." *Shund*, or commercial theater, Soviet Yiddish theater, Yiddish theater in Poland, and drama in the concentration camps and ghettos are thoroughly discussed. Reproductions of original playbills, stage scenes, and cartoons accompany the text.

CYNTHIA A. KLÍMA

Theodicy

Blumenthal, David R., *Facing the Abusing God: A Theology of Protest*, Louisville, Kentucky: Westminster/Knox, 1993

Kushner, Harold S., *When Bad Things Happen to Good People*, New York: Schocken, 1981; London: Pan, 1982

Leaman, Oliver, *Evil and Suffering in Jewish Philosophy* (Cambridge Studies in Religious Traditions, 6), Cambridge and New York: Cambridge University Press, 1995

Levi ben Gershom, *The Commentary of Levi ben Gerson (Gersonides) on the Book of Job*, edited and translated by Abraham Lassen, New York: Bloch, 1946

Maimonides, Moses, *The Guide of the Perplexed*, translated by Shlomo Pines, Chicago: University of Chicago Press, 1963

God is good, and God is all-powerful: these two claims have been axiomatic for Jews, Christians, and Muslims since biblical times. And for just as long, people have been trying to reconcile the two propositions with the harsh realities of life. The world is full of suffering, and much of it appears undeserved and pointless. Why does God sometimes fail or refuse to intervene to stop evil or to save his creatures from anguish? This is the problem of "theodicy," or the justification of the ways of God. In the Bible, this issue constitutes the central theme of the Book of Job, and it is articulated in the cry of the psalmist, "Why do you hide your face, heedless of our misery and our suffering?" (Psalm 44:25).

The debate continued through the rabbinic tradition. Although Rabbi Yannai (second century C.E.) said: "It is not in our power [to explain] the tranquillity of the wicked nor the afflictions of the righteous," there are several attempts in the Talmud to explain suffering. One collection of sayings speaks of three kinds of suffering: punishment for sin, especially for neglect of Torah; "chastisements of love" (see Proverbs 3:12), which are borne in love; and suffering that purges sin, bringing atonement. Life after death, a firm principle of rabbinic belief, compensates for apparent injustice in this world; the righteous suffer as mortals in order to reap greater reward in the hereafter. Some, especially kabbalists, adopted the concept of reincarnation to explain the suffering of the apparently innocent, such as children. The problem of evil is indeed central for Kabbalah, which sees the origin of what appears as evil (although ultimately all derives from the Creator and therefore is good) in the dominance of the divine attribute of justice over that of mercy. In recent times discussion has been stimulated in reaction to the Holocaust, but little has emerged that is new in principle.

LEAMAN has produced what may well be the first overview of the problem of theodicy in Jewish religious philosophy. (It is not a survey of the problem in Jewish religious thought generally, as it contains no more than passing reference to the Talmud or to the midrashic and kabbalistic sources.) Leaman's starting and finishing point is the Book of Job, and even this text is investigated from a philosophical standpoint rather than in terms of traditional exegesis. Through his reading of Job, he draws attention to the relationship between experience, philosophy, and religion; Job does not conclude from innocent suffering that God does not exist, nor does Job perceive that all is well in the world. With this foundation, Leaman offers a critical analysis of the views of Philo, Saadya, Maimonides, Gersonides, Benedict de Spinoza, Moses Mendelssohn, Hermann Cohen, Martin Buber, Franz Rosenzweig, and some post-Holocaust thinkers. Returning to Job for his conclusion,

Leaman contends that a discussion of evil and suffering is really a discussion about relationships with God.

MAIMONIDES was the most influential Jewish religious thinker of the Middle Ages, and this text is his major philosophical testament. In it, he seeks to harmonize the Scriptures as understood in Jewish tradition with philosophy, that is, with the science and thought of Aristotle as mediated through his Islamic translators and interpreters. Maimonides' views are often misrepresented by scholars who seek hidden meanings in his words, or by those who cannot accept that his intentions run counter to current orthodoxy. In his bold discussion of God's providence in book 3 chapters 8–24, he argues that imperfection, hence evil and suffering, lies in the nature of physical matter as subject to generation and corruption. Of the ten concentric spheres that (in Ptolemaic cosmology) make up the universe, only the innermost—the earth—consists of physical matter; because human beings live on this sphere, they share in its material chaos, which lies outside of God's providence. However, human beings also possess souls, which belong to the nonmaterial universe of the upper spheres. By cultivation of the spirit or intellect, their souls—which are the essential and enduring part of them—are united with the active intellect and placed directly within God's providence, immune to evil and suffering and open to the flow of divine knowledge through the "chain of being"; this process enables exceptional people to become prophets.

LEVI BEN GERSHOM (Gersonides) lived in Provence in the 14th century and was among the most important scientists of the Middle Ages. In his commentary on Job, he addresses the problem of theodicy. The message of Job, Gersonides says, is that humans should apply reason, or wisdom, to the understanding of their misfortunes; Job was virtuous but not initially wise. The wise person appreciates that God has created the world in the best possible way, even though this creation has occasional unpleasant side effects. Following Averroës, Gersonides maintains that God, in knowing himself, knows particulars. Consistent with his "dignity," however, God knows them not in detached form, as humans do, but as the necessary result of rational principles; the wise person, understanding this truth, can benefit from special divine providence.

KUSHNER, a Reconstructionist rabbi, presents his deservedly popular book as the work of "a religious man who has been hurt by life." The text is dedicated to the memory of his son, Aaron, a victim of progeria (premature aging) who died just after his 14th birthday. The diagnosis of Aaron's malady and the subsequent unfolding tragedy shook the naive faith of Kushner and his wife in the conventional image of God as an "all-wise, all-powerful parent figure who would treat us as our earthly parents did, or even better . . . and would see to it that we got what we deserved in life." Kushner offers comfort rather than theology. In a key passage, he asserts that God's words to Job (40:9–14) mean that although God wants the righteous to live peaceful, happy lives, and so shares Job's anger at the suffering of the righteous, he is unable to save innocent victims from cruelty and chaos. "God can't do everything," states Kushner in the title of chapter seven, "but he can do some important things." Most importantly, God does not solve problems for humans, but he enables them to cope, and through prayer he gives them strength, patience, and hope. Kushner skillfully draws out the universal relevance of his Jewish sources, although it cannot be said that his rather attenuated God has much in common with the God of the Bible or of Maimonides.

BLUMENTHAL, in this bold and imaginative book, follows his mentor, Abraham J. Heschel, in conceiving of God as "anthropopathic"—sharing human feelings. "God, as understood by the personalist stream of the tradition and experience, is personal. So God too must have a character, sensitivities, an individual history, and a moral capacity. . . ." God is fair; God addresses, and can be addressed by, humankind; God is powerful but not perfect; God is loving; God gets angry; God chooses and is partisan. Blumenthal writes in the wake of a sequence of statements from Holocaust theologians, such as Borowitz and Fackenheim, and precisely at a time when child abuse has become a public issue. A new and shocking image becomes available—that of God in Auschwitz as the abusing parent. Just as a parent does not stop being a parent because he abuses, the abusing God remains God and cannot be rejected. People must acknowledge the relationship and continue to live with God. Is such a God worth calling "God"? Blumenthal thinks so, first, because "the realm of the holy is there"; second, because by using religious and moral language, "humankind may be able to save itself from a fate as bad as, or worse than, the Holocaust." This book issues from the heart, and it will reach the heart. Not for a moment does Blumenthal attempt to lull the reader with easy explanations of messy world conditions or with illusory hopes for the future.

NORMAN SOLOMON

Tithes

Avery-Peck, Alan J., *Mishnah's Division of Agriculture: A History and Theology of Seder Zeraim* (Brown Judaic Studies, no. 79), Chico, California: Scholars Press, 1985

Brooks, Roger, *Support for the Poor in the Mishnaic Law of Agriculture: Tractate Peah* (Brown Judaic Studies, no. 43), Chico, California: Scholars Press, 1983

Haas, Peter J., *A History of the Mishnaic Law of Agriculture: Tractate Maaser Sheni* (Brown Judaic Studies, no. 18), Chico, California: Scholars Press, 1980

Herman, Menahem, *Tithe as Gift: The Institution in the Pentateuch and in Light of Mauss's Prestation Theory* (Distinguished Dissertation Series, 20), San Francisco: Mellen Research University Press, 1992

Jaffee, Martin S., *Mishnah's Theology of Tithing: A Study of Tractate Maaserot* (Brown Judaic Studies, no. 19), Chico, California: Scholars Press, 1981

Scripture designates the tithe as the portion of the produce and animals produced in the land of Israel that is due to God (see, for example, Leviticus 27:30–33; Numbers 18:21–32; Deuteronomy 12, 14:22–29, 26:12–15). Scholarship on the topic addresses either the tithe in the Scripture itself—investigating the passages in their original context—or rab-

binic interpretations of the various tithes, particularly as explicated in the Mishnah.

A biblical study, HERMAN's work interprets the tithe in light of anthropologist Marcel Mauss's theory of prestation. Herman's thesis is that the biblical tithe is best understood not as a tax, but as a form of socially governed gift-exchange ("prestation") in which tangible goods (the tithe) are exchanged for intangible ones (God's protection, blessing, covenant, etc.). After surveying modern critical interpretations of the tithe in Scripture, Herman analyzes the pentateuchal references to the tithe, explains Mauss's gift-exchange theory, and concludes that the tithe was a gift-exchange centered around the covenant between God and the people of Israel.

AVERY-PECK's work is a good place to begin reading on tithing in the Mishnah. This study provides a detailed analysis of the growth and meaning of the mishnaic law of agriculture, and the author offers both a synchronic analysis of the thrust and meaning of the final form of the Order of Agriculture (one of the Mishnah's six fundamental divisions) and a diachronic reconstruction of the various stages of development of the theoretical premises of the law of agriculture. After supplying an overview of the meaning of the final form of this section of the Mishnah, Avery-Peck turns to the component tractates (Peah, Demai, Kilaim, Shebiit, Terumot, Maaserot, Maaser Sheni, Hallah, Orlah, and Bikkurim). Each tractate is introduced, and its thematic units are presented. Building on his evaluations of the individual tractates, the author distinguishes a history of the Mishnah's Order of Agriculture during three time periods: before 70 C.E., the Yavnean period (70 to 140 C.E.), and the Ushan period (140 to 170 C.E.).

Avery-Peck's treatment of the various tractates relies on expositions of the tractates previously published in the Brown Judaic Studies series, particularly those by Brooks, Haas, and Jaffee considered here. These authors, while commenting on different tractates, share a similar approach. They are self-consciously historicist, seeking to illuminate in the manner of their teacher, Jacob Neusner, the social and political circumstances that prompted the theological reflection captured in the Mishnah. Each commentary's centerpiece is an intentionally literal translation of the tractate. This centrality of translation reflects the authors' belief that syntax, formalized literary patterns, and intentional ambiguities are the key to the meaning and interpretation of the tractates.

The commentary on Tractate Peah (the corner-offering for the poor) was written by BROOKS. The premise of this tractate is that the poor are owed a portion of the fruit of the land. This tractate takes up the scriptural references to poor-offerings with respect to the produce in the corner of the field (Leviticus 19:9, 23:22), gleanings (Leviticus 19:9, 23:22), forgotten sheaves (Deuteronomy 24:19), separated grapes (Leviticus 19:10), defective clusters (Leviticus 19:10; Deuteronomy 24:21), and the poor man's tithe (Deuteronomy 26:12). The Mishnah's framers seek to determine the practical implications of the poor's exclusive right to a portion of the crops grown in Israel, guaranteed by the doctrine that God controls the entire land of Israel and is therefore owed tithes, which are to be distributed to those under God's special care—the poor and the priests.

Tractate Ma'aserot (Tithes), commented on by JAFFEE, focuses on two issues: the first, and less important, is the identification of the class of produce that is subject to the tithe; the second, and more pressing, is the question of when a crop is suitable to be tithed and when the tithe must be paid. In Ma'aserot, as in Peah, the framers' answers to these questions are based on the belief that agricultural produce of the land of Israel requires a sacred tax owed to God (Leviticus 27:30). Jaffee argues that the theology of Ma'aserot's thinkers aims to link God to the Israelite farmers by means of the agricultural cycle.

HAAS's commentary on Tractate Ma'aser Sheni (Second Tithe) addresses the agricultural offering that Israelite farmers separate from their harvest and eat in Jerusalem (Deuteronomy 14:22–27). The purpose of the tractate is to establish special restrictions to govern the treatment of this consecrated produce prior to the time it is consumed in Jerusalem. The tractate focuses on two issues: first, it dictates the circumstances under which the tithe can be eaten, and second, it provides a mechanism for the farmer to sell the consecrated produce in order to ease the burden of transportation of the tithe to Jerusalem, and then to use the value of the tithe for the prescribed purpose.

The works of Brooks, Jaffee, and Haas together bring into focus the mishnaic authors' theological and practical understanding of biblical tithes after 70 C.E. The framers of the division of agriculture believed that in spite of the loss of the Jerusalem temple, the people of the land of Israel still owed the biblical tithes to God. The formulation of the laws in the Order of Agriculture establishes the means by which the tithes could be properly paid in the absence of the temple. By focusing on authorial intent and the meaning of a tractate in its original context, these scholars speak to historical questions at the heart of nascent rabbinic Judaism.

SHEILA DUGGER GRIFFITH

Toleration

Erspamer, Peter R., *The Elusiveness of Tolerance: The "Jewish Question" from Lessing to the Napoleonic Wars* (University of North Carolina Studies in the Germanic Languages and Literatures, vol. 117), Chapel Hill: University of North Carolina Press, 1997

Katz, Jacob, *Out of the Ghetto: The Social Background of Jewish Emancipation, 1770–1870,* Cambridge, Massachusetts: Harvard University Press, 1973

Low, Alfred D., *Jews in the Eyes of the Germans: From the Enlightenment to Imperial Germany,* Philadelphia: Institute for the Study of Human Issues, 1979

Sorkin, David, *The Transformation of German Jewry, 1780–1840,* New York: Oxford University Press, 1987; Oxford: Oxford University Press, 1990

Formally, *toleration* means allowance of religions not officially sanctioned by the government or ruler of a nation. Such toleration may take the form of a full equality or it may merely be a grudging forbearance. Historiographically, the word *toleration* has been used to refer to the movement in 18th-century Europe spurred by the Tolerance Debate, which argued the issue of Jewish emancipation.

LOW lauds the accomplishments of the Tolerance Debate in increasing the level of toleration in 18th-century Germany and Austria. Despite the relatively recent publication date of this monograph, Low actually began work on the book during the Third Reich, and his aim was to point out that not all important figures in German history were antisemitic. This was a somewhat daring stance at that time for a native Austrian such as Low.

Low points to Emperor Joseph II of Austria and the Edict of Toleration that the emperor passed in 1782, improving the lot of his Jewish subjects. The provisions of these edicts included abolition of the yellow badges that Jews had been forced to wear outside of the ghettos and the annulment of the dehumanizing body toll placed on Jews and their cattle. Other important provisions included granting Austrian Jews the right to send their children to elementary and secondary schools. Attendance at universities, which had never been forbidden, was now expressly allowed. Jews were allowed to frequent public places of amusement. Most dramatically, they were allowed to learn any trade and to engage in wholesale business under the same conditions as Christian subjects, and they were permitted to establish factories.

Frederick the Great of Prussia pursued a more conservative Jewish policy than Joseph II but indirectly advanced the progress of the Jews when he felt it was in his own economic interest to do so. Wealthy Jews enjoyed his support in helping to build up the Prussian economy, but poorer Jews lived in a state of abject misery. Frederick's Jewish regulations, such as the exorbitant taxation of Jews, smacked of a dislike of the Jewish religion and its adherents. However, Jews who established factories were better able to obtain letters of protection that permitted their residence in Prussia. The Enlightenment had both a positive and a negative effect on Frederick's policy toward Jews. On the one hand, he was influenced by the Judeophobia of Voltaire, a favorite in his court. On the other hand, many of his ministers were influenced by Enlightenment precepts calling for religious tolerance and a separation of church and state. Low points out that Frederick the Great had received the Jewish philosopher Moses Mendelssohn and paid his respects to him, but he fails to mention that Frederick refused to ratify Mendelssohn's nomination to teach at the Royal Academy and therefore killed the appointment.

KATZ discusses the limitations of tolerance, especially for Jewish intellectuals. Jews lived in what Katz calls "a semi-neutral society." Because of the Enlightenment, they were allowed to speculate on abstract questions but were not allowed to voice their opinion on practical political matters.

SORKIN casts toleration in dialectical terms. He views the growth of Jewish rights as part of a quid pro quo whereby Jews were to refashion themselves and give up many of their cultural attributes in exchange for more rights. To the extent that Jewish culture remained a separate entity from German culture, Jews' social integration remained incomplete and Jewish emancipation was only partially successful.

ERSPAMER probes this dialectic posited by Sorkin even further and examines the extent to which gentile proponents of emancipation had their arguments on behalf of Jews undermined by their own incomplete acceptance of Jewish culture. The famous German writer Gotthold Ephraim Lessing was one of the initiators of the Tolerance Debate, but in his pro-emancipatory drama of 1779, *Nathan the Wise*, Nathan is portrayed as both a Jew and a spokesman for the Christian Enlightenment. This imposes contradictions upon him; his effectiveness as a spokesman for the Christian Enlightenment depends on his ability to distance himself from his own Jewish in-group.

This irony appears in the way that Nathan raises his stepdaughter Recha. He brings her up to be part of the multicultural utopia posited by Enlightenment ideals. Nathan is aware that someday Recha will leave him for a broader family setting: the Jew's daughter must herself cease to be a Jew and join a larger circle of humanity. Nathan finds himself in a situation like that of Moses in the Bible: he leads his people (not only Recha, but also the characters Curd, Saladin, and Sittah) to the border of the promised land, but he cannot enter it himself. Utopia is at the same time universal and strangely exclusive. He cannot cease to be a Jew, so he must be excluded from this broader circle of humanity. He is further isolated when his daughter surrenders her Jewishness to enter the broader utopian family. The writings of 18th-century proponents of multiculturalism such as Lessing are beset by cultural fissures. This comes about, for the most part, because multiculturalists seek to enter into dialogue with "Otherness." In order to do so, however, they must first enter into an internal dialogue with themselves, and conceptual fissures inevitably arise because elements of this internal dialogue are often unresolved.

PETER R. ERSPAMER

Tribes, Ten Lost

Adler, Elkan Nathan (editor), *Jewish Travellers* (Broadway Travellers), London: Routledge, 1930; New York: Bloch, 1931; 2nd edition, as *Jewish Travellers: A Treasury of Travelogues from 19 Centuries*, New York: Hermon, 1966

Godbey, Allen H., *The Lost Tribes a Myth: Suggestions towards Rewriting Hebrew History* (Duke University Publications), Durham, North Carolina: Duke University Press, 1930

Lyman, Stanford M., "The Lost Tribes of Israel as a Problem in History and Sociology," *International Journal of Politics, Culture, and Society*, 12(1), Fall 1998

Parfitt, Tudor, *Journey to the Vanished City: The Search for a Lost Tribe of Israel*, London: Hodder and Stoughton, 1992; New York: St. Martin's Press, 1993

Primack, Karen, *Jews in Places You Never Thought Of*, Hoboken, New Jersey: Ktav, 1998

Weil, Shalva et al. (editors), *Beyond the Sambatyon: The Myth of the Ten Lost Tribes*, Tel Aviv: Beth Hatefutsoth, The Nahum Goldman Museum of the Jewish Diaspora, 1991

The fall of the northern kingdom of Israel in 722 B.C.E., as related in 2 Kings 17:5–6, presents the world with one of the great puzzles of Jewish history: What became of the Ten Tribes, traditional descendants of the sons of Jacob, that constituted Israel and were deported with its fall? The southern kingdom of Judah consisted of the two tribes of Judah and Benjamin, and most modern Jews regard themselves as their descendants or identify with the landless religious functionaries of the tribe of Levi. The fates of Reuben, Simeon, Issachar, Zebulun, Menasseh, Ephraim, Dan, Naphtali, Gad, and Asher remain an enigma, however. Certain biblical prophets—above all, Isaiah, Jeremiah, and Ezekiel—express hope that the lost tribes will be restored, while the Apocrypha (Tobit) and Pseudepigrapha (IV Ezra) and Josephus Flavius (*Antiquities*) speculate about where the tribes may have gone. Various passages of rabbinic literature also discuss this topic. The most popular of these texts are Genesis Rabbah 73:6 and Sanhedrin 10:6 in the Palestinian Talmud, in which the mythical river Sambatyon is mentioned as the insuperable border dividing the lost tribes from their fellow Israelites.

The myth continued to be cherished in post-talmudic times and was popular with Jews and Christians alike in Europe throughout the Middle Ages and early modernity. The search for the Ten Lost Tribes received a fresh impetus with the rise of scientific Bible research and ethnography, as well as the political and technical developments of the 19th and 20th centuries that made important biblical sites more accessible to scholars. Certain Zionist groups continue to pursue the answer to this puzzle, for they believe that their mission, the ingathering of the exiles of Israel, and their notion *Klal Israel* (the whole community of Israel) mandates outreach to groups in Asia, Africa, and elsewhere whose identity as descendants of the lost tribes is, to say the least, in question. During the last 2,500 years, the Ten Lost Tribes have been identified with numerous communities worldwide. Some of these communities observe customs that from a contemporary perspective appear vaguely "Jewish," at least in part; others do not. Only a few of the peoples who claim descent from the tribes, such as the Indian Bene Israel and the Ethiopian Beta Israel, have made their way into the Jewish mainstream.

The founding father of the Ten Lost Tribes myth in post-talmudic times is the mysterious Eldad ha-Dani, a traveler who appeared in Cairo, Kairouan (Tunisia), and Spain around 880. ADLER, an intrepid manuscript hunter who acquired several important medieval and early modern Jewish travelogues, compiled a valuable anthology of this literature that includes the most serviceable English translation of Eldad's colorful accounts. Eldad claimed to be a member of the lost tribe of Dan, and he stated that Dan lived together with Naphtali, Gad, and Asher in the mythical land of Havila, "where gold is" (Genesis 2:11), which he locates in Ethiopia. Eldad draws a map of the territories of all the Lost Tribes, locating them mostly in Persia, Babylonia, and Arabia, and Adler points out that Eldad's story is still recited regularly in Persian synagogues. Eldad also vividly describes the Sambatyon river, where dangerous torrential waters run six days a week and an impenetrable fire appears on its banks on the sabbath. His stories were accepted by the Jewish authorities of the places he visited, and they reached central Europe during the Middle Ages. Adler himself argues that unqualified skepticism on the part of modern readers toward these tales is "unjustifiable." Adler also translates travelogues by David Reuveni (c.1500–1535)—who claimed that his brother was Joseph, king of the tribes of Reuben, Gad, and one-half of the tribe of Menasseh—and Benjamin of Tudela—the great 12th-century traveler whose narrative features significant discussion of the question of the tribes. Also included in the anthology is Obadiah de Bertinoro's 15th-century travel diary, which recounts the story of a war between the Ten Tribes and Prester John in Ethiopia.

GODBEY's classic is still by far the most comprehensive and detailed work on "Ten Tribism," as Morris Epstein nicknames the phenomenon in his ironically toned prolegomenon to the reissue of this text. Godbey himself combines ironic distance with an ardent fervor for disclosing the historical reality behind the myths. He argues that there is such a reality, but he goes to great pains to distinguish his own positivistic approach from the naive assumptions of the "lost tribes hunters," who are the objects of many sarcastic attacks in his book. He criticizes travelers who are too hasty to conclude from superficial knowledge of local traditions that certain communities are of Jewish descent, even when the communities themselves protest against this identification—for example, the Muslim Pathans of Afghanistan call themselves Beni-Israel, but they do not consider themselves to be related to the Jews of the region.

Godbey also campaigns against the trends that dominated physical anthropology during his lifetime. Physiognomists of both Jewish and non-Jewish origin studied the facial and physical features of prospective descendants of the Ten Tribes in order to identify "pure Jewish types." In his view, the "lost tribes hunters" were quite incorrect in presuming that they had discovered irrefutable proof of lines of descent from Jacob's lost sons to today's Jews or would-be Jews. To the contrary, he argues, the communities that are allegedly descendants of the Lost Tribes gained this reputation either because of wildly inadequate circumstantial evidence (as in the Pathan case) or because of false genealogical accounts that mask acts of conversion.

Through "careful examination" of the Hebrew Bible and the histories of the communities that are potential descendants of the tribes, Godbey concludes that the "loss" of the Ten Tribes is itself a myth and that the consequences of the deportation of the northern tribes in 722 B.C.E. are overestimated: only a few thousand people were deported from Israel, and there is no reason to assume that they were the biological ancestors of the many communities that have been presumed to be the Lost Tribes. Furthermore, Godbey asserts that there is no evidence that shows historical, ethnological, or religious differences between the southern tribes of Judah and Benjamin and the ten northern tribes. He emphasizes that, in addition to the story of the Ten Tribes, there have been many other instances in which Jewish communities have scattered, thereby producing new dispersed groupings with claims to an Israelite genealogy. Furthermore, Godbey contends that historians have underestimated the importance of Jewish missionary activities. During the last 2,500 years, many groups of people in many places and at many different times have become converts to Judaism, and the beliefs of these isolated communities of descendants of proselytes accordingly reflect different stages of development in the Jewish religion. Thus, the fact that a Jewish group's traditions differ from the rabbinic mainstream by no means necessarily suggests a genealogical connection to the lost tribes. Among the most obvious examples are certain groups of Yemenite Jews, especially from Hadramaut, and the ancient Berber-speaking Jewish communities of the Moroccan Atlas. While Godbey's study exudes a scientific character, he clearly has his biases. He firmly believes in the historical value of biblical accounts and presumes that Christianity develops Judaism to its "most spiritual and ethical heights."

LYMAN analyzes the motivations behind the creation and repeated reinvention of the Ten Lost Tribes myth. Unlike Godbey, he is relatively unconcerned with the "real" histories of the alleged descendants of the Ten Tribes. Instead, he employs a postmodernist epistemology to investigate the meaning of the myth to its believers. He describes his project as a sort of quest to root "the theodicy of Jewish identity" (or survival) in historical context, and he argues that the Lost Tribe descendants are meant to be living proof that obscure or contradictory biblical representations are in fact historically true. He demonstrates that the shape of the myth has changed several times during the course of history. While rabbinic and medieval sources focus on different versions of the Sambatyon story and locate the tribes in remote parts of the Near East and Central Asia, modern mythologists (from Columbus onwards) tend to equate the descendants with existing "exotic and heterodoxical peoples" who are "invested with . . . a complex, sometimes contradictory construction of Jewishness, Jewish history, or Jewish memory." The second part of Lyman's article is dedicated to the Samaritans, "an anomalous peoplehood" claiming descent from Ephraim and Menasseh and continuing to survive as an indigenous and ambiguous Israeli-Palestinian minority. The Samaritans have never left the land of Israel, and their religious practices resemble rabbinic Judaism more closely than do the practices of other groups that have been granted the status of Lost Hebrews. Unlike other heterodox groups, however, the Samaritans have not sought rabbinical acknowledgment, because such a sanction would compromise the Samaritans' claim to the holy Mount Gerizim near Nablus, an ancient Israelite sanctuary and rival to Jerusalem, as well as their claims for the authenticity of their priesthood. The depiction of the Samaritan place in antiquity and brief reviews of sociological theories (such as Max Weber's) that help explain this community's distinctive development are very strong points in Lyman's sober and elegant study.

PRIMACK is a vivid illustration of the well-meaning modern Jewish search for "exotic" communities that may be estranged descendants of the Ten Tribes. The book, which has neither a scientific method nor scientific aims, was published on behalf of two interrelated philanthropic societies, the U.S.-based Kulanu ("All of us") and the Israeli Amishav ("My people returns"). Both organizations have strong Zionist aspirations: they trace "crypto-Jews" worldwide, working to move these groups to Israel and pressuring the Israeli chief rabbinate to acknowledge these potential immigrants as Jewish. Primack describes the efforts to reach the "descendants" of the Lost Tribes, teach them Judaism, bestow upon them religious objects such as Torah scrolls and prayer shawls, and, finally, prepare them for immigration to Israel.

According to Primack, the most impressive success story of Kulanu/Amishav to date concerns the Shinlung of northeast India, a tribal society of approximately 2 million people, 5,000 to 10,000 of whom are said to be actively practicing Judaism. Since the 1950s, this minority has claimed that they are descendants of the tribe of Menasseh and that their ancestors migrated south from China sometime after the 14th century, eventually reaching the Indian states of Mizoram and Manipur, where they were Christianized during the 19th century. Primack's book presents the Shinlung's claim to Israelite descent and describes the 1996 immigration of approximately 200 Shinlung individuals to Israel, where these immigrants had to undergo conversion and were sent to live in a kibbutz in the Gaza strip. Primack also provides accounts of other groups in regions where one would have "never thought of" finding Jewish communities: for example, Incas in Trujillo, Peru, who decided in 1966 to become Jewish; the Abayudaya of Uganda, who started in 1919 to observe Jewish law and customs; a Telugu-speaking community in Andhra Pradesh, India, who claim to be of the tribe of Ephraim; and the Lemba, a tribal society of more than 100,000 persons living in Zimbabwe, Malawi, Mozambique, and South Africa. These groups are not able or willing to prove their descent from the Ten Tribes in a way acceptable by rabbinic authorities, but, as Primack makes clear, the organizations are nevertheless eager to embrace them on the basis of a very broad interpretation of the notion of the Jewish community. Intended as a guide for individuals who wish to support the organizations' activities, the book shows how an ancient myth can appear in modern garb and serve contemporary political goals.

In 1991, Tel Aviv's Diaspora Museum mounted an exhibition on the Lost Tribes myth entitled "Beyond the Sambatyon." In line with the museum's strongly pedagogic slant, pictures and texts were presented, but no actual ethnographical artifacts were included. The catalog (WEIL et al.) is one of very few comprehensive surveys on the Ten Lost Tribes. In a brief and concise manner, all relevant topics and figures connected with the myth are surveyed, and the catalog reproduces most of the pictures from the exhibition. The catalog's contents can be roughly divided into three categories: first, prints, drawings, and manuscripts that refer to the myth in premodern and early modern times. These include frontispieces of old travelogues, such as those anthologized by Adler; the medieval Prester John story about a mythical Christian conqueror who was said to rule over remote Asian or African lands adjacent to the Sambatyon river where the Ten Tribes dwelt; a reference to Shabbetai Tsevi, who based his claim to be the messiah on (among other things) his alleged reign over the Ten Tribes; a portrait of Manasseh ben Israel, the 17th-century Amsterdam rabbi who recounted the stories of a contemporary traveler, Antonio de Montezinos, who claimed to have met South American Indians who were descendants of Reuben and Levi; and references to the theories of the "British Israelites," who assert that the English are of ancient Israelite origin. Second, the catalog includes photographs of Jewish communities whose ancient Israelite origins are mostly acknowledged by contemporary authorities, such as Yemenite, Indian, Bukharan, Uzbek, Georgian, and Ethiopian groups, as well as the now-extinct Chinese Jews and the Samaritans. Third, the catalog presents extraordinary materials related to groups whose affiliations to Judaism are either in doubt or definitely stem from recent acts of conversion, including some of the communities described by Primack.

PARFITT is a prolific author on the issue of Jewish fringe groups. In the late 1980s he visited the Lemba of southern Africa, also mentioned in Primack's book as one of a handful of "exotic" societies hoping for rabbinical acknowledgement. The Lemba represent a fine case study of a historically non-Jewish community struggling to attain a clear-cut Jewish identity. Parfitt met on his journey leaders and "normal" folk, all of whom expressed a conscious desire to be Jews. The Lemba base their claims on historical projections and on observable parallels between their religious practices and those of Judaism. They describe a past in which they were more physically similar to Jews (the Lemba claim that they were once white with "Semitic" features), and they contend that formerly they possessed a sacred literature, which has been lost. Their oral tradition depicts a golden age in the "vanished city" of Sena, a place of undetermined location, and relates a myth of the tribe's migration from northeast Africa or possibly from Yemen. (Parfitt traveled unsuccessfully to the Hadramaut region of Yemen to search for Sena.) Their myths also recount the Lemba's part in the foundation of Greater Zimbabwe, and they assert that the tribe shares a common ancestry with the Beta Israel of Ethiopia. Like them, the Lemba claim descent from the mythical union between King Solomon and the Queen of Sheba, but the Lemba do not seem to identify with any particular lost tribe.

Parfitt also identifies some remarkably detailed similarities between the Lemba cult and customs of the Ethiopian Beta Israel, and he argues that scholars have not yet explained these parallels satisfactorily. The Lemba distinguish certain animals as unclean; they slaughter animals in a way very similar to Jewish custom; they observe rituals of avoidance regarding menstruating women that resemble the purity laws of the Torah; they have ideas (albeit vague) about the holiness of the first day of the new moon; and they practice male circumcision. The Lemba circumcise older boys, not infants, and these acts resemble the initiation rites of other African societies, but the Lemba individuals whom Parfitt interviewed insisted that their ritual was connected to Jewish practice. The lack of a written tradition makes it extremely difficult to trace the historical background of Lemba claims, but Parfitt found many hints that Jewish cultural patterns had only recently been incorporated into Lemba oral tradition. For example, he argues that the Star of David probably first became the symbol of the Lemba Cultural Association of South Africa only after Lemba domestics working for a Jewish family became familiar with the star displayed in the house of their employer. Thus, Parfitt emerges skeptical about the Jewish roots of the Lemba, and he ponders the possibility of Muslim influence upon their tradition. The reader may wish that Parfitt had explained more adequately how Jewishness came to be so strongly inscribed in contemporary Lemba tradition and what Kulanu/Amishav activities may have to do with this development. Additionally, this book does not establish whether the Lemba, or some of them, aspire to emigrate to Israel, as Primack's account suggests. Still, Parfitt's exciting travelogue offers intriguing insights into the creation of a Jewish identity.

MONIKA HUMER

Tsedakah *see* Charity

Tunisia

Awret, Irene, *Days of Honey: The Tunisian Boyhood of Rafael Uzan,* New York: Schocken, 1984

Ben-Sasson, Menahem, "The Jewish Community of Gabès in the 11th Century: Economic and Residential Patterns," in *Communautés juives des marges sahariennes du Maghreb,* edited by Michel Abitbol, Jerusalem: Ben-Zvi Institute, 1982

Deshen, Shlomo, "Southern Tunisian Jewry in the Early 20th Century," in *Jews among Muslims: Communities in the Precolonial Middle East,* edited by Shlomo Deshen and Walter P. Zenner, New York: New York University Press, and Houndmills, Basingstoke, Hampshire: Macmillan, 1996

Laskier, Michael M., "From Hafsia to Bizerte: Tunisia's Nationalist Struggle and Tunisian Jewry, 1952–61," *Mediterranean Historical Review,* 2, 1987

Memmi, Albert, *The Pillar of Salt,* New York: Criterion, 1955; London: Elek, 1956

Rozen, Minna, "The Leghorn Merchants in Tunis and Their Trade with Marseilles at the End of the 17th Century," in *Les relations intercommunautaires juives en Méditerranée occidentale, XIIIe-XXe siècles,* edited by J.L. Miège, Paris: Editions du Centre National de la Recherche Scientifique, 1984

Serels, M. Mitchell, "The Non-European Holocaust: The Fate of Tunisian Jewry," in *Sephardim and the Holocaust,* edited by Solomon Gaon and M. Mitchell Serels, New York: Yeshiva University, 1987

Udovitch, Abraham L. and Lucette Valensi, *The Last Arab Jews: The Communities of Jerba, Tunisia,* New York: Harwood Academic, 1984

The Jews of Tunisia were a heterogeneous group, composed of urban and rural Jews, with the former subdivided between indigenous and Livornese. Most of the community was Westernized under the French Protectorate and has emigrated since the 1950s, mainly to Israel and France, but a relatively high proportion of the Jews on the island of Djerba stayed and kept their traditional way of life. Most of the research on Tunisian Jewry is in Hebrew or French.

A personal view of a small Jewish community is provided by AWRET in her biography of a Tunisian Jew, Rafael Uzan. Born in the Tunisian coastal town of Nabeul, Uzan tells of his boyhood, family and communal relations, education, work as a shoemaker, and relations with the Muslims. Details about festivals, pilgrimages, beliefs, and customs are described as is

the condition of the Jews during World War II and German occupation.

Based primarily on Genizah documents and responsa literature, BEN-SASSON examines the economic life and residential patterns of the Jews of Gabès, in southern Tunisia, in the 11th century, when the region was under the rule of the Ziridis who represented the Fatimids. The involvement of Jews from Gabès in international and local trade is explored as are their agricultural and manufacturing activities.

DESHEN examines the socioeconomic structure and the institutions of the Jewish society of southern Tunisia in the early 20th century, based primarily on rabbinic sources. As a result of its relatively peaceful history and the economic behavior of the Muslim Berber population among whom they lived, the Jews in this region, and especially on the island of Djerba, developed complementary economic patterns that influenced their social, cultural, and institutional life. Because the Berbers operated a network of migrant merchants throughout Tunisia, the Jews entered into local commerce and filled local positions and did not engage during this period in international or itinerant trade. As a result, Djerban Jewry became sedentary, and the local community grew to exercise a high degree of power over its individual members, especially in religious matters.

The impact of the Tunisian national struggle for independence on the Jewish community of Tunisia is examined by LASKIER. Following a survey of the political background, Laskier describes the Jewish communities in the years 1952 to 1956, including an examination of the reasons for and results of the attacks on the Jews of Hafsia in June 1952. The policy of the State of Israel and the Jewish Agency toward Tunisian Jewry during the same period is examined as is Jewish emigration from Tunisia. Developments during the first years of independence are described next, including Zionist activities and government policy. Laskier concludes with a comparison between the Jewish communities of Tunisia, Morocco, and Algeria prior to and following independence.

MEMMI's autobiographical novel describes growing up in the Jewish community of Tunis and covers the period until the late 1940s. His vivid description includes images of the Jewish neighborhood, customs, the Sabbath, feasts, education, family life, adolescence, and World War II and its aftermath. Memmi provides a very personal view of Jewish life in Tunis in the first half of the 20th century.

ROZEN examines the commercial activities of Livornese Jewish merchants in Tunis at the end of the 17th century. Jews and conversos persecuted by the Inquisition settled in large numbers in Leghorn following the privilege granted in 1593 by the grand duke of Tuscany, who guaranteed freedom and security to merchants of all nations and religions who wished to settle and trade there. This community was very mobile and established branches in other important commercial centers, including Tunis. As Tuscan citizens, these merchants benefited from special extraterritorial protection granted by the capitulations treaties. During the 17th and 18th centuries, the Livornese Jews in Tunis were prominent in international trade. Rozen examines their various economic activities, including their involvement in piracy, their relations with the French merchants in Tunis, and the activities of several specific Jewish firms there. She shows how a "triangle of commerce" was formed in the Mediterranean, linking Leghorn, Tunis, and Marseilles, within which the Jewish merchants from Tunis and Leghorn cooperated with the French merchants in Tunis and Marseilles in order to benefit from the same privileges the French enjoyed under Franco-Ottoman agreements.

SERELS shows how the Jews of Tunisia were affected by anti-Jewish legislation and German occupation during World War II. As a French protectorate since 1881, Tunisia came under the Vichy regime with the fall of France in 1940, and anti-Jewish legislation was introduced. Serels details the implications of this legislation for the individual and the community. Following the Allied invasion of North Africa, German and Italian forces regrouped in Tunisia in late 1942, and anti-Jewish operations intensified, sending Jews to concentration and labor camps. Serels details the anti-Jewish legislation and operations across Tunisia until the withdrawal of the Axis forces in May 1943. The regulations, however, were removed by the Allies only in August 1943.

Based on field study conducted in 1978 and 1979, UDOVITCH and VALENSI describes the life of the approximately 1,200 Jews of the two communities of the island of Djerba, who are effectively the last Jewish communities in the Arab world who have preserved their traditional spiritual, social, and economic life. Against the background of their myths of origin, Udovitch and Valensi examine the history of the communities, stressing their persistence in strict observance of religious rulings, often more rigorously construed than elsewhere. Symbols of identity are examined as is the issue of a sacred space, defining special places for Jews and for women. Communal life is described in detail, emphasizing the roles of individuals and committees who provide a largely lay leadership. Other major issues to be examined are family life, including the role of women, and the daily and annual cycles as related to the community as a whole and to men and women separately. The education of men, from its rigorous beginnings for small boys to adult learning and publishing activity, is examined as are the beginnings of girls' formal school education. Udovitch and Valensi also describe the changing roles of Jews in economic life and the implications for Jewish-Muslim relations. The role of the synagogue is examined, especially that of the Ghriba synagogue and the meaning for Djerban Jews of its status as a pilgrimage destination for those who have left the island. Richly illustrated, the book provides an absorbing examination of internal efforts to preserve traditional Jewish life in a changing society.

RACHEL SIMON

U

United States: Community Histories

Cutler, Irving, *The Jews of Chicago: From Shtetl to Suburb,* Urbana: University of Illinois Press, 1996

Dalin, David G. and Jonathan Rosenbaum, *Making a Life, Building a Community: A History of the Jews of Hartford,* New York: Holmes and Meier, 1997

Ehrlich, Walter, *Zion in the Valley: The Jewish Community of St. Louis,* vol. 1: *1807–1907,* Columbia: University of Missouri Press, 1997

Friedman, Murray (editor), *Jewish Life in Philadelphia, 1830–1940,* Philadelphia: Institute for the Study of Human Issues, 1983

Rottenberg, Dan (editor), *Middletown Jews: The Tenuous Survival of an American Jewish Community,* Bloomington: Indiana University Press, 1997

Sandberg, Neil C., *Jewish Life in Los Angeles: A Window to Tomorrow,* Lanham, Maryland: University Press of America, 1986

Sarna, Jonathan D. and Ellen Smith (editors), *The Jews of Boston,* Boston: Combined Jewish Philanthropies of Greater Boston, 1995

Community histories have long been a staple of American Jewish historiography. These histories are diverse, ranging from celebratory anniversary volumes that smooth out the rough edges of the story to scholarly studies that illuminate broad sociological trends as well as the history of the particular local community. In between are a variety of coffee-table books, anthologies, and oral histories. Jewish community history has flourished since the mid-20th century, a development that owes a great deal to the influence of Jacob Rader Marcus, historian, founder, and director of the American Jewish Archives from 1947 to 1995. Marcus not only raised the standard for U.S. Jewish history scholarship, he also encouraged amateur historians to write the stories of their synagogues and communities. In 1953 he published a primer on writing local Jewish history that surveyed the major documentary sources and provided a sample outline. "Do not be disturbed," he wrote, "if you have had no experience in the past writing history. With a little preparation you, too, can write something that is worthwhile and helpful." In the years that followed, Marcus advised many authors and wrote prefaces for some of their works. The American Jewish Historical Society has also supported research and publication of these works, and the Jewish Publication Society published many fine traditional community histories, although university and academic presses have increasingly taken over this task.

DALIN and ROSENBAUM present a well-researched volume with an ambitious agenda. They aim "not only to analyze the history of Hartford Jews and their community, but also to place those data in the larger context of American Jewish history, including the history of Jews and Judaism in Connecticut and New England; ethnic, religious, and urban history; and the discipline of American history in general." The authors are partly successful in meeting these objectives, as they make comparisons with other regions, outline broad social trends, and place Hartford within its regional context. The book overemphasizes institutional history, however, and its survey of women and groups outside the mainstream is too brief. Dalin and Rosenbaum have meticulously documented their research, but the book could use a good general index to complement the name index. On the whole, this book presents a thorough analysis of the community within the course of U.S. Jewish history.

CUTLER offers a general survey of Chicago Jewish history. Despite its colorful and varied history, Jewish Chicago has never been the subject of a good analytical study; previous efforts are dated or narrow in scope. Cutler's contribution, a coffee-table book sprinkled with photographs, only partly addresses the need. He paints the history of the community with broad strokes, from the first settlement of German Jews through the growth of vibrant neighborhoods on Chicago's West Side and finally to migrations north of the city. The salient events, institutions, and people are covered, making this book a good introduction. But the study is marred by flaws in documentation, and the author relies too heavily on secondary sources. Many rich archival collections remain unexplored, and a scholarly treatment of this important Jewish community is still needed.

EHRLICH also addresses a relatively underrepresented community but with more success than Cutler. This history of the Jewish community of St. Louis is a solid contribution that draws on archival sources, newspapers, and oral histories, as well as general history scholarship. Ehrlich's work covers not only religious, economic, and political life but also the role of the Jewish press. The author offers few comparisons to other communities, and the photographs lack documentation, but the book is generally well done.

FRIEDMAN is a well-regarded collection of essays on Jewish Philadelphia. Jewish women's history, often relegated to the margins of the story, is surveyed in an essay by Evelyn Bodek, who traces the roles that Jewish women played in the philanthropic institutions of the city. Other essays cover such important subjects as immigrant workers and unions, the relationship between German Jews and Eastern European Jews in the Jewish Federation, and notable communal leaders such as Isaac Leeser. A final essay draws a comparison between the Jewish communities in Philadelphia and Boston, and similar patterns in the development of philanthropic organizations and synagogues in the two cities are traced.

SARNA and SMITH have produced an essential resource for Boston Jewish history that could serve as a model for other volumes of this kind. Presented in a large, coffee-table-book format, this collection focuses on movements and institutions that have been central to the history of Jewish Boston, including Zionism, philanthropy, and education. An introductory essay by Sarna puts Boston in the context of U.S. Jewish history; the author observes that Boston was different from many other U.S. cities in the 19th century because it was late in developing synagogues and other Jewish institutions and because the tensions between German and East European immigrants in Boston were resolved so quickly. Not one of the essays focuses exclusively on the history of Jewish women in Boston, but the subject is integral to the book.

ROTTENBERG edits a volume that is not a traditional community history but a collection of oral histories. The early studies of "Middletown" by Robert and Helen Lynd (1929, 1937) had almost ignored the existence of the Jewish community in Muncie, Indiana; this volume was published to correct this flaw and to explore the demographic and sociological trends of the Jewish community. The 19 oral histories demonstrate restlessness in the community and evaluate the pervasive effects of change and mobility. The book concludes that in many ways the Jewish community participated in the trends that affected the larger community.

SANDBERG focuses attention on the growing Jewish community of Los Angeles, where, he posits, some national trends become evident earlier than they do in the rest of the country. His book is less a history than a sociological study and is concerned with demographics, religious identity, and the long-term survival of the community. Sandberg's research represents an important category of community study that complements the strengths of a more traditional historical study.

JOY KINGSOLVER

See also New York; United States: General Histories

United States: General Histories

Diner, Hasia, *A Time for Gathering: The Second Migration, 1820–1880* (The Jewish People in America, vol. 2), Baltimore, Maryland: Johns Hopkins University Press, 1992

Faber, Eli, *A Time for Planting: The First Migration, 1654–1820* (The Jewish People in America, vol. 1), Baltimore, Maryland: Johns Hopkins University Press, 1992

Feingold, Henry L., *A Time for Searching: Entering the Mainstream, 1920–1945* (The Jewish People in America, vol. 4), Baltimore, Maryland: Johns Hopkins University Press, 1992

Hertzberg, Arthur, *The Jews in America: Four Centuries of an Uneasy Encounter: A History,* New York: Simon and Schuster, 1989; Chichester, West Sussex: Columbia University Press, 1997

Karp, Abraham J., *Haven and Home: A History of the Jews in America,* New York: Schocken, 1985; as *A History of the Jews in America,* London: Aronson, 1997

Marcus, Jacob Rader, *United States Jewry, 1776–1985,* 4 vols., Detroit, Michigan: Wayne State University Press, 1989–1993

Sachar, Howard M., *A History of the Jews in America,* New York: Knopf, 1992

Shapiro, Edward S., *A Time for Healing: American Jewry since World War II* (The Jewish People in America, vol. 5), Baltimore, Maryland: Johns Hopkins University Press, 1992

Sorin, Gerald, *A Time for Building: The Third Migration, 1880–1920* (The Jewish People in America, vol. 3), Baltimore, Maryland: Johns Hopkins University Press, 1992

Sorin, Gerald, *Tradition Transformed: The Jewish Experience in America* (The American Moment), Baltimore, Maryland: Johns Hopkins University Press, 1997

General histories of the Jews in the United States have often been flawed, but some contributions from the last 15 years of the 20th century have shown more promise. The best of them reflect new directions in historiography and challenge easy generalizations.

The "Jewish People in America" series, taken together, is an insightful and well-written survey of American Jewish history that integrates Jewish women's experiences into the overall picture. FABER's volume, the first in the series, traces the history of early American Jewry from the first permanent Jewish settlement in North America in 1654 to the early republic. Finding in these early years the seeds of later experiments with acculturation and assimilation, Faber sees Jewish communities in this period as testing grounds for ideas of voluntary affiliation and citizenship. In the second volume, DINER traces the history of the first wave of immigrants, documenting the ways in which Old World Judaism was transformed into a new Jewish identity. Her work highlights the role of such organizations as B'nai B'rith, landsmanschaftn, and other types of aid associations. SORIN (1992) draws a distinction between acculturation and assimilation, arguing that as immigrants adjusted to life in the United States, they became acculturated in ways that kept their distinct identity intact. FEINGOLD's volume begins with the antisemitism of the 1920s and moves through the subsequent decades of prosperity and upward mobility, covering developments in education, Zionism, and political involvement. A final chapter presents a balanced and cautious approach to the difficult question of the American response to the Holocaust. SHAPIRO begins with the postwar period and notes increasing assimilation through recent years. His particular slant on these trends becomes evident in the last chapter, in which he takes a despairing view of the future and criticizes changes to traditional definitions of Jewish identity. Some astonishing statements, such as the claim that only a few converts were genuinely attracted to Judaism, are unsupported by documentation.

HERTZBERG has written perhaps the weakest of the books reviewed in this essay. Although his survey is very readable, appealing to a broad public, it is marred by careless research and questionable interpretation. Treatment of women's history is minimal; the chapter entitled "The Invention of the Jewish Mother" relies on tenuous assertions and perpetuates stereotypes. Since this book is written for a general audience, it has no footnotes, which makes his arguments even more problematic. The concluding chapters, which speak of disillusionment and the loss of faith, view recent assimilation as a grave threat to any American Jewish future.

KARP outlines the ways in which Jews seeking a haven in the New World made that world their home, becoming integrated into American society and helping to shape it. His volume functions very well as an introduction to the major themes in American Jewish history, but its brisk pace limits it. Primary documents, inserted into the narrative, help give the story immediacy, but at times readers would benefit from more explanation or context. Contrary to the gloomy predictions favored by many commentators, Karp maintains an upbeat view of the future:

> American Jews' morale for survival is bolstered by their historic experience in America. They are here despite the prophecies of doom pronounced in every generation. And they can look back to ideologies and strategies for survival which made possible the ongoing enterprise of creative Jewish survival in a free and open society.

MARCUS, who did so much to shape contemporary writing about American Jewish history, produced this monumental four-volume set near the end of his career. Reflecting his focus on colonial and 19th-century Jewish history and his interest in Jewish community histories, these volumes trace developments in the United States in the early period, the period ending in 1840, the "Germanic" period (1840 to 1920), and the East European period (1920 to 1985). Recent history is condensed into a relatively brief overview. Marcus's style is lively and readable, his outlook positive: "There can be no question, for the Jew this is the best country, the freest land in the world. . . . There may be misgivings but he faces the future with trust, with confidence, with dogged faith." But for all its virtues, this set needs to be read alongside some of the other, more recent interpretations of American Jewish history.

SACHAR offers an impressive survey of the range of Jewish endeavor in the United States. His encyclopedic history includes cultural, literary, and political movements. In Sachar's opinion, the success of the Jewish people in the New World had reached new heights by the postwar period. "Taking root in America," he writes, "this was a minority people—transformed within human memory into the largest, wealthiest, the most powerful community in Jewish history—that was engrossed no longer with issues of economic security or political toleration. Rather, its preoccupation henceforth was the encouragement, refinement, and apparently limitless enhancement of group identity and creativity." This vision of the future was dissipated by the identity crises of the last three decades of the 20th century. Disagreement over relations with Israel, embarrassing scandals involving a Jewish underworld, and the loss of faith in a unifying purpose all worked together, in Sachar's view, to produce a profound disillusionment.

SORIN (1997) is a thought-provoking analysis of American Jewish history that deserves careful reading. Sorin builds his history on the central role that immigration played in American Jewish history. Skipping lightly over the early period, his interest lies in how successive waves of immigration shaped American Jewish culture. He elaborates on the argument, presented in the Feingold series, that acculturation did not destroy a distinct Jewish identity or destroy the meaning Jews found in their past. Citing what he calls "rejuvenating events," such as the efforts to bring Jews out of the Soviet Union, he argues that Judaism is constantly being redefined. Sorin is able to set Jewish immigration in the context of the acculturation of other ethnic groups, contrasting Jewish experience with that of Hispanic immigrants of the late 20th century. Overall, the Jewish experience in the United States is "the best example of the success of cultural pluralism."

JOY KINGSOLVER

See also United States: Community Histories

V

Vegetarianism

Berman, Louis, *Vegetarianism and the Jewish Tradition*, New York: Ktav, 1982

Bleich, Rabbi J. David, "Vegetarianism and Judaism," *Tradition*, 23(1), Summer 1987

Cohen, Rabbi Alfred, "Vegetarianism from a Jewish Perspective," *Journal of Halacha and Contemporary Society*, 1(2), Fall 1981

Kalechofsky, Roberta (editor), *Judaism and Animal Rights: Classical and Contemporary Responses*, Marblehead, Massachusetts: Micah, 1992

Kalechofsky, Roberta (editor), *Rabbis and Vegetarianism: An Evolving Tradition*, Marblehead, Massachusetts: Micah, 1995

Kalechofsky, Roberta, *Vegetarian Judaism: A Guide for Everyone*, Marblehead, Massachusetts: Micah, 1998

Kalechofsky, Roberta and Rosa Rasiel, *The Jewish Vegetarian Year Cookbook*, Marblehead, Massachusetts: Micah, 1997

Schwartz, Richard H., *Judaism and Vegetarianism*, Smithtown, New York: Exposition, 1982; 2nd edition, Marblehead, Massachusetts: Micah, 1988

Judaism and vegetarianism? Given the importance of animal sacrifices to biblical religion and of carnivorous foodways to the contemporary Jewish folk ethos, one may wonder whether the two can be related. In fact, there has been much Jewish vegetarian activity recently in the United States, Israel, the United Kingdom, and elsewhere, and there is a broad and growing body of literature exploring connections between Judaism and vegetarianism.

SCHWARTZ has written a comprehensive analysis of all aspects of Jewish vegetarianism. The first chapter presents a "vegetarian view of the Bible" that discusses God's first strictly vegetarian dietary law (Genesis 1:29); God's second vegetarian attempt, represented by the manna; and the view of some Jewish scholars that people will again be vegetarians in the time of the Messiah. The next five chapters consider respectively Jewish teachings on compassion for animals; preserving health; protecting the environment and conserving natural resources; helping hungry people; and pursuing peace. Schwartz also discusses how animal-based diets and agriculture seriously violate these teachings. The book addresses 37 questions that are often asked of vegetarians who take the Jew-

ish tradition seriously. These include such favorites as: Do we not have to eat meat on the Sabbath and Jewish festivals? Were we not given dominion over animals? What about animal sacrifices and the hoped-for restoration of the Temple? Jewish vegetarian groups and activities in the United States, Great Britain (where the Jewish Vegetarian Society has its international headquarters), and Israel are reviewed. Also provided are biographies of famous Jewish vegetarians, an annotated bibliography, recipes and food-related suggestions, and action ideas for those who might want to promote vegetarianism.

KALECHOFSKY (1998) uses similar arguments, stressing contradictions between Judaism and the realities of animal agriculture and diets, to assert that vegetarianism is the ideal diet for Jews today, and she provides an additional consideration, the unity of the Jewish people, "kelal Yisrael." In her view, all of kelal Yisrael could once again share meals in each others' homes and at each others' celebrations if all Jews were vegetarians. The chapter on health extensively discusses recent problems related to the consumption of meat, including "mad cow disease," genetic engineering, and recalls of meat because of outbreaks of e.coli and salmonella poisoning. Kalechofsky provides an insightful historical and sociological context in the chapters "Kashrut and Modernity" and "From Living Soul to Animal Machine."

BERMAN provides a less polemical, more psychological analysis than Schwartz and Kalechofsky. The book is relatively short (the main text is only 72 pages long), but there are valuable chapters titled "Slaughter as a Mode of Worship" and "The Dietary Laws as Atonements for Flesh Eating." These chapters speculate that the sacrifices provided a cover for meat eating in a religion that has such strong teachings on compassion for animals, and that the dietary laws substituted for animal sacrifice after the Temple in Jerusalem was destroyed. While vegetarianism is viewed favorably, the author identifies himself as one who, if invited to dinner, would play the "visiting anthropologist" and eat what was served.

KALECHOFSKY (1995) provides thought-provoking essays on Jewish connections to vegetarianism by and about 17 rabbis. The rabbis included in the anthology form a varied group: Orthodox, Conservative, Reform, and Reconstructionist; male and female; modern and of previous generations; and recent converts to vegetarianism as well as long-time proponents. They differ also in their arguments for vegetarianism, although all are based on Jewish values: preserving health; showing compassion to animals; protecting the environment; and sharing with the hungry. Rabbi Everett Gendler's essay offers an additional cogent argument: people are supposed to exult in creation and to join a chorus of all living creatures singing God's praises; but instead, humans, sharply deviating from this mission, have treated their fellow choir members horribly, killing them and consuming their corpses. Particularly powerful is the essay by the former chief rabbi of Ireland, David Rosen, in which he indicates that eating meat is not acceptable today according to halakhah (Jewish law) because of its negative health effects and also because of the cruelty to animals on factory farms.

KALECHOFSKY (1992) provides a wide variety of insightful essays on Jewish teachings related to animal rights and vegetarianism, and she includes two chapters each from the books by Schwartz and Berman. Also reprinted here is the essay by COHEN, an Orthodox scholar who provides a comprehensive overview of the topic. Since he is not a vegetarian, many of his statements that favor vegetarianism are in a sense the more compelling, including his conclusion that "If a person is more comfortable not eating meat, there would be no obligation for him to do so on the Sabbath," and "we may clearly infer that eating meat, even on a Festival, is not mandated by the *halacha*." He also concedes that "if indeed eating meat is injurious to one's health, it is not only permissible but perhaps even mandatory that we reduce our ingestion of an unhealthy product to the minimum level."

In his scholarly overview of vegetarianism, BLEICH, another non-vegetarian Orthodox rabbi, noted scholar of halakhah, and a professor at Yeshiva University, also concludes that Jews need not be vegetarians: "The implication is that meat may be consumed when there is desire and appetite for it as food, but may be eschewed when there is not desire and, *a fortiori*, when it is found to be repugnant," and "Jewish tradition does not command carnivorous behavior."

KALECHOFSKY and RASIEL provide a thoughtful analysis of the connections between vegetarianism and Jewish holidays, along with 170 recipes and many food-related ideas to enhance the joy of the festivals.

RICHARD H. SCHWARTZ

Veneration of Saints, Pilgrimages, and Holy Places

Adler, Elkan Nathan (editor), *Jewish Travellers* (Broadway Travellers), London: Routledge, 1930; New York: Bloch, 1931; 2nd edition, as *Jewish Travellers: A Treasury of Travelogues from 9 Centuries*, New York: Hermon, 1966

Ben-Ami, Issachar, *Ha'aratsat ha-kedoshim be-kerev Yehude Maroko*, 1984; translated as *Saint Veneration among the Jews in Morocco*, Detroit, Michigan: Wayne State University Press, 1998

Ben-Ari, Eyal, "Saints' Sanctuaries in Israeli Development Towns: On a Mechanism of Urban Transformation," *Urban Anthropology and Studies of Cultural Systems and World Economic Development*, 16, Summer 1987

Ben-Ari, Eyal and Yoram Bilu (editors), *Grasping Land: Space and Place in Contemporary Israeli Discourse and Experience* (SUNY Series in Anthropology and Judaic Studies), Albany: State University of New York Press, 1997

Bilu, Yoram, "Dreams and the Wishes of the Saint," in *Judaism Viewed from Within and from Without: Anthropological Studies* (SUNY Series in Anthropology and Judaic Studies), edited by Harvey Goldberg, Albany: State University of New York Press, 1987

Bilu, Yoram and H. Abramovich, "In Search of the Sadiq: Visitational Dreams among Moroccan Jews in Israel," *Psychiatry*, 48

Giller, Pinchas, "Recovering the Sanctity of the Galilee: The Veneration of Sacred Relics in the Classical Kabbalah," *The Journal of Jewish Thought and Philosophy*, 4, 1994

Weingrod, Alex, *The Saint of Beersheba* (SUNY Series in Israeli Studies), Albany: State University of New York Press, 1990

In the modern period, it has been common to portray Judaism as a rootless faith, divested of symbols and without the romanticism of religious shrines. To an important extent, diaspora Judaism certainly did substitute the veneration of texts for the veneration of relics. The resilient portability of text veneration, from its inception in the first Babylonian exile, was able to sustain diaspora culture. Nonetheless, Judaism has a rich history of veneration of graves and shrines, which has seen a burst of new activity in the late 20th century. From the biblical and rabbinic periods, and particularly in the practice of Jewish mysticism, the sacred shrine has been of great importance.

GILLER sets out the underpinnings of veneration of sacred relics in the central kabbalistic works. Giller also addresses the contemporary spread of grave site veneration in the context of other relic-based traditions in Christianity and Buddhism.

The tradition of pilgrimage and of literary reports of these pilgrimages is deeply rooted in Jewish literature of the Middle Ages. A number of these medieval reports have been translated in ADLER, notably that of Benjamin of Tudela, who visited the Holy Land in 1170 and described its sacred places. His description is augmented by the accounts of Petahiah of Regensburg, who also alluded to Persian Jewish traditions that posit the grave sites of 550 "prophets and sages." Petahiah also identified many grave sites in Persia that are venerated by Jews to this day. These accounts are further augmented by the 13th-century accounts of Samuel ben Samson and Menahem ben Peretz ha-Hebroni. Menahem made a point of relying on local traditions and defending their antiquity. There is also a late-13th-century anonymous student of Nahmanides who writes on grave sites, as well as Ashtori ha-Parhi, Ya'akov ben Natanel ha-Cohen, and Moshe Basula from the early part of the 14th century. The late Renaissance and early modern period is represented by the advent of *moreh derekh* (road guide) literature. The first formal *moreh derekh*, compiled by Uri Ben Shim'on, became the widely distributed *Yihus ha-Avot*. It is the first published work on the grave sites of the saints and was translated into Arabic and Ladino.

The establishment of new sacred sites, specifically in the "development towns" of Israel, are documented in BEN-ARI, in BILU, and in BILU and ABRAMOVICH. Bilu's studies emphasize the activities of the Moroccan community, both in Morocco and Israel, as a particularly rich source of religious traditions. Bilu has documented the phenomenon of the translocation of saints from Morocco and elsewhere, who appear to the faithful in visitational dreams. Bilu views this phenomenon as an expression of local identity among new immigrants from Middle Eastern countries. Because such communities were often marginal and economically dependent in the decades following mass migration to Israel, Bilu suggests that the phenomenon is a reflection of a dispossessed community's need to claim the land and thereby validate their presence. A number of important essays on this phenomenon have been collected in BEN-ARI and BILU.

Easily the most important English-language monograph on this topic is BEN-AMI. There are three reasons for this. First, and quite simply, there are no others; perhaps this form of religious expression is so remote from the English-speaking Jewish experience that no book-length studies of the subject have been written in English, nor have any others appeared in English translation, but further studies are clearly needed. Second, Ben-Ami succeeds so well because he brings to his task both the skills of an accomplished folklorist and the local knowledge, as an Israeli of Moroccan origin, to avoid the shortcoming of his chosen discipline, whereby specific facts are often sacrificed to the claims of putatively universal truths to homogenizing effect. Third and most important, he has an extraordinarily big story to break.

When the Frenchified Lithuanian Jewish intellectual Nahum Slouschz traveled through the pre-Sahara at the beginning of the 20th century, he was appalled by one jarring experience that seemed to conflict horribly with the pristine, patriarchal Judaism he had discovered. This was his encounter with an extended family of Syrian origin who manifested extreme violence, not to say evil, and yet were clearly doing a roaring trade as holy men. There was only one construction Slouschz could think to put upon what he saw: the enterprising Abuhasera clan, learning of the successful methods of the self-promoting Galician *zaddikim*, had seen fit to try their luck among the still more susceptible Jews of the mountains and deserts of North Africa. The data amassed by Ben-Ami, however, more than suffices to demonstrate the contrary: that the rebbe cults of the Hasidim, not to mention the older but less crucial traditions of prostration at the graves of patriarchs in the land of Israel or prophets in Mesopotamia, are all of them light and superficial elements in contrast to the place of holy people and holy places—the latter usually sanctified by association with holy people but sometimes intrinsically holy—in the religious life of Moroccan Jewry. Ben-Ami identifies no less than 652 saints actively venerated by Moroccan Jews in the last quarter of the 20th century or at least within the memory of his informants, Moroccan immigrants in Israel. Half of the book constitutes a remarkable *Who's Who*, in which Ben-Ami digests the testimonies he has collected and collates it with published primary and secondary sources. About some of his subjects there is nothing known except a name, while about others there is a great deal of material, whether factual, as in the case of a mainstream rabbinic authority such as Raphael "the Angel" Berdugo, or literary/

legendary, as in the case of a folk hero such as Lala Solica, who elected to die a martyr's death rather than marry the sultan. The remainder of the study is devoted to analysis, with sections on the nomenclature of Moroccan Jewish sainthood, hereditary sanctity, miracles wrought by saints, saints appearing in dreams, pilgrimages, pilgrim hymnody, confraternities responsible for organizing pilgrimages and maintaining shrines, and the relationship between Jews and Muslims at these holy places. Among the multitude of accompanying appendices, along with a map of holy places and an index of folk-motifs, there are lists of Muslim saints venerated by Jews and Jewish saints venerated by Muslims—a scarcely surprising manifestation of the "maraboutism," with its heavily "pagan" and mystical influences, that is the common heritage of rural Moroccans. Ben-Ami concludes with a study of the enduring place of Jewish marabouts in contemporary Israel, and a prime example of this phenomenon forms the subject for WEINGROD's profile.

PINCHAS GILLER

Venice

Bloch, Joshua, *Venetian Printers of Hebrew Books*, New York: New York Public Library, 1932

Calimani, Riccardo, *Storia del Ghetto di Venezia*, Milan: Rusconi, 1985; translated by Katherine Silberblatt Wolfthal as *The Ghetto of Venice*, New York: Evans, 1987

Pullan, Brian, "Venetian Jewry and the Monti di Pietà," in his *Rich and Poor in Renaissance Venice: The Social Institutions of a Catholic State, to 1620*, Cambridge, Massachusetts: Harvard University Press, and Oxford: Blackwell, 1971

Pullan, Brian, *The Jews of Europe and the Inquisition of Venice, 1550–1670*, Oxford: Blackwell, and Totowa, New Jersey: Barnes and Noble, 1983

Ravid, Benjamin, *Economics and Toleration in Seventeenth Century Venice* (Monograph Series, no. 2), Jerusalem: American Academy for Jewish Research, 1978

Ravid, Benjamin, "The Socioeconomic Background of the Expulsion and Readmission of the Venetian Jews, 1571–1573," in *Essays in Modern Jewish History: A Tribute to Ben Halpern*, edited by Frances Malino and Phyllis Cohen Albert, Rutherford, New Jersey: Fairleigh Dickinson University Press, and London: Associated University Presses, 1982

Roth, Cecil, *Venice*, Philadelphia: Jewish Publication Society, 1930

The Jews of Venice have been subjects of both general narrative histories and more documented texts focusing on particular aspects of Jewish life there, including moneylending, the Inquisition, Jews' position in society, and their treatment by the Venetian government. While the first two texts discussed below are perhaps more suitable for the general reader, those that follow are aimed at scholars seeking specific documented information.

ROTH's history of the Jews of Venice was his attempt to "redeem [the Ghetto scene] from the neglect from which it has hitherto suffered." Continually cited by later authors, although not the most scholarly study now available, Roth's work is narrative in tone, with few notes, several illustrations, a very brief bibliography, and an anecdotal style. Roth begins with the arrival of the Jews in antiquity as slaves and traders and ends with Venice's unification with Italy in 1866, focusing on Venice's intolerance and its critical protection of the Jews. Among other subjects, Roth treats the Jews' governing structures, religious organization, daily rituals, entertainment, and education, and their involvement in the arts, alchemy, and gambling. He finishes with the decline and fall of Venice and its Jews as medieval repressive measures again were reinforced against the Jews in the mid–18th century. Because Roth was writing before World War II, his tone is perhaps less tragic than that of the authors who followed. Roth's work pays homage to Jewish life in Venice; it is almost a biography of the Ghetto, enjoyable to read, and still a must for the scholar of Venetian history or the casual inquirer.

CALIMANI's story of the Venetian Ghetto is comprehensive, well organized, and accessible, dated only by his mention of the "shadow of nuclear weapons" at its close. It is, in a way, an updated version of Roth's history, similarly marked by few historical or documentary notes, a narrative style, and an informed tone. Almost a digest of all prior scholarship, this work presents the characters whose lives invigorated the Ghetto (many of whom also were described by Roth 55 years earlier), the status of printing, and the moneylenders and their charters. He cites the scholars he follows while producing a sympathetic chronological portrait of Ghetto life, which he ends by reiterating the Jews' position as aliens denied Italian citizenship, despite their integration into Venetian society by the end of the 19th century. Calimani's likable style draws any reader into the complicated history of the Jews of Venice.

In contrast to these broader, less scholarly texts, RAVID (1982) uses the archives of Venice to shed new light on the 1571 decision to expel Jewish moneylenders from Venice. Convincingly using textual evidence, he proves that this decision, previously thought to have been unanimous, was resisted by government officials. He also highlights early charter renewals to show this was not a sudden change of attitude by the Venetian government. After giving a brief history of Jewish moneylenders' settlement in Venice, he demonstrates that the process of renewing their charter had been tenuous each time around, involving religious and economic tensions and ever-increasing restrictions. He places the events of 1571 in the context of the defeat of the Venetians at Cyprus and antisemitic sentiments that, although always present, were heightened by this event.

RAVID (1978), parts of which began as his dissertation, answers the previous lack of scholarship on Simone Luzzatto's *Discorsi* by using once again documents in the Venetian State Archives. Ravid sees the *Discorsi*, reflecting the Jewish condition in Venice, as responding specifically to the impact of a 1636 robbery by Jews, and as an answer to several anti-Jewish texts of the mid–16th century. Ravid delineates Luzzatto's two-part text: a description of the role of Jews in Venice—especially in the maritime economy—and a defense of Jewish customs and the Jews' friendly attitude toward non-Jews. Ravid reviews the first ten *discorsi* in depth, presenting them as an attempt to maintain the tenuous status of the Jews in Venice by proving their financially important role in the maritime trade; he then briefly glosses over the later discourses, which refute accusations against Jews and their religion. He notes Luzzatto's lack of historical influence but treats the document in a positive light, despite what some readers may find the almost pathetic nature of Luzzatto's text.

PULLAN (1983) draws on documentary evidence from the mid–16th century to 1670, and especially Inquisition records, in a detailed study of those who suffered at the hands of the Inquisition. The three-part study describes first the Inquisition, then various groups of Jews in Venice at the time, and finally the focus of the Inquisition: Jewish converts to Christianity. Pullan defines the unique qualities of the Venetian Inquisition in relation to its counterparts, especially in Spain and Portugal. He explains that in Venice, Jews and Christians were meant to be separated and the Inquisition was used to define that order; anyone indecisive or not accepting the "debased role of Jews" was subject to the Inquisition. The text is fortified by an extensive bibliography, index, and documentation of consulted manuscripts. By using specific individual cases and records, Pullan permits the reader a personal glimpse into history, supported by his strongly documented scholarship of the period in general.

PULLAN's (1971) long study in its entirety examines Venetian history through study of government policy toward the poor. As "innovations in poor relief introduced between the mid–15th and early 17th centuries," Pullan devotes the final third of his study to the Jewish moneylenders and to the pawnshops called *Monti di Pietà*, which were forced to provide inexpensive credit and low-interest loans to the poor. Extremely well documented, Pullan's text provides a comparative study of the Jewish banks and the *Monti di Pietà* over 150 years, revealing the changing nature of Jewish moneylending. In the process he highlights the uncharitable treatment of the Jews in light of the Venetian government's attempts to provide charity to the poor. Pullan again shows that the Venetian government's aim was to preserve the existing social and political order of the Republic, regardless of the treatment of the Jews. He includes an extensive bibliography, index, and notes.

BLOCH's text is a straightforward explanation of the history of Jewish printing in Venice, focusing on the first half of the 16th century. Bloch highlights the contribution of Christian printing pioneer Daniel Bomberg, who established the city's first Hebrew printing press in 1515. He also discusses those who worked with Bomberg and those who inherited his business after his own press ended operations in 1549. Bloch comments on the difficulties Jews encountered when attempting to participate in printing activity in Venice, and he gives a clear history of the craft, citing many books that could be useful both for further study of the history of printing and more broadly of Jews in Venice.

HILARY LIEBERMAN

War and Peace

Artson, Bradley Shavit, *Love Peace and Pursue Peace: A Jewish Response to War and Nuclear Annihilation,* New York: United Synagogue of America, 1988

Hurwitz, Deena, *Walking the Red Line: Israelis in Search of Justice in Palestine,* Philadelphia: New Society, 1992

Landau, Yehezkel, *Violence and the Value of Life in Jewish Tradition* (Oz VeShalom Publications English Language Series, 2), Jerusalem: Oz VeShalom, 1984

Landes, Daniel, *Confronting Omnicide: Jewish Reflections on Weapons of Mass Destruction,* Northvale, New Jersey: Aronson, 1991

Polner, Murray and Naomi Goodman (editors), *The Challenge of Shalom: The Jewish Traditon of Peace and Justice,* Philadelphia: New Society, 1994

Saperstein, David (editor), *Preventing the Nuclear Holocaust: A Jewish Response,* New York: Union of American Hebrew Congregations, 1983

Siegel, Danny, *Family Reunion: Making Peace in the Jewish Community: Sources and Resources from Tanach, Halachah, and Midrash,* Spring Valley, New York: Town House, 1989

Wilcock, Evelyn, *Pacifism and the Jews* (Conflict and Peacemaking), Stroud, Gloucestershire: Hawthorn, 1994

The institution of war and the commandment to pursue peace are discussed in both legal and ethical traditional sources. These subjects take on a special urgency today because of the existence of the State of Israel, because of the deployment of weapons of mass destruction, and because of the rise in interethnic violence all over the world. For this reason, most of the books discussed here concern themselves with contemporary issues as well as with historical and theoretical material. Most of these titles were published by or are distributed through organizations that sponsored their production.

ARTSON's survey of the subject of peace and war is based on Jewish sources from all periods. Beginning with a consideration of such basic issues as the nature of the Jewish heritage, the sources of aggression, and the value of human life, this book systematically covers the issues of warfare and peacemaking. It quotes traditional sources, and Rabbi Artson offers his own commentary on them. This is the most complete work on this subject currently available. The book includes an extensive bibliography.

POLNER and GOODMAN have collected a variety of essays by both activists and intellectuals who have grappled with the difficulties of peacemaking. The opening section, "The Tradition," consists of rabbinic essays by authors from several streams of Judaism. The next two sections, "The Holocaust" and "Israel," are concerned with the two toughest issues to which contemporary Jewish pacifists must respond, while "Reverence for All Life" contains discussions of vegetarianism in the Jewish tradition. The latter part of the book is divided into two long sections: "Saying No to War and Tyranny" and "Testimonies," both of which offer essays by and about activists working against militarism and for peace, including the perspectives of Jewish conscientious objectors from World War I to the present day. The volume has a detailed index and a bibliography.

WILCOCK presents the reader with a series of substantial historical essays on Jewish pacifists and peace activists of the 20th century. The first two chapters deal with Jewish pacifism during World War I in Britain and in the United States, focusing on the careers of John Harris and Rabbi Judah Magnes. Chapters three through five examine Jewish peacemaking in Palestine during the British Mandate. These chapters include not only the expected studies of such well-known figures as Enzo Sereni and Judah Magnes but also a chapter on the ultraorthodox Jews of Jerusalem who opposed Zionism and pursued peaceful relations with their Arab neighbors. The two chapters exploring World War II and the Holocaust are especially remarkable. The first considers Rabbi Abraham Cronbach's insistence on pacifism during a time when such a philosophy might seem unthinkable to any Jew. The second chapter on this period discusses nonviolent resistance by Jews under Nazi rule, including the use of such tactics in the concentration camps; the analysis is a powerful response to the claim that nonviolence can only work in a democracy. The remaining two essays deal with more contemporary issues. The first evaluates Rabbi Abraham Joshua Heschel's opposition to the war in Vietnam, and the second studies Israeli pacifism as exemplified by Natan Hofshi. This book includes an appendix with quotations from biblical and rabbinic sources on war and peace.

SIEGEL is a slim volume that presents to lay readers a compelling argument based on Jewish tradition for the nonviolent resolution of conflict at all levels. Quotations from traditional sources are woven together by the author's commentary, and although the text is less than one hundred pages long, it provides a cogent defense of the ethics of peacemaking.

LANDAU is a brief collection of essays meant for religious Jews who live in Israel or who are concerned with peace-making in Israel. The authors are all Orthodox, and only one is not a rabbi. Contributions to the anthology include "The Morality of Warfare," by Lord Jakobovits, former Chief Rabbi of Great Britain; "Violence and the Value of Life," by Rabbi Emanuel Rackman, president of Bar-Ilan University; and "The Jewish Attitude Towards Peace and War," by Rabbi David Shapiro. The book also offers an annotated collection of quotations on the ethics of warfare compiled by Professor Uriel Simon of Bar-Ilan University.

LANDES brings together essays by rabbis from a wide spectrum of backgrounds on issues pertaining to possible Jewish responses to the topic of weapons of mass destruction. Seeking guidance from an ancient tradition about how to address this contemporary problem, the authors discuss biblical and rabbinic thinking on such matters as cataclysm, the limitations of warfare in Jewish law, and the prohibition on destructiveness even in times of war. The opinions expressed here range from condemnation of the existence of nuclear weapons to justification for such weapons as instruments of justice and security. Most of the authors, however, argue against the stockpiling of nuclear weapons and oppose national security policies that depend on the maintenance of a nuclear threat. This volume was published at the end of the Cold War but continues to be all too relevant.

SAPERSTEIN is a handbook for activists. It is divided into two parts: "Jewish Perspectives" and a "Factual Section." Most of the first section consists of essays on halakhic and aggadic perspectives on war, nuclear war, and nuclear strategy. At the end of this section there is a compendium of statements by U.S. Jewish organizations on nuclear weapons. The latter section is a collection of essays on nuclear weapons issues. Some parts of this section are now out of date, but much of the analysis continues to be valuable as background to the discussions in the first section.

HURWITZ has brought together a collection of brief essays by Israelis, both Jewish and Arab, who work for justice and peace in the State of Israel. Many opinions that are not within the Israeli political mainstream are represented; all of the writers are committed to nonviolence in pursuing their ideals and programs. The volume includes an appendix listing and describing organizations that work for justice and peace within Israel.

PHILIP J. BENTLEY

Weizmann, Chaim 1874–1952

Russian-born British Zionist, first president of Israel

Berlin, Isaiah, *Chaim Weizmann*, London: Weidenfeld and Nicolson, and New York: Farrar, Straus and Cudahy, 1958

Leon, Dan and Yehuda Adin (editors), *Chaim Weizmann: Statesman of the Jewish Renaissance: The Chaim Weizmann Centenary, 1874–1974* (Confrontation Series, no. 3), Jerusalem: Zionist Library, 1974

Litvinoff, Barnet, *Weizmann: Last of the Patriarchs*, London: Hodder and Stoughton, and New York: Putnam, 1976

Reinharz, Jehuda, *Chaim Weizmann: The Making of a Zionist Leader*, New York: Oxford University Press, 1985

Reinharz, Jehuda, *Chaim Weizmann: The Making of a Statesman*, New York: Oxford University Press, 1993

Rose, Norman, *Chaim Weizmann: A Biography*, New York: Viking, 1986; London: Weidenfeld and Nicolson, 1987

Weizmann, Chaim, *Trial and Error: The Autobiography of Chaim Weizmann*, Philadelphia: Jewish Publication Society, and London: Hamilton, 1949

Despite his pivotal role in the formation of Israel, Chaim Weizmann has been considered, in terms of books produced, the least interesting of all the Zionist leaders. Overshadowed by Theodor Herzl, who led the Zionist organization before him, and then by David Ben-Gurion, who shaped the young State of Israel after him, Weizmann has been strangely neglected by historians. He was a leader who championed a "synthetic" approach that combined the practicalities of settlement with international politics. His aversion to ideology and factionalization has appealed neither to the iconography of the left nor to that of the right in Israel as Ben Gurion and Jabotinsky respectively have done. The relative paucity of analytical material about him is belied by Weizmann's crucial 30-year leadership of what he developed from a small and fractious Jewish federation into a foundling state, at the same time establishing himself personally as a chemist of international reknown.

WEIZMANN recognized that he had been responsible for a series of remarkable achievements, and in addition to publishing his autobiography in 1949 he donated his meticulously preserved papers to what would eventually be Yad Chaim Weizmann. Being almost completely blind by the late 1940s, he dictated much of the later part of *Trial and Error* to Maurice Samuels and revised it with his help. Perhaps as a result of this method of production, the book retains an engagingly anecdotal character and offers insight into the way Weizmann thought. As part of a clear and extensive history of his life it includes more detailed accounts of trips and meetings than would interest later biographers because the events were either inconsequential or unverifiable. Despite its occasional unreliability with regard to details, it is a compelling account of the development of Weizmann hand in hand with Zionism.

In his short overview of the achievements of Weizmann, originally given as an address at the Hebrew University in 1957, BERLIN demonstrates the greatness of his subject. Berlin knew Weizmann, and from his perspective as fellow Jew and fellow long-term resident in England one might have expected him to have given a more personal account of the man. In fact it is an explanation of what makes a great man and why Weizmann is such a man. It does analyze Weizmann's achievements in uniting the Jewish people and helping to form a Jewish state as well as Weizmann's passion for England, but more than a philosophical treatise this is a personal testament from a great thinker who knew Weizmann well.

The small volume of essays compiled by LEON and ADIN includes another essay by Berlin that provides a compressed biographical account of Weizmann. The collection also includes articles by two prime ministers of Israel (David Ben-Gurion and Moshe Sharrett), a deputy prime minister (Abba Eban), and Weizmann's closest friend (Meyer Weisgal). The book provides different perspectives from highly eminent people on how Weizmann's attitudes toward science, Zionism, and his friends were all profoundly intertwined. The editors also offer 12 photographs of Weizmann taken between 1880 and 1949 with a series of family members and luminaries that trace his life from childhood to presidency. The final essay, "The Missing Voice" by Meyer Weisgal, is a brief and poignant reminiscence of Weizmann's "low castigating prophetic" voice, and it is followed by a selection of 25 pages of Weizmann's quotations organized according to topic as if to fill in that "missing voice."

LITVINOFF provides a relatively brief and breezy tour of the life and times of Weizmann. He does so by abandoning both the scholarly and the hagiographic approach, adopting instead a familiar tone for the narrative. His style suffers from being anachronistic, sometimes having hindsight, sometimes registering historical surprise, but it has the effect of making Weizmann seem like a friend rather than some distant figure on a pedestal. At times Litvinoff is surprisingly cavalier with small details, and at other times the breadth of the brush strokes with which he paints the historical settings are remarkable. The success of this book is in presenting the mood of the milieus in which Weizmann operated and keeping it a volume of manageable size.

REINHARZ (1985 and 1993) has been writing the belated but scholarly and definitive biography of Weizmann. The first volume begins with the social and historical background of Motol, where Weizmann's parents lived and where he was born, and ends before World War I. The second volume takes up where the first leaves off and reaches into the British mandate but barely into the 1920s. The final book (unfinished at the time of writing) will cover the end of Weizmann's life. Reinharz's research is irreproachable, but the prose is often pedestrian and unnecessarily dense. Each of the volumes is more than 500 pages long, and, although much of the space is taken up by rigorous footnotes and bibliographies, the combination of excessive detail and stolid writing makes this err toward the pedantic side of scholarship. The subtitles, "The Making of a Zionist Leader" and "The Making of a Statesman," suggest the reason for including so much background detail. Reinharz has sacrificed telling the story of Weizmann's life in favor of a comprehensive coverage of its context, but this biography is still a vital resource for any reader interested in the details of Weizmann's life.

The biography written by ROSE was published at almost the same time as the first volume of Reinharz's biography, and it suffers from not having been able to take advantage of the research that Reinharz used. Its 462 pages are, however, well written and interesting to read, and it does have an index and some referencing apparatus. For a good and thoroughly informative read about Weizmann's life, this is the book that strikes the balance between the story and the facts. Rose keeps a distance between himself and his subject without letting Weizmann seem remote. The book does have the annoying tic of repeating the same story with the same brief analysis and wording when an event that had been introduced thematically

is reached chronologically, but it is a small price to pay for a complete and satisfying biography in one volume.

DAN FRIEDMAN

Western Wall

Ben-Dov, M., Mordechay Naor, and Zeev Anner (editors), *Ha-Kotel*, 1981; translated by Raphael Posner as *The Western Wall*, New York: Adama, 1983

Kasher, Menahem M., *Kotel ha-Ma'aravi*, 1972; translated by Charles Wengrov as *The Western Wall: Its Meaning in the Thought of the Sages*, New York: Judaica Press, 1972

Ronnen Safdie, Michal, *The Western Wall*, New York: Hugh Lauter Levin, 1997

For centuries, the Western Wall has served as Judaism's most holy site, where Jews have assembled to mourn the destruction of the Temple, pray, observe festivals, and since 1967, stage national and personal celebrations. Built by Herod in the first century B.C.E., the Western Wall represents part of the retaining wall that surrounded the Temple platform. It is constructed out of large, well-hewn stones, some weighing more than 100 tons. Above the Herodian courses rest smaller stones added in later centuries. The destruction of the Temple in 70 C.E. and subsequent alterations to the Temple Mount left the Western Wall as one of the few architectural remains of the Second Temple. Judaism's deep attachment to the Western Wall was slow to develop. In response to the Bar Kokhba revolt in the second century C.E., the Roman government denied Jews access to Jerusalem and the wall. Other locations such as the Mount of Olives, where Jews could look down into the city and upon the ruins of the Temple, became important venues for worship. Jewish writings from the destruction of the Temple through the Middle Ages contain few references to the Western Wall. The wall's celebrated role in Jewish consciousness emerges in the 16th century when Turkish rulers granted Jews greater access to the site. At the same time, older traditions that spoke of the western wall of the sanctuary as the permanent residence of the *Shekinah*, God's earthly presence, came to be applied to the Western Wall, thereby confirming its sacred character. Subsequent centuries witnessed growing veneration for and conflicts over the wall. A secondary wall was built parallel to the Western Wall in the 16th century, creating a small, enclosed space where Jews worshiped for 400 years, until 1948 when the Old City of Jerusalem fell under Jordanian control. Following the Six Day War in 1967, which returned the Western Wall to Jewish possession, the enclosure wall and many structures immediately opposite the Western Wall were removed, and a large plaza was constructed to allow throngs of worshipers and visitors to experience the wall.

Ben-Dov played an integral role in the excavation of the Temple Mount, including the Western Wall, from 1968 through the 1980s, and the anthology edited by BEN-DOV, NAOR, and ANNER collects 11 essays on various topics related to the Western Wall. The volume offers the most comprehensive study of the wall in English. Chapters one and two, both written by Ben-Dov, report on the history of the wall, its architecture, and the major archaeological investigations conducted in the 19th and 20th centuries. Chapter three summarizes many of the accounts left by travelers who visited the wall in antiquity, the Middle Ages, and the early modern period. Chapter four describes some of the customs associated with the Western Wall and the halakhic decisions regulating proper behavior at the wall. Chapter five relates several folktales connected with the wall. Chapter six recounts early attempts by wealthy Jews to purchase the wall and the violent struggles over the Western Wall among Jews, Arabs, and the British during the Mandatory period. Chapter seven narrates the events surrounding the capture of the wall in 1967 and the initial reactions among Jews to the news that the wall was under Israeli control. Chapter eight describes the plans for building the plaza in front of the Western Wall. Chapter nine examines depictions of the wall in Jewish and Christian arts and crafts. Chapter ten identifies the various flora and fauna that live at the wall. The volume concludes with Ben-Dov's reflections on four historical and contemporary aspects of the stones themselves.

KASHER explores the meaning of the Western Wall particularly after the site came into Israeli possession. He structures his presentation largely in the form of a commentary on passages from a variety of Jewish sources, such as the Bible, rabbinic literature, the Zohar, prayers originally written for recitation at the wall, and those that have come to be used in this manner. Kasher not only recalls how Jews in the past have spoken of the wall, but sees the return of the wall to Jewish control as a unique opportunity to establish the prophesied single congregation of Israel that will herald the ingathering of the exiles and inauguration of the messianic redemption. He notes an early medieval text that suggests that in the messianic age, God will require Jews to make a holy pilgrimage not three times a year, as stipulated in the Bible, but at the beginning of each month. Kasher regards the new custom of worshiping at the wall on Rosh Hodesh, the celebration marking the beginning of a Jewish month, as the fulfillment of this vision.

RONNEN SAFDIE, a professional photographer, has assembled a vivid pictorial essay on life at the Western Wall. Her 135 color photographs are not only elegant, they eloquently capture many of the "stories of the wall." Through her lens, the viewer encounters hasidic men in their black coats and hats, Italian nuns dressed in white, Ethiopian Jews shielding themselves from the sun with brightly colored umbrellas, and Jews at prayer shielding themselves from the rain with their prayer shawls. Ronnen Safdie has captured the young and old, men and women, Jews and non-Jews; those praying; those celebrating festivals, weddings, and bar mitzvahs; and those gathered at the wall in search of healing. Ronnen Safdie's residence in the Jewish Quarter of the Old City overlooking the wall has allowed her to become intimately familiar with the drama that takes place at the wall at all hours of the day and night.

GARY GILBERT

Wiesel, Elie 1928–

Hungarian-born American Holocaust survivor, novelist, and human rights activist

Berenbaum, Michael, *The Vision of the Void: Theological Reflections on the Works of Elie Wiesel*, Middletown, Connecticut: Wesleyan University Press, 1979

Brown, Robert McAfee, *Elie Wiesel, Messenger to All Humanity*, Notre Dame, Indiana: Notre Dame University Press, 1983, revised edition, 1989

Cargas, Harry J., *Responses to Elie Wiesel*, New York: Persea Books, 1978

Estess, Ted L., *Elie Wiesel*, New York: F. Ungar, 1980

Fine, Ellen S., *Legacy of Night, The Literary Universe of Elie Wiesel*, Albany: State University of New York Press, 1982

Rosenfeld, Alvin H. and Irving Greenberg, *Confronting the Holocaust: The Impact of Elie Wiesel*, Bloomington: Indiana University Press, 1978

The novelist and human rights advocate Elie Wiesel is probably the most famous Holocaust survivor currently active in the Western world. Born in Transylvania in 1928, he received a thorough Jewish education. Deported with his family to Auschwitz in 1944, he lost most of his family and was liberated in 1945. His first great work, *Night,* was rejected by a number of publishers until finally accepted in 1960. Since then, Wiesel has written 30 books, received the Nobel Prize for Peace in 1986, and devoted his life to preserving the memory of the victims of the Holocaust. There is now a very large amount of critical and scholarly work on the many facets of Wiesel's writing—his literary techniques, theology, philosophical significance, activism, and impact.

BERENBAUM analyzes the religious and theological implications of Wiesel's work. Beginning with an exposition of Wiesel's trilogy, *Night, Dawn,* and *The Accident,* he charts the increasing crisis of faith of the pious young teenager who was taken to Auschwitz in 1944. Wiesel's journey back to God appears in later novels such as *The Town Beyond The Wall,* in which a friendship between two sufferers reveals God's faint presence in human goodness. In Wiesel's later work, the emphasis is on the struggle against indifference and a rediscovery of the hasidic values of the hallowing of the world and the affirmation of life. Later, in *The Oath,* the protagonist exclaims, "We shall do it [i.e., struggle against indifference] without the help of the Messiah; he is taking too long. We shall start right here." Berenbaum also stresses Wiesel's theme of spiritual madness as wisdom and presents a view of Wiesel as the modern Job, protesting injustice and suffering. For Wiesel the struggle against Auschwitz lies in bearing witness and in Jewish solidarity. Berenbaum concludes that Wiesel has made a great impact on contemporary Jewish theology. Still, Wiesel has produced no ready-made theology of the Holocaust. For him the Holocaust is the ultimate theological challenge. The questions will continue; for now, the only response lies in the struggle against evil.

BROWN, a Protestant theologian, has written a survey of the personal, philosophical, and artistic dimensions of Wiesel's work. His entire book is informed by the theme of a journey—

Wiesel's own journey and the parallel road that the reader must take together with him. Brown has made his own journey, for he states at the outset that the Holocaust is an ethical problem for Christians, since the executioners of the Holocaust were themselves baptized Christians. Brown argues persuasively that with Wiesel storytelling takes on a moral significance, and thus Wiesel becomes a "messenger to all humanity." The book begins with Wiesel's initial message of darkness in Auschwitz and continues with the evolution of Wiesel's novels from themes of escapism and detachment to participation and activism. Wiesel's journeys—back to his hometown of Sighet and back to Torah, Hasidic tradition, and Jewish mysticism—are rendered movingly by Brown. Still, Brown emphasizes, the "silence of God" and the "necessity of contention" with God, as well as return and reconciliation, are important themes in Wiesel's work. The last chapters deal with Christian responsibility and the importance of following Wiesel's journey for mending the world. Brown's work reveals the great impact that Wiesel has had on some prominent Christian thinkers.

Like Brown, CARGAS is a Christian, but a Catholic, and an authority on the Holocaust and its literature. This volume represents a wide-ranging collection of essays on Wiesel by major Jewish and Christian scholars, theologians, and literary critics. Two interviews with Wiesel himself are presented in the beginning and the middle of the volume. This proves to be a good technique, for the first interview prepares the reader for the rich variety of responses to come, while the next conversation sums up the major issues and prepares the ground for the final portion of the book. The essays range from an analysis of *Night,* to the evolution of hope in the subsequent novels, to an important essay by Josephine Knopp on "Wiesel and the Absurd," to analysis of the theological implications of Wiesel's work. The book ends with a fine summary by Cargas on Christian response to Wiesel's work. This volume was compiled in 1978, well before Wiesel received the Nobel Prize for Peace, and it registers the remarkable attention that Wiesel received even at that early date.

ESTESS puts together a very useful survey for the beginner in this volume of the extensive series Modern Literature Monographs. This excellent summary approaches Wiesel primarily as an interrogator—a questioner of himself, of humanity, and of God. It begins with the premise (following Wiesel's own assertion) that the autobiographical novel *Night,* Wiesel's only work to deal with Auschwitz directly, is the foundation of all his later work. The most stimulating chapter in the book is presented as a centerpiece and is titled "The Drama of Interrogation." This chapter explores the endless questions posed by Wiesel that make him a type of "wise man" for the 20th century. The importance of Wiesel as questioner puts him at the core of Jewish tradition. A useful chronology and bibliography round out this useful little book.

FINE has written probably the best book on the literary techniques of Wiesel and the best analysis of *Night* available. The pervasive theme of the book is Wiesel's role in witnessing and bearing witness. All of his protagonists are witnesses, says Fine. Fine suggests that Wiesel has been influenced not only by Jewish mysticism and Hasidism, but also by 20th-century existentialism. An authority on French literature, Fine

demonstrates how the work of Albert Camus, the great existentialist novelist of the absurd, made a significant impact on the young Wiesel. It is often overlooked that all of Wiesel's novels have been written in French, his adopted language. Fine provides many intriguing details in this regard, and looks also at the one exception: the first, much longer Yiddish version of *Night,* written in 1956 and published in Buenos Aires under the title *And The World Remained Silent.* She emphasizes the important theme of the father-son relationship in the novel and analyzes the ending of the book, in which Eliezer looks into a mirror and sees a corpse with piercing eyes staring back at him, as a new beginning, a point of departure where writing and testifying become reasons for living.

ROSENFELD and GREENBERG, an expert on Holocaust literature and a distinguished rabbi and theologian, respectively, compiled this book of essays on Wiesel in 1978, the same year in which Cargas compiled his. This is the perfect supplement to the Cargas volume, presenting material not touched by the other book. Rosenfeld provides an excellent introduction on "The Problematics of Holocaust Literature." The theme of silence is explored by Terrence Des Pres, while the essay by Rosette C. Lamon provides a fascinating story of why and how Wiesel turned to French as the language for his works. Essays by Byron Sherwin and Emil Fackenheim locate Wiesel in Jewish traditions of midrash (commentary or explication) and lamentation. Leo Eitinger, the prominent psychiatrist and authority on Holocaust-related psychiatric trauma, synthesizes his role as healer and survivor and relates this to the work of Wiesel. The final statement by Wiesel himself, "Why I Write," has become Wiesel's famous credo of purpose, and provides a powerful conclusion to this excellent collection: "Why I write? To wrench those victims from oblivion. To help the dead vanquish death."

LEON STEIN

Wisdom Literature

Brenner, Athalya (editor), *A Feminist Companion to Wisdom Literature* (Feminist Companion to the Bible, 9), Sheffield, South Yorkshire: Sheffield Academic Press, 1995

Crenshaw, James L. (editor), *Studies in Ancient Israelite Wisdom* (Library of Biblical Studies), New York: Ktav, 1976

Crenshaw, James L., *Old Testament Wisdom: An Introduction,* Atlanta, Georgia: Knox, 1981; London: SCM, 1982; revised edition, Louisville, Kentucky: Westminster/Knox, 1998

Day, John, Robert P. Gordon, and H.G.M. Williamson (editors), *Wisdom in Ancient Israel: Essays in Honour of J.A. Emerton,* Cambridge and New York: Cambridge University Press, 1995

Gammie, John G. and Leo G. Perdue (editors), *The Sage in Israel and the Ancient Near East,* Winona Lake, Indiana: Eisenbrauns, 1990

Murphy, Roland E., *The Tree of Life: An Exploration of Biblical Wisdom Literature* (Anchor Bible Reference

Library), New York: Doubleday, 1990; 2nd edition, Grand Rapids, Michigan: Eerdmans, 1996

Perdue, Leo G., *Wisdom and Creation: The Theology of Wisdom Literature,* Nashville, Tennessee: Abingdon, 1994

von Rad, Gerhard, *Weisheit in Israel,* 1970; translated by James D. Martin as *Wisdom in Israel,* Nashville, Tennessee: Abingdon, and London: SCM, 1972

Westermann, Claus, *Wurzeln der Weisheit: Die ältesten Sprüche Israels und anderer Völker,* 1990; translated by J. Daryl Charles as *Roots of Wisdom: The Oldest Proverbs of Israel and Other Peoples,* Louisville, Kentucky: Westminster/Knox, and Edinburgh: Clark, 1995

The "Wisdom Literature" of the Bible is best identified negatively: it is the literature that does not address the dominant biblical themes of the election of Israel, covenant, and "salvation history." Instead, it is concerned with universal human experiences, and its theology represents God as the creator and sustainer of the world. The term was originally applied to three books of the Hebrew canon: Proverbs, Job, and Kohelet (Ecclesiastes). Scholars often extend the category to include the books of Ben Sira (Sirach or Ecclesiasticus) and the Wisdom of Solomon, which are considered canonical by Roman Catholic and Eastern Orthodox Christians, as well as a few Psalms. The extent of "wisdom influence" in the rest of the Bible is currently a matter of debate.

MURPHY has written an introduction directed to first-time readers of the wisdom literature, presenting a range of opinions on the most fundamental issues in wisdom scholarship without feeling compelled to resolve every issue. He attempts to cover a great many topics in relatively few pages, however, so the long and complex books of Proverbs and Job receive necessarily light treatment. The discussion of Kohelet is deeper and quite thought-provoking. The chapter on the personification of Wisdom is also very thorough. Murphy's thinking on several key issues has evolved significantly over the years since the publication of the first edition, and these new ideas are summarized in an appendix to the second edition.

CRENSHAW (1981), while not assuming any prior knowledge of the wisdom literature, approaches it from a more philosophical point of view. The introduction and first two chapters situate the wisdom tradition within Israel's intellectual history. Crenshaw provides a remarkably concise explanation of the various forms of proverbs, and he conveys clearly the structure and dominant themes of the Book of Proverbs. His discussion of Job effectively integrates literary and philosophical considerations. It is important to realize that Crenshaw is presenting his own point of view and not necessarily a scholarly consensus. Thus, for example, he portrays Kohelet as a thorough pessimist, disregarding the *carpe diem* theme that other scholars have seen as Kohelet's solution to life's vanity. Nonetheless, his serious engagement with the problems addressed by Israel's sages prepares his readers well to meet the challenges of tackling the wisdom books.

Crenshaw's approach is profoundly influenced by VON RAD's groundbreaking work on the wisdom literature. Von Rad presents Israel's wisdom as a philosophical tradition that developed in school settings. He traces a series of themes through the wisdom literature, rather than treating each book separately. He concludes that for the Israelite sage, creation was an ordered system that called for trust in God; at the same time, human knowledge of the world's order was limited by the mystery of the divine will. Although scholars now dispute some of his basic assumptions—such as the idea that wisdom began as a movement toward secularism, challenging the "pan-sacralism" of Israel's early history, and only later became "theologized"—this book has set the agenda for most subsequent studies of the wisdom literature.

The most serious challenge to this approach to wisdom is WESTERMANN's study, which focuses on the earliest wisdom texts, Proverbs 10–31. He argues that most of these sayings reflect the experience of ordinary people living in small agrarian communities, not that of an elite group of sages. Rather than looking for the origins of Israelite wisdom in the productions of the scribal cultures of the ancient Near East (as biblical scholars are wont to do), he views the proverb as a form of expression typical of preliterate cultures. Westermann's argument depends on hypothetical reconstructions of the original forms of proverbs, since he acknowledges that the present form of most biblical proverbs is literary. Still, he has a valid point that there is little evidence to support von Rad's claim that the wisdom tradition originated in an educational context.

PERDUE sets out to fill a long-standing gap in biblical scholarship: the lack of a comprehensive study of the theology of the wisdom literature. Although creation is generally recognized to be an important wisdom theme, Perdue argues that creation theology accounts for all of the major emphases of the wisdom literature, including its humanism, its interest in order and the relation of human beings to their environment, and its concern with theodicy. The two main thrusts of creation theology are cosmology (the creation of the world) and anthropology (the creation of humanity), which stand in a dialectical relationship throughout the wisdom literature. Perdue successfully illustrates the interplay of these two themes in each of the wisdom books, although he tends to harmonize the outlooks of the very different books.

The remaining books are collections of highly diverse essays, and therefore they can only be described in broad strokes. Most of the studies in CRENSHAW (1976) were already considered classics by the time he assembled them. This book is a valuable introduction to the history of 20th-century scholarship on wisdom, including important contributions by German scholars that are only here translated into English. GAMMIE and PERDUE provide a wide-ranging study of the role of the sage in ancient Israel and its neighboring cultures, as well as the evolution of this role in early Judaism. Thus, the biblical wisdom literature is contextualized both historically and from a cross-cultural perspective. DAY, GORDON, and WILLIAMSON also include a number of essays on the ancient Near Eastern background of Israelite wisdom, but their main focus is the influence of the wisdom tradition on other parts of the Bible, especially the prophets. BRENNER collects studies by feminist scholars on the portrayal of women in the wisdom literature, particularly the "strange woman" in Proverbs 1–9, along with three feminist readings of Job. Hence it is by no means a complete companion to wisdom literature, but readers who are looking for new approaches to biblical texts will find it stimulating.

KARINA MARTIN HOGAN

Wise, Isaac Mayer 1819–1900

Bohemian-born American rabbi and pioneer of Reform Judaism

Heller, James, *Isaac M. Wise: His Life, Work, and Thought*, New York: Union of American Hebrew Congregations, 1965

Knox, Israel, *Rabbi in America: The Story of Isaac M. Wise* (Library of American Biography), Boston: Little Brown, 1957

May, Max, *Isaac Mayer Wise, the Founder of American Judaism: A Biography*, New York: Putnam, 1916

Meyer, Michael, *Response to Modernity: A History of the Reform Movement in Judaism* (Studies in Jewish History), New York: Oxford University Press, 1988

Rubinstein, Aryeh, "Isaac Mayer Wise: A New Approach," *Jewish Social Studies*, Winter–Spring 1977

Silverstein, Alan, *Alternatives to Assimilation: The Response of Reform Judaism to American Culture, 1840–1930* (Brandeis Series in American Jewish History, Culture, and Life), Hanover, New Hampshire: University Press of New England, 1994

Temkin, Sefton, *Isaac Mayer Wise: Shaping American Judaism* (Littman Library of Jewish Civilization), Oxford and New York: Oxford University Press, 1992; as *Creating American Reform Judaism: The Life and Times of Isaac Mayer Wise*, London and Portland, Oregon: Vallentine Mitchell, 1998

Rabbi Isaac Mayer Wise was a pioneer of Reform Judaism in the United States. Wise advocated a union of Jewish congregations, a common prayer book, a rabbinic training institution, and a national rabbinic organization. The establishment of the Hebrew Union College in 1875 was his greatest achievement.

HELLER was one of Wise's successors in the pulpit of Cincinnati's B'nai Yeshurun Congregation. His lengthy work is divided into two major sections. The first is a straightforward, detailed description of Wise's life and achievements. The second portion is a systematic account of his thinking in a number of key areas. Throughout, Wise himself is quoted liberally. Heller has not written a critical biography of Wise; Heller does not fully assess Wise's place in American Jewish or Reform movement history, nor does he evaluate the worth or depth of Wise's ideas. Rather, his painstakingly researched, scrupulously documented, lengthy work is more in the nature of a chronicle. It conveys a good deal of valuable information, especially on Wise's early years, but it is not an objective analysis of its subject. Heller does not conceal his admiration and sympathy for Wise and is at pains to portray him as a moderate, constructive Reformer.

KNOX's balanced and lucid work is a relatively brief narrative of Wise's life, contributions, and thought. Although it includes a useful "Note on Sources," it is lacking in footnotes and is not a scholarly study but rather a helpful introduction to its seminal subject. Chapters seven and eight are the most notable. The former provides a succinct and cogent summary of Wise's philosophy of religion in general and of Judaism in particular. The latter insightfully compares and contrasts Wise's religious stance with that of prominent 19th-century liberal Protestant leaders.

MAY, the grandson of I.M. Wise, wrote the first full-length biography of this immensely influential Reform Jewish pioneer. Although (forgivably) partial, it provides some valuable biographical details. The study also demonstrates how Wise's success was due in no small measure to his indefatigable energy, personal charisma and contacts, and most effective journalistic, organizational, and oratorical abilities. May's theme is to recount Wise's efforts to Americanize Judaism so that it was, "free, progressive, enlightened, united, and respected." In doing so he allows Wise to relate in his own words a good deal of his life and activities. May does not go further than this. As he states in his preface, "I have not attempted to give an estimate of Rabbi Wise as an author and theologian because I am not competent to do so."

MEYER's panoramic and highly regarded book is the most authoritative to date on the history of the Reform movement. His remarks concerning Wise reflect the author's ability clearly to present objective and informed judgments based upon a superb command of historical sources, a penetrating intellect, and well-honed historical sensibility. Meyer succinctly and convincingly analyzes and assesses Wise's character, religious thinking, activities, and legacy to American Judaism. The author recognizes Wise's opportunism and tendency for self-aggrandizement, but also his persistence and clarity of vision. He discusses Wise's radical as well as moderate Reformist tendencies and also pays tribute to Wise's success in working for a strong and self-confident American Judaism.

RUBINSTEIN's polemical article is a critical reassessment of what he terms the traditional portrayal of Wise as an advocate of moderate Reform Judaism, a champion of Jewish unity, and an individual who was beset by jealous, short-sighted, and doctrinaire enemies. Rubinstein argues that Wise was in fact a radical Reformer, provoked more disunity than unity, and made enemies due to his own faults and shortcomings. Rubinstein is highly critical of what he sees as Wise's disdain for consistency, his causistry, self-serving deceptive behavior, and lack of a coherent religious philosophy. He views Wise as essentially an opportunist who tried to be all things to all people, thereby irrevocably tarnishing his accomplishments and reputation.

SILVERSTEIN's goal is to assess the influence of the general American environment on the Reform movement. He emphasizes the broader social and cultural forces, for example those affecting rabbinic function and status, that helped lead to a uniquely American version of Reform Judaism. This focus also stresses the influences emanating at the congregational level, since individual congregations offer concrete examples of the impact of larger trends. One such congregation Silverstein studies in depth is I.M. Wise's B'nai Yeshurun of Cincinnati. With this orientation, Silverstein effectively demonstrates that religious change flows not merely from individual rabbinic and ideological sources but also from the laity of local congregations and larger tendencies. Thus, Wise reflected the desires of his congregants, as well as the influence of Episcopalian and Unitarian bodies, in advocating a national Reform organization. The laity also strongly supported the founding of the Hebrew Union College, which was affected by Protestant denominational college models. This does not mean that Wise and Reform Jews slavishly followed Christian precedents. Rather, they adopted religious patterns and techniques suitable to the American environment.

TEMKIN was a long-time, well-respected scholar of I.M. Wise and the author of *Encyclopaedia Judaica*'s article concerning him (volume 16). Temkin has produced the most recent and the most significant full-length biography of his subject. Comprehensive, penetrating, and thoroughly documented, Temkin's work is arranged chronologically and reflects a sympathetic although not uncritical view of the American reformer. He succeeds in presenting an impressively informed, well-rounded, and balanced picture of the individual who perhaps more than any other successfully adapted Judaism to its American environment. Temkin emphasizes the crucial role Wise's editorship of *The Israelite* newspaper had in establishing him as an American Jewish spokesman and argues convincingly that *Minhag America,* Wise's prayer book, was his most important work. Temkin stresses the ongoing impact of Enlightenment ideas on Wise but notes that his significance lies far more in his concrete pioneering achievements in institution-building than in his theology or scholarship. Throughout his study, Temkin is careful to place Wise within the larger context, both Jewish and general, of his time. He accurately describes Wise's sense of mission, vision, and strength of personality but does not overlook his weaknesses: "It was his persistence that won him the war where his impetuosity lost him may battles."

ELLIOT LEFKOVITZ

Wise, Stephen Samuel 1874–1949
Hungarian-born American rabbi and Zionist leader

Shapiro, Robert D., *A Reform Rabbi in the Progressive Era: The Early Career of Stephen S. Wise* (Harvard Dissertations in American History and Political Science), New York: Garland, 1988

Urofsky, Melvin I., *A Voice That Spoke for Justice: The Life and Times of Stephen S. Wise* (SUNY Series in Modern Jewish History), Albany: State University of New York Press, 1982

Voss, Carl Hermann, *Rabbi and Minister: The Friendship of Stephen S. Wise and John Haynes Holmes,* Cleveland, Ohio: World, 1964; 2nd edition, Buffalo, New York: Prometheus, 1980

Voss, Carl Hermann, "The Lion and the Lamb: An Evaluation of the Life and Work of Stephen S. Wise," *American Jewish Archives,* 21, April 1969

Voss, Carl Hermann (editor), *Stephen S. Wise: Servant of the People,* Philadelphia: Jewish Publication Society, 1969

Wise, Stephen S., *Challenging Years: The Autobiography of Stephen Wise,* New York: Putnam's, 1949; London: East and West Library, 1951

Wise, Stephen S., *The Personal Letters of Stephen Wise,* Boston: Beacon, 1956

Stephen Samuel Wise was a prominent figure in U.S. Jewish life and politics during the first half of the 20th century. Wise was born in Budapest a little more than a year before his family immigrated to the United States and settled in New York. He was ordained by Adolf Jellinek, the Chief Rabbi of Vienna, in 1893 and earned his doctorate from Columbia University in 1902. His first pulpit was at B'nai Jeshurun in New York. In 1899, Wise became the rabbi at Congregation Beth Israel in Portland, Oregon. In 1905, he received a call to preach at Temple Emanu-El. He declined this offer of New York's most prestigious pulpit, but nevertheless he returned permanently to New York the following year. Thereupon, he set about founding the Free Synagogue, telling the *New York Tribune* on 20 October 1906 that in his new institution he would "as its name implies, be free and untrammeled, free to voice without fear, or scruple the high moral and spiritual teaching of the synagogue." Wise remained a flamboyant and controversial leader and emerged as an important spokesman for social justice and Zionism.

WISE (1956) has edited the personal letters of his father to his wife Louise Waterman, his children, his grandson, and John Haynes Holmes (a Protestant minister who participated in interfaith services with Stephen Wise, Sr.). These letters are interesting primary source material on the rabbi, offering a glimpse into his private life. The collection is divided into five parts: 1899 to 1900, which covers the period from the meeting of Wise and Waterman until their marriage; 1901 to 1906, the years in Portland; 1907 to 1918, the founding of the Free Synagogue until the end of World War I; 1919 to 1932, the end of World War I until the rise of Hitler; and 1933 to 1949.

SHAPIRO's study provides a thorough and objective view of the life and career of Wise. The work is broken down into six sections: the education of an U.S. rabbi, the early Zionist career, the early years at the Free Synagogue, from pulpit to politics, and the fight for Americanism and Zionism. Shapiro discusses nearly every significant event in Wise's life and offers ample documentation to support his claims and ideas.

UROFSKY's monumental biography is a heavily biased look at Wise's controversial life. In Urofsky's eyes, Wise was correct in every situation; the author fails to understand that at times Wise's challengers had valid reasons for their objections to his behavior. The work is not entirely useless, however, for Urofsky does provide coverage of all phases of Wise's life.

VOSS's (1969a) article was written on the 20th anniversary of Wise's death. The work highlights Wise's achievements as a rabbi, scholar, and activist. Voss, who knew and worked with Wise, adds some personal notes and discusses Wise as an inspirational contemporary.

VOSS's (1969b) selection of Wise's professional letters is broken down into five sections: "Years of Growth" (1892–1911), "The New Freedoms" (1912–1919), "America at the Crossroads" (1920–1932), "The Lonely Agony" (1933–1939), and

"If I Forget Thee, O Jerusalem" (1940–1949). This work includes an excellent chronology of Wise's life and achievements.

VOSS (1964) is an account of the relationship of Wise and Holmes. In this important study, Voss explores the unusual friendship of a rabbi and a minister and their unique collaboration, describing how their interfaith services led to a tremendous outcry against Wise and were condemned on all sides. Voss discusses other collaborations between Wise and Holmes as well.

WISE (1951) defends his actions in his posthumously published autobiography. As a public figure, he was aware of the fact that many people did not agree with his ideas and ideologies, and he wrote this work to set the record straight on events and to justify his choices. Wise discusses most of the big controversies that surrounded him in his tenure as a public figure. He writes about his Zionist feelings, his ideas on social justice, the founding and workings of the Free Synagogue, his political roles, his public speaking, antisemitism and World War II, Jewish-Christian relations, and interfaith worship.

HAVVA S. CHARM

Wissenschaft des Judentums

Heschel, Susannah, *Abraham Geiger and the Jewish Jesus* (Chicago Studies in the History of Judaism), Chicago: University of Chicago Press, 1998

Meyer, Michael, "Leopold Zunz and the Scientific Ideal," in his *The Origins of the Modern Jew: Jewish Identity and European Culture in Germany, 1749–1824*, Detroit, Michigan: Wayne State University Press, 1967

Schorsch, Ismar, *From Text to Context: The Turn to History in Modern Judaism* (Tauber Institute for the Study of European Jewry Series, 19), Hanover, New Hampshire: University Press of New England, 1994

Wiener, Max, "The Ideology of the Founders of Jewish Scientific Research," *YIVO Annual of Jewish Social Science*, 5, 1950

Wiener, Max, "Abraham Geiger's Conception of the Science of Judaism," *YIVO Annual of Jewish Social Science*, 11, 1956–1957

The movement for a *Wissenschaft des Judentums* (a "science," or scientific approach to the study, of Judaism) arose in Germany in the 1820s. This movement paralleled and took its cue from the rise of historical thinking exemplified by Baron Alexander von Humboldt, Leopold von Ranke, and G.W.F. Hegel in non-Jewish German intellectual and academic circles. Yet at the same time, it exhibited the distinguishing marks of its proponents, who were members of an excluded minority trying to win political emancipation and achieve social integration. Furthermore, the members of the Berlin *Verein für Kultur und Wissenschaft des Judentums* (Association for the Culture and Study of Judaism), who were in large part the architects of the new "critical" study of Jewry, often associated themselves with the movement for reform in Judaism. Although the Verein and its journal devoted to the Wis-

senschaft des Judentums were short-lived, modern and contemporary Jewish studies owes its existence to the intellectual innovation of this Berlin association's founders. Unfortunately, the movement has not been studied extensively in English academic writing; most of the scholarly literature about this topic (as well as the primary sources) are available only to readers of German. While the foci of the secondary works vary, all agree that the Wissenschaft des Judentums was a political and social phenomenon as well as an intellectual endeavor.

MEYER's chapter on Leopold Zunz, whose biography illustrates the greatest achievements of the Wissenschaft des Judentums in its own day, provides a succinct and provocative overview of the political motivations and considerations behind the creation of the new scientific study of Judaism. This chapter contributes to Meyer's case that a productive tension arose from Jewish attempts to participate in German intellectual and political life. In Meyer's view, the goal of Zunz and other like-minded individuals was "to bring Judaism under the aegis of science, to make it respectable by bringing it into the light of *Wissenschaft*," or pure science. Meyer investigates not only the program of Wissenschaft itself, but also the more general social and political circumstances that led to the founding of the Verein and its collapse several years later.

SCHORSCH's monograph is an invaluable contribution to English-language research on the Wissenschaft des Judentums. This volume is the most comprehensive treatment of a subject that is usually relegated to a footnote in other, more general treatments of the modern German-Jewish experience. The political and social contexts for the Verein and Wissenschaft make a necessary appearance on these pages. However, Schorsch primarily focuses on the proponents of Wissenschaft; for this study, the vicissitudes of their biographies stand in place of more wide-ranging historical analysis. This attribute of his book is both its strength and its weakness. While informative about the lives of the Verein members and other individuals associated with or influenced by Wissenschaft, Schorsch's narrative is weakened by its lack of a general or comparative perspective on 19th-century historicism or other socio-intellectual currents. This focus solely on Jewish historicism may explain in part also why he views the Jewish "turn to history" in a uniformly unproblematic light. Nonetheless, his study is a necessary source for any further research on the topic.

WIENER (1950) sets the stage for his discussion of Wissenschaft ideology by comparing the traditional modes by which Jews studied themselves and their past with the "critical" method offered by the Wissenschaft des Judentums. In particular, he questions why Wissenschaft's first object of study was rabbinic, rather than biblical, literature. He argues that it was precisely the feeling of continuity between rabbinic Judaism and the scholars' own time that made that period compelling; the members of the Verein "were groping to find expression for their deepest Jewish interests." That they sought entrance into the halls of Prussian academe instead of becoming rabbis as their fathers had did not call their commitment to Judaism into question. On the contrary, they saw themselves as acting both for the benefit of Jews and Judaism and, at the same time, as acting in accordance with the philosophical spirit of their age, i.e., Hegelian idealism. Wiener would have us understand the Wissenschaft des Judentums as a highly political, even emotional, program rather than the pure science of which the Verein members often spoke.

In his article on Abraham Geiger, WIENER (1956–1957) investigates the Wissenschaft des Judentums through the life of a man who tried not only to craft a new tool for scholarship, but also to live out an ideology based on his intellectual endeavor. Geiger, an important rabbinical figure aligned with the Reform movement, used Wissenschaft to bolster his position that Judaism was "an instrument which would lead to pure humanity." As such, he provides an excellent illustration of a person for whom historical scholarship could serve an agenda whose proponents were accused of radical antihistoricism. Geiger additionally demonstrates the tendency to use scholarship about Judaism as a haven for those who do not or cannot remain within Orthodoxy, which has become only more pronounced through the modern age.

HESCHEL's work, structured around the biography and work of Abraham Geiger, challenges the reader to rethink many of the dichotomies that previously characterized scholars' assessment of the politics of the Wissenschaft des Judentums. Heschel is unwilling to accept either Gershom Scholem's condemnation of the historiographic movement for its assimilationism or Schorsch's paean to the achievements of the movement for its emancipatory aims. Rather, she uses feminist and postcolonial theory to argue that Geiger in particular (and the Wissenschaft des Judentums by extension), like Manet's scandalous *Olympia,* "reversed the gaze" of the dominant Christian majority and forced leaders of Protestant thought to confront the Jewish subaltern in their midst. Heschel breathes new life into an often-stagnant debate through her fruitful use of poststructuralist theory and her examination of the tensions within Protestant, as well as Jewish, intellectual history in 19th-century Germany.

MARA BENJAMIN

See also Jewish Studies

Wolfson, Harry   1887–1974

Lithuanian-born American historian of philosophy

Feuer, Lewis S., "Recollections of Harry Austryn Wolfson," *American Jewish Archives,* 28, 1976
Goldberg, Hillel, *Between Berlin and Slobodka: Jewish Transition Figures from Eastern Europe,* Hoboken, New Jersey: Ktav, 1989
Goldin, Judah, "On the Sleuth of Slobodka and the Cortez of Kabbalah," *American Scholar,* 49, Summer 1980
Harvey, Warren Zev, "Hebraism and Western Philosophy in H.A. Wolfson's Theory of History," *Immanuel,* 14, Spring 1982
Schwarz, Leo W., *Wolfson of Harvard: Portrait of a Scholar,* Philadelphia: Jewish Publication Society, 1978

Harry Wolfson was a celebrated historian of philosophy and a professor of Jewish studies at Harvard University. He was unrivaled as an authority on Hellenistic, patristic, Islamic, scholastic, and Jewish philosophy. His two-volume study *The Philosophy of Spinoza* painstakingly traces the philosopher's medieval sources.

SCHWARZ, who was among Wolfson's earliest students at Harvard and his ardent admirer and friend for some 40 years, has written a full-length encomium of his teacher. He begins by tracing Wolfson's odyssey from his birthplace in Ostrin, Lithuania (the middle name Austryn that Wolfson adopted is an Anglicized variation of the name of this town), to the yeshivah of Slobodka where he honed his knowledge of the Talmud and traditional Jewish learning. Schwarz depicts Wolfson's progress from Slobodka to the Lower East Side of New York City, then to Scranton, Pennsylvania, and on to Harvard, arriving in 1908 during the time of Santayana and the "golden age" of philosophy. There he received both his bachelor's degree and his doctorate in philosophy (1915) and spent the next six decades of his life teaching Jewish studies. In 1925 he was appointed Nathan Littauer Professor of Hebrew Literature and Jewish Philosophy, a chair created especially for him, but his knowledge of all medieval philosophy—Jewish, Christian, Islamic—was unrivaled in the United States at the time.

The chairman of the Semitics department once wrote to Wolfson, "You seem to have developed a new method . . . in the field of medieval philosophy; you trace words and ideas through half a dozen languages, like hunters following a fox, and never returning empty-handed." Wolfson called the analytical method referred to the "Talmudic hypothetico-deductive method of text interpretation," and equated it with the scientific method as it applied to the study of texts. Schwarz explains how it was this traditional Jewish method of text study that Wolfson consciously followed in all his monumental and magisterial studies of Crescas, Spinoza, Philo, the Kalamists (Muslim theologians), and the church fathers, though externally he conformed to all the accepted canons of modern scholarship. Even so, Wolfson's scheme of medieval philosophy begins with a Jew, Philo, in the first century, and ends with a Jew, Spinoza, in the 17th century.

Wolfson had a fine literary style and a knack for making abstruse ideas clear, and Schwarz offers several memorable examples of his considerable expository skills. He explained, for example, the three views on the origin of the soul—those of creation, preexistence, and traducianism—in these terms: "custom-made," "ready-made," and "second-hand." In considering the origin of the universe, Wolfson differentiates between the theories of creation out of preexistent matter, creation ex nihilo, and emanation by comparing the first to a potter who molds his vessel out of clay, the second to a magician pulling rabbits out of a hat, and the third to a spider spinning a web out of itself.

In Schwarz's portrait Wolfson comes through as a likeable personality, not a remote, scholastic recluse. Even the eccentricities that amused his contemporaries (he kept manuscripts in a refrigerator and drafts of his books in the stove of his bachelor apartment) lend a human touch to this eulogistic tribute.

HARVEY offers a perceptive discussion of Judaism's contribution to Western philosophy according to Wolfson's early and mature views.

GOLDBERG maintains that Wolfson's vaunted method of research was taken over from the discourses of Rabbi Moses Mordecai Epstein, who was the senior Talmud lecturer at the yeshivah of Slobodka while Wolfson studied there and who in 1901 published the first volume of his work *Levush Mordecai*, which, he states in the preface, constitutes the record of the lectures that he delivered at the yeshivah. Shorn of embroidery, Goldberg claims that Wolfson at Harvard applied to philosophical texts the critico-conceptual method of Talmud analysis of his teacher in Slobodka, and he offers a lucid point-by-point comparison of the rabbi and the professor that can be readily followed by English readers without rabbinic training.

There is a scholarly consensus that Wolfson had an extraordinary mind, that he was one of the greatest Jewish scholars of the 20th century, and that he wrote magisterial volumes that, though dated, remain standard reference works. What is in dispute is Wolfson the human being and his character. Goldberg portrays Wolfson as an insecure, cynical, distant, and elitist egotist who was interested only in himself and his coterie of cronies. According to Goldberg, Wolfson wrote a number of articles between 1915 and 1921 that were so vile and degenerate that they could only be matched by the scribblings of the antisemitic underworld. Among other things, Wolfson is shown to ridicule Judaism and Jewish ceremonies, poke fun at Jewish beggars, and call Yiddish literature the cesspool of European letters. It emerges that Wolfson's undivided loyalty was to Harvard, not to its Jewish students, and he took no interest in Jewish-related problems at the university. Goldberg further claims that when Harvard instituted a *numerus clausus*, Wolfson was silent; when Harvard refused to offer any positions to Jewish refugee professors during the Nazi era, Wolfson was silent; and when Harvard scheduled admission examinations on Yom Kippur, Wolfson was silent.

Wolfson confessed that he was not troubled by Harvard's procedure, and he characterized those who protested the policy as driven by "outer convenience," while those who violated the Day of Atonement in order to take the examination were driven by "inner duty." Goldberg reports that when Wolfson was old and sick, he occasionally told Jewish visitors: "Those Goyim think Aquinas is a great philosopher; they spend years studying him. I tell you Maimonides is far greater. In two or three days I can study this Aquinas and know him." However this may be, it should be observed that there is no scintilla of all this in his published works. When the Pontifical Institute of Medieval Studies published a *Festschrift* in honor of the great Aquinas scholar Etienne Gilson, Wolfson contributed a learned article titled "St. Thomas on Divine Attributes," which he dedicated "as a token of high regard and admiration for my good friend Professor Gilson."

GOLDIN's essay discusses an article by Professor Gershom Scholem that adds several accusations to Goldberg's indictment. The two most important are that Wolfson snubbed Jewish scholars and coveted Gentile praise. Specifically, in Wolfson's work on Spinoza, Wolfson does not mention Leo Strauss's monumental study, *Spinoza's Critique of Religion*, which had appeared several years before his own two-volume work. Goldin absolves him of this charge, explaining that Wolfson never permitted himself to be deflected from his course for polemical purposes while writing his books. This may be so, but in 1938, when Strauss came to the United States as a refugee, Wolfson did not lift a finger to find him a position (Wolfson's former instructor, Horace Kallen, was successful in finding Strauss employment at the New School), despite the fact that by this time Strauss's contribution to medieval philosophy equaled—or surpassed—that of Wolfson. The second charge Goldin concedes. A word of praise from a learned Jesuit meant more to Wolfson than the accolades of all Jewish scholars, even including Louis Ginzberg, whom he held in high regard.

FEUER was a student of Wolfson who became somewhat estranged from him when Feuer, against Wolfson's advice, joined a radical student protest. They became reconciled, and Wolfson shared his reminiscences with Feuer shortly before Wolfson's death. Feuer's portrait is between the disembodied intellectual plaster saint of Schwarz's hagiography and the Faustian figure portrayed by Goldberg. Feuer sees Wolfson as a lonely bachelor-scholar who toiled away seven days a week for nearly 60 years and who described himself as a "maker of footnotes." Wolfson used to ask Feuer to take him to the movies, where Wolfson routinely fell asleep and on awaking would try to reconstruct the plot just as he tried imaginatively to reconstitute Spinoza's mind. At the train station on the way back to Cambridge, Wolfson would buy all the sensationalistic scandal sheets and girlie magazines, to the great embarrassment of Feuer. For much of his career, Wolfson was *at* Harvard but not quite *of* Harvard; his appointment was on a year-to-year basis. In 1925, after a decade of teaching, Harvard decided that his appointment as an assistant professor would be terminated unless the Jewish community would fund his salary. Luckily a patron was found in the person of Lucius Littauer, who established a chair of Jewish studies at Harvard, and Wolfson was appointed its first incumbent. It is to this fact that Feuer attributes what he interprets, in essence, as Wolfson's insecurity.

JACOB HABERMAN

Women: Biblical

Bal, Mieke, *Lethal Love: Feminist Literary Readings of Biblical Love Stories* (Indiana Studies in Biblical Literature), Bloomington: Indiana University Press, 1987

Bal, Mieke, *Murder and Difference: Gender, Genre, and Scholarship on Sisera's Death* (Indiana Studies in Biblical Literature), Bloomington: Indiana University Press, 1988

Bal, Mieke, *Death and Dissymmetry: The Politics of Coherence in the Book of Judges* (Chicago Studies in the History of Judaism), Chicago: University of Chicago Press, 1988

Brenner, Athalya, *The Israelite Woman: Social Role and Literary Type in Biblical Narrative* (Biblical Seminar Series), Sheffield, South Yorkshire: JSOT, 1985

Brenner, Athalya (editor), *The Feminist Companion to the Bible*, 10 vols., Sheffield, South Yorkshire: Sheffield Academic Press, 1993–1996

Brenner, Athalya, *The Intercourse of Knowledge: On Gendering Desire and "Sexuality" in the Hebrew Bible* (Biblical Interpretation Series, vol. 26), New York: Brill, 1997

Brenner, Athalya and Carole Fontaine, *A Feminist Companion to Reading the Bible: Approaches, Methods and Strategies,* Sheffield, South Yorkshire: Sheffield Academic Press, 1997

Brenner, Athalya and Fokkelien van Dijk Hemmes, *On Gendering Texts: Female and Male Voices in the Hebrew Bible* (Biblical Interpretation Series, vol. 1), New York: Brill, 1993

Camp, Claudia V. and Carole R. Fontaine (editors), *Women, War, and Metaphor: Language and Society in the Study of the Hebrew Bible* (Semeia, 61), Atlanta, Georgia: Scholars Press, 1993

Day, Peggy (editor), *Gender and Difference in Ancient Israel,* Minneapolis, Minnesota: Fortress, 1989

Exum, J. Cheryl, *Fragmented Women: Feminist (Sub)versions of Biblical Narratives* (Journal for the Study of the Old Testament Supplement Series, 163), Sheffield, South Yorkshire: JSOT, and Valley Forge, Pennsylvania: Trinity Press International, 1993

Exum, J. Cheryl, *Plotted, Shot, and Painted: Cultural Representations of Biblical Women* (Journal for the Study of the Old Testament Supplement Series, 215), Sheffield, South Yorkshire: Sheffield Academic Press, 1996

Meyers, Carol, *Discovering Eve: Ancient Israelite Women in Context,* New York: Oxford University Press, 1988

Pardes, Ilana, *Countertraditions in the Bible: A Feminist Approach,* Cambridge, Massachusetts: Harvard University Press, 1992

Trible, Phyllis, *God and the Rhetoric of Sexuality* (Overtures to Biblical Theology, 2), Philadelphia: Fortress, 1978; London: SCM, 1992

Trible, Phyllis, *Texts of Terror: Literary-Feminist Readings of Biblical Narratives* (Overtures to Biblical Theology, 13), Philadelphia: Fortress, 1984

Weems, Renita, *Battered Love: Marriage, Sex, and Violence in the Hebrew Prophets* (Overtures to Biblical Theology), Minneapolis, Minnesota: Fortress, 1995

The last two decades of the 20th century witnessed a veritable explosion of biblical studies concerned with women and gender. The study of the Hebrew Bible has been immeasurably enriched by this new infusion of often brilliant scholarship, and to many it seems that the turn of the millennium must see a long-overdue paradigm shift in the field of biblical studies, due, in no small part, to precisely this body of work.

Athalya Brenner, through her own work, in collaboration with colleagues, and as editor of the premier series of feminist biblical studies, has contributed immensely to the present wealth of material. BRENNER (1993–1996) comprises a vast store of collected essays by a wide range of biblical scholars on diverse aspects of the biblical book(s) to which each volume is devoted. The series includes volumes on Genesis; Exodus through Deuteronomy; Judges; Samuel and Kings; the Latter Prophets; Song of Songs; wisdom literature; Esther, Judith and Susanna; Ruth; and the Hebrew Bible in the New Testament. An introductory collection, edited by BRENNER and FONTAINE and published after the series itself, attempts to provide critical overviews of the theoretical insights, methodological strategies, and disciplinary perspectives that inform the articles in the ten-volume series. One of the most impressive things about the series is the skill and matter-of-factness with which individual authors and the collections themselves effectively integrate traditionally distinct genres of expression and analysis and meld a profoundly activist impulse with conventional (and unconventional) protocols of academic research. Such interventions are the hallmarks of critical feminist scholarship, and this series provides many fine examples of that scholarship at its best.

Two of Brenner's own books chart very nicely the increasing sophistication and depth of work on women and gender in biblical studies. BRENNER (1985) provides a basic introduction to the Bible's female characters and to some of the foundational questions and problems posed by the first generation of feminists who made their way into biblical studies in the academy. She asks both about social institutions and about literary paradigms in exploring how the biblical texts portray and classify female characters and the roles those characters play. Published 12 years later, BRENNER (1997) explores the ways in which "human love, desire and sex . . . are gendered in the Hebrew Bible." Early questions about "what" led to further questions about "how"—the means and the mechanisms by which biblical knowledge about women, men, sex, and desire is created and perpetuated. These latter questions are pursued by Brenner through chapters on linguistic and semantic data, bodies, procreation and contraception, incest, adultery, rape, and what she terms "pornoprophetics"—pornographic elements in the biblical prophetic literature.

The impetus for this latter work was BRENNER and VAN DIJK HEMMES's collaboration. The two friends and scholars have probed all manner of passages from the Bible in examining the extent to which voices of authority in the text—rather than authorship of the text—might be gendered. Brenner provides an introduction; van Dijk-Hemmes follows with a methodological summary and brief essays applying her method to texts ranging from victory and mockery songs through wisdom speeches and prophetic pronouncements, love songs, laments, vows, and prayers, to birth songs and naming speeches. This section is followed in turn by Brenner's close analyses of chapters from Proverbs and Qohelet (Ecclesiates). Finally, each offers an experimental reading of texts of "prophetic pornography," precursors to Brenner's continued work on the subject following van Dijk-Hemmes's untimely death in 1994. The book is a valuable first foray into an extremely complex aspect of biblical interpretation, one that only becomes more intriguing with further critical refinement.

Bal's trilogy came as a revelation (indeed, a revolution) to biblicists from an outsider to the field, and it has been instrumental in shaping the work of an entire rising generation of scholars. Already well known for her work in narratology, Bal applied her formidable intellect to a set of biblical stories—both those found in the Bible and those (in art, literature, children's books, etc.) that are part of the received traditions—and provided a multilayered examination of the interrelated dynamics of dominance, violence, and gender encoded in them. BAL (1987) reconsiders biblical "love stories" in which danger and death have traditionally been assigned the shape of a woman; BAL (1988a) critiques the discipline of biblical scholarship through the careful dissection of academic discourses applied to the different accounts of Sisera's death found in Judges 4–5; and BAL (1988b) juxtaposes the patriarchal coherence of received traditions on the Book of Judges and Bal's own proposed countercoherence that recognizes the centrality of the women's stories and emphasizes the significance of sexual and domestic violence to the book as a whole. Various technical errors scattered throughout these books, and subsequently addressed by professional biblicists, in no way detract from the impressive scope of Bal's project. In all three books, Bal employs psychoanalysis and structuralism/poststructuralism as key hermeneutical tools, a choice that may be off-putting to some; many others will find Bal's theory-laden discourse daunting. While greater accessibility would have made these works even more valuable, they will reward the effort required to understand them.

Cheryl Exum is one of many scholars who have drawn on both Bal's and Brenner's insights in enhancing her own approach to reading stories of biblical women. EXUM (1993) takes a primarily literary approach, with a hefty dose of psycholanalytics, to consider, among other things, the ways in which female biblical characters suffer violence not only physically at the hands of other (male) characters but also textually at the hands of the authors and editors of the traditions. She offers what she calls "feminist (sub)versions" of the texts she reads, neither reclaiming their women nor discarding the texts for their misogyny. EXUM (1996) moves even further into the broad field of cultural studies and, taking her cue from Bal and others, explores several biblical women in their manifestations in film, opera, fine art, and narrative, as objects of a male gaze. She also takes this opportunity to expand on and refine some of her earlier work on the women surrounding Moses in the Exodus stories and to add her own voice to the growing body of work on the violent pornography found in biblical prophecy.

PARDES, likewise, owes a great debt to Bal, with whom she nonetheless takes issue in calling for a more historical approach to the study of biblical women. Pardes blends critiques of prior scholarship on biblical women and her own proposals about method with sustained examples and illustrations of that method applied to the stories of Eve, Rachel and Leah, Zipporah, Ruth, the Shulamite, and Job's wife. Among other strategies, she offers readings of P against J, midrash against Torah, and Song of Songs against prophetic misogyny in her ongoing conversation with these texts and other scholars who study them.

MEYERS offers a historical and social scientific approach to the paradigmatic biblical woman, Eve—both the much-maligned character of the second and third chapters of Genesis and the "everywoman"— the flesh-and-bones peasant of ancient Israel. Several chapters of the book synthesize for the reader significant archaeological data and biblical texts through which Meyers draws her picture of ancient household and family life and the struggle to scratch out a living in the largely barren highlands of early Iron Age Israel. The core of

the book is a retranslation and reinterpretation of Genesis 2–3 in light of the sociological/anthropological models Meyers constructs. Eve, in this reading, becomes a kind of separate but equal partner of Adam, one who shares with him the ever-increasing burden of agricultural and domestic labor, but who suffers as well the disability of increased demands for childbearing ("I will greatly increase your toil and your pregnancies") required for subsistence in the Israelite highlands. Meyers's clear and accessible style and her effort throughout to defend the biblical text against what she terms feminist critics' "misplaced preoccupation with biblical androcentrism" and patriarchy have made this book popular in nonacademic study groups and college classrooms alike.

DAY's anthology comprises a fine collection whose breadth of subject matter is equalled only by the range of methods employed. Each piece offers a brief but deep treatment of a particular question, issue, or text—often setting the Bible in its wider Near Eastern context and in dialogue with other ancient documents and artifacts. Social history and philology stand side-by-side with literary and cultural criticism and folklore studies. Hagar's story finds resonances in the Epic of Gilgamesh, and Jephthah's daughter's "rite of passage" in the Iphegenia and Kore myths. The Israelite's "Queen of Heaven" has a sister in Astarte and Ishtar, and Esther is unveiled as an exemplum to all diaspora Jewry of a feminine nonconfrontational model of effective power. The book is an excellent introduction to the field, is eminently readable, and includes enough footnotes to keep even the hardcore experts engaged.

CAMP and FONTAINE's is another significant anthology that brings together an impressive array of biblical scholars—in this case around a broad but specific topic. The book considers "how metaphor 'works' in the Hebrew Bible, and how such workings both shape and are shaped by social realities" that infuse the lives of women and the cultures of violence that spawn war. Some essays are more focused on theoretical issues of gender and metaphor; most, however, deal with particular texts and tropes in which women, men, sex, and warfare are key elements. Three response essays, one from a linguistic perspective, the other two situated in postmodern psychoanalytic theory (the first of these two by Bal), complete the volume.

Metaphor, sex, and violence are the focus as well of WEEMS's book-length treatment of images of sexual/marital violence in the books of the Prophets. Weems considers, from many angles, the content of the marriage metaphor as a representation of God's relationship with Israel in the books of Hosea, Ezekiel, and Jeremiah, and the ways in which their invocation of battered, humiliated, sexually abused "promiscuous" wives could become a way of talking about divine love—a love inextricably bound up with and expressed through jealousy, terror, and torture. Weems argues that both the prophetic authors and their intended priestly audience were male; and thus the sexualized female body served as a battleground in a power struggle between men. Following very careful and systematic explorations of the rhetorical force and deployment of this metaphor in the ancient Near East, Weems concludes her book with a meditation on how contemporary readers—survivors of sexual and domestic violence, ethicists, theologians, marginalized peoples, liberationists—

can (or cannot) read these texts, and how any work on them must be self-consciously relevant to such readers and their experiences of violence.

Finally, Phyllis Trible's books hold a special place as among the earliest fruits of modern biblical scholarship on women and gender. For many in the present generation of biblical scholars, Trible's work was an introduction to the tools and texts that provided a way to begin to think about women, sexuality, and feminine God language. TRIBLE (1978) and TRIBLE (1984) employ rhetorical criticism as their primary methods and offer close readings of selected texts. As volumes two and 13 of Fortress Press's "Overtures to Biblical Theology" series, the studies often have something of a homiletic quality about them—Trible (1984) began as a series of lectures directed toward "the preaching enterprise in the church." Many of Trible's proposals and conclusions have been seriously challenged by others in the field, and her attempts to rescue the Bible through readings that efface the misogynistic and patriarchal elements, while discovering "original" pro-feminist impulses, have gained for her work a great many supporters and detractors alike.

CYNTHIA M. BAKER

See also Women: Ancient and Modern; Women: Contemporary; Women: Status

Women: Ancient and Modern

Antler, Joyce, *The Journey Home: Jewish Women and the American Century,* New York: Free Press, 1997

Baskin, Judith (editor), *Jewish Women in Historical Perspective,* Detroit, Michigan: Wayne State University Press, 1991, 2nd edition, 1998

Baskin, Judith (editor), *Women of the Word: Jewish Women and Jewish Writing,* Detroit, Michigan: Wayne State University Press, 1994

Glenn, Susan A., *Daughters of the Shtetl: Life and Labor in the Immigrant Generation,* Ithaca, New York: Cornell University Press, 1990

Henry, Sondra and Emily Taitz, *Written Out of History: A Hidden Legacy of Jewish Women Revealed through Their Writings and Letters,* New York: Bloch, 1978; as *Written Out of History: Our Jewish Foremothers,* New York: Biblio, 1990

Hyman, Paula E. and Deborah Dash Moore (editors), *Jewish Women in America: An Historical Encyclopedia,* 2 vols., New York: Routledge, 1997; London: Routledge, 1998

Levine, Amy-Jill (editor), *"Women Like This": New Perspectives on Jewish Women in the Greco-Roman World* (Early Judaism and Its Literature, no. 1), Atlanta, Georgia: Scholars Press, 1991

Lowenthal, Marvin (editor and translator), *The Memoirs of Glückel of Hameln,* New York and London: Harper and Brothers, 1932

Ofer, Dalia and Lenore J. Weitzman, *Women in the Holocaust,* New Haven, Connecticut: Yale University Press, 1998

Sacks, Maurie, *Active Voices: Women in Jewish Culture,* Urbana: University of Illinois Press, 1995

Umansky, Ellen and Dianne Ashton, *Four Centuries of Jewish Women's Spirituality: A Sourcebook,* Boston: Beacon, 1992

Weissler, Chava, *Voices of the Matriarchs: Listening to the Prayers of Early Modern Jewish Women,* Boston: Beacon, 1998

There are a number of good collections and a range of monographs exploring Jewish women's lives and works from antiquity through the present day.

Baskin's two collections have become standard texts in many college-level Judaism and women's studies courses. Each volume presents a fine array of scholarly articles representing a range of academic disciplines and highlighting individual personalities and broader cultural dynamics of different places and periods. The essays are arranged more or less chronologically, and the historical-geographical center of each book is early modern and modern Europe and the United States, with the Middle Ages and the Middle East receiving brief attention in each volume, while antiquity is granted a token nod in BASKIN (1991). (The chronological distribution may reflect the focus of English-language scholarship being undertaken in both Jewish and women's history in general.) Baskin's (1991) usefulness as a textbook is enhanced by its balance of geohistorical and thematic survey articles. Each article provides a small taste of existing scholarship on a period or theme, and the notes provide some direction for further exploration. Select annotated bibliographies would have been a valuable addition. The more substantial volume of the two, BASKIN (1994) offers a similarly useful mixture of general survey articles and articles focused on particular writers or themes. Both volumes present significant primary research by contemporary scholars in a format accessible to a nonspecialist audience.

Another book that seeks to provide a historical survey is HENRY and TAITZ's study. These authors have constructed a running narrative focused on fictional characters and historical Jewish women, beginning with biblical Jewish heroines and concluding with U.S. political and intellectual leaders. The book reads like a popular "who's who" of model Jewish women, and its publication in the late 1970s provided for many readers an introduction to the rich resources available for reconstructing Jewish women's history. The volume will engage young and novice readers, and it contains enough primary source citations to make it a useful reference for the college classroom as well.

Nine of the 11 essays edited by LEVINE examine images of Jewish women in (usually male-authored and sometimes strikingly misogynist) Greco-Roman literature, while the remaining two essays consider evidence about female authorship in antiquity. The quality of critical scholarship and writing in these essays varies widely from very fine to not-so-fine, and an uncritical, apologetic interest appears now and then, most explicitly in Judith Romney Wegner's "Philo's Portrayal of Women—Hebraic or Hellenic?" Nonetheless, the collection does provide a good introduction to the study of images of women in the Jewish pseudepigrapha.

LOWENTHAL renders a great service to modern readers with his translation of the memoirs of Glikl of Hameln, an ordinary, capable, and comfortably wealthy German Jewish woman of the late 17th and early 18th centuries. This account, written by Glikl as a testament to and legacy for her children, combines autobiographical narrative with business records, moralizing exhortations, and prayers, and it is tinged on occasion with the shadows of larger historical events such as the Cossack massacres of Jews in Poland and the rise and fall of Shabbetai Tsevi. Glikl's text is the earliest extant Yiddish memoir by a woman, and it is unsurpassed as a firsthand glimpse into the life of a European Jewish woman of the period.

WEISSLER has likewise filled a significant lacuna with her translation and examination of Yiddish *tkhines*, Ashkenazi prayers (some authored by women) that were created for the pious devotions of women and "men who are like women"— the former were often barred from the classical Hebrew rabbinic literature so highly valued in these early modern Jewish communities, while the latter were uneducated in that tradition. Weissler divides her study into three parts, each comprising both scholarly analysis and extensive quotation of the prayers. Part one introduces the genre and its settings, provides the theoretical frameworks for the study, and considers constructions of gender, bodies, and the spiritual aspirations of women in the *tkhines*. Part two explores mystical overtones and images in some of these prayers, and part three completes the study with a look at the transformation of the *tkhines* in the new world of U.S. Jewish immigrants at the turn of the 20th century. A final essay, titled "The Feminist Scholar and the *Tkhines*," offers Weissler's own reflections on identity and commitments.

A short excerpt from Glikl's memoir and a selection of *tkhines* are included among the impressive store of primary sources compiled and edited by UMANSKY and ASHTON. Spanning the years between 1560 and 1990 and framed by a general introduction and final list of sources, this anthology focuses on the vitally important but inevitably amorphous realm of "spirituality," presented here through the voices of women from many generations and locations. These poems, memoirs, prayers, rituals, meditations, letters, essays, reflections, dedications, and speeches are divided into four chronological categories: "1560–1800: Traditional Voices," "1800–1890: Stronger Voices," "1890–1960: Urgent Voices," and "1960–1990: Contemporary Voices." As the book unfolds, each category comprises progressively more sources and a greater multiplicity of voices; each section is introduced with a carefully crafted introduction that supplies an overall context and a brief background summary of each author and her work(s). Most of this collection consists of excerpts or full pieces published elsewhere, although a number of the most recent contributions were written expressly for this publication. Together, the pieces create a rich sourcebook that lends itself to many settings; the volume will interest scholars, students, practitioners, dreamers, poets, and the merely curious.

In the collection of articles edited by SACKS, one finds a dizzying array of topics and approaches held together, once again, under the general rubric of varied "voices." Thus, the first essay, a rather cursory recital of the standard received wisdom titled "Women as Wives in Rabbinic Literature," is the single entry under the heading of "Male Voices." Sacks's intention here is explicit: she presents this essay "so that readers can later compare what they read with these more expected assertions." Unfortunately, this routine version of rabbinic Judaism is not only uninteresting in itself, it also sets an unnecessarily weak tone for the generally engaging and often insightful articles that follow. Following the collection's less-than-promising start, however, the quality of the analysis improves in the remaining sections of the book, which are loosely organized under the headings of "Public Voices" (articles on early Zionist women and Reform sisterhoods); "Literary Voices" (articles on Grace Aguilar and Holocaust narratives); "Ritual Voices" (pieces on new rituals, bar mitzvah moms, and newly orthodox women); "Folk Voices" (work on Tunisian immigrants to Israel, Orthodox high school girls, and Judeo-Spanish song traditions); and "An Anthropological Voice" (a programmatic and substantive essay by noted anthropologist Susan Starr Sered). There is much intriguing information and analysis here. Moreover, the 11 essays, to varying degrees, model an interdisciplinary, "wholistic," and woman-centered approach to scholarship on Jewish women that enriches this field of inquiry immeasurably.

The world of turn-of-the-20th-century immigrant sweatshops and smaller contract shops is the focus of GLENN's study of first-generation Jews in the United States. The author explores the everyday lives and self-perceptions of young Jewish women workers in the garment industries of the United States' urban centers, and she suggests that the gender divisions of the work environment enabled the women to develop a sense of self-possession and self-esteem that provided a strong base for political organizing, labor union activity, and community building. The book valuably highlights the involvement of Jewish women in the unionization of the garment industry, but it is less strong in its apprehension of the specifically Jewish and Yiddish cultural history of these immigrant women. Glenn's rich synthesis and analysis of a variety of materials make this an excellent overview of an important and fascinating subject.

OFER and WEITZMAN's book is an extremely impressive and invaluable contribution to Holocaust studies, Jewish studies, and gender and women's studies. Included here are essays by the majority of the late 20th century's most capable and articulate scholars on women, gender, and the Holocaust, as well as a handful of survivors' testimonies, which were penned explicitly for this volume and are presented alongside the third-person descriptive and analytical essays that make up the bulk of this collection. The focus of the essays range from Jewish life in prewar Europe and under the growing Nazi movement to life in the ghettos, the resistance, and the camps. Matters and materials examined include diaries and memoirs, institutions and movements, everyday events, coping strategies, and scholarly research on the Holocaust and on Holocaust literature. Information about women and women's experiences is finely woven together with analyses of gendered aspects of torture, suffering, coping, and resistance during the Holocaust, as well as with discussions of the significance of gender for events and stories that followed. The editors provide a compelling general introduction to their project and brief introductions to each section and piece presented in the volume.

ANTLER is a consummate storyteller, and her well-researched, narrative presentation of the lives and times of dozens of 20th-century Jewish women is as readable as it is informative. Antler does not maintain skeptical distance from or offer critical analysis of her subjects; instead, she unabashedly celebrates women who become heroines—big and small—in these tellings of their tales. The author's real contribution is her provision of vivid detail, historical and cultural context, and a sense of the ongoing struggles around identity, community, and commitment exemplified by each of these Jewish women. She highlights well some of the complex gender dynamics inherent in the events and lives she recounts, but she never strays from the laudatory tone that characterizes the work as a whole.

The encyclopedia produced by HYMAN and MOORE is a veritable gold mine of historical and biographical information on a vast number of U.S. Jewish women whose lives or work have had a measurable local, national, or global impact. Discussions of women, the editors note, are strikingly few in most reference works on Jews and Judaism, while the Jewishness of many Jewish women is effaced or disregarded in most reference works on women. This two-volume encyclopedia "rectifies this loss and provides a usable past" for any and all who would make use of its resources. While the vast majority (800) of the entries are biographical, these articles are supplemented by more than 100 topical entries on such subjects as theater, Zionism, anarchists, the Young Women's Hebrew Association, and the labor movement. In their preface, the editors provide a few definitional caveats: "American" refers to the United States and includes immigrants and refugees as well as native-born residents and some émigrés; "Jewish" refers to those born of one or more Jewish parents as well as converts to or from Judaism, including a number of women who rejected any Jewish identity or considered their Judaism irrelevant; and "historical encyclopedia" indicates a focus on the biographies of persons no longer living and the lives of Jewish women over the age of 60 who have already proven to be of historical consequence. The several exceptions to this last rule encompass primarily entertainers, athletes, and prominent women in contemporary national politics. Each article is accompanied by a recommended bibliography and, where appropriate, selected published titles by the person profiled.

CYNTHIA M. BAKER

See also Women: Biblical; Women: Contemporary; Women: Status

Women: Contemporary

Beck, Evelyn Torton, *Nice Jewish Girls: A Lesbian Anthology* (Crossing Press Feminist Series), Trumansburg, New York: Crossing, 1982; revised edition, Boston: Beacon, 1989

Daniel, Ruby and Barbara C. Johnson, *Ruby of Cochin: An Indian Jewish Woman Remembers*, Philadelphia: Jewish Publication Society, 1995

Heschel, Susannah, *On Being a Jewish Feminist*, New York: Schocken, 1983

Kaufman, Debra Renee, *Rachel's Daughters: Newly Orthodox Jewish Women*, New Brunswick, New Jersey: Rutgers University Press, 1991

Kaye/Kantrowitz, Melanie, *The Issue Is Power: Essays on Women, Jews, Violence, and Resistance*, San Francisco: Aunt Lute, 1992

Kaye/Kantrowitz, Melanie and Irena Klepfisz, *The Tribe of Dina: A Jewish Women's Anthology* (Sinister Wisdom, 29/30), Montpelier, Vermont: Sinister Wisdom, 1986; revised edition, Boston: Beacon, 1989

Moore, Tracy (editor), *Lesbiot: Israeli Lesbians Talk about Sexuality, Feminism, Judaism and Their Lives*, London and New York: Cassell, 1995

Piercy, Marge, *He, She, and It: A Novel*, New York: Knopf, 1991

Pogrebin, Letty Cottin, *Deborah, Golda, and Me: Being Female and Jewish in America*, New York: Crown, 1991

Sered, Susan Starr, *Women as Ritual Experts: The Religious Lives of Elderly Jewish Women in Jerusalem*, New York: Oxford University Press, 1992

Sharoni, Simona, *Gender and the Israeli-Palestinian Conflict: The Politics of Women's Resistance* (Syracuse Studies on Peace and Conflict Resolution), Syracuse, New York: Syracuse University Press, 1995

Siegel, Rachel Josefowitz and Ellen Cole (editors), *Celebrating the Lives of Jewish Women: Patterns in a Feminist Sampler* (Haworth Innovations in Feminist Studies), New York: Harrington Park, 1997

The number of available books about contemporary Jewish women's experiences and concerns is substantial and continues to grow. There are several impressive studies that focus on contemporary Jewish women, and yet some of the most interesting and illuminating treatments of the subject come in the form of collections of first-person writings that have appeared over the past few decades.

Compiled and edited while she was still a graduate student at the University of Pennsylvania, HESCHEL's anthology has been a veritable handbook for budding Jewish feminists. BECK's anthology provides a similar "bible" for many Jewish women—lesbian, feminist, and otherwise. KAYE/KANTROWITZ and KLEPFISZ's anthology rounds out this foundational triad of collected writings by and about contemporary women engaged in thinking about, wrestling with, and celebrating many dimensions of Jewish women's experiences. All three books contain a variety of materials. The pieces in Heschel's book are all in essay form, but they range in content from critical analysis to autobiography and personal reflection, from theological manifesto to recipe for ritual. The texts collected by Kaye/Kantrowitz and Klepfisz and by Beck are decidedly more secular in orientation than Heschel's work, with many meditations on ethnic and sexual identity politics and explorations of cultural and political legacies. These latter two volumes feature poetry, fiction, and photographs, as well as essays of various sorts. Each collection is a rich resource in its own right as well as a snapshot of a time that has already become "history." All three volumes stand in similar self-conscious relation to contemporary

Jewish and women's movements, and all seek to provide resources and inspiration for those movements and the myriad communities and commitments that they embrace.

KAYE/KANTROWITZ compiles a collection of the author's own writings, including analytical and activist essays, book reviews, speeches, fiction, and personal reflections that emphasize how violence and power relations reproduce each other on micro and macro levels. Rape and other forms of violence against women, war, racism, antisemitism, and imperialism, as well as intricate and deadly connections among these practices and ideologies, are examined from the self-consciously and explicitly Jewish, American, and female perspective of the author. Written over a 15-year period, these texts also provide a glimpse into the world of both an individual and a wider community of progressive Jewish women confronting the ever more complex networks of oppression and resistance that characterized the late 20th century.

A very different perspective on the world emerges from the stories, songs, recollections, and photographs of Ruby Daniel and her community as captured by DANIEL and JOHNSON. Born and raised in Cochin, in the southern Indian state of Kerala, Daniel is heir to one of the most ancient communities of Jews outside of the Mediterranean and Middle East, and the volume is a wellspring of folklore and family legend presented through the memories of this engaging and articulate informant. The contents are divided into three sections. The first, a reflective autobiography of Daniel's life in India and her move to Israel, includes memories of her childhood and young adulthood, a family history and genealogy, portraits of extended family members, and Daniel's perceptions of other surrounding communities. The second part describes the Cochin Jewish community, its synagogues and other institutions, and its relationships with the local and British colonial ruling powers. In the final section, Daniel provides a holiday calendar complete with colorful descriptions of family and community celebrations of the major Jewish holidays. Photographs and song texts add still more dimensions to the multilayered collage. Johnson's extremely useful and informative footnotes accompany Daniel's narrative and help to explain the historical context, enabling the reader to distinguish between Daniel's individual perceptions and received stereotypes, and addressing how others might have viewed the same events or the practices of neighboring communities. The memoir is a real treasure.

SIEGEL and COLE's collaborative effort presents first-person accounts by dozens of (primarily American) Jewish women reflecting on their histories, upbringings, transformations, and accommodations to their various definitions of Jewish identity. Photographs and short biographies of the contributors add a nice touch to this collection of thoughtful and often conversation-like pieces by women both unknown (such as Elisa Goldberg, a Philadelphia artist) and widely known (such as Susan Weidman Schneider, the editor-in-chief of *Lilith: The Independent Jewish Women's Magazine*, and Lenore Walker, an expert on the psychology of domestic violence). Contributors range from teenagers (such as Elisheva Glass, a sophomore at Ithaca High School in western New York State) to great-grandmothers (including Siegel herself). Almost all of the women are professionals in social work,

psychology, or the humanities, yet each speaks first and foremost as a woman and Jew, often describing her professional and other life choices as outgrowths of dynamics deeply rooted in these two identity categories. There is no apparent organization to the book's presentation; it is, to use the editors' metaphor, a sampler whose patterns lie both above and below its finely textured surface.

Another collection of contemporary Jewish women's stories takes the form of edited transcripts from a U.S.-Israeli oral history project. MOORE and her collaborators have brought together 21 narratives by Israeli lesbians representing, it seems, the most international collection of contemporary Jewish women's voices to date (over half are native-born Israelis, and the remainder are immigrants from all over the Western world). A distinctive feature of this collection of autobiographical accounts is the fact that each piece is edited by a different hand. The reader therefore enjoys the tandem presentation of one woman's oral history through another's selection and arrangement of her material. These pairings are supplemented by brief biographical statements by the editors at the start of the volume. The documentary collection is introduced by a short history of the project, a thumbnail sketch of Israel and its political scene, and an account of the beginnings of lesbian organizing in that context.

POGREBIN interweaves events and stories from her life with deeper reflections on meaning and identity. Her musings are thoughtful, if not profound or enlightening; her analyses and propositions are relatively tame and circumscribed. Pogrebin has a wonderful knack for presenting herself to the reader, warts and all, in the conversational tone that characterizes the book. Among her many recollections are a tribute to her mother, an account of a meeting with Golda Meir, a sermon for her niece's bat mitzvah, a survey of Jewish female images in Hollywood films, and meditations on biblical stories and heroines. The final 100 pages of the book recount experiences and insights Pogrebin gained in dialogue with black and Jewish feminists over many years and describe encounters between Jewish feminist Zionists (including Pogrebin herself) and Palestinian nationalist feminists. Pogrebin's essays in this part of the book convey a very vivid sense of the learned ignorance, misunderstandings, suspicions, and deep resistances such dialogues can reveal, as well as the few glimmers of insight that participants sometimes acquire. Thus, she offers a view of a seemingly intractable, complicated, and deeply frustrating endeavor marked by few successes but impressive for the sheer persistence of the parties involved as they work toward common understanding and peaceful solutions. Pogrebin's mixed-genre monograph is both idiosyncratic and deeply resonant, an ethical autobiography that is at once a cautionary tale and a call to action.

An Israeli professor of peace and conflict resolution, SHARONI presents accounts of Israeli Jewish women's struggles for security and justice juxtaposed with corresponding accounts of Palestinian women and their political work. The combination is provocative and compelling. Sharoni alternates political theory and sociological gender analysis with historical overviews of women's movements, and she supplies a close examination of the lives and political activities of women in the years between the start of the *intifada* and the signing of the Declaration of Principles by the Israeli government and the Palestine Liberation Organization (1987 to 1993). A final chapter considers political alliances between Israeli Jewish women and Palestinian women. Photographs scattered throughout the book provide poignant visual documentation, and a substantial bibliography points to a wealth of related sources.

A rather different community of Israeli women is explored in SERED's ethnographic study of elderly Kurdish and Yemenite immigrants to Israel. Sered's study focuses explicitly on the ritual activities and identifications of sacredness by this community of women. She finds that these women do not merely suffer under the disabilities of divisions and strictures imposed on them in the name of Jewish tradition; they also mobilize some of those same traditional mythologies and practices to create meaning and community that are woman-centered and that value and sanctify the concerns of their everyday lives. Sered allows the women's stories and self-descriptions to reveal the inadequacy of models that assume that male-centered, non-domestic rituals are more important than the often female-centered, domestic (and non-domestic) rituals that mark the "ultimate concerns of life, suffering, and death." This book represents ethnography at its best, and Sered's skill and insight provide an engaging and edifying portrait of a community of Jewish women at the end of their lives and at the height of their creative powers.

Unlike Sered's subjects, who grew up with the constraints and traditions that shaped their lives and identities, the women described by KAUFMAN are "newly-orthodox" Jews. Like Sered, Kaufman presents these women through their own words and from their own perspectives, highlighting concerns that they identify as most important and compelling to them, rather than emphasizing issues that an "outsider" or a male member of their community might expect to take precedence. The bulk of the book is descriptive, but the volume employs a finely-wrought framework of interpretive observations and summaries that downplays neither the patriarchal and often reactionary aspects of Jewish Orthodoxy nor the appearance of reasoned choice in the accounts of the ba'alot teshuvah. The women in this study come primarily from secular or minimally religious backgrounds, and most are young, educated, single women. Perhaps the most interesting insight proffered by Kaufman is that while these women energetically reject "feminism" (which appears as a one-dimensional caricature in their accounts), their own explanations of their choices and their articulations of Orthodox Jewish values frequently employ feminist rhetoric. For example, it is precisely the feminist values of woman's self-possession and control over her body and sexuality that these women displace from "secular" feminism and attribute to Orthodox Judaism. Kaufman's general conclusions, which come at the end of the book, provide a fine summary and raise many intriguing questions about women, gender, Judaism, Orthodoxy, and the study of modern (and postmodern) identity politics.

PIERCY, a prolific poet, essayist, and fiction writer, develops many Jewish characters and themes in her writings. Any number of the female characters in her various works, like Piercy herself, would fall comfortably under the rubric of "contemporary Jewish women." This particular novel stretches the boundaries of this category only slightly by presenting characters from an imagined but not-too-distant future. The protagonists of the story are Shira and her grandmother Malkah, two generations of women who inhabit the "Jewish free town" of Tikva in a time when transglobal corporations have replaced most of the boundaries, functions, and institutions (including ethnic and religious ones) of the now defunct nation states. Masterfully intertwining a vision of an eerily recognizable future with old and new tales of the Golem of Prague and blending Jewish mysticism with feminism and the politics of survival, Piercy creates a fable full of fascinating Jewish women who are themselves as familiar as they are futuristic.

CYNTHIA M. BAKER

See also Feminism; Gender; Women: Ancient and Modern; Women: Biblical; Women: Status; Women's Literature: Modern and Contemporary

Women: Status

Biale, Rachel, Women and Jewish Law: An Exploration of Women's Issues in Halakhic Sources, New York: Schocken, 1984

Brooten, Bernadette J., Women Leaders in the Ancient Synagogue: Inscriptional Evidence and Background Issues (Brown Judaic Studies, no. 36), Chico, California: Scholars Press, 1982

El-Or, Tamar, Educated and Ignorant: Ultraorthodox Jewish Women and Their World, Boulder, Colorado: Rienner, 1994

Grossman, Susan and Rivka Haut (editors), Daughters of the King: Women and the Synagogue: A Survey of History, Halakhah, and Contemporary Realities, Philadelphia: Jewish Publication Society, 1992

Hauptman, Judith, Rereading the Rabbis: A Woman's Voice, Boulder, Colorado: Westview, 1997; Oxford: Westview, 1998

Levitt, Laura, Jews and Feminism: The Ambivalent Search for Home, New York: Routledge, 1997

Peskowitz, Miriam B., Spinning Fantasies: Rabbis, Gender, and History (Contraversions, 9), Berkeley, California, and London: University of California Press, 1997

Swirski, Barbara and Marilyn P. Safir (editors), Calling the Equality Bluff: Women in Israel (Athene Series), New York: Pergamon, 1991

Wegner, Judith Romney, Chattel or Person?: The Status of Women in the Mishnah, New York: Oxford University Press, 1988

As gender studies has emerged as a scholarly discipline and has developed ever more compelling and sophisticated questions, methods, insights, and analyses, categories such as women's "status" and "role" (once rather widely employed) have largely fallen into disuse. Thus it is that only one of the works considered here has "status" in its title—and then only in its subtitle, where it is linked to the very circumscribed domain of early rabbinic law. The rest, for the most part, reframe or reconceive that broad constellation of issues previously blanketed by the concept of status, a concept at once too amorphous and too narrow to be genuinely descriptive of the experience of (Jewish) women across ages, classes, nationalities, ethnicities, and so forth.

BROOTEN's book, despite being unattractively published as an unrevised Harvard dissertation manuscript, has achieved a wide and well-deserved readership both within and outside the academy. Brooten's thesis, that "women served as leaders in a number of synagogues during the Roman and Byzantine periods," was one of the earliest challenges to long-held assumptions about women's exclusion from positions of Jewish communal leadership in antiquity. In part one, Brooten closely examines 19 Latin and Greek inscriptions from tombs and dedicatory plaques in which Jewish women bear such titles as "leader of the synagogue," "mother of the synagogue," "elder," "leader," "fatheress," and "priest." While these inscriptions were known to scholars long before Brooten collected them in her study, each was summarily and uncritically dismissed as merely honorific—that is, unreflective of any authority or active leadership responsibility—when associated with women. The absence of compelling evidence to justify such summary dismissal is well highlighted by Brooten, who also provides insights from literary sources and non-Jewish inscriptions by which to better understand the possible meanings adhering to each title. In part two, Brooten considers related issues; most importantly she asks about the existence of separate women's galleries in ancient synagogues. Again, she demonstrates convincingly both the paucity of evidence for such separated, gendered spaces, and the almost universal presupposition on the part of archaeologists that such spaces must have existed, resulting in a systematic misreading of evidence in order to substantiate that claim. While a historian's caution precludes Brooten's ability to make any positive claims with certainty, her careful scholarship and canny skepticism make for a powerful corrective to scholarship on women driven more by stereotype than by sound analysis.

GROSSMAN and HAUT in a sense pick up where Brooten leaves off. Their book is a wide-ranging anthology spanning ages and continents, genres and disciplines. The editors divide their materials into three sections: "History," "Halakhah," and "Contemporary Realities," much of the latter given over to "Personal Vignettes" and a few newly developed rituals. All the articles are accessible to the general reader, and only a handful offer anything in the way of sustained analysis; the majority are largely descriptive. Description, in fact, is this collection's greatest strength. The reader is offered glimpses into medieval and modern synagogue practices; prayer and purity practices; halakhic and sociological trends; illiterate, semi-literate, and formally educated groups of women; and Iranian, Yemenite, Ashkenazi, hasidic, and havurah communities, among others. Inevitably, the quality of the individual pieces varies greatly, but with so many voices and perspectives included, the book presents an interesting cross-section of women within the communities they continue to build.

WEGNER's book affords a valuable resource for the study of early rabbinic texts and their formulations of women's variable legal status. Drawing on her own extensive legal training,

Wegner delineates the categories of women recognized in the mishnaic system and elucidates the rationale underlying the rabbis' treatment of women as sometimes "chattel," sometimes "person." All women are persons, Wegner argues, as regards public rights and responsibilities and criminal liability. However, three categories of women (minor daughter, wife, and levirate widow) are reduced to chattel in instances in which a man's private proprietary claims to their sexuality are at issue. Wegner's thesis, although well and carefully argued, has real limitations. Her systematic and at times uncritical use of such analytic classifications as "autonomous" and "dependent," "public" and "private," and "chattel" and "person," while useful for clarifying certain important dynamics and issues, has the effect of obscuring many others of at least equal significance. In addition, despite the author's occasional nod toward questions of social practice, the unreflective and inaccurate gender stereotypes that continue to burden much scholarship on this period are widely evident here as well. The book serves as a useful point from which to enter this field of inquiry, but a broader range of analytical tools would have added greatly to its value.

Such analytical tools are employed to good effect in two subsequent books treating the same period and body of texts. HAUPTMAN proposes to read early rabbinic texts from a woman's perspective. More to the point, she reads as a professional talmudist standing squarely within that tradition and employing its native modes of analysis and argumentation. She begins by critiquing others' approaches that, to her mind, do these texts an injustice either by reading individual passages "shorn of their larger contexts" within the rabbinic corpus or by condemning their deeply patriarchal character from the standpoint of contemporary egalitarianism and social justice. The book presents an interesting mix in both its organization and agenda. The chapters are drawn partly from categories created by the mishnaic/talmudic system itself (e.g., *Sotah*, the suspected adulteress, and *Niddah*, menstrual impurity and immersion) and partly from more general legal issues in which women have a stake (e.g., the offering of testimony, rights to inheritance, ritual obligations and exemptions). Similarly, in substance, her careful and close readings of her selected texts move between naming the injustices and disabilities suffered by women within the rabbinic system of law and constructing an apologetic that holds that the rabbis introduced a number of measures "to ameliorate the lot of women" created by the received tradition of biblical legislation. Hauptman is very clear that she is not engaging in social history and that her explorations within the rabbinic legal system may well not reflect common practice of the period. At the same time, however, her arguments about the early rabbis' remedial stance often seem to presuppose practical limitations on women that are not to be found in the Torah itself. On the whole, this fine collection of studies serves as an excellent example of how the talmudic tradition contains within itself dynamic models and methods for creating improvements in women's halakhic status—and why those who continue to embrace talmudic traditions should embrace these impulses as well.

PESKOWITZ's book is, in some respects, more closely focused: it concentrates explicitly on early rabbinic texts, largely legal, involving spinning and spinners. Even so, the study has great depth and critical acuity, as it goes to the heart of questions about how gender norms and hierarchies of power are "naturalized" and rendered invisible through association with repetitive, tedious, mundane activities such as spinning and weaving. Peskowitz explores evidence from a number of literary, archaeological, and artistic sources to flesh out her reading of the rabbinic texts; and she draws on an intriguing array of current cultural studies in reflecting on the "ideological work" of storytelling and the deeply gendered process of history-writing itself.

While examining many of the rabbinic texts also considered by Wegner, Hauptman, and Peskowitz, BIALE's project is expressly contemporary and not historical. Biale does not ask about ancient rabbinic intentions or impulses but rather organizes her book, in digest form, around issues of practical concern to halakhically observant Jewish women. These range from the performance of ritual commandments through marriage, divorce, and abandonment, to sexuality, reproductive choices, domestic violence, and rape (themes revisited and recast by Hauptman). The book's importance is twofold. First, it provides a condensed reference source spanning centuries of debates, dissents, and legal decisions (by Jewish men) that continue to have a profound effect on the lives of many Jewish women. Second, it introduces its readers to the most basic tools of talmudic exegesis and argumentation (tools traditionally denied to women) and calls attention to vital elements of the halakhic process that may hold some promise for those such as Biale and Hauptman who seek to work within that system to promote change. While Biale is a bit too optimistic in her reading of 2,000 years of rabbinic legislation, wherein she sees "a gradual and persistent effort to redress the fundamental imbalance in power between men and women," her book does serve as a useful primer on the long history and perpetuation of that imbalance.

In her Bar Ilan doctoral dissertation, translated from the Hebrew, EL-OR offers a candid illustration of what the exclusion of women from talmudic learning (and its attendant access to power and status in Orthodox Judaism) looks like in a contemporary haredi, or ultraorthodox, community in Israel. El-Or's is an anthropological sketch of the lives of Gur hasidic women with particular analytical attention to the ways in which the gender-segregated educational institutions of the community work to reproduce an exclusively male authority structure wherein knowledge is validated and legitimated only through its ascription to men, while the intellectual capabilities of women are rendered invisible (and undesirable) to both men and the women themselves. El-Or considers this "education for ignorance" a paradox—one of many negotiated by the haredi community in its complicated accommodation to modernity. The paradox does not result from any illusion that education and ignorance are necessarily incompatible, but rather from the disjuncture between the clear aims of this education to keep the women intellectually resistant to non-haredi Israeli and Jewish culture while at the same time excluding them from the intellectual pursuits (talmudic study) that underpin the value system of the community. But these women *are* intellectually engaged and literate, asserts El-Or, and the greatest paradox, as she see it, is that "the women use their literate ignorance as a conscious, emotional, and social means of living as educated Jewish women."

The insights and observations of many other women in Israel are collected by SWIRSKI and SAFIR in a book whose title invokes the Israeli myth of gender equality in order to highlight just how great the social, economic, and legal disparities between men and women (as well as Jews and non-Jews, Ashkenazim and Sephardim) really are. The editors have arranged the 43 essays in this collection into seven sections. These sections address the themes of family, sex and reproduction, militarism, labor, political power, the implications of living in a "Jewish State," the kibbutz and moshav movements, domestic and state-sanctioned violence against women, and feminism in Israel. While the essays are primarily by and about middle-class Jewish (Ashkenazi) Israelis, there are a few pieces by and about Israeli Arab and Sephardi women as well. As the editors themselves acknowledge, many voices and perspectives are missing from this collection, but it is, nonetheless, a rich compendium of biography and statistics, history and ethics, analysis and activism. It serves as an invaluable introduction to Israeli life and politics as experienced and understood by contemporary Israeli women.

LEVITT reconfigures the old question of status in yet another provocative and compelling way as she explores the gendered interplay of modern Judaism, with its troubled rabbinic legacy, and Western liberalism, with its deep investments in colonialism and assimilation. Through a series of critical and very personal readings of a broad range of texts, Levitt scrutinizes her relationship to the promises and limitations of liberalism, feminism, and Judaism—all "places" where she, the granddaughter of Eastern European Jewish immigrants, has sought to find a "home in America." The first half of the book moves from consideration of the *ketubbah* (rabbinic marriage contract) and talmudic rape law, to Napoleonic legislation and Jewish responses to emancipation, to feminist critiques of the sexual contract implicit in liberal civil society and liberal Jewish theology. Part two is an ongoing conversation with Jewish and non-Jewish feminists in an attempt to make audible an explicitly Jewish voice in feminist studies.

CYNTHIA M. BAKER

See also Feminism; Gender; Women: Contemporary; Women's Literature: Modern and Contemporary

Women's Literature: Early Modern

Ashkenazi, Yaakov ben Yitzchak, *Tz'enah Ur'enah: The Classic Anthology of Torah Lore and Midrashic Comment* (ArtScroll Judaica Classics), 3 vols., translated by Miriam Stark Zakon, Brooklyn, New York: Mesorah, 1983–1984

Cardin, Nina Beth (editor and translator), *Out of the Depths I Call to You: A Book of Prayers for the Married Jewish Woman,* Northvale, New Jersey: Aronson, 1992

Freehof, Solomon B., "Devotional Literature in the Vernacular: Judeo-German, Prior to the Reform Movement," *CCAR (Central Conference of American Rabbis) Yearbook,* 33, 1923

Klirs, Tracy Guren (compiler), *The Merit of Our Mothers/Bizkhus imohes: A Bilingual Anthology of Jewish Women's Prayers*, Cincinnati, Ohio: Hebrew Union College Press, 1992

Segal, Agnes Romer, "Yiddish Works on Women's Commandments in the Sixteenth Century," in *Studies in Yiddish Literature and Folklore* (Monograph Series, 7), Jerusalem: Hebrew University, 1986

Tarnor, Norman (compiler and translator), *A Book of Jewish Women's Prayers: Translations from the Yiddish*, Northvale, New Jersey: Aronson, 1995

Weissler, Chava, *Voices of the Matriarchs: Listening to the Prayers of Early Modern Jewish Women*, Boston: Beacon, 1998

Zakutinsky, Ruth (compiler and translator), *Techinas: A Voice from the Heart: "As Only a Woman Can Pray,"* Brooklyn, New York: Aura, 1992

Early modern Jewish women's literature (mid–16th through 18th century) is notable for a flourish of works written in Yiddish. The three major genres represented in this literature are *tehinot*, personal and supplicatory prayers recited by women; *mitsvot nashim*, compilations and digests of laws, especially those edicts incumbent primarily upon women; and translations of and commentaries on the Bible.

The tehinot served as a women's folk liturgy, and they addressed women's lives and concerns. Biblical matriarchs and heroines are invoked in the tehinot in addition to the patriarchs. Numerous tehinot were composed for *Rosh Hodesh* (the new month), a time known as a women's holiday. These prayers frequently emphasize adherence to the three best-known traditional duties pertaining to women—*halah*, tithing of dough; *nidah*, rules pertaining to marriage and family purity; and *hadlakat ha-ner*, lighting candles on the sabbath and holidays. These women's obligations are often referred to by the acronym *HaNaH*, and it is primarily these topics that are addressed in the mitsvot nashim. (The term *HaNaH*, more familiar to English readers as *Hannah*, is also of course the name of the biblical personality who prayed for a child in the Book of Samuel and who serves as a model of Jewish prayer.) The tehinot, mitsvot nashim, and Bible paraphrases were extremely popular and published in numerous editions. Despite their fame as women's literature, most of these works were written by men for women, with the exception of tehinot, which were composed by women as well.

Tehinot were first published in the late 16th century, and editions continue to be issued today. Thus, the time frame of these Yiddish prayers extends beyond the early modern period. The anthologies of tehinot discussed below are generally translations of mid–19th- and early 20th-century editions. Despite these publication dates, however, they include tehinot that were written far earlier. One of these earlier collections, *Shas Tehine Hadoshe*, compiled by Ben-Zion Alfes (1850–1940) in the early 20th century, was relied on extensively as a source of tehinot by both Norman Tarnor and Ruth Zakutinsky (although misidentified by the latter). Alfes's text also is indicative of the vitality of the genre, for he includes tehinot originally written as much as two centuries earlier as well as tehinot that he composed.

CARDIN edits, translates, and provides an introduction to a manuscript of prayers presented by the physician Giuseppe Coen to his wife Yehudit Kutscher Coen in 1786. This collection is distinctive because the prayers are in Hebrew with introductory instructions in Italian. Despite this difference, the topics addressed and the function served by these Hebrew prayers are quite similar to those of the Yiddish tehinot described above. They therefore indicate that the genre of women's prayers was alive outside the Yiddish speaking community, although the Yiddish prayers are better known and documented. Indeed, additional manuscripts of women's prayers in Hebrew from Italy are extant, and internal evidence in these manuscripts suggests that they were frequently passed down from mother to daughter.

FREEHOF's article is the pioneering English-language study of Yiddish tehinot. The introductory portions of the article explore the Jewish legal justification for the use of the vernacular in prayer and the place of spontaneous personal prayer in Judaism. These halakhic concerns are scarcely mentioned in later studies of tehinot. Thus, this initial discussion of tehinot introduces a pattern characteristic of many subsequent investigations of the genre—these studies are serious works, but they are nonetheless framed by the prevailing issues of the times in which they were written. In the case of Freehof, the questions of prayer in the vernacular and innovation in prayer were important topics on the agenda of the Reform movement. The body of Freehof's study focuses on the *Seder Tefilot u-Vakashot*, a standard work of tehinot initially published in the mid–18th century (further identified by Weissler in her work cited here), and Freehof includes English translations of a number of tehinot. His closing topic is the use and influence of Kabbalah on the *tehine* literature.

ASHKENAZI, of Janow, Poland, wrote this text at the beginning of the 17th century. His title derives from the phrase in Song of Songs 3:11: "Go out and see [daughters of Jerusalem]." The text includes a translation of the Pentateuch, weekly *Haftarot*, and the Five Scrolls, intertwined with traditional commentaries and midrashic, aggadic, and mystical material written in Yiddish in a lyrical yet intimate folk style. The first known edition was published in Basel in 1622 and quickly became extremely popular, as the numerous editions subsequently published demonstrate. Known as the *"taytsh humesh"* (vernacular Bible), Ashkenazi's work was widely studied in Jewish households on the Sabbath, particularly by mothers with their children and by groups of women. It is now presented in its entirety in a lucid English version. This is a popular rather than a scholarly edition, which is accessible to most readers, even though it is directed at an audience with a high degree of familiarity with traditional sources. A brief glossary of Hebrew terms is appended. A more extensive list would have opened the work to a wider audience, however.

KLIRS's anthology of tehinot has its origins in her rabbinical thesis, which was revised to make it accessible to general audiences. This bilingual edition has the Yiddish text and the English translation on facing pages. The tehinot were transcribed from the original Yiddish editions and appear in a modern typeface. The volume includes a general introduction to the tehine literature, footnotes explaining unfamiliar references, and a glossary that includes terms that may be unknown to the average reader. A selected bibliography and a list of Yiddish editions from which the tehinot were chosen are also appended to the book.

SEGAL's is the only article available in English on mitsvot nashim. These legal digests were first written c.1475 and became very popular. Versions of mitsvot nashim are currently extant both in manuscript and printed form. Segal compares three different texts written prior to 1602. (Later editions were chiefly reprints or abridgments of these three.) Mitsvot nashim were written by scholars in a readable, enjoyable, popular style. The authors sought to disseminate knowledge and insure adherence to the laws, but they emphasized that their writings applied to standard situations and that any questions that arose from particular circumstances should be referred to a rabbi. Interwoven with the legal rulings is ethical and narrative material from a wide range of Jewish literature. This feature of the mitsvot nashim exposed women to sources they would not otherwise have encountered.

TARNOR selected tehinot and translated them into English. This work contains English only and does not feature the original Yiddish texts of the tehinot. He provides a useful introduction, extensive notes, a short glossary, and a bibliography that includes the titles of the tehine collections from which the tehinot in the book were selected. The tehinot presented here cover the Jewish daily ritual and yearly holiday cycle, as well as tehinot for special occasions—such as "To synagogue the first time after rising from childbed"—and particular requests, among them "Deliverance from bad neighbors."

WEISSLER, the leading scholar in the field, provides an excellent overview of the tehine literature. She is the only contemporary researcher to have gone beyond translation of tehinot to in-depth analysis of them. Her book presents the tehinot in several contexts, namely related religious literature for women, women's spiritual lives, definitions of gender in Ashkenazi Jewry, and the integration of kabbalistic material into mainstream Jewish life. Translations of tehinot, including tehinot written by women, appear throughout the book to illustrate and illuminate Weissler's lively discussion of the genre. The history of the tehine is traced from its origins through its distinct patterns of development in Eastern and Western Europe and subsequent transformation in the United States. The place of the study of tehinot in contemporary feminist scholarship is addressed, as is the much-debated issue of authorship and women's authorial involvement.

Another bilingual anthology of tehinot has been compiled and translated by ZAKUTINSKY. The book opens from right to left, in the manner of a Hebrew book. The English translation is on the left page, facing the original Yiddish texts, reset in modern typeface. In contrast to the other works discussed, Zakutinsky approaches the material as a vehicle for contemporary women's prayer (rather than study, inspiration, or contemplation). Thus, the preface advises that it is preferable to say tehinot in Yiddish rather than English, and a guide to Yiddish pronunciation is included. Although this popular work does not include a glossary, it does contain brief introductory and explanatory materials that help make the prayers accessible even to those who are not familiar with the world of traditional Judaism. Nearly half the book is devoted to tehinot for the Sabbath when the new month is blessed; the remain-

der includes prayers for holidays and for special occasions and situations, among them: "A baby's first tooth" and "For a stepmother."

SHULAMITH Z. BERGER

See also Women; Women's Literature: Modern and Contemporary

Women's Literature: Modern and Contemporary

Baskin, Judith (editor), *Women of the Word: Jewish Women and Jewish Writing,* Detroit, Michigan: Wayne State University Press, 1994

Halio, Jay and Ben Siegel (editors), *Daughters of Valor: Contemporary Jewish American Women Writers,* Newark: University of Delaware Press, 1997

Lichtenstein, Diane, *Writing Their Nations: The Tradition of Nineteenth-Century American Jewish Women Writers,* Bloomington: Indiana University Press, 1992

Shapiro, Ann (editor), *Jewish American Women Writers: A Bio-Bibliographical and Critical Sourcebook,* Westport, Connecticut: Greenwood, 1994

Sokoloff, Naomi, Anne Lapidus Lerner, and Anita Norich (editors), *Gender and Text in Modern Hebrew and Yiddish Literature,* New York: Jewish Theological Seminary of America, 1992

With the development of feminist literary criticism has come an increased interest in the writing of Jewish women. This interest has taken several forms: recovering the works of previously neglected Jewish women writers; seeking out the works of emerging ones; developing critical and theoretical frameworks to understand themes, languages, and styles in women's writing; and examining the role of gender in literature and popular culture.

In the first book-length application of feminist criticism and gender theory to Hebrew and Yiddish literature, SOKOLOFF, LERNER, and NORICH present a collection of essays by a group of feminist literary scholars and creative writers. Noting that the two distinct literary traditions have long been described in gendered terms—with Hebrew, the holy tongue, largely inaccessible to women, and Yiddish, the daily "mother tongue," troped as female—the essayists discuss their interrelatedness as Jewish literature, while placing them also in the context of Western literature. In addition to providing a theoretical framework, the essays focus primarily on the works of women poets, and they also offer reflections by several contemporary women fiction writers, as well as a gender analysis of several male writers.

Taking a more historical approach and spanning a longer period of time, the essays in BASKIN explore the writing of Jewish women in a variety of languages from the Middle Ages to the present. Written by literary scholars, several of the essays focus on individual writers such as Devorah Baron, Anzia Yezierska, Cynthia Ozick, Emma Lazarus, and Maya Bejerano; others explore the image of women in different literary contexts such as medieval Hebrew literature, Yiddish literature, or the writing of S.Y. Agnon. Some of the essays explore broad themes, such as women in the Holocaust and feminism in Israeli writing.

Several studies focus on the writing of Jewish American women writers. LICHTENSTEIN explores the literary tradition of 19th-century Jewish women in America, incorporating a wide spectrum of writing, from private letters and diaries to published works by established poets and writers. Through these writings, she traces women's struggle to assert a dual identity, both Jewish and American, at a time when such multiple loyalties were considered suspect. Responding, like Jewish men, to the pressures of assimilation and additionally to the marginality of gender, Jewish women sought ways to reconcile American and Jewish culture. By constructing a hybrid image of the Jewish woman, melding the mythic ideals of the American "true woman" and the Jewish "mother in Israel," Lichtenstein shows how women's writing staked out a position at once American, Jewish, and female.

SHAPIRO argues that Jewish American women writers have been doubly marginalized, by ethnicity (or religion) and by gender, and largely left out of the American as well as the Jewish literary canon. The essays contained in this volume, written by different literary scholars and covering more than 50 individual poets, playwrights, and fiction writers, trace the development of distinctive themes, concerns, and paradigms in the works of these Jewish American women writers and document their works' critical reception.

Focusing on writing since World War II, with an emphasis on the last quarter of the 20th century, HALIO and SIEGEL's volume of essays by literary scholars traces the growing influence of Jewish American women writers. Examining fiction, drama, and poetry, as well as memoirs and criticism, the collected essays explore the ways in which a broad spectrum of authors have articulated issues connected to Judaism and gender. Topics include representations of the Holocaust in Jewish American women's writing, Jewish fiction in the multicultural context, and the place of Jewishness in writers as diverse as Erica Jong, Pauline Kael, Cynthia Ozick, Adrienne Rich, Anne Roiphe, and Wendy Wasserstein.

SARA R. HOROWITZ

See also Feminism; Gender; Women; Women's Literature: Early Modern

Y

Yemen and the Arabian Peninsula

Ahroni, Reuben, *Yemenite Jewry: Origins, Culture, and Literature* (Jewish Literature and Culture), Bloomington: Indiana University Press, 1986

Ahroni, Reuben, *The Jews of the British Crown Colony of Aden: History, Culture, and Ethnic Relations* (Brill's Series in Jewish Studies, vol. 12), New York: Brill, 1994

Barer, Shlomo, *The Magic Carpet*, New York: Harper, and London: Secker and Warburg, 1952

Caspi, Mishael Masrawi, *Daughters of Yemen*, Berkeley: University of California Press, 1985

Klorman, Bat-Zion Eraqi, *The Jews of Yemen in the Nineteenth Century: A Portrait of a Messianic Community* (Brill's Series in Jewish Studies, vol. 6), New York: Brill, 1993

Koningsveld, P. Sj. van, J. Sadan, and Q. Samarra'i, *Yemenite Authorities and Jewish Messianism: Ahmad ibn Nasir al-Zaydi's Account of the Sabbathian Movement in Seventeenth Century Yemen and Its Aftermath*, Leiden: Leiden University, Faculty of Theology, 1990

Newby, Gordon Darnell, *A History of the Jews of Arabia: From Ancient Times to Their Eclipse under Islam* (Studies in Comparative Religion), Columbia: University of South Carolina Press, 1988

Nini, Yehuda, *The Jews of Yemen, 1800–1914*, Philadelphia: Harwood Academic, 1991

Parfitt, Tudor, *The Road to Redemption: The Jews of the Yemen, 1900–1950* (Brill's Series in Jewish Studies, vol. 17), New York: Brill, 1996

Tobi, Jacob, *West of Aden: A Survey of the Aden Jewish Community*, Netanya: Association for Society and Culture, 1994

One of the oldest diaspora communities, the Jews of Yemen were widely spread across the country, mostly keeping traditional ways of life among the Arabs until their emigration, mainly to Israel, starting in 1892 and peaking in the 1950s. Under British rule since 1839, Adeni Jews were highly Westernized. They are one of the most researched Middle Eastern communities, and much of the published work is in Hebrew, with important scholarship in English as well.

AHRONI (1986) is a comprehensive survey of Jewish life in Yemen. Against the background of Yemen's history and socioeconomic structure, Ahroni examines Yemenite Jewry from antiquity to the end of Ottoman rule in 1914. His survey starts with the biblical period, moving to postbiblical and pre-Islamic times, including the mass Judaization and the Jewish kingdoms of that period. Most of the book deals with the Muslim period: the attitude of Muhammad and Islam toward Yemenite Jews, Jewish literary activity, the impact of the Sabbatian movement on Yemenite Jewry, the exile of the Yemenite Jews to Mauza' in 1679, and developments during the 18th and 19th centuries. Based on an extensive list of publications, the book provides a succinct survey of Jewish life in Yemen through 1914.

AHRONI (1994) focuses on the British period in Aden, starting with an examination of the years preceding the 1839 British conquest. Ahroni then describes the impact of the British occupation on the Jews, the arrival of Jewish refugees from Yemen in the late 1920s and early 1930s, and Muslim-Jewish relations, including the 1932 riots. Special chapters deal with daily life, marriage and divorce, education, and the Judeo-Arabic vernacular. The impact of Zionism, especially in the 1940s, the 1947 riots, and the mass emigration are detailed. This well-researched and annotated study provides a comprehensive overview of the Adeni community.

BARER provides a contemporary description of the mass emigration of Yemeni Jews in the mid-20th century and details their move from all over Yemen to Aden, the airlift to Israel, the involvement of Israeli and other volunteers in the operation, and the arrival in Israel.

CASPI's book is a collection of Yemenite Jewish female poetry and love poetry in the original Judeo-Arabic and Hebrew with English translation. Female poetry was oral and sung at exclusively female gatherings, and it expresses the intimate feelings of women about many private issues, including their attitude toward men and their position in the community in general. Yemenite Jewish female poetry is always in the Judeo-Arabic vernacular and is highly expressive, explicit, and erotic, while men's poetry is often in Hebrew and slightly veiled when it deals with love. The collection is of value to those interested in literature, gender studies, folklore, and linguistics.

KLORMAN examines the Yemeni Jewish messianic movements of the nineteenth century in the context of Jewish and Muslim messianism in general and in Yemen in particular. The Mahdist idea in Islam is examined with reference to its manifestations in Yemen. Similarly, the Sabbatian movement is described, with emphasis on its spread in Yemen. Three 19th-century Jewish messianic movements are discussed, as are the messianic expressions in the waves of Jewish immigration to Palestine from 1881 to 1914. Focusing on this central issue for the Yemenite Jewish community helps explain its uniqueness and even how its internal structure, cultural life, and socioeconomic conditions were shaped by this preoccupation.

KONINGSVELD, SADAN, and SAMARRA'I's work provides a scholarly publication of an Arabic 17th-century text dealing with Jewish messianism in Yemen in 1666 and 1667. The Arabic text is based on oral and written Muslim sources and thus provides a unique perspective on Jewish messianism in Yemen. The book includes a survey of the text, the manuscript, the author, and his purpose. It also provides a historical survey of the waves of messianic outbursts and details of the social and legal aspects of the status of Yemenite Jews in the 17th century. This is followed by a complete translation, edition, and reproduction of the Arabic text. This is a unique opportunity to examine an important phenomenon of Yemenite Judaism as it appeared to the Muslim bystander.

NEWBY's study is a reconstruction of Arabian Jewish history up to the early Islamic period and is based mostly on Muslim sources, which were often hostile to Jews and Judaism due to Jewish resistance to Muhammad and Islam. After defining the region he intends to examine, Newby scrutinizes the legends of the beginnings of the Jewish communities in Arabia. He then discusses the Roman period with special reference to the Jewish kingdom in Yemen under Dhu Nuwas. A central part of the study is devoted to the Jews of Hejaz and the results of their encounter with Muhammad and Islam. Special attention is given to historiographic and methodological issues.

NINI's book focuses mainly on the 19th century, examining the life of the Jewish community as a minority among the Muslims. It opens with a general description of the country, its population, administration, and political developments. Against this background developments within the community are examined, with special reference to communal institutions and leaders and the messianic movements of the 19th century. Nini also examines the relations of Yemenite Jews with Jews outside Yemen and the waves of immigration to Palestine between 1881 and 1914. The study is based on archival and published sources (mostly in Hebrew) and interviews.

Following a short history of the Jews of Yemen, PARFITT focuses on the community during the 20th century. He examines the attitude of the imam and the Muslims in general toward the community, their social, economic, and cultural life, and communal organization. Special attention is paid to the worsening of conditions for the community and the mass migration to Israel through Aden at mid-century. Parfitt utilizes archival sources, including a private archive and memoirs of one of the British participants in the emigration operation, and provides very detailed information on the emigration process.

TOBI's book is an insider's description of the Jewish community of Aden. Aden-born Tobi, who later immigrated to Israel and then to England, describes the history and life of the community. Following a survey of Aden and its Jews until the British conquest of 1839, Tobi examines the organization of the community and its social, economic, and cultural life, with details on the 1947 riots and the emigration that followed. Special attention is given to customs and festivals. With its lively personal description and numerous photographs and documents, this is a useful source on the community.

RACHEL SIMON

Yeshivot: Medieval

Beinart, Haim (editor), *Moreshet Sepharad/The Sephardi Legacy*, 2 vols., Jerusalem: Magnes Press of Hebrew University, 1992

Gil, Moshe, "The Babylonian Yeshivot and the Maghrib in the Early Middle Ages," *Proceedings of the American Academy for Jewish Research*, 57, 1990–1991

Goitein, S.D., *A Mediterranean Society: The Jewish Communities of the Arab World as Portrayed in the Documents of the Cairo Geniza*, vol. 2: *The Community*, Berkeley: University of California Press, 1967

Golb, Norman, *The Jews in Medieval Normandy: A Social and Intellectual History*, Cambridge and New York: Cambridge University Press, 1998

Kanarfogel, Ephraim, "Rabbinic Authority and the Right to Open an Academy in Medieval Ashkenaz," *Michael*, 12, 1991

Kanarfogel, Ephraim, *Jewish Education and Society in the High Middle Ages*, Detroit, Michigan: Wayne State University Press, 1992

Neuman, Abraham, *The Jews in Spain: Their Social, Political and Cultural Life during the Middle Ages*, 2 vols., Philadelphia: Jewish Publication Society, 1942

Pick, Shlomo, "The Jewish Communities of Provence before the Expulsion of 1306," Ph.D. diss., Bar Ilan University, 1996

Every major Jewish center during the Middle Ages boasted a network of talmudic academies. The differences between the centers had to do mostly with the means by which these yeshivot were sustained, the relationship between the yeshivot and the communities including the rights and prerogatives of the academy heads, the contents of the curriculum, and the level of the students. Complicating the picture is the fact that smaller or more informal study halls or adult groups, taught by lesser known figures, often functioned in the same locale or region as more formal or better known yeshivot.

During the geonic period, there were two central academies in Babylonia (Sura and Pumbedita, both of which relocated to Baghdad toward the end of the ninth century) and a central Palestinian academy. In addition to the gaon who headed each of these academies, there was an academic hierarchy of scholars charged with fulfilling various functions. A small number of families dominated the leadership of these well-organized institutions. These academies had two main sources of income: donations, which were sent together with questions addressed to the gaon, and taxes imposed on the communities in areas considered subject to the authority of one yeshivah or another.

GIL traces the connections between the Babylonian and Palestinian yeshivot and the Jewish communities of North Africa. There was a struggle between Palestine and Babylonia for influence on these communities, with Babylonia winning out in the early 11th century. Babylonia's ascendancy may be attributed both to the perceived superiority of its scholars and to the mass migration from Babylonia to the Maghreb. Until the first half of the tenth century, the connection between Babylonia and the Maghreb was almost exclusively through the academy of Sura. Gil presents evidence for the earliest ongoing contacts with Pumbedita. He also highlights the role that the community of Kairwan in Tunisia played in copying and distributing geonic responsa and in raising funds for the academies.

Much additional information about the central Palestinian academy has come to light in material from the Cairo Genizah. In addition to presenting Genizah material on the Gaonate, GOITEIN uses the Genizah documents to sketch a picture of the social and intellectual character of the yeshivot throughout the Middle East during this period. He notes the competition for students between the central or regional schools and the local study halls and attempts to determine the sizes of these different types of schools and the ages of their students. Goitein also traces the different titles of those who administered the various yeshivot. While scientific and philosophical study was popular among Jews in the Muslim world, the yeshivot do not seem to have taught these disciplines; instead, the academies offered only a traditional curriculum of talmudic, halakhic, and biblical studies.

The transition in the 11th century from the heyday of the geonic era to the period of the Rishonim is marked by a migration of Jews to western Europe and the establishment of yeshivot there. NEUMAN, in his social and cultural history of the Jews in medieval Spain, includes a chapter on the academies there. Despite the relative decentralization of authority, many of the issues that were of concern during the geonic period remained, including the means by which to support the schools, forms of communication between major yeshivot and local study halls, and the titles and responsibilities that academy heads were to carry. Neuman traces the leading yeshivot in Spain from the Muslim period through the period of the Christian Reconquista, describing their locations and their heads. Neuman suggests that a number of academies were housed in local synagogues, and he discusses the ways that rabbinic texts were provided to students and the difficulties that occasionally arose in this endeavor.

Several studies in BEINART also deal with the yeshivot in medieval Spain, filling in a number of new details as a result of more recent research. Avraham Grossman provides a comprehensive listing of the most significant academy heads and rabbinic scholars in medieval Spain from the Muslim period through the 15th century. He discusses their works, the nature of their contributions, and the locales and impact of their yeshivot. Contrary to the picture painted by Neuman and others, Yom Tov Assis argues that support and control of the yeshivot in medieval Spain, in both economic and curricular matters, was not the responsibility of a particular city or community. Rather, these initiatives were in the hands of individual scholars and patrons, while "societies" consisting of members drawn from the community, but functioning separately, were established in order to oversee these and other social and cultural services.

KANARFOGEL (1992) focuses on the yeshivot of medieval Ashkenaz but makes a number of comparative assessments in arriving at his conclusions. Ashkenazi society, beginning with the pre-Crusade period, was reluctant to pay advanced-level Torah scholars for their study or even for teaching, except under limited conditions. Although scholars should be aided in earning their livelihoods through business or other pursuits, Ashkenazi Jewry did not even grant tax exemptions for scholars until the late Middle Ages. Andalusian Jewry, on the other hand, typically gave financial support to their scholars, and this continued through the medieval period in Spain, despite the objections of Maimonides (who did advocate tax exemptions for scholars). Spanish and Provençal academies and communities provided stipends and funding for students, while there is almost no evidence of this in Ashkenaz.

In the pre-Crusade period, the Ashkenazi yeshivot were identified with the cities in which they were located (as were the leading European monasteries). As was the case, however, in regard to the cathedral schools and their masters (beginning c.1100), the academies of the tosafists were identified primarily with the head of the academy, not the locale in which they were situated. This may also have been a function, in part, of the dialectical method that was the hallmark of the tosafist academies and that depended in large measure on the intellectual capabilities of the academy head and his students (similar, once again, to the nature of the cathedral schools). In Spain and in Provence, following the pattern of the geonic yeshivot, centers of learning remained the more prominent consideration or means of identification. Communities often appointed the academy heads in Spain, using a formal instrument for this purpose. As KANARFOGEL (1991) demonstrates, the right to open an academy in Ashkenaz was governed not by the tenets of communal government but by the halakhically defined relationship between teachers and students.

Kanarfogel (1992) provides evidence for estimating the size of the tosafist academies. These yeshivot were located, for the most part, in the home of the principal, which meant that the size of an academy probably did not exceed 25. Leading Provençal and Spanish yeshivot, which were housed in synagogues or other specially designated communal structures, appear to have been larger. In additional to discussing the parameters of tosafist dialectic, Kanarfogel shows that biblical studies were not part of the regular curriculum in the academies of high medieval Ashkenaz, which marks another change from the pre-Crusade period.

In his chapter on the yeshivot of Provence in the 12th and 13th centuries, PICK argues that the Provençal academies underwent significant change during the period. In the 12th century, yeshivot catering to the most advanced students were, for the most part, communally maintained and supported. By the end of the 13th century, the academies became more identified with the scholars who headed them, and their focus was more on the discussion of halakhic works and conclusions than on talmudic casuistry. Pick also discusses the structures in which the yeshivot may have been housed.

GOLB suggests that the yeshivot in northern France were founded and maintained by the cities and towns in which they were located. Many of the sources, however, that Golb cites in support of his contention are Spanish or Provençal. Golb also relies on *Sefer Hukkei ha-Torah,* a unique blueprint for setting up a system of elementary education and for the founding of advanced talmudic academies. The place (or region) of origin of this document, however, and whether or not it was actually implemented remain matters of considerable scholarly contention. Finally, Golb believes that the Jewish communal structure discovered by archaeologists at Rouen (the capital of Normandy) is the remains of the communally funded academy characteristic of northern France (rather than a mere synagogue structure), and he advances the argument that this academy was an intellectual center of considerable importance during the 12th and 13th centuries.

EPHRAIM KANARFOGEL

See also Yeshivot: Modern

Yeshivot: Modern

Alon, Gedalyahu, "The Lithuanian Yeshivas," translated by Sid Z. Leiman in *The Jewish Expression,* edited by Judah Goldin, New York: Bantam, 1970

Heilman, Samuel C., *Defenders of the Faith: Inside Ultra-Orthodox Jewry,* New York: Schocken, 1992

Helmreich, William B., *The World of the Yeshiva: An Intimate Portrait of Orthodox Jewry,* New York: Free Press, and London: Collier Macmillan, 1982

Lichtenstein, Aharon, "The Ideology of Hesder," *Tradition,* 19, Fall 1981

Menes, Abraham, "The Yeshivot in Eastern Europe," in *The Jewish People, Past and Present,* vol. 2, New York: Jewish Encyclopedia Handbooks, 1955

Solomon, Norman, *The Analytic Movement: Hayyim Soloveitchik and His Circle* (South Florida Studies in the History of Judaism, no. 58), Atlanta, Georgia: Scholars Press, 1993

Yeshivot (singular, yeshivah) are academies for the advanced study of the Talmud and rabbinic literature. A Russian philosopher of religion once described the yeshivah as a personification of the Hegelian absolute. He was referring not merely to the extraordinary standards of knowledge and memory common among the academies' students, who paradigmatically knew the Talmud so intimately that were one to pierce a volume with a pin they were able to identify the word on each page through which the pin struck. He was also speaking of the intensity of the students' thirst for knowledge, their inner strength, and their self-sacrificing devotion to Torah study, which took priority over all other considerations. Similarly redolent of this consuming involvement, one of the characters in Chaim Grade's engrossing novel, *The Yeshiva,* nostalgically reminisces: "We'll never be able to get the Yeshiva out of our systems."

In his accessible study of the yeshivot in the modern period, MENES succinctly traces the revival of talmudic learning to the influence of the 18th-century Gaon of Vilna. Shortly after the Gaon's death, his disciple, Rabbi Hayim Volozhiner, founded the Volozhin Yeshivah in 1802, marking the beginning of a new epoch in the history of higher Jewish learning in Lithuania and Poland. Menes stresses that Rabbi Hayim was an able administrator, and the fact that only the best students were admitted to the yeshivah enhanced the prestige of the institution. Rabbi Hayim abolished the old custom of "eating days," which dictated that each day the student had to seek his meals in a different household. Instead, students received a modest stipend, which enabled them to live in a frugal but dignified manner. Soon, Menes demonstrates, other yeshivot adopted the model of the Volozhin Yeshivah. The author also discusses the yeshivot of the Musar movement, developed under the impetus of the 19th-century rabbi Israel Salanter Lipkin, where, in addition to the Talmud and its commentaries, moralist literature was studied and great stress was laid on the ethical factor in religious life, and he describes the leading Musar yeshivah, Kenesset Yisrael in Slabodka, near Kovno, Lithuania. Photographs of some of the yeshivot and their heads enhance the essay.

ALON studied at the Slabodka Yeshivah and later taught Talmud and Jewish history at the Hebrew University of Jerusalem. In this essay, which was published shortly after the destruction of the yeshivot by the Nazis, the author emphasizes that the yeshivot are not to be confused with seminaries for the training of rabbis. Rather, he identifies the primary aim of the yeshivot as the study of the Torah both for its own sake and to produce a group of learned Jews to act as a leaven that raises the standards of scholarship and piety in the community at large. In Slabodka, students used to say that "if a student prepared himself for ordination from the very start and studied the dietary laws in *Yoreh Deah,* you could be sure that he was neither gifted or knowledgeable in Torah." Even the followers of the Enlightenment, who aggressively criticized most traditional forms of Jewish life, sang the praises of the yeshivah students for their attachment to study and the search for truth. Alon mentions a hearsay report (happily confirmed later) that 300 students from the Mir Yeshivah, as well as fugitives from other yeshivot, had found wartime refuge in Shanghai, where they studied and taught the Torah with an even greater intensity than before. Indeed, these men plucked from the fire of the Nazi devastation were the pioneers who set up new yeshivot in the United States and, to a lesser extent, in Israel.

HELMREICH is a professor of sociology and Judaic studies at the City University of New York and an observant Jew who studied at several yeshivot. He combines four different approaches in his study of yeshivot in the United States: participant observation; in-depth interviews with the heads of the leading yeshivot, including Rabbis Moshe Feinstein (Mesivta Tifereth Yerushalayim), Shneur Kotler (Lakewood), Yitzchok Hutner (Chaim Berlin), and Joseph B. Soloveitchik (Yeshiva University); statistical information gathered from responses to a detailed questionnaire sent to the alumni of an unnamed yeshiva; and written material from a wide variety of sources, listed in the 11-page bibliography at the end of the book. The final chapters of the book consider whether the yeshivot are successful in reaching their goals. The author's answer is a guarded "yes." Helmreich concludes that the traditional yeshivah movement is here to stay. His statistical survey shows that 91 percent of yeshivah graduates continue to study the Talmud on a regular basis (two out of three do so daily), and an even greater percentage remain strictly Orthodox in their practice. The retention rate in the yeshivot is good, and the vast majority of graduates are committed to sending their children to yeshivot and to transmitting the same life pattern to the next generation. Despite Helmreich's generally sanguine appraisal, he does not overlook certain striking weaknesses and problems, two of which are particularly conspicuous: first, the exclusive emphasis in the curriculum (except at Yeshiva University) on Talmud study leaves the students deficient in such areas as Bible, Jewish history, and even in Hebrew language and grammar. Second, the opposition to secular learning in general, and college attendance in particular, fosters a feeling of insularity and smugness among the students about the superiority of their lifestyle, which is often expressed as intolerance of outsiders.

HEILMAN, an Orthodox Jewish sociologist, supplements Helmreich's study by investigating the ultraorthodox yeshivot in Israel. Heilman uses anthropological participant-observer methods to study the group from within; thus, he identifies with his subjects and their views and then steps back to examine his subjects critically but sympathetically. The study is extremely well written and free from technical jargon.

LICHTENSTEIN's essay is devoted to a type of yeshivah peculiar to the State of Israel. The *hesder* yeshivah reflects a special five-year arrangement through which high school graduates combine approximately 16 months of army service with advanced talmudic studies for the balance of the time. Students at these yeshivot have won the admiration of even vehemently anticlerical elements in Israeli society for their heroism in battle, and they have helped the religious community to avoid the stigma of parasitism that arises when regular yeshivah students acquire draft exemptions. At some of these *hesder* schools, particularly at the academy headed by Lichtenstein in Har Etzion, the level of learning is on a high plane, even if by no means comparable with the attainments common in such traditionalist Israeli yeshivot as Brisk, Hebron, or Ponevezh.

SOLOMON explicates with great success the complex methodology for talmudic studies first employed in the Lithuanian yeshivot that subsequently spread to all traditional academies of talmudic learning. At the end of the 19th century, Rabbi Hayim Soloveitchik and his circle created an impressive system of abstract concepts for understanding the Talmud and halakhah and their inner logic. Solomon compares the work of these talmudists to the analytical approach to jurisprudence first championed by John Austin in England and pursued by Justice Oliver Wendell Holmes in the United States and Hans Kelsen in Europe, although he detects no direct interplay of influence between the Lithuanian talmudists and these jurists. The author also contends that the method has affinities to philosophical analysis, a popular movement in Anglo-American philosophy in the middle of the 20th century that regards all philosophical problems as arising from a misuse of language and proposes that all confusions dissolve once the concepts are clearly analyzed. Many obscure passages in the Talmud do indeed become illuminated by the conceptual method that Solomon investigates. At the same time, however, the exponents of this method paid a price for their neglect of everything outside the "four ells of halakhah" and their dis-

dain of modern historico-critical studies. Their interpretations frequently fail simple historical tests, as when Maimonides, in a responsum unknown to Rabbi Hayim Soloveitchik, anticipates a difficulty raised and cleverly resolved by the latter and explains it away as the careless mistake of a copyist, who misplaced a subordinate clause in the text of Maimonides' Code.

JACOB HABERMAN

See also Yeshivot: Medieval

Yiddish Literature

Harshav, Benjamin, *The Meaning of Yiddish*, Berkeley: University of California Press, 1990
Liptzin, Solomon, *The Maturing of Yiddish Literature*, New York: David, 1970
Miron, Dan, *A Traveler Disguised: A Study in the Rise of Modern Yiddish Fiction in the Nineteenth Century*, New York: Schocken, 1973
Roskies, David G., *A Bridge of Longing: The Lost Art of Yiddish Storytelling*, Cambridge, Massachusetts: Harvard University Press, 1995
Wisse, Ruth R., *The Schlemiel as Modern Hero*, Chicago: University of Chicago Press, 1971

Yiddish literature has been an important part of Jewish cultural expression since the late Middle Ages when Northern European Jews began composing prose and poetry in their patois of Germanic, Hebrew, Slavic, and Romance elements. At the end of the 18th century, a distinct modern Yiddish literature diverged from old Yiddish literature. This division between the modern and the old involved content, style, and even language. Old Yiddish literature employed a stylized and crystallized Yiddish literary language that did not correspond to spoken Yiddish. Modern Yiddish literature, by contrast, employs a new literary Yiddish that is based on spoken dialects.

LIPTZIN's study presents an overview of Yiddish literature in the early 20th century, primarily between 1914 and 1939. He chronicles how Yiddish literature was invigorated by developments in the diaspora in the late 19th and early 20th centuries. Liptzin discusses the various literary movements within Yiddish literature in Europe and the Western hemisphere. At the beginning of each chapter, he helpfully lists the writers associated with the city or area under discussion. He then examines particular authors, focusing on literary style, major works, and significant literary contributions. Liptzin also includes relevant discussions of the historical context and social and political situations that shaped the types of Yiddish literature produced. This agreeable survey of individual Yiddish authors and the centers of creativity (New York, Kiev, Moscow, Minsk, Warsaw) is an excellent primer for anyone interested in the heyday of modern Yiddish literature.

WISSE's theme is the literary character of the *schlemiel* (loser) as depicted in the Yiddish literature of the 20th century. She discusses different aspects of the evolution of this stock character as well as the particular authors who prompted the developments. According to Wisse, the schlemiel represents a coping mechanism in response to a seemingly hostile world. The graver the circumstances and the dimmer the hope, the more the schlemiel transcends those circumstances and provides a valid, albeit unconventional, interpretation of events. Thus, Wisse argues, the schlemiel is the literary hero of a people who choose not to see the world as it is, but as it should be. The study begins with a brief history of the fool in the Jewish folklore of the Middle Ages and then turns to the schlemiel's literary debut in Adalbert von Chamisso's 1813 novel *Peter Schlemihl*. Next, Wisse traces the deepening of the character through the works of Mendele Moykher Sforim, Sholem Aleichem, and I. I. Trunk. Wisse also addresses the impact of the Holocaust on the use of the schlemiel in the work of Isaac Bashevis Singer, the effect of Americanization on the schlemiel, and the perception of the Jew in American literature. The monograph closes with a look at the groundbreaking works of Saul Bellow and the morose, antipathetic views of the schlemiel that prevailed in the 1960s.

As a backdrop for his examination of the writing of Sholem Yankev Abramovitsh, better known as Mendele Moykher Sforim (Mendele the Book Peddler), MIRON describes the literary movements among European Jews in the 19th century. The author explains that his book is about "loss and reinvention." The protagonists are those modern Jews who attempt to salvage supposedly traditional forms of culture for a nontraditional audience. Miron suggests that in this act of drawing on and modifying "traditional" forms, modern Yiddish literature is an act of "creative betrayal" that both draws from and feeds back into the collective life of the people. With great skill, he portrays the rise of Yiddish literature, paying special attention to the works of Sholem Aleichem and I.L. Peretz. After examining how Yiddish gradually supplanted Hebrew as the language of choice for many authors because of the creative freedom it offered, Miron turns to the truism that the determining characteristic of Yiddish literature is that it was written in Yiddish. He discusses the political, social, and psychological elements that made Yiddish a major literary language and highlights the scholastic and political hurdles that impeded the Yiddish literary movement.

The fundamental contribution of HARSHAV's study is his fine examination of Yiddish as a language. In the first part of the book, the author examines the history and nature of Yiddish and considers the various social, political, psychological, and etymological aspects of the language. In the second part, Harshav, like Miron, recounts the history of Yiddish literature. Harshav argues that the impetus of modern Yiddish literature came from the late-19th-century Ashkenazi enlightenment, the Haskalah, which catapulted Yiddish onto the literary stage by encouraging Ashkenazim to embrace the literary genres of their host culture and to become vital components within that culture. Prompted by the Haskalah, Jewish authors began using the Yiddish language and the poetic and prose forms current in their host culture. Harshav emphasizes the difficulties that accompanied the Yiddish writers' attempts to legitimize their use of the Yiddish language and popular writing styles. This section of the book treats European and U.S. Yiddish authors, and Harshav argues that most European authors followed the conventions of Russian poetic style, while U.S. authors attempted to develop their own distinct styles. Harshav's study concludes with an overview of the introspective movement in American Yiddish poetry, emphasizing the poetry of Jacob Glatshteyn.

ROSKIES gives a broad picture of the development of modern Yiddish literature from the stories of Nahman of Bratslav (18th century) to the work of post-Holocaust writers. In his chronological treatment of Rabbi Nahman, Isaac Meir Dik, I. L. Peretz, Sholem Aleichem, Der Nister (Pinkhes Kahanovitsh), Itzik Manger, Singer, and his fellow post-Holocaust authors, Roskies examines the sociological considerations that motivated these writers and their contemporaries to write in particular styles of Yiddish. He surveys the history of Yiddish typography, the characterization of Yiddish as the language of women and the uneducated, the ideological strife between the Haskalah and Hasidism, and the authors' struggles to validate their own use of Yiddish over Hebrew.

KEVIN EDWARD GRIFFITH

Yom Kippur *see* Festivals and Fasts; Sin and Atonement

Z

Zionism

Avineri, Shlomo, *The Making of Modern Zionism: Intellectual Origins of the Jewish State*, New York: Basic Books, and London: Weidenfeld and Nicolson, 1981

Berkowitz, Michael, *Zionist Culture and West European Jewry before the First World War*, Cambridge and New York: Cambridge University Press, 1993

Herzl, Theodor, *Der Judenstaat*, 1896; as *The Jewish State*, London: Nutt, 1896; New York: Maccabaean, 1904

Herzl, Theodor, *Altneuland*, 1902; translated by Lotta Levensohn as *Old-New Land*, New York: Bloch, 1941

Herzl, Theodor, *Theodor Herzls Tagebücher, 1895–1904*, 1922; as *The Diaries of Theodor Herzl*, New York: Grosset and Dunlap, 1956; London: Gollancz, 1958

Laqueur, Walter, *A History of Zionism*, New York: Holt, Rinehart and Winston, and London: Weidenfeld and Nicolson, 1972

Mosse, George L., *Confronting the Nation: Jewish and Western Nationalism* (Tauber Institute for the Study of European Jewry Series, 16), Hanover, New Hampshire: University Press of New England for Brandeis University Press, 1993

Pinsker, Leon, *Autoemancipation! Mahnruf an seine stammesgenossen von einem russischen Juden*, 1882; as *Auto-Emancipation*, New York: Maccabaean, 1906; London: Federation of Zionist Youth, 1937

Reinharz, Jehuda, *Chaim Weizmann* (Studies in Jewish History), New York: Oxford University Press, 1985

Reinharz, Jehuda and Walter Schatzberg (editors), *The Jewish Response to German Culture: From the Enlightenment to the Second World War*, Hanover, New Hampshire: University Press of New England for Clark University, 1985

Reinharz, Jehuda and Anita Shapira (editors), *Essential Papers on Zionism* (Essential Papers on Jewish Studies), New York: New York University Press, 1996

Urofsky, Melvin I., *American Zionism from Herzl to the Holocaust*, Garden City, New York: Anchor, 1975; London: University of Nebraska Press, 1995

Vital, David, *The Origins of Zionism*, Oxford: Clarendon, 1975

Vital, David, *Zionism: The Formative Years*, New York: Oxford University Press, and Oxford: Clarendon, 1982

Vital, David, *Zionism: The Crucial Phase*, New York: Oxford University Press, and Oxford: Clarendon, 1987

Zionism emerged as a political movement committed to the creation of a Jewish state in Palestine in the last decades of the 19th century, when European Jews responded both to the larger currents of romantic nationalism engulfing the continent and to rising antisemitism. Like other 19th-century European romantic nationalists who sought to ground their communal identity in a unified national culture, Zionists asserted that the new Jewish homeland would provide for a return to more pristine Jewish ways of living. As such, Zionism reinvigorated Jewish culture while also refocusing the priorities of that culture on the revival of a Jewish national consciousness. Zionism also inspired a revival of Hebrew as a literary and spoken language. With the founding of the State of Israel, a largely secular Zionist movement slowly incorporated Jewish religious elements into its self-understanding. By the 1970s, Zionism had become a virtually inseparable component of Jewish culture and identity. This essay reviews the views of two early Zionists and several works of history about the Zionist movement.

PINSKER articulates his vision of a Jewish state in response to Russia's pogroms in 1881 and 1882. Pinsker rejects assimilation as a viable response to antisemitism, contending that Jewish culture and tradition make Jews foreigners regardless of the specific European communities in which they reside. Given their unique language and history, Jews can only survive as Jews if they regain their historical sense of national dignity and establish a state to ensure their personal security. Pinsker directs Jewish nationalistic aspirations toward the political and cultural self-liberation of the Jewish community. Along with Herzl's works, Pinsker's treatise should be counted among the cornerstones of modern Zionism.

Herzl, the symbolic father of modern Zionism and an early advocate of a more secular vision of a Jewish homeland, reflects the spirit of the German-Jewish Enlightenment. In Paris as the representative of a liberal Vienna newspaper, he covered the 1894 Dreyfus Affair. Dreyfus—a model of the assimilated Jew and a proud officer of the French military, willing to die for his country—was tried and convicted of treason, a verdict that revealed to Herzl an unexpected layer of virulent antisemitism in French society. In response, he moved away from assimilation, acculturation, and conversion as possible solutions to the so-called Jewish problem. Although unaware of what Pinsker had written a decade earlier, Herzl similarly concludes that antisemitism remains an all-pervasive factor in European culture and a threat to European Jewry. As evident in HERZL (1922), Herzl felt a sense of mission and immediacy as he composed HERZL (1896), in which he places the so-called Jewish problem squarely within the arena of international politics, arguing that the normalization of the Jewish presence in the world would be possible only through the creation of a Jewish state. HERZL (1902) is a novel that envisions a utopia in which Jews cooperate in the utilization of scientific advances and natural resources.

LAQUEUR offers an effective overview of the origins and course of Zionism from the French Revolution through the creation of the State of Israel. He identifies antisemitism as the primary force behind the movement's emergence and also stresses the effects of Zionism on the Arabs. This is primarily a political history; Laqueur does not address cultural or social issues in significant depth.

VITAL's three-volume series (1975, 1982, 1987) delving into Zionism's political and institutional history follows the interpretive model of Vladimir Jabotinsky, arguing that Zionism elevated Jews from the role of objects of history to that of historical actors who guide and shape their own future. Vital's analysis of political issues is considerably deeper than Laqueur's, but like Laqueur, Vital places little emphasis on cultural and intellectual trends. Nevertheless, Vital's work is still considered the classic among overviews of the history of political Zionism.

REINHARZ and SHAPIRA present a massive collection of 31 articles that describe Zionism as a national movement with clear ideological origins, demonstrating that as the movement rejected the Uganda solution, it also distanced itself from the idea of the diaspora. The volume also shows how Zionism's modest successes in Europe in the early 20th century did not prevent splits within the movement or its Americanization, and it explains that Zionism in the land of Israel differed from its European and American counterparts on the question of how to transform long-held national myths into an authentic Jewish state. Five articles explore the Zionists' conflict with the British and Arabs regarding plans for the future of Palestine, and the final four chapters address the emergence of a new and unique Hebrew culture in Palestine.

REINHARZ and SCHATZBERG offer 17 essays that explore Jewish responses to changes in German culture from the Enlightenment through the Second World War; collectively, they provide important background for the history of Zionism. The opening essays outline the attempts by German Jews to assimilate into German society. While Emancipation allowed the possibility of a respectable place within society, German Jews coupled German *Bildung* with social respectability. Within German Jewry, concerted efforts were made to minimize those aspects of Jewish tradition that alienated Jews from German culture and society. Yet as quickly as German Jewry adapted new modes of defining its identity, antisemitic trends in German culture increasingly viewed Jews as social outsiders. Thus, Zionism took hold as some Jews realized the failure of their attempts at assimilation and became motivated to look for new options.

AVINERI's inquiry into the intellectual origins of modern Zionism traces its evolution through the lives of 17 leading Zionists. Beginning with Nachman Krochmal and Heinrich Graetz, European Jewry recovered its sense as a historical force. As Jewish nationalists toyed with contemporary political ideologies and movements, Jewish intellectuals responded to the challenges of modernity, the Enlightenment, and Jewish tradition. Drawing from Pinsker's idea of self-emancipation and Herzl's vision of a Jewish state, some Zionist thinkers placed European Jewry at the crux of a crisis of Western civilization. Nachman Syrkin, Ber Borochov, and Aharon David Gordon reflected the attitudes of Eastern European Jewry and gravitated toward the ideologies of the political left, while Asher Ginzberg, Yehiel Michal Pines, and the more religiously inclined, mingled political Zionism with a sense that the creation of a Jewish state would also be a form of religious fulfillment. Avineri brings Zionism into contemporary history with a discussion of David Ben-Gurion, a leader willing to be ruthless in his pursuit of the power necessary to realize the goals of the Zionist movement. A political pragmatist, Ben-Gurion sought the diplomatic and military alliances in the international arena that would further the realization of Zionist objectives and then protect the nascent Israeli state. In conclusion, Avineri regards Zionism as a permanent revolution: revolutionary in its impact on Jewish identity and permanent in its continued emphasis on Jewish distinctiveness.

MOSSE uses a sophisticated cultural-intellectual perspective to guide his analysis of the interplay of European Jewry and rising nationalism. Within 12 short essays, Mosse traces the rise of European nationalism from the French Revolution through its emergence as the new secular religion. Anchored in Enlightenment thought and pursuing assimilation through education, Western European Jewry failed to recognize that the rise of the German Nazi party was part of a larger shift in European civilization toward anti-intellectualism. Similarly, most European Jews did not sufficiently realize that in an increasingly insecure world, their more humanistic liberalism was at odds with the secular ideologies of the Italian Futurist movement and U.S. culture in general (both of which lauded modern technologies and materialism as symbols of prosperity and power). However, two Zionists of successive generations, Max Nordau and Gershom Scholem, were well aware of the growing gap between Jews and their surrounding societies, and they presented within their studies of Jewish history, culture, and religion a vision of Jewish nationalism that avoided the pitfalls of European nationalism by preserving liberal values. While Mosse's work may not seem as directly related to the rise of political Zionism as the studies of the previously mentioned authors, his careful weaving together of European and Jewish cultural-intellectual history provides a dynamic and original interpretation of the context from which Zionism emerged.

BERKOWITZ focuses on the Zionist movements in Central and Western Europe from 1897 to 1914, stressing their efforts to bring conceptions of Jewish identity closer to the Zionist program. Specifically, Zionists emphasized their commitment to revitalizing Jewish uniqueness, and they integrated middle-class European Jewry's nationalism and hopes for full emancipation with the call for a modernized humanist Judaism. It was this combination of politics and culture within the Zionist ideology that eventually sufficed to motivate Western European Jewry to celebrate the renaissance of Jewish nationalism and to welcome calls for a Jewish state in Palestine.

REINHARZ's well-documented biography of Chaim Weizmann uses a vast array of resources, including personal correspondence, speeches, and press accounts, to follow Weizmann from his emergence as a Zionist leader through his role as Israel's first president. In this important political history, Reinharz describes Weizmann's careful efforts to balance relationships among the leading Zionist personalities involved in the formation of a Jewish state, as well as among Zionist and British policy makers.

UROFSKY turns his talents toward a study of Zionism in the United States and the role played by Louis D. Brandeis in the U.S. movement. Brandeis directed U.S. Zionism to provide financial, moral, and political support for Jewish settlement in Palestine, but—unlike Weizmann—he did little to recruit those seeking to settle in Palestine. As Urofsky interprets it, American Zionism lacked ideological depth. The distance between American and continental European Zionism grew as Europeans criticized the unwillingness of Jews in the United States to break ties with American culture and become more physically involved in the establishment of a Jewish state in Palestine. European Zionists did not understand that their U.S. counterparts perceived a vicarious Zionism to be a means of preserving both a Jewish and an American identity, without violating their commitment to the creation of a Jewish state.

DAVID MEIER

See also Israel, State of: Judaism in; Kibbutz; Zionism, Labor; Zionism, Revisionist

Zionism, Labor

Cohen, Mitchell, *Zion and State: Nation, Class, and the Shaping of Modern Israel*, Oxford and New York: Blackwell, 1987

Kimmerling, Baruch, *Zionism and Economy*, Cambridge, Massachusetts: Schenkman, 1983

Lockman, Zachary, *Comrades and Enemies: Arab and Jewish Workers in Palestine, 1906–1948*, Berkeley: University of California Press, 1996

Merhav, Peretz, *The Israeli Left: History, Problems, Documents*, San Diego, California: Barnes, and London: Tantivy, 1980

Preuss, Walter, *The Jewish Labour Movement in Palestine: Its Aims and Achievements*, Berlin: Verbandsbüro Po'alei Zion, 1928

Preuss, Walter, *The Labour Movement in Israel: Past and Present,* Jerusalem: Mass, 1965

Shafir, Gershon, *Land, Labor, and the Origins of the Israeli-Palestinian Conflict, 1882–1914* (Cambridge Middle East Library, 20), Cambridge and New York: Cambridge University Press, 1989; updated edition, Berkeley: University of California Press, 1996

Shalev, Michael, *Labour and the Political Economy in Israel* (Library of Political Economy), Oxford and New York: Oxford University Press, 1992

If the aim of Zionism was to revive a Jewish national life in Palestine, its realization would have been impossible without the concomitant establishment of a viable Jewish economic life in the country. Unlike most other settler movements, which received economic and military support from colonial rulers, Jewish immigrants were forced to develop their own socioeconomic structures to ensure the burgeoning yishuv's survival and growth. The labor movement played a decisive role in this process, substantially establishing the Jewish economic and security systems first of pre-1948 Palestine and then of Israel.

PREUSS (1928) is a monograph produced for the left-wing Po'alei Zion movement. It describes the labor movement's understanding of Palestine and its indigenous population, which would play a determinant role in the evolution of labor Zionist ideology and practice. The tract explains "the importance of colonizing and opening up new countries by means of labor and not by exploitation. . . . The settlement of backward and undeveloped countries is an integral part of upbuilding a socialist commonwealth."

PREUSS (1965) similarly contends that Palestine's condition as "sparsely populated and neglected" meant that from the beginning "conventional methods of class warfare were inadequate." The goal of the labor movement in the 1920s, then, was to build a new Jewish commonwealth that would ensure for the entire population "a decent existence and maintenance . . . of the civilized standards [of] Eastern Europe."

This combined socialist and colonial ideology profoundly influenced the construction of Zionist, and subsequently Israeli, national identities. Yet their conflation and the effect on pre- and post-1948 policies were not examined by scholars until recently.

For example, MERHAV offers a detailed history of the various components of the Zionist and Israeli "Left," moving chronologically from the foundations of the labor movement in the diaspora through the establishment, union, and dissolution of the numerous parties that emerged in Palestine during the late Ottoman and Mandate periods and finally ending with the gradual demise of labor hegemony in post-1948 Israel, epitomized by the victory of the Likud in 1977. Merhav's analysis attempts to elucidate the lines of development and stages of consolidation of the labor movement, in particular the trend by the Ahdut ha-'Avodah and later Mapai parties toward "reformism" and the compromise of socialist principles for the sake of party unity. Yet Merhav's general avoidance of discussing the Left's conflictual relationship with either its main economic competitor, the Palestinian Arab workers, or its primary ideological adversary, the Revisionist movement, means that the reader cannot contextualize or prioritize the wealth of details presented in his descriptive analysis.

Such lacunae are partially addressed by COHEN, whose central thesis is that the well-known political triumph of the labor movement in the 1930s was accompanied by a self-transformation crucial for shaping the future of Israeli politics in the post-1948 period, that is, the "reification" of the state by the Labor leadership (the term is borrowed from Georg Lukác's reading of Marx). This process was epitomized by Ben-Gurion's concept of *mamlakhtiyut*, which symbolized the move from a desire to create an *am oved,* or working nation in its own state, to the idea of a state standing above all classes as a "thing unto itself."

Under Ben-Gurion's leadership, statism dominated the labor movement, which, with the Histadrut as its "state" apparatus, identified itself with the state rather than identifying the nation's interests with those of the working class. Concomitant with this reification of the state was the positioning of the army as the "key mediator between the individual and the state and society," a development prompted by the centrality of the discourse of security in Zionist and then Israeli politics after 1936. Even more, Ben-Gurion posited that only the army could play the vital role of educating and socializing immigrants from dozens of countries into citizens of a new Israeli nation. In Cohen's view, the ideology of *mamlakhtiyut* sowed the seeds for labor's later defeat by the Right in 1977, which can be understood as the natural realization of the militant, statist worldview that Ben-Gurion's labor and Jabotinsky's "revisionist" ideologies shared, despite their differences in strategy.

If a central tenet of Ben-Gurion's statism was the paramount importance of security, Shafir and Lockman help us understand how the security discourse arose out of the economic competition between Jewish and Arab workers and its relationship to the land question in Palestine. SHAFIR's analysis focuses on the period before World War I, which he sees as the formative period for the ideologies and practices underlying both the Israeli and the Palestinian national movements. His thesis is that before they could exert authority over the growing Zionist community, the agricultural pioneers who would lead the labor movement first had to crystallize their own method of state and nation formation during the period from 1882 to 1914. His investigation demonstrates that the "militant, exclusivist nationalism" that ultimately characterized labor Zionism evolved specifically out of several simultaneous struggles on the behalf of Jewish workers: against the difficulties of adapting to strenuous agricultural labor, against the low wages paid by the Jewish planters, and against the Palestinian workers who accepted wages far below what most Jews could endure. Out of these struggles the concept of "Kibush Avodah," or the "Conquest of Labor," was born.

When by 1909 the Conquest of Labor proved to be an "abysmal failure," the labor movement transformed the object of conquest from the labor market to the land itself. With this new focus on land as the prerequisite for building a socialist Jewish economy, the kibbutz emerged as a primary device for conquering both land and labor for Jews. Shafir's analysis reveals that the two primary conflicts between Arabs and Jews before 1948—labor and land—had their roots in the incipient Zionist labor movement's struggle for survival.

Picking up on Shafir's insights, LOCKMAN attempts to construct a "relational history" of Jews and Arabs in Palestine/Israel, that is, a history that understands that through "mutually formative interactions" both Jewish and Arab communities "shaped one another in complex ways and at many levels." Specifically, Lockman examines the often simultaneously conflictual and cooperative relationship between the Jewish labor movement and the Arab working class (in particular, between Arab and Jewish railway workers), comparing the reality of Arab-Jewish relations to the rhetoric of the Zionist labor leadership and the "conquest of labor," as well as analyzing evolving "security" strategies in the wake of the Arab revolt of 1936 to 1939.

By explaining the relationship between labor Zionist and colonial discourses, Lockman helps us understand the ideology underlying the earlier studies presented above. He argues that a colonialist understanding of Palestine as being "neglected" and its native inhabitants as being "backward" has combined with the language of socialism, class struggle, and international working-class solidarity to create the contradictory (socialist and nationalist) impulses of labor Zionism that to this day characterize the movement's socioeconomic policies and its stances on peace and security.

Kimmerling and Shalev combine the sociological and historiographic approaches of Shafir and Lockman with econometric analyses of the Zionist/Israeli economies during the pre- and post-1948 periods. In so doing, these two authors help us understand the economic ramifications of labor Zionist ideology and policies over time, and they illuminate how evolving economic realities (both internal and worldwide trends) led to fundamental changes in both.

KIMMERLING examines how the Zionist movement managed to accomplish its major goal of establishing a Jewish state despite its "economic nonviability" in comparison to other immigrant-settler societies. Kimmerling analyzes the main streams of Zionist economic ideology and their interaction with the actual economic reality in Palestine/Israel by discussing the processes of change that occurred in Israeli society as it shifted from a model of economic activity anchored in Zionist ideology and the needs of state-building to an economy based on increased industrialization in the decades after achieving sovereignty.

The author begins by explaining that the early labor Zionist "pioneering economy" was distinguished from the economies of other colonial movements because the Zionists lacked abundant and inexpensive land and faced ideological constraints on exploiting the cheap local labor. Kimmerling then shows how this type of economic regime affected the influx of Jewish capital to the country and the resulting development of both the Arab and Jewish sectors of the economy during the Mandate period, particularly through the transfer of this Jewish capital to the Arab sector through land purchases and employment. (Despite labor Zionism's ideological opposition to employing Arab labor, Arabs constituted a significant percentage of the Jewish economy's workforce until 1936.) He also discusses how the Jewish socioeconomic system's dependence on exchange with the Arab sector led Arab leaders to engage in "economic warfare" against Jews in order to cripple the Jewish economy. Like labor Zionism's exclusivist ideology, the attempts to seal off the Arab economy did not achieve long-term success.

The second half of the book examines how sovereignty changed the dynamics of both labor Zionist ideology and the Israeli economy. Like Cohen, Kimmerling discusses the importance of statism for constructing a role for the state as a "rich father," tightly controlling disbursement of the postindependence inflow of foreign capital. Funds were coming from immigrants, the floating of bonds and loans, diaspora contributions, German reparations, and the like, and the state began to act as an "economic (institutional) entrepreneur that tried to develop the economy and to administer a social policy" through selective investments in the private sector. Kimmerling concludes his study by examining the far-reaching changes that occurred in the kibbutz system in the era of sovereignty, particularly the industrialization of the kibbutz economy. This economic change led to a dimming of the ideological role of the kibbutz in Israeli society from its earlier position as "the most original creation of the Zionist enterprise," with its emphasis on building an egalitarian society based on productive physical labor (all of which centered around agriculture). The 1977 Likud victory and the subsequent liberalization and consumerization of the economy signified the diminishing status of the kibbutz and the Labor party hegemony which supported it.

SHALEV provides perhaps the most in-depth analysis of the relationship between labor ideology and economic policy available in English or Hebrew. In line with the methodological focus on labor unions and parties underlying the "new political economy," the book focuses exclusively on the history and policies of the Histadrut and the Mapai party. Shalev begins by addressing how and why the Histadrut deviated from European models of labor organization, particularly in its concern for the realization of national interests in the rural sector rather than the class interests of urban wage-earners. The imbrication of the concerns of labor with Zionist policy demonstrates that the economic dynamics of the meeting between Arabs and Jews in the labor market set into motion both Jewish labor exclusivism and ethnic tension between the two communities. Like Shafir, Shalev finds that these developments began around 1908 as the image of the Jewish laborers underwent ideological transformation from that of wage-earners competing with Arabs to that of settlers struggling to acquire territory.

Shalev also explains why, after 1948, the Arab minority (and, later, Palestinians from the West Bank and Gaza) became incorporated into a segmented labor system rather than participating in a labor market based on upward mobility and full integration. He attributes the emergent labor policies as much to the pursuance by the Histadrut of its perceived labor-market interests as to continued national hostility toward Arabs. The author next evaluates the historical dominance of the Mapai party, attributing its central role to the extensive overlap between the interests of the working and middle classes, the relatively small role of private capital in the Jewish/Israeli economy, and the Mapai's focus on territorial and military expansionism in the postsovereignty era. He concludes that the economic crises of the 1960s and 1970s, along with the incorporation of the Occupied Territories and subsequent militarization of the Israeli economy after 1967, gradually led to changes in economic and political policy and, particularly, to the weakening of the state economy vis-à-vis both domestic business interests and foreign trends. These developments, in turn, weakened the hegemony of both the Histadrut and the Mapai party. In this way, Shalev demonstrates the determinative roles played by both national conflict and worldwide economic developments in the political economy of pre- and postsovereignty Israel.

MARK LEVINE

Zionism, Revisionist

Katz, Shmuel, *Lone Wolf: A Biography of Vladimir (Ze'ev) Jabotinsky*, 2 vols., New York: Barricade, 1996

Laqueur, Walter, "In Blood and Fire: Jabotinsky and Revisionism," in his *A History of Zionism*, New York: Holt, Rinehart and Winston, and London: Weidenfeld and Nicolson, 1972; reprinted with a new introduction, New York: Schocken Books, 1989

Schechtman, Joseph B., *The Vladimir Jabotinsky Story*, vol. 1: *Rebel and Stateman: The Early Years*, New York: Yoseloff, 1956, and vol. 2: *Fighter and Prophet: The Last Years*, New York: Yoseloff, 1961

Schechtman, Joseph B. and Yehuda Benari, *History of the Revisionist Movement*, vol.1: *1925–1930*, Tel-Aviv: Hadar, 1970

Shapiro, Yonathan, *The Road to Power: Herut Party in Israel*, Albany: State University of New York Press, 1991

Shavit, Jacob, *Jabotinsky and the Revisionist Movement, 1925–1948*, London and Totowa, New Jersey: Cass, 1988

Weinbaum, Laurence, *A Marriage of Convenience: The New Zionist Organization and the Polish Government 1936–1939* (East European Monographs, no. 369), New York: Columbia University Press, 1993

Revisionist Zionism began in 1925 as a militant faction within the international Zionist movement. Revisionism's founder, the Russian Zionist orator Vladimir Ze'ev Jabotinsky, called for a revision of the Zionist movement's strategy for achieving a Jewish national home in Palestine, a strategy he regarded as excessively cautious. Jabotinsky's dissatisfaction with the Zionist leadership's responses to Palestinian Arab violence and British policy in Palestine led to the secession of the Revisionists from the Zionist movement in 1935. After Jabotinsky's death, his followers spearheaded the armed Jewish revolt against British forces in Palestine from 1944 to 1947. They subsequently entered the political arena as the Herut Party, forerunner of the contemporary Likud Party in Israel.

The early historiography of Revisionism was the work of movement veterans who tended to portray its activities in uncritical terms. SCHECHTMAN's two-volume biography of Jabotinsky, followed by SCHECHTMAN and BENARI, the first volume of a projected two-volume history of Revisionism (the second volume never appeared), offers a view of the Zionist firebrand and his movement through the eyes of one of his former senior aides. According to Schechtman and Benari, the Revisionists are scorned prophets: if heeded, Jabotinsky's pleas to European Jewry to emigrate en masse to Palestine during the 1930s would have preempted the Holocaust; the Revisionists' early skepticism regarding British intentions was borne out by the subsequent shifts in British policy against Zionism; and the Revisionists' advocacy of a more forceful approach to Palestinian Arab hostility, if adopted, would have checked the violent Arab outbreaks of the 1920s and 1930s. As for the fate of the movement itself, Schechtman and Benari maintain that the Revisionists might well have been elected to lead the world Zionist movement if not for the widely publicized, although ultimately unproved, accusations that several of their members were involved in the assassination of Labor Zionist leader Haim Arlosoroff in 1933, at the pinnacle of Revisionism's popularity.

The first serious critique of the Revisionist movement was that of LAQUEUR. He agrees that Revisionism had strong appeal in the Jewish world, especially among East European Jewish youth. Laqueur further notes that in retrospect there is no doubt the movement "recognized certain basic facts [about Palestine and the situation of European Jewry] earlier and more clearly than other Zionist parties." At the same time, while absolving Jabotinsky himself of his rivals' accusations of fascism, Laqueur is critical of what he regards as "the fascist aberrations of some of his followers," which in Laqueur's view Jabotinsky made no serious effort to combat. Laqueur also takes the Revisionists to task for criticizing British rule in Palestine while offering no alternative allies to whom the Zionist movement might turn.

A partial rejoinder to the latter point is the finding of WEINBAUM that the secret alliance between the Revisionists and the Polish government between 1936 and 1939 resulted in Polish military assistance to the Revisionists' militant underground, as well as Polish aid for Revisionist transports of unauthorized Polish Jewish immigrants to Palestine in defiance of British quota restrictions.

Laqueur concludes that Revisionism, whatever its achievements, is little more than a relic of the Zionist past. While other Zionist factions went on to become a part of contemporary Israeli political culture, "the history of revisionism ends with the death of the leader," he writes. "Jabotinsky left no clear message to be readily applied in the world of the 1970s."

Later historians saw Jabotinsky's legacy in a different light, especially after Jabotinsky's disciples, the Likud Party, were for the first time elected to power in Israel in 1977, five years after Laqueur's assessment appeared. SHAVIT, in contrast to Laqueur, asserts that "no Zionist leader continues to be as relevant for his followers as does Jabotinsky." In Shavit's view, Revisionism "produced a deep-rooted and organic political tradition" that, while for several decades confined to the political opposition, eventually emerged victorious and "became a part of the mainstream of the prevailing Israeli political and ideological reality."

On the specific points of historical controversy, Shavit falls somewhere between Schechtman and Laqueur. Shavit is less convinced than Laqueur as to the influence of fascism within the Revisionist rank and file, regarding the alleged parallels between the Revisionists and European fascists as superficial. At the same time, Shavit finds far less merit than Schechtman in the specifics of the Revisionist platform. "Revisionism offered Zionism a way it could not possibly follow," Shavit contends, maintaining that the gradual building of a Palestinian Jewish society, rather than a political or military struggle or immediate mass immigration, was the key to the realization of Zionist goals.

In SHAPIRO's analysis of the evolution of the Revisionists' Herut Party and the factors leading to its electoral triumph in 1977, the pre–World War II European nationalist movements are said to have been of decisive influence in the shaping of Revisionism. While not quite branding Revisionism fascist, Shapiro contends that Polish nationalism was the model for the development of the Revisionist movement into a "leader party," centered first around Jabotinsky and later Menahem Begin. After Israel's creation in 1948, Herut refrained from developing the favor-doling bureaucracy typical of Israeli political parties and instead emphasized what Shapiro calls "status politics," appealing to those who felt politically or culturally excluded from the Israeli ruling establishment. In the 1970s Herut's regular constituency was supplemented by large numbers of Sephardi Jews—immigrants and children of immigrants from Arab countries—who had suffered discrimination at the hands of the ruling Labor Party. This alliance of traditional Revisionists and Sephardim propelled Jabotinsky's heirs to power.

Although KATZ, like Schechtman, is an alumnus of the Revisionist movement, his 1996 biography of Jabotinsky is a far more serious work of scholarship than Schechtman's, utilizing a wealth of original documents from archives on several continents and covering many aspects of Jabotinsky's life that Schechtman missed. While Schechtman is loath to criticize the Revisionist leader, Katz is more objective and does not mind pointing out Jabotinsky's failings, although he does not find very many of them. Katz believes that historical events such as the Holocaust, Britain's turn against Zionism, and Arab belligerency vindicate the Revisionist view of the Jewish people as trapped in a hostile world where survival has always depended upon strength and assertiveness.

RAFAEL MEDOFF

Zohar

Dan, Joseph, *The Zohar and Its Generation* (Jerusalem Studies in Jewish Thought, vol. 8), Jerusalem: Magnes, 1989

Giller, Pinchas, *The Enlightened Will Shine: Symbolization and Theurgy in the Later Strata of the Zohar* (SUNY Series in Judaica), Albany: State University of New York Press, 1993

Huss, Boaz, "*Sefer ha-Zohar* as a Canonical, Sacred and Holy Text: Changing Perspectives of the Book of Splendor between the Thirteenth and Eighteenth Centuries," *Journal of Jewish Thought and Philosophy*, 7, 1997

Liebes, Yehuda, *Studies in the Zohar* (SUNY Series in Judaica), Albany: State University of New York Press, 1993

Scholem, Gershom, *Major Trends in Jewish Mysticism* (Hilda Strook Lectures), New York: Schocken, 1941; 3rd edition, New York: Schocken, 1954; London: Thames and Hudson, 1955

Tishby, Isaiah and Yeruham Fishel Lachower, *Mishnat ha-Zohar,* 1949; translated by David Goldstein as *The Wisdom of the Zohar* (Littman Library of Jewish Civilization), Oxford and New York: Oxford University Press, 1989

The Zohar is the most important work in Jewish mysticism. Widely circulated in esoteric circles in the Middle Ages and very generally accepted as canonical or sacred among the majority of the world's Jews from the Renaissance through the 19th century, its teachings formed the basis of most subsequent Jewish mysticism. The Zohar is not a single work but a collection of some two dozen separate compositions, comprising in published editions more than 1,200 folios of densely printed Aramaic text. Modern scholars of Kabbalah, such as Gershom Scholem and Isaiah Tishby, posit a process of literary development that can be charted from the confusion of the Zohar's structure. According to this "documentary hypothesis," the mysticism of the Zohar developed from a system based in philosophy to one based in theosophy.

Scholem's earliest research on the Zohar dealt with whether Moses de Leon wrote the Zohar and suggested, idealistically perhaps, that the work's origins were in antiquity and not at the hand of that 13th-century Castilian mystic. Only later did Scholem conclude that de Leon composed the whole text. The essay "The Zohar: The Book and Its Author" in SCHOLEM analyzes the trail of linguistic mistakes and anachronisms that make clear the work's late origins. Busy explaining de Leon's literary method, Scholem neglected to do justice to him as a towering spiritual and artistic genius of the Middle Ages. Scholem maintains that de Leon wrote the main sections of the Zohar, then composed the Hebrew writings for which he claimed authorship. In this way, Scholem explains these works' references to the Zohar.

In his introduction to TISHBY and LACHOWER, Tishby was able to conclude to the contrary that the Zohar was largely written after the Hebrew works of de Leon. This monumental two-volume thematic systematization of the Zohar includes extensive topical introductions to the book's major preoccupations and provides excellent translations of a number of its sections. Tishby's introductions to every section are among the most cogent treatments of kabbalistic material available in English.

LIEBES has made a strong case for multiple authorship of a number of compositions originally credited to Moses de Leon. Liebes associates the origins of this circle of mystics with the gnostic kabbalists of Castile: Bahya ben Asher, Joseph ben Shalom Ashkenazi, and Todros Abulafia. Beyond this analysis, Liebes emphasizes the extent to which the Zohar's authors lost their own identities in the process of developing a new romantic mythos that linked the Galilean mystics of talmudic antiquity directly with the coming messianic age. Liebes also includes English translations of two of his most important articles, "The Messiah of the Zohar" and "How Was the Zohar Written?" In these articles, Liebes addresses issues of the Zohar's authorship, the dominant themes therein, and the underlying rationale for its pseudepigraphical nature.

There has been a flowering of advanced Zohar scholarship in recent years, much of which is encapsulated in DAN, which appears as a volume of the journal *Jerusalem Studies in Jewish Thought,* itself one of the most important venues for relevant scholarship in the last three decades. While most of the contributions to Dan's volume are in Hebrew, these are briefly summarized by Dan in his introduction. Among the important studies published in English in this volume are those by Ronald Kiener on Islam in the Zohar, Stephen Benin on Christian parallels to the Zohar's conception of divine passibility, and Mark Verman on 13th-century kabbalistic practice prior to the appearance of the Zohar.

HUSS addresses the ways in which the Zohar gained status as an essential sacred text in Judaism. GILLER addresses a number of themes in the Zohar's later sections. Both of these works trace the movement of the Zohar from the margins of the Jewish literary heritage to its center.

PINCHAS GILLER

Zoroastrianism and Judaism *see* Dualism

INDEXES

BOOKLIST INDEX

Books and articles discussed in the entries are listed here by author/editor name. The page numbers refer to the booklists themselves, where full publication information is given.

GENERAL INDEX

Page numbers in **bold** indicate subjects with their own entries.

687

NOTES ON CONTRIBUTORS

Howard Tzvi Adelman. Lecturer, Mofet Institute and Achva Academic College, Beer Tuvia. Contributor to *The Expulsion of the Jews: 1492 and After* edited by Raymond Waddington and Arthur Williamson (1994), *Proceedings of the Eleventh World Congress of Jewish Studies* (1994), *Women of the World: Women and Jewish Writing* edited by Judith Baskin (1994), *Gender and Judaism* edited by T. Rudavsky (1995), and *American Historical Association's Guide to Historical Literature* (1995). **Essays:** Authority, Rabbinic and Communal; Education; History: General Histories, Premodern Authors; Human Rights; Israel, Land of: History; Jewish Studies; Literature, Jewish; Marranism; Nasi Family; Renaissance.

Rebecca Alpert. Assistant Professor of Religion and Women's Studies, Temple University, Philadelphia. Author of *Exploring Judaism: A Reconstructionist Approach* (with Jacob Staub, 1986) and *Like Bread on the Seder Plate: Jewish Lesbians and the Transformation of Tradition* (1997). Editor of *The Reconstructionist* (1994–). Contributor to *Tikkun, Shofar, Religious Institutions and Women's Leadership* edited by C. Wessinger (1996), *Judaism since Gender* (1997), and *Religion and Sex in American Public Life* edited by K. Sands (1999). **Essay:** Homosexuality.

Eleanor Amico. Independent scholar. Editor of *Reader's Guide to Women's Studies* (1998). Contributor to *Great Lives from History: American Women* (1995), *Identities in Literature* (1997), *On the Market: Surviving the Academic Job Search*, edited by Christine Boufis and Victoria C. Olsen (1997), *The Encyclopedia of Modern Social Issues* (1997), and *Dictionary of World Biography* (1999). **Essays:** Chosen People; Symbols and Symbolism.

Robert Ash. Doctoral candidate, Department of Sociology, University of Leicester. **Essays:** Great Britain; Secularism.

Shawn Zelig Aster. Doctoral candidate in Biblical Studies, Department of Asian and Middle Eastern Studies, University of Pennsylvania, Philadelphia. **Essays:** Creation; Flora and Fauna of the Bible; Judges, Book of; Kings, Book of; Samuel, Book of.

Fred Astren. Associate Professor, Jewish Studies Program, San Francisco State University, San Francisco, California. Author of *The Jewish Printed Book in India* (1992). Editor of *Papers on Islam and Judaism in Honor of William M. Brinner* (forthcoming). Contributor to *Encyclopedia of the Dead Sea Scrolls* (forthcoming) and *Medieval Encounters*. **Essay:** Karaites.

Cynthia M. Baker. Assistant Professor of Jewish Studies, Department of Religious Studies, Santa Clara University, Santa Clara, California. Editor of *Engendering Knowledge, Engendering Power: Feminism as Theory and Practice* (1992). Contributor to *Anti-Covenant: Counter-Reading Women's Lives in the Hebrew Bible* edited by Mieke Bal (1989), *Shofar, Journal of Medieval and Early Modern Studies, The Encyclopedia of Women and World Religion* edited by Serinity Young (forthcoming), and *Parchments of Gender: Reading the Bodies of Antiquity* edited by Maria Wyke (forthcoming). **Essays:** Am Ha'arets; Women: Biblical; Women: Ancient and Modern; Women: Contemporary; Women: Status.

Carol Bakhos. Visiting Instructor, Department of Religion, Middlebury College, Middlebury, Vermont. **Essay:** Midrash Aggadah.

Pamela Barmash. Rabbi and Assistant Professor, Department of Asian and Near Eastern Languages and Literatures, Program in Jewish and Near Eastern Studies, Washington University, St. Louis, Missouri. **Essays:** Covenant; Sabbath; Targum.

Judith R. Baskin. Professor, Department of Judaic Studies, State University of New York at Albany. Author of *Pharaoh's Counsellors: Job, Jethro and Balaam in Rabbinic and Patristic Tradition* (1983). Editor of *Jewish Women in Historical Perspective* (1991), *Women of the Word: Jewish Women and Jewish Writing* (1994), *Gender and Jewish Studies: A Curriculum Guide* (with Shelly Tenenbaum, 1994), and *Jewish Women in Historical Perspective* (2nd edition, 1998). Contributor to *Jewish History, Association for Jewish Studies Review, Women in Jewish Culture* edited by Maurie Sacks (1995), *Where We Stand: Issues and Debates in Ancient Judaism, Judaism in Late Antiquity* edited by Jacob Neusner and Alan Avery-Peck (1999), and *Judaism in Practice: From the Middle Ages to the Early Modern Period* edited by Lawrence Fine (1999). **Essays:** Divorce; Family.

Leora Batnitzky. Assistant Professor, Department of Religion, Princeton University, Princeton, New Jersey. Author of *Idolatry and Representation: The Philosophy of Franz Rosenzweig*

Reconsidered (forthcoming). Co-editor of *German-Jewish Religious Thought* (special issue of *New German Critique*, 1999). Contributor to *Oxford Journal of Legal Studies, New German Critique, Journal of Jewish Thought and Philosophy, Journal of Religion*, and *Biblicon*. **Essay:** Cohen, Hermann.

Wout Jacques van Bekkum. Professor, History Department, University of Amsterdam, and Lecturer, Hebrew Department, University of Groningen. Author of *The Qedushta'ot of Yehudah according to Genizah Manuscripts* (1988), *A Hebrew Alexander Romance* (1992, 1994), and *Hebrew Poetry from Late Antiquity* (1998). Contributor to *Dispute Poems and Dialogues in the Ancient and Mediaeval Near East* (1991), *Early Christian Poetry* (1993), *Lexicon of Semantics in Four Traditions: Hebrew, Sanskrit, Greek, Arabic* (1997), and *Pre-Modern Encyclopaedic Texts* (1997). **Essay:** Saadia ben Joseph Gaon.

Dean Bell. Associate Dean, Spertus Institute of Jewish Studies, Chicago. Associate Editor of *Shofar* (1997–). Contributor to *Shofar* and *Proceedings of the Patristic, Medieval, and Renaissance Conference* (1997). **Essays:** Anti-Judaism: Middle Ages; Germany: Medieval; Hasidei Ashkenaz; Rabbinic Biography: Medieval; Rabbinic Biography: Early Modern.

Mara Benjamin. Doctoral candidate, Department of Religious Studies, Stanford University, Stanford, California. **Essays:** History: Ideas of; Wissenschaft des Judentums.

Philip J. Bentley. Rabbi and Honorary President, Jewish Peace Fellowship. Contributor to *Judaism, Parabola, Fellowship, The Challenge of Shalom* edited by M. Polner and N. Goodman (1994), *Ecology and the Jewish Spirit* edited by Ellen Bernstein (1997), and *Trees, Earth, and Torah* edited by Arthur Waskow (1999). **Essay:** War and Peace.

Shulamith Z. Berger. Archivist and Curator of Rare Books and Manuscripts, Yeshiva University, New York. Contributor to *Daughters of the King* edited by Rivka Haut and Susan Grossman (1992), *Jewish Women in America: An Historical Encyclopedia* edited by Paula E. Hyman and Deborah Dash Moore (1997), *Conference Proceedings: Di Froyen: Women and Yiddish* (1997), and *Pakn-Treger*. **Essay:** Women's Literature: Early Modern.

Ellen Birnbaum. Resource Information Coordinator, Office for Sponsored Research, Harvard University, Cambridge, Massachusetts. Author of *The Place of Judaism in Philo's Thought: Israel, Jews, and Proselytes* (1996). Editorial board member of Philo of Alexandria Commentary Series. Advisory board member of *The Studia Philonica Annual*. **Essay:** Philo of Alexandria.

Laurie Blumberg. Doctoral candidate, Department of Near Eastern and Judaic Studies, Brandeis University, Waltham, Massachusetts. Contributor to *Encyclopedia of Historians and Historical Review* edited by Kelly Boyd (forthcoming). **Essay:** Antisemitism.

Julia Bock. Librarian, Museum of Jewish Heritage, New York. **Essays:** Baeck, Leo; Hungary.

Philip V. Bohlman. Associate Professor of Music and Jewish Studies, University of Chicago. Author of *The Study of Folk Music in the Modern World* (1988), *"The Land Where Two Streams Flow": Music in the German-Jewish Community of Israel* (1989), and *The World Center for Jewish Music in Palestine 1936–1940: Jewish Musical Life on the Eve of World War II* (1992). Editor of *Ethnomusicology and Modern Music History* (1991), *Comparative Musicology and Anthropology of Music: Essays in the History of Ethnomusicology* (1991), and *Land without Nightingales: Music in the Making of German-America* (1999). Contributor to *Ethnomusicology, Journal of Musicology*, and *Jahrbuch für Volksliedforschung*. **Essays:** Music: Art Music; Music: Ashkenazi Folk Music; Music: Views on Music.

Alfredo Fabio Borodowski. Visiting Assistant Professor of Jewish Philosophy, Jewish Theological Seminary, New York. Contributor to *Proceedings of the Rabbinical Assembly Convention* (1994). **Essay:** Miracles.

S. Daniel Breslauer. Professor, Department of Religious Studies, University of Kansas. Author of *A New Jewish Ethics* (1983), *Covenant and Community in Modern Judaism* (1989), and *Judaism and Civil Religion* (1993). Editor of *Shofar* (1991–) and *Sociological Inquiries* (1995–). Contributing editor, *The Seductiveness of Jewish Myth* (1997). Contributor to *Jewish Thought, Hebrew Studies, Reconstructionist, Shofar*, and *Jewish Spiritual Journeys* edited by Lawrence A. Hoffman and Arnold J. Wolf (1997). **Essays:** Faith; Heschel, Abraham Joshua; Idolatry.

Shannon Burkes. Assistant Professor, Department of Religion, Florida State University, Tallahassee. Author of *Death in Qoheleth and Egyptian Biographies of the Late Period* (1999). Contributor to *Journal for the Study of Judaism*. **Essays:** Death, Burial, and Mourning: Biblical and Talmudic; Five Scrolls.

Deidre Butler. Doctoral candidate and assistant to Chair in Canadian Jewish Studies, Department of Religion, Concordia University, Montreal. Editor of *Journal of Religion and Culture* (1996–98). Contributor to *Journal of Religion and Culture* and *Jewish Women in America: An Historical Encyclopedia* edited by Paula E. Hyman and Deborah Dash Moore (1998). **Essays:** History: General Histories, Modern Authors; History: Modern; Philosophy: Modern.

Hallie Lynn Cantor. Library assistant, Yeshiva University, New York. Co-author of *Double Identity* (with Mayer Bendet, 1989) and *True Identity* (with Mayer Bendet, 1990). Editor of *Search My Heart* (1986), *The Shanghai Connection* (1988), and *The Heroic Struggle* (1999). Associate editor of *Jewish Reader* (1989–93) and *Jewish Homemaker* (1990–96). Contributor to *Jewish Homemaker* and *Association of Jewish Libraries: New York Metropolitan Area Newsletter*. **Essay:** Menahem Mendel of Kotsk.

Havva S. Charm. Research Associate, Library of the Jewish Theological Seminary, New York. **Essay:** Wise, Stephen Samuel.

Judith R. Cohen. Adjunct Graduate Faculty, Department of Music, York University, Toronto. Contributor to *Canadian Folk Music Journal, Musicworks, Jewish Folklore and Ethnology Review, Rivista de Musicología, Canadian Women's Studies, Women and Music in Cross-Cultural Perspective* edited by Ellen Koskoff (1987), *World Music, Politics and Social Change* edited by Simon Frith (1989), *Ballads and Boundaries* edited by James Porter (1995), *Active Voices: Women in Jewish Culture* edited by Maurie Sacks (1995), and *Hommage à Haïm-Vidal Séphiha* edited by Marie-Christine Varol and Winifred Busse (1996). **Essay:** Music: Sephardi Music.

Alan D. Corré. Emeritus Professor of Hebrew Studies, University of Wisconsin–Milwaukee. Author of *Daughter of My People* (1971) and *Icon Programming for Humanists* (1990). Editor of *Understanding the Talmud* (1975), *The Quest for Social Justice II* (1992), and *A Morsel of Bread* (1997). Editorial board member of *Text Technology* (1993–). Contributor to *Journal of Jewish Studies, Jewish Quarterly Review, American Jewish Historical Quarterly, Folklore, Text Technology, Semitic Studies in honor of Wolf Leslau* edited by Alan Kaye (1991), *Contacts between Cultures: West Asia and North Africa* edited by A. Harrak (1992), *Les Juifs d'Espagne: Histoire d'une diaspora 1492–1992* edited by Henry Méchoulan (1992), and *Boundaries of the Ancient Near Eastern World* edited by Meir Lubetsky (1998). **Essays:** Caro, Joseph; Circumcision.

Andrew Davies. Lecturer in Hebrew Bible, Mattersey Hall, Nottinghamshire. Editorial assistant for *Biblical Interpretation* (1996–). Contributor to *They Spoke from God: An Integrative Survey of the Old Testament* edited by William C. Williams (1998). **Essays:** Bible: Criticism; Isaiah, Book of; Prophets, Former and Latter; Prophets, Twelve Minor.

Joseph M. Davis. Assistant Professor of Jewish Thought, Gratz College, Philadelphia. Contributor to *AJS Review* and *Leo Baeck Institute Yearbook.* **Essays:** Judah Loew ben Bezalel; Prague.

Nachum Dershowitz. Professor, Department of Computer Science, Tel-Aviv University. Author of *The Evolution of Programs* (1983) and *Calendrical Calculations* (1997). Editor of *Rewriting Techniques and Applications* (1989) and *Conditional and Typed Rewriting Systems* (1995). Contributor to *IEEE Transactions on Software Engineering, Communications of the ACM, Journal of Symbolic Computation, Machine Intelligence* edited by J.E. Hayes, et al. (1988), and *Software—Practice and Experience.* **Essay:** Calendar.

Eliezer Diamond. Assistant Professor, Department of Talmud and Rabbinics, Jewish Theological Seminary, New York. Contributor to *The Schocken Guide for Jewish Books* edited by Barry Holtz (1992), *Journal for the Study of Judaism, Union Seminary Quarterly Review, Ethics of Consumption* edited by David Crocker and Toby Linden (1998), and *Jewish Quarterly Review.* **Essays:** Asceticism; Talmudic Literature: Introductions; Talmudic Literature: Theology; Talmudic Literature: Hermeneutics.

Marsha Bryan Edelman. Associate Professor of Music and Dean for Academic Affairs, Gratz College, Philadelphia. Editor of *Bibliography of Jewish Music* (1986), *Freedom and Responsibility: Exploring the Challenges of Jewish Continuity* (1998), and *Journal of Synagogue Music* (1998–). Contributor to *Musica Judaica, Shma, Jewish Women in America* edited by Paula Hyman and Deborah Dash Moore (1997), *The Oxford Dictionary of the Jewish Religion* edited by R.J. Zwi Werblowsky and Geoffrey Wigoder (1997), and *Freedom and Responsibility: Exploring the Challenges of Jewish Continuity* edited by Rela Mintz Geffen and Marsha Bryan Edelman (1998). **Essays:** Music: Cantillation; Music: Cantorial Music.

Nehama Edinger. Doctoral candidate, Jewish Theological Seminary, New York. **Essay:** Piyyut.

Laurence L. Edwards. Associate Rabbi, K.A.M. Isaiah Israel Congregation, Chicago. Contributor to *Cross Currents* and *Islamic Identity and the Struggle for Justice* (1996). **Essay:** Maimonidean Controversy.

Avrum Ehrlich. Fellow of Clare Hall, Cambridge University. Author of *Leadership in the Habad Movement* (forthcoming). **Essays:** Habad; Haredim; Sanhedrin, Semikhah, and Rabbinate.

Carl S. Ehrlich. Assistant Professor, Division of Humanities, York University, Toronto. Author of *The Philistines in Transition: A History from ca. 1000–730 B.C.E.* (1996). Editorial board member of *Trumah: Zeitschrift der Hochschule für Jüdische Studien* (1993–95). Contributor to *Zeitschrift des Deutschen Palästina-Vereins, Vetus Testamentum, The Age of Solomon* edited by Lowell K. Handy (1997), *World Religions: The Illustrated Guide* edited by Michael D. Coogan (1998), and *European Judaism* (1998). **Essay:** Onomastics.

David Engel. Skirball Professor of Modern Jewish History, New York University. Author of *In the Shadow of Auschwitz* (1987), *Facing a Holocaust* (1993), and *Between Liberation and Flight* (1996). Editor of *Gal-Ed: On the History of Jews in Poland* (1985–), *Journal of Israeli History* (1997–), and *Polin* (1997–). Co-editor of *Studies in the History of Krakow Jewry* (1998). Contributor to *Zion, Jewish Social Studies, Yad Vashem Studies, Jews in Eastern Poland and the USSR* edited by N. Davis and A. Polonsky (1991), and *The Jews of Poland* edited by I. Bartal and I. Gutman (1997). **Essay:** Poland.

Marc Michael Epstein. Assistant Professor of Religion and Coordinator of Jewish Studies, Vassar College, Poughkeepsie, New York. **Essays:** Architecture, Synagogue: Medieval and Modern; Art: Ceremonial; Iconography; Manuscripts, Hebrew.

Peter R. Erspamer. Lecturer in German, Carroll College, Waukesha, Wisconsin. Author of *The Elusiveness of Tolerance: The "Jewish Question" from Lessing to the Napoleonic Wars* (1997). Contributor to *The Yale Companion to Jewish Writing and Thought in German Culture* edited by Sander L. Gilman and Jack Zipes (1997), *Literature and Ethnic Discrimination* edited by Michael J. Meyer (1997), and *Those Who Resisted the Persecution of the Jews* edited by Ruby Rohrlich (1998). **Essays:** Assimilation; Emden-Eybeschütz Controversy; Haskalah; Herzl, Theodor; Toleration.

Dina Ripsman Eylon. Doctoral candidate, Near and Middle Eastern Civilizations, University of Toronto. Editor of *Women in Judaism* (1997–). Contributor to *Military Women Worldwide* edited by Reina Pennington (1998), and *American National Biography* (1999). **Essays:** Dualism; Hebrew Literature, Modern; Reference Works.

Michael V. Fox. Weinstein-Bascom Professor in Jewish Studies, Hebrew Department, University of Wisconsin. Author of *The Song of Songs and the Ancient Egyptian Love Songs* (1985), *Qohelet and His Contradictions* (1987), *Character and Ideology in the Book of Esther* (1991), *The Redaction of the Books of Esther* (1991), and *Proverbs* (forthcoming). Editor of *Hebrew Studies* (1982–93) and *S.B.L. Dissertation Series* (1994–). Editorial board member of *Journal of Biblical Literature* (1991–96). Co-editor of *Temples, Texts, and Traditions: Essays in Honor of Menahem Haran* (1996). Contributor to *Hebrew Union College Annual, Journal of Biblical Literature, Vetus Testamentum, In Search of Wisdom: Essays in Memory of John Gammie* (1993), and *"You Are My Sister": Essays in Honor of R.E. Murphy* (1997). **Essays:** Ecclesiastes; Proverbs.

Arnold Franklin. Doctoral candidate, Department of Near Eastern Studies, Princeton University, Princeton, New Jersey. **Essays:** Exilarchate; Genizah, Cairo; Geonim; Judeo-Arabic Literature; Muhammad and Judaism; Saadia ben Joseph Gaon; Sephardim; Spain.

Lisbeth S. Fried. Doctoral candidate, Department of Hebrew and Judaic Studies, New York University. Contributor to *Leviticus* by J. Milgrom (forthcoming) and *Eerdman's Bible Dictionary* (forthcoming). **Essays:** Chronicles; Ezra and Nehemiah, Books of.

Dan Friedman. Doctoral candidate, Department of Comparative Literature, Yale University, New Haven, Connecticut. **Essays:** Levinas, Emmanuel; Weizmann, Chaim.

Baruch Frydman Kohl. Senior Rabbi, Beth Tzedec Congregation, Toronto. Editorial board member of *Conservative Judaism* (1984–89). Contributor to *Conservative Judaism, Judaism,* and *Maj'shavot=Pensamientos.* **Essays:** Arama, Isaac; Priesthood: Biblical.

Esther Fuchs. Professor of Judaic Studies, University of Arizona, Tucson. Author of *Encounters with Israeli Authors* (1983), *Cunning Innocence: Irony in the Works of S.Y. Agnon* (1985), *Comic Aspects in S.Y. Agnon's Fiction* (1987), and *Israeli Mythogynies: Women in Contemporary Hebrew Fiction* (1987). Editor of *Women and the Holocaust: Narrative and Representation* (forthcoming) and *Women in Jewish Life and Culture* (special edition of *Shofar*; forthcoming). Contributor to *Who Is Hiding the Truth? Women and Deception in the Hebrew Bible* edited by Adela Y. Collins (1985), *Images of Love and War in Contemporary Israeli Fiction: A Feminist Revision* edited by Helen Cooper, et al. (1989), and *The Characterization of Mothers and Sexual Politics in the Biblical Narrative* edited by Adela Y. Collins (1995). **Essays:** Pappenheim, Bertha; Szold, Henrietta.

Zev Garber. Professor, Department of Jewish Studies, Los Angeles Valley College, Van Nuys, California. Author of *Shoah, The Paradigmatic Genocide: Essays in Exegesis and Eisegesis* (1994). Editor of *Teaching Hebrew Language and Literature at the College Level* (1991), *Perspectives on Zionism* (1994), *Shofar* (1995–), *What Kind of God? Essays in Honor of Richard L. Rubenstein* (1995), *Peace in Deed: Essays in Honor of Harry James Cargas* (1998), and *Academic Approaches to Teaching Jewish Studies* (1999). Contributor to *From Prejudice to Destruction: Western Civilization in the Shadow of Auschwitz* edited by C. Jan Colijn and Marcia Sachs Littell (1995), *Holocaust and Church Struggle: Religion, Power and the Politics of Resistance* edited by Hubert G. Locke and Marcia Sachs Littell (1996), *The Uses and Abuses of Knowledge* edited by Henry F. Knight and Marcia Sachs Littell (1997), *U.S. Holocaust Scholars Write to the Vatican* edited by Harry James Cargas (1998), and *Confronting the Holocaust: A Mandate for the 21st Century* edited by Stephen C. Feinstein, et al. (1998). **Essays:** Holocaust: Responses to the Holocaust; Judaism, Introductions to; Samaritans.

Lloyd P. Gartner. Professor Emeritus of Modern Jewish History, Department of Jewish History, Tel-Aviv University. Author of *A Documentary History of Jewish Education in the United States* (1970), *The Jewish Immigrant in England 1870–1914* (1973), *History of the Jews in Cleveland* (1978), and *The Jewish Community in the United States* (1988). Editorial board of *Societas* (1970–78), *AJS Review* (1985–), and *Modern Judaism* (1983–). Book review editor of *American Jewish Historical Quarterly* (1962–70). Contributor to *American Jewish Historical Quarterly, AJS Review, Transactions of the Jewish Historical Society of England,* and *Jewish History.* **Essays:** Emancipation; New York.

Jane Gerber. Professor, Department of History, Graduate School and University Center of the City University of New York. Author of *Jewish Society in Fez* (1980) and *The Jews of Spain* (1992). Editor of *Jewish Social Studies* (1969–93), *American Jewish History* (1986–96), *Jewish Political Studies* (1988–95), *Authority, Power and Leadership in the Jewish Polity* (1991), and *Sephardic Studies in the University* (1995). Contributor to *Jewish Book Annual* (1981), *Humanities, Reconstructionist, History and Hate* edited by D. Berger (1986), *Judaism* edited by R. Seltzer (1988), and *The Modern Jewish Experience* edited by J. Wertheimer (1993). **Essays:** Muhammad and Judaism; Sephardim; Spain.

Gary Gilbert. Assistant Professor, Department of Philosophy and Religious Studies, Claremont McKenna College, Claremont, California. Editor of *Exploring New Understandings of Theological Scholarship* (1995), and *The Papers of the Henry Luce III Fellows in Theology* (1996). Contributor to *Union Seminary Quarterly Review, Encyclopedia of Theology* edited by Leslie Houlden (1995), *Putting Body and Soul Together* edited by Virginia Wiles, et al. (1997), and *Ancient Judaism VIII* edited by Amy-Jill Levine and Richard Pervo (forthcoming). **Essays:** Jerusalem; Temple and Temple Mount; Western Wall.

Pinchas Giller. Assistant Professor, University of Judaism, Los Angeles. Author of *The Enlightened Will Shine: Symbolization and Theurgy in the Later Strata of the Zohar* (1993) and *Reading the Zohar* (forthcoming). Contributor to *The Tu B'shvat Anthology* edited by Arthur Waskow (forthcoming). **Essays:** Kabbalah: Translations; Kabbalah: Introductions; Luria, Isaac; Veneration of Saints, Pilgrimages, and Holy Places; Zohar.

Aubrey L. Glazer. Doctoral candidate, Department of Jewish Philosophy, Jewish Theological Seminary, New York. Contributor to *Scat!* and *Harthouse Review.* **Essays:** God, Names of; Jabès, Edmond.

Matthew Goff. Doctoral candidate, Divinity School, University of Chicago. Contributor to *Heythrop Journal, Australian Journal of Comedy,* and *Millennial Prophecy Report.* **Essays:** Cemeteries: Antiquity; Lieberman, Saul; Tabernacle.

Matt Goldish. Associate Professor of Jewish and European History, The Ohio State University. Author of *Judaism in the Theology of Sir Isaac Newton* (1998). Contributor to *Journal of Jewish Studies, Studia Rosenthaliana, Jewish Quarterly Review, Science in Context, The Books of Nature and Scripture* edited by J.E. Force and R.H. Popkin (1994), and *Newton and Religion* edited by J.E. Force and R.H. Popkin (1998). **Essays:** Acosta, Uriel; Nieto, David.

Chanita Goodblatt. Senior Lecturer, Department of Foreign Literatures and Linguistics, Ben-Gurion University of the Negev. Contributing editor of *Re-Soundings* (1995–97). Editorial committee member of *PSYART* (1997–). Contributor to *Jerusalem Studies in Jewish Folklore, Prooftexts, Renaissance and Reformation, Dvarim Ahadim, Exemplaria, Israeli Writers Consider the "Outsider"* edited by Leon Yudkin (1993), *Writing, Region and Nation* edited by James A. Davies (1994), *Proceedings of the Eleventh World Congress of Jewish Studies* (1994), and *Walt Whitman Encyclopedia* edited by J.R. LeMaster and Donald D. Kummings (1998). **Essay:** Christian Hebraists.

Sharon Green. Lecturer, Department of Germanic Languages and Literatures, University of Toronto. Author of *Love in Exile: A Key to the Work of S.Y. Agnon* (forthcoming). Co-editor of *And They Will Call Me: Poems from the Holocaust* (1982). Contributor to *Literature and Culture, Encyclopedia of the Novel* edited by Paul Schellinger (1999), and *The Broken Melody: Essays in Memory of Haim Brandwein* edited by Miriam Brandwein (forthcoming). **Essay:** Poetry: Modern Hebrew.

Leonard J. Greenspoon. Philip M. and Ethel Klutznick Chair in Jewish Civilization, Creighton University, Omaha, Nebraska. Author of *Textual Studies in the Book of Joshua* (1983) and *Max Leopold Margolis: A Scholar's Scholar* (1987). Editor of *Ezekiel* (1979, 1983), *VIII Congress of the IOSCS Paris 1992* (1995), *Representations of Jews through the Ages* (1996), *Yiddish Language and Culture: Then and Now* (1997), *Religious Studies Review* (1990–), and *TC* (1995–). Contributor to *Bulletin of the IOSCS, Jewish Quarterly Review, Traditions in*

Transformation edited by B. Halpern and J. Levenson (1981), *Bible Review, Religion and Politics in the Modern World* edited by P. Markl and N. Smart (1985), *Biblical Archaeologist, Hebrew Union College Annual, Septuagint, Scrolls, and Cognate Writings* edited by G. Brooke and B. Lindars (1990), *Anchor Bible Dictionary* edited by D.N. Freedman (1992), *Solomon Goldman Lectures* edited by M. Gruber (1993), and *Judaism.* **Essays:** Hellenism; Hellenistic Literature; Joshua, Book of.

Kevin Edward Griffith. Doctoral candidate, Department of Religious Studies, University of Virginia, Charlottesville. **Essay:** Yiddish Literature.

Sheila Dugger Griffith. Doctoral candidate, Department of Religious Studies, University of Virginia, Charlottesville. **Essay:** Tithes.

Mayer Irwin Gruber. Associate Professor, Department of Bible and Ancient Near East, Ben-Gurion University of the Negev. Author of *Aspects of Nonverbal Communication in the Ancient Near East* (1980), *The Motherhood of God and Other Studies* (1992), *Women in the Biblical World* (1995), and *Rashi's Commentary on Psalms 1–89* (1998). Editor of *Solomon Goldman Lectures* (1993). Editorial board member of *Annual of Rabbinic Judaism.* Contributor to *Biblica, Zeitschrift für die alttestamentliche Wissenschaft, Vetus Testamentum, Studies in Bibliography and Booklore, Journal of Psychology and Judaism, Pomegranates and Golden Bells: Jacob Milgrom Festschrift* edited by David P. Wright, et al. (1995), *Civilizations of the Ancient Near East* edited by Jack M. Sasson (1995), *A Feminist Companion to the Later Prophets* edited by Athalya Brenner (1995), *Cyrus H. Gordon Festschrift* edited by Meir Lubetski, et al. (1998), and *Women's Roles in Ancient Civilizations* edited by Bella Zweig (1998). **Essays:** Humor; Leviticus; Masorah; Numbers, Book of; Psalms; Solomon ben Isaac.

Peter Haas. Associate Professor, Department of Religious Studies, Vanderbilt University, Nashville, Tennessee. Author of *A History of the Mishnaic Law of Agriculture: Maaser Sheni, Translation and Exegesis* (1980), *The Talmud of Babylonia: An American Translation XXXV: Meilah and Tamid* (1987), *Morality after Auschwitz: The Radical Challenge of the Nazi Ethic* (1988), and *Responsa: Literary History of a Rabbinic Genre* (1996). Editor of *Biblical Hermeneutics in Jewish Moral Discourse* (1985) and *Recovering the Role of Women: Power and Authority in Rabbinic Judaism* (1992). Book review editor of *Journal of Reform Judaism* (1991–94). Contributor to *New Perspectives on Ancient Judaism* edited by Jacob Neusner (1987), *Semeia, Religious Studies Review, United Theological Seminary Journal of Theology,* and *Jewish Law Association Studies.* **Essays:** Ethical Wills; Halakhah: Responsa; Reform Judaism.

Jacob Haberman. Rabbi. Author of *Maimonides and Aquinas: A Contemporary Appraisal* (1979). Contributor to *Encyclopaedia Judaica* edited by Cecil Roth (1972), *Yad Le-Heman* edited by Zvi Malachi (1983), *Bitzaron, Journal of Jewish Studies, Judaism, What Is The Purpose of Creation?* edited by

Michael J. Alter (1991), *Mahut,* and *Jewish Quarterly Review.* **Essays:** Ahad Ha'am; Akiba ben Joseph; Death, Burial, and Mourning: Medieval and Modern; Dogmas; Ethical Culture; Frankel, Zacharias; Gordon, Judah Leib; Hirsch, Samson Raphael; ibn Daud, Abraham; Modern Orthodox Judaism; Moses ben Maimon; Neturei Karta; Schechter, Solomon; Soloveitchik, Joseph Baer; Steinberg, Milton; Wolfson, Harry; Yeshivot: Modern.

Schulamith Chava Halevy. Doctoral candidate, Hebrew University of Jerusalem. Author of *Interior Castle: Poems about Being and Being Coerced* (1998). Editor of *Shofar* (special issue, 1999). Contributor to *Midstream, Tradition, Jewish Folklore and Ethnology Review, Pesefas,* and *Línea Directa.* **Essay:** Crypto-Jews, Contemporary.

Eric C. Helmer. Ph.D. in Modern Religious Thought, Boston University. **Essays:** Aristotelianism; Gnosis and Early Mysticism; Identity; Neoplatonism; Sociology of Religion.

Geoffrey Herman. Doctoral candidate, Hebrew University of Jerusalem. Contributor to *Zion* and *Proceedings of the Twelfth World Congress of Jewish Studies.* **Essay:** Priesthood: Post-biblical.

Samuel Herzfeld. Assistant Rabbi, Hebrew Institute of Riverdale, New York. **Essays:** Costume; Dietary Laws.

Richard Hirsh. Rabbi, Executive Director of the Reconstructionist Rabbinical Association, and Faculty Member, Reconstructionist Rabbinical College, Wyncote, Pennsylvania. Editor of *Reconstructionist.* Contributor to *Jewish Exponent.* **Essays:** Kaplan, Mordecai Menahem; Reconstructionist Judaism.

Karina Martin Hogan. Doctoral candidate, Divinity School, University of Chicago. Contributor to *Access Bible* (forthcoming) and *Journal for the Study of Judaism.* **Essays:** Apocrypha and Pseudepigrapha: Translations; Apocrypha and Pseudepigrapha: Introductions; Dead Sea Scrolls; Wisdom Literature.

Leslie J. Hoppe. Professor, Biblical Literature and Languages, Catholic Theological Union, Chicago. Author of *Joshua, Judges* (1982), *What Are They Saying about Biblical Archaeology* (1984), *Being Poor* (1987), *A New Heart* (1991), and *The Synagogues and Churches of Ancient Palestine* (1994). Editor of *Bible Today* (1984–) and *Old Testament Abstracts* (1987–). Contributor to *Biblical Theology Bulletin, Biblical Research, Eglise et Theologie, Biblical and Theological Reflections on the Challenge of Peace* edited by John Pawlikowski and Donald Senior (1984), and *Deuteronomium* edited by Norbert Lohfink (1985). **Essays:** Archaeology; Bible: Introductions; Bible: Reference Tools; Decalogue; Deuteronomy; History: Biblical Israel.

Timothy J. Horner. Doctoral candidate, Wolfson College, Oxford University. Contributing editor of *The Ecole Initiative.* Contributor to *Churchman* (1996). **Essays:** Christian-Jewish Relations: Apologetics and Polemics; Jewish Christians.

Sara R. Horowitz. Associate Professor, Department of English, and Director, Jewish Studies Program, University of Delaware,

Newark. Author of *Voicing the Void: Muteness and Memory in Holocaust Fiction.* Editor of *Kerem, Jewish American Women Writers: A Bio-Bibliographical and Critical Sourcebook* (1994). Contributor to *Cardozo Studies in Law and Literature* (1992), *Holocaust Remembrance: The Shapes of Memory* edited by Geoffrey Hartman (1993), *Women of the World: Jewish Women and Jewish Writing* edited by Judith Baskin (1994), *Judaism since Gender* edited by Miriam Peskowitz and Laura Levitt (1997), and *Spielberg's Holocaust: Critical Perspectives on Schindler's List* edited by Yosefa Loshitzky (1997). **Essays:** Feminism; Holocaust: Literature and Memoirs; Holocaust: Film Treatments; Women's Literature: Modern and Contemporary.

Monika Humer. Librarian, Institute for Jewish Studies, University of Vienna. **Essays:** Lineage; Tribes, Ten Lost.

Charles David Isbell. Instructor of Religious Studies, Louisiana State University. Author of *Introduction to Hebrew* (1975, 1979), *Corpus of the Aramaic Incantation Bowls* (1975), *A Commentary on the Book of Malachi* (1980), *Theological Didactic Drama* (forthcoming). Contributor to *Journal of Near Eastern Studies, Hebrew Annual Review* (1978), *Journal of Central Conference of American Rabbis, Vetus Testamentum,* and *Art and Meaning: Rhetoric in Biblical Literature* (1982). **Essays:** Commandments; Social Ethics.

Martin S. Jaffee. Professor, Jewish Studies and Comparative Religion, University of Washington, Seattle. Author of *Mishnah's Theology of Tithing* (1981), *Talmud of the Land of Israel: Maaserot* (1987), *Talmud of Babylonia: Horayot* (1987), and *Early Judaism* (1997). Editor of *Innovation in Religious Traditions* (1992) and *Readings in Judaism, Christianity, and Islam* (1998). Contributor to *Religion, Journal of Jewish Studies, Journal of the American Academy of Religion, Oral Tradition, Interpreting Judaism in a Postmodern Age* edited by Steven Kepnes (1996), and *Teaching Oral Tradition* edited by John Miles Foley (1998). **Essay:** Oral Tradition.

Julian Jakobovits. Assistant Professor of Medicine, Johns Hopkins University School of Medicine, Baltimore, Maryland. Contributor to *Be Fruitful and Multiply* edited by Richard V. Grazi (1994) and *Neurologist.* **Essay:** Bioethics.

Barbara C. Johnson. Assistant Professor, Department of Anthropology, Ithaca College, Ithaca, New York. Author of *Ruby of Cochin: An Indian Jewish Woman Remembers* (with Ruby Daniel, 1995). Contributor to *Jews of India* edited by Thomas Timberg (1986), *Four Centuries of Jewish Women's Spirituality* edited by Ellen Umansky and Dianne Ashton (1992), *Studies of Indian Jewish Identity* edited by Nathan Katz (1995), *The Jews of India: A Story of Three Communities* edited by Orpa Slapak (1995), *Gender and Race through Education and Political Activism* edited by Dena Shenk (1995), *The Jews of China* edited by Jonathan Goldstein (1998), *Pe'amin,* and *Manushi.* **Essays:** Baghdadi Jews of India; Bene Israel of India; Cochin Jews; India.

Willis Johnson. John Nuveen Instructor, Divinity School, University of Chicago. **Essays:** Body; Libels, Anti-Jewish:

Medieval; Talmudic Literature: Translations; Talmudic Literature: Reference Tools.

Norma Baumel Joseph. Associate Professor, Department of Religion, Concordia University. Contributor to *Celebrating the New Moon: Rosh Hodesh Anthology* edited by Sue Berrin (1996), *A Heart of Wisdom* edited by Sue Berrin (1997), *Celebrating the Lives of Jewish Women: Patterns in a Feminist Sampler* edited by Rachel Siegel and Ellen Cole (1997), *Creating the Jewish Future* (1998), and *Shofar*. **Essays:** Agunah; Feinstein, Moses.

S. Tamar Kamionkowski. Chair, Department of Biblical Civilization, Reconstructionist Rabbinical College. Contributor to *Sermons Seldom Heard* edited by Annie Lally Milhaven (1991) and *Jewish, Alive, and American* edited by Sherry Shulewitz (1998). **Essays:** Esther, Book of; Exodus; Ezekiel, Book of; Ruth, Book of.

Ephraim Kanarfogel. Professor, Department of Jewish History, Yeshiva University, New York. Author of *Jewish Education and Society in the High Middle Ages* (1992) and *"Peering through the Lattices": Mystical, Magical, and Pietistic Dimensions in the Tosafist Period* (1998). Editorial board member of *Jewish Book Annual* (1996–). Contributor to *Proceedings of the American Academy for Jewish Research, Journal of Jewish Thought and Philosophy, AJS Review, Jewish Quarterly Review,* and *Yale Companion to Jewish Writing and Thought in German Culture 1096–1996* edited by Sander Gilman (1997). **Essays:** Abraham ben David of Posquières; Gershom ben Judah; Moses ben Nahman; Yeshivot: Medieval.

Dana Evan Kaplan. Research Fellow, Center for Jewish Studies, University of Wisconsin–Milwaukee. Author of *Jews and Judaism in the New South Africa* (forthcoming) and *American Reform Judaism Today* (forthcoming). Editor of *Contemporary Issues in Reform Judaism* (forthcoming). Contributor to *American Jewish History, Judaism, Tradition, CCAR,* and *American Jewish Archives*. **Essays:** Autonomy, Personal; South Africa.

Gregory Kaplan. Doctoral candidate, Department of Religious Studies, Stanford University, Stanford, California. **Essays:** Abrogation of Law and Custom; Holiness.

Jonathan Karp. Visiting Instructor, Franklin and Marshall College, Lancaster, Pennsylvania. Contributor to *Romantic Russia* (forthcoming). **Essay:** Gentiles.

Paul A. Kay. Associate Professor, Department of Environment and Resource Studies, University of Waterloo, Waterloo, Ontario. Editor of *Problems of and Prospects for Predicting Great Salt Lake Levels* (1985), *The Professional Geographer* (1988–91), and *Great Plains Research* (1991–). Contributor to *Theoretical and Applied Climatology, International Symposium on Water Resources Management in the Middle East* edited by Glenn Stout and Radwan Al-Weshah (1993), *International Workshop on Regional Implications of Future Climate Change* edited by Michael Graber, et al. (1993), *Visions of Land and Community* edited by Harold Brodsky and Robert Mitchell (1997), *Hydrogeography of the Middle East at Peace* edited by Aaron Wolf and Hussein Amery (1998), *Climate Research, Polar Record,* and *Water Resources Development*. **Essays:** Agricultural Laws; Ecology.

James A. Kelhoffer. Instructor, Lutheran School of Theology at Chicago. Contributor to *Biblical Research* and *Ex Auditu*. **Essay:** Art: Late Antiquity.

Menachem Kellner. Wolfson Professor of Jewish Thought, University of Haifa. Author of *Dogma in Medieval Jewish Thought* (1986), *Must a Jew Believe Anything?* (1988), *Maimonides on Human Perfection* (1990), *Maimonides on Judaism and the Jewish People* (1991), and *Maimonides on the Decline of the Generations and the Nature of Rabbinic Authority* (1996). Editor of *Contemporary Jewish Ethics* (1978, 1985), *The Pursuit of the Ideal: Jewish Writings of Steven Schwarzschild* (1990), and *Human Freedom and Moral Responsibility: General and Jewish Perspectives* (with Charles Manekin, 1997). Contributor to *British Journal for the History of Science, Association for Jewish Studies Review, Jewish Political Studies Review, Hebrew Union College Annual, Torah u-Madda Journal, Interpreters of Judaism in the Late Twentieth Century* edited by Steven Katz (1993), *Studies in Halakha and Jewish Thought Presented to Rabbi Professor Emanuel Rackman* edited by M. Beer (1994), *Contemporary Jewish Ethics and Morality* edited by E. Dorff and L. Newman (1995), *Communication in the Jewish Diaspora* edited by S. Menache (1996), and *Hazon Nahum* edited by J. Gurock and Y. Elman (1998). **Essay:** Levi ben Gershom.

Ari Kelman. Doctoral candidate, American Studies Program, New York University. Contributor to *Learn Torah With, Conservative Judaism*. **Essays:** Diaspora; Race, Jews as; Race, Views on.

Joy Kingsolver. Archivist, Chicago Jewish Archives, Spertus Institute of Jewish Studies, Chicago. **Essays:** United States: Community Histories; United States: General Histories.

Samuel Z. Klausner. Professor Emeritus of Sociology, University of Pennsylvania, Philadelphia. Author of *Psychiatry and Religion: A Sociological Study of the New Alliance of Ministers and Psychiatrists* (1964), *On Man in His Environment: Social Scientific Foundations for Research and Policy* (1971), *Eskimo Capitalists: Oil, Politics, and Alcohol* (with Edward Foulks, 1982), and *Succeeding in Corporate America: The Experience of Jewish MBAs* (1989). Editor of *The Study of Total Societies* (1967), *Why Man Takes Chances: Studies in Stress Seeking* (1968), *Religion in the United States* (1968), *Society and Its Physical Environment* (1970), and *Journal for the Scientific Study of Religion* (1964–70). Contributor to *Journal of Educational Psychology, Iyun, Middle East Journal,* and *Archives de Sociologie des Religions*. **Essay:** Apostasy.

Mark Kligman. Assistant Professor of Music, Hebrew Union College-Jewish Institute of Religion, New York. Contributor to *Yivo Annual* (1996), *Religion in Geschichte und Gegenwart* (1998), *Encyclopedia of Judaism* edited by Jacob Neusner (forthcoming), and *Aram Soba* edited by Walter Zenner (forthcoming). **Essay:** Music: Middle Eastern Music.

Cynthia A. Klíma. Assistant Professor, Department of Foreign Languages, State University of New York, Geneseo. Contributor to *Franz Kafka Society of America Yearbook* and *Monatshefte*. **Essays:** Architecture, Synagogue: Late Antiquity; Ben-Gurion, David; Central Europe; Jewish Quarter; Magic and Superstition; Shtetl; Theater.

Rebbeca Kobrin. Doctoral candidate, Department of History, University of Pennsylvania, Philadelphia. **Essay:** Israel, State of: Judaism in Israel.

Samuel S. Kottek. The Harry Friedenwald Chair for History of Medicine, Hebrew University-Hadassah Medical School, Jerusalem. Author of *Medicine and Hygiene in the Works of Flavius Josephus* (1994). Editor of *Moses Maimonides: Physician, Scientist, and Philosopher* (with F. Rosner, 1993), *Medicine and Medical Ethics in Medieval and Early Modern Spain* (with L. García-Ballester, 1996), *Health and Disease in the Holy Land* (with M. Waserman, 1996), and *Korot*. Editorial board member of *Vesalius, Medicina nei Secoli*, and *Israel Journal of Medical Sciences*. Contributor to *Journal of the History of Biology, Bulletin of the International Society for the History of Medicine*, and *Aufstieg und Niedergang der Römischen Welt* edited by W. Haase and H. Temporini (1996). **Essay:** Medicine.

Diane Kriger. Doctoral candidate, Department of Near and Middle Eastern Civilizations, University of Toronto. Editor of *Women in Judaism* (1997–) and *Introducing Tosefta* (forthcoming). Contributor to *Ottawa Law Review* and *The Historical Encyclopedia of World Slavery* edited by Junius P. Rodriguez (1997). **Essay:** Slavery.

Gail Labovitz. Visiting Instructor, Department of Talmud and Rabbinics, Jewish Theological Seminary, New York. Editor of *Mizmor Shir Birkon* (1993) and *Summary Index: The Committee on Jewish Law and Standards* (1994). Contributor to *Proceedings of the Rabbinical Assembly* (1995), *Shofar*, and *Canadian Women's Studies*. **Essays:** Conservative Judaism; Ketubbah.

Hartley Lachter. Doctoral candidate, Skirball Department of Judaic Studies, New York University. **Essay:** Scholem, Gershom.

Ruth Langer. Assistant Professor of Jewish Studies, Theology Department, Boston College. Author of *To Worship Properly: Tensions Between Liturgical Custom and Halakhah in Judaism* (1998). Editor of *CCAR Journal* (1991–96). Contributor to *Proceedings of the American Academy for Jewish Research, Hebrew Union College Annual, Proceedings of the North American Academy of Liturgy*, and *Worship*. **Essays:** Liturgy, History of; Liturgy, Reform; Synagogue.

Yaakov A. Lattes. Rabbi and doctoral candidate, Department of Jewish History, Bar-Ilan University. Contributor to *Jerusalem Letter, Jewish Political Studies Review, La Rassegna Mensile di Israel*, and *Zakhor*. **Essays:** Italy; Luzzatto, Moses Hayyim; Luzzatto, Samuele Davide; Rossi, Azariah dei; Shabbetai Tsevi.

Eric Lawee. Assistant Professor, Division of Humanities, York University, Toronto. Contributor to *Viator, Hebrew Union College Annual, Medieval Studies, AJS Review*, and *Studies in Medieval Jewish History and Literature III* edited by Isadore Twersky and Jay M. Harris (1998). **Essay:** Abravanel, Isaac.

Elliot Lefkovitz. Adjunct Professor of Holocaust Studies, Spertus Institute of Jewish Studies, Chicago, and Adjunct Professor, Department of History, Loyola University of Chicago. Author of *History of Anshe Emet Synagogue* (1976), *The Story of Herman and Maurice Spertus* (1994), and *History of Temple Sholom* (1995). Editor of *Dimensions of the Holocaust* (1990). Contributor to *Encyclopedia Britannica* (1975–76), *World Book Encyclopedia* (1990), and *Journal of American History*. **Essay:** Wise, Isaac Mayer.

Harris Lenowitz. Professor, Department of Languages, University of Utah, Salt Lake City. **Essays:** Bar Kokhba, Simeon; Frank, Jacob Joseph.

Arthur M. Lesley. Associate Professor, Department of Hebrew Language and Literature, Baltimore Hebrew University, Baltimore, Maryland. Contributor to *Prooftexts, Seminar, Ficino and Renaissance Neoplatonism* edited by Konrad Eisenbichler and Olga Zorzi Pugliese (1986), *Renaissance Rereadings: Intertext and Context* edited by Maryanne C. Horowitz, et al. (1988), *Essential Papers on Jewish Culture in Renaissance and Baroque Italy* edited by David B. Ruderman (1992), *The Midrashic Imagination: Jewish Exegesis, Thought and History* edited by Michael Fishbane (1993), and *Storia d'Italia, Annali 11: Gli ebrei in Italia* edited by Corrado Vivanti (1996). **Essays:** Abravanel, Judah; Messer Leon Family.

Alan Levenson. Associate Professor, Cleveland College of Jewish Studies, Cleveland, Ohio. Contributor to *Shofar, Insiders and Outsiders* edited by Dagmar Lorenz and Gabriele Weinberger (1995), *Gender and Judaism* edited by Tamar Rudavsky (1995), *Jewish Social Studies*, and *Judaism*. **Essays:** Buber, Martin; Rosenzweig, Franz.

Mark LeVine. Mellon Postdoctoral Fellow, Department of History, Cornell University, Ithaca, New York. Contributing editor of *Tikkun*. Contributor to *Journal of Palestine Studies, Middle East Report, International Journal of Middle East Studies, Global Norms/Urban Forms*, and *National Identities*. **Essays:** Kibbutz; Zionism, Labor.

Bernard M. Levinson. Berman Family Chair of Jewish Studies and Hebrew Bible and Associate Professor of Classical and Near Eastern Studies, University of Minnesota, Minneapolis. Author of *Deuteronomy and the Hermeneutics of Legal Innovation* (1997). Editor of *Theory and Method in Biblical and Cuneiform Law* (1994). Co-editor of *Gender and Law in the Hebrew Bible and the Ancient Near East* (1998). Editorial board member of *Journal of Biblical Literature, Zeitschrift für Altorientalische und Biblische Rechtsgeschichte*. Contributor to *Harvard Theological Review, Journal of Biblical Literature, "Not in Heaven": Coherence and Complexity in Biblical Narrative* edited by Jason P. Rosenblatt (1991), *Innovation in Religious Traditions: Essays in the Interpretation of Religious Change* edited by Michael A. Williams (1992), *Theory and Method in Biblical and Cuneiform Law* edited by Bernard M. Levinson (1994), and *Bundesdoku-*

ment und Gesetz: Studien zum Deuteronomium edited by Georg Braulik (1995). **Essay**: Bible: Law.

Justin Jaron Lewis. Doctoral candidate, Department of Near and Middle Eastern Civilizations, University of Toronto, and rabbinical student, Academy for Jewish Religion, New York. **Essays**: Folktales; Israel ben Eliezer Ba'al Shem Tov; Levi Isaac of Berdichev; Satmar.

Hilary Lieberman. Doctoral candidate, Department of Italian Language and Literature, Yale University, New Haven, Connecticut. Contributor to *Romance Languages Annual* (1998). **Essays**: Chagall, Marc; Modena, Leone; Venice.

Christopher A. Link. Doctoral candidate, Department of Religion, Boston University. **Essay**: Angels and Demons.

Shari Lowin. Doctoral candidate, Department of Near Eastern Languages and Civilizations, University of Chicago. Contributor to *Hadassah Magazine*. **Essays**: Ba'alei Shem; Geiger, Abraham.

Edith Lubetski. Associate Professor, Library Administration, Stern College for Women, Yeshiva University, New York. Author of *Writings on Jewish History* (1974) and *The Jewish Woman: Recent Books* (1995). Co-author of *Building a Judaica Library Collection* (1983). Associate editor of *Judaica Librarianship* (1983–). Contributor to *Library Resources and Technical Services, Judaica Librarianship,* and *Ten Da'at.* **Essays**: Agnon, Shmuel Yosef; Ozick, Cynthia.

George Mandel. Former Fellow, Oxford Center for Hebrew and Jewish Studies. Author of *Who Was Ben-Yehuda with in Boulevard Montmartre?* (1984). Editor of Eliezer Ben-Yehuda's *A Dream Come True* (1993). **Essay**: Ben-Yehuda, Eliezer.

Alisa Gayle Mayor. Visiting Scholar, Department of Slavic Languages and Literatures, Brown University, Providence, Rhode Island. Contributor to *Study Group on Eighteenth-Century Russia Newsletter* and *Slavic and East European Journal.* **Essays**: Ashkenazim; Cemeteries: Medieval and Modern; Lithuania; Russia.

Rafael Medoff. Visiting Scholar, Jewish Studies Program, State University of New York, Purchase. Author of *The Deafening Silence: American Jewish Leaders and the Holocaust, 1933–1945* (1987) and *Zionism and the Arabs: An American Jewish Dilemma, 1898–1948* (1997). Editorial board of *Menorah Review* (1992–) and *Shofar* (1996–). Contributor to *American Jewish History, Studies in Zionism, Holocaust Studies Annual, American Jewish Archives,* and *Holocaust and Genocide Studies.* **Essay**: Zionism, Revisionist.

David Meier. Associate Professor, Department of Social Sciences, Dickinson State University, Dickinson, North Dakota. Associate editor of *European Studies Journal* (1995–). Contributor to *Confronting the Holocaust* edited by Stephen C. Feinstein (1998) and *Modern Germany* edited by Dieter Buse and Juergen Doerr (1998). **Essays**: Abulafia, Abraham; Zionism.

Marc Miller. Doctoral candidate, Department of Germanic Languages, Columbia University, New York. **Essays**: Bialik,

Hayyim Nahman; Peretz, Isaac Leib; Sholem Aleichem; Singer, Isaac Bashevis.

Victor A. Mirelman. Professor, Spertus Institute of Jewish Studies, Chicago. Author of *En Busqueda de Una Identidad* (1988) and *Jewish Buenos Aires, 1890–1930* (1991). Contributor to *Jewish Social Studies, American Jewish Historical Quarterly, American Jewish Archives,* and *Sephardim in the Americas* edited by Martin A. Cohen and Abraham J. Peck. **Essay**: Latin America and the Caribbean.

Alan Mittelman. Associate Professor, Department of Religion, Muhlenberg College, Allentown, Pennsylvania. Author of *Between Kant and Kabbalah* (1990) and *The Politics of Torah* (1996). Editor of *Jewish Political Studies Review* (1992–1998). Contributor to *First Things* (1996), *The Modern Jewish Experience* edited by Jack Wertheimer (1993), and *European Jewry: Between America and Israel* edited by S. Ilan Troen (1998). **Essay**: Political Theory.

Hillel C. Neuer. Associate at the law firm of Paul, Weiss, Rifkind, Wharton, and Garrison, New York. **Essay**: Creation.

Scott B. Noegel. Assistant Professor, Department of Near Eastern Languages and Civilization, University of Washington, Seattle. Author of *Janus Parallelism in the Book of Job* (1996) and *Nocturnal Secret Ciphers: The Punning Language of Dreams in the Ancient Near East* (1998–). Editor of *Puns and Pundits: Wordplay in the Hebrew Bible and Ancient Near Eastern Literature* (1998–). Contributor to *Acta Sumerologica, Aula Orientalis, Biblica, Journal of Biblical Literature,* and *Zeitschrift für alttestamentliche Wissenschaft.* **Essays**: Ancient Near East; Babylonia; Bible: Hermeneutics; Canaanites; Genesis; Song of Songs.

D.P. O'Brien. Doctoral candidate, Wolfson College, Oxford University. Contributor to *Vetus Testamentum* and *Journal of Early Christian Studies.* **Essays**: Josephus, Flavius; Pharisees; Sadducees.

John T. Pawlikowski. Professor, Department of Historical and Doctrinal Studies, Catholic Theological Union, Chicago. Author of *Catechetics and Prejudice* (1973), *Sinai and Calvary* (1976), *Christ in the Light of the Christian-Jewish Dialogue* (1982), *The Challenge of the Holocaust for Christian Theology* (1982), and *Jesus and the Theology of Israel* (1989). Editor of *Biblical and the Theological Reflections on the Challenge of Peace* (1984), *Economic Justice* (1988), *The Ecological Challenge* (1994), *Journal of Ecumenical Studies, Shofar, New Theology Review,* and *Holocaust and Genocide Studies.* Contributor to *Journal of Ecumenical Studies, Journal of Holocaust and Genocide Studies, Theological Studies, Cross Currents, New Theology Review, The Holocaust as Interruption* edited by Elisabeth Shüssler Fiorenza and David Tracy (1984), *Twenty Years of Jewish-Catholic Relations* edited by Eugene J. Fisher, et al. (1986), *Thinking the Unthinkable* edited by Roger S. Gottlieb (1990), *Introduction to Jewish-Christian Relations* edited by Michael Shermis and Arthur E. Zannoni (1991), and *Visions of the Other* edited by Eugene J. Fisher (1994). **Essays**: Christian-Jewish Relations: Contemporary Dialogue; Jesus and Judaism.

Sarah Pessin. Doctoral candidate, Department of Philosophy, Ohio State University. Contributor to *Journal of the History of Philosophy*. **Essays:** Astrology; Numerology and Numbers.

Sigrid Peterson. Instructor, Department of Religious Studies, University of Pennsylvania, Philadelphia. Contributor to *Ioudaios Review, Religious Studies Review,* and *The Dead Sea Scrolls Fifty Years after Their Discovery* (forthcoming). **Essays:** Ethical and Devotional Literature; History: Talmudic Era.

Lucy K. Pick. John Nuveen Instructor, Divinity School, University of Chicago. Contributor to *Revue Bénédictine* and *Viator.* **Essay:** Crusades.

Judith S. Pinnolis. Reference Librarian for Publications and Training, Goldfarb Library, Brandeis University, Waltham, Massachusetts. Contributor to *Nineteenth-Century American Musical Theater.* **Essay:** Music: American Jewish Music.

Sanford Pinsker. Shadek Professor of Humanities, Franklin and Marshall College, Lancaster, Pennsylvania. Author of *The Schlemiel as Metaphor* (1971), *The Comedy That "Hoits"* (1975), *The Uncompromising Fictions of Cynthia Ozick* (1987), *Understanding Joseph Heller* (1991), and *Jewish-American Fiction, 1917–1987* (1992). Editor of *Philip Roth: Critical Essays* (1982). Co-editor of *Jewish-American Literature and Culture: An Encyclopedia* (1992). Contributor to *Studies in American-Jewish Literature.* **Essays:** American Literature; Black-Jewish Relations in the United States.

Paul A. Rainbow. Professor of New Testament, North American Baptist Seminary, Sioux Falls, South Dakota. Contributor to *Novum Testamentum, Westminster Theological Journal, Journal of Jewish Studies,* and *Bulletin for Biblical Research.* **Essays:** God-Fearers; Paul and Judaism.

Eric Reymond. Doctoral candidate, University of Chicago. **Essay:** Elephantine.

Karyn Riegel. Media and Cultural Programs Director, Bronfman Center for Jewish Life at New York University. Sub-editor of *The Latin American and Latino Annotated International Film Bibliography, 1946–1996* (1999). **Essay:** Film.

Ira Robinson. Professor, Department of Religion, Concordia University, Montreal. Author of *Moses Cordovero's Introduction to Kabbala* (1994). Editor of *Cyrus Adler: Selected Letters* (1985), *An Everyday Miracle: Yiddish Culture in Montreal* (1990), *The Thought of Moses Maimonides* (1990), *The Interaction of Scientific and Jewish Cultures in Modern Times* (1994), *Renewing Our Days: Montreal Jews in the Twentieth Century* (1995), and *Canadian Jewish Studies* (1994–). Contributor to *American Jewish History, Judaism, Canadian Ethnic Studies, American Jewish Archives,* and *Canadian Jewish Studies.* **Essay:** Canada.

James T. Robinson. Doctoral candidate, Department of Near Eastern Languages and Civilizations, Harvard University, Cambridge, Massachusetts. Contributor to *The Encyclopedia of Medieval Hebrew Science and Philosophy* edited by Steven Harvey (forthcoming). **Essay:** Allegory.

Fred Rosner, Professor of Medicine, Mount Sinai School of Medicine, New York, and Director, Department of Medicine, Mount Sinai Services at Queens Hospital Center, Jamaica, New York. Author of *Maimonides' Treatises on Poisons, Hemorrhoids and Coliobitation* (1984), *Modern Medicine and Jewish Ethics* (1986), *Medical Aphorisms of Moses Maimonides* (1989), *Maimonides' Treatise on Asthma* (1993), and *Pioneers in Jewish Medical Ethics* (1997). Editor of *Jewish Bioethics* (1979), *Cancer Investigation* (1981–), *Moses Maimonides: Physician, Scientist and Philosopher* (1993), *Medicine and Jewish Law* (1990, 1993), *Primary Care Update for Ob-Gyns* (1993–), and *Mount Sinai Journal of Medicine* (1994–). Contributor to *Encyclopaedia Judaica* (1972), *Encyclopaedia of Bioethics* (1978), *Current Therapy of Infertility,* and *Current Hematology and Oncology.* **Essays:** Birth Control and Abortion; Euthanasia; Reproductive Technologies.

Jeffrey L. Rubenstein. Associate Professor, Department of Hebrew and Judaic Studies, New York University. Author of *The History of Sukkot in the Second Temple and Rabbinic Periods* (1995). Contributor to *Association of Jewish Studies Review, Hebrew Union College Annual, Jewish Quarterly Review, Harvard Theological Review,* and *Revue Biblique.* **Essays:** Rabbinic Biography: Talmudic; Sukkot.

William D. Rubinstein. Professor of Modern History, University of Wales, Aberystwyth. Author of *The Jews in Australia: A Thematic History, Volume II, 1945–Present* (1991), *Capitalism, Culture, and Decline in Britain, 1750–1990* (1993), *A History of the Jews in the English-Speaking World: Great Britain* (1996), and *The Myth of Rescue* (1997). Editor of *Jews in the Sixth Continent* (1986) and *Journal of the Australian Jewish Historical Society* (1988–95). Editorial board member *Australian Journal of Jewish Studies* (1987–). Contributor to *Past and Present, Jewish Journal of Sociology,* and *Welsh History Review.* **Essays:** Australia and New Zealand; Philosemitism.

Dominic Rudman. Lecturer in Old Testament, Department of Theology and Religious Studies, King's College, London. Contributor to *Journal of Biblical Literature, Journal of Northwest Semitic Languages, Vetus Testamentum, Qohelet in the Context of Wisdom* edited by Anton Schoors (1998), and *Catholic Biblical Quarterly.* **Essays:** Apocalyptic; Eschatology; Jeremiah, Book of.

Leonard Victor Rutgers. Research Fellow of the Royal Dutch Academy of Arts and Sciences, University of Utrecht. Author of *The Jews in Late Ancient Rome* (1995) and *The Hidden Heritage of Diaspora Judaism* (1998). **Essays:** Graetz, Heinrich; History: Second Temple Period; Momigliano, Arnaldo.

Suzanne Rutland. Head, Department of Semitic Studies, University of Sydney. Author of *Seventy-five Years: The History of a Jewish Newspaper* (1970), *Take Heart Again: The Story of a Fellowship of Jewish Doctors* (1983), *Edge of the Diaspora: Two Centuries of Jewish Settlement in Australia* (1988, 1997), *Pages of History: A Century of the Australian Jewish Press* (1995), and *And With One Voice: A History of the New South Wales Jewish Board of Deputies* (1998). Editor of *Aus-*

tralian Jewish Historical Society Journal (1991–), *One Land: Two Peoples* (1993, 1995, 1998), and *Opposite the Lion's Den: A Story of Hiding Dutch Jews* (1996). Contributor to *Australian Journal of Politics and History, Yad Vashem Studies, Leo Baeck Year Book, Australian Journal of Jewish Studies, Australian Jewish Historical Society Journal, The New South Wales Jewish Community: A Survey* (1978), *Jews in the Sixth Continent* (1987), *Australia's Gulf War* (1992), *Minorities* (1995), and *Precious Legacy* (1998). **Essays:** Menasseh ben Israel; Netherlands, The.

Rachel Sabath. Rabbi and Director of Rabbinic Programs, National Jewish Center for Learning and Leadership. Co-author of *Preparing Your Heart for the High Holy Days* (1996) and *Striving Towards Virtue: A Contemporary Guide to Jewish Ethical Behavior* (1996). Contributor to *Shma, Tikkun, Jewish Spectator,* and *Cross Currents.* **Essays:** Continuity; Musar.

Angel Sáenz-Badillos. Professor, Department of Hebrew and Aramaic Studies, Universidad Complutense, Madrid. Author of *Las Tešubot de Dunaš hen Labrat* (1980), *Mahberet Menahem* (1986), *Semu'el ha Nagid, Poemas I Desde el Campo de Batalla* (1988), *A History of the Hebrew Language* (1993), and *Yehuda ha-Levi: Poemas* (1994). Editor of *Homenaje a D. Gonzales Maeso* (1977), *Miscelánea de Estudios Árabes y Hebraicos* (1978), *Homenaje Pérez Castro* (1987), *Poesiá Estrófica* (1989), *Homenaje Díaz Esteban* (1992). Contributor to *Sefarad, Revista de Filología Española, Prooftexts,* and *La Corónica.* **Essays:** ibn Ezra, Abraham; ibn Ezra, Moses; ibn Gabirol, Solomon; ibn Nagrela, Samuel; Judah Halevi; Poetry: Medieval Hebrew.

Ari Salkin-Weiss. Freelance writer, Chicago. **Essays:** Halakhah: Introductions; Reference Works.

Robert B. Salters. Senior Lecturer in Hebrew and Old Testament, University of St. Andrews. Author of *The Commentary of R. Samuel ben Meir on Qohelet* (with Sara Japhet, 1985) and *Jonah and Lamentations* (1994). Contributor to *Vetus Testamentum, Zeitschrift für die Alttestamentliche Wissenschaft, Expository Times, Journal of Jewish Studies, Jewish Quarterly Review, A Word in Season* edited by P.R. Davies and J.D. Martin (1986), *A Dictionary of Biblical Interpretation* edited by R.J. Coggins and J.L. Houlden (1990), and *Rashi et la Culture Juive en France du Nord au Moyen Age* edited by G. Nahon and C. Touati (1997). **Essay:** Lamentations.

Gabriel Sanders. Associate, Leo Baeck Institute, New York. **Essay:** Mendelssohn, Moses.

Jack T. Sanders. Professor Emeritus, Religious Studies Department, University of Oregon. Author of *The New Testament Christological Hymns* (1971), *Ethics in the New Testament* (1975, 1983), *Ben Sira and Demotic Wisdom* (1983), *The Jews in Luke-Acts* (1987), and *Schismatics, Sectarians, Dissidents, Deviants: The First One Hundred Years of Jewish-Christian Relations* (1993). Editor of *Journal of Biblical Literature* (1977–82), *Gnosticism and the Early Christian World* (1990) and *Gospel Origins and Christian Beginnings* (1990). Contributor to *Journal of Biblical Literature, Zeitschrift für die*

neutestamentliche Wissenschaft, Hebrew Union College Annual, Luke-Acts and the Jewish People edited by Joseph Tyson (1988), and *Aufstieg und Niedergang der römischen Welt* edited by Wolfgang Haase (1996). **Essays:** Anti-Judaism: Late Antiquity; Ben Sira, Wisdom of.

Roberta G. Sands. Associate Professor, School of Social Work, University of Pennsylvania, Philadelphia. Author of *Clinical Social Work Practice in Community Mental Health* (1991). Associate Editor of *Social Science Journal* (1987–90). Contributor to *Handbook of American Women's History* edited by A.H. Zophy (1990), *Qualitative Research in Social Work* edited by E. Sherman and W. Reid (1994), *Discourse Processes, Social Work in Education, Families in Society,* and *Clinical Social Work Journal.* **Essay:** Ba'alei Teshuvah.

Marc Saperstein. Professor of Jewish History, Department of History, George Washington University, Washington, D.C. Author of *Decoding the Rabbis* (1980), *Jewish Preaching 1200–1800* (1989), *Moments of Crisis in Jewish-Christian Relations* (1989), and *"Your Voice like a Ram's Horn"* (1996). Editor of *Essential Papers on Messianic Movements and Personalities in Jewish History* (1992). Book review editor of *AJS Review* (1997–). Contributor to *Révue des Études Juives, Jewish Social Studies, Harvard Theological Review, The Land of Israel* edited by Lawrence Hoffman (1986), *Dictionary of the Middle Ages* (1987), *Encyclopedia of Religion* (1987), *Studia Rosenthaliana, Jewish Quarterly Review, Oxford Dictionary of the Jewish Religion* (1996), and *History of Jewish Philosophy* edited by Daniel Frank and Oliver Leaman (1996). **Essays:** Homiletics; Israel, Land of: In Jewish Thought.

Gad B. Sarfatti. Emeritus Professor, Department of Hebrew and Semitic Languages, University Bar-Ilan, Ramat-Gan. Author of *Mathematical Terminology in Hebrew Scientific Literature of the Middle Ages* (1968), *Hebrew Semantics* (1985), and *In the Language of My People* (1997). Editor of *E.Y. Kutscher: Hebrew and Aramaic Studies* (1977), *Studies in Hebrew and Semitic Languages* (1980), and *Hebrew Language Studies* (1983). Contributor to *Leshonenu, Tarbiz, HUCA,* and *Maarav.* **Essays:** Hebrew Alphabet; Hebrew Language.

Isaac Sassoon. Rabbi and Instructor of Talmud, Institute for Traditional Judaism, Teaneck, New Jersey. Author of *Ve-Ha'arev Na.* Editor (with H.P. Salomon) of Uriel da Costa's *Examination of Pharisaic Traditions* (1993) and Antonio José Saraiva's *Inquisicao e Cristaos-Novos* (forthcoming as *The Marrano Factory*). **Essay:** Kingship.

Michael L. Satlow. Assistant Professor, Department of Religious Studies, University of Virginia. Author of *Tasting the Dish: Rabbinic Rhetorics of Sexuality* (1995). Contributor to *Journal of the History of Sexuality, Asceticism* edited by Vincent Wimbush and Richard Valantasis (1995), *Harvard Theological Review, Journal of Biblical Literature,* and *Journal of Jewish Studies.* **Essays:** Gender; Marriage; Sex.

Andrew Schein. Lecturer, Netanyah Academic College. Contributor to *Applied Economics, Judaism,* and *Tradition.* **Essay:** Economic Ideologies.

Stuart Schoenfeld. Associate Professor, Department of Sociology, Glendon College, York University, Toronto. Editor of *Essays in the Social Scientific Study of Judaism and Jewish Society* (1991), and *Journal of Jewish Education* (1992, 1997). Contributor to *Contemporary Jewry, Journal of Jewish Education, Jewish Political Studies Review, Canadian Encyclopedia* (1997), and *Jewish Survival: The Identification Problem at the End of the 20th Century* (1998). **Essay:** Bar Mitzvah and Bat Mitzvah.

Rebecca Schorsch. Doctoral candidate, Divinity School, University of Chicago. **Essay:** Ginzberg, Louis.

Emile G.L. Schrijver. Joods Historisch Museum, Amsterdam. **Essays:** Books and Libraries; Printing, Early Hebrew; Scribes; Script and Scribal Practices.

Richard H. Schwartz. Professor of Mathematics, College of Staten Island, City University of New York. Author of *Judaism and Vegetarianism* (1982, 1988), *Judaism and Global Survival* (1984), and *Mathematics and Global Survival* (1997). Contributor to *Judaism and Animal Rights* edited by Roberta Kalechofsky (1992) and *The Challenge of Shalom* edited by Murray Polner and Naomi Goodman (1994). **Essays:** Animals, Treatment of; Vegetarianism.

Roberta Hanfling Schwartz. Independent scholar and lecturer, Chicago. **Essay:** Glikl of Hameln.

Esther I. Seidel. Lecturer in Jewish Thought, Leo Baeck College, London. Author of *"Jüdische Philosophie" in nichtjüdischer und jüdischer Philosophiegeschichtsschreibung* (1984). Editor of *European Judaism* (1995–), and *Monographien zur Wissenschaft des Judentums* (1995–). Contributing editor of *Nicht durch Geburt allein* (1995), and *Not by Birth Alone* (1997). Contributor to *Biblioteca dell' Archivio di Filosofia: La storia della filosofia ebraica* (1993), *European Judaism, Jewish Identity in Modern Times: Leo Baeck* (1995), *Manna, Ideengeschichte und Wissenschaftsgeschichte* edited by R. Dodel, et al. (1997), *Leo Baeck: Zwischen Geheimnis und Gebot* (1997), and *Das Leben leise wieder lernen* (1997). **Essays:** China; Conversion to Judaism; God, Doctrines and Concepts of; Philosophy: General; Philosophy: Medieval; Spinoza, Baruch de.

Marc B. Shapiro. Weinberg Chair of Judaic Studies, University of Scranton, Scranton, Pennsylvania. Author of *Between the Yeshiva World and Modern Orthodoxy: The Life and Works of Rabbi Jehiel Jacob Weinberg* (1999). Editor of *Collected Writings of Rabbi Jehiel Jacob Weinberg* (1998). Contributor to *Judaism, Torah u-Madda Journal, Tradition, Henoch,* and *Maimonidean Studies.* **Essay:** Rabbinic Biography: Modern.

Brenda J. Shaver. Doctoral candidate, Divinity School, University of Chicago. **Essay:** Daniel, Book of.

Shmuel Shepkaru. Visiting Professor, Department of History, University of Oklahoma. **Essays:** Martyrdom; Suicide.

Ita Sheres. Professor, English and Comparative Literature Department, San Diego State University, San Diego, California. Author of *Dinah's Rebellion: A Biblical Parable for Our Time* (1990) and *The Truth about the Virgin: Sex and Ritual in the Dead Sea Scrolls* (1995). Contributor to *Studies in American Jewish Literature, Soviet Jewish Affairs, Judaism, Centennial Review,* and *Shofar.* **Essay:** Passover.

Hayim Y. Sheynin. Head of Reference Services, Gratz College Library, Philadelphia. Author of *Introduction to the Poetry of Joseph ben Tanhum ha-Yerushalmi and to the History of Its Research, Catalog of Hebrew Incunabula in the Soviet Union,* and *Sephardi Language.* Guest editor of *Jewish Quarterly Review* (special issue in honor of Dr. Leon Nemoy). Editor of *Cataloguing Rules for Oriental Literature.* Editorial board member of *Jewish Quarterly Review.* Contributor to *Acta Orientalia Academiae Scientiarum Hungarica, Hagut Ivrit Bi-Brit ha-Moazot, Jewish Quarterly Review, Sefarad, Community and Culture,* and *Zion.* **Essays:** Crescas, Hasdai; Inquisition; Khazars; Ladino Literature; Languages, Jewish; Lexicographers and Grammarians; Portugal; Provence.

Colin Shindler. Author of *Exit Visa: Detente, Human Rights and the Jewish Emigration Movement in the USSR* (1978), *Ploughshares into Swords? Israelis and Jews in the Shadow of the Intifada* (1991), and *Israel, Likud and the Zionist Dream: Power, Politics, and Ideology from Begin to Netanyahu* (1995). Editor of *Jews in the USSR* (1972–75), *Jewish Quarterly* (1985–94), and *Judaism Today* (1995–). Contributor to *Journalism and the Holocaust 1933–45* (1998) and *Terrorism and Political Violence* (1997). **Essays:** Kahane, Meir; London.

Adina Shoulson. Doctoral candidate, Skirball Department of Hebrew and Judaic Studies, New York University. **Essays:** Johanan ben Zakkai; Krochmal, Nahman.

Edward Silver. Doctoral candidate, Divinity School, University of Chicago. **Essay:** Sin and Atonement.

Rachel Simon. Princeton University, Princeton, New Jersey. Author of *Libya between Ottomanism and Nationalism* (1987) and *Change within Tradition among Jewish Women in Libya* (1992). Editorial board of *Mideast File* (1982, 1986), *On History* (1988), *National Union Catalog of Middle Eastern Microforms* (1989), *MELA Notes* (1995–), and *Jewish Book Annual* (1996–). Contributor to *Alliance Review, Jewish History, Shofar, Africana Journal, Jewish Political Studies Review, Vision and Conflict in the Holy Land* edited by R.I. Cohen (1985), *New Horizons in Sephardic Studies* edited by Y.K. Stillman and G.K. Zucker (1993), *The Jews of the Ottoman Empire* edited by A. Levy (1993), and *Decision Making and Change in the Ottoman Empire* edited by C.E. Farah (1993). **Essays:** Algeria; Egypt and Sudan; Iran, Afghanistan, and Central Asia; Iraq; Libya; Middle East; Morocco; North Africa; Tunisia; Yemen and the Arabian Peninsula.

Alexej Michaelovitch Sivertsev. Doctoral candidate, Skirball Department of Hebrew and Judaic Studies, New York University. **Essay:** Patriarchate.

Abraham Socher. Fellow in the Humanities, Stanford University, Stanford, California. Contributor to *Jewish Social Studies.* **Essay:** Elijah ben Solomon of Vilna.

Adam Sol. Doctoral candidate, Department of English, University of Cincinnati, Cincinnati, Ohio. Poetry Editor of *Indiana Review* (1993–95). Contributor to *Response, Studies in American Jewish Literature, Judaism, Prairie Schooner*, and *Crazyhorse*. Essay: Poetry: American Jewish.

Norman Solomon. Fellow in Modern Jewish Thought, Oxford Centre for Hebrew and Jewish Studies, and Lecturer in Theology, Oxford University. Author of *Judaism and World Religion* (1991), *The Analytic Movement* (1993), and *A Very Short Introduction to Judaism* (1996). Editorial board of *Christian-Jewish Relations* (1985–1991) and *Jewish Journal of Sociology* (1990–). Contributor to *Jewish Law Annual, Maghreb Review, Contemporary Jewish Theology* edited by Dan Cohn-Sherbok (1992), *God, Truth, and Reality* edited A. Sharma (1992), and *The Jubilee Challenge* edited by H. Ucko (1997). Essays: Messiah and Messianism; Science and Religion; Theodicy.

Benjamin D. Sommer. Assistant Professor, Department of Religion, Northwestern University, Evanston, Illinois. Author of *A Prophet Reads Scripture: Allusion in Isaiah 40–66* (1998). Contributor to *Journal of Biblical Literature, Society of Biblical Literature Seminar Papers, New Visions of Isaiah* edited by Marvin Sweeney and Roy Melugin (1996), and *Vetus Testamentum* (1996). Essays: Bible: Theology; Kaufmann, Yehezkel; Pentateuch; Poetry: Biblical; Prophecy.

Nanette Stahl. Judaica Curator, Yale University Library, New Haven, Connecticut. Author of *The First Hebrew Primer to the Bible* (1980) and *Law and Liminality in the Bible* (1995). Essays: Haggadah, Passover; Mendele Moykher Sforim.

Leon Stein. Professor, History and Liberal Studies, Roosevelt University, Chicago. Author of *The Holocaust: A Turning Point for Our Time: A Curriculum for the High Schools of Illinois* (1997). Contributor to *Journal of Central European History, Remembering for the Future* edited by Yehuda Bauer (1988), *Proteus*, and *Problems Unique to the Holocaust* edited by H.J. Cargas (1999). Essays: Germany: Modern; Holocaust: Histories; Libels, Anti-Jewish: Modern; Wiesel, Elie.

Gillian D. Steinberg. Doctoral candidate, Department of English, University of Delaware, Newark. Essays: Nahman of Bratslav; Schoenberg, Arnold.

Simon A. Steiner. Doctoral candidate, Department of Religion, Columbia University, New York. Essay: Hasidic Thought.

Andrew E. Steinmann. Adjunct Professor, Department of Religion, Ashland University, Ashland, Ohio. Author of *Are My Prayers Falling on Deaf Ears?* (1997). Editor of *God's Word* (1995). Contributor to *Journal of Biblical Literature, Vetus Testamentum, Concordia Journal, TC*, and *Fortunate the Eyes That See* edited by Andrew H. Bartelt, et al. (1995). Essays: Bible: Translations; Job, Book of.

Dennis Stoutenburg. Director of Judaic Studies, Providence College, Otterburne, Manitoba. Essay: Festivals and Fasts.

Kenneth Stow. Department of Jewish History, University of Haifa. Author of *Catholic Thought and Papal Jewry Policy* (1977), *The 1007 Anonymous and Papal Sovereignty* (1984), *Alienated Minority* (1992, 1994), and *Jews in Rome* (1995, 1997). Editor of *Jewish History* (1986–) and *The Church and the Jews in the 13th Century By Solomon Grayzel*, (1989). Editorial board member of *Zion* (1995–), *Italia* (1993–), and *Rassegna Mensile d'Israel* (1991–). Contributor to *Renaissance Quarterly, American Historical Review*, and *Biblioteque d'Humanisme e Renaissance*. Essay: History: Medieval.

Adam Sutcliffe. Chaim Lopata Assistant Professor of European Jewish History, Department of History, University of Illinois at Urbana-Champaign. Contributor to *New Voices in Jewish Thought* edited by Robert Rabinowitz (1998), *The Eighteenth Century: Theory and Interpretation* (1998), and *Making Heroes: Exemplary Lives from History* edited by Geoffrey Cubbitt and Allen Warren (1999). Essay: Golem.

Rivka B. Kern Ulmer. Visiting Scholar, Center for Jewish Studies, University of California, Los Angeles. Author of *Tröstet, tröstet mein Volk* (1986), *Rabbinische Responsen zum Synagogenbau* (1990), *The Evil Eye in the Bible and in Rabbinic Literature* (1994), *A Synoptic Edition of Pesiqta Rabbati Based upon All Extant Manuscripts and The Editio Princeps* (1997), and *Talmud Yerushalmi: Ma'aserot, Ma'aser Sheni* (1996). Editor of *Diskussionsbeiträge aus dem Jüdischen Lehrhaus in Frankfurt am Main* (1986) and *Poetry of Rebecca* (1986). Contributor to *Juden in Kassel 1808–1933* (1986), *Linguistica Biblica, Judaism, Encyclopédie Philosophique* (1991), *Zeitschrift für Religions und Geistegeschichte, Proceedings of the Eleventh World Congress of Jewish Studies* (1994), *Theologische Realencyclopädie* (1995), *Journal for the Study of Judaism, Approaches to Ancient Judaism*, and *Annual of Rabbinic Judaism*. Essays: Charity; Mikveh.

Ellen M. Umansky. Carl and Dorothy Bennett Professor of Judaic Studies, Fairfield University, Fairfield, Connecticut. Author of *Lily Montagu and the Advancement of Liberal Judaism: From Vision to Vocation* (1983). Editor of *Lily Montagu: Sermons, Letters, Addresses and Prayers* (1985), *Four Centuries of Jewish Women's Spirituality: A Sourcebook* (with Dianne Ashton, 1992), *Response* (1979–89), *Reconstructionist* (1989–93), *Journal of Jewish Feminist Studies in Religion* (1990–), and *Southern Jewish History* (1997–). Contributor to *Choices in Modern Jewish Thought* edited by Eugene B. Borowitz (1995), *The Americanization of the Jews* edited by Robert Seltzer and Norman Cohen (1995), *Women Rabbis: Exploration and Celebration* edited by Gary Zola (1996), *Jewish Women in Historical Perspective* edited by Judith Baskin (1998), *Feminism and World Religions* edited by Arvind Sharma and Katherine Young (1998), *Conservative Judaism, Journal of Reform Judaism/CCAR Journal, Cross Currents, Modern Judaism*, and *Reconstructionist*. Essay: Montagu, Lily.

Barry D. Walfish. Judaica Specialist, University of Toronto Library. Author of *Esther in Medieval Garb* (1993). Editor of *Moses Kimhi: Commentary on the Book of Job* (1992), *The Frank Talmage Memorial Volume* (1992–93), *Yiddish Panorama* (1995), and Frank Talmage's *Apples of Gold in*

Settings of Silver (1999). Co-editor of *With Reverence for the Word* (forthcoming). Contributor to *Eretz Israel, Israel and the Diaspora: Mutual Relations* edited by Menachem Mor (1991), *The Frank Talmage Memorial Volume, The Bible in Light of Its Interpreters* edited by Sara Japhet (1994), *With Reverence for the Word, Judaica Librarianship, Jewish Quarterly Review, Dor le-Dor,* and *Jewish Studies.* **Essays:** Bible: Medieval Exegesis; Kimhi Family.

Seth Ward. Assistant Professor, Judaic Studies and History, University of Denver, Denver, Colorado. Author of *Synagogues and Churches in Islamic Law* (1984). Editor of *Avoda and Ibada: Liturgy and Ritual in Islamic and Judaic Traditions* (1999) and *Covenant and Chosenness in Mormonism and Judaism* (1999). Editorial board member of *Shofar* (1997–). Contributor to *Bulletin of the School of Oriental and African Studies, Jewish Linguistic Studies, Journal of Ecumenical Studies, Medieval Encounters, Sepphoris in Galilee* (1996), *Islamic Legal Interpretation: Muftis and their Fatwas* (1996), *Yerushalayim ve-Eretz Yisrael,* and *Galilee, Confluence of Cultures* (1999). **Essays:** Islamic-Jewish Relations; Maimonides Family.

Arthur Waskow. Director of the Shalom Center, Philadelphia. Author of *Down-to-Earth Judaism* and *Godwrestling: Round 2.* Co-editor of *Trees, Earth and Torah: A Tu B'Shvat Anthology.* **Essay:** Renewal.

Victoria Waters. Doctoral candidate, Divinity School, University of Chicago. **Essay:** Kook, Abraham Isaac.

Shalva Weil. Department of Education, Ben-Gurion University of the Negev. Editor of *From Cochin to Israel* (1984), *Religious Practices and Beliefs of Ethiopian Jews in Israel* (1989), *One-Parent Families among Ethiopian Immigrants in Israel* (1991), *Ethiopian Jews in the Limelight* (1997), *Roots and Routes: Ethnicity and Migration in Global Perspective* (1999), *Israel Social Science Research* (special issue on Ethiopian Jewry, 1996), World Heritage Press's Hindu-Judaic Studies Series: *Hindu-Jewish Dialogue, International Journal of Hindu Studies, South Asian Anthropology,* and *Journal of Indo-Judaic Studies.* Contributor to *Journal of Comparative Family Studies, Man, Pe'amin, Human Organization,* and

International Journal on Minority and Group Rights. **Essay:** Ethiopia.

David Weinberg. Professor, Department of History, Wayne State University, Detroit, Michigan. Author of *Les Juifs en Paris de 1933 à 1939* (1974), *A Community on Trial: The Jews of Paris in the 1930s* (1977), and *Between Tradition and Modernity: Haim Zhitlowski, Simon Dubnow, Ahad Ha-Am, and the Shaping of Modern Jewish Identity* (1996). Editor of *Shoah* (1971–73). Contributor to *Encyclopedia of the Holocaust* (1989), *Modern Judaism, Max Nordau: Kulturkritik, Transferts culturels européens* (1996), *Patterns of Migration 1850–1914* (1996), and *Tradition Renewed: A History of the Jewish Theological Seminary* edited by Jack Wertheimer (1997). **Essay:** France.

Libby White. Librarian, Jewish Vocational Service, Baltimore, Maryland, and Beth Israel Synagogue, Owings Mills, Maryland. Contributor to *Association of Jewish Libraries Proceedings* (1999), *Association of Jewish Libraries Newsletter, Magazines for Libraries* edited by Bill Katz, and *Funk and Wagnalls New Encyclopedia.* **Essay:** Balkans.

Reena Zeidman. Assistant Professor, Department of Religious Studies, Queen's University, Kingston, Ontario. Contributor to *Approaches to Ancient Judaism,* edited by Jacob Neusner (1995, 1996) and *We Who Can Fly: Poems, Essays and Memories in Honor of Adele Weisman* edited by Elizabeth Green (1997). **Essays:** Midrash Halakhah: Translations; Midrash Halakhah: Introductions.

Walter P. Zenner. Professor of Anthropology and Judaic Studies, State University of New York at Albany. Author of *Minorities in the Middle* (1991). Co-editor of *Urban Life* (with George Gmelch, 1980, 1988, 1996), *Jewish Societies in the Middle East* (with Shlomo Deshen, 1982), *Critical Essays in Israel: Social Issues and Scholarship* (with Russell Stone, 1994), *Jews Among Muslims* (with Shlomo Deshen, 1997), and *Critical Essays on Israeli Society, Religion and Government* (with Kevin Avruch, 1997). Contributor to *Genocide and the Modern Age* edited by Isidor Wallimann and Michael N. Dobkowski (1987), *City and Society, Jewish Journal of Sociology,* and *Israel Affairs.* **Essay:** Syria.